WEEK 01

Contents			Page	Date	Check
Day 01	PART 1	고득점 기출 포인트	02	월 일	☐
Day 02	PART 2	고득점 기출 포인트	10	월 일	☐
Day 03	PART 3, 4	패러프레이징	16	월 일	☐
Day 04	PART 3, 4	시각자료 연계 문제	24	월 일	☐
Day 05	PART 3, 4	의도파악 문제	32	월 일	☐

◀ LC Orientation

MP3 바로듣기   강의 바로보기

1 사람의 동작/상태를 묘사하는 문장

- 주로 be동사 + -ing 형태의 현재진행 시제로 표현됩니다.
- 다양한 동사 표현과 그 발음을 알아 두어야 합니다.

A woman is **kneeling** in a garden.
여자가 정원에서 무릎을 꿇고 있다.

A girl is **watering** some plants.
여자아이가 식물에 물을 주고 있다.

They're **taking care of** a garden.
이들은 정원을 돌보고 있다.

A woman is **wearing** a hat.
여자가 모자를 쓴 상태이다.

필수 암기 정답 문장

다음은 최근 토익에서 자주 출제되는 정답 문장들로, 동사 부분의 표현을 모르면 정답을 고르기 어려우므로 반드시 외워 두세요.

They're **facing** each other.	서로 마주보고 있다.
He's **weighing** a bag on a scale.	저울에 주머니의 무게를 달고 있다.
The men are **shaking hands**.	악수를 하고 있다.
She's **performing** outdoors.	야외에서 공연을 하고 있다.
The woman is **reaching into** a drawer.	서랍에 손을 뻗고 있다.
A man is **arranging** pillows on a couch.	소파 위의 쿠션들을 정리하고 있다.
A woman is **sweeping[mopping]** the floor.	바닥을 쓸고[닦고] 있다.
They're **seated** across from one another.	사람들이 서로 마주보며 앉아 있다.
She's **bending over** some stacked boxes.	쌓여 있는 박스 위로 몸을 구부리고 있다.
A man is **leaning against** a railing.	난간에 기대어 있다.
One of the people is **strolling** down a path.	길을 따라 걷고 있다.
The man is **pushing** a wheelbarrow.	외바퀴 손수레를 밀고 있다.
The men are **unloading** materials from a vehicle.	차량에서 자재를 내리고 있다.
She's **inserting** a plug into an outlet.	플러그를 콘센트에 꽂고 있다.

2 사물/풍경을 묘사하는 문장

- 수동태 표현과 그 발음에 익숙해야 합니다.
- 사물의 상태는 주로 「is/are + p.p.」 또는 「has/have been + p.p.」의 형태로 표현되는데, 둘 다 '~되어 있다'라고 해석하며 의미 차이는 거의 없습니다.
- 다소 생소한 사물의 명칭이 자주 등장하므로 알아 두어야 합니다.

Some boats **are docked** at a pier.
보트들이 부두에 정박해 있다.

Some boats **are tied** to a dock.
보트들이 부두에 묶여 있다.

Some boats have **been secured** to a dock.
보트들이 부두에 고정되어 있다.

A dock has **been built** in a harbor.
부두가 항구에 지어져 있다.

필수 암기 정답 문장

Products <u>are displayed</u> on shelves.
       = are on display, are being displayed

제품들이 선반에 진열되어 있다.

A light fixture <u>is suspended</u> from the ceiling.
      = is hanging

조명 장치가 천장에 매달려 있다.

Tools **are propped against** a wall.
연장들이 벽에 기대어져 있다.

Some books **have been arranged** on shelves.
책들이 선반에 정리되어 있다.

A drawer **has been left open**.
서랍이 열려 있다.

A picnic area **has been set up** outdoors.
피크닉 공간이 야외에 설치되어 있다.

Vehicles **are parked** side by side.
차량들이 나란히 주차되어 있다.

Some lines **have been painted** in a parking area.
주차장에 선들이 그려져 있다.

The tables **are unoccupied**.
테이블들이 비어 있다.

Some bookshelves **are separated** by an aisle.
책장들이 통로로 나뉘어 있다.

A roof of a building **is covered with** snow.
건물 지붕이 눈으로 덮여 있다.

Potted plants **have been placed** in the corner.
화분들이 구석에 놓여 있다.

Some rope **is lying** on the ground.
줄이 땅 위에 놓여 있다.

Some skyscrapers **are overlooking** a harbor.
높은 빌딩들이 항구를 내려다보고 있다.

만점 보장 TIP

사물에 현재 행해지는 동작을 나타내는 「is/are being p.p.」
A wheelbarrow **is being pushed**. 외바퀴 손수레가 밀리고 있다.
Materials **are being moved** across the work area.
자재가 작업장을 가로질러 옮겨지고 있다.

3 만점을 방해하는 함정

▪ '상태'를 진행 중인 '동작'으로 묘사하는 오답

He's putting on a jacket. (X)
재킷을 입는 중이다.

Items are being placed on the shelves. (X)
물건들이 선반에 놓이고 있다.

A railing is being installed. (X)
난간이 설치되고 있다.

예외 Some clothing is being displayed. (O)
옷이 진열되어 있다.

☞ 동사 display는 수동진행형으로
상태를 나타낼 수 있어요.

▪ 주어-동사는 맞는데 뒷부분의 묘사를 틀리게 하는 오답

She's examining some safety glasses. (X)
보호 안경을 자세히 들여다보고 있다.

Some potted plants have been placed on
the table. (X).
화분들이 테이블 위에 놓여 있다.

▪ 구석에 있는 사물을 묘사하는 정답

Some decorations have been mounted on
the wall. (O)
벽에 장식품이 놓여 있다.

Cleaning tools are propped against the
boxes. (O)
청소 도구들이 상자에 기대어 있다.

듣기 전 사진 파악하기

- 등장 인물의 주요 동작을 확인합니다.
- 눈에 띄는 사물의 위치 및 상태를 확인합니다.

 선택지를 들으며 소거하기

- 확실한 오답은 X, 확실한 정답은 O, 애매하거나 나중에 판단하고자 하는 것은 △ 표시하며 듣습니다.
- 반드시 동사를 포함해 그 뒤에 나오는 표현까지 들어야 합니다.
- 듣는 도중 정답이라고 생각되는 선택지가 있어도 끝까지 듣고 확인해야 합니다.

(A) ~~Boxes~~ are stacked on top of each other. X

(B) Some clothes are hanging on a rack. O

(C) A woman is ~~stocking~~ shelves. X

(D) A woman is ~~purchasing~~ an item. X

 최종 정답 선택하기

  ⓐ ● ⓒ ⓓ

 바로 다음 문제 사진 파악하기

- 정답이 너무 헷갈리거나 제대로 못 들었다면 빨리 찍고 다음 문제를 들을 준비를 해야 합니다.

Practice

정답 및 해설 p.42

MP3 바로듣기   강의 바로보기

오늘 학습한 내용을 적용하여 기출 변형 문제들을 풀어보세요.

1.

2.

3.

4.

5.

6.

7.

8.

9.

10.

11.

12.

archway 아치형 길

trail, path 오솔길, 작은 길

driveway 진입로

pavement 포장 도로, 인도

pedestrian 행인

curb 연석

ramp 경사로

dock, pier 부두

railing 난간

awning 차양

bushes 덤불, 관목

patio 야외 테라스

wheelbarrow 외바퀴 손수레

column 기둥

scaffolding (공사장의) 비계

diner 식사 손님

TIP
보통 유리로 되어 있기 때문에 glass case라고 하기도 해요.

display case 진열장

TIP
발음에 유의하세요

aisle 통로

counter (주방의) 조리대

container 용기, 그릇

checkout counter 계산대
cash register 현금 등록기

TIP
자전거 거치대를 bicycle rack이라고 해요.

rack (옷)걸이

rug 깔개

power tool 전동 공구

TIP
동사(삽질하다, 삽으로 뜨다)로도 출제됩니다.

shovel 삽

crate 나무 상자

scale 저울

stool 등받이 없는 의자, 스툴

outlet 콘센트

utensils (주방) 도구

1 의문사 의문문

- 의문사 의문문의 경우 의문사가 무엇이었는지 꼭 기억해야 합니다.
- [When → 시간, 시점], [Where → 위치, 장소, 출처], [Who → 사람, 부서명]으로 답하는 것이 기본이지만 이러한 기본 맥락을 벗어나는 응답에 유의해야 합니다.
- What/Which 의문문에서는 뒤에 오는 명사가 중요하므로 이를 놓치지 않고 들어야 합니다.
- How 의문문은 방법/수단, 선호 사항, 상태, 상황, 의견, 출처, 제안, 정도 등을 묻는 다양한 질문으로 출제됩니다.

Q **When** can I talk to you about the orientation?
오리엔테이션에 대해 언제 얘기할 수 있을까요?

A How about **tomorrow morning**?
내일 아침 어때요?

Q **Where** will we hold the awards ceremony?
어디에서 시상식을 열 건가요?

A It hasn't been decided yet.
아직 결정되지 않았어요.

Q **Who**'s responsible for updating the catalog?
누가 카탈로그 업데이트 작업을 담당하나요?

A What should be changed?
무엇이 변경되어야 하는데요?

Q **What do you think of** this poster design?
이 포스터 디자인에 대해 어떻게 생각하세요?

A It's better than the old one.
이전 것보다 낫네요.

Q **Which caterer** is providing food for the event?
어떤 출장 요리 업체가 행사에 음식을 제공할 건가요?

A **The one** we used last month.
지난달에 이용했던 곳이요.

Q **Why** did Mr. Hwang leave early today?
황 씨는 왜 오늘 일찍 퇴근했나요?

A He had a dental appointment at 4 o'clock.
치과 예약이 4시에 있었어요.

Q **How do I register** for the event?
행사에 등록을 어떻게 하면 되나요?

A By filling out this form.
이 서식을 작성해서요.

Q **How did** the negotiations with ECTA Company go?
ECTA 사와의 협상은 어떻게 되었나요?

A They were successful.
성공적이었어요.

Q **How often** does the shop have a sale?
얼마나 자주 그 상점이 할인을 하나요?

A Once a month.
한 달에 한 번이요.

2 일반 의문문

- Is the building ~? Did you ~? Have you ~? Could you ~?와 같이 Be동사나 조동사로 시작하는 의문문입니다. 조동사 자체보다는 그 뒤에 이어지는 주어-동사의 내용을 주의 깊게 듣는 것이 중요합니다.
- Yes/No로 답하는 것이 일반적이지만, Yes나 No를 포함하지 않는 선택지가 정답이 되는 경우도 많기 때문에 질문과 선택지 사이의 논리 관계를 따져서 정답을 선택해야 합니다.

Q Is the **noise disturbing** you?
A Yes, it is difficult to concentrate.

소음이 당신을 방해하나요?
네, 집중하기가 어렵네요.

Q Are there some **openings** in your **department**?
A I am afraid we are not currently hiring.

당신의 부서에 공석이 좀 있나요?
현재 채용하고 있지 않습니다.

Q Did the **deadline** for the current project **change**?
A Didn't you get the e-mail from your supervisor?

현 프로젝트의 마감기한이 변경되었나요?
당신의 상사로부터 메일을 받지 못했나요?

Q Have the **new catalogues arrived** yet?
A I haven't seen them.

새 카탈로그들이 도착했나요?
전 못 봤는데요.

Q **Can you give me a ride** to the train station?
A Sure, I can do that.

기차역까지 태워다 주시겠어요?
물론이죠, 그렇게 해 드릴 수 있어요.

Q Do you know **who posted** this advertisement?
A Dan Swanson did.

누가 이 광고를 게재했는지 아세요?
댄 스완슨 씨가 했어요.

> 「Do you know + 의문사절?」의 경우, 상대가 알고 있는지를 묻기보다는 의문사절 내용에 해당하는 정보를 요청하는 질문이기 때문에 의문사절의 내용에 대한 직접적인 응답을 하는 경우가 많아요.

만섬 보장 TIP

부정 의문문 안 틀리는 요령

Aren't they ~?, Didn't he ~?, Shouldn't we ~? 등과 같은 부정 의문문이 나왔을 때는 not이 없다고 간주하고 일반 긍정 의문문처럼 해석하세요. 즉, 주어와 동사에 집중해 들으면서 '~하죠?', '~했나요?' 등과 같이 짧은 긍정형으로 파악한 뒤 정답을 선택하면 됩니다.

Q Didn't **you register** for the **webinar** next week?
(→ Did you register~?)
A No, I have plans at that time.

다음 주 인터넷 세미나에 등록했나요?
아뇨, 전 그때 계획이 있어요.

Q Hasn't the **package arrived** yet?
(→ Has the package arrived ~?)
A Yes, we just received it.

그 소포가 도착했나요?
네, 막 그것을 받았어요.

3 선택 의문문

- 「A or B」 형태로 두 개의 선택 사항을 제시하는 선택 의문문에서는 두 개의 선택 사항 중에서 하나를 선택하는 응답이 정답으로 가장 많이 출제됩니다. 둘 다 선택하거나, 둘 다 하지 않거나, 제3의 선택지에 대한 응답, 선택 사항과 관련 없는 응답도 정답으로 출제되고 있으므로 다양한 답변을 익혀 두어야 합니다.

Q Would you rather **complete the report alone**, or do you **need my help**?

A I can handle it myself.

> A or B 선택 사항 중에서 A를 선택하는 답변으로, complete the report alone을 handle it myself라고 표현했어요.
> 같은 의미의 다른 표현을 사용한 고난도 유형입니다.

보고서를 혼자 완성하시겠어요, 아니면 제 도움이 필요하세요?

저 혼자 처리할 수 있습니다.

Q Should I **reserve Room 5 or 6** for the meeting?

A Only Room 3 is available.

회의를 위해 5번 회의실을 예약할까요, 아니면 6번 회의실로 할까요?

3번 회의실만 이용 가능합니다.

Q **Would you like a paper** or **a plastic bag** for your purchases?

A Either is okay.

구입하신 물건에 종이 봉투를 드릴까요, 아니면 비닐 봉투를 드릴까요?

둘 중 아무거나 괜찮아요.

Q Should we **purchase a new printer** or just **repair this one**?

A It depends on our budget.

새 프린터를 구매해야 할까요, 아니면 그냥 이걸 수리해야 할까요?

그건 저희 예산에 달렸어요.

4 평서문, 부가 의문문

- 평서문이 나오면 질문에서 강하게 발음되는 키워드를 중심으로 재빨리 질문 내용을 파악한 뒤, 파악한 내용을 떠올리며 올바르지 않은 응답을 소거해서 정답을 선택해야 합니다.
- 부가 의문문은 평서문 뒤에 꼬리말을 붙인 형태로, '그렇죠?', '맞죠?'라고 해석합니다. 꼬리말은 그 형태가 어떻든지 무시하고, 주어진 문장을 듣되 not이 있어도 모두 긍정문으로 해석해서 문장의 내용이 맞으면 Yes, 아니면 No로 답하는 것이 요령입니다.

Q The **registration** for the **seminar** is due **tomorrow**.

A I'm not planning on going.

세미나 등록이 내일까지예요.

전 갈 계획이 없는데요.

Q **Mr. Gonzales** is in **Shanghai** on business, isn't he?

A Yes, but you can contact him by phone.

곤잘레스 씨가 사업 차 상하이에 계시죠, 그렇죠?

네, 하지만 그에게 전화로 연락하실 수 있어요.

Q The new **Mexican restaurant** requires reservations, right?

A It's only busy on the weekends.

새로 생긴 멕시코 식당은 예약이 필수죠, 맞죠?

거긴 주말에만 붐벼요.

5 고난도 문제 질문-응답 유형

- **Part 2 고난도 문제들의 특징**

  질문 내용에 대해 직접적으로 답하지 않고 돌려 말하는 응답

  질문이 요구하는 정보가 아닌 전혀 다른 제3의 내용으로 응답

  질문에 대한 대답 대신 오히려 질문을 하는 응답

Q	Did you **take notes** during the lecture?	강의 듣는 동안 노트 필기를 했나요?
A	Recording it was allowed.	녹음하는 것이 허용되었어요.

Q	Would you like to **something to drink** while you wait?	기다리시는 동안 마실 것 좀 드릴까요?
A	My friend should be here soon.	제 친구가 곧 올 겁니다.

Q	Do you want to **share a taxi** to the convention center?	컨벤션 센터까지 택시를 같이 탈까요?
A	It's only a few blocks away.	몇 블록만 가면 되는데요.

Q	**When** are you **available** to discuss the business trip?	출장에 대해서 언제 논의 가능하세요?
A	I have a big deadline today.	오늘은 제가 중요한 마감이 있어요.

Q	Is the **new accounting program easy to use**?	새 회계 프로그램은 사용하기 쉽나요?
A	I haven't used it yet.	아직 사용해보지 않았어요

Q	Doesn't your **train depart tonight**?	기차가 오늘밤에 출발하지 않나요?
A	We canceled our trip.	여행을 취소했어요.

Q	**Who's setting up** the conference room?	누가 회의실을 세팅할 거죠?
A	Could you do it this time?	이번엔 당신이 해줄 수 있나요?

Q	**How much** does it **cost to replace** the desks?	책상들을 교체하는 데 비용이 얼마가 드나요?
A	Do you mean the ones in the meeting room?	회의실에 있는 것들 말입니까?

집중력을 최대로 높여 듣기

- 할 수 있는 최대한의 집중력을 발휘하여 질문의 첫 부분을 반드시 들어야 합니다.
- 의문사가 나오면 듣자마자 적어 둡니다. 그래야 나중에 헷갈리지 않아요.

Q. When is Jason planning to start work?

When

선택지를 들으며 소거하기

- 확실한 오답은 X, 확실한 정답은 O, 애매한 것은 △ 표시하며 듣습니다.
- 듣는 도중 정답이라고 생각되는 선택지가 있더라도 끝까지 듣고 확인해야 합니다.

(A) At a marketing company. X
(B) Not until next October. O
(C) Yes, a sales associate. X

> **TIP**
> When을 Where로 착각하면 (A)를 고를 위험이 큽니다. 특히, 영국이나 호주 성우는 Where를 말할 때 /r/ 발음을 거의 하지 않기 때문에 얼핏 들으면 When으로 착각할 수 있어요. 또한, When을 듣고 똑바로 기억해두지 않으면 선택지를 듣다 헷갈려서 잘못된 선택을 하게 될 수 있으니 주의하세요.

최종 정답 선택하기

바로 다음 문제 들을 준비하기

- 정답이 너무 헷갈리거나 잘 듣지 못했다면 빨리 찍고 다음 문제를 들을 준비를 해야 합니다.

Practice

정답 및 해설 p.44

MP3 바로듣기 　 강의 바로보기

오늘 학습한 내용을 적용하여 기출 변형 문제들을 풀어보세요.

1. Mark your answer.　　　　　　　(A) (B) (C)

2. Mark your answer.　　　　　　　(A) (B) (C)

3. Mark your answer.　　　　　　　(A) (B) (C)

4. Mark your answer.　　　　　　　(A) (B) (C)

5. Mark your answer.　　　　　　　(A) (B) (C)

6. Mark your answer.　　　　　　　(A) (B) (C)

7. Mark your answer.　　　　　　　(A) (B) (C)

8. Mark your answer.　　　　　　　(A) (B) (C)

9. Mark your answer.　　　　　　　(A) (B) (C)

10. Mark your answer.　　　　　　　(A) (B) (C)

11. Mark your answer.　　　　　　　(A) (B) (C)

12. Mark your answer.　　　　　　　(A) (B) (C)

13. Mark your answer.　　　　　　　(A) (B) (C)

14. Mark your answer.　　　　　　　(A) (B) (C)

15. Mark your answer.　　　　　　　(A) (B) (C)

16. Mark your answer.　　　　　　　(A) (B) (C)

17. Mark your answer.　　　　　　　(A) (B) (C)

18. Mark your answer.　　　　　　　(A) (B) (C)

19. Mark your answer.　　　　　　　(A) (B) (C)

20. Mark your answer.　　　　　　　(A) (B) (C)

DAY 03

PART 3, 4 패러프레이징

기출 POINT

1 동의어나 상위 개념 어휘를 이용하는 유형

- 토익에서 가장 자주 출제되는 paraphrasing 유형으로, 대화/담화의 표현을 비슷한 의미의 다른 어휘를 이용하여 바꾸어 표현합니다. 토익에 잘 나오는 동의어/상위 개념어를 알아 두세요. (p.22 고득점 특집 참조)

M: I can't give you a cost estimate until I get the exact dimensions of each table. Would you please e-mail me this information?

남: 각 테이블의 정확한 치수를 받을 때까진 견적을 내드릴 수가 없어요. 이 정보를 제게 이메일로 보내 주시겠어요?

Q. 남자가 요구하는 정보는?
→ 몇몇 물건들의 크기

Q. What information does the man ask for?
정답 The sizes of some items

기출 POINT

2 제시된 상황을 요약하는 유형

- 대화/담화에 나온 상황을 종합하여 요약 설명하는 선택지를 찾는 상당히 어려운 유형입니다. 이러한 유형의 문제가 얼마나 나오는지에 따라 Part 3, 4의 난이도가 결정됩니다.

M: I was planning on attending the marketing seminar this Friday but the manager asked me to do a presentation at the board meeting that day.

W: Too bad. You've been looking forward to the seminar so much.

남: 이번 주 금요일 마케팅 세미나에 참석하려고 했는데 과장님께서 그날 이사회 때 발표를 하라고 하셨어요.

여: 안됐군요. 그 세미나를 엄청 기다려왔잖아요.

Q. 남자의 문제는 무엇인가?
→ 일정상의 충돌이 있다.

Q. What is the man's problem?
정답 He has a scheduling conflict.

3 Paraphrasing 감 잡기 QUIZ

- 최근 들어 토익 Part 3, 4의 정답이 paraphrasing되어 나오는 유형이 어려워져서 많은 연습이 필요합니다.
  반드시 문제를 먼저 읽은 후 대화/담화를 듣고 알맞은 답을 골라보세요.

1. What does the man say he will do?

   (A) Review some data

   (B) Send some materials

W: I don't think I can make it to the training session.

M: Don't worry. I can just e-mail you the meeting minutes. Then you'll at least know what we discussed.

W: Thanks. That would be great.

2. What does the man want?

   (A) A sample document

   (B) A product demonstration

W: How's the market report going?

M: I'm struggling. It would be helpful if I could see how it was done last quarter.

W: Oh, I can give you a copy of an old one.

3. What is the problem?

   (A) Some items are missing.

   (B) Some items are out of stock.

M: I'm sorry, we don't have any oak tables available now. We'll get a new shipment next week.

W: Is the floor model available?

M: Let me check with my manager.

4. What are some of the listeners encouraged to do?

   (A) Get some refreshments

   (B) Fill out a survey

Before we begin, let me remind you there will be no break until 7. For those of you here at the lecture room, some light snacks have been set up near the entrance. We will begin in 15 minutes.

5. What can listeners find in Section C?

   (A) Discounted items

   (B) Promotional flyers

Many of our fiction books in Section C are available for half price right now, so make sure you check them out. There are many bestsellers among them, and some have been adapted into award-winning films.

6. What is special about the product?

   (A) It is free to use.

   (B) It is lightweight.

The thing that makes this program so unique is that it can be downloaded from the company's Web site at no cost. Just be sure to download the one that is compatible with your operating system.

정답 및 해설 p.48

대화 듣기 전 문제 읽기

- 3개 문항으로 이루어진 세트의 문제와 선택지를 빠르게 읽고 파악합니다. 시간이 부족하면 문제만이라도 꼭 읽습니다.
- 문제를 읽을 때 주요 키워드에 동그라미로 표시해 둡니다.

- 제안·요청 사항을 묻는 문제가 나오면 누가 누구에게 제안·요청하는 것을 묻는지를 확실히 파악해야 합니다.

 대화 듣기

- 미리 읽은 문제와 관련된 내용을 노려 듣습니다. 이때 문제의 순서와 정답 단서가 나오는 순서는 대부분 일치합니다.
- 대화를 들을 때 시선은 문제와 선택지에 둡니다.

1. What did the man intend to do?
   (A) Come to work late
   (B) Hand in a report early
   (C) Reschedule his meetings
   (D) Work on the weekend

2. Why is the man upset?
   (A) He didn't know about a meeting.
   (B) He has to go out of town suddenly.
   (C) His boss gave him a difficult project.
   (D) His computer will be unavailable.

3. What will the man ask his boss to do?
   (A) Extend a deadline
   (B) Hire an assistant
   (C) Listen to a sales proposal
   (D) Raise his salary

M: I think I'm going to come in to work on Saturday to finish this budget report due on Monday morning.

W: Saturday? Haven't you heard? They're tearing up the floors to lay new LAN cables throughout the office. **You won't be able to use any computer in the office. Everything will be unplugged.**

M: What? I had no idea! **I'd better go ask the boss to let me hand in the report on Tuesday morning** then.

W: Well, I hope she gives you an extension.

- 대화를 듣는 도중 정답이 나오면 문제지에 바로 표시합니다. 답안지 마킹은 리스닝 시험이 모두 끝나고 리딩으로 넘어가기 전에 한꺼번에 합니다.
- 앞부분을 들을 때는 첫 번째 문제를, 중간 부분 들을 때 두 번째 문제를, 끝부분을 들을 땐 세 번째 문제에 시선을 둡니다.
- 단서를 놓친 것 같은 생각이 들면 과감히 다음 문제로 시선을 옮깁니다.

 다음 문제 세트 읽기

- 정답이 너무 헷갈리거나 잘 듣지 못했다면 빨리 찍고 다음 문제 세트를 읽고 들을 준비를 해야 합니다.

1. What did the man intend to do?
   (A) Come to work late
   (B) Hand in a report early
   (C) Reschedule his meetings
   (D) Work on the weekend

2. Why is the man upset?
   (A) He didn't know about a meeting.
   (B) He has to go out of town suddenly.
   (C) His boss gave him a difficult project.
   (D) His computer will be unavailable.

3. What will the man ask his boss to do?
   (A) Extend a deadline
   (B) Hire an assistant
   (C) Listen to a sales proposal
   (D) Raise his salary

4. Where most likely are the speakers?
   (A) At a fitness center
   (B) At an art gallery
   (C) At a university
   (D) At a cooking school

5. According to the woman, why should Mr. Hirst sign up for a membership?
   (A) To attend a performance
   (B) To book classes online
   (C) To receive a free gift
   (D) To leave a comment

6. What does Jason give to Mr. Hirst?
   (A) A course schedule
   (B) A free T-shirt
   (C) A membership card
   (D) An application form

오늘 학습한 내용을 적용하여 기출 변형 문제들을 풀어보세요.

PART 3

1. Where do the speakers most likely work?
   (A) At a sporting goods store
   (B) At a magazine publisher
   (C) At a hardware store
   (D) At a gym

2. What does the man ask the woman about?
   (A) The schedule of a sports tournament
   (B) The experience of staff members
   (C) The number of participants
   (D) The cost of some lessons

3. What will the man do tomorrow?
   (A) Hold a meeting
   (B) Process a delivery
   (C) Clean a work area
   (D) Prepare a survey

4. What does the man say he recently started doing?
   (A) Going to a gym
   (B) Ordering from a restaurant
   (C) Working at an office
   (D) Following a diet

5. What does the man offer to do?
   (A) Prepare a meal
   (B) Lend a book
   (C) Send a Web site link
   (D) Explain a process

6. What problem does the woman mention?
   (A) She has food allergies.
   (B) She has no time to cook.
   (C) She ordered the wrong food.
   (D) She cannot afford a product.

PART 4

7. What is Flex Gym celebrating?
   (A) Installing some machines
   (B) Completing some renovations
   (C) Reaching a target
   (D) Opening a new branch

8. How can the listeners receive a free gift?
   (A) By visiting a Web site
   (B) By referring a new member
   (C) By signing up for a class
   (D) By attending an event

9. What does the speaker say happens on weekends?
   (A) Meals are provided.
   (B) Employees are trained.
   (C) Seminars are held.
   (D) Prices are reduced.

10. What does the listener want to do?
    (A) Train company employees
    (B) Upgrade work computers
    (C) Improve building security
    (D) Promote new services

11. Why will a new project be delayed?
    (A) A supervisor is unavailable.
    (B) A business is relocating.
    (C) Some products are sold out.
    (D) Some tools were not delivered.

12. What does the speaker ask the listener to provide?
    (A) A product catalog
    (B) A business contract
    (C) A delivery address
    (D) A project budget

Paraphrasing 빈출 동의어 표현

Part 3, 4에서 단골로 출제되는 동의어 표현과 상위 개념 어휘를 꼭 외우고 넘어가세요.

- visit (방문하다), come by, stop by (들르다)
- finish (끝내다), complete (완성하다)
- start, begin (시작하다), get A started (A를 시작하다)
- talk to (~에게 얘기하다), speak with (~와 얘기하다)
- start later (나중에 시작하다), postpone (미루다)
- troubleshoot (문제를 해결하다), solve (해결하다)
- dimension (크기, 치수), size (크기)
- go over (검토하다), review (검토하다)
- log on to (접속하다), sign in to (접속하다)
- attend (~에 참석하다), participate in (~에 참가하다)
- sales are down (매출이 줄다), sales are low (매출이 저조하다), sales are decreasing (매출이 줄고 있다)
- look at carefully, examine (자세히 보다)
- give a hand, help, assist (돕다)
- a company (회사), a business (업체)
- carry out, perform (수행하다)
- is not allowed, is not permitted (허용되지 않다), is prohibited (금지되다)
- take notes, write down (적다)
- take a look, go over, review (검토하다)
- come back, return (돌아오다)
- set up a meeting, arrange a meeting, schedule a meeting (회의를 잡다)
- change a date (날짜를 바꾸다), reschedule (일정을 다시 잡다)
- out of stock (재고가 없는), not available (구할 수 없는)
- pick up (비격식: 사다), buy, purchase (구매하다)
- fill out a form, complete a form (서식을 작성하다)
- is loading slowly (느리게 로딩된다), is running slowly (느리게 작동된다)
- change, make a change (변경하다), modify (변경하다, 수정하다)
- stand out (눈에 띄다, 돋보이다), unique (독특한)
- put together, assemble (조립하다)
- affordable (비싸지 않은), reasonable (가격이 합리적인)
- auto shop, car repair shop (차 정비소)
- career fair, job fair (취업 박람회)
- clinic, medical office (치료소, 진료소)
- coupon (쿠폰), voucher (쿠폰, 상품권)

- diet (식단), eating habit (식습관)
- employment, hiring (고용), staffing (직원 채용)
- free, complimentary, no cost, no charge (무료의)
- lost, missing, misplaced (잃어버린, 실종된)
- hand in, turn in, submit (제출하다)
- hand out, pass out, distribute (나눠주다, 배포하다)
- Human Resources, Personnel (인사팀)
- international, overseas (해외의), abroad (해외에)
- launch, release (출시하다)
- luggage, baggage (수하물, 짐)
- new hires, new recruits, new employees, new staff, newcomers (신입사원)
- out of order, broken (고장 난)
- malfunctioning (오작동하는), not working properly (제대로 작동하지 않는)
- take a picture, take a photograph (사진을 찍다)
- advertisement, ad, commercial (광고)
- remove, get rid of, throw away (없애다, 제거하다)
- receipt (영수증), proof of purchase (구매 증거)
- supplies (용품), products, items (제품)
- track (추적하다), monitor (추적 관찰하다)
- workout (운동), fitness (신체 단련), exercise (운동)
- decline, refuse, reject, turn down (거절하다)
- retain personnel, keep employees (직원들의 근속을 유지하다)
- to be offered at a low price (낮은 가격에 제공됨), affordability (적당한 가격으로 구입할 수 있는 것)
- periodically (주기적으로), regularly (정기적으로)
- factory, plant (공장), manufacturing facility (제조 시설)
- call A back, return A's call (A에게 답신 전화를 하다)
- buy a company, acquire a business (회사[업체]를 인수하다)
- research some options, look up some options (선택 가능한 사항들을 조사해보다, 알아보다)
- numbers, figures (수치)
- show A around, give A a tour (A에게 구경시켜주다)
- colleague, coworker (동료)
- understaffed, short-staffed (인원이 부족한)

Paraphrasing 빈출 상위 개념 어휘

- project (프로젝트), painting (페인트칠) → work (일, 작업)
- art supplies (미술용품), vitamins (비타민) → items (물품), products (제품)
- bus, train, taxi (버스, 기차, 택시) → transportation (교통), vehicle (탈 것)
- e-mail (이메일을 보내다), fax (팩스를 보내다), mail (우편으로 보내다), ship (배송하다) → send (보내다)
- part-time designers (시간제 근무 디자이너들) → staff (직원), employees (직원, 사원)
- Chris in the accounting department (회계부의 크리스) → colleague (동료)
- security camera (보안 카메라), projector (프로젝터), photocopier (복사기) → equipment (장비)
- manuals (설명서), instructions (사용 안내서) → materials (자료)
- call (전화하다), e-mail (이메일을 보내다) → contact (연락하다)
- sales figures (매출액) → data (자료), information (정보)
- snack (스낵), drink (음료) → refreshments (다과)
- coffee (커피), juice (주스), soda (탄산 음료) → beverage (음료)
- dinner (저녁식사), lunch (점심식사) → meal (식사)
- be discontinued (단종되다) → unavailable (구매할 수 없는), no longer carry (더 이상 취급하지 않다)
- have a lot of experience (경험이 많다) → be familiar (익숙하다)
- add items to the order (주문에 물품을 추가하다) → update an order (주문을 업데이트하다)
- survey customers (고객 설문조사를 하다) → collect customer feedback (고객 의견을 수집하다)
- hall (홀, 방), convention center (컨벤션 센터) → venue (행사 장소)
- won't turn on (켜지지 않는다), error message (오류 메세지) → is not working (작동되지 않는다)
- a jazz concert (재즈 콘서트) → a musical performance (음악 공연)
- art contest (미술 대회), bicycle race (자전거 경주) → competition (대회, 시합)
- commute (통근하다) → travel (이동하다)
- desk(책상), chair(의자), table(식탁) → furniture (가구)
- handout (유인물), document (문서), packet (꾸러미), papers (서류) → material (자료)
- make more user-friendly (사용자 친화적으로 만들다), upgrade (업그레이드하다) → improve (향상시키다)
- passport (여권), driver's license (운전면허증), ID badge (ID 배지) → identification (신분증)
- pens and notebooks (펜과 공책) → writing supplies (필기구)
- performance (공연), seminar (세미나), conference (학회), job fair (취업 박람회) → event (행사)
- purchase (구매하다) → get (구하다)
- questionnaire (설문지), application (신청서) → form (양식)
- storm (폭풍), heavy snow (폭설) → bad[inclement] weather (좋지 않은 날씨, 악천후)
- swimming pool (수영장), tennis court (테니스장) → facility (시설)
- vendor (상인), manufacturer (제조업자) → provider (제공자)
- 10% off (10% 할인), half price (반값) → discount (할인), special offer (특가 행사)
- baseball game (야구 경기), tennis match (테니스 경기) → sporting event (스포츠 행사)
- name, phone number, and e-mail address (이름, 전화번호, 그리고 이메일 주소) → contact information (연락처 정보)
- open another branch (또 다른 지점을 열다) → expand (확장하다), grow (성장하다)
- estimate (견적서), application (지원서, 신청서), résumé (이력서), reference letter (추천서), contract (계약서) → document (서류)
- name (이름), job (직업), age (나이) → personal information (개인 정보)

가출 POINT

1 표/목록 유형

- 가장 자주 출제되는 시각자료 유형이며, 가격표, 일정표, 주문서, 교통 안내, 메뉴 등이 나옵니다.
  대화/담화에 언급된 단서를 주어진 시각자료 목록에서 찾아 그 옆에 나온 내용과 매칭하면 쉽게 풀 수 있습니다.

• 가격표

Package	Price Per Month
Standard	$19.99
Premium	$24.99
Unlimited	$29.99
Platinum	$39.99

W: 플래티넘 패키지는 너무 비싸니 그 아래 단계인
언리미티드로 할게요.

Q. 여자는 얼마를 지불할 것인가?

• 일정표

September 25 Schedule	
09:00-11:30	Intern Interviews
14:00	
15:00	Board Meeting
16:00	
17:00	Client Teleconference

M: 오전엔 면접이 있고요, 오후에 이사회 끝나고 시간이
납니다.
W: 네 그럼 그때 뵐게요.

Q. 이들은 몇 시에 만날 것인가?

• 층별 안내

Pro Electronics Directory	
1F	Cameras
2F	Mobile phones
3F	Televisions
4F	Computers

W: 스마트폰을 사려고 하는데요 어디로 가야 해요?

Q. 여자는 몇 층으로 갈 것인가?

• 출발/도착 안내

Destination	Departure Time	Status
Chicago	4:20 PM	On time
Los Angeles	7:00 PM	Delayed 30 min.
New York	7:35 PM	Delayed 1 hour
Miami	8:00 PM	On time

M: 나 교통체증 때문에 늦을 것 같아. 어쩌지?
W: 괜찮아. 우리 비행기가 1시간 지연된대.

Q. 이들의 목적지는 어디인가?

필수 어휘

account 계정	price estimate 가격 견적서
item 품목	shareholder's meeting 주주 회의
rate 요금, 가격	conference call 전화 회의
quantity 수량	webinar 웨비나(인터넷상 세미나)
amount 양	itinerary 여행 일정
inventory 재고 (목록)	lunch break 점심 휴게 시간
bill 계산서	tour 견학
invoice 운송장, 구매내역서	directory 안내, 명부
description 설명	extension 내선 번호
order # 주문 번호	departure 출발
product code 제품 고유 번호	arrival 도착
price per person 인당 가격	status 상황
price per month 월별 가격	delayed 지연된
content 목차, 내용물	on schedule 일정대로, 예정대로
cost 비용	canceled 취소된
days overdue 연체 일수	baggage claim 짐 찾는 곳
free shipping 무료 배송	flight number 항공편 번호

2 그래프 유형

- 주로 막대 그래프나 원그래프가 출제되며, 가끔 선 그래프도 등장합니다. 숫자를 언급해서 그에 해당하는 항목을 찾게 하거나, "가장 높은(the highest)", "가장 낮은(the lowest)" 등의 표현을 언급하여 이를 기준으로 단서를 찾게 만듭니다. 난이도 높은 문제의 경우 "두 번째로 높은(the second/next highest)"이 정답 단서로 잘 나옵니다.

• 막대 그래프

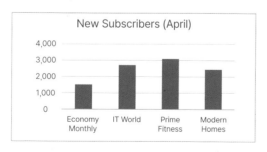

W: 우리 회사 잡지들 중 하나가 이번 달에 2,000명의 신규 구독자를 확보하는 것에 실패했네요. 다음 회의 때 이 잡지에 대해 논의해봅시다.

Q. 어느 잡지에 대해 논의할 것인가?

• 원그래프

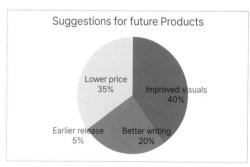

M: 우리 게임 제품의 그래픽을 개선하자는 의견이 가장 많이 나왔는데요, 이에 관해서는 이미 작업이 진행중입니다. 그래서 그 다음으로 많이 나온 의견에 대해 논의해 보려고 합니다.

Q. 무엇에 대해 논의할 것인가?

③ 지도/평면도 유형

- 실내 평면도나 길거리 약도가 자주 출제됩니다. 지도나 약도에서는 next to(~의 옆에), across from
  (~의 맞은 편에)와 같은 위치를 나타내는 전치사구 표현이 결정적 힌트가 되므로 놓치지 않고 들어야 합니다.

• 평면도

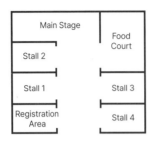

M: 전시 진열대를 예약 하려는데 어디가 좋을까요?

W: 1번 진열대는 이미 예약된데다, 거긴 접수처 옆이라
어수선해요. 푸드코트 맞은편은 어때요?

Q. 여자는 어느 진열대를 추천하는가?

• 약도

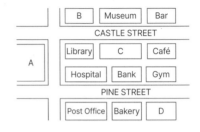

W: 새로 생긴 타코 레스토랑에서 만납시다.
캐슬 스트리트에 있고 박물관 바로 맞은편에 있어요.

Q. 청자는 어디로 갈 것인가?

• 좌석배치도

W: 저는 통로 쪽 좌석(aisle seat)을 원해요.
그런데 화장실 근처는 싫습니다.

Q. 어느 좌석을 선택할 것인가?

• 지하철 노선도

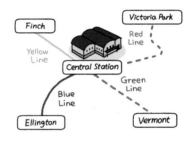

M: 지난 밤 태풍으로 선로가 망가져 블루라인에 대대적인
수리작업이 있을 것입니다. 그래서 일부 지역 주민들은
중앙역에 가는 데 지장이 있을 것 같습니다.

Q. 어느 지역이 영향을 받겠는가?

필수 어휘

route 노선	layout 배치도
trail 산책로, 등산길	hallway 통로
entrance 입구	booth 부스 cf. stall 가판대, 좌판
exit 출구	reception 접수처, 안내데스크
gate 정문, 대문	checkout counter 계산대
aisle seat 통로 쪽 좌석 cf. window seat 창측 좌석	complex 복합건물
parking area[lot] 주차장	directory 층별 안내
city hall 시청	floor 층
floor plan 평면도	business center 비즈니스 센터

4 기타 유형

- 쿠폰이나 티켓, 설명서, 제품 이용 가이드, 업무 흐름도(flow chart), 일기예보, 설문조사, 조리법(recipe) 등 매우 다양한 시각자료가 출제되지만, 대부분 한눈에 파악하기 쉬우므로 요령만 익혀 두면 어렵지 않게 풀 수 있습니다.

• 쿠폰

Grill & Chill 🥩
10% off (Groups of 15+)
Book Rooms for 3 hours!

Expires: July 1	Offer good at All locations

우리 모임 날짜는 7월 5일로 정해졌어요. 참석 인원은 30명입니다. Grill & Chill의 쿠폰은 못 쓸 것 같으니 다른 식당을 찾아봐야 합니다.

Q. 쿠폰을 왜 못 쓰는가?

• 티켓

JetGreen Airlines	🌐
To: Boston	**Seat:** 8D
Flight: J205	
Gate: 33C	
Boarding Time: 09:00	**Departure time:** 09:30

보스턴 행 J205편 비행기에 탑승하시는 여러분께 안내 드립니다. 탑승구가 변경되었습니다. 9시까지 40A 탑승구로 가주시기 바랍니다.

Q. 티켓의 어떤 정보가 바뀌었는가?

• 설명서

Instructions	
Step 1	Click "Change password"
Step 2	Enter new password
Step 3	Click "Done"
Step 4	Restart computer

M: 새 패스워드를 넣었는데 왜 진행이 안되죠?
W: "완료" 버튼을 누르세요.

Q. 남자가 이어서 할 단계는?

• 일기예보

Weather Forecast			
Tuesday	Wednesday	Thursday	Friday
30°C	28°C	26°C	33°C
⛅	🌧️	☀️	☁️

M: 다음 주 수요일엔 하루 종일 비가 오는군요.
W: 일기예보를 보니 그 다음날은 비가 하나도 안 오고 날씨가 좋네요. 그날 만납시다.

Q. 이들은 무슨 요일에 만날 것인가?

필수 어휘

voucher, coupon 쿠폰, 바우처
discount 할인
valid[good] until ~까지 유효한
expiration date 유효기간
expire 만기하다
location 지점
off 할인되어
refund 환불
member 회원 **cf.** nonmember 비회원
ticket holder 티켓 소지자

save 절약
flight 비행편
seat 좌석
gate (공항의) 탑승구
boarding time 탑승 시각
step 단계 (=stage)
process 과정
flow chart 업무 흐름도
instructions 설명서

대화/담화 듣기 전 문제 읽고 시각자료 파악

- 3개 문항으로 이루어진 세트의 문제를 빠르게 읽고 파악합니다.
- 문제를 읽을 때 주요 키워드에 동그라미로 표시해 둡니다.
- 주어진 시각자료를 파악합니다. 문제 읽을 시간이 부족하면 시각자료만이라도 꼭 미리 봐 둬야 합니다.
- 시각자료 연계 문제는 항상 Look at the graphic으로 시작합니다. 시각자료와 해당하는 문제가 어떤 관련이 있는지 생각해봅니다.

TIP

① 다음에 공연할 사람이 누구인지 묻고 있고, 선택지에는 아티스트명이 나와 있습니다.
② 시각자료에서 아티스트명이 있는 곳을 보면 그 옆에 시간 정보가 나와 있습니다.
③ 담화에서 시간 정보가 언급될 것이므로 몇 시가 언급되는지 잘 들었다가 그 시간대에 해당하는 아티스트를 매칭하면 됩니다.

Mountford Park Music Festival	
2:00 P.M.	The Sunny Days
3:30 P.M.	Svetlana Roussev
4:00 P.M.	Jasmin & Lynn
5:30 P.M.	Blinding Lights

1. Look at the graphic. Who will perform at the concert next?

   (A) The Sunny Days
   (B) Svetlana Roussev
   (C) Jasmin & Lynn
   (D) Blinding Lights

2. According to the speaker, why is the music festival special?

3. Why does the speaker ask the listeners to visit a Web site?

대화/담화 듣기

- 미리 읽은 문제와 관련된 내용을 노려 듣습니다.
- 대화/담화를 들을 때 시선은 문제와 선택지에 둡니다.
- 문제의 순서와 정답 단서가 나오는 순서는 대부분 일치하기 때문에 듣는 순서대로 풀면 됩니다.

Thanks for coming out today's music festival in Mountford Park! It's almost 4 P.M., so it's nearly time for our next band to perform on stage. Before they start, I'd like to remind you all about why this event is important. All of the proceeds from today's event, such as ticket sales and food and beverage sales, will go to the local children's charity. So, please make sure you buy some of the delicious food and drink we have provided. The money will be put towards building a new children's library downtown. If you'd like to see a design of the library, you can visit our Web site at www.musicfest.com.

Mountford Park Music Festival	
2:00 P.M.	The Sunny Days
3:30 P.M.	Svetlana Roussev
4:00 P.M.	Jasmin & Lynn
5:30 P.M.	Blinding Lights

- 대화/담화를 듣는 도중 정답이 나오면 문제지에 바로 표시합니다.
- 앞부분을 들을 때는 첫 번째 문제를, 중간 부분 들을 때 두 번째 문제를, 끝부분을 들을 땐 세 번째 문제에 시선을 둡니다.
- 단서를 놓친 것 같은 생각이 들면 과감히 다음 문제로 시선을 옮깁니다.
- 놓친 문제는 맨 마지막에 해결합니다.

1. Look at the graphic. Who will perform at the concert next?
   (A) The Sunny Days
   (B) Svetlana Roussev
   (C) Jasmin & Lynn
   (D) Blinding Lights

2. According to the speaker, why is the music festival special?
   (A) It features local musicians.
   (B) It is raising money for charity.
   (C) It is being broadcast on television.
   (D) It is being held in a historic building.

3. Why does the speaker ask the listeners to visit a Web site?
   (A) To view a building design
   (B) To purchase event tickets
   (C) To enter a competition
   (D) To make a donation

 다음 문제 세트 읽기

- 정답이 너무 헷갈리거나 잘 듣지 못했다면 빨리 찍고 다음 문제 세트를 읽고 들을 준비를 해야 합니다.

오늘 학습한 내용을 적용하여 기출 변형 문제들을 풀어보세요.

PART 3

Delivery Prices	
Next Day	$7.00
2-3 days	$5.50
4-7 days	$4.00
8 or more days	$2.50

STAGE 1	STAGE 2
Market Reserach Study	Planning & Design
STAGE 4	STAGE 3
Testing & Improvements	Prototype Production

1. Where does the conversation most likely take place?

   (A) At a clothing store

   (B) At an electronics store

   (C) At an office supply store

   (D) At a furniture store

4. What type of products does the business most likely produce?

   (A) Construction tools

   (B) Fitness equipment

   (C) Kitchen appliances

   (D) Laptop computers

2. Look at the graphic. How much will the man pay for delivery?

   (A) $7.00

   (B) $5.50

   (C) $4.00

   (D) $2.50

5. Look at the graphic. Which stage in the timeline is the project currently at?

   (A) Stage 1

   (B) Stage 2

   (C) Stage 3

   (D) Stage 4

3. What does the woman offer to do?

   (A) Provide a receipt

   (B) Extend a warranty

   (C) Change an item

   (D) Reduce a price

6. What will the woman do next?

   (A) Meet with shareholders

   (B) Update a schedule

   (C) Send a document

   (D) Make a phone call

PART 4

Wellboro Public Library

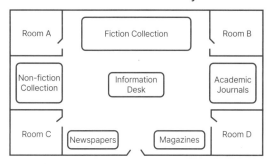

CUSTOMER SURVEY SUGGESTIONS

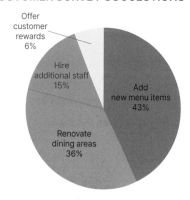

7. What does the speaker thank Shaw Enterprises for?

(A) Funding a project

(B) Providing employees

(C) Donating computers

(D) Renovating a building

8. Look at the graphic. According to the speaker, where can people copy documents?

(A) In Room A

(B) In Room B

(C) In Room C

(D) In Room D

9. What will happen next?

(A) A building tour will be given.

(B) A special guest will be introduced.

(C) A book signing event will be held.

(D) A live performance will take place.

10. Why does the speaker apologize?

(A) A speaker is absent.

(B) A meeting was delayed.

(C) A room is unavailable.

(D) A device has malfunctioned.

11. Look at the graphic. Which customer suggestion is the speaker surprised by?

(A) Add new menu items

(B) Renovate dining areas

(C) Hire additional staff

(D) Offer customer rewards

12. Why does the speaker mention Ms. Ellwood?

(A) To invite her to address the listeners

(B) To thank her for her contribution

(C) To announce a new company executive

(D) To nominate her for an award

기출 POINT ❶ 의도파악 문제 질문 유형

- 의도파악 문제는 딱 다음 세 가지 형태로만 나옵니다. 형태가 뚜렷하게 구분되기 때문에 문제지를 보고 의도파악 문제임을 미리 파악해 해당 부분을 노려 들을 수 있습니다.

- What does the woman **mean when she says**, "I don't think Jeff has any assignments"?
- What does the man **imply when he says**, "I think we can do better"?
- **Why does the man say**, "I have been really busy"?

TIP
이런 문제들이 보이면 문제부터 선택지까지 읽어야 할 텍스트가 많기 때문에 좀더 서둘러야 합니다. 대화를 듣기 전에 주어진 문장에 밑줄을 치고 재빨리 읽으며 해석해 두세요.

기출 POINT ❷ 의도파악 문제의 특징

출제 빈도 및 난이도
Part 3는 한 회당 2문제, Part 4는 3문제가 출제됩니다. 대화/담화가 이어지는 흐름을 파악해야 하고, 선택지가 문장으로 되어 있기 때문에 난이도가 높습니다.

주어진 문장 해석이 다가 아니다!
주어진 문장이 어떤 의미인지 묻는 문제가 절대! 아닙니다. '그 말을 한 의도, 이유, 속뜻'을 묻는 문제이기 때문에 단순히 주어진 문장의 의미만 따져서는 정답을 고를 수 없죠. 오히려, 주어진 문장의 표면적 의미와 가까운 선택지를 고르면 틀리게 됩니다.

대화 상황 및 흐름 파악이 필수
대화 중에 화자가 I have a meeting in the afternoon이라고 말했을 때, 대화 내용이 어떻게 흘러왔는지에 따라 이 말은 '저 오후에 바빠요'라는 의미일 수도 있고, 회의를 요청하는 상대에게 '제가 오후에 회의가 있으니 오전으로 잡읍시다'라는 의도일 수도 있습니다. 이와 같이 화자의 의도를 간파하기 위해서는 대화의 흐름을 이해해야 합니다.

3 의도파악 문제 접근법

- 네 개의 선택지들이 모두 긴 문장으로 제시되기 때문에 일일이 읽고 해석하고 들은 대화 내용을 바탕으로 정답을 고르기까지 많은 시간이 소요됩니다. 때문에 속독 능력이 필요하며, 가장 효과적인 방법은 대화를 듣기 전에 미리 주어진 문장과 함께 네 개 선택지를 미리 읽어 두는 것입니다.

- 듣기 전 문제를 읽을 때는 일일이 해석하는 것이 아니라 키워드만 빠르게 읽도록 합니다.

Q. Why does the woman say, "That's the third time this year"?
올해 세 번째네요

(A) She is disappointed that an employee quit.
실망　　　　　　직원 그만둠

(B) She is impressed with the man's performance.
감동　　　　　　성과

(C) She is dissatisfied with a machine.
불만족　　　　기계

(D) She is pleased to see an increase in sales.
기쁨　　　　　매출증가

M: Hi, Polly. I just tried to print a contract for our new chef, but ① the printer seems to be malfunctioning.

W: I know. I tried to make some copies of our lunch menu this morning, but ① I kept seeing a "System Error" message. That's the third time this year.

M: Well, ② it's about time that we replace it. That one is almost ten years old.

W: ② That's true. Let me go over our budget for this month and see if we can afford a new one.

남: 안녕하세요, 폴리 씨. 제가 지금 막 신임 주방장 계약서를 프린트하려고 했는데 프린터가 안 되는 것 같아요.

여: 알아요. 저도 오늘 오전에 런치 메뉴 사본을 만들려는데 계속 "시스템 오류"라는 메시지만 떴어요. 올해만 세 번째네요.

남: 음, 교체해야 할 때인가 봐요. 그 프린터는 거의 10년이나 되었어요.

여: 맞아요. 이번 달 예산을 검토해 보고 새것을 살 여유가 있는지 볼게요.

TIP
주로 제시 문장 바로 앞에
① 정황적인 중요 단서가 있고, 문장 바로 다음에
② 정답에 쐐기를 박는 핵심 단서가 나오기 때문에
이어지는 내용까지 꼭 챙겨 들어야 안전합니다.

4 의도파악 문제 감 잡기 QUIZ

- 최근 들어 의도파악 문제 내용이 매우 다양해지고 어려워져서 많은 연습이 필요합니다.
- 반드시 문제를 먼저 읽고 인용문을 해석해 본 뒤 대화/담화를 들어야 합니다.

1. What does the woman imply when she says, "I never considered that"?

   (A) A deadline was extended.

   (B) A project was unsuccessful.

   (C) A topic was not discussed.

   (D) An idea was helpful.

W: Hello, Mark. I need your opinion about a new ad I'm working on.

M: Sure. I noticed you haven't turned in your latest design yet. What's holding you up?

W: Well, I like how the product looks, but I'm not sure which font to use for the caption.

M: Well, everyone liked the one you made for the last ad.

W: Hmm... **I never considered that**. Let me see how it looks.

2. Why does the woman say, "I drove today"?

   (A) To express regret

   (B) To offer a ride

   (C) To explain a delay

   (D) To request assistance

W: Are you working late tonight? I didn't think anyone else was still here.

M: I had to finish checking the inventory, but I'm done now.

W: Oh, but look at the time. I think the buses have stopped running.

M: Yeah, I definitely missed the last bus to my home. Do you have any idea how much a taxi to Wooster will cost?

W: I'm not sure, but don't worry about that. **I drove today**.

M: Oh, would you mind taking me home? I'd appreciate it.

3. Why does the speaker say, "it might be a while"?

   (A) He wants the interviews to be thorough.

   (B) He is asking the listeners to wait.

   (C) He is complaining about being busy.

   (D) He is explaining that there aren't many positions.

Today, you'll have a chance to talk to some of our division editors. They'll be able to figure out your area of expertise and find assignments for you that match your strengths, as well as give you more information about the sites you'll be working with. We are a little short-staffed today, so it might be a while. In the meantime, you can make the process a bit smoother by filling out a work history form. You can find them at the back desk.

4. What does the speaker imply when she says, "I hope you're open to other options"?

   (A) A new team will be hired.

   (B) A location might be changed.

   (C) A different item should be used.

   (D) A daily meeting schedule is full.

Hello, Ms. Johnson. This is Claire from Castleview. I'm afraid the price of the carpet you chose jumped up, and if we continue using it on the second floor, we will go over our projected costs. I know you really want to keep within the budget, so I hope you're open to other options. I left a sample of a similar design in your office, so give it a look. I need to finish the carpeting before I can start placing the furniture, so please get back to me with your decision soon.

정답 및 해설 p.58

담화 듣기 전 문제 읽기

- 3개 문항으로 이루어진 세트의 문제와 선택지를 빠르게 읽고 파악합니다. 시간이 부족하면 문제만이라도 꼭 읽습니다.
- 문제를 읽을 때 주요 키워드에 동그라미로 표시해 둡니다.

- 문제 형태를 보고 의도파악 문제임을 알아차렸다면 제시된 문장에 밑줄을 긋고 해석합니다.
- 속독에 자신 있다면 선택지까지 다 읽어 두면 좋지만 그렇지 않으면 일단 제시 문장만이라도 확실히 해석해 두세요.

 담화 듣기

- 미리 읽은 문제와 관련된 내용을 노려 듣습니다. 이때 문제의 순서와 정답 단서가 나오는 순서는 대부분 일치합니다.
- 담화를 들을 때 시선은 문제와 선택지에 둡니다.

1. Who most likely is the speaker?
   (A) A maintenance technician
   (B) A recruitment agent
   (C) A financial advisor
   (D) An interior designer

2. What type of business is being discussed?
   (A) A restaurant
   (B) A theater
   (C) A hotel
   (D) A museum

3. Why does the speaker say, "Now is the time to speak up"?
   (A) To suggest a change
   (B) To complain about noise
   (C) To introduce a guest
   (D) To request feedback

So, I'd like to show you my proposed design for the lobby. As you can see, I have used a modern open design, with minimal furnishings and brightly painted walls. I've also included a variety of artwork on the walls, to give the space a more interesting look. I think the guests will have a good first impression when they arrive to check in at the hotel. Overall, I'm very happy with this design, so I hope you are happy to run with it. If you see any potential problems, now is the time to speak up.

- 담화를 듣는 도중 정답이 나오면 문제지에 바로 표시합니다. 답안지 마킹은 리스닝 시험이 모두 끝나고 리딩으로 넘어가기 전에 한꺼번에 합니다.
- 앞부분을 들을 때는 첫 번째 문제를, 중간 부분 들을 때 두 번째 문제를, 끝부분을 들을 땐 세 번째 문제에 시선을 둡니다.
- 단서를 놓친 것 같은 생각이 들면 과감히 다음 문제로 시선을 옮깁니다.

 다음 문제 세트 읽기

- 정답이 너무 헷갈리거나 잘 듣지 못했다면 빨리 찍고 다음 문제 세트를 읽고 들을 준비를 해야 합니다.

1. Who most likely is the speaker?
   (A) A maintenance technician
   (B) A recruitment agent
   (C) A financial advisor
   (D) An interior designer

2. What type of business is being discussed?
   (A) A restaurant
   (B) A theater
   (C) A hotel
   (D) A museum

3. Why does the speaker say, "Now is the time to speak up"?
   (A) To suggest a change
   (B) To complain about noise
   (C) To introduce a guest
   (D) To request feedback

4. What is the report mainly about?
   (A) Weather conditions
   (B) Local news
   (C) International events
   (D) Road maintenance

5. What will happen this weekend?
   (A) A town fair will take place.
   (B) A music festival will be held.
   (C) A sports tournament will start.
   (D) A shopping center will open.

6. How can listeners enter a competition?
   (A) By filling out an online form
   (B) By purchasing a specific product
   (C) By sending an e-mail
   (D) By calling the radio station

Practice

정답 및 해설 p.60

MP3 바로듣기   강의 바로보기

오늘 학습한 내용을 적용하여 기출 변형 문제들을 풀어보세요.

PART 3

1. What is the conversation mainly about?
   - (A) A job interview
   - (B) An event venue
   - (C) A party menu
   - (D) A guest list

2. What does the woman mean when she says, "The sushi will cost $600"?
   - (A) A discount will be provided.
   - (B) A budget may be exceeded.
   - (C) An order has been delivered.
   - (D) An item was priced incorrectly.

3. What does the man ask about?
   - (A) Delaying a shipment
   - (B) Changing an item
   - (C) Arranging a lunch meeting
   - (D) Using a gift certificate

4. What must new employees do within one month?
   - (A) Meet a sales target
   - (B) Complete a course
   - (C) Purchase some equipment
   - (D) Meet with some managers

5. What does the man ask about?
   - (A) Working on weekends
   - (B) Joining an orientation
   - (C) Submitting a document
   - (D) Receiving a salary

6. Why does the woman say, "We try to prioritize the well-being of staff"?
   - (A) To correct an earlier error
   - (B) To explain a company policy
   - (C) To offer the man a promotion
   - (D) To thank the man for his help

PART 4

7. Why is Dinklage Corporation being celebrated?
   (A) It has released a new product.
   (B) It has opened a new branch.
   (C) It has been in business for 20 years.
   (D) It won an industry award.

8. What most likely is the speaker's profession?
   (A) Accountant
   (B) Web designer
   (C) Architect
   (D) Event planner

9. What does the speaker imply when he says, "I made an exception for Dinklage Corporation"?
   (A) He was previously unaware of a business.
   (B) He was happy to work on a project.
   (C) He plans to launch a new business.
   (D) He waived a consultation fee.

10. What type of company does the speaker work for?
    (A) A construction company
    (B) A department store
    (C) An electronics manufacturer
    (D) A recruitment agency

11. Why does the speaker say, "I've had a word with the suppliers about that already"?
    (A) To suggest a different plan
    (B) To introduce a guest speaker
    (C) To reassure the listeners
    (D) To ask the listeners for feedback

12. What will the listeners do next?
    (A) Watch a presentation
    (B) Read a document
    (C) Test some products
    (D) Contact some suppliers

DAY 01

문제 푸는 순서

(A) 상자들이 차곡차곡 쌓여 있다.
(B) 옷들이 옷걸이에 걸려 있다.
(C) 여자가 선반을 채우고 있다.
(D) 여자가 물건을 구매하고 있다.

해설 (A) 상자들이 쌓여 있는 모습은 보이지 않으므로 오답.
    (B) 여러 벌의 옷들이 옷걸이에 걸려 진열되어 있는 모습을
        묘사한 정답.
    (C) 여자가 선반에 물건을 채우고 있지 않으므로 오답.
    (D) 여자가 옷을 보고 있을 뿐 구매하고 있다고 볼 수 없으므
        로 오답.

어휘 stack ~을 쌓다 on top of each other 차곡차곡
    merchandise 상품 stock ~을 채우다, 갖추다 shelf
    선반 cf. 복수형은 shelves purchase ~을 구매하다

Practice

1. (B)	**2.** (A)	**3.** (A)	**4.** (B)	**5.** (A)	**6.** (D)
7. (A)	**8.** (B)	**9.** (B)	**10.** (C)	**11.** (D)	**12.** (D)

1. (A) A woman is lifting the lid of a box.
    (B) A woman is photocopying a document.
    (C) A copy machine is being fixed.
    (D) Office supplies are stacked behind a woman.

    (A) 여자가 상자 뚜껑을 들어올리고 있다.
    (B) 여자가 문서를 복사하고 있다.
    (C) 복사기가 수리되는 중이다.
    (D) 사무용품들이 여자 뒤에 쌓여 있다.

해설 (A) 여자가 들어올리는 것은 복사기 덮개이므로 오답.
    (B) 문서를 복사하는 모습이므로 정답.
    (C) 복사기를 수리하는 모습이 아니므로 오답.
    (D) 사무용품이 쌓여 있는 모습은 보이지 않으므로 오답.

어휘 lift ~을 들어올리다 lid 뚜껑, 마개 photocopy ~을
    복사하다 copy machine 복사기 fix ~을 고치다, 수리하다
    office supplies 사무용품 stack ~을 쌓다 behind ~의
    뒤에

2. **(A) A ladder is leaning against a building.**
    (B) Some trees are being trimmed.
    (C) Some equipment is being moved into a building.
    (D) They're loading supplies into a vehicle.

(A) 사다리가 건물에 기대어 있다.
(B) 몇몇 나무들이 다듬어지고 있다.
(C) 일부 장비가 건물 안으로 옮겨지고 있다.
(D) 사람들이 물품들을 차량 안에 싣고 있다.

해설 (A) 사진의 좌측에 사다리가 건물에 기대어 있는 모습이 보이므
    로 정답.
    (B) 나무를 다듬고 있는 모습은 보이지 않으므로 오답.
    (C) 장비를 건물 안으로 옮기는 모습은 보이지 않으므로 오답.
    (D) 물품을 차량 안에 싣고 있지 않으므로 오답.

어휘 ladder 사다리 lean against ~에 기대다 trim ~을
    다듬다, 자르다 equipment 장비 move ~을 옮기다 load
    ~을 싣다 supplies 물품 vehicle 차량

3. **(A) Some people have gathered for a presentation.**
    (B) A woman is distributing handouts.
    (C) The windows have been left open.
    (D) A presenter is adjusting a projector.

    (A) 몇몇 사람들이 발표를 듣기 위해 모여 있다.
    (B) 한 여자가 유인물을 나눠주고 있다.
    (C) 창문들이 열려 있다.
    (D) 발표자가 프로젝터를 조정하고 있다.

해설 (A) 사람들이 모여 발표를 듣고 있으므로 정답.
    (B) 유인물을 나눠주는 사람은 없으므로 오답.
    (C) 창이 열린 모습을 확인할 수 없으므로 오답.
    (D) 발표자가 프로젝터를 만지고 있지 않으므로 오답.

어휘 gather 모이다 presentation 발표 distribute ~을
    나눠주다, 배부하다 handout 유인물 be left + 형용사
    ~인 채로 있다 presenter 발표자 adjust ~을 조절하다
    projector 프로젝터

4. (A) The floor is being cleared.
    **(B) Some light fixtures are suspended from a
        ceiling.**
    (C) A door has been left open.
    (D) Some chairs are stacked in a corner.

    (A) 바닥이 치워지고 있다.
    (B) 조명 기구들이 천장에 매달려 있다.
    (C) 문이 열린 채로 있다.
    (D) 몇몇 의자들이 구석에 쌓여 있다.

해설 (A) 바닥은 이미 깨끗이 치워져 있는 상태이고, 치우는 사람이
    보이지 않으므로 오답.
    (B) 천장에 조명 기구들이 매달려 있으므로 정답.
    (C) 문이 열려 있지 않으므로 오답.
    (D) 의자들이 쌓여 있는 모습은 보이지 않으므로 오답.

어휘 floor 바닥 clear ~을 치우다 light fixture 조명 기구 be
    suspended from ~에 매달려 있다 ceiling 천장 stack
    ~을 쌓다 in a corner 구석에

5. (A) The buildings are overlooking water.
(B) Some lampposts are being installed.
(C) Some pedestrians are crossing the street.
(D) A seating area has been set up outside.

(A) 건물들이 강을 내려다보고 있다.
(B) 가로등들이 설치되는 중이다.
(C) 몇몇 보행자들이 길을 건너고 있다.
(D) 야외에 좌석 구역이 설치되어 있다.

해설 (A) 건물들이 강을 내려다보고 있으므로 정답.
(B) 가로등은 이미 설치되어 있으므로 오답.
(C) 보행자들이 길을 건너는 모습은 보이지 않으므로 오답.
(D) 좌석 구역으로 보이는 곳은 없으므로 오답.

어휘 **overlook** ~을 내려다보다 **water** (호수, 강, 바다의) 물
lamppost 가로등 **install** ~을 설치하다 **pedestrian**
보행자, 행인 **cross** ~을 건너다 **seating area** 좌석 구역
set up ~을 설치하다 **outside** 밖에, 야외에(= outdoors)

6. (A) Some people are strolling along the shore.
(B) The stairs lead to the beach.
(C) They're opening a beach umbrella.
(D) The chairs are facing the water.

(A) 몇몇 사람들이 해변을 따라 거닐고 있다.
(B) 계단이 해변으로 이어지고 있다.
(C) 사람들이 비치 파라솔을 펼치고 있다.
(D) 의자들이 바다를 향해 있다.

해설 (A) 해변을 걷는 사람은 보이지 않으므로 오답.
(B) 계단이 보이지 않으므로 오답.
(C) 비치 파라솔이 이미 펼쳐져 있으므로 오답.
(D) 사람들이 앉아 있는 의자가 바다를 향해 있으므로 정답.

어휘 **stroll** 천천히 거닐다 **along the shore** 해변을 따라
stairs 계단(= staircase) **lead to** ~로 이어지다
beach umbrella 비치 파라솔 **face** v. ~을 향하다

7. **(A) They're preparing some food.**
(B) They're tying an apron.
(C) Some plates have been piled in a sink.
(D) Some food is on display in a cafeteria.

(A) 사람들이 음식을 준비하고 있다.
(B) 사람들이 앞치마를 매는 중이다.
(C) 몇몇 접시들이 싱크대에 쌓여 있다.
(D) 구내 식당에 음식이 진열되어 있다.

해설 (A) 주방에서 요리하고 있는 모습이므로 정답.
(B) 앞치마를 이미 착용하고 있으므로 오답.
(C) 싱크대에 접시가 쌓여 있는 모습은 보이지 않으므로 오답.
(D) 음식이 진열된 모습이 아니고, 장소가 부엌이므로 오답.

어휘 **prepare** ~을 준비하다 **tie** ~을 매다, 묶다 **apron** 앞치마
plate 접시 **pile** ~을 쌓다 **sink** 싱크대 **be on display**
진열되어 있다 **cafeteria** 구내 식당

8. (A) Products are being displayed in baskets.
(B) A woman is paying for her purchase.
(C) Some people are waiting in line outside a building.
(D) A vending machine is being used.

(A) 제품들이 바구니에 담겨 진열되어 있다.
(B) 여자가 구매품에 대해 지불하고 있다.
(C) 몇몇 사람들이 건물 밖에서 줄 서서 기다리고 있다.
(D) 자판기가 이용되고 있다.

해설 (A) 제품이 바구니에 담겨 진열되어 있는 모습은 보이지 않으므
로 오답.
(B) 여자가 계산대에서 계산을 하는 모습이므로 정답.
(C) 사람들이 줄을 서 있긴 하지만 건물 밖이 아니므로 오답.
(D) 자판기로 보이는 것은 없으므로 오답.

어휘 **product** 제품 **display** ~을 진열하다 **basket** 바구니
pay for one's purchase 구매품에 대해 지불하다
wait in line 줄 서서 기다리다 **outside** ~의 밖에서
vending machine 자판기

9. (A) The walls are being painted.
(B) Artwork is hanging above some furniture.
(C) The floor is being swept.
(D) Some curtains are being pulled closed.

(A) 벽에 페인트칠이 되고 있다.
(B) 미술품이 가구 위에 걸려 있다.
(C) 바닥이 빗자루로 쓸리고 있다.
(D) 커튼이 쳐지고 있다.

해설 (A) 벽에 페인트칠을 하고 있는 사람이 없으므로 오답.
(B) 소파 위로 큰 미술품이 걸려 있으므로 정답.
(C) 바닥을 쓸고 있는 사람이 보이지 않으므로 오답.
(D) 커튼을 치고 있는 사람이 보이지 않으므로 오답.

어휘 **wall** 벽 **artwork** 미술품, 예술품 **hang** 걸리다 **above**
~의 위에 **furniture** 가구 **floor** 바닥 **sweep** ~을
빗자루로 쓸다 cf. mop ~을 대걸레로 닦다 **pull A closed**
A를 잡아당겨 닫다

10. (A) There's a fountain in front of a building.
(B) A bench is being cleared off.
(C) Some people are relaxing near a fountain.
(D) Some flowers are being planted.

(A) 건물 앞에 분수대가 있다.
(B) 벤치가 깨끗이 치워지고 있다.
(C) 몇몇 사람들이 분수대 근처에서 쉬고 있다.
(D) 꽃들이 심어지고 있다.

해설 (A) 분수대는 있지만 건물이 보이지 않으므로 오답.
(B) 벤치를 치우고 있는 사람은 없으므로 오답.
(C) 분수대 주변에서 휴식을 취하는 사람들이 보이므로 정답.
(D) 꽃들이 이미 심어져 있으므로 오답.

어휘 **fountain** 분수대 **in front of** ~의 앞에 **clear off** ~을

깨끗이 치우다 relax 휴식을 취하다 near ~의 근처에서
plant ~을 심다

11. (A) Some passengers are getting off a ferry.
(B) Some buildings are located behind the hills.
(C) Containers are being unloaded from a ship.
(D) Some boats are docked in a harbor.

(A) 몇몇 승객들이 여객선에서 내리고 있다.
(B) 건물들이 언덕 뒤에 위치해 있다.
(C) 컨테이너들이 배에서 내려지고 있다.
(D) 보트 몇 대가 항구에 정박해 있다.

해설 (A) 내리고 있는 승객들은 보이지 않으므로 오답.
(B) 건물이 보이긴 하지만 언덕 뒤에 위치해 있지 않으므로 오답.
(C) 배에서 컨테이너가 내려지는 모습이 아니므로 오답.
(D) 보트가 항구에 정박해 있는 모습이므로 정답.

어휘 **passenger** 승객 **get off** ~에서 내리다 **ferry** 연락선
be located 위치해 있다 **behind** ~의 뒤에 **hill** 언덕
container 컨테이너 **unload** (짐 등을) 내리다 **be
docked** 정박해 있다 **harbor** 항구

12. (A) She's filling her bag with groceries.
(B) She's bending over to pick up an item.
(C) She's reaching for some merchandise on a shelf.
(D) She's weighing some items on a scale.

(A) 여자가 가방을 식료품으로 채우고 있다.
(B) 여자가 물건을 집기 위해 허리를 숙이고 있다.
(C) 여자가 선반에 있는 제품에 손을 뻗고 있다.
(D) 여자가 물건을 저울에 달고 있다.

해설 (A) 가방에 식료품을 넣는 모습이 아니므로 오답.
(B) 몸을 앞으로 구부린 모습이 아니므로 오답.
(C) 선반에 손을 뻗고 있지 않으므로 오답.
(D) 과일로 보이는 것을 저울에 달고 있으므로 정답.

어휘 **fill A with B** A를 B로 채우다 **grocery** 식료품 **bend
over** 허리를 굽히다, 앞으로 숙이다 **pick up** ~을 집다
item 물건 **reach for** ~에 손을 뻗다 **merchandise** 상품,
제품 **shelf** 선반 **weigh** ~의 무게를 달다 **scale** 저울

DAY 02

PART 2 고득점 기출 포인트

문제 푸는 순서

제이슨 씨는 일을 언제 시작할 계획인가요?
(A) 마케팅 회사에서요.
(B) 내년 10월이나 되어야 해요.
(C) 네, 판매 직원이에요.

해설 (A) 질문의 When을 Where로 착각하면 고르기 쉬운 오답.
(B) 미래의 특정 시점을 말하므로 정답.
(C) 의문사 의문문에 대한 정답으로 Yes/No는 불가.

어휘 **plan to do** ~할 계획이다 **probably** 아마도
sales associate 판매 직원(= sales clerk, sales
representative)

Practice

1. (C)	**2.** (C)	**3.** (A)	**4.** (B)	**5.** (C)	**6.** (B)
7. (A)	**8.** (B)	**9.** (B)	**10.** (A)	**11.** (C)	**12.** (C)
13. (C)	**14.** (A)	**15.** (A)	**16.** (A)	**17.** (B)	**18.** (C)
19. (C)	**20.** (B)				

1. When does the fresh fruit delivery arrive?
(A) She picked it last night.
(B) A delayed order.
(C) Not until next Friday afternoon.

신선한 과일 배송이 언제 도착하죠?
(A) 그녀가 그걸 어젯밤에 땄어요.
(B) 지연된 주문품이요.
(C) 다음 주 금요일 오후는 되어야 해요.

해설 과일 배송이 언제 도착하는지 묻는 When 의문문에 대해 다음
주 금요일 오후나 되어야 한다며 미래 시점을 언급한 (C)가 정답
이다. (A)는 과일 배송이 아니라 대상을 알 수 없는 She에 관해
말하는 오답이다. (B)는 질문에 쓰인 delivery에서 연상 가능한
order를 이용하여 혼동을 유발하는 함정이다.

어휘 **delivery** 배송(품) **pick** (과일, 꽃 등) ~을 따다, 꺾다
delayed 지연된 **order** 주문(품) **Not until + 시점** ~나
되어야 한디

2. Who's giving the keynote speech at the marketing
convention?
(A) It will start at around 9:30.
(B) On January 30.

(C) Check with Paul in Personnel.

누가 마케팅 컨벤션에서 기조 연설을 하나요?
(A) 9시 30분쯤에 시작할 거예요.
(B) 1월 30일이요.
(C) 인사부 폴 씨에게 확인해보세요.

해설 누가 기조 연설자인지 묻는 Who 의문문에 대해 해당 정보를 알고 있는 직원의 이름과 부서를 알려주는 (C)가 정답이다. 간접 응답 유형으로서, 직접적인 답변 대신 관련 정보를 얻을 수 있는 방법을 말해주는 답변이다. (A)와 (B)는 각각 시간과 날짜를 말하고 있으므로 When 의문문에 어울리는 반응이다.

어휘 **give a speech** 연설하다 **keynote** 기조, 주안점 **around** ~쯤 **personnel** 인사부

3. Where can I find Joe Wilson, the head of Human Resources?
(A) Go through the third door on the right.
(B) Yes, he's the supervisor of the department.
(C) I'm glad he got the promotion.

조 윌슨 인사부장님을 어디서 찾을 수 있죠?
(A) 오른편 세 번째 문으로 들어가세요.
(B) 네, 그분이 그 부서의 책임자입니다.
(C) 그분이 승진되어서 기쁩니다.

해설 Where 의문문이므로 특정 위치로 찾아가는 방법을 가르쳐 주는 (A)가 적절한 반응이다. 의문사 의문문이므로 (B)처럼 Yes/No로 대답할 수 없으며, (C)는 승진에 대한 기쁨을 나타내는 말이므로 Where 의문문과 어울리지 않는 답변이다.

어휘 **the head of Human Resources** 인사부장 **go through** ~를 지나가다, 통과하다 **on the right** 오른편에 있는 **supervisor** 책임자, 상사, 감독 **promotion** 승진, 진급

4. Who will be leading the meeting?
(A) It'll be in Conference Room C.
(B) It hasn't been decided yet.
(C) I am honored to meet you.

누가 회의를 진행할 예정인가요?
(A) 회의실 C에서 열릴 것입니다.
(B) 아직 결정되지 않았습니다.
(C) 만나 뵙게 되어 영광입니다.

해설 누가 회의를 진행할 것인지 묻는 Who 의문문에 대해 '아직 결정되지 않았다'고 응답하는 (B)가 정답이다. '모른다', '결정되지 않았다', '다른 사람에게 물어봐라'와 같은 간접 응답이 나올 수 있다는 점도 함께 생각하면서 듣는 것이 좋다.

어휘 **lead** ~을 진행하다, 이끌다 **conference room** 회의실 **be honored to do** ~하게 되어 영광이다

5. Which parking area is for the management?
(A) Approximately 200.

(B) To the national park.
(C) The one behind the building.

어느 주차 구역이 경영진을 위한 곳인가요?
(A) 대략 200개요.
(B) 국립 공원으로요.
(C) 건물 뒤에 있는 것이요.

해설 Which는 명사와 함께 쓰여 선택을 나타내는 의미로 쓰이므로 Which 다음에 이어지는 명사를 함께 잘 들어야 한다. '어느 주차 구역'인지 위치를 묻고 있으므로 대명사 one과 함께 위치 표현으로 답변하는 (C)가 정답이다.

어휘 **parking area** 주차 구역 **management** 경영(진) **approximately** 대략 **national park** 국립공원 **behind** ~ 뒤에

6. Why has the job application deadline been extended?
(A) Yes, the personnel manager.
(B) We haven't had many applicants.
(C) Three positions at our main branch.

입사 지원 마감 기한이 왜 연장된 거죠?
(A) 네, 인사부장님이요.
(B) 지원자가 많지 않았습니다.
(C) 우리 본점에 있는 세 가지 직책이요.

해설 입사 지원 마감일이 연장된 이유를 묻는 Why 의문문이므로 지원자가 많지 않았다는 사실을 알리는 (B)가 정답이다. (A)는 의문사 의문문에 어울리지 않는 Yes로 답변하는 오답이며, (C)는 job application과 연관성 있게 들리는 Three positions를 활용한 오답으로 How many 의문문에 어울리는 답변이다.

어휘 **job application** 입사 지원(서), 구직 지원(서) **deadline** 마감기한 **extend** ~을 연장하다 **personnel manager** 인사부장 **applicant** 지원자 **position** 직책, 일자리 **main branch** 본점

7. How did you find your new job?
(A) I went to a recruiting agency.
(B) About a couple of days ago.
(C) I left it in my desk.

새 직장을 어떻게 찾았어요?
(A) 채용 대행 업체에 갔어요.
(B) 약 이틀 전에요.
(C) 제가 그걸 제 책상에 넣어 두었어요.

해설 새 직장을 구한 방법을 묻는 How 의문문이므로 채용 대행 업체에 갔다는 말로 일자리를 찾은 구체적인 방법을 알려주는 (A)가 정답이다. (B)는 과거 시점 표현이므로 When 의문문에 어울리는 응답이다. (C)는 질문에 쓰인 find(찾다)에서 연상 가능한 상황인 left it in my desk(책상 안에 두었다)를 이용해 혼동을 유발하는 함정이다.

어휘 **recruiting agency** 채용 대행 업체 **about** 약, 대략 **a couple of** 둘의, 두 개의, 두 사람의 **leave** ~을 놓다, 두다

8. How long does it take to get to Detroit from here?
(A) It's been a long time since I've seen them.
(B) Six hours by car.
(C) Around 4 P.M.

여기서 디트로이트까지 가는 데 얼마나 걸리죠?
(A) 그 사람들을 본 지 오래되었어요.
(B) 자동차로 여섯 시간이요.
(C) 오후 네 시쯤이요.

해설 「How long ~?」은 지속 시간이나 기간을 묻는 의문문이며, 디트로이트까지 가는 데 걸리는 시간을 묻고 있으므로 Six hours라는 소요 시간을 말한 (B)가 정답이다.

어휘 **How long does it take to do?** ~하는 데 (시간이) 얼마나 걸리나요? **get to** ~로 가다, ~에 도착하다 **It's been a long time since** ~한 지 오래 되었다, ~한 지 오랜만이다 **around** ~쯤

9. How often do you visit your parents?
(A) Along the coastal road.
(B) About twice a year.
(C) Their visit was cut short.

부모님을 얼마나 자주 방문하세요?
(A) 해안도로를 따라서요.
(B) 대략 일 년에 두 번이요.
(C) 그분들의 방문은 짧았어요.

해설 「How often ~?」 의문문은 '얼마나 자주 ~하는가'라는 의미로 빈도를 물을 때 사용하므로 횟수로 대답하는 (B)가 정답이다.

어휘 **along** (도로 등) ~을 따라 **coastal** 해안의 **about** 약, 대략 **cut short** 서둘러 끝내다

10. Has your manager authorized your vacation leave request?
(A) I haven't actually asked him yet.
(B) Thanks. I really appreciate it.
(C) He wants to take a trip to India.

당신 부서장님께서 당신의 휴가 신청서를 승인해 주셨나요?
(A) 실은 아직 여쭤 보지 않았습니다.
(B) 고맙습니다. 정말로 감사드려요.
(C) 그는 인도로 여행을 떠나고 싶어 해요.

해설 Has로 시작하는 일반 의문문으로, 부서장이 휴가를 승인해주었는지 확인하는 질문에 대해 아직 물어보지 않았다는 말로 승인 여부를 알 수 없는 상황임을 나타내는 (A)가 정답이다.

어휘 **authorize** ~을 승인하다 **vacation leave request** 휴가 신청(서) **actually** 실은, 사실은 **appreciate** ~에 대해 감사하다 **take a trip to** ~로 여행 가다, 출장 가다

11. Did you read about the new exhibit?
(A) I'll leave at 5.
(B) I spoke with him earlier.
(C) Yes, it sounds fascinating.

새로운 전시회에 관한 글을 읽어 보셨나요?
(A) 저는 5시에 나갈 겁니다.
(B) 제가 아까 그분과 얘기했어요.
(C) 네, 대단히 흥미로운 것 같아요.

해설 일반 의문문으로 전시회 관련 글을 읽어 봤는지 확인하는 질문이므로 긍정을 나타내는 Yes와 함께 글에 대한 자신의 의견을 언급하는 (C)가 정답이다.

어휘 **exhibit** 전시회, 전시품 **leave** 나가다, 떠나다 **it sounds + 형용사** ~한 것 같다 **fascinating** 대단히 흥미로운, 매력적인

12. Has the mail arrived yet?
(A) No. They're in the bottom drawer.
(B) We're going as fast as we can.
(C) No. Are you expecting something?

혹시 우편물이 도착했나요?
(A) 아니요. 그것들은 맨 아래 서랍에 있어요.
(B) 저희는 가능한 한 빨리 가고 있어요.
(C) 아니요. 뭐 기다리는 거라도 있으세요?

해설 우편물 도착 여부를 묻는 일반 의문문이다. 이에 대해 부정을 나타내는 No와 함께 기다리는 우편물이라도 있는지 되묻는 (C)가 정답이다.

어휘 **bottom** 맨 아래의 **drawer** 서랍 **as ~ as one can** 가능한 한 ~한[~하게] **expect** (오기로 되어 있는 대상) ~을 기다리다

13. Is this year's trade fair going to be in Peru?
(A) I don't know anyone in our office.
(B) They have a good trade relationship.
(C) Why don't you ask Tara in Marketing?

올해 무역 박람회가 페루에서 열리는 건가요?
(A) 저는 우리 사무실에 아는 사람이 아무도 없어요.
(B) 그들은 좋은 무역 관계를 맺고 있습니다.
(C) 마케팅부의 타라 씨에게 물어보는 게 어때요?

해설 올해 무역 박람회가 페루에서 열리는지 확인하는 일반 의문문에 대해 그 정보를 확인할 수 있는 방법으로 마케팅부의 타라 씨에게 물어보도록 권하는 (C)가 정답이다. 「Why don't you ~?」는 '~하는 게 어때요?'를 뜻하는 제안 표현으로 직접적인 답변 대신 다른 방법을 권할 때 자주 쓰인다. 이처럼 확인하기 위해 묻는 일반 의문문에 대해 Yes/No를 생략하고 되묻거나 대안을 제시하는 등 여러 유형으로 답변하는 것이 가능하다는 점을 기억해 두면 좋다.

어휘 **trade fair** 무역 박람회 **relationship** 관계 **Why don't you ~?** ~하는 게 어때요?

14. Did you send out the notices about the new vacation policy?
(A) I thought you were supposed to do it.
(B) I'll make a hotel reservation then.

(C) To work on the poster designs.

새 휴가 정책에 관한 공지들을 발송하셨나요?
(A) 전 당신이 하기로 되어 있는 줄 알았어요.
(B) 그럼 제가 호텔을 예약할게요.
(C) 포스터 디자인 작업을 하기 위해서요.

해설 새 휴가 정책에 관한 공지들을 발송했는지 확인하는 일반 의문문이므로 상대방이 하기로 되어 있는 줄 알았다는 말로 발송하지 않았음을 나타내는 (A)가 정답이다.

어휘 send out ~을 발송하다 notice 공지 policy 정책, 방침 be supposed to do ~하기로 되어 있다, ~할 예정이다 make a reservation 예약하다 work on ~에 대한 작업을 하다

15. Aren't you going to Dr. Brown's retirement party?
(A) Yes, but I'll be a little late.
(B) No, I won't retire for another five years.
(C) There was a huge crowd.

브라운 박사님 퇴임식에 가시지 않나요?
(A) 네, 하지만 저는 좀 늦을 거예요.
(B) 아뇨, 저는 앞으로 5년 동안 은퇴하지 않을 것입니다.
(C) 엄청 많은 사람들이 있었어요.

해설 행사 참석 여부를 묻는 부정 의문문이므로 긍정을 의미하는 Yes와 함께 좀 늦을 것 같다는 말로 추가 정보를 제시하는 (A)가 정답이다. (B)는 질문에 쓰인 retirement와 일부 발음이 같은 retire를 이용해 혼동을 유발하는 답변으로 자신의 은퇴 시점을 말하고 있어 질문의 의도에 맞지 않는 오답이다.

어휘 retirement 은퇴, 퇴임 retire 은퇴하다 another + 숫자 ~만큼 더 huge 엄청난, 거대한 crowd 사람들, 군중

16. Why don't you ask for a two-day break from work?
(A) I already did that.
(B) He's been very busy recently.
(C) For about one week.

이틀 동안의 업무 휴가를 요청해 보는 게 어때요?
(A) 이미 그렇게 했어요.
(B) 그분은 최근에 아주 바쁘셨어요.
(C) 약 일주일 동안이요.

해설 「Why don't you ~?」는 '~하는 게 어때요?'라는 의미로 제안할 때 사용하며, 시작 부분의 Why만 듣고 이유를 묻는 질문과 혼동하지 말아야 한다. 이 질문에서는 이틀 동안 휴가를 내도록 제안하고 있으므로 휴가를 내는 일을 that으로 지칭해 그렇게 했다는 의미를 나타내는 (A)가 정답이다.

어휘 Why don't you ~? ~하는 게 어때요? ask for ~을 요청하다 break 휴가, 휴식 recently 최근에

17. Could you cover my shift at the restaurant this Saturday?
(A) Yes, we open at 9 A.M. on weekends.
(B) I'm afraid I have plans with my family.

(C) Maybe we should make a reservation.

이번 주 토요일에 제 레스토랑 교대 근무를 대신해 주실 수 있으세요?
(A) 네, 저희는 주말마다 오전 9시에 문을 엽니다.
(B) 유감스럽지만 가족과 함께 하는 계획이 있어서요.
(C) 아마 우리가 예약을 해야 할 겁니다.

해설 「Could you ~?」로 시작하는 요청 의문문으로 대신 근무할 수 있는지 묻는 것에 대해 다른 계획이 있음을 알리는 말로 거절의 뜻을 나타내는 (B)가 정답이다. (A)는 수락을 뜻하는 Yes 뒤에 이어지는 말이 요청 사항과 어울리지 않는 내용이며, (C)는 restaurant에서 연상 가능한 자리 예약을 언급한 오답이다.

어휘 cover ~을 대신하다 shift 교대 근무(조) on weekends 주말마다 I'm afraid (that) (부정적인 일에 대해) 유감스럽지만 ~입니다 make a reservation 예약하다

18. Do you have the tickets for tonight's performance, or do you still have to buy them?
(A) No, she can't play.
(B) The newly released film.
(C) I bought them two days ago.

오늘밤 공연 입장권을 갖고 계신가요, 아니면 여전히 구입하셔야 하나요?
(A) 아뇨, 그분은 연주할 수 없어요.
(B) 새로 개봉한 영화요.
(C) 이틀 전에 샀어요.

해설 입장권을 갖고 있는지, 아니면 사야 하는지 묻는 선택 의문문이므로 tickets를 them으로 지칭해 이틀 전에 샀다는 의미로 입장권을 갖고 있다는 뜻을 나타낸 (C)가 정답이다.

어휘 performance 공연, 연주(회) play 연주하다, 공연하다 release ~을 개봉하다, 공개하다, 출시하다

19. The gym has another branch in Boston, doesn't it?
(A) It's an old machine.
(B) About a membership rate.
(C) Yes, there's one downtown.

그 체육관은 보스턴에 지점이 하나 더 있지 않나요?
(A) 그건 오래된 기계입니다.
(B) 회비에 관해서요.
(C) 네, 시내에 하나 있어요.

해설 보스턴에 지점이 하나 더 있는지 확인하는 부가 의문문이므로 긍정을 의미하는 Yes와 함께 branch를 대명사 one으로 받아 시내에 하나 있다는 말을 덧붙인 (C)가 정답이다. (A)와 (B)는 gym에서 연상 가능한 machine과 membership rate을 각각 이용한 오답이다.

어휘 gym 체육관 another 또 다른 하나의 branch 지점, 지사 membership 회원권, 회원 자격 rate 요금 downtown 시내에

20. I just received the annual earnings report.

(A) At the beginning of the year.

(B) The sales figures are impressive, right?

(C) He earns a high salary.

제가 막 연간 수익 보고서를 받았습니다.

(A) 올해 초예요.

(B) 매출 수치가 인상적이죠?

(C) 그분은 높은 연봉을 받습니다.

해설 자신이 막 연간 수익 보고서를 받았음을 알리는 평서문에 대해 그 보고서에 포함된 매출 수치의 특성에 대해 되묻는 (B)가 정답이다. (A)는 시점 표현이므로 When 의문문에 어울리는 반응이며, (C)는 earnings와 일부 발음이 같은 earns를 이용해 혼동을 유발하는 함정이다.

어휘 annual 연간의, 연례적인 earnings 수익, 소득 at the beginning of ~ 초에, ~가 시작될 때 sales 매출, 판매, 영업 figure 수치, 숫자 impressive 인상적인 earn ~을 벌다, 얻다

DAY 03

PART 3, 4 패러프레이징

감 잡기 QUIZ

Question 1 refers to the following conversation.

여: 전 교육 시간에 못 갈 것 같아요.

남: 걱정 마세요. 제가 회의록을 이메일로 보내 드릴 수 있어요. 그러면 당신은 최소한 우리가 논의했던 것을 알 거예요.

여: 고마워요. 그러면 정말 좋겠네요.

어휘 make it to ~에 제때 가다 training session 교육 시간 minutes 회의록 at least 최소한 | review ~을 검토하다 material 자료

1. 남자는 무엇을 할 것이라고 말하는가?

(A) 자료를 검토한다.

(B) 자료를 보낸다.

Question 2 refers to the following conversation.

여: 시장 보고서가 어떻게 진행되어가나요?

남: 힘겹게 하는 중이에요. 지난 분기에 그게 어떤 식으로 되었는지 보면 도움이 될 텐데요.

여: 아, 제가 예전 것 한 부를 드릴 수 있어요.

어휘 How's A going? A가 어떻게 진행되고 있나요? struggle 몸부림치다, 힘겹게 애쓰다 quarter 분기 copy 사본 | demonstration 시연

2. 남자는 무엇을 원하는가?

(A) 샘플 문서

(B) 제품 시연

Question 3 refers to the following conversation.

남: 죄송합니다. 저희는 현재 구매 가능한 참나무 탁자들이 없습니다. 다음 주에 새로 배송을 받을 거예요.

여: 전시품은 구매 가능한가요?

남: 저희 매니저님께 확인해 보겠습니다.

어휘 available 이용 가능한, 구매 가능한 shipment 배송(물) floor model 전시품 | missing 분실된 out of stock 재고가 없는

3. 무엇이 문제인가?

(A) 몇몇 제품들이 분실되었다.

(B) 몇몇 제품들이 재고가 없다.

Question 4 refers to the following talk.

시작하기에 앞서, 7시까지는 쉬는 시간이 없음을 알려 드립니다. 이곳 강의실에 계시는 분들을 위해 입구 근처에 가벼운 간식이 차려져 있습니다. 15분 후에 시작하도록 하겠습니다.

어휘 remind A (that) A에게 ~라고 상기시키다 break 휴식 시간 light snack 가벼운 간식 set up ~을 설치하다, 차리다 entrance 입구 in + 시간 ~ 후에

4. 몇몇 청자들에게 무엇을 할 것이 권장되는가?

(A) 다과를 먹을 것

(B) 설문을 작성할 것

Question 5 refers to the following announcement.

지금 C구역의 많은 소설책들이 반값에 구매 가능하오니, 꼭 확인해보시기 바랍니다. 그 중에는 베스트셀러 작품들이 다수 있고, 일부는 상을 받은 영화로 각색되기도 하였습니다.

어휘 fiction 소설 for half price 반값에 make sure 반드시 ~하다 check out 흥미로운 것을 살펴보다, 알아보다 adapt ~을 영화로 각색하다 award-winning 상을 받은 film 영화 | discounted 할인된 promotional 홍보의 flyer 전단

5. 청자들은 C구역에서 무엇을 찾을 수 있는가?

(A) 할인 제품

(B) 홍보 전단

Question 6 refers to the following advertisement.

이 프로그램이 매우 특별한 점은 회사의 웹 사이트에서 무료로 다운로드 될 수 있다는 점입니다. 단, 여러분의 운영 시스템과 호환되는 것을 다운로드 받도록 하세요.

어휘 unique 독특한, 특별한 **at no cost** 무료로 **be sure to do** 반드시 ~하다 **compatible with** ~와 호환되는 **operating system** 운영 시스템 | **lightweight** 가벼운

5. 제품에 대해 무엇이 특별한가?
(A) 무료로 사용할 수 있다.
(B) 가볍다.

문제 푸는 순서

Questions 1-3 refer to the following conversation.

남: 저는 토요일에 회사에 출근해서 월요일 오전까지 마감인 이 예산 보고서를 끝내려고 합니다.
여: 토요일에요? 아직 못 들으셨어요? 사무실 전체에 랜선을 새로 깔아야 해서 바닥을 뜯어낸답니다. 사무실에서 컴퓨터를 전혀 쓸 수 없을 거예요. 모든 전원을 뽑아 놓을 거니까요.
남: 뭐라고요? 저는 전혀 몰랐네요! 그럼 부장님에게 가서 보고서를 화요일 오전까지 낼 수 있게 해달라고 해야겠네요.
여: 그럼, 부장님께서 기한을 연장해 주길 바랍니다.

어휘 **due + 일시** ~까지 하기로 예정된 **get A done** A를 하다, 마치다 **tear up** ~을 뜯다, 찢다 **lay** ~을 놓다, 두다 **LAN cable** 랜선 **throughout** ~ 도처에, ~ 전체에 걸쳐 **unplugged** 전원이 뽑힌 **ask A to do** A에게 ~할 것을 요청하다 **boss** 상사 **hand in** ~을 제출하다 **extension** 기한 연장

1. 남자는 무엇을 할 작정이었는가?
(A) 회사에 늦게 오기
(B) 보고서를 일찍 제출하기
(C) 회의 일정을 다시 잡기
(D) 주말에 일하기

해설 남자가 하려고 한 일이 무엇인지 묻고 있다. 남자의 첫 대사에서 주말에 나와 보고서 작성을 완료할 생각이라고(I'm going to come in to work on Saturday to finish this budget report) 밝히고 있으므로 정답은 (D)가 된다.

어휘 **intend to do** ~할 의도이다 **reschedule** ~의 일정을 다시 잡다

Paraphrase work on Saturday → Work on the weekend

2. 남자는 왜 기분이 상했는가?
(A) 중요한 회의에 대해 알지 못했다.
(B) 갑자기 타지로 가야 한다.

(C) 상사가 어려운 프로젝트를 주었다.
(D) 컴퓨터를 쓸 수 없을 것이다.

해설 남자의 기분이 상한 것은 여자의 말을 듣고 난 이후이므로, 이유는 여자의 대사에서 알 수 있다. 남자가 주말에 컴퓨터를 사용할 수 없게 되었기 때문이라고(You won't be able to use any computer in the office)하므로 정답은 (D)임을 알 수 있다.

어휘 **upset** 기분이 상한 **go out of town** 타지에 나가다 **unavailable** 이용할 수 없는

Paraphrase won't be able to use → unavailable

3. 남자는 상사에게 무엇을 할 것을 요청할 것인가?
(A) 마감일을 연장할 것
(B) 조수를 고용할 것
(C) 영업관련 제안에 대해 들을 것
(D) 급여를 인상할 것

해설 제안이나 요청 사항을 묻는 문제는 주로 대화의 마지막 부분에 나온다. 여기서도 남자의 마지막 대사에 드러나 있다. 보고서를 월요일이 아닌 화요일에 제출하게 해달라고 요청하겠다고(I'd better go ask the boss to let me hand in the report on Tuesday morning) 하므로 (A)가 정답이다.

어휘 **deadline** 마감일 **hire** ~을 고용하다 **assistant** 비서, 조수 **proposal** 제안서 **raise** ~을 올리다, 인상하다 **salary** 급여

Practice

1. (A)	**2.** (B)	**3.** (D)	**4.** (D)	**5.** (C)	**6.** (B)
7. (C)	**8.** (D)	**9.** (C)	**10.** (C)	**11.** (B)	**12.** (D)

Questions 1-3 refer to the following conversation.

W: Adam, can I ask you something?
M: Of course. 1 **I'm just restocking our tennis equipment displays.**
W: Those have been selling well recently. In fact, that's what I wanted to talk about. What do you think about starting a program to teach people the basics of tennis?
M: Hmm... I wouldn't be against it, but my main concern would be how many people we would be able to use as instructors. 2 **Do we have anyone on our staff who has actually played on a tennis team?**
W: Several, actually, including me.
M: Oh. In that case, 3 **let's start by conducting a survey to see how many customers are interested. I'll put together some questions tomorrow.**

W: Okay, thanks! Let me know if I can be of any assistance.

여: 애덤 씨, 뭐 좀 여쭤 봐도 될까요?

남: 물론입니다. 저는 그저 우리 테니스 장비 진열품을 다시 채워 넣는 중입니다.

여: 그 제품들이 최근에 계속 잘 판매되고 있죠. 실은, 그 부분과 관련해서 얘기하고 싶었어요. 사람들에게 테니스의 기초를 가르쳐 주는 프로그램을 시작하는 것에 대해 어떻게 생각하세요?

남: 흠… 반대는 하지 않겠지만, 가장 큰 우려 사항은 우리가 얼마나 많은 사람들을 강사로 이용할 수 있을까 하는 점입니다. 우리 직원 중에 누구든 실제로 테니스 팀에서 뛰어본 적이 있는 사람이 있나요?

여: 사실, 여러 명 있어요, 저를 포함해서요.

남: 아. 그렇다면, 얼마나 많은 고객들이 관심이 있는지 알아볼 수 있는 설문 조사를 실시하는 것으로 시작해 봐요. 제가 내일 몇몇 질문들을 정리해 볼게요.

여: 좋아요, 감사합니다! 제가 무엇이든 도와 드릴 수 있다면 말씀해 주세요.

어휘 restock (제품, 재고 등) ~을 다시 채우다, ~을 보충하다 equipment 장비 recently 최근에 in fact 실은, 실제로 teach A B A에게 B를 가르치다 basics 기초, 기본 be against ~에 반대하다 main 가장 큰, 주된, 중요한 concern 우려, 걱정 be able to do ~할 수 있다 instructor 강사 actually 실제로, 사실 several 여러 명, 여러 개 including ~을 포함해 in that case (앞서 언급된 것에 대해) 그렇다면, 그런 경우라면 by (방법) ~하는 것으로, ~함으로써 conduct ~을 실시하다, ~을 수행하다 survey 설문 조사(지) interested 관심 있는 put together (이것저것 모아) ~을 정리하다, ~을 준비하다 let A know A에게 알리다 be of assistance 도움이 되다

---

1. 화자들이 어디에서 근무하고 있을 것 같은가?
(A) 스포츠 용품 매장에서
(B) 잡지 출판사에서
(C) 철물점에서
(D) 체육관에서

해설 화자들의 근무 장소를 묻는 문제의 경우, 업체 이름이나 건물 이름, 특정 업무나 활동, 제공 서비스 등과 관련된 정보를 통해 단서를 파악해야 한다. 남자가 대화 초반부에 테니스 장비 진열품을 다시 채워 넣는 중이라고(I'm just restocking our tennis equipment displays) 언급하고 있는데, 이는 스포츠 용품을 판매하는 곳의 직원이 하는 일에 해당되므로 (A)가 정답이다.

어휘 goods 제품, 상품 publisher 출판사

---

2. 남자가 여자에게 무엇에 관해 묻는가?
(A) 스포츠 토너먼트의 일정
(B) 직원들의 경험

(C) 참가자의 숫자
(D) 일부 강습의 비용

해설 남자가 무엇에 관해 묻는지 묻고 있으므로 남자의 말에 집중해 의문문 또는 ask, wonder, curious, want to know, tell me 등 궁금증이나 정보 전달 요청과 관련된 표현을 통해 제시되는 정보를 들어야 한다. 대화 중반부에 남자가 직원들 중에 누구든 실제로 테니스 팀에서 뛰어본 사람이 있는지(Do we have anyone on our staff who has actually played on a tennis team?) 묻는 부분이 있다. 이는 직원들의 경기 경험과 관련해 묻는 것이므로 (B)가 정답이다.

어휘 participant 참가자 cost 비용

Paraphrase anyone on our staff who has actually played on a tennis team
→ experience of staff members

---

3. 남자가 내일 무엇을 할 것인가?
(A) 회의를 개최하는 일
(B) 배송을 처리하는 일
(C) 업무 공간을 청소하는 일
(D) 설문 조사를 준비하는 일

해설 남자가 내일 무엇을 할 것인지 묻고 있으므로 남자의 말에 집중해 들어야 하며, 질문에 제시된 시점 표현 tomorrow와 함께 계획이나 앞으로의 일정, 제안 사항 등을 알리는 부분을 놓치지 말아야 한다. 남자가 대화 후반부에 설문 조사를 실시하는 것으로 시작하자는 말과 함께 내일 질문들을 정리하겠다고(~ let's start by conducting a survey ~ I'll put together some questions tomorrow) 알리고 있다. 이는 설문 조사를 준비하는 과정에 해당되므로 (D)가 정답이다.

어휘 hold ~을 개최하다, ~을 열다 process ~을 처리하다 prepare ~을 준비하다

Paraphrase survey / put together some questions
→ Prepare a survey

Questions 4-6 refer to the following conversation.

W: Hi, Bert. I'm going to order some pizza for everyone in the office. What kind of toppings would you like?

M: Thanks, but I think I'll skip the pizza. **4 I just started following a new diet. I'm trying to get in shape.**

W: Oh, no problem! So what kind of things are you eating?

M: It's a Mediterranean diet, with lots of fish and vegetables. **5 I found it on a Web site. I could forward the link to you,** if you're interested.

W: Sure! I'd love to try it. But, **6 the problem is I'm too busy to cook at home.** That's why I end up ordering takeout food so often.

여: 안녕하세요, 버트 씨. 제가 사무실에 계신 모든 분을 위해 피자를 좀 주문하려고 합니다. 어떤 종류의 토핑을 원하시나요?

남: 말씀은 감사하지만, 저는 피자를 건너뛸 생각입니다. 막 새로운 다이어트를 하기 시작했거든요. 몸매를 가꾸려 하는 중입니다.

여: 아, 괜찮습니다! 그럼, 어떤 종류의 것들을 드시나요?

남: 이게 지중해식 식사인데, 생선과 채소가 많이 들어 갑니다. 한 웹 사이트에서 찾았어요. 그 링크를 전송해 드릴 수 있습니다, 관심 있으시면요.

여: 물론이죠! 정말 해 보고 싶네요. 하지만, 문제는 제가 집에서 요리하기엔 너무 바쁘다는 점입니다. 그게 바로 제가 결국 포장 음식을 그렇게 자주 주문하게 되는 이유죠.

어휘 order ~을 주문하다 would like ~을 원하다, ~로 하고 싶다 skip ~을 건너뛰다 follow ~을 따라 하다, ~을 따르다 diet 다이어트, 식습관 try to do ~하려 하다 get in shape 몸매를 가꾸다 Mediterranean 지중해의 forward A to B A를 B에게 전송하다 interested 관심 있는 would love to do 꼭 ~하고 싶다 too A to do ~하기엔 너무 A한 That's why 그게 바로 ~하는 이유입니다 end up -ing 결국 ~하게 되다 takeout food 포장 음식

4. 남자는 자신이 최근에 무엇을 하기 시작했다고 말하는가?
(A) 체육관에 가는 일
(B) 레스토랑에서 주문하는 일
(C) 사무실에서 근무하는 일
(D) 다이어트를 하는 일

해설 남자가 최근에 무엇을 하기 시작했다고 말하는지 묻고 있으므로 남자의 말에 집중해 들어야 하며, 질문에 제시된 recently 또는 이와 유사한 가까운 과거 시점 표현과 함께 언급되는 정보를 놓치지 말아야 한다. 대화 초반부에 남자가 막 새로운 다이어트를 하기 시작했다고(I just started following a new diet) 알리고 있으므로 (D)가 정답이다.

어휘 recently 최근에

5. 남자가 무엇을 하겠다고 제안하는가?
(A) 식사를 준비하는 일
(B) 책을 빌려 주는 일
(C) 웹 사이트 링크를 보내는 일
(D) 한 과정을 설명하는 일

해설 남자가 무엇을 하겠다고 제안하는지 묻고 있으므로 남자의 말에 집중해 제안 표현과 함께 제시되는 정보를 들어야 한다. 대화 중반부에 남자가 자신이 찾은 웹 사이트를 언급하면서 그 링크를 전송해 줄 수 있다고(I found it on a Web site. I could forward the link to you ~) 제안하고 있으므로 (C)가 정답이다.

어휘 offer to do ~하겠다고 제안하다 prepare ~을 준비하다 lend ~을 빌려 주다 explain ~을 설명하다 process (처리) 과정

Paraphrase Web site / forward the link
→ Send a Web site link

6. 여자가 어떤 문제를 언급하는가?
(A) 음식 알레르기가 있다.
(B) 요리할 시간이 없다.
(C) 엉뚱한 음식을 주문했다.
(D) 제품을 구입할 여유가 없다.

해설 여자가 어떤 문제를 언급하는지 묻고 있으므로 여자의 말에 집중해 부정적인 정보를 찾아야 한다. 여자가 대화 마지막 부분에 집에서 요리하기엔 너무 바쁘다는(~ the problem is I'm too busy to cook at home) 문제를 알리고 있는데, 이는 요리할 시간이 없다는 뜻이므로 (B)가 정답이다.

어휘 cannot afford (금전적, 시간적으로) ~에 대한 여유가 없다

Paraphrase too busy to cook → has no time to cook

Questions 7-9 refer to the following announcement.

Good morning, Flex Gym members. We are very happy to announce some good news. We have been trying to boost our membership this year, and we are delighted that **7 we have finally reached our goal of having five hundred members!** To celebrate this, we are hosting a party on Friday evening, and all members are welcome to attend. **8 Anyone who comes to the party will receive a free gym bag.** We hope to see you all there! And don't forget, **9 every weekend we are offering seminars on healthy eating and nutrition.** If you'd like to register, please speak to a staff member.

안녕하세요, 플렉스 짐 회원 여러분. 몇 가지 좋은 소식을 공지해 드리게 되어 대단히 기쁩니다. 저희가 올해 회원 규모를 늘리기 위해 계속 노력해 왔으며, 500명의 회원 보유라는 **목표에 미침내 도달하게 되어** 기쁘게 생각합니다. 이를 기념하기 위해, 저희가 금요일 저녁에 파티를 주최하므로, 모든 회원 여러분께서는 얼마든지 참석하셔도 좋습니다. 파티에 오시는 분은 누구든 무료 체육관 가방을 받으시게 될 것입니다. 여러분 모두 그 자리에서 뵙기를 바랍니다! 그리고 잊지 마셔야 하는 점은, 매주 주말에 저희가 건강에 좋은 식사 및 영양에 관한 세미나를 제공한다는 사실입니다. 등록하고자 하시는 분은, 직원에게 말씀하시기 바랍니다.

어휘 try to do ~하기 위해 노력하다, ~하려 하다 boost ~을 늘리다, ~을 증대하다, ~을 촉진하다 membership 회원 규모, 회원 자격 finally 마침내, 결국 reach ~에 도달하다, ~에 이르다 celebrate ~을 기념하다, ~을 축하하다 host ~을 주최하다 be welcome to do 얼마든지 ~해도 좋다, ~하는 것을 환영하다 attend 참석하다 receive ~을 받다 free 무료의 forget 잊다 offer ~을 제공하다 nutrition 영양 would like to do ~하고자 하다, ~하고 싶다

register 등록하다

7. 플렉스 짐이 무엇을 기념하는가?
(A) 몇몇 기계를 설치한 것
(B) 몇몇 개조 공사를 완료한 것
(C) 목표에 도달한 것
(D) 신규 지점을 개장한 것

해설 플렉스 짐이 무엇을 기념하는지 묻고 있으므로 이 업체 이름과 함께 언급되는 긍정적인 정보를 찾아야 한다. 담화 초반부에 화자가 500명의 회원을 보유하는 목표에 마침내 도달했다는(~ we have finally reached our goal of having five hundred members) 사실을 알리고 있으므로 (C)가 정답이다.

어휘 install ~을 설치하다 complete ~을 완료하다 renovation 개조, 보수 branch 지점, 지사

Paraphrase reached our goal → Reaching a target

8. 청자들이 어떻게 무료 선물을 받을 수 있는가?
(A) 웹 사이트를 방문함으로써
(B) 신규 회원을 소개함으로써
(C) 강좌에 등록함으로써
(D) 행사에 참석함으로써

해설 무료 선물이 언급되는 부분에서 그 제공 방식과 관련된 정보를 파악해야 한다. 화자가 담화 중반부에 파티에 오는 사람은 누구든 무료 체육관 가방을 받을 것이라고(Anyone who comes to the party will receive a free gym bag) 언급하고 있다. 이는 행사에 참석하기만 하면 무료 선물을 받는다는 뜻이므로 (D)가 정답이다.

어휘 refer ~을 소개하다, ~을 추천하다 sign up for ~에 등록하다, ~을 신청하다

Paraphrase Anyone who comes to the party → By attending an event

9. 화자가 주말마다 무슨 일이 일어난다고 말하는가?
(A) 식사가 제공된다.
(B) 직원이 교육 받는다.
(C) 세미나가 개최된다.
(D) 가격이 할인된다.

해설 주말마다 무슨 일이 일어난다고 말하는지 묻고 있으므로 질문에 제시된 weekends와 함께 언급되는 정보를 찾아야 한다. 화자가 담화 후반부에 매주 주말에 건강에 좋은 식사 및 영양에 관한 세미나를 제공한다고(~ every weekend we are offering seminars on healthy eating and nutrition) 알리고 있다. 이는 주말마다 세미나가 개최된다는 뜻이므로 (C)가 정답이다.

어휘 provide ~을 제공하다 train ~을 교육하다 hold ~을 개최하다, ~을 열다 reduce ~을 할인하다, ~을 감소시키다, ~을 줄이다

Paraphrase every weekend we are offering seminars → Seminars are held

Questions 10-12 refer to the following telephone message.

Hello, Ms. Crawford. This is Jonathan from Hartman Security Solutions returning your call. You mentioned in your message that **10** **you want to enhance security at your business by having some cameras installed.** That's certainly something we can help you with. However, we won't be able to start on this task until the beginning of next month. **11** **We're currently relocating to new premises, and this process will disrupt our work for about a week.** In the meantime, **12** **could you send me a summary of how much money you have available for the project?** That way, I can choose suitable devices and equipment.

안녕하세요, 크로포드 씨. 저는 귀하께 답신 전화 드리는 하트먼 씨큐리티 솔루션즈의 조너선입니다. 귀하께서는 메시지를 통해 몇몇 카메라를 설치해 놓는 방법으로 업체의 보안을 강화하고 싶으시다고 언급하셨습니다. 이는 분명 저희가 도움을 드릴 수 있는 부분입니다. 하지만, 저희는 다음 달 초나 되어야 이 일을 시작할 수 있을 것입니다. 저희가 현재 새로운 부지로 이전하고 있는데, 이 과정이 약 일주일 동안 저희 업무에 지장을 줄 것입니다. 그 사이에, 프로젝트를 위해 얼마를 이용하실 수 있는지에 대한 요약 내용을 저에게 보내 주시겠습니까? 그렇게 하시면, 적합한 기기와 장비를 선택할 수 있습니다.

어휘 return one's call ~의 전화에 답신하다 mention that ~라고 언급하다 enhance ~을 강화하다, ~을 향상시키다 business 업체, 회사, 사업 by (방법) ~하는 방법으로, ~함으로써 have A p.p. A를 ~해 놓다, A를 ~되게 하다 install ~을 설치하다 help A with B B에 대해 A를 돕다 however 하지만, 그러나 not A until B B나 되어야 A하다 be able to do ~할 수 있다 task 일, 업무 currently 현재, 지금 relocate to ~로 이전하다 premises 부지, 구내 process 과정 disrupt ~에 지장을 주다, ~을 방해하다 in the meantime 그 사이에, 그러는 동안 summary 요약(본) have A available 이용할 수 있는 A를 갖고 있다 that way 그렇게 하면, 그런 방법으로 suitable 적합한, 어울리는 device 기기, 장치 equipment 장비

10. 청자는 무엇을 하고 싶어 하는가?
(A) 회사 직원을 교육하는 일
(B) 업무용 컴퓨터를 업그레이드하는 일
(C) 건물 보안을 향상시키는 일
(D) 새로운 서비스를 홍보하는 일

해설 화자는 담화 초반부에 청자가 카메라 설치를 통해 업체의 보안을 강화하기를 원한다고 말한(~ you want to enhance security at your business by having some cameras installed) 사실

을 밝히고 있다. 이는 업체가 있는 건물의 보안을 향상시키는 일을 의미하므로 (C)가 정답이다.

어휘 train ~을 교육하다 improve ~을 향상시키다, ~을 개선하다 promote ~을 홍보하다

Paraphrase enhance security at your business
→ Improve building security

11. 새로운 프로젝트가 왜 지연될 것인가?
(A) 책임자가 시간이 나지 않는다.
(B) 업체가 이전하는 중이다.
(C) 일부 제품이 품절된 상태이다.
(D) 일부 공구가 배송되지 않았다.

해설 지연 사실을 알리는 부분에서 그 이유를 파악해야 한다. 담화 중반부에 화자가 현재 새로운 부지로 이전하는 중이라고(We're currently relocating to new premises ~) 알리면서 이 일로 인해 업무에 지장을 받을 것이라고 말하므로 (B)가 정답이다.

어휘 supervisor 책임자, 상사, 감독 unavailable (사람) 시간이 나지 않는, (사물) 이용할 수 없는 sold out 품절된, 매진된 tool 공구, 도구

Paraphrase relocating to new premises
→ business is relocating

12. 화자가 청자에게 무엇을 제공하도록 요청하는가?
(A) 제품 카탈로그
(B) 사업 계약서
(C) 배송 주소
(D) 프로젝트 예산

해설 화자가 담화 후반부에 프로젝트에 대해 얼마나 많은 비용을 이용할 수 있는지에 대한 요약 내용을 보내 달라고(~ could you send me a summary of how much money you have available for the project?) 요청하는 부분이 있다. 이는 프로젝트 예산 규모를 확인하고자 요청하는 말이므로 (D)가 정답이다.

어휘 contract 계약(서) budget 예산

Paraphrase how much money you have available for the
project → project budget

DAY 04

PART 3,4 시각자료 연계 문제

문제 푸는 순서

Questions 1-3 refer to the following talk.

오늘 마운트포드 공원에서 열리는 음악 축제에 와 주셔서 감사합니다! 거의 오후 4시가 다 되었으니 저희 다음 밴드가 무대에서 연주할 시간이 되었네요. 시작하기에 앞서, 여러분께 이 행사가 왜 중요한지에 대해 말씀드리겠습니다. 오늘 행사의 모든 수익금, 예를 들어 티켓 매출과 식음료 매출 같은 것들이 지역 아동 자선단체로 갈 것입니다. 그러니, 저희가 제공해드린 맛있는 음식과 음료를 꼭 구매해주시기 바랍니다. 이 수익금은 시내에 새로운 아동 도서관을 짓는 데 사용될 것입니다. 도서관 디자인을 보고 싶으시면 저희 웹 사이트 www.musicfest.com을 방문해 주세요.

마운트포드 공원 음악 축제	
오후 2:00	The Sunny Days
오후 3:30	Svetlana Roussev
오후 4:00	Jasmin & Lynn
오후 5:30	Blinding Lights

어휘 almost 거의(= nearly) perform 공연하다, 연주하다 on stage 무대에서 remind A about B A에게 B에 대해 상기시키다 proceeds 수익금 sales 판매, 매출 beverage 음료 local 지역의 children's charity 자선 단체 make sure 확실히 ~하도록 하다 delicious 맛있는 be put towards (비용의 일부가) ~에 보태지다 downtown 시내에

1. 시각자료를 보시오. 누가 콘서트에서 다음으로 공연할 것인가?
(A) The Sunny Days
(B) Svetlana Roussev
(C) Jasmin & Lynn
(D) Blinding Lights

해설 시각자료를 먼저 파악하고 문제와 어떤 연관성이 있는지 미리 감을 잡아야 한다. 시각자료를 보면 시간대별로 음악가 이름이 함께 나와 있고, 선택지에는 음악가 이름이 나열되어 있으므로 담화에서는 시간 표현이 언급될 것을 예상할 수 있다. 언급되는 시간 표현을 잘 듣고 그에 해당하는 음악가를 고르면 된다. 담화 첫 부분에서 4시가 거의 다 되었으니 다음 밴드가 공연할 차례라고 안내하고(It's almost 4 P.M., so it's nearly time for our next band to perform ~) 있다. 시각자료에서 오후 4시에 해당하는 음악가를 확인하면 (C)가 정답임을 알 수 있다.

2. 화자에 따르면 왜 음악 축제가 특별한가?
(A) 지역 음악가들이 특별히 출연한다.
(B) 자선 단체를 위해 모금하고 있다.
(C) 텔레비전에 방송되고 있다.
(D) 역사적인 건물에서 열리고 있다.

해설 이 행사가 중요한 이유를 말해주겠다고 한 뒤 모든 수익금이 아이들을 위한 자선단체로 간다는(All of the proceeds from today's event, ~ will go to the local children's charity) 사실을 전하고 있다. 따라서 이를 자선단체를 위해 모금하고(raise money) 있다고 표현한 (B)가 정답이다.

어휘 feature v. ~을 특별히 포함하다 raise money 모금하다 broadcast ~을 방송하다 be held 열리다, 개최되다

Paraphrase proceeds from today's event, ~ will go to the local children's charity
→ raising money for charity

3. 화자는 왜 청자들에게 웹 사이트를 방문하라고 하는가?
(A) 건물 디자인을 보기 위해
(B) 행사 티켓을 구매하기 위해
(C) 대회에 참가하기 위해
(D) 기부를 하기 위해

해설 담화 마지막에 If you'd like to see a design of the library, you can visit our Web site at www.musicfest.com이라고 말하며 도서관 디자인을 보고 싶어 하는 사람들에게 웹 사이트 방문을 권하고 있다.

어휘 view ~을 보다 enter ~에 참가하다 competition 대회, 시합 make a donation 기부하다 cf. donation 기부

Practice

1. (D)	2. (A)	3. (C)	4. (C)	5. (D)	6. (C)
7. (C)	8. (C)	9. (A)	10. (B)	11. (B)	12. (B)

Questions 1-3 refer to the following conversation and chart.

M: Excuse me. **1** I'd like to purchase this sofa for my new apartment.
W: No problem! That's one of our most popular sofas. Where is your apartment located? We will deliver the item for you. Here's our list of delivery prices.
M: I actually live in a town around 50 kilometers from the city. But, **2** I'd like to receive the item by tomorrow. I'm happy to pay a higher charge.
W: Sure. We can arrange that for you. By the way, **3** I could change the cushions that come with the sofa, if you prefer a different style.
M: No, thanks. I like the ones that are on display.

남: 실례합니다. 제가 새 아파트에서 쓰기 위해 이 소파를 구입하고자 합니다.
여: 알겠습니다! 그 제품은 가장 인기 있는 저희 소파들 중의 하나입니다. 아파트가 어디에 위치해 있나요? 저희가 제품을 배달해 드리겠습니다. 여기 저희 배달 가격 목록입니다.
남: 제가 사실 시에서 약 50킬로미터 떨어진 곳에 있는 마을에 살고 있어요. 하지만, 제품을 내일까지 받았으면 합니다. 기꺼이 더 높은 요금을 지불하겠습니다.
여: 좋습니다. 그렇게 조치해 드릴 수 있습니다. 그건 그렇고, 소파에 딸려 있는 쿠션을 바꿔 드릴 수 있습니다, 다른 스타일을 선호하시면요.
남: 아뇨, 괜찮습니다. 진열되어 있는 것이 마음에 듭니다.

배달 요금	
익일	7.00 달러
2-3일	5.50 달러
4-7일	4.00 달러
8일 이상	2.50 달러

어휘 would like to do ~하고자 하다, ~하고 싶다 popular 인기 있는 be located 위치해 있다 actually 사실, 실은 around 약, 대략 receive ~을 받다 by (기한) ~까지 charge (청구) 요금 arrange ~을 조치하다, ~을 조정하다, ~을 마련하다 by the way (화제 전환 시) 그건 그렇고, 그런데 come with ~에 딸려 있다 prefer ~을 선호하다 on display 진열되어 있는, 전시되어 있는

1. 대화가 어디에서 진행되고 있을 것 같은가?
(A) 의류 매장에서
(B) 전자 제품 매장에서
(C) 사무용품 매장에서
(D) 가구 매장에서

해설 남자가 대화를 시작하면서 특정 소파를 this sofa로 지칭해 그것을 구입하고 싶다(I'd like to purchase this sofa ~) 알리고 있다. 이는 가구 제품 매장에서 할 수 있는 말에 해당되므로 (D)가 정답이다.

어휘 clothing 의류, 옷 electronics 전자 제품

Paraphrase sofa → furniture

2. 시각자료를 보시오. 남자가 배달에 얼마나 많은 비용을 지불할 것인가?
(A) $7.00
(B) $5.50
(C) $4.00
(D) $2.50

해설 대화 중반부에 남자가 제품을 내일까지 받고 싶다고(I'd like to

receive the item by tomorrow) 알리고 있다. 시각자료에서 익일 배송에 해당되는 첫 번째 줄에 요금이 $7.00로 표기되어 있으므로 (A)가 정답이다.

3. 여자가 무엇을 하겠다고 제안하는가?
(A) 영수증을 제공하는 일
(B) 품질 보증 기간을 연장하는 일
(C) 제품을 변경하는 일
(D) 가격을 할인하는 일

해설 여자가 무엇을 하겠다고 제안하는지 묻고 있으므로 여자의 말에 집중해 제안 표현과 함께 제시되는 정보를 찾아야 한다. 대화 후반부에 여자가 소파에 딸려 있는 쿠션을 바꿔 줄 수 있다고(~ I could change the cushions that come with the sofa ~) 제안하고 있는데, 이는 제품을 변경하는 일에 해당되므로 (C)가 정답이다.

어휘 offer to do ~하겠다고 제안하다 provide ~을 제공하다 receipt 영수증 extend ~을 연장하다 warranty 품질 보증(서) reduce ~을 할인하다, ~을 줄이다

Paraphrase change the cushions that come with the sofa
→ Change an item

Questions 4-6 refer to the following conversation and timeline.

M: Hi, Ella. Our shareholders have requested a progress update on **4** **the new range of refrigerators we are developing.** What should I tell them?

W: Well, **5** **our engineers just finished producing the prototype, and we've moved on to the next stage now.** That will probably continue for at least one week.

M: Sounds good. Do you have any reports I can show to our shareholders?

W: Yes, **6** **there's an extensive report on the previous stage.** I'll e-mail it to you immediately.

남: 안녕하세요, 엘라 씨. 주주들께서 우리가 개발하고 있는 새로운 냉장고 제품군에 대한 작업 진행 정보를 요청하셨어요. 제가 뭐라고 말씀드려야 하죠?

여: 음, 우리 엔지니어들이 시제품 생산을 막 끝마쳤고, 현재 다음 단계로 넘어간 상태입니다. 이 단계가 아마 최소 일주일은 지속될 겁니다.

남: 좋습니다. 제가 주주들께 보여 드릴 수 있는 어떤 보고서라도 갖고 계신가요?

여: 네, 이전 단계에 관한 광범위한 보고서가 있습니다. 제가 즉시 이메일로 보내 드리겠습니다.

1단계	2단계
시장 조사 연구	기획 및 디자인
4단계	3단계
테스트 및 개선	시제품 생산

어휘 shareholder 주주 request ~을 요청하다, ~을 요구하다 progress (작업 등의) 진행, 진척 range 제품군, 종류, 범위 refrigerator 냉장고 develop ~을 개발하다 produce ~을 생산하다 prototype 시제품 move on to (과정) ~로 넘어가다, ~로 나아가다 continue 지속되다 at least 최소한, 적어도 extensive 광범위한, 폭넓은 previous 이전의, 과거의 immediately 즉시 research 조사, 연구 study 연구 improvement 개선, 향상

4. 업체에서 어떤 종류의 제품을 생산할 것 같은가?
(A) 건설 도구
(B) 피트니스 장비
(C) 주방 기기
(D) 노트북 컴퓨터

해설 어떤 종류의 제품을 생산할 것 같은지 묻고 있으므로 제품 명칭이나 특징 등과 관련된 정보를 찾아야 한다. 남자가 대화 초반부에 소속 회사를 we로 지칭해 현재 개발 중인 새 냉장고 제품군을 (~ the new range of refrigerators we are developing) 언급하고 있으므로 (C)가 정답이다.

어휘 construction 건설, 공사 tool 도구, 공구 equipment 장비 appliance (가전) 기기

Paraphrase refrigerators → Kitchen appliances

5. 시각자료를 보시오. 프로젝트가 현재 진행표의 어느 단계에 해당되는가?
(A) 1단계
(B) 2단계
(C) 3단계
(D) 4단계

해설 작업 순서도가 제시되는 시각자료 문제의 경우, 각 순서에 해당되는 일을 미리 확인해두는 것이 좋으며, 특정 작업을 기준으로 앞뒤 순서에 해당되는 일을 파악하는 방식으로 단서가 제시될 수 있으므로 유의해야 한다. 대화 중반부에 여자가 시제품 생산을 막 끝마쳐서 현재 다음 단계로 넘어간 상태라고(~ just finished producing the prototype, and we've moved on to the next stage now) 알리고 있다. 시각자료에서 시제품 생산을 뜻하는 Prototype Production이 STAGE 3에 해당되며, 그 다음 단계로 넘어갔다고 했으므로 STAGE 4인 (D)가 정답이다.

어휘 timeline 진행표, 일정표 currently 현재, 지금

6. 여자가 곧이어 무엇을 할 것인가?
(A) 주주들과 만나는 일
(B) 일정표를 업데이트하는 일
(C) 문서를 보내는 일
(D) 전화를 거는 일

해설 특정 화자가 곧이어 할 일을 묻는 경우, 대부분 대화 후반부에 단서가 제시되며, 계획이나 일정, 제안 등과 관련된 말을 통해 단서를 파악할 수 있다. 대화 맨 마지막 부분에 여자가 보고서를 언급하면서 이메일로 즉시 보내겠다고(~ there's an extensive report on the previous stage. I'll e-mail it to you immediately) 알리고 있으므로 (C)가 정답이다.

어휘 meet with (약속하고) ~와 만나다 make a phone call 전화하다

Paraphrase report / mail it to you → Send a document

Questions 7-9 refer to the following talk and map.

It's my great pleasure to welcome you all to the opening of Wellboro Public Library. I'd like to start by **7** **thanking Shaw Enterprises for giving us ten desktop computers for our IT Lounge.** We really appreciate your generosity. Now, let me briefly describe the library's facilities. Well, apart from the IT Lounge, which is at the back near the fiction collection, **8** **we also have a photocopier room, which is just next to the newspaper section.** But first, **9** let's go inside and take a look around the library so you can see our book collections. Please follow me.

웰보로 공공 도서관의 개장식에 오신 모든 분을 맞이하게 되어 대단히 기쁩니다. 저희 IT 라운지에 10대의 데스크톱 컴퓨터를 전달해 주신 쇼 엔터프라이즈 사에 감사 드리는 것으로 시작하고자 합니다. 저희는 그 너그러움에 정말 감사 드립니다. 이제, 도서관 시설물을 간단히 설명해 드리겠습니다. 음, 소설 소장 구역 근처의 뒤쪽에 있는 IT 라운지 외에도, 신문 구역 바로 옆에, 복사실도 있습니다. 하지만 먼저, 여러분께서 저희 도서 소장품을 보실 수 있도록 도서관 내부로 들어가서 한 번 둘러 보겠습니다. 저를 따라 오시기 바랍니다.

웰보로 공공 도서관

A번 방	소설 소장 구역	B번 방
비소설 소장 구역	안내 데스크	학술 저널
C번 방　신문	잡지	D번 방

어휘 by (방법) ~하는 것으로, ~함으로서 appreciate ~에 대해 감사하다 generosity 너그러움, 관대함 let me do 제가 ~해 드리겠습니다 briefly 간단히, 잠시 describe ~을 설명하다, ~을 묘사하다 facility 시설(물) apart from ~ 외에도, ~을 제외하고 near ~ 근처에 fiction 소설 collection 소장(품), 수집(품) photocopier 복사기 next to ~ 옆에 section 구역, 구획, 부분, 부문 take a look around ~을 한 번 둘러 보다 follow ~을 따라 가다 non-fiction 비소설의 academic journal 학술 저널

7. 화자가 무엇에 대해 쇼 엔터프라이즈에 감사하는가?
(A) 프로젝트에 자금을 제공한 것
(B) 직원을 제공한 것
(C) 컴퓨터를 기증한 것
(D) 건물을 개조한 것

해설 무엇에 대해 쇼 엔터프라이즈에 감사하는지 묻고 있으므로 이 업체 이름 및 감사 표현이 언급되는 부분에서 그 이유를 찾아야 한다. 담화 초반부에 화자가 IT 라운지에 10대의 데스크톱 컴퓨터를 전달해 준 쇼 엔터프라이즈 사에 감사한다는(~ thanking Shaw Enterprises for giving us ten desktop computers for our IT Lounge) 말을 전하고 있으며, 이는 컴퓨터를 기증한 것으로 볼 수 있으므로 (C)가 정답이다.

어휘 fund v. ~에 자금을 제공하다 provide ~을 제공하다 donate ~을 기증하다, ~을 기부하다 renovate ~을 개조하다, ~을 보수하다

Paraphrase giving us ten desktop computers
→ Donating computers

8. 시각자료를 보시오. 화자의 말에 따르면, 사람들이 어디에서 문서를 복사할 수 있는가?
(A) A번 방에서
(B) B번 방에서
(C) C번 방에서
(D) D번 방에서

해설 건물 안내도나 거리 지도 등이 시각 자료로 제시되는 경우, 특정 위치를 찾아야 하므로 출발점을 비롯해 이동 방식, 위치 관계를 나타내는 동사와 전치사 등에 특히 유의해 들어야 한다. 화자가 담화 후반부에 복사실이 신문 구역 바로 옆에 위치해 있다는(~ we also have a photocopier room, which is just next to the newspaper section) 사실을 밝히고 있다. 시각 자료에서 왼쪽 하단에 Newspapers로 표기된 구역에 있고, 그 바로 옆에 위치한 방이 C이므로 (C)가 정답이다.

9. 곧이어 무슨 일이 있을 것인가?
(A) 건물 견학 시간이 제공될 것이다.
(B) 특별 손님이 소개될 것이다.
(C) 도서 사인회 행사가 개최될 것이다.
(D) 라이브 공연이 열릴 것이다.

해설 화자가 담화 맨 마지막 부분에 도서관 안으로 들어가서 한 번

둘러 보자고(~ let's go inside and take a look around the library ~) 제안하고 있다. 이는 건물을 견학하는 일을 의미하므로 (A)가 정답이다.

어휘 introduce ~을 소개하다, ~을 도입하다 book signing 도서 사인회 hold ~을 개최하다, ~을 열다 performance 공연, 연주(회) take place (일, 행사 등이) 열리다, 개최되다, 발생되다

Paraphrase go inside and take a look around the library
→ building tour will be given

Questions 10-12 refer to the following excerpt from a meeting and pie chart.

Okay, let's begin the meeting. **10 I'm sorry that we are starting 15 minutes later than planned**, but we had to wait for our Plymouth branch workers to arrive. So, we have been surveying our customers for the past two months, and we specifically asked them to suggest ways they would like us to improve our business. As you can see from the chart, the most popular suggestion is to expand our menus. However, **11 what I found most surprising is that 36 percent of customers made this other suggestion**. Before we discuss the customer feedback in depth, **12 I'd like to thank Ms. Ellwood for organizing this useful survey.**

좋습니다, 회의를 시작하겠습니다. 계획보다 15분 늦게 시작하게 되어 죄송하지만, 우리 플리머스 지점 직원들께서 도착하시기를 기다려야 했습니다. 자, 우리가 지난 2개월 동안 우리 고객들을 대상으로 계속 설문 조사해 왔으며, 우리는 특히 고객들께 우리 회사를 개선하기를 원하시는 방법을 제안하도록 요청 드렸습니다. 차트에서 보실 수 있다시피, 가장 일반적인 제안 사항이 우리 메뉴를 확대하는 것입니다. 하지만, 제가 가장 놀랍다고 생각한 것은 36퍼센트의 고객들께서 이렇게 다른 제안을 하셨다는 점입니다. 우리가 고객 의견을 깊이 있게 논의하기에 앞서, 이 유용한 설문 조사를 마련해 주신 엘우드 씨께 감사드리고자 합니다.

고객 설문 조사 제안 사항

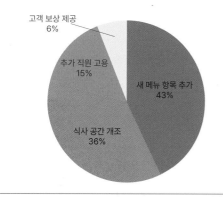

고객 보상 제공
6%

추가 직원 고용
15%

식사 공간 개조
36%

새 메뉴 항목 추가
43%

어휘 than planned 계획보다 branch 지점, 지사 arrive 도착하다 survey v. ~에게 설문 조사하다 n. 설문 조사(지) past 지난, 과거의 specifically 특히, 구체적으로 ask A to do A에게 ~하도록 요청하다 suggest ~을 제안하다 would like A to do A에게 ~하기를 원하다 improve ~을 개선하다, ~을 향상시키다 popular 일반적인, 대중적인 suggestion 제안, 의견 expand ~을 확대하다, ~을 확장하다 however 하지만, 그러나 find A B A를 B하다고 생각하다 surprising 놀라게 하는 discuss ~을 논의하다, ~을 이야기하다 feedback 의견 in depth 깊이 있게, 심층적으로 organize ~을 마련하다, ~을 준비하다 useful 유용한 reward 보상 hire ~을 고용하다 additional 추가적인 renovate ~을 개조하다, ~을 보수하다 add ~을 추가하다

10. 화자가 왜 사과하는가?
(A) 연사가 불참한 상태이다.
(B) 회의가 지연되었다.
(C) 방을 이용할 수 없다.
(D) 기기가 오작동했다.

해설 질문에 제시된 apologize나 sorry, I'm afraid, unfortunately 등과 같이 사과 또는 유감을 나타내는 표현과 함께 언급되는 정보를 찾아야 한다. 화자가 담화를 시작하면서 사과의 말과 함께 계획보다 15분 늦게 회의를 시작하게 된 점을(I'm sorry that we are starting 15 minutes later than planned ~) 이유로 언급하고 있으므로 (B)가 정답이다.

어휘 absent 불참한, 부재 중인, 결근한 delay ~을 지연시키다 unavailable 이용할 수 없는 device 기기, 장치 malfunction 오작동하다

Paraphrase starting 15 minutes later than planned
→ delayed

11. 시각자료를 보시오. 화자가 어느 고객 제안 사항에 놀라워하는가?
(A) 새 메뉴 항목 추가
(B) 식사 공간 개조
(C) 추가 직원 고용
(D) 고객 보상 제공

해설 차트나 그래프가 시각자료로 제시되는 경우, 각 항목의 수치 표현 및 이를 비교하는 내용이 대화 중에 언급될 수 있다는 점에 유의하면서 듣는 것이 좋다. 화자가 담화 후반부에 36퍼센트의 고객이 제안한 것이 놀라웠다고(~ what I found most surprising is that 36 percent of customers made this other suggestion) 언급하고 있다. 시각자료에서 왼쪽 아래에 36%로 표기된 항목이 Renovate dining area이므로 (B)가 정답이다.

12. 화자가 왜 엘우드 씨를 언급하는가?
(A) 청자들에게 연설하도록 요청하기 위해
(B) 기여에 대해 감사하기 위해

(C) 신임 회사 임원을 발표하기 위해
(D) 상에 대한 후보로 지명하기 위해

해설 담화 맨 마지막 부분에 화자가 유용한 설문 조사를 마련해 준 엘우드 씨에게 감사하다는(I'd like to thank Ms. Ellwood for organizing this useful survey) 말을 전하고 있다. 이는 설문 조사를 통해 고객 의견을 파악하는 데 기여한 것에 대한 감사의 인사에 해당되므로 (B)가 정답이다.

어휘 invite A to do A에게 ~하도록 요청하다 address v. ~에게 연설하다 contribution 기여, 공헌 executive 임원, 이사 nominate A for B A를 B에 대한 후보로 지명하다

Paraphrase thank Ms. Ellwood for organizing this useful survey → thank her for her contribution

DAY 05

PART 3,4 의도 파악 문제

감 잡기 QUIZ

Question 1 refers to the following conversation.

> 여: 안녕하세요, 마크 씨. 제가 지금 작업 중인 새 광고에 관해 당신의 의견이 필요합니다.
> 남: 그럼요. 아직 당신의 최신 디자인을 제출하지 않았다는 것을 알고 있습니다. 왜 지체되는 거죠?
> 여: 음, 제품이 보여지는 방식은 마음에 들어요, 하지만 자막에 어느 서체를 활용해야 할지 여전히 확실하지 않습니다.
> 남: 저, 모든 사람들이 지난 번 광고에 당신이 만들었던 것을 마음에 들어 했어요.
> 여: 흠... 그건 한 번도 고려해 보지 않았어요. 그게 어떻게 보일지 확인해 볼게요.

어휘 Would you mind -ing? ~해 주시겠어요? help A with B B에 대해 A를 돕다 opinion 의견 ad 광고 work on ~을 맡아 작업하다 be happy to do 기꺼이 ~하다 notice (that) ~임을 알아차리다 turn in ~을 제출하다 latest 최신의 hold A up A를 지체시키다 how A looks A의 모습, A가 보이는 방식 font 서체 caption 자막 consider ~을 고려하다 | deadline 마감기한 extend ~을 연장하다 unsuccessful 성공적이지 못한 helpful 도움이 되는, 유익한

1. 여자가 "그건 한 번도 고려하지 않았어요"라고 말할 때 암시하는 것은 무엇인가?
   (A) 마감기한이 연장되었다.

(B) 프로젝트가 성공적이지 못했다.
(C) 화제가 논의되지 않았다.
(D) 아이디어가 도움이 되었다.

해설 남자가 모든 이들이 지난 번 광고에 여자가 만들었던 것을 마음에 들어 했다고(everyone liked the one you made for the last ad) 말한 것에 대한 반응으로 쓰인 말이다. 바로 그 다음에 그게 어떻게 보일지 확인해 보겠다는(Let me see how it looks) 말한 것을 통해 남자가 말한 대로 하려 한다는 것을 알 수 있으므로 이를 아이디어가 도움이 되었다는 말로 바꿔 표현한 (D)가 정답이다.

Question 2 refers to the following conversation.

> 여: 오늘밤에 늦게까지 일하세요? 다른 누군가가 아직 여기 있을 줄은 몰랐어요.
> 남: 재고 목록을 확인하는 일을 끝마쳐야 했지만, 지금 다 완료되었습니다.
> 여: 아, 하지만 시간을 보세요. 버스 운행이 종료되었을 것 같아요.
> 남: 네, 분명 제 집으로 가는 막차를 놓쳤습니다. 우스터로 가는 택시비가 얼마나 할지 아시나요?
> 여: 확실하지 않지만, 걱정하지 마세요. 저는 오늘 운전해서 왔어요.
> 남: 아, 저를 집에 데려다 주시겠어요? 감사드립니다.

어휘 work late 늦게까지 일하다 anyone else 다른 누군가 finish -ing ~하는 것을 끝마치다 inventory 재고 (목록) stop -ing ~하는 것을 멈추다 run 운행하다 definitely 분명히, 틀림없이 miss ~을 놓치다 Do you have any idea ~? ~인지 아시나요? cost ~의 비용이 들다 worry about ~에 대해 걱정하다 drive 차를 몰고 오다, 가다 would you mind -ing? ~해주시겠어요? appreciate ~에 대해 감사하다 | express ~을 표현하다 regret 유감(의 뜻) offer a ride 차로 태워 주다 explain ~을 설명하다 delay 지연, 지체 request ~을 요청하다 assistance 도움

2. 여자는 왜 "저는 오늘 운전해서 왔어요"라고 말하는가?
   (A) 유감을 표현하기 위해
   (B) 차로 태워 주기 위해
   (C) 지연 상황을 설명하기 위해
   (D) 도움을 요청하기 위해

해설 여자가 걱정하지 말라는 말과 함께(don't worry about that) 해당 문장을 말하고 있고, 뒤이어 남자가 그에 대해 감사하다고 (Oh, would you mind taking me home? I'd appreciate it) 말하고 있다. 이는 여자가 차로 태워주겠다고 제안하는 것에 대해 감사하는 내용이므로 (B)가 정답이다.

Question 3 refers to the following talk.

> 오늘, 여러분께서는 저희 부서 편집자 몇 분과 이야기를 나눌 수 있는 기회를 갖게 되실 것입니다. 이분들께서는 여러분의 전문 영역을 알아내 드릴 수 있을 것이며, 여러분 각자의 장점에 어울리는 일을 찾아 주실 뿐만 아니라 여러분께서 함께 일하시게 될 곳들에 관한 더 많은 정보도 제공해 주실 것입니다. 저희가 오늘 약간 일손이 부족한 관계로, 시간이 조금 걸릴 수도 있습니다. 그 사이에, 여러분께서는 근무 경력 관련 양식을 작성해 주시면 조금 더 순조롭게 과정이 진행되도록 만드실 수 있습니다. 이 양식은 뒤쪽의 책상에서 찾아보실 수 있습니다.

어휘 have a chance to do ~할 기회를 갖다 division (회사 등의) 부, 과 editor 편집자 figure out ~을 알아내다 area of expertise 전문 영역 assignment (할당된) 일, 임무 match ~에 어울리다 strength 장점, 강점 as well as ~뿐만 아니라 short-staffed 일손이 부족한 a while 잠시, 잠깐 in the meantime 그 사이에, 그러는 동안 make A 형용사 A를 ~하게 만들다 process 과정 smoother 더 순조로운 fill out ~을 작성하다 work history 근무 경력 form 양식 | thorough 철저한, 빈틈 없는 complain about ~에 대해 불만을 제기하다 explain that ~임을 설명하다 position 일자리, 직책

3. 화자가 "시간이 조금 걸릴 수도 있습니다"라고 말하는 이유는 무엇인가?
(A) 면접이 철저하게 진행되기를 원하고 있다.
(B) 청자들에게 대기하도록 요청하고 있다.
(C) 바쁜 것에 대해 불만을 제기하고 있다.
(D) 일자리가 많지 않다는 점을 설명하고 있다.

해설 오늘 일손이 조금 부족하다면서(We are a little short-staffed today) 이 말을 하는데, 일 처리가 조금 늦어질 수도 있으니 기다려 달라는 의미로 사용된 것이다. 따라서 대기하도록 요청한다는 의미로 쓰인 (B)가 정답이다.

Question 4 refers to the following telephone message.

> 안녕하세요, 존슨 씨. 저는 <캐슬뷰>에서 전화 드리는 클레어입니다. 유감스럽게도 귀하께서 선택하신 카펫의 가격이 뛰어올랐으며, 2층에도 같은 것을 계속 사용할 경우, 예상 비용을 초과하게 될 것입니다. 귀하께서는 꼭 예산 범위 내에 머물러 있기를 원하신다는 점을 알고 있기 때문에 다른 선택권에 대해서도 마음을 열고 고려해 보시기를 바랍니다. 제가 귀하의 사무실에 유사한 디자인으로 된 샘플을 갖다 놓았으므로 한 번 확인해 보십시오. 가구를 들여 놓는 작업을 시작하기 전에 카펫 설치 작업을 완료해야 하므로 곧 귀하의 결정과 함께 제게 다시 연락 주시기 바랍니다.

어휘 jump up 뛰어 오르다 continue -ing 계속 ~하다 go over ~을 초과하다 projected 예상된 keep within ~ 이내로 유지하다 budget 예산 be open to ~에 대해 마음을 열다 option 선택권 leave A in B A를 B에 놓다, 두다 similar 유사한 give it a look 한 번 보다

place ~을 놓다, 두다 get back to ~에게 다시 연락하다 decision 결정 soon 곧, 머지 않아 hire ~을 고용하다 location 위치, 지점 item 제품, 물품 full 꽉 찬, 가득 찬

4. 화자가 "다른 선택권에 대해서도 마음을 열고 고려해 보시기를 바랍니다."라고 말할 때 암시하는 것은 무엇인가?
(A) 새로운 팀이 고용될 것이다.
(B) 위치가 변경될 수도 있다.
(C) 다른 제품이 사용되어야 한다.
(D) 일일 회의 일정이 꽉 찼다.

해설 청자가 선택한 카펫이 예산을 초과하기 때문에 다른 선택권에 대해 마음을 열고 고려해 보라고 말한 뒤, 유사한 디자인으로 된 샘플을 가져다 두었으니 확인해 보라고(I left a sample of a similar design ~ so give it a look) 하는 것으로 보아, 다른 선택권에 대해 고려해 보라는 말은 예산에 맞추기 위해 다른 카펫 제품을 이용해야 한다는 뜻임을 알 수 있다. 따라서 (B)가 정답이다.

문제 푸는 순서

Questions 1-3 refer the following excerpt from a meeting.

> 그럼, 여러분께 제안된 로비 디자인을 보여드리겠습니다. 보시다시피, 저는 현대적인 개방형 디자인을 사용하였으며, 가구를 최소화하고 밝은 색으로 벽을 칠했습니다. 또한 공간에 보다 흥미로운 모습을 주기 위해 벽에 다양한 종류의 그림을 걸었습니다. 제 생각에 손님들이 호텔에 체크인 하러 도착하실 때 좋은 첫 인상을 받게 되실 것 같습니다. 전체적으로 저는 이 디자인에 만족하는데요, 여러분들도 기꺼이 이 디자인을 받아들이시면 좋겠습니다. 잠재적인 문제점들이 보이신다면, 지금이 바로 말씀해 주실 때입니다.

어휘 proposed 제안된 modern 현대적인 open 열린, 개방형의 minimal 아주 적은, 최소의 furnishing 가구, 비품 brightly 밝게 include ~을 포함시키다 a variety of 다양한 종류의 artwork 미술품, 예술 작품 look 모습, 외관 first impression 첫인상 overall 대체로, 전반적으로 be happy with ~을 마음에 들어 하다 be happy to do 기꺼이 ~하다 run with (생각·방법을) 받아들이다, 이용하기 시작하다 potential 잠재적인 speak up 거리낌없이 말하다

1. 화자는 누구일 것 같은가?
(A) 유지보수 기술자
(B) 채용 대리인
(C) 재정 고문
(D) 인테리어 디자이너

해설 자신이 담당한 로비 디자인을 보여주면서 현대적인 개방형에 가구를 최소화하고 밝은 색으로 벽을 칠했다는 디자인상의 특징을 설명하고 있으므로 화자는 인테리어 디자이너일 것으로 추측할 수 있다. 따라서 (D)가 정답이다.

어휘 maintenance 유지 보수 technician 기술자 recruitment 채용 agent 대리인, 중개상 financial 재정의 advisor 고문, 조언자

2. 어떤 유형의 업체가 논의되고 있는가?
(A) 식당
(B) 극장
(C) 호텔
(D) 박물관

해설 담화 중반부에 호텔에 체크인하러 온 손님들이 좋은 첫인상을 받게 될 것이라고(~ guests will have a good first impression when they arrive to check in at the hotel) 말하는 데서 논의의 대상이 되는 업체는 호텔임을 알 수 있다. 따라서 (C)가 정답이다.

어휘 business 업체

3. 화자는 왜 "지금이 바로 말씀해 주실 때입니다"라고 말하는가?
(A) 변경 사항을 제안하기 위해
(B) 소음에 대해 불만을 제기하기 위해
(C) 손님을 소개하기 위해
(D) 의견을 요청하기 위해

해설 소개한 디자인에 혹시라도 잠재적인 문제가 보인다면 지금 말해 달라고 하는 것은 디자인에 대한 의견을 달라는 뜻이므로 (D)가 정답이다.

어휘 complain about ~에 대해 불만을 제기하다 introduce ~을 소개하다 request ~을 요청하다 feedback 의견

Practice

1. (C)	**2.** (B)	**3.** (B)	**4.** (B)	**5.** (A)	**6.** (B)
7. (B)	**8.** (C)	**9.** (B)	**10.** (C)	**11.** (C)	**12.** (B)

Questions 1-3 refer to the following conversation.

W: Hi, Mr. Goldman. I'm calling from the catering company you hired **1** for your office party. **I tried to get a hold of the menu items you requested.**

M: Oh, will you be able to provide the sushi platter?

W: We could, but **2** **we are really trying to stay within the budget you gave us.** The sushi will cost $600.

M: I think we can afford that. Also, **3** I wanted to ask if we could swap the corn soup with some miso soup.

W: Sure. That won't be a problem.

여: 안녕하세요, 골드먼 씨. 귀하께서 사무실 파티를 위해 고용하신 출장 요리 제공 업체에서 전화 드렸습니다. 제가 귀하께서 요청하신 메뉴 제품들을 구해 보려 했습니다.

남: 아, 초밥 모음 요리를 제공해 주실 수 있는 건가요?

여: 해 드릴 순 있지만, 저희에게 제공해 주신 예산에서 정말로 벗어나지 않게 하려 하고 있습니다. 초밥 비용이 600달러가 될 겁니다.

남: 저희가 그 정도는 감당할 수 있을 것 같아요. 그리고, 옥수수 수프를 미소 수프로 바꿀 수 있을지 여쭤 보고 싶었어요.

여: 물론입니다. 그건 문제 없을 겁니다.

어휘 catering 출장 요리 제공(업) hire ~을 고용하다 try to do ~하려 하다, ~하려 노력하다 get a hold of ~을 구하다, ~을 찾아내다 request ~을 요청하다, ~을 요구하다 be able to do ~할 수 있다 provide ~을 제공하다 platter 큰 접시, 큰 접시에 나오는 모음 요리 stay within ~에서 벗어나지 않다 budget 예산 cost ~의 비용이 들다 can afford (시간적, 금전적으로) ~을 감당할 수 있다, ~에 대한 여유가 있다 ask if ~인지 물어 보다 swap A with B A를 B로 바꾸다

1. 대화가 주로 무엇에 관한 것인가?
(A) 구직 면접
(B) 행사 개최 장소
(C) 파티 메뉴
(D) 손님 명단

해설 여자가 대화 초반부에 상대방인 남자의 사무실 파티 및 남자가 요청한 메뉴 제품을 언급한(~ for your office party. I tried to get a hold of the menu items you requested) 뒤로 특정 음식과 관련해 이야기하고 있으므로 (C)가 정답이다.

어휘 venue 개최 장소, 행사장

2. 여자가 "초밥 비용이 600달러가 될 겁니다"라고 말할 때 무엇을 의미하는가?
(A) 할인이 제공될 것이다.
(B) 예산이 초과될 수 있다.
(C) 주문품이 배송되었다.
(D) 제품 가격이 부정확하게 책정되었다.

해설 여자가 대화 중반부에 남자가 제공한 예산에서 벗어나지 않게 하려 한다고(~ we are really trying to stay within the budget you gave us) 언급하면서 '초밥 비용이 600달러가 될 겁니다'라고 말하는 흐름이다. 이는 초밥 비용이 많이 나오는 것에 따라 비용을 예산 범위 내에서 유지하지 못할 가능성이 있음을 뜻하는 말이므로 (B)가 정답이다.

어휘 provide ~을 제공하다 exceed ~을 초과하다 order 주문(품) priced 가격이 책정된 incorrectly 부정확하게

3. 남자가 무엇에 관해 묻는가?
(A) 배송을 지연시키는 일

(B) 제품을 변경하는 일

(C) 오찬 모임을 마련하는 일

(D) 상품권을 사용하는 일

해설 대화 후반부에 남자가 옥수수 수프를 미소 수프로 바꿀 수 있을지 물어보고 싶었다고(I wanted to ask if we could swap the corn soup with some miso soup) 알리고 있으므로 제품 변경을 뜻하는 (B)가 정답이다.

어휘 delay ~을 지연시키다, ~을 미루다 arrange ~을 마련하다, ~을 조치하다 gift certificate 상품권

Paraphrase swap the corn soup with some miso soup
→ Changing an item

Questions 4-6 refer to the following conversation.

W: Before we finish your interview, I'd like to discuss **4** our health and safety course. All of our new employees must complete it within their first month of employment.

M: No problem. I know that safety is important in a factory. By the way, if I get this job, **5** will I need to work on Saturdays or Sundays?

W: **6** It's our policy that staff are never asked to work any hours outside of their normal schedules. We try to prioritize the well-being of staff.

여: 면접 끝마치기 전에, 저희 보건 안전 과정을 이야기해 드리고자 합니다. 모든 저희 신입 사원은 반드시 고용 첫 달 내에 그 과정을 완료해야 합니다.

남: 좋습니다. 안전이 공장 내에서 중요하다는 점을 알고 있습니다. 그건 그렇고, 제가 이 일자리를 얻게 되면, 매주 토요일이나 일요일에 근무해야 하나요?

여: 직원들이 정규 업무 일정 외에는 어떤 시간이든 절대 일하도록 요청 받지 않는다는 것이 저희 정책입니다. 저희는 지원들의 복지를 우선시하려 하고 있습니다.

어휘 discuss ~을 이야기하다, ~을 논의하다 health and safety 보건 안전 complete ~을 완료하다 within ~ 이내에 employment 고용, 취업 by the way (화제 전환 시) 그건 그렇고, 그런데 will need to do ~해야 할 것이다 policy 정책 be asked to do ~하도록 요청 받다 outside of ~ 외에, ~을 벗어나서 normal 정규의, 정상의, 보통의 try to do ~하려 하다, ~하려 노력하다 prioritize ~을 우선시하다 well-being 복지, 행복

4. 신입 사원들은 한 달 내에 무엇을 반드시 해야 하는가?

(A) 판매 목표를 충족하는 일

(B) 한 가지 과정을 완료하는 일

(C) 일부 장비를 구입하는 일

(D) 몇몇 책임자들과 만나는 일

해설 질문에 제시된 new employees 및 within one month가 언급되는 부분에서 단서를 찾아야 한다. 여자가 대화 초반부에 보건 안전 과정을 언급하면서 신입 사원이 반드시 고용 첫 달에 그 과정을 완료해야 한다고(~ our health and safety course. All of our new employees must complete it within their first month of employment) 알리고 있으므로 (B)가 정답이다.

어휘 meet (요구, 조건 등) ~을 충족하다 sales 판매(량), 영업, 매출 purchase ~을 구입하다 equipment 장비 meet with (약속하고) ~와 만나다

5. 남자가 무엇에 관해 묻는가?

(A) 주말마다 근무하는 것

(B) 오리엔테이션에 참가하는 것

(C) 서류를 제출하는 것

(D) 연봉을 받는 것

해설 남자가 무엇에 관해 묻는지 묻고 있으므로 남자의 말에 집중해 의문문 또는 ask, wonder, curious, want to know, tell me 등 궁금증이나 정보 전달 요청과 관련된 표현을 통해 제시되는 정보를 찾아야 한다. 대화 중반부에 남자가 매주 토요일이나 일요일에 근무해야 하는지(~ will I need to work on Saturdays or Sundays?) 묻고 있으므로 (A)가 정답이다.

어휘 join ~에 참가하다, ~에 합류하다 submit ~을 제출하다, ~을 내다 receive ~을 받다

Paraphrase work on Saturdays or Sundays
→ Working on weekends

6. 여자가 왜 "저희는 직원들의 복지를 우선시하려 하고 있습니다."라고 말하는가?

(A) 앞서 나타난 오류를 바로잡기 위해

(B) 회사 정책을 설명하기 위해

(C) 남자를 승진시키기 위해

(D) 남자에게 도움에 대해 감사하기 위해

해설 여자가 대화 후반부에 직원들이 정규 업무 일정 외에는 절대 일하도록 요청 받지 않는다는 정책을(It's our policy that staff are never asked to work any hours outside of their normal schedules) 언급하면서 '직원들의 복지를 우선시하려 하고 있습니다'라고 알리는 흐름이다. 이는 자신이 언급한 근무 관련 정책을 만든 이유를 설명하는 말에 해당되므로 (B)가 정답이다.

어휘 correct ~을 바로잡다, ~을 고치다 explain ~을 설명하다 offer A B A에게 B를 제공하다 promotion 승진, 홍보, 판촉

Questions 7-9 refer to the following talk.

> **[7]** I am very honored to be invited to speak at this grand opening of Dinklage Corporation's brand new branch office. **[8]** I was approached by Dinklage Corporation 2 years ago to design their new building, and the original blueprints I created are on display in the lobby. I'm proud of how well the project turned out, and I'm delighted that the structure stands out from all other buildings in the area. **[9]** Many companies have asked me to work with them over the years, and I always turn down their offers. But, I made an exception for Dinklage Corporation.
>
> 딘클리지 코퍼레이션의 완전히 새로운 지사의 이 개장 기념 행사에서 연설하도록 요청 받게 되어 대단히 영광스럽게 생각합니다. 저는 2년 전에 딘클리지 코퍼레이션으로부터 새 건물을 설계해 달라는 제의를 받았으며, 제가 만든 원본 설계도가 로비에 진열되어 있습니다. 저는 이 프로젝트가 얼마나 좋은 결과로 나타났는지 자랑스럽게 생각하며, 이 건축물이 지역 내의 다른 모든 건물들 사이에서 두드러진다는 사실이 기쁩니다. 많은 회사들이 수년 동안에 걸쳐 저에게 함께 일하도록 요청해 왔는데, 저는 항상 그 제안을 거절합니다. 하지만, 딘클리지 코퍼레이션은 예외였습니다.

어휘 **be honored to do** ~해서 영광스럽게 생각하다 **be invited to do** ~하도록 요청 받다 **brand new** 완전히 새로운 **branch office** 지사 **approach** (제의 등을 위해) ~에게 접촉하다, ~에게 다가가다 **original** 원본의, 원래의, 독창적인 **blueprint** 설계도, 청사진 **create** ~을 만들어 내다 **on display** 진열 중인, 전시 중인 **be proud of** ~을 자랑스러워하다 **turn out** (결과로서) 드러나다, 판명되다, 되어가다 **be delighted that** ~해서 기쁘다 **structure** 건축물, 구조물 **stand out from** ~ 중에서 두드러지다, ~ 사이에서 눈에 띄다 **ask A to do** A에게 ~하도록 요청하다 **over the years** 수년 동안에 걸쳐 **turn down** ~을 거절하다 **offer** 제안, 제공 **make an exception for** ~은 예외로 하다

7. 딘클리지 코퍼레이션이 왜 축하 받고 있는가?
(A) 신제품을 출시했다.
(B) 새 지사를 열었다.
(C) 영업한 지 20년째가 되었다.
(D) 업계에서 주는 상을 받았다.

해설 화자가 담화를 시작하면서 딘클리지 코퍼레이션의 완전히 새로운 지사의 개장 기념 행사에서 연설하게 되어 영광이라고(~ to speak at this grand opening of Dinklage Corporation's brand new branch office) 언급하고 있으므로 (B)가 정답이다.

어휘 **celebrate** ~을 축하하다, ~을 기념하다 **release** ~을 출시하다, ~을 발매하다 **industry** 업계 **award** 상

8. 화자의 직업이 무엇일 것 같은가?
(A) 회계사
(B) 웹 디자이너
(C) 건축가
(D) 행사 기획자

해설 담화 초반부에 화자가 딘클리지 코퍼레이션으로부터 새 건물을 설계해 달라는 제의를 받은 사실을(I was approached by Dinklage Corporation 2 years ago to design their new building ~) 언급하고 있다. 이는 건축가가 하는 일에 해당되므로 (C)가 정답이다.

어휘 **profession** 직업

9. 화자가 "딘클리지 코퍼레이션은 예외였습니다"라고 말할 때 무엇을 암시하는가?
(A) 전에는 한 업체를 알지 못했다.
(B) 프로젝트를 맡아 일해서 기뻤다.
(C) 새로운 사업을 시작할 계획이다.
(D) 상담 비용을 철회했다.

해설 화자가 담화 후반부에 많은 회사들이 수년 동안에 걸쳐 함께 일하도록 요청했지만 거절했다고(Many companies have asked me to work with them over the years, and I always turn down their offers) 말하면서 '딘클리지 코퍼레이션은 예외였습니다'라고 알리는 흐름이다. 이는 기꺼이 딘클리지 코퍼레이션과 일하고자 했다는 뜻으로 일종의 기쁨을 나타내는 말에 해당되므로 (B)가 정답이다.

어휘 **be unaware of** ~을 알지 못하다 **previously** 이전에, 과거에 **work on** ~을 맡아 일하다 **plan to do** ~할 계획이다 **launch** ~을 시작하다, ~을 출시하다 **waive** ~을 철회하다, ~을 포기하다

Questions 10-12 refer to the following excerpt from a meeting.

> Let's begin this meeting by discussing ways to promote **[10]** our new lines of laptops and cell phones to potential suppliers. Our sales strategy is going to be focused on the new features we have added to these latest lines. We especially want you to emphasize how easy the new devices are to use. Now, **[11]** some of you might be worried that we don't have any full working models to demonstrate yet. I've had a word with the suppliers about that already. As long as you follow the sales pitch, the suppliers should be interested. **[12]** I gave each of you a copy of the pitch, and I'd like you all to take a look at it now.
>
> 잠재 공급업체들에게 우리의 새 노트북 컴퓨터 및 휴대전화기 제품군을 홍보할 방법을 이야기하는 것으로 이번 회의를 시작해 보겠습니다. 우리의 영업 전략은 이 최신 제품군에 추가한 새로운 특징들에 초점이 맞춰지게 될 것입니다. 우리는 특히 여러분께

서 새로운 기기들이 사용하기 얼마나 쉬운지 강조해 주시기를 원합니다. 자, 여러분 중 일부는 우리가 시연할 완전히 작동되는 어떤 모델도 아직 갖고 있지 않다는 사실이 걱정스러우실 수도 있습니다. 제가 이미 그 부분과 관련해 공급업체들과 이야기 나눴습니다. 여러분께서 구매 권유 전략을 따르시기만 하면, 공급업체들이 관심을 가질 것입니다. 제가 여러분 각자에게 이 구매 권유 전략을 한 부씩 나눠 드렸으며, 여러분 모두 지금 한 번 확인해 보시기 바랍니다.

어휘 promote ~을 홍보하다 line 제품군, 종류 potential 잠재적인 supplier 공급업체, 공급업자 sales 영업, 판매(량), 매출 strategy 전략 be focused on ~에 초점이 맞춰지다 feature 특징, 기능 add A to B A를 B에게 추가하다 latest 최신의 especially 특히 want A to do A에게 ~하기를 원하다 emphasize ~을 강조하다 device 기기, 장치 be worried that ~라는 점을 걱정하다 full 완전한, 전적인, 모든, 최대의 working 작동하는 demonstrate ~을 시연하다, ~을 시범 보이다 have a word with ~와 이야기 나누다 as long as ~하기만 하면, ~하는 한 follow ~을 따르다, ~을 따라 하다 sales pitch 구매 권유 전략, 구매 권유 행위 interested 관심 있는 would like A to do A에게 ~하기를 원하다 take a look at ~을 한 번 보다

10. 화자가 어떤 종류의 회사에서 근무하는가?
(A) 건설 회사
(B) 백화점
(C) 전자 제품 제조사
(D) 채용 대행사

해설 담화 초반부에 화자가 소속 회사를 our로 지칭하면서 제품을 our new lines of laptops and cell phones라고 언급하고 있으므로 (C)가 정답이다.

Paraphrase laptops and cell phones → electronics

11. 화자가 왜 "제가 이미 그 부분과 관련해 공급업체들과 이야기 나눴습니다"라고 말하는가?
(A) 다른 계획을 제안하기 위해
(B) 초청 연사를 소개하기 위해
(C) 청자들을 안심시키기 위해
(D) 청자들에게 의견을 요청하기 위해

해설 화자가 담화 중반부에 시연할 수 있는 완전히 작동되는 어떤 모델도 갖고 있지 않다는 사실을 청자들 중 일부가 걱정할 수 있다고(~ some of you might be worried that we don't have any full working models to demonstrate yet) 언급하면서 '이미 그 부분과 관련해 공급업체들과 이야기 나눴습니다'라고 말하는 흐름이다. 이는 이미 이야기된 부분이기 때문에 걱정할 필요가 없다는 뜻에 해당되는 말이므로 이러한 의미로 쓰인 (C)가 정답이다.

어휘 introduce ~을 소개하다, ~을 도입하다 reassure ~을

안심시키다 ask A for B A에게 B를 요청하다 feedback 의견

12. 청자들이 곧이어 무엇을 할 것인가?
(A) 발표를 보는 일
(B) 문서를 읽는 일
(C) 일부 제품을 테스트하는 일
(D) 일부 공급업체에 연락하는 일

해설 담화 맨 마지막 부분에 화자가 구매 권유 전략을 한 부씩 나눠 준 사실을 말하면서 청자들에게 지금 한 번 확인해 보도록(I gave each of you a copy of the pitch, and I'd like you all to take a look at it now) 권하고 있으므로 (B)가 정답이다.

어휘 presentation 발표(회) contact ~에게 연락하다

Paraphrase copy of the pitch / take a look at it
→ Read a document

시원스쿨 LAB

해설 바로보기 ▶

TOEIC

Test of English for International Communication

TEST 1

실전 모의고사 1

LISTENING TEST

In the Listening test, you will be asked to demonstrate how well you understand spoken English. The entire Listening test will last approximately 45 minutes. There are four parts, and directions are given for each part. You must mark your answers on the separate answer sheet. Do not write your answers in your test book.

PART 1

Directions: For each question in this part, you will hear four statements about a picture in your test book. When you hear the statements, you must select the one statement that best describes what you see in the picture. Then find the number of the question on your answer sheet and mark your answer. The statements will not be printed in your test book and will be spoken only one time.

Statement (D), "They are taking photographs," is the best description of the picture, so you should select answer (D) and mark it on your answer sheet.

1.

2.

GO ON TO THE NEXT PAGE

3.

4.

5.

6.

GO ON TO THE NEXT PAGE →

PART 2

Directions: You will hear a question or statement and three responses spoken in English. They will not be printed in your test book and will be spoken only one time. Select the best response to the question or statement and mark the letter (A), (B), or (C) on your answer sheet.

7. Mark your answer on your answer sheet.

8. Mark your answer on your answer sheet.

9. Mark your answer on your answer sheet.

10. Mark your answer on your answer sheet.

11. Mark your answer on your answer sheet.

12. Mark your answer on your answer sheet.

13. Mark your answer on your answer sheet.

14. Mark your answer on your answer sheet.

15. Mark your answer on your answer sheet.

16. Mark your answer on your answer sheet.

17. Mark your answer on your answer sheet.

18. Mark your answer on your answer sheet.

19. Mark your answer on your answer sheet.

20. Mark your answer on your answer sheet.

21. Mark your answer on your answer sheet.

22. Mark your answer on your answer sheet.

23. Mark your answer on your answer sheet.

24. Mark your answer on your answer sheet.

25. Mark your answer on your answer sheet.

26. Mark your answer on your answer sheet.

27. Mark your answer on your answer sheet.

28. Mark your answer on your answer sheet.

29. Mark your answer on your answer sheet.

30. Mark your answer on your answer sheet.

31. Mark your answer on your answer sheet.

PART 3

Directions: You will hear some conversations between two or more people. You will be asked to answer three questions about what the speakers say in each conversation. Select the best response to each question and mark the letter (A), (B), (C) or (D) on your answer sheet. The conversations will not be printed in your test book and will be spoken only one time.

32. What type of product are the speakers discussing?

(A) Computer keyboards
(B) Wireless earphones
(C) Portable speakers
(D) Rechargeable batteries

33. What aspect of the product is the man surprised about?

(A) Its appearance
(B) Its weight
(C) Its packaging
(D) Its accessories

34. What does the man suggest doing?

(A) Updating a Web site
(B) Changing a product design
(C) Submitting a report
(D) Arranging a presentation

35. What activity is scheduled for the morning?

(A) A training workshop
(B) A product demonstration
(C) A press conference
(D) A workplace inspection

36. What do the men say they would like to do?

(A) Check their e-mails
(B) Return to their office
(C) Print some documents
(D) Distribute handouts

37. What does the woman say is a standard policy?

(A) Wearing identification tags
(B) Putting on safety equipment
(C) Signing a visitor's book
(D) Attending an orientation

38. Who is the woman?

(A) A customer service agent
(B) An IT technician
(C) A store manager
(D) A Web site designer

39. What does the man say is his goal?

(A) Attracting more customers
(B) Making a process easier
(C) Reducing customer complaints
(D) Designing new products

40. What is the man going to do next?

(A) Visit a Web site
(B) Provide a tour
(C) Present some designs
(D) Discuss survey results

41. Why is the woman calling?

(A) To place an order
(B) To ask for directions
(C) To confirm a reservation
(D) To update a schedule

42. What does the woman imply when she says, "June 20 is two weeks away"?

(A) She has an appointment on June 20.
(B) She has plenty of time to complete a task.
(C) She does not want to wait that long.
(D) She will contact the man at a later time.

43. What will the man do next?

(A) Ship some produce
(B) Offer a different item
(C) Calculate a discount
(D) Check a schedule

GO ON TO THE NEXT PAGE

44. Where does the conversation most likely take place?

(A) At a college
(B) At a fitness club
(C) At a library
(D) At a restaurant

45. What will be delivered today?

(A) Some uniforms
(B) Some books
(C) Some food
(D) Some furniture

46. Why will the man be unable to work late today?

(A) He will attend a family event.
(B) He has a job interview.
(C) He needs to return a recent purchase.
(D) He has a dental appointment.

47. What type of business is the woman opening?

(A) A modeling agency
(B) A clothing design company
(C) A cosmetics store
(D) A jewelry manufacturing firm

48. Why does the man say he is proud of Bluesky Photography?

(A) It completes all projects on time.
(B) It offers competitive rates.
(C) It has received an industry award.
(D) It uses innovative technology.

49. What are the speakers going to do next?

(A) Prepare a cost estimate
(B) Examine some images
(C) Change a product design
(D) Take some photographs

50. Why does the man say, "It'll be my first time"?

(A) To extend an invitation
(B) To seek some advice
(C) To explain a delay
(D) To express gratitude

51. What does the man hope that the event attendees will do?

(A) Watch a video clip
(B) Arrive early
(C) Interview for a job
(D) Bring a résumé

52. Why does the woman suggest contacting Karl?

(A) He will attend a job fair.
(B) He is hiring new staff.
(C) He can update a Web site.
(D) He has an event schedule.

53. What type of business do the speakers most likely work for?

(A) A public relations firm
(B) A beverage company
(C) A sportswear manufacturer
(D) A health spa

54. What new strategy does the man propose?

(A) Redesigning a Web site
(B) Advertising on television
(C) Purchasing a rival company
(D) Using celebrity endorsements

55. What does the woman say is necessary?

(A) A training workshop
(B) A board meeting
(C) A deadline extension
(D) An advance payment

56. What is the purpose of the conversation?

(A) To review production figures
(B) To approve a project proposal
(C) To compare some employees
(D) To discuss a staff survey

57. What does the company want to purchase?

(A) Computers
(B) Furniture
(C) Uniforms
(D) Software

58. What will the speakers do next Monday?

(A) Purchase some equipment
(B) Hold some interviews
(C) Place an advertisement
(D) Make an announcement

59. Where most likely are the speakers?

(A) At a bus terminal
(B) At a hotel
(C) At an airport
(D) At a train station

60. What are the speakers preparing for?

(A) A product demonstration
(B) A job interview
(C) A grand opening event
(D) A financial audit

61. What will the speakers most likely do next?

(A) Board a vehicle
(B) Check a travel itinerary
(C) Present some tickets
(D) Visit a different location

Children's Festival Event Map

Area 1 Magic Show	**Area 2** Face Painting
Area 4 Ring Toss	**Area 3** Fishing Game

62. Who most likely are the speakers?

(A) Library staff
(B) Toy store employees
(C) Maintenance workers
(D) Public school teachers

63. Look at the graphic. Where will a snack stand be placed?

(A) In Area 1
(B) In Area 2
(C) In Area 3
(D) In Area 4

64. Why will the woman most likely talk to Sandra?

(A) To get a snack
(B) To update a flyer
(C) To review a process
(D) To schedule an appointment

GO ON TO THE NEXT PAGE

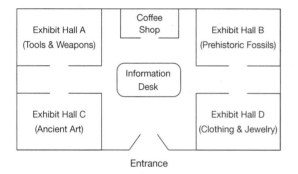

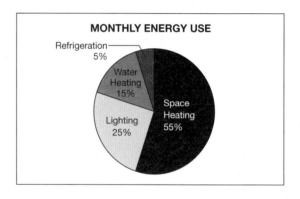

65. Why is the man visiting the history museum?

(A) To apply for a job
(B) To join a guided tour
(C) To plan a future trip
(D) To deliver an exhibit

66. Look at the graphic. Which exhibit hall does the woman say is currently closed?

(A) Exhibit Hall A
(B) Exhibit Hall B
(C) Exhibit Hall C
(D) Exhibit Hall D

67. What does the woman suggest doing?

(A) Attending a special event
(B) Talking to her supervisor
(C) Taking an information pamphlet
(D) Coming back tomorrow

68. What type of business do the speakers most likely own?

(A) A factory
(B) A grocery store
(C) A restaurant
(D) A shipping company

69. Look at the graphic. Which percentage of the energy use is the woman concerned about?

(A) 5%
(B) 15%
(C) 25%
(D) 55%

70. What does the man say he will do?

(A) Install some equipment
(B) Tidy a workspace
(C) Research some prices
(D) Check an inventory

PART 4

Directions: You will hear some talks given by a single speaker. You will be asked to answer three questions about what the speaker says in each talk. Select the best response to each question and mark the letter (A), (B), (C), or (D) on your answer sheet. The talks will not be printed in your test book and will be spoken only one time.

71. Where do the listeners work?

    (A) At a bookstore
    (B) At a sports arena
    (C) At a library
    (D) At a department store

72. According to the speaker, what is the purpose of an event?

    (A) To attract customers
    (B) To raise money
    (C) To provide education
    (D) To thank employees

73. What will the listeners receive for volunteering?

    (A) A cash bonus
    (B) A store membership
    (C) A gift voucher
    (D) A day off work

74. What will Axon Enterprises do this winter?

    (A) Expand into foreign markets
    (B) Renovate its manufacturing plant
    (C) Launch a new product line
    (D) Merge with another company

75. What does Axon Enterprises manufacture?

    (A) Computer software
    (B) Medical equipment
    (C) Construction tools
    (D) Mobile phones

76. Why should the listeners visit a Web site?

    (A) To place advance orders
    (B) To register for an event
    (C) To read a press release
    (D) To view job vacancies

77. Who is Annabel Chong?

    (A) A Web site designer
    (B) A fashion designer
    (C) An interior designer
    (D) A packaging designer

78. What will the listeners do on the tour?

    (A) Watch a video clip
    (B) Meet with Ms. Chong
    (C) Visit a manufacturing facility
    (D) Create some products

79. Why does the speaker say, "don't be shy"?

    (A) To suggest that the listeners apply for a job
    (B) To inform the listeners about a group activity
    (C) To praise the listeners for their hard work
    (D) To encourage the listeners to ask questions

80. What event is being celebrated?

    (A) A manager's retirement
    (B) A company expansion
    (C) A new sales record
    (D) A product launch

81. According to the speaker, what will the company do in July?

    (A) Relocate its headquarters
    (B) Start a marketing campaign
    (C) Launch a Web site
    (D) Hire additional staff

82. What will happen next?

    (A) A projector will be set up.
    (B) An award will be presented.
    (C) Some documents will be distributed.
    (D) Some refreshments will be served.

GO ON TO THE NEXT PAGE

83. What type of event are the listeners attending?

(A) A shareholders meeting
(B) A trade show
(C) A grand opening
(D) A training workshop

84. Who is Lawrence Russell?

(A) A professor
(B) A business owner
(C) An event organizer
(D) An author

85. According to the speaker, why will Lawrence Russell arrive late?

(A) He is speaking at another event.
(B) He had a transportation delay.
(C) He is eating breakfast.
(D) He went to the wrong location.

86. What is the speaker mainly discussing?

(A) Rent adjustments
(B) Building improvements
(C) Parking policies
(D) Employment opportunities

87. What does the speaker mean when she says, "This couldn't have happened without you"?

(A) The listeners will receive rewards.
(B) A project will be temporarily suspended.
(C) The listeners' feedback was invaluable.
(D) Some volunteers are required for a task.

88. What does the speaker encourage the listeners to do?

(A) Look at some pictures
(B) Inspect a room
(C) Check a schedule
(D) Sign up for an event

89. According to the speaker, which type of milk is selling poorly?

(A) Low-fat milk
(B) Flavored milk
(C) Lactose-free milk
(D) High-calcium milk

90. Which department do the listeners most likely work in?

(A) Human resources
(B) Advertising
(C) Finance
(D) Sales

91. What will the listeners probably do tomorrow morning?

(A) Attend a staff meeting
(B) Come to work early
(C) Send some ideas
(D) Contact some consumers

92. Where does the speaker work?

(A) At a research facility
(B) At a manufacturing plant
(C) At a construction site
(D) At a hardware store

93. Why does the speaker say, "it's not enough"?

(A) To request a deadline extension
(B) To suggest increasing security measures
(C) To explain an increase in expenses
(D) To increase an order of supplies

94. What does the speaker want to discuss at a future meeting?

(A) Installing some devices
(B) Recruiting additional staff
(C) Providing extra training
(D) Delaying a project

Florida Orange Farm - Department Managers	
Lionel Jeffries	Finance & Payroll
Jeff Nichols	Growing & Harvesting
Marty Planer	Packing & Distribution
Paul Mooney	Sales & Marketing

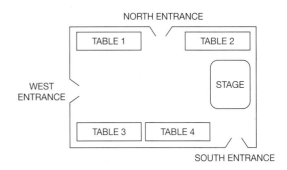

95. What does the speaker say about the listeners' hotel?

(A) It is located in a downtown area.
(B) It offers reasonable room rates.
(C) It includes a swimming pool.
(D) It is known for its delicious food.

96. Why might an activity be canceled?

(A) Because some machinery broke down
(B) Because poor weather is expected
(C) Because a staff member is unavailable
(D) Because a business is closing early

97. Look at the graphic. Who is the speaker?

(A) Lionel Jeffries
(B) Jeff Nichols
(C) Marty Planer
(D) Paul Mooney

98. What is the main purpose of the call?

(A) To request some information
(B) To provide an update on service
(C) To suggest delaying an event
(D) To inform a client about a menu change

99. Look at the graphic. Which table of food is the speaker concerned about?

(A) Table 1
(B) Table 2
(C) Table 3
(D) Table 4

100. What does the speaker say he will do?

(A) Move to a different room
(B) Speak to a manager
(C) Send a photograph
(D) Have a table repaired

This is the end of the Listening test. Turn to Part 5 in your test book.

GO ON TO THE NEXT PAGE

READING TEST

In the Reading test, you will read a variety of texts and answer several different types of reading comprehension questions. The entire Reading test will last 75 minutes. There are three parts, and directions are given for each part. You are encouraged to answer as many questions as possible within the time allowed. You must mark your answers on the separate answer sheet. Do not write your answers in your test book.

PART 5

Directions: A word or phrase is missing in each of the sentences below. Four answer choices are given below each sentence. Select the best answer to complete the sentence. Then mark the letter (A), (B), (C), or (D) on your answer sheet.

101. All new employees should ------- to the human resources office to receive a work uniform.

(A) report
(B) reporter
(C) reports
(D) reporting

102. Guests are offered a cold beverage and a snack ------- arrival at our hotel.

(A) during
(B) within
(C) between
(D) upon

103. Mr. Jackson met with an old colleague of ------- visiting Boston for a technology conference.

(A) he
(B) him
(C) his
(D) himself

104. The board members had ------- selected a new COO by the time Ms. Dickson decided to apply for the position.

(A) already
(B) besides
(C) apart
(D) very

105. Outdoor Elite's hiking boots are ------- than cheaper brands of footwear.

(A) durably
(B) durable
(C) more durable
(D) durability

106. Ms. Levinson will pay the outstanding balance for her annual home energy bills ------- a week.

(A) which
(B) within
(C) almost
(D) by

107. Driving time between the airport and the downtown area will drastically decrease ------- the new elevated freeway is opened.

(A) once
(B) in case
(C) still
(D) not only

108. Due to an extensive landscaping project, Mont Royale Botanical Garden is only partially ------- at the moment.

(A) accessibility
(B) accessible
(C) access
(D) accessing

109. The payroll manager informed all employees ------- the new pay date will be the 10th of each month.

(A) when
(B) so
(C) that
(D) what

110. When assembling the model aircraft, handle the pieces ------- to avoid accidentally breaking them.

(A) gently
(B) gentle
(C) gentlest
(D) gentleness

111. The new office manager will not ------- any latenesses or unexplained absences from staff.

(A) dictate
(B) ascertain
(C) concern
(D) tolerate

112. To find out the full ------- for any of our computers, please speak with one of our sales representatives.

(A) specific
(B) specifically
(C) specifies
(D) specifications

113. All visitors to the baseball stadium are ------- to dispose of any glass bottles they are carrying before entering the venue.

(A) desired
(B) required
(C) considered
(D) refused

114. ------- released at only a limited number of movie theaters, *The Leaves of Summer* went on to be one of the most popular movies of the year.

(A) Original
(B) Originally
(C) Origin
(D) Originate

115. During the first ------- of the housing development project, several old buildings at the site will be demolished.

(A) outcome
(B) view
(C) deposit
(D) phase

116. Mr. Carrell was pleased to see that the ------- tenant had left the apartment in excellent condition.

(A) likely
(B) early
(C) consequent
(D) former

117. Based on online testimonials, most clients are extremely impressed by the ------- level of EZ Repair's technicians.

(A) experienced
(B) experiences
(C) experience
(D) experiencing

118. Renovating the waiting room at the health clinic is unfortunately ------- longer than expected.

(A) making
(B) delaying
(C) placing
(D) taking

119. The company founder has decided to postpone the relocation of the head office until ------- in the year.

(A) later
(B) forward
(C) gradually
(D) nearby

120. A marketing survey ------- that most consumers now prefer to order groceries through mobile applications rather than visit a store.

(A) has indicated
(B) indicating
(C) indicate
(D) has been indicated

GO ON TO THE NEXT PAGE

121. Both potential destinations for the company excursion seem appealing, although neither the beach resort ------- the mountain resort offers a corporate discount.

(A) not
(B) but
(C) nor
(D) and

122. Swifty's latest lines of sportswear are becoming very popular, particularly ------- teenagers.

(A) among
(B) against
(C) until
(D) below

123. As part of his seminar on diversity and inclusion, Roger Blackcroft recommends that people expose ------- to new cultures and experiences.

(A) they
(B) themselves
(C) their
(D) theirs

124. ------- the safety inspector's report, our factory has failed to meet the government's minimum standard for workplace safety.

(A) Whereas
(B) According to
(C) Because
(D) Instead of

125. Once the ------- to our menu have been finalized, kitchen staff will be trained on how to cook the new dishes.

(A) amends
(B) amending
(C) amendments
(D) amended

126. The annual National Health Conference ------- medical professionals together to discuss a wide variety of important health issues.

(A) resumes
(B) brings
(C) conveys
(D) asserts

127. The judging panel members ------- for almost two hours before deciding on the winner of the dance contest.

(A) deliberated
(B) awarded
(C) designated
(D) affirmed

128. Morningside Bakery ------- the necessary vendor permit to serve food from a booth during the town fair.

(A) obtain
(B) obtained
(C) obtaining
(D) will be obtained

129. Ms. Moreno has chosen May 10 as the ------- date for the company's customer service training, although it may need to be changed.

(A) likable
(B) continual
(C) tentative
(D) affirmative

130. Mr. Richardson has seen ------- improvement in staff productivity since introducing the employee incentive program.

(A) rather
(B) little
(C) nothing
(D) few

PART 6

Directions: Read the texts that follow. A word, phrase, or sentence is missing in parts of each text. Four answer choices for each question are given below the text. Select the best answer to complete the text. Then mark the letter (A), (B), (C) or (D) on your answer sheet.

Questions 131-134 refer to the following notice.

For the attention of all Slater Health Foods staff:

As part of our ongoing efforts ------- improving our services, we are launching our redesigned
            131.
Web site next week. Our customers will now be able to purchase products through our Web

store as soon as they set up a customer ------- online. In order to assist our customers with
                                        132.
setting this up, we will be sending those on our mailing list an e-mail this week. This will contain

a ------- that they can click to take them to our customer settings page. Once they enter a few
    133.
details, they will be ready to start buying items online. -------. Please let our customers know
                                                          134.
about this change whenever you chat with them in the store.

131. (A) to continue
     (B) continues
     (C) continued
     (D) in continuing

132. (A) accounting
     (B) account
     (C) accounted
     (D) accountings

133. (A) piece
     (B) set
     (C) member
     (D) link

134. (A) You may fill out the form if you wish to join
         the mailing list.
     (B) Some products are currently out of stock
         due to a delivery error.
     (C) We are confident this will prove to be very
         successful.
     (D) Slater Health Foods is known for its
         generous discounts.

GO ON TO THE NEXT PAGE

Questions 135-138 refer to the following article.

Betty's BBQ Wins Again

PHOENIX (December 10) - In the latest edition of the annual Arizona Good Food Guide, Betty's BBQ has been named the Best Family Restaurant for the third ------- year. Betty Grundy, who
135.
opened the restaurant almost 15 years ago, accepted the award at a ceremony last weekend. The restaurant's kitchen team joined ------- onstage to thank the judges and voters.
136.

Ms. Grundy took the opportunity to introduce Gus Walker and Juan Chavez. -------. Mr. Walker
137.
and Mr. Chavez have more than 30 years of experience in the restaurant industry between them, and are considered experts in barbecued food. ------- the restaurant's typical pork, beef, and
138.
chicken dishes, they will also be preparing a new range of menu items using buffalo meat.

---

135. (A) successively
(B) successive
(C) succeeds
(D) succeed

136. (A) it
(B) her
(C) some
(D) any

137. (A) Betty's BBQ is known for its delicious sauces.
(B) Competition in the restaurant industry is on the rise.
(C) Both of them are new to Betty's BBQ.
(D) Award nominees will be announced this week.

138. (A) Provided
(B) Despite
(C) Instead of
(D) Along with

Questions 139-142 refer to the following advertisement.

Is your company looking to fill job vacancies? Here at *The Midtown Gazette* we are expanding our classified jobs section in order to help employers ------- with potential job candidates. You

139.

can advertise in our ------- for very reasonable rates, starting from only $10 per day for the

140.

smallest ad space we offer.

To place an advertisement in our newspaper, visit www.midtowngazette.com/advertisements and fill out the appropriate form. You will need to provide details of your business, including contact details and the business reference number. -------. We provide a wide range of packages that our

141.

advertisers can choose from, and you can even place a half-page or full-page ad. -------, these

142.

may only be run on a weekly or one-off basis rather than a daily basis.

139. (A) connecting
(B) connects
(C) connected
(D) connect

140. (A) subscription
(B) convention
(C) publication
(D) merchandise

141. (A) Successful applicants will be invited to interview for the role.
(B) Subscribing to the newspaper is a very simple process.
(C) Next, upload the advertisement that you want us to run.
(D) Many employers are struggling to fill vacancies these days.

142. (A) However
(B) Consequently
(C) For example
(D) On the contrary

GO ON TO THE NEXT PAGE

Questions 143–146 refer to the following Web page.

The Atreus Software Suite can ------- improve the management and operation of businesses in a
143.
wide selection of fields. Our software began as a simple word processing program, but we have

enhanced it over the past few years. Now, we believe that it is not only a ------- alternative to the
144.
leading business management software packages, but close to becoming the best of all.

The current version combines excellent word processing, spreadsheet, database, and
presentation programs with innovative teleconferencing and project management applications.
-------. To download a free 14-day trial, please click the link below. We are confident that Atreus
145.
Software Suite ------- your expectations!
146.

---

143. (A) harshly
  (B) doubtfully
  (C) markedly
  (D) dutifully

144. (A) viable
  (B) concerned
  (C) diligent
  (D) grateful

145. (A) We hope you enjoyed the trial version of
    our product.
  (B) The software suite will be launched early
    next year.
  (C) Additional features are likely to be offered
    in future versions.
  (D) Atreus will begin hiring new employees
    immediately.

146. (A) exceeded
  (B) had exceeded
  (C) will exceed
  (D) is exceeding

PART 7

Directions: In this part you will read a selection of texts, such as magazine and newspaper articles, e-mails, and instant messages. Each text or set of texts is followed by several questions. Select the best answer for each question and mark the letter (A), (B), (C), or (D) on your answer sheet.

Questions 147-148 refer to the following invoice.

FIRST CHOICE

CLIENT INVOICE

Payable by: Faraday Advertising Inc.

Date and Time of Service: November 3, 9:30 A.M. – 12:30 P.M.

Pick-up Address: 113 Pitcher Avenue, Buffalo, NY - Faraday Advertising (Current Head Office)

Delivery Address: 2029 Maitland Drive, Buffalo, NY - Faraday Advertising (New Head Office)

Item Type	Quantity	Price per item	Cost
Office chair	28	$5.00	$140.00
Desk (large)	14	$15.00	$210.00
File cabinet	6	$12.00	$72.00
Bookshelf	5	$10.00	$50.00
		Total Amount Payable (due by November 2):	$472.00

First Choice provides high-quality packing materials and guarantees that no damage will be caused to items during shipping. If you have any inquiries regarding this invoice or our service, please call us at (014)-555-1042.

---

147. What type of business most likely is First Choice?

(A) A recruitment firm
(B) A cleaning service
(C) A moving company
(D) An office supply store

148. What information is NOT included in the invoice?

(A) How to contact First Choice
(B) How many employees will provide service
(C) The number of items involved in the service
(D) When the client's payment is due

GO ON TO THE NEXT PAGE

Questions 149-150 refer to the following e-mail.

To:	Eva Daniels <evadaniels@homemail.com>
From:	Craig Brand <cbrand@luxorrealty.com>
Date:	November 5
Subject:	Order #59878
Attachment:	property map

Dear Ms. Daniels,

Thank you for your interest in the property located at 512 Byers Road. As you requested, I have scheduled a viewing for you on Saturday, November 18, at 10:30 a.m. I will meet you outside the property and show you around myself. The property is currently undergoing some minor renovations, so I'm afraid there might be some equipment and building materials scattered around. You should be able to find a parking space on Byers Road without any difficulty. Please don't forget to check the map that I have included with this message. It will help you to find the property and plan the quickest route.

Regards,

Craig Brand
Property Agent
Luxor Realty

149. What is the main purpose of the e-mail?

(A) To apologize for some building work
(B) To recommend some properties
(C) To confirm an appointment
(D) To explain a procedure

150. What is Ms. Daniels reminded to do?

(A) Obtain a parking permit
(B) Check an attachment
(C) Submit a payment
(D) Visit a Web site

To: all_members@lifefitgym.com
From: info@lifefitgym.com
Date: July 15
Subject: Important announcement

Greetings!

We hope you are enjoying the lovely summer weather! Over the next couple of months, there will be several changes here at Life Fit Gym. These changes are all designed to improve our amenities and provide better service to our valued members. Starting July 25, members will receive two free personal training sessions instead of one when they refer a friend for a membership. We decided to improve this policy in order to bring in more new members.

Also, we will be enlarging Fitness Room 3 in early August and moving our spinning classes into there from Fitness Room 2. This is due to the increasing popularity of our spinning classes. In addition, Fitness Rooms 1 and 4 will be undergoing remodeling throughout August. New flooring and mirrored wall paneling will be installed in order to improve the appearance of the rooms.

We hope you will all be happy with the changes!

Best wishes,

The Life Fit Gym Team

---

151. Why was the e-mail sent?

(A) To invite members to a special event
(B) To promote a new series of fitness classes
(C) To celebrate the success of a business
(D) To inform members about a policy change

152. Where are spinning classes currently held?

(A) Fitness Room 1
(B) Fitness Room 2
(C) Fitness Room 3
(D) Fitness Room 4

GO ON TO THE NEXT PAGE

Questions 153-154 refer to the following text message chiain.

Oscar Munoz [8:24 A.M.] Jana, I just wanted to thank you for supervising my sales team while I was away at the conference yesterday.

Jana Draper [8:26 A.M.] It's the least I could do. You covered for me twice last month!

Oscar Munoz [8:28 A.M.] I guess you're right! So, did everything run smoothly?

Jana Draper [8:31 A.M.] Yes, although I did have a slight problem with Becky. She arrived late in the morning, and came back late from her lunch break.

Oscar Munoz [8:33 A.M.] Oh, that's not like her. Did she explain what the problem was?

Jana Draper [8:35 A.M.] She apologized, but she didn't really have a valid excuse. Perhaps you should speak with her today.

Oscar Munoz [8:36 A.M.] Yes, I'll ask her about it during my team meeting. Thanks for letting me know.

153. At 8:26 A.M., what does Ms. Draper mean when she writes, "It's the least I could do"?

(A) She was pleased to attend a conference.
(B) She is disappointed with some sales figures.
(C) She worked late at the office yesterday.
(D) She was happy to help out Mr. Munoz.

154. What is suggested about Becky?

(A) She will meet with Ms. Draper today.
(B) She is normally on time for work.
(C) She recently took a day off.
(D) She is Mr. Munoz's team leader.

Questions 155-157 refer to the following memo.

To: Yeats Corporation Staff
From: Karl Styger, HR Manager
Subject: Louise Gunning (Assistant Payroll Manager)
Date: June 28

As most of you already know, Louise Gunning will soon be stepping down from her role as our Assistant Payroll Manager. Louise has worked with us for almost 10 years, and we appreciate all the hard work she has put in during her time with us. Her final work day will be July 31, and we are currently seeking a suitable replacement.

In line with our new approach of focusing on employee welfare and career advancement, we will not be advertising this vacancy externally. Instead, we encourage any Yeats Corporation employees who are interested in the role to apply directly by submitting a résumé and cover letter to the HR office. Applicants should have some relevant work experience and a broad knowledge of payroll operations. Yeats Corporation will provide full on-the-job training.

The successful applicant will work in the payroll department at our head office from 9 a.m. to 5:30 p.m., Monday through Friday, with occasional Saturday/Sunday work when necessary. He or she will report directly to Hugh Amblin, Payroll Manager, and be required to attend weekly management meetings.

155. What is the main purpose of the memo?

(A) To introduce a new assistant manager
(B) To describe proposed changes to a hiring policy
(C) To invite staff to a retirement party
(D) To announce an employment opportunity

156. What is suggested about Yeats Corporation?

(A) It recently opened a new branch.
(B) It advertises jobs on its Web site.
(C) It offers a competitive monthly wage.
(D) It values its current employees.

157. What is indicated about the payroll department?

(A) It is closed on national holidays.
(B) It is sometimes open on weekends.
(C) It runs a weekly training workshop.
(D) It is currently managed by Karl Styger.

GO ON TO THE NEXT PAGE

Questions 158-160 refer to the following Web page.

http://www.pierrotartgallery.com/exhibitions/upcoming

New Exhibit: Color Forest (September 10 - October 10)
Artist: Trisha Castanet

Opening in the East Wing on September 10, Color Forest is sure to captivate all visitors to Pierrot Art Gallery. — [1] —. Created by renowned artist Trisha Castanet, the exhibition is comprised of one thousand plants and flowers intricately sculpted from iron and placed in a large tray of white sand in the middle of the room. When visitors first enter the exhibit space, all of the plants and flowers will appear black. — [2] —. As visitors slowly move around the exhibit, the objects will appear to burst into color. — [3] —. To achieve this effect, Castanet painted only the sides and reverse of each sculpture, and carefully positioned them so that they all appear to bloom simultaneously. — [4] —.

Trisha Castanet was born in Lisbon, Portugal, and later attended London's prestigious Hadley College of Modern Art. Her career has spanned almost 20 years, and her works have been influenced by the rural landscapes of the many countries in which she has resided over the years. For instance, Color Forest draws inspiration from the tulip fields of Rotterdam, where she has been based for the past 4 years. Admission to the exhibit costs $8 and includes a color brochure and audio guide.

158. What is indicated about the Color Forest exhibit?

(A) It will be on display for one month.
(B) It has been shown in several countries.
(C) It will be located in an outdoor area.
(D) It took two decades to create.

159. What is suggested about Trisha Castanet?

(A) She taught at a well-known art college.
(B) She has exhibited paintings of landscapes.
(C) She has lived in various regions.
(D) She will give a talk at the gallery.

160. In which of the positions marked [1], [2], [3], and [4] does the following sentence best belong?

"However, there is more to the exhibit than initially meets the eye."

(A) [1]
(B) [2]
(C) [3]
(D) [4]

Questions 161-163 refer to the following brochure.

IDEAL SOLUTIONS
1139 Stanley Road,
Toronto, ON, M3C 0E3

Ideal Solutions has over 20 years of experience in organizing a wide range of corporate and personal gatherings such as wedding receptions, company banquets, and grand openings. We provide a full range of services, including the following:

- Initial consultation to ascertain the client's needs and goals
- Decoration of rooms, including balloons and floral arrangements
- Provision of catering using our in-house team of chefs
- Printing of invitations, flyers, posters, and other materials
- Various entertainment options such as live musicians, magicians, and acrobats

We pride ourselves on our reliable and professional service and we always exceed our clients' expectations. We also guarantee that our prices cannot be beat. Our rates are lower than all our competitors', and we offer generous discounts to returning clients. Furthermore, no other company in our field can compete with us when it comes to prompt, dependable customer service.

If you are interested in hiring us for the first time, or simply wish to find out more about what we can do for you, go to www.idealsolutions.ca. If you are an existing client and would like to hire us again, please call our management team directly at (705)-555-0135.

---

161. What type of business is Ideal Solutions?

(A) A marketing agency
(B) A renovation company
(C) An event planning firm
(D) A printing shop

162. How does Ideal Solutions differ from other companies in its field?

(A) Its service is more affordable.
(B) It provides a free consultation.
(C) It offers a corporate discount.
(D) It operates in a wider area.

163. How can new clients get information about Ideal Solutions' services?

(A) By reading a flyer
(B) By visiting a Web site
(B) By calling a telephone number
(D) By attending an upcoming event

GO ON TO THE NEXT PAGE

Questions 164-167 refer to the following information.

Innomax Business Skills Development Seminars

Any Merryweather Inc. staff that are interested in attending this year's seminars should read the following information. In previous years, employees have found the event to be highly beneficial, and we strongly encourage our employees to consider registering.

1. Seminar Details: The seminars are hosted by Innomax and will take place on Saturday, May 17 and Sunday, May 18. Each day will consist of four two-hour seminars covering a wide range of topics such as IT skills, project management, and customer service. As in previous years, all sessions will be held at Langley Business Institute in Philadelphia. Each seminar requires a $30 registration fee and will be led by an individual who has vast experience in his or her respective field.

2. Registration: Employees who are interested in attending one or more seminars should contact Ms. Martino in our HR office for assistance. Merryweather will cover the cost of one seminar per employee. Additional seminars must be paid for by employees. Please ensure that you register no later than March 31.

3. Transportation/Accommodation: Merryweather Inc. will assist staff attending the seminars by providing transportation and accommodation. Buses will run from our head office to Philadelphia on May 17 and May 18, departing at 8 a.m and returning at 5 p.m. We will reserve rooms for staff at any hotel in Philadelphia, provided the nightly rate does not exceed $120. Please inform Ms. Martino of your requirements when registering.

4. Eligibility: Please be advised that only full-time staff are invited to attend the seminars. We plan to provide our other staff members with equally beneficial training opportunities later in the year.

164. What is indicated about the seminars?

(A) They will take place in several different venues.
(B) They will be held over a three-day period.
(C) They have been attended by Merryweather staff before.
(D) They are sponsored by Merryweather Inc.

165. What are interested individuals required to do?

(A) Obtain authorization from their department manager
(B) Provide receipts to Ms. Martino
(C) Register for seminars by May 17
(D) Pay for additional seminars themselves

166. According to the information, why might accommodation requests be rejected?

(A) A seminar is already fully booked.
(B) A reservation date is unavailable.
(C) A room rate is too high.
(D) A hotel is located outside the downtown area.

167. What is suggested about part-time employees?

(A) They will be provided with transportation.
(B) They are unable to attend the seminars.
(C) They must pay more than full-time employees.
(D) They receive a discount on event registration.

Questions 168-171 refer to the following text message chain.

Roy Barrister [10:07 A.M.]	Maggie, Norman... I think we might have a problem.
Maggie Chen [10:08 A.M.]	Oh, no. What's up?
Roy Barrister [10:10 A.M.]	Geraldine Swain, the singer who's supposed to give the first performance of the day, hasn't even shown up at the event site yet.
Maggie Chen [10:11 A.M.]	You're kidding! Isn't she supposed to go on stage at 10:30?
Roy Barrister [10:13 A.M.]	Exactly. We advertised that the first act will perform at that time, so we can't disappoint all the attendees.
Noman Kyles [10:15 A.M.]	She mentioned that she felt ill during the rehearsal yesterday. Maybe that has something to do with it. Maggie, don't you have her manager's contact number? Why don't you give him a call?
Maggie Chen [10:17 A.M.]	I was just thinking that. I'll let you both know what I find out. In the meantime, try to find a performer who is willing to go on in her place.

168. Where most likely is Mr. Barrister?

(Λ) Λt a movie premiere
(B) At a comedy show
(C) At an art exhibition
(D) At a music festival

169. At 10:11 A.M., why does Ms. Chen most likely say, "You're kidding"?

(A) She finds some information amusing.
(B) She disagrees with Mr. Barrister.
(C) She wants Mr. Barrister to work harder.
(D) She is surprised by some news.

170. What is indicated about Mr. Kyles?

(A) He is scheduled to perform at an event.
(B) He spoke with Ms. Swain yesterday.
(C) He has been feeling unwell recently.
(D) He knows where Ms. Swain is.

171. What will Ms. Chen most likely do next?

(A) Call Ms. Swain's manager
(B) Make an announcement
(C) Change an event schedule
(D) Give a performance

GO ON TO THE NEXT PAGE

Questions 172-175 refer to the following advertisement.

Come Fly With Altus Airways

Altus Airways was recently voted the number one airline in the world for the third consecutive year. — [1] —. We were praised for the high quality of food we have always provided to our passengers, as well as our impeccable safety record. — [2] —. This year, we were also recognized for the changes we made to the entertainment systems in our aircraft. These now boast larger, more advanced screens and a more extensive range of TV shows, movies, and games. — [3] —. Another reason to choose Altus Airways for your next trip is our excellent customer service. — [4] —. From our Web site to our check-in procedure to our in-flight services, we aim to exceed your expectations in every way.

Altus Airways serves all major destinations within the United States and around the world, as well as a large number of remote locations. Over the next few months, we intend to introduce new flights to places such as Greenland and Sri Lanka, serving these countries for the first time. For more information about our flight routes and services, please visit our Web site at www.altusairways.com.

172. The word "recognized" in paragraph 1, line 3, is closest in meaning to

(A) mirrored
(B) commended
(C) identified
(D) advertised

173. According to the advertisement, what has Altus Airways recently improved for its passengers?

(A) Its safety measures
(B) Its check-in procedure
(C) Its in-flight meals
(D) Its entertainment systems

174. What is suggested about Altus Airways?

(A) It is based in Greenland.
(B) It plans to add new flight destinations.
(C) It offers discounts on several flight routes.
(D) It recently conducted a passenger survey.

175. In which of the positions marked [1], [2], [3], and [4] does the following sentence best belong?

"Since our founding 26 years ago, none of our airplanes have been involved in a crash."

(A) [1]
(B) [2]
(C) [3]
(D) [4]

GO ON TO THE NEXT PAGE

Walking Tour of Littlehampton

Full-day walking tour of Littlehampton, July 14, 9:15 A.M. to 4:30 P.M. We recommend bringing a sun hat, sunscreen, and an umbrella so that you are prepared for any unexpected weather conditions. Please inform us in advance if you have any specific dietary requirements.

TOUR ITINERARY

9:15 A.M.	Depart from Littlehampton Tourist Information Center
9:30 A.M.	Sightseeing Location 1: Littlehampton Botanical Gardens
11:00 A.M.	Sightseeing Location 2: St. Michael's Cathedral
12:30 P.M.	Lunch in Grandview Park (Packed lunches provided)
1:30 P.M.	Sightseeing Location 3: Littlehampton Petting Zoo
3:30 P.M.	Sightseeing Location 4: Little Wharf Seafood Market
4:30 P.M.	Arrive back at Littlehampton Tourist Information Center

To:	Edith Connolly <econnolly@lpc.com>
From:	Harry Jacobsen <hjacobsen@worldmail.net>
Subject:	Regarding our conversation
Date:	July 15

Dear Ms. Connolly,

I really enjoyed chatting to you while I was on the walking tour of Littlehampton yesterday. The tour itself was excellent from beginning to end. Having never been to your town before, I had no idea it was home to so many wonderful sightseeing places. I particularly liked our stop at your place of work. It was fascinating to see how you and your team of volunteers care for all the animals there, and I was very impressed with your commitment to your work.

During our discussion, you mentioned that your organization is dependent on fundraising and donations. I would be interested in providing a cash gift of five thousand dollars in order to help you and your staff achieve your goals this year. Hopefully, this will allow you to repair the broken equipment you mentioned and purchase new equipment. Please let me know the best way to transfer this sum to you.

I look forward to hearing from you.

Regards,

Harry Jacobsen

176. What can be inferred from the tour itinerary?

(A) Food is provided to participants.
(B) Tours may be cancelled due to bad weather.
(C) Tour groups will travel by bus.
(D) Some sightseeing locations are unavailable.

177. Where did Mr. Jacobsen most likely meet Ms. Connolly?

(A) At Sightseeing Location 1
(B) At Sightseeing Location 2
(C) At Sightseeing Location 3
(D) At Sightseeing Location 4

178. What is suggested about Mr. Jacobsen?

(A) He plans to move to Littlehampton.
(B) He is a former colleague of Ms. Connolly.
(C) He was visiting Littlehampton for the first time.
(D) He was disappointed with the walking tour.

179. In the e-mail, the word "achieve" in paragraph 2, line 3, is closest in meaning to

(A) succeed
(B) attain
(C) set
(D) evaluate

180. What does Mr. Jacobsen ask Ms. Connolly to do in his e-mail?

(A) Provide some information
(B) Inquire about a job
(C) Schedule a meeting
(D) Offer to volunteer

GO ON TO THE NEXT PAGE

ROCOCO BISTRO - SET MENUS

Italian Experience (3 Courses, $28 per person)
Appetizer: Garlic bread or salad
Main Course: Pasta or pizza
Dessert: Gelato or lemon cake
Availability: Monday through Sunday, 12:00 P.M. to 7 P.M.

British Sunday Dinner (4 Courses, $32 per person)
Appetizer: Prawn cocktail or melon balls
Main Courses: Roast chicken with vegetables and cheese selection with crackers
Dessert: Sticky toffee pudding or fruit cake
Availability: Only Sundays, 3:00 P.M. to 7 P.M.

Spanish Fiesta (4 Courses, $36 per person)
Appetizer: Mixed olives or bread with dip
Main Courses: Seafood paella and Spanish omelet
Dessert: Ice cream or cheesecake
Availability: Mondays, Wednesdays, and Fridays, 2:00 P.M. to 7:00 P.M.

Asian Medley (5 Courses, $42 per person)
Appetizer: Spring rolls or prawn toast
Main Courses: Pad Thai, bibimbap, and roast duck
Dessert: Sweet rice cake or pineapple cake
Availability: Tuesdays, Thursdays, Saturdays, and Sundays, 3:00 P.M. to 7:00 P.M.

---

http://www.besteatsboston.com/userreviews/19189

BEST EATS BOSTON - Restaurant Reviews

Restaurant: Rococo Bistro
Date: Thursday, September 15

Review: My most recent trip to Rococo Bistro prompted me to make an account and post my first review here. The food there simply gets better and better. Yesterday I dined there with some friends and we all ordered one of the restaurant's set menus. All four courses were absolutely delicious, and the service was amazing as well. The restaurant was surprisingly busy considering it was a weekday, but our waiter, Steve, was very attentive to our needs. If I had any minor criticism, it's that the tables in the dining area could be spaced a little farther apart. It can feel quite cramped at busy times, and the noise from nearby diners makes it a little hard to have a conversation.

Review Submitted By: Peter DeVito

181. What is indicated about Rococo Bistro?

    (A) It primarily serves British food.
    (B) It operates in four locations.
    (C) It offers discounts to groups.
    (D) It is open seven days a week.

182. When does Rococo Bistro most likely open?

    (A) 12:00 P.M.
    (B) 2:00 P.M.
    (C) 3:00 P.M.
    (D) 7:00 P.M.

183. What can be inferred about Mr. DeVito?

    (A) He visited Rococo Bistro with work colleagues.
    (B) He lives nearby Rococo Bistro.
    (C) He has posted several reviews of Rococo Bistro.
    (D) He regularly dines at Rococo Bistro.

184. How much did Mr. DeVito most likely pay for his meal?

    (A) $28 per person
    (B) $32 per person
    (C) $36 per person
    (D) $42 per person

185. What aspect of Rococo Bistro does Mr. DeVito think could be improved?

    (A) Its service
    (B) Its prices
    (C) Its food
    (D) Its layout

GO ON TO THE NEXT PAGE

Questions 186-190 refer to the following memo, e-mail, and report.

To: All Nyman Manufacturing Employees
From: Darren Beckham, General Operations Manager
Subject: Important date
Date: August 16

All staff please note that a team of technicians from Sylen Security will visit our factory on Wednesday, August 23, from 10 a.m. to 12 p.m. Once they arrive, our security manager will show them around and assist them with anything they need. Please be advised that the team may need to temporarily disrupt our workflow while performing the necessary installation work. We appreciate your cooperation while the work is underway.

Darren

E-Mail Message

To: Darren Beckham <dbeckham@nymaninc.com>
From: Cassie Wong <cwong@sylensecurity.com>
Subject: Schedule conflict
Date: August 17

Dear Mr. Beckham,

With regret, our team will not be able to perform the work originally scheduled for August 23 at your factory. This is due to an unfortunate scheduling error. We appreciate your understanding, and I hope you will agree to reschedule the work for another day. We would be able to perform the work on Monday, August 21, from 11 a.m. to 1 p.m., Thursday, August 24, from 1 p.m. to 3 p.m., or Friday, August 25, from 3 p.m. to 5 p.m. Please let me know your preference.

As an apology for the rescheduling, we are prepared to offer you a 5 percent discount on the installation costs.

I look forward to hearing from you.

Best wishes,

Cassie Wong,
Installations Team Leader

SYLEN SECURITY

INSTALLATION REPORT

Nyman Manufacturing
3527 Stonebridge Road, Elfburg
Installation date: August 24
Team leader: Cassie Wong

Details of Work: Our team arrived on schedule and we were greeted by Clint Ridley, who gave us a brief tour of the factory and showed us where our work would be carried out.

We began by installing the CCTV cameras around the factory and in the reception area of Nyman Manufacturing's administration building. All work was completed swiftly by our work team, and a full test was performed to ensure the equipment operated perfectly. Mr. Ridley was very impressed with the performance of the cameras. Next, we installed the fingerprint scanner at the factory entrance. Although the system is functioning, I noted that the software is an older version than we originally advertised to the client, so I plan to go back early next month to update it.

186. What is the main purpose of the memo?

(A) To describe a new security procedure
(B) To request volunteers for a project
(C) To announce a new employee incentive program
(D) To inform staff about some upcoming work

187. In the e-mail, the word "prepared" in paragraph 2, line 1, is closest in meaning to

(A) likely
(B) willing
(C) potential
(D) grateful

188. At what time did Ms. Wong most likely arrive at Nyman Manufacturing's factory?

(A) 10:00 a.m.
(B) 11:00 a.m.
(C) 1:00 p.m.
(D) 3:00 p.m.

189. What is suggested about Mr. Ridley?

(A) He has experience in installing devices.
(B) He is Nyman Manufacturing's security manager.
(C) He is a former employee of Sylen Security.
(D) He submitted a report to Ms. Wong.

190. What does the report indicate about Ms. Wong?

(A) She has worked with Nyman Manufacturing several times.
(B) She did not accompany the installation work team.
(C) She was unable to complete a camera installation.
(D) She intends to return to the factory in September.

GO ON TO THE NEXT PAGE

To:	Alan Jones <ajones@xenonelectronics.com>
From:	Barbara Winkler <bwinkler@xenonelectronics.com>
Subject:	Product Launch
Date:	March 17

Hi Alan,

I know you have been very busy arranging the launch of our company's new mobile phone in April, and I thought you might appreciate some advice regarding the official launch event. I know that several very important shareholders and investors will be attending the launch, and that it is important that everything runs smoothly and efficiently. Therefore, I'd like to suggest contacting Zoom Catering to provide food and refreshments to our guests.

Zoom Catering not only provides outstanding food, but also a corporate discount to repeat clients. Considering we used them for our year-end banquet last year, we should be entitled to a lower rate for this service. I realize you may already have a different catering firm in mind, but please consider Zoom as an option. Just keep in mind that many of our guests do not eat meat, and some have food allergies we need to accommodate. For instance, the CEO of Diver Investment is highly allergic to peanuts, and the president of Crick Financial will require several dairy-free options.

Good luck with the arrangements, and let me know if you need any assistance.

Regards,

Barbara

Zoom Catering
Edmonton, Alberta

With over 25 years of experience in catering corporate events of all sizes, Zoom Catering can guarantee you a premium service at an affordable rate.

Contact us today to take advantage of the various services we can provide for your event:
- Customization of event menus to suit all guests (including a wide range of meat-free dishes)
- Team of up to ten catering staff to provide excellent service to your guests
- Free tea, coffee, soft drinks, and mineral water for all guests (we are not licensed to serve alcohol)
- Decoration of dining area and tables (including floral centerpieces, folded napkins, and tablecloths)

Contact our team of helpful staff at 555-6611 to reserve your luxurious feast today!

Zoom Catering
April 7

Dear Ms. Ness,

We have spoken with Alan Jones of Xenon Electronics regarding your specific dietary requirements, and we are pleased to inform you that the majority of dishes being served during today's event are peanut-free. Only two dishes contain peanuts - the chicken satay and the pad Thai - both of which have been placed on a separate table spaced far away from the other dishes. Please let us know if we can assist you in any way. Although I will need to leave before the product launch begins, one of my colleagues will be happy to help you.

Sincerely,

Beatrice Ferry
Zoom Catering

191. What is the purpose of the e-mail?

(A) To invite Mr. Jones to an upcoming event
(B) To suggest delaying a product launch
(C) To provide assistance with arrangements
(D) To compare two potential event caterers

192. What makes Zoom Catering an appropriate business for the event?

(A) Its vegetarian menu
(B) Its affordable prices
(C) It experience in the field
(D) It catering team size

193. According to the advertisement, what is not provided by Zoom Catering?

(A) Personalized menus
(B) Table decorations
(C) Alcoholic beverages
(D) Serving staff

194. For what company does Ms. Ness most likely work?

(A) Crick Financial
(B) Diver Investment
(C) Xenon Electronics
(D) Zoom Catering

195. What is true about Ms. Ferry?

(A) She suggested an alternative to the chicken satay.
(B) She has arranged to meet with Ms. Ness.
(C) She prepared all of the catering dishes herself.
(D) She will not be present at the product launch.

GO ON TO THE NEXT PAGE

Questions 196-200 refer to the following notice, advertisement, and e-mail.

To:	All Bar-B-Q Burger Staff
From:	Frank Doyle
Date:	May 2
Subject:	Summer Special Offers

Dear Employees,

This summer, we are planning to introduce a new range of special offers in an effort to boost our sales and profits. These offers will be implemented in all branches of Bar-B-Q Burger, and full training will be provided to staff prior to their launch. In addition, each branch will receive appropriate marketing materials, including posters and flyers, to promote the offers.

The first offer is a buy-one-get-one-free (BOGOF) offer on all our Extra Large Meals. Based on our projections, despite offering a free meal worth $8.99, this offer will draw in 10 percent more customers and result in a net profit over the busy June-August period. The second special offer will also run from June until August, and this one will be applied to our children's menu. With every children's meal, we will be giving away a complimentary toy. The toy will be an action figure, and there will be five different figures, each one depicting one of the Bar-B-Q Burger characters from our popular TV commercials. We encourage all staff to promote these offers to customers whenever possible.

Please be advised that the details of the special offers may still be changed before they are officially introduced on June 1. Full details will be provided by your branch manager in the last week of May.

Frank Doyle
Marketing Manager
Bar-B-Q Burger

Bar-B-Q Burger
Take Advantage of Our Incredible Special Offers This Summer!

Buy one Extra Large Meal and get another one for free!

Whenever you buy any Extra Large Meal from our menu, we'll give you another one completely free! You can either order the second meal along with the first one or take a voucher that can be redeemed at any branch of Bar-B-Q Burger before August 31.

Purchase a meal from the children's menu and your child receives a free gift! From June 1, all children's meals will come with a colorful story book about all of the popular Bar-B-Q characters! Each month we will offer a different book, so children can try to complete the entire set of three.

Available from June 1 to August 31.

To: Frank Doyle <fdoyle@barbqburger.com>
From: Carissa Sandoval <csandoval@barbqburger.com>
Date: September 12
Subject: Summer Special Offers Evaluation

Hi Frank,

I've been going over the sales figures for the June to August period, and I'm pleased to see that both special offers were very successful. Our projections regarding the BOGOF special offer proved to be highly accurate. Our profits on those meals almost doubled compared with last summer. Having spoken to the board members, it is likely that we will bring back this special offer from December to February.

The special offer on children's meals was also a great success, although it was disappointing that we had to end the offer two weeks earlier than planned due to a shortage of gifts. We have received assurances from the supplier that this will not happen in the future should we decide to run the special offer again.

The board members have requested that you join the meeting at headquarters next month to congratulate you on your hard work. Please contact me at your earliest possible convenience and I will allocate a travel budget for you.

Regards,

Carissa Sandoval, Finance Manager
Bar-B-Q Burger

196. What is the purpose of the notice?

(A) To inform staff of upcoming changes
(B) To introduce new menu items to customers
(C) To congratulate employees for reaching a goal
(D) To seek feedback from staff about a marketing strategy

197. What can be inferred about Bar-B-Q Burger?

(A) It has hired a new marketing manager.
(B) It recently opened new branches.
(C) It advertises its products on television.
(D) It receives fewer customers in summer.

198. What aspect of the special offer for children was changed after May 2?

(A) The size of the meal
(B) The duration of the offer
(C) The menu items involved
(D) The type of free gift

199. What does Ms. Sandoval indicate about Bar-B-Q Burger in her e-mail?

(A) It extended the BOGOF offer by an extra month.
(B) It will work with a different supplier in the future.
(C) Its special offers were less successful than expected.
(D) It ran out of story books in August.

200. What will happen at Bar-B-Q Burger in October?

(A) A new special offer will begin.
(B) A marketing budget will be increased.
(C) Mr. Doyle will attend a meeting.
(D) Ms. Sandoval will give a presentation.

Stop! This is the end of the test. If you finish before time is called,
you may go back to Parts 5, 6, and 7 and check your work.

토익학습지 실전편
실전 모의고사 1 정답 및 스크립트

정답

PART 1

1. (A)　**2.** (C)　**3.** (D)　**4.** (B)　**5.** (B)　**6.** (A)

PART 2

7. (C)　**8.** (C)　**9.** (B)　**10.** (C)　**11.** (B)　**12.** (C)　**13.** (A)　**14.** (A)　**15.** (B)　**16.** (A)　**17.** (B)　**18.** (B)　**19.** (A)　**20.** (C)　**21.** (A)
22. (A)　**23.** (B)　**24.** (C)　**25.** (B)　**26.** (C)　**27.** (B)　**28.** (A)　**29.** (A)　**30.** (C)　**31.** (B)

PART 3

32. (C)　**33.** (B)　**34.** (D)　**35.** (D)　**36.** (C)　**37.** (A)　**38.** (D)　**39.** (B)　**40.** (C)　**41.** (A)　**42.** (C)　**43.** (C)　**44.** (B)　**45.** (C)　**46.** (D)
47. (D)　**48.** (C)　**49.** (B)　**50.** (B)　**51.** (D)　**52.** (C)　**53.** (B)　**54.** (D)　**55.** (B)　**56.** (D)　**57.** (B)　**58.** (D)　**59.** (C)　**60.** (A)　**61.** (D)
62. (A)　**63.** (B)　**64.** (B)　**65.** (C)　**66.** (D)　**67.** (B)　**68.** (B)　**69.** (C)　**70.** (C)

PART 4

71. (C)　**72.** (B)　**73.** (C)　**74.** (D)　**75.** (B)　**76.** (D)　**77.** (B)　**78.** (C)　**79.** (D)　**80.** (B)　**81.** (D)　**82.** (C)　**83.** (D)　**84.** (D)　**85.** (B)
86. (B)　**87.** (C)　**88.** (A)　**89.** (D)　**90.** (B)　**91.** (C)　**92.** (C)　**93.** (B)　**94.** (A)　**95.** (C)　**96.** (B)　**97.** (C)　**98.** (B)　**99.** (B)　**100.** (B)

PART 5

101. (A)　**102.** (D)　**103.** (C)　**104.** (A)　**105.** (C)　**106.** (B)　**107.** (A)　**108.** (B)　**109.** (C)　**110.** (A)　**111.** (D)　**112.** (D)
113. (B)　**114.** (B)　**115.** (D)　**116.** (D)　**117.** (C)　**118.** (D)　**119.** (A)　**120.** (A)　**121.** (C)　**122.** (A)　**123.** (B)　**124.** (B)
125. (C)　**126.** (B)　**127.** (A)　**128.** (B)　**129.** (C)　**130.** (B)

PART 6

131. (A)　**132.** (B)　**133.** (D)　**134.** (C)　**135.** (B)　**136.** (B)　**137.** (C)　**138.** (D)　**139.** (D)　**140.** (C)　**141.** (C)　**142.** (A)
143. (C)　**144.** (A)　**145.** (C)　**146.** (C)

PART 7

147. (C)　**148.** (B)　**149.** (C)　**150.** (B)　**151.** (D)　**152.** (B)　**153.** (D)　**154.** (B)　**155.** (D)　**156.** (D)　**157.** (B)　**158.** (A)
159. (C)　**160.** (B)　**161.** (C)　**162.** (A)　**163.** (B)　**164.** (C)　**165.** (D)　**166.** (C)　**167.** (B)　**168.** (D)　**169.** (D)　**170.** (B)
171. (A)　**172.** (B)　**173.** (D)　**174.** (D)　**175.** (B)　**176.** (A)　**177.** (C)　**178.** (C)　**179.** (B)　**180.** (A)　**181.** (D)　**182.** (A)
183. (D)　**184.** (C)　**185.** (D)　**186.** (D)　**187.** (B)　**188.** (C)　**189.** (B)　**190.** (D)　**191.** (C)　**192.** (A)　**193.** (C)　**194.** (B)
195. (D)　**196.** (A)　**197.** (C)　**198.** (D)　**199.** (D)　**200.** (C)

Part 1

1.   (A) She's packing a suitcase.
   (B) She's closing some curtains.
   (C) She's folding a blanket.
   (D) She's putting on a hat.

2.   (A) The man is sliding his wallet into his pocket.
   (B) The woman is putting groceries in the shopping cart.
   (C) The man is making a payment with his card.
   (D) The woman is attaching price tags to some merchandise.

3.   (A) The woman is handing out some brochures.
   (B) The woman is bending down to pick up a book.
   (C) The woman is walking through a doorway.
   (D) The woman is resting her hand on some books.

4.   (A) A man is loading materials onto a cart.
   (B) A man is pushing a wheelbarrow.
   (C) A woman is sweeping a walkway.
   (D) A woman is putting away some tools.

5.   (A) They're holding a metal handrail.
   (B) They're going up a staircase.
   (C) They're stepping into a street.
   (D) They're carrying backpacks.

6.   (A) Some motorbikes have been parked in a row.
   (B) Some tires are being repaired.
   (C) Some vehicles are being driven up a ramp.
   (D) Some parking spaces are being resurfaced.

Part 2

7.   How much do these multivitamins cost?
   (A) That sounds like a bargain.
   (B) Only two per day.
   (C) They're 25 dollars.

8.   Are you going to the dentist today or tomorrow?
   (A) At the new dental clinic.
   (B) Sure, I'll schedule an appointment.
   (C) Tomorrow at 10 o'clock.

9.   Why were you late for the meeting?
   (A) Thanks, it was informative.
   (B) Because I was with a client.
   (C) Right after lunch.

10.   Would you like something to read while you wait?
    (A) I really enjoyed that book.
    (B) For at least 30 minutes.
    (C) A magazine would be nice.

11.   When should I come back to pick up my ID card?
    (A) Yes, we'll mail it.
    (B) In two days.
    (C) For security reasons.

12.   Do you think our regular diners will like our new menu?
    (A) I'll try the lobster, thanks.
    (B) We can accommodate 50 diners.
    (C) Yes, it's better than ever.

13.   How do I apply for a branch transfer?
    (A) Where do you want to go?
    (B) That's our main branch office.
    (C) You can move it over here.

14.   Can I help you file all those documents?
    (A) I'd be grateful if you did.
    (B) Have you found it?
    (C) No, I haven't completed it.

15.   Mr. Haskin is being promoted this month, isn't he?
    (A) I doubt that I'm qualified.
    (B) No, not until January.
    (C) It's on sale for half price.

16.   How many languages does Lucinda speak?
    (A) She's fluent in three.
    (B) That's up to her.
    (C) She used to live abroad.

17.   Didn't they clean our office windows?
    (A) A new operating system.
    (B) Yes, only yesterday.
    (C) We have a great view.

18.   Who's in charge of buying the coffee for the break room?
    (A) We'll take a break in five minutes.
    (B) I believe that's Alan's job.
    (C) I prefer the dark roast blend.

19.   Where can I find an extra stapler?
    (A) You can borrow mine.
    (B) Just these pages, please.
    (C) I already did.

20.   Excuse me, when can we check in?
    (A) For three days.
    (B) A double room on the top floor.
    (C) We're still preparing your room.

21.   I'd like to have Rachel supervise our new branch office.
    (A) I'm sure she could handle it.

(B) No, she's not here today.

(C) You've done an excellent job.

22. Will the performance be streamed online or only shown on TV?

(A) We still haven't decided.

(B) Turn to Channel 10.

(C) That was an amazing concert.

23. We should repair the photocopier beside the reception desk.

(A) Did you make me a copy?

(B) It was fixed this morning.

(C) Just go down this corridor.

24. Who's going to interview the applicants for the sales positions?

(A) Yes, around ten representatives.

(B) Can I still apply for a job?

(C) I thought that was your responsibility.

25. I heard you just moved into a nice new apartment.

(A) There are some places downtown.

(B) You should come for a visit.

(C) The elevator is at the end of the hall.

26. Which employee won the sales competition?

(A) Brian can do that for you.

(B) I'm not a big fan of sports.

(C) We're still counting the figures.

27. Are the products in this store always so cheap?

(A) No, you need to pay in cash.

(B) There's a special sale this week.

(C) Let's buy two then.

28. The new IT technician is really knowledgeable, isn't he?

(A) Well, he has 20 years of experience.

(B) Maybe I can help you.

(C) I think he's in the maintenance office.

29. We've received a lot of applications for the factory manager vacancy.

(A) It's certainly an attractive position.

(B) I'm afraid we don't have any vacancies.

(C) You should submit it by the end of this week.

30. Why are the heating units making so much noise?

(A) Please turn down the volume.

(B) Yes, it's getting hot in here.

(C) They probably need to be inspected.

31. Weren't the old office desks thrown out already?

(A) The marketing department.

(B) They're being picked up tomorrow.

(C) The new ones look great.

Part 3

Questions 32-34 refer to the following conversation.

M: Miranda, how are the designs coming along for our new line of portable speakers? You're in charge of that project, right?

W: That's right, and they're looking great! We've listened to customer feedback and made many improvements compared with our previous models. I have a prototype right here. Take a look.

M: Wow, you've done a great job! I can't believe how light it is! This will definitely make it easy for people to carry them around.

W: Yes, I'm really proud of that. I think customers will be surprised, too.

M: Why don't we organize a presentation for the board members? I'm sure they'd like an update on the product development.

Questions 35-37 refer to the following conversation with three speakers.

W: Hi, Peter and Kostas. I'm Rhonda, the operations manager here at Sisco Manufacturing. I'll be showing you around the factory during this morning's inspection.

M1: It's nice to meet you. Before we get started, could we quickly use a computer? Our office printer is broken, so I wasn't able to print the inspection forms.

M2: Yes, I need to print out a copy of our health and safety checklist, too.

W: Of course! First, please put on these visitor ID tags. That's a standard policy for anyone coming into our buildings.

Questions 38-40 refer to the following conversation.

W: Hello, Mr. Royle. I'm Diane from Blitz Web Design. I'm here about your work request.

M: Thanks for coming in, Diane. Our Web site really needs some professional help.

W: Well, I've helped quite a few firms in the clothing industry. What exactly are you looking for?

M: My main goal is to simplify the way in which customers make purchases through our online store. Many of them log out from the checkout page because they're confused.

W: That's definitely something I can help with. You said

you'd already prepared a few design ideas on paper, right?

M: Yes. Let me show you those, and you can give me your opinion.

Questions 41-43 refer to the following conversation.

M: Thank you for calling Frank's Fresh Produce. How may I help you?

W: Hi, I'd like to purchase around 30 kilograms of blueberries for my smoothie store. Would you be able to provide that amount?

M: Please hold for a moment while I check our stock. For an order of that size, we'll be able to deliver it on June 20.

W: June 20 is two weeks away.

M: Well, another option would be to send you half now and half later, and lower the price a little. Let me just figure out what kind of price reduction I could offer you.

Questions 44-46 refer to the following conversation.

W: Thanks for sweeping and mopping all our exercise rooms, Steve. They're going to look perfect when our new gym members arrive for their orientation classes.

M: My pleasure.

W: Can you help out with one more thing? We're having some sandwiches delivered for the orientation, and I need you to arrange them on some tables.

M: No problem. What time will they be delivered?

W: They should arrive around 10 o'clock.

M: Okay, but just to let you know, I won't be able to work late today. I have to see my dentist at 5:30 to have a filling replaced.

W: I understand. I'll make sure you can leave by 5.

Questions 47-49 refer to the following conversation.

M: Hi, Ms. Tarrant. I've been expecting you. Welcome to Bluesky Photography.

W: Thanks. As I mentioned over the phone, I'm starting a jewelry making business. I'm mostly hoping to sell my items online, so it's important that I have excellent images of them to show to potential customers.

M: Well, Bluesky Photography has a lot of experience in creating promotional images for merchandise. In fact, I'm proud to say we received a prize for Best Commercial Photographs just last year.

W: I'm happy to hear that! So, I can safely assume your images are very high quality, right?

M: Of course! Why don't you view some samples in the catalog here?

Questions 50-52 refer to the following conversation.

M: Hi, Becky. I know you've represented our company at previous job fairs. Well, I've been given that responsibility this year, and I'm not sure what I'm doing. It'll be my first time.

W: Well, it's pretty easy. When I attended those events, I made sure I took along a lot of pamphlets and flyers to hand out to attendees.

M: Thanks, I'll do that. And, our CEO told me I should try to get a lot of résumés from the event attendees, so I really hope they remember to bring one along.

W: Hmm... It might be a good idea to speak to Karl. He can add a reminder to our Web site so that the attendees don't forget.

Questions 53-55 refer to the following conversation.

W: Gary, I'm thinking about how we can improve the marketing strategy for our company's latest line of sports drinks. Do you have any ideas?

M: Well, the consumers who drink our products are generally fans of sports and exercise. So, how about getting famous athletes to endorse our products in our ads?

W: Don't you think our budget is a little too small for that?

M: Well, you might be right. But, we could try to request an increase.

W: Okay, I'll need to arrange a meeting with our board members then. In the meantime, try to figure out how much you think it might cost.

Questions 56-58 refer to the following conversation with three speakers.

M1: Have you both looked over the surveys we asked employees to take part in last month? The feedback we've gotten could really help us to boost productivity and workplace morale.

M2: Yes, the survey responses seem very interesting. As we expected, it looks like the company's plan to buy better desks and chairs is popular with our workers.

M1: Yes, and the survey results also indicate that we should create more clubs and activity groups for staff.

W: Well, let's think of some ideas for clubs this week. Then we can announce them at the staff meeting next Monday morning.

Questions 59-61 refer to the following conversation.

W: Hi, Gordon. Sorry I'm late, but the traffic was terrible. Did you already check in and get your boarding pass?

M: Not yet. Our flight has been delayed by two hours. So, I've just been sitting in this computer lounge and going over our product demonstration plan for tomorrow.

W: Well, that's a good way to use our time while we wait. This demonstration is so important. We really need to impress the potential investors.

M: Exactly. Without their financial support, we might not be able to launch our product.

W: Hmm… It's a little noisy in here, though. How about moving to a different spot to discuss our strategy?

M: Sure. There's a coffee shop over there that's pretty empty.

W: Sounds good to me.

Questions 62-64 refer to the following conversation and map.

M: Hey, Megumi! Are you done with the planning for our library's Children's Summer Festival?

W: Hi, Pete. Actually, I'm trying to fit in a snack stand in one of our library's areas, but I'm not sure which area to put it in.

M: Well, why don't we put it in the face painting area? I don't think that area needs as much space as we initially assigned to it.

W: You're probably right. I'll put it there. By the way, have you seen Sandra? The event flyer should mention that snacks will be available for purchase.

M: I think she's using the computer lab to finalize the flyer design now.

Questions 65-67 refer to the following conversation and museum map.

W: Welcome to Ashville History Museum. Can I help you with anything?

M: Hello, I'm a college professor, and I'm planning to bring my students here on a trip. I'm just here today to check what exhibits you have.

W: No problem. Well, we have four large exhibit halls, but I'm afraid our clothing and jewelry hall is currently closed for remodeling.

M: That's a pity. I was really hoping to show those exhibits to my students. Will it reopen anytime soon?

W: Not for at least a month. But, you could try speaking to my manager about it. He might be able to arrange for you to see at least some of the items.

Questions 68-70 refer to the following conversation and pie chart.

W: Larry, I need to speak with you about our monthly energy use here at Greenfield Grocery. I think there are ways we could cut down on energy.

M: What do you have in mind?

W: Well, I feel like we are using far too much energy on lighting right now. Why don't we have more windows installed? The natural light would really brighten up the place.

M: That's a great idea. I'll contact some window companies today and ask for some cost estimates.

W: Thanks. Let me know what you find out.

Part 4

Questions 71-73 refer to the following excerpt from a meeting.

Before we wrap up this brief meeting, I'd like to remind you all about the Family Fun Day we will be holding here at the library next weekend. We will have several fun activities for children and adults, such as face painting, story reading, and quizzes with exciting prizes. Our aim is to take the proceeds from ticket sales and donations and use that money to expand our children's reading area. Anyone who wishes to volunteer during the event will receive a $20 gift coupon for Manley Department Store.

Questions 74-76 refer to the following broadcast.

In local business news, Portland-based Axon Enterprises announced yesterday that it will merge with rival firm Polaris Corporation this winter. Axon is the country's leading manufacturer of medical devices such as MRI machines, thermometers, and stethoscopes. The two companies aim to combine their strengths on new research and development projects, while creating an additional ten thousand jobs across the United States. New positions have already been posted online, so if you are interested, visit Axon's Web site right away.

Questions 77-79 refer to the following tour information.

It's my pleasure today to give you all a tour of Chong Fashion House, where the world-renowned designer Annabel Chong creates all her clothing. As you are all studying to follow in Ms. Chong's footsteps, we hope this tour helps to inspire you! I'm going to take you around our offices first so that you can see where we come up with concepts and plan projects. Then we'll visit the manufacturing building, where you'll see how our workers make our garments. And, don't be shy. The workers will be happy to explain various techniques and tools to you.

Questions 80-82 refer to the following speech.

Good morning, everyone. Today we are here to celebrate our company's successful growth across North America. We just finalized the purchase of new facilities in Toronto, Chicago, and Dallas, and this will help us to significantly expand our operations. We are currently advertising vacancies for these new locations, and we plan to recruit around 2,000 workers in July. Now, before we celebrate with a catered lunch, I'm going to hand out some revenue and cost projections for the next few years. Please take a moment to review them.

Questions 83-85 refer to the following introduction.

Welcome to our annual workshop on customer service training. This two-day event will start this morning with a talk from our keynote speaker. Lawrence Russell is a leading expert on meeting the needs of consumers, and he has written five best-selling books on the subject. He'll talk to you about new trends in consumer expectations, and ways in which businesses can keep customers satisfied. Unfortunately, however, Mr. Russell's flight was a little behind schedule, so his talk will be delayed by about 30 minutes. In the meantime, please enjoy some coffee and muffins.

Questions 86-88 refer to the following speech.

I'd like to start this tenants' association meeting by talking about some ways in which our apartment building will be improved over the next few months. First, the building manager has listened to our complaints and agreed to install a secure entry system at the main door. He has also listened to our feedback regarding the fitness room. He'll have the broken equipment repaired or replaced, and also renovate the room. This couldn't have happened without you. I have some pictures here of equipment we can request. Take a look and let me know what you think.

Questions 89-91 refer to the following talk.

Good afternoon, everyone. I've been looking at the report I received from our sales department, and it seems that all of our milk products are selling well, apart from our milk that is high in calcium. So, I'd like you all to boost the poor sales of this product by coming up with some advertisements that we can use on TV, online, and in printed publications. These ads need to attract consumers by really showing the benefits of the product. I'll expect you all to think about it this evening, and then e-mail some concepts to me when you get to work tomorrow morning.

Questions 92-94 refer to the following telephone message.

Hi, Ms. Walsh. This is Michael, the site manager for the Riley Building construction project. I'm calling to tell you that we're having some issues with security here at the site. It seems like some tools have been removed during the night, and this is going to cause a work delay and an increase in expenses. We have a couple of security guards patrolling at night, but it's not enough. I think it would be best if we have some CCTV cameras installed to enhance security. Hopefully we can talk about this when we meet on Wednesday.

Questions 95-97 refer to the following announcement and table.

Good morning. I'm glad you all flew down here to Florida to view our orange farm. I hope you had a pleasant stay in the hotel we booked for you. We specifically chose one with a pool so you could have a swim and cool down after your long trip. Now, I'm afraid the outdoor part of the tour today might have to be canceled, because the forecast calls for a severe storm. However, you'll still have lots to see inside our packing and distribution facility, where I am the supervisor. But, first, you're going to go with my colleague and learn more about our annual profits.

Questions 98-100 refer to the following telephone message and map.

Hi, I'm calling from Gold Star Catering. As you requested, I'm at the venue with my team setting up the food for your company's year-end celebration. Everything is looking great, and we are on schedule to begin serving at 6 P.M. However, I'm worried about the table of food you asked us to set up near the north entrance. I don't think it's safe having it so close to the stage, as there are lots of electrical cables there. I'll talk to the supervisor here at the venue and see if he can tidy up the cables. If not, it might be a good idea to move the table.

해설 바로보기 ▶

TOEIC

Test of English for International Communication

TEST 2

실전 모의고사 2

LISTENING TEST

In the Listening test, you will be asked to demonstrate how well you understand spoken English. The entire Listening test will last approximately 45 minutes. There are four parts, and directions are given for each part. You must mark your answers on the separate answer sheet. Do not write your answers in your test book.

PART 1

Directions: For each question in this part, you will hear four statements about a picture in your test book. When you hear the statements, you must select the one statement that best describes what you see in the picture. Then find the number of the question on your answer sheet and mark your answer. The statements will not be printed in your test book and will be spoken only one time.

Statement (D), "They are taking photographs," is the best description of the picture, so you should select answer (D) and mark it on your answer sheet.

1.

2.

GO ON TO THE NEXT PAGE

3.

4.

5.

6.

GO ON TO THE NEXT PAGE →

PART 2

Directions: You will hear a question or statement and three responses spoken in English. They will not be printed in your test book and will be spoken only one time. Select the best response to the question or statement and mark the letter (A), (B), or (C) on your answer sheet.

7. Mark your answer on your answer sheet.

8. Mark your answer on your answer sheet.

9. Mark your answer on your answer sheet.

10. Mark your answer on your answer sheet.

11. Mark your answer on your answer sheet.

12. Mark your answer on your answer sheet.

13. Mark your answer on your answer sheet.

14. Mark your answer on your answer sheet.

15. Mark your answer on your answer sheet.

16. Mark your answer on your answer sheet.

17. Mark your answer on your answer sheet.

18. Mark your answer on your answer sheet.

19. Mark your answer on your answer sheet.

20. Mark your answer on your answer sheet.

21. Mark your answer on your answer sheet.

22. Mark your answer on your answer sheet.

23. Mark your answer on your answer sheet.

24. Mark your answer on your answer sheet.

25. Mark your answer on your answer sheet.

26. Mark your answer on your answer sheet.

27. Mark your answer on your answer sheet.

28. Mark your answer on your answer sheet.

29. Mark your answer on your answer sheet.

30. Mark your answer on your answer sheet.

31. Mark your answer on your answer sheet.

PART 3

Directions: You will hear some conversations between two or more people. You will be asked to answer three questions about what the speakers say in each conversation. Select the best response to each question and mark the letter (A), (B), (C) or (D) on your answer sheet. The conversations will not be printed in your test book and will be spoken only one time.

32. Where most likely are the speakers?

(A) At an airport
(B) On a train
(C) At a catering company
(D) In a restaurant

33. What does the man say his company is now providing?

(A) Seasonal discounts
(B) Entertainment services
(C) Complimentary food
(D) Exclusive memberships

34. Why does the woman prefer staying in her seat?

(A) It is very comfortable.
(B) It is close to the bathroom.
(C) It has a nice view.
(D) It has space for her belongings.

35. Where does the man work?

(A) At a restaurant
(B) At a warehouse
(C) At a travel agency
(D) At a fresh produce store

36. What disadvantage is mentioned about the product?

(A) It is unsuitable for cooking.
(B) It is more expensive than other products.
(C) It takes a week to be delivered.
(D) It includes an import fee.

37. What will the woman do next?

(A) Provide contact details
(B) Call a supplier
(C) Examine some products
(D) Pay for a purchase

38. Who most likely are the speakers?

(A) Delivery drivers
(B) Engineers
(C) Caterers
(D) Interior designers

39. What is scheduled to happen at 2 P.M.?

(A) An event will finish.
(B) A delivery will arrive.
(C) A musical performance will start.
(D) A speech will be given.

40. What does the woman say she will do next?

(A) Arrange some tables
(B) Park a vehicle
(C) Install some devices
(D) Contact a CEO

41. What problem does the woman inform the man about?

(A) A screen has been damaged.
(B) A cell phone will not turn on.
(C) Some software has stopped working.
(D) Some phone batteries will not charge.

42. What aspect of a product does the woman say is important?

(A) The price
(B) The size
(C) The durability
(D) The color

43. What does the man imply when he says, "We can hardly keep them on the shelves"?

(A) The woman should consider other models.
(B) Some items are difficult to display.
(C) Some shelves need to be repaired.
(D) A product is popular with customers.

GO ON TO THE NEXT PAGE

44. Where do the speakers most likely work?

(A) At a beverage company
(B) At a renovation company
(C) At a catering company
(D) At a marketing company

45. What problem does the woman mention?

(A) Some items were damaged.
(B) Some employees are absent.
(C) Some suppliers are too far away.
(D) Some clients have complained.

46. What does Ray say he will research?

(A) The availability of a product
(B) The popularity of a brand
(C) The cost of a project
(D) The benefits of a business location

47. What are the speakers discussing?

(A) An installation plan
(B) A customer survey
(C) A sales contest
(D) An advertising strategy

48. Where do the speakers work?

(A) At a health clinic
(B) At a supermarket
(C) At a sports stadium
(D) At a fitness club

49. What will happen on Friday?

(A) Prizes will be awarded.
(B) New staff will be hired.
(C) A meeting will be held.
(D) A discount will be offered.

50. What is the main topic of the conversation?

(A) A new tourist attraction
(B) A grand opening event
(C) A landscaping project
(D) An urban development plan

51. According to the woman, what are some residents concerned about?

(A) Property prices
(B) Traffic congestion
(C) Construction noise
(D) Lack of public transport

52. What does the woman ask the man to do?

(A) Attend a meeting
(B) Speak with residents
(C) Extend a deadline
(D) Submit a design

53. According to the man, what will the speakers' company do next week?

(A) Repair some equipment
(B) Hire new employees
(C) Release sales figures
(D) Open a new facility

54. What does the woman suggest?

(A) Assigning mentors
(B) Hosting a training seminar
(C) Scheduling interviews
(D) Inviting a guest speaker

55. What does the man say he will do?

(A) Organize an event
(B) Offer a promotion
(C) Set a training schedule
(D) Make an announcement

56. What are the speakers discussing?

(A) Scheduling a meeting
(B) Replacing devices
(C) Relocating a business
(D) Changing suppliers

57. What is the woman concerned about?

(A) A project deadline
(B) A spending budget
(C) An employment contract
(D) A hiring policy

58. What does the man say would result from a change?

(A) Fewer work delays would occur.
(B) Customers would be more satisfied.
(C) Monthly profits would increase.
(D) Staff would have more time off work.

---

59. What does the factory most likely produce?

(A) Construction tools
(B) Exercise equipment
(C) Home furnishings
(D) Security devices

60. What does the woman ask the man about?

(A) The cost of materials
(B) The size of an order
(C) The start date of a project
(D) The destination of a shipment

61. Why does the woman say, "The end of the week is fine"?

(A) To suggest rescheduling a meeting
(B) To thank the man for a deadline extension
(C) To request some time off from work
(D) To turn down an offer of assistance

Name:
Jane Smith

Employee ID Number:
2987

Department Number:
0126

Security Reference Number: 4827 9379 0012
● ●

62. Look at the graphic. Which number will the woman enter?

(A) 2987
(B) 0126
(C) 4827
(D) 0012

63. What happened last month?

(A) A new company facility opened.
(B) An inspection was carried out.
(C) A construction project began.
(D) A training session was held.

64. Why will the man send a memo to employees?

(A) To thank them for their hard work
(B) To invite them to an event
(C) To inform them about a process
(D) To request volunteers

GO ON TO THE NEXT PAGE

Thursday Meeting Schedule	
Room 301	9:00 A.M.
Room 302	10:00 A.M.
Room 303	11:00 A.M.
Room 304	1:00 P.M.

Eberon Inc. Fundraising Event	
Tent 1 Games & Activities	Tent 2 Snacks & Beverages
Tent 3 Music & Comedy	Tent 4 Donations & Information

65. Which industry do the speakers most likely work in?

(A) Construction
(B) Finance
(C) Publishing
(D) Software

66. What will the woman do by the end of the day?

(A) Authorize a payment
(B) Change a meeting schedule
(C) Finalize a budget proposal
(D) Contact some clients

67. Look at the graphic. When will a meeting be held?

(A) At 9:00 A.M.
(B) At 10:00 A.M.
(C) At 11:00 A.M.
(D) At 1:00 P.M.

68. What was the woman surprised about?

(A) The number of staff volunteers
(B) The amount of money raised
(C) A recent newspaper article
(D) An advertisement for an event

69. Look at the graphic. Which tent does the man say he will work in?

(A) Tent 1
(B) Tent 2
(C) Tent 3
(D) Tent 4

70. What will be discussed with the event planner later?

(A) Performance schedules
(B) Game prizes
(C) Admission fees
(D) Tent sizes

PART 4

Directions: You will hear some talks given by a single speaker. You will be asked to answer three questions about what the speaker says in each talk. Select the best response to each question and mark the letter (A), (B), (C), or (D) on your answer sheet. The talks will not be printed in your test book and will be spoken only one time.

71. Who is taking part in a city's competition?

(A) Graphic designers
(B) International tourists
(C) Local students
(D) Council members

72. Where will the winning logo be unveiled?

(A) At a fundraising event
(B) At a grand opening
(C) At a city parade
(D) At a press conference

73. What can the listeners do on a Web site?

(A) Sign up for an event
(B) Make a donation
(C) Complete a form
(D) View some designs

74. What type of event are the listeners attending?

(A) A staff orientation
(B) A product launch
(C) A community celebration
(D) A recruitment fair

75. Where are the listeners asked to go later?

(A) To a training session
(B) To a company's booth
(C) To a security office
(D) To a parking area

76. What will be distributed to the listeners?

(A) Pamphlets
(B) Coupons
(C) Free samples
(D) Order forms

77. What field does the speaker most likely work in?

(A) IT consulting
(B) Real estate
(C) Interior design
(D) Event management

78. What does the speaker ask the listener to provide?

(A) A floor plan
(B) A rental agreement
(C) Some directions
(D) Some photographs

79. Why does the speaker say, "make this your top priority"?

(A) To recommend a purchase
(B) To correct an earlier error
(C) To encourage swift action
(D) To make a change to a schedule

80. Where does the announcement most likely take place?

(A) At a restaurant
(B) At a department store
(C) At a hotel
(D) At a factory

81. According to the speaker, what will happen on Saturday?

(A) A renovation project will start.
(B) An inspection will be carried out.
(C) Some equipment will be repaired.
(D) Some employees will be hired.

82. What does the speaker ask the listeners to do?

(A) Install some devices
(B) Tidy up the break room
(C) Review some procedures
(D) Attend a training class

GO ON TO THE NEXT PAGE

83. Who is the speaker?

(A) A park ranger
(B) A landscape gardener
(C) A city council member
(D) A financial consultant

84. Why does the speaker say, "that was the easy part"?

(A) To suggest changing a procedure
(B) To indicate that more funding is required
(C) To acknowledge that there are challenges ahead
(D) To thank the listeners for their assistance

85. What does the speaker say will happen in April?

(A) Some walls will be constructed.
(B) Some flowers will be planted.
(C) A park will reopen to visitors.
(D) A building will be enlarged.

86. What is the main focus of the tour?

(A) Traditional art
(B) Historical buildings
(C) Local wildlife
(D) Natural scenery

87. What does the speaker say he will provide for the listeners?

(A) Waterproof clothing
(B) Trail maps
(C) Bottled water
(D) Packed lunches

88. Who was Henry Masters?

(A) A sculptor
(B) An inventor
(C) A painter
(D) A photographer

89. What does the speaker ask the listeners to do at the main gate?

(A) Sign a visitor's book
(B) Put on an identification tag
(C) Read some guidelines
(D) Take some protective gear

90. What does the speaker mean when he says, "Feel free to stop me at any time"?

(A) He is willing to reschedule a tour.
(B) He understands that a deadline is tight.
(C) He is happy to answer questions.
(D) He will provide his contact details.

91. What will the listeners most likely do after lunch?

(A) View some products
(B) Speak with an executive
(C) View a video clip
(D) Fill out some forms

92. Where does the speaker most likely work?

(A) At a car showroom
(B) At vehicle factory
(C) At a car rental firm
(D) At an auto shop

93. What is the speaker discussing?

(A) Changing a policy
(B) Recruiting additional staff
(C) Offering new services
(D) Conducting a survey

94. What should the listeners advise customers to do?

(A) Make an advance booking
(B) Sign up for a membership
(C) Read an information manual
(D) Leave an online comment

Department Managers - Extension List	
Dave Bassett	Ext. 428
Lois Grant	Ext. 538
Sahid Mitra	Ext. 281
Lesley Findlay	Ext. 354

95. What department does the speaker work in?

(A) Customer service
(B) Human resources
(C) Information Technology
(D) Accounting

96. What problem is the speaker discussing?

(A) High monthly expenses
(B) Increased customer complaints
(C) Low employee productivity
(D) Reduced demand for products

97. Look at the graphic. Who does the speaker say some employees should contact?

(A) Dave Bassett
(B) Lois Grant
(C) Sahid Mitra
(D) Lesley Findlay

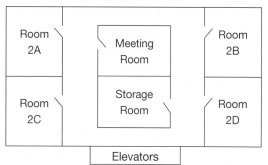

Floor Plan - 2nd Floor

98. Why is the speaker unhappy with her current office?

(A) It is far from her coworkers.
(B) It is too noisy.
(C) It is not spacious enough.
(D) It is in poor condition.

99. Look at the graphic. Which room does the speaker offer to take?

(A) Room 2A
(B) Room 2B
(C) Room 2C
(D) Room 2D

100. According to the speaker, what needs to be submitted by Wednesday?

(A) A transfer request
(B) A security deposit
(C) A building lease
(D) An approval form

This is the end of the Listening test. Turn to Part 5 in your test book.

GO ON TO THE NEXT PAGE

READING TEST

In the Reading test, you will read a variety of texts and answer several different types of reading comprehension questions. The entire Reading test will last 75 minutes. There are three parts, and directions are given for each part. You are encouraged to answer as many questions as possible within the time allowed. You must mark your answers on the separate answer sheet. Do not write your answers in your test book.

PART 5

Directions: A word or phrase is missing in each of the sentences below. Four answer choices are given below each sentence. Select the best answer to complete the sentence. Then mark the letter (A), (B), (C), or (D) on your answer sheet.

101. ------- at Hilltop Bistro often praise Chef Marceau's delicious salad dressings.

(A) Dines
(B) Dining
(C) Diner
(D) Diners

102. The business management class Mr. Richardson ------- is no longer available in the evening.

(A) attendees
(B) attending
(C) to attend
(D) was attending

103. A public forum ------- all local residents will be held on November 22 at City Hall.

(A) for
(B) since
(C) through
(D) until

104. Jackal Software is hoping to hire an ------- tutor to teach some employees the Japanese language.

(A) experience
(B) experiences
(C) experienced
(D) experiencing

105. Mr. Longford's main duty is to help recently-hired employees ------- to their new roles.

(A) adapt
(B) apply
(C) perform
(D) submit

106. A close friend of ------- plans to publish her first novel by the end of the year.

(A) me
(B) my
(C) myself
(D) mine

107. The quickest way to reach Salisbury Convention Center from the airport is ------- shuttle bus.

(A) for
(B) to
(C) in
(D) by

108. The new shopping mall in Richmont will open for business on ------- March 21 or March 28.

(A) either
(B) soon
(C) also
(D) yet

109. Our financial ------- suggests slightly increasing the delivery charge on our customers' food orders.

(A) advised
(B) advisor
(C) advising
(D) advises

110. At Lancet Manufacturing, meetings between managers typically last ------- longer than those involving the entire workforce.

(A) such
(B) so
(C) much
(D) very

111. Mr. Trent voided the warranty on his laptop computer when he ------- removed some of the internal components.

(A) mistake
(B) mistaken
(C) mistakenly
(D) mistook

112. Positions in the research laboratory at Biogen North are very ------- to new biotechnology graduates.

(A) attraction
(B) attract
(C) attractive
(D) attracting

113. By gradually lowering the price of the house at 135 Salter Street, the real estate agent believed that it would ------- be purchased.

(A) proficiently
(B) barely
(C) eventually
(D) initially

114. The One World Foundation sends donors a monthly ------- on the charity's various worldwide projects.

(A) update
(B) payment
(C) collection
(D) recruitment

115. Until the traffic signals are fully installed and -------, Dryford Avenue will remain closed to all vehicles.

(A) functions
(B) functional
(C) functionality
(D) functioned

116. Last Thursday's ------- about our advertising strategy resulted in several innovative ideas that we plan to use.

(A) discussion
(B) discussing
(C) discussed
(D) discuss

117. In his role as the regional manager of Apricot Electronics, Mr. Driscoll is ------- for more than 500 sales representatives.

(A) tenable
(B) affordable
(C) possible
(D) responsible

118. ------- technical difficulties, the livestream of the film awards ceremony cut out for almost 15 minutes.

(A) As long as
(B) Due to
(C) Because
(D) However

119. Big Top Burgers regularly engages with customers on social media to boost ------- online presence.

(A) its
(B) them
(C) theirs
(D) itself

120. Lotus Spa's Premier Package includes a choice of seven different treatments, ------- on a customer's preferences.

(A) regarding
(B) alternating
(C) relying
(D) depending

GO ON TO THE NEXT PAGE

121. The audience members ------- exited the concert venue when the fire alarm sounded.

(A) extremely
(B) limitedly
(C) minutely
(D) rapidly

122. Ms. Bannister has allocated more money to ------- the company's upcoming line of office furniture.

(A) repair
(B) promote
(C) select
(D) invest

123. Gary Benson, following on from his successful debut album, plans ------- his next album in a remote cabin in the woods.

(A) recording
(B) have recorded
(C) record
(D) to record

124. The CEO of Milton Enterprises ------- owns seven expensive sports cars and will purchase another one later this year.

(A) plenty
(B) already
(C) alike
(D) least

125. Passengers are reminded to check in baby strollers and other oversized baggage ------- boarding the airplane.

(A) prior to
(B) and
(C) last
(D) otherwise

126. The subscription cancellation ------- was simplified with the addition of an online cancellation button on the company's Web site.

(A) orientation
(B) procedure
(C) appointment
(D) referral

127. All of our investors will be offered an ------- tour of the new restaurant one week before it opens.

(A) absolute
(B) exclusive
(C) overt
(D) increased

128. Saber Corporation's annual profits have improved ------- since the new sales manager was hired.

(A) substantial
(B) to substantiate
(C) substantially
(D) substantiate

129. At the staff training workshop, employees were ------- up according to which department they work in.

(A) brought
(B) elevated
(C) carried
(D) divided

130. PC Depot employs a team of ------- ready to help customers with any computer repairs or improvements.

(A) technical
(B) technicalities
(C) technicians
(D) technically

Directions: Read the texts that follow. A word, phrase, or sentence is missing in parts of each text. Four answer choices for each question are given below the text. Select the best answer to complete the text. Then mark the letter (A), (B), (C) or (D) on your answer sheet.

Questions 131-134 refer to the following Web page.

Formosa Resort - General Information

At Formosa Resort, our guests can stay in a Standard Room, Deluxe Room, or Premier Room. ------- includes at least one king-sized bed and offers an outstanding view of the ocean. Our
131.
resort is known not only for its comfortable rooms, but ------- for its wide range of amenities
132.
and activities. Guests can enjoy our beautiful outdoor swimming pool and well-equipped fitness center, and children in particular will love our game room and miniature golf course. If you would like to plan a day trip, the staff in our tourist information center ------- tours to several local
133.
landmarks such as Jade Valley Amusement Park and the Mount Shan Nature Preserve. -------.
134.
Schedules and pricing can be found by clicking the Day Trips tab at the top of the page.

131. (A) Theirs
(B) Each
(C) Another
(D) Either one

132. (A) nearly
(B) ever
(C) regularly
(D) also

133. (A) did arrange
(B) can arrange
(C) had arranged
(D) are arranging

134. (A) We hope you enjoyed your stay at Formosa Resort.
(B) Please note that advanced booking is advised.
(C) Thank you for providing feedback on our tours.
(D) Our guest rooms start from only $70 per night.

GO ON TO THE NEXT PAGE

Questions 135-138 refer to the following article.

Urban Development Project to Begin in Akerville

Akerville City Council announced yesterday that it intends to launch a large-scale urban development project at Blackcroft Industrial Park.

One of the main aims of the project is to convert the abandoned Rossco warehouse into a shopping mall and movie theater. The warehouse, ------- as Rossco Steel Inc.'s main storage
135.
facility for around 35 years, will be partially demolished and then extensively renovated. -------.
136.
Once complete, the building will house approximately 250 businesses and ------- a 10-screen
137.
cinema.

Akerville's mayor, Laura McDonald, predicts that the project will create over one thousand new jobs and significantly boost the local economy. At a recent press conference, ------- promised
137.
this was the first of many big changes coming to the city.

135. (A) to serve
(B) had served
(C) and is serving
(D) which had served

136. (A) Rossco is one of the largest employers in Akerville.
(B) The work is expected to take roughly two years.
(C) Council members plan to vote on the project early next month.
(D) Local residents are disappointed about the mall's closure.

137. (A) propose
(B) preview
(C) boast
(D) access

138. (A) we
(B) she
(C) who
(D) it

Questions 139-142 refer to the following notice.

For the attention of all EDK Manufacturing Staff

Please be advised that work on the factory floor will be temporarily disrupted on Friday afternoon due to the ------- of our new fire alarm and fire extinguishing systems. This fire drill will help us
139.
ascertain the effectiveness of the newly installed equipment.

We will not be giving you advance warning of when the fire alarm will be triggered. -------. Calmly
140.
yet quickly follow our evacuation route and assemble in the parking lot at the rear of the factory. The extinguishing system will then spray ------- areas with a specialized fire suppression gas.
141.
Staff must remain outdoors ------- the factory supervisor informs them that it is safe to return to
142.
their workstations.

---

139. (A) relocation
(B) posting
(C) building
(D) testing

140. (A) Fires have become an increasing concern in the manufacturing industry.
(B) Investigators are still working to determine the source of the fire.
(C) When it sounds, immediately turn off any machinery at your workspace.
(D) Remember to check the batteries in all smoke alarms on a regular basis.

141. (A) vacated
(B) vacates
(C) to vacate
(D) vacating

142. (A) from
(B) always
(C) so that
(D) until

GO ON TO THE NEXT PAGE

Questions 143-146 refer to the following article.

Middlevale Music Festival Set to Return

Music fans were left disappointed when the Middlevale Music Festival did not take place last summer for the first time since the first event was held in 2011. The event was cancelled due to the demolition of Middlevale Concert Hall, and the event organizers have spent the last year searching for an alternate venue. -------, they found a suitable site for the concert at Almond
143.
Campgrounds.

-------. Not only will the event be held outdoors for the first time, but it will take place over three
144.
days rather than two. This means that a larger number of musicians ------- on stage during the
145.
festival. As such, the price of ------- will increase from $100 to $130 this year. Tickets can be
146.
purchased at www.middlevalemusicfestival.com or from various vendors in the city.

143. (A) For instance
(B) Eventually
(C) On the other hand
(D) Previously

144. (A) This year's festival will differ in many ways from previous ones.
(B) Event organizers hope to find a suitable venue by the end of June.
(C) The event has seen a significant decrease in popularity over the years.
(D) Reviews of this year's festival have been highly positive so far.

145. (A) will be performing
(B) will be performed
(C) were performing
(D) to perform

146. (A) installation
(B) enrollment
(C) admission
(D) relocation

PART 7

Directions: In this part you will read a selection of texts, such as magazine and newspaper articles, e-mails, and instant messages. Each text or set of texts is followed by several questions. Select the best answer for each question and mark the letter (A), (B), (C), or (D) on your answer sheet.

Questions 147-148 refer to the following coupon.

Nutriburst Protein Milkshakes - 30% Off!

Nutriburst is celebrating the launch of two new flavors of protein milkshakes: Mint Chocolate and Mixed Berries. Although we produce a wide variety of health foods and supplements, we are largely known for our range of best-selling protein milkshakes. This coupon can be redeemed at any retailer that stocks our products and entitles you to 30 percent off a 2.2 kg tub of any flavor of milkshake, including our two newest flavors. It cannot be used to purchase products that are already discounted or along with any other vouchers.

Expiry date: April 30

147. What is suggested about Nutriburst?

(A) It is offering a discount on all products.
(B) Its Mixed Berries milkshake is its best-selling flavor.
(C) It is opening two new retail locations.
(D) Its older milkshake flavors are popular.

148. What is true about the coupon?

(A) It must be used by a certain date.
(B) It must be redeemed at an online store.
(C) It can only be used for specific milkshake flavors.
(D) It can be used in conjunction with other special offers.

Questions 149-150 refer to the following advertisement.

Whirlwind 600 Stove

Combining advanced technology with elegant design

$799.99

Appliance features:

Whirlwind Induction: Provides fast, safe heating (only for pots and pans made from cast iron, enamel cast iron, or stainless steel)

Flexicook: Merge two or more cooking zones of the stovetop for more space and flexibility while cooking with different sizes of cookware

Surfacto Plus: Wipe away spills and pieces of food with ease thanks to our advanced Surfacto Plus surface coating

EZ Touch Slider: Easily adjust cooking temperature with our advanced touch slider control system

Chef Control: Choose melting/simmering options with one touch of a button for maximum convenience

149. What is indicated about the Whirlwind 600 Stove?

(A) It is currently available at a discounted price.

(B) It is covered by an extended warranty.

(C) It should be used with specific cookware.

(D) It comes with complimentary pots and pans.

150. What does the Surfacto Plus feature allow users to do?

(A) Adjust the size of each cooking zone

(B) Clean the appliance easily

(C) Change the temperature settings quickly

(D) Activate a simmering function

To: Rick Garrett <rgarrett@fitworld.com>

From: Troy Sandler <tsandler@elitegym.com>

Subject: Welcome to the gym!

Date: April 5

Dear Mr. Garrett,

We are glad you have decided to become a member of Elite Gym! When you signed up for your membership, you mentioned to our sales manager Mr. Tarbuck that you might be interested in signing up for personal training sessions. As such, Mr. Tarbuck has passed on your details to me and I would like to offer you a trial session, just so you can get an idea of how I could help you. If you are happy with how the trial session goes, you would be able to meet with me two or three times a week to work toward your fitness goals. If you'd like to find out what other members have said about my techniques and how much I have helped my clients, you should visit our Web site and view my profile page. Please feel free to contact me directly at 555-0194 if you are interested, or you can ask for me the next time you visit the gym.

Regards,

Troy Sandler

151. Who most likely is Mr. Sandler?

(A) A sales manager
(B) A personal trainer
(C) A recruitment agent
(D) A new gym member

152. Why is Mr. Garrett advised to visit a Web site?

(A) To upgrade a membership
(B) To view a class schedule
(C) To see pictures of a gym
(D) To read member reviews

GO ON TO THE NEXT PAGE

Questions 153-154 refer to the following text message chain.

Katie Pryce [4:04 P.M.]
Hi, Craig. I heard you're flying out to Pittsburgh to meet one of our new clients on Thursday.

Craig Lonegan [4:05 P.M.]
That's right. I'm trying to arrange accommodation, and a restaurant for a lunch meeting, but I have no idea what to choose.

Katie Pryce [4:07 P.M.]
I used to work in Pittsburgh. I know the city really well.

Craig Lonegan [4:08 P.M.]
Oh, really? Well, any tips you can provide would be greatly appreciated.

Katie Pryce [4:09 P.M.]
Sure! If I were you, I'd stay at the Grand Osprey Hotel on 12th Avenue. It's downtown, but easily accessible from the airport. And for your meeting, let me get back to you later tonight.

153. At 4:07 P.M., what does Ms. Pryce most likely mean when she writes, "I used to work in Pittsburgh"?

(A) She has extensive experience in her field.
(B) She can provide Mr. Lonegan with assistance.
(C) She plans to accompany Mr. Lonegan on her trip.
(D) She recommends planning a trip to Pittsburgh.

154. What information will Ms. Pryce likely send to Mr. Lonegan this evening?

(A) A restaurant name
(B) A meeting schedule
(C) A hotel phone number
(D) A flight itinerary

The 5th Annual Montreaux Film Festival
Important Announcement

For the past few years, our small organization has had the pleasure of hosting the Montreaux Film Festival, showing more than 100 amazing films to attendees! However, despite the popularity of the event, we are struggling financially and may be unable to host it this year. As such, we are looking for interested individuals and businesses who may wish to sponsor this year's festival for a small fee.

We are offering you a unique opportunity to advertise your products and services in our event program and on various promotional banners, flyers, and posters at either of our usual screening locations. All that we ask is that you donate a minimum of $250 that will be used to organize this year's event. Assuming we manage to raise enough money, we will host the event on August 15 and 16. All sponsors will receive VIP tickets allowing free entry to any film showing. VIP guests will also have an opportunity to hang out in the backstage VIP areas where you will have an opportunity to meet some of the stars of the films being shown.

If you are interested in supporting us, please call us at (408) 555-0124 or send an e-mail to management@montreauxfest.com.

Edwin Coppell, President
Montreaux Film Society

---

155. What is the purpose of the notice?

(A) To encourage festival submissions
(B) To attract film society members
(C) To announce a schedule change
(D) To seek event sponsors

156. What is suggested about the film festival?

(A) It includes international movies.
(B) It normally lasts for one week.
(C) It did not take place last year.
(D) It is held at two different venues.

157. What is indicated about VIP guests?

(A) They will receive free refreshments.
(B) They will have a chance to meet actors.
(C) They will pay a reduced ticket fee.
(D) They will be assigned priority seating.

GO ON TO THE NEXT PAGE

Questions 158-160 refer to the following announcement.

Yarrow Public Library

All members should note that starting June 1, it will no longer be possible to use the library terminals to reserve books. The terminals have been in place for almost twenty years, and they are severely outdated. Instead of using the terminals to place a hold on books, members should use the library's new Web site at www.yarrowpubliclibrary.com. — [1] —. On the Web site, you should log in by entering your membership number. You will then be prompted to choose a unique password. — [2] —. In order to reserve specific books, you should then click the Database tab at the top of the page. You can search for specific titles by book name, author name, publishing year, and serial number. — [3] —. Once you have found the book you are looking for, click on the database entry and then click reserve. — [4] —. You will then be asked to enter the date on which you would like to reserve the title and the borrowing duration.

Please note that books in our fiction and non-fiction sections can now be borrowed for a maximum of three weeks instead of two. Journals and academic textbooks may be borrowed for up to two weeks instead of one.

---

158. What is the purpose of the announcement?

(A) To explain a new procedure
(B) To announce a library closure
(C) To request the return of books
(D) To invite members to an event

159. What is suggested about Yarrow Public Library?

(A) It will install new terminals in June.
(B) It has sent Web site passwords to members.
(C) It recently added new books to its collection.
(D) It has extended its borrowing times.

160. In which of the positions marked [1], [2], [3], and [4] does the following sentence best belong?

"Make sure to choose something that nobody else could guess."

(A) [1]
(B) [2]
(C) [3]
(D) [4]

Questions 161-163 refer to the following directions.

SUPERVAX 300

Thank you for purchasing the Supervax 300 vacuum cleaner!

To operate the device, press down on the foot pedal and recline the handle, causing the stabiliser wheels to be raised. Turn the device on by pressing the power button on the front of the handle. When you are finished vacuuming, return the vacuum cleaner to an upright position and the stabiliser wheels will automatically drop. Always remember to use the convenient handle to lift and move the vacuum cleaner around with ease.

In order to take care of your vacuum cleaner and avoid any malfunctions, please refer to the following guidance. Never use any lubricants, cleaning agents, polishes, or air fresheners on any part of the device, as these may damage the components. Also, be aware that the Supervax 300 is fitted with a thermal cut-out system. If any part of the vacuum cleaner becomes blocked, the device may overheat and automatically shut off. If this happens, turn off and unplug the vacuum cleaner and allow it to cool before attempting to check filters for blockages. Always store the vacuum cleaner indoors. Exposure to temperatures below 0°c will damage electrical wiring in the device.

If you have any problems with your Supervax 300, you should contact one of our agents for help. The quickest way is to visit our Web site at www.supervaxappliances.com and click on the Live Chat button. Our customer service agents are available 24 hours a day, 7 days a week. You may also reach us by sending a message to support@supervax.com. We aim to respond to e-mails within three working days. Our call center agents can also assist you from Monday to Friday, 9 a.m. to 6 p.m. Call us at 555-0137. Please check the serial number on your device before contacting us for assistance.

---

161. What is indicated about the Supervax 300?

(A) It comes with several accessories.
(B) It is easy to carry.
(C) It has detachable wheels.
(D) It has a rechargeable battery.

162. According to the directions, what may cause the vacuum cleaner to turn off?

(A) A loose filter
(B) A faulty power cable
(C) An uneven floor surface
(D) An increase in temperature

163. What is NOT mentioned as a method for seeking assistance?

(A) Chatting with an agent online
(B) Contacting customer support by e-mail
(C) Calling a telephone number
(D) Consulting a troubleshooting guide

GO ON TO THE NEXT PAGE

Questions 164-167 refer to the following article.

William Grogan, the developer of the globally popular mobile phone app Smart Park, wasn't always the celebrated business owner and entrepreneur that he is today. In his early 20s, he started driving a taxi after he dropped out of Dillon University halfway through a degree in computer programming. — [1] —. Over the next ten years, he noticed that it was increasingly difficult for drivers to find places to park in urban areas. In his hometown of San Diego in particular, drivers would spend an average of 40 minutes looking for a spot. It was this experience that inspired him to use his programming expertise to develop the Smart Park application for mobile phones.

Launched in all major app stores two years ago, Smart Park quickly became a huge hit, with more than 5 million downloads in its first year. The app utilizes advanced navigation software that allows users to find available spaces in any city in the world. In addition, it provides useful information about parking fees, traffic congestion levels, and auto theft probability in given areas. — [2] —. Mr. Grogan developed the application with assistance from two friends, and he now runs a company that employs more than 250 workers. — [3] —. "I can't believe what a success Smart Park has turned out to be," Mr. Grogan recently said. "And this is just the beginning, as we have lots of exciting new developments planned for next year."

What Mr. Grogan is referring to is the launch of Smart Park V2, which is scheduled for release next February. — [4] —. This new version will feature more detailed city maps and an improved user interface. As with the current version, the V2 will be available as a free app, with the option for users to pay $5.99 to remove advertising and unlock certain features.

164. What was Mr. Grogan's first job?

(A) Computer programmer
(B) Urban planner
(C) App developer
(D) Taxi driver

165. What change has Mr. Grogan identified in cities?

(A) Increased traffic congestion
(B) Fewer available parking spaces
(C) More litter in urban parks
(D) Increased usage of public transportation

166. What is true about the Smart Park mobile application?

(A) It became widely known through online advertising.
(B) It was not popular immediately after release.
(C) A new version of it will be launched next year.
(D) Mr. Grogan developed it on his own.

167. In which of the marked [1], [2], [3], and [4] does the following sentence best belong?

"Such data allows users to avoid neighborhoods known for high crime rates."

(A) [1]
(B) [2]
(C) [3]
(D) [4]

Questions 168-171 refer to the following online chat discussion.

Penny Larkin [11:11 A.M.]	Hey, Norm and Gloria... I have two new ideas for things we could organize for staff at our company's team-building workshop. I'd like to know what you think.
Gloria Martinez [11:12 A.M.]	Of course! What do you have in mind?
Penny Larkin [11:14 A.M.]	Well, the first activity is a survival challenge, where teams will compete to build the best shelter using only the branches and plants they can find in the forest.
Norm Jillett [11:15 A.M.]	I like the sound of that. It would really require excellent teamwork.
Penny Larkin [11:17 A.M.]	That's what I was thinking. And I also want to arrange a navigation challenge, where teams have to find a prize in the forest using a map, a compass, and some general directions.
Gloria Martinez [11:18 A.M.]	We did something similar at my previous company. It was a great success, and all the staff enjoyed it. I think we should organize both activities. What do you think, Norm?
Norm Jillett [11:21 A.M.]	Absolutely! So what should we do to help you with that, Penny?
Penny Larkin [11:22 A.M.]	Well, I was hoping you could purchase the items we'll need for the navigation challenge. And, Gloria, I'd like you to prepare a full schedule of activities and distribute it among our employees.
Gloria Martinez [11:23 A.M.]	No problem. I'll have it done by the end of the day.
Norm Jillett [11:24 A.M.]	Sure. I'll get on it right now and let you know once I'm done.

168. Why did Ms. Larkin send the message to her colleagues?

(A) To invite them on a company excursion
(B) To suggest changing an event location
(C) To discuss the agenda for a meeting
(D) To ask their opinions on event activities

169. At 11:15 A.M., what does Mr. Jillett most likely mean when he writes, "I like the sound of that"?

(A) He will be available to attend an event.
(B) He has heard good reviews about a venue.
(C) He supports Ms. Larkin's suggestion.
(D) He has experience in organizing events.

170. What is implied about the team-building workshop?

(A) It will take place outdoors.
(B) It is held every year.
(C) It costs money to attend.
(D) It includes an awards ceremony.

171. What will Mr. Jillett probably do next?

(A) Prepare an event schedule
(B) Hold a staff meeting
(C) Buy some compasses
(D) Visit a workshop venue

GO ON TO THE NEXT PAGE

Questions 172-175 refer to the following article.

Attention All Runners!

Hollybrook, July 24 – On Saturday, August 10, the Hollybrook Foundation will be hosting its annual fun run in Templeton Forest, and the registration period starts today. As in previous years, the event will include two different runs: a 3-kilometer course for children and casual runners, and a 10-kilometer course for more experienced participants. Registration costs $7.50 for adults and $3.50 for children aged 15 and under. All proceeds will go toward the foundation's various community projects. Race winners will receive prizes such as gift certificates for local stores and restaurants.

Hollybrook Foundation's president, Judith Lowe, recently discussed the organization's goals over the next few years. "We are working on several projects with the aim of improving amenities within the Hollybrook community", said Ms. Lowe. "For instance, the money we raise from this year's fun run will be used to repair and renovate the children's library on Main Street, which is badly in need of improvement after the storms and flooding we experienced earlier this year."

To register for the event, interested individuals should visit www.hollybrookfunrun.com and complete an online registration form. Alternatively, forms can be filled out in person at the foundation's head office at 13 Ruby Avenue, which is open Monday through Friday, 9 a.m. to 6 p.m. Businesses or individuals who are simply interested in donating money to the foundation are encouraged to e-mail the president directly at jlowe@hollybrook.org.

172. What type of event will be held in Hollybrook in August?

(A) An outdoor concert
(B) A grand opening event
(C) A fundraising contest
(D) A community fair

173. What will some event participants receive?

(A) Restaurant vouchers
(B) Cash prizes
(C) Free refreshments
(D) Library memberships

174. What is suggested about the children's library?

(A) It has suffered from water damage.
(B) It has been closed for one year.
(C) Its book collection will be expanded.
(D) It will be moved to a new location.

175. According to the article, why might an individual e-mail Ms. Lowe?

(A) To make a complaint
(B) To register for an event
(C) To request directions
(D) To provide a donation

GO ON TO THE NEXT PAGE

Questions 176-180 refer to the following advertisement and e-mail.

Diego's Salsa Dancing
2098 Sherman Avenue, Vancouver
555-0124

If you are looking for a fun, energetic activity to enjoy, then come on down to Diego's Salsa Dancing! We are reopening on October 1 after extensive remodeling, and our dance studio has been improved in several ways. Not only can it accommodate more people now, but it has new mirrored walls and new flooring. We are offering various classes during the October to December period, and registration begins on September 1. Sign up before September 15 and get your first two classes completely free! When you enroll, you will receive a complimentary pair of dancing shoes, a username and password for our Web site and its archive of salsa music and dance videos, and a voucher for 10 percent off your meals at Diego's Tacos, located next door to the dance studio.

October-December Classes:
- Introduction to Salsa: If you are completely new to salsa dancing, this is the class for you! Learn the basic dance moves in a fun, welcoming environment. Classes are held on Tuesdays and Thursdays, from 7 P.M. to 9 P.M.
- Intermediate 1: For those who have already mastered the basics, this class introduces some more sophisticated dance moves. Classes are held on Mondays and Wednesdays, from 7 P.M. to 9 P.M.
- Intermediate 2: Identical to our other intermediate class, but held in the morning to accommodate those who are busy in the evening. Classes are held on Mondays and Thursdays, from 6:30 A.M. to 8:30 A.M.
- Advanced Salsa: For experienced salsa dancers who want to challenge themselves by learning the most advanced moves. Classes are held on Fridays, from 7 P.M. to 9 P.M.

To: kcapshaw@mailone.ca
From: dgonzalez@diegossalsa.com
Date: September 14
Subject: Salsa classes
Attachment: Class_schedule

Dear Ms. Capshaw,

I'm delighted that you have chosen to sign up for salsa classes at my dance school. I have received your initial payment and added you to the class list. I really look forward to seeing you next month. When you arrive for your first class on Monday evening, I will provide you with all of the benefits that come with class enrollment. If you have any questions about the classes, please do not hesitate to contact me.

Regards,

Diego Gonzalez
Owner and Dance Instructor
Diego's Salsa Dancing/Diego's Tacos

176. What is indicated about Diego's Salsa Dancing?

(A) It is located above a restaurant.
(B) It has recently opened a new branch.
(C) It has been closed for renovations.
(D) It is hosting a grand opening event.

177. What is NOT mentioned as a benefit of enrollment?

(A) Free footwear
(B) Web site access
(C) Music CDs
(D) Discounted food

178. Why did Mr. Gonzalez send an e-mail to Ms. Capshaw?

(A) To inform her of a schedule change
(B) To suggest joining a dance class
(C) To confirm her registration
(D) To request an additional payment

179. Which class will Ms. Capshaw most likely attend?

(A) Introduction to Salsa
(B) Intermediate 1
(C) Intermediate 2
(D) Advanced Salsa

180. What is indicated about Ms. Capshaw?

(A) Her home is near the dance school.
(B) Her first two classes will be free.
(C) She has eaten at Diego's Tacos before.
(D) She will attend classes in September.

GO ON TO THE NEXT PAGE

For the Attention of the Press
Contact person: ghodgson@gardenburger.com (Gareth Hodgson, PR Manager, Garden Burger)

COLUMBUS, December 3 – Garden Burger is taking a new approach to attract more customers to its 23 locations throughout Ohio. We have listened closely to feedback from our customers, and we believe that now is the time to add several new sandwiches and burgers to our menu. As with all of our current products, the new items will be low in fat and salt, and high in protein and fiber, compared with all other fast food restaurant chains.

Throughout January, we will be inviting customers to participate in tasting sessions in order to finalize which new sandwiches and burgers we will offer in our stores. We plan to test out 15 potential additions, and based on comments from participants during the tasting sessions, we will choose the eight most popular items. If you are interested in participating, please e-mail our customer relations manager, who will be leading the sessions. Send a brief introduction about yourself to crmanager@gardenburger.com.

Garden Burger opened its first restaurant in Cleveland almost 11 years ago and now operates branches throughout Ohio, from Akron to Columbus. Our newest outlet is due to open for business in Toledo in early February. The changes to our menu will take effect in all branches in March.

E-Mail Message

To: Linda Berkeley <lberkeley@gardenburger.com>
From: Helen Sharpe <helensharpe@globenet.com>
Subject: January session
Date: February 2

Dear Ms. Berkeley,

As you may remember, I took part in the sessions last month at Garden Burger's headquarters in Cleveland. I enjoyed the experience, and I was proud to be a part of it. And, of course, I'm really looking forward to trying the items when your newest branch opens in my hometown next week! I am writing to you as I have yet to receive the restaurant vouchers that you said would be e-mailed to all session attendees. As a huge fan of your food, I was hoping to receive the vouchers by now. Could you please let me know when I can expect them?

Best wishes,

Helen Sharpe

181. According to the press release, what is Garden Burger planning to do?

(A) Recruit new employees
(B) Close several branches
(C) Launch a marketing campaign
(D) Introduce menu items

182. What is suggested about Garden Burger?

(A) It is cheaper than its competitors.
(B) Its food is relatively healthy.
(C) It operates branches worldwide.
(D) Its ingredients are produced locally.

183. What are attendees of the sessions in January be required to do?

(A) Undergo training
(B) Provide feedback
(C) Pay a registration fee
(D) Sign a contract

184. What does the e-mail suggest about Ms. Sharpe?

(A) She is Ms. Berkeley's supervisor.
(B) She distributed menu vouchers to attendees.
(C) She led a session at Garden Burger's headquarters.
(D) She regularly eats at Garden Burger.

185. Where does Ms. Sharpe probably live?

(A) In Columbus
(B) In Cleveland
(C) In Toledo
(D) In Akron

GO ON TO THE NEXT PAGE

Gigawatt Computing

Gigawatt Computing is one of the leading manufacturers of all-in-one desktop computers in the United States. All of our computers include cutting-edge technology and components and come equipped with an extensive range of programs and applications. Please note that antivirus packages must be purchased separately. Take a look at four of the most prominent features that help Gigawatt computers stand out from the crowd.

1. Powerful Performance – Boot up in seconds at lightning-fast speed with 512GB SSD storage, and easily handle numerous tasks simultaneously thanks to our award-winning Phoenix 8 processor. DDR4 RAM allows our computers to run reliably at faster speeds, providing a performance boost for everything, from multi-tasking on office projects to playing games.

2. Maximum Entertainment – Our devices provide you with the best seats right in your own house. Our computer speakers are wrapped in acoustic fabric and custom tuned by audio experts to deliver incredible sound quality. Easily stream music from your smartphone with Gigawatt Audio Stream. Enjoy your favorite movies on our Full-HD display, offering a vibrant 1920 x 1080 resolution.

3. Stylish Design – Boasting a micro-edge display, a sleek and slim design, and leather accents, our computers are designed to look modern and sophisticated. Conveniently placed ports on the side and back of the device allow for easy access and fewer visible cables.

4. Complete Privacy – Stream and browse carefree with a pop-up privacy camera that tucks safely away when not in use. Take advantage of our advanced privacy and security settings to ensure nobody can access your computer.

To: Lance Plunkett <lplunkett@gigawatt.com>
From: Lily Myers <lmyers@segundamarketing.com>
Subject: New work computers
Date: June 4

Dear Mr. Plunkett,

Thank you so much for responding to the questions in my earlier e-mail. Your detailed explanation about where the USB ports are located on the computers was very helpful. It seems as though the computers would be perfectly suited for Segunda Marketing employees, so we have placed a bulk order on your Web site.

I did note that the computers do not come with any pre-installed anti-virus software, so I was hoping you could recommend the best anti-virus package for large businesses. We would be purchasing it for around 25 computers, and we would be willing to pay up to $50 per computer on an annual basis. Another important factor is customer support. We would not only be looking for a company that offers phone and e-mail support, but also the option to speak with a customer agent live online. Thank you in advance for any assistance you can provide.

Best wishes,

Lily Myers
Segunda Marketing

Best Antivirus Packages for Businesses

If you are a business owner and want to ensure that all of your computers and files are completely secure, it is crucial that you purchase a reliable antivirus package immediately. Our experts have compiled a list of the four best packages for businesses. All of them offer superb protection and come at a reasonable price. Please note, however, that the below packages cannot be purchased only for one device; they must be purchased for at least five devices.

Antivirus Packages	Price per device (One Year)	Support Types
Safescan	$54.99	Phone, E-mail, Live Chat
Byteprotect	$45.99	E-mail, Live Chat
Ironsystem	$54.99	Phone, E-mail
Complock	$45.99	Phone, E-mail, Live Chat

186. What is indicated about Gigawatt Computing?

(A) It has expanded into global markets.
(B) It manufactures laptop computers.
(C) It has won a technology award.
(D) It is hosting a product launch event.

187. Why did Ms. Myers send Mr. Plunkett the e-mail?

(A) To request computer repairs
(B) To report a problem with a Web site
(C) To make a change to an order
(D) To request some advice

188. What feature of Gigawatt computers did Ms. Myers and Mr. Plunkett discuss by e-mail?

(A) Feature 1
(B) Feature 2
(C) Feature 3
(D) Feature 4

189. According to the information, what is true of the four anti-virus packages?

(A) They were developed by the same company.
(B) They require a minimum purchase.
(C) They can be paid for on a monthly basis.
(D) They are currently being discounted.

190. What antivirus package would best meet the needs of Segunda Marketing employees?

(A) Safescan
(B) Byteprotect
(C) Ironsystem
(D) Complock

GO ON TO THE NEXT PAGE

Upcoming Renovation Work at Kapersky Corporation

In February, Kapersky Corporation's offices will undergo a significant transformation. A remodeling team will be decorating our offices Monday through Friday, in order to modernize and improve our work environment. We have contracted Gillies Interiors to carry out the renovation work - a company that has more than 25 years of experience in designing and remodeling corporate workspaces.

Each department will be repainted in vibrant colors which have been shown to boost worker morale and performance, which should result in a higher work rate in our staff. In addition, floor tiles will be removed and replaced with carpets in order to make our offices quieter overall. Finally, new desks and chairs will be set up and the layouts of some departments will be altered so that employees will be able to discuss projects more easily with one another. The work team will arrive one day prior to the first day of renovations in order to measure the offices and set up some equipment. A renovation schedule has been created and will be handed out to all staff at the weekly meeting this Friday. We apologize for any disruption this work will cause, but we assure you that the results will be worth it.

Kapersky Corporation Renovation Schedule

Renovation Work by Department

February 5th	Monday	Accounting
February 6th	Tuesday	Sales
February 7th	Wednesday	Human Resources
February 8th	Thursday	Marketing
February 9th	Friday	Public Relations

While work is underway, you may be asked to temporarily work in a different office. If you have any queries, please contact Mr. Carlson in Human Resources.

To:	Mike Carlson, Human Resources Manager
From:	Lisa Brannigan
Subject:	Office Renovations
Date:	February 5

Hi Mr. Carlson,

According to the renovation schedule, work will be carried out in my department tomorrow, and I'm a little concerned about how this may affect my work. I am currently working on a very important project, and the completion deadline is this Thursday. I know that employees are being temporarily moved while their respective departments are being renovated, but I could still hear a lot of noise coming from the Accounting Department today, and I found it very distracting. I'd be a lot more productive working on my laptop at home tomorrow, so I was hoping you could approve that for me.

I hope to hear from you soon.

Regards,

Lisa Brannigan

191. What is NOT mentioned as a benefit of the renovations?

(A) Lower expenditures
(B) Increased productivity
(C) Reduced noise
(D) Improved communication

192. What does the notice indicate about the renovation schedule?

(A) It was created by Mr. Carlson.
(B) It is likely to be changed.
(C) It will be posted on a notice board.
(D) It will be distributed among employees.

193. What most likely will happen on February 4?

(A) Walls will be painted.
(B) Equipment will be moved.
(C) Rooms will be measured.
(D) Lunch breaks will be extended.

194. In which department does Ms. Brannigan probably work?

(A) Accounting
(B) Sales
(C) Marketing
(D) Public Relations

195. What is one purpose of Ms. Brannigan's e-mail?

(A) To suggest merging departments
(B) To request a remote working day
(C) To extend a project deadline
(D) To thank Mr. Carlson for his assistance

GO ON TO THE NEXT PAGE

Questions 196-200 refer to the following brochure and e-mails.

Huntly National Park

Campgrounds and Amenities

Located approximately 40 kilometers north of Boulder, Colorado, the 270,000-acre Huntly National Park boasts more than 60 picturesque mountain peaks, and over 100 hiking trails. The park attracts over 4 million visitors per year and features various amenities such as three visitor centers, several public restrooms, and free parking at several of the most popular trailheads. The park also contains four well-developed, spacious campgrounds, each with a clean, drinkable water supply, which are well-suited to corporate excursions and events.

The Red Campground can accommodate groups of up to 25 individuals, and tents can be rented for an additional fee. If you need to rent tents, but require a larger space, then you may wish to make a booking at the Green Campground, which is suitable for groups of up to 45. For group bookings where on-site tent rental is not required, up to 35 visitors can stay in the Blue Campground, while the Yellow Campground can accommodate a maximum of 55 individuals.

To make a group booking at one of our campgrounds, please speak with our park manager, Ryan Cresswell, at our main visitor center at River Rapids Trailhead. You may also reach him at 555-0134 or rcresswell@hnp.com.

To: Angela Matheson
From: Frank Hubbard
Subject: Team-building Workshop
Date: July 18

Hi Angela,

As you requested, I contacted Great Outdoors on Main Street about renting 12 four-person tents for your upcoming team-building workshop. The manager of the store responded to my e-mail and assured me this would be no problem, and we just need to let him know the dates on which you will need them.

Also, I visited Huntly National Park over the weekend in order to check out the campgrounds and amenities there. I spoke with Ryan Cresswell, the park manager, and he showed me around. As you suspected, the campground you were keen to book would be perfect for your group of 45 employees. According to Mr. Cresswell, the campground is available for your group booking on the following dates: August 6 to August 9; August 29 to September 1; and September 22 to September 25. Having spoken with the park manager, I believe this latter option would be the best choice, as the temperature would be cooler and there would be fewer mosquitoes and flies at that time.

If you are happy to go ahead with the campground booking, please let me know your preferred dates and I will get the site reserved for you.

Frank

To:	Frank Hubbard
From:	Angela Matheson
Subject: Re:	Team-building Workshop
Date:	July 18

Hi Frank,

Thanks so much for making those arrangements with the tent rental company and for checking out the campground. As you suggested, it would make sense to hold the workshop at a time when the temperature is more pleasant and there are fewer insects. So, I'd appreciate it if you could go ahead and finalize the campground reservation for me. You have been a tremendous help with this event, so I'm happy to give you an extra day of paid vacation. Please let me know when you would like to use this.

Angela

196. What does the brochure mention about the Huntly National Park?

(A) It has recently opened a new visitor center.
(B) It includes hiking trails of various difficulties.
(C) It is situated to the south of Boulder, Colorado.
(D) It receives a large number of visitors annually.

197. Who most likely is Mr. Hubbard?

(A) A park manager
(B) A Great Outdoors employee
(C) A personal assistant
(D) A client of Ms. Matheson

198. How did Mr. Hubbard obtain information about equipment rental?

(A) By sending an e-mail
(B) By visiting a store
(C) By calling a phone number
(D) By checking a Web site

199. Where will Ms. Matheson's team-building workshop most likely be held?

(A) At the Red Campground
(B) At the Green Campground
(C) At the Blue Campground
(D) At the Yellow Campground

200. When will Ms. Matheson's team-building workshop most likely start?

(A) On August 6
(B) On August 29
(C) On September 22
(D) On September 25

Stop! This is the end of the test. If you finish before time is called, you may go back to Parts 5, 6, and 7 and check your work.

토익학습지 실전편
실전 모의고사 2 정답 및 스크립트

정답

PART 1

1. (A)　**2.** (C)　**3.** (D)　**4.** (C)　**5.** (D)　**6.** (B)

PART 2

7. (B)　**8.** (C)　**9.** (C)　**10.** (B)　**11.** (C)　**12.** (B)　**13.** (C)　**14.** (A)　**15.** (C)　**16.** (B)　**17.** (A)　**18.** (A)　**19.** (C)　**20.** (A)　**21.** (B)
22. (C)　**23.** (A)　**24.** (B)　**25.** (B)　**26.** (A)　**27.** (C)　**28.** (A)　**29.** (A)　**30.** (C)　**31.** (C)

PART 3

32. (B)　**33.** (C)　**34.** (C)　**35.** (D)　**36.** (C)　**37.** (A)　**38.** (C)　**39.** (D)　**40.** (A)　**41.** (A)　**42.** (B)　**43.** (D)　**44.** (C)　**45.** (D)　**46.** (A)
47. (C)　**48.** (D)　**49.** (C)　**50.** (D)　**51.** (B)　**52.** (D)　**53.** (B)　**54.** (A)　**55.** (D)　**56.** (D)　**57.** (B)　**58.** (A)　**59.** (D)　**60.** (B)　**61.** (D)
62. (D)　**63.** (B)　**64.** (C)　**65.** (B)　**66.** (C)　**67.** (C)　**68.** (A)　**69.** (D)　**70.** (D)

PART 4

71. (C)　**72.** (D)　**73.** (D)　**74.** (B)　**75.** (B)　**76.** (A)　**77.** (B)　**78.** (D)　**79.** (C)　**80.** (D)　**81.** (B)　**82.** (C)　**83.** (B)　**84.** (C)　**85.** (B)
86. (D)　**87.** (C)　**88.** (C)　**89.** (D)　**90.** (C)　**91.** (B)　**92.** (C)　**93.** (A)　**94.** (D)　**95.** (C)　**96.** (C)　**97.** (B)　**98.** (C)　**99.** (D)　**100.** (D)

PART 5

101. (D)　**102.** (D)　**103.** (A)　**104.** (C)　**105.** (A)　**106.** (D)　**107.** (D)　**108.** (A)　**109.** (B)　**110.** (C)　**111.** (C)　**112.** (C)
113. (C)　**114.** (A)　**115.** (B)　**116.** (A)　**117.** (D)　**118.** (B)　**119.** (A)　**120.** (D)　**121.** (D)　**122.** (B)　**123.** (D)　**124.** (B)
125. (A)　**126.** (B)　**127.** (B)　**128.** (C)　**129.** (D)　**130.** (C)

PART 6

131. (B)　**132.** (D)　**133.** (B)　**134.** (B)　**135.** (D)　**136.** (B)　**137.** (C)　**138.** (B)　**139.** (D)　**140.** (C)　**141.** (A)　**142.** (D)
143. (B)　**144.** (A)　**145.** (A)　**146.** (C)

PART 7

147. (D)　**148.** (A)　**149.** (C)　**150.** (B)　**151.** (B)　**152.** (D)　**153.** (B)　**154.** (A)　**155.** (D)　**156.** (D)　**157.** (B)　**158.** (A)
159. (D)　**160.** (B)　**161.** (B)　**162.** (D)　**163.** (D)　**164.** (D)　**165.** (B)　**166.** (C)　**167.** (B)　**168.** (D)　**169.** (C)　**170.** (A)
171. (C)　**172.** (C)　**173.** (A)　**174.** (A)　**175.** (D)　**176.** (C)　**177.** (C)　**178.** (C)　**179.** (B)　**180.** (B)　**181.** (D)　**182.** (C)
183. (B)　**184.** (D)　**185.** (C)　**186.** (C)　**187.** (D)　**188.** (C)　**189.** (B)　**190.** (D)　**191.** (A)　**192.** (D)　**193.** (C)　**194.** (B)
195. (B)　**196.** (D)　**197.** (C)　**198.** (A)　**199.** (B)　**200.** (C)

Part 1

1.
  (A) She's kneeling on the floor.
  (B) She's holding a basket.
  (C) She's opening a machine door.
  (D) She's folding some towels.

2.
  (A) A car has been parked in a garage.
  (B) A bicycle has been mounted on a vehicle.
  (C) A car door is being left open.
  (D) A tire is being inflated.

3.
  (A) He's buttoning a shirt.
  (B) He's looking for paper in a cabinet.
  (C) He's opening the lid of a photocopier.
  (D) He's using a touch screen.

4.
  (A) The people are setting up a tent.
  (B) The people are building a campfire.
  (C) The people are having some snacks.
  (D) The people are unloading camping gear.

5.
  (A) The arch is decorated with flowers.
  (B) A brick wall is being painted.
  (C) A door has been left open.
  (D) Some potted plants have been placed outside.

6.
  (A) Scaffolding is being removed.
  (B) A roof is under construction.
  (C) Some workers are carrying a ladder.
  (D) Some workers are pushing a wheelbarrow.

Part 2

7. Did the board members approve the deadline extension?
  (A) A marketing campaign.
  (B) No, not yet.
  (C) There's no proof.

8. Where do we store the employee uniforms?
  (A) The store closes at 5.
  (B) Some new work shirts.
  (C) In the HR department.

9. When should my food order arrive at my office?
  (A) From the sandwich shop.
  (B) Yes, it should.
  (C) No later than 1 P.M.

10. You contacted the supplier about the invoice, didn't you?
  (A) Just some office supplies.
  (B) Yes, I called them yesterday.
  (C) A part-time contract.

11. Would you like green beans or mushrooms with your steak?
  (A) Let's sit on the patio.
  (B) Medium-rare, thanks.
  (C) I'll take the green beans.

12. Wasn't Ms. Lester at the fundraiser last night?
  (A) A local charity organization.
  (B) No, she was working late.
  (C) We raised $5,000.

13. How many employees will be attending the training workshop?
  (A) No, they'll travel by bus.
  (B) Because our sales are too low.
  (C) Around forty, I think.

14. Where can I catch a bus to the hospital?
  (A) Sorry, but I'm not from around here.
  (B) It's about a 30-minute journey.
  (C) Two tickets, please.

15. You're demonstrating the product at the convention, right?
  (A) No, I got it online.
  (B) The technology industry.
  (C) It's not ready to show yet.

16. Don't you want to take a day off from work?
  (A) He has a doctor's appointment.
  (B) Yes, but my manager won't allow it.
  (C) At an accounting firm.

17. Who turned on the air conditioner?
  (A) I was feeling hot.
  (B) Press the red button.
  (C) No, it's my turn.

18. We should order business cards with our contact details to give to clients.
  (A) That's a good idea.
  (B) You can call me later.
  (C) Where did you put them?

19. What if we postponed the street parade until next month?
  (A) That's a shame.
  (B) It's held every year.
  (C) It's too late to reschedule it.

20. I heard that Bobby has asked for a branch transfer.
  (A) He changed his mind in the end.
  (B) There's a branch in Bathgate.
  (C) You'll need approval from a manager.

21. Why can't I view the file you e-mailed to me?
(A) It's definitely a nice view.
(B) You need to enter a password.
(C) Maybe it's in my junk folder.

22. Would you like me to get some drinks for everyone?
(A) I really enjoyed them.
(B) No, I don't have any plans.
(C) Mary's already at the coffee shop.

23. When are the safety inspectors arriving?
(A) Anytime now.
(B) In the factory.
(C) Yes, I guess so.

24. Let's practice our presentation when you have time.
(A) You've really improved.
(B) I'm not busy right now.
(C) What present did you buy?

25. How can I get my suit cleaned before tomorrow?
(A) Tomorrow works fine for me.
(B) There's a dry cleaner nearby.
(C) It looks really good on you.

26. Will the work schedule be posted this morning or sometime after lunch?
(A) Check again at around 2.
(B) I brought food with me today.
(C) A 9 to 5 shift.

27. Who showed interest in volunteering at the job fair?
(A) That would be a great help.
(B) What would I have to do?
(C) A few people from the sales team.

28. Why was the opening night of the play postponed?
(A) The theater has been flooded.
(B) Actually, I'd love to go and see it.
(C) By April 10th at the latest.

29. Are you flying to our Los Angeles branch office tomorrow?
(A) I was planning on taking a train.
(B) The annual board meeting.
(C) It will be my first time there.

30. The food in this restaurant needs more seasoning.
(A) No, I'm already full.
(B) This is our busiest season.
(C) Would you like to speak to the chef?

31. What's our deadline for repairing the bridge across the river?
(A) There's an alternative route you could use.

(B) No more than ten thousand dollars.
(C) The work must be done by mid-June.

Part 3

Questions 32-34 refer to the following conversation.

W: Excuse me, sir. When will we arrive at the station?

M: Hmm... we still have about an hour to go.

W: Oh, really? In that case, I might go to the buffet car for some food. Will they accept a credit card?

M: Actually, our rail company just began offering a new service, in partnership with a catering firm. So, all the sandwiches and soups are free for passengers.

W: Wow, that's nice! Actually, I wonder if I could order the food and stay in my seat. I'm really enjoying seeing all the scenery out this window.

M: Of course! Just tell me what you'd like, and I'll be back with it in a few minutes.

Questions 35-37 refer to the following conversation.

W: Excuse me, can you help? I'm looking for some durian. I tried some during my recent trip to Indonesia, and I loved it. A friend recommended your store because you stock a lot of exotic fruits here.

M: That's right. But, we don't typically sell much durian. I can order some for you from our overseas supplier, but delivery will take about a week. Would that still be okay?

W: That's fine. I'll leave you my name and phone number. You can just give me a quick call when it arrives.

Questions 38-40 refer to the following with three speakers.

M1: We only have one hour to set up all the display tables and prepare all the food for the Redman Corporation office party. Jason, you give me a hand with all the main dishes. And Louise, you get all the snacks and appetizers ready.

M2: One hour is not a lot of time to set up such a large buffet.

M1: I know, but at 2 P.M., the company's CEO will speak to all his staff in this room, so we need to be ready before then.

W: Well, there's no time to waste. I'll set up all the tables around the room, and you guys can start bringing in all the food from the van.

Questions 41-43 refer to the following conversation.

W: Excuse me. I bought this mobile phone here last month. But, the screen is already scratched, just from keeping the phone in my pocket. Is there any way to fix it?

M: I'm afraid not, but you could buy a phone case to stop it from happening again. We have a very large selection over here.

W: That's a good idea. But, it's important that it's not too big and bulky, because I do normally keep my phone in my pocket. Oh, how about this model here?

M: Well, that's the one I was going to recommend, and it's the last one we have in stock. We can hardly keep them on the shelves.

W: Okay, then I'd better take this one today.

Questions 44-46 refer to the following conversation with three speakers.

W: Hi, Lukas and Ray. I'd like to talk to you about some of the feedback we've had from clients about our food.

M1: Sure, what is it?

W: Well, we've had complaints from several clients about the new salad dressing we are using. They say it tastes far too salty, and that we should change back to the original one.

M1: I guess we could go back to the old one. But, didn't the manufacturer announce it was planning to discontinue that dressing? I think you told me that, Ray.

M2: That's what I heard. Well, I'll do some searches online today and see if it's still possible to purchase that salad dressing. If not, we'll need to try a different one.

Questions 47-49 refer to the following conversation.

M: Hi, Cathy. Did you hear that there's going to be a sales contest throughout January? Whoever attracts the most new gym members will get a cash bonus.

W: That's a great idea! We've been struggling to attract new members to our fitness club, so this will motivate everyone to try harder. Did our manager mention how much the cash bonus will be?

M: No, but I heard he'll tell us all of the details at our staff meeting this week. Don't forget that it will be held at 8 A.M. this Friday instead of 9 A.M.

Questions 50-52 refer to the following conversation.

W: Good morning, Mr. Archer. I'm glad you had time to meet me here at the area we plan to develop. I'd like to hear your ideas.

M: Well, the key to effective urban development is giving the community what it needs. So, I plan to create a

commercial shopping district, plus several recreational facilities.

W: That sounds perfect. Now, some local residents have expressed concern about the plan. They are worried that a lot of new stores will cause traffic congestion in the area.

M: That's understandable. But, my plan includes measures to avoid any congestion.

W: Great! Would you be able to draft a design for the area and send it to me by Friday? I'd like to show it to the other council members.

Questions 53-55 refer to the following conversation.

M: Hi, Nancy. I wanted to talk to you about the new salespeople we will be recruiting next week. In the past, when workers have joined our company, it has taken them a while to settle in and perform well. How can we fix that?

W: Well, I've been thinking about that, and it might be a good idea to assign a senior employee to each new worker. The senior employees could be their mentors and give them helpful advice.

M: I love that idea! I'll announce that at our next staff meeting and find out who is interested in volunteering for that role.

Questions 56-58 refer to the following conversation.

W: Adam, you mentioned in the meeting that you think we should use a new supplier for our office supplies. What's wrong with the current one?

M: Their deliveries are never on time these days. So, I think we should switch to Gibson Stationery.

W: I see. But didn't we decide that their prices were a little high? I'm concerned that we'll go over our spending budget if we switch to them.

M: Well, the price isn't that much higher, actually. And, in the long term, because deliveries would arrive on time, we wouldn't have so many delays with our work projects.

Questions 59-61 refer to the following conversation.

M: Harriet, The Primrose Hotel has just placed an order with our factory. They're improving hotel security and want us to provide several CCTV cameras for their gym, parking area, and main lobby.

W: We should be able to handle that. How many cameras do they need in total?

M: The initial order is for twenty. They'd prefer to have them by the end of the week, and I don't think we have twenty in stock right now. Shall I assign some workers to help you speed up production?

W: The end of the week is fine. If it seems like we're struggling, I'll let you know.

Questions 62-64 refer to the following conversation and badge.

W: Excuse me, Tom. I'm having a problem using my card to open the door of the research facility.

M: Oh, we installed new keypad entry systems to increase security. Scanning your card won't work anymore.

W: So, do I just enter my employee ID number?

M: No. Do you see this long security reference number at the bottom? Just enter the last four digits of that.

W: Okay, got it. I guess we made some changes after we had our security inspection last month.

M: Exactly. I think I'd better send a memo to all staff later today, explaining what they need to do in order to open these doors.

Questions 65-67 refer to the following conversation and schedule.

M: Hi, Tricia. Have you finished the cost analysis of Eastwick Corporation's new project? They're waiting to see if we can reduce their overall expenses.

W: Actually, I'm still making some changes to their budget proposal. I have a few details to finish off, but I should be done before the end of the day.

M: No problem. Please let me know once everything is ready.

W: Of course. By the way, what time are we supposed to meet with the clients on Thursday?

M: Just check the schedule on the notice board. We are meeting them in room 303, but I can't remember the exact time.

Questions 68-70 refer to the following conversation and table.

W: Hi, Mike. I must say, I'm surprised by how many employees have volunteered to help out with our company's fundraising event.

M: Yes, I'm glad so many people are interested in making the event a success.

W: Most of them want to work in the tent where the musicians and comedians will perform, but we need to persuade more of them to help out with taking donations and providing information.

M: Well, that's the tent I'll be working in during the event. I'll try to convince some people to help me out.

W: Good. Don't forget we have a meeting with the event planner later. She'll be able to tell us how big each tent will be, and how many workers they'll accommodate.

Part 4

Questions 71-73 refer to the following broadcast.

Good evening. You're watching the local news on Channel 5. Regent City Council has been considering several thousand designs submitted by local school and college students, and they will soon choose one to be the official logo of the city. The competition winner, and his or her logo design, will be announced and unveiled during a press conference at City Hall on March 15. The new logo is part of the city's plan to boost local tourism. A shortlist of the fifty best logo designs can be viewed on the council's Web page, along with the details of each designer.

Questions 74-76 refer to the following talk.

Good morning, everyone! I'm the lead product designer at Meteor Electronics, and it's my pleasure today to show you our newest cell phone model: the Meteor S6. The phone officially launches today, and I'll be demonstrating all of its innovative features during my presentation. Later, you can visit the Meteor Electronics booth in the main hall to purchase one at a special price, only today. Now, let's begin. My colleague Henry is going to hand out brochures first. These include product specifications and details about new features.

Questions 77-79 refer to the following telephone message.

Hello, Mr. Simpkins. This is Jean calling from Tayfront Property. As you know, we are currently listing your home on our Web site, but we haven't received any offers yet. I think homebuyers would be more interested if you were able to add more images to the listing. So, I'd appreciate it if you could take a few high-quality pictures and send them to me by e-mail. As previously arranged, your listing will only be online for one more month, so make this your top priority. Thank you.

Questions 80-82 refer to the following announcement.

Before you all start work on our assembly lines today, I'd like to make a quick announcement. On Saturday, a safety inspector will be coming to check all of our manufacturing machines and tools. He will also be observing each of you and how you perform certain actions during your work shift. So, it's especially important that you follow all of our safety procedures perfectly. I have put these procedures up on the notice board in the break room. Please look them over when you have a chance.

Questions 83-85 refer to the following excerpt from a meeting.

It's a pleasure to be here today to give a presentation to the city council's parks and recreation department. I'm Barbara Maxwell, the senior gardener for the landscaping project to improve Beaumont Park. I'm delighted to inform you that the first phase of the project has been completed ahead of schedule. We have expanded the park boundary and planted hedges around the perimeter. But, that was the easy part. The real work starts with the planting of the central rose garden. Throughout March, we will prepare the flowerbeds and build the rock walls, and the roses will be planted in the middle of April.

Questions 86-88 refer to the following tour information.

Thank you for joining this tour of the beautiful Mount Pascal National Park. I'm going to guide you along some fairly easy trails, where you'll get to see many beautiful views of the surrounding mountains and valleys. Along the way, you'll see spectacular waterfalls and impressive rock formations. When we stop for a break at around 10 A.M., I'll hand out bottles of water. It will be quite hot today, so it's important to stay hydrated. Our first stop will be the ridge where Henry Masters produced many of his most popular oil paintings in the 1930s. So, let's get going.

Questions 89-91 refer to the following talk.

I'm happy to welcome you all to MK Manufacturing's main factory. We hope that today's tour will encourage you to invest in our expanding business. Now, while passing through the main gate, make sure you pick up a pair of protective glasses and a hard hat. You'll see a lot of complicated machinery and processes today, and these might require further explanation. Feel free to stop me at any time. Following the tour, we'll have lunch in the cafeteria, and then you'll meet with our CEO to discuss potential investment opportunities.

Questions 92-94 refer to the following announcement.

I'd like to discuss a change that we are planning to implement starting next month. Here at Besty Car Hire, it has always been our policy that customers can drop off vehicles at any of our branches. However, they will no longer be able to do this. Instead, they must return vehicles to the branch where they were originally picked up. I think most customers will understand our reasons for making the change. However, if any of them complain, please advise them to visit our Web site and leave a review on our customer feedback page.

Questions 95-97 refer to the following excerpt from a meeting and contact list.

Let's begin this meeting with all of our IT staff by discussing our company's new Web chat software. Management had us install this program last month hoping that it would improve communication between departments and project members. However, we have found that it has caused a decrease in staff productivity, as too many employees are using it for general chit-chat and gossip. As a result, those found to be misusing the software have been temporarily banned. These employees will need to call extension 538 in order to regain access to the program.

Questions 98-100 refer to the following telephone message and floor plan.

Hi, Mr. Grainger. I'm calling to request that my office be moved to one of the rooms on the recently-renovated second floor of our building. The office I'm in at the moment just isn't big enough for all the documents I need to handle, so I'd appreciate more space. I've been looking at the floor plan for the second floor, and I'd be happy to take the office that's situated opposite from the door to the storage room. According to head office, I need to get an approval form from you, and then hand it in before Wednesday. I really appreciate your assistance.

시원스쿨 토익학습지 실전편

초판 1쇄 발행 2023년 1월 2일
초판 2쇄 발행 2023년 11월 10일

지은이 시원스쿨어학연구소
펴낸곳 (주)에스제이더블유인터내셔널
펴낸이 양홍걸 이시원

홈페이지 www.siwonschool.com
주소 서울시 영등포구 국회대로74길 12 시원스쿨
교재 구입 문의 02)2014-8151
고객센터 02)6409-0878

ISBN 979-11-6150-656-2 13740
Number 1-110207-18190407-06

시원스쿨
토익학습지
—
실전편

시원스쿨 LAB

TOEIC

Test of English for International Communication

TEST 3

해설 바로보기 ▶

TOEIC

Test of English for International Communication

TEST 3

실전 모의고사 3

MP3 바로듣기

강의 바로보기

LISTENING TEST

In the Listening test, you will be asked to demonstrate how well you understand spoken English. The entire Listening test will last approximately 45 minutes. There are four parts, and directions are given for each part. You must mark your answers on the separate answer sheet. Do not write your answers in your test book.

PART 1

Directions: For each question in this part, you will hear four statements about a picture in your test book. When you hear the statements, you must select the one statement that best describes what you see in the picture. Then find the number of the question on your answer sheet and mark your answer. The statements will not be printed in your test book and will be spoken only one time.

Statement (D), "They are taking photographs," is the best description of the picture, so you should select answer (D) and mark it on your answer sheet.

1.

2.

GO ON TO THE NEXT PAGE

3.

4.

5.

6.

GO ON TO THE NEXT PAGE

PART 2

Directions: You will hear a question or statement and three responses spoken in English. They will not be printed in your test book and will be spoken only one time. Select the best response to the question or statement and mark the letter (A), (B), or (C) on your answer sheet.

7. Mark your answer on your answer sheet.

8. Mark your answer on your answer sheet.

9. Mark your answer on your answer sheet.

10. Mark your answer on your answer sheet.

11. Mark your answer on your answer sheet.

12. Mark your answer on your answer sheet.

13. Mark your answer on your answer sheet.

14. Mark your answer on your answer sheet.

15. Mark your answer on your answer sheet.

16. Mark your answer on your answer sheet.

17. Mark your answer on your answer sheet.

18. Mark your answer on your answer sheet.

19. Mark your answer on your answer sheet.

20. Mark your answer on your answer sheet.

21. Mark your answer on your answer sheet.

22. Mark your answer on your answer sheet.

23. Mark your answer on your answer sheet.

24. Mark your answer on your answer sheet.

25. Mark your answer on your answer sheet.

26. Mark your answer on your answer sheet.

27. Mark your answer on your answer sheet.

28. Mark your answer on your answer sheet.

29. Mark your answer on your answer sheet.

30. Mark your answer on your answer sheet.

31. Mark your answer on your answer sheet.

Directions: You will hear some conversations between two or more people. You will be asked to answer three questions about what the speakers say in each conversation. Select the best response to each question and mark the letter (A), (B), (C) or (D) on your answer sheet. The conversations will not be printed in your test book and will be spoken only one time.

32. Why is the woman calling the man?

(A) To explain an application process
(B) To discuss a construction project
(C) To request some documents
(D) To confirm a job interview

33. What does the man want to know?

(A) Which entrance to use
(B) Where to park his vehicle
(C) What time he should arrive
(D) How to find a building

34. What does the woman say a receptionist will provide?

(A) A building map
(B) An identification tag
(C) A meeting schedule
(D) A parking permit

35. Where do the speakers most likely work?

(A) At a department store
(B) At a sports stadium
(C) At a restaurant
(D) At a museum

36. According to the man, what should be changed?

(A) Business hours
(B) A floor plan
(C) Some lighting
(D) Some prices

37. What is the woman disappointed about?

(A) A staff incentive plan
(B) A remodeling concept
(C) The size of a budget
(D) The timeline of a project

38. What most likely is the woman's job?

(A) Recruitment manager
(B) Interior designer
(C) Real estate agent
(D) Furniture store worker

39. What does the man say will happen next month?

(A) A sales promotion
(B) A staff orientation
(C) A grand opening event
(D) A company merger

40. What will the woman do next?

(A) Return to her workplace
(B) Calculate a price
(C) Review a document
(D) Tour a building

41. What field do the speakers work in?

(A) Human resources
(B) Electrical engineering
(C) Technical support
(D) Automobile sales

42. What does the man suggest the woman do?

(A) Look for jobs online
(B) Purchase a new vehicle
(C) Update her résumé
(D) Attend a career fair

43. Why is the woman excited about her new house?

(A) It was recently renovated.
(B) It is conveniently located.
(C) It has a swimming pool.
(D) It is affordable to rent.

GO ON TO THE NEXT PAGE

44. What is the conversation mainly about?

(A) A new product line
(B) A seasonal sale
(C) New staff training
(D) Job vacancies

45. What is Ryan's job?

(A) Ordering new supplies of stock
(B) Handling customer complaints
(C) Creating marketing campaigns
(D) Supervising a device repair service

46. What does the woman say happens once a month?

(A) Promotions are offered.
(B) Seminars are held.
(C) Discounts are applied.
(D) Employees are hired.

47. How do the speakers know each other?

(A) They grew up in the same neighborhood.
(B) They played sports together.
(C) They worked for the same business.
(D) They went to college together.

48. What position is the woman pursuing?

(A) Accountant
(B) Journalist
(C) Teacher
(D) Engineer

49. What does the woman mean when she says, "You won't regret it"?

(A) She is happy to provide a reference to the man.
(B) She thinks the man should attend an event.
(C) She recommends that the man enroll in a course.
(D) She will allow the man to borrow some materials.

50. What did the speakers design last week?

(A) A bus station
(B) An airport building
(C) An apartment complex
(D) A shopping center

51. What is the woman concerned about?

(A) Compiling some data
(B) Transporting materials
(C) Exceeding a budget
(D) Meeting a deadline

52. What will the man probably do next?

(A) Order some supplies
(B) Revise a blueprint
(C) Contact a client
(D) Send a payment

53. Where does the woman work?

(A) At a fashion magazine
(B) At a manufacturing plant
(C) At a dry cleaner
(D) At a clothing store

54. What does the woman ask about?

(A) The cost of a project
(B) The date of an event
(C) The name of a business
(D) The fee for equipment rental

55. What does the man say he will do?

(A) Compare some companies
(B) Submit some ideas
(C) Provide a discount
(D) Reschedule a meeting

56. What are the speakers mainly discussing?
(A) A financial audit
(B) A staff training session
(C) A product demonstration
(D) A grand opening event

57. Why does the man say, "She's usually reliable"?
(A) To praise a worker
(B) To express surprise
(C) To agree with a suggestion
(D) To delegate a task

58. What will the woman do next?
(A) Order new products
(B) Show some images
(C) Examine a room
(D) Check a schedule

---

59. Where do the speakers most likely work?
(A) At a health clinic
(B) At a public library
(C) At a sportswear store
(D) At fitness center

60. What aspect of a project is Wendy concerned about?
(A) The time frame
(B) The budget
(C) The product design
(D) The advertising

61. What does the man say about the mobile app?
(A) It will be launched next month.
(B) It will be easy to use.
(C) It will boost customer satisfaction.
(D) It will be free to download.

October 11 Afternoon Schedule Jake Simpson	
1:00 PM	Intern Interviews
2:00 PM	
3:00 PM	
4:00 PM	Board Meeting
5:00 PM	
6:00 PM	Client Teleconference
7:00 PM	

62. Where most likely do the speakers work?
(A) At a department store
(B) At a moving company
(C) At an architectural firm
(D) At a Web design company

63. What problem does the woman mention?
(A) A cost is too high.
(B) A client is not satisfied.
(C) Some materials are unavailable.
(D) Some documents were not printed.

64. Look at the graphic. When will the speakers most likely meet?
(A) At 2:00 PM
(B) At 3:00 PM
(C) At 5:00 PM
(D) At 7:00 PM

GO ON TO THE NEXT PAGE

Coffee Table Designs

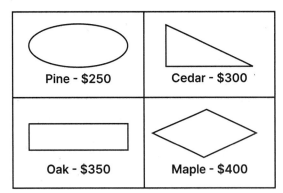

Pine - $250	Cedar - $300
Oak - $350	Maple - $400

New Customers

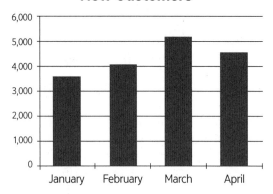

65. What can customers do at the store?

(A) Have their products repaired
(B) Customize their products
(C) Learn how to make furniture
(D) Recycle their old furniture

66. Look at the graphic. Which shape does the woman want her coffee table to be?

(A) Oval
(B) Triangle
(C) Rectangle
(D) Diamond

67. What will the man probably do next?

(A) Order new stock
(B) Provide a catalog
(C) Take payment details
(D) Show a product

68. What is the purpose of the conversation?

(A) To review customer complaints
(B) To discuss a sales approach
(C) To choose an event venue
(D) To consider a hiring strategy

69. Look at the graphic. Which month does the woman mention?

(A) January
(B) February
(C) March
(D) April

70. What does the woman suggest doing?

(A) Updating a handbook
(B) Arranging a training class
(C) Revising a Web site
(D) Offering bonuses to staff

Directions: You will hear some talks given by a single speaker. You will be asked to answer three questions about what the speaker says in each talk. Select the best response to each question and mark the letter (A), (B), (C), or (D) on your answer sheet. The talks will not be printed in your test book and will be spoken only one time.

71. Where is the announcement taking place?

(A) At travel agency
(B) At a subway station
(C) At a national park
(D) At a bus terminal

72. Why is the announcement being made?

(A) A lost item has been found.
(B) A building is closing early.
(C) An event has been canceled.
(D) A route is unavailable.

73. Where does the speaker tell some listeners to go?

(A) To a main entrance
(B) To a customer service desk
(C) To a ticket booth
(D) To a parking lot

74. What maintenance work will be done?

(A) Some new lighting will be installed.
(B) Some elevators will be repaired.
(C) A room will be repainted.
(D) An Internet server will be backed up.

75. What will the listeners be allowed to do on Monday?

(A) Take an early break
(B) Miss a regular meeting
(C) Move their work desks
(D) Work from home

76. What does the speaker offer to do for the listeners?

(A) Organize a staff outing
(B) Extend a work deadline
(C) Provide discount coupons
(D) Increase overtime pay

77. What kind of organization does the speaker work for?

(A) An educational institute
(B) A historical society
(C) A conservation group
(D) A charitable foundation

78. What does the speaker imply when she says, "we'd be out all day"?

(A) A tour might be canceled.
(B) A weather forecast is pleasing.
(C) A distance is too far to walk.
(D) A rest stop has been scheduled.

79. What does the speaker remind the listeners about?

(A) Cold temperatures
(B) Steep cliffs
(C) Dangerous wildlife
(D) Rocky ground

80. What does the company produce?

(A) Health supplements
(B) Sports clothing
(C) Exercise equipment
(D) Kitchen appliances

81. According to the speaker, what did Edward Fisher receive?

(A) A branch transfer
(B) A budget increase
(C) An industry award
(D) A job promotion

82. What does the company plan to do this week?

(A) Launch a Web site
(B) Design new products
(C) Survey some customers
(D) Offer some discounts

GO ON TO THE NEXT PAGE

83. Where does the announcement take place?

(A) At a restaurant
(B) At a movie theater
(C) At a sports stadium
(D) At an art gallery

84. What does the speaker say is available in the lobby?

(A) Event programs
(B) Vouchers
(C) Refreshments
(D) Audio guides

85. What was recently completed?

(A) A building expansion
(B) A device installation
(C) A training program
(D) A customer survey

86. Who most likely is the speaker?

(A) A newspaper editor
(B) A public relations manager
(C) A TV network executive
(D) A university lecturer

87. What does the speaker say is surprising about Lance Redfield?

(A) His academic qualifications
(B) His award-winning works
(C) His scientific contributions
(D) His personal wealth

88. What does the speaker need a volunteer to do?

(A) Interview a guest
(B) Carry out research
(C) Create a work schedule
(D) Post a job advertisement

89. Who most likely are the listeners?

(A) Real estate agents
(B) Tenants' association members
(C) Construction company staff
(D) City council members

90. According to the speaker, what change has recently been made?

(A) Some traffic lights have been installed.
(B) Some street signs have been replaced.
(C) A parking lot has been expanded.
(D) New roads have been opened.

91. Why does the speaker say, "it's important that the work is done well"?

(A) To praise some workers
(B) To request some assistance
(C) To explain the reason for a delay
(D) To announce a job opportunity

92. What industry is the speaker most likely an expert in?

(A) Customer service
(B) Accounting
(C) Marketing
(D) Human resources

93. According to the speaker, what happened last month?

(A) His TV show began airing.
(B) His latest book was published.
(C) He started a business.
(D) He won an industry award.

94. Why does the speaker say, "They typically don't last long"?

(A) To explain why a workshop will finish early
(B) To stress the importance of using the Internet
(C) To give advice on seeking job opportunities
(D) To describe his past business accomplishments

Activity	Location
Health & Safety Training	Room 4
Tour of Departments	Various
Customer Service Presentation	Room 10
Uniform Assignment	HR Office

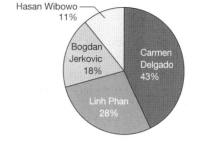

95. Where do the listeners most likely work?

(A) At a hotel
(B) At a hospital
(C) At a post office
(D) At a grocery store

96. What is the speaker pleased about?

(A) A work schedule
(B) A building renovation
(C) A company policy
(D) A job application

97. Look at the graphic. What will the listeners do at 1 P.M.?

(A) Learn about safety
(B) Tour a building
(C) Watch a presentation
(D) Receive uniforms

98. What kind of organization are the listeners members of?

(A) A book club
(B) A sailing crew
(C) A cycling group
(D) A climbing group

99. Look at the graphic. According to the speaker, which person will be invited to give a talk?

(A) Carmen Delgado
(B) Linh Phan
(C) Bogdan Jerkovic
(D) Hasan Wibowo

100. What does the speaker ask the listeners to do?

(A) Recruit more members
(B) Use a sign-up sheet
(C) Suggest a venue
(D) Sell some tickets

This is the end of the Listening test. Turn to Part 5 in your test book.

GO ON TO THE NEXT PAGE

READING TEST

In the Reading test, you will read a variety of texts and answer several different types of reading comprehension questions. The entire Reading test will last 75 minutes. There are three parts, and directions are given for each part. You are encouraged to answer as many questions as possible within the time allowed. You must mark your answers on the separate answer sheet. Do not write your answers in your test book.

PART 5

Directions: A word or phrase is missing in each of the sentences below. Four answer choices are given below each sentence. Select the best answer to complete the sentence. Then mark the letter (A), (B), (C), or (D) on your answer sheet.

101. Please contact our mortgage advisor ------- your initial consultation.

(A) schedule
(B) scheduled
(C) to schedule
(D) will schedule

102. The jungle safari tour is the most popular outdoor ------- near Golden Bay Resort.

(A) active
(B) activity
(C) actively
(D) activities

103. Because of a problem with our mailing list database, some promotional flyers might not ------- our customers this month.

(A) arrive
(B) continue
(C) gather
(D) reach

104. Mr. Hauer, our marketing director, will present ------- proposed advertising strategy at the companywide meeting next Thursday.

(A) he
(B) him
(C) his
(D) himself

105. Data from the first phase of clinical trials is ------- being compiled by Dr. Findlay and her team of researchers.

(A) currently
(B) previously
(C) lastly
(D) evenly

106. The assembly instructions for the chest of drawers are ------- and easy to follow.

(A) cheap
(B) sturdy
(C) partial
(D) clear

107. Ms. Wright decided to sell her home in the expensive Glendale neighborhood and move into an ------- priced apartment downtown.

(A) affordably
(B) affording
(C) affordable
(D) afforded

108. According to the local tour company, the statue outside Mayberry Park was created ------- 1678.

(A) onto
(B) down
(C) at
(D) around

109. Non-club members are ------- to use the courts at Bixby Tennis Club on Tuesdays and Thursdays.

(A) welcome
(B) relative
(C) advanced
(D) precise

110. Business students who have trouble finding the class schedule should be informed that ------- is the one on the middle noticeboard.

(A) their
(B) theirs
(C) they
(D) themselves

111. ------- Ms. Khan's résumé is rather impressive, she has not been offered a job interview in over four months.

(A) Although
(B) Because
(C) In case
(D) However

112. Colson Boulevard will be closed to all vehicles ------- April 7 until April 10 due to road resurfacing.

(A) since
(B) when
(C) from
(D) over

113. The office manager is pleased that the new intern is ------- improving at his duties.

(A) poorly
(B) mutually
(C) gradually
(D) hardly

114. Our diners often ask our wait staff for wine recommendations ------- choosing one to accompany their meal.

(A) also
(B) before
(C) next
(D) whereas

115. Ms. Parker's recently published book on economics has received very high ------- from critics.

(A) praising
(B) praised
(C) to praise
(D) praise

116. ------- has Mr. Cochrane managed to achieve as many sales as he did this month.

(A) Rarer
(B) Rarest
(C) Rarely
(D) Rarity

117. Our head chef will ------- his pasta sauce recipe in response to customer complaints that it was too salty.

(A) launch
(B) alter
(C) confirm
(D) employ

118. According to a recent podcast episode, shareholders of Sleek Computing have lost ------- in the company's founder and CEO.

(A) innovation
(B) application
(C) honesty
(D) confidence

119. The HR manager believes that offering advanced training to existing employees is more ------- than hiring new staff.

(A) benefit
(B) beneficial
(C) benefits
(D) benefiting

120. ------- properties are being developed in the Carlsbad neighborhood and will be available for viewing in August.

(A) Tenable
(B) Affordable
(C) Adjustable
(D) Relatable

GO ON TO THE NEXT PAGE

121. ------- each training workshop, attendees will be asked to complete and submit a feedback form.

(A) Above
(B) Following
(C) Opposite
(D) Without

122. Shelby Corgan was fired by the sales manager because she provided ------- information to a customer.

(A) mislead
(B) misleads
(C) misleading
(D) to mislead

123. Rita Waller's handmade furniture is easily recognizable by the intricate carvings ------- its edges.

(A) within
(B) into
(C) from
(D) along

124. Everyone participating in the team-building session will be given a one-hour ------- for lunch.

(A) budget
(B) expense
(C) break
(D) departure

125. It is recommended to keep cover letters ------- and informative, so avoid writing lengthy letters filled with unnecessary details.

(A) concise
(B) durable
(C) continuous
(D) rapid

126. An experienced volunteer to help new employees settle into their roles ------- by the HR manager.

(A) seeking
(B) sought
(C) was sought
(D) used to seek

127. *Couture Magazine* is currently offering a 2-month trial ------- in an effort to attract new readers.

(A) subscription
(B) association
(C) prescription
(D) allocation

128. The battery of the Psion X5 electric car is highly advanced and can be charged ------- there is a charging station.

(A) wherever
(B) quickly
(C) according to
(D) without

129. A large number of people have applied for the customer service agent vacancies and we will interview ------- who meet the minimum job requirements.

(A) what
(B) any
(C) which
(D) somebody

130. During the city's anniversary celebrations, the ------- of Slurpy Smoothies offered a 50% discount on all large beverages.

(A) mayor
(B) customer
(C) performer
(D) proprietor

PART 6

Directions: Read the texts that follow. A word, phrase, or sentence is missing in parts of each text. Four answer choices for each question are given below the text. Select the best answer to complete the text. Then mark the letter (A), (B), (C) or (D) on your answer sheet.

Questions 131-134 refer to the following advertisement.

Regala Publishing Job Vacancy - Graphic Designer

We are currently seeking an experienced individual to join the graphic design department at Regala Publishing. Applications are being accepted ------- and the submission deadline is May
131.
29. ------- can find out more about our company, including our products and services, by visiting
132.
www.regalapublishing.ca.

The successful candidate's main work duties will largely focus on the design of covers and illustrations ------- used in our various publications. We are seeking an individual with at least
133.
two years of experience in a graphic design role and a degree in a relevant subject. -------.
134.
Successful applicants will be invited to interview for the position the week starting June 10.

131. (A) now
(B) likewise
(C) there
(D) instead

132. (A) It
(B) You
(C) They
(D) Everyone

133. (A) can be
(B) that are
(C) and being
(D) that had been

134. (A) Regala Publishing prints a wide range of magazines.
(B) We can confirm that we have received your application.
(C) To apply, please send your résumé to hr@ regala.com.
(D) Thank you for your interest in the advertised vacancy.

GO ON TO THE NEXT PAGE

Questions 135-138 refer to the following memo.

To: Western Fried Chicken Branch Managers
Subject: Menu changes
Date: December 28

Good morning,

As you all know, several notable changes to our menu were ------- at the recent companywide
                                                            135.
management meeting. By introducing our King Fillet Burger one month earlier than planned, we

expect to greatly increase profits. All branches will begin selling the item on February 1. -------.
                                                                                    136.
Accordingly, promotional materials will be distributed among all branches within the next week.

Another thing we agreed on is the change of pricing to our meal offers. At the moment, a

medium meal is priced at $6.99 and a large meal is $8.99. ------- these prices will be changed to
                                                          137.
$6.49 and $8.49, respectively. The new prices will come into effect before the end of this month,

and we believe this will draw in more customers. Please feel free to contact me with any other

------- on how we might be able to improve our business.
138.

---

135. (A) served
(B) decided
(C) talked
(D) consumed

136. (A) Sales have increased significantly since
the item went on sale.
(B) This means we only have one month to
advertise the product.
(C) Some customers have complained about
the product's taste.
(D) The Ludlow branch is typically our most
profitable location.

137. (A) Before
(B) Soon
(C) After all
(D) That is

138. (A) suggesting
(B) suggested
(C) suggestions
(D) suggests

Questions 139-142 refer to the following article.

Ridgeback 200 – The Next Step in Hiking Boot Technology

The new Ridgeback 200 hiking boots are 100 percent waterproof and are made from advanced materials that completely block any ------- from entering the boots. Furthermore, the reinforced
                                       139.
rubber soles are highly ------- and are guaranteed to last for at least 2 years, even with heavy
                         140.
use.

The boots retail for only $129.95 and can be found at most well-known camping supply stores and sporting goods stores. Alternatively, visit our Web site at www.ridgebackbootsonline.com to view our full range of products. Any boots ------- through our Web site come with an extra set of
                                                          141.
shoelaces and a free water bottle. -------.
                                   142.

---

139. (A) faults
(B) dust
(C) light
(D) moisture

140. (A) assertive
(B) cheap
(C) durable
(D) customizable

141. (A) purchasers
(B) are purchasing
(C) purchased
(D) to purchase

142. (A) We apologize for the current issues affecting our Web site.
(B) We know you will not regret buying these outstanding boots.
(C) We plan to open several new retail stores in the near future.
(D) We would be happy to refund you for the damaged hiking boots.

GO ON TO THE NEXT PAGE

Questions 143-146 refer to the following Web page.

Trenton Town Council – Clothing Donation

We are delighted to announce that our annual clothing donation event will take place on Saturday, July 11, and Sunday, July 12. As always, we encourage all local residents to donate any ------- that they no longer require, provided they are still in wearable condition. Collection
143.
bins have been set up in the parking lot next to Hawley's Drugstore, and donors will not be required ------- any fee to enter the lot.
144.

Before dropping off any clothing, please ensure that it is not ripped or torn and make sure that it has been ------- prior to drop-off. Items that are defective or dirty will not be accepted. As
145.
in previous years, donated items will be distributed accordingly among the town's homeless shelters and orphanages. -------. We hope to see many of you next weekend!
146.

---

143. (A) devices
(B) garments
(C) properties
(D) cosmetics

144. (A) to pay
(B) paying
(C) payment
(D) have paid

145. (A) bought
(B) washed
(C) worn
(D) afforded

146. (A) This is a great opportunity to help your local community.
(B) A full schedule of performers can be found on our Web site.
(C) Damaged goods may be returned at any time for a full refund.
(D) Last year, Trenton Town Council raised over $25,000 for a local charity.

PART 7

Directions: In this part you will read a selection of texts, such as magazine and newspaper articles, e-mails, and instant messages. Each text or set of texts is followed by several questions. Select the best answer for each question and mark the letter (A), (B), (C), or (D) on your answer sheet.

Questions 147-148 refer to the following information.

Fresh Grub Co. - A New Food Subscription Service

Are you feeling uninspired in the kitchen? Do you want to try a wide range of foods from all over the world? Then subscribe to Fresh Grub Co. today and enjoy our weekly deliveries of various delicious meals. Each week, we send out a new themed box of ingredients, from Indian curries to Italian pastas, along with easy-to-follow recipes.

When you subscribe via our Web site at www.freshgrubco.ca, you will receive your first box for only $4.99. You may choose to receive vegetarian boxes or regular boxes. After your first box, you will pay the standard rate of $9.99 per week. This represents an excellent value for money, as our ingredients and recipes are designed to help you create a meal for three.

Your third monthly box from us comes with a Golden Ticket that you can pass on to a friend to encourage them to try out our food. With this special voucher, they will be able to sign up and receive their first box for free. If they enjoy their trial box, their subsequent boxes will be billed at the standard weekly rate.

147. What is true according to the information?

(A) Vegetarian boxes are more expensive.
(B) Boxes are delivered on a monthly basis.
(C) Recipes can be viewed on a Web site.
(D) Prices increase after the first box.

148. What is the purpose of the Golden Ticket?

(A) To receive a specific box
(B) To enter a competition
(C) To upgrade a current subscription
(D) To refer someone to a service

GO ON TO THE NEXT PAGE

Questions 149-150 refer to the following notice.

Burnley Apartments
Important Information

Dear residents,

Please be advised that there will be a couple of upcoming changes taking effect in the apartment building, beginning Monday, March 5.

First, the south entrance will no longer be available for entering and leaving the building. Many of you have reported issues with the keycard entry system at that door, and our maintenance manager will eventually replace this with an updated system. In the meantime, this door will remain locked. Please enter the building via Main Street for the time being.

In addition, the opening hours of our swimming pool will be changed from 8 a.m. - 9 p.m. to 9 a.m. - 7 p.m. Unfortunately, we do not currently have enough swimming pool attendants to staff the pool during the extended hours.

149. Who most likely issued the notice?

(A) A building supervisor
(B) An apartment tenant
(C) A maintenance manager
(D) A swimming pool attendant

150. What is suggested about Burnley Apartments?

(A) It does not have any elevators.
(B) It has several vacant apartments.
(C) It recently enlarged its swimming pool.
(D) It has more than one entrance.

Questions 151-152 refer to the following e-mail.

To: All Employees, Britannia Sports
From: Jeff Foster
Date: November 16
Subject: Podcast episode

Dear Staff,

As many of you know, Britannia Sports has been running advertisements on the popular sports podcast First Place. We were very excited about this opportunity, as the podcast has become hugely popular since launching in April and now attracts more than 500,000 listeners per week. Unfortunately, the hosts of the podcast recently made an error when discussing our returns and refunds policy. They stated that we offer a two-week money-back guarantee, but as you all know, we only offer full refunds on items returned within one week of purchase.

As a result of this mistake, you may encounter some customers who expect to be refunded more than one week after making a purchase. In such cases, please inform them that this is only possible within seven days, and apologize for the misleading podcast segment. If a customer is not satisfied with this explanation, you may also offer a $5 gift voucher as a token of goodwill. If you have any questions, please contact your branch manager.

Regards,

Jeff Foster,
Regional Manager, Britannia Sports

151. What is stated about the First Place podcast?

(A) It has been struggling to increase the number of listeners.
(B) It provided inaccurate information about a company.
(C) It has been offering listeners Britannia Sports gift vouchers.
(D) It recently featured Jeff Foster as a special guest.

152. What does Mr. Foster ask the e-mail recipients to do?

(A) Provide partial refunds after one week
(B) Attend a meeting with a branch manager
(C) Explain a policy to customers
(D) Promote the podcast to potential listeners

GO ON TO THE NEXT PAGE

Questions 153-154 refer to the following text message chain.

Lynda Booker [11:25 A.M.] Hi, Gary. I'm just checking if you're on your way to meet our new client for lunch.

Gary Forgan [11:26 A.M.] Yes, but I can't actually remember which stop you said to get off at.

Lynda Booker [11:28 A.M.] Just get off at the downtown terminal. The restaurant where you are meeting the client is right across the road from there.

Gary Forgan [11:29 A.M.] Oh, perfect! But, I think it would have been faster taking the subway.

Lynda Booker [11:30 A.M.] Perhaps. But you'd have a longer walk from the station to the restaurant.

Gary Forgan [11:31 A.M.] You've got a point.

153. Where most likely is Mr. Forgan when he writes to Ms. Booker?

(A) In a subway car
(B) In a rental car
(C) On an airplane
(D) On a bus

154. At 11:31 A.M., what does Mr. Forgan most likely mean when he writes, "You've got a point"?

(A) He believes he will be on time for a meeting.
(B) He disagrees with Ms. Booker's suggestion.
(C) He is glad he does not have far to walk.
(D) He is grateful to Ms. Booker for her assistance.

Questions 155-157 refer to the following article.

The Maidstone Gazette

Tourism Development Committee Announces Big Changes

By George Stanforth

(November 4) – Maidstone City Council recently unveiled the first designs for its new nationwide campaign to attract more tourists to the city. – [1] –. During a press conference, Reginald Brent, head of the council's Tourism Development Committee, discussed several upcoming changes to the city's branding and advertising. – [2] –.

One of the most significant changes will be the replacement of the city's long-standing logo, which depicts the popular local landmark Maidstone Cathedral. – [3] –. In its place, the council will use a new logo and mascot named Morris the Moose, which is designed to appeal to children and reflect the large moose population that inhabits the local region. – [4] –. The character was selected as the winner of a local contest among schoolchildren, many of whom submitted designs for the city's new logo.

Starting January 1, Morris the Moose will be featured on a wide range of new promotional materials such as tourism brochures, guide books, and billboards. It will also be displayed prominently on the city's Web site and appear in several new television advertisements. Mr. Brent said, "We believe this rebranding will rejuvenate our local tourism industry, and we expect to see an immediate improvement once the campaign begins in January."

155. What is the purpose of the article?

(A) To announce the closure of a tourist attraction
(B) To celebrate an increase in local tourism
(C) To report on a marketing campaign
(D) To introduce a new city council member

156. What is indicated about Morris the Moose character?

(A) It was unveiled in the Maidstone Gazette.
(B) It was created by a child.
(C) It will serve as a temporary logo.
(D) It will be displayed at Maidstone Cathedral.

157. In which of the positions marked [1],[2],[3] and [4] does the following sentence best belong?

"The building has been used to promote the city for almost two decades."

(A) [1]
(B) [2]
(C) [3]
(D) [4]

GO ON TO THE NEXT PAGE

Questions 158-160 refer to the following notice.

Acorn Hotel

Important Notice!

Please remember that our gym will be closed from April 12 to April 17 while it is being redecorated. New flooring is being laid and the walls will be repainted by maintenance workers during this time. When you are checking in our guests, you must inform them about the temporary closure and apologize for the inconvenience. Also, let them know that once the gym reopens on April 18, it will once again be accessible around-the-clock. Exercise classes with our qualified instructors will also resume on the 18th.

We will be holding a brief reopening ceremony in the evening on the final day of the remodeling work. All staff and guests are welcome to attend. Refreshments will be provided.

---

158. For whom is the notice most likely intended?

(A) Hotel guests
(B) Front desk staff
(C) Maintenance workers
(D) Gym instructors

159. What is suggested about the hotel's gym?

(A) It will have new equipment installed in it.
(B) It requires a membership card.
(C) It is typically open 24 hours a day.
(D) It is located on the first floor.

160. What will probably happen on April 17?

(A) Gym classes will begin.
(B) A celebration will be held.
(C) Remodeling work will start.
(D) A special guest will arrive.

Questions 161-163 refer to the following article.

Technology Company Set to Move Head Office

(February 7) - San Diego-based technology company Spitfire Enterprises recently announced its plans to relocate its headquarters to San Francisco this summer. Spitfire founder and president Juan Ortega said that the move will benefit the company in a variety of ways. Not only will it bring the company closer to many of its current clients, but it will also allow the company to provide a larger workspace for its ever-expanding workforce.

The new head office, which is situated on Sullivan Avenue, was previously used as a warehouse and administration building by Eagle Packed Foods. The building had remained unoccupied ever since Eagle went out of business eight years ago, and its condition had deteriorated over the years. Spitfire has invested a rumored $3 million dollars into the remodeling and restoration of the building, and the work is scheduled for completion in June.

Gabriela Interiors, based in downtown San Francisco, was offered the contract to renovate the building after an intense bidding war among design firms. According to Mr. Ortega, "We were very impressed with the proposal put forward by Gabriela Interiors' lead designer, Casey Atkins." He added, "One of the key factors in our decision was that Mr. Atkins guaranteed he could complete the project under budget, without making any sacrifices regarding the quality of the building materials or the attractiveness of the design." Spitfire Enterprises aims to begin full operations in the building as soon as the work is complete.

161. Why is Spitfire Enterprises relocating its headquarters?

(A) It needs to accommodate an increasing number of employees.
(B) It hopes to seek opportunities to connect with new clients.
(C) Its current head office building is in poor condition.
(D) Its employees mainly live in San Francisco.

162. What is suggested about Spitfire Enterprises?

(A) It is collaborating on a project with Eagle Packed Foods.
(B) It is currently based in downtown San Francisco.
(C) It has undergone several previous expansions.
(D) It will move its operations to San Francisco in June.

163. Why was Gabriela Interiors awarded a business contract?

(A) It has worked with Spitfire Enterprises before.
(B) It can complete some work before a specific date.
(C) It has promised not to exceed an expense limit.
(D) It is known for the high quality of its building materials.

GO ON TO THE NEXT PAGE

Questions 164-167 refer to the following e-mail.

To: Chris Manson <cmanson@mailfirst.net>
From: Edward Lang <elang@livingwell.com>
Date: March 25
Subject: Living Well (13th Avenue)

Dear Mr. Manson,

I was very disappointed to read your e-mail regarding your recent experience at our Living Well location on 13th Avenue. We always strive to stock the freshest, most nutritious products in our stores, so I was truly sorry to hear that the Oatgrain Cereal Bars you purchased were three months out of date. — [1] —. I have contacted all branch managers and instructed them to take more care when maintaining inventory to ensure that this error does not happen again in the future. You mentioned that you are currently a Living Well member, and I would like to offer you the opportunity to change from Standard to VIP at no extra charge. This would mean that you would receive free shipping on any orders you make online and also a 10 percent discount on all purchases. — [2] —. I hope that this will restore your confidence in Living Well. — [3] —.

Furthermore, I would like to offer you a full refund for the out-of-date products you purchased. At your earliest convenience, please provide your bank account information and I will be happy to transfer the payment to you. — [4] —. If you wish to discuss the matter further, you may contact me directly at 555-9285.

Sincerely,

Edward Lang, Regional Manager
Living Well

164. What is the purpose of the e-mail?

(A) To recommend new products
(B) To respond to a complaint
(C) To explain a procedure
(D) To offer advice to an employee

165. What type of business most likely is Living Well?

(A) A magazine company
(B) A fitness center
(C) A health food store
(D) An event planning agency

166. What is offered as a solution to the problem?

(A) A replacement product
(B) A gift certificate
(C) A complimentary gift
(D) A membership upgrade

167. In which of the positions marked [1], [2], [3] and [4] does the following sentence best belong?

"We typically check our products every two or three days."

(A) [1]
(B) [2]
(C) [3]
(D) [4]

Questions 168-171 refer to the following online chat discussion.

Cecilia Kramer [9:11 A.M.]	Hi, guys. I'd just like to get an update on how things are going with the TV commercials and Web site ads for our upcoming line of sportswear. Fiona, you mentioned you had some good news about the commercials, right?
Fiona Findlay [9:14 A.M.]	That's right! I've been negotiating with the basketball star Nathan Cosgrove. He has agreed to star in our commercials and endorse our products, because he loves that we give 2 percent of each sale to charity.
George Amstell [9:15 A.M.]	Glad to hear that!
Arnold Levy [9:17 A.M.]	I figured he would! He's involved with a lot of good causes.
Fiona Findlay [9:20 A.M.]	And it gets better. He agreed to do it for half of the fee we initially offered.
Cecilia Kramer [9:21 A.M.]	That's amazing news! And how are we getting on with the ads we'll be putting on Web sites and social media?
George Amstell [9:22 A.M.]	Well, I've been finalizing the designs, and they're ready now. We just need to negotiate with people representing the social media platforms we hope to run them on.
Arnold Levy [9:24 A.M.]	Actually, I just heard back from Mark Curbishley, and he has already agreed to run them for a fair price.
Cecilia Kramer [9:25 A.M.]	Great! I'll let our investors know that everything is on schedule for our launch then. Keep me updated, everyone.

168. What are the writers mainly discussing?
(A) A grand opening event
(B) An advertising campaign
(C) A new Web site design
(D) A sports competition

169. At 9:17 A.M., what does Mr. Levy most likely mean when he writes "I figured he would?"
(A) He expected Mr. Cosgrove to agree to a proposal.
(B) He is surprised about Mr. Cosgrove's involvement.
(C) He would prefer to meet with Mr.Cosgrove in person.
(D) He thinks Mr. Cosgrove will demand a high fee.

170. What has Mr. Amstell been doing?
(A) Filming a TV commercial
(B) Changing a Web site layout
(C) Meeting with potential investors
(D) Designing online ads

171. Who most likely is Mr. Curbishley?
(A) A graphic designer
(B) A social media representative
(C) A sports agent
(D) A financial consultant

GO ON TO THE NEXT PAGE

Questions 172-175 refer to the following article.

Music News

SEATTLE (August 11) - Bridget Starr, the popular singer-songwriter known for hits such as Heart on Fire and Go My Own Way, announced yesterday that she is quitting the music industry in favor of pursuing an acting career. Ms. Starr grew up in Seattle before moving to Houston, Texas to attend the Lone Star Institute of Music(LSIM). After graduating, she then relocated to Phoenix, Arizona, where she began playing her music to impressed audiences in the city's clubs and concert halls. Eventually, she moved to Portland where she was offered her first record deal with Pacifica Music.

While Ms. Starr's debut album received favorable reviews, it was not until her second album, Starlit Drive, that she attained worldwide fame. She met experienced songwriter Rick Daniels in Portland, and the pair worked together on many of the compositions that were included on Starlit Drive. The album sold more than 20 million copies around the world, receiving several awards, and the pair continued their songwriting partnership on three subsequent albums. However, according to Ms. Starr, her passion for music has dwindled over the years, and she will no longer be recording new music or performing live for her millions of fans. Instead, she has moved back to her hometown to work with an acting coach in order to prepare for some upcoming roles she has already been offered. Ms. Starr said, "Ever since I was a child, I have dreamed of starring in movies, and I feel that now is the time to pursue my dreams."

172. What is the purpose of the article?

(A) To report on Ms. Starr's recent award win
(B) To announce Ms. Starr's upcoming album
(C) To report on Ms. Starr's change of career
(D) To describe Ms. Starr's musical style

173. The word "attained" in paragraph 2, line 2, is closest in meaning to

(A) sought
(B) affirmed
(C) exceeded
(D) achieved

174. What is indicated about Mr. Daniels?

(A) He collaborated with Ms. Starr on numerous songs.
(B) He has recently retired from the music industry.
(C) He was one of Ms. Starr's teachers at LSIM.
(D) He has written several songs for film soundtracks.

175. Where does Ms. Starr currently live?

(A) In Texas
(B) In Seattle
(C) In Phoenix
(D) In Houston

GO ON TO THE NEXT PAGE

Questions 176-180 refer to the following e-mail and expense report.

To: David Carpenter <dcarpenter@flashcorp.net>
From: Rebecca Mellor <rebecca@etonbistro.com>
Subject: Re: Table Booking at Eton Bistro
Date: December 7

Dear Mr. Carpenter,

I am very sorry to tell you that our Percival Street location is unable to provide a private dining room for your staff Christmas meal on December 23 as requested. Unfortunately, all of the private dining rooms at that branch were booked up several weeks in advance. Please allow me to recommend two other options that you may wish to consider. If you still wish to hold your staff dinner at our Percival Street restaurant, we could offer you the following reservation options:

| Private Dining Room | Percival Street | Seating: 25 people | Date: December 22 | Time: 6:30 P.M. - 9:00 P.M. |
| Large Patio Table | Percival Street | Seating: 20 people | Date: December 23 | Time: 7:00 P.M. - 9:30 P.M. |

Alternatively, even though our Barlow Avenue location is significantly further from your office, we would be able to offer the following booking:

| Private Dining Room | Barlow Avenue | Seating: 25 people | Date: December 22 | Time: 6:00 P.M. - 8:30 P.M. |

Both locations can provide the Christmas Dinner set menu (appetizer, main course, dessert), and drinks are available at an additional cost. If anyone in your group has specific dietary requirements, we can change any course on the menu to suit them. Please contact us right away at 555-0134 so that we can make suitable arrangements for you and your colleagues. We look forward to serving you at Eton Bistro.

Kind regards,

Rebecca Mellor

Flash Corporation
Business Expense Report
Employee Name: David Carpenter
Position: Branch Manager
Total expenses claimed: $2,350
Please provide a brief description of the expense:
The above expenses covered the cost of the branch office Christmas meal, which took place in a Private Dining Room at Eton Bistro on December 22. The meal was attended by 22 staff members from Flash Corporation's Lincoln branch office. Each employee enjoyed the Christmas Dinner set menu and drinks. A bus was rented to transport employees from the branch office to Eton Bistro on Barlow Avenue. While I was occupied with urgent work matters that evening, my assistant manager Chris Dyer ensured that the meal did not go over our assigned budget, and he passed on all relevant receipts, which you will find attached.

176. What is the purpose of the e-mail?

(A) To suggest an alternative arrangement
(B) To recommend a new seasonal menu
(C) To confirm a customer's restaurant booking
(D) To request a deposit for a reservation

177. What is indicated about the Christmas Dinner set menu?

(A) It includes four courses.
(B) It can be customized.
(C) It is unavailable at certain locations.
(D) It comes with complimentary drinks.

178. What did Mr. Carpenter most likely do after receiving the e-mail?

(A) Visited the restaurant
(B) Spoke with his employees
(C) Viewed a menu
(D) Made a phone call

179. What does the expense report indicate about Mr. Carpenter?

(A) He drove a rented bus to Eton Bistro.
(B) He has dined at Eton Bistro several times.
(C) He was unable to attend the company meal.
(D) He exceeded a spending limit on December 22.

180. What time did Flash Corporation staff most likely leave Eton Bistro?

(A) 7:00 P.M.
(B) 8:30 P.M.
(C) 9:00 P.M.
(D) 9:30 P.M

GO ON TO THE NEXT PAGE

Questions 181-185 refer to the following advertisement and form.

Crowe Academy of Performing Arts(CAPA)

Summer Seminar on Acting and Filmmaking

If you are an aspiring actor, screenwriter, or director, you will undoubtedly enjoy this year's summer seminar on July 24th. Previous summer seminars focusing on dance and music proved to be very popular, and we are confident that this year's event will also be a huge success. To register for the seminar, please visit our Web site at www.capa.com/summerseminar and complete a sign-up form. Registration costs $75 per person and includes access to all three presentations as well as a free lunch and refreshments. We are delighted to have three special guest presenters participating in this year's event, each of whom has worked in the movie industry for a number of years and has been involved with several successful projects.

Three talks will be given during the upcoming seminar:

- "The Importance of Movement and Speech in Acting" (Speaker: Loretta Singh, Actor)

- "Screenwriting: Adapting Novels to Film" (Speaker: Gary Davies, Screenwriter)

- "The Essentials of Film Direction" (Speaker: Kara Jackson, Director)

If you encounter any problems when signing up, you may contact our event coordinator, Maggie Cole, directly at mcole@capa.com. Ms. Cole will be happy to help you complete the process. We politely request that all seminar attendees fill out a comment form on our Web site after the event. This helps us to continue improving our seminars.

---

www.capa.com/summerseminar/commentform/8279

Thank you, Nigel Lean, for attending our recent seminar. Please complete the form below and submit it to our customer service team. We would appreciate your feedback on the following aspects of the seminar you attended.

Quality of Presentations	Poor ☐	Average ☐	Good ☐	Excellent ☑
Customer Service Standard	Poor ☐	Average ☑	Good ☐	Excellent ☐
Usefulness of Event Web site	Poor ☐	Average ☐	Good ☑	Excellent ☐

Which seminar talk did you enjoy the most and why?

All of the talks were excellent and informative, particularly the one provided by Ms. Jackson. She discussed many issues that will help me to get my career in the industry off the ground. Her work has been a huge inspiration to me, and I hope I can follow in her footsteps.

Is there any aspect of the seminar that you think should be improved?

While I thought the talks were all interesting and that the event provided a good value for the money, I would suggest that it be held somewhere else in future. The building is very old and accessibility for wheelchair users is extremely limited. Furthermore, the acoustics in the auditorium are rather poor. I was seated near the back of the room, and I often struggled to hear the speakers.

Click HERE to submit.

181. What is suggested about the seminar?

(A) It may only be attended by CAPA members.

(B) It is held on an annual basis.

(C) It lasts for three days.

(D) It takes place in several venues.

182. According to the advertisement, why should readers contact Ms. Cole?

(A) To accept an invitation to talk at the event

(B) To discuss issues with registration

(C) To inquire about upcoming CAPA events

(D) To request a seminar feedback form

183. What is mentioned about the presenters?

(A) They have extensive experience in their fields.

(B) They have won industry awards.

(C) They are former students of CAPA.

(D) They will take questions from the attendees.

184. What is suggested about Mr. Lean?

(A) He has acted in motion pictures.

(B) He has written several movie scripts.

(C) He has attended many events at CAPA.

(D) He is interested in directing films.

185. What aspect of the seminar does Mr. Lean suggest changing?

(A) The venue

(B) The price

(C) The schedule

(D) The topics

GO ON TO THE NEXT PAGE

Questions 186-190 refer to the following letters and invoice.

March 8
Crawford Books
672 Osterman Avenue, Calgary, AB, T2P 2M5

Dear Ms. Crawford,

I am an avid reader, so I was very intrigued when a friend of mine recently told me about your bookstore. I have only lived in Calgary for four months, and I had been struggling to find a good bookstore with a wide selection of paperbacks and hardbacks. When I checked out your Web site, I was amazed by your extensive selection of books, and I placed an order for five titles immediately. I was delighted that they were delivered within two days, but I was rather disappointed to find that the condition of one of the books is quite poor. Some of the pages of the book by Mary Wolecki have obvious bends and creases, and there is a small tear in the front cover. Of course, this has left me unsure about whether or not I will make a second order from your business.

I do not plan to return the book, but I would be grateful if you could offer an explanation.

Kind regards,

Grace Lim

CUSTOMER'S INVOICE

Crawford Books
672 Osterman Avenue, Calgary, AB, T2P 2M5
Customer name: Ms. Grace Lim
Purchase date: March 8

Book Title	Author	Book Type	Price
Solar Eclipse	Jacob Meester	Paperback	$9.49
Endless Summer	Mary Wolecki	Paperback	$6.95
A History of Cooking	Anthony Braun	Hardback	$14.95
Little Secrets	Cara DeLonge	Paperback	$10.49
Art of the Egyptians	Clive Greene	Hardback	$15.95
		TOTAL	$67.83 ($5 delivery fee added)

If you are dissatisfied with any of the items you purchased, you may request your money back within 21 days of the purchase date.

March 12

Ms. Grace Lim

1107 Monaghan Street, Calgary, AB, T3Q 3RG

Dear Ms. Lim,

I was very sorry to receive your letter and read that you were disappointed with one of your purchases. It is important to note that we sell both new and used books, and the title you mentioned was actually a pre-owned copy, as stated on the Web site at the time of purchase. All of our new and used books are checked thoroughly by me before they are sold, and they must meet certain criteria with regards to their condition. It is quite common for used books to come with minor flaws, and this is typically reflected in their pricing. I hope this explanation will satisfy you and that you will return as a customer of Crawford Books.

Also, while I was checking the invoice, you were charged full price for the hardback book on Art of the Egyptians, even though this book was being offered at 50%-off at the time of your purchase. As such, I have issued a full refund for this title as a gesture of goodwill. I am truly sorry about the error, and I hope we have an opportunity to serve you again soon.

Sincerely,

Jenny Crawford
Crawford Books

---

186. What can be inferred about Ms. Lim from her letter?

(A) She visited Crawford Books in person.
(B) She has written several books.
(C) She is a new customer to Crawford Books.
(D) She received a discount on her purchases.

187. What book does Ms. Lim refer to in her letter?

(A) Solar Eclipse
(B) Endless Summer
(C) A History of Cooking
(D) Little Secrets

188. What is suggested about Crawford Books?

(A) It operates in multiple branch locations.
(B) It primarily sells hardback books.
(C) It offers free shipping.
(D) It will not provide refunds after three weeks.

189. What is stated in the second letter?

(A) Ms. Lim's card was overcharged.
(B) Ms. Lim was sent the wrong books.
(C) Ms. Crawford inspects all products prior to shipping.
(D) Ms. Crawford will offer a discount on Ms. Lim's next order.

190. How much will Ms. Lim most likely be refunded?

(A) $6.95
(B) $10.49
(C) $14.95
(D) $15.95

GO ON TO THE NEXT PAGE

Laguna Design Company

Laguna Design Company has over a decade of experience in interior design and renovation. Our experienced team of professionals can handle any project, from home improvements to large-scale commercial remodeling.

We have been based in Los Angeles for the past 13 years, and we are delighted to finally open another branch in San Francisco. As part of a special promotion to celebrate the opening of this new location, clients based in San Francisco will receive 10 percent off all costs related to work projects. This limited-time offer will run from March 1 to April 30.

Examples of our work, and more details about the services we provide can be found on our Web site at www.lagunadesignco.com. If you wish to schedule an initial consultation, please contact us at sales@lagunadesign.com.

Laguna Design Company

Client name: Brian Hanna
Client's address: 409 Seaford Boulevard, San Francisco, CA 94105
Dates of work: Initial consultation (March 23) / Work performed (April 3 - April 7)
Work details: Wall painting, wall papering, light fixture installation, carpet laying, kitchen repairs
Work team leader: Brigette Cooke

Breakdown of costs:
- Initial consultation: $100
- Repairs: $275
- Labor: $550
- Materials: $1,460

Outstanding balance: $2,385.00
Payment due by: April 30

If you have any questions regarding your invoice, please contact our accounts manager at irisdriscoll@lagunadesign.com.

To:	Brian Hanna <bhanna@homeweb.com>
From:	Iris Driscoll <irisdriscoll@lagunadesign.com>
Date:	April 12
Subject:	Work project

Dear Mr. Hanna,

Thank you for making the payment for the work conducted on your home. I'm glad to hear that you are delighted with the results of our design and renovation work. With regard to your recent e-mail regarding your invoice, you are correct that there was an error in the billing. I have discussed the matter with our sales manager, and he has confirmed that you were offered a free consultation due to the extensive nature and high costs of the work project. As such, this fee will be returned to you immediately. Please allow two or three days for this to show up in your bank account.

Kind regards,

Iris Driscoll
Accounts Manager
Laguna Design Company

191. What is indicated about Laguna Design Company?

(A) It has been in business for twenty years.
(B) It just launched a second branch.
(C) It recently hired new employees.
(D) It offers reduced rates to returning clients.

192. What can be inferred about Mr. Hanna?

(A) He is renovating several properties.
(B) He has recently moved to San Francisco.
(C) He submitted a payment to Ms. Cooke.
(D) He received a discount on services.

193. What is the main purpose of the e-mail?

(A) To request a payment from a client
(B) To address a client's query
(C) To confirm the completion of some work
(D) To set up a consultation with a client

194. In the e-mail, the phrase "conducted" in paragraph 1, line 1, is closest in meaning to

(A) scheduled
(B) assured
(C) transported
(D) performed

195. What payment will be returned to Mr. Hanna?

(A) $100
(B) $275
(C) $550
(D) $1,460

GO ON TO THE NEXT PAGE

Questions 196-200 refer to the following instant message, e-mail, and article.

Johnny Chambers (11:33 A.M.)

Hi, Gina. As you know, we'll be officially launching our advertising campaign for this year's Prism Music Festival in one week. Some of the musicians we hoped to announce in our first line-up have not yet responded to confirm their appearance. Could you please get in touch with their mangers or representatives to confirm they will be taking part? On the posters and advertisements, we are hoping to include at least eight confirmed acts on the Red Stage(Pop Music), six on the Blue Stage(Rock Music), and four on the Green Stage(Electronic Music). We need a signed contract from each artist before we can confirm their appearance in our marketing materials. Also, please remind all artist representatives that due to our budget limitations, only the headline acts on each stage will receive free transportation and accommodation during the festival. Thanks.

To: ginabayne@prismfestival.com
From: sedmonds@artistrep.com
Date: May17
Subject: Mr. Astin's Performance

Dear Ms. Bayne,

My apologies for the delay in getting back to you regarding the musician I represent, Tobias Astin. Having spoken to Mr. Astin about the Prism Music Festival, I am delighted to inform you that he is very excited to perform for his fans at the event. With regards to the scheduling options you proposed, Mr. Astin would prefer to play during the 6:45 P.M. to 7:45 P.M. time slot on the Green Stage, just before the headline act.

I have looked over the contract you sent, and discussed it with Mr. Astin, and we are happy with the appearance fee that you are offering. Unfortunately, Mr. Astin is currently on tour, and due to return in a couple of days. Once he is back, I will have him sign a copy and ensure that this is sent back to you immediately. Also, we are looking forward to seeing the posters you will be creating to advertise the festival line-up. If you could send us a copy, we would be very grateful.

Kind regards,

Stuart Edmonds

First Line-up of Prism Music Festival Announced

Prism Events, organizers of the popular annual Prism Music Festival, have finally announced some of the performers scheduled to appear at this year's event. Around 60,000 music fans are expected to attend the event, which will take place on July 21 at Corgan Park in downtown Carson City. Tickets go on sale 9 A.M. on June 1, and can be purchased by visiting www.prismevents.com. Due to the expected popular demand, tickets will be limited to three per person.

Among the acts that are confirmed so far, the one that has generated the most excitement is James Silberman, who will be headlining the Red Stage and playing hits from his two platinum-selling albums. Other popular acts set to perform include Tobias Astin and Jennifer Diaz. Prism Events plans to announce the full line-up sometime around the end of June.

196. What is suggested about Mr. Astin?

(A) He has appeared at the festival before.
(B) He recently released a new album.
(C) He has spoken directly with Ms. Bayne.
(D) He plays electronic music.

197. Why did Mr. Edmonds write the e-mail?

(A) To suggest a schedule change
(B) To describe Mr. Astin's music
(C) To recommend an event performer
(D) To confirm Mr. Astin's interest

198. What will Mr. Edmonds soon be sending to Ms. Bayne?

(A) An event schedule
(B) A signed contract
(C) An appearance fee
(D) A festival poster

199. What is suggested about Mr. Silberman?

(A) He will receive free accommodation.
(B) He has collaborated on some music with Mr. Astin.
(C) His performance can be viewed on a Web site.
(D) He will give the opening performance at the event.

200. What is NOT mentioned in the article?

(A) The estimated attendance
(B) The event date
(C) The ticket price
(D) The festival location

Stop! This is the end of the test. If you finish before time is called,
you may go back to Parts 5, 6, and 7 and check your work.

토익학습지 실전편
실전 모의고사 3 정답 및 스크립트

PART 1

1. (C)　**2.** (A)　**3.** (D)　**4.** (D)　**5.** (C)　**6.** (D)

PART 2

7. (B)　**8.** (C)　**9.** (A)　**10.** (A)　**11.** (C)　**12.** (A)　**13.** (C)　**14.** (A)　**15.** (B)　**16.** (A)　**17.** (C)　**18.** (C)　**19.** (A)　**20.** (B)　**21.** (C)
22. (B)　**23.** (B)　**24.** (C)　**25.** (C)　**26.** (A)　**27.** (B)　**28.** (B)　**29.** (B)　**30.** (A)　**31.** (C)

PART 3

32. (D)　**33.** (A)　**34.** (B)　**35.** (D)　**36.** (C)　**37.** (C)　**38.** (B)　**39.** (D)　**40.** (D)　**41.** (D)　**42.** (A)　**43.** (B)　**44.** (C)　**45.** (D)　**46.** (B)
47. (D)　**48.** (C)　**49.** (C)　**50.** (B)　**51.** (C)　**52.** (C)　**53.** (D)　**54.** (A)　**55.** (B)　**56.** (C)　**57.** (B)　**58.** (B)　**59.** (D)　**60.** (B)　**61.** (C)
62. (C)　**63.** (B)　**64.** (C)　**65.** (B)　**66.** (D)　**67.** (D)　**68.** (B)　**69.** (C)　**70.** (A)

PART 4

71. (B)　**72.** (D)　**73.** (B)　**74.** (B)　**75.** (A)　**76.** (C)　**77.** (C)　**78.** (C)　**79.** (D)　**80.** (C)　**81.** (D)　**82.** (A)　**83.** (B)　**84.** (C)　**85.** (B)
86. (C)　**87.** (C)　**88.** (B)　**89.** (B)　**90.** (A)　**91.** (C)　**92.** (C)　**93.** (A)　**94.** (B)　**95.** (D)　**96.** (B)　**97.** (C)　**98.** (A)　**99.** (B)　**100.** (C)

PART 5

101. (C)　**102.** (B)　**103.** (D)　**104.** (C)　**105.** (A)　**106.** (D)　**107.** (A)　**108.** (D)　**109.** (A)　**110.** (B)　**111.** (A)　**112.** (C)
113. (C)　**114.** (B)　**115.** (D)　**116.** (C)　**117.** (B)　**118.** (D)　**119.** (B)　**120.** (B)　**121.** (B)　**122.** (C)　**123.** (C)　**124.** (C)
125. (A)　**126.** (C)　**127.** (A)　**128.** (A)　**129.** (B)　**130.** (D)

PART 6

131. (A)　**132.** (B)　**133.** (B)　**134.** (C)　**135.** (B)　**136.** (B)　**137.** (B)　**138.** (C)　**139.** (D)　**140.** (C)　**141.** (C)　**142.** (B)
143. (B)　**144.** (A)　**145.** (B)　**146.** (A)

PART 7

147. (D)　**148.** (D)　**149.** (A)　**150.** (D)　**151.** (B)　**152.** (C)　**153.** (D)　**154.** (C)　**155.** (C)　**156.** (B)　**157.** (C)　**158.** (B)
159. (C)　**160.** (B)　**161.** (A)　**162.** (D)　**163.** (C)　**164.** (B)　**165.** (C)　**166.** (D)　**167.** (A)　**168.** (B)　**169.** (A)　**170.** (D)
171. (B)　**172.** (C)　**173.** (D)　**174.** (A)　**175.** (B)　**176.** (A)　**177.** (B)　**178.** (D)　**179.** (C)　**180.** (B)　**181.** (B)　**182.** (B)
183. (A)　**184.** (D)　**185.** (A)　**186.** (C)　**187.** (B)　**188.** (D)　**189.** (C)　**190.** (D)　**191.** (B)　**192.** (D)　**193.** (B)　**194.** (D)
195. (A)　**196.** (D)　**197.** (D)　**198.** (B)　**199.** (A)　**200.** (C)

Part 1

1. (A) She's emptying a shopping basket.
(B) She's pushing a shopping cart.
(C) She's facing shelving units.
(D) She's paying at a cash register.

2. (A) He's buttoning his shirt.
(B) He's polishing a mirror.
(C) He's hanging a jacket on a rack.
(D) He's folding some laundry.

3. (A) A man is repairing a light fixture.
(B) A man is assembling some shelves.
(C) Some tools have been left on a chair.
(D) A tool set has been laid out.

4. (A) Some people are watering plants.
(B) Some people are sitting around a fountain.
(C) Trees are being planted along the fence.
(D) A fence is surrounding a fountain.

5. (A) A basket is being emptied.
(B) A motorcycle is being repaired
(C) A man is loading boxes onto a vehicle.
(D) A man is putting on a safety helmet.

6. (A) A sign is being hung above a display.
(B) A cash register is in the corner of a store.
(C) Some cartons have been stacked on the floor.
(D) Some shelves have been stocked with a variety of items.

Part 2

7. Where is the closest furniture store?
(A) Yes, a new dining table.
(B) It's just across the street.
(C) We close at 6 P.M.

8. Who's assembling the bookshelves we ordered?
(A) From the Web site.
(B) Delivery was free.
(C) Mr. Randolph is.

9. Would you like to review the survey results?
(A) I already did.
(B) Two hundred customers.
(C) It's a wonderful view.

10. How are the scented candles selling?
(A) Much better than expected.
(B) Sure, I'll send them today.
(C) In several stores.

11. Who will be joining the business luncheon?
(A) The reservation is for noon.
(B) The food was impressive.
(C) Just a few supervisors.

12. What's the lifespan of these batteries?
(A) Approximately 5 years.
(B) Try replacing them.
(C) We have some in the drawer.

13. When did you submit your application form?
(A) A part-time position.
(B) To the HR department.
(C) I applied last Wednesday.

14. I wouldn't recommend staying at that hotel.
(A) But it's had a lot of good reviews.
(B) Try to get a deluxe room.
(C) No, this is my first time here.

15. I could send you an estimate for our landscaping service.
(A) No, he's an interior designer.
(B) I'd appreciate that.
(C) A detailed project plan.

16. These ink cartridges won't fit in our printer.
(A) Stacey purchased those.
(B) Print some extra ones.
(C) There's space by the door.

17. Will you be able to place the job advertisement today?
(A) Thanks for coming in to interview.
(B) No, I saw it in the newspaper.
(C) Yes, I'm working on it now.

18. Why was the training workshop canceled?
(A) That's what I heard.
(B) Please register by April 3.
(C) Because the instructor is too busy.

19. What's the start date for the road resurfacing work?
(A) I'm not sure when it is.
(B) There are too many potholes.
(C) That won't take too long.

20. What machine setting should I wash these clothes on?
(A) Yes, they're ready for pick-up.
(B) I'd check the user manual.
(C) Because we need to clean them.

21. Are you flying to New York this weekend or next weekend?

(A) You can change your ticket online.
(B) Yes, usually once a month.
(C) I delayed my trip until next weekend.

22. Do you need me to come into work early tomorrow?
(A) A department meeting.
(B) Well, we have a lot to do.
(C) The subway is the quickest way.

23. Didn't you get a warranty on your laptop?
(A) It's the latest model.
(B) Yes, for two years.
(C) That's a great deal.

24. Why don't you try fixing the monitor yourself?
(A) I appreciate your help.
(B) To request a quote for repairs.
(C) I don't have a clue how to do it.

25. David is taking our new client out for lunch today, right?
(A) I'd prefer a different restaurant.
(B) Thanks, but I already made plans.
(C) He won't have enough time.

26. What size of a discount should we offer on our summer dresses?
(A) How about 15 percent?
(B) A brand-new clothing line.
(C) Yes, I got them half-price.

27. How can I find Mr. Boyle's e-mail address?
(A) Okay, I'll wait for your message.
(B) I have his business card.
(C) Yes, he does.

28. I'll call our landlord about our late rent payment.
(A) No, it's on the 25th.
(B) He won't be very pleased.
(C) Around $700 per month.

29. A lot of diners have complained about our salad dressing.
(A) It must be delicious then.
(B) I'll try out a new recipe.
(C) A choice of salad or soup.

30. This singer has an amazing voice, doesn't he?
(A) He's really talented.
(B) I've been taking lessons.
(C) Maybe there's a technical problem.

31. Weren't you planning to build an addition to your house?
(A) It comes fully furnished.

(B) On the corner of Main and 5th.
(C) I don't think I can afford to.

Part 3

Questions 32-34 refer to the following conversation.

W: Hello, this is Clarissa Main calling from CJ Construction. I'd just like to confirm that you'll be coming in for your job interview with us at 10 A.M. tomorrow.

M: Yes, thanks for the reminder. Oh, I was wondering something. I know that the CJ Construction building is very large and has several entrances. Can you tell me which door I should go to?

W: It's best to come in through the north entrance. The receptionist there will then tell you where to go. She'll also give you a visitor's ID tag that you should wear while you're in the building.

Questions 35-37 refer to the following conversation.

W: Mark, I'm glad we have a break before the next tours begin. Oh, did you hear about the renovation plan? Apparently, the museum management is going to add new flooring to all the exhibit halls.

M: Yeah, it sounds like a good plan. I hope they also make some improvements to the lighting. A lot of our exhibits are not lit well enough, so they don't look attractive or interesting to visitors.

W: That's true, but unfortunately, management has a very limited budget for the renovations. So, they might not be able to afford it right now.

Questions 38-40 refer to the following conversation.

M: Thanks for meeting me here at our offices. We're hoping you can come up with some ideas to improve the layout of our workspace. If you can provide a good design, we can begin renovations immediately.

W: Well, I can see that you're not using your space efficiently right now. I think you'll need to make several changes to the layout and furnishings.

M: What would you suggest that we do? Our company is merging with another firm next month, and we'll need more space for our new workers.

W: First of all, I'll need to have a look at all of the different rooms in the building, so I'd appreciate it if you could show me around.

Questions 41-43 refer to the following conversation.

W: Tim, as you know, I'm leaving our car showroom to move to Ipswich next month. I know you lived there for a few years, so do you know any employers who might be hiring car salespeople?

M: Well, I worked at a car showroom in Ipswich, but I think it closed down. If I were you, I'd just search online for vacancies. There must be plenty of jobs available.

W: I've been looking, but I haven't found much so far.

M: Have you already found a house in Ipswich?

W: Yes, and I'm so excited to move into it. It's right in the city center, so it's close to everything.

Questions 44-46 refer to the following conversation with three speakers.

W: Hi, Derek. Welcome to our team here at Computer World.

M1: Hi. I'm looking forward to my first day. I know we sell a wide range of electronics, but I'm also interested in learning about the device repair service here.

W: Of course. Ryan's the supervisor of that department.

M2: Hello, Derek. After lunch, I'll be teaching you how to repair various devices in my department.

M1: I'm looking forward to it, Ryan. I know a little bit about repairs, but I'm sure you can teach me a lot.

W: You'll also find out about our skill development seminars that we offer every month. These will help you to learn a wide variety of advanced skills.

Questions 47-49 refer to the following conversation.

M: Penny, I didn't expect to bump into you! We haven't seen each other since we graduated from college. How are you doing?

W: Well, I struggled to find a job for a while, so I decided to enroll in a one-year course to become a teacher. It's been going really well so far.

M: That's great! And will it be easy to get a job at the end of the course?

W: Yes, everyone who completes the course is guaranteed a local teaching position.

M: Wow! Maybe I should consider enrolling, too.

W: You won't regret it.

Questions 50-52 refer to the following conversation.

M: Hi, how are you doing with the final blueprint? You know the one for the new airport terminal we designed last week?

W: It's almost finished. I'm just having a bit of trouble including all the features the client requested.

M: Well, it is going to be the largest terminal at the airport once it opens. So, it will be expected to contain a lot of amenities and features.

W: Yes, but the client is asking for too much. I'm concerned we'll go over our proposed budget if I include everything they requested.

M: Don't worry. I'm just about to call the client, actually. I'll let them know that the project might cost a little bit more than expected.

Questions 53-55 refer to the following conversation.

W: Hello. As I mentioned earlier, I'd like to hire you to create a professional Web site for my clothing store.

M: Well, I have a lot of experience in that. What features do you want to include in the Web site?

W: It will need to show all of my products, and I'd like it to include a Web store where customers can make purchases online. How much would you charge for a project like that?

M: It depends on the design, but it would be between $6,000 and $10,000. And, there will be additional charges if you require regular site maintenance.

W: I think I can afford that. I'm looking forward to seeing some of your ideas for the site.

M: Great. Well, I'll come up with some concepts and send them to you by the end of the week.

Questions 56-58 refer to the following conversation.

M: Tina, the potential investors will be here in an hour to see us demonstrate our new products. Have they been sent here from the factory yet?

W: I just took them out of the packaging. They weren't packed securely, and it seems that they've been damaged during shipping.

M: Emma was in charge of packaging the products. She's usually reliable.

W: I guess she didn't have a lot of time to do it.

M: How bad is the damage, anyway? Did you take any pictures?

W: Yes, I have some here. Take a look.

Questions 59-61 refer to the following conversation with three speakers.

W1: When we last met, we talked about creating a mobile app that our members can use to schedule exercise classes and training sessions here at our gym. How's that going, Wendy?

W2: I've been working with the app developer, and we've run into a few problems. It seems that the app will be more expensive to create than we thought. I'm worried that our budget isn't large enough.

M: Well, Wendy, the mobile app is going to help us make our customers more satisfied, so I think it's an important project for us. So, just tell the app developer we are happy to pay a little more in order to make the app a success.

Questions 62-64 refer to the following conversation and schedule.

W: Hey, Jake. I was just wondering whether you have any free time this afternoon. I'd like to discuss the blueprints for the Highman Department Store project.

M: Hi, Jenny. I'll be busy conducting interviews for intern positions after lunchtime today. It might take a while. Is there a problem?

W: Yes, I'm afraid so. I showed the blueprints to the client, and he was quite disappointed with the design features we included. He also wants us to use different building materials.

M: I see. Well, I'll have to go to the board meeting later today, but let's meet right after that in my office. Please bring a copy of the designs.

Questions 65-67 refer to the following conversation and product list.

M: Welcome to Woodman Custom Furniture. Are you looking for something specific?

W: Hi, I'm hoping to buy a unique coffee table for my new home. I heard that customers can design their own pieces of furniture here.

M: That's right. We let customers choose the type of wood they want, and the design they like. Here's an example of some of our coffee table designs.

W: I love the shape of the maple coffee table, but it's a little too pricey for me. Would it be possible to have that shape of table, but with a cheaper wood?

M: Of course! In fact, I have one like that in stock now. Follow me and you can take a look.

Questions 68-70 refer to the following conversation and bar graph.

M: Hailey, I want to ask you about the new sales script your team has been using since January. Has this helped them to sign up new customers? Should we use this approach in all branches?

W: I think so. It has been really effective in attracting new customers. Actually, we signed up more than 5,000 new customers for our services in one month.

M: That's amazing! Have the sales team members found it easy to use?

W: Yes, but it did take them some time to learn the sales script. It might be a good idea to add it to our employee handbook so that staff can refer to it whenever they need to.

Part 4

Questions 71-73 refer to the following announcement.

Attention, all passengers intending to take the green line to City Hall Station. Due to an unexpected problem with a section of track between Fairway Street and City Hall, you will be unable to travel that subway route. You should either transfer to another line at Fairway Street or take another mode of transport from there. For anyone who has already purchased a ticket to take the green line to City Hall, you may visit the customer service desk to request a refund.

Questions 74-76 refer to the following announcement.

I'd just like to remind you all that some engineers will be coming to fix our elevators on Monday morning. There will be quite a lot of noise in the office, starting from 11 A.M., so you're allowed to go for lunch one hour earlier than usual on that day. Now, I know some of you normally like to eat a packed lunch at your desks. So, I'm going to provide you all with coupons that you can use to get money off at some local restaurants that day. Just let me know where you would like to eat.

Questions 77-79 refer to the following information.

Good morning, and welcome to our tour of Indigo Valley. Today I'll be showing you some of the local wildlife that we here at the national conservation group work hard to protect. We're starting at Bowford Forest, where several endangered species of birds and mammals live. We will eventually reach Angel Waterfall, but we'll need to use jeeps to go that far. If we were to try that on foot, we'd be out all day. Now, please remember to be careful while walking through the forest. The trail can be a bit rocky, so take care not to fall.

Questions 80-82 refer to the following excerpt from a meeting.

Let's begin today's staff meeting with some good news. I'm pleased to inform you all that sales of our fitness machines are steadily increasing. In fact, we've temporarily run out of stock for our treadmills and exercise bikes. Edward Fisher's expertise in sales has helped a lot. He recently got promoted to regional sales manager and it was well deserved. And, we expect sales to grow further from here. This week, we'll be opening our new business homepage to make it easier for customers to buy our products online.

Questions 83-85 refer to the following announcement.

Welcome, everyone, to the first night of the Ashbury Film Festival. Before you take your seats for the first movie showing, please remember that we do not allow food inside the cinema. You are, of course, welcome to purchase snacks and beverages in the lobby and enjoy them there before and after the showing. In addition, we're pleased to inform you that the installation of our advanced surround sound speakers was recently completed. We're sure you'll enjoy the improved audio quality this evening.

Questions 86-88 refer to the following excerpt from a meeting.

I wanted to meet with you all today to discuss some new ideas for documentaries and programs we could air on our television network. Since our network mostly covers topics related to nature and history, I thought it would be a good idea to make a show about Lance Redfield, the renowned explorer and botanist. I'm sure our viewers would be surprised to learn about his valuable contributions to science over the past three decades. Of course, I would need one of you to begin researching Mr. Redfield's life and career. Who would be happy to volunteer for that?

Questions 89-91 refer to the following talk.

I'm pleased that the tenants' association has given me this opportunity to discuss the council's ongoing road maintenance in the neighborhood. I understand that, as local residents, you are disappointed with how long the work has taken. We have put new traffic lights at the junction of Main Street and South Road, and we are almost finished resurfacing both roads. We assure you that the work will be done by the end of this week. I know you expected everything to be finished last week. Please understand it's important that the work is done well.

Questions 92-94 refer to the following talk.

Welcome to this training workshop on how to promote and advertise your products or services. You may recognize me from the TV show, Business Guru, which started airing last month. On the show, I share tips on marketing, and I'll be discussing many of those tips with you here today. For instance, some new companies don't appreciate how crucial it is to build a strong Internet presence for their business. They typically don't last long. So, let's look at some ways you can make your own businesses succeed.

Questions 95-97 refer to the following talk and schedule.

Good morning, everyone. Welcome to your orientation day here at Smartfood Supermarket. We have several activities scheduled for you today as part of your first day of training. Most of the activities will take place in different rooms right here in our training center. As you can probably see, the center has just been renovated, and I'm really happy with the way it turned out. In a moment, I'll hand you over to our HR manager, who will give you a talk on health and safety. I'll see you again at 1 P.M., when we'll meet in Room 10 for one of the training activities.

Questions 98-100 refer to the following excerpt from a meeting and pie chart.

Good afternoon! Thanks for coming to this meeting of our book club. As you recall, we took a vote recently on who we should invite to give a talk for our organization's anniversary celebration. I put the results into this pie chart here. So, clearly, the most popular option was Carmen Delgado, but she's going to be out of the country at that time. However, the second-most popular speaker is able to attend! I hope that all of you can make it to next month's event, because it's going to be very exciting. Now, I'm open to ideas on where to hold it, so please feel free to make a recommendation.

WEEK 02

Contents			Page	Date	Check
Day 01	PART 5	고난도 문법 완전 정복 1	02	월 일	☐
Day 02	PART 5	고난도 문법 완전 정복 2	08	월 일	☐
Day 03	PART 6	고난도 유형 완전 정복	14	월 일	☐
Day 04	PART 7	고난도 단일지문 완전 정복	20	월 일	☐
Day 05	PART 7	고난도 다중지문 완전 정복	28	월 일	☐

◀ RC Orientation

명사 선택지가 두 개 이상의 명사로 구성될 때 알맞은 명사 고르기

선택지가 단수와 복수명사 형태로 주어질 때는 빈칸 앞의 부정관사 또는 수량형용사를 보고 수 일치되는 명사를 정답으로 고르면 되고, 가산과 불가산명사 형태로 주어질 때는 빈칸 앞에 부정관사가 없다면 무조건 불가산명사를 정답으로 고르면 됩니다.

> Several [policy / **policies**] in our company are outdated and are being reviewed by the executives.
> 우리 회사에서 몇몇 정책들은 너무 오래되었으며, 임원들에 의해 검토되고 있다.
>
> [Participant / **Participation**] in the workshop is free of charge and open to the public.
> 워크숍 참석은 무료이며, 대중에게 개방된다.

명사 알맞은 복합명사 고르기

복합명사에서 주로 뒤의 명사 자리가 빈칸으로 출제되며, 동사와의 의미 연결이 부자연스럽거나 빈칸 뒤에 제시된 동사와 수 일치가 되지 않는 등의 오류를 단서로 알맞은 명사를 고를 수 있습니다.

> Bad weather is likely to **cause price** [**increases** / increased] for groceries this year.
> 올해는 좋지 않은 날씨가 식료품의 가격 상승을 유발할 수도 있다.
>
> Traffic [**delays** / to delay] **are** expected due to heavy rains, so start earlier tomorrow.
> 폭우로 인해 교통 체증이 예상되므로, 내일은 일찍 출발하도록 하세요.

토익 빈출 복합명사

sales representative 영업사원
workplace safety 작업장 안전
price reductions 가격 인하

product distribution 상품 유통
job openings 구인
marketing strategies 마케팅 전략

만점 보장 TIP

복합명사 문제에서 선택지에 두 개의 명사가 제시되는 경우

복합명사를 고르는 문제에서 선택지에 두 개의 명사가 제시되는 경우 ① 수 일치 ② 사람명사 vs. 행위명사 ③ 사람명사 vs. 사물명사 등의 방법으로 빈칸에 들어갈 알맞은 명사를 고를 수 있습니다.

The **building** [manager / **management**] **office** requested that tenants keep their pets quiet.
건물 관리사무소는 입주자들이 애완동물을 조용하게 해줄 것을 요청했다.

대명사 알맞은 부정대명사 고르기

부정대명사 문제는 사람 또는 사물을 나타내는 알맞은 대명사를 선택하거나, 뒤에 「of the 명사」 구조와 함께 쓰일 수 있는 수량 부정대명사들이 주로 출제됩니다.

To meet the high demand, [**everyone** / something] must **work** on weekends during March.
높은 수요를 맞추기 위해, 3월 동안에 모두가 주말 근무를 해야 한다.

Roy Farm has [**one** / every] **of the longest histories** of meat processing in the world.
로이 팜은 육가공 분야에서 역사가 세계에서 가장 긴 업체들 중 하나이다.

As [**none** / no] **of the seminars** conflict with my work schedule, I can attend any of them.
세미나들 중에 아무것도 내 근무 일정과 충돌하지 않으므로, 나는 그것들 중 어느 것이든 참석할 수 있다.

「of the 명사」 구조와 함께 쓰이는 수량 부정대명사

one[neither, either, each, none] + of the + 복수명사
all[many, several, most, some, both] + of the + 복수명사

형용사 알맞은 수량·부정형용사 고르기

토익에서 형용사 문제는 주로 형용사 품사 찾기 유형 또는 수량형용사와 부정형용사가 수식하는 명사와의 수 일치 유형으로 출제됩니다. 형용사 자리인 빈칸 뒤에 있는 명사를 보고 함께 쓰일 수 있는 수량형용사와 부정형용사의 종류를 알아두어야 합니다.

Our hygiene policy requires staff to wash their hands [**every** / several] **60 minutes**.
우리의 위생 정책은 직원들이 60분마다 손을 씻도록 요구하고 있다.

[**Any** / All] **diner** conscious of their weight can find many healthy foods at our restaurant.
체중에 신경을 쓰는 고객은 누구든 저희 식당에서 많은 건강한 음식을 찾으실 수 있습니다.

토익 빈출 수량형용사

단수명사 수식	every 모든	each 각각의	another 또 하나의	one 하나의
복수명사 수식	several 여럿의 a lot of 많은 numerous 수많은	many 많은 all 모든 every + 복수 시간명사 ~마다 (주기적 행위)	a few 몇몇의 most 대부분의	some 몇몇의 few 거의 없는
불가산명사 수식	much 많은 a lot of 많은	a little 약간의 all 모든	little 거의 없는 most 대부분의	some 약간의

토익 빈출 부정형용사

단수명사 수식	another 또 하나의 any 어떤 ~이든 the other 나머지
복수명사 수식	other 다른 some 일부의 any 어떤 ~이든 the other 나머지 both 두 ~ 모두
불가산명사 수식	some 어떤 any 어떤 ~이든

분사 분사구문에서 알맞은 분사의 형태 넣기

토익에서 분사는 분사구문 내에서 알맞은 분사의 형태를 넣는 유형 또는 분사의 시제를 고르는 유형으로 출제됩니다. 분사구문은 아래 예문과 같이 분사구문의 접속사 뒤에 주어가 생략되고 동사를 현재분사 또는 과거분사로 바꾸어 나타낸 형태를 가집니다.

Remember to check the details of the contract **when** [**revising** / revised] it.
계약서를 수정할 때 세부사항을 확인하는 것을 명심하십시오.
↳ = you revise

Your smartphone may fail to function properly **if** [exposing / **exposed**] to extreme temperatures.
귀하의 스마트폰은 극한 기온에 노출되는 경우 제대로 기능하지 못할 수도 있습니다.
↳ = it is exposed

분사구문이 주절과 동일한 시제라면 단순시제(-ing 또는 p.p.)를 사용하고, 주절보다 앞선 시제라면 완료시제(Having p.p. 또는 Having been p.p.)를 사용하면 됩니다.

[**Having worked** / Working] with us **for many years**, Mr. Walker **has** a deep understanding of our business.
우리와 수년간 같이 일을 해왔기 때문에, 워커 씨는 우리 사업을 깊이 이해하고 있다.

[**Having failed** / Failing] to meet safety requirements, Funplay's new line of children's toys **was not released** onto the market last month.
안전 기준 요건을 충족하지 못했기 때문에, 펀플레이 사의 새로운 아동용 완구 제품들은 지난달 시장에 출시되지 않았다.

 타동사의 수동태 분사구문은 과거분사 뒤에 명사 목적어가 올 수 없습니다. 따라서 분사구문을 묻는 문제에서 선택지로 타동사의 현재분사와 과거분사가 제시되었고, 빈칸 뒤에 명사 목적어가 없다면 과거분사가 정답입니다. 이때 과거분사 앞에 being이 생략되는 것에 유의해야 합니다.

As [stating / **stated**] **in the earlier e-mail**, we will cease operations as of May 31.
이전의 이메일에서 언급된 바와 같이, 우리는 5월 31일부로 영업을 중단할 것입니다.

Mr. Reynolds has displayed tremendous commitment and diligence since [**joining** / joined] **the company** about 18 months ago.
레이놀즈 씨는 약 18개월 전에 입사한 이래로 엄청난 헌신과 근면함을 보여주었다.

필수 암기 분사형 전치사

아래 분사들은 전치사로 쓰임이 굳어진 것으로, 전치사로 암기해두면 문제 풀이 시간을 단축하는 데 큰 도움이 됩니다.

concerning ~에 관련하여	compared to ~에 비하여
regarding ~에 관하여	considering ~을 감안하면
based on ~에 기반하여	beginning (with/on/in) ~부터
starting (with/on/in) ~부터	following ~ 후에
including ~을 포함해	excluding ~을 제외하고
according to ~에 따르면	owing to ~ 때문에
given ~을 감안하면	notwithstanding ~임에도 불구하고

[**Compared** / Comparing] **to** other divisions, we have recorded the highest profits.
다른 부서들에 비해, 우리가 가장 높은 수익을 거두었다.

오늘 학습한 내용을 적용하여 아래 기출 변형 문제들을 풀어보세요.

MEMO

1   In order to apply for the position, employees must first request a
    ------- from their department manager.
    (A) referring
    (B) referred
    (C) referral
    (D) refer

2   We regret to inform you that, due to a recent policy change, new
    employees will receive ------- after a three-month trial period.
    (A) benefited
    (B) benefits
    (C) benefiting
    (D) beneficiaries

3   Workers interested in receiving additional training should
    contact ------- in the personnel department to learn about
    upcoming workshops.
    (A) who
    (B) them
    (C) anyone
    (D) something

4   For more inquiries regarding job ------- here at our company, visit
    our homepage at www.solartech.com.
    (A) open
    (B) opens
    (C) openly
    (D) openings

5   When ------- with tight deadlines, Mr. Heinz has proved himself
    capable of meeting them.
    (A) face
    (B) faces
    (C) faced
    (D) facing

MEMO

6   ------- has to stop by Heilman's Bakery on Fern Street to pick up
the cake for Mr. Vaughn's retirement party.
(A) Someone
(B) Us
(C) They
(D) Those

7   When you proofread the articles, please mark ------- spelling
errors in the text using a red pen.
(A) both
(B) many
(C) every
(D) any

8   As ------- in the Building Department's inspection report, the
old Morse Theater requires extensive structural reinforcement
and renovation.
(A) indicated
(B) indication
(C) indicate
(D) indicating

9   ------- customer comment cards, Pascal's French Bistro should
consider lowering the prices of its appetizers.
(A) According to
(B) Providing that
(C) In the event that
(D) Because

10 Flight attendants must make sure that ------- of the
passengers has securely fastened their seatbelt.
(A) every
(B) all
(C) each
(D) much

기출 POINT

동사 4형식 동사의 알맞은 수동태 형태 넣기

send, offer, award, issue, grant, vote 등 4형식 동사에서 사람이 주어인 수동태의 과거분사는 뒤에 명사를 동반합니다. 사물이 주어일 때는 과거분사 뒤에 전치사를 동반하는 형태의 문장이 제시됩니다.

> Only disabled **employees** will be [<u>**granted**</u> / granting] **access** to the new parking area.
> 장애를 지닌 직원들에게만 새로운 주차 구역의 이용권한이 주어질 것입니다.

기출 POINT

동사 보어 자리에서 분사와 형용사 구분하기

동사의 태에서 가장 어려운 부분은 보어 자리에 올 수 있는 분사(현재분사/과거분사), 형용사, 그리고 명사를 구분하는 것입니다. 특히 토익에서는 분사와 형용사가 보어 자리에 자주 제시되는데 외형상 두 가지 모두 답이 될 수 있기 때문에, 주어와의 관계를 파악하여 정답을 골라야 합니다.

> We all agreed that the **inventory system** was [disrupted / <u>**disruptive**</u>] to prompt delivery.
> 우리 모두가 재고 시스템이 신속한 배송을 저해한다는 데 동의했다.

기출 POINT

부사 고난도 부사 자리 찾기

부사는 형용사, 분사, 동사, 동명사 외에도 부사, 전치사구, 절, 분사구문 앞에 위치해 이들을 수식할 수 있습니다. 특히, particularly(특히), exclusively(오직, 독점적으로) 등 대상을 특정하는 부사들은 전치사구를 수식합니다.

> Today's presentation will deal [exclusive / <u>**exclusively**</u>] with our new product.
> 오늘의 설명회는 오직 우리의 신제품만을 다룰 것입니다.

accordingly(따라서), otherwise(그렇지 않으면), thereby(그로 인해)와 같은 부사는 앞 절의 내용을 받아서 다음 절 또는 분사구문을 연결할 수 있지만, 쓰이는 위치가 서로 달라 구분해서 사용됩니다. accordingly는 주로 연결되는 절의 끝에, otherwise는 연결되는 절의 동사 앞 또는 끝에, 그리고 thereby는 연결되는 분사구문의 앞에 사용됩니다.

> Half of our workers will work from home, [<u>**thereby**</u> / elsewhere] **reducing operating expenses.**
> 우리 직원의 절반이 재택근무를 할 것이며, 그로 인해, 운영 비용이 줄어들 것입니다.

만점 보장 TIP

명사(구)를 수식할 수 있는 부사

아래 부사들은 명사(구) 앞에 위치해 명사(구)를 수식할 수 있기 때문에 다른 부사들과 구분해서 알아 두어야 합니다.

| only 오직 | even 심지어 | formerly 전에 ~였던, ~출신의 | specifically 특히 |

[Later / **Formerly**] a prominent economist, Mr. Madison is now the CEO of Lion Financial.
저명한 경제학자 출신인 메디슨 씨는 현재 리온 금융사의 대표이사이다.

접속사 알맞은 부사절 접속사 고르기

Wh + ever 부사절 접속사는 '(아무리) ~라 할지라도' 혹은 '어떤 ~든지'의 의미를 갖습니다. Wh + ever는 문장 내에서 부사 역할을 하기 때문에 완전한 문장과 함께 쓰입니다.

> whenever (= no matter when) 언제라 할지라도, 언제든지
> wherever (= no matter where) 어디라 할지라도, 어디든지
> however (= no matter how) 얼마나 ~할지라도, 얼마나 ~하든지
>
> * however는 형용사/부사와 함께 쓰이며, 이 경우 형용사/부사 바로 앞에 위치합니다.

Our premium member cards can be used [**wherever** / whichever] other credit cards are accepted.
저희 프리미엄 회원 카드는 다른 신용카드들이 받아들여지는 곳이라면 어디에서든 사용될 수 있습니다.

[**However** / Rather] slowly our reader base grows, our magazine is still collecting more advertising revenue.
우리 독자층이 아무리 더디게 증가하더라도, 우리 잡지는 여전히 더 많은 광고 수익을 거둬 들이고 있다.

whether는 부사절과 명사절을 모두 이끌 수 있는 접속사인데, 부사절 접속사로 쓰일 경우 뒤에 or가 함께 사용됩니다. Whether A or B는 'A이든 B이든 상관없이'라고 해석하며, 주로 or를 보고 빈 칸에 whether를 고르는 유형으로 출제됩니다.

[**Whether** / Either] you pay in cash or by credit card, you will receive store points that can be used for rewards.
현금으로 지불하든 또는 신용카드로 하든 상관없이, 보상 판매에 대해 사용하실 수 있는 매장 포인트를 받게 되실 것입니다.

전치사 알맞은 시간 · 장소 관련 전치사 고르기

전치사 throughout과 across는 범위 내 모든 지역을 언급하는 전치사입니다. throughout과 across 뒤에 장소 명사가 위치하면 '~전역에 걸쳐, ~ 도처에'라는 의미를 나타냅니다. 특히, throughout의 경우, throughout the summer(여름 내내)이라는 시간적 의미도 기억해 놓는 것이 좋습니다.

> A variety of events will be taking place [**throughout** / toward] the city.
> 다양한 행사들이 도시 전역에 걸쳐 열릴 것이다.

필수 암기 「동사 + 전치사」 짝꿍

아래 동사들은 방향의 전치사 to/from과 함께 자주 출제되는 동사들입니다. 짝꿍으로 암기해두면 문제 풀이 시간을 단축하는 데 큰 도움이 됩니다.

- submit / donate / deliver / ship / offer / relocate / move + 목적어 + to + 명사
  (명사)에게 (목적어)를 제출하다 / 기부하다 / 배달하다 / 운송하다, 보내다 / 제공하다 / 이전하다 / 이동하다

> Trax Sportswear will **relocate** its main office [**to** / as] Michigan.
> 트랙스 스포츠웨어는 본사를 미시간으로 이전할 것이다.

- obtain / receive / purchase / order / eliminate + 목적어 + from + 명사
  (명사)로부터 (목적어)를 얻다 / 받다 / 구매하다 / 주문하다 / 제거하다

> Ms. Dekker **has received** a coupon [**from** / in] the store.
> 데커 씨는 그 가게로부터 쿠폰 한 장을 받았다.

전치사 알맞은 이유 전치사 고르기

이유 전치사들은 어떤 일이 일어난 것의 원인이나 이유를 나타냅니다. 빈칸에 이유 전치사가 필요하다면 '~때문에' 또는 '~덕택에'라는 뜻을 가진 전치사 중 문맥에 어울리는 것을 정답으로 고르면 됩니다.

> due to, owing to, because of, on account of ~때문에, ~로 인해   thanks to ~ 덕택에

> The company picnic **has been cancelled** [**due to** / such as] bad weather.
> 회사의 야유회는 악천후로 인해 취소되었다.

전치사 알맞은 동반·제외 전치사 고르기

아래 전치사들은 동반 또는 제외의 뜻을 나타내는 전치사들입니다. 토익 전치사 문제는 의미 연결 관계를 묻는 유형이 주로 출제되므로 각 전치사의 뜻을 정확히 알고 있어야 합니다.

동반	with ~와 함께, ~와의, ~을 가지고
	along with ~와 함께, ~에 덧붙여
	together with ~와 함께
	including ~을 포함하여
제외	without ~없이, ~가 없다면
	aside from ~은 별도로 하고
	except (for) ~을 제외하고
	excluding ~을 제외하고
	apart from ~ 외에

Mr. Willy has arranged a meeting [**with** / along] the marketing director.
윌리 씨는 마케팅 부장과의 회의 일정을 잡았다.

No one [along with / **except**] Mr. Houde can access the confidential data.
호드 씨 외에 누구도 기밀 자료에 접근할 수 없다.

전치사 알맞은 주제 전치사 고르기

아래 전치사들은 모두 '~에 관한'이라는 의미를 가진 전치사들입니다. 빈칸 뒤에 특정 정보의 내용을 나타내는 명사구가 제시되어 있다면 주제 전치사를 정답으로 고르면 됩니다. 토익에서 주제 전치사로 가상 많이 쓰이는 about 외에 그와 농일한 뜻을 가진 다른 전치사들도 꼭 암기해 두어야 합니다.

> about, regarding, concerning, on, as to, pertaining to, related to, with regard [respect] to, in regard [respect] to ~에 관한

This document contains sensitive information [beside / **about**] the company's finances.
이 서류는 회사의 재무에 관한 민감한 정보를 담고 있다.

오늘 학습한 내용을 적용하여 아래 기출 변형 문제들을 풀어보세요.

MEMO

1 In accordance with our policy, you will ------- a refund for the bouquet of flowers that you received three days late.
(A) issue
(B) to issue
(C) have issued
(D) be issued

2 ------- you want to gain muscle or just lose weight, Fitness Clinic can create an appropriate program for you.
(A) Plus
(B) Either
(C) Rather
(D) Whether

3 Each of these plant specimens requires specific soil conditions, so be sure to label each one -------.
(A) wherever
(B) hardly
(C) accordingly
(D) never

4 Supervisors at Plebbs Manufacturing conduct weekly performance evaluations for each new factory worker ------- the worker's first two months of employment.
(A) along
(B) toward
(C) throughout
(D) between

5 Dana Sullivan ------- the Player of the Year by the Women's Soccer Association three years in a row.
(A) had been voting
(B) has been voted
(C) to be voting
(D) having voted

6 The charity met its fundraising goal of $10,000 ------- a
   substantial donation from Emmet Chemicals.
   (A) as well as
   (B) overall
   (C) thanks to
   (D) even if

7 Most customers who responded to our survey were ------- with
   the new menu we introduced last week.
   (A) satisfaction
   (B) satisfied
   (C) satisfying
   (D) satisfactory

8 The hiring committee has yet to obtain a letter of
   recommendation ------- your previous employer, Mr. Vorhees.
   (A) over
   (B) behind
   (C) out of
   (D) from

9 Vehicles may be parked ------- our building residents can find
   space.
   (A) whoever
   (B) wherever
   (C) whatever
   (D) whichever

10 Labor organizations asked the government to provide citizens
   with more education, ------- raising the skill levels of potential
   workers.
   (A) whereas
   (B) in order that
   (C) thereby
   (D) if only

PART 6 고난도 유형 완전 정복

강의 바로보기

기출 POINT

접속부사 문맥 내 인과 관계를 파악해 알맞은 접속부사 넣기

인과 접속부사는 앞 문장의 내용을 근거로 발생하게 될 결과를 연결합니다.

Therefore 그러므로, 따라서	As a result 그 결과	Accordingly 그에 따라서
Consequently 결국	Thus 그리하여	In short 한 마디로, 요약해서
After all 결국	Eventually 결국	To that end 그 목적으로
For that reason 그런 이유로	In the end 결국	

예제 인과 접속부사

Welcome to Littleton Business Networking Association (LBNA). It is a policy of the LBNA to include contact information for our members in our online directory. -------, we would like you to check that all your listed details are accurate and fully complete. Should you notice that any details need to be updated, you can make all necessary revisions on our Web site yourself. To sign up to receive our monthly newsletter, please check the appropriate box beside your listing in the online directory.

(A) Nonetheless   (B) Therefore
(C) Otherwise   (D) Conversely

① **빈칸 앞 문장 해석**
   정책상 온라인 주소록에 회원 연락처가 들어갑니다.
   ⇒ 사실

② **빈칸 뒤 문장 해석**
   주소록 정보가 맞는지 그리고 다 채워져 있는지 확인하십시오.
   ⇒ 요청사항

③ **빈칸 앞뒤 문장 의미 관계 파악**
   앞 문장을 근거로 회원에게 확인을 요청하고 있으므로 인과 관계입니다.

④ **정답 선택**
   선택지 중 인과 관계를 나타내는 접속부사 (B) Therefore가 정답입니다.

문맥파악: 어휘 문맥을 파악해 알맞은 어휘 고르기

Part 6에서 출제되는 어휘 문제는 다음과 같이 4가지 유형으로 출제됩니다.

- **첫 문장에 단서가 있는 경우**
  Part 6 지문에서 첫 문장은 글의 주제나 종류, 그리고 전체 흐름을 파악할 수 있기 때문에 항상 읽는 것이 좋습니다.

- **지시어/접속부사가 있는 경우**
  빈칸이 포함된 문장에 지시어 this/that/such, 대명사, 정관사, 소유격 등이 있는 경우, 앞 문장의 문맥을 살펴 해당 대상을 찾아야 하고, 접속부사가 있는 경우에는 빈칸 앞뒤 문장과의 의미 관계를 확인해 알맞은 어휘를 골라야 합니다.

- **빈칸 뒤 문장에 단서가 있는 경우**
  빈칸이 포함된 문장에 지시어나 접속부사 같은 정답의 단서를 찾을 수 없는 경우, 보통 빈칸 뒤 문장에 단서가 있는 경우가 많습니다. 특히, 첫 문제가 어휘 문제인 경우, 대부분 바로 다음 문장에 단서가 주어집니다.

- **전체 맥락을 파악해야 하는 경우**
  가장 고난도 유형으로, 지문의 여러 부분을 읽고 그 내용을 종합적으로 이해해야 합니다. 따라서, 어휘 문제의 정답 단서를 바로 찾을 수 없는 경우, 다른 문제들을 먼저 풀이하면서 전체 맥락을 파악한 후 다시 시도하는 것이 좋습니다.

예제 전체 맥락을 파악해야 하는 경우

Dover Public Library, a primarily government-funded institution, **will receive a private donation of $1.2 million from Clarence Mandelson, president of the internationally successful Mandelson Enterprises**, to expand the building and improve its amenities.

Mr. Mandelson, whose contribution will be invaluable to the future of the library, made the announcement on Wednesday morning. He has promised to donate $1.2 million of his own personal fortune in order to renovate and expand the building.

The funding from Mr. Mandelson will be ------- in four phases, with the first installment scheduled to be received by the library's board of directors on September 15. The board intends to use the first donation to double the size of the General Reference section.

(A) paid out
(B) added up
(C) cut back
(D) checked out

① **빈칸 근처 단서 찾기**
빈칸 근처에 단서가 없다면 다른 문제를 먼저 풀면서 전체 맥락을 파악합니다.
⇒ 공공 도서관이 개인 기부금을 받게 됨

② **빈칸 문장 해석**
돈이 4단계로 ------- 예정이며, 맨델슨 씨로부터 첫 입금액을 9월 15일에 받게 될 것입니다.

③ **정답 선택**
문맥상 돈을 받는 행위와 부합하는 동사가 필요하므로 '지불되다'라는 의미인 (A) paid out이 정답입니다.

문맥파악: 문장삽입 문맥을 파악해 알맞은 문장 넣기

Part 6에서 문장삽입 문제는 아래 4가지 유형으로 출제됩니다.

- **지시어/대명사가 단서인 경우**
  this, the, its, there, such와 같은 지시어/대명사가 선택지에 포함되어 있다면 빈칸 앞 문장과의 연결 관계를 파악하면 됩니다.

- **접속부사가 단서인 경우**
  선택지에 however, therefore, if so, also 등의 접속부사가 있다면 해당 문장을 먼저 해석한 후, 빈칸 앞 문장과의 문맥상 연결 논리를 비교하면 됩니다.

- **빈칸 뒤 부연설명이 있는 경우**
  삽입될 문장을 더 구체적으로 설명하는 내용이 빈칸 다음 부분에 이어지는 유형으로, 흐름을 정확히 이해해야 풀 수 있습니다. 선택지에 지시어, 대명사, 정관사, 접속부사 등의 단서가 없는 경우, 빈칸 뒤 문장을 먼저 읽고 이를 설명하는 키워드가 포함된 선택지를 고르면 됩니다.

- **앞뒤 문맥을 살펴야 하는 경우**
  빈칸의 앞뒤를 모두 읽어야 알맞은 문장을 삽입할 수 있는 유형은 특별한 단서가 없는 경우, 제시된 상황이 전개되는 순서를 파악해야 합니다. 이때, 문제 풀이 시간이 많이 소모되므로 다른 3문제를 먼저 풀면서 전체 흐름을 파악한 후 푸는 것이 좋습니다.

예제 빈칸 뒤 부연설명이 있는 경우

MovePro Inc.
Meeting Minutes (Thursday, May 14)

The May 14 meeting was led by Carla DeVos. The main issue discussed during the meeting was the proposed expansion of MovePro Inc. Ms. DeVos emphasized the need for the company to expand its operations in order to remain the industry leader amid increasing competition. -------. **It seems that the annual budget for this year may not be sufficient for the company's plans to grow.** As a result, the board members agreed that potential sources of additional investment should be discussed at the following week's meeting.

(A) Next, she detailed new policies that will be implemented.
(B) The board members congratulated Ms. DeVos on her achievements.
(C) She noted the challenges MovePro must overcome in order to evolve.
(D) She will meet with the chairman of Swift Shipper to discuss the merger.

① **빈칸 뒤 문장 파악**
연간 예산이 회사의 발전 계획에 비해 충분하지 않음

② **빈칸에 필요한 내용 파악**
회사의 확장 사업 예산이 부족한 상황을 묘사할 수 있는 문장이 필요합니다.

③ **정답 선택**
예산 부족 상황을 도전 과제(the challenges)로 묘사한 (C)가 정답입니다.

예제 | 앞뒤 문맥을 살펴야 하는 경우

MEMORANDUM
Date: November 17
To: All Bertrand Corporation Staff

The computers in our IT suites are scheduled for software upgrades from November 22 to November 26. Please be advised that you can expect some computers to be unavailable while the upgrade is being carried out.

-------. A notice will be posted on each department's notice board by 9 A.M. throughout the week, and this will tell you which IT suites have computers available on each day.

(A) Availability of computers will change on a daily basis.
(B) Turn in your electronic devices for upgrades by Friday.
(C) Internet services will be limited during this time.
(D) First, move all important files to an external drive.

① 빈칸 앞 문장 파악
  컴퓨터 소프트웨어 업그레이드로 컴퓨터 사용 불가

② 빈칸 뒤 문장 파악
  공지 게시판을 통해 이용 가능한 컴퓨터실 안내를 게시할 예정

③ 정답 선택
  선택지 중 컴퓨터 사용 가능성과 관련된 사항을 나타낸 (A)가 정답입니다.

Part 6 시제 문제 출제 패턴 총정리

Part 6에서 선택지가 동사의 다양한 시제로 이루어져 있다면, 시간표현이나 빈칸 앞뒤 문장의 시제를 보고 알맞은 시제를 골라야 합니다. 이때, 지문에 제시된 날짜를 단순 비교하는 쉬운 유형부터 특정 단서 없이 지문의 전체 흐름을 파악하여 알맞은 시제를 고르는 고난도 유형까지 골고루 출제됩니다. Part 6 시제 문제는 아래에 제시된 4가지 유형으로 출제됩니다.

- **첫 문장에 단서가 있는 경우**
  지문의 첫 문장 또는 첫 단락에 사용된 동사의 시제를 단서로 빈칸의 시제를 파악할 수 있는 유형입니다.

- **지문에 제시된 날짜를 비교하는 경우**
  편지나 이메일 상단에 쓰인 날짜와 지문 내 제시된 날짜를 비교하는 유형입니다.

- **지문의 종류가 단서인 경우**
  공지, 회람, 발표 유형의 지문은 미래의 일을 알려주므로 미래시제가 정답일 확률이 높고, 광고의 경우, 자사가 제공하는 또는 미래에 제공할 서비스/제품 등을 알리는 것이 목적이므로 현재/현재완료/미래시제를 정답으로 선택하면 됩니다.

- **전체 흐름을 파악해야 하는 경우**
  제시된 지문을 모두 읽고 빈칸에 들어갈 동사의 알맞은 시제를 골라야 하는 유형으로, 문제 풀이 시간이 가장 많이 소요되는 고난도 유형입니다. 모든 문장을 정확히 해석하기보다는 문장 내 중요 키워드 위주로 시점을 파악해야 합니다.

Practice

정답 및 해설 P.42

강의 바로보기

오늘 학습한 내용을 적용하여 아래 기출 변형 문제들을 풀어보세요.

Questions 1-4 refer to the following instructions.

MEMO

Classic Toys & Collectibles Company

Star Force Action Figures

All of our products are in perfect condition, but we cannot be responsible for any damage caused during shipping. -------, it is **1** your responsibility to check the condition of items when they arrive, and contact us immediately should you notice any defects. All our Star Force toys come in their ------- packaging and have never **2** been handled. Several toys include accessories such as vehicles, weapons, or alternative outfits.

------- may have been sold separately, and accordingly, they may **3** be sent to you in a separate package after you make a purchase. If you wish to treat Star Force toys as an investment, it is important to care for each item in an appropriate manner. -------. This way, the **4** items can be maintained in excellent condition, and their estimated worth will continue to increase.

---

1. (A) Finally
   (B) Otherwise
   (C) Even though
   (D) Therefore

2. (A) original
   (B) vague
   (C) approximate
   (D) likely

3. (A) Neither
   (B) Various
   (C) These
   (D) What

4. (A) To do so, consult our enclosed guide.
   (B) Some items may require assembly.
   (C) Our complete line can be viewed online.
   (D) Doing this may devalue the item.

MEMO

Questions 5-8 refer to the following memo.

To: All Flicks Cinema Movie Club Members

The founders of the Flicks Cinema Movie Club plan to meet on October 2 to discuss changes to our ticketing policy for future film showings. As you know, a suggestion was made at the last meeting ------- a limited number of guest cinema tickets.

5

-------, club members are able to obtain three extra guest tickets
6
for each scheduled movie club film showing at Flicks Cinema. However, with the increase in the number of club members, and the subsequent increase in the number of guests, many club members have had to miss out due to all tickets being sold out. -------.
7
Therefore, it has been proposed that we limit the number of guest tickets that can be provided in order to ensure that there are -------
8
tickets for club members.

The outcome of the meeting will be announced in the next cinema club newsletter on October 6.

5   (A) designate
     (B) designates
     (C) designated
     (D) to designate

6   (A) Eventually
     (B) Immediately
     (C) Currently
     (D) Formerly

7   (A) New members may enroll on our Web site.
     (B) Obviously, this is unfair to our loyal club members.
     (C) Foreign films tend to be the most popular.
     (D) However, tickets are still available for later showings.

8   (A) ample
     (B) earnest
     (C) attentive
     (D) proficient

사실확인 지문과 선택지를 비교해 언급되지 않은(NOT) 내용 확인하기

사실확인 유형 중 NOT 유형은 단서가 분산되어 있어 시간을 많이 소요하므로, 다른 문제들을 먼저 풀고 지문의 내용이 파악이 된 후에 푸는 것이 좋습니다. 지문의 표현이 질문과 선택지에서 그대로 제시되지 않고 패러프레이징되는 경우가 많으므로 유의해야 합니다.

예제 NOT 유형

We at Neptune Yachts are delighted to announce that **we are currently preparing to receive 10 new deluxe vessels** at our Redfern Wharf location. The finishing touches were put on these boats last week and they left the Italian shipyard yesterday.

The five new Faretti 700 yachts are 24 meters in length, and include 1800 horsepower twin engines. **The five new Faretti 850 yachts are 20 meters in length**, and include 1400 horsepower twin engines. All models come equipped with life jackets and personal flotation devices as standard.

Speak with a Neptune Yachts sales representative today to place an advance order. **All yachts will be ready for viewing and purchase from May 12.**

Q. What information is NOT included in the advertisement?
(A) The date that the new boats will be on sale
(B) The number of new vessels available
(C) The approximate price of each new model
(D) The general size of the new yachts

① **문제 유형 확인**
   문제에서 NOT included를 보고 사실확인 문제임을 알 수 있습니다.

② **선택지 먼저 읽기**
   (A) date - on sale 판매 날짜
   (B) number - vessels available 판매 가능한 선박 수
   (C) price - model 모델 가격
   (D) size - yachts 요트 크기

③ **지문과 선택지 대조**
   (A) purchase from May 12
   (B) preparing to receive 10 new deluxe vessels
   (C) 언급 X
   (D) are 24 meters in length, are 20 meters in length

④ **정답 선택**
   지문에 언급된 (A), (B), (D)를 소거하고 언급되지 않은 (C)를 정답으로 선택합니다.

Paraphrasing

be ready for viewing and purchase 보고 구매할 수 있도록 준비되다 → be on sale 판매되다

기출 POINT

추론 지문을 기반으로 언급되지 않은 내용 추론하기

추론 유형은 지문을 꼼꼼히 해석해 숨은 사실을 이끌어내야 하므로 고난도 문제에 속합니다. 지문의 내용이 패러프레이징되어 선택지에 정답으로 제시되는 경우도 있어 유의해야 합니다.

예제 추론 유형

Promote your services in a Jolly Inasal Restaurant!

Why promote a service in a restaurant?
It is well-known that the promotion of local services in restaurants is one of the most common and direct methods of advertising in the Philippines. Restaurants usually operate all year round and are frequented by lots of foreign tourists. **Therefore, you will greatly benefit from restaurant advertisements that serve as an affordable means for attracting tourists.**

Why choose Jolly Inasal?
Jolly Inasal is one of the largest restaurant chains in the Philippines and has branches in several of the Philippines' busiest tourist resorts. Most of these destinations have numerous Jolly Inasal branches. A Jolly Inasal restaurant is open 24 hours a day and receives around one thousand customers a day. And, if you leave flyers or business cards by the cash register, they will be easily seen by anyone paying for their meal.

Q. For whom is the information most likely intended?
(A) Job seekers
(B) Restaurant owners
(C) Tour operators
(D) Travelers

① 문제 유형 확인
문제에서 most likely를 보고 추론 유형임을 확인합니다.

② 선택지 먼저 읽기
(A) 구직자들
(B) 식당 주인들
(C) 투어 여행업자들
(D) 여행객들

③ 지문 내용 파악
첫 번째 문단에 '관광객들을 끌어들이는 저렴한 수단인 식당 광고로 이득을 볼 것이다'라는 내용이 언급되어 있습니다.

④ 정답 선택
지문에 있는 내용을 기반으로 관광 관련 업종 사람들이 대상임을 추론할 수 있습니다. 따라서 (C)가 정답입니다.

Paraphrasing

will greatly benefit from restaurant advertisements that serve as an affordable means for attracting tourists
관광객을 끌어들이는 홍보 수단으로 이득을 볼 것이다
→ Tour operators 투어 여행업자

의도파악 화자가 말한 표현의 문맥 속 의미 찾기

의도파악 유형에서 인용구는 주로 긍정/동의 또는 부정/거절의 표현들이 자주 출제됩니다.

- No problem. / Don't bother. 괜찮아요. 바쁘지 않아요.
- Sounds good. / Good point. 좋은 생각이에요.
- Certainly. / Why not? 당연하죠.
- I couldn't agree more. / You can say that again. / You have a point. 동감이에요.
- I wish I could. 저도 할 수 있으면 좋겠어요.
- I doubt it. 그렇지 않을 겁니다.
- That won't work for me. 저에게는 해당이 되지 않아요.
- I don't know. 잘 모르겠어요.
- No way. 안됩니다.

예제 의도파악 유형

> **Technical Support Agent (9:42 A.M.)**
> Thank you for contacting Mesa Electronics! What may I assist you with?
>
> **Joe Carter (9:43 A.M.)**
> I bought a tablet computer, and it was delivered this morning. However, I've been unable to switch it on since it arrived. It's the Mesa Delta 2.
>
> **Technical Support Agent (9:45 A.M.)**
> Okay. Now, to power on that tablet, you need to hold the button for at least 5 seconds.
>
> **Joe Carter (9:46 A.M.)**
> I should've known! Let me try that... (pause) It worked! Thanks for your help!
>
> Q. At 9:46 A.M., what does Mr. Carter most likely mean when he writes, "I should've known"?
> (A) He had never thought about pressing the button long.
> (B) He believes some instructions are unclear.
> (C) He has already tried the agent's suggestion.
> (D) He is disappointed about the service.

① **문제 유형 확인**

문제에서 인용구를 보고 의도파악 문제라는 것을 파악합니다.

② **지문에서 인용구 위치 찾기**

지문에서 제시된 메시지 전송 시간과 인용구가 언급된 곳을 찾고 문맥을 파악합니다.

③ **인용구 앞 또는 뒤 문맥 파악**

인용구가 있는 문장 앞부분에서 전원 버튼을 일정 시간 동안 누르고 있어야 된다고 말하는 부분이 있는데, 인용구가 이에 대한 답변인 것을 알 수 있습니다.

④ **정답 선택**

"알았어야 했는데"라는 말은 버튼을 오래 누르는게 해결책일 줄은 생각도 못했다는 뜻이므로 (A)가 정답입니다.

(Paraphrasing)

hold the button for at least 5 seconds 버튼을 적어도 5초 동안 누르고 있다
→ pressing the button long 버튼을 오래 누르다

문장삽입 문맥을 파악해 알맞은 문장 넣기

문장삽입 유형 문제의 정답 단서는 보통 주어진 문장 또는 주어진 문장 뒤에 위치한 문장에서 등장합니다. 하지만, 단서 없이 논리적 판단으로 풀어야 하는 문제도 종종 출제되므로 유의해야 합니다.

- 지시대명사/지시형용사: this, that, these, those, such, each → 바로 앞 문장에서 가리키는 대상 찾기
- 인칭대명사: they, it, she, he → 앞 문장에서 사람 명사/이름이 나오는지 확인
- 접속부사: therefore, however, thus, also, yet → 해석을 통해 앞뒤 문장의 논리 관계 확인
- 정관사: the + 명사 → 앞 문장에서 해당 명사 찾기
- 시간부사구: after, before, prior to, and then, first → 시간 순서대로 내용이 나열되었는지 확인

예제 문장삽입 유형

To: Farraday Telecom Employees

As employees of Farraday Telecom, you will be able to receive our home entertainment package at discounted rates if you sign up during May. – [1] –. Our Top Premium package includes high speed Internet service and cable television with all premium channels. – [2] –. **It costs $30 per month for one television, and $45 a month for two televisions.** Households with more than two televisions should contact the sales office to check the other savings available. – [3] –.

The package includes the fastest Internet connection speeds and access to over 200 channels. Upon installation, you will also receive two free tickets for Henley Cineplex. – [4] –.

Call the sales office to schedule installation to receive this special discount.

Q. In which of the positions marked [1], [2], [3], and [4] does the following sentence best belong?

"Prices vary depending on the number of televisions you wish to have the services installed on."

(A) [1]
(B) [2]
(C) [3]
(D) [4]

① **문제 유형 확인**
   문제에서 주어진 문장을 보고 문장삽입 문제라는 것을 확인합니다.

② **제시된 문장 읽기**
   제시된 문장을 먼저 읽습니다. 비용이 텔레비전 대수에 따라 달라진다는 내용입니다.

③ **지문에서 관련 내용 찾기**
   지문에서 가격이 나온 부분을 찾습니다. 첫 번째 문단 중반부에 costs, $30, $45 가 보입니다.

④ **정답 선택**
   지문의 단서 문장은 문제에 제시된 문장의 예시에 해당합니다. 따라서, 상세 비용을 언급한 문장보다 앞에 나와야 하므로 (B)가 정답입니다.

(Paraphrasing)

cost v. 비용이 ~이다 → price n. 가격

Practice

정답 및 해설 P.45

강의 바로보기

오늘 학습한 내용을 적용하여 아래 기출 변형 문제들을 풀어보세요.

Questions 1-3 refer to the following article.

Local Eatery Receives Overdue Recognition

by Cyrus Deacon

Greenview - In its latest Web article, Foodlovers.com ranked Greenview's very own Big Bone Steakhouse at number three on its list of Top Five Steak Restaurants in Benbow County. According to Foodlovers.com, Big Bone Steakhouse was selected because not only does it serve high-grade, delicious beef, but its generous portions are almost double the size of those offered by its competitors. From T-bone, ribeye, and sirloin beefsteaks, to pork chops and chicken wings, Big Bone Steakhouse has something for everyone.

The proprietor of Big Bone Steakhouse, Gus Brubaker, was overjoyed to hear that his restaurant had been included on the list. When I asked him how he felt about it, he said, "I am delighted that my business has been recognized as one of the leading steak restaurants in the county. Magdalena Grill and Ray's Surf'N Turf have been in business much longer than we have, so I'm not surprised they took the top two places on the list."

---

1 Why was Big Bone Steakhouse included on the list compiled by Foodlovers.com?

(A) It is one of the most affordable steak restaurants in the region.

(B) It offers a wider selection of side dishes than its competitors.

(C) It focuses on providing meat that is produced locally.

(D) It serves larger steaks than other restaurants in the county.

2 What is NOT indicated about Big Bone Steakhouse?

(A) It provides vegetarian options.

(B) It is based in Greenview.

(C) It serves various types of meat.

(D) It is owned by Gus Brubaker.

3 What can be inferred about Magdalena Grill?

(A) It allows diners to join a membership plan.

(B) It is not a brand-new establishment.

(C) It does not offer chicken or pork.

(D) It is not as profitable as Big Bone Steakhouse.

Questions 4-6 refer to the following e-mail.

To: Gloria Costa <gcosta@stormit.com>
From: David Wallace <dwallace@stormit.com>
Date: September 2
Subject: Super Sync Drive

Dear Ms. Costa,

Since January this year, the Corporate Accounts Department has been using Super Sync Drive, or SSD, a cloud storage service that allows users to securely store and share encrypted files. As you know, on August 26, I explained this service to all of our new employees during the orientation session and mentioned that everyone will need to sign up for this service in order to be able to access and share any client-related file.

Our security policy requires everyone to take advantage of SSD, so as a new employee, you must register for the service on your first day of work. As such, if you come in on September 4, please create your user name and password straight away by visiting www.supersyncdrive.com, entering our company's unique identification code (56927BA), and following the instructions provided. As soon as you have created a profile and logged in, you will be able to access all corporate account records dating back to March 1 of this year.

If you encounter any difficulties when using SSD, please direct your problems to Jonathan Schulz.

Regards,

David Wallace

---

4   What is the purpose of the e-mail?
   (A) To schedule a meeting
   (B) To remind staff to back up files
   (C) To outline a mandatory training session
   (D) To request that a task be completed

5   When was Ms. Costa first told about Super Sync Drive?
   (A) On March 1
   (B) On August 26
   (C) On September 4
   (D) On September 5

6   What is suggested about the new user names and passwords?
   (A) They will be assigned to staff by Mr. Wallace.
   (B) They are necessary to use the computers.
   (C) They are required to check old records.
   (D) They should be changed on a monthly basis.

Questions 7-9 refer to the following online chat discussion.

Nina Kramer [10:15 A.M.]
Can you all please update me on how the preparations are going for the department store's big opening day celebration?

Amy Styles [10:16 A.M.]
Well, you'll all be pleased to know that the city council finally approved the concert we plan to hold outside the main entrance.

Phoebe Long [10:17 A.M.]
That's great!

Grant Munson [10:18 A.M.]
It's about time! We applied for the performance permit back in April.

Amy Styles [10:19 A.M.]
Yes, and it took me a while to convince the local residents' committee that the volume wouldn't be too high and bothersome.

Phoebe Long [10:21 A.M.]
I finalized all the decorations for the celebration. I have a team of decorators putting them in place right now.

Grant Munson [10:22 A.M.]
And I've been talking to talent agents who represent some actors. I'm pretty confident that Ryan Esper will be available to say a few words and cut the ribbon at the entrance.

Nina Kramer [10:23 A.M.]
Excellent! His new show is pulling in millions of viewers. Okay, team, please keep me updated.

---

7 What are the writers discussing?
  (A) A department store sale
  (B) A grand opening event
  (C) A product launch
  (D) A staff excursion

8 At 10:18 A.M., what does Mr. Munson most likely mean when he writes, "It's about time"?
  (A) He had doubts that the council would issue a permit.
  (B) He thinks a concert should start at an earlier time.
  (C) He is worried about an imminent deadline.
  (D) He had expected a decision to be made sooner.

9 What were local residents concerned about?
  (A) Increased prices
  (B) Traffic congestion
  (C) Safety issues
  (D) Excessive noise

Questions 10-12 refer to the following excerpt from a brochure.

WHITE SANDS RESORT
ACCOMODATIONS & ACTIVITIES

White Sands Resort consists of ten beautiful beach huts that include either an electric fan or full air conditioning, plus modern bathroom facilities. We provide 18 hours of electricity per day, which is 2 hours more than other resorts in the region, from 10 A.M. – 4 A.M.

Each beach hut has a large balcony and provides a spectacular view across the sea to a diverse array of islands. White Sands Resort is located on the eastern coast of Palawan, far from major civilized areas, so you can have a chance to truly appreciate the beautiful, peaceful environment without any interruptions. — [1] —.

During high tide, you can swim in the sea just outside the beach huts, and there are other places for swimming and snorkeling just 200 meters up the beach. — [2] —. We rent out snorkeling and diving gear, kayaks, and jet skis.

You could also hire one of our mountain bikes and tour the eastern mountains of Palawan, or hire a boat so that you can sail to a quiet beach to have a picnic and enjoy the wonderful scenery.

We would also be happy to arrange "island hopping" tours for you. These last for either 3 hours or 6 hours, and include a delicious lunch consisting of freshly-caught, barbecued fish and a wide range of local fruits. — [3] —. Please note that it is compulsory to make a contribution of $5 toward the EPF(Environmental Preservation Fund) before embarking on a tour. — [4] —.

10 What is indicated about the beach huts?

(A) They all contain an air conditioning unit.

(B) They include modern cooking facilities.

(C) They are located near a mountain.

(D) They sometimes receive no power.

11 What is NOT mentioned as a rental option at White Sands Resort?

(A) Bicycles

(B) Hiking gear

(C) Diving equipment

(D) Boats

12 In which of the positions marked [1], [2], [3], and [4] does the following sentence best belong?

"This will be expertly prepared by your boatman while you explore the beach."

(A) [1]

(B) [2]

(C) [3]

(D) [4]

DAY 05

강의 바로보기

기출 POINT

이중지문 두 개의 지문에서 정답 단서를 종합하여 연계문제 정답 찾기

이중지문에서 1~2문제는 반드시 첫째 지문과 둘째 지문을 모두 보고 풀어야 하는 연계 문제로 출제됩니다. 따라서, 한 지문에서 확실한 정답의 단서를 찾을 수 없다면, 다른 지문에서 추가적인 정답 단서를 찾은 후, 두 단서를 종합하여 정답을 골라야 합니다.

▪ **이중지문 문제 풀이 순서**

① **주제/목적, 세부사항, 동의어 유형 먼저 풀기**

첫째 지문의 초반부 또는 상대적으로 적은 부분만 읽고 정답을 찾을 수 있는 주제/목적, 세부사항, 동의어 유형의 문제를 먼저 풉니다.

② **사실확인, 추론 문제는 나중에 풀기**

사실확인 또는 추론 유형은 패러프레이징을 거치거나 지문에서 직접적인 정답 단서를 찾을 수 없기 때문에 나중에 푸는 것이 좋습니다. 또한, 질문에 NOT이 포함되어 있다면 지문과 선택지를 하나하나 대조해야 하므로 문제풀이 시간이 많이 소요됩니다. 따라서 비교적 쉬운 유형을 먼저 해결하고 나서 푸는 것이 좋습니다.

③ **연계문제는 마지막으로 풀기**

질문에 suggested, implied, inferred, most likely 등이 들어가는 추론 유형은 연계문제일 가능성이 매우 높습니다. 또한, 선택지가 같은 종류의 명사, 숫자, 날짜, 고유명사 등으로 이루어져 있다면, 연계문제일 확률이 높으므로 마지막으로 푸는 것이 좋습니다.

To: Kristofer Jones <kjones@tmail.net>
From: Kelly Hawking
            <khawking@bakercellularphones.com>
Subject: Order Number 289422
Date: October 5

Thank you for ordering a Sweetair mobile phone. Your new smart phone will come fully equipped with a wall charger, automobile charger, and a computer cable. As a free gift for spending over $500, you will also receive a protective case and a package of screen protectors.

Your item is scheduled for delivery on October 16, but please understand that you qualify for our rush delivery offer. For only $6.50, you can get your merchandise a week sooner, on October 9. To take advantage of this special offer, you must reply by October 6, after which the offer will expire. Thank you again for purchasing an item from Baker Cellular Phones.

Sincerely,

Kelly Hawking
Customer Sales

To: Kelly Hawking <khawking@bakercellularphones.com>
From: Kristofer Jones <kjones@tmail.net>
Subject: Re: Order Number 289422
Date: October 6

Please change my delivery to the rush option and charge my credit card accordingly. I would also like to inform you that I want the phone delivered to my business. Please ignore the "ship to" address that I listed on the form when I placed my original online order. Thank you.

Q. When will Mr. Jones most likely receive his item?
   (A) On October 5
   (B) On October 6
   (C) On October 9
   (D) On October 16

① **문제 유형 확인**
   선택지가 같은 종류의 날짜로 구성되어 있으므로 연계문제일 가능성이 높습니다.

② **문제의 키워드 파악**
   문제의 키워드는 Mr. Jones, receive, item입니다.

③ **첫째 지문 단서 찾기**
   첫째 지문에서 일반배송은 10월 16일, 빠른 배송 옵션을 선택하면 10월 9일에 물건을 받을 수 있다고 했으므로 추가 단서가 필요합니다.

④ **둘째 지문 단서 찾기 및 정답 선택**
   둘째 지문에서 배송 방식을 결정하는 추가 단서를 찾습니다. 첫 문장에서 빠른 배송 옵션으로 변경해달라고 요청하므로 (C)가 정답입니다.

Paraphrasing

get 받다 → receive 받다
merchandise 상품 → item 상품
sooner 더 일찍 → the rush option 빠른 옵션

삼중지문 세 개의 지문에서 정답 단서를 종합하여 연계문제 정답 찾기

삼중지문 유형의 경우, 이중지문보다 읽어야 할 지문의 양이 조금 많아졌을 뿐 문제풀이 방법은 동일합니다. 패러프레이징에 유의하며 [주제/목적, 세부사항, 동의어 문제 → 사실확인/추론 문제 → 연계문제] 순으로 풀면 됩니다. 삼중지문의 연계문제는 두 번째 또는 세 번째 문제가 첫째 지문과 둘째 지문의 연계문제로, 네 번째 또는 다섯 번째 문제가 둘째 지문과 셋째 지문의 연계문제로 출제되는 경향이 있습니다.

예제 삼중지문 연계문제 유형

Kenting Science Institute (KSI) has the following positions opening in London.

Senior Research Scientist (Wandsworth Facility)
· Bachelor's degree in a science-related field
· Three or more years of experience conducting scientific research in a laboratory

1 **Laboratory Technician (Camden Town Facility)**
· Knowledge of laboratory equipment
· Setting up, cleaning, maintenance, and repair of all laboratory equipment

If you would like to apply for either of these positions, please contact the human resources manager at tfranck@ksi.com.

To: Tobias Franck <tfranck@ksi.com>
From: Isobel White <isobelwhite@tmail.com>
Subject: Laboratory Technician

Dear Mr. Franck,

2 I noticed your advertisement in Modern Scientist Magazine for a laboratory technician. I feel that the nature of the work is perfectly suited to my background, and **1** I live just a short walk from the facility. For the past 18 months, I have been working as a sales representative for the laboratory equipment distributor Medsales Midwest, where I have gained comprehensive knowledge about all the devices we handle. Additionally, I obtained a college diploma in microbiology this year, and the course afforded me a chance to get hands-on experience using laboratory equipment.

Sincerely,

Isobel White

Q1

① **문제 유형 확인**

질문에 inferred가 들어가는 추론 유형은 연계문제일 가능성이 매우 높습니다.

② **선택지 먼저 읽기**

(A) writes - magazine 잡지에 글을 씀
(B) graduated 18 months ago
　　18개월 전 졸업
(C) currently lives Camden Town
　　현재 캠덴 타운에 거주
(D) worked - institute before
　　전에 여기서 일했음

③ **문제의 키워드가 있는 지문 내용 파악**

문제 키워드 Ms. White를 지문에서 찾으니 둘째 지문의 발신인입니다. 지문 초반에 실험실 기사직에 대해 언급하며 그 시설과 가까운 곳에 살고 있다고 말하고 있습니다.

④ **추가 단서 찾기 및 정답 선택**

첫째 지문을 보니 실험실 기사직의 근무지가 Camden Town 시설이므로 (C)가 정답입니다.

Kenting Science Institute (KSI)
Work Schedule Information

Senior Research Scientists
· Flexible schedule, depending on project stage.
  Morning work or afternoon work throughout the week.
  Occasional weekend work.

Laboratory Technicians
· Weekday shift work required. **2** Equipment should be cleaned and set up for the following day between 5 P.M. and 8 P.M., Monday through Friday, every week. Technicians work 3 shifts a week.

Q1. What can be inferred about Ms. White?
  (A) She writes for a magazine.
  (B) She graduated 18 months ago.
  (C) She currently lives in Camden Town.
  (D) She has worked at the institute before.

Q2. If her job application is successful, when will Ms. White be required to work?
  (A) Weekday mornings
  (B) Weekday afternoons
  (C) Weekday evenings
  (D) Weekend evenings

Q2

① **문제 유형 확인**

선택지가 같은 종류의 명사로 구성되어 있으므로 연계문제일 가능성이 높습니다.

② **문제의 키워드 파악**

문제의 키워드는 when, Ms. White, work입니다.

③ **문제의 키워드가 있는 지문 내용 파악**

둘째 지문 초반에서 화이트 씨가 지원한 직무는 실험실 기사직임을 알 수 있습니다.

④ **추가 단서 찾기 및 정답 선택**

근무 일정이 나온 셋째 지문에서 기사직 근무시간을 확인하면 평일 오후 5-8시이므로 (C)가 정답입니다.

(**Paraphrasing**)

live a short walk from ~에서 조금만 걸으면 되는 곳에 살다 → live in ~에 살다
between 5 P.M. and 8 P.M. 오후 5시에서 8시 사이에 → evening 저녁
Monday through Friday 월요일부터 금요일 → weekday 주중

오늘 학습한 내용을 적용하여 아래 기출 변형 문제들을 풀어보세요.

Questions 1-5 refer to the following advertisement and e-mail.

One-to-One Tours

When you are traveling in Mexico, make the most of your limited time in this beautiful country by contacting One-to-One Tours. Our customers can enjoy:

- Private tours with a knowledgeable local guide
- Discounts on selected local accommodations
- Airport pick-ups and transportation to hotels
- Lower admission costs at local tourist sites and landmarks
- Complimentary bottled water available at all times
- Tips on the best restaurants with the most affordable prices

We offer private tours around four of Mexico's most popular tourist destinations. The tour guides named below are very knowledgeable about their respective cities.

Mexico City: Adrianna Alvarez   **Monterrey:** Fernando Barrera
Guadalajara: Javier Zavala   **Morelia:** Esperanza Reyna

We would advise customers to make a reservation at least three weeks in advance. Bookings can be made online at www.onetoonetours.com.

To: Customer Service Department <customerservices@onetoone.com>
From: Brittany Schwarz <bschwarz@catanmail.com>
Subject: Private tour
Date: November 15

Dear Sir or Madam,

I chose to take advantage of your service earlier this month based on the many positive customer testimonials I read on your Web site. I was very excited to take my first private tour, but I am sorry to say that I will have second thoughts about contacting your company in the future.

To begin with, Mr. Zavala was more than 45 minutes late in picking me up from the airport. Then, following a brief stop for lunch, I was dropped off at my hotel to find that I was booked into a smoking room, not a non-smoking room as requested. Throughout the remainder of my 3-day tour of the city, I received barely any information from my guide regarding the historic buildings I visited. Also, most of the sites we went to refused to accept the discount coupons, pointing out that they had already expired. Frankly, this was embarrassing and unacceptable.

1 What is NOT offered by One-to-One Tours in its advertisement?
(A) Reduced hotel rates
(B) Deals on tourist attractions
(C) Discounts on local meals
(D) Free beverages

2 What does One-to-One Tours encourage customers to do?
(A) E-mail tour guides directly to make a reservation
(B) Reserve a three-week tour of cities in Mexico
(C) Recommend the private tours to their acquaintances
(D) Book their private tour a few weeks before traveling

3 Why did Ms. Schwarz write the e-mail?
(A) To express thanks for a service
(B) To report an error in an itinerary
(C) To request a refund
(D) To register a complaint

4 In the e-mail, the word "following", in paragraph 2, line 1, is closest in meaning to
(A) leading to
(B) prior to
(C) subsequent to
(D) according to

5 What is suggested about Ms. Schwarz?
(A) She found out about One-to-One Tours from a family member.
(B) She previously went on a private tour of Monterrey.
(C) She spent time sightseeing in Guadalajara.
(D) She had originally requested a smoking room.

Questions 6-10 refer to the following e-mails and chart.

To: Shaun Dillinger; Meryl Houseman; Raul Gonzales; Selina Moretz
From: Darius Lautner
Subject: Record of sales (Apr-Jul)
Date: Friday, August 7

Greetings everyone,

I have attached the sales report for the last few months, which was compiled over the past week by our accounting manager, Ms. Tibbs. I would like to discuss this in detail with you at Monday's meeting, but I'll take this opportunity to point out some noteworthy trends and figures.

The figures listed for coffee are our highest since the opening of the business last year. This was to be expected, as we have been aggressively marketing our new varieties. As you will be able to see, the month during which sales of coffee were highest coincides with the time when we ran the billboard advertisements throughout the downtown area.

Next, please take a look at the sales for muffins. To be honest, these figures fall far below our expectations. In an effort to boost sales, we will begin a new 'Beverage & Muffin' promotion on September 1. We can discuss this strategy in depth next week.

Please familiarize yourselves with the report over the weekend so that we can have a productive meeting on Monday.

Darius

Kalimantan Coffee Shop
Record of Product Sales: April ~ July

	April	May	June	July
Coffee	$16,340	$17,750	$17,150	$18,230
Tea	$9,510	$9,250	$8,750	$8,700
Muffins	$8,200	$7,840	$8,340	$7,560
Bagels	$9,530	$8,560	$8,940	$9,250

To: Darius Lautner
From: Lucy Tibbs
Subject: Sales Figures Error
Date: Monday, August 10

Good morning, Darius,

I just realized that I made a mistake when I was recording the figures for the recent sales report that I sent to you. Please refer to the chart and change the figure $8,340 to $8,560. I forgot to add the sales for the final day of that period. Sorry for the inconvenience!

Lucy

6   What is the purpose of the first e-mail?
    (A) To discuss certain items on a sales report
    (B) To propose new ideas for advertising
    (C) To recommend that Ms. Tibbs be promoted
    (D) To explain why sales figures have been falling

7   According to the first e-mail, what will most likely happen on September 1?
    (A) A new line of beverages will be launched.
    (B) Employees will attend a training workshop.
    (C) New sales strategies will be employed.
    (D) Customers will be given a complimentary item.

8   When most likely did the business run a series of billboard advertisements?
    (A) In April
    (B) In May
    (C) In June
    (D) In July

9   For which item did Ms. Tibbs make a mistake when calculating sales figures?
    (A) Coffee
    (B) Tea
    (C) Muffins
    (D) Bagels

10 In the second e-mail, the word "recording" in paragraph 1, line 1, is closest in meaning to
    (A) listening
    (B) collaborating
    (C) initiating
    (D) documenting

DAY 01

PART 5 | 고난도 문법 완전 정복 1

Practice

1. (C)	**2.** (B)	**3.** (C)	**4.** (D)	**5.** (C)	**6.** (A)
7. (D)	**8.** (A)	**9.** (A)	**10.** (C)		

1.

정답 (C)

해석 그 직책에 지원하기 위해서, 직원들은 반드시 가장 먼저 소속 부서장에게 추천을 요청해야 한다.

해설 부정관사 a와 전치사 from 사이에 빈칸이 있으므로 빈칸은 부정관사 a와 함께 쓰일 수 있는 명사 자리이다. 따라서 (C) referral이 정답이다.

어휘 apply for ~에 지원하다 request ~을 요청하다 referral 추천, 소개, 위탁 refer ~을 맡기다, 참조하게 하다

2.

정답 (B)

해석 최근의 정책 변경으로 인해, 신입직원들은 3개월간의 수습 기간 후에 복지 혜택을 받게 될 것임을 알려드리게 되어 유감스럽게 생각합니다.

해설 타동사 receive의 뒤에 위치한 빈칸은 목적어 역할을 할 명사 자리이므로 명사인 (B) benefits와 (D) beneficiaries 중에서 정답을 골라야 한다. 직원이 회사로부터 받을 수 있는 것은 복지 혜택이므로 '복지 혜택'이라는 의미의 사물명사 (B) benefits가 정답이다.

어휘 regret to do ~하게 되어 유감으로 생각하다 due to ~로 인해, ~ 때문에 trial period 수습 기간 benefit v. 이득을 보다, 유익하다 n. 복지 혜택, 이득 beneficiary 수혜자

3.

정답 (C)

해석 추가 교육을 받는 데 관심이 있는 직원들은 곧 있을 워크숍에 대해 알아보시려면 인사팀 누구에게나 연락하십시오.

해설 빈칸에는 연락 대상으로 사람을 나타내는 단어가 들어가야 하므로 부서의 소속원들 중 '아무나'를 가리키는 부정대명사 (C) anyone이 정답이다. (B) them이 빈칸에 들어갈 경우에 주어 Workers와 연락 대상이 같게 되므로 오답이다.

어휘 interested in ~에 관심 있는 learn about ~에 대해 알다 upcoming 곧 있을, 다가오는

4.

정답 (D)

해석 여기 저희 회사에서의 공석과 관련하여 더 많은 문의사항에 대해서는, www.solartech.com으로 저희 홈페이지를 방문해주십시오.

해설 빈칸 앞에 위치한 가산명사 job 앞에 부정관사가 없으므로 빈칸에 또 다른 명사가 와 job과 복합명사를 구성해야 한다. 따라서 job과 함께 '공석, 일자리'라는 의미로 쓰이는 (D) openings가 정답이다.

어휘 regarding ~와 관련하여 job opening 채용, 공석 openly 솔직하게, 터놓고

5.

정답 (C)

해석 빠듯한 마감시한에 직면했을 때, 헤인즈 씨는 자신이 일정을 맞출 능력이 있다는 것을 증명했다.

해설 접속사 When 뒤에는 절이 와야 하는데, 주어가 없고 전치사구만 있으므로 분사구문이 되어야 한다. 선택지에서 분사는 (C) faced와 (D) facing이고, 동사 face가 타동사인데 빈칸 뒤에 명사 목적어 없이 전치사구만 나타나 있으므로 과거분사 (C) faced가 정답이다.

어휘 faced with ~에 직면한 tight (일정 등) 빠듯한, 꽉 짜인 prove oneself + 형용사 자신이 ~하다는 것을 입증하다 capable of -ing ~할 능력이 있는

6.

정답 (A)

해석 누군가가 펀 스트리트에 위치한 헤일맨 베이커리에 들러서 본 씨의 은퇴 기념 파티에 필요한 케이크를 가져 와야 한다.

해설 빈칸 뒤로 동사와 전치사구, 그리고 to부정사구가 이어져 있으므로 빈칸이 주어 자리임을 알 수 있다. 따라서 목적격 대명사인 (B) Us는 오답이며, 동사 has와 수 일치가 되지 않는 복수 대명사 (C) They도 오답이다. (A) Someone과 (D) Those 중 누군가 한 사람만 가면 되는 상황이므로 (A) Someone이 정답이다.

어휘 stop by ~에 들르다 pick up ~을 가져 오다, 가져 가다 retirement 은퇴, 퇴직

7.

정답 (D)

해석 기사를 교정할 때, 붉은색 펜을 사용해 기사 내의 모든 철자 오류를 표시해 주십시오.

해석 동사 mark의 목적어로 쓰인 복수명사 spelling errors를 수식

하면서 '모든, 어떠한'의 뜻을 나타내는 형용사 (D) any가 정답
이다.

어휘 proofread ~을 교정하다 mark ~을 표기하다 spelling
error 철자 오류

8.

정답 (A)

해석 건축관리국의 조사 보고서에 밝혀진 바와 같이, 낡은 모스 극장
은 대규모 구조물 보강과 수리를 필요로 한다.

해설 빈칸이 속한 절에 주어와 동사가 없으므로 분사구문의 형태가
되어야 한다. 타동사 indicate가 들어갈 자리 뒤에 목적어가 없
으므로 빈칸에는 수동을 의미하는 과거분사 (A) indicated가
정답이다.

어휘 as ~처럼 indicate ~라고 밝히다 Building
Department (관공서) 건축관리국 inspection 조사, 검
사 extensive 대규모의, 폭넓은 structural 구조의, 건축의
reinforcement 보강 indication 지표, 암시

9.

정답 (A)

해석 고객 의견 카드에 따르면, 파스칼 프렌치 비스트로 식당은 전채
요리의 가격을 내리는 것을 고려해 봐야 한다.

해설 빈칸 뒤에 customer comment cards라는 명사가 있으므로
이 명사를 목적어로 취할 수 있는 분사형 전치사 (A) According
to가 정답이다. 나머지 선택지들은 모두 절을 이끌어야 하는 접
속사들이므로 오답이다.

어휘 according to ~에 따르면 customer comment card
고객 의견 카드 providing that ~라는 것을 조건으로 하여
in the event that ~할 경우에

10.

정답 (C)

해석 승무원들은 각 승객들이 안전벨트를 안전하게 착용했는지 반드
시 확인해야 한다.

해석 빈칸 다음에 「of the + 복수명사」가 있으므로 형용사로만 쓰이
는 (A) every, 불가산명사와 쓰이는 (D) much는 우선 소거한
다. 나머지 선택지들은 모두 「of the + 복수명사」의 구조와 함
께 쓰일 수 있는데, that절의 동사 has가 단수 동사이므로 (C)
each가 정답이다.

어휘 flight attendant 승무원 make sure that 반드시 ~하다,
~인지 확인하다 securely 안전하게 fasten ~을 묶다, 잠
그다

DAY 02

Practice

1. (D)	2. (D)	3. (C)	4. (C)	5. (B)	6. (C)
7. (B)	8. (D)	9. (B)	10. (C)		

1.

정답 (D)

해석 저희 정책에 따라, 귀하께서는 3일 늦게 받으신 꽃다발에 대해
환불을 받게 되실 것입니다.

해설 조동사 will 뒤에는 동사원형이 쓰여야 하는 자리이므로 (B) to
issue는 우선 소거한다. 동사 issue는 3형식 동사와 4형식 동사
로 모두 쓰일 수 있는데, 문장의 주어인 you는 환불을 받는 대상
(고객)이어야 하므로 두 개의 목적어 중 사람 목적어가 주어 자리
로 이동한 것을 알 수 있다. 따라서, issue가 4형식 동사로 쓰인
상태에서 목적어 한 개가 주어 자리로 이동한 수동태 구조가 되
어야 알맞으므로 (D) be issued가 정답이다.

어휘 in accordance with ~에 따라 issue a refund 환불해
주다 bouquet of flowers 꽃다발, 부케

2.

정답 (D)

해석 근육을 만들고 싶으신 분이든, 아니면 단지 살을 빼고 싶으신 분
이든, 피트니스 클리닉은 여러분을 위해 적절한 프로그램을 만들
어 드릴 수 있습니다.

해설 빈칸은 빈칸 이하에 주어와 동사를 각각 포함한 두 개의 절을 연
결할 접속사 자리이고, 빈칸 뒤에 or가 있으므로 부사절 접속사
인 (D) Whether가 정답이다.

어휘 whether A or B A이든 B이든 gain ~을 얻다 lose
weight 살을 빼다 appropriate 적절한 rather 오히려

3.

정답 (C)

해석 이 식물 표본들은 각각 특정한 토양 조건을 필요로 하므로, 그에
따라 각각의 식물에 꼭 이름을 붙이도록 해야 한다.

해설 우선 빈칸 앞까지의 문장 구성이 완전하므로 빈칸은 부사 자리
이다. 절을 이끄는 접속사 (A) wherever를 제외한 나머지 부사
들 중에서, 문장 맨 마지막에 올 수 있으면서 '그에 따라'라는 결
과의 의미를 나타내는 (C) accordingly가 정답이다.

어휘 specimen 견본, 표본 specific 특정한, 구체적인 soil 토양 be sure to do 꼭 ~하다 label v. 이름을 붙여 분류하다, 라벨로 나타내다 accordingly 그에 따라서, 적절히 hardly 거의 ~않다

4.

정답 (C)

해석 플렙스 제조사의 관리자들은 각각의 신입 공장 근로자의 입사 후 처음 2개월 내내 매주 실적 평가를 진행한다.

해설 빈칸 앞뒤에 명사구가 제시되어 있으므로 빈칸은 전치사 자리인데, 빈칸 뒤에 기간 표현이 있으므로 이와 어울려 '~내내'라는 의미로 사용되는 기간 전치사 (C) throughout이 정답이다.

어휘 conduct ~을 수행하다 performance 실적 evaluation 평가 employment 고용

5.

정답 (B)

해석 다나 설리반 씨는 3년 연속으로 여자 축구 협회에 의해 올해의 선수로 선정되었다.

해설 선택지가 4형식 동사 vote의 다양한 형태로 구성되어 있고, 빈칸 앞으로 목적어가 각각 1개씩 제시되어 있다. 사람 목적어가 주어 자리에 있으므로 수동태 (B) has been voted가 정답이다.

어휘 vote A B A를 B로 선정하다, 뽑다 in a row 연속으로

6.

정답 (C)

해석 그 자선 단체는 에밋 화학공업 사에서 기부한 상당한 금액 덕분에 1만 달러의 기금 마련 목표를 충족했다.

해설 빈칸 앞에 주어와 동사가 포함된 절이 있고 빈칸 뒤에는 명사구와 전치사구만 위치한 구조이다. 따라서 빈칸 뒤에 위치한 명사구를 이끌 전치사가 필요하므로 선택지에서 유일한 전치사이면서 기금 마련 목표를 충족할 수 있었던 이유를 나타내는 (C) thanks to가 정답이다.

어휘 charity 자선 (단체) fundraising 기금 마련(활동) thanks to ~ 덕분에, ~ 때문에 substantial 상당한 as well as ~뿐만 아니라 overall a. 전반적인 ad. 전반적으로 even if 비록 ~라 하더라도

7.

정답 (B)

해석 설문 조사에 응답했던 대부분의 고객들은 우리가 지난주에 출시했던 새로운 메뉴에 만족했다.

해설 빈칸이 be동사 were와 전치사 with 사이에 위치해 있으므로 빈칸은 주격보어 자리이다. 새로운 메뉴에 대해 만족감을 느끼는 주체가 사람명사 customers이므로 과거분사 (B) satisfied가

정답이다.

어휘 respond to ~에 응답하다 satisfied 만족한 introduce ~을 출시하다, 소개하다 satisfaction 만족 satisfying 만족감을 주는 satisfactory 만족할 만한

8.

정답 (D)

해석 채용 위원회는 귀하의 이전 고용주인 부히스 씨로부터 아직 추천서를 받지 못했습니다.

해설 선택지가 모두 전치사이고 빈칸 앞뒤에 명사구들이 위치해 있으므로 이 명사구들 사이의 의미 관계를 가장 잘 나타낼 수 있는 전치사를 찾아야 한다. 따라서 동사 obtain과 어울려서 '~로부터'라는 의미로 출처를 나타낼 때 사용하는 (D) from이 정답이다.

어휘 hiring committee 채용 위원회 have yet to do 아직 ~하지 못하다 obtain ~을 받다, 획득하다 a letter of recommendation 추천서 employer 고용주

9.

정답 (B)

해석 우리 건물 입주자들이 공간을 찾을 수 있는 곳이라면 어디든지 주차가 가능합니다.

해설 빈칸 앞뒤로 주어와 동사를 갖춘 완전한 구성의 절이 있으므로 빈칸은 접속사 자리이다. 따라서 완전한 절과 함께 사용하는 (B) wherever가 정답이다.

어휘 vehicle 차량 resident 입주자, 주민 space 공간

10.

정답 (C)

해석 노동 단체들은 시민들에게 교육을 더 많이 제공하고, 그로 인해 잠재적 근로자들의 능력 수준을 향상시키도록 정부에 요청했다.

해설 빈칸 앞에는 주어와 동사, 목적어, 그리고 목적보어를 갖춘 완전한 구성의 절이, 빈칸 뒤에는 현재분사구문이 있으므로 분사구문을 연결할 수 있는 부사 (C) thereby가 정답이다.

어휘 labor organization 노동 단체 ask A to do A가 ~하도록 요청하다 thereby 그로 인해 raise ~ 을 향상시키다, 끌어올리다 whereas ~인 반면, 한편 if only 오직 ~이기만 하면

DAY 03

PART 6 고난도 유형 완전 정복

예제 인과 접속부사

리틀턴 비즈니스 네트워킹 협회(LBNA) 가입을 환영합니다. 온라인 주소록에 회원 연락처를 넣는 것이 LBNA의 정책입니다. 따라서, 기재된 귀하의 모든 상세정보가 정확하며 빠진 것이 없는지 확인하시기 바랍니다. 업데이트될 정보가 있다면, 웹 사이트에서 직접 필요한 수정을 하실 수 있습니다. 저희 월간 소식지를 받도록 등록하시려면, 온라인 주소록에서 귀하의 정보란 옆의 해당 박스를 체크하시기 바랍니다.

(A) 그럼에도 불구하고   **(B) 따라서**
(C) 그렇지 않으면   (D) 역으로

어휘   include ~을 포함하다 contact information 연락처 directory 주소록 accurate 정확한 fully complete 빠짐없이 완료된 should you + 동사 혹시 ~라면 notice that ~임을 발견하다 make a revision 수정하다 oneself 직접, 스스로 sign up to do ~하도록 등록하다 monthly newsletter 월간 소식지 appropriate 적절한, 알맞은 beside ~의 옆에 listing 등록 정보

예제 전체 맥락을 파악해야 하는 경우

주로 정부의 재정 지원을 받는 기관인 도버 공공 도서관이 건물을 확장하고 편의시설을 개선하기 위해 세계적으로 성공한 기업인 맨델슨 사의 회장 클라렌스 맨델슨 씨로부터 120만 달러의 개인 기부금을 받을 예정입니다.

도서관의 미래에 매우 중요한 기부를 하게 될 맨델슨 씨는 수요일 오전에 그에 대해 발표했습니다. 그는 도서관 건물 보수 및 확장 공사를 할 수 있도록 사비로 120만 달러를 기부하기로 약속했습니다.

멘델슨 씨가 기부하는 자금은 네 단계로 지급될 것이며, 처음 지급되는 금액은 9월 15일에 도서관 이사회가 수령할 예정입니다. 이사회는 첫 기부금을 일반 참조 도서 구역의 규모를 두 배로 늘리는 데 사용할 계획입니다.

(A) 지급될 것이며   (B) 합산할 것이며
(C) 축소할 것이며   (D) 확인할 것이며

어휘   government-funded 정부가 자금을 지원하는 institution 기관, 단체 expand ~을 확장하다 amenities 편의시설 contribution 기부(금) invaluable 매우 소중한 fortune 재산 funding 자금 (제공) phase 단계, 국면

예제 빈칸 뒤 부연설명이 있는 경우

무브프로 주식회사
회의록 (5월 14일, 목요일)

5월 14일 회의는 칼라 데보스 씨께서 진행하셨습니다. 회의 중에 논의된 주요 사안은 우리 무브프로 주식회사에 대해 제안된 사업 확장이었습니다. 데보스 씨께서는 심화되는 경쟁 속에서 업계의 선두 자리를 유지하기 위해 회사의 사업을 확장해야 하는 필요성을 강조하셨습니다. 데보스 씨는 우리 무브프로 사가 발전하기 위해 극복해야 하는 도전 과제들을 언급해 주셨습니다. 올해의 연간 예산은 회사의 성장 계획에 대해 충분하지 않을 것 같습니다. 결과적으로, 이사회는 다음 주에 열릴 회의에서 추가 투자액을 얻을 수 있는 잠재적인 공급원이 논의되어야 한다는 점에 동의했습니다.

(A) 다음으로, 데보스 씨가 시행 예정인 새로운 정책들을 상세히 설명했습니다.
(B) 이사회는 데보스 씨의 성취에 관한 축하 인사를 전했습니다.
(C) 데보스 씨는 우리 무브프로 사가 발전하기 위해 극복해야 하는 도전 과제들을 언급해 주셨습니다.
(D) 데보스 씨는 합병에 대해 논의하기 위해 스위프트 쉬퍼 사의 의장과 만날 것입니다.

어휘   meeting minutes 회의록 be led by ~가 진행하다, 이끌다 expansion (사업) 확장, 확대 emphasize ~을 강조하다 expand ~을 확장하다, 확대하다 operation 사업, 운영 amid ~ 사이에서, ~하는 가운데에 sufficient 충분한 agree that ~라는 점에 동의하다 source 공급원, 원천 investment 투자(액) following 다음의

예제 앞뒤 문맥을 살펴야 하는 경우

회람
날짜: 11월 17일
수신: 벌트랜드 사 전 직원

우리 컴퓨터실 내의 컴퓨터들을 대상으로 11월 22일부터 11월 26일까지 소프트웨어 업그레이드가 진행될 예정입니다. 이 업그레이드 작업이 진행되는 동안 일부 컴퓨터들이 사용될 수 없을 것으로 예상된다는 점에 유의하시기 바랍니다.

컴퓨터 사용 가능 여부는 매일 변경됩니다. 해당 주 내내 각 부서의 공지 게시판에 오전 9시까지 메시지가 게시될 것이며, 이 메시지를 통해 매일 어느 컴퓨터실에 있는 컴퓨터가 사용 가능한지 알 수 있을 것입니다.

(A) 컴퓨터 사용 가능 여부는 매일 변경됩니다.
(B) 업그레이드 작업을 위해 금요일까지 귀하의 전자기기를 제출하십시오.

(C) 이 시간 동안 인터넷 서비스가 제한될 것입니다.

(D) 우선, 모든 중요한 파일들을 외부 드라이브에 옮기십시오.

어휘 IT suite 컴퓨터실 be scheduled for ~이 예정되다 Please be advised that ~라는 점에 유의하십시오 expect A to do A가 ~할 것으로 예상하다 unavailable 이용할 수 없는 while ~하는 동안 carry out ~을 실시하다, 시행하다 availability 사용 가능성 on a daily basis 하루 단위로, 매일 throughout (기간) ~에 걸쳐 turn in ~을 제출하다 external drive 외장 드라이브

Practice

1. (D) 2. (A) 3. (C) 4. (A) 5. (D) 6. (C)
7. (B) 8. (A)

1-4.

클래식 완구 & 골동품 회사
스타 포스 액션 피규어

모든 저희 제품들은 완벽한 상태이지만, 배송 중에 발생되는 어떠한 손상에 대해서도 책임을 지지 않습니다. 1 따라서, 제품이 도착하면 그 상태를 확인하는 것은 여러분의 책임이며, 어떠한 결함이든지 발견하시는 경우에 즉시 저희에게 연락 주시기 바랍니다. 저희의 모든 스타 포스 완구 제품들은 2 최초의 포장 용기에 담겨 출시되며, 한 번도 사용되지 않은 것입니다. 여러 완구 제품에는 자동차와 무기, 또는 교체용 복장들과 같은 부대용품들이 포함되어 있습니다.

3 이 제품들은 별도로 판매되었을 수도 있으므로 구입하신 후에 별도의 배송 물품으로 발송될 수 있습니다. 스타포스 완구 제품을 투자 대상으로 취급하기를 원하실 경우, 각 제품을 적절한 방법으로 관리하시는 것이 중요합니다. 4 그렇게 하기 위해서, 동봉해 드린 저희 가이드를 참고하시기 바랍니다. 이 방법을 통해, 해당 제품은 훌륭한 상태로 유지될 수 있으며, 예상 가치는 지속적으로 오를 것입니다.

어휘 action figure 액션 피규어(가상의 캐릭터를 재현한 조형물) in perfect condition 완벽한 상태인 damage 손상, 피해 cause ~을 초래하다, 유발하다 shipping 배송 responsibility 책임 immediately 즉시 notice ~을 알아채다, 인식하다 defect 결함 handle (손으로) ~을 사용하다, 다루다 weapon 무기 alternative 대체하는 outfit 복장, 옷 may have p.p. ~했을 수도 있다 separately 별도로, 따로 accordingly 그에 따라, 그러므로 separate 별도의, 분리된 make a purchase 구매하다 treat A as B A를 B로 취급하다, 대하다 investment 투자 (대상) care for ~을 관리하다, 돌보다 in an appropriate manner 적절한 방법으로 this way 이렇게 함으로써, 이와 같은 방법으로 maintain ~을 유지하다 estimated 예상된

worth 가치

1.

정답 (D)

해설 빈칸 앞에서 배송 중에 발생되는 손상에 대해서는 책임을 지지 않는다고 알리고 있고, 빈칸 뒤에는 제품의 상태를 확인하는 것이 상대방의 책임이라고 언급하고 있다. 이는 상대방에게 책임이 있음을 공지하기 위한 일종의 이유와 결과에 해당되는 내용이므로 '따라서, 그러므로'라는 의미로 인과 관계를 나타낼 때 사용하는 (D) Therefore가 정답이다.

어휘 finally 마침내, 마지막으로 otherwise 그렇지 않으면 even though 비록 ~이기는 하지만

2.

정답 (A)

해설 빈칸에 쓰일 형용사는 포장 용기를 뜻하는 packaging을 수식해 그 특성이나 상태를 나타내야 한다. 바로 뒤에 한 번도 사용되지 않았다는 말이 있으므로 처음 그대로의 상태를 의미하는 (A) original이 정답이다.

어휘 vague 모호한 approximate 근사치의, 대략적인 likely 가능성 있는, ~할 것 같은

3.

정답 (C)

해설 문장 맨 앞에 빈칸이 있고 바로 뒤에 동사 may have been sold가 위치해 있으므로 빈칸은 주어 자리이다. (B) Various를 제외한 나머지 선택지들이 주어 역할을 할 수 있는 것인데, 빈칸에 쓰일 것은 바로 앞에 언급된 accessories를 대신해야 하므로 '이것들'을 의미하는 대명사 (C) These가 정답이다.

어휘 neither (A nor B) (A도 B도) 둘 다 아니다 various 다양한

4.

정답 (A)

해석 (A) 그렇게 하기 위해서, 동봉해 드린 저희 가이드를 참고하시기 바랍니다.
(B) 일부 제품은 조립 과정을 필요로 할 수 있습니다.
(C) 저희의 모든 제품 종류는 온라인으로 확인해 보실 수 있습니다.
(D) 이렇게 하는 것은 제품의 가치를 떨어뜨릴 수 있습니다.

해설 빈칸 앞에 제품을 적절한 방법으로 관리해야 한다는 말이 있으므로 이를 To do so로 표현해 가이드를 참고하라고 알리는 내용을 담은 (A)가 정답이다.

어휘 consult ~을 참고하다, 찾아 보다 enclosed 동봉된 assembly 조립 complete 완전한, 모든 line (제품) 종류, 군 view ~을 보다 devalue ~의 가치를 떨어뜨리다

5-8.

수신: 모든 플릭스 시네마 무비 클럽 회원

플릭스 시네마 무비 클럽 설립자들이 10월 2일에 향후 영화 상영회에 대한 매표 정책상의 변화를 논의하기 위해 모일 계획입니다. 아시다시피, 지난번 회의에서 제한된 숫자의 초대 손님 극장 관람권을 5 지정하기 위한 제안이 이뤄졌습니다.

6 현재, 클럽 회원들은 플릭스 시네마에서 상영하는 각각의 예정된 무비 클럽 영화에 대해 세 장의 추가 초대 손님 관람권을 얻을 수 있습니다. 하지만, 클럽 회원 숫자의 증가와 그에 따른 초대 손님들의 숫자 증가가 발생되면서, 모든 입장권이 매진됨으로 인해 많은 클럽 회원들이 그 기회를 놓쳐야 했습니다. 7 분명히, 이는 충실한 우리 클럽 회원들에게 불공평한 일입니다. 따라서, 클럽 회원들을 위한 8 충분한 입장권이 존재하도록 보장하기 위해 제공될 수 있는 초대 손님 관람권의 숫자를 제한하도록 제안되었습니다.

회의 결과는 10월 6일에 나올 다음 시네마 클럽 소식지에 공지될 것입니다.

어휘 founder 설립자, 창립자 discuss ~을 논의하다 ticketing 매표 showing 상영회 make a suggestion 제안하다 designate ~을 지정하다 a limited number of 제한된 숫자의 scheduled 예정된 subsequent 그 다음의, 그 뒤에 일어나는 miss out 기회를 놓치다 be proposed that ~하도록 제안되다 ensure that ~임을 보장하다, 반드시 ~하도록 하다 outcome 결과

5.

정답 (D)

해설 빈칸 앞에 이미 문장의 동사 was made가 쓰여 있으므로 빈칸에는 준동사가 와야 한다. 또한, 빈칸 이하 부분은 지난 회의에서 제안이 이뤄진 목적을 나타내야 알맞으므로 목적을 말할 때 사용하는 to부정사 (D) to designate이 정답이다.

6.

정답 (C)

해설 빈칸이 속한 문장은 현재시제 동사 are와 함께 회원들이 현재 일반적으로 얻고 있는 추가 입장권 수량을 말하는 내용을 담고 있다. 따라서 현재의 상황을 나타낼 때 사용하는 부사 (C) Currently가 정답이다.

어휘 formerly 이전에

7.

정답 (B)

해석 (A) 신입 회원들은 우리 웹 사이트에서 등록할 수 있습니다.
(B) 분명히, 이는 충실한 우리 클럽 회원들에게 불공평한 일입니다.

(C) 외국 영화들이 가장 인기가 많은 경향이 있습니다.
(D) 하지만, 나중에 있을 상영회에 대한 입장권이 여전히 구매 가능합니다.

해설 빈칸 앞 문장에 많은 클럽 회원들이 손해를 본 사실이 언급되어 있으므로 이러한 사실을 this로 지칭해 충실한 회원들에게 불공평하게 적용되고 있음을 알리는 (B)가 정답이다.

어휘 enroll 등록하다 unfair 불공평한 loyal 충실한

8.

정답 (A)

해설 빈칸은 회원들을 위한 입장권 수량과 관련해 보장해야 하는 일을 나타내는 that절에 속해 있다. 앞서 회원들이 얻는 입장권의 부족 문제가 언급되어 있으므로 모든 회원들을 위한 입장권이 적정량 존재해야 한다는 의미가 되어야 자연스럽다. 따라서 '충분한'을 뜻하는 (A) ample이 정답이다.

어휘 ample 충분한 earnest 성실한, 진심 어린 attentive 주의를 기울이는, 배려하는 proficient 능숙한, 숙련된

DAY 04

PART 7 · 고난도 단일지문 완전 정복

예제 NOT 유형

저희 넵튠 요트 사가 현재 레드펀 와프 지점에서 10척의 새로운 디럭스형 선박을 인도받기 위해 준비하고 있다는 사실을 알려드리게 되어 기쁩니다. 지난주에 이 보트들에 대한 마무리 작업이 이뤄졌으며, 어제 이탈리아의 조선소를 떠났습니다.

다섯 척의 새로운 파레티 700 요트들은 길이는 24미터이며, 1,800 마력의 트윈 엔진을 포함하고 있습니다. 다섯 척의 새로운 파레티 850 요트들은 길이가 20미터이며, 1,400 마력의 트윈 엔진을 포함하고 있습니다. 모든 모델이 구명조끼와 개인 부유 기구를 표준으로 갖추고 생산됩니다.

오늘 저희 넵튠 요트 영업사원과 말씀 나누셔서 사전 주문하시기 바랍니다. 모든 요트는 5월 12일부터 보고 구매하실 수 있게 준비가 될 것입니다.

Q. 광고에 무슨 정보가 포함되어 있지 않은가?
(A) 새로운 보트들이 판매되는 날짜
(B) 구매 가능한 새 선박의 숫자
(C) 각 새 모델의 대략적인 가격
(D) 새로운 요트들의 전반적인 크기

어휘 prepare to do ~할 준비를 하다 vessel 선박 location 지점, 위치 put finishing touches on ~에 마무리 작업을

하다, 마무리 손질을 하다 **equipped with** ~을 갖춘 **floatation device** (물에서 떠 있기 위한) 부유 기구 **as standard** 표준으로, 기본으로 **representative** 직원 **place an advance order** 사전 주문하다 **viewing** 둘러 보기 **on sale** 판매 중인 **approximate** 대략적인

예제 **추론 유형**

졸리 이나살 레스토랑에서 귀사의 서비스를 홍보하세요!

왜 레스토랑에서 서비스를 홍보해야 하는가?
레스토랑에서 진행하는 지역 내 서비스의 홍보가 필리핀에서 가장 흔하면서 직접적인 광고 방법들 중 하나라는 사실은 잘 알려져 있습니다. 레스토랑은 일반적으로 일년 내내 운영되며, 많은 외국인 관광객들이 자주 드나드는 곳입니다. 그러므로, 귀사는 관광객들을 끌어들이는 저렴한 수단인 레스토랑 광고를 통해 상당한 이득을 볼 것입니다.

왜 졸리 이나살을 선택해야 하는가?
졸리 이나살은 필리핀에서 가장 규모가 큰 레스토랑 체인들 중 하나이며, 필리핀에서 가장 분주한 여러 휴양지에 지점을 보유하고 있습니다. 대부분의 이 여행지들에 다수의 졸리 이나살 지점이 있습니다. 졸리 이나살 레스토랑은 하루 24시간 영업하며, 하루에 약 1천 명의 고객을 받습니다. 그리고, 계산대 옆에 전단이나 명함을 놓아 두시면, 식사 비용을 지불하시는 모든 분께서 쉽게 보시게 될 것입니다.

Q. 정보가 누구를 대상으로 할 가능성이 가장 큰가?
(A) 구직자들
(B) 레스토랑 소유주들
(C) 여행사들
(D) 여행객들

어휘 **promote** ~을 홍보하다 **direct** 직접적인 **method** 방법 **operate** 운영되다 **all year round** 일년 내내, 연중으로 **frequent** v. ~에 자주 다니다 **therefore** 그러므로, 따라서 **serve as** ~로서 역할을 하다 **affordable** 가격이 알맞은 **means** 수단 **attract** ~을 끌어들이다 **tourist resort** 휴양지 **destination** 여행지, 목적지 **flyer** 전단 **job seeker** 구직자 **tour operator** 여행사

예제 **의도파악 유형**

기술 지원 담당 직원 (오전 9:42)
메사 일렉트로닉스에 연락 주셔서 감사합니다! 무엇을 도와 드릴까요?

조 카터 (오전 9:43)
제가 태블릿 컴퓨터를 한 대 구입했고, 오늘 아침에 배송되었습니다. 하지만, 도착한 이후로 계속 전원을 켤 수 없습니다. 메사 델타 2 모델입니다.

기술 지원 담당 직원 (오전 9:45)
좋습니다. 자, 그 태블릿의 전원을 켜려면, 버튼을 최소한 5초 동

안 누르고 있어야 합니다.

조 카터 (오전 9:46)
알았어야 했는데! 한 번 해 볼 게요... (잠시 정적) 작동됐어요! 도와 주셔서 감사합니다!

Q. 오전 9시 46분에, 카터 씨가 "I should've known"이라고 쓸 때 의도한 것은 무엇인가?
(A) 버튼을 오래 누르는 것은 생각도 못했다.
(B) 일부 설명이 불명확하다고 생각한다.
(C) 이미 직원의 제안 사항을 시도해 봤다.
(D) 서비스에 대해 실망하고 있다.

어휘 **technical support** 기술 지원 **agent** 직원, 대리인 **power on** ~의 전원을 켜다 **hold** ~을 누르고 있다 **should have p.p.** ~했어야 했다 **work** 작동되다 **instructions** 설명, 안내 **unclear** 불명확한, 불분명한 **suggestion** 제안, 의견 **be disappointed about** ~에 대해 실망하다

예제 **문장삽입 유형**

수신: 패러데이 텔레콤 전 직원

패러데이 텔레콤 직원으로서, 여러분께서는 5월 중으로 신청하시면 할인된 요금으로 홈 엔터테인먼트 패키지 서비스를 받으실 수 있을 것입니다. ─ [1] ─. 우리 톱 프리미엄 패키지는 고속 인터넷 서비스와 모든 프리미엄 채널이 있는 케이블 텔레비전을 포함합니다. ─ [2] ─. 텔레비전 한 대에 매달 30달러의 비용이, 두 대의 텔레비전에 대해서는 매달 45달러의 비용이 들어갑니다. 두 대가 넘는 텔레비전이 있는 가정은 영업부에 연락하셔서 이용 가능한 다른 할인 혜택이 있는지 확인해 보셔야 합니다. ─ [3] ─.

이 패키지는 가장 빠른 인터넷 연결 속도와 200개가 넘는 채널에 대한 이용 서비스를 포함합니다. 설치 시에, 헨리 시네플렉스 무료 입장권 2장도 받으시게 됩니다. ─ [4] ─.

영업부에 전화하셔서 이 특별 할인 서비스를 받으실 수 있도록 설치 일정을 잡아 보시기 바랍니다.

Q. [1], [2], [3], [4]로 표기된 위치들 중에서, 다음 문장이 들어가기에 가장 적절한 곳은 어디인가?

"가격은 해당 서비스가 설치되기를 원하는 텔레비전 수에 따라 다릅니다."

(A) [1]
(B) [2]
(C) [3]
(D) [4]

어휘 **rate** 요금 **savings** 절약, 할인 **access to** ~에 대한 이용, 접근 **upon** ~할 시에, ~하는 대로 **installation** 설치 **vary** 다르다, 다양하다 **depending on** ~에 따라, ~에 달려 있는

Practice

1. (D)	2. (A)	3. (B)	4. (D)	5. (B)	6. (C)
7. (B)	8. (D)	9. (D)	10. (D)	11. (B)	12. (C)

1-3.

늦게나마 인정 받고 있는 지역 음식점
작성자, 사이러스 디콘

그린뷰 - 자체 최신 웹 기사에서, 푸드러버스 닷컴이 벤보우 카운티 내 최고의 스테이크 레스토랑 다섯 곳에 대한 목록에서 2(B) 바로 그린뷰에서만 찾아 볼 수 있는 빅 본 스테이크하우스를 3위에 올려 놓았습니다. 푸드러버스 닷컴에 따르면, 1 빅 본 스테이크하우스가 선정된 이유는 우수한 등급의 맛있는 소고기를 제공할 뿐만 아니라 그 넉넉한 양이 여러 경쟁업체에서 제공하는 것보다 거의 두 배에 달하는 크기 때문이기도 했습니다. 2(C) 티본과 꽃등심, 그리고 등심 스테이크에서부터, 폭찹과 치킨 윙에 이르기까지, 빅 본 스테이크하우스에는 모든 사람을 위한 것이 있습니다.

2(D) 빅 본 스테이크하우스의 소유주 거스 브루바커 씨는 자신의 레스토랑이 이 목록에 포함되었다는 사실을 듣고 뛸 듯이 기뻐했습니다. 제가 그 기분이 어땠는지 물어 봤을 때, 그분은 이렇게 말했습니다. "제 업체가 카운티 내에서 손꼽히는 스테이크하우스 레스토랑들 중 하나로 인정받았다는 점이 기쁩니다. 3 막달레나 그릴과 레이즈 서프 앤 터프가 저희보다 훨씬 더 오래 영업해왔기 때문에, 저는 그곳들이 목록에서 가장 높은 두 개의 순위를 차지했다는 사실은 놀랍지 않습니다."

어휘 eatery 음식점, 식당 overdue 이미 행해졌어야 할, 기한이 지난 recognition 인정 rank v. ~을 순위에 올리다 select ~을 선정하다 serve (음식) ~을 제공하다, 내오다 generous 넉넉한, 후한 portion (제공되는) 양, 1인분 double the + 명사 ~의 두 배인 proprietor 소유주 overjoyed 뛸 듯이 기쁜 recognize ~을 인정하다 leading 손꼽히는, 선도적인 be in business 영업하다

1. 빅 본 스테이크하우스는 왜 푸드러버스 닷컴이 정리한 목록에 포함되었는가?
  (A) 지역 내에서 가장 가격이 알맞은 스테이크 레스토랑들 중 하나이다.
  (B) 경쟁업체들보다 더 다양한 종류의 곁들임 요리를 제공한다.
  (C) 지역적으로 생산된 고기를 제공하는 데 초점을 맞춘다.
  (D) 카운티 내에서 다른 레스토랑들보다 더 큰 스테이크를 제공한다.

정답 (D)

해설 빅 본 스테이크하우스가 3위에 선정된 이유가 언급되는 첫 단락에, 우수한 등급의 맛있는 소고기를 제공할 뿐만 아니라 그 넉넉한 양이 여러 경쟁업체에서 제공하는 것보다 거의 두 배

에 달하는 크기 때문이기도 했다고(because not only does it serve high-grade, delicious beef, but its generous portions are almost double the size of those offered by its competitors) 알려져 있다. 따라서 더 큰 스테이크를 제공한다는 것을 언급한 (D)가 정답이다.

어휘 compile (자료 등) ~을 모아 정리하다 affordable 가격이 알맞은 a wider selection of 더 다양한 종류의 side dish 곁들임 요리

2. 빅 본 스테이크하우스에 관해 언급되지 않은 것은 무엇인가?
  (A) 채식주의자를 위한 옵션을 제공한다.
  (B) 그린뷰에 본사를 두고 있다.
  (C) 다양한 종류의 고기를 제공한다.
  (D) 거스 브루바커 씨가 소유하고 있다.

정답 (A)

해설 첫 단락 시작 부분의 그린뷰에서만 찾아볼 수 있는 빅 본 스테이크하우스를 언급한(Greenveiw's very own Big Bone Steakhouse) 부분에서 (B)를, 티본과 꽃등심, 그리고 등심 스테이크에서부터, 폭찹과 치킨 윙에 이르기까지 다양한 종류의 고기를 제공한다는(From T-bone, ribeye, and sirloin beefsteaks, to pork chops and chicken wings) 부분에서 (C)를, 그리고 두 번째 단락의 빅 본 스테이크하우스의 소유주 거스 브루바커 씨를 언급한(The proprietor of Big Bone Steakhouse, Gus Brubaker) 부분에서 (D)도 확인 가능하다. 하지만 채식주의자를 위한 옵션과 관련된 정보는 제시되어 있지 않으므로 (A)가 정답이다.

어휘 be based in ~에 본사를 두다, ~을 기반으로 하다

3. 막달레나 그릴에 관해 유추할 수 있는 것은 무엇인가?
  (A) 식사 손님들에게 회원제에 가입할 수 있게 해 준다.
  (B) 완전히 새로운 시설이 아니다.
  (C) 닭고기 또는 돼지고기를 제공하지 않는다.
  (D) 빅 본 스테이크하우스만큼 수익성이 좋지는 않다.

정답 (B)

해설 막달레나 그릴이 언급되는 두 번째 단락에, 브루바커 씨의 인터뷰 내용으로 막달레나 그릴과 레이즈 서프 앤 터프가 자신의 업체보다 훨씬 더 오래 영업해 왔다고(Magdalena Grill and Ray's Surf'N Turf have been in business much longer than we have) 언급되어 있다. 이는 막달레나 그릴이 오래된 곳임을 나타내는 것이므로 (B)가 정답이다.

어휘 diner 식사 손님 membership plan 회원 약정 brand-new 완전히 새로운 establishment (학교, 식당, 병원 등의) 시설(물) profitable 수익성이 좋은

4-6.

수신: 글로리아 코스타 <gcosta@stormit.com>
발신: 데이빗 월러스 <dwallace@stormit.com>
날짜: 9월 2일
제목: 슈퍼 싱크 드라이브

코스타 씨께,

올해 1월 이후로, 기업 계정 관리부에서는 사용자에게 암호화된 파일을 안전하게 저장하고 공유할 수 있게 해 주는 클라우드 저장 서비스인 슈퍼 싱크 드라이브, 즉 SSD를 이용해 오고 있습니다. 아시다시피, **5** 8월 26일에, 제가 오리엔테이션 시간 중에 모든 우리 신입 사원들에게 이 서비스를 설명해 드렸으며, 모든 사람이 어떤 고객 관련 파일이든 이용하고 공유할 수 있도록 이 서비스에 등록해야 한다고 언급해 드렸습니다.

4 5 우리 보안 정책에 의해 모든 사람이 SSD를 이용해야 하므로, 신입 사원으로서, 귀하께서는 반드시 근무 첫 날 이 서비스에 등록하셔야 합니다. 따라서, 9월 4일에 출근하시면, www.supersyncdrive.com을 방문해 우리 회사의 고유 식별 코드(56927BA)를 입력한 다음, **6** 제공되는 안내를 따라 곧바로 사용자 이름과 비밀번호를 생성하시기 바랍니다. 프로필을 만들고 로그인하시는 대로, 올해 3월 1일까지 거슬러 올라가는 모든 기업 계정 기록에 접속하실 수 있을 것입니다.

SSD를 이용하시면서 어떤 어려움이든 접하시게 되면, 조나단 슐츠 씨께 문제점을 전달하시기 바랍니다.

안녕히 계십시오.

데이비드 월러스

어휘 corporate 기업의 storage 저장, 보관 securely 안전하게 store ~을 저장하다, 보관하다 encrypted 암호화된 access ~을 이용하다, ~에 접근하다 A-related A와 관련된 require A to do A에게 ~하도록 요구하다 take advantage of ~을 이용하다 register for ~에 등록하다 as such 따라서, 그런 이유로 straight away 곧바로, 즉시 unique identification code 고유 식별 코드 as soon as ~하는 대로, ~하자마자 date back to (날짜 등) ~까지 거슬러 올라가다 encounter ~을 접하다, 맞닥뜨리다 direct A to B A를 B에게 전달하다

4. 이메일의 목적은 무엇인가?
(A) 회의 일정을 정하는 것
(B) 직원들에게 파일을 백업하도록 상기시키는 것
(C) 의무 교육 시간을 간략히 설명하는 것
(D) 업무가 완료되도록 요청하는 것

정답 (D)

해설 배경 설명에 해당되는 첫 단락에 이어, 두 번째 단락에서 보안 정책에 의해 모든 사람이 SSD를 이용해야 하므로 신입 사원인 상대방에게 반드시 근무 첫 날 이 서비스에 등록해야 한다고(you must register for the service on your first day of work) 알리고 있다. 이는 이 일이 반드시 완료되어야 한다는 뜻이므로

(D)가 정답이다.

어휘 remind A to do A에게 ~하도록 상기시키다 outline ~을 간략히 설명하다 mandatory 의무적인 task 업무 complete ~을 완료하다

5. 코스타 씨는 언제 처음 슈퍼 싱크 드라이브에 관한 이야기를 들었는가?
(A) 3월 1일에
(B) 8월 26일에
(C) 9월 4일에
(D) 9월 5일에

정답 (B)

해설 첫 단락에 8월 26일에 있었던 오리엔테이션 시간 중에 해당 서비스를 모든 신입 사원들에게 설명한(on August 26, I explained this service to all of our new employees) 사실과 함께, 두 번째 단락 첫 문장에 신입 사원인 상대방에게 등록하도록(as a new employee, you must register for the service) 알리고 있으므로 (B)가 정답이다.

6. 새 사용자 이름과 비밀번호에 관해 암시된 것은 무엇인가?
(A) 월러스 씨에 의해 직원들에게 배정될 것이다.
(B) 컴퓨터를 사용하는 데 필수적이다.
(C) 오래된 기록을 확인하는 데 필요하다.
(D) 한 달 단위로 변경되어야 한다.

정답 (C)

해설 사용자 이름과 비밀번호가 언급되는 두 번째 단락 마지막에, 안내를 따라 사용자 이름과 비밀번호를 생성해 프로필을 만들고 로그인하면 올해 3월 1일까지 거슬러 올라가는 모든 기업 계정 기록에 접속할 수 있다고(please create your user name and password ~ As soon as you have created a profile and logged in, you will be able to access all corporate account records dating back to March 1 of this year) 알리고 있다. 따라서 사용자 이름과 비밀번호를 만들어 과거의 기록을 확인할 수 있다는 것을 알 수 있으므로 (C)가 정답이다.

어휘 assign ~을 배정하다, 할당하다 on a monthly basis 한 달 단위로, 매달

7-9.

니나 크레이머 [오전 10:15]
7 여러분 모두 저에게 백화점의 성대한 개장일 축하 행사에 대한 준비 작업이 어떻게 되어가고 있는지 소식 좀 전해 주시겠어요?

에이미 스타일즈 [오전 10:16]
저, 여러분 모두 시 의회에서 드디어 우리가 중앙 출입구 밖에서 개최하려고 계획하고 있는 콘서트를 승인했다는 사실을 알면 기쁘실 거예요.

피비 롱 [오전 10:17]
아주 잘됐네요!

그랜트 먼슨 [오전 10:18]

그럴 때도 됐어요! 8 우리가 지난 4월에 그 공연 허가서를 신청했잖아요.

에이미 스타일즈 [오전 10:19]

네, 그리고 9 그 소리가 너무 크고 성가시지 않을 거라고 제가 지역 주민 자치회를 설득하는 데 시간이 한참 걸렸죠.

피비 롱 [오전 10:21]

저는 그 축하 행사에 필요한 모든 장식을 최종 완료했어요. 지금 장식을 제자리에 갖춰 놓고 있는 장식 전문가들로 구성된 팀이 있어요.

그랜트 먼슨 [오전 10:22]

그리고 저는 몇몇 배우들을 대표하는 연기자 대리인들과 계속 얘기해 오고 있습니다. 저는 라이언 에스퍼 씨가 몇 마디 말씀도 해 주시고 입구에서 리본도 자를 시간이 있으실 거라고 꽤 확신합니다.

니나 크레이머 [오전 10:23]

훌륭해요! 그분의 새 프로그램이 수백 만 명의 시청자들을 끌어들이고 있잖아요. 좋아요, 팀원 여러분, 저에게 계속 소식 전해주세요.

어휘 update A on B B에 관해 A에게 새로운 소식을 전하다 preparation 준비 council 의회 approve ~을 승인하다 It's about time 때가 되었다 permit 허가서 take A B to do ~하는 데 A에게 B의 시간이 걸리다 convince ~을 설득하다 bothersome 성가신, 귀찮은 decorator 장식 전문가 put A in place A를 제자리에 갖춰 놓다, 설치하다 agent 대리인, 직원 represent ~을 대표하다, 대리하다 pull in ~을 끌어들이다 viewer 시청자

7. 메시지 작성자들은 무엇을 이야기하고 있는가?
(A) 백화점 세일 행사
(B) 대대적인 개장 행사
(C) 제품 출시
(D) 직원 야유회

정답 (B)

해설 크레이머 씨가 채팅을 시작하면서 백화점의 성대한 개장일 축하 행사에 대한 준비 작업이 어떻게 되어 가고 있는지 알려 달라고(how the preparations are going for the department store's big opening day celebration?) 물은 뒤로 그 진행 상황과 관련된 내용으로 채팅이 이어지고 있다. 따라서 개장 행사가 주제임을 알 수 있으므로 (B)가 정답이다.

어휘 launch 출시, 공개 excursion 야유회, 짧은 여행

8. 오전 10시 18분에, 먼슨 씨가 "It's about time"이라고 썼을 때, 그가 의도한 것은 무엇인가?
(A) 의회가 허가증을 발급해 줄 것인지에 대해 의구심이 있었다.
(B) 콘서트가 더 이른 시점에 시작되어야 한다고 생각한다.
(C) 임박한 마감 시한에 대해 걱정하고 있다.
(D) 결정이 더 빨리 내려질 것으로 기대했었다.

정답 (D)

해설 먼슨 씨가 "그럴 때도 됐죠"라고 말하면서 자신들이 지난 4월에 그 공연 허가서를 신청했다는(We applied for the performance permit back in April) 말을 덧붙이고 있다. 이는 공연에 대한 허가가 늦게 결정되었다는 의미로서 더 빨리 결정되었어야 했다는 의도를 담고 있는 말이다. 따라서 (D)가 정답이다.

어휘 have doubts that ~라는 점에 의구심을 갖다 issue v. ~을 발급하다 imminent 임박한

9. 지역 주민들은 무엇에 대해 우려하고 있는가?
(A) 인상된 가격
(B) 교통 혼잡
(C) 안전 문제
(D) 과도한 소음

정답 (D)

해설 오전 10시 19분에 스타일즈 씨가 소리가 너무 크고 성가시지 않을 거라고 지역 주민 자치회를 설득하는 데 시간이 한참 걸렸다는(it took me a while to convince the local residents' committee that the volume wouldn't be too high and bothersome) 말을 하고 있는데, 이는 주민들이 지나친 소음 문제를 우려하고 있다는 뜻이므로 (D)가 정답이다.

어휘 congestion 혼잡 excessive 과도한

10-12.

화이트 샌즈 리조트
숙박 및 활동

화이트 샌즈 리조트는 현대적인 욕실 시설에 더해 선풍기 또는 전체 에어컨을 포함하는 10개의 아름다운 해변 오두막으로 구성되어 있습니다. 10 저희는 하루에 오전 10시부터 오전 4시까지 18시간의 전기를 공급해 드리고 있으며, 이는 지역 내 다른 리조트들보다 2시간이 더 많습니다.

각 해변 오두막은 대형 발코니가 있으며, 바다를 가로질러 아주 다양한 섬들이 장관을 이루는 경관을 제공합니다. 저희 화이트 샌즈 리조트는 개발이 이뤄진 주요 지역들에서 멀리 떨어진 팔라완 동쪽 해변에 위치해 있으므로, 어떠한 방해도 없이 아름답고 평화로운 환경을 진정으로 감상하실 수 있는 기회를 가지실 수 있습니다. ─ [1] ─.

만조 동안에는, 해변 오두막 바로 밖에 있는 바다에서 수영하실 수 있으며, 해변에서 불과 200미터 거리에서 수영 및 스노클링하실 수 있는 다른 장소들도 있습니다. ─ [2] ─. 11(C) 저희는 스노클링 및 다이빙 장비, 카약, 그리고 제트 스키를 대여해 드리고 있습니다.

또한 11(A) 저희 산악 자전거들 중 한 대를 빌려 팔라완 동쪽 산들을 여행하시거나, 조용한 해변이 있는 곳으로 항해해 소풍을 하고 멋진 경치를 즐기실 수 있도록 11(D) 보트를 빌리실 수도 있습니다.

저희는 또한 여러분을 위해 기꺼이 "여러 섬을 둘러 보는" 투어도 마련해 드릴 것입니다. **12** 이는 3시간 또는 6시간 동안 지속되며, 갓 잡아 바비큐 과정을 거친 생선과 아주 다양한 지역 과일로 구성된 맛있는 점심 식사를 포함합니다. − [3] −. 투어를 떠나시기 전에 EPF(환경 보호 기금)에 5달러를 기부하시는 것이 의무라는 점에 유의하시기 바랍니다. − [4] −.

어휘 accommodation 숙박 consist of ~로 구성되다 spectacular 장관을 이루는 a diverse array of 아주 다양한(= a wide range of) civilized 개발이 이뤄진 truly 진정으로 appreciate ~을 감상하다, ~의 진가를 알아보다 interruption 방해, 지장 high tide 만조 rent out ~을 대여해 주다 scenery 경치, 풍경 arrange ~을 마련하다, 조치하다 island hopping 여러 섬 둘러 보기, 이 섬 저 섬으로 다니기 freshly-caught 갓 잡은 compulsory 의무적인 make a contribution 기부하다 embark on ~을 시작하다, ~에 착수하다

10. 해변 오두막에 관해 언급된 것은 무엇인가?
(A) 전부 에어컨 기기를 포함한다.
(B) 현대적인 요리 설비를 포함한다.
(C) 산 근처에 위치해 있다.
(D) 때때로 전기가 들어오지 않는다.

정답 (D)

해설 첫 단락에 하루에 오전 10시부터 오전 4시까지 18시간의 전기를 공급한다는(We provide 18 hours of electricity per day) 말이 쓰여 있는데, 이는 전기가 공급되지 않는 시간대가 있다는 뜻이므로 (D)가 정답이다.

어휘 unit (하나의) 기기, 장치

11. 화이트 샌즈 리조트의 대여 옵션으로 언급되지 않은 것은 무엇인가?
(A) 자전거
(B) 등산 장비
(C) 다이빙 장비
(D) 보트

정답 (B)

해설 세 번째 단락에 스노클링 및 다이빙 장비, 카약 그리고 제트 스키를 대여해준다는(We rent out snorkeling and diving gear) 부분에서 (C)를, 산악 자전거들 중 한대를 빌릴 수 있다는(You could also hire one of our mountain bikes) 부분에서 (A)를, 그리고 보트를 빌릴 수도 있다는(hire a boat) 부분에서 (D)도 확인할 수 있다. 하지만 등산 장비 대여와 관련된 정보는 찾아볼 수 없으므로 (B)가 정답이다.

12. [1], [2], [3], [4]로 표기된 위치들 중에서, 다음 문장이 들어가기에 가장 적절한 곳은 어디인가?

"이는 여러분께서 해변을 탐험하시는 동안 보트 운전사에 의해 전문적으로 준비될 것입니다."

(A) [1]
(B) [2]
(C) [3]
(D) [4]

정답 (C)

해설 제시된 문장은 앞서 언급된 특정한 것을 가리키는 This와 함께 그것이 보트 운전사에 의해 준비된다는 의미를 나타내므로 This로 가리킬 수 있는 단수명사로서 보트 운전사가 준비할 수 있는 대상이 언급된 문장을 찾아야 한다. 따라서 맛있는 점심 식사를 뜻하는 a delicious lunch가 언급된 문장 뒤에 위치한 [3]에 들어가 점심 식사가 준비되는 방식을 알리는 흐름이 되어야 알맞으므로 (C)가 정답이다.

어휘 expertly 전문적으로 explore ~을 탐험하다

DAY 05

PART 7 고난도 다중지문 완전 정복

예제 이중지문 연계문제 유형

수신: 크리스토퍼 존스 <kjones@tmail.net>
발신: 켈리 호킹 <khawking@bakercellularphones.com>
제목: 주문 번호 289422
날짜: 10월 5일

스위트에어 휴대전화기를 주문해 주셔서 감사 드립니다. 귀하의 새 스마트폰은 벽면 충전기와 차량용 충전기, 그리고 컴퓨터 연결 케이블이 모두 갖춰져 나옵니다. 500달러 넘게 소비하시는 것에 대한 무료 선물로, 보호용 케이스와 스크린 보호 필름 패키지도 받으시게 됩니다.

귀하의 제품은 10월 16일에 배송될 예정이지만, 귀하께서 저희 빠른 배송 제공 서비스에 대한 자격이 있으시다는 점을 알아 두시기 바랍니다. 불과 6.50달러에, 일주일 더 빠른 10월 9일에 상품을 받아 보실 수 있습니다. 이 특별 제공 서비스를 이용하시려면, 반드시 10월 6일까지 답장해 주셔야 하며, 그 이후에는 이 제공 서비스가 만료됩니다. 베이커 휴대전화 매장에서 제품 구입해 주신 것에 대해 다시 한번 감사드립니다.

안녕히 계십시오.

켈리 호킹
고객 판매부

어휘 come equipped with ~가 갖춰져서 나오다 fully 전부, 완전히 charger 충전기 qualify for ~에 대한 자격이 있다 merchandise 상품 take advantage of ~을 이용하다 reply 답장하다 expire 만료되다

수신: 켈리 호킹 <khawking@bakercellularphones.com>
발신: 크리스토퍼 존스 <kjones@tmail.net>
제목: 회신: 주문 번호 289422
날짜: 10월 6일

제 배송을 빠른 것으로 변경해 주시고, 그에 따라 제 신용카드로 비용 청구해 주시기 바랍니다. 또한, 제 회사로 전화기가 배송되었으면 합니다. 제가 처음에 온라인으로 주문했던 양식에 기재한 "배송지" 주소는 무시하시기 바랍니다. 감사합니다.

어휘 charge ~로 비용을 청구하다 accordingly 그에 따라 ignore ~을 무시하다

Q. 존스 씨는 언제 자신의 제품을 받을 것 같은가?
(A) 10월 5일에
(B) 10월 6일에
(C) 10월 9일에
(D) 10월 16일에

예제 **삼중지문 연계문제 유형**

켄팅 과학 연구소(KSI)에 다음과 같이 런던에서 근무하는 공석 직책이 있습니다.

수석 연구 과학자 (원즈워스 시설)
· 과학 관련 분야의 학사 학위 소지자
· 3년 이상 실험실에서 과학 연구를 수행해 본 경력 보유자

실험실 기사 (캠든 타운 시설)
· 실험실 장비에 대한 지식 소유자
· 모든 실험 장비에 대한 설치, 세척, 유지 관리, 그리고 수리가 가능한 자

이 직책들 중 하나에 지원하고자 하시는 분들께서는, tfranck@ksi.com으로 연구소 인사부장에게 연락하시기 바랍니다.

어휘 following 다음의, 아래의 Bachelor's degree 학사 학위 A-related A와 관련된 conduct ~을 수행하다, 실시하다 maintenance 유지 관리 either of ~ 둘 중의 하나

수신: 토비아스 프랭크 <tfranck@ksi.com>
발신: 이소벨 화이트 <isobelwhite@tmail.com>
제목: 실험실 기사

프랭크 씨께,

모던 사이언티스트 매거진에서 실험실 기사를 찾는 귀사의 광고를 보게 되었습니다. 저는 그 업무의 성격이 제 배경에 완벽히 어울린다고 생각하며, 저는 해당 시설에서 도보로 가까운 거리에 살고 있습니다. 지난 18개월 동안, 저는 실험실 장비 유통 업체인 메드세일즈 미드웨스트 사의 영업 사원으로 근무해 오고 있었으며, 그곳에서 저는 저희가 다루는 모든 기기에 관한 포괄적인 지식을 얻었습니다. 게다가, 저는 올해 대학에서 미생물학 졸업장을

받았으며, 그 학업 과정은 저에게 실험실 장비를 이용한 실무 경험을 얻을 기회를 제공해 주었습니다.

안녕히 계십시오.

이소벨 화이트

어휘 notice ~을 알아차리다, 인식하다 nature 성격, 특성 be suited to ~에 어울리다, 적합하다 distributor 유통 업체 comprehensive 포괄적인, 종합적인 handle ~을 다루다, 처리하다 diploma 졸업장, 수료증 microbiology 미생물학 afford A B A에게 B를 제공하다 hands-on experience 실무 경험

켄팅 과학 연구소(KSI)
업무 일정 정보

수석 연구 과학자
· 프로젝트 단계에 따른 탄력적인 일정. 일주일에 걸쳐 오전 근무 또는 오후 근무. 때때로 주말 근무.

실험실 기사
· 주중 교대 근무 필요. 장비는 매주 월요일에서 금요일까지 다음 날을 위해 오후 5시에서 8시 사이에 세척되고 설치되어야 합니다. 기사들은 일주일에 3교대 근무로 일합니다.

어휘 flexible 탄력적인, 유연한 depending on ~에 따라, ~에 달려 있는 throughout ~ 동안에 걸쳐, ~ 내내 occasional 때때로 있는 shift 교대 근무(조)

Q1. 화이드 씨에 관해 무엇을 유추할 수 있는가?
(A) 한 잡지를 위해 글을 쓴다.
(B) 18개월 전에 졸업했다.
(C) 현재 캠든 타운에 살고 있다.
(D) 해당 연구소에서 전에 일한 적이 있다.

Q2. 화이트 씨의 구직 지원이 성공적이라면, 언제 근무해야 할 것인가?
(A) 주중 오전마다
(B) 주중 오후마다
(C) 주중 저녁마다
(D) 주말 저녁마다

Practice

1. (C) **2.** (D) **3.** (D) **4.** (C) **5.** (C) **6.** (A)
7. (C) **8.** (D) **9.** (C) **10.** (D)

1-5.

원-투-원 투어

멕시코에서 여행하실 때, 저희 원-투-원 투어에 연락하셔서 이 아름다운 나라에서 여러분의 제한된 시간을 최대로 활용해 보십시오. 저희 고객들께서 즐기실 수 있는 것은 다음과 같습니다.

• 박식한 현지 가이드와 함께 하는 개인 투어
• 1(A) 엄선된 지역 숙박 시설에 대한 할인
• 공항 픽업 및 호텔로 이동하는 교통편
• 1(B) 지역 관광지 및 명소에서의 낮은 입장료
• 1(D) 항상 이용 가능한 무료 생수
• 가장 가격이 알맞은 최고의 레스토랑들에 대한 팁

저희는 멕시코에서 가장 인기 있는 관광지 네 곳을 돌아 보는 개인 투어를 제공해 드리고 있습니다. 아래에 이름이 기재된 투어 가이드들은 각각의 도시에 관해 아주 많은 지식을 지니고 있습니다.

멕시코 시티: 아드리아나 알바레즈
몬테레이: 페르난도 바레라
5 **과달라하라:** 하비에르 자발라
모렐리아: 에스페란자 레이나

2 저희는 고객들께 최소 3주 전에 미리 예약하시도록 권해 드리고 있습니다. 예약은 www.onetoonetours.com에서 온라인으로 하실 수 있습니다.

어휘 make the most of ~을 최대한 활용하다
knowledgeable 박식한, 아는 것이 많은 selected 엄선된 complimentary 무료의 affordable 가격이 알맞은 destination 목적지, 여행지 respective 각각의 advise A to do A에게 ~하도록 권하다 in advance 미리, 사전에

수신: 고객 서비스부 <customerservices@onetoone.com>
발신: 브리타니 슈월츠 <bschwarz@catanmail.com>
제목: 개인 투어
날짜: 11월 15일

관계자께,

제가 귀사의 웹 사이트에서 읽은 많은 긍정적인 고객 추천 후기를 바탕으로 이번 달 초에 귀사의 서비스를 이용하기로 결정했습니다. 저는 첫 개인 투어를 하게 되어 매우 흥분되었지만, 3 제가 나중에 귀사에 연락하는 것을 다시 생각해 보겠다는 말씀을 드리게 되어 유감스럽습니다.

첫 번째로, 5 자발라 씨는 공항에서 저를 태우러 오시는 데 있어 45분 넘게 늦으셨습니다. 그런 다음, 점심 식사를 위해 잠깐 들른 4 후에, 저를 호텔에 내려 주셨을 때 요청 드린 대로 금연 객실이 아닌 흡연 객실로 예약되었다는 사실을 알게 되었습니다. 나머지 3일간의 제 도시 투어 기간 내내, 저는 제가 방문했던 역사적인

건물들에 관해 가이드로부터 어떤 정보도 거의 듣지 못했습니다. 또한, 제가 갔던 대부분의 도시들은 할인 쿠폰을 받기를 거절하면서, 이미 만료되었다는 점을 지적했습니다. 솔직히, 이는 당황스럽고 받아들일 수 없었습니다.

어휘 based on ~을 바탕으로 customer testimonial 고객 추천 후기 have second thoughts about ~에 대해 다시 생각해 보다 to begin with 첫 번째로, 가장 먼저 following ~ 후에 brief stop 잠깐 들름 drop off ~을 내려 주다 barely 거의 ~ 않다 regarding ~에 관해 refuse to do ~하기를 거절하다 point out that ~임을 지적하다 expire 만료되다 embarrassing 당황스러운 unacceptable 받아들일 수 없는

1. 광고에서 원-투-원 투어에 의해 제공되지 않는 것은 무엇인가?
(A) 할인된 호텔 요금
(B) 관광 명소에 대한 서비스
(C) 현지 식사에 대한 할인
(D) 무료 음료

정답 (C)

해설 첫 지문에서 엄선된 지역 숙박 시설에 대한 할인 혜택을 즐길 수 있다는(Discounts on selected local accommodations) 부분에서 (A)를, 지역 관광지 및 명소에서의 낮은 입장료 혜택이 명시된 (Money off local tourist sites and landmarks) 부분에서 (B)를, 무료 생수를 이용할 수 있다는(Complimentary bottled water) 부분에서 (D)도 확인할 수 있다. 하지만 식사에 대한 할인 정보는 언급되어 있지 않으므로 (C)가 정답이다.

어휘 reduced 할인된 deal 제공 서비스, 거래 attraction 명소, 인기 장소

2. 원-투-원 투어는 고객들에게 무엇을 하도록 권장하는가?
(A) 투어 가이드에게 직접 이메일을 보내 예약하는 일
(B) 멕시코에서 3주 동안의 도시 투어를 예약하는 일
(C) 지인들에게 개인 투어를 추천해 주는 일
(D) 여행 몇 주 전에 개인 투어를 예약하는 일

정답 (D)

해설 첫 지문 마지막 부분에 최소 3주 전에 미리 개인 투어를 예약하도록 권한다고(We would advise customers to make a reservation for a private tour at least three weeks in advance) 언급되어 있으므로 (D)가 정답이다.

어휘 acquaintance 지인, 아는 사람

3. 슈월츠 씨는 왜 이메일을 썼는가?
(A) 서비스에 대해 감사를 표하기 위해
(B) 일정표의 오류를 알리기 위해
(C) 환불을 요청하기 위해
(D) 불만을 제기하기 위해

정답 (D)

해설 두 번째 지문 첫 단락에 나중에 또 연락하는 것을 다시 생각해 보겠다는 말을 하게 되어 유감스럽다고(I am sorry to say that I will have second thoughts about contacting your company in future) 말하면서 공항 픽업과 호텔 객실, 쿠폰 이용 등과 관련해 불편했던 점들을 언급하고 있다. 따라서 (D)가 정답이다.

어휘 itinerary 일정(표) request ~을 요청하다 register a complaint 불만을 제기하다

4. 이메일에서, 두 번째 단락, 첫 번째 줄의 단어 "following"과 의미가 가장 가까운 것은 무엇인가?
(A) ~로 이어지는
(B) ~에 앞서
(C) ~ 다음에
(D) ~에 따라

정답 (C)

해설 해당 문장에서 following 뒤에 명사구 a brief stop for lunch가 목적어로 쓰여 점심 식사를 위해 잠깐 들른 일을 말하고 있으며, 앞뒤의 내용으로 보아 공항 픽업과 점심 식사, 호텔 도착으로 이어지는 일을 순서대로 말하고 있다는 것을 알 수 있다. 따라서 '점심 식사 후에'라는 순서를 나타내기 위해 following이 쓰인 것이므로 '~ 다음에'를 뜻하는 (C) subsequent to가 정답이다.

5. 슈월츠 씨에 관해 암시된 것은 무엇인가?
(A) 가족을 통해 원-투-원 투어에 관해 알게 되었다.
(B) 이전에 몬테레이 개인 투어를 떠났다.
(C) 과달라하라에서 관광하면서 시간을 보냈다.
(D) 처음에 흡연 객실을 요청했다.

정답 (C)

해설 두 번째 지문 두 번째 단락에 자발라 씨가 공항에 태우러 오는 데 있어 45분 넘게 늦었다는(Mr. Zavala was more than 45 minutes late in picking me up from the airport) 말이 쓰여 있는데, 첫 지문 후반부에 자발라 씨가 과달라하라 지역 투어 가이드라는(Guadalajara: Javier Zavala) 정보가 쓰여 있으므로 (C)가 정답이다.

어휘 spend time -ing ~하면서 시간을 보내다 sightsee 관광하다

6-10.

수신: 숀 딜린저; 메릴 하우스먼; 라울 곤잘레스; 셀리나 모레츠
발신: 다리우스 로트너
제목: 판매 기록 (4월-7월)
날짜: 8월 7일, 금요일

안녕하세요, 여러분,

6 제가 지난 몇 개월 동안에 대한 판매 보고서를 첨부해 드렸는데, 이는 지난 한 주 동안에 걸쳐 우리 회계부장님이신 팁스 씨에 의해 정리되었습니다. 저는 월요일에 있을 회의 시간에 여러분과 함께 이것을 상세히 논의하고 싶지만, 6 이 이메일을 빌어 몇 가지 주목할 만한 경향 및 수치를 짚어 보는 기회로 삼고자 합니다.

커피에 대해 기재된 수치가 작년에 업체를 개업한 이후로 가장 높습니다. 이는 예상되었던 점이었는데, 우리의 새 제품 종류를 공격적으로 마케팅해 오고 있기 때문입니다. 여러분도 보실 수 있겠지만, 8 커피 판매량이 가장 높았던 달이 우리가 시내 지역 전체에 걸쳐 옥외 광고판을 운영했던 시기와 일치합니다.

다음으로, 머핀 판매량을 한 번 보시기 바랍니다. 솔직히, 이 수치는 우리의 기대치보다 훨씬 아래에 있습니다. 7 판매량을 증대하기 위한 노력의 일환으로, 우리는 9월 1일에 '음료 & 머핀' 촉진행사를 시작할 것입니다. 우리는 다음 주에 이 전략을 깊이 있게 논의할 수 있습니다.

우리가 월요일에 생산적인 회의를 할 수 있도록 주말 동안에 걸쳐 이 보고서 내용을 숙지하시기 바랍니다.

다리우스

어휘 compile (자료 등을 모아) ~을 정리하다 in detail 상세히 take A opportunity to do A를 ~하는 기회로 삼나 point out ~을 짚고 넘어가다, 지적하다 noteworthy 주목할 만한 aggressively 공격적으로 coincide with (시기 등이) ~와 일치하다, ~와 동시에 일어나다 billboard advertisement 옥외 광고(판) fall far below ~보다 훨씬 낮은 수준에 해당되다 expectation 기대(치) boost ~을 증대하다, 촉진하다 in depth 깊이 있게 familiarize oneself with ~을 숙지하다, ~에 익숙해 지도록 하다 productive 생산적인

킬리만탄 커피 매장
제품 판매 기록: 4월 ~ 7월

	4월	5월	6월	8 7월
8 커피	$16,340	$17,750	$17,150	8 $18,230
차	$9,510	$9,250	$8,750	$8,700
9 머핀	$8,200	$7,840	9 $8,340	$7,560
베이글	$9,530	$8,560	$8,940	$9,250

어휘 realize that ~임을 알아차리다, 깨닫다 make a mistake 실수하다 refer to ~을 참고하다 inconvenience 불편

6. 첫 번째 이메일의 목적은 무엇인가?
(A) 판매 보고서상의 특정 제품들에 대해 논의하는 것
(B) 광고에 대한 새로운 아이디어를 제안하는 것
(C) 팁스 씨가 승진되도록 추천하는 것
(D) 왜 판매 수치가 하락하고 있는지 설명하는 것

정답 (A)

해설 첫 지문 첫 단락에 지난 몇 개월 동안에 대한 판매 보고서를 첨부한(I have attached the sales report for the last few months) 사실과 함께 몇 가지 주목할 만한 경향 및 수치를 짚어 보겠다고(I'll take this opportunity to point out some noteworthy trends and figures) 언급하면서 제품과 관련된 분석 내용을 말하고 있다. 따라서 판매 보고서의 제품에 관해 논의하는 것이 목적임을 알 수 있으므로 (A)가 정답이다.

7. 첫 번째 이메일에 따르면, 9월 1일에 무슨 일이 있을 것 같은가?
(A) 새로운 음료 제품군이 출시될 것이다.
(B) 직원들이 교육 워크숍에 참석할 것이다.
(C) 새로운 판매 전략이 활용될 것이다.
(D) 고객들에게 무료 제품이 제공될 것이다.

정답 (C)

해설 9월 1일이라는 시점이 제시되는 첫 지문 세 번째 단락에, 판매량을 증대하기 위한 노력의 일환으로 9월 1일에 '음료 & 머핀' 판촉 행사를 시작할 것이라고(In an effort to boost sales, we will begin a new 'Beverage & Muffin' promotion on September 1) 알리고 있다. 이는 새로운 판매 전략을 이용하는 일이 시작된다는 말이므로 (C)가 정답이다.

어휘 launch ~을 출시하다 employ ~을 활용하다, 이용하다 complimentary 무료의

8. 해당 업체는 언제 일련의 옥외 광고판을 운영했을 것 같은가?
(A) 4월에

(B) 5월에
(C) 6월에
(D) 7월에

정답 (D)

해설 첫 지문 두 번째 단락에, 커피 판매량이 가장 높았던 달이 시내 지역 전체에 걸쳐 옥외 광고판을 운영했던 시기와 일치한다고 (the month during which sales of coffee were highest coincides with the time when we ran the billboard advertisements) 쓰여 있으므로, 커피 판매액이 가장 높은 달을 찾아야 한다. 두 번째 지문 도표에서 액수가 가장 높은 달이 $18,230로 쓰여 있는 7월이므로(July, $18,230) (D)가 정답이다.

9. 팁스 씨는 판매 수치를 계산할 때 어느 제품에 대해 실수했는가?
(A) 커피
(B) 차
(C) 머핀
(D) 베이글

정답 (C)

해설 세 번째 지문에 팁스 씨가 실수한 사실과 함께 $8,340라는 수치를 $8,560으로 변경하도록 요청하는 말이 쓰여 있는데, 두 번째 지문 도표에서 $8,340라는 액수는 머핀 6월 판매 액수(June, $8,340)이므로 (C)가 정답이다.

10. 두 번째 이메일에서, 첫 번째 단락, 첫 번째 줄의 단어 "recording"과 의미가 가장 가까운 것은 무엇인가?
(A) 듣는
(B) 협업하는
(C) 시작하는
(D) 기록하는

정답 (D)

해설 세 번째 지문의 해당 문장에서 was recording 뒤에 목적어로 the figures for the recent sales report라는 말이 쓰여 있다. 따라서 recording은 '기록하다'라는 의미를 나타내기 위해 사용된 단어임을 알 수 있으므로 '문서에 기록하다'라는 의미로 쓰이는 동사 document의 분사형 (D) documenting이 정답이다.

WEEK 03

	Contents	Page	Date	Score (맞은 개수)
Day 01	LC Half Test	02	월 일	/50
Day 02	RC Half Test	08	월 일	/50
Day 03	LC Half Test	22	월 일	/50
Day 04	RC Half Test	28	월 일	/50
Day 05	LC Half Test	42	월 일	/50

PART 1

Directions: For each question in this part, you will hear four statements about a picture in your test book. When you hear the statements, you must select the one statement that best describes what you see in the picture. Then find the number of the question on your answer sheet and mark your answer. The statements will not be printed in your test book and will be spoken only one time.

1.

2.

PART 2

Directions: You will hear a question or statement and three responses spoken in English. They will not be printed in your test book and will be spoken only one time. Select the best response to the question or statement and mark the letter (A), (B), or (C) on your answer sheet.

3. Mark your answer on your answer sheet.

4. Mark your answer on your answer sheet.

5. Mark your answer on your answer sheet.

6. Mark your answer on your answer sheet.

7. Mark your answer on your answer sheet.

8. Mark your answer on your answer sheet.

9. Mark your answer on your answer sheet.

10. Mark your answer on your answer sheet.

11. Mark your answer on your answer sheet.

12. Mark your answer on your answer sheet.

13. Mark your answer on your answer sheet.

14. Mark your answer on your answer sheet.

15. Mark your answer on your answer sheet.

16. Mark your answer on your answer sheet.

17. Mark your answer on your answer sheet.

18. Mark your answer on your answer sheet.

19. Mark your answer on your answer sheet.

20. Mark your answer on your answer sheet.

PART 3

Directions: You will hear some conversations between two or more people. You will be asked to answer three questions about what the speakers say in each conversation. Select the best response to each question and mark the letter (A), (B), (C) or (D) on your answer sheet. The conversations will not be printed in your test book and will be spoken only one time.

21. What are the speakers mainly discussing?

    (A) A seasonal sale
    (B) A staff orientation
    (C) A remodelling project
    (D) A work schedule

22. What has caused a problem?

    (A) A printer malfunctioned.
    (B) A delivery arrived late.
    (C) A document was misplaced.
    (D) An employee made an error.

23. What is the man going to do next?

    (A) Lead a training class
    (B) Speak with employees
    (C) Order some supplies
    (D) Open a store

24. Where does the woman work?

    (A) At an antique store
    (B) At a radio station
    (C) At a movie production studio
    (D) At an online auction site

25. Why does the man say, "I only posted it fifteen minutes ago"?

    (A) To explain a mistake
    (B) To reject a request
    (C) To request some advice
    (D) To express surprise

26. What does the woman ask the man to do?

    (A) Attend a meeting
    (B) Reduce a price
    (C) Collaborate on a project
    (D) Extend a deadline

27. What is Emily congratulated for?

    (A) Negotiating a contract
    (B) Relocating to a new branch
    (C) Reaching a sales target
    (D) Winning an award

28. What will happen this month?

    (A) A job opportunity will be offered.
    (B) A new product will be launched.
    (C) A store promotion will begin.
    (D) A training workshop will take place.

29. What does the man want to do?

    (A) Apply for a position
    (B) Have a device repaired
    (C) Purchase a computer
    (D) Learn about some software

30. What does the man mention about his train ride?

    (A) The train departed late.
    (B) The train broke down.
    (C) His destination was wrong.
    (D) His seat was changed.

31. What does the woman say about Northern Rail?

    (A) It has a good reputation.
    (B) It is offering a new service.
    (C) It provides staff discounts.
    (D) It was recently founded.

32. What does the woman give to the man?

    (A) A ticket
    (B) A refund
    (C) A document
    (D) A beverage

Art Gallery Exhibitions	
Jenny Hurlock	Digital media
Andre Guzman	Wildlife photography
Emma Alcock	Bronze sculpture
Jeremy Choi	Watercolor painting

33. Where do the speakers most likely work?

(A) At a supermarket
(B) At a restaurant
(C) At a beverage company
(D) At a museum

34. Why is the woman concerned?

(A) She forgot to purchase a ticket.
(B) She has to work this afternoon.
(C) She does not have much money.
(D) She did not dress appropriately.

35. Look at the graphic. Which artist's exhibition does the man recommend?

(A) Jenny Hurlock
(B) Andre Guzman
(C) Emma Alcock
(D) Jeremy Choi

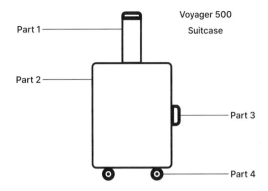

Voyager 500 Suitcase

36. What does the woman say is happening this month?

(A) A store is having a closing down sale.
(B) A discount is being offered on a specific brand.
(C) New product ranges are being launched.
(D) Free delivery is available on all purchases.

37. What concern does the man have about Travelpro products?

(A) They are too expensive.
(B) They are not durable.
(C) They have limited storage capacity.
(D) They only come in one color.

38. Look at the graphic. What part of the Voyager 500 suitcase does the woman emphasize?

(A) Part 1
(B) Part 2
(C) Part 3
(D) Part 4

PART 4

Directions: You will hear some talks given by a single speaker. You will be asked to answer three questions about what the speakers say in each conversation. Select the best response to each question and mark the letter (A), (B), (C) or (D) on your answer sheet. The conversations will not be printed in your test book and will be spoken only one time.

39. Where is the talk being given?

(A) At a convention center
(B) At a resort
(C) At a shopping mall
(D) At a restaurant

40. What will take place today?

(A) A street parade
(B) A musical performance
(C) A job fair
(D) A food festival

41. What does the speaker suggest the listeners do?

(A) Use a shuttle bus
(B) Make a reservation
(C) Take some coupons
(D) Purchase a ticket

42. What is the news report mainly about?

(A) A newly-opened restaurant
(B) An employment opportunity
(C) A home moving service
(D) A local business owner

43. What does the speaker imply when he says, "Quick Grub employs over fifty drivers"?

(A) A business is currently hiring.
(B) A company has grown significantly.
(C) An error was made in a previous report.
(D) A training program has been effective.

44. According to the speaker, who is Ms. Lowell planning to work with?

(A) A marketing manager
(B) An interior designer
(C) Financial consultants
(D) Application developers

45. What is the message mostly about?

(A) A business deal
(B) A company policy
(C) A training session
(D) A safety inspection

46. Why does the speaker say, "there are 100 presentation slides!"?

(A) To request assistance with preparing a presentation
(B) To suggest postponing a company event
(C) To explain why an activity will run longer than expected
(D) To thank the listener for help with a task

47. What will the speaker give to some employees?

(A) Meal vouchers
(B) ID tags
(C) Job descriptions
(D) Packed lunches

Pattern 1   Pattern 2   Pattern 3   Pattern 4

48. What did the company do last year?

(A) It recruited additional staff.
(B) It increased production of items.
(C) It expanded into overseas markets.
(D) It discontinued some products.

49. Look at the graphic. Which pattern of cushion is the most popular?

(A) Pattern 1
(B) Pattern 2
(C) Pattern 3
(D) Pattern 4

50. According to the speaker, what has the IT team been doing?

(A) Repairing office computers
(B) Responding to customer inquiries
(C) Enhancing Web site security
(D) Creating an online store

READING TEST

In the Reading test, you will read a variety of texts and answer several different types of reading comprehension questions. The entire Reading test will last 75 minutes. There are three parts, and directions are given for each part. You are encouraged to answer as many questions as possible within the time allowed. You must mark your answers on the separate answer sheet. Do not write your answers in your test book.

PART 5

Directions: A word or phrase is missing in each of the sentences below. Four answer choices are given below each sentence. Select the best answer to complete the sentence. Then mark the letter (A), (B), (C), or (D) on your answer sheet.

1. The finance manager has asked that the travel expense receipts be submitted at ------- earliest convenience.

   (A) you
   (B) your
   (C) yours
   (D) yourself

2. The newly-revised version of the Beijing Travel Guide features ------- for tour itineraries and restaurants.

   (A) recommendation
   (B) recommendations
   (C) recommending
   (D) recommended

3. Results ------- surveys conducted by our marketing team indicate that most consumers believe our products are overpriced.

   (A) out
   (B) up
   (C) into
   (D) from

4. When visiting Beijing's most famous food street, foreign tourists can ------- countless local dishes that they could never try at home.

   (A) sample
   (B) samples
   (C) sampled
   (D) sampling

5. Mr. Trank is happy to take either the Westway Airways or the Swiftjet flight, ------- one is cheaper.

   (A) both
   (B) whichever
   (C) enough
   (D) anybody

6. Although the Borealis 800 laptop computer is priced similarly to competing models, it is ------- more powerful.

   (A) notice
   (B) noticed
   (C) noticing
   (D) noticeably

7. We invite all job seekers to submit an application form ------- they have at least six months of experience in a retail environment.

(A) in case
(B) unless
(C) according to
(D) as long as

8. At least 200 people applied for the financial manager position, but ------- lacked the necessary qualifications.

(A) yet
(B) every
(C) much
(D) many

9. The ------- real estate brochure details the spacious luxury homes available on Long Island, New York.

(A) enclosure
(B) enclosing
(C) enclosed
(D) enclose

10. ------- Dr. Meaney, the plans for expansion will be delayed until further studies can be conducted.

(A) As well as
(B) Such as
(C) According to
(D) Aside from

11. Please be aware that, due to unforeseen circumstances, there will be a slight ------- to the conference program.

(A) modification
(B) explanation
(C) organization
(D) illustration

12. Photographer Joshua Davies ------- his latest work during last week's exhibition at the Bellevue Gallery of Visual Arts.

(A) present
(B) will present
(C) was presented
(D) presented

13. If you have difficulty operating your new rice cooker, please check the ------- troubleshooting guide on our Web site.

(A) helps
(B) helped
(C) helpful
(D) helpfully

14. ------- Mr. Selleck had demonstrated good leadership and communication abilities, he was offered a position as a team leader.

(A) Until
(B) Because
(C) While
(D) Unless

15. The anti-virus program on our work computers is updated ------- to keep them safe from malicious software.

(A) frequently
(B) suddenly
(C) nearly
(D) barely

16. Building permit requests submitted ------- approval must be accompanied by a project cost specification.

(A) unless
(B) over
(C) from
(D) for

PART 6

Directions: Read the texts that follow. A word, phrase, or sentence is missing in parts of each text. Four answer choices for each question are given below the text. Select the best answer to complete the text. Then mark the letter (A), (B), (C) or (D) on your answer sheet.

Questions 17-20 refer to the following advertisement.

Morgan Bank Customers

From next month, you will be able to register online for our brand new Internet banking program! It doesn't matter whether you have a high-interest savings account or a checking account; all customers are eligible for this ------- .
                                                    17.

------- . Of course, it may require a few minutes of your time to set up a user name and password,
  18.
but once that has been completed, you are almost ready to begin banking online. A customer service representative will ------- you as soon as your online account has been authorized and you will be able
                        19.
to use ------- from that point onwards.
      20.

For more details, pick up an information pamphlet at any branch of Morgan Bank, or visit our Web site at www.morganbank.com.

17. (A) service
    (B) event
    (C) building
    (D) feedback

18. (A) Some additional charges may apply.
    (B) Come in today to create your new bank account.
    (C) It is very easy to sign up.
    (D) User access will be temporarily suspended for site maintenance.

19. (A) respond
    (B) introduce
    (C) present
    (D) notify

20. (A) them
    (B) it
    (C) some
    (D) his

Dear Sir or Madam,

My company is planning to have a year-end banquet to celebrate what has been a very successful year for us so far. Approximately 150 of our staff will attend. The Beverly Hotel has been recommended to me by a number of my colleagues. --------, I have some reservations about whether you will be able to
21.
meet our requirements.

I have concerns that your function rooms may not be -------- for our needs. Specifically, we would
22.
like to find a large room that includes a stage and audio/visual equipment, including a public address system, a projector, a laptop, and a screen.

If you could send me detailed information about your function rooms, it would be much appreciated. I am particularly interested in your banquet hall, which I believe is the largest and best equipped of the rooms. --------. I would be happy -------- a reply from you at your earliest possible convenience, as we
23.   **24.**
would like to book a venue by the end of this month. Thank you in advance for your help.

Peter Quinn

21. (A) However
    (B) Therefore
    (C) Furthermore
    (D) Similarly

22. (A) total
    (B) opposite
    (C) adequate
    (D) able

23. (A) However, another room should be fine if it has already been reserved.
    (B) As a result, you might not have enough staff to handle the catering.
    (C) Stage lighting would also be useful but isn't necessary.
    (D) My employees and I had a wonderful evening there.

24. (A) would receive
    (B) to receive
    (C) being received
    (D) to have been received

PART 7

Directions: In this part you will read a selection of texts, such as magazine and newspaper articles, e-mails, and instant messages. Each text or set of texts is followed by several questions. Select the best answer for each question and mark the letter (A), (B), (C), or (D) on your answer sheet.

Questions 25-26 refer to the following notice.

To: All Mulberry Fashion Head Office Staff
From: Beverly Gunn, Chairwoman and CEO

It is my pleasure to announce that the board of directors has selected our current Head of Domestic Sales, Margot Duchovny, to take over as European Sales Director when Bianca Bing retires in April.

Approximately 10 years ago, she took a position at Mulberry, and was immediately assigned to our Paris office. Later, she was transferred to the San Francisco office, and finally to our head office. Her enthusiasm for fashion and her proficiency in sales management make her a true asset to our company.

It is also important that we commemorate the many invaluable contributions that Ms. Bing made to Mulberry over the years, so we have organized for us to all get together on March 30 at the Magnolia Restaurant. If you have any questions about the event, call my assistant, Nia Goldberg, at extension 331. For more details, contact the head of human resources, Benjamin Gunn, at extension 306.

25. What is the purpose of the notice?

(A) To report on sales figures
(B) To request that a task be completed
(C) To explain a policy change
(D) To notify staff of a personnel change

26. Why will an event be held on March 30?

(A) To welcome a new executive
(B) To announce European sales projections
(C) To choose a suitable replacement
(D) To recognize an employee's accomplishments

Join the Cork Residents Association (CRA)

The Cork Residents Association provides you with a way to directly influence and discuss issues that affect our town. By joining the CRA, you will be able to hear about proposed community events, plans for urban development, and issues affecting our schools and hospitals before these matters are officially announced to the general public.

As well as being able to discuss these issues at monthly CRA meetings, you will receive a weekly newsletter, titled The Cork Bulletin. This publication contains articles written by our members, a list of dates for future community events, reports on local fundraising efforts, and news about special offers available at stores in town.

If you are interested in becoming a member of the association, please e-mail Doris Wentworth at secretary@cra.com and she will add your name to our list immediately.

27. What is being advertised?
   (A) A local magazine
   (B) An upcoming meeting
   (C) A community group
   (D) An urban development plan

28. What are interested individuals encouraged to do?
   (A) Obtain membership by e-mail
   (B) Purchase a ticket for a town event
   (C) Submit an article to a newspaper
   (D) Contact local store owners

29. What are CRA members NOT likely to be informed about?
   (A) Local healthcare news
   (B) Construction proposals
   (C) Shopping discounts
   (D) Work opportunities

The Roachford Evening News
City Council Finally Announces Transit Plans

August 8

After months of negotiations with transit officials and construction firms, Roachford City Council has formally authorized a plan to add new bus lines throughout the city. Starting next month, several roads that run from the downtown area out to the city's various suburbs will be widened and resurfaced to accommodate new bus lanes and routes. — [1] —. Residents have long held the opinion that the city's bus network is not sufficiently extensive, so the new routes will come as good news to most local people. — [2] —.

Additionally, the central city bus terminal will receive a fleet of fifteen additional vehicles to be used on the aforementioned routes. — [3] —. Bus fares and monthly/yearly passes will remain at the same prices for buses on all routes. — [4] —.

To view a diagram of the new transit routes and to find out more information about fares and bus schedules, visit www.roachfordtransit.com.

---

30. What does the article mainly discuss?

(A) The unveiling of a new bus terminal
(B) Efforts to improve a transportation system
(C) Plans to alleviate downtown traffic congestion
(D) An increase in the price of bus tickets

31. According to the article, what can people do on the Web site?

(A) Print discounted travel passes
(B) Check a construction schedule
(C) Leave feedback about the council's plans
(D) View a map of proposed bus routes

32. In which of the positions marked [1], [2], [3], and [4] does the following sentence best belong?

"In an effort to reduce pollution, the buses will all be electric."

(A) [1]
(B) [2]
(C) [3]
(D) [4]

Questions 33-36 refer to the following online chat discussion.

Hudgens Corporation Intranet
Chat Client v.2.2
Logged in as: Esther Moffatt (Sales Department)

Esther Moffatt:	(3:03 P.M.)	How do you all feel about catching the new Brad Kane movie at the cinema after work?
Sidney Walker:	(3:05 P.M.)	I'm free tonight.
Olly Edwards:	(3:07 P.M.)	Same here.
Lucy Forbes:	(3:09 P.M.)	I wish I could, but I'll be staying late to phone applicants about coming for interviews next week. Let me know how the movie is tomorrow!
Esther Moffatt:	(3:12 P.M.)	That's a shame, Lucy. What positions are you trying to fill in your department?
Lucy Forbes:	(3:14 P.M.)	We're looking for a corporate tax manager and a payroll assistant. Ms. Grantham has told me to call around twenty applicants this evening.
Olly Edwards:	(3:15 P.M.)	Wow! That's a lot of phone calls. Do you want a hand with that?
Lucy Forbes:	(3:16 P.M.)	I'd appreciate it. Have you had any experience in calling job candidates?
Olly Edwards:	(3:17 P.M.)	Sure, I've helped my department manager with that in the past.
Lucy Forbes:	(3:17 P.M.)	Well, that would be great. Thanks, Olly.
Sidney Walker:	(3:19 P.M.)	Will you be holding the interviews in our brand new conference room?
Lucy Forbes:	(3:21 P.M.)	Not unless someone wants to let me use their time slot. It's fully booked all day Monday.
Esther Moffatt:	(3:22 P.M.)	You can use mine. I was just going to use it for a team meeting.
Lucy Forbes:	(3:23 P.M.)	Great! Just let me know what time I can use the room.

33. At 3:05 P.M., what does Mr. Walker most likely mean when he says, "I'm free tonight"?

(A) He wants to watch a different movie.
(B) He has a free cinema ticket.
(C) He likes Ms. Moffat's idea.
(D) He would prefer to reschedule a trip.

34. What is suggested about the job candidates?

(A) They will be coming to the company today.
(B) They will be interviewed by Mr. Edwards.
(C) They have been contacted by e-mail.
(D) They applied for positions in Accounting.

35. What is implied about Ms. Grantham?

(A) She has submitted an application.
(B) She is a payroll assistant.
(C) She is Ms. Forbes's manager.
(D) She plans to watch a movie.

36. Who has made a reservation to use the conference room?

(A) Ms. Moffat
(B) Mr. Walker
(C) Mr. Edwards
(D) Ms. Forbes

To: All sales department staff
From: Jonas Olsson, Sales Manager
Subject: Teambuilding event
Date: Wednesday, July 5

As you know, Konex Telecommunications' annual teambuilding event will take place on Saturday, July 22. After listening to your complaints regarding the previous year's events, the management team met and discussed ways to do things differently this year. In an effort to provide a more stimulating environment, we decided that the event will no longer be held at the convention center near the head office. It has been moved to an outdoor area at the Evergreen Valley Farm. Everything else about the event, including the activity itinerary we discussed at Tuesday's meeting, remains largely unchanged.

All sales department staff are required to participate in this excursion. Members of staff from our three other branch offices will also be in attendance, as will representatives from Corporate Challenge, the company that organized the event activities. At the end of the day, we will all assemble at a nearby restaurant for dinner, where company founder Arnold Lundgren will talk to everyone about current company goals. A shuttle bus will be provided on the day of the event. If you wish to take advantage of this, write your name on the form on the notice board. Finally, you're all welcome to e-mail me with any questions.

37. Why was the memo sent?

(A) To discuss negative feedback about an event

(B) To ask for suggestions about a group activity

(C) To announce a new venue for an event

(D) To request a change of the event date

38. What is indicated about Mr. Olsson?

(A) He is the founder of Konex Telecommunications.

(B) He attended a meeting about the event.

(C) He will attend a convention next Tuesday.

(D) He helped to organize some event activities.

39. The word "assemble" in paragraph 2 line 4 is closest in meaning to

(A) converse

(B) build

(C) compile

(D) gather

40. What are event attendees asked to do?

(A) Contact a representative from Corporate Challenge

(B) Add their name to a list if they require transportation

(C) Send an e-mail to Mr. Lundgren if they have any queries

(D) Attend a meeting at a different branch office

Questions 41-45 refer to the following e-mails.

To:	George Halliburton <ghalliburton@swiftrealty.com>
From:	Serena Jolie <sjolie@mymail.com>
Subject:	Problem with Plumbing
Date:	March 7

Dear Mr. Halliburton,

Since last night, there has been no water coming out of my kitchen faucet, and the water pressure in my bathroom has been extremely low. I tried calling the building manager this morning, because he told me previously that the building has an agreement with a specific plumbing company. However, he didn't answer his phone, so I asked my neighbor, Walter Timmins, what I should do. He informed me that you offered him assistance on one occasion when he had a problem with his heating. I remembered that your assistant, Lisa Jenkins, wrote down your e-mail address for me when I was in your office last month. Hopefully, you can advise me on what I should do about the plumbing.

Best wishes,

Serena Jolie
Apartment 612
Santa Monica Apartments

To: Serena Jolie <sjolie@mymail.com>
From: George Halliburton <ghalliburton@swiftrealty.com>
Subject: Re: Problem with Plumbing
Date: March 7

Dear Serena,

I'm sorry to hear about the problem in your apartment. The building manager, Mario Gonzalez, is normally the person who takes care of repairs, or calls a specialist out to make the repairs. Unfortunately, he is currently on vacation. The building has a business arrangement with Handy Plumbing, situated nearby on Nestor Boulevard. I am an acquaintance of the manager there, so I'll get in touch with him on his cell phone. Afterwards, I'll e-mail you to let you know what time he will be coming round to fix your water. I'm sorry that I forgot to leave you my business card when you signed the housing lease at my office. You can reach me at 555-8282 anytime.

Regards,

George Halliburton

41. In the first e-mail, what is indicated about the problem in Ms. Jolie's apartment?

(A) It has happened before.
(B) It became worse this morning.
(C) It has affected other tenants.
(D) It started yesterday.

42. Who most likely did Ms. Jolie attempt to contact first about the problem?

(A) Walter Timmins
(B) George Halliburton
(C) Mario Gonzalez
(D) Lisa Jenkins

43. In the second e-mail, the word "normally" in paragraph 1, line 2, is closest in meaning to

(A) regularly
(B) ordinarily
(C) fortunately
(D) certainly

44. Who most likely is Mr. Halliburton?

(A) A building tenant
(B) A local plumber
(C) A real estate agent
(D) A building manager

45. How does Mr. Halliburton offer to help Ms. Jolie?

(A) By visiting a business location
(B) By coming to her apartment
(C) By speaking to his supervisor
(D) By making a phone call

Questions 46-50 refer to the following article, information, and text message.

THIS WEEKEND AT THE BOX OFFICE!

Cinephile Weekly
By Amy Swann

This weekend (July 12-13), *Alien Invasion* maintained its position atop the box office rankings table, thanks to highly positive reviews and an innovative marketing campaign. Another reason for the film's success is its impressive cast, which includes recent award winners Dwayne Robinson and Kayla Davitt.

Earth Tremors also continued its successful run at the box office this weekend, taking in an impressive $89 million despite being released over three weeks ago. Film critics are unanimous in their opinion that the film accurately portrays the interesting characters and exciting plot of the source novel, which was written by acclaimed author Mark Burroughs.

Lastly, *Upside Down* was not only the most successful new release this weekend ($91.4 million), but also the most successful new release of the month. What is especially notable is the fact that its production company was only set up near the end of last year, and *Upside Down* is the company's first ever movie release.

US Box Office Rankings

This Weekend: July 12 - July 13

Rank(Last Week)	Title	Production Company	Weekend Gross	Total Gross
1 (1)	Alien Invasion	Pacifica	$106.5M	$403M
2 (-)	Upside Down	Mobius Films	$91.4M	$91.4M
3 (2)	Super Sleuth	Indica	$13.2M	$77.6M
4 (3)	Earth Tremors	Pacifica	$8.9M	$133M
5 (-)	Cyborg Girl	Olsen	$6.1M	$6.1M

Note: Olsen Pictures' new movie was a limited release, showing at only 350 theaters throughout the country and taking in $6.1 million at the box office. It will receive a full nationwide release next weekend.

To: Patricia Yates
Date: July 14
From: Michael Ritchie

Hi Patricia...

Well, I have to agree! You were right about the movie. It's a shame I couldn't join you to see it on Saturday, but I had some time yesterday afternoon. Wow! I'm not surprised it's already topping the box office rankings on its opening weekend. Oh... while I was at the cinema, I saw a trailer for a new film that I think we should go and see. It was only shown at a few cinemas this past weekend, but it's already at number 5 in the box office rankings. Check out the trailer and let me know if you feel like going to see it this weekend. (8:56 P.M.)

46. What is Ms. Swann's article mainly about?

(A) Movies that are currently in development
(B) The worldwide success of *Alien Invasion*
(C) The financial performance of recent films
(D) Films nominated for upcoming awards

47. What is suggested about *Earth Tremors* in the article?

(A) It was directed by Mark Burroughs.
(B) It has won awards recently.
(C) It has been adapted from a book.
(D) It features two very popular actors.

48. What is indicated about Mobius Films?

(A) It is releasing a movie next month.
(B) It is a relatively new company.
(C) Its film broke a box office record.
(D) It collaborated with Pacifica.

49. What can be inferred about Ms. Yates?

(A) She was unable to go to the cinema last weekend.
(B) She has recently watched *Alien Invasion*.
(C) She recommended a cinema to Mr. Ritchie.
(D) She normally goes to the cinema every weekend.

50. What film does Mr. Ritchie most likely want to watch this weekend?

(A) Upside Down
(B) Super Sleuth
(C) Earth Tremors
(D) Cyborg Girl

DAY 03

LC Half Test

제한 시간 30분

MP3 바로듣기

강의 바로보기

정답 및 해설 p. 26

PART 1

Directions: For each question in this part, you will hear four statements about a picture in your test book. When you hear the statements, you must select the one statement that best describes what you see in the picture. Then find the number of the question on your answer sheet and mark your answer. The statements will not be printed in your test book and will be spoken only one time.

1.

2.

PART 2

Directions: You will hear a question or statement and three responses spoken in English. They will not be printed in your test book and will be spoken only one time. Select the best response to the question or statement and mark the letter (A), (B), or (C) on your answer sheet.

3. Mark your answer on your answer sheet.

4. Mark your answer on your answer sheet.

5. Mark your answer on your answer sheet.

6. Mark your answer on your answer sheet.

7. Mark your answer on your answer sheet.

8. Mark your answer on your answer sheet.

9. Mark your answer on your answer sheet.

10. Mark your answer on your answer sheet.

11. Mark your answer on your answer sheet.

12. Mark your answer on your answer sheet.

13. Mark your answer on your answer sheet.

14. Mark your answer on your answer sheet.

15. Mark your answer on your answer sheet.

16. Mark your answer on your answer sheet.

17. Mark your answer on your answer sheet.

18. Mark your answer on your answer sheet.

19. Mark your answer on your answer sheet.

20. Mark your answer on your answer sheet.

PART 3

Directions: You will hear some conversations between two or more people. You will be asked to answer three questions about what the speakers say in each conversation. Select the best response to each question and mark the letter (A), (B), (C) or (D) on your answer sheet. The conversations will not be printed in your test book and will be spoken only one time.

21. Why is the man calling?

    (A) To reschedule an appointment
    (B) To promote new services
    (C) To discuss some repairs
    (D) To seek some advice

22. What does the woman say will happen this afternoon?

    (A) A safety inspection
    (B) A client meeting
    (C) Some job interviews
    (D) Some training seminars

23. What should the woman do before the man arrives?

    (A) Clear an area
    (B) Sign a form
    (C) Turn off a device
    (D) Send a payment

24. Where most likely are the speakers?

    (A) At a clothing store
    (B) At an office supply store
    (C) At a health food store
    (D) At an electronics store

25. What does the woman ask about?

    (A) Business locations
    (B) Color choices
    (C) Item availability
    (D) Warranty length

26. What does the man say the woman can do on Wednesday?

    (A) Browse new product lines
    (B) Become a store member
    (C) Request a discount
    (D) Make a payment

27. What have the speakers received?

    (A) An overdue payment
    (B) A promotional offer
    (C) A menu for an event
    (D) An invoice from a supplier

28. What does the woman imply when she says, "We use it in a lot of dishes"?

    (A) She wants to change some recipes.
    (B) She thinks the man's idea is poor.
    (C) She will show the man some alternatives.
    (D) She is pleased with a product's popularity.

29. What does the woman suggest?

    (A) Comparing some prices
    (B) Introducing new dishes
    (C) Hiring additional workers
    (D) Discontinuing a menu item

30. What product are the speakers discussing?

    (A) A tablet computer
    (B) A pair of headphones
    (C) A smart watch
    (D) A game console

31. Why is the product's design being changed?

    (A) To extend its battery life
    (B) To reduce its power usage
    (C) To decrease its weight
    (D) To improve its water resistance

32. What does the woman ask Ross to do?

    (A) Send a product sample
    (B) Arrange a meeting
    (C) Train some employees
    (D) Submit a report

Title	Author
General Pepper's Team	Nahid Shirazi
Hey, Judith!	Tuan Pham
A Bluebird's Song	Vasiliki Samaras
Blueberry Fields	Armen Krikorian

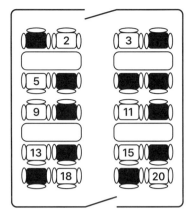

33. What did the woman forget to do?

   (A) Pay a late fee
   (B) Sign up for an event
   (C) Place a book on hold
   (D) Renew her membership card

34. Look at the graphic. Who is the woman's favorite author?

   (A) Nahid Shirazi
   (B) Tuan Pham
   (C) Vasiliki Samaras
   (D) Armen Krikorian

35. According to the man, what will take place next weekend?

   (A) A book signing event
   (B) A writing workshop
   (C) A charity collection
   (D) A fundraiser

36. What event are the speakers preparing for?

   (A) A product launch
   (B) A training seminar
   (C) A fundraising event
   (D) A career fair

37. What does the woman ask the man to help with?

   (A) Printing a pamphlet
   (B) Collecting some products
   (C) Advertising an event
   (D) Setting up a stage

38. Look at the graphic. Which seats will the speakers choose?

   (A) Seats 2 and 3
   (B) Seats 5 and 9
   (C) Seats 9 and 13
   (D) Seats 11 and 15

PART 4

Directions: You will hear some talks given by a single speaker. You will be asked to answer three questions about what the speakers say in each conversation. Select the best response to each question and mark the letter (A), (B), (C) or (D) on your answer sheet. The conversations will not be printed in your test book and will be spoken only one time.

39. Who most likely are the listeners?

   (A) Apartment managers
   (B) Scientific researchers
   (C) Graphic designers
   (D) Staff recruiters

40. What type of product is the speaker discussing?

   (A) A communication system
   (B) A construction tool
   (C) A staff uniform
   (D) A security device

41. What will the listeners do next?

   (A) Watch a demonstration
   (B) Tour a facility
   (C) Receive keycards
   (D) Separate into groups

42. Where does the speaker work?

   (A) At a travel agency
   (B) At an accounting firm
   (C) At a hotel
   (D) At a restaurant

43. Why is the speaker calling?

   (A) To discuss a trip itinerary
   (B) To request some information
   (C) To provide feedback on a proposal
   (D) To reschedule a presentation

44. What does the speaker mean when she says, "we won't be doing any sightseeing"?

   (A) A tour is no longer offered.
   (B) A schedule will be full.
   (C) Some tickets are too expensive.
   (D) Some attractions are closed.

45. Who most likely are the listeners?

   (A) Restaurant managers
   (B) Advertising executives
   (C) Product designers
   (D) Factory supervisors

46. What is the speaker mainly discussing?

   (A) Biodegradable bags
   (B) Recycled furniture
   (C) Green energy
   (D) Reusable straws

47. Why does the speaker think a product will be popular?

   (A) It will have an attractive appearance.
   (B) It will be cheap to purchase.
   (C) It will come in a variety of sizes.
   (D) It will be easily portable.

Sales Summary	
Furniture (Without Extended Warranty)	32
Furniture (With Extended Warranty)	17
Appliances (Without Extended Warranty)	38
Appliances (With Extended Warranty)	21

48. Why does the speaker congratulate the listener?

(A) She recently transferred to the head office.
(B) She was promoted to sales manager.
(C) Her job application was accepted.
(D) Her branch broke a company record.

49. Look at the graphic. Which number needs to be corrected?

(A) 32
(B) 17
(C) 38
(D) 21

50. What does the speaker advise the listener to do?

(A) Submit a document
(B) Check an e-mail
(C) Review a warranty
(D) Contact a customer

READING TEST

In the Reading test, you will read a variety of texts and answer several different types of reading comprehension questions. The entire Reading test will last 75 minutes. There are three parts, and directions are given for each part. You are encouraged to answer as many questions as possible within the time allowed. You must mark your answers on the separate answer sheet. Do not write your answers in your test book.

PART 5

Directions: A word or phrase is missing in each of the sentences below. Four answer choices are given below each sentence. Select the best answer to complete the sentence. Then mark the letter (A), (B), (C), or (D) on your answer sheet.

1. Fleet Accounting hopes to ------- a part-time office assistant to help with general duties.

    (A) determine
    (B) advertise
    (C) recruit
    (D) lead

2. Hotel guests can book the scuba diving course and temple tour ------- or as part of a discounted package.

    (A) separates
    (B) separation
    (C) separating
    (D) separately

3. The chairman of the tennis club asked Mary Hampton whether ------- would be interested in becoming the club's treasurer.

    (A) herself
    (B) she
    (C) hers
    (D) her

4. Martyn usually arrives at the office much ------- than any of the other employees at Grayson Design.

    (A) earliest
    (B) earlier
    (C) early
    (D) the earliest

5. The head of the human resources department will be leading an ------- for new recruits at the training center in Bancroft.

    (A) orientation
    (B) orienting
    (C) orientations
    (D) oriented

6. Employees can learn about a wide variety of career advancement opportunities ------- our monthly newsletter.

    (A) around
    (B) between
    (C) under
    (D) through

7. Although it has received several surprisingly negative reviews, the new movie by Artem Popov is likely to ------- win awards.

    (A) ahead
    (B) still
    (C) very
    (D) after

8. Customers must retain and provide a proof of purchase ------- return a product to Denham Department Store.

    (A) so
    (B) but
    (C) in addition to
    (D) in order to

9. At this time, bids ------- publicly by Catasauqua Area School District for a contract to install and maintain new boilers in the region's many schools.

    (A) are accepting
    (B) are being accepted
    (C) accept
    (D) have accepted

10. ------- he decided to move to downtown Chicago, Mr. Cassidy lived in a beautiful house overlooking a lake.

    (A) Since
    (B) Before
    (C) Rather
    (D) Whether

11. Ms. Arterton is ------- with employees who offer to work an extra shift during the busy festive period.

    (A) impressive
    (B) impress
    (C) impressed
    (D) impressing

12. Ms. Martinez was eventually able to find the set of keys she dropped with ------- from several passers-by.

    (A) assist
    (B) assistance
    (C) assistant
    (D) assisted

13. The company president decided to offer the customer care supervisor position to Cheryl Arnett, ------- her lack of experience in management.

    (A) because
    (B) instead
    (C) despite
    (D) moreover

14. The star player of the Milford United plans to retire ------- the team wins the championship this year.

    (A) even if
    (B) at least
    (C) in case
    (D) away from

15. Paul Garfield, the orchestra's longest-serving member, ------- as one of the most talented musicians in the world.

    (A) regards
    (B) to regard
    (C) regarding
    (D) is regarded

16. The bridge over Nantwich River is ------- closed to cyclists and pedestrians due to strong crosswinds.

    (A) previously
    (B) individually
    (C) lastly
    (D) temporarily

PART 6

Directions: Read the texts that follow. A word, phrase, or sentence is missing in parts of each text. Four answer choices for each question are given below the text. Select the best answer to complete the text. Then mark the letter (A), (B), (C) or (D) on your answer sheet.

Questions 17-20 refer to the following letter.

Dear sir/madam,

Thank you for contacting me regarding Ms. Tina Matthews. I can absolutely ------- Ms. Matthews for
17.
the accounting assistant position she has applied for at your firm. Ms. Matthews ------- at Penforth
18.
Manufacturing's headquarters in Swindon. Her primary role here is to assist the finance manager with
staff payroll and department budgets. She has shown an outstanding work ethic during her time here,
and we consider her a valuable team member. I have no doubt that she would be a great ------- to any
19.
corporation she works for throughout her career. -------.
20.

Sincerely,

Gareth Evans

Personnel Manager

Penforth Manufacturing

17. (A) recruit
    (B) remember
    (C) request
    (D) recommend

18. (A) employs
    (B) employed
    (C) is employed
    (D) was employed

19. (A) asset
    (B) outcome
    (C) decision
    (D) effort

20. (A) Please don't hesitate to contact me if you
        have any questions.
    (B) Ms. Matthews will begin her new job on the
        first day of October.
    (C) I appreciate your assistance with the
        recruitment process.
    (D) In conclusion, I feel Ms. Matthews is fully
        deserving of the promotion.

Questions 21-24 refer to the following advertisement.

Klattenburg Nature Walks invites you to sign up for our relaxing yet invigorating walk around the picturesque hills and meadows that ------- the town of Klattenburg!
21.

Our walks start at Bergen Farm by the Eisel River, and we set off along a pleasant footpath leading to Weiss Mountain. During the walk, our local tour guides will point out some of the beautiful flowers that have made this area so popular. -------. People are often attracted by their unique, sweet scent, but
22.
please refrain from picking any of them.

Around noon, we will take a break and enjoy a delicious picnic lunch of bread, cheese and ham. This gives you an opportunity to rest ------- enjoying the stunning views of the countryside.
23.

After the picnic, we will carry on towards Klattenburg Meadow, where you will be able ------- some of
24.
the deer that are native to the area.

21. (A) surrounding
    (B) surround
    (C) surrounds
    (D) to surround

22. (A) The walk takes about four hours and
        covers a lot of ground.
    (B) Feel free to ask your guide about anything
        you see.
    (C) A few of these grow only in the lush
        meadows in this region.
    (D) It is highly recommended to wear sturdy
        hiking boots.

23. (A) while
    (B) however
    (C) whereas
    (D) yet

24. (A) observing
    (B) observe
    (C) have observed
    (D) to observe

PART 7

Directions: In this part you will read a selection of texts, such as magazine and newspaper articles, e-mails, and instant messages. Each text or set of texts is followed by several questions. Select the best answer for each question and mark the letter (A), (B), (C), or (D) on your answer sheet.

Questions 25-26 refer to the following advertisement.

<u>Do you like working outdoors</u>
<u>and speaking to new people?</u>

If so, then Loktite Corporation may have the perfect job for you! Loktite is the leading manufacturer of plastic storage containers that are used in millions of homes worldwide to keep food fresh. Our products are scientifically proven to provide the highest level of freshness.

In an effort to reach even more new customers, our "street team" of salespeople frequently visits neighborhoods to demonstrate our products and assist local residents in making an order. If you think you might like to join our street team, simply come on down to the Loktite careers day on March 15 and have an interview with one of our branch managers. The event will be held at Gorley Conference Center from 10 a.m. until 5 p.m.

25. What position is being advertised?
    (A) A production line worker
    (B) A sales representative
    (C) A scientific researcher
    (D) A branch manager

26. What are interested individuals encouraged to do?
    (A) Attend a recruitment event
    (B) Submit an application form
    (C) Visit Loktite's head office
    (D) Call a conference center

Questions 27-29 refer to the following e-mail.

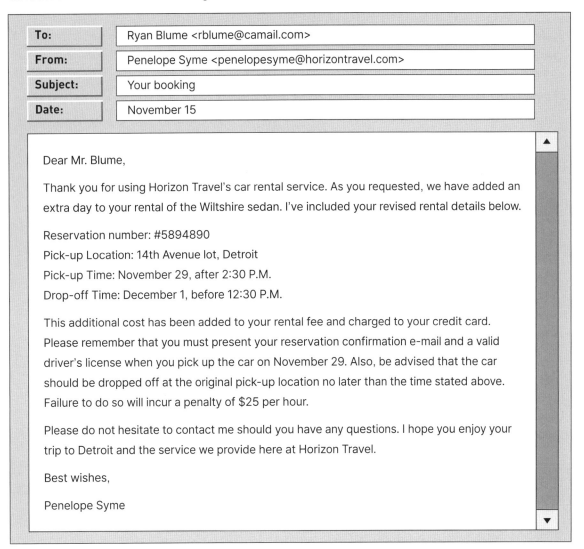

To:	Ryan Blume <rblume@camail.com>
From:	Penelope Syme <penelopesyme@horizontravel.com>
Subject:	Your booking
Date:	November 15

Dear Mr. Blume,

Thank you for using Horizon Travel's car rental service. As you requested, we have added an extra day to your rental of the Wiltshire sedan. I've included your revised rental details below.

Reservation number: #5894890
Pick-up Location: 14th Avenue lot, Detroit
Pick-up Time: November 29, after 2:30 P.M.
Drop-off Time: December 1, before 12:30 P.M.

This additional cost has been added to your rental fee and charged to your credit card. Please remember that you must present your reservation confirmation e-mail and a valid driver's license when you pick up the car on November 29. Also, be advised that the car should be dropped off at the original pick-up location no later than the time stated above. Failure to do so will incur a penalty of $25 per hour.

Please do not hesitate to contact me should you have any questions. I hope you enjoy your trip to Detroit and the service we provide here at Horizon Travel.

Best wishes,

Penelope Syme

27. Why was the e-mail sent?
(A) To outline a business trip itinerary
(B) To detail equipment rental policies
(C) To announce a new service
(D) To confirm arrangements for a vehicle

28. What is indicated about Mr. Blume?
(A) He has extended a rental period.
(B) He is a regular customer of Horizon Travel.
(C) He is visiting Detroit for the first time.
(D) He received a discount on a service.

29. According to the e-mail, what is Mr. Blume required to show when he arrives at the 14th Avenue lot?
(A) A payment receipt
(B) A driver's license
(C) A membership card
(D) A parking permit

July 19
Ms. Lucy Cooper
7212 Bradley Street
Louisville, KY 40204

Dear Ms. Cooper,

Did you realize that you can now pay your monthly electricity bills online? Since July 1, more and more of our customers have been signing up for an online account in order to take advantage of this useful new service. You can enjoy the following advantages:

▸ Pay your bills online quickly and securely using your credit card
▸ Log in to our Web site to view your current electricity rate and latest meter reading
▸ Receive 10 percent off selected appliances in our online store
▸ Protect the environment by switching to paperless billing to reduce waste
▸ Receive notifications by e-mail when your bill payment is late

Signing up for an online account could not be easier. Simply go to www.midvaleelectric.com and click on the tab that says "Pay Your Bills Online" to register for this service. We already have our customers' home addresses, meter readings, and electricity usage plans in our system, so all we need from you is your name and your Midvale Electric ID number.

Sincerely,

Jennifer Turner
Customer Service
Midvale Electric Company

---

30. What is the main purpose of the letter?

(A) To advertise a new company
(B) To request a bill payment
(C) To promote a new service
(D) To explain a billing error

31. What is NOT mentioned as a benefit of paying bills online?

(A) Reduction of wasted paper
(B) Lower electricity rates
(C) Discounts on online purchases
(D) E-mail alerts for overdue bills

32. What information must be provided in order to sign up for an online account?

(A) A recent meter reading
(B) A credit card number
(C) A home address
(D) A customer ID number

Questions 33-36 refer to the following announcement.

Residents of San Andreas have a unique opportunity to attend an interesting event this coming Saturday afternoon. The purpose of the event is to give residents a taste of the services provided by a highly-specialized and relatively uncommon company. Treasures & Trinkets may have just opened for business in San Andreas, but its stores in other cities have helped the company to gain a strong reputation for its team of experienced antiques specialists and its valuation services. — [1] —.

Visitors will be able to bring along old items, such as family heirlooms, and have them examined by Treasures & Trinkets' experts, who have specialized backgrounds in furniture, ceramics, jewelry, and art, among other things. — [2] —. Treasures & Trinkets representatives will give customers a bit of background about the items, offer an approximate valuation, and recommend how much the item should be insured for. — [3] —.

Booths and tents will be set up in Brayford Park in the historic Barrettown neighborhood of San Andreas. — [4] —. Those who are unable to attend can visit the store from Monday to Friday or go to www. treasuresandtrinkets.com, where they can submit pictures and receive an online valuation and history of an item. Tips on how you can become an appraiser and antiques expert are also available on our site.

33. What event is being held in Brayford Park?

   (A) A market offering local arts and crafts
   (B) A demonstration of a company's products
   (C) An appraisal of potentially valuable items
   (D) An exhibition of antiques found in the area

34. What is indicated about Treasures & Trinkets?

   (A) It provides insurance coverage for special items.
   (B) It recently opened a new store in San Andreas.
   (C) It specializes in the restoration of artifacts.
   (D) It is currently accepting donations from residents.

35. What is provided on the Web site?

   (A) Tips on taking care of old objects
   (B) Photographs of well-known antiques
   (C) Directions to business locations
   (D) Information on learning a new skill

36. In which of the positions marked [1], [2], [3] and [4] does the following sentence best belong?

   "The public can visit these booths for free from 1 P.M. to 6 P.M."

   (A) [1]
   (B) [2]
   (C) [3]
   (D) [4]

Carol Brent [10:25 A.M.]

Larry… Are you free right now? I need your opinion on our fleet of vehicles.

Larry Gallagher [10:26 A.M.]

My next meeting isn't until 11.

Carol Brent [10:28 A.M.]

Well, I've noticed that we've been turning away business because we just don't have enough trucks to deal with large relocation jobs. Don't you think we should expand the fleet?

Larry Gallagher [10:31 A.M.]

It's already been taken care of. I approved the purchase of five more heavy-cargo trucks a few days ago. They'll be here on our lot by the time you get back from your travels.

Carol Brent [10:33 A.M.]

I'm glad to hear it! And, I look forward to seeing them after my trip to Kingston.

Larry Gallagher [10:34 A.M.]

Another thing… on Tuesday, I spoke with a business owner who had requested our services before. I informed him that we're now in a position to help.

Carol Brent [10:36 A.M.]

That sounds great. The more business, the better!

37. At 10:26 A.M., what does Mr. Gallagher most likely mean when he writes, "My next meeting isn't until 11"?

(A) He would like Ms. Brent to join a meeting.
(B) He will make a change to his work schedule.
(C) He has time to give Ms. Brent some feedback.
(D) He plans to arrive early for a work appointment.

38. What type of business do Mr. Gallagher and Ms. Brent work for?

(A) A vehicle manufacturer
(B) A moving company
(C) An auto shop
(D) A car showroom

39. What is suggested about Ms. Brent?

(A) She recently joined the business.
(B) She is an experienced driver.
(C) She is concerned about expenditure.
(D) She is planning to take a trip.

40. What did Mr. Gallagher do earlier in the week?

(A) He met with some investors.
(B) He helped Ms. Brent choose some vehicles.
(C) He contacted a potential client.
(D) He recruited a new employee.

Questions 41-45 refer to the following memo and article.

To: All Board Members
From: Quincy Theroux
Subject: Steve Blake
Date: September 10

Fellow Members of the Board,

I'm sending this message just to go over the main points that we decided to include in the press release that we will submit to media outlets later today. After announcing Steve Blake's resignation, we will mention my temporary appointment as CEO and I will express my gratitude for Steve's hard work. Steve has indicated to us that he does not mind if we also mention his reason for leaving. He has prepared a quote that will also be included in the press release. Please remember that any subsequent questions from the press should be directed to the president of the committee responsible for finding us a new CEO.

Thank you,

Quincy Theroux
Chairman
Zenco Corporation

A CHANGE IN ZENCO CORPORATION

(September 11) Zenco Corporation's board of directors today announced that Steve Blake will step down as chief executive officer, effective October 1. Quincy Theroux, chairman of the board, will serve as temporary CEO while a search is conducted to find a permanent replacement. Mr. Blake will be appointed as president and CEO of a large international shipping company on November 1.

"We are extremely grateful to Steve for the leadership he has shown over the past ten years. In that time, the company has grown rapidly and doubled its profits," said Mr. Theroux. "We hope Steve achieves even more success in the next stage of his career."

"The things we have achieved at Zenco have helped the company to become the leading online education service in the United Kingdom," said Mr. Blake. "I'm very proud of all our accomplishments and I'm grateful for the support I have received from my fellow board members."

Melinda Dillinger, the president of the nomination and governance committee, is leading the search for Mr. Blake's replacement and has asked executive recruitment expert Tristan Murphy to assist her with the search. They hope to fill the position by the end of this year.

41. What is the main purpose of Mr. Theroux's memo?

   (A) To inform colleagues about a hiring decision
   (B) To finalize the details of an announcement
   (C) To request that board members attend a meeting
   (D) To explain the reason for Mr. Blake's resignation

42. In the memo, the word "express" in paragraph 1, line 3 is closest in meaning to

   (A) facilitate
   (B) pursue
   (C) expedite
   (D) convey

43. Who will be responsible for handling questions from the press?

   (A) Steve Blake
   (B) Quincy Theroux
   (C) Melinda Dillinger
   (D) Tristan Murphy

44. What is indicated about Zenco Corporation in the article?

   (A) It is planning to hire more employees this month.
   (B) It is involved in the global shipping of packages.
   (C) It has doubled its earnings in the past decade.
   (D) It has recently launched online classes.

45. By what date does Zenco Corporation expect to appoint a new CEO?

   (A) October 1
   (B) October 31
   (C) November 1
   (D) December 31

City of Eureka, IL
Meeting of the Mayor and City Council Members - Monday, April 1

Roll Call (Mark 'X' if in attendance)

Meeting chaired by: James Hallman (Mayor of Eureka) X

Council members:

Burt Bulmer	Nina Delson	Roy Grainger X	Susie Loudon X
Sarah Masters	Gareth Hart X	Barry Cobb X	Colin Watts
Tom Benson (Fire Chief) X	Paul Carter (Police Chief) X	Kristi Carr (City Planner) X	

Permitted absences: Due to the ongoing issues affecting residents following last week's storms and flooding, Councilman Bulmer, Councilman Watts, and Councilwoman Masters have been officially excused from this meeting.

Meeting Agenda – April 1

Item	Approximate Time	Overview
A	8:45 a.m. – 9:00 a.m.	Review of the minutes of last month's meeting
B	9:00 a.m. – 9:20 a.m.	Presentation by the City Planner regarding the replanting of trees along Slater Avenue
C	9:20 a.m. – 9:50 a.m.	Talk on payment of council members' expenses for the upcoming trip to the Illinois Infrastructure Conference
D	9:50 a.m. – 10:15 a.m.	Proposal to use money budgeted for the Main Street maintenance fund for the landscaping of Byers Park
E	10:15 a.m. – 10:35 a.m.	Talk and presentation by the Fire Chief regarding the fire department's request for new vehicles
F	10:35 a.m. – 11:00 a.m.	Brief discussion led by Barry Cobb on potential sites for holding this summer's Eurekafest outdoor concert

To: Mayor James Hallman <jhallman@eurekagov.com>
From: Gareth Hart <ghart@eurekagov.com>
Date: April 4
Subject: Meeting Follow-up

Dear Mayor Hallman,

Thank you for leading the very rewarding meeting on April 1. I found our discussion about Main Street and Byers Park to be highly beneficial and productive. However, as you may have noticed, I had to leave the room for around twenty minutes at 9:30 A.M., so I missed most of that session. I hope you and I can find some time to discuss that topic when we meet for lunch tomorrow.

Best regards,

Gareth Hart

46. What is indicated about the city of Eureka?

(A) Its council members meet on a weekly basis.
(B) It has recently appointed new city officials.
(C) It will soon undergo a period of expansion.
(D) It has experienced inclement weather.

47. Which council member was absent from the meeting without authorization?

(A) Barry Cobb
(B) Sarah Masters
(C) Nina Delson
(D) Colin Watts

48. Which agenda item will feature a presentation from Tom Benson?

(A) Item B
(B) Item C
(C) Item D
(D) Item E

49. What topic does Mr. Hart wish to discuss with Mayor Hallman?

(A) The urgent need for road repairs in Eureka
(B) Travel expenses for an upcoming trip
(C) Possible locations for a music performance
(D) The reallocation of some budget funds

50. In the e-mail, the word "highly" in paragraph 1, line 2, is closest in meaning to

(A) severely
(B) overly
(C) profitably
(D) exceedingly

DAY 05

LC
Half Test

30 min
제한 시간 30분

MP3 바로듣기

강의 바로보기

정답 및 해설 p. 51

PART 1

Directions: For each question in this part, you will hear four statements about a picture in your test book. When you hear the statements, you must select the one statement that best describes what you see in the picture. Then find the number of the question on your answer sheet and mark your answer. The statements will not be printed in your test book and will be spoken only one time.

1.

2.

PART 2

Directions: You will hear a question or statement and three responses spoken in English. They will not be printed in your test book and will be spoken only one time. Select the best response to the question or statement and mark the letter (A), (B), or (C) on your answer sheet.

3. Mark your answer on your answer sheet.

4. Mark your answer on your answer sheet.

5. Mark your answer on your answer sheet.

6. Mark your answer on your answer sheet.

7. Mark your answer on your answer sheet.

8. Mark your answer on your answer sheet.

9. Mark your answer on your answer sheet.

10. Mark your answer on your answer sheet.

11. Mark your answer on your answer sheet.

12. Mark your answer on your answer sheet.

13. Mark your answer on your answer sheet.

14. Mark your answer on your answer sheet.

15. Mark your answer on your answer sheet.

16. Mark your answer on your answer sheet.

17. Mark your answer on your answer sheet.

18. Mark your answer on your answer sheet.

19. Mark your answer on your answer sheet.

20. Mark your answer on your answer sheet.

PART 3

Directions: You will hear some conversations between two or more people. You will be asked to answer three questions about what the speakers say in each conversation. Select the best response to each question and mark the letter (A), (B), (C) or (D) on your answer sheet. The conversations will not be printed in your test book and will be spoken only one time.

21. What does the man say he is considering doing?
    (A) Eating more healthily
    (B) Joining a fitness center
    (C) Applying for a new job
    (D) Purchasing exercise equipment

22. What type of event does the woman mention?
    (A) A staff orientation
    (B) A seasonal sale
    (C) A grand opening
    (D) A sports contest

23. What does the woman explain to the man?
    (A) How to obtain a membership
    (B) How to locate a business
    (C) How to check a schedule
    (D) How to access a Web site

24. What are the speakers mainly discussing?
    (A) An overseas expansion
    (B) A branch merger
    (C) A landscaping project
    (D) An employment opportunity

25. Which aspect of a building is most important to the speakers?
    (A) A spacious parking lot
    (B) Modern facilities
    (C) A convenient location
    (D) Low rental costs

26. What does the woman say she forgot to tell the man about?
    (A) A deadline
    (B) A meeting date
    (C) A staff bonus
    (D) A budget

27. What are the men picking up?
    (A) Sports equipment
    (B) Furniture
    (C) Office supplies
    (D) Uniforms

28. What problem are the men discussing?
    (A) An order is incorrect.
    (B) A business is closed.
    (C) A product is damaged.
    (D) An address is wrong.

29. What does the woman suggest the men do?
    (A) Call a store owner
    (B) Visit a different location
    (C) Cancel an order
    (D) Wait a little longer

30. What type of event are the speakers planning?
    (A) A company trip
    (B) A training seminar
    (C) A recruitment event
    (D) An annual dinner

31. What does the woman like about a location?
    (A) Its size
    (B) Its convenience
    (C) Its affordability
    (D) Its food

32. Why does the woman say, "we have a decent budget this year"?
    (A) To praise the man's efforts
    (B) To reassure the man
    (C) To suggest a budget revision
    (D) To express surprise

Ayling Culinary School Beginner Baking Classes	
Monday	5:00 P.M.
Wednesday	7:30 A.M. 6:30 P.M.
Friday	6:00 P.M.

33. What is the man concerned about?

(A) A school is too far away.
(B) Some classes may be full.
(C) A parking lot is too small.
(D) Some fees are too high.

34. Look at the graphic. Which class time does the woman refer to?

(A) 5:00 P.M.
(B) 7:30 A.M.
(C) 6:30 P.M.
(D) 6:00 P.M.

35. What does the man suggest?

(A) Checking a schedule
(B) Contacting a school
(C) Sharing transportation
(D) Having a meal

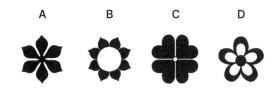

A　　　B　　　C　　　D

36. What were customers invited to do?

(A) Enter a competition
(B) Attend a grand opening event
(C) Sign up for a membership
(D) Take part in a survey

37. What will the speakers do next week?

(A) Create a catalog
(B) Launch a Web site
(C) Offer a discount
(D) Distribute flyers

38. Look at the graphic. Which logo design will the speakers use?

(A) Logo A
(B) Logo B
(C) Logo C
(D) Logo D

PART 4

Directions: You will hear some talks given by a single speaker. You will be asked to answer three questions about what the speakers say in each conversation. Select the best response to each question and mark the letter (A), (B), (C) or (D) on your answer sheet. The conversations will not be printed in your test book and will be spoken only one time.

39. Who most likely is the speaker?

   (A) A factory manager
   (B) A fashion designer
   (C) A shoe salesperson
   (D) A marketing specialist

40. Why are more samples needed?

   (A) To distribute to social media users
   (B) To prove the high quality of a product
   (C) To encourage people to join a membership
   (D) To give to customers who spend a certain amount

41. What will the listeners do next?

   (A) Tour a facility
   (B) Watch a slideshow
   (C) Meet with a celebrity
   (D) Sign a business contract

42. What type of product is being advertised?

   (A) A sleeping bag
   (B) A backpack
   (C) A tent
   (D) A bed

43. What does the speaker say is unique about a product?

   (A) It can be easily washed.
   (B) It is highly durable.
   (C) It is lightweight.
   (D) It has extra padding.

44. How can the listeners receive a complimentary item?

   (A) By entering a code online
   (B) By signing up for a membership
   (C) By joining a mailing list
   (D) By visiting a store in person

45. What does the speaker mean when he says, "Dalebrook has a lot of excellent restaurants"?

   (A) There are several potential event venues.
   (B) A town is receiving more tourists.
   (C) There are many new job opportunities.
   (D) A choice was not easy to make.

46. According to the speaker, what will Holly's receive?

   (A) A tax exemption
   (B) A certificate
   (C) A trophy
   (D) A plaque

47. What does the speaker invite the listeners to do?

   (A) Applaud an award winner
   (B) Sample some menu items
   (C) Join him on the stage
   (D) Make their way to the entrance

Average Customer Rating

48. Who most likely is Mr. Berger?

    (A) An engineer
    (B) An architect
    (C) An interior designer
    (D) A landscaper

49. Look at the graphic. Which device did the
    speaker choose?

    (A) Blade 3000
    (B) Whizz 550
    (C) Flyer 1000
    (D) Phase 200

50. What does the speaker offer to do?

    (A) Check an invoice
    (B) Send an image
    (C) Assemble a product
    (D) Increase a budget

시원스쿨LAB

DAY 01　LC Half Test

1. (B)	**2.** (A)	**3.** (B)	**4.** (C)	**5.** (A)
6. (C)	**7.** (C)	**8.** (B)	**9.** (B)	**10.** (A)
11. (B)	**12.** (C)	**13.** (A)	**14.** (C)	**15.** (B)
16. (A)	**17.** (A)	**18.** (A)	**19.** (B)	**20.** (B)
21. (D)	**22.** (D)	**23.** (B)	**24.** (C)	**25.** (D)
26. (B)	**27.** (C)	**28.** (A)	**29.** (D)	**30.** (D)
31. (A)	**32.** (D)	**33.** (B)	**34.** (D)	**35.** (B)
36. (B)	**37.** (B)	**38.** (D)	**39.** (B)	**40.** (D)
41. (C)	**42.** (D)	**43.** (B)	**44.** (D)	**45.** (C)
46. (C)	**47.** (A)	**48.** (B)	**49.** (A)	**50.** (D)

Part 1

1.
(A) She's looking out the window.
(B) She's holding a mobile phone.
(C) She's sipping from a cup.
(D) She's purchasing some food.

(A) 여자가 창문 밖을 내다보고 있다.
(B) 여자가 휴대전화기를 붙잡고 있다.
(C) 여자가 컵에 든 것을 조금씩 마시고 있다.
(D) 여자가 일부 음식을 구입하고 있다.

해설 (A) 여자의 시선이 창문 밖을 향하고 있지 않으므로 오답.
(B) 여자가 손으로 휴대전화기를 붙잡고 있는 자세를 취하고 있으므로 정답.
(C) 여자가 컵에 든 것을 마시는 자세를 취하고 있지 않으므로 오답.
(D) 여자가 음식을 구입하는 상황이 아니므로 오답.

어휘 **look out** ~의 밖을 내다보다 **hold** ~을 붙잡다, ~을 쥐다, ~을 들다 **sip from** ~을 조금씩 마시다, ~을 홀짝거리다 **purchase** ~을 구입하다

2.
(A) A wooden structure has been built outside.
(B) A construction crew is working on a building.
(C) Some ladders are leaning against a wall.
(D) Construction equipment is lifting tree branches.

(A) 목재 구조물이 외부에 지어져 있다.
(B) 공사장 인부들이 건물에 대해 작업하고 있다.
(C) 몇몇 사다리가 한쪽 벽에 기대어져 있다.
(D) 공사 장비가 나뭇가지들을 들어올리고 있다.

해설 (A) 목재 구조물이 외부 공간에 지어져 있는 상태이므로 정답.

(B) 작업 중인 공사장 인부들을 찾아볼 수 없으므로 오답.
(C) 벽에 기대어져 있는 사다리를 찾아볼 수 없으므로 오답.
(D) 공사 장비가 나뭇가지가 아닌 목재를 들어올리고 있으므로 오답.

어휘 **wooden** 목재의, 나무로 된 **structure** 구조(물) **crew** (함께 일하는) 작업자들, 팀, 조 **work on** ~에 대해 작업하다 **ladder** 사다리 **lean against** ~에 기대다 **equipment** 장비 **lift** ~을 들어올리다 **branch** 나뭇가지

Part 2

3. When would you like to have your dental appointment?
(A) At the dentist's office.
(B) At 3 o'clock on Thursday.
(C) Just a regular cleaning.

언제 치과 예약을 잡으시겠어요?
(A) 치과에서요.
(B) 목요일 3시요.
(C) 그냥 주기적인 세정이요.

해설 언제 치과 예약을 잡고 싶은지 묻고 있으므로 특정 시점을 나타내는 표현으로 답변하는 (B)가 정답이다. (A)는 dental과 발음이 유사한 dentist를 활용해 혼동을 유발하는 오답이다.

어휘 **would like to do** ~하기를 원하다, ~하고자 하다 **dental** 치과의, 치아의 **appointment** 예약, 약속 **dentist** 치과 의사 **regular** 주기적인, 정기적인, 보통의, 일반적인 **cleaning** 세정, 세척, 청소

4. Do you need the client's e-mail address?
(A) Check your junk folder.
(B) It's in the business district.
(C) No, I saved it on my computer.

그 고객의 이메일 주소가 필요하신가요?
(A) 정크 메일 폴더를 확인해 보세요.
(B) 그건 상업 지구에 있습니다.
(C) 아뇨, 제 컴퓨터에 저장해 두었어요.

해설 특정 고객의 이메일 주소가 필요한지 묻고 있으므로 부정을 뜻하는 No와 함께 the client's e-mail address를 it로 지칭해 컴퓨터에 저장했다는 말로 고객의 이메일 주소가 필요하지 않은 이유를 알리는 (C)가 정답이다. (A)는 e-mail에서 연상 가능한 junk folder를 활용해 혼동을 유발하는 오답이다.

어휘 **junk folder** 정크 메일 폴더 **district** 지구, 구역 **save** ~을 저장하다

5. Who is allowed to use the company credit card?

(A) Only the supervisors.
(B) We just accept cash.
(C) I doubt it.

누가 회사 법인 카드를 이용하도록 허용되나요?
(A) 오직 책임자들만요.
(B) 저희는 현금만 받습니다.
(C) 그렇지 않을 거예요.

해설 누가 회사 법인 카드를 이용하도록 허용되는지 묻고 있으므로 그 대상자에 해당되는 직책으로 답변하는 (A)가 정답이다. (B)는 credit card에서 연상 가능한 cash를 활용해 혼동을 유발하는 오답이다.

어휘 **be allowed to do** ~하도록 허용되다 **supervisor** 책임자, 상사, 감독 **accept** ~을 받아들이다, ~을 수락하다 **doubt** ~을 확신하지 못하다, ~을 의심하다

6. This week's sales have improved, right?

(A) They're half-price right now.
(B) A wide range of products.
(C) Yes, but not by much.

이번 주 판매량이 향상된 게 맞죠?
(A) 그것들이 지금은 반값이에요.
(B) 아주 다양한 제품이요.
(C) 네, 하지만 많이는 아니예요.

해설 이번 주 판매량이 향상된 게 맞는지 묻고 있으므로 긍정을 뜻하는 Yes와 함께 그 차이가 많지는 않다는 말을 덧붙인 (C)가 정답이다. (A)와 (B)는 sales에서 연상 가능한 half-price와 products를 각각 활용해 혼동을 유발하는 오답이다.

어휘 **sales** 판매(량), 영업, 매출 **improve** 개선되다, 향상되다, ~을 개선하다, ~을 향상시키다 **a wide range of** 아주 다양한 **by** (차이) ~만큼, ~ 정도

7. Have you been introduced to our new manager yet?

(A) Mr. Parker does, I think.
(B) I'm hoping to be promoted.
(C) Yes, we met at lunchtime.

혹시 우리 신임 부장님께 소개 인사하셨나요?
(A) 파커 씨께서 하시는 것 같아요.
(B) 전 승진되기를 바라고 있습니다.
(C) 네, 점심 시간에 만나 뵀습니다.

해설 신임 부장에게 소개했는지 묻고 있으므로 긍정을 뜻하는 Yes와 함께 언제 만나서 소개했는지 알리는 말을 덧붙인 (C)가 정답이다. (A)와 (B)는 new manager에서 연상 가능한 사람 이름 Mr. Parker와 promoted를 각각 활용해 혼동을 유발하는 오답이다.

어휘 **introduce** ~을 소개하다 **hope to do** ~하기를 바라다

promote ~을 승진시키다, ~을 홍보하다

8. Why is the street parade postponed?

(A) That's on Tenth Avenue.
(B) Because of the weather forecast.
(C) Sorry, we can't wait any longer.

거리 퍼레이드가 왜 연기된 거죠?
(A) 10번 애비뉴에서 합니다.
(B) 일기 예보 때문예요.
(C) 죄송하지만, 저희는 더 이상 기다릴 수 없어요.

해설 거리 퍼레이드가 왜 연기된 것인지 묻고 있으므로 Why와 어울리는 Because of와 함께 일기 예보를 이유로 언급한 (B)가 정답이다. (A)는 street에서 연상 가능한 Tenth Avenue를, (C)는 postponed에서 연상 가능한 can't wait any longer를 각각 활용해 혼동을 유발하는 오답이다.

어휘 **postpone** ~을 연기하다, ~을 미루다 **not ~ any longer** 더 이상 ~ 않다

9. Doesn't the package at the reception desk need to be sent?

(A) Yes, she's the receptionist.
(B) Thanks. I almost forgot.
(C) Probably some office supplies.

안내 데스크에 있는 배송 물품이 보내져야 하지 않나요?
(A) 네, 그분은 안내 담당 직원입니다.
(B) 감사합니다. 깜빡 잊을 뻔했어요.
(C) 아마 몇몇 사무용품일 거예요.

해설 안내 데스크에 있는 배송 물품이 보내져야 하지 않는지 묻고 있으므로 그 사실을 알려준 것에 대한 감사 인사와 함께 깜빡 잊을 뻔했다는 말을 덧붙인 (B)가 정답이다. (A)는 reception과 발음이 유사한 receptionist를 활용해 혼동을 유발하는 답변으로, Yes 뒤에 이어지는 말이 배송 물품 발송과 관련 없는 오답이다.

어휘 **package** 배송 물품, 포장물, 소포 **reception desk** 안내 데스크, 접수 데스크 **receptionist** 안내 담당 직원, 접수 담당 직원 **supplies** 용품, 물품

10. Who took the pictures for that article you wrote for the magazine?

(A) A photographer named Gary Brown.
(B) Yes, he's an excellent writer.
(C) I rarely read anything these days.

그 잡지를 위해 작성하신 기사에 필요하셨던 사진들을 누가 찍었나요?
(A) 개리 브라운이라는 이름의 사진 작가요.
(B) 네, 그분은 훌륭한 작가입니다.
(C) 저는 요즘 좀처럼 아무것도 읽지 않아요.

해설 잡지용 기사에 필요했던 사진을 누가 찍었는지 묻고 있으므로 특정 사진 작가의 이름을 밝히는 (A)가 정답이다. (B)는 의문사 의문문에 맞지 않는 Yes로 답변하는 오답이며, (C)는 magazine에서 연상 가능한 read를 활용해 혼동을 유발하는 오답이다.

어휘 **take a picture** 사진을 찍다 **photographer** 사진 작가 **named A** A라는 이름의 **rarely** 좀처럼 ~ 않다

11. How often should the filters in the air conditioning unit be cleaned?

(A) It's getting warm in here.
(B) Randy knows more about that.
(C) There's a mop in the closet.

에어컨 기기의 필터를 얼마나 자주 세척해야 하나요?
(A) 이 안이 점점 따뜻해지고 있어요.
(B) 랜디 씨가 그것에 관해 더 잘 알아요.
(C) 벽장에 대걸레가 있어요.

해설 에어컨 기기의 필터를 얼마나 자주 세척해야 하는지 묻고 있으므로 세척하는 일을 that으로 지칭해 랜디 씨가 더 잘 안다는 말로 관련 정보를 확인할 수 있는 방법을 알리는 (B)가 정답이다. (A)는 air conditioning에서 연상 가능한 getting warm을, (C)는 cleaned에서 연상 가능한 mop을 각각 활용해 혼동을 유발하는 오답이다.

어휘 **air conditioning unit** 에어컨 기기, 냉방 장치 **get 형용사** ~한 상태가 되다 **mop** 대걸레 **closet** 벽장, 찬장

12. You have a long commute to the office, don't you?

(A) At the train station.
(B) The building across from here.
(C) It's the worst part of my day.

사무실까지 통근하시는 시간이 길지 않으신가요?
(A) 기차역에서요.
(B) 이곳 맞은편에 있는 건물이요.
(C) 제 하루 중에서 가장 끔찍한 부분이죠.

해설 사무실까지 통근하는 시간이 길지 않은지 묻고 있으므로 그 시간을 It로 지칭해 가장 끔찍하다는 말로 통근 시간이 아주 길다는 뜻을 나타낸 (C)가 정답이다. (B)는 office에서 연상 가능한 building을 활용해 혼동을 유발하는 오답이다.

어휘 **commute** 통근 **across from** ~ 맞은편에, ~ 건너편에 **worst** 가장 나쁜, 최악의

13. What should we prepare for Saturday's hiking trip?

(A) Make sure you bring water.
(B) By doing some warm-up stretches.
(C) It was a scenic trail.

토요일에 있을 등산 여행을 위해 우리가 뭘 준비해야 하죠?

(A) 반드시 물을 챙겨오도록 하세요.
(B) 준비 운동을 위한 스트레칭을 하는 것으로요.
(C) 경치 좋은 등산로였어요.

해설 토요일에 있을 등산 여행을 위해 뭘 준비해야 하는지 묻고 있으므로 물을 꼭 챙겨오라고 당부하며 준비물을 알리는 (A)가 정답이다. (B)는 prepare에서 연상 가능한 warm-up stretches를, (C)는 hiking trip에서 연상 가능한 scenic trail을 각각 활용해 혼동을 유발하는 오답이다.

어휘 **prepare** ~을 준비하다 **make sure (that)** 반드시 ~하도록 하다, ~하는 것을 확실히 해 두다 **by** (방법) ~하는 것으로, ~함으로써 **warm-up** 준비 운동 **scenic** 경치가 좋은 **trail** 등산로, 산길

14. Don't you need a permit to park here?

(A) Sure, go ahead.
(B) It's a really nice park.
(C) Not after 7 P.M.

이곳에 주차하려면 허가증이 필요하지 않은가요?
(A) 물론이죠, 어서 하세요.
(B) 정말 멋진 공원이에요.
(C) 오후 7시 이후엔 아닙니다.

해설 특정 장소에 주차하는 데 허가증이 필요하지 않은지 묻고 있으므로 오후 7시 이후에는 아니라는 말로 7시 이후에는 허가증 없이 주차할 수 있다는 뜻을 나타낸 (C)가 정답이다. (B)는 park의 다른 의미(주차하다, 공원)를 활용해 혼동을 유발하는 오답이다.

어휘 **permit** 허가증 **park** v. 주차하다 n. 공원 **go ahead** 어서 하세요, 먼저 하세요

15. Do you want a room with a beach view or a view of the pool?

(A) A walk along the beach sounds nice.
(B) It makes no difference to me.
(C) You can check in at 2 P.M.

해변 경관이 보이는 객실을 원하시나요, 아니면 수영장 경관이 보이는 객실을 원하시나요?
(A) 해변을 따라 걷는 산책이 아주 좋은 것 같아요.
(B) 저는 아무래도 좋습니다.
(C) 오후 2시에 체크인하실 수 있습니다.

해설 해변 경관이 보이는 객실을 원하는지, 아니면 수영장 경관이 보이는 객실을 원하는지 묻는 선택 의문문에 아무래도 좋다는 말로 어느 쪽이든 상관없다는 뜻을 나타낸 (B)가 정답이다. (A)는 beach를 반복한 답변으로, 객실 선택과 관련 없는 산책에 대한 의견을 말하는 오답이며, (C)는 room에서 연상 가능한 check in을 활용해 혼동을 유발하는 오답이다.

어휘 **view** 경관, 전망 **along** (길 등) ~을 따라 **sound 형용사** ~한 것 같다, ~하게 들리다 **make no difference** 차이가 없다, 문제가 되지 않는다

16. Would you like me to reserve first class seats for your business trip?

   (A) Haven't you checked our budget recently?
   (B) A window seat is fine.
   (C) It was a direct flight.

출장 가시는 데 제가 일등석으로 예매해 드릴까요?
(A) 최근에 우리 예산을 확인해 보시지 않았나요?
(B) 창가 좌석이면 됩니다.
(C) 직항편이었어요.

해설 상대방이 이용할 일등석 좌석을 질문자 자신이 예매해도 될지 묻는 데 대해 예산을 확인해보지 않았는지 되묻는 것으로 일등석 예매가 불가능한 상황임을 의미하는 (A)가 정답이다. (B)는 seat를 반복한 답변으로, 비용 문제가 걸려 있는 일등석 좌석 예매 여부를 묻는 질문에 맞지 않는 오답이며, (C)는 first class seats와 business trip에서 연상 가능한 direct flight을 활용해 혼동을 유발하는 오답이다.

어휘 **Would you like me to do?** 제가 ~해 드릴까요? **reserve** ~을 예약하다 **budget** 예산 **recently** 최근에 **direct flight** 직항편

17. Where are we moving our headquarters office to?

   (A) Somewhere in Austin.
   (B) The off switch.
   (C) You've been there too?

우리 본사 사무실을 어디로 옮기는 건가요?
(A) 오스틴 어딘가로요.
(B) 끄는 스위치요.
(C) 당신도 그곳에 가보셨어요?

해설 본사 사무실을 어디로 옮기는지 묻고 있으므로 대략적인 위치를 나타내는 말로 답변하는 (A)가 정답이다. (B)는 office와 일부 발음이 유사한 off switch를 활용해 혼동을 유발하는 오답이다.

어휘 **somewhere** 어딘가에, 어딘가로 **headquarters** 본사 **have been there** 그곳에 가본 적이 있다

18. What kind of food should we serve at the awards ceremony?

   (A) Not everyone eats meat.
   (B) Thank you for nominating me.
   (C) Yes, the venue looks great.

우리가 시상식에서 어떤 종류의 음식을 제공해야 하나요?
(A) 모든 사람이 고기를 먹는 건 아닙니다.
(B) 저를 후보로 지명해 주셔서 감사합니다.
(C) 네, 행사장이 아주 좋아 보여요.

해설 시상식에서 어떤 종류의 음식을 제공해야 하는지 묻고 있으므로 모든 사람이 고기를 먹는 것은 아니라는 말로 채식 메뉴의 필요성을 알리는 (A)가 정답이다. (B)는 awards에서 연상 가능한 nominating을 활용해 혼동을 유발하는 오답이며, (C)는

의문사 의문문에 맞지 않는 Yes로 답변하는 오답이다.

어휘 **serve** (음식 등) ~을 제공하다, ~을 내오다 **awards ceremony** 시상식 **nominate** ~을 후보로 지명하다 **venue** 행사장, 개최 장소 **look 형용사** ~하게 보이다, ~한 것 같다

19. Those new shoes look really comfortable.

   (A) On the bottom shelf.
   (B) Damon Footwear is known for that.
   (C) Alright, I'll wait here.

저 새 신발이 정말 편해 보여요.
(A) 아래쪽 선반에요.
(B) 데이먼 풋웨어가 그걸로 알려져 있죠.
(C) 알겠어요, 여기서 기다릴게요.

해설 특정 신발이 정말 편해 보인다는 의견을 말하고 있으므로 그러한 특징을 that으로 지칭해 데이먼 풋웨어가 그런 신발로 알려져 있다는 말로 일종의 동의를 나타내는 (B)가 정답이다.

어휘 **look 형용사** ~하게 보이다, ~한 것 같다 **comfortable** 편한 **bottom** 아래쪽의, 하단의 **shelf** 선반, 진열대 **be known for** ~로 알려져 있다

20. Did you use our building's parking garage?

   (A) Some reserved spaces.
   (B) I took a taxi.
   (C) Excuse me, but you can't park here.

저희 건물 주차장을 이용하셨나요?
(A) 몇몇 지정 공간이요.
(B) 저는 택시를 탔어요.
(C) 실례지만, 여기 주차하시면 안됩니다.

해설 건물 주차장을 이용했는지 묻고 있으므로 택시를 탔다는 말로 주차장을 이용하지 않았다는 뜻을 나타낸 (B)가 정답이다. (A)는 parking garage에서 연상 가능한 reserved spaces를 활용해 혼동을 유발하는 오답이며, (C)는 parking과 발음이 유사한 park을 활용해 혼동을 유발하는 답변이다.

어휘 **parking garage** 주차장 **reserved** 지정된, 예약된 **take** (교통편) ~을 타다, ~을 이용하다 **park** v. 주차하다

Part 3

Questions 21-23 refer to the following conversation.

W: Good morning, Dave. Oh, **21** why are you putting up a new shift schedule for our full-time workers? Didn't Simon do that yesterday?

M: Yes, but **22** he completely forgot that we need more staff to work over the busy Christmas period. So, I had to add a few more shifts to the schedule and print it again.

W: **22** That's not like him to make a mistake like that. I'm glad you've fixed it.

M: No problem. Now **23** I'm going to ask a few of our part-time staff whether they can do a few extra shifts, too.

W: Great idea. Our store is going to be really busy.

여: 안녕하세요, 데이브 씨, 아, 왜 우리 정규직 직원들을 위한 새 교대 근무 일정표를 게시하시는 건가요? 사이먼 씨께서 어제 하시지 않았나요?

남: 네, 하지만 바쁜 크리스마스 기간에 걸쳐 근무할 추가 직원이 필요하다는 사실을 완전히 잊으셨어요. 그래서, 제가 일정표에 몇몇 교대 근무를 더 추가해서 다시 출력해야 했습니다.

여: 그런 실수를 하시다니 사이먼 씨답지 않네요. 바로잡으셨다니 다행입니다.

남: 별 말씀을요. 이제 몇몇 시간제 근무 직원들에게도 추가 교대 근무를 할 수 있는지 물어보려고 합니다.

여: 아주 좋은 생각이에요. 우리 매장이 정말 바빠질 거예요.

어휘 **put up** ~을 게시하다, ~을 부착하다 **shift** 교대 근무(조) **completely** 완전히, 전적으로 **forget that** ~임을 잊다 **over** ~ 동안에 걸쳐 **add A to B** A를 B에 추가하다 **make a mistake** 실수를 저지르다 **fix** ~을 바로잡다, ~을 고치다 **whether** ~인지 (아닌지) **extra** 추가의, 별도의

21. 화자들은 주로 무엇을 이야기하고 있는가?
(A) 계절 할인 행사
(B) 직원 오리엔테이션
(C) 개조 공사 프로젝트
(D) 근무 일정

해설 대화의 주제나 목적은 대체로 초반부에 드러날 가능성이 높으므로 대화가 시작될 때 특히 집중해 들어야 한다. 여자가 대화 시작 부분에 왜 남자가 새 교대 근무 일정표를 게시하고 있는지 (why are you putting up a new shift schedule ~?) 이유를 물은 뒤로 변경된 근무 일정표를 게시하는 이유와 관련해 이야기하고 있으므로 (D)가 정답이다.

어휘 **seasonal** 계절의 **remodeling** 개조 공사, 리모델링

Paraphrase new shift schedule
→ work schedule

22. 무엇이 문제를 초래했는가?
(A) 프린터가 오작동했다.
(B) 배송 물품이 늦게 도착했다.
(C) 문서가 분실되었다.
(D) 직원이 실수를 저질렀다.

해설 무엇이 문제를 초래했는지 묻는 경우, 문제의 원인에 해당되는 좋지 못한 일을 언급하므로 부정적인 정보를 말하는 부분을 통해 단서를 파악해야 한다. 대화 중반부에 남자가 사이먼 씨를 he로 지칭해 이 사람이 잊은 것을(he completely forgot that ~) 알리자, 여자가 그런 실수를 했다는 것이 믿기지 않는다는(That's not like him to make a mistake like that) 말을 하고 있으므로 (D)가 정답이다.

어휘 **cause** ~을 초래하다, ~을 야기하다 **malfunction** 오작동 하다 **delivery** 배송(품) **arrive** 도착하다 **misplace** ~을 분실하다, ~을 둔 곳을 잊다 **make an error** 실수를 저지르 다

23. 남자는 곧이어 무엇을 할 것인가?
(A) 교육 강좌를 진행하는 일
(B) 직원들과 이야기하는 일
(C) 몇몇 용품을 주문하는 일
(D) 매장을 여는 일

해설 특정 화자가 곧이어 할 일을 묻는 경우, 대부분 대화 후반부에 단서가 제시되며, 계획이나 일정, 제안 등과 관련된 말을 통해 단서를 파악할 수 있다. 대화 후반부에 남자가 몇몇 시간제 근무 직원들에게도 추가 교대 근무를 할 수 있는지 물어보려고 한다고(I'm going to ask a few of our part-time staff whether they can do a few extra shifts, too) 알리고 있는데, 이는 그 직원들과 이야기하는 일을 의미하므로 (B)가 정답이다.

어휘 **lead** ~을 진행하다, ~을 이끌다 **training** 교육, 훈련 **order** ~을 주문하다 **supplies** 용품, 물품

Paraphrase ask a few of our part-time staff
→ Speak with employees

Questions 24-26 refer to the following conversation.

M: Hi, this is William Fisher.

W: Hello, I'm Mary Shilling, and **24** I'm calling from Goldberg Film Productions. **25** I just noticed your online post saying that you're selling a vintage guitar.

M: Oh, really? I only posted it fifteen minutes ago.

W: Well, we've been looking for this type of guitar for a long time. We'd like to buy it to use it in an upcoming movie we're making, but **26** we're hoping you could lower the price a little. Would it be possible?

M: Hmm... I suppose I could.

남: 안녕하세요, 윌리엄 피셔입니다.

여: 안녕하세요, 저는 메리 쉴링이며, 골드버그 영화사에서 전화 드렸습니다. 골동품 기타를 판매하신다고 쓰신 온라인 게시물을 막 봤습니다.

남: 아, 정말로요? 불과 15분 전에 게시했는데요.

여: 음, 저희가 오랫동안 이런 종류의 기타를 계속 찾고 있었습니다. 저희가 제작 중인 신작 영화에 사용할 수 있게 구입했으면 하는데, 가격을 조금 낮춰 주실 수 있기를 바라고 있습니다. 가능하실까요?

남: 흠... 그럴 수 있을 것 같아요.

어휘 **notice** ~을 알게 되다, ~에 주목하다 **post** n. 게시물 v. ~을 게시하다 **vintage** 골동품의, 고전적인, 오래된 가치가 있는 **look for** ~을 찾다 **upcoming** 다가오는, 곧 있을 **lower** v. ~을 낮추다, ~을 내리다 **a little** 조금, 약간 **suppose (that)** ~라고 생각하다

24. 여자는 어디에서 일하는가?
(A) 골동품 매장에서
(B) 라디오 방송국에서
(C) 영화 제작사에서
(D) 온라인 경매 사이트에서

해설 특정 화자의 근무 장소를 묻는 문제의 경우, 업체 이름이나 건물 이름, 특정 업무나 활동, 제공 서비스 등과 관련된 정보를 통해 단서를 파악해야 한다. 여자가 대화 초반부에 자신의 이름과 함께 골드버그 영화사에서 전화했다고 알리는 것으로(I'm calling from Goldberg Film Productions) 자신의 근무 장소를 언급하고 있으므로 (C)가 정답이다.

어휘 **antique** 골동품 **auction** 경매

Paraphrase Film Productions
→ movie production studio

25. 남자는 왜 "불과 15분 전에 게시했는데요"라고 말하는가?
(A) 실수를 설명하기 위해
(B) 요청을 거절하기 위해
(C) 일부 조언을 요청하기 위해
(D) 놀라움을 표현하기 위해

해설 여자가 대화 초반부에 남자가 골동품 기타를 판매한다고 쓴 온라인 게시물을 막 봤다고(I just noticed your online post saying that you're selling a vintage guitar) 알리자, 남자가 '불과 15분 전에 게시했어요'라고 언급하는 흐름이다. 이는

게시물을 올린 지 얼마 되지도 않았는데 그것을 보고 바로 연락한 것에 대한 놀라움을 나타내는 말이므로 (D)가 정답이다.

어휘 **reject** ~을 거절하다 **request** n. 요청 v. ~을 요청하다 **express** (생각, 감정 등) ~을 표현하다

26. 여자는 남자에게 무엇을 하도록 요청하는가?
(A) 회의에 참석하는 일
(B) 가격을 할인하는 일
(C) 프로젝트를 공동 작업하는 일
(D) 마감기한을 연장하는 일

해설 여자가 무엇을 하도록 요청하는지 묻고 있으므로 여자의 말에 집중해 요청 표현과 함께 제시되는 정보를 찾아야 한다. 여자가 대화 후반부에 가격을 조금 낮춰 줄 수 있기를 바란다는 말과 함께 그것이 가능할지(we're hoping you could lower the price a little. Would it be possible?) 묻고 있으므로 (B)가 정답이다.

어휘 **attend** ~에 참석하다 **reduce** ~을 할인하다, ~을 감소시키다 **collaborate** 공동 작업하다, 협업하다 **extend** ~을 연장하다 **deadline** 마감기한

Paraphrase lower the price
→ Reduce a price

Questions 27-29 refer to the following conversation with three speakers.

W1: **27** Congratulations, Emily! You've already met your target for computer sales this month. I don't think anyone at our branch has sold fifty laptops in three weeks before.

W2: Oh, really? I'm happy to hear that.

W1: Actually, **28** our store will be advertising a sales manager vacancy later this month. I think you should apply for it.

W2: I'd love to! But, do you think I'd be suited for a management role?

W1: Yes, definitely.

W2: Oh, hold on a moment while I assist this customer. What can I do for you, sir?

M: Hi, I bought a laptop here last month, but **29** I don't understand how to use the software. Can you help me out?

여1: 축하합니다, 에밀리 씨! 벌써 이번 달 컴퓨터 판매량 목표를 충족하셨네요. 우리 지점에서 이전에 그 누구도 3주 만에 50대의 노트북 컴퓨터를 판매한 적이 없었던 것 같아요.

여2: 아, 그래요? 그 말씀을 듣게 되어 기쁩니다.

여1: 실은, 우리 매장에서 이번 달 후반에 영업 관리자 공석을 광고할 예정입니다. 그 자리에 지원하시면 좋을 것 같아요.

여2: 꼭 그렇게 하고 싶어요! 하지만, 제가 관리자 역할에 어울린다고 생각하세요?

여1: 네, 당연합니다.

여2: 아, 제가 이 고객님을 도와 드리는 동안 잠시만 기다려 주세요. 무엇을 도와 드릴까요, 고객님?

남: 안녕하세요, 제가 지난 달에 이 노트북 컴퓨터를 구입했는데, 소프트웨어 사용법이 이해가 되지 않아서요. 저 좀 도와주실 수 있으세요?

어휘 **meet** (요구, 조건 등) ~을 충족하다 **target** 목표 **sales** 판매(량), 영업, 매출 **branch** 지점, 지사 **actually** 실은, 사실 **advertise** ~을 광고하다 **vacancy** 공석, 빈자리 **apply for** ~에 지원하다, ~을 신청하다 **be suited for** ~에 어울리다, ~에 적합하다 **management role** 관리자 역할, 책임자 역할 **definitely** (강한 긍정) 당연하죠, 물론이죠 **hold on a moment** 잠시 기다리세요 **while** ~하는 동안 **assist** ~을 돕다 **how to do** ~하는 방법 **help A out** A를 돕다

27. 에밀리 씨는 무엇에 대해 축하 받는가?

(A) 계약을 협상한 것
(B) 신규 지점으로 자리를 옮긴 것
(C) 판매 목표에 도달한 것
(D) 상을 받은 것

해설 에밀리 씨가 무엇에 대해 축하 받는지 묻고 있으므로 에밀리 씨의 이름과 함께 축하의 인사를 전할 때 그 이유를 파악해야 한다. 여자 한 명이 대화 시작 부분에 축하 인사와 함께 에밀리 씨의 이름을 부르면서 벌써 이번 달 컴퓨터 판매량 목표를 충족했다고(Congratulations, Emily! You've already met your target for computer sales ~) 알리고 있으므로 (C)가 정답이다.

어휘 **be congratulated for** ~에 대해 축하 받다 **negotiate** ~을 협의하다, ~을 협상하다 **contract** 계약(서) **relocate to** ~로 옮기다, ~로 이전하다 **reach** ~에 도달하다, ~에 이르다 **win an award** 상을 받다

Paraphrase met your target for computer sales
→ Reaching a sales target

28. 이번 달에 무슨 일이 있을 것인가?

(A) 일자리 기회가 제공될 것이다.
(B) 신제품이 출시될 것이다.
(C) 매장 판촉 행사가 시작될 것이다.
(D) 교육 워크숍이 개최될 것이다.

해설 질문에 제시된 시점 표현 this month가 제시되는 부분에서 단서를 찾아야 한다. 여자 한 명이 대화 중반에 이번 달 후반에 영업 관리자 공석을 광고한다고(our store will be advertising a sales manager vacancy later this month) 알리고 있다. 이는 일자리 기회가 제공된다는 말과 같

으므로 (A)가 정답이다.

어휘 **happen** 일어나다, 발생하다 **opportunity** 기회 **offer** ~을 제공하다, ~을 제안하다 **launch** ~을 출시하다, ~을 시작하다 **promotion** 판촉 (행사), 홍보, 승진 **take place** (일, 행사 등이) 개최되다, 일어나다, 발생되다

Paraphrase will be advertising a sales manager vacancy
→ A job opportunity will be offered.

29. 남자는 무엇을 하고 싶어 하는가?

(A) 일자리에 지원하는 일
(B) 기기를 수리 받는 일
(C) 컴퓨터를 구입하는 일
(D) 일부 소프트웨어에 관해 아는 일

해설 남자의 말에 집중해 희망 사항 등을 알리는 부분에서 단서를 파악해야 한다. 대화 맨 마지막 부분에 남자가 소프트웨어 사용법을 모르겠다는 말과 함께 도와 달라고(I don't understand how to use the software. Can you help me out?) 묻고 있으므로 (D)가 정답이다.

어휘 **have A p.p.** A를 ~되게 하다, A를 ~해놓다 **device** 기기, 장치 **learn about** ~에 대해 알아보다, 배우다

Questions 30-32 refer to the following conversation.

W: Hi, Bob. I didn't expect you to arrive on time.

M: Well, the train ride was smooth, apart from one thing.

W: Oh, what happened?

M: Well, **30** I had paid for a first class seat, but the rail company had overbooked. So, **30** I ended up sitting in economy class.

W: You booked your ticket through **31** Northern Rail, right? That company is highly regarded and normally gets great reviews.

M: Yes, so I don't know why they made an error. Anyway, I'm ready to get going. Are you parked just outside the station?

W: That's right. **32** And here... I bought you a coffee. You can enjoy that before we set off.

여: 안녕하세요, 밥 씨. 제때 도착하실 거라고 예상하지 못했어요.
남: 음, 기차 운행이 순조로웠어요, 한 가지만 제외하면요.
여: 아, 무슨 일이 있었나요?
남: 그게, 제가 일등석 요금을 지불했는데, 철도회사에서 초과 예약이 되었어요. 그래서, 결국 이코노미 좌석에 앉게 되었죠.
여: 노던 레일을 통해서 티켓을 예매하신 게 맞죠? 그 회사는 높이 평가되고 있고 일반적으로 이용 후기도 아주 좋은 곳인데요.

남: 네, 그래서 저도 그곳에서 왜 실수했는지 모르겠어요. 어쨌든, 저는 갈 준비가 되어 있습니다. 역 바로 바깥쪽에 주차하셨나요?

여: 그렇습니다. 그리고 여기... 제가 커피 사왔어요. 출발하기 전에 드시면 됩니다.

어휘 **expect A to do** A가 ~할 것으로 예상하다 **arrive** 도착하다 **on time** 제때 **ride** (차량 등의) 운행, 타고 가기 **smooth** 순조로운 **apart from** ~을 제외하고, ~외에는 **overbook** 초과 예약되다 **end up -ing** 결국 ~하게 되다 **book** ~을 예약하다 **highly regarded** 높이 평가 받는 **normally** 일반적으로, 보통 **review** 후기, 평가, 의견 **make an error** 실수하다 **anyway** 어쨌든 **be ready to do** ~할 준비가 되다 **get going** (계속) 가다, 출발하다, 떠나다 **set off** 출발하다

30. 남자는 열차 운행과 관련해 무엇을 언급하는가?
(A) 열차가 늦게 출발했다.
(B) 열차가 고장 났다.
(C) 목적지가 틀렸다.
(D) 좌석이 변경되었다.

해설 대화 중반부에 남자가 원래 일등석 티켓을 구입했는데 초과 예약 문제로 인해 결국 이코노미 좌석에 앉았다고(I had paid for a first class seat ~ I ended up sitting in economy class) 알리고 있다. 이는 좌석이 변경되는 일을 겪었다는 뜻이므로 (D)가 정답이다.

어휘 **depart** 출발하다, 떠나다 **break down** 고장 나다 **destination** 목적지, 도착지

Paraphrase paid for a first class seat / ended up sitting in economy class
→ seat was changed

31. 여자는 노던 레일과 관련해 무슨 말을 하는가?
(A) 좋은 평판을 지니고 있다.
(B) 새로운 서비스를 제공하고 있다.
(C) 직원 할인을 제공한다.
(D) 최근에 설립되었다.

해설 대화 중반부에 여자가 노던 레일을 언급한 뒤로 높이 평가되면서 이용 후기도 아주 좋은 곳이라고(~ Northern Rail, right? That company is highly regarded and normally gets great reviews) 말하고 있다. 이는 회사 평판이 아주 좋다는 뜻이므로 (A)가 정답이다.

어휘 **reputation** 평판, 명성 **offer** ~을 제공하다(= provide) **recently** 최근에 **found** ~을 설립하다

Paraphrase highly regarded / gets great reviews
→ has a good reputation

32. 여자는 남자에게 무엇을 주는가?
(A) 티켓

(B) 환불 금액
(C) 문서
(D) 음료

해설 여자의 말에 집중해 전달이나 제공 등과 관련된 표현과 함께 언급하는 정보를 찾아야 한다. 대화 맨 마지막 부분에 여자가 물건을 건넬 때 사용하는 here과 함께 남자에게 줄 커피를 샀다고 (And here... I bought you a coffee) 알리고 있으므로 (D)가 정답이다.

어휘 **refund** 환불(액)

Paraphrase coffee → beverage

Questions 33-35 refer to the following conversation and information.

W: It's so lucky that we both have a day off today. We've been working long shifts all week, and it's nice to finally have a break.

M: I know! **33** We've never had this many diners. I guess they all heard about our new menu options. Almost everyone has been ordering the new dishes.

W: They're definitely popular! Well, what are we doing with our day off today? I hope it's something indoors. **34** I didn't wear warm clothes, and it's much colder than I expected.

M: Well, **35** why don't we go and see the photography exhibition in this art gallery? I heard that it's a fantastic exhibition.

여: 오늘 저희 둘 모두 휴무여서 정말 다행이에요. 이번 주 내내 장시간 교대 근무를 했는데, 드디어 쉬게 되어 좋네요.

남: 맞아요! 우리가 이렇게 많은 식사 손님을 받았던 적은 없었어요. 제 생각엔 그분들 모두가 우리의 새 메뉴에 대해 들은 것 같아요. 거의 모든 분들이 신메뉴를 주문하셨잖아요.

여: 그것들은 확실히 인기가 있어요! 음, 오늘 휴무에 우리는 무엇을 할까요? 전 실내에서 하는 거면 좋겠어요. 제가 따뜻한 옷을 입지 않았는데, 제 예상보다 훨씬 더 춥네요.

남: 음, 이 미술관에 사진 전시회를 관람하러 가는 건 어때요? 굉장한 전시회라고 들었어요.

미술관 전시회	
제니 헐록	디지털 미디어
안드레 구즈만	야생 동식물 사진
엠마 알콕	청동 조각상
제레미 최	수채화

어휘 **day off** 휴무, 휴일 **shift** 교대 근무 **have a break** 잠시 휴식을 취하다 **diner** 식사 손님 **definitely** 분명히, 확실히 **indoors** 실내의 **photography** 사진 **exhibition** 전시(회)

art gallery 미술관 fantastic 환상적인, 엄청난, 굉장한
wildlife 야생 동식물 bronze sculpture 청동 조각상
watercolor painting 수채화

33. 화자들은 어디에서 일하겠는가?

(A) 슈퍼마켓에서
(B) 레스토랑에서
(C) 음료 회사에서
(D) 박물관에서

해설 대화 초반에 여자가 이번 주 내내 장시간 교대 근무를 했지
만 하루 쉬게 돼서 좋다고 말하자, 남자가 이렇게 많은 식사 손
님을 받았던 적은 없었다고(We've never had this many
diners ~) 말하며 신메뉴에 대해 들은 것 같다고 언급하는 부
분을 통해 화자들이 근무하는 장소가 레스토랑임을 알 수 있다.
따라서 (B)가 정답이다. diner가 '식사 손님'을 의미하므로 주의
해야 한다.

34. 여자는 왜 우려하는가?

(A) 티켓을 구입하는 것을 잊어버렸다.
(B) 오늘 오후에 일을 해야 한다.
(C) 돈이 많지 않다.
(D) 옷을 알맞게 입지 않았다.

해설 대화 중반부에 여자가 휴무인 오늘 실내 활동을 하면 좋겠다고
말하면서 자신이 따뜻한 옷을 입지 않았는데 생각보다 더 춥다
는 것을 이유로 언급하고 있으므로 여자가 우려하는 이유가 옷
을 따뜻하게, 즉 알맞게 입지 않았기 때문임을 알 수 있다. 따라
서 (D)가 정답이다.

어휘 **forget to do** ~하는 것을 잊어버리다 **dress** 옷을 입다
appropriately 알맞게, 적절하게

Paraphrase didn't wear warm clothes / much colder than I
expected
→ did not dress appropriately

35. 시각자료를 보시오. 남자는 어느 예술가의 전시회를 권하는가?

(A) 제니 헐록
(B) 안드레 구즈만
(C) 엠마 알콕
(D) 제레미 최

해설 대화 후반부에 실내 활동을 하고 싶다는 여자의 말에 남자
가 미술관의 사진 전시회를 관람하는 것은 어떠겠냐고 제
안하고(why don't we go and see the photography
exhibition in this art gallery?) 있다. 도표에서 '사진
(photography)'이 표기된 항목의 예술가 이름은 Andre
Guzman이므로 (B)가 정답이다.

Questions 36-38 refer to the following conversation and
diagram.

M: Can you help me? I'd like to buy a new suitcase
today, but I can't decide which one to get. There
are so many to choose from in your store.

W: I'd be happy to help you. Well, **36** for this month
only, our store is offering 15 percent off on all
Travelpro brand suitcases.

M: **37** That's tempting, but I've found that
Travelpro products break very easily due to
their cheap materials.

W: In that case, how about this **38** Voyager 500
model? **38** It will last for several years, and it's
very easy to move around, because its wheels
are specially designed for multi-directional
movement.

남: 저를 도와주시겠어요? 오늘 새 여행 가방을 사려고 하는데, 어
느 것으로 살지 결정하지 못하겠어요. 이 매장에 선택할 수 있
는 게 정말 많네요.
여: 도와드리게 되어 기쁩니다. 음, 이번 달 한정으로, 저희 매장은
모든 트래블프로 브랜드 여행 가방에 15 퍼센트 할인을 제공해
드립니다.
남: 그건 솔깃하네요, 하지만 트래블프로 상품들이 값싼 재료 때문
에 매우 쉽게 고장 난다는 걸 알게 됐어요.
여: 그렇다면, 이 보이저 500 모델은 어떠세요? 오랫동안 사용할
수 있고, 바퀴들이 다방향 움직임을 목적으로 특별히 고안되었
기 때문에 움직이기 아주 쉽습니다.

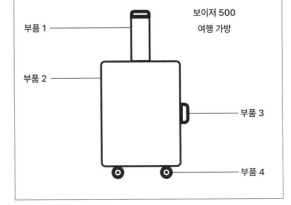

어휘 **suitcase** 여행 가방 **offer** ~을 제공하다 **tempting** 솔깃
한 **find** ~을 알게 되다 **break** 고장 나다 **due to** ~때문
에 **cheap** 저렴한, 값싼 **material** 재료 **in that case** 그
런 경우라면, 그렇다면 **last** v. 오래가다, 지속되다 **move
around** 움직이다, 돌아다니다 **wheel** 바퀴 **specially** 특
히 **designed** 고안된 **multi-directional** 다방향의, 여러
방향의 **movement** 움직임, 이동

36. 여자는 이번 달에 무슨 일이 일어날 것이라고 말하는가?

(A) 상점이 점포 정리 세일을 한다.
(B) 특정 브랜드에 할인이 제공된다.
(C) 신제품군이 출시된다.
(D) 모든 구매에 무료 배송이 이용 가능하다.

해설 this month가 핵심어이므로 이 표현이 언급될 때 집중해서 듣도록 한다. 대화 중반부에 여자가 this month를 언급하면서 모든 트래블프로 브랜드의 여행 가방에 15퍼센트 할인을 제공할 것이라고(for this month only, ~ is offering 15 percent off on all Travelpro brand suitcases) 말한다. 따라서 이를 특정 브랜드에 할인이 제공될 것이라고 패러프레이징한 (B)가 정답이다.

어휘 **closing down sale** 점포 정리 세일 **offer** ~을 제공하다 **specific** 특정한 **range** 범위, ~군 **launch** ~을 출시하다 **available** 이용 가능한 **purchase** n. 구매(품)

Paraphrase is offering 15 percent off on all Travelpro brand suitcases
→ A discount is being offered on a specific brand.

37. 남자는 트래블프로 제품에 대해 어떤 우려를 하고 있는가?

(A) 너무 비싸다.
(B) 내구성이 없다.
(C) 저장 용량이 한정되어 있다.
(D) 한 가지 색상으로만 나온다.

해설 남자가 트래블프로 제품을 언급하는 부분에 집중해서 들어야 한다. 대화 중반부에 남자가 트래블프로 여행 가방에 대한 할인은 솔깃하지만 값싼 재료 때문에 매우 쉽게 고장 난다는 걸 알게 됐다고(That's tempting, but I've found that Travelpro products break very easily due to their cheap materials) 말한다. 따라서, 매우 쉽게 고장 난다는 것을 내구성이 없다는 말로 표현한 (B)가 정답이다.

어휘 **concern** 걱정, 우려 **expensive** 비싼 **durable** 내구성이 있는 **limited** 제한된, 한정적인 **storage** 저장 **capacity** 용량, 수용력

Paraphrase break very easily → not durable

38. 시각자료를 보시오. 여자는 보이저 500 여행 가방의 어떤 부품을 강조하는가?

(A) 부품 1
(B) 부품 2
(C) 부품 3
(D) 부품 4

해설 여자가 가방에 대해 언급하는 부분에 집중해서 어떤 부분을 강조하는지 들어야 한다. 대화 후반부에 여자가 보이저 500 모델에 관해 바퀴들이 다방향 움직임을 목적으로 특별히 고안되었기 때문에 움직이기 쉽다고(~ it's very easy to move around, because its wheels are specially designed for multi-directional movement) 말하며 남자에게 해당 모델을 추천하고 있다. 시각자료에서 바퀴는 Part 4에 해당하

므로 (D)가 정답이다.

어휘 **emphasize** ~을 강조하다

Part 4

Questions 39-41 refer to the following talk.

I hope you have all had a great time during this company training workshop in Cornwall. And, I'm sure you took advantage of all the fantastic amenities **39** at this resort. Some of you have mentioned that you're planning to stay for one more night before returning to work on Monday. Well, you'll be pleased to know **40** there's a festival being held in Cornwall today, with delicious foods from all over the world. And **41** you can get some free meal coupons from this resort, so you should definitely take those if you plan to attend the event.

여러분 모두 이곳 콘월에서 열린 사내 교육 워크숍 중에 아주 좋은 시간 보내셨기를 바랍니다. 그리고, 분명 이 리조트의 모든 환상적인 편의시설을 이용하셨으리라 생각합니다. 여러분 중 일부가 월요일에 회사로 복귀하기 전에 하룻밤 더 머무를 계획이라고 언급해 주셨습니다. 음, 오늘 콘월에서, 전 세계 각지에서 온 맛있는 음식과 함께 개최되는 축제가 있다는 사실을 아시면 기쁘실 것입니다. 그리고 이 리조트에서 몇몇 무료 식사 쿠폰을 받으실 수 있으므로, 이 행사에 참석하실 계획이시라면 꼭 받아가시기 바랍니다.

어휘 **take advantage of** ~을 이용하다 **amenities** 편의시설 **mention that** ~라고 언급하다 **plan to do** ~할 계획이다 **return to** ~로 복귀하다, ~로 돌아가다 **be pleased to do** ~해서 기쁘다 **hold** ~을 개최하다, ~을 열다 **definitely** 꼭, 반드시, 분명히, 확실히 **attend** ~에 참석하다

39. 담화는 어디에서 진행되고 있는가?

(A) 컨벤션 센터에서
(B) 리조트에서
(C) 쇼핑몰에서
(D) 레스토랑에서

해설 담화가 진행되는 장소를 묻고 있으므로 건물 이름, 행사 이름, 특정 업무나 활동, 제공 서비스 등과 관련된 정보를 통해 단서를 파악해야 한다. 화자가 담화 초반부에 at this resort라는 말로 현재 있는 장소를 언급하고 있으므로 (B)가 정답이다.

40. 오늘 무슨 일이 있을 것인가?

(A) 거리 퍼레이드
(B) 음악 공연
(C) 직업 박람회

(D) 음식 축제

해설 오늘 무슨 일이 있을 것인지 묻고 있으므로 질문에 제시된 today 또는 '오늘'에 해당되는 시점 표현이 언급되는 부분에서 단서를 파악해야 한다. 담화 중반부에 화자가 전 세계 각지에서 온 맛있는 음식과 함께 개최되는 축제가 있다고(there's a festival being held in Cornwall today, with delicious foods from all over the world) 알리고 있으므로 (D)가 정답이다.

어휘 take place (일, 행사 등이) 일어나다, 발생되다, 개최되다 performance 공연, 연주(회) fair 박람회, 축제 마당

41. 화자는 청자들에게 무엇을 하도록 권하는가?
(A) 셔틀버스를 이용하는 일
(B) 예약하는 일
(C) 몇몇 쿠폰을 가져가는 일
(D) 티켓을 구입하는 일

해설 권장 또는 제안 표현과 함께 제시되는 정보를 들어야 한다. 담화 후반부에 화자가 무료 식사 쿠폰을 언급하면서 그것을 꼭 가져가라고(you can get some free meal coupons from this resort, so you should definitely take those) 권하고 있으므로 (C)가 정답이다.

어휘 make a reservation 예약하다

Paraphrase free meal coupons / take those
→ Take some coupons

Questions 42-44 refer to the following conversation.

You're listening to the local news report on WKRT Radio. 42 43 Next, we have a special report about a local entrepreneur. Last summer, Tina Lowell started a food delivery business called Quick Grub with only five drivers. Now, after only 9 months, Quick Grub employs over fifty drivers. Customers place orders through Ms. Lowell's Web site, and then she has their food delivered to them. In order to make her business even more convenient, 44 Ms. Lowell plans to collaborate with developers to create a mobile phone app, which is expected to launch by the end of the year.

여러분께서는 WKRT 라디오의 지역 뉴스 보도를 청취하고 계십니다. 다음 순서는, 지역 기업가에 관한 특집 보도입니다. 지난 여름, 티나 로웰 씨는 겨우 5명의 기사와 함께 퀵 그럽이라는 음식 배달 사업을 시작했습니다. 현재, 불과 9개월 밖에 지나지 않았지만, 퀵 그럽은 50명이 넘는 기사를 고용하고 있습니다. 고객들이 로웰 씨의 웹 사이트를 통해 주문하고 나면, 로웰 씨가 음식을 배달시킵니다. 사업을 훨씬 더 편리하게 만들기 위해, 로웰 씨는 휴대전화 앱을 만들 수 있는 개발업자들과 협업할 계획이며, 이는 올 연말까지 출시될 것으로 예상됩니다.

어휘 local 지역의, 현지의 entrepreneur 기업가 called A A라고 부르는, A라는 employ ~을 고용하다 place an order 주문하다 then 그런 다음, 그때, 그럼, 그렇다면 have A p.p. A를 ~되게 하다, A를 ~해놓다 in order to do ~하기 위해 make A B A를 B인 상태로 만들다 even (비교급 수식) 훨씬 convenient 편리한 collaborate with ~와 협업하다, ~와 공동 작업하다 developer 개발업자, 개발업체 create ~을 만들어 내다 be expected to do ~할 예정이다 launch 출시되다, 시작되다

42. 뉴스 보도는 주로 무엇에 관한 것인가?
(A) 새롭게 개장한 레스토랑
(B) 취업 기회
(C) 이사 서비스
(D) 지역 업체 소유주

해설 화자가 담화 시작 부분에 지역 기업가에 관해 보도한다고 알리면서 티나 로웰 씨가 시작한 사업을 소개하고 있다(Next, we have a special report about a local entrepreneur. ~ Tina Lowell started a food delivery business ~). 이는 지역 업체 소유주가 담화 주제임을 알리는 말이므로 (D)가 정답이다.

어휘 employment 취업, 고용 opportunity 기회 owner 소유주, 주인

Paraphrase local entrepreneur
→ local business owner

43. 화자가 "퀵 그럽은 50명이 넘는 기사를 고용하고 있습니다."라고 말할 때 무엇을 암시하는가?
(A) 업체가 현재 직원을 고용하는 중이다.
(B) 회사가 상당히 성장했다.
(C) 이전의 보도에서 실수가 있었다.
(D) 교육 프로그램이 효과적이었다.

해설 화자가 담화 초반부에 티나 로웰 씨가 겨우 5명의 기사와 함께 음식 배달 사업을 시작한(Tina Lowell started a food delivery business called Quick Grub with only five drivers) 사실을 알린 뒤로, 불과 9개월 만에 '50명이 넘는 기사를 고용하고 있다'고 언급하는 흐름이다. 이는 회사가 빠르게 성장했음을 나타내는 말이므로 (B)가 정답이다.

어휘 currently 현재 hire (직원 등을) 고용하다 grow 성장하다 significantly 상당히, 많이 make an error 실수하다 previous 이전의 training 교육 effective 효과적인

44. 화자의 말에 따르면, 로웰 씨가 누구와 함께 일할 계획인가?
(A) 마케팅 책임자
(B) 실내 디자이너
(C) 재무 컨설턴트
(D) 애플리케이션 개발자

해설 담화 후반부에 화자는 로웰 씨가 휴대전화 앱을 만들 수 있는 개발자들과 협업할 계획이라고(Ms. Lowell plans to collaborate with developers to create a mobile phone app) 알리고 있으므로 (D)가 정답이다.

어휘 **financial** 재무의, 재정의, 금융의 **consultant** 컨설턴트, 상담 전문가

Paraphrase developers to create a mobile phone app → Application developers

Questions 45-47 refer to the following telephone message.

Hi, Claire. **45** I'm leading the new employee orientation at our training center today. Everything is prepared, so I'll be starting the session at 10 a.m. like you requested. But I doubt I'll be finished by 12. I've been looking at the health and safety presentation, which management asked me to give, and there are 100 presentation slides! So, **46** I've had to cancel the lunch reservation we made for our new staff, because we'd never make it to the restaurant on time. Instead, **47** I'll just give them vouchers that they can exchange for food in our cafeteria.

안녕하세요, 클레어 씨. 제가 오늘 교육 센터에서 신입 사원 오리엔테이션을 진행합니다. 모든 것이 준비되어 있어서, 요청하신 대로 오전 10시에 그 시간을 시작할 예정입니다. 하지만, 제가 12시까지 끝마칠 것 같지 않습니다. 경영진이 저에게 제공하도록 요청한 보건 및 안전 발표 내용을 계속 살펴봤는데, 100개나 되는 발표 슬라이드가 있습니다! 그래서, 신입 사원들을 위해 우리가 예약한 점심 식사를 취소해야 했는데, 우리가 절대로 제시간에 그 레스토랑에 가지 못할 것이기 때문입니다. 대신, 그냥 우리 구내식당에서 음식으로 교환할 수 있는 쿠폰을 제공하겠습니다.

어휘 **lead** ~을 진행하다, ~을 이끌다 **prepared** 준비되어 있는 **session** (특정 활동을 위한) 시간 **request** 요청하다 **doubt (that)** ~라고 생각하지 않다, ~임을 의심하다 **presentation** 발표 (자료) **management** 경영진 **make a reservation** 예약하다 **make it to** ~로 가다 **on time** 제시간에 **instead** 대신(에) **voucher** 쿠폰, 상품권 **exchange A for B** A를 B로 교환하다 **cafeteria** 구내식당

45. 메시지는 주로 무엇에 관한 것인가?
   (A) 사업 거래
   (B) 회사 정책
   (C) 교육 시간
   (D) 안전 점검

해설 화자가 담화를 시작하면서 오늘 교육 센터에서 신입 사원 오리

엔테이션을 진행한다고(I'm leading the new employee orientation at our training center today) 알린 뒤로 그 시간의 운영과 관련해 이야기하고 있으므로 (C)가 정답이다.

어휘 **deal** 거래 (조건), 계약 **policy** 정책 **inspection** 점검, 검사

Paraphrase employee orientation at our training center → training session

46. 화자는 왜 "100개나 되는 발표 슬라이드가 있습니다!"라고 말하는가?
   (A) 발표를 준비하는 데 대한 도움을 요청하기 위해
   (B) 회사 행사를 연기하는 것을 제안하기 위해
   (C) 한 가지 활동이 왜 예상보다 더 오래 진행될지 설명하기 위해
   (D) 청자에게 업무를 도와준 것에 대해 감사하기 위해

해설 화자가 담화 중반부에 '100개나 되는 발표 슬라이드가 있다'고 언급한 뒤로, 신입 사원들을 위해 예약한 점심 식사를 취소해야 했다는 사실과 함께 절대로 제시간에 그 레스토랑에 가지 못할 것이라고(I've had to cancel the lunch reservation ~ we'd never make it to the restaurant on time) 알리고 있다. 이는 발표라는 활동이 오래 진행될 것이라는 뜻이므로 (C)가 정답이다.

어휘 **request** ~을 요청하다 **assistance with** ~에 대한 도움, 지원 **prepare** ~을 준비하다 **suggest -ing** ~하도록 제안하다 **postpone** ~을 연기하다, ~을 미루다 **explain** ~을 설명하다 **run** 진행되다 **than expected** 예상보다 **task** 업무, 일

47. 화자는 일부 직원들에게 무엇을 줄 것인가?
   (A) 식권
   (B) 사원증
   (C) 직무 설명서
   (D) 점심 도시락

해설 화자가 일부 직원들에게 무엇을 줄 것인지 묻고 있으므로 질문에 제시된 give 또는 provide, offer, send 등과 같이 전달이나 제공과 관련된 표현이 제시되는 부분에 단서를 찾아야 한다. 담화 맨 마지막 부분에 화자가 구내식당에서 음식으로 교환할 수 있는 쿠폰을 제공하겠다고(I'll just give them vouchers that they can exchange for food in our cafeteria) 알리고 있는데, 이는 식권을 제공하겠다는 뜻이므로 (A)가 정답이다.

어휘 **description** 설명, 묘사

Paraphrase vouchers that they can exchange for food in our cafeteria → Meal vouchers

Questions 48-50 refer to the following excerpt from the meeting and presentation slide.

Let's start this meeting by looking at our line of cushions. **48** Last year, we doubled production of our cushions in order to meet the rising demand for them. As you can see on the slide, we currently have four cushion patterns. Sales for each cushion pattern are all quite high, but **49** our bestselling pattern by far is the zigzag one. Our customers really like how eye-catching that pattern is. We expect sales to increase even further once we open **50** our online store on our Web site. Our IT team has been working hard to create that, and it should be ready to launch in March.

우리의 쿠션 제품 라인을 살펴보는 것으로 이번 회의를 시작해 보겠습니다. 작년에, 우리는 증가하는 수요를 충족하기 위해 우리 쿠션의 생산을 두 배로 늘렸습니다. 슬라이드에서 보실 수 있는 것처럼, 우리는 현재 네 가지 쿠션 패턴이 있습니다. 각 쿠션 패턴에 대한 판매량이 모두 상당히 높기는 하지만, 우리의 베스트셀러 패턴은 단연 지그재그 모양으로 된 것입니다. 우리 고객들께서는 그 패턴이 시선을 사로잡는 걸 정말 마음에 들어 하고 계십니다. 우리 웹 사이트에 온라인 매장을 여는 대로 판매량이 훨씬 더 많이 증가할 것으로 예상합니다. 우리 IT팀이 이것을 만들기 위해 계속 열심히 노력하고 있으며, 3월에 개시할 준비가 될 것입니다.

 패턴 1   패턴 2   패턴 3   패턴 4

어휘 by (방법) ~하는 것으로, ~함으로써 double v. ~을 두 배로 하다 production 생산, 제작 in order to do ~하기 위해 meet (요구, 조건 등) ~을 충족하다 rising 증가하는, 상승하는 demand 수요 currently 현재 sales 판매(량), 매출, 영업 quite 상당히, 꽤 by far 단연 eye-catching 시선을 사로잡는 expect A to do A가 ~할 것으로 예상하다 increase 증가하다, 오르다 even (비교급 수식) 훨씬 further 더 많이, 한층 더 once (일단) ~하는 대로, ~하자 마자 create ~을 만들어 내다 be ready to do ~할 준비가 되다 launch 개시하다, 시작하다, 출시하다

48. 회사는 작년에 무엇을 했는가?
(A) 추가 직원을 모집했다.
(B) 제품 생산량을 늘렸다.
(C) 해외 시장으로 사업을 확장했다.
(D) 일부 제품을 단종했다.

해설 질문에 제시된 시점 표현 last year가 제시되는 부분에서 단서를 찾아야 한다. 담화 초반부에 화자가 작년에 쿠션의 생산을

두 배로 늘린(Last year, we doubled production of our cushions ~) 사실을 언급하고 있으므로 (B)가 정답이다.

어휘 recruit ~을 모집하다 additional 추가적인 expand into (사업 등) ~로 확장하다 overseas 해외의 discontinue ~을 단종하다

Paraphrase doubled production of our cushions → increased production of items

49. 시각자료를 보시오. 어느 패턴의 쿠션이 가장 인기 있는가?
(A) 1번 패턴
(B) 2번 패턴
(C) 3번 패턴
(D) 4번 패턴

해설 제품 소개 등을 위한 기호나 그림 등이 제시되는 시각자료 문제의 경우, 각 항목의 특징적인 요소를 미리 확인해 두는 것이 좋으며, 항목별로 각 선택지와 짝을 이루는 특징이 담화 중에 단서로 제시된다는 점에 유의해야 한다. 담화 중반부에 화자가 베스트셀러 제품이 지그재그 모양으로 된 것이라고(our bestselling pattern by far is the zigzag one) 알리고 있다. 시각자료에서 지그재그 패턴이 들어간 제품은 맨 왼쪽에 있는 Pattern 1이므로 (A)가 정답이다.

50. 화자의 말에 따르면, IT팀은 무엇을 계속 하고 있는가?
(A) 사무실 컴퓨터를 수리하는 일
(B) 고객 문의에 대응하는 일
(C) 웹 사이트 보안을 강화하는 일
(D) 온라인 매장을 만드는 일

해설 IT팀이 언급되는 부분에서 업무나 프로젝트와 관련된 정보를 찾아야 한다. 화자가 담화 후반부에 웹 사이트상의 온라인 매장을 언급하면서 IT팀이 그것을 만들고 있다고(~ our online store on our Web site. Our IT team has been working hard to create that ~) 알리고 있으므로 (D)가 정답이다.

어휘 repair ~을 수리하다 respond to ~에 대응하다, ~에 응답하다 inquiry 문의 enhance ~을 강화하다, ~을 향상시키다 security 보안

DAY 02 RC Half Test

1. (B)	**2.** (B)	**3.** (D)	**4.** (A)	**5.** (B)
6. (D)	**7.** (D)	**8.** (D)	**9.** (C)	**10.** (C)
11. (A)	**12.** (D)	**13.** (C)	**14.** (B)	**15.** (A)
16. (D)	**17.** (A)	**18.** (C)	**19.** (D)	**20.** (B)
21. (A)	**22.** (C)	**23.** (A)	**24.** (B)	**25.** (D)
26. (D)	**27.** (C)	**28.** (A)	**29.** (D)	**30.** (B)
31. (D)	**32.** (C)	**33.** (C)	**34.** (D)	**35.** (C)
36. (A)	**37.** (C)	**38.** (B)	**39.** (D)	**40.** (C)
41. (D)	**42.** (C)	**43.** (B)	**44.** (C)	**45.** (A)
46. (C)	**47.** (C)	**48.** (B)	**49.** (B)	**50.** (D)

Part 5

1.
정답 (B)

해석 재무팀장은 여러분이 출장 경비 영수증을 가능한 빠른 시점에 제출할 것을 요청했습니다.

해설 전치사 at의 목적어에 해당하는 명사구 earliest convenience를 수식해야 하므로 소유격 대명사 (B) your가 정답이다.

어휘 finance 재무, 재정 ask that ~할 것을 요청하다 expense 지출(비용) receipt 영수증 submit ~을 제출하다 at one's earliest convenience 가능한 빨리

2.
성답 (B)

해석 새롭게 개정된 베이징 여행 가이드 버전은 여행 일정 및 레스토랑에 대한 추천 사항을 특징으로 한다.

해설 빈칸은 타동사인 features의 목적어 역할을 명사 자리이다. 여기서 목적어는 추천 행위가 아니라 가이드 책자 내의 정보에 해당하는 '추천 사항'을 의미해야 한다. 따라서 가산 명사 recommendation이 빈칸에 올 수 있는데 빈칸 앞에 부정관사가 없으므로 복수명사 (B) recommendations가 정답이다.

어휘 revise ~을 개정하다, ~을 수정하다 feature ~을 특징으로 하다 itinerary 일정(표) recommendation 추천 (사항), 추천서 recommend ~을 추천하다

3.
정답 (D)

해석 우리 마케팅팀이 실시한 설문 조사에서 얻은 결과에 따르면 대부분의 소비자들은 우리 제품들이 너무 비싸다고 생각하는 것으로 나타나 있다.

해설 빈칸 앞뒤에 위치한 명사 Results와 surveys가 각각 '결과'와 '설문 조사'를 뜻하므로 '설문 조사에서 얻은 결과'와 같은 의미가 구성되어야 자연스럽다. 따라서, surveys가 정보를 얻은 출처에 해당되므로 '~에서, ~로부터'라는 뜻의 (D) from이 정답이다.

어휘 result 결과(물) survey 설문 조사(지) conduct ~을 실시하다, ~을 수행하다 indicate that ~인 것으로 나타나다, ~임을 가리키다 overpriced 너무 비싼, 가격이 너무 비싸게 매겨진

4.
정답 (A)

해석 베이징에서 가장 유명한 식당가를 방문할 때, 해외 관광객들은 집에서 절대 먹어볼 수 없는 수많은 현지 요리를 맛볼 수 있다.

해설 조동사 can 뒤에 위치한 빈칸은 동사원형이 필요한 자리이므로 (A) sample이 정답이다.

어휘 countless 수많은 local 현지의, 지역의 try ~을 먹어보다, ~을 시도해보다 sample v. ~을 맛보다, ~을 시식하다

5.
정답 (B)

해석 트랭크 씨는 웨스트웨이 에어웨이즈 또는 스위프트제트 두 곳의 항공편 중에서 어느 쪽이든 더 저렴한 것을 기꺼이 이용한다.

해설 빈칸 뒤에 대명사 주어 one과 동사 is로 이어지는 절이 쓰여 있어 이 절을 이끌 수 있는 접속사가 빈칸에 필요하므로 선택지에서 유일한 접속사인 (B) whichever가 정답이다.

어휘 take (교통편) ~을 이용하다, ~을 타다 either A or B A 또는 B 둘 중의 하나 both (A and B) (A와 B) 둘 모두 whichever 어느 쪽이든 ~하는

6.
정답 (D)

해석 보렐리스 800 노트북 컴퓨터가 경쟁 모델들과 유사하게 가격이 책정되어 있기는 하지만, 눈에 띄게 더 강력하다.

해설 be동사 is와 비교급 형용사 형태의 보어 more powerful 사이에 위치한 빈칸은 이 비교급 형용사를 수식할 부사가 필요한 자리이므로 (D) noticeably가 정답이다.

어휘 priced 가격이 책정된 similarly (to) (~와) 유사하게 competing 경쟁하는 notice v. ~에 주목하다, ~임을 알아차리다 n. 주목, 공지 noticeably 눈에 띄게, 현저히

7.
정답 (D)

해석 소매업종에서 최소 6개월간 근무한 경력만 있다면 지원서를 제출해 보시기를 모든 구직자분들께 말씀드립니다.

해설 빈칸 앞뒤에 주어와 동사가 포함된 절이 각각 있으므로 빈칸에 접속사가 필요하다. 빈칸 다음의 절이 구직 지원에 필요한 조건으로 판단할 수 있으므로 '~하는 한, ~이기만 하면'이라는 뜻의 (D) as long as가 정답이다.

어휘 invite A to do A에게 ~할 것을 청하다 job seeker 구직자 application form 지원서 as long as ~하는 한, ~이기만 하면 at least 최소한 retail 소매(업) in case ~의 경우

8.
정답 (D)

해석 최소 200명의 사람들이 그 재무팀장 직책에 지원하기는 했지만, 많은 이들이 필수 자격 요건이 부족했다.

해설 빈칸이 접속사 but과 동사 lacked 사이에 위치하고 있으므로 빈칸은 이 절의 주어 자리이며, 앞서 언급된 복수명사구 200 people을 대신할 대명사가 쓰여 이들의 자격 부족을 나타내는 의미가 되어야 알맞으므로 복수명사를 대신할 수 있는 대명사 (D) many가 정답이다.

어휘 apply for ~에 지원하다, ~을 신청하다 financial 재무의, 금융의 position 직책, 일자리 lack A A가 부족하다 necessary 필수의, 필요한 qualifications 자격 요건

9.
정답 (C)

해석 동봉된 부동산 안내책자는 뉴욕의 롱 아일랜드에 있는 넓고 호화로운 주택들을 상세히 설명하고 있습니다.

해설 빈칸이 정관사와 명사 사이에 있으므로 이 명사를 수식할 수 있으면서 형용사의 역할을 할 수 있는 분사가 와야 한다. 현재분사 (B) enclosing과 과거분사 (C) enclosed 중에서 골라야 하는데 부동산 안내책자는 사람에 의해 동봉되는 대상이므로 수동의 의미를 나타내는 (C) enclosed가 정답이다.

어휘 enclosed 동봉된 real estate 부동산, 부동산 중개업 detail n. 세부내용 v. ~을 상세히 알리다, 열거하다 spacious 넓은 enclosure 동봉 enclose ~을 동봉하다

10.
정답 (C)

해석 미니 박사에 따르면, 확장 계획은 추가적인 조사가 실시될 수 있을 때까지 연기될 것이다.

해설 빈칸 뒤에 제시된 사람 이름은 확장 계획이 연기될 것이라는 내용의 출처를 나타내는 것이 의미상 가장 자연스럽다. 따라서 '~에 따르면'이라는 의미의 출처를 나타내는 전치사 (C) According to가 정답이다.

어휘 according to ~에 따르면 expansion 확장 further 추가적인, 더 conduct ~을 실시하다 as well as ~은 물론이고, ~외에도 such as 예를 들면 aside from ~을 제외하면

11.
정답 (A)

해석 예상치 못한 상황으로 인해, 회의 프로그램에 약간의 변경이 이루어질 것이라는 점을 알려드립니다.

해설 빈칸 바로 앞에 있는 형용사 slight의 수식을 받아 의미상 알맞은 어휘를 골라야 한다. 빈칸 앞에 '예상치 못한 상황'이 제시되어 있는데, 이로 인해 '회의 프로그램에 약간의 변경'이 필요할 수 있으므로 (A) modification이 정답이다.

어휘 unforeseen 예상치 못한 circumstance 상황 slight 약간의 modification 수정, 변경 explanation 설명 illustration 삽화

12.
정답 (D)

해석 사진가 조슈아 데이비스 씨는 지난주에 벨뷰 시각 예술 갤러리에서 있었던 전시회에서 자신의 최근 작품을 전시했다.

해설 빈칸 다음에 동사의 목적어가 있으므로 수동태 (C) was presented를 먼저 소거한다. 빈칸 뒤에 작품을 전시한 시점이 과거임을 나타내는 last week's exhibition이 있으므로 과거시제 (D) presented가 정답이다.

어휘 photographer 사진가 present v. ~을 제시하다, 보여주다 latest 최근의, 최신의 exhibition 전시(회) visual art 시각 예술

13.
정답 (C)

해석 새로 구입하신 전기 밥솥을 작동하시는 데 문제가 있을 경우, 저희 웹 사이트에서 도움이 되는 문제 해결 가이드를 확인해 보시기 바랍니다.

해설 정관사 the와 명사구 troubleshooting guide 사이에 위치한 빈칸은 이 명사구를 수식할 형용사가 필요한 자리이므로 (C) helpful이 정답이다.

어휘 have difficulty -ing ~하는 데 문제가 있다 operate ~을 작동하다, ~을 운영하다 troubleshooting 문제 해결, 고장 수리 helpfully 도움이 되게

14.
정답 (B)

해석 셀렉 씨가 훌륭한 리더십과 의사 소통 능력을 보여주었기 때문에, 그는 팀장 직책을 제안받았다.

해설 선택지가 모두 부사절 접속사이므로 해석을 통해 의미상 알맞은 것을 고르면 된다. 뛰어난 능력을 보인 것이 팀장 자리를 제안받은 이유로 판단할 수 있으므로 '~ 때문에'라는 의미의 (B) Because가 정답이다.

어휘 demonstrate ~을 보여 주다, (능력 등) 발휘하다 position 직책, 일자리 until (지속) ~할 때까지 while ~하는 동안, ~인 반면에 unless ~가 아니라면

15.

정답 (A)

해석 우리 업무용 컴퓨터에 설치된 바이러스 방지 프로그램은 악성 소프트웨어로부터 컴퓨터를 안전하게 유지하기 위해 자주 업데이트된다.

해설 선택지가 모두 다른 부사로 구성되어 있으므로 해석을 통해 알맞은 어휘를 골라야 한다. 빈칸에 들어갈 부사는 빈칸 바로 앞에 위치한 동사 is updated를 수식해 바이러스 방지 프로그램의 업데이트 방식과 관련된 의미를 나타내야 한다. 또한, 현재시제로 쓰인 동사와 의미가 어울려야 하므로 (A) frequently가 정답이다.

어휘 anti-virus 바이러스 방지의 keep A B A를 B한 상태로 유지하다 malicious 악성의, 악의적인 frequently 자주, 빈번히 suddenly 갑자기 nearly 거의 barely 거의 ~ 않다

16.

정답 (D)

해석 승인을 받기 위해 제출되는 건축 허가 신청서에는 사업비 사양서가 동봉되어야 합니다.

해설 빈칸에는 빈칸 뒤에 있는 명사 approval을 목적어로 취할 수 있는 전치사가 와야 하므로 접속사 (A) unless를 먼저 소거한다. 제출하는 것은 승인을 목적으로 하기 때문에 빈칸에는 '~을 위하여'라는 목적의 뜻을 나타내는 (D) for가 정답이다.

어휘 permit n. 허가증 v. ~을 허락하다 request n. 신청 v. ~을 신청하다 approval 승인, 찬성 be accompanied by ~을 동반하다 specification 사양서 unless ~하지 않는 한, 만약 ~이 아니라면

Part 6

17-20.

모건 은행 고객 여러분

다음 달부터, 여러분께서는 완전히 새로운 저희 인터넷 뱅킹 프로그램에 온라인으로 등록하실 수 있게 됩니다! 이자가 높은 저축 계좌를 갖고 계시든, 아니면 당좌 예금 계좌를 갖고 계시든 상관없으며, 모든 고객들께서 이 **17** 서비스에 대한 자격을 지니고 계십니다.

18 등록하는 일은 아주 간단합니다. 물론, 사용자 이름과 비밀번호를 설정하시는 데 몇 분의 시간이 필요하실 수도 있지만, 일단 그 부분이 완료되기만 하면, 온라인 뱅킹을 시작하실 준비가 거의 되신 것입니다. 여러분의 온라인 계정이 승인되는 대로 고객 서비스 직원이 여러분께 **19** 통보해 드릴 것이며, 그 시점 이후로 계속 **20** 그것을 사용하실 수 있게 됩니다.

더욱 상세한 정보를 원하시면, 모건 은행 전 지점에서 정보 안내 책자를 가져가시거나, 저희 웹 사이트 www.morganbank.com을 방문하시기 바랍니다.

어휘 register 등록하다 brand new 완전히 새로운 It doesn't matter 상관없다, 중요치 않다 high-interest 이자가 높은, 고금리의 savings account 저축 계좌 checking account 당좌 예금 계좌 be eligible for ~에 대한 자격이 있다 require ~을 필요로 하다 set up ~을 설정하다, 설치하다 once 일단 ~하기만 하면 complete ~을 완료하다 representative 직원 as soon as ~하는 대로, ~하자마자 authorize ~을 승인하다 from A onwards A 이후로 계속

17.

정답 (A)

해설 선택지가 모두 다른 명사로 구성되어 있으므로 해석을 통해 알맞은 어휘를 골라야 한다. 빈칸에 들어갈 명사는 빈칸 앞에 위치한 this와 함께 앞서 언급된 특정 대상을 대신해야 하는데, 고객들이 무엇에 대해 자격을 지니고 있는지를 나타내야 한다. 앞서 새 인터넷 뱅킹 프로그램을 소개하는 문장들이 쓰여 있으므로 이를 한 단어로 가리킬 수 있는 명사로 '서비스'를 의미하는 (A) service가 정답이다.

18.

정답 (C)

해석 (A) 약간의 추가 요금이 적용될 수도 있습니다.
(B) 오늘 찾아 오셔서 새 은행 계좌를 만드시기 바랍니다.
(C) 등록하는 일은 아주 간단합니다.
(D) 사이트 유지관리 작업으로 인해 사용자 접근이 일시적으로 중단될 것입니다.

해설 빈칸 뒤에 사용자 이름과 비밀번호를 설정하는 데 몇 분 걸릴 수도 있다는 사실이 언급되어 있는데, 이는 등록 과정에서 발생 가능한 일이다. 따라서 사용자 등록과 관련된 내용을 담은 문장이 빈칸에 쓰여야 흐름이 자연스러우므로 (C)가 정답이다.

어휘 charge (청구) 요금 apply 적용되다 access 접근, 이용 temporarily 일시적으로 suspend ~을 중단하다, 유예하다

19.

정답 (D)

해설 온라인 계정이 승인되는 대로 고객 서비스 직원이 고객(you)을 상대로 할 수 있는 일을 나타낼 동사가 빈칸에 쓰여야 한다. 따라서 승인이 된 사실을 고객에게 알리는 과정을 거치는 것이 자연스러우므로 '~에게 통보하다, 알리다'를 의미하는 (D) notify가 정답이다.

어휘 respond (to) (~에) 반응하다, 대응하다 present ~을 제시하다, 발표하다

20.

정답 (B)

해설 빈칸에는 to부정사로 쓰인 동사 use의 목적어로서 사용 대상이 되는 것을 나타낼 대명사가 와야 한다. 따라서 바로 앞에 언급된

온라인 계정(your online account)이 사용 대상이 되어야 알맞으므로 단수명사를 대신하는 (B) it이 정답이다.

21-24.

관계자께,

저희 회사가 지금까지 저희에게 매우 성공적이었던 한 해를 기념하기 위해 연말 연회를 여는 것을 계획 중입니다. 약 150명의 저희 직원이 참석할 것입니다. 많은 제 동료 직원들에 의해 더 베벌리 호텔이 저에게 추천되었습니다. **21** 하지만, 귀 호텔에서 저희 요구 조건을 충족해 주실 수 있을지에 대해 몇몇 걱정거리가 있습니다.

저는 그곳의 연회실들이 저희가 필요로 하는 사항에 대해 **22** 충분하지 않을 수도 있다는 우려를 갖고 있습니다. 특히, 저희는 장내 방송 설비, 프로젝터, 노트북 컴퓨터, 그리고 스크린을 포함해 무대 및 시청각 장비를 포함하는 대형 공간을 찾고자 합니다.

귀 호텔의 연회장에 관한 상세정보를 저에게 보내주실 수 있다면, 대단히 감사할 것입니다. 저는 특히 그곳의 연회 홀에 관심이 있는데, 그곳의 공간들 중에서 가장 크고 잘 갖춰진 곳이라고 생각하기 때문입니다. **23** 하지만, 그곳이 이미 예약되어 있다면 다른 공간도 괜찮을 것입니다. 저희가 이달 말까지 행사장을 예약하기를 원하기 때문에 가급적 빨리 답장을 **24** 받을 수 있다면 기쁠 것입니다. 미리 도움에 대해 감사 드립니다.

피터 퀸

어휘 **year-end** 연말의 **approximately** 약, 대략 **attend** ~에 참석하다 **colleague** 동료 (직원) **have reservations about** ~에 대해 걱정거리가 있다, 의구심이 있다 **meet** ~을 충족하다 **requirement** 요구 조건, 필요 조건 **concern** 우려, 걱정 **function room** 연회장, 행사장 **adequate** 충분한 **specifically** 특히, 구체적으로(= particularly) **audio/visual equipment** 시청각 장비 **public address system** 장내 방송 설비 **equipped** 갖춰진 **at your earliest possible convenience** 가급적 빨리 **venue** 행사장 **in advance** 미리, 사전에

21.

정답 (A)

해설 빈칸 앞 문장에는 많은 동료들이 추천해 주었다는 긍정적인 정보가, 빈칸 뒤에는 걱정거리가 있다는 부정적인 말이 쓰여 있다. 따라서 대조적인 내용이 제시되는 흐름임을 알 수 있으므로 '하지만'이라는 의미로 대조나 반대를 나타내는 접속부사 (A) However가 정답이다.

어휘 **therefore** 따라서, 그러므로 **furthermore** 더욱이 **similarly** 유사하게, 마찬가지로

22.

정답 (C)

해설 빈칸 앞 단락 마지막 문장에 몇몇 걱정거리가 있다고 언급한 것과 관련된 우려 사항을 말하는 문장이 되어야 자연스럽다. 따라

서 필요로 하는 것에 대해 충분하지 않을 수 있다는 의미가 되어야 알맞으므로 '충분한'을 뜻하는 (C) adequate이 정답이다.

23.

정답 (A)

해석 **(A) 하지만, 그곳이 이미 예약되어 있다면 다른 공간도 괜찮을 것입니다.**
(B) 결과적으로, 출장 요리 업무를 처리할 직원이 충분치 않을 수도 있을 것입니다.
(C) 무대 조명 또한 유용할 수 있겠지만, 필수는 아닙니다.
(D) 저희 직원들과 저는 그곳에서 아주 멋진 저녁 시간을 보냈습니다.

해설 빈칸 앞 문장에 연회용 홀에 특히 관심이 있음을 밝히면서 그곳이 가장 좋은 공간임을 언급하고 있다. 즉 그곳을 이용하고 싶다는 뜻을 나타내는 것이며, 이 홀을 it으로 지칭해 이미 예약이 되어 있어 이용하지 못할 경우에 대한 대안을 알리는 (A)가 정답이다.

어휘 **as a result** 결과적으로 **handle** ~을 처리하다, 다루다 **catering** 출장 요리 제공(업)

24.

정답 (B)

해설 빈칸 앞에 위치한 would be happy는 to부정사와 결합해 '~하면 기쁠 것이다, 기꺼이 ~할 것이다' 등의 의미를 나타내므로 (B) to receive가 정답이다.

Part 7

25-26.

수신: 멀베리 패션 본사 전 직원
발신: 베벌리 건, 회장 및 대표이사

25 비앙카 빙 씨께서 4월에 은퇴하시면 유럽 영업 담당 이사직을 맡도록 이사회에서 현재 우리의 국내 영업 책임자인 마고 듀코브니 씨를 선임했다는 사실을 알려 드리게 되어 기쁩니다.

약 10년 전에, 듀코브니 씨는 우리 멀베리 사에서 직책 하나를 맡아, 우리 회사의 파리 지사로 즉시 파견되었습니다. 이후에, 듀코브니 씨는 샌프란시스코 지사로, 그리고 마지막으로 우리 본사로 전근되었습니다. 패션에 대한 그녀의 열정과 영업 관리에 있어서의 업무 숙련도가 그녀를 우리 회사의 진정한 인재로 만들어주고 있습니다.

26 또한 오랜 기간에 걸쳐 빙 씨께서 우리 멀베리 사에 공헌해오신 많은 소중한 일들을 기념하는 것도 중요하므로, 3월 30일에 우리가 모두 매그놀리아 레스토랑에서 함께 하는 자리를 마련해 두었습니다. 이 행사에 관해 어떤 질문이든 있으실 경우, 제 비서 니아 골드버그 씨에게 내선번호 331번으로 전화하시기 바랍니다. 추가 상세 정보를 원하시는 분은, 내선번호 306번으로 벤자민 건 인사부장님께 연락하십시오.

어휘 **board of directors** 이사회 **select** ~을 선임하다, 선택하다 **take over as** ~로서 자리를 맡다 **retire** 은퇴하다 **immediately** 즉시 **be assigned to** ~로 파견되다, 배치되다 **be transferred to** ~로 전근되다 **enthusiasm** 열정 **proficiency** 숙련(도), 능숙함 **asset** 인재, 자산 **commemorate** ~을 기념하다 **invaluable** 소중한 **make contributions** 공헌하다, 기여하다 **organize** ~을 마련하다, 조직하다 **extension** 내선전화(번호)

25. 공지의 목적은 무엇인가?
(A) 영업 수치에 관해 보고하는 것
(B) 한 가지 업무가 완료되도록 요청하는 것
(C) 정책 변동을 설명하는 것
(D) 직원들에게 인사 이동을 알리는 것

정답 (D)

해설 첫 단락에 비앙카 빙 씨의 은퇴와 유럽 영업 담당 이사직을 맡도록 마고 듀코브니 씨를 선임함(Margot Duchovny, to take over as European Sales Director when Bianca Bing retires in April) 사실 두 가지를 언급하고 있다. 이는 인사 이동을 알리는 것이므로 (D)가 정답이다.

어휘 **figure** 수치, 숫자 **request that** ~하도록 요청하다 **policy change** 정책 변동 **notify A of B** A에게 B를 알리다

26. 왜 3월 30일에 행사가 개최되는가?
(A) 신임 이사를 맞이하기 위해
(B) 유럽에서의 영업 전망을 발표하기 위해
(C) 적합한 후임자를 선택하기 위해
(D) 한 직원의 업적을 인정하기 위해

정답 (D)

해설 3월 30일이라는 날짜가 제시되는 세 번째 단락에, 오랜 기간에 걸쳐 빙 씨가 회사에 공헌해 온 많은 소중한 일들을 기념한다고(It is also important that we commemorate the many invaluable contributions that Ms. Bing made ~ get together on March 30 at the Magnolia Restaurant) 알리고 있다. 이는 그 동안의 공헌을 기리는 일, 즉 빙 씨의 업적을 인정하기 위한 일이므로 (D)가 정답이다.

어휘 **executive** 이사, 임원 **projection** 전망 **replacement** 후임(자), 대체(자) **recognize** ~을 인정하다 **accomplishment** 업적, 성취

27-29.

코크 주민 자치회 (CRA) 가입

27 저희 코크 주민 자치회는 우리 도시에 영향을 주는 사안들을 논의하고 직접적으로 영향을 미칠 수 있는 방법을 여러분께 제공해 드립니다. CRA에 가입함으로써, 여러분께서는 제안된 지역 사회 행사와 29(B) 도시 개발 계획, 그리고 우리 도시의 29(A) 학교 및 병원에 영향을 주는 사안들에 관해 이러한 일들이 일반 대중에게 공식적으로 알려지기 전에 들어 보실 수 있게 됩니다.

월례 CRA 회의에서 이러한 사안들을 논의하실 수 있을 뿐만 아니라, <코크 회보>라는 제목의 주간 소식지도 받아 보시게 됩니다. 이 간행물은 회원들이 작성한 기사와 앞으로 있을 지역 사회 행사 날짜 목록, 지역 모금 운동에 관한 보도, 그리고 도시 내 여러 매장에서 이용 가능한 29(C) 특가 행사에 관한 소식을 포함합니다.

28 자치회 회원이 되시는 데 관심이 있으실 경우, secretary@cra.com으로 도리스 웬트워스 씨에게 이메일을 보내시면, 이분께서 즉시 저희 명단에 여러분의 성함을 추가해 드릴 것입니다.

어휘 **association** 협회, ~회 **influence** ~에 영향을 미치다 (= affect) **proposed** 제안된 **urban development** 도시 개발 **issue** 사안, 문제 **matter** 일, 문제 **the general public** 일반 대중 **titled A** A라는 제목의 **publication** 간행물, 출판물 **fundraising** 모금, 기금 마련 **effort** (대대적인) 운동, 노력 **special offer** 특가 (제품)

27. 무엇이 광고되고 있는가?
(A) 지역 잡지
(B) 곧 있을 회의
(C) 지역 사회 단체
(D) 도시 개발 계획

정답 (C)

해설 첫 번째 단락에 코크 주민 자치회는 우리 도시에 영향을 주는 사안들을 논의하고 직접적으로 영향을 미칠 수 있는 방법을 제공한다고(The Cork Residents Association provides you with a way to directly influence and discuss issues that affect our town) 알리면서 회원 가입과 관련된 정보를 제공하고 있다. 따라서 지역 사회 단체에 관한 광고임을 알 수 있으므로 (C)가 정답이다.

어휘 **upcoming** 곧 있을, 다가오는

28. 관심 있는 사람들은 무엇을 하도록 권장되는가?
(A) 이메일로 회원 자격을 얻는 일
(B) 도시 내 행사 입장권을 구매하는 일
(C) 신문사에 기사를 제출하는 일
(D) 지역 매장 소유주들에게 연락하는 일

정답 (A)

해설 마지막 단락에 자치회 회원이 되는 데 관심이 있으면 secretary@cra.com으로 도리스 웬트워스 씨에게 이메일을 보내도록(If you are interested in becoming a member of the association, please e-mail Doris Wentworth at secretary@cra.com) 권하고 있다. 이는 이메일을 통해 회원 자격을 얻는 일을 가리키므로 (A)가 정답이다.

어휘 **be encouraged to do** ~하도록 권장되다, 장려되다

29. CRA 회원들이 안내 받지 못할 가능성이 있는 것은 무엇인가?
(A) 지역 의료 서비스 소식
(B) 공사 제안
(C) 쇼핑 할인

(D) 취업 기회

정답 (D)

해설 회원들에게 제공되는 소식과 관련해, 첫 단락의 도시 개발 계획 (plans for urban development)에서 (B)를, 학교 및 병원에 영향을 주는 사안들(issues affecting our schools and hospital)에서 (A)를 확인할 수 있다. 또한, 두 번째 단락의 특가 행사에 관한 소식(news about special offers)에서 (C)도 확인 가능하다. 하지만 취업 기회와 관련된 정보는 지문에 제시되어 있지 않으므로 (D)가 정답이다.

어휘 **be likely to do** ~할 가능성이 있다 **inform** ~에게 통보하다, 알리다 **healthcare** 의료

30-32.

더 로치포드 이브닝 뉴스
시의회, 마침내 교통 계획을 발표하다

8월 8일

수개월에 걸친 교통 당국자 및 건설 업체들과의 협의 끝에, 로치포드 시의회가 도시 전역에 새로운 버스 노선들을 추가하는 계획을 공식 승인했습니다. 다음 달부터, 30 시내 지역에서 도시의 다양한 교외 지역으로 뻗어 나가는 여러 도로들이 새로운 버스 전용 차로 및 경로를 수용하기 위해 확장되고 재포장될 것입니다. — [1] —. 주민들은 도시의 버스 노선망이 충분히 광범위하지 않다는 의견을 오랫동안 고수해 왔기 때문에, 새로운 경로들이 대부분의 지역 사람들에게 좋은 소식으로 다가올 것입니다. — [2] —.

32 추가로, 도시 중심 지역의 버스 터미널이 위에 언급한 경로에서 이용될 15대의 추가 차량을 받게 될 것입니다. — [3] —. 버스 요금 및 월간/연간 승차권은 모든 경로의 버스에 대해 동일 가격으로 유지됩니다. — [4] —.

31 새로운 교통 경로에 대한 도표를 확인해 보시고 요금 및 버스 운행 일정에 관한 추가 정보를 알아보시려면, www. roachfordtransit.com을 방문하시기 바랍니다.

어휘 **council** 의회 **transit** 교통, 운송 **negotiation** 협의, 협상 **official** n. 당국자, 관계자 **formally** 공식적으로, 정식으로 **authorize** ~을 승인하다, ~을 인가하다 **run** (길 등이) 뻗어 있다, 이어지다 **suburb** 교외 지역 **widen** ~을 확장하다, ~을 넓히다 **resurface** (도로 등) ~을 재포장하다 **accommodate** ~을 수용하다 **hold the opinion that** ~라는 의견을 유지하다 **sufficiently** 충분히 **extensive** 광범위한, 폭넓은 **additionally** 추가로 **fleet** (한 단체가 소유한) 전체 차량, 비행기, 선박 **aforementioned** 위에서 언급한 **pass** 승차권, 이용권

30. 기사가 주로 무엇을 이야기하고 있는가?
(A) 새로운 버스 터미널의 공개
(B) 교통 시스템을 개선하기 위한 노력
(C) 시내 교통 혼잡을 완화하기 위한 계획
(D) 버스 티켓 가격의 인상

정답 (B)

해설 첫 단락에 버스 노선 추가 계획이 승인된 사실과 함께 시내 지역에서 도시의 다양한 교외 지역으로 뻗어 나가는 여러 도로들이 새로운 버스 전용 차로 및 경로를 수용하기 위해 확장되고 재포장될 것이라고(several roads that run from the downtown area ~ will be widened and resurfaced to accommodate new bus lanes and routes) 알리고 있다. 이는 교통 시스템을 개선하는 일에 해당되므로 (B)가 정답이다.

어휘 **unveiling** (첫) 공개, 선보임 **improve** ~을 개선하다, ~을 향상시키다 **transportation** 교통, 운송 **alleviate** ~을 완화하다 **traffic congestion** 교통 혼잡

31. 기사 내용에 따르면, 사람들이 웹 사이트에서 무엇을 할 수 있는가?
(A) 할인된 교통 승차권을 출력하는 일
(B) 공사 일정을 확인하는 일
(C) 의회의 계획에 관한 의견을 남기는 일
(D) 제안된 버스 경로 안내도를 확인하는 일

정답 (D)

해설 웹 사이트가 언급된 마지막 단락에 새로운 교통 경로에 대한 도표를 확인하고 요금 및 버스 운행 일정에 관한 추가 정보를 알아보려면 웹 사이트를 방문하라고(To view a diagram of the new transit routes ~ visit www.roachfordtransit.com) 알리고 있다. 따라서, 둘 중 하나에 해당되는 버스 경로 안내도를 확인하는 일을 뜻하는 (D)가 정답이다.

어휘 **leave** ~을 남기다 **proposed** 제안된

32. [1], [2], [3], [4]로 표기된 위치들 중에서, 다음 문장이 들어가기에 가장 적절한 곳은 어디인가?

"오염을 줄이기 위한 노력의 일환으로, 이 버스들은 모두 전기 차량이 될 것입니다."

(A) [1]
(B) [2]
(C) [3]
(D) [4]

정답 (C)

해설 제시된 문장은 특정 버스를 가리키는 the buses와 함께 그 버스들이 오염을 줄이기 위해 전기 차량이 될 것이라는 의미를 담고 있다. 따라서, 버스 터미널에 제공되는 15대의 추가 차량을 언급한 문장 뒤에 위치한 [3]에 들어가 그 특징을 알리는 흐름이 되어야 자연스러우므로 (C)가 정답이다.

어휘 **in an effort to do** ~하기 위한 노력의 일환으로 **reduce** ~을 줄이다, ~을 감소시키다 **pollution** 오염

33-36.

허진스 코퍼레이션 인트라넷
챗 클라이언트 v.2.2
로그인한 사용자: 에스더 모펫 (영업부)

에스터 모펫: (오후 3:03) <u>33</u> 퇴근 후에 극장에서 새 브래드 케인 영화 보러 가는 거 다들 어떠세요?

시드니 워커: (오후 3:05) 저는 오늘 저녁에 시간 있어요.

올리 에드워즈: (오후 3:07) 저도요.

루시 포브스: (오후 3:09) 저도 가고 싶긴 한데, 다음 주에 있을 면접을 보러 오는 일과 관련해 지원자들에게 전화해야 해서 늦게까지 있을 예정이에요. 그 영화 어떤지 내일 알려주세요!

에스터 모펫: (오후 3:12) 아쉽네요, 루시 씨. 당신 부서에 어떤 자리를 충원하시려는 거죠?

루시 포브스: (오후 3:14) <u>34</u> 법인세 관리 책임자와 급여 관리 담당 보조를 찾고 있어요. <u>35</u> 그랜섬 씨께서 저에게 오늘 저녁에 지원자 약 20명에게 전화하라고 말씀하셨어요.

올리 에드워즈: (오후 3:15) 와우! 전화 횟수가 많네요. 그 일 좀 도와 드릴까요?

루시 포브스: (오후 3:16) 그럼 감사하겠습니다. 구직 지원자들에게 전화해 보신 경험이 한 번이라도 있으세요?

올리 에드워즈: (오후 3:17) 그럼요, 전에 그런 일에 대해 저희 부장님을 도와 드린 적이 있어요.

루시 포브스: (오후 3:17) 음, 그럼 아주 좋을 것 같아요. 고마워요, 올리 씨.

시드니 워커: (오후 3:19) 완전히 새로운 우리 대회의실에서 그 면접을 개최하실 예정이신가요?

루시 포브스: (오후 3:21) 누군가가 저에게 자신의 시간대를 이용하게 해주지 않으면 불가능해요. 월요일에 하루 종일 예약이 꽉 차 있어요.

에스터 모펫: (오후 3:22) <u>36</u> 제 시간을 이용하셔도 됩니다. 저는 그냥 팀 회의를 위해 이용할 생각이었거든요.

루시 포브스: (오후 3:23) 잘됐네요! 몇 시에 제가 그 방을 이용할 수 있는지 알려만 주세요.

어휘 **sales** 영업, 매출 **How do you feel about ~?** ~은 어떠세요? **catch** ~을 보다, ~을 관람하다 **applicant** 지원자 **let A know** A에게 알리다 **That's shame** 아쉽네요, 안 됐네요 **position** 일자리, 직책 **fill** ~을 충원하다, ~을 채우다 **look for** ~을 찾다 **corporate tax** 법인세 **payroll** 급여 관리, 급여 대상자 명단 **assistant** 보조, 비서 **around** 약, 대략 **hand** 도움(의 손길) **appreciate** ~에 대해 감사하다 **hold** ~을 개최하다, ~을 열다 **brand new** 완전히 새로운 **Not unless** ~하지 않는다면 아니다, ~가 아니라면 안 된다 **let A do** A에게 ~하게 하다 **time slot** 시간대 **fully** 완전히, 전적으로 **booked** 예약된

---

33. 오후 3시 5분에, 워커 씨가 "I'm free tonight"이라고 말할 때 무엇을 의미할 것 같은가?

(A) 다른 영화를 보고 싶어 한다.
(B) 무료 영화 입장권이 있다.
(C) 모펫 씨의 아이디어를 마음에 들어 한다.
(D) 출장 일정을 재조정하고 싶어 한다.

정답 (C)

해설 3시 3분 메시지에 모펫 씨가 퇴근 후에 극장에서 새 브래드 케인 영화 보러 가는 게 어떤지(How do you all feel about catching the new Brad Kane movie?) 묻는 것에 대해 워커 씨가 '오늘 저녁에 시간 있어요'라고 대답하는 흐름이다. 이는 저녁에 시간이 있어서 함께 영화 보러 갈 수 있다는 뜻으로써 그 아이디어가 마음에 든다는 동의를 나타내는 말이므로 (C)가 정답이다.

어휘 **would prefer to do** ~하고 싶다, ~하고자 하다 **reschedule** ~의 일정을 재조정하다

34. 구직 지원자들과 관련해 암시된 것은 무엇인가?

(A) 오늘 회사로 올 예정이다.
(B) 에드워즈 씨가 면접 볼 것이다.
(C) 이메일로 연락 받았다.
(D) 회계팀 직책에 지원했다.

정답 (D)

해설 구직 지원자 면접과 관련해 이야기하던 포브스 씨가 3시 14분 메시지에 법인세 관리 책임자와 급여 관리 담당 보조를 찾고 있다고(We're looking for a corporate tax manager and a payroll assistant) 언급하고 있다. 이는 회계 관련 업무로서, 회계팀 직책에 지원한 사람들을 찾는다는 것을 알 수 있으므로 (D)가 정답이다.

어휘 **contact** ~에게 연락하다 **apply for** ~에 지원하다, ~을 신청하다

35. 그랜섬 씨와 관련해 암시된 것은 무엇인가?

(A) 지원시를 제출했다.
(B) 급여 관리 업무 보조이다.
(C) 포브스 씨의 부서장이다.
(D) 영화를 볼 계획이다.

정답 (C)

해설 그랜섬 씨의 이름이 언급되는 3시 14분 메시지에 포브스 씨가 그랜섬 씨로부터 오늘 저녁에 지원자에게 연락하는 일을 하도록 전달 받은 사실을 말하고 있다. 이를 통해 두 사람이 상사와 부하 직원의 관계에 있음을 알 수 있으므로 (C)가 정답이다.

어휘 **submit** ~을 제출하다 **application** 지원(서), 신청(서)

36. 누가 대회의실을 이용하기 위해 예약했는가?

(A) 모펫 씨
(B) 워커 씨
(C) 에드워즈 씨
(D) 포브스 씨

정답 (A)

해설 대회의실 이용과 관련해, 3시 22분 메시지에 모펫 씨가 자신의 시간대를 이용하라고 알리면서 그저 팀 회의를 위해 이용할 생각이었다고(You can use mine. I was just going to use it for a team meeting) 언급하고 있어 모펫 씨가 대회의실을 예약한 상태임을 알 수 있으므로 (A)가 정답이다.

어휘 make a reservation 예약하다

37-40.

수신: 영업부 전 직원
발신: 조나스 올슨, 영업부장
제목: 팀 단합 행사
날짜: 7월 5일 수요일

아시다시피, 우리 코넥스 통신회사의 연례 팀 단합 행사가 7월 22일, 토요일에 개최됩니다. 예년의 행사들과 관련된 여러분의 불만 사항을 들은 후에, **38** 경영진이 모여 올해는 다르게 진행할 방법을 논의했습니다. 더욱 흥미를 불러일으킬 수 있는 환경을 제공하기 위한 노력으로, **37** 저희는 이 행사가 더 이상 본사 근처에 있는 컨벤션 센터에서 개최되지 않을 것이라는 결정을 내렸습니다. 이번 행사는 에버그린 밸리 팜에 있는 야외 공간으로 옮겨졌습니다. 우리가 화요일 회의에서 논의한 활동 일정을 포함해 이 행사와 관련된 그 외의 모든 것은 대부분 변경되지 않은 상태로 유지됩니다.

영업부 전 직원은 이번 야유회에 참가해야 합니다. 세 곳의 다른 우리 지사에 근무하는 직원들 또한 참석할 것이며, 이번 행사 활동을 마련한 회사인 코퍼레이트 챌린지의 직원들도 참석할 것입니다. 그날 하루를 마칠 때, 우리는 모두 저녁 식사를 위해 근처의 레스토랑에 **39** 모일 것이며, 그곳에서 회사 창립자이신 아놀드 룬드그렌 씨께서 모든 사람에게 현재 회사의 목표에 관해 말씀해 주실 것입니다. **40** 행사 당일에 셔틀 버스가 제공될 것입니다. 이를 이용하기를 원하시는 경우, 알림판의 양식에 성함을 작성해 주시기 바랍니다. 마지막으로, 여러분 모두 얼마든지 이메일로 저에게 어떤 질문이든 하셔도 좋습니다.

어휘 annual 연례의, 해마다의 take place (일, 행사 등이) 개최되다, 발생되다 regarding ~와 관련해 stimulating 흥미를 불러 일으키는, 자극이 되는 no longer 더 이상 ~ 않다 itinerary 일정(표) be required to do ~해야 하다 excursion 야유회, 짧은 여행 in attendance 참석한 representative 직원 assemble 모이다 nearby 근처의 take advantage of ~을 이용하다 notice board 알림판 be welcome to do 얼마든지 ~해도 좋다

37. 회람이 왜 발송되었는가?
(A) 행사에 관한 부정적인 의견에 대해 논의하기 위해
(B) 단체 활동에 관한 제안을 요청하기 위해
(C) 행사를 위한 새로운 장소를 알리기 위해
(D) 행사 날짜의 변경을 요청하기 위해

정답 (C)

해설 첫 단락에 해당 행사가 더 이상 본사 근처에 있는 컨벤션 센터에서 개최되지 않을 것이라는 결정을 내린 사실을(the event will no longer be held at the convention center near the head office) 알리면서 새로운 장소 및 관련 세부 정보를 제공하고 있다. 따라서 새로운 행사 장소를 알리는 것이 목적임을 알 수 있으므로 (C)가 정답이다.

어휘 ask for ~을 요청하다 suggestion 의견, 제안 venue (행사 등의) 장소

38. 올슨 씨에 관해 언급된 것은 무엇인가?
(A) 코넥스 통신회사의 창립자이다.
(B) 해당 행사에 관한 회의에 참석했다.
(C) 다음 주 화요일에 한 컨벤션에 참석할 예정이다.
(D) 여러 행사 활동을 조직하는 데 도움이 되었다.

정답 (B)

해설 첫 번째 단락에 경영진이 모여 올해 행사를 다르게 진행할 방법을 논의했다고(the management team met and discussed) 언급되어 있고, 그 뒤 문장에서 경영진을 '저희 (we)'라고 언급하였으므로 올슨 씨는 관련 회의에 참석했음을 알 수 있다. 따라서 (B)가 정답이다.

39. 두 번째 단락, 네 번째 줄의 단어 "assemble"과 의미가 가장 가까운 것은 무엇인가?
(A) 대화하다
(B) 짓다, 구축하다
(C) (자료 등을) 편집하다
(D) 모이다

정답 (D)

해설 제시된 단어 assemble 앞뒤의 내용을 보면, 행사가 끝나고 모든 사람들이 근처에 있는 레스토랑에서 하는 일을 나타낸다는 것을 알 수 있다(we will all ~ at a nearby restaurant for dinner). 따라서 다같이 모여 식사하는 자리가 마련된다는 것을 알 수 있으므로 '모이다'를 뜻하는 (D) gather가 정답이다.

40. 행사 참석자들은 무엇을 하도록 요청 받는가?
(A) 코퍼레이트 챌린지의 직원에게 연락하는 일
(B) 교통편이 필요할 경우에 각자의 이름을 명단에 추가하는 일
(C) 어떤 문의사항이든 있을 경우에 룬드그렌 씨에게 이메일을 보내는 일
(D) 다른 지사에서 열리는 회의에 참석하는 일

정답 (B)

해설 두 번째 단락 후반부에, 셔틀 버스가 제공된다는 말과 함께 이를 이용하기를 원하면 알림판의 양식에 이름을 작성하도록(A shuttle bus will be provided on the day of the event. If you wish to take advantage of this, write your name on the form) 요청하고 있으므로 (B)가 정답이다.

어휘 attendee 참석자 be asked to do ~하도록 요청 받다 require ~을 필요로 하다 query 문의, 질문

41-45.

> **수신:** 조지 핼리버튼 <ghalliburton@swiftrealty.com>
> **발신:** 세레나 졸리 <sjolie@mymail.com>
> **제목:** 배관 문제
> **날짜:** 3월 7일
>
> 핼리버튼 씨께,
>
> **41** 어젯밤 이후로, 제 주방 수도꼭지에서는 물이 전혀 나오지 않고 있고, 욕실 수압은 대단히 낮습니다. **42** 제가 오늘 아침에 건물 관리 책임자에게 한 번 전화해 봤는데, 이분께서 전에 저에게 건물이 특정 배관 업체와 계약을 맺었다고 얘기해 주셨기 때문입니다. 하지만, 전화를 받지 않으셔서, 제 이웃인 월터 티민스 씨께 어떻게 해야 하는지 여쭤 봤습니다. 이분께서 난방 문제를 겪으셨을 때 귀하께서 한 차례 도움을 제공해 주셨다고 알려 주셨습니다. 제가 지난달에 귀하의 사무실에 갔을 때 귀하의 비서이신 리사 젠킨스 씨께서 귀하의 이메일 주소를 적어 주셨던 게 기억 났습니다. 배관 문제와 관련해 제가 어떻게 해야 하는지 조언해 주실 수 있기를 바랍니다.
>
> 안녕히 계십시오.
>
> 세레나 졸리
> 612호
> 산타 모니카 아파트

어휘 plumbing 배관 faucet 수도꼭지 extremely 대단히, 매우 previously 이전에, 과거에 agreement 계약(서), 합의(서) specific 특정한, 구체적인 inform A that A에게 ~라고 알리다 offer A B A에게 B를 제공하다 assistance 도움, 지원 on one occasion 한 차례 assistant 비서, 조수 hopefully 희망하여, 바라건대

> **수신:** 세레나 졸리 <sjolie@mymail.com>
> **발신:** 조지 핼리버튼 <ghalliburton@swiftrealty.com>
> **제목:** 회신: 배관 문제
> **날짜:** 3월 7일
>
> 세레나 씨께,
>
> 귀하의 아파트에 나타난 문제에 관해 듣게 되어 유감입니다. **42** 건물 관리 책임자이신 마리오 곤잘레스 씨는 **43** 일반적으로 수리 문제를 처리하시거나, 수리 작업을 하기 위해 전문가를 부르는 일을 하시는 분입니다. 안타깝게도, 이분께서 현재 휴가 중이십니다. 건물은 근처의 네스터 블리바드에 자리잡고 있는 핸디 플러밍과 거래 계약이 되어 있습니다. **45** 제가 그곳 책임자와 아는 사이이기 때문에, 이분 휴대전화로 연락해 보겠습니다. 그 후에, 몇 시에 귀하의 수도 문제를 바로잡으러 들르실 수 있을지 이메일을 보내 알려 드리겠습니다. **44** 제 사무실에서 주택 임대 계약서에 서명하셨을 때 제 명함을 남겨 드린다는 걸 깜빡 잊어서 죄송합니다. 555-8282번으로 언제든지 저에게 연락하시면 됩니다.
>
> 안녕히 계십시오.
>
> 조지 핼리버튼

어휘 normally 일반적으로, 보통 take care of ~을 처리하다, ~을 다루다 call A out (급한 상황에서) A를 부르다, A를 호출하다 specialist 전문가 currently 현재 business arrangement 거래 계약, 사업 합의 situated on ~에 자리잡고 있는, ~에 위치한 nearby 근처에 acquaintance 아는 사람, 지인 get in touch with ~와 연락하다 afterwards 그 후에, 나중에 let A know A에게 알리다 come around 들르다, 찾아 오다 leave A B A에게 B를 남기다 lease 임대 계약(서) reach ~에게 연락하다

41. 첫 번째 이메일에서, 졸리 씨 아파트의 문제와 관련해 언급된 것은 무엇인가?

(A) 전에도 일어난 적이 있었다.
(B) 오늘 아침에 악화되었다.
(C) 다른 세입자들에게 영향을 미쳤다.
(D) 어제 시작되었다.

정답 (D)

해설 첫 번째 이메일 시작 부분에 어젯밤 이후로 주방 수도꼭지에서는 물이 전혀 나오지 않고 있고 욕실 수압은 대단히 낮다는 (Since last night, there has been no water coming) 문제를 알리는 말이 쓰여 있다. 이는 어제 문제가 발생되었다는 뜻이므로 (D)가 정답이다.

어휘 worse 악화된, 더 나쁜 affect ~에 영향을 미치다 tenant 세입자

42. 졸리 씨가 문제와 관련해 누구에게 처음 연락하려 시도했을 것 같은가?

(A) 월터 티민스
(B) 조지 핼리버튼
(C) 마리오 곤잘레스
(D) 리사 젠킨스

정답 (C)

해설 첫 번째 지문 초반부에 문제 상황을 언급한 직후에 오늘 아침에 건물 관리 책임자에게 전화한(I tried calling the building manager this morning) 사실을 알리고 있다. 이와 관련해, 두 번째 지문 시작 부분에 건물 관리 책임자의 이름이 마리오 곤잘레스라고(The building manager, Mario Gonzalez) 쓰여 있으므로 (C)가 정답이다.

어휘 attempt to do ~하려 시도하다

43. 두 번째 이메일에서, 첫 번째 단락, 두 번째 줄의 단어 "normally"와 의미가 가장 가까운 것은 무엇인가?

(A) 주기적으로
(B) 일반적으로
(C) 다행히
(D) 분명히

정답 (B)

해설 해당 문장에서 normally가 쓰인 앞뒤 부분을 읽어 보면, 현재 시제 동사(is, takes, calls)가 쓰여 있어 건물 관리 책임자인 마리오 곤잘레스 씨가 평소에 하는 일을 설명하고 있다는 것을 알

수 있다. 따라서, 일반적으로 늘 하는 일을 말하기 위해 현재시제 동사와 어울리는 normally가 쓰였다는 것을 알 수 있으므로 '일반적으로' 등을 뜻하는 또 다른 부사 (B) ordinarily가 정답이다.

44. 핼리버튼 씨가 누구일 것 같은가?
(A) 건물 세입자
(B) 지역 배관공
(C) 부동산 중개업자
(D) 건물 관리 책임자

정답 (C)

해설 핼리버튼 씨가 작성한 이메일인 두 번째 지문 후반부에 자신의 사무실에서 상대방인 세레나 씨가 주택 임대 계약서에 서명한 일을(when you signed the housing lease at my office) 언급하는 말이 쓰여 있다. 이는 부동산 중개업을 하는 사람이 하는 일에 해당되므로 (C)가 정답이다.

어휘 plumber 배관공 real estate 부동산

45. 핼리버튼 씨가 어떻게 졸리 씨를 돕겠다고 제안하는가?
(A) 사업 지점 한 곳을 방문함으로써
(B) 아파트로 찾아감으로써
(C) 상사에게 이야기함으로써
(D) 전화를 함으로써

정답 (D)

해설 핼리버튼 씨가 작성한 이메일인 두 번째 지문 중반부에 자신이 거래 계약이 되어 있는 업체의 책임자에게 휴대전화로 연락하겠다고(I am an acquaintance of the manager there, so I'll get in touch with him on his cell phone) 알리는 말이 쓰여 있으므로 (D)가 정답이다.

어휘 offer to do ~하겠다고 제안하다 by (방법) ~함으로써, ~해서 location 지점, 위치 supervisor 상사, 감독 make a phone call 전화하다

46-50.

이번 주말의 박스 오피스

시네파일 위클리
작성자, 에이미 스완

이번 주말에(7월 12일-13일), 46 <에일리언 인베이전>이 대단히 긍정적인 평가 및 혁신적인 마케팅 캠페인 덕분에, 박스 오피스 순위표에서 최상위 자리를 유지했습니다. 이 영화가 성공한 또 다른 이유는 인상적인 출연진인데, 여기에는 최근의 수상자인 드웨인 로빈슨과 카일라 다빗이 포함되어 있습니다.

46 <어스 트레머스>도 3주도 더 이전에 개봉되었음에도 불구하고 8천 9백만 달러를 거둬 들이면서, 이번 주말에 박스 오피스에서 성공적인 행보를 이어갔습니다. 영화 평론가들은 이 영화가 47 찬사를 받고 있는 작가 마크 버로우즈의 원작 소설에 등장하는 인물들과 줄거리를 정확하게 묘사하고 있다는 데 모두 의견을 같이 하고 있습니다.

마지막으로, 46 <업사이드 다운>은 이번 주말에 가장 큰 성공을 거둔 개봉작일뿐만 아니라(91.4백만 달러), 이번 달에 가장 큰 성공을 거둔 개봉작입니다. 특히 주목할 만한 점은 48 이 작품의 제작사가 불과 작년 연말 무렵에 설립되었다는 사실이며, <업사이드 다운>은 이 회사 최초의 영화 개봉작입니다.

어휘 maintain ~을 유지하다 position 자리, 위치 atop ~의 맨 위에, ~의 꼭대기에 rakings table 순위표 thanks to ~ 덕분에, ~ 때문에 highly 대단히, 매우 positive 긍정적인 review 평가, 후기 innovative 혁신적인 impressive 성공적인 cast 출연진 include ~을 포함하다 recent 최근의 award winner 수상자 continue ~을 계속하다 run 행보, 진행, 운영, 운행 despite ~에도 불구하고 release v. ~을 개봉하다, ~을 출시하다 n. 개봉(작), 출시 critic 평론가 unanimous 모두 뜻이 같은, 만장일치의 accurately 정확히 portray ~을 묘사하다 plot 줄거리 source 원천, 근원, 출처 acclaimed 찬사를 받는 not only A, but also B A뿐만 아니라 B도 especially 특히 notable 주목할 만한 the fact that ~라는 사실 set up ~을 설립하다, ~을 설치하다, ~을 마련하다 near the end of ~의 끝 무렵에

미국 박스 오피스 순위

이번 주말: 7월 12일 - 7월 13일

순위 (지난주)	제목	제작사	주말 수익	총 수익
49 1 (1)	49 에일리언 인베이전	퍼시피카	$106.5 백만	$403 백만
2 (-)	48 업사이드 다운	48 뫼비우스 필름	$91.4 백만	$91.4 백만
3 (2)	슈퍼 슬루스	인디카	$13.2 백만	$77.6 백만
4 (3)	어스 트레머스	퍼시피카	$8.9 백만	$133 백만
50 5 (-)	50 사이보그 걸	올센	$6.1 백만	$6.1 백만

참고: 올센 픽처스의 신작 영화는 제한적인 개봉작으로서, 전국에 걸쳐 불과 350개의 극장에서 상영되면서 박스 오피스에서 6백 1십만 달러를 거둬 들였습니다. 이 작품은 다음 주말에 전국에서 완전히 개봉될 것입니다.

어휘 gross 수익 limited 제한된 throughout (장소) ~ 전역에 걸쳐, (기간) ~ 동안 내내 receive a release 개봉되다 nationwide 전국적인

49 수신: 파트리샤 예이츠

날짜: 7월 14일

발신: 마이클 리치

안녕하세요, 파트리샤 씨...

음, 동의해야겠네요! 그 영화와 관련해 당신 말이 맞았어요. **49** 토요일에 함께 보러 갈 수 없어서 아쉬웠지만, 제가 어제 오후에 시간이 좀 있었어요. 와우! **49** 개봉 첫 주말에 이미 박스 오피스 순위에서 1위를 차지했다는 게 놀랍지 않네요. 아... 제가 극장에 있는 동안, 우리가 함께 보러 가야 한다고 생각하는 새 영화의 예고편을 봤어요. 바로 지난 주말에 몇몇 영화관에서만 상영되었는데도, **50** 이미 박스 오피스 순위의 5위에 있어요. 그 예고편을 확인해 보시고 이번 주말에 보러 가시고 싶은 생각이 드실지 알려 주세요. (오후 8시 56분)

어휘 It's a shame (that) ~해서 아쉽다, ~해서 안타깝다 join A to do A와 함께 ~하다 top ~에서 1위에 오르다 trailer 예고편

46. 스완 씨의 기사가 주로 무엇에 관한 것인가?
(A) 현재 제작 진행 중인 영화들
(B) <에일리언 인베이전>의 세계적인 성공
(C) 최신 영화들의 금전적 성과
(D) 곧 있을 시상식의 후보로 지명될 영화들

정답 (C)

해설 첫 지문에 단락마다 서로 다른 작품의 박스 오피스 순위와 수익을 언급해(*Alien Invasion* maintained its position atop the box office rankings table / *Earth Tremors* ~ taking in an impressive $89 million / *Upside Down* ~ ($91.4 million)) 주말 흥행 성적을 알리고 있으므로 (C)가 정답이다.

어휘 currently 현재 in development (제작, 개발 등이) 진행 중인 nominate ~을 후보로 지명하다 upcoming 곧 있을, 다가오는

47. 기사에서 <어스 트레머스>와 관련해 암시된 것은 무엇인가?
(A) 마크 버로우즈 씨가 감독했다.
(B) 최근에 상을 받았다.
(C) 책에서 각색되었다.
(D) 두 명의 아주 인기 있는 배우들을 특징으로 한다.

정답 (C)

해설 기사인 첫 지문에서 <어스 트레머스> 관련 정보가 제시된 두 번째 단락에 작가 마크 버로우즈의 원작 소설에 등장하는 인물들과 줄거리를 정확하게 묘사하고 있다는 점이(the film accurately portrays the characters and plot of the source novel by acclaimed author Mark Burroughs) 언급되어 있다. 이를 통해 그 소설을 각색해 영화로 제작했다는 사실을 알 수 있으므로 (C)가 정답이다.

어휘 win an award 상을 받다, 수상하다 adapt ~을 각색하다, ~을 개작하다 feature ~을 특징으로 하다

48. 뫼비우스 필름과 관련해 언급된 것은 무엇인가?
(A) 다음 달에 영화를 한 편 개봉한다.
(B) 비교적 새로운 회사이다.
(C) 그곳의 영화가 박스 오피스 기록을 경신했다.
(D) 퍼시피카와 공동 작업했다.

정답 (B)

해설 뫼비우스 필름은 두 번째 지문에 제시된 도표에서 2위에 오른 작품 <업사이드 다운>의 제작사로(Upside Down, Mobius Films) 표기되어 있다. 이 작품과 관련해, 첫 지문 마지막 단락에 <업사이드 다운>의 제작사가 불과 작년 연말 무렵에 설립된 사실이(its production company was only set up near the end of last year) 쓰여 있어 비교적 새로운 회사임을 알 수 있으므로 (B)가 정답이다.

어휘 relatively 비교적, 상대적으로

49. 예이츠 씨와 관련해 유추할 수 있는 것은 무엇인가?
(A) 지난 주말에 영화를 보러 갈 수 없었다.
(B) 최근에 <에일리언 인베이전>을 봤다.
(C) 극장 한 곳을 리치 씨에게 추천했다.
(D) 평소에 주말마다 영화를 보러 간다.

정답 (B)

해설 예이츠 씨의 이름은 문자 메시지인 세 번째 지문 상단의 수신인 항목에서 찾아볼 수 있으며, 이 지문 초반부에 예이츠 씨와 토요일에 함께 영화를 보러 가지 못한 사실과 그 영화가 박스 오피스 순위에서 1위를 차지한 사실이(It's a shame I couldn't join you to see it on Saturday, ~ it's already topping the box office rankings on its opening weekend) 언급되어 있다. 두 번째 지문에 제시된 도표에 <에일리언 인베이전>이 1위로 표기되어 있어 예이츠 씨가 주말에 이 작품을 봤다는 사실을 알 수 있으므로 (B)가 정답이다.

어휘 be unable to do ~할 수 없다 normally 평소에, 보통, 일반적으로

50. 리치 씨가 이번 주말에 어떤 영화를 보고 싶어할 것 같은가?
(A) <업사이드 다운>
(B) <슈퍼 슬루스>
(C) <어스 트레머스>
(D) <사이보그 걸>

정답 (D)

해설 세 번째 지문 후반부에 리치 씨가 주말에 보고 싶은 영화를 이야기하면서 박스 오피스 순위의 5위에 있다는(it's already at number 5 in the box office rankings) 사실을 밝히고 있다. 두 번째 지문에 제시된 도표에 <사이보그 걸>이 5위에 표기되어 있으므로 (D)가 정답이다.

DAY 03 LC Half Test

1. (D)	**2.** (A)	**3.** (A)	**4.** (C)	**5.** (B)
6. (A)	**7.** (B)	**8.** (C)	**9.** (A)	**10.** (A)
11. (C)	**12.** (C)	**13.** (B)	**14.** (B)	**15.** (A)
16. (A)	**17.** (B)	**18.** (B)	**19.** (B)	**20.** (A)
21. (C)	**22.** (B)	**23.** (A)	**24.** (B)	**25.** (C)
26. (D)	**27.** (D)	**28.** (B)	**29.** (A)	**30.** (C)
31. (D)	**32.** (B)	**33.** (A)	**34.** (D)	**35.** (C)
36. (D)	**37.** (B)	**38.** (C)	**39.** (B)	**40.** (D)
41. (A)	**42.** (A)	**43.** (A)	**44.** (B)	**45.** (C)
46. (D)	**47.** (A)	**48.** (D)	**49.** (D)	**50.** (B)

Part 1

1. (A) Some microphones are being installed.
(B) The monitors have been turned off.
(C) A woman is speaking at a podium.
(D) A woman is adjusting some equipment.

(A) 몇몇 마이크가 설치되고 있다.
(B) 모니터들이 꺼져 있는 상태이다.
(C) 여자가 강단에서 연설하고 있다.
(D) 여자가 일부 장비를 조정하고 있다.

해설 (A) 여자가 마이크를 설치하는 동작을 하고 있지 않으므로 오답.
(B) 모니터들이 켜져 있는 상태이므로 오답.
(C) 여자가 강단에 서서 연설하는 자세를 취하고 있지 않으므로 오답.
(D) 여자가 손으로 장비를 조정하는 자세를 취하고 있으므로 정답.

어휘 install ~을 설치하다 turn off ~을 끄다 podium 강단, 연단 adjust ~을 조정하다, ~을 조절하다 equipment 장비

2. **(A) A portion of the roof is unfinished.**
(B) Some roofing materials are being removed by a crane.
(C) A construction worker is climbing up a ladder.
(D) Some ladders are lying across a construction site.

(A) 지붕의 일부분이 완성되지 않은 상태이다.
(B) 일부 지붕 공사용 자재가 크레인에 의해 치워지고 있다.
(C) 공사장 인부가 사다리 위로 올라가고 있다.

(D) 몇몇 사다리들이 공사 현장을 가로질러 놓여 있다.

해설 (A) 지붕의 가운데 부분이 아직 완성되지 않은 상태이므로 정답.
(B) 사진 속에 크레인이 보이지 않으므로 오답.
(C) 사람들이 사다리 위로 올라가는 동작을 하고 있지 않으므로 오답.
(D) 사다리가 공사장에 놓여 있지 않으므로 오답.

어휘 portion 일부, 부분 unfinished 완성되지 않은 roofing 지붕 공사 material 자재, 재료, 물품 remove ~을 치우다, ~을 없애다 climb up ~ 위로 올라가다 ladder 사다리 lie (사물이) 놓여 있다 across ~을 가로질러, ~에 걸쳐 construction 공사 site 현장, 부지, 장소

Part 2

3. When will the annual bonuses be awarded to staff?

(A) Probably around the 20th.
(B) He's won several awards.
(C) No, for all employees.

연례 보너스가 언제 직원들에게 지급될 건가요?
(A) 아마 20일쯤일 거예요.
(B) 그분이 여러 상을 받았어요.
(C) 아뇨, 전 직원을 대상으로요.

해설 연례 보너스가 언제 직원들에게 지급될지 묻고 있으므로 대략적인 시점으로 답변하는 (A)가 정답이다. (B)는 award를 반복한 답변으로서, award의 다른 의미(주다, 상)를 활용해 혼동을 유발하는 오답이며, (C)는 의문사 의문문에 맞지 않는 No로 답변하는 오답이다.

어휘 annual 연례적인, 해마다의 award ~을 제공하다, ~을 수여하다 around ~쯤, ~ 무렵에 win an award 상을 받다 several 여럿의, 몇몇의

4. Where do you normally shop for your clothes?
(A) On the weekends.
(B) No, I haven't been there.
(C) I prefer to buy them online.

보통 어디서 옷을 쇼핑하세요?
(A) 매주 주말에요.
(B) 아뇨, 저는 그곳에 가본 적이 없어요.
(C) 온라인에서 구입하는 걸 선호합니다.

해설 보통 어디서 옷을 쇼핑하는지 묻고 있으므로 clothes를 them으로 지칭해 자신이 선호하는 구입 방식을 언급하는 (C)가 정답

이다. (B)는 의문사 의문문에 맞지 않는 No로 답변하는 오답이다.

어휘 **normally** 보통, 일반적으로 **prefer to do** ~하는 것을 선호하다

5. Why is the new staff orientation being moved to the 10th?

(A) In the company training center.
(B) There was a schedule conflict.
(C) We'll need more chairs then.

신입 사원 오리엔테이션이 왜 10일로 옮겨지는 거죠?
(A) 회사 교육 센터에서요.
(B) 일정 충돌 문제가 있었어요.
(C) 그럼 의자가 더 필요할 겁니다.

해설 신입 사원 오리엔테이션이 왜 10일로 옮겨지는지 묻고 있으므로 일정 충돌 문제가 있었다는 말로 개최 날짜가 바뀐 이유를 언급하는 (B)가 정답이다. (A)는 orientation에서 연상 가능한 training을 활용해 혼동을 유발하는 오답이다.

어휘 **schedule conflict** 일정 충돌, 일정상의 겹침 **then** 그럼, 그렇다면, 그때, 그런 다음

6. Should we go over the survey results now?
(A) Yes, let's take a look.
(B) I'll go there by bus.
(C) About 20 questions.

우리가 지금 설문 조사 결과를 검토해야 할까요?
(A) 네, 한 번 살펴봅시다.
(B) 저는 그곳에 버스로 갈 거예요.
(C) 약 20개의 질문이요.

해설 지금 설문 조사 결과를 검토해야 하는지 묻고 있으므로 동의를 뜻하는 Yes와 함께 살펴보도록 제안하며 질문에 답하는 (A)가 정답이다. (B)는 go를 반복한 답변으로서, go의 다른 의미(검토하다, 가다)를 활용해 혼동을 유발하는 오답이나.

어휘 **go over** ~을 검토하다, ~을 살펴보다 **survey** 설문 조사(지) **result** 결과(물) **take a look** 한 번 보다 **about** 약, 대략

7. How do I register for the IT skills workshop?
(A) My laptop works fine now.
(B) By going to the HR office.
(C) That's a new electronics store.

IT 기술 워크숍에 어떻게 등록하나요?
(A) 제 노트북 컴퓨터가 지금은 잘 작동됩니다.
(B) 인사부에 가시면 됩니다.
(C) 그곳은 새 전자 제품 매장이에요.

해설 IT 기술 워크숍에 어떻게 등록하는지 묻고 있으므로 방법을 나타낼 때 사용하는 전치사 By와 함께 등록 업무를 처리하는 부

서로 가라고 알리는 (B)가 정답이다. (A)는 IT에서 연상 가능한 laptop 및 workshop과 일부 발음이 같은 work를 활용해 혼동을 유발하는 오답이다.

어휘 **register for** ~에 등록하다 **work** (기계 등) 작동되다 **by** (방법) ~해서, ~함으로써 **HR** 인사(부) **electronics** 전자 제품

8. Should I buy tickets for the new horror movie or the action one?

(A) It was really enjoyable, thanks.
(B) I haven't seen it yet.
(C) I definitely prefer action films.

신작 공포 영화 입장권을 구입할까요, 아니면 액션 영화로 할까요?
(A) 정말 즐거웠어요, 감사합니다.
(B) 저는 아직 그걸 보지 못했어요.
(C) 저는 확실히 액션 영화를 선호해요.

해설 신작 공포 영화와 액션 영화 중에서 어느 영화에 대한 입장권을 구입할지 묻는 선택 의문문에 대해 확실히 액션 영화를 선호한다는 말로 원하는 영화 장르를 직접적으로 언급한 (C)가 정답이다. (B)는 movie에서 연상 가능한 have seen을 활용해 혼동을 유발하는 오답이다.

어휘 **enjoyable** 즐거운 **definitely** (강조) 확실히, 분명히 **prefer** ~을 선호하다

9. You often go to the gym on Fourth Avenue, right?
(A) That one closed last month.
(B) There are lots of new members.
(C) No, I'm busy today.

4번 애비뉴에 있는 체육관에 자주 가시는 게 맞죠?
(A) 그곳은 지난 달에 문을 닫았어요.
(B) 신규 회원이 많이 있어요.
(C) 아뇨, 저는 오늘 바쁩니다.

해설 4번 애비뉴에 있는 체육관에 자주 가는 게 맞는지 묻는 데 대해 the gym on Fourth Avenue를 That one으로 지칭해 문을 닫았다는 말로 그곳에 가지 않는다는 뜻을 나타낸 (A)가 정답이다. (B)는 go to the gym에서 연상 가능한 new members를 활용해 혼동을 유발하는 오답이다.

어휘 **gym** 체육관

10. My driving lesson has been delayed until Wednesday.

(A) Let's do something today then.
(B) The instructor is very experienced.
(C) I'd prefer to take the train.

제 운전 교습이 수요일로 미뤄졌습니다.
(A) 그럼 우리 오늘 뭔가 해요.
(B) 그 강사는 경험이 아주 많아요.

(C) 저는 기차를 타고 싶어요.

해설 운전 교습이 수요일로 미뤄졌다는 사실을 알리고 있으므로 그에 따른 영향으로 교습을 받지 않는 오늘 뭔가 하도록 제안하는 (A)가 정답이다. (B)는 lesson에서 연상 가능한 instructor를, (C)는 driving에서 연상 가능한 train을 각각 활용해 혼동을 유발하는 오답이다.

어휘 **delay** ~을 미루다, ~을 연기하다 **then** 그럼, 그렇다면, 그때, 그런 다음 **instructor** 강사 **experienced** 경험 많은 **would prefer to do** ~하고 싶다, ~하고자 하다 **take** (교통편) ~을 타다, ~을 이용하다

11. Where did the instruction manual for this photocopier go?

(A) I'll make a few more copies.
(B) Well, that was easy.
(C) Check your desk drawer.

이 복사기 사용 설명서가 어디로 간 거죠?
(A) 제가 몇 부 더 복사할게요.
(B) 음, 그건 쉬운 일이었어요.
(C) 당신 책상 서랍을 확인해 보세요.

해설 복사기 사용 설명서가 어디로 갔는지 묻고 있으므로 이 설명서를 찾을 수 있는 방법으로 책상 서랍을 확인해 보도록 제안하는 (C)가 정답이다. (A)는 photocopier과 일부 발음이 같은 copies를 활용해 혼동을 유발하는 오답이다.

어휘 **instruction manual** 사용 설명서, 취급 설명서 **photocopier** 복사기 **make a copy** 복사하다 **drawer** 서랍

12. Would you mind showing me briefly how to use this software?

(A) That's a really popular show.
(B) He's installing it on all computers.
(C) I'll give you a quick demonstration.

이 소프트웨어를 사용하는 방법 좀 간단히 알려주시겠어요?
(A) 그건 정말 인기 있는 프로그램이죠.
(B) 그분이 모든 컴퓨터에 그걸 설치하고 있어요.
(C) 제가 간단히 시범 보여 드릴게요.

해설 소프트웨어를 사용하는 방법을 간단히 알려달라고 요청하고 있으므로 그 방법에 해당되는 것으로서 시범을 보여주겠다고 알리는 (C)가 정답이다. (A)는 show의 다른 의미(알려주다, 프로그램)를, (B)는 software에서 연상 가능한 computers를 각각 활용해 혼동을 유발하는 오답이다.

어휘 **Would you mind -ing?** ~해 주시겠어요? **briefly** 간단히, 짧게 **how to do** ~하는 방법 **install** ~을 설치하다 **demonstration** 시범, 시연(회)

13. I don't know how to get this window open.
(A) Normally from 9 until 6.

(B) It's cool enough in here already.
(C) Barry locked the door.

이 창문을 여는 방법을 모르겠어요.
(A) 보통 9시에서 6시까지요.
(B) 이곳은 이미 충분히 시원해요.
(C) 배리 씨가 그 문을 잠갔어요.

해설 창문을 여는 방법을 모르겠다고 알리는 말에 이미 충분히 시원하다는 말로 굳이 창문을 열 필요가 없다는 뜻을 나타낸 (B)가 정답이다. (C)는 window와 open에서 연상 가능한 locked the door를 활용해 혼동을 유발하는 오답이다.

어휘 **get A B** A를 B한 상태로 만들다 **normally** 보통, 일반적으로 **lock** ~을 잠그다

14. The inventory check is next week, isn't it?
(A) Sorry, we don't accept personal checks.
(B) Yes, after we close on Monday.
(C) The proposal wasn't very strong.

재고 물품 조사가 다음 주에 있지 않나요?
(A) 죄송하지만, 저희가 개인 수표는 받지 않습니다.
(B) 네, 월요일에 문을 닫은 후에요.
(C) 그 제안이 그렇게 강력하진 않았어요.

해설 재고 물품 조사가 다음 주에 있지 않은지 묻고 있으므로 긍정을 뜻하는 Yes와 함께 해당 조사가 실시되는 시점을 알리는 (B)가 정답이다. (A)는 check를 반복한 답변으로서, check의 다른 의미(조사, 수표)를 활용해 혼동을 유발하는 오답이다.

어휘 **inventory** 재고(품), 재고 목록 **accept** ~을 받아들이다, ~을 수락하다 **check** n. 수표 **proposal** 제안(서)

15. How soon can you start working here?
(A) As early as next Monday.
(B) In the HR Department.
(C) It's a reasonable commute.

얼마나 빨리 이곳에서 근무를 시작하실 수 있죠?
(A) 이르면 다음 주 월요일이요.
(B) 인사부에서요.
(C) 적당한 통근 거리네요.

해설 얼마나 빨리 근무를 시작할 수 있는지 묻고 있으므로 가장 빠른 미래 시점으로 답변하는 (A)가 정답이다. (B)와 (C)는 각각 working에서 연상 가능한 부서명 HR Department와 commute를 활용해 혼동을 유발하는 오답이다.

어휘 **as A as B** B만큼 A하게 **HR** 인사(부) **reasonable** 적당한, 합리적인, 가격이 알맞은 **commute** 통근 (거리)

16. What products should we give out as cosmetics samples?

(A) Just the lipstick this time.
(B) Thanks, but I already have one.

(C) Yes, that sounds like a good idea.

화장품 샘플로 어떤 제품을 나눠줘야 할까요?
(A) 이번엔 그냥 립스틱만요.
(B) 감사합니다만, 제가 이미 하나 갖고 있어요.
(C) 네, 좋은 아이디어인 것 같아요.

해설 화장품 샘플로 어떤 제품을 나눠줘야 하는지 묻고 있으므로 특정 종류의 제품을 언급하는 (A)가 정답이다. (C)는 의문사 의문문에 맞지 않는 Yes로 답변하는 오답이다.

어휘 give out ~을 나눠주다 cosmetics 화장품 sound like ~인 것 같다, ~인 것처럼 들리다

17. Would you mind helping me set up the meeting room?

(A) Yes. We met him last month.
(B) Not at all. Let me just finish this e-mail.
(C) I think it was over around 5 P.M.

회의실을 준비하는 일 좀 도와주시겠어요?
(A) 네. 우리는 그분을 지난달에 만났습니다.
(B) 물론입니다. 이 이메일 쓰는 것만 마치고요.
(C) 그건 오후 5시쯤에 끝난 것 같아요.

해설 「Would you mind -ing?」는 상대방에게 정중하게 요청하는 표현으로, 동사 mind가 지닌 의미(~을 꺼리다)의 특성상 수락을 나타낼 때 No, not at all 또는 Certainly not 등과 같이 부정어를 사용한다는 점에 주의해야 한다. 따라서, 수락을 나타내는 Not at all과 함께 이메일을 작성하는 일을 완료하고 돕겠다는 뜻을 나타내는 (B)가 정답이다.

어휘 **Would you mind -ing?** ~해 주시겠어요? cf. mind ~을 꺼리나, 싫어하다 **set up** ~을 준비하다, 설치하다 **be over** 끝나다 **around** ~쯤

18. Who's taking over as the department head?

(A) Yes, I'm going to miss working with her.
(B) It's in our newsletter.
(C) On the application form.

누가 그 부서장 자리를 이어받는 건가요?
(A) 네, 그분과 함께 일했던 게 그리울 거예요.
(B) 우리 소식지에 나와 있어요.
(C) 지원서에요.

해설 누가 부서장 자리를 이어받는지 묻고 있으므로 회사 소식지에 나와 있다는 말로 관련 정보를 파악할 수 있는 방법을 알리는 (B)가 정답이다. (A)는 의문사 의문문에 맞지 않는 Yes로 답변하는 오답이다.

어휘 **take over** 이어받다, 인수하다 **department head** 부서장 **miss -ing** ~한 것을 그리워하다 **application** 지원(서), 신청(서) **form** 양식, 서식

19. I'd like to have these pants shortened, please.

(A) I've got some spare parts.
(B) We don't do alterations here.
(C) A formal business suit.

이 바지 길이를 줄이고 싶습니다.
(A) 저에게 몇몇 여분의 부품이 있어요.
(B) 저희가 이곳에선 수선을 하지 않습니다.
(C) 비즈니스 정장이요.

해설 바지 길이를 줄이고 싶다고 알리는 말에 대해 수선을 하지 않는다는 말로 줄여줄 수 없다는 뜻을 나타낸 (B)가 정답이다. (A)는 pants와 발음이 유사한 parts를, (C)는 pants에서 연상 가능한 suit를 각각 활용해 혼동을 유발하는 오답이다.

어휘 **have A p.p.** A를 ~되게 하다, A를 ~해놓다 **shorten** ~을 줄이다, ~을 짧게 하다 **spare** 여분의, 예비용의 **part** 부품 **alteration** 수선, 개조, 변경 **formal suit** 정장

20. This weekend will be our busiest time of the year.

(A) We'd better ask more staff to work.
(B) He never has any free time.
(C) No, let's go somewhere quieter.

이번 주말이 일년 중에서 가장 바쁜 때가 될 겁니다.
(A) 더 많은 직원에게 근무하도록 요청하는 게 좋겠어요.
(B) 그분은 전혀 여유 시간이 없으세요.
(C) 아뇨, 더 조용한 곳으로 갑시다.

해설 이번 주말이 일년 중에서 가장 바쁠 것이라는 사실을 알리고 있으므로 그에 대한 조치로서 더 많은 직원들에게 근무를 요청하는 일을 언급한 (A)가 정답이다. (B)는 time을 반복한 답변으로서, 대상을 알 수 없는 He의 상황에 관해 말하고 있으므로 핵심에서 벗어난 오답이다.

어휘 **had better do** ~하는 게 좋다 **ask A to do** A에게 ~하도록 요청하다 **somewhere** 어딘가로, 어딘가에

Part 3

Questions 21-23 refer to the following conversation.

M: Hi, this is Toby calling from Wayfield Plumbing. I just heard your message about **21** the leaking pipe in your office ceiling. I could be there by 11 A.M. to fix it, if that suits you.

W: Thanks, that would be perfect! As I mentioned when I called, **22** an important client will be coming to our office for a meeting this afternoon. So, we really need this problem to be fixed quickly.

M: I'm sure it won't take me too long. **23** Just make sure that you move everything away from the area where the problem is. I'll need some space in order to do my work.

남: 안녕하세요, 저는 웨이필드 플러밍에서 전화 드리는 토비입니다. 귀하의 사무실 천장에서 물이 새는 파이프와 관련해 남기신 메시지를 막 들었습니다. 제가 오전 11시까지 그곳에 가서 고칠 수 있습니다, 그래도 괜찮으시면요.

여: 감사합니다, 그럼 완벽할 거예요! 제가 전화 드렸을 때 언급해 드린 바와 같이, 중요한 고객께서 오늘 오후에 회의하러 저희 사무실로 오실 예정입니다. 그래서, 이 문제가 정말 신속히 바로잡혀야 합니다.

남: 분명 시간이 그렇게 오래 걸리지 않을 겁니다. 문제가 생긴 곳에서 반드시 모든 것을 치워 놓으시기만 하면 됩니다. 제가 작업을 하려면 공간이 좀 필요할 겁니다.

어휘　leaking (물, 가스 등이) 새는, 누출되는　ceiling 천장　by (기한) ~까지　fix ~을 고치다, ~을 바로잡다　suit ~에게 적합하다, ~에게 어울리다　mention 언급하다　quickly 신속히, 빨리　take A B(시간) A에게 B만큼의 시간이 걸리다　make sure that 반드시 ~하도록 하다, ~하는 것을 확실히 해 두다　move A away from B B에서 A를 치워 놓다　in order to do ~하려면, ~하기 위해

21. 남자는 왜 전화하는가?

(A) 예약 일정을 재조정하기 위해
(B) 새로운 서비스를 홍보하기 위해
(C) 수리 작업을 논의하기 위해
(D) 약간의 조언을 구하기 위해

해설　남자가 대화 초반부에 천장에 물이 새는 문제를 언급하면서 11시까지 고치러 갈 수 있다고 알린 뒤로(~ the leaking pipe in your office ceiling. I could be there by 11 A.M. to fix it ~), 그 수리 작업과 관련해 이야기하고 있으므로 (C)가 정답이다.

어휘　reschedule ~의 일정을 재조정하다　appointment 예약, 약속　promote ~을 홍보하다, ~을 촉진하다, ~을 승진시키다　discuss ~을 논의하다, ~을 이야기하다　repair 수리　seek ~을 구하다, ~을 찾다

22. 여자는 오늘 오후에 무슨 일이 있을 것이라고 말하는가?

(A) 안전 점검
(B) 고객 회의
(C) 일부 구직자 면접
(D) 일부 교육 세미나

해설　여자의 말에 집중해 this afternoon이라는 시점이 제시되는 부분에서 단서를 찾아야 한다. 대화 중반부에 여자가 중요한 고객이 오늘 오후에 회의를 하기 위해 온다고(~ an important client will be coming to our office for a meeting this afternoon) 알리고 있으므로 (B)가 정답이다.

어휘　inspection 점검, 검사

23. 남자가 도착하기 전에 여자는 무엇을 해야 하는가?

(A) 한 곳을 치우는 일
(B) 양식에 서명하는 일
(C) 기기를 끄는 일
(D) 지불 금액을 보내는 일

해설　남자가 도착하기 전에 여자는 무엇을 해야 하는지 묻고 있으므로 특정 행위와 관련해 언급하는 일을 찾는 데 집중해야 한다. 대화 마지막 부분에 남자가 문제가 생긴 곳에서 모든 것을 치워 놓으라고(Just make sure that you move everything away from the area ~) 알리고 있으므로 (A)가 정답이다.

어휘　clear ~을 치우다, ~을 깨끗하게 하다　form 양식, 서식　turn off ~을 끄다　device 기기, 장치　payment 지불(액)

Paraphrase　move everything away from the area
　　　　　　→ Clear an area

Questions 24-26 refer to the following conversation.

M: Can I help you find anything in particular? **24** We sell a wide range of stationery, and we have a discount on folders and binders right now.

W: Actually, my company needs some large sheets of paper for drawing blueprints on. We normally get A-Zero paper here, but **25** I can't find it today. Do you have any?

M: Oh, we stopped stocking that size, because we barely sold any of it. I could place an order for you, though. How many sheets do you want?

W: Around 200 should be perfect. Thanks.

M: No problem. **26** It should be delivered to our store on Wednesday. You can pay for it when you come back to get it.

남: 무엇이든 특별히 찾으시는 게 있으시면 도와 드릴까요? 저희가 아주 다양한 문구 제품을 판매하고 있는데, 지금 폴더와 바인더를 할인해 드리고 있습니다.

여: 실은, 저희 회사에서 설계도를 그릴 큰 용지가 좀 필요합니다. 저희가 보통 이곳에서 A0 용지를 구입하는데, 오늘은 찾을 수가 없네요. 조금이라도 남은 게 있나요?

남: 아, 저희가 그 사이즈를 갖춰 놓는 것을 중단했는데, 거의 판매하지 못하다시피 했기 때문입니다. 하지만, 주문해 드릴 수 있습니다. 몇 장이나 원하시나요?

여: 200장 정도면 아주 좋을 거예요. 감사합니다.

남: 별 말씀을요. 수요일에 저희 매장으로 배송될 겁니다. 가지러 다시 오실 때 비용을 지불하시면 됩니다.

어휘　help A do ~하도록 A를 돕다　in particular 특별히　a wide range of 아주 다양한　stationery 문구 제품　actually 실은, 사실　a sheet of paper 종이 한 장　draw ~을 그리다　blueprint 설계도, 청사진　normally 보통, 일

반적으로 **stock** (재고로) ~을 갖춰 놓다 **barely ~ any** 거의 ~않다시피 하다 **place an order** 주문하다 **though** (문장 끝이나 중간에서) 하지만 **around** 약, 대략 **pay for** ~에 대한 비용을 지불하다

24. 화자들은 어디에 있을 것 같은가?
   (A) 의류 매장에
   (B) 사무용품 매장에
   (C) 건강 식품 매장에
   (D) 전자 제품 매장에

해설 대화 초반부에 남자가 아주 다양한 문구 제품을 판매한다는 말과 함께 지금 폴더와 바인더를 할인한다고(We sell a wide range of stationery, and we have a discount on folders and binders right now) 알리고 있다. 이는 사무용품 매장에서 판매하는 제품에 해당되므로 (B)가 정답이다.

   Paraphrase stationery / folders and binders
   → office supply

25. 여자는 무엇에 관해 묻는가?
   (A) 영업 지점
   (B) 색상 선택권
   (C) 제품 구입 가능성
   (D) 품질 보증 기간

해설 여자가 대화 중반부에 특정 제품을 찾을 수 없다는 말과 함께 남은 게 있는지(~ I can't find it today. Do you have any?) 묻고 있다. 이는 제품을 구입할 수 있는지를 문의하는 말에 해당되므로 (C)가 정답이다.

어휘 **location** 지점, 위치 **availability** 구입 가능성, 이용 가능성 **warranty** 품질 보증(서) **length** 시간, 기간

26. 남자는 여자가 수요일에 무엇을 할 수 있다고 말하는가?
   (A) 신제품 라인을 둘러보는 일
   (B) 매장 회원이 되는 일
   (C) 할인율을 요청하는 일
   (D) 비용을 지불하는 일

해설 남자의 말에 집중해 on Wednesday라는 시점 표현과 함께 언급되는 일을 파악해야 한다. 대화 맨 마지막 부분에 남자가 수요일에 매장으로 배송된다는 말과 함께 다시 올 때 비용을 지불하면 된다고(It should be delivered to our store on Wednesday. You can pay for it when you come back to get it) 알리고 있으므로 (D)가 정답이다.

어휘 **browse** ~을 둘러보다 **make a payment** 비용을 지불하다

   Paraphrase pay for it
   → Make a payment

Questions 27-29 refer to the following conversation.

W: Jamie, **27** I just got an e-mail from our spice supplier with an invoice for the ingredients we ordered last month. It seems like some of their prices have gone up.

M: Oh, let me check the invoice. Yes, the price of the coriander has almost doubled. **28** Maybe we should stop ordering it for our restaurant.

W: Well... We use it in a lot of dishes.

M: Good point. We'd have to make a lot of changes to our menu.

W: **29** How about looking at the prices from other suppliers? Then, we could just choose the cheapest one and place an order with them.

여: 제이미 씨, 우리가 지난 달에 주문한 재료에 대해 거래 내역서와 함께 양념 공급업체에서 보낸 이메일을 막 받았어요. 일부 가격이 인상된 것 같아요.
남: 아, 제가 거래 내역서를 확인해 볼게요. 네, 고수 가격이 거의 두 배로 올랐네요. 아마 우리 레스토랑을 위해 그걸 주문하는 걸 중단해야 할 것 같아요.
여: 음... 우리가 그걸 많은 요리에 이용하고 있어요.
남: 좋은 지적입니다. 우리가 메뉴를 많이 변경해야 할 거예요.
여: 다른 공급업체들의 가격을 살펴보는 건 어떨까요? 그런 다음, 가장 저렴한 곳만 선택하면 그곳에 주문할 수 있을 거예요.

어휘 **spice** 양념 **supplier** 공급업체, 공급업자 **invoice** 거래 내역서 **ingredient** (음식) 재료, 성분 **order** ~을 주문하다 **It seems like** ~인 것 같다 **let me do** 제가 ~할게요 **coriander** 고수 **double** v. 두 배가 되다 **Good point** 좋은 지적입니다 **make a change to** ~을 변경하다 **How about -ing?** ~하는 건 어때요? **then** 그런 다음, 그 후에, 그때, 그렇다면 **place an order with** ~에게 주문하다

27. 화자들은 무엇을 받았는가?
   (A) 기한이 지난 지불 금액
   (B) 판촉용 제공 서비스
   (C) 행사용 메뉴
   (D) 공급업체에서 보낸 거래 내역서

해설 화자들이 무엇을 받았는지 묻고 있으므로 receive나 get처럼 받는 행위를 나타내는 동사 또는 give, provide, send, e-mail 등과 같이 전달이나 제공과 관련된 동사가 제시되는 부분에서 단서를 찾아야 한다. 여자가 대화 시작 부분에 공급업체에서 거래 내역서를 포함해 보낸 이메일을 받았다고(I just got an e-mail from our spice supplier with an invoice ~) 알리고 있으므로 (D)가 정답이다.

어휘 **overdue** 기한이 지난, 벌써 했어야 할 **payment** 지불(액)

promotional 판촉의, 홍보의 offer 제공(되는 것)

28. 여자가 "우리가 그걸 많은 요리에 이용하고 있어요"라고 말할 때 무엇을 암시하는가?

(A) 일부 조리법을 변경하고 싶어 한다.
(B) 남자의 아이디어가 좋지 못하다고 생각한다.
(C) 남자에게 몇몇 대안을 알려줄 것이다.
(D) 제품의 인기에 만족하고 있다.

해설 남자가 대화 중반부에 주문하는 것을 중단해야 할 것 같다고(Maybe we should stop ordering it for our restaurant) 알리자, 여자가 '많은 요리에 이용하고 있다'고 말하는 흐름이다. 이는 많은 요리에 들어가는 것이기 때문에 주문을 중단할 수 없다는 뜻으로 남자의 아이디어가 좋지 않다는 의미를 나타내는 말에 해당되므로 (B)가 정답이다.

어휘 recipe 조리법 alternative n. 대안 be pleased with ~에 만족하다, ~에 기뻐하다 popularity 인기

29. 여자는 무엇을 제안하는가?

(A) 몇몇 가격을 비교하는 일
(B) 새로운 요리를 도입하는 일
(C) 추가 직원을 고용하는 일
(D) 메뉴 품목 생산을 중단하는 일

해설 대화 마지막 부분에 여자가 다른 공급업체들의 가격을 살펴보면 어떨지(How about looking at the prices from other suppliers?) 제안하고 있다. 이는 다른 업체의 가격을 비교해 보자는 뜻이므로 (A)가 정답이다.

어휘 compare ~을 비교하다 introduce ~을 도입하다, ~을 소개하다 additional 추가적인 discontinue (생산을) 중단하다

Paraphrase looking at the prices from other suppliers
→ Comparing some prices

Questions 30-32 refer to the following conversation with three speakers.

W: Hi, Ross and Marty. I'm just checking in with you to get an update on the new devices we're developing. For a start, 30 **how are things going with our new smart watch?**

M1: Well, we just finished testing it. When we submerged it in water, the product's touch screen stopped working. So, we are still working on it.

M2: Right. 31 **We need to change the design to ensure that the product is fully waterproof, as we're going to advertise.** I think we'll have it ready by the middle of next week.

W: No problem. 32 **Ross, can you schedule a meeting for next Friday with our investors? They'll want to see our progress.**

M1: Okay, I'll set that up right away.

여: 안녕하세요, 로스 씨 그리고 마티 씨. 우리가 개발하고 있는 새 기기에 관한 정보를 얻고자 두 분께 알아보는 중입니다. 우선, 우리의 새 스마트 시계는 어떻게 되어가고 있나요?
남1: 음, 막 테스트를 마쳤습니다. 물속에 넣었을 때, 제품의 터치 스크린이 작동을 멈췄어요. 그래서, 여전히 그에 대한 작업을 하고 있습니다.
남2: 맞아요. 이 제품이 반드시 완전 방수가 되도록 디자인을 변경해야 해요, 우리가 광고하려고 하는 대로요. 제 생각에 저희가 다음 주 중반까지는 그걸 완성해야 해요.
여: 좋습니다. 로스 씨, 다음 주 금요일로 우리 투자자들과 함께 하는 회의 일정 좀 잡아 주시겠어요? 그분들께서 우리의 진행 상황을 확인해 보고 싶으실 거예요.
남1: 네, 곧바로 잡아 드릴게요.

어휘 check in with ~에게 알아보다, ~와 접촉하다 device 기기, 장치 develop ~을 개발하다 for a start 우선 how are things going with ~? ~는 어떻게 되어가고 있나요? submerge (물 등에) ~을 넣다, ~을 잠기게 하다 work (기계 등이) 작동되다 work on ~에 대한 작업을 하다 ensure that 반드시 ~하도록 하다, ~하는 것을 확실히 해 두다 fully 완전히, 전적으로 waterproof 방수인 advertise 광고하다 have A ready A를 준비하다, A가 다 준비되도록 하다, A가 완성되도록 하다 investor 투자자 progress 진행 상황, 진척 set A up A의 일정을 잡다, A를 마련하다 right away 곧바로, 즉시

30. 화자들은 무슨 제품을 이야기하고 있는가?

(A) 태블릿 컴퓨터
(B) 헤드폰
(C) 스마트 시계
(D) 게임기

해설 제품 명칭이나 특징적인 요소가 언급되는 부분에서 단서를 찾아야 한다. 여자가 대화 시작 부분에 새 스마트 시계가 어떻게 되어가고 있는지(how are things going with our new smart watch?) 물은 뒤로, 이 제품의 개발 과정과 관련해 이야기하고 있으므로 (C)가 정답이다.

31. 제품 디자인은 왜 변경되는가?

(A) 배터리 수명을 늘리기 위해
(B) 전력 사용량을 줄이기 위해
(C) 무게를 감소시키기 위해
(D) 방수 기능을 개선하기 위해

해설 남자 한 명이 대화 중반부에 제품이 반드시 완전 방수가 되도록 디자인을 변경해야 한다고(We need to change the design to ensure that the product is fully waterproof ~) 알리고 있으므로 (D)가 정답이다.

어휘 **extend** ~을 늘리다, ~을 연장하다 **reduce** ~을 줄이다, ~을 감소시키다(= decrease) **improve** ~을 개선하다, ~을 향상시키다 **water resistance** 방수

Paraphrase to ensure that the product is fully waterproof
→ To improve its water resistance

32. 여자는 로스 씨에게 무엇을 하도록 요청하는가?

(A) 제품 샘플을 보내는 일
(B) 회의 일정을 잡는 일
(C) 일부 직원을 교육하는 일
(D) 보고서를 제출하는 일

해설 여자가 대화 후반부에 로스 씨의 이름을 부르면서 다음 주 금요일로 투자자들과 함께 하는 회의 일정을 잡아줄 것을 요청하고 (Ross, can you schedule a meeting for next Friday with our investors?) 있으므로 (B)가 정답이다.

어휘 **arrange** ~을 마련하다, ~을 조치하다, ~의 일정을 잡다 **submit** ~을 제출하다

Paraphrase schedule a meeting → Arrange a meeting

Questions 33-35 refer to the following conversation and list of books.

W: Hi, I came in to look for a book, but I just remembered that **33** **I forgot to pay an overdue charge from the last one I borrowed.** Here's my membership card.

M: Here it is. It looks like you owe $1.25. Once you pay that, you can check out books again.

W: Okay, here you go. And **34** **do you have a copy of** *Blueberry Fields*? **It's my favorite author's latest book.**

M: Yes, on that display there. Also, **35** **next weekend our library will be hosting a special event for charity. We'll be collecting used books, clothes, and toys if you have any that you'd like to donate.**

여: 안녕하세요, 제가 책을 한 권 찾아보러 왔는데, 제가 지난번에 빌린 것의 연체 요금을 지불하는 걸 잊었다는 게 막 기억났어요. 여기 제 회원 카드입니다.
남: 여기 있습니다. 1.25달러를 지불하셔야 하는 것 같습니다. 지불하시는 대로, 다시 도서를 대출하실 수 있습니다.
여: 좋아요, 여기 있습니다. 그리고 <블루베리 필드> 책이 있나요? 제가 가장 좋아하는 작가의 최신 도서입니다.

남: 네, 저기 저쪽 진열대에 있습니다. 그리고, 다음 주말에 저희 도서관에서 특별 자선 행사를 주최할 예정입니다. 기부하시고자 하는 것이 있으시면 저희가 중고 도서와 의류, 그리고 장난감을 모을 예정입니다.

제목	작가
제너럴 페퍼스 팀	나히드 쉬라지
헤이, 주디스!	투안 팜
블루버드 송	바실리키 사마라스
블루베리 필드	아르멘 크리코리언

어휘 **forget to do** ~하는 것을 잊다 **overdue** 연체된, 기한이 지난 **charge** 청구 요금 **borrow** ~을 빌리다 **It looks like** ~인 것 같다, ~인 것처럼 보이다 **owe** ~을 갚아야 하다, ~을 빚지고 있다 **once** (일단) ~하는 대로, ~하자마자 **favorite** 가장 좋아하는 **author** 작가 **latest** 최신의 **display** 진열(품), 전시(품) **host** ~을 주최하다 **charity** 자선 (행위), 자선 단체 **collect** ~을 모으다, ~을 수집하다 **used** 중고의 **donate** ~을 기부하다

33. 여자는 무엇을 하는 것을 잊었는가?

(A) 연체료를 지불하는 일
(B) 행사에 등록하는 일
(C) 책을 보류해 놓는 일
(D) 회원 카드를 갱신하는 일

해설 여자의 말에서 질문에 제시된 forget과 함께 언급되는 정보를 찾아야 한다. 여자가 대화 시작 부분에 자신이 빌린 책에 대한 연체료를 지불하는 것을 잊었다는 사실을(~ I forgot to pay an overdue charge from the last one I borrowed) 언급하고 있으므로 (A)가 정답이다.

어휘 **late fee** 연체료 **sign up for** ~에 등록하다, ~을 신청하다 **place A on hold** A를 보류하다 **renew** ~을 갱신하다

Paraphrase overdue charge
→ late fee

34. 시각자료를 보시오. 여자가 가장 좋아하는 작가는 누구인가?

(A) 나히드 쉬라지
(B) 투안 팜
(C) 바실리키 사마라스
(D) 아르멘 크리코리언

해설 여자가 대화 중반부에 <블루베리 필드> 책이 있는지 물으면서 자신이 가장 좋아하는 작가의 최신 도서라고(~ do you have a copy of *Blueberry Fields*? It's my favorite author's latest book) 알리고 있다. 시각자료에서 맨 아랫줄에 Blueberry Fields의 작가 이름이 Armen Krikorian으로 표기되어 있으므로 (D)가 정답이다.

35. 남자의 말에 따르면, 다음 주말에 무슨 일이 있을 것인가?

(A) 도서 사인회
(B) 글쓰기 워크숍
(C) 자선 행사용 물품 수집
(D) 모금 행사

해설 질문에 According to the man이라고 쓰여 있는 경우, 남자의 말에 집중해 단서를 찾아야 하며, 다음 주말에 있을 일을 묻고 있으므로 next weekend라는 시점 표현과 함께 언급되는 정보를 찾아야 한다. 대화 후반부에 남자가 다음 주말에 특별 자선 행사를 주최한다는 말과 함께 중고 도서와 의류, 그리고 장난감을 모을 것이라고 (~ next weekend our library will be hosting a special event for charity. We'll be collecting used books, clothes, and toys ~) 알리고 있다. 이는 자선 행사를 위한 물품을 수집한다는 뜻이므로 (C)가 정답이다.

어휘 **take place** (일, 행사 등이) 일어나다, 발생되다, 개최되다 **collection** 수집, 수거, 모음 **fundraiser** 모금 행사

Paraphrase charity / We'll be collecting
→ charity collection

Questions 36-38 refer to the following conversation and bus seating chart.

W: Ernie, **36** we're almost prepared for the career fair we're participating in this weekend. I just had our company's information pamphlets printed, so there are only a few things left to do.

M: Do you need a hand with anything?

W: Actually, **37** we need to take some of our products to the event, and I need someone to pick those up from our warehouse.

M: No problem. I can go there after lunch.

W: Great. And, I was just about to book our seats on the train. Let's take a look at the available seats on the Web site. **38** I'd prefer a window seat with a table.

M: Same here. Look, **38** we can each have a window seat, facing one another. Those seats would be perfect for us.

여: 어니 씨, 우리가 이번 주말에 참가하는 취업 박람회에 대한 준비가 거의 다 되었습니다. 제가 막 우리 회사의 정보 안내 책자를 인쇄해 두었기 때문에, 남은 일이 몇 가지 밖에 되지 않습니다.

남: 뭐든 도움이 필요하신 게 있나요?

여: 실은, 우리의 몇몇 제품을 행사장으로 가져가야 하는데, 창고에서 받아올 사람이 필요합니다.

남: 좋습니다. 제가 점심 식사 후에 갈 수 있어요.

여: 잘됐네요. 그리고, 제가 우리 기차 좌석을 막 예약하려던 참이었어요. 웹 사이트에 이용 가능한 좌석을 함께 확인해 봐요. 저는 탁자가 있는 창가 좌석이 좋아요.

남: 저도요. 여기, 우리가 서로 마주보면서 각자 창가 좌석에 앉을 수 있어요. 그 좌석들이 우리에게 딱 알맞을 거예요.

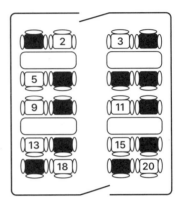

어휘 **be prepared for** ~에 대해 준비되어 있다 **career fair** 취업 박람회 **participate in** ~에 참가하다 **have A p.p.** A를 ~되게 하다, A를 ~해놓다 **pamphlet** 안내 책자, 팸플릿 **there is A left** A가 남아 있다 **need a hand with** ~에 도움이 필요하다 **actually** 실은, 사실 **take A to B** A를 B로 가져가다, A를 B로 데려가다 **pick A up** A를 가져오다, A를 가져가다 **warehouse** 창고 **be about to do** 막 ~하려는 참이다 **book** ~을 예약하다 **take a look at** ~을 한 번 보다 **available** 이용 가능한, 구입 가능한 **would prefer** ~로 하고 싶다, ~을 원하다 **Same here** (동의) 저도요 **face** v. ~을 마주보다 **one another** 서로

36. 화자들은 어떤 행사를 준비하고 있는가?

(A) 제품 출시회
(B) 교육 세미나
(C) 모금 행사
(D) 취업 박람회

해설 화자들이 준비하고 있는 행사가 무엇인지 묻고 있으므로 특정 행사 명칭이나 행사 주제, 관련 활동 등이 언급되는 부분에서 단서를 찾아야 한다. 여자가 대화를 시작하면서 이번 주말에 참가하는 취업 박람회에 대한 준비가 거의 다 되었다고 (~ we're almost prepared for the career fair we're participating in this weekend) 알리고 있으므로 (D)가 정답이다.

어휘 **prepare for** ~을 준비하다 **launch** 출시(회), 공개, 개시 **training** 교육, 훈련 **fundraising** 모금, 자금 조달

37. 여자는 남자에게 무엇을 돕도록 요청하는가?

(A) 안내 책자를 인쇄하는 일
(B) 일부 제품을 가져오는 일

(C) 행사를 광고하는 일
(D) 무대를 설치하는 일

해설 여자가 대화 중반부에 남자에게 행사장에 가져가야 하는 제품을 언급하면서 창고에서 그것들을 받아올 사람이 필요하다는 말로(~ we need to take some of our products to the event, and I need someone to pick those up from our warehouse) 도움을 요청하고 있으므로 (B)가 정답이다.

어휘 **help with** ~하는 것을 돕다 **collect** ~을 가져오다, ~을 수거하다 **advertise** ~을 광고하다 **set up** ~을 설치하다, ~을 마련하다

Paraphrase some of our products / pick those up
→ Collecting some products

38. 시각자료를 보시오. 화자들은 어느 좌석을 선택할 것인가?
(A) 좌석 2와 3
(B) 좌석 5와 9
(C) 좌석 9와 13
(D) 좌석 11과 15

해설 좌석 안내도나 배치도 등이 제시되는 시각자료 문제의 경우, 전치사구나 동사 등과 같이 위치 관계를 나타내는 표현에 특히 집중해 들어야 한다. 대화 후반부에 여자가 창가 좌석이 좋다고 알리자(I'd prefer a window seat with a table), 남자가 서로 마주보면서 각자 창가에 앉을 수 있는 곳을(we can each have a window seat, facing one another) 언급하고 있다. 시각자료에서 탁자를 사이에 두고 창가에 앉아 서로 마주볼 수 있는 위치에 해당되는 좌석은 왼편 아래쪽에 9번과 13번으로 표기된 좌석이므로 (C)가 정답이다.

Part 4

Questions 39-41 refer to the following excerpt from a meeting.

Good afternoon, everyone. I'm Mark Lewis from Gosford Security Services. **39** I'm here at your research laboratory today to explain how to use **40** the new door entry device we installed here this morning. **40** This security equipment is very advanced, and has several features. It will only permit access to those whose fingerprint and retina scans are entered into the system. So, you'll need to scan those today. Now, it's probably easier if **41** I just show you how to use the scanner first. Please come closer and take a look.

안녕하세요, 여러분. 저는 고스포드 보안 서비스의 마크 루이스입니다. 저는 오늘 아침에 저희가 이곳에 설치해 드린 새 출입문 기기를 이용하는 방법을 설명해 드리기 위해 오늘 여러분의 연구 실험실에 왔습니다. 이 보안 장비는 매우 고급 제품이며, 여러 가지

특징이 있습니다. 오직 지문과 망막 스캔 정보가 시스템에 입력되어 있는 사람들만 출입을 허용합니다. 따라서, 오늘 그것들을 스캔하셔야 할 것입니다. 자, 제가 먼저 스캐너를 이용하는 방법을 알려 드리기만 하면 아마 더 쉬울 것입니다. 더 가까이 오셔서 한 번 확인해 보시기 바랍니다.

어휘 **research** 연구, 조사 **laboratory** 실험실 **how to do** ~하는 방법 **device** 기기, 장치 **install** ~을 설명하다 **equipment** 장비 **advanced** 고급의, 발전된, 진보한 **several** 여럿의, 몇몇의 **feature** 특징, 기능 **permit** ~을 허용하다 **access** 접근 (권한), 이용 (권한) **those** (수식어와 함께) ~하는 사람들 **fingerprint** 지문 **retina** 망막 **enter A into B** A를 B에 입력하다 **close** ad. 가까이 a. 가까운 **take a look** 한 번 보다

39. 청자들은 누구일 것 같은가?
(A) 아파트 관리인들
(B) 과학 연구원들
(C) 그래픽 디자이너들
(D) 직원 모집 담당자들

해설 화자가 담화 초반부에 청자들을 your로 지칭해 청자들이 있는 연구 실험실에 와 있다고(I'm here at your research laboratory ~) 알리고 있으므로 (B)가 정답이다.

어휘 **recruiter** (직원 등의) 모집 담당자

40. 화자는 어떤 종류의 제품을 이야기하고 있는가?
(A) 통신 시스템
(B) 공사 도구
(C) 직원 유니폼
(D) 보안 기기

해설 담화 초반부에 화자가 새로운 출입문 기기를(the new door entry device) 이용하는 방법을 설명한다고 알리면서 이를 보안 장비를 뜻하는 This security equipment로 지칭하고 있으므로 (D)가 정답이다.

어휘 **communication** 통신, 의사 소통 **tool** 도구, 공구

Paraphrase door entry device / security equipment
→ security device

41. 청자들은 곧이어 무엇을 할 것인가?
(A) 시연을 보는 일
(B) 시설을 둘러보는 일
(C) 키카드를 받는 일
(D) 여러 조로 나뉘는 일

해설 담화 맨 마지막 부분에 화자가 스캐너 사용법을 보여주는 일을 언급하면서 가까이 와서 보도록 권하고 있다(~ I just show you how to use the scanner first. Please come closer and take a look). 이는 자신이 시연하는 것을 보도록 권하는 말에 해당되므로 (A)가 정답이다.

어휘 **demonstration** 시연(회), 시범 **tour** v. ~을 둘러보다, ~을 견학하다 **facility** 시설(물) **receive** ~을 받다 **keycard** 키카드(카드식 열쇠) **separate into** ~로 나뉘다, 분리되다

[Paraphrase] show you how / take a look
→ Watch a demonstration

Questions 42-44 refer to the following telephone message.

Hi, Rodrigo. **43** I've finalized everything for our trip to visit our client in London to present our financial proposal to them. This is a very important business deal for **42** our accounting firm, so everything has to go smoothly. Our flight will depart from Manchester at 7 a.m. and land in London around 8. We'll check in at our hotel and then go straight to our client's offices. We'll have several meetings and presentations over the two days we'll spend in London. **44** We might have time in our schedule for a nice meal at a restaurant, but I'm sorry to say we won't be doing any sightseeing.

안녕하세요, 로드리고 씨. 런던의 우리 고객사를 방문해 우리의 재무 제안서를 발표하기 위한 출장에 필요한 모든 것을 최종 확정했습니다. 우리 회계 법인에 매우 중요한 사업 거래이므로, 모든 일이 순조롭게 진행되어야 합니다. 우리 항공편이 오전 7시에 맨체스터에서 출발해 8시쯤 런던에 착륙할 것입니다. 우리 호텔에 체크인한 다음, 고객사의 사무실로 곧장 가게 됩니다. 런던에서 보낼 이틀 동안에 걸쳐 여러 회의와 발표 시간이 있을 것입니다. 우리 일정에 레스토랑에서 맛있는 식사를 할 시간은 있을지도 모르겠지만, 관광은 전혀 하지 못할 것이라는 말씀을 드리게 되어 죄송합니다.

어휘 **finalize** ~을 최종 확정하다 **present** ~을 발표하다, ~을 제시하다 **financial** 재무의, 재정의 **proposal** 제안(서) **deal** 거래 (조건), 거래 제품 **accounting firm** 회계 법인 **go smoothly** 순조롭게 진행되다 **depart** 출발하다, 떠나다 **land** v. 착륙하다 **then** 그런 다음, 그 후에, 그렇다면, 그때 **go straight** 곧장 가다 **several** 여럿의, 몇몇의 **presentation** 발표(회) **over** ~ 동안에 걸쳐 **sightseeing** 관광

42. 화자는 어디에서 일하는가?

(A) 여행사에서
(B) 회계 법인에서
(C) 호텔에서
(D) 레스토랑에서

해설 담화 초반부에 화자가 자신의 소속 업체를 our accounting firm이라고 지칭하고 있으므로 (B)가 정답이다.

43. 화자는 왜 전화하는가?

(A) 출장 일정을 이야기하기 위해
(B) 일부 정보를 요청하기 위해
(C) 제안에 관한 의견을 제공하기 위해
(D) 발표 일정을 재조정하기 위해

해설 화자가 전화하는 이유를 묻는 것은 담화 주제를 묻는 것이며, 주제나 목적은 대체로 초반부에 드러날 가능성이 높으므로 담화가 시작될 때 특히 집중해 들어야 한다. 화자가 담화 초반부에 런던 고객사를 방문하는 출장에 필요한 모든 것을 확정했다고(I've finalized everything for our trip to visit our client in London ~) 언급한 뒤로 항공편 시간과 런던에서의 동선 등과 관련해 이야기하고 있다. 이는 출장 일정을 이야기하는 것이므로 (A)가 정답이다.

어휘 **itinerary** 일정(표) **request** ~을 요청하다 **provide** ~을 제공하다 **feedback** 의견 **reschedule** ~의 일정을 재조정하다

44. 화자가 "관광은 전혀 하지 못할 것입니다"라고 말할 때 무엇을 의미하는가?

(A) 투어가 더 이상 제공되지 않는다.
(B) 일정이 꽉 차게 될 것이다.
(C) 몇몇 입장권이 너무 비싸다.
(D) 몇몇 명소가 문을 닫았다.

해설 담화 후반부에 화자가 레스토랑에서 맛있는 식사를 할 시간은 있을지도 모른다고(We might have time in our schedule for a nice meal at a restaurant ~) 언급하면서 '관광은 전혀 하지 못할 것이다'라고 알리는 흐름이다. 이는 식사 시간을 제외하면 출장 업무와 관련된 일정이 꽉 차서 관광할 여유가 없을 것이라는 뜻을 나타내는 말이므로 (B)가 정답이다.

어휘 **no longer** 더 이상 ~않다 **offer** ~을 제공하다 **attraction** 명소, 인기 장소

Questions 45-47 refer to the following excerpt from a meeting.

Good morning, everyone. I gathered you all for this meeting because **45** I want you to begin designing our next product. As you know, most businesses have stopped offering plastic straws when they sell beverages to customers. Some of them offer paper ones, which can be thrown away without harming the environment. But **46** how about straws that people can use again and again? A straw made of bamboo would last for a long time, and **47** its smooth, sophisticated look would be popular with consumers. So, I'd like to see your ideas before the end of the day.

안녕하세요, 여러분. 제가 여러분 모두를 이 회의에 소집한 이유는 여러분께서 우리의 다음 제품을 디자인해주시기를 원하기 때문입니다. 아시다시피, 대부분의 업체들이 고객들에게 음료를 판매할 때 플라스틱 빨대를 제공하는 것을 중단했습니다. 그들 중 일부는 종이로 된 것을 제공하고 있는데, 그것들은 환경에 해를 끼치지 않고 버려질 수 있습니다. 하지만 사람들이 몇 번이고 다시 사용할 수 있는 빨대가 있으면 어떨까요? 대나무로 만든 빨대는 오랫동안 지속될 것이며, 그 매끈하면서 세련된 모습은 소비자들에게 인기 있을 것입니다. 따라서, 오늘 일과 종료 전까지 여러분의 아이디어를 확인해 보고자 합니다.

어휘 **gather** ~을 소집하다, ~을 모으다 **stop -ing** ~하는 것을 멈추다 **straw** 빨대 **throw away** ~을 버리다 **without -ing** ~하지 않고, ~하지 않은 채 **harm** v. ~에 해를 끼치다 **how about A?** A는 어떤가요? **made of** ~로 만들어진 **bamboo** 대나무 **last** v. 지속되다 **smooth** 매끈한, 부드러운 **sophisticated** 세련된, 정교한 **be popular with** ~에게 인기 있다 **consumer** 소비자

45. 청자들은 누구일 것 같은가?
(A) 레스토랑 매니저들
(B) 광고 관련 임원들
(C) 제품 디자이너들
(D) 공장 관리 책임자들

해설 담화 초반부에 화자가 청자들을 you로 지칭해 회사의 다음 제품을 디자인해 주기를 원한다고(~ I want you to begin designing our next product) 알리고 있다. 이는 제품을 디자인하는 사람들에게 할 수 있는 말에 해당되므로 (C)가 정답이다.

어휘 **advertising** 광고 (활동) **executive** 임원, 이사 **supervisor** 책임자, 상사, 감독

46. 화자는 주로 무엇을 이야기하고 있는가?
(A) 생분해성 봉지
(B) 재활용 가구
(C) 친환경 에너지
(D) 재사용 가능한 빨대

해설 담화 중반부에 화자가 사람들이 몇 번이고 다시 사용할 수 있는 빨대가 있으면 어떨지 질문하면서(how about straws that people can use again and again?) 그런 제품이 지니는 장점을 이야기하고 있으므로 (D)가 정답이다.

어휘 **biodegradable** 생분해성의(미생물에 의해 환경 친화적으로 분해됨) **recycled** 재활용된 **green** 친환경의 **reusable** 재사용 가능한

Paraphrase straws that people can use again and again
→ Reusable straws

47. 화자는 왜 제품이 인기 있을 것이라고 생각하는가?
(A) 매력적인 모습을 지닐 것이다.
(B) 구입하기 저렴할 것이다.
(C) 다양한 크기로 나올 것이다.
(D) 쉽게 휴대할 수 있을 것이다.

해설 질문에 제시된 popular 또는 이와 유사한 like, favorite, famous 등의 표현이 제시되는 부분에서 단서를 찾아야 한다. 담화 후반부에 화자가 대나무 빨대의 매끈하면서 세련된 모습이 소비자들에게 인기 있을 것이라고(its smooth, sophisticated look would be popular with consumers) 알리고 있다. 이는 매력적인 모습으로 인해 인기 있을 것이라는 말이므로 (A)가 정답이다.

어휘 **attractive** 매력적인 **appearance** 모습, 외관 **a variety of** 다양한 **portable** 휴대할 수 있는

Paraphrase smooth, sophisticated look
→ attractive appearance

Questions 48-50 refer to the following telephone message and sales summary.

Hi, Barbara. This is Colin calling from the head office. First of all, **48** well done! I saw that the Shepperton branch broke the record for most sales last month. Congratulations! Now, the main reason I'm calling is that you inquired about your sales summary for this month. You're right that there's an error. **49** My database confirms that it should show 24 sales of appliances with the extended warranty, in addition to 38 without the warranty. So, **50** I amended your summary and e-mailed it to you. Please check that you have received it and get back to me if you have any questions. Thank you.

안녕하세요, 바바라 씨. 저는 본사에서 전화 드리는 콜린입니다. 가장 먼저, 수고 많으셨습니다! 셰퍼튼 지점이 지난 달에 최다 판매량 기록을 깬 것을 확인했습니다. 축하드립니다! 자, 제가 전화 드리는 주된 이유는 이달 판매량 요약 정보에 관해 문의하셨기 때문입니다. 오류가 있다고 하신 말씀이 맞습니다. 제 데이터베이스에 따르면 품질 보증 서비스가 없는 38개의 제품과 더불어 연장된 품질 보증 서비스가 포함된 24개의 가전 기기 판매량이 보여야 하는 것으로 확인됩니다. 따라서, 요약 정보를 수정해 이메일로 보내 드렸습니다. 받으셨는지 확인하신 다음, 어떤 질문이든 있으시면 저에게 다시 연락 주십시오. 감사합니다.

판매량 요약	
가구 (연장된 품질 보증 미포함)	32
가구 (연장된 품질 보증 포함)	17
가전 기기 (연장된 품질 보증 미포함)	38
가전 기기 (연장된 품질 보증 포함)	21

어휘 **head office** 본사 **branch** 지점, 지사 **break the record** 기록을 깨다 **sales** 판매(량), 영업, 매출 **inquire about** ~에 관해 문의하다 **summary** 요약(본) **confirm that** ~임을 확인해주다 **appliances** 가전 기기 **extended** (기간 등이) 연장된 **warranty** 품질 보증(서) **in addition to** ~뿐만 아니라, ~ 외에도 **amend** ~을 수정하다 **get back to** ~에게 다시 연락하다

48. 화자는 왜 청자에게 축하 인사를 하는가?
(A) 최근에 본사로 전근했다.
(B) 영업부장으로 승진되었다.
(C) 구직 지원서가 접수되었다.
(D) 소속 지점이 회사 기록을 깼다.

해설 축하 인사를 하는 이유를 묻고 있으므로 축하의 말과 함께 언급되는 이유를 통해 단서를 파악해야 한다. 보통 축하한다는 말을 한 후에 이유를 말할 것이라 예상하지만, 이유를 먼저 언급한 후에 축하한다는 말을 하는 경우도 있으므로 주의해야 한다. 담화 초반부에 화자가 수고했다는 말과 축하한다는 말 사이에 셰퍼튼 지점이 지난 달에 최다 판매량 기록을 깬 것을 확인했다고(well done! I saw that the Shepperton branch broke the record for most sales last month. Congratulations!) 알리고 있으므로 (D)가 정답이다.

어휘 **congratulate** ~에게 축하 인사를 하다 **recently** 최근에 **transfer to** ~로 전근하다 **promote** ~을 승진시키다 **application** 지원(서), 신청(서) **accept** ~을 받아들이다, ~을 수락하다

49. 시각자료를 보시오. 어느 숫자가 바로잡혀야 하는가?
(A) 32
(B) 17
(C) 38
(D) 21

해설 담화 후반부에 화자가 연장된 품질 보증 서비스가 포함된 24개의 가전 기기 판매량이 보여야 한다고(~ it should show 24 sales of appliances with the extended warranty ~) 알리고 있다. 시각자료에서 제목 아래의 네 번째 항목에 연장된 품질 보증 포함 가전 기기가 21개로 표기되어 있는데, 담화에서 연장된 품질 보증 서비스가 포함된 가전 기기가 24개라고 했으므로 (D)가 정답이다.

어휘 **correct** ~을 바로잡다, ~을 정정하다

50. 화자는 청자에게 무엇을 하도록 권하는가?
(A) 문서를 제출하는 일
(B) 이메일을 확인하는 일
(C) 품질 보증서를 살펴보는 일
(D) 고객에게 연락하는 일

해설 담화 후반부에 화자가 요약 정보를 수정해 이메일로 보냈다는 말과 함께 그것을 받았는지 확인하도록(I amended your summary and e-mailed it to you. Please check that

you have received it ~) 권하고 있으므로 (B)가 정답이다.

어휘 **advise A to do** A에게 ~하도록 권하다 **submit** ~을 제출하다 **review** ~을 살펴보다, ~을 검토하다 **contact** ~에게 연락하다

Paraphrase e-mailed it to you / check that you have received it → Check an e-mail

DAY 04 RC Half Test

1. (C)	**2.** (D)	**3.** (B)	**4.** (B)	**5.** (A)
6. (D)	**7.** (B)	**8.** (D)	**9.** (B)	**10.** (B)
11. (C)	**12.** (B)	**13.** (C)	**14.** (A)	**15.** (D)
16. (D)	**17.** (D)	**18.** (C)	**19.** (A)	**20.** (A)
21. (B)	**22.** (C)	**23.** (A)	**24.** (D)	**25.** (B)
26. (A)	**27.** (D)	**28.** (A)	**29.** (B)	**30.** (C)
31. (B)	**32.** (D)	**33.** (C)	**34.** (B)	**35.** (D)
36. (D)	**37.** (C)	**38.** (B)	**39.** (D)	**40.** (C)
41. (B)	**42.** (D)	**43.** (A)	**44.** (C)	**45.** (D)
46. (D)	**47.** (C)	**48.** (D)	**49.** (B)	**50.** (D)

Part 5

1.
정답 (C)

해석 플릿 어카운팅은 일반적인 업무를 도울 시간제 사무 보조 직원을 모집하기를 바라고 있다.

해설 선택지가 모두 다른 동사로 구성되어 있어 해석을 통해 알맞은 어휘를 골라야 한다. 빈칸에 들어갈 동사는 회사 측에서 앞으로 일어나기를 바라는 일로서 업무를 도울 보조 직원과 관련해 할 수 있는 행위를 나타내야 하므로 '~을 모집하다'를 뜻하는 (C) recruit이 정답이다.

어휘 hope to do ~하기를 바라다 assistant 보조, 비서 duty 업무, 직무 determine ~을 밝혀내다, ~을 결정하다 recruit ~을 모집하다 lead ~을 이끌다

2.
정답 (D)

해석 호텔 손님들께서는 스쿠버 다이빙 코스와 사찰 투어를 별도로 또는 할인된 패키지의 일부로 예약하실 수 있습니다.

해설 빈칸 앞에 주어와 동사, 그리고 명사구 목적어가 이어져 있는 완전한 절이 있으므로 빈칸 뒤에는 or로 연결된 as 전치사구와 마찬가지로 부가적인 역할을 할 부사가 빈칸에 쓰여야 한다. 따라서 (D) separately가 정답이다.

어휘 temple 사찰, 절 as part of ~의 일부로, ~의 일환으로 separate v. 분리되다, ~을 분리하다 a. 분리된, 별도의, 따로 떨어진 separation 분리, 구분 separately 별도로, 따로

3.
정답 (B)

해석 그 테니스 클럽의 회장은 메리 햄튼 씨에게 클럽 회계 담당자가 되는 데 관심이 있을지 물어봤다.

해설 주어와 동사가 포함된 절을 이끄는 접속사 whether와 동사 would be 사이에 빈칸이 위치해 있으므로 빈칸은 whether절의 주어 자리이다. 따라서 주격 대명사 (B) she가 정답이다.

어휘 chairman 회장, 의장 whether ~인지 (아닌지) be interested in ~에 관심이 있다 treasurer 회계 담당자

4.
정답 (B)

해석 마틴 씨는 보통 그레이슨 디자인 사의 다른 어떤 직원들보다 훨씬 더 일찍 사무실에 도착한다.

해설 빈칸에는 빈칸 앞에 있는 부사 much의 수식을 받음과 동시에 빈칸 뒤에 위치한 than과 짝을 이룰 수 있는 것이 와야 한다. 따라서 비교급 부사 (B) earlier가 정답이다.

어휘 usually 보통, 일반적으로 much (비교급 수식) 훨씬

5.
정답 (A)

해석 인사부장님께서 밴크로프트의 교육 센터에서 신입 사원들을 대상으로 하는 오리엔테이션을 진행하실 예정입니다.

해설 빈칸은 부정관사 an의 수식을 받음과 동시에 동사 be leading의 목적어 역할을 할 단수명사 자리이므로 (A) orientation이 정답이다.

어휘 human resources department 인사부 lead ~을 진행하다, ~을 이끌다 new recruit 신입 사원 orient ~을 적응시키거나, ~의 방향을 설정하나

6.
정답 (D)

해석 직원들께서는 우리 월간 소식지를 통해 아주 다양한 승진 기회에 관해 아실 수 있습니다.

해설 선택지가 모두 전치사로 구성되어 있고, 빈칸 뒤에 위치한 명사구 our monthly newsletter가 직원들이 승진 기회와 관련해 알 수 있는 수단으로 볼 수 있으므로 '~을 통해'라는 의미로 수단이나 매체 등을 나타낼 때 사용하는 (D) through가 정답이다.

어휘 a wide variety of 아주 다양한 career advancement 승진 around ~ 주위에, ~ 전역에 between (A and B) (A와 B) 사이에 through ~을 통해, ~을 통과해

7.

정답 (B)

해석 여러 가지 놀라울 정도로 부정적인 평가를 받기는 했지만, 아르템 포포프의 신작 영화는 여전히 상을 받을 가능성이 있다.

해설 빈칸이 to부정사를 구성하는 to와 동사원형 win 사이에 있으므로 동사 앞에 위치해 동사를 수식할 수 있는 부사 (B) still이 정답이다.

어휘 receive ~을 받다 surprisingly 놀라울 정도로 negative 부정적인 be likely to do ~할 가능성이 있다 win an award 상을 받다, 수상하다 ahead (시간·공간상으로) 앞으로, 앞에 still 여전히, 그럼에도 불구하고

8.

정답 (D)

해석 고객들은 덴햄 백화점에 제품을 반품하기 위해서 반드시 구매 입증 서류를 보관했다가 제공해야 한다.

해설 빈칸 앞에 이미 주어와 동사가 있으므로 빈칸 뒤에 나온 동사원형은 준동사 형태로 쓰여야 한다. 또한, 빈칸 앞의 내용이 반품을 위해 제공해야 하는 것을 나타내므로 빈칸에는 동사원형과 결합해 '~하기 위해'라는 의미로 목적을 나타내는 (D) in order to가 정답이다.

어휘 retain ~을 보관하다, 보유하다 a proof of purchase 구매 증명서, 영수증 in order to do ~하기 위해 in addition to ~에 더해, ~ 외에도

9.

정답 (B)

해석 현재, 지역의 많은 학교에 새 보일러를 설치하고 유지 보수하는 계약을 위해 카타사우쿠아 교육구에서 공개적으로 입찰을 받고 있다.

해설 주어 bids 뒤로 문장의 동사가 없으므로 빈칸은 문장의 동사 자리이다. 그런데 선택지에 제시된 타동사 accept의 목적어가 뒤에 없으므로 수동태 (B) are being accepted가 정답이다.

어휘 at this time 현재, 지금, 이번에는 bid 입찰 publicly 공개적으로 school district 교육구 contract 계약(서) install ~을 설치하다 maintain ~을 유지 보수하다

10.

정답 (B)

해석 시카고 시내로 이사하기로 결정하기 전에, 캐시디 씨는 호수가 내려다보이는 아름다운 주택에 살았다.

해설 문장 중간에 위치한 콤마를 기준으로 앞뒤에 각각 주어와 동사가 포함된 절이 하나씩 쓰여 있으므로 빈칸은 이 절들을 연결할 접속사 자리이다. 또한, '시카고로 이사하기로 결정하기 전에, ~에 살았다'와 같은 의미가 되어야 자연스러우므로 '~하기 전에'를 뜻하는 접속사 (B) Before가 정답이다.

어휘 overlook (건물 등이) ~을 내려다보다 since ~한 이후로, ~하기 때문에 rather 다소, 약간, 오히려 whether ~인지

(아닌지), ~와 상관없이

11.

정답 (C)

해석 아터튼 씨는 바쁜 축제 기간 중에 추가 교대 근무로 일하겠다고 제안하는 직원들에 대해 깊은 인상을 받았다.

해설 빈칸 앞뒤에 각각 위치한 be동사와 전치사 with는 과거분사 impressed와 결합해 '~에 깊은 인상을 받다'라는 의미를 나타내므로 (C) impressed가 정답이다.

어휘 be impressed with ~에 깊은 인상을 받다 extra 추가의, 여분의 shift 교대 근무(조) festive 축제의 impressive 인상적인 impress ~에게 깊은 인상을 남기다

12.

정답 (B)

해석 마르티네즈 씨는 여러 행인들의 도움으로 자신이 떨어뜨렸던 열쇠 꾸러미를 결국 찾을 수 있었다.

해설 빈칸은 전치사 with의 목적어 역할을 할 명사 자리이며, '사람들의 도움으로'와 같은 의미가 되어야 자연스러우므로 돕는 행위를 나타내는 명사 (B) assistance가 정답이다.

어휘 eventually 결국, 마침내 drop ~을 떨어뜨리다 passer-by 행인, 지나가는 사람 assist ~을 돕다, ~을 지원하다 assistance 도움, 지원 assistant 보조, 조수, 비서

13.

정답 (C)

해석 사장님께서 셰릴 아넷 씨의 관리직 경험 부족에도 불구하고 그분께 고객 관리 책임자 직책을 제안하기로 결정하셨다.

해설 빈칸은 빈칸 뒤에 위치한 명사구 her lack of experience in management를 목적어로 취할 전치사 자리이다. 따라서, 선택지에서 유일하게 전치사인 (C) despite이 정답이다.

어휘 offer ~을 제안하다, ~을 제공하다 supervisor 책임자, 감독 position 직책, 일자리 lack 부족 management 관리(직), 경영, 운영 instead 대신 despite ~에도 불구하고 moreover 더욱이, 게다가

14.

정답 (A)

해석 밀포드 유나이티드의 그 스타 선수는 설사 팀이 올해 챔피언 결정전에서 승리한다 하더라도 은퇴할 계획이다.

해설 빈칸 앞뒤로 주어와 동사가 각각 포함된 절이 하나씩 쓰여 있으므로 빈칸은 이 절들을 연결할 접속사 자리이다. 또한, '설사 우승한다 하더라도 은퇴할 계획이다'와 같은 의미가 구성되어야 자연스러우므로 '설사 ~라 하더라도'를 뜻하는 접속사 (A) even if가 정답이다.

어휘 retire 은퇴하다 championship 챔피언 결정전, 선수권 대회 even if 설사 ~라 하더라도 in case (that) ~할 경우에 (대비해) away from ~로부터 멀리, ~에서 떠나서

15.

정답 (D)

해석 그 오케스트라에서 가장 오래 재직한 단원인 폴 가필드 씨는 전 세계에서 가장 능력 있는 음악가들 중 한 명으로 여겨진다.

해설 빈칸 앞에는 주어와 주어를 수식하기 위해 콤마로 삽입된 명사구가, 빈칸 뒤에는 전치사구가 있으므로 빈칸이 동사 자리임을 알 수 있다. 동사 regard는 타동사로서 목적어를 필요로 하는데, 빈칸 뒤에 목적어가 없으므로 수동태가 되어야 한다. 따라서 (D) is regarded가 정답이다.

어휘 longest-serving 가장 오래 재직한, 가장 오래 활동한 talented 능력 있는, 재능 있는 regard A as B A를 B로 여기다

16.

정답 (D)

해석 낸트위치 강을 가로지르는 다리가 강한 옆바람으로 인해 자전거를 타는 사람 및 보행자를 대상으로 일시적으로 폐쇄된 상태이다.

해설 선택지가 모두 다른 부사로 구성되어 있으므로 해석을 통해 알맞은 어휘를 골라야 한다. 다리가 폐쇄되는 방식과 관련된 의미를 나타내어 '강한 바람으로 인해 일시적으로 폐쇄된 상태이다'와 같은 의미가 되어야 자연스러우므로 '일시적으로, 임시로'를 뜻하는 (D) temporarily가 정답이다.

어휘 pedestrian 보행자 due to ~로 인해, ~ 때문에 crosswind 옆바람 previously 이전에, 과거에 individually 개별적으로 lastly 마지막으로, 최종적으로 temporarily 일시적으로, 임시로

Part 6

17-20.

관계자께,

티나 매튜스 씨와 관련해 저에게 연락 주셔서 감사합니다. 매튜스 씨가 귀사에 지원하신 회계 담당 보조 직책에 대해 전적으로 **17** 추천해 드릴 수 있습니다. 매튜스 씨는 스윈든에 위치한 펜포스 제조사의 본사에 **18** 고용되어 있습니다. 이 곳에서의 주된 역할은 직원 급여 및 부서별 예산 업무에 대해 재무부장님을 돕는 것입니다. 매튜스 씨는 이곳에서 근무한 기간 중에 뛰어난 직업 의식을 보여 주었으며, 저희는 소중한 팀원으로 여기고 있습니다. 저는 의심의 여지없이 매튜스 씨가 직장 생활 전반에 걸쳐 근무하게 될 어떤 회사에서도 훌륭한 **19** 인재가 될 것이라고 생각합니다. **20** 어떤 질문이든 있으시면 주저하지 마시고 저에게 연락 주십시오.

안녕히 계십시오.

가레스 에반스
인사부장
펜포스 제조회사

어휘 regarding ~와 관련해 absolutely 전적으로, 완전히 accounting 회계 apply for ~에 지원하다 headquarters 본사 primary 주된 assist A with B B에 대해 A를 돕다 payroll 급여 (명단) outstanding 뛰어난, 우수한 work ethic 직업 의식 valuable 소중한 have no doubt that ~라는 점에 의심의 여지가 없다 throughout ~ 전반에 걸쳐

17.

정답 (D)

해설 선택지가 모두 다른 동사로 구성되어 있으므로 해석을 통해 알맞은 어휘를 골라야 한다. 빈칸 뒤에 지문 전반적으로 매튜스 씨가 근무 기간 중에 뛰어난 직업 의식을 보여 주었다는 사실과 소중한 팀원으로 여겨진다는 점 등이 제시되어 있다. 따라서 새로운 회사에 지원한 매튜스 씨를 추천한다는 흐름이 되어야 자연스러우므로 '~을 추천하다'를 뜻하는 (D) recommend가 정답이다.

어휘 recruit ~을 모집하다

18.

정답 (C)

해설 빈칸 뒤에 위치한 문장에 현재시제 동사 is와 함께 매튜스 씨가 현재 하고 있는 일을 설명하고 있으므로 현재 고용되어 있는 상태임을 나타내는 현재시제 동사가 빈칸에 쓰여야 한다. 또한, 선택지에 제시된 타동사 employ 뒤에 목적어가 없으므로 현재시제 수동태인 (C) is employed가 정답이다.

19.

정답 (A)

해설 선택지가 모두 다른 명사로 구성되어 있으므로 해석을 통해 의미상 알맞은 것을 골라야 한다. 빈칸이 속한 that절의 주어 she는 매튜스 씨를 가리키므로 사람명사가 빈칸에 와야 한다. 따라서 '인재, 자산' 등의 의미로 사람에 대해 사용할 수 있는 (A) asset이 정답이다.

어휘 outcome 결과

20.

정답 (A)

해석 (A) 어떤 질문이든 있으시면 주저하지 마시고 저에게 연락 주십시오.
(B) 매튜스 씨는 10월 1일에 새로운 일을 시작할 것입니다.
(C) 모집 과정에 대한 귀하의 도움에 감사드립니다.
(D) 결론적으로, 저는 매튜스 씨가 전적으로 승진 자격이 있다고 생각합니다.

해설 지문 전체적으로 함께 근무해 온 매튜스 씨가 새로운 회사에 지원한 사실과 함께 매튜스 씨의 장점을 설명하는 것으로 해당 직책에 추천하는 내용이 제시되어 있다. 따라서 추천인의 입장에서 매튜스 씨와 관련된 추가 정보가 필요할 경우에 연락해 달라는 의미로 마지막 인사를 전하는 흐름이 되어야 자연스러우므

로 (A)가 정답이다.

어휘 assistance with ~에 대한 도움 recruitment 모집 process 과정 in conclusion 결론적으로, 마지막으로 fully 전적으로, 완전히 deserving of ~에 대한 자격이 있는, ~을 받을 만한

21-24.

클래튼버그 네이처 웍스가 클래튼버그 마을을 **21** 둘러싸고 있는 그림 같은 여러 언덕과 목초지 주변에서 진행되는 편안하면서도 활기를 북돋워주는 산책 행사에 등록하시도록 여러분들을 초대합니다!

저희 산책 행사는 이젤 강 옆에 위치한 베르겐 농장에서 시작되며, 바이스 산으로 이어지는 기분 좋은 오솔길을 따라 출발합니다. 산책 중에, 우리 지역의 투어 가이드들이 이 구역을 아주 인기 있게 만들어준 몇몇 아름다운 꽃들을 가리켜 드릴 것입니다. **22** 이것들 중 몇몇은 오직 이 지역의 무성한 목초지에서만 자랍니다. 사람들은 자주 그 독특하고 달콤한 향에 이끌리지만, 어떤 것이든 꺾는 일을 삼가시기 바랍니다.

정오 즈음에, 휴식을 취하면서 빵과 치즈, 그리고 햄으로 구성된 맛있는 피크닉 도시락을 즐길 것입니다. 이 시간은 아주 멋진 시골 풍경을 **23** 즐기는 동안 휴식할 수 있는 기회를 제공해 드립니다.

피크닉 후에, 클래튼버그 목초지 쪽으로 계속 이동할 것이며, 이곳에서 이 지역 토종 사슴 몇 마리를 **24** 관찰하실 수 있을 것입니다.

어휘 invite A to do A를 ~하도록 초대하다 relaxing 마음을 편하게 해주는 A yet B A하면서도 B한 invigorating 활기를 북돋워주는 picturesque 그림 같은 meadow 목초지 surround ~을 둘러싸다 set off 출발하다 footpath 오솔길 lead to ~로 이어지다 point out ~을 가리키다 lush 무성한 attract ~을 끌어들이다 scent 향기 refrain from -ing ~하는 것을 삼가다 stunning 아주 멋진, 굉장히 아름다운 carry on towards ~ 쪽으로 계속 가다 native to ~ 토종인, ~ 토박이인

21.
정답 (B)

해설 빈칸이 명사구 the picturesque hills and meadows를 뒤에서 수식하는 관계대명사 that 바로 뒤에 위치해 있으므로 that절의 동사 자리임을 알 수 있다. 관계대명사가 수식하는 명사구가 복수이므로 복수동사 (B) surround가 정답이다.

22.
정답 (C)

해석 (A) 이 산책 행사는 약 4시간이 걸리며, 광범위하게 진행됩니다.
(B) 여러분께서 보시는 어떤 것에 관해서든 가이드에게 마음껏 질문하시기 바랍니다.
(C) 이것들 중 몇몇은 오직 이 지역의 무성한 목초지에서만 자랍니다.

(D) 튼튼한 등산화를 착용하시도록 적극 권장됩니다.

해설 빈칸 뒤에 독특하고 달콤한 향에 이끌려도 어떤 것도 꺾지 말라고 당부하는 말이 쓰여 있으므로 앞서 언급된 아름다운 꽃들의 중요성과 관련된 문장이 빈칸에 쓰여야 흐름이 자연스럽다. 따라서 오직 해당 지역에서만 자란다는 의미를 지닌 (C)가 정답이다.

어휘 cover a lot of ground 광범위하게 진행되다 It is highly recommended to do ~하는 것이 적극 권장되다 sturdy 튼튼한

23.
정답 (A)

해설 빈칸 앞에는 주어, 동사, 두 개의 목적어가 있고, 그 뒤에는 빈칸과 enjoying이 이끄는 분사구가 이어져 있다. 따라서 빈칸에는 분사구와 쓰일 수 있는 접속사가 와야 하는데 '멋진 풍경을 즐기는 동안 쉴 기회를 제공해준다'와 같은 의미가 되어야 자연스러우므로 '~하는 동안'을 뜻하는 (A) while이 정답이다.

24.
정답 (D)

해설 빈칸 앞에 위치한 be able은 to부정사와 결합해 '~할 수 있다'라는 의미를 나타내므로 (D) to observe가 정답이다.

Part 7

25-26.

25 야외에서 근무하는 것과
새로운 사람들과 이야기하는 것을 좋아하십니까?

만약 그러시다면, 록타이트 사가 여러분과 딱 맞는 일자리를 가지고 있을 수 있습니다! 록타이트 사는 음식을 신선하게 보관하기 위해 전 세계 수백 만 가정에서 사용되는 플라스틱 용기를 제조하는 최고의 업체입니다. 저희 상품은 최고의 신선함을 제공하는 데 있어 과학적으로 증명되었습니다.

훨씬 더 많은 새로운 고객을 만나기 위한 노력으로, **25** 저희 영업 부서의 '길거리 팀'은 회사 상품을 선보이고 주문을 하는 데 있어 지역 주민들을 돕고자 인근 지역들을 자주 방문합니다. 만약 저희 길거리 팀에 합류하고 싶은 생각이 있다면, **26** 그저 3월 15일 록타이트 채용의 날에 오셔서 저희 지점장 중 한 분과 면접을 보시기 바랍니다. 행사는 골리 컨퍼런스 센터에서 오전 10시부터 오후 5시까지 개최될 것입니다.

어휘 outdoors 야외에서 corporation 기업 leading 선도적인 manufacturer 제조업체 storage 보관 worldwide 전 세계적으로 scientifically proven 과학적으로 입증된 frequently 자주 demonstrate ~을 보여주다 assist ~을 돕다 branch manager 지점장

25. 어떤 직책이 광고되고 있는가?

    (A) 생산 라인 직원
    (B) 영업 직원
    (C) 과학 연구원
    (D) 지점장

정답 (B)

해설 지문의 제목을 통해 광고에서 언급되는 채용 자리가 야외에서 근무하는 것 및 새로운 사람들과 이야기하는 것과(Do you like working outdoors and speaking to new people?) 관련되어 있음을 알 수 있다. 또한, 두 번째 문단에 영업직원들로 된 길거리 팀에(our "street team" of salespeople) 합류하길 원하는 사람들을 대상으로 글을 쓰고 있다는 것을 알 수 있으므로 (B)가 정답이다.

어휘 **sales representative** 영업 직원 **scientific** 과학적인

26. 관심 있는 사람들은 무엇을 하도록 권장되는가?

    (A) 채용 행사에 참석하는 일
    (B) 지원서를 제출하는 일
    (C) 록타이트의 본사를 방문하는 일
    (D) 컨퍼런스 센터에 전화하는 일

정답 (A)

해설 두 번째 문단 마지막 부분에 록타이트 채용의 날에 오라고 (simply come on down to the Loktite careers day on March 15) 권하고 있으므로 채용 행사를 언급한 (A)가 정답이다.

어휘 **recruitment** 채용 **application form** 지원서 **head office** 본사

27-29.

수신: 라이언 블룸 <rblume@camail.com>
발신: 페넬로페 사임 <penelopesyme@horizontravel.com>
제목: 귀하의 예약
날짜: 11월 15일

블룸 씨께,

저희 호라이즌 여행사의 자동차 대여 서비스를 이용해 주셔서 감사합니다. 27 28 요청하신 바와 같이, 저희가 귀하의 윌트셔 승용차 대여 서비스에 별도로 하루를 추가해 드렸습니다. 귀하의 수정된 대여 상세 정보를 아래와 같이 포함해 드렸습니다.

예약 번호: #5894890
29 수령 장소: 디트로이트, 14번가 차고
수령 시간: 11월 29일, 오후 2:30 이후
반납 시간: 12월 1일, 오후 12:30 이전

이에 대한 추가 비용이 귀하의 대여 요금에 합산되어 귀하의 신용카드로 청구되었습니다. 29 11월 29일에 차량을 수령할 때 반드시 예약 확인 이메일과 유효한 운전면허증을 제시하셔야 한다는 점을 기억하시기 바랍니다. 또한, 해당 차량이 늦어도 위에 기재된 시간까지 원래의 수령 장소로 반납되어야 한다는 점도 유의하십시

오. 이렇게 하시지 못할 경우에 시간당 25달러의 벌금이 발생할 것입니다. 어떠한 질문이든 있으시면 주저하지 마시고 저에게 연락 주십시오. 디트로이트로 떠나시는 여행 및 이곳 호라이즌 여행사에서 저희가 제공해 드리는 서비스를 즐기실 수 있기를 바랍니다.

안녕히 계십시오.

페넬로페 사임

어휘 **rental** 대여, 임대 **request** ~을 요청하다 **revised** 수정된 **reservation** 예약 **pick-up** 가져가기, 가져오기 **drop-off** 갖다 놓기 **charge** ~을 청구하다 **present** ~을 제시하다 **confirmation** 확인(서) **valid** 유효한 **pick up** ~을 가져가다, 가져오다 **be advised that** ~라는 점에 유의하다 **drop off** ~을 갖다 놓다, 내려 놓다 **no later than** 늦어도 ~까지는 **stated above** 위에 쓰여 있는 **failure to do** ~하지 못함 **incur** ~을 발생시키다 **penalty** 벌금

27. 왜 이메일이 보내졌는가?

    (A) 출장 일정을 간략히 설명하기 위해
    (B) 장비 대여 정책을 상세히 설명하기 위해
    (C) 새로운 서비스를 알리기 위해
    (D) 차량 예약을 확인해 주기 위해

정답 (D)

해설 첫 번째 문단에 상대방이 요청한 대로 윌트셔 승용차 대여 서비스에 별도로 하루를 추가했다는(As you requested, we have added an extra day to your rental of the Wiltshire sedan) 사실과 함께 예약 차량 이용과 관련된 정보를 제공하는 것으로 내용이 전개되고 있으므로 (D)가 정답이다.

어휘 **outline** ~을 간략히 설명하다 **itinerary** 일정(표) **detail** ~을 상세히 설명하다 **equipment** 장비 **arrangement** 계약, 예정

28. 블룸 씨에 관해 언급된 것은 무엇인가?

    (A) 대여 기간을 연장했다.
    (B) 호라이즌 여행사의 단골 고객이다.
    (C) 처음으로 디트로이트를 방문한다.
    (D) 서비스에 대해 할인을 받았다.

정답 (A)

해설 블룸 씨는 이 이메일의 수신인이며, 첫 번째 문단에 요청대로 윌트셔 승용차 대여 서비스에 별도로 하루를 추가했다는(As you requested, we have added an extra day to your rental of the Wiltshire sedan) 사실이 언급되어 있으므로 블룸 씨가 차량 대여 기간을 하루 연장했음을 알 수 있다. 따라서 (A)가 정답이다.

어휘 **extend** ~을 연장하다, 늘리다 **regular customer** 단골 고객

29. 이메일에 따르면, 블룸 씨가 14번가 차고에 도착할 때 무엇을 보여 주어야 하는가?

(A) 비용 지불 영수증
(B) 운전면허증
(C) 회원증
(D) 주차 허가증

정답 (B)

해설 14번가 차고는 지문 중반부에 차량 수령 장소로(Pick-up Location: 14th Avenue lot, Detroit) 언급되어 있고, 그 아래 단락에 11월 29일에 차량을 수령할 때 반드시 예약 확인 이메일과 유효한 운전면허증을 제시하라고(Please remember that you must present your reservation confirmation e-mail and a valid driver's license) 알리고 있다. 따라서 언급된 두 개 중 하나인 (B)가 정답이다.

어휘 arrive 도착하다 payment 지불(금) permit 허가증

30-32.

7월 19일
루시 쿠퍼
브래들리 스트리트 7212번지
루이빌, 켄터키 40204

쿠퍼 씨께,

30 매달 전기요금을 이제는 온라인으로 결제하실 수 있다는 것을 알고 계셨습니까? 7월 1일부터, 30 이 유용한 새로운 서비스를 이용하기 위해 더욱 많은 고객 분들께서 온라인 계정을 등록하고 계십니다. 귀하께서는 다음과 같은 혜택을 누리실 수 있습니다:

▶ 신용카드를 사용하시어 온라인상에서 빠르고 안전하게 청구서 요금을 결제하실 수 있습니다.
▶ 웹 사이트에 로그인하시어 귀하의 실시간 전기 요금과 최근 미터 검침 정보를 확인하실 수 있습니다.
▶ 31(C) 온라인 상점에서 엄선된 기기에 10퍼센트 할인을 받으실 수 있습니다.
▶ 31(A) 쓰레기를 줄이기 위해 종이를 사용하지 않는 청구서로 전환하시면 환경을 보호하실 수 있습니다.
▶ 31(D) 결제가 미납될 때 이메일로 알림을 받으실 수 있습니다.

온라인 계정 등록은 이보다 더 쉬울 수 없습니다. 간단하게 www.midvaleelectric.com으로 들어가셔서 "청구 요금 온라인 결제" 탭을 클릭하시어 이 서비스에 등록하시면 됩니다. 저희가 이미 고객 주소, 미터 검침 정보, 그리고 전기 사용 계획을 시스템에 보유하고 있으니 32 저희가 필요한 것은 고객님의 성함과 미드베일 전기 ID 번호입니다.

안녕히 계십시오.

제니퍼 터너
고객 서비스부
미드베일 전기 회사

어휘 realize ~을 깨닫다, 알다 electricity 전기 bill 청구서 sign up for ~을 신청하다, 가입하다 in order to do ~하기 위해 take advantage of ~을 이용하다 useful

유용한 advantage 혜택 securely 안전하게 current 현재의 latest 최근의, 최신의 meter reading 미터 검침 appliance 용품, 기기 protect ~을 보호하다 switch to ~로 전환하다 paperless 종이를 쓰지 않는 reduce ~을 줄이다 notification 알림 payment 결제 simply 단지, 간단하게 register for ~에 등록하다 usage 사용량

30. 편지의 주목적은 무엇인가?
(A) 새로운 기업을 광고하는 것
(B) 청구서 지불을 요청하는 것
(C) 새로운 서비스를 홍보하는 것
(D) 청구 오류를 설명하는 것

정답 (C)

해설 지문 첫 문장에서 매월 전기요금을 이제부터 온라인으로 결제할 수 있다는(Did you realize that you can now pay your monthly electricity bills online?) 사실을 알려주면서 유용한 새로운 서비스에 대해(take advantage of this useful new service) 말하고 있다. 따라서 새로운 서비스를 알리는 것이 목적임을 알 수 있으므로 (C)가 정답이다.

어휘 advertise ~을 광고하다 promote ~을 홍보하다 error 오류, 잘못

31. 온라인 결제의 혜택으로 언급되지 않은 것은?
(A) 종이 낭비 감소
(B) 전기 요금 절약
(C) 온라인 구매 할인
(D) 연체된 청구액 이메일 알림

정답 (B)

해설 두 번째 문단에 세 번째 항목의 온라인 상점(our online store)에서 10 퍼센트 할인을 받을 수 있다는 것에서 (C)를, 네 번째 항목의 쓰레기를 줄인다는(reduce waste) 것에서 (A)를, 마지막 항목 결제가 늦는 경우 이메일로 알림을 받을 수 있다는(receive notifications by e-mail when your bill payment is late) 것에서 (D)를 찾을 수 있다. 따라서 지문에 언급되지 않은 (B)가 정답이다.

어휘 benefit 혜택 wasted 낭비된, 버려지는 rate 요금 alert 경고, 알림 overdue 연체된, 기한이 지난

32. 온라인 계정에 등록하기 위해 반드시 제공되어야 하는 정보는 무엇인가?
(A) 최근 계량기 검침 기록
(B) 신용카드 번호
(C) 집 주소
(D) 회원 ID 번호

정답 (D)

해설 마지막 문단의 마지막 문장에 온라인 계정을 만들기 위해 이름과 회원 ID 번호가 필요하다고(all we need from you is your name and your Midvale Electric ID number) 언급하고 있으므로 (D)가 정답이다.

어휘 **provide** 제공하다 **in order to do** ~하기 위해 **sign up for** ~에 등록하다

33-36.

> 산 안드레아스 주민들께서는 다가오는 이번 주 토요일 오후에 흥미로운 행사에 참석하실 수 있는 특별한 기회가 있습니다. 이 행사의 목적은 대단히 전문화되어 있으면서 비교적 흔치 않은 회사에서 제공하는 서비스를 경험하실 수 있는 기회를 주민 여러분께 드리는 것입니다. **34** '트레저스 & 트링키츠'가 산 안드레아스에서는 막 영업을 위해 문을 연 것일 수 있지만, 다른 여러 도시에 위치한 매장들은 경험 많은 골동품 전문가들로 구성된 팀과 가치 평가 서비스로 인해 회사가 훌륭한 명성을 얻는 데 있어 도움이 되어 왔습니다. — [1] —.
>
> **33** 방문객들께서는 집안의 가보 같은 오래된 물품을 지참하고 오셔서, 다른 여러 물건들 가운데에서도 가구와 도자기, 장신구, 그리고 예술품에 대해 전문적인 배경 지식을 지니고 있는 '트레저스 & 트링키츠'의 전문가들에게 검증 받으실 수 있을 것입니다. — [2] —. '트레저스 & 트링키츠' 직원들이 물품들과 관련된 약간의 배경 지식을 고객 여러분께 전해 드리고, 대략적인 가치 평가 정보를 제공해 드리며, 그 물품에 대해 어느 정도 액수의 보험을 들어야 하는지 추천해 드릴 것입니다. — [3] —.
>
> **33** **36** 산 안드레아스의 역사적인 바렛타운 지역에 있는 브레이포드 공원에 부스와 텐트가 설치될 것입니다. — [4] —. 참석하실 수 없는 분들께서는 월요일부터 금요일까지 매장을 방문하시거나 www.treasuresandtrinkets.com에 가 보실 수 있으며, 여기서 사진을 제출해 온라인으로 가치 평가와 물품의 역사에 관한 정보를 받아 보실 수 있습니다. **35** 감정 전문가 및 골동품 전문가가 될 수 있는 방법에 관한 팁도 저희 사이트에서 찾아 보실 수 있습니다.

어휘 **highly-specialized** 대단히 전문화된 **relatively** 비교적, 상대적으로 **uncommon** 흔치 않은 **gain a reputation for** ~로 명성을 얻다 **experienced** 경험 많은 **antique** 골동품 **valuation** 가치 평가 **bring along** ~을 지참하고 오다 **heirloom** 가보 **examine** ~을 검사하다, 조사하다 **representative** 직원 **approximate** 대략적인 **be insured for** ~의 액수로 보험에 들다 **appraiser** 감정인

33. 브레이포드 공원에서 무슨 행사가 개최되는가?
  (A) 지역 예술품과 공예품을 제공하는 시장
  (B) 회사 제품의 시연회
  (C) 잠재적으로 가치 있는 물품에 대한 감정
  (D) 지역 내에서 발굴된 골동품 전시회

정답 (C)

해설 브레이포드 공원은 세 번째 단락에 부스와 텐트가 설치되는 곳으로(Booths and tents will be set up in Brayford Park) 언급되어 있다. 시설물이 설치되는 이유는 두 번째 단락에 제시된 것과 같이 집안의 가보 같은 오래된 물품을 갖고 와서 가구와 도자기, 장신구, 그리고 예술품에 대해 전문적인 배경 지식을 지니고 있는 전문가들에게 점검 받는(Visitors will be able

to bring along old items, such as family heirlooms, and have them examined by Treasures & Trinkets' experts) 행사를 열기 위해서이다. 이는 잠재적으로 높은 가치를 지니고 있을 수 있는 물품들에 대한 감정을 받는 것이므로 (C)가 정답이다.

어휘 **demonstration** 시연(회) **appraisal** 감정, 평가 **valuable** 가치 있는

34. '트레저스 & 트링키츠'에 관해 무엇이 언급되는가?
  (A) 특별한 물품에 대해 보험 보장 서비스를 제공한다.
  (B) 최근 산 안드레아스에 매장을 열었다.
  (C) 공예품의 복원을 전문으로 한다.
  (D) 현재 주민들로부터 기부를 받고 있다.

정답 (B)

해설 첫 단락에 '트레저스 & 트링키츠'가 산 안드레아스에서는 막 영업을 위해 문을 연 것일 수 있다고(Treasures & Trinkets may have just opened for business in San Andreas) 알리는 말이 쓰여 있는데, 이는 산 안드레아스에서 문을 연 지 얼마 되지 않았다는 뜻이므로 (B)가 정답이다.

어휘 **insurance coverage** 보험 보장 **specialize in** ~을 전문으로 하다 **restoration** 복원, 복구 **artifact** 공예품, 인공 유물 **accept a donation** 기부를 받다

35. 웹 사이트에서 무엇이 제공되는가?
  (A) 오래된 물건을 관리하는 팁
  (B) 잘 알려진 골동품 사진
  (C) 여러 사업 지점으로 찾아가는 길 안내
  (D) 새로운 기술을 배우는 것에 관한 정보

정답 (D)

해설 웹 사이트가 언급되는 마지막 단락에, 감정 전문가 및 골동품 전문가가 될 수 있는 방법에 관한 팁도 사이트에서 찾아 볼 수 있다고(Tips on how you can become an appraiser and antiques expert are also available on our site) 알리고 있다. 이는 새로운 기술을 배우는 것과 관련된 정보를 얻을 수 있다는 뜻이므로 (D)가 정답이다.

어휘 **take care of** ~을 관리하다, 돌보다 **well-known** 잘 알려진

36. [1], [2], [3], [4]로 표기된 위치들 중에서, 다음 문장이 들어 가기에 가장 적절한 곳은 어디인가?

  "일반인들은 오후 1시부터 오후 6시까지 무료로 이 부스들을 방문할 수 있습니다."

  (A) [1]
  (B) [2]
  (C) [3]
  (D) [4]

정답 (D)

해설 제시된 문장은 앞서 언급된 부스들을 these booths라고 가리키면서 일반인들(The public)이 해당 부스를 방문할 수 있는

시간 및 비용과 관련된 정보를 제공하고 있다. 따라서 부스 설치 장소를 알리는 문장 뒤에 위치한 [4]에 들어가 부스 이용 관련 정보를 제공하는 문맥이 되어야 알맞으므로 (D)가 정답이다.

37-40.

> **캐롤 브렌트** [오전 10:25]
> 래리 씨... **37** 지금 시간 괜찮으세요? 우리가 보유한 차량들과 관련해 당신 의견이 필요합니다.
>
> **래리 갤러거** [오전 10:26]
> 제 다음 회의가 11시나 되어야 있습니다.
>
> **캐롤 브렌트** [오전 10:28]
> 음, **38** 우리가 그저 대규모 이사 업무를 처리할 트럭이 충분하지 않다는 이유로 계속 거래를 거절해 오고 있다는 사실을 알게 되었습니다. 우리가 보유 차량을 확대해야 한다고 생각하지 않으세요?
>
> **래리 갤러거** [오전 10:31]
> 그 부분은 이미 처리되었어요. 제가 며칠 전에 5대의 추가 대형 화물 트럭의 구입을 승인했습니다. **39** 출장에서 돌아오실 때쯤이면 이곳 우리 주차장에 와 있을 겁니다.
>
> **캐롤 브렌트** [오전 10:33]
> 그 말씀을 듣게 되어 기쁩니다! 그리고, 어서 킹스턴 출장을 마치고 그것들을 보고 싶군요.
>
> **래리 갤러거** [오전 10:34]
> 한 가지 더 말씀 드리자면... **40** 화요일에, 전에 우리 서비스를 요청하신 적이 있었던 업체 소유주 한 분과 이야기를 나눴습니다. 그분께 우리가 이제 도와 드릴 수 있는 입장이 되었다고 알려 드렸어요.
>
> **캐롤 브렌트** [오전 10:36]
> 아주 잘된 것 같습니다. 거래가 더 많을수록 더 좋죠!

어휘 **fleet** (한 단체가 소유한) 전체 차량, 비행기, 선박 **vehicle** 차량 **not until** ~나 되어야 하다 **turn away** ~을 거절하다 **deal with** ~을 처리하다, ~에 대처하다(= take care of) **relocation** 이사, 이전 **expand** ~을 확대하다, ~을 확장하다 **approve** ~을 승인하다 **heavy-cargo** 대형 화물의 **lot** 주차장 **by the time** ~할 때쯤이면 **get back from** ~에서 돌아오다 **owner** 소유주, 주인 **request** ~을 요청하다 **inform A that** A에게 ~라고 알리다 **in a position to do** ~할 수 있는 입장에 있는

37. 오전 10시 26분에, 갤러거 씨가 "My next meeting isn't until 11."이라고 쓸 때 무엇을 의미할 것 같은가?
    (A) 브렌트 씨가 회의에 참석하기를 원한다.
    (B) 자신의 업무 일정을 변경할 것이다.
    (C) 브렌트 씨에게 일부 의견을 제공할 시간이 있다.
    (D) 업무 관련 약속에 일찍 도착할 계획이다.

정답 (C)

해설 10시 25분 메시지에서 브렌트 씨가 갤러거 씨에게 지금 시간

이 괜찮은지 물으면서 의견이 필요하다고(Are you free right now? I need your opinion on our fleet of vehicles) 알리자, 갤러거 씨가 '다음 회의가 11시나 되어야 있습니다'라고 대답하는 흐름이다. 이는 11시에 있을 회의에 가기 전까지 시간이 있어서 의견을 말할 수 있다는 뜻이므로 (C)가 정답이다.

어휘 **would like A to do** A에게 ~하기를 원하다 **make a change to** ~을 변경하다 **arrive** 도착하다 **appointment** 약속, 예약

38. 갤러거 씨와 브렌트 씨는 어떤 종류의 업체에서 일하는가?
    (A) 차량 제조사
    (B) 이사 전문 회사
    (C) 자동차 수리소
    (D) 자동차 전시장

정답 (B)

해설 브렌트 씨가 10시 28분에 작성한 메시지에 소속 회사를 we로 지칭해 대규모 이사 업무를 처리할 트럭이 충분하지 않다는 사실을(we just don't have enough trucks to deal with large relocation jobs) 언급하는 부분이 있다. 이는 이사 전문 회사에서 일하는 직원이 할 수 있는 말에 해당되므로 (B)가 정답이다.

어휘 **manufacturer** 제조사 **auto shop** 자동차 수리소 **showroom** 전시장, 전시실

39. 브렌트 씨와 관련해 암시된 것은 무엇인가?
    (A) 최근에 회사에 입사했다.
    (B) 경험 많은 기사이다.
    (C) 지출 비용을 우려하고 있다.
    (D) 출장을 갈 계획이다.

정답 (D)

해설 갤러거 씨가 10시 31분에 작성한 메시지에 브렌트 씨가 출장에서 돌아오는 시점을 언급하는(by the time you get back from your travels) 말을 하고 있고, 그 다음 메시지에서 브렌트 씨가 출장을 마치고 새로 들어올 차량들을 보고 싶다고(I look forward to seeing them after my trip to Kingston) 언급하고 있으므로 브렌트 씨가 곧 출장을 떠난다는 사실을 알 수 있으므로 (D)가 정답이다.

어휘 **recently** 최근에 **experienced** 경험 많은 **be concerned about** ~을 우려하다 **expenditure** 지출 (비용) **take a trip** 출장을 떠나다, 여행 가다

40. 갤러거 씨가 이번 주 초에 무엇을 했는가?
    (A) 몇몇 투자자를 만났다.
    (B) 몇몇 차량을 선택하도록 브렌트 씨를 도왔다.
    (C) 잠재 고객에게 연락했다.
    (D) 신입 직원을 모집했다.

정답 (C)

해설 갤러거 씨가 10시 34분에 작성한 메시지를 보면, 전에 자사의 서비스를 요청한 적이 있었던 업체 소유주 한 명과 화요일에 이

야기를 나눈 사실과 함께 그 사람에게 이제 도움을 줄 수 있다고 알린(on Tuesday, I spoke with a business owner who had requested our services before. I informed him that we're now in a position to help) 사실을 언급하고 있다. 이는 회사 서비스를 이용할 잠재적인 고객의 입장에 있는 사람과 연락해 이야기한 것을 의미하므로 (C)가 정답이다.

어휘 **meet with** (약속하고) ~를 만나다 **investor** 투자자 **contact** ~에게 연락하다 **potential** 잠재적인 **recruit** ~을 모집하다

41-45.

수신: 이사회 전 이사님들
발신: 퀸시 서루
제목: 스티브 블레이크 씨
날짜: 9월 10일

동료 이사님들께,

41 우리 회사에서 오늘 이따가 언론 매체에 제출할 보도 자료에 포함하기로 결정한 주요 사항들을 살펴보고자 이 메시지를 보내 드립니다. 스티브 블레이크 씨의 사임을 발표한 후에, 저의 대표이사 임시 선임을 언급하고 나면, 제가 스티브 씨의 노고에 대해 감사의 뜻을 **42** 표할 것입니다. 스티브 씨께서는 떠나시는 이유를 언급해도 상관없으시다는 뜻을 우리에게 나타내셨습니다. 스티브 씨께서는 보도 자료에 포함될 인용문도 준비하셨습니다. **43** 기자단에서 나오는 그 이후의 어떤 질문이든 우리에게 신임 대표이사님을 찾아 주시는 일을 책임지고 계신 위원회장님께 전달되어야 한다는 점도 기억해 주시기 바랍니다.

감사합니다.

퀸시 서루
회장
젠코 코퍼레이션

어휘 **go over** ~을 살펴보다, ~을 검토하다 **include** ~을 포함하다 **press release** 보도 자료 **submit** ~을 제출하다 **media outlet** 언론 매체 **resignation** 사임 **mention** ~을 언급하다 **temporary** 임시의, 일시적인 **appointment** 선임, 임명 **express** (생각·감정 등) ~을 표현하다 **gratitude** 감사(의 뜻) **indicate to A that** A에게 ~라는 뜻을 나타내다 **leave** 떠나다, 그만두다 **quote** 인용문 **subsequent** 그 이후의, 그 다음의 **direct** ~을 전달하다 **committee** 위원회

젠코 코퍼레이션의 변화

(9월 11일) 젠코 코퍼레이션의 이사회는 스티브 블레이크 씨가 10월 1일부로 대표이사직에서 물러날 것이라고 오늘 발표했습니다. 이사회 회장인 퀸시 서루 씨가 정식 후임자를 찾기 위한 조사 작업이 실시되는 동안 임시 대표이사직을 수행할 것입니다. 블레이크 씨는 11월 1일에 한 대형 국제 배송 회사의 사장이자 대표이사로서 선임될 것입니다.

"**44** 저희는 스티브 씨께서 지난 10년 동안에 걸쳐 보여주신 리더십에 대해 대단히 감사하게 생각합니다. 그 기간에, 회사가 빠르게 성장하면서 수익이 두 배로 늘었습니다,"라고 서루 씨가 밝혔습니다. "저희는 스티브 씨께서 경력의 다음 단계에서 훨씬 더 큰 성공을 이루시기를 바랍니다."

"저희가 젠코 사에서 이룬 것들이 이 회사가 영국 내에서 선도적인 온라인 교육 서비스 업체가 되는 데 도움을 주었습니다,"라고 블레이크 씨가 밝혔습니다. "저는 우리의 모든 성과가 매우 자랑스러우며, 동료 이사님들로부터 받은 지원에 대해 감사하게 생각합니다."

43 후보 지명 및 관리 위원회장이신 멜린다 딜린저 씨가 블레이크 씨의 후임자 조사 작업을 이끌고 있으며, 임원 모집 전문가 트리스탄 머피 씨에게 그 조사 작업을 지원하도록 요청한 상태입니다. **45** 이들은 올 연말까지 해당 직책을 충원하기를 바라고 있습니다.

어휘 **board of directors** 이사회, 이사진 **step down as** ~의 자리에서 물러나다 **effective + 시점** ~부터, ~부터 시행되어 **serve as** ~로 재직하다, ~의 역할을 하다 **conduct** ~을 실시되다, ~을 수행하다 **permanent** 정식의, 영구적인 **replacement** 후임(자), 대체(자) **appoint** ~을 선임하다, ~을 임명하다 **extremely** 대단히, 매우 **double** ~을 두 배로 만들다 **profit** 수익 **achieve** ~을 이루다, ~을 달성하다 **leading** 선도적인, 손꼽히는 **be proud of** ~을 자랑스러워하다 **accomplishment** 성과, 업적, 성취 **support** 지원, 후원 **nomination** 후보 지명 **governance** 관리, 통제 **committee** 위원회 **executive** 임원, 이사 **recruitment** (직원 등의) 모집 **assist A with B** B에 대해 A를 돕다 **fill** ~을 충원하다, ~을 채우다 **position** 직책, 일자리

41. 서루 씨가 작성한 회람의 주 목적은 무엇인가?
(A) 동료들에게 고용 결정을 알리는 것
(B) 발표 내용의 세부 사항을 최종 확정하는 것
(C) 이사들에게 회의에 참석하도록 요청하는 것
(D) 블레이크 씨의 사임에 대한 이유를 설명하는 것

정답 (B)

해설 서루 씨가 작성한 첫 번째 지문 시작 부분에 오늘 언론 매체에 제출할 보도 자료에 포함하기로 결정한 주요 사항들을 살펴보기 위해 메시지를 보낸다고(to go over the main points that we decided to include in the press release) 알리고 있다. 이는 보도 자료를 통해 발표하는 내용의 세부적인 정보를 짚어보면서 최종 확정하는 것을 의미하므로 (B)가 정답이다.

어휘 colleague 동료 (직원) hiring 고용 finalize ~을 최종 결정하다 details 세부 사항, 상세 정보 request that ~하도록 요청하다 explain ~을 설명하다 resignation 사임

42. 회람에서, 첫 번째 단락, 세 번째 줄의 단어 "express"와 의미가 가장 가까운 것은 무엇인가?

(A) 용이하게 하다
(B) 추구하다
(C) 더 신속히 처리하다
(D) 전달하다

정답 (D)

해설 해당 문장에서 express 뒤에 '감사, 고마움'을 뜻하는 명사 gratitude가 목적어로 쓰여 있어 express가 감사의 마음을 표현한다는 의미를 지닌다는 것을 알 수 있다. 이는 그러한 생각이나 감정을 전달한다는 말과 같으므로 '전달하다'를 뜻하는 (D) convey가 정답이다.

43. 누가 언론의 질문을 처리하는 일을 책임질 것인가?

(A) 스티브 블레이크 씨
(B) 퀸시 서루 씨
(C) 멜린다 딜린저 씨
(D) 트리스탄 머피 씨

정답 (C)

해설 언론의 질문을 처리하는 일과 관련된 정보가 제시된 첫 지문 후반부에 어떤 질문이든 신임 대표이사를 찾는 일을 책임지고 있는 위원회장에게 전달되어야 한다고(any subsequent questions from the press should be directed to the president of the committee responsible for finding us a new CEO) 알리는 말이 쓰여 있다. 또한, 이 위원회장과 관련해, 두 번째 지문 마지막 단락에 후보 지명 및 관리 위원회장인 멜린다 딜린저 씨가 그 대표이사 후임자를 찾는 일을 이끌고 있다고(Melinda Dillinger, the president of the nomination and governance committee) 언급하고 있으므로 (C)가 정답이다.

어휘 be responsible for ~을 책임지다 handle ~을 처리하다, ~을 다루다

44. 기사에서 젠코 코퍼레이션과 관련해 언급된 것은 무엇인가?

(A) 이번 달에 더 많은 직원들을 고용할 계획이다.
(B) 포장 물품의 해외 배송과 관련되어 있다.
(C) 지난 10년 동안 수익을 두 배로 늘렸다.
(D) 최근 여러 온라인 강좌를 출시했다.

정답 (C)

해설 두 번째 지문 두 번째 단락에 지난 10년 동안 회사가 빠르게 성장한 사실과 수익이 두 배로 늘어난 사실이(over the past ten years. In that time, the company has grown rapidly and doubled its profits) 언급되어 있으므로 (C)가 정답이다.

어휘 be involved in ~와 관련되다 shipping 배송, 선적

package 포장 물품, 소포 earnings 수익, 소득 decade 10년 launch ~을 출시하다, 시작하다

45. 젠코 코퍼레이션은 며칠까지 신임 대표이사를 선임할 것으로 예상하는가?

(A) 10월 1일
(B) 10월 31일
(C) 11월 1일
(D) 12월 31일

정답 (D)

해설 두 번째 지문 마지막 문장에 블레이크 씨의 후임자가 맡게 될 신임 대표이사직을 the position으로 지칭해 연말까지 그 직책을 충원하기를 바라고 있다는(They hope to fill the position by the end of this year) 말이 쓰여 있다. 따라서 (D)가 정답이다.

어휘 expect to do ~할 것으로 예상하다, ~할 것으로 기대하다

46-50.

유레카 시, IL
시장 및 시의원 회의 – 4월 1일, 월요일

출석 확인 (출석한 경우 'X' 표시하시오)
회의 주관: 제임스 홀먼 (유레카 시장) X

의원:

버트 벌머 X	**47** 니나 델스	로이 그레인저 X	수지 루던 X
새라 매스터즈	가레스 하트 X	배리 콥 X	콜린 와츠
48 톰 벤슨 (소방서장) X	폴 카터 (경찰서장) X		
크리스티 카 (도시 계획 책임) X			

불참 허용 대상: **46** 지난주에 있었던 폭풍과 침수 피해 후에 주민들에게 계속 영향을 미치는 문제들로 인해, **47** 벌머 의원과 와츠 의원, 그리고 매스터즈 의원이 이번 회의에서 공식적으로 제외되었습니다.

어휘 mayor 시장 council 의회 roll call 출석 확인 in attendance 출석한, 참석한 chair v. ~을 주관하다, ~의 의장을 맡다 permitted 허용된 absence 부재, 결석 due to ~로 인해, ~때문에 ongoing 계속되는 affect ~에 영향을 미치다 following ~ 후에 flooding 침수, 홍수 officially 공식적으로, 정식으로 be excused from ~에서 제외되다, ~에서 면제되다

어휘 **agenda** 안건, 의제 **approximate** 대략적인 **overview** 개요 **minutes** 회의록 **regarding** ~와 관련된 **replanting** 다시 심기 **expense** 지출 (비용) **upcoming** 다가오는, 곧 있을 **proposal** 제안(서) **budget** v. ~의 예산을 세우다 **maintenance** 시설 관리, 유지 관리 **fund** 기금, 자금 **landscaping** 조경 **request** 요청 **brief** 간략한, 짧은 **potential** 잠재적인 **site** 부지, 현장 **hold** ~을 개최하다, ~을 열다

어휘 **follow-up** 후속 조치 **lead** ~을 진행하다, ~을 이끌다 **rewarding** 보람 있는 **find A to be B** A를 B하다고 생각하다 **highly** 대단히, 매우 **beneficial** 유익한, 이로운 **productive** 생산적인 **may have p.p.** ~했을 수도 있다

notice 알게 되다, 알아차리다 **leave** ~에서 나가다, ~에서 떠나다 **around** 약, 대략 **miss** ~을 놓치다, ~을 빠트리다 **session** (특정 활동을 위한) 시간 **discuss** ~을 이야기하다, ~을 논의하다

46. 유레카 시와 관련해 언급된 것은 무엇인가?
(A) 의원들이 일주일 단위로 모인다.
(B) 최근에 새로운 시 관계자를 선임했다.
(C) 곧 확장 공사 기간을 거칠 것이다.
(D) 좋지 못한 날씨를 겪었다.

정답 (D)

해설 첫 지문 마지막 단락에 지난주에 있었던 폭풍과 침수 피해 후에 주민들에게 계속 영향을 미치는 문제들이 있다고(Due to the ongoing issues affecting residents following last week's storms and flooding) 알리는 말이 쓰여 있으므로 이러한 어려움을 언급한 (D)가 정답이다.

어휘 **on a weekly basis** 일주일 단위로, 매주 **recently** 최근에 **appoint** ~을 선임하다, ~을 임명하다 **official** n. 관계자, 당국자 **undergo** ~을 거치다, ~을 겪다 **expansion** 확장, 확대 **inclement weather** 좋지 못한 날씨, 악천후

47. 어느 의원이 승인 없이 회의에 불참했는가?
(A) 배리 콥
(B) 새라 매스터즈
(C) 니나 델슨
(D) 콜린 와츠

정답 (C)

해설 첫 지문 마지막 단락에 벌머 의원과 와츠 의원, 그리고 매스터즈 의원이 회의에서 공식적으로 제외되었다고(Councilman Bulmer, Councilman Watts, and Councilwoman Masters have been officially excused from this meeting) 알리고 있다. 이와 관련해, 바로 위 단락에 출석 표기가 되어 있지 않은 의원들 중에서 니나 델슨(Nina Delson) 씨가 공식적으로 제외된 의원에 포함되어 있지 않으므로 (C)가 정답이다.

어휘 **absent** 부재 중인, 빠진, 결석한 **authorization** 승인, 인가

48. 어느 안건이 톰 벤슨의 발표를 특징으로 할 것인가?
(A) 항목 B
(B) 항목 C
(C) 항목 D
(D) 항목 E

정답 (D)

해설 톰 벤슨이라는 이름은 첫 지문 중간 단락의 'Tom Benson (Fire Chief)'에 소방서장이라고 표기된 부분에서 찾아 볼 수 있다. 그리고, 두 번째 지문의 E 항목에 소방서의 요청 사항 및 소방서장의 발표가(Talk and presentation by the Fire Chief) 언급되어 있으므로 (D)가 정답이다.

49. 하트 씨는 어떤 주제를 홀먼 시장과 논의하기를 바라는가?

    (A) 유레카의 긴급 도로 수리 필요성

    (B) 다가오는 출장에 필요한 지출 비용

    (C) 음악 공연을 열 가능성이 있는 장소

    (D) 일부 예산 자금의 재배정

정답 (B)

해설 세 번째 지문 후반부에, 9시 30분에 진행되던 시간을 놓친 사실과 함께 그 주제와 관련해 이야기하고 싶다는(I had to leave the room for around twenty minutes at 9:30 A.M., ~ I hope you and I can find some time to discuss that topic) 뜻을 알리고 있다. 두 번째 지문에서 9시 30분에 해당되는 시간에 진행된 C 항목의 개요가 '일리노이 사회기반 시설 컨퍼런스 출장에 필요한 의원 지출 비용 지급에 관한 논의(Talk on payment of council members' expenses for the upcoming trip to the Illinois Infrastructure Conference)'이므로 (B)가 정답이다.

어휘 **urgent** 긴급한 **repair** 수리 **expense** 지출 (비용), 경비 **location** 장소, 지점, 위치 **reallocation** 재배정, 재할당 **budget** 예산

50. 이메일에서, 첫 번째 단락, 두 번째 줄의 단어 "highly"와 의미가 가장 가까운 것은 무엇인가?

    (A) 극심하게

    (B) 지나치게

    (C) 수익성 있게

    (D) 대단히

정답 (D)

해설 해당 문장에서 부사 highly는 '대단히, 매우' 등의 의미로 바로 뒤에 위치한 형용사 beneficial과 productive를 수식해 강조하는 역할을 한다. 따라서, 이와 동일한 의미로 쓰이는 (D) exceedingly가 정답이다.

DAY 05 LC Half Test

1. (C)	**2.** (D)	**3.** (B)	**4.** (A)	**5.** (A)
6. (C)	**7.** (C)	**8.** (A)	**9.** (A)	**10.** (C)
11. (C)	**12.** (C)	**13.** (A)	**14.** (A)	**15.** (B)
16. (A)	**17.** (B)	**18.** (C)	**19.** (B)	**20.** (B)
21. (B)	**22.** (C)	**23.** (A)	**24.** (B)	**25.** (C)
26. (D)	**27.** (D)	**28.** (B)	**29.** (D)	**30.** (A)
31. (D)	**32.** (B)	**33.** (B)	**34.** (D)	**35.** (D)
36. (D)	**37.** (B)	**38.** (C)	**39.** (D)	**40.** (A)
41. (B)	**42.** (C)	**43.** (D)	**44.** (A)	**45.** (C)
46. (D)	**47.** (A)	**48.** (D)	**49.** (C)	**50.** (B)

Part 1

1.
(A) The woman is looking at a computer monitor.
(B) The woman is typing on a keyboard.
(C) The woman is leaning on her elbow.
(D) The woman is painting a picture.

(A) 여자가 컴퓨터 모니터를 보고 있다.
(B) 여자가 키보드로 타자를 치고 있다.
(C) 여자가 팔꿈치로 기대고 있다.
(D) 여자가 그림을 그리고 있다.

해설 (A) 여자의 시선이 모니터를 향해 있지 않으므로 오답.
(B) 여자가 타자를 치는 동작을 하고 있지 않으므로 오답.
(C) 여자가 오른쪽 팔꿈치를 탁자에 대고 기댄 상태로 있으므로 정답.
(D) 여자가 그림을 그리는 동작을 하고 있지 않으므로 오답.

어휘 **type on a keyboard** 키보드로 타자를 치다 **lean on one's elbow** 팔꿈치로 기대다

2.
(A) A television has been set on a desk.
(B) A lamp has been attached to the wall.
(C) Some plants are hanging above a table.
(D) Some chairs are facing a television screen.

(A) 텔레비전이 책상에 놓여 있다.
(B) 전등이 벽에 부착된 상태로 있다.
(C) 몇몇 식물들이 탁자 위쪽에 매달려 있다.
(D) 몇몇 의자들이 텔레비전 화면을 향해 있다.

해설 (A) 텔레비전이 놓여 있는 위치가 책상이 아니므로 오답.
(B) 전등이 벽에 부착된 상태가 아니므로 오답.
(C) 식물이 매달려 있는 상태가 아니므로 오답.
(D) 의자들이 텔레비전을 향해 있는 상태로 놓여 있으므로 정답.

어휘 **set** ~을 놓다, ~을 설치하다 **attach A to B** A를 B에 부착하다, A를 B에 붙이다 **plant** 식물 **hang** 매달리다, 걸리다 **above** (분리된 위치) ~ 위쪽에 **face** v. ~을 향하다, ~을 마주보다

Part 2

3. Where's the post office?
(A) My office is on the second floor.
(B) Beside the museum.
(C) Let's send it by mail.

우체국이 어디 있나요?
(A) 제 사무실은 2층에 있습니다.
(B) 박물관 옆에요.
(C) 그걸 우편으로 보냅시다.

해설 우체국이 어디 있는지 묻고 있으므로 위치 표현으로 답변하는 (B)가 정답이다. (A)는 office를 반복한 답변으로서, 위치 표현이 포함되어 있기는 하지만 우체국 위치가 아니므로 오답이며, (C)는 post office에서 연상 가능한 mail을 활용해 혼동을 유발하는 오답이다.

어휘 **beside** ~ 옆에 **by mail** 우편으로

4. Who's picking up the coffees this morning?
(A) Annie said she'd get them.
(B) No, I don't have a copy.
(C) The café downstairs.

누가 오늘 아침에 커피를 가져오나요?
(A) 애니 씨가 가져올 거라고 했어요.
(B) 아뇨, 서는 사본이 없어요.
(C) 아래층에 있는 카페요.

해설 오늘 아침에 커피를 누가 가져오는지 묻고 있으므로 coffees를 them으로 지칭해 그 일을 하는 사람의 이름을 밝히는 (A)가 정답이다. (B)는 coffee와 발음이 유사한 copy를, (C)는 coffee에서 연상 가능한 café를 각각 활용해 혼동을 유발하는 오답이다.

어휘 **pick up** ~을 가져오다, ~을 가져가다 **downstairs** 아래층에

5. Why did Charlie clock out and leave after the lunch break?
(A) Because he has a dental appointment.
(B) Sometime in the afternoon.
(C) Yes, it was delicious.

찰리 씨가 왜 점심 시간 후에 퇴근 시간을 기록하고 가셨나요?
(A) 치과 예약이 있으시기 때문입니다.
(B) 오후 중으로요.
(C) 네, 맛있었습니다.

해설 찰리 씨가 왜 점심 시간 후에 퇴근 시간을 기록하고 갔는지 묻고 있으므로 이유를 나타낼 때 사용하는 Because와 함께 치과 예약이 있다는 말로 일찍 퇴근한 이유를 밝히는 (A)가 정답이다. (B)는 after the lunch와 일부 발음이 유사하면서 연상하기 쉬운 afternoon을 활용한 오답이다. (C)는 의문사 의문문에 맞지 않는 Yes로 답변하고 있으므로 오답이다.

어휘 **clock out** 퇴근 시간을 기록하다 **leave** 나가다, 떠나다, 그만두다 **dental** 치과의, 치아의 **appointment** 예약, 약속

6. Have you received your quarterly bonus yet?
(A) Thanks, it was helpful.
(B) Based on your sales over that period.
(C) It gets added to our paychecks.

혹시 분기 보너스를 받으셨나요?
(A) 고마워요, 도움이 되었습니다.
(B) 그 기간에 걸친 당신 판매량을 바탕으로요.
(C) 우리 급여에 추가됩니다.

해설 분기 보너스를 받았는지 묻고 있으므로 quarterly bonus를 It으로 지칭해 급여에 추가된다는 말로 지급 방식을 알리는 (C)가 정답이다. (A)는 감사의 말에 해당되는 Thanks 뒤에 이어지는 말이 보너스 수령 여부와 관련 없는 말이며, (B)는 bonus에서 연상 가능한 Based on your sales를 활용해 혼동을 유발하는 오답이다.

어휘 **receive** ~을 받다 **quarterly** 분기의 **helpful** 도움이 되는, 유익한 **based on** ~을 바탕으로, ~을 기반으로 **over** ~ 동안에 걸친 **get p.p.** ~되다, ~된 상태가 되다 **add A to B** A를 B에 추가하다 **paycheck** 급여 수표, 급여 명세서

7. Can you speed up the file transfer?
(A) He moved to the Camden branch.
(B) The employee records.
(C) This is as fast as it goes.

파일 전송 속도를 높여주실 수 있으세요?
(A) 그분은 캠든 지사로 옮기셨어요.
(B) 직원 기록이요.
(C) 원래 이 정도 빠르기입니다.

해설 파일 전송 속도를 높일 수 있는지 요청하는 말에 대해 원래 속도가 그렇다는 말로 더 높일 수 없다는 뜻을 나타낸 (C)가 정답이다. (A)는 transfer에서 연상 가능한 moved를, (B)는 file에서 연상 가능한 records를 각각 활용해 혼동을 유발하는 오답이다.

어휘 **speed up** ~의 속도를 높이다 **transfer** 전송, 전근, 이동 **branch** 지사, 지점 **as A as it goes** 원래 A한 정도인, 더 A할 수 없는

8. When can you review the proposal from Booker Financial?
(A) I was just getting around to it.
(B) Someone from Accounting.
(C) On page 6.

부커 파이낸셜의 제안서를 언제 검토하실 수 있으신가요?
(A) 막 그걸 볼 시간이 났어요.
(B) 회계부의 누군가요.
(C) 6페이지에요.

해설 부커 파이낸셜의 제안서를 언제 검토할 수 있는지 묻고 있으므로 proposal을 it으로 지칭해 그 일에 대한 시간이 막 났다는 말로 이제 검토하기 시작했다는 뜻을 나타내는 (A)가 정답이다. (B)는 Financial에서 연상 가능한 Accounting을 활용해 혼동을 유발하는 오답이다.

어휘 **review** ~을 검토하다, ~을 살펴보다 **proposal** 제안(서) **get around to** ~할 시간이 나다, ~할 여유가 생기다 **Accounting** 회계부

9. Let me try calling the landlord one more time.
(A) Maybe he turned his phone off.
(B) Can I have your number?
(C) This month's rent is due.

제가 집주인에게 한 번 더 전화해 보도록 할게요.
(A) 아마 그분이 전화기를 꺼놓았을 거예요.
(B) 당신 전화번호 좀 알려 주시겠어요?
(C) 이번 달 월세 지불 기한이 됐어요.

해설 자신이 직접 집주인에게 한 번 더 전화해 보겠다고 알리는 말에 대해 landlord를 he로 지칭해 집주인이 전화기를 꺼놨을 거라는 말로 통화하기 어려울 것임을 의미하는 (A)가 정답이다. (B)는 calling에서 연상 가능한 number를, (C)는 landlord에서 연상 가능한 month's rent를 각각 활용해 혼동을 유발하는 오답이다.

어휘 **try -ing** (한 번) ~하는 것을 시도해 보다 **landlord** 집주인 **turn A off** A를 끄다 **rent** 월세, 집세 **due** 지불 기한이 된, 하기로 되어 있는

10. I have to visit a client in Denver next week.
(A) A great place for a vacation.
(B) Visiting hours end at 8 o'clock.
(C) Don't forget to report your travel expenses.

제가 다음 주에 덴버에 계신 고객을 방문해야 합니다.
(A) 휴가 장소로 아주 좋은 곳이죠.
(B) 면회 시간이 8시에 종료됩니다.
(C) 출장 경비를 보고하시는 일을 잊지 마세요.

해설 다음 주에 덴버에 있는 고객을 방문해야 한다는 사실을 알리는 말에 대해 그와 관련된 정책으로서 출장 경비를 잊지 말고 보고하도록 상기시키는 말에 해당되는 (C)가 정답이다. (A)는 visit에서 연상 가능한 place for a vacation을, (B)는 visit과 일부 발음이 유사한 Visiting을 각각 활용해 혼동을 유발하는 오

답이다.

어휘 **vacation** 휴가 **forget to do** ~하는 것을 잊다 **expense** 경비, 지출 (비용)

---

11. What time are the decorators starting the painting?
(A) White walls would look best.
(B) I'm ready if you are.
(C) Sometime after lunch.

장식업자들이 몇 시에 페인트칠을 시작하나요?
(A) 흰색 벽이 가장 좋아 보일 거예요.
(B) 당신만 준비되면 됩니다.
(C) 점심 시간 지나서 오후 중으로요.

해설 장식업자들이 몇 시에 페인트칠을 시작하는지 묻고 있으므로 대략적인 미래 시점으로 답변하는 (C)가 정답이다. (A)는 painting에서 연상 가능한 White walls를 활용해 혼동을 유발하는 오답이다.

어휘 **decorator** 장식업자, 장식 전문가 **look 형용사** ~하게 보이다, A한 것 같다

---

12. Did this restaurant start using a new recipe for vegetable soup?
(A) Oh, I'm already full.
(B) Let's double our order.
(C) They do taste a bit different.

이 레스토랑이 야채 수프에 새 조리법을 이용하기 시작한 건가요?
(A) 아, 저는 이미 배불러요.
(B) 우리 주문량을 두 배로 늘립시다.
(C) 분명 맛이 좀 다르네요.

해설 현재 있는 레스토랑에서 브레드스틱에 새 조리법을 이용하기 시작한 것인지 묻고 있으므로 breadsticks를 They로 지칭해 분명 맛이 좀 다르다는 말로 새 조리법을 이용한 것으로 추정된다는 의미를 나타낸 (C)가 정답이다. (A)는 restaurant과 breadsticks에서 연상 가능한 full을 활용해 혼동을 유발하는 오답이다.

어휘 **recipe** 조리법 **vegetable** 야채 **full** 배부른 **double** v. ~을 두 배로 늘리다 **taste A** A한 맛이 나다 **a bit** 조금, 약간

---

13. Hasn't this magazine subscription ended?
(A) There's one month left.
(B) I rarely read these days.
(C) Yes, that's the latest issue.

이 잡지 구독 기간이 끝나지 않았나요?
(A) 한 달 남았어요.
(B) 저는 요즘 좀처럼 독서하지 않아요.
(C) 네, 그게 최신 호입니다.

해설 잡지 구독 기간이 끝나지 않았는지 묻고 있으므로 한 달 남았다는 말로 아직 구독 기간이 끝나지 않았다는 의미를 나타낸 (A)가 정답이다. (B)와 (C)는 magazine에서 연상 가능한 read와 issue를 각각 활용해 혼동을 유발하는 오답이다.

어휘 **subscription** 구독, 서비스 이용 **there's A left** A가 남아 있다, 남은 A가 있다 **rarely** 좀처럼 ~ 않다 **latest** 최신의 **issue** (출판물의) 호

---

14. Our amusement park's new rollercoaster is really popular.
(A) I think the advertisements helped.
(B) You need to be a certain height to ride it.
(C) Yes, let's go there this weekend.

우리 놀이공원의 새 롤러코스터가 정말 인기 있어요.
(A) 제 생각엔 광고가 도움이 되었던 것 같아요.
(B) 그걸 타려면 특정 키가 되어야 합니다.
(C) 네, 이번 주말에 그곳에 갑시다.

해설 소속 놀이공원의 새 롤러코스터가 정말 인기 있다는 사실을 알리는 말에 대해 그 이유와 관련해 광고가 도움이 되었던 것 같다는 의견을 밝히는 (A)가 정답이다. (B)는 rollercoaster에서 연상 가능한 certain height to ride it을 활용해 혼동을 유발하는 오답이며, (C)는 동의를 뜻하는 Yes 뒤에 이어지는 말이 인기 상승과 관련 없는 내용이므로 오답이다.

어휘 **amusement park** 놀이공원 **popular** 인기 있는 **advertisement** 광고 **certain** 특정한, 일정한 **ride** ~을 타다

---

15. Wouldn't it be easier to take a taxi to the company's headquarters?
(A) No, the driver got lost on the way.
(B) I'm just used to getting there by train.
(C) The CEO said I have to be there.

그 회사의 본사로 택시를 타고 가는 게 더 쉽지 않을까요?
(A) 아뇨, 기사님께서 도중에 길을 잃으셨어요.
(B) 저는 그냥 기차로 그곳에 가는 게 익숙해요.
(C) 대표이사님께서 제가 거기 있어야 한다고 하셨어요.

해설 특정 회사의 본사로 택시를 타고 가는 게 더 쉽지 않을지 묻고 있으므로 the company's headquarters를 there로 지칭해 기차로 가는 게 익숙하다는 말로 택시를 타지 않겠다는 뜻을 나타낸 (B)가 정답이다. (A)는 taxi에서 연상 가능한 driver을 활용해 혼동을 유발하는 오답으로, 부정을 뜻하는 No 뒤에 택시를 탈 것인지에 대한 생각과 관련 없는 말이 이어지고 있으므로 어울리지 않는 반응이다.

어휘 **It would be easier to do** ~하는 게 더 쉬울 것이다 **take** (교통편) ~을 타다, ~을 이용하다 **headquarters** 본사 **get lost** 길을 잃다 **on the way** (이동하는) 도중에 **be used to -ing** ~하는 데 익숙하다 **get there** 그곳에 가다

16. The parking lot is free, isn't it?
(A) **No, but it's not expensive.**
(B) There should be a park near the building.
(C) I'll have some time later today.

그 주차장은 무료이지 않나요?
(A) **아뇨, 하지만 비싸진 않습니다.**
(B) 그 건물 근처에 공원이 있을 거예요.
(C) 제가 오늘 이따가 시간이 좀 있을 겁니다.

해설 주차장이 무료인지 확인하는 부가 의문문에 대해 부정을 뜻하는 No와 함께 비싸지 않다는 정보를 덧붙이는 (A)가 정답이다. (B)는 질문에 쓰인 parking과 발음이 유사한 park를 이용해 혼동을 유발하는 오답이며, (C)는 free의 다른 의미(무료의, 시간이 있는)를 이용해 free와 연관성 있게 들리는 have some time으로 혼동을 유발하는 답변이다.

어휘 **parking lot** 주차장 **free** 무료의, 시간이 있는 **near** ~ 근처에 **have some time** 시간이 좀 있다 **later today** 오늘 이따가

17. Aren't you coming to the meeting that's about to start?
(A) A group of shareholders.
(B) **Claire is filling in for me.**
(C) That should be enough, thanks.

막 시작하려고 하는 회의에 가시지 않나요?
(A) 주주들로 구성된 그룹이요.
(B) **클레어 씨가 제 대신 갑니다.**
(C) 그거면 충분할 거예요, 감사합니다.

해설 막 시작하려고 하는 회의에 가지 않는지 묻고 있으므로 클레어 씨가 자신을 대신한다는 말로 가지 않는다는 뜻을 나타낸 (B)가 정답이다. (A)는 meeting에서 회의 참석 대상자로 연상 가능한 shareholders를 활용해 혼동을 유발하는 오답이다.

어휘 **be about to do** 막 ~하려는 참이다 **shareholder** 주주 **fill in for** ~을 대신하다

18. Did you get an information sheet or should I print you another one?
(A) That's good to know.
(B) The printer was fixed earlier.
(C) **Mr. Hanlon gave me one.**

정보 안내지를 받으셨나요, 아니면 제가 한 장 더 출력해 드릴까요?
(A) 잘 알겠습니다.
(B) 프린터가 아까 수리되었어요.
(C) **핸런 씨께서 한 장 주셨어요.**

해설 정보 안내지를 받았는지, 아니면 자신이 한 장 더 출력해서 줄지 묻고 있으므로 information sheet을 one으로 지칭해 핸런이라는 사람이 한 장 주었다는 말로 안내지를 받았다는 뜻을 나타낸 (C)가 정답이다. (A)는 선택 의문문과 관련 없는 응답이

며, (B)는 print와 발음이 일부 유사한 printer을 활용한 오답이다.

어휘 **sheet** (종이 등의) 한 장 **another** 또 다른 하나의 **That's good to know** 잘 알겠습니다, 잘됐네요, 다행이네요 **fix** ~을 수리하다

19. How often does the bus come?
(A) He usually commutes by bus.
(B) **About every 20 minutes.**
(C) The box was sent this morning.

그 버스가 얼마나 자주 오나요?
(A) 그분은 평소에 버스로 통근해요.
(B) **약 20분마다 한 번씩이요.**
(C) 그 상자는 오늘 아침에 보냈어요.

해설 특정 버스가 얼마나 자주 오는지 묻고 있으므로 대략적인 빈도를 나타내는 말로 답변하는 (B)가 정답이다. every는 시간이나 길이 등을 나타내는 복수명사와 결합해 '~마다 한 번씩, 매 ~에' 등을 의미한다. (A)는 bus를 반복한 답변으로서, 대상을 알 수 없는 He의 통근 방법을 말하고 있어 핵심에서 벗어난 오답이며, (C)는 bus와 발음이 유사한 box를 활용해 혼동을 유발하는 오답이다.

어휘 **usually** 평소에, 보통, 일반적으로 **commute** 통근하다 **about** 약, 대략

20. Does this arch design seem suitable for the building's entrance?
(A) Here's a copy of the key.
(B) **I don't see any problems with these blueprints.**
(C) Which exit did you take?

이 아치형 디자인이 그 건물 출입구에 적합한 것 같으세요?
(A) 여기 복사한 열쇠입니다.
(B) **저는 이 설계도에 어떤 문제도 보이지 않아요.**
(C) 어느 출구를 이용하셨나요?

해설 아치형 디자인이 건물 출입구에 적합한 것 같은지 묻고 있으므로 그 디자인이 그려져 있는 설계도를 these blueprints로 지칭해 어떤 문제도 보이지 않는다는 말로 디자인이 건물 출입구에 적합하다는 의미를 나타낸 (B)가 정답이다. (A)와 (C)는 building's entrance에서 연상 가능한 a copy of the key와 exit를 각각 활용해 혼동을 유발하고 있다.

어휘 **arch** 아치형 구조물 **seem** 형용사 ~한 것 같다, ~하게 보이다 **suitable for** ~에 적합한, ~에 어울리는 **blueprint** 설계도, 청사진 **exit** 출구

Part 3

Questions 21-23 refer to the following conversation.

M: Hi, Charlotte. **21** I heard you just signed up for a membership at the new gym. I'm thinking about doing that, too.

W: You should! **22** They're having their official opening celebration this weekend. Anyone can turn up and try out the equipment for free, and even watch some demonstrations by the instructors.

M: I'll check it out. Anyway, **23** tell me how to become a member. Can I do it online?

W: No, you'll need to do it in person. Just turn up this weekend and speak with one of the staff. And, make sure you bring ID and a credit card.

남: 안녕하세요, 샬럿 씨. 새로 생긴 체육관에 회원으로 막 등록하셨다는 얘기를 들었어요. 저도 그렇게 할까 생각 중이에요.

여: 하세요! 이번 주말에 그곳에서 정식 개장 기념 행사를 열어요. 누구든 가서 무료로 장비를 시험해 볼 수 있고, 심지어 강사들이 진행하는 몇몇 시연회도 볼 수 있어요.

남: 확인해 보겠습니다. 어쨌든, 회원이 되는 방법 좀 알려 주세요. 온라인으로 할 수 있나요?

여: 아뇨, 직접 가서 하셔야 할 거예요. 그냥 이번 주말에 가셔서 직원들 중 한 명과 이야기하세요. 그리고, 반드시 신분증과 신용 카드를 챙겨 가도록 하세요.

어휘 **sign up for** ~에 등록하다, ~을 신청하다 **gym** 체육관 **official** 정식의, 공식적인 **celebration** 기념 행사, 축하 행사 **turn up** 나타나다, 모습을 보이다 **try out** ~을 시험해 보다 **equipment** 장비 **for free** 무료로 **demonstration** 시연(회), 시범 **instructor** 강사 **check A out** A를 확인해 보다 **anyway** 어쨌든 **how to do** ~하는 방법 **in person** 직접 (가서) **make sure (that)** 반드시 ~하도록 하다, ~하는 것을 확실히 해 두다

21. 남자는 무엇을 하는 것을 고려하고 있다고 말하는가?
(A) 더 건강하게 음식을 먹는 일
(B) 피트니스 센터에 가입하는 일
(C) 새로운 일자리에 지원하는 일
(D) 운동 장비를 구입하는 일

해설 남자가 자신의 생각이나 계획 등을 밝히는 부분에서 단서를 찾아야 한다. 남자가 대화를 시작하면서 상대방인 여자가 새로 생긴 체육관에 회원으로 막 등록했다는 얘기를 들은 사실과 자신도 그렇게 하는 것을 생각하고 있다고(I heard you just signed up for a membership at the new gym. I'm thinking about doing that, too) 알리고 있으므로 (B)가 정

답이다.

어휘 **consider -ing** ~하는 것을 고려하다 **healthily** 건강하게, 건강에 좋게 **join** ~에 가입하다, ~에 합류하다 **apply for** ~에 지원하다, ~을 신청하다 **exercise** 운동

Paraphrase signed up for a membership at the new gym → Joining a fitness center

22. 여자는 어떤 종류의 행사를 언급하는가?
(A) 직원 오리엔테이션
(B) 계절 할인 행사
(C) 개장 기념 행사
(D) 스포츠 대회

해설 여자가 특정 행사 명칭이나 관련 세부 활동 등을 말하는 부분에서 단서를 찾아야 한다. 여자가 대화 중반부에 자신이 가입한 체육관의 정식 개장 기념 행사가 열린다는(They're having their official opening celebration this weekend) 사실을 알리고 있으므로 (C)가 정답이다.

어휘 **seasonal** 계절적인, 계절에 따른

Paraphrase official opening celebration → grand opening

23. 여자는 남자에게 무엇을 설명하는가?
(A) 회원 자격을 얻는 방법
(B) 업체 위치를 찾는 방법
(C) 일정을 확인하는 방법
(D) 웹 사이트를 이용하는 방법

해설 여자가 남자에게 무엇을 설명하는지 묻고 있으므로 여자의 말에 집중해 들어야 하며, Part 3 대화에서는 상대방의 요청이나 제안에 따라 하게 되는 일을 묻는 경우도 흔하므로 남자의 말에도 함께 귀 기울여 듣는 것이 좋다. 대화 후반부에 남자가 회원이 되는 방법을 알려 달라고 말하면서 온라인으로 할 수 있는지(tell me how to become a member. Can I do it online?) 묻자, 여자가 그 방법과 관련해 설명하고 있으므로 (A)가 정답이다.

어휘 **obtain** ~을 얻다, ~을 획득하다 **locate** ~의 위치를 찾다 **access** ~을 이용하다, ~에 접근하다

Paraphrase how to become a member → How to obtain a membership

Questions 24-26 refer to the following conversation.

W: Magnus, **24** our landscaping company is going to merge two of our smallest branches this year. The CEO has put you and I in charge of overseeing the move and ensuring it goes smoothly.

M: Oh, that's quite a big responsibility.

W: Yes, and the first thing we need to do is find a bigger building for the employees from both branches. We'll be closing the two current buildings as part of the move.

M: I see. Well, **25** I think we need to find a building that's located close to major highways, so that it's convenient for our workers to visit clients.

W: I agree. That's very important. Oh, **26** I forgot to tell you, the CEO has allocated one million dollars for us to use on this project.

여: 매그너스 씨, 우리 조경 회사가 올해 우리 지사들 중 가장 작은 두 곳을 통합할 예정입니다. 대표이사님께서 당신과 저에게 그 조치를 감독하고 반드시 순조롭게 진행되도록 하는 일의 책임을 맡기셨어요.
남: 아, 상당히 중요한 책임이네요.
여: 네, 그리고 우리가 해야 하는 첫 번째 일은 두 지사에 모두 속한 직원들이 근무할 더 큰 건물을 찾는 것입니다. 우리가 이 조치의 일환으로 두 곳이 현재 위치한 건물들을 닫게 될 겁니다.
남: 알겠습니다. 음, 제 생각엔 우리가 주요 고속도로들과 가까운 곳에 위치한 건물을 찾아야 할 것 같은데, 그래야 우리 직원들이 고객들을 방문하기 편리합니다.
여: 동의해요. 아주 중요한 부분이죠. 아, 말씀 드리는 걸 잊은 게 있는데, 대표이사님께서 이 프로젝트에 사용하라고 우리에게 1백만 달러를 할당해 주셨어요.

어휘 **landscaping** 조경 **merge** ~을 통합하다, ~을 합병하다 **branch** 지사, 지점 **put A in charge of B** A에게 B에 대한 책임을 맡기다 **oversee** ~을 감독하다 **move** 조치, 움직임 **ensure (that)** 반드시 ~하도록 하다, ~하는 것을 확실히 해 두다 **go smoothly** 순조롭게 진행되다 **quite** 상당히, 꽤 **responsibility** 책임 **both** 둘 모두의 **current** 현재의 **as part of** ~의 일환으로, ~의 일부로 **be located** 위치해 있다 **close to** ~와 가까이 **so that** (결과) 그래야, 그러므로 (목적) ~하도록 **convenient** 편리한 **agree** 동의하다 **forget to do** ~하는 것을 잊다 **allocate** ~을 할당하다, ~을 배정하다

24. 화자들은 주로 무엇을 이야기하고 있는가?
(A) 해외 사업 확장
(B) 지사 통합
(C) 조경 프로젝트
(D) 취업 기회

해설 대화의 주제나 목적은 대체로 초반부에 드러날 가능성이 높으므로 대화가 시작될 때 특히 집중해 들어야 한다. 여자가 대화를 시작하면서 올해 지사들 중 가장 작은 두 곳을 통합할 예정이라고(our landscaping company is going to merge two of our smallest branches this year) 알린 뒤로 그 일의 진행 순서와 관련해 이야기하고 있으므로 (B)가 정답이다.

어휘 **overseas** 해외의 **expansion** 확장, 확대 **merger** 통합, 합병 **employment** 취업, 고용 **opportunity** 기회

Paraphrase merge two of our smallest branches → branch merger

25. 건물의 어떤 측면이 화자들에게 가장 중요한가?
(A) 널찍한 주차장
(B) 현대적인 시설
(C) 편리한 위치
(D) 낮은 임대 비용

해설 건물의 어떤 측면이 화자들에게 가장 중요한지 묻고 있으므로 특징적인 요소를 말하거나 강조하는 점을 파악해야 한다. 대화 후반부에 남자가 주요 고속도로들과 가까운 곳에 위치한 건물을 찾아야 직원들에게 편리하다고(I think we need to find a building that's located close to major highways, so that it's convenient for our workers to visit clients) 알리고 있는데, 이는 편리한 위치의 중요성을 말하는 것이므로 (C)가 정답이다.

어휘 **aspect** 측면, 양상 **spacious** 널찍한 **parking lot** 주차장 **facility** 시설(물) **rental** 임대, 대여

Paraphrase find a building that's located close to major highways → convenient location

26. 여자는 남자에게 무엇에 관해 이야기하는 것을 잊었다고 말하는가?
(A) 마감기한
(B) 회의 날짜
(C) 직원 보너스
(D) 예산

해설 여자가 무엇에 관해 이야기하는 것을 잊었다고 말하는지 묻고 있으므로 여자의 말에 집중해 단서를 파악해야 한다. 대화 후반부에 여자가 깜빡 잊은 것이 있다고 알리면서 대표이사가 프로젝트에 사용하도록 1백만 달러를 할당한 사실을(I forgot to tell you, the CEO has allocated one million dollars for us to use on this project) 알리고 있다. 이는 프로젝트의 예산 규모를 알리는 말이므로 (D)가 정답이다.

Paraphrase has allocated one million dollars for us to use on this project → budget

Questions 27-29 refer to the following conversation with three speakers.

M1: We've been parked outside the store for almost an hour waiting `27` to pick up the work shirts and pants we ordered.

M2: `28` They should be open by now. Let's call Maggie at the head office and check the store's business hours.

W: A1 Work Apparel. How can I help?

M1: Hi, Maggie. It's Liam and Frank here. Any idea when the supplier will open his store today?

W: I'll check. Oh, it seems that they open later on Mondays. `29` Hang on for another 15 minutes and the owner should arrive.

남1: 우리가 주문한 업무용 셔츠와 바지를 가져가려고 기다리면서 거의 한 시간 동안 이 매장 밖에서 주차해 놓고 있었어요.
남2: 지금쯤 문을 열어야 하는데요. 본사에 있는 매기 씨에게 전화해서 이 매장 영업 시간을 확인해 봐요.
여: A1 워크 어패럴입니다. 무엇을 도와 드릴까요?
남1: 안녕하세요, 매기 씨. 저희는 리암과 프랭크입니다. 공급업자가 오늘 언제 매장 문을 여는지 아시는 거라도 있으세요?
여: 확인해 볼게요. 아, 매주 월요일은 더 늦게 여는 것 같아요. 15분만 더 기다려 보시면, 소유주가 도착할 겁니다.

어휘 **park** ~을 주차하다 **pick up** ~을 가져가다, ~을 가져오다 **order** ~을 주문하다 **by now** 지금쯤 **head office** 본사 **business hours** 영업 시간 **supplier** 공급업자, 공급업체 **it seems that** ~인 것 같다, ~인 것처럼 보이다 **hang on** 기다리다, 대기하다 **owner** 소유주, 주인

27. 남자들은 무엇을 가져가는가?
(A) 스포츠 장비
(B) 가구
(C) 사무용품
(D) 유니폼

해설 남자들이 무엇을 가져가는지 묻고 있으므로 남자들이 어떤 특정 물품을 언급하는지 파악하는 데 집중해야 한다. 남자 한 명이 대화 시작 부분에 자신들이 주문한 업무용 셔츠와 바지를 가져가기 위해(to pick up the work shirts and pants we ordered) 기다리고 있는 상황임을 언급하고 있으므로 (D)가 정답이다.

어휘 **equipment** 장비 **supplies** 용품, 물품

Paraphrase work shirts and pants
→ Uniforms

28. 남자들은 어떤 문제를 이야기하고 있는가?
(A) 주문이 부정확하다.
(B) 업체가 문을 닫은 상태이다.
(C) 제품이 손상된 상태이다.
(D) 주소가 잘못되어 있다.

해설 남자들이 어떤 문제를 이야기하고 있는지 묻고 있으므로 남자들의 말에서 부정적인 정보를 파악하는 데 집중해야 한다. 대화 초반부에 남자 한 명이 업체를 They로 지칭해 지금쯤 문을 열어야 한다고(They should be open by now) 언급하고 있는데, 이는 문을 닫은 상태일 때 문제를 겪는 상황에서 할 수 있는 말이므로 (B)가 정답이다.

어휘 **order** 주문(품) **incorrect** 부정확한 **damaged** 손상된, 피해를 입은

29. 여자는 남자들에게 무엇을 하도록 권하는가?
(A) 매장 소유주에게 전화하는 일
(B) 다른 지점을 방문하는 일
(C) 주문을 취소하는 일
(D) 조금 더 기다리는 일

해설 여자의 말에 집중해 권고 또는 제안 표현과 함께 제시되는 정보를 찾아야 한다. 대화 맨 마지막 부분에 여자가 15분 더 기다리면 소유주가 도착할 것이라고(Hang on for another 15 minutes and the owner should arrive) 알리고 있으므로 (D)가 정답이다.

어휘 **location** 지점, 위치

Paraphrase Hang on for another 15 minutes
→ Wait a little longer

Questions 30-32 refer to the following conversation.

M: I'm really looking forward to `30` organizing this year's employee trip with you, Martina.

W: It will be a fun task! And, I'm glad you'll be helping me. Let's start off by choosing a good location. My top choice would be `31` Fairview Resort at Silver Lake. It offers a lot of fun activities, and `31` its three restaurants are known for their delicious dishes.

M: It has a good reputation, but `32` can we afford it? It's a lot more expensive than the places we stayed at in previous years.

W: Well, we have a decent budget this year.

M: Oh, that's good to know!

남: 당신과 함께 올해의 직원 여행을 준비하는 일을 정말로 고대하고 있습니다, 마르티나 씨.

여: 재미있는 업무가 되겠네요! 그리고, 저를 도와주시게 된다니 기
쁩니다. 좋은 장소를 선택하는 것으로 시작해 봐요. 제가 생각
하는 최고의 선택권은 실버 레이크에 있는 페어뷰 리조트일 거
예요. 재미있는 활동을 많이 제공하고, 거기 있는 세 곳의 레스
토랑이 맛있는 요리로 알려져 있어요.

남: 평판이 좋은 곳이기는 하지만, 우리가 감당할 수 있을까요? 우
리가 예년에 머물렀던 곳들보다 훨씬 더 비싸잖아요.

여: 음, 우리가 올해는 준수한 예산을 보유하고 있어요.

남: 아, 잘됐네요!

어휘 **look forward to -ing** ~하기를 고대하다 **organize** ~을
준비하다, ~을 조직하다 **task** 업무, 일 **start off** 시작하다
location 장소, 지점, 위치 **choice** 선택(권) **be known
for** ~로 알려져 있다 **reputation** 평판, 명성 **afford** (금전
적으로) ~을 감당하다, ~할 여유가 있다 **a lot** (비교급 수식)
훨씬 **previous** 이전의, 과거의 **decent** (수준, 질 등) 준수
한, 꽤 괜찮은 **budget** 예산

30. 화자들은 어떤 종류의 행사를 계획하고 있는가?

(A) 회사 여행
(B) 교육 세미나
(C) 직원 모집 행사
(D) 연례 저녁 회식

해설 화자들이 어떤 종류의 행사를 계획하고 있는지 묻고 있으므
로 특정 행사 명칭이나 관련 세부 활동 등과 같은 특징을 파악
하는 데 집중해야 한다. 남자가 대화 초반부에 여자와 함께 올
해의 직원 여행을 준비하는 일을(organizing this year's
employee trip) 언급하고 있으므로 (A)가 정답이다.

어휘 **training** 교육, 훈련 **recruitment** (직원 등의) 모집
annual 연례적인, 해마다의

Paraphrase this year's employee trip
→ company trip

31. 여자는 한 장소와 관련해 무엇을 마음에 들어 하는가?

(A) 규모
(B) 편리성
(C) 가격 적절성
(D) 음식

해설 여자가 한 장소와 관련해 무엇을 마음에 들어 하는지 묻고 있
으므로 특정 장소를 언급하는 부분에서 설명하는 장점이
나 특징을 파악해야 한다. 대화 중반부에 여자가 한 리조트
를 언급하면서 그곳의 특징과 관련해 맛있는 요리로 알려져
있다는(~ Fairview Resort at Silver Lake. ~ its three
restaurants are known for their delicious dishes) 사
실을 알리고 있으므로 (D)가 정답이다.

Paraphrase delicious dishes
→ food

32. 여자는 왜 "우리가 올해는 준수한 예산을 보유하고 있어요"라
고 말하는가?

(A) 남자의 노력을 칭찬하기 위해
(B) 남자를 안심시키기 위해
(C) 예산 수정을 제안하기 위해
(D) 놀라움을 표현하기 위해

해설 남자가 대화 후반부에 특정 장소를 감당할 수 있을지 물으면
서 훨씬 비싼 곳임을 언급하자(can we afford it? It's a lot
more expensive ~), 여자가 '올해는 준수한 예산을 보유하고
있다'고 알리는 흐름이다. 이는 남자에게 비용 문제를 걱정할 필
요가 없다는 의미로 안심시키는 말에 해당되므로 (B)가 정답이
다.

어휘 **praise** ~을 칭찬하다 **effort** 노력 **reassure** ~을 안심시
키다 **suggest** ~을 제안하다, ~을 권하다 **revision** 수정,
변경 **express** (생각, 감정 등) ~을 표현하다

Questions 33-35 refer to the following conversation and
schedule.

W: Danny, would you be interested in signing up
for baking classes with me at Ayling Culinary
School? It just opened a branch across the
street from our office, and it's a good chance to
learn something new.

M: Sure! That sounds fun. **33** But will there be any
spaces left in the classes? I know the school is
pretty popular.

W: Actually, I checked, and **34** they still have
spaces for their Friday classes. But, we'd
better sign up today.

M: Let's do it. And **35** maybe we can have dinner
together after our class ends.

여: 대니 씨, 저와 함께 에일링 요리 학원의 제과 강좌에 등록하는
데 관심이 있으신가요? 우리 사무실 길 건너편에 막 지점을 하
나 열었는데, 뭔가 새로운 걸 배울 수 있는 좋은 기회예요.

남: 좋아요! 재미있을 것 같아요. 하지만 그 강좌에 조금이라도 남
은 자리가 있을까요? 그 학원이 꽤 인기 있는 것으로 알고 있어
서요.

여: 실은, 제가 확인해 봤는데, 금요일 강좌에 여전히 자리가 있어
요. 하지만, 오늘 등록하는 게 좋을 거예요.

남: 그렇게 합시다. 그리고 아마 수업이 끝난 후에 함께 저녁 식사
도 할 수 있을 거예요.

에일링 요리 학원 초보자 제과 강좌	
월요일	오후 5:00
수요일	오전 7:30
	오후 6:30
금요일	오후 6:00

어휘 **sign up for** ~에 등록하다, ~을 신청하다 **baking** 제과
branch 지점, 지사 **across** ~ 건너편에, ~ 맞은편에
there be A left A가 남아 있다, 남은 A가 있다 **pretty** 꽤,
아주 **actually** 실은, 사실 **had better do** ~하는 게 좋다

33. 남자는 무엇에 대해 우려하는가?

(A) 학원이 너무 멀리 떨어져 있다.

(B) 일부 강좌가 꽉 찰 수도 있다.

(C) 주차장이 너무 작다.

(D) 일부 요금이 너무 높다.

해설 질문에 제시된 concerned 또는 worried 같은 말이나 의구
심 또는 불안감을 표현하는 말이 언급되는 부분에서 단서를 찾
아야 한다. 대화 중반부에 남자가 강좌에 남는 자리가 있을지
(But will there be any spaces left in the classes?) 묻
고 있는데, 이는 강좌가 꽉 찰 수 있다는 우려에서 비롯된 말이
므로 (B)가 정답이다.

어휘 **be concerned about** ~에 대해 우려하다 **far away**
멀리 떨어진 **parking lot** 주차장 **fee** 요금, 수수료

34. 시각자료를 보시오. 여자는 어느 강좌 시간을 언급하는가?

(A) 오후 5시

(B) 오전 7시 30분

(C) 오후 6시 30분

(D) 오후 6시

해설 도표가 제시되는 시각자료 문제의 경우, 각 항목의 명칭을 미
리 확인해 두는 것이 좋으며, 항목별로 각 선택지와 짝을 이루
는 정보가 대화 중에 단서로 제시된다는 점에 유의해야 한다. 대
화 후반부에 여자가 금요일 강좌에 여전히 자리가 있다고(they
still have spaces for their Friday classes) 알리고 있다.
시각자료에서 금요일 강좌가 표기된 맨 아래칸에 시간이 6:00
P.M.으로 쓰여 있으므로 (D)가 정답이다.

어휘 **refer to** ~을 언급하다

35. 남자는 무엇을 제안하는가?

(A) 일정표를 확인하는 일

(B) 학원에 연락하는 일

(C) 교통편을 함께 이용하는 일

(D) 식사하는 일

해설 남자의 말에 집중해 제안 표현과 함께 제시되는 정보를 찾아
야 한다. 대화 맨 마지막 부분에 남자가 수업이 끝난 후에 함
께 저녁 식사도 할 수 있을 것이라고(maybe we can have
dinner together after our class ends) 언급하고 있으므
로 (D)가 정답이다.

어휘 **contact** ~에 연락하다 **share** ~을 함께 하다, ~을 공유하
다 **transportation** 교통(편)

Paraphrase have dinner

→ Having a meal

Questions 36-38 refer to the following conversation and design.

> **W:** Mitch, **36** we asked all our customers to participate in a survey last month. Have you had a chance to look over the forms they submitted?
>
> **M:** Yes, and their feedback was very useful.
>
> **W:** I'm glad to hear that!
>
> **M:** Yes, and I'm glad we asked for opinions on which logo we should use for our flower shop. **37** Now we can add it to our new Web site when it goes online next week.
>
> **W:** Exactly! Can I see the logos we were considering, and which one our customers preferred?
>
> **M:** Sure, take a look. **38** Most of our customers chose the one with the four heart-shaped petals, and I agree with them.
>
> **W:** Oh, that's my favorite, too. Let's definitely go with that one then.

여: 미치 씨, 우리가 지난 달에 모든 고객들께 설문 조사에 참가하
도록 요청 드렸어요. 그분들께서 제출하신 양식을 살펴보실
기회가 있으셨나요?

남: 네, 그리고 그분들 의견이 아주 유용했어요.

여: 그 말씀을 들으니 기쁘네요!

남: 네, 그리고 우리 꽃집에 어느 로고를 사용해야 하는지에 관한
의견을 요청 드려서 다행입니다. 이제 우리의 새 웹 사이트가
다음 주에 온라인 상태가 되면 그걸 추가할 수 있어요.

여: 맞아요! 우리가 고려하던 로고들을 볼 수 있나요, 그리고 우리
고객들께서 어느 것을 선호했나요?

남: 그럼요, 한 번 보세요. 대부분의 우리 고객들께서 네 개의 하
트 모양 꽃잎으로 된 것을 선택하셨는데, 저도 같은 생각입니
다.

여: 아, 저도 그게 가장 마음에 들어요. 그럼 확실히 이것으로 하도
록 해요.

A	B	C	D

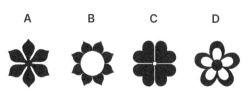

어휘 **participate in** ~에 참가하다 **survey** 설문 조사(지)
have a chance to do ~할 기회가 있다 **look over** ~을
살펴보다, ~을 검토하다 **form** 양식, 서식 **submit** ~을 제
출하다 **feedback** 의견 **useful** 유용한 **ask for** ~을 요

청하다 **opinion** 의견 **add A to B** A를 B에 추가하다 **go online** 온라인 상태가 되다 **Exactly** (강한 동의) 맞아요, 바로 그거예요 **consider** ~을 고려하다 **prefer** ~을 선호하다 **take a look** 한 번 보다 **A-shaped** A 모양으로 된 **petal** 꽃잎 **agree with** ~에 동의하다 **favorite** 가장 좋아하는 것 **definitely** 확실히, 분명히 **go with** (결정) ~로 하다 **then** 그럼, 그렇다면, 그런 다음, 그때

36. 고객들은 무엇을 하도록 요청받았는가?
(A) 경연대회에 참가하는 일
(B) 개장 기념 행사에 참석하는 일
(C) 회원으로 등록하는 일
(D) 설문 조사에 참가하는 일

해설 여자가 대화를 시작하면서 모든 고객에게 설문 조사에 참가하도록 요청한 사실을(we asked all our customers to participate in a survey last month) 언급하고 있으므로 (D)가 정답이다.

어휘 **be invited to do** ~하도록 요청 받다 **enter** ~에 참가하다 **competition** 경연대회, 경기대회 **attend** ~에 참석하다 **sign up for** ~에 등록하다, ~을 신청하다 **take part in** ~에 참가하다

Paraphrase participate in a survey
→ Take part in a survey

37. 화자들은 다음 주에 무엇을 할 것인가?
(A) 카탈로그를 만드는 일
(B) 웹 사이트를 시작하는 일
(C) 할인을 제공하는 일
(D) 전단을 배부하는 일

해설 화자들이 다음 주에 무엇을 할 것인지 묻고 있으므로 next week라는 시점 표현과 함께 언급되는 정보를 찾아야 한다. 남자가 대화 중반부에 자신들의 새 웹 사이트가 다음 주에 온라인 상태가 된다고(Now we can add it to our new Web site when it goes online next week) 알리고 있다. 이는 다음 주에 새 웹 사이트가 시작된다는 뜻이므로 (B)가 정답이다.

어휘 **create** ~을 만들어 내다 **launch** ~을 시작하다, ~을 출시하다 **distribute** ~을 배부하다, ~을 나눠주다 **flyer** 전단

Paraphrase our new Web site when it goes online
→ Launch a Web site

38. 시각자료를 보시오. 화자들은 어느 로고 디자인을 사용할 것인가?
(A) 로고 A
(B) 로고 B
(C) 로고 C
(D) 로고 D

해설 제품 소개 등을 위한 기호나 그림 등이 제시되는 시각자료 문제의 경우, 각 항목의 특징적인 요소를 미리 확인해 두는 것이 좋으며, 항목별로 각 선택지와 짝을 이루는 특징이 대화 중에 단

서로 제시된다는 점에 유의해야 한다. 대화 후반부에 남자가 대부분의 고객들이 네 개의 하트 모양 꽃잎으로 된 것을 선택한 사실과 자신도 그에 동의한다는(Most of our customers chose the one with the four heart-shaped petals, and I agree with them) 말을 하고 있다. 시각자료에서 C에 해당되는 그림이 네 개의 하트 모양 꽃잎으로 구성되어 있으므로 (C)가 정답이다.

Part 4

Questions 39-41 refer to the following excerpt from a meeting.

Thank you for coming to **39** this marketing meeting. I've been working on the ad campaign for your new line of shoes. I think that there is one really important thing that you can do to increase interest and sales, but **40** I'm going to need more samples in order to do that. My plan is to give out those samples to some high-profile social media personalities, and have them reach out to their followers to tell them what they like about your shoes. This can be surprisingly effective. Now, **41** I've prepared some slides to show you. They break down the differences between recent campaigns that used this tactic versus those that did not. **41** Here's the first one.

이번 마케팅 회의 시간에 오신 것에 대해 감사드립니다. 제가 여러분의 새로운 신발 제품 라인에 필요한 광고 캠페인 작업을 계속 해오고 있습니다. 저는 여러분께서 사람들의 관심과 판매량을 끌어올리기 위해 하실 수 있는 정말로 중요한 한 가지 사항이 있다고 생각하지만, 그렇게 하기 위해서는 샘플이 더 많이 필요할 것입니다. 제 계획은 그 샘플들을 사람들의 높은 관심을 받는 몇몇 소셜 미디어 유명인들에게 나눠준 다음, 여러분의 신발 제품과 관련해 무엇이 마음이 드는지 이야기할 수 있도록 팔로워들에게 다가가게 하는 것입니다. 이는 놀라울 정도로 효과적일 수 있습니다. 자, 제가 여러분께 보여드릴 몇몇 슬라이드를 준비했습니다. 여기에 이러한 전략을 활용한 최근의 광고 캠페인과 그렇지 않았던 것들 사이의 차이점들이 분류되어 있습니다. 여기 그 첫 번째입니다.

어휘 **work on** ~에 대한 작업을 하다 **ad** 광고 **line** 제품 라인, 제품군 **increase** ~을 끌어올리다, ~을 증가시키다 **interest** 관심 **sales** 판매(량), 매출, 영업 **in order to do** ~하기 위해, ~하려면 **give out** ~을 나눠주다 **high-profile** 사람들의 높은 관심을 받는, 이목을 끄는 **personality** 유명인, 개성, 성격 **have A do** A에게 ~하게 하다 **reach out to** ~에게 다가가다, ~와 접촉하다 **surprisingly** 놀라울 정도로 **effective** 효과적인 **prepare** ~을 준비하다 **break down** ~을 분류하다, ~을 상세 항목으로 보여주다 **difference** 차이점 **recent** 최근

의 **tactic** 전략, 전술 **A versus B** (경기, 경쟁 등) A 대 B

39. 화자는 누구일 것 같은가?
(A) 공장 관리 책임자
(B) 패션 디자이너
(C) 신발 영업사원
(D) 마케팅 전문가

해설 화자가 담화 시작 부분에 마케팅 회의임을 밝히면서 신발 제품 라인에 필요한 광고 캠페인 작업을 계속 하고 있다고(this marketing meeting. I've been working on the ad campaign for your new line of shoes) 알리고 있다. 이는 마케팅을 전문으로 하는 사람이 할 수 있는 일에 해당되므로 (D)가 정답이다.

어휘 **salesperson** 영업사원 **specialist** 전문가

40. 샘플이 왜 더 많이 필요한가?
(A) 소셜 미디어 이용자들에게 나눠주기 위해
(B) 제품의 높은 품질을 증명하기 위해
(C) 사람들에게 회원으로 가입하도록 권하기 위해
(D) 특정 금액을 소비하는 고객들에게 제공하기 위해

해설 샘플이 왜 더 많이 필요한지 묻고 있으므로 샘플과 관련해 말하는 부분에서 함께 언급되는 이유를 찾아야 한다. 담화 중반부에 화자가 샘플이 더 많이 필요하다고 밝히면서 몇몇 소셜 미디어 유명인들에게 나눠줄 생각이라고(I'm going to need more samples in order to do that. My plan is to give out those samples to some high-profile social media personalities ~) 알리고 있으므로 (A)가 정답이다.

어휘 **distribute** ~을 나눠주다, ~을 배부하다 **prove** ~을 증명하다 **encourage A to do** A에게 ~하도록 권하다 **join** ~에 가입하다, ~에 합류하다 **certain** 특정한, 일정한 **amount** 금액, 액수

Paraphrase give out those samples to some high-profile social media personalities
→ distribute to social media users

41. 청자들은 곧이어 무엇을 할 것 같은가?
(A) 시설을 둘러보는 일
(B) 슬라이드쇼를 보는 일
(C) 유명인과 만나는 일
(D) 사업 계약서에 서명하는 일

해설 담화 후반부에 화자가 청자들에게 보여줄 슬라이드를 준비했다고 알리면서(I've prepared some slides to show you) 첫 번째 것을 소개하는(Here's the first one) 말을 하고 있으므로 (B)가 정답이다.

어휘 **tour** v. ~을 둘러보다, ~을 견학하다 **facility** 시설(물) **celebrity** 유명인 **contract** 계약(서)

Questions 42-44 refer to the following advertisement.

> If you are planning a camping trip, or even just want to sleep outside in your own back yard, **42** consider buying a Pinnacle tent today. You won't find a better quality product at such an affordable price. Our tent differs from others on the market because **43** it includes an additional padded layer of Pinnacle's high-quality memory foam, ensuring that you have a comfortable sleep. Visit your local camping supply store or our Web site at www.pinnacletent.com to make a purchase. If you order through our Web site, **44** put in the code PINNACLE10 to receive a free mug with your order.
>
> 캠핑 여행을 계획하고 계시거나, 심지어 그저 자택 뒷마당의 옥외 공간에서라도 주무시기를 원하시는 경우, 오늘 피너클 텐트 구입을 고려해 보십시오. 이 정도로 알맞은 가격에 더 나은 고급 제품을 찾지 못하실 것입니다. 저희 텐트가 시중에 나와 있는 다른 제품들과 다른 이유는 한 겹 더 패드 처리된 저희 피너클의 고품질 메모리 폼을 포함하고 있어서, 편안하게 수면하시도록 보장해 드리기 때문입니다. 여러분의 지역 내 캠핑 용품 매장을 방문하시거나 저희 웹 사이트 www.pinnacletent.com을 방문해 구입하시기 바랍니다. 저희 웹 사이트를 통해 주문하시는 경우, 코드 번호 PINNACLE10을 입력하시면 주문품과 함께 무료 머그잔을 받으시게 됩니다.

어휘 **plan** ~을 계획하다 **consider -ing** ~하는 것을 고려하다 **quality** a. 고급의, 질 좋은 **affordable** (가격이) 알맞은, 구입할 수 있는 **differ from** ~와 다르다 **on the market** 시중에 나와 있는 **include** ~을 포함하다 **additional** 추가적인 **padded** 패드 처리된, 패드를 덧댄 **layer** 겹, 층, 막 **high-quality** 고품질의 **memory foam** 메모리 폼(스펀지의 한 종류) **ensure that** ~임을 보장하다, 반드시 ~하도록 하다 **comfortable** 편안한 **local** 지역의, 현지의 **supply** n. 용품, 물품 **make a purchase** 구입하다 **put in** ~을 입력하다 **mug** 머그잔

42. 어떤 종류의 제품이 광고되고 있는가?
(A) 침낭
(B) 배낭
(C) 텐트
(D) 침대

해설 담화 초반부에 화자가 오늘 피너클 텐트 구입을 고려해 보라고 (consider buying a Pinnacle tent today) 알린 뒤로 텐트 제품 관련 사항을 설명하고 있으므로 (C)가 정답이다.

어휘 **advertise** ~을 광고하다

43. 화자는 제품과 관련해 무엇이 특별하다고 말하는가?

(A) 쉽게 세척할 수 있다.
(B) 내구성이 매우 뛰어나다.
(C) 무게가 가볍다.
(D) 추가 패드가 있다.

해설 제품의 특징이나 장점 등을 소개하는 부분에서 단서를 찾아야한다. 담화 중반부에 화자가 추가로 한 겹 더 패드 처리된 고품질 메모리 폼을 포함하고 있다는(it includes an additional padded layer of Pinnacle's high-quality memory foam) 특징을 설명하고 있으므로 (D)가 정답이다.

어휘 **unique** 특별한, 독특한 **durable** 내구성이 좋은 **lightweight** 가벼운, 경량의 **extra** 추가의, 여분의

Paraphrase includes an additional padded layer of Pinnacle's high-quality memory foam
→ has extra padding

44. 청자들은 어떻게 무료 제품을 받을 수 있는가?

(A) 온라인으로 코드를 입력함으로써
(B) 회원으로 등록함으로써
(C) 우편물 수신자 명단에 가입함으로써
(D) 직접 매장을 방문함으로써

해설 무료 제품 및 그 방법과 관련된 정보가 제시되는 부분에서 단서를 찾아야 한다. 담화 후반부에 화자가 웹 사이트에서 주문할 때 코드 번호 PINNACLE10을 입력하면 주문품과 함께 무료 머그 잔을 받는다고(put in the code PINNACLE10 to receive a free mug with your order) 알리고 있으므로 (A)가 정답이다.

어휘 **complimentary** 무료의 **sign up for** ~에 등록하다, ~을 신청하다 **join** ~에 가입하다, ~에 합류하다 **mailing list** 우편물 수신자 명단 **in person** 직접 (가서)

Paraphrase put in the code PINNACLE10
→ entering a code

Questions 45-47 refer to the following talk.

As the mayor of Dalebrook, I'm pleased to announce our Local Restaurant of the Year. 45 After much deliberation, the judging panel finally chose a winner among the nominees. And as I'm sure most of you know, Dalebrook has a lot of excellent restaurants. However, in the end, one business stood out from the rest on account of its exceptional food and high service standards. 46 Our winner is Holly's, and the business will receive a special plaque that it can display at its entrance. Now, 47 let's have a warm round of applause for the owner of the restaurant, Holly Jacobs.

데일브룩의 시장으로서, 저는 '올해의 지역 식당'을 발표하게 되어 기쁩니다. 심사숙고 끝에, 심사위원단이 마침내 지명된 후보들 사이에서 수상 식당을 선택했습니다. 그리고 분명 여러분 대부분께서 아시다시피, 데일브룩에는 훌륭한 식당들이 많습니다. 하지만, 결국, 한 곳의 업체가 탁월한 음식 및 높은 서비스 기준으로 인해 나머지 업체들보다 두드러지게 되었습니다. 수상 식당은 '홀리스'이며, 이 업체는 입구에 진열할 수 있는 특별 상패를 받게 될 것입니다. 자, 함께 이 식당의 소유주이신 홀리 제이콥스 씨께 뜨거운 박수 보내 주시기 바랍니다.

어휘 **mayor** 시장 **local** 지역의, 현지의 **deliberation** 숙고, 심의 **judging panel** 심사위원단 **choose** ~을 선택하다 **winner** 수상자, 당첨자, 우승자 **nominee** 지명된 후보 **however** 하지만, 그러나 **in the end** 결국, 결과적으로 **stand out from** ~보다 두드러지다, ~보다 눈에 띄다 **the rest** 나머지 **on account of** ~로 인해, ~ 때문에 **exceptional** 탁월한, 특출한, 우수한 **standard** 기준, 표준 **plaque** 상패 **display** ~을 진열하다, ~을 전시하다 **have a warm round of applause** 뜨거운 박수를 보내다 **owner** 소유주, 주인

45. 화자가 "데일브룩에는 훌륭한 식당들이 많습니다"라고 말할 때 무엇을 의미하는가?

(A) 여러 잠재적인 행사 개최 장소가 있다.
(B) 도시가 관광객을 더 많이 받고 있다.
(C) 새로운 구직 기회가 많이 있다.
(D) 선택하는 일이 쉽지 않았다.

해설 담화 초반부에 화자가 심사숙고 끝에 심사위원단이 마침내 지명된 후보들 사이에서 수상 식당을 선택했다고(After much deliberation, the judging panel finally chose a winner among the nominees) 언급한 뒤에 '데일브룩에 훌륭한 식당이 많다'고 말하는 흐름이다. 이는 훌륭한 식당이 많아서 그 중에서 한 곳을 선택하는 일이 어려웠다는 뜻을 나타내는 말이므로 (D)가 정답이다.

어휘 **potential** 잠재적인 **venue** 개최 장소, 행사장 **opportunity** 기회

46. 화자의 말에 따르면, 홀리스는 무엇을 받을 것인가?

(A) 면세 혜택
(B) 증명서
(C) 트로피
(D) 상패

해설 홀리스가 무엇을 받을 것인지 묻고 있으므로 홀리스라는 명칭이 제시되는 부분에서 receive, get, be provided, be offered, be sent 등과 같이 받거나 제공되는 일을 나타내는 동사와 함께 언급되는 것을 찾아야 한다. 담화 후반부에 화자는 수상 식당이 홀리스임을 알리면서 상패를 받는다고(Our winner is Holly's, and the business will receive a special plaque ~) 언급하고 있으므로 (D)가 정답이다.

어휘 **exemption** 면제, 공제 **certificate** 증명서, 자격증, 수료증

47. 화자는 청자들에게 무엇을 하도록 요청하는가?

(A) 수상자에게 박수 치는 일
(B) 일부 메뉴 품목을 시식하는 일
(C) 함께 무대에 오르는 일
(D) 입구 쪽으로 가는 일

해설 화자가 청자들에게 무엇을 하도록 요청하는지 묻고 있으므로 요청 표현과 함께 제시되는 정보를 찾아야 한다. 화자가 담화 맨 마지막 부분에 홀리스라는 식당의 소유주인 홀리 제이콥스 씨에게 뜨거운 박수를 보내도록(let's have a warm round of applause for the owner of the restaurant, Holly Jacobs) 요청하고 있으므로 (A)가 정답이다.

어휘 **applaud** v. ~에게 박수 치다 **make one's way to** ~로 나아가다

> **Paraphrase** have a warm round of applause
> → Applaud

Questions 48-50 refer to the following telephone message and graph.

---

48 Hi, Mr. Berger. I know you're busy planting the new trees at Farmuir Park right now, but I just wanted to confirm that I bought the new hedge-trimming device for you, as you requested. I compared some of the top-rated devices on the market before making the purchase. I didn't get the one with the highest average customer rating, however, as it was way over our budget. So, 49 I got the one with the second-highest rating instead. Anyway, 50 I'd be happy to forward a picture of it to you, if you want to check it out.

안녕하세요, 베르거 씨. 지금 파무어 파크에서 새 나무들을 심으시느라 바쁘시다는 것은 알지만, 요청하신 바와 같이, 필요하신 새 생울타리 손질용 기기를 구입했다는 사실을 확인해 드리고 싶었습니다. 구입하기 전에 시중에 나와 있는 몇몇 최고 평점을 받은 기기들을 비교했습니다. 하지만, 가장 높은 평균 고객 평점을 받은 것을 구입하진 않았는데, 우리 예산을 너무 많이 초과했기 때문입니다. 그래서, 대신 두 번째로 높은 평점을 받은 것으로 구입했습니다. 어쨌든, 확인해 보시길 원하시면, 기꺼이 이 제품 사진을 전송해 드리겠습니다.

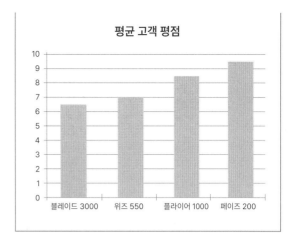

평균 고객 평점

어휘 **be busy -ing** ~하느라 바쁘다 **plant** v. (나무 등) ~을 심다 **confirm that** ~임을 확인해 주다 **hedge-trimming** 생울타리 손질용의 **device** 기기, 장치 **request** 요청하다 **compare** ~을 비교하다 **top-rated** 가장 높은 점수를 받은, 최고 순위에 오른, 최고 등급을 받은 **on the market** 시중에 나와 있는 **make a purchase** 구입하다 **average** 평균의 **rating** 평점, 등급 **way** (강조) 너무, 아주, 훨씬 **budget** 예산 **instead** 대신 **anyway** 어쨌든 **forward** ~을 전송하다 **check A out** A를 확인해 보다

48. 베르거 씨는 누구일 것 같은가?

(A) 엔지니어
(B) 건축가
(C) 실내 디자이너
(D) 조경 전문가

해설 특정 인물의 신분을 묻는 문제의 경우, 그 사람의 이름과 함께 단체 이름이나 건물 이름, 특정 업무나 활동, 전문 분야, 제공 서비스 등과 관련된 정보가 반드시 제시되므로 이를 통해 단서를 파악해야 한다. 화자가 담화 시작 부분에 베르거 씨의 이름을 부르면서 공원에서 나무를 심느라 바쁜 상태임을 안다고(Hi, Mr. Berger. I know you're busy planting the new trees at Farmuir Park ~) 언급하고 있다. 이는 조경 분야에 종사하는 사람이 할 수 있는 일에 해당되므로 (D)가 정답이다.

49. 시각자료를 보시오. 화자는 어느 기기를 선택했는가?

(A) 블레이드 3000
(B) 위즈 550
(C) 플라이어 1000
(D) 페이즈 200

해설 그래프나 차트가 제시되는 시각자료 문제의 경우, 특히 수치 표현을 비교하기 위해 최상급이나 비교급 표현, 또는 서수를 활용한 표현이 잘 쓰이므로 이 부분에 유의하는 것이 좋다. 담화 후반부에 화자가 두 번째로 높은 평점을 받은 것으로 구입했다고(I got the one with the second-highest rating instead) 알리고 있다. 시각자료에서 두 번째로 평점이 높은 제품은 오른

쪽에서 두 번째에 표기된 Flyer 1000이므로 (C)가 정답이다.

50. 화자는 무엇을 하겠다고 제안하는가?

(A) 거래 내역서를 확인하는 일
(B) 이미지를 보내는 일
(C) 제품을 조립하는 일
(D) 예산을 늘리는 일

해설 화자가 무엇을 하겠다고 제안하는지 묻고 있으므로 제안 표현과 함께 제시되는 정보를 찾아야 한다. 담화 맨 마지막 부분에 화자가 기꺼이 제품 사진을 전송하겠다고(I'd be happy to forward a picture of it to you ~) 알리고 있으므로 (B)가 정답이다.

어휘 **offer to do** ~하겠다고 제안하다 **invoice** 거래 내역서 **assemble** ~을 조립하다

Paraphrase forward a picture
→ Send an image

WEEK 04

Contents	Page	Date	Score (맞은 개수)
Day 01 RC Half Test	02	월 일	/50
Day 02 LC Half Test	16	월 일	/50
Day 03 RC Half Test	22	월 일	/50
Day 04 LC Half Test	36	월 일	/50
Day 05 RC Half Test	42	월 일	/50

READING TEST

In the Reading test, you will read a variety of texts and answer several different types of reading comprehension questions. The entire Reading test will last 75 minutes. There are three parts, and directions are given for each part. You are encouraged to answer as many questions as possible within the time allowed. You must mark your answers on the separate answer sheet. Do not write your answers in your test book.

PART 5

Directions: A word or phrase is missing in each of the sentences below. Four answer choices are given below each sentence. Select the best answer to complete the sentence. Then mark the letter (A), (B), (C), or (D) on your answer sheet.

1. The hotel's private beach does not receive many visitors because it is not ------- accessible to guests.

   (A) easy
   (B) easily
   (C) easier
   (D) easiest

2. Liz Grey will announce ------- retirement during the company's year-end banquet on December 20.

   (A) she
   (B) her
   (C) hers
   (D) herself

3. Because he was overseas on a business trip, Mr. Tucker sent his ------- to the newly appointed CEO by e-mail.

   (A) congratulations
   (B) congratulate
   (C) congratulating
   (D) congratulatory

4. ------- next Monday, employees will be required to submit a daily work report to their department manager.

   (A) Effectively
   (B) Effectiveness
   (C) Effective
   (D) Effects

5. A recent survey shows ------- the city's most prominent landmarks are attracting more tourists than ever before.

   (A) that
   (B) this
   (C) what
   (D) those

6. Word of Dr. Banks's resignation spread rapidly as she had many ------- in the industry.

   (A) acquainted
   (B) acquainting
   (C) acquaintance
   (D) acquaintances

7. The Carter Bridge will reopen to traffic on October 5 ------- seven months of repair work.
(A) after
(B) between
(C) further
(D) along

8. Preparing ------- on his business trip, Mr. Young assigned several tasks to his employees.
(A) departed
(B) departing
(C) to depart
(D) departs

9. When ordering supplies, you must be ------- and ensure you only purchase items that we absolutely need.
(A) selecting
(B) select
(C) selective
(D) to select

10. The drastic fall in tourism following the closure of Bridgend Art Museum indicates ------- how crucial the museum was to the local economy.
(A) along
(B) just
(C) near
(D) alike

11. We will check the building blueprint thoroughly ------- it has been submitted by the architect.
(A) then
(B) while
(C) due to
(D) as soon as

12. The new novel that Ann Paterson plans to publish this year is the ------- book in the author's successful Magic Monsters series.
(A) absolute
(B) separate
(C) entire
(D) final

13. ------- a reduction in costs for most of its perfumes' ingredients, Penelope Cosmetics has increased prices by over fifty percent.
(A) Although
(B) Neither
(C) Despite
(D) As

14. The experiment ------- all day Wednesday in Dr. Shin's laboratory on the second floor.
(A) conducts
(B) has conducted
(C) was conducted
(D) are conducted

15. Taylor O'Neil is an award-winning sculptor ------- work has been exhibited in several of the world's most prominent galleries.
(A) during
(B) prior to
(C) whose
(D) as well as

16. The printing of the posters for the music festival has been delayed, but they should be ------- around town next week.
(A) used up
(B) applied for
(C) put up
(D) carried on

PART 6

Directions: Read the texts that follow. A word, phrase, or sentence is missing in parts of each text. Four answer choices for each question are given below the text. Select the best answer to complete the text. Then mark the letter (A), (B), (C) or (D) on your answer sheet.

Questions 17-20 refer to the following article.

Car Manufacturer Set to Open New Plant

Toledo (April 3) - During a recent press conference, the CEO of Royston Motors announced that the car manufacturer plans to open a new factory in Toledo early next year. Royston has rapidly emerged as a leading company in the domestic ------- industry, due in large part to the high sales of its popular
17.
Royston Segue sedan. The firm's CEO, Brian Redmond, believes the factory will create an ------- 800
18.
jobs in Toledo.

The new factory in Toledo will mainly be used to manufacture Royston's upcoming Polaris model. The plant's assembly lines will be ------- with the very latest technology to ensure maximum operating
19.
efficiency. -------. Mr. Redmond hopes that the factory will be able to produce over 500,000 vehicles
20.
per year, making it the company's most profitable facility.

17. (A) healthcare
(B) financial
(C) agricultural
(D) automotive

18. (A) estimation
(B) estimate
(C) estimated
(D) estimating

19. (A) received
(B) equipped
(C) contained
(D) insured

20. (A) Manufacturing of the Polaris will soon be discontinued.
(B) Inspectors recently inspected the defective machinery.
(C) In turn, this will enable an increased rate of production.
(D) Royston is known for its excellent customer support.

Questions 21-24 refer to the following e-mail.

To: <Mailing List>

From: <info@digitalmarketplace.com>

Subject: Become a Digital Marketplace Member

Date: May 6

Dear sir/madam,

With over 500,000 household products to choose from, Digital Marketplace is your best choice ------- **21.** online. We offer an amazing range of items, from home furnishings and appliances to cleaning products and cookware. Our prices cannot be beat, and we offer complimentary ------- **22.** on all orders within the city limits of Seattle.

-------. **23.** Members receive discounts on various items and a free full-color product catalog every two months. In addition, by signing up for a Digital Marketplace membership, you ------- **24.** invitations to various special sales events and product launches. Simply follow this link to sign up: www. digitalmarketplace.com/join.

21. (A) shops
    (B) for shopping
    (C) who shopped
    (D) by having shopped

22. (A) payment
    (B) training
    (C) removal
    (D) delivery

23. (A) Membership allows you to take advantage of several benefits.
    (B) To renew your membership, follow these instructions.
    (C) We value feedback from all of our members.
    (D) Please note that your membership is due to expire this month.

24. (A) have received
    (B) would receive
    (C) are receiving
    (D) to receive

PART 7

Directions: In this part you will read a selection of texts, such as magazine and newspaper articles, e-mails, and instant messages. Each text or set of texts is followed by several questions. Select the best answer for each question and mark the letter (A), (B), (C), or (D) on your answer sheet.

Questions 25-26 refer to the following e-mail.

To:	Keith Caputo <kcaputo@ballouagency.com>
From:	Dora Winslow <dwinslow@ballouagency.com
Subject:	Bed of Roses Anniversary
Date:	May 9

Hi Keith,

As I'm sure you know, we are planning to celebrate the 10-year anniversary of Magnus Dahl's best-seller, *Bed of Roses*. Mr. Dahl was this agency's first ever client, and he remains the most successful of all the writers we represent. I'd like to present him with a token of our appreciation during the banquet we are organizing for next Saturday. I have attached a list of suitable gifts with the approximate price range for each, as well as the names of stores where each item may be found. I'd like you to take care of this for me.

You can either pay for the item yourself and be reimbursed later, or obtain a company credit card from my assistant, Meredith Long, on the fourth floor of our office building.

Thank you,

Dora Winslow
Client Relations Manager
Ballou Literary Agency

25. Who most likely is Magnus Dahl?

(A) A book critic
(B) An author
(C) A company founder
(D) An assistant

26. What does Ms. Winslow ask Mr. Caputo to do?

(A) Reserve a venue
(B) Order some food
(C) Contact a client
(D) Purchase a gift

Questions 27-29 refer to the following letter.

October 17

Dear Ms. Wiseau,

Mont-Royal Badminton Club has been expanding rapidly, and we have an increasing amount of administrative and management duties. — [1] —. In November, we plan to change the structure of our management team and assign one of our club members to the newly created position of Assistant Club Secretary. I was very impressed with your willingness to cover for our badminton instructor last month. Members of the beginners group informed me that they found your instruction very beneficial. — [2] —. This kind of attitude shows that you are an ideal candidate for an official role on the club committee, so I would like to offer you the position of Assistant Club Secretary.

— [3] —. As this is a matter that requires discretion, I request that you do not discuss it with other club members until I have received your formal decision in writing. — [4] —.

Best regards,

Paul Theroux
Club Secretary, Mont-Royal Badminton Club

---

27. What will happen at the badminton club next month?
    (A) The club will attempt to attract new members.
    (B) A new badminton instructor will be hired.
    (C) The Assistant Club Secretary will resign.
    (D) There will be a restructuring of club management.

28. What can be inferred about Ms. Wiseau?
    (A) She renewed her club membership in October.
    (B) She is directly involved with the club's finances.
    (C) She taught a badminton class in September.
    (D) She attended an interview with Mr. Theroux.

29. In which of the positions marked [1], [2], [3], and [4] does the following sentence best belong?

    "We do not plan to advertise this position and would rather appoint someone internally."

    (A) [1]
    (B) [2]
    (C) [3]
    (D) [4]

Core Zen Yoga
New Member Registration Form Starting January 1st

Every month, we accept new members here at Core Zen Yoga! Our classes help you to strengthen and stimulate your body and mind. No matter how old you are, how strong you are, or how flexible you are, Core Zen Yoga has a yoga class that will perfectly match your needs and capabilities. Our Beginner class meets every Monday, Tuesday, Thursday, and Saturday. Our Intermediate class meets every Tuesday, Wednesday, and Sunday. Our advanced class takes place on Fridays and Saturdays.

Please complete this form and give it to a Core Zen Yoga staff member.

Name: Becky Masters
Class: Intermediate Level
Address: 398 Ferris Street, Boston, MA 02115
E-mail: bmasters@usmail.com

Please specify which membership package you would prefer:
___ January Only (1-month trial package) - $89
___ January 1 to February 28 - $169
___ January 1 to March 31 - $239
_X_ January 1 to April 30 - $289

30. What is suggested about Core Zen Yoga?
   (A) It has several locations in Boston.
   (B) It primarily teaches advanced yoga.
   (C) It is currently hiring new staff.
   (D) It welcomes members of all ages.

31. How often will Ms. Masters most likely attend the class?
   (A) Once a week
   (B) Twice a week
   (C) Three times a week
   (D) Four times a week

32. How much does a 3-month membership cost?
   (A) $89
   (B) $169
   (C) $239
   (D) $289

Questions 33-36 refer to the following online chat discussion.

[3:14 P.M.] Boris Lansing

How are the arrangements coming along for our firm's year-end dinner? All the board members will attend, so we need to book somewhere special.

[3:16 P.M.] Miranda Sawyer

Well, Mr. Lansing, I'm sorry to say that we still haven't made a reservation.

[3:17 P.M.] Olivia DeRossi

Yes, we were hoping to book a room at Dillinger's Bistro, but it turns out that it's fully booked.

[3:18 P.M.] Boris Lansing

That's typical.

[3:21 P.M.] Miranda Sawyer

And it might be the only place that has a private room large enough to fit all our employees.

[3:22 P.M.] Olivia DeRossi

Oh... I saw an advertisement online recently for a huge new restaurant on Fourth Avenue. Maybe I can print out its menu online.

[3:23 P.M.] Boris Lansing

That's a good idea, Olivia. Once you've done that, let us know. We can get together and check out its food.

[3:24 P.M.] Miranda Sawyer

Sounds good to me. Send me a message when you're ready, Olivia.

---

33. What are the writers mainly discussing?

(A) A board meeting
(B) A restaurant expansion
(C) A staff meal
(D) An awards ceremony

34. At 3:18 p.m., what does Mr. Lansing imply when he writes, "That's typical"?

(A) He is disappointed with a restaurant menu.
(B) He knows that Dillinger's Bistro is popular.
(C) He disagrees with Ms. DeRossi's suggestion.
(D) He often dines at Dillinger's Bistro.

35. What is suggested about Dillinger's Bistro?

(A) It operates branches in several locations.
(B) It recently underwent renovations.
(C) It can accommodate large groups.
(D) It does not require advance reservations.

36. What will Ms. DeRossi most likely do next?

(A) Visit a restaurant
(B) Order some food
(C) Print out a map
(D) Check a Web site

BLUE WAVE INC.
APPOINTS NEW CEO

Toronto, January 21 – Blue Wave Inc. made an announcement yesterday that Selina Riley will be appointed as the company's new chief executive officer. Ms. Riley has over 35 years of experience in product development and has received much recognition for the unique and creative designs she has come up with for many of Blue Wave's smart phones and tablet computers. Her efforts and contributions have enabled Blue Wave to become one of the most prominent and successful producers of electronic devices in the world.

Ms. Riley had a long and successful career even before joining Blue Wave. After graduating, she spent four years in the product development department at Moniko Corporation and a further seven years at Pizarro Enterprises. During her time at Pizarro, she rapidly rose to the position of assistant department manager and was later appointed as department manager. After resigning from her position in order to have a baby, she later joined Bravetech Inc., where she served briefly as a design expert and consultant, and was eventually recruited by Blue Wave Inc.

37. What is Ms. Riley known for?

   (A) Her commitment to customer service
   (B) Her experience in advertising
   (C) Her skill at managing employees
   (D) Her innovative product designs

38. What type of business is Blue Wave Inc.?

   (A) A telecommunications firm
   (B) A financial consultancy
   (C) A Web design company
   (D) An electronics manufacturer

39. At which company did Ms. Riley begin her career?

   (A) Blue Wave Inc.
   (B) Moniko Corporation
   (C) Pizarro Enterprises
   (D) Bravetech Inc.

40. What happened during Ms. Riley's time at Pizarro Enterprises?

   (A) She helped to rapidly increase sales.
   (B) She collaborated with Bravetech Inc.
   (C) She received at least two promotions.
   (D) She recruited several managers.

Short Story Contest at the 7th Annual Williamsburg Literary Festival Sponsored by the Creative Writers Association (CWA)

The Creative Writers Association is now calling on all local writers to apply to participate in a short story contest, which will be running as part of the 7th Annual Williamsburg Literary Festival. The aim of the contest, and indeed that of the festival itself, is to highlight local literary talent and provide exposure and support to these aspiring writers. All of this year's festival events will take place in Williamsburg Community Center and the town's public library from July 27 to August 6. Excerpts from shortlisted short story entries will be read in the latter venue on August 3 and August 4, and the stories will be published online in their entirety for everyone to read.

Only short stories that have not been published elsewhere will be accepted. Stories should either be uploaded at www.cwa.org/festival/contest or sent as an e-mail attachment to writingcontest@cwa.org. Documents must be received by July 20 at the latest. The judging panel will then decide on a final shortlist and notifications will be sent out to successful participants by July 26.

The CWA will arrange for a stage to be erected for the short story readings. Winners chosen from the 15-21 age group will read excerpts on the first of the two aforementioned days, while those in the 21-and-over category will read on the following day.

For full details and guidelines about the contest, please visit the Creative Writers Association Web site. Alternatively, you may contact the head of the judging panel, Ms. Henderson, directly at 555-8334.

To: Creative Writers Association <members@cwa.org>
From: Bobby Shaye <bshaye@culturex.com>
Date: July 26
Subject: Short Story Readings

Dear CWA Members,

Thank you for choosing to shortlist my work as one of the finalists in this year's writing contest. Actually, this will be the first time that any of my work has been read by anyone, so I was a little nervous about submitting my story, *In a Glass House*. I originally started writing down ideas for the story after graduating from university and moving to Williamsburg almost a decade ago, but it wasn't until earlier this year that I was inspired to go back to it and finish it off. After working in advertising for several years, I have now decided to turn my attention towards becoming an established author. I would much rather make a living doing something that I have a passion for. I'm looking forward to meeting some of you when I arrive to give my reading. Thank you again for this wonderful opportunity.

Sincerely,

Bobby Shaye

41. What is indicated about the Williamsburg Literary Festival?

(A) It will take place entirely in the public library.
(B) It is sponsored by a leading publisher.
(C) It highlights the work of renowned authors.
(D) It seeks to celebrate local talent.

42. What information is NOT mentioned in the announcement?

(A) The writing credentials of the CWA judging panel members
(B) The date when the shortlisted writers will be contacted
(C) How to submit work for the consideration of the judging panel
(D) The schedule for the readings of shortlisted short stories

43. When will Mr. Shaye most likely arrive at the public library?

(A) July 27
(B) August 3
(C) August 4
(D) August 6

44. What is suggested about Mr. Shaye?

(A) He has met with Ms. Henderson.
(B) He was unsure about the contest guidelines.
(C) He intends to pursue a new career.
(D) He was born in Williamsburg.

45. What is true about Mr. Shaye's submitted work?

(A) It was first started earlier this year.
(B) It has never been read by the general public.
(C) It is about events that took place in the local area.
(D) It was published in a university magazine.

Questions 46-50 refer to the following invoice and e-mails.

Argento Computer Supplies - INVOICE #13442

Ordered on: October 13	Shipping date: October 15	Expected arrival date: October 18

BILL TO:	SHIP TO:
Mr. Clive Owen	Ms. Maggie Spalding
Company Headquarters	Customer Service Call Center
Pulsar Telecom Inc.	Pulsar Telecom Inc.
4434 Smithson Street	6698 Ellington Drive
Baltimore, MD 21255	Columbia, MD 21044

Product Name	Product Code	Product Price	Quantity Purchased	Sub-Total Cost
Astra Wireless Keyboard	#A875	$15.99	18	$287.82
Dietrich Swivel Office Chair	#A349	$34.95	10	$349.50
Horizon 20-inch Monitor	#B238	$69.99	8	$559.92
Sonica Headphones (+ Mic)	#A337	$14.95	14	$209.30
Astra Corded Mouse	#B613	$13.99	10	$139.90
			SHIPPING FEE	$75.00
			TOTAL COST	$1621.44

To:	Clive Owen <cliveowen@pulsartelecom.com>
From:	Joshua Randall <jrandall@argentocomp.com>
Subject:	Order #13442
Date:	October 18

Dear Mr. Owen,

Unfortunately, the Sonica headphones that you ordered are sold out at this time, and we are not expecting a new shipment until early next month. I attempted to call you regarding this issue, but you seem to have mistakenly provided an incorrect telephone number. I amended your order to include 14 sets of Computek Z9 headphones instead. These headphones normally retail at $16.95 per set. If you wish to return any items, please let me know.

Sincerely,

Joshua Randall

To: Joshua Randall <jrandall@argentocomp.com>
From: Clive Owen <cliveowen@pulsartelecom.com>
Subject: Re: Order #13442
Date: October 18

Mr. Randall,

Thank you for the fast shipping and the high quality of the computer monitors and office chairs. However, I am not satisfied with the headphones you offered as a replacement for the out-of-stock model. They do not actually include a microphone, which is vital for the telephone operators in our call center. I will return these to you and wait for the other model to come back in stock. Also, I made a mistake when I originally selected the Astra items. I should have ordered the wireless version of that manufacturer's mouse. Therefore, I will return the corded ones immediately and pay the extra money required for the wireless models.

Regards,

Clive Owen
General Operations Manager
Pulsar Telecom Inc. Headquarters

46. What is NOT true about the order made by Pulsar Telecom Inc.?

(A) It was initially placed on October 13.
(B) It will be delivered to a location in Baltimore.
(C) It was paid for by Clive Owen.
(D) It includes a variety of electronic goods.

47. What action did Mr. Randall take?

(A) He increased the specified quantity of a particular item.
(B) He arranged for a shipping charge to be removed.
(C) He sent Mr. Owen a duplicate copy of his invoice.
(D) He substituted an item with a more expensive one.

48. In the first e-mail, the word "expecting" in paragraph 1, line 2, is closest in meaning to

(A) preparing
(B) receiving
(C) stocking
(D) anticipating

49. What does Mr. Owen say about the replacement items he received?

(A) They were damaged during shipping.
(B) They are extremely well designed.
(C) They do not meet his needs.
(D) They were delivered later than expected.

50. Which item did Mr. Owen order by mistake?

(A) Product #A875
(B) Product #A349
(C) Product #B238
(D) Product #B613

PART 1

Directions: For each question in this part, you will hear four statements about a picture in your test book. When you hear the statements, you must select the one statement that best describes what you see in the picture. Then find the number of the question on your answer sheet and mark your answer. The statements will not be printed in your test book and will be spoken only one time.

1.

2.

PART 2

Directions: You will hear a question or statement and three responses spoken in English. They will not be printed in your test book and will be spoken only one time. Select the best response to the question or statement and mark the letter (A), (B), or (C) on your answer sheet.

3. Mark your answer on your answer sheet.

4. Mark your answer on your answer sheet.

5. Mark your answer on your answer sheet.

6. Mark your answer on your answer sheet.

7. Mark your answer on your answer sheet.

8. Mark your answer on your answer sheet.

9. Mark your answer on your answer sheet.

10. Mark your answer on your answer sheet.

11. Mark your answer on your answer sheet.

12. Mark your answer on your answer sheet.

13. Mark your answer on your answer sheet.

14. Mark your answer on your answer sheet.

15. Mark your answer on your answer sheet.

16. Mark your answer on your answer sheet.

17. Mark your answer on your answer sheet.

18. Mark your answer on your answer sheet.

19. Mark your answer on your answer sheet.

20. Mark your answer on your answer sheet.

PART 3

Directions: You will hear some conversations between two or more people. You will be asked to answer three questions about what the speakers say in each conversation. Select the best response to each question and mark the letter (A), (B), (C) or (D) on your answer sheet. The conversations will not be printed in your test book and will be spoken only one time.

21. What does the woman ask the man about?
    (A) Apartment rent
    (B) Parking availability
    (C) Meeting space
    (D) Renovation costs

22. What problem does the woman have?
    (A) She cannot access her apartment.
    (B) She lost a colleague's contact details.
    (C) She is late in submitting some work.
    (D) Her office is closed this weekend.

23. What does the man suggest the woman do?
    (A) Contact her coworkers
    (B) Move to a new apartment
    (C) Change a work schedule
    (D) Talk to a building manager

24. What are the speakers discussing?
    (A) A product range
    (B) A Web site design
    (C) A building blueprint
    (D) A corporate logo

25. What type of company do the speakers work for?
    (A) An interior design company
    (B) An Internet provider
    (C) An event planning firm
    (D) A hardware store

26. What does the woman recommend?
    (A) Enlarging a design
    (B) Using specific colors
    (C) Printing some copies
    (D) Surveying customers

27. What problem does the woman report?
    (A) A manual was not received.
    (B) An item will not function properly.
    (C) An Internet connection is too slow.
    (D) A Web site is inaccessible.

28. What information does the man request from the woman?
    (A) The name of the person who served her
    (B) The Web site password
    (C) The specific item name
    (D) Her phone number

29. What will the woman probably do next?
    (A) Return the product
    (B) Follow the manual instructions
    (C) Talk with a specialist
    (D) Find a Web page

30. Where most likely are the speakers?
    (A) At a hospital
    (B) At a convention
    (C) At a museum
    (D) At a community center

31. What type of event will the man go to tomorrow?
    (A) A musical performance
    (B) An awards ceremony
    (C) A work dinner
    (D) A sports tournament

32. Why does the woman say, "each talk will be uploaded online"?
    (A) To explain a procedure
    (B) To correct a mistake
    (C) To make a suggestion
    (D) To reject an idea

Model	Maximum Capacity
Berry	2
Rowan	4
Spring	6
Horizon	10

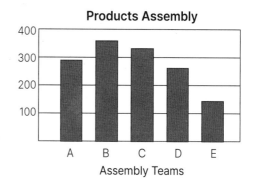

Products Assembly

33. What kind of product does the woman's workplace sell?

(A) Children's toys
(B) Camping supplies
(C) Storage containers
(D) Home furnishings

34. Look at the graphic. Which model will the man buy?

(A) Berry
(B) Rowan
(C) Spring
(D) Horizon

35. What is the man concerned about?

(A) The quality
(B) The delivery
(C) The assembly
(D) The price

36. What is mainly being discussed?

(A) A machine installation
(B) An employee incentive plan
(C) A productivity problem
(D) A new range of products

37. Look at the graphic. Which assembly team is being discussed?

(A) Team B
(B) Team C
(C) Team D
(D) Team E

38. What does the woman say she will do next?

(A) Extend a deadline
(B) Speak with a manager
(C) Inspect a machine
(D) Schedule a training session

PART 4

Directions: You will hear some talks given by a single speaker. You will be asked to answer three questions about what the speakers say in each conversation. Select the best response to each question and mark the letter (A), (B), (C) or (D) on your answer sheet. The conversations will not be printed in your test book and will be spoken only one time.

39. Where does the announcement take place?

(A) At a community center
(B) At a gym
(C) At an apartment building
(D) At a park

40. What new service does the speaker mention?

(A) Personal training programs
(B) Repairs and maintenance
(C) Rental of sports equipment
(D) Advice on healthy eating

41. How can club members get more information?

(A) By reading a newsletter
(B) By checking a notice board
(C) By speaking with a chairman
(D) By attending an orientation session

42. According to the speaker, where was an item advertised?

(A) In a newspaper ad
(B) At an electronics store
(C) In a catalogue
(D) At an auction

43. What does the speaker imply when he says, "the operating system's default language was Russian"?

(A) He wants to trade one item for another.
(B) He is impressed with some software.
(C) He does not want to ship an item to Russia.
(D) He cannot understand Russian.

44. What does the speaker ask the listener to do?

(A) Reduce the price of an item
(B) Contact a supplier
(C) E-mail him an invoice
(D) Send him an additional item

45. What type of product is being discussed?

(A) An electronic device
(B) A piece of furniture
(C) An item of clothing
(D) A computer program

46. What does the speaker say she will give the listeners?

(A) A product sample
(B) An information pamphlet
(C) A market research report
(D) A magazine article

47. What are the listeners asked to think about?

(A) The location of a launch event
(B) The cost of the product
(C) A new product design
(D) A marketing plan

	Poor	Satisfactory	Execllent
LOCATION	✔	☐	☐
STAFF	☐	☐	✔
FOOD	☐	☐	✔
AMENITIES	☐	✔	☐

48. Who is the message most likely for?

(A) A hotel employee
(B) A magazine writer
(C) A former guest
(D) A food critic

49. What does the speaker say he has sent to the listener?

(A) A brochure
(B) A tourist map
(C) A discount coupon
(D) An invoice

50. Look at the graphic. Which category does the speaker want to discuss?

(A) Location
(B) Staff
(C) Food
(D) Amenities

READING TEST

In the Reading test, you will read a variety of texts and answer several different types of reading comprehension questions. The entire Reading test will last 75 minutes. There are three parts, and directions are given for each part. You are encouraged to answer as many questions as possible within the time allowed. You must mark your answers on the separate answer sheet. Do not write your answers in your test book.

PART 5

Directions: A word or phrase is missing in each of the sentences below. Four answer choices are given below each sentence. Select the best answer to complete the sentence. Then mark the letter (A), (B), (C), or (D) on your answer sheet.

1. Mr. Harker is certain that the ------- with Drummond Corporation's board members progressed well.

   (A) negotiators
   (B) negotiations
   (C) negotiated
   (D) negotiates

2. Technicians are performing maintenance on the computer network, and access to e-mail ------- unavailable until tomorrow.

   (A) was
   (B) are being
   (C) has been
   (D) will be

3. Mr. Smith plans to finish the project that he is currently working on before ------- requests a raise.

   (A) he
   (B) himself
   (C) him
   (D) his

4. The servers at Montcalm Restaurant are known for their skill in ------- the most suitable wine to complement each dish.

   (A) selection
   (B) selected
   (C) selecting
   (D) selective

5. New tenants are advised to check the condominium announcement board ------- after moving into an apartment.

   (A) frequency
   (B) frequented
   (C) frequently
   (D) frequents

6. The client has asked Mr. Wilson for the ------- timeframe for completion of the construction project.

   (A) estimated
   (B) estimating
   (C) estimation
   (D) estimates

7. All Lumber King sales staff will be given ------- to attend the Sell More Products seminar.

   (A) permitted
   (B) permission
   (C) permit
   (D) permissive

8. ------- moving to Morningside three months ago, Ms. Connolly has spent more than $10,000 on home renovations.

   (A) Since
   (B) Except
   (C) During
   (D) Where

9. The CEO opted to hire a cheaper catering company for this year's staff party to leave ------- money for hiring live entertainment.

   (A) gradual
   (B) proficient
   (C) competent
   (D) sufficient

10. Several high-rise apartment blocks have recently been built in Berryfield, which was ------- an industrial area.

    (A) alternatively
    (B) intermittently
    (C) occasionally
    (D) formerly

11. Ticket ------- for next month's technology convention will be overseen by the HR manager.

    (A) allocate
    (B) allocates
    (C) allocation
    (D) allocating

12. Customers of Floyd Bank should take note that transactions made ------- the period of March 12 to March 15 may not appear immediately on account statements.

    (A) while
    (B) during
    (C) under
    (D) above

13. A valid driving license is a ------- for anyone applying for the delivery driver position.

    (A) requirement
    (B) fulfillment
    (C) recognition
    (D) contribution

14. Mr. Chatworth is committed to making the college course schedules ------- for students with busy lives.

    (A) flexed
    (B) flexibility
    (C) more flexibly
    (D) more flexible

15. Prices for our scuba diving courses depend upon the size and experience level ------- the group.

    (A) as
    (B) about
    (C) before
    (D) of

16. Tenants may decorate their condominium and perform minor renovations, ------- approval is given by the landlord.

    (A) along with
    (B) according to
    (C) provided that
    (D) regardless of

PART 6

Directions: Read the texts that follow. A word, phrase, or sentence is missing in parts of each text. Four answer choices for each question are given below the text. Select the best answer to complete the text. Then mark the letter (A), (B), (C) or (D) on your answer sheet.

Questions 17-21 refer to the following product information.

Thank you for purchasing the Xenon Electronics XE500 65-inch LED television. Please register the product on ------- Web site at www.xenonelectronics.com/productregistration. This will allow us to
        17.
provide you with the highest quality of support and maintenance. You will need to enter information from your receipt as well as the product's serial number. -------. The registration process only takes a
                                                                                                18.
few minutes.

By registering your product, you will activate its extended 3-year warranty. -------, the television will
                                                                                       19.
be covered for technical faults and accidental damage for three years from the original purchase date. Please take note of the customer support number on our Web site and do not hesitate ------- us if you
                                                                                                        20.
have any problems with your purchase.

17. (A) its
    (B) our
    (C) your
    (D) their

18. (A) Please bring the receipt with you when returning it.
    (B) Replacement parts can be ordered online.
    (C) You can find this on the back of the television.
    (D) Try our troubleshooting guide to solve the problem.

19. (A) In contrast
    (B) Afterwards
    (C) Similarly
    (D) However

20. (A) contacting
    (B) contact
    (C) to contact
    (D) contacted

Questions 21-24 refer to the following article.

Beer Company Pressured to Change Policy

May 16 - Beer365, a craft beer subscription service, has finally agreed to change its cancellation policy and procedure starting next month. Currently, members must call the company directly if they wish to cancel a monthly subscription, but ------- they will be given the option to cancel easily online.
21.

The current cancellation procedure has been criticized for several reasons. -------, callers are often
22.
placed on hold for more than an hour before they finally speak with an agent. Also, the cancellation hotline is only operational between 9 A.M. and 5 P.M., Monday through Friday, making it ------- for
23.
many people to call. According to Beer365 founder Kate Jones, "We listened to our customers, and we always strive to give them what they want." -------.
24.

---

21. (A) lately
    (B) soon
    (C) almost
    (D) nearly

22. (A) However
    (B) As a result
    (C) For example
    (D) On the other hand

23. (A) inconvenienced
    (B) inconveniently
    (C) inconvenience
    (D) inconvenient

24. (A) Customers have responded favorably to
        the new range of products.
    (B) As such, several new telephone agents will
        be hired in the coming weeks.
    (C) Beer365 has garnered a strong reputation
        for its innovative marketing methods.
    (D) An option to end subscriptions will be
        added to the Web site on June 1.

PART 7

Directions: In this part you will read a selection of texts, such as magazine and newspaper articles, e-mails, and instant messages. Each text or set of texts is followed by several questions. Select the best answer for each question and mark the letter (A), (B), (C), or (D) on your answer sheet.

Questions 25-26 refer to the following text message chain.

Mohinder Singh [9:24 A.M.]
Rachel, I wanted to ask you something about the changes you asked me to make to the presentation and garnish of our pork chop dish.

Rachel Sanders [9:25 A.M.]
Sure, Mohinder, what is it?

Mohinder Singh [9:27A.M.]
Would you prefer that I pour the mustard sauce on top of the red onion garnish, or to the side of the chops?

Rachel Sanders [9:29 A.M.]
I'd like to check both styles and see what looks best. But, I won't get to the restaurant until lunchtime.

Mohinder Singh [9:30 A.M.]
I suppose it can wait until we open. But, the first group of diners is booked for 11:15.

Rachel Sanders [9:31 A.M.]
Why wait? Just take a picture of the two dishes next to one another and send it to me.

Mohinder Singh [9:32 A.M.]
You got it. Just give me about thirty minutes.

Rachel Sanders [9:33 A.M.]
Great. I'll get back to you and let you know what I think.

Mohinder Singh [9:35 A.M.]
No problem. Talk to you soon.

---

25. Who most likely is Mr. Singh?

(A) A restaurant owner
(B) A cashier
(C) A chef
(D) A grocery store worker

26. At 9:32 A.M., what does Mr. Singh most likely mean when he writes, "You got it"?

(A) He will meet Ms. Sanders at a restaurant.
(B) He has sent a file to Ms. Sanders.
(C) He will take a photograph of some food.
(D) He has changed some menu items.

Lush Green Company

Making your home or business beautiful!

Here at Lush Green, we understand that the first thing people see when visiting your home or business is often the garden and outdoor areas. We can provide various professional services that will make these areas more attractive and impressive. Not only can we plant the bushes and trees of your choice and expertly sculpt them to your liking, but we can also install water features and centerpieces such as fountains, bird baths, and ponds. Lush Green has over two decades of experience in the industry and counts some of the largest corporations in the UK among its clients. We operate Monday through Saturday and can start work as early as 6 a.m. and finish work as late as 8 p.m.

If you are interested in scheduling a time for us to visit your home or workplace to discuss your vision and requirements, call us directly at 555-7759. Our offices are based in central Branford, but we can also provide services in several surrounding towns and cities. Further details about our services, our service area, and our rates can be found at www.lushgreenco.co.uk.

27. What type of business is Lush Green Company?

(A) An interior design firm
(B) A landscaping service
(C) A construction corporation
(D) An environmental foundation

28. What is NOT indicated about Lush Green Company?

(A) It has worked with many important companies.
(B) It has been in business for more than twenty years.
(C) It provides services seven days a week.
(D) It deals with both residences and businesses.

29. According to the advertisement, how can potential customers arrange a consultation?

(A) By visiting an office in Branford
(B) By logging into a Web site
(C) By sending an e-mail to Lush Green
(D) By calling a phone number

Evangeline's Cajun Bistro

8724 Blue Bayou Street, New Orleans, LA 70119

At Evangeline's Cajun Bistro, we aim to serve authentic Southern cuisine in a relaxed setting at affordable prices. Many exciting changes have recently occurred at our main branch and at our new Bayside Road location. The Shrimp Etouffee we introduced in March has already become a firm favorite with our regular diners, as has the Eggplant Pirogue added in April. The most exciting addition in May was our Stuffed Catfish, which has already replaced our famous Blackened Redfish as our best-selling entrée. Your feedback allows us to continually improve the standards of cuisine and service we provide. Please take a moment to complete this comment form and hand it to your server.

Diner's name: Simon Villeneuve
Date/Time of visit: May 27, 7:30 p.m.
Appetizer ordered: Fried Green Tomatoes
Entrée ordered: Stuffed Pork Chop
Side dishes ordered: Alligator Sausage
Dessert ordered: Banana Fritters

Additional comments:

As always, the stuffed pork chop was succulent and delicious. However, I'm not sure why it took almost 45 minutes to cook such a simple dish as fried green tomatoes. This wasn't the case when I last ordered it here. Although the car park was full when I visited, there were plenty of spaces on the street outside the restaurant.

---

30. What is the main purpose of the form?

(A) To invite customers to a grand opening
(B) To inform diners about future menu changes
(C) To solicit opinions from customers
(D) To provide directions to a new restaurant

31. What menu item was most recently added to the menu?

(A) Blackened Redfish
(B) Shrimp Etouffee
(C) Stuffed Catfish
(D) Eggplant Pirogue

32. What can be inferred about Mr. Villeneuve from the form?

(A) He ordered one of the restaurant's new dishes.
(B) He was visiting the restaurant for the first time.
(C) He waited a long time to receive his appetizer.
(D) He failed to find a parking space near the restaurant.

Questions 33-36 refer to the following memo.

Dear Ms. Fines,

Welcome to the neighborhood and thank you for joining the Oceanview Tenants Association. We hope you'll enjoy living here and find following the tenant guidelines easy and helpful in keeping our neighborhood great. The tenants association meets on the 10th day of every month in apartment 2. We encourage all members of the tenants association to attend these meetings and to exchange contact information with other tenants to discuss neighborhood issues, or in case of emergencies. You can also find copies of the Oceanview Apartments newsletter at our monthly meetings.

The staff of Oceanview Apartments takes care of most of the maintenance, but as a tenant you will also have some responsibilities. All tenants must comply with the following guidelines:
- Place any garbage in the appropriately marked area
- Separate recyclable items into the provided bins
- Inform any visitors that they must park in the guest parking area

Additionally, we hope you will come to our next monthly meeting to introduce yourself to the rest of the tenants association. Welcome to the neighborhood again, Ms. Fines, and we hope to be good neighbors with you.

Tessie Cole
President, Oceanview Tenants Association

33. What is the purpose of the memo?
(A) To ask the receiver to give a presentation
(B) To request that a rent payment be made
(C) To relate the process for membership
(D) To detail duties for a resident

34. How often does the Oceanview Tenants Association meet?
(A) Every week
(B) Every two weeks
(C) Every month
(D) Every year

35. With whom is Ms. Fines expected to stay in regular contact?
(A) The president of the association
(B) Oceanview staff
(C) Newsletter writers
(D) Oceanview tenants

36. What is Ms. Fines encouraged to do within a month?
(A) Introduce herself at a meeting
(B) Invite guests to her apartment
(C) Separate recyclable items from her garbage
(D) Apply for a leadership position

September 12

Ms. Rhonda Ogilvie

501 Stratford Road

Dundee, Scotland, UK

DD5 7PS

Dear Ms. Ogilvie,

After careful deliberation among board members here at Manning Diagnostics Inc., we are delighted to announce that you have been selected to assume the role of lab technician, starting from Monday, October 1. — [1] —. We have already received reference letters from your former employers, and you submitted copies of your university degrees and transcripts along with your resume and application form on August 14. — [2] —.

Once you begin working here, we will ask that you set up an account with Forbes Savings Bank in order to receive your wages. — [3] —. Our human resources department requires that all new staff members receive a tour of the laboratories and undergo basic health and safety training before starting work at our facility. Please choose a day that is suitable for you and let me know at your earliest possible convenience. — [4] —. I have enclosed two copies of your contract. Please sign both of them and bring one copy with you on your first official day of work.

Sincerely,

Harold Reid

Chief Science Officer

Manning Diagnostics Inc.

37. Why was the letter sent to Ms. Ogilvie?

(A) To request that she attend an interview
(B) To ask her to submit necessary documents
(C) To offer her a position of employment
(D) To confirm the receipt of her application form

38. What is suggested about Manning Diagnostics Inc.?

(A) It operates in more than one business location.
(B) It is currently attempting to fill several positions.
(C) It has recently appointed new board members.
(D) It prefers that staff use the same financial institution.

39. What is Ms. Ogilvie asked to do before the end of September?

(A) Submit her banking details
(B) Attend a training session
(C) Send a signed contract
(D) Contact a former employer

40. In which of the positions marked [1], [2], [3], and [4] does the following sentence best belong?

"There was a lot of interest in the vacancy, but you stood out among the other applicants."

(A) [1]
(B) [2]
(C) [3]
(D) [4]

To:	Elizabeth Banks <elizbanks@halomail.com>
From:	Rodney Falwell <gamanager@moorfield.co.uk>
Subject:	Congratulations on Your Wedding
Date:	May 19

Dear Ms. Banks,

Thank you for choosing Moorfield Manor as the venue for your beautiful wedding on May 14. I truly hope that you enjoyed your special day and the services we provided. Our well-sculpted grounds and gardens provided the perfect backdrop for your ceremony. The photographs that were taken next to the water fountain out front of the building looked exceptionally elegant. I hope that you, your husband, and your 200+ guests enjoyed all of the food that they were served in the Grand Dining Room. It is unfortunate that we currently only provide on-site accommodation for the bride and groom, but I trust that the rooms at the nearby Olive Hotel were more than satisfactory for your guests.

Our head wedding coordinator, Ann Underwood, has asked me to convey her best wishes to you. We would appreciate it if you could send us an e-mail detailing exactly what you thought about our venue, our food, our staff, and our overall event planning performance.

Sincerely,

Rodney Falwell
General Affairs Manager
Moorfield Manor

To: Rodney Falwell <gamanager@moorfield.co.uk>
From: Elizabeth Banks <elizbanks@halomail.com>
Subject: Re: Congratulations on Your Wedding
Date: May 20

Dear Mr. Falwell,

We had a fantastic day at Moorfield Manor, and we couldn't have been happier with the stunning venue and gardens. We were also very impressed with the enthusiasm and politeness of all staff members. The food was very delicious, and our guests especially liked the wedding cake you provided. However, the thing that pleased my husband and I most was the care and attention we received from your head wedding coordinator. She was always present to ensure things were going smoothly.

If I had to identify some features which could use some improvement, I would probably say the parking area and the lack of shuttle buses running between the train station and the manor. These were just minor issues and did very little to lessen our opinion of your venue and service. In fact, a friend of mine recently got engaged and is wondering where to have her wedding. I'll be sure to tell her all about my personal experience at Moorfield Manor.

Warmest regards,

Elizabeth Banks

41. What is the purpose of the first e-mail?

(A) To confirm the reservation of a wedding venue
(B) To advertise a new range of wedding packages
(C) To request feedback on provided services
(D) To express gratitude for a wedding gift

42. What is NOT mentioned as a current feature of Moorfield Manor?

(A) An outdoor water feature
(B) A variety of guest bedrooms
(C) A spacious dining room
(D) A landscaped garden

43. What impressed Ms. Banks most about Moorfield Manor?

(A) The convenience of the shuttle bus system
(B) The high quality of the catering service
(C) The attentiveness shown by Ms. Underwood
(D) The interior design of the dining area

44. In the second e-mail, the word "lack" in paragraph 2, line 2, is closest in meaning to

(A) delay
(B) absence
(C) reduction
(D) removal

45. What is indicated about Ms. Banks?

(A) She was not happy with her overall experience.
(B) She was very impressed with her room at the Olive Hotel.
(C) She invited several guests from overseas to her wedding.
(D) She will recommend the venue to an acquaintance.

Questions 46-50 refer to the following notice, letter, and article.

Casting Call for "A Better Universe"

- A new movie to be directed by Wesley Finch -

Auditions to be held on Saturday, April 19

8:30 a.m. to 6:30 p.m.

Big Star Theater

4602 Willow Boulevard, Sacramento, CA 95814

April 3

Mr. Edward Walcott

6009 Wisteria Road

Redding, CA 96003

Dear Edward,

I'm sure you probably already know that Los Angeles-based Goldberg Movie Productions is due to start casting for a new movie. They have announced open auditions throughout California, with the first ones taking place in San Diego and San Francisco on April 5 and April 15, respectively. However, you'll be pleased to hear that there's also an audition being held in your hometown on April 19. I know that would be a much more convenient location for you, because it's not far from your new home in Redding. I understand that you wanted to take a break from acting in order to spend more time with your family, but I truly think that the lead role in this movie would be perfect for you.

Best wishes,

Harvey Fierstein

A&R Manager

Solid Gold Actors Agency

Sacramento Entertainment Magazine – April Issue
Auditions Begin for Science Fiction Movie

Goldberg Movie Productions is now inviting all aspiring performers to attend an open audition at the Big Star Theater in downtown Sacramento. The production company is casting several roles for *A Better Universe*, which is a big-budget sci-fi movie written by Steven Hendry. Mr. Hendry won acclaim from film critics for his last screenwriting effort, the action film *End of the Line*. Shooting of the movie is expected to commence sometime in July.

If you think you would be suitable for a role in the movie, you should go down to the theater on April 19 and speak with the director and the casting manager. You will be required to act out some scenes from the film while reading from a current draft of the movie script. Take your portfolio with you, which should include some professional headshots and full-body pictures.

46. For whom is the notice intended?
    (A) Film directors
    (B) Movie critics
    (C) Actors
    (D) Writers

47. Why did Mr. Fierstein send the letter?
    (A) To request more information about an upcoming film
    (B) To encourage a client to compete for a role
    (C) To express his interest in attending an audition
    (D) To advise Mr. Walcott to take a break from working

48. In which city did Mr. Walcott most likely grow up?
    (A) San Diego
    (B) Redding
    (C) Los Angeles
    (D) Sacramento

49. What is indicated about *A Better Universe*?
    (A) Steven Hendry will star in the film.
    (B) It is the director's debut movie.
    (C) It will premiere in the Big Star Theater.
    (D) Filming will begin in the summer.

50. What should interested individuals do on April 19?
    (A) Meet with Wesley Finch
    (B) Submit references from former employers
    (C) Register on a Web site
    (D) Attend a photography session

PART 1

Directions: For each question in this part, you will hear four statements about a picture in your test book. When you hear the statements, you must select the one statement that best describes what you see in the picture. Then find the number of the question on your answer sheet and mark your answer. The statements will not be printed in your test book and will be spoken only one time.

1.

2.

PART 2

Directions: You will hear a question or statement and three responses spoken in English. They will not be printed in your test book and will be spoken only one time. Select the best response to the question or statement and mark the letter (A), (B), or (C) on your answer sheet.

3. Mark your answer on your answer sheet.

4. Mark your answer on your answer sheet.

5. Mark your answer on your answer sheet.

6. Mark your answer on your answer sheet.

7. Mark your answer on your answer sheet.

8. Mark your answer on your answer sheet.

9. Mark your answer on your answer sheet.

10. Mark your answer on your answer sheet.

11. Mark your answer on your answer sheet.

12. Mark your answer on your answer sheet.

13. Mark your answer on your answer sheet.

14. Mark your answer on your answer sheet.

15. Mark your answer on your answer sheet.

16. Mark your answer on your answer sheet.

17. Mark your answer on your answer sheet.

18. Mark your answer on your answer sheet.

19. Mark your answer on your answer sheet.

20. Mark your answer on your answer sheet.

PART 3

Directions: You will hear some conversations between two or more people. You will be asked to answer three questions about what the speakers say in each conversation. Select the best response to each question and mark the letter (A), (B), (C) or (D) on your answer sheet. The conversations will not be printed in your test book and will be spoken only one time.

21. Who most likely is the woman?

    (A) A customer
    (B) A delivery person
    (C) A shop clerk
    (D) A newspaper writer

22. What does the man say about the coupon?

    (A) He did not know about it.
    (B) He used it at another store.
    (C) He thinks it already expired.
    (D) He will use it next week.

23. What does the woman suggest the man do?

    (A) Speak to the manager
    (B) Buy some more items
    (C) Sign up for a membership
    (D) Come back later

24. Where do the speakers most likely work?

    (A) At a farm
    (B) At a restaurant
    (C) At a grocery store
    (D) At a delivery service

25. What document do the speakers refer to?

    (A) A schedule
    (B) An invoice
    (C) A recipe
    (D) A résumé

26. Why does the man say, "I'd like to hear what Mr. Hines thinks"?

    (A) To delay a decision
    (B) To recommend an employee
    (C) To assign a task
    (D) To accept a suggestion

27. Where is the conversation taking place?

    (A) In a movie theater
    (B) In a concert hall
    (C) In a music store
    (D) In an instrument shop

28. What problem does Charlene mention?

    (A) An item has sold out.
    (B) A delivery was rescheduled.
    (C) A price is higher than advertised.
    (D) A service is no longer available.

29. What does the man offer to do?

    (A) Provide a refund
    (B) Include a delivery service
    (C) Contact a supplier
    (D) Reserve an item

30. What are the speakers mainly discussing?

    (A) Hiring a new IT manager
    (B) Organizing a training session
    (C) Upgrading some software
    (D) Purchasing new computers

31. What is the man concerned about?

    (A) The cost of a service
    (B) The date of a project deadline
    (C) The size of a product
    (D) The price of some equipment

32. Why does the woman recommend Melton IT?

    (A) It has the lowest prices.
    (B) It offers a discount.
    (C) It is located nearby.
    (D) Its staff is friendly.

The Kipper Cow Dessert Bar

··

Today's Menu

Choco Volcano Cake	······	$4.50
Cheese Cake	······	$5.50
Red Velvet	······	$6.50
5-Layer Cake	······	$7.50

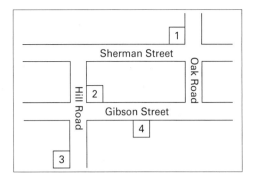

33. Why did the man's friend recommend the restaurant?

(A) It is located nearby.
(B) It is owned by a famous chef.
(C) It has fun commercials.
(D) It uses organic ingredients.

34. What does the woman say about the carrot cake?

(A) It isn't available by the slice.
(B) It is a seasonal item.
(C) It contains nuts.
(D) It is currently sold out.

35. Look at the graphic. How much does the man's dish cost?

(A) $4.50
(B) $5.50
(C) $6.50
(D) $7.50

36. Where does the man most likely work?

(A) At a bank
(B) At a travel agency
(C) At a bus terminal
(D) At a hotel

37. Look at the graphic. Which ATM does the man recommend?

(A) ATM 1
(B) ATM 2
(C) ATM 3
(D) ATM 4

38. What will the man most likely do next?

(A) Give some directions
(B) Process a payment
(C) Check a bank card
(D) Look for an umbrella

PART 4

Directions: You will hear some talks given by a single speaker. You will be asked to answer three questions about what the speakers say in each conversation. Select the best response to each question and mark the letter (A), (B), (C) or (D) on your answer sheet. The conversations will not be printed in your test book and will be spoken only one time.

39. What kind of business do the listeners most likely work for?
   (A) A clothing store
   (B) A bank
   (C) A restaurant
   (D) A laundry service

40. What is the purpose of the meeting?
   (A) To train new employees
   (B) To plan a sales event
   (C) To improve customer services
   (D) To announce a policy change

41. Why does the speaker say, "the document was just made this morning"?
   (A) To offer an excuse
   (B) To criticize a mistake
   (C) To recognize an achievement
   (D) To prioritize an issue

42. What is being discussed?
   (A) The downsizing of the company
   (B) The training of new employees
   (C) The renovation of a store
   (D) The opening of a new headquarters

43. According to the speaker, what is surprising?
   (A) A competitor has increased its sales.
   (B) Online profits have fallen rapidly.
   (C) Certain stores have been successful.
   (D) International sales are rising.

44. What will Carol Morrison most likely do?
   (A) Organize a meeting with clients
   (B) Conduct a training session
   (C) Survey some customers
   (D) Help to relocate staff

45. What is the speaker preparing to do?
   (A) Take a tour
   (B) Write an article
   (C) Attend a lecture
   (D) Evaluate some employees

46. What does the speaker request?
   (A) An employee list
   (B) An expense report
   (C) A newspaper
   (D) A restaurant menu

47. Why does the speaker say, "there will be an in-flight meal service"?
   (A) To explain an expense
   (B) To complain about a flight length
   (C) To request a seat upgrade
   (D) To turn down a suggestion

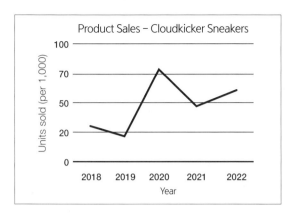

Product Sales – Cloudkicker Sneakers

48. According to the speaker, what will happen next month?

(A) An employee will retire.
(B) A company will close.
(C) A promotional campaign will start.
(D) A product will be released.

49. Look at the graphic. Which year will the meeting focus on?

(A) 2018
(B) 2019
(C) 2020
(D) 2021

50. What will the listeners do next?

(A) Schedule a deadline
(B) Watch a video
(C) Try a product
(D) Listen to a presentation

READING TEST

In the Reading test, you will read a variety of texts and answer several different types of reading comprehension questions. The entire Reading test will last 75 minutes. There are three parts, and directions are given for each part. You are encouraged to answer as many questions as possible within the time allowed. You must mark your answers on the separate answer sheet. Do not write your answers in your test book.

PART 5

Directions: A word or phrase is missing in each of the sentences below. Four answer choices are given below each sentence. Select the best answer to complete the sentence. Then mark the letter (A), (B), (C), or (D) on your answer sheet.

1. The board members agree that the biggest ------- of the office manager is his inability to delegate tasks efficiently.

    (A) weak
    (B) weakly
    (C) weakness
    (D) weaken

2. At Smith Accounting, ------- clientele are offered a beverage and a snack upon arrival.

    (A) every
    (B) all
    (C) each
    (D) one

3. A considerable percentage of the Magitek Software's annual budget ------- for overseas advertising.

    (A) is reserving
    (B) has been reserved
    (C) has reserved
    (D) reserved

4. The CEO has called for employees from different departments to assist one ------- in order to meet the impending deadline.

    (A) the others
    (B) another
    (C) others
    (D) other

5. Our white wines are ------- the perfect accompaniment to the fresh seafood dishes on our menu.

    (A) normally
    (B) fairly
    (C) casually
    (D) evenly

6. Staff members are reminded to submit their vacation leave requests ------- the last working day of this month.

    (A) by
    (B) over
    (C) against
    (D) at

7. The parking area at the Richmond Community Center will undergo renovations this month, so its employees should make other transportation ------.

(A) arrange
(B) arranging
(C) arrangements
(D) arranges

8. ------ Five-Star Catering is known for its high-quality food, several of its recent clients have been dissatisfied with the dishes provided.

(A) Because
(B) However
(C) As if
(D) While

9. Nellysan Industries announced its purchase of an Egyptian-based chocolate company, ------ its plans for expansion into North Africa.

(A) confirm
(B) confirming
(C) confirmed
(D) is confirming

10. Multinational companies must make an effort to understand the customs of each country in ------ they set up branch offices.

(A) when
(B) whose
(C) where
(D) which

11. By implementing an employee incentive program, we can ------ boost staff morale but also increase overall productivity.

(A) not only
(B) much
(C) both
(D) even if

12. New employees must complete a comprehensive training program to learn how to use ------ equipment properly.

(A) protect
(B) protected
(C) protecting
(D) protective

13. During the tour of the factory, shareholders will watch several employees demonstrate ------ to use the assembly line machinery.

(A) who
(B) what
(C) how
(D) that

14. All genres of film ------ documentaries are shown at the annual Hoplite Festival.

(A) opposite
(B) toward
(C) along
(D) except

15. The seminar instructor usually incorporates diagrams in her presentations ------ what she is describing to attendees.

(A) illustrated
(B) is illustrating
(C) illustrates
(D) to illustrate

16. Sales of Fun Furniture products have increased ------ since the store renovation and the introduction of newer products.

(A) considerably
(B) considerable
(C) considering
(D) considered

Directions: Read the texts that follow. A word, phrase, or sentence is missing in parts of each text. Four answer choices for each question are given below the text. Select the best answer to complete the text. Then mark the letter (A), (B), (C) or (D) on your answer sheet.

Questions 17-20 refer to the following review.

On the Stage

By Jasmine Bluth

August 13 – *My Fair Lady* at the Sandville Community Arts Center

This new production of *My Fair Lady* at the Sandville Community Arts Center is one to rival the best of Broadway. Local actors Sandra Boyd and Harrison Frock take on the roles of Eliza Doolitle and Professor Higgins in this version of the well-loved stage classic. The stars of the show ------- by a
17.
talented group of supporting actors, who all reside in the local Sandville area.

In the musical, Professor Higgins attempts to teach Eliza Doolittle ------- she needs to know in order to
18.
become a sophisticated lady. From her speech and her clothing to the way she holds her fork, Eliza is schooled in upper class behavior, allowing her to fit in among London's rich aristocrats.

The show runs from August 10 to September 30. -------. Whether you attend a matinee or an evening
19.
showing, the experience is sure to be -------.
20.

17. (A) are accompanied
    (B) are accompanying
    (C) would have accompanied
    (D) will accompany

18. (A) whoever
    (B) whichever
    (C) whenever
    (D) whatever

19. (A) However, the next planned production is
       Oklahoma.
    (B) Tickets can be purchased online at www.
       scac.org or at the venue's box office.
    (C) In fact, this version draws heavily from the
       highly popular film.
    (D) Bob Hicok has returned to direct yet
       another Sandville community play.

20. (A) talkative
    (B) entertaining
    (C) historical
    (D) prominent

To: LisaTennant@acemail.net

From: Brett_Stark@lolafurnishings.com

Subject: Re: My recent purchase

Attachment: Exchange form

Dear Ms. Tennant,

I was very disappointed to find out ------- the mahogany dining table you ordered from our Web site
21.
arrived with a scratch on the surface. We will send one of our employees to your location to collect the

------- item. Please complete the attached exchange form and give it to our worker when he arrives. A
22.
replacement table will then be shipped to you within a few days. -------, Lola Furnishings can offer you
23.
a full refund for the item. If this is what you would prefer, please call me at 555-3982 and I will make

the necessary arrangements. -------. We hope you will continue shopping at Lola Furnishings for years
24.
to come!

Sincerely,

Brett Stark

Customer Service Manager

Lola Furnishings

---

21. (A) that
    (B) so
    (C) it
    (D) about

22. (A) damaged
    (B) incorrect
    (C) harmful
    (D) accidental

23. (A) Eventually
    (B) Regrettably
    (C) Occasionally
    (D) Alternatively

24. (A) I am delighted that you found our services
        to be satisfactory.
    (B) Thank you for your prompt response to my
        inquiry.
    (C) Our range of products is the most extensive
        in the country.
    (D) Please accept my apologies for this
        inconvenience.

PART 7

Directions: In this part you will read a selection of texts, such as magazine and newspaper articles, e-mails, and instant messages. Each text or set of texts is followed by several questions. Select the best answer for each question and mark the letter (A), (B), (C), or (D) on your answer sheet.

Questions 25-26 refer to the following text message chain.

ISMAN ALI [6:16 P.M.]
Hi, Craig. I checked my schedule for tomorrow and I'll have some free time at 10:30 in the morning to discuss the Elliot Building project.

CRAIG KANE [6:18 P.M.]
Great. We have a few things to go over. Did you check your e-mail?

ISMAN ALI [6:20 P.M.]
Yes, I got the blueprints. Thanks. They look quite impressive.

CRAIG KANE [6:21 P.M.]
I'm pleased with the work I've done on them, but the client, Mr. Rosewood, has asked for some last-minute alterations.

ISMAN ALI [6:23 P.M.]
Really? That could affect our project deadlines.

CRAIG KANE [6:24 P.M.]
Without a doubt. So, I'd like your input tomorrow about the best way to handle this.

ISMAN ALI [6:25 P.M.]
No problem. We'll figure out a way to compromise and keep the client happy.

25. What is suggested about Mr. Kane?

(A) He had to reschedule a meeting with Mr. Ali.
(B) He is planning to contact an architect.
(C) He sent some documents to Mr. Ali.
(D) He will visit the Eliot Building tomorrow.

26. At 6:24 P.M., what does Mr. Kane mean when he writes, "Without a doubt"?

(A) He is concerned about a work schedule.
(B) He would like to discuss a matter in person.
(C) He believes Ms. Rosewood will change her mind.
(D) He wants to change some building blueprints.

Questions 27-29 refer to the following e-mail.

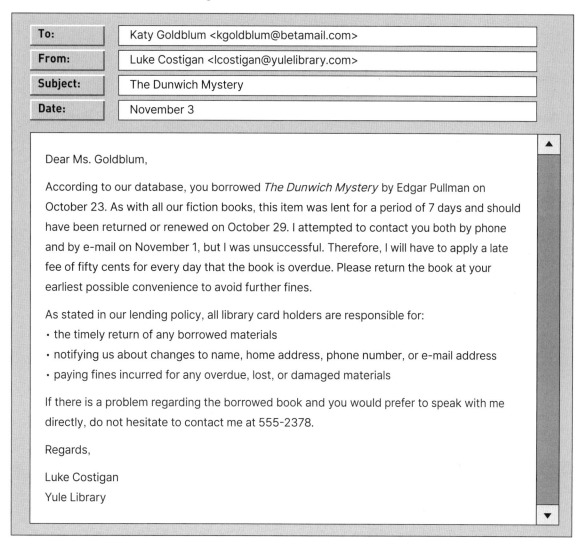

To:	Katy Goldblum <kgoldblum@betamail.com>
From:	Luke Costigan <lcostigan@yulelibrary.com>
Subject:	The Dunwich Mystery
Date:	November 3

Dear Ms. Goldblum,

According to our database, you borrowed *The Dunwich Mystery* by Edgar Pullman on October 23. As with all our fiction books, this item was lent for a period of 7 days and should have been returned or renewed on October 29. I attempted to contact you both by phone and by e-mail on November 1, but I was unsuccessful. Therefore, I will have to apply a late fee of fifty cents for every day that the book is overdue. Please return the book at your earliest possible convenience to avoid further fines.

As stated in our lending policy, all library card holders are responsible for:
• the timely return of any borrowed materials
• notifying us about changes to name, home address, phone number, or e-mail address
• paying fines incurred for any overdue, lost, or damaged materials

If there is a problem regarding the borrowed book and you would prefer to speak with me directly, do not hesitate to contact me at 555-2378.

Regards,

Luke Costigan
Yule Library

27. Why did Mr. Costigan send the e-mail?
   (A) To inform a customer about a new book
   (B) To apologize for a database error
   (C) To explain a new borrowing procedure
   (D) To issue a reminder to a customer

28. When was Ms. Goldblum's book originally due back to the library?
   (A) On October 23
   (B) On October 29
   (C) On November 1
   (D) On November 3

29. What is indicated about library card holders at Yule Library?
   (A) They can borrow materials for a maximum of two weeks.
   (B) They can reserve books through the library's Web site.
   (C) They should renew memberships on an annual basis.
   (D) They should report changes in personal information.

A Reminder for All Kermode Media Employees

Dear staff,

Please do not forget that a fire drill will be held in our building on Friday, May 17. The exact time of the drill is unknown, but it will definitely take place before noon. If this interrupts any tasks you are working on, I can approve an extension.

Management is hoping to see a massive improvement this month. — [1] —. Approximately 10 percent of employees failed to evacuate the building within five minutes during last month's drill. — [2] —. We had a similar result in both March and February. Our performance has been consistently below the recommended government safety standards.

When you hear the fire alarm, use the staircases instead of the elevators and exit out of the main entrance to our building. — [3] —. If you have any questions, please speak to me or your supervisor. — [4] —.

Thank you,

Gillian Miller

---

30. Who most likely put up the notice?

(A) A fire chief
(B) A building resident
(C) A department manager
(D) A government official

31. What is NOT indicated about the fire drill?

(A) It usually takes place every month.
(B) It will be held in the morning.
(C) Staff should evacuate within 5 minutes.
(D) Staff should use the elevators.

32. In which of the positions marked [1], [2], [3], and [4] does the following sentence best belong?

"Do not go back inside under any circumstances until the drill is over."

(A) [1]
(B) [2]
(C) [3]
(D) [4]

Leading Automotive Firm

Facing Difficulties

By Lionel Peterson

(September 1) - Devona Motors Inc. announced yesterday that it has officially requested the return of nearly 595,000 sedans due to a power-steering issue. The move applies to the Devona Libra and the Devona Argo, both of which were launched in February.

A spokesperson for Devona explained that a faulty electrical connection has the potential to disable electric power-steering, causing drivers to lose control. Devona originally claimed that the defect has not resulted in any injuries, but more than 50 incidents have been reported by insurance companies. These incidents involve the abovementioned Devona models hitting curbs and roadside objects due to the steering defect, causing several drivers to hurt their neck, back, or shoulders.

The American Traffic Safety Organization (ATSO) began investigating the power-steering issue in April when it started receiving complaints from dealerships and motorists. Devona rejected ATSO's initial recommendations that affected models be recalled, arguing in a May letter to the organization that the number of complaints was too low to justify such drastic action.

The automotive firm also issued a technical report to car dealerships in June in an effort to cover up the defect. However, due to the growing number of complaints and pressure from the ATSO, the firm had no choice but to recall the cars and publicly admit that the power-steering problem is a genuine danger to motorists.

---

33. What is the article mainly about?

(A) A delay in a production process
(B) A problem with manufacturing machinery
(C) A new technology in specific cars
(D) A recall of defective vehicles

34. What can be inferred about the Devona Argo cars?

(A) They were released onto the market one year ago.
(B) Some of them include an outdated braking system.
(C) They were found to be less safe than the Devona Libra cars.
(D) Some of them have been involved in accidents.

35. What is suggested about Devona Motors Inc.?

(A) It intends to cease all production in its manufacturing plants.
(B) It has been fined by the American Traffic Safety Organization.
(C) It did not immediately admit that there was a problem.
(D) It sent letters to individuals who had purchased its products.

36. When did ATSO first become aware of the technical fault?

(A) In February
(B) In April
(C) In May
(D) In June

To: All department managers <managerlist@iversen.com>
From: Bernard Huddlestone <bhuddlestone@iversen.com>
Date: Tuesday, April 6
Subject: Good news

It is my pleasure to inform you all about a pleasing development. Our negotiations with Jagten Technologies have ended successfully, with the Copenhagen-based firm agreeing to lend its expertise by working collaboratively with us on our new cell phone model. This was an extremely important deal for us to sign in order for us to keep on schedule and finish the first stage of product design and development by August.

Jagten is renowned in the electronics industry for its ability to prolong battery life in devices and minimize internal heating. We placed a high priority on such matters, as our customers have voiced concerns over the short battery life and high temperatures of our previous models. I am now confident that these issues will be adequately addressed. I have truly appreciated your endeavors over the past few weeks, and I would like to do something to reward you. Therefore, I am planning to take you all out for dinner next Friday.

I'll send a follow-up e-mail later today with more details. Please try to clear room in your schedules, because this is no less than you deserve.

Bernard Huddlestone
Chief Operations Officer, Iversen Incorporated

37. For whom is the e-mail intended?

   (A) Product designers at Jagten Technologies
   (B) Executives at Jagten Technologies
   (C) Customers of Iversen Incorporated
   (D) Supervisors at Iversen Incorporated

38. Why is Mr. Huddlestone pleased?

   (A) A crucial business deal was made.
   (B) A product development stage was
       completed.
   (C) An innovative product has been released.
   (D) A merger was successfully carried out.

39. According to the e-mail, what does Mr. Huddlestone expect his company to do in the near future?

   (A) Collaborate with several firms
   (B) Change a product's appearance
   (C) Resolve some customer complaints
   (D) Design a rechargeable battery

40. What are the e-mail recipients invited to do?

   (A) Join a company committee
   (B) Offer suggestions for a meal
   (C) Submit nominations for an award
   (D) Attend a celebratory event

Agate Electronics – Current Vacancies

Digital Media Manager (Position #0060)

Applicants must have at least 10 years of experience in the field of digital advertising. The successful applicant will be responsible for developing Agate's online advertising campaigns.

Engineering Lab Technician (Position #0061)

Applicants must have at least 1 year of experience (preferably 2 years) working in an electronic engineering lab. This position involves shift rotation over the course of a 7-day working week.

Senior Production Designer (Position #0062)

Applicants must have at least 5 years of experience in production design. The successful applicant must have impeccable production skills (color, layout, fonts). Submission of a portfolio is required.

Software Engineer (Position #0063)

Applicants must have at least 18 months of software development experience and a firm understanding of all common programming languages.

Although applicants' university degrees will be taken into consideration, we are more interested in finding individuals who have enthusiasm and experience. Please e-mail your résumé to Lee Staunton at employment@agateinc.com, and indicate which position you are interested in.

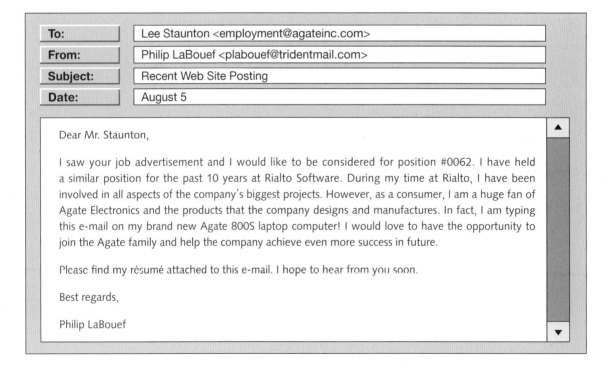

To:	Lee Staunton <employment@agateinc.com>
From:	Philip LaBouef <plabouef@tridentmail.com>
Subject:	Recent Web Site Posting
Date:	August 5

Dear Mr. Staunton,

I saw your job advertisement and I would like to be considered for position #0062. I have held a similar position for the past 10 years at Rialto Software. During my time at Rialto, I have been involved in all aspects of the company's biggest projects. However, as a consumer, I am a huge fan of Agate Electronics and the products that the company designs and manufactures. In fact, I am typing this e-mail on my brand new Agate 800S laptop computer! I would love to have the opportunity to join the Agate family and help the company achieve even more success in future.

Please find my résumé attached to this e-mail. I hope to hear from you soon.

Best regards,

Philip LaBouef

41. Which position requires the least amount of experience?

(A) Software Engineer
(B) Engineering Lab Technician
(C) Senior Production Designer
(D) Digital Media Manager

42. What can be inferred about Agate Electronics from the advertisement?

(A) It manufactures a wide range of kitchen appliances.
(B) It has recently opened a new business location.
(C) It normally focuses on the domestic market.
(D) It values experience over academic achievements.

43. What is the purpose of Mr. LaBouef's e-mail?

(A) To inquire about an application process
(B) To express interest in a position
(C) To recommend a colleague for a job
(D) To point out an error in a Web site posting

44. What is indicated about the job that Mr. LaBouef mentions in his e-mail?

(A) It may require some weekend shifts.
(B) Applicants must send examples of past work.
(C) Applicants will be asked to take a practical test.
(D) It requires extensive knowledge of online advertising.

45. In the e-mail, the word "time" in paragraph 1, line 2, is closest in meaning to

(A) duration
(B) background
(C) renewal
(D) employment

Questions 46-50 refer to the following letters and Web page.

Mr. Josef Moskowitz
4003 Meadow Drive
Syracuse, NY 13245

Dear Mr. Moskowitz,

The Arkadia Film Festival is scheduled to take place in Rochester in the first week of July and we still have vacancies for two qualified individuals on the judging panel. Among this year's featured films, we have the latest blockbuster movie by acclaimed Swedish director Jonas Brolin and lots of promising movies from Europe, the Middle East, and Asia. Our panel of judges includes actors, directors, and film critics who have extensive experience in the movie industry. As the senior professor of film studies at Carlton College, you would also be perfectly suited to fill such a role.

Please let me know if this offer interests you. If it does, then I will send you an information pack that contains everything you will need to know about the event and your responsibilities.

Best regards,

Beatrice Jones
Co-founder
Arkadia Film Festival

http://www.arkadiafilmfest.com

| American Films | **European Films** | Middle Eastern Films | Asian Films |

Arkadia Film Festival (July 8 – July 11)

July 8	July 9
Bed of Roses (France)	Mountain Escape (Norway)
Bremen Tales (Germany)	Persona Non Grata (Italy)
Fabuleux Destin (France)	Secreto (Spain)

July 10	July 11
Mi Madre (Spain)	Trés Jours (France)
Eagles of Warsaw (Poland)	Brothers' Bond (Sweden)
Je T'aime (France)	The White Cockade (Scotland)

Ms. Beatrice Jones
551 Denham Street
Rochester, NY 14614

Dear Ms. Jones,

It would be my pleasure to take you up on your offer. There is one problem that may affect my ability to participate. Under no circumstances will I be able to show up on the opening day of the festival, because I will be out of state attending my daughter's wedding on that day. Hopefully, this will not pose too much of a problem. I would be able to meet with you on the following day and view the films that I may have missed.

I look forward to hearing from you. Please feel free to call me at 555-8837.

Best wishes,

Josef Moskowitz

---

46. What is the main purpose of the first letter?

(A) To announce award nominees
(B) To confirm that a movie is eligible for judging
(C) To extend an invitation to join a panel
(D) To request that an event schedule be changed

47. Who is Josef Moskowitz?

(A) A film director
(B) A theater actor
(C) A movie critic
(D) A college lecturer

48. When will Jonas Brolin's film most likely be shown?

(A) On July 8
(B) On July 9
(C) On July 10
(D) On July 11

49. What is Mr. Moskowitz intending to do on July 8?

(A) Attend a family event
(B) Meet with Ms. Jones
(C) Watch some movies
(D) Announce an award winner

50. In the second letter, the word "pose" in paragraph 1, line 3, is closest in meaning to

(A) configure
(B) present
(C) display
(D) stand

시원스쿨 LAB

1. (B)	**2.** (B)	**3.** (A)	**4.** (C)	**5.** (A)
6. (D)	**7.** (A)	**8.** (C)	**9.** (C)	**10.** (B)
11. (D)	**12.** (D)	**13.** (C)	**14.** (C)	**15.** (C)
16. (C)	**17.** (D)	**18.** (C)	**19.** (B)	**20.** (C)
21. (B)	**22.** (D)	**23.** (A)	**24.** (B)	**25.** (B)
26. (D)	**27.** (D)	**28.** (C)	**29.** (C)	**30.** (D)
31. (C)	**32.** (C)	**33.** (C)	**34.** (B)	**35.** (C)
36. (D)	**37.** (D)	**38.** (D)	**39.** (B)	**40.** (C)
41. (D)	**42.** (A)	**43.** (C)	**44.** (C)	**45.** (B)
46. (B)	**47.** (D)	**48.** (D)	**49.** (C)	**50.** (D)

Part 5

1.

정답 (B)

해석 그 호텔 소유의 해변은 손님들이 쉽게 접근할 수 없기 때문에 방문객을 많이 받지 않는다.

해설 빈칸이 동사와 형용사 보어 사이에 위치해 있으므로 빈칸은 형용사를 앞에서 수식할 부사 자리이다. 따라서 (B) easily가 정답이다.

어휘 **private** 개인 소유의, 사적인, 민간의 **receive** ~을 받다 **accessible to A** A가 접근 가능한, A가 이용 가능한 **easily** 쉽게, 수월하게

2.

정답 (B)

해석 리즈 그레이 씨께서 12월 20일에 있을 회사 연말 연회 중에 은퇴를 발표하실 것입니다.

해설 빈칸이 동사와 명사 목적어 사이에 위치해 있으므로 빈칸은 명사를 수식할 수 있는 소유격 대명사 자리이다. 따라서 (B) her가 정답이다.

어휘 **announce** ~을 발표하다, 알리다 **retirement** 은퇴 **year-end** 연말의 **banquet** 연회

3.

정답 (A)

해석 터커 씨가 출장으로 해외에 있었기 때문에, 그는 신임 대표이사에게 이메일로 축하 인사를 전했다.

해설 빈칸이 소유격 대명사와 전치사 사이에 있으므로 빈칸은 소유격 대명사의 수식을 받을 명사 자리이다. 따라서 (A)

congratulations가 정답이다.

어휘 **congratulations** 축하(의 말) **newly appointed** 새로 임명된 **congratulate** ~에게 축하하다 **congratulatory** 축하의

4.

정답 (C)

해석 다음 주 월요일부터 시행되는 것으로서, 직원들께서는 소속 부서장님께 일일 업무 보고서를 제출하셔야 할 것입니다.

해설 빈칸 뒤에 위치한 미래 시점 표현 next Monday는 앞으로 직원들이 해야 하는 일과 관련된 정책 하나가 시행되는 시점임을 알 수 있다. 따라서, 시점 표현과 결합해 '~부터 시행되는' 등의 의미를 나타낼 때 사용하는 (C) Effective가 정답이다.

어휘 **be required to do** ~해야 하다, ~할 필요가 있다 **submit** ~을 제출하다 **effectively** 효과적으로 **effectiveness** 유효성, 효과적임 **effective** 효과적인, (시점 표현과 함께) ~부터 시행되는 **effect** 효과, 영향

5.

정답 (A)

해석 최근의 설문 조사는 도시에서 가장 유명한 명소들이 과거 그 어느 때보다 더 많은 관광객들을 끌어들이고 있다는 것을 보여준다.

해설 빈칸 앞에는 주어와 동사가, 빈칸 뒤에는 주어와 동사가 포함된 하나의 절이 있으므로 빈칸부터 문장 끝까지가 타동사 shows의 목적어 역할을 하는 명사절이 되어야 한다. 따라서 명사절을 이끌 수 있는 접속사 (A) that과 (C) what 중에서 골라야 하는데, 빈칸 뒤의 절의 구성이 완전하므로 (A) that이 정답이다.

어휘 **recent** 최근의 **survey** n. 설문 조사 **show that** ~임을 보여주다 **prominent** 유명한, 눈에 띄는 **landmark** 명소, 주요 건물 **attract** ~을 끌어들이다

6.

정답 (D)

해석 뱅스 박사의 사직 소식이 빠르게 퍼져 나갔는데, 그녀는 업계에 많은 지인들이 있었기 때문이었다.

해설 빈칸이 형용사와 전치사구 사이에 있으므로 빈칸은 형용사의 수식을 받을 수 있는 명사 자리이다. 선택지에서 명사는 (C) acquaintance와 (D) acquaintances인데, 복수 수량 형용사 many의 수식을 받아야 하므로 복수명사 (D) acquaintances가 정답이다.

어휘 **word** 소문 **resignation** 사직, 퇴사 **spread** 퍼지다 **rapidly** 신속하게, 빠르게 **acquaint** v. ~을 익히 알게 하다 **acquaintance** 지인

7.

정답 (A)

해석 카터 브리지가 7개월 동안의 수리 작업 후에 10월 5일에 차량들을 대상으로 재개통될 것이다.

해설 빈칸에는 빈칸 뒤에 위치한 명사구 seven months를 목적어로 취할 전치사가 필요하며, 수리 작업 끝에 다시 개통된다는 의미가 되어야 자연스러우므로 '~ 후에'를 뜻하는 (A) after가 정답이다.

어휘 repair 수리 between prep. ~ 사이에 ad. 그 사이에 further ad. 더 멀리, 한층 더 a. 더 먼, 더 깊이 있는 along prep. (길 등) ~을 따라 ad. 앞으로, 함께

8.

정답 (C)

해석 출장을 떠날 준비를 하면서, 영 씨는 여러 업무를 자신의 직원들에게 맡겼다.

해설 빈칸 앞에 분사로 쓰인 동사 prepare는 to부정사를 목적어로 취해 '~할 준비를 하다'라는 의미를 나타내므로 (C) to depart가 정답이다.

어휘 prepare to do ~할 준비를 하다 assign ~을 맡기다 task 업무, 일 depart 떠나다, 출발하다

9.

정답 (C)

해석 용품을 주문하실 때, 반드시 주의해서 선택하셔야 하며, 우리가 전적으로 필요로 하는 제품들만 꼭 구입하도록 하십시오.

해설 빈칸 앞에 be동사가 있으므로 동사원형 (B) select를 제외하고 나머지 선택지 중에서 정답을 골라야 한다. be동사의 보어 역할을 하면서 사람 주어의 행동을 보충 설명해줄 수 있는 형용사 (C) selective가 정답이다.

어휘 supplies 용품, 물품 selective 주의해서 고르는, 선택적인 ensure (that) 꼭 ~하도록 하다 absolutely 전적으로, 절대적으로

10.

정답 (B)

해석 브리젠드 미술관의 폐쇄 후에 나타난 관광 산업의 급격한 붕괴는 이 미술관이 지역 경제에 얼마나 중요했는지를 단적으로 나타낸다.

해설 빈칸이 동사와 동사의 목적어 역할을 하는 how가 이끄는 명사절 사이에 위치해 있으므로 이 사이에 위치해 목적어를 강조하는 역할을 할 수 있는 부사 (B) just가 정답이다.

어휘 drastic 급격한 fall in ~의 붕괴, ~의 하락, ~의 감소 following ~ 후에 closure 폐쇄, 폐업 indicate ~을 나타내다, ~을 가리키다 crucial 아주 중요한, 중대한 near ad. 가까이 a. 가까운 prep. ~ 가까이에 alike ad. 비슷하게, (둘 다) 똑같이 a. 비슷한

11.

정답 (D)

해석 우리는 건물 설계도가 건축가에 의해 제출 완료되는 대로 그것을 철저히 확인할 것이다.

해설 빈칸 앞뒤에 주어와 동사를 포함한 절이 각각 있으므로 빈칸에 이 두 절을 연결할 접속사가 필요하다. 설계도가 제출되는 대로 확인한다는 의미가 되어야 알맞으므로 '~하는 대로, ~하자마자'를 뜻하는 (D) as soon as가 정답이다.

어휘 blueprint 설계도, 도면 thoroughly 철저히, 빈틈없이 as soon as ~하는 대로, ~하자마자 then 그러면, 그런 다음에 while ~하는 동안, ~인 반면에 due to ~ 때문에, ~로 인해

12.

정답 (D)

해석 앤 피터슨 씨가 올해 출간할 계획인 신간 소설은 이 작가의 성공적인 매직 몬스터즈 시리즈의 마지막 권이다.

해설 선택지가 모두 형용사로 구성되어 있어 해석을 통해 알맞은 어휘를 골라야 한다. 빈칸 뒤에 시리즈물이라는 말이 쓰여 있어 그 일부에 해당되는 책 한 권임을 의미할 수 있는 형용사가 빈칸에 쓰여야 자연스러우므로 '마지막의, 최종의'를 뜻하는 (D) final이 정답이다.

어휘 novel 소설 publish ~을 출간하다 author 작가, 저자 absolute 완전한, 절대적인 separate a. 분리된, 별도의 entire 전체의

13.

정답 (C)

해석 대부분의 향수 원료 비용이 감소했음에도 불구하고, 페넬로페 화장품은 50퍼센트가 넘게 가격을 인상했다.

해설 선택지가 접속사와 전치사로 구성되어 있으므로 문장 구조를 확인해야 한다. '향수 원료 비용 감소'와 '가격 인상'이라는 상반된 내용을 연결하려면 '~에도 불구하고'를 의미하는 양보접속사 또는 전치사가 필요한데, 빈칸 뒤에 명사구가 있으므로 전치사 (C) Despite가 정답이다.

어휘 despite ~에도 불구하고 reduction 감소, 축소 ingredient 원료 production 생산 although ~에도 불구하고 neither 어느 것도 아닌 as ~로서, ~이기 때문에

14.

정답 (C)

해석 실험은 2층에 있는 신 박사의 실험실에서 수요일에 하루 종일 실시되었다.

해설 선택지에 제시된 동사 conduct가 '~을 실시하다'라는 뜻을 가진 타동사인데 빈칸 뒤의 all day Wednesday가 그 대상이 될 수 없으므로 빈칸에는 수동태가 와야 한다. 주어가 단수이므로 단수 형태의 수동태 (C) was conducted가 정답이다.

어휘 experiment 실험 conduct ~을 실시하다, 수행하다

laboratory 실험실

15.

정답 (C)

해석 테일러 오닐 씨는 상을 받은 조각가로, 그의 작품은 세계에서 가장 훌륭한 여러 갤러리에서 전시되고 있다.

해설 빈칸 뒤의 내용은 테일러 오닐 씨에 대해 설명하는 절이며, 빈칸 바로 뒤에 제시된 work는 그의 작품을 나타내므로 소유 관계를 나타내면서 절을 이끄는 소유격 관계대명사 (C) whose가 정답이다.

어휘 award-winning 상을 받은 sculptor 조각가 exhibit ~을 전시하다 prominent 훌륭한 as well as ~에 더하여, ~뿐만 아니라

16.

정답 (C)

해석 그 음악 축제에 필요한 포스터 인쇄 작업이 지연되기는 했지만, 다음 주에 마을 전역에 부착되어야 한다.

해설 선택지가 모두 다른 동사의 과거분사형으로 구성되어 있으므로 해석을 통해 알맞은 어휘를 골라야 한다. 빈칸이 속한 절의 주어가 앞서 언급된 posters를 가리키므로 행사 포스터의 활용 등과 관련된 의미를 나타내야 한다. 또한, 빈칸 뒤에 위치한 전치사구와 어울려 '마을 전역에 부착되다'와 같은 의미가 되어야 자연스러우므로 '~을 부착하다'를 뜻하는 (C) put up이 정답이다.

어휘 printing 인쇄, 출력 delay ~을 지연시키다, ~을 미루다 around ~ 전역에, ~ 곳곳에 use up ~을 다 쓰다, ~을 완전히 소모하다 apply for ~에 지원하다, ~을 신청하다 put up ~을 부착하다, ~을 게시하다 carry on ~을 계속하다

Part 6

17-20.

> 새 공장 개장 예정인 자동차 제조사
>
> 톨레도 (4월 3일) - 최근 있었던 기자 회견 중에, 로이스턴 모터스의 대표이사는 내년 초에 이 자동차 제조사가 톨레도에 새로운 공장을 개장할 예정이라고 발표했습니다. 로이스턴 사는 주로 자사의 인기 있는 로이스턴 세그웨이 승용차의 높은 판매량으로 인해 국내 **17** 자동차 업계에서 손꼽히는 회사로 빠르게 떠올랐습니다. 이 회사의 브라이언 레드먼드 대표이사는 이 공장이 톨레도 지역에서 **18** 대략 800개의 일자리를 창출할 것으로 생각하고 있습니다.
>
> 톨레도 지역의 새 공장은 로이스턴 사에서 곧 출시하는 폴라리스 모델을 제조하는 데 주로 이용될 것입니다. 이 공장의 조립 라인은 최대 가동 효율을 보장하기 위해 최신 기술력을 **19** 갖추게 될 것입니다. **20** 결국, 이는 생산 비율의 증가를 가능하게 해줄 것입니다. 레드먼드 씨는 이 공장이 매년 50만 대가 넘는 차량

을 생산해, 회사에서 가장 수익성이 뛰어난 시설이 될 수 있기를 바라고 있습니다.

어휘 manufacturer 제조사 set to do ~할 예정인 recent 최근의 press conference 기자 회견 emerge as ~로 떠오르다 leading 손꼽히는, 선도적인 domestic 국내의 industry 업계 due to ~로 인해 in large part 주로, 대부분 sales 판매(량), 매출 mainly 주로 manufacture ~을 제조하다 upcoming 곧 있을, 다가오는 assembly 조립 ensure ~을 보장하다 operating efficiency 가동 효율, 운영 효율 produce ~을 생산하다 vehicle 차량 profitable 수익성이 있는 facility 시설(물)

17.

정답 (D)

해설 선택지가 모두 다른 형용사로 구성되어 있으므로 해석을 통해 알맞은 어휘를 골라야 한다. 빈칸은 바로 뒤에 있는 명사 industry를 수식해 문장의 주어인 로이스턴 사가 어느 업계에 속해 있는지를 나타내야 한다. 앞선 문장에 Royston Motors라는 명칭과 car manufacturer라는 말이 쓰여 있어 자동차 업계에 속한 것을 알 수 있으므로 '자동차의'를 뜻하는 (D) automotive가 정답이다.

어휘 healthcare 의료의 financial 재정의, 금융의 agricultural 농업의 automotive 자동차의

18.

정답 (C)

해설 빈칸이 부정관사와 숫자 표현 사이에 위치해 있으므로 숫자 표현 앞에 쓰여 '대략적인, 추정된' 등을 뜻하는 형용사 (C) estimated가 정답이다.

어휘 estimation 추정, 추산, 판단 estimate v. ~을 추정하다 n. 추정, 견적(서) estimated 대략적인, 추정된

19.

정답 (B)

해설 빈칸이 be동사 및 전치사 with 사이에 위치해 있으므로 이 구조와 어울리는 과거분사가 필요하다. 빈칸 앞뒤 부분의 내용으로 볼 때 공장 조립 라인에 최신 기술이 포함되거나 적용된다는 의미가 구성되어야 자연스러운데, 이는 조립 라인이 갖추게 되는 특징적인 요소에 해당되므로 '~을 갖춘'이라는 뜻의 (B) equipped가 정답이다.

어휘 equip (A with B) (A에게 B를) 갖춰주다 contain ~을 포함하다, ~을 담고 있다 insure ~을 보험에 들다, ~을 보증하다

20.

정답 (C)

해석 (A) 폴라리스의 제조가 곧 중단될 것입니다.

(B) 조사관들이 최근 결함이 있는 기계를 조사했습니다.

(C) 결국, 이는 생산 비율의 증가를 가능하게 해줄 것입니다.

(D) 로이스턴은 훌륭한 고객 지원 서비스로 알려져 있습니다.

해설   빈칸 앞에 위치한 문장에 공장 조립 라인에 최대 가동 효율을 보장하는 최신 기술이 쓰인다는 말이 제시되어 있으므로 결과를 말할 때 사용하는 In turn과 함께 그러한 기술의 적용에 따른 결과로서 생산 비율의 증가가 가능해진다는 점을 알리는 (C)가 정답이다.

어휘   **discontinue** ~을 중단하다, ~을 단종하다 **inspector** 조사관 **defective** 결함이 있는 **in turn** 결국, 결과적으로 **enable** ~을 가능하게 하다 **rate** 비율, 요금, 속도, 등급 **be known for** ~로 알려지다

21-24.

> 수신: <발송 대상자 명단>
> 발신: <info@digitalmarketplace.com>
> 제목: 디지털 마켓플레이스 회원이 되어 보십시오
> 날짜: 5월 6일
>
> 여러분께,
>
> 선택하실 수 있는 가정용 제품을 50만개 넘게 보유하고 있는, 저희 디지털 마켓플레이스는 온라인에서 **21** 쇼핑하시는 데 있어 최고의 선택입니다. 저희는 가정용 가구와 가전 기기에서부터 청소용 제품과 조리 기구에 이르기까지 놀라울 정도로 다양한 제품을 제공해 드립니다. 저희 가격은 누구도 넘어설 수 없으며, 시애틀 시 경계 내에 해당되는 모든 주문에 대해 무료 **22** 배송 서비스를 제공해 드립니다.
>
> **23** 회원 자격으로 인해 여러분께서는 여러 혜택을 이용하실 수 있습니다. 회원이 되시면 다양한 제품에 대한 할인 서비스 및 두 달에 한 번씩 완전히 컬러로 된 무료 제품 카탈로그를 받습니다. 추가로, 디지털 마켓플레이스 회원 자격을 신청하시면, 다양한 특별 할인 행사 및 제품 출시 행사 초대장도 **24** 받으실 것입니다. 다음 링크를 따라 가입하시기만 하면 됩니다: www.digitalmarketplace.com/join.

어휘   **household** 가정 **choose from** ~에서 선택하다 **an amazing range of** 놀라울 정도로 다양한 **furnishings** 가구, 집기 **appliance** (가전) 기기 **cookware** 조리 기구 **complimentary** 무료의 **order** 주문(품) **limits** 경계 **receive** ~을 받다 **various** 다양한 **in addition** 추가로, 게다가 **sign up for** ~을 신청하다, ~에 등록하다 **invitation** 초대(장) **launch** 출시, 시작

21.

정답   (B)

해설   빈칸 앞에 디지털 마켓플레이스가 최고의 선택이라는 말이 쓰여 있으므로 빈칸 이하는 무엇에 대한 선택인지 그 대상이나 목적을 나타내야 가장 자연스럽다. 따라서, '~하는 데 있어, ~을 위해' 등의 의미로 choice와 함께 그 대상이나 목적을 나타낼

때 사용하는 전치사 for와 동명사가 결합된 (B) for shopping이 정답이다.

22.

정답   (D)

해설   빈칸은 동사 offer의 목적어 자리이므로 회사 측에서 무료로 제공할 수 있는 서비스에 해당되는 명사가 쓰여야 한다. 또한, 빈칸 뒤에 그 제공 범위에 해당되는 지역이 언급되어 있어 특정 지역 내에서의 이동과 관련된 서비스를 나타내야 하므로 '배송, 배달'을 뜻하는 (D) delivery가 정답이다.

어휘   **payment** 지불(액) **training** 교육, 훈련 **removal** 제거, 없앰

23.

정답   (A)

해석   **(A) 회원 자격으로 인해 여러분께서는 여러 혜택을 이용하실 수 있습니다.**
(B) 회원 자격을 갱신하시려면, 이 안내를 따르시기 바랍니다.
(C) 저희는 모든 회원 여러분의 의견을 소중히 여깁니다.
(D) 귀하의 회원 자격이 이번 달에 만료될 예정이라는 점에 유의하십시오.

해설   빈칸 뒤에 이어지는 문장들을 읽어 보면, 회원들에게 제공되는 몇 가지 혜택이 언급되어 있다. 따라서, 이러한 혜택을 누릴 수 있다는 사실을 알리며 도입 문장의 역할을 하는 (A)가 정답이다.

어휘   **A allow B to do** A로 인해 B가 ~할 수 있다, A가 B에게 ~할 수 있게 해주다 **take advantage of** ~을 이용하다 **benefit** 혜택, 이점 **renew** ~을 갱신하다 **instructions** 안내, 설명, 지시 **value** v. ~을 소중히 여기다, ~을 가치 있게 생각하다 **note that** ~라는 점에 유의하다 **be due to do** ~할 예정이다 **expire** 만료되다

24.

정답   (B)

해설   빈칸 앞뒤 부분의 내용으로 볼 때, 빈칸이 속한 문장에서 말하는 초대장을 받는 일은 회원으로 가입한 이후에 발생 가능한 일이라는 것을 알 수 있다. 따라서, '~할 것이다, ~일 것이다'와 같은 의미로 가정 또는 상상에 따른 결과 등을 말할 때 사용하는 조동사 would가 포함된 (B) would receive가 정답이다.

Part 7

25-26.

> **수신:** 키스 카푸토 <kcaputo@ballouagency.com>
> **발신:** 도라 윈슬로우 <dwinslow@ballouagency.com>
> **제목:** <베드 오브 로지스> 기념일
> **날짜:** 5월 9일
>
> 안녕하세요, 키스 씨.
>
> 분명 당신이 알고 있다시피, 우리는 **25** 매그너스 달 씨의 베스트셀러인 <베드 오브 로지스>의 10주년 기념일을 축하할 계획 중에 있습니다. 달 씨는 우리 회사의 첫 고객이자 **25** 우리가 대표하는 모든 작가들 중 가장 성공한 작가로 남아 있습니다. 전 그분께 다음 주 토요일에 우리가 준비하고 있는 연회가 진행되는 동안 감사 표시를 전하고 싶습니다. **26** 적합한 선물들을 적은 목록을 첨부하였으며, 여기에는 각 물건을 찾을 수 있는 가게의 이름뿐만 아니라 각 물건의 대략적인 가격대가 포함되어 있습니다. 이를 처리해 주신다면 좋겠습니다.
>
> 직접 물건값을 지불하고 나중에 변제를 받거나, 또는 우리 회사 건물 4층에 있는 제 비서 메러디스 롱 씨로부터 회사의 신용카드를 받아가셔도 됩니다.
>
> 감사합니다.
>
> 도라 윈슬로우
> 고객관리팀장
> 벌루 출판 에이전시

어휘 celebrate ~을 축하하다 anniversary 기념일 agency 대리점, 서비스 제공기관 first ever client 가장 첫 고객 remain 남아 있다 represent ~을 대표하다 a token of one's appreciation 감사의 표시 banquet 연회 attach ~을 첨부하다 suitable 적합한 approximate 대략적인, 대략의 range 범위 take care of ~을 처리하다 reimburse ~을 변제하다, 배상하다 assistant 비서, 조수

25. 매그너스 달 씨는 누구인가?
(A) 도서 평론가
(B) 작가
(C) 기업 창립자
(D) 비서

정답 (B)

해설 첫 번째 문단 첫 문장에서 언급된 베스트셀러와 그 다음 문장에서 회사가 대표하는 모든 작가들 중 가장 성공적인 사람(he remains the most successful of all the writers we represent)이라는 부분을 통해 작가임을 유추할 수 있으므로 (B)가 정답이다.

어휘 critic 평론가 author 작가 founder 설립자, 창립자

26. 윈슬로우 씨는 카푸토 씨에게 무엇을 하기를 요구하는가?
(A) 장소를 예약할 것
(B) 음식을 주문할 것
(C) 고객에게 연락할 것
(D) 선물을 구매할 것

정답 (D)

해설 첫 번째 문단 마지막 문장에서 키스 씨에게 이를 처리해주면 좋겠다는(I'd like you to take care of this for me) 부분에서 this가 지칭하는 것을 파악해야 한다. 그 앞 문장에서 선물 목록과 가격대, 물품을 구매할 수 있는 장소를 언급하고 있어 상대방에게 선물을 구매해 줄 것을 요청하고 있는 것을 알 수 있으므로 (D)가 정답이다.

어휘 reserve ~을 예약하다 venue 장소 contact ~에게 연락하다 purchase ~을 구매하다

27-29.

> **27 28** 10월 17일
>
> 와이소 씨께,
>
> 우리 몬트로얄 배드민턴 동호회가 계속 빠르게 규모가 확장되면서, 행정 및 운영 업무의 양이 점점 늘어나고 있습니다. — [1] —. **27** 11월에, 우리는 운영팀의 구조를 바꾸고 동호회 회원들 중 한 분께 동호회 부총무라는 새롭게 만든 직책을 배정할 계획입니다. 저는 **28** 지난달에 귀하께서 우리 배드민턴 강사를 대신하시겠다고 하셨던 의지에 매우 깊은 인상을 받았습니다. 초보자 그룹 구성원들께서 저에게 귀하의 지도가 매우 유익하다고 생각하셨다는 사실을 알려 주셨습니다. — [2] —. 이러한 태도는 귀하께서 우리 동호회 위원회의 공식적인 역할에 대해 이상적인 후보자임을 나타내는 것이므로, 귀하께 동호회 부총무 직책을 제안해 드리고자 합니다.
>
> — [3] —. **29** 이는 신중함을 필요로 하는 사안이므로, 제가 서면으로 귀하의 공식 결정을 전달 받을 때까지 동호회의 다른 회원들께 이야기하시지 않도록 요청 드립니다. — [4] —.
>
> 안녕히 계십시오.
>
> 폴 서루
> 동호회 총무, 몬트로얄 배드민턴 동호회

어휘 expand (규모, 사업 등이) 확장되다, 확대되다 increasing 점점 더 많은, 늘어나는 administrative 행정의 management 운영(진), 관리 assign A to B A에게 B를 배정하다, A에게 B를 맡기다 be impressed with ~에 깊은 인상을 받다 willingness to do ~하려는 의지 cover for ~을 대신하다 inform A that A에게 ~라고 알리다 find A B A를 B하다고 생각하다 instruction 지도, 가르침, 설명 beneficial 유익한 attitude 태도, 마음가짐 ideal 이상적인 candidate 후보자, 지원자 official 공식적인, 정식의(= formal) offer A B A에게 B를 제안하다, A에게 B를 제공하다 matter 사안, 문제 require ~을 필요

로 하다 **discretion** 신중함 **request that** ~하도록 요청하다 **decision** 결정 **in writing** 서면으로

27. 다음 달에 배드민턴 동호회에 무슨 일이 있을 것인가?
(A) 동호회에서 신규 회원을 끌어들이려 시도할 것이다.
(B) 새 배드민턴 강사가 고용될 것이다.
(C) 동호회 부총무가 물러날 것이다.
(D) 동호회 운영진이 개편될 것이다.

정답 (D)

해설 지문 상단에 작성 날짜가 October 17로 쓰여 있어 질문에서 말하는 다음 달은 11월임을 알 수 있다. 첫 단락 초반부에 11월에 운영팀의 구조를 바꾼다고(In November, we plan to change the structure of our management team) 언급하고 있는데, 이는 운영진을 개편한다는 뜻이므로 (D)가 정답이다.

어휘 **attempt to do** ~하려 시도하다 **attract** ~을 끌어들이다 **resign** 물러나다, 사임하다 **restructuring** 개편, 구조 조정

28. 와이소 씨와 관련해 유추할 수 있는 것은 무엇인가?
(A) 10월에 동호회 회원 자격을 갱신했다.
(B) 동호회의 재무와 직접적으로 관련되어 있다.
(C) 9월에 배드민턴 수업을 가르쳤다.
(D) 서루 씨와 갖는 면접 자리에 참석했다.

정답 (C)

해설 와이소 씨의 이름은 지문 상단에 수신인으로 표기된 부분에서 찾아볼 수 있으며, 첫 단락 중반부에 와이소 씨를 your로 지칭해 상대방이 지난달에 배드민턴 강사의 역할을 대신한 일이(your willingness to cover for our badminton instructor last month) 언급되어 있다. 지문 상단의 작성 날짜가 October 17로 쓰여 있어 지난달에 해당되는 9월에 대신 배드민턴을 가르쳤다는 사실을 알 수 있으므로 (C)가 정답이다.

어휘 **renew** ~을 갱신하다 **be involved with** ~와 관련되다 **finance** 재무, 재정

29. [1], [2], [3], [4]로 표기된 위치들 중에서, 다음 문장이 들어가기에 가장 적절한 곳은 어디인가?

"우리는 이 직책을 광고하지 않을 계획이며, 내부에서 누군가를 선임하고자 합니다."

(A) [1]
(B) [2]
(C) [3]
(D) [4]

정답 (C)

해설 제시된 문장은 앞서 언급된 특정 직책을 this position으로 지칭해 그 직책을 광고하지 않고 내부에서 자체적으로 선임하려 한다는 의미를 나타낸다. 따라서, 해당 직책인 the position of Assistant Club Secretary를 제안하는 문장 및 그러한 선임 계획을 this로 지칭해 주의 사항을 알리는 문장 사이에 위치한

[3]에 들어가 부총무 직책에 대한 선임 방식을 언급하는 흐름이 되어야 자연스러우므로 (C)가 정답이다.

어휘 **would rather do** ~하고자 하다, ~하고 싶다 **appoint** ~을 선임하다, ~을 임명하다 **internally** 내부적으로

30-32.

코어 젠 요가
1월 1일부터 시작하는 신규 회원 등록서

매달, 코어 젠 요가에서는 신규 회원을 모집합니다! 저희의 요가 수업은 당신의 신체와 정신을 강화시키고 활성화시키는 데 도움이 됩니다. **30** 여러분의 나이, 힘, 혹은 유연성과 상관없이, 코어 젠 요가에는 여러분의 필요와 능력에 완벽하게 맞는 요가 수업이 있습니다. 초급반은 매주 월, 화, 목, 토요일에 모이며, **31** 중급반은 매주 화, 수, 일요일에 만납니다. 상급반 강좌는 금요일과 토요일마다 열립니다.

이 양식을 작성 완료하시고 코어 젠 요가 직원에게 주세요.

이름: 베키 매스터즈
31 강좌: 중급 레벨
주소: 매사추세츠 02115, 보스턴, 페리스 스트리트 398번지
이메일: bmasters@usmail.com

귀하가 선호하는 멤버십 패키지를 명시해 주시기 바랍니다.
____ 1월 한정(1개월 체험 패키지) - 89달러
____ 1월 1일부터 2월 28일까지 - 169달러
32 1월 1일부터 3월 31일까지 - 239달러
 X 1월 1일부터 4월 30일까지 - 289달러

어휘 **registration** 등록, 가입 **form** 양식, 서류 **strengthen** ~을 강화하다, 튼튼하게 하다 **stimulate** ~을 활성화시키다 **flexible** 유연한 **match** ~에 맞다, 어울리다 **needs** 필요(로 하는 것) **capability** 능력 **intermediate** 중급의 **advanced** 고급의, 상급의 **specify** ~을 명시하다 **trial** (무료)체험

30. 코어 젠 요가와 관련해 암시된 것은?
(A) 보스턴에 여러 지점이 있다.
(B) 주로 상급 요가를 가르친다.
(C) 현재 새로운 직원을 채용하고 있다.
(D) 모든 연령대의 회원을 환영한다.

정답 (D)

해설 지문 초반부에 코어 젠 요가는 나이, 힘, 유연성에 상관없이 회원을 모집하고 있다는 것을(No matter how old you are, how strong you are, or how flexible you are, Core Zen Yoga has a yoga class) 알 수 있다. 따라서 (D)가 정답이다.

어휘 **location** 지점, 지사 **primarily** 주로 **currently** 현재 **hire** ~을 고용하다

31. 매스터즈 씨는 수업에 얼마나 자주 참석할 것으로 보이는가?

    (A) 일주일에 한 번
    (B) 일주일에 두 번
    (C) 일주일에 세 번
    (D) 일주일에 네 번

정답 (C)

해설 매스터즈 씨가 작성한 지문 중반부 강좌 항목에 중급반이라고 (Class: Intermediate Level) 적혀 있는데, 지문 초반부에 중급반 수업은 매주 화요일, 수요일, 일요일에 모인다고 쓰여있으므로(Our Intermediate class meets every Tuesday, Wednesday, and Sunday) 일주일에 세 번 참석할 것임을 알 수 있다. 따라서 (C)가 정답이다.

어휘 **How often ~?** 얼마나 자주 ~? **attend** ~에 참석하다

32. 3개월 멤버십의 비용은 얼마인가?

    (A) 89달러
    (B) 169달러
    (C) 239달러
    (D) 289달러

정답 (C)

해설 지문 후반부에 1월 1일부터 3월 31일까지 3개월 기간의 가격은 239달러로(January 1 to March 31 - $239) 나타나 있으므로 (C)가 정답이다.

어휘 **cost** ~의 비용이 들다

33-36.

> **[오후 3:14] 보리스 랜싱**
> 33 우리 회사의 연말 저녁 만찬 행사 준비는 어떻게 되어가고 있나요? 모든 이사님들께서 참석하실 것이기 때문에, 어딘가 특별한 곳을 예약해야 합니다.
>
> **[오후 3:16] 미란다 소여**
> 음, 랜싱 씨, 말씀 드리기 죄송하지만 여전히 예약을 하지 못했습니다.
>
> **[오후 3:17] 올리비아 데로시**
> 네, 34 저희가 딜린저스 비스트로에 공간을 하나 예약할 수 있기를 바랐지만, 예약이 꽉 찬 것으로 드러났습니다.
>
> **[오후 3:18] 보리스 랜싱**
> 그런 일이 일반적이죠.
>
> **[오후 3:21] 미란다 소여**
> 그리고 35 그곳이 우리 전 직원에게 적합할 정도로 충분히 넓은 개별 공간이 있는 유일한 곳일지도 모릅니다.
>
> **[오후 3:22] 올리비아 데로시**
> 아... 제가 최근에 온라인에서 4번가에 새로 생긴 엄청 큰 레스토랑에 대한 광고를 봤어요. 36 아마 제가 온라인에서 그곳 메뉴를 출력할 수 있을 겁니다.

> **[오후 3:23] 보리스 랜싱**
> 36 좋은 생각입니다, 올리비아 씨. 일단 그 일을 완료하시는 대로, 저희에게 알려 주세요. 우리가 함께 모여서 그곳 음식을 확인해 볼 수 있을 거예요.
>
> **[오후 3:24] 미란다 소여**
> 저는 좋습니다. 준비되시면 메시지 보내 주세요, 올리비아 씨.

어휘 **How is A coming along?** A는 어떻게 되어가고 있나요? **arrangement** 준비, 조치 **year-end** 연말의 **board member** 이사, 임원 **attend** ~에 참석하다 **book** ~을 예약하다 **make a reservation** 예약하다 **it turns out that** ~인 것으로 드러나다 **fully** 완전히, 전적으로, 모두 **typical** 일반적인, 전형적인 **fit** (크기 등이) ~에 적합하다, ~에 알맞다 **advertisement** 광고 **recently** 최근에 **huge** (크기, 정도 등이) 엄청난 **once** 일단 ~하는 대로, ~하자마자 **let A know** A에게 알리다 **get together** 함께 모이다

33. 메시지 작성자들이 주로 무엇을 이야기하고 있는가?

    (A) 이사회 회의
    (B) 레스토랑 확장 공사
    (C) 직원 회식
    (D) 시상식

정답 (C)

해설 오후 3시 14분에 랜싱 씨가 보낸 첫 번째 메시지에 회사의 연말 저녁 만찬 행사 준비가 어떻게 되어가고 있는지(How are the arrangements coming along for our firm's year-end dinner?) 물은 뒤로, 그 준비 상황과 관련해 이야기하고 있으므로 (C)가 정답이다.

어휘 **board** 이사회 **expansion** 확장, 확대

34. 오후 3시 18분에, 랜싱 씨가 "That's typical"이라고 쓸 때 무엇을 암시하는가?

    (A) 레스토랑 메뉴에 실망한 상태이다.
    (B) 딜린저스 비스트로가 인기 있다는 것을 알고 있다.
    (C) 데로시 씨의 제안에 동의하지 않는다.
    (D) 딜린저스 비스트로에서 자주 식사한다.

정답 (B)

해설 3시 17분에 데로시 씨가 딜린저스 비스트로에 공간을 하나 예약할 수 있기를 바랐지만 예약이 꽉 찬 상태라고 알린 것에 대해 랜싱 씨가 '그런 일이 일반적이다'라고 반응하는 흐름이다. 이는 딜린저스 비스트로가 원래 인기가 많아서 예약이 꽉 차는 일이 흔하다는 사실을 알고 있다는 뜻이므로 (B)가 정답이다.

어휘 **be disappointed with** ~에 실망하다 **disagree with** ~에 동의하지 않다 **suggestion** 제안, 의견 **dine** 식사하다

35. 딜린저스 비스트로와 관련해 암시된 것은 무엇인가?

    (A) 여러 곳에 지점을 운영하고 있다.
    (B) 최근에 개조 공사를 거쳤다.

(C) 대규모 단체 손님을 수용할 수 있다.

(D) 사전 예약을 필요로 하지 않는다.

정답 (C)

해설 3시 21분 메시지에 소여 씨가 딜린저스 비스트로를 it으로 지칭해 그곳이 전 직원에게 적합할 정도로 충분히 넓은 개별 공간이 있는 유일한 곳일 것이라고(it might be the only place that has a private room large enough to fit all our employees) 언급하는 말이 있다. 이는 한 회사의 전 직원을 수용할 수 있을 정도로 크다는 뜻이므로 수용 규모와 관련된 (C)가 정답이다.

어휘 operate ~을 운영하다, ~을 가동하다 branch 지점, 지사 location 장소, 지점, 위치 undergo ~을 거치다, ~을 겪다 renovation 개조, 보수 accommodate ~을 수용하다 require ~을 필요로 하다 advance 사전의, 미리 하는

36. 데로시 씨가 곧이어 무엇을 할 것 같은가?

(A) 레스토랑을 방문하는 일

(B) 일부 음식을 주문하는 일

(C) 지도를 출력하는 일

(D) 웹 사이트를 확인하는 일

정답 (D)

해설 데로시 씨가 3시 22분 메시지에 온라인에서 새 레스토랑의 메뉴를 출력할 수 있다고(Maybe I can print out its menu online) 알리자, 곧이어 랜싱 씨가 좋은 생각이라는 말로 동의하면서 그 일을 완료하는 대로 알려 달라고(Once you've done that, let us know) 언급하고 있다. 따라서, 데로시 씨가 온라인에서 메뉴를 출력하기 위해 웹 사이트를 확인할 것으로 생각할 수 있으므로 (D)가 정답이다.

어휘 order ~을 주문하다 print out ~을 출력하다

37-40.

> **블루 웨이브 주식회사**
> **새로운 대표이사를 임명하다**
>
> 토론토, 1월 21일 – 어제 블루 웨이브 주식회사는 셀리나 라일리 씨가 새로운 대표이사로 임명될 것임을 발표하였다. **37** 라일리 씨는 35년 이상의 상품 개발 경력을 가지고 있고, 블루 웨이브의 많은 **38** 스마트폰과 태블릿 컴퓨터에 대해 생각해 낸 **37** 독특하고 창의적인 디자인으로 크게 업적을 인정 받았다. **38** 그녀의 노력과 공헌은 블루 웨이브가 세계에서 가장 유명하고 성공적인 전자기기 생산회사 중의 하나가 될 수 있게 하였다.
>
> 라일리 씨는 심지어 블루 웨이브에 합류하기 전에 이미 길고 성공적인 경력을 가지고 있었다. **39** 졸업 후, 그녀는 4년간 모니코 코퍼레이션의 상품 개발 부서에 근무하였으며 이후 7년간 피사로 엔터프라이즈에서 근무하였다. **40** 피사로 엔터프라이즈에서 그녀는 빠르게 부서의 차장 직책으로 고속 승진하였으며 그 이후에 부장으로 임명되었다. 출산으로 인해 자리에서 물러난 후 나중에 브레이브테크 주식회사에 입사하여 잠시 디자인 전문가와 자문 위원으로 근무하였고, 결국 블루 웨이브 주식회사에 채용되었다.

어휘 be appointed as ~로 임명되다 make an announcement 발표하다 chief executive officer(CEO) 대표이사, 최고 경영자 receive (much) recognition for ~로 (크게) 업적을 인정받다 come up with ~을 생각해 내다 effort 노력 contribution 공헌 enable A to do A가 ~하는 것을 가능하게 하다 prominent 유명한 career 직장 경력 corporation 대기업, 법인 enterprise 기업, 회사 rapidly 빠르게 resign 사임하다 serve 근무하다 briefly 잠시 expert 전문가 eventually 결국

37. 라일리 씨는 무엇으로 알려져 있는가?

(A) 고객 서비스에 대한 헌신

(B) 광고 분야에서의 경력

(C) 직원 관리 기술

(D) 혁신적인 제품 디자인

정답 (D)

해설 첫 번째 문단 두 번째 문장부터 라일리 씨에 대한 정보가 언급되어 있는데 독특하고 창의적인 디자인 개발로 인정을 받았다는 말이(Ms. Riley has over 35 years of experience in product development and has received much recognition for the unique and creative designs) 쓰여 있으므로 (D)가 정답이다.

어휘 commitment 헌신 experience 경력, 경험 skill 능력, 기술 manage ~을 관리하다 innovative 혁신적인

38. 블루 웨이브 주식회사는 어떠한 유형의 회사인가?

(A) 통신회사

(B) 금융 컨설팅 회사

(C) 웹 디자인 회사

(D) 전자기기 제조 회사

정답 (D)

해설 첫 번째 문단 중반부에 라일리 씨의 업적에 대해 설명을 하면서 회사에서 스마트폰과 태블릿 컴퓨터를 개발했다고(she has come up with for many of Blue Wave's smart phones and tablet computers) 소개하고 있고, 그 다음 문장에서도 가장 유명하고 성공적인 전자기기 생산 회사 중 하나가 되었다는(to become one of the most prominent and successful producers of electronic devices in the world) 사실을 밝히고 있으므로 (D)가 정답이다.

어휘 telecommunication (이동) 통신 manufacturer 제조회사, 제조업체

39. 라일리 씨가 직장 경력을 시작한 곳은 어느 회사인가?

(A) 블루 웨이브 주식회사

(B) 모니코 코퍼레이션

(C) 피사로 엔터프라이즈

(D) 브레이브테크 주식회사

정답 (B)

두 번째 문단에 라일리 씨가 졸업 후 제일 먼저 모니코 코퍼레이션의 상품 개발 부서에서 4년간 근무했다는(After graduating, she spent four years in the product development department at Moniko Corporation) 내용이 나와 있으므로 (B)가 정답이다.

40. 라일리 씨가 피사로 사에 있을 때 무슨 일이 있었는가?

    (A) 매출을 급속히 증가시키는 데 도움이 되었다.
    (B) 브레이브테크 주식회사와 협력했다.
    (C) 적어도 2번의 승진을 했다.
    (D) 몇몇의 부서장들을 채용했다.

정답 (C)

해설 두 번째 문단 중반부에서 라일리 씨가 피사로 사에서 근무할 동안 부서의 차장으로 승진되었고, 그 이후 부장으로 임명되었다는(During her time at Pizarro, she rapidly rose to the position of assistant department manager and was later appointed as department manager) 말이 있는데, 이는 최소한 두 번의 승진을 했음을 알 수 있다. 따라서 (C)가 정답이다.

어휘 **increase** ~을 증가시키다 **collaborate** 협력하다 **at least** 최소한, 적어도 **promotion** 승진 **recruit** ~을 모집하다, 채용하다

41-45.

제7회 연례 윌리엄스버그 문학 축제에서 열리는
단편 소설 콘테스트
창작가 협회(CWA) 후원

창작가 협회는 현재 모든 지역 작가들에게 제7회 연례 윌리엄스 버그 문학 축제의 일부 행사로 진행되는 단편 소설 콘테스트에 참가하도록 지원하시기를 요청 드리고 있습니다. **41** 실제 이 축제 자체의 목적이기도 한 이 콘테스트의 목적은 지역의 재능 있는 문학 작가를 집중 조명하고, 장차 작가가 되려는 분들에게 노출 및 지원을 제공해 드리는 것입니다. 올해 열리는 축제의 모든 행사는 7월 27일부터 8월 6일까지 윌리엄스버그 지역 문화 센터와 시 공공 도서관에서 개최됩니다. **42(D)** **43** 최종 후보에 오른 단편 소설 참가작에서 발췌한 내용이 후자의 행사장에서 8월 3일과 4일에 낭송되며, 그 소설들은 모든 사람이 읽을 수 있도록 전체 내용이 온라인에 실릴 것입니다.

45 오직 다른 곳에서 출판되지 않았던 단편 소설만 접수될 것입니다. **42(C)** 소설 작품은 www.cwa.org/festival/contest에서 업로드되거나, 이메일 첨부 문서로 writingcontest@cwa.org로 보내져야 합니다. 서류는 늦어도 반드시 7월 20일까지 접수되어야 합니다. 그 후 심사위원단이 최종 후보를 결정할 것이며, **42(B)** 통과하신 참가자들께 7월 26일까지 통지서가 발송될 것입니다. 저희 CWA가 단편 소설 낭송 행사를 위한 무대가 세워지도록 준비할 것입니다. 15세에서 21세 그룹에서 선정된 수상자들은 위에 말씀 드린 이틀 중 첫 번째 날에 발췌 내용을 낭송하게 되며, **43** 21세 초과 연령 부문에서 수상하신 분들은 다음 날 낭송하실 것입니다.

이번 콘테스트에 관한 모든 상세 정보 및 가이드라인을 보시려면, 창작가 협회 웹 사이트를 방문하시기 바랍니다. 또는, 심사위원장이신 헨더슨 씨께 555-8334번으로 직접 연락하셔도 됩니다.

어휘 **short story** 단편 소설 **call on A to do** A에게 ~하도록 요청하다 **run** 진행되다, 운영되다 **as part of** ~의 일부분으로, ~의 일환으로 **aim** 목적 **highlight** ~을 집중 조명하다 **talent** 재능 있는 사람 **exposure** 노출 **aspiring** 장차 ~가 되려는 **excerpt** 발췌 내용 **shortlist** v. ~을 최종 후보에 올리다 n. 최종 후보 명단 **entry** 참가작, 출품작 **the latter** (앞서 언급된 둘 중) 후자의 **in one's entirety** 전체로 **elsewhere** 다른 곳에서 **accept** ~을 받아들이다 **attachment** 첨부(된 것) **at the latest** 늦어도 **notification** 통지(서) **arrange for A to do** A가 ~하도록 준비하다, 조치하다 **aforementioned** 위에서 언급한 **alternatively** 또는, 그렇지 않으면

수신: 창작가 협회 <members@cwa.org>
발신: 바비 쉐이 <bshaye@culturex.com>
날짜: 7월 26일
제목: 단편 소설 낭송

CWA 회원 여러분,

45 올해의 글쓰기 콘테스트에서 결선 진출 작품들 중의 하나로 제 작품이 최종 후보에 오르도록 선택해 주셔서 감사합니다. 사실, 이번이 누군가에 의해 어떤 제 작품이든 읽히는 것이 처음이기 때문에, 저는 제 소설 <우리 집에서>를 제출하는 게 조금 긴장되었습니다. **43** 제가 거의 10년 전에 대학교를 졸업하고 윌리엄스버그로 이사한 후에 이 소설에 대한 아이디어를 처음 적어 놓기 시작했지만, 올해 초가 되어서야 다시 그 작업을 진행해 끝마치도록 영감을 얻었습니다. **44** 수년 동안 광고계에서 일한 후에, 저는 이제 인정 받는 작가가 되는 것에 눈을 돌리기로 결정했습니다. 제가 열정을 지니고 있는 뭔가를 하면서 살아가고 싶은 생각이 큽니다. 제가 낭송을 위해 도착할 때 여러분 중 몇몇 분을 만나 뵙기를 고대하고 있습니다. 이 멋진 기회에 대해 다시 한번 감사 드립니다.

안녕히 계십시오.

바비 쉐이

어휘 **finalist** 결선 진출 작품, 결선 진출자 **not until A that B** A가 되어서야 B하다 **inspired** 영감을 얻은 **finish A off** A를 끝마치다 **turn one's attention towards** ~로 눈을 돌리다, 관심을 돌리다 **established** 인정 받는, 자리 잡은 **would much rather do** ~하고 싶은 마음이 크다 **make a living** 살아가다, 생계를 꾸리다 **passion** 열정

41. 윌리엄스버그 문학 축제에 관해 명시된 것은 무엇인가?

    (A) 전체적으로 공공 도서관에서 개최될 것이다.
    (B) 선도적인 출판사에 의해 후원 받는다.
    (C) 유명 작가들의 작품을 집중 조명한다.
    (D) 지역의 재능 있는 사람들을 기리기 위한 것이다.

정답 (D)

해설 첫 지문 첫 단락에 지역의 재능 있는 문학 작가를 집중 조명하고 장차 작가가 되려는 사람들에게 노출 및 지원을 제공해 주는 것이라고(The aim of the contest, and indeed that of the festival itself, is to highlight local literary talent and provide exposure and support to these aspiring writers) 그 목적을 언급하고 있으므로 (D)가 정답이다.

어휘 **entirely** 전체적으로, 전적으로 **renowned** 유명한 **seek to do** ~하기를 추구하다

---

42. 공지에서 언급되지 않은 정보는 무엇인가?
(A) CWA 심사위원들의 저작 관련 자격
(B) 최종 후보에 오른 작가들이 연락 받는 날짜
(C) 심사위원단의 심사를 위해 작품을 제출하는 방법
(D) 최종 후보에 오른 단편 소설 낭독 일정

정답 (A)

해설 첫 지문 첫 단락 마지막 부분에 최종 후보에 오른 단편 소설 참가작에서 발췌한 내용이 8월 3일과 4일에 낭송된다는(will be read in the latter venue on August 3 and August 4) 부분에서 (D)를, 두 번째 단락 초반부에 소설 작품이 특정 홈페이지에 업로드되거나 이메일로 보내져야(Stories should either be uploaded ~ or sent as an e-mail attachment to writingcontest@cwa.org) 한다는 부분에서 (C)를, 그리고 통과한 지원자들에게 7월 26일까지 통지서가 발송될 것이라는(notifications will be sent out to successful participants by July 2) 부분에서 (B)를 확인할 수 있다. 하지만 심사위원들의 자격과 관련된 정보는 제시되어 있지 않으므로 (A)가 정답이다.

이휘 **credentials** 자격(증) **consideration** 심사, 고려

---

43. 쉐이 씨는 언제 공공 도서관에 도착할 것 같은가?
(A) 7월 27일
(B) 8월 3일
(C) 8월 4일
(D) 8월 6일

정답 (C)

해설 첫 지문 첫 단락과 세 번째 단락에, 8월 3일과 4일이 낭송 날짜라는(will be read in the latter venue on August 3 and August 4) 점과 21세 초과 연령 부문 수상자는 두 번째 날에 낭송한다는 점이(while those in the 21-and-Over category will read on the following day) 쓰여 있다. 그리고 두 번째 지문 중반부에 쉐이 씨가 10년 전에 대학을 졸업한 사실이(after graduating from university and moving to Williamsburg almost a decade ago) 언급되어 있어 21세 초과 연령 부문에 해당된다는 것을 알 수 있으므로 8월 4일에 낭송한다는 점도 알 수 있다. 따라서 (C)가 정답이다.

---

44. 쉐이 씨에 관해 암시된 것은 무엇인가?
(A) 헨더슨 씨를 만난 적이 있다.
(B) 콘테스트 가이드라인에 대해 확실히 알지 못했다.
(C) 새로운 경력을 추구할 계획이다.
(D) 윌리엄스버그에서 태어났다.

정답 (C)

해설 두 번째 지문 후반부에 수년 동안 광고계에서 일한 끝에 인정 받는 작가가 되는 것에 눈을 돌리기로 결정했다는(After working in advertising for several years, I have now decided to turn my attention towards becoming an established author) 말이 있는데, 이는 새로운 경력을 추구하는 것을 뜻하므로 (C)가 정답이다.

어휘 **intend to do** ~할 계획이다, 작정이다 **pursue** ~을 추구하다

---

45. 쉐이 씨가 제출한 작품에 대해 사실인 것은 무엇인가?
(A) 올해 초에 처음 시작되었다.
(B) 일반 대중에 의해 한 번도 읽힌 적이 없다.
(C) 지역 내에서 발생된 사건들에 관한 것이다.
(D) 대학 잡지에 실렸다.

정답 (B)

해설 두 번째 지문 시작 부분에 올해의 글쓰기 콘테스트에서 결선 진출 작품들 중의 하나로 자신의 작품이 최종 후보에 오르도록 선택된(Thank you for choosing to shortlist my work as one of the finalists) 사실이 쓰여 있고, 첫 지문 두 번째 단락에 참가작이 다른 곳에서 출판되지 않은 것이어야 한다고(Only short stories that have not been published elsewhere will be accepted) 알리고 있다. 따라서 쉐이 씨의 작품은 한 번도 출판되어 읽힌 적이 없다는 것을 알 수 있으므로 (B)가 정답이다.

어휘 **the general public** 일반 대중

46-50.

아르젠토 컴퓨터 용품 - 거래 내역서 #13442		
46(A) 주문 날짜: 10월 13일	배송 날짜: 10월 15일	예상 도착 날짜: 10월 18일

46(C) 비용 청구 주소: 클라이브 오웬 씨 회사 본사 펄사 텔레콤 주식회사 스미스 스트리트 4434번지 볼티모어, MD 21255	배송 주소: 매기 스폴딩 씨 고객 서비스 콜 센터 펄사 텔레콤 주식회사 엘링턴 드라이브 6698번지 컬럼비아, MD 21044

제품명	제품 코드	제품 가격	구매 수량	소계
46(D) 애스트라 무선 키보드	#A875	$15.99	18	$287.82
디트리히 사무용 회전 의자	#A349	$34.95	10	$349.50
46(D) 호라이즌 20인치 모니터	#B238	$69.99	8	$559.92
46(D) 47 소니카 헤드폰(+마이크)	#A337	47 $14.95	14	$209.30
46(D) 50 애스트라 유선 마우스	50 #B613	$13.99	10	$139.90
			배송 요금	$75.00
			총계	$1621.44

어휘 invoice 거래 내역서 order ~을 주문하다 shipping 배송
expected 예상되는 arrival 도착 headquarters 본사
quantity 수량 sub-total 소계의 swivel chair 회전 의
자 corded 유선의, 줄이 달린

수신: 클라이브 오웬 <cliveowen@pulsartelecom.com>
발신: 조슈아 랜덜 <jrandall@argentocomp.com>
제목: 제품 주문 #13442
날짜: 10월 18일

오웬 씨께,

유감스럽게도, 귀하께서 주문하신 소니카 헤드폰이 현재 품절된 상
태이며, 저희가 다음 달 초나 되어야 새 배송 물품을 받을 것으로
48 예상하고 있습니다. 이 문제와 관련해 전화 드리려고 했으나, 실
수로 부정확한 전화 번호를 제공해 주신 것 같습니다. 47 대신 컴퓨
터테크 Z9 헤드폰 14세트를 포함하도록 귀하의 주문을 수정해 드렸
습니다. 이 헤드폰은 일반적으로 세트당 16.95달러에 소매 판매
됩니다. 어떤 제품이든 반품하시기를 바라시는 경우, 저에게 알려
주십시오.

안녕히 계십시오.

조슈아 랜덜

어휘 unfortunately 유감스럽게도, 안타깝게도 at this time
현재, 지금 not A until B B나 되어야 A하다 expect
~을 예상하다, ~을 기대하다 shipment 배송(품)
attempt to do ~하려 시도하다 regarding ~와 관련해
seem to have p.p. ~했던 것 같다 mistakenly 실수로
amend ~을 수정하다, ~을 변경하다 include ~을 포함하

다 instead 대신 normally 일반적으로, 보통 retail 소매
판매되다 return ~을 반품하다, ~을 반납하다

수신: 조슈아 랜덜 <jrandall@argentocomp.com>
발신: 클라이브 오웬 <cliveowen@pulsartelecom.com>
제목: 회신: 제품 주문 #13442
날짜: 10월 18일

랜덜 씨께,

빠른 배송을 비롯해 고품질의 컴퓨터 모니터와 사무용 의자에 대
해 감사 드립니다. 하지만, 49 품절된 모델에 대한 대체품으로서
제공해 주신 헤드폰이 만족스럽지 않습니다. 실제로 마이크를 포
함하고 있지 않은데, 이는 저희 콜 센터 내의 전화 상담원들에게 필
수적입니다. 이 제품들을 귀하께 반품해 드리고 원래의 모델이 재
고로 다시 들어오기를 기다리겠습니다. 그리고, 50 제가 처음에
애스트라 제품을 선택했을 때 실수를 했습니다. 그 제조사의 마우
스에 대해 무선 버전을 주문했어야 했습니다. 따라서, 즉시 유선 제
품을 반품하고 무선 모델에 필요한 추가 비용을 지불하겠습니다.

안녕히 계십시오.

클라이브 오웬
총무부장
펄사 텔레콤 주식회사 본사

어휘 be satisfied with ~에 만족하다 offer ~을 제공하다
replacement 대체(품), 교체(품) out-of-stock 품절
된 actually 실제로, 사실 vital 필수적인 telephone
operator 전화 상담원 come back in stock 다시 재고
로 들어오다 make a mistake 실수하다 originally 원래,
애초에 select ~을 선택하다 should have p.p. ~했어
야 했다 therefore 따라서, 그러므로 immediately 즉시
required 필요한, 필수의

46. 펄사 텔레콤 주식회사가 주문한 사항과 관련해 사실이 아닌 것
은 무엇인가?

(A) 10월 13일에 처음 주문이 이뤄졌다.
(B) 볼티모어에 있는 지점으로 배송될 것이다.
(C) 클라이브 오웬 씨가 비용을 지불했다.
(D) 다양한 전자 제품을 포함한다.

정답 (B)

해설 첫 지문 상단의 주문 날짜: 10월 13일(Ordered on: October
13) 부분에서 (A)를, 바로 아래에 표기된 비용 청구 주소: 클라
이브 오웬 씨(BILL TO: Mr. Clive Owen) 부분에서 (C)를, 그
리고 아래의 도표에서 제품명 항목에 제시된 키보드, 모니터, 헤
드폰, 마우스(Keyboard, Monitor, Headphones, Mouse)
에서 다양한 전자 제품을 포함한다고 언급한 (D)를 확인할 수
있다. 하지만 오른쪽 상단에 배송 주소가 컬럼비아(Columbia)
로 쓰여 있으므로 (B)가 정답이다.

어휘 initially 처음에 place v. (주문 등) ~을 하다 location 지
점, 위치 electronic goods 전자 제품

47. 랜덜 씨가 어떤 조치를 취했는가?

(A) 특정 제품의 명시된 수량을 늘렸다.
(B) 배송 요금이 없어지도록 조치했다.
(C) 오웬 씨에게 거래 내역서 복사본을 보냈다.
(D) 한 제품을 더 비싼 것으로 대신했다.

정답 (D)

해설 두 번째 지문 중반부에 컴퓨테크 Z9 헤드폰 14세트를 대신 포함하도록 주문을 수정한 사실과 함께 세트당 16.95달러에 소매 판매된다고(I amended your order to include 14 sets of Computek Z9 headphones instead. These headphones normally retail at $16.95 per set) 알리고 있다. 첫 번째 지문 하단의 도표에서 네 번째 항목인 소니카 헤드폰(Sonica Headphones)의 제품 가격이 $14.95로 표기되어 있어 더 비싼 제품으로 대체했다는 사실을 알 수 있으므로 (D)가 정답이다.

어휘 **specified** 명시된 **particular** 특정한, 특별한 **arrange for A to do** A가 ~하도록 조치하다 **charge** 청구 요금 **duplicate** 복사본의 **substitute A with B** A를 B로 대신하다

48. 첫 번째 이메일에서, 첫 번째 단락, 두 번째 줄의 단어 "expecting"과 의미가 가장 가까운 것은 무엇인가?

(A) 준비하는
(B) 받는
(C) 재고로 갖추는
(D) 예상하는

정답 (D)

해설 해당 문장에서 동사 are expecting 뒤에 새로운 배송을 뜻하는 new shipment와 시점을 나타내는 early next month가 쓰여 있다. 따라서, 새로운 배송 물품이 들어올 것으로 예상하는 시점을 말하고 있다는 것을 알 수 있으므로 '예상하다, 기대하다' 등을 뜻하는 동사 anticipate의 현재분사 (D) anticipating이 정답이다.

49. 오웬 씨는 자신이 받은 대체 제품과 관련해 무슨 말을 하는가?

(A) 배송 중에 손상되었다.
(B) 대단히 잘 디자인되어 있다.
(C) 필요로 하는 점을 충족하지 못한다.
(D) 예상보다 더 늦게 배송되었다.

정답 (C)

해설 세 번째 지문 초반부에 대체 제품으로 보내준 것이 만족스럽지 못하다는 말과 함께 필수 요소인 마이크를 포함하고 있지 않다고(I am not satisfied with the headphones you offered ~ They do not actually include a microphone, which is vital for the telephone operators in our call center) 알리고 있다. 이는 오웬 씨 회사 측에서 필요로 하는 점을 충족하지 못한다는 뜻이므로 (C)가 정답이다.

어휘 **extremely** 대단히, 매우 **meet** (요구, 조건 등) ~을 충족하다 **than expected** 예상보다

50. 오웬 씨가 어느 제품을 실수로 주문했는가?

(A) 제품 #A875
(B) 제품 #A349
(C) 제품 #B238
(D) 제품 #B613

정답 (D)

해설 세 번째 지문 후반부에 주문상의 실수를 언급하면서 무선 버전의 마우스를 주문했어야 했다고(I made a mistake when I originally selected the Astra items. I should have ordered the wireless version of that manufacturer's mouse) 알리고 있다. 첫 번째 지문 하단의 도표에서 마우스 제품의 번호가 마지막 줄에 표기된 #B613이므로 (D)가 정답이다.

어휘 **by mistake** 실수로

DAY 02 LC Half Test

1. (D)	**2.** (B)	**3.** (B)	**4.** (C)	**5.** (B)
6. (A)	**7.** (B)	**8.** (C)	**9.** (A)	**10.** (C)
11. (B)	**12.** (C)	**13.** (B)	**14.** (A)	**15.** (C)
16. (C)	**17.** (B)	**18.** (A)	**19.** (B)	**20.** (A)
21. (C)	**22.** (D)	**23.** (D)	**24.** (D)	**25.** (C)
26. (B)	**27.** (B)	**28.** (C)	**29.** (D)	**30.** (B)
31. (A)	**32.** (C)	**33.** (B)	**34.** (B)	**35.** (C)
36. (C)	**37.** (D)	**38.** (B)	**39.** (D)	**40.** (C)
41. (B)	**42.** (A)	**43.** (D)	**44.** (D)	**45.** (A)
46. (B)	**47.** (D)	**48.** (C)	**49.** (A)	**50.** (D)

Part 1

1. (A) The man is loading some boxes onto a truck.
(B) Some walls are being repainted.
(C) The man is clearing off some tables.
(D) A broom has been propped against a wall.

(A) 남자가 몇몇 상자들을 트럭에 싣는 중이다.
(B) 몇몇 벽들이 다시 페인트칠되는 중이다.
(C) 남자가 몇몇 탁자들을 깨끗이 치우는 중이다.
(D) 빗자루 하나가 벽에 기대어져 있다.

해설 (A) 상자를 트럭에 싣는 동작을 하는 것이 아니므로 오답.
(B) 벽을 페인트칠하는 동작을 하는 것이 아니므로 오답.
(C) 탁자를 치우는 동작을 하는 것이 아니므로 오답.
(D) 빗자루 하나가 벽에 기대어져 있는 모습을 묘사하고 있으므로 정답.

어휘 **load A onto B** A를 B에 싣다 **repaint** ~을 다시 페인트칠하다 **clear off** ~을 깨끗이 치우다 **broom** 빗자루 **be propped against** ~에 기대어져 있다

2. (A) There are chairs next to the couch.
(B) A flower arrangement has been set on the table.
(C) A window is being opened.
(D) Lights have been suspended above a chair.

(A) 소파 옆에 의자들이 있다.
(B) 꽃 장식이 탁자 위에 놓여 있다.
(C) 창문이 열리는 중이다.
(D) 조명들이 의자 위쪽에 매달려 있다.

해설 (A) 사진 속에서 소파(couch)를 찾아볼 수 없으므로 오답.
(B) 꽃 장식이 탁자 중앙에 놓여 있는 모습을 묘사하고 있으므

로 정답.
(C) 창문을 여는 동작을 하는 사람을 찾아볼 수 없으므로 오답.
(D) 의자 위쪽에 매달려 있는 조명(Lights)을 찾아볼 수 없으므로 오답.

어휘 **next to** ~옆에 **couch** 소파 **flower arrangement** 꽃 장식 **set** ~을 놓다, 설치하다 **light** 조명 **suspend** ~을 매달다 **above** (분리된 위치) ~ 위쪽에

Part 2

3. When is the last shipment of books arriving?
(A) I wouldn't recommend driving there.
(B) In about three weeks.
(C) You should book your hotel first.

마지막 도서 배송 물품이 언제 도착하죠?
(A) 그곳에 차를 몰고 가는 건 권하지 않겠어요.
(B) 약 3주 후에요.
(C) 호텔을 먼저 예약하셔야 해요.

해설 When 의문문으로 시점을 묻고 있으므로 대략적인 미래 시점을 말하는 (B)가 정답이다. (A)는 질문에 쓰인 arriving과 발음이 유사한 driving을 이용한 오답이다. (C)는 book의 다른 의미(책, 예약하다)를 이용한 오답으로, 호텔 예약은 질문과 전혀 관련 없는 내용이다.

어휘 **shipment** 배송(품) **recommend -ing** ~하는 것을 권하다 **in 기간** ~ 후에 **about** 약, 대략 **book** v. ~을 예약하다

4. What did Mr. Otto say about your vacation request?
(A) No, two weeks off.
(B) At the hotel.
(C) He didn't approve it.

오토 씨가 당신의 휴가 요청에 대해 뭐라고 얘기하던가요?
(A) 아뇨, 2주간 쉬어요.
(B) 호텔에서요.
(C) 그분께서 승인해 주지 않으셨어요.

해설 휴가 요청에 대해 오토 씨가 한 말이 무엇이었는지 묻는 What 의문문이므로 승인해 주지 않았다고 말한 (C)가 정답이다. 의문사 의문문은 Yes/No 로 대답할 수 없으므로 (A)는 오답이며, (B)는 장소 표현이므로 Where 의문문에 어울리는 응답이다.

어휘 **request** 요청(서) **off** 휴무인 **approve** ~을 승인하다

5. Are there extra plastic bags for my purchases?

(A) Here is your receipt.
(B) Sure, please take this one.
(C) In aisle 6.

제 구입품을 담을 여분의 비닐 봉지가 있나요?
(A) 여기 영수증 있습니다.
(B) 물론이죠, 이걸로 가져 가세요.
(C) 6번 통로에요.

해설 「Are there ~?」 일반 의문문으로 여분의 비닐 봉지가 있는지 확인하고 있으므로 긍정을 나타내는 Sure 및 plastic bag을 대신하는 one과 함께 특정한 것을 가져가도록 권하는 (B)가 정답이다. (A)는 질문에 쓰인 purchases에서 연상 가능한 receipt를 이용해 혼동을 유발하는 오답이다. (C)는 특정 제품을 찾을 수 있는 위치에 해당되는 말이므로 질문의 의도에 맞지 않는 답변이다.

어휘 **extra** 여분의, 별도의 **plastic bag** 비닐 봉지 **purchase** n. 구매(품) **receipt** 영수증 **aisle** 통로

6. Wasn't Betty at the sales conference in Osaka last month?

(A) I didn't see her there.
(B) Sales were down last quarter.
(C) On the second floor.

베티 씨가 지난 달에 오사카에서 열린 영업 컨퍼런스에 참석하지 않았나요?
(A) 거기서 그분을 보지 못했어요.
(B) 매출이 지난 분기에 떨어졌어요.
(C) 2층에요.

해설 베티 씨가 지난 달에 오사가에서 열린 영업 건퍼런스에 침석하지 않았는지 확인하는 부정 의문문에 대해 베티 씨를 her로 지칭해 그곳에서 보지 못한 사실을 말하는 (A)가 정답이다. (B)는 질문에 쓰인 sales를 반복한 답변으로 질문의 의도에 맞지 않는 반응이며, (C)는 위치 표현이므로 Where 의문문에 어울리는 답변이다.

어휘 **sales** 영업, 매출, 판매 **quarter** 분기

7. Where do you want me to put these boxes?
(A) I put the mail on your desk.
(B) Just leave them by the door.
(C) He knows what's inside the boxes.

이 상자들을 제가 어디에 두기를 원하세요?
(A) 제가 그 우편물을 당신 책상에 두었습니다.
(B) 그냥 문 옆에 놓아 주세요.
(C) 그가 그 상자들 안에 들어있는 것을 알고 있습니다.

해설 위치를 묻는 Where 의문문으로 상자를 둘 곳을 묻고 있으므로 특정 위치를 알려 주는 (B)가 정답이다. (A)도 위치 전치사구 on your desk를 포함하고 있지만 우편물을 놓아 둔 곳을 말하고 있으므로 질문의 의도에 맞지 않는 오답이다. (C)는 상자를 놓을 위치가 아니라 대상을 알 수 없는 He에 대해 말하고 있

으므로 오답이다.

어휘 **put** ~을 놓다, 두다(= leave) **by** ~ 옆에 **inside** ~ 안에

8. When do we start interviewing job candidates?
(A) Wow, congratulations!
(B) Several college graduates.
(C) The position's been filled.

우리가 언제 구직 지원자들을 면접 보는 일을 시작하나요?
(A) 와우, 축하합니다!
(B) 여러 대학 졸업생들이요.
(C) 그 직책이 충원되었어요.

해설 언제 구직 지원자들을 면접 보는 일을 시작하는지 묻는 데 대해 해당 직책을 The position으로 지칭해 충원되었다는 말로 면접 보는 일을 할 필요가 없음을 의미하는 (C)가 정답이다. (A)와 (B)는 interviewing job candidates에서 연상 가능한 축하 인사 congratulations와 지원자 college graduates를 각각 활용해 혼동을 유발하는 오답이다.

어휘 **candidate** 지원자, 후보자 **graduate** n. 졸업생 **position** 직책, 일자리 **fill** ~을 충원하다, ~을 채우다

9. How do I apply for an annual membership at your fitness center?

(A) Just sign up at the front desk.
(B) About my job application.
(C) That doesn't fit you well.

당신 피트니스 센터의 연간 회원권은 어떻게 신청하죠?
(A) 접수 데스크에서 등록하시면 됩니다.
(B) 제 구직 지원에 관해서요.
(C) 그건 당신에게 잘 맞지 않네요.

해설 연간 회원권의 신청 방법을 묻는 How 의문문이므로 접수 데스크에서 등록하라고 알리는 (A)가 정답이다. (B)는 질문에 쓰인 apply와 연관성 있게 들리는 명사 application을 이용해 혼동을 유발하는 답변이며, (C)는 질문에 쓰인 fitness와 일부 발음이 같은 fit을 이용해 혼동을 유발하는 답변이다.

어휘 **apply for** ~을 신청하다, ~에 지원하다 **annual** 연간의, 연례적인 **sign up (for)** (~에) 등록하다, 신청하다 **front desk** 접수 데스크 **application** 지원(서), 신청(서) **fit** v. (크기 등이) ~에 맞다, 어울리다

10. This folding bike isn't as lightweight as I thought it would be.

(A) That's a great idea.
(B) Let's turn on the lights.
(C) Would you like me to carry it?

이 접이식 자전거가 제가 생각했던 것만큼 가볍지 않아요.
(A) 아주 좋은 아이디어입니다.
(B) 조명을 켜 봅시다.
(C) 제가 들어 드릴까요?

해설 자전거의 무게가 가볍지 않음을 알리는 평서문에 대해 대신 들어 주겠다고 제안하는 의미를 담은 (C)가 정답이다. (A)는 상대방의 의견에 동의할 때 사용하는 말이므로 어울리지 않는 반응이며, (B)는 질문에 쓰인 lightweight과 일부 발음이 같은 lights를 이용해 혼동을 유발하는 오답이다.

어휘 **folding bike** 접이식 자전거 **as A as B** B만큼 A한 **lightweight** 가벼운, 경량의 **turn on** ~을 켜다 **Would you like me to do?** 제가 ~해 드릴까요? **carry** ~을 들고 다니다, 옮기다, 휴대하다

11. Do you know who might be suitable to lead the meeting?

(A) It will be held in that room.
(B) I think Jason could do it.
(C) Only top quality products.

누가 회의를 진행하기에 적합할 지 아시나요?
(A) 그건 저 방에서 개최될 거예요.
(B) 제이슨 씨가 할 수 있을 것 같아요.
(C) 오직 최고 품질의 제품들만요.

해설 Do로 시작하는 일반 의문문이지만 핵심은 who이다. 이 질문은 회의를 진행하기에 적합한 사람을 묻고 있으므로 사람 이름이 직접적으로 언급된 (B)가 정답이다. (A)는 질문에 쓰인 meeting에서 연상 가능한 회의 진행 장소를 말하는 것으로 혼동을 유발하는 오답이다.

어휘 **suitable** 적합한 **lead** ~을 진행하다, 이끌다 **hold** ~을 개최하다, 열다 **top quality** 최고 품질의

12. How many chairs will we need for the banquet?

(A) Eric will chair the meeting.
(B) I enjoyed the speech.
(C) We're not sure yet.

연회에 얼마나 많은 의자가 필요할까요?
(A) 에릭 씨가 회의를 주재할 겁니다.
(B) 저는 그 연설이 즐거웠어요.
(C) 저희는 아직 확실치 않아요.

해설 「How many ~?」로 시작하는 의문문으로 필요한 의자의 수량을 묻고 있지만, 특정 수량 대신 '잘 모르겠다'라는 말로 답변하는 (C)가 정답이다. (A)는 chair의 다른 의미(의자, 주재하다)를 이용해 혼동을 유발하는 오답이다. (B)는 banquet에서 연상 가능한 speech를 이용해 혼동을 유발하는 답변으로 필요한 의자 수량과 관련 없는 오답이다.

어휘 **banquet** 연회 **chair** v. ~을 주재하다 **speech** 연설

13. Would you like to come to the product demonstration?

(A) In the new laboratory.
(B) Who else is attending?
(C) No, he's not able to come.

제품 시연회에 오시고 싶으세요?
(A) 새로운 실험실에서요.
(B) 또 누가 참석하나요?
(C) 아뇨, 그는 올 수 없어요.

해설 '~하고 싶으세요?'를 뜻하는 「Would you like to do?」 의문문으로 제품 시연회에 오고 싶은지 정중하게 묻는 것에 대해 긍정이나 부정을 나타내는 대신 누가 참석하는지 확인하기 위해 되묻는 (B)가 정답이다. (C)는 거절을 뜻하는 No 뒤에 이어지는 말이 질문의 의도에 맞지 않는 오답이다.

어휘 **demonstration** 시연(회), 시범 **laboratory** 실험실 **attend** ~에 참석하다

14. Should I go over my report with Ms. Coleman before presenting it?

(A) I don't think she's in today.
(B) The presentation was excellent.
(C) On the 10 o'clock news.

제 보고서를 제출하기 전에 콜먼 씨와 검토해야 하나요?
(A) 오늘 그분이 출근하지 않은 것 같아요.
(B) 발표가 정말 훌륭했어요.
(C) 10시 뉴스에서요.

해설 콜먼 씨와 함께 보고서를 검토해야 하는지 확인하는 Should 의문문에 대해 '그렇다' 혹은 '아니다'라는 대답 대신 그 사람이 출근하지 않은 것 같다는 말로 검토 작업을 할 수 없다는 뜻을 나타낸 (A)가 정답이다. (B)는 질문에 쓰인 presenting과 발음이 유사한 presentation을 이용해 혼동을 유발하는 답변이며, (C)는 report에서 연상 가능한 news를 이용해 혼동을 유발하는 오답이다.

어휘 **go over** ~을 검토하다 **present** v. ~을 제출하다, 제공하다 **presentation** 발표

15. I was very pleased to hear about Ms. Vonn's promotion.

(A) Who do you think will be chosen?
(B) I placed an advertisement in the paper.
(C) Yes, she definitely deserves it.

저는 본 씨의 승진 얘기를 듣고 아주 기뻤습니다.
(A) 누가 선정되어야 한다고 생각하세요?
(B) 제가 신문에 광고를 하나 냈습니다.
(C) 네, 그분은 분명히 그럴 만한 자격이 있으십니다.

해설 본 씨의 승진에 관해 듣고 기뻤다는 의견을 말하는 평서문에 대해 동의를 나타내는 Yes와 함께 Ms. Vonn을 she로 지칭해 그 사람이 그럴 만한 자격이 있다는 말을 덧붙인 (C)가

정답이다. (A)는 질문에 쓰인 promotion에서 연상 가능한 chosen(선정된)을 이용해 혼동을 유발하는 답변이며, (B)는 질문에 쓰인 pleased와 발음이 유사하게 들리는 placed를 이용해 혼동을 유발하는 오답이다.

어휘 **be pleased to do** ~해서 기쁘다 **promotion** 승진 **place an advertisement** 광고를 내다 **definitely** 분명히 **deserve** ~에 대한 자격이 있다, ~을 받을 만하다

16. Who has the new test results?
(A) Right after lunch.
(B) I didn't get a high score.
(C) Probably the development team.

누가 새로운 테스트 결과를 가지고 있나요?
(A) 점심 식사 직후에요.
(B) 저는 높은 점수를 받지 못했습니다.
(C) 아마 개발팀일 거예요.

해설 누가 테스트 결과를 가지고 있는지 묻는 Who 의문문에 대해 특정 부서명으로 대답한 (C)가 정답이다. (A)는 시점 표현이므로 When 의문문에 적절한 답변이며, (B)는 질문에 쓰인 test에서 연상 가능한 score를 이용해 혼동을 유발하는 오답이다.

어휘 **result** 결과(물) **right after** ~ 직후에 **score** 점수 **probably** 아마 **development** 개발

17. You're coming into the office on Saturday, right?
(A) Okay, thanks for the invitation!
(B) Not if I finish this report today.
(C) It should fit in here.

토요일에 사무실로 나오시는 게 맞죠?
(A) 좋아요, 초대해 주셔서 감사합니다!
(B) 제가 오늘 이 보고서를 끝내면 그렇지 않아요.
(C) 여기에 맞을 겁니다.

해설 토요일에 사무실로 나오는 게 맞는지 묻고 있으므로 오늘 보고서를 끝내는 것을 조건으로 언급해 그에 따라 결정될 수 있다는 뜻을 나타낸 (B)가 정답이다. (A)는 coming에서 연상 가능한 감사 인사 thanks for the invitation을 활용해 혼동을 유발하는 오답이다.

어휘 **invitation** 초대(장) **fit** (크기, 모양 등이) 들어맞다

18. Which airline should we take for our trip to Canada?
(A) The company already booked a flight.
(B) At Pearson Airport.
(C) I'm looking forward to it, too.

캐나다 출장을 위해 우리가 어느 항공사를 이용해야 할까요?
(A) 회사에서 이미 항공편을 예약했어요.
(B) 피어슨 공항에서요.
(C) 저도 그것을 고대하고 있습니다.

해설 항공사 선택과 관련된 Which 의문문에 대해 회사 측에서 이미 항공편을 예약했다는 말로 어느 항공사를 선택할지 생각할 필요가 없음을 알리는 (A)가 정답이다. (B)는 장소 표현으로서 airline에서 연상 가능한 airport를 이용한 오답이며, (C)는 trip에 초점에 맞춰 답변자 자신의 기대감을 나타내는 오답이다.

어휘 **airline** 항공사 **trip** 출장, 여행 **book** ~을 예약하다 **flight** 항공편 **look forward to** ~을 고대하다

19. We should check for any errors in these blueprints.
(A) Building designs, I think.
(B) Wendy already reviewed them.
(C) Yes, for a new shopping mall.

이 설계도에 어떤 오류라도 있는지 확인해 봐야 합니다.
(A) 제 생각에는 건물 디자인 같아요.
(B) 웬디 씨가 이미 검토했어요.
(C) 네, 새로운 쇼핑몰을 위해서요.

해설 설계도에 오류가 있는지 확인해야 한다고 제안하는 평서문에 대해 웬디 씨가 이미 검토했다는 말로 확인할 필요가 없음을 알리는 (B)가 정답이다. (A)는 질문에 쓰인 blueprints(설계도)에서 연상 가능한 building designs를 이용해 혼동을 유발하는 오답이며, (C)는 긍정을 나타내는 Yes 뒤에 이어지는 말이 오류 확인과 관련 없는 내용이다.

어휘 **check for** ~가 있는지 확인하다 **blueprint** 설계도, 청사진 **review** ~을 검토하다

20. Do you think we can leave now or should we wait a bit?
(A) It depends on the traffic.
(B) You can leave it here, thanks.
(C) A bit earlier next time.

우리가 지금 출발해도 될 것 같으세요, 아니면 조금 더 기다려야 하나요?
(A) 교통 상황에 따라 달라요.
(B) 그거 여기에 두세요, 감사합니다.
(C) 다음에는 좀 더 일찍요.

해설 지금 출발해도 되는지, 아니면 조금 더 기다려야 하는지 묻는 선택 의문문인데, 둘 중 하나를 선택하는 대신 교통 상황에 따라 다르다는 말로 조건을 언급한 (A)가 정답이다. (B)와 (C)는 질문에 쓰인 leave와 a bit을 각각 반복해 혼동을 유발하는 답변으로 질문의 의도에 맞지 않는 오답이다.

어휘 **leave** 출발하다, 떠나다, ~을 놓다, 두다 **a bit** 조금, 약간 **depend on** ~에 따라 다르다, ~에 달려 있다

Part 3

Questions 21-23 refer to the following conversation.

> W: Hi, Mike. **21** Do you know whether our apartment building has any empty rooms that would be suitable for a meeting?
>
> M: Actually, I'm not really sure. Why do you ask?
>
> W: Well, **22** my colleagues and I want to work on a presentation this weekend, but our office will be closed for renovations. We'd rather not go to a public place due to the noise.
>
> M: Well, there might be an empty room down in the basement, but I'm not sure whether there are tables or chairs. **23** You should ask Mr. Harding, the building supervisor. He'll know if the room is suitable.
>
> W: Thanks, I'll do that now.
>
> ---
>
> 여: 안녕하세요, 마이크 씨. 우리 아파트 건물에 회의용으로 적합할 만한 어떤 빈 방이든 있는지 아세요?
> 남: 실은, 확실히 알지 못합니다. 왜 물어 보시는 건가요?
> 여: 저, 제 동료 직원들과 제가 이번 주말에 있을 발표 작업을 하고 싶은데, 저희 사무실이 개조 공사 때문에 문을 닫아요. 저희가 소음 때문에 공공 장소에 가고 싶지 않아서요.
> 남: 저, 지하로 내려가시면 빈 공간이 하나 있을 수도 있는데, 탁자나 의자가 있는지 잘 모르겠어요. 건물 관리인인 하딩 씨에게 물어보세요. 그 공간이 적합한지 그분께서 아실 거예요.
> 여: 고마워요, 지금 그렇게 할게요.

어휘 **whether** ~인지 (아닌지) **suitable for** ~에 적합한, 어울리는 **colleague** 동료 (직원) **work on** ~에 대한 작업을 하다 **presentation** 발표 **renovation** 개조, 보수 **would rather do** ~하고 싶다 **public place** 공공 장소 **due to** ~ 때문에 **noise** 소음 **basement** 지하(실)

21. 여자는 남자에게 무엇에 관해 묻는가?
(A) 아파트 임대료
(B) 주차장 이용 가능성
(C) 회의 장소
(D) 개조 공사 비용

해설 대화를 시작하면서 여자가 아파트 건물에 회의용으로 적합한 어떤 빈 방이든 있는지(Do you know whether our apartment building has any empty rooms that would be suitable for a meeting?) 묻고 있다. 이는 회의 장소로 쓸 곳이 있는지 묻는 것이므로 (C)가 정답이다.

어휘 **rent** 임대료, 월세 **availability** 이용 가능성
Paraphrase empty rooms that would be suitable for a meeting
→ Meeting space

22. 여자는 무슨 문제점이 있는가?
(A) 자신의 아파트에 출입할 수 없다.
(B) 동료 직원의 연락처를 잃어버렸다.
(C) 어떤 작업물을 제출하는 데 늦었다.
(D) 자신의 사무실이 이번 주말에 문을 닫는다.

해설 문제점을 묻고 있으므로 부정적인 정보를 찾아야 한다. 대화 중반부에 여자가 주말에 동료와 해야 하는 작업이 있는데 사무실이 개조 공사 때문에 문을 닫는다고(our office will be closed for renovations) 알리고 있다. 따라서 이를 언급한 (D)가 정답이다.

어휘 **access** ~에 접근하다, ~을 이용하다 **contact details** 연락처 **submit** ~을 제출하다

23. 남자는 여자에게 무엇을 하도록 제안하는가?
(A) 동료 직원들에게 연락하는 일
(B) 새 아파트로 이사하는 일
(C) 업무 일정을 변경하는 일
(D) 건물 관리인에게 얘기하는 일

해설 대화 맨 마지막에 남자가 건물 매니저인 하딩 씨에게 물어보라고(You should ask Mr. Harding, the building supervisor) 제안하면서 그 사람이 이용 적합성과 관련해 알고 있을 것이라고 언급하고 있다. 따라서 (D)가 정답이다.

어휘 **contact** ~에게 연락하다 **coworker** 동료 (직원)
Paraphrase ask Mr. Harding, the building supervisor
→ Talk to a building manager

Questions 24-26 refer to the following conversation with three speakers.

> M1: Leanne, **24** we appreciate your stopping by to look over our designs for the new company logo. We're looking forward to hearing your thoughts.
>
> M2: Exactly. So, here are some designs. We need to choose the best one and present it to the board members this Friday. What do you think?
>
> W: Well, this one would be best for our firm. **25** As an event planning company, we need a logo that's distinctive and modern.
>
> M1: That's my favorite too. Do you think we should keep the same colors that our company has always used?
>
> W: Absolutely. Our clients recognize our colors in our advertisements, so **26** you should stick

with blue and green like we always have.

M2: Thanks for your feedback. After a few small changes, I think we'll be ready.

남1: 린, 회사의 새 로고에 필요한 우리 디자인을 살펴보실 수 있도록 들러 주셔서 감사드립니다. 당신의 생각을 들어 볼 수 있기를 기대하고 있습니다.

남2: 맞아요. 자, 여기 디자인이 있습니다. 가장 좋은 것을 선택해서 이번 주 금요일에 이사진에 제출해야 합니다. 어떻게 생각하세요?

여: 저, 이것이 우리 회사에 가장 잘 맞을 것 같아요. 행사 기획 회사로서, 우리는 독특하고 현대적인 로고가 필요합니다.

남1: 저도 그게 가장 마음에 듭니다. 우리 회사가 항상 사용해 오던 것과 같은 색상들을 유지해야 한다고 생각하시나요?

여: 당연하죠. 우리 고객들께서는 우리 광고에서 회사의 색상들을 인식하시기 때문에 우리가 항상 사용하는 것과 같은 청색과 녹색을 유지해야 합니다.

남2: 의견 주셔서 감사합니다. 몇 가지 작은 수정 작업을 거치고 나면, 준비가 될 것 같습니다.

어휘 **appreciate one's doing** ~가 …한 것에 감사하다 **stop by** 들르다 **look over** ~을 살펴보다, 검토하다 **look forward to -ing** ~하기를 고대하다 **thought** 생각, 의견 **Exactly** (긍정의 답변으로) 맞습니다, 바로 그렇습니다 **present A to B** A를 B에 제출하다, 제시하다 **board members** 이사진 **be best for** ~에 가장 잘 맞다, 적합하다 **firm** 회사 **event planning** 행사 기획 **distinctive** 독특한 **favorite** 가장 마음에 드는 것, 가장 좋아하는 것 **keep** ~을 유지하다 **Absolutely** (동의, 허락을 나타내어) 당연하죠, 물론이죠 **recognize** ~을 인식하다 **stick with** ~을 유지하다, 고수하다 **feedback** 의견 **a few** 몇몇의

24. 화자들은 무엇에 관해 이야기하고 있는가?
(A) 제품 종류
(B) 웹 사이트 디자인
(C) 건물 설계도
(D) 기업 로고

해설 남자 한 명이 대화를 시작하면서 회사의 새 로고에 필요한 디자인을 살펴볼 수 있도록 들러줘서 감사하다는 인사와 함께 의견을 들어 보고 싶다고(we appreciate your stopping by to look over our designs for the new company logo. ~) 말한다. 따라서 회사의 로고가 핵심 내용임을 알 수 있으므로 (D)가 정답이 된다.

어휘 **range** (제품) 종류, 범위 **blueprint** 설계도, 도면 **corporate** 기업의

25. 화자들은 무슨 종류의 회사에서 근무하는가?
(A) 인테리어 디자인 회사
(B) 인터넷 서비스 제공 업체

(C) 행사 기획 전문 회사
(D) 철물점

해설 대화 중반부에 여자가 자신이 일하는 회사와 관련해 행사 기획 업체라고(As an event planning company, we need a logo ~) 언급하는 부분을 통해 (C)가 정답임을 알 수 있다.

어휘 **work for** ~에서 근무하다 **provider** 제공 업체 **hardware store** 철물점

26. 여자는 무엇을 권하는가?
(A) 디자인을 확대할 것
(B) 특정 색상들을 활용할 것
(C) 몇 부 인쇄할 것
(D) 고객들에게 설문 조사를 할 것

해설 대화 후반부에 여자는 항상 사용하는 청색과 녹색을 유지해야 한다고(you should stick with blue and green like we always have) 권하고 있는데, 이는 특정한 색상만 사용해야 한다는 말이므로 (B)가 정답이 된다.

어휘 **enlarge** ~을 확대하다 **specific** 특정한, 구체적인 **copy** 1부, 1장, 사본 **survey** ~에게 설문 조사를 하다

Paraphrase stick with blue and green like we always have
→ Using specific colors

Questions 27-29 refer to the following conversation.

W: Hi, **27** I just received a Wi-Fi router that I ordered online from you. I've been trying for the last hour to connect it to my Internet, but I can't figure it out. The manual doesn't seem to be helping me.

M: Okay, I'm sorry about that. **28** Can you tell me which one you ordered? And I'll see if I can get someone to instruct you how to do it over the phone.

W: I have a TIME-JEST 30. To be honest, I have problems following specialists over the phone. **29** Can you direct me to a help page on the Internet? And I'll try to fix the problem myself.

M: Sure, I can do that for you. We have a very clear Frequently Asked Questions page on our Web site. There's a link to it on the bottom right corner of the homepage.

여: 안녕하세요, 그쪽에서 온라인으로 주문한 와이파이 중계기를 방금 받았어요. 지난 한 시간 동안 그걸 인터넷에 연결시키려고 해봤는데 모르겠어요. 설명서가 도움이 안 되는 것 같네요.

남: 알겠습니다, 그러셨다니 유감입니다. 어떤 것을 주문했는지 말씀해주시겠습니까? 그럼 전 하는 방법을 전화상으로 알려줄 수 있는 사람을 찾을 수 있는지 알아보겠습니다.

여: 타임-제스트 30을 가지고 있습니다. 솔직히 말해서, 저는 전화 상으로 전문가들이 말하는 걸 따라가는 게 어려워요. 저를 인 터넷상의 도움말 페이지로 안내해 주시겠습니까? 그러면 제가 문제를 혼자서 해결해 볼게요.

남: 물론이죠, 그렇게 해드릴 수 있습니다. 저희 웹 사이트에 아주 명확한 FAQ 페이지가 있어요. 홈페이지 맨 밑에 오른쪽 구석 에 거기로 가는 링크가 있습니다.

어휘 **Wi-Fi router** 와이파이 중계기 **connect A to B** A를 B에 연결하다 **figure out** ~을 알아내다 **manual** 설명서 **seem to do** ~하는 것 같다 **see if** ~인지 알아보다 **get A to do** A가 ~하도록 하다 **instruct A B** A에게 B를 가르치다, 알려주다 **over the phone** 전화상으로 **to be honest** 솔직히 말해서 **have problems -ing** ~하는 데 문제를 겪다 **follow** (충고·지시 등을) 따르다 **specialist** 전문가 **direct A to B** A를 B로 안내하다 **help page** 도움 말 페이지 **fix the problem** 문제를 해결하다 **clear** 명백 한, 분명한 **Frequently Asked Questions** 자주 묻는 질 문들(= FAQ) **bottom** 맨 아래

27. 여자는 어떤 문제를 알리는가?
(A) 설명서를 받지 못했다.
(B) 제품이 제대로 작동하지 않는다.
(C) 인터넷 연결이 너무 느리다.
(D) 웹 사이트 접속이 안 된다.

해설 첫 대사에서 여자는 온라인으로 주문해 받은 와이파이 중 계기가 인터넷에 연결이 안 된다는(I just received a Wi-Fi router that I ordered online from you. I've been trying for the last hour to connect it to my Internet) 문제점을 말하고 있다. 기기가 작동이 잘 안되는 상황이므로 (B)가 정답이다. Internet이 언급되었다고 해서 무작정 (C)를 골라선 안 된다.

어휘 **properly** 제대로 **connection** 연결 **inaccessible** 접근 할 수 없는

28. 남자는 여자에게 어떤 정보를 요청하는가?
(A) 여자에게 서비스를 제공한 사람의 이름
(B) 웹 사이트 비밀번호
(C) 특정 제품의 이름
(D) 여자의 전화번호

해설 와이파이 중계기를 제대로 작동시키지 못하고 있는 여자에게 남자는 Can you tell me which one you ordered라고 묻 는다. 무엇을 주문했는지 말해달라고 묻는 것은 주문한 제품명 을 알려 달라는 뜻이므로 (C)가 정답이다.

어휘 **serve** ~에게 서비스를 제공하다

29. 여자는 곧이어 무엇을 할 것인가?
(A) 제품을 반품한다.
(B) 설명서의 안내를 따른다.

(C) 전문가와 이야기한다.
(D) 웹 페이지를 찾는다.

해설 여자가 인터넷상의 도움말 페이지를 알려달라고 요청하고(Can you direct me to a help page on the Internet) 이에 남 자가 FAQ 페이지를 보는 방법을 안내하고 있다. 이로부터 여자 는 웹 사이트의 FAQ 페이지를 찾아볼 것임을 알 수 있으므로 (D)가 정답이다.

어휘 **return** ~을 반환하다, 돌려주다 **instruction** 지시
Paraphrase a help page on the Internet
→ a Web page

Questions 30-32 refer to the following conversation.

M: Excuse me. **30** What time is Dr. Lee's speech for the medical convention this evening? I'm wondering if I have time for dinner.

W: I'm sorry. You must have the wrong information. Her keynote speech will be tomorrow night.

M: Oh, that's too bad. **31** I have to leave the convention early tomorrow. I have tickets to the orchestra.

W: I see. But, each talk will be uploaded online. **32** Let me write down the Web site address for you.

남: 실례합니다. 오늘 저녁에 있을 리 박사님의 의학 컨벤션 연설이 몇 시죠? 제가 저녁 식사할 시간이 있을지 궁금해서요.

여: 죄송합니다. 잘못된 정보를 알고 계신 게 틀림없습니다. 그분의 기조 연설은 내일 밤입니다.

남: 아, 정말 아쉽네요. 제가 내일 일찍 컨벤션 장소를 떠나야 해요. 오케스트라 공연 입장권이 있거든요.

여: 알겠습니다. 하지만, 각 연설이 온라인으로 업로드될 겁니다. 제가 웹 사이트 주소를 적어 드리겠습니다.

어휘 **wonder if** ~인지 궁금하다 **must** ~하는 것이 틀림없다 **keynote speech** 기조 연설 **leave** ~을 떠나다 **write down** ~을 적다

30. 화자들은 어디에 있겠는가?
(A) 병원에
(B) 컨벤션 장소에
(C) 박물관에
(D) 지역 문화 센터에

해설 대화 시작 부분에 남자가 오늘 저녁에 있을 리 박사의 의학 컨 벤션 연설 시간을 물으면서 자신이 식사할 시간 여유가 있을지 궁금해 하고 있다(What time is Dr. Lee's speech for the medical convention this evening? I'm wondering if I have time for dinner). 이는 컨벤션 개최 장소에서 할 수 있는 말에 해당되므로 (B)가 정답이다.

31. 남자는 내일 어떤 종류의 행사에 갈 것인가?

(A) 음악 공연
(B) 시상식
(C) 저녁 회식
(D) 스포츠 경기

해설 '내일'이라는 시점이 제시되는 중반부에, 남자가 내일 컨벤션 장소를 떠난다는 말과 함께 오케스트라 입장권이 있다고(I have to leave the convention early tomorrow. I have tickets to the orchestra) 알리고 있다. 이는 음악 공연을 가리키므로 (A)가 정답이다.

어휘 **performance** 공연, 연주(회) **awards ceremony** 시상식

Paraphrase orchestra
  → musical performance

32. 여자는 왜 "각 연설이 온라인으로 업로드될 겁니다"라고 말하는가?

(A) 절차를 설명하기 위해
(B) 실수를 바로잡기 위해
(C) 제안하기 위해
(D) 아이디어를 거절하기 위해

해설 대화 마지막에 여자가 '각 연설이 온라인으로 업데이트될 것이다'라고 알리면서 자신이 웹 사이트 주소를 적어 주겠다고(Let me write down the Web site address for you) 말하는 상황이다. 이는 온라인으로 연설을 확인하도록 제안하는 것이므로 (C)가 정답이다.

어휘 **explain** ~을 설명하다 **procedure** 절차 **correct** v. ~을 바로잡다 **make a suggestion** 제안하다 **reject** ~을 거절하다

Questions 33-35 refer to the following conversation and table.

W: Welcome to Alpine Outdoor Goods. Are you looking for anything specific?

M: Well, **33** my wife and I want to take our son on a camping trip, so I'm looking for a tent we could use.

W: You came to the right place then. We have a few different sizes. What maximum capacity would be best for you?

M: I don't want one that's too big. **34** One that can accommodate up to four people would suit us perfectly.

W: Take a look at this list of popular models. I think this one would be perfect.

M: Great! And **35** is it fairly easy to assemble? I've never had to set one up before, so I'm a bit worried.

W: It's simple. You won't have any problems.

여: 알파인 아웃도어 용품점에 오신 것을 환영합니다. 특별히 찾고 계신 것이라도 있으세요?

남: 저, 아내와 제가 아들을 데리고 캠핑 여행을 떠나고 싶어서, 저희가 이용할 수 있는 텐트를 찾고 있습니다.

여: 그러시면 제대로 찾아 오셨습니다. 저희는 몇 가지 다른 사이즈가 있습니다. 어떤 최대 수용 인원으로 된 것이 가장 적합할까요?

남: 너무 큰 것은 원하지 않습니다. 최대 네 명까지 수용할 수 있는 것이 저희에게 완벽하게 어울릴 겁니다.

여: 인기 모델들을 담은 이 목록을 한 번 확인해 보세요. 저는 이것이 완벽할 것 같아요.

남: 아주 좋아요! 그리고 조립하기 꽤 쉬운가요? 전에 한 번도 설치했어야 했던 적이 없어서, 약간 걱정이 되어서요.

여: 간단합니다. 어떤 문제도 없을 겁니다.

모델	최대 수용 인원
베리	2
로완	4
스프링	6
호라이즌	10

어휘 **specific** 특정한, 구체적인 **then** 그럼, 그렇다면 **maximum capacity** 최대 수용 인원 **accommodate** ~을 수용하다 **up to** 최대 ~까지 **suit** ~에게 어울리다, 적합하다 **take a look at** ~을 한 번 보다 **fairly** 꽤, 아주, 상당히 **assemble** ~을 조립하다 **set A up** A를 설치하다 **a bit** 약간, 조금 **worried** 걱정하는

33. 여자의 근무 장소에서 어떤 종류의 제품을 판매하는가?

(A) 아동용 장난감
(B) 캠핑 용품
(C) 저장용 용기
(D) 가정용 가구

해설 대화 초반부에 남자가 원하는 제품을 언급하면서 '아내와 제가 아들을 데리고 캠핑 여행을 떠나고 싶어서, 저희가 이용할 수 있는 텐트를 찾고 있습니다(my wife and I want to take our son on a camping trip, so I'm looking for a tent we could use)'라고 알리고 있다. 따라서 캠핑 용품을 판매하는 매장임을 알 수 있으므로 (B)가 정답이다.

어휘 **storage** 저장, 보관 **container** 용기, 그릇 **furnishing** 가구, 비품

Paraphrase tent → Camping supplies

34. 시각자료를 보시오. 남자는 어느 모델을 구입할 것인가?

    (A) 베리
    (B) 로완
    (C) 스프링
    (D) 호라이즌

해설 남자가 자신이 원하는 텐트의 크기를 언급하는 중반부에 최대 네 명까지 수용할 수 있는 것이 좋겠다고(One that can accommodate up to four people would suit us perfectly) 알리고 있다. 도표에서 최대 수용 인원이 4로 표기된 제품이 Rowan이므로 (B)가 정답이다.

35. 남자는 무엇에 대해 우려하는가?

    (A) 품질
    (B) 배송
    (C) 조립
    (D) 가격

해설 대화 후반부에 남자가 조립하기 쉬운지 물으면서 한 번도 해 본 적이 없어서 걱정된다고(is it fairly easy to assemble? I've never had to set one up before, so I'm a bit worried) 알리고 있으므로 (C)가 정답이다.

어휘 **be concerned about** ~에 대해 우려하다 **quality** 품질, 질 **assembly** 조립 (작업)

Questions 36-38 refer to the following conversation and graph.

M: Excuse me, Ms. Watkins. 36 **I'd like to talk to you about the productivity of one of the assembly teams in our factory.** Do you have time to look at this graph?

W: Certainly. Is there some kind of problem on the assembly line?

M: Well, as you can see, 37 **one of our teams assembled less than two hundred products yesterday.** That's way below the daily production target.

W: I see. Well, 38 **I'll talk to the supervisor of that team straight away and tell him to motivate his workers.** We can't afford to fall behind schedule. Our new product line is due to be launched next month.

남: 실례합니다, 왓킨스 씨. 우리 공장에 있는 조립 팀들 중 한 곳의 생산성에 관해 얘기 좀 했으면 합니다. 이 그래프를 한 번 보실 시간이 있으신가요?
여: 그럼요. 조립 라인에 무슨 문제라도 있나요?
남: 저, 보시다시피, 우리 팀들 중의 하나가 어제 200개가 채 되

지 않는 제품을 조립했습니다. 이는 일일 생산 목표보다 훨씬 더 낮은 것입니다.
여: 알겠습니다. 그럼, 제가 그 팀의 책임자와 지금 바로 얘기를 해서 소속 직원들에게 동기 부여를 하도록 말씀 드릴게요. 우리는 일정보다 뒤처져 있을 여유가 없습니다. 우리의 새로운 제품 라인이 다음 달에 출시될 예정이니까요.

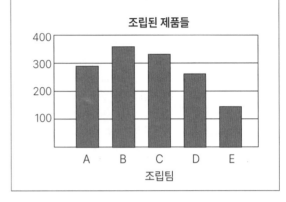

조립된 제품들

어휘 **productivity** 생산성 **assembly** 조립 **Certainly** 그럼요, 물론이죠, 당연합니다 **some kind of** 일종의, 뭔가 **assemble** ~을 조립하다 **less than** ~ 미만의, ~가 채 되지 않는 **way** (강조) 훨씬 **below** ~ 보다 낮은 **daily** 매일의 **production target** 생산 목표 **supervisor** 책임자, 부서장 **straight away** 지금 바로 **tell A to do** A에게 ~하도록 말하다 **motivate** ~에게 동기 부여를 하다, 격려하다 **can't afford to do** ~할 여유가 없다 **fall behind schedule** 일정보다 뒤처지다 **product line** 제품 라인, 제품군 **be due to do** ~할 예정이다 **launch** ~을 출시하다, 공개하다

36. 무엇이 주로 논의되고 있는가?

    (A) 기계 설치 작업
    (B) 직원 인센티브 제도
    (C) 생산성 관련 문제
    (D) 새로운 종류의 제품들

해설 대화의 주제를 묻는 문제이므로 대화가 시작될 때 특히 집중해 들어야 한다. 남자가 대화를 시작하면서 공장 내 조립 팀들 중 한 곳의 생산성에 관해 얘기하고 싶다고(I'd like to talk to you about the productivity of one of the assembly teams in our factory) 언급하고 있으므로 (C)가 정답이다.

어휘 **installation** 설치 **incentive** 인센티브, 장려금, 보상책 **range** (제품) 종류, 범위

37. 시각자료를 보시오. 어느 조립 팀에 관해 이야기되고 있는가?

    (A) B팀
    (B) C팀
    (C) D팀
    (D) E팀

해설 대화 중반부에 남자가 대상이 되는 조립 팀의 특성과 관련해

어제 200개가 채 되지 않는 제품을 조립했다고(one of our teams assembled less than two hundred products yesterday) 말하고 있다. 시각자료에서 200개 미만을 기록한 팀이 E로 표기되어 있으므로 (D)가 정답이다.

38. 여자는 곧이어 무엇을 할 것이라고 말하는가?
(A) 마감기한을 연장하는 일
(B) 책임자와 이야기하는 일
(C) 기계를 점검하는 일
(D) 교육 시간 일정을 정하는 일

해설 대화 후반부에 여자가 해당 팀의 책임자와 지금 바로 얘기를 해서 소속 직원들에게 동기 부여를 하겠다고(I'll talk to the supervisor of that team straight away ~) 말하고 있으므로 이에 대해 언급한 (B)가 정답이다.

어휘 **extend** ~을 연장하다 **deadline** 마감기한 **inspect** ~을 점검하다, 조사하다 **session** (특정 활동을 위한) 시간

Paraphrase talk to the supervisor of that team
→ Speak with a manager

Part 4

Questions 39-41 refer to the following announcement.

> **39** I'm delighted to be here this morning to officially open Acorn Park's three new public tennis courts. In addition to the courts, there is also **40** a new rental office just inside the main entrance of the clubhouse. This means that people who don't own their own equipment can rent tennis rackets and balls and enjoy the new courts. Now that the number of courts has increased from three to six, the tennis club will meet more frequently for practice sessions. **41**
> If you're a member of the tennis club, you can find a full schedule of sessions on the notice board inside the clubhouse, as well as important announcements and other news.

오늘 아침 이곳 에이콘 공원에 3개의 새로운 공공 테니스 경기장을 공식 개장하는 현장에 있게 되어 기쁩니다. 경기장 뿐만 아니라, 클럽하우스 중앙 출입구의 바로 안쪽에는 새로운 대여 사무소도 있습니다. 이는 자신만의 장비가 없는 사람들이 테니스 라켓과 공을 빌려 새로운 경기장에서 즐거운 시간을 보낼 수 있다는 것을 의미합니다. 경기장이 3개에서 6개로 늘어났기 때문에, 연습 시간을 위해 테니스 클럽에서 더 자주 만날 것입니다. 테니스 클럽의 회원이시라면, 클럽하우스 내의 게시판에서 중요한 공지와 다른 소식 뿐만 아니라 전체 시간 일정표도 보실 수 있습니다.

어휘 **be delighted to do** ~하게 되어 기쁘다 **officially** 공식

적으로 **in addition to** ~뿐만 아니라 **own** ~을 소유하다 **equipment** 장비 **rent** ~을 빌리다, 대여하다 **now that** ~이기 때문에 **the number of** ~의 수 **increase from A to B** A에서 B로 증가하다 **frequently** 자주 **notice board** 게시판

39. 담화는 어디에서 이루어지는가?
(A) 커뮤니티 센터에서
(B) 체육관에서
(C) 아파트 건물에서
(D) 공원에서

해설 담화의 첫 부분에서 Acorn Park의 새로운 테니스 경기장을 개장하는 현장에 있게 되어 기쁘다(I'm delighted to be here this morning to officially open Acorn Park's three new public tennis courts)고 말하는 것으로 보아, 화자는 현재 Acorn Park에 있음을 알 수 있다. 따라서 정답은 (D)이다.

40. 화자는 어떤 새로운 서비스를 언급하는가?
(A) 개인 훈련 프로그램
(B) 수리 및 유지 보수
(C) 스포츠 장비의 대여
(D) 건강한 식생활에 대한 조언

해설 테니스 경기장 뿐만 아니라 새로 추가된 대여 사무소를 언급하면서, 개인 장비가 없는 사람들이 테니스 라켓과 테니스 공을 빌릴 수 있다고 안내하고 있다. 따라서 정답은 (C)이다.

어휘 **personal** 개인적인 **repairs** 수리 **maintenance** 유지 보수 **rental** 대여 **advice** 조언

Paraphrase rent → rental
tennis rackets and balls → sports equipment

41. 클럽의 회원들은 어떻게 정보를 더 얻을 수 있는가?
(A) 소식지를 읽음으로써
(B) 게시판을 확인함으로써
(C) 회장과 대화함으로써
(D) 오리엔테이션에 참석함으로써

해설 화자는 클럽 회원들이 추가 정보를 클럽하우스 내의 게시판에서 얻을 수 있다고(If you're a member of the tennis club, you can find a full schedule of sessions on the notice board inside the clubhouse, as well as important announcements and other news) 안내하므로 정답은 (B)이다. 참고로, notice board와 비슷한 뜻으로 토익에도 자주 나오는 bulletin board를 함께 알아 두면 좋다.

어휘 **newsletter** 소식지

Questions 42-44 refer to the following telephone message.

Hi. This is Kenneth Grimes. **42** I bought the Kipperware computer that you had posted in the local newspaper. You were very friendly when we met, and the computer appears to be in great condition. However, when I turned it on, the operating system's default language was Russian. **43** To change it, I need to have the original install disk. **44** Would you be able to send it to me? I don't have time to drive all the way to your side of the city again. Thanks.

안녕하세요. 저는 케네스 그라임스입니다. 저는 귀하께서 지역 신문에 게시하셨던 키퍼웨어 컴퓨터를 구입한 사람입니다. 만나 뵈었을 때 귀하께서는 매우 친절하셨으며, 이 컴퓨터가 매우 훌륭한 상태인 것 같습니다. 그런데 제가 이 컴퓨터를 켰을 때, 운영 시스템의 디폴트 언어가 러시아어였습니다. 이것을 변경하기 위해, 원본 설치 디스크가 필요합니다. 이 디스크를 제게 좀 보내주시겠습니까? 도시 내에서 귀하께서 계신 쪽까지 제가 다시 한 번 차를 몰고 갈 만한 시간이 없습니다. 감사합니다.

어휘 post ~을 게시하다 friendly 친절한 appear to do ~한 것 같다 in great condition 아주 좋은 상태인 turn A on A를 켜다, 틀다 operating system 운영 시스템 default language 디폴트 언어 original 원본의, 처음의 install disk 설치 디스크 all the way to ~까지 쭉, 계속

42. 화자에 따르면, 물품은 어디에 광고되었는가?
(A) 신문 광고에
(B) 전자 제품 매장에
(C) 제품 카탈로그에
(D) 경매 행사에

해설 제품이 광고된 곳을 묻고 있는데, 담화 시작 부분에 지역 신문에 상대방이 게시한 컴퓨터를 구입했다고(I bought the Kipperware computer that you had posted in the local newspaper.) 알리고 있으므로 (A)가 정답이다.

어휘 advertise ~을 광고하다 ad 광고 electronics 전자 제품 auction 경매

43. 화자가 "운영 시스템의 디폴트 언어가 러시아어였습니다"라고 말할 때 암시하는 것은 무엇인가?
(A) 한 가지 제품을 다른 것과 교환하고 싶어 한다.
(B) 일부 소프트웨어 대해 깊은 인상을 받았다.
(C) 러시아로 제품을 배송하고 싶어 하지 않는다.
(D) 러시아어를 이해할 수 없다.

해설 질문에 포함된 문장은 "운영 시스템의 디폴트 언어가 러시아어이다"라는 의미로 해석할 수 있다. 담화에서 이 말 바로 다

음에 이것을 변경하려면 원본 설치 디스크가 필요하다고(To change it, I need to have the original install disk) 알리고 있다. 이는 해당 언어를 이해 가능한 것으로 바꾸기 위한 조치로 생각할 수 있으므로 (D)가 정답임을 알 수 있다.

어휘 trade A for B A를 B로 교환하다, 바꾸다 be impressed with ~에 대해 깊은 인상을 받다 ship ~을 배송하다, 선적하다

44. 화자는 청자에게 무엇을 하도록 요청하는가?
(A) 제품에 대한 가격을 낮출 것
(B) 공급업체에 연락할 것
(C) 자신에게 이메일로 거래 내역서를 보낼 것
(D) 자신에게 추가 제품을 보낼 것

해설 화자가 요청하는 일을 찾아야 하므로 화자의 말에서 요청 관련 표현이 제시되는 부분에서 단서를 파악해야 한다. 담화 후반부에 원본 설치 디스크를 언급하면서 그것을 보내 달라고(Would you be able to send it to me?) 요청하고 있다. 이는 앞서 자신이 구입했다고 언급하는 컴퓨터 외에 추가적인 물품을 요청하는 것이므로 이에 대해 말한 (D)가 정답이다.

어휘 reduce ~을 낮추다, 감소시키다 contact ~에게 연락하다 supplier 공급업체 invoice 거래 내역서 additional 추가적인 item 제품, 물품

Questions 45-47 refer to the following excerpt from a meeting.

I'd like to first of all thank everyone for attending this meeting. **45** The reason I have you all here is to show you the new phone design that we will be releasing next year. It's been developed a lot quicker than I expected, and I wanted to make sure you all see it before the media hears about it. Before you leave today, **46** I'm going to give you all a pamphlet that outlines all the features of the phone. What we don't have is a marketing strategy, and that's where you all come in. **47** I want you to go home and think about how we can attract attention to this new product. If any of you come up with something, send me an e-mail and I'll get right back to you.

먼저 이 회의에 참석해주신 모든 분들께 감사드립니다. 여러분 모두를 이곳에 모신 이유는 내년에 출시할 새 전화기 디자인을 보여드리기 위해서입니다. 예상했던 것보다 훨씬 빨리 개발되어, 언론이 제품에 대해 듣기 전에 여러분 모두 꼭 보셨으면 합니다. 오늘 나가시기 전에, 여러분 모두에게 전화기의 모든 기능을 설명하는 소책자를 드릴 것입니다. 우리에게 없는 것은 마케팅 전략인데, 이 점이 바로 여러분 모두가 관여하게 되는 부분입니다. 여러분은 댁에 가셔서 어떻게 하면 이 신제품에 대해 사람들

의 관심을 끌 수 있을지를 생각해보시기 바랍니다. 여러분 중 누구든지 뭔가 생각나면 제게 이메일을 보내주세요. 그럼 제가 바로 답변을 드리겠습니다.

어휘 **first of all** 우선 **thank A for -ing** A에게 ~한 것에 대해 감사하다 **reason** 이유 **have you all here** 여러분 모두를 이곳에 오게 하다 **show A B** A에게 B를 보여주다 **release** ~을 출시하다 **develop** ~을 개발하다 **a lot quicker than I expected** 예상했던 것보다 훨씬 빨리 **make sure** 확실히 ~하도록 하다 **media** 미디어, 언론 **leave** 떠나다, 나가다 **pamphlet** 소책자 **outline** v. ~을 간단히 설명하다 **feature** 기능, 특색 **what we don't have** 우리가 갖고 있지 않은 것 **marketing strategy** 마케팅 전략 **come in** 관여하다 **attract attention to** ~로 관심을 끌다 **come up with** ~을 생각해 내다, 떠올리다 **get right back to** ~에게 다시 바로 연락하다

45. 어떤 종류의 제품이 논의되고 있는가?
(A) 전자 기기
(B) 가구 한 점
(C) 의류 제품
(D) 컴퓨터 프로그램

해설 화자는 내년 출시 예정인 새 전화기 제품의 디자인을 보여주는 것이 회의의 목적이라고 밝히며 신제품 마케팅에 대한 아이디어를 구하고 있다. 따라서 이 담화에서 논의되는 것은 new phone임을 알 수 있다. 이를 electronic device라고 다르게 표현한 (A)가 정답이다.

어휘 **electronic** 전자의 **device** 장치, 장비 **item** 제품, 품목 **clothing** 의류
Paraphrase new phone → electronic device

46. 화자는 청자들에게 무엇을 주겠다고 말하는가?
(A) 제품 샘플
(B) 정보 소책자
(C) 시장 조사 보고서
(D) 잡지 기사

해설 담화 중반부에 화자는 I'm going to give you all a pamphlet that outlines all the features of the phone 이라고 말하고 있다. 새 전화기 제품의 특징을 안내하는 소책자를 주겠다고 하므로 (B)가 정답이다.

어휘 **market research** 시장 조사

47. 청자들에게 무엇에 대해 생각해볼 것을 요청하는가?
(A) 출시 행사 장소
(B) 제품 가격
(C) 신제품 디자인
(D) 마케팅 계획

해설 담화 끝부분에 화자는 청중들에게 집에 돌아가 신제품이 사람들의 관심을 끌게 할 방법을 생각해 볼 것을(I want you

to go home and think about how we can attract attention to this new product) 당부하고 있다. how we can attract attention to this new product와 뜻이 통하는 것은 (D) marketing plan이다.

어휘 **location** 장소, 지점 **launch** n. (제품 등의) 출시 **cost** 비용
Paraphrase how we can attract attention to this new product
→ marketing plan

Questions 48-50 refer to the following telephone message and survey.

Hello, **48** this is Gregory Doyle, the guest services manager at the Prescott Hotel. Thank you for completing a comment card before checking out. I have your card in front of me now, and I just wanted to ask you for some further information so that we can improve the overall guest experience at the hotel. I completely understand your reason for ranking our location so low. Prescott Hotel actually has other hotels in more convenient locations. **49** I have mailed you a brochure with more information about these, in case you wish to stay with us again in future. **50** What I really want to talk to you about is the category you ranked as satisfactory on the card. I'd be grateful if you could return my call to discuss this. Thank you.

안녕하세요, 저는 프레스코트 호텔 고객 서비스 매니저인 그레고리 도일입니다. 체크아웃 하시기 전에 고객 평가 카드를 작성해 주셔서 감사합니다. 지금 제 앞에 고객님의 카드가 있는데요, 저희 호텔에서 전반적인 고객 경험을 향상시킬 수 있도록 몇 가지 추가 정보를 고객님께 여쭤보고 싶었습니다. 저는 고객님께서 저희 위치에 대해 그렇게 낮은 점수를 주신 이유를 전적으로 이해하고 있습니다. 사실 프레스코트 호텔은 더 편리한 장소에 다른 지점 호텔들을 갖고 있습니다. 고객님께서 나중에 다시 저희와 함께 머물기를 원하시는 경우를 대비해서, 저는 고객님께 이곳들과 관련된 더 많은 정보가 담긴 안내책자를 우편으로 보내드렸습니다. 제가 정말로 고객님께 말씀드리고 싶은 것은 카드에 만족함이라고 등급을 매긴 부분입니다. 이 부분을 논의하기 위해 제게 답신 전화를 주시면 감사하겠습니다. 감사합니다.

	나쁨	만족	매우 만족
위치	✔		
직원			✔
음식			✔
편의시설		✔	

어휘 **guest** 고객, 손님 **complete** ~을 끝마치다, 작성하다

comment 의견, 평 check out 체크아웃하다, 비용을 지
불하고 나가다 further information 추가 정보 overall
전반적인 experience 경험 completely 완전히 rank
(등급 등) ~을 매기다 actually 실은 convenient 편리한
location 장소, 위치 in case ~할 경우를 대비해서
category 항목, 범주 grateful 감사히 여기는 poor 형편
없는 satisfactory 만족스러운 amenities 편의시설들

48. 메시지는 누가 대상일 것 같은가?
    (A) 호텔 직원
    (B) 잡지 기자
    (C) 이전 고객
    (D) 음식 평론가

해설 담화 초반부에 화자가 호텔 매니저임을 밝히면서 상대방이
      호텔에서 체크아웃 했다는 말이 나오는 것으로(~ at the
      Prescott Hotel. ~ before checking out) 볼 때, 메시지의
      대상은 이전에 머물렀던 고객임을 알 수 있으므로 정답은 (C)이
      다.

어휘 **former** 이전의 **critic** 평론가

49. 화자는 청자에게 무엇을 보냈다고 말하는가?
    (A) 안내 책자
    (B) 여행자 지도
    (C) 할인 쿠폰
    (D) 거래 내역서

해설 담화 중반부에 I have mailed you a brochure라고 알리면
      서 안내 책자를 보낸 사실을 밝히고 있으므로 정답은 (A)이다.

어휘 **invoice** 거래 내역서

50. 시각자료를 보시오. 화자는 어느 항목에 대해 논의하고 싶어 하
    는가?
    (A) 위치
    (B) 직원
    (C) 음식
    (D) 편의시설

해설 화자는 담화 후반부에 What I really want to talk to you
      about is the category you ranked as satisfactory on
      the card라는 말로 '만족'이라고 등급을 매긴 카테고리에 대해
      얘기하고 싶다고 알리고 있다. 시각자료에서 '만족'에 표시된 항
      목이 Amenities이므로 (D)가 정답이다.

어휘 **amenities** 편의시설

DAY 03 RC Half Test

1. (B)	**2.** (D)	**3.** (A)	**4.** (C)	**5.** (C)
6. (A)	**7.** (B)	**8.** (A)	**9.** (D)	**10.** (D)
11. (C)	**12.** (B)	**13.** (A)	**14.** (D)	**15.** (D)
16. (C)	**17.** (B)	**18.** (C)	**19.** (B)	**20.** (C)
21. (B)	**22.** (C)	**23.** (D)	**24.** (C)	**25.** (C)
26. (C)	**27.** (B)	**28.** (C)	**29.** (D)	**30.** (C)
31. (C)	**32.** (C)	**33.** (D)	**34.** (C)	**35.** (D)
36. (A)	**37.** (C)	**38.** (D)	**39.** (B)	**40.** (A)
41. (C)	**42.** (B)	**43.** (C)	**44.** (B)	**45.** (D)
46. (C)	**47.** (B)	**48.** (D)	**49.** (D)	**50.** (A)

Part 5

1.

정답 (B)

해석 하커 씨는 드럼몬드 주식회사의 이사진과의 협상이 잘 진행되었다고 확신하고 있다.

해설 빈칸이 정관사와 전치사 사이에 위치해 있으므로 빈칸은 명사 자리이다. 따라서 명사인 (A) negotiators와 (B) negotiations 중에서 하나를 골라야 하는데 that절의 주어로서 동사 progressed와 의미가 어울려야 하므로 '협상'을 의미하는 (B) negotiations가 정답이다.

어휘 **be certain that** ~임을 확신하다 **negotiation** 협상 **progress** 진행되다, 진척되다 **negotiator** 협상가 **negotiate** ~을 협상하다

2.

정답 (D)

해석 기술자들이 컴퓨터 네트워크 유지 보수 작업을 수행 중이며, 내일까지는 이메일을 이용할 수 없을 것입니다.

해설 선택지에 be동사의 여러 시제가 제시되어 있으므로 알맞은 시제를 고르는 문제임을 알 수 있다. 빈칸 뒤에 미래시제 단서 표현 until tomorrow가 있으므로 (D) will be가 정답이다.

어휘 **technician** 기술자 **perform** ~을 수행하다 **maintenance** 유지 보수 **access to** ~의 이용, ~로의 접근 **unavailable** 이용 불가능한

3.

정답 (A)

해석 스미스 씨는 급여 인상을 요청하기 전에 현재 진행 중인 프로젝트를 끝낼 계획이다.

해설 빈칸 다음에 제시된 requests는 명사와 동사로 모두 쓰이는데 requests 다음에 명사가 바로 이어지고 있으므로 여기서는 동사로 쓰였다는 것을 알 수 있다. 따라서 문장의 주어 역할을 할 수 있는 주격 대명사 (A) he가 정답이다.

어휘 **currently** 현재 **work on** ~에 대한 일을 하다 **request** v. ~을 요구하다 n. 요구 **raise** 급여 인상

4.

정답 (C)

해석 몽캄 식당에 근무하는 종업원들은 각 음식을 보완해 주기에 가장 적합한 와인을 고르는 능력으로 알려져 있다.

해설 빈칸이 전치사 바로 뒤에 위치해 있으므로 빈칸에는 명사와 동명사가 올 수 있다. 그런데 빈칸 뒤에 명사구가 이어져 있으므로 이 명사구를 목적어로 취할 수 있는 동명사 (C) selecting이 정답이다.

어휘 **be known for** ~으로 알려져 있다 **select** ~을 고르다, 선택하다 **suitable** 적합한 **complement** v. ~을 보완하다 **selection** 선택(한 것) **selective** 선택적인, 가리는

5.

정답 (C)

해석 새로운 세입자들께서는 아파트로 입주하신 후에 자주 아파트 공지 안내판을 확인하시기 바랍니다.

해설 빈칸 앞에 주어와 동사, to부정사구가 이미 구성이 완전하므로 빈칸은 부사 지리이다. 따라시 (C) frequently가 정답이다.

어휘 **tenant** 세입자 **be advised to do** ~하시기 바랍니다, ~하시도록 권해 드립니다 **condominium** 아파트 **announcement** 공지, 발표 **frequency** 빈도, 빈번함 **frequent** a. 잦은, 빈번한 v. ~에 자주 가다 **frequently** 자주, 빈번히

6.

정답 (A)

해석 그 고객은 윌슨 씨에게 공사 프로젝트의 완료에 대한 대략적인 진행 일정을 요청했다.

해설 빈칸이 정관사와 명사 사이에 위치해 있으므로 빈칸은 명사를 수식할 형용사 자리이다. 따라서 (A) estimated가 정답이다.

어휘 **ask A for B** A에게 B를 요청하다 **timeframe** 진행 일정, 진행 기간 **estimated** 대략적인, 추정되는 **estimate** v. ~을 추정하다, ~을 추산하다 n. 추정(치), 견적(서)

estimation 추정(치), 판단, 평가

7.
정답 (B)

해석 럼버 킹 사의 모든 영업사원들은 '더 많은 상품을 판매하기' 세미나에 참가하도록 허락 받을 것이다.

해설 빈칸 앞에 위치한 동사가 두 개의 목적어를 가지는 give의 수동태이고, 받는 사람인 sales staff가 주어 자리에 있으므로 빈칸에는 주어지는 대상을 나타내는 명사가 와야 한다. 선택지에서 명사는 불가산명사 (B) permission과 가산명사 (C) permit인데 빈칸 앞에 부정관사가 없으므로 (B) permission이 정답이다.

어휘 give A permission to do A에게 ~하는 것을 허락하다 permit v. ~을 허락하다, 허가하다 n. 허가증 permissive 허용하는

8.
정답 (A)

해석 3개월 전에 모닝사이드로 이사한 이후로, 코널리 씨는 주택 개조 공사에 1만 달러가 넘는 돈을 소비해 왔다.

해설 주절에 현재완료시제 동사와 함께 1만 달러가 넘는 돈을 소비해온 사실이 쓰여 있어 three months ago가 가리키는 과거 시점이 그 시작점인 것으로 볼 수 있으므로 '~ 이후로'라는 뜻의 전치사 (A) Since가 정답이다.

어휘 renovation 개조, 보수 since ~ 이후로 except ~을 제외하고, ~ 외에는 during ~ 중에, ~ 동안

9.
정답 (D)

해석 대표이사님께서는 라이브 공연을 이용하는 데 드는 충분한 비용을 남겨두기 위해 올해의 직원 파티에 더 저렴한 출장 요리 회사를 고용하기로 선택하셨다.

해설 선택지가 모두 다른 형용사로 구성되어 있으므로 해석을 통해 알맞은 어휘를 골라야 한다. 빈칸에는 바로 뒤에 위치한 명사를 수식해 라이브 공연을 위해 남겨두는 비용 규모와 관련된 의미를 나타내야 하므로 '충분한'을 뜻하는 (D) sufficient가 정답이다.

어휘 opt to do ~하기로 선택하다 catering 출장 요리 제공(업) live entertainment 라이브 공연 gradual 점차적인 proficient 능숙한 competent 유능한, (충분한) 능력을 갖춘 sufficient 충분한

10.
정답 (D)

해석 최근에 베리필드 지역에 몇몇 고층 아파트 단지가 건설되었는데, 이 지역은 이전에 공업 지역이었다.

해설 특정 지역의 현재와 과거의 모습을 비교하는 내용으로, 과거시제 동사와 함께 바로 앞에 위치한 지역의 과거에 대해 설명하는 관계사절에 빈칸이 있으므로 '과거에, 이전에'라는 뜻의 (D) formerly가 정답이다.

어휘 high-rise 고층의 apartment block 아파트 단지 recently 최근에 alternatively 대안으로, 대신하여 intermittently 간헐적으로 occasionally 때때로 formerly 과거에, 이전에

11.
정답 (C)

해석 다음 달에 열리는 기술 컨벤션에 대한 입장권 배정이 인사부장님에 의해 관리될 것입니다.

해설 빈칸 앞에 제시된 명사 Ticket과 빈칸 그리고 전치사구가 이어져 있고, 문장의 동사가 제시되어 있다. 따라서 Ticket과 함께 빈칸은 주어 역할을 해야 하는데 빈칸에는 명사가 들어가야 하므로 (C) allocation이 정답이다. 동명사 (D) allocating도 명사 역할을 할 수 있지만 타동사가 동명사가 되려면 뒤에 목적어가 필요하므로 오답이다.

어휘 oversee ~을 관리하다, 감독하다 HR 인사(부) allocate ~을 배정하다, 할당하다 allocation 배정, 할당

12.
정답 (B)

해석 플로이드 은행의 고객들께서는 3월 12일부터 3월 15일까지의 기간 동안 이루어진 거래가 거래 명세서에 바로 나타나지 않을 수도 있다는 점을 유념하시기 바랍니다.

해설 선택지가 전치사와 접속사로 구성되어 있으므로 문장 구조를 분석해야 한다. 빈칸 뒤에 위치한 명사구가 거래가 이뤄진 기간을 나타내므로 기간 전치사 (B) during이 정답이다.

어휘 take note 주목하다 transaction 거래 during ~동안 appear 나타나다 immediately 즉시 account statement 거래 명세서 while ~하는 동안 under ~아래로, ~미만으로 above ~위로, ~이상으로

13.
정답 (A)

해석 유효한 운전 면허증은 누구든 배송 기사 직책에 지원하시는 분께 필수 조건이다.

해설 선택지가 모두 다른 명사로 구성되어 있으므로 해석을 통해 알맞은 어휘를 골라야 한다. 빈칸 앞에 제시된 유효한 운전 면허증이 빈칸 뒤에 제시된 배송 기사 직책에 지원하는 사람에게 꼭 갖춰야 하는 요건이므로 '필수 조건, 필수 사항'이라는 뜻의 (A) requirement가 정답이다.

어휘 valid 유효한 driving license 운전 면허증 apply for ~에 지원하다 delivery 배송 position 직책, 자리 requirement 필수 조건, 필수 사항 fulfillment 이행, 실현, 성취 recognition 인지, 인정 contribution 공헌, 기여

14.

정답 (D)

해석 챗워스 씨는 바쁜 삶을 사는 학생들을 위해 대학 수업 과정 일정을 더욱 탄력적으로 만드는 데 전념하고 있다.

해설 빈칸 앞에 동명사로 쓰인 동사 make는 5형식 동사로서 뒤에 목적어와 목적보어를 가진다. 따라서 빈칸은 목적보어 자리인데 수업 일정의 운영 상태와 관련된 의미가 되어야 하므로 형용사 (D) more flexible이 정답이다.

어휘 **be committed to -ing** ~하는 데 전념하다, ~하는 데 헌신하다 **make A B** A를 B하게 만들다 **flexed** 구부러진, 몸이 풀린 **flexibility** 탄력성, 유연성 **flexibly** 탄력적이게, 유연하게 **flexible** 탄력적인, 유연한

15.

정답 (D)

해석 저희 스쿠버 다이빙 강좌에 대한 가격은 해당 그룹의 규모 및 경험 수준에 따라 다릅니다.

해설 빈칸 앞뒤에 위치한 명사구들의 의미로 볼 때, '그룹의 규모 및 경험 수준'이라는 의미로 특정 그룹이 지닌 특성을 말하는 내용이 되어야 자연스러우므로 '~의' 등의 의미로 소유나 소속, 구성 요소 등을 말할 때 사용하는 (D) of가 정답이다.

어휘 **depend upon** ~에 따라 다르다, ~에 달려 있다 **as** (자격, 신분 등) ~로서, (유사성) ~처럼, ~만큼

16.

정답 (C)

해석 세입자들은 건물 소유주에 의해 승인을 받는다면, 각자의 아파트를 장식하고 가벼운 개조 작업을 실시할 수 있다.

해설 빈칸 앞뒤에 각각 주어와 동사가 포함된 절이 있으므로 빈칸에는 이 두 절을 연결할 접속사가 필요하다. 따라서 선택지 중 유일한 접속사 (C) provided that이 정답이다.

어휘 **tenant** 세입자 **condominium** 아파트 **minor** 가벼운, 사소한 **renovation** 개조, 보수 **provided that** (만일) ~라면 **approval** 승인, 허가 **landlord** 건물 소유주, 집주인 **along with** ~와 함께 **according to** ~에 따르면 **regardless of** ~에 상관 없이

Part 6

17-20.

제논 일렉트로닉스 XE500 65인치 LED 텔레비전을 구입해 주셔서 감사합니다. **17** 저희 웹 사이트 www.xenonelectronics.com/productregistration에 해당 제품을 등록해 주시기 바랍니다. 이를 통해 저희가 귀하께 최고 수준의 지원 및 유지 관리 서비스를 제공해 드릴 수 있을 것입니다. 갖고 계신 영수증의 정보뿐만 아니라 제품 일련 번호도 입력하셔야 할 것입니다. **18** 이는 텔레비전 뒷면에서 찾으실 수 있습니다. 등록 과정은 불과

몇 분밖에 걸리지 않습니다.

귀하의 제품을 등록하시는 것으로, 연장된 3년 기간의 품질 보증 서비스를 활성화하시게 됩니다. **19** 그 후에, 귀하의 텔레비전은 최초의 구입일로부터 3년 동안 기술적인 결함 및 돌발적인 손상에 대한 서비스가 보장될 것입니다. 저희 웹 사이트에 나와 있는 고객 지원 번호에 주목하시기 바라며, 귀하의 구입 제품에 어떤 문제든 발생하는 경우에 주저하지 마시고 저희에게 **20** 연락 주십시오.

어휘 **register** ~을 등록하다 **A allow B to do** A로 인해 B가 ~할 수 있다, A가 B에게 ~할 수 있게 해주다 **provide A with B** A에게 B를 제공하다 **support** 지원, 후원 **maintenance** 유지 관리, 시설 관리 **as well as** ~뿐만 아니라 …도 **registration** 등록 **process** 과정 **take** ~의 시간이 걸리다 **activate** ~을 활성화시키다, ~을 가동시키다 **extended** 연장된 **warranty** 품질 보증(서) **cover** (보험 등이) ~을 보장하다, (비용 등에 대해) ~을 충당하다 **fault** 결함, 흠 **accidental** 돌발적인, 우연한 **take note of** ~에 주목하다, ~을 받아 적다 **hesitate to do** ~하기를 주저하다, ~하기를 망설이다

17.

정답 (B)

해설 빈칸 뒤에 제시된 웹 사이트는 그 다음 문장에 쓰여 있는 us와 같이 이 제품 정보를 작성한 회사의 웹 사이트이다. 따라서, us와 동일 대상을 지칭하는 1인칭 소유격대명사가 빈칸에 쓰여야 알맞으므로 (B) our가 정답이다.

18.

정답 (C)

해석 (A) 반품하실 때 영수증을 지참하고 오시기 바랍니다.
(B) 교체 부품은 온라인에서 주문하실 수 있습니다.
(C) 이는 텔레비전 뒷면에서 찾으실 수 있습니다.
(D) 문제를 해결하시려면 저희 문제 해결 가이드를 한 번 확인해 보십시오.

해설 빈칸 앞에 영수증의 정보와 제품 일련 번호를 입력해야 한다는 말이 쓰여 있다. 따라서, 제품 일련 번호를 의미하는 the product's serial number를 this로 지칭해 이 번호를 확인할 수 있는 방법을 알리는 (C)가 정답이다.

어휘 **return** ~을 반품하다, ~을 반납하다 **replacement** 교체(품), 대체(품) **part** 부품 **troubleshooting** 문제 해결, 고장 수리 **solve** ~을 해결하다

19.

정답 (B)

해설 빈칸 앞에는 제품을 등록하면 3년 기간의 품질 보증 서비스가 시작된다는 말이, 빈칸 뒤에는 3년 동안 보장되는 서비스를 설명하는 말이 쓰여 있다. 이는 보증 서비스가 시작되고 나중에 발생 가능한 일을 차례로 알리는 흐름에 해당되므로 '그 후에, 나중에'라는 의미로 순서를 나타낼 때 사용하는 (B) Afterwards

가 정답이다.

어휘 **in contrast** 반대로, 그에 반해서 **afterwards** 그 후에, 나중에 **similarly** 유사하게, 마찬가지로 **however** 하지만, 그러나

20.

정답· (C)

해설 빈칸 앞에 위치한 동사 hesitate은 to부정사와 결합해 '~하기를 주저하다, ~하기를 망설이다'를 의미하므로 (C) to contact가 정답이다.

어휘 **contact** ~에게 연락하다

21-24.

> **정책 변경 압박을 받고 있는 맥주 회사**
>
> 5월 16일 - 수제 맥주 정기 배송 서비스 업체인 비어365가 마침내 다음 달부터 자사의 취소 정책 및 절차를 변경하는 데 동의했습니다. 현재, 회원들은 월간 정기 배송 서비스를 취소하고자 하는 경우에 반드시 이 회사에 직접 전화해야 하지만, **21** 곧 온라인에서 손쉽게 취소할 수 있는 선택권이 제공될 것입니다.
>
> 현재의 취소 절차는 여러 이유로 비난 받아 왔습니다. **22** 예를 들어, 전화를 건 사람은 흔히 한 시간 넘게 대기 상태에 놓여 있은 후에야 마침내 직원과 이야기합니다. 또한, 취소 직통 전화가 오직 월요일부터 금요일, 오전 9시에서 오후 5시 사이에만 운영되고 있어, 많은 사람들이 전화하는 것을 **23** 불편하게 만들고 있습니다. 비어365의 설립자 케이트 존스 씨의 말에 따르면, "저희는 고객 여러분의 말씀에 귀 기울였으며, 원하시는 것을 제공해 드리기 위해 항상 애쓰고 있습니다." **24** 정기 배송 서비스를 종료할 수 있는 선택권은 6월 1일에 웹 사이트에 추가될 것입니다.

어휘 **pressured to do** ~하도록 압박 받는 **policy** 정책 **agree to do** ~하는 데 동의하다 **cancellation** 취소 **procedure** 절차 **currently** 현재 **cancel** ~을 취소하다 **current** 현재의 **criticize A for B** B에 대해 A를 비난하다 **be placed on hold** 대기 상태에 놓이다 **agent** 직원, 대리인 **hotline** 직통 전화 **operational** 운영되는, 가동되는 **make it A for B to do** B가 ~하는 것을 A하게 만들다 **founder** 설립자, 창립자 **strive to do** ~하기 위해 애쓰다

21.

정답 (B)

해설 빈칸이 속한 but절에 미래시제 동사와 함께 앞으로 온라인에서 손쉽게 취소할 수 있는 선택권이 제공될 것이라고 알리는 말이 쓰여 있다. 따라서, 미래시제 동사와 어울리는 부사로서 '곧, 머지 않아'라는 의미로 가까운 미래에 발생되는 일임을 말할 때 사용하는 (B) soon이 정답이다.

어휘 **lately** 최근에, 근래에 **nearly** 거의

22.

정답 (C)

해설 빈칸 뒤에 전화를 건 사람이 한 시간 넘게 대기한 후에야 직원과 이야기한다는 말이 쓰여 있다. 이는 빈칸 앞에 위치한 문장에서 말하는 여러 비난 이유의 한 가지 예시에 해당되는 것으로 볼 수 있으므로 '예를 들어'라는 의미로 예시를 말할 때 사용하는 (C) For example이 정답이다.

어휘 **however** 하지만, 그러나 **as a result** 결과적으로 **on the other hand** 반면에, 한편

23.

정답 (D)

해설 빈칸 앞에 분사로 쓰여 있는 동사 make는 「make it A for B to do」의 구조로 쓰여 'B가 ~하는 것을 A하게 만들다'라는 의미를 나타낸다. 여기서 A에는 형용사 보어가, B에는 to부정사의 행위 주체를 나타내는 명사가 각각 쓰이므로 형용사인 (D) inconvenient가 정답이다.

어휘 **inconvenience** n. 불편함 v. ~를 불편하게 하다 **inconveniently** 불편하게 **inconvenient** 불편한

24.

정답 (D)

해석 (A) 고객들은 새로운 종류의 제품에 대해 호의적으로 반응했습니다.
(B) 따라서, 여러 신입 전화 상담원이 앞으로 몇 주 동안에 걸쳐 고용될 것입니다.
(C) 비어365는 자사의 혁신적인 마케팅 방식으로 뛰어난 명성을 얻었습니다.
(D) 정기 배송 서비스를 종료할 수 있는 선택권은 6월 1일에 웹 사이트에 추가될 것입니다.

해설 빈칸 앞 문장들을 읽어 보면 첫 단락에서 시행된다고 언급한 온라인 취소 선택권이 도입되는 배경을 설명하고 있다. 따라서 곧 도입되는 온라인 취소 선택권의 시행과 관련된 의미를 지닌 문장이 쓰여야 자연스러우므로 그 선택권의 시행 날짜를 알리는 (D)가 정답이다.

어휘 **respond to** ~에 반응하다, ~에 대응하다 **favorably** 호의적으로 **range** 종류, 제품군 **as such** 따라서, 그러므로 **garner** ~을 얻다 **reputation** 명성, 평판 **innovative** 혁신적인 **method** 방식, 방법

Part 7

25-26.

> **모힌더 싱 [오전 9:24]**
> 레이첼 씨, **25** 저에게 우리 폭 찹 요리의 제공 방식과 장식 요소에 대해 적용하도록 요청하셨던 변경 사항과 관련해 여쭤보고 싶은 것이 있었습니다.

레이첼 샌더스 [오전 9:25]
좋아요, 모힌더 씨, 그게 뭔가요?

모힌더 싱 [오전 9:27]
제가 머스터드 소스를 자색 양파 위에 붓는 게 좋으세요, 아니면 폭 찹 옆에 붓는 게 좋으신가요?

레이첼 샌더스 [오전 9:29]
두 가지 스타일을 모두 확인해서 무엇이 가장 좋아 보이는지 알아보고 싶어요. 하지만, 제가 점심 시간이나 되어야 레스토랑에 갈 겁니다.

모힌더 싱 [오전 9:30]
우리가 문을 열 때까지 기다릴 수 있을 것 같아요. 하지만, 첫 식사 손님 그룹이 11시 15분으로 예약되어 있습니다.

레이첼 샌더스 [오전 9:31]
왜 기다리시죠? 26 그냥 서로 나란히 놓은 두 가지 요리 사진을 찍어서 저에게 보내 주세요.

모힌더 싱 [오전 9:32]
그렇게 하겠습니다. 약 30분 정도만 시간을 주세요.

레이첼 샌더스 [오전 9:33]
좋습니다. 제가 다시 연락 드려서 어떻게 생각하는지 알려 드릴게요.

모힌더 싱 [오전 9:35]
알겠습니다. 곧 다시 얘기하시죠.

어휘   make a change to ~을 변경하다 ask A to do A에게 ~하도록 요청하다 presentation 제공 방식, 표현 방식 garnish 장식(물) pour ~을 붓다, ~을 따르다 would like to do ~하고 싶다, ~하고자 하다 not A until B B나 되어야 A하다 get to ~로 가다, ~에 도착하다 suppose (that) ~라고 생각하다 be booked for (시간, 날짜 등) ~로 예약되어 있다 next to ~ 옆에 one another 서로 You got it 그렇게 하겠습니다, 알겠습니다 about 약, 대략 get back to ~에게 다시 연락하다

25. 싱 씨는 누구일 것 같은가?
(A) 레스토랑 소유주
(B) 계산 담당 직원
(C) 요리사
(D) 식료품점 직원

정답   (C)

해설   싱 씨가 처음 작성한 메시지에 자신에게 폭 찹 요리의 제공 방식과 장식 요소에 대해 적용하도록 요청한 변경 사항을(the changes you asked me to make to the presentation and garnish of our pork chop dish) 언급하는 말이 쓰여 있다. 이는 요리사가 할 수 있는 일에 해당되므로 (C)가 정답이다.

어휘   owner 소유주, 주인 grocery store 식료품점

26. 오전 9시 32분에, 싱 씨가 "You got it"이라고 쓸 때 무엇을 의미하는 것 같은가?
(A) 레스토랑에서 샌더스 씨를 만날 것이다.
(B) 샌더스 씨에게 파일을 보냈다.
(C) 일부 음식의 사진을 촬영할 것이다.
(D) 일부 메뉴 품목을 변경했다.

정답   (C)

해설   질문에 제시된 You got it이라는 말은 '그렇게 하겠습니다, 알겠습니다' 등의 의미로 동의나 수락 등을 나타낼 때 사용하는 말이다. 9시 31분 메시지에서 샌더스 씨가 서로 나란히 놓은 두 가지 요리 사진을 찍어서 자신에게 보내 달라고 요청한 것에 대해 그렇게 하겠다고 동의하면서 30분 정도만 시간을 달라고 부탁하고 있으므로 (C)가 정답이다.

어휘   take a photograph of ~을 사진 촬영하다

27-29.

러쉬 그린 사

28(D) 여러분의 가정 또는 회사를 아름답게 가꿔 드립니다!

저희 러쉬 그린은, 사람들이 여러분의 가정이나 회사를 방문할 때 종종 가장 먼저 보는 것이 정원과 실외 공간이라는 것을 알고 있습니다. 저희는 이러한 공간을 더 매력적이고 인상적인 공간으로 만들어줄 다양한 전문적인 서비스를 제공합니다. 27 선택하신 관목과 나무를 심고 마음에 드시도록 전문적으로 가꾸어 드리는 것뿐만이 아니라, 인공폭포 및 분수대, 새 물통, 또는 연못 등과 같은 중앙 장식물을 설치해 드립니다. 러쉬 그린은 업계에서 28(B) 20년 이상의 경험이 있으며 28(A) 영국의 가장 큰 몇몇 기업들도 고객으로 맞이하고 있습니다. 28(C) 저희 영업시간은 월요일부터 토요일까지이며, 아주 이른 오전 6시에 시작해 저녁 8시나 되어야 영업이 끝납니다.

29 만약 저희와 일정을 잡고, 저희가 가정이나 일터에 방문하여, 비전과 요건에 대해 이야기하고 싶으시다면 555-7759로 바로 연락 주십시오. 저희 사무실은 브랜포드 중심에 위치해 있지만 주위의 여러 농네와 시내에도 서비스를 제공하고 있습니다. 저희 서비스 및 서비스 구역 그리고 비용에 대한 추가 상세 정보는 www.lushgreenco.co.uk에서 보실 수 있습니다.

어휘   professional 전문적인 attractive 매력적인 impressive 인상적인 expertly 훌륭하게 sculpt ~을 조각하다 install ~을 설치하다 water feature 인공폭포 centerpieces 중앙부 장식 industry 산업 discuss ~을 의논하다 vision 비전 requirement 요건 surrounding 주변의

27. 러쉬 그린 사는 무슨 종류의 회사인가?
(A) 인테리어 디자인 회사
(B) 조경 서비스업체
(C) 건설 기업
(D) 환경 재단

정답 **(B)**

해설 첫 단락 초반부에 관목과 나무를 심고 전문적으로 가꾸어 주는 것뿐만 아니라, 중앙 장식물을 설치해 준다고(Not only can we plant the bushes and trees of your choice and expertly sculpt them to your liking, but we can also install water features and centerpieces) 회사를 소개하고 있다. 따라서 (B)가 정답이다.

어휘 **corporation** 기업 **environment** 환경 **foundation** 재단

---

28. 러쉬 그린 사에 대해 언급되지 않은 것은?

(A) 여러 중요 기업들과 일해 왔다.
(B) 20년 이상 동안 사업을 해왔다.
(C) 일주일 내내 서비스를 제공한다.
(D) 주거지 및 기업체를 모두 대상으로 한다.

정답 **(C)**

해설 첫 문단 마지막 문장에 러쉬 그린 사의 영업시간이 월요일부터 토요일까지라고(We operate Monday through Saturday) 나타나 있으므로 (C)가 정답이다. 20년 이상의 경험이 있다는(Lush Green has over two decades of experience in the industry) 부분에서 (B)를, 영국의 가장 큰 기업들도 고객으로 맞이하고 있다는(counts some of the largest corporations in the UK among its clients) 부분에서 (A)를, 광고 부제목에서 가정 또는 회사를 아름답게 가꿔준다는(Making your home or business beautiful!) 부분에서 (D)를 찾을 수 있다.

어휘 **be in business** 사업을 하다, 운영하다 **deal with** ~을 대하다, 다루다

---

29. 광고에 따르면, 잠재적인 고객은 어떻게 상담 일정을 잡을 수 있는가?

(A) 브랜포드에 있는 사무실에 방문해서
(B) 웹 사이트에 로그인해서
(C) 러쉬 그린 사에 이메일을 보내서
(D) 전화를 걸어서

정답 **(D)**

해설 마지막 문단 첫 문장에서 일정을 잡고, 가정이나 일터에 방문하여, 비전과 요건에 대해 이야기하고 싶다면 555-7759로 연락달라는(If you are interested in scheduling a time for us to visit your home or workplace to discuss your vision and requirements, call us directly at 555-7759) 부분에서 전화를 통하여 상담을 잡을 수 있다는 것을 알 수 있다. 따라서 (D)가 정답이다.

어휘 **potential** 가능성이 있는, 잠재적인

30-32.

에반젤린 케이준 비스트로
블루 바이우 가, 8724 번지 뉴올리언스, 로스앤젤레스 70119

에반젤린 케이준 비스트로는 남부 정통 요리를 편안한 분위기에 알맞은 가격으로 제공하는 것을 목표로 하고 있습니다. 저희 본점과 새로 생긴 베이사이드 로드 지점에서는 최근 많은 흥미진진한 변화가 있었습니다. 3월에 선보인 새우 에투페는 4월에 추가된 가지 피로그와 마찬가지로 벌써 단골 고객들에게 확고한 인기 메뉴가 되었습니다. **31** 가장 흥미로운 5월의 추가 메뉴는 저희의 '속을 채운 메기 요리'였는데, 그것은 이미 저희 매장에서 가장 잘 팔리는 주요리로서 유명한 연어 구이를 대체했습니다. 여러분의 의견은 저희가 제공하는 요리와 서비스의 기준을 지속적으로 향상시킬 수 있게 합니다. **30** 잠시 시간을 내셔서 이 의견 양식을 작성하시고 종업원에게 전달하여 주십시오.

고객 성함: 사이먼 빌뇌브
방문일/시간: 5월 27일, 오후 7시 30분
32 **주문한 에피타이저:** 녹색 토마토 튀김
주문한 메인 요리: 돼지고기 갈비
주문한 사이드 메뉴: 악어 소시지
주문한 디저트: 바나나 튀김

기타 의견:
항상 그렇듯이 돼지고기 갈비는 육즙이 많고 맛있었습니다. **32** 하지만 녹색 토마토 튀김 같은 간단한 요리가 왜 거의 45분이 걸렸는지 모르겠습니다. 지난번에 주문했을 때에는 그러지 않았습니다. 방문하였을 때 주차장은 꽉 차 있었지만 식당 밖의 길가에 충분한 공간이 있었습니다.

어휘 **aim to do** ~하는 것을 목표로 하다 **authentic** 정통의, 진짜인, 진품인 **cuisine** 요리 **relaxed** 편안한, 여유 있는 **setting** 배경, 장소 **etouffee** 에투페, 찜 요리 **eggplant** 가지 **pirogue** 피로그(반으로 잘라 카누모양으로 구운 요리) **stuffed** 채워진 **catfish** 메기 **replace** ~을 교체하다, 대체하다 **blackened** 검게 그을린, 구운 **redfish** 연어(수컷) **entree** 앙트레(코스 요리 중 주요리) **continually** 지속적으로, 꾸준히 **comment form** 의견 양식 **pork chop** 돼지 갈비살 **fritter** 튀김 **succulent** 즙이 많은 **car park** 주차장 **plenty of** 충분한

---

30. 이 양식의 주된 목적은 무엇인가?

(A) 고객들을 개업식에 초대하는 것
(B) 앞으로 있을 메뉴 변경에 대해 식당 손님에게 알리는 것
(C) 고객의 의견을 요청하는 것
(D) 새로운 식당으로 가는 방향을 알려주는 것

정답 **(C)**

해설 첫 단락 마지막 문장을 읽어보면 의견 양식을 작성하여 제출해 달라는(Please take a moment to complete this comment form and hand it to your server) 요청이 담겨 있다. 따라서 고객들에게 의견을 부탁한다는 (C)가 정답이다.

어휘 **grand opening** 개업식 **diner** 식당 손님, 식사를 하는 사람 **solicit** ~을 요청하다, 간청하다 **direction** 방향

31. 어떤 메뉴 품목이 메뉴에 가장 최근에 추가되었는가?

    (A) 연어 구이
    (B) 새우 에투페
    (C) 속을 채운 메기 요리
    (D) 가지 피로그

정답 (C)

해설 첫 단락 중반부에 3월과 4월에 추가된 요리를 언급하면서 5월의 추가 메뉴인 속을 채운 메기 요리도 함께 언급했으므로(The Shrimp Etouffee we introduced in March ~ as has the Eggplant Pirogue added in April. The most exciting addition in May was our Stuffed Catfish) (C)가 정답이다.

어휘 **added to** ~에 추가된

32. 이 양식에서 빌뇌브 씨에 대해 유추할 수 있는 것은 무엇인가?

    (A) 식당의 새로운 요리 중 하나를 주문했다.
    (B) 식당을 처음으로 방문하는 중이었다.
    (C) 애피타이저를 받기 위해 오래 기다렸다.
    (D) 식당 가까이에 있는 주차 공간을 찾지 못했다.

정답 (C)

해설 마지막 문단에서 빌뇌브 씨는 녹색 토마토 튀김 같은 간단한 요리가 왜 거의 45분이 걸렸는지 모르겠다고(I'm not sure why it took almost 45 minutes to cook such a simple dish as fried green tomatoes) 언급했고, 두 번째 문단에서 빌뇌브 씨가 시킨 에피타이저가 녹색 토마토 튀김인 것을(Appetizer ordered: Fried Green Tomatoes) 알 수 있으므로 (C)가 정답이다.

어휘 **appetizer** 애피타이저, 전채요리 **fail to do** ~하는 것을 실패하다, ~하지 못하다 **parking space** 주차 공간, 주차장

33-36.

파인즈 씨께,

우리 지역에 오신 것을 환영하며, 오션뷰 입주자 협회에 가입하신 것에 대해 감사드립니다. 이곳에서 즐겁게 거주하시기 바라며, **33** 우리 지역을 훌륭하게 유지하는 데 있어 입주자 가이드 라인을 따르는 일이 쉽고 유익하게 생각되시기를 바랍니다. **34** 저희 입주자 협회는 2동 아파트에서 매달 10일에 모임을 갖습니다. 저희는 입주자 협회의 모든 회원들께 이 회의에 참석하셔서 지역 관련 사안을 논의하시거나 긴급 상황의 경우에 대비해 **35** 다른 입주자들과 연락처를 교환하시도록 권해 드리고 있습니다. 또한 월례 회의 시간에 오션뷰 아파트 소식지도 찾아 보실 수 있습니다.

오션뷰 아파트 직원들이 대부분의 시설 관리를 처리하고 있지만, 입주자로서 여러분께도 몇 가지 책임이 있습니다. 모든 입주자들은 반드시 다음 가이드라인을 준수해야 합니다.

- 모든 쓰레기를 적절하게 표기된 구역에 놓아 주십시오.
- 제공된 통에 재활용 물품을 분리해 넣으십시오.
- 모든 방문자에게 반드시 방문자 주차 구역에 주차해야 한다는 점

을 알리십시오. 추가로, **36** 저희는 귀하께서 다음 번 월례 회의 시간에 오셔서 입주자 협회의 나머지 분들께 귀하를 소개하실 수 있기를 바랍니다. 파인즈 씨, 다시 한번 우리 지역에 오신 것을 환영하며, 귀하와 좋은 이웃이 될 수 있기를 바랍니다.

테시 콜
회장, 오션뷰 입주자 협회

어휘 **neighborhood** 지역, 인근 **join** ~에 가입하다, 합류하다 **tenant** 입주자 **association** 협회 **encourage A to do** A에게 ~하도록 권하다, 장려하다 **in case of** ~의 경우에 (대비해) **take care of** ~을 처리하다, 다루다 **maintenance** 시설 관리, 유지 관리 **responsibility** 책임 **comply with** ~을 준수하다, 따르다 **place** v. ~을 놓다, 두다 **appropriately** 적절하게, 알맞게 **marked** 표기된 **separate** ~을 분리하다 **bin** 통, 쓰레기통 **neighbor** 이웃

33. 회람의 목적은 무엇인가?

    (A) 수신인에게 발표를 하도록 요청하는 것
    (B) 임대료가 지불되도록 요청하는 것
    (C) 회원 자격에 필요한 과정을 이야기하는 것
    (D) 주민 대상 의무들을 상세히 설명하는 것

정답 (D)

해설 첫 단락에 해당 지역을 훌륭하게 유지하는 데 있어 입주자 가이드라인을 따르는 일이 쉽고 유익하게 생각되기를 바란다고(We hope you'll enjoy living here and find following the tenant guidelines easy and helpful in keeping our neighborhood great) 알리면서 준수해야 할 사항들을 설명하고 있다. 이는 주민들이 해야 하는 의무적인 일들을 설명하는 것이므로 (D)가 정답이다.

어휘 **ask A to do** A에게 ~하도록 요청하다 **receiver** 수신인 **give a presentation** 발표하다 **request that** ~하도록 요청하다 **make a payment** 지불하다 **relate** ~을 이야기하다 **process** 과정 **duty** 의무, 지무

34. 오션뷰 입주자 협회는 얼마나 자주 만나는가?

    (A) 일주일에 한 번
    (B) 격주에 한 번
    (C) 한 달에 한 번
    (D) 일 년에 한 번

정답 (C)

해설 첫 단락에 입주자 협회가 2동 아파트에서 매달 10일에 모임을 갖는다고(The tenants association meets on the 10th day of every month in apartment 2) 알리고 있으므로 (C)가 정답이다.

35. 파인즈 씨는 누구와 주기적으로 연락하고 지낼 것으로 예상되는가?

　　(A) 해당 협회 회장
　　(B) 오션뷰 직원들
　　(C) 소식지 작성자들
　　(D) 오션뷰 입주자들

정답　(D)

해설　첫 단락에 입주자 협회 회의에 참석해 다른 입주자들과 연락처를 교환하도록 권하고 있다고(We encourage all members of the tenants association to attend these meetings and to exchange contact information with other tenants) 알리고 있으므로 (D)가 정답이다.

어휘　**be expected to do** ~할 것으로 예상되다 **stay in regular contact with** ~와 주기적으로 연락하고 지내다

36. 파인즈 씨는 한 달 내로 무엇을 하도록 권장되는가?

　　(A) 회의에서 자신을 소개하는 일
　　(B) 자신의 아파트로 손님들을 초대하는 일
　　(C) 자신의 쓰레기에서 나오는 재활용 물품들을 분리하는 일
　　(D) 지도부 직책에 지원하는 일

정답　(A)

해설　마지막 단락에 상대방에게 다음 번 월례 회의 시간에 와서 입주자 협회의 나머지 사람들께 소개할 수 있기를 바란다고(we hope you will come to our next monthly meeting to introduce yourself to the rest of the tenants association) 알리고 있으므로 (A)가 정답이다.

어휘　**be encouraged to do** ~하도록 권장되다 **garbage** 쓰레기 **leadership** 지휘부, 지도부

37-40.

> 9월 12일
> 론다 오길비 씨
> 스트랫포드 로드 501번지
> 던디, 스코틀랜드, UK
> DD5 7PS
>
> 오길비 씨께,
>
> 이곳 저희 매닝 다이어그노스틱스 주식회사의 이사진 사이에서 심사숙고한 끝에, **37 39 40** 귀하께서 10월 1일, 월요일부터 실험실 기술자 직책을 맡으시도록 선택되셨다는 사실을 알려 드리게 되어 기쁩니다. — [1] —. 저희가 이미 귀하의 이전 고용주들께 보내주신 추천서를 받았으며, 귀하께서는 8월 14일에 이력서 및 지원서와 함께 대학 학위 및 성적 증명서 사본을 제출하셨습니다. — [2] —.
>
> **38** 일단 이곳에서 근무를 시작하시는 대로, 급여를 받으실 수 있게 귀하께 포브스 저축 은행에 계좌를 하나 마련하시도록 요청 드릴 것입니다. — [3] —. **39** 저희 인사부는 모든 신입 직원들께 저희 시설에서 업무를 시작하시기 전에 실험실을 견학하고 기본적인

> 보건 안전 교육 과정을 거치시도록 요구하고 있습니다. 귀하께 적합한 날짜를 선택하셔서 가급적 빨리 저에게 알려 주시기 바랍니다. — [4] —. 제가 귀하의 계약서를 2부 동봉해 드렸습니다. 두 계약서에 모두 서명하신 다음, 첫 공식 출근일에 1부를 지참하고 오시기 바랍니다.
>
> 안녕히 계십시오.
>
> 해럴드 레이드
>
> 수석 과학 담당관
> 매닝 다이어그노스틱스 주식회사

어휘　**deliberation** 숙고 **announce that** ~임을 알리다, ~라고 발표하다 **select** ~을 선택하다 **assume** (책임 등) ~을 맡다 **reference letter** 추천서 **former** 이전의, 과거의, 전직 ~의 **employer** 고용주 **transcript** 성적 증명서 **along with** ~와 함께 **résumé** 이력서 **once** 일단 ~하는 대로, ~하자마자 **ask that** ~하도록 요청하다 **set up** ~을 마련하다, ~을 설정하다, ~을 설치하다 **account** 계좌, 계정 **wage** 급여, 임금 **require that** ~하도록 요구하다 **laboratory** 실험실 **undergo** ~을 거치다, ~을 겪다 **facility** 시설(물) **be suitable for** ~에게 적합하다, ~에게 어울리다 **let A know** A에게 알리다 **at your earliest possible convenience** 가급적 빨리 **enclose** ~을 동봉하다 **contract** 계약(서) **official** 공식적인, 정식의

37. 편지가 왜 오길비 씨에게 보내졌는가?

　　(A) 면접 시간에 참석하도록 요구하기 위해
　　(B) 필수 서류를 제출하도록 요청하기 위해
　　(C) 취업 자리를 제안하기 위해
　　(D) 지원서 접수를 확인해 주기 위해

정답　(C)

해설　첫 단락에 오길비 씨에게 실험실 기술자 직책을 맡도록 선택된 사실을 알린다는 말이(you have been selected to assume the role of lab technician, starting from Monday, October 1) 쓰여 있다. 이는 일자리를 제안한다는 뜻을 나타내는 말이므로 (C)가 정답이다.

어휘　**attend** ~에 참석하다 **necessary** 필수의, 필요한 **offer A B** A에게 B를 제안하다, A에게 B를 제공하다 **employment** 취업, 고용 **receipt** 받음, 수령, 영수증

38. 매닝 다이어그노스틱스 주식회사와 관련해 암시된 것은 무엇인가?

　　(A) 한 곳이 넘는 사업 지점을 운영하고 있다.
　　(B) 현재 여러 직책을 충원하려 시도하고 있다.
　　(C) 최근 신임 이사들을 선임했다.
　　(D) 직원들에게 같은 금융 기관을 이용하게 하는 것을 선호한다.

정답　(D)

해설　두 번째 단락에 일을 시작하는 대로 포브스 저축 은행에 급여를 받을 수 있는 계좌를 하나 만들도록 요청할 것이라고(we will ask that you set up an account with Forbes Savings Bank in order to receive your wages) 알리고 있다. 이는 소속 직원들에게 동일하게 요청하는 사항으로 볼 수 있으므로 (D)가 정답이다.

어휘 **operate** ~을 운영하다, ~을 가동하다 **location** 지점, 위치 **currently** 현재 **attempt to do** ~하려 시도하다 **recently** 최근 **appoint** ~을 선임하다, ~을 임명하다 **financial** 금융의, 재무의 **institution** 기관, 협회

39. 오길비 씨가 9월 말이 되기 전에 무엇을 하도록 요청 받는가?
(A) 금융 상세 정보를 제출하는 일
(B) 교육 시간에 참석하는 일
(C) 서명한 계약서를 보내는 일
(D) 이전의 고용주에게 연락하는 일

정답 (B)

해설 9월 말은 첫 단락에서 오길비 씨의 근무 시작일로 언급하는 10월 1일이(starting from Monday, October 1) 되기 직전의 시점이다. 이 시점과 관련해, 두 번째 단락에 인사부에서 모든 신입 직원들에게 업무를 시작하기 전에 실험실을 견학하고 기본적인 보건 안전 교육 과정을 거치도록 요구한다고(all new staff members receive a tour of the laboratories and undergo basic health and safety training before starting work at our facility) 알리는 말이 쓰여 있어 오길비 씨가 9월 말까지 이 두 가지를 완료해야 한다는 것을 알 수 있으므로 둘 중 하나인 교육 과정 참석을 언급한 (B)가 정답이다.

어휘 **details** 상세 정보, 세부 사항 **training** 교육, 훈련 **session** (특정 활동을 위한) 시간

40. [1], [2], [3], [4]로 표기된 위치들 중에서, 다음 문장이 들어가기에 가장 적절한 곳은 어디인가?

"해당 공석에 대한 관심이 많았지만, 귀하께서 다른 지원자들 사이에서 돋보이셨습니다."

(A) [1]
(B) [2]
(C) [3]
(D) [4]

정답 (A)

해설 제시된 문장은 특정 공석을 the vacancy로 지칭해 그 자리에 대한 관심이 많았지만 다른 지원자들 사이에서 돋보였다는 의미를 나타내는데, 이는 오길비 씨가 합격한 이유에 해당되는 것으로 볼 수 있다. 따라서, 합격 사실을 알리는 문장 뒤에 위치한 [1]에 들어가 그 이유를 알리는 흐름이 되어야 자연스러우므로 (A)가 정답이다.

어휘 **interest in** ~에 대한 관심 **vacancy** 공석, 빈 자리 **stand out** 돋보이다, 두드러지다, 눈에 띄다 **applicant** 지원자, 신청자

41-45.

수신: 엘리자베스 뱅크스 <elizbanks@halomail.com>
발신: 로드니 폴웰 <gamanager@moorfield.co.uk>
제목: 결혼식 축하드립니다
날짜: 5월 19일

뱅크스 씨께,

5월 14일에 있었던 귀하의 아름다운 결혼식 행사장으로 무어필드 메이너를 선택해 주셔서 감사드립니다. 귀하의 특별했던 하루 및 저희가 제공해 드린 서비스가 즐거우셨기를 진심으로 바랍니다. **42(D)** 잘 조각된 저희 구내와 정원이 귀하의 기념 행사에 완벽한 배경을 제공해 드렸습니다. **42(A)** 건물 앞쪽 바깥에 위치한 분수대 옆에서 촬영한 사진들은 특별히 고급스러워 보였습니다. 저는 귀하 및 귀하의 남편 분, 그리고 **42(C)** 200명이 넘는 손님께서 그랜드 다이닝 룸에서 제공 받으신 모든 음식을 즐기셨기를 바랍니다. 저희가 현재 오직 신랑 신부만 대상으로 현장 숙소를 제공해 드리고 있어 유감스럽게 생각하지만, 근처에 위치한 올리브 호텔의 객실들이 귀하의 손님들께 더없이 만족스러우셨으리라 믿습니다.

저희 **43** 결혼 행사 진행 책임자 앤 언더우드 씨께서 귀하께 축복의 말씀 전해 드리도록 요청하셨습니다. **41** 저희 행사장과 음식, 직원들, 그리고 전반적인 행사 기획 능력과 관련해 정확히 어떻게 생각하셨는지 자세히 설명하시는 이메일을 보내 주실 수 있다면 감사하겠습니다.

안녕히 계십시오.

로드니 폴웰
총무부장
무어필드 메이너

어휘 **venue** 행사장, 개최 장소 **well-sculpted** 잘 조각된 **grounds** 구내 **backdrop** 배경(막) **next to** ~ 옆에 **water fountain** 분수대 **exceptionally** 특별히, 유난히 **elegant** 고급스러운, 우아한 **serve A B** (음식 등) A에게 B를 제공하다 **unfortunate** 유감스러운, 불운한 **currently** 현재 **on-site** 현장의, 현지의 **bride and groom** 신랑 신부 **nearby** 근처의 **satisfactory** 만족스러운 **coordinator** 진행 책임자, 편성 책임자 **convey** ~을 전하다, ~을 전달하다 **exactly** 정확히 **overall** 전반적인 **planning** 기획

수신: 로드니 폴웰 <gamanager@moorfield.co.uk>
발신: 엘리자베스 뱅크스 <elizbanks@halomail.com>
제목: 회신: 결혼식 축하드립니다
날짜: 5월 20일

폴웰 씨께,

저희는 무어필드 메이너에서 환상적인 하루를 보냈으며, 굉장히 아름다운 행사장 및 정원과 함께 더 행복할 수는 없었을 것입니다. 저희는 또한 모든 직원 분들의 열정과 정중함에도 매우 깊은 인상을 받았습니다. 음식은 아주 맛있었는데, 제공해 주신 웨딩 케이크

를 저희 손님들께서 특히 마음에 들어 하셨습니다. 하지만, **43** 제 남편과 저를 가장 기쁘게 했던 것은 저희가 결혼 행사 진행 책임자로부터 받았던 배려와 관심이었습니다. 이분께서는 반드시 모든 일이 순조롭게 진행되도록 하시기 위해 항상 자리를 지키고 계셨습니다.

약간 개선할 수도 있겠다 싶은 몇몇 특징을 확인해 드려야 한다면, 아마 주차 구역 및 기차역과 그 저택 사이를 운행하는 셔틀버스의 **44** 부족함을 말씀 드려야 할 것 같습니다. 이것들은 단지 사소한 문제였으며, 행사장 및 서비스에 대한 저희 의견을 약화시키는 데 거의 영향이 없었습니다. 사실, **45** 제 친구 한 명이 최근에 약혼했는데, 어디서 결혼식을 해야 할지 궁금해 하고 있습니다. 저는 분명 무어필드 메이너에서의 제 개인적인 경험에 관해 모두 이야기해 줄 것입니다.

안녕히 계십시오.

엘리자베스 뱅크스

어휘 **could have p.p.** ~할 수 있었을 것이다 **stunning** 굉장히 아름다운, 아주 멋진 **enthusiasm** 열정, 열의 **politeness** 정중함, 공손함 **please** ~을 기쁘게 하다 **care** 배려, 주의, 관심 **attention** 관심, 주목 **present** 자리에 있는, 참석한 **ensure (that)** 반드시 ~하도록 하다, ~임을 확실히 해두다 **go smoothly** 순조롭게 진행되다 **identify** ~을 확인하다, ~을 식별하다 **improvement** 개선, 향상 **lack** 부족, 결핍 **run** 운행되다, 운영되다 **manor** 저택 **do little** 거의 영향이 없다, 별 효과가 없다 **lessen** ~을 약화시키다, ~을 줄이다 **get engaged** 약혼하다 **wonder** ~을 궁금해하다

41. 첫 번째 이메일의 목적은 무엇인가?
(A) 결혼식 행사장 예약을 확인해 주는 것
(B) 새로운 종류의 결혼식 패키지 서비스를 광고하는 것
(C) 제공된 서비스에 관한 의견을 요청하는 것
(D) 결혼식 선물에 대해 감사의 마음을 표하는 것

정답 (C)

해설 첫 번째 지문의 첫 단락에서 과거에 진행된 결혼식 및 관련 서비스 이용과 관련해 이야기하는 배경 설명을 하고 있으며, 두 번째 단락에서 행사장과 음식, 직원들, 그리고 전반적인 행사 기획 능력과 관련해 정확히 어떻게 생각했는지 자세히 설명하는 이메일을 보내 달라는 말로(We would appreciate it if you could send us an e-mail detailing exactly what you thought about) 글의 목적을 나타내고 있으므로 (C)가 정답이다.

어휘 **confirm** ~을 확인해 주다 **reservation** 예약 **range** 종류, 범위, 제품군 **request** ~을 요청하다 **express** (생각, 감정 등) ~을 표현하다 **gratitude** 감사(의 마음)

42. 무어필드 메이너가 현재 지닌 특징으로 언급되지 않은 것은 무엇인가?
(A) 옥외 인공 분수

(B) 다양한 손님용 침실
(C) 널찍한 식사 공간
(D) 조경 작업이 된 정원

정답 (B)

해설 첫 지문 첫 단락의 잘 조각된 저희 구내와 정원(Our well-sculpted grounds and gardens) 부분에서 (D)를, 건물 앞쪽 바깥에 위치한 분수대(the water fountain) 부분에서 (A)를, 200명이 넘는 손님들께서 그랜드 다이닝 룸에서 제공받은 모든 음식을 즐겼기를 바란다는(200+ guests enjoyed all of the food that they were served in the Grand Dining Room) 부분에서 (C)를 확인할 수 있다. 하지만 손님들이 근처의 올리브 호텔 객실을 이용했다는 말이 쓰여 있어 손님들을 위한 침실은 특징에 해당되지 않으므로 (B)가 정답이다.

어휘 **water feature** 인공 분수, 수경 시설 **a variety of** 다양한 **spacious** 널찍한 **landscape** ~에 조경 작업을 하다

43. 무엇이 무어필드 메이너와 관련해 뱅크스 씨에게 가장 깊은 인상을 남겼는가?
(A) 셔틀버스 시스템의 편리함
(B) 고품질 출장 요리 서비스
(C) 언더우드 씨가 보여준 세심함
(D) 식사 공간의 실내 디자인

정답 (C)

해설 두 번째 지문 첫 단락에 가장 기뻤던 것이 결혼 행사 진행 책임자로부터 받았던 배려와 관심이었다는(the thing that pleased my husband and I most was the care and attention we received from your head wedding coordinator) 말이 쓰여 있다. 이와 관련해 첫 지문 두 번째 단락에 결혼 행사 진행 책임자의 이름이 앤 언더우드라고(Our head wedding coordinator, Ann Underwood) 쓰여 있으므로 (C)가 정답이다.

어휘 **impress** ~에게 깊은 인상을 남기다 **convenience** 편리함 **catering** 출장 요리 제공(업) **attentiveness** 세심함, 배려심

44. 두 번째 이메일에서, 두 번째 단락, 두 번째 줄의 단어 "lack"과 의미가 가장 가까운 것은 무엇인가?
(A) 지연
(B) 부재
(C) 감소
(D) 제거

정답 (B)

해설 lack은 '부족, 결핍' 등을 뜻하는 명사로서, 이 문장에서는 셔틀버스가 존재하지 않는다는 의미를 나타내기 위해 사용되었으므로 '부재, 없음' 등을 뜻하는 (B) absence가 정답이다.

45. 뱅크스 씨와 관련해 언급된 것은 무엇인가?
(A) 자신의 전반적인 경험에 만족하지 못하고 있다.
(B) 올리브 호텔의 객실에 매우 깊은 인상을 받았다.
(C) 여러 해외 손님들을 자신의 결혼식에 초대했다.

(D) 행사장을 아는 사람에게 추천할 것이다.

정답 (D)

해설 두 번째 지문 두 번째 단락에 친구 한 명이 최근에 약혼했는데 어디서 결혼식을 해야 할지 궁금해하고 있다는 말과 함께 무어 필드 메이너에서의 개인적인 경험에 관해 모두 이야기해 줄 것이라고 (a friend of mine recently got engaged ~ tell her all about my personal experience at Moorfield Manor) 알리고 있다. 이는 친구에게 그 행사장에서 결혼하도록 추천하겠다는 뜻을 나타내는 말이므로 (D)가 정답이다.

어휘 **from overseas** 해외로부터 **acquaintance** 아는 사람, 지인

46-50.

"어 베터 유니버스" 배우 오디션 공고

46 50 *- 웨슬리 핀치 감독의 신작 영화 -*
46 48 4월 19일, 토요일에 오디션 개최 예정
오전 8시 30분부터 오후 6시 30분까지

빅 스타 극장
윌로우 블리바드 4602번지, **48** 새크라멘토, CA 95814

어휘 **casting call** 배우 오디션 공고 **hold** ~을 개최하다, ~을 열다

4월 3일
에드워드 월콧 씨
위스테리아 로드 6009번지
레딩, CA 96003

에드워드 씨께,

로스앤젤레스에 본사를 둔 골드버그 영화사가 신작 영화를 위해 캐스팅을 시작할 예정이라는 사실을 아마 이미 알고 계실 거라고 분명히 생각합니다. 캘리포니아 전역에서 열리는 공개 오디션을 공지했는데, 첫 오디션이 4월 5일과 4월 15일에 각각 샌디에이고와 샌프란시스코에서 개최됩니다. 하지만, **48** 4월 19일에 당신의 고향에서 개최되는 오디션도 있다는 사실을 들으시면 기쁘실 것입니다. 그곳이 훨씬 더 편리한 장소일 것이라는 사실을 알고 있는데, 레딩에 위치한 당신의 새 집에서 멀지 않기 때문입니다. 가족과 함께 더 많은 시간을 보내시기 위해 연기를 잠시 쉬시기를 원하셨던 것으로 알고 있지만, **47** 이 영화의 주인공 배역이 당신에게 완벽할 것이라고 진심으로 생각합니다.

안녕히 계십시오.

하비 피어스타인
A&R 매니저
47 솔리드 골드 배우 에이전시

어휘 **A-based** A에 본사를 둔, A를 기반으로 하는 **be due to do** ~할 예정이다 **casting** 캐스팅, 배역 선정 **take place** (일, 행사 등이) 개최되다, 발생되다 **respectively** 각각

---

convenient 편리한 **location** 장소, 지점 **far from** ~에서 멀리 있는 **take a break from -ing** ~하는 것을 잠시 쉬다 **truly** 진심으로, 진정으로 **lead role** 주인공 배역

새크라멘토 엔터테인먼트 매거진 - 4월호
공상 과학 영화 오디션 시작되다

골드버그 영화사가 현재 새크라멘토 시내에 위치한 빅 스타 극장에서 열리는 공개 오디션에 참석하도록 모든 연기자 지망생에게 요청하고 있습니다. 이 제작사는 거액의 예산이 투입되는 스티븐 헨드리 각본의 공상 과학 영화 <어 베터 유니버스>에 필요한 여러 배역을 캐스팅합니다. 헨드리 씨는 마지막 각본 활동이었던 액션 영화 <엔드 오브 더 라인>으로 영화 평론가들의 찬사를 받았습니다. **49** 이 영화의 촬영은 7월 중에 시작될 것으로 예상됩니다.

이 영화의 배역에 적합할 것이라고 생각하시는 분이시라면, **50** 4월 19일에 해당 극장으로 찾아 가셔서 감독 및 캐스팅 매니저와 이야기 나눠 보시기 바랍니다. 이 영화 대본의 현재 초안을 읽으시면서 영화 속의 몇몇 장면을 연기해 보셔야 할 것입니다. 포트폴리오를 챙겨 가시기 바라며, 몇몇 전문적인 얼굴 사진 및 전신 사진을 포함해야 합니다.

어휘 **aspiring** ~을 지망하는, 장차 ~가 되려는 **attend** ~에 참석하다 **big-budget** 거액의 예산이 투입되는 **win acclaim** 찬사를 받다 **critic** 평론가, 비평가 **screenwriting** 각본을 쓰는 일 **shooting** 촬영 **be expected to do** ~할 것으로 예상되다 **commence** 시작되다 **be suitable for** ~에 적합하다, ~에 어울리다 **be required to do** ~해야 하다, ~할 필요가 있다 **act out** ~을 연기해 보이다 **current** 현재의 **draft** 초안 **script** 대본 **include** ~을 포함하다 **headshot** 얼굴 사진

46. 공지가 누구를 대상으로 하는가?
(A) 영화 감독
(B) 영화 평론가
(C) 배우
(D) 작가

정답 (C)

해설 첫 번째 지문 상단에 신작 영화(A new movie)라는 말과 함께 오디션이 개최된다고(Auditions to be held) 쓰여 있다. 따라서, 배우들을 대상으로 하는 오디션 공지임을 알 수 있으므로 (C)가 정답이다.

어휘 **be intended for** ~을 대상으로 하다

47. 피어스타인 씨가 왜 편지를 보냈는가?
(A) 다가오는 영화와 관련된 더 많은 정보를 요청하기 위해
(B) 고객에게 배역을 위해 경쟁하도록 권하기 위해
(C) 오디션 참석에 대한 관심을 표현하기 위해
(D) 월콧 씨에게 일을 잠시 쉬도록 조언하기 위해

정답 (B)

해설 두 번째 지문 마지막 부분에 골드버그 영화사의 신작 영화 주

인공 역할이 상대방인 에드워드 월콧 씨에게 완벽할 것으로 생각한다고(I truly think that the lead role in this movie would be perfect for you) 알리고 있다. 또한, 지문 하단에 피어스타인 씨의 소속 회사가 배우 에이전시(Solid Gold Actors Agency)로 쓰여 있는 것으로 볼 때, 고객의 입장에 있는 배우 에드워드 월콧 씨에게 그 배역을 위해 오디션을 보도록 권하는 말이라는 것을 알 수 있으므로 (B)가 정답이다.

어휘 request ~을 요청하다 upcoming 다가오는, 곧 있을 encourage A to do A에게 ~하도록 권하다 compete 경쟁하다 interest in ~에 대한 관심 attend ~에 참석하다 advise A to do A에게 ~하도록 조언하다

48. 월콧 씨가 어느 도시에서 성장했을 것 같은가?
(A) 샌디에이고
(B) 레딩
(C) 로스앤젤레스
(D) 새크라멘토

정답 (D)

해설 두 번째 지문 중반부에 4월 19일에 월콧 씨의 고향에서 개최되는 오디션도 있다는 사실을 언급하고 있다(there's also an audition being held in your hometown on April 19). 이 날짜는 첫 지문에 제시된 오디션 날짜이며(Auditions to be held on Saturday, April 19), 아래쪽에 그 장소와 함께 도시 이름이 Sacramento로 표기되어 있으므로 (D)가 정답이다.

어휘 grow up 성장하다, 자라다

49. <어 베터 유니버스>와 관련해 언급된 것은 무엇인가?
(A) 스티븐 헨드리 씨가 영화의 주연을 맡을 것이다.
(B) 해당 감독의 데뷔 영화이다.
(C) 빅 스타 극장에서 시사회를 할 것이다.
(D) 촬영이 여름에 시작될 것이다.

정답 (D)

해설 세 번째 지문 첫 단락에 <어 베터 유니버스>와 관련해 설명하면서 이 영화를 the movie로 지칭해 촬영이 7월 중에 시작될 것으로 예상된다는(Shooting of the movie is expected to commence sometime in July) 정보를 전하고 있으므로 (D)가 정답이다.

어휘 star v. 주연을 맡다 premiere v. 시사회를 하다 filming 촬영

50. 관심 있는 사람들이 4월 19일에 무엇을 해야 하는가?
(A) 웨슬리 핀치 씨와 만나는 일
(B) 과거의 고용주가 작성한 추천서를 제출하는 일
(C) 웹 사이트에 등록하는 일
(D) 사진 촬영 시간에 참석하는 일

정답 (A)

해설 세 번째 지문 두 번째 단락에 관심 있는 사람들에게 4월 19일에 해당 극장으로 가서 감독 및 캐스팅 매니저와 이야기해 보도록(you should go down to the theater on April 19 and speak with the director and the casting manager) 권하고 있다. 이는 해당 영화 감독 및 캐스팅 매니저와 만나는 일을 의미하는데, 첫 지문 상단에 감독 이름이 웨슬리 핀치라고(A new movie to be directed by Wesley Finch) 쓰여 있으므로 (A)가 정답이다.

어휘 individual n. 사람, 개인 meet with (약속하고) ~와 만나다 reference 추천서, 추천인 former 과거의, 이전의, 전직 ~의 employer 고용주 register 등록하다 photography 사진 촬영(술)

DAY 04 LC Half Test

1. (D)	**2.** (B)	**3.** (C)	**4.** (B)	**5.** (A)
6. (B)	**7.** (C)	**8.** (B)	**9.** (A)	**10.** (B)
11. (C)	**12.** (B)	**13.** (C)	**14.** (B)	**15.** (A)
16. (B)	**17.** (C)	**18.** (C)	**19.** (A)	**20.** (A)
21. (C)	**22.** (A)	**23.** (D)	**24.** (B)	**25.** (A)
26. (A)	**27.** (C)	**28.** (B)	**29.** (D)	**30.** (C)
31. (A)	**32.** (B)	**33.** (A)	**34.** (D)	**35.** (B)
36. (D)	**37.** (B)	**38.** (D)	**39.** (B)	**40.** (C)
41. (A)	**42.** (A)	**43.** (C)	**44.** (D)	**45.** (A)
46. (A)	**47.** (D)	**48.** (A)	**49.** (C)	**50.** (B)

Part 1

1.　(A) Some trees are being cut down.
　　(B) A man is clearing off some tables.
　　(C) Some people are planting a garden.
　　(D) Picnic tables have been arranged in a row.

　　(A) 몇몇 나무들이 잘려 쓰러지는 중이다.
　　(B) 한 남자가 몇몇 탁자를 깨끗이 치우는 중이다.
　　(C) 몇몇 사람들이 뜰에 식물을 심는 중이다.
　　(D) 피크닉 테이블들이 일렬로 배치되어 있다.

해설　(A) 나무를 자르는 동작을 하는 사람을 찾아볼 수 없으므로 오답.
　　(B) 탁자를 치우는 사람을 찾아볼 수 없으므로 오답.
　　(C) 식물을 심는 동작을 하는 사람을 찾아볼 수 없으므로 오답.
　　(D) 피크닉 테이블들이 일렬로 설치되어 있는 상태를 묘사하고 있으므로 정답.

어휘　cut down ~을 잘라 쓰러트리다　clear off ~을 깨끗이 치우다　plant a garden 뜰에 식물을 심다　arrange ~을 배치하다, 정렬하다　in a row 일렬로

2.　(A) Some boats are passing under a bridge.
　　(B) The buildings are overlooking water.
　　(C) The boats are all identical in size and shape.
　　(D) Some people are walking near a harbor.

　　(A) 몇몇 보트들이 다리 밑을 지나는 중이다.
　　(B) 건물들이 물을 내려다보고 있다.
　　(C) 보트들이 모두 크기와 모양이 같다.
　　(D) 몇몇 사람들이 항구 근처에서 걷는 중이다.

해설　(A) 다리 밑을 지나는 보트는 찾아볼 수 없으므로 오답.
　　(B) 건물들이 물을 내려다보는 위치에 세워져 있는 모습을 묘사

하고 있으므로 정답.
　　(C) 크기와 모양이 동일한 보트들을 찾아볼 수 없으므로 오답.
　　(D) 사람들의 모습은 보이지 않으므로 오답.

어휘　pass 지나가다　overlook (건물 등이) ~을 내려다보다　identical 동일한　shape 모양　near ~ 근처에서　harbor 항구

Part 2

3.　Which of these is my sandwich?
　　(A) I've already eaten.
　　(B) Sure, let's go.
　　(C) Whichever one you want.

　　이 중에 어느 것이 제 샌드위치인가요?
　　(A) 전 이미 먹었어요.
　　(B) 물론이죠, 갑시다.
　　(C) 어느 것이든 당신이 원하는 것이요.

해설　Which of these ~?는 '이 중에 어떤 것'이라는 의미이다. 어떤 것이 자신의 샌드위치인지 묻는 질문에 대해 '원하는 것이라면 어떤 것이든'이라는 의미로 아무거나 가져가라는 뜻인 (C)가 정답이다. 여기서 one은 질문에 나온 sandwich를 대신한 대명사이다. 참고로, Which 의문문에서는 대명사 one이 들어간 문장이 정답으로 많이 출제되고 있다.

어휘　already 이미, 벌써　whichever 어느 쪽이든 ~한 것

4.　Should I make some flyers?
　　(A) A flight to Sydney.
　　(B) Yes. That would be great.
　　(C) It arrives at 4.

　　제가 전단을 좀 만들어야 하나요?
　　(A) 시드니로 가는 항공편이요.
　　(B) 네. 그렇게 하면 아주 좋을 거예요.
　　(C) 그건 4시에 도착합니다.

해설　전단을 만들어야 하는지 확인하는 Should 의문문이므로 긍정을 나타내는 Yes와 함께 그렇게 하는 것이 좋겠다고 동의하는 말을 덧붙인 (B)가 정답이다. (A)와 (C)는 각각 질문에 쓰인 flyers의 발음에서 연상 가능한 flight과 arrives를 이용해 혼동을 유발하는 오답이다.

어휘　flyer 전단　flight 항공편

5.　I'll wait for you outside the theater at 6:30 this evening.
　　(A) Great. I'll see you there.

(B) I think they're on their way.

(C) It's a popular movie.

오늘 저녁 6시 30분에 극장 밖에서 당신을 기다릴게요.

(A) 좋습니다. 그곳에서 뵐게요.

(B) 그분들께서 오시는 중일 거예요.

(C) 인기 있는 영화입니다.

해설 저녁 6시 30분에 만날 장소를 알리는 평서문에 대해 긍정을 나타내는 Great과 함께 그곳에서 보자는 말을 덧붙인 (A)가 정답이다. (B)는 대상을 알 수 없는 they를 언급한 오답이며, (C)는 질문에 쓰인 theater에서 연상 가능한 popular movie를 이용해 혼동을 유발하는 오답이다.

어휘 **wait for A** A를 기다리다 **outside** ~ 바깥에 **on one's way** 오는 중, 가는 중인

6. When will the posters be ready?

(A) I don't think red is the best color.

(B) Hasn't Sarah already prepared them?

(C) There was nothing in today's post.

포스터가 언제 준비되죠?

(A) 빨간색이 가장 좋은 색상은 아닌 것 같아요.

(B) 새라 씨가 이미 준비하지 않았나요?

(C) 오늘 우편물에는 아무것도 없었습니다.

해설 When 의문문으로 포스터 준비 시점을 묻고 있지만 새라 씨가 이미 준비하지 않았냐며 되묻는 (B)가 정답이다. When 의문문에 대해 항상 정확한 시점으로 답변하는 선택지만 정답이 되는 것이 아니므로 주의해야 한다. (A)는 질문에 언급된 ready와 발음이 비슷한 red를 이용한 오답이며, (C)도 질문에 언급된 poster와 발음이 비슷한 post를 이용한 오답이다.

어휘 **poster** 포스터, 벽보 **prepare** ~을 준비하다 **post** n. 우편(함), 우편물

7. Did you fax the evaluation forms?

(A) I don't think anyone has fixed it.

(B) No more than three business days.

(C) I thought you had taken care of that already.

평가 양식을 팩스로 보냈나요?

(A) 아무도 그걸 고치지 않은 것 같습니다.

(B) 영업일로 3일 내로요.

(C) 그건 당신이 이미 처리하신 걸로 생각했어요.

해설 평가 양식을 팩스로 보냈는지 묻는 일반 의문문에 대해 상대방이 이미 처리한 줄 알았다는 말로 자신이 할 필요가 없었음을 나타내는 (C)가 정답이다. (A)는 질문에 쓰인 fax와 발음이 유사한 fixed를 이용해 혼동을 유발하는 오답이다.

어휘 **fax** v. ~을 팩스로 보내다 **evaluation** 평가(서) **form** 양식, 서식 **fix** ~을 고치다, 바로잡다 **no more than + 숫자** ~ 이내, ~ 이하 **business day** 영업일 **take care of** ~을 처리하다, 다루다

8. Ms. Boyd has the receipts for her business trip, doesn't she?

(A) A client meeting in Taiwan.

(B) I think they're on her desk.

(C) There are plenty of seats left.

보이드 씨가 출장 영수증들을 갖고 계시지 않나요?

(A) 타이완에서 열리는 고객 회의요.

(B) 그것들이 그분 책상에 있는 것 같습니다.

(C) 남아 있는 좌석이 많이 있습니다.

해설 보이드 씨가 영수증들을 갖고 있는지를 확인하는 부가 의문문이므로 receipts를 they로 지칭해 그 사람의 책상에 있을 것이라고 알리는 (B)가 정답이다. (A)는 질문에 쓰인 business trip에서 연상 가능한 client meeting을 이용한 오답이며, (C)도 trip에서 연상 가능한 plenty of seats를 활용한 오답이다.

어휘 **receipt** 영수증 **business trip** 출장 **There is A left** 남아 있는 A가 있다 **plenty of** 많은

9. Could I use that photocopier after you're finished with it?

(A) Sure, but it might take a while.

(B) In the Marketing Department.

(C) I made additional copies.

그 복사기를 다 쓰시고 나면 제가 사용해도 될까요?

(A) 그럼요, 하지만 시간이 좀 걸릴 수도 있어요.

(B) 마케팅 부서에서요.

(C) 제가 추가 사본들을 만들었습니다.

해설 「Could I ~?」로 시작하는 요청 의문문으로, 다음 순서로 복사기를 써도 되는지 묻고 있으므로 긍정을 나타내는 Sure와 함께 시간이 좀 걸릴 수도 있다는 말을 덧붙인 (A)가 정답이다. (B)는 장소 표현이므로 Where 의문문에 어울리는 답변이며, (C)는 질문에 쓰인 photocopier와 일부 발음이 유사한 copies를 이용해 혼동을 유발하는 오답이다.

어휘 **photocopier** 복사기 **be finished with** ~을 다 끝내다, 완료하다 **take a while** 시간이 좀 걸리다 **make a copy** 복사하다 **additional** 추가적인

10. This message from Mr. Barnes is quite confusing.

(A) Sometime this afternoon.

(B) I don't understand it, either.

(C) Thanks for clearing that up.

반스 씨께서 보내신 이 메시지가 꽤 헷갈려요.

(A) 오늘 오후 중으로요.

(B) 저도 이해가 되지 않아요.

(C) 그것을 깨끗하게 정리해 주셔서 감사합니다.

해설 반스 씨의 메시지가 헷갈린다는 의견을 말하는 평서문에 대해 자신도 이해할 수 없다는 말로 동의를 나타내는 (B)가 정답이

다. (A)는 대략적인 시점을 말하는 표현이므로 When 의문문에 어울리는 반응이며, (C)는 감사 표현이므로 메시지가 헷갈린다는 의견에 대한 반응으로 어울리지 않는 답변이다.

어휘 **quite** 꽤, 상당히 **confusing** 헷갈리게 하는, 혼란스럽게 하는 **either** (부정문에서) ~도, 마찬가지로 **clear up** ~을 깨끗이 정리하다, 치우다

11. Who's in charge of ordering paper for the printer?
(A) The article has many errors.
(B) Mr. Baker gave a speech about the problem.
(C) I'm not, anyway.

프린터 용지를 주문하는 일을 누가 맡고 있죠?
(A) 그 기사는 오류가 많습니다.
(B) 베이커 씨가 그 문제에 대해 연설했습니다.
(C) 어쨌든 저는 아닙니다.

해설 용지 주문 담당자가 누구인지 묻는 Who 의문문에 대해 자신은 아니라는 의미를 나타내는 (C)가 정답이다. (B)는 사람 이름을 언급하기는 하지만 용지 주문 담당자가 아니라 연설한 사람을 말하고 있으므로 오답이다. Who 의문문에 대해 사람 이름을 언급하는 선택지를 기계적으로 고르지 않도록 유의한다.

어휘 **be in charge of** ~을 맡다, 책임지고 있다 **article** 기사 **error** 오류 **give a speech** 연설하다 **anyway** 어쨌든

12. Would you like this shirt or a bigger one?
(A) Yes, I have quite a few.
(B) What sizes do you have?
(C) It's the largest one we have.

이 셔츠가 좋으세요, 아니면 더 큰 게 좋으세요?
(A) 네, 전 꽤 많이 갖고 있어요.
(B) 어떤 사이즈들이 있나요?
(C) 그게 저희가 갖고 있는 가장 큰 것입니다.

해설 현재 보여주는 셔츠를 원하는지, 아니면 더 큰 것을 원하는지 묻는 선택 의문문에 대해 어떤 사이즈들이 있는지 되묻는 것으로 더 큰 사이즈를 선택할 생각이 있음을 나타내는 (B)가 정답이다. (A)는 답변자 자신의 보유 수량을 말하는 답변이므로 질문의 의도에 맞지 않는 오답이며, (C)는 질문에 쓰인 bigger one에서 연상 가능한 largest one을 이용해 혼동을 유발하는 오답이다.

어휘 **Would you like ~?** ~을 원하시나요?, ~가 좋으세요? **quite a few** 꽤 많은 것, 상당수

13. Do you know why Mee-Sun hasn't been in the office today?
(A) She seems qualified.
(B) Because she arrived early.
(C) I think she's on holiday.

미선 씨가 오늘 계속 사무실에 없는 이유를 아세요?
(A) 그분은 자격이 있는 것으로 보입니다.

(B) 그분이 일찍 도착했기 때문입니다.
(C) 그분이 휴가 중인 것 같아요.

해설 Do로 시작하는 의문문이지만 의문사 why가 핵심이므로 Why 의문문을 푸는 경우와 마찬가지로 의문사 뒤에 이어지는 내용을 파악하는 데 집중해야 한다. 미선 씨가 왜 사무실에 없는지 묻고 있으므로 휴가 중인 것 같다는 말로 자신이 생각하는 이유를 알리는 (C)가 정답이다. (B)는 why와 어울리는 Because로 시작하는 답변이지만, 뒤에 이어지는 내용이 미선 씨의 부재와 관련 없는 말이므로 오답이다.

어휘 **qualified** 자격이 있는, 적격인 **be on holiday** 휴가 중이다

14. Have you made any progress with the window displays?
(A) The new range of winter clothing.
(B) Yes, but we need to work on them some more.
(C) It's a really nice place.

창가 제품 진열 작업이 좀 진척되었어요?
(A) 새로운 종류의 겨울 의류 제품이요.
(B) 네, 하지만 조금 더 작업해야 합니다.
(C) 정말 좋은 곳입니다.

해설 제품 진열 작업이 진척되었는지 확인하는 일반 의문문에 대해 긍정을 나타내는 Yes와 함께 해야 할 것이 조금 더 있다는 말로 아직 완료되지 않았음을 알리는 (B)가 정답이다. (A)는 질문에 쓰인 window displays에서 연상 가능한 winter clothing을 이용한 오답이며, (C)는 displays와 발음이 유사하게 들리는 place를 이용해 혼동을 유발하는 오답이다.

어휘 **make progress with** ~을 진척시키다 **display** 진열(품) **range** (제품 등의) 종류, 범위 **clothing** 의류 **work on** ~에 대한 작업을 하다 **some more** 조금 더

15. You're going to Seattle soon, aren't you?
(A) Yes, my flight is at 1 P.M.
(B) It's not that far.
(C) No, she didn't.

곧 시애틀로 가실 예정이시지 않나요?
(A) 네, 제 비행기가 오후 1시에 있습니다.
(B) 그렇게 멀지 않습니다.
(C) 아뇨, 그분은 그러지 않았어요.

해설 시애틀로 곧 갈 예정인지 확인하는 부가 의문문에 대해 긍정을 나타내는 Yes와 함께 출발 시간을 덧붙이는 (A)가 정답이다. (B)는 거리와 관련된 말이므로 How far 또는 How long 의문문에 어울리는 답변이며, (C)는 부정을 나타내는 No 뒤에 자신이 아니라 대상을 알 수 없는 she에 대해 말하는 오답이다.

어휘 **that** ad. 그렇게, 그만큼 **far** 멀리 있는

16. Will the monthly meeting be held here or at the headquarters?

(A) He wanted to discuss the budget limit.
(B) It's taking place in this building.
(C) At the beginning of May.

월례 회의가 이곳에서 개최되나요, 아니면 본사에서 개최되나요?
(A) 그분은 예산 한도를 논의하고 싶어 했습니다.
(B) 이 건물에서 개최됩니다.
(C) 5월 초에요.

해설 월례 회의가 이곳에서 개최되는지, 아니면 본사에서 개최되는지 묻는 선택 의문문이므로 이 건물에서 열린다고 알리는 (B)가 정답이다. (C)는 질문에 쓰인 monthly에서 연상할 수 있는 시점 표현을 이용해 혼동을 유발하는 오답이다.

어휘 **monthly** 월간의, 매월의 **hold** ~을 개최하다, 열다 **headquarters** 본사, 본부 **discuss** ~을 논의하다, 이야기하다 **budget** 예산 **limit** 한도, 한계 **take place** (일, 행사 등이) 발생되다, 개최되다

17. How are we going to finish the remodeling on time?

(A) The designer recommended it.
(B) At two o'clock.
(C) Actually, we are almost done.

우리가 어떻게 제때 개조 작업을 끝낼 수 있을까요?
(A) 디자이너가 그것을 추천했어요.
(B) 2시에요.
(C) 실은, 거의 끝났어요.

해설 개조 작업을 어떻게 제때 끝낼 지 묻는 How 의문문인데, 구체적인 방법을 제시하는 대신 거의 끝났다는 말로 현재의 상황을 알림으로써 그 방법을 생각할 필요가 없음을 나타내는 (C)가 정답이다. (B)는 질문에 쓰인 time에서 연상 가능한 시간을 말해 혼동을 유발하는 답변이다.

어휘 **on time** 제때 **recommend** ~을 추천하다, 권하다 **done** (일을) 끝낸, 완료한

18. Hasn't the furniture been delivered yet?

(A) That sofa is nice.
(B) I think delivery is free of charge.
(C) No, it'll get here tomorrow.

그 가구가 아직 배송되지 않은 건가요?
(A) 저 소파가 아주 좋네요.
(B) 배송은 무료인 것 같습니다.
(C) 안 왔어요, 내일 이곳에 도착할 거예요.

해설 가구의 배송 여부를 확인하는 부정 의문문이므로 부정을 의미하는 No와 함께 내일 배송된다는 사실을 덧붙이는 (C)가 정답이다. (A)는 질문에 쓰인 furniture에서 연상 가능한 sofa를

언급한 오답이며, (B)는 delivered와 발음이 유사한 delivery를 이용해 혼동을 유발하는 오답이다.

어휘 **deliver** ~을 배송하다 **yet** 아직 **delivery** 배송(품) **free of charge** 무료인 **get here** 이곳에 도착하다, 오다

19. Will Ms. Orwell pick up her order before we close?

(A) She'll stop by tomorrow.
(B) Never mind. I don't want any more.
(C) At the new clothing store downtown.

우리가 문을 닫기 전에 오웰 씨께서 주문품을 가져 가실까요?
(A) 그분은 내일 들를 거예요.
(B) 신경 쓰지 마세요. 저는 더 이상 원하지 않습니다.
(C) 시내에 있는 새 의류 매장에서요.

해설 문을 닫기 전에 오웰 씨가 주문품을 가지러 올 것인지 묻는 Will 의문문에 대해 부정을 나타내는 No를 생략한 채로 내일 들를 거라는 말로 오늘 오지 않는다는 뜻을 나타낸 (A)가 정답이다. (B)의 Never mind는 '신경 쓸 것 없다, 괜찮다'는 의미이며, 오웰 씨가 아닌 답변자 자신의 상황을 말하는 것이므로 오답이다.

어휘 **pick up** ~을 가져가다, 가져오다 **stop by** 들르다 **Never mind** 신경 쓰지 마세요, 괜찮아요 **downtown** ad. 시내에

20. Let's use the private dining room instead of the main hall.

(A) But there are too many guests coming.
(B) Did you receive an invitation?
(C) We have 280 guest rooms at our hotel.

중앙 홀 대신 개별 식사 공간을 이용하도록 합시다.
(A) 하지만 오실 손님들이 너무 많습니다.
(B) 초대장을 받으셨나요?
(C) 저희 호텔에는 280개의 객실이 있습니다.

해설 중앙 홀이 아닌 개별 식사 공간을 이용하자고 제안하는 말에 대해 손님이 많이 올 것이라는 말로 동의할 수 없음을 의미하는 (A)가 정답이다. (B)와 (C)는 질문에 쓰인 dining room과 연관성 있게 들리는 invitation과 guest rooms를 각각 이용해 혼동을 유발하는 오답이다.

어휘 **private** 개별적인, 사적인 **dining room** 식사 공간 **instead of** ~ 대신에 **invitation** 초대(장)

Part 3

Questions 21-23 refer to the following conversation.

W: So, **21** that comes to eighty-eight dollars and fifty cents. Did you get one of our coupons from the newspaper today? **21** It will give you twenty percent off all household goods purchased this weekend.

M: **22** Really? No, I don't have one. I bought today's paper and I read it from cover to cover, but I didn't see a coupon. Which section was it in?

W: It's on the back page, next to our advertisement. We will be running the same special offer every week, but on different products. **23** If you go home quickly and get the coupon, I'll refund twenty percent of the total price when you return.

여: 자, 다 해서 88달러 50센트입니다. 오늘 신문에서 저희 쿠폰들 중 하나를 얻으셨습니까? 그 쿠폰으로 이번 주말에 구매하시는 모든 생활용품에 대해 20퍼센트 할인 받으실 수 있습니다.

남: 정말요? 아뇨, 가지고 있지 않아요. 오늘 신문을 사서 처음부터 끝까지 읽었는데 쿠폰은 못 봤어요. 어느 섹션에 있었는데요?

여: 뒷면에 있습니다, 저희 광고 바로 옆에요. 똑같은 특가 행사를 매주 할 예정이긴 한데요, 다른 제품들에 대해서 할 겁니다. 댁에 빨리 가셔서 쿠폰을 가져오실 수 있으면 돌아오셨을 때 총액에서 20퍼센드를 환불해 드리겠습니다.

어휘 **come to + 액수** (총액이) ~가 되다 **coupon** 쿠폰
twenty percent off 20퍼센트 할인 **household**
goods 생활용품 **from cover to cover** 처음부터 끝까
지 **section** 섹션, (신문의) 난 **back page** 뒷면 **next to**
~ 바로 옆에 **run** ~을 운영하다 **special offer** 특가 행사
refund v. ~을 환불해주다 **total price** 총 가격

21. 여자는 누구이겠는가?
(A) 고객
(B) 배달원
(C) 상점 점원
(D) 신문기자

해설 대화 초반부에 여자가 계산대에서 총 구매액을 말해주며 생활
용품 할인 쿠폰 이용에 대한 안내를 해 주는 것으로 보아 여자
는 상점의 점원임을 알 수 있으므로 (C)가 정답이다.

어휘 **clerk** 점원

22. 남자는 쿠폰에 대해 뭐라고 말하는가?
(A) 그것에 대해 몰랐다.
(B) 다른 매장에서 사용했다.
(C) 이미 만료되었다고 생각한다.
(D) 다음 주에 사용할 것이다.

해설 여자가 오늘 신문에서 쿠폰을 얻었는지 묻자 남자는 신문을 사
서 읽었지만 쿠폰을 보지 못했다고(I bought today's paper
and I read it from cover to cover, but I didn't see a
coupon) 말한다. 이로부터 남자는 쿠폰에 대해 알지 못했음
을 알 수 있다. 따라서 (A)가 정답이다.

어휘 **expire** (기간 등이) 만료되다

23. 여자는 남자에게 무엇을 할 것을 제안하는가?
(A) 매니저와 얘기할 것
(B) 물건을 더 살 것
(C) 회원으로 등록할 것
(D) 나중에 다시 올 것

해설 쿠폰을 가지고 있지 않은 남자에게 여자는 집에 가서 가져오면
20%를 할인해 주겠다고(If you go home quickly and get
the coupon, I'll refund twenty percent of the total
price when you return) 말하고 있다. 이는 쿠폰을 가지고
다시 올 것을 제안하는 것이므로 (D)가 정답이다.

어휘 **sign up for** ~에 등록하다 **membership** 회원자격
come back 돌아오다(= return)

Paraphrase return → Come back

Questions 24-26 refer to the following conversation.

M: Hey, Taylor. **24** Is one of today's lunch specials a salad? We received a large order of lettuce in this morning's delivery.

W: I noticed that, too. **25** Let's check the kitchen calendar to see what's planned for today.

M: Hmm... it looks like we only have the usual specials. Maybe our supplier made a mistake.

W: Well, we've been discussing adding more vegetarian options, so **26** why don't we include a garden salad on today's menu?

M: I'd like to hear what Mr. Hines thinks. He should be here soon.

W: Right. Let's wait for him.

남: 안녕하세요, 테일러 씨. 오늘 점심 특선 중의 하나가 샐러드인
가요? 오늘 아침 배송에 주문량이 많은 상추를 받았거든요.

여: 저도 그렇다는 걸 알았어요. 오늘 무엇이 계획되어 있는지 주방
일정표를 확인해 봅시다.

남: 흠... 그저 평소와 같은 특선들만 있는 것 같은데요. 아마 우리
공급 업체에서 실수한 것 같네요.

여: 저, 우리가 더 많은 채식 선택권을 추가하는 것을 계속 이야기
해 오고 있으니까, 오늘 메뉴에 가든 샐러드를 포함하는 건 어
떠세요?

남: 하인즈 씨가 어떻게 생각하는지 듣고 싶군요. 곧 여기로 올 거
예요.

여: 그렇죠. 그럼 하인즈 씨를 기다려 봐요.

어휘 **special** 특선 요리 **order** 주문(품) **notice** ~을 알아차리
다 **calendar** 일정표 **plan** ~을 계획하다 **it looks like**
~인 것 같다 **usual** 평소의, 보통의, 늘 있는 **supplier** 공
급 업체 **make a mistake** 실수하다 **add** ~을 추가하다
include ~을 포함하다

24. 화자들은 어디에서 일하고 있을 것 같은가?
   (A) 농장에서
   (B) 레스토랑에서
   (C) 식료품점에서
   (D) 배달 서비스 업체에서

해설 대화를 시작하면서 남자가 오늘 점심 특선 중의 하나가 샐러드
인지(Is one of today's lunch specials a salad?) 묻고 있
다. 이는 음식점에서 일하는 직원이 할 수 있는 말이므로 (B)가
정답이다.

25. 화자들은 무슨 문서를 언급하는가?
   (A) 일정표
   (B) 거래 내역서
   (C) 영수증
   (D) 이력서

해설 대화 중반부에 여자가 오늘 무엇이 계획되어 있는지 주방 일정
표를 확인해 보자고(Let's check the kitchen calendar to
see what's planned for today) 제안하고 있으므로 (A)가
정답이다.

어휘 **refer to** ~을 언급하다

Paraphrase kitchen calendar
         → schedule

26. 남자는 왜 "하인즈 씨가 어떻게 생각하는지 듣고 싶군요"라고
말하는가?
   (A) 결정을 미루기 위해
   (B) 직원을 추천하기 위해
   (C) 일을 배정하기 위해
   (D) 제안을 수락하기 위해

해설 대화 후반부에 여자가 오늘 메뉴에 가든 샐러드를 포함하는

건 어떤지(why don't we include a garden salad on
today's menu?) 묻자, 남자가 '하인즈 씨 생각을 듣고 싶다'고
대답하는 상황이다. 이는 하인즈 씨 의견을 들어보고 결정하겠
다는 뜻이므로 (A)가 정답이다.

어휘 **delay** ~을 미루다 **suggestion** 제안, 의견 **assign** ~을
배정하다, 할당하다 **task** 일, 업무 **support** ~을 지지하다,
지원하다 **decision** 결정

Questions 27-29 refer to the following conversation with
three speakers.

W1: Excuse me, **27** I'm looking for the new record
   by Miles Peterson. Do you have it in stock?

M: I think we should have it. He's the jazz pianist,
   right?

W1: That's right. I tried looking in the jazz section
   already, but I can't find it.

M: Hmm... Let me check with my coworker. **28**
   Charlene, did we get a delivery of new records
   today?

W2: **28** We were supposed to, but it was changed
   to tomorrow instead. The roads are too icy
   today.

M: Oh, I see. Miss, **29** I could hold back one of the
   copies of the record for you when they arrive
   tomorrow.

W1: That would be great. Thank you! I'll come in to
   get it in the afternoon.

여1: 실례합니다, 마일스 피터슨의 새 앨범을 찾고 있습니다. 재고
가 있나요?

남: 있는 것 같습니다. 그분께서 재즈 피아니스트이신 것이 맞죠?

여1: 맞습니다. 제가 이미 재즈 코너에 가서 한 번 살펴봤는데, 찾을
수가 없네요.

남: 흠... 제 동료 직원에게 확인해 보겠습니다. 살린 씨, 오늘 새 앨
범 배송 물품들이 들어왔나요?

여2: 그럴 예정이었지만, 대신 내일로 변경되었습니다. 오늘 도로
가 너무 미끄러워서요.

남: 아, 알겠습니다. 고객님, 내일 그 앨범이 도착하면 제가 한 장 따
로 보관해 드릴 수 있습니다.

여1: 그렇게 해 주시면 좋겠어요. 감사합니다! 오후에 구입하러 오
겠습니다.

어휘 **have A in stock** A가 재고로 있다 **try -ing** 한 번 ~해 보
다 **look in** ~을 살펴 보다, 확인해 보다 **check with** ~
에게 확인하다 **coworker** 동료 직원 **delivery** 배송(품)
be supposed to do ~할 예정이다, ~하기로 되어 있다

instead 대신 icy (길이) 미끄러운, 빙판길인 hold back
~을 따로 보관하다, 빼 놓다 come in to do ~하러 오다

27. 대화는 어디에서 이뤄지고 있는가?
(A) 극장에서
(B) 콘서트 홀에서
(C) 음반 매장에서
(D) 악기 상점에서

해설 여자 한 명이 대화 시작 부분에 Miles Peterson의 새 앨범
을 찾고 있다고(I'm looking for the new record by Miles
Peterson) 말하는 부분을 통해 음반을 판매하는 매장에 있다
는 것을 알 수 있으므로 (C)가 정답이다.

어휘 **take place** (일, 행사 등) 발생되다, 일어나다
instrument 악기

28. 샬린 씨는 무슨 문제점을 언급하는가?
(A) 제품이 품절되었다.
(B) 배송 일정이 재조정되었다.
(C) 가격이 광고된 것보다 더 높다.
(D) 서비스를 더 이상 이용할 수 없다.

해설 Charlene이라는 이름과 함께 부정적인 정보가 제시되는 부
분이 있음을 예상하고 들어야 한다. 대화 중반부에 남자가
Charlene이라는 이름과 함께 새 배송 물품이 들어왔는지 묻
자(Charlene, did we get a delivery of new records
today?) 여자 한 명이 곧바로 내일로 변경되었다고(~ but it
was changed to tomorrow instead) 대답하고 있다. 따라
서, 배송 일정이 재조정되었다는 의미로 쓰인 (B)가 정답이다.

어휘 **sold out** 품절된, 매진된 **reschedule** ~의 일정을 재조정
하다 **than advertised** 광고된 것보다 **no longer** 더 이
상 ~ 않다 **available** 이용 가능한
Paraphrase it was changed to tomorrow instead
→ was rescheduled

29. 남자는 무엇을 하겠다고 제안하는가?
(A) 환불을 제공하는 일
(B) 배송 서비스를 포함하는 일
(C) 공급업체에 연락하는 일
(D) 제품을 따로 남겨 두는 일

해설 대화 후반부에 남자가 내일 앨범이 도착하면 따로 한 장 보관
해 두겠다고(I could hold back one of the copies of the
record for you ~) 제안하고 있으므로 제품을 따로 남겨 둔다
는 의미로 쓰인 (D)가 정답이다.

어휘 **refund** 환불 **include** ~을 포함하다 **contact** ~에게 연락
하다 **supplier** 공급업체 **reserve** ~을 따로 남겨 두다, 예
약하다
Paraphrase hold back one of the copies of the record for
you
→ Reserve an item

Questions 30-32 refer to the following conversation.

M: Excuse me, Ms. Della. I need to ask you
something. **30** We are having a lot of problems
with the computers in my office, but the
computers in your office seem to have very
few problems. Did you have someone upgrade
the programs on yours?

W: Actually, we did. I know of an excellent IT
company called Regent IT, so I called them
two years ago when all of our computers were
running slow.

M: I see. Maybe I should do the same. **31** But I'm
a bit worried about the price. We've made so
many purchases this year that I can't afford to
spend much more.

W: In that case, **32** I would suggest calling Melton
IT instead. I heard they offer 20 percent off to
all new customers.

남: 실례합니다, 델라 씨. 뭐 좀 여쭤볼 것이 있어요. 저희 사무실의
컴퓨터들엔 문제가 많은데 당신 사무실의 컴퓨터들은 거의 없
는 것 같아요. 누군가에게 당신 컴퓨터들의 프로그램을 업그레
이드하도록 했나요?
여: 사실은 그렇게 했어요. 제가 리젠트 IT라는 좋은 IT 회사를 알
고 있어서 2년 전에 저희가 쓰던 모든 컴퓨터들이 느리게 작동
되었을 때 그쪽에 전화했었거든요.
남: 그렇군요. 저도 그렇게 해야겠어요. 하지만 가격이 좀 걱정이네
요. 올해 구매를 너무 많이 해서 더 지출할 여유가 없어요.
여: 그런 경우라면, 대신 멜튼 IT에 전화해 볼 것을 추천 드려요. 거
긴 모든 신규 고객들에게 20% 할인해 준다고 들었어요.

어휘 **ask A B** A에게 B를 물어보다 **seem to do** ~하는 것 같다
have very few problems 문제가 거의 없다 **have A
upgrade** A를 시켜 ~을 업그레이드하게 하다 **actually**
사실상 **know of** ~에 관해서 (간접적으로) 알다 **called**
+ 이름 ~라는 이름의, ~라고 불리는 **run slow** 느리게 작
동하다 **do the same** 똑같은 일을 하다 **a bit** 약간 **be**
worried about ~에 대해 걱정하다 **price** 가격 **make**
a purchase 구매를 하다 **so 형용사/부사 that절** 너무 ~
해서 …이다 **can't afford to do** ~할 (금전적·시간적) 여
유가 없다 **spend** ~을 지출하다 **in that case** 그 경우에
suggest -ing ~할 것을 제안하다 **offer A to B** A를 B에
게 제공하다 **20 percent off** 20% 할인

30. 화자들은 주로 무엇에 대해 이야기하고 있는가?
(A) 새로운 IT 매니저 고용
(B) 교육 연수 준비
(C) 소프트웨어 업그레이드

(D) 새 컴퓨터 구매

해설 대화 초반부에 남자가 컴퓨터 문제를 언급하면서 여자가 누군가에게 시켜 프로그램을 업그레이드했는지(Did you have someone upgrade the programs ~) 물은 뒤로 컴퓨터 프로그램 업그레이드에 대해 이야기하고 있으므로 (C)가 정답이다.

어휘 hire ~을 고용하다 organize ~을 조직하다, 준비하다 training session 교육 연수

31. 남자는 무엇에 대해 걱정하는가?
(A) 서비스 비용
(B) 프로젝트 마감일
(C) 제품 크기
(D) 일부 장비의 가격

해설 be concerned about은 '~에 대해 걱정하다'라는 뜻이므로 남자의 대사 중에 이와 비슷한 의미의 표현이 나오는지 귀기울여 듣도록 한다. 대화 중반부에서 남자는 자신도 IT 업체에 연락해 업그레이드를 해야겠다면서 But I'm a bit worried about the price라고 말한다. 가격에 대해 걱정이 된다는 것은 대화 내용상 IT 업체가 제공해줄 서비스 비용에 대해 걱정하는 것이므로 (A)가 정답이다.

어휘 be concerned[worried] about ~에 대해 걱정하다 deadline 마감기한 equipment 장비

32. 여자는 왜 멜튼 IT를 추천하는가?
(A) 가격이 가장 싸다.
(B) 할인을 해준다.
(C) 근처에 위치해 있다.
(D) 직원들이 친절하다.

해설 대화 마지막에서 여자는 가격을 고민하는 남자에게 Melton IT를 추천하며 I heard they offer 20 percent off to all new customers라는 장점을 덧붙이고 있다. 추천한 업체가 신규 고객에게 20% 할인을 해준다고 하므로 이와 의미가 통하는 (B)가 정답이다.

어휘 discount 할인 be located 위치해 있다 nearby ad. 인근에, 가까운 곳에 friendly 친절한
Paraphrase offer 20 percent off → offers a discount

Questions 33-35 refer to the following conversation and menu.

W: Hi! Welcome to the Kipper Cow Dessert Bar! Do you know what you'd like to order?

M: Oh, I need a minute. **33** My friend said I should give this place a try since I live right down the road. **34** She always raves about the carrot cake, but I don't see it in the display.

W: Well, she's right. **34** It is very popular, so it actually sold out earlier. We only bake a limited amount each day to guarantee the freshness.

M: Ah, I see. Well, what do you like here?

W: Me? **35** I'm particularly fond of the cheese cake. It's creamy and sweet, and it comes with your choice of fruit jam.

M: **35** Sounds delicious. I'll take one slice.

여: 안녕하세요! 키퍼 카우 디저트 바에 오신 것을 환영합니다! 무엇을 주문하고 싶으신지 확인해 보셨나요?
남: 아, 잠깐만 시간을 주세요. 제가 길 바로 저편에 살고 있기 때문에 이곳에 한 번 와 봐야 한다고 제 친구가 말해 주었어요. 그 친구는 항상 이곳의 당근 케이크를 극찬했는데, 진열되어 있는 것을 볼 수 없네요.
여: 저, 그분 말씀이 맞습니다. 그 제품은 너무 인기가 많아서 실은 아까 품절되었습니다. 저희는 신선함을 보장하기 위해 매일 한정된 수량만 굽습니다.
남: 아, 알겠습니다. 저, 이곳에서 무엇을 마음에 들어 하시나요?
여: 저요? 저는 치즈 케이크를 특히 좋아합니다. 크림 같으면서 달콤하고, 직접 선택하시는 과일 잼이 딸려 나옵니다.
남: 맛있을 것 같네요. 한 조각 주세요.

키퍼 카우 디저트 바

....

오늘의 메뉴

초코 볼케이노 케이크	......	4.50달러
치즈 케이크	......	5.50달러
레드 벨벳	......	6.50달러
5단 케이크	......	7.50달러

어휘 need a minute 잠깐 시간이 필요하다 give A a try A를 시도해 보다 since ~이므로 right down the road 길 바로 저편에 rave about ~을 극찬하다 display 진열(대), 진열품 actually 실은, 사실은 sell out 품절

되다, 매진되다 **limited** 한정된, 제한된 **amount** 수량 **guarantee** ~을 보장하다 **freshness** 신선함 **be fond of** ~을 좋아하다 **particularly** 특히, 특별히 **creamy** 크림 같은 **come with** ~가 딸려 있다, 함께 나오다 **one's choice of** ~가 직접 선택한 **sound 형용사** ~한 것 같다, ~한 것처럼 들리다

33. 남자의 친구는 왜 해당 레스토랑을 추천했는가?

(A) 근처에 위치해 있다.
(B) 유명한 요리사가 소유하고 있다.
(C) 재미있는 광고 방송을 한다.
(D) 유기농 재료를 사용한다.

해설 대화 초반부에 남자가 길 바로 저편에 살고 있기 때문에 이 곳에 한 번 와 봐야 한다고 친구가 말한 것을 언급하고 있으므로(My friend said I should give this place a try since I live right down the road) 거리상의 근접함이라는 특성을 말한 (A)가 정답이다.

어휘 **be located nearby** 근처에 위치해 있다 **own** ~을 소유하다 **commercial** 광고 방송 **organic** 유기농의 **ingredient** 재료, 성분

34. 여자는 당근 케이크에 관해 무슨 말을 하는가?

(A) 조각으로 구입할 수 없다.
(B) 계절 제품이다.
(C) 견과류를 포함하고 있다.
(D) 현재 품절된 상태이다.

해설 당근 케이크가 언급되는 부분이 있음을 예상하고 들어야 한다. 대화 중반부에 남자가 당근 케이크를 언급하자(She always raves about the carrot cake) 바로 뒤이어 여자가 인기가 많아서 이미 품절되었다고 말하므로(It is very popular, so it actually sold out earlier) 현재 품절 상태인 것을 언급한 (D)가 정답이다.

어휘 **available** 구입 가능한, 이용 가능한 **seasonal** 계절의 **contain** ~을 포함하다 **nuts** 견과류 **currently** 현재

35. 시각자료를 보시오. 남자의 음식은 비용이 얼마인가?

(A) 4.50달러
(B) 5.50달러
(C) 6.50달러
(D) 7.50달러

해설 대화 후반부에 여자가 치즈 케이크를 좋아한다는 말과 함께 (I'm particularly fond of the cheese cake) 그 특징을 설명하자 남자가 맛있을 것 같다면서 그것으로 한 조각 달라고 (Sounds delicious. I'll take one slice) 요청하고 있다. 시각자료에서 치즈 케이크의 가격으로 5.50달러가 제시되어 있으므로 (B)가 정답이다.

어휘 **dish** 음식, 요리 **cost** ~의 비용이 들다

Questions 36-38 refer to the following conversation and map.

M: Hello, Ms. Walters. **36** I hope you're enjoying your stay here. Is your room comfortable enough for you?

W: Yes, it's great! Actually, I was wondering if there's an ATM nearby where I could withdraw some money.

M: Here... This local map is free for all guests. There are a few ATMs marked on it.

W: Thanks! I only have my bank card from home, though. So, I need a machine that will take foreign cards.

M: Well, **37** the ATM on the corner of Gibson Street and Hill Road definitely accepts foreign bank cards. It's about a 10-minute walk from here.

W: I'll try that one. But, it's raining, and **38** I don't have an umbrella.

M: Hold on a moment. **38** We have one you can use.

남: 안녕하세요, 월터스 씨. 이곳에서 즐겁게 머무르고 계시기를 바랍니다. 객실이 충분히 편안하신가요?

여: 네, 아주 좋아요! 실은, 제가 돈을 좀 인출할 수 있는 ATM이 근처에 있는지 궁금했어요.

남: 여기... 이 지역 안내도가 모든 고객들께 무료입니다. 몇몇 ATM이 표기되어 있습니다.

여: 감사합니다! 하지만, 제가 집에서 가져온 은행 카드만 갖고 있어요. 그래서, 해외 카드를 받는 기계가 필요해요.

남: 저, 깁슨 스트리트와 힐 로드가 만나는 모퉁이에 있는 ATM이 분명 해외 은행 카드도 받습니다. 여기서 걸어서 약 10분 거리입니다.

여: 그곳에 한 번 가 볼게요. 하지만, 비가 내리고 있는데, 제가 우산이 없어요.

남: 잠시 기다려 주십시오. 저희에게 사용하실 수 있는 것이 있습니다.

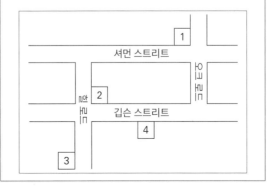

어휘 **comfortable** 편안한 **wonder if** ~인지 궁금하다
nearby 근처에 **withdraw** (돈 등) ~을 인출하다, 꺼내
다 **free** 무료인 **mark** ~을 표기하다 **on the corner of
A and B** A와 B가 만나는 모퉁이에 **definitely** 분명히
accept ~을 받아들이다, 수용하다 **about** 약, 대략 **Hold
on a moment** 잠시만 기다려 주세요.

36. 남자는 어디에서 일할 것 같은가?
(A) 은행에서
(B) 여행사에서
(C) 버스 터미널에서
(D) 호텔에서

해설 대화 시작 부분에 남자가 즐겁게 머무르고 있는지, 그리고 객실
이 충분히 편안한지 묻고 있다(I hope you're enjoying your
stay here. Is your room comfortable enough for
you?). 이는 숙박 업소 직원이 할 수 있는 말이므로 (D)가 정답
이다.

37. 시각자료를 보시오. 남자는 어느 ATM을 권하는가?
(A) ATM 1
(B) ATM 2
(C) ATM 3
(D) ATM 4

해설 여자가 원하는 특정 ATM과 관련해, 대화 중반부에 남자가 깁
슨 스트리트와 힐 로드가 만나는 모퉁이에 있는 ATM이 분
명 해외 은행 카드도 받는다고(the ATM on the corner
of Gibson Street and Hill Road definitely accepts
foreign bank cards) 알리고 있다. 지도에서 Gibson
Street와 Hill Road로 표기된 거리가 서로 만나는 모퉁이에
해당되는 것이 2번이므로 (B)가 정답이다.

어휘 **recommend** ~을 권하다, 추천하다

38. 남자는 곧이어 무엇을 할 것 같은가?
(A) 길 안내를 해 주는 일
(B) 지불 비용을 처리하는 일
(C) 은행 카드를 확인하는 일
(D) 우산을 찾는 일

해설 대화 후반부에 여자가 우산이 없다고(I don't have an
umbrella) 말하자, 남자는 여자가 사용할 수 있는 게 있다고
(We have one you can use) 말해주고 있다. 이는 우산을
하나 찾아 주겠다는 뜻이므로 (D)가 정답이다.

어휘 **directions** 길 안내 **process** ~을 처리하다 **payment**
지불(금)

Part 4

Questions 39-41 refer to the following talk.

Over the past month, a few of our local branches
have been receiving complaints about the quality
of our customer service. **39** Here at Harmony
Bank, we pride ourselves on providing attentive
and thorough customer care, so this is a huge
problem. Therefore, **40** today's meeting will be
about how we can prevent any further complaints
in this area. I've handed out a report that contains
different issues clients have called in, and we'll
work in groups to come up with proper solutions to
them. Keep in mind, the document was just made
this morning. **41** I've already found a mistake on
the first page.

지난 한 달 동안, 몇몇 우리 지역 내 지점에서 우리 고객 서비스의
수준에 관한 불만을 접수해 왔습니다. 우리 하모니 은행에서는 세
심하고 철저한 고객 관리 서비스를 제공하는 것을 자랑스럽게 여
기고 있기 때문에 이는 매우 큰 문제입니다. 따라서, 오늘 회의는
우리 지역에서 더 이상의 불만 사항이 발생하는 것을 방지할 수 있
는 방법에 관한 회의가 될 것입니다. 고객들께서 전화로 알려 오신
여러 다른 문제들을 담은 보고서를 나눠 드렸는데, 이 문제들에 대
한 적절한 해결책을 내놓을 수 있도록 그룹으로 나눠 진행하겠습
니다. 명심하셔야 할 부분은, 이 문서가 오늘 아침에 막 만들어졌
는 점입니다. 저는 이미 첫 페이지에서 실수를 발견했습니다.

어휘 **over** ~ 동안에 걸쳐 **a few of** 몇몇의 **local** 지역의, 현지
의 **branch** 지점, 지사 **complaint** 불만, 불평 **quality** 수
준, 질, 품질 **pride oneself on** ~을 자랑스러워하다
attentive 세심한, 배려하는 **thorough** 철저한
customer care 고객 관리 **huge** 엄청난, 막대한
prevent ~을 방지하다, 막다 **further** 추가의 **hand out**
~을 나눠 주다, 배부하다 **contain** ~을 포함하다 **issue** 문
제, 사안 **call in** 전화로 알리다 **come up with** (아이디어
등) ~을 내놓다, 생각해 내다 **proper** 적절한 **solution** 해
결책 **keep in mind** 명심하다

39. 청자들은 무슨 종류의 업체에서 근무하고 있을 것 같은가?
(A) 의류 매장
(B) 은행
(C) 레스토랑
(D) 세탁소

해설 담화 초반부에 화자는 Here at Harmony Bank라는 말로 은
행에 근무하는 사람임을 나타내고 있으므로 (B)가 정답임을 알
수 있다.

어휘 **work for** ~에서 근무하다 **clothing** 의류 **laundry** 세탁물

40. 회의의 목적은 무엇인가?

(A) 신입 직원들을 교육하는 것
(B) 세일 행사를 계획하는 것
(C) 고객 서비스를 개선하는 것
(D) 정책의 변화를 발표하는 것

해설 화자는 담화 초반부에 회의를 여는 배경을 먼저 설명한 후에 중반부에 가서야 그 목적을 언급하고 있다. 오늘 회의가 더 이상의 불만 사항이 발생하는 것을 방지할 수 있는 방법에 관한 회의가 될 것이라는(today's meeting will be about how we can prevent any further complaints in this area) 말로 회의의 목적을 알리고 있다. 이는 불만 사항을 줄이기 위한 방법을 찾으려는 것인데, 결국 고객 서비스를 개선하려는 것과 같으므로 (C)가 정답이다.

어휘 **policy** 정책, 방침

41. 화자는 왜 '이 문서가 오늘 아침에 막 만들어졌다는 점입니다'라고 말하는가?

(A) 변명을 말하기 위해
(B) 실수를 비난하기 위해
(C) 업적을 인정하기 위해
(D) 한 가지 문제를 우선적으로 처리하기 위해

해설 '문서가 오늘 아침에 막 만들어졌다'는 말 바로 다음에 화자가 이미 첫 페이지에서 실수를 발견했다고(I've already found a mistake on the first page) 알리는 것으로 보아 급하게 만든 문서에 대해 이해해 줄 것을 당부하기 위해 한 말임을 알 수 있다. 따라서 변명을 말하기 위해서라는 의미로 쓰인 (A)가 정답이다.

어휘 **offer an excuse** 변명하다 **criticize** ~을 비난하다, 비판하다 **recognize** ~을 인정하다 **achievement** 업적, 성취 **prioritize** ~을 우선시하다, 우선적으로 처리하다

Questions 42-44 refer to the following excerpt from a meeting.

I have a very important issue to speak about before we adjourn this morning's meeting. **42** As of next month, we will be closing five of our locations south of the city. Now that most of our business is coming through online sales, our physical locations have become less necessary. **43** What has come as a bit of a shock, however, is how well the stores in the north are doing. So, we have decided to keep them going - at least for now. For my management team here today, I'm going to ask you all to **44** e-mail your staffing requirements to our HR manager, Carol Morrison, so we can find new positions at northern stores for those who are currently working in the southern stores.

오늘 오전 회의를 휴회하기 전에 한 가지 매우 중요한 사안에 대해 말씀드리고자 합니다. 다음 달로, 시 남부의 5개 매장 문을 닫을 것입니다. 대부분의 우리 사업이 온라인 판매를 통해 이루어지므로, 실제 매장들은 그 필요성이 줄어들게 되었습니다. 그런데 조금 놀랄 만한 것은 북부 지역의 매장들이 얼마나 잘 유지되고 있는지 입니다. 그래서, 우리는 최소한 지금으로선 그 매장들을 그대로 두기로 결정했습니다. 오늘 여기 오신 운영진 여러분께 알려드리건대, 여러분의 직원 배치 관련 요건을 인사팀장인 캐롤 모리슨 씨에게 이메일로 보내주시길 요청드리려고 합니다. 그럼 저희는 현재 남부 지역의 매장에서 근무 중인 직원들이 북부 지역의 매장에서 맡을 수 있는 새 직책들을 찾을 수 있을 것입니다.

어휘 **adjourn** ~을 휴회하다, 미루다 **as of + 일시** ~부로, ~부터 **location** 영업소, 지점 **now that** ~이니까 **a business comes through online sales** 온라인 판매를 통해 사업이 이루어지다 **physical** 물리적인, 실체가 있는 **necessary** 필요한 **what has come as a bit of a shock** 다소 충격으로 다가온 것, 다소 충격적인 것 **how well A is doing** A가 얼마나 잘 되고 있는지 **keep A going** A가 지속되게 하다 **at least** 적어도 **for now** 지금으로서는 **management team** 운영진, 경영팀 **e-mail A to B** A를 B에게 이메일로 보내다 **staffing** 직원 배치 **requirement** 요건, 필요 조건 **HR manager** 인사부장 cf. HR = Human Resources **position** 직책 **northern** a. 북부의 cf. **southern** 남부의 **those who** ~하는 사람들 **currently** 현재

42. 무엇이 논의되고 있는가?

(A) 회사 규모 축소
(B) 신입 직원 교육
(C) 매장 개조 공사
(D) 새 본사 오픈

해설 담화 도입부에서 매장 일부를 닫을 예정이라고(As of next month, we will be closing five of our locations south of the city) 밝히고 있다. 이후는 매장을 닫는 이유와 그에 따른 준비사항에 대한 내용이다. 따라서 이 담화에서 논의되고 있는 주제로 알맞은 것은 (A)이다. 일부 매장 문을 닫는 것(closing five of our locations)을 규모 축소(downsizing)라고 다르게 표현하였다.

어휘 **downsizing** 규모 축소, 인력 감축 **renovation** 개조 공사 **headquarters** 본사

Paraphrase closing five of our locations
→ downsizing

43. 화자에 따르면, 무엇이 놀라운가?

(A) 경쟁사의 매출이 올랐다.
(B) 온라인 수익이 빠르게 떨어졌다.
(C) 어떤 매장들은 성공적이었다.
(D) 해외 매출이 오르고 있다.

해설 surprising이 핵심어이므로 화자가 놀랍다고 말하는 부분을 주의 깊게 들어야 한다. 이 담화에서는 surprising, surprised 등의 표현 대신 What has come as a bit of a shock라는 표현을 이용해 놀라움을 표하고 있다. 화자가 놀라워하는 것은 매출이 주로 온라인에서 발생해 오프라인 매장들을 줄여야 하는 상황에서 북부 매장들이 잘 되고 있다는 점 (how well the stores in the north are doing)이므로 (C)가 정답이다.

어휘 competitor 경쟁사 profit 수익, 이윤 fall 떨어지다 rapidly 빠르게 certain 어떤 rise v. 오르다

Paraphrase doing well → successful

44. 캐롤 모리슨 씨는 무엇을 할 가능성이 큰가?
(A) 고객과의 회의를 마련한다.
(B) 교육 연수를 실시한다.
(C) 일부 고객들을 설문 조사한다.
(D) 직원들을 재배치하는 것을 돕는다.

해설 Carol Morrison이 핵심어이므로 이 이름이 언급되는 곳을 주의 깊게 듣는다. 담화 마지막 부분에, 인사 담당자인 Carol Morrison에게 이메일로 직원 배치 관련 요건들을 보내라고 당부하는 내용이 나오는데, 그렇게 해서 곧 문을 닫는 남부 매장 직원들을 북부 매장에서 근무하게 하는 방안을 찾겠다고 (so we can find new positions at northern stores for those who are currently working in the southern stores) 하므로, Carol Morrison이 하게 될 일은 직원 재배치를 돕는 일임을 알 수 있다. 따라서 (D)가 정답이다.

어휘 organize ~을 조직하다, 마련하다 conduct ~을 실시하다 survey v. ~을 설문 조사하다 help to do ~하도록 돕다 relocate ~을 재배치하다, 이동시키다

Questions 45-47 refer to the following phone message.

Hello, Claire. This is Lucas calling about 45 the factory tour I'll be taking tomorrow. Really, I'll only be checking out the new equipment, so you don't need to prepare anything special for me. 46 The only item I need is a list of the current employees and their positions. 47 You also mentioned going to a restaurant after picking me up at the airport. Well, there will be an in-flight meal service. So, I'll see you tomorrow.

안녕하세요, 클레어 씨. 내일 제가 하게 될 공장 견학과 관련해 전화 드리는 루카스입니다. 실제로, 저는 오직 새로운 장비만을 확인할 것이기 때문에, 저를 위해 어떤 특별한 것도 준비하실 필요는 없습니다. 제가 필요한 유일한 것은 현재 근무 중인 직원들과 그들의 직책을 담은 목록입니다. 귀하께서는 또한 공항에 차로 저를 데리러 오신 후에 레스토랑으로 가는 것도 언급해 주셨습니다. 저, 기내 식사 서비스가 있을 것입니다. 그럼, 내일 뵙겠습니다.

어휘 take a tour 견학하다 check out ~을 확인하다 equipment 장비 prepare ~을 준비하다 item 물품, 항목 current 현재의 position 직책, 자리 mention ~을 언급하다 pick up ~을 차로 데리러 가다 in-flight 기내의 meal 식사

45. 화자는 무엇을 하기 위해 준비하는 중인가?
(A) 견학하는 일
(B) 기사를 작성하는 일
(C) 강연에 참석하는 일
(D) 일부 직원들을 평가하는 일

해설 화자가 준비하는 일을 묻고 있으므로 화자의 말에서 계획과 관련된 일이나 미래 표현 등이 제시되는 부분에서 단서를 찾아야 한다. 담화를 시작하면서 화자는 자신이 내일 하게 될 공장 견학(the factory tour I'll be taking tomorrow)을 언급하고 있으므로 (A)가 정답임을 알 수 있다.

어휘 article (신문 등의) 기사 evaluate ~을 평가하다

46. 화자는 무엇을 요청하는가?
(A) 직원 목록
(B) 지출 비용 보고서
(C) 신문
(D) 레스토랑 메뉴

해설 담화 중반부에 남자는 자신이 필요로 하는 것과 관련해, 현재 근무 중인 직원들과 그들의 직책을 담은 목록이 필요하다는(The only item I need is a list of the current employees and their positions) 말로 요청 사항을 전달하고 있으므로 (A)가 정답이다.

어휘 expense 지출 (비용)

47. 화자는 왜 "기내 식사 서비스가 있을 것입니다"라고 말하는가?
(A) 지출 비용을 설명하기 위해
(B) 비행 시간에 관해 불평하기 위해
(C) 좌석 업그레이드를 요청하기 위해
(D) 제안을 거절하기 위해

해설 해당 문장은 담화 후반부에 화자가 상대방이 공항에서 자신을 차로 태워 레스토랑으로 가는 것을 언급했다고(~ going to a restaurant after picking me up at the airport) 알리는 말 다음에 들을 수 있다. 즉 기내 식사로 해결할 수 있으니 굳이 레스토랑에 갈 필요가 없음을 나타내는 것이므로 상대방의 제안에 대한 거절의 뜻을 나타내는 말이라는 것을 알 수 있다. 따라서 (D)가 정답이다.

어휘 complain about ~에 대해 불평하다 length 지속 시간 turn down ~을 거절하다

Questions 48-50 refer to the following talk and graph.

Good afternoon, everyone. **48** I know I won't be head of sales until Mr. Han officially retires next month, but in the meantime, I'd like us to go ahead and prepare for future projects. So, let's get familiar with our top product's recent performance. On this graph, you can see that we sold around 50,000 units last year, which is respectable, but **49** one year in particular was very successful. Today, I want us to figure out what made that year different. The commercials we were running at the time got a lot of publicity, so **50** let's review them in a video I've put together. Just watch it and think about what made the commercials stand out.

안녕하세요, 여러분. 다음 달에 한 씨께서 공식적으로 퇴직하셔야 제가 영업부장이 된다는 점을 알고 있기는 하지만, 그 사이에 우리가 일을 진행해 앞으로의 프로젝트들을 준비했으면 합니다. 따라서 우리의 최고 제품이 최근에 보여준 성과에 대해 파악해 봅시다. 이 그래프에서, 우리가 작년에 약 5만 개의 제품을 판매했다는 점을 알 수 있으며, 이는 꽤 괜찮기는 하지만, 한 해가 특히 매우 성공적이었습니다. 오늘, 저는 무엇이 그 한 해를 다르게 만들었는지를 우리가 알아낼 수 있기를 바랍니다. 당시에 우리가 냈던 광고 방송들이 많은 홍보 효과를 가져다 주었기 때문에, 제가 준비해 온 동영상을 통해 함께 검토해 보겠습니다. 그냥 시청하시면서 무엇이 이 광고 방송들을 눈에 띄게 만들었는지에 관해 생각해 보시기 바랍니다.

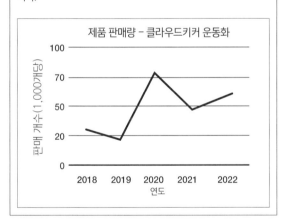

제품 판매량 – 클라우드키커 운동화

판매 개수(1,000개당)

연도: 2018 2019 2020 2021 2022

48. 화자의 말에 따르면, 다음 달에 무슨 일이 있을 것인가?
(A) 직원이 퇴직할 것이다.
(B) 회사가 문을 닫을 것이다.
(C) 홍보 캠페인이 시작될 것이다.
(D) 제품이 출시될 것이다.

해설 다음 달이라는 시점이 질문의 핵심이므로 다음 달이라는 미래 시점과 함께 언급되는 일을 찾아야 한다. 담화를 시작하면서 화자는 다음 달에 Han 씨가 공식적으로 퇴직해야 자신이 영업부장이 된다고(I know I won't be head of sales until Mr. Han officially retires next month) 알리고 있으므로 한 직원의 퇴직을 언급한 (A)가 정답이다.

어휘 **promotional** 홍보의, 판촉의 **release** ~을 출시하다

49. 시각자료를 보시오. 회의는 어느 해에 초점을 맞출 것인가?
(A) 2018년
(B) 2019년
(C) 2020년
(D) 2021년

해설 담화 중반부에 화자는 특정한 한 해가 특히 매우 성공적이었고 오늘 그 이유를 알아볼 수 있기를 바란다고(one year in particular was very successful. Today, I want us to figure out what made that year different) 알리고 있다. 따라서 시각자료에서 가장 매출이 높았던 해에 관해 이야기한다는 것을 일 수 있으므로 (C)가 정답이다.

어휘 **focus on** ~에 초점을 맞추다

50. 청자들은 곧이어 무엇을 할 것인가?
(A) 마감시한 일정을 정할 것이다.
(B) 동영상을 시청할 것이다.
(C) 제품을 시험 사용해 볼 것이다.
(D) 발표를 들을 것이다.

해설 담화의 마지막에 화자는 자신이 준비해 온 동영상을 통해 함께 검토해 보고 시청하는 동안 동영상 속의 광고가 지닌 특징을 생각해 보도록(let's review them in a video I've put together. Just watch it and think about what made the commercials stand out) 당부하고 있다. 따라서 (B)가 정답임을 알 수 있다.

어휘 **schedule** ~의 일정을 정하다 **deadline** 마감기한 **try** ~을 시험 삼아 해 보다 **presentation** 발표(회)

DAY 05　RC Half Test

1. (C)	**2.** (B)	**3.** (B)	**4.** (B)	**5.** (A)
6. (A)	**7.** (C)	**8.** (D)	**9.** (B)	**10.** (D)
11. (A)	**12.** (D)	**13.** (C)	**14.** (D)	**15.** (D)
16. (A)	**17.** (A)	**18.** (D)	**19.** (B)	**20.** (B)
21. (A)	**22.** (A)	**23.** (D)	**24.** (D)	**25.** (C)
26. (A)	**27.** (D)	**28.** (B)	**29.** (D)	**30.** (C)
31. (D)	**32.** (C)	**33.** (D)	**34.** (D)	**35.** (C)
36. (B)	**37.** (D)	**38.** (A)	**39.** (C)	**40.** (D)
41. (B)	**42.** (D)	**43.** (D)	**44.** (D)	**45.** (D)
46. (C)	**47.** (D)	**48.** (D)	**49.** (A)	**50.** (B)

Part 5

1.
정답　(C)

해석　이사회는 그 부서장의 가장 큰 단점이 업무를 효율적으로 위임하지 못하는 무능력함이라는 데 동의하고 있다.

해설　빈칸이 최상급 형용사와 전치사 사이에 위치해 있으므로 빈칸은 최상급 형용사의 수식을 받을 명사가 필요한 자리이다. 따라서 (C) weakness가 정답이다.

어휘　inability to do ~하지 못하는 무능함　delegate ~을 위임하다　efficiently 효율적으로　weakly 약하게, 힘없이　weakness 단점, 약점　weaken v. 약화되다, ~을 약화시키다

2.
정답　(B)

해석　스미스 어카운팅 사에서는, 모든 고객들에게 도착 즉시 음료와 간식이 제공된다.

해설　빈칸 뒤에 복수동사가 있으므로 clientele이 복수명사임을 알 수 있다. 따라서 복수명사를 수식할 수 있는 복수 수량 형용사 (B) all이 정답이다.

어휘　clientele 고객들　offer A B A에게 B를 제공하다　beverage 음료　upon ~ 즉시, ~하자마자　arrival 도착

3.
정답　(B)

해석　매기텍 소프트웨어 사의 연간 예산의 상당 부분이 해외 광고를 위해 비축되었다.

해설　동사 reserve는 '~을 남겨 두다, 비축하다'라는 의미로 쓰이는

타동사인데, 빈칸 뒤에 목적어가 없으므로 수동태로 쓰여야 한다. 따라서 (B) has been reserved가 정답이다.

어휘　considerable 상당한　annual 연간의, 연례의　budget 예산　overseas 해외의　reserve ~을 남겨 두다, 비축하다

4.
정답　(B)

해석　대표이사는 임박한 마감시한을 맞추기 위해 다른 부서에 근무하는 직원들에게 서로 도와주는 것을 요청했다.

해설　빈칸 앞의 one과 함께 to부정사로 쓰인 assist의 목적어 역할을 해야 하므로 '서로'라는 뜻으로 one과 함께 쓰이는 (B) another가 정답이다.

어휘　call for ~을 요청하다　assist ~을 돕다　one another 서로　meet the deadline 마감시한을 맞추다　impending 임박한

5.
정답　(A)

해석　저희 화이트 와인들은 일반적으로 저희 메뉴의 신선한 해산물 요리에 곁들이기에 완벽합니다.

해설　빈칸 앞에 현재시제 동사가 쓰여 있어 업체에서 보유한 화이트 와인들이 지닌 일반적인 특성을 나타내는 문장임을 알 수 있으므로 '일반적으로, 보통'이라는 의미로 현재시제 동사와 어울려 쓰이는 (A) normally가 정답이다.

어휘　accompaniment 곁들이는 것, 딸려 있는 것　normally 일반적으로, 보통　fairly 꽤, 상당히, 공정하게　casually 무심코, (복장 등) 간편하게　evenly 고르게, 균등하게

6.
정답　(A)

해석　직원들께서는 이번 달 마지막 근무일까지 각자의 휴가 요청서를 제출해야 한다는 점을 명심하시기 바랍니다.

해설　선택지가 모두 전치사로 구성되어 있으므로 빈칸 앞뒤의 내용을 파악한다. 빈칸 앞에 휴가 요청서를 제출하라는 말이 쓰여 있어 빈칸 뒤에 제시된 시점이 그 제출 기한임을 알 수 있다. 따라서, '~까지'라는 의미로 기한을 나타낼 때 사용하는 (A) by가 정답이다.

어휘　be reminded to do ~하는 것을 명심하다, ~하도록 상기되다　vacation leave 휴가　request 요청(서)　by (기한) ~까지　over (위치, 이동 등) ~을 넘어, ~ 전체에 걸쳐, (기간) ~ 동안에 걸쳐　against ~에 반대하여, ~에 기대어

7.

정답 (C)

해석 리치몬드 커뮤니티 센터 주차장이 이번 달에 보수공사를 하기 때문에 그곳 직원들은 다른 교통편을 마련해야 한다.

해설 빈칸 앞에 위치한 복수 수량형용사 other와 어울리는 복수명사구가 구성되어야 하므로 명사 transportation과 어울려 복합명사를 구성하는 복수명사 (C) arrangements가 정답이다.

어휘 parking area 주차장 undergo ~을 겪다 renovation 보수, 수리 transportation 운송, 교통 arrangement 마련, 준비

8.

정답 (D)

해석 파이브 스타 케이터링은 질 높은 음식 메뉴로 잘 알려져 있지만, 최근에 몇몇 고객들은 제공된 음식에 만족하지 못했다.

해설 빈칸에는 콤마를 기준으로 제시된 두 개의 절을 연결할 수 있는 접속사가 와야 한다. 음식의 질이 높은 것으로 유명하다는 내용과 최근에 고객들이 만족하지 못했다는 내용은 대조적인 의미를 나타내므로 '~이지만, ~인 한편'이라는 의미로 쓰이는 (D) While이 정답이다.

어휘 be known for ~로 유명하다 high-quality 질 높은 recent 최근의 be dissatisfied with ~에 불만족하다 as if 마치 ~인 것처럼

9.

정답 (B)

해석 넬리산 공업사는 이집트에 기반을 둔 한 초콜릿 회사 매입을 발표했는데, 이는 북아프리카 지역으로의 사업 확장 계획을 확인해주는 것이었다.

해설 이미 문장의 동사 announced가 있으므로 분사 형태가 빈칸에 와야 하는데, 빈칸 바로 뒤에 위치한 명사구를 목적어로 취할 수 있는 현재분사 (B) confirming이 정답이다.

어휘 announce ~을 발표하다, 알리다 Egyptian-based 이집트에 기반을 둔 expansion 확장

10.

정답 (D)

해석 다국적 기업들은 반드시 지사를 설립하는 각 국가의 풍습을 이해하도록 노력해야 한다.

해설 빈칸이 전치사와 주어 사이에 위치해 있는데, 선택지의 관계사들 중에서 전치사의 목적어 역할을 하면서 관계사절을 이끌 수 있는 (D) which가 정답이다.

어휘 multinational company 다국적 기업 make an effort to do ~하도록 노력하다 custom 풍습, 관습 set up ~을 설립하다, 설치하다 branch office 지사

11.

정답 (A)

해석 직원 인센티브 프로그램을 시행함으로써, 우리는 직원들의 사기를 촉진할 수 있을 뿐만 아니라, 전반적인 생산성도 증대할 수 있다.

해설 빈칸 뒤를 보면 boost와 increase라는 두 개의 동사가 but also로 연결되어 있는데, but also는 not only와 짝을 이뤄 상관 접속사를 구성하므로 (A) not only가 정답이다.

어휘 implement ~을 시행하다 boost ~을 촉진하다, 신장시키다 morale 사기, 의욕 not only A but also B A뿐만 아니라 B도 overall 전반적인 productivity 생산성

12.

정답 (D)

해석 신입 사원들은 보호 장비를 제대로 사용하는 법을 배우기 위해 반드시 종합 교육 프로그램을 완료해야 한다.

해설 빈칸에는 to부정사의 목적어 역할을 하면서 빈칸 뒤에 있는 명사 equipment를 수식할 수 있는 것이 와야 한다. 구조상 분사와 형용사가 빈칸에 올 수 있는데, 보호를 목적으로 하는 장비의 속성을 나타내야 하므로 형용사 (D) protective가 정답이다.

어휘 complete v. ~을 완료하다 comprehensive 포괄적인, 종합적인 protective equipment 보호 장비 properly 제대로, 알맞게 protect ~을 보호하다

13.

정답 (C)

해석 그 공장 견학 중에, 주주들은 여러 직원들이 조립 라인 기계를 이용하는 방법을 시연하는 모습을 지켜볼 것이다.

해설 타동사 demonstrate의 목적어로 to부정사가 제시되었는데, to부정사 뒤의 구조가 완전하므로 의문부사인 (C) how가 정답이다. 의문대명사인 (A) who와 (B) what은 불완전한 구조를 이끄므로 오답이며, (D) that은 to부정사를 이끌 수 없으므로 정답이 될 수 없다.

어휘 shareholder 주주 watch A do A가 ~하는 것을 지켜보다 demonstrate ~을 시연하다, 시범을 보이다 assembly 조립

14.

정답 (D)

해석 다큐멘터리를 제외한 모든 장르의 영화들이 연례 홉라이트 축제에서 상영된다.

해설 선택지가 모두 다른 전치사로 구성되어 있으므로 빈칸 앞뒤에 제시된 명사의 의미를 파악해야 한다. 빈칸 앞의 명사구는 '모든 장르의 영화'라는 의미로 전체 범위를 아우르는 의미를 나타내는데 빈칸 뒤에 다큐멘터리라는 특정 장르가 별도로 언급되어 있으므로 제외 대상을 뜻한다는 것을 알 수 있다. 따라서 '~을 제외하고'라는 의미로 쓰이는 (D) except가 정답이다.

어휘 genre 장르 except ~을 제외하고 show ~을 상영하다,

상연하다 **opposite** ~의 건너편에, 맞은편에 **toward** (이동) ~을 향해 (목적) ~을 위해 **along** (길 등) ~을 따라

15.

정답 (D)

해석 그 세미나 강사는 자신이 참석자들에게 설명하는 것을 분명히 보여주기 위해 일반적으로 발표 내용에 도표를 포함한다.

해설 빈칸이 속한 주절에 이미 동사가 쓰여 있으므로 빈칸에는 동사가 올 수 없고, 빈칸 뒤부분이 발표 내용에 도표를 포함하는 목적을 나타내야 자연스러우므로 '~하기 위해'라는 의미로 목적을 말할 때 사용하는 to부정사 (D) to illustrate이 정답이다.

어휘 **incorporate** ~을 포함하다 **diagram** 도표 **presentation** 발표(회) **describe** ~을 설명하다 **attendee** 참석자 **illustrate** ~을 분명히 보여주다, ~에 삽화를 넣다

16.

정답 (A)

해석 펀 가구사의 제품의 매출이 매장 보수 공사 및 더 새로운 상품 도입 이후로 상당히 증가했다.

해설 빈칸 뒤에 명사가 없으므로 동사 increase가 자동사로 사용되어 빈칸 앞 절이 완전한 것을 알 수 있다. 따라서 빈칸에는 자동사를 수식할 수 있는 부사 (A) considerably가 정답이다.

어휘 **considerably** 상당히 **renovation** 수리, 개축 **introduction** 도입, 소개 **considerable** 상당한 **consider** ~을 고려하다

Part 6

17-20.

무대 위에서
작성자, 재스민 블러스

8월 13일 – 샌드빌 지역 문화 아트 센터에서 열리는 <마이 페어 레이디>

샌드빌 지역 문화 아트 센터에서 열리는 이 새로운 공연물 <마이 페어 레이디>는 브로드웨이 최고의 작품에 비할 만한 공연입니다. 지역 배우 샌드라 보이드와 해리슨 프록이 많은 사랑을 받은 이 고전 무대 작품의 이번 버전에서 일라이자 두리틀과 히긴스 교수 역할을 맡습니다. 이번 공연의 두 주인공은 모두 샌드빌 지역 내에 거주하고 있는 재능 있는 조연 배우들을 **17** 동반합니다.

이 뮤지컬에서, 히긴스 교수는 일라이자 두리틀에게 세련된 여성이 되기 위해 알아야 하는 **18** 무엇이든 가르치려 합니다. 말투와 복장에서부터 포크를 붙잡는 방식에 이르기까지, 일라이자는 상류층의 행동 방식으로 교육 받으며, 자신을 런던의 부유한 귀족 사이에서 어울릴 수 있게 만듭니다.

이 공연은 8월 10일부터 9월 30일까지 진행됩니다. **19** 입장권은 www.scac.org에서 온라인으로 또는 공연장 매표소에서 구입하실 수 있습니다. 낮 상연 시간에 참석하시든, 아니면 저녁 상연 시간에 참석하시든 상관없이, 그 경험은 분명 **20** 즐거울 것입니다.

어휘 **production** 제작(된 작품) **rival** v. ~에 비하다, ~와 필적하다 **take on the role of** ~의 역할을 맡다 **well-loved** 많은 사랑을 받은 **be accompanied by** ~을 동반하다 **talented** 재능 있는 **supporting actor** 조연 배우 **reside in** ~에 거주하다 **attempt to do** ~하려 시도하다 **sophisticated** 세련된 **school** v. ~을 교육하다 **upper class** 상류층 **fit in** 어울리다 **aristocrat** 귀족 **run** 진행되다, 운영되다 **venue** 공연장, 행사장 **matinee** 낮 상연 시간 **be sure to do** 분명 ~하다

17.

정답 (A)

해설 선택지에 제시된 동사 accompany는 타동사인데, 빈칸 뒤에 목적어 없이 전치사가 있으므로 수동태 동사가 쓰여야 한다. 따라서 (A) are accompanied가 정답이다.

18.

정답 (D)

해설 빈칸 앞뒤의 내용으로 보아 '~가 되기 위해 알아야 하는 무엇이든 가르치다'와 같은 의미가 되어야 알맞으므로 '~하는 무엇이든'이라는 뜻으로 쓰이는 (D) whatever가 정답이다.

19.

정답 (B)

해석 (A) 하지만, 다음으로 계획된 공연 작품은 <오클라호마>입니다.
 (B) 입장권은 www.scac.org에서 온라인으로 또는 공연장 매표소에서 구입하실 수 있습니다.
 (C) 사실, 이 버전은 대단히 인기 많은 영화에서 많은 부분을 차용한 것입니다.
 (D) 밥 히콕 씨가 또 다른 샌드빌 지역 연극을 연출하기 위해 돌아왔습니다.

해설 빈칸 앞에는 공연 기간을 알리는 말이, 빈칸 뒤에는 낮 공연이든 저녁 공연이든 상관없이 좋은 경험이 될 것이라는 말이 쓰여 있다. 따라서 공연 관람 방법과 관련된 정보를 담은 문장이 빈칸에 쓰여야 흐름이 자연스러우므로 입장권 구입 방법을 설명하는 (B)가 정답이다.

어휘 **planned** 계획된 **draw heavily from** ~에서 많이 차용하다 **highly** 대단히, 매우 **direct** ~을 연출하다, 감독하다 **yet another** 또 다른 하나의

20.

정답 (B)

해설 선택지가 모두 다른 형용사로 구성되어 있어 해석을 통해 알
맞은 어휘를 골라야 한다. 빈칸에 쓰일 형용사는 주어 the
experience의 특징을 나타내야 하는데, 여기서 말하는 '경험'
은 공연 관람 경험을 의미하므로 '즐거움을 주는'을 뜻하는 (B)
entertaining이 정답이다.

어휘 talkative 수다스러운 prominent 두드러진, 중요한
entertaining 즐거움을 주는

21-24.

수신: LisaTennant@acemail.net
발신: Brett_Stark@lolafurnishings.com
제목: 회신: 저의 최근 구매품
첨부: 교환용 양식

테넌트 씨께,

귀하께서 저희 웹 사이트를 통해 주문하신 마호가니 식탁이 표면
에 흠집이 있는 채로 **21** 도착했다는 사실을 알게 되어 매우 실망
스럽습니다. 저희가 귀하의 자택으로 직원들 중 한 명을 보내 **22**
손상된 제품을 수거해 드릴 것입니다. 첨부해 드린 교환용 양식
을 작성 완료하셔서 저희 직원이 도착하면 전해 주시기 바랍니다.
교체 식탁이 그 후에 며칠 내로 귀하께 배송될 것입니다. **23** 또
는, 저희 롤라 퍼니싱스에서 해당 제품에 대해 전액 환불을 제공해
드릴 수도 있습니다. 이것이 귀하께서 원하시는 것일 경우, 555-
3982번으로 저에게 전화 주시면 제가 필요한 조치를 취해 드리겠
습니다. **24** 이와 같은 불편함에 대해 사과드립니다. 저희는 귀하
께서 앞으로도 계속 저희 롤라 퍼니싱스에서 쇼핑하시기를 바랍니
다!

안녕히 계십시오.

브렛 스타크
고객 서비스부장
롤라 퍼니싱스

어휘 recent 최근의 exchange 교환 disappointed 실망한
surface 표면 collect ~을 수거하나, 모으나 complete
~을 작성 완료하다 attached 첨부된 replacement 교체
(품) full refund 전액 환불 would prefer ~을 원하다,
~하고 싶다 make an arrangement 조치하다, 마련하다

21.

정답 (A)

해설 빈칸 뒤에 주어와 동사가 포함된 절이 이어져 있으므로 빈칸에
는 접속사가 필요한데, 동사 find out은 that절을 목적어로 취
하므로 (A) that이 정답이다.

22.

정답 (A)

해설 선택지가 모두 다른 형용사로 구성되어 있으므로 해석을 통해
알맞은 어휘를 골라야 한다. 빈칸 앞뒤에 위치한 정관사와 명사
item은 앞 문장에서 흠집이 있는 채로 도착한 주문품을 가리킨

다. 따라서 이러한 상태를 나타낼 수 있는 '손상된, 피해를 입은'
등을 뜻하는 (A) damaged가 정답이다.

어휘 incorrect 부정확한, 잘못된 accidental 우연한, 돌발적인
damaged 손상된, 피해를 입은

23.

정답 (D)

해설 빈칸 앞에는 제품을 교체하는 방법이, 빈칸 뒤에는 전액 환불을
제공하는 방법이 제시되어 있다. 이는 문제 해결을 위해 선택 가
능한 두 가지 다른 방법들을 말하는 흐름이므로 '또는, 그렇지
않으면'이라는 의미로 선택을 나타내는 (D) Alternatively가
정답이다.

어휘 eventually 마침내, 결국 regrettably 유감스럽게도, 안
타깝게도 occasionally 때때로 alternatively 또는, 그
렇지 않으면

24.

정답 (D)

해석 (A) 귀하께서 저희 서비스가 만족스럽다고 생각하셨다니 기쁩
니다.
(B) 제 문의 사항에 대한 즉각적인 대응에 감사드립니다.
(C) 저희 제품 범위는 전국에서 가장 폭넓습니다.
(D) 이와 같은 불편함에 대해 사과드립니다.

해설 앞서 지문 전체적으로 결함 제품에 대한 조치를 설명하는 내용
이 제시되어 있으므로 이러한 상황을 this inconvenience로
지칭해 사과의 말을 전하는 (D)가 정답이다.

어휘 find A to be B A를 B하다고 생각하다 satisfactory
만족스러운 prompt 즉각적인 response 대응, 반응
inquiry 문의 extensive 폭넓은, 광범위한

Part 7

25-26.

이스만 알리 [오후 6:16]
안녕하세요, 크레이그 씨. 제 내일 일정을 확인해 봤는데, 오전 10
시 30분에 엘리엇 빌딩 프로젝트를 논의할 여유 시간이 좀 있을 겁
니다.

크레이그 케인 [오후 6:18]
잘됐네요. 우리가 검토해야 할 사항이 몇 가지 있습니다. **25** 이메
일은 확인해 보셨나요?

이스만 알리 [오후 6:20]
25 네, 설계도를 받았습니다. 감사합니다. 상당히 인상적인 것같
습니다.

크레이그 케인 [오후 6:21]
저는 제가 그에 대해 완료한 작업이 만족스러운데, 고객이신 로즈
우드 씨께서 마지막 순간에 몇 가지 변경을 요청하셨어요.

이스만 알리 [오후 6:23]
그래요? **26** 그럼 우리 프로젝트 마감 기한에도 영향을 미칠 수 있겠네요.

크레이그 케인 [오후 6:24]
의심의 여지가 없죠. 그래서, 이를 처리할 가장 좋은 방법과 관련해 내일 당신 의견을 듣고자 합니다.

이스만 알리 [오후 6:25]
좋습니다. 절충해서 계속 고객을 만족시킬 수 있는 방법을 알아내게 될 겁니다.

어휘 **go over** ~을 검토하다, ~을 살펴보다 **blueprint** 설계도, 청사진 **look A** A한 것 같다, A하게 보이다 **impressive** 인상적인 **be pleased with** ~에 만족하다, ~에 기뻐하다 **ask for** ~을 요청하다 **last-minute** 마지막 순간의 **alteration** 변경 **affect** ~에 영향을 미치다 **Without a doubt** 의심의 여지가 없다 **input** 의견, 조언(의 제공) **handle** ~을 처리하다, ~을 다루다 **figure out** ~을 알아내다, ~을 파악하다 **compromise** 절충하다 **keep A B** 계속 A를 B한 상태로 유지하다

25. 케인 씨와 관련해 암시된 것은 무엇인가?
   (A) 알리 씨와의 회의 일정을 재조정해야 했다.
   (B) 한 건축가에게 연락할 계획을 세우고 있다.
   (C) 알리 씨에게 일부 문서를 보냈다.
   (D) 내일 엘리엇 빌딩을 방문할 것이다.

정답 (C)

해설 6시 18분 메시지에 케인 씨가 알리 씨에게 이메일을 확인했는지 묻자(Did you check your e-mail?), 알리 씨가 그렇다는 말과 함께 설계도를 받았다고(Yes, I got the blueprints) 언급하고 있다. 이는 케인 씨가 이메일로 문서 파일을 보냈음을 나타내는 말에 해당되므로 (C)가 정답이다.

어휘 **reschedule** ~의 일정을 재조정하다

26. 오후 6시 24분에, 케인 씨가 "Without a doubt"이라고 쓸 때 무엇을 의미하는가?
   (A) 업무 일정을 우려하고 있다.
   (B) 직접 가서 한 가지 사안을 논의하고자 한다.
   (C) 로즈우드 씨가 마음을 바꿀 것으로 생각한다.
   (D) 몇몇 건물 설계도를 변경하고 싶어 한다.

정답 (A)

해설 알리 씨가 6시 23분에 프로젝트 마감 기한에도 영향을 미칠 수 있겠다고(That could affect our project deadlines) 언급하자, 케인 씨가 '의심의 여지가 없습니다'라고 대답하는 흐름이다. 이는 당연히 마감 기한에 영향을 미친다는 의미로 그러한 업무 일정 변동에 대해 우려의 뜻을 나타내는 말에 해당되므로 (A)가 정답이다.

어휘 **be concerned about** ~을 우려하다 **matter** 사안, 문제 **in person** 직접 (가서)

27-29.

┌───┐
수신: 케이티 골드브럼 <kgoldblum@betamail.com>
발신: 루크 코스티간 <lcostigan@yulelibrary.com>
제목: <던위치 미스터리>
날짜: 11월 3일

골드브럼 씨께,

저희 데이터베이스에 따르면, **27** 회원님은 10월 23일에 에드가 풀만의 <던위치 미스터리>를 대여하셨습니다. **27** 저희의 모든 소설 책이 그렇듯이, 이 책은 7일간 대여되었고 **28** 10월 29일에 반납되거나 연장이 되었어야 합니다. 11월 1일에 회원님께 전화와 이메일을 통해 연락을 취하였으나 연락이 닿지 않았습니다. 그러므로, 연체된 시점에서 매일 50센트의 연체료를 적용해야 할 것입니다. 최대한 빠른 시일 내에 책을 반납하시어 더 이상의 벌금을 피하십시오.

저희 대여 방침에 명시되어 있듯이, 모든 도서관 카드 소지자는 다음과 같은 책임이 있습니다:
- 대여한 물품의 기한 내 반납
- **29** 이름, 집 주소, 전화번호 또는 이메일 주소 변경에 대한 알림
- 모든 연체, 분실 또는 손상된 물품에 대해 발생되는 벌금 납부

대여하신 도서에 관련한 문제가 있어 저와 직접 이야기하고 싶으시다면, 망설이지 마시고 555-2378로 연락 주십시오.

안녕히 계세요.

루크 코스티간
율 도서관
└───┘

어휘 **according to** ~에 따르면 **borrow** ~을 빌리다 **fiction** 소설 **lend** ~을 빌려주다 **return** ~을 돌려주다 **renew** ~을 갱신하다 **attempt to do** ~하려고 시도하다 **apply** ~을 적용하다 **late fee** 연체료 **overdue** 기한이 지난, 연체된 **avoid** ~을 피하다 **fine** 벌금 **be responsible for** ~에 책임이 있다 **timely** 때에 맞춘 **notify** 알리다 **incur** (비용을) 발생시키다 **regarding** ~에 관하여 **directly** 직접, 곧바로

27. 코스티간 씨가 이메일을 보낸 이유는 무엇인가?
   (A) 고객에게 새로운 책을 알리기 위해
   (B) 데이터베이스 오류에 대해 사과하기 위해
   (C) 새로운 대여 절차를 설명하기 위해
   (D) 고객에게 독촉장을 발부하기 위해

정답 (D)

해설 첫번째 단락에서 코스티간 씨는 소설 책의 대여 기간이 7일임을 언급하며 대여한 책을 고객이 아직 반납하지 않았음을(this item was lent for a period of 7 days and should have been returned or renewed on October 29) 말하고 있다. 따라서 책의 대여 기간이 지났음을 상기시켜 준다는 내용의 독촉장을 보낸다는 의미로 쓰인 (D)가 정답이다.

어휘 **apologize for** ~에 대해 사과하다 **procedure** 절차

issue ~을 발부하다, 발표하다 reminder 상기시키는 것, 독촉장

28. 골드브럼 씨의 책이 원래 도서관에 반납되어야 하는 예정일은 언제였는가?

(A) 10월 23일
(B) 10월 29일
(C) 11월 1일
(D) 11월 3일

정답 (B)

해설 첫 번째 단락 두 번째 문장에서 10월 29일에 반납되거나 연장이 되었어야 했다고(should have been returned or renewed on October 29) 알리고 있으므로 (B)가 정답이다.

어휘 originally 원래

29. 율 도서관의 카드 소지자에 대해 명시된 것은 무엇인가?

(A) 최대 2주 동안 물품을 대여할 수 있다.
(B) 도서관 웹 사이트를 통해 책을 예약할 수 있다.
(C) 1년 주기로 회원권을 갱신해야 한다.
(D) 개인 정보 변경 사항을 알려야 한다.

정답 (D)

해설 두 번째 단락의 세 가지 항목 중 두 번째 항목을 보면 이름, 집 주소, 전화번호 또는 이메일 변경에 대한 알림이(notifying us about changes to name, home address, phone number, or e-mail address) 카드 소지자의 의무임을 언급하고 있으므로 (D)가 정답이다.

어휘 holder 소지자 reserve ~을 예약하다 on an annual basis 1년 주기로, 1년마다 report ~을 보고하다, 알리다

30-32.

> **커모드 미디어 전 직원에게 전하는 공지**
>
> 직원 여러분께,
>
> 31(A) 소방 훈련이 5월 17일, 금요일에 우리 건물에서 열린다는 사실을 잊지 마시기 바랍니다. 이 훈련의 정확한 시간은 알려지지 않은 상태이지만, 31(B) 분명 정오가 되기 전에 진행될 것입니다. 30 이것이 여러분께서 일하고 계시는 어떤 업무든 지장을 주는 경우, 제가 기간 연장을 승인해 드릴 수 있습니다.
>
> 경영진에서는 이번 달에 아주 크게 개선된 모습을 볼 수 있기를 바라고 있습니다. — [1] —. 약 10퍼센트의 직원들이 지난달에 있었던 훈련에서 31(C) 5분 내에 건물에서 대피하시지 못했습니다. — [2] —. 31(A) 3월과 4월에도 모두 유사한 결과가 나타났습니다. 우리 회사의 성적이 정부 권장 안전 기준에 지속적으로 미치지 못하고 있습니다.
>
> 32 화재 경보기 소리를 들으시면, 엘리베이터 대신 계단을 이용하셔서 우리 건물의 정문 밖으로 나가십시오. — [3] —. 어떤 질문이든 있으시면, 저 또는 소속 부서장님께 말씀하시기 바랍니다. — [4] —.

감사합니다.

질리언 밀러

어휘 reminder (상기시키기 위한) 공지, 메시지 forget that ~임을 잊다 fire drill 소방 훈련 exact 정확한 unknown 알려지지 않은 definitely 분명히, 확실히 take place (일, 행사 등이) 발생되다, 개최되다 interrupt ~에 지장을 주다, ~을 방해하다 work on ~에 대한 일을 하다 approve ~을 승인하다 extension (기간) 연장 massive 아주 큰, 엄청난 improvement 개선, 향상 approximately 약, 대략 fail to do ~하지 못하다 evacuate ~에서 대피하다 consistently 지속적으로 recommended 권장되는 staircases 계단 instead of ~ 대신 exit 나가다 supervisor 책임자, 감독

30. 누가 공고를 게시했을 것 같은가?

(A) 소방서장
(B) 건물 주민
(C) 부서장
(D) 정부 관계자

정답 (C)

해설 첫 번째 단락에 질리언 밀러 씨가 자신을 I로 지칭해 어떤 업무든 지장을 받는 경우에 자신이 기간 연장을 승인해 줄 수 있다고 알리는 말이 쓰여 있다. 이는 책임자의 역할을 하는 사람이 갖고 있는 권한에 해당되므로 부서장을 뜻하는 (C)가 정답이다.

어휘 put up ~을 게시하다, ~을 부착하다 official n. 관계자, 당국자

31. 소방 훈련과 관련해 언급되지 않은 것은 무엇인가?

(A) 일반적으로 매달 진행된다.
(B) 오전에 개최될 것이다.
(C) 직원들이 5분 내에 대피해야 한다.
(D) 직원들이 엘리베이터를 이용해야 한다.

정답 (D)

해설 첫 단락에 훈련 개최 날짜인 5월 17일, 금요일과(on Friday, May 17) 두 번째 단락에서 3월 및 4월 훈련 결과를(We had a similar result in both March and February) 말하는 부분에서 (A)를 확인할 수 있다. 또한, 첫 단락에 정오가 되기 전에 진행될 것이라는(it will definitely take place before noon) 부분에서 (B)를, 두 번째 단락에 5분 내에 대피해야 한다는(evacuate the building within five minutes) 부분에서 (C)를 확인할 수 있다. 하지만 마지막 단락에 계단을 이용하라고 알리고 있으므로 (D)가 정답이다.

어휘 usually 일반적으로, 보통 hold ~을 개최하다, ~을 열다

32. [1], [2], [3], [4]로 표기된 위치들 중에서, 다음 문장이 들어가기에 가장 적절한 곳은 어디인가?

"어떤 상황에 처하시게 되든 훈련이 종료될 때까지 내부로 다시 들어가지 마십시오."

(A) [1]

(B) [2]

(C) [3]

(D) [4]

정답　(C)

해설　제시된 문장은 어떤 상황이든 훈련이 끝날 때까지 안으로 다시 들어가지 말라는 의미를 지니고 있다. 이는 계속 밖에 머물러 있어야 한다는 뜻으로서, 건물 밖으로 나가는 방법을 알리는 문장 뒤에 위치한 [3]에 들어가 밖으로 나간 후에 해야 하는 일을 말하는 흐름이 되어야 자연스러우므로 (C)가 정답이다.

어휘　under any circumstances 어떤 상황에 처하더라도, 어떤 일이 있더라도

33-36.

일류 자동차 회사,
난관에 직면하다
리오넬 피터슨 작성

(9월 1일) - ▨33 어제 데보나 자동차 회사는 동력 조향 장치 문제로 인해 거의 59만 5천 대의 승용차에 대한 회수를 공식적으로 요청했다고 발표했다. 이러한 조치는 데보나 리브라와 데보나 아르고에 적용되며, 두 모델 모두 2월에 출시되었다.

데보나 자동차의 대변인은 전기 연결 결함으로 인해 전기 동력 조향 장치가 작동하지 않아, 그 결과 운전자가 차량을 통제하지 못할 가능성이 있다고 설명했다. 데보나 자동차는 ▨35 처음에 결함으로 인한 어떠한 부상도 발생하지 않았다고 주장했으나, 50건 이상의 사고가 보험회사들에 의해 신고되었다. ▨34 이러한 사고에는 위에서 언급한 데보나 차량이 조향 장치 결함으로 인해 연석과 길가 물체들에 부딪혔고, 그 결과 몇몇 운전자들은 목, 허리, 어깨 등에 부상을 입었다는 내용이 포함되어 있다.

▨36 미국 교통 안전 기구(ATSO)는 대리점과 운전자들부터 불만이 접수되기 시작한 4월에 동력 조향 장치 문제에 대한 조사를 시작하였다. 데보나 사는 영향을 받는 모델들을 회수해야 한다는 ATSO의 초기 권고를 거절하면서, 5월에 그 기관에 보낸 편지에서 불만의 숫자가 너무 적어서 이러한 급격한 조치를 정당화할 수 없다고 주장했다.

이 자동차 회사는 또한 결함을 감추기 위한 노력으로 6월에 차량 대리점에 기술 보고서를 발행했다. 그러나 점점 증가하는 불만 제기의 횟수와 ATSO의 압박으로 인해, 이 회사는 차량들을 회수하고 공개적으로 동력 조향 장치 문제가 운전자에게 진정으로 위험할 수 있다는 사실을 인정할 수밖에 없었다.

어휘　leading 선도하는, 대표하는 automotive 자동차의 announce ~을 발표하다 officially 공식적으로 nearly 거의 power-steering 동력 조향 장치 move 조치, 행동 apply to ~에 적용되다 launch ~을 출시하다 spokesperson 대변인 faulty 결함이 있는 electrical

전기의 disable ~을 무능하게 하다, 쓸모 없게 하다 electric 전기의 claim ~을 주장하다 defect 결함 result in ~인 결과를 낳다 injury 부상 incident 사고 abovementioned 위에서 언급한 curb 연석 roadside 길가 investigate ~을 조사하다 dealership 대리점 recall ~을 회수하다 justify ~을 정당화 하다 drastic 급격한 cover up ~을 숨기다 have no choice but to do ~할 수밖에 없다 publicly 공개적으로 admit ~을 인정하다 genuine 진짜의, 순수한

33. 기사는 주로 무엇에 관한 내용인가?

(A) 생산 과정의 지연

(B) 제조 기계의 문제

(C) 특정 차량에 대한 신기술

(D) 결함 있는 차량의 회수

정답　(D)

해설　첫 문단에서 데보나 사가 자동차의 동력 조향 장치 문제로 인해 자동차를 회수할 것을 공식적으로 요청했다고 언급하고 (Devona Motors Inc. announced yesterday that it has officially requested the return of nearly 595,000 sedans due to a power-steering issue) 있으므로 (D)가 정답이다.

어휘　delay 지연 manufacturing 제조 machinery 기계 defective 결함 있는 vehicle 차량, 탈 것

34. 데보나 아르고 자동차에 관해 유추할 수 있는 것은 무엇인가?

(A) 1년 전에 시장에 출시되었다.

(B) 일부 차량은 구식 브레이크 시스템을 포함한다.

(C) 데보나 리브라 자동차보다 덜 안전하다고 밝혀졌다.

(D) 일부 차량은 사고와 관련이 있었다.

정답　(D)

해설　두 번째 단락에 데보나 차량이 조향 장치 결함으로 인해 연석과 길가 물체들에 부딪혔고 그 결과 몇몇 운전자들은 목, 허리, 어깨 등에 부상을 입었다는 내용이 포함되어 있다는(These incidents involve the abovementioned Devona models ~ causing several drivers to hurt their neck, back, or shoulders) 부분에서 일부 모델이 사고와 관련이 있었음을 확인할 수 있다. 따라서 (D)가 정답이다.

어휘　release ~을 출시하다 outdated 구식의 be involved in ~와 관련되어 있다

35. 데보나 자동차 회사와 관련해 암시된 것은 무엇인가?

(A) 제조공장에서 모든 생산을 중단할 예정이다.

(B) 미국 교통 안전 기구에 의해 벌금이 부과되었다.

(C) 문제가 있다는 것을 즉각적으로 인정하지 않았다.

(D) 상품을 구매한 사람들에게 편지를 보냈다.

정답　(C)

해설　두 번째 단락에 데보나 사가 처음에 결함으로 인한 어떠한 부상도 발생하지 않았다고 주장했다는(Devona originally claimed that the defect has not resulted in any injuries) 내용이 제시되어 있으므로 (C)가 정답이다.

어휘 **intend to do** ~할 의도이다, 계획이다 **cease** ~을 정지하다, 멈추다 **fine** 벌금을 부과하다 **admit** ~을 인정하다

36. ATSO가 기술적 결함을 처음 알게 된 것은 언제인가?
(A) 2월에
(B) 4월에
(C) 5월에
(D) 6월에

정답 **(B)**

해설 세 번째 단락 첫 번째 문장에 미국 교통 안전 기구(ATSO)가 대리점과 운전자들부터 불만이 접수되기 시작한 4월에 동력 조향 장치 문제에 대한 조사를 시작하였다는(The American Traffic Safety Organization (ATSO) began investigating ~ in April when it started receiving complaints from) 내용을 통해 4월에 기술적 결함을 알게 된 것을 알 수 있다. 따라서 (B)가 정답이다.

어휘 **technical** 기술적인 **fault** 결함

37-40.

37 **수신:** 모든 부서장들 <managerlist@iversen.com>
발신: 버나드 허들스톤 <bhuddlestone@iversen.com>
날짜: 4월 6일 화요일
제목: 좋은 소식

여러분 모두에게 기분 좋은 일 한 가지에 관해 알려 드리게 되어 기쁩니다. 38 재그텐 테크놀로지와의 협상이 성공적으로 마무리되어, 코펜하겐에 본사를 둔 이 업체가 우리의 새 휴대전화 모델에 대해 우리와 협력함으로써 그곳의 전문 지식을 제공하는 데 합의했습니다. 이는 우리가 일정에 맞춰 8월까지 제품 디자인 및 개발의 첫 단계를 완료하기 위해 서명해야 했던 대단히 중요한 계약이었습니다.

재그텐 사는 전자제품 업계에서 기기 내의 배터리 수명을 늘리고 내부의 열을 최소화하는 능력으로 유명한 곳입니다. 우리는 이러한 문제들에 대해 최우선 순위를 두었는데, 39 우리 고객들이 이전의 우리 모델들이 지닌 짧은 배터리 수명 및 높은 온도 문제에 대해 우려의 목소리를 냈기 때문입니다. 저는 이제 이 문제들이 적절하게 처리될 것이라고 확신합니다. 저는 지난 몇 주 동안에 걸친 여러분의 노력에 대해 진심으로 감사드리며, 여러분께 보상해 드리기 위해 뭔가 해드리고자 합니다. 따라서, 40 저는 다음 주 금요일에 여러분 모두를 모시고 나가 저녁 회식 자리를 가질 계획입니다.

제가 오늘 이따가 추가 상세 정보를 담은 후속 이메일을 보내 드리겠습니다. 이는 다름 아닌 여러분이 누려야 마땅한 것이므로 40 일정표에서 공간을 비워두도록 하시기 바랍니다.

버나드 허들스톤
최고 운영 책임자, 37 이베르센 주식회사

어휘 **inform A about B** A에게 B에 관해 알리다
development (새롭게 전개된) 일, (제품 등의) 개발

negotiation 협상, 협의 **A-based** A에 본사를 둔 **agree to do** ~하기로 합의하다 **lend one's expertise** 전문 지식을 제공하다 **collaboratively** 협력하여, 합작으로 **keep A on schedule** A를 일정에 맞추다 **prolong** ~을 늘리다, 연장하다 **internal** 내부의 **place a high priority on** ~에 최우선 순위를 두다 **voice concerns over** ~에 대해 우려의 목소리를 내다 **temperature** 온도 **appreciate** ~에 대해 감사하다 **endeavor** 노력, 시도 **follow-up** 후속의 **clear room in** ~에서 공간을 비워두다 **no less than A deserve** 다름 아닌 A가 누려야 마땅한 것

37. 이메일은 누구를 대상으로 하는가?
(A) 재그텐 테크놀로지의 제품 디자이너들
(B) 재그텐 테크놀로지의 이사들
(C) 이베르센 주식회사의 고객들
(D) 이베르센 주식회사의 부서장들

정답 **(D)**

해설 이메일 상단의 수신인 항목에 모든 부서장들(To: All department managers)이라고 쓰여 있고, 하단의 작성자 이름 옆에 소속 회사 이름이 '이베르센 주식회사(Iversen Incorporated)'라고 적혀 있으므로 (D)가 정답이다.

어휘 **executive** 이사, 임원

38. 허들스톤 씨는 왜 기뻐하는가?
(A) 중대한 사업 계약이 이뤄졌다.
(B) 한 가지 제품 개발 단계가 완료되었다.
(C) 한 가지 혁신적인 제품이 출시되었다.
(D) 합병이 성공적으로 실시되었다.

정답 **(A)**

해설 첫 단락에 재그텐 테크놀로지와의 협상이 성공적으로 마무리되어 새 휴대전화 모델에 대해 협력함으로써 그곳의 전문 지식을 제공하는 데 합의했다고(Our negotiations with Jagten Technologies have ended successfully, with the Copenhagen-based firm agreeing to lend its expertise by working collaboratively with us) 알리고 있다. 이는 두 회사 사이에서 사업 협력 계약이 이뤄졌다는 뜻이므로 (A)가 정답이다.

어휘 **crucial** 중대한 **innovative** 혁신적인 **release** ~을 출시하다, 공개하다 **merger** 합병 **carry out** ~을 실시하다, 수행하다

39. 이메일에 따르면, 허들스톤 씨는 자신의 회사가 가까운 미래에 무엇을 하기를 기대하는가?
(A) 여러 업체들과 협업하는 일
(B) 한 제품의 외관을 변경하는 일
(C) 몇몇 고객 불만사항을 해결하는 일
(D) 재충전 가능한 배터리를 고안하는 일

정답 **(C)**

해설 두 번째 단락에 고객들이 짧은 배터리 수명과 높은 온도에 우려의 목소리를 냈다고 언급하면서, 이 문제들이 적절히 처리될 것

이라고(our customers have voiced concerns over the short battery life ~ these issues will be adequately addressed) 말하고 있으므로 (C)가 정답이다.

어휘 **appearance** 외관, 겉모습 **resolve** ~을 해결하다 **rechargeable** 재충전 가능한

40. 이메일 수신자들은 무엇을 하도록 요청받는가?
(A) 회사 위원회에 가입하는 일
(B) 식사 제안을 하는 일
(C) 상에 대한 지명 후보를 제출하는 일
(D) 축하 행사에 참석하는 일

정답 (D)

해설 두 번째 단락 마지막에 다음 주 금요일에 이메일 수신인 모두를 데리고 가 저녁 회식 자리를 가질 계획이라고(Therefore, I am planning to take you all out for dinner next Friday) 알린 후, 마지막 단락에서 일정을 꼭 비워 놓도록 당부하고 있다. 이는 축하하기 위한 자리에 참석하도록 요청하는 것이므로 (D)가 정답이다.

어휘 **recipient** 수신자, 받는 사람 **be invited to do** ~하도록 요청 받다 **suggestion** 의견, 제안 **submit** ~을 제출하다 **nomination** 후보 지명 **celebratory** 축하하는, 기념하는

41-45.

애거트 일렉트로닉스 – 현 공석

디지털 미디어 관리 책임자 (직책 #0060)
지원자는 반드시 디지털 광고 분야에서 최소 10년의 경력을 지니고 있어야 합니다. 합격한 지원자는 저희 애거트 사의 온라인 광고 캠페인 개발을 책임지게 될 것입니다.

공학 실험실 기사 (직책 #0061)
41 지원자는 반드시 전자 공학 실험실에서 최소 1년간(2년 선호) 근무한 경력을 지니고 있어야 합니다. 이 직책은 7일 동안의 일주일 근무 과정에 걸친 순환 교대 근무를 수반합니다.

수석 제품 디자이너 44 (직책 #0062)
지원자는 반드시 최소 5년의 제품 디자인 경력을 지니고 있어야 합니다. 합격한 지원자는 반드시 흠잡을 데 없는 생산 기술(색상, 배치, 서체)을 지니고 있어야 합니다. **44** 포트폴리오 제출은 필수입니다.

소프트웨어 엔지니어 (직책 #0063)
지원자는 반드시 최소 18개월의 소프트웨어 개발 경력 및 모든 일반적인 프로그래밍 언어에 대한 탄탄한 이해를 지니고 있어야 합니다.

42 지원자들의 대학 학위가 고려되긴 하겠지만, 저희는 열정과 경험을 지닌 분들을 찾는 데 더 관심이 있습니다. 여러분의 이력서를 employment@agateinc.com으로 리 스턴튼 씨께 보내시기 바라며, 어느 직책에 관심이 있으신지 표기해 주십시오.

어휘 **current** 현재의 **vacancy** 공석, 빈 자리 **applicant** 지

원자, 신청자 **at least** 최소한, 적어도 **field** 분야 **be responsible for** ~에 대한 책임을 지다 **lab** 실험실 **preferably** 선호하여 **involve** ~을 수반하다 **shift** 교대 근무(조) **rotation** 순환, 교대, 회전 **impeccable** 흠 잡을 데 없는 **submission** 제출(하는 것) **required** 필수인, 필요한 **firm** 탄탄한, 확고한, 견실한, 굳은 **take A into consideration** A를 고려하다 **be interested in** ~에 관심이 있다 **enthusiasm** 열정, 열의 **résumé** 이력서 **indicate** ~을 표기하다, ~을 가리키다

수신: 리 스턴튼 <employment@agateinc.com>
발신: 필립 라부에프 <plabouef@tridentmail.com>
제목: 최근의 웹 사이트 게시물
날짜: 8월 5일

스턴튼 씨께,

43 44 저는 귀사의 구인 광고를 확인해 봤으며, 직책 #0062에 대해 고려되었으면 합니다. 저는 10년간 리얼토 소프트웨어 사에서 유사한 직책을 유지해 왔습니다. 리얼토 사에서 보낸 **45** 시간 중에, 저는 이 회사에서 가장 큰 프로젝트들의 모든 측면에 관여해 왔습니다. 하지만, 소비자로서, 저는 애거트 일렉트로닉스 및 귀사에서 디자인하고 제조하는 제품의 엄청난 팬입니다. 실제로, 저는 완전히 새로운 제 애거트 800S 노트북 컴퓨터로 이 이메일을 작성하고 있습니다! 저는 애거트 사의 가족으로 함께 하면서 회사가 앞으로 훨씬 더 큰 성공을 이루는 데 도움이 될 수 있는 기회를 꼭 얻었으면 합니다.

이 이메일에 제 이력서를 첨부해 드렸으니 확인해 보시기 바랍니다. 곧 소식 전해주시기를 바랍니다.

안녕히 계십시오.

필립 라부에프

어휘 **recent** 최근의 **posting** 게시물 **consider** ~을 고려하다 **hold** ~을 유지하다, ~을 보유하다 **be involved in** ~에 관여하다, ~에 참여하다 **aspect** 측면, 양상 **consumer** 소비자 **huge** 엄청난 **manufacture** ~을 제조하다 **in fact** 실제로, 사실 **brand new** 완전히 새로운 **opportunity to do** ~할 수 있는 기회 **join** ~와 함께 하다, ~에 합류하다 **achieve** ~을 이루다, ~을 달성하다 **attach A to B** A를 B에 첨부하다, A를 B에 부착하다

41. 어느 직책이 가장 적은 경력을 필요로 하는가?
(A) 소프트웨어 엔지니어
(B) 공학 실험실 기사
(C) 수석 제품 디자이너
(D) 디지털 미디어 관리 책임자

정답 (B)

해설 첫 지문의 두 번째 항목인 공학 실험실 기사에 대한 자격 요건에 최소 1년의 경력을 지니고 있어야 한다고(Applicants must have at least 1 year of experience) 쓰여 있는 것이 네 가지 직책의 필수 경력 중 가장 짧은 기간이므로 (B)가 정답이다.

42. 광고에서 애거트 일렉트로닉스와 관련해 유추할 수 있는 것은 무엇인가?

(A) 아주 다양한 주방 기기를 제조한다.
(B) 최근에 새로운 사업 지점을 열었다.
(C) 일반적으로 국내 시장에 초점을 맞춘다.
(D) 학업적 성취보다 경력을 더 소중하게 생각한다.

정답 (D)

해설 첫 지문 마지막 단락에 지원자들의 대학 학위가 고려되긴 하지만 열정과 경험을 지닌 사람을 찾는 데 더 관심이 있다는 (Although applicants' university degrees will be taken into consideration, we are more interested in finding individuals who have enthusiasm and experience) 말이 쓰여 있다. 이는 학업적인 배경보다 경력이 더 중요하다는 뜻이므로 (D)가 정답이다.

어휘 appliances (가전) 기기 location 지점, 위치 normally 일반적으로, 보통 focus on ~에 초점을 맞추다 domestic 국내의 value v. ~을 소중하게 생각하다 achievement 성취, 달성, 업적

43. 라부에프 씨가 보낸 이메일의 목적은 무엇인가?

(A) 지원 과정에 관해 문의하는 것
(B) 한 직책에 대한 관심을 표현하는 것
(C) 한 일자리에 동료를 추천하는 것
(D) 웹 사이트 게시물의 오류를 지적하는 것

정답 (B)

해설 두 번째 지문 첫 단락에 상대방 회사의 구인 광고를 확인한 사실과 함께 직책 #0062에 대해 고려되기를 원한다고(I saw your job advertisement and I would like to be considered for position #0062) 알리는 말이 쓰여 있다. 따라서 (B)가 정답이다.

어휘 inquire about ~에 관해 문의하다 application 지원(서), 신청(서) process 과정 express (생각, 감정 등) ~을 표현하다 colleague 동료 (직원) point out ~을 지적하다

44. 라부에프 씨가 자신의 이메일에서 말하는 일자리와 관련해 언급된 것은 무엇인가?

(A) 몇몇 주말 교대 근무를 필요로 할 수도 있다.
(B) 지원자가 반드시 과거 업무의 예시를 보내야 한다.
(C) 지원자가 실무 테스트를 거치도록 요청 받을 것이다.
(D) 온라인 광고에 대한 폭넓은 지식을 필요로 한다.

정답 (B)

해설 두 번째 지문 첫 단락에 라부에프 씨는 직책 #0062에 대해 고려되기를 원한다고(I would like to be considered for position #0062) 알리고 있다. 첫 번째 지문에서 #0062로 표기된 세 번째 직책에 포트폴리오 제출이 필수라는 (Submission of a portfolio is required) 말이 쓰여 있는데, 이는 과거의 작업물 등을 확인할 수 있는 자료를 제출해야 한다는 뜻이므로 (B)가 정답이다.

어휘 past 과거의, 지난 be asked to do ~하도록 요청 받다

practical 실질적인, 현실적인 extensive 폭넓은, 광범위한

45. 이메일에서, 첫 번째 단락, 두 번째 줄의 단어 "time"과 의미가 가장 가까운 것은 무엇인가?

(A) 지속 기간
(B) 배경
(C) 갱신
(D) 고용

정답 (D)

해설 해당 문장에서 time이 속한 전치사구 During my time at Rialto는 앞선 문장에서 라부에프 씨가 10년 동안 다녔던 회사라고 언급한 리얼토 사에서 보낸 기간을 나타낸다. 이는 그곳에 고용된 기간을 말하는 것이므로 '고용' 등을 뜻하는 (D) employment가 정답이다.

46-50.

조세프 모스코위츠 씨
메도우 드라이브 4003 번지
시러큐스, NY 13245

모스코위츠 씨께,

아카디아 영화제가 7월 첫 번째 주에 로체스터에서 개최될 예정이며, [46] 저희 심사위원단에 자격을 갖추신 두 분에 대한 공석이 여전히 있습니다. 올해 특징을 이루는 영화들 중에는, 찬사를 받고 있는 [48] 스웨덴 감독 조나스 브롤린의 최신 블록버스터 영화 및 유럽과 중동, 그리고 아시아의 기대되는 영화들이 많습니다. 저희 심사위원단은 영화계에서 폭넓은 경험을 지니고 계신 배우와 감독, 그리고 영화 평론가들을 포함합니다. [47] 칼턴 대학교의 영화학과 선임 교수로서, [46] 귀하께서도 이러한 역할을 수행하시는 데 완벽히 어울리실 것입니다.

이 제안이 관심 있으신지 저에게 알려 주시기 바랍니다. 그러실 경우, 행사 및 귀하의 책임과 관련해 알아 두셔야 할 모든 것을 담고 있는 안내 책지 묶음을 보내 드리겠습니다.

안녕히 계십시오.

베아트리체 존스
공동 설립자
아카디아 영화제

어휘 be scheduled to do ~할 예정이다 take place (일, 행사 등) 개최되다, 일어나다, 발생되다 vacancy 공석 qualified 자격을 갖춘, 적격인 judging panel 심사위원단 featured 특징을 이루는 latest 최신의 acclaimed 찬사를 받는 promising 기대되는, 유망한 critic 평론가 extensive 폭넓은, 광범위한 be suited to do ~하는 데 어울리다, ~하는 데 적합하다 fill (역할 등) ~을 수행하다, ~을 충족하다 offer 제안, 제공 information pack 안내 책자 묶음 contain ~을 담고 있다, ~을 포함하다 responsibility 책임

미국 영화	**유럽 영화**	중동 영화	아시아 영화

49 아카디아 영화제 (7월 8일 – 7월 11일)

7월 8일 베드 오브 로즈 (프랑스) 브레멘 테일즈 (독일) 페뷜루 데스틴 (프랑스)	**7월 9일** 마운틴 이스케이프 (노르웨이) 페르소나 논 그라타 (이탈리아) 세크레토 (스페인)
7월 10일 미 마드레 (스페인) 이글스 오브 바르샤바 (폴란드) 쥬뗌므 (프랑스)	**48 7월 11일** 트헤 주흐 (프랑스) **48** 브라더즈 본드 (스웨덴) 화이트 코케이드 (스코틀랜드)

베아트리체 존스 씨
데넘 스트리트 551번지
로체스터, NY 14614

존스 씨께,

기쁜 마음으로 귀하의 제안을 받아들이겠습니다. 제 참가 가능성에 영향을 미칠 수 있는 문제가 한 가지 있습니다. **49** 어떠한 일이 있어도 제가 영화제 개막일에는 갈 수 없는데, 그날 제 딸 결혼식에 참석해야 해서 다른 주에 가 있을 것이기 때문입니다. 이것이 너무 큰 문제를 **50** 제기하지 않기를 바랍니다. 그 다음 날 귀하를 만나 뵙고 제가 놓쳤을 수도 있는 영화들을 확인해 볼 수 있을 것입니다.

연락 주실 수 있기를 고대합니다. 언제든지 저에게 555-8837번으로 전화 주시기 바랍니다.

안녕히 계십시오.

조세프 모스코위츠

어휘 **take A up on A's offer** A의 제안을 받아들이다 **affect** ~에 영향을 미치다 **participate** 참가하다 **under no circumstances** 어떠한 일이 있어도 ~ 않다 **show up** 나타나다, 모습을 드러내다 **attend** ~에 참석하다 **hopefully** 희망하여, 기대하여 **pose** (문제, 위협 등) ~을 제기하다, ~을 일으키다 **following** 다음의, 그 후의 **view** ~을 보다 **may have p.p.** ~했을 수도 있다 **miss** ~을 놓치다, ~을 지나치다 **look forward to -ing** ~할 수 있기를 고대하다

46. 편지의 주 목적은 무엇인가?
(A) 수상 후보 지명자들을 알리는 것
(B) 한 영화가 심사 대상 자격이 있음을 확인해 주는 것
(C) 위원단에 합류하도록 초청하는 것
(D) 행사 일정이 변경되도록 요청하는 것
정답 (C)

해설 첫 번째 지문 첫 단락에 영화제 심사위원단에 공석이 있다는 사실과 함께(we still have vacancies for two qualified individuals on the judging panel) 상대방인 모스코위츠 씨가 그 역할에 적합할 것이라고(you would also be perfectly suited to fill such a role) 알리는 말이 이 단락 초반부와 후반부에 쓰여 있다. 이는 심사위원단에 합류해 심사위원의 역할을 하도록 초대하는 말에 해당되므로 (C)가 정답이다.

어휘 **nominee** 후보 지명자 **be eligible for** ~에 대한 자격이 있다 **extend an invitation** 초청하다, 초청장을 보내다 **request that** ~하도록 요청하다

47. 조세프 모스코위츠 씨는 누구인가?
(A) 영화 감독
(B) 연극 배우
(C) 영화 평론가
(D) 대학 교수
정답 (D)

해설 첫 지문 첫 단락에 모스코위츠 씨를 칼튼 대학교의 영화학과 선임 교수라고(As the senior professor of film studies at Carlton College) 언급하고 있으므로 (D)가 정답이다.

어휘 **theater** 연극, 희곡, 극장 **lecturer** 교수, 강사

48. 조나스 브롤린 씨의 영화가 언제 상영될 것 같은가?
(A) 7월 8일에
(B) 7월 9일에
(C) 7월 10일에
(D) 7월 11일에
정답 (D)

해설 조나스 브롤린 씨의 이름은 첫 지문 첫 단락에 스웨덴 감독이라고(Swedish director Jonas Brolin) 언급하는 부분에서 찾아볼 수 있다. 그리고 두 번째 지문의 일정표에서 스웨덴 영화 작품이 오른쪽 아래에 표기된 7월 11일에(July 11, Brothers' Bond (Sweden)) 포함되어 있으므로 (D)가 정답이다.

49. 모스코위츠 씨가 7월 8일에 무엇을 할 계획인가?
(A) 가족 행사에 참석하는 일
(B) 존스 씨와 만나는 일
(C) 몇몇 영화를 보는 일
(D) 수상자를 발표하는 일
정답 (A)

해설 질문에 언급된 7월 8일이라는 날짜는 두 번째 지문 상단에 영화제 개막일로 표기되어 있다(Arkadia Film Festival (July 8 – July 11)). 그리고 이 개막일과 관련해, 세 번째 지문 중반부에 모스코위츠 씨가 어떠한 일이 있어도 영화제 개막일에는 갈 수 없다는 말과 함께 그 이유로 그날 딸 결혼식에 참석해야 한다고(Under no circumstances will I be able to show up on the opening day ~ attending my daughter's wedding on that day) 알리고 있다. 이는 가족 행사에 참석하는 일을 의미하므로 (A)가 정답이다.

어휘 **intend to do** ~할 계획이다, ~할 작정이다

50. 두 번째 편지에서, 첫 번째 단락, 세 번째 줄의 단어 "pose"와 의미가 가장 가까운 것은 무엇인가?

(A) 설정하다
(B) 야기하다
(C) 진열하다
(D) 세우다

정답 (B)

해설 해당 문장에서 주어 this는 앞 문장에서 딸 결혼식에 참석해야 해서 개막일에 가지 못한다고 언급한 일을 가리킨다. 그리고 동사 pose 뒤에 '너무 큰 문제'를 뜻하는 명사구가 쓰여 있어 개막일에 가지 못하는 것이 큰 문제를 일으키지 않기를 바란다는 의미임을 알 수 있다. 따라서, pose가 문제를 발생시킨다는 의미로 쓰였다는 것을 알 수 있으므로 부정적인 일과 관련해 '야기하다' 등을 뜻하는 (B) present가 정답이다.

시원스쿨LAB

WEEK 05

정답 및 해설 p. 02

PART 1

Directions: For each question in this part, you will hear four statements about a picture in your test book. When you hear the statements, you must select the one statement that best describes what you see in the picture. Then find the number of the question on your answer sheet and mark your answer. The statements will not be printed in your test book and will be spoken only one time.

1.

2.

PART 2

Directions: You will hear a question or statement and three responses spoken in English. They will not be printed in your test book and will be spoken only one time. Select the best response to the question or statement and mark the letter (A), (B), or (C) on your answer sheet.

3. Mark your answer on your answer sheet.

4. Mark your answer on your answer sheet.

5. Mark your answer on your answer sheet.

6. Mark your answer on your answer sheet.

7. Mark your answer on your answer sheet.

8. Mark your answer on your answer sheet.

9. Mark your answer on your answer sheet.

10. Mark your answer on your answer sheet.

11. Mark your answer on your answer sheet.

12. Mark your answer on your answer sheet.

13. Mark your answer on your answer sheet.

14. Mark your answer on your answer sheet.

15. Mark your answer on your answer sheet.

16. Mark your answer on your answer sheet.

17. Mark your answer on your answer sheet.

18. Mark your answer on your answer sheet.

19. Mark your answer on your answer sheet.

20. Mark your answer on your answer sheet.

PART 3

Directions: You will hear some conversations between two or more people. You will be asked to answer three questions about what the speakers say in each conversation. Select the best response to each question and mark the letter (A), (B), (C) or (D) on your answer sheet. The conversations will not be printed in your test book and will be spoken only one time.

21. What are the speakers discussing?
    (A) A company outing
    (B) A consumer trend
    (C) A market research report
    (D) A conference schedule

22. What is the problem?
    (A) Some names are not listed correctly.
    (B) A product sample has been misplaced.
    (C) Some invitations were not sent out.
    (D) An application form is incomplete.

23. What does the woman say she did yesterday?
    (A) Took part in a survey
    (B) Sent a list of names
    (C) Made a copy
    (D) Contacted a supplier

24. What are the speakers working on?
    (A) A product catalogue
    (B) A company Web site
    (C) A store advertisement
    (D) A packaging design

25. What does the man say about the company book club?
    (A) The members are getting a discount.
    (B) The members are visiting a store.
    (C) The members are ordering new books.
    (D) The members are conducting a survey.

26. Why does the woman say, "Robert can handle it"?
    (A) To request additional help
    (B) To approve of a new hire
    (C) To express disappointment about the man's efforts
    (D) To permit the man's absence

27. Why did the woman most likely contact the man's company?
    (A) To order a replacement item
    (B) To request some repairs
    (C) To complain about a service
    (D) To have a new bath installed

28. What does the man say about the woman's building?
    (A) Many tenants have reported a problem.
    (B) It recently had new pipes installed.
    (C) Some of its foundations have become weak.
    (D) It had its water supply temporarily cut off.

29. What will the woman do this weekend?
    (A) Go to her friend's apartment
    (B) Eat a meal at a restaurant
    (C) Have some guests over
    (D) Remodel her bathroom

30. Why are the speakers meeting?
    (A) For a job interview
    (B) For a training session
    (C) For a facility tour
    (D) For a sales presentation

31. What most likely is the man's profession?
    (A) Financial advisor
    (B) Recruitment manager
    (C) Safety inspector
    (D) Marketing director

32. What does the man say he likes about the company?
    (A) Its product range
    (B) Its training methods
    (C) Its recycling policies
    (D) Its advanced equipment

Clark's Deli	
Black Olives	$7.50
Tuna Salad	$9.50
Sliced Ham	$6.99
Tomato Soup	$5.99
Total	$29.98

Thanks for shopping
at Clark's Deli!

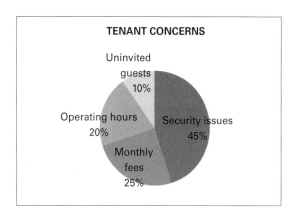

33. What problem does the woman mention?

(A) She was sent the wrong product.
(B) A special discount was not offered.
(C) An item was damaged in transit.
(D) One of her purchases is missing.

34. Look at the graphic. What amount will be refunded to the woman?

(A) $7.50
(B) $9.50
(C) $6.99
(D) $5.99

35. What will the man probably do next?

(A) Send a payment
(B) Speak to a coworker
(C) Order new stock
(D) Deliver a product

36. What type of facility is being discussed?

(A) A fitness room
(B) A swimming pool
(C) A parking lot
(D) A business center

37. Look at the graphic. What tenant concern would the man like to discuss?

(A) Security issues
(B) Monthly fees
(C) Operating hours
(D) Uninvited guests

38. What will the woman most likely do next?

(A) Survey the tenants
(B) Present a project budget
(C) Distribute documents
(D) Put up a notice

PART 4

Directions: You will hear some talks given by a single speaker. You will be asked to answer three questions about what the speakers say in each conversation. Select the best response to each question and mark the letter (A), (B), (C) or (D) on your answer sheet. The conversations will not be printed in your test book and will be spoken only one time.

39. What industry does the speaker work in?

    (A) Architecture
    (B) Print journalism
    (C) Hospitality
    (D) Broadcasting

40. Why does the speaker say, "I think there was a miscommunication"?

    (A) To respond to a missed phone call
    (B) To recommend an additional meeting
    (C) To revise an earlier message
    (D) To indicate disapproval of a project

41. What does the speaker suggest the listener do?

    (A) Take a few days off
    (B) Read an article
    (C) Hire a new employee
    (D) Visit a work site

42. What kind of business is Ginivers?

    (A) An online bookstore
    (B) A hardware store
    (C) An electronics store
    (D) A convenience store

43. What does Ginivers offer for technology enthusiasts?

    (A) A product trial area
    (B) A guide book
    (C) A free electronic device
    (D) A monthly catalog

44. What does the advertisement say about online orders?

    (A) They incur no delivery charge.
    (B) They are eligible for a discount.
    (C) They are shipped within five days.
    (D) They include free giftwrapping.

45. Who most likely are the listeners?

    (A) Accountants
    (B) Safety experts
    (C) Web designers
    (D) Event organizers

46. What does the speaker mean when he says, "We expect more from you!"?

    (A) He plans to hire more employees.
    (B) He is disappointed in the listeners.
    (C) He is apologizing for the heavy workload.
    (D) He hopes the listeners are satisfied.

47. What will the listeners do tomorrow?

    (A) Attend a training session
    (B) Contact some customers
    (C) Work additional hours
    (D) Repair some equipment

48. What does the speaker thank the listeners for?

(A) Writing positive reviews
(B) Attending a store opening
(C) Enrolling in a writing course
(D) Purchasing a book

49. Look at the graphic. Which topic will the speaker cover this morning?

(A) Handling Difficult Situations
(B) Making People Like You
(C) Cooperating Well With Others
(D) Becoming an Effective Leader

50. What does the speaker say about the second part of the book reading session?

(A) It will be held in an outdoor location.
(B) It will be presented by a different author.
(C) Refreshments will be available to attendees.
(D) Copies of the book will be signed.

DAY 02

RC
Half Test

40 min

제한 시간 40분

강의 바로보기

정답 및 해설 p. 16

READING TEST

In the Reading test, you will read a variety of texts and answer several different types of reading comprehension questions. The entire Reading test will last 75 minutes. There are three parts, and directions are given for each part. You are encouraged to answer as many questions as possible within the time allowed. You must mark your answers on the separate answer sheet. Do not write your answers in your test book.

PART 5

Directions: A word or phrase is missing in each of the sentences below. Four answer choices are given below each sentence. Select the best answer to complete the sentence. Then mark the letter (A), (B), (C), or (D) on your answer sheet.

1. The bus ride from Serene Resort to Mount Rapids will take approximately five hours, with one ------- 30-minute stop.

    (A) scheduled
    (B) scheduling
    (C) schedule
    (D) schedules

2. At his retirement dinner, Mr. Speck was given an expensive wristwatch in ------- of his 30 years of service.

    (A) recognizes
    (B) recognizing
    (C) recognition
    (D) recognize

3. In order to discuss important issues more frequently, the department managers now meet ------- Tuesdays and Thursdays.

    (A) on
    (B) next
    (C) into
    (D) behind

4. The technician recommends that employees clean the air conditioner's filter ------- three days.

    (A) nearly
    (B) most
    (C) previous
    (D) every

5. Employees at Heelflip Software ------- to take a pay cut in order to prevent the closure of the company.

    (A) agreeing
    (B) to agree
    (C) agreement
    (D) have agreed

6. A ramp at the main entrance of the building will make your realty office more ------- to handicapped customers.

    (A) accessed
    (B) accessible
    (C) accessing
    (D) access

7. The hybrid strawberry plant that can grow in desert conditions is the ------- of substantial research and experimentation.

(A) product
(B) producer
(C) produced
(D) producing

8. Job seekers should take the online aptitude test by ------- and should not refer to notes or textbooks.

(A) they
(B) themselves
(C) them
(D) their

9. Any students ------- in applying for the summer internship at Voller Law Firm should send an e-mail to Franck Voller directly.

(A) directed
(B) experienced
(C) interested
(D) concerned

10. All complaints about products and shipping problems are ------- handled by our customer support team.

(A) efficient
(B) more efficient
(C) efficiency
(D) efficiently

11. The city council held a public forum to ask ------- residents were in favor of the proposed shopping mall.

(A) although
(B) since
(C) whether
(D) both

12. In order to maintain a steady pace of operation, replace the batteries ------- the power level falls to 5 percent.

(A) by contrast
(B) in summary
(C) whenever
(D) rather than

13. Midland Biotech tests all applicants in various skills to help managers ------- the capabilities of job candidates.

(A) evolve
(B) determine
(C) assume
(D) doubt

14. Departmental work schedules must be received ------- Friday if they are to be posted on the notice board over the weekend.

(A) upon
(B) beside
(C) before
(D) next to

15. The Knowles Advising Group works with large corporations and ------- provides consultations for small firms.

(A) faintly
(B) abruptly
(C) rarely
(D) permanently

16. ------- brought up by local residents at the town meeting will be passed on directly to Mayor Swanson in a report.

(A) Editions
(B) Issues
(C) Attendances
(D) Materials

PART 6

Directions: Read the texts that follow. A word, phrase, or sentence is missing in parts of each text. Four answer choices for each question are given below the text. Select the best answer to complete the text. Then mark the letter (A), (B), (C) or (D) on your answer sheet.

Questions 17-20 refer to the following e-mail.

To: Maria Diaz <mdiaz@bramblesbistro.com>
From: Freddie Moore <fmoore@bramblesbistro.com>
Subject: New Supplier
Date: August 10

Hi Maria,

As you know, I have been looking into other options for purchasing fresh produce for our restaurant ------- ongoing problems with our current supplier. After carrying out some research, I think we
17.
should choose Greenwood Farm. The farm is known ------- high quality fruit and vegetables at very
18.
reasonable prices.

I have scheduled a meeting with the owner of Greenwood Farm for next Tuesday, and I am confident we will ------- an agreement on the terms of a business contract. Assuming everything goes smoothly,
19.
we should be doing business with them starting next month. -------. Please inform our staff members
20.
of this exciting change during today's meeting.

Regards,

Freddie Moore, Owner
Brambles Bistro

---

17. (A) despite
    (B) although
    (C) because of
    (D) as far as

18. (A) it provided
    (B) and providing
    (C) that provides
    (D) for providing

19. (A) serve
    (B) reach
    (C) carry
    (D) assume

20. (A) This will solve the problems we have
       experienced with our supply.
    (B) I hope that the closure of the restaurant will
       only be temporary.
    (C) As such, I think we should increase the size
       of our ongoing order.
    (D) I'm pleased that you have decided to
       accept the position.

---

57 Fairfax Boulevard
San Francisco, CA 94104

Dear Mr. Wyatt,

As the founder of the One Love Foundation, I'd like ------- you about a series of fundraising events
                                                   21.
we have planned for this summer. You are one of our long-time members, so I think you are the right
person to help us to organize the events. -------, you could assist us by soliciting donations from local
                                                   22.
businesses within San Francisco.

The first event we are planning is a concert that ------- in Montague Park sometime during July and
                                                        23.
feature at least 50 well-known bands and singers. This will require a large amount of advance planning,
so we are assembling a team of foundation members who have had experience in organizing relatively
large events. I recall that you were an asset to our team last year when we arranged the bake sale at
City Plaza. -------.
        24.

Yours sincerely,

Abigail Glover, Founder
One Love Foundation

---

21. (A) informed
    (B) informing
    (C) to inform
    (D) information

22. (A) Nevertheless
    (B) Alternatively
    (C) Therefore
    (D) Afterwards

23. (A) was held
    (B) is holding
    (C) has been held
    (D) will be held

24. (A) Proceeds from the bake sale were used for
        various good causes.
    (B) Please let me know whether you can help
        out with our upcoming events.
    (C) Thank you once again for your recent hard
        work and commitment.
    (D) Concert tickets are expected to go on sale
        during the first month of June.

PART 7

Directions: In this part you will read a selection of texts, such as magazine and newspaper articles, e-mails, and instant messages. Each text or set of texts is followed by several questions. Select the best answer for each question and mark the letter (A), (B), (C), or (D) on your answer sheet.

Questions 25-26 refer to the following memo.

MEMORANDUM

To: All Gilligan Manufacturing Staff
Date: August 23
Subject: Plan for Saturday

Dear Staff,

The excursion to Bayley Beach this weekend will be going ahead as planned, despite the cancelation of the beach concert that was scheduled to take place. Janet Osborne has spoken to the manager of the Seaview Hotel and received an excellent corporate discount on rooms there. She will be booking some buses for us on Thursday, and handing out a list of planned group activities on Friday. You have all been working so hard, so I hope to see you all at the beach for some well-deserved fun and relaxation.

Regards,

John Ledley

---

25. Why was the memo sent?
    (A) To discuss an incentive plan for employees
    (B) To inform staff of Saturday's work schedule
    (C) To explain why an event has been canceled
    (D) To confirm details of a company outing

26. What is Janet Osborne planning to do on Thursday?
    (A) Contact a hotel manager
    (B) Reserve an event venue
    (C) Arrange transportation
    (D) Distribute an activity schedule

Questions 27-29 refer to the following e-mail.

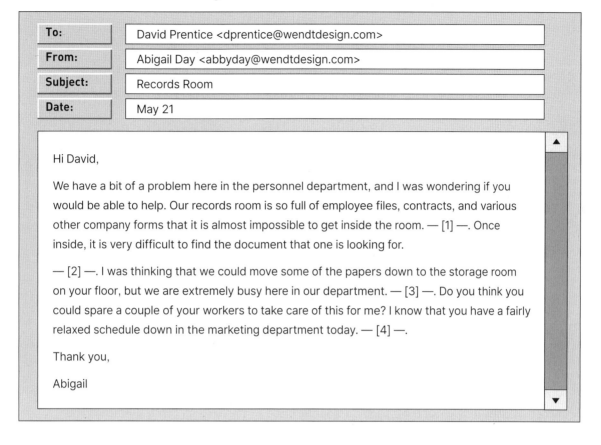

To: David Prentice <dprentice@wendtdesign.com>

From: Abigail Day <abbyday@wendtdesign.com>

Subject: Records Room

Date: May 21

Hi David,

We have a bit of a problem here in the personnel department, and I was wondering if you would be able to help. Our records room is so full of employee files, contracts, and various other company forms that it is almost impossible to get inside the room. — [1] —. Once inside, it is very difficult to find the document that one is looking for.

— [2] —. I was thinking that we could move some of the papers down to the storage room on your floor, but we are extremely busy here in our department. — [3] —. Do you think you could spare a couple of your workers to take care of this for me? I know that you have a fairly relaxed schedule down in the marketing department today. — [4] —.

Thank you,

Abigail

27. What problem does Ms. Day mention?

(A) She cannot unlock the door to the records room.
(B) She has misplaced an important document.
(C) She requires more storage space.
(D) She failed to meet a deadline.

28. What does Ms. Day ask Mr. Prentice to do?

(A) Reschedule a department meeting
(B) Submit some employee files
(C) Lend a hand in the marketing department
(D) Send workers to the personnel department

29. In which of the positions marked [1], [2], [3] and [4] does the following sentence best belong?

"It doesn't help that we are also incredibly short-staffed today."

(A) [1]
(B) [2]
(C) [3]
(D) [4]

Questions 30-32 refer to the following advertisement.

Job Vacancy #603 - Cleaning Operative

Mulgrew Inc. is looking to recruit a Cleaning Operative, who will report to the Facilities Manager. The successful candidate will be responsible for providing a variety of cleaning services at a specific site.

Key Duties:

- Sweeping, mopping, and vacuuming
- Wiping, dusting, and polishing of light fixtures and furniture
- Emptying waste bins, removing rubbish to collection areas
- Monitoring stocks of cleaning products and ordering items whenever necessary
- Carrying out duties in accordance with safety guidelines and policies
- Reporting all accidents and dangerous occurrences to the Facilities Manager

Key Requirements:

- Previous cleaning experience is advantageous, but not essential
- The ability to perform work duties well both independently and as part of a team
- An enthusiastic approach to your work and excellent timekeeping

Mulgrew Inc. is a leading commercial and residential cleaning services company that operates in numerous cities throughout the US and Canada. We place an emphasis on client satisfaction and expect all of our employees to provide a consistently high standard of service. To apply for the above position, please visit www.mulgrewinc.com.

---

30. What is NOT indicated as one of the job duties?

(A) Purchasing cleaning products
(B) Disposing of trash
(C) Repairing furniture
(D) Following safety procedures

31. According to the advertisement, what is a requirement of job applicants?

(A) They must have a background in cleaning.
(B) They must possess an academic qualification.
(C) They must be willing to have a flexible schedule.
(D) They must be able to work well on their own.

32. What can be inferred about Mulgrew Inc.?

(A) Its headquarters are based in Canada.
(B) It requires staff to undergo regular training.
(C) It provides services to corporate clients.
(D) It is trying to fill several job vacancies.

Questions 33-36 refer to the following online chat discussion.

Morrow, Colin <9:41 A.M.>

Janet, have you tried to access our Web site yet this morning? I'm trying to update our property listings, but the page won't load at all.

Ferrier, Janet <9:42 A.M.>

Hold on a moment. Hmm... I see what you mean. Perhaps Roger knows something about it. I'll add him.

Morrow, Colin <9:44 A.M.>

Hi, Roger. Do you have any idea what's wrong with our homepage?

Smeaton, Roger <9:46 A.M.>

Oh, I've taken it down temporarily while I change the layout, and it's taking time to get it done.

Ferrier, Janet <9:47 A.M.>

I told you so.

Morrow, Colin <9:49 A.M.>

So how can I add some new properties to our page? The clients are expecting them to go on the market starting from today.

Smeaton, Roger <9:50 A.M.>

I'm afraid you'd better let them know that our Web site will not be available until noon.

Morrow, Colin <9:51 A.M.>

Okay, I'll do that right away.

33. Where do the writers most likely work?

(A) At a construction company
(B) At an online supermarket
(C) At an architectural firm
(D) At a real estate agency

34. At 9:47 A.M., what does Ms. Ferrier imply when she writes, "I told you so"?

(A) She wants Mr. Smeaton to provide more details.
(B) She will help Mr. Morrow with a task.
(C) She has already revised a listing.
(D) She is already aware of a problem.

35. What can be suggested about Mr. Smeaton?

(A) He is the owner of the business.
(B) He has knowledge of Web design.
(C) He will repair some equipment.
(D) He will work late this evening.

36. What will Mr. Morrow probably do next?

(A) Check the homepage
(B) Visit some properties
(C) Contact some clients
(D) Reschedule an appointment

ENWAY ONLINE LANGUAGE INSTITUTE (EOLI)
COURSE INFORMATION (Course #0029)

Course name: Business Spanish

Course start dates: January 5, March 2, May 3, July 1, September 2, November 4

Course duration: 4 weeks (intensive course) or 8 weeks (regular course)

Lessons per week: 5 (8-week course) or 10 (4-week course)

Lesson duration: 50 minutes

Minimum level requirement: Intermediate

Course instructors: Jean Young and Juan Jose Jimenez

Course fee: Registered Enway Students - $675 / Non-registered - $750

To enroll, please click HERE to download a printable enrollment form, and then send the completed form along with the appropriate course fee to: Enway Online Language Institute, 607 West Monroe Street, Phoenix, AZ 85007.

Anyone who enrolls in this course will receive a selection of class materials, including sample business presentations, contracts, and journal articles. Lists of specific business vocabulary will also be provided.

37. Where would the information most likely be found?

    (A) In a business journal
    (B) In a promotional flyer
    (C) On a notice board
    (D) On a Web page

38. What is indicated about Enway Online Language Institute?

    (A) It is a recently established business.
    (B) It was founded by Ms. Young and Mr. Jimenez.
    (C) It operates a business location in Phoenix.
    (D) It is currently seeking new language instructors.

39. What is NOT true about Course #0029?

    (A) Beginners are unable to enroll in the course.
    (B) Enrollees can choose from multiple start dates.
    (C) Intensive course students will receive 5 lessons per week.
    (D) Each regular course lesson will last for less than one hour.

40. What is available only to pre-registered Enway students?

    (A) An increased number of classes
    (B) A discount on the course fee
    (C) A longer course duration
    (D) A variety of free course materials

Urgently Seeking Sales Representatives
POLTRAXIS INC.

Poltraxis Inc. is looking to solidify its position as a market leader by expanding its sales force and enlarging its client base. We wish to build a team of pharmaceutical sales representatives to support and promote our popular lines of diabetes treatments and insulin-based products. Sales representatives will report to Poltraxis Inc.'s regional sales managers in Haymarket, Calton, Leith, and Marchmont.

Job Requirements

- Two years of pharmaceutical sales experience required
- A proven track record of sales success
- Ability to learn, understand, and explain complex information
- Technical aptitude and computer skills are essential

Please send your résumé, a recommendation letter from a former employer, a copy of your national insurance card/driver's license, and a completed application form directly to the manager of the region in which you would like to work: Bob Kienzle (Calton), Susan Kinney (Marchmont), Debra Holloway (Haymarket), and Scott Arthurs (Leith). Application forms and e-mail addresses can be found at www.poltraxis.co.uk/recruitment.

To: Debra Holloway <dholloway@poltraxis.co.uk>
From: Nick Matlock <nmatlock@xcelmail.com>
Subject: Job application
Date: August 13

Dear Ms. Holloway,

I am writing to apply for one of the sales representative positions advertised in The Newtown Tribune on August 12th. I would specifically like to work in your branch office, as I just moved to your region from Marchmont. I have attached a copy of my résumé along with my application form. However, I'm afraid my previous employer is currently overseas, so there might be a slight delay in obtaining and submitting a reference letter. A scan of my driver's license is also attached. If you require any additional documents, please let me know. I hope to hear from you soon.

Sincerely,

Nick Matlock

41. In what type of industry are the positions being advertised?

   (A) Software
   (B) Electronics
   (C) Medical
   (D) Real estate

42. What is suggested about Poltraxis Inc.?

   (A) It is hiring regional sales managers.
   (B) It has experienced a decline in business.
   (C) It is preparing to release new products.
   (D) It is hoping to attract new clients.

43. What is NOT listed as a job requirement?

   (A) Experience in managing a team
   (B) Evidence of previous high sales
   (C) Proficiency in using computers
   (D) An ability to discuss difficult concepts

44. What required document was Mr. Matlock unable to send?

   (A) A résumé
   (B) A letter of reference
   (C) An application form
   (D) A copy of his ID

45. In which branch office will Mr. Matlock most likely work if he is hired?

   (A) Calton
   (B) Leith
   (C) Marchmont
   (D) Haymarket

Clarke County Occupational Safety Association (CCOSA)

Professional Workshop (Saturday, March 12 - Sunday, March 13) - Willowbrook Convention Center

SESSION	ROOM	DAY ONE	DAY TWO
1	1A	Hazard Identification & Risk Assessment	Reducing Musculoskeletal Disorders in Office Workers
2	2A	Fire Prevention Procedures	Handling Potentially Dangerous Substances
3	1B	Exercises You Can Do at Your Office Desk	Eye and Vision Disorders in Computer Operators
4	2B	Advances in Non-slip Floor Coverings	Preventing Workplace Violence
5	1A	Hidden Hazards in the Workplace	How to Evacuate Buildings in the Event of a Fire

To:	Richard Fitzpatrick <rfitzpatrick@ccosa.com>
From:	Kiefer Matthews <kmatthews@ccosa.com>
Subject:	Thanks Again
Date:	March 9
Attachment:	speakerinfo.doc

Hi Richard,

I just wanted to tell you again how grateful I am that you have offered to fill in at this weekend's workshop. When Ray called me last night to inform me he'd be unable to lead his session, I thought I'd never find a replacement. With your background in optometry, you will be the perfect person to give the talk. As I mentioned on the phone, you'll be compensated for your time.

Also, you asked about the other speakers who have agreed to give talks at the workshop, so I've attached some additional information that wasn't included on the original agenda.

All the best,

Kiefer Matthews
CCOSA President

CCOSA Professional Workshop
Speaker Information

Session 1: 9:00 a.m. – 10:30 a.m. / Arnold Johnson (Day 1) / Lisa Greene (Day 2)

Session 2: 10:30 a.m. – 12:00 p.m. / Ben Hansen (Day 1) / Elizabeth Hale (Day 2)

Session 3: 1:00 p.m. – 2:30 p.m. / Lisa Greene (Day 1) / Ray Williamson (Day 2)

Session 4: 2:30 p.m. – 4:30 p.m. / Arnold Johnson (Day 1) / Mary Swan (Day 2)

Session 5: 4:30 p.m. – 6:00 p.m. / Mary Swan (Day 1) / Ben Hansen (Day 2)

46. What is the workshop mainly about?

    (A) Global healthcare developments
    (B) Healthy eating and nutrition
    (C) Advances in modern technology
    (D) Workplace health and safety

47. When will the talk on evacuation procedures end?

    (A) At 12:00 p.m.
    (B) At 2:30 p.m.
    (C) At 4:30 p.m.
    (D) At 6:00 p.m.

48. In the e-mail, the phrase "fill in" in paragraph 1, line 1, is closest in meaning to

    (A) complete
    (B) submit
    (C) register
    (D) substitute

49. What will Mr. Fitzpatrick most likely discuss during the workshop?

    (A) Floor coverings
    (B) Hazardous substances
    (C) Vision disorders
    (D) Office exercises

50. Who is NOT scheduled to speak in Room 1A?

    (A) Ben Hansen
    (B) Elizabeth Hale
    (C) Lisa Greene
    (D) Arnold Johnson

PART 1

Directions: For each question in this part, you will hear four statements about a picture in your test book. When you hear the statements, you must select the one statement that best describes what you see in the picture. Then find the number of the question on your answer sheet and mark your answer. The statements will not be printed in your test book and will be spoken only one time.

1.

2.

PART 2

Directions: You will hear a question or statement and three responses spoken in English. They will not be printed in your test book and will be spoken only one time. Select the best response to the question or statement and mark the letter (A), (B), or (C) on your answer sheet.

3. Mark your answer on your answer sheet.

4. Mark your answer on your answer sheet.

5. Mark your answer on your answer sheet.

6. Mark your answer on your answer sheet.

7. Mark your answer on your answer sheet.

8. Mark your answer on your answer sheet.

9. Mark your answer on your answer sheet.

10. Mark your answer on your answer sheet.

11. Mark your answer on your answer sheet.

12. Mark your answer on your answer sheet.

13. Mark your answer on your answer sheet.

14. Mark your answer on your answer sheet.

15. Mark your answer on your answer sheet.

16. Mark your answer on your answer sheet.

17. Mark your answer on your answer sheet.

18. Mark your answer on your answer sheet.

19. Mark your answer on your answer sheet.

20. Mark your answer on your answer sheet.

PART 3

Directions: You will hear some conversations between two or more people. You will be asked to answer three questions about what the speakers say in each conversation. Select the best response to each question and mark the letter (A), (B), (C) or (D) on your answer sheet. The conversations will not be printed in your test book and will be spoken only one time.

21. Why is the man calling?

(A) To ask how long a delivery will take
(B) To change the details of an order
(C) To inquire about a special offer
(D) To ask about an extra charge

22. What problem does the woman mention?

(A) A delivery address was incorrect.
(B) A store is closing earlier than usual.
(C) A payment was unsuccessful.
(D) An item is currently unavailable.

23. What does the woman offer to do?

(A) Deliver a different item
(B) Provide a discount
(C) Increase the size of an order
(D) Call the man back

24. What is mainly being discussed?

(A) A hotel reservation
(B) A flight itinerary
(C) Transportation options
(D) Tour packages

25. What does Harry suggest?

(A) Renting a vehicle
(B) Postponing a trip
(C) Visiting a Web site
(D) Changing hotels

26. What will the woman probably do next?

(A) Purchase bus tickets
(B) Speak with some clients
(C) Contact a hotel manager
(D) Work on a presentation

27. What is the woman's area of expertise?

(A) Art history
(B) Technology development
(C) Web design
(D) Video production

28. What does the man ask the woman to do?

(A) Reveal new information
(B) Post instructions online
(C) Respond to listeners' calls
(D) Visit the show again

29. Why does the woman say, "you'll have to try it out for yourself"?

(A) To offer a free demonstration of a device
(B) To increase consumer interest in a product
(C) To defend the poor sales of a device
(D) To explain her absence from an event

30. Why is the woman calling?

(A) To purchase tennis equipment
(B) To cancel a reservation
(C) To book a sporting venue
(D) To inquire about a membership

31. What does the man suggest the woman do?

(A) Bring some equipment
(B) Change the booking time
(C) Pay with a credit card
(D) Come to a location early

32. What does the man offer to do?

(A) Extend the business hours
(B) Provide free equipment
(C) Give an entry fee discount
(D) Send a list of services

| Laundry Room | 402 | 404 |
| 401 | Elevator / Stairs | 403 |

Belmont Bank - Savings Accounts	
Standard Savings $ Minimum Balance - $10	Extra Savings $$ Minimum Balance - $100
Enhanced Savings $$$ Minimum Balance - $500	Premier Savings $$$$ Minimum Balance - $5,000

33. Who most likely is the man?

(A) A landlord
(B) A maintenance crew member
(C) A hotel guest
(D) A front desk clerk

34. Look at the graphic. Which room is the woman staying in?

(A) 401
(B) 402
(C) 403
(D) 404

35. What does the woman remind the man about?

(A) A necessary repair
(B) A transportation arrangement
(C) A laundry service
(D) A flight time

36. Why does the man want to open a savings account?

(A) He wants to travel overseas.
(B) He hopes to purchase a new vehicle.
(C) He is planning to buy property.
(D) He needs to pay school tuition fees.

37. Look at the graphic. Which savings account will the man most likely choose?

(A) Standard Savings
(B) Extra Savings
(C) Enhanced Savings
(D) Premier Savings

38. What does the woman say comes with a new savings account?

(A) A discount voucher
(B) A check book
(C) A coffee mug
(D) A monthly newsletter

PART 4

Directions: You will hear some talks given by a single speaker. You will be asked to answer three questions about what the speakers say in each conversation. Select the best response to each question and mark the letter (A), (B), (C) or (D) on your answer sheet. The conversations will not be printed in your test book and will be spoken only one time.

39. Where does the speaker work?

(A) At a recording studio
(B) At a record store
(C) At an instrument shop
(D) At a fabric retailer

40. What does the speaker say he has done?

(A) Placed an order
(B) Increased a bill amount
(C) Consulted a professional
(D) Compared a price

41. What does the speaker offer?

(A) Store credit
(B) Home delivery
(C) A special discount
(D) A training session

42. What type of product is the Bulb Buddy?

(A) A tablet computer
(B) A light fixture
(C) A gardening tool
(D) A kitchen utensil

43. According to the speaker, what makes the product unique?

(A) It comes with extra parts.
(B) It is rechargeable.
(C) It includes a warranty.
(D) It has various functions.

44. Why does the speaker say, "You won't find them in any stores"?

(A) To announce a product recall
(B) To emphasize the product's popularity
(C) To promote a new Web site
(D) To encourage listeners to call

45. According to the speaker, what will take place tomorrow?

(A) A store opening
(B) A product demonstration
(C) A training session
(D) A team-building event

46. Who is Mr. Jones?

(A) A product developer
(B) A new supervisor
(C) A potential buyer
(D) A financial consultant

47. What will the listeners do later today?

(A) Attend a lecture
(B) Design some posters
(C) Speak to some clients
(D) Meet with a supervisor

Recreation Program Budget	
Program	Cost
Pilates Class	$750
Flag Football League	$900
Softball Team	$1,100
Annual Hiking Trip	$2,000

48. Look at the graphic. Which program does the speaker say takes the least time?

(A) Pilates class
(B) Flag Football League
(C) Softball Team
(D) Annual Hiking Trip

49. What solution does the speaker propose?

(A) Charging participation fees
(B) Increasing a budget
(C) Extending working hours
(D) Expanding program choices

50. What does the speaker ask the listeners to do?

(A) Distribute a survey
(B) Donate some funds
(C) Work over the weekend
(D) Organize an event

READING TEST

In the Reading test, you will read a variety of texts and answer several different types of reading comprehension questions. The entire Reading test will last 75 minutes. There are three parts, and directions are given for each part. You are encouraged to answer as many questions as possible within the time allowed. You must mark your answers on the separate answer sheet. Do not write your answers in your test book.

PART 5

Directions: A word or phrase is missing in each of the sentences below. Four answer choices are given below each sentence. Select the best answer to complete the sentence. Then mark the letter (A), (B), (C), or (D) on your answer sheet.

1. Mr. Ruddock ------- updates software on the company's computers to ensure they are protected from viruses.

   (A) regular
   (B) more regular
   (C) regularly
   (D) regularity

2. Mr. Depp's considerable knowledge of ------- sales makes him ideally suited to become the new store manager.

   (A) retailing
   (B) retailer
   (C) retailed
   (D) retail

3. If you have any complaints about public services, please contact ------- local council member.

   (A) you
   (B) your
   (C) yours
   (D) yourself

4. Please ------- whether you wish to renew your subscription to our magazine by calling us at 555-0989.

   (A) confirmation
   (B) confirmed
   (C) confirm
   (D) confirms

5. To increase his chances of promotion, Mr. Maguire has ------- in a management training course.

   (A) attended
   (B) recommended
   (C) proposed
   (D) enrolled

6. The college district is the perfect location for your jumbo pretzel store, ------- will easily attract many students.

   (A) who
   (B) which
   (C) what
   (D) they

7. Since beginning her role as the general office manager, Ms. Perkins has been praised for her effective leadership -------.

(A) capableness
(B) capable
(C) capably
(D) capabilities

8. Graham Office Supplies recently ------- to terminate its contract with White Fountain Company after several late payments.

(A) decides
(B) decided
(C) to decide
(D) will decide

9. Strenco Corporation's new employee incentive scheme does not take effect ------- the beginning of next year.

(A) yet
(B) under
(C) until
(D) when

10. The restaurant being constructed opposite Lafeside Theater will ------- various dishes originating from Central America.

(A) consume
(B) serve
(C) advise
(D) replace

11. The Sunflower Hotel is ------- located close to both a beautiful white sand beach and the city's famous shopping area.

(A) gradually
(B) conveniently
(C) substantially
(D) nearly

12. The final match of the tennis tournament was postponed ------- rain showers were much heavier than expected.

(A) because
(B) unless
(C) as such
(D) in order that

13. Several highly qualified individuals have applied for the Senior Web Designer ------- at Markies Frozen Foods.

(A) location
(B) deadline
(C) audition
(D) role

14. A meeting has been set up with a small team of the company's accountants ------- its chief financial officer.

(A) but rather
(B) as well as
(C) even though
(D) if only

15. Mr. Lowell has collaborated ------- an experienced interior designer to improve the appearance of the hotel lobby.

(A) with
(B) to
(C) at
(D) for

16. ------- an appropriate venue is found this week, the company banquet will have to be rescheduled for sometime next month.

(A) Unless
(B) Therefore
(C) Otherwise
(D) Instead

PART 6

Directions: Read the texts that follow. A word, phrase, or sentence is missing in parts of each text. Four answer choices for each question are given below the text. Select the best answer to complete the text. Then mark the letter (A), (B), (C) or (D) on your answer sheet.

Questions 17-20 refer to the following memo.

To: All Biosystems Inc. Staff

From: Alan Arnold, Laboratory Manager

Date: November 6

Please be aware that we are introducing new security measures next week. ------- Monday, November
17.
11, you will be required to enter a numeric code on a keypad when entering our main research building.

This system is being installed to prevent unauthorized individuals from accessing the -------. On
18.
several occasions, visitors have accidentally entered our research labs, and we need to stop this from

happening.

------- the door entry system, we are going to issue identity tags to all Biosystems Inc. employees.
19.
These must be worn at all times while you are working. Please visit the security office as soon as you

arrive on Monday morning to obtain your identity tag and numeric door code. -------.
20.

17. (A) Effective
    (B) Effect
    (C) To effect
    (D) Effectively

18. (A) feature
    (B) position
    (C) route
    (D) facility

19. (A) Just as
    (B) In contrast
    (C) Along with
    (D) Compared with

20. (A) The faults in the security system will be
        repaired next week.
    (B) We appreciate your cooperation in keeping
        our workplace secure.
    (C) Please inform us if you are unable to attend
        the training workshop.
    (D) The new waste disposal procedure must
        be followed by all staff.

To: Sally Sturgess

From: Guest Services

Subject: Your Recent Stay at Gleneagles Resort

Date: November 25

Attachment: Room Voucher

Dear Ms. Sturgess,

We are terribly sorry to hear about the problems you ------- during your stay at Gleneagles Resort
                                                         21.
from November 19 to November 21. Please be assured that the used towels and the unchanged

bedding you found in your room are not representative of the high standards of service on which our

resort has built its reputation. ------- of our rooms are equipped with fresh towels and bedding before
                                  22.
guests are allowed to check in. We apologize for the -------. We would be happy to provide you with
                                                      23.
a complimentary one-night stay at our resort, including a meal at our Italian restaurant, Santini's. The

next time you reserve a room at our resort, simply print out the voucher attached to this e-mail and

present it to the front desk staff upon checking in. -------.
                                                     24.

Sincerely,

Oscar Plimpton

21. (A) encounter
    (B) encountered
    (C) to encounter
    (D) will have encountered

22. (A) Most
    (B) Some
    (C) All
    (D) Whole

23. (A) addition
    (B) delay
    (C) reduction
    (D) inconvenience

24. (A) The resort is conveniently located in the
        commercial district.
    (B) Most of our guests are satisfied with this
        new service.
    (C) However, one of our staff members
        promptly addressed the matter.
    (D) Once again, I apologize for the poor
        standard of service you received.

PART 7

Directions: In this part you will read a selection of texts, such as magazine and newspaper articles, e-mails, and instant messages. Each text or set of texts is followed by several questions. Select the best answer for each question and mark the letter (A), (B), (C), or (D) on your answer sheet.

Questions 25-26 refer to the following notice.

Barnaby's Market
Fresh Local Produce

We value your feedback!

Here at Barnaby's Market, we always strive to provide the highest quality of fresh fruit and vegetables for our customers. We want to hear what you think about our product ranges so that we can continue to meet your needs. Before leaving the store today, please ask a cashier for a customer comment card. This just takes a moment to fill out, and can be dropped in the box at the store exit. On June 30, we will randomly choose three comment cards from the box. Those who submitted the three selected comment cards will receive a complimentary basket of delicious fresh fruits. This offer applies to both members and nonmembers of Barnaby's Market.

Kindest regards,

Barnaby Fotheringham Store Manager

---

25. What is the purpose of the notice?

    (A) To notify customers about new products
    (B) To thank customers for their patronage
    (C) To attract new customers to a business
    (D) To solicit opinions from customers

26. What will some customers receive for free?

    (A) A gift voucher for Barnaby's
    (B) A selection of produce
    (C) A meal at a restaurant
    (D) A store membership

To:	Gerard Sutcliffe <gsutcliffe@belcherinc.com>
From:	Edwina Stark <csmanager@mormontpark.com>
Subject:	Mormont Park Has Reopened
Date:	September 8

Dear Mr. Sutcliffe,

This summer, we made many changes at our restaurant. We redesigned and renovated our dining area, installed various new kitchen appliances, and allowed our chefs to introduce new dishes to the menu. — [1] —. Since reopening this month, we have received much positive feedback from our diners. — [2] —. We have not seen you at our restaurant for a while, so I thought I would take this opportunity to contact you directly to let you know that we are once again open for business. — [3] —.

Please let us know whether you would like to make a reservation with us sometime this month. If you do make a booking this month, we would be happy to provide a free glass of wine to each member of your dining group. — [4] —. I am certain that you will be impressed with the high quality and reasonable prices of our new ranges of appetizers and desserts.

Please call 555-7623 if you wish to make a lunch or dinner reservation.

Best regards,

Edwina Stark
Customer Service Manager
Mormont Park Restaurant

27. Why was the e-mail sent to Mr. Sutcliffe?

(A) To update him on the progress of renovations
(B) To invite him to a grand opening event
(C) To inform him about an employment opportunity
(D) To encourage him to make a booking

28. What is NOT a change mentioned by Ms. Stark?

(A) The hiring of new chefs
(B) The addition of new menu items
(C) The redesign of the restaurant's interior
(D) The installation of devices

29. In which of the positions marked [1], [2], [3], and [4] does the following sentence best belong?

"Moreover, food critic James Gordon gave us a 5-star review in the latest issue of *Food Monthly*."

(A) [1]
(B) [2]
(C) [3]
(D) [4]

The Fourth Annual
DEO Championship
Gaming Series

The Digital Evolution Organization (DEO) is pleased to announce its 4th Championship Gaming Series, which will take place from Friday, March 11 to Monday, March 14. As always, this tournament will bring together the best video game players from around the world as they compete to win cash prizes.

When the event was held in Tokyo, Japan, last year, the first prize of $250,000 USD was won by Gyung-don Jang, a professional gamer from South Korea. The runner-up prize of $100,000 was awarded to Kun Jian Ho of Singapore. At this year's event in Taipei, Taiwan, the prize money will be double that of last year.

Over the first three days, contestants will be playing three different games: Star Fleet 2, Galaxy Fighters, and Army of Heroes. On the fourth and final day of the event, the head of DS Software, Takeda Miyazaki, will present his company's much-anticipated upcoming game, Star Fleet 3. For details on schedules and entry requirements, visit www.deo.com/championships.

30. What is indicated about this year's event?

(A) It will last for two days.
(B) It will be broadcast online.
(C) It will be hosted by Gyung-don Jang.
(D) It will be held in Taiwan.

31. How much money will this year's runner-up competitor most likely receive?

(A) $100,000
(B) $200,000
(C) $250,000
(D) $500,000

32. On which day will Takeda Miyazaki give a presentation?

(A) Monday
(B) Friday
(C) Saturday
(D) Sunday

Questions 33-36 refer to the following online chat discussion.

Fred Yorke [10:11 A.M.]	Gillian! Are you at the warehouse right now?
Gillian Jacobsen [10:12 A.M.]	I'm on my way there at the moment.
Fred Yorke [10:14 A.M.]	I didn't bring enough fertilizer for the lawn here at the Foster Road job. Now I'm too busy to go all the way to the warehouse to get some.
Gillian Jacobsen [10:16 A.M.]	Let me just bring Roy in on this. He's at the warehouse now. What amount are you looking for?
Fred Yorke [10:17 A.M.]	Twenty-five kilograms would be enough. Can you manage that, Roy?
Roy Benton [10:18 A.M.]	Let me check. Hmm...Not even close.
Fred Yorke [10:19 A.M.]	Oh, dear. I really need it to finish the job, or the client will be really upset.
Gillian Jacobsen [10:21 A.M.]	Well, I'm stopping by the warehouse to load a truck for the hedge trimming jobs on Fairbanks Crescent and Muir Boulevard. But, before I go to those, I could stop by the Whatts Avenue store and get you what you need.
Fred Yorke [10:22 A.M.]	That would be fantastic. Make sure it's the Truegrow Plus type.
Roy Benton [10:23 A.M.]	Sorry I couldn't help, Fred.

33. What type of business does Mr. Yorke probably work for?

(A) An interior design firm
(B) A shipping company
(C) A landscaping firm
(D) A hardware store

34. At 10:18 A.M., what does Mr. Benton imply when he writes, "Not even close"?

(A) A project is running behind schedule.
(B) A job location is too far away.
(C) A vehicle Mr. Yorke needs is unavailable.
(D) An item is in limited supply.

35. Where does Ms. Jacobsen say she will go next?

(A) To Muir Boulevard
(B) To Foster Road
(C) To Whatts Avenue
(D) To Fairbanks Crescent

36. What does Mr. Yorke ask Ms. Jacobsen to do?

(A) Make contact with a client
(B) Retain the receipt from a purchase
(C) Select a particular brand
(D) Place an order for materials

LYNCH SPORTS CENTER
1113 Morley Road, Deerhurst Hills, Edgewood
Tel: 555-7236

Located on the outskirts of the city, Lynch Sports Center is the best place in the suburbs for anyone who enjoys sports and exercise. Having just recently opened, we are still offering 20 percent discounts on new memberships, so do not hesitate – come along and sign up today!

Our sports center is equipped with brand new state-of-the-art amenities and equipment. We have a large pool on the first floor, as well as a sports hall that is used for badminton, basketball, and volleyball. Our second floor includes four tennis courts, and we have three additional courts outside for warm seasons. We also have an outdoor playing field for team sports such as football and soccer. The field is available from March through October and the grass is trimmed on a regular basis in order to keep the playing surface in perfect condition. Due to high demand, bookings are required.

Lynch Sports Center Opening Times:
• Tuesday to Thursday: 8:00 a.m. – 10:30 p.m.
• Friday to Saturday: 8:00 a.m. – 11:00 p.m.
• Sunday: 10:00 a.m. – 9:30 p.m.

Although non-members may also use our facilities, members receive lower rates on all sports hall/ court/field bookings and equipment rental. So, take advantage of our discount on memberships, which is only available until the end of July.

37. What is the purpose of the information?

    (A) To announce the relocation of a sports center
    (B) To notify members about a temporary closure
    (C) To advertise a brand of sportswear
    (D) To promote a new recreation facility

38. What is NOT indicated about Lynch Sports Center?

    (A) It is open seven days a week.
    (B) It has an indoor swimming pool.
    (C) It has three outdoor tennis courts.
    (D) It is located in a suburban area.

39. What is suggested about the outdoor playing field?

    (A) It is not available in October.
    (B) It must be reserved in advance.
    (C) It has an artificial surface.
    (D) It may only be used by members.

40. What will most likely happen on August 1?

    (A) Opening times will change.
    (B) Rental rates will decrease.
    (C) A special offer will be unavailable.
    (D) A new sports hall will open.

Auto News Monthly
Eleganta Motors Preparing to Launch New Model

(London, October 30) The new luxury sedan manufactured by London-based Eleganta Motors is destined to become extremely popular, especially in the business world. With its stylish design and its 5.8 liter V8 engine, Eleganta's Greenwich Town Car promises to be both powerful and sophisticated.

Eleganta Motors CEO Isobel Arnott said, "The Greenwich Town Car is the ideal car for business executives and high-flyers. Its interior is more spacious than any other car in its class, and we have used ultra-premium leather for the seats. The car's best features are its state-of-the-art Precision-X satellite navigation system and its "A-HALT" automatic braking system, which provides a new standard in driver safety."

The Greenwich Town Car will be available for purchase worldwide starting from the first week in December.

To:	Edward Linus <elinus@blytheeng.com>
From:	Alex Murphy <amurphy@blytheeng.com>
Date:	November 17
Subject:	Our Company Cars

Dear Mr. Linus,

I'm working on our budget for next year, and we actually have a lot more money than we expected. Our profits this year have been unprecedented, and this will allow us to improve key areas of our business. One thing that we can improve upon is our fleet of company cars. I'd like you to approve the purchase of six luxury sedans that we can start using in January. I recommend that we purchase Greenwich Town Cars, which is the latest model manufactured by Eleganta Motors.

Our fleet of cars still primarily consists of the outdated Jespen Mark V models manufactured by Agutter Motors. By upgrading our vehicles to Greenwich Town Cars, we would surely impress all of our clients from overseas when we send drivers to pick them up from the airport and then drive them around the city.

I will await your decision regarding my Greenwich Town Car suggestion. Assuming that you give me your approval, I will contact Elaganta Motors as soon as the new model is released and inform them that we wish to purchase six cars.

Best regards,

Alex Murphy
Chief Accounting Manager, Blythe Engineering

41. What is NOT indicated about the Greenwich Town Car?

   (A) It has yet to be released onto the market.
   (B) It features new navigation technology.
   (C) It has a larger interior than other similar models.
   (D) It includes a state-of-the-art audio system.

42. In the article, the word "standard" in paragraph 2, line 4, is closest in meaning to

   (A) alternative
   (B) regulation
   (C) benchmark
   (D) innovation

43. What is the purpose of the e-mail?

   (A) To request authorization to make a purchase
   (B) To describe the features of a new car model
   (C) To explain the main points of a budget plan
   (D) To suggest ways to increase company profits

44. What is implied about Blythe Engineering in the e-mail?

   (A) It currently uses several cars manufactured by Eleganta Motors.
   (B) Its visiting clients expect transportation to be provided.
   (C) It worked collaboratively with Agutter Motors on a project.
   (D) Its executives regularly travel overseas on business trips.

45. When does Mr. Murphy intend to place an order with Eleganta Motors?

   (A) In October
   (B) In November
   (C) In December
   (D) In January

Come on Down to View my Designer Wedding Dresses!

Throughout April, I, Giselle Rossi, will be celebrating the opening of my new store, Wedding Dresses by Giselle! My new store is located on the corner of 10th and Granville in downtown Chicago, and it will be open from 9 a.m. to 6 p.m., Monday through Saturday. I have been designing and manufacturing custom-made dresses for over two decades, and I will also have an extensive collection of ready-to-wear gowns on display at my store.

All dress fitting appointments must be made at least 48 hours in advance. This can be done by phone, by e-mail, or by making a reservation on my Web site. Alternatively, you can just stop by my store! You can arrange a fitting for any day of the week except for Sundays. Please check out my dresses at www.dressesbygiselle.com or call my store directly at 555-3789.

Wedding Dresses by Giselle

When you come in for a dress fitting in April,
you will receive one of the following complimentary gifts!

- Anyone fitted for a dress from last year's Fall Couture line will receive a free mascara and foundation kit.
- Anyone fitted for a dress from my new Spring Couture line will receive a pair of matching pearl earrings at no extra cost.
- Anyone who is fitted for a ready-to-wear gown will get a discount of 5 percent.
- Bridesmaids will each get a free glass of champagne when they come in for a fitting.

To: Giselle Rossi <grossi@giselle.com>

From: Helena Maxwell <hmaxwell@flymail.net>

Date: March 23

Subject: Your Collection

Dear Ms. Rossi,

I am planning to marry my fiancé in September and I would love to wear a Giselle dress on our special day. I'm prepared to spend a little extra and purchase a dress from your new Spring Couture line, which I had the pleasure of seeing on the catwalk during fashion week in New York City last month. I also recently attended a wedding in Indianapolis, and the bride looked absolutely stunning in your couture dress, although I believe that particular one was from your Fall line.

I was very happy to learn that you have relocated your business from its original home in Los Angeles. I don't live far from your new location on 10th and Granville, so it will be very convenient for me to stop by for a fitting. Would 2 p.m. on April 3rd be okay?

Best regards,

Helena Maxwell

---

46. In the advertisement, the word "extensive" in paragraph 1, line 4, is closest in meaning to

(A) spacious
(B) vast
(C) prolonged
(D) exclusive

47. According to the advertisement, what is NOT true about dress fitting appointments?

(A) They must be requested at least two days beforehand.
(B) They can be booked by visiting the business.
(C) They can be set up using an Internet site.
(D) They may only take place on a weekday.

48. What does the e-mail suggest about Ms. Rossi?

(A) She got married in Indianapolis earlier this year.
(B) She designed a dress for Ms. Maxwell in the past.
(C) She will attend Ms. Maxwell's upcoming wedding.
(D) She recently showed her work at a fashion show.

49. What will Ms. Maxwell probably receive on the day of her dress fitting?

(A) A 5 percent discount
(B) A complimentary makeup kit
(C) A free pair of earrings
(D) A glass of champagne

50. Where does Ms. Maxwell want her dress fitting to take place?

(A) In Los Angeles
(B) In New York City
(C) In Chicago
(D) In Indianapolis

DAY 05

LC
Half Test

제한 시간 30분

MP3 바로듣기

강의 바로보기

정답 및 해설 p. 51

PART 1

Directions: For each question in this part, you will hear four statements about a picture in your test book. When you hear the statements, you must select the one statement that best describes what you see in the picture. Then find the number of the question on your answer sheet and mark your answer. The statements will not be printed in your test book and will be spoken only one time.

1.

2.

PART 2

Directions: You will hear a question or statement and three responses spoken in English. They will not be printed in your test book and will be spoken only one time. Select the best response to the question or statement and mark the letter (A), (B), or (C) on your answer sheet.

3. Mark your answer on your answer sheet.

4. Mark your answer on your answer sheet.

5. Mark your answer on your answer sheet.

6. Mark your answer on your answer sheet.

7. Mark your answer on your answer sheet.

8. Mark your answer on your answer sheet.

9. Mark your answer on your answer sheet.

10. Mark your answer on your answer sheet.

11. Mark your answer on your answer sheet.

12. Mark your answer on your answer sheet.

13. Mark your answer on your answer sheet.

14. Mark your answer on your answer sheet.

15. Mark your answer on your answer sheet.

16. Mark your answer on your answer sheet.

17. Mark your answer on your answer sheet.

18. Mark your answer on your answer sheet.

19. Mark your answer on your answer sheet.

20. Mark your answer on your answer sheet.

PART 3

Directions: You will hear some conversations between two or more people. You will be asked to answer three questions about what the speakers say in each conversation. Select the best response to each question and mark the letter (A), (B), (C) or (D) on your answer sheet. The conversations will not be printed in your test book and will be spoken only one time.

21. Where do the speakers work?

    (A) At a bookstore
    (B) At a supermarket
    (C) At a restaurant
    (D) At a fitness center

22. What will happen this week?

    (A) Discounts will be offered.
    (B) Workers will be hired.
    (C) Equipment will be purchased.
    (D) New products will be sold.

23. What will the woman probably do in the afternoon?

    (A) Interview job applicants
    (B) Attend an event
    (C) Place an advertisement
    (D) Create a training program

24. What most likely is Karen's area of expertise?

    (A) Public relations
    (B) Accounting
    (C) Web design
    (D) Staff training

25. What does the man want to review with Karen?

    (A) Survey feedback
    (B) Workplace regulations
    (C) Sales statistics
    (D) Employee benefits

26. Why has the orientation been postponed?

    (A) A room is unavailable.
    (B) A supervisor is absent.
    (C) Some equipment is damaged.
    (D) A scheduling conflict has occurred.

27. Why is the woman calling?

    (A) To request a travel brochure
    (B) To suggest a meeting time
    (C) To cancel a holiday
    (D) To organize a vacation

28. Why is Ms. White unavailable to help the woman?

    (A) She is traveling in Mexico.
    (B) She moved to another office.
    (C) She quit her job.
    (D) She is on a business trip.

29. What does the man suggest the woman do?

    (A) Go to a different store
    (B) Talk with a different travel agent
    (C) Send an e-mail to Ms. White
    (D) Choose a different destination

30. Where is the conversation taking place?

    (A) At a bus station
    (B) At a car rental agency
    (C) At a factory
    (D) At a hotel

31. What does the man imply when he says, "Your reservation is for Thursday, December 17"?

    (A) An appointment has been postponed.
    (B) A service is available.
    (C) A deadline is approaching.
    (D) A mistake has been made.

32. What will the woman probably do next?

    (A) Check a train schedule
    (B) Reschedule a meeting
    (C) Ask for permission
    (D) Provide a credit card

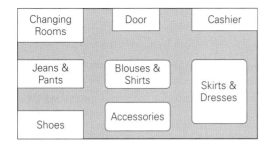

Quick Troubleshooting Guide
Eclipse KSE Series

"On"(Normal)   Error #13   Error #19   Error #23   Error #37

33. What are the speakers mainly discussing?

(A) A seasonal sale
(B) A defective item
(C) A job vacancy
(D) A discount voucher

34. What recently happened at the store?

(A) Renovations were completed.
(B) A manager was hired.
(C) Merchandise was delivered.
(D) An opening event was held.

35. Look at the graphic. Which section of the store will the woman probably go to next?

(A) Jeans & Pants
(B) Blouses & Shirts
(C) Skirts & Dresses
(D) Accessories

36. Who most likely is the woman?

(A) A computer technician
(B) A store manager
(C) A customer service representative
(D) A television show producer

37. Look at the graphic. Which error are the speakers discussing?

(A) Error #13
(B) Error #19
(C) Error #23
(D) Error #37

38. What will the man do in the afternoon?

(A) Visit a Web site
(B) Go to a store
(C) Call a technician
(D) Purchase a warranty

PART 4

Directions: You will hear some talks given by a single speaker. You will be asked to answer three questions about what the speakers say in each conversation. Select the best response to each question and mark the letter (A), (B), (C) or (D) on your answer sheet. The conversations will not be printed in your test book and will be spoken only one time.

39. Who is the speaker?

(A) A business owner
(B) A restaurant employee
(C) A chef
(D) A tour guide

40. According to the speaker, what is happening this week?

(A) A new restaurant is hiring staff.
(B) A drink is being sold at a discount.
(C) A two-for-one special is being offered.
(D) A new menu is being introduced.

41. How can listeners receive a free drink?

(A) By attending a weekend party
(B) By using a credit card
(C) By ordering a chef's special
(D) By becoming a member

42. What type of merchandise does the store sell?

(A) Luggage
(B) Gardening tools
(C) Electronics
(D) Furniture

43. Why have store displays been rearranged?

(A) To decorate for a holiday
(B) To allow space for renovations
(C) To promote a special sale
(D) To increase product visibility

44. What does the speaker imply when she says, "everyone wants them"?

(A) Another store offered a lower price.
(B) An order cannot be filled.
(C) Many workers have asked for time off.
(D) A product has not been released yet.

45. Who most likely is the speaker?

(A) A theater employee
(B) A business owner
(C) A charity founder
(D) A movie director

46. Why does the speaker say, "I hope you brought your wallets!"?

(A) To inform the listeners that a service is expensive
(B) To remind the listeners to take their personal belongings
(C) To recommend that the listeners purchase a ticket
(D) To encourage the listeners to make a donation

47. What will the listeners probably do next?

(A) Watch a video clip
(B) Look at a menu
(C) Enjoy a live performance
(D) Listen to another speaker

Record of Personal Expense	
Purchase	Cost
Gasoline	$80
Lodgings	$240
Promotional Items	$90
Food	$120
	Total: $530

48. What did the listener do last week?

(A) He had a vacation.
(B) He hired new employees.
(C) He attended a job fair.
(D) He upgraded some computers.

49. Look at the graphic. Which amount needs to be confirmed?

(A) $80
(B) $240
(C) $90
(D) $120

50. What does the speaker say was e-mailed to employees?

(A) A contact list
(B) Membership details
(C) A purchasing policy
(D) Job responsibilities

시원스쿨 LAB

1. (C)	**2.** (D)	**3.** (C)	**4.** (C)	**5.** (C)
6. (B)	**7.** (C)	**8.** (A)	**9.** (C)	**10.** (C)
11. (C)	**12.** (C)	**13.** (A)	**14.** (A)	**15.** (C)
16. (A)	**17.** (C)	**18.** (A)	**19.** (B)	**20.** (C)
21. (C)	**22.** (A)	**23.** (B)	**24.** (A)	**25.** (B)
26. (D)	**27.** (B)	**28.** (A)	**29.** (C)	**30.** (C)
31. (A)	**32.** (C)	**33.** (D)	**34.** (D)	**35.** (B)
36. (A)	**37.** (B)	**38.** (C)	**39.** (A)	**40.** (D)
41. (A)	**42.** (C)	**43.** (A)	**44.** (B)	**45.** (C)
46. (B)	**47.** (C)	**48.** (D)	**49.** (B)	**50.** (A)

Part 1

1. (A) File folders have been put on a shelf.
(B) Tables are being arranged in an office.
(C) Some chairs are unoccupied.
(D) Some documents are being collected.

(A) 파일 폴더들이 선반에 놓여 있다.
(B) 탁자들이 한 사무실에 정렬되고 있다.
(C) 몇몇 의자들이 비어 있는 상태이다.
(D) 몇몇 서류들이 수거되는 중이다.

해설 (A) 선반에 놓여 있는 폴더들을 찾아볼 수 없으므로 오답.
(B) 탁자를 정렬하는 동작을 하는 사람은 없으므로 오답.
(C) 탁자마다 빈 의자가 놓여 있는 상태를 묘사하고 있으므로 정답.
(D) 서류를 수거하는 동작을 하는 사람을 찾아볼 수 없으므로 오답.

어휘 **put** ~을 놓다, 두다 **arrange** ~을 정렬하다, 정리하다 **unoccupied** 비어 있는, 점유되지 않은 **collect** ~을 수거하다, 모으다

2. (A) One of the men is operating heavy machinery.
(B) A wheelbarrow is being positioned near a column.
(C) A shovel has been placed on a tool rack.
(D) The men are wearing safety vests.

(A) 남자들 중 한 명이 중장비를 작동하는 중이다.
(B) 외바퀴 손수레가 기둥 근처에 놓여지는 중이다.
(C) 삽 하나가 공구 걸이에 놓여 있다.
(D) 남자들이 안전 조끼를 착용한 상태이다.

해설 (A) 중장비를 작동하는 사람은 없으므로 오답.

(B) 외바퀴 손수레가 기둥 근처에 놓이는 상황이 아니므로 오답.
(C) 공구 걸이에 놓여 있는 삽을 찾아볼 수 없으므로 오답.
(D) 작업 중인 남자들이 모두 안전 조끼를 착용한 상태를 묘사하고 있으므로 정답.

어휘 **operate** ~을 작동하다, 조종하다 **heavy machinery** 중장비 **wheelbarrow** 외바퀴 손수레 **position** v. ~을 두다, 위치시키다 **column** 기둥 **shovel** 삽 **place** v. ~을 두다, 놓다 **tool rack** 공구 걸이 **safety vest** 안전 조끼

Part 2

3. Who did Ms. Bonnet have lunch with?
(A) During the lunch time.
(B) Next Friday.
(C) Someone from the sales team.

누가 보넷 씨와 함께 점심 식사를 했죠?
(A) 점심 시간 중에요.
(B) 다음주 금요일이요.
(C) 영업팀 사람이요.

해설 보넷 씨와 함께 점심 식사를 한 사람이 누구인지 묻는 Who 의문문으로, 특정 이름이나 직책을 언급하는 대신 부정대명사를 포함해 영업팀 사람이라고 답변한 (C)가 정답이다. (A)는 질문에 쓰인 lunch를 반복 사용한 오답이며, (B)는 미래 시점 표현이므로 When 의문문에 적절한 응답이다.

4. Where did Austin leave the invoices?
(A) He left the company last week.
(B) 500 dollars.
(C) Check in the top drawer.

오스틴 씨가 어디에 거래 내역서들을 두었나요?
(A) 그는 지난주에 회사를 그만뒀어요.
(B) 500 달러예요.
(C) 맨 위 서랍을 확인해 보세요.

해설 거래 내역서의 보관 위치를 묻는 Where 의문문이므로 확인 가능한 위치 표현으로 답변하는 (C)가 정답이다. (A)는 질문에 쓰인 동사 leave의 과거형 left를 이용한 함정 오답이며, (B)는 거래내역서에서 연상 가능한 금액을 언급해 혼동을 유발하는 선택지이다.

어휘 **leave** ~을 두다, ~을 놓다, ~을 그만두다, ~에서 떠나다 **invoice** 거래내역서 **drawer** 서랍

5. Hasn't the delivery truck been loaded yet?
(A) We offer express delivery.
(B) It's free to download.

(C) No, we're still working on it.

배송 트럭에 아직도 짐이 다 실리지 않았나요?
(A) 저희는 신속 배송 서비스를 제공합니다.
(B) 그건 무료로 다운로드 할 수 있습니다.
(C) 아뇨, 저희가 여전히 작업 중입니다.

해설 배송 트럭에 아직도 짐이 다 실리지 않았는지 확인하는 부정 의
문문에 대해 부정을 뜻하는 No와 함께 해당 업무를 it으로 받
아 여전히 작업 중이라는 말로 짐이 다 실리지 않았음을 알리는
(C)가 정답이다. (A)는 delivery를 반복해 혼동을 유발하는 오
답이며, (B)는 loaded와 발음이 유사한 download를 이용한
오답이다.

어휘 **delivery** 배송(품) **load** ~에 짐을 싣다, 적재하다
express 특급의, 급행의 **free** 무료의 **work on** ~에 대한
작업을 하다

6. What's the registration deadline?
(A) The batteries are dead.
(B) Two weeks from today.
(C) On the corner of Broad Street and Millstream
Way.

등록 마감기한이 언제죠?
(A) 배터리들이 다 닳았어요.
(B) 오늘부터 2주 후요.
(C) 브로드 스트리트와 밀스트림 웨이가 만나는 모퉁이에요.

해설 What의 의미를 정확히 파악하기 위해 뒤에 이어지는 말에 집
중해 들어야 한다. What 뒤에 등록 마감기한을 뜻하는 명사구
가 쓰여 있는데, 이는 언제인지 묻는 질문이므로 2주 후라는 미
래 시점 표현으로 답변한 (B)가 정답이다. (A)는 deadline과
일부 발음이 같은 dead를 이용해 혼동을 유발하는 답변이며,
(C)는 위치 표현이므로 Where 의문문에 어울리는 반응이다.

어휘 **registration** 등록 **deadline** 마감기한 **dead** (기기 등이)
수명이 다 된, 작동하지 않는 **on the corner of A and B**
A와 B가 만나는 모퉁이에

7. Which font should I use for the headline?
(A) At the bottom of each page.
(B) Yes, I read it earlier.
(C) Use a unique one.

제목에 어느 서체를 사용해야 하나요?
(A) 각 페이지 하단에요.
(B) 네, 아까 그걸 읽어 봤어요.
(C) 독특한 것을 사용하세요.

해설 Which font라는 말과 함께 어느 서체를 사용해야 하는지 묻
는 의문문에 대해 font를 대명사 one으로 받아 독특한 것을
사용하도록 알리는 (C)가 정답이다. (A)는 위치 표현이므로
Where 의문문에 어울리는 답변이며, (B)는 의문사 의문문에
어울리지 않는 Yes로 답변한 오답이다.

어휘 **font** 서체 **headline** (신문 등의) 제목, 헤드라인 **at the
bottom of** ~의 하단에, 밑부분에 **unique** 독특한, 특별한

8. Shouldn't we get permission before leaving the
office early?
(A) I was going to ask Mr. Ramirez.
(B) Can you apply for the permit?
(C) Okay, I'll leave them in the back.

사무실에서 일찍 나가기 전에 허락을 받아야 하지 않나요?
(A) 제가 라미레즈 씨에게 요청하려고 했어요.
(B) 그 허가증을 신청해 주시겠어요?
(C) 알겠어요, 제가 그것들을 뒤쪽에 놓아 둘게요.

해설 사무실에서 일찍 나가기 전에 허락을 받아야 하지 않는지 확인
하는 부정 의문문이므로 허락을 받기 위해 요청하려 했다고 답
변하는 (A)가 정답이다. (B)는 질문에 쓰인 permission과 발
음이 유사한 permit 을, (C)는 leaving의 원형인 leave를 각
각 이용해 혼동을 유발하는 오답이다.

어휘 **get permission** 허락을 얻다 **leave** ~에서 나가다, 떠나
다, ~을 놓아 두다 **apply for** ~을 신청하다, ~에 지원하다
permit 허가증

9. We're receiving our new business cards this week,
right?
(A) Some new cars.
(B) The company's logo.
(C) I didn't hear anything.

우리가 이번 주에 새로운 명함을 받는 것이 맞죠?
(A) 일부 새로운 차량들이요.
(B) 회사 로고요.
(C) 저는 아무 얘기도 듣지 못했어요.

해설 이번 주에 새로운 명함을 받는 것인지 확인하는 부가 의문문
에 대해 자신은 알지 못한다는 의미를 나타내는 말로 답변하는
(C)가 정답이다. (A)는 질문에 쓰인 cards와 발음이 유사하게
들리는 cars를 이용한 오답이며, (B)는 business cards에서
연상 가능한 company's logo를 이용해 혼동을 유발하는 답
변이다.

어휘 **receive** ~을 받다 **business card** 명함

10. How much does it cost to get in?
(A) They said it would take more time.
(B) Those items should be paid for in cash.
(C) Less than 5 dollars.

입장하는 데 비용이 얼마나 드나요?
(A) 그 사람들이 더 많은 시간이 걸릴 거라고 했어요.
(B) 그 물품들에 대해 현금으로 지불되어야 합니다.
(C) 5달러 미만이요.

해설 How much 뒤로 동사 cost가 쓰이면 금액을 묻는 질문이

므로 구체적인 액수를 밝히는 (C)가 정답이다. (A)는 How much와 연관성 있게 들리는 소요 시간을 말하는 것으로 혼동을 유발하는 오답이며, (B)는 질문에 쓰인 cost에서 연상 가능한 paid, cash를 이용해 혼동을 유발하는 답변이다.

어휘 **get in** 들어가다, 입장하다 **cost** (비용이) 들다 **pay for** ~에 대한 값을 지불하다 **in cash** 현금으로 **less than** ~보다 적게[적은]

11. Will our study be published before the conference?
(A) At the United Hotel.
(B) An analysis of popular ads.
(C) No, not until after.

우리 연구가 컨퍼런스 전에 출간될까요?
(A) 유나이티드 호텔에서요.
(B) 인기 있는 광고들에 대한 분석 내용입니다.
(C) 아뇨, 그 이후에나 될 거예요.

해설 연구 내용이 출간되는 대략적인 시점을 확인하는 Will 의문문이므로 부정을 나타내는 No와 함께 컨퍼런스 이후에나 나올 거라는 말을 덧붙인 (C)가 정답이다. (A)는 장소 표현이므로 Where 의문문에 어울리는 반응이며, (B)는 질문에 쓰인 study(연구)에서 연상 가능한 analysis(분석)를 이용해 혼동을 유발하는 답변으로 연구 주제에 해당되는 말이므로 오답이다.

어휘 **study** 연구 **publish** ~을 출판하다 **analysis** 분석(한 내용) **ad** 광고(= advertisement) **not until after** (앞서 언급된 특정 시점에 대해) 그 이후나 되어야 한다

12. When are these taxes due?
(A) They're way too high.
(B) The train is due in ten minutes.
(C) By the end of next week.

이 세금의 납부 기한이 언제죠?
(A) 그것들은 너무 많이 높습니다.
(B) 그 기차가 10분 후에 출발할 예정입니다.
(C) 다음 주 말까지요.

해설 세금을 언제까지 내야 하는지 그 기한을 묻는 When 의문문이다. 따라서 '다음 주 말까지'라는 특정 미래 시점을 말하는 (C)가 적절한 응답이다. (A)는 taxes에서 연상 가능한 금액을 이용한 함정이다. (B)는 질문에 쓰인 due를 반복하여 혼동을 주는 선택지로, 세금과 관련 없는 기차 출발 시점을 말하는 오답이다.

어휘 **tax** 세금 **due** ~가 기한인, ~에 예정된 **way too** 너무 많이 cf. **way** (강조) 너무, 아주 **in** 시간 ~ 후에 **by** (기한) ~까지

13. What would you like to do this afternoon?
(A) How about having a coffee together?
(B) No, it takes place before noon.

(C) I have a date tomorrow.

오늘 오후에 뭐 하고 싶으세요?
(A) 함께 커피 마시는 건 어때요?
(B) 아뇨, 그건 정오 전에 개최돼요.
(C) 내일 데이트 약속이 있어요.

해설 What 의문문으로 상대방에게 오후에 하고 싶은 일이 무엇인지 묻고 있으므로 함께 하고 싶은 일을 제안하는 (A)가 정답이다. 오늘 오후에 할 일을 묻고 있으므로 내일 있을 약속을 말하는 (C)는 어울리지 않는 반응이다.

어휘 **How about -ing?** ~하는 건 어때요? **take place** (행사, 일 등이) 개최되다, 발생되다

14. Have the transfer requests been submitted?
(A) We just sent the last ones.
(B) We did not receive your submission.
(C) He wants to move to another branch.

전근 신청서가 제출되었나요?
(A) 저희가 마지막 것들을 막 보냈습니다.
(B) 저희는 당신의 제출물을 받지 못했습니다.
(C) 그는 다른 지사로 전근하고 싶어 합니다.

해설 Have/Has로 시작하는 일반 의문문은 이미 완료된 일이나 경험을 물을 때 주로 사용한다. 전근 신청서가 제출되었는지 묻는 질문에 대해 requests를 대신하는 ones와 함께 마지막 신청서들을 보냈다고 알리는 (A)가 정답이다. (B)는 질문에 쓰인 submitted와 발음이 비슷한 submission을 이용해 혼동을 유발하는 오답이며, (C)는 transfer와 관련 있게 들리는 move to another branch를 이용한 오답이다.

어휘 **transfer** 전근, 이전 **request** 요청(서) **submit** ~을 제출하다 **receive** ~을 받다 **submission** 제출(물) **branch** 지사, 지점

15. Why is Oscar leaving our law firm?
(A) Yes, in January next year.
(B) He's the most qualified to lead us.
(C) He wants to spend time traveling.

오스카 씨가 왜 우리 법률회사를 그만두는 거죠?
(A) 네, 내년 1월에요.
(B) 그분께서 우리를 이끌어 가시는 데 가장 적격이십니다.
(C) 여행을 하시면서 시간을 보내고 싶어 하세요.

해설 오스카 씨가 회사를 그만두는 이유를 묻는 Why 의문문이므로 오스카 씨를 He로 지칭해 그 사람이 하고 싶어 하는 일을 언급한 (C)가 정답이다. (A)는 의문사 의문문에 맞지 않는 Yes로 답변하는 오답이며, (B)는 앞으로 함께 일할 가능성이 있는 사람을 대상으로 할 수 있는 말이므로 질문의 의도에 어울리지 않는 반응이다.

어휘 **leave** ~을 그만두다, ~에서 떠나다 **law firm** 법률회사 **qualified** 적격인, 자격을 갖춘 **lead** ~을 이끌다 **spend time -ing** ~하면서 시간을 보내다

16. This year's film festival wasn't well-attended, was it?

   (A) We should've advertised more.
   (B) It's at the Gainley Theater.
   (C) At 7 P.M. every day.

올해 열린 영화제에 참석한 사람들이 많지 않았죠?
(A) 우리가 더 많이 광고했어야 했어요.
(B) 게인리 극장에서 합니다.
(C) 매일 오후 7시에요.

해설 영화제에 참석자가 적었다는 사실을 확인하는 부가 의문문에 대해 더 많이 광고했어야 한다는 말로 동의하는 (A)가 정답이다. (B)는 질문에 쓰인 film에서 연상 가능한 theater를 활용한 오답으로 Where 의문문에 어울리는 답변이며, (C)는 시간 표현이므로 When 의문문에 어울리는 반응이다.

어휘 **well-attended** 사람들이 많이 참석한 **should have p.p.** ~했어야 했다

17. Won't Mr. Grant be designing the festival posters this year?

   (A) Several popular musicians.
   (B) He'll be signing it this week.
   (C) Actually, he's busy with other things.

그랜트 씨가 올해 축제 포스터들을 디자인하는 것 아닌가요?
(A) 여러 인기 있는 음악가들이요.
(B) 그분이 이번 주에 그것에 서명할 예정입니다.
(C) 사실, 그분은 다른 일들로 바빠요.

해설 그랜트 씨가 축제 포스터들을 디자인하는 것인지 확인하는 부정 의문문이므로 다른 일로 바쁘다는 말로 디자인 작업을 할 수 없는 상황임을 알리는 (C)가 정답이다. (A)는 질문에 쓰인 festival에서 연상 가능한 musicians를 이용한 오답이며, (B)는 질문에 쓰인 designing과 발음이 비슷한 signing을 이용해 혼동을 유발하는 답변이다.

어휘 **sign** ~에 서명하다 **be busy with** ~로 바쁘다

18. How do you like the new copy machine?

   (A) It's hard to use so far.
   (B) At the coffee shop.
   (C) He will be out of the office tomorrow.

새 복사기가 마음에 드시나요?
(A) 지금까진 사용하기 어려워요.
(B) 커피 전문점에서요.
(C) 그는 내일 사무실에 있지 않을 거예요.

해설 「How do you like ~?」는 특정 대상이 마음에 드는지 묻는 의문문으로 상대방의 의견을 묻는 것과 같다. 따라서 새 복사기가 아직 사용하기 어렵다는 의견을 밝힌 (A)가 정답이다. (B)는 질문에 쓰인 copy와 발음이 유사한 coffee를 이용해 혼동을 유발하는 답변이다. (C)는 copy machine과 연관성 있게 들리는 office를 이용해 혼동을 유발하는 답변이다.

어휘 **hard** 어려운 **so far** 지금까지 **out of the office** 사무실에 없는

19. Sales of our new desserts have been lower than we hoped.

   (A) We hope so, too.
   (B) I know. It's disappointing.
   (C) It's on sale for ten percent off.

우리의 새 디저트에 대한 매출이 우리가 희망했던 것보다 더 낮습니다.
(A) 저희도 그렇기를 바랍니다.
(B) 알고 있습니다. 실망스럽네요.
(C) 그건 10퍼센트 할인 판매 중입니다.

해설 디저트 제품의 매출이 낮았던 사실을 알리는 평서문에 대해 그것이 실망스럽다는 의견을 제시하는 (B)가 정답이다. (A)와 (C)는 hope 및 sales를 각각 반복해 혼동을 유발하는 오답으로, 디저트 제품 매출이 낮은 사실을 말하는 것에 대한 반응으로 어울리지 않는 답변이다.

어휘 **sales** 매출, 판매(량) **disappointing** 실망스러운 **on sale** 판매 중인 **off** 할인된

20. Why weren't you at the company dinner yesterday?

   (A) Yes, and it was great to see you there.
   (B) Sorry, but I'm afraid we're running late.
   (C) I went to a birthday party for my cousin instead.

왜 어제 회사 회식에 안 왔어요?
(A) 네, 그리고 그곳에서 뵈어서 정말 좋았어요.
(B) 죄송하지만, 저희가 늦을 것 같아요.
(C) 대신 제 사촌의 생일 파티에 갔어요.

해설 의문사 Why로 시작하는 의문문은 의문사 자체보다 뒤에 이어지는 내용에 더 집중해 들어야 한다. 회식에 오지 않은 이유를 묻고 있으므로 회식 대신 가야 했던 다른 일을 말하는 것으로 회식에 참석하지 못한 이유를 밝히는 (C)가 정답이다. (A)는 의문사 의문문에 맞지 않는 Yes로 답변하는 오답이며, (B)는 과거의 회식 참석이 아니라 현재 늦는 상황을 알리는 말이므로 질문의 의도에 맞지 않는 반응이다.

어휘 **I'm afraid (that)** (부정적인 일에 대해) ~인 것 같다, 유감스럽지만 ~이다 **be running late** 약속 시간에 늦다 **instead** 대신

Part 3

Questions 21-23 refer to the following conversation.

> M: I was just looking over **21** the report you submitted detailing the market research you carried out, and it seems that there is some information missing.
>
> W: Well, I took great care to include all of the information that you requested, so I'm surprised that there is anything missing. Can you tell me what I forgot to include?
>
> M: The majority of it is fine, but **22** you left out the first names of the participants in the customer survey. You were supposed to include each person's full name.
>
> W: Oh, I forgot to mention that **23** I faxed you a full list of the participants yesterday, so you can refer to that if you need to get their full details or contact them with follow-up questions.
>
> ---
>
> 남: 당신이 실시한 시장 조사 내용을 자세히 담아 제출한 보고서를 검토하고 있던 중이었는데, 일부 정보가 빠져 있는 것 같습니다.
>
> 여: 저, 요청하셨던 모든 정보를 넣으려고 신경을 많이 썼는데 빠진 것이 있다니 놀랍습니다. 제가 무엇을 포함시키는 걸 잊었는지 말씀해 주시겠어요?
>
> 남: 대부분 문제가 없지만, 고객 설문 조사 참가자들의 이름을 넣지 않으셨는데요. 각 참가자의 성명을 모두 넣으셔야 했어요.
>
> 여: 아, 제가 말씀드리는 것을 깜빡 했는데요, 제가 어제 모든 참가자 명단을 팩스로 보내드려서, 참가자에 대한 모든 세부 정보를 파악해야 하거나 후속 질문을 위해 연락할 필요가 있으시면 참고할 수 있으세요.

어휘 **look over** ~을 살펴보다, 검토하다 **detail** v. ~을 상세하게 서술하다 n. 세부 사항 **carry out** ~을 수행하다 **it seems that** ~인 것 같다 **missing** 빠진, 분실한 **take care** 조심하다, 주의하다 **include** ~을 포함하다 **request** ~을 요청하다 **forget to do** ~할 것을 잊어버리다 **the majority of** ~의 대부분 **leave out** ~을 생략하다, 제외하다 **participant** n. 참가자 **survey** 설문 조사 **be supposed to do** ~하기로 되어 있다 **mention** ~을 언급하다 **refer to** ~을 참고하다 **contact** ~에게 연락하다 **follow-up** 후속의

21. 화자들은 무엇을 논의하고 있는가?
(A) 회사 야유회
(B) 소비자 트렌드
(C) 시장 조사 보고서
(D) 회의 일정

해설 대화 주제는 주로 초반에 드러나므로 첫 문장에 집중해야 하며, 명사 위주로 키워드를 파악해 주제를 찾아야 한다. the report 와 market research에서 (C)가 주제임을 알 수 있다.

22. 무엇이 문제인가?
(A) 일부 이름이 목록에 정확하게 기입되지 않았다.
(B) 제품 샘플을 잃어버렸다.
(C) 몇몇 초대장이 발송되지 않았다.
(D) 지원서가 미완성이다.

해설 문제점에 대해 언급할 때 I'm afraid that ~, I'm worried[concerned] that ~, but, however 등과 같이 부정적인 상황을 나타내거나 대화의 흐름을 바꾸는 표현이 주로 사용된다는 점을 기억하자. 남자의 두 번째 말 The majority of it is fine, but 이후에 문제점이 언급되고 있는데, 남자가 말하는 you left out the first names of the participants 라는 문제점을 다른 말로 바꾸어 쓴 (A)가 정답이다.

어휘 **list** v. ~을 목록에 기입하다, 명부에 올리다 **correctly** 정확하게, 제대로 **misplace** ~을 잘못 두다, 둔 곳을 잊어버리다 **application form** 지원서 **incomplete** 완성되지 않은

Paraphrase you left out the first names of the participants
→ Some names are not listed correctly.

23. 여자는 어제 무엇을 했다고 말하는가?
(A) 설문조사에 참가했다.
(B) 명단을 보냈다.
(C) 복사를 했다.
(D) 공급업체에 연락했다.

해설 여자가 어제 무엇을 했다고 말하는지를 묻고 있으므로 여자의 대사 중 특정 시점 yesterday가 언급되는 곳을 제대로 들어야 한다. 대화의 마지막 부분에서 여자는 어제 팩스로 참가자들의 명단을 보냈다고(I faxed you a full list of the participants yesterday) 하므로 (B)가 정답이다.

어휘 **take part in** ~에 참가하다 **make a copy** 복사하다 **supplier** 공급자, 공급업체

Paraphrase faxed you a full list of the participants
→ Sent a list of names

Questions 24-26 refer to the following conversation.

> W: I can't wait to show our clients **24** the progress we've made on their product catalogue. We've put a lot of time into it, and I think they'll really appreciate our attention to detail.
>
> M: I'm sure they'll love it. The photographer we used was amazing, too. The photos look really professional.

W: Yeah. It was a good decision to hire him.

M: Oh, before I forget. **25** You know I'm a part of the company book club? Well, there's a famous writer giving a lecture at Hamilton Bookstore Tuesday at 2 o'clock, and the club is going to it. **26** Do you mind if I take that afternoon off?

W: Hmm.. **26** we have a meeting on Friday we need to prepare for, but Robert can handle it.

여: 저는 고객들께 우리가 그분들을 위해 만든 제품 카탈로그에 대한 진척 상황을 빨리 알려 드리고 싶어요. 우리가 이 작업에 많은 시간을 들였기 때문에 세부적인 부분까지 신경 쓴 것을 진심으로 인정해 주실 거라고 생각해요.

남: 분명히 아주 마음에 들어 하실 겁니다. 우리가 이용한 사진가도 아주 놀라운 분이었어요. 사진들이 정말로 전문적으로 보여요.

여: 네. 그분을 고용한 것은 좋은 결정이었어요.

남: 아, 제가 잊기 전에 말씀드릴 것이 있어요. 제가 회사의 독서 동호회에 속해 있다는 것을 알고 계시죠? 저, 화요일 2시에 해밀턴 서점에서 유명한 작가 한 분이 진행하는 강연이 있는데, 동호회에서 그곳에 갈 예정이에요. 그날 오후에 휴무를 신청해도 괜찮을까요?

여: 흠... 우리가 준비해야 하는 회의가 금요일에 있기는 하지만 로버트 씨가 그 일을 처리할 수 있어요.

어휘 **can't wait to do** 빨리 ~하고 싶다 **make progress** 진척시키다, 진행하다 **product catalogue** 제품 카탈로그 **put A into B** A를 B에 쏟아붓다, 두자다 **appreciate** ~을 인정하다, ~의 진가를 알아보다 **attention to** ~에 대한 주의, 주목, 관심, 돌봄 **detail** 세부 사항 **photographer** 사진가 **amazing** 놀라운 **look** 형용사 ~하게 보이다 **professional** 전문적인 **decision** 결정 **hire** ~을 고용하다 **forget** 잊다 **book club** 독서 동호회 **give a lecture** 강연하다 **Do you mind if ~?** ~해도 괜찮을까요? **take A off** A만큼 쉬다, 휴가를 내다 **prepare for** ~을 준비하다 **handle** ~을 처리하다

24. 화자들은 무슨 작업을 맡아 하고 있는가?

(A) 제품 카탈로그
(B) 회사의 웹 사이트
(C) 상점 광고
(D) 포장지 디자인

해설 대화 시작 부분에 여자가 고객들을 위해 만든 제품 카탈로그에 대한 진척 상황(the progress we've made on their product catalogue)을 언급하는 내용을 통해 (A)가 정답임을 알 수 있다.

어휘 **work on** ~을 맡아 작업하다 **advertisement** 광고 **packaging** 포장(지)

---

25. 남자는 회사의 독서 동호회에 관해 무슨 말을 하는가?

(A) 회원들이 할인을 받는다.
(B) 회원들이 매장 한 곳을 방문한다.
(C) 회원들이 새로운 책들을 주문하고 있다.
(D) 회원들이 설문 조사를 실시하고 있다.

해설 남자가 말하는 독서 동호회가 핵심이므로 남자의 말에서 이 동호회 이름이 제시되는 부분에 특정 정보가 제시될 것임을 예상하고 들어야 한다. 대화 중반부에 남자는 자신이 독서 동호회 회원임을 언급하면서(I'm a part of the company book club) 동호회가 Hamilton Bookstore에서 열리는 강연에 간다고(~ a lecture at Hamilton Bookstore Tuesday at 2 o'clock, and the club is going to it) 말하고 있다. 따라서 회원들이 서점 한 곳을 방문할 예정임을 알 수 있으므로 (B)가 정답이다.

어휘 **get a discount** 할인을 받다 **conduct** ~을 실시하다 **survey** 설문 조사

26. 여자는 왜 "로버트 씨가 그 일을 처리할 수 있어요"라고 말하는가?

(A) 추가적인 도움을 요청하기 위해
(B) 신규 채용자에 대해 승인하기 위해
(C) 남자의 노력에 대해 실망감을 표현하기 위해
(D) 남자의 부재를 허용해 주기 위해

해설 해당 문장은 바로 앞서 남자가 요청하는 휴무에 대한(Do you mind if I take that afternoon off?) 답변으로 들을 수 있는 말이다. 여자는 회의가 있다는 말과 함께(we have a meeting on Friday we need to prepare for, but.. ~) Robert가 그것을 처리할 수 있다고 말하고 있는데, 이는 결국 남자의 요청을 받아들이는 것과 같다. 따라서 남자의 부재를 허용한다는 의미로 쓰인 (D)가 정답이 된다.

어휘 **request** ~을 요청하다 **additional** 추가적인 **approve of** ~을 승인하다 **new hire** 신규 채용자 **express** ~을 표현하다 **disappointment** 실망(감) **effort** 노력 **permit** ~을 허용하다 **absence** 부재, 결근

Questions 27-29 refer to the following conversation.

M: Hello. I'm James from Goldman Plumbing. **27** You called our office this morning about your bathroom. Is there a problem with your pipes?

W: I'm so glad you are here. Thanks for coming quickly. The problem started last night and **27** we haven't been able to take a shower since. We really need it fixed.

M: I see. Actually, **28** there have been many problems with the pipes in this building. Many of your neighbors have reported the same thing. I'll take a look, but I think this is a problem affecting the whole building.

W: Okay, I understand. But, please have a look, just in case. **29 I have some friends coming over for a dinner party this coming Saturday, so I really need the bathroom problems to be fixed before they arrive.**

남: 안녕하세요. 전 골드만 배관의 제임스입니다. 오늘 오전에 욕실에 대해 저희 사무실로 전화 주셨죠. 댁의 배관 파이프에 문제가 있나요?

여: 오신 걸 보니 너무 반가워요. 빨리 와주셔서 감사합니다. 문제는 어젯밤에 생겼고요, 그 이후로 샤워도 못하고 있어요. 정말 꼭 수리를 받아야 해요.

남: 알겠습니다. 실은 이 건물의 파이프에 문제가 많습니다. 많은 이웃들이 같은 문제를 알려왔어요. 제가 들여다보긴 하겠지만, 이건 건물 전체에 영향을 미치는 문제인 것 같습니다.

여: 알겠습니다. 하지만 혹시 모르니 한 번 봐주세요. 돌아오는 토요일에 친구들이 저녁 식사 파티에 오거든요. 그래서 친구들이 도착하기 전에 욕실 문제가 꼭 해결되었으면 해요.

어휘 plumbing (건물의) 배관, 배관작업 bathroom 욕실 take a shower 샤워하다 since ad. 그 이후로 need A (to be) fixed A가 수리되어야 한다, 바로 잡혀야 한다 I see 알겠습니다 actually 실은 take[have] a look 살펴보다 affect ~에 영향을 끼치다 whole 전체의 just in case 만약을 위해 come over 놀러오다, 찾아오다

27. 여자는 남자의 회사에 왜 연락했겠는가?
   (A) 교체품을 주문하기 위해
   (B) 수리를 요청하기 위해
   (C) 서비스에 대해 불만을 제기하기 위해
   (D) 새 욕조를 설치하기 위해

해설 대화 처음에 남자가 자신을 배관회사 직원이라고 소개하며 여자가 욕실 파이프 문제로 전화했음을 확인하고 있다. 이에 여자가 샤워도 못하고 있다며 이 문제가 꼭 해결되어야 한다고(We really need it fixed) 말한다. 이로부터 여자는 파이프 수리를 요청하기 위해 전화했다는 것을 알 수 있으므로 (B)가 정답이다.

어휘 order ~을 주문하다 replacement 교체 repair n. 수리 complain about ~에 대해 불평하다 have A p.p. A가 ~되도록 하다 bath 욕조

28. 남자는 여자의 건물에 대해 뭐라고 말하는가?
   (A) 많은 세입자들이 문제를 알렸다.
   (B) 최근에 새 파이프를 설치했다.
   (C) 건물 토대 일부가 약해졌다.
   (D) 물 공급을 일시적으로 중단시켰다.

해설 남자의 대사 중 building이 언급되는 곳에 집중한다. 남자는 이 건물에 수도관 문제가 많다며 이웃들도 같은 문제를 알려왔다고(there have been many problems with the

pipes in this building. Many of your neighbors have reported the same thing) 말하고 있다. 이 점에 대해 언급하면서 your neighbors를 tenants로 paraphrasing한 (A)가 정답이다.

어휘 tenant 세입자 recently 최근에 foundations (pl.) 건물의 토대 cut A off A를 단절시키다 supply 공급 temporarily 일시적으로, 임시로

Paraphrase your neighbors
   → tenants

29. 여자는 이번 주말에 무엇을 할 것인가?
   (A) 친구의 아파트에 간다.
   (B) 식당에서 식사를 한다.
   (C) 몇몇 손님을 맞이한다.
   (D) 욕실을 개조한다.

해설 this weekend가 핵심어이므로 여자의 대사 중 이 표현이 언급되는 부분을 잘 듣도록 한다. 대화 마지막 여자의 말 중에서 I have some friends coming over for a dinner party this coming Saturday가 힌트이다. this weekend를 this coming Saturday라고 표현한 것을 알아차려야 한다. 이번 토요일에 친구들이 파티하러 오기로 했다고 하므로 (C)가 정답이다.

어휘 meal 식사 have A over A를 손님으로 맞이하다 remodel ~을 개조하다

Paraphrase have some friends coming over
   → Have some guests over

Questions 30-32 refer to the following conversation with three speakers.

W1: Hi, Mr. Young. I'm Cathy Harper, the general operations manager here at JX Chemicals. This is our head of production, Lisa Rodriguez, and **30 we'll be showing you around the manufacturing plant this morning.**

M: Good morning. I'm happy to be here.

W2: Thanks for coming. **31 We're looking forward to hearing your suggestions on ways we can reduce operating costs and increase our profits** here at our company.

M: Well, I'm here to help. **32 I'm already impressed with your policies on reusing paper and other recyclable materials.** And, I'm sure I'll find numerous other ways to improve your finances.

W1: We hope so. Now, if you'd like to follow us, we'll take a look at our main assembly line.

여1: 안녕하세요, 영 씨. 저는 캐시 하퍼이며, 이곳 JX 케미컬즈의 총무부장입니다. 이분은 저희 생산 책임자이신 리사 로드리게즈 씨이며, 저희가 오늘 아침에 귀하께 제조 공장을 견학시켜 드릴 것입니다.

남: 안녕하세요. 이곳에 오게 되어 기쁩니다.

여2: 와 주셔서 감사합니다. 저희가 이곳 저희 회사에서 운영 비용을 줄이고 수익을 늘릴 수 있는 방법에 관한 귀하의 의견을 들어 볼 수 있기를 고대하고 있습니다.

남: 저, 저는 도움을 드리기 위해 이곳에 왔습니다. 저는 이미 종이 및 기타 재활용 물품을 다시 사용하는 귀사의 정책에 깊은 인상을 받았습니다. 그리고, 분명 귀사의 재무 상태를 개선할 다수의 다른 방법들을 찾을 것입니다.

여1: 저희도 그러기를 바랍니다. 자, 저희를 따라오시면, 함께 저희 주요 조립 라인을 보시게 될 겁니다.

어휘 **general operations manager** 총무부장 **head** 책임자, 장 **show A around B** A에게 B를 견학시켜주다(= give A a tour of B) **manufacturing plant** 제조 공장 **look forward to -ing** ~하기를 고대하다 **suggestion** 의견, 제안 **reduce** ~을 줄이다, 감소시키다 **operating costs** 운영 비용 **increase** ~을 늘리다, 증가시키다 **profit** 수익 **be impressed with** ~에 깊은 인상을 받다 **policy** 정책, 방침 **recyclable** 재활용 가능한 **material** 물품, 재료, 자료 **numerous** 다수의, 수많은 **improve** ~을 개선하다, 향상시키다 **finance** 재무, 재정 **follow** ~을 따라 가다 **take a look at** ~을 한번 보다 **assembly** 조립

30. 화자들은 왜 만나고 있는가?
(A) 구직 면접을 위해
(B) 교육 시간을 위해
(C) 시설 견학을 위해
(D) 영업 발표를 위해

해설 대화 초반부에 여자 한 명이 남자에게 자신들이 제조 공장을 견학시켜 줄 것이라고(we'll be showing you around the manufacturing plant this morning) 하므로 (C)가 정답이다.

어휘 **facility** 시설(물) **sales** 영업, 판매, 매출 **presentation** 발표

Paraphrase show you around the manufacturing plant → facility tour

31. 남자의 직업은 무엇일 것 같은가?
(A) 재무 상담 전문가
(B) 채용 책임자
(C) 안전 조사관
(D) 마케팅 이사

해설 대화 중반부에 여자 한 명이 운영 비용을 줄이고 수익을 늘릴 수 있는 방법에 관한 남자의 의견을 듣고 싶다고(We're looking forward to hearing your suggestions on ways we can reduce operating costs and increase

our profits) 알리고 있다. 이는 재무 상담과 관련된 일이므로 (A)가 정답이다.

어휘 **profession** 직업 **financial** 재무의, 재정의 **advisor** 상담 전문가, 자문 **recruitment** 채용, 모집 **inspector** 조사하는 사람

32. 남자는 회사에 대해 무엇이 마음에 든다고 말하는가?
(A) 제품 범위
(B) 교육 방식
(C) 재활용 정책
(D) 고급 장비

해설 남자가 마음에 드는 것을 묻고 있으므로 남자가 말하는 긍정적인 정보를 찾아야 한다. 대화 후반부에 남자가 이미 종이 및 기타 재활용 물품을 다시 사용하는 정책에 깊은 인상을 받았다고(I'm already impressed with your policies on reusing paper and other recyclable materials) 하므로 (C)가 정답이다.

어휘 **range** 범위, 종류 **method** 방식 **advanced** 고급의, 진보한 **equipment** 장비

Questions 33-35 refer to the following conversation and receipt.

M: Hi, thanks for calling Clark's Deli. How can I help you?

W: Well, I came into the deli this morning to purchase a few items, but **33** when I got home I realized one of the items I paid for wasn't in my bag.

M: **34** Oh, I'm sorry about that, ma'am. Which item was it?

W: **34** It was the soup. I have my receipt here, and I was definitely charged for it.

M: Hmm... I think our new worker forgot to put it in the bag. I'd be happy to give you a refund the next time you come into the store.

W: Thanks, I appreciate it. And **35** maybe you should ask the worker to be more careful next time.

M: **35** Yes, I'll do that right away.

남: 안녕하세요, 클라크 델리에 전화 주셔서 감사합니다. 무엇을 도와드릴까요?

여: 저, 제가 오늘 아침에 몇 가지 제품을 구입하러 귀하의 조리 식품 매장에 갔었는데, 집에 돌아왔을 때 제가 비용을 지불한 제품들 중의 하나가 가방이 들어 있지 않았다는 것을 알게 되었습니다.

남: 아, 그런 일이 있으셨다니 유감입니다, 고객님. 그것이 어느 제품이었죠?

여: 수프였어요. 여기 영수증을 갖고 있는데, 이 제품에 대해 분명히 비용이 청구되었어요.

남: 흠... 아마 저희 신입 직원이 그 제품을 가방에 넣어 드리는 것을 잊은 것 같습니다. 다음 번에 저희 매장으로 오실 때 기꺼이 환불을 해 드리겠습니다.

여: 고맙습니다, 그렇게 해 주신다니 감사합니다. 그리고 그 직원에게 다음 번에는 좀 더 신중하게 일하도록 요청하셔야 할 것 같아요.

남: 네, 지금 바로 그렇게 하겠습니다.

클라크 델리

블랙 올리브	7.50달러
참치 샐러드	9.50달러
슬라이스 햄	6.99달러
토마토 수프	5.99달러
총액	29.98달러

클라크 델리를
이용해주셔서 감사합니다!

어휘 **come into** ~로 들어가다 **deli** 조리 식품 매장 **realize (that)** ~임을 알게 되다 **pay for** ~의 비용을 지불하다 **receipt** 영수증 **definitely** 분명히, 확실히 **charge A for B** A에게 B에 대한 비용을 청구하다 **forget to do** ~하는 것을 잊다 **put A in B** A를 B에 넣다 **give A a refund** A에게 환불해 주다 **the next time + 절** 다음 번에 ~할 때 **appreciate** ~에 대해 감사하다 **careful** 신중한, 조심하는 **right away** 지금 바로, 당장

33. 여자는 무슨 문제점을 언급하는가?
(A) 엉뚱한 제품을 배송 받았다.
(B) 특별 할인이 제공되지 않았다.
(C) 한 제품이 운송 중에 손상되었다.
(D) 구입 제품 하나가 빠져 있다.

해설 대화 시작 부분에 여자가 자신이 구매한 제품 하나가 집에 갔을 때 가방에 들어 있지 않았음을 알게 되었다고(when I got home I realized one of the items I paid for wasn't in my bag) 말하고 있다. 따라서 구매 제품이 빠져 있다는 의미로 쓰인 (D)가 정답이다.

어휘 **wrong** 잘못된, 틀린, 엉뚱한 **damaged** 손상된 **in transit** 운송 중에 **missing** 빠진, 없는, 분실된

Paraphrase one of the items I paid for
→ one of her purchases
wasn't in my bag
→ missing

34. 시각자료를 보시오. 여자에게 얼마의 액수가 환불될 것인가?
(A) 7.50 달러
(B) 9.50달러
(C) 6.99달러
(D) 5.99달러

해설 여자에게 환불되는 액수를 묻고 있으므로 시각자료에 제시된 제품 명칭에 초점을 맞춰 들어야 한다. 대화 중반부에 남자가 빠져 있는 제품이 무엇이었는지 묻는 질문에 대해(Oh, I'm sorry about that, ma'am. Which item was it?) 여자가 수프였다고(It was the soup) 대답하고 있다. 시각자료에 수프의 가격이 5.99 달러로 쓰여 있으므로 (D)가 정답이다.

어휘 **amount** 액수, 금액 **refund** ~을 환불해 주다

35. 남자는 곧이어 무엇을 할 것 같은가?
(A) 비용을 송금한다.
(B) 동료 직원에게 이야기한다.
(C) 새로운 재고품을 주문한다.
(D) 제품 하나를 배송한다.

해설 대화 후반부에 여자가 한 직원에게 다음 번에 더 신중하게 일하도록 요청하라고 부탁하자(maybe you should ask the worker to be more careful next time) 남자가 지금 바로 그렇게 하겠다고(Yes, I'll do that right away) 대답하고 있다. 따라서 동료 직원에게 이야기한다는 의미로 쓰인 (B)가 정답임을 알 수 있다.

어휘 **payment** (지불) 비용 **coworker** 동료 직원 **stock** 재고(품)

Questions 36-38 refer to the following conversation and pie chart.

M: 36 Let's review the plans for the proposed construction of the gym in the basement of the apartment building. Tracey, did you bring the surveys that our tenants filled out?

W: Yes, and most tenants are very excited about having a room where they can exercise. However, judging from the survey responses, the tenants are most worried about security.

M: Well, we're installing personal lockers, so there's nothing for them to worry about. So, 37 let's move on to the next biggest concern the tenants have and talk about that.

W: Sure. Actually, 38 I made several copies of this chart that shows a breakdown of the main concerns.

M: Great work! If you don't mind, 38 please pass out a copy to each member of the tenants association before we continue.

남: 아파트 건물 지하로 제안된 체육관 공사 계획을 검토해 봅시다. 트레이시 씨, 우리 세입자들이 작성한 설문 조사지를 갖고 오셨나요?

여: 네, 그리고 대부분의 세입자들이 운동할 수 있는 공간이 생기는 것에 대해 아주 들떠 있어요. 하지만, 설문 조사 답변으로 판단해 볼 때, 세입자들이 대부분 보안에 대해 걱정하고 있어요.

남: 저, 우리가 개인 사물함을 설치하기 때문에, 그분들이 걱정할 것이 전혀 없습니다. 그럼, 세입자들이 그 다음으로 갖고 있는 가장 큰 우려 사항으로 넘어가서 얘기해 봅시다.

여: 좋아요. 실은, 세분화된 주요 우려 사항을 보여주는 이 차트 사본을 여러 장 만들었어요.

남: 아주 잘 하셨어요! 괜찮으시면, 계속 얘기하기 전에 세입자 협회의 각 회원에게 한 장씩 나눠주시기 바랍니다.

세입자 우려 사항

- 불청객 10%
- 영업 시간 20%
- 보안 문제 45%
- 월간 요금 25%

어휘 **review** ~을 검토하다, 살펴보다 **proposed** 제안된 **construction** 공사, 건설 **basement** 지하(실) **survey** 설문 조사(지) **tenant** 세입자 **fill out** ~을 작성하다 **exercise** 운동하다 **judge from** ~을 통해 판단하다 **response** 답변, 응답 **be worried about** ~에 대해 걱정하다 **install** ~을 설치하다 **concern** 우려 **make a copy of** ~의 사본을 만들다, ~을 복사하다 **breakdown** 세분화, 명세(서) **pass out** ~을 나눠주다 **association** 협회 **continue** 계속하다 **uninvited** 초대되지 않은

36. 어떤 종류의 시설이 이야기되고 있는가?
(A) 피트니스 룸
(B) 수영장
(C) 주차장
(D) 비즈니스 센터

해설 대화 시작 부분에 남자가 아파트 건물 지하로 제안된 체육관 공사 계획을 검토해 보자고(Let's review the plans for the proposed construction of the gym in the basement of the apartment building) 말하면서 체육관 시설을 짓는 것과 관련된 내용으로 대화가 진행되고 있다. 따라서 (A)가 정답이다.

어휘 **facility** 시설(물)

Paraphrase gym
→ fitness room

37. 시각자료를 보시오. 남자는 어떤 세입자 우려 사항을 이야기하고 싶어하는가?
(A) 보안 문제
(B) 월간 요금
(C) 운영 시간
(D) 불청객

해설 대화 중반부에 남자는 두 번째로 가장 큰 우려 사항으로 넘어가 얘기하자고(let's move on to the next biggest concern the tenants have and talk about that) 제안하고 있다. 그래프에서 두 번째로 높은 비율로 표기된 것이 25%에 해당되는 Monthly fees이므로 (B)가 정답이다.

38. 여자는 곧이어 무엇을 할 것 같은가?
(A) 세입자들에게 설문 조사하는 일
(B) 프로젝트 예산을 제시하는 일
(C) 문서를 배부하는 일
(D) 공지를 게시하는 일

해설 대화 후반부에 여자가 차트 사본을 여러 장 만들었다고(I made several copies of this chart that shows a breakdown of the main concerns) 알리자, 남자가 그것을 회원들에게 나눠주라고(please pass out a copy to each member of the tenants association before we continue) 말하고 있다. 이는 해당 복사본을 배부하라는 뜻이므로 (C)가 정답이다.

어휘 **survey** v. ~에게 설문 조사하다 **present** ~을 제시하다, 발표하다 **budget** 예산 **distribute** ~을 배부하다, 나눠주다 **put up** ~을 게시하다, 내걸다 **notice** 공지, 알림

Paraphrase pass out a copy to each member
→ Distribute documents

Part 4

Questions 39-41 refer to the following telephone message.

Hi, Howard. It's Dominique. **39** I spent the morning going over your initial designs for the Ellsworth Foundation's new building, and I have some feedback for you. I think there was a miscommunication. **40** The Ellsworth Foundation gave very specific guidelines for the building's style and arrangement, but you included a lot of your own ideas. I'm sorry I didn't oversee your work more. I know you spent a lot of time on this already. **41** You should take the rest of the week off, though. Then you can come back ready to restart the project. I'll see you on Monday.

안녕하세요, 하워드 씨. 도미니크입니다. 저는 엘스워즈 재단의 새 건물에 대한 귀하의 디자인 초안을 검토하면서 오전 시간을 보냈는데, 귀하께 말씀 드릴 의견이 있습니다. 제 생각에는 잘못된 의사 전달이 있었던 것 같습니다. 엘스워즈 재단은 해당 건물의 스타일 및 배치에 대해 아주 구체적인 가이드라인을 제공해 주었지만, 귀하께서는 본인의 아이디어를 많이 포함하셨습니다. 귀하께서 작업하신 것을 더 많이 관리해 드리지 못해 죄송합니다. 귀하께서 이 작업에 이미 많은 시간을 쏟으셨다는 것을 알고 있습니다. 하지만 귀하께서는 이번 주의 나머지 시간을 쉬셔야 합니다. 그래야 프로젝트를 다시 시작하실 준비가 되어 돌아오실 수 있습니다. 그럼 월요일에 뵙겠습니다.

어휘 spend A -ing ~하는 데 A의 시간을 소비하다 go over ~을 검토하다 initial 처음의, 초기의 feedback 의견 miscommunication 잘못된 의사소통 specific 구체적인 arrangement 배치, 배열 include ~을 포함하다 one's own 자기 자신의 oversee (제대로 되는지) 관리하다, 감독하다 take A off A만큼 쉬다 the rest of ~의 나머지 ready to do ~할 준비가 된

39. 화자는 무슨 업계에서 근무하는가?
(A) 건축
(B) 출판 저널리즘
(C) 접객업
(D) 방송

해설 화자가 일하는 업계를 묻고 있으므로 특정 업무나 활동 또는 서비스 등과 관련된 표현이 제시되는 부분에서 단서를 찾아야 한다. 담화 시작 부분에 화자가 Ellsworth Foundation의 새 건물에 대한 상대방의 디자인 초안을 검토했다고(I spent the morning going over your initial designs for the Ellsworth Foundation's new building) 알리는 내용을 통해 (A)가 정답임을 알 수 있다.

어휘 industry 업계 hospitality (호텔 등의) 접객업

40. 화자는 왜 "제 생각에는 잘못된 의사 전달이 있었던 것 같습니다"라고 말하는가?
(A) 받지 못한 전화에 대해 답변하기 위해
(B) 추가 회의를 권하기 위해
(C) 이전에 받은 메시지를 수정하기 위해
(D) 프로젝트가 마음에 들지 않음을 나타내기 위해

해설 해당 문장은 담화의 초반부에 들을 수 있는데, 바로 뒤이어 Ellsworth Foundation가 제공한 구체적인 가이드라인과 달리 자신만의 아이디어를 많이 포함했다는(The Ellsworth Foundation gave very specific guidelines ~, but you included a lot of your own ideas) 말을 들을 수 있다. 이는 허용 가능한 상태의 작업이 아님을 의미하는 것이므로 (D)가 정답임을 알 수 있다.

어휘 respond to ~에 답변하다, 응답하다 missed (전화 통화) 받지 못한, 놓친 additional 추가의 revise ~을 수정하다, 개정하다 indicate ~을 나타내다, 가리키다 disapproval

못마땅함, 반감

41. 화자는 청자에게 무엇을 하도록 제안하는가?
(A) 며칠 휴식을 취할 것
(B) 기사 하나를 읽어 볼 것
(C) 신입 사원 한 명을 고용할 것
(D) 작업 장소를 방문할 것

해설 담화의 후반부에 화자는 이번 주의 나머지 시간을 쉬도록 제안하고 있으므로(You should take the rest of the week off, though) 며칠 휴식을 취한다는 의미로 쓰인 (A)가 정답이다.

어휘 article (신문 등의) 기사 work site 작업 장소, 근무지

Questions 42-44 refer to the following advertisement.

Are you sick of newspapers, books, and magazines? If so, come to Ginivers! **42** We have the largest range of electronic reading devices in the country, so we are confident that we can satisfy all your technology needs. **43** We even have a practice area where serious fans of technology can use and play with most of our electronic devices. And if you can't come into the store, we have an online store where you can buy all our products from the comfort of your own home. And **44** if you do choose to buy from our online store, you'll receive a five percent discount off any item.

신문, 책, 잡지가 지겨우십니까? 그렇다면 지니버스로 오세요! 저희는 전국에서 가장 다양한 종류의 전자책 단말기들을 보유하고 있으므로 귀하의 모든 기술적 필요 사항을 만족시켜드릴 자신이 있습니다. 저희는 기술에 진지한 관심을 갖고 계신 분들이 저희 전자 기기들의 대부분을 이용해보고 작동해볼 수 있는 시범 이용 구역도 갖추고 있습니다. 그리고 매장에 오실 수 없다면 여러분 댁에서 편안하게 저희의 모든 제품을 구매하실 수 있는 온라인 매장이 있습니다. 그리고 저희 온라인 매장에서 구매하시기로 선택하시면 모든 제품에 대해 5%의 할인을 받으실 수 있습니다.

어휘 be sick of ~에 싫증나다, ~이 지겹다 if so 만일 그렇다면 have the largest range of 가장 많은 종류의 ~을 보유하다 electronic reading device 전자책 단말기 in the country 국내에서 be confident that ~라고 확신하다 satisfy ~을 만족시키다 technology needs 기술 관련 필요사항 practice area 시범 사용 구역 serious 진지한 electronic devices 전자 기기 online store 온라인 매장 product 제품 from the comfort of one's own home ~의 집에서 편안하게 choose to do ~하기로 선택하다 receive a 5 percent discount off any item 그 어떤 물건에 대해서도 5% 할인을 받다

42. 지니버스는 어떤 종류의 업체인가?

    (A) 온라인 서점
    (B) 철물점
    (C) 전자제품점
    (D) 편의점

해설 광고 첫 부분에서 Ginivers라는 매장을 언급하며 We have the largest range of electronic reading devices 라고 소개하고 있다. 전자책 단말기(electronic reading devices)를 취급할 만한 곳은 (C)이다.

어휘 **hardware store** 철물점

43. 지니버스는 기술 제품 애호가들에게 무엇을 제공하는가?

    (A) 제품 시범 이용 구역
    (B) 안내 책자
    (C) 무료 전자 기기
    (D) 월간 카탈로그

해설 질문의 핵심어 technology enthusiasts를 담화에서는 serious fans of technology라고 표현하고 있다. 이들에 대해 말하면서 기술 제품에 관심이 많은 사람들이 제품을 사용해 볼 수 있는 시범 이용 구역을 갖추고 있다고(We even have a practice area where serious fans of technology can use and play with most of our electronic devices)하므로 (A)가 정답이다.

어휘 **trial** 시범 이용, 무료 체험 **monthly** 월간의

Paraphrase practice area
      → product trial area

44. 광고는 온라인 주문에 대해 뭐라고 말하는가?

    (A) 배송비가 발생하지 않는다.
    (B) 할인을 받을 수 있다.
    (C) 5일 이내에 배송된다.
    (D) 무료 선물 포장을 포함한다.

해설 online orders가 핵심이므로 이와 관련 있는 표현이 언급 되는 곳에 귀 기울인다. 담화 후반부에 온라인 매장이 소개되고 있는데, 이곳에 모든 제품들을 갖추고 있으며, 무엇을 구매하든 5% 할인을 해주겠다고(if you do choose to buy from our online store, you'll receive a five percent discount off any item) 한다. 따라서 (B)가 정답이다.

어휘 **incur** ~을 발생시키다 **delivery charge** 배송비 **be eligible for** ~을 받을 자격이 있다 **ship** v. ~을 배송하다 **within 5 days** 5일 이내에 **include** ~을 포함하다 **giftwrapping** 선물 포장 (재료)

Questions 45-47 refer to the following excerpt from a meeting.

> I gathered you all here this morning to discuss a problem we've been having with our online store. Several customers have reported that the pictures accompanying our listed products are not the correct pictures. **45** Your team handles all Web site content for Bex Sportswear, so **46** this issue is something you must be held responsible for. We expect more from you! In order to fix the issues with our online catalog, **47** I'd like all of you to stay late tomorrow night. So, please keep working on the images until 8:30 P.M. That should give you ample time to fix all the problems.

우리 온라인 매장에 대해 겪고 있는 문제점을 논의하기 위해 오늘 아침 이곳으로 여러분 모두를 소집했습니다. 여러 고객들께서 우리 목록에 올려져 있는 제품에 동반된 사진들이 정확한 사진들이 아니라고 알려주셨습니다. 여러분이 속해 있는 팀이 우리 벡스 스포츠 의류사의 웹 사이트에 있는 모든 내용을 처리하기 때문에 이 사안은 여러분께서 반드시 책임져 주셔야 하는 일입니다. **우리는 여러분으로부터 더 많은 것을 기대하고 있습니다!** 우리 온라인 카탈로그의 문제점들을 바로잡기 위해서, 저는 여러분 모두가 내일 밤에 늦게까지 남아 주시기를 바랍니다. 그래서 오후 8시 30분까지 이미지들에 대한 작업을 계속해 주시기 바랍니다. 이렇게 하시면 모든 문제점들을 바로잡는 데 충분한 시간을 가지실 수 있을 것입니다.

어휘 **gather** ~을 소집하다, 모으다 **report that** ~라고 알리다, 보고하다 **accompany** ~에 동반되다 **listed** 목록에 올려진, 기재된 **correct** 정확한, 올바른 **handle** ~을 처리하다 **content** 내용(물) **issue** 사안, 문제 **hold A responsible for B** A에게 B에 대한 책임을 지우다 **expect** ~을 기대하다, 예상하다 **in order to do** ~하기 위해 **fix** ~을 바로잡다, 고치다 **would like A to do** A에게 ~하기를 원하다 **stay late** 늦게까지 남아 있다 **keep -ing** 계속 ~하다 **work on** ~을 맡아 작업하다 **until** (지속) ~까지 **ample** 충분한

45. 청자들은 누구일 것 같은가?

    (A) 회계사들
    (B) 안전 전문가들
    (C) 웹 디자이너들
    (D) 행사 조직 담당자들

해설 화자는 회의를 하게 된 배경을 먼저 설명한 후, 담화 중반부에 가서 청자들이 소속된 팀이 모든 웹 사이트 내용을 처리한다고 (Your team handles all Web site content) 알리고 있다. 이를 통해 청자들은 웹 디자이너들임을 알 수 있으므로 (C)가 정답이다.

어휘 **accountant** 회계사 **expert** 전문가 **organizer** 조직자, 주최자

46. 화자가 "우리는 여러분으로부터 더 많은 것을 기대하고 있습니다"라고 말할 때 의미하는 것은 무엇인가?

(A) 더 많은 직원들을 고용할 계획이다.
(B) 청자들에게 실망한 상태이다.
(C) 과중한 업무량에 대해 사과하고 있다.
(D) 청자들이 만족하기를 바라고 있다.

해설 해당 문장은 담화 중반부에 청자들이 반드시 책임져야 하는 일이라고(this issue is something you must be held responsible for) 언급한 다음에 들을 수 있다. 즉 앞서 언급한 문제점과 관련해 청자들이 제대로 책임지고 처리하지 못한 것에 대해 한 말에 해당하므로 이를 실망한 상태라는 말로 표현한 (B)가 정답이다.

어휘 **be disappointed in** ~에 실망하다 **apologize for** ~에 대해 사과하다 **heavy workload** 과중한 업무량 **satisfied** 만족한

47. 청자들은 내일 무엇을 할 것인가?

(A) 교육 시간에 참석한다.
(B) 일부 고객들에게 연락한다.
(C) 추가 근무를 한다.
(D) 일부 장비를 수리한다.

해설 tomorrow라는 시점 표현이 제시되는 부분에서 단서를 찾아야 한다. 화자는 담화 후반부에 내일 밤에 늦게까지 남아 주기를 바란다는 말과 함께(I'd like all of you to stay late tomorrow night) 오후 8시 30분까지 이미지들에 대한 작업을 계속해 달라고 요청하고 있다. 이는 추가 근무를 하는 것을 의미하므로 (C)가 정답이다.

어휘 **session** (특정 활동을 위한) 시간 **contact** ~에게 연락하다 **work additional hours** 추가 근무를 하다 **equipment** 장비

Questions 48-50 refer to the following excerpt from a book reading and chapter list.

Hello, ladies and gentlemen. I'm glad so many of you have come along to the bookstore to hear me read from my new release, *Become a Better You*. Before we begin, **48** I can see that many of you have bought a copy of my book. Thanks a lot. It means a lot to me. When I wrote this book, my intention was to help as many people as possible, and I hope I've succeeded. To start today's reading, **49** I'd like to skip the first chapter and go straight to chapter 2. Oh, the owner of the bookstore has told me that the sun will come out after lunch, so **50** we'll be moving up to the rooftop garden for the second part of my reading. Okay, let's begin.

안녕하세요, 신사 숙녀 여러분. 저는 이렇게 많은 분들께서 제 신작 <더 나은 당신이 되기>를 제가 낭독해 드리는 것을 들으러 서점까지 와 주셔서 기쁘게 생각합니다. 시작하기 전에, 많은 분들께서 제 책을 구입하신 것을 알 수 있습니다. 대단히 감사합니다. 이는 제게 아주 뜻 깊은 일입니다. 제가 이 책을 썼을 때, 제 의도는 가능한 한 많은 분들을 돕는 것이었고, 제가 성공을 거두었기를 바라고 있습니다. 오늘의 낭독 행사를 시작하면서, 첫 번째 챕터는 건너 뛰고 두 번째 챕터로 곧바로 넘어가고자 합니다. 아, 이 서점의 사장님께서 점심 식사 후에 해가 날 것이라고 말씀해 주셨기 때문에, 제 낭독 행사의 2부는 옥상의 정원으로 옮겨서 진행하겠습니다. 자, 시작해 보겠습니다.

더 나은 당신이 되기
존 해니티 저

챕터 1: 어려운 상황에 대처하기
챕터 2: 사람들이 당신을 좋아하게 만들기
챕터 3: 타인들과 잘 협력하기
챕터 4: 유능한 리더 되기

어휘 **come along to** ~로 오다, 가다 **hear A do** A가 ~하는 것을 듣다 **release** 출시(된 것), 공개 **see that** ~임을 알다, 확인하다 **a copy of** ~의 1권, 1부, 1장 **mean a lot to** ~에게 큰 의미가 되다 **intention** 의도, 계획 **as many A as possible** 가능한 한 많은 A **succeed** 성공하다 **skip** ~을 건너뛰다 **go straight to** ~로 곧바로 가다 **owner** 소유주 **tell A that** A에게 ~라고 말하다 **come out** 나오다 **move up to** ~로 올라가다 **rooftop** 옥상 **handle** ~에 대처하다, ~을 다루다, 처리하다 **situation** 상황 **make A do** A가 ~하게 만들다 **cooperate with** ~와 협력하다 **effective** (사람이) 유능한

48. 화자는 무엇에 대해 청자들에게 감사하는가?

(A) 긍정적인 후기를 작성한 것
(B) 매장 개업식에 참석한 것
(C) 작문 강좌에 등록한 것
(D) 책을 구입한 것

해설 담화 시작 부분에 많은 사람들이 자신의 책을 구입한 것을 알 수 있다고(I can see that many of you have bought a copy of my book) 말한 후에 감사의 인사를 전하고 있다. 따라서 책을 구입한 것이 그 이유임을 알 수 있으므로 (D)가 정답이다.

어휘 **thank A for B** B에 대해 A에게 감사하다 **positive** 긍정적인 **review** (이용) 후기, 평가, 의견 **enroll in** ~에 등록하다 **purchase** ~을 구입하다

49. 시각자료를 보시오. 화자는 오늘 아침에 무슨 주제를 다룰 것인가?

(A) 어려운 상황에 대처하기
(B) 사람들이 당신을 좋아하게 만들기
(C) 타인들과 잘 협력하기
(D) 유능한 리더 되기

해설 챕터별 주제를 찾아야 하므로 시각자료에서 챕터의 순서 및 주제 내용을 미리 확인해 둔 후에 들어야 한다. 담화 후반부에 첫 번째 챕터를 건너뛰고 두 번째 챕터로 곧장 넘어가겠다고 (I'd like to skip the first chapter and go straight to chapter 2) 알리고 있으므로 시각자료에서 두 번째 챕터에 해당되는 주제인 (B)가 정답이다.

어휘 **cover** (주제 등) ~을 다루다

50. 화자는 도서 낭독 시간의 두 번째 파트에 관해 무슨 말을 하는가?

(A) 옥외에 있는 장소에서 열릴 것이다.
(B) 다른 작가에 의해 제공될 것이다.
(C) 참석자들이 다과를 이용할 수 있을 것이다.
(D) 책마다 사인을 해 줄 것이다.

해설 낭독 행사의 두 번째 파트가 질문의 핵심이므로 이 명칭이 제시되는 부분이 있다는 것을 예상하고 들어야 한다. 담화 후반부에 옥상에 있는 정원에서 행사의 두 번째 파트를 진행할 것이라고(we'll be moving up to the rooftop garden for the second part of my reading) 알리고 있다. 따라서 행사 장소와 관련해 옥상에 있는 정원과 같은 의미에 해당되는 '옥외에 있는 장소'가 언급된 (A)가 정답이다.

어휘 **session** (특정 활동을 위한) 시간 **hold** (행사 등) ~을 개최하다, 열다 **location** 장소, 위치, 지점 **present** ~을 제공하다, 제시하다, 발표하다 **author** 작가, 저자 **refreshments** 다과 **available to** ~가 이용 가능한 **attendee** 참석자 **sign** ~에 사인해 주다

Paraphrase rooftop garden
→ outdoor location

DAY 02　RC Half Test

Part 5

1.

정답　(A)

해석　세렌느 리조트에서 라피즈 산으로 가는 버스 여행은 한 차례 예정된 30분의 정차 시간을 포함해 약 5시간이 소요될 것이다.

해설　빈칸이 형용사 역할을 하는 숫자 표현과 명사구 사이에 위치해 있으므로 빈칸은 명사구를 수식하는 형용사 자리이다. 그런데 선택지에 형용사가 없으므로 형용사의 역할을 대신할 수 있는 분사 중에서 정답을 골라야 하는데, 정차 일정은 사람에 의해 정해지는 대상이므로 수동의 의미를 나타낼 수 있는 과거분사 (A) scheduled가 정답이다.

어휘　take ~의 시간이 걸리다　approximately 약, 대략

2.

정답　(C)

해석　은퇴 기념 저녁 만찬에서, 스펙 씨는 30년 간의 재직에 대한 공로를 인정 받아 비싼 손목시계를 받았다.

해설　빈칸이 전치사 in과 of 사이에 위치해 있으므로 빈칸은 전치사 in의 목적어 역할을 할 명사 자리이다. 따라서 (C) recognition 이 정답이다.

어휘　retirement 은퇴　in recognition of ~에 대한 공로를 인정해, ~에 대한 표창으로　recognize ~을 인정하다, ~을 표창하다

3.

정답　(A)

해석　중요한 사안들을 더 자주 논의하기 위해, 부서장님들은 이제 매주 화요일과 목요일에 모인다.

해설　빈칸이 바로 뒤에 'A and B'의 구조로 위치한 요일을 목적어로

취할 전치사 자리이므로 요일을 목적어로 취할 수 있는 전치사 (A) on이 정답이다.

어휘　discuss ~을 논의하다, ~을 이야기하다　issue 사안, 문제　frequently 자주, 빈번히　into (이동) ~ 안으로, (변화 등) ~로　behind prep. (위치) ~ 뒤에, (진행 등) ~보다 뒤처져 ad. 뒤에

4.

정답　(D)

해석　기술자는 직원들이 3일마다 에어컨의 필터를 청소하도록 권장했다.

해설　동사 recommend의 목적어 역할을 하는 that절이 완전하므로 빈칸 이하는 부사의 역할을 해야 한다. 따라서 빈칸 뒤에 위치한 three days와 함께 '~마다'라는 의미로 주기를 나타낼 때 사용하는 (D) every가 정답이다.

어휘　technician 기술자　recommend that ~하도록 권장하다, 추천하다　nearly 거의　most a. 가장 많은, 대부분의 ad. 가장 많이　previous 이전의

5.

정답　(D)

해석　힐플립 소프트웨어 사의 직원들은 회사의 폐업을 막기 위해 급여 삭감을 받아들이는 데 동의했다.

해설　빈칸 앞에 명사와 전치사구가 있고, 빈칸 뒤에는 to부정사와 목적을 나타내는 in order to가 이끄는 구만 있으므로 빈칸 은 동사 자리이다. 따라서 선택지 중 유일한 동사인 (D) have agreed가 정답이다.

어휘　pay cut 급여 삭감　prevent ~을 막다, 방지하다　closure 폐업, 폐쇄　agreement 합의(서), 계약(서)

6.

정답　(B)

해석　건물 중앙 출입구의 경사로는 장애가 있으신 고객들께서 귀하의 부동산 사무실을 더 잘 이용하실 수 있도록 만들어 드릴 것입니다.

해설　빈칸 앞에 위치한 동사 make는 5형식 동사로서 「make + 목적어 + 목적격보어」의 구조로 쓰이므로 목적어 뒤에 위치한 빈칸에 목적격보어로 쓰일 수 있는 형용사 (B) accessible이 정답이다.

어휘　ramp 경사로　realty 부동산　handicapped 장애가 있는　accessible 이용 가능한, 접근 가능한　access n. 접근, 이용 v. ~에 접근하다, ~을 이용하다

7.

정답 (A)

해석 사막 기후 조건에서도 자랄 수 있는 교배종 딸기는 상당한 연구와 실험의 결과물이다.

해설 빈칸이 정관사와 전치사 사이에 위치해 있으므로 명사 자리이다. 선택지 중 명사는 (A) product와 (B) producer인데 빈칸에는 문장의 주어인 딸기를 나타낼 수 있는 것이 들어가야 하므로 사물 명사 (A) product가 정답이다.

어휘 **hybrid** 교배종의 **substantial** 상당한, 중대한 **product** 결과물, 제품 **producer** 생산자 **produce** ~을 생산하다

8.

정답 (B)

해석 구직자들은 스스로 온라인 적성 시험을 치러야 하며, 메모나 교재를 참조하지 말아야 한다.

해설 빈칸 앞에 전치사가 있으므로 빈칸은 전치사의 목적어 역할을 할 수 있는 대명사가 필요하다. 또한, 행위 주체자에 해당하는 주어 Job seekers 자신을 가리켜야 하므로 재귀대명사 (B) themselves가 정답이다.

어휘 **job seeker** 구직자 **aptitude** 적성, 소질 **by oneself** 스스로, 혼자서 **refer to** ~을 참조하다

9.

정답 (C)

해석 볼러 로펌의 여름 인턴 프로그램에 지원하는 데 관심이 있는 학생은 누구든 프랑크 볼러 씨에게 직접 이메일을 보내야 한다.

해설 빈칸 뒤에 위치한 전치사 in과 어울릴 수 있으면서 어떤 학생이 인턴 프로그램에 지원하기 위해 이메일을 보내야 하는지를 나타낼 수 있는 형용사가 필요하므로 in과 함께 '~에 관심이 있는'이라는 의미를 구성하는 (C) interested가 정답이다.

어휘 **apply for** ~에 지원하다, ~을 신청하다 **directly** 직접, 곧장, 즉시 **directed** 안내된, 지시에 따른, 통제된 **experienced** 경험 많은 **concerned** 우려하는

10.

정답 (D)

해석 제품 및 배송 문제와 관련된 모든 불만 사항이 저희 고객 지원팀에 의해 효율적으로 처리됩니다.

해설 수동태 동사를 구성하는 be동사 are와 과거분사 handled 사이에 위치한 빈칸은 이 과거분사를 앞에서 수식할 부사 자리이므로 (D) efficiently가 정답이다.

어휘 **shipping** 배송 **handle** ~을 처리하다, ~을 다루다 **efficient** 효율적인 **efficiency** 효율(성) **efficiently** 효율적으로

11.

정답 (C)

해석 제안된 쇼핑몰에 대해 주민들이 찬성하는지를 묻기 위해 시 의회가 공청회를 개최했다.

해설 to부정사로 사용된 동사 ask 뒤에 빈칸이 있고 그 뒤로 주어와 동사가 포함된 절이 이어져 있다. 따라서, 빈칸 이하 부분의 절이 타동사 ask의 목적어 역할을 하는 명사절이 되어야 알맞으므로 명사절 접속사 (C) whether가 정답이다.

어휘 **public forum** 공청회 **ask whether** ~인지 아닌지 묻다 **in favor of** ~에 찬성하는 **proposed** 제안된

12.

정답 (C)

해석 일정한 작동 속도를 유지하기 위해, 전원 상태가 5퍼센트로 떨어질 때마다 배터리를 교체하시기 바랍니다.

해설 빈칸 앞에는 명령문 구조의 절이 있고, 빈칸 뒤에는 주어와 동사를 포함한 절이 있으므로 빈칸은 이 두 개의 절을 연결할 접속사 자리이다. 따라서 선택지 중 유일한 접속사인 (C) whenever가 정답이다.

어휘 **maintain** ~을 유지하다 **steady** 일정한, 꾸준한 **pace** 속도 **operation** 가동, 작동, 운영 **fall to** ~로 떨어지다, 줄어들다 **by contrast** 대조적으로 **in summary** 요컨대, 요약하자면 **rather than** ~하지 않고, ~하는 대신

13.

정답 (B)

해석 미드랜드 바이오테크는 구직 지원자들의 역량을 밝혀내도록 관리자들을 돕기 위해 다양한 기술을 지닌 모든 지원자들을 테스트한다.

해설 선택지가 모두 다른 동사로 구성되어 있으므로 해석을 통해 알맞은 어휘를 골라야 한다. 관리자들이 구직 지원자들의 역량과 관련해 할 수 있는 일에 해당되는 의미를 나타내야 하므로 '~을 밝혀내다, ~을 결정하다' 등을 뜻하는 (B) determine이 정답이다.

어휘 **various** 다양한 **capability** 역량, 능력 **evolve** 발전하다, ~을 발전시키다 **determine** ~을 밝혀내다, ~을 결정하다 **assume** ~라고 생각하다, (역할 등) ~을 맡다 **doubt** ~을 의심하다, ~라고 생각하지 않다

14.

정답 (C)

해석 부서의 업무 일정이 주말 동안 게시판에 공지되려면 반드시 금요일 전에 제출되어야 합니다.

해설 빈칸 뒤에 특정한 일이 완료되어야 하는 시점을 나타내는 명사가 있으므로 '~ 이전에'라는 의미로 쓰이는 (C) before가 정답이다.

어휘 **departmental** 부서의 **post** ~을 게시하다 **over the weekend** 주말에 걸쳐 **beside** ~옆에 **next to** ~ 옆에

15.

정답 (C)

해석 놀레스 자문 그룹은 대기업들과 함께 일하고, 소기업들에게는 상담 서비스를 거의 제공하지 않는다.

해설 선택지가 모두 부사로 구성되어 있어 해석을 통해 알맞은 부사를 골라야 한다. 빈칸 앞에 대기업들과 함께 일한다는 내용과 접속사 and 뒤에 작은 회사들에게 상담을 제공한다는 상반된 내용이 나와 있으므로 부정을 나타내는 부사 (C) rarely가 정답이다.

어휘 corporation 기업, 회사 rarely 거의 ~않다 faintly 희미하게, 어렴풋이 abruptly 갑작스럽게 permanently 영구히, 불변으로

16.

정답 (B)

해석 지역 주민들께서 주민 회의 시간에 제기하신 사안들이 보고서의 형태로 스완슨 시장님께 직접 전달될 것입니다.

해설 선택지가 모두 다른 명사로 구성되어 있으므로 해석을 통해 알맞은 어휘를 골라야 한다. 빈칸에 쓰일 명사는 지역 주민들이 회의 시간에 제기할 수 있는 것을 나타내야 하므로 '사안, 문제'를 뜻하는 (B) Issues가 정답이다.

어휘 bring up ~을 제기하다, (말, 의견 등) ~을 꺼내다 pass A on to B A를 B에게 전달하다 edition (출판물 등의) 판, 호 attendance 참석, 참석자 수

Part 6

17-20.

수신: 마리아 디아즈 <mdiaz@bramblesbistro.com>
발신: 프레디 무어 <fmoore@bramblesbistro.com>
제목: 새로운 공급업체
날짜: 8월 10일

안녕하세요, 마리아 씨,

아시다시피, 우리의 현 공급업체에서 계속되는 문제들 **17** 때문에 우리 레스토랑에 필요한 신선한 농산물을 구입하는 데 대한 다른 선택권들을 계속 살펴보고 있습니다. 조사를 좀 실시한 끝에, 우리가 그린우드 팜을 선택해야 한다고 생각합니다. 이 농장은 아주 합리적인 가격에 고품질 과일과 채소를 **18** 제공하는 것으로 알려져 있습니다.

제가 다음 주 화요일로 그린우드 팜의 소유주와 갖는 회의 일정을 잡아두었으며, 사업 계약서의 조항들에 대해 합의에 **19** 이를 것으로 확신합니다. 모든 것이 순조롭게 진행된다는 가정 하에, 우리는 다음 달부터 이곳과 거래를 하게 될 것입니다. **20** 이는 우리가 물품 공급에 대해 겪어 왔던 문제들을 해결해줄 것입니다. 오늘 있을 회의 시간에 이 흥미로운 변동 사항을 직원들께 알리시기 바랍니다.

안녕히 계십시오.

프레디 무어, 소유주
브램블스 비스트로

어휘 supplier 공급업체 look into ~을 살펴보다, ~을 조사하다 produce n. 농산물 ongoing 계속되는 current 현재의 carry out ~을 실시하다, ~을 수행하다 reasonable 합리적인 agreement 합의(서) term (계약 등의) 조항, 조건 contract 계약(서) assuming (that) ~라는 가정 하에, 가령 ~라면 go smoothly 순조롭게 진행되다 inform A of B A에게 B를 알리다

17.

정답 (C)

해설 빈칸 앞뒤에 명사구가 있으므로 빈칸은 전치사 자리이다. ongoing problems는 물품 구입과 관련해 다른 선택권을 살펴보게 된 이유로 볼 수 있으므로 '~ 때문에'라는 의미로 이유를 말할 때 사용하는 (C) because of가 정답이다.

어휘 despite ~에도 불구하고 although (비록) ~이기는 하지만 as far as ~만큼 멀리

18.

정답 (D)

해설 빈칸 앞에 수동태로 쓰인 동사 be known은 전치사 for와 결합해 '~로 알려져 있다'라는 의미를 나타내므로 for와 동명사로 구성된 (D) for providing이 정답이다.

19.

정답 (B)

해설 빈칸 뒤에 '합의' 등을 뜻하는 명사가 쓰여져 있는데, 이는 앞선 문장에서 언급한 회의를 통해 달성하고자 하는 목표에 해당되는 것으로 볼 수 있으므로 '~에 이르다, ~에 도달하다'를 뜻하는 (B) reach가 정답이다.

어휘 serve (음식 등) ~을 제공하다, ~에게 서비스를 제공하다 reach ~에 이르다, ~에 도달하다 carry ~을 나르다, ~을 휴대하다 assume ~라고 생각하다, ~라고 추정하다

20.

정답 (A)

해석 **(A) 이는 우리가 물품 공급에 대해 겪어 왔던 문제들을 해결해줄 것입니다.**
(B) 저는 레스토랑의 폐쇄가 그저 일시적인 일이기를 바랍니다.
(C) 따라서, 저는 우리가 계속되는 주문의 규모를 늘려야 한다고 생각합니다.
(D) 귀하께서 해당 직책을 수락하시기로 결정하셔서 기쁩니다.

해설 빈칸 앞에 새로 찾은 회사와의 계약 협의가 순조롭게 진행되면 다음 달부터 거래를 하게 된다는 말이 쓰여 있다. 따라서, 거래를 시작하는 일과 관련된 문장이 빈칸에 쓰여야 알맞으므로 거

래를 시작하는 일을 This로 지칭해 앞선 단락에서 언급한 것과 같은 문제를 해결하게 된다는 말로 새로운 거래 시작에 따른 긍정적인 영향을 알리는 (A)가 정답이다.

어휘 solve ~을 해결하다 supply n. 물품 공급(품) temporary 일시적인, 임시의 as such 따라서, 그러므로 accept ~을 수락하다, ~을 받아들이다 position 직책, 일자리

21-24.

페어팩스 불리바드 57번지
샌프란시스코, CA 94104

와이어트 씨께,

'원 러브 파운데이션'의 창립자로서, 저는 저희가 이번 여름으로 계획한 일련의 기금 마련 행사에 관해 귀하께 21 알려 드리고자 합니다. 귀하께서는 저희 장기 회원들 중 한 분이시므로, 저는 귀하가 이 행사들을 주최하도록 도움을 주실 적임자라고 생각합니다. 22 또는, 샌프란시스코 내에 위치한 지역 업체들에게 기부를 요청하는 것으로 저희에게 도움을 주실 수도 있습니다.

저희가 계획 중인 첫 번째 행사는 몬태규 공원에서 7월 중으로 23 개최될 콘서트이며, 최소 50팀의 잘 알려진 밴드와 가수들이 특별 출연합니다. 이는 아주 많은 사전 기획 작업을 필요로 할 것이므로, 비교적 큰 행사들을 주최하는 데 있어 경험을 지니고 계신 재단 회원들로 구성된 팀을 꾸리는 중입니다. 저는 저희가 시티 플라자에서 제과제품 판매 행사를 마련했던 작년에 귀하께서 저희 팀에 귀중한 인재이셨던 사실이 기억납니다. 24 다가오는 저희 행사에 도움을 주실 수 있으신지 저에게 알려 주시기 바랍니다.

안녕히 계십시오.

아비가일 글로버, 창립자
원 러브 파운데이션

어휘 founder 창립자, 설립자 a series of 일련의 fundraising 기금 마련, 모금 alternatively 또는, 그렇지 않으면 solicit ~을 요청하다, 간청하다 feature v. ~을 특별 출연시키다, 특징으로 하다 a large amount of 아주 많은 (양의) advance planning 사전 기획 assemble ~을 집합시키다, 모으다 foundation 재단 relatively 비교적, 상대적으로 recall that ~임을 기억하다, 회상하다 asset 인재, 자산 arrange ~을 마련하다, 준비하다 upcoming 다가오는, 곧 있을

21.

정답 (C)

해설 빈칸 앞에 있는 'd like는 would like를 줄여 쓴 것이며, would like는 to부정사와 결합해 '~하고자 하다, ~하고 싶다'라는 의미를 나타내므로 (C) to inform이 정답이다.

22.

정답 (B)

해설 빈칸 앞에는 행사를 주최하는 데 도움을 제공해 달라는 문장이, 빈칸 뒤에는 업체에 기부를 요청하는 것으로 도움을 제공할 수 있다는 말이 쓰여 있다. 이는 도움을 제공하는 데 있어 선택 가능한 방법을 언급하는 흐름에 해당되므로 '또는, 그렇지 않으면'이라는 의미로 선택을 나타낼 때 사용하는 접속부사 (B) Alternatively가 정답이다.

어휘 nevertheless 그럼에도 불구하고 therefore 그러므로, 따라서 afterwards 나중에, 그 뒤로

23.

정답 (D)

해설 빈칸 앞에 위치한 주절에 현재진행형 동사와 함께 현재 콘서트를 계획 중이라고 알리고 있으므로 개최 시점이 미래임을 알 수 있다. 또한, 빈칸이 속한 that절이 수식하는 concert는 사람에 의해 개최되는 것이므로 선택지에 제시된 동사 hold가 수동태로 쓰여야 한다. 따라서 미래시제 수동태의 형태인 (D) will be held가 정답이다.

24.

정답 (B)

해석 (A) 해당 제과제품 판매 행사를 통해 얻은 수익은 여러 좋은 목적을 위해 쓰였습니다.
(B) 다가오는 저희 행사에 도움을 주실 수 있으신지 저에게 알려 주시기 바랍니다.
(C) 귀하께서 최근 보여주신 노고와 헌신에 대해 다시 한번 감사 드립니다.
(D) 콘서트 입장권이 6월 첫째 주 중에 판매에 돌입할 것으로 예상됩니다.

해설 지문 전체적으로 현재 계획 중인 행사에 대해 도움을 제공할 수 있는 방법 등을 설명하고, 상대방의 과거 경험을 언급하는 내용이 제시되어 있다. 따라서 앞으로 열릴 행사에 대해 도움 제공하도록 다시 한번 당부하는 의미를 담은 문장이 쓰여야 자연스러우므로 (B)가 정답이다.

어휘 proceeds 수익(금) cause n. 목적, 대의 help out with ~에 도움을 주다 commitment 헌신 go on sale 판매에 돌입하다

Part 7

25-26.

회람

수신: 길리건 매뉴팩처링 사의 전 직원
날짜: 8월 23일
제목: 토요일 계획

직원 분들께,

개최하기로 예정되어 있었던 해변 콘서트는 취소되었지만 **25** 이번 주말 베일리 해변으로 가는 여행은 계획대로 진행될 것입니다. 자넷 오스본 씨가 씨뷰 호텔 매니저와 상의한 뒤 그 곳 객실에 대해 엄청난 기업 할인을 받았습니다. **26** 오스본 씨는 목요일에 우리 버스 몇 대를 예약해 줄 것이며, 금요일에는 계획된 단체 활동 목록을 나눠 주실 겁니다. 여러분 모두 정말 열심히 일을 해오셨기에, 그에 따른 즐거움과 휴식을 누릴 충분한 자격이 있으시므로 저는 여러분 모두를 해변에서 만나길 바랍니다.

안녕히 계십시오.

존 레들리

어휘 manufacturing 제조 excursion 여행 go ahead 진행되다 despite ~임에도 불구하고 cancelation 취소 be scheduled to do ~할 예정이다 take place 개최되다, 일어나다 receive a discount on ~에 대한 할인을 받다 corporate discount 기업 할인 well-deserved 충분한 자격이 있는 relaxation 휴식

25. 회람은 왜 전송되었는가?
(A) 직원 성과급 제도를 논의하기 위해
(B) 토요일 근무 일정을 직원들에게 통지하기 위해
(C) 행사가 취소된 이유를 설명하기 위해
(D) 회사 여행 세부사항을 확인하기 위해

정답 (D)

해설 지문 전반적으로 베일리 해변으로 가는 여행에 대한 자세한 정보가(The excursion to Bayley Beach this weekend will be going ahead as planned) 나와있다. 기업 할인을 받았다는 정보와 버스 예약, 계획된 단체 활동에 대한 내용들은 모두 여행에 대한 세부사항이므로 (D)가 정답이다.

어휘 incentive plan 성과급 제도 inform A of B A에게 B에 대해 알리다, 통지하다 work schedule 근무 일정 confirm ~을 확인하다 outing 여행, 야유회

26. 자넷 오스본 씨는 목요일에 무엇을 할 계획인가?
(A) 호텔 매니저에게 연락한다.
(B) 행사 장소를 예약한다.
(C) 교통수단을 마련한다.
(D) 활동 일정표를 배부한다.

정답 (C)

해설 지문 중반부에 자넷 오스본 씨가 목요일에 버스 예약을 해 줄 것이라는(She will be booking some buses for us on Thursday) 내용이 있다. 따라서 (C)가 정답이다.

어휘 arrange ~을 마련하다 transportation 교통 수단 distribute ~을 배부하다

27-29.

수신: 데이빗 프렌티스 <dprentice@wendtdesign.com>
발신: 애비게일 데이 <abbyday@wendtdesign.com>
제목: 기록 보관실
날짜: 5월 21일

안녕하세요, 데이빗 씨,

28 이곳 저희 인사부에 문제가 좀 있는데, 도와 주실 수 있을지 궁금합니다. **27** 저희 기록 보관실이 직원 파일과 계약서, 그리고 기타 다양한 회사 양식들로 너무 가득 차 있어서 이 보관실 안으로 들어가는 게 거의 불가능합니다. — [1] —. 일단 안에 들어가면, 찾고 있는 문서를 발견하기 매우 어렵습니다.

— [2] —. 저희가 일부 서류를 근무하고 계시는 층에 있는 보관실로 내려 보낼 수 있을 거라고 생각하고 있었는데, **29** 이곳 저희 부서가 현재 대단히 바쁩니다. — [3] —. **28** 저를 위해 이 문제를 처리할 수 있도록 당신 부서의 직원 두 명을 내어주실 수 있을 것 같으신가요? 오늘 그쪽 마케팅부가 일정이 꽤 느긋한 것으로 알고 있습니다. — [4] —.

감사합니다.

애비게일

어휘 wonder if ~인지 궁금하다 so A that B 너무 A해서 B하다 be full of ~로 가득하다 contract 계약(서) once 일단 ~하면, ~하는 대로 storage 보관, 저장 extremely 대단히, 매우 spare ~을 내어주다, ~을 빌려 주다 take care of ~을 처리하다, ~을 다루다 fairly 꽤, 상당히 relaxed 느긋한

27. 데이 씨가 어떤 문제를 언급하는가?
(A) 기록 보관실 문을 열 수 없다.
(B) 중요한 문서를 둔 곳을 잊었다.
(C) 더 많은 보관 공간을 필요로 한다.
(D) 마감 기한을 충족하지 못했다.

정답 (C)

해설 첫 번째 단락에 기록 보관실이 다양한 문서들로 가득 차 있어서 보관실 안으로 들어가는 게 거의 불가능하다는(Our records room is so full of employee files, contracts, and various other company forms that it is almost impossible to get inside the room) 상황을 알리고 있다. 이는 더 많은 보관 공간이 필요하다는 말이므로 (C)가 정답이다.

어휘 unlock ~을 열다, ~을 해제하다 misplace ~을 둔 곳을 잊다, ~을 분실하다 fail to do ~하지 못하다 meet (요구, 조건 등) ~을 충족하다

28. 데이 씨가 프렌티스 씨에게 무엇을 하도록 요청하는가?
(A) 부서 회의 일정을 재조정하는 일
(B) 일부 직원 파일을 제출하는 일
(C) 마케팅부에 도움을 제공하는 일
(D) 인사부로 직원을 보내는 일

정답 (D)

해설 두 번째 단락에 데이 씨가 상대방 부서의 직원을 보내줄 수 있는지 묻는 것으로(Do you think you could spare a couple of your workers to take care of this for me?) 도움을 요청하고 있으며, 첫 단락에 자신의 부서가 인사부라고(here in the personnel department) 언급하고 있으므로 (D)가 정답이다.

어휘 ask A to do A에게 ~하도록 요청하다 reschedule ~의 일정을 재조정하다 lend a hand 도움을 주다

29. [1], [2], [3], [4]로 표기된 위치들 중에서, 다음 문장이 들어가기에 가장 적절한 곳은 어디인가?

"저희가 오늘 믿을 수 없을 정도로 일손이 부족하다는 점도 도움이 되지 않습니다."

(A) [1]
(B) [2]
(C) [3]
(D) [4]

정답 (C)

해설 제시된 문장은 유사한 추가 정보를 말할 때 사용하는 also와 함께 일손이 부족하다는 점도 문제임을 알리는 의미를 지니고 있다. 따라서, 이와 유사한 정보로서 소속 부서가 현재 대단히 바쁘다고 언급하는 문장(but we are extremely busy here in our department) 뒤에 위치한 [3]에 들어가 두 가지 유사한 정보를 나란히 제공하는 흐름이 되어야 자연스러우므로 (C)가 정답이다.

어휘 It doesn't help that ~라는 점이 도움이 되지 않는다 incredibly 믿을 수 없을 정도로 short-staffed 일손이 부족한, 직원이 부족한

30-32.

> **일자리 공석 # 603 – 청소원**
>
> 멀그루 주식회사는 설비 관리자의 지시를 받으며 근무할 청소원을 모집 중입니다. 합격하신 분은 특정 장소에서 다양한 청소 서비스 제공을 담당하게 됩니다.
>
> **주요 업무:**
> • 쓸기, 걸레질, 진공 청소기 청소하기
> • 조명 기구와 가구 닦기, 먼지 털기, 광택 내기
> • 30(B) 쓰레기통 비우기, 수거 공간으로 쓰레기 치우기

• 청소용품의 재고 관리와 필요할 때마다 30(A) 물품 주문하기
• 30(D) 안전 지침과 정책에 따른 직무 수행하기
• 설비 관리자에게 모든 사고와 위험한 상황들 보고하기

주요 자격요건:
• 과거의 청소 업무 경력은 우대되지만, 필수적이지 않음
• 31 단독으로 그리고 팀의 일원으로서 업무를 잘 수행할 수 있는 능력
• 일에 대한 열정적인 마인드와 뛰어난 시간관리

멀그루 주식회사는 미국과 캐나다 전역에 걸쳐 여러 도시에서 운영하는 최고의 32 기업 및 주택 청소 서비스 기업입니다. 저희는 고객만족을 중요하게 생각하며, 직원들은 지속적으로 높은 수준의 서비스를 제공할 것입니다. 위 직책에 지원하려면, www.mulgrewinc.com을 방문하시기 바랍니다.

어휘 look to do ~할 생각을 하다 report to (직장에서) ~의 지시를 받다, ~에게 업무 보고를 하다 specific 구체적인, 특정한 sweep ~을 쓸다 mop 걸레질 하다, 닦다 vacuum (진공청소기로) 청소하다 wipe 닦다 dust 먼지를 제거하다 polish 광택을 내다, 윤기 있게 닦다 light fixture 조명 기구 rubbish 쓰레기 carry out ~을 수행하다, 실행하다 in accordance with ~에 따라 occurrence 발생, 발생하는 것 advantageous 이로운, 유리한 independently 단독으로, 독립적으로 enthusiastic 열정적인 timekeeping 시간 관리 leading 선도의, 일류의 throughout ~의 전역에 place an emphasis on ~을 중요하게 여기다, ~을 강조하다 consistently 일관적으로, 지속적으로

30. 담당 업무 중 하나로 명시되지 않은 것은 무엇인가?
(A) 청소 용품 구매하기
(B) 쓰레기 처리하기
(C) 가구 수리하기
(D) 안전 절차 준수하기

정답 (C)

해설 주요 업무가 언급되어 있는 두 번째 문단의 세 번째 항목인 쓰레기통 비우기(Emptying waste bins, removing rubbish)에서 (B)를, 네 번째 항목인 물품 주문하기(ordering items) 부분에서 (A)를, 다섯 번째 항목인 안전 지침과 정책에 따라 직무 수행하기(Carrying out duties in accordance with safety guidelines and policies)에서 (D)가 명시되었음을 알 수 있다. 따라서 지문에 언급되지 않은 (C)가 정답이다.

어휘 dispose of ~을 처리하다, 처분하다 procedure 절차

31. 광고에 따르면, 지원자의 자격요건은 무엇인가?
(A) 청소 분야에 경험을 가지고 있어야 한다.
(B) 학업적인 자격을 갖추고 있어야 한다.
(C) 유동적인 근무시간을 받아들일 의향이 있어야 한다.
(D) 혼자서 일을 잘할 수 있어야 한다.

정답 (D)

해설 주요 자격요건을 제시하고 있는 세 번째 문단 두 번째 항목에 독립적으로 일할 수 있는 능력이(The ability to perform work duties well both independently) 언급되어 있으므로 (D)가 정답이다.

어휘 background in ~에서의 경력, 경험 possess ~을 가지고 있다, 소유하다 qualification 자격 be willing to do 기꺼이 ~하다, ~할 의향이 있다 flexible 유동적인 on one's own 혼자서, 단독으로

32. 멀그루 주식회사에 대해 유추할 수 있는 것은?
(A) 본사는 캐나다에 있다.
(B) 직원들로 하여금 정기적인 교육을 받도록 한다.
(C) 기업 고객들에게 서비스를 제공한다.
(D) 여러 개의 공석을 충원하기 위해 노력 중이다.

정답 (C)

해설 마지막 단락에 멀그루 주식회사가 기업 및 주택 청소 서비스를 제공하는 기업이라고(commercial and residential cleaning services company) 소개하고 있으므로 (C)가 정답이다.

어휘 be based in ~를 기반으로 하다 undergo ~을 겪다, 받다 corporate client 기업 고객 fill ~을 채우다

33-36.

> **모로우, 콜린 <오전 9:41>**
> 제닛 씨, 혹시 오늘 아침에 우리 웹 사이트에 접속하려 해 보셨나요? 33 제가 우리 건물 목록을 업데이트하려는 중인데, 페이지가 전혀 뜨지 않네요.
>
> **페리어, 재닛 <오전 9:42>**
> 잠시만요. 흠... 무슨 말씀이신지 알겠어요. 아마 로저 씨가 뭔가 알고 계실 거예요. 제가 로저 씨를 추가할게요.
>
> **모로우, 콜린 <오전 9:44>**
> 안녕하세요, 로저 씨. 우리 홈페이지에 무슨 일이 있는 건지 알고 계신 거라도 있나요?
>
> **스미튼, 로저 <오전 9:46>**
> 아, 34 35 제가 배치를 변경하는 동안 일시적으로 내려 두었습니다. 그런데 끝내는 데 시간이 좀 걸리네요.
>
> **페리어, 재닛 <오전 9:47>**
> 제가 그럴 거라고 했잖아요.
>
> **모로우, 콜린 <오전 9:49>**
> 그럼 제가 우리 페이지에 어떻게 몇개의 새 건물을 추가할 수 있죠? 33 고객들께서 오늘부터 시장에 공개될 것으로 예상하고 계세요.
>
> **스미튼, 로저 <오전 9:50>**
> 36 우리 웹 사이트가 정오까지 이용할 수 없을 것이라고 그분들께 알려 드리시는 게 좋을 것 같습니다.
>
> **모로우, 콜린 <오전 9:51>**
> 36 알겠어요, 당장 그렇게 할게요.

어휘 access ~에 접속하다, ~을 이용하다 property 건물, 부동산 Hold on a moment 잠시만요 what's wrong with ~에 무슨 일이 있는지, ~에 뭐가 문제인지 take A down A를 내려 놓다, A를 분해하다, A를 해체하다 temporarily 일시적으로, 임시로 layout 배치, 구획 take time to do ~하는 데 시간이 걸리다 get A done A를 끝마치다 I'm afraid (부정적인 일에 대해) ~인 것 같습니다, 유감이지만 ~입니다 had better do ~하는 게 좋다 not A until B B나 되어야 A하다 available 이용 가능한

33. 메시지 작성자들이 어디에서 근무할 것 같은가?
(A) 건설 회사에서
(B) 온라인 슈퍼마켓에서
(C) 건축 회사에서
(D) 부동산 중개업체에서

정답 (D)

해설 모로우 씨가 9시 41분에 작성한 메시지에는 자사의 건물 목록을(our property listings) 언급하는 말이 쓰여 있고, 9시 49분 메시지에는 건물들을 뜻하는 properties를 them으로 지칭해 그것들이 시장에 공개되는 것을 고객들이 기대하고 있다는(The clients are expecting them to go on the market starting) 말이 쓰여 있다. 따라서 메시지 작성자들이 부동산 중개와 관련된 일을 하는 사람들이라는 것을 알 수 있으므로 (D)가 정답이다.

어휘 architectural 건축의 real estate 부동산 agency 중개업체, 대행사

34. 오전 9시 47분에, 페리어 씨가 "I told you so"라고 쓸 때 무엇을 암시하는가?
(A) 스미튼 씨에게 추가 상세 정보 제공을 원하고 있다.
(B) 한 가지 일에 대해 모로우 씨를 도울 것이다.
(C) 이미 목록을 수정해 두었다.
(D) 이미 그 문제를 알고 있다.

정답 (D)

해설 9시 46분에 스미튼 씨가 자사 홈페이지 문제의 원인과 관련해 자신이 배치를 변경하는 동안 일시적으로 내려 두었고, 작업을 끝내는 데 시간이 조금 걸린다고(I've taken it down temporarily while I change the layout, and it's taking time to get it done) 알리자, 페리어 씨가 이미 작업 시간이 조금 걸릴 것이라는 문제 상황을 알고 있다는 뜻으로 하는 말에 해당되므로 (D)가 정답이다.

어휘 details 상세 정보, 세부 사항 help A with B B에 대해 A를 돕다 revise ~을 수정하다, ~을 변경하다

35. 스미튼 씨와 관련해 유추할 수 있는 것은 무엇인가?
(A) 해당 업체의 소유주이다.
(B) 웹 디자인 관련 지식을 갖고 있다.
(C) 일부 장비를 수리할 것이다.
(D) 오늘 저녁에 늦게까지 일할 것이다.

정답 (B)

해설 9시 46분에 메시지에 스미튼 씨가 자사 홈페이지와 관련해 배치를 변경하는 일을 하고 있다는(while I change the layout) 말이 쓰여 있다. 이는 웹 디자인 업무를 맡고 있으며, 그와 관련된 지식을 갖고 있는 것으로 볼 수 있으므로 (B)가 정답이다.

어휘 knowledge 지식 repair ~을 수리하다 equipment 장비

36. 모로우 씨가 곧이어 무엇을 할 것 같은가?
(A) 홈페이지를 확인하는 일
(B) 일부 건물을 방문하는 일
(C) 일부 고객에게 연락하는 일
(D) 예약 일정을 재조정하는 일

정답 (C)

해설 9시 50분 메시지에 스미튼 씨가 앞서 언급된 고객들(clients)을 them으로 지칭해 문제와 관련된 정보를 그 사람들에게 알리는 게 좋겠다고(I'm afraid you'd better let them know) 말하자, 모로우 씨가 당장 그렇게 하겠다고(Okay, I'll do that right away) 동의하고 있다. 따라서 모로우 씨가 해당 고객들에게 곧장 연락할 것으로 생각할 수 있으므로 (C)가 정답이다.

어휘 reschedule ~의 일정을 재조정하다 appointment 예약, 약속

37-40.

엔웨이 어학원(EOLI)
강의 정보(강의 #0029)

강의명: 비즈니스 스페인어

강의 시작일: 1월 5일, 3월 2일, 5월 3일, 7월 1일, 9월 2일, 11월 4일

39 강의 기간: 4주 (집중반) 또는 8주 (정규반)

39 주당 수업 횟수: 5회 (8주 강좌) 또는 10회 (4주 강좌)

수업 시간: 50분

최소 기준 조건: 중급자

강사: 진 영과 후안 호세 히메네스

40 수업료: 엔웨이 등록 학생 - 675달러 / 미등록 학생 - 750달러

등록을 원하시면, **37** 여기를 클릭하여 출력 가능한 등록 양식을 다운로드하신 다음 **38** 웨스트 먼로 스트리트 607번지, 피닉스, 애리조나 주 85007 엔웨이 온라인 어학원의 주소로 완성된 양식과 해당 수업료를 함께 보내주시기 바랍니다.

이 강의에 등록하는 모든 분은 비즈니스 발표 샘플과 계약서 샘플, 잡지기사 샘플을 포함한 다양한 수업 자료를 받게 될 것입니다. 특정 비즈니스 어휘 목록 또한 제공될 것입니다.

어휘 institute 기관 duration (지속)기간 intensive 집중적인 intermediate 중급의 registered 등록된 printable 출력 가능한 enrollment form 등록 양식 along with ~와 함께 completed form 완성된 양식 appropriate 적절한 enroll in ~에 등록하다 a selection of 다양한 contract 계약서 specific 구체적인, 특정한

37. 이 안내문은 어디서 볼 수 있을 것 같은가?
(A) 비즈니스 저널에서
(B) 홍보용 전단에서
(C) 알림 게시판에서
(D) 웹 페이지에서

정답 (D)

해설 두 번째 문단에 여기를 클릭하여 출력 가능한 양식을 다운받으라는(please click HERE to download a printable enrollment form) 문장에서 인터넷상의 웹 페이지에서 볼 수 있는 글임을 알 수 있으므로 (D)가 정답이다.

어휘 journal 잡지 promotional flyer 홍보용 전단 notice board 게시판

38. 엔웨이 온라인 어학원에 대해 명시된 것은?
(A) 최근에 설립된 업체이다.
(B) 영 씨와 히메네스 씨에 의해서 설립되었다.
(C) 피닉스에서 업체를 운영하고 있다.
(D) 현재 새로운 언어 강사를 구하고 있다.

정답 (C)

해설 두 번째 단락에 등록 양식과 수업료를 보내라고 하는 주소가 웨스트 먼로 스트리트 607번지, 피닉스, 애리조나 주 85007 엔웨이 온라인 어학원(Enway Online Language Institute, 607 West Monroe Street, Phoenix, AZ 85007)이라고 쓰여 있으므로 피닉스에 위치해 있다는 것을 알 수 있다. 따라서 (C)가 정답이다.

어휘 found ~을 설립하다 operate ~을 운영하다 seek ~을 구하다 instructor 강사

39. 강의 #0029에 대하여 사실이 아닌 것은?
(A) 초보자는 강의 등록이 불가능하다.
(B) 등록한 사람은 여러 시작일 중에서 선택할 수 있다.
(C) 집중반 학생은 주당 5회 수업을 받을 것이다.
(D) 각 정규반 수업은 1시간 미만으로 지속될 것이다.

정답 (C)

해설 첫 번째 문단 강의 기간 항목과 주당 수업 횟수 항목에서 8주 강좌 정규반 학생들은 5회 수업을, 4주 집중반 학생들은 10회 수업이라고 되어 있으므로 집중반 학생들은 주당 10회의 수업이 정해져 있다는 것을 알 수 있다. 따라서 (C)가 정답이다.

어휘 last 지속되다

40. 엔웨이에 사전 등록한 학생들만 가능한 것은 무엇인가?

(A) 수업 수의 증가
(B) 수강료 할인
(C) 더 긴 강의 기간
(D) 다양한 무료 강의 자료

정답 (B)

해설 첫 번째 문단의 수업료 항목에서(Registered Enway Students - $675 / Non-registered - $750)라고 언급되어 있으므로 이미 등록이 된 학생들은 할인을 받는다는 사실을 알 수 있다. 따라서 (B)가 정답이다.

41-45.

영업 사원 긴급 구인
폴트랙시스 주식회사

저희 폴트랙시스 주식회사는 ▣42 영업 인력을 확대하고 고객 층을 넓힘으로써 시장 선두 주자로서의 입지를 공고히 하고자 합니다. ▣41 저희는 인기 있는 저희 당뇨병 치료제 및 인슐린 기반 제품 라인을 지원하고 홍보할 제약 영업 사원들로 팀을 구성하기를 바라고 있습니다. 영업 사원들은 헤이마켓과 칼튼, 리스, 그리고 마치몬트에 계신 저희 폴트랙시스 주식회사 지부장님들께 업무 보고를 하게 될 것입니다.

자격 요건
• 2년 간의 제약 영업 경력 필수
• ▣43(B) 영업 성공 실적 입증 기록
• ▣43(D) 복잡한 정보를 습득해 이해하고 설명할 수 있는 능력
• ▣43(C) 기술적 소질 및 컴퓨터 활용 능력은 필수입니다

이력서와 이전 고용주의 추천서, 국가에서 발급한 보험 카드 또는 운전 면허증 사본, 그리고 작성 완료된 지원서를 근무하시고자 하는 지역의 지부장님께 직접 보내시기 바랍니다: 밥 킨즐(칼튼), 수전 키니(마치몬트), ▣45 데브라 할러웨이(헤이마켓), 그리고 스캇 아서스(리스). 지원서 및 이메일 주소는 www.poltraxis.co.uk/recruitment에서 찾아 보실 수 있습니다.

어휘 urgently 긴급히 look to do ~하고자 하다, ~할 계획이다 solidify ~을 공고히 하다, ~을 굳건히 하다 expand ~을 확대하다, ~을 확장하다(= enlarge) force 인력 client base 고객 층 pharmaceutical 제약의, 약학의 diabetes 당뇨병 treatment 치료(제) A-based A 기반의 regional 지역의, 지방의 requirement 요건, 필수 조건 required 필수인, 필요로 하는 proven 입증된, 증명된 track record 실적 explain ~을 설명하다 complex 복잡한 aptitude 소질, 적성 recommendation letter 추천서 former 이전의, 과거의, 전직 ~의 insurance 보험 completed 완료된 application 지원(서), 신청(서) region 지역

수신: 데브라 할러웨이 <dholloway@poltraxis.co.uk>
발신: 닉 매틀록 <nmatlock@xcelmail.com>
제목: 구직 지원
날짜: 8월 13일

▣45 할러웨이 씨께,

저는 8월 12일에 더 뉴타운 트리뷴에 광고된 영업 사원 직책들 중 하나에 지원하고자 이메일을 씁니다. ▣45 저는 특히 귀하의 지사에서 근무하기를 원하는데, 제가 마치몬트에서 이 지역으로 막 이사했기 때문입니다. 제 지원서와 함께 이력서를 한 부 첨부해 드렸습니다. 하지만, ▣44 유감스럽게도 이전의 제 고용주께서 현재 해외에 계시기 때문에, 추천서를 받아 제출하는 데 약간의 지연 문제가 있을 수도 있습니다. 스캔한 제 운전 면허증도 첨부해 드렸습니다. 어떤 추가 서류든 필요로 하시는 경우, 알려 주시기 바랍니다. 곧 연락 주시기를 바랍니다.

안녕히 계십시오.

닉 매틀록

어휘 apply for ~에 지원하다, ~을 신청하다 specifically 특히, 구체적으로 attach ~을 첨부하다, ~을 부착하다 along with ~와 함께 previous 이전의, 과거의 currently 현재 overseas 해외에 있는 slight 약간의 delay 지연, 지체 obtain ~을 얻다 reference letter 추천서 require ~을 필요로 하다 additional 추가적인

---

41. 어떤 종류의 업계에 속한 직책이 광고되고 있는가?

(A) 소프트웨어
(B) 전자 제품
(C) 의학
(D) 부동산

정답 (C)

해설 첫 지문 첫 단락에 당뇨병 치료제 및 인슐린 기반 제품 라인과 관련된 제약 영업 사원을 언급하고 있어(pharmaceutical sales representatives to support and promote our popular lines of diabetes treatments and insulin-based products) 의학 업계에 속한 회사가 낸 광고임을 알 수 있으므로 (C)가 정답이다.

42. 폴트랙시스 주식회사와 관련해 암시된 것은 무엇인가?

(A) 영업 지부장들을 고용하고 있다.
(B) 사업 침체를 겪어 왔다.
(C) 신제품 출시를 준비하고 있다.
(D) 신규 고객을 끌어들이기를 바라고 있다.

정답 (D)

해설 첫 지문 첫 단락에 영업 인력을 확대하고 고객 층을 넓혀(by expanding its sales force and enlarging its client base) 시장 선두 주자로서의 입지를 확고하게 하려 한다고 알리는 말이 쓰여 있다. 이는 새로운 고객을 끌어들이는 일을 가리키므로 (D)가 정답이다.

어휘 **experience** ~을 겪다, ~을 경험하다 **decline in** ~의 침체, ~의 하락 **prepare to do** ~할 준비를 하다 **release** ~을 출시하다, ~을 발매하다 **attract** ~을 끌어들이다

43. 자격 요건으로 기재되지 않은 것은 무엇인가?

(A) 팀을 관리해 본 경험
(B) 과거의 높은 판매량에 대한 증거
(C) 능숙한 컴퓨터 활용 능력
(D) 어려운 개념을 이야기할 수 있는 능력

정답 (A)

해설 자격 요건이 제시된 첫 지문 두 번째 단락에서 영업 성공 실적 입증 기록을(proven track record of sales success) 통해 과거의 높은 판매량에 대한 증거를 뜻하는 (B)를, 복잡한 정보를 습득해 이해하고 설명할 수 있는 능력(Ability to learn, understand, and explain complex information)에서 (D)를, 그리고 기술적 소질 및 컴퓨터 활용 능력은 필수라는 (computer skills are essential) 부분에서 (C)를 확인할 수 있다. 하지만 팀을 관리해 본 경험과 관련된 요건은 제시되어 있지 않으므로 (A)가 정답이다.

어휘 **evidence** 증거(물) **proficiency in** ~의 능숙함

44. 매틀록 씨는 어떤 필수 서류를 보낼 수 없었는가?

(A) 이력서
(B) 추천서
(C) 지원서
(D) 신분증 사본

정답 (B)

해설 두 번째 지문 중반부에 이전의 고용주가 현재 해외에 있어서 추천서를 받아 제출하는 데 약간의 지연 문제가 있을 수도 있다고(there might be a slight delay in obtaining and submitting a reference letter) 알리는 말이 쓰여 있으므로 (B)가 정답이다.

45. 매틀록 씨는 고용되는 경우에 어느 지사에서 근무할 것 같은가?

(A) 칼튼
(B) 리스
(C) 마치몬트
(D) 헤이마켓

정답 (D)

해설 두 번째 지문 초반부에 할러웨이 씨의 지사에서 근무하고 싶다는(I would specifically like to work in your branch office) 의사를 나타내고 있다. 이와 관련해, 첫 지문 마지막 단락에 할러웨이 씨가 헤이마켓에 근무하는 것으로(Debra Holloway (Haymarket)) 표기되어 있으므로 (D)가 정답이다.

46-50.

클라크 카운티 직업 안전 협회 (CCOSA)

전문 워크숍 (3월 12일, 토요일 - 3월 13일, 일요일)
- 윌로우브룩 컨벤션 센터

시간	장소	1일차	2일차
50 1	**50** 1A	**46** 위험 요소 식별 및 위험성 평가	사무직 직장인들의 근골격계 장애 줄이기
2	2A	**46** 화재 예방 절차	잠재적으로 위험한 물체 처리하기
49 3	1B	**46** 사무실 책상에서 할 수 있는 운동	**49** 컴퓨터 사용자들의 눈 및 시력 장애
4	2B	미끄럼 방지 바닥 덮개의 발전	직장 내 폭력 예방
47 50 5	**50** 1A	직장 내에 숨어 있는 위험 요소	**47** 화재 발생 시 건물에서 대피하는 법

어휘 **occupational** 직업의 **hazard** 위험 (요소) **identification** 식별, 확인 **assessment** 평가 **prevention** 예방 **procedure** 절차 **advance** 발전, 진보 **non-slip** 미끄럼 방지의 **covering** 덮개, 깔개 **musculoskeletal** 근골격계의 **disorder** 장애 **substance** 물체, 물질 **vision** 시력 **operator** 조작하는 사람 **prevent** ~을 예방하다 **violence** 폭력 **evacuate** ~에서 대피하다 **in the event of** ~의 경우에

수신: 리차드 피츠패트릭 <rfitzpatrick@ccosa.com>
발신: 키퍼 매튜스 <kmatthews@ccosa.com>
제목: 다시 한번 감사합니다
날짜: 3월 9일
첨부: 연설자정보.doc

안녕하세요, 리차드 씨,

이번 주말에 있을 워크숍에서 **48** 대신해 주시겠다고 제안해 주셔서 얼마나 감사하게 생각하는지 다시 한번 말씀 드리고 싶었습니다. **49** 레이 씨께서 어젯밤에 저에게 본인 시간을 진행하실 수 없을 거라고 알리시기 위해 전화하셨을 때, 대체하실 분을 절대 찾지 못할 거라고 생각했습니다. 시력 검사에 대한 경험이 있으시기 때문에, 귀하께서는 그 연설을 하시기에 완벽한 분이실 겁니다. 제가 전화로 언급해 드렸다시피, 귀하의 시간에 대해 보상 받으시게 될 것입니다.

또한, 워크숍에서 연설을 하기로 동의하신 나머지 연사 분들에 관해 물어 보셨기 때문에, 원래의 일정표에 포함되어 있지 않았던 일부 추가 정보를 첨부해 드렸습니다.

안녕히 계십시오.

키퍼 매튜스
CCOSA 회장

어휘 grateful 감사하게 생각하는 fill in (근무 등을) 대신하다 inform A (that) A에게 ~라고 알리다 lead ~을 진행하다, ~을 이끌다 replacement 대체(자), 후임 optometry 시력 검사 give a talk 연설하다 mention ~을 언급하다 compensate A for B A에게 B에 대해 보상하다 additional 추가적인 include ~을 포함하다 agenda 일정표, 의제, 안건

CCOSA 전문 워크숍
연사 정보

50 시간 1: 오전 9:00 – 오전 10:30 / 아놀드 존슨 (1일차) / 리사 그린 (2일차)

시간 2: 오전 10:30 – 오후 12:00 / 벤 한센 (1일차) / 엘리자베스 헤일 (2일차)

49 시간 3: 오후 1:00 – 오후 2:30 / 리사 그린 (1일차) / 49 레이 윌리엄슨 (2일차)

시간 4: 오후 2:30 – 오후 4:30 / 아놀드 존슨 (1일차) / 메리 스완 (2일차)

47 50 시간 5: 오후 4:30 – 오후 6:00 / 메리 스완 (1일차) / 벤 한센 (2일차)

---

46. 워크숍이 주로 무엇에 관한 것인가?
(A) 전 세계의 의료 발전
(B) 건강에 좋은 식사와 영양
(C) 현대 기술의 발전
(D) 직장 내 보건과 안전

정답 (D)

해설 첫 번째 지문에서 위험 요소 식별 및 위험성 평가(Hazard Identification & Risk Assessment), 화재 예방 절차(Fire Prevention Procedures), 사무실에서 할 수 있는 운동(Exercises You Can Do at Your Office Desk) 등이 소주제로 제시되어 있는 것으로 볼 때, 직장 내의 보건 및 안전과 관련된 워크숍임을 알 수 있으므로 (D)가 정답이다.

어휘 development 발전, 개발 nutrition 영양

47. 대피 절차에 관한 연설이 언제 종료될 것인가?
(A) 오후 12시에
(B) 오후 2시 30분에
(C) 오후 4시 30분에
(D) 오후 6시에

정답 (D)

해설 첫 번째 지문에 화재 발생 시의 대피 방법이(How to Evacuate Buildings in the Event of a Fire) 오른쪽 하단에 2일차의 5번 시간으로 표기되어 있다. 이 시간과 관련해, 세 번째 지문 마지막 줄에 5번 시간의 종료 시점이 오후 6시로(Session 5: 4:30 p.m. – 6:00 p.m.) 표기되어 있으므로 (D)가 정답이다.

어휘 evacuation 대피 procedure 절차

48. 이메일에서, 첫 번째 단락, 첫 번째 줄의 표현 "fill in"과 의미가 가장 가까운 것은 무엇인가?
(A) 완료하다
(B) 제출하다
(C) 등록하다
(D) 대체하다

정답 (D)

해설 해당 문장에서 fill in이 속한 that절은 이메일 수신인인 리차드 씨가 워크숍에서 무엇을 하겠다고 제안했는지를 나타낸다. 바로 다음 문장에 레이 씨가 자신의 시간을 진행할 수 없다고 알린 사실과 함께 대체할 사람을 찾지 못할 줄 알았다고 언급하는 것으로 볼 때, 리차드 씨가 레이 씨의 시간을 대신 맡겠다고 제안한 것으로 생각할 수 있으므로 '대체하다'를 뜻하는 (D) substitute가 정답이다.

49. 피츠패트릭 씨가 워크숍 중에 무엇을 이야기할 것 같은가?
(A) 바닥 덮개
(B) 위험한 물체
(C) 시력 장애
(D) 사무실 내 운동

정답 (C)

해설 두 번째 지문 첫 단락에서 수신인인 리차드 피츠패트릭 씨가 레이 씨의 시간을 대신한다는 사실을 알 수 있고(When Ray called me last night to inform me he'd be unable to lead his session, I thought I'd never find a replacement), 마지막 지문의 세 번째 줄에 레이 씨가 2일차의 3번 시간에 배정된 것을 확인할 수 있다(Session 3: 1:00 p.m. – 2:30 p.m. / Lisa Greene (Day 1) / Ray Williamson (Day 2)). 이와 관련해, 첫 지문에 2일차 3번 시간의 주제가 '컴퓨터 사용자들의 눈 및 시력 장애(Eye and Vision Disorders in Computer Operators)'로 쓰여 있으므로 (C)가 정답이다.

50. 1A호실에서 연설할 예정이 아닌 사람은 누구인가?
(A) 벤 한센
(B) 엘리자베스 헤일
(C) 리사 그린
(D) 아놀드 존슨

정답 (B)

해설 첫 번째 지문에 첫 줄의 1번 시간과 마지막 줄의 5번 시간에 대한 장소가 1A로 표기되어 있다. 이 시간들과 관련해, 마지막 지문의 첫 줄에 1번 시간의 연설자가 아놀드 존슨 씨와 리사 그린 씨로(Session 1: ~ Arnold Johnson (Day 1) / Lisa Greene (Day 2)), 마지막 줄에 5번 시간의 연설자가 메리 스완 씨와 벤 한센 씨로(Session 5: ~ Mary Swan (Day 1) / Ben Hansen (Day 2)) 각각 표기되어 있다. 이 네 사람에 해당되지 않는 연설자가 엘리자베스 헤일 씨이므로 (B)가 정답이다.

1. (D)	**2.** (D)	**3.** (A)	**4.** (A)	**5.** (A)
6. (C)	**7.** (A)	**8.** (A)	**9.** (B)	**10.** (A)
11. (A)	**12.** (B)	**13.** (A)	**14.** (A)	**15.** (C)
16. (C)	**17.** (B)	**18.** (C)	**19.** (A)	**20.** (A)
21. (A)	**22.** (C)	**23.** (B)	**24.** (C)	**25.** (C)
26. (D)	**27.** (B)	**28.** (A)	**29.** (B)	**30.** (C)
31. (D)	**32.** (B)	**33.** (D)	**34.** (C)	**35.** (B)
36. (B)	**37.** (C)	**38.** (B)	**39.** (C)	**40.** (B)
41. (B)	**42.** (D)	**43.** (C)	**44.** (D)	**45.** (B)
46. (C)	**47.** (D)	**48.** (D)	**49.** (A)	**50.** (A)

Part 1

1.　(A) The yard has been left unattended.
　　(B) Flowers have been planted in pots.
　　(C) A gardening tool is being picked up.
　　(D) The garden is being taken care of.

　　(A) 뜰이 방치된 상태로 남아 있다.
　　(B) 꽃들이 여러 화분에 심어져 있다.
　　(C) 원예 도구가 들어올려지는 중이다.
　　(D) 정원이 관리되는 중이다.

해설　(A) 여자가 작업하는 모습으로 볼 때 정원이 방치된 상태로 볼 수 없으므로 오답.
　　(B) 여러 화분에 꽃이 심어져 있는 모습을 찾아볼 수 없으므로 오답.
　　(C) 여자가 이미 도구를 들고 있는 상태이므로 오답.
　　(D) 정원에 초점을 맞춰 사람에 의해 관리되고 있는 상황을 묘사하고 있으므로 정답.

어휘　**be left unattended** 방치된 채로 있다　**plant** v. ~을 심다　**pot** 단지, 항아리, 냄비　**gardening tool** 원예 도구　**pick up** ~을 집어 들다　**take care of** ~을 관리하다, 돌보다

2.　(A) An outdoor area is crowded with people.
　　(B) Some trees are being planted.
　　(C) Some chairs are being stacked next to a table.
　　(D) A pathway is paved with stones.

　　(A) 야외 공간이 사람들로 분주한 상태이다.
　　(B) 몇몇 나무들이 심어지는 중이다.
　　(C) 몇몇 의자들이 한 탁자 옆에 쌓이는 중이다.
　　(D) 보도가 돌로 포장되어 있다.

해설　(A) 사람들로 분주한 상태가 아니므로 오답.
　　(B) 나무를 심는 동작을 하는 사람을 찾아볼 수 없으므로 오답.
　　(C) 의자들을 쌓는 동작을 하는 사람을 찾아볼 수 없으므로 오답.
　　(D) 돌을 깔아 보도를 포장한 상태를 묘사하고 있으므로 정답.

어휘　**be crowded with** ~로 분주하다　**plant** v. ~을 심다　**stack** ~을 쌓다, 쌓아 올리다　**next to** ~ 옆에　**pathway** 보도　**pave** (도로 등) ~을 포장하다

Part 2

3.　How can I get reimbursed for the flight tickets?
　　(A) Give your receipts to Ms. Blake.
　　(B) I flew back to India.
　　(C) I think so.

　　항공권에 대해 어떻게 환급 받을 수 있나요?
　　(A) 블레이크 씨에게 영수증을 제출하세요.
　　(B) 저는 비행기를 타고 인도로 돌아왔습니다.
　　(C) 저는 그렇게 생각합니다.

해설　How 뒤에 '환급 받다'를 뜻하는 get reimbursed가 쓰였으므로 환급 받는 방법을 묻는 의문문임을 알 수 있다. 따라서, 비용을 환급 받는 데 필요한 영수증을 제출하라고 알리는 (A)가 정답이다. (B)는 질문에 쓰인 flight에서 연상 가능한 flew를 이용해 혼동을 유발하는 오답이며, (C)는 동의를 나타낼 때 사용하는 말이므로 질문의 의도에 맞지 않는다.

어휘　**get reimbursed for** ~에 대한 비용을 환급 받다　**flight ticket** 항공권　**receipt** 영수증　**fly back to** 비행기를 타고 ~로 돌아오다, 돌아가다 cf. fly-flew-flown

4.　Is that area reserved for visitors?
　　(A) I'm not sure. Let me check.
　　(B) No, I will not be going.
　　(C) The guests are arriving soon.

　　저 구역은 방문객 전용이죠?
　　(A) 잘 모르겠어요. 확인해 볼게요.
　　(B) 아뇨, 전 가지 않을 겁니다.
　　(C) 손님들이 곧 도착할 거예요.

해설　한 구역이 방문객 전용인지 확인하는 일반 의문문에 대해 잘 모르겠다며 확인해 보겠다는 말로 간접적으로 답변한 (A)가 정답이다. (C)는 질문에 쓰인 visitors에서 연상 가능한 guests를 이용해 혼동을 유발하는 오답이다.

어휘　**reserved** 예약된, 지정된

5. Don't you have an appointment with the marketing manager?

(A) Yes, I'm leaving for it now.
(B) I don't know anything about marketing.
(C) No, I am the sales manager.

마케팅 부장님과 약속이 있으시지 않나요?
(A) 맞습니다, 지금 그 일로 나갑니다.
(B) 저는 마케팅에 대해 아무것도 모릅니다.
(C) 아뇨, 저는 영업부장입니다.

해설 마케팅 부장님과 약속이 있지 않은지 묻는 부정 의문문에 대해 긍정을 나타내는 Yes와 함께 appointment를 it으로 지칭해 그 일 때문에 나간다는 말을 덧붙인 (A)가 정답이다. (B)는 질문에 쓰인 marketing을, (C)는 manager를 각각 반복한 답변으로 마케팅 부장과의 약속과 관련 없는 오답이다.

어휘 **have an appointment with** ~와 약속이 있다 **leave** 나가다, 떠나다 **sales** 영업, 판매, 매출

6. Where is the nearest shopping mall?

(A) Every other Tuesday.
(B) About 5 or 6 dollars.
(C) Down the street from my office.

가장 가까운 쇼핑몰이 어디에 있나요?
(A) 격주로 화요일마다요.
(B) 대략 5~6달러요.
(C) 제 사무실에서 길을 따라 쭉 내려가시면 됩니다.

해설 쇼핑몰의 위치를 묻는 Where 의문문이므로 쇼핑몰로 찾아가는 방법을 가르쳐 주는 (C)가 정답이다. '격주로 화요일마다'를 뜻하는 (A)는 빈도를 묻는 How often 의문문에 어울리는 답변이며, (B)는 금액을 말하고 있으므로 How much 의문문에 어울리는 반응이다.

어휘 **every other Tuesday** 격주로 화요일마다 **about** 약, 대략 **down the street** 거리를 따라

7. I can't find the new intern's reference letters.

(A) Ask her to provide them again.
(B) It is a good job opportunity.
(C) The post office is across the road.

신입 인턴 직원의 추천서를 찾을 수가 없어요.
(A) 다시 제출해 달라고 요청하세요.
(B) 좋은 취업 기회입니다.
(C) 우체국은 길 건너편에 있습니다.

해설 신입 인턴 직원의 추천서를 찾을 수 없다는 평서문에 대해 new intern을 her로 지칭해 다시 제출하도록 요청하라고 권하는 (A)가 정답이다. (B)는 질문에 쓰인 intern과 연관성 있게 들리는 job opportunity를 이용한 오답이며, (C)는 질문에 쓰인 letters에서 연상 가능한 post office를 이용한 오답이다.

어휘 **reference letter** 추천서 **provide** ~을 제공하다 **job opportunity** 취업 기회 **across** ~ 건너편에

8. When will that antique car in the garage be restored?

(A) Once all the parts arrive.
(B) At the hardware store.
(C) Yes, it was a nice drive.

차고에 있는 골동품 자동차가 언제 복구될까요?
(A) 모든 부품이 도착하는 대로요.
(B) 철물점에서요.
(C) 네, 아주 멋진 드라이브였어요.

해설 자동차 수리 시점을 묻는 When 의문문에 대해 시간 접속사 Once를 이용해 '부품이 도착하는 대로'라는 말로 대략적인 시점을 말한 (A)가 정답이다. (B)는 장소 표현이므로 Where 의문문에 적절한 답변이다. (C)는 car에서 연상 가능한 drive를 이용한 오답이다.

어휘 **antique** a. 골동품인 n. 골동품 **garage** 차고 **restore** ~을 복구하다, 복원하다 **once** ~하는 대로, ~하자마자 **part** 부품 **hardware store** 철물점

9. Should we arrange a lunch meeting with our clients?

(A) I agree. It was a good plan.
(B) They want it to be quick.
(C) The product launch went smoothly.

우리 고객들과 함께 하는 오찬 모임을 마련해야 할까요?
(A) 동의합니다. 그건 좋은 계획이었어요.
(B) 그분들께서는 그것이 신속히 진행되기를 원하세요.
(C) 제품 출시 행사가 순조롭게 진행되었습니다.

해설 고객들과의 오찬 모임을 준비해야 하는지 확인하는 Should 의문문이므로 clients를 they로, lunch meeting을 it으로 지칭해 고객들이 오찬 모임의 신속한 주최를 원한다고 알리는 (B)가 정답이다. (A)는 과거에 있었던 일에 대한 의견인데, 질문은 앞으로 해야 하는 일을 묻고 있으므로 어울리지 않는 답변이다. (C)는 질문에 쓰인 lunch와 발음이 거의 비슷한 launch를 이용해 혼동을 유발하는 오답이다.

어휘 **arrange** ~을 마련하다, 조치하다 **client** 고객, 의뢰인 **agree** 동의하다 **want A to do** A에게 ~하기를 원하다 **quick** 빠른, 신속한 **launch** 출시, 공개 **go smoothly** 순조롭게 진행되다

10. Have you made me an extra copy of the contract?

(A) I left it on your desk.
(B) What do you take in your coffee?
(C) One hundred should be enough.

저에게 계약서 추가 사본을 만들어 주셨었나요?
(A) 책상에 놓아 드렸습니다.
(B) 커피에 무엇을 넣어서 드시죠?
(C) 100장이면 충분할 겁니다.

해설 계약서 추가 사본을 만들어서 자신에게 주었는지 확인하는 일반 의문문에 대해 책상에 놓아 두었다는 말로 사본을 만들어 주었음을 의미하는 (A)가 정답이다. (B)는 copy와 발음이 유사하게 들리는 coffee를 이용한 오답이며, (C)는 copy에서 연상 가능한 사본 수량을 말하는 오답이다.

어휘 **make A B** A에게 B를 만들어 주다 **a copy of** 사본, 한 부, 한 장 **extra** 추가의, 별도의 **contract** 계약(서) **leave A on B** A를 B에 놓다, 두다 **take** ~을 먹다, 섭취하다 **enough** 충분한

---

11. What was the topic of your presentation?
(A) Domestic sales.
(B) Right next to the conference room.
(C) About an hour or so.

당신의 발표 주제가 무엇이었나요?
(A) 국내 영업이요.
(B) 대회의실 바로 옆에요.
(C) 약 한 시간 정도요.

해설 What 의문문은 의문사 자체보다 그 뒤에 이어지는 내용을 듣는 것이 더 중요하므로 What was the topic까지는 꼭 들어야 한다. 발표 주제를 묻고 있으므로 국내 영업(Domestic sales)이라는 말로 특정 주제를 직접 언급하고 있어 질문에 어울리는 답변을 한 (A)가 정답이다. (B)는 presentation에서 연상 가능한 conference room을 이용한 함정으로, 위치 표현으로 답변하고 있으므로 Where 의문문에 어울리는 반응이다. (C)는 대략적인 소요 시간을 나타내므로 How long 의문문에 어울리는 답변이다.

어휘 **presentation** 발표 **domestic** 국내의 **sales** 영업, 판매 **right** (강조) 바로 **or so** (수량, 시간 표현 뒤에서) ~ 정도, ~ 쯤

---

12. Weren't you going to replace that office chair?
(A) No, I tried a different place.
(B) I figured I'd just keep it.
(C) An office furniture store.

그 사무용 의자를 교체하려던 것 아니었어요?
(A) 아뇨, 다른 곳에 한 번 가봤어요.
(B) 그냥 계속 사용하기로 했습니다.
(C) 사무용 가구 매장이요.

해설 사무실 의자를 교체할 생각이 아니었는지 묻는 부정 의문문이므로 No를 생략한 채로 의자를 그냥 갖고 있기로 했다는 말로 교체하지 않는다는 뜻을 나타낸 (B)가 정답이다. (A)는 질문에 쓰인 replace와 발음이 유사한 place를 이용해 혼동을 유발하는 답변이며, (C)는 질문에 쓰인 office를 반복한 답변으로 의자 교체 여부와 관련 없는 오답이다.

어휘 **replace** ~을 교체하다 **try** ~을 한번 해보다 **figure (that)** ~라고 생각하다, 판단하다

---

13. Could you take a look at this project proposal?
(A) Sorry, I'm just on my way out.
(B) No, I didn't take it.
(C) I've never seen her before.

이 프로젝트 제안서 좀 한 번 봐 주시겠어요?
(A) 죄송하지만, 제가 막 나가는 길이라서요.
(B) 아뇨, 저는 가져 가지 않았어요.
(C) 저는 전에 그분을 한 번도 본 적이 없습니다.

해설 「Could you ~?」로 시작하는 요청 의문문이므로 사과의 말과 함께 지금 나가는 중이라 요청을 수락할 수 없다는 말을 덧붙인 (A)가 정답이다. (B)는 질문에 쓰인 take를 반복해 혼동을 유발하는 답변으로, No 뒤에 이어지는 말이 수락 또는 거절과 관련이 없으므로 No만 듣고 혼동하지 않도록 유의해야 한다. (C)는 대상을 알 수 없는 her를 언급한 오답이다.

어휘 **take a look at** ~을 한 번 보다 **proposal** 제안(서) **on one's way out** 나가는 길인 **take** ~을 가져가다

---

14. Which singer did you like the most?
(A) They were all excellent.
(B) I'm afraid I forgot the song titles.
(C) Mostly ballads.

당신은 어느 가수가 가장 마음에 들었나요?
(A) 전부 훌륭했어요.
(B) 곡 제목들을 잊어버린 것 같아요.
(C) 대체로 발라드요.

해설 Which singer로 시작되어 어느 가수가 가장 마음에 들었는지 묻는 의문문에 대해 모두 훌륭했다는 말로 답변하는 (A)가 정답이다. (B)와 (C)는 모두 singer에서 연상 가능한 song과 ballads를 각각 이용해 혼동을 유발하는 오답이다.

어휘 **the most** 가장 (많이) **I'm afraid (that)** (부정적인 일에 대해) ~인 것 같다 **forget** ~을 잊다 **mostly** 대체로, 대부분

---

15. Can you fix the photocopier, or are you leaving soon?
(A) You've fixed quite a meal today.
(B) He's gone for the day.
(C) I have some time now.

복사기를 고쳐 주실 수 있으세요, 아니면 곧 나가시나요?
(A) 당신이 오늘 진수성찬을 준비했군요.
(B) 그분은 오늘 퇴근했어요.
(C) 지금 시간이 좀 있습니다.

해설 복사기를 고쳐줄 수 있는지 아니면 곧 나가봐야 하는지 묻는 선택 의문문에 대해 시간이 있다는 말로 고쳐줄 수 있다는 뜻을 나타내는 (C)가 정답이다. (A)는 질문에 쓰인 fix의 다른 의미 (고치다-준비하다)를 이용해 혼동을 유발하는 오답이며, (B)는 대상을 알 수 없는 He에 대해 말하는 오답이다.

어휘 **photocopier** 복사기 **fix** ~을 고치다, 준비하다 **quite a meal** 진수성찬 cf. quite a 상당한, 대단한 **have gone for the day** 퇴근하다

16. Does the factory supervisor know that Mr. Yates is stopping by today?

(A) Tomorrow would suit me better.

(B) We can stop for a bit.

(C) You'd better remind him.

공장 책임자께서 오늘 예이츠 씨께서 들르신다는 것을 알고 계신가요?

(A) 저에게는 내일이 더 잘 맞을 것 같습니다.

(B) 저희는 잠시 멈출 수 있습니다.

(C) 그분께 상기시켜 드리는 게 좋겠어요.

해설 예이츠 씨가 들른다는 사실을 공장 책임자가 알고 있는지 확인하는 일반 의문문에 대해 그 책임자를 him으로 지칭해 상기시켜 주도록 권하는 (C)가 정답이다. (A)는 today와 연관성 있게 들리는 tomorrow를 이용해 혼동을 유발하는 오답이며, (B)는 질문에 쓰인 stop을 반복한 오답이다.

어휘 **supervisor** 책임자, 부서장, 상사 **stop by** (잠시) 들르다 **suit** ~에게 잘 맞다, 적합하다 **for a bit** 잠깐 동안 **had better do** ~하는 게 좋다 **remind** ~에게 상기시키다

17. I'd like you to present an award at our music awards ceremony.

(A) He definitely deserved to win.

(B) I'd be honored to do so.

(C) Yes, it was an enjoyable evening.

저는 귀하께서 저희 음악 시상식에서 시상해 주셨으면 합니다.

(A) 그분은 분명히 받을 자격이 있었습니다.

(B) 그렇게 하게 된다면 영광일 것입니다.

(C) 네, 즐거운 저녁 시간이었습니다.

해설 시상식에서 시상해 달라고 요청하는 평서문이므로 시상하는 일을 do so로 바꿔 표현해 그렇게 하면 영광일 것이라고 답변하는 (B)가 정답이다. (A)는 질문에 쓰인 awards에서 연상 가능한 win(상을 받다)을 이용해 혼동을 유발하는 오답이며, (C)는 수락을 나타내는 Yes 뒤에 이어지는 말이 과거의 일에 대한 내용이므로 어울리지 않는 반응이다.

어휘 **would like A to do** A에게 ~하길 원하다 **present** ~을 수여하다, 제공하다 **award** 상 **awards ceremony** 시상식 **definitely** 분명히, 확실히 **deserve to do** ~할 자격이 있다, ~할 만하다 **win** (상 등) ~을 받다, 타다 **be honored to do** ~해서 영광이다 **enjoyable** 즐거운

18. What do you think about the new chief editor?

(A) We've been introduced.

(B) I knew about it.

(C) She's highly qualified.

신임 편집장님에 대해 어떻게 생각하세요?

(A) 저희는 소개되었습니다.

(B) 저는 그것에 대해 알고 있었습니다.

(C) 그분은 매우 뛰어난 자격을 지니고 있어요.

해설 「What do you think about ~?」은 어떤 대상에 대해 상대방의 생각을 물을 때 사용하므로 의견이나 평가 등을 말하는 답변이 정답으로 자주 등장한다. 신임 편집장에 대한 생각을 묻고 있으므로 그 사람의 자격과 관련된 평가에 해당되는 (C)가 정답이다.

어휘 **chief editor** 편집장 **introduce** ~을 소개하다 **highly** 매우, 대단히 **qualified** 자격이 있는, 적격의

19. Won't Food Express be hired to cater our grand opening reception?

(A) The manager will make that decision.

(B) We open on August 10.

(C) It's on the far side of the lobby.

푸드 익스프레스 사가 우리 개장식 축하 연회에 출장 요리를 제공하도록 고용되는 것 아닌가요?

(A) 부장님께서 그 결정을 내리실 겁니다.

(B) 저희는 8월 10일에 문을 엽니다.

(C) 그것은 로비 저쪽 끝에 있습니다.

해설 특정 업체의 고용 여부를 묻는 부정 의문문에 대해 부장이 결정할 것이라는 말로 아직 고용 여부를 알 수 없음을 알리는 (A)가 정답이다. (B)는 opening과 일부 발음이 유사한 open을 이용해 혼동을 유발하는 오답이며, (C)는 reception에서 연상 가능한 lobby를 이용한 오답이다.

어휘 **hire** ~을 고용하다 **cater** v. ~에 출장 요리를 제공하다 **reception** 축하 연회, (호텔 등의) 프런트, 접수처 **make a decision** 결정하다 **on the far side of** ~의 저쪽 편에, 저쪽 끝에

20. Would you prefer a window seat or one on the aisle?

(A) I have no preference.

(B) To see the scenic view.

(C) I'll set up a projector

창가 좌석이 좋으세요, 아니면 통로 쪽 좌석이 좋으세요?

(A) 특별히 선호하는 건 없습니다.

(B) 좋은 경치를 보기 위해서요.

(C) 제가 프로젝터를 설치할게요.

해설 좌석 위치와 관련된 두 가지 선택 사항을 제시하는 선택 의문문에 대해 특별히 선호하는 게 없다는 말로 답변하는 (A)가 정답이다. 이처럼 선택 의문문에 대해 어느 것이든 상관없다는 의미

를 나타내는 말이 정답인 경우가 종종 있으므로 기억해 두는 것이 좋다. 유사한 의미로 쓰이는 It doesn't matter(상관없어요), I don't care(저는 상관하지 않아요) 등도 함께 알고 있으면 좋다.

어휘 **prefer** ~을 선호하다 **aisle** 통로 **preference** 선호(하는 것) **scenic** 경치가 좋은 **view** n. 경치, 전망 **set up** ~을 설치하다

Part 3

Questions 21-23 refer to the following conversation.

M: Hello. **21** I ordered a pepperoni pizza from your Web site, and I'd like to find out when it will arrive. It's already been one hour since I placed the order.

W: Oh, that's strange. Let me just check our database. Ah, I can see that you did make the order, but **22** I'm afraid your credit card was declined.

M: In that case, why didn't you call me or send me a text message? We have been waiting a long time for our pizza.

W: I'm sorry about that, but we've been really busy this evening. **23** I'll take a note of your name, and you can get five dollars off the next time you call to order a pizza.

남: 안녕하세요. 제가 귀사의 웹 사이트에서 페퍼로니 피자를 주문했는데, 언제 도착할지 알고 싶습니다. 제가 주문을 한 지 벌써 1시간이나 되어서요.

여: 아, 이상한 일이네요. 저희 데이터베이스를 확인해 보겠습니다. 아, 고객님께서 분명히 주문하신 것은 확인할 수 있지만, 신용카드가 거절되었습니다.

남: 그런 경우라면, 왜 제게 전화를 주시든지 아니면 문자 메시지를 보내시지 않으셨죠? 저희는 오랫동안 피자가 오기를 기다렸어요.

여: 죄송합니다만, 저희가 오늘 저녁에 정말로 계속 바빴습니다. 제가 고객님의 성함을 적어 두었다가 다음 번에 피자 주문을 위해 전화주실 때 5달러를 할인 받으실 수 있도록 해 드리겠습니다.

어휘 **find out** ~을 알아 내다, 파악하다 **since** ~한 이후로 **place an order** 주문하다 **see that** ~임을 알다, 확인하다 **I'm afraid (that)** (부정적인 일에 대해) ~한 것 같다 **decline** ~을 거절하다 **in that case** 그런 경우라면, 그렇다면 **text message** 문자 메시지 **wait a long time for** ~을 오래 기다리다 **take a note of** ~을 적어 두다 **get A off** A를 할인 받다 **the next time + 절** 다음 번에 ~할 때

21. 남자는 왜 전화를 하는가?

(A) 배달이 얼마나 걸릴지 묻기 위해
(B) 주문의 세부 사항을 변경하기 위해
(C) 특가 서비스에 관해 문의하기 위해
(D) 추가 요금에 관해 문의하기 위해

해설 전화의 목적은 대체로 대화 초반부에 먼저 제시되므로 대화가 시작될 때 특히 집중해야 한다. 남자가 대화를 시작하면서 피자를 주문했는데 언제 도착할지 알고 싶다(I ordered a pepperoni pizza ~ I'd like to find out when it will arrive)고 말하고 있으므로 (A)가 정답임을 알 수 있다.

어휘 **how long A will take** A가 얼마나 걸릴지 **details** 세부 사항, 상세 정보 **inquire about** ~에 관해 문의하다 **special offer** 특가 서비스 **extra** 추가의, 별도의 **charge** (청구) 요금

22. 여자는 무슨 문제점을 언급하는가?

(A) 배송 주소가 부정확하다.
(B) 매장이 평소보다 일찍 문을 닫는다.
(C) 비용 지불이 되지 않았다.
(D) 물품이 현재 구매 불가능하다.

해설 여자는 대화 중반부에 피자 주문과 관련해 상대방의 신용카드가 거절되었다는 문제점을 말하고 있으므로(I'm afraid your credit card was declined) 이를 비용 지불이 되지 않았다는 말로 표현한 (C)가 정답이다.

어휘 **incorrect** 부정확한, 틀린 **than usual** 평소보다 **payment** 비용 (지불) **unsuccessful** 성공적이지 못한 **currently** 현재 **unavailable** 구매 불가능한

Paraphrase your credit card was declined
→ A payment was unsuccessful.

23. 여자는 무엇을 하겠다고 제안하는가?

(A) 다른 제품을 배달하는 일
(B) 할인을 제공하는 일
(C) 주문의 규모를 늘리는 일
(D) 남자에게 다시 전화하는 일

해설 대화의 마지막 부분에서 여자는 이름을 적어 두었다가 다음 번에 피자 주문을 위해 전화를 할 때 5달러를 할인 받을 수 있도록 하겠다(I'll take a note of your name, and you can get five dollars off the next time you call to order a pizza)고 제안하고 있으므로 할인 제공이라는 말로 간단히 표현한 (B)가 정답이다.

어휘 **provide** ~을 제공하다 **increase** ~을 늘리다, 증가시키다 **call A back** A에게 다시 전화하다

Paraphrase you can get five dollars off
→ Provide a discount

Questions 24-26 refer to the following conversation with three speakers.

W: Hi, guys. Our flights and hotel rooms are booked for our business trip to China, but **24** we still don't know how to get from the airport to our hotel.

M1: **24** I was thinking that we should just rent a car once we arrive. **25** What do you think, Harry?

M2: **25** Well, why don't we take a look at the hotel's Web site? It probably has information about how to get there easily from the airport.

W: That's a good idea. They might even provide a free shuttle. Dave, **26** why don't you do that while I finish off the presentation we're giving to our clients?

M1: Okay. I'll let both of you know what I find online.

여: 안녕하세요, 여러분. 중국으로 떠나는 우리 출장에 필요한 항공편과 호텔 객실은 예약이 되어 있는데, 공항에서 우리 호텔로 가는 방법은 아직 알지 못하고 있습니다.
남1: 저는 우리가 도착하는 대로 차를 한 대 빌려야 한다고 생각하고 있었어요. 어떻게 생각하세요, 해리?
남2: 저, 그 호텔 웹 사이트를 한 번 확인해 보는 건 어떨까요? 아마 공항에서 그곳까지 쉽게 갈 수 있는 방법에 관한 정보가 있을 거예요.
여: 좋은 생각이에요. 심지어 무료 셔틀버스를 제공할 수도 있어요. 데이브, 제가 우리 고객들을 대상으로 할 예정인 발표 준비를 끝마치는 동안 그 일 좀 해 주시겠어요?
남1: 알겠습니다. 제가 온라인으로 찾아본 것을 두 분께 알려 드릴게요.

어휘 **book** ~을 예약하다 **business trip** 출장 **how to do** ~하는 방법 **get from A to B** A에서 B로 가다, 이동하다 **rent** ~을 대여하다 **once** (일단) ~하는 대로, ~하자마자 **why don't we ~?** ~하는 건 어때요? **take a look at** ~을 한 번 보다 **probably** 아마 **easily** 쉽게, 편리하게 **even** 심지어 (~도) **provide** ~을 제공하다 **free** 무료의 **shuttle** 셔틀버스 **while** ~하는 동안 **finish off** ~을 끝마치다, 마무리하다 **give a presentation** 발표하다 **let A know** A에게 알리다 **find** ~을 찾다

24. 무엇이 주로 논의되고 있는가?
(A) 호텔 예약
(B) 항공편 일정
(C) 교통편 선택권
(D) 투어 패키지

해설 대화 시작 부분에 여자가 공항에서 호텔로 가는 방법은 아직 알지 못한다고(we still don't know how to get from the airport to our hotel) 말하자 남자 한 명이 차를 대여하는 것을 제안하고 있다(I was thinking that we should just rent a car once we arrive). 따라서 교통편을 선택하는 일에 관한 대화임을 알 수 있으므로 (C)가 정답이 된다.

어휘 **reservation** 예약 **itinerary** 여행 일정(표) **transportation** 교통편 **option** 선택(권)

25. 해리 씨는 무엇을 제안하는가?
(A) 차량을 대여할 것
(B) 출장을 연기할 것
(C) 웹 사이트를 방문할 것
(D) 호텔을 변경할 것

해설 Harry 씨가 제안하는 일을 묻고 있으므로 Harry라는 이름이 언급된 다음에 반응하는 사람이 제안하는 일을 찾아야 한다. 대화 중반부에 남자 한 명이 Harry의 생각을 묻는 질문을 하자(What do you think, Harry?) 다른 남자가 호텔 웹 사이트를 한 번 확인해 보는 건 어떨지(Well, why don't we take a look at the hotel's Web site?) 제안하고 있다. 따라서 웹 사이트 방문을 의미하는 (C)가 정답이다.

어휘 **postpone** ~을 연기하다

Paraphrase take a look at the hotel's Web site
→ Visiting a Web site

26. 여자는 곧이어 무엇을 할 것 같은가?
(A) 버스 티켓을 구입한다.
(B) 일부 고객들과 얘기한다.
(C) 호텔 매니저에게 연락한다.
(D) 발표에 대한 작업을 한다.

해설 대화 마지막에 여자가 남자 한 명에게 고객들을 대상으로 하는 발표 준비를 하는 동안 앞서 서로 언급한 일을 해 달라고 묻고 있으므로(why don't you do that while I finish off the presentation we're giving to our clients?) 발표 작업을 말한 (D)가 정답임을 알 수 있다.

어휘 **contact** ~에게 연락하다 **work on** ~을 맡아 일하다

Questions 27-29 refer to the following conversation.

M: This is Corey Rutter, host of the *Plugged-In Podcast*. With me today is **27** tech-innovator Aya Sasaki, lead designer of the Starwave 4. Aya, tell us a bit about this device.

W: I'm extremely proud of it. The Starwave 4 improves on every aspect of the previous model.

M: Its development has been very secretive. **28** Is there anything new you can tell us?

W: Well, anyone interested in high-quality video editing should be excited. But that's all for now; you'll have to try it out for yourself. **29** It will be available next week.

남: 저는 플러그드 인 팟캐스트의 진행자인 코리 러터입니다. 오늘 저와 함께 하실 분은 스타웨이브 4의 선임 디자이너이자 기술 혁신가이신 아야 사사키 씨입니다. 아야 씨, 저희에게 이 기기에 관해 조금 말씀해 주시죠.

여: 저는 이 제품이 너무나 자랑스럽습니다. 스타웨이브 4는 이전 모델이 지닌 모든 측면을 능가합니다.

남: 이 제품의 개발 과정은 매우 비밀스러웠습니다. 저희에게 말씀해 주실 새로운 것이 있으신가요?

여: 저, 고품질 동영상 편집에 관심이 있으신 분들이시라면 누구나 흥분되실 겁니다. 하지만 지금으로서는 이것이 말씀드릴 수 있는 전부이며, 직접 사용해 보셔야 할 겁니다. 이 제품은 다음 주에 구매 가능합니다.

어휘 host (방송 프로그램 등의) 진행자 tech-innovator 기술 혁신가 lead designer 선임 디자이너 a bit 조금, 약간 device 기기, 장치 extremely 대단히, 매우, 극히 be proud of ~을 자랑스러워하다 improve 개선되다, 발전하다 aspect 측면, 양상 previous 이전의 development 개발, 발전 secretive 비밀스러운 anyone + 수식어구 ~하는 사람은 누구나 high-quality 고품질의 editing 편집 for now 지금으로서는, 당분간은 try A out (시험 삼아) A를 사용해 보다 for oneself 직접, 스스로 available 구매 가능한

27. 여자의 전문 분야는 무엇인가?
(A) 미술사
(B) 기술 개발
(C) 웹 디자인
(D) 동영상 제작

해설 대화 시작 부분에 남자가 여자를 소개하면서 Starwave 4의 선임 디자이너이자 기술 혁신가라고(tech-innovator Aya Sasaki, lead designer of the Starwave 4) 말하면서 해당 기기에 관해 얘기해 달라고 부탁하고 있으므로(Aya, tell us a bit about this device) 기술 개발을 의미하는 (B)가 정답임을 알 수 있다.

어휘 area of expertise 전문 분야 art history 미술사 production 제작, 생산

28. 남자는 여자에게 무엇을 하도록 요청하는가?
(A) 새로운 정보를 공개할 것
(B) 온라인으로 설명을 게시할 것
(C) 청취자들의 전화에 응답할 것
(D) 프로그램을 다시 방문할 것

해설 남자의 말에서 요청 관련 표현이 제시되는 부분에서 단서를 파

악해야 한다. 남자는 대화 중반부에 제품과 관련해 말해 줄 새로운 것이 있는지(Is there anything new you can tell us?) 묻고 있으므로 이를 새로운 정보 공개라는 말로 표현한 (A)가 정답이다.

어휘 reveal ~을 공개하다, 밝히다, 드러내다 post ~을 게시하다 instructions 설명, 안내, 지시 respond to ~에 응답하다, 대응하다

29. 여자는 왜 "직접 사용해 보셔야 할 겁니다"라고 말하는가?
(A) 기기에 대한 무료 시연회를 제공하기 위해
(B) 제품에 대한 소비자들의 관심을 높이기 위해
(C) 기기의 저조한 매출을 변호하기 위해
(D) 자신이 행사에 부재했던 것을 설명하기 위해

해설 "직접 사용해 봐야 한다"는 말에 이어 다음 주에 구매 가능할 것(It will be available next week)이라고 말하고 있으므로 제품 구매를 유도하기 위해 사용된 문장이라는 것을 알 수 있다. 이는 소비자들의 관심을 끌기 위한 방법에 해당되는 것이므로 이와 같은 의미로 쓰인 (B)가 정답이 된다.

어휘 demonstration 시연(회) increase ~을 높이다, 증가 시키다 consumer 소비자 interest in ~에 대한 관심 defend ~을 변호하다, 옹호하다 poor 저조한, 형편 없는 absence 부재, 자리에 없음

Questions 30-32 refer to the following conversation.

W: Hello, **30** I'm calling in regard to your tennis courts. Could I please reserve two of your courts for April 26? We would like to start playing at around 3 P.M., please.

M: Sure. Let me just check our schedule for that time. Well, it seems we are booked until 3:30 P.M. that day. I'll book you in for that time, but **31** I suggest you arrive early as the group before you will probably finish early.

W: Okay, thanks a lot. Do you have rackets and balls for rent?

M: We do. And if you pay today, we have a special offer available. **32** We have free racket and ball rental for bookings for two or more courts.

여: 안녕하세요, 테니스 코트에 관해 문의하려고 전화 드립니다. 4월 26일에 2개 코트를 예약할 수 있을까요? 저희는 오후 3시 경에 경기를 시작하려고 합니다.

남: 물론입니다. 제가 그 날짜의 스케줄을 확인해 보도록 하겠습니다. 음, 그 날은 오후 3시 30분까지 예약이 있는 것 같습니다. 그 시간으로 예약해 드리겠습니다. 하지만 앞의 그룹이 일찍 경기를 끝낼 수도 있으니 미리 도착하시길 바랍니다.

여: 알겠습니다. 정말 감사합니다. 대여할 수 있는 라켓과 볼이 있나요?

남: 있습니다. 그리고 오늘 비용을 지불하시면 특별한 혜택을 이용하실 수 있습니다. 2개 이상 코트를 예약하신 분들께는 테니스 라켓과 공을 무료로 대여해 드립니다.

어휘 **in regard to** ~에 관하여 **reserve** ~을 예약하다 **booked** 예약이 된 **book A in** A의 이름을 예약 명부에 올리다 **probably** 아마도 **racket** 라켓 **rent** 대여 **available** 이용 가능한 **rental** 대여 **special offer** 특별 혜택 **booking** 예약

30. 여자는 왜 전화하는가?
(A) 테니스 장비를 구입하기 위해
(B) 예약을 취소하기 위해
(C) 운동할 장소를 예약하기 위해
(D) 회원권에 대해 문의하기 위해

해설 전화 건 목적이 드러나는 여자의 첫 대사 I'm calling in regards to your tennis courts. Could I please reserve two of your courts for April 26?를 들어보면 테니스 코트를 예약하기 위해서임을 알 수 있으므로 정답은 (C)가 된다.

어휘 **venue** (행사) 장소 **inquire about** ~에 대해 문의하다

Paraphrase reserve two of your courts
→ book a sporting venue

31. 남자는 여자에게 무엇을 할 것을 제안하는가?
(A) 장비를 가지고 올 것
(B) 예약 시간을 변경할 것
(C) 신용카드로 지불할 것
(D) 장소에 일찍 도착할 것

해설 남자가 제안하는 바는 I suggest ~ 다음에 드러난다. you arrive early as the group before you will probably finish early에서 테니스 코트에 일찍 오라고 제안하고 있으므로 정답은 (D)가 된다.

Paraphrase arrive early
→ Come to a location early

32. 남자는 무엇을 하겠다고 하는가?
(A) 영업 시간을 연장한다.
(B) 무료 장비를 제공한다.
(C) 입장료를 할인해 준다.
(D) 서비스 목록을 보내준다.

해설 남자의 마지막 대사 We have free racket and ball rental for bookings를 들어보면 라켓과 공을 무료로 대여해 주겠다고 하므로 정답은 (B)가 된다.

Paraphrase racket and ball
→ equipment

Questions 33-35 refer to the following conversation and floor plan.

M: Good evening, Ms. Lowell. **33** How are you enjoying your stay?

W: Well, the room is comfortable, and it has a great view of the park. I haven't been sleeping well, though.

M: Oh, I'm sorry to hear that. What's the problem?

W: **34** There's a lot of noise from the elevator, and it runs all through the night. You've probably heard this complaint before, though, since **34** my room shares a wall with it.

M: Actually, this is new information. I'd offer to change your room, but we're fully booked.

W: Oh, don't worry about it. **35** Just don't forget about the airport shuttle I reserved for tomorrow morning.

M: Of course. It will pick you up at 6:45 A.M.

남: 안녕하세요, 로웰 씨. 숙박하시면서 즐거운 시간 보내고 계신가요?
여: 저, 객실은 편안하고, 공원 풍경이 아주 잘 보입니다. 하지만 잠을 잘 자지 못하고 있어요.
남: 아, 그 말씀을 듣게 되어 유감입니다. 무슨 문제라도 있으신가요?
여: 엘리베이터에서 소음이 많이 나는데다 밤새도록 운행되고 있어요. 그런데 제 객실이 엘리베이터와 벽이 맞닿아 있기 때문에 아마 전에 같은 불만 사항을 들어 보신 적이 있으셨을 것 같아요.
남: 실은, 이번에 처음 듣는 얘기입니다. 객실을 변경해 드리고 싶기는 하지만 현재 예약이 꽉 차 있습니다.
여: 아, 걱정하지 마세요. 제가 내일 아침으로 예약한 공항 셔틀 버스에 대해서만 잊지 말아 주셨으면 합니다.
남: 물론입니다. 오전 6시 45분에 버스가 모셔다 드릴 겁니다.

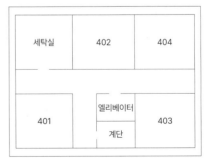

어휘 **stay** 숙박, 머무름 **comfortable** 편안한, 쾌적한 **have a great view of** ~의 풍경이 아주 잘 보이다 **though** (문장 끝이나 중간에서) 하지만, 그런데 **noise** 소음 **run** 운행하다 **all through the night** 밤새도록 **probably** 아마 **complaint** 불만 **share A with B** A를 B와 공유하다, 나눠 갖다 **actually** 실은, 사실은 **offer to do** ~하겠다고 제안하다 **fully booked** 예약이 꽉 찬 **worry about** ~에 대해 걱정하다 **forget about** ~에 대해 잊다 **airport shuttle** 공항 셔틀 버스 **reserve A for B** A를 B의 날짜로 예약하다 **pick up** ~을 차로 데리러 가다, 태워 주다 **laundry** 세탁물

33. 남자는 누구일 것 같은가?
(A) 건물주
(B) 시설 관리팀 직원
(C) 호텔 손님
(D) 프론트 데스크 직원

해설 남자의 신분을 묻고 있으므로 특정 업무나 활동 또는 서비스 등과 관련된 표현이 제시되는 부분에서 단서를 찾아야 한다. 대화를 시작하면서 남자가 즐겁게 숙박하고 있는지 묻고 있는데 (How are you enjoying your stay?) 이는 호텔의 프론트 데스크에 근무하는 직원이 객실 손님에게 물어볼 수 있는 말이므로 (D)가 정답이 된다.

어휘 **landlord** 건물주 **maintenance** 시설 관리, 유지 관리 **clerk** 직원, 점원

34. 시각자료를 보시오. 여자는 어느 객실에 머무르고 있는가?
(A) 401
(B) 402
(C) 403
(D) 404

해설 배치도에서 각 공간의 명칭을 미리 확인해 두는 것이 좋으며, 위치 관계를 나타내는 전치사구에 주의해 들어야 한다. 대화 중반부에 여자가 엘리베이터에서 소음이 많이 나고 있고(There's a lot of noise from the elevator) 자신의 객실이 엘리베이터와 맞닿아 있다고(my room shares a wall with it) 알리는 부분에서 여자의 객실 위치를 확인할 수 있다. 시각자료에서 엘리베이터 바로 옆에 있는 객실 번호가 403이므로 (C)가 정답이다.

35. 여자는 남자에게 무엇에 대해 상기시키는가?
(A) 필요한 수리 작업
(B) 교통편에 대한 조치
(C) 세탁 서비스
(D) 항공편 시간

해설 여자의 말에서 당부나 제안 등을 나타내는 표현이 제시되는 부분에서 단서를 찾아야 한다. 대화 후반부에 여자가 내일 아침으로 예약한 공항 셔틀 버스에 대해서만 잊지 말아 달라고(Just don't forget about the airport shuttle I reserved for ~) 당부하고 있으므로 교통편에 대한 조치를 뜻하는 (B)가 정

답이다.

어휘 **remind A about B** A에게 B에 대해 상기시키다 **necessary** 필요한, 필수의 **repair** 수리 **transportation** 교통편 **arrangement** 준비, 마련, 조치 **flight** 항공편

Questions 36-38 refer to the following conversation and information.

W: Welcome to Belmont Bank. How can I help you this morning?

M: Hi, **36** I'd like to open a high interest savings account to help me save up to buy my first car. Which one would you recommend?

W: We have a few to choose from. Can you tell me the minimum balance you can maintain? You know, the higher the minimum balance, the higher the interest rate.

M: Well, I don't get paid that much, but **37** I'm sure I'll always have a balance of at least $500.

W: Okay. Well, here's a flip chart showing the minimum monthly balance for our most popular savings accounts.

M: Oh, great. And **38** are there any benefits that come with opening a savings account?

W: **38** You'll get a personal check book, but I'm afraid that's it.

M: That's fine. Thanks for the information.

여: 벨몬트 은행에 오신 것을 환영합니다. 오늘 아침에 무엇을 도와 드릴까요?
남: 안녕하세요, 제가 첫 자동차를 구입하는 데 저축할 수 있도록 도움이 될 고이자 저축 계좌를 개설하고 싶습니다. 어느 것을 추천해 주실 수 있으세요?
여: 저희에게 선택 가능한 몇 가지가 있습니다. 유지하실 수 있는 최소 잔액을 말씀해 주시겠습니까? 그러니까, 최소 잔액이 높을수록 이율이 높습니다.
남: 저, 제가 급여를 그렇게 많이 받지는 않지만, 분명 항상 최소 500달러는 잔액을 갖고 있을 거예요.
여: 좋습니다. 그럼, 가장 인기 있는 저희 저축 계좌들에 대한 최소 월간 잔액을 보여 주는 플립 차트가 여기 있습니다.
남: 아, 잘됐네요. 그럼 저축 계좌를 개설하는 데 딸린 어떤 혜택이라도 있나요?
여: 개인 수표책을 받으시게 되는데, 그게 전부인 것 같습니다.
남: 괜찮습니다. 정보 알려 주셔서 감사합니다.

벨몬트 은행 - 저축 계좌	
스탠다드 저축 계좌 $ 최소 잔액 - $10	엑스트라 저축 계좌 $$ 최소 잔액 - $100
인핸스드 저축 계좌 $$$ 최소 잔액 - $500	프리미어 저축 계좌 $$$$ 최소 잔액 - $5,000

어휘 **interest** 이자 **savings account** 저축 계좌 **help A do** A가 ~하는 것을 돕다 **save up** 저축하다, 모으다 **recommend** ~을 추천하다, 권하다 **choose from** ~에서 선택하다 **minimum** 최소의, 최저의 **balance** 잔액, 잔고 **maintain** ~을 유지하다 **interest rate** 금리, 이율 **get paid** 급여를 받다 **that much** 그렇게 많이 **at least** 최소한, 적어도 **flip chart** (넘기면서 보는) 플립 차트 **benefit** 혜택 **come with** ~에 딸려 있다 **check book** (수표 용지를 철한) 수표책 **that's it** 그게 전부다

36. 남자는 왜 저축 계좌를 개설하고 싶어하는가?
(A) 해외로 여행을 가고 싶어한다.
(B) 새 차량을 구입하기를 바라고 있다.
(C) 부동산을 구입할 계획이다.
(D) 학교 등록금을 내야 한다.

해설 대화 초반부에 남자가 자신의 첫 자동차를 구입하는 데 저축할 수 있는 계좌를 개설하고 싶다고(I'd like to open a high interest savings account to help me save up to buy my first car) 알리고 있으므로 (B)가 정답이다.

어휘 **overseas** 해외로 **vehicle** 차량 **plan to do** ~할 계획이다 **property** 건물, 부동산 **tuition fee** 등록금

Paraphrase buy my first car
→ purchase a new vehicle

37. 시각자료를 보시오. 남자가 어느 저축 계좌를 선택할 것 같은가?
(A) 스탠다드 저축 계좌
(B) 엑스트라 저축 계좌
(C) 인핸스드 저축 계좌
(D) 프리미어 저축 계좌

해설 대화 중반부에 남자가 최소 500달러의 잔액을 갖고 있을 거라고(I'm sure I'll always have a balance of at least $500) 언급하는데, 도표에서 이 액수로 표기된 항목이 왼쪽 하단에 위치한 Enhanced Savings이므로 (C)가 정답이다.

38. 여자는 신규 저축 계좌에 무엇이 딸려 있다고 말하는가?
(A) 할인 쿠폰
(B) 수표책
(C) 커피 머그컵
(D) 월간 소식지

해설 대화 후반부에 여자가 저축 계좌를 개설하는 데 딸린 어떤 혜택이라도 있는지(are there any benefits that come with opening a savings account?) 묻자, 남자가 개인 수표책을 받는다고(You'll get a personal check book) 말하므로 (B)가 정답이다.

어휘 **voucher** 쿠폰, 상품권

Part 4

Questions 39-41 refer to the following telephone message.

Good afternoon, Ms. Andrews. **39** It's Pete Hampton from *Midtown Music*. I figured out why your guitar wouldn't stay in tune, and it was an easy fix. I just had to restring it with some lighter nylon strings. **40** I added them to the repair cost, so the bill will be a little higher than we discussed. If you'd like, **41** I can deliver your guitar to your home after I leave the shop since you live nearby. Just call back and let me know.

안녕하세요, 앤드류스 씨. 저는 미드타운 뮤직의 피트 햄튼입니다. 귀하의 기타가 왜 음정이 맞지 않는 상태로 있는지 알아 냈으며, 이는 쉽게 고칠 수 있는 것이었습니다. 단지 더 가벼운 나일론 기타 줄로 바꿔 끼우기만 하면 되는 것이었습니다. 제가 이 가격을 수리비에 추가했으므로, 청구서 금액이 논의했던 것보다 약간 더 높을 것입니다. 괜찮으시다면, 귀하께서 근처에 거주하고 계시기 때문에 제가 매장에서 퇴근한 후에 댁으로 기타를 배달해 드릴 수 있습니다. 제게 다시 전화 주셔서 알려 주시기 바랍니다.

어휘 **figure out** ~을 알아내다, 해결하다 **stay in tune** (악기 등) 음정이 맞는 상태로 있다 **easy fix** 쉽게 고칠 수 있는 것 **restring** ~의 줄을 바꾸다 **light** 가벼운 **string** 줄, 끈 **add A to B** A를 B에 추가하다, 더하다 **repair cost** 수리비 **bill** 청구서, 계산서 **deliver A to B** A를 B로 배달하다 **leave** ~에서 나가다, 떠나다 **since** ~이므로 **nearby** 근처에 **call back** 다시 전화하다 **let A know** A에게 알리다

39. 화자는 어디에서 근무하는가?
(A) 녹음 스튜디오
(B) 음반 매장
(C) 악기 매장
(D) 섬유 소매점

해설 화자의 근무 장소를 묻는 문제이므로 담화 중에 언급되는 특정 업체의 이름이나 업무 활동, 서비스 등과 관련된 내용을 파악해야 한다. 담화 초반부에 화자는 자신이 Midtown Music에 근무한다는 말과 함께, 기타가 왜 음정이 맞지 않는 상태로 있는지 알아냈다고(I figured out why your guitar wouldn't stay in tune) 알리고 있으므로 악기 매장을 뜻하는 (C)가 정답이다.

어휘 record store 음반 매장 instrument 악기 fabric 섬유,
직물

40. 화자는 자신이 무엇을 했다고 말하는가?

　(A) 주문을 했다.
　(B) 청구서 액수를 늘렸다.
　(C) 전문가에게 상의했다.
　(D) 가격을 비교했다.

해설　화자 자신이 한 일을 묻고 있으므로 과거 시제나 현재 완료 시제
　　　동사와 함께 과거 시점의 일로 언급하는 내용을 찾아야 한다.
　　　담화 중반부에 특정 가격을 수리비에 추가했고 청구서 금액이
　　　약간 더 높을 것이라고(I added them to the repair cost,
　　　so the bill will be a little higher ~) 말한 것에 대해 언급한
　　　(B)가 정답이다.

어휘　place an order 주문하다 consult ~에게 상의하다
　　　professional 전문가 compare ~을 비교하다

　Paraphrase added them to the repair cost
　　　　　　 → Increased a bill amount

41. 화자는 무엇을 제공하는가?

　(A) 매장 포인트
　(B) 자택 배달 서비스
　(C) 특별 할인
　(D) 교육 시간

해설　화자가 제공하는 것을 찾아야 하므로 화자 자신이 해주겠다
　　　고 언급하는 부분이 있음을 예상하고 들어야 한다. 담화 마지
　　　막에 집으로 기타를 배달해 줄 수 있다고(I can deliver your
　　　guitar to your home ~) 알리는 부분에 대해 자택 배달이라
　　　는 말로 표현한 (B)가 정답이다.

어휘　store credit 매장 포인트

　Paraphrase deliver your guitar to your home
　　　　　　 → Home delivery

Questions 42-44 refer to the following advertisement.

---

42 Do you get tired of chopping up onions and
bulbs of garlic when you're preparing a meal?
If so, then you probably need the Bulb Buddy!
Our product uses stainless steel blades and an
innovative cutting function to help you chop
ingredients quickly and effortlessly. And, 43 unlike
other similar products on the market, the Bulb
Buddy comes with a warranty. If you purchase
one today, we will offer you a guarantee that it will
work well for the next five years. 44 To purchase
a Bulb Buddy, call us now at 555-8276. You won't
find them in any stores. So, don't hesitate. Take
advantage of this incredible offer, and get a Bulb
Buddy today.

식사 준비를 하실 때 양파와 통마늘을 잘게 써는 것이 지겨우신가
요? 그러시다면, 여러분은 벌브 버디가 필요하실 수도 있습니다!
저희 제품은 스테인리스 스틸 칼날과 혁신적인 절단 기능을 활용
해 음식 재료를 빠르고 힘들지 않게 썰도록 도와 드립니다. 그리고
시중에 나와 있는 다른 유사 제품들과는 달리, 벌브 버디에는 품질
보증서가 딸려 있습니다. 오늘 구입하실 경우, 앞으로 5년 동안 제
대로 기능을 할 것이라는 점을 여러분께 보장해 드립니다. 벌브 버
디를 구입하시려면, 555-8276으로 지금 전화 주세요. 어느 매장
에서도 이 제품을 찾아보실 수 없을 것입니다. 따라서, 주저하지 마
십시오. 이 믿기 힘든 제공 서비스를 이용하셔서, 오늘 벌브 버디를
구입해 보세요.

어휘　get tired of ~하는 것을 지겨워하다 chop up ~을 잘게
　　　썰다 onion 양파 bulb of garlic 통마늘 prepare ~을
　　　준비하다 meal 식사 If so 그렇다면 stainless steel
　　　스테인리스 스틸 blade 칼날 innovative 혁신적인
　　　function 기능, 성능 help A do A가 ~하는 것을 돕다
　　　ingredient 재료, 성분 quickly 빠르게 effortlessly 힘
　　　들이지 않고, 쉽게 unlike ~와 달리 similar 유사한 on
　　　the market 시중에 나와 있는 come with ~가 딸려 있다
　　　warranty 품질 보증(서) purchase ~을 구입하다 offer
　　　A B A에게 B를 제공하다 a guarantee that ~라는 보증
　　　hesitate 주저하다, 망설이다 take advantage of ~을
　　　이용하다 incredible 믿기 힘든 offer 제공(되는 것), 제안

42. 벌브 버디는 무슨 종류의 제품인가?

　(A) 태블릿 컴퓨터
　(B) 조명 기구
　(C) 원예 도구
　(D) 주방 용품

해설　Bulb Buddy가 질문의 핵심이므로 이 명칭과 함께 제시되는
　　　정보를 파악하는 데 집중해야 한다. 담화 시작 부분에 화자가 식
　　　사 준비를 할 때 양파와 통마늘을 잘게 써는 것이 지겨운지 질
　　　문을 던지는 부분에서 음식 조리와 관련된 제품임을 알 수 있
　　　다(Do you get tired of chopping up onions and bulbs
　　　of garlic when you're preparing a meal? If so, then
　　　you probably need the Bulb Buddy!). 따라서 주방 용품
　　　을 뜻하는 (D)가 정답임을 알 수 있다.

어휘　light fixture 조명 기구 gardening 원예 tool 도구, 공구
　　　kitchen utensil 주방 용품

43. 화자의 말에 따르면, 무엇이 해당 제품을 특별하게 만드는가?

　(A) 추가 부품이 딸려 있다.
　(B) 재충전이 가능하다.
　(C) 품질 보증서가 포함되어 있다.
　(D) 다양한 기능이 있다.

해설　제품을 특별하게 만드는 이유를 묻고 있으므로 다른 제품과 구
　　　별되는 기능이나 특징 등이 제시되는 부분에서 단서를 찾아야
　　　한다. 담화 중반부에 화자는 유사 제품들과 달리 Bulb Buddy

에는 품질 보증서가 딸려 있다고(unlike other similar products on the market, the Bulb Buddy comes with a warranty) 알리고 있다. 따라서 이와 같은 특징을 언급한 (C)가 정답이다.

어휘 **extra** 추가의, 별도의 **part** 부품 **rechargeable** 재충전 가능한 **include** ~을 포함하다 **various** 다양한

44. 화자는 왜 "어느 매장에서도 이 제품을 찾아보실 수 없을 것입니다"라고 말하는가?

(A) 제품 회수를 알리기 위해
(B) 제품의 인기를 강조하기 위해
(C) 새로운 웹 사이트를 홍보하기 위해
(D) 청자들에게 전화하도록 권하기 위해

해설 해당 문장은 담화 후반부에 화자가 특정 전화번호와 함께 전화를 걸어 제품을 구매하는 방법(To purchase a Bulb Buddy, call us now at 555-8276)을 소개한 후에 들을 수 있는 말이다. 따라서 제품 구매를 위해 전화하도록 권하기 위해 한 말이라는 것을 알 수 있으므로 (D)가 정답이다.

어휘 **recall** 회수, 리콜 **emphasize** ~을 강조하다 **popularity** 인기 **promote** ~을 홍보하다 **encourage A to do** A에게 ~하도록 권하다, 장려하다

Questions 45-47 refer to the following excerpt from a meeting.

Well, I hope you are all ready for **45** tomorrow afternoon. Mr. Jones should arrive at 2 P.M., and **45** we will demonstrate our products to him after some refreshments. As you know, Mr. Jones is very interested in our new range of photocopiers, and this is our chance to truly impress him. **46** If he likes what he sees, he will purchase thousands of units to be sold in his chain of electronics stores. It's very important that each of you know what your role is tomorrow. So, **47** later on today, you'll all meet with the product development manager, who will assign you specific tasks such as speaking, demonstrating, or preparing handouts.

그럼, 여러분 모두가 내일 오후를 위해 준비되었기를 바랍니다. 존스 씨는 오후 2시에 도착할 것이며, 다과 후에 존스 씨에게 우리 제품을 시연할 것입니다. 아시다시피, 존스 씨는 우리 회사의 새 복사기 제품군에 대해 큰 관심을 가지고 계시기 때문에, 이번 행사는 존스 씨에게 정말로 깊은 인상을 심어줄 수 있는 기회입니다. 존스 씨가 보게 될 제품들을 마음에 들어 하실 경우, 그분의 전자제품 체인 매장에서 판매될 수 있도록 수천 대의 제품을 구입하실 겁니다. 여러분 각자가 내일 맡을 역할을 파악하는 것은 매우 중요합니다. 그래서 오늘 이따가, 여러분 모두가 제품 개발 부장님을 만날 것이며, 부장님께서 발표와 제품 시연, 또는 유인물 준비 등과 같은 구체적인 임무를 배정해 드릴 겁니다.

어휘 **be ready for** ~에 대한 준비가 되다 **demonstrate** ~을 시연하다 **refreshments** 다과 **range** 제품군, 종류 **photocopier** 복사기 **truly** 정말로, 진정으로 **impress** ~에게 (깊은) 인상을 남기다 **thousands of** 수천의 **unit** (상품의) 한 개, 한 대 **electronics store** 전자제품 매장 **role** 역할 **later on today** 오늘 이따가 **meet with** (약속하여) ~와 만나다 **product development** 제품 개발 **assign A B** A에게 B를 배정하다, 할당하다 **such as** ~와 같은 **prepare** ~을 준비하다 **handout** 유인물

45. 화자에 따르면, 내일 무슨 일이 있을 것인가?

(A) 매장 개장식
(B) 제품 시연
(C) 교육 프로그램
(D) 팀워크 구축 행사

해설 담화 초반에 tomorrow가 언급되고 있다. 내일의 행사와 관련하여 Mr. Jones가 오후에 도착하고, 그때 그에게 제품 시연을 한다고(we will demonstrate our products to him) 알리고 있으므로 (B)가 정답임을 알 수 있다.

어휘 **opening** 개장(식) **team-building** 팀워크 구축

46. 존스 씨는 누구인가?

(A) 제품 개발자
(B) 신임 부서장
(C) 잠재 구매자
(D) 재무 컨설턴트

해설 Mr. Jones가 언급되는 이후를 잘 듣는다. 화자의 말에 따르면, Mr. Jones가 화자의 복사기 제품들에 관심이 많으며, 제품 시연회를 계기로 그에게 깊은 인상을 심어주어야 한다고 한다. 그리고 그가 제품들을 마음에 들어 하면 수천 대를 구매할 것이라고(If he likes what he sees, he will purchase thousands of units to be sold in his chain of electronics stores) 말하는 데서 그가 잠재 구매자임을 확인할 수 있으므로 (C)가 정답이다.

어휘 **supervisor** 부서장, 책임자 **potential** 잠재적인 **financial** 재무의, 재정

47. 오늘 이따가 청자들은 무엇을 할 것인가?

(A) 강연에 참석한다.
(B) 포스터를 디자인한다.
(C) 일부 고객들에게 이야기한다.
(D) 부서장과 만난다.

해설 later today가 핵심어이다. 화자는 담화 마지막 부분에서 오늘 오후에 각자에게 특정 업무를 할당해 줄 제품 개발 부장을 만나게 될 것이라고(So, later on today, you'll all meet with the product development manager, who will assign you specific tasks) 공지하고 있다. Product development manager, who will assign you specific tasks를 supervisor라고 표현한 (D)가 정답이다.

어휘 **lecture** 강연(회)

Paraphrase manager → supervisor

Questions 48-50 refer to the following excerpt from a meeting and budget report.

As you all know, keeping our employees healthy and happy is important to this company, but we need to make sure we don't spend too much on this initiative. Therefore, we need to cut back on the recreation budget. **48 I thought we could just cut out the most expensive program, but that program also takes the least amount of time per quarter.** It doesn't affect our overall productivity as much. **49 Another option could be to add a small participation cost to each program.** This might not be a popular move, though. To help us decide, **50 please hand out these surveys to your department staff members,** and then return them to me.

아시다시피, 우리 직원들을 건강하고 행복하게 해 드리는 것이 회사에게 있어 중요한 일이지만, 이 계획에 대해 반드시 너무 많은 비용을 소비하지 않도록 해야 합니다. 따라서, 우리는 레크리에이션 관련 예산을 감축해야 합니다. 저는 우리가 그저 가장 비용이 많이 드는 프로그램을 없애기만 하면 된다고 생각했었는데, 그 프로그램은 또한 분기마다 가장 적은 시간이 걸리는 프로그램입니다. 이는 우리의 전반적인 생산성에 그렇게 많이 영향을 미치지 않습니다. 또 다른 선택권은 각 프로그램에 약간의 참가비를 추가하는 것이 될 수 있습니다. 하지만 이는 사람들이 좋아하지 않는 방법일 수 있습니다. 우리가 결정하는 데 도움이 될 수 있도록, 여러분의 부서 직원들에게 이 설문 조사 양식을 나눠주신 후에, 저에게 다시 되돌려 주시기 바랍니다.

레크리에이션 프로그램 예산	
프로그램	비용
필라테스 수업	750달러
플래그 풋볼 경기	900달러
소프트볼 팀	1,100달러
연례 등산 행사	2,000달러

어휘 **keep A 형용사** A를 ~하게 유지하다 **make sure (that)** 반드시 ~하도록 하다 **spend A on B** (시간, 돈) A를 B에 소비하다 **initiative** 계획, 운동 **therefore** 따라서, 그러므로 **cut back on** ~을 줄이다, 감축하다 **recreation** 레크리에이션, 오락 **budget** 예산 **cut out** ~을 빼다, 삭제하다 **the least amount of time** 가장 적은 시간 **per quarter** 각 분기당 **affect** ~에 영향을 미치다 **overall** 전반적인 **productivity** 생산성 **as much** 그렇게 많이 **option** 선택권 **add A to B** A를 B에 추가하다 **participation cost** 참가비 **move** 조치, 방법 **though** (문장 끝이나, 중간에서) 하지만 **hand out** ~을 나눠주다,

배부하다 **survey** 설문조사(지) **staff member** 직원 **return A to B** A를 B에게 돌려주다 **annual** 연례의, 해마다의

48. 시각자료를 보시오. 화자는 어느 프로그램이 가장 적은 시간이 걸린다고 말하는가?

(A) 필라테스 강좌
(B) 플래그 풋볼 리그
(C) 소프트볼 팀
(D) 연례 등산 여행

해설 가장 적은 시간이 걸리는 프로그램을 찾아야 하는데, 시각자료에 비용만 제시되어 있으므로 담화에서 비용과 관련된 내용이 단서로 제시될 것임을 예상하고 들어야 한다. 담화 중반부에 가장 비용이 많이 드는 프로그램이 분기마다 가장 적은 시간이 걸리는 프로그램이라고(I thought we could just cut out the most expensive program, but that program also takes the least amount of time per quarter) 알리고 있다. 시각자료에서 가장 비용이 많이 드는 것이 Annual Hiking Trip이므로 (D)가 정답이 된다.

49. 화자는 무슨 해결책을 제안하는가?

(A) 참가비를 부과하는 것
(B) 예산을 늘리는 것
(C) 근무 시간을 연장하는 것
(D) 프로그램 선택권을 확대하는 것

해설 담화 후반부에 화자는 또 다른 선택권으로 각 프로그램에 약간의 참가비를 추가하는 것을 언급하고 있으므로(Another option could be to add a small participation cost to each program) 참가비 부과를 의미하는 (A)가 정답이다.

어휘 **propose** ~을 제안하다 **charge** ~을 부과하다, 청구하다 **extend** ~을 연장하다 **expand** ~을 확대하다, 확장하다 **choice** 선택권

Paraphrase add a small participation cost → Charging participation fees

50. 화자는 청자들에게 무엇을 하도록 요청하는가?

(A) 설문 조사 양식을 나눠줄 것
(B) 자금을 기부할 것
(C) 주말 동안 근무할 것
(D) 행사를 조직할 것

해설 화자의 말 중 요청 관련 표현이 제시되는 부분에서 단서를 파악해야 한다. 담화 후반부에 각 부서의 직원들에게 설문 조사 양식을 나눠주도록(please hand out these surveys to your department staff members) 요청하고 있으므로 이에 대해 언급한 (A)가 정답이다.

어휘 **distribute** ~을 나눠주다, 배부하다 **donate** ~을 기부하다 **fund** 자금 **over** ~동안에 걸쳐 **organize** ~을 조직하다, 준비하다

Paraphrase hand out → distribute

1. (C)	**2.** (D)	**3.** (B)	**4.** (C)	**5.** (D)
6. (B)	**7.** (D)	**8.** (B)	**9.** (C)	**10.** (B)
11. (B)	**12.** (A)	**13.** (D)	**14.** (B)	**15.** (A)
16. (A)	**17.** (A)	**18.** (D)	**19.** (C)	**20.** (B)
21. (B)	**22.** (C)	**23.** (D)	**24.** (C)	**25.** (D)
26. (B)	**27.** (D)	**28.** (A)	**29.** (B)	**30.** (D)
31. (B)	**32.** (A)	**33.** (C)	**34.** (D)	**35.** (C)
36. (C)	**37.** (D)	**38.** (A)	**39.** (B)	**40.** (C)
41. (D)	**42.** (C)	**43.** (A)	**44.** (B)	**45.** (C)
46. (B)	**47.** (D)	**48.** (D)	**49.** (C)	**50.** (C)

Part 5

1.

정답   (C)

해석   러독 씨는 반드시 바이러스로부터 보호되도록 하기 위해 회사의 컴퓨터의 소프트웨어를 주기적으로 업데이트한다.

해설   주어와 동사 사이에 위치한 빈칸은 동사를 앞에서 수식할 부사 자리이므로 (C) regularly가 정답이다.

어휘   ensure (that) 반드시 ~하도록 하다, ~하는 것을 확실히 해두다 regular 주기적인, 보통의 regularly 주기적으로, 정기적으로 regularity 주기적임, 정기적임

2.

정답   (D)

해석   뎁 씨가 지닌 소매 영업에 관한 상당한 지식은 그를 신임 지점장이 되는 데 더할 나위 없이 적합한 사람으로 만들어 준다.

해설   전치사 of와 명사 sales 사이에 빈칸이 있으므로 빈칸은 명사를 수식하는 형용사 또는 복합명사를 구성하는 또 다른 명사가 필요하다. 따라서 sales와 함께 '소매 영업'이라는 의미를 나타내는 복합명사를 구성할 수 있는 명사 (D) retail이 정답이다.

어휘   considerable 상당한 knowledge 지식 retail n. 소매(업) v. ~을 소매 판매하다 ideally 더할 나위 없이 suited 적합한, 어울리는 retailing 소매업 (활동) retailer 소매업체, 소매업자

3.

정답   (B)

해석   공공 서비스와 관련해 어떤 불만 사항이든 있으실 경우, 여러분의 지역 의회 의원에게 연락하십시오.

해설   빈칸이 동사와 명사구 목적어 사이에 위치해 있으므로 빈칸은 명사구를 수식할 수 있는 단어가 필요한 자리이다. 따라서 소유격 대명사 (B) your가 정답이다.

어휘   complaint 불만, 불평 public 공공의, 대중의 contact ~에게 연락하다 council member 의회 의원

4.

정답   (C)

해석   저희에게 555-0989로 전화하셔서 저희 잡지에 대한 구독 기간을 갱신하기를 원하시는지 확인해 주시기 바랍니다.

해설   빈칸이 Please 뒤에 있으므로 빈칸은 Please와 함께 명령문을 이끌 동사원형이 필요한 자리이다. 따라서 (C) confirm이 정답이다.

어휘   renew ~을 갱신하다 subscription 구독 (기간) confirmation 확인 (편지)

5.

정답   (D)

해석   승진 가능성을 높이기 위해, 매과이어 씨는 관리자 교육 과정에 등록했다.

해설   선택지가 모두 다른 과거분사로 구성되어 있으므로 해석을 통해 알맞은 어휘를 골라야 하는데 빈칸 뒤의 전치사 in과 어울리는 것을 골라야 한다. 승진 가능성을 높이기 위해 특정 교육 과정에 대해 할 수 있는 일을 나타내는 어휘가 필요하므로 '등록하다'를 뜻하는 enroll의 과거분사 (D) enrolled가 정답이다.

어휘   chance 가능성 promotion 승진, 홍보 attend ~에 참석하다 propose ~을 제안하다 enroll in ~에 등록하다

6.

정답   (B)

해석   대학가는 귀하의 점보 프레첼 매장을 열기에 완벽한 위치이며, 귀하의 가게는 쉽게 많은 학생들을 끌어들일 것입니다.

해설   주어와 동사가 포함된 절 뒤로 빈칸과 동사가 바로 이어지는 구조이다. 따라서, 불완전한 절을 이끌 관계대명사가 필요한데, 빈칸 앞에 사물 선행사가 있으므로 (B) which가 정답이다.

어휘   district 구역 location 위치, 장소 easily 쉽게, 용이하게 attract ~을 끌어들이다

7.

정답   (D)

해석   총무부장으로서의 역할을 시작한 이후로, 퍼킨스 씨는 효과적인 리더십 능력으로 칭찬 받아 왔다.

해설   명사 leadership 뒤에 위치한 빈칸에 리더십과 관련해 칭찬을 받은 이유를 나타낼 수 있는 또 다른 명사가 들어가 leadership과 복합명사를 구성해야 알맞으므로 '능력, 역량'을

뜻하는 (D) capabilities가 정답이다.

어휘 since ~한 이후로 general office manager 총무부장 praise A for B B에 대해 A를 칭찬하다 capableness 할 수 있음 capable ~할 수 있는, 유능한 capably 유능하게, 훌륭하게 capability 능력, 역량

8.

정답 (B)

해석 여러 번의 체납이 발생한 끝에 그래함 사무용품 사는 최근에 화이트 파운틴 사와의 계약을 파기하기로 결정했다.

해설 빈칸 앞에 문장의 주어와 부사가 있고 뒤에는 to부정사가 있으므로 빈칸이 동사 자리임을 알 수 있다. 동사가 아닌 (C) to decide를 소거하면 나머지 선택지가 모두 다른 시제로 구성되어 있으므로 문장에서 시점 단서를 찾아 풀어야 한다. 따라서 빈칸 앞에 있는 recently와 함께 쓰이는 과거시제 (B) decided가 정답이다.

어휘 recently 최근에 terminate ~을 파기하다 contract n. 계약(서) late payment 체납, 지불 연체

9.

정답 (C)

해석 스트렌코 사의 신입사원 장려금 지급 계획은 내년 초까지는 실행되지 않을 것이다.

해설 빈칸 뒤에 명사구가 있으므로 빈칸은 전치사 자리이다. 또한, 이 명사구가 시점을 나타내므로 시점 명사구를 목적어로 취하는 (C) until이 정답이다.

어휘 scheme 계획, 책략 take effect 실행되다, 효력을 발휘하다

10.

정답 (B)

해석 라페사이드 극장 맞은편에 지어지고 있는 레스토랑은 중앙 아메리카에서 유래한 다양한 음식을 제공할 것이다.

해설 선택지가 모두 다른 동사로 구성되어 있으므로 해석을 통해 알맞은 어휘를 골라야 한다. 빈칸에 쓰일 어휘는 레스토랑 측에서 음식과 관련해 할 수 있는 일을 나타내야 하므로 음식에 대해 '~을 제공하다, ~을 내오다'를 뜻하는 (B) serve가 정답이다.

어휘 opposite ~의 맞은편에, ~의 건너편에 originate from ~에서 유래하다, ~에서 시작되다 consume ~을 소비하다, ~을 먹다 serve (음식 등) ~을 제공하다, ~을 내오다 advise ~을 조언하다, ~에게 조언하다

11.

정답 (B)

해석 선플라워 호텔은 아름다운 흰 백사장과 시의 유명 쇼핑 구역에 모두 가까운 곳에 편리하게 위치해 있다.

해설 선택지가 모두 부사이므로 해석을 통해 의미상 알맞은 어휘를 골라야 한다. 해석상 호텔이 두 구역에 모두 가깝게 위치해 있다

는 것이 자연스러우므로 위치와 관련해 '편리하게'라는 의미로 쓰이는 (B) conveniently가 정답이다.

어휘 conveniently 편리하게 be located close to ~에 가깝게 위치해 있다 gradually 점차 substantially 상당히 nearly 거의

12.

정답 (A)

해석 그 테니스 토너먼트의 마지막 경기가 연기되었는데, 소나기가 예상보다 훨씬 더 심했기 때문이었다.

해설 빈칸 앞뒤로 주어와 동사를 포함한 절이 있으므로 빈칸은 접속사 자리이다. '소나기가 심했기 때문에 경기가 연기되었다'와 같은 의미가 구성되어야 자연스러우므로 '~하기 때문에'라는 뜻으로 이유를 말할 때 사용하는 (A) because가 정답이다.

어휘 postpone ~을 연기하다, ~을 미루다 rain shower 소나기 heavy (정도, 양 등이) 심한, 많은 than expected 예상보다 unless ~하지 않는다면, ~가 아니라면 as such 따라서, 그러므로 in order that ~하기 위해, ~할 수 있도록

13.

정답 (D)

해석 매우 뛰어난 자격을 갖춘 여러 사람들이 마키스 프로즌 푸드 사의 수석 웹 디자이너 역할에 지원했다.

해설 선택지가 모두 다른 명사로 구성되어 있으므로 해석을 통해 알맞은 어휘를 골라야 한다. 빈칸에 쓰일 명사는 바로 앞에 위치한 직책 the Senior Web Designer와 어울려 사람들이 지원 가능한 일자리 등을 나타내야 하므로 '역할, 임무' 등을 뜻하는 (D) role이 정답이다.

어휘 highly 매우, 대단히, 아주 qualified 자격을 갖춘, 적격의 apply for ~에 지원하다, ~을 신청하다 location 지점, 위치, 장소 audition 오디션 role 역할, 직무

14.

정답 (B)

해석 회사의 최고 재무 이사 뿐만 아니라, 회사 회계사들로 구성된 소규모 팀도 참석하는 회의가 예정되어 있다.

해설 빈칸 앞뒤에 명사구가 있으므로 두 개의 명사구를 병렬 구조로 연결할 수 있는 (B) as well as가 정답이다.

어휘 set up ~을 마련하다 accountant 회계사, 회계 담당 직원 chief financial officer 최고 재무 이사 even though 비록 ~이지만, ~라 하더라도

15.

정답 (A)

해석 로웰 씨는 호텔 로비의 외관을 개선하기 위해 경험 많은 실내 디자이너와 공동 작업했다.

해설 선택지가 모두 전치사로 구성되어 있고 빈칸 앞에 현재완료시제로 쓰여 있는 동사 collaborate가 있으므로 이 동사와 어울

려 쓰이면서 공동 작업하는 사람을 말할 때 쓰이는 (A) with가 정답이다.

어휘 **experienced** 경험 많은 **improve** ~을 개선하다, ~을 향상시키다 **appearance** 외관, 겉모습

16.

정답 (A)

해석 적당한 장소를 이번 주에 찾지 못할 경우, 사내 연회는 다음 달 중으로 일정이 재조정되어야 할 것이다.

해설 콤마 앞뒤로 주어와 동사를 포함한 두 개의 절이 있으므로 빈칸은 접속사 자리이다. 따라서, 선택지에서 유일한 접속사인 (A) Unless가 정답이다.

어휘 **appropriate** 적당한, 적절한 **venue** 장소 **banquet** 연회 **be rescheduled for** ~로 일정이 재조정되다 **unless** ~가 아니라면 **therefore** 그러므로 **otherwise** 그렇지 않으면 **instead** 대신에

Part 6

17-20.

수신: 바이오시스템즈 주식회사 전 직원
발신: 앨런 아놀드, 연구소장
날짜: 11월 6일

우리가 다음 주에 새로운 보안 조치를 도입한다는 점에 유의하시기 바랍니다. 11월 11일 월요일에 **17** 시행되는 것으로서, 여러분께서는 우리의 주 연구소 건물에 출입하실 때 키패드에 숫자 코드를 입력하셔야 할 것입니다. 이 시스템은 승인되지 않은 사람이 이 **18** 시설에 접근하는 것을 방지하기 위해 설치됩니다. 몇 차례나, 방문객들이 실수로 우리 연구소에 출입한 바 있으며, 우리는 이런 일이 발생되는 것을 막아야 합니다.

이 출입문 **19** 시스템과 함께, 바이오시스템즈 주식회사 전 직원 여러분께 사원증을 발급할 예정입니다. 이는 반드시 업무 중에 항상 착용하셔야 합니다. 월요일 아침에 도착하시는 대로 경비실을 방문하셔서 각자의 사원증과 숫자 출입문 코드를 받으시기 바랍니다. **20** 우리 업무 장소를 안전하게 유지하는 데 있어 여러분의 협조에 감사 드립니다.

어휘 **laboratory** 연구소, 실험실(= lab) **be aware that** ~임에 유의하다, ~임을 알고 있다 **measures** 절차 **numeric** 숫자의 **prevent A from -ing** A가 ~하는 것을 방지하다, A가 ~하는 것을 막다(= stop A from -ing) **access** ~에 접근하다, ~을 이용하다 **occasion** 때, 기회, 행사 **accidentally** 실수로, 우연히 **issue** v. ~을 발급하다, ~을 지급하다 **identity** 신분, 신원 **at all times** 항상 **as soon as** ~하는 대로, ~하자마자 **obtain** ~을 받다, ~을 얻다

17.

정답 (A)

해설 앞선 문장에 새로운 보안 조치를 도입한다는 말이 쓰여 있어 빈칸 뒤에 위치한 날짜와 요일이 그 시행 시점임을 알 수 있다. 따라서, 시점 표현과 결합해 '~부터 시행되는'이라는 의미를 나타내는 (A) Effective가 정답이다.

어휘 **effective** 효과적인, (시점 표현과 함께) ~부터 시행되는 **effect** n. 효과, 영향 v. ~에 영향을 미치다, (결과로서) ~을 일으키다 **effectively** 효과적으로

18.

정답 (D)

해설 빈칸에 쓰일 명사는 동명사 accessing의 목적어로서 출입 또는 이용이 가능한 대상을 나타내야 하므로 앞선 문장에 언급된 main research building이 그 대상임을 알 수 있다. 따라서, 이 건물을 대신할 수 있는 명사가 빈칸에 쓰여야 하므로 '시설(물)'을 뜻하는 (D) facility가 정답이다.

어휘 **feature** 특징, 기능 **position** 직책, 일자리 **route** 노선, 경로 **facility** 시설(물)

19.

정답 (C)

해설 빈칸은 바로 뒤에 위치한 명사구 the door entry system을 목적어로 취할 전치사 자리이다. 또한, 그 뒤에 또 다른 보안 조치를 소개하는 내용이 쓰여 있어 추가적인 정보를 언급하는 의미가 구성되어야 알맞으므로 '~와 함께'라는 의미로 추가 사항을 알릴 때 사용하는 (C) Along with가 정답이다.

어휘 **just as** 꼭 ~처럼 **in contrast** 반대로, 그에 반해서 **along with** ~와 함께 **compare with** ~에 비해, ~와 비교해

20.

정답 (B)

해석 (A) 이 보안 시스템의 결함이 다음 주에 수리될 것입니다.
(B) 우리 업무 장소를 안전하게 유지하는 데 있어 여러분의 협조에 감사 드립니다.
(C) 이 교육 워크숍에 참석하실 수 없는 경우에 저희에게 알려 주십시오.
(D) 새로운 쓰레기 처리 절차가 반드시 전 직원에 의해 준수되어야 합니다.

해설 지문 전체적으로 새로운 보안 조치를 소개하면서 그 시행 방식과 관련해 설명하는 내용을 담고 있다. 따라서, 지문 맨 마지막에 위치한 빈칸에 그러한 조치의 시행과 관련해 언급하면서 글을 마무리하는 문장이 쓰여야 알맞으므로 회사의 안전을 유지하는 것에 대한 협조에 감사하다는 말로 인사하는 (B)가 정답이다.

어휘 **fault** 결함, 흠 **appreciate** ~에 대해 감사하다 **cooperation** 협조, 협력 **secure** 안전한 **inform** ~에게 알리다 **attend** ~에 참석하다 **disposal** 처리, 처분

procedure 절차 follow ~을 준수하다, ~을 따르다

21-24.

수신: 샐리 스터게스
발신: 고객 서비스부
제목: 귀하의 최근 글렌이글스 리조트 숙박
날짜: 11월 25일
첨부: 객실 쿠폰

스터게스 씨께,

귀하께서 11월 19일부터 11월 21일까지 저희 글렌이글스 리조트에서 머무르시는 동안 **21** 접하셨던 문제점들에 관한 이야기를 듣게 되어 대단히 유감입니다. 귀하께서 객실에서 발견하신 사용된 타월과 교체되지 않은 침구는 저희 리조트가 그 동안 명성을 쌓아온 높은 수준의 서비스를 대표하는 것이 아니라는 사실을 거듭 말씀드립니다. 저희 객실 **22** 모두는 고객들께서 체크인 하시도록 허용되기 전에 깨끗한 타월과 침구를 갖춥니다. 저희는 이러한 **23** 불편함에 대해 사과 드립니다. 저희는 기꺼이 저희 이탈리안 레스토랑인 산티니즈에서의 식사를 포함해 리조트 1일 무료 숙박 서비스를 제공해 드리겠습니다. 다음 번에 저희 리조트 객실을 예약하실 때, 이 이메일에 첨부된 쿠폰을 출력하셔서 체크인하실 때 프런트 데스크 직원에게 제시하시기만 하면 됩니다. **24** 다시 한번, 귀하께서 받으신 좋지 못한 수준의 서비스에 대해 사과 드립니다.

안녕히 계십시오.

오스카 플림턴

어휘 voucher 쿠폰, 상품권 encounter ~을 접하다, ~와 맞닥뜨리다 Please be assured that ~임을 거듭 말씀 드립니다, ~라는 점에 안심하시기 바랍니다 bedding 침구 be representative of ~을 대표하다 build one's reputation ~의 명성을 쌓다 be equipped with ~을 갖추고 있다 complimentary 무료의 reserve ~을 예약하다 attached 첨부된 upon -ing ~하는 순간에, ~하자마자

21.

정답 (B)

해설 빈칸 앞에 제시되어 있는 you 이하 부분이 the problems를 수식하는 관계대명사절이 되어야 하므로 주어 you 뒤에 위치한 빈칸은 동사 자리이다. 또한, 숙박 기간으로 제시된 November 19 to November 21가 상단의 이메일 작성 날짜 November 25보다 과거 시점에 해당되므로 과거시제 동사가 쓰여야 한다. 따라서 (B) encountered가 정답이다.

22.

정답 (C)

해설 빈칸 뒤에 제시되는 내용을 보면 일반적으로 객실에 깨끗한 상태의 물품이 구비된다는 사실이 쓰여 있다. 이는 모든 객실을 대상으로 행해지는 일이어야 하며, 「of + 복수명사구」의 수식을

받을 수 있으면서 '~의 모두'를 의미할 때 사용하는 (C) All이 정답이다.

어휘 whole n. 전체

23.

정답 (D)

해설 빈칸에 쓰일 명사는 전치사 for의 목적어로서 사과의 말을 전하는 이유를 나타내야 한다. 앞서 고객인 상대방이 객실에서 사용된 타월과 교체되지 않은 침구를 발견한 사실이 쓰여 있으므로 이러한 경험을 대신할 명사로 '불편함'을 뜻하는 (D) inconvenience가 정답이다.

어휘 addition 추가(되는 것) delay 지연, 지체 reduction 감소, 할인

24.

정답 (D)

해석 (A) 리조트가 상업 지구 내에 편리하게 위치해 있습니다.
(B) 대부분의 저희 고객들께서는 이 신규 서비스에 만족하고 계십니다.
(C) 하지만, 저희 직원들 중 한 명이 그 문제를 즉시 처리했습니다.
(D) 다시 한번, 귀하께서 받으신 좋지 못한 수준의 서비스에 대해 사과 드립니다.

해설 앞서 지문 전체적으로 고객인 상대방에게 과거 시점에 숙박하면서 겪은 좋지 못한 경험에 대해 사과하고 그에 대한 보상을 제공하겠다는 내용이 쓰여 있다. 따라서 그러한 좋지 못한 경험을 the poor standard of service you received로 가리켜 사과의 말을 전하는 의미를 담은 (D)가 정답이다.

어휘 be conveniently located in ~에 편리하게 위치해 있다 commercial district 상업 지구 promptly 즉시, 즉각적으로 address v. (문제 등) ~을 처리하다, 다루다

Part 7

25-26.

바너비 마켓
신선한 지역 농산물

25 여러분의 의견을 소중하게 생각합니다!

저희 바너비 마켓에서는, 고객님들께 최고 품질의 신선한 과일과 야채를 제공하기 위해 항상 노력합니다. 저희 마켓은 계속해서 고객 여러분의 요구를 충족시켜 드릴 수 있도록 저희 제품군에 대해 어떠한 의견을 가지고 계신지 듣고 싶습니다. 오늘 매장을 떠나시기 전에, 계산원에게 **25** 고객 의견 카드를 요청하십시오. 작성하시는 데 잠깐이면 되고, 매장 출구에 위치한 상자에 넣어주시면 됩니다. 6월 30일에, 저희가 상자에서 무작위로 3장의 의견 카드를 뽑을 것입니다. 선정된 3장의 의견 카드를 제출하신 분들은 **26** 맛있고 신선한 과일 바구니를 무료로 받으실 겁니다. 이 행사는 바

너비 마켓의 회원 및 비회원에게 모두 해당됩니다.

감사합니다.

바너비 포서링엄 지점 매니저

어휘 local produce 지역 농산물 value ~을 소중히 여기다 strive to do ~하는데 매진하다, 노력하다 quality 품질 product ranges 물품 내역, 제품군 meet one's needs ~의 요구를 충족시키다 cashier 계산원 comment card 의견 카드 take + 시간 ~만큼 (시간)이 걸리다 moment 잠깐 fill out ~을 작성하다 randomly 무작위로 complimentary 무료의 apply to ~에 해당되다, 적용되다

25. 공지의 주된 목적은 무엇인가?
　(A) 고객에게 신제품에 대해 알리기 위해
　(B) 고객의 상점 애용에 대해 감사하기 위해
　(C) 매장에 새로운 고객을 끌어들이기 위해
　(D) 고객들로부터 의견을 요청하기 위해

정답 (D)

해설 부제목에서 고객의 의견을 소중히 여긴다는(We value your feedback) 내용과 지문 중반부에 고객 의견 카드를 작성해 달라는 내용이(please ask a cashier for a customer comment card) 언급되고 있으므로 (D)가 정답이다.

어휘 notify ~을 알리다, 통지하다 patronage 애용 attract ~을 끌어들이다 solicit A from B B로부터 A를 간청하다, 요청하다

26. 일부 고객들은 무료로 무엇을 받게 되는가?
　(A) 바나비 상품권
　(B) 여러 종류의 농산물
　(C) 레스토랑에서의 식사
　(D) 매장 회원권

정답 (B)

해설 지문 후반부에 선정된 3장의 의견 카드를 작성한 사람에게는 무료의 맛있고 신선한 과일 바구니를 준다고(Those who submitted the three selected comment cards will receive a complimentary basket of delicious fresh fruits) 언급되어 있다. 따라서 과일을 농산물로 바꿔 표현한 (B)가 정답이다.

어휘 for free 무료로 gift voucher 상품권 a selection of 다양한, 여러 종류의

27-29.

수신: 제라드 섯클리프 <gsutcliffe@belcherinc.com>
발신: 에드위나 스타크 <csmanager@mormontpark.com>
제목: 모몬트 파크가 재개장했습니다
날짜: 9월 8일

섯클리프 씨께,

올 여름에, 저희는 저희 레스토랑에 많은 변화를 주었습니다. 저희는 **28(C)** 식사 공간을 다시 디자인하고 개조했으며, **28(D)** 다양한 새 주방 기기를 설치했고, 저희 요리사들에게 메뉴에 **28(B)** 새 요리를 도입할 수 있게 해 드렸습니다. — [1] —. **29**

이번 달에 재개장한 이후로, 저희는 식사 손님들로부터 많은 긍정적인 의견을 받아 왔습니다. — [2] —. 저희 레스토랑에서 한동안 귀하를 뵙지 못했기 때문에, 이번 기회를 빌어 저희가 다시 한번 문을 열고 영업 중이라는 사실을 귀하께 알려 드리기 위해 직접 연락 드려야겠다는 생각이 들었습니다. — [3] —.

27 이번 달 중으로 저희 쪽에 예약을 하실 생각이신지 알려 주시기 바랍니다. 이번 달에 분명히 예약하시는 경우, 함께 식사하시는 그룹에 속하신 각각의 분들께 기꺼이 무료 와인 한 잔을 제공해 드리겠습니다. — [4] —. 귀하께서 새로운 종류의 저희 애피타이저 및 디저트의 높은 품질과 합리적인 가격에 깊은 인상을 받으시리라 확신합니다.

점심 또는 저녁 식사 예약을 하시고자 하는 경우에 555-7623번으로 전화 주시기 바랍니다.

안녕히 계십시오.

에드위나 스타크
고객 서비스부장
모몬트 파크 레스토랑

어휘 make a change 변화를 주다, 변경하다 install ~을 설치하다 appliance 기기, 기구 introduce ~을 도입하다, ~을 소개하다 diner 식사 손님 for a while 한동안 take this opportunity to do 이번 기회를 빌어 ~하다 whether ~인지 (아닌지) make a reservation 예약하다(= make a booking) be certain that ~임을 확신하다 be impressed with ~에 깊은 인상을 받다 reasonable 합리적인 range 종류, 제품군

27. 왜 섯클리프 씨에게 이메일이 보내졌는가?
　(A) 개조 공사 진행 상황에 관한 알리기 위해
　(B) 개장 기념 행사에 초대하기 위해
　(C) 고용 기회와 관련해 알리기 위해
　(D) 예약하도록 권하기 위해

정답 (D)

해설 첫 번째 단락에서 그 동안 있었던 개조 공사와 관련된 소식을 전하고, 두 번째 단락에서 이번 달 중으로 예약을 할 생각이 있는지 알려 달라고(Please let us know whether you would like to make a reservation with us sometime this month) 요청하고 있다. 이는 재개장한 레스토랑을 예약해 다시 방문하도록 권하는 말에 해당되므로 (D)가 정답이다.

어휘 progress 진행 상황, 진척 renovation 개조, 보수 inform ~에게 알리다 employment 고용, 취업 encourage A to do A에게 ~하도록 권하다

28. 스타크 씨가 언급하는 변화가 아닌 것은 무엇인가?

(A) 새로운 요리사의 고용
(B) 새로운 메뉴 품목의 추가
(C) 레스토랑 실내의 재디자인
(D) 기기의 설치

정답 (A)

해설 첫 번째 단락에 식사 공간을 다시 디자인했다는(We redesigned and renovated our dining area) 부분에서 (C)를, 그리고 다양한 새 주방 기기를 설치했다는(installed various new kitchen appliances) 부분에서 (D)를, 새 요리를 도입할 수 있게 했다는(allowed our chefs to introduce new dishes) 부분에서 (B)를 확인할 수 있다. 하지만 새로운 요리사의 고용과 관련된 정보는 제시되어 있지 않으므로 (A)가 정답이다.

어휘 hiring 고용 addition 추가(하는 것) installation 설치

29. [1], [2], [3], [4]로 표기된 위치들 중에서, 다음 문장이 들어가기에 가장 적절한 곳은 어디인가?

"게다가, 음식 평론가 제임스 고든 씨께서는 <월간 푸드> 최신호에서 저희에게 별 5개의 평점을 주셨습니다."

(A) [1]
(B) [2]
(C) [3]
(D) [4]

정답 (B)

해설 제시된 문장은 유사한 추가 정보를 말할 때 사용하는 Moreover와 함께 음식 평론가 제임스 고든이 별 5개의 평점을 준 사실을 말하고 있다. 따라서 레스토랑 평가와 관련된 문장으로서 손님들로부터 많은 긍정적인 의견을 받았다고 알리는 문장 뒤에 위치한 [2]에 들어가 레스토랑 평가와 관련된 정보를 추가로 언급하는 흐름이 되어야 자연스러우므로 (B)가 정답이다.

어휘 moreover 게다가, 더욱이 critic 평론가, 비평가 latest 최신의 issue (출판물 등의) 호

30-32.

제4회 연례
DEO 게임 시리즈 챔피언십

디지털 발전 기구(DEO)는 32 3월 11일 금요일부터 3월 14일 월요일까지 열리는 제4회 게임 시리즈 챔피언십을 발표하게 되어 기쁩니다. 언제나 그렇듯이, 이 대회는 세계 최고의 비디오 게임 선수들이 상금을 타기 위해 경쟁하기 때문에, 그들을 한곳으로 불러들일 것입니다.

이 행사가 지난해 일본, 도쿄에서 개최되었을때, 1등 상금인 25만 달러가 한국의 프로게이머인 장경돈 씨에게 돌아갔습니다. 31 2등 상금인 10만 달러는 싱가포르의 쿤 지안 호씨가 차지했습니다. 30 대만의 타이페이에서 열리는 올해 행사에는 31 상금이 지난해의 두 배가 될 것입니다.

행사의 첫 3일 동안, 대회 참가자들은 <스타 플릿 2>, <갤럭시 파이터즈>, 그리고 <아미 오브 히어로즈>의 세 가지 다른 게임을 할 것입니다. 32 행사의 4일차이자 마지막 날에, DS소프트웨어의 회장인 타케다 미야자키 씨가 그의 회사에서 많은 기대를 받고 있는 신작 게임인 <스타 플릿 3>에 대해 발표를 할 것입니다. 일정에 대한 세부 사항 및 참가 조건에 대해서는 www.deo.com/championships에 방문하시기 바랍니다.

어휘 be pleased to do ~하게 되어 기쁘다 announce ~을 발표하다 take place 발생하다, 개최되다 compete 경쟁을 펼치다 runner-up 2등, 2인자 contestant 참가자 head 회장, 책임자 much-anticipated 많은 기대를 받는 entry requirement 참가 조건

30. 올해의 행사에 대해 언급된 것은 무엇인가?
(A) 이틀 동안 지속될 것이다.
(B) 온라인 상으로 중계될 것이다.
(C) 장경돈 씨에 의해 주최될 것이다.
(D) 대만에서 열릴 것이다.

정답 (D)

해설 두 번째 단락 마지막 문장에 올해 대회가 대만에서 열린다는 사실이(At this year's event in Taipei, Taiwan) 언급되어 있으므로 (D)가 정답이다.

어휘 last 지속되다 broadcast ~을 방송하다 host ~을 주최하다

31. 올해의 2등 참가자는 얼마의 상금을 받을 것 같은가?
(A) $100,000
(B) $200,000
(C) $250,000
(D) $500,000

정답 (B)

해설 두 번째 문단에서 지난해보다 올해의 상금이 2배가 되었다고(the prize money will be double that of last year) 언급하고 있으므로 작년 2등 상금인 $100,000의 2배인 (B)가 정답이다.

32. 타케다 미야자키 씨가 발표하는 요일은 언제인가?
(A) 월요일
(B) 금요일
(C) 토요일
(D) 일요일

정답 (A)

해설 마지막 단락에 행사 마지막 날 타케다 미야자키 씨가 발표를 할 예정임을(On the fourth and final day of the event, the head of DS Software, Takeda Miyazaki, will present) 알리고 있으며, 첫 번째 단락에 제시된 행사 기간에서 마지막 날은 3월 14일 월요일이므로 (A)가 정답이다.

어휘 give a presentation 발표하다

33-36.

> **프레드 요크 [오전 10:11]** 질리안 씨! 지금 창고에 계신가요?
>
> **질리안 제이콥슨 [오전 10:12]** 지금 그곳으로 가는 길이에요.
>
> **프레드 요크 [오전 10:14]** **33** 제가 이곳 포스터 로드 작업에 잔디용 비료를 충분히 가져 오지 않았어요. 제가 지금 너무 바빠서 창고까지 먼 길을 가 좀 가져올 틈이 없어요.
>
> **질리안 제이콥슨 [오전 10:16]** 제가 그냥 로이 씨를 이 대화창에 초대할게요. 지금 창고에 계시거든요. 찾으시는 양이 얼마나 되죠?
>
> **프레드 요크 [오전 10:17]** **34** 25킬로그램이면 충분할 겁니다. 처리해 주실 수 있으세요, 로이 씨?
>
> **로이 벤튼 [오전 10:18]** 확인해 볼게요. 흠... 어림도 없습니다.
>
> **프레드 요크 [오전 10:19]** 아, 이런. 작업을 마치려면 정말 필요해요, 그렇지 않으면 고객께서 정말 화내실 거예요.
>
> **질리안 제이콥슨 [오전 10:21]** 음, 제가 페어뱅크스 크레센트와 뮤어 블리바드의 생울타리 손질 작업을 위해 트럭에 실을 게 있어서 창고에 들르는 중이에요. 하지만, 제가 이 두 곳에 가기 전에, **35** 왓츠 에비뉴 매장에 들러서 필요하신 것을 사다 드릴 수 있을 거예요.
>
> **프레드 요크 [오전 10:22]** 그럼 아주 좋을 것 같아요. **36** 반드시 트루그로우 플러스 종류여야 합니다.
>
> **로이 벤튼 [오전 10:23]** 도와 드리지 못해서 죄송합니다, 프레드 씨.

어휘 **warehouse** 창고 **fertilizer** 비료 **lawn** 잔디(밭) **would rather (not) do** ~하고 싶다(하고 싶지 않다) **go all the way to** ~까지 먼 길을 가다 **bring A in on B** A를 B에 끌어들이다, A를 B에 참여시키다 **manage** ~을 해내다, ~을 감당하다 **Not even close** (수량, 진행, 기대 등) 어림도 없다, 아직 멀었다, 훨씬 못 미친다 **stop by** ~에 들르다 **load** (짐 등을) ~에 싣다 **hedge** 생울타리 **trimming** 손질, 다듬기

33. 요크 씨가 어떤 종류의 업체에서 일하고 있는 것 같은가?

(A) 실내 디자인 회사
(B) 배송 회사
(C) 조경 회사
(D) 철물점

정답 (C)

해설 요크 씨가 10시 14분에 작성한 메시지에 자신이 현재 있는 포스터 로드에서 진행하는 작업에 필요한 잔디용 비료를 충분히 가져 오지 않았다고(I didn't bring enough fertilizer for the lawn here at the Foster Road job) 알리는 말이 쓰여 있다. 이는 조경 작업을 하는 사람이 할 수 있는 말에 해당되므로 (C)가 정답이다.

어휘 **landscaping** 조경 (작업)

34. 오전 10시 18분에, 벤튼 씨가 "Not even close"라고 쓸 때 무엇을 암시하는가?

(A) 프로젝트가 일정보다 뒤처져 진행되고 있다.
(B) 작업 장소가 너무 멀리 있다.
(C) 요크 씨가 필요한 차량이 이용 불가능하다.
(D) 제품이 공급량이 제한되어 있다.

정답 (D)

해설 Not even close는 수량과 관련해 말할 경우에는 '어림도 없다' 등을 의미한다. 이 지문에서는 요크 씨가 10시 17분에 25킬로그램이면 충분할 거라고 알리면서 처리해 줄 수 있는지 묻는 것에 대한 답변으로서 그 정도의 양을 전혀 제공할 수 없다는 뜻이므로 (D)가 정답이다.

어휘 **run** 진행되다, 운영되다 **behind schedule** 일정보다 뒤처져 **unavailable** 이용할 수 없는 **supply** 공급(량)

35. 제이콥슨 씨가 곧이어 어디로 갈 것이라고 말하는가?

(A) 뮤어 블리바드로
(B) 포스터 로드로
(C) 와츠 애비뉴로
(D) 페어뱅크스 크레센트로

정답 (C)

해설 10시 21분 메시지에 제이콥슨 씨가 페어뱅크스 크레센트와 뮤어 블리바드에 작업하러 가기 전에 왓츠 에비뉴 매장에 먼저 들를 수 있다고(before I go to those, I could stop by the Whatts Avenue store and buy you what you need) 알리고 있다. 따라서 (C)가 정답이다.

36. 요크 씨가 제이콥슨 씨에게 무엇을 하도록 요청하는가?

(A) 고객에게 연락하는 일
(B) 구매 영수증을 보관하는 일
(C) 특정 브랜드를 선택하는 일
(D) 재료를 주문하는 일

정답 (C)

해설 요크 씨가 10시 22분에 작성한 메시지에 반드시 트루그로우 플러스 종류여야 한다고(Make sure it's the Truegrow Plus type) 알리는 말이 쓰여 있는데, 이는 특정 브랜드의 제품을 구입하도록 당부하는 말에 해당되므로 (C)가 정답이다.

어휘 **make contact with** ~에게 연락하다 **retain** ~을 보유하다, ~을 유지하다 **select** ~을 선택하다 **particular** 특정한

37-40.

> **린치 스포츠 센터**
> 몰리 로드 1113번지, 디어허스트 힐스, 엣지우드
> 전화: 555-7236
>
> 도시 외곽에 위치한 린치 누구든 스포츠 센터는 스포츠와 운동을 즐기는 사람을 위해 교외에 위치한 최고의 장소입니다. **37** 최근에

개업한 후, 저희는 여전히 신규 회원에게 20퍼센트 할인을 해 드리고 있으니 오셔서 오늘 등록하세요!

저희 스포츠 센터는 최신식의 편의시설과 장비를 갖추고 있습니다. 저희는 1층에 커다란 수영장을 가지고 있으며, 뿐만 아니라 배드민턴, 농구, 그리고 배구를 위해 이용되는 스포츠 홀도 있습니다. 2층은 4개의 테니스 코트를 포함하고 있으며, 저희는 따뜻한 계절에 사용되는 야외에 3개의 추가 코트를 가지고 있습니다. 저희는 또한 미식축구 축구와 같은 팀 스포츠를 위한 야외 경기장도 가지고 있습니다. 이 경기장은 3월에서 10월까지 사용 가능하며, 경기장 표면을 완벽한 상태로 유지하기 위해 잔디는 정기적으로 손질됩니다. **39** 높은 수요로 인해 예약은 필수입니다.

린치 스포츠 센터 운영 시간:

- **38** 화요일에서 목요일: 오전 8시 – 오후 10시 30분
- 금요일에서 토요일: 오전 8시 – 오후 11시
- 일요일: 오전 10시 – 오후 9시 30분

비회원도 저희 시설을 이용할 수 있지만, 회원들은 모든 스포츠홀, 코트, 경기장 예약과 장비 대여에 대해 더 낮은 요금을 받습니다. 그러므로 회원권 할인을 이용하시기 바라며, **40** 이는 7월 말까지만 유효합니다.

어휘 **outskirt** 변두리, 외곽 **suburbs** 변두리, 교외 **be equipped with** ~을 갖추고 있다 **state-of-the-art** 최신의, 최첨단의 **amenities** 편의시설, 오락시설 **as well as** 뿐만 아니라 **playing field** 스포츠 경기장 **trim** ~을 자르다, 다듬다 **on a regular basis** 정기적으로 **surface** 표면 **due to** ~로 인해, ~ 때문에 **demand** 수요 **facility** 시설 **rate** 요금 **take advantage of** ~을 이용하다

37. 이 정보의 목적은 무엇인가?
(A) 스포츠 센터의 이전을 알리기 위해서
(B) 일시적인 폐쇄에 대해 회원들에게 통보하기 위해서
(C) 스포츠 의류 브랜드를 광고하기 위해서
(D) 새로운 레크리에이션 시설을 홍보하기 위해서

정답 (D)

해설 첫 번째 단락에 최근에 문을 연 스포츠센터에서 신입회원에 대한 할인을 진행하며 등록을 권장하는 내용을(Having just recently opened, we are still offering 20 percent discounts on new memberships) 확인할 수 있으므로 (D)가 정답이다.

어휘 **relocation** 이전, 재배치 **notify** ~을 통보하다, 알리다 **recreation** 오락, 여흥

38. 린치 스포츠 센터에 대해 명시되지 않은 것은?
(A) 일주일에 7일 문을 연다.
(B) 실내 수영장이 있다.
(C) 3개의 야외 테니스 코트가 있다.
(D) 교외 지역에 위치해 있다.

정답 (A)

해설 세 번째 문단에 제시된 운영시간을 보면 화요일에서 목요일, 금요일과 토요일, 일요일의 운영시간은 나와 있지만, 월요일의 운영시간은 나와 있지 않으므로 주 6일 운영한다는 것을 알 수 있다. 따라서 (A)가 정답이다.

어휘 **indoor** 실내의 **suburban** 교외의

39. 야외 경기장에 대해 암시된 것은 무엇인가?
(A) 10월에는 사용 불가능하다.
(B) 반드시 미리 예약이 되어야 한다.
(C) 인공적인 표면을 가지고 있다.
(D) 회원들에 의해서만 사용될 수 있다.

정답 (B)

해설 두 번째 단락 중반부에 야외 경기장에 대한 수요가 높기 때문에 예약이 필수라는(Due to high demand, bookings are required) 내용이 언급되어 있으므로 (B)가 정답이다.

어휘 **in advance** 미리, 앞서 **artificial** 인공적인

40. 8월 1일에 무슨 일이 있을 것 같은가?
(A) 운영시간이 변경될 것이다.
(B) 대여료가 낮아질 것이다.
(C) 특별 제공 서비스가 이용 불가능할 것이다.
(D) 새로운 스포츠 홀이 개관할 것이다.

정답 (C)

해설 마지막 단락에 회원권 할인이 7월 말까지 가능하다고 했으므로(take advantage of our discount on memberships, which is only available until the end of July) 8월 1일에는 이 회원권 할인을 이용할 없다는 것을 유추할 수 있다. 따라서 (C)가 정답이다.

어휘 **rental rate** 대여료 **offer** 할인

41-45.

월간 자동차 뉴스
엘레갠타 모터스 신모델 출시 준비 중

41(A) (런던, 10월 30일) 런던에 본사를 둔 앨레갠타 모터스에서 제조하는 새 고급 승용차가 특히 재계에서 대단히 큰 인기를 얻게 될 것이 틀림없습니다. 세련된 디자인 및 5.8리터 V8 엔진을 통해, 앨레갠타의 그린위치 타운 카는 강력함과 세련됨을 모두 갖추게 될 것으로 보입니다.

엘라갠타 모터스의 이소벨 아넷 대표이사는 다음과 같이 밝혔습니다, "그린위치 타운 카는 비즈니스 임원 및 성공한 사업가에게 이상적인 자동차입니다. **41(C)** 실내는 동종의 다른 어떤 자동차보다 더 넓으며, 저희는 좌석에 최고급 가죽을 사용했습니다. 이 자동차의 가장 뛰어난 특징은 **41(B)** 최신 프리시즌-X 위성 내비게이션 시스템과 자동 "정차" 브레이크 시스템이며, 이는 운전자 안전에 있어 새로운 **42** 기준을 제공합니다."

41(A) **45** 그린위치 타운 카는 12월 첫째 주부터 전 세계에서 구입 가능하게 될 것입니다.

어휘 launch ~을 출시하다, ~을 시작하다 manufacture ~을 제조하다 be destined to do ~하는 것이 틀림 없다, ~할 운명이다 extremely 대단히, 매우 especially 특히 both A and B A와 B 둘 모두 sophisticated 세련된 ideal 이상적인 executive 임원, 이사 high-flyer 성공한 사업가 spacious 널찍한 in one's class 동종의 ultra-premium 최고급의 satellite 위성 available 이용 가능한, 구입 가능한 worldwide 전 세계에서, 전 세계적으로

수신: 에드워드 라이너스 <elinus@blytheeng.com>
발신: 알렉스 머피 <amurphy@blytheeng.com>
날짜: 11월 17일
제목: 우리 회사 차량

라이너스 씨께,

제가 우리의 내년 예산 작업을 하는 중인데, 사실 우리가 예상한 것보다 자금을 더 많이 보유하고 있습니다. 올해 우리 수익이 전례 없는 상태였기 때문에, 이로 인해 우리가 사업의 핵심 영역들을 개선할 수 있을 것입니다. 한 가지 우리가 개선할 수 있는 대상이 우리가 보유한 회사 차량들입니다. **43** 우리가 1월에 이용하기 시작할 수 있는 여섯 대의 고급 승용차 구입을 승인해 주셨으면 합니다. 저는 그린위치 타운 카를 구입하도록 권해 드리고 싶은데, 이 차량이 엘레갠타 모터스에서 제조하는 최신 모델입니다.

우리 회사 차량은 여전히 주로 애거터 모터스에서 제조한 구식 제스펜 마크 V 모델들로 구성되어 있습니다. 우리 차량을 그린위치 타운 카로 업그레이드함으로써, **44** 우리가 해외에서 오시는 모든 고객들을 태워 드리러 공항으로 기사를 보낸 다음, 도시 곳곳으로 모셔다 드릴 경우에 분명 깊은 인상을 남기게 될 것입니다.

그린위치 타운 카 제안과 관련된 결정을 기다리고 있겠습니다. 저에게 승인해 주신다는 가정 하에, **45** 새로운 모델이 출시되는 대로 엘레갠타 모터스에 연락해 우리가 여섯 대의 자동차를 구입하고자 한다는 사실을 알리겠습니다.

안녕히 계십시오.

알렉스 머피
회계 관리 부장, 블라이드 엔지니어링

어휘 work on ~에 대한 작업을 하다 actually 사실, 실은, 실제로 unprecedented 전례 없는 improve ~을 개선하다, ~을 향상시키다 fleet (한 단체가 보유한) 전체 차량/항공기/선박 approve ~을 승인하다 latest 최신의 primarily 주로 consist of ~로 구성되다 outdated 구식의, 오래된 surely 분명히 from overseas 해외로부터 pick A up A를 차에 태우러 가다, A를 차로 데려 오다 await ~을 기다리다 regarding ~와 관련해 suggestion 제안, 의견 assuming that ~라는 가정 하에, ~한다면 approval 승인 as soon as ~하는 대로, ~하자마자 release ~을 출시하다, ~을 발매하다

41. 그린위치 타운 카와 관련해 언급되지 않은 것은 무엇인가?
(A) 아직 시장에 출시되지 않았다.

(B) 새로운 내비게이션 기술을 특징으로 한다.
(C) 다른 유사 모델들보다 실내가 더 넓다.
(D) 최신 오디오 시스템을 포함한다.

정답 (D)

해설 첫 지문의 작성 날짜(London, October 30)와 동일 지문 마지막 문장의 출시 날짜를(The Greenwich Town Car will be available ~ from the first week in December) 통해 아직 출시되지 않았음을 뜻하는 (A)를 확인할 수 있다. 또한, 두 번째 단락에 언급된 최신 내비게이션 기술과(its state-of-the-art Precision-X satellite navigation system) 넓은 실내를(more spacious than any other car in its class) 통해 (B)와 (C)도 확인할 수 있다. 하지만 최신 오디오 시스템과 관련된 정보는 제시되어 있지 않으므로 (D)가 정답이다.

어휘 have yet to do 아직 ~하지 않았다 feature v. ~을 특징으로 하다 include ~을 포함하다

42. 기사에서, 두 번째 단락, 네 번째 줄의 단어 "standard"와 의미가 가장 가까운 것은 무엇인가?
(A) 대안
(B) 규제
(C) 기준(점)
(D) 혁신(성)

정답 (C)

해설 standard가 포함된 which절은 앞서 주절에 언급된 브레이크 시스템을 수식해 그 시스템이 운전자 안전과 관련해 새롭게 제공하는 것을 가리킨다. 좋은 시스템이 갖춰지면 관련된 기능이나 서비스의 수준이 높아지는 것으로 생각할 수 있는데, 이는 새로운 기준을 제공하는 것과 같으므로 '기준'을 뜻하는 (C) benchmark가 정답이다.

43. 이메일의 목적은 무엇인가?
(A) 제품을 구입하도록 승인을 요청하는 것
(B) 새로운 자동차 모델의 특징을 설명하는 것
(C) 예산 계획의 요점들을 설명하는 것
(D) 회사 수익을 늘릴 수 있는 방법들을 제안하는 것

정답 (A)

해설 두 번째 지문 첫 번째 단락에 1월에 이용하기 시작할 수 있는 여섯 대의 고급 승용차 구입을 승인해 주었으면 좋겠다고(I'd like you to approve the purchase of six luxury sedans) 요청하는 부분이 목적에 해당되므로 (A)가 정답이다.

어휘 authorization 승인, 인가 main point 요점 suggest ~을 제안하다

44. 이메일에서 블라이드 엔지니어링과 관련해 암시된 것은 무엇인가?
(A) 현재 엘레갠타 모터스에서 제조한 여러 자동차를 이용하고 있다.
(B) 방문 고객들이 교통편을 제공 받을 것으로 예상한다.
(C) 애거터 모터스와 공동으로 프로젝트를 작업했다.
(D) 임원들이 주기적으로 해외 출장을 떠난다.

정답 (B)

해설 두 번째 지문 두 번째 단락에 해외에서 오는 고객들을 태우러 공항으로 기사를 보내고 도시 곳곳으로 데려 가는 일이(all of our clients from overseas when we send drivers to pick them up from the airport and then drive them around the city) 언급되어 있다. 이는 블라이드 엔지니어링을 방문하는 고객들이 교통편을 제공 받을 수 있다는 뜻이므로 (B)가 정답이다.

어휘 **currently** 현재 **expect A to do** A가 ~한 것으로 예상하다 **collaboratively** 공동으로 **regularly** 주기적으로 **travel overseas on a business trip** 해외로 출장을 떠나다

45. 머피 씨가 언제 엘레간타 모터스에 주문할 계획인가?
(A) 10월에
(B) 11월에
(C) 12월에
(D) 1월에

정답 (C)

해설 두 번째 지문 마지막 단락에 새로운 모델이 출시되는 대로 엘레간타 모터스에 연락해 여섯 대의 자동차를 구입하고자 한다는 사실을 알리겠다는(I will contact Elaganta Motors as soon as the new model is released and inform them that we wish to purchase six cars) 말이 쓰여 있다. 그 출시 시점과 관련해 첫 지문 마지막 문장에 12월부터 구입 가능하다는(The Greenwich Town Car will be available for purchase ~ from the first week in December) 정보가 제시되어 있으므로 (C)가 정답이다.

어휘 **intend to do** ~할 계획이다, ~할 작정이다

46-50.

어서 오셔서 제 고급 웨딩 드레스를 살펴보세요!

4월 한 달 농안에 걸쳐, 저 지젤 로시가 새로운 매장 '웨딩 드레스 바이 지젤'의 개장을 기념할 예정입니다! **50** 새로운 제 매장은 시카고 시내에서 10번가와 그랜빌가가 만나는 모퉁이에 위치해 있으며, 월요일부터 토요일, 오전 9시부터 오후 6시까지 문을 엽니다. 저는 20년 넘게 주문 제작 드레스를 디자인하고 제조해 왔으며, 제 매장에 **46** 광범위한 기성복 여성 드레스 컬렉션도 진열해 놓을 것입니다.

47(A) 모든 드레스 가봉 예약은 반드시 적어도 48시간 전에 미리 이뤄져야 합니다. 이는 전화, 이메일, 또는 **47(C)** 제 웹 사이트상의 예약을 통해 하실 수 있습니다. 아니면, **47(B)** 그냥 제 매장에 들르셔도 됩니다! 매주 일요일을 제외하고 일주일 중 어느 요일이든 가봉 시간을 잡으실 수 있습니다. www.dressesbygiselle.com에서 제 드레스들을 확인해 보시거나 555-3789번으로 제 매장에 직접 전화 주시기 바랍니다.

어휘 **Come on down to do** 어서 오셔서 ~하세요 **view** ~을

보다 **throughout** (기간) ~ 동안에 걸쳐, (장소) ~ 전역에 걸쳐 **custom-made** 주문 제작의, 맞춤 제작의 **have A on display** A를 진열해 놓다, A를 전시해 놓다 **extensive** 광범위한, 폭넓은 **ready-to-wear** 기성복의 **gown** 여성 드레스 **fitting** 가봉(양복 등을 맞출 때 제대로 맞는지 보기 위해 대강 꿰매어 하는 작업), 피팅(구입 전에 미리 입어 보는 것) **make an appointment** 예약하다(= make a reservation) **in advance** 미리, 사전에 **alternatively** (대안을 말할 때) 또는, 아니면 **stop by** ~에 들르다 **arrange** ~의 일정을 잡다, ~을 조치하다 **except for** ~을 제외하고

웨딩 드레스 바이 지젤

4월에 드레스 가봉을 위해 오시는 경우, 다음 무료 선물들 중 하나를 받으시게 될 것입니다!

◆ 작년의 가을 쿠튀르 라인에 속한 드레스를 가봉하시는 모든 분께서 무료 마스카라와 파운데이션 세트를 받으시게 됩니다.
◆ **49** 새로운 제 봄 쿠튀르 라인에 속한 드레스를 가봉하시는 모든 분께서 그에 어울리는 진주 귀걸이를 무료로 받으시게 됩니다.
◆ 기성복 여성 드레스를 가봉하시는 모든 분께서 5퍼센트 할인을 받으시게 됩니다.
◆ 신부 들러리들께서 가봉하시러 오시는 경우에는 각자 무료 샴페인 한 병을 받으시게 됩니다.

어휘 **following** 다음의, 아래의 **complimentary** 무료의(= free) **fitted for** ~을 가봉하는 **matching** 어울리는 **at no extra cost** 추가 비용 없이, 무료로 **bridesmaid** 신부 들러리

수신: 지젤 로시 <grossi@giselle.com>
발신: 헬레나 맥스웰 <hmaxwell@flymail.net>
날짜: 3월 23일
제목: 귀하의 컬렉션

로시 씨께,

제가 9월에 약혼자와 결혼할 계획이라서 저희의 특별한 날에 지젤 드레스를 꼭 입고 싶습니다. 저는 비용을 좀 더 많이 들여서 **48** **49** 귀하의 새로운 봄 쿠튀르 라인에 속한 드레스를 구입할 준비가 되어 있는데, 이는 제가 지난달에 뉴욕 시에 있었던 패션 위크 행사 중에 무대에 오른 것을 보는 즐거움이 있었던 드레스입니다. 제가 최근에 인디애나폴리스에서 있었던 결혼식에도 참석했는데, 신부가 귀하의 쿠튀르 드레스를 입은 모습이 정말 굉장히 아름다워 보였지만, 그 특정 드레스는 귀하의 가을 제품 라인에 속한 것 같습니다.

귀하의 업체를 원래의 자리에 있던 로스앤젤레스에서 이전하셨다는 사실을 알게 되어 매우 기뻤습니다. **50** 제가 10번가와 그랜빌가가 만나는 곳에 위치한 귀하의 새 매장에서 멀지 않은 곳에 살고 있기 때문에, 가봉을 위해 들르기 매우 편리할 것입니다. 4월 2일 오후 2시에 시간이 괜찮으실까요?

안녕히 계십시오.

헬레나 맥스웰

어휘 **fiancé** 약혼자 **be prepared to do** ~할 준비가 되어 있다 **spend extra** 더 많은 돈을 들이다, 추가로 소비하다 **catwalk** 패션 쇼 무대 **recently** 최근에 **bride** 신부 **absolutely** 정말로, 완전히, 전적으로 **stunning** 굉장히 아름다운, 아주 멋진 **particular** 특정한 **relocate** ~을 이전하다 **location** (매장 등의) 지점, 위치, 장소

46. 광고에서, 첫 번째 단락, 네 번째 줄의 단어 "extensive"와 의미가 가장 가까운 것은 무엇인가?

(A) 널찍한
(B) 엄청난
(C) 장기적인
(D) 독점적인

정답 (B)

해설 해당 문장에서 형용사 extensive가 수식하는 collection of ready-to-wear gowns는 디자이너가 자신의 매장에 진열해 놓는 드레스 제품 컬렉션을 가리킨다. 따라서, extensive는 제품의 보유 규모를 나타내야 하는데, 제품 선택의 폭이 넓다는 점을 장점으로 말하는 내용이 되어야 자연스러우므로 '엄청난, 방대한' 등을 뜻하는 (B) vast가 정답이다.

47. 광고 내용에 따르면, 드레스 가봉 예약과 관련해 사실이 아닌 것은 무엇인가?

(A) 반드시 적어도 이틀 전에 미리 요청되어야 한다.
(B) 업체를 방문해서 예약할 수 있다.
(C) 인터넷 사이트를 이용해 일정을 잡을 수 있다.
(D) 오직 평일에만 진행될 수 있다.

정답 (D)

해설 첫 지문 두 번째 단락에 적어도 48시간 전에 미리 요청해야 한다는(All dress fitting appointments must be made at least 48 hours in advance) 부분에서 (A)를, 웹 사이트상으로 예약할 수 있다는(by making a reservation on my Web site) 부분에서 (C)를, 그리고 그냥 매장에 들러도 된다는 (Alternatively, you can just stop by my store) 부분에서 (B)를 확인할 수 있다. 하지만 같은 단락에 일요일을 제외하고 어느 요일이든 예약할 수 있다는 말이 쓰여 있으므로 평일에만 가능하다는 뜻을 나타내는 (D)가 정답이다.

어휘 **beforehand** 미리, 사전에 **set up** ~의 일정을 잡다, ~을 마련하다 **take place** (일, 행사 등이) 진행되다, 개최되다

48. 이메일에서 로시 씨와 관련해 암시하는 것은 무엇인가?

(A) 올해 초에 인디애나폴리스에서 결혼했다.
(B) 과거에 맥스웰 씨를 위해 드레스를 디자인했다.
(C) 다가오는 맥스웰 씨의 결혼식에 참석할 것이다.
(D) 최근 패션 쇼에서 자신의 작품을 선보였다.

정답 (D)

해설 세 번째 지문 첫 단락에 작성자인 맥스웰 씨가 로시 씨의 새로운 봄 쿠튀르 라인에 속한 드레스를 구입하려 한다는 말과 함께 지난달에 뉴욕 시에서 있었던 패션 위크 행사 중에 무대에 오른 것을 본 사실을(your new Spring Couture line, which I had the pleasure of seeing on the catwalk during fashion week in New York City last month) 언급하고 있다. 이는 로시 씨가 최근 열린 패션 쇼에서 자신의 드레스를 선보였다는 뜻이므로 (D)가 정답이다.

어휘 **get married** 결혼하다 **upcoming** 다가오는, 곧 있을

49. 맥스웰 씨가 드레스 가봉 작업 당일에 무엇을 받을 것 같은가?

(A) 5퍼센트 할인 서비스
(B) 무료 메이크업 세트
(C) 무료 귀걸이
(D) 삼페인 한 병

정답 (C)

해설 세 번째 지문 첫 단락에 로시 씨의 새로운 봄 쿠튀르 라인에 속한 드레스를 구입하려 한다는 말이(I'm prepared to spend a little extra and purchase a dress from your new Spring Couture line) 쓰여 있다. 이 제품 라인과 관련해, 두 번째 지문 두 번째 항목에 봄 쿠튀르 라인에 속한 드레스를 가봉하면 진주 귀걸이를 무료로 받는다고(Anyone fitted for a dress from my new Spring Couture line will receive a pair of matching pearl earrings) 알리고 있으므로 (C)가 정답이다.

50. 맥스웰 씨가 어디에서 드레스 가봉 작업이 진행되기를 원하는가?

(A) 로스앤젤레스에서
(B) 뉴욕 시에서
(C) 시카고에서
(D) 인디애나폴리스에서

정답 (C)

해설 세 번째 지문 두 번째 단락에 맥스웰 씨가 10번가와 그랜빌가가 만나는 곳에 위치한 로시 씨의 새 매장에서 멀지 않은 곳에 살고 있어서 가봉을 위해 들르기 매우 편리할 것이라고(I don't live far from your new location on 10th and Granville, so it will be very convenient) 알리고 있다. 이 위치는 첫 번째 지문 첫 단락에 로시 씨의 시카고 매장이 있는 곳으로(My new store is located on the corner of 10th and Granville in downtown Chicago) 언급되어 있으므로 (C)가 정답이다.

1. (C)	**2.** (C)	**3.** (A)	**4.** (A)	**5.** (C)
6. (A)	**7.** (C)	**8.** (B)	**9.** (C)	**10.** (B)
11. (A)	**12.** (A)	**13.** (C)	**14.** (B)	**15.** (B)
16. (A)	**17.** (C)	**18.** (B)	**19.** (A)	**20.** (C)
21. (C)	**22.** (B)	**23.** (D)	**24.** (C)	**25.** (A)
26. (B)	**27.** (D)	**28.** (C)	**29.** (B)	**30.** (B)
31. (D)	**32.** (C)	**33.** (D)	**34.** (C)	**35.** (A)
36. (C)	**37.** (C)	**38.** (B)	**39.** (B)	**40.** (C)
41. (D)	**42.** (C)	**43.** (D)	**44.** (B)	**45.** (C)
46. (D)	**47.** (A)	**48.** (C)	**49.** (C)	**50.** (B)

Part 1

1.
(A) They are standing at a cash register.
(B) The fruits are all being wrapped.
(C) An assortment of fruit is being displayed.
(D) A woman is pushing a shopping cart.

(A) 사람들이 현금 등록기 앞에 서 있다.
(B) 과일들이 모두 포장되는 중이다.
(C) 다양한 종류의 과일이 진열되어 있다.
(D) 한 여자가 쇼핑 카드를 밀고 있다.

해설   (A) 현금 등록기를 찾아볼 수 없으므로 오답.
(B) 과일을 포장하는 동작을 하는 사람이 없으므로 오답.
(C) 다양한 종류의 과일들이 진열되어 있는 상태를 묘사하고 있으므로 정답.
(D) 여자가 카트를 미는 동작을 하고 있지 않으므로 오답.

어휘   **cash register** 현금 등록기 **wrap** ~을 포장하다 **an assortment of** 다양한 종류의 **display** v. ~을 진열하다

2.
(A) Passengers are standing on the deck of a ship.
(B) Some people are passing through an arch.
(C) Some people are walking toward a ship.
(D) A ship is approaching the shore.

(A) 승객들이 배 갑판 위에 서 있다.
(B) 몇몇 사람들이 아치형 구조물을 통과하고 있다.
(C) 몇몇 사람들이 배를 향해 걸어가고 있다.
(D) 배 한 척이 해안으로 다가가는 중이다.

해설   (A) 갑판 위에 서 있는 승객들을 찾아볼 수 없으므로 오답.
(B) 아치형 구조물(an arch)을 찾아볼 수 없으므로 오답.
(C) 정박된 배를 향해 걸어가고 있는 사람들을 묘사하고 있으므

로 정답.
(D) 배가 이미 정박해 있는 상태이므로 오답.

어휘   **deck** 갑판 **pass** 지나가다 **through** ~를 통해, 통과해 **arch** 아치형 구조물 **toward** ~ 쪽으로 **approach** ~로 다가가다, 다가오다 **shore** 해안, 물가

Part 2

3. Where can I see tomorrow's schedule of concerts?
(A) It's on our Web site.
(B) Probably around 5 P.M.
(C) I saw it last time.

어디에서 내일 콘서트 일정표를 볼 수 있죠?
(A) 저희 웹 사이트에 있습니다.
(B) 아마 오후 5시쯤일 거예요.
(C) 저는 지난번에 그것을 봤어요.

해설   어디에서 콘서트 일정표를 볼 수 있는지 묻는 Where 의문문이므로 해당 정보를 확인할 수 있는 웹 사이트를 언급한 (A)가 정답이다. (B)는 시점 표현이므로 When 의문문에 적절한 응답이다. (C)는 답변자 자신이 과거 시점에 본 사실을 말하고 있어 일정표를 볼 수 있는 곳을 묻는 질문의 의도에 맞지 않는 오답이다.

어휘   **schedule** 일정(표) **probably** 아마도 **around** ~쯤

4. Who can I talk to about signing up for a class?
(A) Use the online registration form.
(B) Ms. Smith came in earlier than usual.
(C) To learn computer programming.

강좌에 등록하는 일과 관련해 누구와 이야기할 수 있을까요?
(A) 온라인 등록 양식을 이용하세요.
(B) 스미스 씨가 평소보다 일찍 왔어요.
(C) 컴퓨터 프로그래밍을 배우기 위해서요.

해설   강좌 등록에 관해 얘기할 수 있는 담당자를 묻는 Who 의문문이지만, 사람 이름이나 직책 등의 정보 대신 온라인 등록 양식을 이용하면 된다는 말로 간접적으로 응답한 (A)가 정답이다. (B)는 사람 이름을 언급하고 있지만 등록 업무 담당자가 아니라 스미스 씨의 도착 시점을 말하고 있으므로 오답이다. (C)는 질문에 쓰인 class에서 연상 가능한 동사 learn을 이용하여 혼동을 유발하는 오답이다.

어휘   **sign up for** ~에 등록하다, ~을 신청하다 **registration** 등록 **form** 양식, 서식 **than usual** 평소보다 **learn** ~을 배우다

5. Did we meet our sales target for the month of September?
(A) I think you're right.
(B) At the end of the month.
(C) I'm sure Mr. Schneider will know.

우리가 9월 한 달 동안 매출 목표를 달성했나요?
(A) 당신 말이 맞는 것 같아요.
(B) 이 달 말에요.
(C) 분명 슈나이더 씨가 알 겁니다.

해설 매출 목표의 달성 여부를 묻는 일반 의문문에 대해 해당 정보를 알고 있을 만한 사람을 알리는 것으로 간접적으로 답변하는 (C)가 정답이다. (A)는 상대방의 말에 동의할 때 사용하는 말이므로 어울리지 않는 답변이다. (B)는 자칫 달성 시점을 말하는 것으로 착각할 수 있지만, 미래 시점에 해당되는 표현이므로 과거의 일을 묻는 질문에 어울리지 않는 오답이다.

어휘 **meet** (조건 등) ~을 충족하다

6. Would you like a paper or a plastic bag for your purchases?
(A) Either is fine with me.
(B) Soup and salad, please.
(C) This toy is made of plastic.

구매품에 대해 종이 봉지를 원하세요, 아니면 비닐 봉지를 원하세요?
(A) 둘 중 아무거나 좋습니다.
(B) 수프와 샐러드로 주세요.
(C) 이 장난감은 플라스틱으로 만들어졌어요.

해설 두 가지 선택 사항을 제시하는 선택 의문문에 대해 '둘 중 아무거나 좋다'라는 말로 답변하는 (A)가 정답이다. 제시된 선택 사항 중 하나를 고르는 답변을 하는 것이 아니라 either를 이용해 '둘 중 아무거나 좋다'고 대답하는 선택지는 정답일 확률이 매우 높다. (C)는 질문에 쓰인 plastic을 반복해 혼동을 유발하는 답변으로, 질문의 의도에 전혀 맞지 않는 오답이다.

어휘 **plastic bag** 비닐 봉지 **purchase** n. 구매(품) **either** 둘 중 아무거나 **be made of** ~로 만들어져 있다

7. When is Sheryl coming over?
(A) The seminar was last Friday.
(B) She was late for her appointment.
(C) Sometime next week.

셰릴 씨가 언제 이쪽으로 오죠?
(A) 그 세미나는 지난주 금요일이었어요.
(B) 그분은 예약에 늦었습니다.
(C) 다음 주 중으로요.

해설 When 의문문으로 셰릴이 오는 시점을 묻고 있으므로 대략적인 미래 시점으로 답변하는 (C)가 정답이다. (A)도 시점 표현을 포함하고 있지만 질문과 맞지 않는 과거 시점이며, 세미나에 관해 말하고 있으므로 오답이다. (B)도 질문과 맞지 않는 과거 시

점이다. 이렇게 When 의문문에 대한 정답을 고를 때 주어와 동사 시제 파악에도 주의를 기울여야 한다.

어휘 **come over** 이쪽으로 오다, 건너 오다 **be late for** ~에 늦다 **appointment** 예약, 약속

8. Didn't Mr. Finley tell you to cancel the order?
(A) No, I can't buy it.
(B) Yes, but he changed his mind.
(C) Yes, in chronological order.

핀리 씨가 당신에게 그 주문을 취소하라고 말하지 않았나요?
(A) 아뇨, 저는 그것을 살 수 없습니다.
(B) 네, 하지만 그분께서 생각을 바꾸셨어요.
(C) 네, 연대순으로요.

해설 핀리 씨가 특정 주문을 취소하라고 말하지 않았는지 확인하는 부정 의문문이므로 긍정을 의미하는 Yes라고 말한 후, 그 사람이 생각을 바꾸었다는 말을 덧붙이는 (B)가 정답이다. (A)는 질문에 쓰인 order에서 연상 가능한 buy를 이용해 혼동을 유발하는 오답이며, (C)는 질문에 쓰인 order의 다른 의미(주문, 순서)를 활용한 답변으로, 질문의 의도에 맞지 않는 오답이다.

어휘 **tell A to do** A에게 ~하라고 말하다 **order** n. 주문(품), 순서 **change one's mind** ~의 마음을 바꾸다 **in chronological order** 연대순으로

9. Would you like to reschedule the interview for tomorrow?
(A) Yes, that position has been filled.
(B) It certainly is a lovely view.
(C) Actually, today's better for me.

면접 일정을 내일로 재조정하고 싶으세요?
(A) 네, 그 직책은 충원되었어요.
(B) 정말 너무 멋진 경치예요.
(C) 사실, 전 오늘이 더 좋아요.

해설 「Would you like to do?」는 '~하고 싶으세요?'라는 의미이며, 면접일을 내일로 변경하고 싶은지 묻고 있으므로 내일보다 오늘이 더 좋다는 뜻을 나타내는 (C)가 정답이다. (A)는 긍정을 나타내는 Yes 뒤에 이어지는 내용이 일정 재조정과 관련된 질문의 의도에 맞지 않는 반응이며, (B)는 질문에 쓰인 interview의 일부 발음에 해당되는 view를 이용한 오답이다.

어휘 **reschedule A for 일시** A의 일정을 ~로 재조정하다 **fill** ~을 충원하다, 채우다 **position** 직책, 일자리 **lovely** 훌륭한, 아주 멋진 **view** 경치, 경관, 시야, 견해

10. Have the new uniforms been delivered to your branch yet?
(A) Staff must dress appropriately.
(B) I've been off for a few days.
(C) Delivery is available for an extra charge.

혹시 새 유니폼이 당신 지사로 배송되었나요?
(A) 직원들은 반드시 적절하게 갖춰 입어야 합니다.

(B) 제가 며칠 동안 휴무였습니다.

(C) 배송 서비스는 추가 요금을 내시면 이용하실 수 있습니다.

해설   새로운 유니폼이 배송되었는지 확인하는 일반 의문문에 대해 며칠 동안 휴무였다는 말로 배송 여부를 알지 못한다는 뜻을 나타내는 (B)가 정답이다. (A)는 uniforms과 연관성 있게 들리는 dress를 이용한 오답이며, (C)는 delivered와 유사하게 들리는 delivery를 이용해 배송 조건을 말하는 답변이므로 질문에 맞지 않는 오답이다.

어휘   **branch** 지사, 지점 **yet** (의문문에서) 혹시, 벌써 **dress** v. 복장을 갖춰 입다 **appropriately** 적절하게 **off** 휴무인 **delivery** 배송(품) **available** 이용 가능한 **extra** 추가의, 별도의 **charge** (청구) 요금

---

11. What's this badge for?
  (A) You need it to get into the conference.
  (B) It wasn't that bad.
  (C) Karen used to live there.

이 배지는 무엇에 쓰는 것이죠?
  (A) 컨퍼런스에 입장하는 데 필요합니다.
  (B) 그렇게 나쁘지 않았어요.
  (C) 카렌이 전에 거기 살았어요.

해설   「What is + 명사 + for?」는 용도나 목적을 묻는 질문이다. 따라서 this badge가 어디에 쓰이는지 묻는 것이므로, 컨퍼런스에 입장할 때 필요하다는 말로 그 용도를 설명하는 (A)가 정답이다. (B)는 badge와 발음이 비슷한 bad를 이용해 혼동을 유발하는 선택지이다.

어휘   **get into** ~로 들어가다 **used to do** 전에 ~하곤 했다

---

12. Does this product require assembly?
  (A) Some, but it's fairly simple.
  (B) Yes, this logo symbolizes our company.
  (C) No, you have to put it together first.

이 제품은 조립 과정이 필요한가요?
  (A) 일부요, 하지만 아주 간단합니다.
  (B) 네, 이 로고는 저희 회사를 상징합니다.
  (C) 아뇨, 그것을 먼저 조립하셔야 합니다.

해설   제품을 조립할 필요가 있는지 확인하는 일반 의문문이므로 이에 대해 일부만 그렇다고 말하면서 아주 간단하다는 사실을 덧붙인 (A)가 정답이다. (C)는 부정을 나타내는 No라고 말한 뒤에 이어지는 내용이 조립 과정이 필요하다는 뜻을 나타내고 있어 앞뒤가 맞지 않으므로 오답이다.

어휘   **require** ~을 필요로 하다 **assembly** 조립 **fairly** 꽤, 아주 **symbolize** ~을 상징하다 **put A together** A를 조립하다

---

13. What kind of job does Mr. Leonard do?
  (A) He's discussing it with Linda Smith.
  (B) He's skilled enough to get the job.
  (C) Mostly public relations.

레오나드 씨는 어떤 종류의 일을 하시나요?
  (A) 그분이 린다 스미스 씨와 그것을 논의하고 있어요.
  (B) 그분은 그 일을 맡기에 충분히 숙련되어 있어요.
  (C) 주로 홍보 관련된 일이요.

해설   특정 인물이 하는 일을 묻는 What 의문문이므로 '주로 홍보 관련된 일'이라는 말로 직접적으로 업무의 종류를 말한 (C)가 정답이다. (A)와 (B)는 모두 관련 있는 답변처럼 들리지만 특정 업무의 종류를 말하는 것이 아니므로 오답이다.

어휘   **discuss** ~을 논의하다, 이야기하다 **skilled** 숙련된, 능숙한 **enough to do** (형용사 뒤에서) ~하기에 충분히 **mostly** 주로, 대부분 **public relations** 홍보

---

14. Why is our inventory so low this month?
  (A) Towards the end of December.
  (B) A shipment has been delayed.
  (C) If there's a demand for it.

이번 달에 우리 재고 물량이 왜 이렇게 적은 거죠?
  (A) 12월말 무렵에요.
  (B) 배송이 지연되었습니다.
  (C) 그것에 대한 수요가 있다면요.

해설   Why 의문문으로 재고 물량이 적은 이유를 묻고 있으므로 배송이 지연되었다는 말로 아직 물품을 받지 못한 상황임을 알리는 (B)가 정답이다. (A)는 질문에 쓰인 this month와 연관성 있게 들리는 December를 이용해 혼동을 유발하는 오답이다.

어휘   **inventory** 재고 (목록) **towards** ~ 무렵에, ~경에 **shipment** 배송(품) **delay** ~을 지연시키다 **demand for** ~에 대한 수요

---

15. Should I start the information session now or wait until more people come in?
  (A) They have been informed.
  (B) We have a lot to deal with, so let's begin.
  (C) I'm waiting for the sales figures to come out.

제가 설명회를 지금 시작해야 하나요, 아니면 더 많은 사람들이 올 때까지 기다려야 하나요?
  (A) 그분들은 통보 받았습니다.
  (B) 우리가 다뤄야 할 내용이 많기 때문에, 시작합시다.
  (C) 저는 매출 수치가 나오기를 기다리고 있습니다.

해설   설명회를 지금 시작할지, 아니면 좀 더 기다릴지를 묻는 선택 의문문에 대해 다룰 내용이 많다는 말과 함께 지금 시작하는 것을 선택한 (B)가 정답이다. (A)는 질문에 쓰인 information과 발음이 유사한 informed를 이용해 혼동을 유발하는 오답이며, (C)는 질문에 쓰인 wait를 반복한 답변으로 질문의 의도에 맞지 않는 오답이다.

어휘   **information session** 설명회 **inform** ~에게 알리다, 통보하다 **deal with** ~을 다루다, 처리하다 **sales** 영업, 판매, 매출 **figure** 수치, 숫자

16. Will I be able to get reimbursed for the flight tickets?
(A) Give your receipts to Ms. Shirley.
(B) Let me check if we can go by airplane.
(C) So do I.

제가 항공권에 대해 환급 받을 수 있을까요?
(A) 영수증을 셜리 씨에게 드리세요.
(B) 우리가 비행기로 갈 수 있는지 확인해 볼게요.
(C) 저도 그렇습니다.

해설 항공권을 구입한 비용을 환급 받을 수 있을지 확인하는 Will 의문문이므로 Yes를 생략한 채로 환급 받기 위한 구체적인 방법을 말하는 (A)가 정답이다. (B)는 질문에 쓰인 flight에서 연상 가능한 by airplane을 이용해 혼동을 유발하는 답변으로 환급 여부와 관련 없는 오답이며, (C)는 현재시제 일반 동사가 쓰인 문장에 대해 동일한 상황임을 알릴 때 사용하는 말이므로 질문의 의도에 맞지 않는 답변이다.

어휘 **get reimbursed for** ~에 대한 비용을 환급 받다 **flight ticket** 항공권, 비행기표 **receipt** 영수증 **Let me check if** ~인지 확인해 보겠습니다 **by airplane** 비행기로

17. What business did you choose to sponsor our event?
(A) At the Marriott Theater next month.
(B) Yes, Mr. Smith will be attending.
(C) I'm still waiting to talk to some of them.

저희 행사를 후원하기 위해 어떤 업체를 선정하셨나요?
(A) 다음 달에 매리어트 극장에서요.
(B) 네, 스미스 씨께서 참석하실 예정입니다.
(C) 몇몇 곳들과 얘기하기 위해 여전히 기다리는 중입니다.

해설 What business로 시작해 선정한 업체의 종류나 특성을 묻는 의문문에 대해 여전히 얘기를 나누는 중이라는 말로 아직 선정하지 않았음을 알리는 (C)가 정답이다. (A)는 장소 표현이므로 Where 의문문에 어울리는 답변이며, (B)는 의문사 의문문에 맞지 않는 Yes로 대답하는 오답이다.

어휘 **business** 업체, 회사 **choose** ~을 선정하다, 결정하다 **sponsor** ~을 후원하다 **attend** ~에 참석하다

18. Which of today's island tours should I sign up for?
(A) The tour starts at 9 A.M.
(B) They're canceled due to the storm.
(C) It'll last for half a day.

오늘의 섬 투어 중에서 제가 어느 것을 신청해야 하나요?
(A) 그 투어는 오전 9시에 시작합니다.
(B) 그것들이 폭풍우 때문에 취소되었습니다.
(C) 반나절 동안 지속될 겁니다.

해설 자신이 선택할 투어를 묻는 Which 의문문이므로 tours를 They로 지칭해 취소되었다는 말로 선택할 수 없음을 알리

는 (B)가 정답이다. (A)는 투어 시작 시점을 말하고 있으므로 When 의문문에 어울리는 답변이며, (C)는 지속 시간을 나타내므로 How long 의문문에 어울리는 응답이다.

어휘 **sign up for** ~을 신청하다, ~에 등록하다 **due to** ~ 때문에 **storm** 폭풍우 **last** v. 지속되다 **half a day** 반나절

19. Wasn't Ms. Jennings supposed to arrive for her dental check-up at 11 A.M.?
(A) She changed her appointment to a later time.
(B) Yes, let's check the flight details.
(C) Great. I'll meet you there.

제닝스 씨가 치과 검진을 위해 오전 11시에 도착하기로 되어 있지 않았나요?
(A) 그분이 나중 시간으로 예약을 변경했습니다.
(B) 네, 항공편 관련 상세 정보를 확인해 봅시다.
(C) 좋아요. 그럼 거기서 뵐게요.

해설 제닝스 씨가 치과 검진을 위해 오전 11시에 도착하기로 되어 있지 않았는지 확인하는 부정 의문문이므로 예약 시간을 나중으로 변경했다는 말로 11시에 오지 않는다는 뜻을 나타내는 (A)가 정답이다. (B)는 질문에 쓰인 check-up의 일부 발음에 해당되는 check를 이용해 혼동을 유발하는 답변이다. (C)는 제닝스 씨의 예약 상황이 아닌 답변자 자신의 약속 장소를 말하는 답변이므로 오답이다.

어휘 **be supposed to do** ~하기로 되어 있다, ~할 예정이다 **check-up** 검진 **appointment** 예약, 약속 **flight** 항공편, 비행 **details** 상세 정보, 세부 사항

20. The chairs should be in place before the orientation participants arrive.
(A) At least twenty new staff members.
(B) You can place them on my desk. Thanks.
(C) I'll have Alex do it right now.

오리엔테이션 참가자들이 도착하기 전에 의자들이 제자리에 있어야 합니다.
(A) 적어도 20명의 신입 사원들이요.
(B) 그것들을 제 책상 위에 놓아 두시면 됩니다. 감사합니다.
(C) 알렉스 씨에게 지금 바로 그렇게 하라고 얘기하겠습니다.

해설 오리엔테이션 참가자들이 오기 전에 의자들이 제자리에 있어야 한다고 알리는 평서문에 대해 그 일을 it으로 지칭해 알렉스 씨에게 하도록 시키겠다고 말하는 (C)가 정답이다. (A)는 인원수를 말하는 답변이므로 How many 의문문에 어울리는 답변이며, (B)는 질문에 쓰인 place의 다른 의미(자리, 놓다)를 이용해 혼동을 유발하는 답변으로, 의자들을 놓는 위치로 어울리지 않는 오답이다.

어휘 **in place** 제자리에 있는 **participant** 참가자 **at least** 적어도, 최소한 **place** ~을 놓다, 두다 **have A do** A에게 ~하게 하다 **right now** 지금 바로

Part 3

Questions 21-23 refer to the following conversation.

M: Rachel, 21 I'm so happy about how popular our pizza store is getting. Diners are really enjoying our menu options and the fresh ingredients we use.

W: Yes, and 22 after the new servers are hired this week, we'll be able to serve all our customers more quickly.

M: You're right. Oh, that reminds me. I'd like to make sure our employees are well prepared, so 23 I was hoping you could make a program for a two-day training session.

W: 23 Sure, I can do that. I should have some spare time this afternoon.

남: 레이첼 씨, 우리 피자 매장이 얼마나 인기를 얻고 있는지에 대해 너무 기쁩니다. 식사 손님들께서 우리 메뉴 옵션과 우리가 사용하는 신선한 재료를 정말로 즐기고 계세요.
여: 네, 그리고 이번 주에 신입 종업원들이 고용되고 나면, 더욱 신속하게 모든 고객들께 서비스를 제공해 드릴 수 있을 거예요.
남: 맞습니다. 아, 그 말씀을 하시니까 생각나네요. 저는 우리 직원들이 반드시 잘 준비되도록 하고 싶어서, 당신이 이틀 간의 교육 시간에 대한 프로그램을 만들어 주실 수 있기를 바라고 있었어요.
여: 좋아요, 그렇게 할 수 있어요. 제가 오늘 오후에 여유 시간이 좀 있을 거예요.

어휘 **get 형용사** ~한 상태가 되다 **ingredient** (음식) 재료 **server** 종업원 **hire** ~을 고용하다 **be able to do** ~할 수 있다 **serve** ~에게 서비스를 제공하다 **remind** ~에게 상기시키다 **make sure (that)** 반드시 ~하도록 하다 **prepared** 준비된 **training** 교육 **session** (특정 활동을 위한) 시간 **spare time** 여유 시간

21. 화자들은 어디에서 일하는가?
(A) 서점에서
(B) 슈퍼마켓에서
(C) 레스토랑에서
(D) 피트니스 센터에서

해설 대화를 시작하면서 남자가 자신들의 피자 매장이 인기 있어서 기쁘다는(I'm so happy about how popular our pizza store is getting) 말과 함께 식사 손님들의 반응을 언급하고 있다. 이를 통해 피자 레스토랑이 대화 장소임을 알 수 있으므로 (C)가 정답이다.

Paraphrase pizza store
→ restaurant

22. 이번 주에 무슨 일이 있을 것인가?
(A) 할인이 제공될 것이다.
(B) 직원들이 고용될 것이다.
(C) 장비가 구입될 것이다.
(D) 신제품이 판매될 것이다.

해설 '이번 주'라는 시점이 언급되는 중반부에 여자가 '이번 주에 신입 종업원들이 고용되고 나면(after the new servers are hired this week)'이라는 말을 하고 있으므로 (B)가 정답이다.

어휘 **offer** ~을 제공하다 **equipment** 장비

Paraphrase new servers
→ workers

23. 여자는 오후에 무엇을 하겠는가?
(A) 구직 지원자들을 면접 보는 일
(B) 행사에 참석하는 일
(C) 광고를 내는 일
(D) 교육 프로그램을 만드는 일

해설 대화 후반부에 남자가 여자에게 이틀 간의 교육 시간에 대한 프로그램을 만들어 줄 수 있기를 바라고 있었다고(I was hoping you could make a program for a two-day training session) 말하자, 여자가 오늘 오후에 할 수 있다고 답변하고 있으므로 (D)가 정답이다.

어휘 **job applicant** 구직 지원자 **attend** ~에 참석하다 **place an advertisement** 광고를 내다 **create** ~을 만들어 내다

Paraphrase make a program for a two-day training session
→ Create a training program

Questions 24-26 refer to the following conversation with three speakers.

W1: 24 Hi, Karen. Donald and I were just making sure that you're settling in well here at Bryce Food Packaging. With your impressive qualifications, 24 we're hoping you're going to greatly improve our Web site.

M: And another thing... 25 I'd like to run through some survey comments we received about our current site. When are you free today?

W2: Well, I think I'll be pretty busy today. 26 The orientation for new staff begins at 10 A.M.

W1: Oh, didn't you get the memo? 26 It was rescheduled for Friday because the personnel manager is off sick with the flu. Your schedule should be pretty clear today.

여1: 안녕하세요, 캐런 씨. 도널드 씨와 제가 우리 브라이스 식품 포장 사에서 당신이 잘 적응하고 있으신지 확인하고 있었어요. 인상 깊은 자격을 지니고 계시니, 저희는 당신이 우리 웹 사이트를 크게 개선해 주기를 바라고 있습니다.

남: 그리고 한 가지 더 말씀드리자면... 현재 우리 사이트에 관해 전해 받은 설문 조사 의견을 빨리 살펴보고자 합니다. 오늘 언제 시간이 되시나요?

여2: 저, 오늘은 제가 아주 바쁠 것 같습니다. 신입 직원들을 위한 오리엔테이션이 오전 10시에 시작됩니다.

여1: 아, 메모를 받지 못하셨나요? 인사부장님께서 독감 때문에 병가를 내셔서 금요일로 일정이 재조정되었습니다. 오늘 당신의 일정은 꽤 여유로울 겁니다.

어휘 **settle in** 적응하다 **impressive** 인상적인 **qualification** 자격 (요건) **greatly** 크게, 대단히 **improve** ~을 개선하다, 향상시키다 **run through** 빨리 ~을 살펴보다 **survey** 설문 조사 **comment** 의견 **current** 현재의 **free** 시간이 나는 **pretty** 아주, 매우 **reschedule** ~의 일정을 재조정하다 **personnel manager** 인사부장 **be off sick** 병가를 내다 **flu** 독감 **clear** (방해, 지장 등이) 전혀 없는, 자유로운

24. 캐런 씨의 전문 영역은 무엇일 것 같은가?
(A) 홍보
(B) 회계
(C) 웹 디자인
(D) 직원 교육

해설 Karen 씨의 전문 영역을 묻고 있으므로 Karen이라는 이름이 제시되는 부분에서 특정 업무와 관련된 정보를 찾아야 한다. 대화 시작 부분에 여자 한 명이 Karen에게 인사하면서 웹 사이트를 크게 개선해 주기를 바라고 있다고(we're hoping you're going to greatly improve our Web site) 알리는 부분이 단서이다. 이와 같은 일에 해당되는 선택지로 웹 디자인을 뜻하는 (C)가 정답이다.

어휘 **area of expertise** 전문 영역 **public relations** 홍보 **accounting** 회계 **training** 교육

25. 남자는 캐런 씨와 함께 무엇을 검토하고 싶어 하는가?
(A) 설문 조사 의견
(B) 근무지 내 규정
(C) 매출 통계 자료
(D) 직원 혜택

해설 남자가 함께 검토하고 싶어 하는 것이 질문의 핵심이므로 남자의 말에서 검토 작업과 관련된 바람이 제시되는 내용이 있음을 예상하고 들어야 한다. 대화 중반부에 남자가 설문 조사 의견을 빨리 살펴보고자 한다는 말로(I'd like to run through some survey comments) 자신의 바람을 나타내는 부분을 통해 (A)가 정답임을 알 수 있다.

어휘 **workplace** 근무지, 작업장 **regulation** 규정, 규제 **statistics** 통계 (자료) **benefit** 혜택, 이득

26. 오리엔테이션은 왜 연기되었는가?
(A) 회의실을 이용할 수 없다.
(B) 책임자가 부재 중이다.
(C) 일부 장비가 손상되었다.
(D) 일정 상의 충돌이 발생했다.

해설 오리엔테이션이 연기된 이유를 묻고 있으므로 해당 행사가 연기된 사실과 함께 그 이유가 언급될 것임을 예상하고 들어야 한다. 대화 후반부에 오리엔테이션 일정이 언급된 뒤로 여자 한 명이 인사부장이 독감 때문에 병가를 내서 금요일로 일정이 재조정되었다고(It was rescheduled for Friday because the personnel manager is off sick with the flu) 말하고 있다. 이는 해당 행사를 맡은 사람이 자리에 없다는 뜻이므로 책임자의 부재를 언급한 (B)가 정답이다.

어휘 **postpone** ~을 연기하다, 미루다 **unavailable** 이용할 수 없는 **supervisor** 책임자, 부서장, 감독관 **absent** 부재 중인, 자리에 없는 **equipment** 장비 **damaged** 손상된 **scheduling conflict** 일정상의 충돌 **occur** 발생하다, 일어나다

Questions 27-29 refer to the following conversation.

W: Hi, 27 I'm looking to book a holiday in Mexico this coming summer. I usually speak with Joanne White. Is she available to talk?

M: Unfortunately, 28 Joanne is no longer working at this office. Actually, she recently left our agency to have her first child.

W: Ah, okay. I'm happy to hear that. I know that she has wanted to have a child for a while. I really wish she were here to help me though, as she always found me the cheapest price.

M: We were disappointed to lose her, too. She was one of the best staff members we ever had. 29 You should talk with Gary. He looks after all of our best clients and has been in the industry now for fifteen years.

여: 안녕하세요, 이번 돌아오는 여름에 멕시코에서 보낼 휴가를 예약하려고 알아보고 있어요. 전 평소에 조앤 화이트 씨와 상담하는데요. 그분과 얘기할 수 있나요?

남: 안타깝지만, 조앤 씨는 이제 이곳 사무실에서 근무하지 않습니다. 사실 그분은 최근 첫 아이를 출산하기 위해 회사를 그만 두었어요.

여: 아, 알겠습니다. 그 말을 들으니 반갑네요. 그분이 한동안 아이를 갖고 싶어했다는 걸 알거든요. 그분이 늘 제게 가장 싼 가격을 찾아줬기 때문에 여기 있으면서 절 도와줬으면 하는 마음은 있지만요.

남: 저희도 그분이 떠나서 안타까웠답니다. 저희와 함께 했던 가장 우수한 직원들 중 한 명이었거든요. 게리 씨와 상담해보세요. 그가 저희의 우수 고객들을 담당하고 있고, 이 업계에서 15년째 근무하고 있어요.

어휘 **book a holiday** 휴가를 예약하다 **recently** 최근에 **leave** ~을 떠나다, 그만두다 **I wish she were here** 그녀가 여기 있으면 좋겠다 **find A B** A에게 B를 찾아주다 **be disappointed to do** ~해서 실망하다 **look after** ~을 돌보다, 처리하다 **industry** 업계

27. 여자는 왜 전화하는가?
(A) 여행 책자를 요청하기 위해
(B) 회의 시간을 제안하기 위해
(C) 휴가를 취소하기 위해
(D) 휴가를 준비하기 위해

해설 전화 건 이유나 목적은 대화의 초반부에 드러난다. 따라서 전화 건 사람의 첫 대사를 집중해서 들어야 한다. 대화 초반부에 여자가 I'm looking to book a holiday in Mexico this coming summer라며 용건을 밝히고 있다. 휴가를 예약하고 싶다고 하므로 (D)가 정답이다.

어휘 **brochure** (안내) 책자 **organize** ~을 준비하다, 조직하다

28. 화이트 씨는 왜 여자를 도울 수 없는가?
(A) 멕시코에서 여행 중이다.
(B) 다른 사무실로 이사했다.
(C) 일을 그만두었다.
(D) 출장 중이다.

해설 Ms. White가 언급되는 부분을 잘 듣도록 한다. 여자가 늘 하던 대로 Joanne White 씨와 얘기하고 싶다고 하자 남자가 Joanne is no longer working at this office. Actually, she recently left our firm to have her first child라고 알려주고 있다. 아이를 낳기 위해 회사를 그만두었다는 것이다. 이 내용과 의미가 통하는 선택지는 (C)이다.

어휘 **be on a business trip** 출장 중이다

Paraphrase left our firm
→ quit her job

29. 남자는 여자에게 무엇을 하라고 제안하는가?
(A) 다른 매장으로 갈 것
(B) 다른 여행사 직원과 얘기할 것
(C) 화이트 씨에게 이메일을 보낼 것
(D) 다른 목적지를 고를 것

해설 마지막 대사에서 남자는 You should talk with Gary. He looks after all of our best clients and has been in the industry now for fifteen years라며 다른 직원을 소개시켜 주고 있다. Gary라는 직원이 우수 고객을 관리하고 경험도 많으니 그와 얘기하라는 것이다. 휴가를 예약하고 싶다는 여자의

말에서 남자가 일하는 곳은 여행사임을 알 수 있으므로 (B)가 정답이다. Gary를 a different travel agent라고 표현했다.

어휘 **destination** 목적지

Questions 30-32 refer to the following conversation.

M: Good morning! **30** Welcome to One Road Car Rentals. How can I help you?

W: Hi. **30** **31** I reserved a compact car to pick up this morning. My name is Ally Martin.

M: Let me check... Your reservation is for Thursday, December 17.

W: Oh, no. I need to drive to Belleville this afternoon for a factory inspection, and there aren't any buses or trains that go there.

M: Well, we have a luxury car available now, but it's more expensive.

W: **32** Let me call my office to confirm the extra cost. I'll just be a minute.

남: 안녕하세요! 원 로드 자동차 렌탈에 오신 것을 환영합니다. 무엇을 도와 드릴까요?
여: 안녕하세요. 제가 소형 자동차를 오늘 아침에 가져가는 것으로 예약했어요. 제 이름은 앨리 마틴입니다.
남: 확인해 보겠습니다... 고객님의 예약은 12월 17일 목요일로 되어 있습니다.
여: 아, 안돼요. 제가 공장 점검 때문에 오늘 오후에 벨빌로 차를 운전해서 가야 하는데, 그곳으로 가는 버스나 기차가 하나도 없어요.
남: 저, 저희에게 지금 이용하실 수 있는 고급 자동차가 한 대 있기는 하지만, 더 비쌉니다.
여: 제가 추가 비용을 확정 받을 수 있게 제 사무실에 전화해 볼게요. 잠깐이면 될 거예요.

어휘 **reserve** ~을 예약하다 **compact car** 소형 자동차 **pick up** ~을 가져가다, 가져오다 **reservation** 예약 **inspection** 점검, 조사 **available** 이용 가능한 **confirm** ~을 확인하다 **extra** 추가의, 별도의

30. 어디에서 대화가 이뤄지고 있는가?
(A) 버스 정류장에서
(B) 자동차 대여 업체에서
(C) 공장에서
(D) 호텔에서

해설 대화 시작 부분에 남자가 Welcome to One Road Car Rentals라고 업체 이름을 알리고 있고, 여자도 가져 갈 차량을 예약했다고(I reserved a compact car to pick up this morning) 언급하는 것을 통해 자동차 대여 업체에서 이뤄지는 대화임을 알 수 있으므로 (B)가 정답이다.

어휘 **take place** (일, 행사 등이) 발생되다, 개최되다 **rental** 대여, 임대 **agency** 업체, 대행사

31. 남자가 "고객님의 예약은 12월 17일 목요일로 되어 있습니다"라고 말할 때 암시하는 것은 무엇인가?

(A) 예약이 연기되었다.
(B) 서비스를 이용할 수 있다.
(C) 마감기한이 다가오고 있다.
(D) 실수가 발생되었다.

해설 여자가 오늘 아침에 가져갈 차량을 예약했다고(I reserved a compact car to pick up this morning) 말한 것에 대해 '예약이 12월 17일 목요일로 되어 있다'고 알리고 있다. 이는 예약할 때 실수를 해 잘못 예약했음을 말하는 것이므로 (D)가 정답이다.

어휘 **appointment** 예약, 약속 **postpone** ~을 연기하다, 미루다 **available** 이용할 수 있는 **deadline** 마감 기한 **approach** 다가오다 **make a mistake** 실수하다

32. 여자는 곧이어 무엇을 할 것 같은가?

(A) 기차 일정표를 확인하는 일
(B) 회의 일정을 재조정하는 일
(C) 허락을 요청하는 일
(D) 신용카드를 제공하는 일

해설 대화 마지막에 여자가 추가 비용을 확정받을 수 있게 자신의 사무실에 전화해 보겠다고(Let me call my office to confirm the extra cost) 알리고 있는데, 이는 허락을 받으려는 것이므로 (C)가 정답이다.

어휘 **reschedule** ~의 일정을 재조정하다 **ask for** ~을 요청하다 **permission** 허락, 허가

Paraphrase call my office to confirm the extra cost
→ Ask for permission

Questions 33-35 refer to the following conversation and floor plan.

W: Excuse me, **33** I printed out this coupon from your Web site last month. I'm wondering if it's still valid.

M: Hmm... let's see. Yes, sure. You can use that here to get 20 percent off any item before the end of April. And **34** we just got a huge shipment of new products yesterday.

W: Oh, I'm happy to hear that. I'm hoping to buy something from the new line that you are advertising on your flyers right now.

M: No problem. **35** You'll find that line in the clothing section just in front of the changing rooms. Let me know if you need any help finding anything.

여: 실례합니다, 제가 지난 달에 귀사의 웹 사이트에서 이 쿠폰을 출력했습니다. 여전히 유효한지 궁금해서요.

남: 흠... 어디 보자. 네, 그렇습니다. 4월말이 되기 전에 이곳에서 사용하시면 어떤 물품이든지 20퍼센트 할인 받으실 수 있습니다. 그리고 신제품을 실은 엄청난 배송 물품이 어제 막 들어왔습니다.

여: 아, 그 말씀을 들으니 기쁘네요. 지금 전단을 통해 광고하고 계신 신제품 라인에서 뭔가 구입할 수 있기를 바라고 있습니다.

남: 별 말씀을요. 탈의실 바로 앞쪽에 있는 의류 코너에서 그 신제품 라인을 찾아보실 수 있습니다. 제품을 찾으시는 데 도움이 필요하시면 제게 알려 주시기 바랍니다.

어휘 **print out** ~을 출력하다, 인쇄하다 **wonder if** ~인지 궁금하다 **valid** 유효한 **get 20 percent off** ~에서 20퍼센트 할인 받다 **huge** 엄청난, 막대한 **shipment** 배송(품), 선적(품) **hope to do** ~하기를 바라다 **line** 제품 라인, 제품군 **advertise** ~을 광고하다 **flyer** 전단 **clothing section** 의류 코너 **in front of** ~의 앞에 **changing room** 탈의실 **cashier** 계산대

33. 화자들은 주로 무엇에 관해 이야기하고 있는가?

(A) 계절 세일 행사
(B) 결함이 있는 제품
(C) 구인 자리
(D) 할인 쿠폰

해설 대화 주제를 묻고 있으므로 대화가 시작되는 부분에 특히 집중해 들어야 한다. 여자가 대화를 시작하면서 자신이 웹 사이트에서 출력한 쿠폰이 여전히 유효한지 궁금하다고 문의하자(I printed out this coupon from your Web site last month. I'm wondering if it's still valid) 남자가 할인을 받을 수 있는 쿠폰임을 언급하고 있다. 따라서 할인 쿠폰을 의미하는 (D)가 정답이다.

어휘 **seasonal** 계절의 **defective** 결함이 있는 **vacancy** 공석, 빈 자리 **voucher** 쿠폰, 상품권

Paraphrase coupon
→ voucher

34. 매장에서 최근에 무슨 일이 있었는가?

(A) 개조 공사가 완료되었다.
(B) 매니저 한 명이 고용되었다.
(C) 상품이 배송되었다.
(D) 개장 기념 행사가 열렸다.

해설 최근이라는 과거 시점이 질문의 핵심이므로 질문에 포함된 recently를 비롯해 가까운 과거를 나타내는 시점 표현이 제시되는 부분에서 단서를 찾아야 한다. 대화 중반부에 남자가 신제품을 실은 배송 물품이 어제 막 들어왔다는 말로(we just got a huge shipment of new products yesterday) 가까운 과거 시점에 있었던 일을 말하고 있다. 따라서 상품 배송을 의미하는 (C)가 정답이다.

어휘 **renovation** 개조, 보수 **complete** ~을 완료하다 **hire** ~을 고용하다 **merchandise** 상품 **deliver** ~을 배송하다 **be held** (행사 등이) 열리다, 개최되다

Paraphrase we just got a huge shipment of new products → Merchandise was delivered.

35. 시각자료를 보시오. 여자는 곧이어 매장의 어느 코너로 갈 것 같은가?

(A) 청바지와 바지
(B) 블라우스와 셔츠
(C) 스커트와 드레스
(D) 액세서리

해설 배치도에서 각 코너의 명칭 및 위치 관계를 먼저 확인한 후에 이동 방향을 알리는 정보에 유의해 들어야 한다. 여자가 원하는 제품 구입과 관련해 남자가 대화 후반부에 탈의실 바로 앞쪽에 있는 의류 코너에서 찾아볼 수 있다고(You'll find that line in the clothing section just in front of the changing rooms) 말하고 있다. 시각자료에서 탈의실 바로 앞쪽에 있는 코너는 Jeans & Pants이므로 (A)가 정답이다.

Questions 36-38 refer to the following conversation and indicator.

W: Hello, 36 this is the Eclipse Electronics technical support line. My name is Allison. How can I help you?

M: I recently bought an Eclipse KSE500 television at a local department store. It's been working well for a week, but now it won't turn on.

W: Hmm... What happens when you press the power button?

M: Usually there's a ring of light that appears all around the button, but 37 now only the bottom half of the circle lights up briefly.

W: I see. That indicates that it's an error with the

internal power supply. It won't be an easy fix.

M: I'm glad I got the warranty then. 38 I'll just take it back to the store this afternoon.

여: 안녕하세요, 이클립스 전자 회사 기술 지원 전화 서비스입니다. 제 이름은 앨리슨입니다. 무엇을 도와 드릴까요?

남: 제가 최근에 지역 백화점에서 이클립스 KSE500 텔레비전을 구입했습니다. 일주일 동안은 잘 작동되었는데, 현재는 켜지지 않고 있어요.

여: 흠... 전원 버튼을 누르시면 무슨 일이 생기나요?

남: 보통은 버튼 주변 전체에 원형으로 불이 들어오는데, 지금은 그 원 모양의 아래쪽 절반에만 잠깐 불이 켜져요.

여: 알겠습니다. 그 표시는 내부 전력 공급에 오류가 있음을 나타냅니다. 간단한 수리 작업은 아닙니다.

남: 그렇다면 품질 보증서가 있어서 다행이네요. 오늘 오후에 매장으로 다시 가져 가겠습니다.

간단한 문제 해결 가이드
이클립스 KSE 시리즈

"켜짐"(정상)　오류#13　오류#19　오류#23　오류#37

어휘 **technical support** 기술 지원 **recently** 최근에 **department store** 백화점 **work** (기계 등이) 작동되다 **turn on** 켜지다 **happen** 발생되다, 일어나다 **press** ~을 누르다 **usually** 보통, 일반적으로 **appear** 나타나다, 보이다 **all around** ~의 주변 전체에 **bottom** 아래, 하단 **circle** 원형, 동그라미 **light up** 불이 들어오다 **briefly** 잠시 **indicate that** ~임을 나타내다 **internal** 내부의 **power supply** 전력 공급 **fix** 수리 **warranty** 품질 보증(서) **then** 그렇다면, 그럼 **take A back to B** A를 B로 다시 가져 가다 **troubleshooting** 문제 해결, 문제 진단 **normal** 정상의

36. 여자는 누구일 것 같은가?

(A) 컴퓨터 기술자
(B) 매장 매니저
(C) 고객 서비스 직원
(D) 텔레비전 프로그램 제작자

해설 대화를 시작하면서 여자가 Eclipse Electronics 기술 지원 전화 서비스에 전화했다고(this is the Eclipse Electronics technical support line) 말하고 있으므로 여자의 신분으로 고객 서비스 직원을 뜻하는 (C)가 정답임을 알 수 있다.

어휘 **technician** 기술자 **representative** 직원

37. 시각자료를 보시오. 화자들은 어느 오류에 관해 이야기하고 있는가?

(A) 13번 오류
(B) 19번 오류
(C) 23번 오류
(D) 37번 오류

해설 화자들이 이야기하는 오류를 묻고 있으므로 특정 오류 상태에 해당되는 표시 방법을 설명하는 부분을 찾아야 한다. 대화 중반부에 남자가 자신이 겪는 문제점과 관련해 원 모양의 아래쪽 절반에만 잠깐 불이 켜진다고(now only the bottom half of the circle lights up briefly) 말하고 있다. 시각자료에서 이와 같은 표시 상태에 해당되는 것이 23번 오류이므로 (C)가 정답이다.

38. 남자는 오후에 무엇을 할 것인가?

(A) 웹 사이트를 방문한다.
(B) 매장으로 간다.
(C) 기술자에게 전화한다.
(D) 품질 보증 서비스를 구입한다.

해설 남자가 오후에 할 일을 묻고 있으므로 남자의 말에서 오후라는 시점 표현과 함께 제시되는 정보를 파악해야 한다. 대화의 끝부분에 남자가 오늘 오후에 매장으로 다시 가져 가겠다고(I'll just take it back to the store this afternoon) 말하고 있으므로 매장으로 찾아 가는 일을 언급한 (B)가 정답이다.

Part 4

Questions 39-41 refer to the following talk.

Hello. Welcome to Jade Garden. **39** I'm George and I'll be your server for the evening. To get things started, I'll introduce you to one of our specials. Jade Garden is famous in this city for its sirloin steak and special mushroom sauce. **40** And for this week only, if you order one, you will receive another one free. Also, just for today, **41** if you sign up as a member of Jade Garden, you'll get a free drink of your choice the next time you visit us. I'll hand you each a form with your menus.

안녕하세요. 제이드 가든에 오신 것을 환영합니다. 제 이름은 죠지이며, 오늘 저녁 여러분의 담당 종업원입니다. 가장 먼저, 저희 특별 요리 중 한 가지를 소개해 드리겠습니다. 저희 제이드 가든은 이 도시에서 설로인 스테이크와 특제 버섯 소스로 유명합니다. 그리고 이번주에 한해, 하나를 주문하시면 무료로 스테이크를 하나 더 드립니다. 또한 오늘 하루에 한해, 저희 제이드 가든 회원으로 등록하시면, 다음 번에 방문하실 때 원하시는 음료를 무료로 드실 수 있습니다. 메뉴와 함께 여러분 각자에게 가입 양식을 나눠 드리겠습니다.

어휘 server 종업원 to get things started 가장 먼저 말씀 드리자면 introduce A to B A에게 B를 소개하다 special n. 특별 요리 sirloin steak 설로인(등심) 스테이크 mushroom 버섯 order ~을 주문하다 free ad. 무료로 sign up as a member of ~의 회원으로 등록하다, 가입 신청하다 get a free drink 무료로 음료를 받다 of one's choice ~가 원하는 것을 선택해 the next time + 절 다음 번에 ~할 때 hand A B A에게 B를 나눠주다 form n. 양식, 서식

39. 화자는 누구인가?

(A) 매장 소유주
(B) 레스토랑 직원
(C) 요리사
(D) 여행 가이드

해설 화자는 자신을 your server for the evening이라고 소개하며 식당의 특별 메뉴(sirloin steak and special mushroom sauce) 및 그와 관련된 행사에 대해 안내하고 있다. 따라서 이 화자는 식당 직원일 것이라고 추측할 수 있으므로 정답은 (B)이다.

어휘 business 매장, 업체, 회사

40. 화자에 따르면, 이번 주에 무슨 일이 있을 것인가?

(A) 새 레스토랑이 직원을 채용한다.
(B) 음료가 할인된 가격에 판매되고 있다.
(C) 하나의 가격에 두 개를 받는 특별 서비스가 제공된다.
(D) 새로운 음식 메뉴가 소개되고 있다.

해설 this week이 핵심어이므로 이 표현이 언급되는 곳에 귀 기울이도록 한다. 담화 중반부에서 화자는 for this week only, if you order one, you will receive another one free라고 안내하고 있다. 이번 주에 한해서 1+1 행사를 한다고 하므로 (C)가 정답이다.

어휘 hire ~을 채용하다 at a discount 할인된 가격에 two for one 하나의 가격으로 두 개를 받는 offer ~을 제공하다 introduce ~을 소개하다, 도입하다

Paraphrase if you order one, you will receive another one free → a two-for-one special

41. 청자들은 어떻게 무료 음료를 받을 수 있는가?

(A) 주말 파티에 참석함으로써
(B) 신용카드를 이용함으로써
(C) 주방장 추천 요리를 주문함으로써
(D) 회원이 됨으로써

해설 담화 마지막 부분에 a free drink가 언급되고 있다. 회원으로 등록하면 무료 음료를 받을 수 있다고(if you sign up as a member of Jade Garden, you'll get a free drink of your choice ~) 하므로, 무료 음료를 받을 수 있는 방법은 (D)임을 알 수 있다.

어휘 chef's special 주방장 추천 요리

Paraphrase sign up as a member
　　　　　→ becoming a member

Questions 42-44 refer to the following excerpt from a meeting.

This staff meeting will mostly focus on **42** the rearrangement of the electronics department to get ready for the holiday shopping season. You'll notice the biggest change is that our most popular items, like **42** TVs and sound systems, have been moved to the back of the store. **43** Now, customers will walk through the store and see more of our other merchandise, hopefully increasing overall sales. Oh, and **44** we still don't have any Yorbit Gamestations in stock. I placed an order for more last month, but everyone wants them. We'll just have to wait, and in the meantime, encourage shoppers to buy a competing brand.

이번 직원 회의는 주로 연휴 쇼핑 시즌에 대한 준비로 전자 제품 코너를 재배치한 작업에 초점을 맞출 것입니다. 여러분은 TV와 음향 시스템 등과 같이 우리의 가장 인기 있는 제품들이 매장 뒤쪽으로 옮겨졌다는 점이 가장 큰 변화라는 것을 알게 될 것입니다. 이제, 고객들은 매장을 지나 다니면서 우리의 다른 상품을 더 많이 보게 될 것이며, 이로 인해 전반적인 매출이 증대되기를 바라고 있습니다. 오, 그리고 우리는 여전히 요빗 게임스테이션 제품을 재고로 전혀 갖고 있지 않습니다. 제가 지난 달에 추가 제품을 주문했지만, 모든 분들께서 이 제품을 원하고 계십니다. 우리는 기다릴 수밖에 없으며, 그 사이에 쇼핑객들에게 경쟁 브랜드의 제품을 구입하도록 권해 드려야 할 것입니다.

어휘 focus on ~에 초점을 맞추다 rearrangement 재배치 electronics 전자 제품 get ready for ~에 대해 준비하다 holiday shopping season 연휴 쇼핑 시즌 notice ~임을 알아차리다, 인식하다 sound system 음향 시스템 be moved to ~로 옮겨지다 walk through ~을 걸어 지나다니다 merchandise 상품 hopefully 희망하여, 바라건대 overall 전반적인 sales 매출, 판매(량) have A in stock A를 재고로 갖고 있다 place an order 주문하다 in the meantime 그 사이에, 그러는 동안 encourage A to do A에게 ~하도록 권하다 competing 경쟁하는

42. 매장에서 무슨 종류의 상품을 판매하는가?
(A) 여행 가방
(B) 원예 도구
(C) 전자 제품
(D) 가구

해설 담화 시작 부분에 화자는 전자 제품 코너를 재배치한 일(the rearrangement of the electronics department)을 언급하고 있고, 뒤이어 TV와 음향 시스템(TVs and sound systems)을 예로 들고 있다. 따라서 전자 제품을 뜻하는 (C)가 정답이다.

어휘 luggage 여행 가방 gardening 원예 tool 도구, 공구

43. 매장 진열품들이 왜 재배치되었는가?
(A) 휴일을 위해 장식하기 위해
(B) 개조 공사를 위한 공간을 만들기 위해
(C) 특별 세일 행사를 홍보하기 위해
(D) 제품의 가시성을 높이기 위해

해설 매장 진열품들이 재배치된 이유를 묻고 있으므로 재배치 작업 및 그 이유나 효과 등이 언급될 것임을 예상하고 들어야 한다. 담화 중반부에 고객들이 매장을 다니면서 다른 상품을 더 많이 보시게 될 것이라고(Now, customers will walk through the store and see more of our other merchandise) 알리고 있다. 이는 고객들의 눈에 더 잘 보이게 만든 것이므로 제품의 가시성을 높이기 위해서라는 의미로 쓰인 (D)가 정답이다.

어휘 decorate 장식하다 allow space for ~에 대한 공간을 만들다, 확보하다 renovation 개조, 보수 promote ~을 홍보하다 visibility 가시성, 눈에 잘 보임

44. 화자가 "모든 분들께서 이 제품을 원하고 계십니다"라고 말할때 암시하는 것은 무엇인가?
(A) 다른 매장에서 더 낮은 가격을 제공했다.
(B) 주문이 충족될 수 없다.
(C) 많은 직원들이 휴무를 요청했다.
(D) 제품이 아직 출시되지 않았다.

해설 해당 문장은 담화 후반부에 들을 수 있는데, Yorbit Gamestations 제품을 재고로 전혀 갖고 있지 않아서 지난 달에 추가 제품을 주문했다고(we still don't have any Yorbit Gamestations in stock. I placed an order for more last month) 알리는 말 다음에 제시되고 있다. 따라서 많은 사람들이 원하고 있기 때문에 물품을 확보할 수 없음을 의미하는 말이라는 것을 알 수 있으므로 주문이 충족될 수 없다는 뜻으로 쓰인 (B)가 정답이 된다.

어휘 fill an order 주문을 충족하다, 이행하다 ask for ~을 요청하다 time off 휴무 release ~을 출시하다

Welcome to the Rockman Theater, everyone. I'm delighted to see so many people here in attendance tonight. **45 As the founder of the One World Foundation, it gives me great pleasure to host tonight's fundraising banquet.** We have invited many special guests to this evening's event, from movie stars and athletes to some of the most successful business people in the country. **46 The purpose of tonight's event is to receive donations for our various charity projects.** I hope you brought your wallets! Now, before we begin serving the banquet, **47 I'd like you all to watch a short film** that shows the many good causes we are involved in around the world. Thanks.

락맨 극장에 오신 것을 환영합니다, 여러분. 오늘밤에 이렇게 많은 분들께서 이곳을 찾아보신 것을 보게 되어 기쁩니다. 원 월드 재단의 설립자로서, 오늘밤의 기금 마련 연회를 주최하는 일은 제게 대단한 기쁨을 선사해 줍니다. 오늘 저녁의 행사를 위해 영화 배우와 운동 선수들에서부터 전국에서 가장 성공한 몇몇 사업가들에 이르기까지 여러 특별 손님들을 초청했습니다. 오늘밤 행사의 목적은 저희가 진행하는 다양한 자선 프로젝트에 대한 기부금을 모금하는 것입니다. 여러분께서 지갑을 가져오셨기를 바랍니다! 자, 연회에 필요한 음식을 제공하는 일을 시작하기 전에, 저희가 전 세계에서 관여하고 있는 여러 자선 활동들을 보여주는 짤막한 동영상을 여러분 모두가 봐주셨으면 합니다. 감사합니다.

어휘 **be delighted to do** ~해서 기쁘다 **in attendance** 참석한, 출석한 **founder** 설립자 **host** ~을 주최하다 **fundraising** 기금 마련 **banquet** 연회 **invite** ~을 초대하다 **athlete** 운동 선수 **business people** 사업가들 **purpose** 목적 **donation** 기부(금) **various** 다양한 **charity** 자선 (활동) **bring** ~을 가져오다 **wallet** 지갑 **serve** ~에 음식을 제공하다 **would like A to do** A에게 ~하기를 원하다 **good cause** 자선 활동, 좋은 일, 대의 **be involved in** ~에 관여하다, 관련되어 있다

45. 화자는 누구일 것 같은가?
(A) 극장 직원
(B) 사업가
(C) 자선 단체 설립자
(D) 영화 감독

해설 담화를 시작하면서 화자는 자신을 One World Foundation의 설립자라고 소개하고 있고(As the founder of the One World Foundation) 오늘밤에 열리는 기금 마련 연회를 주최하게 되어 기쁘다고(it gives me great pleasure to host tonight's fundraising banquet) 덧붙이고 있다. 따라서 자선 사업을 하는 단체의 설립자라는 것을 알 수 있으므로 (C)가 정답이다.

어휘 **business owner** 사업가 **movie director** 영화 감독

46. 화자는 왜 "여러분께서 지갑을 가져오셨기를 바랍니다"라고 말하는가?
(A) 청자들에게 한 가지 서비스가 비용이 많이 든다고 알리기 위해
(B) 청자들에게 각자의 개인 소지품들을 챙기도록 상기시키기 위해
(C) 청자들에게 티켓을 구입하도록 권하기 위해
(D) 청자들에게 기부금을 내도록 권하기 위해

해설 해당 문장은 담화 중반부에 화자가 행사의 목적이 다양한 자선 프로젝트에 대한 기부금을 모금하는 것이라고(The purpose of tonight's event is to receive donations for our various charity projects) 알린 후에 들을 수 있다. 따라서 기부금을 내도록 권하기 위한 말이라는 것을 알 수 있으므로 이와 같은 의미로 쓰인 (D)가 정답이다.

어휘 **inform A that** A에게 ~라고 알리다 **remind A to do** A에게 ~하도록 상기시키다 **belongings** 소지품 **recommend that** ~하도록 권하다, 추천하다 **encourage A to do** A에게 ~하도록 권하다, 장려하다 **make a donation** 기부하다, 기부금을 내다

47. 청자들은 곧이어 무엇을 할 것 같은가?
(A) 동영상을 시청한다.
(B) 메뉴를 확인한다.
(C) 라이브 공연을 즐긴다.
(D) 다른 연설자의 말을 듣는다.

해설 담화 후반부에 화자는 식사에 앞서 짧은 동영상을 봐 주기를 원한다고(I'd like you all to watch a short film ~) 제안하고 있다. 따라서 동영상 시청을 뜻하는 (A)가 정답이다.

어휘 **performance** 공연

Questions 48-50 refer to the following telephone message and expense sheet.

Hello, Mr. Harris. I'm Eva Vance from the accounting department. I just have a question about the reimbursement sheet from **48 your trip to the talent recruitment fair last week.** I've looked at your submitted form and the receipts you supplied, but it doesn't quite add up. **49 You spent money on promotional items that you gave away, but it looks like you wrote down 20 dollars more than the amount I obtained from the receipts.** Could you double check for me? And in the future, can you make purchases such as this using the company account at Every-Mart? **50 I e-mailed the membership account name and password to all employees last month.** Please use it from now on.

안녕하세요, 해리스 씨. 저는 회계부의 에바 반스입니다. 귀하께서 지난주에 인재 채용 박람회장으로 떠나셨던 출장에서 발생된 비용에 대한 환급 신청서와 관련해 질문이 있습니다. 귀하께서 제출해 주신 양식과 제공해 주신 영수증들을 살펴봤는데, 합산 금액이 꽤 맞지 않습니다. 귀하께서는 사람들에게 나눠주신 홍보 물품에 대해 비용을 소비하셨는데, 제가 영수증을 바탕으로 총계를 낸 액수보다 20달러를 더 기재하신 것 같습니다. 다시 한 번 확인해 주시겠습니까? 그리고 향후에 이와 같은 것을 에브리-마트에서 구매하실 때는 회사 계정을 이용해주시겠습니까? 제가 지난달에 회원 계정명과 비밀번호를 전 직원에게 보냈습니다. 앞으로는 그것을 이용해 주십시오.

개인 경비 기록	
구매	비용
휘발유	80달러
숙박	240달러
홍보물	90달러
음식	120달러
	총액: 530달러

어휘 accounting 회계 reimbursement 비용 환급 sheet 양식, 문서, 서류 talent recruitment fair 인재 채용 박람회 submit ~을 제출하다 form 양식, 서식 receipt 영수증 supply ~을 제공하다 spend money on ~에 비용을 소비하다 add up 말이 되다, 앞뒤가 맞다 promotional 홍보의, 판촉의 item 물품, 제품 give away ~을 나눠주다 it looks like ~한 것 같다 write down ~을 기재하다, 적어 놓다 amount 액수 obtain 얻다, 획득하다 double check ~을 다시 한번 확인하다 make a purchase 구매하다 such as ~와 같은 account 계정, 계좌 from now on 앞으로는 expense 지출 (비용) gasoline 휘발유 lodging 숙소

48. 청자는 지난주에 무엇을 했는가?
(A) 휴가를 떠났다.
(B) 신입 사원들을 고용했다.
(C) 직업 박람회에 참석했다.
(D) 일부 컴퓨터들을 업그레이드했다.

해설 질문에 제시된 지난주라는 시점이 핵심이므로 이 시점 표현이 제시되는 부분에서 단서를 찾아야 한다. 담화 초반부에 상대방이 지난주에 인재 채용 박람회장으로 출장을 갔다는 사실을 (your trip to the talent recruitment fair last week) 언급하고 있으므로 직업 박람회 참석을 의미하는 (C)가 정답이다.

어휘 vacation 휴가 job fair 직업 박람회

49. 시각자료를 보시오. 어느 액수가 확인되어야 하는가?
(A) 80달러
(B) 240달러
(C) 90달러
(D) 120달러

해설 확인되어야 하는 액수가 질문의 핵심이므로 담화 중에 잘못된 액수로 된 항목이 언급될 것임을 예상하고 들어야 한다. 담화 중반부에 사람들에게 나눠 준 홍보 물품에 대해 비용을 소비했고 화자 자신이 계산한 것보다 20달러를 더 기재한 것 같다고 (You spent money on promotional items ~ it looks like you wrote down 20 dollars more ~) 알리고 있다. 따라서 시각자료에서 홍보 물품에 해당되는 비용인 (C)가 정답이다.

어휘 confirm ~을 확인해주다

50. 화자는 직원들에게 무엇이 이메일로 보내졌다고 말하는가?
(A) 연락처 목록
(B) 회원 상세 정보
(C) 구매 관련 정책
(D) 직무 정보

해설 이메일로 보내진 것이 질문의 핵심이므로 이메일에 포함된 대상이 제시될 것임을 예상하고 들어야 한다. 담화 후반부에 회원 계정 이름과 비밀번호를 전 직원에게 이메일로 발송했다고 (I e-mailed the membership account name and password ~) 알리고 있으므로 회원 상세 정보를 뜻하는 (B)가 정답임을 알 수 있다.

어휘 contact 연락(처) details 상세 정보 policy 정책, 방침 job responsibility 직무, 책무

Paraphrase membership account name and password
→ Membership details

시원스쿨 **LAB**

WEEK 06

Contents	Page	Date	Score (맞은 개수)
Day 01 RC Half Test	02	월 일	/50
Day 02 LC Half Test	16	월 일	/50
Day 03 RC Half Test	22	월 일	/50
Day 04 LC Half Test	36	월 일	/50
Day 05 RC Half Test	42	월 일	/50

READING TEST

In the Reading test, you will read a variety of texts and answer several different types of reading comprehension questions. The entire Reading test will last 75 minutes. There are three parts, and directions are given for each part. You are encouraged to answer as many questions as possible within the time allowed. You must mark your answers on the separate answer sheet. Do not write your answers in your test book.

PART 5

Directions: A word or phrase is missing in each of the sentences below. Four answer choices are given below each sentence. Select the best answer to complete the sentence. Then mark the letter (A), (B), (C), or (D) on your answer sheet.

1. Mr. Howard asked his secretary to find a suitable ------- near the airport for his business trip.

   (A) accommodated
   (B) accommodation
   (C) accommodates
   (D) accommodate

2. Mr. Bellamy ------- Brightman Corporation seven years ago after leaving his position at Finnegan Tech Inc.

   (A) founded
   (B) would found
   (C) founds
   (D) had been founded

3. Green World Foundation has informed us of an ------- method for distributing our goods throughout the country.

   (A) alternative
   (B) alternated
   (C) alternating
   (D) alternator

4. Reserve your tickets for Milton Music Festival ------- to avoid missing the biggest event of the year.

   (A) still
   (B) often
   (C) today
   (D) always

5. Hamran Auto Detailing Services provides complimentary interior ------- for anyone who brings their car in for repairs.

   (A) cleaning
   (B) cleanest
   (C) cleaned
   (D) clean

6. Please refer to the product manual ------- your printer cannot connect wirelessly to your computer.

   (A) if
   (B) besides
   (C) toward
   (D) unless

7. Ms. Benitez is ------- to hear that Professor Jackman has agreed to deliver a speech at this year's medical conference.

(A) pleasure
(B) pleasing
(C) pleased
(D) please

8. The Indy Press Gallery is located just ------- the Rainy Day Bakery on Hudson Boulevard.

(A) into
(B) over
(C) among
(D) past

9. Most hotel guests tend to dine at our poolside restaurant ------- our rooftop one.

(A) rather than
(B) in short
(C) as a result of
(D) by all means

10. Employee morale at our factory has continued to fall, ------- among night shift workers.

(A) particular
(B) particularly
(C) particularize
(D) particularity

11. According to the CEO, the financial status of Saxon Pharmaceuticals is ------- than its quarterly figures would imply.

(A) stable
(B) more stable
(C) more stably
(D) most stable

12. When choosing wine to accompany a meal, select ------- that complements the taste of the food.

(A) it
(B) another
(C) this
(D) one

13. Mike Luther's documentary about fast food is one of the most highly ------- films of the past year.

(A) concerned
(B) regarded
(C) performed
(D) applied

14. Digital Plaza stocks ------- such as cases and screen covers for most mobile phone models.

(A) accessories
(B) repairs
(C) technicians
(D) applications

15. Bautista Airlines ------- passengers to take advantage of its complimentary blankets, pillows, and sleeping masks.

(A) inquires
(B) achieves
(C) attracts
(D) encourages

16. Ms. Koumas is thinking of exchanging her automobile ------- a newer model.

(A) for
(B) on
(C) into
(D) by

PART 6

Directions: Read the texts that follow. A word, phrase, or sentence is missing in parts of each text. Four answer choices for each question are given below the text. Select the best answer to complete the text. Then mark the letter (A), (B), (C) or (D) on your answer sheet.

Questions 17-20 refer to the following letter.

Dear Taco City customers,

We regret to inform you that there is a temporary shortage of the salsa and guacamole ------- dishes
17.
are typically served with. -------, our regular supplier is experiencing a stock shortage, and this may
18.
last for several days.

If you are ordering a dish that is typically accompanied by salsa or guacamole, please consider some
suitable -------. We can offer you sour cream, chili sauce, or cheese dip instead. We apologize for this
19.
inconvenience and appreciate your understanding.

-------.
20.

17. (A) and
    (B) that
    (C) from
    (D) among

18. (A) Finally
    (B) Therefore
    (C) For instance
    (D) Unfortunately

19. (A) locations
    (B) ingredients
    (C) incentives
    (D) substitutions

20. (A) We hope you enjoyed your meal.
    (B) Our menu will return to normal next week.
    (C) Please provide feedback on our new menu.
    (D) The new dishes are available at all
        branches.

Attention: All Morrigan Grocery Staff

Training Seminars (Sunday, March 29, 8:00 A.M. and 9:00 P.M.)

We will be running two seminars ------- the new self-checkout systems that are being installed
                                    21.
next week. All employees need to be knowledgeable about the new devices so that they can assist

customers whenever necessary. -------. Please make sure that you attend one of the seminars.
                                22.

If you are unable to attend either seminar, you must contact our human resources manager in advance.

We ------- to arrange a third seminar for those who cannot attend on March 29. Please note that this
     23.
------- is extremely important as it will provide you with the knowledge you need to help our customers.
 24.

21. (A) regarding
    (B) through
    (C) in case of
    (D) along with

22. (A) We apologize for the technical issues
       affecting the checkouts.
    (B) Our customers have had difficulty in using
       the new system.
    (C) The sessions will be held in the upstairs
       meeting room.
    (D) If you wish to apply, please visit our Web
       site.

23. (A) strived
    (B) strive
    (C) to strive
    (D) will strive

24. (A) revision
    (B) equipment
    (C) training
    (D) target

PART 7

Directions: In this part you will read a selection of texts, such as magazine and newspaper articles, e-mails, and instant messages. Each text or set of texts is followed by several questions. Select the best answer for each question and mark the letter (A), (B), (C), or (D) on your answer sheet.

Questions 25-26 refer to the following text message chain.

NEIL FRANCIS (5:12 P.M.)

Hey, Louise. I still have lots left to do here at the office. There's no way I'll be finishing on time.

LOUISE ELLIOT (5:14 P.M.)

Oh, that's too bad. Well, I can cancel our reservation at Magnolia Restaurant and make another one. How's Friday for you?

NEIL FRANCIS (5:15 P.M.)

It's hard to say. I'm afraid that some other urgent tasks might come up. Maybe we should just postpone it completely this week. How about next Monday?

LOUISE ELLIOT (5:17 P.M.)

That works for me. I know you have the annual sales report to work on this week.

NEIL FRANCIS (5:18 P.M.)

Yes, there's so much work to do. Thanks for understanding!

25. What is suggested about the writers?

(A) They will both stay late at the office.
(B) They are collaborating on a sales report.
(C) They will meet for lunch on Friday.
(D) They had made a plan for a meal.

26. At 5:15 P.M., what does Mr. Francis most likely mean when he writes, "It's hard to say"?

(A) He has forgotten a restaurant name.
(B) He has never eaten at Magnolia Restaurant.
(C) He requires Ms. Elliot's assistance.
(D) He is unsure of his schedule.

To:	Leroy Howlett <lhowlett@promail.com>
From:	Ella Moffat <emoffat@griswold.com>
Subject:	Kingfisher Bed Frame
Date:	November 8

Dear Mr. Howlett,

I am responding to the e-mail you sent to our customer service team on November 6. I understand that you came into our store last month and purchased the Kingfisher Solid Oak Bed Frame for your new apartment, and you were told that the item would be delivered within 7 working days. I'm very sorry that you have not yet received the item. I have checked our records and I can confirm that your payment went through our system successfully. However, a mistake in our warehouse department resulted in your order being erased from our system.

Once again, I am truly sorry for the inconvenience this has caused you. You originally paid a total of $325.99, including a fee for standard shipping. As our way of apologizing, I will refund the original shipping fee to your credit card and mark your bed frame for expedited shipping at no extra charge. You will receive it in 2 or 3 days.

Kindest regards,

Ella Moffat
Customer Service Manager
Griswold Home Furnishings

27. Why did Mr. Howlett most likely contact Griswold Home Furnishings?

(A) To apologize for a delivery delay
(B) To ask about a store's new inventory
(C) To inquire about a recent order
(D) To complain about a faulty product

28. What is NOT indicated about Mr. Howlett?

(A) He purchased an item by credit card.
(B) He recently moved into a new home.
(C) He is a regular customer at the store.
(D) He visited the store in October.

29. What does Ms. Moffat say she will do?

(A) Upgrade a shipping service
(B) Provide a full product refund
(C) Send replacement parts
(D) Have an item repaired

Daisy Chain Boutique
3491 Morrow Road
Boulder, CO 80302

Since opening last year, Daisy Chain has become Boulder's premier fashion boutique, and we are happy to announce to our customers that we are slashing our prices this month! We need more space for our incoming winter stock, so all of our remaining summer items will be on sale until September 30th. Everything must go!

All summer dresses will be marked down by 25 percent!
Selected pants and jeans will be discounted by up to 35 percent!
Our colorful T-shirts will all be on sale at 50 percent off!
Blouses and shorts will all be available at between 20 and 30 percent off!

Store members may use their membership cards to obtain an additional 10 percent discount on sale items. Also, if you spend $200 or more in our store, we will include a bracelet of your choice at no extra cost. For details about our product lines and business hours, visit www.daisyfashion.com.

---

30. Why is Daisy Chain Boutique having a sale?

(A) It is celebrating its grand opening.
(B) It is having trouble attracting customers.
(C) It is going out of business.
(D) It is making room for new products.

31. What type of product is available at a half price?

(A) Dresses
(B) T-shirts
(C) Pants
(D) Blouses

32. How can customers receive a free gift?

(A) By purchasing a specific product
(B) By signing up for a store membership
(C) By making a purchase on the Web site
(D) By spending a certain amount of money

To: Medical Research Division
From: Sandra Kernigan, General Manager
Date: July 12

DKL Associates has decided to participate again in the yearly medical convention in London from July 27 to 30. Currently, we are looking for volunteers to work at DKL's booth.

From time to time, our volunteers receive highly technical medical questions. For this reason, we need staff in medical research who can work in five-hour blocks. Staff members who took part in our most recent study on medicine for back pain are especially needed. This convention provides a chance to expand your knowledge about the various medical fields that DKL specializes in. Anyone interested is asked to contact Mr. Peter Clark before July 19.

We are aware that some of you may not be familiar with techniques on promoting DKL's services, so this will be addressed at a mandatory workshop being held next week for volunteers. Specific services to be showcased at the convention include:

• Medical file management
• Developing electronic prescription software
• Medical referral Web site operations

We will also emphasize our plan to publish fewer medical digests and textbooks. By limiting printed publications, DKL can focus on promoting itself as a global leader in online medical publications. DKL insists that everyone visiting our booth be made fully aware of this.

33. For whom is the memo intended?
    (A) All newly-hired employees
    (B) Executives of an association
    (C) Staff in a specific division
    (D) Guest speakers at a convention

34. What is required of the individuals who participate in the convention?
    (A) They must have worked at prior conventions.
    (B) They must be trained as sales professionals.
    (C) They must contribute writings.
    (D) They must attend a special session.

35. What will convention volunteers NOT be asked to do?
    (A) Lead seminars on medicine
    (B) Work five hours at a time
    (C) Answer challenging questions
    (D) Discuss software for prescriptions

36. What is indicated as a company goal?
    (A) Producing online publications
    (B) Hiring medical experts
    (C) Opening an office abroad
    (D) Filming a TV documentary

The Cortana Hotel
Calle 98 Via 104, Pavas, San Jose, Costa Rica

Mr. Joe Salvetti
1078 Palm Boulevard
Miami, FL 33125

Dear Mr. Salvetti,

I was very sorry to read your letter regarding your recent stay at our hotel. The Cortana Hotel prides itself on its reputation for providing impeccable service to its guests. Therefore, I felt much regret when I learned that you had encountered several issues while staying here. I am glad you brought these problems to my attention in your letter.

With regard to the room you received, I am truly sorry for the confusion. The reason you were given a Standard Room is that a computer error led to us overbooking some of our Deluxe Rooms. Of course, you were only charged at the standard rate. Also, I apologize that we were unable to store your luggage for you on your check-in day. I understand that you arrived in San Jose much earlier than the check-in time of 2 p.m., but our hotel does not have enough space to store luggage for guests. — [1] —.

Lastly, I cannot apologize enough for the unfortunate delay with our airport shuttle bus service. — [2] —. We were all terribly sorry to hear that you were forced to take a later flight to Miami and pay a charge for changing your ticket. — [3] —.

In an attempt to make things up to you, we invite you to stay with us again. — [4] —. Management has approved that you are entitled to a complimentary 6-night/7-day stay, which you can take advantage of at any time of year. During this stay, you will be allowed to eat at our restaurant free of charge. Please give us another chance to show you how important our guests are to us.

Kindest regards,

Rosalita Perez
Guest Relations Manager
The Cortana Hotel

37. Why did Ms. Perez write the letter?

   (A) To explain why a hotel's rates have increased
   (B) To inform Mr. Salvetti that no rooms are available
   (C) To describe a hotel's new check-in policy
   (D) To respond to a former guest's complaints

38. What can be inferred about Mr. Salvetti?

   (A) He was overcharged for his room.
   (B) He lost his luggage during his trip.
   (C) He missed his scheduled flight.
   (D) He received a room upgrade.

39. What does Ms. Perez offer to Mr. Salvetti?

   (A) A gift certificate for a hotel restaurant
   (B) A discount on regular room rates
   (C) A free week-long stay at the hotel
   (D) A partial refund of his hotel expenses

40. In which of the positions marked [1], [2], [3], and [4] does the following sentence best belong?

   "Typically, these run on an hourly basis without any problems."

   (A) [1]
   (B) [2]
   (C) [3]
   (D) [4]

SMAS Film Festival Ends With Awards Show

Santa Monica, California (September 3) - The Santa Monica Arts Society (SMAS) held its annual film festival from August 29 to September 2, and the final night of the event was dominated by an awards ceremony to honor exceptional films shown during the festival. In addition to the many awards handed out to actors, event organizers also awarded the Kubrick Prize for film direction, the Deakins Prize for cinematography, and the Mamet Prize for screenwriting.

SMAS members were not the only ones responsible for making nominations at the festival this year. The organization assembled a panel of famous movie stars and well-respected directors to help choose which movies should be considered for the awards. The youngest of this year's award winners, Timothy J. Pelletier, 25, grew up here in Santa Monica and graduated from Roseangle Film School, although he is now based in West Hollywood. This recent award is one of several he has received since taking his first job in the movie business three years ago.

October 4

Timothy J. Pelletier
135 Ritz Apartments,
8896 Sunset Boulevard, West Hollywood, CA 90069

Dear Mr. Pelletier,

First of all, I would like to congratulate you on winning the Mamet Prize at the SMAS Film Festival last month. I greatly admired the work you did on the movie and I thoroughly think that you deserved to win the award. My movie production company has recently acquired the rights to the best-selling novel, *A Paler Shade of Grey*, and we are currently seeking skilled individuals to help us to adapt this successful book into a profitable motion picture. I believe that you would be a perfect fit for this project. We have already attracted two of the most popular actors working in the business today: Ellen Lee and Chris Ellison.

I'd like to arrange a meeting with you so that we can discuss this potential working relationship face to face in more detail. Please call me at 555-3777 at your earliest possible convenience.

Best regards,

Agatha Cruz
Chief Executive Officer
Cruz Evert Films Inc.

41. What is true about the SMAS Film Festival?

    (A) It lasted for seven days.
    (B) It focuses on international cinema.
    (C) It included an awards show on August 29.
    (D) It is held on a yearly basis.

42. Who was NOT involved in choosing nominees for the movie awards?

    (A) Movie producers
    (B) Actors
    (C) SMAS members
    (D) Directors

43. What is indicated about Mr. Pelletier?

    (A) He graduated from film school last year.
    (B) He has been recognized for his previous work.
    (C) He spent much of his childhood in West Hollywood.
    (D) He was unable to attend the recent SMAS Film Festival.

44. Why did Ms. Cruz send the letter to Mr. Pelletier?

    (A) To obtain the rights to a piece of literature
    (B) To recommend that he attend an audition
    (C) To invite him to work on an upcoming project
    (D) To inform him that his job application was successful

45. For what did Mr. Pelletier win an award?

    (A) Acting
    (B) Screenwriting
    (C) Film direction
    (D) Cinematography

Novalife Serviced Apartments

- True Comfort and Elegance in the Heart of Osaka –

Thank you for choosing to stay at the Novalife Serviced Apartments. Our building serves as a convenient base for people visiting the city for sightseeing, as well as those attending conferences at the nearby convention center. Our fitness center is open from 7 A.M. until 9 P.M. and is equipped with a full range of exercise machines and equipment, while our supermarket is open 24 hours a day. You can also take the elevator up to our rooftop area, which has been professionally landscaped and boasts a variety of flowers, bushes, and trees.

The Novalife Serviced Apartments building is situated within walking distance of numerous department stores, restaurants, and fashion boutiques, most of which are listed in the complimentary Novalife magazine that you will find in your apartment. If you require transportation information, a Novalife worker at the reception desk will be happy to assist you. You may use our reasonably-priced WiFi by entering your apartment number on our Web page at www.novalifeapartments.com/services.

---

www.novalifeapartments.com/services   — ☐ X

Guest Name:	Brian Finnegan
E-mail Address:	b_finnegan@homemail.net
Tel. Number:	555-8376

Preferred Payment Method:	Credit Card	¬▼
Credit Card Issuer:	VivaCard	¬▼
Card Number:	****-****-****-4180	

Please enter your apartment number below and click 'Continue' to complete the Activation Process. Thank you for using Novalife's services. We will do all we can to ensure that you have a pleasant and memorable stay.

CONTINUE

To:	Brian Finnegan <b_finnegan@homemail.net>
From:	Ray Tanaka <raytanaka@novalife.com>
Subject:	Please accept my apologies
Date:	October 8

Mr. Finnegan,

In response to your recent e-mail, please allow me to express my apologies on behalf of Novalife Serviced Apartments. Unfortunately, we have had to reduce our operating hours, and we are now accessible from 7 A.M. to 10 P.M. The reason for this is that necessary renovation work will be carried out during the night. Full round-the-clock accessibility will be restored by October 11th. Once again, I am sorry for the inconvenience, and I would appreciate your understanding regarding this matter.

Sincerely,

Ray Tanaka
Reception Desk Manager

46. In the information, the word "boasts" in paragraph 1, line 5, is closest in meaning to

(A) exceeds
(B) contains
(C) praises
(D) recommends

47. According to the information, how can guests find out about dining options in the area?

(A) By speaking with a reception desk worker
(B) By logging into the Novalife Web site
(C) By checking in the local newspaper
(D) By reading a free publication

48. What is suggested about the Novalife Serviced Apartments building?

(A) It includes a convention center.
(B) It offers an airport shuttle bus service.
(C) It is situated near a busy commercial district.
(D) It provides reserved parking to its residents.

49. What can be inferred about Mr. Finnegan?

(A) His credit card was declined.
(B) He received a room discount online.
(C) He ordered room service through a Web site.
(D) He paid to connect to the Internet.

50. What did Mr. Finnegan most likely complain about in his e-mail?

(A) A fitness center
(B) A rooftop area
(C) An apartment
(D) A grocery store

PART 1

Directions: For each question in this part, you will hear four statements about a picture in your test book. When you hear the statements, you must select the one statement that best describes what you see in the picture. Then find the number of the question on your answer sheet and mark your answer. The statements will not be printed in your test book and will be spoken only one time.

1.

2.

PART 2

Directions: You will hear a question or statement and three responses spoken in English. They will not be printed in your test book and will be spoken only one time. Select the best response to the question or statement and mark the letter (A), (B), or (C) on your answer sheet.

3. Mark your answer on your answer sheet.

4. Mark your answer on your answer sheet.

5. Mark your answer on your answer sheet.

6. Mark your answer on your answer sheet.

7. Mark your answer on your answer sheet.

8. Mark your answer on your answer sheet.

9. Mark your answer on your answer sheet.

10. Mark your answer on your answer sheet.

11. Mark your answer on your answer sheet.

12. Mark your answer on your answer sheet.

13. Mark your answer on your answer sheet.

14. Mark your answer on your answer sheet.

15. Mark your answer on your answer sheet.

16. Mark your answer on your answer sheet.

17. Mark your answer on your answer sheet.

18. Mark your answer on your answer sheet.

19. Mark your answer on your answer sheet.

20. Mark your answer on your answer sheet.

PART 3

Directions: You will hear some conversations between two or more people. You will be asked to answer three questions about what the speakers say in each conversation. Select the best response to each question and mark the letter (A), (B), (C) or (D) on your answer sheet. The conversations will not be printed in your test book and will be spoken only one time.

21. Where is this conversation most likely taking place?
    (A) At a cell phone outlet
    (B) At a publishing company
    (C) At a warehouse
    (D) At an office supply store

22. What will happen the following day?
    (A) A delivery will arrive.
    (B) A new worker will be hired.
    (C) A printer will be repaired.
    (D) A sale will begin.

23. What does the man say about the product?
    (A) It was being offered at a discount.
    (B) It has been discontinued.
    (C) It is high quality.
    (D) It is missing a price tag.

24. Where do the speakers agree to go?
    (A) To a parking lot
    (B) To a restaurant
    (C) To a subway station
    (D) To a client meeting

25. What does the woman imply when she says, "we just hired twelve new people"?
    (A) Some training will be required.
    (B) A budget has been reduced.
    (C) Some mistakes will likely occur.
    (D) A department has been successful.

26. What does the woman ask the man about?
    (A) Providing some feedback
    (B) Adding a payment method
    (C) Attending a workshop
    (D) Designing a Web page

27. What position is Ryan interviewing for?
    (A) Furniture salesman
    (B) Clothing designer
    (C) Interior decorator
    (D) Quality assurance manager

28. What does the woman tell Ryan to bring?
    (A) A writing sample
    (B) A diploma
    (C) Product samples
    (D) A letter of recommendation

29. What does Ryan ask about?
    (A) Flexible hours
    (B) Vacation time
    (C) Store locations
    (D) Commission options

30. What are the speakers mainly discussing?
    (A) A security device
    (B) A cell phone application
    (C) A training session
    (D) A computer program

31. What will employees receive by e-mail tomorrow?
    (A) An instruction guide
    (B) A user name
    (C) A serial number
    (D) A password

32. What does the woman say is an advantage of Buckler V2?
    (A) It rarely breaks down.
    (B) It updates automatically.
    (C) It comes with a guarantee.
    (D) It can be easily customized.

Gift Voucher

10% off all refrigerators
20% off all rice cookers
30% off all microwaves
50% off all kettles

Train	Destination	Departure Time
325	Oshawa	2:00 P.M.
346	Kingston	2:15 P.M.
257	Montreal	2:30 P.M.
465	Ottawa	3:00 P.M.

33. What does the woman say she did last week?

   (A) She renovated a property.
   (B) She launched a business.
   (C) She moved into a new home.
   (D) She purchased an appliance.

34. Look at the graphic. What discount will the woman receive?

   (A) 10%
   (B) 20%
   (C) 30%
   (D) 50%

35. How can the woman obtain a free gift?

   (A) By spending a certain amount
   (B) By purchasing a warranty
   (C) By completing a form
   (D) By showing a membership card

36. Why is a train delayed?

   (A) Some debris is blocking a track.
   (B) Bad weather is expected.
   (C) A ticketing error has occurred.
   (D) A technical problem needs to be fixed.

37. Look at the graphic. Which departure time will the man change?

   (A) 2:00 P.M.
   (B) 2:15 P.M.
   (C) 2:30 P.M.
   (D) 3:00 P.M.

38. What does the man ask the woman to do?

   (A) Go to a station platform
   (B) Make an announcement
   (C) Speak with a train driver
   (D) Issue new tickets to passengers

PART 4

Directions: You will hear some talks given by a single speaker. You will be asked to answer three questions about what the speakers say in each conversation. Select the best response to each question and mark the letter (A), (B), (C) or (D) on your answer sheet. The conversations will not be printed in your test book and will be spoken only one time.

39. Where is the speaker calling from?

    (A) A hardware store
    (B) A clothing manufacturer
    (C) A catering company
    (D) An online bookstore

40. What caused the problem?

    (A) A Web site wasn't updated.
    (B) A payment was insufficient.
    (C) A delivery was lost.
    (D) A sale had ended.

41. What is the listener advised to do?

    (A) Make an additional payment
    (B) Return some merchandise
    (C) Cancel an order
    (D) Choose a different item

42. Why does the speaker congratulate Rodger?

    (A) He was awarded a promotion.
    (B) He signed a new client.
    (C) He was hired by a large company.
    (D) He created a marketing plan.

43. According to the speaker, what does Johnson's Marketing hope to do?

    (A) Establish new branch offices
    (B) Purchase another company
    (C) Attract more foreign businesses
    (D) Hold a marketing conference

44. What does the speaker ask about?

    (A) The location of an upcoming workshop
    (B) The details of a recently signed contract
    (C) The most convenient time for a meeting
    (D) The best way to contact the listener

45. What is the main topic of the meeting?

    (A) A customer complaint
    (B) A product's development
    (C) A web site review
    (D) A photo shoot

46. What feature of the product does the speaker mention?

    (A) Easy portability
    (B) Additional accessories
    (C) Adjustable lighting
    (D) Enhanced zoom

47. What does the speaker imply when she says, "the battery life is under an hour"?

    (A) Customers should charge the battery at home.
    (B) The battery should last longer.
    (C) Extra batteries will be sold.
    (D) The battery uses advanced technology.

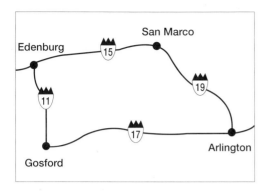

48. What is the report mainly about?

   (A) A fundraising event
   (B) A city's founding celebration
   (C) A store's grand opening
   (D) An upcoming music festival

49. Look at the graphic. Which highway is being
    repaired?

   (A) Highway 11
   (B) Highway 15
   (C) Highway 17
   (D) Highway 19

50. Why are listeners advised to call the radio
    station?

   (A) To enter a contest
   (B) To get directions
   (C) To speak with a guest
   (D) To register for an event

READING TEST

In the Reading test, you will read a variety of texts and answer several different types of reading comprehension questions. The entire Reading test will last 75 minutes. There are three parts, and directions are given for each part. You are encouraged to answer as many questions as possible within the time allowed. You must mark your answers on the separate answer sheet. Do not write your answers in your test book.

PART 5

Directions: A word or phrase is missing in each of the sentences below. Four answer choices are given below each sentence. Select the best answer to complete the sentence. Then mark the letter (A), (B), (C), or (D) on your answer sheet.

1. Mr. Norris will consider implementing the proposed expansion strategy after evaluating ------- potential benefits.

   (A) they
   (B) it
   (C) them
   (D) its

2. The owners of Bitburg Manufacturing ------- to reduce operating costs by hiring a new factory supervisor.

   (A) intend
   (B) intending
   (C) intentional
   (D) intentionally

3. The ------- investigating the cause of the river pollution have identified three possible sources.

   (A) researchers
   (B) researching
   (C) researches
   (D) research

4. Employees who are promoted from ------- the department are exempt from the computer skills proficiency test.

   (A) after
   (B) into
   (C) above
   (D) within

5. The Falcon Run at Alpen Ski Resort is incredibly steep and dangerous, ------- it unsuitable for inexperienced skiers.

   (A) make
   (B) makes
   (C) making
   (D) made

6. Without this software, we cannot guarantee the security of our database, ------- can we guarantee that the information you supply will not be intercepted.

   (A) or
   (B) and
   (C) but
   (D) nor

7. All agricultural workers are required to watch videos on workplace ------- before operating any equipment.

(A) safe
(B) safely
(C) safer
(D) safety

8. In order to achieve the best taste possible, you must ------- monitor the temperature of the sauce.

(A) vigilantly
(B) vigilant
(C) vigilance
(D) vigil

9. Mr. Forbes visited several potential event venues to decide ------- is the most suitable for the banquet.

(A) either
(B) another
(C) anything
(D) which

10. The new casual clothing policy has ------- that employees are more productive when they are dressed more comfortably.

(A) prepared
(B) shown
(C) designated
(D) preferred

11. Sirius Electronics is planning to hire a marketing expert to ------- the company's international brand recognition.

(A) refer
(B) boost
(C) endorse
(D) assimilate

12. Mr. Arnott and Ms. Villa have been practicing their talks all morning ------- their presentation goes smoothly.

(A) so that
(B) provided that
(C) as well as
(D) because

13. The Village Hotel provides ------- bathroom products, coffee, and mineral water in all guest rooms.

(A) compliment
(B) complimented
(C) complimentary
(D) compliments

14. The financial consultant has recommended that we ------- the budget that is allocated for business trip expenses.

(A) lower
(B) lowered
(C) are lowering
(D) to lower

15. The fitness center will be closed to all members ------- the new exercise machines are being installed.

(A) before
(B) during
(C) while
(D) unless

16. ------- the afternoon rain showers, the charity fundraiser at Holden Park still raised over $10,000.

(A) On the other hand
(B) As a matter of fact
(C) Notwithstanding
(D) Eventually

PART 6

Directions: Read the texts that follow. A word, phrase, or sentence is missing in parts of each text. Four answer choices for each question are given below the text. Select the best answer to complete the text. Then mark the letter (A), (B), (C) or (D) on your answer sheet.

Questions 17-20 refer to the following notice.

For the attention of all Merryweather Inc. Staff:

Please note that we have changed our policy regarding customer refunds for delayed deliveries. Starting today, refunds will only be ------- for orders that are at least 7 days late. Previously, we
      17.
refunded customers whenever an order was 4 days late. This change was deemed ------- due
                                                                               18.
to problems with the courier service we work with, and also due to the upcoming busy Christmas shopping season.

Unfortunately, this may result in an increased number of customer -------. Please be understanding
                                                                  19.
when dealing with angry customers who demand a refund for deliveries that are a few days late. Apologize and explain why they are not eligible for a refund. -------. We appreciate your understanding
                                                        20.
and hard work.

17. (A) spent
    (B) played
    (C) issued
    (D) stocked

18. (A) necessarily
    (B) necessary
    (C) necessity
    (D) necessitate

19. (A) purchases
    (B) complaints
    (C) memberships
    (D) surveys

20. (A) You have all been trained on how to handle such situations.
    (B) The new policy will take effect early next month.
    (C) Your refund will be processed within five working days.
    (D) Customers can take advantage of the offers by visiting our Web site.

To: Terry Richardson <trichardson@mymail.net>

From: Beluga Hotel <customerservices@beluga.com>

Subject: Your Reservation

Date: July 2

Mr. Richardson,

Thank you for making a reservation at Beluga Hotel! We see you -------- a Family Room for your three-
                                                              21.
night stay. This room includes one king-sized bed and two single beds, with an option to add an extra

folding bed. --------. We are here to make your stay as pleasurable as possible, and we are always
            22.
happy to help.

When checking in, please show your booking reference number to our front desk staff. You will be

asked to pay a $100 security deposit to cover any accidental damage to the room. As per our policy,

we will need to make a photocopy of your passport --------.
                                                  23.

Please do not -------- to let us know if there is anything else we can do to make your stay more
             24.
comfortable.

Customer Service

Beluga Hotel

21. (A) chooses
    (B) will choose
    (C) chosen
    (D) have chosen

22. (A) We hope you had a comfortable stay.
    (B) You may book this room through our Web
        site.
    (C) The room includes the following features.
    (D) Please let us know if you require one.

23. (A) after all
    (B) recently
    (C) as well
    (D) still

24. (A) limit
    (B) hesitate
    (C) refrain
    (D) postpone

PART 7

Directions: In this part you will read a selection of texts, such as magazine and newspaper articles, e-mails, and instant messages. Each text or set of texts is followed by several questions. Select the best answer for each question and mark the letter (A), (B), (C), or (D) on your answer sheet.

Questions 25-26 refer to the following e-mail.

To: Emma Samson (esamson@bizzmag.ca)
From: Tony Mowbray (tmowbray@bizzmag.ca)
Subject: Farmers' Market Article
Date: March 30

Hi Emma,

I'm writing about the town's annual farmers' market, which will take place on April 4th and 5th. I know that it will run from 9 a.m. on Saturday to 7 p.m. on Sunday, and that it is expected to attract at least 10,000 people over the weekend. But, do you know where it is being held this year? I wrote down that it will take place on Carlson Street, but I heard a rumor that the organizers are moving it to a new site. I'd appreciate your help. The deadline for my article is in one hour.

Thanks,

Tony
Staff Writer
Bizz Magazine

25. Why did Mr. Mowbray send the e-mail to Ms. Samson?

(A) To provide some help
(B) To extend an invitation
(C) To request assistance
(D) To promote an event

26. What is suggested about the farmer's market?

(A) It is a monthly event.
(B) It is becoming less popular.
(C) It will be held at two locations.
(D) It will be featured in a magazine.

Wedding Tips for Men: Tip #3
By Kirk Hemsworth

Cost is the primary factor when choosing your wedding formalwear. Rented tuxedos cost between 15% and 35% of the price of a new one, and tuxedos generally cost between $350 and $550. For most people, renting will be the best option, so let's focus on that.

- Shop around until you find the right formalwear store for you. The store should update its stock regularly, take your measurements properly, and give you a professional tuxedo fitting.
- The store owner should listen to you. If he insists on showing you garments that do not interest you, politely say, "No, thank you," and find a different store.
- The store should be able to supply you with all the accessories you'll need: bow tie, cufflinks, suspenders, and shoes. Make sure that you ask for these to be included in the rental.
- Finally, have all your groomsmen rent their tuxedos from the same shop as you, so you'll all match perfectly. When I did this last year, the store even provided a discount. Arrange fittings and reserve their tuxedos at least one month before your wedding.

27. For what situation is the information most likely intended?

(A) Repairing clothing
(B) Choosing an event venue
(C) Hiring a vehicle
(D) Renting a suit

28. What is NOT a recommendation given by Mr. Hemsworth?

(A) Check out several locations
(B) Request various accessories
(C) Take your own measurements
(D) Make a reservation in advance

29. What can be inferred about Mr. Hemsworth?

(A) He will attend a friend's wedding.
(B) He owns a formalwear store.
(C) He got married last year.
(D) He owns a tuxedo.

Questions 30-32 refer to the following article.

Northridge (April 24) – The Northridge Department of Transportation recently approved a proposal to widen a frequently congested major road by Interstate 63. As such, construction work on Dorris Road is scheduled to start early next month and finish by the beginning of the summer.

Many citizens and people who have seen first-hand the horrors of the Dorris Road traffic are certainly pleased that the department has finally approved the proposal after months of citizens petitioning for the roadwork.

"It's good to see that our hard work finally paid off," said Mr. James Lee, a post office worker. "We've really been suffering because of all the traffic. I mean, it's not horrible all the time, but when it is, a normally 10-minute drive takes over an hour." Francis Begon, a city bus driver, had this to say: "Everyone who owns a car knows that you shouldn't take that road, but what can we do, all other roads into the city are just as bad. And the city bus station is located on Dorris, so I can't even avoid it. I just hope the construction makes the traffic better."

Although construction work may cause even more traffic in the area, Mayor Freeman assures drivers that the work will mainly be done late at night, when there is much less traffic. He also advises drivers to take other roads to alleviate the traffic congestion on Dorris Road.

---

30. What is the purpose of the article?

(A) To take a poll on residents' opinions on a road
(B) To describe a plan to make improvements to a road
(C) To tell drivers to drive slowly on an accident-prone road
(D) To explain the reason for road traffic

31. According to the article, what is located on Dorris Road?

(A) A construction company
(B) A transportation office
(C) A bus station
(D) A post office

32. What does Mayor Freeman advise people to do?

(A) Use public transportation
(B) Take different routes
(C) Drive more slowly
(D) Stay home when possible

Questions 33-36 refer to the following online chat discussion.

[Jensen, David]: (2:15 P.M.)
Hi, Lee. I met with our shareholders this morning, and they responded negatively to the boxes and wrappers we designed for our products.

[Fielding, Lee]: (2:17 P.M.)
How come? The marketing team worked very hard on those designs.

[Jensen, David]: (2:18 P.M.)
They feel that the packaging won't help our products to stand out on the supermarket shelves.

[Fielding, Lee]: (2:19 P.M.)
Just a moment, I'll add Penelope from Marketing…

(Penelope Reyes invited to chat window)

[Jensen, David]: (2:21 P.M.)
Hi, Penelope. Our shareholders disliked the box and wrapper designs and have requested some modifications.

[Reyes, Penelope]: (2:23 P.M.)
My team worked overtime to produce those designs. To be honest, I don't think anything should be changed.

[Fielding, Lee]: (2:25 P.M.)
I hear you. So, the three of us should get together and try to reach a compromise.

[Reyes, Penelope]: (2:26 P.M.)
Fine with me. Let's try to figure this out.

[Jensen, David]: (2:27 P.M.)
Great idea. I'll book one of the conference rooms for this afternoon.

33. What is the discussion mainly about?
    (A) The launch of some new products
    (B) A change to online advertising
    (C) A decline in customer satisfaction
    (D) The design of some packaging

34. What problem did the shareholders mention?
    (A) Customers would prefer simpler designs.
    (B) Materials might cost too much.
    (C) Products might not be noticeable.
    (D) Companies are becoming more competitive.

35. At 2:25 P.M., what does Mr. Fielding imply when he writes, "I hear you"?
    (A) He would like to speak to Ms. Reyes in person.
    (B) He was informed about some plans earlier.
    (C) He does not fully understand a proposal.
    (D) He understands that Ms. Reyes is disappointed.

36. What will the writers do later today?
    (A) Meet with shareholders
    (B) Present some new products
    (C) Attempt to solve a problem
    (D) Make changes to a work schedule

To: Max Cowell <maxcowell@cjinc.com>

From: Olivia Crowe <ocrowe@cjinc.com>

Subject: Mark Kendall and Tina Winslow

Date: December 20

Mr. Cowell,

You mentioned at last week's management meeting that each department manager should consider which staff members are most deserving of an award this year. — [1] —.

My first choice is Mark Kendall. — [2] —. He was hired by our company right after his graduation 3 years ago, and he has become a valued member of our marketing team. This year, he was responsible for an incredibly successful market research study we carried out throughout the country. — [3] —. He has spoken openly of his desire to eventually become a team leader here at our firm. I will also nominate Tina Winslow. She has been with us for almost 5 years now and she leads a team of six online marketers. — [4] —. Her promotional campaigns and advertising strategies have been directly responsible for our significant increase in overall earnings over the past 12 months.

I'm sure that both employees will be overjoyed when you call them up to the stage and give them their awards at the year-end banquet on December 29th.

Regards,

Olivia

37. What does Ms. Crowe imply about Mr. Kendall?

    (A) He has worked for several companies.
    (B) He has a qualification in online marketing.
    (C) He has won awards for his work.
    (D) He has a strong ambition to succeed.

38. What is NOT indicated about Ms. Winslow?

    (A) She has helped the company become more profitable.
    (B) She has received a promotion during the past year.
    (C) She is responsible for managing other employees.
    (D) She has worked at the firm for longer than Mr. Kendall has.

39. Who will most likely present an award on December 29?

    (A) Olivia Crowe
    (B) Mark Kendall
    (C) Tina Winslow
    (D) Max Cowell

40. In which of the positions marked [1], [2], [3], and [4] does the following sentence best belong?

    "After giving it some thought, I have finalized my choices."

    (A) [1]
    (B) [2]
    (C) [3]
    (D) [4]

Rocky Trails Company
7677 Seymour Avenue, Billings, MN 59107

We stock all kinds of goods, from portable gas stoves and frying pans, to tents and sleeping bags, to the finest waterproof jackets, pants, and hiking boots. We are also proud to announce the launch of four new lines of hiking backpacks:

· **Peregrine:** Aeropro ventilation system. HDPE plastic frame
  Sizes: 25L, 28L, 30L, 32L, 36L / **Colors:** Black/Grey, Blue/Grey, Blue/Green

· **Eagle:** Aeromax ventilation system. Aluminum frame
  Sizes: 32L, 34L, 36L, 38L, 40L / **Colors:** Blue/Grey, Red/Grey, Blue/Red

· **Buzzard:** Aeropro ventilation system. Aluminum frame
  Sizes: 36L, 40L, 45L, 50L, 55L / **Colors:** Blue/Green, Blue/Grey, Black/Grey

· **Falcon:** Aeromax ventilation system. Aluminum frame
  Sizes: 40L, 45L, 50L, 55L, 65L, 70L / **Colors:** Black/Grey, Red/Grey, Green/Black

All backpacks in the above lines include a chest strap, side pockets, a rain cover, and a padded waist strap. To view pictures of our backpacks, visit www.rockytrailsmontana.com.

Rocky Trails Company
Customer Service Department
7677 Seymour Avenue, Billings, MN 59107

Dear sir/madam,

I recently purchased a hiking backpack from your new product line, and I thought you might be interested in hearing my opinion about it. I have used the bag during two hikes in poor weather conditions and it performed superbly. The 36L size provided ample room for my extra gear and my food. The lightweight aluminum frame fit my back extremely well and provided me with maximum comfort at all times. Also, the material seems very strong, and I particularly like the stylish black and grey colors. In short, I'm very pleased with this backpack.

Best wishes,

Regina Porter

41. What type of merchandise is NOT mentioned
    in the advertisement?

    (A) Camping furniture
    (B) Cooking equipment
    (C) Sleeping bags
    (D) Waterproof clothing

42. What is indicated about the Falcon backpacks?

    (A) They do not include a rain cover.
    (B) They are available in six different colors.
    (C) They utilize an Aeropro ventilation system.
    (D) They come in larger sizes than other
        backpacks.

43. What is the main purpose of the letter?

    (A) To complain about a recent purchase
    (B) To request information about an item
    (C) To suggest ways to improve a backpack
    (D) To praise the quality of a product

44. In the letter, the word "ample" in paragraph 1,
    line 3, is closest in meaning to

    (A) sufficient
    (B) excessive
    (C) variable
    (D) numerous

45. Which type of backpack did Ms. Porter most
    likely purchase?

    (A) Peregrine
    (B) Eagle
    (C) Buzzard
    (D) Falcon

GoJuice Corporation

GoJuice is rapidly becoming one of the most popular sports/energy beverages in the United Kingdom. We currently sell hundreds of thousands of units to supermarkets, convenience stores, and fitness centers every month. By purchasing bulk orders directly from GoJuice Corporation, you can receive a lower price per unit, increasing your profit margins when you sell GoJuice to your customers.

GoJuice beverages are even more beneficial than water when they are drank during or after exercise. Not only does GoJuice prevent dehydration, but it also helps the body to absorb fluids and increases the body's energy levels. Our best-selling flavors are orange and strawberry. Current flavors are kiwi and lemon, with our new acai flavor due for release on April 1.

GoJuice Corporation
ORDER SUMMARY

Deliver to:
Gary Sherman
RPM Gym & Sports Center
212 Bayville Avenue

Bill to:
Ms. Sharon Goldberg
(Accounts Manager)
RPM Gym & Sports Center

Order Number	Order Date	Sales Rep	Shipping Date	Delivery Date
#0927	04/23	Clifford Curtis	04/25	04/29

Product ID	Description	Quantity	Unit Price	Total Price
#1057	Strawberry GoJuice	250	$0.49	$122.50
#1059	Acai GoJuice Plus	100	$0.59	$59.00
#1095	Kiwi GoJuice Plus	200	$0.69	$138.00
#1097	Orange GoJuice	600	$0.49	$294.00
			Total	$648.50

All shipments are subject to an additional flat $35 delivery charge. Customers holding GoJuice memberships are eligible to receive free shipping.

To: Gary Sherman <gsherman@rpm.com>

From: Sharon Goldberg <sgoldberg@rpm.com>

Subject: Beverage Order

Date: April 29

Hi Gary,

I'm just e-mailing you to let you know that I ordered more GoJuice drinks for the gym and they should be arriving at the main entrance on April 29. It's a shame that we have to pay a delivery fee every time we order. Perhaps I should look into ways of getting that removed for future orders. I'd like you or one of the other instructors to receive the order and bring the shipping invoice to the finance office.

Thank you,

Sharon Goldberg
RPM Gym & Sports Center

---

46. Who is the information most likely intended for?

(A) Members of a fitness center
(B) Customers at a supermarket
(C) Staff at GoJuice Corporation
(D) Businesses that sell beverages

47. What is indicated about GoJuice Corporation in the information?

(A) It distributes its products worldwide.
(B) Its products should be consumed before exercise.
(C) It offers a complimentary gift to new customers.
(D) It provides discounts on large orders.

48. Which product was released in April?

(A) Product #1097
(B) Product #1057
(C) Product #1095
(D) Product #1059

49. What can be inferred about Ms. Goldberg?

(A) She is a fitness instructor at a sports center.
(B) She spoke to Clifford Curtis on April 25th.
(C) She does not have a GoJuice membership.
(D) She places beverage orders on a monthly basis.

50. In the e-mail, the word "ways" in paragraph 1, line 3, is closest in meaning to

(A) offers
(B) approaches
(C) streets
(D) entrances

PART 1

Directions: For each question in this part, you will hear four statements about a picture in your test book. When you hear the statements, you must select the one statement that best describes what you see in the picture. Then find the number of the question on your answer sheet and mark your answer. The statements will not be printed in your test book and will be spoken only one time.

1.

2.

PART 2

Directions: You will hear a question or statement and three responses spoken in English. They will not be printed in your test book and will be spoken only one time. Select the best response to the question or statement and mark the letter (A), (B), or (C) on your answer sheet.

3. Mark your answer on your answer sheet.

4. Mark your answer on your answer sheet.

5. Mark your answer on your answer sheet.

6. Mark your answer on your answer sheet.

7. Mark your answer on your answer sheet.

8. Mark your answer on your answer sheet.

9. Mark your answer on your answer sheet.

10. Mark your answer on your answer sheet.

11. Mark your answer on your answer sheet.

12. Mark your answer on your answer sheet.

13. Mark your answer on your answer sheet.

14. Mark your answer on your answer sheet.

15. Mark your answer on your answer sheet.

16. Mark your answer on your answer sheet.

17. Mark your answer on your answer sheet.

18. Mark your answer on your answer sheet.

19. Mark your answer on your answer sheet.

20. Mark your answer on your answer sheet.

PART 3

Directions: You will hear some conversations between two or more people. You will be asked to answer three questions about what the speakers say in each conversation. Select the best response to each question and mark the letter (A), (B), (C) or (D) on your answer sheet. The conversations will not be printed in your test book and will be spoken only one time.

21. What are the speakers mainly discussing?

    (A) A business appointment
    (B) A company policy
    (C) A job interview
    (D) A training course

22. What is the woman's problem?

    (A) She has to conduct an interview.
    (B) She has a lunch date in 10 minutes.
    (C) She will be late for the meeting.
    (D) She has a scheduling conflict.

23. What does the man offer to do?

    (A) Meet with a potential client
    (B) Lead an important meeting
    (C) Write down the details of a meeting
    (D) Talk to management

24. What type of event are the speakers planning to attend?

    (A) A concert
    (B) A movie premiere
    (C) A play
    (D) A sports game

25. Why is the man concerned?

    (A) He does not know how to find the venue.
    (B) He read some negative reviews online.
    (C) He has a conflict in his schedule.
    (D) He thinks the event might be sold out.

26. What is mentioned about Miranda's cousin?

    (A) He will give a performance.
    (B) He will accompany the speakers.
    (C) He works in a ticket office.
    (D) He is an event organizer.

27. Why is the woman calling the man?

    (A) To request technical help
    (B) To discuss a project
    (C) To find a lost item
    (D) To plan a meal

28. What does the woman mean when she says, "A candidate is arriving shortly for an interview"?

    (A) She is unprepared for a meeting.
    (B) She cannot be disturbed right now.
    (C) She is unsure of a decision.
    (D) She wants the man to hurry.

29. What does the woman say about the interview?

    (A) It will be at another location.
    (B) It will be held over the Internet.
    (C) It will start after working hours.
    (D) It will not last long.

30. Where most likely does the woman work?

    (A) At a real estate agency
    (B) At a financial institution
    (C) At an electricity company
    (D) At an appliance store

31. What does the man decide to do?

    (A) Extend a subscription
    (B) Reschedule a meeting
    (C) Make a payment by credit card
    (D) Visit a business location

32. What will be sent to the man?

    (A) A monthly account statement
    (B) A membership card
    (C) An information pamphlet
    (D) A payment receipt

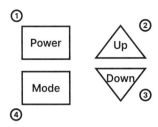

33. What are the speakers discussing?

(A) A computer lab
(B) A career fair
(C) An Internet provider
(D) A building renovation

34. What does the woman say she was worried about?

(A) Loud distractions
(B) Low registration
(C) A tight deadline
(D) High expenses

35. Look at the graphic. Which button will the man press?

(A) Button 1
(B) Button 2
(C) Button 3
(D) Button 4

Guest Invoice	
Breakfast - Rooftop Buffet	$15
Room Service - Dinner Menu	$22
Lunch - Poolside Restaurant	$18
Room Mini Bar/Snacks	$11
Total:	$66

36. Who most likely is the man?

(A) A hotel guest
(B) A kitchen employee
(C) A receptionist
(D) A travel agent

37. Look at the graphic. Which amount on the invoice will be removed?

(A) $15
(B) $22
(C) $18
(D) $11

38. What will the man do at 10:30?

(A) Take a flight
(B) Have a meal
(C) Meet a friend
(D) Join a tour

PART 4

Directions: You will hear some talks given by a single speaker. You will be asked to answer three questions about what the speakers say in each conversation. Select the best response to each question and mark the letter (A), (B), (C) or (D) on your answer sheet. The conversations will not be printed in your test book and will be spoken only one time.

39. Where is the announcement being made?

(A) At a train station
(B) At an airport
(C) At a department store
(D) At a bus station

40. What does the speaker ask listeners to do?

(A) Purchase another ticket
(B) Submit complaints online
(C) Retrieve their luggage
(D) Wait in a designated area

41. According to the speaker, what will be distributed?

(A) Free meals
(B) Hotel vouchers
(C) Pre-paid phone cards
(D) Information booklets

42. What is the purpose of the message?

(A) To review a meeting
(B) To change a schedule
(C) To correct an error
(D) To interview an applicant

43. What does the speaker imply when she says, "the publishing date is next month"?

(A) All of the work is finished.
(B) A decision must be made soon.
(C) A date has been pushed back.
(D) Another project is scheduled to start.

44. What most likely will the speaker do next?

(A) Check a previous project
(B) Make a phone call
(C) Meet with a client
(D) Update a web site

45. Who mostly likely are the listeners?

(A) Mechanical engineers
(B) Delivery drivers
(C) Warehouse workers
(D) Train operators

46. What is the topic of the meeting?

(A) Addressing employee complaints
(B) Improving customer service
(C) Meeting shipment deadlines
(D) Introducing a new machine

47. What will the listeners do next?

(A) Watch a video
(B) Test a product
(C) Complete a survey
(D) Memorize a script

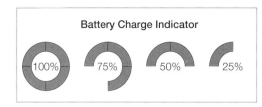

Battery Charge Indicator

100%   75%   50%   25%

48. What is the purpose of the call?

(A) To make a complaint
(B) To offer assistance
(C) To cancel a meeting
(D) To express gratitude

49. What will the speaker do this afternoon?

(A) Instruct new staff
(B) Attend an interview
(C) Visit a doctor
(D) Plan a vacation

50. Look at the graphic. What battery charge does the speaker's cell phone currently have?

(A) 25 percent
(B) 50 percent
(C) 75 percent
(D) 100 percent

READING TEST

In the Reading test, you will read a variety of texts and answer several different types of reading comprehension questions. The entire Reading test will last 75 minutes. There are three parts, and directions are given for each part. You are encouraged to answer as many questions as possible within the time allowed. You must mark your answers on the separate answer sheet. Do not write your answers in your test book.

PART 5

Directions: A word or phrase is missing in each of the sentences below. Four answer choices are given below each sentence. Select the best answer to complete the sentence. Then mark the letter (A), (B), (C), or (D) on your answer sheet.

1. Due to a mechanical fault, there will be a 20-minute ------- to the departure of the 2:35 train to Manchester.

   (A) delays
   (B) delay
   (C) to delay
   (D) delayed

2. Sales of Melon King's refreshing fruit smoothies ------- increase during the humid summer months.

   (A) cleanly
   (B) spaciously
   (C) approximately
   (D) frequently

3. Ms. Hendricks will be traveling overseas ------- month, so Mr. Lipman will temporarily supervise her employees.

   (A) whole
   (B) near
   (C) all
   (D) last

4. ------- Mr. Brennan was hired last summer, he has already received three promotions at Skylark Software.

   (A) Before
   (B) Until
   (C) Since
   (D) Whether

5. All of our electrical appliances come ------- against accidental damage for a period of 18 months.

   (A) guarantees
   (B) guaranteed
   (C) guaranteeing
   (D) guarantee

6. Factory workers must ------- clean all assembly line machinery at the end of each daily shift.

   (A) possibly
   (B) hopefully
   (C) intentionally
   (D) thoroughly

7. Due to the delay, passengers with connecting flights will disembark before ------- who are arriving at their final destination.

(A) anyone
(B) whichever
(C) them
(D) those

8. New team members often find themselves ------- on their coworkers for their first few weeks in the factory.

(A) dependable
(B) depend
(C) dependent
(D) dependence

9. Visiting shareholders are given the chance to tour the Randall Motors factory to see ------- our vehicles are manufactured.

(A) during
(B) about
(C) how
(D) whom

10. Mr. Jeon has a few concerns ------- revenue projections for the upcoming year.

(A) onto
(B) between
(C) regarding
(D) next

11. ------- the building blueprints have been finalized, construction will begin on the new multi-story car park.

(A) Soon
(B) Then
(C) Later
(D) Once

12. During the street festival, the parking lot on Ford Street will be open from 8 A.M. to 11 P.M. ------- its usual operating hours.

(A) instead of
(B) from
(C) in case
(D) between

13. The staff members were very excited ------- the CEO announced that a new pay raise would take effect next month.

(A) what
(B) where
(C) when
(D) which

14. The Wilson Community Library offers a service ------- members to renew books through the Web site.

(A) allow
(B) allowance
(C) allowing
(D) allows

15. 'No Littering' signs have been placed ------- Pittsburgh as part of a new environmental initiative.

(A) against
(B) except
(C) throughout
(D) upon

16. The Longhorn Community Center successfully raised a large amount of money, most of ------- was allocated for the improvement of local parks.

(A) which
(B) whose
(C) whom
(D) them

PART 6

Directions: Read the texts that follow. A word, phrase, or sentence is missing in parts of each text. Four answer choices for each question are given below the text. Select the best answer to complete the text. Then mark the letter (A), (B), (C) or (D) on your answer sheet.

Questions 17-20 refer to the following advertisement.

Get Paid For Your Opinion!

Resolute Marketing is currently seeking enthusiastic individuals to ------- our market research team in
 17.
Los Angeles. As a member of the team, you will be asked to visit a wide variety of businesses to try out

their products and services. We then ask you to submit ------- of your experiences as a consumer. You
 18.
will need to rate each business based on factors such as product quality, customer service standard,

and overall value for money.

We ------- all costs involved during your market research duties, and you will also be paid $25 for each
 19.
business you visit. You must have a valid driving license and a bank account to apply for this position.

-------. If you are interested in becoming a market researcher at Resolute Marketing, please call our HR
 20.
team at (013)-555-3498 today!

17. (A) register
    (B) respond
    (C) visit
    (D) join

18. (A) evaluates
    (B) evaluated
    (C) evaluations
    (D) evaluate

19. (A) cover
    (B) affirm
    (C) limit
    (D) refer

20. (A) Many local businesses are currently hiring
        new employees.
    (B) Bank transfers will be made on the last
        Friday of each month.
    (C) Please inform us if you are unable to submit
        the report on time.
    (D) We are delighted to offer you a role in our
        market research team.

Questions 21-24 refer to the following e-mail.

To: Poppy Reed <preed@argolisinc.com>

From: Colin Chapman <cchapman@argolisinc.com>

Subject: Upcoming convention

Date: September 8

Hi Poppy,

I'm pleased to inform you that I have asked Mr. Horowitz ------- you join me at the technology
                21.

convention on September 16. We originally thought you would need to stay in the office to lead the

staff orientation, but we came up with an alternative arrangement. -------. So, I'm very excited that you
                22.

can help me represent Argolis Inc. at the convention.

We need to register for the convention ------- through the Web site. Please make sure that you do that
           23.

before the end of today. If you need any assistance with it, please let me know. I'm sure you will enjoy

the ------- and find it to be a beneficial experience.
   24.

Regards,

Colin

---

21. (A) to let
    (B) let
    (C) lets
    (D) was let

22. (A) Our HR manager will handle that by herself.
    (B) Please complete one section a week.
    (C) I would probably call the client.
    (D) You can always adjust the volume.

23. (A) then
    (B) even if
    (C) after all
    (D) in advance

24. (A) training
    (B) event
    (C) promotion
    (D) tour

PART 7

Directions: In this part you will read a selection of texts, such as magazine and newspaper articles, e-mails, and instant messages. Each text or set of texts is followed by several questions. Select the best answer for each question and mark the letter (A), (B), (C), or (D) on your answer sheet.

Questions 25-26 refer to the following text message chain.

Patrick Reed [9:11 A.M.]
Hey, Martha... I'm on my way to DX Electronics Convention in Portland, but I left my company ID badge on my desk. Would you mind sending me a photo of it? I'll need to show it at the venue.

Martha Shay [9:14 A.M.]
✓ Image File Received. Open or Save As

Martha Shay [9:15 A.M.]
There you are. Oh, by the way, I took a call from Annie in Accounting. She said she had better get your receipts on time this time.

Patrick Reed [9:17 A.M.]
I won't let her down! Anyway, I want to be reimbursed for my expenses straight away.

Martha Shay [9:18 A.M.]
Okay. Enjoy the convention!

25. Who most likely is Martha?

(A) A convention organizer
(B) A photographer
(C) An accounting manager
(D) A colleague of Patrick's

26. At 9:17 A.M., what does Patrick imply when he writes, "I won't let her down"?

(A) He plans to keep his expenses low.
(B) He will ask Annie for advice.
(C) He will meet a submission deadline.
(D) He will meet Annie at a convention.

Questions 27-29 refer to the following letter.

September 20

Mr. Vernon Anderson

Anderson & Fring Inc.

2996 Bismarck Drive

Minneapolis, MN 55423

Dear Mr. Anderson,

I am the director of personnel at Grazer Packed Meats Inc. and I am writing to you on behalf of our founder and CEO, Harold Plummer. Grazer Packed Meats Inc. is a locally-based meat packing company specializing in the distribution of meat products to clients throughout the United States and Europe.

In recent months, we have been involved in a legal dispute regarding the health and safety policies at our plant. Although this has not directly impacted our earnings, it has negatively affected our company's reputation.

Mr. Plummer suggested that we hire a professional agency to strengthen the public image of our business. I recall reading an article in *The Minneapolis Times* last year that described Anderson & Fring as the most effective public relations firm in the country, so you are the first company I have contacted about this. I would like to set up a meeting with you, or with one of your representatives. Please contact me at 555-6671 to discuss this.

Yours sincerely,

Craig Brewster

Director of Personnel,

Grazer Packed Meats Inc.

27. What is indicated about Grazer Packed Meats Inc.?

(A) It has experienced a decline in profits.
(B) It was founded by Mr. Brewster.
(C) It exports its products overseas.
(D) It operates several meat packing plants.

28. What does Mr. Brewster want Anderson & Fring Inc. to do?

(A) Conduct a health and safety inspection
(B) Improve his company's reputation
(C) Assist in the distribution of products
(D) Reduce his firm's annual expenditure

29. How did Mr. Brewster first hear about Anderson & Fring?

(A) His CEO recommended the company to him.
(B) He saw an advertisement on the Internet.
(C) He spoke with one of Mr. Anderson's employees.
(D) He read an article in a newspaper.

Questions 30-32 refer to the following notice.

Break Room Refrigerator

Several disputes have occurred recently regarding the proper use of the break room refrigerator. Many employees have contacted me with their concerns and asked me to clarify our refrigerator policies.

You should label any item you place in the refrigerator. Pens and post-it notes have been provided on top of the refrigerator so that you can label your items. Any perishable item intended to be shared among all employees should be labeled 'For Everyone.' Please also include your name and the date on which the item was initially placed in the refrigerator. Stick a note on the front of the fridge stating, 'Help yourself to <item name>.'

A refrigerator cleaning schedule has been attached to the side of the refrigerator. Any perishable food that is not eaten or removed from the refrigerator by 6 p.m. on Friday will be thrown away by the person cleaning the refrigerator. Perishable foods include: meat, poultry, fish, eggs, dairy products, fruits, and vegetables. Condiments, dressings, and sauces will be thrown away periodically, based on their 'use by' date.

30. Why most likely was the notice posted?
(A) To address problems with faulty appliances
(B) To request suggestions from employees
(C) To respond to complaints made by staff
(D) To inform staff about a break room renovation

31. What can be found on top of the refrigerator?
(A) A list of stored items
(B) Bags for storing food
(C) Labeling materials
(D) A cleaning schedule

32. What is probably NOT a type of food that will be thrown away every Friday?
(A) Ketchup
(B) Chicken
(C) Orange
(D) Egg salad

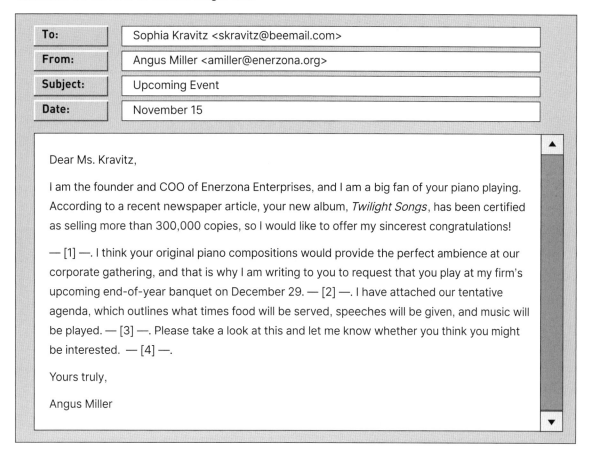

To: Sophia Kravitz <skravitz@beemail.com>

From: Angus Miller <amiller@enerzona.org>

Subject: Upcoming Event

Date: November 15

Dear Ms. Kravitz,

I am the founder and COO of Enerzona Enterprises, and I am a big fan of your piano playing. According to a recent newspaper article, your new album, *Twilight Songs*, has been certified as selling more than 300,000 copies, so I would like to offer my sincerest congratulations!

— [1] —. I think your original piano compositions would provide the perfect ambience at our corporate gathering, and that is why I am writing to you to request that you play at my firm's upcoming end-of-year banquet on December 29. — [2] —. I have attached our tentative agenda, which outlines what times food will be served, speeches will be given, and music will be played. — [3] —. Please take a look at this and let me know whether you think you might be interested. — [4] —.

Yours truly,

Angus Miller

---

33. What is the main purpose of the letter?

(A) To congratulate an outstanding employee
(B) To advertise an upcoming concert
(C) To request tickets for a performance
(D) To book the services of a musician

34. What is NOT stated about Sophia Kravitz?

(A) She composes her own music.
(B) She plays several instruments.
(C) She recently released an album.
(D) She has been featured in a publication.

35. What did Mr. Miller include with the e-mail?

(A) A business contract
(B) A payment receipt
(C) An event schedule
(D) A concert ticket

36. In which of the positions marked [1], [2], [3], and [4] does the following sentence best belong?

"I have a proposal that I feel you might be interested in."

(A) [1]
(B) [2]
(C) [3]
(D) [4]

Talent Search Canada
TV Show
Seeking Participants

The first ever season of Talent Search Canada will be shown on the Saturn Broadcasting Network on Wednesdays and Saturdays. The show will consist of 22 regular one-hour episodes and one special 3-hour episode for the season finale. While the final episode will be filmed in front of an expected audience of 8,000 fans in Toronto, the majority of episodes will take place at SBN's studios in Ottawa. The creators of the show hope to attract tens of thousands of hopeful participants from as far afield as Vancouver and Halifax. The judging panel will be comprised of the following successful figures from the world of entertainment:

• Erik Mourinho (Owner of Down Low Records, a Los Angeles-based record label)
• Carla Ramirez (Renowned dancer and choreographer of several hit Broadway shows)
• Jacob Northup (Award-winning television and movie star known for his comedic roles)

Those of you who are interested in taking part have a number of options. You can e-mail a video of you performing your particular talent to talentsearch@sbn.ca, sign up directly via the SBN Web site at www.sbncanada.ca, or show up at one of the many auditions scheduled to take place in cities all over the country.

37. What is suggested about Talent Search Canada?

    (A) It will be aired once a week.
    (B) It has received over eight thousand applications.
    (C) It will run for a total of twenty-two episodes.
    (D) It is a brand new television show.

38. In which city will Talent Search Canada primarily be filmed?

    (A) Toronto
    (B) Vancouver
    (C) Halifax
    (D) Ottawa

39. Who will be a member of the judging panel?

    (A) A singer
    (B) A movie director
    (C) An actor
    (D) A theater owner

40. What is NOT mentioned as a way for potential participants to apply?

    (A) Attending an audition
    (B) Registering online
    (C) Calling a hotline
    (D) Sending a video clip

Questions 41-45 refer to the following Web page information and e-mail.

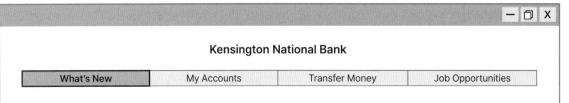

Kensington National Bank

| What's New | My Accounts | Transfer Money | Job Opportunities |

Announcing Individual Checking Elite!

Kensington National Bank now offers a new account, Individual Checking Elite. This account offers many rewards over our Basic Checking account including higher interest rates and more options for transferring money.

Until the end of May, we are inviting our account holders to switch their Basic Checking accounts into Individual Checking Elite accounts without any change fees. Furthermore, those who make the switch will benefit from a discounted fee of only $6 per month for the first year. After one year, the charge will increase to the standard Individual Checking Elite rate of $9.50 each month.

For more information or to sign up for this offer, talk to one of our account representatives at 888-555-1222.

To: <customers@kengsingtonnationalbank.com>
From: <vdole@campbellsdeli.com>
Subject: New checking account
Date: May 3

Yesterday, I opened an Individual Checking Elite account, and I thought that the money in my Basic Checking account would be transferred into the new account at the time of enrollment. However, when I access my online banking page, I see that my balance is $0 for the Individual Checking Elite account. Could you please explain to me why my money wasn't deposited into my new account?

I appreciate your help.

Victor Dole

41. What is the purpose of the web page information?

    (A) To announce a change to a banking charge
    (B) To explain online banking services
    (C) To advertise a new checking account
    (D) To announce a business partnership

42. What is stated about the fee?

    (A) It will be lower during the first year.
    (B) Customers can pay it early.
    (C) It is lower than charges at other banks.
    (D) Customers can choose their payment date.

43. What is Mr. Dole worried about?

    (A) Someone logged into his online account.
    (B) He was billed too much for a fee.
    (C) He cannot change his online password.
    (D) His funds were not deposited into his new account.

44. What is most likely true about Mr. Dole?

    (A) He did not pay an account change fee.
    (B) His fee has been raised.
    (C) He will close his account.
    (D) He is a new customer of Kensington National Bank.

45. In the e-mail, the word "balance" in paragraph 1, line 3 is closest in meaning to

    (A) equality
    (B) amount
    (C) average
    (D) stability

Questions 46-50 refer to the following e-mails and notice.

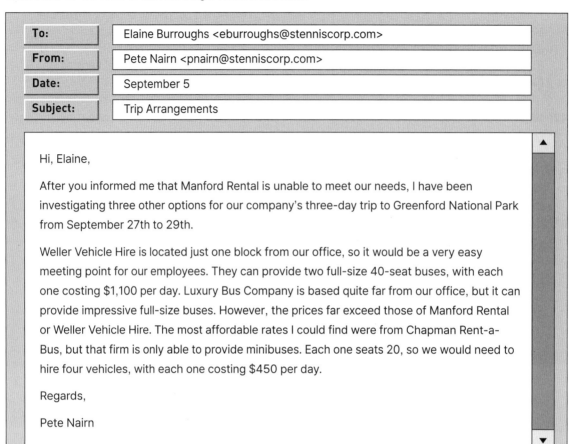

To:	Elaine Burroughs <eburroughs@stenniscorp.com>
From:	Pete Nairn <pnairn@stenniscorp.com>
Date:	September 5
Subject:	Trip Arrangements

Hi, Elaine,

After you informed me that Manford Rental is unable to meet our needs, I have been investigating three other options for our company's three-day trip to Greenford National Park from September 27th to 29th.

Weller Vehicle Hire is located just one block from our office, so it would be a very easy meeting point for our employees. They can provide two full-size 40-seat buses, with each one costing $1,100 per day. Luxury Bus Company is based quite far from our office, but it can provide impressive full-size buses. However, the prices far exceed those of Manford Rental or Weller Vehicle Hire. The most affordable rates I could find were from Chapman Rent-a-Bus, but that firm is only able to provide minibuses. Each one seats 20, so we would need to hire four vehicles, with each one costing $450 per day.

Regards,

Pete Nairn

To: Pete Nairn <pnairn@stenniscorp.com>
From: Elaine Burroughs <eburroughs@stenniscorp.com>
Date: September 6
Subject: Re: Trip Arrangements

Hi, Pete,

I really appreciate all the research you've carried out. We used Manford Rental for last year's trip, so it's unfortunate that they have no buses available this year. I think our best option would be to book the two full-size buses offered by the company located near our workplace. We anticipate that between 65 and 75 staff members will be coming on our company trip, so this option will fulfill our requirements. Also, I was less than satisfied with the service and vehicles provided by Chapman Rent-a-Bus a couple of years ago.

Elaine

Stennis Corporation Company Excursion

Staff, we are pleased to announce that a company trip has been planned for later this month. Buses will depart from our main parking lot at 8:00 A.M. on September 27th and reach Greenford National Park by approximately 11 A.M. We will return at around 7 P.M. on September 28th. A company-wide e-mail detailing the schedule and activities that have been planned for the trip will be sent to you by the end of this week. In the meantime, if you have any questions, please contact Elaine Burroughs in Personnel.

Thank you,

The Management

46. What is indicated about Chapman Rent-a-Bus?

   (A) It is located near Luxury Bus Company.
   (B) It specializes in providing 40-seat buses.
   (C) It offers relatively inexpensive prices.
   (D) It only has a total of four vehicles.

47. What is suggested about Ms. Burroughs?

   (A) She has rented vehicles from Luxury Bus Company before.
   (B) She has experience in dealing with Chapman Rent-a-Bus.
   (C) She believes that Mr. Nairn should hire four buses.
   (D) She used to be an employee at Manford Rental.

48. In the second e-mail, the word "book" in paragraph 1, line 3, is closest in meaning to

   (A) reserve
   (B) note
   (C) publish
   (D) inquire

49. What company does Ms. Burroughs recommend?

   (A) Manford Rental
   (B) Weller Vehicle Hire
   (C) Luxury Bus Company
   (D) Chapman Rent-a-Bus

50. What can be inferred about the company trip?

   (A) The destination was changed.
   (B) The month was changed.
   (C) The duration was changed.
   (D) The type of transportation was changed.

시원스쿨 **LAB**

정답 및 해설

1. (B)	**2.** (A)	**3.** (A)	**4.** (C)	**5.** (A)
6. (A)	**7.** (C)	**8.** (D)	**9.** (A)	**10.** (B)
11. (B)	**12.** (D)	**13.** (B)	**14.** (A)	**15.** (D)
16. (A)	**17.** (B)	**18.** (D)	**19.** (D)	**20.** (B)
21. (A)	**22.** (C)	**23.** (D)	**24.** (C)	**25.** (D)
26. (D)	**27.** (C)	**28.** (C)	**29.** (A)	**30.** (D)
31. (B)	**32.** (D)	**33.** (C)	**34.** (D)	**35.** (A)
36. (A)	**37.** (D)	**38.** (D)	**39.** (C)	**40.** (B)
41. (D)	**42.** (A)	**43.** (B)	**44.** (C)	**45.** (B)
46. (B)	**47.** (D)	**48.** (C)	**49.** (D)	**50.** (D)

Part 5

1.

정답　(B)

해석　하워드 씨는 출장을 위해 공항 근처에 있는 적합한 숙박 시설을 찾도록 비서에게 요청했다.

해설　빈칸은 바로 앞에 위치한 형용사 suitable의 수식을 받음과 동시에, to부정사로 쓰인 동사 find의 목적어 역할을 할 명사 자리이므로 (B) accommodation이 정답이다.

어휘　ask A to do A에게 ~하도록 요청하다　secretary 비서　suitable 적합한, 알맞은　accommodate ~을 수용하다　accommodation 숙박 시설, 숙소

2.

정답　(A)

해석　벨라미 씨는 피니건 테크 사에서 퇴사한 후, 7년 전에 브라이트만 회사를 설립했다.

해설　빈칸 뒤에 seven years ago라는 과거시점 표현이 있으므로 빈칸에 과거시점을 나타내는 동사가 필요한데, 빈칸 뒤에 목적어가 있으므로 능동태인 (A) founded가 정답이다.

어휘　found ~을 설립하다　corporation 법인, 회사　position 직책, 일자리

3.

정답　(A)

해석　그린 월드 재단은 우리 상품을 전국적으로 유통시키는 것에 대한 대체 방안을 우리에게 알려 주었다.

해설　빈칸이 부정관사와 명사 사이에 위치해 있으므로 빈칸에 명사를 수식할 형용사가 들어가야 한다. 따라서 (A) alternative가 정답이다.

어휘　inform A of B A에게 B를 알리다　alternative a. 대체 가능한, 대안이 되는 n. 대안　distribute ~을 유통시키다, 배부하다　alternate v. ~을 번갈아 하다, 번갈아 일어나다 a. 번갈아 하는　alternator 교류 발전기

4.

정답　(C)

해석　올해 가장 큰 행사를 놓치시는 일을 피하실 수 있도록 오늘 밀튼 음악 축제 입장권을 예매하세요.

해설　선택지가 모두 다른 부사로 구성되어 있는데 빈칸에 쓰일 부사는 올해 가장 큰 행사를 놓치지 않도록 입장권을 예매하는 방식과 관련된 의미를 나타내야 한다. 따라서 가능한 한 빨리 예매하도록 권하는 말이 되어야 자연스러우므로 가장 빠른 시점에 해당되는 '오늘'을 뜻하는 (C) today가 정답이다.

어휘　reserve ~을 예약하다　avoid -ing ~하는 것을 피하다

5.

정답　(A)

해석　햄랜 자동차 디테일링 서비스 사는 수리를 위해 차량을 가져오는 고객 누구에게나 무료 실내 청소 서비스를 제공한다.

해설　빈칸 앞에 타동사 provides와 두 개의 형용사가 있고, 빈칸 뒤에 전치사가 있으므로 빈칸에는 형용사의 수식을 받으며 타동사의 목적어 역할을 할 명사 자리이다. 따라서 (A) cleaning이 정답이다.

어휘　complimentary 무료의　cleaning 청소　bring in ~을 가지고 오다, 들여오다

6.

정답　(A)

해석　프린터가 컴퓨터에 무선으로 연결될 수 없는 경우에 제품 설명서를 참고하시기 바랍니다.

해설　빈칸 앞뒤로 명령문과 주어와 동사가 포함된 절이 쓰여 있으므로 빈칸은 접속사 자리이다. 또한, '프린터가 컴퓨터에 무선으로 연결될 수 없는 경우에 제품 설명서를 참고하십시오'와 같은 의미가 구성되어야 자연스러우므로 '~하는 경우에, ~라면'을 뜻하는 (A) if가 정답이다.

어휘　refer to ~을 참고하다　connect to ~에 연결되다　besides prep. ~ 외에(도), ~을 제외하고 ad. 뿐만 아니라, 그 외에도　toward (이동, 방향 등) ~ 쪽으로, ~을 향해, (목적) ~을 위해　unless ~하지 않는다면, ~가 아니라면

7.

정답　(C)

해석　베니테즈 씨는 잭맨 교수가 올해의 의료 컨퍼런스에서 연설을

하기로 합의했다는 소식을 듣고 기뻐하고 있다.

해설 빈칸이 be동사와 to부정사 사이에 위치해 있으므로 빈칸은 be 동사와 결합하는 동사의 주격보어 자리인데, 사람 주어의 감정 을 나타내야 하므로 과거분사 형태인 (C) pleased가 정답이 다.

어휘 **be pleased to do** ~해서 기쁘다 **agree to do** ~하기로 합의하다 **deliver a speech** 연설하다 **pleasure** 기쁨, 즐거움 **pleasing** 기쁘게 하는 **please** ~을 기쁘게 하다

8.

정답 (D)

해석 인디 프레스 갤러리는 허드슨 불리바드에 있는 레이니 데이 제 과점을 바로 지난 곳에 위치해 있다.

해설 빈칸에는 빈칸 앞에 위치한 is located와 어울려 위치 관계를 나타낼 전치사가 필요한데, 길거리 상에서의 위치를 나타내야 하므로 '~을 지난, ~을 지나서' 등의 의미로 쓰이는 (D) past가 정답이다.

어휘 **be located past** ~을 지난 곳에 위치해 있다 **into** ~ 안으 로 **among** ~ 사이에, ~ 중에서

9.

정답 (A)

해석 대부분의 호텔 손님들께서는 우리 옥상에 있는 것이 아닌 수영 장 가장자리에 있는 레스토랑에서 식사하시는 경향이 있습니 다.

해설 빈칸에는 빈칸 뒤에 쓰인 명사구를 목적어로 취할 전치사가 필 요하며, '옥상에 있는 것이 아닌 수영장 가장자리에 있는 레스토 랑에서 식사하는 경향이 있다'와 같은 의미가 구성되어야 자연 스러우므로 '~가 아니라, ~ 대신' 등을 뜻하는 (A) rather than 이 정답이다.

어휘 **tend to do** ~하는 경향이 있다 **dine** 식사하다 **rather than** ~가 아니라, ~ 대신 **in short** 요컨대 **by all means** 무슨 수를 써서라도, 기어코

10.

정답 (B)

해석 우리 공장 직원들의 사기가 계속해서 떨어져 왔으며, 특히 야간 교대 근무 직원들 사이에서 그래왔다.

해설 주어와 동사가 포함된 하나의 절이 끝나고 콤마와 함께 among 이 이끄는 전치사구가 추가된 구조이다. 따라서 빈칸에는 빈 칸 뒤의 전치사구를 수식할 수 있는 부사가 쓰여야 하므로 (B) particularly가 정답이다.

어휘 **morale** 사기, 의욕 **particularly** 특히 **among** ~ 사이에 서 **shift** 교대 근무 **particularize** ~을 자세히 다루다, 특 별한 예를 들다 **particularity** 특이성

11.

정답 (B)

해석 색슨 제약회사의 대표이사에 따르면, 회사의 재정 상태는 분기 별 수치가 의미하는 것보다 더 안정적인 상황이다.

해설 빈칸 앞에 be동사가 있으므로 빈칸은 주격보어 자리이다. 따라 서 빈칸에는 형용사가 와야 하는데 빈칸 뒤에 제시된 than과 짝 을 이뤄 비교의 의미를 나타내야 하므로 (B) more stable이 정답이다.

어휘 **according to** ~에 따르면 **status** 상황, 상태 **stable** 안 정적인 **quarterly** 분기의 **imply** ~을 의미하다, 암시하다 **stably** 안정적으로

12.

정답 (D)

해석 식사에 곁들일 와인을 선택하실 때, 음식의 맛을 보완해주는 것 을 선택하십시오.

해설 빈칸에 쓰일 대명사는 앞서 언급된 wine 중 한 가지를 의미해 야 하므로 앞서 언급된 것과 동일한 종류에 속하는 불특정한 하 나를 말할 때 사용하는 (D) one이 정답이다.

어휘 **accompany** ~에 곁들이다, ~을 동반하다 **select** ~을 선 택하다, ~을 선정하다 **complement** v. ~을 보완하다

13.

정답 (B)

해석 패스트푸드에 관한 마이크 루더의 다큐멘터리는 지난 한 해 동 안 가장 높이 평가된 영화들 중 하나이다.

해설 선택지가 모두 다른 과거분사로 구성되어 있으므로 해석을 통 해 알맞은 어휘를 골라야 한다. 빈칸에 쓰일 과거분사는 부사 highly의 수식을 받을 수 있으면서 영화 작품의 특징과 관련된 이미지를 나타내야 하므로 highly와 함께 '높이 평가되는'이라는 뜻으로 쓰이는 (B) regarded가 정답이다.

어휘 **highly** (수준 등) 높이, 매우 **concerned** 우려하는 **regarded** 간주되는, 여겨지는 **apply** 지원하다, 신청하다, ~을 적용하다

14.

정답 (A)

해석 디지털 플라자는 대부분의 휴대전화기 모델에 대한 케이스와 화면 커버 같은 부대용품을 갖추고 있다.

해설 선택지가 모두 다른 명사로 구성되어 있으므로 해석을 통해 알 맞은 어휘를 골라야 한다. 빈칸에 쓰일 명사는 such as와 함께 언급된 명사 cases와 screen covers를 하나로 아우를 수 있 는 범주에 해당되는 것이어야 하므로 '부대용품'을 뜻하는 (A) accessories가 정답이다.

어휘 **stock** v. (재고로) ~을 갖추다 **accessories** 부대용품 **application** 지원(서), 적용, 애플리케이션

15.

정답 (D)

해석 바우티스타 항공사는 승객들에게 무료 담요와 베개, 그리고 수

면 마스크를 이용하도록 권장한다.

해설 빈칸 뒤에 「목적어 + to do」의 구조가 이어져 있으므로 이와 같은 구조와 결합해 '~에게 …하도록 권하다, 장려하다'라는 의미를 나타낼 때 사용하는 (D) encourages가 정답이다.

어휘 encourage A to do A에게 ~하도록 권하다, 장려하다 take advantage of ~을 이용하다 complimentary 무료의 inquire 문의하다 attract ~을 끌어 들이다

16.

정답 (A)

해석 코우마스 씨는 자신의 자동차를 더 신형 모델로 바꾸려고 생각 중이다.

해설 선택지가 모두 다른 전치사로 구성되어 있는데, 동사 exchange와 함께 교환 대상을 나타낼 때 전치사 for를 사용하므로 (A) for가 정답이다.

어휘 exchange A for B A를 B로 바꾸다 automobile 자동차

Part 6

17-20.

타코 시티 고객 여러분께,

저희는 음식과 일반적으로 함께 제공되는 **17** 것으로서 살사와 과카몰리의 일시적인 부족 문제가 발생된 상태임을 알려 드리게 되어 유감스럽게 생각합니다. **18** 안타깝게도, 저희 고정 공급업체가 재고 부족 문제를 겪고 있으며, 이는 며칠 동안 지속될 수 있습니다.

일반적으로 살사 또는 과카몰리가 곁들여지는 음식을 주문하시는 경우, 몇몇 적절한 **19** 대체품을 고려해 보시기 바랍니다. 저희는 대신 사우어 크림, 칠리 소스, 또는 치즈 딥을 제공해 드릴 수 있습니다. 저희는 이러한 불편함에 대해 사과 드리며, 여러분의 양해에 감사 드립니다.

20 저희 메뉴는 다음 주에 정상 운영으로 돌아갈 것입니다.

어휘 regret to do ~해서 유감이다 inform A that A에게 ~라고 알리다 temporary 일시적인, 임시의 shortage 부족 typically 일반적으로, 전형적으로 serve (음식 등) ~을 제공하다, ~을 내오다 supplier 공급업체 last v. 지속되다 accompany ~을 곁들이다, ~을 동반하다 consider ~을 고려하다 suitable 적절한, 적합한 instead 대신 apologize for ~에 대해 사과하다 appreciate ~에 대해 감사하다

17.

정답 (B)

해설 빈칸 뒤에 주어와 동사가 포함된 절이 쓰여 있으므로 이 절을 이끌 수 있는 접속사가 빈칸에 쓰여야 한다. 또한, 빈칸 이하 부분

은 전치사 with의 목적어가 빠진 불완전한 구조이고, 그 의미로 보아 빈칸 앞에 위치한 명사 salsa and guacamole를 수식하는 관계사절이 되어야 한다는 것을 알 수 있으므로 불완전한 절을 이끄는 접속사 중 하나인 관계대명사 (B) that이 정답이다.

18.

정답 (D)

해설 빈칸 뒤에 공급업체가 재고 부족 문제를 겪고 있어서 앞선 문장에서 언급한 문제가 며칠 지속될 수 있다는 사실을 알리는 말이 쓰여 있다. 이는 부정적인 상황에 대한 원인과 그에 따른 영향을 말하는 흐름이므로 '안타깝게도, 유감스럽게도'와 같은 의미로 부정적인 일에 관한 정보를 알리는 (D) Unfortunately가 정답이다.

어휘 finally 마침내, 마지막으로 therefore 따라서, 그러므로 for instance 예를 들어 unfortunately 안타깝게도, 유감스럽게도

19.

정답 (D)

해설 빈칸에 쓰일 명사는 동사 consider의 목적어로서, 앞선 단락에서 현재 이용할 수 없는 상황임을 알린 살사와 과카몰리가 포함되는 음식을 주문하는 경우에 고려하도록 권하는 대상을 나타내야 한다. 따라서, 살사와 과카몰리 대신 이용 가능한 것을 가리킬 수 있는 명사가 필요하므로 '대체품'을 의미하는 (D) substitutions가 정답이다.

어휘 ingredient (음식 등의) 재료, 성분 incentive 보상책, 장려 정책 substitution 대체(품), 대용(품)

20.

정답 (B)

해석 (A) 저희는 여러분의 식사가 즐거우셨기를 바랍니다.
(B) 저희 메뉴는 다음 주에 정상 운영으로 돌아갈 것입니다.
(C) 새로운 저희 메뉴에 관한 의견을 제공해 주시기 바랍니다.
(D) 새로운 음식이 전 지점에서 이용 가능합니다.

해설 지문 전체적으로 살사와 과카몰리를 이용할 수 없는 상황임을 알리면서 그에 대한 대안을 언급하는 내용으로 지문이 전개되고 있다. 지문 마지막 부분에 빈칸이 위치해 있으므로 글을 마무리하는 성격을 지니면서 살사와 과카몰리의 제공과 관련된 정보를 담고 있는 문장이 와야 한다. 따라서 다음 주에 정상 운영된다는 의미로 살사와 과카몰리를 다시 이용할 수 있는 시점을 알리는 (B)가 정답이다.

어휘 return to normal 정상으로 돌아가다 available 이용 가능한, 구입 가능한

21-24.

모리건 식료품점 전 직원에게 알립니다.

교육 세미나 (3월 29일, 일요일, 오전 8시와 오후 9시)

우리는 다음 주에 설치되는 새로운 셀프 계산대 **21** 시스템과 관련된 세미나를 두 차례 진행할 예정입니다. 전 직원 여러분께서는 필요할 때마다 고객들을 도와 드릴 수 있도록 이 새로운 기기에 관해 많은 것을 알고 계셔야 합니다. **22** 이 시간들은 위층 회의실에서 개최될 것입니다. 반드시 세미나 시간들 중 하나에 참석하시기 바랍니다.

두 차례의 세미나 중 어느 한쪽이든 참석하실 수 없는 경우, 반드시 미리 우리 인사부장님께 연락하셔야 합니다. 우리는 3월 29일에 참석하실 수 없는 분들을 위해 세 번째 세미나를 마련하기 위해 **23** 노력할 것입니다. 이 **24** 교육이 여러분께 우리 고객들을 도와 드리는 데 필요하신 지식을 제공해 드릴 것이기 때문에 대단히 중요하다는 점에 유의하시기 바랍니다.

어휘 run ~을 진행하다, ~을 운영하다 checkout 계산대 install ~을 설치하다 knowledgeable 아는 것이 많은, 박식한 so that (목적) ~하도록 assist ~을 돕다, ~을 지원하다 whenever necessary 필요할 때마다 attend ~에 참석하다 be unable to do ~할 수 없다 either 둘 중 하나의 contact ~에게 연락하다 human resources 인사(부) in advance 미리, 사전에 arrange ~을 마련하다, ~을 조정하다 note that ~라는 점에 유의하다, ~임에 주목하다 extremely 대단히, 매우

21.

정답 (A)

해설 선택지가 모두 다른 전치사로 구성되어 있어 해석을 통해 알맞은 어휘를 골라야 한다. 빈칸 앞에는 두 번의 세미나가, 빈칸 뒤에는 새로운 계산 시스템이 쓰여 있어 이 새로운 시스템이 세미나의 주제인 것으로 볼 수 있다. 따라서, '~와 관련해'라는 의미로 **주**제니 연관성을 말할 때 사용하는 (A) regarding이 정답이다.

어휘 regarding ~와 관련해 through ~을 통해, ~을 거쳐, (장소) ~ 전역에, (기간) ~ 동안 내내 in case of ~의 경우에 along with ~와 함께

22.

정답 (C)

해석 (A) 해당 계산대에 영향을 미치는 기술적인 문제에 대해 사과드립니다.
(B) 우리 고객들께서 새로운 시스템을 이용하시는 데 문제를 겪으셨습니다.
(C) 이 시간들은 위층 회의실에서 개최될 것입니다.
(D) 지원하고자 하시는 경우, 저희 웹 사이트를 방문하십시오.

해설 빈칸 앞에 위치한 문장들이 새로운 셀프 계산대 시스템과 관련된 세미나가 열린다는 사실과 이 행사를 여는 목적을 설명하고

있다. 따라서, 이 행사의 개최와 관련된 정보를 담은 문장이 빈칸에 필요하므로 two seminars를 대신하는 The sessions와 함께 행사 개최 장소를 알리는 (C)가 정답이다.

어휘 apologize for ~에 대해 사과하다 affect ~에 영향을 미치다 have difficulty in -ing ~하는 데 문제를 겪다 hold ~을 개최하다 apply 지원하다, 신청하다

23.

정답 (D)

해설 주어와 빈칸 뒤로 to부정사와 전치사구만 이어져 있으므로 빈칸이 동사 자리임을 알 수 있다. 또한, 빈칸이 속한 문장에서 말하는 세 번째 세미나는 앞선 단락에서 다음 주(next week)라는 미래 시점으로 언급된 3월 29일에 열리는 두 번의 세미나에 참석하지 못하는 사람들을 위해 더 나중의 미래 시점에 열리는 행사이다. 따라서 (D) will strive가 정답이다.

어휘 strive 노력하다, 애쓰다

24.

정답 (C)

해설 빈칸 뒤에 고객들을 돕는 데 필요한 지식을 제공하기 때문에 대단히 중요하다는 말이 쓰여 있다. 이는 지문 전체적으로 설명하는 세미나의 중요성을 말하는 것이며, 직원들에게 지식을 제공한다는 말을 통해 교육 행사임을 알 수 있으므로 '교육, 훈련'을 의미하는 (C) training이 정답이다.

어휘 revision 수정, 변경 target 목표(물), 대상

Part 7

25-26.

닐 프랜시스 (오후 5:12)
안녕하세요, 루이스 씨. 제가 여전히 이곳 사무실에서 할 일이 많이 남아 있습니다. 제가 제때 끝마칠 방법이 없습니다.

루이스 엘리엇 (오후 5:14)
아, 너무 아쉽네요. 음, **25** 제가 우리 매그놀리아 레스토랑 예약을 취소한 다음, 다시 할 수 있습니다. **26** 금요일 어떠세요?

닐 프랜시스 (오후 5:15)
말씀 드리기 어려워요. 뭔가 다른 긴급한 업무가 튀어나올 수도 있을 것 같아서요. 아마 이번 주에는 그냥 완전히 미뤄야 할 거예요. 다음 주 월요일은 어떠세요?

루이스 엘리엇 (오후 5:17)
저는 괜찮습니다. 이번 주에 작업하셔야 하는 연간 매출 보고서가 있다는 걸 알고 있습니다.

닐 프랜시스 (오후 5:18)
네, 할 게 너무 많네요. 이해해 주셔서 감사합니다!

어휘 have A left to do 해야 할 A가 남아 있다 on time 제때

I'm afraid that (부정적인 일에 대해) ~인 것 같다, 유감이지만 ~이다 **urgent** 긴급한 **task** 업무, 일 **come up** 나타나다, 발생되다 **postpone** ~을 연기하다, ~을 미루다 **completely** 완전히, 전적으로 **That works for me** (제안 등에 대해) 저는 좋아요 **annual** 연간의, 연례적인 **work on** ~에 대한 작업을 하다

25. 메시지 작성자들과 관련해 암시된 것은 무엇인가?

(A) 두 사람 모두 사무실에 늦게까지 있을 것이다.

(B) 매출 보고서를 함께 작업하고 있다.

(C) 금요일에 점심 식사를 위해 만날 것이다.

(D) 식사를 하기 위한 계획을 세웠다.

정답 (D)

해설 프랜시스 씨가 할 일이 많아 시간이 나지 않는다고 알리자, 엘리엇 씨가 5시 14분에 작성한 메시지를 통해 아쉬움을 나타내면서 매그놀리아 레스토랑 예약을 취소하겠다고(I can cancel our reservation at Magnolia Restaurant) 언급하고 있다. 이는 함께 식사하기 위해 레스토랑을 예약했음을 의미하는 말에 해당되므로 (D)가 정답이다.

어휘 **collaborate on** ~에 대해 협업하다, ~을 공동 작업하다 **make a plan** 계획을 세우다

26. 오후 5시 15분에, 프랜시스 씨가 "It's hard to say"라고 쓸 때 무엇을 의미할 것 같은가?

(A) 레스토랑 이름을 잊어버렸다.

(B) 매그놀리아 레스토랑에서 한 번도 식사한 적이 없었다.

(C) 엘리엇 씨에게 도움을 요청하고 있다.

(D) 자신의 일정에 대해 확실하지 않다.

정답 (D)

해설 엘리엇 씨가 5시 14분에 현재의 예약을 취소한다고 알리면서 금요일은 시간이 어떤지(How's Friday for you?) 묻는 것에 대해 '말씀 드리기 어려워요'라고 대답하는 흐름이다. 이는 그때 시간이 날지 알 수 없다는 뜻으로서, 일정이 확실하지 않다는 말에 해당되므로 (D)가 정답이다.

어휘 **require** ~을 요청하다 **be unsure of** ~에 대해 확실하지 않다

27-29.

수신: 르로이 하울렛 <lhowlett@promail.com>
발신: 엘라 모펏 <emoffat@griswold.com>
제목: 킹피셔 침대 프레임
날짜: 28(D) 11월 8일

하울렛 씨께,

27 귀하께서 11월 6일에 저희 고객서비스팀으로 보내신 이메일에 대한 답신입니다. 귀하께서는 28(D) 지난달 저희 매장을 방문하시어 28(B) 새로운 아파트에 사용할 27 킹피셔 솔리드 오크 침대 프레임을 구매하셨으며, 이 제품이 영업일 7일 이내로

배송될 것이라고 들으셨을 겁니다. 27 아직까지 해당 제품을 수령하지 못하고 계신 점에 대해 매우 유감스럽게 생각합니다. 저희 기록을 제가 확인해보니 지불도 저희 시스템을 통해 성공적으로 마치신 것을 확인할 수 있었습니다. 그러나 저희 창고 관리 부서의 실수로 귀하의 주문이 자사 시스템에서 삭제되어 있었습니다.

다시 한번, 이 일로 인해 불편을 끼쳐드려 진심으로 사과 말씀 드립니다. 귀하께서는 원래 일반 배송 비용을 포함하여 총 325.99달러를 지불하셨습니다. 사과의 의미로 원래의 배송 비용을 귀하의 28(A) 신용 카드로 환불해드리고, 29 추가 비용 없이 귀하께서 주문하신 침대 프레임에 긴급 배송 표기를 해 드리겠습니다. 이틀 내지 삼일 이내로 해당 상품을 수령하실 수 있을 것입니다.

안녕히 계십시오.

엘라 모펏 드림
고객서비스팀 매니저
그리월드 홈 퍼니싱스

어휘 **respond to** ~에 응답하다 **payment** 지불 **warehouse department** 창고 관리 부서 **result in** ~라는 결과를 초래하다 **erase** ~을 삭제하다 **inconvenience** 불편 **standard shipping** 일반 배송 **apologize** ~에 대해 사과하다 **refund** ~을 환불하다 **expedited shipping** 긴급 배송 **at no extra charge** 추가 비용 없이

27. 하울렛 씨는 왜 그리월드 홈 퍼니싱스 사에 연락했을 것 같은가?

(A) 배송 지연에 대해 사과하기 위해

(B) 매장의 새로운 재고품에 대해 문의하기 위해

(C) 최근의 주문에 대해 문의하기 위해

(D) 결함이 있는 제품에 대해 불만을 제기하기 위해

정답 (C)

해설 첫 문장에서 11월 6일에 하울렛 씨가 고객 서비스팀에게 이메일을 보냈음을 알 수 있으며, 이어지는 문장을 통해 물품 구매 후 아직 상품을 받지 못한 상태임을(I'm very sorry that you have not yet received the item) 확인할 수 있다. 따라서 배송 받지 못한 물건에 관해 이메일을 썼을 것임을 유추할 수 있으므로 (C)가 정답이다.

어휘 **delay** 지연 **inventory** 재고, 재고품 **inquire about** ~에 대해 문의하다 **faulty** 결함이 있는

28. 하울렛 씨에 대해 명시되지 않은 것은 무엇인가?

(A) 신용 카드로 제품을 구매했다.

(B) 최근에 새로운 집으로 이사했다.

(C) 매장의 단골 고객이다.

(D) 10월에 매장을 방문했다.

정답 (C)

해설 이메일 상단의 날짜가 11월 8일인 것과 지문 초반부에 지난달에 매장을 방문했다는(you came into our store last month) 부분에서 10월에 방문한 점을 언급한 (D)를, 새로운 아파트에서 사용할 것이라는(for your new apartment) 부분에서 (B)

를, 두 번째 문단의 신용카드로 환불해 주겠다는(refund the original shipping fee to your credit card) 부분에서 (A)를 찾을 수 있다. 따라서 언급되지 않은 (C)가 정답이다.

어휘 regular customer 단골 고객

29. 모펏 씨는 자신이 무엇을 할 것이라고 말하는가?
 (A) 배송서비스를 업그레이드하는 일
 (B) 제품에 대해 전액 환불을 해주는 일
 (C) 대체 부품을 보내는 일
 (D) 제품을 수리해주는 일

정답 (A)

해설 두 번째 단락 후반부에 추가 비용 없이 주문한 제품에 긴급 배송 표기를 해주겠다는(mark your bed frame for expedited shipping at no extra charge) 제안을 하고 있으므로 (A)가 정답이다.

어휘 replacement 대체(품)

30-32.

데이지 체인 부티크
3491 모로우 로드
볼더, 콜로라도 80302

작년에 개업한 이후로, 데이지 체인은 볼더에서 최고의 패션 부티크가 되었으며, 저희 고객들에게 저희가 이번 달에 가격을 대폭 낮출 것이라는 소식을 알려드리게 되어 기쁩니다! 30 저희는 입고될 겨울용 재고품을 위해 더 많은 공간이 필요하므로 저희에게 남아있는 모든 여름 물품들은 9월 30일까지 할인 판매될 것입니다. 모든 것을 처분합니다!

모든 여름 드레스는 25퍼센트 가격 인하될 것입니다!
선별된 바지와 청바지는 최대 35퍼센트까지 할인될 것입니다!
31 다양한 색의 티셔츠는 모두 50퍼센트 할인 판매됩니다!
블라우스와 반바지는 모두 20퍼센트에서 30퍼센트 사이에 구입 가능할 것입니다!

매장 회원은 할인 품목에 10퍼센트 추가 할인을 얻기 위해 회원 카드를 사용해도 됩니다. 또한, 32 저희 매장에서 200달러 이상을 소비하시는 경우, 저희가 추가 비용 없이 선택하신 팔찌를 포함시켜 드립니다. 저희의 제품 라인과 영업 시간에 대한 자세한 사항을 원하신다면, www.daisyfashion.com으로 방문하시기 바랍니다.

어휘 boutique 부티크, 양품점 premier 최고의 slash 대폭 줄이다 incoming 들어오는, 입고되는 stock 재고품 on sale 할인 판매되는 mark down 가격을 인하하다 discount ~을 할인하다 available 구입 가능한 obtain ~을 얻다, 획득하다 additional 추가적인, 추가의 bracelet 팔찌 at no extra cost 추가 비용 없이, 무료로

30. 데이지 체인 부티크가 할인 판매를 하는 이유는 무엇인가?
 (A) 개업을 기념하고 있다.

(B) 고객을 유치하는 데 어려움을 겪고 있다.
 (C) 폐업할 것이다.
 (D) 새로운 상품들을 위한 공간을 만들고 있다.

정답 (D)

해설 첫 단락에서 겨울 재고품이 들어올 것을 대비하여 좀 더 많은 공간이 필요해서 여름 상품을 할인 판매할 것이라고(We need more space for our incoming winter stock, so all of our remaining summer items will be on sale until September 30th) 쓰여 있으므로 (D)가 정답이다.

어휘 have trouble -ing ~하는 데 어려움을 겪다 go out of business 폐업하다 room 공간

31. 절반의 가격으로 구입 가능한 상품의 종류는 무엇인가?
 (A) 드레스
 (B) 티셔츠
 (C) 바지
 (D) 블라우스

정답 (B)

해설 두 번째 문단에서 다양한 색의 티셔츠가 50퍼센트 할인 판매된다고(Our colorful T-shirts will all be on sale at 50 percent off) 알리고 있으므로 (B)가 정답이다.

32. 고객은 어떻게 무료 선물을 받을 수 있는가?
 (A) 특정 상품을 구입함으로써
 (B) 매장 회원으로 등록함으로써
 (C) 웹 사이트에서 구매함으로써
 (D) 일정 금액을 소비함으로써

정답 (D)

해설 마지막 단락에 매장에서 200달러 이상 소비하면 추가 비용 없이 팔찌를 받을 수 있다고(if you spend $200 or more in our store, we will include a bracelet of your choice at no extra cost) 언급하고 있으므로 (D)가 정답이다.

어휘 specific 특정한, 구체적인 certain 일정한

33-36.

---

33 **수신:** 의학연구부
발신: 샌드라 커니건, 총무부장
날짜: 7월 12일

DKL 어소시에이츠는 7월 27일부터 30일까지 런던에서 열리는 연례 의학 컨벤션에 다시 한번 참가하기로 결정했습니다. 현재, 우리는 DKL 부스에서 일할 자원봉사자를 찾고 있습니다.

때때로, 35(C) 우리 자원봉사자들은 매우 전문적인 의학 관련 질문을 받습니다. 이런 이유로, 33 35(B) 우리는 5시간 단위로 일하실 수 있는 의학연구부 직원이 필요합니다. 요즘 의약품에 대한 우리의 가장 최근 연구에 참여했던 직원들이 특별히 필요합니다. 이 컨벤션은 우리 DKL 사가 전문으로 하고 있는 다양한 의학 분야에 관한 여러분의 지식을 넓힐 수 있는 기회를 제공해 줍니다. 관심

있으신 분은 누구든 7월 19일 전에 피터 클라크 씨에게 연락하시기를 요청 드립니다.

34 우리는 여러분 중 일부가 우리 DKL 사의 서비스를 홍보하는 기술에 익숙하지 않을 수 있다는 점을 알고 있기 때문에, 이 부분이 자원봉사자들을 위해 다음 주에 개최되는 의무적인 워크숍에서 처리될 것입니다. 컨벤션에서 선보이게 될 특정 서비스에는 다음이 포함됩니다.

- 의학 파일 관리
- **35(D)** 전자식 처방전 소프트웨어 개발
- 의학 서비스 소개 웹 사이트 운영

우리는 또한 의학 다이제스트 및 교재를 더 적게 출판하는 계획을 강조할 것입니다. **36** 인쇄 출판물을 제한함으로써, 우리 DKL 사는 온라인 의학 출판물에 있어 세계적인 선두주자로서 홍보하는 데 초점을 맞출 수 있습니다. 우리 DKL 사는 우리 부스를 방문하는 모든 사람이 이러한 점을 전적으로 인식하도록 만들어야 한다고 주장하는 바입니다.

어휘 **from time to time** 때때로 **highly** 대단히, 매우 **block** (시간, 공간 등의) 구간, ~대 **back pain** 요통 **expand** ~을 넓히다, 확대하다 **field** 분야 **specialize in** ~을 전문으로 하다 **be asked to do** ~하도록 요청 받다 **be familiar with** ~에 익숙하다, ~을 잘 알다 **address** v. (문제 등) ~을 처리하다, 다루다 **mandatory** 의무적인 **specific** 특정한, 구체적인 **showcase** v. ~을 선보이다 **prescription** 처방전 **referral** 소개, 위탁 **emphasize** ~을 강조하다 **digest** n. (문학 작품, 시사 문제 등의) 다이제스트, 요약집 **publication** 출판(물) **insist that** ~라고 주장하다

33. 이 회람은 누구를 대상으로 하는가?
(A) 새로 고용된 모든 직원들
(B) 협회의 임원진
(C) 특정 부서의 직원들
(D) 컨벤션의 초청 연사들

정답 (C)

해설 지문 상단의 수신인 항목에 의학연구부(To: Medical Research Division)라고 쓰여 있고, 두 번째 단락에 행사장에서 일할 사람으로 의학연구부 직원이 필요하다고(we need staff in medical research) 알리고 있다. 따라서 이 부서의 직원들이 수신 대상임을 알 수 있으므로 (C)가 정답이다.

어휘 **intended for** ~을 대상으로 하는 **newly-hired** 새롭게 고용된 **association** 협회 **division** (단체 등의) 부, 과

34. 컨벤션에 참가하는 사람들에게 요구되는 것은 무엇인가?
(A) 반드시 이전의 컨벤션에서 일했어야 한다.
(B) 반드시 영업 전문가로서 교육 받아야 한다.
(C) 반드시 글을 기고해야 한다.
(D) 반드시 특별 시간에 참석해야 한다.

정답 (D)

해설 세 번째 단락에 일부 직원이 회사의 서비스를 홍보하는 기술에 익숙하지 않을 수 있다는 점을 언급하면서 이 부분이 자원 봉사자들을 위해 다음 주에 개최되는 의무적인 워크숍에서 처리된다고(We are aware that some of you may not be familiar with techniques on promoting DKL's services, so this will be addressed at a mandatory workshop) 알리고 있다. 이는 의무적으로 워크숍 시간에 참석해야 한다는 사실을 말하는 것이므로 (D)가 정답이다.

35. 컨벤션 자원봉사자들이 요청 받지 않을 일은 무엇인가?
(A) 의학에 관한 세미나를 진행하는 일
(B) 한번에 5시간 근무하는 일
(C) 까다로운 질문에 답변하는 일
(D) 처방전 소프트웨어에 대해 논의하는 일

정답 (A)

해설 두 번째 단락의 자원봉사자들이 매우 전문적인 의학 질문들을 받는다는(our volunteers receive highly technical medical questions) 부분에서 (C)를, 5시간 단위로 일할 수 있는 직원이 필요하다는(who can work in five-hour blocks) 부분에서 (B)를 확인할 수 있다. 또한, 네 번째 단락 두 번째 항목의 전자식 처방전 소프트웨어 개발(Developing electronic prescription software)에서 (D)도 확인할 수 있다. 하지만 세미나를 진행하는 일과 관련된 정보는 제시되어 있지 않으므로 (A)가 정답이다.

어휘 **challenging** 까다로운, 힘든

36. 무엇이 회사의 목표로 언급되는가?
(A) 온라인 출판물을 제작하는 일
(B) 의학 전문가를 고용하는 일
(C) 해외에 사무소를 개소하는 일
(D) TV 다큐멘터리를 촬영하는 일

정답 (A)

해설 마지막 단락에 인쇄 출판물을 제한함으로써 온라인 의학 출판물에 있어 세계적인 선두주자로서 홍보하는 데 초점을 맞출 수 있다고(By limiting printed publications, DKL can focus on promoting itself as a global leader in online medical publications) 알리고 있다. 이는 온라인 출판물 제작에 집중하겠다는 뜻이므로 (A)가 정답이다.

어휘 **abroad** 해외에

37-40.

더 코타나 호텔
칼 98 비아 104, 파바스, 산호세, 코스타리카

조 살베티 씨
팜 블리바드 1078번지
마이애미, FL 33125

살베티 씨께,

37 저희 호텔에서의 최근 숙박과 관련된 귀하의 편지를 읽고 매우 유감스러웠습니다. 저희 더 코타나 호텔은 고객들께 흠 잡을 데 없는 서비스를 제공해 드리는 것에 대한 명성을 자랑스럽게 여기고 있습니다. 따라서, 귀하께서 이곳에서 숙박하신 동안 여러 문제를 접하셨다는 사실을 알게 되었을 때 대단히 유감스러웠습니다. 귀하께서 저에게 편지로 이 문제들에 대해 주목하게 해 주셔서 기쁘게 생각합니다.

귀하께서 받으신 객실과 관련해, 혼란스럽게 해 드려 대단히 죄송합니다. 귀하께서 스탠다드 객실을 제공 받으신 이유는 컴퓨터 오류로 인해 저희가 일부 디럭스 객실을 초과 예약하는 일로 이어졌기 때문입니다. 당연히, 귀하께는 스탠다드 요금만 청구되었습니다. 또한, 체크인 당일에 귀하의 짐을 보관해 드릴 수 없었던 점도 사과 드립니다. 귀하께서 체크인 시간인 오후 2시보다 훨씬 더 일찍 산호세에 도착하신 것으로 알고 있지만, 저희 호텔은 고객 분들을 위해 짐을 보관할 공간이 충분하지 않습니다. — [1] —.

마지막으로, **40** 저희 공항 셔틀버스 서비스의 유감스러운 지연 문제에 대해 아무리 사과의 말씀 드려도 부족할 것입니다. — [2] —. **38** 귀하께서 어쩔 수 없이 마이애미로 떠나는 더 늦은 항공편을 이용하시면서 항공권 변경을 위해 요금을 지불하셔야 했다는 말씀을 듣고 저희는 모두 대단히 죄송한 마음이었습니다. — [3] —.

이런 일들에 대해 귀하께 보상해 드리기 위해, 다시 저희 호텔에서 숙박하시기를 요청 드립니다. — [4] —. **39** 귀하께서 무료 6박 7일 숙박에 대한 자격이 있으시다고 저희 경영진에서 승인했으며, 이는 연중 언제든지 이용하실 수 있습니다. 이 숙박 중에, 귀하께서는 무료로 저희 레스토랑에서 식사하시도록 허용되실 것입니다. 고객들께서 저희에게 얼마나 중요한지를 보여드릴 수 있는 기회를 한번 더 주시기 바랍니다.

안녕히 계십시오.

로살리타 페레즈
고객 관리부장
더 코타나 호텔

어휘 **regarding** ~와 관련해(= with regard to) **pride oneself on** ~을 자랑스러워하다 **reputation** 명성, 평판 **impeccable** 흠 잡을 데 없는 **regret** 유감, 후회 **encounter** ~을 접하다, ~와 맞닥뜨리다 **bring A to one's attention** ~에게 A에 주목하게 하다, A를 ~에게 알리다 **confusion** 혼란, 혼동 **charge** v. ~에게 청구하다 n. 청구 요금 **rate** 요금, 비율, 등급 **store** ~을 보관하다, ~을

저장하다 **unfortunate** 유감스러운, 불운한 **terribly** 대단히, 극심하게, 몹시 **be forced to do** 어쩔 수 없이 ~해야 하다 **in an attempt to do** ~하기 위해, ~하기 위한 시도로 **make A up to B** A에 대해 B에게 보상하다 **approve that** ~임을 승인하다 **be entitled to** ~에 대한 자격이 있다 **complimentary** 무료의 **take advantage of** ~을 이용하다 **be allowed to do** ~하도록 허용되다 **free of charge** 무료로

37. 페레즈 씨가 왜 편지를 썼는가?
(A) 호텔 요금이 왜 인상되었는지 설명하기 위해
(B) 살베티 씨에게 이용 가능한 객실이 없다는 점을 알리기 위해
(C) 호텔의 새로운 체크인 정책을 설명하기 위해
(D) 이전 고객의 불만 사항에 대응하기 위해

정답 (D)

해설 첫 단락 시작 부분에 편지의 수신인인 고객이 최근 숙박과 관련해 보낸 편지를 읽고 매우 유감스러웠다고(I was very sorry to read your letter regarding your recent stay at our hotel) 알린 뒤로, 상대방이 숙박 중에 겪은 문제와 그에 대한 보상 방법을 이야기하고 있다. 이는 고객이 편지를 통해 제기한 불만 사항에 대응하는 것이므로 (D)가 정답이다.

어휘 **inform A that** A에게 ~라고 알리다 **policy** 정책, 방침 **respond to** ~에 대응하다, ~에 답변하다 **former** 이전의, 과거의, 전직 ~의

38. 살베티 씨와 관련해 유추할 수 있는 것은 무엇인가?
(A) 객실에 대해 요금이 과다 청구되었다.
(B) 여행 중에 짐을 분실했다.
(C) 예정된 항공편을 놓쳤다.
(D) 객실 업그레이드 서비스를 받았다.

정답 (C)

해설 세 번째 단락에 살베티 씨가 어쩔 수 없이 마이애미로 떠나는 더 늦은 항공편을 이용하면서 항공권 변경을 위해 요금을 지불한 사실을 들은(to hear that you were forced to take a later flight to Miami and pay a charge for changing your ticket) 내용이 쓰여 있다. 이는 예약한 비행기를 타지 못해 다른 비행기로 변경했음을 의미하는 말이므로 (C)가 정답이다.

어휘 **overcharge** ~에게 과다 청구하다

39. 페레즈 씨가 살베티 씨에게 무엇을 제공하는가?
(A) 호텔 레스토랑용 상품권
(B) 일반 객실 요금에 대한 할인
(C) 호텔에서의 일주일 무료 숙박
(D) 호텔 지출 비용에 대한 부분 환불

정답 (C)

해설 마지막 단락에 살베티 씨에게 무료 6박 7일 숙박에 대한 자격이 있다고 경영진에서 승인한(Management has approved that you are entitled to a complimentary 6-night/7-day stay) 사실을 알리고 있다. 이는 무료 숙박 서비스를 제공하겠다는 뜻이므로 (C)가 정답이다.

어휘 **gift certificate** 상품권 **partial** 부분적인 **expense** 지출 (비용), 경비

40. [1], [2], [3], [4]로 표기된 위치들 중에서, 다음 문장이 들어가기에 가장 적절한 곳은 어디인가?

"일반적으로, 이것들은 아무런 문제 없이 한 시간 단위로 운영됩니다."

(A) [1]
(B) [2]
(C) [3]
(D) [4]

정답 (B)

해설 제시된 문장은 앞서 언급된 복수명사를 대신하는 these와 함께 일반적으로 한 시간 단위로 운영된다는 사실을 알리는 의미를 담고 있다. 따라서 이러한 방식으로 운영할 수 있는 것으로서 공항 셔틀버스 서비스를 언급한 문장 뒤에 위치한 [2]에 들어가 셔틀버스들을 these로 지칭해 그 버스들의 운영 방식과 관련해 알리는 흐름이 되어야 자연스러우므로 (B)가 정답이다.

어휘 **typically** 일반적으로, 전형적으로 **run** 운영되다, 진행되다 **on an hourly basis** 한 시간 단위로, 한 시간마다

41-45.

panel 위원단 well-respected 높이 평가 받는, 크게 존경 받는 be based in ~을 기반으로 하다 recent 최근의

SMAS 영화제가 시상식과 함께 종료되다

산타 모니카, 캘리포니아 (9월 3일) - 41 산타 모니카 예술 협회(SMAS)가 8월 29일부터 9월 2일까지 연례 영화제를 개최했으며, 이 행사의 마지막 날 밤은 영화제 기간에 상영된 훌륭한 영화들을 기리는 시상식이 지배했습니다. 배우들에게 수여된 많은 상뿐만 아니라, 행사 주최 측에서 영화 연출 부문에 대해 큐브릭 상을, 촬영 부문에 대해 디킨즈 상을, 그리고 45 각본 부문에 대해 마멧 상을 수여했습니다.

42(C) SMAS 회원들이 올해 이 영화제에서 후보를 지명하는 책임을 진 유일한 사람들은 아니었습니다. 협회 측에서 어느 영화들이 여러 상에 대해 고려되어야 하는지 선택하는 데 도움이 될 수 있도록 42(B) 42(D) 유명 영화 스타들과 높이 평가 받는 영화 감독들로 위원단을 구성했습니다. 올해의 수상자들 중 최연소인 25세의 티모시 J. 펠르티어 씨는 이곳 산타 모니카에서 성장해 로즈앵글 영화 학교를 졸업했지만, 지금은 웨스트 할리우드를 기반으로 활동하고 있습니다. 43 최근에 받은 이 상이 그가 3년 전에 영화계에서 첫 일자리를 얻은 이후로 받은 여러 상들 중 하나입니다.

어휘 **dominate** ~을 지배하다, ~을 장악하다 **honor** ~을 기리다, ~에게 영예를 주다 **exceptional** 훌륭한, 예외적인 **organizer** 주최자, 조직자 **cinematography** 촬영(술) **screenwriting** 각본, 시나리오 **make a nomination** 후보를 지명하다 **assemble** ~을 구성하다, ~을 집합시키다

10월 4일

티모시 J. 펠르티어

리츠 아파트 135호,
선셋 블리바드 8896번지, 웨스트 할리우드, CA 90069

펠르티어 씨께,

가장 먼저, 지난달에 있었던 SMAS 영화제에서 45 마멧 상을 수상하신 것에 대해 축하 인사 드리고자 합니다. 저는 그 영화에 대해 작업하신 것에 대단히 감탄했으며, 전적으로 그 상을 받으실 만한 자격이 있으셨다고 생각합니다. 제 영화 제작사가 최근 베스트셀러 소설 <페일러 쉐이드 오브 그레이>에 대한 저작권을 획득했으며, 44 저희가 현재 성공을 거둔 이 책을 수익성 좋은 영화 작품으로 각색하는 데 도움을 주실 수 있는 숙련된 분을 찾고 있습니다. 저는 귀하께서 이 프로젝트에 완벽히 어울리시는 분이실 것이라고 생각합니다. 저희가 이미 요즘 업계에서 활동 중이신 가장 인기 있는 배우들 중 두 분인 엘렌 리 씨와 크리스 엘리슨 씨를 섭외했습니다.

저는 직접 대면한 자리에서 더 자세히 이 잠재적인 업무 관계를 논의할 수 있도록 귀하와 함께 하는 회의를 마련하고자 합니다. 가급적 빨리 저에게 555-3777번으로 전화 주시기 바랍니다.

안녕히 계십시오.

아가사 크루즈
대표이사
크루즈 에버트 필름 주식회사

어휘 **congratulate A on B** B에 대해 A를 축하하다 **win** (상 등) ~을 받다, ~을 타다 **admire** ~에 감탄하다 **thoroughly** 전적으로, 완전히 **deserve to do** ~할 만한 자격이 있다, 마땅히 ~해야 하다 **acquire** ~을 획득하다 **skilled** 숙련된, 능숙한 **adapt A into B** A를 B로 각색하다, A를 B로 개작하다 **profitable** 수익성이 있는 **motion picture** 영화 **perfect fit** 완벽히 어울리는 사람 **arrange** ~을 마련하다, ~을 조치하다 **so that** (목적) ~하도록 **relationship** 관계 **face to face** 직접 대면하여 **in detail** 자세히 **at one's earliest possible convenience** 가급적 빨리

41. SMAS 영화제와 관련해 사실인 것은 무엇인가?
(A) 7일 동안 지속되었다.
(B) 해외 영화에 초점을 맞춘다.
(C) 8월 29일에 열린 시상식을 포함했다.
(D) 일년 단위로 개최된다.

정답 (D)

해설 첫 지문 첫 단락 시작 부분에 산타 모니카 예술 협회(SMAS)가 8월 29일부터 9월 2일까지 연례 영화제를 개최한(The Santa Monica Arts Society (SMAS) held its annual film festival) 사실이 쓰여 있다. 여기서 말하는 연례 영화제 (annual film festival)는 해마다 개최되는 영화제임을 뜻하므로 (D)가 정답이다.

어휘 last v. 지속되다 focus on ~에 초점을 맞추다 on a yearly basis 일년 단위로, 매년

42. 누가 영화 시상식 후보 지명자들을 선택하는 데 관련되어 있지 않은가?

(A) 영화 제작자들
(B) 배우들
(C) SMAS 회원들
(D) 감독들

정답 (A)

해설 첫 지문 두 번째 단락에 SMAS 회원들이 올해 이 영화제에서 후보를 지명하는 책임을 진 유일한 사람들은 아니었다는 (SMAS members were not the only ones) 부분에서 (C)를, 유명 영화 스타들과 높이 평가 받는 영화 감독들로 위원단을 구성했다는 (a panel of famous movie stars and well-respected directors) 부분에서 (B)와 (D)를 확인할 수 있다. 하지만 영화 제작자들과 관련된 정보는 제시되어 있지 않으므로 (A)가 정답이다.

어휘 be involved in ~에 관련되어 있다 nominee 후보 지명자

43. 펠르티어 씨와 관련해 언급된 것은 무엇인가?

(A) 작년에 영화 학교를 졸업했다.
(B) 이전의 작품에 대해 인정 받았다.
(C) 웨스트 할리우드에서 대부분의 어린 시절을 보냈다.
(D) 최근에 열린 SMAS 영화제에 참석할 수 없었다.

정답 (B)

해설 첫 지문 두 번째 단락 후반부에 펠르티어 씨가 3년 전에 영화계에서 첫 일자리를 얻은 이후로 여러 상들을 받은 사실이 쓰여 있다(is one of several he has received since taking his first job in the movie business three years ago). 이는 이전의 작업물에 대해 인정 받았음을 의미하는 말이므로 (B)가 정답이다.

어휘 recognize ~을 인정하다, ~을 표창하다 previous 이전의, 과거의

44. 크루즈 씨는 왜 펠르티어 씨에게 편지를 보냈는가?

(A) 한 가지 문학 작품에 대한 권리를 얻기 위해
(B) 오디션에 참석하도록 권하기 위해
(C) 곧 있을 프로젝트를 맡아 작업하도록 요청하기 위해
(D) 취업 지원이 성공적이었음을 알리기 위해

정답 (C)

해설 두 번째 지문 첫 단락에 책 하나를 영화 작품으로 각색할 사람을 찾고 있다는 말과 함께 상대방인 펠르티어 씨가 이 프로젝트에 완벽히 어울릴 것이라고(we are currently seeking skilled individuals to help us to adapt this successful book into a profitable motion picture. I believe that you

would be a perfect fit for this project) 알리고 있다. 이는 그 프로젝트를 맡아 작업하도록 요청하는 말에 해당되므로 (C)가 정답이다.

어휘 obtain ~을 얻다 invite A to do A에게 ~하도록 요청하다 upcoming 곧 있을, 다가오는 inform A that A에게 ~라고 알리다

45. 펠르티어 씨는 무엇에 대해 상을 받았는가?

(A) 연기
(B) 각본
(C) 영화 연출
(D) 촬영

정답 (B)

해설 두 번째 지문 첫 단락 시작 부분에 마멧 상을 수상한 것에 대해 축하한다는(congratulate you on winning the Mamet Prize) 말이 쓰여 있다. 이 상과 관련해, 첫 지문 첫 단락에 각본 부문에 대해 마멧 상을 수여했다는(the Mamet Prize for screenwriting) 말이 쓰여 있어 펠르티어 씨가 각본상을 받았다는 사실을 알 수 있으므로 (B)가 정답이다.

46-50.

노바라이프 고급 임대 아파트
- 오사카 중심부에서 누리는 진정한 편안함과 고급스러움 -

저희 노바라이프 고급 임대 아파트에서 머무르시기로 결정해 주셔서 감사합니다. 저희 건물은 관광을 위해 저희 도시를 방문하시는 분들뿐만 아니라, 근처의 컨벤션 센터에서 개최되는 컨퍼런스에 참석하시는 분들께도 편리한 거처의 역할을 합니다. 저희 피트니스 센터는 오전 7시부터 오후 9시까지 개장하고, 모든 종류의 운동 기계 및 장비를 갖추고 있으며, **50** 저희 슈퍼마켓은 하루 24시간 영업합니다. 또한 엘리베이터를 이용하셔서 옥상 구역으로 올라가실 수도 있으며, 이곳은 전문적으로 조경 작업이 되어 다양한 꽃과 관목, 그리고 나무들을 **46** 자랑합니다.

47 48 저희 노바라이프 고급 임대 아파트 건물은 다수의 백화점과 레스토랑, 그리고 패션 부티크에 걸어서 갈 수 있는 거리에 자리잡고 있으며, 그 대부분은 아파트 내에서 찾으시게 될 무료 노바라이프 잡지에 기재되어 있습니다. 교통 정보가 필요하실 경우, 노바라이프 안내 데스크 직원이 기꺼이 도와 드릴 것입니다. **49** 저희 웹 페이지 www.novalifeapartments.com/services에서 아파트 호수를 입력하시면 합리적인 가격의 와이파이도 이용하실 수 있습니다.

어휘 serviced apartment 고급 임대 아파트 comfort 편안함 elegance 고급스러움, 우아함 serve as ~의 역할을 하다 base 거처, 거점 sightseeing 관광 as well as ~뿐만 아니라 …도 nearby 근처의 be equipped with ~을 갖추고 있다 landscape ~에 조경 작업을 하다 boast ~을 자랑하다 bush 관목 be situated 자리잡고 있다, 위치해 있다 within walking distance of ~에서 걸어서 갈 수 있는 거리에 있는 list ~을 기재하다, ~을 목록

에 올리다 **complimentary** 무료의 **reasonably** 합리적
으로 **priced** 가격이 책정된

---

www.novalifeapartments.com/services

투숙객 성명:	브라이언 피네건	
이메일 주소:	b_finnegan@homemail.net	
전화 번호:	555-8376	

선호하는 지불 방식:	신용카드	¬▼
신용카드 발급업체:	비바카드	¬▼
카드 번호:	****-****-****-4180	

49 아래에 아파트 호수를 입력하신 다음, '계속하기' 버튼을 클릭
해 활성화 과정을 완료하십시오. 노바라이프 서비스를 이용해 주
셔서 감사합니다. 반드시 즐겁고 기억에 남는 숙박이 되도록 최선
을 다하겠습니다.

계속하기

어휘 **preferred** 선호하는 **complete** ~을 완료하다
activation 활성화 **ensure that** 반드시 ~하도록 하다,
~임을 확실히 해두다 **memorable** 기억에 남을 만한

수신: 브라이언 피네건 <b_finnegan@homemail.net>
발신: 레이 타나카 <raytanaka@novalife.com>
제목: 사과의 말씀 드립니다
날짜: 10월 8일

피네건 씨께,

50 귀하의 최근 이메일에 대한 답변으로, 저희 노바라이프 고급
임대 아파트를 대표해 사과의 말씀 전해 드리고자 합니다. 유감스
럽게도, 저희가 운영 시간을 줄여야 했던 관계로, 현재 오전 7시부
터 오후 10시까지 출입 가능합니다. 그 이유는 필수 개조 공사가
야간에 실시될 것이기 때문입니다. **50** 완전한 24시간 출입은 10
월 11일에 재개될 것입니다. 다시 한 번, 불편함에 대해 사과 드리
며, 이 문제와 관련해 양해해 주시면 감사하겠습니다.

안녕히 계십시오.

레이 타나카
안내 데스크 팀장

어휘 **Please accept my apologies** 사과의 말씀 드립니다 **in
response to** ~에 대한 답변으로, ~에 대응해 **recent** 최
근의 **express** (생각, 감정 등) ~을 표현하다 **on behalf
of** ~을 대표해, ~을 대신해 **unfortunately** 유감스럽게도,
안타깝게도 **accessible** 출입 가능한, 이용 가능한 **carry
out** ~을 실시하다, ~을 수행하다 **full** 완전한, 전적인, 최대
의 **round-the-clock** 24시간의 **accessibility** 출입 (가
능성), 이용 (가능성) **restore** ~을 재개하다, ~을 복구하다
appreciate ~에 대해 감사하다 **regarding** ~와 관련해
matter 문제, 사안

---

46. 정보에서, 첫 번째 단락, 다섯 번째 줄의 단어 "boasts"와 의미
가 가장 가까운 것은 무엇인가?

(A) 초과하다
(B) 포함하다
(C) 칭찬하다
(D) 추천하다

정답 (B)

해설 해당 문장에서 boasts가 속한 which절은 바로 앞에 위치한
our rooftop area를 설명하는 역할을 하므로 boasts의 목적
어로 쓰인 a variety of flowers, bushes, and trees가 그곳
에 있는 다양한 꽃과 관목, 그리고 나무들을 가리킨다는 것을 알
수 있다. 이는 그 공간이 포함하는 특징적인 요소를 말하는 것이
므로 '포함하다' 등을 뜻하는 (B) contains가 정답이다.

47. 정보 내용에 따르면, 손님들이 어떻게 해당 지역에서 식사 선택
권과 관련해 알아볼 수 있는가?

(A) 안내 데스크 직원과 이야기함으로써
(B) 노바라이프 웹 사이트에 로그인함으로써
(C) 지역 신문에서 확인함으로써
(D) 무료 출판물을 읽음으로써

정답 (D)

해설 첫 지문 두 번째 단락에 해당 아파트가 여러 백화점과 레스토
랑, 그리고 패션 부티크에서 가까운 거리에 있다는 말과 함
께 그런 곳들이 무료 노바라이프 잡지에 기재되어 있다고
(numerous department stores, restaurants, and
fashion boutiques, most of which are listed in the
complimentary Novalife magazine) 알리고 있다. 따라서,
무료로 제공되는 출판물을 통해 식사 장소와 관련된 정보를 얻
을 수 있다는 점을 알 수 있으므로 (D)가 정답이다.

어휘 **find out about** ~에 관해 알아보다, ~에 관해 파악하다
publication 출판(물)

48. 노바라이프 고급 임대 아파트 건물과 관련해 암시된 것은 무엇
인가?

(A) 컨벤션 센터를 포함하고 있다.
(B) 공항 셔틀버스 서비스를 제공한다.
(C) 분주한 상업 지구와 가까운 곳에 자리잡고 있다.
(D) 입주민에게 지정 주차 공간을 제공한다.

정답 (C)

해설 첫 지문 두 번째 단락에 해당 아파트가 여러 백화점과 레스토랑,
그리고 패션 부티크에서 가까운 거리에 있다고(The Novalife
Serviced Apartments building is situated within
walking distance of numerous department stores,
restaurants, and fashion boutiques) 알리는 말이 쓰여 있
다. 이를 통해 그러한 건물들이 모여 있는 곳, 즉 분주한 상업 지
구와 가깝다는 사실을 알 수 있으므로 (C)가 정답이다.

어휘 **include** ~을 포함하다 **be situated** 자리잡고 있다,
위치해 있다 **commercial district** 상업 지구 **reserved
parking** 지정 주차 (공간)

49. 피네건 씨와 관련해 유추할 수 있는 것은 무엇인가?

(A) 신용카드 사용이 거절되었다.

(B) 온라인에서 객실 할인을 받았다.

(C) 웹 사이트를 통해 룸 서비스를 주문했다.

(D) 인터넷에 접속하기 위해 비용을 지불했다.

정답 (D)

해설 첫 지문 두 번째 단락에 특정 웹 페이지 주소를 언급하면서 그 곳에서 아파트 호수를 입력하면 합리적인 가격으로 와이파이도 이용할 수 있다고 알리는(you may use our reasonably-priced WiFi by entering your apartment number on our Web page) 말이 쓰여 있다. 이러한 과정과 관련해, 두 번째 지문 하단에 아파트 호수를 입력하고 '계속하기' 버튼을 클릭하면 활성화된다고 쓰여 있어(Please enter your apartment number below and click 'Continue' to complete the Activation Process) 와이파이 서비스를 이용하기 위해 비용을 지불했음을 알 수 있으므로 (D)가 정답이다.

어휘 **decline** ~을 거절하다 **connect to** ~에 접속하다, ~에 연결되다

50. 피네건 씨가 이메일로 무엇과 관련해 불만을 제기했을 것 같은가?

(A) 피트니스 센터

(B) 옥상 공간

(C) 아파트

(D) 식료품점

정답 (D)

해설 세 번째 지문 첫 문장을 통해 상대방인 피네건 씨가 이미 최근에 이메일을 보냈다는 사실을 알 수 있다. 이와 관련해, 이 지문 중반부에 완전한 24시간 출입이 10월 11일에 재개된다고 알리고 있는데(Full round-the-clock accessibility will be restored by October 11th), 이는 첫 번째 지문 첫 단락에 슈퍼마켓이 하루 24시간 영업한다고(our supermarket is open 24 hours a day) 언급되어 있는 부분과 연결되는 정보이다. 따라서, 피네건 씨가 슈퍼마켓을 24시간 이용하지 못하는 상황과 관련해 이메일을 보냈던 것으로 볼 수 있으므로 (D)가 정답이다.

DAY 02 · LC Half Test

1. (C)	**2.** (D)	**3.** (A)	**4.** (A)	**5.** (B)
6. (A)	**7.** (C)	**8.** (B)	**9.** (B)	**10.** (A)
11. (B)	**12.** (A)	**13.** (A)	**14.** (C)	**15.** (C)
16. (A)	**17.** (C)	**18.** (C)	**19.** (A)	**20.** (B)
21. (D)	**22.** (A)	**23.** (A)	**24.** (C)	**25.** (D)
26. (B)	**27.** (A)	**28.** (D)	**29.** (B)	**30.** (D)
31. (C)	**32.** (B)	**33.** (C)	**34.** (C)	**35.** (C)
36. (D)	**37.** (B)	**38.** (B)	**39.** (B)	**40.** (A)
41. (D)	**42.** (B)	**43.** (A)	**44.** (C)	**45.** (B)
46. (C)	**47.** (B)	**48.** (C)	**49.** (C)	**50.** (A)

Part 1

1.
(A) A mountain path leads into the water.
(B) People are hiking in the mountains.
(C) A fence runs along the edge of the road.
(D) Shadows are being cast on the road.

(A) 산길이 물가로 이어져 있다.
(B) 사람들이 산에서 하이킹하고 있다.
(C) 울타리가 도로 가장자리를 따라 뻗어 있다.
(D) 도로에 그늘이 드리워져 있다.

해설 (A) 물 쪽으로 이어져 있는 길을 찾아볼 수 없으므로 오답.
(B) 사람들을 찾아볼 수 없으므로 오답.
(C) 도로를 따라 물가와 경계를 이루는 울타리가 세워져 있는 모습을 묘사하고 있으므로 정답.
(D) 그늘을 찾아볼 수 없으므로 오답.

어휘 **path** 길, 이동로 **lead to** ~로 이어지다 **run** (길 등이) 뻗어 있다, 이어지다 **along** (길 등) ~을 따라 **edge** 가장자리 **cast a shadow** 그늘을 드리우다

2.
(A) A pathway is being paved.
(B) One of the men is getting into a vehicle.
(C) Buildings are lining both sides of a street.
(D) A construction crew is working on a building.

(A) 보도가 포장되는 중이다.
(B) 남자들 중 한 명이 차량에 승차하는 중이다.
(C) 건물들이 거리 양쪽 면에 늘어서 있다.
(D) 한 공사 작업팀이 건물에 대해 작업하는 중이다.

해설 (A) 보도(pathway)를 포장하는 작업을 하는 것이 아니므로 오답.

(B) 승차하는 사람을 찾아볼 수 없으므로 오답.
(C) 거리 양쪽 면에 늘어서 있는 건물들을 찾아볼 수 없으므로 오답.
(D) 건물 공사 현장에서 인부들이 작업하는 모습을 묘사하고 있으므로 정답.

어휘 **pathway** 보도 **pave** ~을 포장하다 **get into** ~에 들어가다 **vehicle** 차량 **line** v. 늘어서 있다 **construction** 공사, 건설 **crew** (함께 작업하는) 팀, 조

Part 2

3. When can I expect to receive the furniture I ordered?

(A) Within 10 business days.
(B) It was more expensive than I expected.
(C) On the company's Web site.

제가 주문한 가구를 언제 받게 될 거라고 예상하면 될까요?
(A) 영업일로 10일 이내에요.
(B) 그건 제가 예상했던 것보다 더 비쌌습니다.
(C) 회사의 웹 사이트에서요.

해설 「When can I expect to ~?」는 '~하는 것을 언제쯤으로 예상하면 될까요?'라는 의미로 시점을 물어보는 완곡한 표현이다. '주문한 가구를 받을 수 있는 시점'을 묻는 질문에 within과 함께 대략적인 시점으로 답하는 (A)가 정답이다. 여기서 business days는 공휴일과 주말을 제외한 영업일, 즉 평일을 의미한다.

어휘 **business day** 영업일

4. Will you be able to pick up our clients from the airport in two hours?

(A) Only if I get my report finished.
(B) How about tomorrow?
(C) It was a 4-hour flight.

2시간 후에 공항에서 우리 고객들을 모셔올 수 있으시겠어요?
(A) 제가 보고서를 끝내야만 가능합니다.
(B) 내일은 어떤가요?
(C) 4시간 비행이었습니다.

해설 「Will you be able to ~?」는 '~할 수 있나요?'라는 의미로 미래 시점에 어떠한 일이 가능한지에 대한 여부를 묻는 질문이다. 이에 대해 가능/불가능 여부를 밝히는 답변이 일반적이지만 어려운 문제의 경우 only if를 통해 가능한 조건을 제시하는 답변이 정답이 되기도 한다. 따라서 보고서를 끝내야만 2시간 후에 고객을 픽업하러 갈 수 있다는 말로 질문에 답하는 (A)가 정답

이다.

어휘 **only if** ~해야만, ~할 경우에 한해 **get A finished[done]** A를 마치다 **flight** 비행

5. Why will the auditorium be closed tomorrow?
(A) No, it's free.
(B) They're doing repair work.
(C) Just a week ago.

강당이 내일 왜 문을 닫죠?
(A) 아뇨, 무료예요.
(B) 수리 작업을 해요.
(C) 불과 일주일 전에요.

해설 강당이 문을 닫는 이유를 묻는 Why 의문문이므로 '수리 작업을 할 예정이다'라는 말로 그 이유를 말하는 (B)가 정답이다. (A)는 의문사 의문문에 맞지 않는 No로 답변하는 오답이며 (C)는 과거 시점 표현이므로 When 의문문에 어울리는 응답이다.

어휘 **auditorium** 강당 **free** 무료인 **repair** 수리

6. Isn't your assignment due on the first of the month?
(A) No, not until the 10th.
(B) His duties seem to be challenging.
(C) Yes, I was the first one here.

당신에게 할당된 업무가 1일이 기한이죠?
(A) 아뇨, 10일이나 되어야 합니다.
(B) 그분의 직무들은 힘든 일인 것 같아요.
(C) 네, 여기서 제가 첫 번째였어요.

해설 할당된 업무 기한이 1일까지였는지 확인하는 부정 의문문이므로 부정을 의미하는 No와 함께 정확한 시점을 덧붙이는 것으로 잘못된 정보를 바로잡아주는 (A)가 정답이다. (B)는 대상을 알 수 없는 His를 언급해 그 사람의 업무 특성을 말하는 내용이므로 질문의 의도에 맞지 않는 오답이며, (C)는 질문에 쓰인 first를 반복해 혼동을 유발하는 답변이다.

어휘 **assignment** 할당(된 일), 배정(된 일) **due + 시점** ~가 기한인 **not until + 시점** ~나 되어야 **seem 형용사** ~인 것 같다 **challenging** 힘든, 어려운, 도전적인

7. Do you mind if I borrow your phone?
(A) It'd be better to e-mail me.
(B) No, she hasn't called.
(C) I'm afraid I left it in my office.

당신 전화기를 빌려도 괜찮을까요?
(A) 제게 이메일을 보내는 것이 더 좋을 거예요.
(B) 아뇨, 그녀는 전화하지 않았어요.
(C) 아무래도 제가 그걸 사무실에 두고 온 것 같아요.

해설 「Do you mind if I ~?」는 '제가 ~해도 괜찮을까요?'라는 뜻으로 허락을 구하는 질문이다. 승낙 여부를 말하는 답변을 고르는 것이 일반적이나, 때로는 승낙/거부를 할 때 우회적으로 돌려서 말하는 경우가 있다. 전화기를 두고 왔다는 말로 빌려줄 수 없다는 것을 우회적으로 표현하고 있으므로 (C)가 정답이다.

어휘 **Do you mind if ~?** ~해도 괜찮을까요? **I'm afraid ~** (유감스럽게도) ~인 것 같다 **leave** (물건 등을) 두고 오다[가다]

8. I guess you'd prefer to sit outside on the patio.
(A) No, I'd prefer the cream pasta.
(B) Yes, the weather is lovely today.
(C) There were a large number of guests.

당신은 야외 테라스에 앉길 원하시겠군요.
(A) 아뇨, 전 크림 파스타를 원합니다.
(B) 네, 오늘 날씨가 참 좋네요.
(C) 손님들이 많이 오셨어요.

해설 평서문은 워낙 다양한 상황에 대해 말하기 때문에 답변으로 정해진 유형이 없다. 문장을 듣고 재빨리 어떤 상황인지 파악해 그에 맞게 대답하는 것을 골라야 하기 때문에 순발력이 더욱 필요하다. '당신은 테라스 자리에 앉길 원하시겠군요'라는 말에 Yes라고 동의하며 날씨가 좋다고 덧붙이는 (B)가 정답이다.

어휘 **prefer to do** ~하는 것을 선호하다 **patio** 테라스 **lovely** 사랑스러운, 좋은 **a number of** 많은, 다수의

9. Who's covering for you on your day off?
(A) To New Jersey.
(B) Sean said he could.
(C) No, I don't think so.

누가 당신 휴무일에 당신 업무를 대신하죠?
(A) 뉴저지로요.
(B) 션 씨가 할 수 있다고 했어요.
(C) 아뇨, 전 그렇게 생각하지 않아요.

해설 cover의 의미를 모르거나 알아듣지 못했다고 하더라도 질문이 시작되는 부분의 Who만 잘 들으면 정답을 고를 수 있다. '누구'를 묻는 Who 의문문이므로 Sean이라는 특정 인물의 이름을 언급하는 (B)가 정답이다. (A)는 행선지를 말하고 있으므로 Where 의문문에 어울리는 대답이며, (C)처럼 의문사 의문문에 Yes/No로 대답하는 답변은 바로 오답 처리한다.

어휘 **cover** (업무 등을) 대신하다 **day off** 휴무일

10. That plant needs to get more sunlight.
(A) Why don't you put it near the window?
(B) The manufacturing plant is in Boston.
(C) Let's go to the beach this weekend.

저 식물은 더 많은 햇빛을 받을 필요가 있습니다.
(A) 그걸 창가에 두는 것이 어때요?
(B) 제조 공장은 보스턴에 있습니다.
(C) 이번 주말에 해변에 갑시다.

해설 plant라는 단어는 '식물'이라는 뜻도 있고 '공장'이라는 뜻도 있다. 주어진 문장에서 햇빛(sunlight)이 더 필요하다고 했으므로, 이 문장의 plant는 '식물'을 의미한다는 것을 알 수 있다. 식물에 햇빛이 더 필요하다는 말에 식물을 창가로 옮길 것을 제안하며 답하는 (A)가 정답이다. (B)는 plant의 서로 다른 의미(식물, 공장)를 이용한 오답이며, (C)는 질문과 전혀 관련 없는 내용의 오답이다.

어휘 **plant** 식물, 공장 **sunlight** 햇빛 **manufacturing plant** 제조 공장 **beach** 해변

11. Mr. Lee recently moved to a new apartment, didn't he?

(A) He works in the Sales Department.
(B) Yes. He lives on Holt Street now.
(C) You can move them over there. Thanks.

리 씨가 최근에 새로운 아파트로 이사하지 않았나요?
(A) 그분은 영업부에서 근무합니다.
(B) 맞아요. 지금 홀트 스트리트에 살고 계세요.
(C) 저기 저쪽으로 그것들을 옮기시면 됩니다. 고맙습니다.

해설 리 씨가 새로운 아파트로 이사했는지 확인하는 부가 의문문에 대해 긍정을 나타내는 Yes와 함께 현재 거주하는 지역을 구체적으로 덧붙여 말한 (B)가 정답이다. (A)는 질문에 쓰인 apartment와 일부 발음이 유사한 department를 이용한 오답이며, (C)는 질문에 쓰인 move를 반복해 혼동을 유발하는 답변이다.

어휘 **recently** 최근에 **move to** ~로 이사하다 **Sales Department** 영업부 **move** ~을 옮기다 **over there** 저기 저쪽에, 바로 저쪽에

12. What time does the train arrive?

(A) It should be here in 5 minutes.
(B) I think you should lead the training.
(C) No, I'm not too busy.

기차가 몇 시에 도착하죠?
(A) 5분 후에 여기 올 겁니다.
(B) 당신이 그 교육을 진행해야 한다고 생각해요.
(C) 아뇨, 전 그렇게 바쁘지 않아요.

해설 질문의 핵심은 What time(몇 시)이다. 기차 도착 시간을 묻는 질문이므로 '5분 후'라는 가까운 미래 시점으로 답변하는 (A)가 정답이다. '~ 후에'라는 의미로 자주 출제되는 「in + 시간/기간」 표현을 알아 둬야 한다. (B)는 질문에 쓰인 train과 발음이 유사한 training을 이용해 혼동을 유발하는 오답이며, (C)처럼 의문사 의문문에 Yes/No로 대답하는 답변은 바로 오답 처리한다.

어휘 **in 시간/기간** ~ 후에 **lead** ~을 이끌다, 진행하다 **training** 교육, 훈련

13. There are far too many documents to file this

morning.

(A) Maybe we should ask for some assistance.
(B) It's only a short distance from here.
(C) Yes, I watched that documentary recently.

오늘 아침에 정리해야 할 문서가 너무 많아요.
(A) 도움을 요청해야 할 것 같아요.
(B) 여기서 짧은 거리일 뿐입니다.
(C) 네, 저는 그 다큐멘터리를 최근에 보았습니다.

해설 far은 '거리가 먼' 외에도 '아주, 몹시, 훨씬'이라는 의미를 가지고 있어 far too many는 '너무도 많은'이라고 해석한다. 정리해야 할 문서가 너무 많다는 말에 '도움을 요청해야 할 것 같아요'라는 말로 응답하는 (A)가 정답이다. 질문의 far를 거리 개념으로 이해할 경우 distance를 언급하는 (B)를 고르기 쉬우므로 주의해야 하며, (C)는 documents와 일부 발음이 비슷한 documentary를 이용한 오답이다.

어휘 **ask for** ~을 요청하다, 부탁하다 **assistance** 도움, 보조 **distance** 거리 **recently** 최근에

14. Is breakfast still being served or did it finish at 11?

(A) A table for six, thanks.
(B) I finished my entire meal.
(C) You can still order it.

아침식사가 여전히 제공되는 중인가요, 아니면 11시에 종료되었나요?
(A) 6인용 테이블로요, 감사합니다.
(B) 저는 모든 식사를 끝마쳤습니다.
(C) 아직 주문할 수 있습니다.

해설 아침식사가 아직 제공되는지(still being served) 또는 종료되었는지(did it finish) 묻는 선택 의문문이다. 이에 대해 '아직 주문할 수 있어요'라는 말로 질문의 still being served를 paraphrasing하여 답하는 (C)가 정답이다.

어휘 **serve** (음식을) 제공하다, 내오다 **entire** 전체의

15. Power to the neighborhood's been restored, hasn't it?

(A) I moved there last month.
(B) That's my favorite store.
(C) Yes, everything's been fixed.

우리 지역으로 들어오는 전기가 복구되지 않았나요?
(A) 저는 지난 달에 그곳으로 이사했어요.
(B) 그곳이 제가 가장 좋아하는 매장입니다.
(C) 네, 모든 것이 고쳐졌어요.

해설 전기가 복구된 것이 맞는지 확인하는 부가 의문문이므로 긍정을 나타내는 Yes와 함께 모두 고쳐졌다는 말을 덧붙이는 (C)가 정답이다. (B)는 restored와 일부 발음이 같은 store를 이용해 혼동을 유발하는 오답이며, (A)는 neighborhood에서 연상 가능한 moved there를 이용한 오답이다.

어휘 power 전기, 전력 neighborhood 지역, 인근, 이웃 restore ~을 복구하다 favorite 가장 좋아하는 fix ~을 고치다, 바로잡다

16. What's the monthly newsletter called?

(A) Check the front page.
(B) She called me last month.
(C) It's been delivered.

그 월간 소식지가 뭐라고 불리나요?
(A) 1면을 확인해 보세요.
(B) 그녀가 지난달에 저에게 전화했어요.
(C) 그건 배송되었습니다.

해설 be called는 '~라고 불리다'라는 뜻으로 명칭 등을 말할 때 사용한다. 이 질문에서는 월간 소식지의 명칭을 묻고 있으므로 그 명칭을 직접 말하는 대신 1면을 확인해 보라고 간접적으로 응답한 (A)가 정답이다. (B)는 질문에 쓰인 동사 call을 반복한 답변인데, call의 서로 다른 의미(부르다, 전화하다)를 이용해 혼동을 유발하는 답변이다.

어휘 monthly 월간의, 매달의 newsletter 소식지 call A B A를 B라고 부르다 front page (신문 등의) 1면 deliver ~을 배송하다

17. The laboratory is in our new company headquarters.

(A) OK, raise it to fifty percent.
(B) For both product research and testing.
(C) Which street is that located on?

실험실은 저희 회사의 새 본사에 있습니다.
(A) 좋습니다, 그걸 50%로 올려주세요.
(B) 제품 조사와 테스트 둘 모두를 위해서입니다.
(C) 그게 어느 거리에 위치해 있죠?

해설 실험실이 새 본사에 있다는 정보를 전달하는 평서문이다. 이에 대해 본사가 어디에 위치해 있는지 물어보며 응답하는 (C)가 정답이다. (A)는 it이 무엇인지 불분명하며, (B)는 laboratory와 관련 있게 들리지만 제시된 문장의 핵심 내용(실험실이 본사에 있다)과 관련이 없다.

어휘 laboratory 실험실 headquarters 본사 raise 올리다 product research 제품 조사 be located 위치해 있다

18. How much time is needed for an international shipment?

(A) Five days ago.
(B) At around 3 P.M.
(C) At least two weeks.

해외 배송에 얼마나 많은 시간이 필요한가요?
(A) 5일 전에요.
(B) 오후 3시쯤에요.
(C) 적어도 2주요.

해설 「How much time ~?」은 얼마나 많은 시간이 걸리는지, 즉 기간을 묻는 의문문이다. 이 질문에서는 해외 배송에 걸리는 시간을 묻고 있으므로 At least와 함께 대략적인 기간으로 질문에 답하는 (C)가 정답이다. (A)와 (B)는 모두 기간이 아닌 시점 표현이므로 When 의문문에 적절한 응답이다.

어휘 shipment 배송(품) at least 적어도, 최소한 around ~쯤

19. Would you like to enroll in our advanced yoga class?

(A) I doubt I'm experienced enough.
(B) At least 70 new students.
(C) We normally meet twice a week.

요가 상급반에 등록하시겠어요?
(A) 제가 경험이 충분할지 모르겠습니다.
(B) 적어도 70명의 새로운 학생들입니다.
(C) 우리는 보통 일주일에 두 번씩 만납니다.

해설 「Would you like to ~?」는 '~하시겠습니까?'라는 뜻으로 무엇을 할 것을 정중히 권유/제안하는 표현이다. 이에 대한 대답으로는 수락이나 거절의 표현이 오는 것이 어울린다. 따라서 '경험이 충분한 것 같지 않다'는 말로 요가 상급반 등록에 대해 망설임을 표현하며 질문에 답하는 (A)가 정답이다. (B)는 질문의 enroll in과 class에서 연상되는 학생 수를 언급한 오답이며, (C)는 질문과 관련 없는 내용을 언급하는 오답이다.

어휘 advanced 상급의, 고급의 doubt 확신하지 못하다 normally 보통

20. I thought there was an ATM around here.

(A) Yes, this area has the best places to eat.
(B) There's one inside the convenience store.
(C) I've lived here my whole life.

저는 이곳 주변에 ATM이 한 대 있다고 생각했어요.
(A) 네, 이 지역에는 최고의 먹거리 장소들이 있습니다.
(B) 편의점 안에 하나 있습니다.
(C) 저는 일생 동안 이곳에서 살아왔습니다.

해설 제시된 문장은 'ATM이 여기 있는 줄 알았다 (그런데 없다)'는 의미이다. 이에 대해 편의점 안에 ATM이 한 대 있다고 말하며 질문에 답하는 (B)가 정답이다. (A)는 긍정을 나타내는 Yes 뒤에 이어지는 말이 ATM과 관련 없으며, (C)도 제시문의 here를 동일하게 사용하였으나 제시문과 관련 없는 내용이므로 오답이다.

어휘 ATM 현금자동입출금기(= Automated Teller Machine) around here 이 주변에 inside ~의 안에 convenience store 편의점 one's whole life 일생 동안

Part 3

Questions 21-23 refer to the following conversation.

> **M:** Hey, Brenda, it looks like we're almost out of product number 893X7, **24** the black ink for ink jet printers. **25** Could you put that on your list for tomorrow's warehouse delivery?
>
> **W:** 893X7. Got it. They're really selling out fast. I remember filling the shelves with those just last week.
>
> **M:** **26** Well, they've been on sale this week, at 15 percent off. I guess people were stocking up while the price was lower.
>
> **W:** You're probably right. OK, I have it on the list. Is there anything else we need from the warehouse tomorrow?
>
> ----
>
> 남: 브렌다 씨, 893X7 제품이 거의 다 떨어진 것 같은데, 잉크젯 프린터에 쓰는 까만 색 잉크예요. 내일 창고에서 배달시킬 목록에 그 제품을 적어주겠어요?
> 여: 893X7. 알겠습니다. 정말 빨리 팔리네요. 제 기억으론 바로 지난 주에 그것들을 선반에 채워 놓은 것 같은데요.
> 남: 그게, 이번 주에 15퍼센트 할인했잖아요. 사람들이 값이 더 쌀 때 사서 비축해 놓으려고 했던 것 같아요.
> 여: 그렇겠군요. 자, 목록에 올렸어요. 이밖에 우리가 내일 창고에서 필요로 하는 게 또 있나요?

어휘 **be out of** ~이 다 떨어지다 **almost** 거의 **put A on the list** A를 명단에 올리다, 기입하다 **warehouse** 창고 **delivery** 배송, 배달 **Got it.** (구어) 알았습니다. **remember -ing** ~한 것을 기억하다 **fill A with B** A를 B로 채우다 **be on sale** 할인 판매되다 **stock up** 많이 사서 비축하다 **price** 가격 **lower** 더 낮은 **have A on the list** A를 목록에 포함시키다

21. 이 대화가 이뤄지고 있는 장소는 어디이겠는가?
(A) 휴대폰 할인점
(B) 출판사
(C) 창고
(D) 사무용품점

해설 대화 초반부에 결정적인 힌트가 있다. black ink for ink jet printers(잉크젯 프린터용 검정 잉크)를 취급할 만한 곳은 사무용품점일 것이므로 (D)가 정답이다.

어휘 **outlet** 할인점 **office supply** 사무용품

22. 다음 날 어떠한 일이 있을 것인가?
(A) 배송품이 도착할 것이다.

(B) 새로운 직원이 채용될 것이다.
(C) 프린터가 수리될 것이다.
(D) 할인이 시작될 것이다.

해설 대화 초반부에 남자가 Could you put that on your list for tomorrow's warehouse delivery?라고 묻는 데서 내일 배송이 될 것이라는 사실을 알 수 있으므로 정답은 (A)가 된다.

어휘 **following day** 다음날 **hire** ~을 고용하다, 채용하다 **repair** ~을 고치다, 수리하다

Paraphrase tomorrow's warehouse delivery
→ A delivery will arrive.

23. 남자는 제품에 대해 뭐라고 말하는가?
(A) 할인가로 제공되고 있었다.
(B) 단종되었다.
(C) 품질이 뛰어나다.
(D) 가격표가 없다.

해설 제품에 대해 남자가 하는 말을 묻는 문제이므로 남자의 대사에 귀 기울여야 한다. 대화 중반부에서 남자는 잉크에 대해 Well, they've been on sale this week, at 15 percent off라고 한다. 15퍼센트 할인 중이었다는 말이므로 (A)가 정답이다.

어휘 **at a discount** 할인해서 **discontinue** ~을 중단하다, 단종시키다 **quality** 질, 품질 **price tag** 가격표 **miss** ~이 없다, ~을 빠트리다

Questions 24-26 refer to the following conversation.

> **W:** Doug, is that you?
>
> **M:** Tara! It's been a long time. Are you heading home? **24** Let's walk to the subway together.
>
> **W:** **24** Sure, that will give us a chance to catch up.
>
> **M:** So, what were you doing down here? Isn't your office on the 10th floor?
>
> **W:** Yes, but my department will be relocated to this floor. I wanted to get a quick look at my new workspace.
>
> **M:** **25** You were promoted to sales director last year, right? I hear sales have been great.
>
> **W:** Well, we just hired twelve new people. We're hoping to enter international markets soon. Oh, do you still work on our online store?
>
> **M:** Yes. Why?
>
> **W:** **26** Do you think it would be possible to provide a payment option for customers overseas?
>
> ----

여: 더그 씨, 당신 맞죠?

남: 타라 씨! 오랜만이에요. 집으로 가시는 길이에요? 함께 지하철 역으로 걸어가죠.

여: 좋아요, 그렇게 하면 그동안의 얘기를 할 수 있는 기회가 될 거예요.

남: 그럼 이쪽에 내려와서 뭘 하고 계셨어요? 당신 사무실이 10층에 있지 않나요?

여: 네, 하지만 제 부서가 이 층으로 이전될 거예요. 새로운 제 업무 공간을 잠깐 한 번 보고 싶었어요.

남: 작년에 영업부장으로 승진되신 게 맞죠? 매출이 계속 아주 좋다는 얘기를 듣고 있어요.

여: 저, 저희가 막 12명의 신입 사원을 고용했어요. 우리가 곧 여러 해외 시장으로 진입하기를 바라고 있거든요. 아, 여전히 우리 온라인 매장에서 일하고 계신가요?

남: 네. 왜 그러시죠?

여: 해외에 있는 고객들을 위한 비용 지불 선택권을 제공하는 게 가능할 것 같으세요?

어휘 **It's been a long time** 오랜만입니다 **head** 향하다, 가다 **catch up** 그동안의 얘기를 하다 **department** 부서 **relocate** ~을 이전하다, 옮기다 **get a quick look at** ~을 잠깐 한 번 보다 **promote** ~을 승진시키다 **sales** 영업, 매출, 판매 **hire** ~을 고용하다 **provide** ~을 제공하다 **payment** 지불(금) **overseas** ad. 해외에 a. 해외의

24. 화자들은 어디로 가는 데 동의하는가?
(A) 주차장으로
(B) 레스토랑으로
(C) 지하철 역으로
(D) 고객 회의 장소로

해설 대화 초반부에 남자가 함께 지하철 역으로 걸어 가자고(Let's walk to the subway together) 제안하는 것에 대해 Sure 라고 여자가 긍정의 답변을 하고 있으므로 (C)가 정답이다.

어휘 **agree to do** ~하는 데 동의하다

25. 여자가 "저희가 막 12명의 신입 사원을 고용했어요"라고 말할 때 암시하는 것은 무엇인가?
(A) 일부 교육이 필요할 것이다.
(B) 예산이 감소되었다.
(C) 몇몇 실수가 발생될 가능성이 있을 것이다.
(D) 부서가 성공적이었다.

해설 대화 중반부에 남자가 상대방이 영업부장으로 승진된 것이 맞는지 확인하는 질문과 함께 매출이 아주 좋다고(You were promoted to sales director last year, right? I hear sales have been great) 언급하자, 여자가 '막 12명의 신입 사원을 고용했다'고 알리는 상황이다. 이는 여자가 맡은 부서가 아주 잘 운영되고 있음을 나타내는 것이므로 (D)가 정답이다.

어휘 **require** ~을 필요로 하다 **budget** 예산 **reduce** ~을 감소시키다, 줄이다 **likely** 가능성 있는 **occur** 발생되다

26. 여자는 남자에게 무엇에 관해 묻는가?
(A) 일부 의견을 제공하는 일
(B) 비용 지불 방법을 추가하는 일
(C) 워크숍에 참석하는 일
(D) 웹 페이지를 고안하는 일

해설 대화 맨 마지막에 여자가 해외에 있는 고객들을 위해 비용 지불 선택권 하나를 제공하는 게 가능할지(Do you think it would be possible to provide a payment option for customers overseas?) 묻고 있다. 이는 해외 고객을 위한 비용 지불 방법을 추가하는 일에 대한 의견을 묻는 것이므로 (B)가 정답이다.

어휘 **feedback** 의견 **add** ~을 추가하다 **attend** ~에 참석하다 **design** ~을 고안하다

Paraphrase provide a payment option
→ Adding a payment method

Questions 27-29 refer to the following conversation with three speakers.

M1: Hi, Ryan. We're glad you could come in today. Looking at your résumé, I see you've already spent some time in the retail industry. **27** Do you have any experience with selling furniture?

M2: Well, I've mostly worked in clothing stores, but I've been a shift manager since last winter.

W: OK, that's helpful. **28** Would you be able to provide a recommendation letter from the general manager about your experience?

M2: Sure, I can bring one in for you. May I ask a question, though?

M1: **29** What's on your mind, Ryan?

M2: **29** What's your company's vacation policy for new employees? I'll need some time off next month for my brother's wedding.

남1: 안녕하세요, 라이언 씨. 오늘 오실 수 있어서 기쁩니다. 이력서를 살펴 보니까 소매 판매 업계에서 이미 일을 하신 적이 있으신 것을 확인할 수 있습니다. 가구를 판매하는 일과 관련된 경험이 있으신가요?

남2: 저, 저는 대부분 의류 매장에서 근무했었지만, 지난 겨울 이후로 교대 근무 책임자로 일해 왔습니다.

여: 좋아요, 그건 도움이 되겠어요. 경력과 관련해서 총 책임자로부터 추천서를 받아 제출해 주실 수 있으신가요?

남2: 그럼요, 한 부 가져올 수 있습니다. 그런데 질문을 하나 드려도 될까요?

남1: 무엇인가요, 라이언 씨?
남2: 신입 사원들에 대한 귀사의 휴가 정책은 어떤가요? 제가 다음 달에 동생 결혼식 때문에 휴가 신청을 해야 해서요.

어휘 résumé 이력서 see (that) ~임을 알게 되다, 확인하다 retail 소매 판매 industry 업계 clothing 의류 shift 교대 근무(조) since ~ 이후로 helpful 도움이 되는 recommendation letter 추천서 general manager 총 책임자, 총 지배인 bring A in A를 가져오다 though (문장 끝이나 중간에서) 하지만, 그런데 What's on your mind? 무슨 일인가요?, 무슨 생각 중인가요? vacation 휴가 policy 정책 time off 휴가, 휴무

27. 라이언 씨는 무슨 직책에 대해 면접을 보는 중인가?
(A) 가구 영업 사원
(B) 의류 디자이너
(C) 인테리어 장식 담당자
(D) 품질 보증 책임자

해설 면접을 보는 직책을 묻고 있으므로 업무적인 특성과 관련된 정보부터 찾아야 한다. 대화 시작 부분에 남자 한 명이 Ryan을 부르면서 가구를 판매하는 일과 관련된 경험이 있는지(Do you have any experience with selling furniture?) 묻고 있으므로 가구 영업 사원을 의미하는 (A)가 정답이 된다.

어휘 salesman 영업 사원 decorator 장식 담당자, 장식 전문가 quality assurance 품질 보증

28. 여자는 라이언 씨에게 무엇을 가져오라고 말하는가?
(A) 작문 샘플
(B) 수료증
(C) 제품 샘플
(D) 추천서

해설 여자가 가져오라고 말하는 것이 질문의 핵심이므로 여자의 말에서 뭔가를 가져오도록 요청하는 표현을 통해 단서를 찾아야 한다는 것을 알 수 있다. 대화 중반부에 여자가 경력과 관련해서 추천서를 받아 제출하도록 요청하고 있으므로(Would you be able to provide a recommendation letter ~) 추천서를 뜻하는 (D)가 정답이다.

어휘 tell A to do A에게 ~하라고 말하다 diploma 수료증 letter of recommendation 추천서

29. 라이언 씨는 무엇에 관해 묻는가?
(A) 유동적인 근무 시간
(B) 휴가
(C) 매장 위치
(D) 수수료 선택권

해설 Ryan 씨가 묻는 내용을 찾아야 하므로 Ryan 씨가 누구인지 잘 듣고 그가 질문하는 내용의 핵심을 파악해야 한다. 대화 마지막에 한 남자가 무엇을 생각하고 있는지(What's on your mind, Ryan?) Ryan 씨에게 묻자, 바로 뒤이어 다른 남자가 신

입 사원들에 대한 회사의 휴가 정책을 묻고 있으므로 (What's your company's vacation policy for new employees?) 휴가를 의미하는 (B)가 정답임을 알 수 있다.

어휘 flexible 유동적인, 탄력적인 location 위치, 지점 commission 수수료 option 선택권

Questions 30-32 refer to the following conversation.

W: Hi, Ben. **30** We've just finished installing Buckler V2, our new anti-virus software. Now every employee's computer is protected against viruses and other harmful programs.

M: Great. So, our workers won't need to set anything up when they arrive at the office in the morning?

W: Actually, **31** they'll need to enter a product serial number so that they can download a final update. I'll send that to them by e-mail first thing tomorrow.

M: Thanks. Will our workers need to update the program regularly?

W: No. **32** One of the best things about Buckler V2 is its automatic monthly updates, so there's nothing that your workers need to do themselves.

여: 안녕하세요, 벤 씨. 저희가 방금 저희의 새 바이러스 방지 소프트웨어인 버클러 V2를 설치하는 일을 끝마쳤습니다. 이제 모든 직원의 컴퓨터가 바이러스와 기타 유해한 프로그램으로부터 보호되고 있습니다.
남: 아주 좋습니다. 그럼, 저희 직원들이 아침에 사무실에 도착할 때 어떤 것도 설치할 필요가 없는 거죠?
여: 실은, 최종 업데이트를 다운로드하실 수 있도록 제품일련번호를 입력하셔야 할 겁니다. 제가 내일 아침에 가장 먼저 그것을 이메일로 직원들께 보내 드리겠습니다.
남: 감사합니다. 저희 직원들이 주기적으로 프로그램을 업데이트해야 할까요?
여: 아뇨. 버클러 V2와 관련해 가장 좋은 점들 중의 하나가 자동 월간 업데이트이기 때문에, 귀하의 직원들께서 직접 하셔야 하는 건 아무것도 없습니다.

어휘 install ~을 설치하다 anti-virus 바이러스 방지의 protect A against B B로부터 A를 보호하다 harmful 유해한 set A up A를 설치하다 arrive 도착하다 serial number 일련번호 so that ~하도록 first thing tomorrow 내일 아침에 가장 먼저 regularly 주기적으로 oneself (부사처럼 쓰여) 직접, 스스로

30. 화자들은 주로 무엇을 이야기하고 있는가?

    (A) 보안 기기

    (B) 휴대전화 애플리케이션

    (C) 교육 시간

    (D) 컴퓨터 프로그램

해설   대화 시작 부분에 여자가 새 바이러스 방지 소프트웨어인 버클러 V2를 설치하는 일을 끝마쳤다고(We've just finished installing Buckler V2, our new anti-virus software) 알린 뒤로, 이 소프트웨어의 사용과 관련된 내용으로 대화가 진행되고 있다. 따라서 (D)가 정답이다.

어휘   **device** 기기, 장치 **training** 교육 **session** (특정 활동을 위한) 시간

Paraphrase anti-virus software

        → computer program

31. 직원들이 내일 이메일로 무엇을 받을 것인가?

    (A) 안내 가이드

    (B) 사용자 이름

    (C) 일련번호

    (D) 비밀번호

해설   여자가 대화 중반부에 '내일'이라는 시점을 언급하면서, 직원들이 입력해야 하는 일련번호를 내일 아침에 보내겠다고(they'll need to enter a product serial number ~ I'll send that to them by e-mail first thing tomorrow) 알리고 있다. 따라서 (C)가 정답이다.

어휘   **instruction** 안내, 설명, 지시

32. 여자는 무엇이 버클러 V2의 장점이라고 말하는가?

    (A) 좀처럼 고장 나지 않는다.

    (B) 자동으로 업데이트된다.

    (C) 품질 보증서가 딸려 있다.

    (D) 쉽게 맞춤 설정될 수 있다.

해설   대화 맨 마지막에 여자가 버클러 V2와 관련해 가장 좋은 점들 중의 하나가 자동 월간 업데이트라고(One of the best things about Buckler V2 is its automatic monthly updates) 알리고 있으므로 (B)가 정답이다.

어휘   **advantage** 장점, 이점 **rarely** 좀처럼 ~ 않다 **break down** 고장 나다 **come with** ~가 딸려 있다, ~을 포함하다 **guarantee** 품질 보증(서) **customize** ~을 맞춤 설정하다, 맞춤 제작하다

Paraphrase automatic monthly updates

        → updates automatically

Questions 33-35 refer to the following conversation and coupon.

M: Good morning. Can I help you find any specific products?

W: Yes, please. `33` I just moved into a new apartment last week, and I need to buy a lot of appliances for it. Today I'm looking for an affordable microwave. Oh, and a friend gave me this voucher for your store.

M: Well, `34` we have this excellent microwave here for only 50 dollars. And, by using your voucher, you'll pay even less.

W: Oh, `34` that sounds perfect. I'll take it then.

M: Great! Now, `35` if you take a moment to fill out a store membership form, I'll be able to add a complimentary set of plates to your purchase.

남: 안녕하세요. 어떤 특정 제품이든 찾으시도록 도와 드릴까요?

여: 네, 부탁합니다. 제가 지난 주에 막 새 아파트로 이사했기 때문에, 집에 필요한 가전기기를 많이 구입해야 합니다. 오늘은 가격이 알맞은 전자레인지를 찾고 있어요. 아, 그리고 제 친구가 이 매장에서 쓸 수 있는 이 상품권도 주었습니다.

남: 음, 여기 겨우 50달러에 판매하는 훌륭한 이 전자레인지가 있습니다. 그리고, 갖고 계신 상품권을 사용하시면, 훨씬 더 적은 금액을 지불하시게 됩니다.

여: 아, 완벽한 것 같아요. 그럼 이걸로 할게요.

남: 아주 좋습니다! 지금, 잠시 시간 내셔서 매장 회원 가입 양식을 작성하시면, 구매 제품에 무료 접시 세트를 추가해 드릴 수 있습니다.

상품권
모든 냉장고 10% 할인
모든 전기 밥솥 20% 할인
모든 전자레인지 30% 할인
모든 주전자 50% 할인

어휘   **specific** 특정한, 구체적인 **appliances** 가전기기 **look for** ~을 찾다 **affordable** 가격이 알맞은, 저렴한 **microwave** 전자레인지 **voucher** 상품권, 쿠폰 **even** (비교급 수식) 훨씬 **take** ~을 가져가다 **then** 그럼, 그렇다면, 그런 다음, 그때 **take a moment to do** 잠시 시간 내서 ~하다 **fill out** ~을 작성하다 **form** 양식, 서식 **be able to do** ~할 수 있다 **add A to B** A를 B에 추가하다 **complimentary** 무료의 **purchase** 구매(품)

33. 여자가 지난 주에 무엇을 했다고 말하는가?

    (A) 건물을 개조했다.

    (B) 사업을 시작했다.

(C) 새 집으로 이사했다.
(D) 가전기기를 구입했다.

해설 여자의 말에 집중해 단서를 파악해야 하며, 질문에 제시된 시점 표현 last week이 제시되는 부분을 놓치지 않고 듣는 것이 중요하다. 대화 초반부에 여자가 I just moved into a new apartment last week이라는 말로 지난 주에 새 아파트로 이사했다고 알리고 있으므로 (C)가 정답이다.

어휘 renovate ~을 개조하다, ~을 보수하다 property 건물, 부동산 launch ~을 시작하다, ~을 출시하다

[Paraphrase] moved into a new apartment
→ moved into a new home

---

34. 시각자료를 보시오. 여자가 어떤 할인 서비스를 받을 것인가?
(A) 10%
(B) 20%
(C) 30%
(D) 50%

해설 대화 중반부에 남자가 we have this excellent microwave here for only 50 dollars라는 말로 50달러에 판매하는 전자레인지를 소개하자, 여자가 that sounds perfect. I'll take it then이라는 말로 구매 의사를 밝히고 있다. 시각자료의 세 번째 줄에 30% off all microwaves와 같이 전자레인지의 할인 비율이 30%라고 표기되어 있으므로 (C)가 정답이다.

---

35. 여자가 어떻게 무료 선물을 받을 수 있는가?
(A) 일정 금액을 소비함으로써
(B) 품질 보증 서비스를 구입함으로써
(C) 양식을 작성 완료함으로써
(D) 회원 카드를 보여줌으로써

해설 남자가 대화 맨 마지막 부분에 if you take a moment to fill out a store membership form, I'll be able to add a complimentary set of plates to your purchase라고 알리면서 매장 회원 가입 양식을 작성하면 무료 접시 세트를 추가하겠다고 언급하고 있으므로 (C)가 정답이다.

어휘 obtain ~을 받다, ~을 획득하다 free 무료의 certain 일정한, 특정한 amount 금액, 액수 warranty 품질 보증(서) complete ~을 완료하다

[Paraphrase] fill out a store membership form
→ completing a form

Questions 36-38 refer to the following conversation and information.

W: Hi, Allan. I've just heard that one of the trains due to depart soon will be delayed by one hour. **36** The engineers are still working to fix a mechanical fault.

M: Okay, **37** I'll make a change to the departure board now. Which train is it?

W: **37** It's number 346 headed to Kingston.

M: Got it. I'll update the board. **38** Would you mind announcing the delay over the public address system? There are already a lot of passengers waiting to board that train.

여: 안녕하세요, 앨런 씨. 곧 출발할 예정인 열차들 중 하나가 1시간 지연될 거라는 얘기를 막 들었어요. 엔지니어들이 기계적인 결함을 바로잡기 위해 여전히 작업 중입니다.
남: 네, 지금 출발 안내 전광판을 변경할게요. 어느 열차인가요?
여: 킹스턴으로 향하는 346번 열차입니다.
남: 알겠습니다. 전광판을 업데이트할게요. 장내 방송 시스템으로 이 지연 문제를 공지해 주시겠어요? 그 기차에 탑승하기 위해 대기하고 계신 승객들이 이미 많이 있습니다.

열차	도착지	출발 시간
325	오샤와	오후 2:00
346	킹스턴	오후 2:15
257	몬트리올	오후 2:30
465	오타와	오후 3:00

어휘 due to do ~할 예정인 depart 출발하다, 떠나다 delay v. ~을 지연시키다 n. 지연, 지체 by (차이) ~ 정도, ~만큼 fix ~을 바로잡다, ~을 고치다 fault 결함 make a change to ~을 변경하다 departure board 출발 안내 전광판 headed to ~로 향하는 over (수단 등) ~로, ~을 통해 public address system 장내 방송 시스템 passenger 승객 board ~에 탑승하다 destination 도착지, 목적지

---

36. 열차가 왜 지연되는가?
(A) 일부 쓰레기가 철로를 가로막고 있다.
(B) 좋지 못한 날씨가 예상된다.
(C) 매표상의 오류가 발생되었다.
(D) 기술적인 문제가 바로잡혀야 한다.

해설 열차가 왜 지연되는지 묻고 있는데, 이런 질문의 경우에 해당 문제를 언급하는 부분에 문제 발생 원인이 함께 제시되므로 이 정보를 찾는 데 집중해야 한다. 대화 초반부에 여자가 열차 지연 문제를 언급하면서 The engineers are still working to fix a mechanical fault라는 말로 엔지니어들이 기계적인 결함을 바로잡기 위해 작업 중이라고 알리고 있다. 이는 기술적인 문제가 열차 지연의 원인임을 알리는 말에 해당되므로 (D)가 정답이다.

어휘 debris 쓰레기, 잔해 block ~을 가로막다 expect ~을 예상하다 ticketing 매표 occur 발생되다, 일어나다

[Paraphrase] mechanical fault
→ technical problem

37. 시각자료를 보시오. 남자가 어느 출발 시간을 변경할 것인가?

(A) 오후 2:00
(B) 오후 2:15
(C) 오후 2:30
(D) 오후 3:00

해설 남자가 대화 중반부에 I'll make a change to the departure board now. Which train is it?라고 언급하는 부분에서 출발 안내 전광판을 변경하겠다는 말과 함께 어느 열차인지 묻자, 여자가 It's number 346 headed to Kingston와 같이 킹스턴행 346번 열차임을 알리고 있다. 시각자료에 킹스턴행 346번 열차의 출발 시간이 두 번째 줄에 2:15 P.M.이라고 쓰여 있으므로 (B)가 정답이다.

38. 남자가 여자에게 무엇을 하도록 요청하는가?

(A) 역 승강장으로 가는 일
(B) 공지를 하는 일
(C) 기관사와 이야기하는 일
(D) 승객들에게 새 승차권을 발급하는 일

해설 남자의 말에 집중해 요청 표현과 함께 제시되는 정보를 찾아야 한다. 대화 후반부에 남자가 Would you mind announcing the delay over the public address system?이라는 말로 장내 방송 시스템으로 지연 문제를 공지하도록 요청하고 있으므로 (B)가 정답이다.

어휘 **make an announcement** 공지하다, 발표하다
issue ~을 발급하다, ~을 지급하다

Paraphrase announcing the delay
→ Make an announcement

Part 4

Questions 39-41 refer to the following telephone message.

Hello, Ms. Bailey. **39** I'm calling from Grey and Parker Menswear regarding your online order from yesterday. I'm looking at your order now, and there is a slight problem. **39** You ordered a number of shirts from our online store, and most of them were sent out this morning. However, one of the items you ordered was a blue and white striped shirt in a French cut. I'm sorry, but this shirt is out of stock right now. **40** The system should not have allowed the purchase to go through, but, unfortunately, one of our staff did not update the site this week. **41** Could you go onto the Web site now and select another shirt you like? We'll have it sent out immediately. I'm sorry about this inconvenience.

안녕하세요, 베일리 씨. 어제 귀하께서 온라인으로 주문하신 물품과 관련해 그레이 앤 파커 남성복에서 전화 드렸습니다. 고객님의 주문서를 지금 보고 있는데요, 작은 문제가 하나 있습니다. 저희 온라인 매장에서 여러 벌의 셔츠를 주문하셨고, 대부분의 제품들은 오늘 아침에 발송되었습니다. 그런데, 주문하신 제품 중의 하나가 프랑스식 재단으로 된 블루 앤 화이트 줄무늬 셔츠입니다. 죄송하지만, 이 셔츠는 현재 재고가 없습니다. 온라인 시스템에서 제품 구매가 진행되지 못하게 했어야 했지만, 안타깝게도 저희 직원 중의 한 명이 이번 주에 사이트를 업데이트하지 않았습니다. 지금 웹 사이트에 가셔서 맘에 드시는 다른 셔츠로 선택해 주시겠습니까? 선택하신 제품은 즉시 배송해 드리겠습니다. 불편을 끼쳐 드려 죄송합니다.

어휘 **regarding** ~와 관련해 **order** n. 주문(품) v. ~을 주문하다 **slight** 작은, 약간의 **a number of** 많은 수의 **striped shirt** 줄무늬 셔츠 **cut** n. 재단 (상태) **out of stock** 재고가 없는 **should have p.p.** ~했어야 했다 **allow** ~을 허용하다 **purchase** n. 구매(품) **go through** 이루어지다, 성사되다 **unfortunately** 안타깝게도, 불행히도 **go onto the site** 사이트를 방문하다 **select** ~을 선택하다 **have A p.p.** A가 ~되게 하다 **immediately** 즉시 **inconvenience** 불편함

39. 화자는 어디에서 전화를 거는가?

(A) 철물점
(B) 의류 제조사
(C) 출장요리업체
(D) 온라인 서점

해설 화자가 담화 첫 부분 인사말에서 소속 업체를 밝히고 있으나 (I'm calling from Grey and Parker Menswear) 순식간에 지나가기 때문에, 좀 더 듣고 판단하도록 한다. 이후에 제시되는 You ordered a number of shirts from our online store, ~에서 의류 제품과 물품 주문, 그리고 배송에 대한 내용이 나오는 것으로 볼 때 (B)가 정답임을 알 수 있다.

어휘 **catering** 출장요리(서비스)

40. 무엇이 문제를 일으켰는가?

(A) 웹 사이트가 업데이트되지 않았다.
(B) 지불 금액이 충분하지 않았다.
(C) 배송 제품이 사라졌다.
(D) 세일 기간이 끝났다.

해설 problem의 원인을 묻고 있으므로 담화에서 부정적인 내용이 제시될 것임을 알 수 있다. 화자는 고객이 주문한 제품 중의 하나가 재고가 없음(this shirt is out of stock right now)을 밝히면서 그럼에도 불구하고 주문이 가능했던 이유를 The system should not have allowed the purchase to go through, but, unfortunately, one of our staff did not update the site this week와 같이 알리고 있다. 결국 직원의 실수로 업데이트되지 않은 것이 문제의 원인이므로 (A)가 정답이다.

어휘 payment 지불(금액) insufficient 불충분한 delivery 배송(품) end 끝나다

41. 청자는 무엇을 하라는 권고를 받는가?
(A) 추가 비용을 지불할 것
(B) 일부 상품을 반품할 것
(C) 주문을 취소할 것
(D) 다른 제품을 고를 것

해설 청자가 권고 받는 내용을 묻는 문제이므로 화자의 말에서 권고나 제안 등의 표현이 제시되는 부분을 찾아야 한다. 화자는 재고가 없는 제품이 주문될 수 있었던 일련의 과정을 설명한 후에 마지막 부분에 가서 Could you go onto the site now and select another shirt you like?와 같이 Could you ~?를 이용해 다른 제품을 고를 것을 권고하고 있으므로 (D)가 정답이다.

어휘 additional 추가의 merchandise 상품 item 물품, 품목

Paraphrase select another shirt
→ Choose a different item

Questions 42-44 refer to the following telephone message.

Hello, Rodger. It's Mike Dunleavy here. I'm the chief financial officer here at the firm. **42** I heard you just completed the signing of Maxine Cosmetics. Well done. It's a great new client for us. **43** I've been on the board here at Johnson's Marketing for five years, and I think this might be our biggest client yet. **43** I spoke to the other board members today, and we all agreed that we want our company to sign even more clients from overseas. I'd really like you to come and meet with me and the rest of the board and discuss your strategies with us. **44** What time would be best for you? We can work around your busy schedule.

안녕하세요, 로저 씨. 마이크 던리비입니다. 저는 이곳 회사에서 최고재무이사직을 맡고 있습니다. 당신이 막 맥신 화장품 사와의 계약을 완료하셨다고 들었습니다. 정말 잘 하셨습니다. 이 회사는 우리에게 아주 좋은 새 고객사입니다. 저는 5년째 이곳 존슨 마케팅 사의 이사회에 속해 있는데요, 아마 이 회사가 지금까지 중에서 가장 큰 고객사일 것으로 생각됩니다. 오늘 이사회의 다른 임원들에게 이야기를 했는데, 저희 모두 우리 회사가 훨씬 더 많은 해외의 고객사들과 계약을 맺기를 원한다는 점에 동의했습니다. 저희는 당신이 꼭 오셔서 저를 비롯한 나머지 이사회 임원들을 만나 당신의 전략에 대해 논의할 수 있기를 바랍니다. 언제 시간이 가장 괜찮으신지요? 바쁘신 시간을 피해 뵐 수 있습니다.

어휘 chief financial officer 최고재무이사(CFO) firm n. 회

사 complete v. ~을 완료하다 signing 서명, 계약 Well done 잘 하셨어요 on the board 이사회에 속한 yet (최상급과 함께) 지금까지 중에서 board member 이사회 임원 agree that ~라는 점에 동의하다 sign v. ~와 계약하다, 서명하다 from overseas 해외의, 해외로부터의 the rest of ~의 나머지 strategy 전략 work around ~을 피해 일하다

42. 화자는 왜 로저 씨를 축하하는가?
(A) 승진되었다.
(B) 새로운 고객과 계약했다.
(C) 대기업에 채용되었다.
(D) 마케팅 계획을 만들어 냈다.

해설 Rodger는 이 메시지의 수신인이다. 담화 초반의 I heard you just completed the signing of Maxine Cosmetics. Well done. It's a great new client for us라는 말로 새로운 고객사와 계약을 맺은 것을 칭찬하고 있으므로 (B)가 정답이다.

어휘 be awarded a promotion 승진되다 create ~을 만들어 내다

43. 화자에 따르면, 존슨 마케팅 사가 희망하는 일은 무엇인가?
(A) 새로운 지사들을 세우는 것
(B) 또 다른 회사를 매입하는 것
(C) 더 많은 해외 기업들을 끌어들이는 것
(D) 마케팅 컨퍼런스를 개최하는 것

해설 화자는 자신이 Johnson's Marketing의 이사회 임원이며, 이사회 임원들 모두 더 많은 해외 고객사들과 계약을 맺고 싶어한다고(I spoke to the other board members today, and we all agreed that we want our company to sign even more clients from overseas) 언급하고 있다. 이는 더 많은 해외 기업을 끌어들이는 일을 의미하므로 (C)가 정답이다.

어휘 establish ~을 세우다, 설립하다 branch office 지사, 지부 attract ~을 끌어들이다 foreign business 해외 기업 hold (행사 등) ~을 열다, 개최하다

Paraphrase sign even more clients from overseas
→ attract more foreign businesses

44. 화자는 무엇에 대해 묻는가?
(A) 곧 있을 워크샵 장소
(B) 최근에 서명한 계약서의 상세 정보
(C) 만날 수 있는 가장 편리한 시간
(D) 청자에게 연락할 수 있는 가장 좋은 방법

해설 담화 마지막 부분에서 화자는 만나서 이야기 나누고 싶다며 언제가 가장 좋을지를(What time would be best for you?) 묻는다. 즉 만날 수 있는 가장 편리한 시간을 묻는 것이므로 (C)가 정답이다.

어휘　location 위치, 지점　upcoming 곧 있을, 다가오는　details 상세 사항　contract n. 계약(서)　convenient 편리한　contact ~에게 연락하다

Questions 45-47 refer to the following talk.

> All right, everyone. **45** We have a lot to discuss today about the development of the new EDT digital camera. We want this camera to be marketed at a competitive price, but we still want it to be appealing to professional photographers. To that end, we are adding in a lot of special features. For example, **46** we're including advanced lighting options to give the user more control over light settings. **47** Due to these extra features, though, the battery life is under an hour. So our design team will be focusing on that problem this month.

> 좋습니다, 여러분. 우리는 오늘 새 EDT 디지털 카메라 제품의 개발과 관련해 논의할 것이 많이 있습니다. 우리는 이 카메라가 경쟁력 있는 가격에 출시되기를 원하지만, 여전히 전문 사진가들의 마음을 끌 수 있기를 원하기도 합니다. 이와 같은 목표를 위해, 우리는 많은 특별 기능들을 추가할 것입니다. 예를 들어, 사용자에게 빛과 관련된 설정에 대해 더 많은 조절 기능을 제공해 주기 위해 개선된 명암 선택권을 포함할 것입니다. 하지만 이와 같은 추가 기능들로 인해, 배터리 수명은 한 시간 미만입니다. 따라서 우리 디자인 팀은 이번 달에 그와 같은 문제에 초점을 맞출 것입니다.

어휘　market ~을 시장에 내놓다, 출시하다　competitive 경쟁력 있는　appealing to ~의 마음을 끄는　professional 전문적인　photographer 사진가　to that end 그 목표를 위해　add in ~을 추가하다, 포함하다　feature 기능, 특징　include ~을 포함하다　advanced 개선된, 나아진, 진보한　lighting (사진 등의) 명암, 조명　option 선택권　give A B A에게 B를 주다　control over ~에 대한 조절, 제어, 통제　setting 설정, 환경　though (문장 중간이나 끝에서) 하지만　due to ~로 인해　extra 추가의, 별도의　under ~ 미만의　focus on ~에 초점을 맞추다

45. 회의의 주제는 무엇인가?
(A) 고객 불만 사항
(B) 제품의 개발
(C) 웹 사이트 의견
(D) 사진 촬영

해설　담화의 주제를 묻고 있으므로 담화가 시작될 때 특히 집중해 핵심 정보를 파악해야 한다. 담화 시작 부분에 새 EDT 디지털 카메라 제품의 개발과 관련해 논의할 것이 많다고(We have a lot to discuss today about the development of the new EDT digital camera) 알리는 것을 통해 (B)가 정답임을 알 수 있다.

어휘　complaint 불만　review 의견, 평가, 후기　photo shoot 사진 촬영

46. 화자는 제품의 무슨 특징을 언급하는가?
(A) 편리한 휴대성
(B) 추가적인 부대용품
(C) 조절 가능한 명암
(D) 강화된 줌 기능

해설　제품의 특징을 묻는 문제이므로 특정 기능과 관련된 정보가 제시될 것임을 예상하고 들어야 한다. 담화 중반부에 빛과 관련된 환경에 대해 더 많은 조절 기능을 제공해 주기 위해 개선된 명암 선택권을 포함할 것이라고(we're including advanced lighting options to give the user more control over light settings) 말로 특징을 설명하고 있다. 이는 조절 가능한 명암 기능을 말하는 것이므로 이와 같은 의미로 쓰인 (C)가 정답이 된다.

어휘　mention ~을 언급하다　portability 휴대 가능함　additional 추가적인　accessories 부대용품　adjustable 조절 가능한　enhanced 강화된, 증대된

47. 화자가 "배터리 수명은 한 시간 미만입니다"라고 말할 때 암시하는 것은 무엇인가?
(A) 고객들이 집에서 배터리를 충전해야 한다.
(B) 배터리가 더 오래 지속되어야 한다.
(C) 별도의 배터리가 판매될 것이다.
(D) 배터리가 진보된 기술을 이용한다.

해설　"배터리 수명이 한 시간 미만이다"는 담화 후반부에 추가 기능으로 인한(Due to these extra features) 배터리 상태를 나타내는 말로 언급되어 있다. 그 다음에 디자인 팀이 이 문제에 초점을 맞출 것이라고 하는 것으로 보아 배터리 수명이 더 늘어나야 한다는 것을 강조하는 말에 해당되므로 (B)가 정답임을 알 수 있다.

어휘　charge ~을 충전하다　last 지속되다　longer 더 오래　extra 별도의, 추가의

Questions 48-50 refer to the following radio broadcast and map.

> You're tuned in to *Radio Santosa*, and I'm your host, Jimmy Munez. This weekend, **48** we're all excited about the opening of the brand new Montoya Department Store in downtown Edenburg. To celebrate its first day in business, there will be lots of special discounts at the store, as well as some live music performances. If you're planning to drive to Edenburg from out of town, remember that **49** the highway between Gosford and Arlington is currently closed for repairs. Now, **50** for a chance to win a $50 discount voucher for the store, call us now at 555-3876.

여러분께서는 라디오 산토사를 청취하고 계시며, 저는 진행자인 지미 뮤네즈입니다. 이번 주말에, 에덴버그 시내에 완전히 새로운 몬토야 백화점이 개장하는 것에 대해 우리 모두가 들떠 있습니다. 이 백화점의 영업 첫날을 기념하기 위해, 라이브 음악 공연뿐만 아니라 매장에서 제공하는 많은 특별 할인 서비스가 있을 것입니다. 도시 외부 지역으로부터 에덴버그까지 차량을 운전해 가실 계획이신 경우, 고스포드와 알링턴 사이에 있는 고속도로가 현재 수리 작업으로 인해 폐쇄되어 있다는 점을 기억해 두시기 바랍니다. 자, 해당 매장에서 사용할 수 있는 50달러 상당의 할인 쿠폰을 받으실 수 있는 기회를 얻으려면, 지금 저희에게 555-3876으로 전화 주시기 바랍니다.

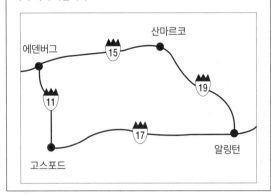

어휘   **be tuned in to** ~을 청취하다, ~에 채널을 맞추다
host (방송 등의) 진행자 **brand new** 완전히 새로운
celebrate ~을 기념하다, 축하하다 **in business** 영업 중인 **as well as** ~뿐만 아니라 **performance** 공연, 연주
plan to do ~할 계획이다 **drive to** ~로 차를 몰고 가다
from out of ~의 바깥으로부터 **remember that** ~임을 기억하다 **between A and B** A와 B사이에 **currently** 현재 **closed** 폐쇄된, 문을 닫은 **repair** 수리 **win** (상, 상품 등) ~을 받다, 타다 **voucher** 쿠폰, 상품권

48. 방송 보도는 주로 무엇에 관한 것인가?
(A) 기금 마련 행사
(B) 도시의 설립 기념 행사
(C) 매장의 개장식
(D) 다가오는 음악 축제

해설   화자는 간단히 자신을 소개한 후에 Edenburg 시내에 새로 개장하는 Montoya Department Store를 언급하면서 이와 관련된 행사 정보를 말하고 있다(~ the opening of the brand new Montoya Department Store in downtown Edenburg). 따라서 매장의 개장식을 의미하는 (C)가 정답이다.

어휘 **fundraising** 기금 마련 **founding** 설립, 창립
celebration 기념 행사, 축하 행사 **upcoming** 다가오는, 곧 있을

49. 시각자료를 보시오. 어느 고속도로가 수리 중인가?
(A) 11번 고속도로
(B) 15번 고속도로
(C) 17번 고속도로
(D) 19번 고속도로

해설   수리 중인 고속도로를 묻고 있으므로 수리 작업과 관련된 정보가 있다는 점을 예상하고 들어야 하며, 지도가 제시되어 있으므로 위치 표현에 주의해 들어야 한다. 화자는 담화 후반부에 Gosford와 Arlington 사이에 있는 고속도로가 현재 수리 작업으로 인해 폐쇄되어 있다고(the highway between Gosford and Arlington is currently closed for repairs) 알리고 있다. 시각자료에서 Gosford와 Arlington 사이에 위치한 도로 번호는 17이므로 (C)가 정답이다.

50. 청자들은 왜 라디오 방송국으로 전화하도록 권해지는가?
(A) 경품 행사에 참가하기 위해
(B) 길 안내 정보를 얻기 위해
(C) 초대 손님과 이야기하기 위해
(D) 행사에 등록하기 위해

해설   청자들이 방송국으로 전화해야 하는 이유를 묻고 있으므로 담화 중에 전화를 걸도록 권하는 부분이 있음을 예상하고 들어야 한다. 담화 마지막 부분에 50달러 상당의 할인 쿠폰을 받을 수 있는 기회를 얻으려면 지금 전화하라고 알리고 있는데(for a chance to win a $50 discount voucher for the store, call us now at 555-3876) 이는 경품 행사에 참가하는 것을 뜻하므로 (A)가 정답이다.

어휘 **enter** ~에 참가하다, 가입하다 **contest** 경품 행사, 경연대회 **directions** 길 안내 (정보) **register for** ~에 등록하다

DAY 03 RC Half Test

1. (D)	**2.** (A)	**3.** (A)	**4.** (D)	**5.** (C)
6. (D)	**7.** (D)	**8.** (A)	**9.** (D)	**10.** (B)
11. (B)	**12.** (A)	**13.** (C)	**14.** (A)	**15.** (C)
16. (C)	**17.** (C)	**18.** (B)	**19.** (B)	**20.** (A)
21. (D)	**22.** (D)	**23.** (C)	**24.** (B)	**25.** (C)
26. (D)	**27.** (D)	**28.** (C)	**29.** (C)	**30.** (B)
31. (C)	**32.** (B)	**33.** (D)	**34.** (C)	**35.** (D)
36. (C)	**37.** (D)	**38.** (B)	**39.** (D)	**40.** (A)
41. (A)	**42.** (D)	**43.** (D)	**44.** (A)	**45.** (C)
46. (D)	**47.** (D)	**48.** (D)	**49.** (C)	**50.** (B)

Part 5

1.
정답 (D)

해석 노리스 씨는 제안된 확장 전략의 잠재적 혜택을 평가한 후에 이를 시행하는 것을 고려할 것이다.

해설 빈칸 앞에 동명사가 있고, 빈칸 뒤에 명사구가 있으므로 빈칸에는 동명사의 목적어 역할을 하는 명사구를 수식할 소유격 대명사가 와야 한다. 따라서 (D) its가 정답이다.

어휘 consider -ing ~하는 것을 고려하다 implement v. ~을 시행하다, 실시하다 proposed 제안된 expansion 확장, 확대 strategy 전략 evaluate ~을 평가하다 benefit 혜택

2.
정답 (A)

해석 비트버그 제조사의 소유주들은 신임 공장 관리 책임자를 고용함으로써 운영비를 줄일 생각이다.

해설 빈칸 앞에는 주어가, 빈칸 뒤에는 to부정사구와 전치사구만 있으므로 빈칸은 문장의 동사 자리이다. 따라서 (A) intend가 정답이다.

어휘 operating costs 운영비 supervisor 책임자, 상사, 감독 intend to do ~할 생각이다, ~할 작정이다 intentional 의도적인, 고의적인 intentionally 의도적으로, 고의로

3.
정답 (A)

해석 강물 오염의 원인을 조사하던 조사원들이 가능성 있는 세 가지 근원을 밝혀냈다.

해설 빈칸이 정관사와 분사 사이에 위치해 있으므로 빈칸은 분사의 수식을 받을 명사 자리이다. 선택지 중 명사는 (A) researchers 와 (D) research인데, 조사하는 행위의 주체를 나타낼 사람 명사가 필요한 자리이므로 '조사원' 등을 뜻하는 명사 (A) researchers가 정답이다.

어휘 investigate ~을 조사하다 pollution 오염 identify ~을 밝혀내다, ~을 결정하다 source 근원, 원천

4.
정답 (D)

해석 부서 내부에서 승진된 직원들은 컴퓨터 활용 능력 시험에서 면제된다.

해설 빈칸 앞에 위치한 전치사 from과 함께 '부서 내부에서'라는 의미를 구성할 수 있는 또 다른 전치사가 와야 하므로 (D) within 이 정답이다.

어휘 promote ~을 승진시키다 be exempt from ~에서 면제되다

5.
정답 (C)

해석 알펜 스키 리조트의 팔콘 런은 믿을 수 없을 정도로 가파르고 위험하며, 이로 인해 미숙한 스키어들에게 부적합하다.

해설 빈칸 앞에 주어와 동사가 포함된 절이 있고, 문장에 접속사가 없으므로 빈칸에는 동사가 올 수 없다. 따라서 분사가 들어가 빈칸 이하 부분이 분사구문의 구조가 되어야 알맞으며, 빈칸 뒤에 목적어 it이 쓰여 있어 목적어를 취할 수 있는 현재분사가 필요하므로 (C) making이 정답이다.

어휘 incredibly 믿을 수 없을 정도로 steep 가파른 unsuitable 적합하지 않은, 알맞지 않은 inexperienced 미숙한, 경험이 부족한

6.
정답 (D)

해석 이 소프트웨어가 없다면, 저희 데이터베이스의 보안 상태를 보장할 수 없으며, 귀하께서 제공하시는 정보가 차단되지 않을 것이라 보장할 수도 없습니다.

해설 선택지가 모두 등위접속사로 구성되어 있는데, 빈칸 뒤에 조동사와 주어가 도치된 구조가 제시되어 있으므로 부정어 (D) nor 가 정답이다.

어휘 guarantee ~을 보장하다 security 보안 supply ~을 제공하다 intercept ~을 차단하다, 가로채다

7.
정답 (D)

해석 모든 농장 근로자들은 어떤 장비든 작동하기 전에 작업장 안전에 대한 영상을 시청해야 한다.

해설 빈칸 앞에 있는 단수 가산명사 workplace는 부정관사 a가 필요하므로 전치사 on의 목적어가 될 수 없다. 따라서 workplace와 함께 복합명사를 이룰 불가산명사 (D) safety가 정답이다.

어휘 agricultural 농업의 be required to do ~해야 한다 workplace 작업장, 일터 operate ~을 작동하다

8.
정답 (A)

해석 가능한 한 최고의 맛을 이뤄내기 위해, 반드시 한시도 방심하지 말고 소스의 온도를 관찰하셔야 합니다.

해설 빈칸이 조동사와 동사 사이에 위치해 있으므로 빈칸은 동사를 수식할 부사 자리이다. 따라서 (A) vigilantly가 정답이다.

어휘 the best A possible 가능한 한 최고의 A vigilantly 한시도 방심하지 않고, 경계하여 vigilant 조금도 방심하지 않는, 경계하는 vigilance 경계, 감시 vigil 밤샘, 철야

9.
정답 (D)

해석 포브스 씨는 어느 곳이 연회에 가장 적합한지 결정하기 위해 여러 잠재적인 행사장을 방문했다.

해설 빈칸 앞에는 완전한 구성의 절이 있고, to부정사 to decide 뒤에 주어 없이 동사로 시작되는 불완전한 절이 쓰여 있으므로 빈칸에는 불완전한 절을 이끌면서 접속사의 역할을 할 수 있는 것이 필요하다. 따라서 관계대명사 (D) which가 정답이다.

어휘 venue 행사장, 개최 장소 suitable 적합한, 알맞은

10.
정답 (B)

해석 새로운 평상복 정책에 따르면 직원들이 더 편안하게 옷을 착용할 때 더 생산적인 것으로 나타났다.

해설 빈칸 뒤에 that이 이끄는 절이 있어 이 절을 목적어로 취할 수 있는 동사의 과거분사가 빈칸에 필요하다. 따라서 동사 show의 과거분사인 (B) shown이 정답이다.

어휘 casual clothing 평상복 productive 생산적인 dressed 옷을 입은 designate ~을 지정하다, ~을 지명하다

11.
정답 (B)

해석 시리우스 일렉트로닉스는 회사의 국제적인 브랜드 인지도를 드높이기 위해 마케팅 전문가를 고용할 계획을 세우고 있다.

해설 빈칸에 쓰일 동사는 to부정사를 구성해 마케팅 전문가를 고용하려는 목적으로서 회사의 브랜드 인지도와 관련된 변화를 나타내야 하므로 '~을 드높이다' 등을 의미하는 (B) boost가 정답이다.

어휘 recognition 인지(도), 인식, 인정 refer ~을 참고하다, ~을 조회하다, ~을 소개하다, ~을 맡기다 boost ~을 드높이다, ~을 촉진하다 endorse (유명인이) ~을 광고하다 assimilate ~을 동화시키다, ~을 받아들이다

12.
정답 (A)

해석 아노트 씨와 빌라 씨는 자신들의 발표가 순조롭게 진행되도록 오전 내내 자신들의 발표 내용을 계속 연습하고 있다.

해설 빈칸 앞뒤에 주어와 동사가 포함된 절이 쓰여 있으므로 빈칸은 접속사 자리이다. 또한, '발표가 순조롭게 진행되도록 계속 연습하고 있다'와 같은 의미가 구성되어야 자연스러우므로 '~하도록'이라는 뜻으로 목적을 나타낼 때 사용하는 (A) so that이 정답이다.

어휘 go smoothly 순조롭게 진행되다 so that (목적) ~하도록, (결과) 그래서, 그러므로 provided that ~한다면 as well as ~뿐만 아니라 …도, ~만큼 잘

13.
정답 (C)

해석 빌리지 호텔은 모든 객실에서 무료 욕실 제품, 커피, 그리고 미네랄 워터를 제공한다.

해설 동사 provides와 'A, B, and C'의 구조로 나열된 명사들 사이에 위치한 빈칸은 이 명사들을 앞에서 수식할 형용사가 필요한 자리이므로 (C) complimentary가 정답이다.

어휘 compliment v. ~을 칭찬하다 n. 칭찬 complimentary 무료의

14.
정답 (A)

해석 그 재무 컨설턴트는 우리에게 출장 지출 비용으로 할당된 예산을 낮추도록 권했다.

해설 동사 recommended의 목적어 역할을 하는 that절의 주어 뒤에 위치한 빈칸은 that절의 동사 자리이다. recommend와 같이 권고, 제안, 명령, 요구 등을 나타내는 동사의 목적어 역할을 하는 that절의 동사는 동사원형을 사용하므로 (A) lower가 정답이다.

어휘 allocate ~을 할당하다, ~을 배정하다 expense 지출 (비용), 경비

15.
정답 (C)

해석 새 운동기구들이 설치되는 동안 모든 회원들을 대상으로 피트니스 센터가 문을 닫을 것이다.

해설 빈칸 앞뒤로 주어와 동사를 포함한 절이 위치해 있으므로 빈칸은 접속사 자리이다. 기기를 설치하는 기간 동안 문을 닫는다는 의미가 되어야 자연스러우므로 '~하는 동안'이라는 의미로 쓰이는 (C) while이 정답이다.

어휘 **while** ~하는 동안 **install** ~을 설치하다

16.

정답 (C)

해석 오후의 소나기에도 불구하고, 홀든 공원에서 열린 자선 기금 마련 행사는 그래도 1만 달러가 넘는 금액을 모금했다.

해설 빈칸과 콤마 사이에 명사구만 위치해 있으므로 빈칸은 전치사 자리이다. 따라서 선택지 중 유일한 전치사인 (C) Notwithstanding이 정답이다.

어휘 **notwithstanding** ~에도 불구하고 **rain shower** 소나기 **charity** 자선 (활동) **fundraiser** 기금 마련 행사, 모금 행사 **raise** (자금 등) ~을 모금하다 **on the other hand** 다른 한편으로는, 반면에 **as a matter of fact** 사실, 실은 **eventually** 마침내, 결국

Part 6

17-20.

메리웨더 주식회사 전 직원에게 알립니다.

우리가 지연 배송에 대한 고객 환불과 관련된 정책을 변경했다는 점에 유의하시기 바랍니다. 오늘부터, 환불 금액은 오직 최소 7일 늦은 주문품에 대해서만 **17** 지급될 것입니다. 과거에는, 주문품이 4일 늦을 때마다 고객들께 환불해 드렸습니다. 이러한 변화는 우리가 거래하는 택배 서비스 회사의 문제들로 인해, 그리고 다가오는 바쁜 크리스마스 쇼핑 시즌으로 인해서도 **18** 필수적인 것으로 여겨집니다.

유감스럽게도, 이는 고객 **19** 불만 사항의 수가 증가하는 결과를 낳을 수 있습니다. 며칠 늦는 배송 물품에 대해 환불을 요구하는 화가 난 고객들에게 대처하실 때 이해심을 발휘해 주시기 바랍니다. 사과의 말씀을 드리고 왜 환불 자격이 되지 않는지 설명해 드리시기 바랍니다. **20** 여러분께서는 모두 이러한 상황을 처리하는 방법을 교육 받으셨습니다. 여러분의 양해와 노고에 감사 드립니다.

어휘 **note that** ~라는 점에 유의하다, ~임에 주목하다 **regarding** ~와 관련해 **at least** 최소한, 적어도 **previously** 과거에, 이전에 **whenever** ~할 때마다 **be deemed A** A한 것으로 여겨지다 **courier** 택배 회사 **upcoming** 다가오는, 곧 있을 **result in** ~라는 결과를 낳다, ~을 초래하다 **understanding** 이해심이 있는, 이해하는 **deal with** ~에 대처하다, ~을 다루다 **demand** ~을 요구하다 **be eligible for** ~에 대한 자격이 있다 **appreciate** ~에 대해 감사하다

17.

정답 (C)

해설 빈칸에 쓰일 어휘는 '환불(액)'을 뜻하는 주어 refunds와 관련

해 할 수 있는 행위에 해당되는 의미를 나타내야 하므로 '~을 지급하다' 등을 뜻하는 issue의 과거분사인 (C) issued가 정답이다.

어휘 **issue** v. ~을 지급하다, ~을 발급하다 **stock** v. ~을 재고로 갖추다, ~을 채워 넣다

18.

정답 (B)

해설 빈칸 앞에 수동태로 쓰여 있는 동사 be deemed는 형용사 또는 명사와 결합해 '~한 것으로 여겨지다'라는 의미를 나타낸다. 또한, 주어가 가리키는 변화의 특성과 관련된 의미가 구성되어야 자연스러우므로 형용사인 (B) necessary가 정답이다.

어휘 **necessarily** 필수적으로, 반드시 **necessity** 필요(성), 필수품 **necessitate** ~을 필요하게 만들다

19.

정답 (B)

해설 빈칸에 쓰일 명사는 바로 앞에 위치한 customer와 복합명사를 구성해 증가할 수 있는 것을 나타내야 한다. 빈칸 뒤에 위치한 문장에 화가 난 고객들에 대한 대처 방법이 언급되는 것으로 볼 때 고객 불만의 증가 가능성을 말하는 문장이 되어야 자연스러우므로 '불만, 불평'을 뜻하는 (B) complaints가 정답이다.

20.

정답 (A)

해석 (A) 여러분께서는 모두 이러한 상황을 처리하는 방법을 교육 받으셨습니다.
(B) 새로운 정책은 다음 달 초부터 시행될 것입니다.
(C) 귀하의 환불은 영업일로 5일 내에 처리될 것입니다.
(D) 고객들께서는 저희 웹 사이트를 방문하시면 해당 제공 서비스를 이용하실 수 있습니다.

해설 빈칸 앞에 자격이 되지 않는 고객들의 환불 요청에 대처하는 방법이 쓰여 있으므로 그러한 상황을 such situations로 지칭해 직원들이 대처 방법에 관해 이미 교육을 받았다는 말로 어떻게 대처해야 하는지 잘 알고 있을 것이라는 의미를 담은 (A)가 정답이다.

어휘 **handle** ~을 처리하다, ~을 다루다 **take effect** 시행되다, 발효되다 **process** v. ~을 처리하다 **take advantage of** ~을 이용하다

21-24.

수신: 테리 리차드슨 <trichardson@mymail.net>
발신: 벨루가 호텔 <customerservices@beluga.com>
제목: 귀하의 예약
날짜: 7월 2일

리차드슨 씨께,

저희 벨루가 호텔에 예약해 주셔서 감사합니다! 귀하께서 3박의

숙박을 위해 패밀리 룸을 21 선택하신 것으로 알고 있습니다.

이 객실은 킹 사이즈 침대 하나와 싱글 침대 두 개를 포함하고 있으며, 여분의 접이식 침대를 추가하실 수 있는 선택권이 있습니다. 22 하나 필요하실 경우에 저희에게 알려 주십시오. 저희는 귀하의 숙박을 가능한 한 즐겁게 만들어 드리기 위해 대기하고 있으며, 언제나 기꺼이 도와 드리겠습니다.

체크인하실 때, 저희 프런트 데스크 직원에게 귀하의 예약 조회 번호를 보여 주시기 바랍니다. 객실에 대한 어떠한 돌발적인 손상에 대한 비용을 충당하기 위해 100달러의 보증금을 지불하시도록 요청 받으실 것입니다. 저희 정책에 따라, 귀하의 23 여권도 복사해야 할 것입니다.

귀하의 숙박을 더욱 편안하게 만들어 드리기 위해 저희가 해 드릴 수 있는 다른 어떤 것이든 있으시면 24 주저하지 마시고 저희에게 알려 주시기 바랍니다.

고객 서비스부

벨루가 호텔

어휘 **add** ~을 추가하다 **folding** 접이식의 **as A as possible** 가능한 한 A한 **pleasurable** 즐거운 **reference number** 조회 번호, 참조 번호 **be asked to do** ~하도록 요청 받다 **security deposit** 보증금 **cover** (비용 등) ~을 충당하다 **accidental** 돌발적인, 우연한 **as per** ~에 따라 **policy** 정책 **make a photocopy of** ~을 복사하다 **comfortable** 편안한

21.

정답 (D)

해설 동사 see의 목적어 역할을 하는 that절에서 주어 you와 빈칸 뒤로 명사구와 전치사구만 쓰여 있어 빈칸이 that절의 동사 자리임을 알 수 있다. 또한, 앞선 문장에 예약한 것에 대해 감사하다는 말이 쓰여 있어 빈칸 뒤에 위치한 a Family Room을 이미 선택해 예약한 것으로 볼 수 있으므로 과거에 완료된 일의 상태가 현재까지 지속되는 경우에 사용하는 현재완료시제 동사 (D) have chosen이 정답이다.

22.

정답 (D)

해석 (A) 편안한 숙박 되셨기를 바랍니다.
(B) 저희 웹 사이트를 통해 이 객실을 예약하실 수 있습니다.
(C) 그 객실은 다음과 같은 특징을 포함합니다.
(D) 하나 필요하실 경우에 저희에게 알려 주십시오.

해설 빈칸 앞 문장에 여분의 접이식 침대를 추가할 수 있는 선택권이 있다는 말이 쓰여 있으므로 an extra folding bed를 대신하는 대명사 one과 함께 하나 필요하면 알려 달라는 말로 접이식 침대의 이용 방법을 언급하는 (D)가 정답이다.

어휘 **following** 다음의, 아래의 **feature** 특징

23.

정답 (C)

해설 빈칸이 속한 문장에서 말하는 여권 복사는 앞선 문장에서 언급한 보증금 지불과 함께 체크인할 때 해야 하는 일들 중의 하나로 볼 수 있다. 따라서, 유사한 정보를 추가로 알리는 흐름임을 알 수 있으므로 '~도, 또한' 등의 의미로 추가 정보를 말할 때 사용하는 (C) as well이 정답이다.

어휘 **after all** 결국, 어쨌든 **as well** ~도, 또한

24.

정답 (B)

해설 빈칸에 쓰일 동사는 바로 뒤에 위치한 to부정사와 결합할 수 있는 자동사여야 하며, 필요한 것이 있을 경우에 호텔 측에 알리는 일과 관련해 하지 말라고 당부하는 일을 말해야 하므로 to부정사와 결합해 '~하기를 주저하다'라는 의미를 나타낼 때 사용하는 (B) hesitate이 정답이다.

어휘 **refrain (from)** (~을) 삼가다, 자제하다 **postpone** ~을 연기하다, ~을 미루다

Part 7

25-26.

수신: 엠마 삼손 (esamson@bizzmag.ca)
발신: 토니 모브레이 (tmowbray@bizzmag.ca)
제목: 농산물 직판장 기사
날짜: 3월 30일

안녕하세요, 엠마 씨,

저는 4월 4일과 5일에 열릴 26 마을 연례 농산물 직판장에 관한 기사를 쓰고 있습니다. 저는 그 행사가 토요일 오전 9시부터 일요일 오후 7시까지 운영될 것이라고 알고 있으며, 주말 동안 최소 10,000명의 사람들을 끌어들일 것이라고 예상된다는 것을 알고 있습니다. 25 하지만, 올해에 이 행사가 어디서 열리는지 아시나요? 저는 그것이 칼슨 스트리트에서 열릴 것이라고 써 두었는데, 행사 주최자들이 새로운 장소로 옮길 것이라는 소문을 들었습니다. 25 당신이 도와주시면 감사하겠습니다. 제 기사의 마감 시간은 한 시간 이후입니다.

감사합니다.

토니
26 전속기자
비즈 매거진

어휘 **take place** 열리다, 개최되다 **run** 운영되다 **attract** ~을 끌어들이다 **at least** 최소한, 적어도 **be held** 열리다, 개최되다 **rumor** 소문 **site** 장소 **appreciate** ~에 대해 감사하다 **staff writer** 전속 기자, 전속 작가

25. 모브레이 씨가 삼손 씨에게 이메일을 보낸 이유는 무엇인가?

(A) 도움을 주기 위해
(B) 초대하기 위해
(C) 도움을 요청하기 위해
(D) 행사를 홍보하기 위해

정답 (C)

해설 지문 중반부에서 토니 씨가 엠마 씨에게 행사 장소에 대한 정보를 요청하고(do you know where it is being held this year?) 있으므로 (C)가 정답이다.

어휘 provide ~을 제공하다 extend an invitation 초대하다, 초청하다 promote ~을 홍보하다

26. 농산물 직판장에 대해 암시된 것은 무엇인가?

(A) 월간 행사이다.
(B) 인기가 떨어지고 있다.
(C) 두 곳의 장소에서 열릴 것이다.
(D) 잡지에 특집으로 실릴 것이다.

정답 (D)

해설 첫 문장에서 모브레이 씨가 농산물 직판장에 대한 글을 쓰고 있다고 언급하는데(I'm writing about the town's annual farmers' market) 이메일 하단의 정보에 잡지사의 기자임이(Staff Writer, Bizz Magazine) 나타나 있으므로 (D)가 정답이다.

어휘 feature ~을 특집으로 하다

27-29.

남성들을 위한 결혼 팁: 세 번째 이야기
커크 햄스워스 작성

27 결혼 예복을 선택할 때 비용은 중요한 요소입니다. 대여한 턱시도는 새로 사는 턱시도 가격의 15~35 퍼센트 사이이며, 일반적으로 턱시도는 350달러에서 550달러 사이의 가격입니다. **27** 대부분의 사람들에게, 대여가 최고의 선택일 것이므로 이 부분에 초점을 맞춰 보겠습니다.

• **28(A)** 자신에게 맞는 예복 매장을 찾을 때까지 여러 매장을 다녀 보십시오. 그런 매장은 정기적으로 재고를 새로 들여놓고, 정확하게 여러분의 치수를 재고, 여러분에게 전문적인 턱시도 착용 서비스를 제공해주는 곳이어야 합니다.
• 매장 주인은 여러분의 말에 귀 기울이는 사람이어야 합니다. 만약 매장 주인이 당신이 관심이 없는 의상만 보여주려고 한다면, 정중하게 "아니오, 괜찮습니다"라고 말하고, 다른 매장을 찾으십시오.
• 매장은 나비넥타이, 커프스 단추, 멜빵, 신발 등 여러분이 필요한 모든 액세서리를 제공할 수 있어야 합니다. **28(B)** 반드시 이것들이 대여에 포함되도록 요청하십시오.
• 마지막으로, 모든 신랑 들러리들이 자신들의 턱시도를 여러분과 같은 매장에서 대여하도록 하셔야, 여러분들은 모두 완벽하게 잘 어울릴 것입니다. **29** 작년에 제가 이렇게 했을 때, 그 매장은 할인까지 해주었습니다. 피팅을 준비하고 **28(D)** 턱시도를 예약하는 것을 적어도 결혼식 한 달 전에 하십시오.

어휘 formalwear 정장, 예복 tuxedo 턱시도 rented 대여한 shop around 여기저기 둘러보다 stock 재고 take one's measurements ~의 치수를 재다 insist on ~을 고집하다, 요구하다 garment 의상 supply A with B A에게 B를 제공하다, 공급하다 bow tie 나비넥타이 cufflinks 커프스 단추 suspenders 멜빵 groomsman 신랑 들러리

27. 정보는 어떤 상황을 목적으로 할 것 같은가?

(A) 옷 수선하기
(B) 행사 장소 선택하기
(C) 차량 임대하기
(D) 의상 대여하기

정답 (D)

해설 첫 번째 단락에서 예복을 언급하며 대부분의 사람들에게 대여는 최고의 선택이라고(renting will be the best option) 말하고 있으므로 (D)가 정답이다.

어휘 be intended for ~를 위한 것이다 venue 장소 suit 정장, 옷

28. 햄스워스 씨가 추천하지 않은 것은 무엇인가?

(A) 여러 장소를 확인할 것
(B) 다양한 액세서리를 요청할 것
(C) 자신의 신체 치수를 스스로 측정할 것
(D) 사전에 예약할 것

정답 (C)

해설 두 번째 문단 첫 번째 항목에서 맞는 예복 매장을 찾을 때까지 여러 매장을 다녀보라는(Shop around until you find the right formalwear store for you) 부분에서 (A)를, 세 번째 항목에서 액세서리들이 대여에 포함되는지 확실히 하라는(Make sure that you ask for these to be included in the rental) 부분에서 (B)를, 예약은 최소한 결혼식 한 달 전에 해달라는(reserve their tuxedos at least one month before your wedding) 부분에서 (D)를 찾을 수 있다. 따라서 지문에 언급되지 않은 (C)가 정답이다.

어휘 give a recommendation 추천하다 check out ~을 확인하다 in advance 미리

29. 햄스워스 씨에 대해 추론할 수 있는 것은 무엇인가?

(A) 친구의 결혼식에 참석할 것이다.
(B) 예복 매장을 소유하고 있다.
(C) 작년에 결혼했다.
(D) 턱시도를 소유하고 있다.

정답 (C)

해설 마지막 단락에 작년에 이 정보의 작성자인 햄스워스 씨가 이용했을 때 매장에서 할인을 해주었다는(When I did this last year, the store even provided a discount) 부분에서 작년에 본인 결혼식을 위해 턱시도 대여 서비스를 이용했음을 알 수 있으므로 (C)가 정답이다.

어휘 get married 결혼하다 own ~을 소유하다

30-32.

노스리지 (4월 24일) - **30** 노스리지 교통국이 최근 63번 주간 고속도로 옆에 위치한 자주 혼잡해지는 주요 도로 한 곳을 확장하자는 제안을 승인했습니다. 이에 따라, 도리스 로드에 대한 공사 작업이 다음 달 초에 시작되어 초여름까지 완료될 예정입니다.

직접적으로 도리스 로드의 교통량이 주는 공포를 경험해 온 많은 시민들과 사람들은 해당 도로 공사에 대해 수 개월 동안 시민들이 탄원서를 낸 끝에 교통국이 마침내 제안을 승인했다는 사실에 분명 기뻐하고 있습니다.

"우리의 노력이 마침내 결실을 맺었다는 사실을 알게 되어 좋습니다,"라고 우체국 직원인 제임스 리 씨는 말했습니다. "우리는 그 모든 교통량 때문에 정말로 고통 받아 오고 있었습니다. 제 말은, 항상 끔찍한 것은 아니지만, 보통 차로 10분이 걸리는 거리가 1시간 넘게 걸릴 때 그렇습니다." 시내 버스 기사인 프랜시스 비건 씨는 다음과 같이 밝혔습니다. "자동차를 소유하고 있는 모든 사람이 그 도로를 이용하지 말아야 한다는 사실을 알고 있지만, 우리가 뭘 할 수 있을지도 모르지만, 도시로 향하는 다른 모든 도로들도 그만큼 좋지 않습니다. 그리고 **31** 시내 버스 정류장이 도리스 로드에 위치해 있기 때문에, 심지어 저는 피할 수도 없습니다. 저는 그저 그 공사가 교통량을 더 좋게 만들어주기를 바라고 있습니다."

비록 공사 작업이 그 구역에 훨씬 더 심한 교통량을 야기할 수도 있지만, 프리먼 시장은 운전자들에게 그 작업이 교통량이 훨씬 더 적은 늦은 밤 시간에 주로 이뤄질 것이라고 확언하고 있습니다. 또한 **32** 운전자들에게 도리스 로드의 교통 혼잡을 완화할 수 있게 여러 다른 도로를 이용하도록 권하고 있습니다.

어휘 approve ~을 승인하다 widen ~을 확장하다, 넓히다 frequently 자주, 빈번히 congested 혼잡한 as such 그에 따라, 그러므로 be scheduled to do ~할 예정이다 first-hand 직접적으로 petition v. 탄원하다 pay off 결실을 맺다 all the time 항상 avoid ~을 피하다 cause ~을 야기하다, 초래하다 assure A that A에게 ~라고 확언하다, 장담하다 alleviate ~을 완화하다

30. 기사의 목적은 무엇인가?
(A) 한 도로에 대한 주민들의 의견을 여론 조사하는 것
(B) 한 도로를 개선하려는 계획을 설명하는 것
(C) 운전자들에게 사고가 나기 쉬운 도로에서 서행하도록 말하는 것
(D) 도로 교통량에 대한 이유를 설명하는 것

정답 (B)

해설 첫 단락에 노스리지 교통국이 최근 자주 혼잡해지는 주요 도로 한 곳을 확장하자는 제안을 승인한(The Northridge Department of Transportation recently approved a proposal to widen a frequently congested major road) 사실을 언급하면서, 그 도로 확장과 관련된 정보를 전하는 것으로 내용이 전개되고 있다. 이는 도로를 개선하는 일에 해

당되므로 (B)가 정답이다.

어휘 take a poll 여론 조사하다 make improvements 개선하다, 향상시키다 accident-prone 사고가 나기 쉬운

31. 기사에 따르면, 도리스 로드에 무엇이 위치해 있는가?
(A) 건설회사
(B) 교통 관리실
(C) 버스 정류장
(D) 우체국

정답 (C)

해설 세 번째 단락 후반부에 시내 버스 정류장이 도리스 로드에 위치해 있다는(And the city bus station is located on Dorris) 사실이 쓰여 있으므로 (C)가 정답이다.

32. 프리먼 시장은 사람들에게 무엇을 하도록 권하는가?
(A) 대중 교통을 이용하는 일
(B) 다른 경로를 이용하는 일
(C) 더 천천히 운전하는 일
(D) 가급적 집에 머물러 있는 일

정답 (B)

해설 마지막 단락에서 시장이 운전자들에게 도리스 로드의 교통 혼잡을 완화할 수 있게 여러 다른 도로를 이용하도록 권하고 있다는(He also advises drivers to take other roads to alleviate the traffic congestion on Dorris Road) 내용이 쓰여 있으므로 (B)가 정답이다.

어휘 public transportation 대중 교통 route 경로, 노선 when possible 가급적, 가능한 한

33-36.

[젠슨, 데이빗]: (오후 2:15)
안녕하세요, 리 씨. 제가 오늘 아침에 우리 주주들과 만났는데, **33** 이분들께서 우리가 제품을 위해 디자인한 상자와 포장지들에 대해 부정적으로 반응하셨어요.

[필딩, 리]: (오후 2:17)
어째서요? 마케팅팀에서 그 디자인들에 대해 아주 열심히 작업했는데요.

[젠슨, 데이빗]: (오후 2:18)
34 그 제품 포장이 슈퍼마켓 선반에서 우리 제품을 돋보이게 하는 데 도움이 되지 않을 거라고 생각하고 계세요.

[필딩, 리]: (오후 2:19)
잠시만요, 제가 마케팅팀의 페넬로페 씨를 추가할게요...

(페넬로페 레예스 님이 대화창에 초대되었습니다)

[젠슨, 데이빗]: (오후 2:21)
안녕하세요, 페넬로페 씨. 우리 주주들께서 상자 및 포장지 디자인을 마음에 들어 하지 않으셔서 몇 가지 수정을 요청하셨습니다.

[레예스, 페넬로페]: (오후 2:23)
35 저희 팀이 초과 근무를 하면서 그 디자인들을 만들었습니다. 솔직히, 저는 어떤 것도 변경되어야 한다는 생각은 들지 않아요.

[필딩, 리]: (오후 2:25)
저도 그렇습니다. 그래서, 36 우리 세 사람이 한 자리에 모여서 합의에 이르도록 해야 합니다.

[레예스, 페넬로페]: (오후 2:26)
저는 좋아요. 36 이 문제를 해결해 보도록 하죠.

[젠슨, 데이빗]: (오후 2:27)
아주 좋은 생각입니다. 36 제가 오늘 오후로 회의실들 중 하나를 예약할게요.

어휘 shareholder 주주 respond to ~에 반응하다, ~에 대응하다 wrapper 포장지 How come? 어째서요?, 왜요? stand out 돋보이다, 눈에 띄다 modification 수정, 변경 work overtime 초과 근무하다 to be honest 솔직히 (말하면) I hear you (동의의 의미로) 저도요, 제 말이요 get together 모이다 reach ~에 이르다, ~에 도달하다 compromise 합의, 타협, 절충 figure A out A를 해결하다, A를 파악하다, A를 알아보다

33. 채팅은 주로 무엇을 말하고 있는가?
(A) 일부 신제품의 출시
(B) 온라인 광고에 대한 변경
(C) 고객 만족도의 하락
(D) 일부 포장지의 디자인

정답 (D)

해설 젠슨 씨가 첫 번째 메시지에서 주주들을 만난 사실과 함께 제품을 위해 디자인한 상자와 포장지에 대해 주주들이 부정적인 반응을 보였다고(they responded negatively to the boxes and wrappers we designed for our products) 알린 뒤로 그 디자인과 관련해 이야기하고 있으므로 (D)가 정답이다.

어휘 launch 출시, 공개, 시작 decline in ~의 하락, 감소 satisfaction 만족(도)

34. 주주들이 어떤 문제를 언급했는가?
(A) 고객들이 더 단순한 디자인을 선호할 것이다.
(B) 소재가 너무 많은 비용이 들 수도 있다.
(C) 제품이 눈에 띄지 못할 수도 있다.
(D) 회사들이 더 경쟁적인 상태가 되어가고 있다.

정답 (C)

해설 2시 18분에 젠슨 씨가 작성한 메시지에 주주들을 They로 지칭해 제품 포장이 슈퍼마켓 선반에서 제품을 돋보이게 하는 데 도움이 되지 않을 거라는(They feel that the packaging won't help our products to stand out) 생각을 밝히고 있다. 이는 제품이 눈에 띄지 않는 문제를 말하는 것이므로 (C)가 정답이다.

어휘 material 소재, 재료, 물품 cost ~의 비용이 들다

noticeable 눈에 띄는, 주목할 만한, 두드러진 competitive 경쟁적인

35. 오후 2시 25분에, 필딩 씨가 "I hear you"라고 쓸 때 무엇을 암시하는가?
(A) 레예스 씨와 직접 만나서 이야기하고 싶어 한다.
(B) 일부 계획과 관련해 더 일찍 통보 받았다.
(C) 제안 사항을 완전히 이해하지 못하고 있다.
(D) 레예스 씨가 실망한 것을 이해하고 있다.

정답 (D)

해설 2시 23분 메시지에 레예스 씨가 팀에서 초과 근무를 하면서까지 디자인들을 만든 사실과 어떤 것도 변경되어야 한다는 생각이 들지 않는다고(I don't think anything should be changed) 밝히자, 필딩 씨가 '저도요, 제 말이요' 등의 의미로 동의를 나타내는 흐름이다. 힘들게 만든 디자인이 주주들을 만족시키지 못한 것에 대해 레예스 씨가 아무것도 변경할 필요가 없다는 말로 실망감을 나타내는 것에 대해 공감하는 말에 해당되므로 (D)가 정답이다.

어휘 in person 직접 (만나서) inform ~에게 알리다 fully 완전히, 전적으로, 최대로

36. 메시지 작성자들이 오늘 이후에 무엇을 할 것인가?
(A) 주주들과 만나는 일
(B) 일부 신제품을 발표하는 일
(C) 문제를 해결하려 하는 일
(D) 근무 일정을 변경하는 일

정답 (C)

해설 필딩 씨가 2시 25분 메시지에 함께 모여 합의에 이르도록 해 보자고(the three of us should get together and try to reach a compromise) 제안한 뒤로, 레예스 씨와 젠슨 씨가 각각 해당 문제를 해결하자는(Let's try to figure this out) 말과 오늘 오후로 회의실을 하나 예약하겠다는(I'll book one of the conference rooms for this afternoon) 말을 하고 있다. 이는 오후에 문제 해결 방법을 찾겠다는 뜻이므로 (C)가 정답이다.

어휘 present ~을 발표하다, ~을 제시하다 solve ~을 해결하다 make a change to ~을 변경하다

37-40.

수신: 맥스 코웰 <maxcowell@cjinc.com>
발신: 올리비아 크로우 <ocrowe@cjinc.com>
제목: 마크 켄달과 티나 윈슬로우
날짜: 12월 20일

39 코웰 씨께,

지난주에 있었던 경영진 회의 시간에 40 각 부서장이 올해 어느 직원들이 상을 받을 만한 가장 뛰어난 자격을 지니고 있는지 고려해 봐야 한다고 언급하셨습니다. ─ [1] ─.

40 제 첫 번째 선택은 마크 켄달 씨입니다. — [2] —. 이분은 **38(D)** 3년 전에 졸업하신 직후에 우리 회사에 고용되었으며, 저희 마케팅팀의 소중한 일원이 되었습니다. 올해, 이분은 저희가 전국에 걸쳐 실시해 믿을 수 없을 정도로 성공적이었던 시장 조사 연구를 책임지셨습니다. — [3] —. **37** 이분은 이곳 우리 회사에서 결국 팀장이 되겠다는 바람을 공개적으로 밝히신 바 있습니다. 저는 또한 티나 윈슬로우 씨도 후보로 지명하겠습니다. 이분은 현재 **38(D)** 거의 5년 동안 저희와 함께 해 왔으며, **38(C)** 6명의 온라인 마케팅 담당자들로 구성된 팀을 이끌고 있습니다. — [4] —. **38(A)** 이분의 홍보 캠페인과 광고 전략들은 지난 12개월 동안에 걸친 전체적인 수익의 상당한 증가에 대한 직접적인 원인이었습니다.

39 12월 29일에 있을 연말 연회에서 두 직원을 모두 무대로 호명하셔서 시상하시면 분명 크게 기뻐할 것입니다.

안녕히 계십시오.

올리비아

어휘 **mention that** ~라고 언급하다 **management** 경영(진), 운영(진) **department manager** 부서장 **deserving of** ~을 받을 만한 (자격이 있는) **valued** 소중한, 귀중한 **be responsible for** (사람) ~을 책임지다, (사물) ~에 대한 원인이다 **incredibly** 믿을 수 없을 정도로 **carry out** ~을 실시하다, ~을 수행하다 **speak openly of** ~을 공개적으로 밝히다 **desire to do** ~하고자 하는 바람 **eventually** 결국, 끝내 **nominate** ~을 후보로 지명하다 **significant** 상당한, 많은 **overall** 전반적인 **earnings** 수익, 소득 **overjoyed** 크게 기뻐하는 **year-end** 연말의

37. 크로우 씨가 켄달 씨와 관련해 암시하는 것은 무엇인가?
(A) 여러 회사에서 근무한 적이 있다.
(B) 온라인 마케팅에 대한 자격이 있다.
(C) 자신의 일에 대해 상을 받은 적이 있다.
(D) 성공하고자 하는 당찬 포부를 지니고 있다.

정답 (D)

해설 두 번째 단락 중반부에 켄달 씨가 회사에서 팀장이 되겠다는 바람을 공개적으로 밝힌 적이 있다고(He has spoken openly of his desire to eventually become a team leader here at our firm) 알리는 말이 쓰여 있다. 이를 통해 켄달 씨가 성공에 대한 욕심이 있다는 것을 알 수 있으므로 (D)가 정답이다.

어휘 **qualification** 자격 (요건) **win an award** 상을 받다 **ambition** 포부, 야망

38. 윈슬로우 씨와 관련해 언급되지 않은 것은 무엇인가?
(A) 더욱 수익성이 좋아지도록 회사에 도움을 주었다.
(B) 지난 1년 동안 승진된 적이 있다.
(C) 다른 직원들을 관리하는 책임을 맡고 있다.
(D) 켄달 씨보다 더 오래 회사에서 근무해 왔다.

정답 (B)

해설 두 번째 단락에 마크 켄달 씨가 3년 전에 졸업 직후 회사에 고용됐다는(He was hired by our company right after his graduation 3 years ago)부분과 티나 슬로우 씨가 5년 동안 함께 해왔다는(She has been with us for almost 5 years now) 부분에서 (D)를, 6명의 마케팅 담당자들로 구성된 팀을 이끌고 있다는(she leads a team of six online marketers) 부분에서 (C)를, 그리고 윈슬로우 씨의 홍보 캠페인과 광고 전략들이 전체적인 수익 증가의 원인이었다고(Her promotional campaigns and advertising strategies have been directly responsible for our significant increase in overall earnings) 언급하는 부분에서 (A)를 확인할 수 있다. 하지만 승진과 관련된 정보는 제시되어 있지 않으므로 (B)가 정답이다.

어휘 **profitable** 수익성이 있는 **promotion** 승진, 홍보, 판촉

39. 12월 29일에 누가 시상할 것 같은가?
(A) 올리비아 크로우 씨
(B) 마크 켄달 씨
(C) 티나 윈슬로우 씨
(D) 맥스 코웰 씨

정답 (D)

해설 마지막 단락에 이 이메일의 수신인인 코웰 씨를 you로 지칭해 직원들을 무대로 호명해 시상한다고(when you call them up to the stage and give them their awards) 알리는 말이 쓰여 있으므로 (D)가 정답이다.

40. [1], [2], [3], [4]로 표기된 위치들 중에서, 다음 문장이 들어가기에 가장 적절한 곳은 어디인가?

"어느 정도 생각해 본 끝에, 제 선택을 최종 확정했습니다."

(A) [1]
(B) [2]
(C) [3]
(D) [4]

정답 (A)

해설 제시된 문장은 자신의 선택과 관련해 최종 결정을 내린 사실을 알리는 의미를 담고 있다. 따라서 어느 직원이 상을 받아야 하는지 고려해 봐야 한다는 사실이 언급된 문장과 첫 번째 선택 대상인 켄달 씨를 언급하는 문장 사이에 위치한 [1]에 들어가 후보자와 관련해 최종 결정을 내렸음을 밝히면서 첫 번째 선택 대상을 말하는 흐름이 되어야 자연스러우므로 (A)가 정답이다.

어휘 **give A a thought** A에 대해 생각해 보다 **finalize** ~을 최종 결정하다

41-45.

로키 트레일스 컴퍼니
세이모어 애비뉴 7677번지, 빌링스, MN 59107

41(B) 41(C) 41(D) 저희는 휴대용 가스레인지와 프라이팬에서부터, 텐트와 침낭, 최상급 방수 재킷과 바지, 그리고 등산화에 이르기까지 모든 종류의 제품을 갖추고 있습니다. 저희는 또한 네 가지 새로운 등산용 배낭 제품 라인의 출시를 알려 드리게 되어 자랑스럽게 생각합니다.

- 페리그린: 에어로프로 통풍 시스템. HDPE 플라스틱 프레임
  크기: 25L, 28L, 30L, 32L, 36L / **색상:** 블랙/그레이, 블루/그레이, 블루/그린

- 이글: 에어로맥스 통풍 시스템. 알루미늄 프레임
  크기: 32L, 34L, 36L, 38L, 40L / **색상:** 블루/그레이, 레드/그레이, 블루/레드

- 버저드: 에어로프로 통풍 시스템. **45** 알루미늄 프레임
  크기: **45** 36L, 40L, 45L, 50L, 55L / **색상:** 블루/그린, 블루/그레이, **45** 블랙/그레이

- 팔콘: 에어로맥스 통풍 시스템. 알루미늄 프레임
  42 크기: 40L, 45L, 50L, 55L, 65L, 70L / **색상:** 블랙/그레이, 레드/그레이, 그린/블랙

상기 제품라인에 속하는 모든 배낭은 가슴 끈과 측면 주머니, 우천용 커버, 그리고 패드 처리된 허리 끈을 포함합니다. 저희 배낭 사진을 확인해 보시려면, www.rockytrailsmontana.com을 방문하시기 바랍니다.

어휘 stock (재고로) ~을 갖추다, ~을 취급하다 goods 제품, 상품 portable 휴대용의 be proud to do ~해서 자랑스럽다 ventilation 통풍, 환기 strap 끈 padded 패드 처리가 된 view ~을 보다

로키 트레일스 컴퍼니
고객 서비스부
세이모어 애비뉴 7677번지, 빌링스, MN 59107

관계자께,

제가 최근 귀사의 신제품 라인에 속한 등산용 배낭을 구입했는데, 이에 관한 제 의견을 들어 보시는 데 관심이 있으실 수도 있겠다고 생각했습니다. **43** 제가 좋지 못한 기상 조건에서 두 차례 등산하는 동안 이 배낭을 이용했고, 기가 막히게 좋은 기능을 보였습니다. **45** 36L의 크기는 여분의 장비 및 음식물에 대한 **44** 충분한 공간을 제공했습니다. **45** 경량 알루미늄 프레임은 제 등에 대단히 잘 들어맞았고, 항상 최상의 편안함을 제공해 주었습니다. 또한, 소재가 매우 튼튼한 것 같고, 특히 세련된 **45** 블랙과 그레이 색상이 마음에 듭니다. 간단히 말씀 드려서, 저는 이 배낭에 매우 만족합니다.

안녕히 계십시오.

레지나 포터

어휘 recently 최근 condition 조건, 상태 superbly 기가 막히게, 매우 뛰어나게 ample 충분한 extra 여분의, 추가의 gear 장비 lightweight 경량의 fit (크기, 모양 등이) ~에 잘 맞다 extremely 대단히, 매우 comfort 편안함 at all times 항상 particularly 특히 in short 간단히 말해서, 요컨대 be pleased with ~에 만족하다, ~에 기뻐하다

41. 어떤 종류의 상품이 광고에서 언급되지 않는가?
  (A) 캠핑용 가구
  (B) 조리 기구
  (C) 침낭
  (D) 방수 의류

정답 (A)

해설 첫 지문 첫 단락에 휴대용 가스레인지와 프라이팬에서부터, 텐트와 침낭, 최상급 방수 재킷과 바지, 그리고 등산화에 이르기까지 모든 종류의 제품을 갖추고 있다는(We stock all kinds of goods, from portable gas stoves and frying pans, to tents and sleeping bags, to the finest waterproof jackets, pants, and hiking boots) 내용에서 (B), (C), (D)를 모두 확인할 수 있다. 하지만 캠핑용 가구에 해당되는 제품은 제시되어 있지 않으므로 (A)가 정답이다.

42. 팔콘 배낭과 관련해 언급된 것은 무엇인가?
  (A) 우천용 커버를 포함하지 않는다.
  (B) 여섯 가지 다른 색상으로 구입 가능하다.
  (C) 에어로프로 통풍 시스템을 활용한다.
  (D) 다른 배낭들보다 더 큰 크기로 나온다.

정답 (D)

해설 첫 지문 하단에 팔콘 제품의 크기가 40L, 45L, 50L, 55L, 65L, 70L로(Size: 40L, 45L, 50L, 55L, 65L, 70L) 표기되어 있어 나머지 배낭 제품들보다 더 크게 나온다는 것을 알 수 있으므로 (D)가 정답이다.

어휘 available 구입 가능한, 이용 가능한 utilize ~을 활용하다

43. 편지의 주 목적은 무엇인가?
  (A) 최근의 구입 제품에 관해 불만을 제기하는 것
  (B) 한 제품에 관한 정보를 요청하는 것
  (C) 배낭을 개선할 수 있는 방법을 제안하는 것
  (D) 한 제품의 품질을 칭찬하는 것

정답 (D)

해설 두 번째 지문 초반부에 자신이 구입한 배낭 제품이 좋지 못한 기상 조건에도 아주 좋은 기능을 보였다고(I have used the bag during two hikes in poor weather conditions and it performed superbly) 언급한 뒤로 어떤 점이 좋았는지 설명하고 있으므로 (D)가 정답이다.

어휘 recent 최근의 request ~을 요청하다 suggest ~을 제안하다 improve ~을 개선하다, ~을 향상시키다 praise ~을 칭찬하다

44. 편지에서, 첫 번째 단락, 세 번째 줄의 단어 "ample"과 의미가 가장 가까운 것은 무엇인가?

    (A) 충분한
    (B) 과도한
    (C) 가변적인
    (D) 다수의

정답 (A)

해설 해당 문장에서 ample이 부정관사 없이 쓰일 경우에 공간을 뜻하는 명사 room을 수식하고 있고, 그 뒤에 추가 장비와 음식을 의미하는 말이 쓰여 있다. 따라서 ample이 배낭 공간의 넉넉함을 나타내는 형용사임을 알 수 있고, 이는 공간이 충분하다는 의미로 생각할 수 있으므로 '충분한'을 뜻하는 (A) sufficient가 정답이다.

45. 포터 씨가 어떤 종류의 배낭을 구입했을 것 같은가?

    (A) 페리그린
    (B) 이글
    (C) 버저드
    (D) 팔콘

정답 (C)

해설 두 번째 지문 중반부에서 후반부에 걸쳐 포터 씨가 구입한 제품으로 특징으로 36L의 크기와(36L size) 경량 알루미늄 프레임(lightweight aluminum frame), 그리고 블랙과 그레이 색상이(stylish black and grey colors) 언급되어 있다. 첫 번째 지문에서 이 세 가지 특징을 모두 포함하는 제품이 세 번째로 제시된 Buzzard이므로 (C)가 정답이다.

46-50.

> **고주스 코퍼레이션**
>
> 저희 고주스가 영국에서 빠르게 가장 인기 있는 스포츠/에너지 음료들 중 하나가 되어가고 있습니다. 저희는 현재 매달 슈퍼마켓과 편의점, 그리고 피트니스 센터에 수십 만 개의 제품을 판매하고 있습니다. **46 47** 저희 고주스 코퍼레이션에서 직접 대량 주문품을 구입하시면, 개당 더 낮은 가격으로 받아, 고객들께 고주스를 판매하실 때 수익 폭을 높이실 수 있습니다.
>
> 저희 고주스 음료는 운동 중에 또는 후에 마시면 물보다 훨씬 더 유익합니다. 고주스가 탈수를 예방해 줄 뿐만 아니라, 몸이 액체를 흡수하는 데 도움도 드리고 신체 에너지 수준도 높여 드립니다. 저희 베스트셀러 맛은 오렌지와 딸기 맛입니다. 현재의 맛은 키위와 레몬이며, **48** 새로운 아사이 맛이 4월 1일에 출시될 예정입니다.

어휘 **rapidly** 빠르게 **beverage** 음료 **hundreds of thousands of** 수십 만의 **unit** (제품, 기기 등의) 한 개, 한 대 **bulk** 대량의 **per** ~당, ~마다 **profit** 수익 **margin** 폭, 차이, 여지, 한도 **beneficial** 유익한, 이로운 **not only A but also B** A뿐만 아니라 B도 **prevent** ~을 예방하다, ~을 막다 **dehydration** 탈수 **absorb** ~을 흡수하다 **fluid** 액체 **flavor** 맛, 풍미 **due** ~할 예정인 **release** 출시, 발매

> ### 고주스 코퍼레이션
> ### 주문 요약
>
> **배송지:**   **청구서 수신:**
>
> 게리 셔먼   샤론 골드버그 씨
> RPM 짐 & 스포츠 센터   (회계팀장)
> 베이빌 애비뉴 212번지 짐 & 스포츠 센터

주문 번호	주문 날짜	영업 사원	발송 날짜	배송 날짜
#0927	04/23	클리포드 커티스	04/25	04/29

제품 ID	설명	수량	개당 가격	총 가격
#1057	딸기 고주스	250	$0.49	$122.50
48 #1059	**48** 아사이 고주스 플러스	100	$0.59	$59.00
#1095	키위 고주스 플러스	200	$0.69	$138.00
#1097	오렌지 고주스	600	$0.49	$294.00
			총액	$648.50

> **모든 배송은 추가로 고정 35달러의 배송 요금 대상입니다. 49** 고주스 회원 자격을 보유하고 계신 고객들께서는 무료 배송 서비스를 받으실 수 있는 자격이 있으십니다.

어휘 **summary** 요약(본) **bill** 청구서, 계산서 **account** 회계, 계좌, 계정 **sales rep** 영업 사원 **description** 설명 **quantity** 수량 **be subject to** ~의 대상이 되다, ~을 조건으로 하다 **flat** (요금 등이) 고정의, 균일한 **charge** (청구) 요금 **be eligible to do** ~할 자격이 있다

> **수신:** 게리 셔먼 <gsherman@rpm.com>
> **발신:** 샤론 골드버그 <sgoldberg@rpm.com>
> **제목:** 음료 주문
> **날짜:** 4월 29일
>
> 안녕하세요, 게리 씨,
>
> 제가 체육관에 필요한 고주스 음료를 더 주문했고 4월 29일에 정문에 도착할 것이라는 사실을 알려 드리고자 이메일 보냅니다. **49** 우리가 주문할 때마다 배송 요금을 지불해야 한다는 점이 아쉽습니다. 아마 제가 앞으로의 주문에 대해 그 요금을 없앨 **50** 방법들을 살펴봐야 할 것 같습니다. 당신 또는 다른 강사 분들 중 한 분이 주문품을 받아 배송 내역서를 재무팀에 갖다 주셨으면 합니다.
>
> 감사합니다.
>
> 샤론 골드버그
> RPM 짐 & 스포츠 센터

어휘 **It's a shame that** ~라는 점이 아쉽다, ~해서 안타깝다 **every time** 주어 + 동사 ~할 때마다 **look into** ~을 살펴보다, ~을 조사하다 **get A p.p.** A를 ~되게 하다, A를 ~해 놓다 **instructor** 강사 **invoice** 거래 내역서 **finance** 재무, 재정

46. 정보가 누구를 대상으로 하는가?

(A) 피트니스 센터 회원들

(B) 슈퍼마켓에 있는 고객들

(C) 고주스 코퍼레이션에서 일하는 직원들

(D) 음료를 판매하는 업체들

정답 (D)

해설 첫 지문 첫 단락에 개당 더 낮은 가격으로 받아 고객들에게 고 주스를 판매할 때 수익 폭을 높일 수 있다는(you can receive a lower price per unit, increasing your profit margins when you sell GoJuice to your customers) 말이 쓰여 있 다. 이는 해당 음료를 납품 받아 고객들에게 판매하는 소매업체 등을 대상으로 하는 말에 해당되므로 (D)가 정답이다.

어휘 **be intended for** ~을 대상으로 하다

47. 정보에서 고주스 코퍼레이션과 관련해 언급된 것은 무엇인가?

(A) 전 세계적으로 제품을 유통시킨다.

(B) 제품을 운동 전에 마셔야 한다.

(C) 신규 고객에게 무료 선물을 제공한다.

(D) 대량 주문에 대해 할인을 제공한다.

정답 (D)

해설 첫 지문 첫 단락에 고주스 코퍼레이션을 통해 대량으로 구입 하면 개당 더 낮은 가격으로 받을 수 있다고(By purchasing bulk orders directly from GoJuice Corporation, you can receive a lower price per unit) 언급되어 있다. 이는 대량 주문 시의 할인 혜택을 설명하는 것이므로 (D)가 정답이 다.

어휘 **distribute** ~을 유통시키다 **consume** ~을 마시다, ~을 먹다, ~을 소비하다 **complimentary** 무료의

48. 4월에 어느 제품이 출시되었는가?

(A) 제품 #1097

(B) 제품 #1057

(C) 제품 #1095

(D) 제품 #1059

정답 (D)

해설 첫 지문 마지막 문장에 새로운 아사이 맛이 4월 1일에 출시된다 고(with our new acai flavor due for release on April 1) 쓰여 있다. 이 제품과 관련해, 두 번째 지문의 도표 두 번째 줄에 해당 제품 번호가 #1059로 표기되어(#1059, Acai GoJuice Plus) 있으므로 (D)가 정답이다.

어휘 **release** ~을 출시하다, ~을 발매하다

49. 골드버그 씨와 관련해 유추할 수 있는 것은 무엇인가?

(A) 스포츠 센터의 피트니스 강사이다.

(B) 클리포드 커티스 씨와 4월 25일에 이야기했다.

(C) 고주스 회원 자격을 보유하고 있지 않다.

(D) 한 달 단위로 음료를 주문한다.

정답 (C)

해설 세 번째 지문 중반부에 주문할 때마다 배송 요금을 지불해야 한 다는 점이 아쉽다는(It's a shame that we have to pay a delivery fee every time we order) 말이 쓰여 있다. 또한, 두 번째 지문 하단에 고주스 회원은 무료로 배송 받을 자격이 있 다고(Customers holding GoJuice memberships are eligible to receive free shipping) 언급하고 있어 매번 배송 요금을 지불하는 골드버그 씨는 회원이 아니라는 것을 알 수 있 으므로 (C)가 정답이다.

어휘 **on a monthly basis** 한 달 단위로, 매달

50. 이메일에서, 첫 번째 단락, 세 번째 줄의 단어 "ways"와 의미가 가장 가까운 것은 무엇인가?

(A) 제안

(B) (접근) 방식

(C) 거리

(D) 입구

정답 (B)

해설 해당 문장에서 ways는 동사 look into의 목적어로서 살펴보는 대상에 해당된다. 또한, 앞 문장에서 언급한 배송 요금을 that으 로 지칭해 그것을 없애는 일이 언급되어 있는 것으로 볼 때, 그 렇게 할 수 있는 '방법'을 살펴봐야 한다는 의미임을 알 수 있으 므로 '(접근) 방식'을 뜻하는 (B) approaches가 정답이다.

1. (C)	**2.** (A)	**3.** (C)	**4.** (C)	**5.** (A)
6. (C)	**7.** (C)	**8.** (C)	**9.** (B)	**10.** (B)
11. (C)	**12.** (A)	**13.** (C)	**14.** (A)	**15.** (C)
16. (C)	**17.** (C)	**18.** (C)	**19.** (A)	**20.** (C)
21. (A)	**22.** (D)	**23.** (C)	**24.** (C)	**25.** (D)
26. (C)	**27.** (C)	**28.** (B)	**29.** (D)	**30.** (C)
31. (D)	**32.** (C)	**33.** (A)	**34.** (B)	**35.** (C)
36. (A)	**37.** (C)	**38.** (D)	**39.** (A)	**40.** (D)
41. (B)	**42.** (A)	**43.** (B)	**44.** (B)	**45.** (C)
46. (D)	**47.** (A)	**48.** (C)	**49.** (A)	**50.** (A)

Part 1

1.
(A) Curtains are being pulled closed.
(B) Pillows have been arranged on the bed.
(C) A patterned rug has been placed on the floor.
(D) A couch is being lifted for cleaning.

(A) 커튼이 당겨져 닫히는 중이다.
(B) 베개들이 침대 위에 정렬되어 있다.
(C) 무늬가 있는 양탄자가 바닥에 놓여 있다.
(D) 소파가 청소를 위해 들어올려지고 있다.

해설 (A) 커튼을 치는 사람을 찾아볼 수 없으므로 오답.
(B) 베개들이 정리되어 놓여 있는 곳이 침대가 아니므로 오답.
(C) 무늬가 있는 양탄자가 바닥에 놓여 있는 모습을 묘사하고 있으므로 정답.
(D) 소파를 들어 올리는 사람을 찾아볼 수 없으므로 오답.

어휘 be pulled closed 당겨져 닫히다 pillow 베개 arrange ~을 정렬하다, 배치하다 patterned 무늬가 있는 rug 양탄자 place v. ~을 놓다, 두다 couch 소파 lift ~을 들어올리다 cleaning 청소, 세척

2.
(A) A pier protrudes into the water.
(B) Some people are stepping onto a boat.
(C) People are strolling along the edge of the water.
(D) The roof of the building is being fixed.

(A) 물이 있는 쪽으로 부두가 돌출되어 있다.
(B) 몇몇 사람들이 보트에 오르는 중이다.
(C) 사람들이 물가를 따라 거닐고 있는 중이다.
(D) 건물 지붕이 수리되는 중이다.

해설 (A) 바닷물 쪽으로 부두가 돌출되어 있는 모습을 묘사하고 있으므로 정답.
(B) 보트에 오르는 사람들을 찾아볼 수 없으므로 오답.
(C) 물가를 따라 거닐고 있는 사람들을 찾아볼 수 없으므로 오답.
(D) 건물 지붕이 수리되는 모습을 찾아볼 수 없으므로 오답.

어휘 protrude 돌출되다, 튀어나오다 step onto ~에 올라서다 stroll 거닐다, 산책하다 along (길 등) ~을 따라 edge 가장자리 fix ~을 고치다, 수리하다

Part 2

3. How long did the survey take?
(A) About working conditions.
(B) Take an online survey.
(C) Over a week.

설문 조사하는 데 얼마나 오래 걸렸나요?
(A) 근무 조건에 관해서요.
(B) 온라인 설문 조사를 하세요.
(C) 일주일 넘게요.

해설 「How long ~?」은 '얼마나 오래 ~하나요?'라는 의미로 지속 시간이나 기간을 물을 때 사용한다. 설문 조사가 얼마나 오래 걸렸는지 묻고 있으므로 대략적인 기간을 나타내는 (C)가 정답이다. (A)는 설문 조사의 주제에 해당되는 답변이므로 오답이며, (B)는 질문에 언급된 survey를 반복해 혼동을 유발하는 오답이다.

어휘 survey 설문 조사(지) take ~의 시간이 걸리다, ~을 취하다, 선택하다 working conditions 근무 조건 over ~ 넘게

4. What kind of benefits do you provide for your employees?
(A) The changes have been quite beneficial to the firm.
(B) Yes, I heard that the company treats its staff well.
(C) Generous vacation leave and bonuses.

직원들을 위해 어떤 종류의 혜택을 제공하시나요?
(A) 그 변화가 회사에 상당히 유익했어요.
(B) 네, 그 회사가 직원을 잘 대우해준다고 들었습니다.
(C) 넉넉한 휴가와 보너스가 있습니다.

해설 benefits는 '회사에서 제공하는 혜택 또는 복리후생'을 의미하므로 직원들을 위해 제공하는 혜택의 종류에 관해 답하는 것을 정답으로 골라야 한다. 따라서 휴가와 보너스를 언급하

며 복리후생의 종류로 질문에 답하는 (C)가 정답이다. (C)에서 generous는 '넉넉한, 많은'이라는 의미로 휴가(vacation leave)와 보너스(bonuses)가 많다는 것을 나타낸다.

어휘 **benefits** (주로 복수) 복리후생, 혜택 **beneficial** 이익이 되는, 이로운 **firm** 회사 **staff** 직원 **generous** 넉넉한, 후한 **leave** 휴가

5. Can you help me set up this product display, or do you have customers to serve?

    (A) I have some time right now.

    (B) The service here is excellent.

    (C) The new range of cosmetic products.

제가 이 진열 제품을 설치하는 것을 도와줄 수 있나요, 아니면 응대해야 할 손님이 있으신가요?
(A) 저는 지금 시간이 좀 있어요.
(B) 이곳의 서비스는 훌륭합니다.
(C) 다양한 새로운 화장품입니다.

해설 선택 사항인 A와 B가 각각 문장으로 구성된 난이도 높은 문제이지만, or 전의 문장만 제대로 들어도 답을 고를 수 있다. 도와줄 수 있는지 여부를 묻는 질문에 '지금 시간이 있다'는 말로 A(도와줄 수 있다)를 선택하여 답하는 (A)가 정답이다. (B)는 질문의 serve와 관련된 어휘를, (C)는 질문에 나온 어휘를 그대로 활용한 오답이다.

어휘 **set up** ~을 설치하다, 마련하다 **display** 진열 **serve** ~을 응대하다, (음식 등을) 제공하다, 내다 **range** (상품의) 세트, 제품군 **cosmetic product** 화장품

6. What's the projected budget for the trip to New York?

    (A) The project is not finished, is it?

    (B) They're meeting in January.

    (C) We need about $3,000.

뉴욕으로 가는 여행에 필요한 예상 예산이 얼마나 될까요?
(A) 그 프로젝트는 아직 안 끝나지 않았나요?
(B) 그들은 1월에 만날 거예요.
(C) 우리는 약 3,000달러가 필요해요.

해설 의문사 What 뒤에 이어지는 projected budget이 '예상되는 예산'을 뜻하므로 How much 의문문과 같은 의미를 나타낸다. 따라서 대략적인 액수로 답한 (C)가 정답이다. What's the projected budget이 비용 수준을 묻는 질문이라는 것을 이해하지 못하면 질문에 쓰인 project가 반복되는 (A)를 고르거나 trip과 관련된 의미를 지니는 (B)를 고르는 실수를 할 수 있다.

어휘 **projected** 예상되는 **budget** 예산 **about** 약, 대략

7. How much farther is it to the convention center?

    (A) Tickets are 20 dollars.

    (B) Around five thousand people.

    (C) Just a few blocks.

컨벤션 센터까지 얼마나 더 가야 하나요?
(A) 표는 20달러입니다.
(B) 약 5천 명의 사람들입니다.
(C) 몇 블록만 더요.

해설 「How much farther ~?」는 '얼마나 더 ~?'라는 의미로 거리를 묻는 질문이므로, 거리를 나타내는 표현이나 걸리는 시간 등으로 대답하는 것이 적절하다. 따라서 '몇 블록만 더 가면 된다, 단지 몇 블록 떨어져 있다'고 말하는 (C)가 정답이다. How much만 듣고 성급하게 가격을 말하는 (A)를 고르지 않도록 유의한다. (B)는 convention center를 듣고 참석자 수를 떠올려 고르게 만드는 함정이다.

어휘 **farther** 더 먼 (cf. far의 비교급) **convention center** 컨벤션 센터 (회의, 전시장, 숙박 시설이 집중된 지역 또는 종합 빌딩) **a few** 몇몇의

8. Wasn't there a schedule attached to the e-mail yesterday?

    (A) Attendance is required.

    (B) We're behind schedule.

    (C) Sorry, I haven't checked.

어제 이메일에 첨부된 일정표가 있지 않았나요?
(A) 참석은 필수입니다.
(B) 우리는 예정보다 늦어진 상태입니다.
(C) 죄송해요, 확인하지 못했습니다.

해설 이메일에 첨부된 일정표가 있지 않았는지 확인하는 부정 의문문에 대해 미안하다는 말과 함께 확인하지 못해서 알지 못한다는 말을 덧붙인 (C)가 정답이다. (A)는 질문 내용과 관련 없는 오답이며, (B)는 질문에 쓰인 schedule을 반복한 답변으로, 일정표 첨부 여부가 아니라 일의 진행 상황을 말하는 오답이다.

어휘 **attached** 첨부된 **attendance** 출석, 참석 **required** 필수의, 필요한 **behind schedule** 예정보다 늦은

9. You've distributed all the pay slips, haven't you?

    (A) It's available in all major retailers.

    (B) I asked Phil to do that.

    (C) Yes, I get paid on a monthly basis.

당신이 모든 급여 명세서를 배부하시지 않았나요?
(A) 그것은 모든 주요 소매업체에서 구입 가능합니다.
(B) 필 씨에게 그것을 해달라고 부탁했습니다.
(C) 네, 저는 월 단위로 급여를 받습니다.

해설 급여 명세서를 배부하였는지 확인하는 부가 의문문이다. 이에 대해 배부했다면 Yes, 아니라면 No로 답하는 것이 기본이나, Yes/No를 생략하고 질문 내용에 맞는 대답을 하기도 한다. 따라서 No를 생략하고 급여 명세서 배부를 제3자인 필 씨에게 해달라고 부탁했다고 말하며 질문에 답하는 (B)가 정답이다. (A)는 it이 무엇인지 불분명하고 내용도 질문과 관련 없으며, (C)는 pay slip에서 연상 가능한 내용(get paid on a monthly basis)으로 혼동을 유발하는 오답이다.

어휘 **distribute** ~을 배부하다, 나누어주다 **pay slip** 급여 명세서 **available** 구입 가능한, 이용할 수 있는 **retailer** 소매상, 소매업체 **get paid** 급여를 받다 **on a monthly basis** 월 단위로, 매월

10. What is the best way to have this stain removed from this shirt?
    (A) We straightened everything up before we went home.
    (B) You'd better take it to a dry cleaner.
    (C) Take the next right and go straight for three blocks.

이 셔츠에서 얼룩을 제거하는 가장 좋은 방법이 뭔가요?
(A) 저희가 집에 가기 전에 모두 깨끗이 정리했습니다.
(B) 세탁소에 가져 가시는 게 좋겠어요.
(C) 다음 모퉁이에서 우회전 한 다음, 세 블록 직진하세요.

해설 얼룩을 지우는 방법을 묻고 있으므로 세탁소에 가져가 보라고 권하며 질문에 답하는 (B)가 정답이다. (A)는 질문에 쓰인 stain과 발음이 유사한 straighten을 이용해 혼동을 유발하는 오답이며, (C)는 질문에 쓰인 way로 인해 길을 묻는 질문으로 착각하는 경우에 잘못 고를 수 있는 오답이다.

어휘 **have A p.p.** A를 ~되게 하다 **stain** 얼룩 **remove** ~을 제거하다, 없애다 **straighten up** ~을 깨끗이 정리하다 **had better + 동사원형** ~하는 게 좋다 **dry cleaner** 세탁소 **take a right** 우회전하다 **go straight** 직진하다

11. Is there a quicker method for accessing patient records?
    (A) You can use the express bus.
    (B) Yes, he sure has a lot of patience.
    (C) Not until we start using a database.

환자 기록을 볼 수 있는 더 빠른 방법이 있나요?
(A) 급행 버스를 이용할 수 있어요.
(B) 네, 그는 확실히 참을성이 많아요.
(C) 데이터베이스를 이용하기 시작해야 가능해요.

해설 질문을 알아듣기도 어렵고 답변을 고르기도 어려운 문제이다. patient records(환자 기록)를 더 빠르게 볼 수 있는 방법이 있는지 여부를 묻는 질문이므로 기본적으로 Yes/No로 답해야 하지만 Yes/No를 생략하고 방법의 유무를 나타내는 말이 답변으로 올 수 있다. 따라서 No를 생략하고 Not until을 사용해 조건을 언급하며 질문에 답하는 (C)가 정답이다.

어휘 **quicker** 더 빠른 **method** 방법 **access** ~에 접근하다 **patient** 환자 **express bus** 급행 버스 **patience** 참을성, 인내심 **not until** ~ 전까지는 아니다, ~가 되어서야 비로소

12. Why don't you ask for a discount on this jacket?
    (A) This is already the sale price.

    (B) Count it again.
    (C) It's supposed to be cold today.

이 재킷 할인을 요청해보는 것이 어때요?
(A) 이것이 이미 할인된 가격이에요.
(B) 다시 세어보세요.
(C) 오늘은 추울 거예요.

해설 할인을 요청해 보라는 제안에 대해 이미 할인된 가격이라는 말로 간접적으로 거절하는 (A)가 정답이다. (B)는 discount와 유사하게 들리는 count를 이용한 오답이며, (C)는 jacket에서 연상되는 cold를 이용한 오답이다.

어휘 **ask for** ~을 요청하다 **sale price** 세일가, 할인가 **count** 세어 보다 **be supposed to do** ~하기로 되어 있다, 해야 한다

13. The number of applicants for the job has been surprising.
    (A) A job in the marketing department.
    (B) No, I haven't had time to order supplies.
    (C) Well, it's a really desirable position.

그 일자리에 지원한 사람들의 숫자는 놀라웠어요.
(A) 마케팅 부서의 일자리입니다.
(B) 아니요, 저는 물품을 주문할 시간이 없었습니다.
(C) 음, 그건 정말 탐나는 자리이거든요.

해설 제시된 문장은 '일자리에 지원한 지원자의 숫자가 놀라울 정도로 많았다'는 의미이다. 이에 대한 적절한 답변으로, 지원자의 수가 많은 것에 대한 이유를 말하는 (C)가 정답이다. (A)는 질문에 나온 job을 이용해 혼동하게 만든 오답이며, (B)는 질문의 surprising과 선택지의 supplies의 유사한 발음을 이용한 오답이다.

어휘 **the number of** ~의 숫자[수치] **applicant** 지원자, 신청자 **supplies** 물품, 용품 **desirable** 탐나는, 매력적인 **position** 직책, 자리

14. Do you want to go grocery shopping at the Empire Mall?
    (A) Does it even have a supermarket?
    (B) The cosmetics department is on the second floor.
    (C) Of course we did.

엠파이어 쇼핑몰에 식료품 사러 갈래요?
(A) 그곳에 슈퍼마켓도 있어요?
(B) 화장품 코너는 2층에 있어요.
(C) 물론 우린 그랬죠.

해설 쇼핑몰에 식료품을 사러 가고 싶은지 의향을 묻는 질문이다. 이에 대해 긍정이나 부정의 대답을 하는 대신, the Empire Mall을 그곳(it)이라고 지칭하여 그곳에 슈퍼마켓도 있는지 되물으며 질문에 답하는 (A)가 정답이다. 참고로, 반문하는 대답은 정답일 확률이 매우 높다. (B)는 shopping에서 연상되는

department를 활용한 오답이며, (C)는 Of course로 긍정을 나타냈으나 뒤에 이어지는 말이 의향을 묻는 질문 내용과 관련 없는 오답이다.

어휘 **go grocery shopping** 식료품 쇼핑을 가다 **cosmetics** 화장품

15. What qualifications are required for the marketer position?

(A) It's right across the street.
(B) Yes, it's fine now.
(C) They're listed on the company Web site.

마케팅 담당자 직책에 어떤 자격 요건이 필요한가요?
(A) 길 바로 건너편에 있어요.
(B) 네, 그게 지금은 괜찮아요.
(C) 그것들은 회사 웹 사이트에 게시되어 있습니다.

해설 What qualifications가 핵심이므로 이 부분을 놓치지 않아야 정답을 고를 수 있다. 마케팅 담당자 직책에 필요한 자격 요건을 묻는 질문에 특정 자격 요건을 직접 알려주는 대신 회사 웹 사이트에 나와 있다고 우회적으로 응답한 (C)가 정답이다. 이렇게 특정 정보를 요청하는 질문에 대해 그것을 알 수 있는 장소나 방법, 또는 사람을 알려주는 대답도 종종 정답으로 등장한다는 점을 알아 두는 것이 좋다.

어휘 **qualification** 자격 (요건) **require** ~을 요구하다, 필요로 하다 **position** 직책, 자리 **list** ~을 기재하다, 목록에 올리다 **right across the street** 길 바로 건너편에

16. Did you receive a party invitation or should I send another one?

(A) I'm only inviting close friends.
(B) At Peking Chinese restaurant.
(C) I didn't get anything yet.

당신은 파티 초대장을 받았나요, 아니면 제가 하나 더 보내드려야 하나요?
(A) 저는 가까운 친구들만 초대할 것입니다.
(B) 페킹 중식당에서 합니다.
(C) 저는 아직 아무것도 받지 못했습니다.

해설 선택 의문문이므로 주어진 선택사항이 무엇인지를 파악해야 한다. 즉 초대장을 받았는지(receive a party invitation) 아니면 한 장 보내줘야 하는지(send another one)를 묻고 있으므로 둘 중 하나를 택해 답하거나 다른 대안을 제시하는 응답을 골라야 한다. 따라서 '아무것도 못 받았다'는 말로 send another one을 선택하는 (C)가 정답이다.

어휘 **invitation** 초대(장)

17. The Web page describing our inventory is missing some items.

(A) Mr. Chase invented most of them.
(B) It uses more electricity than we expected.
(C) It should be updated by tomorrow.

우리 물품 목록을 설명하는 웹 페이지에 몇 가지 품목들이 빠져 있어요.
(A) 체이스 씨가 그것들의 대부분을 발명했습니다.
(B) 그것은 우리가 기대했던 것보다 더 많은 전기를 사용합니다.
(C) 그것은 내일까지 업데이트되어야 합니다.

해설 웹 페이지에 몇 가지 품목이 빠져 있다는 정보를 알리는 평서문이다. 이에 대해 빠져 있는 몇 가지 품목들이 내일까지 업데이트되어야 한다는 말로 제시문에 답하는 (C)가 정답이다. (A)는 inventory와 발음이 비슷한 invented를 이용한 오답이며, (B)는 제시문의 내용과 관련 없는 오답이다.

어휘 **describe** 묘사하다, 설명하다 **miss** ~을 빠트리다, ~이 없다 **invent** ~을 발명하다 **electricity** 전기 **update** ~을 업데이트하다, 갱신하다

18. Should we put up Christmas decorations in our office this year?

(A) The new carpet looks nice.
(B) A lot of people were invited last year.
(C) We'd better check with Mr. Kane first.

올해 우리는 사무실에 크리스마스 장식을 달아야 하나요?
(A) 새 카펫이 멋지네요.
(B) 지난해에 많은 사람들이 초대되었어요.
(C) 케인 씨에게 먼저 확인하는 것이 좋을 것 같습니다.

해설 사무실에 장식을 해야 할지 묻는 질문에 대해 Yes/No로 바로 답하는 대신 제3자(Kane)에게 확인하는 것이 좋겠다는 말로 답하는 (C)가 정답이다. (A)는 Christmas decorations와 관련 없는 내용이며, (B)는 내용과 시제 모두 맞지 않는 오답이다.

어휘 **put up** ~을 게시하다, 걸다 **Christmas decorations** 크리스마스 장식 **had better + 동사원형** ~하는 것이 낫다 **check with + 사람** ~에게 확인해보다

19. Why haven't more apples been put out on display yet?

(A) We're going to do it when we are less busy.
(B) At the front entrance of the store, please.
(C) They are grown at a local farm.

왜 아직도 더 많은 사과들이 진열되어 있지 않은 거죠?
(A) 우리가 덜 바쁠 때 그 일을 할 것입니다.
(B) 매장의 정문 앞에 부탁 드립니다.
(C) 그것들은 지역 농장에서 재배됩니다.

해설 이유를 묻는 의문사 Why로 시작하는 부정 의문문 형태로, 동사 부분이 현재완료 시제(have + p.p.)의 부정 형태에 수동태(be + p.p.)로 되어 있어 어려운 질문 형태이다. 사과가 아직도 더 진열되지 못한 이유를 묻는 질문에 그 이유를 직접 말하는 대신 덜 바쁠 때 작업(it)할 것이라는 말로 질문에 답하는 (A)가

정답이다.

어휘 **put out** ~을 내놓다 **on display** 진열된 **grow** ~을 재배하다, 기르다 **less** 덜 ~한 **front entrance** 정문

20. I'm sure that I've met the new sales manager somewhere before.

(A) He'll be in a meeting until 5.
(B) We'll be hiring a new one this week.
(C) Probably at the conference last year.

전에 신임 영업부장님을 어딘가에서 만난 적이 있다고 확신해요.
(A) 그는 5시까지 회의 중일 것입니다.
(B) 우리는 이번 주에 새로운 분을 고용할 거예요.
(C) 아마 작년에 열린 컨퍼런스일 거예요.

해설 평서문은 의문사가 없기 때문에 문장의 의도를 단번에 파악하기 어렵다. 주어와 동사 부분을 집중적으로 듣고 화자의 의도가 무엇인지 파악한 후 그에 알맞은 답을 골라야 한다. 확실한 장소는 기억나지 않지만 신임 영업부장을 어디선가 만났던 것이 틀림없다는 말에 작년 컨퍼런스일 것이라는 추측으로 답하는 (C)가 정답이다. (A)와 (B)는 the new sales manager을 각각 He와 a new one으로 지칭했다고 볼 수 있지만, 과거의 만남 여부와 관련 없는 오답이다.

어휘 **somewhere** 어딘가에서

Part 3

> **W:** Hi, Mark. **22** Are you on your way to the meeting? It's in 10 minutes.
>
> **M:** Ah, the meeting about next year's possible merger? Yes, I'm going there now. Do you want to go together?
>
> **W:** Management said **22** it was compulsory, but **21 22** I have an appointment with a potential client in 10 minutes. If it goes well, it will mean a lot of money for the company. What should I do?
>
> **M:** **21** You should definitely go to your appointment. I think management would prefer to have you making us money than attending the meeting. **23** If you want, I can take some notes and share them with you later.

여: 안녕하세요, 마크 씨. 회의에 가는 길이세요? 10분 후에 있잖아요.
남: 아, 내년에 있을지도 모르는 합병에 대한 회의 말이죠? 네, 지금 가는 길이에요. 같이 갈래요?

여: 경영진이 필히 참석해야 하는 회의라고 말했지만 제가 10분 후에 잠재 고객과 약속이 있어서요. 일이 잘 되면 회사에 아주 큰 금전적 이익이 될 텐데. 어떻게 해야 하죠?
남: 당연히 약속에 가야죠. 경영진도 당신이 회의에 참석하기보단 우리에게 돈을 벌어다 주는 걸 좋아할 걸요. 원하면 내가 필기를 해서 나중에 당신과 그 내용을 공유할 수 있어요.

어휘 **be on one's way to** ~로 가는 길이다 **merger** 합병 **management** 경영진 **compulsory** 의무적인, 필수의 **have an appointment with** ~와 약속이 있다 **potential client** 잠재 고객 **go well** (일 등이) 잘 되다 **mean** ~을 의미하다 **definitely** 당연히, 확실히 **prefer to do** ~하는 것을 선호하다 **take notes** 노트 필기를 하다 **share A with B** A를 B와 나누다, 공유하다

21. 화자들은 주로 무엇에 대해 이야기하고 있는가?
(A) 업무 약속
(B) 회사 정책
(C) 취업 면접
(D) 교육 과정

해설 회의에 의무적으로 참석해야 하는데 여자가 고객과 중요한 약속이 있는 상황이다. 이러한 상황에 대해 여자가 남자의 의견을 구하고, 남자는 약속에 가는 것이 좋겠다고 권하고 있다. 따라서 이들이 이야기하고 있는 주제는 '여자가 고객과 만나기로 한 약속'이라고 할 수 있으므로 (A)가 정답이다.

어휘 **policy** 정책, 방침

Paraphrase an appointment with a potential client
→ A business appointment

22. 여자의 문제는 무엇인가?
(A) 면접을 진행해야 한다.
(B) 10분 후에 점심 데이트가 있다.
(C) 회의에 늦을 것이다.
(D) 일정이 겹친다.

해설 여자의 두 번째 대사에서 알 수 있다. 10분 뒤에 열릴 회의에 의무적으로 참석해야 하는데, 같은 시간에 고객과 중요한 약속이 있는 상황으로, 이에 대해 어떻게 해야 하는지 고민하고 있다. 이러한 여자의 문제를 한 마디로 요약하면 '일정이 겹친다'이므로 (D)가 정답이다.

어휘 **conduct** ~을 수행하다 **have a scheduling conflict** 일정이 겹치다

23. 남자는 무엇을 해주겠다고 하는가?
(A) 잠재 고객을 만난다.
(B) 중요한 회의를 주재한다.
(C) 회의 세부 내용을 적는다.
(D) 경영진과 얘기한다.

해설 대화 맨 마지막에서 남자는 여자에게 고객과의 약속에 가라며

회의 내용을 필기해 보여주겠다고(If you want, I can take some notes and share them with you later) 제안하고 있다. 따라서 (C)가 정답이다.

어휘 lead ~을 이끌다 write down ~을 적다 detail 세부 사항, 세부 정보

Paraphrase take some notes
→ Write down the details

Questions 24-26 refer to the following conversation with three speakers.

W1: **24** I'm really looking forward to the opening night of the play at Bastion Theater. Are we all still planning to go together?

W2: Of course! I've been wanting to see it for a long time. It got great reviews in New York last month.

M: I'm still interested in going, too. **25** But, haven't we left a little late to get tickets? There might not be any left.

W1: Oh, don't worry about that. **26** Miranda already reserved us three in advance. Isn't that right?

W2: **26** Yes, my cousin works in the theater's box office, so he was able to set some aside for us.

M: Oh, that's great news! I'm sure we're going to have a great time.

여1: 저는 배스티언 극장에서 있을 연극 공연의 개막일 저녁이 정말로 많이 기대돼요. 우리 모두 여전히 함께 갈 계획인 거죠?
여2: 물론이죠! 저는 오랫동안 그 공연을 보고 싶었어요. 지난 달에 뉴욕에서 아주 뛰어난 평가를 받았어요.
남: 저도 그곳에 가는 데 여전히 관심이 있기는 해요. 하지만 입장권을 구매하기에는 조금 늦게 나선 것 아닌가요? 하나도 남아 있지 않을 수도 있어요.
여1: 아, 그건 걱정하지 마세요. 이미 미란다 씨가 우리를 위해 미리 3장 예매해 두었어요. 그렇지 않아요?
여2: 네, 제 사촌이 그 극장의 매표소에서 근무하고 있어서, 우리를 위해 몇 장 따로 남겨 둘 수 있었어요.
남: 아, 아주 좋은 소식이네요! 분명 아주 즐거운 시간을 보낼 수 있을 거예요.

어휘 look forward to -ing ~을 고대하다 play 연극 for a long time 오랫동안 review 평가, 의견, 후기 leave 떠나다, 출발하다 worry about ~에 대해 걱정하다 reserve A B A에게 B를 예약해 주다 in advance 미리

---

box office 매표소 set A aside A를 따로 남겨 두다, 확보해 두다

24. 화자들은 무슨 종류의 행사에 참석할 계획인가?
   (A) 콘서트
   (B) 영화 시사회
   (C) 연극 공연
   (D) 스포츠 경기

해설 행사의 종류를 파악해야 하므로 특정 행사 명칭이나 제품 및 서비스 등과 같이 특징적인 요소가 드러나는 정보를 찾아야 한다. 대화를 시작하면서 여자 한 명이 Bastion Theater에서 있을 연극 공연의 개막일 저녁이 정말로 많이 기대된다고(I'm really looking forward to the opening night of the play at Bastion Theater) 말하고 있으므로 (C)가 정답이다.

어휘 movie premiere 영화 시사회

25. 남자는 왜 걱정하는가?
   (A) 행사장을 찾는 방법을 알지 못한다.
   (B) 온라인으로 일부 부정적인 후기를 읽었다.
   (C) 자신의 일정이 겹친다.
   (D) 행사가 매진될 수도 있다고 생각하고 있다.

해설 남자의 말에서 걱정 관련 표현이나 부정적인 정보가 제시되는 부분을 찾아야 한다. 남자가 대화 중반부에 입장권을 구매하기에는 좀 늦게 나선 것이 아닌지 물으면서 하나도 남아 있지 않을 수도 있다고(But, haven't we left a little late to get tickets? There might not be any left) 걱정하는 부분을 언급하고 있다. 이는 행사가 매진될까 걱정하는 것이므로 (D)가 정답이다.

어휘 venue 행사장 negative 부정적인 conflict (일정 상의) 겹침, 충돌 sold out 매진되다, 품절되다

26. 미란다 씨의 사촌에 관해 무엇이 언급되는가?
   (A) 공연을 할 것이다.
   (B) 화자들과 동행할 것이다.
   (C) 매표소에서 근무한다.
   (D) 행사 조직자이다.

해설 Miranda의 사촌이 질문의 핵심이므로 이 내용이 언급되는 부분에 집중해 들어야 한다. 대화 후반부에 여자 한 명이 Miranda라는 이름과 함께 이미 표를 예매했다고(Miranda already reserved us three in advance) 알리자 바로 뒤이어 다른 여자가 자신의 사촌이 매표소에서 근무한다고(Yes, my cousin works in the theater's box office) 답변하고 있다. 따라서 매표소에서 근무하는 사실을 언급한 (C)가 정답이다.

어휘 give a performance 공연하다 accompany ~와 동행하다, ~을 동반하다 organizer 조직자, 주최자

Questions 27-29 refer to the following conversation.

W: Hello, Eugene! It's Louise from Advertising. **27** I think I left my ID badge in your office after lunch. Do you see it?

M: Hmm... give me a moment. Oh, I found it. I'll bring it right up.

W: That's OK. A candidate is arriving shortly for an interview. **28** I'll just drop by your office after I finish. I don't need it until later anyway.

M: Sure, I'll be here. Is the interview for the art director position? I thought it had already been filled.

W: Yeah, we actually already made our decision to just promote from within the company. **29** It was too late to cancel this interview, though, so it will be brief. I'll see you in a little bit.

여: 안녕하세요, 유진 씨! 저는 광고부의 루이스입니다. 제가 점심 식사 후에 당신의 사무실에 사원증을 놓고 온 것 같아요. 혹시 보이시나요?
남: 흠... 잠시만요. 오, 찾았어요. 지금 바로 갖다 드릴게요.
여: 괜찮아요. 면접 때문에 지원자 한 명이 곧 도착할 거예요. 면접을 마친 후에 사무실로 들를게요. 어쨌든 이따가까지 필요하진 않거든요.
남: 좋습니다, 저는 여기 있을 거예요. 그 면접이 미술 감독 직책에 대한 것인가요? 저는 그 자리가 이미 충원되었다고 생각했어요.
여: 네, 사실 회사 내부에서 사람을 승진시키기로 이미 결정을 내렸습니다. 하지만 이 면접을 취소하기에는 너무 늦어서, 간단하게 할 겁니다. 잠시 후에 뵙겠습니다.

어휘 **ID badge** 사원증 **give me a moment** 잠시만요 **bring A up** A를 갖다 주다 **right** 바로 **candidate** 지원자, 후보자 **shortly** 곧, 머지 않아 **drop by** ~에 들르다 **until later** 이후에, 나중까지 **anyway** 어쨌든 **art director** 미술 감독 **fill** (자리 등) ~을 충원하다, 채우다 **actually** 사실은, 실은 **make one's decision** 결정을 내리다 **promote** 승진시키다 **from within** ~의 내부로부터 **too 형용사 to do** ~하기에는 너무 …한 **though** (문장 중간이나 끝에서) 하지만 **brief** 간단한, 잠시 동안의 **in a little bit** 잠시 후에, 조금 후에

27. 여자는 왜 남자에게 전화를 거는가?
(A) 기술적인 도움을 요청하기 위해
(B) 프로젝트를 논의하기 위해
(C) 분실한 물품을 찾기 위해
(D) 식사 계획을 세우기 위해

해설 여자가 전화를 거는 목적을 묻고 있으므로 대화가 시작될 때 여자의 말에 집중해 들어야 한다. 대화 시작 부분에 여자는 점심 식사 후에 상대방의 사무실에 사원증을 놓고 온 것 같다고 말하면서 그것이 보이는지 묻고 있으므로(I think I left my ID badge in your office after lunch. Do you see it?) 분실 물품을 찾기 위해서라는 의미로 쓰인 (C)가 정답이다.

어휘 **technical** 기술적인 **lost** 분실한 **item** 물품, 제품 **meal** 식사

28. 여자가 "면접 때문에 지원자 한 명이 곧 도착할 거예요"라고 말할 때 무엇을 의미하는가?
(A) 회의에 대한 준비가 되어 있지 않다.
(B) 지금 당장은 방해를 받으면 안 된다.
(C) 결정에 대해 확실치 않다.
(D) 남자가 서둘러 주기를 원하고 있다.

해설 대화 중반부에 여자는 이 말과 함께 면접을 마친 후에 상대방의 사무실로 들르겠다고(I'll just drop by your office after I finish) 말하고 있으므로 당장은 면접에 집중해야 한다는 의미로 쓰인 문장임을 알 수 있다. 따라서 이와 유사한 의미로 지금은 방해를 받으면 안 된다는 뜻으로 쓰인 (B)가 정답이 된다.

어휘 **be unprepared for** ~에 대한 준비가 되어 있지 않다 **disturb** ~을 방해하다 **be unsure of** ~가 확실치 않다 **decision** 결정 **hurry** 서두르다

29. 여자는 면접과 관련해 무엇이라고 말하는가?
(A) 다른 장소에서 있을 것이다.
(B) 인터넷 상에서 이뤄질 것이다.
(C) 업무 시간 이후에 시작될 것이다.
(D) 오래 지속되지 않을 것이다.

해설 면접과 관련해 여자가 언급한 내용을 묻고 있으므로 면접 진행 상의 특징이 제시될 것임을 미리 예상하고 들어야 한다. 대화 후반부에 여자는 면접을 취소하기에는 너무 늦어서 간단하게 할 것이라고(It was too late to cancel this interview, though, so it will be brief) 말하고 있으므로 이와 유사한 의미에 해당되는 (D)가 정답이다.

어휘 **location** 위치, 지점 **be held** (행사 등이) 열리다, 개최되다 **over the Internet** 인터넷 상에서 **working hours** 업무 시간 **last** v. 지속되다

Paraphrase it will be brief
→ It will not last long.

Questions 30-32 refer to the following conversation.

M: Hello, I moved into an apartment recently, and **30** I just received my first electricity bill from your company. Can I pay that over the phone by credit card?

W: I'm afraid not, sir. There are two methods available to you. You can go to our Web site and pay it online, or **31** if there's a **Renshaw Energy Store** nearby, you can stop by there with your bill.

M: Oh, **31** there's one that's just a five-minute drive from here, so I'll just do that then.

W: I'm glad I could help. By the way, **32** would you like me to mail you a pamphlet describing the benefits of paying your bills online?

M: Sure, that would be nice.

W: No problem. It should arrive by the end of this week.

남: 안녕하세요, 제가 최근에 한 아파트로 이사했는데, 귀사로부터 첫 번째 전기세 고지서를 막 받았습니다. 신용카드를 이용해서 전화로 이 요금을 지불할 수 있나요?

여: 그렇게 하실 수 없을 것 같습니다, 고객님. 이용하실 수 있는 두 가지 방법이 있습니다. 저희 웹 사이트로 가셔서 온라인으로 지불하시거나, 근처에 렌쇼 에너지 스토어가 있을 경우, 고지서를 갖고 그곳에 들르시면 됩니다.

남: 아, 이곳에서 5분 정도 차를 타고 가면 되는 거리에 한 곳이 있으니까, 그럼 그렇게 할게요.

여: 제가 도와드릴 수 있어서 기쁩니다. 그건 그렇고, 온라인으로 비용을 지불하시는 것에 대한 혜택을 설명하는 팸플릿을 우편으로 발송해 드려도 될까요?

남: 그럼요, 그렇게 해 주시면 좋겠어요.

여: 알겠습니다. 이번 주 말까지는 도착할 겁니다.

어휘 **move into** ~로 이사해 들어가다 **recently** 최근에 **electricity bill** 전기세 고지서 **over the phone** 전화상으로 **I'm afraid not** 그렇지 않을 것 같습니다 **method** 방법 **available to** ~가 이용 가능한 **nearby** 근처에 **stop by** ~에 들르다 **five-minute drive** 차로 5분 거리의 **then** 그럼, 그렇다면 **by the way** (화제 전환 시) 그건 그렇고 **would like A to do** A에게 ~하기를 원하다 **pamphlet** 팸플릿, 안내 책자 **describe** ~을 설명하다 **benefit** 혜택, 이득

30. 여자는 어디에서 근무하고 있을 것 같은가?
(A) 부동산 중개업소에서
(B) 금융 기관에서
(C) 전기 서비스 회사에서
(D) 가전 기기 매장에서

해설 대화 시작 부분에 남자가 상대방인 여자의 회사로부터 전기세 고지서를 받은 사실을 언급하고 있으므로(I just received my first electricity bill from your company) 전기 서비스 회사를 뜻하는 (C)가 정답임을 알 수 있다.

어휘 **real estate agency** 부동산 중개업소 **financial institution** 금융 기관 **appliance** 가전 기기

31. 남자는 무엇을 하기로 결정하는가?
(A) 서비스 가입 기간을 연장하는 일
(B) 회의 일정을 재조정하는 일
(C) 신용카드로 비용을 지불하는 일
(D) 사업 지점을 방문하는 일

해설 대화 중반부에 여자가 근처에 Renshaw Energy Store가 있을 경우 고지서를 갖고 그곳에 가면 된다고(if there's a Renshaw Energy Store nearby, you can stop by there with your bill) 말하자 남자가 그렇게 하겠다고(~, so I'll just do that then) 동의하고 있으므로 사업 지점 방문을 뜻하는 (D)가 정답임을 알 수 있다.

어휘 **extend** ~을 연장하다 **subscription** 서비스 가입, (정기) 구독 **reschedule** ~의 일정을 재조정하다 **make a payment** 비용을 지불하다 **business location** 사업 지점

Paraphrase Renshaw Energy Store / stop by
→ Visit a business location

32. 남자에게 무엇이 보내질 것인가?
(A) 월간 계좌 이용 내역서
(B) 회원 카드
(C) 안내 팸플릿
(D) 지불 영수증

해설 남자에게 보내지는 것이 질문의 핵심이므로 발송되는 물품이나 자료 등이 있음을 예상하고 들어야 한다. 대화 후반부에 여자가 온라인으로 비용을 지불하는 것에 대한 혜택을 설명하는 팸플릿을 우편으로 발송해도 될지 묻는 질문에 대해(would you like me to mail you a pamphlet ~) 남자가 Sure라고 동의하고 있으므로 안내 팸플릿을 의미하는 (C)가 정답이다.

어휘 **monthly** 월간의, 달마다의 **account** 계좌, 계정 **statement** 내역서, 명세서 **receipt** 영수증

Questions 33-35 refer to the following conversation and control panel.

M: Hi, Nicole. You know, **33** I think our library's new computer lab is working out really well. I've been getting lots of positive feedback from members here at our library.

W: I agree. Honestly, **34** I was a bit worried at first because I didn't think that we would meet our goal of getting members to register for classes. I assumed that most of them had tablets or laptops in their rooms that they would use instead.

M: Well, fortunately, it all worked out. But, shouldn't we keep it cool in there?

W: You're right. With all the people using it, the room must have gotten warmer than expected. The thermostat is on the wall there.

M: 35 The down button, right? Got it!

남: 안녕하세요, 니콜 씨. 있잖아요, 전 우리 도서관의 새 컴퓨터실이 정말로 잘 되어가고 있는 것 같아요. 이곳 우리 도서관의 회원들에게서 긍정적인 의견을 계속 많이 받고 있어요.

여: 동의해요. 솔직히, 저는 처음에 좀 걱정했는데, 회원들을 강좌에 등록시키는 일에 대해 목표를 충족할 거라고 생각하지 않았거든요. 그분들 대부분이 각자의 방에 대신 이용할 만한 태블릿 컴퓨터나 노트북 컴퓨터를 갖고 계신다고 생각했어요.

남: 음, 다행히, 전부 잘 되었어요. 그런데, 그곳을 시원하게 유지해야 하지 않을까요?

여: 맞아요. 모든 사람이 이용하면서, 그 방이 틀림없이 예상보다 더 더워졌을 거예요. 온도 조절 장치가 저쪽 벽에 있습니다.

남: 다운 버튼 맞죠? 됐습니다!

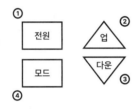

① 전원
② 업
③ 다운
④ 모드

어휘 lab 실험실 work out (well) 잘 되어가다 positive 긍정적인 feedback 의견 agree 동의하다 honestly 솔직히 a bit 조금, 약간 worried 걱정하는 meet (요구, 조건 등) ~을 충족하다 get A to do A에게 ~하게 하다 register for ~에 등록하다 assume that ~라고 생각하다, ~라고 추정하다 instead 대신 fortunately 다행히 keep A B A를 B한 상태로 유지하다 with A -ing A가 ~하면서, A가 ~한 채로 must have p.p. 틀림없이 ~했을 것이다, ~한 것이 분명하다 get 형용사 ~한 상태가 되다 than expected 예상보다 thermostat 온도 조절 장치

33. 화자들이 무엇을 이야기하고 있는가?
   (A) 컴퓨터실
   (B) 취업 박람회
   (C) 인터넷 제공업체
   (D) 건물 개조 공사

해설 대화의 주제나 목적은 대체로 초반부에 드러날 가능성이 높으므로 대화가 시작될 때 특히 집중해 들어야 한다. 대화 초반부에 남자가 자신들이 근무하는 도서관의 새 컴퓨터실이 정말로 잘 되어가고 있는 것 같다고(I think our library's new computer lab is working out really well) 알린 뒤로 이 컴퓨터실의 운영과 관련해 이야기하고 있으므로 (A)가 정답이

다.

어휘 career fair 취업 박람회 provider 제공업체, 제공업자 renovation 개조, 보수

34. 여자가 무엇을 걱정했다고 말하는가?
   (A) 시끄러운 방해 요소
   (B) 낮은 등록자 수
   (C) 빡빡한 마감기한
   (D) 높은 지출 비용

해설 대화 중반부에 여자가 회원들을 강좌에 등록시키는 일에 대해 목표를 충족할 것 같지 않아서 걱정했다고(I was a bit worried ~ I didn't think that we would meet our goal of getting members to register for classes) 알리고 있다. 이는 강좌 등록자 수가 낮을까 걱정했다는 뜻이므로 (B)가 정답이다.

어휘 distraction 집중을 방해하는 것, 지장을 주는 것 registration 등록, 등록자 수 tight (비용, 기한 등이) 빡빡한, 빠듯한 deadline 마감기한 expense 지출 (비용)
   Paraphrase didn't think that we would meet our goal of getting members to register
   → Low registration

35. 시각자료를 보시오. 남자가 어느 버튼을 누를 것인가?
   (A) 1번 버튼
   (B) 2번 버튼
   (C) 3번 버튼
   (D) 4번 버튼

해설 각 버튼의 명칭과 위치, 모양을 먼저 확인한 다음, 대화 중에 버튼 명칭이나 특징적인 요소를 언급하는 부분에서 단서를 찾아야 한다. 남자가 대화 맨 마지막 부분에 다운 버튼을 언급하면서 곧바로 됐다고(The down button, right? Got it!) 말하고 있다. 시각자료에서 오른쪽 아래에 Down이라고 표기된 버튼이 3번이므로 (C)가 정답이다.

Questions 36-38 refer to the following conversation and bill.

M: Good morning. 36 I'd like to check out of my room, please.

W: Good morning, sir. I have a copy of your invoice for hotel expenses here. Please check it and let me know if there are any errors.

M: Okay, let's see... Hmm, 37 it seems you've charged me for lunch at the poolside restaurant, but I paid for that in cash.

W: Oh, I'm sorry. 37 I'll remove that charge and have a new invoice printed out for you now.

M: Thanks. **38** I'm supposed to go on a tour of local attractions at 10:30, so I hope this won't take too long.

남: 안녕하세요. 제 객실에서 체크아웃 하려고 합니다.

여: 안녕하세요, 고객님. 여기 호텔 이용 지출액에 대한 내역서가 한 부 있습니다. 확인하신 다음, 오류가 있으면 저에게 알려 주시기 바랍니다.

남: 네, 보겠습니다... 흠, 수영장 옆에 있는 레스토랑에서 했던 점심 식사에 대해 요금을 청구하신 것 같은데, 제가 현금으로 지불했습니다.

여: 아, 죄송합니다. 지금 그 청구 요금을 삭제하고 새 내역서를 출력해 드리겠습니다.

남: 감사합니다. 제가 10시 30분에 지역 명소 투어를 가기로 되어 있어서, 이게 너무 오래 걸리지 않기를 바랍니다.

고객 이용 내역서	
아침 식사 - 옥상 뷔페	$15
룸 서비스 - 저녁 식사 메뉴	$22
점심 식사 - 수영장 옆 레스토랑	$18
룸 미니 바/스낵	$11
총액:	$66

어휘 **check out of** ~에서 체크아웃하다 **invoice** 이용 내역서, 거래 내역서 **let A know if** A에게 ~인지 알리다 **let's see** (확인하거나 기억을 떠올릴 때) 어디 보자, 어디 한 번 봅시다 **it seems (that)** ~인 것 같다, ~인 것처럼 보이다 **charge** v. ~에게 요금을 청구하다 n. 청구 요금 **pay for** ~에 대한 비용을 지불하다 **remove** ~을 없애다, ~을 제거하다 **be supposed to do** ~하기로 되어 있다, ~할 예정이다 **local** 지역의, 현지의 **attraction** 명소, 인기 장소 **take long** 오래 걸리다 **rooftop** 옥상

36. 남자는 누구일 것 같은가?

(A) 호텔 손님
(B) 주방 직원
(C) 접수 직원
(D) 여행사 직원

해설 남자가 대화를 시작하면서 여자에게 객실에서 체크아웃하겠다고(I'd like to check out of my room, please) 알리고 있는데, 이는 호텔 손님이 호텔 직원에게 할 수 있는 말에 해당되므로 (A)가 정답이다.

37. 시각자료를 보시오. 이용 내역서의 어느 금액이 삭제될 것인가?

(A) $15
(B) $22
(C) $18
(D) $11

해설 대화 중반부에 남자가 수영장 옆에 있는 레스토랑에서 점심 식사한 것에 대해 요금을 청구했다는(it seems you've

charged me for lunch at the poolside restaurant) 말과 함께 현금으로 이미 지불한 사실을 알리자, 여자가 그 청구 요금을 삭제하겠다고(I'll remove that charge) 답변하고 있다. 시각자료에서 Poolside restaurant이 표기된 세 번째 줄에 기재된 요금이 $18이므로 (C)가 정답이다.

38. 남자가 10시 30분에 무엇을 할 것인가?

(A) 비행기를 타는 일
(B) 식사하는 일
(C) 친구를 만나는 일
(D) 투어에 합류하는 일

해설 남자가 10시 30분에 무엇을 할 것인지 묻고 있으므로 10시 30분이라는 시점 표현이 제시되는 부분에서 단서를 찾아야 한다. 남자가 대화 맨 마지막 부분에 10시 30분에 지역 명소 투어를 가기로 되어 있다고(I'm supposed to go on a tour of local attractions at 10:30) 알리고 있으므로 (D)가 정답이다.

Paraphrase go on a tour of local attractions
→ Join a tour

Part 4

Questions 39-41 refer to the following announcement.

We are sorry to announce that **39** the 10:40 P.M. FastTrak train to Boston has been canceled due to weather conditions. At this time, **40** we ask that all FastTrak travelers leave the boarding platform and wait in the second floor main hall. Since this is the last train of the night, **41** a FastTrak representative will come and hand out one-night vouchers for the nearby Country Inn hotel. Additionally, you can use your current ticket for any Boston-bound train departing tomorrow morning, though, in most cases, only standing room will be available.

보스턴으로 향하는 오후 10시 40분 패스트트랙 열차가 기상 상태로 인해 취소되었음을 알려 드리게 되어 유감스럽게 생각합니다. 현재, 모든 패스트트랙 이용 여객객들께서는 탑승 승강장에서 나오셔서 2층 대합실에서 대기하시도록 요청 드립니다. 이 열차가 오늘 밤 막차이므로, 패스트트랙 소속 직원이 나와 근처의 컨트리 인 호텔에서 사용하실 수 있는 1박 쿠폰을 나눠드릴 것입니다. 추가로, 대부분의 경우, 오직 서서 가는 공간만 이용 가능하겠지만, 현재 갖고 계신 티켓은 내일 아침에 보스턴을 향해 출발하는 어느 열차에 대해서도 사용하실 수 있습니다.

어휘 **due to** ~로 인해 **weather conditions** 기상 상태 **leave** ~에서 나가다, 떠나다 **boarding** 탑승 **platform** 승강장 **representative** 직원 **hand out** ~을 나눠주다

voucher 쿠폰, 상품권 **nearby** 근처의 **additionally** 추가로 **current** 현재의 **bound** ~을 향하는, ~행의 **depart** 출발하다 **though** (비록) ~이기는 하지만 **in most cases** 대부분의 경우에

39. 공지는 어디에서 이뤄지고 있는가?

(A) 기차역에서
(B) 공항에서
(C) 백화점에서
(D) 버스 터미널에서

해설 담화 시작 부분에 Boston으로 향하는 오후 10시 40분 FastTrak 열차가 취소되었다고(the 10:40 P.M. FastTrak train to Boston has been cancelled) 알리는 부분을 통해 담화가 이뤄지고 있는 장소가 기차역임을 알 수 있으므로 (A)가 정답이다.

어휘 **make an announcement** 공지하다, 발표하다, 알리다

40. 화자는 청자들에게 무엇을 하도록 요청하는가?

(A) 티켓을 한 장 더 구입할 것
(B) 온라인으로 불만 사항을 제출할 것
(C) 각자의 수하물을 찾아 갈 것
(D) 지정된 구역에서 대기할 것

해설 화자가 요청하는 일을 찾아야 하므로 화자의 말에서 요청 관련 표현이 제시되는 부분에서 단서를 파악해야 한다. 담화 초반부에 탑승 승강장에서 나와 2층 대합실에서 대기하도록(we ask that all FastTrak travelers ~ and wait in the second floor main hall) 요청하고 있으므로 지정된 구역에서 대기하는 일을 언급한 (D)가 정답이다.

어휘 **complaint** 불만 **retrieve** ~을 다시 찾아가다, 회수하다 **luggage** 수하물, 짐 **designated** 지정된

Paraphrase wait in the second floor main hall
→ Wait in a designated area

41. 화자의 말에 따르면, 무엇을 나눠줄 것인가?

(A) 무료 식사
(B) 호텔 쿠폰
(C) 선불 전화 카드
(D) 안내 소책자

해설 나눠주는 것이 무엇인지 묻고 있으므로 질문에 제시된 distribute을 비롯해 제공과 관련된 표현이 제시되는 부분에서 단서를 찾아야 한다. 담화 중반부에 Country Inn hotel에서 사용할 수 있는 1박 쿠폰을 나눠준다고(~ and hand out one-night vouchers for the nearby Country Inn hotel) 언급하고 있으므로 (B)가 정답이다.

어휘 **distribute** ~을 나눠주다, 배부하다 **pre-paid** 선불된

Questions 42-44 refer to the following telephone message.

Hello, it's Rachel. **42** I just wanted to go over everything we discussed this morning. Most importantly, **43** we're still deciding on the last two stories to be included in the Best New Authors collection. And remember, the publishing date is next month. Then, since the revising work has been quite hectic, you asked me to recruit another editor. **44** So after this, I'll call the guy who worked with us last time. And... that's about it. If everything goes smoothly, we should stay on schedule.

안녕하세요, 저는 레이첼입니다. 저는 오늘 아침에 우리가 논의했던 모든 사항들을 점검해 보고 싶었습니다. 가장 중요한 것으로, 우리는 여전히 최고의 신규 작가 컬렉션에 포함시킬 마지막 두 가지 소설을 정하는 중입니다. 그리고 기억하셔야 하는 점은 출판 날짜가 다음 달입니다. 그래서, 수정 작업이 상당히 많이 바빴기 때문에, 제게 편집자를 한 명 더 모집하도록 요청해 주셨습니다. 그래서 이 전화 메시지를 남긴 후에, 제가 지난 번에 우리와 함께 일했던 남자분께 전화를 드릴 것입니다. 그리고... 대략 이 정도입니다. 모든 일이 순조롭게 진행된다면, 우리는 일정에 맞출 수 있을 것입니다.

어휘 **go over** ~을 점검하다, 다시 살피다 **most importantly** 가장 중요하게 **decide on** ~을 결정하다 **story** 소설, 이야기 **include** ~을 포함하다 **publishing** 출판, 발간 **then** 그래서, 그렇다면 **since** ~이므로 **revising work** 수정 작업 **quite** 상당히, 꽤 **hectic** 아주 바쁜 **ask A to do** A에게 ~하도록 요청하다 **recruit** ~을 모집하다 **another** 또 다른 한 명의 **editor** 편집자 **last time** 지난 번에 **that's about it** (말을 마무리할 때) 대략 이 정도입니다, 대충 그렇습니다 **smoothly** 순조롭게 **stay on schedule** 일정에 맞추다, 일정대로 진행하다

42. 메시지의 목적은 무엇인가?

(A) 회의 내용을 검토하는 것
(B) 일정을 변경하는 것
(C) 오류를 수정하는 것
(D) 지원자를 면접하는 것

해설 담화의 주제를 묻고 있으므로 담화가 시작될 때 특히 집중해 핵심 정보를 파악해야 한다. 화자는 오늘 아침에 논의했던 모든 사항들을 점검해 보고 싶다고(I just wanted to go over everything we discussed this morning) 알리면서 담화를 시작하고 있으므로 회의 내용 검토를 의미하는 (A)가 정답이다.

어휘 **correct** ~을 수정하다, 바로잡다 **applicant** 지원자

Paraphrase go over everything we discussed
→ review a meeting

43. 화자가 "출판 날짜가 다음 달입니다"라고 말할 때 암시하는 것은 무엇인가?

(A) 모든 일이 완료된 상태이다.
(B) 결정이 곧 내려져야 한다.
(C) 날짜가 뒤로 미뤄졌다.
(D) 또 다른 프로젝트가 시작될 예정이다.

해설 해당 문장은 담화 중반부에 들을 수 있으며, 여전히 Best New Authors 컬렉션에 포함시킬 마지막 두 가지 소설을 정하는 중이라고(we're still deciding on the last two stories to be included ~) 알리는 말 다음에 제시되고 있다. 따라서 빨리 해당 사항을 결정해야 한다는 의미로 쓰인 말이라는 것을 알 수 있으므로 (B)가 정답이 된다.

어휘 make a decision 결정을 내리다 push back ~을 뒤로 미루다 be scheduled to do ~할 예정이다

44. 화자는 곧이어 무엇을 할 것 같은가?

(A) 이전의 프로젝트를 확인한다.
(B) 전화를 건다.
(C) 고객과 만난다.
(D) 웹 사이트를 업데이트한다.

해설 담화 후반부에 전화 메시지를 남긴 후에 지난 번에 함께 일했던 남자에게 전화를 할 것이라고(So after this, I'll call the guy who worked with us last time) 말하고 있으므로 (B)가 정답임을 알 수 있다.

어휘 previous 이전의 make a phone call 전화를 걸다 meet with (약속하여) ~와 만나다

Questions 45-47 refer to the following talk.

Good afternoon. Today, 45 46 I want to talk to you all about the new Roadhog Forklifts we'll be using in the warehouse. I know you are all experienced operators, but these machines have a few big differences we should all be aware of. These models feature faster speeds and heavier lift capacities, and while these are welcome upgrades, they have the potential to cause large accidents if misused. On the other hand, there are also some new safety improvements that we'll discuss. Before we start, 47 we'll watch an introductory video that should cover all of the basics.

안녕하세요. 오늘, 저는 여러분 모두에게 우리가 창고에서 사용할 예정인 새로운 로드혹 지게차에 관해 말씀드리고자 합니다. 저는 여러분 모두가 경험 많은 기계 운전자들이라는 것을 알고 있지만, 이 기계들은 우리 모두가 알고 있어야 하는 몇 가지 큰 차이점들이 있습니다. 이 모델들은 더 빠른 속도와 더 무거운 것을 들어 올리는 기능을 특징으로 하는데, 이와 같은 부분이 반가운 업그레이드인 반면에, 잘못 사용될 경우에 대형 사고를 초래할 잠

재성이 있습니다. 다른 한편으로 생각해 보면, 우리가 논의해야 할 몇몇 새로운 안전 개선 사항들도 있다는 의미입니다. 시작하기 전에, 모든 기본적인 사항들을 다룰 제품 소개용 동영상을 시청하시겠습니다.

어휘 warehouse 창고 experienced 경험 많은 operator (기계 등의) 운전자 difference 차이점 be aware of ~을 알고 있다, 인식하다 feature ~을 특징으로 하다 lift 들어 올리기 capacity 기능, 용량, 수용력 welcome 반가운, 환영 받는 have the potential to do ~할 잠재성이 있다 cause ~을 초래하다 accident 사고 misuse ~을 오용하다, 남용하다 on the other hand 다른 한편으로는 improvement 개선, 향상 introductory 소개용의 cover (주제 등) ~을 다루다 basics 기본 사항, 기초 사항

45. 청자들은 누구일 것 같은가?

(A) 기계 공학자들
(B) 배송 기사들
(C) 창고 직원들
(D) 열차 기관사들

해설 담화 시작 부분에 자신들이 창고에서 사용할 기계(the new Roadhog Forklifts we'll be using in the warehouse)를 언급하는 것으로 보아 창고 직원들임을 알 수 있으므로 (C)가 정답이다.

어휘 mechanical engineer 기계 공학자 train operator 열차 기관사

46. 회의의 주제는 무엇인가?

(A) 직원 불만 사항을 처리하는 것
(B) 고객 서비스를 개선하는 것
(C) 배송 마감일을 충족하는 것
(D) 새로운 기계를 소개하는 것

해설 화자는 담화 시작 부분에 창고에서 사용할 예정인 새로운 Roadhog Forklifts에 관해 이야기할 것이라고(I want to talk to you all about the new Roadhog Forklifts we'll be using in the warehouse) 알리고 있으므로 새로운 기계 소개를 의미하는 (D)가 정답이 된다.

어휘 address ~을 처리하다, 다루다 complaint 불만 improve ~을 개선하다, 향상시키다 meet ~을 충족하다 deadline 마감기한 introduce ~을 소개하다

Paraphrase talk to you all about the new Roadhog Folklifts → Introducing a new machine

47. 청자들은 곧이어 무엇을 할 것인가?

(A) 동영상을 볼 것이다.
(B) 제품을 테스트할 것이다.
(C) 설문지를 작성 완료할 것이다.
(D) 대본을 암기할 것이다.

해설 담화의 끝부분에 모든 기본적인 사항들을 다룰 제품 소개용 동영상을 볼 것이라고(we'll watch an introductory video that ~) 알리고 있으므로 이에 대해 언급한 (A)가 정답이다.

어휘 complete ~을 작성 완료하다 survey 설문 조사(지) memorize ~을 암기하다, 외우다 script 원고, 대본

Questions 48-50 refer to the following telephone message and diagram.

Hi, Norman. This is Fiona calling from Bridger Corporation. 48 49 I know we had planned to get together this afternoon to discuss a potential project collaboration, but I'm afraid I won't be able to make it. One of my colleagues has called in sick, and 49 I'll need to substitute for him as the lead instructor at our orientation for new workers. Let's try to chat later today to make an alternative arrangement. 50 My cell phone is already down to one bar of battery, though, so please respond to me by e-mail later, in case my phone is off. Sorry for the inconvenience.

안녕하세요, 노먼 씨. 저는 브릿저 코퍼레이션에서 전화 드리는 피오나입니다. 잠재적인 프로젝트 협업 문제를 논의하기 위해 오늘 오후에 모임을 갖기로 계획했었다는 것을 알고 있기는 하지만, 참석할 수 없을 것 같습니다. 제 동료 직원들 중의 한 명이 병가를 내는 바람에 저희 신입 사원들을 위한 오리엔테이션 시간에 지도 강사로서의 역할을 대신 맡아야 합니다. 오늘 이따가 얘기를 나눠서 대체 일정을 정했으면 합니다. 그런데 제 휴대전화기에 이미 배터리가 한 칸 밖에 남지 않아서 제 전화기가 꺼져 있을 경우에 대비해 나중에 이메일로 제게 답변해 주시기 바랍니다. 불편함을 끼쳐 드려 죄송합니다.

배터리 충전 표시

| 100% | 75% | 50% | 25% |

어휘 get together 모이다, 만나다 potential 잠재적인 collaboration 협업 make it 가다, 도착하다 colleague 동료 직원 call in sick (전화로) 병가를 내다 substitute for ~을 대체하다, 대신하다 lead instructor 지도 강사 chat 얘기를 나누다 make an arrangement 일정을 정하다, 조정하다 alternative 대체하는, 대안의 down 줄어든, 낮아진 though (문장 끝이나 중간에서) 하지만 respond to ~에 답변하다, 응답하다 in case (that) ~의 경우에 대비해 off 꺼진, 기능을 멈춘 inconvenience 불편함 charge 충전 indicator 표시(등), 계기(반)

48. 전화의 목적은 무엇인가?
(A) 불만을 제기하는 것
(B) 도움을 제공하는 것
(C) 회의를 취소하는 것
(D) 감사를 표현하는 것

해설 담화를 시작하면서 화자는 오늘 오후에 모임을 갖기로 계획했었지만, 참석할 수 없을 것 같다고(I know we had planned to get together this afternoon ~, but I'm afraid I won't be able to make it) 알리고 있다. 이는 계획되어 있던 회의를 취소해야 한다는 것을 의미하는 말이므로 (C)가 정답이 된다.

어휘 make a complaint 불만을 제기하다 assistance 도움 express (감정 등) ~을 표현하다 gratitude 감사(의 마음)

Paraphrase get together / won't be able to make it
→ cancel a meeting

49. 화자는 오늘 오후에 무엇을 할 것인가?
(A) 신입 사원들을 교육한다.
(B) 면접에 참석한다.
(C) 의사를 방문한다.
(D) 휴가를 계획한다.

해설 오늘 오후라는 미래 시점이 질문의 핵심이므로 질문에 포함된 this afternoon을 비롯해 가까운 미래를 나타내는 시점 표현이 제시되는 부분에서 단서를 찾아야 한다. 담화 시작 부분에 오늘 오후의 회의 일정 취소를 언급한 화자는 그 이유로 신입 사원들을 위한 오리엔테이션 시간에 강사로서의 역할을 해야 한다고(I'll need to substitute for him as the lead instructor at our orientation for new workers) 알리고 있다. 따라서 신입 사원 교육을 의미하는 (A)가 정답이 된다.

어휘 instruct ~을 교육하다, 가르치다

Paraphrase substitute / as the lead instructor / for new workers
→ Instruct new staff

50. 시각자료를 보시오. 화자의 휴대전화기는 현재 어느 정도의 배터리 충전 상태를 나타내는가?

(A) 25퍼센트
(B) 50퍼센트
(C) 75퍼센트
(D) 100퍼센트

해설 배터리 충전 상태를 나타내는 비율 및 막대 표시가 시각자료로 제시되어 있는데, 화자는 담화 후반부에 휴대전화기에 이미 배터리가 한 칸 밖에 남지 않았다고(My cell phone is already down to one bar of battery) 알리고 있다. 시각자료에서 한 칸에 해당되는 비율은 25%이므로 (A)가 정답임을 알 수 있다.

1. (B)	**2.** (D)	**3.** (C)	**4.** (C)	**5.** (B)
6. (D)	**7.** (D)	**8.** (C)	**9.** (C)	**10.** (C)
11. (D)	**12.** (A)	**13.** (C)	**14.** (C)	**15.** (C)
16. (A)	**17.** (D)	**18.** (C)	**19.** (A)	**20.** (B)
21. (A)	**22.** (A)	**23.** (D)	**24.** (B)	**25.** (D)
26. (C)	**27.** (C)	**28.** (B)	**29.** (D)	**30.** (C)
31. (C)	**32.** (A)	**33.** (D)	**34.** (B)	**35.** (C)
36. (A)	**37.** (D)	**38.** (D)	**39.** (C)	**40.** (C)
41. (C)	**42.** (A)	**43.** (D)	**44.** (A)	**45.** (B)
46. (C)	**47.** (B)	**48.** (A)	**49.** (B)	**50.** (C)

Part 5

1.

정답 (B)

해석 기술적인 결함으로 인해, 맨체스터행 2시 35분 기차의 출발이 20분 지연될 것이다.

해설 빈칸 앞에 있는 20-minute라는 숫자 표현은 형용사이므로 빈칸은 이 형용사의 수식을 받을 명사 자리이다. 또한, 빈칸 앞에 부정관사가 있으므로 단수명사 (B) delay가 정답이다.

어휘 **mechanical** 기술적인 **fault** 결함, 실수, 결점 **delay** n. 지연 v. ~을 미루다, 연기하다 **departure** 출발

2.

정답 (D)

해석 멜론 킹에서 나온 상큼한 과일 스무디 제품의 매출은 습도가 높은 여름 기간에 흔히 증가한다.

해설 선택지가 모두 부사로 이루어져 있으므로 해석을 통해 알맞은 어휘를 골라야 한다. 빈칸 뒤에 동사 increase가 있으므로 이와 어울리는 부사를 찾아야 하는데, 이 문장은 현재시제 동사를 사용해 반복되는 일을 나타내고 있으므로 빈도부사 (D) frequently가 정답이다.

어휘 **refreshing** 상쾌하게 만드는 **frequently** 흔히, 자주 **humid** 습도가 높은 **cleanly** 청결히 **spaciously** 넓게 **approximately** 약, 대략

3.

정답 (C)

해석 헨드릭스 씨께서 한 달 내내 해외로 출장 가실 예정이므로, 리프먼 씨께서 일시적으로 그분의 직원들을 관리하실 것입니다.

해설 빈칸이 속한 절이 주어와 동사, 부사로 구성되어 있어 완전한 구조이므로 빈칸과 month가 부사의 역할을 해야 한다. 또한, 미래시제 동사와 어울리는 미래 시점 표현이 구성되어야 알맞으므로 month와 결합해 '한 달 내내'라는 의미를 나타내는 부사구를 구성하는 (C) all이 정답이다.

어휘 **oversea** 해외로, 해외에 **temporarily** 일시적으로, 임시로 **supervise** ~을 관리하다, ~을 감독하다 **whole** 전체의, 모든 **near** a. 가까운 ad. 가까이 prep. ~ 가까이에, ~ 근처에 v. ~에 접근하다

4.

정답 (C)

해석 브레넌 씨가 지난 여름에 고용된 이후로, 스카이라크 소프트웨어에서 벌써 세 번이나 승진되었다.

해설 선택지가 모두 접속사이므로 해석을 통해 알맞은 것을 골라야 한다. 콤마 뒤에 위치한 절에 현재완료시제 동사가 쓰여 있으므로 빈칸이 속한 절에서 쓰인 과거 시점 표현 last summer가 시작점임을 알 수 있다. 따라서 '~한 이후로'라는 의미로 과거의 시작점을 말할 때 사용하는 (C) Since가 정답이다.

어휘 **receive a promotion** 승진되다 **until** (지속) ~할 때까지 **since** ~한 이후로, ~하기 때문에 **whether** ~인지 (아닌지), ~와 상관없이

5.

정답 (B)

해석 모든 저희 전자 제품은 돌발적인 손상에 대해 18개월 동안 품질 보증이 됩니다.

해설 빈칸 앞에 동사 come이 쓰여 있으므로 빈칸은 동사 자리가 아니며, 동사 come은 형용사 또는 과거분사와 결합해 '~한 상태가 되다, ~한 상태로 나오다' 등을 의미하므로 과거분사 (B) guaranteed가 정답이다.

어휘 **electrical appliances** 전자 제품, 가전 제품 **against** ~에 대비하여, ~에 반대하여 **accidental** 돌발적인, 우연한 **guarantee** ~의 품질을 보증하다, ~을 보장하다

6.

정답 (D)

해석 공장 직원들은 반드시 각각의 일일 교대 근무 종료 시에 모든 조립 라인 기계를 철저하게 닦아야 한다.

해설 선택지가 모두 다른 부사로 구성되어 있으므로 해석을 통해 알맞은 어휘를 골라야 한다. 빈칸에 쓰일 부사는 바로 뒤에 위치한 동사 clean을 수식해 근무 종료 시에 조립 라인 기계를 닦는 방식을 나타내야 하므로 '철저하게' 등을 뜻하는 (D) thoroughly가 정답이다.

어휘 **assembly** 조립 **shift** 교대 근무(조) **hopefully** 희망하

여, 바라건대 **intentionally** 의도적으로, 고의로
thoroughly 철저하게, 꼼꼼히

~ 위로

7.

정답 (D)

해석 연착 때문에, 연결 항공편을 이용하는 탑승객들이 이곳이 최종 목적지에 도착할 사람들보다 먼저 내릴 것입니다.

해설 빈칸 뒤 관계대명사절의 수식을 받아 '~하는 사람들'이라는 의미로 전치사 before의 목적어 역할을 할 대명사가 빈칸에 필요하다. 따라서 (A) anyone과 (D) those 중에서 하나를 골라야 하는데, 빈칸 뒤에 쓰인 복수 동사 are과 수 일치해야 하므로 (D) those가 정답이다.

어휘 **due to** ~로 인해, ~ 때문에 **delay** 지연, 연착
connecting flight 연결 항공편 **disembark** 내리다

8.

정답 (C)

해석 신입 팀원들은 종종 공장에 들어온 첫 몇 주 동안 자신이 동료들에게 의존하고 있음을 알게 된다.

해설 빈칸 앞에 5형식 동사 find와 목적어가 있으므로 빈칸은 형용사 목적보어 자리이다. 따라서 선택지 중 형용사는 (A) dependable과 (C) dependent 두 개인데, 빈칸 뒤에 위치한 전치사 on과 어울리는 (C) dependent가 정답이다.

어휘 **find oneself + 형용사** 자신이 ~임을 알다 **dependent on** ~에 의존적인 **dependable** 의지할 수 있는 **depend (on)** (~에) 의존하다 **dependence** 의존

9.

정답 (C)

해석 방문 중인 주주들에게 우리 랜달 모터스 공장의 차량들이 어떻게 제조되는지 볼 수 있도록 공장을 견학할 기회가 주어졌다.

해설 빈칸 다음에 주어와 수동태 동사로 구성된 절이 있으므로 전치사인 (A) during과 (B) about은 소거한다. 빈칸 뒤에 완전한 구조의 절이 있고, 동사 see의 목적어 역할을 할 수 있는 (C) how가 정답이다.

어휘 **shareholder** 주주 **tour** ~을 견학하다, 둘러보다
vehicle 차량, 탈 것 **manufacture** ~을 제조하다

10.

정답 (C)

해석 전 씨는 다가오는 해의 수익 예측과 관련해 몇 가지 우려하는 부분이 있다.

해설 선택지가 모두 전치사로 구성되어 있으므로 빈칸 앞뒤 명사의 의미 관계를 파악해야 한다. 빈칸 앞뒤에 제시된 명사 concerns와 revenue projections를 '~와 관련해'라는 뜻으로 자연스럽게 연결하는 (C) regarding이 정답이다.

어휘 **concern** 우려, 관심 **regarding** ~와 관련해 **revenue** 수익 **projection** 예측 **upcoming** 다가오는, 곧 있을 **onto**

11.

정답 (D)

해석 일단 건물 설계도가 최종 확정되면, 여러 층으로 된 새로운 주차 건물의 공사가 시작될 것이다.

해설 콤마를 기준으로 앞뒤에 주어와 동사가 포함된 두 개의 절이 있으므로 이를 연결할 수 있는 접속사 (D) Once가 정답이다.

어휘 **blueprint** 설계도, 도면 **finalize** ~을 최종 확정하다
multi-story 여러 층의 **soon** 곧, 머지 않아 **then** 그러고 나서, 그 후에 **later** 나중에

12.

정답 (A)

해석 거리 축제 중에, 포드 스트리트에 있는 주차장은 평상시의 운영 시간 대신에 오전 8시부터 오후 11시까지 개방될 것이다.

해설 빈칸 앞에는 축제 기간 동안 주차장이 영업을 하는 시간을, 빈칸 뒤에는 평상시의 운영 시간이 있으므로 운영 시간이 일시적으로 변동된 것임을 나타내는 문장이 되어야 한다. 따라서 '~ 대신에'라는 의미로 쓰이는 (A) instead of가 정답이다.

어휘 **during** ~ 중에, 동안 **instead of** ~ 대신에, ~하지 않고 **operating hour** 운영 시간, 영업 시간 **in case** ~의 경우에

13.

정답 (C)

해석 대표이사님께서 새로운 급여 인상이 다음 달부터 시행될 것이라고 발표하셨을 때 직원들이 매우 흥분했다.

해설 '대표이사가 ~라고 발표했을 때 직원들이 매우 흥분했다'와 같은 의미가 구성되어야 자연스러우므로 '~할 때'라는 의미로 완전한 절을 이끄는 (C) when이 정답이다.

어휘 **announce that** ~라고 발표하다, ~라고 알리다 **pay raise** 급여 인상 **take effect** 시행되다, 발효되다

14.

정답 (C)

해석 윌슨 커뮤니티 도서관은 회원들에게 웹 사이트를 통해 도서의 대출을 연장할 수 있는 서비스를 제공합니다.

해설 빈칸 앞에 주어와 동사, 목적어로 구성된 완전한 절이 있고, 빈칸 뒤에 접속사 없이 명사와 to부정사구가 있으므로 빈칸은 준동사 자리이다. 따라서 빈칸 뒤의 명사 members를 목적어로 취하면서 빈칸 앞에 위치한 명사 service를 수식할 수 있는 현재분사 (C) allowing이 정답이다.

어휘 **allow A to do** A에게 ~하는 것을 허용하다 **renew** ~을 연장하다, 갱신하다 **through** ~을 통해

15.

정답 (C)

해석 '쓰레기 투기 금지' 표지판이 새로운 환경보호 운동의 일환으로 피츠버그 전역에 걸쳐 배치되었다.

해설 선택지가 모두 전치사로 구성되어 있으므로 빈칸 뒤에 제시된 명사의 특성을 파악해야 한다. 빈칸 뒤에 제시된 명사 Pittsburgh는 넓은 장소에 해당되는 도시이므로 '~ 전역에 걸쳐'라는 의미로 쓰이는 (C) throughout이 정답이다.

어휘 No Littering 쓰레기 투기 금지 place ~을 배치하다, 놓다, 두다 initiative (문제 해결 등을 위한) 운동 against ~에 반대해, ~에 기대어 except ~을 제외하고 upon ~ 하자마자, ~ 위에

16.

정답 (A)

해석 롱혼 커뮤니티 센터는 성공적으로 많은 액수의 자금을 마련했는데, 이 자금의 대부분은 지역 공원을 개선하는 데 할당되었다.

해설 빈칸 뒤의 내용으로 보아 most of의 대상이 되는 것은 바로 앞에 위치한 a large amount of money이므로 빈칸에 들어갈 관계대명사로 앞 문장에 제시된 사물을 가리킬 수 있는 (A) which가 정답이다.

어휘 raise (자금 등) ~을 마련하다 a large amount of 많은 양의 allocate ~을 할당하다 improvement 개선, 향상

Part 6

17-20.

여러분의 의견에 대해 보수를 지급해 드립니다!

저희 레졸루트 마케팅이 현재 로스앤젤레스에 위치한 저희 시장 조사팀에 **17** 합류하실 열정적인 분을 찾고 있습니다. 이 팀의 일원으로서, 여러분께서는 아주 다양한 업체를 방문해 그곳의 제품과 시비스를 테스트해 보도록 요성 받으시게 될 것입니다. 저희가 그 후에 소비자의 입장에서 여러분의 경험에 대한 **18** 평가서를 제출하도록 요청 드립니다. 여러분께서는 품질과 고객 서비스 기준, 그리고 전반적인 가성비 같은 요소들을 바탕으로 각 업체를 평가하셔야 할 것입니다.

저희가 여러분의 시장 조사 업무 중에 수반되는 모든 비용을 **19** 부담해 드리며, 방문하시는 각 업체에 대해 25달러의 비용도 지급 받으시게 될 것입니다. 이 직책에 지원하시려면 반드시 유효한 운전 면허증과 은행 계좌를 보유하고 계셔야 합니다. **20** 은행 계좌 이체는 매달 마지막 금요일에 이뤄질 것입니다. 저희 레졸루트 마케팅의 시장 조사 담당 직원이 되시는 데 관심이 있으실 경우, 오늘 (013)-555-3498번으로 저희 인사팀에 전화 주시기 바랍니다!

어휘 get paid 보수를 지급 받다, 급여를 지급 받다 seek ~을 찾다, ~을 구하다 enthusiastic 열정적인, 열심인 be asked to do ~하도록 요청 받다 a wide variety of 아주

다양한 business 업체, 회사 try out ~을 테스트해 보다 then 그 후에, 그때 rate ~을 평가하다, ~의 평점을 매기다 based on ~을 바탕으로, ~을 기반으로 overall 전반적인 value for money 가성비, 비용 대비 가치 involved 수반된, 관련된 duty 업무, 직무 valid 유효한 position 직책, 일자리 HR 인사(팀)

17.

정답 (D)

해설 빈칸 앞에 레졸루트 마케팅이라는 회사에서 열정적인 사람을 찾는다는 말이 쓰여 있어 시장 조사팀에서 일할 직원을 구한다는 사실을 알 수 있다. 이는 해당 팀에 새롭게 합류하는 것과 같으므로 '~에 합류하다, ~에 입사하다' 등을 뜻하는 (D) join이 정답이다.

어휘 register 신청하다, 등록하다 respond 대응하다, 응답하다 join ~에 합류하다, ~에 입사하다

18.

정답 (C)

해설 빈칸 바로 앞에 to부정사로 쓰인 동사 submit이 있어 빈칸은 이 동사의 목적어로서 제출 대상이 되는 사물을 나타낼 명사가 필요한 자리이므로 (C) evaluations가 정답이다.

어휘 evaluate ~을 평가하다 evaluation 평가(서)

19.

정답 (A)

해설 빈칸 앞에 위치한 주어 We는 이 구인 광고를 내는 회사를 가리키며, 빈칸 뒤에 업무 중에 수반되는 모든 비용을 의미하는 명사구가 쓰여 있다. 따라서 회사에서 모든 비용을 처리해준다는 의미가 구성되어야 자연스러우므로 비용 등과 관련해 '~을 부담하다, ~을 충당하다'를 뜻하는 (A) cover가 정답이다.

어휘 cover (비용 등) ~을 부담하다, ~을 충당하다 affirm ~을 단언하다, ~을 주장하다 refer 언급하다, ~을 참고하게 하다

20.

정답 (B)

해석 (A) 많은 지역 업체들이 현재 신입 직원을 고용하고 있습니다.
(B) 은행 계좌 이체는 매달 마지막 금요일에 이뤄질 것입니다.
(C) 해당 보고서를 제때 제출하실 수 없는 경우에 저희에게 알려 주십시오.
(D) 저희는 귀하께 저희 시장 조사팀 내의 역할을 제공해 드리게 되어 기쁩니다.

해설 빈칸 앞에 직원에게 지급되는 비용을 설명하면서 직책에 지원하기 위한 자격 요건으로 유효한 운전 면허증과 은행 계좌를 갖고 있어야 한다는 말이 쓰여 있다. 따라서 해당 비용의 지급 및 은행 계좌와 관련된 정보를 담은 문장으로서 비용 지급 방법과 시점을 알리는 (B)가 정답이다.

어휘 bank transfer 은행 계좌 이체 inform ~에게 알리다 be unable to do ~을 할 수 없다 on time 제때

21-24.

> 수신: 파피 리드 <preed@argolisinc.com>
> 발신: 콜린 채프먼 <cchapman@argolisinc.com>
> 제목: 다가오는 컨벤션
> 날짜: 9월 8일
>
> 파피 씨께,
>
> 제가 호로비츠 씨께 9월 16일에 열리는 기술 컨벤션 행사에서 당신을 저와 함께 [21] 하게 해달라고 요청 드렸다는 사실을 알려 드리게 되어 기쁩니다. 저희는 원래 당신이 직원 오리엔테이션을 진행하기 위해 사무실에 계셔야 할 것이라고 생각했지만, 대안이 되는 조치가 생각났습니다. [22] 우리 인사부장님께서 혼자 그 일을 처리하실 것입니다. 따라서, 저는 당신이 컨벤션에서 아르골리스 주식회사를 대표하도록 저를 도와주실 수 있다는 사실이 흥분됩니다.
>
> 우리는 웹 사이트를 통해 [23] 미리 컨벤션에 등록해야 합니다. 반드시 오늘 하루가 끝나기 전에 그렇게 하시도록 하십시오. 그에 대해 어떤 도움이든 필요하시면, 저에게 알려 주십시오. 분명 [24] 행사를 즐거워하실 것이며, 유익한 경험이라고 생각하시게 될 것입니다.
>
> 안녕히 계십시오.
>
> 콜린

어휘 upcoming 다가오는, 곧 있을 inform A that A에게 ~라고 알리다 originally 원래, 애초에 lead ~을 진행하다, ~을 이끌다 come up with (아이디어 등) ~을 생각해내다, ~을 떠올리다 alternative 대안의 arrangement 조치, 준비, 마련 represent ~을 대표하다 make sure that 반드시 ~하도록 하다, ~임을 확실히 해두다 assistance 도움, 지원 find A to be B A를 B라고 생각하다 beneficial 유익한, 이로운

21.

정답 (A)

해설 빈칸이 속한 that절에 동사 have asked가 이미 쓰여 있으므로 빈칸이 동사 자리가 아니라는 것을 알 수 있다. 따라서 준동사가 와야 하므로 선택지 중 유일한 준동사 형태인 (A) to let이 정답이다.

22.

정답 (A)

해석 **(A) 우리 인사부장님께서 혼자 그 일을 처리하실 것입니다.**
(B) 일주일에 한 부분씩 완료하시기 바랍니다.
(C) 제가 아마 그 고객께 전화 드릴 겁니다.
(D) 언제든지 음량을 조절하실 수 있습니다.

해설 빈칸 앞 문장에 상대방이 직원 오리엔테이션을 진행하기 위해 사무실에 있어야 하는 것으로 생각했다는 말과 함께 그 문제에 대한 대안에 해당되는 조치가 생각났다는 말이 쓰여 있다. 따라

서 직원 오리엔테이션(staff orientation)을 지칭하는 that과 함께 인사부장이 혼자 처리할 것이라는 말로 이 문제를 해결할 수 있는 조치가 무엇인지 알리는 (A)가 정답이다.

어휘 handle ~을 처리하다, ~을 다루다 by oneself 혼자, 자기 힘으로 adjust ~을 조절하다, ~을 조정하다

23.

정답 (D)

해설 빈칸 앞에는 컨벤션에 등록해야 한다는 말이, 빈칸 뒤에는 그 방법을 알리는 전치사구가 쓰여 있다. 따라서 등록 방식과 관련된 말이 빈칸에 들어가야 자연스러우므로 '미리, 사전에'라는 의미로 대략적인 등록 시점을 알리는 (D) in advance가 정답이다.

어휘 then 그럼, 그런 다음 even if 설사 ~라 하더라도 after all 결국, 어쨌든 in advance 미리, 사전에

24.

정답 (B)

해설 빈칸에 쓰일 명사는 동사 enjoy의 목적어로서 즐길 수 있는 대상을 나타내야 하며, 앞선 문장에 언급된 the convention이 그 대상이어야 의미가 자연스러우므로 이를 대신할 수 있는 명사로서 '행사'를 뜻하는 (B) event가 정답이다.

어휘 promotion 승진, 홍보, 판촉

Part 7

25-26.

> **패트릭 리드 [오전 9:11]**
> 안녕하세요, 마사 씨... 제가 포틀랜드에서 열리는 DX 일렉트로닉스 컨벤션에 가는 길인데, [25] 책상에 제 사원증을 놓고 왔습니다. 그 사진을 저에게 좀 보내 주실 수 있으세요? 행사장에서 제시해야 해서요.
>
> **마사 셰이 [오전 9:14]**
> √ 이미지 파일 받음. 열기 또는 다른 이름으로 저장
>
> **마사 셰이 [오전 9:15]**
> 여기 있습니다. 아, 그건 그렇고, 제가 회계팀의 애니 씨로부터 전화를 받았어요. [26] 이분이 이번엔 당신의 영수증들을 제때 받는 게 좋겠다고 하시더라고요.
>
> **패트릭 리드 [오전 9:17]**
> 실망시켜 드리지 않을 겁니다! 어쨌든, 저도 곧바로 제 지출 비용을 환급 받고 싶거든요.
>
> **마사 셰이 [오전 9:18]**
> 알겠습니다. 컨벤션 잘 다녀 오세요!

어휘 on one's way to ~로 가는 길인, ~로 오는 길인 leave ~을 놓고 오다 Would you mind -ing? ~해 주시겠어요? venue 행사장, 개최 장소 receive ~을 받다 There you are (뭔가 전달할 때) 여기 있습니다 **by the way** (화제 전환 시) 그건 그렇고, 그런데 **Accounting** 회계팀 **had better do** ~하는 게 좋다 **receipt** 영수증 **on time** 제때 **let A down** A를 실망시키다 **anyway** 어쨌든 **reimburse** ~을 환급해 주다 **expense** 지출 (비용), 경비 **straight away** 곧바로, 즉시

25. 마사 씨가 누구일 것 같은가?

(A) 컨벤션 주최자
(B) 사진가
(C) 회계팀장
(D) 패트릭 씨의 동료

정답 (D)

해설 패트릭 씨가 9시 11분에 작성한 첫 메시지에 책상에 자신의 사원증을 놓고 왔다고 알리면서 그 사진을 보내 달라고 마사 씨에게 부탁하고(I left my company ID badge on my desk. Would you mind sending me a photo of it?) 있다. 이는 회사 사무실에서 근무 중인 동료 직원에게 할 수 있는 말에 해당되므로 (D)가 정답이다.

어휘 **organizer** 주최자, 조직자 **colleague** 동료 (직원)

26. 오전 9시 17분에, 패트릭 씨가 "I won't let her down"이라고 쓸 때 무엇을 암시하는가?

(A) 자신의 지출 비용을 낮게 유지할 계획이다.
(B) 애니 씨에게 조언을 요청할 것이다.
(C) 제출 마감 기한을 충족할 것이다.
(D) 컨벤션에서 애니 씨를 만날 것이다.

정답 (C)

해설 9시 15분 메시지에 마사 씨가 회계팀 애니 씨의 전화를 받았다는 말과 함께 그 사람이 이번엔 영수증들을 제때 받는 게 좋겠다고 말한 사실을(She said she had better get your receipts on time this time) 알리자, 패트릭 씨가 '그분을 실망시키지 않을 겁니다'라고 반응하고 있다. 이는 제때 영수증을 제출하겠다는 뜻이므로 (C)가 정답이다.

어휘 **keep A B** A를 B한 상태로 유지하다 **ask A for B** A에게 B를 요청하다 **meet** (요구, 조건 등) ~을 충족하다 **submission** 제출(하는 것)

27-29.

9월 20일
버논 앤더슨 씨
앤더슨 & 프링 주식회사
비스마르크 드라이브 2996번지
미니애폴리스, 미네소타 55423

앤더슨 씨께,

저는 그라츠 육가공 주식회사의 인사부장이며, 저희의 창립자이자 대표이사인 헤롤드 플러머 씨를 대신하여 편지를 쓰고 있습니다.

그라츠 육가공 주식회사는 **27** 육류 제품을 미국과 유럽 전역에 있는 고객에게 유통하는 것을 전문으로 하는 지역 기반의 정육 회사입니다.

최근 몇 개월 동안, 저희는 공장에서의 보건 안전 정책에 관련한 법적 분쟁에 연루되어 있었습니다. 비록 이것이 저희의 수익에 직접적으로 영향을 끼치지 않았지만, 저희 회사의 명성에 부정적인 영향을 미쳤습니다.

28 플러머 씨는 저희 기업의 이미지를 강화하기 위해 전문적인 대행사를 고용해야 한다고 제안하였습니다. **29** 저는 작년에 앤더슨 & 프링 사를 국내에서 가장 유능한 홍보회사라고 설명한 <미니애폴리스 타임즈>의 기사를 읽었던 것이 기억나서, 이와 관련해 가장 먼저 귀사에 연락을 취한 것입니다. 저는 귀하나 대표자 중의 한 분과 회의를 마련하고 싶습니다. 이를 논의하기 위해 555- 6671로 연락해주시기 바랍니다.

안녕히 계십시오.

크레이그 브루스터
인사부장
그랏츠 육가공 주식회사

어휘 **director of personnel** 인사부장 **on behalf of** ~을 대신하여 **locally-based** 지역 기반의, 현지에 기반을 둔 **meat packing** 정육의, 육류를 도축하는 **specialize in** ~을 전문으로 하다 **distribution** 유통, 배분 **throughout** 전역에 걸쳐 **be involved in** ~에 연루되다 **legal** 법적인 **dispute** 분쟁, 논란 **regarding** ~에 관한 **impact** ~에 영향을 미치다 **earning** 소득, 수입 **affect** ~에 영향을 주다 **reputation** 명성, 평판 **agency** 대행사, 대리점 **strengthen** ~을 강화하다 **recall** ~을 기억해내나, 상기하다 **public relations** 홍보 **representative** 대표자, 대리인

27. 그라츠 육가공 주식회사에 대해 명시된 것은 무엇인가?

(A) 수익의 감소를 겪어 왔다.
(B) 브루스터 씨에 의해 창립되었다.
(C) 자사의 상품을 해외로 수출한다.
(D) 여러 육류 포장 공장을 운영하고 있다.

정답 (C)

해설 첫 번째 문단 마지막 부분에 육류 제품을 미국과 유럽 전역에 있는 고객에게 유통하는 것을 전문으로 하는 정육 회사라고 (Grazer Packed Meats Inc. is a locally-based meat packing company specializing in the distribution of meat products to clients throughout the United States and Europe) 설명하고 있으므로 (C)가 정답이다.

어휘 **decline** 감소 **profit** 수익, 수입 **export** ~을 수출하다 **overseas** 해외로 **operate** ~을 운영하다, 가동하다

28. 브루스터 씨는 앤더슨 & 프링 주식회사가 무엇을 해 주기를 원하는가?

(A) 보건 안전 검사를 실시하는 것
(B) 소속 회사의 평판을 향상시켜주는 것
(C) 상품의 유통을 지원하는 것
(D) 소속 회사의 연간 지출을 감소시키는 것

정답 (B)

해설 세 번째 문단에 플러머 씨가 기업의 이미지를 강화하기 위해 전문적인 대행사를 고용해야 한다고 제안했다는(Mr. Plummer suggested that we hire a professional agency to strengthen the public image of our business) 내용이 제시되어 있으므로 (B)가 정답이다.

어휘 conduct ~을 수행하다, 실시하다 inspection 검사, 점검 improve ~을 향상시키다, 개선시키다 reputation 명성 expenditure 지출, 비용

29. 브루스터 씨는 앤더슨 & 프링 주식회사에 대해 어떻게 처음 듣게 되었는가?

(A) 자신의 대표이사가 그 회사를 추천하였다.
(B) 인터넷에서 광고를 보았다.
(C) 앤더슨 씨의 직원들 중 한명과 이야기를 나누었다.
(D) 신문에서 기사를 읽었다.

정답 (D)

해설 마지막 문단에 작년에 앤더슨 & 프링 사를 국내에서 가장 유능한 홍보회사라고 설명한 <미니애폴리스 타임즈>의 기사를 읽었던 기억이 있다고(I recall reading an article in *The Minneapolis Times* last year that described Anderson & Fring as the most effective public relations firm in the country) 언급하고 있으므로 신문 기사에서 회사에 대해 처음 접하게 되었음을 알 수 있다. 따라서 (D)가 정답이다.

30-32.

휴게실 냉장고

30 최근 휴게실 냉장고의 적절한 사용에 관하여 몇 가지 논란이 발생하였습니다. 많은 직원들이 걱정스런 마음으로 제게 연락을 하여 냉장고 규정을 명확히 해 줄 것을 부탁하였습니다.

여러분이 냉장고에 넣으시는 그 어떠한 물건이든 라벨을 써서 붙이셔야 합니다. **31** 여러분이 자신의 물건에 라벨로 표기할 수 있도록 펜과 포스트잇 메모지가 냉장고 위에 제공되어 있습니다. 모든 직원들과 함께 나눌 목적으로 사온 부패하기 쉬운 음식은 '모두를 위한 것'이라고 라벨을 붙여 주십시오. 또한 여러분의 이름과 그 음식이 냉장고에 놓여진 최초의 날짜를 포함해 주십시오. 냉장고 앞에 "<제품명> 마음껏 드세요."라고 적어서 붙여 놓으시면 됩니다.

냉장고 청소 일정은 냉장고 옆면에 붙어 있습니다. **32** 금요일 저녁 6시까지 먹거나 냉장고에서 치워지지 않은 부패하기 쉬운 음식은 냉장고 청소 담번에 의해 버려질 것입니다. 부패하기 쉬운 음식에는 육류, 가금류, 생선, 달걀, 유제품, 과일, 그리고 채소가 포함됩니다. 양념과 드레싱 그리고 소스는 유통기한에 따라 주기적으로 버려질 것입니다.

어휘 break room 휴게실 dispute 논란 occur 발생하다 concern 걱정 clarify ~을 명확하게 하다 label ~에 라벨을 붙이다 perishable 잘 상하는, 부패하기 쉬운 intend to do ~할 의도이다 initially 최초로, 처음에 help oneself (음식을) 마음껏 즐기다, 마음껏 먹다 poultry 가금류의 고기 condiment 양념 dairy product 유제품 throw away ~을 버리다 periodically 주기적으로 use by date 유효기한, 유통기한

30. 공지문이 게시된 이유는 무엇일 것 같은가?

(A) 결함이 있는 가전제품에 대한 문제를 다루기 위해서
(B) 직원들에게 제안을 요청하기 위해서
(C) 직원들의 불평에 대해 응답하기 위해서
(D) 휴게실 개조 공사에 대해 직원들에게 알리기 위해서

정답 (C)

해설 첫 문단에서 최근 휴게실 냉장고의 적절한 사용에 관하여 몇 가지 논란이 발생하였고, 많은 직원들이 냉장고 규정을 명확히 해 줄 것을 부탁하였다고(Several disputes have occurred ~ asked me to clarify our refrigerator policies) 말하고 있다. 따라서 이에 대한 응답으로 공지를 올렸다고 유추할 수 있으므로 (C)가 정답이다.

어휘 address (문제를) 다루다, 처리하다 faulty 결함이 있는 respond to ~에 응답하다, ~에 답변하다

31. 냉장고 위에서 발견할 수 있는 것은 무엇인가?

(A) 저장되어 있는 제품 목록
(B) 음식을 저장하기 위한 가방
(C) 라벨 표기용 물품
(D) 청소 일정표

정답 (C)

해설 두 번째 문단에 라벨로 표기할 수 있도록 펜과 포스트잇 메모지가 냉장고 위에 제공되어 있다고(Pens and post-it notes have been provided on top of the refrigerator so that you can label your items) 정보를 알리고 있으므로 (C)가 정답이다.

어휘 stored 저장된 material 자재, 물건

32. 매주 금요일마다 버려질 음식의 종류가 아닌 것은?

(A) 케첩
(B) 닭고기
(C) 오렌지
(D) 계란 샐러드

정답 (A)

해설 마지막 문단에서 특정 시간까지 먹거나 치워지지 않은 부패하기 쉬운 음식은 버려질 것이라고 하며, 부패하기 쉬운 음식에는 육류, 가금류, 생선, 달걀, 유제품, 과일, 그리고 채소가 포함된다고(Any perishable food that is not eaten or removed ~ Perishable foods include: meat, poultry, fish, eggs, dairy products, fruits, and vegetables) 그 종류를 나열하고 있으므로 이에 포함되지 않은 (A)가 정답이다.

33-36.

> **수신:** 소피아 크래비츠 <skravitz@beemail.com>
> **발신:** 앵거스 밀러 <amiller@enerzona.org>
> **제목:** 다가오는 행사
> **날짜:** 11월 15일
>
> 크래비츠 씨께,
>
> 저는 에너조나 엔터프라이즈의 설립자이자 최고 운영 책임자이며, 귀하의 피아노 연주를 아주 좋아하는 팬입니다. **34(D)** 최근의 신문 기사에 따르면, **34(C)** 귀하의 새 앨범 <트와일라이트 송즈>가 30만장이 넘게 판매된 것으로 인증되었기 때문에, 진심으로 축하의 말씀 드리고자 합니다!
>
> — [1] —. **36** 저는 **34(A)** 귀하의 원작 피아노 곡들이 저희 기업 모임 행사에서 완벽한 분위기를 제공할 것이라고 생각하며, **33** 그것이 바로 다가오는 12월 29일에 있을 저희 회사의 연말 연회에서 연주해 주시도록 요청 드리기 위해 이메일을 쓰는 이유입니다. — [2] —. **35** 제가 잠정적인 일정표를 첨부해 드렸는데, 여기에 몇 시에 음식이 제공되고 연설이 진행되는지, 그리고 음악이 연주될지 간략히 설명되어 있습니다. — [3] —. 이를 한 번 살펴보시고 귀하께서 생각하시기에 관심이 있으실지 알려 주시기 바랍니다. — [4] —.
>
> 안녕히 계십시오.
>
> 앵거스 밀러

어휘 upcoming 다가오는, 곧 있을 COO 최고 운영 책임자 according to ~에 따르면 certify ~을 인증하다, ~을 증명하다 offer one's sincerest congratulations 진심으로 축하의 말을 전하다 composition 작곡(한 곡), 음악 작품 ambience 분위기 corporate 기업의 gathering 모임 banquet 연회 attach ~을 첨부하다, ~을 부착하다 tentative 잠정적인 agenda 일정(표), 의제, 안건 outline ~을 간략히 설명하다 serve (음식 등) ~을 제공하다, ~을 내오다 take a look at ~을 한 번 보다

33. 편지의 주 목적은 무엇인가?
(A) 뛰어난 직원을 축하하는 것
(B) 다가오는 콘서트를 광고하는 것
(C) 공연 입장권을 요청하는 것
(D) 음악가의 서비스를 예약하는 것

정답 (D)

해설 두 번째 단락에서 12월 29일에 있을 회사 연말 연회에서 연주하도록 요청하기 위해 이메일을 쓴다고(I am writing to you to request that you play at my firm's upcoming end-of-year banquet on December 29) 알리고 있는데 이는 상대방인 피아노 연주자에게 일종의 서비스를 제공하도록 미리 요청하는 것이므로 (D)가 정답이다.

어휘 outstanding 뛰어난, 우수한 performance 공연, 연주(회)

34. 소피아 크래비츠 씨와 관련해 언급되지 않은 것은 무엇인가?
(A) 직접 자신의 음악을 작곡한다.
(B) 여러 가지 악기를 연주한다.
(C) 최근에 앨범을 발매했다.
(D) 출판물에 특집으로 실렸다.

정답 (B)

해설 두 번째 단락에서 상대방의 원작 피아노 곡들을 언급하는 (I think your original piano compositions would provide) 부분을 통해 (A)를, 첫 번째 단락의 새 앨범 <트와일라이트 송즈>(your new album, Twilight Songs) 부분에서 (C)를, 그리고 같은 문장에서 최근에 실린 기사를 언급하는 (According to a recent newspaper article) 부분에서 (D)를 확인할 수 있다. 하지만 여러 가지 악기를 연주하는 것과 관련된 정보는 제시되어 있지 않으므로 (B)가 정답이다.

어휘 compose ~을 작곡하다 one's own 자신만의 recently 최근에 release ~을 발매하다, ~을 출시하다 feature ~을 특집으로 싣다, ~을 특징으로 하다

35. 밀러 씨가 이메일에 무엇을 포함했는가?
(A) 사업 계약서
(B) 지불 영수증
(C) 행사 일정표
(D) 콘서트 티켓

정답 (C)

해설 두 번째 단락에 잠정적인 일정표를 첨부했다고(I have attached our tentative agenda) 알리는 내용이 쓰여 있으므로 (C)가 정답이다.

어휘 contract 계약(서) payment 지불(액) receipt 영수증

36. [1], [2], [3], [4]로 표기된 위치들 중에서, 다음 문장이 들어가기에 가장 적절한 곳은 어디인가?

"귀하께서 관심이 있으실 수도 있다고 생각하는 제안이 한 가지 있습니다."

(A) [1]
(B) [2]
(C) [3]
(D) [4]

정답 (A)

해설 제시된 문장은 상대방이 관심을 가질 만한 제안이 하나 있다고 알리는 의미를 지니고 있다. 이는 제안이나 요청을 할 때 상세 정보를 제공하기에 앞서 도입부 역할을 하는 문장에 해당되므로 크래비츠 씨에게 요청하고자 하는 일의 상세 정보가 제시된 문장 앞에 위치한 [1]에 들어가 그러한 일을 제안하려 한다고 언급하는 흐름이 되어야 자연스럽다. 따라서 (A)가 정답이다.

37-40.

> **탤런트 발굴 캐나다**
> **TV쇼**
> **참가자 모집**
>
> **37** <탤런트 발굴 캐나다>의 사상 첫 시즌이 새턴 방송 네트워크에서 매주 수요일과 토요일에 방송될 것입니다. 쇼는 1시간 길이의 정규 에피소드 22회와 시즌 피날레를 위한 3시간 길이의 특별 에피소드 1회로 구성될 것입니다. 마지막 에피소드가 토론토에서 예상 인원 8,000명의 팬들 앞에서 촬영되는 반면에, **38** 대다수의 에피소드는 오타와의 SBN 스튜디오에서 진행될 것입니다. 이 쇼의 제작자들은 밴쿠버나 핼리팩스처럼 멀리 떨어진 곳에서 온 희망에 찬 수만 명의 참가자들을 끌어오기를 바라고 있습니다. 심사위원단은 연예계에서 성공한 다음의 인사들로 구성될 것입니다.
>
> - 에릭 무리뉴 (다운 로우 레코드 대표, 로스앤젤레스에 본사를 둔 음반 제작사)
> - 칼라 라미레스 (유명한 댄서이자 여러 개의 브로드웨이 히트작 안무가)
> - 제이콥 노섭 (**39** 상을 수상한 경력이 있는 코믹한 역할로 알려진 텔레비전 및 영화 스타)
>
> 참가하는 데에 관심이 있으신 분들께는 여러 선택 방법이 있습니다. **40** 여러분의 특정한 재능을 선보이는 동영상을 talentsearch@sbn.ca에 이메일로 보내주시거나 SBN 웹 사이트 www.sbncanada.ca를 통해 직접 등록하실 수 있으며, 또는 전국의 도시에서 열릴 예정인 많은 오디션 중의 한 곳에 참여하실 수도 있습니다.

어휘 **seek** ~을 찾다 **consist of** ~로 구성되다 **finale** 피날레, 마지막 부분 **film** ~을 촬영하다 **expected** 예상되는 **majority** 대다수 **attract** ~을 끌다, 불러오다 **far afield** 멀리 떨어져 **judge** 심사위원 **panel** 집단 **be comprised of** ~로 구성되다 **choreographer** 안무가 **award-winning** 상을 받은 **sign up** 등록하다, 가입하다 **via** ~을 통해서, ~을 경유하여 **show up** 나타나다

37. <탤런트 발굴 캐나다>에 대해 암시되는 것은 무엇인가?
(A) 매주 한 번 방영될 것이다.
(B) 8천장이 넘는 지원서를 받았다.
(C) 총 22회에 걸쳐 진행될 것이다.
(D) 새로운 텔레비전 쇼이다.

정답 (D)

해설 첫 번째 단락 첫 문장에 <탤런트 발굴 캐나다>의 첫 시즌이 방송될 것이라는(The first ever season of Talent Search Canada will be shown) 문구를 통해 해당 프로그램이 곧 시작할 새로운 텔레비전 쇼인 것을 알 수 있다. 따라서 (D)가 정답이다.

어휘 **be aired** 방송되다 **application** 지원(서), 신청(서) **brand new** 완전 새로운

38. 어느 도시에서 주로 <탤런트 발굴 캐나다>가 촬영될 것인가?
(A) 토론토
(B) 밴쿠버
(C) 핼리팩스
(D) 오타와

정답 (D)

해설 첫 번째 단락 중반부에 대다수의 에피소드가 오타와에 있는 스튜디오에서 진행될 것이라고(the majority of episodes will take place at SBN's studios in Ottawa) 언급되어 있으므로 (D)가 정답이다.

어휘 **primarily** 주로

39. 누가 심사위원이 될 것인가?
(A) 가수
(B) 영화감독
(C) 배우
(D) 극장 소유자

정답 (C)

해설 두 번째 문단에 상을 수상한 경력이 있는 영화배우도 심사위원단에 포함될 것임을(Award-winning television and movie star known for his comedic roles) 알 수 있으므로 (C)가 정답이다.

40. 잠재적 참가자들이 지원하는 방법으로서 언급되지 않은 것은 무엇인가?
(A) 오디션에 참석하는 것
(B) 온라인으로 등록하는 것
(C) 서비스 상담전화로 전화하는 것
(D) 비디오 영상을 보내는 것

정답 (C)

해설 마지막 단락에 관심이 있는 사람들은 동영상을 이메일로 보내거나 웹 사이트를 통해 직접 등록할 수 있으며, 또는 전국 여러 도시에서 열릴 오디션 중의 한 곳에 참여할 수도 있다는(You can e-mail a video of you performing ~ or show up at one of the many auditions) 문장을 통해 (A)와 (B) 그리고 (D)를 찾을 수 있다. 하지만 서비스 상담전화로 전화하는 것은 언급되어 있지 않으므로 (C)가 정답이다.

어휘 **potential** 잠재적인 **register** 등록하다

41-45.

> **켄싱턴 국립 은행**
>
> | 새로운 소식 | 내 계좌 | 계좌 이체 | 직원 채용 |
> |---|---|---|---|
>
> **개인 당좌 예금 엘리트를 알려 드립니다!**
>
> **41** 켄싱턴 국립 은행은 현재 새로운 계좌인 개인 당좌 예금 엘리트를 제공해 드리고 있습니다. 이 계좌는 저희 기본 당좌 예금 계좌에 비해 더 높은 이자율과 계좌 이체에 대해 더 많은 옵션을 포함한 많은 보상을 제공해 드립니다.

5월 말까지, **44** 저희는 저희 계좌 보유 고객들께 어떠한 변경 수수료 없이 기본 당좌 예금 계좌에서 개인 당좌 예금 엘리트로 전환하시기를 요청 드립니다. **42** 더욱이, 전환하시는 분들께서는 첫 1년 동안 매달 불과 6달러 밖에 되지 않는 할인된 수수료 혜택을 보시게 될 것입니다. 1년 후에는, 해당 청구 금액이 매달 표준 개인 당좌 예금 엘리트 요금인 9.50달러로 오를 것입니다.

추가 정보를 원하시거나 이 제공 서비스를 신청하시려면, 888-555-1222번으로 저희 계좌 관리 담당 직원들 중 한 명과 이야기 나누시기 바랍니다.

어휘 **transfer money** 계좌 이체하다 **checking (account)** 당좌 예금 계좌 **reward** 보상 **interest rate** 이자율 **invite A to do** A에게 ~하도록 요청하다 **switch A into B** A를 B로 전환하다 **benefit from** ~로부터 혜택을 보다, 이득을 얻다 **standard** 표준의, 일반적인 **representative** 직원

수신: <customers@kensingtonnationalbank.com>
발신: <vdole@campbellsdeli.com>
제목: 신규 당좌 예금 계좌
날짜: 5월 3일

44 어제, 저는 개인 당좌 예금 엘리트 계좌를 개설했으며, 제 기본 당좌 예금 계좌에 있는 돈이 등록 시에 새로운 계좌로 이체될 것이라고 생각했습니다. 하지만, 제 온라인 뱅킹 페이지에 접속하면, **43** 제 개인 당좌 예금 엘리트 계좌에 대한 **45** 잔액이 0달러인 것으로 보입니다. 제 돈이 왜 새로운 계좌로 입금되지 않았는지 저에게 설명해 주시겠습니까?

도와 주셔서 감사 드립니다.

빅터 돌

어휘 **at the time of** ~할 시에 **enrollment** 등록 **access** ~에 접속하다, ~을 이용하다 **balance** 잔액, 잔고 **deposit** ~을 입금하다 **appreciate** ~에 대해 감사하다

41. 웹 페이지 정보의 목적은 무엇인가?
(A) 은행 수수료의 변경을 알리는 것
(B) 온라인 뱅킹 서비스를 설명하는 것
(C) 새로운 당좌 예금 계좌를 광고하는 것
(D) 사업 제휴를 알리는 것

정답 (C)

해설 첫 지문 첫 단락에 켄싱턴 국립 은행이 현재 새로운 계좌인 개인 당좌 예금 엘리트를 제공하고 있다고(Kensington National Bank now offers a new account, Individual Checking Elite) 알리면서 해당 당좌 예금 서비스와 관련된 정보를 알리고 있다. 따라서 당좌 예금 서비스 홍보가 목적임을 알 수 있으므로 (C)가 정답이다.

어휘 **banking charge** 은행 수수료 **business partnership** 사업 제휴

42. 수수료에 관해 언급된 것은 무엇인가?
(A) 첫 1년 동안 더 낮을 것이다.
(B) 고객들이 일찍 지불할 수 있다.
(C) 다른 은행의 청구 요금보다 더 낮다.
(D) 고객들이 지불 날짜를 선택할 수 있다.

정답 (A)

해설 첫 지문 두 번째 단락에 전환 고객들에게 첫 1년 동안 매달 불과 6달러 밖에 되지 않는 할인된 수수료 혜택이 제공되고 1년 후에는 9.50달러로 오른다고(Furthermore, those who make the switch will benefit from a discounted fee of only $6 ~ increase to the standard Individual Checking Elite rate of $9.50 each month) 알리고 있다. 따라서 첫 1년 동안 더 낮은 수수료가 부과되는 것이므로 이를 언급한 (A)가 정답이다.

43. 돌 씨는 무엇에 대해 걱정하고 있는가?
(A) 누군가가 자신의 온라인 계정에 로그인했다.
(B) 수수료에 대해 너무 많이 청구 받았다.
(C) 자신의 온라인 비밀번호를 변경할 수 없다.
(D) 자신의 돈이 새 계좌로 입금되지 않았다.

정답 (D)

해설 두 번째 지문에 개인 당좌 예금 엘리트 계좌에 대한 잔액이 0달러라는 말과 함께 돈이 왜 새로운 계좌로 입금되지 않았는지 설명해 달라고(I see that my balance is $0 for the Individual Checking Elite account. Could you please explain to me why my money wasn't deposited into my new account?) 묻고 있으므로 (D)가 정답이다.

어휘 **bill** ~에게 청구서를 보내다 **fund** 돈, 자금

44. 돌 씨에 관해 무엇이 사실일 것 같은가?
(A) 계좌 변경 수수료를 지불하지 않았다.
(B) 자신의 수수료가 인상되었다.
(C) 자신의 계좌를 닫을 것이다.
(D) 켄싱턴 국립 은행의 신규 고객이다.

정답 (A)

해설 두 번째 지문 첫 문장에 어제 개인 당좌 예금 엘리트 계좌를 개설했다는(Yesterday, I opened an Individual Checking Elite account) 사실이 쓰여 있고, 첫 지문 두 번째 단락에 어떠한 변경 수수료 없이 기본 당좌 예금 계좌에서 개인 당좌 예금 엘리트로 전환할 수 있다는(to switch their Basic Checking accounts into Individual Checking Elite accounts without any change fees) 말이 언급되어 있다. 따라서 돌 씨는 변경 수수료를 지불하지 않았다는 것을 알 수 있으므로 (A)가 정답이다.

어휘 **raise** ~을 인상하다, 끌어 올리다

45. 이메일에서, 첫 번째 단락, 세 번째 줄의 단어 "balance"와 의미가 가장 가까운 것은 무엇인가?
(A) 균등

(B) 액수
(C) 평균
(D) 안정

정답 (B)

해설 해당 문장은 계좌에 balance가 0달러로 나타나 있다는 의미를 나타낸다. 즉 계좌 잔액이 0달러라는 뜻이므로 balance가 잔액 또는 잔고를 가리킨다는 것을 알 수 있으며, 이는 '액수'와 같은 말이므로 (B) amount가 정답이다.

46-50.

수신: 일레인 버로우스 <eburroughs@stenniscorp.com>
발신: 피트 네언 <pnairn@stenniscorp.com>
날짜: 9월 5일
제목: 여행 준비

안녕하세요, 일레인 씨,

맨포드 렌탈이 우리의 요구를 충족할 수 없다는 사실을 저에게 알려 주신 후, **50** 9월 27일부터 29일까지 그린포드 국립 공원으로 떠나는 3일 간의 우리 회사 여행을 위해 세 가지 다른 선택지를 계속 조사하고 있었습니다.

49 웰러 비히클 하이어가 우리 사무실에서 바로 한 블록 떨어진 곳에 위치해 있기 때문에, 우리 직원들에게 아주 쉬운 모임 지점이 될 겁니다. 이곳은 두 대의 40석 대형 버스를 제공할 수 있고, 각각 하루에 1,100달러의 비용이 듭니다. 럭셔리 버스 컴퍼니는 우리 사무실에서 꽤 먼 곳을 기반으로 하지만, 인상적인 대형 버스를 제공할 수 있습니다. 하지만, 가격이 맨포드 렌탈 또는 웰러 비히클 하이어의 가격을 훨씬 초과합니다. **46** 제가 찾을 수 있었던 가장 저렴한 요금은 채프먼 렌트-어-버스에서였는데, 이 회사는 오직 소형 버스만 제공할 수 있습니다. 각각 좌석이 20석이기 때문에, 네 대의 차량을 빌려야 할 것이며, 각각 하루에 450달러의 비용이 듭니다.

안녕히 계십시오.

피트 네언

어휘 arrangement 준비, 마련, 조치 investigate ~을 조사하다 with A -ing A가 ~하면서, A가 ~하는 채로 cost ~의 비용이 들다 be based 기반으로 하다, 본사가 있다 quite 꽤, 상당히 far from ~에서 먼 impressive 인상적인 exceed ~을 초과하다 affordable 저렴한, 가격이 알맞은 rate 요금, 비율, 속도 seat v. ~의 좌석이 있다, ~을 앉힐 수 있다 hire (돈을 내고) ~을 빌리다, (사람) ~을 고용하다

수신: 피트 네언 <pnairn@stenniscorp.com>
발신: 일레인 버로우스 <eburroughs@stenniscorp.com>
날짜: 9월 6일
제목: 회신: 여행 준비

안녕하세요, 피트 씨,

실시하신 모든 조사에 대해 정말 감사 드립니다. 우리가 작년 여행에 맨포드 렌탈을 이용했기 때문에, 그곳에 올해 이용 가능한 버스가 없다는 게 아쉽습니다. **49** 우리에게 최고의 선택권은 우리 근무지에서 가까운 곳에 위치한 회사에서 제공하는 두 대의 대형 버스를 **48** 예약하는 것이 될 거라고 생각합니다. 65명에서 75명 사이의 직원들이 우리 회사 여행에 올 예정인 것으로 예상하고 있기 때문에, 이 선택권이 우리의 요건을 충족할 것입니다. 또한, **47** 저는 2년 전에 채프먼 렌트-어-버스에서 제공한 서비스와 차량이 결코 만족스럽지 않았습니다.

일레인

어휘 appreciate ~에 대해 감사하다 carry out ~을 실시하다, ~을 수행하다 It's unfortunate that ~라는 점이 아쉽다, ~해서 유감이다 have A available 이용 가능한 A가 있다 near ~에서 가까이 anticipate that ~라고 예상하다 fulfill ~을 충족하다, ~을 이행하다 requirement 요건, 필수 조건 less than 결코 ~ 않다

스테니스 코퍼레이션 회사 야유회

직원 여러분, 회사 여행이 이달 하순으로 계획되어 있다는 사실을 알려 드리게 되어 기쁩니다. 버스가 9월 27일 오전 8시에 우리 회사의 본관 주차장에서 출발해 대략 오전 11시까지 그린포드 국립 공원에 도착할 것입니다. **50** 우리는 9월 28일 오후 7시쯤 돌아올 것입니다. 이 여행을 위해 계획된 일정 및 활동을 자세히 설명하는 회사 전체 이메일이 이번 주말까지 여러분께 발송될 것입니다. 그 사이에, 어떤 질문이든 있으시면, 인사부의 일레인 버로우스 씨에게 연락하시기 바랍니다.

감사합니다.

경영진

어휘 excursion 야유회 announce that ~임을 알리다, ~라고 발표하다 depart 출발하다 reach ~에 도착하다, ~에 이르다 approximately 약, 대략 around ~쯤, 약, 대략 company-wide 회사 전체의 detail v. ~을 자세히 설명하다 in the meantime 그 사이에, 그러는 동안

46. 채프먼 렌트-어-버스와 관련해 언급된 것은 무엇인가?
(A) 럭셔리 버스 컴퍼니 근처에 위치해 있다.
(B) 40석 버스를 제공하는 것을 전문으로 한다.
(C) 비교적 비싸지 않은 가격을 제공한다.
(D) 오직 총 네 대의 차량만 보유하고 있다.

정답 (C)

해설 첫 지문 두 번째 단락에 가장 저렴한 요금이 채프먼 렌트-어-

버스에 있었다는(The most affordable rates I could find were from Chapman Rent-a-Bus) 말이 쓰여 있어 이곳의 요금이 비싸지 않다는 사실을 알 수 있으므로 (C)가 정답이다.

어휘 **specialize in** ~을 전문으로 하다 **relatively** 비교적, 상대적으로 **inexpensive** 비싸지 않은

47. 버로우스 씨와 관련해 암시된 것은 무엇인가?
(A) 예전에 럭셔리 버스 컴퍼니에서 차량을 대여한 적이 있었다.
(B) 채프먼 렌트-어-버스를 대해 본 경험이 있다.
(C) 네언 씨가 네 대의 버스를 빌려야 한다고 생각한다.
(D) 전에 맨포드 렌탈의 직원이었다.

정답 (B)

해설 두 번째 지문 마지막 문장에 2년 전에 채프먼 렌트-어-버스에서 제공한 서비스와 차량이 결코 만족스럽지 않았다는(I was less than satisfied with the service and vehicles provided by Chapman Rent-a-Bus a couple of years ago) 사실이 언급되어 있다. 이는 버로우스 씨가 채프먼 렌트-어-버스라는 업체를 접한 사실이 있음을 의미하는 말이므로 (B)가 정답이다.

어휘 **rent** ~을 대여하다, ~을 임대하다 **deal with** ~을 상대하다, ~을 처리하다 **used to do** 전에 ~했다

48. 두 번째 이메일에서, 첫 번째 단락, 세 번째 줄의 단어 "book"과 의미가 가장 가까운 것은 무엇인가?
(A) 예약하다
(B) 주목하다
(C) 출판하다
(D) 문의하다

정답 (A)

해설 해당 문장은 이용하려는 업체와 관련해 가장 좋은 선택권이라고 생각하는 것을 말하는 내용을 담고 있으며, to부정사로 쓰인 동사 book 뒤에 위치한 명사구 the two full-size buses는 앞으로 있을 회사 여행에 필요한 차량을 가리킨다. 따라서 그러한 차량을 예약한나는 의미가 되어야 가장 자연스러우므로 '예약하다'를 뜻하는 (A) reserve가 정답이다.

49. 버로우스 씨가 어떤 회사를 추천하는가?
(A) 맨포드 렌탈
(B) 웰러 비히클 하이어
(C) 럭셔리 버스 컴퍼니
(D) 채프먼 렌트-어-버스

정답 (B)

해설 두 번째 지문에 버로우스 씨는 근무지에서 가까운 곳에 위치한 회사에서 제공하는 두 대의 대형 버스를 예약하는 것이 최선이라고 생각한다는(I think our best option would be to book the two full-size buses offered by the company located near our workplace) 뜻을 나타내고 있다. 이는 첫 지문 두 번째 단락에서 웰러 비히클 하이어가 한 블록 거리에 있

어서 직원들이 모이기 쉽고 두 대의 대형 버스를 제공할 수 있다고 알리는(Weller Vehicle Hire is located just one block from our office, ~ They can provide two full-size 40-seat buses) 부분과 일치하는 정보이므로 (B)가 정답이다.

50. 회사 여행과 관련해 유추할 수 있는 것은 무엇인가?
(A) 목적지가 변경되었다.
(B) 해당 달이 변경되었다.
(C) 기간이 변경되었다.
(D) 교통 수단이 변경되었다.

정답 (C)

해설 첫 지문 첫 단락에는 9월 27일부터 29일까지 그린포드 국립 공원으로 떠나는 3일 간의 여행이라고(our company's three-day trip to Greenford National Park from September 27th to 29th) 쓰여 있는데, 세 번째 지문 중반부에는 9월 27일에 출발해 9월 28일 오후 7시쯤 돌아올 것이라고(We will return at around 7 P.M. on September 28th) 알리고 있다. 따라서 여행 기간이 애초의 계획보다 짧아졌다는 것을 알 수 있으므로 (C)가 정답이다.

어휘 **destination** 목적지, 도착지 **duration** (지속) 기간, 시간

시원스쿨 **LAB**

WEEK 07

	Contents	Page	Date	Score (맞은 개수)
Day 01	LC+RC Half Test	02	월 일	/100
Day 02	LC+RC Half Test	22	월 일	/100
Day 03	LC+RC Half Test	42	월 일	/100
Day 04	LC+RC Half Test	62	월 일	/100
Day 05	LC+RC Half Test	82	월 일	/100

PART 1

Directions: For each question in this part, you will hear four statements about a picture in your test book. When you hear the statements, you must select the one statement that best describes what you see in the picture. Then find the number of the question on your answer sheet and mark your answer. The statements will not be printed in your test book and will be spoken only one time.

1.

2.

PART 2

Directions: You will hear a question or statement and three responses spoken in English. They will not be printed in your test book and will be spoken only one time. Select the best response to the question or statement and mark the letter (A), (B), or (C) on your answer sheet.

3. Mark your answer on your answer sheet.

4. Mark your answer on your answer sheet.

5. Mark your answer on your answer sheet.

6. Mark your answer on your answer sheet.

7. Mark your answer on your answer sheet.

8. Mark your answer on your answer sheet.

9. Mark your answer on your answer sheet.

10. Mark your answer on your answer sheet.

11. Mark your answer on your answer sheet.

12. Mark your answer on your answer sheet.

13. Mark your answer on your answer sheet.

14. Mark your answer on your answer sheet.

15. Mark your answer on your answer sheet.

16. Mark your answer on your answer sheet.

17. Mark your answer on your answer sheet.

18. Mark your answer on your answer sheet.

19. Mark your answer on your answer sheet.

20. Mark your answer on your answer sheet.

PART 3

Directions: You will hear some conversations between two or more people. You will be asked to answer three questions about what the speakers say in each conversation. Select the best response to each question and mark the letter (A), (B), (C) or (D) on your answer sheet. The conversations will not be printed in your test book and will be spoken only one time.

21. What is the topic of the conversation?

(A) A maintenance contract
(B) An expense report
(C) A travel company convention
(D) A business deal

22. What problem does the man mention?

(A) The contracts have no signatures.
(B) The client's company has gone bankrupt.
(C) The documents are different.
(D) The client will buy a different company.

23. What does the woman say she will do?

(A) Discuss the issue with the client
(B) Cancel the business agreement
(C) Organize a meeting with her employees
(D) Print another copy of the document

---

24. What are the speakers mainly discussing?

(A) A group of new workers
(B) A change in company policy
(C) A plan to lay off employees
(D) A new office space

25. What problem does the woman mention?

(A) A dispute between group members
(B) An increase in company spending
(C) The mistakes made by the staff
(D) The speed of some employees

26. What will the woman probably do next week?

(A) Apply for another job
(B) Attend a sales workshop
(C) Arrange a training session
(D) Recruit extra employees

---

27. What are the speakers mainly discussing?

(A) A business merger
(B) A factory expansion
(C) A foreign client
(D) A company policy

28. What does the man say about Madigan Shipping?

(A) It may provide a discount.
(B) It is no longer in business.
(C) It is based overseas.
(D) It has changed its rates.

29. What does the woman mean when she says, "Then it won't be a problem"?

(A) She thinks a price is reasonable.
(B) She is satisfied with a time frame.
(C) She can perform several tasks.
(D) She will find another shipping company.

---

30. What problem does the company have?

(A) It is behind schedule on a project.
(B) It is failing to meet its sales targets.
(C) It has received complaints from customers.
(D) It is struggling to attract investors.

31. What does the woman suggest?

(A) Creating a marketing plan
(B) Hiring a consultant
(C) Participating in an event
(D) Training new employees

32. What does the woman ask Bobby to do?

(A) Place an advertisement
(B) Contact some clients
(C) Select team members
(D) Calculate an annual budget

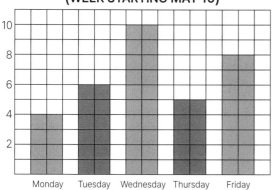

**NUMBER OF LATE EMPLOYEES
(WEEK STARTING MAY 10)**

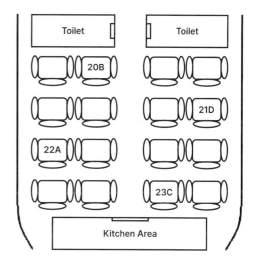

33. Where most likely do the speakers work?

(A) At a restaurant
(B) At a factory
(C) At a health clinic
(D) At an appliance store

34. Look at the graphic. When did bad weather occur?

(A) On Tuesday
(B) On Wednesday
(C) On Thursday
(D) On Friday

35. What does the man suggest?

(A) Changing the length of work shifts
(B) Providing bonuses to employees
(C) Giving some workers a financial penalty
(D) Recruiting new staff members

36. Where is the conversation taking place?

(A) At a departure gate
(B) At a check-in counter
(C) On an airplane
(D) At a travel agency

37. Look at the graphic. What is the woman's seat number?

(A) 20B
(B) 21D
(C) 22A
(D) 23C

38. What does the man mention about the woman's baggage?

(A) It is missing a tag.
(B) It looks very expensive.
(C) It has been misplaced.
(D) It is heavier than what is allowed.

PART 4

Directions: You will hear some talks given by a single speaker. You will be asked to answer three questions about what the speakers say in each conversation. Select the best response to each question and mark the letter (A), (B), (C) or (D) on your answer sheet. The conversations will not be printed in your test book and will be spoken only one time.

39. What is the talk mainly about?

(A) A system failure
(B) A software upgrade
(C) A computer model change
(D) A financial audit

40. According to the speaker, what will take place on Tuesday?

(A) Company desks will be cleared.
(B) Documents will be converted into electronic files.
(C) New staff will begin working.
(D) Files will be removed from computers.

41. What must employees do this week?

(A) Move to a new location
(B) Buy new computers
(C) Fill out a questionnaire
(D) Go to a meeting

42. Where does the speaker probably work?

(A) At a bicycle shop
(B) At a manufacturing plant
(C) At a car rental agency
(D) At a doctor's clinic

43. What does the speaker imply when he says, "And, that was just the start"?

(A) He is impressed with some work.
(B) He found several other problems.
(C) He wants assistance with a new project.
(D) He finished a job quickly.

44. What does the speaker say he has done?

(A) Sent an invoice
(B) Postponed an order
(C) Provided a refund
(D) Shipped an item

45. Who most likely are the listeners?

(A) Fitness instructors
(B) Potential investors
(C) Interior designers
(D) New gym members

46. What can be found next to the changing room entrance?

(A) Towels
(B) Beverages
(C) Lockers
(D) T-shirts

47. Why does the speaker say, "Please keep this in mind"?

(A) To recommend an exercise class
(B) To emphasize a business policy
(C) To announce a special promotion
(D) To ask the listeners for their opinions

6th Floor - Games / Toys
5th Floor - Furniture
4th Floor - Electronics
3rd Floor - Sportswear
2nd Floor - Menswear
1st Floor - Womenswear

48. Why is the speaker calling?

(A) To arrange a product demonstration
(B) To request some repairs
(C) To inquire about a project schedule
(D) To reschedule an interview

49. Look at the graphic. Where is the speaker's office most likely located?

(A) On the 1st Floor
(B) On the 2nd Floor
(C) On the 3rd Floor
(D) On the 4th Floor

50. What does the speaker mention about the furniture department?

(A) It has several vacancies.
(B) It was moved to a different floor.
(C) It is being renovated.
(D) It is holding a special sale.

This is the end of the Listening test. Turn to Part 5 in your test book.

READING TEST

In the Reading test, you will read a variety of texts and answer several different types of reading comprehension questions. The entire Reading test will last 75 minutes. There are three parts, and directions are given for each part. You are encouraged to answer as many questions as possible within the time allowed. You must mark your answers on the separate answer sheet. Do not write your answers in your test book.

PART 5

Directions: A word or phrase is missing in each of the sentences below. Four answer choices are given below each sentence. Select the best answer to complete the sentence. Then mark the letter (A), (B), (C), or (D) on your answer sheet.

51. Factory production ------- by 20% due to less demand last year.

   (A) reduce
   (B) reducing
   (C) was reduced
   (D) reduced

52. Leto Timepieces is a well-established company that creates completely ------- watches that are 100 percent waterproof.

   (A) reliable
   (B) reliability
   (C) reliably
   (D) relying

53. In ------- to unexpectedly low ticket sales, the event organizers decided to move the concert to a smaller venue.

   (A) respond
   (B) responds
   (C) response
   (D) responded

54. As technology continues to develop rapidly, people are going online to shop much more ------- than they used to.

   (A) frequency
   (B) frequent
   (C) frequently
   (D) frequence

55. Unlike other department managers, Ms. Fawcett would rather create the monthly work schedule -------.

   (A) hers
   (B) her
   (C) herself
   (D) her own

56. The board members ------- several submissions for the company's new logo before choosing Melissa Dixon's design.

   (A) evaluated
   (B) evaluating
   (C) to evaluate
   (D) evaluation

57. The health inspector had several ------- about the Redwood Diner's outdated refrigeration unit.

(A) concern
(B) concerns
(C) concerned
(D) concerning

58. Products that are damaged during shipping may be returned to the ------- address for a full refund.

(A) follow
(B) follower
(C) followed
(D) following

59. Ashforth Campground offers a wide range of teambuilding ------- for corporate excursions.

(A) requests
(B) tickets
(C) activities
(D) exceptions

60. In his latest painting, *Wind Over Valley*, Pierre Mondeau has ------- to incorporate his own artistic style with traditional styles.

(A) attempted
(B) completed
(C) persuaded
(D) recognized

61. All attendees are advised to be ------- of others by turning off their mobile phones during the performance.

(A) considerate
(B) consideration
(C) considerably
(D) considerable

62. WJE Engineering announced this morning ------- Mr. Fillmore has been appointed as Director of Sales.

(A) that
(B) what
(C) because
(D) while

63. The guest speaker will be ------- for audience questions at the end of the seminar.

(A) fulfilled
(B) available
(C) generous
(D) extended

64. Please contact Mr. Nishioka ------- you need immediate assistance with registration.

(A) so as
(B) rather than
(C) if
(D) in order that

65. The survey indicated that ------- 3 out of 10 professional tennis player s prefer to use our brand of rackets.

(A) approximately
(B) approximate
(C) approximation
(D) approximates

66. Employment applications will not be processed ------- contact information for listed references.

(A) only
(B) except
(C) without
(D) unless

PART 6

Directions: Read the texts that follow. A word, phrase, or sentence is missing in parts of each text. Four answer choices for each question are given below the text. Select the best answer to complete the text. Then mark the letter (A), (B), (C) or (D) on your answer sheet.

Questions 67-70 refer to the following memo.

To: All Front Desk Staff

From: Brian Corden, Maintenance Manager

Subject: Lobby Elevators

Date: September 17

I am writing to update you ------- the issues our guests have been experiencing when using the
          67.
elevators in the lobby, particularly when they try to go to the upper floors of the hotel. The maintenance

team is attempting to solve this problem, but it may take them a couple of days. -------, I'd like to
                                                                              68.
suggest a temporary fix to make sure that our guests are not inconvenienced by this matter. All guests

who need to reach the upper floors will be permitted to use the service elevator next to the hotel

kitchens. -------. This employee will direct guests to the elevator and assist them with any ------- they
          69.   **70.**
may have.

Please explain this situation to our guests when they are checking in for their stay.

Thank you,

Brian

---

67. (A) regard
(B) regards
(C) regarded
(D) regarding

68. (A) For example
(B) In the meantime
(C) Conversely
(D) Otherwise

69. (A) As a result, dinner services will have to be postponed.
(B) A concierge will be stationed at the front desk accordingly.
(C) Repair men will also be travelling back and forth to the 8th floor, though.
(D) In addition, the stairwell is still available.

70. (A) problems
(B) refunds
(C) answers
(D) practices

Questions 71-74 refer to the following e-mail.

To: Alex Chen <achen@zoomma.com>

From: Angela Tippett <atippett@techmarket.com>

Date: April 30

Subject: Your purchase

We are grateful that you chose to shop at Technology Market Online, the best source for electronics on the Internet. This e-mail ------- receipt of your recent payment.
       71.

-------. However, when you ordered the Lazer V3-571G laptop computer, you neglected to indicate
72.
which color you would prefer. We would appreciate it if you could address this issue by making a

------- at your earliest possible convenience. The model that you ordered is available in Midnight Black
73.
or Cherry Red. After you have informed us, you will receive an updated confirmation e-mail ------- an
                                                74.
explanation of how to track your item by entering its serial number on our site.

Please don't hesitate to ask me any other questions, should you have any.

Sincerely,

Angela Tippett
Customer Service Agent, Technology Market Online

---

71. (A) acknowledging
    (B) acknowledgement
    (C) acknowledge
    (D) acknowledges

72. (A) We regret to inform you that the item is no longer in stock.
    (B) Your item is almost ready for shipping.
    (C) The credit card you provided could not be charged.
    (D) Several other offers are available during our Summer Sales event.

73. (A) purchase
    (B) selection
    (C) contract
    (D) complaint

74. (A) so that
    (B) even if
    (C) along with
    (D) if only

PART 7

Directions: In this part you will read a selection of texts, such as magazine and newspaper articles, e-mails, and instant messages. Each text or set of texts is followed by several questions. Select the best answer for each question and mark the letter (A), (B), (C), or (D) on your answer sheet.

Questions 75-76 refer to the following text message chain.

REGINA LONG	[11:35 A.M.]	Hey Troy. I'm on my way to Grover Bistro. What time did you book the table for?
TROY JACKSON	[11:37 A.M.]	Oh, there'll be lots of spaces.
REGINA LONG	[11:38 A.M.]	Well, I hope you're right! I don't want to wait around to be seated.
TROY JACKSON	[11:40 A.M.]	It'll be fine. But, you may have to wait a few minutes on me. I'm just about to leave now.
REGINA LONG	[11:41 A.M.]	Okay, no problem. I'll just order a drink and browse some Web sites while I wait.

75. At 11:37 A.M., what does Mr. Jackson mean when he writes, "there'll be lots of spaces"?

(A) He wants to invite some friends
(B) He thinks it will be easy to park.
(C) He has not made a reservation.
(D) He will check his schedule.

76. What is suggested about Ms. Long?

(A) She has been to the bistro several times.
(B) She will wait outside the bistro for Mr. Jackson.
(C) She will arrive at the bistro before Mr. Jackson.
(D) She will check directions on a Web site.

Questions 77-79 refer to the following article.

July 14th (Loneburg) - Following several months of discussions concerning the historical importance of the Greenwood Theater, the city council has finally made a decision regarding its fate. — [1] —. On Saturday, July 20, the theater will be torn down using explosives and heavy construction machinery. The site of the Greenwood Theater will be cleared by November 1 and will later be used as the site of the brand new Hackney Telecom headquarters. — [2] —.

The Greenwood Theater, originally known as the Pavilion Theater, opened in 1965 and enjoyed two decades of popularity and success. — [3] —. However, insufficient investment led to its closure in the early-1990s. There was an attempt to revive the venue in 2001, but it was closed again indefinitely after it was flooded in 2002. Despite being long since abandoned, the attractive building is still regarded as a town landmark and many locals will be sorry to see it go on July 20th. — [4] —.

77. What is the article mainly about?

    (A) The construction of a new theater
    (B) The relocation of a firm's headquarters
    (C) The life of a successful local resident
    (D) The planned demolition of a building

78. What is NOT indicated about the Greenwood Theater?

    (A) It originally had a different name.
    (B) It experienced funding difficulties.
    (C) It enjoyed great success in the 1990s.
    (D) It was shut down on two occasions.

79. In which of the positions marked [1], [2], [3], and [4] does the following sentence best belong?

    "It was even used to host several high-profile film festivals."

    (A) [1]
    (B) [2]
    (C) [3]
    (D) [4]

To: Brenda Davenport, Human Resources
From: Johnathan Brewer, Warehouse Manager
Date: August 11
Subject: Parking problems

Ms. Davenport,

This is Jonathan Brewer, head of our Warehouse and Shipping Department. As I'm sure you know, last week's storm caused significant damage to the roof of our warehouse. Because of this, we will have to empty portions of our warehouse while construction crews make repairs. The construction crews will arrive on Friday, September 4, and they will work through Tuesday, September 8.

Employees should be aware of the following change in procedure. Because we have to empty the warehouse to make room for construction crews, shipments cannot be processed until after completion. If your clients need anything, it should be shipped before or after the construction.

Also, the construction crews will bring in lots of heavy equipment, so employees will not be able to park in our parking lot until the day after the work is finished. Instead, they may park along Ashcott Avenue or at the Brice Hotel. As such, employees may need to leave for work earlier than they usually do.

Thank you for your time. Please forward this to all employees as soon as possible.

Regards,

Johnathan Brewer

---

80. What needs to be repaired as a result of the storm?

    (A) The assembly line machinery
    (B) The warehouse roof
    (C) The shipping area
    (D) The parking lot

81. What are employees encouraged to do during the repairs?

    (A) Clean their own workstations
    (B) Reschedule shipping dates
    (C) Volunteer for a construction project
    (D) Find an alternative parking space

82. What day can employees return to their normal morning routines?

    (A) Monday
    (B) Tuesday
    (C) Wednesday
    (D) Friday

Questions 83-86 refer to the following e-mail.

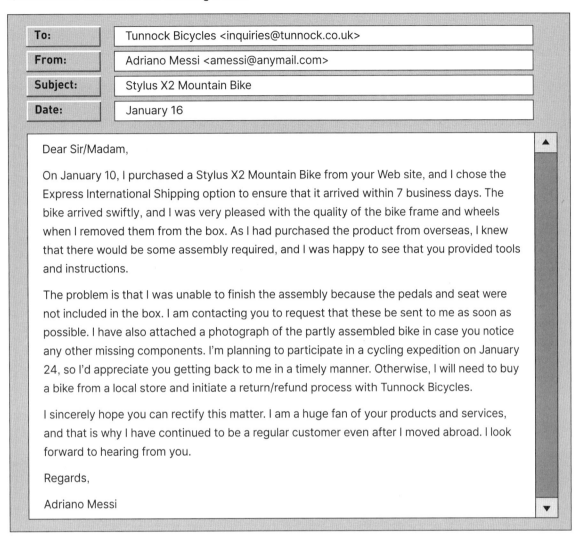

To: Tunnock Bicycles <inquiries@tunnock.co.uk>

From: Adriano Messi <amessi@anymail.com>

Subject: Stylus X2 Mountain Bike

Date: January 16

Dear Sir/Madam,

On January 10, I purchased a Stylus X2 Mountain Bike from your Web site, and I chose the Express International Shipping option to ensure that it arrived within 7 business days. The bike arrived swiftly, and I was very pleased with the quality of the bike frame and wheels when I removed them from the box. As I had purchased the product from overseas, I knew that there would be some assembly required, and I was happy to see that you provided tools and instructions.

The problem is that I was unable to finish the assembly because the pedals and seat were not included in the box. I am contacting you to request that these be sent to me as soon as possible. I have also attached a photograph of the partly assembled bike in case you notice any other missing components. I'm planning to participate in a cycling expedition on January 24, so I'd appreciate you getting back to me in a timely manner. Otherwise, I will need to buy a bike from a local store and initiate a return/refund process with Tunnock Bicycles.

I sincerely hope you can rectify this matter. I am a huge fan of your products and services, and that is why I have continued to be a regular customer even after I moved abroad. I look forward to hearing from you.

Regards,

Adriano Messi

83. What is the main purpose of the e-mail?

(A) To complain that a product was delivered late
(B) To inquire about some missing parts
(C) To commend a business for its excellent products
(D) To request that his bicycle be repaired

84. What has Mr. Messi attached to his e-mail?

(A) A diagram
(B) A warranty
(C) An invoice
(D) An image

85. What will Mr. Messi do if the company fails to respond swiftly?

(A) Reschedule a cycling trip
(B) Make an official complaint
(C) Refuse to make a payment
(D) Purchase a different bicycle

86. What is implied about Mr. Messi?

(A) He has worked for Tunnock Bicycles.
(B) He received a discount on his purchase.
(C) He bought a product from Tunnock Bicycles.
(D) He intends to make a payment to Tunnock Bicycles on January 24.

August 2
Mr. Vernon Ayers
Ayers Systems Inc.
Wyatt Technology Park, Denver

Dear Mr. Ayers,

I am delighted that you have agreed to lead a product design workshop at one of our upcoming TKS Technology Conferences. You will be reimbursed for your expenses via your online account in addition to receiving $55 per hour.

As previously discussed, we would like you to lead the workshop at our final summer conference on Saturday, August 15. You may confirm your participation by calling our HR Department manager, Les Selleck, at 555-3674. If you are unable to participate in the summer conference, please inform Mr. Selleck as soon as possible. We will then make alternative arrangements for you to lead a workshop at our first fall conference on Saturday, September 5.

You should submit the reimbursement form to our accounting team no more than three days after your appearance at the conference. At that time, you must also include all relevant receipts for accommodation and travel. Meals are not covered under our reimbursement policy.

To assist you with your preparations for your role at the conference, we would like to put you in touch with Ms. Gillian Bowers, who performed the same role at each of our spring conferences. You may reach her at gbowers@livetek.com. Please be aware that finalized conference schedules for both of the aforementioned events will be sent to you on August 8.

If you have any questions, please direct them to our HR manager.

Best regards,

Angela Baker
Head Organizer, TKS Technology Conference

87. What is NOT mentioned about the TKS Technology Conference?

(A) It will be held several times this year.
(B) It offers an hourly payment to workshop leaders.
(C) It provides complimentary meals to participants.
(D) It covers hotel and transportation costs.

88. What is true about Ms. Bowers?

(A) She has led a product design workshop before.
(B) She will give a talk at the upcoming TKS Technology Conference.
(C) She is currently employed at Ayers Systems Inc.
(D) She works in a human resources department.

89. When will Mr. Ayers officially be informed of the full conference schedules?

(A) On August 2
(B) On August 8
(C) On August 15
(D) On September 2

90. What is suggested about Mr. Ayers?

(A) He will be reimbursed for his expenses in cash.
(B) He is not likely to participate in the summer workshop.
(C) He is likely to contact the accounting team before the conference.
(D) He will receive some advice from Gillian Bowers.

To:	Bob Watanabe <bwatanabe@sushiagogo.com>
From:	Deborah Mara <debmara@morinthent.com>
Subject:	Shareholders Meeting (June 29)
Date:	June 9

Dear Mr. Watanabe,

Thank you for agreeing to cater our shareholders meeting at Morinth Enterprises. Unlike the previous time you catered an event for us, this event will be taking place in our main conference room on the 26th floor, and not in our training center on the 29th floor. I will arrange for you and your staff to have access to the service elevator so that you don't need to try to fit all your equipment into the regular ones beside the reception desk.

I was wondering if you would allow my assistant, Callum Stewart, to visit your business to sample some of your new food items. He would be able to stop by between noon and 2 p.m. any day during the week starting June 16. You can get in touch with him by sending an e-mail to cstewart@morinthent.com. I'm looking forward to seeing you on the day of our shareholders meeting.

Best regards,

Deborah Mara
Chief Executive Officer
Morinth Enterprise

To: Deborah Mara <debmara@morinthent.com>
From: Bob Watanabe <bwatanabe@sushiagogo.com>
Subject: Re: Shareholders Meeting (June 29)
Date: June 10

Dear Ms. Mara,

I'm really looking forward to making your meeting an enjoyable affair, and I'm confident that everyone at the event will love our new range of delicacies. I'll be coordinating and cooking at your gathering in person, and the head of my highly-trained wait staff, Daniel Hartigan, will also be there to assist. Regarding meeting with your assistant, I have some free time in my schedule on June 18, so I will contact him today to make arrangements.

Best wishes,

Bob Watanabe
Owner and Head Chef
Sushi-A-Go-Go Catering

91. Why did Ms. Mara send the first e-mail?

(A) To invite a shareholder to meeting
(B) To inquire about new catering menus
(C) To discuss details of a business deal
(D) To express gratitude for a recent meal

92. What should Mr. Watanabe do upon arrival at Morinth Enterprises?

(A) Register at a reception desk
(B) Use a special elevator
(C) Go directly to the 29th floor
(D) Meet Ms. Mara's assistant

93. When will Ms. Mara and Mr. Watanabe meet?

(A) On June 9
(B) On June 16
(C) On June 18
(D) On June 29

94. Who most likely is Daniel Hartigan?

(A) A head chef
(B) A business owner
(C) A food server
(D) A company shareholder

95. What will Mr. Watanabe do on June 18?

(A) Show a menu to Ms. Mara
(B) Open a new business location
(C) Prepare some food samples
(D) Send an e-mail to Mr. Stewart

Technology Mag – Featured Review (Senzfield Nexon X)

By Emily Park

Senzfield's new device marks a step forward in the company's efforts to compete with Epona Inc.'s range of G-star devices.

The Nexon X's screen is bright, vibrant, and a joy to view. However, when it comes to overall aesthetic design, the Nexon X is somewhat lacking in innovation. With regard to size and weight, Senzfield has achieved some success. Measuring 247.1mm x 177.1mm x 6.1mm, the Nexon X is thinner than its nearest rival, the Epona G-star 3, and noticeably lighter as well, weighing only 653 grams. The Nexon X's battery will last for at least one full day. However, the device's built-in 8-megapixel camera is disappointing - the image quality is clearly not on par with that provided by a smartphone or a dedicated camera.

Despite a few flaws, this is an impressive gadget that is priced at a very reasonable $199.99, significantly less than several rival tablets. For in-depth product specifications, please visit www.senzfield.com/nexonx/specs.

---

www.senzfield.com/nexonx/specs

SENZFIELD ELECTRONICS

TABLETS			
Nexon 2		Processor	Zolt Core 1.3GHz
Nexon 3		Operating System	Top Hat OS v5.1
Nexon X		Memory	RAM: 1 GB / ROM 16 GB
Shift 230		Battery	Usage Time: 24 hours
Xenon G		Dimensions	247.1 mm x 177.5 mm x 6.4 mm
Xenon GS		Weight	1.44 lbs (653g)
		Camera	8-megapixel
		Retail Price	$199.99

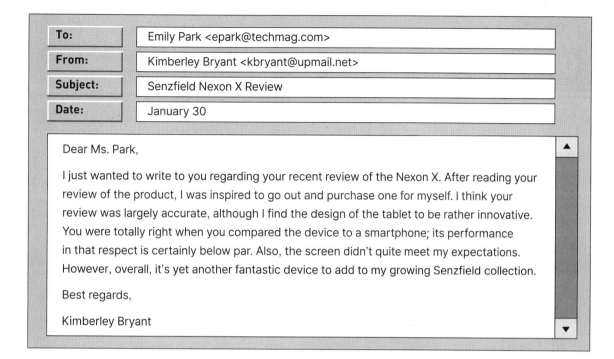

To:	Emily Park <epark@techmag.com>
From:	Kimberley Bryant <kbryant@upmail.net>
Subject:	Senzfield Nexon X Review
Date:	January 30

Dear Ms. Park,

I just wanted to write to you regarding your recent review of the Nexon X. After reading your review of the product, I was inspired to go out and purchase one for myself. I think your review was largely accurate, although I find the design of the tablet to be rather innovative. You were totally right when you compared the device to a smartphone; its performance in that respect is certainly below par. Also, the screen didn't quite meet my expectations. However, overall, it's yet another fantastic device to add to my growing Senzfield collection.

Best regards,

Kimberley Bryant

96. In the product review, the word "clearly" in paragraph 2, line 6 is closest in meaning to

(A) transparently
(B) emptily
(C) obviously
(D) sharply

97. What is NOT indicated about the Nexon X?

(A) It has a larger screen than the Epona G-star 3.
(B) Its battery holds a charge for at least 24 hours.
(C) It weighs less than the Epona G-star 3.
(D) It is cheaper than some similar devices.

98. What information is stated incorrectly in the review?

(A) The weight of the device
(B) The resolution of the camera
(C) The device's typical retail price
(D) The dimensions of the device

99. What point do Ms. Bryant and Ms. Park agree on about the product?

(A) Its design is highly innovative.
(B) Its screen is not bright enough.
(C) Its camera is of poor quality.
(D) Its processor is very powerful.

100. What can be inferred about Ms. Bryant?

(A) She regrets purchasing a Nexon X.
(B) She has posted a product review online.
(C) She owns several Senzfield products.
(D) She collaborated with Ms. Park on an article.

DAY 02

LC+RC Half Test

제한 시간 60분

MP3 바로듣기

강의 바로보기

정답 및 해설 p. 27

PART 1

Directions: For each question in this part, you will hear four statements about a picture in your test book. When you hear the statements, you must select the one statement that best describes what you see in the picture. Then find the number of the question on your answer sheet and mark your answer. The statements will not be printed in your test book and will be spoken only one time.

1.

2.

PART 2

Directions: You will hear a question or statement and three responses spoken in English. They will not be printed in your test book and will be spoken only one time. Select the best response to the question or statement and mark the letter (A), (B), or (C) on your answer sheet.

3. Mark your answer on your answer sheet.

4. Mark your answer on your answer sheet.

5. Mark your answer on your answer sheet.

6. Mark your answer on your answer sheet.

7. Mark your answer on your answer sheet.

8. Mark your answer on your answer sheet.

9. Mark your answer on your answer sheet.

10. Mark your answer on your answer sheet.

11. Mark your answer on your answer sheet.

12. Mark your answer on your answer sheet.

13. Mark your answer on your answer sheet.

14. Mark your answer on your answer sheet.

15. Mark your answer on your answer sheet.

16. Mark your answer on your answer sheet.

17. Mark your answer on your answer sheet.

18. Mark your answer on your answer sheet.

19. Mark your answer on your answer sheet.

20. Mark your answer on your answer sheet.

PART 3

Directions: You will hear some conversations between two or more people. You will be asked to answer three questions about what the speakers say in each conversation. Select the best response to each question and mark the letter (A), (B), (C) or (D) on your answer sheet. The conversations will not be printed in your test book and will be spoken only one time.

21. Where does the man most likely work?

    (A) At a household appliance store
    (B) At a home cleaning service
    (C) At a maintenance office
    (D) At a grocery store

22. According to the man, what does the woman need to do?

    (A) Restart a device
    (B) Download an app
    (C) Pay a service charge
    (D) Schedule some repairs

23. What event does the man mention?

    (A) An online gift giveaway
    (B) An art competition
    (C) A local festival
    (D) A special sale

24. What does the man want to do?

    (A) Start a business
    (B) Buy a house
    (C) Renovate a property
    (D) Purchase a vehicle

25. What does the woman mention about the Web site she used?

    (A) It features several photographs.
    (B) It has the most extensive listings.
    (C) It has recently been updated.
    (D) It offers the cheapest deals.

26. What does the woman recommend?

    (A) Visiting a real estate agency
    (B) Checking a weekend publication
    (C) Signing up to receive a newsletter
    (D) Speaking to one of her colleagues

27. What is the woman trying to do?

    (A) Renew a membership
    (B) Change a password
    (C) Purchase a textbook
    (D) Sign up for a course

28. What does the man imply when he says, "That's certainly strange"?

    (A) He does not understand the woman's question.
    (B) He believes prices are listed incorrectly.
    (C) He thinks a Web site may be malfunctioning.
    (D) He is surprised that a product has sold out.

29. What does the man offer to do for the woman?

    (A) Provide a discount
    (B) Update her personal details
    (C) Explain a schedule
    (D) Send her a form

30. Where is the conversation taking place?

    (A) In a library
    (B) In a restaurant
    (C) In a health food shop
    (D) In a book store

31. What will the woman do this weekend?

    (A) Host a gathering
    (B) Go on a vacation
    (C) Join a cooking class
    (D) Attend a performance

32. What does Toby recommend?

    (A) Making a reservation
    (B) Coming back next week
    (C) Rescheduling a shipment
    (D) Visiting a different branch

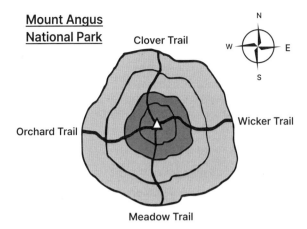

Mount Angus National Park

Clover Trail

Orchard Trail

Wicker Trail

Meadow Trail

N
W E
S

33. Where is the conversation taking place?

(A) In a parking lot
(B) In an information office
(C) At a travel agency
(D) On a mountain trail

34. Look at the graphic. Which trail is temporarily closed?

(A) Clover Trail
(B) Orchard Trail
(C) Meadow Trail
(D) Wicker Trail

35. What will the woman probably do next?

(A) Meet her friends
(B) Examine a map
(C) Purchase snacks
(D) Return to her car

Ticket Counter	Popcorn	Beverages	Hot Dogs	Restroom
	Screen 1	Screen 2	Screen 3	Screen 4
Door				

36. What are the speakers mainly discussing?

(A) A job opportunity
(B) A movie schedule
(C) A newly-released film
(D) A special offer

37. What does the woman say about the movie theater?

(A) It has been very busy recently.
(B) It has added a new screen.
(C) It is being renovated.
(D) It is closing down soon.

38. Look at the graphic. Which screen will the man go to?

(A) Screen 1
(B) Screen 2
(C) Screen 3
(D) Screen 4

PART 4

Directions: You will hear some talks given by a single speaker. You will be asked to answer three questions about what the speakers say in each conversation. Select the best response to each question and mark the letter (A), (B), (C) or (D) on your answer sheet. The conversations will not be printed in your test book and will be spoken only one time.

39. According to the speaker, what is the business known for?

(A) Famous coffee
(B) Delicious sweets
(C) Hardware items
(D) City tours

40. What can tour members do at the visitor center?

(A) Speak to experts
(B) Purchase a guidebook
(C) Receive free samples
(D) Watch a video

41. Why should the listener press 3?

(A) To ask questions
(B) To reserve a venue
(C) To hear the message again
(D) To get directions

42. Where is the talk taking place?

(A) At a retirement dinner
(B) At an awards ceremony
(C) At a staff orientation
(D) At an opening celebration

43. Who most likely is Jay Landry?

(A) A business owner
(B) An actor
(C) A keynote speaker
(D) A singer

44. Why does the speaker say, "It'll be worth the wait"?

(A) To apologize for the delay
(B) To express gratitude to the listeners
(C) To explain a schedule change
(D) To make the listeners excited

45. What is the purpose of the call?

(A) To respond to a colleague
(B) To request assistance
(C) To recommend a supplier
(D) To review an annual budget

46. What does the speaker mean when he says, "We just don't have the funds"?

(A) He is worried about sales figures.
(B) He cannot approve a request.
(C) He has misplaced some money.
(D) He is waiting to receive information.

47. What does the speaker say he will do in April?

(A) Promote some employees
(B) Extend a work contract
(C) Launch a marketing campaign
(D) Reconsider a decision

```
ADRIFT AIRWAYS – RATINGS

IN-FLIGHT MEAL      ★★
SEAT COMFORT        ★★★★★
ENTERTAINMENT       ★★★★
SHOPPING            ★★★
```

48. Who most likely is the listener?

(A) An airline customer
(B) A magazine writer
(C) A customer service manager
(D) A business owner

49. What is the speaker concerned about?

(A) Modifying a fleet of planes
(B) Advertising a new range of services
(C) Losing customers to competitors
(D) Reducing the number of complaints

50. Look at the graphic. What aspect of the airline will the speaker discuss tomorrow?

(A) In-flight meal
(B) Seat comfort
(C) Entertainment
(D) Shopping

This is the end of the Listening test. Turn to Part 5 in your test book.

READING TEST

In the Reading test, you will read a variety of texts and answer several different types of reading comprehension questions. The entire Reading test will last 75 minutes. There are three parts, and directions are given for each part. You are encouraged to answer as many questions as possible within the time allowed. You must mark your answers on the separate answer sheet. Do not write your answers in your test book.

PART 5

Directions: A word or phrase is missing in each of the sentences below. Four answer choices are given below each sentence. Select the best answer to complete the sentence. Then mark the letter (A), (B), (C), or (D) on your answer sheet.

---

51. Ms. Lorimer was thirty minutes late for her dental appointment because of ------- traffic congestion.

(A) heavy
(B) heavily
(C) heaviest
(D) heaviness

52. Matthew and Diana plan to put ------- home up for sale and move to the suburbs next year.

(A) they
(B) them
(C) their
(D) theirs

53. Apollon Inc. keeps job satisfaction high by ------- its employees with various incentive gifts.

(A) reward
(B) rewards
(C) rewarding
(D) rewarded

54. The upcoming seminars at Bridgerton Institute should appeal to anyone who is interested ------- computer programming.

(A) on
(B) in
(C) at
(D) by

55. All company work files will be backed up ------- the technicians perform network maintenance.

(A) over
(B) before
(C) so that
(D) even

56. The *Millborough Daily News* ------- published an article about the mayor's election win.

(A) timely
(B) quickly
(C) formerly
(D) extremely

57. Hill Street Coffee House offers more than 50 ------- of coffee originating from all over the world.

(A) varying
(B) varieties
(C) various
(D) varies

58. The grounds of the country club are ------- after by an experienced team of landscape gardeners.

(A) looked
(B) look
(C) looking
(D) to look

59. Opened 10 years -------, the ice-skating rink has become increasingly popular with local residents.

(A) once
(B) ago
(C) long
(D) when

60. To avoid serious accidents, all refinery workers should follow standard safety ------- at work.

(A) procedures
(B) developments
(C) categories
(D) qualifications

61. Spritz Furnishings just launched a new line of ------- office furniture to prevent muscle and joint pain.

(A) intrinsic
(B) ergonomic
(C) intangible
(D) extroverted

62. BlueSky Company produces ------- priced clothing and footwear designed for camping and hiking.

(A) reason
(B) reasoned
(C) reasonable
(D) reasonably

63. Ms. Simpson has given ------- an extended deadline for completing the market research survey.

(A) we
(B) us
(C) our
(D) ourselves

64. Please create a company handbook ------- new employees can learn about our policies.

(A) so that
(B) in order to
(C) because of
(D) as well as

65. Construction work to enlarge the main hall of the Ashberg Convention Center will be carried out ------- the next eight months.

(A) above
(B) over
(C) along
(D) with

66. The last week of December is ------- many firms will most likely notice a surge in overall consumer spending.

(A) what
(B) why
(C) how
(D) when

PART 6

Directions: Read the texts that follow. A word, phrase, or sentence is missing in parts of each text. Four answer choices for each question are given below the text. Select the best answer to complete the text. Then mark the letter (A), (B), (C) or (D) on your answer sheet.

Questions 67-70 refer to the following advertisement.

Zander Printing -------- all your promotional materials an eye-catching and professional appearance. We
            67.
specialize in the design and production of flyers, posters, invitations and brochures for a diverse -------
                                                                                                    68.
of corporate clients.

When you use our services, you also have the option to obtain a VIP membership. As a member, you
can take advantage of our express service, which means you can have your orders completed in half
the normal time. -------. On bulk orders, you may receive up to 30 percent off the total cost of your
            69.
order, and you can order smaller items such as business cards and invitations at half price.

To find out more ------- our services and membership plans, call us today at (031)-555-0129.
            70.

67. (A) gave
    (B) will give
    (C) would have given
    (D) has given

68. (A) limit
    (B) portion
    (C) menu
    (D) range

69. (A) Zander Printing works with many well-
        known corporate clients.
    (B) Thank you for placing your order with our
        sales team.
    (C) Moreover, membership provides you with
        several discounts.
    (D) For example, we can provide pamphlets for
        tours and events.

70. (A) upon
    (B) from
    (C) about
    (D) due to

To: katysloane@gomail.com

From: colinmaxwell@officemax.com

Date: July 16

Subject: Re: Missing order

Dear Ms. Sloane,

I just read your message regarding the two Betatech photocopiers you ordered from us on July 8. You are correct: as per our policy, your items should have been delivered within 7 business days. I was very surprised to learn that you have not received them yet. ------- 71. , we allow a maximum of 5 business days for deliveries. ------- 72. . According to this document, your goods were damaged in transit, and returned to our warehouse by the delivery company. We had to wait for two more copiers to come in, and these were sent out to you yesterday. Should the order still not have arrived by July 20, please ------- 73. us. Please accept my utmost apologies. We often have problems with our current shipping company. I'm sorry to say it, but this type of issue is becoming quite ------- 74. , and we will have to take action to address this.

Sincerely,

Colln Maxwell

Office Max Supplies

71. (A) As always
    (B) After all
    (C) In that case
    (D) In conclusion

72. (A) We can confirm that we have received your payment.
    (B) Please refer to our policy on shipping and ordering.
    (C) Unfortunately, the goods you requested are no longer on sale.
    (D) I was able to locate the monthly shipping schedule.

73. (A) contacted
    (B) to contact
    (C) contacting
    (D) contact

74. (A) welcome
    (B) beneficial
    (C) typical
    (D) affordable

PART 7

Directions: In this part you will read a selection of texts, such as magazine and newspaper articles, e-mails, and instant messages. Each text or set of texts is followed by several questions. Select the best answer for each question and mark the letter (A), (B), (C), or (D) on your answer sheet.

Questions 75-76 refer to the following advertisement.

COOL OFF THIS SUMMER
AT SPLISH SPLASH CANYON!

Splish Splash Canyon, operated by Action Ridge Inc., provides an ideal setting for you to keep cool while enjoying the sunshine. Our multi-million-dollar water park was first opened in 1989, and today it boasts a wide variety of attractions. We have the country's fastest water slide, the country's longest rafting course, a massive wave pool, several outstanding restaurants, and an outdoor stage where concerts take place every weekend. All-day parking is inexpensive and life jackets are available for rent.

To celebrate the start of a new summer season of fun and adventure at Splish Splash Canyon, we are pleased to announce the details of our brand new summer season pass, available from June 1!

For only $79.99, season pass holders will receive:
· Unlimited admission to the park from June 1 to August 31
· A 15% discount on all food and beverages
· A 10% discount on all gift shop purchases
· One complimentary admission for a guest per month
· Free access to the miniature golf course and go karts
· Free use of the shuttle bus service running to/from Yorkton Bus Terminal

And if you buy two or more season passes, each pass will cost only $69.99!

Visit www.splishsplashcanyon.com to find out more and to purchase your pass today!

75. What is the main purpose of the advertisement?
   (A) To publicize a new tourist destination
   (B) To describe the history of a water park
   (C) To announce new park attractions
   (D) To promote a special seasonal offer

76. What benefit will visitors receive for purchasing a Splish Splash Canyon season pass?
   (A) Lower fees for concert tickets
   (B) A complimentary gift
   (C) Use of a transportation service
   (D) Year-round access to the park

Questions 77-79 refer to the following online chat discussion.

Sandy	[2:14 P.M.]	Hey, Alec... The Customer Service team will be relocating to our building on the 24th. We still need to decide on the best location for them.
Alec	[2:20 P.M.]	I was discussing the situation with Frank yesterday and he made a good suggestion. Shipping and Receiving has the largest square footage in the facility and it is located on the first floor, right next to the food processing facility. It would be the most functional and convenient location for them.
Sandy	[2:22 P.M.]	Are you saying that we should divide the room in half?
Alec	[2:25 P.M.]	Yes. Shipping and Receiving could remain closest to our entrance, and Customer Service should work closely with them.
Sandy	[2:30 P.M.]	That might not work out. The Wi-Fi is unreliable in that section of the room. That is why no computers are currently set up there. Customer Service requires high speed Internet access at all times.
Alec	[2:35 P.M.]	That's an easy fix. I could call a technician to install a wireless router to boost the signal. In fact, my 4:00 meeting just got canceled, so I will get in touch with the necessary department then. I will let you know how it goes.
Sandy	[2:39 P.M.]	Great. Thanks.

77. What is indicated about the company?

(A) It is seeking new employees.
(B) It is moving a department.
(C) It is switching Internet providers.
(D) It is purchasing new computers.

78. What did Frank say about the Customer Service team members?

(A) They have complained about the Internet connection.
(B) They will replace the Shipping and Receiving staff.
(C) They will arrive on the 24th.
(D) They should be situated on the first floor.

79. At 2:30 P.M., what does Sandy mean when she writes, "That might not work out"?

(A) She believes the Customer Service staff are unproductive.
(B) She thinks a room is unsuitable for Customer Service.
(C) She recommends changing the date of a project.
(D) She would prefer to work in Shipping and Receiving.

To: All staff

From: Oliver Carruthers

Subject: Annual staff party

Date: October 29

Greetings,

We are all winding down as we approach the end of the fiscal year. I trust that each of you is looking forward to a well-deserved break. As a team, we have had a very productive year and on behalf of the management here at PQR Enterprises, I would like to invite you to our annual staff party for an opportunity to get to know your colleagues better in a relaxed environment. You all deserve it!

The event will be held in the ballroom at Reitman Hotel on November 8 at 6:00 P.M. It will be catered by Stonewall Catering. Entertainment will be provided by the Reitman Hotel Band, as well as the popular comedian Wayne Rally.

We understand that many of you have children, which makes it difficult to attend evening functions. Because we hope to accommodate as many of you as possible, we have hired childcare staff who will provide free babysitting on the night of the party. Children will be fed a healthy meal which will be followed by a family movie. Qualified babysitters will be there to attend to the children's needs. After the movie, there will be games and arts and crafts to keep the youngsters entertained until their parents are ready to go home.

We sincerely hope to see everyone there!

---

80. What is the main purpose of the e-mail?

   (A) To congratulate the team on a successful fiscal year
   (B) To invite staff to a celebratory company party
   (C) To inform staff that they will receive an extra bonus
   (D) To request childcare services during a staff party

81. What is NOT mentioned as something the children will enjoy?

   (A) A movie
   (B) Music
   (C) Games
   (D) Arts and crafts

82. What can be inferred about Mr. Carruthers?

   (A) He is planning a monthly meeting.
   (B) He is concerned about sales.
   (C) He plans to hire new employees.
   (D) He represents management.

Construction Set to Begin on the MJ Megamall

(February 26) - Milton James Holdings Inc. announced yesterday that the construction of the MJ Megamall is set to get underway in April. The venture had been delayed after residents of Daletown, the proposed location of the mall, protested against the construction plan. Many of them believe that the inevitable rise in the number of motorists will result in packed city streets and a lack of available parking spaces. However, these residents were ultimately unsuccessful in their efforts to stop the project, which will cost in excess of $850 million.

The CEO of Milton James Holdings Inc., Mr. William Jones, has attempted to ease such fears on a number of occasions by stressing that the mall's parking lot has an impressive capacity of 6,700 vehicles. — [1] —. The massive shopping center will include numerous attractions as well as hundreds of retail outlets. Although plans to build an aquarium were scrapped, shoppers will still be able to enjoy films at a 12-screen cinema, go ice skating, and play 18 holes on the miniature golf course. — [2] —.

Milton James Holdings Inc. will hold an official press conference next month to announce more details about the MJ Megamall. — [3] —. The company's CEO will answer most questions, with assistance from the senior architect who worked on the project. — [4] —. The first commercial retailers are expected to move in approximately two years from now.

83. Why did local residents oppose the construction of MJ Megamall?

(A) It will cause property prices to rise.
(B) It will increase traffic congestion.
(C) It will harm local businesses.
(D) It will cost too much money.

84. What will NOT be a feature of the new shopping mall?

(A) A movie theater
(B) An ice rink
(C) An aquarium
(D) A golfing area

85. What is expected to happen in March?

(A) Mr. Jones will meet with concerned residents.
(B) Construction of the MJ Megamall will begin.
(C) Mr. Jones will attend a press conference.
(D) Retailers will move into the MJ Megamall.

86. In which of the positions marked [1], [2], [3], and [4] does the following sentence best belong?

"Each of the new amenities will require a separate admission fee."

(A) [1]
(B) [2]
(C) [3]
(D) [4]

Questions 87-90 refer to the following interview.

Inni Hamor, winner of last year's Best New Author Award, recently had a chance to speak with this year's winner Kara Gall about her new book, *Trying To Tie*.

Q: Ms. Gall, you recently came into the writing scene, and your first book, *Trying To Tie*, instantly became a great hit. I personally had the pleasure of reading your book, but can you tell us more about what the book is about for those who didn't have the chance to take a look yet?

A: Sure, Mr. Hamor. The book, actually, believe it or not, contains things that I've seen kids go through when I used to be a high school teacher. The story follows the protagonist, Charlie Wensill, as he copes with all kinds of issues and problems that he has growing up in a bad part of the city.

Q: What was one of the main reasons of doing this type of writing?

A: Well, as I think back on it, I think I just wanted to give teenagers something they could read and relate to. It's always being said, but being a teen really is an important period in someone's life. The things that we go through as a teenager really set the groundwork for what kind of person we become when we grow older.

Q: You certainly reached the hearts of many readers with the book. It has seen great success. And with that, do you plan on writing another similar story?

A: I get asked that a lot, and I'm sorry to say that I have no plans for another book. I'm actually preoccupied at the moment with speaking at schools to help kids like the one in my book stay in school, and even do well in school.

87. Who most likely is the intended audience for Trying to Tie?

(A) Parents
(B) Teenagers
(C) Toddlers
(D) Teachers

88. What was Ms. Gall's previous profession?

(A) A journalist
(B) A teacher
(C) A school principal
(D) A publisher

89. What is suggested about Mr. Hamor?

(A) He has not yet read Ms. Gall's book.
(B) He wrote an award-winning book.
(C) He teaches English at a school.
(D) He co-wrote a book with Ms. Gall.

90. What does Ms. Gall's current project involve?

(A) Speaking to students at schools
(B) Researching topics for a story
(C) Conducting seminars for young authors
(D) Teaching handicapped students

Brumpton Gazette

These days, Liza Tetley often finds herself elbow-deep in cookie dough, chocolate chips, nuts, and raisins. Her rapidly growing business, Tetley's Tea Shop, offers a wide variety of teas and coffees, but it is the freshly-made cookies that have people lining up along the street. Drawing on her childhood experiences of baking with her mother, the owner of this shop has created sweet treats that are apparently adored by locals and tourists alike.

Ms. Tetley, who served as a successful advertising executive for several years, has almost doubled the shop's number of customers since adding her homemade cakes and cookies to the menu. In an effort to generate interest among customers, she does not stick only to traditional varieties, and often experiments with flavors such as cherry-mint and orange-almond cookies. "Actually, I've always baked my own cakes and cookies at home, even in recent years while I was still working in an office," she says. "In the end, the urge to open my shop led to me resigning from my job, and my experience in business has actually helped me in my new venture."

Customers stopping by Tetley's Tea Shop give the proprietor high marks for both her endless hard work and her dedication to baking cookies fresh and on-site. While many shops close through the winter months once the tourist season ends, Tetley's Tea Shop still boasts a long line of local residents who are eager to get their hands on a warm, soft cookie. With such loyal clientele, it should come as no surprise that Ms. Tetley has plans to open a second business location.

Tetley's Tea Shop is located in downtown Brumpton near exit 3 of Sawyer subway station and opposite from the Channing Cross bus stop.

To:	Liza Tetley <manager@tetleyteashop.com>
From:	Mark Bauer <mbauer@prismad.com>
Subject:	Recent Article
Date:	December 10

Hello Liza,

I just finished reading the piece in yesterday's Brumpton Gazette, and it really sounds like your business is doing well. I'm so happy for you! I promise I'll drop by soon to try a few things on your menu! We still talk about you fondly here at the office, and we all miss collaborating with you on projects for our clients. Apart from that, things are going well here, and we will soon need to hire some additional staff to handle our new clients. I hope to see you soon!

Best wishes,

Mark

91. What is suggested about Ms. Tetley?

   (A) She is involved in her family's business.
   (B) She creates unique varieties of cookies.
   (C) She has just opened a second business location.
   (D) She plans to place an advertisement.

92. In the article, the word "marks" in paragraph 3, line 1, is closest in meaning to

   (A) prices
   (B) regulations
   (C) ratings
   (D) standards

93. What is NOT indicated about Tetley's Tea Shop?

   (A) It closes during the winter season.
   (B) It is easily accessible by public transportation.
   (C) It has become increasingly popular.
   (D) It sells other foods apart from cookies.

94. Why did Mr. Bauer send the e-mail?

   (A) To request that Ms. Tetley attend a meeting
   (B) To ask Ms. Tetley for assistance with a new client
   (C) To ask if Ms. Tetley is hiring new staff
   (D) To congratulate Ms. Tetley on her success

95. Where most likely does Mr. Bauer work?

   (A) At a publishing company
   (B) At a food manufacturer
   (C) At a financial services firm
   (D) At an advertising agency

To:	Dianne Sangster <dsangster@dukehotel.com>
From:	Edward Barr <ebarr@dukehotel.com>
Subject:	Staff uniforms
Date:	February 8

Dear Ms. Sangster,

I have attached a list of the work uniforms I have chosen for our staff here at the Duke Hotel. All of these uniforms consist of high-quality garments manufactured by Bellman Work Attire, and I think they match perfectly with the style of our hotel.

The uniforms will be handed out to all staff during the orientation period, which starts on February 21 and ends on February 25. Therefore, it is imperative that the items all arrive here before the first day of orientation. If at all possible, I'd like to receive Item #4823 as soon as possible, as those workers will begin work one week earlier than the other staff. I would prefer to avoid any potential setbacks as we approach our hotel's grand opening day on March 1.

Please get in touch with me if you have any questions.

Best regards,

Edward Barr, General Manager
The Duke Hotel

UNIFORMS REQUIRED:

Front Desk Staff (Male): #1186 High Button Wool Vest & Pants
Front Desk Staff (Female): #4214 Single Breasted Suit Coat & Skirt
Housekeeping Staff: #4823 Microfiber Cleaning Tunic
Restaurant Wait Staff: #R45 Banded Collar Shirt & Vest

To:	Edward Barr <ebarr@dukehotel.com>
From:	Dianne Sangster <dsangster@dukehotel.com>
Subject: Re:	Staff uniforms
Date:	February 9

Dear Mr. Barr,

While I do agree that the High Button Wool Vests & Pants and the Single Breasted Suit Coats & Skirts are good choices for those staff members, I'm wondering if the material might be too warm. It would be very difficult for staff to perform their duties effectively if they feel too hot and stuffy. What do you think?

I can order all the uniforms you picked out except for the Banded Collar Shirts & Vests. For some reason, Bellman recently discontinued those items, but Simpson has garments that are almost exactly the same. Should I order from them instead? I'm sure I'll have all the uniforms ready by February 15, long before the orientation begins.

Best regards,

Dianne Sangster, Human Resources Manager
The Duke Hotel

---

96. Why did Mr. Barr contact Ms. Sangster?

(A) To inform her of his preferences
(B) To explain an orientation schedule
(C) To confirm that he will visit the hotel
(D) To arrange a meeting with her

97. In the first e-mail, the word "approach" in paragraph 2, line 5 is closest in meaning to

(A) progress
(B) calculate
(C) strategize
(D) near

98. According to Mr. Barr, what items are required most urgently?

(A) High Button Wool Vests & Pants
(B) Single Breasted Suit Coats & Skirts
(C) Microfiber Cleaning Tunics
(D) Banded Collar Shirts & Vests

99. What is Ms. Sangster concerned about?

(A) Project delays
(B) Employee comfort
(C) Scheduling conflicts
(D) Staff recruitment

100. For which group of employees is Mr. Barr's choice not available?

(A) Male Front Desk Staff
(B) Female Front Desk Staff
(C) Housekeeping Staff
(D) Restaurant Wait Staff

PART 1

Directions: For each question in this part, you will hear four statements about a picture in your test book. When you hear the statements, you must select the one statement that best describes what you see in the picture. Then find the number of the question on your answer sheet and mark your answer. The statements will not be printed in your test book and will be spoken only one time.

1.

2.

PART 2

Directions: You will hear a question or statement and three responses spoken in English. They will not be printed in your test book and will be spoken only one time. Select the best response to the question or statement and mark the letter (A), (B), or (C) on your answer sheet.

3. Mark your answer on your answer sheet.

4. Mark your answer on your answer sheet.

5. Mark your answer on your answer sheet.

6. Mark your answer on your answer sheet.

7. Mark your answer on your answer sheet.

8. Mark your answer on your answer sheet.

9. Mark your answer on your answer sheet.

10. Mark your answer on your answer sheet.

11. Mark your answer on your answer sheet.

12. Mark your answer on your answer sheet.

13. Mark your answer on your answer sheet.

14. Mark your answer on your answer sheet.

15. Mark your answer on your answer sheet.

16. Mark your answer on your answer sheet.

17. Mark your answer on your answer sheet.

18. Mark your answer on your answer sheet.

19. Mark your answer on your answer sheet.

20. Mark your answer on your answer sheet.

PART 3

Directions: You will hear some conversations between two or more people. You will be asked to answer three questions about what the speakers say in each conversation. Select the best response to each question and mark the letter (A), (B), (C) or (D) on your answer sheet. The conversations will not be printed in your test book and will be spoken only one time.

21. What kind of business does the man own?

    (A) A law firm
    (B) A hardware store
    (C) A real estate agency
    (D) An auto repair shop

22. Why does the man want to move his business?

    (A) To reduce expenses
    (B) To have more space
    (C) To shorten a commute
    (D) To be closer to his clientele

23. What will the woman most likely do next?

    (A) Check her schedule
    (B) Calculate some costs
    (C) Provide some property listings
    (D) Review a business proposal

24. Where do the speakers most likely work?

    (A) At a travel agency
    (B) At an airport
    (C) At a train station
    (D) At a car rental firm

25. What does the man ask the woman about?

    (A) A preferred destination
    (B) A venue for an event
    (C) The location of a document
    (D) The cost of a flight ticket

26. What does the woman say is happening this month?

    (A) A customer survey is being carried out.
    (B) A property is being converted into offices.
    (C) Some computer software is being upgraded.
    (D) A new filing system is being implemented.

27. Where most likely does the woman work?

    (A) At a pharmacy
    (B) At an accounting firm
    (C) At a fitness center
    (D) At a dental clinic

28. What does the woman say about Dr. Jennings?

    (A) He is attending an event.
    (B) He has retired from his job.
    (C) He is looking for new clients.
    (D) He will receive an award.

29. Why does the woman say, "Dr. Chalmers has been with us for more than a decade"?

    (A) To recommend a colleague for promotion
    (B) To offer the man reassurance
    (C) To advise the man to contact Dr. Chalmers
    (D) To provide an excuse for an error

30. Who most likely are George and Isabella?

    (A) Auto shop mechanics
    (B) Potential car buyers
    (C) Real estate agents
    (D) Financial advisors

31. What are George and Isabella planning to do next month?

    (A) Move to a new home
    (B) Take a trip overseas
    (C) Renovate a property
    (D) Start a new business

32. What is mentioned about the manufacturer?

    (A) It is a relatively new company.
    (B) It makes a wide variety of products.
    (C) It has a good reputation.
    (D) It provides discounts to first-time buyers.

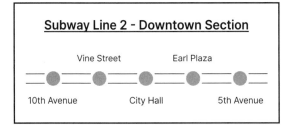

Subway Line 2 - Downtown Section

Vine Street · Earl Plaza

10th Avenue · City Hall · 5th Avenue

Interview Schedule
-Afternoon-

James Swift	1:30 PM
Tina Maynard	2:15 PM
Danny Keenan	3:00 PM
Jill Stone	3:45 PM

33. Where is the conversation most likely taking place?

(A) In a subway station
(B) In parking garage
(C) On a street
(D) On a train

34. Why is the man concerned?

(A) He has lost a ticket.
(B) He cannot find an ATM.
(C) He is running late for an appointment.
(D) His vehicle has broken down.

35. Look at the graphic. Which station will the man probably get off at?

(A) 10th Avenue
(B) Vine Street
(C) City Hall
(D) Earl Plaza

36. What are the speakers mainly discussing?

(A) Hiring strategies
(B) Sales figures
(C) Travel plans
(D) Company policies

37. Look at the graphic. Who will not attend an interview this afternoon?

(A) James Swift
(B) Tina Maynard
(C) Danny Keenan
(D) Jill Stone

38. What will the man bring to the woman's office?

(A) Résumés
(B) Tickets
(C) Contracts
(D) Pamphlets

PART 4

Directions: You will hear some talks given by a single speaker. You will be asked to answer three questions about what the speakers say in each conversation. Select the best response to each question and mark the letter (A), (B), (C) or (D) on your answer sheet. The conversations will not be printed in your test book and will be spoken only one time.

39. Where does the speaker most likely work?

    (A) A marketing company
    (B) An electronics company
    (C) An accounting firm
    (D) An Internet provider

40. What has the company recently done?

    (A) Designed a new product
    (B) Taken over another firm
    (C) Created a series of advertisements
    (D) Hired new product developers

41. According to the speaker, what will the listeners do in the next few weeks?

    (A) Organize a convention
    (B) Help new staff to settle in
    (C) Collaborate on a project
    (D) Conduct a market research study

42. Where is the announcement taking place?

    (A) On an airplane
    (B) On a boat
    (C) In a hotel
    (D) At a travel agency

43. Why does the speaker say, "It normally costs 40 dollars"?

    (A) To apologize for a price change
    (B) To promote a new service
    (C) To announce a seasonal sale
    (D) To encourage participation

44. What are interested individuals advised to do?

    (A) Check a schedule
    (B) Present a ticket
    (C) Fill out a form
    (D) Talk to an employee

45. What type of event is being introduced?

    (A) A fundraiser
    (B) A theatrical performance
    (C) A grand opening
    (D) An awards ceremony

46. What does the speaker mean when she says, "I'm sure some of them are familiar to you"?

    (A) The listeners were given information about the films.
    (B) The special guests are well-known.
    (C) The event organizers are grateful to the listeners.
    (D) The listeners should introduce themselves.

47. According to the speaker, what will happen after the event?

    (A) A meal will be served.
    (B) A concert will take place.
    (C) A film will be shown.
    (D) An announcement will be made.

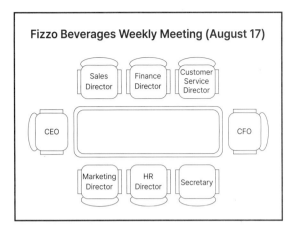

Fizzo Beverages Weekly Meeting (August 17)

48. What is the main purpose of the call?

    (A) To discuss meeting topics
    (B) To request assistance
    (C) To announce a room change
    (D) To extend an invitation

49. What problem does the speaker mention?

    (A) A director cannot attend the meeting.
    (B) Some renovations are behind schedule.
    (C) Some equipment has malfunctioned.
    (D) A project has been unsuccessful.

50. Look at the graphic. What most likely is the listener's job title?

    (A) CEO
    (B) Secretary
    (C) Sales Director
    (D) Finance Director

This is the end of the Listening test. Turn to Part 5 in your test book.

READING TEST

In the Reading test, you will read a variety of texts and answer several different types of reading comprehension questions. The entire Reading test will last 75 minutes. There are three parts, and directions are given for each part. You are encouraged to answer as many questions as possible within the time allowed. You must mark your answers on the separate answer sheet. Do not write your answers in your test book.

PART 5

Directions: A word or phrase is missing in each of the sentences below. Four answer choices are given below each sentence. Select the best answer to complete the sentence. Then mark the letter (A), (B), (C), or (D) on your answer sheet.

51. Most individuals who took part in our recent survey ------- with our products and services.

(A) are satisfying
(B) were satisfying
(C) are satisfied
(D) have satisfied

52. ------- Ms. Dewar's guidance, the marketing team created an innovative international advertising campaign.

(A) Under
(B) Now
(C) Instead
(D) While

53. Ms. Lee's event ------- was delivered to the wrong address, so she did not attend Mr. Forster's retirement dinner.

(A) invitations
(B) inviting
(C) invited
(D) invitation

54. According to one art expert, the recently-discovered portraits were ------- painted by the reclusive artist Joe Moot.

(A) liking
(B) likely
(C) likelihood
(D) liked

55. Wakefield Bank is ------- developing a new electronic banking application for mobile phone users.

(A) previously
(B) currently
(C) severely
(D) frequently

56. To meet the publishing deadline for the latest edition, Mr. Knowles finished the editing by ------- over the holiday.

(A) he
(B) him
(C) himself
(D) his own

57. In order to adapt to modern dining trends, many restaurants ------- offering more vegetarian options in the last few years.

(A) will begin
(B) have begun
(C) will have begun
(D) to begin

58. A final decision on the relocation of ATR Communications will be ------- this afternoon.

(A) regarded
(B) shut
(C) made
(D) assisted

59. ------- next Monday, Big Taco customers will be given the option to upgrade a large meal to an extra large meal.

(A) Begin
(B) Begins
(C) Begun
(D) Beginning

60. -------, none of this year's nominees at the British Film Awards have won an award before.

(A) Surprisingly
(B) Surprise
(C) Surprised
(D) Surprising

61. The third-floor cafeteria will be closed for a prolonged ------- while renovation work is underway.

(A) period
(B) minute
(C) lapse
(D) meeting

62. Money has been ------- for the professional development program, but the company director is not willing to proceed with its implementation until next year.

(A) budgeted
(B) budgeting
(C) budget
(D) budgets

63. Anyone ------- orders stationery from Delta Office Supplies normally receives his or her items within 48 hours.

(A) whomever
(B) whom
(C) whose
(D) who

64. Customers with faulty laptops can visit our technical support centers in Allerton or Farnham, ------- is more convenient.

(A) whichever
(B) everyone
(C) other
(D) both

65. ------- you are unable to attend tomorrow's workshop, please make sure the enclosed form is returned by this Friday.

(A) Whether
(B) Even if
(C) Nevertheless
(D) Yet

66. ------- the retail locations operated by Greenway Grocery, the branch in Westpark Mall is the most profitable.

(A) During
(B) To
(C) Above
(D) Of

PART 6

Directions: Read the texts that follow. A word, phrase, or sentence is missing in parts of each text. Four answer choices for each question are given below the text. Select the best answer to complete the text. Then mark the letter (A), (B), (C) or (D) on your answer sheet.

Questions 67-70 refer to the following notice.

All Grandview Condominiums Tenants

Please take note that the communal swimming pool will be closed for urgent repairs from April 4 to April 8. The ------- will take place between 10 A.M. and 5 P.M. each day.
67.

------- the swimming pool is under repair, please make sure that children are kept away from the area
68.
for their own safety. -------. In addition, tenants are advised to remove any valuable belongings from
69.
the storage room, as the repair crew may need to use this space to temporarily store some equipment.

These repairs are necessary to ensure that the swimming pool ------- with city regulations. We
70.
appreciate your patience and understanding.

67. (A) work
(B) event
(C) tour
(D) contest

68. (A) Even
(B) During
(C) While
(D) Yet

69. (A) Your feedback has helped us to improve our amenities.
(B) We offer children's swimming lessons every Wednesday.
(C) A lifeguard will be present at the pool at all times.
(D) There will be several potentially dangerous tools on site.

70. (A) to comply
(B) compliance
(C) complies
(D) complying

Questions 71-74 refer to the following advertisement.

Private Dining Rooms Available for Hire

Bonetti's Restaurant is celebrating the opening of its new private dining rooms! A spectacular lakeside dining experience could be ------- ! All private dining rooms ------- picturesque views of Bennett Lake.
71.   72.
You can enjoy a variety of freshly-caught seafood and our locally-sourced ingredients in total privacy.
We also have a mouth-watering selection of desserts. -------, you may not have any room left to try
73.
them! Bonetti's Restaurant prides itself on its very generous portion sizes, so you might be full after

your main course! Our private dining rooms can be booked for groups of up to 25 people. ------- . We
74.
hope to serve you soon at Bonetti's Restaurant!

Andrew Bonnetti (555-0097), Restaurant Manager

---

71. (A) many
(B) yours
(C) mine
(D) others

72. (A) featured
(B) featuring
(C) feature
(D) have featured

73. (A) However
(B) Therefore
(C) Similarly
(D) Consequently

74. (A) All of them praised our impressive selection
of dishes.
(B) We expect the renovation to be finished by
the end of the month.
(C) These can be customized to meet your
dietary requirements.
(D) Larger parties may be accommodated in
special circumstances.

PART 7

Directions: In this part you will read a selection of texts, such as magazine and newspaper articles, e-mails, and instant messages. Each text or set of texts is followed by several questions. Select the best answer for each question and mark the letter (A), (B), (C), or (D) on your answer sheet.

Questions 75-76 refer to the following coupon.

WILSON'S COMPUTER STORE

This coupon entitles the bearer to receive a one-time discount on a single-item purchase.

With this card, you may receive 10 percent off any of our laptops and home PCs, 20 percent off any monitors, or 15 percent off our new lines of portable hard drives.

Computer keyboards, headsets, and speakers are not included in this offer. This coupon can be used at all Wilson's Computer Store branches, and must be used before the end of December.

---

75. What is NOT being offered at a discount?

(A) Laptop computers
(B) Computer keyboards
(C) External hard drives
(D) Desktop computers

76. What is indicated about Wilson's Computer Store?

(A) It will open a new branch in December.
(B) It has multiple business locations.
(C) It sells both new and used products.
(D) It is promoting a new line of computers.

Rebecca Carlton, CEO
Volkom Enterpises

Dear Ms. Carlton,

I recently noticed the Chief Financial Officer (CFO) vacancy advertised in the May issue of the Long Beach Business Journal. As you can see from my enclosed résumé, I have over twenty years of business and finance experience. I was employed in the Accounting Department at Pendell Corporation for five years before being moved to the Finance Department. After helping to cut the company's costs by 18 percent within my first year in the department, I was promoted to Financial Manager at the firm's San Francisco headquarters, where for the next six years I was responsible for strategic planning and budgeting of company finances.

I went on to join Wiley Construction Inc. as the Director of Finance at its head office in San Diego nine years ago. In my time there as a director, I have played a key role in establishing and implementing a novel finance operating model, which has allowed the company to make more accurate financial projections and to allocate funds more efficiently.

I would appreciate it if you could give me the opportunity to speak with you in person so that we can discuss my experience and suitability for the role in more detail. I will be patiently awaiting your response.

Sincerely,

Nathan Pogba

---

77. According to the letter, why did Mr. Pogba receive a promotion at Pendell Corporation?

(A) He helped the company to increase its annual revenue.
(B) He created an innovative financial model.
(C) He contributed to the lowering of the firm's expenditures.
(D) He increased the company's customer base.

78. How long has Mr. Pogba been working for Wiley Construction Inc.?

(A) 5 years
(B) 6 years
(C) 9 years
(D) 20 years

79. Why is Mr. Pogba writing to Ms. Carlton?

(A) To suggest collaborating on a project
(B) To offer his services as a consultant
(C) To request more information
(D) To set up an appointment

To: WalterSpiegel@whcc.com

From: AlisonRiley@gomail.com

Date: August 19

Subject: Wrong charges

Dear Mr. Spiegel,

I am a country club member who is part of the Social Membership plan, which includes pool usage, tennis lessons, and use of the exercise facilities. — [1] —. However, I am currently looking at my bill for the period of May to July and I see that I have been charged $965. Unless I am mistaken, this is the fee normally applied to those who sign up for a Corporate Membership. — [2] —.

At no time since joining the country club eight months ago have I upgraded my membership. — [3] —. If you take a moment to check your computer database, I'm sure you will see that this is the case. Up until this point, I have been very impressed with the country club and its facilities, not to mention your department's attentiveness to members. — [4] —. I intend to remain a member of your country club for years to come, so I would appreciate it if you could amend the bill for the period of May to July and send a new one out. Please do not hesitate to contact me at 555 –1192 should you require any information.

I would greatly appreciate it if you could resolve this matter swiftly. Thank you.

Sincerely,

Alison Riley

---

80. Why was the e-mail sent?

(A) To inquire about membership options
(B) To give thanks for good service
(C) To request access to facilities
(D) To complain about a charge

81. What does Ms. Riley request that the country club do?

(A) Issue a full refund
(B) Extend a payment deadline
(C) Upgrade her membership
(D) Send her a revised bill

82. In which of the positions marked [1], [2], [3] and [4] does the following sentence best belong?

"I typically pay $820 per quarter in order to receive full access to these benefits."

(A) [1]
(B) [2]
(C) [3]
(D) [4]

Questions 83-86 refer to the following advertisement.

Posted: September 1

Commercial Unit Available in Downtown Toronto
Rent: $4,500/month

A large commercial space in the Silverlake Shopping Center will be vacated at the end of this month. A new tenant may open for business in the unit on October 1. It is conveniently located on the first floor near the western entrance, resulting in heavy footfall and a high number of potential customers. It is also just a short distance from busy areas such as the event stage and food court. It is very rare to find a vacancy in this shopping center, and these commercial spaces are highly desirable.

The 290,000-square-meter Silverlake Shopping Center is more expansive than the other malls in the downtown area, and it attracts the highest number of consumers. The unit has ample room for any product displays you wish to set up, and it comes with numerous adjustable shelves. All store owners renting commercial space in the mall are assigned a designated space in the parking lot adjacent to the building.

Silverlake Shopping Center store owners also receive a generous discount at the Piccadilly Movie Theater located on the 5th floor of the shopping center. The unit can be viewed on alternate Sundays when the mall is closed: first on Sunday, September 7, and then two weeks later on Sunday, September 21. To arrange a viewing or to obtain more information, please e-mail propertyoffice@silverlake.com.

---

83. When will the unit be available for rent?

(A) On September 1
(B) On September 7
(C) On September 21
(D) On October 1

84. What is suggested about the commercial space?

(A) It has recently been renovated.
(B) It is comprised of several rooms.
(C) It is on the 5th floor of the mall.
(D) It is close to dining establishments.

85. What is indicated about the Silverlake Shopping Center?

(A) It is the tallest structure in the downtown area.
(B) It is larger than other local shopping centers.
(C) It currently has numerous vacant commercial units.
(D) It is closed for business every weekend.

86. What comes with the commercial unit?

(A) A membership card
(B) Product displays
(C) Free movie tickets
(D) A parking space

Questions 87-90 refer to the following online chat discussion.

[9:30 A.M.]

Nick: Hey guys, what's up?

[9:31 A.M.]

Ron: I don't know. Tom invited us.

[9:38 A.M.]

Tom: Hi, guys! Sorry for the delay! I had some emergencies to handle. I got a text from Alison. She says her bus broke down and she will be late coming in today.

[9:39 A.M.]

Nick: Oh no! I was depending on her to do the presentation for the new clients.

[9:40 A.M.]

Ron: I know! And they are arriving in half an hour.

[9:41 A.M.]

Nick: Tom, why don't you give them a tour of the office and take them to meet the company president first?

[9:41 A.M.]

Ron: That should take up forty-five minutes or so.

[9:42 A.M.]

Tom: Okay! After that, perhaps you two can take them to the coffee shop downstairs as well.

[9:43 A.M.]

Ron: That sounds terrific! Alison should be here by then.

[9:43 A.M.]

Nick: It will also give the clients a chance to see how we work.

87. What are the writers mainly discussing?

    (A) What to do about a bus route change
    (B) Where to have a coffee break
    (C) How to handle a schedule delay
    (D) When to meet their former coworker

88. When will the clients arrive?

    (A) In 15 minutes
    (B) In 30 minutes
    (C) In 45 minutes
    (D) In 60 minutes

89. What does Nick ask Tom to do?

    (A) Take the clients to lunch
    (B) Give a presentation
    (C) Explain a delay
    (D) Show the clients around

90. At 9:40 A.M., what does Ron imply when he writes, "I know!"?

    (A) He knows how to solve the problem.
    (B) He is concerned about a presentation.
    (C) He received a text from Alison a moment ago.
    (D) He is well prepared for a client meeting.

Restaurant Review - Mahogany Bistro

By: Sarah Alford

The building at 1236 Ocean Drive in Portland, Maine, has housed no fewer than six businesses in the last eight years. Some of these, such as the Crispy Lobster House and Nemo's Seafood Buffet, lasted only one year before going out of business.

However, the Mahogany Bistro is the newest tenant and early signs indicate that this restaurant may become a success. First, Mahogany belongs to the same ownership group that provided start-up funding for L'Aventino and Ten on 10th, two of the best reviewed eateries in nearby Lewistown. Also, last month's addition of several attractive decorative touches, including a large fireplace, has transformed the once unexceptional venue into a sophisticated dining space.

Chef Peter Masterson, formerly of L'Aventino, clearly specializes in appetizers. The sea bass with radish was outstanding, as were the scallops marinated in lemon juice, which I noticed several other diners ordering. Only the Caesar salad fell short due to its slightly soggy lettuce. While the main courses may not be as impressive as the appetizers, the grilled pork chops were still quite good. To top it all off, the restaurant boasts an excellent house cocktail list, an extensive selection of locally-brewed beers, and friendly servers who are attentive at all times to the needs of the diners.

To:	Sarah Alford <sarahalford@mainetimes.com>
From:	Josh Hewitt <jhewitt@gotmail.com>
Subject:	Mahogany Bistro Review
Date:	April 11

Dear Ms. Alford,

I really enjoyed reading your review in The Maine Times yesterday, and I agree that the Mahogany Bistro is a great addition to the local dining scene. Although I've only eaten there one time, I'd recommend that you try the penne pasta for your main course next time. I chose that dish instead of the pork ribs, and I think it was a good choice. I was pleased to see you mention the appetizer with the lemon marinade. I ordered the same thing, and it was excellent.

I look forward to reading your next review!

Best wishes,

Josh Hewitt

91. What is mentioned about the Mahogany Bistro?

(A) It has been open for business for one year.
(B) It is located next to Crispy Lobster House.
(C) It has multiple business locations.
(D) It has recently undergone renovations.

92. What is stated about Chef Masterson?

(A) He is a cofounder of Mahogany Bistro.
(B) He was previously employed in Lewistown.
(C) He currently works at two restaurants.
(D) He has won awards for his cooking.

93. What can be inferred about Ms. Alford?

(A) She recommended the scallops to the other diners.
(B) She preferred the main courses over the appetizers.
(C) She thought the Caesar salad was worthy of praise.
(D) She was impressed with the variety of beverages.

94. In the e-mail, the word "try" in paragraph 1, line 3, is closest in meaning to

(A) propose
(B) endeavor
(C) prepare
(D) sample

95. Which dish did Mr. Hewitt most likely order?

(A) The sea bass dish
(B) The scallop dish
(C) The Caesar salad
(D) The pork ribs

Fiesta Tropico Resort - August Guest Activities
All activities are free of charge for guests unless otherwise stated.

When?	What?	Who?
Every Monday/ Wednesday	**Scuba Diving Lesson:** Explore the beautiful underwater world beneath the waves surrounding El Nido.	Led by Olly Galvez
Every Tuesday/Friday	**Fire Dancing on the Beach:** Your instructor will teach you the graceful art of traditional fire dancing.	Led by Isla Agustin
Every Wednesday/ Saturday	**Island Hopping Tour:** Experience numerous small islands around El Nido and have lunch on your boat.	Led by Ricky Reyes
Every Thursday/Sunday	**Filipino Cooking:** Learn to cook local Filipino dishes. (Total cost of ingredients added to guests' bill.)	Led by Martin Alonzo

Please visit the Guest Activities Office to obtain detailed timetables and to register.

To:	Activities Team Members <activitiesteam@fiestatropico.com>
From:	Jenny Kim <jennykim@fiestatropico.com>
Subject:	Important developments
Date:	August 1

Hi everyone,

I'd like to draw your attention to this month's activities program. I've just found out that Isla Agustin and Martin Alonzo will be attending an advanced training workshop from August 7 to August 13, so they'll be unavailable to lead their respective activities during that time. Therefore, I will lead Isla's activities and Jane Gonzales will lead Martin's. Once Isla and Martin come back to work on August 14, everything will continue as normal.

Regards,

Jenny Kim
Activities Team Manager
Fiesta Tropico Resort

Fiesta Tropico Resort

Name: Cathy Beringer

Date: August 15

Number of guests: 4

Date of stay: August 8 – August 12

Feedback:

I'd like to thank you for the excellent service you provided at your resort. I recently stayed there with my family, and we all had so much fun taking part in the activities on offer. I was unable to join the excursion with Mr. Reyes, but my traveling companions seemed to have a great time. My husband and I thought the fire dancing class was a lot of fun, and he is planning to utilize some of the skills he learned in Ms. Gonzales's class in our kitchen at home. Also, my mom and dad had a great time with Mr. Galvez. They will use all of his tips and techniques during their trip to Bali in October.

---

96. When does an activity that includes an extra charge take place?

(A) Every Wednesday
(B) Every Friday
(C) Every Saturday
(D) Every Sunday

97. What is the purpose of the e-mail?

(A) To recommend two new staff members
(B) To outline some schedule changes
(C) To encourage staff to attend a workshop
(D) To introduce new activities for guests

98. In the e-mail, the phrase "found out" in paragraph 1, line 1, is closest in meaning to

(A) searched for
(B) located
(C) looked at
(D) learned

99. Who taught Ms. Beringer how to perform a fire dance?

(A) Mr. Galvez
(B) Ms. Kim
(C) Mr. Reyes
(D) Mr. Alonzo

100. What are Ms. Beringer's parents most likely intending to do in Bali?

(A) Take a tour of some islands
(B) Learn local dances
(C) Enjoy some scuba diving
(D) Make traditional food

DAY 04

LC+RC
Half Test

제한 시간 60분

MP3 바로듣기

강의 바로보기

정답 및 해설 p. 76

PART 1

Directions: For each question in this part, you will hear four statements about a picture in your test book. When you hear the statements, you must select the one statement that best describes what you see in the picture. Then find the number of the question on your answer sheet and mark your answer. The statements will not be printed in your test book and will be spoken only one time.

1.

2.

PART 2

Directions: You will hear a question or statement and three responses spoken in English. They will not be printed in your test book and will be spoken only one time. Select the best response to the question or statement and mark the letter (A), (B), or (C) on your answer sheet.

3. Mark your answer on your answer sheet.

4. Mark your answer on your answer sheet.

5. Mark your answer on your answer sheet.

6. Mark your answer on your answer sheet.

7. Mark your answer on your answer sheet.

8. Mark your answer on your answer sheet.

9. Mark your answer on your answer sheet.

10. Mark your answer on your answer sheet.

11. Mark your answer on your answer sheet.

12. Mark your answer on your answer sheet.

13. Mark your answer on your answer sheet.

14. Mark your answer on your answer sheet.

15. Mark your answer on your answer sheet.

16. Mark your answer on your answer sheet.

17. Mark your answer on your answer sheet.

18. Mark your answer on your answer sheet.

19. Mark your answer on your answer sheet.

20. Mark your answer on your answer sheet.

PART 3

Directions: You will hear some conversations between two or more people. You will be asked to answer three questions about what the speakers say in each conversation. Select the best response to each question and mark the letter (A), (B), (C) or (D) on your answer sheet. The conversations will not be printed in your test book and will be spoken only one time.

21. What event does the man plan to attend?

    (A) A music festival
    (B) A sports event
    (C) A community fair
    (D) An art exhibition

22. Why is the woman surprised?

    (A) A performance has been canceled.
    (B) An event has been relocated.
    (C) Tickets are still available.
    (D) Parking will be free.

23. What should the woman do by the end of the day?

    (A) Decide on seats
    (B) Apply for a membership
    (C) Check a Web site
    (D) Buy the man a ticket

24. Who most likely is the man?

    (A) A supermarket employee
    (B) A coffee shop owner
    (C) A restaurant worker
    (D) A store cleaner

25. Why does the man apologize?

    (A) The customer was overcharged.
    (B) A delivery address was incorrect.
    (C) He prepared the wrong food.
    (D) An order is not ready yet.

26. What will the woman do next?

    (A) Visit another business
    (B) Speak to a supervisor
    (C) Cancel the order
    (D) Make a copy of a receipt

27. Why is the woman going to Baltimore?

    (A) For a performance
    (B) For an audition
    (C) For a client meeting
    (D) For a family vacation

28. What does the man say about the dining car?

    (A) It does not serve breakfast.
    (B) It only serves meals reserved in advance.
    (C) It is more expensive than regular seating.
    (D) It takes a long time for the food to be served.

29. What does the man mean when he says, "the train to Baltimore doesn't leave for another half hour"?

    (A) A departure board is inaccurate.
    (B) An engine malfunction has occurred.
    (C) The woman has time to get some food.
    (D) The woman should take an express train.

30. What type of event are the speakers attending?

    (A) A music concert
    (B) A theater play
    (C) A sports competition
    (D) A film festival

31. Why is traffic bad in the downtown area?

    (A) An accident has occurred.
    (B) Some buildings are being constructed.
    (C) A street is being repaired.
    (D) Some roads are closed for an event.

32. What is the woman concerned about?

    (A) Purchasing a ticket
    (B) Meeting a performer
    (C) Locating a venue
    (D) Finding a parking spot

Cottages for Rent	Rate per Night	Number of Beds
Daisy Cottage	$200	3
Juniper Cottage	$300	4
Ivy Cottage	$400	6
Pine Cottage	$500	7

33. What are the speakers discussing?

(A) A training seminar
(B) A company trip
(C) A client visit
(D) A property renovation

34. Why is the man concerned?

(A) Inclement weather is expected.
(B) A building requires repairs.
(C) Transportation is unavailable.
(D) A budget may be inadequate.

35. Look at the graphic. Which cottage will the woman most likely choose?

(A) Daisy Cottage
(B) Juniper Cottage
(C) Ivy Cottage
(D) Pine Cottage

Vacant Space Left #1	Vendor: Bob's Burgers	Vendor: Fruit Smoothies	Vacant Space Left #4

MAIN STREET

Vendor: Frozen Yogurt	Vacant Space Right #2	Vacant Space Right #3	Vendor: Jumbo Pretzels

36. What type of product does the man want to sell?

(A) Beverages
(B) Clothing
(C) Snack foods
(D) Posters

37. Look at the graphic. In which vacant space would the man like to set up his stall?

(A) Left #1
(B) Left #4
(C) Right #2
(D) Right #3

38. What does the woman ask the man to do?

(A) Attend a meeting
(B) Provide product samples
(C) Complete a form
(D) Present an ID

PART 4

Directions: You will hear some talks given by a single speaker. You will be asked to answer three questions about what the speakers say in each conversation. Select the best response to each question and mark the letter (A), (B), (C) or (D) on your answer sheet. The conversations will not be printed in your test book and will be spoken only one time.

39. What is the topic of Mr. Denton's talk?

(A) An electrical appliance
(B) A new car model
(C) A navigation system
(D) A manufacturing plant

40. Who is the intended audience for the talk?

(A) Marketing executives
(B) Automobile engineers
(C) Media professionals
(D) Focus group members

41. What is the audience invited to do?

(A) Go to the lobby after the talk
(B) Ask questions during the presentation
(C) Pick up an information packet
(D) Join an environmental organization

42. What type of product is being discussed?

(A) A kitchen appliance
(B) An audio device
(C) An exercise machine
(D) A construction tool

43. What does the speaker mean when he says, "It hasn't helped"?

(A) Customers are having difficulty.
(B) Products are being delivered late.
(C) Employees require further training.
(D) A procedure has been beneficial.

44. What will the speaker probably do next?

(A) Distribute a document
(B) Demonstrate a product
(C) Introduce a colleague
(D) Discuss a customer survey

45. What department does the speaker work in?

(A) Human resources
(B) Web design
(C) Marketing
(D) Administration

46. What problem does the speaker mention?

(A) A deadline cannot be extended.
(B) A design was submitted late.
(C) An incorrect font was used.
(D) A package has not arrived.

47. Why does the speaker say, "I know you have a lot going on right now"?

(A) To inquire about the listener's schedule
(B) To suggest postponing a work task
(C) To express regret for making a request
(D) To ask the listener to attend a meeting

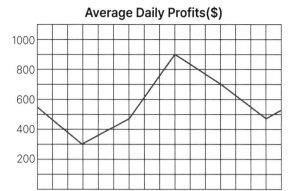

Average Daily Profits($)

48. Look at the graphic. Which month is the speaker discussing?

    (A) February
    (B) March
    (C) April
    (D) May

49. What will the business do next month?

    (A) Open another store
    (B) Release new products
    (C) Hire more employees
    (D) Enlarge a display area

50. What does the speaker ask the listeners to do?

    (A) Attend a training class
    (B) Survey customers
    (C) Provide suggestions
    (D) Review sales figures

This is the end of the Listening test. Turn to Part 5 in your test book.

READING TEST

In the Reading test, you will read a variety of texts and answer several different types of reading comprehension questions. The entire Reading test will last 75 minutes. There are three parts, and directions are given for each part. You are encouraged to answer as many questions as possible within the time allowed. You must mark your answers on the separate answer sheet. Do not write your answers in your test book.

PART 5

Directions: A word or phrase is missing in each of the sentences below. Four answer choices are given below each sentence. Select the best answer to complete the sentence. Then mark the letter (A), (B), (C), or (D) on your answer sheet.

51. Dillon Home Interiors has a large selection of furniture designed for ------- who reside in small condominiums.

    (A) those
    (B) these
    (C) them
    (D) they

52. A full seating chart for the event venue is available ------- online on our Web site.

    (A) to view
    (B) view
    (C) viewing
    (D) views

53. Replacing the old machinery with brand new machines has greatly improved the manufacturing plant's operating -------.

    (A) efficient
    (B) efficiently
    (C) more efficient
    (D) efficiency

54. Management announced that the winner of this year's work efficiency contest ------- a 500-dollar bonus.

    (A) granted
    (B) granting
    (C) was granted
    (D) has granted

55. Many companies in Cookville are in ------- need of security personnel for their warehouses.

    (A) urgency
    (B) urgently
    (C) urgent
    (D) urgencies

56. The urban planning department has finally allocated funds for the leveling ------- the uneven sidewalks on Hirst Avenue.

    (A) with
    (B) of
    (C) out
    (D) through

57. The CEO mentioned that the two companies have ------- collaborated on billboard advertising projects.

(A) traditions
(B) traditional
(C) traditionally
(D) traditionalism

58. Any queries about our company's new sales commission structure should be ------- to Ms. Cochrane in the HR team.

(A) limited
(B) asserted
(C) followed
(D) directed

59. ------- the special bonus is normally given only to full-time employees, part-time workers will also receive it this year.

(A) Although
(B) Until
(C) Whether
(D) Moreover

60. Thanks to decreasing -------, Rashid's Dry Cleaner has experienced a sharp rise in the number of customers it serves.

(A) competition
(B) competed
(C) competitive
(D) competitor

61. Once the client has decided which appetizers and main dishes he wants us to provide, he will consider ------- options for desserts.

(A) another
(B) either
(C) several
(D) whichever

62. Volunteering at the animal shelter and playing the piano in a local jazz band are ------- his many hobbies.

(A) among
(B) considering
(C) regarding
(D) about

63. The vast majority of people these days prefer to use a credit card ------- pay in cash.

(A) only if
(B) rather than
(C) in case
(D) so that

64. ------- did Mr. Cohle gather all the financial data, but he also entered it into the spreadsheet himself.

(A) Not only
(B) In addition
(C) Besides
(D) Above

65. We advise all employers to proofread job vacancy advertisements carefully prior to ------- them on our Web site.

(A) posted
(B) posts
(C) post
(D) posting

66. To ensure that your entry is ------- accepted after the submission deadline, please contact the contest organizing committee directly by phone.

(A) more
(B) still
(C) very
(D) enough

PART 6

Directions: Read the texts that follow. A word, phrase, or sentence is missing in parts of each text. Four answer choices for each question are given below the text. Select the best answer to complete the text. Then mark the letter (A), (B), (C) or (D) on your answer sheet.

Questions 67-70 refer to the following notice.

Welcome to Trinity Advertising's third annual staff conference. -------. With such a large number of
67.
employees attending, we will be keeping to a ------- timetable during the event to ensure that we
68.
complete all of our activities on time.

Keeping this in mind, we ask you to ------- from missing any scheduled events. You should all already
69.
know how vital it is to attend each one.

Tonight, we will gather in the ballroom for a formal dinner followed by our annual awards ceremony.
Tomorrow, there will be a series of speakers and workshops. We apologize that no lunch will be
provided in between the workshops. -------, sandwiches and beverages may be purchased from the
70.
vending machines in the lobby.

67. (A) We hope your stay with us has been an
        enjoyable one.
    (B) Please give a warm welcome to our guests
        and make them feel at home.
    (C) Allow me to describe some of the topics
        that will be discussed during the event.
    (D) We are set to break previous records with
        over 500 staff attending this year.

68. (A) rigorous
    (B) various
    (C) numerous
    (D) hazardous

69. (A) obtain
    (B) refrain
    (C) prevent
    (D) mind

70. (A) For instance
    (B) In addition
    (C) However
    (D) Otherwise

Questions 71-74 refer to the following article.

Dulwich Tourism Figures Soaring

DULWICH (December 28) - Local hotel and restaurant owners ------- a significant increase in business
$\overline{71.}$
in Dulwich. Ever since the Magic World amusement park opened in June, visitors have been flocking
to the town to visit the new attraction. According to the tourist information office, more than 500,000
tourists visited Dulwich between July and December. -------. Experts expect this upward trend to
$\overline{72.}$
continue moving into next year.

The boom in tourism has had a positive effect on local businesses ------- hotels and restaurants. Mitch
$\overline{73.}$
Haskin, owner of The Oakfield Hotel, attributes the rise in tourism not only to the opening of Magic
World, but also to Dulwich Town Council's increased focus on -------. According to Mr. Haskin, "The
$\overline{74.}$
online advertisements and promotional campaigns created by the council have directly benefitted all
businesses in Dulwich."

71. (A) experiencing
    (B) are experiencing
    (C) will experience
    (D) would experience

72. (A) Dulwich is known for several historical
        landmarks.
    (B) The town council has promised to assist
        struggling businesses.
    (C) Magic World will reopen in March after the
        work has been completed.
    (D) This is triple the number recorded in the
        first half of the year.

73. (A) throughout
    (B) between
    (C) such as
    (D) ahead of

74. (A) hiring
    (B) investing
    (C) marketing
    (D) construction

PART 7

Directions: In this part you will read a selection of texts, such as magazine and newspaper articles, e-mails, and instant messages. Each text or set of texts is followed by several questions. Select the best answer for each question and mark the letter (A), (B), (C), or (D) on your answer sheet.

Questions 75-76 refer to the following text message chain.

GARETH BOULD	(12:40 P.M.)	Hi, Vicki. I'm still at the printing shop waiting for the presentation handouts. Can you start getting things set up for the presentation? The laptop is in my office, and the slides are saved in the documents folder.
VICKI MOONEY	(12:41 P.M.)	On it.
GARETH BOULD	(12:43 P.M.)	Excellent. The presentation won't begin until 2:30 P.M., but I want to make sure the laptop is in the room and the slides are all ready to show.
VICKI MOONEY	(12:44 P.M.)	The presentation will be in the third floor conference room, won't it?
GARETH BOULD	(12:46 P.M.)	Yes, and then we'll give the potential investors a tour of the research laboratory. They won't be able to access it when they first arrive. We'll need to take them to the security office for ID badges first.
VICKI MOONEY	(12:47 P.M.)	Oh, of course. Right, I'll start getting things organized.
GARETH BOULD	(12:48 P.M.)	I appreciate it, Vicki. I'll be back soon.

75. At 12:41 P.M., what does Ms. Mooney most likely mean when she writes, "On it"?

(A) She is able to lend Mr. Bould a hand.
(B) She is sure some handouts will be ready.
(C) She is positive that the laptop is in the office.
(D) She thinks Mr. Bould's presentation will be a success.

76. Where most likely is Ms. Mooney going next?

(A) To a security office
(B) To a printing company
(C) To a conference room
(D) To a research laboratory

Questions 77-79 refer to the following memo.

To: All Siegfried Corporation Staff
From: Norman Falkous
Subject: Papaya 6X Smartphone Event
Date: March 22

Dear Staff,

I'd like to inform you all of an exciting opportunity to witness one of the industry leaders unveiling its latest gadget. Tamiya Electronics is holding an industry event on April 15 to mark the release of the Papaya 6X smartphone. The event is bound to be very interesting, especially for those involved in product development and marketing. Of course, we worked alongside Tamiya to help develop its cutting-edge touch screen technology, so we are very proud to see the product finally enter the market.

As a token of appreciation for our contributions, Tamiya Electronics has provided us with 25 guest passes for the event, and these will be allocated on a first-come, first-served basis. For all those who are interested, please make sure to inform me by the end of the month. We need to submit a full list of attendees to Tamiya by April 8. It will serve as an inspiration to those of us here at Siegfried Corporation who dream of becoming a market leader like Tamiya Electronics.

Regards,

Norman Falkous

---

77. What is the purpose of this memo?

(A) To suggest that workers attend an event
(B) To express gratitude to product developers
(C) To outline a project schedule to employees
(D) To remind staff to purchase event tickets

78. The word "bound" in paragraph 1, line 3, is closest meaning to

(A) firm
(B) restrained
(C) certain
(D) forced

79. When should the employees notify Mr. Falkous about attending the event?

(A) By March 31
(B) By April 8
(C) By April 15
(D) By April 30

Blazecom Cable & Internet Service Subscription Renewal
Make sure you continue to receive uninterrupted service!

Customer Name: Mr. Jordan Cranston

Home Address: 552 Spalding Drive, Orlando, FL 32803

Tel. Number: 301-555-3907

E-mail Address: jcranston@blazecom.net

Customer Signature: Jordan Cranston

First Payment Due Upon Renewal: $99.99

Standard Package: $89.99 per month This 12-month package includes 96 cable TV channels and our fastest Internet. Subscribers can enjoy the following: - HD Channels at no extra charge - Free Roam TV on your mobile devices - Up to 150 Mbps download speed - $10 credit on Blazecom merchandise	**Premium Package:** $109.99 per month This 18-month package includes 122 cable TV channels and our fastest Internet. In addition to the standard package's offerings, you will receive access to our full library of Box Office movies at no extra charge.

Technical support hotline: Our technical support team is available to all customers 24 hours a day, seven days a week. Call 555-3892.

Box Office movies: Charges for movies that are purchased through our Box Office service will be added to each monthly bill for those without a Premium Package.

80. What is implied about Mr. Cranston?

   (A) He inquired about a new cable TV package.
   (B) He has experienced problems with an Internet connection.
   (C) He currently has a subscription with Blazecom.
   (D) He has recently moved to a new home address.

81. What is NOT part of the Standard Package?

   (A) The option to watch TV on a cell phone
   (B) Access to more than 100 television channels
   (C) A maximum download speed of 150 Mbps
   (D) Credit on Blazecom products

82. What additional benefit can a customer receive by upgrading from Standard to Premium?

   (A) A faster Internet speed
   (B) Free Box Office movies
   (C) Online technical support
   (D) A warranty on hardware

Questions 83-86 refer to the following online review.

Fiesta Cruise Line's newest vessel, the 3,785-passenger Fiesta Gemini, is undoubtedly the company's most impressive ship yet. Following the cruise industry's latest trends, Fiesta has expanded its eating and entertainment offerings on the Gemini, giving passengers more choices than ever before.

I can sum my 10-night cruise up by saying: "So much to do, so little time!" Among my favorite activities were the mini-golf course, the bowling alley, and the IMAX movie theater. I also loved the magic show and acrobatics show on the main stage in the events auditorium, but I missed the comedy show due to my busy schedule. — [1] —.

The quantity and quality of live music on offer was very impressive. After years of gradually reducing the amount of live music on its ships, Fiesta has listened to passenger feedback and re-introduced concerts. You'll find live bands on the Top Deck Plaza, in the many bars, and even in the casino! — [2] —.

If the ship has any real weakness, it's the breakfast buffet in the main dining room. — [3] —. I felt that the menu repeated items too often, and many of them were not as fresh as they should have been. But my favorite thing about the Gemini was the friendly crew. — [4] —. From the housekeeping staff to the people organizing the activities, everyone always greeted me with a warm smile.

Reviewed By: Greta Mansell

---

83. What is suggested about the Fiesta Gemini cruise ship?

(A) It is a recent addition to the fleet.
(B) It visits destinations all over the world.
(C) It has received several industry awards.
(D) Its passenger cabins have been remodeled.

84. What is NOT an activity that Ms. Mansell enjoyed during her cruise?

(A) Watching a movie
(B) Attending a music performance
(C) Playing mini-golf
(D) Listening to a comedian

85. What does Ms. Mansell think should be improved?

(A) The cleanliness of the cabins
(B) The dining room menu
(C) The outdoor seating areas
(D) The amount of live music

86. In which of the positions marked [1], [2], [3], and [4] does the following sentence best belong?

"Many of them got to know our names within just days of meeting us."

(A) [1]
(B) [2]
(C) [3]
(D) [4]

Optimized for the Outdoors

Recent research has concluded that human beings are more suited to working and living outside than we realize. Some interesting facts are coming to light.

We all know that tribal peoples lived mostly outside, as did the earliest farmers and workers. Until the advent of electricity, people's lives were ruled largely by cycles of daylight and dark, and no one worked far from a window. It appears that we have evolved to do our best when we maintain some link to the great outdoors. Several studies recently conducted show this.

One study examined the effect of crowded city streets on the brain. Subjects were asked to walk for an hour along a busy street while others were instructed to walk in a large park for an hour. When their brains were mapped immediately afterward, it was shown that those who had walked in the park had less activity in the areas of the brain that show anxiety.

Another study showed that in inner-city slum areas, just the presence of a few trees will lower the rates of violent crime in the area. In particular, the rates for reported family violence decrease.

It seems that we need green, growing things in our environment in order for our minds and brains to function well. Employers and business owners would do well to remember this.

87. The word "maintain" in paragraph 2, line 3, is closest in meaning to

(A) repair
(B) keep
(C) believe
(D) claim

88. What is mentioned about the time before electricity was invented?

(A) Workers were given more breaks.
(B) People were evolving faster.
(C) Windows were more important.
(D) Workplaces were less comfortable.

89. In what section of a newspaper would the article most likely be found?

(A) Gardening
(B) Business
(C) Real estate
(D) Travel

90. What does the article suggest happens when people are around trees?

(A) They find it easier to sleep.
(B) Their brain function speeds up.
(C) They produce a higher quality of work.
(D) They become less aggressive.

August 17
Hotel Manager
Verdant Hotel, 552 Fielding Drive
Indianapolis, IN 46225

Dear sir/madam,

I stayed at your hotel last week, checking in on August 11th and checking out on August 14th. Unfortunately, I was not satisfied with the dry cleaning service provided at your establishment. I handed in my business suit for cleaning, but when it was sent back to my room, I noticed that there was a large stain on the breast pocket. I mentioned this to the front desk manager, Ms. Richards, and she instructed the dry cleaner manager to clean the garment again. However, Mr. Perez's efforts were unsuccessful, and I had no choice but to visit a formalwear store to purchase a new suit before my business meeting at 1 p.m.

Although I appreciate Mr. Perez's efforts to rectify the situation, the damage to my suit meant that I ended up paying $300 for a new one. Because only my jacket was damaged, I only ask to be compensated $200 for the jacket, even though the full suit originally cost me $400 in total.

Sincerely,

Richard Waller

To:	Richard Waller <rwaller@berninc.com>
From:	Simon Henley <shenley@verdanthotel.com>
Subject:	Suit Compensation
Date:	August 21

Dear Mr. Waller,

Please accept my apologies regarding the recent issue you experienced at my hotel. This not only caused you a great inconvenience, but also a significant expense. Even though you are only seeking compensation of $200 for the suit jacket, I would like to reimburse you the original total cost of the full suit that was damaged. I will send you a check later today.

Sincerely,

Simon Henley
Manager, Verdant Hotel

91. What is the main purpose of the letter?

    (A) To praise a business
    (B) To describe a problem
    (C) To cancel a reservation
    (D) To complain about a price

92. For how long did Mr. Waller stay at the Verdant Hotel?

    (A) For two nights
    (B) For three nights
    (C) For four nights
    (D) For five nights

93. Who most likely is Mr. Perez?

    (A) A clothing store manager
    (B) A front desk manager
    (C) A hotel manager
    (D) A dry cleaner manager

94. In the e-mail, the word "seeking" in paragraph 1, line 3, is closest in meaning to

    (A) looking
    (B) requesting
    (C) finding
    (D) endeavoring

95. How much money will Mr. Henley send to Mr. Waller?

    (A) $100
    (B) $200
    (C) $300
    (D) $400

To:	Cycle Trader Pro <inquiries@ctp.com>
From:	Des Earnhardt <desearnhardt@realmail.com>
Subject:	Available motorcycles
Date:	October 16

Hello,

I'm hoping you can help me find a specific type of motorcycle. What I'm searching for is a classic Vanguard motorcycle, preferably manufactured between 1978 and 1987. That was the kind of motorcycle I learned to ride on. The cycle should be black and have an engine size of 1,340 cc. I don't mind whether it's an Evol or V-Head engine. Also, I don't want a cycle that has been ridden for too many miles. It should have a mileage of less than 20,000. Finally, I don't want to spend more than $10,000. I look forward to receiving your reply. Thanks in advance!

Des Earnhardt

CYCLE TRADER PRO
5167 Arnott Street, Rutland, VT 05701
Tel: 555-8276

Come on down to Cycle Trader Pro and take a look at our wide selection of motorbikes! For example, we currently have these four amazing Vanguard motorcycles available for purchase!

	Year of Manufacture	Engine Size	Engine Type	Approximate Mileage	Body Color	Price
Vanguard Road King	1986	1,340	V-Head	26,400	Black	$9,200
Vanguard Elektra	1983	1,340	Evol	14,100	Black	$9,400
Vanguard Hard Grip	1981	1,340	Evol	9,700	Silver	$8,200
Vanguard Bison	1979	1,200	V-Head	13,200	Black	$7,100

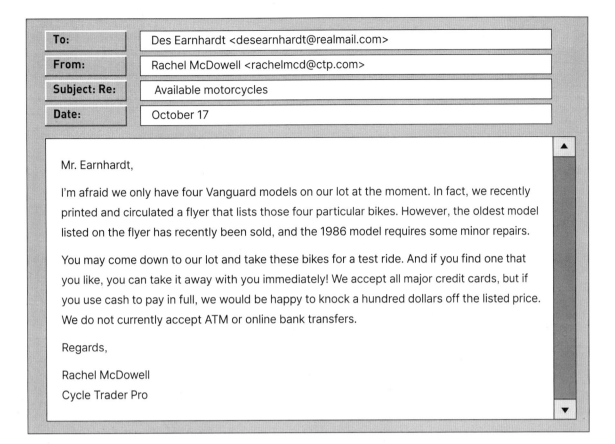

To: Des Earnhardt <desearnhardt@realmail.com>

From: Rachel McDowell <rachelmcd@ctp.com>

Subject: Re: Available motorcycles

Date: October 17

Mr. Earnhardt,

I'm afraid we only have four Vanguard models on our lot at the moment. In fact, we recently printed and circulated a flyer that lists those four particular bikes. However, the oldest model listed on the flyer has recently been sold, and the 1986 model requires some minor repairs.

You may come down to our lot and take these bikes for a test ride. And if you find one that you like, you can take it away with you immediately! We accept all major credit cards, but if you use cash to pay in full, we would be happy to knock a hundred dollars off the listed price. We do not currently accept ATM or online bank transfers.

Regards,

Rachel McDowell

Cycle Trader Pro

---

96. What can be inferred about Mr. Earnhardt?

(A) He lives far from Cycle Trader Pro's business location.
(B) He has sent several e-mails to Cycle Trader Pro.
(C) He is looking for a model that he is used to.
(D) He has experienced technical faults with his motorcycle.

97. Which of the models listed on the flyer would Mr. Earnhardt most likely be interested in?

(A) Road King
(B) Elektra
(C) Hard Grip
(D) Bison

98. In the second e-mail, the word "circulated" in paragraph 1, line 2, is closest in meaning to

(A) enveloped
(B) surrounded
(C) published
(D) distributed

99. What is indicated about the Vanguard Bison?

(A) It was recently modified.
(B) Its price has been reduced.
(C) It is in need of repairs.
(D) It is no longer available.

100. How can Mr. Earnhardt receive a discount on a motorcycle?

(A) By using a specific credit card
(B) By paying via bank transfer
(C) By making an online purchase
(D) By paying the full price in cash

DAY 05 LC+RC Half Test

PART 1

Directions: For each question in this part, you will hear four statements about a picture in your test book. When you hear the statements, you must select the one statement that best describes what you see in the picture. Then find the number of the question on your answer sheet and mark your answer. The statements will not be printed in your test book and will be spoken only one time.

1.

2.

PART 2

Directions: You will hear a question or statement and three responses spoken in English. They will not be printed in your test book and will be spoken only one time. Select the best response to the question or statement and mark the letter (A), (B), or (C) on your answer sheet.

3. Mark your answer on your answer sheet.

4. Mark your answer on your answer sheet.

5. Mark your answer on your answer sheet.

6. Mark your answer on your answer sheet.

7. Mark your answer on your answer sheet.

8. Mark your answer on your answer sheet.

9. Mark your answer on your answer sheet.

10. Mark your answer on your answer sheet.

11. Mark your answer on your answer sheet.

12. Mark your answer on your answer sheet.

13. Mark your answer on your answer sheet.

14. Mark your answer on your answer sheet.

15. Mark your answer on your answer sheet.

16. Mark your answer on your answer sheet.

17. Mark your answer on your answer sheet.

18. Mark your answer on your answer sheet.

19. Mark your answer on your answer sheet.

20. Mark your answer on your answer sheet.

PART 3

Directions: You will hear some conversations between two or more people. You will be asked to answer three questions about what the speakers say in each conversation. Select the best response to each question and mark the letter (A), (B), (C) or (D) on your answer sheet. The conversations will not be printed in your test book and will be spoken only one time.

21. Who does the woman say she has to meet with?

    (A) A Web site designer
    (B) A gym equipment provider
    (C) A marketing director
    (D) A health club owner

22. What event are the speakers preparing for?

    (A) A product demonstration
    (B) An end-of-year celebration
    (C) A sports competition
    (D) A monthly sale

23. Where is the event being publicized?

    (A) On the Internet
    (B) On a radio show
    (C) On a billboard
    (D) On television

24. What does the man ask about the car?

    (A) How long the car has been on the market
    (B) Where the car is located
    (C) When the car was made
    (D) Whether the car has been sold

25. What is unique about the car?

    (A) It is very rare.
    (B) Its color is unusual.
    (D) It is very expensive.
    (D) It has been restored.

26. What will the man probably do tomorrow?

    (A) Test drive a car
    (B) Post an advertisement
    (C) Cancel an appointment
    (D) Deliver an order

27. Where most likely are the speakers?

    (A) At an electronics store
    (B) At a technology expo
    (C) At a print shop
    (D) At a computer repair shop

28. What does the woman imply when she says, "we're closing in 20 minutes"?

    (A) Business have been slow.
    (B) The man can complete a purchase online.
    (C) A decision should be made quickly.
    (D) Another store is still open.

29. What does the woman suggest?

    (A) Using a delivery service
    (B) Purchasing a warranty
    (C) Paying with a credit card
    (D) Signing up for a store membership

30. What are the speakers working on?

    (A) An animated movie
    (B) A television show
    (C) A video game
    (D) A music video

31. What are the women waiting on?

    (A) Some voice recordings
    (B) A purchase confirmation
    (C) A product review
    (D) Some computer hardware

32. What does the man say he will do?

    (A) Extend a deadline
    (B) Increase a budget
    (C) Make a press release
    (D) Contact an agency

Receipt	
Half-day Package	— $55
Instruction fee	— $15
Shoe rental	— $10
Insurance	— $8
Total: $88	

33. What did the man recently do?

(A) Started a business
(B) Booked a trip
(C) Purchased shoes
(D) Organized a company event

34. Look at the graphic. What amount will be removed from the receipt?

(A) $55
(B) $15
(C) $10
(D) $8

35. What does the woman recommend?

(A) Registering for insurance
(B) Eating a meal
(C) Renting a vehicle
(D) Watching a video

Smitty's Pizza – Daily Deals for October			
Tuesday	**Wednesday**	**Thursday**	**Friday**
Pepperoni	Barbeque	Hawaiian	Deluxe Supreme

36. Why does the woman call?

(A) To inquire about an order
(B) To check the store hours
(C) To request a catering service
(D) To ask for a discount

37. What problem does the man mention?

(A) An order is incorrect.
(B) A computer system is down.
(C) An address is not included.
(D) An employee is absent.

38. Look at the graphic. According to the calendar, what day is it?

(A) Tuesday
(B) Wednesday
(C) Thursday
(D) Friday

PART 4

Directions: You will hear some talks given by a single speaker. You will be asked to answer three questions about what the speakers say in each conversation. Select the best response to each question and mark the letter (A), (B), (C) or (D) on your answer sheet. The conversations will not be printed in your test book and will be spoken only one time.

39. What is the topic of the workshop?

    (A) Searching for employment
    (B) Learning an artistic skill
    (C) Decorating one's home
    (D) Running a small business

40. What impressed the speaker about the workshop participants?

    (A) The good attitude they all have
    (B) The speed with which they work
    (C) Their skill at communicating effectively
    (D) Their ability to perform a difficult technique

41. What will the participants most likely do next?

    (A) Complete a survey
    (B) Go out to socialize
    (C) Present some work
    (D) Pay for a course

42. Who most likely are the listeners?

    (A) Business owners
    (B) Athletes
    (C) Reporters
    (D) Sports fans

43. Why does the man say, "they're selling quickly"?

    (A) To describe a business's success
    (B) To suggest new products are very popular
    (C) To encourage the listeners to act soon
    (D) To recommend an alternative

44. According to the man, why should the listeners visit a Web site?

    (A) To request a refund
    (B) To view a schedule
    (C) To check for updates
    (D) To purchase some merchandise

45. What does the speaker mean when she says, "it has been raining hard all day"?

    (A) An extra fee will be charged to finish on time.
    (B) Some work cannot be done as scheduled.
    (C) A sports competition could not be held.
    (D) Additional equipment will be needed.

46. According to the speaker, what will small flags be used for?

    (A) To specify the property line
    (B) To show support for a team
    (C) To designate plant locations
    (D) To warn people not to enter an area

47. What does the speaker want the listener to send her?

    (A) A revised schedule
    (B) A signed contract
    (C) A down payment
    (D) A property map

Wibley's Grocery
-"Family, Friends, and Food"

Weekly Specials

Soft Touch Tissues	Free with Coupon*
Delmore Sharp Cheddar	10% off
Ripple's Hot Chips	Buy 2, Get 1 Free
Stoke's Shaving Cream	15% off

* Limit one per customer

48. According to the speaker, what change will be implemented next month?

(A) New products will be sold.
(B) Another location will open.
(C) Store hours will be extended.
(D) A delivery service will begin.

49. Look at the graphic. Which product has an incorrect offer?

(A) Soft Touch Tissues
(B) Delmore Sharp Cheddar
(C) Ripple's Hot Chips
(D) Stoke's Shaving Cream

50. What is mentioned about Rodney Wells?

(A) He is a new manager.
(B) He is giving away free samples.
(C) He is working in the deli.
(D) He is retiring soon.

This is the end of the Listening test. Turn to Part 5 in your test book.

READING TEST

In the Reading test, you will read a variety of texts and answer several different types of reading comprehension questions. The entire Reading test will last 75 minutes. There are three parts, and directions are given for each part. You are encouraged to answer as many questions as possible within the time allowed. You must mark your answers on the separate answer sheet. Do not write your answers in your test book.

PART 5

Directions: A word or phrase is missing in each of the sentences below. Four answer choices are given below each sentence. Select the best answer to complete the sentence. Then mark the letter (A), (B), (C), or (D) on your answer sheet.

51. Every year, our full-time employees attend a thirty-minute ------- of their work performance.

   (A) review
   (B) reviews
   (C) to review
   (D) reviewed

52. By ------- promoting the latest book, the publisher expects to increase its sales.

   (A) active
   (B) most active
   (C) actively
   (D) more active

53. In his monthly magazine column, economist Giles Dawkins ------- spending trends in the retail sector.

   (A) analysis
   (B) analyzer
   (C) analyzes
   (D) analyzing

54. Students from ------- universities will be able to apply for internships at the Faith Corporation this summer.

   (A) various
   (B) variously
   (C) variety
   (D) variation

55. The budget for the city's 150th birthday celebrations was reviewed by an experienced ------- from Caldwell Financial.

   (A) account
   (B) accounting
   (C) accountant
   (D) accountants

56. ------- the three-month trial period, most new employees are offered permanent positions with the company.

   (A) Follow
   (B) Follows
   (C) Followed
   (D) Following

57. For the duration of the remodeling project, affected employees will be relocated ------- other departments.

(A) on
(B) to
(C) as
(D) for

58. ------- the article was received after the March 15 deadline, it will not be featured in the April edition of the architecture journal.

(A) Since
(B) As if
(C) Nearly
(D) Even

59. Any new advertisers seeking to purchase space in our magazine are asked to consult our ------- for submission, available on our Web site.

(A) issues
(B) references
(C) guidelines
(D) resources

60. These days, ATMs are commonly found in local convenience stores ------- in supermarkets and shopping malls.

(A) as well as
(B) even though
(C) whether
(D) in order to

61. To attract new members, Benny's Gym ------- offers one-day trial memberships to people walking by the building.

(A) recently
(B) occasionally
(C) previously
(D) hardly

62. Visitors to our swimming pool may ------- their belongings in the lockers in our changing rooms.

(A) secure
(B) attain
(C) request
(D) preserve

63. Despite unfavorable weather conditions, last week's 'Peace, Love & Music Together' event was ------- attended.

(A) well
(B) quite
(C) most
(D) every

64. ------- she has worked at Paragon Inc. for almost 20 years, Ms. Gilchrist has never been offered a supervisory role at the firm.

(A) Once
(B) Despite
(C) Because
(D) Although

65. Even though Martin Cross and Jenny Yu often disagree over marketing strategies, ------- respect the focus and creativity the other brings to a project.

(A) another
(B) both
(C) either
(D) less

66. With only a few days left until the announcement of the winner of the CWA Literary Award, judges have to decide ------- author released the best book this year.

(A) about
(B) whom
(C) on
(D) which

PART 6

Directions: Read the texts that follow. A word, phrase, or sentence is missing in parts of each text. Four answer choices for each question are given below the text. Select the best answer to complete the text. Then mark the letter (A), (B), (C) or (D) on your answer sheet.

Questions 67-70 refer to the following article.

New York, 15 October – Freeville Film Studios Ltd. reported a record profit for the third quarter with a rise of 35 percent. The ------- in revenue can be attributed to the company's recent purchase of rival
67.
movie studio, Starlight Pictures Ltd. Since the merger deal, Freeville Film Studios ------- the largest film
68.
studio in North America. -------, the outlook for the industry as a whole is not so bright. Despite the
69.
upswing in profits, the slow economy has led to a decrease in movie theater attendance. -------.
70.

67. (A) downturn
    (B) increase
    (C) leveling
    (D) development

68. (A) became
    (B) will become
    (C) had become
    (D) has become

69. (A) Nonetheless
    (B) Likewise
    (C) For example
    (D) As a result

70. (A) As a result, the company has recently decided to postpone its expansion plan until next year.
    (B) The new film is expected to be released in time for the beginning of the holiday season.
    (C) Freeville Film Studios just can't seem to make a wrong decision.
    (D) It remains to be seen if Starlight Pictures will continue to be competitive.

Questions 71-74 refer to the following memo.

To: All Birdhouse Publishing Employees

From: Karen Chamberlain, CEO

Dear Staff,

Birdhouse Publishing is carrying out a survey of all ------- in order to find out everyone's hobbies and
                                                          71.
interests. This will be sent to you by e-mail shortly after the weekly meeting this Thursday. -------.
                                                                                                72.
Please make sure that you complete this form and return it to the HR department by 5 P.M. on Friday.

In the past, our company had several groups that allowed staff to come together and enjoy various
activities such as badminton, hiking, and cycling. These helped team members to bond, ------- job
                                                                                         73.
satisfaction and productivity. We hope the new groups will have a similar effect!

Once the HR department has received all forms, the data will be compiled and assessed. The HR
manager will ------- announce which activities have been chosen for our staff.
              74.

Regards,

Karen

71. (A) suppliers
    (B) publications
    (C) clients
    (D) employees

72. (A) More information about these new
        products will be provided at the meeting.
    (B) If you require any time off work, please
        inform us at least 2 days in advance.
    (C) Our ultimate goal is to use the data to
        create various social clubs.
    (D) However, the meeting may be moved to
        the third floor conference room.

73. (A) boosting
    (B) boosted
    (C) boosts
    (D) had boosted

74. (A) quite
    (B) then
    (C) instead
    (D) otherwise

PART 7

Directions: In this part you will read a selection of texts, such as magazine and newspaper articles, e-mails, and instant messages. Each text or set of texts is followed by several questions. Select the best answer for each question and mark the letter (A), (B), (C), or (D) on your answer sheet.

Questions 75-76 refer to the following memo.

To: All Marketing Department Staff Members

Subject: Computing Workshops

Date: November 14

Good morning,

I have just had a meeting with Roger Lawson in the IT department. We discussed the upcoming computing workshops and decided that it would be best for us to push our session back by a couple of weeks. As you are all aware, we have some pressing deadlines this month here in the marketing department. Therefore, the customer service department will now attend the workshops the week starting November 24, and we will attend them the week starting December 1. I will send you all a more detailed message about the new workshop schedule via our company messaging system, so please look out for that and let me know if you have any questions about the workshops.

Thanks,

May Knight
Marketing Manager
Cosgrove Foods Inc.

---

75. What is the purpose of the memo?
    (A) To notify staff about planned computer maintenance
    (B) To request feedback from staff about a training session
    (C) To inform employees about a schedule change
    (D) To discuss the merging of two departments

76. What are staff members advised to do?
    (A) Register online for a workshop
    (B) Send a message to Mr. Lawson
    (C) Choose their preferred date
    (D) Check their company messages

We are always happy to receive donations!

Norwood Country Manor & Gardens is committed to ensuring that visitors are able to access all of the rooms in the manor at no cost, including the grand ballroom, the library, and the main dining room, which houses several valuable works of art. In order to continually restore and maintain the interior of the manor, we depend partly on the generous donations of our patrons. If you are willing to assist us with the upkeep of the building by becoming a patron, please speak with a staff member at the information desk in the grand ballroom.

Patronage brings you a variety of perks, such as substantial savings on all items in our gift shop, a special book of historical photographs of Norwood Manor, and an invitation to the gala held each year in the gardens. You can find out more about the benefits of patronage by visiting our Web site at www.norwoodmanor.co.uk.

77. Where would the flyer most likely be handed out?
    (A) In an academic institute
    (B) In an art gallery
    (C) In a historical building
    (D) In a public library

78. What is stated about the interior of the building?
    (A) It is free to enter.
    (B) It was recently renovated.
    (C) It contains antique furniture.
    (D) Some rooms are inaccessible.

79. What is NOT mentioned as a benefit received by patrons?
    (A) An event invitation
    (B) A book of photography
    (C) A gift shop discount
    (D) A Web site user account

Bellingham's
Now also at 454 Torrance Drive (Next to Pastel Art Supplies)
Pittsburgh, PA 15213
555-9237

Business hours:
9 A.M. to 5 P.M., Monday to Friday
9 A.M. to 6 P.M., Saturdays

Free crystal flower vase when you spend over $100
(Kingsway Plaza Store Only)

To celebrate this store's first week in business:
15% off all rugs and carpets
20% off curtains (plain linen only)
25% off all picture frames

The above discounts will be offered from May 2 to May 8.

For only $30 per year, you can sign up for the Bellingham's
customer rewards card and receive an additional 5% off all purchases
made at our Torrance Drive location or our flagship store on Bertrand Street!

Also, until May 8, order any item of bedding
directly from www.bellinghams.com and get 10% off!

---

80. What type of merchandise does Bellingham's sell?

(A) Building materials
(B) Home furnishings
(C) Art supplies
(D) Flowers

81. What is indicated about Bellingham's?

(A) It has stores in more than one city.
(B) It opens seven days a week.
(C) Its merchandise is second-hand.
(D) It is opening a new location.

82. For which item will the customers get an online-only discount?

(A) A bathroom rug
(B) A decorative vase
(C) A bed cover
(D) A set of curtains

Ms. Regine Butler, Director
Urban Neon Clothing Company

Dear Ms. Butler,

I am sure that I speak for everyone here at the One Love Foundation when I say we owe you a debt of gratitude. — [1] —. We were delighted that you and your company were able to contribute garments for us to use in our fashion show at Guildford Community Center last weekend. — [2] —.

Last year, and the year before that, we struggled to solicit clothing contributions from popular clothing designers. — [3] —. As a result, the turnout was below our expectations and the event could hardly be described as a success in terms of ticket sales. — [4] —. Generous contributions from high-profile companies such as yours enabled us to raise the ticket price this year and attract even more guests, thereby helping us to raise more funds to distribute among our usual selection of local charities.

Sincerely, many thanks for your support of our endeavors.

Best wishes,

Daniel Alonso, Events Coordinator

83. Why was the letter written?

(A) To respond to a recent inquiry
(B) To ask a company for a contribution
(C) To promote a fundraising organization
(D) To express thanks for assistance

84. Who most likely is Ms. Butler?

(A) A director of a local charity
(B) A member of One Love Foundation
(C) An executive at a clothing firm
(D) A manager at a community center

85. According to the letter, how was this year's event different from previous events?

(A) It had relatively poor ticket sales.
(B) It was held in a different location.
(C) It involved a higher number of charities.
(D) It was more expensive to attend.

86. In which of the positions marked [1], [2], [3] and [4] does the following sentence best belong?

"The event was a great success and we raised a large amount of funds for local charities."

(A) [1]
(B) [2]
(C) [3]
(D) [4]

Questions 87-90 refer to the following online chat discussions.

Bob Bowban	[3:43 P.M.]	Hello, welcome to Fine Paper, Inc. How may I help you?
Janice Sims	[3:43 P.M.]	Hi, Bob. I'm hoping you can help me with a paper order I made last week.
Bob Bowban	[3:44 P.M.]	Sure. May I please have your order number?
Janice Sims	[3:44 P.M.]	It's 99554620.
Bob Bowban	[3:44 P.M.]	Thank you. One moment please. I will access the order details.
Bob Bowban	[3:46 P.M.]	Ok, I see that you placed an order for 5 cases of white cardstock on February 4.
Janice Sims	[3:47 P.M.]	Yes. The order was supposed to be delivered yesterday, but I haven't received it. Can you help?
Bob Bowban	[3:48 P.M.]	Absolutely. If it's ok with you, I'll invite the shipping manager to join the chat.
Janice Sims	[3:48 P.M.]	That would be great.
Demi Dimitrov	[3:51 P.M.]	Hi, this is Demi. What seems to be the problem?
Bob Bowban	[3:51 P.M.]	Hi Demi. Ms. Sims ordered some cardstock a few days ago and it hasn't been delivered yet.
Demi Dimitrov	[3:51 P.M.]	Give me just a moment and I'll find out what's going on.
Janice Sims	[3:51 P.M.]	Thank you!
Demi Dimitrov	[3:54 P.M.]	Okay, it appears that the truck broke down yesterday and they were unable to complete the deliveries on time. The driver expects to have your order to you by 5:00 P.M. Is that ok?
Janice Sims	[3:55 P.M.]	I need to leave for the day soon, but our receptionist will be able to take the delivery.
Bob Bowban	[3:55 P.M.]	Sounds good. I'll send you a confirmation report by e-mail tomorrow morning.

87. Why does Ms. Sims contact Fine Paper Inc.?

(A) To ask for a discount on paper
(B) To learn more about paper products
(C) To find out about a missing order
(D) To purchase paper products

88. At 3:48 P.M., what does Mr. Bowban mean when he says, "Absolutely"?

(A) He will consider Ms. Sims' suggestion.
(B) He can guarantee fast shipping.
(C) He is confirming the location of a package.
(D) He is willing to assist Ms. Sims.

89. When does the delivery driver expect to arrive at Ms. Sims' workplace?

(A) In 5 minutes
(B) In about one hour
(C) In the morning
(D) Tomorrow afternoon

90. What does Ms. Sims say about the suggested delivery arrangement?

(A) Her office will be closed by 5:00 P.M.
(B) A staff member will receive the package.
(C) She wants the driver to arrive sooner.
(D) She will meet the driver in another area.

Okra Corporation - Adventure Weekend

On Saturday, May 16, and Sunday, May 17, all employees will travel to Lerner Campgrounds to participate in Okra Corporation's annual Adventure Weekend. This is a fun event that takes place in May every year and is intended to improve communication and interaction between all of our workers. Previous events have been extremely effective in strengthening relationships between team members.

Accommodation/Meals

All event attendees will stay in the large cabins situated at Lerner Campground. Each cabin accommodates between 10 and 12 individuals. Breakfast, lunch, and dinner will be provided at no extra expense to staff.

Activities

Several group and individual activities will take place. These include soccer, volleyball, dodgeball, kayaking, and water skiing. Winning teams will be given trophies and rewards. Each day will end with an inspirational talk by a special guest. Any department supervisors who are willing to help coordinate the event should contact Nina Simmons in the general affairs department.

To:	Nina Simmons <nsimmons@okracorp.net>
From:	Grant Wood <gwood@okracorp.net>
Subject:	Adventure Weekend
Date:	April 27

Hi Nina,

Everyone here in the marketing department is really looking forward to the Adventure Weekend next month. You mentioned that you need people to volunteer to be event coordinators and, despite my lack of experience, I would like to do it.

As I'm sure you know, I wasn't present at the previous Adventure Weekend because I hadn't yet joined the company at that time. Therefore, I would appreciate it if you could forward me the employee records for the individuals who will be joining us from the telephone sales office. It would be nice for me to at least know their names, faces, and positions before meeting them for the first time at Lerner Campgrounds.

I hope to hear from you soon.

Grant

91. According to the notice, what is the purpose of the event?

   (A) To attract new customers to the business
   (B) To provide additional training to workers
   (C) To welcome new recruits to the company
   (D) To encourage teamwork among employees

92. What is NOT expected to happen at the event?

   (A) Motivational speeches will be given.
   (B) A musical performance will take place.
   (C) Complimentary meals will be provided.
   (D) Prizes will be awarded to the best teams.

93. In the notice, the word "accommodates" in paragraph 2, line 2, is closest in meaning to

   (A) stays
   (B) keeps
   (C) holds
   (D) carries

94. What can be inferred about Mr. Wood?

   (A) He is experienced in organizing company outings.
   (B) He works in the same department as Ms. Simmons.
   (C) He has a background in telephone sales.
   (D) He has worked at Okra for less than one year.

95. What does Mr. Wood request?

   (A) Directions to the event location
   (B) A schedule of event activities
   (C) Information about staff members
   (D) Ms. Simmons' contact details

Questions 96-100 refer to the following Web page, press release, and e-mail.

www.circusofbeijing.com/home			
HOME	MEMBERS	TOUR DATES	TICKETS

The Circus of Beijing includes a wide variety of specialty acts in its performances, from trapeze artists to kung-fu masters. The principal performers in the circus are all highly trained Chinese acrobats, with Sun Hanchao being one of the most widely known and highly respected performers in his home country. The performances on our upcoming UK tour, from June 17 to June 27, will be directed by the organization's chief artistic coordinator, Yang Tenglong, and accompanied by Mongolian composer Tamir Altasan's rousing orchestral score.

Since being founded in 2007 by Gao Zhipeng, the Circus of Beijing has given performances in over 120 cities, in countries as far-flung as Peru and Finland. The group's performers and management team have won numerous awards over the years. Most notably, Liao Lisheng was recognized for his breathtaking laser and light show when he was presented with the Pavlov Award of Excellence last year.

FOR RELEASE TO THE PRESS
Contact: Zhang Liu
zhangliu@beijingcircus.com

(June 6) – All dates on the Circus of Beijing's upcoming tour of the United Kingdom sold out within only a few days of being announced, so the performance group has decided to add four extra dates in order to meet demand. The tour was originally scheduled to begin on June 17 in Birmingham and end on June 27 in London, but it will now continue until July 4. Please see the additional dates below:

Date	Location	Venue
June 28	Edinburgh	Murray Bridge Stadium
June 30	Newcastle	Wilkes Convention Center
July 2	Manchester	Thorpe City Park
July 4	York	Northam Convention Center

To:	Grant Moore <gmoore@epco.com>
From:	Debbie Donaldson <ddonaldson@epco.com>
Date:	June 28
Subject:	Circus of Beijing performance

Hi Grant,

I was speaking with Rod earlier, and we both decided we'd like to go and see the Circus of Beijing at Thorpe City Park on Friday. Would you fancy coming with us? The park is only a few blocks from the office, so our plan is to take a quick taxi there after we leave work. I heard there are plenty of hot dog and burger stands at the venue, so we don't need to stop off anywhere for dinner.

I heard that it's the most impressive circus performance in the world these days. Actually, apart from the performers, the circus is supposed to include the most amazing laser show. I read about the man responsible for creating all the light effects in Global Experience Magazine recently. It should be spectacular! Let me know if you're interested.

Debbie

96. What is mentioned about Sun Hanchao?

(A) He was one of the founders of the Circus of Beijing.
(B) He is regarded as one of the best acrobats in China.
(C) He was presented with an excellence award last year.
(D) He is responsible for directing circus performances.

97. What is indicated about the Circus of Beijing's upcoming tour?

(A) It will start around one week later than originally scheduled.
(B) It will require the group to travel to more than 120 cities.
(C) It will include several performances in Finland and Peru.
(D) It will feature music written by a Mongolian composer.

98. On the Web page, the word "recognized" in paragraph 2, line 3, is closest in meaning to

(A) illustrated
(B) honored
(C) outlined
(D) featured

99. Who did Ms. Donaldson read about in a magazine article?

(A) Yang Tenglong
(B) Tamir Altasan
(C) Gao Zhipeng
(D) Liao Lisheng

100. Where is Ms. Donaldson's workplace most likely located?

(A) In Edinburgh
(B) In Newcastle
(C) In Manchester
(D) In York

시원스쿨 LAB

LC

1. (B)	**2.** (C)	**3.** (B)	**4.** (B)	**5.** (B)
6. (C)	**7.** (B)	**8.** (A)	**9.** (B)	**10.** (B)
11. (A)	**12.** (A)	**13.** (C)	**14.** (A)	**15.** (C)
16. (C)	**17.** (B)	**18.** (B)	**19.** (A)	**20.** (C)
21. (D)	**22.** (C)	**23.** (A)	**24.** (A)	**25.** (D)
26. (C)	**27.** (C)	**28.** (B)	**29.** (B)	**30.** (D)
31. (C)	**32.** (C)	**33.** (A)	**34.** (D)	**35.** (C)
36. (B)	**37.** (A)	**38.** (D)	**39.** (B)	**40.** (D)
41. (C)	**42.** (A)	**43.** (B)	**44.** (A)	**45.** (B)
46. (C)	**47.** (B)	**48.** (D)	**49.** (D)	**50.** (C)

RC

51. (C)	**52.** (A)	**53.** (C)	**54.** (C)	**55.** (C)
56. (A)	**57.** (B)	**58.** (D)	**59.** (C)	**60.** (A)
61. (A)	**62.** (A)	**63.** (B)	**64.** (C)	**65.** (A)
66. (C)	**67.** (D)	**68.** (B)	**69.** (B)	**70.** (A)
71. (D)	**72.** (B)	**73.** (B)	**74.** (C)	**75.** (C)
76. (C)	**77.** (D)	**78.** (C)	**79.** (C)	**80.** (B)
81. (D)	**82.** (C)	**83.** (B)	**84.** (D)	**85.** (D)
86. (C)	**87.** (C)	**88.** (A)	**89.** (B)	**90.** (D)
91. (C)	**92.** (B)	**93.** (D)	**94.** (C)	**95.** (C)
96. (C)	**97.** (A)	**98.** (D)	**99.** (C)	**100.** (C)

Part 1

1.
(A) They are exiting the automobile.
(B) Some cars have been parked along the road.
(C) A car is being driven down the road.
(D) Some bicycles are leaning against a wall.

(A) 사람들이 자동차에서 내리고 있다.
(B) 몇몇 자동차들이 도로를 따라 주차되어 있다.
(C) 자동차가 도로를 따라 주행되고 있다.
(D) 몇몇 자전거들이 벽에 기대어 있다.

해설 (A) 차에서 내리는 사람을 찾아볼 수 없으므로 오답.
(B) 자동차들이 도로를 따라 주차되어 있는 상태이므로 정답.
(C) 도로에서 달리는 자동차를 찾아볼 수 없으므로 오답.
(D) 벽에 기대어져 있는 자전거를 찾아볼 수 없으므로 오답.

어휘 **exit** ~에서 나가다 **automobile** 자동차 **park** v. ~을 주차하다 **along** (길 등) ~을 따라 **lean against** ~에 기대다

2.
(A) Potted plants are growing on the balcony.
(B) Curtains have been pulled shut.
(C) Lights are hanging above the tables.
(D) All of the seats are occupied.

(A) 화분에 담긴 식물들이 발코니에서 자라고 있다.
(B) 커튼이 당겨져 닫혀 있다.
(C) 조명이 테이블 위쪽에 매달려 있다.
(D) 모든 좌석이 이용 중이다.

해설 (A) 화분에 담긴 식물이 있는 곳이 발코니가 아니므로 오답.
(B) 커튼을 찾아볼 수 없으므로 오답.
(C) 테이블마다 위쪽에 전등이 매달려 있는 상태이므로 정답.
(D) 좌석이 비어 있는 상태이므로 오답.

어휘 **potted plant** 화분에 담긴 식물 **be pulled shut** (커튼 등이 당겨져) 닫혀 있다 **hang** 매달리다, 걸리다 **occupied** 이용 중인, 점유된

Part 2

3. When does the mail usually arrive?
(A) No, it's Sunday today.
(B) By noon at the latest.
(C) To Memphis.

우편물이 보통 언제 도착하나요?
(A) 아뇨, 오늘은 일요일입니다.
(B) 늦어도 정오까지요.
(C) 멤피스로요.

해설 우편물이 언제 도착하는지 묻고 있으므로 '늦어도 정오까지'라는 시점 표현으로 답변하는 (B)가 정답이다. (A)는 의문사 의문문에 맞지 않는 No로 답변하는 오답이며, (C)는 목적지를 나타내는 답변이므로 오답이다.

어휘 **usually** 보통, 일반적으로 **arrive** 도착하다 **by** (기한) ~까지 **at the latest** 늦어도

4. Who's setting up the new accounting software?
(A) Thanks, but I can take care of it.
(B) My assistant, Lucy Jones.
(C) The data was incorrect.

누가 새로운 회계 소프트웨어를 설치하나요?
(A) 감사합니다만, 제가 처리할 수 있습니다.
(B) 제 비서인 루시 존스 씨요.
(C) 그 데이터는 부정확했어요.

해설 누가 새로운 회계 소프트웨어를 설치하는지 묻고 있으므로

담당자의 직책과 이름을 언급하는 (B)가 정답이다. (A)는 상대방의 제안에 거절하는 표현이므로 오답이며, (C)는 질문의 software에서 연상 가능한 data를 활용해 혼동을 유발하는 오답이다.

어휘 set up ~을 설치하다, ~을 설정하다 accounting 회계 (부) take care of ~을 처리하다, ~을 다루다 assistant 비서, 보조 incorrect 부정확한

5. Did Alanna request these documents again?
(A) Please leave them on my desk.
(B) Actually, it was John this time.
(C) I documented all of my changes.

앨라나 씨가 이 문서들을 또 요청했나요?
(A) 제 책상 위에 두세요.
(B) 사실, 이번엔 존 씨였습니다.
(C) 제가 제 변경 사항들을 모두 기록했습니다.

해설 앨라나 씨가 특정 문서들을 또 요청했는지 묻는 데 대해 이번에는 존 씨였다는 말로 다른 사람이 요청했음을 의미하는 (B)가 정답이다. (A)는 documents에서 연상 가능한 leave와 desk를, (C)는 document의 서로 다른 의미(문서, 기록하다)를 각각 활용해 혼동을 유발하는 오답이다.

어휘 leave ~을 남겨 두다 document v. ~을 문서로 기록하다

6. What did you think of the soup?
(A) I was thinking of having a sandwich.
(B) Yes, I hope we find a table.
(C) It could have used more salt.

그 수프가 어떠셨나요?
(A) 전 샌드위치를 먹을까 생각하고 있었어요.
(B) 네, 우리가 테이블을 찾으면 좋겠어요.
(C) 소금을 더 사용할 수 있었을 것 같아요.

해설 수프 맛이 어땠는지 묻고 있으므로 '소금이 더 들어갔으면 좋겠다'는 말로 음식 맛과 관련된 구체적인 의견을 밝히는 (C)가 정답이다. (A)는 soup에서 연상 가능한 sandwich를 이용해 혼동을 유발하는 오답이며, (B)는 의문사 의문문에 맞지 않는 Yes로 답변하는 오답이다.

어휘 What do you think of ~? ~가 어떤가요? could have p.p. ~할 수 있었을 것이다

7. Shouldn't you print copies of the contract?
(A) I reviewed the terms of the contract.
(B) Yes, I'm looking for paper now.
(C) We bought a new 3D printer.

계약서 사본을 출력하셔야 하지 않나요?
(A) 제가 계약서 조항을 검토했습니다.
(B) 네, 지금 용지를 찾고 있어요.
(C) 우리가 새 3D 프린터를 구입했어요.

해설 계약서 사본을 출력해야 하지 않는지 묻고 있으므로 긍정을 뜻하는 Yes와 함께 출력할 종이를 찾고 있다고 덧붙이는 (B)가 정답이다. (A)는 질문에 언급된 contract를 반복한 답변으로 사본 출력 여부와 관련 없는 오답이며, (C)는 질문에 언급된 print와 일부 발음이 유사한 printer을 이용한 오답이다.

어휘 contract 계약(서) review ~을 검토하다, ~을 살펴보다 terms (계약 등의) 조항, 조건

8. Why weren't you at the staff dinner last night?
(A) I thought it was tonight.
(B) We haven't picked a restaurant yet.
(C) I'll do it this evening.

어제 저녁에 왜 직원 회식에 오지 않았나요?
(A) 오늘 저녁인 줄 알았어요.
(B) 아직 식당을 고르지 못했어요.
(C) 제가 오늘 저녁에 그걸 할게요.

해설 직원 회식에 왜 오지 않았는지 묻고 있으므로 staff dinner를 it으로 지칭해 회식이 열리는 시점을 오늘로 잘못 알고 있었다는 말로 그 이유를 말하는 (A)가 정답이다. (B)와 (C)는 dinner에서 연상 가능한 restaurant과 evening을 각각 활용해 혼동을 유발하는 오답이다.

어휘 pick ~을 고르다, ~을 선택하다

9. Aren't you bringing copies of your résumé to the career fair?
(A) Let's have coffee afterwards.
(B) I'm planning to.
(C) Perhaps you should.

채용 박람회에 이력서 사본들을 가져가시지 않나요?
(A) 그 후에 커피를 마십시다.
(B) 그럴 계획이에요.
(C) 아마 그러셔야 할 거예요.

해설 채용 박람회에 이력서를 가져가지 않는지 확인하기 위해 묻고 있으므로 그럴 계획이라는 말로 이력서를 가져간다는 뜻을 나타낸 (B)가 정답이다. 질문에 쓰인 동사 bring 이하 부분이 동일하게 반복되는 것을 피하기 위해 to부정사의 to까지만 말하고 생략한 구조이다. (A)는 copies와 발음이 유사한 coffee를 활용해 혼동을 유발하는 오답이며, (C)는 답변자 자신의 이력서 지참 여부를 말하는 것이 아니라 오히려 질문자에게 할 일을 말하고 있으므로 핵심에서 벗어난 오답이다.

어휘 résumé 이력서 career fair 채용 박람회 afterwards 그 후에, 나중에 plan to do ~할 계획이다

10. You haven't seen the guest list for the party, have you?
(A) Let's invite Steven Park.
(B) Didn't I give it back to you?
(C) Thanks. I'll see you there.

파티 초대 손님 명단을 보시지 못한 게 맞죠?
(A) 스티븐 박 씨를 초대합시다.
(B) 제가 그걸 당신께 돌려드리지 않았나요?
(C) 감사합니다. 거기서 뵙겠습니다.

해설 초대 손님 명단을 보지 못한 게 맞는지 묻고 있으므로 guest list를 it으로 지칭해 질문자에게 돌려주지 않았는지 확인하기 위해 되묻는 (B)가 정답이다. 방법이나 해결책 등과 관련해 되묻는 말이 정답으로 자주 등장하므로 질문과의 의미 관계를 재빨리 파악할 수 있는 상황 판단력을 길러야 한다. (A)와 (C)는 질문의 guest list, party 등에서 연상 가능한 invite와 see you there를 각각 활용해 혼동을 유발하는 오답이다.

11. Would you like to read this newspaper?
(A) Thanks, but I read it on my way to work today.
(B) Sorry. I'm such a slow reader.
(C) I thought that was classified information.

이 신문 읽어 보시겠어요?
(A) 감사합니다만, 오늘 출근하는 길에 읽었어요.
(B) 미안해요. 제가 읽는 속도가 느립니다.
(C) 저는 그게 기밀 정보라고 생각했어요.

해설 신문을 읽고 싶은지 묻고 있으므로 감사의 말과 함께 이미 읽어 봤다고 알리는 것으로 정중히 거절 의사를 밝히는 (A)가 정답이다. (B)는 read와 발음이 유사한 reader를 활용해 혼동을 유발하는 오답이며, (C)는 신문을 읽는 것과 관련된 답변자 자신의 의사와 관련 없는 오답이다.

어휘 **Would you like to do?** ~하시겠어요? **on one's way to** ~로 오는 길에, ~로 가는 길에 **classified** 기밀의

12. Why are you moving out west to Los Angeles?
(A) For a business opportunity.
(B) It's a really long movie.
(C) In three weeks.

왜 로스엔젤레스가 있는 서쪽으로 이사하시나요?
(A) 사업 기회를 위해서요.
(B) 정말 긴 영화네요.
(C) 3주 후에요.

해설 특정 지역으로 이사하는 이유를 묻고 있으므로 이유를 말할 때 사용하는 전치사 For와 함께 사업 기회를 언급하는 (A)가 정답이다. (B)는 moving과 발음이 유사한 movie를 활용해 혼동을 유발하는 오답이며, (C)는 가까운 미래에 해당되는 시점 표현이므로 오답이다.

어휘 **move out to** ~로 이사하다 **opportunity** 기회 **in** 기간 ~ 후에

13. My interview is on the opposite side of the city.
(A) Actually, I prefer living outside the city.
(B) Well, I'm sorry you don't share my view.
(C) You should make sure you set off early.

제 면접이 도시의 반대편에서 있어요.
(A) 사실, 전 시외 지역에 사는 걸 선호합니다.
(B) 음, 제 의견에 동의하지 않으신다니 유감이네요.
(C) 반드시 일찍 출발하도록 하세요.

해설 면접을 보는 곳이 도시 반대편이라는 말로 멀리 가야 한다는 뜻을 나타내는 말에 대해 일찍 출발하라고 조언하는 (C)가 정답이다. (A)는 city가 반복된 답변으로 면접 장소와 관련 없는 오답이며, (B)는 interivew와 일부 발음이 같은 view를 활용해 혼동을 유발하는 오답이다.

어휘 **on the opposite side of** ~의 반대편에 **actually** 사실, 실은 **prefer -ing** ~하는 것을 선호하다 **share one's view** ~의 의견에 동의하다 **make sure** 반드시 ~하도록 하다, ~임을 확실히 해두다 **set off** 출발하다, 떠나다

14. Should we keep waiting for Ms. Sullivan or start the meeting without her?
(A) She should arrive in a moment.
(B) Yes, I waited over an hour.
(C) Please keep them in the supply room.

설리반 씨를 계속 기다려야 하나요, 아니면 그녀 없이 회의를 시작해야 하나요?
(A) 금방 오실 거예요.
(B) 네, 저는 한 시간 넘게 기다렸어요.
(C) 그것들을 비품실에 보관해 주세요.

해설 설리반 씨를 계속 기다려야 하는지 아니면 설리반 씨 없이 회의를 시작해야 하는지 묻고 있으므로 Ms. Sullivan을 She로 지칭해 곧 도착할 것이라는 말로 설리반 씨를 계속 기다려야 한다는 뜻을 나타내는 (A)가 정답이다.

어휘 **keep -ing** 계속 ~하다 **in a moment** 곧, 잠시 후에 **supply room** 비품실, 물품실

15. How often does the soccer team play?
(A) It's a good way to stay fit.
(B) The new sports stadium.
(C) Every Saturday.

그 축구팀이 얼마나 자주 경기를 하나요?
(A) 건강을 유지하는 좋은 방법이에요.
(B) 새로운 스포츠 경기장이요.
(C) 매주 토요일에 합니다.

해설 How often과 함께 빈도를 묻고 있으므로 '매주 토요일'이라는 말로 반복 주기를 언급하는 (C)가 정답이다. (A)와 (B)는 각각 soccer에서 연상 가능한 stay fit과 sports stadium을 활용해 혼동을 유발하는 오답이다.

어휘 **How often ~?** 얼마나 자주 ~? **way to do** ~하는 방법 **stay fit** 건강을 유지하다 **every** 매 ~, ~마다

16. Where will your stall be at the town fair?

(A) All kinds of snacks.

(B) Next weekend.

(C) Near the entrance.

마을 축제 마당에서 어디에 당신 가판대가 위치하나요?

(A) 모든 종류의 간식이요.

(B) 다음 주말에요.

(C) 입구 근처에요.

해설 가판대가 어디에 위치할 것인지 묻고 있으므로 특정 위치를 나타내는 표현으로 대답하는 (C)가 정답이다. (B)는 When 의문문에 어울리는 시점 표현이므로 오답이다.

어휘 **stall** 가판대, 좌판 **fair** 축제 마당, 박람회 **near** ~ 근처에

17. How should the quarterly market report be presented?

(A) The sportswear market.

(B) Ask Mr. Shiraz what he prefers.

(C) About the upcoming presentation.

분기 시장 보고서가 어떻게 발표되어야 하나요?

(A) 스포츠 의류 시장이요.

(B) 쉬라즈 씨께 무엇을 선호하시는지 물어보세요.

(C) 다가오는 발표와 관련해서요.

해설 분기 시장 보고서가 어떻게 제시되어야 하는지 묻고 있으므로 쉬라즈 씨에게 무엇을 선호하는지 물어보라는 말로 관련 정보를 확인할 수 있는 방법을 알리는 (B)가 정답이다. (A)는 market을 반복한 답변으로 보고서 제시 방식과 관련 없는 오답이며, (C)는 present와 발음이 유사한 presentation을 활용해 혼동을 유발하는 오답이다.

어휘 **quarterly** 분기의 **present** ~을 발표하다, ~을 제시하다, ~을 제공하다 **prefer** ~을 선호하다 **upcoming** 다가오는, 곧 있을

18. Did you buy a one-year warranty for your computer?

(A) It takes two hours to get there.

(B) I purchased a two-year one.

(C) No, I'd prefer a newer model.

당신 컴퓨터를 위해 1년 기간의 품질 보증 서비스를 구입하셨나요?

(A) 그곳에 가는 데 두 시간이 걸립니다.

(B) 전 2년짜리를 구입했어요.

(C) 아뇨, 전 더 새로운 모델이 좋습니다.

해설 1년 기간의 품질 보증 서비스를 구입했는지 묻고 있으므로 warranty를 one로 대신해 2년짜리로 구입했다고 알리는 (B)가 정답이다. (A)는 이동 소요 시간을 말하고 있으므로 핵심에서 벗어난 오답이며, (C)는 computer에서 연상 가능한 newer model을 활용해 혼동을 유발하는 오답이다.

어휘 **warranty** 품질보증(서) **take** ~의 시간이 걸리다 **purchase** ~을 구입하다 **would prefer A** A가 좋다, A로 하고 싶다

19. Do you want to go out for lunch now or in an hour?

(A) I'll need to compile this data first.

(B) Ms. Cobb takes an hour for lunch.

(C) I ate here when it first opened.

지금 점심 식사하러 나가고 싶으신가요, 아니면 한 시간 후에 나가고 싶으신가요?

(A) 저는 이 자료를 먼저 정리해야 할 겁니다.

(B) 콥 씨는 점심 식사하시는 데 한 시간이 걸려요.

(C) 저는 이곳이 처음 문을 열었을 때 와서 식사했어요.

해설 지금 점심 식사하러 나갈 건지, 아니면 한 시간 후에 갈 것인지 묻고 있으므로 먼저 끝마쳐야 하는 일이 있다는 말로 나중에 가겠다는 뜻을 나타내는 (A)가 정답이다. (B)는 다른 사람이 점심 식사하는 데 소요되는 시간을 말하고 있어 핵심에서 벗어난 오답이며, (C)는 식사 시점과 관련 없는 오답이다.

어휘 **in 시간** ~ 후에 **compile** (자료 등을 모아) ~을 정리하다

20. The instructions for entering spreadsheet data are extremely confusing.

(A) The date hasn't been set yet.

(B) You can enter through the side entrance.

(C) They're going to be simplified.

스프레드시트 데이디 입력에 대한 설명이 너무 헷갈려요.

(A) 날짜가 아직 정해지지 않았어요.

(B) 옆쪽 출입문을 통해서 들어가실 수 있어요.

(C) 간소화될 예정입니다.

해설 데이터 입력에 대한 설명이 너무 헷갈린다는 사실을 알리는 말에 대해 instructions를 They로 지칭해 간소화될 것이라는 말로 해결 방법을 알리는 (C)가 정답이다. (A)는 data와 발음이 유사한 date를, (B)는 enter의 다른 의미를(입력하다, 들어가다) 각각 활용해 혼동을 유발하는 오답이다.

어휘 **instructions** 설명, 안내, 지시 **spreadsheet** 스프레드시트(표를 이용한 입력 프로그램) **extremely** 너무, 대단히, 매우 **confusing** 헷갈리게 하는, 혼란스럽게 만드는 **simplify** ~을 간소화하다

Part 3

Questions 21-23 refer to the following conversation.

M: Excuse me, Ms. Cartwright. I'm sorry, but **21** there seems to be a problem with the business deal we have going through next week. Can you have a look at the contracts for me?

W: Yes, sure. You mean the Daniels account, right? It was in regards to a travel company takeover, if I remember correctly.

M: Yes, that's the one. **22** If you take a close look at the contracts, you'll notice that some dates and figures differ between our client's contract and the other company's contract. I'm not sure what happened.

W: That's a significant problem. Can you e-mail the contracts to me right away? I had better take a look at them. **23** This takeover is important to Mr. Daniels' company, so I'll let him know about this problem immediately.

남: 실례합니다. 카트라이트 씨. 죄송하지만, 우리가 다음 주에 성사될 사업 거래에 문제가 있는 것 같습니다. 제 대신 계약서들을 한 번 확인해 주시겠어요?

여: 네, 물론이죠. 다니얼스 고객사 말씀하시는 것 맞죠? 그건 여행사 인수와 관련된 것이었어요, 제 기억이 정확하다면요.

남: 네, 그곳 맞습니다. 계약서들을 자세히 살펴보면, 우리 고객사의 계약서와 나머지 회사의 계약서 사이에 일부 날짜와 수치가 다르다는 점을 아시게 될 겁니다. 무슨 일이 있었던 건지 모르겠어요.

여: 그건 중대한 문제네요. 그 계약서들을 즉시 저에게 이메일로 보내주시겠어요? 확인해 보는 것이 낫겠어요. 이 인수는 다니엘스 씨의 회사에 중요한 일이기 때문에, 그분께 이 문제와 관련해 즉시 알리겠습니다.

어휘 **there seems to be A** A가 있는 것 같다 **deal** 거래 **have A -ing** A를 ~하게 하다 **go through** (계약 등이) 성사되다 **have a look at** ~을 한 번 보다 **contract** 계약(서) **account** 고객, 거래처, 계정, 계좌 **in regards to** ~와 관련된 **takeover** (기업의) 인수 **take a close look at** ~을 자세히 한 번 보다 **notice that** ~임을 알게 되다, ~임을 알아차리다 **figure** 수치, 숫자 **differ** 다르다 **significant** 중대한 **had better do** ~하는 편이 낫다 **let A know** A에게 알리다 **immediately** 즉시

21. 대화의 주제가 무엇인가?
(A) 시설 관리 계약
(B) 지출 보고서
(C) 한 여행사의 총회
(D) 사업 거래

해설 대화 초반부에 남자가 사업 거래에 문제가 있음을 상대방에게 알리면서(there seems to be a problem with the business deal ~) 계약서를 확인해줄 수 있는지(Can you have a look at the contracts for me?) 물은 뒤로 그 문제와 관련해 이야기하고 있다. 따라서, 사업 거래가 대화 주제임을 알 수 있으므로 (D)가 정답이다.

어휘 **maintenance** 시설 관리, 유지 관리 **expense** 지출 (비용), 경비

22. 남자가 어떤 문제를 언급하는가?
(A) 계약서에 서명이 없다.
(B) 고객의 회사가 파산했다.
(C) 문서들이 다르다.
(D) 고객이 다른 회사를 매입할 것이다.

해설 대화 중반부에 남자가 두 계약서의 날짜와 수치가 다르다는(~ you'll notice that some dates and figures differ between our client's contract and the other company's contract) 말로 문제를 언급하고 있다. 이는 문서상의 정보가 다르다는 의미이므로 (C)가 정답이다.

어휘 **go bankrupt** 파산하다

Paraphrase some dates and figures differ between our client's contract and the other company's contract
→ The documents are different.

23. 여자는 자신이 무엇을 할 것이라고 말하는가?
(A) 고객과 문제를 논의하는 일
(B) 사업 계약을 취소하는 일
(C) 자신의 직원들과 회의를 준비하는 일
(D) 문서 사본을 한 부 더 출력하는 일

해설 대화 후반부에 여자가 문제와 관련해 고객에게 즉시 알리겠다고(~ so I'll let him know about this problem immediately) 언급하고 있다. 이는 고객과 해당 문제를 논의하겠다는 의미이므로 (A)가 정답이다.

어휘 **agreement** 계약(서), 합의(서) **organize** ~을 마련하다, ~을 조직하다

Paraphrase let him know about this problem immediately
→ Discuss the issue with the client

Questions 24-26 refer to the following conversation.

M: Jessica! **24** What do you think of our new employees? I know you have been working with them very closely.

W: To be honest, **25** I have an issue with how the new group has been working. They are definitely motivated, and they all have good attitudes, **25** but the pace at which they work has not been so impressive. We are a busy company, and presently they are working far too slow.

M: It's true. They are very slow at the moment. But I think we need to give them some time to adjust. I think in a few weeks they will be as fast as everyone else.

W: Yes, you are right. I should be patient. **26** Maybe next week I'll organize a training session for the group so that I can offer some advice on how to increase speed and efficiency.

남: 제시카 씨! 우리 신입 직원들에 대해 어떻게 생각하세요? 그분들과 아주 가깝게 근무하고 계신 거 알아요.

여: 솔직히, 신입 직원 분들이 일하고 있는 방식과 관련해서 문제가 있어요. 분명히 의욕적이고 모두 업무 태도도 좋지만, 업무를 처리하는 속도가 그렇게 인상적이지는 않아요. 우리 회사는 바쁜 곳인데, 현재 그분들은 너무 많이 느리게 일하고 계세요.

남: 사실이에요. 지금은 정말 느리죠. 하지만 우리가 그분들에게 적응할 시간을 좀 줘야 할 것 같아요. 제 생각에 몇 주 후면 다른 모든 사람처럼 빨라질 거예요.

여: 네, 맞는 말씀이에요. 제가 인내심을 가져야겠죠. 아마 다음 주에 그분들을 대상으로 업무 속도와 효율을 높이는 법에 관해 조언을 제공해 드릴 수 있도록 교육 시간을 마련하게 될 겁니다.

어휘 **closely** 가깝게, 긴밀하게, 밀접하게 **to be honest** 솔직히 **have an issue with** ~에 문제가 있다 **definitely** 분명히, 틀림없이 **motivated** 의욕적인, 동기가 부여된 **attitude** 태도 **pace** 속도 **impressive** 인상적인 **presently** 현재, 지금 **far too** 형용사 너무 많이 ~한 **at the moment** 지금, 현재 **adjust** 적응하다 **as A as B** B만큼 A한 **organize** ~을 마련하다, 조직하다 **so that** (목적) ~하도록 **how to do** ~하는 법 **increase** ~을 늘리다, ~을 증가시키다 **efficiency** 효율(성)

24. 화자들이 주로 무엇을 논의하고 있는가?
(A) 신입 직원들
(B) 사내 정책의 변화
(C) 직원 해고 계획
(D) 새로운 사무 공간

해설 대화 초반부에 남자가 여자에게 신입 직원들에 대해 어떻게 생각하는지 물은 뒤로(What do you think of our new employees?), 화자들이 신입 직원들과 관련해 각자의 의견을 밝히는 것으로 대화가 전개되고 있다. 따라서, 신입 직원들이 대화 주제임을 알 수 있으므로 (A)가 정답이다.

어휘 **policy** 정책, 방침 **plan to do** ~하려는 계획 **lay off** ~을 해고하다
Paraphrase new employees
→ A group of new workers

25. 여자가 어떤 문제를 언급하는가?
(A) 팀원들 사이의 논쟁
(B) 회사 지출 비용의 증가
(C) 직원들이 저지른 실수들
(D) 일부 직원들의 업무 속도

해설 여자가 어떤 문제를 언급하는지 묻고 있으므로 여자의 말에서 부정적인 정보를 파악해야 한다. 여자가 대화 중반부에 신입 직원들이 일하는 방식에 문제가 있다고(I have an issue with how the new group has been working) 말하면서 그들이 일하는 속도가 너무 느리다는(but the pace at which they work has not been so impressive. We are a busy company, and presently they are working far too slow) 설명을 덧붙이고 있다. 따라서, 이러한 문제에 해당되는 (D)가 정답이다.

어휘 **dispute** 논쟁, 분쟁 **spending** 지출
Paraphrase working far too slow
→ speed of some employees

26. 여자가 다음 주에 무엇을 할 것 같은가?
(A) 다른 일자리에 지원하는 일
(B) 영업 워크숍에 참석하는 일
(C) 교육 시간을 준비하는 일
(D) 추가 직원을 모집하는 일

해설 여자가 다음 주에 무엇을 할 것인지 묻고 있으므로 미래 시점 표현 next week과 함께 언급되는 계획이나 일정 등과 관련된 정보를 찾아야 한다. 대화 후반부에 여자는 다음 주에 교육 시간을 마련할 것이라는(Maybe next week I'll organize a training session for the group ~) 계획을 알리고 있으므로 (C)가 정답이다.

어휘 **apply for** ~에 지원하다 **attend** ~에 참석하다 **arrange** ~을 마련하다
Paraphrase organize a training session
→ Arrange a training session

Questions 27-29 refer to the following conversation.

W: Hi, Vince. **27** I just received an e-mail from our new Chinese client. They're expecting the first shipment of our tablet computers to arrive within a week. Do you think we'll be able to meet their expectations?

M: I'm not sure. They're based so far away, and they've ordered a huge shipment. Also, **28** we used to use Madigan Shipping for our overseas orders, but they recently went out of business. So, I contacted Fillmore Packages, and they said **29** it will take two weeks to send the order.

W: Then it won't be a problem. **29** I'll give the client a call and explain the reason for the delay in shipping.

여: 안녕하세요, 빈스 씨. 제가 중국의 신규 고객사로부터 방금 이메일을 받았어요. 그쪽에서는 일주일 내로 우리 태블릿 컴퓨터의 첫 배송이 도착할 것으로 예상하고 있어요. 우리가 그쪽의 기대치를 충족할 수 있을 거라고 생각하세요?

남: 잘 모르겠습니다. 그 고객사는 아주 멀리 떨어진 곳에 본사를 두고 있는데, 엄청난 양의 배송 물품을 주문했어요. 그리고, 우리가 전에는 해외 주문에 대해 매디건 배송 회사를 이용했지만, 이곳이 최근에 폐업했어요. 그래서, 제가 필모어 패키지스 사에 연락했는데, 주문품을 보내는 데 2주가 걸릴 거라고 하더라고요.

여: 그럼 문제가 되진 않을 겁니다. 제가 고객사에 전화해서 배송 지연에 대한 이유를 설명할게요.

어휘 **expect A to do** A가 ~할 것으로 예상하다 **meet** (요구, 조건 등) ~을 충족하다 **expectation** 기대(치) **be based** 본사를 두고 있다, 기반으로 하다 **order** v. ~을 주문하다 n. 주문(품) **used to do** 전에 ~하곤 했다 **overseas** 해외의 **recently** 최근에 **go out of business** 폐업하다 **contact** ~에 연락하다 **take** ~의 시간이 걸리다 **then** 그럼, 그렇다면, 그때, 그 후에 **give A a call** A에게 전화하다 **explain** ~을 설명하다 **delay** 지연, 지체

27. 화자들이 주로 무엇을 이야기하고 있는가?
(A) 기업 합병
(B) 공장 확장
(C) 해외 고객
(D) 회사 정책

해설 대화 초반부에 여자가 중국의 신규 고객사로부터 이메일을 받았다고(I just received an e-mail from our new Chinese client) 알리면서 이 고객사의 주문 사항과 관련해 이야기하고 있으므로 (C)가 정답이다.

어휘 **merger** 합병 **expansion** 확장, 확대 **policy** 정책, 방침

28. 남자가 매디건 배송 회사와 관련해 무슨 말을 하는가?
(A) 할인을 제공해 줄 수 있다.
(B) 더 이상 영업하지 않는다.
(C) 해외에 본사를 두고 있다.
(D) 자사의 요금을 변경했다.

해설 Madigan Shipping이 핵심이므로 대화 중에 이 명칭이 제시되는 부분에서 단서를 찾아야 한다. 대화 중반부에 남자가 매디건 배송 회사를 언급하면서 그곳이 원래 이용하던 업체였지만 최근에 폐업했다고(~ we used to use Madigan Shipping ~ but they recently went out of business) 알리고 있다. 이는 더 이상 영업하지 않는다는 뜻이므로 (B)가 정답이다.

어휘 **no longer** 더 이상 ~ 않다 **be in business** 영업하다 **overseas** ad. 해외에 **rate** 요금, 비율, 등급, 속도

Paraphrase they recently went out of business
→ It is no longer in business.

29. 여자가 "그럼 문제가 되진 않을 겁니다"라고 말할 때 무엇을 의미하는가?
(A) 가격이 적정하다고 생각하고 있다.
(B) 기간에 대해 만족하고 있다.
(C) 여러 가지 업무들을 수행할 수 있다.
(D) 다른 배송 회사를 찾을 것이다.

해설 질문에 제시된 문장은 주문품을 보내는 데 2주가 걸릴 거라는(it will take two weeks to send the order) 남자의 말에 대한 여자의 반응이다. 이 문장을 말한 후에 고객에게 전화해서 배송 지연에 대한 이유를 설명하겠다고(I'll give the client a call and explain the reason for the delay in shipping) 말하는 것으로 보아, 배송 기간이 2주가 걸려도 괜찮다는 뜻으로 쓰인 말이라는 것을 알 수 있다. 따라서, 이에 해당되는 의미를 지닌 (B)가 정답이다.

어휘 **reasonable** (가격이) 적정한, 합리적인 **be satisfied with** ~에 만족하다 **time frame** 기간 **perform** ~을 수행하다, ~을 실시하다 **task** 업무, 일

Questions 30-32 refer to the following conversation with three speakers.

M1: The most important thing to discuss today is our company's lack of funding. **30** I'm getting worried that we haven't received much interest from investors.

W: Yes, it's clear that **30** we need to find other ways to let people know about our firm. So, umm... **31** I think it'd be a great idea to take part in the upcoming global retail convention. Bobby, you've represented us at conventions before, right?

M2: That's right, and I'd be happy to do it again.

W: Great. **32** I'd like you to start putting together a team of staff who'll accompany you to the convention. Try to choose your best salespeople.

M2: No problem. I'll get on it right away.

남1: 오늘 논의해야 할 가장 중요한 것은 우리 회사의 자금 부족 문제입니다. 저는 우리가 투자자들로부터 많은 관심을 받지 못해 왔다는 점이 걱정됩니다.
여: 네, 사람들에게 우리 회사에 관해 알릴 수 있는 다른 방법들을 찾아봐야 한다는 것이 분명합니다. 따라서, 음... 다가오는 세계적인 소매업 컨벤션에 참가하는 게 좋은 아이디어일 거라고 생각합니다. 바비 씨, 예전에 열렸던 컨벤션에서 우리 회사를 대표하셨던 것이 맞죠?
남2: 그렇습니다, 그리고 기꺼이 다시 한 번 그렇게 하고 싶습니다.
여: 잘됐네요. 컨벤션에 동행하실 직원들로 팀을 구성하는 일을 시작해 주셨으면 합니다. 최고의 영업사원들로 선정하도록 노력해 주시기 바랍니다.
남2: 알겠습니다. 곧바로 시작하겠습니다.

어휘 **lack of** ~의 부족 **funding** 자금 (제공) **get worried that** ~라는 점이 걱정되다 **receive** ~을 받다 **interest** 관심 **investor** 투자자 **it's clear that** ~라는 점이 분명하다 **let A know** A에게 알리다 **take part in** ~에 참가하다 **upcoming** 다가오는, 곧 있을 **retail** 소매(업) **represent** ~을 대표하다 **would like A to do** A에게 ~하기를 원하다 **put together** ~을 구성하다, 준비하다, ~을 조립하다 **accompany A to B** A를 동반해 B에 가다 **choose** ~을 선택하다 **get on** ~을 시작하다, ~에 착수하다 **right away** 곧바로, 당장

30. 회사에 무슨 문제가 있는가?
(A) 한 프로젝트에 대해 일정이 뒤처져 있다.
(B) 매출 목표를 충족하지 못하고 있다.
(C) 고객들로부터 불만 사항을 받아 왔다.
(D) 투자자들을 유치하는 데 고전하고 있다.

해설 회사의 문제를 묻고 있으므로 회사의 상황과 관련해 부정적인 표현이 제시되는 부분에서 단서를 찾아야 한다. 남자 한 명이 대화 초반부에 투자자들로부터 많은 관심을 받지 못해 왔다는 사실이 걱정된다고(~ we haven't received much interest from investors) 말하자, 여자가 회사에 관해 알릴 수 있는 다른 방법들을 찾아야 한다는 말을(~ we need to find other ways to let people know about our firm) 덧붙이고 있다. 이는 투자자들을 유치하는 데 어려움을 겪고 있는 것이므로 (D)가 정답이다.

어휘 **behind schedule** 일정이 뒤처진 **fail to do** ~하지 못하다 **meet** (요구, 조건 등) ~을 충족하다 **complaint** 불만 **struggle** 고전하다, 힘겨워하다 **attract** ~을 유치하다, 끌

어들이다
Paraphrase we haven't received much interest from investors
→ It is struggling to attract investors.

31. 여자가 무엇을 제안하는가?
(A) 마케팅 계획을 만드는 것
(B) 자문 위원을 고용하는 것
(C) 한 행사에 참가하는 것
(D) 신입 사원들을 교육하는 것

해설 대화 중반부에 여자가 사람들에게 회사에 대해 알려야 한다고 말하면서 소매업 컨벤션에 참가하는 것이 좋겠다고(I think it'd be a great idea to take part in the upcoming global retail convention) 제안하고 있으므로 (C)가 정답이다.

어휘 **create** ~을 만들어내다 **hire** ~을 고용하다 **consultant** 자문 위원, 상담 전문가 **participate in** ~에 참가하다

Paraphrase take part in the upcoming global retail convention
→ Participating in an event

32. 여자는 바비 씨에게 무엇을 하도록 요청하는가?
(A) 광고를 내는 일
(B) 일부 고객들에게 연락하는 일
(C) 팀 구성원들을 선정하는 일
(D) 연간 예산을 계산하는 일

해설 여자가 요청하는 일을 묻고 있으므로 여자의 말에서 요청 관련 표현이 제시되는 부분을 통해 단서를 파악해야 한다. 대화 중반부에 여자가 바비 씨를 부르면서 질문한 후, 그 남자가 대답한 내용과 관련해 컨벤션에 갈 직원들로 팀을 구성하는 일을 시작해 달라고(I'd like you to start putting together a team of staff ~) 요청하고 있다. 따라서, 팀원들을 선정하는 일을 뜻하는 (C)가 정답이다.

어휘 **place an advertisement** 광고를 내다 **contact** ~에게 연락하다 **select** ~을 선정하다 **calculate** ~을 계산하다

Paraphrase putting together a team of staff
→ Select team members

Questions 33-35 refer to the following conversation and chart.

W: Ray, **33** I'm becoming concerned about how many of our kitchen staff and servers are coming in late for their shifts these days.

M: Oh, is it starting to become a problem? We're approaching our busiest season, so we need all our workers to be on time.

W: I agree. Look at the chart for last week... Ten people arrived late on Wednesday, and **34** eight people were late on the day that we had the heavy rainfall.

M: That's not good. **35** Why don't we have staff who arrive late for their work shift pay a fine? That would stop them from coming in late.

여: 레이 씨, 저는 요즘에 얼마나 많은 우리 주방 직원 및 종업원들이 각자의 교대 근무 시간에 늦게 오는지에 대해 우려하고 있어요.

남: 아, 그게 문제가 되기 시작하고 있나요? 우리가 가장 바쁜 시즌과 가까워지고 있기 때문에, 모든 직원들에게 제 시간에 오게 할 필요가 있어요.

여: 동의합니다. 지난주에 대한 이 차트를 좀 보세요... 10명이 수요일에 늦게 도착했고, 폭우가 내렸던 날에는 8명이 지각했어요.

남: 좋지 않네요. 각자의 교대 근무 시간에 늦게 도착하는 직원들에게 벌금을 내도록 하면 어떨까요? 그렇게 하면 늦게 오는 것을 막을 수 있을 거예요.

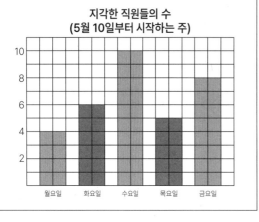

지각한 직원들의 수
(5월 10일부터 시작하는 주)

어휘 concerned about ~에 대해 우려하는 server 종업원, 웨이터 come in late for ~에 지각하다, 늦게 오다 shift 교대 근무(조) approach ~와 가까워지다, ~에 다가가다 need A to do A가 ~할 필요가 있다 on time 제시간에 agree 동의하다 have A do A에게 ~하게 하다 pay a fine 벌금을 내다 stop A from -ing A가 ~하는 것을 막다, A에게 ~하지 못하게 하다

---

33. 화자들이 어디에서 근무할 것 같은가?
(A) 레스토랑에서
(B) 공장에서
(C) 진료소에서
(D) 가전 기기 매장에서

해설 대화 초반부에 여자가 주방 직원 및 종업원들의 교대 근무 시간에 대해 걱정이 되고 있다고(~ how many of our kitchen staff and servers are coming in late ~) 말하고 있다. 주방 직원과 종업원들이 일하는 곳은 음식점이므로 (A)가 정답이다.

34. 시각자료를 보시오. 언제 악천후가 발생했는가?
(A) 화요일에
(B) 수요일에
(C) 목요일에
(D) 금요일에

해설 악천후가 발생한 요일이 질문의 핵심이므로 좋지 않은 기상 상태가 발생한 시점과 관련된 정보를 찾아야 한다. 대화 중반부에 여자가 폭우가 내린 날에 8명이 지각했다고(~ eight people were late on the day that we had the heavy rainfall) 알리고 있다. 시각자료에 8명으로 표기된 요일이 맨 오른쪽에 위치한 Friday이므로 (D)가 정답이다.

어휘 occur 발생하다, 일어나다

35. 남자가 무엇을 제안하는가?
(A) 교대 근무의 지속 시간을 변경하는 것
(B) 직원들에게 보너스를 제공하는 것
(C) 일부 직원들에게 벌금을 부과하는 것
(D) 신입 사원들을 모집하는 것

해설 남자가 제안하는 일을 묻고 있으므로 남자의 말에서 제안 관련 표현이 제시되는 부분을 파악해야 한다. 남자가 대화 후반부에 근무 시간에 늦게 도착하는 직원들에게 벌금을 물리는 것이 어떤지(Why don't we have staff who arrive late for their work shift pay a fine?) 제안하고 있으므로 이러한 방법을 언급한 (C)가 정답이다.

어휘 length 시간 길이 make A do A를 ~하게 만들다 financial penalty 벌금 recruit ~을 모집하다

Paraphrase have staff who arrive late for their work shift pay a fine
→ Giving some workers a financial penalty

Questions 36-38 refer to the following conversation and seating chart.

M: Good morning, ma'am. Welcome to Singapore Air. **36** May I see your passport and ticket confirmation, please?

W: Here you are.

M: Thanks. We have four seats left in business class. Which one would you like? You can see the available seats on my screen.

W: Hmm... **37** I'd like the aisle seat that's close to the restroom, please.

M: Certainly. Now, **36** could you please place your suitcase on the conveyor belt?

W: Okay.

M: Oh, **38** I'm afraid it exceeds the weight limit. You'll need to pay an excess baggage fee of $50.

W: That's no problem. Hold on a moment.

남: 안녕하십니까, 고객님. 싱가포르 항공에 오신 것을 환영합니다. 여권과 항공권 확인서를 보여 주시겠습니까?

여: 여기 있습니다.

남: 감사합니다. 비즈니스 클래스에는 네 개의 좌석이 남아 있습니다. 어느 것으로 하시겠습니까? 제 화면에서 이용 가능한 좌석들을 확인해 보실 수 있습니다.

여: 흠... 화장실과 가까운 곳에 있는 복도 쪽 좌석으로 하고 싶어요.

남: 좋습니다. 이제, 컨베이어 벨트에 여행 가방을 올려 놓아 주시겠습니까?

여: 네.

남: 아, 중량 제한을 초과하는 것 같습니다. 초과 수하물 요금이 50달러를 지불하셔야 할 겁니다.

여: 알겠습니다. 잠시만요.

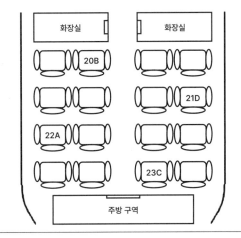

어휘 passport 여권 confirmation 확인(서) have A left A가 남아 있다 would like ~로 하고 싶다, ~을 원하다 available 이용 가능한 aisle 복도 close to ~와 가까운 Certainly (긍정의 답변으로) 좋습니다, 그럼요, 물론이죠 place A on B A를 B에 놓다 suitcase 여행 가방 I'm afraid (부정적인 일에 대해) ~인 것 같습니다, 유감이지만 ~입니다 exceed ~을 초과하다 weight limit 중량 제한 excess baggage fee 초과 수하물 요금 Hold on a moment 잠시만 기다려 주세요

36. 대화가 어디에서 이뤄지고 있는가?
(A) 출발 탑승구에서
(B) 체크인 카운터에서
(C) 기내에서
(D) 여행사에서

해설 대화 초반부에 남자가 여권과 항공권 확인서를 보여 달라고 요청하는(May I see your passport and ticket confirmation, please?) 부분이나 중반부에 여행 가방을 컨베이어 벨트에 올려 달라고 묻는(~ place your suitcase on the conveyor belt?) 것으로 볼 때 공항에서 탑승 전에 수속을 밟는 상황임을 알 수 있다. 따라서, 해당 업무가 진행되는 장소인 (B)가 정답이다.

어휘 take place 발생되다, 일어나다 departure 출발, 떠남 travel agency 여행사

37. 시각자료를 보시오. 여자의 좌석 번호는 무엇인가?
(A) 20B
(B) 21D
(C) 22A
(D) 23C

해설 배치도가 제시되는 문제에서는 이동 방식 및 위치 관계를 나타내는 동사나 형용사, 전치사에 특히 주의해 들어야 한다. 대화 중반부에 여자가 화장실과 가까운 곳에 있는 복도 쪽 좌석으로 달라고(I'd like the aisle seat that's close to the restroom, please) 요청하고 있다. 시각자료에서 왼쪽 상단에 위치한 20B가 화장실과 가까운 복도 쪽 좌석에 해당되므로 (A)가 정답이다.

38. 남자가 여자의 수하물과 관련해 무엇을 언급하는가?
(A) 이름표가 빠져 있다.
(B) 매우 비싸 보인다.
(C) 분실되었다.
(D) 허용된 것보다 무겁다.

해설 여자의 수하물과 관련해 남자가 하는 말이 핵심이므로 남자의 말에서 수하물 관련 정보가 제시될 것임을 예상하고 들을 수 있다. 대화 후반부에 남자가 중량 제한을 초과하는 것 같다는 말과 함께 초과 수하물 요금인 50달러를 지불해야 한다고(I'm afraid it exceeds the weight limit. You'll need to pay an excess baggage fee of $50) 알리고 있다. 중량 제한

을 초과한다는 것은 기준보다 무겁다는 의미이므로 (D)가 정답이다.

어휘 miss ~을 빠트리다, 놓치다 misplace ~을 잃어 버리다, ~을 둔 곳을 잊다 allow ~을 허용하다

Paraphrase exceeds the weight limit
→ heavier than what is allowed

Part 4

Questions 39-41 refer to the following excerpt from a meeting.

Thank you, everyone, for coming. You have probably already heard that **39** we are installing new software on all of our office computers this week. **40** The new system will be installed on Wednesday morning, and will be up and running on your computers by the time you get to work. We hope the transition takes place without any problems. **40** The day before this transition, we will take all the important files from your computers and store them on a hard drive or USB flash drive. That way, nothing will be lost. And to ensure that everything has gone smoothly, **41** please complete a survey by the end of this week so that we can check the effectiveness of the new system.

이 자리에 오신 여러분 모두에게 감사드립니다. 이번 주에 우리의 모든 사무용 컴퓨터에 새로운 소프트웨어를 설치한다는 얘기를 아마 이미 들으셨을 겁니다. 새로운 시스템이 수요일 아침에 설치될 것이며, 업무를 시작하실 때쯤이면 여러분의 컴퓨터에서 가동되고 있을 겁니다. 저희는 이와 같은 변경 작업이 아무런 문제없이 진행되길 바라고 있습니다. 이 변경 작업을 하기 전날에, 여러분의 컴퓨터에서 중요한 파일들을 꺼내서 다른 하드 드라이브나 USB 플래시 드라이브에 저장할 것입니다. 그렇게 하면, 아무 것도 분실되지 않을 것입니다. 그리고 반드시 모든 작업이 순조롭게 진행되도록 하기 위해, 저희가 새 시스템의 효과를 확인해볼 수 있도록 이번 주말까지 설문 조사지를 작성 완료해 주시기 바랍니다.

어휘 install ~을 설치하다 up and running 가동되는, 작동 중인 by the time ~할 때쯤이면 get to work 일을 시작하다, 출근하다 transition 변경, 변환, 과도기 take place 일어나다, 발생되다 store v. ~을 저장하다, ~을 보관하다 That way 그렇게 하면, 그런 방법으로 lost 분실된, 사라진 ensure that 반드시 ~하도록 하다, ~임을 확실히 해두다 go smoothly 순조롭게 진행되다 complete ~을 완료하다 survey 설문 조사(지) by (기한) ~까지 so that (목적) ~하도록 effectiveness 효과

39. 담화가 주로 무엇에 관한 것인가?
(A) 시스템 오류
(B) 소프트웨어 업그레이드
(C) 컴퓨터 모델 교체
(D) 재무 감사

해설 담화의 주제를 묻는 문제이므로 초반부에 집중해 들어야 한다. 화자가 담화 초반부에 이번 주에 모든 사무용 컴퓨터에 새로운 소프트웨어를 설치할 거라고(~ we are installing new software on all of our office computers this week) 말한 후에, 이와 관련된 일정과 작업 방식 등을 설명하고 있다. 새로운 소프트웨어 설치는 업그레이드하는 것과 같으므로 (B)가 정답이다.

어휘 failure 오류, 고장 financial 재무의, 재정의 audit (회계) 감사

Paraphrase installing new software
→ A software upgrade

40. 화자의 말에 따르면, 화요일에 무슨 일이 있을 것인가?
(A) 회사의 책상마다 물건이 치워질 것이다.
(B) 문서들이 전자 파일로 변환될 것이다.
(C) 새 직원들이 근무를 시작할 것이다.
(D) 파일들이 컴퓨터에서 제거될 것이다.

해설 특정 시점인 Tuesday가 핵심이므로 해당 요일이 언급되는 부분을 놓치지 않는 것이 중요하다. 그런데 이 담화에서는 화요일이 직접적으로 제시되는 것이 아니라 수요일을 먼저 말한 다음(The new system will be installed on Wednesday morning), 그 뒤에 '해당 변경 작업 전날(The day before this transition)'이라는 말로 화요일을 간접적으로 나타내고 있다. 그날 컴퓨터에서 파일들을 꺼내 다른 하드 드라이브나 USB 드라이브에 저장할 것이라고(~ we will take all the important files from your computers ~) 알리고 있으므로 파일들을 컴퓨터에서 제거하는 일을 뜻하는 (D)가 정답이다.

어휘 take place 일어나다, 발생하다 clear ~을 치우다 convert A into B A를 B로 변환하다, A를 B로 전환하다 remove A from B A를 B에서 제거하다, A를 B에서 없애다

Paraphrase take all the important files from your computers
→ Files will be removed from computers.

41. 직원들이 이번 주에 무엇을 반드시 해야 하는가?
(A) 새로운 곳으로 이전하는 일
(B) 새 컴퓨터를 구입하는 일
(C) 설문지를 작성하는 일
(D) 회의에 참석하는 일

해설 this week이라는 기간에 직원들이 반드시 해야 하는 일을 묻고 있으므로 this week과 함께 요청 사항이나 당부 사항이 제시될 것으로 예상해 볼 수 있다. 화자가 담화 후반부에 이번 주

말까지라는 기한과 함께 설문지를 작성 완료해야 한다고
(~ please complete a survey by the end of this
week) 알리고 있으므로 (C)가 정답이다.

어휘 **location** 장소, 지점, 위치 **fill out** (서류 등) ~을 작성하다
questionnaire 설문지

Paraphrase complete a survey
→ Fill out a questionnaire

Questions 42-44 refer to the following telephone
message.

Good morning, Ms. Tomkins. This is Josh calling
from Cycle City. **42** I took a look at the Anaconda
mountain bike you brought in for repairs
yesterday. Wow, you really did some damage to
it when you had your accident last week. The first
thing I noticed is that the entire frame is bent out
of shape. And, that was just the start. **43** I'm sorry
to tell you this, but if I repair all of the damages,
it might cost you more than the price of a brand
new model. **44** I've created an invoice and
e-mailed it to you. Please check the figures and
then let me know whether you want me to proceed
with the work. Thanks.

안녕하세요. 탐킨스 씨. 저는 사이클 시티의 조쉬입니다. 어제 수리
작업을 위해 가져 오셨던 아나콘다 산악 자전거를 한 번 살펴 봤습니
다. 와우, 지난 주에 사고를 당하셨을 때 정말로 많이 손상되었습니
다. 제가 가장 먼저 주목했던 것은 전체 프레임의 형태가 뒤틀려
구부러져 있다는 점입니다. 그리고, 이는 시작에 불과했습니다. 이
런 말씀드리기 죄송하지만, 제가 이 모든 손상 부분들을 수리할 경
우, 완전히 새로운 모델의 가격보다 더 많은 비용이 들지도 모릅니
다. 제가 비용 내역서를 만들어서 귀하께 이메일로 보내 드렸습니
다. 수치를 확인해 보신 다음, 저에게 이 작업을 진행하기를 원하시
는지 알려 주시기 바랍니다. 감사합니다.

어휘 **take a look at** ~을 한 번 보다 **repair** n. 수리 v. ~을 수리
하다 **do damage to** ~을 손상시키다, ~에 피해를 입히다
notice ~을 주목하다, ~을 알아차리다 **entire** 전체의
frame 프레임, 골격 **bend** ~을 구부리다 **out of shape**
형태가 뒤틀린 **cost A B** A에게 B의 비용을 들이게 하다
brand new 완전히 새로운 **create** ~을 만들어내다
invoice 비용 내역서, 거래 내역서 **figure** 수치, 숫자
whether ~인지 (아닌지) **want A to do** A에게 ~하기를
원하다 **proceed with** ~을 진행하다, ~을 계속하다

42. 화자가 어디에서 일할 것 같은가?
(A) 자전거 매장에서
(B) 제조 공장에서
(C) 자동차 대여소에서

(D) 진료소에서

해설 화자가 담화 초반부에 상대방이 어제 수리 작업을 위해 가져온
아나콘다 산악 자전거를 살펴 봤다고(I took a look at the
Anaconda mountain bike you brought in for repairs
yesterday) 알리고 있으므로 자전거 수리가 가능한 장소인
(A)가 정답이다.

43. 화자가 "그리고, 이는 시작에 불과했습니다"라고 말할 때 암시
하는 것은 무엇인가?
(A) 일부 작업에 대해 깊은 인상을 받았다.
(B) 여러 가지 다른 문제들을 발견했다.
(C) 새로운 프로젝트에 대해 도움을 원한다.
(D) 빨리 일을 끝마쳤다.

해설 화자가 자전거와 관련된 문제를 언급한 후에 해당 문장과 함
께 모든 손상 부분들을 수리할 경우에 완전히 새로운 모델의
가격보다 더 많은 비용이 들 것이라고(~ if I repair all of the
damages, it might cost you more than the price of a
brand new model) 말하고 있다. 이는 문제가 너무 많아 수
리 비용이 아주 많이 든다는 뜻을 나타내는 것이므로 (B)가 정
답이다.

어휘 **be impressed with** ~에 대해 깊은 인상을 받다

44. 화자는 자신이 무엇을 했다고 말하는가?
(A) 비용 내역서를 발송하는 일
(B) 주문을 연기하는 일
(C) 환불을 제공하는 일
(D) 물품을 배송하는 일

해설 현재완료시제 동사 has done과 함께 과거 시점에 한 일을 묻
고 있으므로 동일한 시제로 된 동사와 함께 지난 일을 언급하는
부분을 찾아야 한다. 담화 후반부에 화자가 비용 내역서를 만들
어서 이메일로 보낸 상태라고(I've created an invoice and
e-mailed it to you) 알리고 있으므로 (A)가 정답이다.

어휘 **postpone** ~을 연기하다 **order** 주문(품) **refund** 환불
(액)

Paraphrase created an invoice and e-mailed it to you
→ Sent an invoice

Questions 45-47 refer to the following talk.

45 Before today's orientation begins, I want to talk to you all about the footwear policy here at the gym. Whenever you come in for a workout, **46** please remove your outdoor shoes and place them in one of the lockers just beside the entrance to the changing rooms. **47** We recently laid new flooring, and we would like to keep it in excellent condition. Please keep this in mind. Now, if you come with me to the main fitness room, our head instructor, Gerry Manford, will show you how to perform some basic warm-up exercises.

오늘 오리엔테이션이 시작되기에 앞서, 여러분 모두에게 이곳 저희 체육관의 신발 관련 정책에 관해 말씀 드리고자 합니다. 운동을 위해 오실 때마다, 야외용 신발을 벗으신 다음, 탈의실로 들어가는 입구 바로 옆에 있는 사물함 중의 하나에 신발을 넣어 주시기 바랍니다. 저희가 최근에 바닥재를 새로 깔았기 때문에, 훌륭한 상태를 유지하고자 합니다. 이 점을 명심하시기 바랍니다. 이제, 저와 함께 중앙 피트니스 룸으로 가시면, 저희 수석 강사이신 게리 맨포드 씨께서 몇몇 기본 워밍업 운동을 하는 방법을 알려드릴 것입니다.

어휘 **policy** 정책, 방침 **whenever** ~할 때마다 **come in for** ~하러 오다 **workout** 운동 **remove** ~을 벗다, ~을 제거하다 **place A in B** A를 B에 넣다 **beside** ~ 옆에 **recently** 최근에 **lay flooring** 바닥재를 깔다 **would like to do** ~하고자 하다, ~하고 싶다 **keep A in excellent condition** A를 훌륭한 상태로 유지하다 **keep A in mind** A를 명심하다 **show A how to do** A에게 ~하는 법을 알려 주다 **warm-up exercise** 워밍업 운동

45. 청자들이 누구일 것 같은가?
(A) 피트니스 강사들
(B) 잠재 투자자들
(C) 실내 디자이너들
(D) 체육관 신규 회원들

해설 담화 초반부에 화자가 오리엔테이션에 앞서 체육관 신발 관련 정책에 관해 이야기하려 한다고(Before today's orientation begins, I want to talk to you all about the footwear policy here at the gym) 말하고 있다. 이는 체육관에 새로 가입한 회원들에게 할 수 있는 말이므로 (D)가 정답임을 알 수 있다.

46. 탈의실 입구 옆에서 무엇을 찾아볼 수 있는가?
(A) 타월
(B) 음료
(C) 사물함
(D) 티셔츠

해설 탈의실 입구 옆이라는 위치가 핵심이므로 해당 위치 표현이 제시되는 부분에서 단서를 찾아야 한다. 담화 중반부에 화자가 신발 보관 장소와 관련해 탈의실로 들어가는 입구 바로 옆에 있는 사물함(~ one of the lockers just beside the entrance to the changing rooms)을 언급하고 있으므로 (C)가 정답이다.

47. 화자는 왜 "이 점을 명심하시기 바랍니다"라고 말하는가?
(A) 운동 강좌를 하나 추천하기 위해
(B) 업체의 방침 한 가지를 강조하기 위해
(C) 특별 판촉 행사를 알리기 위해
(D) 청자들에게 의견을 요청하기 위해

해설 담화 중반부에 화자가 특정 위치에 야외용 신발을 벗어서 보관하도록 요청하면서 그 이유를 언급한(~ please remove your outdoor shoes and place them in ~ we would like to keep it in excellent condition) 후에 해당 문장을 말하고 있다. 질문에 제시된 문장에서 '이것(this)'은 밖에서 신던 신발을 사물함에 보관해야 한다는 방침을 가리키며, 이와 같은 방침을 지키도록 강조하기 위해 명심하라고 알리는 상황임을 알 수 있으므로 (B)가 정답이다.

어휘 **emphasize** ~을 강조하다 **promotion** 판촉 (행사), 홍보, 승진 **ask A for B** A에게 B를 요청하다

Questions 48-50 refer to the following telephone message and building directory.

Hi, this is a message for Anthony Kim. I spoke with you this morning and **48** asked you to come in tomorrow to interview for the assistant manager position. However, due to a conflict in my schedule, I'll need you to come in on Wednesday at 6 P.M. instead. I'm really sorry for the inconvenience. **49** Just come on up to the electronics department and look for my office at the back, just next to the checkout desk. I apologize in advance for the noise in our department store. **50** We are remodeling the furniture department upstairs, so there may be some drilling and hammering during our meeting.

안녕하세요, 이 메시지는 앤서니 킴 씨께 전해 드리는 것입니다. 제가 오늘 아침에 귀하와 이야기를 나누면서 내일 부매니저 직책에 대한 면접을 보러 오시도록 요청 드렸습니다. 하지만, 제 일정상의 충돌 문제로 인해, 대신 수요일 오후 6시에 와 주셔야 할 것입니다. 불편을 끼쳐 드려 대단히 죄송합니다. 전자 기기 매장 층으로 올라오신 후에, 뒤쪽 계산대 바로 옆에 있는 제 사무실로 찾아 오시기만 하시면 됩니다. 저희 백화점 내의 소음에 대해 미리 사과의 말씀드립니다. 저희가 위층에 있는 가구 매장을 개조하는 중이어서 만나 뵙는 중에 드릴 및 망치 작업이 진행되는 중일 수 있습니다.

6층 - 게임기 / 장난감
5층 - 가구
4층 - 전자 기기
3층 - 스포츠 의류
2층 - 남성 의류
1층 - 여성 의류

어휘 **position** 직책, 일자리 **however** 하지만, 그러나 **due to** ~로 인해, ~ 때문에 **conflict in a schedule** 일정 상의 충돌, 겹치는 일정 **need A to do** A가 ~해야 하다 **inconvenience** 불편 **electronics** 전자 기기 **department** (백화점의) 매장 **next to** ~ 옆에 **checkout desk** 계산대 **apologize for** ~에 대해 사과하다 **in advance** 미리, 사전에 **remodel** ~을 개조하다 **drilling** 드릴 작업 **hammering** 망치 작업

48. 화자가 왜 전화를 거는가?
(A) 제품 시연회를 준비하기 위해
(B) 일부 수리 작업을 요청하기 위해
(C) 프로젝트 일정에 관해 문의하기 위해
(D) 면접 일정을 재조정하기 위해

해설 전화를 거는 이유는 주로 담화 시작 부분에 제시되므로 담화가 시작될 때 특히 집중해야 한다. 화자가 상대방에게 내일 면접을 보러 오도록 요청했었는데, 일정상의 충돌 문제로 인해 대신 수요일 오후 6시에 오도록(~ due to a conflict in my schedule, I'll need you to come in on Wednesday at 6 P.M. instead) 알리고 있다. 이는 면접 일정을 재조정하겠다는 뜻이므로 (D)가 정답이다.

어휘 **arrange** ~을 준비하다, ~의 일정을 정하다 **inquire about** ~에 관해 문의하다 **reschedule** ~의 일정을 재조정하다

Paraphrase come in on Wednesday at 6 P.M. instead
→ reschedule

49. 시각자료를 보시오. 화자의 사무실이 어디에 위치해 있을 것 같은가?
(A) 1층에
(B) 2층에
(C) 3층에
(D) 4층에

해설 대화 중반부에 화자가 전자 기기 매장이 있는 층으로 올라온 후에 뒤쪽 계산대 바로 옆에 있는 자신의 사무실로 찾아 오라고(Just come on up to the electronics department and look for my office at the back ~) 알리고 있다. 시각자료에서 전자 기기 매장이 있는 층은 4층이므로 (D)가 정답이다.

50. 화자가 가구 매장과 관련해 무엇을 언급하는가?
(A) 여러 공석이 있다.
(B) 다른 층으로 옮겨졌다.
(C) 현재 개조되는 중이다.
(D) 특별 세일 행사를 열고 있다.

해설 가구 매장이 질문의 핵심이므로 해당 명칭이 제시되는 부분에 집중해 들어야 한다. 담화 후반부에 화자가 위층에 있는 가구 매장을 개조하고 있다고(We are remodeling the furniture department upstairs ~) 알리고 있으므로 이와 같은 의미에 해당되는 (C)가 정답이다.

어휘 **vacancy** 공석, 빈 자리 **renovate** ~을 개조하다, ~을 보수하다 **hold** ~을 열다, ~을 개최하다

Paraphrase are remodeling
→ is being renovated

Part 5

51.
정답 (C)
해석 지난해에는 적은 수요로 인해 공장 생산량이 20% 감축되었다.
해설 빈칸 앞에 주어가 있고, 빈칸 뒤에 전치사구만 있으므로 빈칸은 동사 자리이다. 주어인 공장 생산량은 회사가 인위적으로 결정하는 요소이므로 수동태 (C) was reduced가 정답이다.
어휘 **production** 생산량, 생산 **reduce** ~을 줄이다, 줄어들다 **due to** ~ 때문에 **demand** 수요

52.
정답 (A)
해석 레토 타임피시스 사는 100퍼센트 방수가 되는 완전히 믿을 만한 시계 제품을 만드는 확실히 자리를 잡은 회사이다.
해설 빈칸이 부사와 명사 사이에 위치해 있으므로 빈칸은 부사의 수식을 받음과 동시에 명사를 수식할 형용사 자리이다. 따라서 (A) reliable이 정답이다.
어휘 **well-established** 확실히 자리를 잡은 **completely** 완전히, 전적으로 **reliable** 믿을 만한, 믿을 수 있는 **reliability** 신뢰성 **reliably** 믿을 수 있게, 확실히 **rely** 신뢰하다, 믿다

53.
정답 (C)
해석 예기치 못하게 저조한 입장권 판매량에 대한 대응으로, 행사 주최 측에서 콘서트를 더 작은 행사장으로 옮기기로 결정했다.
해설 빈칸이 전치사 In과 to 사이에 위치해 있으므로 빈칸이 In의 목적어 역할을 할 명사 자리이다. 따라서 (C) response가 정답이다.
어휘 **unexpectedly** 예기치 못하게, 뜻밖에 **venue** 행사장, 개최 장소 **respond** 대응하다, 반응하다 **response** 대응, 반응

54.

정답 (C)

해석 기술이 지속적으로 빠르게 발전하면서, 사람들이 과거보다 훨씬 더 자주 온라인으로 쇼핑하고 있다.

해설 빈칸이 much more와 than 사이에 위치해 있으므로 빈칸은 비교급을 구성할 형용사 또는 부사가 필요한 자리이다. 그런데 빈칸에 쓰일 단어는 to shop을 수식해야 하므로 자동사를 수식할 수 있는 부사 (C) frequently가 정답이다.

어휘 **rapidly** 빠르게 **go online** 온라인으로 접속하다 **frequently** 자주 **used to do** (과거에) 한때 ~했었다 **frequency** 빈도, 잦음 **frequent** a. 잦은, 빈번한 v. ~에 자주 다니다 **frequence** 주파수

55.

정답 (C)

해석 다른 부서장들과는 달리, 포세트 씨는 오히려 자신이 직접 월간 업무 일정을 만든다.

해설 빈칸 앞에 주어와 동사, 그리고 목적어가 있는 완전한 구성의 문장이 있으므로 '직접, 혼자'라는 의미로 부사적으로 쓰이는 재귀대명사 (C) herself가 정답이다.

어휘 **department manager** 부서장 **rather** ad. 오히려, 다소, 약간 **work schedule** 업무 일정 **oneself** (부사적으로) 직접, 혼자

56.

정답 (A)

해석 이사회가 멜리사 딕슨 씨의 디자인을 선택하기에 앞서 회사의 새 로고에 대한 여러 제출 작품을 평가했다.

해설 빈칸 앞에는 주어, 빈칸 뒤에는 명사구와 전치사구만 있으므로 빈칸은 동사 자리이다. 따라서 선택지에서 유일한 동사 형태인 (A) evaluated가 정답이다.

어휘 **board members** 이사회 **submission** 제출(하는 것) **evaluate** ~을 평가하다 **evaluation** 평가(서)

57.

정답 (B)

해석 위생 조사관은 레드우드 식당의 오래된 냉각장치에 대해 몇 가지 우려를 지니고 있다.

해설 빈칸 앞에 복수명사를 수식하는 복수 수량형용사 several이 있으므로 빈칸에는 복수명사가 와야 한다. 따라서 (B) concerns가 정답이다.

어휘 **health inspector** 위생 조사관 **concern** n. 걱정, 우려 v. ~을 걱정스럽게 만들다 **outdated** 오래된, 구식의 **refrigeration** 냉각, 냉장 **concerning** ~에 관련된

58.

정답 (D)

해석 배송 중에 손상된 제품은 전액 환불을 받으실 수 있도록 다음 주소로 반품하시면 됩니다.

해설 빈칸이 정관사와 명사 사이에 있으므로 빈칸은 명사를 수식할 형용사 자리이다. 따라서 (D) following이 정답이다.

어휘 **shipping** 배송 **refund** 환불(액) **follow** ~을 따르다, ~을 준수하다 **follower** 따르는 사람, 추종자 **following** a. 다음의, 아래의 n. 다음(에 말하는 것), 아래(에서 말하는 것) prep. ~ 후에

59.

정답 (C)

해석 애쉬포스 캠프장은 기업 야유회에 필요한 아주 다양한 팀 빌딩 활동을 제공한다.

해설 선택지가 모두 다른 명사로 구성되어 있으므로 해석을 통해 알맞은 어휘를 골라야 하는데, 빈칸에 쓰일 명사는 바로 앞에 위치한 teambuilding과 결합해 캠프장에서 기업 행사를 위해 제공 가능한 것을 나타내야 하므로 '활동'을 뜻하는 (C) activities가 정답이다.

어휘 **a wide range of** 아주 다양한 **corporate** 기업의 **excursion** 야유회 **request** 요청(서) **exception** 예외

60.

정답 (A)

해석 피에르 몬두는 그의 최근 그림인 '계곡을 넘는 바람'에서 자신만의 예술 양식을 전통 양식과 혼합시키려 시도했다.

해설 선택지가 모두 다른 과거분사로 구성되어 있고, 빈칸 뒤에 to부정사가 있으므로 선택지 중에 to부정사를 목적어로 가지는 동사 attempt의 과거분사형 (A) attempted가 정답이다.

어휘 **latest** 최근의, 최신의 **attempt to do** ~하려고 시도하다 **incorporate A with B** A를 B와 통합시키다, 혼합하다 **artistic** 예술적인 **persuade** ~을 설득하다, 납득시키다 **recognize** ~을 인정하다

61.

정답 (A)

해석 모든 참석자들은 공연 동안 휴대폰 전원을 꺼서 다른 분들을 배려해 주시기 바랍니다.

해설 빈칸은 be동사의 보어 역할을 하는 형용사 자리이므로 (A) considerate와 (D) considerable 중에서 답을 골라야 한다. (A)는 '사려 깊은, 배려하는'이라는 뜻이고, (D)는 '(양이나 정도가) 상당한'이라는 뜻이므로 문맥상 타인을 배려하는 행위를 나타낼 수 있는 (A) considerate가 정답이다.

어휘 **be advised to do** ~하시기 바랍니다 **considerate** 사려 깊은, 배려하는 **considerably** 많이, 상당히

62.

정답 (A)

해석 WJE 엔지니어링 사는 오늘 오전에 필모어 씨가 영업이사에 임

명됐다고 발표했다.

해설 빈칸 앞에 있는 동사 announced는 타동사이므로 뒤에 목적어가 필요한데 빈칸 뒤에 주어와 동사를 포함한 절이 있으므로 빈칸은 명사절 접속사 자리이다. 따라서 (A) that과 (B) what 중 정답을 골라야 하는데 빈칸 뒤에 완전한 구성의 절이 있으므로 (A) that이 정답이다.

어휘 announce that ~을 발표하다 appoint ~을 임명하다 director 이사, 본부장

63.

정답 (B)

해석 그 초청 연사는 세미나 종료 시에 청중들의 질문에 답변할 시간이 있을 것이다.

해설 선택지가 모두 다른 형용사로 구성되어 있으므로 해석을 통해 알맞은 어휘를 골라야 한다. 빈칸에 쓰일 형용사는 초청 연사가 세미나 종료 시에 청중들의 질문에 대해 답변하는 일의 발생 가능성과 관련된 의미를 나타내야 하므로 '시간이 나는'을 뜻하는 (B) available이 정답이다.

어휘 audience 청중, 관객, 시청자들 fulfilled 성취감을 느끼는, 만족하는 generous 아낌 없는, 후한 extended 연장된

64.

정답 (C)

해석 등록에 있어 즉각적인 도움이 필요하시다면 니시오카 씨에게 연락하시기 바랍니다.

해설 빈칸 앞뒤로 두 개의 절이 있으므로 빈칸은 접속사 자리인데, 빈칸 뒤의 내용이 니시오카 씨에게 연락을 해야 하는 조건에 해당되므로 '만약 ~면'처럼 조건의 의미를 나타내는 접속사 (C) if가 정답이다.

어휘 if 만약 ~면 immediate 즉각적인 assistance 도움 registration 등록

65.

정답 (A)

해석 설문 조사는 프로 테니스 선수 10명 중 약 3명이 우리 브랜드의 라켓을 즐겨 사용한다는 것을 나타냈다.

해설 빈칸 앞에 명사절 접속사 that이 있고, 빈칸 뒤에 주어와 동사 그리고 목적어를 갖춘 완전한 절이 있으므로 빈칸은 부사 자리이다. 따라서 '대략'이라는 의미로 3이라는 숫자 표현을 수식할 수 있는 (A) approximately가 정답이다.

어휘 indicate that ~임을 나타내다 approximately 약, 대략 out of ~ 중에 racket 라켓 approximation 어림, 추정 approximate 어림 잡다, 추정하다

66.

정답 (C)

해석 추천인 명단에 연락처가 없으면 구직 신청서가 처리되지 않을

것이다.

해설 선택지가 전치사와 접속사로 구성되어 있으므로 문장 구조를 먼저 분석해야 한다. 빈칸 앞에는 주어와 동사가 포함된 절이, 빈칸 뒤에는 명사구와 전치사구가 있으므로 빈칸은 전치사 자리인데 해석상 '연락처가 없으면 구직 신청서가 처리되지 않을 것이다'라는 뜻이 자연스러우므로 '~가 없으면, ~없이'라는 뜻의 (C) without이 정답이다.

어휘 employment application 구직 신청서 process ~을 처리하다 contact information 연락처 reference 추천인 except ~를 제외하고 unless ~하지 않으면

Part 6

67-70.

수신: 모든 프런트 데스크 직원
발신: 브라이언 코덴, 시설관리팀장
제목: 로비 엘리베이터
날짜: 9월 17일

우리 고객들께서 로비에서 엘리베이터를 이용하실 때, 특히 호텔 고층으로 올라가려 하실 때 계속 겪어오고 있는 67 문제와 관련해 여러분께 알려드리기 위해 이메일을 씁니다. 우리 시설관리팀은 이 문제점을 해결해보려 하고 있지만, 며칠 걸릴 수도 있습니다. 68 그러는 동안, 저는 우리 고객들께서 이 문제로 인해 반드시 불편함을 겪지 않도록 하기 위해 임시 방편을 제안하고자 합니다. 고층에 도달해야 하는 모든 고객들께 호텔 주방 옆에 위치한 서비스용 엘리베이터를 이용하도록 허용될 것입니다. 69 그에 따라 안내 담당 직원이 프런트 데스크에 배치될 것입니다. 이 직원이 고객들을 해당 엘리베이터로 안내하고, 고객들께서 겪을 수 있는 어떤 70 문제점에 대해서든 도움을 드릴 것입니다.

고객들께서 숙박을 위해 체크인하실 때 이러한 상황을 설명해 드리십시오.

감사합니다.

브라이언

어휘 regarding ~와 관련해 particularly 특히 upper 위쪽의 attempt to do ~하려 하다 take A 시간 A에게 ~의 시간이 걸리다 in the meantime 그러는 동안, 그 사이에 temporary fix 임시 방편 be inconvenienced by ~로 인해 불편을 겪다 be permitted to do ~하도록 허용되다 concierge (호텔의) 안내 담당 직원 station v. ~을 배치하다 accordingly 그에 따라, 그에 맞춰 direct A to B A를 B로 안내하다

67.

정답 (D)

해설 빈칸 앞에는 대명사가, 빈칸 뒤에는 명사구가 있으므로 빈칸은 전치사 자리이다. 따라서 (D) regarding이 정답이다.

어휘 regard v. (~을 …로) 여기다, 간주하다 n. 관련

68.
정답 (B)

해설 빈칸이 속한 문장은 앞 문장에서 문제를 해결하는 데 며칠 걸릴 것이라고 말한 기간 중에 활용 가능한 해결책을 언급하고 있다. 따라서 '그러는 동안, 그 사이에'를 뜻하는 접속부사가 쓰여야 알맞으므로 (B) In the meantime이 정답이다.

어휘 for example 예를 들어 conversely 정반대로, 역으로 otherwise 그렇지 않으면, 그 외에는

69.
정답 (B)

해석 (A) 결과적으로, 저녁 식사 서비스가 연기되어야 할 것입니다.
(B) 그에 따라 안내 담당 직원이 프런트 데스크에 배치될 것 입니다.
(C) 하지만 수리 기사들 또한 8층을 오가게 될 것입니다.
(D) 추가로, 계단 공간은 여전히 이용 가능합니다.

해설 빈칸 앞 문장에 고객들이 임시로 서비스용 엘리베이터를 이용하는 방법이 언급되어 있고, 빈칸 다음 문장에서 특정 직원을 This employee로 지칭하고 있다. 따라서 This employee에 해당되는 A concierge를 포함해 이 직원이 서비스용 엘리베이터를 이용하는 고객들을 대상으로 하게 될 일을 알리는 (B)가 정답이다.

어휘 as a result 결과적으로 postpone ~을 연기하다 travel back and forth to ~로 오가다 though ad. (문장 끝이나 중간에서) 하지만 stairwell 계단 공간(건물 내에 계단이 따로 마련된 공간)

70.
정답 (A)

해설 선택지가 모두 다른 명사로 구성되어 있으므로 해석을 통해 알맞은 어휘를 골라야 한다. 그런데 빈칸은 「assist A with B」의 구조에서 전치사 with의 목적어로서 도움이 제공되는 일을 나타낸다. 고객들이 임시로 서비스용 엘리베이터를 이용하면서 겪게 될 문제점에 대해 도움을 준다는 의미가 되어야 알맞으므로 '문제점'을 뜻하는 (A) problems가 정답이다.

어휘 practice 관행, 연습, 실행

71-74.

수신: 알렉스 첸 <achen@zoomma.com>
발신: 안젤라 티펫 <atippett@techmarket.com>
날짜: 4월 30일
제목: 귀하의 구매

온라인 최고의 전자제품 매장인 테크놀로지 마켓 온라인을 이용해 주셔서 감사합니다. 본 이메일은 귀하께서 최근에 지불한 금액을 **71** 알려드리기 위한 것입니다.

72 귀하의 제품은 배송 준비가 거의 다 되었습니다. 그런데 귀하께서 레이저 V3-571G 노트북 컴퓨터를 주문하실 때 어떤 색상을 선호하시는지 표시하지 않으셨습니다. 가능한 한 빨리 **73** 선택을 하셔서 이 문제를 처리해 주시면 감사하겠습니다. 귀하께서 주문하신 모델은 미드나잇 블랙이나 체리 레드 색상이 가능합니다. 저희 쪽에 알려주신 후에 새로운 확인 이메일을 받아보실 수 있으며, 일련번호를 저희 사이트에 입력해 배송물품을 추적하는 방법에 대한 설명도 **74** 함께 보내드리겠습니다.

기타 문의사항이 있으시면 주저하지 마시고 제게 문의하시기 바랍니다.

안녕히 계십시오.

안젤라 티펫
고객서비스 사원, 테크놀로지 마켓 온라인

어휘 enrollment 등록 receipt 수취, 받음 neglect to do ~하는 것을 잊다, 소홀히 하다 indicate ~을 표기하다 prefer ~을 선호하다 appreciate it if ~하시면 감사하겠습니다 address v. (문제 등) ~을 처리하다, 해결하다 make a selection 선택하다 at one's earliest possible convenience 가능한 한 빨리 confirmation 확인 explanation 설명 serial number 일련번호 don't hesitate to do 주저하지 말고 ~하세요 should you have any 혹시 ~가 있으실 경우에

71.
정답 (D)

해설 빈칸이 주어와 명사 목적어 사이에 위치해 있으므로 빈칸이 동사 자리임을 알 수 있다. 따라서 (C) acknowledge와 (D) acknowledges 중에서 답을 골라야 하는데, This e-mail이 단수명사이므로 단수동사 (D) acknowledges가 정답이다.

어휘 acknowledge (편지 등) ~을 받았음을 알리다 acknowledgement 받았음을 알림, 승인(서)

72.
정답 (B)

해석 (A) 그 제품이 더 이상 재고가 없다는 점을 알려 드리게 되어 유감입니다.
(B) 귀하의 제품은 배송 준비가 거의 다 되었습니다.
(C) 귀하께서 제공해 주신 신용카드에는 비용이 청구될 수 없었습니다.
(D) 여름 세일 행사 기간 동안 여러 다른 제공 서비스들이 이용 가능합니다.

해설 빈칸 앞을 보면 비용을 지불했다고 하고, 빈칸 뒤에는 제품 주문 시 색상을 선택하지 않아 이 문제를 해결해달라는 내용이 이어지고 있다. 따라서 제품이 아직 발송되지 않았음을 알 수 있으므로 상대방의 제품을 지칭하는 Your item과 함께 배송 준비 상태를 알리는 (B)가 정답이다.

어휘 regret to do ~하게 되어 유감이다 no longer 더 이상 ~

않다 **in stock** 재고가 있는 **charge** ~에 비용을 청구하다, 부과하다

73.
정답 (B)

해설 선택지가 모두 다른 명사로 구성되어 있으므로 해석을 통해 알맞은 어휘를 골라야 한다. 앞 문장에서 노트북 컴퓨터를 구매할 때 색상을 표기하지 않았다고 알려주고 있고, 뒤에서는 미드나잇 블랙과 체리 레드 색상이 제시되고 있다. 즉 두 가지 색상 가운데 '선택'을 하라는 의미이므로 (B) selection이 정답이다.

74.
정답 (C)

해설 빈칸 앞뒤에 동사 receive의 목적어에 해당하는 두 개의 명사구가 있으므로 빈칸은 이 명사구들을 연결할 전치사 자리이다. 따라서 선택지 중 유일한 전치사인 (C) along with가 정답이다.

어휘 **so that** (목적) ~할 수 있도록, (결과) 그러므로 **even if** 비록 ~ 이더라도 **along with** ~와 함께 **if only** 오직 ~이기만 하면

Part 7

75-76.

레지나 롱 [오전 11:35]
안녕하세요, 트로이 씨. 제가 그로버 비스트로에 가는 길이에요. **75** 몇 시로 테이블을 예약하셨나요?

트로이 잭슨 [오전 11:37]
아, 그곳에 자리가 많이 있을 겁니다.

레지나 롱 [오전 11:38]
음, 당신 말이 맞기를 바랍니다! 지리에 앉을 때까지 빈둥대면서 기다리고 싶지 않거든요.

트로이 잭슨 [오전 11:40]
괜찮을 겁니다. 하지만, 몇 분 정도 저를 기다리셔야 할 수도 있습니다. 지금 막 나가려는 참이라서요.

레지나 롱 [오전 11:41]
알겠어요, 괜찮습니다. **76** 기다리는 동안 음료 한 잔 주문해서 몇몇 웹 사이트나 둘러보고 있을게요.

어휘 **on one's way to** ~로 가는 길인, ~로 오는 길인 **wait around** 빈둥대며 기다리다 **be seated** 앉다, 착석하다 **may have to do** ~해야 할 수도 있다 **be about to do** 막 ~하려는 참이다 **browse** ~을 둘러보다

75.
오전 11시 37분에, 잭슨 씨가 "There'll be lots of spaces"라고 쓸 때 무엇을 의미하는가?

(A) 몇몇 친구를 초대하고 싶어 한다.
(B) 주차하기 쉬울 거라고 생각한다.
(C) 예약을 하지 않았다.
(D) 자신의 일정표를 확인할 것이다.

정답 (C)

해설 11시 35분 메시지에 롱 씨가 몇 시로 테이블을 예약했는지(What time did you book the table for?) 묻는 것에 대해 잭슨 씨가 '자리가 많이 있을 것이다'라고 대답하는 흐름이다. 이는 자리가 많을 것이기 때문에 굳이 예약할 필요가 없다는 의미를 나타내는 말이므로 (C)가 정답이다.

어휘 **park** 주차하다 **make a reservation** 예약하다

76.
롱 씨와 관련해 암시된 것은 무엇인가?

(A) 해당 비스트로에 여러 번 가 본 적이 있다.
(B) 해당 비스트로 밖에서 잭슨 씨를 기다릴 것이다.
(C) 잭슨 씨보다 먼저 해당 비스트로에 도착할 것이다.
(D) 웹 사이트에서 길 안내 정보를 확인할 것이다.

정답 (C)

해설 11시 41분 메시지에 롱 씨가 잭슨 씨를 기다리는 동안 음료를 한 잔 주문해서 웹 사이트를 둘러보고 있겠다고(I'll just order a drink and browse some Web sites while I wait) 알리고 있다. 이는 잭슨 씨보다 먼저 도착해서 기다리는 동안 하려는 일을 말하는 것이므로 (C)가 정답이다.

어휘 **have been to** ~에 가 본 적이 있다 **directions** 길 안내

77-79.

7월 14일 (론버그) - 그린우드 극장의 역사적 중요성과 관련된 수개월 간의 논의 끝에, 시의회가 마침내 그 운명과 관련해 결정을 내렸습니다. — [1] —. **77** 7월 20일, 토요일에, 이 극장은 폭발물과 건설 중장비를 활용해 철거될 것입니다. 그린우드 극장 부지는 11월 1일까지 치워질 것이며, 이후에 완전히 새로운 해크니 텔레콤 본사 부지로 쓰일 것입니다. — [2] —.

그린우드 극장은, **78(A)** 원래 파빌리온 극장이라고 알려졌던 곳으로서, **79** 1965년에 개관했으며, 20년 동안 인기와 성공을 누렸습니다. — [3] —. 하지만, **78(B)** 불충분한 투자로 인해 **78(D)** 1990년대 초에 폐관하기에 이르렀습니다. 이 장소를 2001년에 되살리려는 시도가 있었지만, **78(D)** 2002년에 침수 피해를 당한 후에 다시 한번 무기한 폐쇄되었습니다. 버려진 이후로 오랜 시간이 지났음에도 불구하고, 이 매력적인 건물은 여전히 시의 명소로 여겨지고 있으며, 많은 지역 주민들은 안타까운 마음으로 이곳이 7월 20일에 사라지는 모습을 보게 될 것입니다. — [4] —.

어휘 **following** ~ 후에 **concerning** ~와 관련해(= regarding) **importance** 중요성 **fate** 운명 **tear down** ~을 철거하다 **explosive** n. 폭발물 **heavy machinery** 중장비 **site** 부지, 장소, 현장 **clear** ~을 치우다 **headquarters** 본사 **known as** ~라고 알려진 **decade** 10년 **popularity** 인기 **insufficient** 불충분한 **investment** 투자(금) **lead** to ~에 이르다, ~로 이어지다 attempt to do ~하려는 시도 revive ~을 되살리다, ~을 회복시키다 venue (행사 등의) 장소, 개최지 indefinitely 무기한으로 flooded 침수 피해를 입은 despite ~에도 불구하고 abandon ~을 버리다 be regarded as ~로 여겨지다 landmark 명소, 인기 장소 see A do A가 ~하는 모습을 보다

77. 기사는 주로 무엇에 관한 것인가?
(A) 새로운 극장의 건설
(B) 한 회사의 본사 이전
(C) 성공한 한 지역 주민의 삶
(D) 계획된 건물 철거

정답 (D)

해설 지문 초반부에 그린우드 극장의 운명이 결정된 사실과 함께 철거될 예정임을(On Saturday, July 20, the theater will be torn down using explosives and heavy construction machinery) 알린 뒤로, 철거 작업 일정과 해당 부지의 활용과 관련해 설명하고 있으므로 (D)가 정답이다.

어휘 relocation (위치) 이전 demolition 철거

78. 그린우드 극장과 관련해 언급되지 않은 것은 무엇인가?
(A) 원래 다른 명칭을 지니고 있었다.
(B) 자금 관련 문제를 겪었다.
(C) 1990년대에 큰 성공을 누렸다.
(D) 두 차례 폐쇄되었다.

정답 (C)

해설 두 번째 단락에서 원래 파빌리온 극장이라고 알려졌던 곳이었다는(originally known as the Pavilion Theater) 부분에서 (A)를, 같은 단락에서 불충분한 투자로 인해 1990년대 초에 폐관하기에 이르렀다는(insufficient investment led to its closure in the early-1990s) 부분에서 (B)와, (D)를, 추가로 2002년에 침수 피해를 당한 후에 다시 한번 무기한 폐쇄되었다는(it was closed again indefinitely after it was flooded in 2002) 부분에서 (D)를 다시 한번 확인할 수 있다. 하지만 1965년에 개관한 이후의 20년 동안 큰 인기와 성공을 누렸다고 쓰여 있으므로 (C)가 정답이다.

어휘 funding 자금 (제공) shut down ~을 폐쇄하다 occasion 때, 기회, 행사

79. [1], [2], [3], [4]로 표기된 위치들 중에서, 다음 문장이 들어가기에 가장 적절한 곳은 어디인가?

"그곳은 심지어 사람들의 이목을 끄는 여러 영화제를 개최하는 데 이용되기도 했습니다."

(A) [1]
(B) [2]
(C) [3]
(D) [4]

정답 (C)

해설 제시된 문장은 앞서 언급된 단수 사물명사를 대신하는 It 및 과

거시제 동사 was와 함께 과거에 사람들의 이목을 끄는 여러 영화제를 주최하는 데 이용된 사실을 말하고 있다. 따라서 그린우드 극장이 인기 있었던 시기를 언급하는 문장 뒤에 위치한 [3]에 들어가 인기 있는 명소의 역할을 했을 당시에 주최한 행사를 말하는 것으로 얼마나 인기 있었는지를 나타내는 흐름이 되어야 자연스러우므로 (C)가 정답이다.

어휘 host ~을 주최하다 high-profile 사람들의 이목을 끄는

80-82.

수신: 브렌다 대븐포트, 인사팀
발신: 조나단 브루어, 창고 관리자
날짜: 8월 11일
주제: 주차 문제

대븐포트 씨,

저는 저희 창고 선적 부서의 부장인 조나단 브루어입니다. 아시다시피 **80** 지난주의 폭풍우로 인해 저희 창고 지붕이 크게 파손되었습니다. 이 때문에 건설 인부들이 수리를 하는 동안 창고의 일부를 비워야 할 것 같습니다. **82** 건설 인부들은 9월 4일 금요일에 도착할 것이고, 그들은 9월 8일 화요일까지 일할 것입니다.

직원들은 다음과 같은 절차의 변화를 알고 있어야 합니다. 건설 인부들이 일할 공간을 마련하기 위해 창고를 비워야 하기 때문에, 공사가 끝날 때까지 물품 배송은 처리될 수 없습니다. 만약 당신의 고객들이 뭔가 필요한 것이 있다면, 공사 전이나 후에 배송되어야 합니다.

또한, 건설 인부들이 많은 중장비를 가지고 올 예정이어서 **81** 공사가 끝나는 날까지 직원들은 주차장에 주차할 수 없게 됩니다. 대신에 애쉬콧 에비뉴나 브라이스 호텔에 주차할 수 있습니다. 이에 따라, 직원들은 평소보다 일찍 출근해야 할 수도 있습니다.

시간 내 주셔서 감사합니다. 가능한 한 빨리 모든 직원에게 이 내용을 전달해 주십시오.

안녕히 계십시오.

조나단 브루어

어휘 significant 상당한, 중대한 empty 비우다 portion 부분, 몫 be aware of ~을 알다 procedure 절차 make room for ~을 위한 공간을 마련하다 process ~을 가공하다, 처리하다 completion 완료 heavy equipment 중장비 leave for work 출근하다 forward ~을 전달하다

80. 폭풍우의 결과로 수리되어야 하는 것은 무엇인가?
(A) 조립라인 기계류
(B) 창고 지붕
(C) 선적 구역
(D) 주차장

정답 (B)

해설 첫 번째 문단에 지난주의 폭풍우로 인해 창고 지붕이 크게

파손되었다고(last week's storm caused significant damage to the roof of our warehouse) 언급되어 있으므로 손상되어 수리될 필요가 있는 곳은 창고의 지붕임을 알 수 있다. 따라서 (B)가 정답이다.

81. 수리작업 동안 직원들은 무엇을 하라고 권고되는가?
(A) 자신의 작업대를 깨끗이 하라고
(B) 선적 일자를 재조정하라고
(C) 공사 프로젝트를 위해 자원하라고
(D) 대체 주차장을 찾아 보라고

정답 (D)

해설 세 번째 문단에 직원들은 공사 기간 동안 주차를 할 수 없다고 하면서, 특정 도로변과 호텔을 대안으로 제시하고 있다 (employees will not be able to park in our parking lot ~Instead, they may park along Ashcott Avenue or at the Brice Hotel). 따라서 이는 대체 주차장을 찾으라는 말로 이해할 수 있으므로 (D)가 정답이다.

어휘 **workstation** 작업대 **alternative** 대신하는, 대안(의)

82. 직원들은 무슨 요일에 정상적인 오전 일정으로 돌아갈 수 있는가?
(A) 월요일
(B) 화요일
(C) 수요일
(D) 금요일

정답 (C)

해설 첫 번째 단락 후반부에 9월 4일 금요일에 도착해서, 9월 8일 화요일까지 쭉 일한다고(The construction crew will arrive on Friday, September 4, and they will work through Tuesday, September 8) 알리고 있다. 따라서 수요일부터 정상적 일정으로 돌아갈 수 있음을 알 수 있으므로 (C)가 정답이다.

83-86.

수신: 투녹 자전거 사 <inquiries@tunnock.co.uk>
발신: 아드리아누 메시 <amessi@anymail.com>
제목: 스타일러스 X2 산악 자전거
날짜: 1월 16일

담당자님께,

1월 10일에 저는 귀사의 웹 사이트에서 스타일러스 X2 산악자전거를 구매하였으며, 영업일로 7일 내에 확실히 도착하도록 특급 국제 배송 옵션을 선택하였습니다. 자전거는 신속하게 도착하였고, 박스에서 자전거를 꺼내 보고 자전거의 프레임과 바퀴의 품질에 매우 기뻤습니다. 제가 해외에서 이 상품을 구매하였기 때문에, 자전거를 조립해야 한다는 점을 알고 있었으며, 제공해 주신 도구와 설명서를 보게 되어 기뻤습니다.

83 문제는 제가 조립을 완료할 수가 없었다는 것인데 그 이유는 페달과 안장이 박스에 포함되어 있지 않았기 때문입니다. 가능한

한 빨리 저에게 이것들을 보내주실 것을 요청하기 위해 연락 드립니다. 다른 부품이 빠진 것을 알아보실 수도 있으니 **84** 부분적으로 조립된 제 자전거 사진을 동봉해 드립니다. 저는 1월 24일에 자전거 여행에 참가할 예정입니다. **85** 그래서 때에 맞춰 저에게 보내주시면 감사하겠습니다. 그렇지 않으면 이 지역의 자전거 가게에서 자전거를 사야 할 것이며, 투녹 자전거 사는 반환/환불 절차를 시작해야 할 것입니다.

저는 진심으로 귀사가 이 문제를 바로잡아 주실 수 있길 바랍니다. 저는 귀사의 제품과 서비스에 대한 열렬한 팬이고 **86** 그것이 제가 해외로 이사를 온 이후에도 계속해서 단골 고객으로 이용해온 이유입니다. 답변 기다리겠습니다.

안녕히 계십시오.

아드리아누 메시

어휘 **ensure** 반드시 ~하게 하다 **business day** 영업일(공휴일 제외) **swiftly** 신속하게, 빠르게 **request** ~을 요청하다 **as soon as possible** 가능한 한 빨리 **in case** ~한 경우에 대비하여 **expedition** 여행, 탐험 **in a timely manner** 때에 맞게, 적절한 시기에 **otherwise** 그렇지 않으면 **initiate** ~을 시작하다, 착수하다 **sincerely** 진심으로, 진정으로 **rectify** ~을 바로잡다, 시정하다 **abroad** 해외로

83. 이메일의 주된 목적은 무엇인가?
(A) 상품이 늦게 배달된 것에 항의하기 위해서
(B) 누락된 부품에 대해 문의하기 위해서
(C) 우수한 상품에 대해 회사를 칭찬하기 위해서
(D) 자신의 자전거 수리를 요청하기 위해서

정답 (B)

해설 두 번째 단락에서 가능한 한 빨리 이것들 즉, 박스에 포함되지 않은 페달과 안장을 보내줄 것을 요청하기 위해 연락한다는(I am contacting you to request that these be sent to me as soon as possible) 부분에 이메일의 목적이 제시되어 있다. 따라서 (B)가 정답이다.

어휘 **inquire** 문의하다, 알아보다 **part** 부품 **commend** ~을 칭찬하다

84. 메시 씨가 이메일에 첨부한 것은 무엇인가?
(A) 도표
(B) 품질 보증서
(C) 송장
(D) 이미지

정답 (D)

해설 두 번째 단락에서 다른 부품이 빠진 것을 알아보실 수 있으니 부분적으로 조립된 자전거 사진을 동봉한다고(I have also attached a photograph of the partly assembled bike in case you notice any other missing components) 알리고 있다. 따라서 (D)가 정답이다.

어휘 **diagram** 도표, 도해 **warranty** 품질 보증서 **invoice** 송장, 청구서

85. 자전거 회사가 신속하게 답변하지 않는다면, 메시 씨가 취할 행동은 무엇인가?

(A) 자전거 여행 일정을 재조정한다.
(B) 정식으로 불만을 제기한다.
(C) 결제를 거부한다.
(D) 다른 자전거를 구입한다.

정답 (D)

해설 두 번째 단락 후반부에서 행사 참가를 위해 때에 맞춰 배송을 해달라고 요청하면서 그렇지 않다면 다른 자전거 가게에서 자전거를 사야 할 것이라고(I'd appreciate you getting back to me in a timely manner. Otherwise, I will need to buy a bike from a local store) 언급하고 있다. 따라서 (D)가 정답이다.

어휘 **reschedule** 일정을 재조정하다 **make a complaint** 불만을 제기하다 **refuse** ~을 거절하다, 거부하다 **make a payment** 결제하다, 지불하다

86. 메시 씨에 대해 알 수 있는 것은 무엇인가?

(A) 투녹 자전거 사에서 일한 적이 있다.
(B) 구매품에 대한 할인을 받았다.
(C) 투녹 자전거 사에서 상품을 구매했다.
(D) 1월 24일에 투녹 자전거 사에게 대금을 지불할 계획이다.

정답 (C)

해설 마지막 단락에서 메시 씨가 해외로 이사 온 이후에도 단골이었음을(that is why I have continued to be a regular customer even after I moved abroad) 알리는 부분이 있다. 따라서 (C)가 정답이다.

어휘 **former** 이전의 **intend to do** ~할 작정이다, ~할 의도이다

87-90.

8월 2일
버논 에어즈
에어즈 시스템즈 주식회사
와트 테크놀로지 파크, 덴버

에어즈 씨께,

다가오는 저희 TKS 테크놀로지 컨퍼런스들 중 하나에서 **88** 제품 디자인 워크숍을 진행하시는 데 동의해 주셔서 기쁩니다. 귀하께서는 **87(B)** 시간당 55달러를 받으시는 것뿐만 아니라 귀하의 온라인 계좌를 통해 지출 비용에 대해서 환급도 받으시게 될 것입니다.

이전에 논의한 바와 같이, 저희는 귀하께서 8월 15일, 토요일에 있을 **87(A)** 마지막 여름 컨퍼런스에서 워크숍을 진행해 주셨으면 합니다. 555-3674번으로 저희 레스 셀렉 인사부장님께 전화하셔서 참가를 확정해 주시면 됩니다. 여름 컨퍼런스에 참가하실 수 없

는 경우, 가능한 한 빨리 셀렉 부장님께 알리시기 바랍니다. 저희가 그 후에 9월 5일, 토요일에 있을 **87(A)** 첫 번째 가을 컨퍼런스에서 열리는 워크숍을 진행하실 수 있도록 대안을 마련해 드리겠습니다.

컨퍼런스에 참석하신 후 3일 이내에 저희 회계팀으로 비용 환급 양식을 제출하셔야 합니다. 그때, 반드시 **87(D)** 숙박 시설 및 이동에 대한 모든 관련 영수증도 포함하셔야 합니다. 저희 비용 환급 정책에 따라 식비는 충당해 드리지 않습니다.

88 90 컨퍼런스에서의 역할에 대한 준비 과정에 도움을 드리기 위해, 각각의 저희 봄 컨퍼런스에서 동일한 역할을 수행하셨던 질리언 바워스 씨를 소개시켜 드리고자 합니다. gbowers@livetek.com으로 이분께 연락하시면 됩니다. **89** 위에 언급해 드린 두 가지 행사 모두에 대해 최종 확정된 컨퍼런스 일정표가 8월 8일에 귀하께 발송될 것이라는 점에 유의하시기 바랍니다.

어떤 질문이든 있으시면, 저희 인사부장님께 전달하시기 바랍니다.

안녕히 계십시오.

앤젤라 베이커
행사 주최 책임자, TKS 테크놀로지 컨퍼런스

어휘 **upcoming** 다가오는, 곧 있을 **reimburse A for B** B에 대해 A에게 비용을 환급해주다 **expense** 지출 (비용) 경비 **via** ~을 통해 **previously** 이전에, 과거에 **participation** 참가 **participate in** ~에 참가하다 **make an arrangement** 마련하다, 조치하다, 조정하다 **alternative** 대안의, 대체하는 **accounting** 회계 **no more than** ~ 이내에, ~가 채 되지 않는, ~에 지나지 않는 **appearance** 참석, 등장, 나타남 **relevant** 관련된 **cover** (비용 등) ~을 충당하다, ~을 부담하다 **under** ~에 따라, ~ 하에 있는, ~에 영향을 받는 **preparation** 준비 **put A in touch with B** A를 B에게 소개시켜주다, A를 B에게 연락되도록 해주다 **reach** ~에게 연락하다 **be aware that** ~라는 점에 유의하다 **finalized** 최종 확정된 **aforementioned** 위에서 언급한 **direct** (질문 등) ~을 전달하다

87. TKS 테크놀로지 컨퍼런스와 관련해 언급되지 않은 것은 무엇인가?

(A) 일년에 여러 차례 개최될 것이다.
(B) 워크숍 진행자들에게 시급을 제공할 것이다.
(C) 참가자들에게 무료 식사를 제공한다.
(D) 호텔 및 교통 비용을 부담한다.

정답 (C)

해설 두 번째 단락에 마지막 여름 컨퍼런스(our final summer conference)와 첫 번째 가을 컨퍼런스(our first fall conference) 부분에서 일년에 여러 번 개최된다는 뜻으로 쓰인 (A)를, 첫 번째 단락에 시간당 55달러를 받게 될 것이라는 (receiving $55 per hour) 부분에서 (B)를, 세 번째 단락의 숙박과 이동에 대한 모든 영수증도 포함해야 한다는(you must also include all relevant receipts for accommodation and travel) 부분에서 (D)를 확인할 수 있다. 하지만 세 번째 단락에 식비는 충당해주지 않는다고(Meals are not covered under our reimbursement policy) 쓰여 있으므로 (C)가 정답이다.

어휘 **hourly payment** 시급 **leader** 진행자, 이끄는 사람 **complimentary** 무료의

88. 바워스 씨와 관련해 사실인 것은 무엇인가?
(A) 이전에 제품 디자인 워크숍을 진행한 적이 있었다.
(B) 다가오는 TKS 테크놀로지 컨퍼런스에서 강연할 것이다.
(C) 현재 에어즈 시스템즈 주식회사에 고용되어 있다.
(D) 인사부에서 근무하고 있다.

정답 (A)

해설 네 번째 단락에서 바워스 씨를 이 편지를 받는 에어즈 씨와 동일한 역할을 봄 컨퍼런스에서 수행한 사람이라고 소개하고 있다 (Ms. Gillian Bowers, who performed the same role at each of our spring conferences). 그리고 첫 단락에 에어즈 씨가 컨퍼런스에서 제품 디자인 워크숍을 진행하는 데 동의했다는(lead a product design workshop) 말이 쓰여 있어 바워스 씨가 봄 컨퍼런스에서 제품 디자인 워크숍을 진행한 것으로 볼 수 있으므로 (A)가 정답이다.

어휘 **give a talk** 강연하다, 연설하다 **upcoming** 다가오는, 곧 있을 **currently** 현재

89. 에어즈 씨가 언제 완전한 컨퍼런스 일정을 정식으로 통보 받을 것인가?
(A) 8월 2일에
(B) 8월 8일에
(C) 8월 15일에
(D) 9월 2일에

정답 (B)

해설 네 번째 단락에 앞서 언급한 두 가지 행사 모두에 대해 최종 확정된 컨퍼런스 일정표가 8월 8일에 발송될 것이라고 (finalized conference schedules for both of the aforementioned events will be sent to you on August 8) 알리고 있으므로 (B)가 정답이다.

어휘 **officially** 정식으로, 공식적으로 **be informed of** ~을 통보 받다

90. 에어즈 씨와 관련해 암시된 것은 무엇인가?
(A) 현금으로 자신의 지출 비용에 대해 환급 받을 것이다.
(B) 여름 워크숍에 참가하지 않을 가능성이 있다.
(C) 컨퍼런스에 앞서 회계팀에 연락할 가능성이 있다.
(D) 질리언 바워스 씨로부터 조언을 얻을 것이다.

정답 (D)

해설 네 번째 단락에 에어즈 씨가 컨퍼런스에서 할 역할에 대해 준비하는 데 도움이 될 수 있도록 봄 컨퍼런스에서 동일한 역할을 했던 질리언 바워스 씨를 소개해 주겠다고(To assist

you with your preparations for your role at the conference, we would like to put you in touch with Ms. Gillian Bowers) 알리는 말이 쓰여 있다. 이를 통해 에어즈 씨가 바워스 씨에게 연락해 도움을 받는 과정에서 관련 조언을 얻을 가능성이 있는 것으로 볼 수 있으므로 (D)가 정답이다.

어휘 **be likely to do** ~할 가능성이 있다 **contact** ~에게 연락하다 **advice** 조언

91-95.

수신: 밥 와타나베 <bwatanabe@sushiagogo.com>
발신: 데보라 마라 <debmara@morinthent.com>
제목: **93** 주주 총회 (6월 29일)
날짜: 6월 9일

와타나베 씨께,

저희 모린스 엔터프라이즈에서 열리는 주주 총회에 출장 요리를 제공하는 데 동의해 주셔서 감사합니다. **91** 이전에 저희에게 출장 요리를 제공해 주셨던 때와 달리, 이번 행사는 29층에 위치한 저희 교육 센터가 아니라, 26층에 위치한 저희 대회의실에서 개최될 예정입니다. 귀하 및 귀하의 직원들께서 안내 데스크 옆에 있는 일반 엘리베이터에 모든 장비를 맞춰 넣으시려 할 필요가 없도록 **92** 서비스 전용 엘리베이터를 이용하실 수 있게 조치해 드리겠습니다.

95 제 비서인 캘럼 스튜어트 씨에게 귀하의 업체를 방문해 몇몇 새 음식 제품을 시식하게 해 주실 수 있는지 궁금했습니다. 이분께서 6월 16일부터 시작되는 일주일 중에 어느 요일이든 정오에서 오후 2시 사이에 들르실 수 있을 것입니다. cstewart@morinthent.com으로 이메일 보내셔서 이분과 연락하실 수 있습니다. **93** 저희 주주 총회 당일에 뵐 수 있기를 고대하고 있습니다.

안녕히 계십시오.

데보라 마라
대표이사
모린스 엔터프라이즈

어휘 **shareholder** 주주 **cater** v. ~에 출장 요리를 제공하다 **unlike** ~와 달리 **take place** (일, 행사 등이) 개최되다, 일어나다, 발생되다 **arrange for A to do** A가 ~할 수 있도록 조치하다 **have access to** ~을 이용할 수 있다, ~에 접근할 수 있다 **fit A into B** A를 B에 맞춰 넣다 **regular** 일반의, 정규의, 주기적인 **wonder if** ~인지 궁금하다 **sample** v. ~을 시식하다 **stop by** 들르다 **get in touch with** ~와 연락하다

수신: 데보라 마라 <debmara@morinthent.com>
발신: 밥 와타나베 <bwatanabe@sushiagogo.com>
제목: **회신**: 주주 총회 (6월 29일)
날짜: 6월 10일

마라 씨께,

귀사의 회의를 즐거운 행사로 만들 수 있기를 정말로 고대하고 있으며, 행사에 참석하시는 모든 분께서 맛있는 저희 새로운 음식 제품군을 아주 마음에 들어 하시리라 확신합니다. 제가 직접 귀사의 모임에 가서 업무를 조정하고 요리할 예정이며, **94** 뛰어난 교육을 받은 저희 종업원들을 이끄는 팀장 대니얼 하티건 씨께서도 지원해 주시러 그곳에 가실 것입니다. **95** 귀하의 비서를 만나는 일과 관련해서는, 제 6월 18일 일정에 여유 시간이 좀 있으므로, 오늘 연락 드려서 조치하도록 하겠습니다.

안녕히 계십시오.

밥 와타나베
소유주 및 주방장
스시-에이-고-고 케이터링

어휘 make A B A를 B하게 만들다 affair 일, 문제, 사건 be confident that ~임을 확신하다 delicacy 맛있는 것, 진미 coordinate ~을 조정하다, 편성하다 gathering 모임 in person 직접 (가서) highly-trained 뛰어난 교육을 받은, 고도로 훈련된 wait staff 종업원 have free time 여유 시간이 있다 make an arrangement 조치하다, 준비하다

91. 마라 씨가 왜 첫 번째 이메일을 보냈는가?
(A) 주주를 회의에 초대하기 위해
(B) 새로운 출장 요리 메뉴에 관해 문의하기 위해
(C) 사업 거래의 세부 사항을 이야기하기 위해
(D) 최근의 식사에 대해 감사의 뜻을 표현하기 위해

정답 (C)

해설 첫 번째 이메일 첫 단락에 행사가 개최되는 장소가 과거와 다르다는 사실과 함께(Unlike the previous time you catered an event for us, this event will be taking place in our main conference room on the 26th floor) 그에 따른 엘리베이터 이용 방법을 설명하고 있다. 이는 모린스 엔터프라이즈의 주주 총회에 출장 요리를 제공하기로 한 사업 거래와 관련된 세부 사항을 이야기하는 것이므로 (C)가 정답이다.

어휘 inquire about ~에 관해 문의하다 catering 출장 요리 제공(업) express (생각, 감정 등) ~을 표현하다 gratitude 감사(의 뜻) recent 최근의

92. 와타나베 씨가 모린스 엔터프라이즈에 도착하자마자 무엇을 해야 하는가?
(A) 안내 데스크에서 등록하는 일
(B) 특수 엘리베이터를 이용하는 일
(C) 29층으로 곧장 가는 일
(D) 마라 씨의 비서를 만나는 일

정답 (B)

해설 첫 지문 첫 단락에 와타나베 씨가 건물에 도착하면 서비스 전용 엘리베이터를 이용할 수 있게 조치해주겠다고(I will arrange for you and your staff to have access to the service elevator) 알리고 있으므로 (B)가 정답이다.

어휘 register 등록하다

93. 마라 씨와 와타나베 씨가 언제 만날 것인가?
(A) 6월 9일에
(B) 6월 16일에
(C) 6월 18일에
(D) 6월 29일에

정답 (D)

해설 첫 지문 두 번째 단락에 마라 씨가 와타나베 씨에게 주주 총회 당일에 만날 수 있기를 고대한다고(I'm looking forward to seeing you on the day of our shareholders meeting) 알리고 있다. 또한, 이 지문 상단의 제목란에 주주 총회 날짜가 6월 29일로(Shareholders Meeting (June 29)) 표기되어 있으므로 (D)가 정답이다.

94. 대니얼 하티건 씨가 누구일 것 같은가?
(A) 주방장
(B) 업체 소유주
(C) 음식 제공 담당자
(D) 회사 주주

정답 (C)

해설 두 번째 지문 중반부에 뛰어난 교육을 받은 종업원들을 이끄는 팀장이라고(the head of my highly-trained wait staff, Daniel Hartigan) 소개하고 있다. 이는 음식을 제공하는 일을 하는 종업원들을 이끄는 사람이라는 뜻이므로 (C)가 정답이다.

95. 와타나베 씨가 6월 18일에 무엇을 할 것인가?
(A) 마라 씨에게 메뉴를 보여 주는 일
(B) 새 사업 지점을 여는 일
(C) 일부 음식 샘플을 준비하는 일
(D) 스튜어트 씨에게 이메일을 보내는 일

정답 (C)

해설 두 번째 지문 후반부에 와타나베 씨가 마라 씨의 비서를 만날 시간이 나는 날이라고(Regarding meeting with your assistant, I have some free time in my schedule on June 18) 6월 18일을 언급하고 있다. 이는 첫 지문 두 번째 단락에서 마라 씨가 자신의 비서에게 와타나베 씨 업체의 새 음식을 시식하게 할 수 있는지(allow my assistant, Callum Stewart, to visit your business to sample some of your new food items) 묻는 일과 관련된 일정이다. 따라서 와타나베 씨가 6월 18일에 시식을 위한 음식 샘플을 준비할 것으로 생각할 수 있으므로 (C)가 정답이다.

어휘 location 지점, 위치 prepare ~을 준비하다

96-100.

어휘 featured 특집의, 특징을 이루는 mark a step forward 진일보한 것에 해당되다 compete with ~와 경쟁하다 vibrant 선명한, 생동감 있는 when it comes to ~의 측면에 있어, ~와 관련해서는 overall 전반적인 aesthetic 미적인 somewhat 다소 with regard to ~와 관련해 measure 규격이 ~이다, 치수가 ~이다 noticeably 두드러지게, 주목할 만하게 as well ~도, 또한 weigh 무게가 ~이다 last v. 지속되다 built-in 내장된 disappointing 실망하게 만드는 clearly 분명히, 확실히 on par with ~와 동등한 수준인 dedicated 전용의 despite ~에도 불구하고 flaw 단점, 결점 gadget (소형) 기기, 장치 be priced at ~로 가격이 책정되다 significantly 상당히, 많이 in-depth 상세한, 깊이 있는 specifications 사양

어휘 operating system 운영 시스템 dimensions 규격 retail 소매(업)

어휘 regarding ~와 관련해 be inspired to do ~하고 싶은 생각이 들다, ~하도록 영감을 얻다 for oneself 직접, 스스로 largely 대체로, 주로 accurate 정확한 find A to be B A를 B하다고 생각하다 rather 오히려, 다소 totally 전적으로, 완전히 compare A to B A를 B와 비교하다 in that respect 그런 면에서, 그런 점에서 certainly 확실히, 분명히 below par 수준 이하인, 표준 이하인 meet (요구, 조건 등) ~을 충족하다 expectation 기대(치) yet another (지금까지의 것에 이은) 또 다른 하나의 growing 늘어나는

96. 제품 평가에서, 두 번째 단락, 여섯 번째 줄에 있는 단어 "clearly"와 의미가 가장 가까운 것은 무엇인가?

(A) 투명하게
(B) 공허하게
(C) 명백하게
(D) 날카롭게

정답 (C)

해설 해당 문장에서 부사 clearly는 be동사 is와 부정어 not 사이에 위치해 '분명히, 확실히'와 같은 의미로 문장의 내용을 강조하는 역할을 한다. 따라서, 이와 유사한 의미로 쓰이는 (C) obviously가 정답이다.

97. 넥슨 X와 관련해 언급되지 않은 것은 무엇인가?

(A) 에포나 G-스타 3보다 화면이 더 크다.
(B) 배터리가 최소 24시간 동안 충전 상태를 유지한다.
(C) 에포나 G-스타 3보다 무게가 덜 나간다.
(D) 몇몇 유사 기기들보다 더 저렴하다.

정답 (A)

해설 첫 지문 두 번째 단락에서 에포나 G-스타 3보다 더 얇고, 두드러지게 더 가볍기도 하다는(the Nexon X is thinner than its nearest rival, the Epona G-star 3, and noticeably lighter as well) 부분에서 (C)를, 넥슨 X의 배터리가 최소 하루 종일 지속된다는(The Nexon X's battery will last for at least one full day) 부분에서 (B)를, 마지막 단락에 여러 경쟁 태블릿보다 더 저렴한 기기라는(significantly less than several rival tablets) 부분에서 (D)를 확인할 수 있다. 하지만 에포나 G-스타 3와 화면 크기를 비교하는 정보는 제시되어 있지 않으므로 (A)가 정답이다.

어휘 **hold a charge** 충전 상태를 유지하다

---

98. 제품 평가에서 어떤 정보가 부정확하게 제시되는가?
  (A) 기기 무게
  (B) 카메라 해상도
  (C) 기기의 일반 소매가
  (D) 기기 규격

정답 (D)

해설 첫 지문 두 번째 단락에 제품 규격이 247.1mm x 177.1mm x 6.1mm라고 언급되어 있는데(Measuring 247.1mm x 177.1mm x 6.1mm), 이는 두 번째 지문 중간 부분에 제시된 규격 247.1 mm x 177.5 mm x 6.4 mm와 다르므로 (D)가 정답이다.

어휘 **state** ~을 제시하다, ~을 말하다 **incorrectly** 부정확하게
  resolution 해상도 **typical** 일반적인, 전형적인

---

99. 브라이언트 씨와 박 씨는 제품과 관련해 어떤 점에 대해 의견이 일치하는가?
  (A) 디자인이 대단히 혁신적이다.
  (B) 화면이 충분히 밝지 않다.
  (C) 카메라가 품질이 좋지 못하다.
  (D) 프로세서가 매우 강력하다.

정답 (C)

해설 세 번째 지문 중반부에 해당 기기를 스마트폰과 비교한 것에 대해 전적으로 옳다는 말로(You were totally right when you compared the device to a smartphone) 동의한다는 뜻을 나타내는 말이 쓰여 있다. 첫 지문 두 번째 단락에 8메가픽셀의 카메라가 실망스럽다는 말과 함께 이미지 품질이 스마트폰 또는 전용 카메라가 제공하는 것과 동등한 수준은 아니라는(the image quality is clearly not on par with that provided by a smartphone) 말이 쓰여 있어 카메라 품질이 좋지 않다는 점에 서로 의견이 일치하는 것으로 볼 수 있으므로 (C)가 정답이다.

어휘 **agree on** ~에 대해 의견이 일치하다, ~에 대해 동의하다
  highly 대단히, 매우

---

100. 브라이언트 씨와 관련해 유추할 수 있는 것은 무엇인가?
  (A) 넥슨 X를 구입한 것을 후회하고 있다.
  (B) 제품 평가를 온라인에 게시했다.

(C) 여러 센즈필드 제품을 소유하고 있다.
  (D) 박 씨와 공동으로 기사를 작성했다.

정답 (C)

해설 세 번째 지문 마지막 문장에 점점 늘어나고 있는 자신의 센즈필드 수집품에 추가할 수 있는 또 다른 환상적인 기기라는(it's yet another fantastic device to add to my growing Senzfield collection) 말이 쓰여 있다. 이는 이미 여러 센즈필드 제품을 수집해 보유하고 있다는 뜻이므로 (C)가 정답이다.

어휘 **regret -ing** ~한 것을 후회하다 **post** ~을 게시하다
  own ~을 소유하다

LC

1. (D)	**2.** (D)	**3.** (C)	**4.** (B)	**5.** (C)
6. (C)	**7.** (C)	**8.** (A)	**9.** (A)	**10.** (A)
11. (B)	**12.** (B)	**13.** (B)	**14.** (B)	**15.** (B)
16. (A)	**17.** (A)	**18.** (A)	**19.** (C)	**20.** (B)
21. (A)	**22.** (B)	**23.** (A)	**24.** (B)	**25.** (A)
26. (B)	**27.** (D)	**28.** (C)	**29.** (D)	**30.** (D)
31. (A)	**32.** (D)	**33.** (B)	**34.** (B)	**35.** (C)
36. (D)	**37.** (D)	**38.** (C)	**39.** (B)	**40.** (C)
41. (A)	**42.** (D)	**43.** (B)	**44.** (D)	**45.** (A)
46. (B)	**47.** (D)	**48.** (B)	**49.** (C)	**50.** (D)

RC

51. (A)	**52.** (C)	**53.** (C)	**54.** (B)	**55.** (B)
56. (B)	**57.** (B)	**58.** (A)	**59.** (B)	**60.** (A)
61. (B)	**62.** (D)	**63.** (B)	**64.** (A)	**65.** (B)
66. (D)	**67.** (B)	**68.** (D)	**69.** (C)	**70.** (C)
71. (A)	**72.** (D)	**73.** (D)	**74.** (C)	**75.** (D)
76. (C)	**77.** (B)	**78.** (D)	**79.** (B)	**80.** (B)
81. (B)	**82.** (D)	**83.** (B)	**84.** (C)	**85.** (C)
86. (B)	**87.** (B)	**88.** (B)	**89.** (B)	**90.** (A)
91. (B)	**92.** (C)	**93.** (A)	**94.** (D)	**95.** (D)
96. (A)	**97.** (D)	**98.** (C)	**99.** (B)	**100.** (D)

Part 1

1.
(A) She's stocking shelves with merchandise.
(B) She's trying on a jacket.
(C) Some merchandise is being unpacked.
(D) Some clothes are hanging on a rack.

(A) 여자가 선반에 상품을 채우고 있다.
(B) 여자가 재킷을 착용해 보고 있다.
(C) 몇몇 상품이 꾸러미에서 꺼내지고 있다.
(D) 몇몇 의류가 옷걸이에 걸려 있다.

해설 (A) 여자가 선반에 상품을 채우는 동작을 하고 있지 않으므로 오답.
(B) 여자가 재킷을 입어 보는 동작을 하고 있지 않으므로 오답.
(C) 상품을 꺼내는 동작을 하는 사람을 찾아볼 수 없으므로 오답.
(D) 옷들이 옷걸이에 걸려 있는 상태이므로 정답.

어휘 stock v. (상품, 재고 등) ~을 채우다, ~을 갖춰 놓다 try on ~을 한 번 착용해 보다 merchandise 물품, 상품 unpack (꾸러미, 상자 등에서) ~을 꺼내다, ~을 풀어 놓다 hang 걸리다, 매달리다 rack ~걸이, 거치대

2.
(A) Some musicians are unpacking their equipment.
(B) Some instruments are displayed at an outdoor market.
(C) One of the men is setting up a microphone stand.
(D) One of the men is wearing sunglasses.

(A) 몇몇 음악가들이 장비를 꺼내고 있다.
(B) 몇몇 악기들이 야외 시장에 진열되어 있다.
(C) 남자들 중 한 명이 마이크 스탠드를 설치하고 있다.
(D) 남자들 중 한 명이 선글라스를 착용한 상태이다.

해설 (A) 음악가들이 장비를 꺼내는 동작을 하고 있지 않으므로 오답.
(B) 야외 시장을 배경으로 하는 사진이 아니며, 악기들이 진열된 상태도 아니므로 오답.
(C) 마이크 스탠드가 이미 설치된 상태이므로 오답.
(D) 두 남자들 중 오른쪽 남자가 선글라스를 착용한 상태이므로 정답.

어휘 unpack (꾸러미, 상자 등에서) ~을 꺼내다, ~을 풀어 놓다 equipment 장비 instrument 악기, 기구 display ~을 진열하다, ~을 전시하다 outdoor 야외의, 실외의 set up ~을 설치하다 wear (상태) ~을 착용하다

Part 2

3. When will Arnold replace the empty ink cartridges in this printer?
(A) The new machine is better than the old one.
(B) I need to make additional copies.
(C) I thought he did it already.

아놀드 씨가 언제 이 프린터의 빈 잉크 카트리지를 교체하시나요?
(A) 새 기계가 이전 것보다 더 좋습니다.
(B) 제가 추가로 복사해야 해요.
(C) 이미 하셨다고 생각했어요.

해설 아놀드 씨가 언제 프린터의 빈 잉크 카트리지를 교체하는지 묻는 것에 대해 Arnold 씨를 he로, 교체하는 일을 did it으로 각각 대신해 이미 한 줄 알았다는 말로 답변하는 (C)가 정답이다. 미래 시점의 일을 묻는 질문이지만, 이렇게 과거 시점에 완료된

줄 알았다는 말로 잘못 알고 있는 정보를 언급하는 답변도 종종 정답으로 제시된다는 점에 유의해야 한다. (A)와 (B)는 printer 에서 연상 가능한 machine과 copies를 활용해 혼동을 유발 하는 오답이다.

어휘　replace ~을 교체하다　make a copy 복사하다
additional 추가의

4.　Where's the nearest pharmacy?
(A) It has a larger variety of products.
(B) Down the street near the grocery store.
(C) You can borrow mine.

가장 가까운 약국이 어디에 있나요?
(A) 그곳에 아주 더 다양한 종류의 제품들이 있어요.
(B) 길 저쪽 식료품점 근처예요.
(C) 제 것을 빌려 가셔도 돼요.

해설　가장 가까운 약국이 어디에 있는지 묻고 있으므로 위치를 나타 내는 전치사구로 답변하는 (B)가 정답이다. (A)와 (C)는 약국 의 위치와 전혀 관련 없는 내용이므로 오답이다.

어휘　pharmacy 약국　a large variety of 아주 다양한
down (길 등) ~ 저쪽에, ~을 따라　grocery store 식료품 점　borrow ~을 빌리다

5.　Which of these fabrics is the best match with the new carpets?
(A) Doesn't it make more sense to choose the carpets at another time?
(B) Yes, I haven't watched such an exciting match in years.
(C) I have no idea about this kind of thing.

이 직물들 중 어느 것이 새 카펫과 가장 잘 어울리나요?
(A) 다음 번에 카펫을 고르는 게 더 낫지 않을까요?
(B) 네, 수년 동안 그토록 흥미진진한 시합을 보지 못했어요.
(C) 전 이런 것에 대해 잘 알지 못해요.

해설　새 카펫과 가장 잘 어울리는 직물을 묻는 데 대해 특정 직물을 말하는 대신 잘 모르겠다는 말로 답변하는 (C)가 정답이다. '잘 모릅니다,' '~에게 물어보세요,' '아직 결정되지 않았습니다' 등 과 같은 회피성 답변은 정답 확률이 높은 편이므로 관련 표현들 을 미리 기억해 두는 것이 좋다. (A)는 carpets를 반복 사용한 답변으로 질문의 핵심에서 벗어난 오답이며, (B)는 의문사 의문 문에 어울리지 않는 Yes로 답변한 오답이다.

어휘　fabric 직물, 천　match n. 잘 어울리는 것, 시합　make sense 이치에 맞다, 말이 되다, 이해가 되다　at another time 다음 번에　in years 수년 동안　have no idea about ~에 대해 알지 못하다

6.　How do I make an international call from the office phone?
(A) Call me back.

(B) He is in charge.
(C) Just dial the numbers.

사무실 전화로 어떻게 국제 전화를 걸죠?
(A) 저에게 답신 전화 주세요.
(B) 그가 책임지고 있습니다.
(C) 그냥 번호만 누르시면 됩니다.

해설　사무실 전화로 어떻게 국제 전화를 거는지 묻고 있으므로 번호 를 누르기만 하면 된다는 말로 구체적인 방법을 알려주는 (C)가 정답이다. (A)는 call을 반복 사용한 답변으로 질문의 핵심에서 벗어난 오답이며, (B)는 책임자를 말하는 내용이므로 어울리지 않는 오답이다.

어휘　make a call 전화를 걸다　call A back A에게 답신 전화 하다　in charge 책임지고 있는, 맡고 있는　dial the numbers 번호를 누르다

7.　Is David going to the restaurant opening?
(A) You can check their business hours online.
(B) His restaurant is on Eliza Street.
(C) No, he has an assignment to finish.

데이빗 씨가 그 레스토랑 개업식에 가는 건가요?
(A) 그곳의 영업 시간을 온라인으로 확인하실 수 있어요.
(B) 그의 레스토랑이 엘리자 스트리트에 있어요.
(C) 아뇨, 그는 끝마쳐야 할 업무가 있어요.

해설　데이빗 씨가 레스토랑 개장식에 가는지 묻고 있으므로 부정을 의미하는 No와 함께 개장식에 가지 못하는 이유를 설명하는 (C)가 정답이다. (A)는 restaurant opening에서 연상 가능 한 business hours를 활용해 혼동을 유발하는 오답이며, (B) 는 질문의 restaurant을 반복 사용한 답변으로 레스토랑 위치 를 말하고 있으므로 질문의 핵심에서 벗어난 오답이다.

어휘　business hours 영업 시간　assignment (할당된) 업무, 일

8.　Why did Mario transfer to the Calgary office?
(A) To be nearer to his parents.
(B) He moved down to the third floor.
(C) I've never been there before.

마리오 씨가 왜 캘거리 지사로 전근하셨나요?
(A) 부모님과 더 가까이 있기 위해서요.
(B) 그는 아래쪽 3층으로 옮겼어요.
(C) 저는 전에 그곳에 가본 적이 없어요.

해설　마리오 씨가 왜 캘거리 지사로 전근했는지 묻고 있으므로 목적 을 나타내는 To부정사구로 부모님과 더 가까이 있기 위해서라 는 말로 답변한 (A)가 정답이다. (B)는 transfer에서 연상 가 능한 동사 move를 활용해 혼동을 유발하는 답변으로 Where 의문문에 어울리는 위치를 말하고 있어 오답이며, (C)는 마리오 씨가 아닌 답변자 자신의 경험을 말하는 내용이므로 오답이다.

어휘　transfer to ~로 전근하다　be near to ~와 가까이 있다

9. Don't we have to take everything out of the storeroom?

(A) No, only the old files.
(B) Where are they kept?
(C) It's on the fourth floor.

우리가 보관실에 있는 것을 전부 꺼내야 하지 않나요?
(A) 아뇨, 오래된 파일들만요.
(B) 그것들이 어디에 보관되어 있죠?
(C) 4층에 있습니다.

해설 보관실의 물건을 모두 꺼내야 하는지 묻고 있으므로 부정을 나타내는 No와 함께 꺼내야 할 특정 물건을 언급하는 (A)가 정답이다. (B)는 보관된 장소를 되묻는 말에 해당되므로 질문의 핵심에서 벗어난 오답이다. (C)는 Where 의문문에 어울리는 위치를 말하는 답변이므로 오답이다.

어휘 take A out of B B에서 A를 꺼내다 storeroom 보관실, 저장고 keep ~을 보관하다

10. Weren't we supposed to participate in a fundraising event today?

(A) I forgot to schedule it.
(B) Yes, I suppose he's right.
(C) I received it yesterday.

우리가 오늘 기금 마련 행사에 참가하기로 되어 있지 않았나요?
(A) 제가 그 일정을 잡는 것을 잊었어요.
(B) 네, 그의 말이 맞는 것 같아요.
(C) 제가 어제 그걸 받았어요.

해설 오늘 기금 마련 행사에 참가하기로 되어 있지 않았는지 묻는 데 대해 a fundraising event를 it로 지칭해 그 일정을 잡지 못했다는 말로 참가할 수 없다는 뜻을 나타낸 (A)가 정답이다. (B)는 긍정을 나타내는 Yes 뒤에 행사 참가 여부와 관련 없는 he에 관해 말하고 있으므로 오답이다. (C)는 today에서 연상 가능한 yesterday와 함께 과거 시점에 믿기 받은 사실을 말하고 있으므로 오답이다.

어휘 be supposed to do ~하기로 되어 있다, ~해야 하다 participate in ~에 참가하다 fundraising 기금 마련, 모금 forget to do ~하는 것을 잊다 suppose (that) ~라고 생각하다 receive ~을 받다

11. Why don't you rent a car during the conference in Seattle?

(A) Because I attended last year.
(B) I don't think it is necessary.
(C) No, this is my first time here.

시애틀에서 열리는 컨퍼런스 행사 중에 차를 한 대 대여하시는 건 어때요?
(A) 저는 작년에 참석했기 때문이에요.
(B) 그게 필요할 것 같지 않아요.
(C) 아뇨, 저는 이곳이 처음이에요.

해설 차를 한 대 빌리는 것을 제안하고 있으므로 a car를 it으로 지칭해 필요하지 않은 것 같다는 말로 거절의 뜻을 나타낸 (B)가 정답이다. (A)는 이유를 묻는 Why 의문문에 어울리는 답변이므로 오답이며, (C)는 거절을 뜻하는 No 뒤에 이어지는 말이 자동차 대여와 관련 없는 오답이다. 참고로, Why don't you/I/we로 시작하는 질문은 모두 제안을 나타낸다는 점을 미리 기억해 두는 것이 좋다.

어휘 Why don't you ~? ~하시는 게 어때요? rent ~을 대여하다 attend 참석하다 necessary 필요한, 필수의

12. Would you like to attend a workshop for sales representatives next month?

(A) I'm shopping for a birthday present.
(B) It depends on when it is.
(C) The sales are up by 15% this year.

다음 달에 영업 사원 대상 워크숍에 참석하시겠어요?
(A) 생일 선물을 사려고 쇼핑 중이에요.
(B) 그게 언제인지에 따라 달라요.
(C) 올해 매출이 15% 증가했어요.

해설 영업 사원 대상 워크숍에 참석할 것인지 묻는 데 대해 workshop을 it으로 지칭해 행사가 열리는 시점에 따라 다르다는 말로 조건을 먼저 언급하는 (B)가 정답이다. (A)는 workshop과 발음이 일부 유사한 shopping을, (C)는 sales를 각각 활용해 혼동을 유발하는 답변으로 둘 모두 질문의 핵심에서 벗어난 오답이다.

어휘 Would you like to do? ~하시겠어요? attend ~에 참석하다 sales representative 영업 사원 present n. 선물 depend on ~에 따라 다르다, ~에 달려 있다 sales 매출, 판매(량), 영업 by (차이) ~ 정도, ~만큼

13. Have we made more money this month than last month?

(A) I don't think we can afford it.
(B) I haven't seen the figures yet.
(C) It will be launched in September.

우리가 지난 달보다 이번 달에 더 많은 수익을 올렸나요?
(A) 우린 그럴 여유가 없을 것 같습니다.
(B) 아직 수치를 확인해 보지 않았습니다.
(C) 그건 9월에 출시될 겁니다.

해설 이번 달에 더 많은 수익을 올렸는지 묻는 데 대해 아직 수치를 확인하지 않아서 알 수 없다는 뜻을 나타낸 (B)가 정답이다. (A)는 money에서 연상 가능한 afford를 활용한 오답이며, (C)는 제품 출시 또는 일의 시작과 관련된 시점을 말하고 있으므로 질문의 핵심에서 벗어난 오답이다.

어휘 make money 수익을 올리다, 돈을 벌다 afford (시간, 금전적으로) ~에 대한 여유가 있다 figure 수치, 숫자 launch ~을 출시하다, ~을 시작하다

14. When were these rooms last painted?

    (A) There's plenty of room.

    (B) The office manager would know.

    (C) A nice shade of green.

이 방들이 언제 마지막으로 페인트칠이 되었나요?
(A) 공간이 많습니다.
(B) 사무실 책임자께서 아실 겁니다.
(C) 아주 멋진 초록색 빛깔입니다.

해설 언제 마지막으로 페인트칠이 되었는지 묻고 있으므로 책임자가 알고 있을 것이라는 말로 관련 정보를 확인할 수 있는 방법을 알리는 (B)가 정답이다. (A)는 room의 또 다른 의미(공간)를, (C)는 painted와 연관성 있게 들리는 green을 각각 활용해 혼동을 유발하는 오답이다.

어휘 **paint** v. ~을 페인트로 칠하다 **plenty of** 많은, 풍부한
room (관사 없이) 공간 **shade** 빛깔, 색조

15. I'll print out a copy of next week's work schedule for you.

    (A) The printer on the third floor.

    (B) Thanks for your help.

    (C) I try to work out three times a week.

다음 주 근무 일정을 한 부 출력해 드릴게요.
(A) 3층에 있는 프린터요.
(B) 도와 주셔서 감사합니다.
(C) 저는 일주일에 세 번 운동하려고 해요.

해설 특정 문서를 출력해 주겠다고 제안하는 말에 대해 감사의 뜻을 전하는 (B)가 정답이다. (A)는 print와 발음이 유사한 printer를, (C)는 work의 서로 다른 의미(근무, 운동하다)를 각각 활용해 혼동을 유발하는 오답이다.

어휘 **print out** ~을 출력하다, 인쇄하다 **try to do** ~하려 하다
work out 운동하다

16. The dentist has been working quite a long time on that patient.

    (A) Yes, he's taking longer than I expected.

    (B) Your appointment was rescheduled.

    (C) He's been a dentist for 14 years.

치과 의사 선생님께서 저 환자를 꽤 오랫동안 치료하고 계시네요.
(A) 네, 제가 예상한 것보다 시간이 더 오래 걸리시네요.
(B) 예약 일정이 재조정되었습니다.
(C) 14년 동안 치과 의사로 일해 오신 분이세요.

해설 의사가 오랫동안 한 명의 환자를 치료하고 있다는 말에 대해 답변자 자신의 예상보다 시간이 더 오래 걸리고 있다는 말로 동조하는 (A)가 정답이다. (B)는 dentist 및 patient에서 연상 가능한 appointment를 활용해 혼동을 유발하는 오답이며, (C)는 dentist를 반복한 답변으로 경력 기간을 말하고 있으므로 질문의 핵심에서 벗어난 오답이다.

어휘 **quite a long time** 꽤 오랜 시간 cf. quite 꽤, 상당히
expect 예상하다, 기대하다 **appointment** 예약, 약속
reschedule ~의 일정을 재조정하다

17. Why wasn't Elizabeth at the sales workshop?

    (A) She had a prior engagement.

    (B) The first workshop will run for two hours.

    (C) Yes, she made a great deal of sales.

엘리자베스 씨가 왜 영업 워크샵에 오지 않은 거죠?
(A) 선약이 있었대요.
(B) 첫 번째 워크숍이 두 시간 동안 진행될 겁니다.
(C) 네, 그분은 많은 영업 실적을 냈어요.

해설 엘리자베스 씨가 왜 영업 워크샵에 오지 않았는지 묻고 있으므로 Elizabeth를 She로 지칭해 선약이 있었다는 말로 그 이유를 밝히는 (A)가 정답이다. (B)는 workshop을, (C)는 sales를 각각 반복 활용한 답변으로 엘리자베스 씨의 불참 이유와 관련 없는 오답이다.

어휘 **sales** 영업, 판매(량), 매출 **prior engagement** 선약
run 진행되다, 운영되다 **a great deal of** 많은 (양의)

18. Do you think I should take an umbrella on the hike today?

    (A) It's not supposed to rain.

    (B) Starting at 10 a.m.

    (C) Is it a difficult route?

오늘 하이킹에 제가 우산을 가져가야 한다고 생각하세요?
(A) 비가 오진 않을 거예요.
(B) 오전 10시부터요.
(C) 어려운 경로인가요?

해설 우산을 가져가야 하는지를 묻고 있으므로 비가 오지는 않을 것이라는 말로 우산을 가져갈 필요가 없음을 알리는 (A)가 정답이다. (B)는 시작 시점을 나타내는 말이므로 오답이며, (C)는 hike에서 연상 가능한 route를 활용해 혼동을 유발하는 오답이다.

어휘 **be supposed to do** ~하기로 되어 있다, ~해야 하다
starting (시점 표현과 함께) ~부터 **route** 경로, 노선

19. Would you rather do the cooking yourself or use a caterer?

    (A) Yes, I am hungry.

    (B) I think Peter used it.

    (C) I'd prefer doing it myself.

직접 요리를 하시고 싶으신가요, 아니면 출장 요리 업체를 이용하시고 싶으신가요?
(A) 네, 저는 배가 고파요.
(B) 피터 씨가 그걸 이용한 거 같아요.
(C) 제가 직접 하는 게 더 좋겠어요.

해설 요리를 직접 할 것인지, 아니면 출장 요리 업체를 이용할 것인지 묻고 있으므로 직접 하고 싶다는 뜻을 나타낸 (C)가 정답이다. (A)는 cooking에서 연상 가능한 hungry를 활용한 오답이며, (B)는 use를 반복한 답변으로 피터 씨와 관련된 일을 말하고 있으므로 질문의 핵심에서 벗어난 오답이다.

어휘 **Would you rather do?** ~하고 싶으세요?, ~하시겠어요? **oneself** (부사처럼 쓰여) 직접 **caterer** 출장 요리 업체 **prefer -ing** ~하는 게 더 좋다, ~하는 것을 선호하다

20. That was the most boring book I've read in the past few months.

(A) I'm still working on writing the conclusion.
(B) It's strange that it received so much praise.
(C) It was released in August.

그건 제가 지난 몇 달 동안 읽은 가장 지루한 책이었어요.
(A) 전 여전히 결말을 작성하는 작업을 하고 있어요.
(B) 그게 그렇게 많은 찬사를 받은 게 이상해요.
(C) 그건 8월에 출시되었어요.

해설 특정 도서를 That으로 지칭해 최근 읽은 가장 지루한 책이었다는 의견을 말하는 데 대해 찬사를 받은 이유를 모르겠다는 말로 우회적으로 동의의 뜻을 전하는 (B)가 정답이다. (A)와 (C)는 book에 연상 가능한 writing과 released를 각각 활용해 혼동을 유발하는 오답이다.

어휘 **boring** 지루하게 만드는 **work on** ~에 대한 작업을 하다 **conclusion** 결말, 결론 **It's strange that** ~라는 게 이상하다 **receive** ~을 받다 **praise** 찬사, 칭찬 **release** ~을 출시하다, ~을 발매하다

Part 3

Questions 21-23 refer to the following conversation.

M: Thank you for calling 21 Home Goods. How can I help you?

W: Hi, I'm calling because I can't connect my smartphone to 21 the air conditioning unit that I bought at your store last week.

M: Our units should be compatible with all mobile devices. 22 First you'll need to download the mobile app, though.

W: Oh, okay. Here it is.

M: It should give you step-by-step instructions to follow.

W: Thanks, I think I've got it now.

M: By the way, 23 did you know that we're doing a special event? If you leave some feedback on

our Web site, you'll be entered into a drawing for a wide selection of prizes.

남: 홈 굿즈에 전화 주셔서 감사합니다. 무엇을 도와 드릴까요?
여: 안녕하세요, 제가 지난 주에 그쪽 매장에서 구입한 에어컨에 제 스마트폰을 연결할 수 없어서 전화드렸어요.
남: 저희 제품들은 모든 모바일 기기와 호환이 될 텐데요. 먼저 모바일용 앱을 다운로드해야 하긴 하지만요.
여: 아, 그렇군요. 여기 있네요.
남: 따라서 하실 수 있는 단계별 설명을 제공해 드릴 겁니다.
여: 고맙습니다, 이제 된 것 같아요.
남: 그런데, 저희가 특별 행사를 하고 있다는 것 알고 계셨나요? 저희 웹 사이트에 의견을 남겨 주시면, 아주 다양한 경품 추첨 행사에 응모되실 것입니다.

어휘 **connect A to B** A를 B에 연결하다 **unit** (기기의) 한 대 **be compatible with** ~와 호환되다 **device** 기기, 장치 **though** (문장 끝이나 중간에서) 하지만 **step-by-step** 단계별로 하는, 단계적인 **instructions** 안내, 설명 **follow** ~을 따라 하다, ~을 따르다 **by the way** (화제 전환 시) 그런데, 그건 그렇고 **be entered into** ~에 응모되다 **drawing** 추첨 행사 **a wide selection of** 아주 다양한 **prize** 상, 상품, 경품

21. 남자가 어디에서 근무할 것 같은가?
(A) 가전 기기 매장에서
(B) 주택 청소 서비스 업체에서
(C) 관리 사무소에서
(D) 식료품점에서

해설 대화 초반부에 남자가 전화를 받으면서 소속 업체를 밝히고 있고(Thanks for calling Home Goods), 여자가 남자의 매장에서 에어컨을 구입한 사실을(~ the air conditioning unit that I bought at your store ~) 언급하고 있다. 이를 통해 남자가 소속된 매장에서 에어컨을 판매한다는 것을 알 수 있으므로 가전 기기 매장을 뜻하는 (A)가 정답이다.

22. 남자의 말에 따르면, 여자가 무엇을 해야 하는가?
(A) 기기를 다시 시작하는 일
(B) 앱을 다운로드하는 일
(C) 서비스 요금을 지불하는 일
(D) 일부 수리 일정을 잡는 일

해설 대화 중반부에 남자가 자사의 상품이 모든 모바일 장치와 호환이 가능하다고 알리면서 앱을 먼저 다운로드해야 한다고(First you'll need to download the mobile app ~) 언급하고 있으므로 (B)가 정답이다.

23. 남자가 어떤 행사를 언급하는가?
(A) 온라인 선물 증정 행사
(B) 미술 경연 대회

(C) 지역 축제
(D) 특별 할인 행사

해설 남자가 언급하는 행사를 묻고 있으므로 남자가 행사 관련 표현을 언급하는 부분에 집중해 들어야 한다. 대화 후반부에 남자가 특별 행사를 언급하면서 웹 사이트에 의견을 남기면 경품 추첨 행사에 응모된다고(If you leave some feedback on our Web site, you'll be entered into a drawing for a wide selection of prizes) 알리고 있다. 이는 온라인에서 경품을 증정하는 행사임을 뜻하는 말이므로 (A)가 정답이다.

어휘 giveaway 증정(품) competition 경연 대회, 경기 대회 local 지역의, 현지의

Paraphrase Web site / drawing for a wide selection of prizes
→ An online gift giveaway

Questions 24-26 refer to the following conversation.

M: Hello, Ms. Lincoln. It's good to see you. I wonder if you could help me with something. 24 I'm thinking about finding a new place for me and my family, but I'm not sure where to start. How did you find your home when you were looking last year?

W: It's easy. Have you ever heard of realestate.com? 25 It's a great Web site for people looking to purchase new homes. I used it to speed up my search for a place. 25 The places listed on there are accompanied by lots of pictures and information.

M: Oh, that sounds convenient, although I think there might be a problem. I don't have a lot of money to use for a down payment.

W: I see. Well, 26 if I were you, I would simply look at a newspaper on the weekend. They advertise businesses that offer good deals on loans. I think *The Sunday Mail* is the most useful one.

남: 안녕하세요, 링컨 씨. 만나서 반갑습니다. 저 좀 도와주실 수 있는지 궁금합니다. 제가 가족들과 함께 살 새 집을 찾아보려고 생각 중인데, 어디서부터 시작해야 할지 모르겠어요. 작년에 알아보러 다니실 때 어떻게 집을 구하셨나요?

여: 어렵지 않아요. realestate.com이라고 들어보셨어요? 새 집을 구하려고 알아보는 사람들에게 아주 좋은 웹 사이트예요. 제가 집을 빨리 찾고 싶어서 이 사이트를 이용했어요. 거

기에 목록으로 나와 있는 집들에 대해서 많은 사진들과 정보가 함께 올라와 있어요.

남: 아, 편리한 것 같긴 하지만, 제 생각에 문제가 하나 있을지도 모르겠네요. 저는 계약금으로 쓸 돈이 많지 않아요.

여: 알겠어요. 음, 저라면, 그냥 주말에 신문을 확인해 볼 것 같아요. 신문이 괜찮은 대출 조건을 제공하는 업체들을 광고하잖아요. 제 생각엔 <선데이 메일>이 가장 유용한 신문인 것 같아요.

어휘 wonder if ~인지 궁금하다 help A with B B에 대해 A를 돕다 look to do ~하길 바라다, ~하길 기대하다 purchase ~을 구입하다 speed up ~의 속도를 높이다 list ~을 목록에 올리다 be accompanied by ~이 동반되다 convenient 편리한 although 비록 ~이지만 down payment 계약금, 선금 if I were you 저라면, 내가 너라면 advertise ~을 광고하다 deal 거래 조건, 거래 제품 loan 대출

24. 남자가 무엇을 하고 싶어 하는가?
(A) 사업을 시작하는 일
(B) 주택을 구입하는 일
(C) 건물을 개조하는 일
(D) 차량을 구입하는 일

해설 대화 초반부에 남자가 가족과 함께 살 집을 구하려고 하는데(I'm thinking about finding a new place for me and my family ~) 방법을 잘 모르겠다며 여자에게 작년에 어떻게 집을 구했는지 묻고 있으므로 (B)가 정답이다.

25. 여자는 자신이 이용했던 웹 사이트와 관련해 무슨 말을 하는가?
(A) 여러 사진들을 특징으로 한다.
(B) 가장 광범위한 목록이 있다.
(C) 최근에 업데이트되었다.
(D) 가장 저렴한 구매 조건을 제공한다.

해설 대화 중반부에 여자가 웹 사이트 한 곳을 언급하면서 목록에 나와 있는 집들에 대해서 많은 사진과 정보가 함께 올라와 있다고(The places listed on there are accompanied by lots of pictures and information) 알리고 있다. 따라서, 이를 언급한 (A)가 정답이다.

어휘 feature v. ~을 특징으로 하다 extensive 광범위한, 폭넓은 listing 목록 recently 최근에

Paraphrase lots of pictures
→ several photographs

26. 여자가 권하는 일은 무엇인가?
(A) 부동산 중개소를 방문하는 것
(B) 주말에 발간되는 출판물을 확인하는 것
(C) 소식지를 받아볼 수 있도록 신청하는 것
(D) 자신의 동료들 중 한 명과 이야기하는 것

해설 대화 후반부에 여자가 자신이라면 주말 신문을 확인해 볼
　　 것이라고(~ if I were you, I would simply look at a
　　 newspaper on the weekend) 권하고 있다. 주말 신문은 주
　　 말에 발간되는 출판물이므로 이를 언급한 (B)가 정답이다.

어휘 **real estate agency** 부동산 중개소 **publication** 출판
　　 (물) **sign up** 신청하다, 등록하다 **colleague** 동료

　　 Paraphrase look at a newspaper on the weekend
　　　　　　　　→ Checking a weekend publication

Questions 27-29 refer to the following conversation.

W: Hello, **27** I'd like to register for the Spanish
　 Speaking course at your institute. But, **28**
　 every time I click on the registration button
　 on your Web site, I just get sent back to the
　 welcome page. Can you help?

M: That's certainly strange. Do you see any error
　 messages after you click the button?

W: No, I don't. My friend tried it on her laptop and
　 she encountered the same problem.

M: Hmm... I'll notify our IT team about it. In the
　 meantime, **29** I can e-mail you an application
　 directly. You can just fill it out and bring it to our
　 institute with the course fee.

여: 안녕하세요, 그쪽 학원의 스페인어 말하기 강좌에 등록하려고
　 합니다. 하지만, 제가 웹 사이트에서 등록 버튼을 클릭할 때마
　 다, 환영 인사 페이지로 되돌아 가기만 합니다. 좀 도와 주시겠
　 어요?

남: 분명 이상한 일이네요. 버튼을 클릭하신 후에 어떤 에러 메시
　 지라도 보이시나요?

여: 아뇨, 그렇지 않아요. 제 친구도 자신의 노트북 컴퓨터에서 시
　 노해 봤는데, 같은 문제에 직면했어요.

남: 흠... 그와 관련해서 저희 IT 팀에 알리겠습니다. 그 사이에, 제
　 가 이메일로 신청서를 직접 보내 드리겠습니다. 작성하신 후에
　 수강료와 함께 저희 학원으로 가져오시기만 하시면 됩니다.

어휘 **would like to do** ~하고자 하다, ~하고 싶다 **register
　　 for** ~에 등록하다 **institute** 학원, 기관, 단체 **get p.p.**
　　 ~한 상태가 되다 **send A back to B** A를 B로 되돌려 보
　　 내다 **encounter** ~에 직면하다, ~와 맞닥뜨리다 **notify
　　 A about B** A에게 B에 관해 알리다 **in the meantime**
　　 그 사이에, 그러는 동안 **application** 신청(서), 지원(서)
　　 directly 직접, 곧장 **fill A out** A를 작성하다 **course fee**
　　 수강료

27. 여자가 무엇을 하려 하는가?
　　 (A) 회원 자격을 갱신하는 일
　　 (B) 비밀번호를 변경하는 일
　　 (C) 교재를 구입하는 일
　　 (D) 강좌에 등록하는 일

해설 대화 초반부에 여자가 스페인어 말하기 강좌에 등록하려고
　　 한다고(I'd like to register for the Spanish Speaking
　　 course at your institute) 알리고 있으므로 (D)가 정답
　　 이다.

어휘 **renew** ~을 갱신하다 **purchase** ~을 구입하다
　　 textbook 교재 **sign up for** ~에 등록하다

　　 Paraphrase register for the Spanish Speaking course
　　　　　　　　→ Sign up for a course

28. 남자가 "분명 이상한 일이네요"라고 말할 때 암시하는 것은 무
　　 엇인가?
　　 (A) 여자의 질문을 이해하지 못하고 있다.
　　 (B) 가격이 부정확하게 기재되어 있다고 생각한다.
　　 (C) 웹 사이트가 오작동하고 있을 수 있다고 생각한다.
　　 (D) 제품이 품절되어서 놀라워하고 있다.

해설 해당 문장은 대화 초반부에 여자가 등록 버튼을 클릭할 때마다
　　 환영 인사 페이지로 되돌아 간다고(~ every time I click on
　　 the registration button on your Web site, I just get
　　 sent back to the welcome page) 알리는 것에 대한 반응
　　 이다. 남자가 해당 문장과 함께 어떤 에러 메시지든 보이는지 묻
　　 는 것으로 볼 때, 시스템 오작동 여부를 염두에 두고 한 말임을
　　 알 수 있으므로 (C)가 정답이다.

어휘 **list** v. ~을 목록에 기재하다 **incorrectly** 부정확하게
　　 malfunction v. 오작동하다, 제대로 작동하지 않다 **sell
　　 out** 품절되다, 매진되다

29. 남자가 여자를 위해 무엇을 하겠다고 제안하는가?
　　 (A) 할인을 제공하는 일
　　 (B) 여자의 개인 상세 정보를 업데이트하는 일
　　 (C) 일정을 설명해 주는 일
　　 (D) 여자에게 양식을 보내는 일

해설 남자가 여자에게 제안하는 일을 묻고 있으므로 남자의 말에
　　 서 제안 관련 표현이 제시되는 부분을 파악해야 한다. 대화 후
　　 반부에 남자는 여자가 겪고 있는 문제의 해결 방법으로 신청
　　 서를 이메일로 바로 보내 주겠다고(I can e-mail you an
　　 application directly) 제안하고 있으므로 이를 언급한 (D)가
　　 정답이다.

어휘 **offer to do** ~하겠다고 제안하다 **details** 상세 정보, 세부
　　 사항 **explain** ~을 설명하다 **form** 양식, 서식

　　 Paraphrase e-mail you an application
　　　　　　　　→ Send her a form

Questions 30-32 refer to the following conversation with three speakers.

W: Excuse me, **30** I'm looking for a book on Indonesian cooking by Juanita Chen. It's called *Java Gourmet*.

M1: Oh, **30** I'm afraid we just sold the last copy this morning.

W: That's too bad. **31** I'm having people over for a dinner party this Saturday, and I wanted to try some of Ms. Chen's recipes.

M1: Hold on while I check with my manager. **32** Toby, are we expecting any copies of *Java Gourmet* this week?

M2: No, sorry. Our next delivery isn't until next Monday.

W: I see. Well, I guess I'll just try to cook a different dish then.

M2: Wait... **32** why don't you try our other store on Parish Street? They have a much larger cooking selection than we do.

W: Okay, I'll try there. Thanks for your help!

여: 실례합니다, 주아니타 첸 씨가 쓴 인도네시아 요리에 관한 책을 찾고 있습니다. 제목이 <자바 고메>입니다.

남1: 아, 저희가 오늘 아침에 마지막 한 권을 판매한 것 같습니다.

여: 너무 아쉽네요. 제가 이번 주 토요일에 저녁 식사 파티를 위해 사람들을 초대하는데, 첸 씨의 몇몇 조리법들을 시도해 보고 싶었거든요.

남1: 제가 매니저님께 확인해 보는 동안 잠시 기다려 주세요. 토비 매니저님, 이번 주에 <자바 고메>라는 책이 들어올 예정인가요?

남2: 아뇨, 죄송합니다. 다음 번 배송이 다음 주 월요일이나 되어야 해요.

여: 알겠습니다. 음, 그럼 그냥 다른 음식을 요리해 봐야 할 것 같네요.

남2: 잠시만요... 패리쉬 스트리트에 있는 저희 다른 지점에 한 번가 보시면 어떨까요? 그곳에는 저희보다 훨씬 더 많은 종류의 요리책들이 있습니다.

여: 네, 그곳에 한 번 가 볼게요. 도와주셔서 감사합니다!

어휘 **look for** ~을 찾다 **named A** 제목이 A인, A라고 부르는 **I'm afraid** (부정적인 일에 대해) ~인 것 같습니다, 유감이지만 ~입니다 **have A over** A를 초대하다, A를 손님으로 맞이하다 **recipe** 조리법 **Hold on** 잠시 기다려 주세요 **expect** (오기로 한 것) ~을 기다리다 **not until** ~나 되어야 하다 **then** 그럼, 그렇다면, 그때, 그런 다음 **selection** 종류, 선택 (가능한 것)

30. 대화가 어디에서 이뤄지고 있는가?
  (A) 도서관에서
  (B) 레스토랑에서
  (C) 건강 식품 매장에서
  (D) 서점에서

해설 대화 초반부에 여자가 인도네시아 요리에 관한 책을 찾고 있다고 알리면서 책 이름을 언급하자(~ I'm looking for a book on Indonesian cooking by Juanita Chen. It's called *Java Gourmet*), 남자 한 명이 오늘 아침에 마지막 한 권을 판매했다고(I'm afraid we just sold the last copy this morning) 알리고 있다. 이는 책을 판매하는 곳, 즉 서점에서 들을 수 있는 내용이므로 (D)가 정답이다.

31. 여자가 이번 주말에 무엇을 할 것인가?
  (A) 모임을 주최하는 일
  (B) 휴가를 떠나는 일
  (C) 요리 강좌에 참가하는 일
  (D) 공연에 참석하는 일

해설 이번 주말(this weekend)이라는 시점이 핵심이므로 해당 시점 표현이 제시되는 부분에서 단서를 찾아야 한다. 대화 중반부에 여자가 이번 주 토요일에 저녁 식사 파티를 위해 사람들을 초대할 예정이라고(I'm having people over for a dinner party this Saturday) 알리는 부분을 통해 모임을 주최한다는 사실을 알 수 있으므로 (A)가 정답이다.

어휘 **host** ~을 주최하다 **gathering** 모임 **join** ~에 참가하다, ~에 가입하다, ~와 함께 하다 **attend** ~에 참석하다 **performance** 공연, 연주(회)

Paraphrase having people over for a dinner party
        → Host a gathering

32. 토비 씨가 무엇을 권하는가?
  (A) 예약을 하는 것
  (B) 다음 주에 다시 오는 것
  (C) 배송 일정을 재조정하는 것
  (D) 다른 지점을 방문하는 것

해설 토비 씨가 권하는 일을 묻고 있으므로 '토비'라는 이름과 함께 권고나 제안 관련 표현이 제시되는 부분에서 집중해 들어야 한다. 대화 중반부에 한 남자가 토비 씨를 부르면서 요리책의 입고 상황에 대해 묻자, 다른 남자가 다음 주 월요일이나 돼야 들어온다는 말과 함께 자사의 다른 매장에 가 보도록 권하고(~ why don't you try our other store on Parish Street?) 있으므로 (D)가 정답이다.

어휘 **make a reservation** 예약하다 **reschedule** ~의 일정을 재조정하다 **branch** 지점, 지사

Paraphrase try our other store on Parish Street
        → Visiting a different branch

Questions 33-35 refer to the following conversation and map.

M: Welcome to Mount Angus National Park. Can I help you with anything?

W: Hi, **33** I just wanted to stop by the office to pick up a map and some information pamphlets before I start hiking.

M: No problem! Here you are. But you should take note that **34** the trail that starts on the west side of the mountain is closed this month for repairs.

W: Oh, that's okay. I'll be starting at the Meadow Trail entrance, just next to the parking lot.

M: That's a beautiful trail, but it's a little steep and dangerous. Are you hiking alone, or with friends?

W: My friends are on their way now. **35** I'm just going to buy some food and drink from the convenience store next door before they arrive. Thanks for your help!

남: 마운트 앵거스 국립공원에 오신 것을 환영합니다. 제가 도와드릴 일이라도 있을까요?

여: 안녕하세요, 제가 등산을 시작하기 전에 안내 사무소에 들러 지도와 몇몇 정보 안내 책자를 가져 가고 싶었습니다.

남: 알겠습니다! 여기 있습니다. 하지만 산의 서쪽 면에서 시작되는 등산로가 수리 작업 때문에 이번 달에 폐쇄되어 있다는 점에 유의하셔야 합니다.

여: 아, 괜찮습니다. 저는 주차장 바로 옆에 있는 메도우 트레일 입구에서 출발할 예정입니다.

남: 그곳이 아름다운 등산로이기는 하지만, 약간 가파르고 위험합니다. 혼자 등산하시나요, 아니면 친구분들과 함께 하시나요?

여: 제 친구들이 지금 오는 중입니다. 친구들이 도착하기 전에 옆에 있는 편의점에서 음식과 마실 것을 좀 사려고 합니다. 도와주셔서 감사합니다!

마운트 앵거스 국립공원

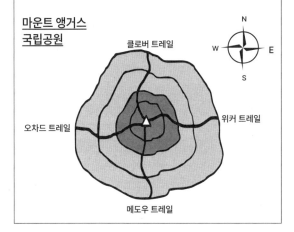

어휘 stop by ~에 들르다 pick up ~을 가져 가다, ~을 가져 오다 pamphlet 안내 책자 take note that ~라는 점에 유의하다 trail 등산로 on the west side of ~의 서쪽 면에 있는 closed 폐쇄된 repair 수리 entrance 입구 next to ~ 옆에 parking lot 주차장 steep 가파른 on one's way 오는 중인, 가는 중인 convenience store 편의점 next door 옆 건물에, 옆 집에 arrive 도착하다

33. 대화가 어디에서 이뤄지고 있는가?
(A) 주차장에서
(B) 안내소에서
(C) 여행사에서
(D) 등산로에서

해설 대화 초반부에 여자가 등산을 시작하기 전에 사무소에 들러 지도와 정보 안내 책자를 가져 가려 한다고(I just wanted to stop by the office to pick up a map and some information pamphlets ~) 알리고 있다. 따라서, 해당 자료를 받아 갈 수 있는 안내 사무소인 (B)가 정답이다.

34. 시각자료를 보시오. 어느 등산로가 일시적으로 폐쇄되어 있는가?
(A) 클로버 트레일
(B) 오차드 트레일
(C) 메도우 트레일
(D) 위커 트레일

해설 일시적으로 폐쇄된 곳이 질문의 핵심이므로 이와 관련된 표현이 제시되는 부분에서 단서를 찾아야 한다. 대화 중반부에 남자가 서쪽 면에서 시작되는 등산로가 수리 작업 때문에 이번 달에 폐쇄되어 있다고(~ the trail that starts on the west side of the mountain is closed this month for repairs) 알리고 있다. 시각자료에서 서쪽 면에 위치한 곳이 Orchard Trail이므로 (B)가 정답이다.

어휘 temporarily 일시적으로, 임시로

35. 여자가 곧이어 무엇을 할 것 같은가?
(A) 친구들을 만나는 일
(B) 지도를 살펴보는 일
(C) 간식을 구입하는 일
(D) 자동차로 돌아가는 일

해설 대화 후반부에 여자가 자신의 친구들이 도착하기 전에 옆에 있는 편의점에서 음식과 마실 것을 살 예정이라고(I'm just going to buy some food and drink from the convenience store next door before they arrive) 말하고 있으므로 (C)가 정답이다. 이는 친구들이 도착하기 전에 하는 일이므로, 대화를 듣는 동안 일의 순서를 명확하게 파악하는 것이 중요하다.

어휘 examine ~을 살펴보다, ~을 점검하다 purchase ~을 구입하다 return to ~로 돌아가다

Paraphrase buy some food and drink
→ Purchase snacks

Questions 36-38 refer to the following conversation and floor plan.

M: One ticket for *Police Force 3*, please. And, **36** I read that all tickets are only one dollar today. Is that right?

W: **36** Yes, that's true. Unfortunately, **37** the movie theater will shut down permanently next Wednesday, so this is our last weekend in business. That's why we're offering such cheap tickets today and tomorrow.

M: Oh, I'm really sorry to hear that. I've been watching films here for over two decades. Which screen should I go to for today's movie?

W: Just go down this hallway. **38** It's the screen directly across from the hot dog counter. If you reach the restroom, then you've gone too far.

남: <폴리스 포스 3> 입장권 1장 주세요. 그리고 오늘 모든 입장권이 1달러라고 쓰여 있는 것을 봤어요. 맞나요?

여: 네, 사실입니다. 안타깝게도, 저희 극장이 다음 주 수요일에 완전히 문을 닫게 되어서, 이번 주말에 마지막 영업을 합니다. 그것이 바로 오늘과 내일 입장권을 그렇게 저렴하게 제공하는 이유입니다.

남: 아, 그 얘기를 듣게 되어 정말 유감입니다. 제가 이곳에서 20년 넘게 영화를 봐 왔거든요. 오늘 영화는 어느 상영관으로 가야 하죠?

여: 이 복도를 따라 가시기만 하면 됩니다. 핫도그 판매대 바로 맞은편에 있는 상영관입니다. 화장실 있는 곳까지 도달하시게 된다면, 너무 멀리 가신 것입니다.

티켓 판매대	팝콘	음료	핫도그		화장실
출입구	1관	2관	3관	4관	

어휘 **unfortunately** 안타깝게도, 아쉽게도 **shut down** 문을 닫다 **permanently** 영구적으로, 완전히 **in business** 영업을 하는 **offer** ~을 제공하다 **decade** 10년 **down** (길 등) ~을 따라, ~ 저쪽에 **hallway** 복도 **directly across from** ~의 바로 맞은편에 있는 **reach** ~에 도달하다, ~에 이르다 **too far** 너무 멀리

36. 화자들이 주로 무엇에 관해 이야기하고 있는가?
(A) 구직 기회
(B) 영화 상영 일정
(C) 새로 개봉한 영화
(D) 특가 제공

해설 남자가 대화를 시작하면서 오늘 모든 입장권이 1달러라고 쓰여 있는 것을 봤다는 말과 함께 이에 대해 확인하는 질문을 하고(I read that all tickets are only one dollar today. Is that right?) 있다. 뒤이어 여자가 긍정의 표현과 함께 그 이유를 언급하고 있으므로 이에 해당하는 (D)가 정답이다.

어휘 **opportunity** 기회 **newly-released** 새로 개봉한, 새로 출시한 **special offer** 특가 제공, 특별 할인

Paraphrase all tickets are only one dollar
→ special offer

37. 여자가 극장과 관련해 무슨 말을 하는가?
(A) 최근에 매우 바빴다.
(B) 새로운 상영관을 추가했다.
(C) 현재 개조 공사 중이다.
(D) 곧 폐업할 예정이다.

해설 여자가 극장에 관해 말하는 정보를 찾아야 하므로 여자의 말에서 극장의 상황이 언급될 것임을 예상하고 들을 수 있다. 대화 중반부에 여자가 다음 주 수요일에 극장이 완전히 문을 닫는다고(~ the movie theater will shut down permanently next Wednesday) 알리고 있으므로 (D)가 정답이다.

어휘 **recently** 최근에 **add** ~을 추가하다 **renovate** ~을 개조하다, ~을 보수하다 **close down** 폐업하다, 문을 닫다

Paraphrase the movie theater will shut down permanently next Wednesday
→ It is closing down soon.

38. 시각자료를 보시오. 남자가 어느 상영관으로 갈 것인가?
(A) 1관
(B) 2관
(C) 3관
(D) 4관

해설 배치도가 시각자료로 제시되어 있으므로 이동 방식 및 특정 위치와 관련된 동사나 전치사 등에 특히 주의해 들어야 한다. 대화 후반부에 여자가 남자에게 핫도그 판매대 바로 맞은편에 있는 상영관이라고(It's the screen directly across from the hot dog counter) 알리고 있다. 시각자료에서 핫도그 판매대 바로 맞은편에 있는 상영관이 Screen 3으로 표기되어 있으므로 (C)가 정답이다.

Part 4

Questions 39-41 refer to the following recorded message.

Thank you for calling Manton Confectionery Factory. **39** Our factory is renowned for producing some of the most delicious candies on the planet. Our business hours are from 8:30 to 4, excluding holidays and weekends. If you wish to join one of our famous tours, please reserve a place before you arrive as we are usually fully booked up. And you'll be pleased to know that our tours conclude with a stop at **40** our visitor center, where free sweets will be handed out. **41** If you have any further inquires, please press 3 to speak to a member of our staff. Thank you for calling Manton Confectionery Factory.

맨튼 제과 공장에 전화 주셔서 감사합니다. 저희 공장은 세상에서 몇몇 가장 맛있는 사탕 제품을 만드는 것으로 유명합니다. 저희 영업 시간은 휴일과 주말을 제외하고 오전 8시 30분부터 오후 4시까지입니다. 유명한 저희 견학 프로그램들 중 하나에 참가하길 원하실 경우, 보통은 저희가 예약이 꽉 차게 되므로 도착하시기 전에 자리를 예약하시기 바랍니다. 그리고 저희 견학 시간이 무료 사탕 과자 제품을 나눠 드리는 방문객 센터에 들르는 것으로 마무리된다는 점을 알게 되시면 기쁘실 겁니다. 어떤 추가 문의 사항이든 있으시면, 3번을 눌러 저희 직원과 통화하시기 바랍니다. 맨튼 제과 공장에 전화 주셔서 감사합니다.

어휘 **confectionary** 사탕 과자의, 과자 제조의 **be renowned for** ~로 유명하다 **on the planet** 세상에서 **excluding** ~은 제외하고 **join** ~에 참가하다, ~에 합류하다 **reserve** ~을 예약하다 **arrive** 도착하다 **usually** 일반적으로, 보통 **be fully booked up** 예약이 꽉 차다 **conclude with** ~로 끝나다 **free** 무료의 **hand out** ~을 나눠주다 **further** 추가의, 한층 더 한 **inquiry** 문의

39. 화자의 말에 따르면, 업체가 무엇으로 알려져 있는가?
   (A) 유명한 커피
   (B) 사탕 과자류
   (C) 철물 용품
   (D) 시내 투어

해설 화자가 담화 초반부에 업체와 관련해 세상에서 가장 맛있는 사탕을 만드는 것으로 유명하다는 말로(Our factory is renowned for producing some of the most delicious candies on the planet) 소개하고 있다. 이를 통해 맛있는 사탕 제품을 만드는 것으로 알려져 있다는 사실을 알 수 있으므로 (B)가 정답이다.

어휘 **sweets** 사탕 과자류, 단 것

Paraphrase candies → sweets

40. 투어 참가자들이 방문객 센터에서 무엇을 할 수 있는가?
   (A) 전문가들과 이야기하는 일
   (B) 가이드북을 구입하는 일
   (C) 무료 샘플을 받는 일
   (D) 동영상을 시청하는 일

해설 담화에서 visitor center가 언급될 때 집중해 들어야 한다. 담화 중반부에 화자가 방문객 센터를 언급하면서 무료로 나눠 주는 과자 제품을 받게 될 것이라고(~ our visitor center, where free sweets will be handed out) 알리고 있으므로 (C)가 정답이다.

어휘 **expert** 전문가

Paraphrase free sweets will be handed out
   → Receive free samples

41. 청자가 왜 3번을 눌러야 하는가?
   (A) 질문을 하기 위해서
   (B) 행사장을 예약하기 위해서
   (C) 메시지를 다시 듣기 위해서
   (D) 길 안내 정보를 얻기 위해서

해설 담화 후반부에 화자는 기타 문의사항이 있으면 3번을 눌러 직원과 통화하라고(If you have any further inquires, please press 3 to speak to a member of our staff) 말하고 있다. 따라서 3번을 누르는 이유는 질문이 있기 때문이므로 (A)가 정답이다.

어휘 **reserve** ~을 예약하다 **venue** 행사장, 개최 장소 **directions** 길 안내

Questions 42-44 refer to the following talk.

It's my pleasure to welcome all of you to today's big event. In just a few moments, **42** we'll welcome our special guest to cut the ribbon and officially open the brand new Lloyd's Department Store. I'm sure you all know our special guest, **43** Jay Landry, as the star of several award-winning TV shows and blockbuster movies. Unfortunately, Mr. Landry has been slightly delayed, but he should be with us shortly to begin the proceedings. **44** Once the doors open, you'll all be welcome to go inside and begin shopping. It'll be worth the wait. For now, please enjoy the music and free refreshments.

오늘 이렇게 중요한 행사에 여러분 모두를 맞이하게 되어 기쁘게 생각합니다. 잠시 후에, 특별 손님을 모셔 리본을 자르고 공식적으로 완전히 새로운 로이즈 백화점을 개장하겠습니다. 오늘 특별 손님이신 제이 랜드리 씨는 여러 상을 받은 TV 프로그램 및 블록버스터 영화에 출연하신 스타라는 점을 여러분 모두가 분명히 알고 계실 것입니다. 아쉽게도, 랜드리 씨의 일정이 조금

지체되긴 했지만, 곧 함께 자리하셔서 행사를 시작하시게 될 것입니다. 개장하는 대로, 여러분 모두 마음껏 입장하셔서 쇼핑을 시작하셔도 좋습니다. 기다리신 보람이 있으실 것입니다. 일단, 음악과 무료 다과를 즐기시기 바랍니다.

어휘 in just a few moments 잠시 후에 officially 공식적으로, 정식으로 brand new 완전히 새로운 several 여럿의, 몇몇의 award-winning 상을 받은, 수상 경력이 있는 unfortunately 아쉽게도, 유감스럽게도 slightly 조금, 약간 delayed 지체된, 지연된 shortly 곧, 머지 않아 proceeding 행사, 일련의 행위들 be welcome to do 마음껏 ~해도 좋다, ~하는 것을 환영하다 worth 명사 ~의 가치가 있는 for now 일단은, 지금으로서는 free 무료의 refreshments 다과

42. 담화가 어디에서 이뤄지고 있는가?
(A) 은퇴 기념 저녁 만찬에서
(B) 시상식 행사장에서
(C) 직원 오리엔테이션 장소에서
(D) 개장 기념 행사장에서

해설 담화 초반부에 화자가 리본을 자르고 공식적으로 새 로이즈 백화점을 개장할 예정이라고(~ to cut the ribbon and officially open the brand new Lloyd's Department Store) 알리고 있으므로 개장 기념 행사장을 뜻하는 (D)가 정답이다.

어휘 retirement 은퇴, 퇴직 celebration 기념 행사, 축하 행사

43. 제이 랜드리 씨가 누구일 것 같은가?
(A) 사업가
(B) 배우
(C) 기조 연설자
(D) 가수

해설 제이 랜드리라는 이름이 제시되는 부분에서 함께 언급되는 정보에 집중해 들어야 한다. 담화 중반부에 화자가 제이 랜드리라는 이름을 언급하면서 여러 TV 프로그램 및 블록버스터 영화에 출연한 스타라고(~ as the star of several award-winning TV shows and blockbuster movies) 소개하고 있다. 따라서, 제이 랜드리 씨가 배우임을 알 수 있으므로 (B)가 정답이다.

44. 화자가 왜 "기다리신 보람이 있으실 것입니다"라고 말하는가?
(A) 지연 문제에 대해 사과하기 위해
(B) 청자들에게 감사의 뜻을 전하기 위해
(C) 일정 변경을 설명하기 위해
(D) 청자들을 들뜨게 만들기 위해

해설 해당 문장은 담화 후반부에 개장하자마자 모두 입장해서 쇼핑을 시작해도 좋다고(Once the doors open, you'll all be welcome to go inside and begin shopping) 알린 후에 들을 수 있는 말이다. 따라서, 쇼핑에 대한 기대감을 갖게 하기

위해 사용된 말이라는 것을 알 수 있으므로 이러한 의미를 지닌 (D)가 정답이다.

어휘 apologize for ~에 대해 사과하다 express (생각, 감정 등) ~을 표현하다 gratitude 감사(하는 마음) explain ~을 설명하다

Questions 45-47 refer to the following telephone message.

> Good morning, Tracy. This is Dennis from the finance department. **45** I received your message about purchasing new work uniforms for the hotel staff. I understand what you're saying, and I do agree that attractive uniforms help to present a good image of our hotel. **46** I really wish I were able to authorize the purchase. The thing is... We just don't have the funds. We've had a decline in the number of guests staying at our hotel, and we're just coming up to our quietest period of the year. Let's talk about this again in the spring. **47** Once the tourism season starts in April, I'll think about this issue again and let you know if we can afford new uniforms.
>
> ⎯⎯⎯⎯⎯⎯⎯⎯⎯⎯⎯⎯⎯⎯⎯⎯⎯
>
> 안녕하세요, 트레이시 씨. 저는 재무팀의 데니스입니다. 호텔 직원들을 위한 새 업무용 유니폼을 구입하는 일에 관한 당신의 메시지를 받았습니다. 무슨 말씀이신지 이해하고 있으며, 매력적인 유니폼이 우리 호텔의 좋은 이미지를 전달하는 데 도움이 된다는 점에 적극 동의합니다. 제가 이 구입 건을 승인해 드릴 수 있다면 정말 좋겠습니다. 문제는... 우리에게 자금이 없습니다. 우리 호텔에서 숙박하시는 고객들의 숫자가 감소되어 왔으며, 일년 중에서 가장 한산한 기간으로 접어 들고 있습니다. 봄에 이 문제와 관련해 다시 이야기해 봅시다. 4월에 관광철이 시작되는 대로, 이 사안을 다시 생각해 보고 우리가 새 유니폼을 구입할 여유가 있는지 알려 드리겠습니다.

어휘 finance 재무, 재정 receive ~을 받다 purchase ~을 구입하다 agree that ~라는 점에 동의하다 attractive 매력적인 present ~을 전달하다, ~을 제시하다 be able to do ~할 수 있다 authorize ~을 승인하다 fund 자금 decline in ~의 감소 come up to ~로 다가가다 once (일단) ~하는 대로, ~하자마자 issue 사안, 문제 let A know A에게 알리다 can afford (시간, 금전적으로) ~에 대한 여유가 있다

45. 전화의 목적은 무엇인가?
(A) 동료 직원에게 답변하는 것
(B) 도움을 요청하는 것
(C) 공급업체를 추천하는 것
(D) 연간 예산을 검토하는 것

해설 담화 초반부에 화자가 새 업무용 유니폼을 구입하는 일에 관한 상대방의 메시지를 받았다고(I received your message about purchasing new work uniforms for the hotel staff) 알리고 있다. 이는 상대방이 앞서 보낸 메시지를 읽고 그에 대한 답변을 하는 경우에 할 수 있는 말이므로 (A)가 정답이다.

어휘 respond to ~에 답변하다, 응답하다 colleague 동료 (직원) assistance 도움, 지원 supplier 공급업체, 공급업자 review ~을 검토하다 annual 연간의, 해마다의 budget 예산

46. 화자가 "우리에게 자금이 없습니다"라고 말할 때 의미하는 것은 무엇인가?

(A) 매출 수치에 대해 걱정하고 있다.
(B) 요청 사항을 승인할 수 없다.
(C) 돈을 잃어버렸다.
(D) 정보를 받기를 기다리고 있다.

해설 해당 문장은 담화 중반부에 화자 자신이 해당 구입 건을 승인해 줄 수 있다면 좋겠다고(I really wish I were able to authorize the purchase) 알린 후에 이어지고 있다. 이는 승인해 줄 수 없는 이유로서 자금 부족 문제를 언급하는 흐름에 해당되므로 (B)가 정답이다.

어휘 sales 매출, 영업, 판매(량) figure 수치, 숫자 approve ~을 승인하다 request 요청, 요구 misplace ~을 잃어버리다, ~을 둔 곳을 잊다

47. 화자가 4월에 무엇을 할 것이라고 말하는가?
(A) 일부 직원들을 승진시키는 일
(B) 근로 계약서를 연장하는 일
(C) 마케팅 캠페인을 시작하는 일
(D) 결정 사항을 재고하는 일

해설 4월에 할 일이 질문의 핵심이므로 4월이라는 시점 표현이 제시되는 부분에서 단서를 찾아야 한다. 담화 후반부에 화자가 4월에 관광철이 시작되는 대로 이 사안을 다시 생각해 보겠다고(Once the tourism season starts in April, I'll think about this issue again) 알리고 있다. 이는 결정 사항을 재고하는 일을 의미하므로 (D)가 정답이다.

어휘 promote ~을 승진시키다 extend ~을 연장하다 contract 계약(서) launch ~을 시작하다, 출시하다 reconsider ~을 재고하다 decision 결정

Paraphrase think about this issue again
→ Reconsider a decision

Questions 48-50 refer to the following telephone message and review.

Hi, William. I'm looking at the annual Sky King Airline Ratings for this year, and I'm disappointed with the scores. **48** As you're in charge of customer service here at Adrift Airways, I'd like you to take measures to improve some aspects of our service. **49** I'm getting increasingly worried that customers will stop choosing us and opt for one of our rivals instead. **50** We are already taking steps to improve the meals on our flights, so I know that rating will improve over the next 12 months. But, **50** I'd like to talk to you about the next lowest rating at our meeting tomorrow.

안녕하세요, 윌리엄 씨. 제가 매년 발표되는 스카이 킹 항공사 올해 평점을 보는 중인데, 점수가 실망스럽습니다. 당신이 우리 애드리프트 항공사의 고객 서비스를 책임지고 있기 때문에, 우리 서비스의 몇몇 측면들을 개선할 수 있는 조치를 취해 주셨으면 합니다. 저는 고객들이 우리를 선택하지 않고 경쟁사들 중의 한 곳을 대신 선택할까 점점 더 걱정이 많아지고 있습니다. 이미 우리 기내에서의 식사 서비스를 개선하기 위한 조치를 취하고 있으므로 이 항목의 평점이 앞으로 12개월 동안에 걸쳐 향상될 것으로 생각합니다. 하지만 내일 있을 회의에서 그 다음으로 가장 낮은 평점에 관해 당신과 이야기해 보고자 합니다.

애드리프트 항공사 – 평점	
기내식	★★
좌석의 편안함	★★★★★
오락 서비스	★★★★
쇼핑	★★★

어휘 annual 연간의, 해마다의 rating 평점, 등급, 순위 be disappointed with ~에 대해 실망하다 in charge of ~을 책임지고 있는 would like A to do A에게 ~하기를 원하다 take measures 조치를 취하다(= take steps) improve ~을 개선하다, 개선되다 aspect 측면, 양상 increasingly 점점 더 choose ~을 선택하다(= opt for) instead 대신 the next lowest 그 다음으로 가장 낮은 in-flight 기내의 comfort 편안함

48. 청자가 누구일 것 같은가?
(A) 항공사 이용 고객
(B) 잡지 기자
(C) 고객 서비스 책임자
(D) 사업가

해설 청자의 신분을 묻고 있으므로 상대방을 지칭하는 말과 함께 특정 직책이나 업무 관련 표현이 제시되는 부분을 찾아야 한

다. 담화 초반부에 화자가 상대방을 가리켜 Adrift Airways의 고객 서비스를 책임지고 있다고(As you're in charge of customer service here at Adrift Airways ~) 알리고 있으므로 (C)가 정답이다.

49. 화자가 무엇에 대해 우려하고 있는가?
(A) 보유 항공기들을 개조하는 것
(B) 새로운 종류의 서비스들을 광고하는 것
(C) 경쟁사들에게 고객들을 빼앗기는 것
(D) 불만 사항의 숫자를 줄이는 것

해설 화자가 담화 중반부에 고객들이 자신의 회사 대신 경쟁사들 중 한 곳을 선택할까 점점 더 걱정이 된다고(I'm getting increasingly worried that customers will stop choosing us and opt for one of our rivals instead) 알리고 있다. 이는 경쟁사에게 고객을 빼앗기는 문제를 의미하므로 (C)가 정답이다.

어휘 modify ~을 개조하다, ~을 변경하다 fleet (한 업체가 보유한) 전체 비행기/차량/선박 advertise ~을 광고하다 range 종류, 제품군 lose A to B A를 B에게 빼앗기다 competitor 경쟁사, 경쟁자 reduce ~을 줄이다, 감소시키다

Paraphrase customers will stop choosing us and opt for one of our rivals instead
→ Losing customers to competitors

50. 시각자료를 보시오. 화자가 내일 항공사의 어떤 측면에 관해 논의할 것인가?
(A) 기내식
(B) 좌석의 편안함
(C) 오락 서비스
(D) 쇼핑

해설 담화 후반부에 화자가 내일 있을 회의에서 두 번째로 낮은 평점을 받은 항목에 관해 이야기하고 싶다고(I'd like to talk to you about the next lowest rating at our meeting tomorrow) 알리고 있다. 시각자료에서 평점이 가장 낮은 항목은 별 표기가 두 개인 기내식(IN-FLIGHT MEAL)이고, 두 번째로 낮은 항목이 별 표기가 세 개인 쇼핑(SHOPPING)이므로 (D)가 정답이다.

Part 5

51.
정답 (A)
해석 로리머 씨는 극심한 교통 혼잡 때문에 자신의 치과 예약 시간에 30분 늦었다.
해설 빈칸이 전치사와 명사구 사이에 위치해 있으므로 명사구를 수식할 형용사 자리이다. 따라서 (A) heavy가 정답이다.
어휘 dental 치과의 appointment 예약, 약속 heavy (정도, 양 등이) 심한, 많은 heavily (정도, 양 등이) 심하게, 세게 heaviness 무거움, 무게

52.
정답 (C)
해석 매튜 씨와 다이애나 씨는 내년에 자신들의 집을 매각용으로 내놓고 교외 지역으로 이사할 계획이다.
해설 빈칸이 to부정사로 쓰인 동사 put과 명사 사이에 위치해 있으므로 명사를 수식할 수 있는 소유격 대명사 (C) their가 정답이다.
어휘 put A up for sale A를 팔려고 내놓다 suburbs 교외 지역

53.
정답 (C)
해석 아폴론 주식회사는 다양한 보상 제도 선물로 직원들에게 보상함으로써 업무 만족도를 높게 유지한다.
해설 빈칸이 전치사와 명사구 사이에 위치해 있으므로 빈칸에는 이 명사구를 목적어로 취함과 동시에 전치사의 목적어 역할을 할 수 있는 동명사가 필요한 자리이므로 (C) rewarding이 정답이다.
어휘 satisfaction 만족(도) by (방법) ~함으로써, ~해서 incentive 보상책, 장려 정책, 격려금 reward ~에게 보상하다

54.
정답 (B)
해석 곧 있을 브리저튼 협회의 세미나들은 컴퓨터 프로그래밍에 관심이 있는 사람들이 누구든 매력적으로 느껴야 한다.
해설 빈칸 앞에 위치한 is interested는 전치사 in과 결합해 '~에 관심이 있다'라는 의미를 나타내므로 (B) in이 정답이다.
어휘 upcoming 곧 있을, 다가오는 appeal to ~에게 매력적이다, ~의 관심을 끌다 be interested in ~에 관심이 있다

55.
정답 (B)
해석 모든 회사 업무 파일은 기술자들이 네트워크 유지 관리 작업을 실시하기 전에 백업될 것입니다.

해설 빈칸 앞뒤로 주어와 동사가 포함된 절이 있으므로 빈칸은 접속사 자리이다. 또한, '기술자들이 유지 관리 작업을 실시하기 전에 파일이 백업될 것이다'와 같은 의미가 구성되어야 자연스러우므로 '~하기 전에'를 뜻하는 (B) before가 정답이다.

어휘 back up (파일 등) ~을 백업하다, (사람, 일 등) ~을 도와주다, ~을 지원하다 maintenance 유지 관리, 시설 관리 so that (목적) ~하도록, (결과) 그래서

56.

정답 (B)

해석 <밀버로우 데일리 뉴스>는 시장의 당선에 관한 기사를 빠르게 실었다.

해설 선택지가 모두 다른 부사로 구성되어 있어 해석을 통해 알맞은 어휘를 골라야 한다. 빈칸에 들어갈 부사는 기사를 실은 방식과 관련된 의미를 나타내야 하므로 '빠르게'를 뜻하는 (B) quickly가 정답이다.

어휘 publish (기사 등) ~을 싣다, ~을 출간하다 election 선거 timely 때에 알맞은, 시기 적절한 formerly 이전에, 과거에 extremely 극도로, 대단히

57.

정답 (B)

해석 힐 스트리트 커피 하우스는 전 세계 각지에서 나오는 50가지가 넘는 종류의 커피를 제공한다.

해설 빈칸이 형용사의 역할을 하는 숫자 표현 50과 전치사 of 사이에 위치해 있으므로 빈칸은 형용사의 수식을 받을 명사 자리이다. 따라서 (B) varieties가 정답이다.

어휘 originate from -에서 나오다, ~에서 비롯되다 varying 변화하는, 바뀌는 variety 종류, 품종 vary 서로 다르다, 바뀌다

58.

정답 (A)

해석 그 컨트리 클럽의 부지는 경험 많은 정원사들로 구성된 팀에 의해 관리된다.

해설 동사 look은 전치사 after와 결합해 '~을 관리하다, ~을 돌보다' 등을 의미하는데, 빈칸 뒤에 위치한 after 뒤에 목적어가 나타나 있지 않아 look after가 수동태로 쓰여야 한다는 것을 알 수 있으므로 과거분사 (A) looked가 정답이다.

어휘 grounds 부지, 구내 experienced 경험 많은 landscape gardener 정원사 look after ~을 관리하다, ~을 돌보다

59.

정답 (B)

해석 10년 전에 개장된, 그 아이스 스케이팅 링크는 지역 주민들에게 점점 더 많은 인기를 얻어 왔다.

해설 빈칸 앞에 기간을 나타내는 10 years가 쓰여 있으므로 기간 표

현과 결합해 '~ 전에'라는 의미로 과거 시점을 가리킬 때 사용하는 (B) ago가 정답이다.

어휘 increasingly 점점 더 popular with ~에게 인기 있는 once 한 번, (과거의) 한 때

60.

정답 (A)

해석 심각한 사고를 피하기 위해서, 모든 정제소 근로자들은 작업 중에 표준 안전 절차를 따라야 한다.

해설 선택지가 모두 다른 명사로 구성되어 있으므로 해석을 통해 알맞은 어휘를 골라야 한다. 동사 follow의 목적어 역할을 할 수 있으면서 빈칸 앞에 제시된 명사 safety와 함께 쓰여 심각한 사고를 피하기 위해 준수해야 할 것을 나타내야 하므로 '절차'라는 뜻의 (A) procedures가 정답이다.

어휘 serious 심각한 refinery 정제소, 정제기구 at work 일하는 중인, 작업 중인 development 발전, 개발 qualification 자격 요건

61.

정답 (B)

해석 스프리츠 퍼니싱스가 근육 및 관절 통증을 예방하는 인체 공학적인 사무용 가구의 새로운 제품 라인을 막 출시했다.

해설 선택지가 모두 다른 형용사로 구성되어 있으므로 해석을 통해 알맞은 어휘를 골라야 한다. 빈칸에 쓰일 형용사는 근육 및 관절 통증을 예방한다는 특징과 어울리는 의미를 지녀야 하므로 '인체 공학적인'을 뜻하는 (B) ergonomic이 정답이다.

어휘 prevent ~을 예방하다, ~을 방지하다 joint 관절 intrinsic 본질적인, 고유한 ergonomic 인체 공학적인 intangible 무형의, 손으로 만질 수 없는 extroverted 외향적인

62.

정답 (D)

해석 블루스카이 사는 캠핑과 하이킹을 위해 디자인된 합리적인 가격의 의류와 신발을 생산한다.

해설 빈칸이 동사와 목적어 역할을 하는 명사를 수식하는 분사 사이에 위치해 있다. 따라서 빈칸에는 과거분사 priced를 수식할 부사가 쓰여야 하므로 (D) reasonably가 정답이다.

어휘 reasonably 합리적으로, 저렴하게 priced 가격이 책정된 reason n. 이유, 근거 v. (근거를 바탕으로) 추론하다, 판단하다

63.

정답 (B)

해석 심슨 씨는 우리가 시장 연구 조사를 완료하는 마감시한을 연장해 주었다.

해설 빈칸 앞에 쓰인 동사 give는 두 개의 목적어를 필요로 하고, 빈칸 뒤에 사물 목적어 an extended deadline이 제시되어 있

으므로 빈칸은 사람 목적어 자리이다. 따라서 목적격 대명사 (B) us가 정답이다.

어휘 extended 연장된 complete ~을 완료하다 survey (설문) 조사

64.

정답 (A)

해석 신입사원들이 우리의 정책에 관해 배울 수 있도록 회사의 편람을 만들어 주십시오.

해설 빈칸 앞에는 명령문으로 된 절이, 빈칸 뒤에는 주어와 동사가 포함된 절이 위치해 있으므로 빈칸은 접속사 자리이다. 따라서 선택지에서 유일한 접속사인 (A) so that이 정답이다.

어휘 company handbook 회사의 편람 so that (목적) ~할 수 있도록, (결과) 그 결과, 그러므로 learn about ~에 관해 배우다, 알게 되다

65.

정답 (B)

해석 에쉬베르그 컨벤션 센터의 대강당을 확장하기 위한 건설 공사가 향후 8개월 동안 이행될 것입니다.

해설 선택지가 모두 다른 전치사로 구성되어 있으므로 빈칸 뒤에 제시된 명사의 특성을 살펴봐야 한다. 빈칸 뒤에 기간을 나타내는 명사가 있으므로 기간 명사와 함께 쓰여 '~동안'이라는 뜻을 나타내는 (B) over가 정답이다.

어휘 construction work 건설 공사 enlarge ~을 확장하다 carry out ~을 이행하다, 수행하다

66.

정답 (D)

해석 12월 마지막 주는 많은 회사들이 전반적인 소비자 지출의 급등을 아마도 알아차릴 시기이다.

해설 선택지가 관계사로 구성되어 있고, 빈칸 뒤에 완전한 구조의 절이 있으므로 빈칸은 관계부사 자리이다. 그런데 빈칸 앞 주어가 '12월 마지막 주'라는 시간을 나타내고 있으므로 빈칸 앞에 선행사 the time이 생략됐다는 것을 알 수 있다. 따라서 (D) when이 정답이다.

어휘 notice ~을 알아채다 surge 급등, 급상승 overall 전반적인 spending 지출

Part 6

67-70.

저희 잰더 프린팅은 여러분의 모든 홍보용 자료에 시선을 사로잡는 전문적인 모습을 67 제공해 드립니다. 저희는 아주 다양한 68 종류의 기업 고객들을 대상으로 전단과 포스터, 초대장, 그리고 안내 책자의 디자인 및 제작을 전문으로 합니다.

여러분께서 저희 서비스를 이용하실 때, VIP 회원 자격을 얻으실 수 있는 선택권도 있습니다. 회원으로서, 여러분께서는 저희 특급 서비스를 이용하실 수 있으며, 이는 일반적인 시간의 절반에 해당되는 시간에 주문이 완료될 수 있다는 의미입니다. 69 게다가, 회원 자격이 여러분께 여러 가지 할인을 제공해 드립니다. 대량 주문에 대해, 주문품 총액에 대해 최대 30퍼센트의 할인을 받으실 수 있으며, 절반 가격에 명함과 초대장 같은 더 작은 제품도 주문하실 수 있습니다.

저희 서비스 및 회원 70 약정과 관련해 더 많은 것을 알아보시려면, 오늘 (031)-555-0129번으로 저희에게 전화 주십시오.

어휘 promotional 홍보의 eye-catching 시선을 사로잡는, 눈길을 끄는 appearance 모습, 외관 specialize in ~을 전문으로 하다 flyer 전단 brochure 안내 책자, 소책자 diverse 다양한 option to do ~할 수 있는 선택권 obtain ~을 얻다, ~을 획득하다 take advantage of ~을 이용하다 express 특급의, 급행의 complete ~을 완료하다 half the 명사 ~의 절반 bulk 대량의 up to 최대 ~의 find out ~을 알아보다, ~을 파악하다

67.

정답 (B)

해설 빈칸 뒤에 이어지는 문장 및 다음 단락에 쓰여 있는 문장의 동사들이 현재시제 또는 가능성을 나타내는 조동사 can을 포함한 형태로 쓰여 업체의 일반적인 특징 및 고객이 이용 가능한 서비스를 소개하고 있다. 따라서 빈칸이 속한 문장에서 말하는 '시선을 사로잡는 전문적인 모습을 제공하는 일'은 업체의 일반적인 특징이거나 앞으로 이용할 수 있는 일에 해당되어야 하므로 앞으로의 일을 나타내는 미래시제 (B) will give가 정답이다.

어휘 would have p.p. ~했을 것이다

68.

정답 (D)

해설 빈칸 앞뒤에 위치한 형용사 diverse 및 「of + 복수명사」 구조와 어울리는 명사가 필요하므로 '종류' 등의 의미로 이 둘과 함께 다양성이나 폭넓은 선택 범위 등을 말할 때 사용하는 (D) range가 정답이다.

어휘 portion 부분, 분량, 1인분 range 종류, 제품군

69.

정답 (C)

해석 (A) 저희 잰더 프린팅은 잘 알려진 많은 기업 고객들과 함께 합니다.

(B) 저희 영업팀에 주문해 주셔서 감사 드립니다.

(C) 게다가, 회원 자격이 여러분께 여러 가지 할인을 제공해 드립니다.

(D) 예를 들어, 저희는 투어 및 행사에 필요한 팸플릿을 제공해 드릴 수 있습니다.

해설 빈칸 앞에 VIP 회원이 누릴 수 있는 혜택이 한 가지 언급되어 있으므로 '게다가, 더욱이'라는 의미로 추가 정보를 말할 때 사용하는 Moreover와 함께 또 다른 혜택을 추가로 알리는 역할을 하는 (C)가 정답이다.

어휘 **well-known** 잘 알려진 **place one's order with** ~에게 주문하다 **moreover** 게다가, 더욱이 **pamphlet** 팸플릿, 안내 책자

70.

정답 (C)

해설 빈칸 앞에 더 많은 것을 알아보라는 말이 쓰여 있어 빈칸 뒤에 위치한 명사구 our services and membership plans가 그 대상에 해당된다는 것을 알 수 있다. 따라서, '~에 관해, ~와 관련해'라는 의미로 대상이나 주제, 관련성 등을 나타낼 때 사용하는 (C) about이 정답이다.

어휘 **upon** ~하는 즉시, ~하자마자 **due to** ~로 인해, ~ 때문에

71-74.

수신: katysloane@gomail.com
발신: colinmaxwell@officemax.com
날짜: 7월 16일
제목: 회신: 빠진 주문품

슬론 씨께,

귀하께서 7월 8일에 저희를 통해 주문하신 베타테크 복사기 두 대와 관련된 귀하의 메시지를 방금 읽었습니다. 귀하의 말씀이 옳으며, 저희 정책에 따라, 귀하의 제품들이 영업일로 7일 이내에 배송되었어야 했습니다. 아직 그것들을 받지 못하셨다는 사실을 알고 매우 놀랐습니다. **71** 늘 그렇듯이, 저희는 배송에 대해 영업일로 최대 5일까지 감안하고 있습니다. **72** 제가 월간 배송 일정표를 찾아낼 수 있었습니다. 이 문서에 따르면, 귀하의 상품은 운송 중에 손상되어 배송회사에 의해 저희 창고로 반품되었습니다. 저희는 복사기 두 대가 더 들어오기를 기다려야 했으며, 이 제품들은 어제 귀하께 보내졌습니다. 주문품이 7월 20일까지 여전히 도착하지 않을 경우, 저희에게 **73** 연락 주시기 바랍니다. 귀하께 깊은 사과의 말씀 드립니다. 저희가 현 배송회사와 자주 문제를 겪습니다. 말씀 드리기 죄송하지만, 이러한 종류의 문제가 꽤 **74** 일반적인 일이 되어가고 있어서, 이를 처리하기 위해 저희가 조치를 취해야 할 것입니다.

안녕히 계십시오.

콜린 맥스웰
오피스 맥스 서플라이즈

어휘 **missing** 사라진, 빠진, 없는 **regarding** ~와 관련해 **as per** ~에 따라 **should have p.p.** ~했어야 했다 **a maximum of** 최대 ~의 **as always** 늘 그렇듯이 **locate** ~의 위치를 찾아내다 **in transit** 운송 중인 **utmost** 최고의, 최상의 **take action** 조치를 취하다 **address** v. (문제 등) ~을 처리하다, 다루다

71.

정답 (A)

해설 빈칸과 콤마 뒤에 위치한 문장이 현재시제 동사 allow와 함께 일반적으로 발생되는 일을 말하는 내용을 담고 있으므로 '늘 그렇듯이'를 뜻하는 (A) As always가 정답이다.

어휘 **after all** 결국에는, 어쨌든 **in that case** 그런 경우에 **in conclusion** 결론으로서, 마지막으로

72.

정답 (D)

해석 (A) 저희가 귀하의 지불액을 받았음을 확인해 드릴 수 있습니다.

(B) 배송 및 주문과 관련해 저희 정책을 참고하시기 바랍니다.

(C) 안타깝게도, 귀하께서 요청하신 상품이 더 이상 판매되지 않습니다.

(D) 제가 월간 배송 일정표를 찾아낼 수 있었습니다.

해설 빈칸 뒤 문장에 '이 문서에 따르면'이라는 말로 특정 문서에 담긴 내용을 바탕으로 운송 관련 정보를 알리는 말이 쓰여 있다. 따라서 this document에 해당되는 것으로서 운송 관련 정보를 확인할 수 있는 the monthly shipping schedule을 포함해 그 일정표를 찾은 사실을 언급하는 (D)가 정답이다.

어휘 **refer to** ~을 참고하다 **request** ~을 요청하다 **no longer** 더 이상 ~ 않다 **on sale** 판매 중인

73.

정답 (D)

해설 빈칸 앞에 please가 있으므로 이와 함께 명령문 구조를 이루는 동사원형 (D) contact가 정답이다.

74.

정답 (C)

해설 빈칸이 속한 but절의 주어 this type of issue는 앞 문장에서 현 배송 업체와 자주 발생된다고 말한 문제를 가리킨다. 따라서 자주 발생되는 상황과 어울리는 형용사 보어가 빈칸에 쓰여야 자연스러우므로 '일반적인, 전형적인'을 의미하는 (C) typical이 정답이다.

어휘 **beneficial** 유익한, 도움이 되는 **affordable** 가격이 알맞은, 구입 가능한

Part 7

75-76.

올 여름은 스플리쉬 스플래쉬 캐니언에서
더위를 날려보세요!

액션 리지 주식회사가 운영하는 스플리쉬 스플래쉬 캐니언은 햇빛을 즐기는 것과 동시에 여러분을 시원하게 해줄 수 있는 이상적인 환경을 제공합니다. 수백 만 달러 규모의 저희 워터파크는 1989년에 처음으로 개장하였으며, 오늘날 매우 다양한 관광명소를 자랑하고 있습니다. 저희는 국내에서 가장 속도가 빠른 워터 슬라이드와 가장 긴 급류 코스, 거대한 파도 풀, 여러 뛰어난 레스토랑, 그리고 주말마다 콘서트가 열리는 야외 무대도 가지고 있습니다. 일일 주차는 저렴하며, 구명 조끼는 대여 가능합니다.

스플리쉬 스플래쉬 캐니언에서의 즐거움과 모험이 있는 새로운 여름 시즌의 시작을 기념하여 75 6월 1일부터 구입 가능한 저희의 완전 새로운 여름 시즌 패스의 상세 정보를 알려드리게 되어 기쁩니다!

단 79.99 달러로, 시즌 패스 구매자는 다음의 혜택을 받으실 수 있습니다.
· 7월 1일부터 8월 31일까지 공원 무제한 입장
· 모든 음식과 음료 15% 할인
· 기프트샵 구매품 10% 할인
· 월 1회 동반 1인 무료
· 미니골프 코스와 고카트 무료 입장
· 76 요크톤 버스 터미널 왕복 셔틀버스 무료 이용

그리고 만약 2개 이상의 시즌 패스를 구입하신다면, 각 패스의 가격은 단 69.99 달러가 될 것입니다!

더 많은 내용을 알아보고 오늘 시즌 패스를 구매하시려면 www.splishsplashcanyon.com을 방문하시기 바랍니다!

어휘 operate ~을 운영하다 ideal 이상적인 multi-million-dollar 수백만 달러 규모의 boast ~을 뽐내다, 자랑하다 rafting 래프팅, 급류타기 massive 거대한 outstanding 우수한 life jacket 구명조끼 for rent 대여의, 대여용으로 announce ~을 발표하다, 알리다 brand new 완전 새로운 holder 소유자, 가지고 있는 사람 unlimited 무제한의 admission 입장 complimentary 무료의

75. 광고의 주된 목적은 무엇인가?
(A) 새로운 관광지를 알리는 것
(B) 워터파크의 역사를 설명하는 것
(C) 공원의 새로운 명소를 알리는 것
(D) 특별 계절 할인을 홍보하는 것

정답 (D)

해설 두 번째 문단에 6월 1일부터 구입 가능한 새로운 여름 시즌 패스의 상세 정보를 알려드리게 되어 기쁘다고(we are pleased

to announce the details of our brand new summer season pass, available from June 1) 말하고 있으므로 혜택의 세부 사항 홍보를 언급한 (D)가 정답이다.

어휘 publicize ~을 광고하다, 널리 알리다 tourist destination 관광지 promote ~을 홍보하다

76. 스플리쉬 스플래쉬 캐니언 시즌 패스를 구매하는 데에 있어 방문객들은 어떤 혜택을 받게 될 것인가?
(A) 더 낮은 콘서트 티켓 요금
(B) 무료 선물
(C) 교통 서비스 이용
(D) 1년 공원 입장권

정답 (C)

해설 방문객들이 받을 혜택들이 언급된 세 번째 문단 마지막 항목에 요크톤 버스 터미널 왕복 셔틀버스 이용이 무료라고(Free use of the shuttle bus service running to/from Yorkton Bus Terminal) 언급되어 있으므로 무료 교통수단을 언급한 (C)가 정답이다.

어휘 fee 요금 transportation 교통 access 접근, 입장

77-79.

샌디 [오후 2:14]
77 안녕하세요, 알렉 씨... 24일에 고객 서비스팀이 우리 건물로 이전할 거예요. 우리는 여전히 그들에게 가장 적합한 위치를 결정해야 해요.

알렉 [오후 2:20]
78 그 상황을 어제 프랭크 씨와 논의했는데, 그가 좋은 제안을 했어요. 선적과 하역 부서가 이 시설 내에서 가장 넓은 부분을 차지하고 있고, 그것은 식품 가공 시설 바로 옆 1층에 위치하고 있어요. 그 곳이 그들에게 가장 실용적이고 편리한 위치가 될 거예요.

샌디 [오후 2:22]
그 공간을 절반으로 나눠야 한다는 거예요?

알렉 [오후 2:25]
네. 선적과 하역 부서는 입구에서 가장 가까운 곳에 남아 있을 수 있고, 고객 서비스 부서는 그들과 긴밀하게 작업해야 하니까요.

샌디 [오후 2:30]
그것은 잘 안될 수도 있어요. 79 그 방의 구역에서는 와이파이가 잘 안 터져요. 그것이 바로 현재 그곳에 컴퓨터가 설치되어 있지 않은 이유예요. 고객 서비스 부서는 항상 고속 인터넷 연결이 필요해요.

알렉 [오후 2:35]
그건 쉽게 해결 가능해요. 신호를 증대시킬 무선 라우터를 설치하기 위해 기술자를 부를 수 있어요. 사실, 방금 4시 회의가 취소되어서, 제가 그때 필요한 부서에게 연락을 할게요. 어떻게 되어가는지 알려 드릴게요.

샌디 [오후 2:39]
좋아요. 고마워요.

어휘 relocate ~을 이전하다 square footage 제곱 피트, 평방 피트 processing 가공, 처리 functional 기능적인, 실용적인 divide ~을 나누다 in half 절반으로 remain close to ~에 가까이 있다 work closely with ~와 긴밀히 협력하다 work out 해결하다, 만들어 내다 unreliable 신뢰할 수 없는 at all times 늘, 항상 fix 해결책 boost ~을 증대하다 router 중계 장치, 라우터

77. 이 회사에 대해서 알 수 있는 것은 무엇인가?
(A) 신입 직원들을 구하고 있다.
(B) 한 부서를 이동시키고 있다.
(C) 인터넷 제공업체를 바꾸고 있다.
(D) 새 컴퓨터들을 구매하고 있다.

정답 (B)

해설 샌디 씨의 첫번째 메시지에서 고객 서비스팀이 이전할 것(The Customer Service team will be relocating to)이라는 내용이 언급되어 있으므로 (B)가 정답이다.

어휘 seek ~을 찾다, 구하다 move ~을 이동시키다 switch ~을 교환하다, 대체하다

78. 프랭크 씨가 고객서비스 팀원들에 대해서 언급한 것은 무엇인가?
(A) 그들이 인터넷 연결에 대해서 불평을 했다.
(B) 그들이 선적과 하역 부서 직원들을 대체하게 될 것이다.
(C) 그들은 24일날 도착할 것이다.
(D) 그들은 1층에 위치해야만 한다.

정답 (D)

해설 두 번째 메시지에서 알렉 씨가 어제 프랭크 씨와 논의한 것을 언급하며, 선적 및 하역 부서가 1층에 식품 가공 시설 옆에 크게 자리잡고 있는데, 이 공간이 고객 서비스팀에게 가장 실용적이고 편리한 위치가 될 것이라고(Shipping and Receiving has the largest square footage in the facility ~ It would be the most functional and convenient location for them) 말하고 있다. 따라서 프랭크 씨가 고객 서비스팀이 1층에 위치해야 한다고 생각하고 있으므로 (D)가 정답이다.

어휘 replace ~을 대체하다 be situated 위치하다

79. 오후 2시 30분에 샌디 씨가 "That might not work out"라고 말한 의미는 무엇인가?
(A) 고객 서비스 직원들이 생산적이지 않다고 생각한다.
(B) 어떤 방이 고객 서비스 부서에 적합하지 않다고 생각한다.
(C) 프로젝트 날짜를 변경하는 것을 권장한다.
(D) 선적 및 하역 부서에서 일하기를 원한다.

정답 (B)

해설 제시된 메시지 바로 앞 내용을 살펴보면 프랭크 씨가 고객 서비

스팀이 1층으로 이전하는 것을 동의하고 있다. 그런데 이에 대해 샌디 씨가 그 방의 와이파이가 좋지 않아서 컴퓨터가 설치되어 있지 않다고(The Wi-Fi is unreliable in that sections of the room. That is why no computers are currently set up there) 언급하고 있다. 따라서 샌디 씨는 1층의 공간이 고객 서비스팀에게 적절하지 않다는 것을 말한 것이므로 (B)가 정답이다.

어휘 unproductive 비생산적인 unsuitable 적합하지 않은

80-82.

수신: 전 직원
82 **발신:** 올리버 카루더스
주제: 연례 직원 파티
날짜: 10월 29일

안녕하세요,

우리는 모두 회계연도 말이 다가옴에 따라 긴장이 풀려가고 있습니다. 여러분 모두가 마땅한 휴식을 기대하고 있으리라 믿습니다. 팀으로서 우리는 매우 생산적인 한 해를 가졌고, **82** 이곳 PQR 사의 경영진을 대신해서, **80** 여러분의 동료들을 편안한 환경에서 더 잘 알 수 있는 기회를 제공하기 위해 여러분을 연례 직원 파티에 초대하고 싶습니다. 여러분 모두 그럴 자격이 있습니다!

이 행사는 11월 8일 오후 6시에 라이트만 호텔의 연회장에서 열릴 예정입니다. 스톤월 케이터링에서 음식을 준비할 것입니다. 파티는 인기 있는 코미디언 웨인 랠리 씨뿐만 아니라 라이브만 호텔 밴드에 의해 제공될 것입니다.

저희는 여러분들 중 많은 사람들이 아이를 가지고 있기 때문에 저녁 행사에 참여하는 것이 어렵다는 것을 이해합니다. 저희는 가능한 한 많은 사람들을 수용하고 싶기 때문에, 파티가 열리는 날 밤에 무료로 아이를 봐줄 수 있는 육아 담당인을 고용했습니다. 아이들은 건강에 좋은 식사를 제공 받을 것이고 그 다음에는 가족 영화가 상영될 것입니다. 자격을 갖춘 육아 담당인들이 그곳에 와서 아이들이 필요한 것들을 돌봐 줄 것입니다. **81** 영화가 끝난 후에는, 부모들이 집에 갈 준비가 될 때까지 아이들을 즐겁게 해줄 수 있는 게임과 공예가 있습니다.

그 곳에서 모두를 뵙게 되기를 진심으로 바랍니다!

어휘 wind down 이완하다, 태업이 풀리다, 긴장을 풀다 fiscal year 회계연도 well-deserved 마땅한 on behalf of ~을 대신하여 relaxed 편안한 deserve ~을 누릴 자격이 있다 cater ~에게 음식을 공급하다 function 행사 accommodate ~을 수용하다 feed ~을 먹이다 be followed by ~이 이어지다 arts and crafts 공예 youngster 아이, 청소년 keep A entertained A를 계속 즐겁게 하다

80. 이 이메일의 주요 목적은 무엇인가?

    (A) 팀에게 성공적 회계연도에 대한 축하를 하려고

    (B) 직원들을 회사 축하 파티에 초대하려고

    (C) 직원들이 추가 보너스를 받을 것임을 알리려고

    (D) 직원 파티를 하는 동안 육아 서비스를 요청하려고

정답 (B)

해설 첫 번째 문단 후반부에서 연례 직원 파티에 초대하고 싶다고 (invite you to our annual staff party) 밝히고 있다. 따라서 이메일의 목적은 파티 초대임을 알 수 있으므로 (B)가 정답이다.

어휘 celebratory 축하의 inform ~을 알리다 request ~을 요청하다

81. 아이들이 즐기게 되는 것으로 언급되지 않은 것은 무엇인가?

    (A) 영화

    (B) 음악

    (C) 게임

    (D) 미술과 공예

정답 (B)

해설 세 번째 문단에서 영화가 끝난 후에 부모들이 집에 갈 준비가 될 때까지 아이들을 즐겁게 해줄 수 있는 게임과 공예가 있을 것이라는(After the movie, there will be games and arts and crafts to keep the youngsters entertained until their parents are ready to go home) 정보를 제시하고 있으므로 이 중 언급되지 않은 (B)가 정답이다.

82. 카루더스 씨에 대해서 추론할 수 있는 것은 무엇인가?

    (A) 그는 월간 회의를 계획 중이다.

    (B) 그는 매출에 대해 걱정한다.

    (C) 그는 신규 직원을 고용할 계획이다.

    (D) 그는 경영진을 대표한다.

정답 (D)

해설 첫 번째 문단에서 이메일을 보낸 목적을 설명하며 이곳 경영진을 대신해서(on behalf of the management here)라는 말이 언급되어 있고, 지문 상단에 발신인이 올리버 카루더스(From: Oliver Carruthers)이므로 (D)가 정답이다.

어휘 concerned 걱정하는 represent ~을 대표하다

83-86.

공사 개시 예정인 MJ 메가몰

85 (2월 26일) - 밀튼 제임스 홀딩스 주식회사는 MJ 메가몰의 공사가 4월에 진행될 예정이라고 어제 발표했습니다. 이 신규 사업은 이 몰에 대해 제안된 장소인 데일타운의 주민들이 공사 계획에 대해 항의한 뒤로 지연된 바 있습니다. 83 많은 주민들은 운전자 수의 불가피한 증가로 인해 도시 거리가 가득 차고 이용 가능한 주차 공간이 부족해지는 결과를 낳을 것이라고 생각합니다. 하지만, 이 주민들은 8억 5천만 달러가 넘는 비용이 투입되는 이 프로젝트를 막기 위한 노력에 있어 궁극적으로 성공하지 못했습니다.

---

85 밀튼 제임스 홀딩스 주식회사의 대표이사인 윌리엄 존스 씨는 이 몰의 주차장이 6,700대라는 인상적인 차량 수용 규모를 갖게 된다는 점을 강조하는 것으로 수 차례 그러한 우려를 진정시키기 위해 시도했습니다. — [1] —. 이 거대한 쇼핑 센터는 다수의 인기 장소뿐만 아니라 수백 개의 소매점도 포함할 것입니다. 수족관을 지으려던 계획이 폐기되기는 했지만, 쇼핑객들은 여전히 84(A) 84(B) 84(D) 86 12개의 상영관이 있는 극장에서 영화를 즐기고, 아이스 스케이트를 타러 갈 수 있으며, 미니 골프 코스에서 18개 홀 경기를 할 수도 있을 것입니다. — [2] —.

85 밀튼 제임스 홀딩스 주식회사는 MJ 메가몰에 관한 더 많은 상세 정보를 알리기 위해 다음 달에 공식 기자 회견을 개최할 것입니다. — [3] —. 85 이 회사의 대표이사가 이 프로젝트를 맡아 작업한 수석 건축가의 도움을 받아 대부분의 질문에 답변할 것입니다. — [4] —. 첫 상업 소매업체들이 지금으로부터 약 2년 후에 입점할 것으로 예상됩니다.

어휘 set to do ~할 예정인 underway 진행 중인 venture (모험적인) 신규 사업 protest against ~에 대해 항의하다 inevitable 불가피한 motorist 운전자 result in ~라는 결과를 낳다, ~을 초래하다 packed 가득 찬 ultimately 궁극적으로, 결국 in excess of ~을 넘는, ~을 초과하는 attempt to do ~하려 시도하다 ease ~을 진정시키다, ~을 완화하다 fear 우려, 두려움 on a number of occasions 수 차례, 여러 번 stress that ~임을 강조하다 capacity 수용 규모 massive 거대한 attraction 인기 장소, 명소 as well as ~뿐만 아니라 ···도 retail outlet 소매점 scrap (계획 등) ~을 폐기하다 press conference 기자 회견 architect 건축가 commercial 상업적인 retailer 소매업체, 소매업자

83. 지역 주민들이 왜 MJ 메가몰의 공사에 반대했는가?

    (A) 부동산 가격이 오르도록 초래할 것이다.

    (B) 교통 혼잡을 증가시킬 것이다.

    (C) 지역 업체들에게 해가 될 것이다.

    (D) 너무 많은 비용이 들 것이다.

정답 (B)

해설 많은 주민들이 첫 단락에 운전자 수의 불가피한 증가로 인해 도시 거리가 가득 차고 이용 가능한 주차 공간이 부족해지는 결과를 낳을 것으로 생각한다고(the inevitable rise in the number of motorists will result in packed city streets and a lack of available parking spaces) 쓰여 있다. 이는 교통 혼잡 문제가 커지는 것에 대한 우려를 의미하므로 (B)가 정답이다.

어휘 oppose ~에 반대하다 cause A to do A에게 ~하도록 초래하다 property 부동산, 건물 harm ~에 해가 되다

84. 새 쇼핑몰의 특징이 되지 않는 것은 무엇인가?

    (A) 극장

    (B) 아이스 링크

    (C) 수족관

(D) 골프 연습장

정답 (C)

해설 두 번째 단락 후반부에 12개의 상영관이 있는 극장에서 영화를 즐기고, 아이스 스케이트를 탈 수 있으며, 미니 골프 코스에서 18개 홀 경기를 할 수 있다고(shoppers will still be able to enjoy films at a 12-screen cinema, go ice skating, and play 18 holes on the miniature golf course) 설명한 부분에서 (A)와 (B), 그리고 (D)를 모두 확인할 수 있다. 하지만 같은 문장에 수족관을 짓는 계획은 폐기되었다고 쓰여 있으므로 (C)가 정답이다.

---

85. 3월에 무슨 일이 있을 것으로 예상되는가?
(A) 존스 씨가 우려하는 주민들과 만날 것이다.
(B) MJ 메가몰의 공사가 시작될 것이다.
(C) 존스 씨가 기자 회견에 참석할 것이다.
(D) 소매업체들이 MJ 메가몰에 입점할 것이다.

정답 (C)

해설 지문 시작 부분에 현재 날짜가 2월 26일로(February 26) 표기되어 있어, 질문에 언급된 3월은 다음 달에 해당된다. 이 시점과 관련해, 세 번째 단락에 다음 달에 기자 회견을 연다는 (Milton James Holdings Inc. will hold an official press conference next month) 말과 함께 대표이사가 프로젝트 관련 질문에 답변한다고(The company's CEO will answer most questions) 알리고 있고, 두 번째 단락에 대표이사 이름이 윌리엄 존스라고(The CEO of Milton James Holdings Inc., Mr. William Jones) 쓰여 있다. 따라서 존스 씨가 3월에 열리는 기자 회견에 참석한다는 것을 알 수 있으므로 (C)가 정답이다.

어휘 meet with (약속하고) ~와 만나다 concerned 우려하는, 걱정하는

---

86. [1], [2], [3], [4]로 표기된 위치들 중에서, 다음 문장이 들어가기에 가장 적절한 곳은 어디인가?

"각각의 새 편의시설은 별도의 입장료를 필요로 할 것입니다."

(A) [1]
(B) [2]
(C) [3]
(D) [4]

정답 (B)

해설 제시된 문장은 앞서 언급된 특정 편의시설 각각을 Each of the new amenities로 지칭해 입장료와 관련된 정보를 제공하고 있다. 따라서 극장과 스케이트장, 골프장 등의 특정 시설을 설명하는 문장 뒤에 위치한 [2]에 들어가 각 시설의 이용 방법과 관련된 입장료 정보를 제공하는 흐름이 되어야 자연스러우므로 (B)가 정답이다.

어휘 amenities 편의시설 require ~을 필요로 하다 separate 별도의, 분리된 admission fee 입장료

87-90.

> **89** 작년의 최고 신인 작가상 수상자인 이니 하모르 씨가 최근 올해의 수상자인 카라 골 씨와 골 씨의 신규 도서 <트라잉 투 타이>에 관해 이야기 나눌 기회가 있었습니다.
>
> **Q:** 골 씨, 최근 작가 세계에 발을 들이셨고, 첫 번째 도서인 <트라잉 투 다이>가 즉시 대단한 히트 작품이 되었습니다. 저는 개인적으로 이 책을 읽는 것이 즐거웠지만, 아직 읽어 볼 기회가 없었던 분들을 위해 이 책이 무엇에 관한 것인지를 저희에게 조금 더 말씀해 주시겠습니까?
>
> **A:** 물론이죠, 하모르 씨. 이 책은, 사실, 믿으실지 모르겠지만, **88** 제가 고등학교 교사였을 때 아이들이 겪는 것을 봐 왔던 일들을 담고 있습니다. 이야기는 주인공인 찰리 웬실이 도시의 어두운 곳에서 자라면서 겪는 모든 종류의 사건과 문제에 대처해 나가는 모습을 따라 갑니다.
>
> **Q:** 이런 종류의 글쓰기를 하시는 주된 이유 중 하나가 무엇인가요?
>
> **A:** 저, 제가 돌이켜 생각해 보니까, **87** 저는 그저 십대들에게 그들이 읽을 수 있고 관련 지을 수 있는 것을 주고 싶어했던 것 같아요. 사람들이 항상 하는 말이지만, 십대가 된다는 건 정말 누군가의 삶에서 중요한 시기입니다. 우리가 십대로서 거치는 것들이 정말로 우리가 더 나이가 들었을 때 어떤 종류의 사람이 되는지에 대한 토대를 만들어 줍니다.
>
> **Q:** 그 책으로 많은 독자들의 마음에 다가간 게 분명합니다. 그 책이 대단한 성공을 이뤘어요. 그리고, 그러한 성공과 함께, 또 다른 유사한 이야기를 쓰실 계획이 있으신가요?
>
> **A:** 그 질문을 많이 받고 있는데, 또 다른 책에 대한 계획은 없다는 점을 말씀 드리게 되어 유감입니다. **90** 제가 사실 제 책 속의 주인공 같은 아이들이 학교에 계속 머무르고 심지어 학교 생활을 잘 할 수 있도록 돕기 위해 현재 여러 학교에서 강연하느라 여념이 없습니다.

어휘 scene ~계, 분야 instantly 즉시 take a look 한 번 보다 believe it or not 믿을지 모르겠지만 go through ~을 겪다, 거치다 protagonist 주인공 cope with ~에 대처하다 think back on ~에 대해 돌이켜 생각하다 relate to ~와 관련 짓다 set the groundwork 토대를 세우다 reach ~에 도달하다, 이르다 get asked that a lot 그 질문을 많이 받다 preoccupied 여념이 없는, 몰두해있는 at the moment 현재

---

87. 누가 <트라잉 투 타이>의 대상 독자일 가능성이 가장 큰가?
(A) 학부모들
(B) 십대들
(C) 유아들
(D) 교사들

정답 (B)

해설 두 번째 답변에 십대들이 읽을 수 있고 관련 지을 수 있는 것을 주고 싶어했던 것 같다고(I think I just wanted to give teenagers something they could read and relate to)

알리고 있으므로 십대들이 대상 독자인 것으로 볼 수 있다. 따라서 (B)가 정답이다.

어휘 intended 대상이 되는, 의도된 audience 독자, 관객, 청중, 시청자 toddler 유아

88. 골 씨의 이전 직업은 무엇이었는가?
(A) 기자
(B) 교사
(C) 학교 교장
(D) 출판인

정답 (B)

해설 첫 번째 답변에 골 씨 자신이 이전에 고등학교 교사였을 때 아이들이 겪는 것을 봐 온 일들을 책에 담았다고(contains things that I've seen kids go through when I used to be a high school teacher) 밝히고 있다. 따라서 (B)가 정답이다.

어휘 profession 직업

89. 하모르 씨에 관해 암시된 것은 무엇인가?
(A) 아직 골 씨의 책을 읽어 보지 않았다.
(B) 상을 받은 책을 집필했다.
(C) 학교에서 영어를 가르친다.
(D) 골 씨와 책 한 권을 공동 집필했다.

정답 (B)

해설 지문이 시작되는 첫 번째 문장에 이니 하모르 씨가 작년의 최고 신인 작가상 수상자라고(Inni Hamor, winner of last year's Best New Author Award) 소개하고 있다. 이는 책을 집필해 상을 받았다는 뜻이므로 (B)가 정답이다.

어휘 award-winning 상을 받은, 수상 경력이 있는 co-write ~을 공동 집필하다

90. 골 씨의 현재 프로젝트는 무엇을 포함하는가?
(A) 여러 학교에서 학생들에게 강연하는 일
(B) 한 가지 이야기에 대한 주제를 조사하는 일
(C) 젊은 작가들을 위한 세미나를 실시하는 일
(D) 장애가 있는 학생들을 가르치는 일

정답 (A)

해설 지문 맨 마지막 문장에 골 씨가 자신의 책 속 주인공 같은 아이들이 학교에 계속 머무르고 학교 생활을 잘 할 수 있도록 돕기 위해 현재 여러 학교에서 강연하느라 여념이 없다고(I'm actually preoccupied at the moment with speaking at schools to help kids) 알리고 있으므로 (A)가 정답이다.

어휘 conduct ~을 실시하다, 수행하다 handicapped 장애가 있는

91-95.

브럼튼 가제트

요즘, 리자 테틀리 씨는 쿠키 반죽과 초콜릿 칩, 견과류, 그리고 건포도에 몰두해 있는 자신을 자주 보게 됩니다. 빠르게 성장하고 있는 리자 씨의 업체, 테틀리즈 티 숍은 아주 다양한 차와 커피를 제공하지만, 사람들을 거리를 따라 줄지어 늘어서게 만드는 것은 갓 구운 쿠키입니다. 어머니와 함께 굽던 어린 시절의 경험을 바탕으로, 이 매장의 소유주는 지역 주민들과 관광객들 모두에게 분명 똑같이 사랑 받는 달콤한 먹거리를 만들어냈습니다.

95 수년 동안 성공적인 광고 이사로 재직했던 테틀리 씨는 메뉴에 홈메이드 케이크와 쿠키를 추가한 이후로 매장의 손님 숫자를 거의 두 배로 늘렸습니다. 고객들 사이에서 관심을 불러 일으키기 위한 노력의 일환으로, 전통적인 종류만 고집하는 것이 아니라, **91** 체리-민트 그리고 오렌지-아몬드 쿠키 같은 맛으로 종종 실험하기도 합니다. "사실, 저는 집에서 저만의 케이크와 쿠키를 항상 구워 왔고, 심지어 제가 사무실에서 여전히 근무하면서 최근 몇 년 동안에도 그렇게 해 왔어요,"라고 리자 씨는 말합니다. "결국, 제 매장을 열기 위한 욕구가 제 직장에서의 퇴사로 이어졌고, 제 비즈니스 관련 경험이 실제로 새로운 사업에 있어 저에게 도움이 되어 왔습니다."

테틀리즈 티 숍에 들르는 고객들은 리즈 씨의 끝없는 노력 및 신선하게 그리고 현장에서 쿠키를 굽는 데에 대한 헌신 모두에 대해 이 소유주에게 높은 **92** 점수를 줍니다. **93** 일단 관광 시즌이 끝나면 많은 매장들이 겨울 기간 내내 문을 닫는 반면, 테틀리즈 티 숍은 따뜻하고 부드러운 쿠키를 손에 넣기를 간절히 바라는 지역 주민들이 늘어선 긴 줄을 여전히 자랑합니다. 이렇게 충성스러운 고객층으로 인해, 테틀리 씨가 두 번째 사업 지점을 개장할 계획을 갖고 있는 것도 전혀 놀라운 일이 아닙니다.

테틀리즈 티 숍은 브럼튼 시내 소여 지하철역 3번 출구 근처, 채닝 크로스 버스 정류장 맞은편에 위치해 있습니다.

어휘 elbow-deep in ~에 몰두한, ~에 빠진 draw on ~을 바탕으로 하다, ~에 의존하다 treat 특별한 것, 선물, 한턱 apparently 분명 adore ~을 아주 좋아하다 A and B alike A와 B 둘 모두 똑같이 serve as ~로서 재직하다, ~의 역할을 하다 generate interest among ~ 사이에서 관심을 불러 일으키다 stick to ~을 고집하다, ~을 고수하다 urge to do ~하고 싶은 욕구, 충동 venture (모험적) 사업 stop by ~에 들르다 proprietor 소유주 dedication to -ing ~하는 데 대한 헌신, 전념 on-site 현장의 boast ~을 자랑하다 get one's hands on ~을 손에 넣다 clientele 고객 층 come as no surprise 전혀 놀랍지 않다

수신: 리자 테틀리 <manager@tetleyteashop.com>
발신: 마크 바우어 <mbauer@prismad.com>
제목: 최근의 기사
날짜: 12월 10일

안녕하세요. 리자 씨,

94 어제 나온 브럼튼 가제트에 실린 기사를 막 다 읽어 봤는데, 당신 매장이 정말로 잘 되어 가고 있는 것 같아요. 잘 돼서 너무 기쁩니다! 제가 곧 들러서 메뉴에 있는 몇 가지를 한 번 먹어 보겠다고 약속 드릴게요! 우리는 여전히 이곳 사무실에서 당신에 대해 애정을 갖고 이야기하고 있으며, 95 우리 모두는 우리 고객들을 위한 프로젝트에 당신과 함께 작업하던 때를 그리워하고 있어요. 그 외에, 이곳에서의 일들도 잘 되어 가고 있어서, 우리가 곧 신규 고객들을 맡을 몇몇 추가 직원을 고용해야 합니다.

곧 뵐 수 있기를 바랍니다!

안녕히 계십시오.

마크

어휘 **piece** (글, 그림, 음악 등의) 한 점, 작품 **drop by** 들르다 **fondly** 애정을 갖고 **apart from** ~ 외에(도) **handle** ~을 다루다, 처리하다

91. 테틀리 씨에 관해 암시된 것은 무엇인가?
(A) 가족 운영 사업에 관련되어 있다.
(B) 독특한 종류의 쿠키를 만든다.
(C) 두 번째 사업 지점을 막 개업했다.
(D) 광고를 낼 계획이다.

정답 (B)

해설 첫 지문 두 번째 단락에 체리-민트 그리고 오렌지-아몬드 쿠키 같은 맛으로 종종 실험하기도 한다는(often experiments with flavors such as cherry-mint and orange-almond cookies) 말이 쓰여 있는데, 이는 독특한 쿠키도 만든다는 뜻이므로 (B)가 정답이다.

어휘 **be involved in** ~에 관련되어 있다 **unique** 독특한, 특별한 **place an advertisement** 광고를 내다

92. 기사에서, 세 번째 단락, 첫 번째 줄의 단어 "marks"와 의미가 가장 가까운 것은 무엇인가?
(A) 가격
(B) 규제
(C) 평점
(D) 기준

정답 (C)

해설 해당 문장에서 marks를 수식하는 형용사로 high가 쓰여 있고, 고객들이 테틀리 씨의 노력과 헌신에 대해 주는 것으로 언급되어 있다. 즉, 노력하고 헌신하는 모습에 높은 점수를 준다는 의미로 생각할 수 있으므로 점수와 유사한 의미로 '평점'을 뜻하는 (C) ratings가 정답이다.

93. 테틀리즈 티 숍에 관해 언급되지 않은 것은 무엇인가?
(A) 겨울철에는 문을 닫는다.
(B) 대중 교통으로 쉽게 접근할 수 있다.
(C) 점점 더 인기가 많아졌다.
(D) 쿠키 외에 다른 음식도 판매한다.

정답 (A)

해설 첫 지문 세 번째 단락에 관광 시즌이 끝나면 많은 매장들이 겨울 기간 내내 문을 닫지만, 테틀리즈 티 숍은 따뜻하고 부드러운 쿠키를 손에 넣기를 간절히 바라는 지역 주민들이 늘어선 긴 줄을 자랑한다고(While many shops close through the winter months once the tourist season ends, Tetley's Tea Shop still boasts a long line of local residents) 언급되어 있으므로 (A)가 정답이다.

어휘 **easily accessible** 쉽게 접근할 수 있는 **public transportation** 대중 교통 **increasingly** 점점 더

94. 바우어 씨는 왜 이메일을 보냈는가?
(A) 테틀리 씨가 회의에 참석하도록 요청하기 위해
(B) 테틀리 씨에게 신규 고객에 대한 도움을 요청하기 위해
(C) 테틀리 씨가 신입 직원을 고용하고 있는지 묻기 위해
(D) 성공에 대해 테틀리 씨를 축하해 주기 위해

정답 (D)

해설 두 번째 지문 시작 부분에 브럼튼 가제트에 실린 기사를 읽은 사실과 테틀리 씨의 매장이 정말로 잘 되어 가고 있는 것 같아서 너무 기쁘다는 말이(I just finished reading the piece in yesterday's Brumpton Gazette, and it really sounds like your business is doing well. I'm so happy for you) 쓰여 있으므로 성공에 대한 축하를 의미하는 (D)가 정답이다.

95. 바우어 씨는 어디에서 일하고 있을 것 같은가?
(A) 출판사에서
(B) 식품 제조사에서
(C) 금융 서비스 업체에서
(D) 광고 대행사에서

정답 (D)

해설 두 번째 중반부에 고객들을 위한 프로젝트에 테틀리 씨와 함께 작업하던 때를 그리워하고 있다는(we all miss collaborating with you on projects for our clients) 말이 쓰여 있고, 첫 지문 두 번째 단락에 테틀리 씨가 수년 동안 성공적인 광고 이사로 재직했다고(Ms. Tetley, who served as a successful advertising executive for several years) 알리는 말이 있으므로 광고 업체를 뜻하는 (D)가 정답이다.

어휘 **manufacturer** 제조사 **financial** 금융의, 재무의 **agency** 대행사, 회사

96-100.

수신: 다이앤 생스터 <dsangster@dukehotel.com>
발신: 에드워드 바 <ebarr@dukehotel.com>
제목: 직원 유니폼
날짜: 2월 8일

생스터 씨께,

96 이곳 듀크 호텔의 우리 직원들을 위해 제가 선택한 근무용 유니폼 목록을 첨부해 드렸습니다. 이 유니폼들은 모두 벨맨 워크 어타이어 사에서 제조한 고품질 의복들로 구성되어 있으며, 우리 호텔의 스타일과 완벽하게 어울린다고 생각합니다.

이 유니폼들은 오리엔테이션 기간 중에 전 직원에게 지급될 것이며, 이는 2월 21일에 시작되어 2월 25일에 종료됩니다. 따라서, 반드시 이 제품들이 모두 오리엔테이션 첫째 날 전에 이곳으로 도착해야 합니다. 가능하다면, 98 저는 가급적 빨리 4823번을 받아보고 싶은데, 그 직원들이 나머지 직원들보다 일주일 더 빨리 근무를 시작할 것이기 때문입니다. 저는 어떠한 잠재적 차질도 피하고자 하는데, 3월 1일에 있을 우리 호텔의 개장식이 97 다가오고 있기 때문입니다.

어떤 질문이든 있으시면 저에게 연락 주시기 바랍니다.

안녕히 계십시오.

에드워드 바, 총무부장
더 듀크 호텔

어휘 attach ~을 첨부하다 consist of ~로 구성되다 garment 의복, 복장 hand out ~을 나눠주다 if at all possible 가능하다면 as soon as possible 가급적 빨리, 가능한 한 빨리 setback 차질 approach ~에 다가가다, 다가오다 get in touch with ~에게 연락하다

필요한 유니폼:

프런트 데스크 직원 (남성): #1186 하이 버튼 울 조끼 & 바지
프런트 데스크 직원 (여성): #4214 싱글 브레스티드 정장 코트 & 치마
98 객실 관리 직원: #4823 극세사 청소용 튜닉
100 레스토랑 종업원: #R45 밴디드 칼라 셔츠 & 조끼

어휘 required 필요한, 필수의 housekeeping 객실 관리

수신: 에드워드 바 <ebarr@dukehotel.com>
발신: 다이앤 생스터 <dsangster@dukehotel.com>
제목: 회신: 직원 유니폼
날짜: 2월 9일

바 씨께,

하이 버튼 울 조끼 & 바지 및 싱글 브레스티드 정장 코트 & 치마가 해당 직원들에게 좋은 선택이라는 데 분명 동의하기는 하지만, 그 재질이 너무 따뜻할 수도 있을지 궁금합니다. 99 직원들이 너무 덥거나 답답하게 느끼면 효과적으로 업무를 수행하는 것

이 아주 어려울 수 있습니다. 어떻게 생각하세요?

100 저는 밴디드 칼라 셔츠 & 조끼를 제외하고 골라 주신 모든 유니폼을 주문할 수 있습니다. 어떤 이유에선지, 벨맨에서 최근 그 제품을 단종했지만, 심슨 사에 거의 정확히 동일한 의복이 있습니다. 대신 그쪽에서 주문할까요? 저는 분명 오리엔테이션이 시작되기 한참 전인 2월 15일까지 모든 유니폼을 준비시켜 둘 것입니다.

안녕히 계십시오.

다이앤 생스터, 인사부장
더 듀크 호텔

어휘 agree that ~임에 동의하다 wonder if ~인지 궁금하다 duty 업무, 직무 effectively 효과적으로 stuffy (공기가 안 통해) 답답한 pick out ~을 고르다 except for ~을 제외하고 discontinue ~을 단종하다 have A ready A를 준비시키다

96. 바 씨는 왜 생스터 씨에게 연락했는가?
  (A) 자신이 선호하는 것을 알리기 위해
  (B) 오리엔테이션 일정을 설명하기 위해
  (C) 해당 호텔을 방문할 것임을 확인해 주기 위해
  (D) 함께 하는 회의 시간을 마련하기 위해

정답 (A)

해설 첫 지문 첫 단락에 듀크 호텔의 직원들을 위해 자신이 선택한 근무용 유니폼 목록을 첨부했다고(I have attached a list of the work uniforms I have chosen for our staff here at the Duke Hotel) 알리면서 유니폼과 관련된 선호도를 설명하고 있으므로 (A)가 정답이다.

어휘 preference 선호(하는 것) arrange ~을 마련하다, 조치하다

97. 첫 번째 이메일에서, 두 번째 단락, 다섯 번째 줄의 단어 "approach"와 의미가 가장 가까운 것은 무엇인가?
  (A) 진척되다
  (B) 계산하다
  (C) 전략을 세우다
  (D) 가까워지다

정답 (D)

해설 해당 문장에서 동사 approach의 목적어로 호텔의 개장일을 의미하는 our hotel's grand opening day가 쓰여 있다. 따라서 개장되는 시점에 다가가고 있다는 의미로 쓰인 말이라는 것을 알 수 있으므로 '가까워지다'라는 의미로 동사로도 쓰이는 (D) near가 정답이다.

98. 바 씨에 따르면, 어떤 제품이 가장 긴급하게 필요한가?
  (A) 하이 버튼 울 조끼 & 바지
  (B) 싱글 브레스티드 정장 코트 & 치마
  (C) 극세사 청소용 튜닉
  (D) 밴디드 칼라 셔츠 & 조끼

정답 (C)

해설 첫 지문 두 번째 단락에 가급적 빨리 4823번을 받아 보고 싶다는(I'd like to receive Item #4823 as soon as possible) 말이 쓰여 있고, 두 번째 지문에 4823번이 극세사 청소용 튜닉(Housekeeping Staff: #4823 Microfiber Cleaning Tunic)으로 표기되어 있으므로 (C)가 정답이다.

어휘 **urgently** 긴급하게

99. 생스터 씨는 무엇에 대해 우려하는가?

(A) 프로젝트 지연
(B) 직원들의 편의
(C) 일정상의 충돌
(D) 직원 모집

정답 (B)

해설 세 번째 지문 첫 단락에 직원들이 너무 덥거나 답답하게 느끼면 효과적으로 업무를 수행하는 것이 아주 어려울 수 있다고 말하면서(It would be very difficult for staff to perform their duties effectively if they feel too hot and stuffy) 상대방의 의견을 묻고 있다. 이는 직원들의 업무상 편의와 관련된 내용이므로 (B)가 정답이다.

어휘 **comfort** 편의, 편안함 **conflict** 충돌, 상충 **recruitment** 모집

100. 바 씨의 선택이 구매 불가능한 것은 어느 그룹의 직원들에 대한 것인가?

(A) 남성 프런트 데스크 직원
(B) 여성 프런트 데스크 직원
(C) 객실 관리 직원
(D) 레스토랑 종업원

정답 (D)

해설 세 번째 지문 두 번째 단락에 밴디드 칼라 셔츠 & 조끼를 제외하고 골라 준 모든 유니폼을 주문할 수 있다고(I can order all the uniforms you picked out except for the Banded Collar Shirts & Vests) 언급되어 있으며, 두 번째 지문에서 이 제품이 레스토랑 종업원용이라는(Restaurant Wait Staff: #R45 Banded Collar Shirt & Vest) 것을 알 수 있으므로 (D)가 정답이다.

DAY 03 LC+RC Half Test

Part 1

1.
(A) A lobby is being decorated.
(B) A pathway is being paved.
(C) They are trying on sunglasses.
(D) They are seated next to each other.

(A) 로비가 꾸며지는 중이다.
(B) 길이 포장되는 중이다.
(C) 사람들이 선글라스를 착용해 보고 있다.
(D) 사람들이 서로 나란히 앉아 있다.

해설 (A) 로비가 꾸며지고 있지 않으므로 오답.
(B) 길이 포장되고 있지 않으므로 오답.
(C) 두 사람 모두 선글라스를 이미 착용한 상태이므로 오답.
(D) 두 사람이 서로 나란히 앉아 있는 모습을 묘사한 정답.

어휘 **decorate** ~을 장식하다 **pave** (도로 등) ~을 포장하다
try on (한 번) ~을 착용해 보다 **next to each other**
서로 나란히

2.
(A) Boats are docked along the pier.
(B) A lamppost is located near the train tracks.
(C) Trees are being planted along the water's edge.
(D) Passengers are boarding a ship.

(A) 보트들이 부두를 따라 정박해 있다.
(B) 가로등이 기차 선로 근처에 위치해 있다.
(C) 나무들이 물가를 따라 심어지고 있다.
(D) 승객들이 배에 탑승하고 있다.

해설 (A) 보트 여러 척이 부두를 따라 정박해 있으므로 정답.
(B) 기차 선로를 찾아볼 수 없으므로 오답.
(C) 나무를 심는 동작을 하는 사람이 보이지 않으므로 오답.
(D) 배에 탑승하는 사람을 찾아볼 수 없으므로 오답.

어휘 **dock** ~을 정박시키다 **along** (길 등) ~을 따라 **pier** 부두
be located at ~에 위치해 있다 **plant** ~을 심다 **edge**
가장자리 **board** ~에 탑승하다

Part 2

3. Who's in charge of taking notes at this meeting?
(A) The secretary might know about that.
(B) No, by cash.
(C) They're Mr. Park's.

누가 이 회의에서 기록을 담당하고 있나요?
(A) 비서가 그에 관해 알고 있을 겁니다.
(B) 아니요, 현금으로요.
(C) 그것들은 박 씨의 것입니다.

해설 회의 내용 기록을 담당하는 사람이 누구인지 묻는 Who 의문
문에 대해 그 일에 관해 아는 사람을 말하는 것으로 관련 정보
를 파악할 수 있는 방법을 알리는 (A)가 정답이다. (B)는 의문사
의문문에 맞지 않는 No로 답변하고 있으므로 오답이며, (C)는
소유 주체를 말하는 내용이므로 오답이다.

어휘 **be in charge of** ~을 담당하다 **take notes** 기록하다
secretary 비서

4. When do you expect them to respond to our offer?
(A) They promised to get back to us by Friday.
(B) We've offered them everything they asked for.
(C) You can't expect just anyone to give us money.

그들이 언제 우리 제안에 응답할 것으로 예상하시나요?

(A) 금요일까지 다시 연락 준다고 약속했어요.
(B) 우리는 그들이 요청했던 모든 것을 제공했습니다.
(C) 단순히 누군가가 우리에게 돈을 줄 거라고 기대할 순 없어요.

해설 제안에 대한 응답을 들을 수 있는 시점을 묻는 When 의문문에 대해 연락을 주기로 한 시점으로 답변하는 (A)가 정답이다. (B)와 (C)는 offer과 expect를 각각 반복 사용한 답변으로, 시점과 관련 없는 내용이므로 질문의 핵심에서 벗어난 오답이다.

어휘 expect A to do A가 ~할 것으로 예상하다 offer n. 제안 v. ~을 제공하다, ~을 제안하다 respond to ~에 응답하다, ~에 대응하다 promise to do ~할 것을 약속하다 get back to ~에게 다시 연락하다

5. How long have you been head of this department?
(A) It takes longer than you'd think.
(B) Ever since I got hired.
(C) Yesterday was the due date.

얼마나 오래 이 부서의 책임자로 계셨나요?
(A) 당신 생각보다 더 오래 걸려요.
(B) 제가 고용된 이후로 계속이요.
(C) 어제가 만기일이었어요.

해설 부서장으로 재직했던 기간을 묻는 How long 의문문에 대해 명확한 기간을 말하는 대답 대신 '~이후로 계속'을 뜻하는 Ever since를 이용하여 '고용된 이후로 계속'이라는 말로 대략적인 기간으로 답변한 (B)가 정답이다. (A)는 How long이 소요 시간을 의미할 때 할 수 있는 답변에 해당되므로 오답이다.

어휘 head 책임자, 장 take long 오래 걸리다 ever since ~한 이후로 계속 hire ~을 고용하다 due date (특히 지불과 관련된) 만기일

6. What's the purpose of calling ahead of time?
(A) Because I didn't wear a watch today.
(B) Six o'clock, unless there has been a change.
(C) To confirm that we're going to be there.

미리 전화하는 목적이 무엇인가요?
(A) 제가 오늘 시계를 차고 있지 않아서요.
(B) 6시요, 변경되지 않았다면요.
(C) 우리가 거기로 간다는 걸 확인해 주려고요.

해설 미리 전화하는 목적이 무엇인지 묻는 What 의문문에 대해 목적을 나타낼 때 사용하는 to부정사구로 답변하는 (C)가 정답이다. (A)와 (C)는 time에서 연상 가능한 watch와 Six o'clock을 각각 활용해 혼동을 유발하는 답변으로, 질문 내용과 관련 없는 오답이다.

어휘 ahead of time 미리 unless ~가 아니라면, ~하지 않는다면 confirm that ~임을 확인해 주다

7. Is Susan going to give a speech or did she decide

against it?
(A) She hasn't told me.
(B) They are against the idea.
(C) She did an excellent job.

수잔 씨가 연설을 하시는 건가요, 아니면 하시지 않기로 결정하셨나요?
(A) 아직 제게 알려주시지 않았어요.
(B) 그들은 그 의견에 반대합니다.
(C) 그녀가 정말 훌륭히 해냈어요.

해설 특정 인물이 연설을 하기로 결정했는지를 묻는 선택 의문문이다. 이에 대해 아직 들은 바가 없다는 말로 결정 사항에 대해 알지 못하는 상태라는 의미를 나타내는 (A)가 정답이다. (B)는 against를 반복 사용한 오답이다. (C)는 Susan을 She로 지칭했다고 판단할 수 있지만 뒤에 이어지는 말이 연설 진행과 관련된 결정과 관련 없으므로 오답이다.

어휘 give a speech 연설하다 decide against ~하지 않기로 결정하다 do an excellent job 훌륭히 해내다

8. Why did you arrange a computer training session for Monday?
(A) I want to start using new software.
(B) Because the current ones are too old.
(C) The operation manual.

왜 월요일로 컴퓨터 교육 시간을 잡으셨어요?
(A) 새 소프트웨어를 사용하기 시작하고 싶어서요.
(B) 현재의 것들이 너무 오래되었기 때문이죠.
(C) 사용 설명서요.

해설 컴퓨터 교육 시간을 월요일로 잡은 이유를 묻는 Why 의문문이다. 이에 대해 Because를 생략하고 이유를 말하는 (A)가 정답이다. (B)는 Because를 사용했지만 특정 요일로 컴퓨터 교육 시간을 잡은 이유와 관련 없는 내용이므로 오답이다.

어휘 arrange A for 시점 A의 일정을 ~로 잡다 training 교육, 훈련 session (특정 활동을 하는) 시간 current 현재의 operation manual 사용 설명서, 안내 책자

9. Is the shipment being delivered today?
(A) It won't arrive until tomorrow.
(B) He was supposed to be here by noon.
(C) Over there, near the sofa.

배송품이 오늘 전달되나요?
(A) 내일이나 되어야 도착할 거예요.
(B) 그가 정오까지 여기 오기로 되어 있었어요.
(C) 저기 저쪽에, 소파 근처에요.

해설 배송품이 오늘 오는지 묻는 질문에 대해 특정 미래 시점과 함께 언제 도착하는지 알리는 (A)가 정답이다. (B)는 배송품이 아니라 대상을 알 수 없는 He에 관해 말하고 있으므로 오답이며, (C)는 Where 의문문에 어울리는 응답이므로 오답이다.

어휘 **shipment** 배송(품) **not A until B** B나 되어야 A하다 **arrive** 도착하다 **be supposed to do** ~하기로 되어 있다, ~할 예정이다 **by** (기한) ~까지 **near** ~ 근처에

10. You wouldn't happen to have a pen and paper, would you?

(A) I think those papers were filed.
(B) I'll check in my bag.
(C) Write my number down, too.

혹시 펜과 종이를 가지고 계시지 않나요?
(A) 그 문서들은 파일로 정리된 것 같아요.
(B) 제 가방을 확인해 볼게요.
(C) 제 전화번호도 적어 두세요.

해설 펜과 종이를 갖고 있는지 묻는 부가 의문문에 가방을 확인해 보겠다는 말로 소지 여부를 파악할 방법을 말하는 것으로 대답하는 (B)가 정답이다. (A)는 소지 여부와 관련 없는 오답이며, (C)는 pen과 paper를 통해 연상 가능한 행위인 write down(적다)를 활용해 혼동을 유발하는 오답이다.

어휘 **happen to do** 혹시 ~하다 **file** v. ~을 파일로 정리하다

11. Would you please fill out this form before you take your prescription?

(A) At the pharmacy.
(B) Can I use your pen?
(C) Yes, I've been there before.

처방약을 가져가시기 전에 이 양식을 작성해 주시겠어요?
(A) 약국에서요.
(B) 펜을 좀 써도 될까요?
(C) 네, 예전에 그곳에 가 본 적 있어요.

해설 양식을 작성해 달라고 요청하는 의문문에 대해 수락 또는 거절하는 대신 양식 작성에 필요한 펜을 빌릴 수 있는지 되묻는 (B)가 정답이다. (A)는 prescription에서 연상 가능한 pharmacy를 활용한 오답이다.

어휘 **fill out** ~을 작성하다 **form** 양식, 서식 **prescription** 조제(약), 처방(전) **pharmacy** 약국

12. Shouldn't you ask Mr. Donald if you can leave early tomorrow?

(A) I have a dental appointment.
(B) No, it isn't.
(C) Oh, I already did.

내일 일찍 퇴근하실 수 있는지 도널드 씨께 여쭤봐야 하지 않나요?
(A) 치과 예약이 있어요.
(B) 아뇨, 그렇지 않아요.
(C) 아, 이미 그렇게 했어요.

해설 상대방이 내일 하게 될 일과 관련해 누군가에게 허락을 받도록

제안하는 부정 의문문이다. 이에 대해 일반 동사 ask를 대신해 과거 시점에 했다는 뜻을 나타내는 did를 활용해 답변하는 (C)가 정답이다. (B)는 부정을 나타내는 No 뒤에 불명확한 주어 it과 일반 동사 ask를 대신할 수 없는 is가 쓰여 있으므로 오답이다.

어휘 **ask A if** A에게 ~인지 묻다 **leave** 떠나다, 나가다 **dental** 치과의 **appointment** 예약, 약속

13. Has Dr. Foster looked at the results of the test or should I send them to him now?

(A) The results came out good.
(B) Yes, I saw him today.
(C) Why don't you ask him?

포스터 박사님께서 테스트 결과를 보셨나요, 아니면 지금 제가 박사님께 보낼까요?
(A) 결과가 좋게 나왔어요.
(B) 네, 저는 오늘 박사님을 뵈었어요.
(C) 박사님께 여쭤보는 게 어때요?

해설 특정 인물이 테스트 결과를 확인했는지, 아니면 자신이 그 사람에게 보내야 하는지 묻는 선택 의문문이다. 이에 대해 당사자에게 직접 물어보도록 권하는 (C)가 정답이다. (A)는 results를 반복한 답변으로서 결과의 내용과 관련된 말이므로 오답이며, (B)는 두 개의 다른 질문이 제시되는 소수의 선택 의문문을 제외하고 대부분의 일반 선택 의문문에 맞지 않는 Yes로 답변하고 있으므로 오답이다.

어휘 **result** 결과 **come out good** 좋게 나타나다

14. Are you planning on recruiting extra people to work in the advertising department?

(A) Not in the near future, no.
(B) Just a résumé and a cover letter.
(C) I submitted my application.

광고부에서 근무할 추가 인력을 고용하실 계획인가요?
(A) 아뇨, 당분간은 아닙니다.
(B) 이력서와 자기소개서만요.
(C) 전 지원서를 제출했습니다.

해설 추가 인력을 고용할 계획인지 묻는 질문에 대해 당분간은 아니라는 말로 가까운 시일 내에 고용할 계획이 없음을 의미하는 (A)가 정답이다. (B)와 (C)는 recruiting에서 연상할 수 있는 résumé, cover letter, 그리고 application(지원서)을 활용한 답변으로서, 질문 내용과 관련 없는 오답이다.

어휘 **plan on -ing** ~할 계획이다 **recruit** ~을 채용하다 **extra** 추가의, 여분의 **advertising** 광고 (활동) **résumé** 이력서 **cover letter** 자기소개서 **submit** ~을 제출하다 **application** 지원(서), 신청(서)

15. You have to update the payroll before the end of the month.

(A) Yes, I deposited it on the 30th.

(B) I'll keep that in mind.
(C) I'm asking for a raise.

월말 전에 급여 관련 사항을 업데이트하셔야 합니다.
(A) 네, 30일에 그 금액을 입금했어요.
(B) 명심하고 있겠습니다.
(C) 급여 인상을 요청하는 겁니다.

해설 상대방에게 해야 할 일을 미리 알려주는 내용의 평서문이다. 이에 대해 해당 업무를 that으로 지칭하여 명심하겠다는 말로 대답하는 (B)가 정답이다. (A)는 긍정을 나타내는 Yes 뒤에 관련 없는 내용을 말하는 오답이며, (C)는 질문의 payroll에서 연상 가능한 raise(급여 인상)를 활용한 오답이다.

어휘 **payroll** 급여 대상자 명단, 급여 지불 총액 **deposit** ~을 입금하다, ~을 예금하다 **keep A in mind** A를 명심하다 **ask for** ~을 요청하다 **raise** 급여 인상

16. This labeling and filing should have been completed a week ago.

(A) It's harder than it looks.
(B) Seven days is too long.
(C) That's two weeks from now.

이 라벨 작업과 파일 정리 작업은 일주일 전에 완료되었어야 했어요.
(A) 그 일이 보기보다 더 어려워요.
(B) 7일은 너무 길어요.
(C) 그건 지금부터 2주 후입니다.

해설 특정 업무가 일주일 전에 끝났어야 했다는 의견을 말하는 평서문이다. 이에 대해 보기보다 더 어렵다는 말로 일을 완료하지 못한 이유를 말하는 (A)가 정답이다. (B)와 (C)는 a week ago와 연관성 있게 들리는 seven days와 two weeks from now를 각각 활용해 혼동을 유발하는 오답이다.

어휘 **label** v. 라벨을 붙이다 **should have p.p.** ~했어야 했다 **complete** ~을 완료하다

17. Are you attending any of the fundraising events?
(A) Meeting Room B.
(B) The donations from our clients.
(C) Yes, the one Rob is organizing.

어떤 기금 마련 행사라도 참석하시나요?
(A) B 회의실이요.
(B) 우리 고객들의 기부금이요.
(C) 네, 롭 씨가 준비하고 있는 것이요.

해설 어떤 기금 마련 행사라도 참석하는지 묻는 질문에 긍정을 나타내는 Yes와 함께 특정 인물이 준비하는 것이라는 말로 참여할 행사를 구체적으로 설명하는 (C)가 정답이다. (A)는 Where 의문문에 적절한 응답이며, (B)는 fundraising에서 연상 가능한 donation을 이용한 오답이다.

어휘 **fundraising event** 기금 마련 행사 **donation** 기부(금) **organize** ~을 준비하다, 조직하다

18. Have you chosen a design for the new logo?
(A) I think that's a wise decision.
(B) Yes, it was lower than expected.
(C) I'm still giving it some thought.

새 로고에 대한 디자인을 선택하셨어요?
(A) 제 생각에 그건 현명한 결정인 것 같아요.
(B) 네, 예상했던 것보다 더 낮아요.
(C) 여전히 생각하는 중이에요.

해설 새 로고를 위한 디자인을 결정했는지를 묻는 질문에 여전히 생각 중이라는 말로 아직 결정하지 못했음을 알리는 (C)가 정답이다. (A)는 that이 지칭하는 것을 알 수 없으므로 오답이며, (B)는 긍정을 나타내는 Yes 뒤에 디자인과 관련 없는 내용이 이어지고 있으므로 오답이다.

어휘 **choose** ~을 선택하다 **decision** 결정 **than expected** 예상했던 것보다 **give A a thought** A에 대해 생각해 보다

19. Was the interview done over the phone, or did you travel to Busan?

(A) They e-mailed me to ask me to attend in person.
(B) Let's have a conference call this Friday.
(C) It didn't go as well as I had expected.

면접이 전화상으로 이뤄졌나요, 아니면 부산으로 가셨나요?
(A) 그쪽에서 직접 참석하라고 요청하는 이메일을 제게 보냈어요.
(B) 이번 금요일에 전화 회의를 합시다.
(C) 제가 예상했던 것만큼 잘 되지 않았어요.

해설 면접 방식을 묻는 선택 의문문에 대해 직접 참석하라는 내용의 이메일을 받았다는 말로 부산으로 직접 갔다는 뜻을 나타낸 (A)가 정답이다. (B)는 phone에서 연상 가능한 conference call을 이용한 오답이다. (C)는 어떤 일의 결과를 말할 때 할 수 있는 말이므로 면접 방식을 묻는 선택 의문문과 관련 없는 오답이다.

어휘 **over the phone** 전화상으로 **travel to** ~로 이동하다, 여행하다 **ask A to do** A에게 ~하도록 요청하다 **attend** 참석하다 **in person** 직접 (가서) **conference call** 전화 회의 **go well** 잘 되다 **as A as B** B만큼 A하게 **expect** 예상하다

20. I thought this machine was going out for repairs.
(A) Well, we decided it was better to go earlier.
(B) I'll call the workshop to see if they're finished.
(C) Actually, this one is newly out of the box.

저는 이 기계가 수리 받으러 가는 줄 알았는데요.
(A) 음, 우리는 더 일찍 가는 게 좋겠다고 결정했어요.
(B) 수리소에 전화해서 일을 다 마쳤는지 확인해 볼게요.
(C) 실은, 이건 상자에서 새로 꺼낸 거예요.

해설 기계가 수리되는 것으로 알고 있었다는 사실을 전하는 평서문
이다. 이에 대해 같은 종류의 것을 나타내는 this one과 함께
상자에서 새로 꺼낸 것이라는 말로 새 제품임을 알리는 (C)가
정답이다. (A)는 go를 반복 사용한 오답이며, (B)는 machine
과 repairs에서 연상 가능한 workshop과 함께 작업 진행과
관련해 문의하는 상황에서 할 수 있는 말이므로 기계가 아직 수
리 받으러 가지 않은 것과는 관련 없는 오답이다.

어휘 go out for ~하러 가다 repair 수리 decide (that) ~라
고 결정하다 workshop 수리소, 작업장 see if ~인지 확
인하다 actually 실은, 사실

Part 3

Questions 21-23 refer to the following conversation.

M: Good morning, Ms. Devlin. As we discussed on
the phone, **21** I'm looking for a new location to
move my car repair shop to. I don't want it to
be too far away, though.

W: Well, let's see what we can find. First, **22** why
have you decided to move your business?

M: **22** As it is, there's only enough space to
service two customers at a time. I need
something a little wider so I can hire some
more staff and take on more customers.

W: I see. And you said you still want to stay within
the city limits of Minneapolis, right?

M: Yes, if possible. Do you have anything like that?

W: Of course! **23** Let me show you all the listings
for sites that meet your criteria.

남: 안녕하세요, 데블린 씨. 전화상으로 논의한 바와 같이, 제 자동
차 정비소를 옮길 새로운 장소를 찾고 있습니다. 하지만 너무
멀지는 않았으면 좋겠어요.
여: 그럼, 어떤 곳을 찾을 수 있는지 알아보죠. 우선, 사업장을 왜
옮기기로 결정하셨나요?
남: 지금은, 한 번에 두 분의 고객에게 서비스를 제공할 정도로 충
분한 공간만 있어요. 직원을 더 고용해서 더 많은 고객들을 받
을 수 있도록 조금 더 넓은 공간이 필요해요.
여: 알겠습니다. 그리고 여전히 미니애폴리스 시 경계 내에 머무르
기를 원하신다고 말씀하셨던 게 맞죠?
남: 네, 가능하다면요. 어디든 그런 곳이 있나요?
여: 물론입니다! 귀하의 기준을 충족시키는 장소들에 대한 모든 목
록을 보여드리겠습니다.

어휘 discuss 논의하다 look for ~을 찾다 location 위치, 장
소 repair 수리 though (문장 끝이나 중간에서) 하지만
decide to do ~하기로 결정하다 as it is 지금 상황에서

는 service v. ~에게 서비스를 제공하다 hire ~을 고용하
다 take on ~을 떠맡다 stay within ~안에 머무르다, ~
을 벗어나지 않다 city limit 도시의 경계 listing 목록, 명
단 site 장소 meet one's criteria ~의 기준을 충족시키
다, ~의 기준에 맞다

21. 남자는 어떤 종류의 사업체를 소유하고 있는가?
(A) 법률 회사
(B) 철물점
(C) 부동산 중개소
(D) 자동차 수리소

해설 대화 초반부에 남자가 인사를 하면서 자신의 자동차 정비소
를 옮길 새로운 장소를 찾고 있다고(I'm looking for a new
location to move my car repair shop to) 말하고 있다.
이를 통해 남자가 소유한 사업체가 자동차 수리소임을 알 수 있
으므로 (D)가 정답이다.

Paraphrase car repair shop
→ auto repair shop

22. 남자는 왜 사업체를 이전하고 싶어 하는가?
(A) 비용을 절감하기 위해
(B) 더 많은 공간을 갖기 위해
(C) 통근 시간을 줄이기 위해
(D) 고객들과 더 가까워지기 위해

해설 대화 중반부에 여자가 사업체를 옮기고 싶은 이유를 묻자, 남자
가 지금은 한 번에 두 명의 고객을 응대할 수 있는 정도의 공간
만 있어서 직원을 고용해 더 많은 고객들을 받을 수 있도록 더
넓은 공간이 필요하다고(~ there's only enough space to
service two customers at a time. I need something
a little wider ~) 이유를 말하고 있다. 따라서, 사업체를 이전
하기 원하는 이유는 더 많은 공간을 갖기 위해서라는 사실을 알
수 있으므로 (B)가 정답이다.

어휘 reduce ~을 절감하다, 줄이다 shorten ~을 줄이다, 짧게
하다 commute n. 통근 (시간) clientele 고객들

23. 여자는 곧이어 무엇을 할 것 같은가?
(A) 일정을 확인하는 일
(B) 비용을 계산하는 일
(C) 몇몇 부동산 목록을 제공하는 일
(D) 사업 제안서를 검토하는 일

해설 대화 후반부에 여자가 남자에게 그의 기준을 충족하는 장소의
목록을 보여주겠다고(Let me show you all the listings
for sites that meet your criteria) 말하고 있다. 이는 부동
산 목록을 보여주는 일이므로 (C)가 정답이다.

어휘 calculate ~을 계산하다, 산출하다 property 부동산, 건
물 proposal 제안(서) provide ~을 제공하다

Paraphrase Let me show you all the listings for sites
→ Provide some property listings

Questions 24-26 refer to the following conversation.

M: Excuse me, Katherine. **24** The Macklin family is coming in this morning to arrange their flights. **24** **25** Do you remember where they want to travel to?

W: **24** Yes. I think they are planning to go to China. I've put all their forms into a file on your computer. You should be able to see it on your desktop.

M: Oh, okay. I can see it. I didn't know you had put it there. Thank you.

W: That's fine. **26** We are changing all our paper files into computer files this month, remember? I had a feeling you didn't have time, so I started to convert some of yours yesterday.

남: 실례합니다, 캐서린 씨. 매클린 씨 가족이 오늘 아침에 항공편을 예약하러 방문할 예정입니다. 그들이 어디로 여행을 떠나길 원하는지 기억하시나요?

여: 네. 제 생각엔 중국으로 갈 계획이신 것 같아요. 그 가족들에 대한 모든 양식을 당신의 컴퓨터에 파일로 저장해 뒀어요. 컴퓨터로 확인해 보실 수 있을 겁니다.

남: 아, 알겠어요. 보이네요. 여기에 저장해 두신 줄 몰랐어요. 감사합니다.

여: 별 말씀을요. 이번 달에 회사에서 종이로 된 모든 파일들을 컴퓨터 파일로 바꾸는 중인데, 기억하시죠? 시간이 없으실 것 같다는 생각에, 어제 당신 종이 파일의 일부를 변환하기 시작했죠.

어휘 arrange ~의 일정을 잡다, ~을 조치하다 plan to do ~할 계획이다 put A into B A를 B에 넣어 놓다 form 양식, 서식 be able to do ~할 수 있다 convert ~을 변환하다

24. 화자들은 어디에서 근무할 것 같은가?
(A) 여행사에서
(B) 공항에서
(C) 기차역에서
(D) 렌터카 회사에서

해설 대화 초반부에 남자가 매클린 씨 가족이 오늘 오전에 항공편을 예약하러 방문할 예정이라면서 그들이 어디로 떠나길 원하는지(The Macklin family is coming in this morning to arrange their flights. Do you remember where they want to travel to?) 묻자 여자가 목적지를 말해주며 모든 양식을 컴퓨터에 파일로 저장해 뒀다고(I think they are planning to go to China. I've put all their forms into a file on your computer) 대답하고 있다. 이를 통해 화자들이 여행 일정을 예약하는 곳, 즉 여행사에서 근무하는 것으로 판단할 수 있으므로 (A)가 정답이다.

25. 남자는 여자에게 무엇에 대해 묻는가?
(A) 선호하는 여행 장소
(B) 행사 개최지
(C) 서류 위치
(D) 항공권 가격

해설 대화 초반부에 남자가 고객(the Macklin family)이 원하는 여행 장소에 대해 여자에게 질문하고(Do you remember where they want to travel to?) 있다. 이를 통해 고객이 선호하는 여행 장소를 묻고 있음을 알 수 있으므로 (A)가 정답이다.

어휘 preferred 선호되는 venue 개최지, 장소

Paraphrase where they want to travel to
→ A preferred destination

26. 여자는 이번 달에 무슨 일이 일어나고 있다고 말하는가?
(A) 고객 설문 조사가 실시되고 있다.
(B) 건물 한 곳이 사무실로 개조되고 있다.
(C) 일부 컴퓨터 소프트웨어가 업그레이드되고 있다.
(D) 새로운 파일 보관 시스템이 실행되고 있다.

해설 대화 후반부에서 여자가 이번 달에 모든 종이 파일들을 컴퓨터 파일로 바꾸는 중이라고(We are changing all our paper files into computer files this month) 알리고 있다. 이는 새로운 파일 보관 시스템을 실행하는 것이므로 (D)가 정답이다.

어휘 carry out ~을 실시하다, 실행하다 property 건물, 부동산 convert A into B A를 B로 개조하다 implement v. ~을 실시하다, 실행하다

Questions 27-29 refer to the following conversation.

M: Hello, this is David Kramer calling. **27** I'd like to make an appointment for tomorrow to have a tooth extracted. I normally see Dr. Jennings.

W: Hi, Mr. Kramer. I'm afraid **28** Dr. Jennings is out of town at a dentistry conference this week. I can book you an appointment with Dr. Chalmers instead.

M: Oh, **29** I'm not too sure about that. I'm only really comfortable seeing Dr. Jennings.

W: Well, Dr. Chalmers has been with us for more than a decade. He's even won awards in the industry for his excellent work.

M: Okay, that sounds good to me then. When can I come in to see him?

W: Please be here by 2 P.M. tomorrow.

남: 여보세요, 저는 데이비드 크레이머입니다. 내일 치아를 뽑을 수 있도록 예약을 하려고 합니다. 보통 제닝스 선생님을 뵙고 있습니다.

여: 안녕하세요, 크레이머 씨. 제닝스 선생님께서는 이번 주에 치과 의학 컨퍼런스 때문에 다른 지역에 가 계십니다. 대신 차머스 선생님으로 예약 시간을 잡아 드릴 수 있습니다.

남: 아, 그렇게 하는 것에 대해 확신이 서질 않네요. 저는 제닝스 선생님에게서 치료 받을 경우에만 정말로 편하거든요.

여: 음, 차머스 선생님께서는 10년 넘게 저희와 함께 해 오셨습니다. 심지어 훌륭한 업적으로 업계에서 상도 받으셨습니다.

남: 알겠습니다, 그렇다면 괜찮을 것 같네요. 그분을 뵈러 언제 갈 수 있죠?

여: 내일 오후 2시까지 오시기 바랍니다.

어휘 make an appointment 예약하다 have A p.p. A를 ~되게 하다 extract ~을 뽑다, 추출하다 out of town 다른 지역에 있는 dentistry 치과 의학 book an appointment A에게 예약 시간을 잡아주다 instead 대신 comfortable 편한, 편안한 decade 10년 win an award 상을 받다 that sounds good to me (앞선 언급된 말에 대해) 괜찮을 것 같습니다 by (기한) ~까지

27. 여자는 어디에서 근무할 것 같은가?
(A) 약국에서
(B) 회계 법인에서
(C) 피트니스 센터에서
(D) 치과에서

해설 대화 초반부에 남자가 여자에게 내일 치아를 뽑을 수 있도록 예약을 하려고 한다고(I'd like to make an appointment for tomorrow to have a tooth extracted) 알리고 있으므로 여자의 근무 장소는 치과임을 알 수 있다. 따라서 (D)가 정답이다.

28. 여자는 제닝스 씨에 관해 무슨 말을 하는가?
(A) 행사에 참석 중이다.
(B) 직장에서 은퇴했다.
(C) 신규 고객들을 찾고 있다.
(D) 상을 받을 것이다.

해설 여자의 말 중 Dr. Jennings라는 이름이 제시되는 부분에서 단서를 파악해야 한다. 대화 초반부에 여자는 제닝스 선생님이 이번 주에 치과 의학 컨퍼런스 때문에 다른 지역에 가 있다고(Dr. Jennings is out of town at a dentistry conference this week) 알리고 있다. 따라서 (A)가 정답이다.

어휘 retire from ~에서 퇴직하다, 은퇴하다
Paraphrase is out of town at a dentistry conference → is attending an event

29. 여자가 "차머스 선생님께서는 10년 넘게 저희와 함께 해 오셨습니다"라고 말하는 이유는 무엇인가?
(A) 동료 직원을 승진 대상으로 추천하기 위해
(B) 남자를 안심시키기 위해
(C) 차머스 씨에게 연락하도록 남자에게 권하기 위해
(D) 실수에 대해 변명하기 위해

해설 해당 문장은 대화 중반부에 남자가 차머스(Chalmers) 선생님에게 진료받는 것에 대해 확신이 서지 않고 제닝스 선생님이 더 편하다고(I'm not too sure about that. I'm only really comfortable seeing Dr. Jennings) 말한 것에 대한 반응으로 쓰인 말이다. 여자가 해당 문장을 말한 이후에 차머스 선생님의 훌륭한 업적을 알리고 있는 것으로 볼 때, 확신이 서지 않는 남자를 안심시키기 위한 목적으로 한 말이라는 것을 알 수 있으므로 (B)가 정답이다.

어휘 reassurance 확신, 안심 advise A to do A에게 ~하도록 권하다, 조언하다 contact ~에게 연락하다 excuse for ~에 대한 변명

Questions 30-32 refer to the following conversation with three speakers.

M1: Thanks for coming back, **30** George and Isabella. You seemed very interested in the Westman 5-door sedan yesterday. Are you back to take it for another test drive?

W: No, we definitely like the vehicle, but we have a few questions about it before we go any further.

M2: Right. **31** We're moving to a place in the suburbs next month, so we'll need a vehicle that's fuel efficient.

M1: Well, this one definitely gets good gas mileage. In fact, it's one of the most fuel-efficient models in our showroom.

M2: Great! And is Westman regarded as a reliable manufacturer?

M1: Of course! **32** When it comes to making sedans, Westman is known as the best in the business.

남1: 다시 찾아 주셔서 감사합니다, 조지 씨 그리고 이사벨라 씨. 두 분께서는 어제 웨스트먼 5도어 세단에 대단히 관심 있어 보이셨습니다. 다시 한 번 시운전해 보시기 위해 오신 건가요?

여: 아니요, 저희는 그 차량이 분명히 마음에 들기는 하지만, 일을 더 진행하기 전에 몇 가지 질문이 있어서요.

남2: 맞아요. 저희가 다음 달에 교외 지역에 있는 곳으로 이사를 가기 때문에, 연비가 좋은 차량이 필요할 거예요.

남1: 음, 이 차량은 분명히 좋은 연비를 보여 줍니다. 실제로, 저희 전시장에서 가장 연비가 뛰어난 모델들 중의 하나입니다.

남2: 잘됐네요! 그리고 웨스트먼 사는 믿을 만한 제조사로 여겨지는 곳인가요?

남1: 물론입니다! 세단 차량 생산에 관해서라면, 웨스트먼 사는 업계 내에서 최고로 알려져 있습니다.

어휘 seem 형용사 ~한 것처럼 보이다 take A for a test drive A를 시운전하러 가다 definitely 분명히 vehicle 차량 go further 일을 진행하다, 진척시키다 suburbs 교외 지역 fuel-efficient 연비가 좋은 gas mileage 연비 be regarded as ~로 여겨지다 reliable 믿을 만한 manufacturer 제조사 when it comes to ~에 관해서라면 be known as ~라고 알려져 있다

30. 조지와 이사벨라는 누구이겠는가?
(A) 자동차 수리소의 정비사
(B) 잠재적인 차량 구매자
(C) 부동산 중개업자
(D) 재정 자문가

해설 특정 인물이 누구인지 묻는 질문의 경우, 이름과 함께 제시되는 정보에 집중해야 한다. 대화 시작 부분에 남자 한 명이 이들의 이름을 부르고, 어제 웨스트먼 5도어 세단에 대단히 관심 있어 보였다고 말하면서 다시 한 번 시운전해 보러 온 것인지(You seemed very interested in the Westman 5-door sedan yesterday. Are you back to take it for another test drive?) 묻고 있다. 이는 차량을 구매하려는 사람에게 할 수 있는 말이므로 (B)가 정답이다.

어휘 mechanic 정비사 potential 잠재적인 real estate agent 부동산 중개업자 financial 재정의, 재무의 advisor 자문, 상담 전문가

31. 조지와 이사벨라는 다음 달에 무엇을 할 계획인가?
(A) 새로운 집으로 이사한다.
(B) 해외로 여행을 떠난다.
(C) 건물을 개조한다.
(D) 새로운 사업을 시작한다.

해설 대화 중반부에 남자 한 명이 다음 달에 교외 지역에 있는 곳으로 이사를 간다고(We're moving to a place in the suburbs next month) 알리고 있다. 이는 새로운 집으로 이사하는 것이므로 (A)가 정답이다.

어휘 overseas 해외로 renovate ~을 개조하다, 보수하다 property 건물, 부동산

32. 해당 제조사에 관해 무엇이 언급되는가?
(A) 비교적 새로운 회사이다.
(B) 아주 다양한 제품을 만든다.
(C) 좋은 평판을 얻고 있다.
(D) 첫 구매 고객에게 할인을 제공한다.

해설 제조사에 관해 언급되는 정보를 찾아야 하므로 회사의 상황과 관련된 부분이 있음을 예상하고 들어야 한다. 대화 후반부에 남자 한 명이 웨스트먼 사가 믿을 만한 제조사인지 묻는 질문에 대해 다른 남자가 웨스트먼 사는 업계 내에서 최고로 알려져 있다고(~ Westman is known as the best in the business) 알리고 있다. 이는 좋은 평판을 얻고 있는 것이므로 (C)가 정답이다.

어휘 relatively 비교적, 상대적으로 a wide variety of 아주 다양한 have a good reputation 좋은 평판을 얻다

Paraphrase Westman is known as the best in the business.
→ It has a good reputation.

Questions 33-35 refer to the following conversation and subway map.

M: Excuse me, can you tell me how to get to the Sky One Building? 33 I've been walking along 12th Avenue for 30 minutes, but I can't find it anywhere.

W: The Sky One Building? I'm sorry to tell you this, but that's on the corner of 7th and Sunset.

M: Oh, no! 34 I'm supposed to be at a meeting there by 11 A.M., and I don't think I can make it on time. Can you tell me the quickest way to get there?

W: You'd be best to take the subway. There's a station a little further up this street.

M: Thanks for your help. And, 35 where should I get off the train?

W: Sorry, but I can't remember the name of the station. But, 35 it's the stop in between City Hall and 5th Avenue.

남: 실례합니다, 스카이 원 빌딩으로 가는 방법 좀 알려 주시겠어요? 제가 12번가를 따라 30분째 걷고 있는데, 어디에서도 찾을 수가 없네요.

여: 스카이 원 빌딩이요? 이런 말씀드리기 죄송하지만, 7번가와 선셋 가가 만나는 모퉁이에 있어요.

남: 아, 이런! 제가 그곳에서 열리는 회의에 오전 11시까지 가기로 되어 있는데, 제시간에 갈 수 있을지 모르겠네요. 그곳으로 가는 가장 빠른 방법 좀 알려 주시겠어요?

여: 지하철을 타시는 게 가장 좋을 거예요. 이 거리를 따라 조금만 더 가시면 역이 하나 있어요.

남: 도와 주셔서 감사합니다. 그리고, 어디에서 내려야 하죠?

여: 죄송하지만, 그 역의 이름은 기억이 나질 않네요. 하지만 시청과 5번가 사이에 있는 역이에요.

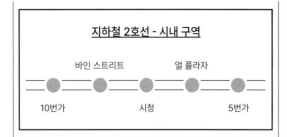

지하철 2호선 - 시내 구역

바인 스트리트　　　　　얼 플라자

10번가　　　　　시청　　　　　5번가

어휘 how to do ~하는 방법 get to ~로 가다 along (길 등) ~을 따라 on the corner of A and B A와 B가 만나는 모퉁이에 be supposed to do ~하기로 되어 있다, ~할 예정이다 make it 가다, 도착하다 on time 제때 a little further 조금 더 up (길 등을 따라) ~의 앞쪽에, 저쪽에 get off ~에서 내리다 in between A and B A와 B 사이에

33. 대화는 어디에서 이루어지고 있겠는가?
(A) 지하철 역에서
(B) 주차장에서
(C) 거리에서
(D) 열차에서

해설 대화 시작 부분에 남자가 자신이 찾는 건물과 관련해 12번가를 따라 30분째 걷고 있다고(I've been walking along 12th Avenue for 30 minutes ~) 알리고 있다. 따라서, 두 사람이 거리에서 만나 이야기를 나누고 있음을 알 수 있으므로 (C)가 정답이다.

34. 남자는 왜 걱정하는가?
(A) 티켓을 분실했다.
(B) 현금 자동 인출기를 찾을 수 없다.
(C) 약속 시간에 늦었다.
(D) 자신의 차량이 고장 났다.

해설 남자가 걱정하는 이유를 찾아야 하므로 남자의 말에서 걱정 관련 표현이나 부정적인 정보가 제시되는 부분을 파악해야 한다. 대화 중반부에 남자는 회의에 오전 11시까지 가기로 되어 있는데 제 시간에 갈 수 있을지 모르겠다고(I'm supposed to be at a meeting there by 11 A.M., and I don't think I can make it on time) 말하며 자신이 걱정하는 바를 나타내고 있다. 이는 약속 시간에 늦은 것을 의미하므로 (C)가 정답이다.

어휘 ATM(Automated Teller Machine) 현금 자동 인출기 run late for ~에 늦다, 지각하다

Paraphrase I don't think I can make it on time
→ is running late for an appointment

35. 시각자료를 보시오. 남자는 어느 역에서 내릴 것 같은가?
(A) 10번가
(B) 바인 스트리트
(C) 시청
(D) 얼 플라자

해설 대화 후반부에 남자가 어디서 내려야 하는지 묻자, 여자가 내려야 하는 역의 위치와 관련해 시청과 5번가 사이에 있는 역이라고(it's the stop in between City Hall and 5th Avenue) 언급하고 있다. 시각자료에서 해당 위치는 Earl Plaza이므로 (D)가 정답이다.

Questions 36-38 refer to the following conversation and schedule.

W: Hi, William. **36** I was wondering if you have some free time today to go over the itinerary for our business trip to Japan.

M: Oh, right. We still need to book our accommodations and transportation. Hmm... I have some time to discuss it this afternoon, but... aren't you busy holding interviews for the sales position?

W: Well, **37** my 3 o'clock interviewee has canceled due to illness, so I'm free at that time.

M: Great! **38** I'll stop by your office with some brochures I picked up. We can take a look at them together.

여: 안녕하세요, 윌리엄 씨. 일본으로 떠나는 우리 출장에 대한 일정표를 검토해 보실 시간이 오늘 있으신지 궁금합니다.
남: 아, 맞네요. 우리는 여전히 숙소와 교통편을 예약해야 하죠. 흠... 오늘 오후에 그 일을 이야기할 수 있는 시간이 있기는 하지만... 영업직에 대한 면접을 실시하시느라 바쁘시지 않으요?
여: 음, 3시 면접자가 질병으로 인해 취소했기 때문에, 그때 시간이 있어요.
남: 잘됐네요! 제가 가져온 안내 책자를 가지고 당신 사무실에 들를게요. 이 책자들을 함께 살펴볼 수 있을 거예요.

면접 일정 -오후-	
제임스 스위프트	오후 1시 30분
티나 메이너드	오후 2시 15분
대니 키넌	오후 3시
질 스톤	오후 3시 45분

어휘 wonder if ~인지 궁금하다 go over ~을 검토하다 itinerary 여행 일정(표) accommodation 숙소 transportation 교통편 discuss ~을 이야기하다, ~을 논의하다 hold ~을 열다, 개최하다 sales position 영업직 interviewee 면접 대상자 cancel 취소하다 due to ~로 인해 illness 질병, 병고 stop by ~에 들르다 brochure 안내 책자 pick up ~을 가져오다 take a look at ~을 한 번 보다

36. 화자들은 주로 무엇에 관해 이야기하고 있는가?
- (A) 채용 전략
- (B) 매출 수치
- **(C) 출장 계획**
- (D) 회사 방침

해설　대화 초반부에 여자가 일본으로 떠나는 출장에 대한 일정표를 검토해 볼 시간이 있는지(I was wondering if ~ to go over the itinerary for our business trip to Japan) 남자에게 물은 후 회의 시간을 정하는 것에 관해 나머지 대화가 진행되고 있다. 이는 출장 계획을 의미하므로 (C)가 정답이다.

Paraphrase　itinerary for our business trip
　　　　　→ Travel plans

37. 시각자료를 보시오. 누가 오늘 오후 면접에 참석하지 않을 것인가?
- (A) 제임스 스위프트
- (B) 티나 메이너드
- **(C) 대니 키넌**
- (D) 질 스톤

해설　선택지에 사람 이름이 기재돼 있으므로 대화에서 면접 시간과 관련해 제시되는 정보에 집중해 들어야 한다. 대화 중반부에 여자가 3시 면접자가 아파서 취소를 했다고(my 3 o'clock interviewee has canceled due to illness) 알리고 있다. 시각자료에서 면접이 3시로 예정된 사람은 대니 키넌(Danny Keenan)이므로 (C)가 정답이다.

38. 남자는 여자의 사무실로 무엇을 가져 갈 것인가?
- (A) 이력서
- (B) 티켓
- (C) 계약서
- **(D) 안내 책자**

해설　남자가 여자의 사무실로 가져 가려는 것을 묻고 있으므로 남자가 물품을 언급하는 부분에 집중해 들어야 한다. 대화 후반부에 남자가 자신이 가져온 안내 책자를 갖고 여자의 사무실로 들르겠다고(I'll stop by your office with some brochures I picked up) 알리고 있으므로 (D)가 정답이다.

Paraphrase　brochures → pamphlets

Part 4

Questions 39-41 refer to the following excerpt from a talk.

I have an exciting announcement to make for everyone. Over the past decade, **39** we have become a leader in the computer manufacturing industry, and now we hope to enter the cell phone market. **40** Just this last week, our engineers came up with a design for our exciting new phone, and we hope it will become an international success. So, you might be wondering why I asked you all to come here today. **41** Well, over the next few weeks, you will all be involved in developing an advertisement campaign for the new phone. Both the campaign and the phone will be officially unveiled to the press at next month's technology convention.

여러분 모두에게 알려드릴 흥미로운 공지가 하나 있습니다. 지난 10년간, 우리는 컴퓨터 제조업계에서 선두를 달려온 회사였으며, 이제 휴대전화 시장에 진입하고자 합니다. 바로 지난 주에, 우리 회사의 엔지니어들이 우리의 흥미로운 새 휴대전화기 디자인 안을 내놓았으며, 우리는 이것이 세계적으로 성공을 거둘 수 있기를 바라고 있습니다. 자, 여러분들께서는 제가 왜 오늘 여러분 모두를 이곳으로 오시라고 요청을 드렸는지 궁금하실 겁니다. 음, 앞으로 몇 주 동안, 여러분 모두 새 휴대전화 제품에 대한 광고 캠페인 개발 업무에 참여하시게 될 것입니다. 광고 캠페인과 휴대전화 모두 다음 달에 있을 기술 컨벤션을 통해 언론에 공식적으로 공개될 예정입니다.

어휘　announcement 공지, 발표　over (기간) ~에 걸쳐　decade 10년　manufacturing 제조　industry 업계　come up with (의견, 해답 등) ~을 내놓다, 제시하다　success 성공　wonder ~을 궁금해 하다　be involved in ~에 참여하다, ~에 관여하다　develop ~을 개발하다　advertisement 광고　officially 공식적으로　unveil ~을 공개하다　the press 언론

39. 화자는 어디에서 근무하겠는가?
- (A) 마케팅 회사
- **(B) 전자제품 회사**
- (C) 회계 법인
- (D) 인터넷 공급업체

해설　담화 초반부에 화자는 자신의 회사를 소개하면서 컴퓨터 제조의 선두 업체가 되었고 휴대폰 시장에 진출하기를 바란다고(we have become a leader in the computer manufacturing industry ~ enter the cell phone market) 있다. 이를 통해 화자의 회사는 전자제품 관련 업체임을 알 수 있으므로 (B)가 정답이다.

어휘 electronics 전자제품 provider 공급업체[업자]

40. 회사는 최근에 무엇을 했는가?
    (A) 신제품을 디자인했다.
    (B) 다른 회사를 인수했다.
    (C) 일련의 광고를 만들어냈다.
    (D) 신입 제품 개발자들을 고용했다.

해설 회사가 최근에 한 일을 묻는 질문이므로 가까운 과거 시점
    에 있었던 일을 언급하는 부분을 찾아 그 내용을 파악해야 한
    다. 화자는 담화 중반부에 지난 주에 엔지니어들이 새로운 휴
    대폰 사업에 필요한 제품 디자인 안을 내놓았다고(Just last
    week, our engineers came up with a design for our
    exciting new phone) 말하고 있다. 이는 새로운 제품을 디자
    인한 것이므로 (A)가 정답이다.

어휘 take over (기업 등) ~을 인수하다 a series of 일련의
    create ~을 만들어내다 hire ~을 고용하다

41. 화자에 따르면, 앞으로 몇 주 동안 청자들은 무엇을 할 것인가?
    (A) 컨벤션을 준비하는 일
    (B) 신입 직원들이 적응하도록 돕는 일
    (C) 프로젝트를 공동 작업하는 일
    (D) 시장 연구 조사를 시행하는 일

해설 앞으로 몇 주 동안 할 일을 묻고 있으므로 이 기간 표현 및 미
    래 시제 동사로 청자들이 하게 될 일을 언급하는 부분에 집중
    해 들어야 한다. 담화 후반부에 화자가 앞으로 몇 주 동안 청자
    들이 새 휴대전화 제품에 대한 광고 캠페인 개발 업무에 참여하
    게 될 것이라고(over the next few weeks, you will all be
    involved in developing an advertisement campaign
    for the new phone) 말하고 있다. 이는 공동으로 하나의 프
    로젝트를 작업하는 것을 의미하므로 (C)가 정답이다.

어휘 organize ~을 준비하다, 조직하다 settle in 자리잡다, 정
    착하다 collaborate on ~을 공동으로 작업하다, 합작하다
    conduct ~을 시행하다 market research study 시장
    연구 조사

`Paraphrase` you will all be involved in developing an
           advertisement campaign
           → Collaborate on a project

Questions 42-44 refer to the following announcement.

Attention, guests. **42** We hope you are enjoying your stay here. We would like to inform you that we have two empty spaces left on our island cruise, which will depart from the beach at 10 A.M. **42** **43** Two other hotel guests purchased the tickets, but it turns out that they are unable to go on the cruise. Instead of asking for a refund, they will kindly let two other guests take their places on the boat. So, **43** don't miss out on this fantastic opportunity. It normally costs 40 dollars. **44** If you are interested in the cruise, please speak with a staff member at the front desk by 9 A.M.

고객 여러분께 알립니다. 이곳에서 즐겁게 머무르시는 중이기를 바랍니다. 해변에서 오전 10시에 출발하는 저희 섬 여객선에 두 곳의 빈 자리가 남아 있다는 점을 알려 드리고자 합니다. 두 분의 호텔 투숙객들이 티켓을 구입하셨지만, 여객선에 탑승하시지 못하는 것으로 드러났습니다. 환불을 요청하시는 대신, 그분들께서는 친절하게도 여객선 내 자신들의 자리를 다른 두 분의 고객들께서 이용하시도록 하실 것입니다. 따라서, 이 환상적인 기회를 놓치지 마시기 바랍니다. 이는 보통 40달러의 비용이 듭니다. 여객선 이용에 관심 있으신 분들께서는, 오전 9시까지 프런트 데스크에 있는 직원에게 말씀해 주시기 바랍니다.

어휘 stay 머무름, 숙박 would like to do ~하고자 하다, ~하
    고 싶다 inform A that A에게 ~라고 알리다 have A p.p.
    ~된 A가 있다, A를 ~되게 하다 cruise 여객선 depart
    from ~에서 출발하다 it turns out that ~인 것으로 밝혀
    지다, 드러나다 be unable to do ~할 수 없다 instead
    of ~ 대신 ask for ~을 요청하다 refund 환불 take
    one's place ~의 자리를 차지하다 miss out on ~을 놓
    치다 opportunity 기회 be ineterested in ~에 관심이
    있다

42. 공지는 어디에서 이뤄지고 있는가?
    (A) 기내에서
    (B) 선상에서
    (C) 호텔에서
    (D) 여행사에서

해설 담화 초반부에 화자가 즐겁게 머무르고 있는 중이기를 바란다
    는 말과 함께, 두 명의 다른 호텔 고객들이 티켓을 구입했다가
    이용하지 못하게 된 여객선 서비스에 대해 알리고(Two other
    hotel guests purchased the tickets ~) 있다. 따라서, 호
    텔에서 여객선 서비스를 이용하도록 알리기 위해 공지를 하는
    상황임을 알 수 있으므로 (C)가 정답이다.

43. 화자는 왜 "이는 보통 40달러의 비용이 듭니다"라고 말하는가?

(A) 가격 변동에 대해 사과하기 위해
(B) 새로운 서비스를 홍보하기 위해
(C) 계절 세일 행사를 알리기 위해
(D) 참여를 장려하기 위해

해설 해당 문장은 담화 중반부에 환상적인 기회를 놓치지 말라고 당부하는(don't miss out on this fantastic opportunity) 말 다음에 들을 수 있다. 이를 통해 좋은 기회를 이용하도록 권하기 위해 쓰인 말이라는 것을 알 수 있으므로 (D)가 정답이다.

어휘 apologize for ~에 대해 사과하다 promote ~을 홍보하다 seasonal 계절의 encourage ~을 장려하다, 권하다 participation 참여, 참가

44. 관심 있는 사람들은 무엇을 하도록 권유 받는가?

(A) 일정표를 확인하는 일
(B) 티켓을 제시하는 일
(C) 양식을 작성하는 일
(D) 직원에게 말하는 일

해설 관심 있는 사람들이 권유 받는 일에 대한 질문이므로 권고나 제안 관련 표현이 제시되는 부분에서 단서를 찾아야 한다. 화자가 담화 후반부에 관심 있는 사람들은 오전 9시까지 프런트 데스크에 있는 직원에게 말해야 한다고(If you are interested in the cruise, please speak with a staff member at the front desk by 9 A.M.) 알리고 있다. 이는 직원에게 말하는 일을 의미하므로 (D)가 정답이다.

어휘 individual 사람, 개인 be advised to do ~하도록 권유 받다 present ~을 제시하다, 보여 주다 fill out ~을 작성하다 form 양식, 서식

Paraphrase speak with a staff member
→ Talk to an employee

Questions 45-47 refer to the following talk.

45 Welcome to this evening's Independent Film Awards Banquet at the Rosenfeld Theater. Tonight's event will celebrate and recognize the brightest new talents in the world of independent cinema. 46 We have many special guests here to present prizes to the deserving winners. I'm sure some of them are familiar to you. 46 For example, renowned director Magnus Karlsson will be presenting the Film of the Year Prize at the end of the night. And, 47 once the event has ended, you're all encouraged to stick around to enjoy a screening of his new documentary.

로즌펠드 극장에서 열리는 오늘밤의 독립 영화 시상식 연회에 오신 것을 환영합니다. 오늘밤의 행사는 독립 영화계에서 가장 빛나는 새로운 인재들을 축하하고 인정하는 자리가 될 것입니다. 많은 특별 손님들께서 자격이 있는 수상자들에게 시상을 해 주시기 위해 이 자리에 와 계십니다. 분명 이분들 중 일부는 여러분도 잘 알고 계실 겁니다. 예를 들어, 유명 영화 감독이신 매그너스 칼슨 씨께서 오늘밤 행사의 마지막에 올해의 영화상을 시상하실 예정입니다. 그리고 행사가 종료되는 대로, 여러분 모두 자리에 남아서 이분의 새로운 다큐멘터리 작품 상영을 즐기시기를 권해 드립니다.

어휘 recognize ~을 인정하다, 표창하다 talent 인재, 재능 (있는 사람) in the world of ~계에서 independent cinema 독립 영화 present ~을 주다, 제시하다 deserving 자격이 있는, 받을 만한 winner 수상자 be familiar to ~에게 잘 알려지다 renowned 유명한 director 영화 감독 stick around (다른 곳으로 가지 않고) 같은 곳에 있다 screening 상영(회)

45. 어떤 종류의 행사가 소개되고 있는가?

(A) 기금 마련 행사
(B) 연극 공연
(C) 개장 기념 행사
(D) 시상식

해설 담화 시작 부분에 화자는 오늘밤의 독립 영화 시상식 연회에 온 것을 환영한다고(Welcome to this evening's Independent Film Awards Banquet~) 말하면서 청자들에게 인사하고 있다. 이를 통해 시상식이 소개되고 있음을 알 수 있으므로 (D)가 정답이다.

Paraphrase Awards Banquet
→ awards ceremony

46. 화자가 "분명 이분들 중 일부는 여러분도 잘 알고 계실 겁니다"라고 말할 때 의미하는 것은 무엇인가?

(A) 청자들에게 영화 관련 정보가 주어졌다.
(B) 특별 손님들이 잘 알려진 사람들이다.
(C) 행사 주최측에서 청자들에게 감사하고 있다.
(D) 청자들이 각자 자신을 소개해야 한다.

해설 많은 특별 손님들이 수상자들에게 시상을 하기 위해 이 자리에 와 있다고(We have many special guests here to present prizes to the deserving winners) 알리면서 해당 문장을 말한 뒤, 유명 영화 감독을 예로 들고(For example, renowned director Magnus Karlsson) 있다. 이를 통해 특별 손님들이 유명 인사임을 강조한 말이라는 것을 알 수 있으므로 이에 해당되는 의미를 지닌 (B)가 정답이다.

어휘 well-known 잘 알려진 organizer 주최자, 조직자 be grateful to ~에게 감사하다 introduce ~을 소개하다

47. 화자의 말에 따르면, 행사 후에 무슨 일이 있을 것인가?

(A) 식사가 제공될 것이다.

(B) 콘서트가 열릴 것이다.
(C) 영화가 상영될 것이다.
(D) 공지가 있을 것이다.

해설 담화에서 행사가 끝난 시점에 있을 일로 언급되는 것을 찾아야 한다. 화자가 담화 후반부에 행사가 종료되는 대로 자리에 남아 다큐멘터리 작품 상영을 즐기기를(once the event has ended ~ to enjoy a screening of his new documentary) 권하고 있다. 따라서, 행사가 종료된 후에는 영화가 상영될 것임을 알 수 있으므로 (C)가 정답이다.

어휘 **serve** (음식 등) ~을 제공하다, 내오다 **take place** 일어나다, 발생하다

Paraphrase enjoy a screening of his new documentary → A film will be shown.

Questions 48-50 refer to the following telephone message and seating chart.

Hi, Brenda, this is Mark calling. I stopped by your office, but you must've already left for the day. **48** I just wanted to let you know that tomorrow morning's meeting has been moved from Conference Room A to Conference Room C. I didn't realize that **49** the overhead projector and speakers in Room A are not working right now and are scheduled to be repaired later this week. This is an important meeting, and most of Fizzo Beverage's department heads will be in attendance. **50** You'll be sitting next to the HR Director, just opposite the Customer Service Manager. Please make sure that you take notes of all the important points we discuss. Thanks.

안녕하세요, 브렌다 씨, 저는 마크입니다. 제가 당신의 사무실에 들렀는데, 이미 퇴근하신 것이 분명했습니다. 저는 내일 아침에 있을 회의가 대회의실 A에서 대회의실 C로 옮겨졌다는 사실을 알려드리고 싶었습니다. 대회의실 A에 있는 오버헤드 프로젝터와 스피커가 현재 작동되지 않아서 이번 주 후반에 수리될 예정이라는 점을 알지 못했습니다. 이번 회의는 중요한 시간이며, 대부분의 피조 음료 회사 소속 부서장님들께서 참석하실 것입니다. 당신은 인사부장님 옆자리이자 고객 서비스 부장님 바로 맞은편 자리에 앉게 되실 것입니다. 우리가 논의하는 모든 중요한 요점들을 반드시 기록해 두시기 바랍니다. 감사합니다.

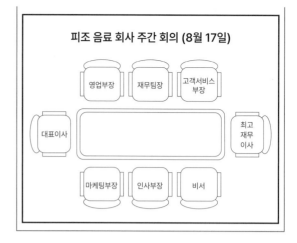

피조 음료 회사 주간 회의 (8월 17일)

영업부장 / 재무팀장 / 고객서비스부장 / 대표이사 / 최고재무이사 / 마케팅부장 / 인사부장 / 비서

어휘 **stop by** ~에 들르다 **must have p.p.** ~한 것이 분명하다, 틀림 없다 **leave for the day** 퇴근하다 **let A know that** A에게 ~임을 알리다 **be moved from A to B** A에서 B로 옮겨지다 **overhead projector** 오버헤드 프로젝터 **work** (기계가) 작동되다 **be scheduled to do** ~할 예정이다 **repair** ~을 수리하다 **department head** 부서장 **in attendance** 참석한, 출석한 **just opposite** ~의 바로 맞은편에 **make sure that** 반드시 ~하도록 하다 **take notes of** ~을 적어 두다, 메모하다 **director** 이사, 부장 **CEO(Chief Exective Officer)** 최고 경영자, 대표이사 **CFO(Chief Finance Officer)** 최고재무이사 **secretary** 비서

48. 전화의 주 목적은 무엇인가?
(A) 회의 주제들을 이야기하는 것
(B) 도움을 요청하는 것
(C) 장소 변경을 알리는 것
(D) 초대를 하는 것

해설 담화 초반부에 화자는 인사를 한 후에 내일 아침에 있을 회의 장소가 옮겨졌다는 사실을 알려 주려 했다고(I just wanted to let you know that tomorrow morning's meeting has been moved from Conference Room A to Conference Room C) 언급하고 있다. 따라서, 장소 변경을 알리는 것이 전화의 목적임을 알 수 있으므로 (C)가 정답이다.

어휘 **extend an invitation** 초대하다, 초대장을 보내다

49. 화자는 무슨 문제점을 언급하는가?
(A) 한 부서장이 회의에 참석할 수 없다.
(B) 일부 개조 공사가 일정에 뒤쳐져 있다.
(C) 일부 장비가 제대로 작동하지 않고 있다.
(D) 한 프로젝트가 성공적이지 못했다.

해설 화자가 언급하는 문제점을 찾아야 하므로 부정적인 정보가 제시되는 부분에서 단서를 파악해야 한다. 담화 중반부에 화자가 오버헤드 프로젝터와 스피커가 작동되지 않아서 이번 주 후반에 수리될 예정이라는 문제점을(~ the overhead projector and speakers in Room A are not working right now ~)

알리고 있다. 이는 일부 장비가 제대로 작동하지 않고 있다는 의미이므로 (C)가 정답이다.

어휘 renovation 개조, 보수 behind schedule 일정에 뒤처진 equipment 장비 malfunction 제대로 작동하지 않다

Paraphrase the overhead projector and speakers / are not working
→ equipment has malfunctioned

50. 시각자료를 보시오. 청자의 직책은 무엇이겠는가?
(A) 대표이사
(B) 비서
(C) 영업부장
(D) 재무팀장

해설 담화 후반부에 화자가 상대방에게 인사부장 옆 자리이자 고객 서비스 팀장 바로 맞은편 자리에 앉게 될 것이라고(You'll be sitting next to the HR Director, just opposite the Customer Service Manager) 알리고 있다. 시각자료에서 해당 위치에 Secretary라고 표기되어 있으므로 (B)가 정답이다.

Part 5

51.
정답 (C)

해석 우리의 최근 설문 조사에 참가한 대부분의 사람들이 우리 제품과 서비스에 만족하고 있다.

해설 빈칸 뒤에 위치한 전치사 with는 be satisfied 구조와 결합해 '(사람이) ~에 만족하다'라는 의미를 나타내므로 (C) are satisfied가 정답이다.

어휘 take part in ~에 참가하다 recent 최근의 satisfy ~을 만족시키다 satisfied (사람이) 만족한

52.
정답 (A)

해석 듀어 씨의 지도 하에, 마케팅팀이 혁신적인 국제 광고 캠페인을 만들어냈다.

해설 빈칸 뒤에 명사구가 위치해 있어 명사구를 목적어로 취하는 전치사가 빈칸에 쓰여야 알맞으므로 선택지에서 유일한 전치사인 (A) Under가 정답이다.

어휘 guidance 지도, 안내 innovative 혁신적인 under (관리, 감독 등) ~ 하에 instead 대신 while ~하는 동안, ~인 반면

53.
정답 (D)

해석 리 씨의 행사 초대장이 엉뚱한 주소로 전달되었기 때문에, 포스터 씨의 은퇴 기념 만찬에 참석하지 않았다.

해설 빈칸 뒤에 위치한 동사의 의미로 볼 때, 빈칸 앞에 위치한 명사 event는 전달의 대상으로 맞지 않으므로 빈칸에 전달 가능한 것을 나타내는 또 다른 명사가 들어가 event와 복합명사를 구성해야 한다는 것을 알 수 있다. 또한, 단수동사 was delivered와 수 일치되는 단수명사가 필요하므로 (D) invitation이 정답이다.

어휘 retirement 은퇴 invitation 초대(장) invite ~을 초대하다

54.
정답 (B)

해석 한 미술 전문가의 말에 따르면, 최근 발견된 초상화들은 아마 은둔 미술가인 조 무트에 의해 그려졌을 것이다.

해설 수동태 동사를 구성하는 be동사와 과거분사 painted 사이에 위치한 빈칸은 과거분사를 수식할 부사가 필요한 자리이므로 (B) likely가 정답이다.

어휘 according to ~에 따르면 recently 최근 discover ~을 발견하다 portrait 초상화 reclusive 은둔한, 속세를 떠난 likely ad. 아마 a. ~할 가능성이 있는, ~할 것 같은 likelihood 가능성, 있음직함

55.
정답 (B)

해석 웨이크필드 은행은 현재 휴대전화 이용자들을 위해 새로운 전자 금융 애플리케이션을 개발하고 있다.

해설 현재진행시제 동사를 구성하는 be동사와 현재분사 developing 사이에 빈칸이 위치해 있으므로 '현재, 지금'이라는 의미로 현재진행시제 동사와 함께 사용하는 (B) currently가 정답이다.

어휘 electronic banking 전자 금융 (시스템) previously 이전에, 과거에 currently 현재, 지금 severely 극심하게, 심각하게 frequently 자주, 빈번히

56.
정답 (C)

해석 최신 호에 대한 출간 마감일을 지키기 위해, 노레스 씨는 휴일 동안에 혼자 편집 작업을 완료했다.

해설 선택지가 대명사로 구성되어 있고, 전치사 by 뒤에 빈칸이 있으므로 by와 결합해 '혼자, 스스로'라는 의미를 구성할 때 사용하는 재귀대명사 (C) himself가 정답이다.

어휘 meet the deadline 마감시한을 맞추다 publishing 출간, 발간 latest 최신의 edition (잡지 등의) 호, 판 editing 편집 by oneself 혼자, 스스로

57.
정답 (B)

해석 현대적인 식사 경향에 적응하기 위해, 많은 레스토랑들이 지난 몇 년 동안에 채식주의자를 위한 선택권을 더 많이 제공하기 시작했다.

해설 In order to 구문 뒤로 주어와 빈칸, 그리고 동명사구만 있으므로 빈칸은 문장의 동사 자리이다. 과거에서 현재까지 이어지는 기간을 의미하는 시간부사구 in the last few years가 있으므로 동사의 시제는 현재완료시제여야 한다. 따라서 (B) have begun이 정답이다.

어휘 adapt to ~에 적응하다 modern 현대적인 dining 식사 vegetarian 채식주의자 option 선택권

58.

정답 (C)

해석 ATR 커뮤니케이션즈의 위치 이전에 대한 최종 결정이 오늘 오후에 내려질 것이다.

해설 명사 decision은 동사 make와 결합해 '결정을 내리다'라는 의미를 나타낸다. 따라서 decision이 주어 자리로 이동한 수동태 문장에서 '결정이 내려지다'와 같은 수동의 의미를 구성하려면 make가 과거분사로 쓰여야 하므로 (C) made가 정답이다.

어휘 decision 결정 relocation (위치) 이전, 이사 regard ~을 …라고 여기다, ~을 평가하다

59.

정답 (D)

해석 다음 주 월요일부터, 빅 타코 고객들께 라지 사이즈 식사를 엑스트라 라지 사이즈 식사로 업그레이드하실 수 있는 선택권이 제공될 것입니다.

해설 빈칸 바로 뒤에 시점 표현 next Monday가 쓰여 있으므로 시점 표현과 결합해 '~부터 (시작되어)'라는 시작 시점의 의미를 나타낼 때 사용하는 (D) Beginning이 정답이다.

어휘 option to do ~할 수 있는 선택권 beginning + 시점 ~부터 (시작되어)

60.

정답 (A)

해석 놀랍게도, 올해의 브리티시 영화상 후보들 중 누구도 이전에 상을 받은 적이 없었다.

해설 콤마와 함께 문장 맨 앞에 위치한 빈칸은 문장 전체를 수식하는 역할을 할 부사가 쓰여야 하는 자리이므로 (A) Surprisingly가 정답이다.

어휘 nominee (상 등의) 후보, 지명된 사람 win an award 상을 받다 surprisingly 놀랍게도 surprise ~을 놀라게 하다 surprised (사람이) 놀란 surprising 놀라게 만드는

61.

정답 (A)

해석 3층에 있는 구내식당이 개조 공사가 진행되는 동안 장기간 폐쇄될 것입니다.

해설 빈칸은 전치사 for의 목적어로서 '장기적인' 등을 뜻하는 prolonged와 어울리는 기간을 나타내야 자연스러우므로 '기간, 시기' 등을 의미하는 (A) period가 정답이다.

어휘 prolonged 장기적인, 오래 계속되는 while ~하는 동안 underway 진행 중인 lapse (시간의) 경과, 추이

62.

정답 (A)

해석 직업 개발 프로그램에 대한 비용 예산이 세워졌지만, 회사의 이사는 내년까지 프로그램 시행에 착수하려 하지 않는다.

해설 budget은 명사와 동사로 모두 사용 가능한데, 명사일 경우에 의미가 자연스럽지 않으므로 오답이다. 따라서 빈칸은 has been과 함께 현재완료시제를 구성하는 동사의 일부가 되어야 하는데, 빈칸 다음에 목적어가 없으므로 수동태를 나타내는 과거분사 (A) budgeted가 정답이다.

어휘 professional development program 직업 개발 프로그램 be willing to do 기꺼이 ~하다 proceed with ~에 착수하다, 진행하다 implementation 시행, 이행

63.

정답 (D)

해석 델타 사무용품에서 문구 제품을 주문하는 분들은 누구나 보통 48시간 이내에 제품을 수령한다.

해설 선택지가 관계사로 구성되어 있고, 빈칸이 문장의 주어와 관계사절의 동사 자리에 위치해 있으므로 빈칸은 문장의 주어 Anyone을 수식할 수 있는 주격 관계대명사 자리이다. 따라서, (D) who가 정답이다.

어휘 stationery 문구 normally 보통, 일반적으로

64.

정답 (A)

해석 노트북 컴퓨터에 결함이 있는 고객들은 알러톤이나 판햄에 있는 저희 기술 지원 센터 중에서 더 편리한 곳을 방문하시면 됩니다.

해설 빈칸 앞에는 주어와 동사를 포함한 완전한 절이, 빈칸 다음에는 동사와 형용사가 이어지고 있으므로 이 절은 추가 설명을 위해 덧붙여진 부사절인 것으로 판단할 수 있으며, 접속사 없이 이 절을 이끌 수 있는 복합관계대명사 (A) whichever가 정답이다.

어휘 faulty 결함이 있는 technical support 기술 지원

65.

정답 (B)

해석 만약 내일 워크숍에 참석하지 못한다 할지라도, 동봉된 양식을 이번 주 금요일까지 꼭 보내주시기 바랍니다.

해설 빈칸은 주어와 동사를 포함한 두 절을 연결할 접속사가 필요한 자리이다. 선택지에서 접속사 Whether는 or가 동반되어야 하고, Yet은 접속사로 쓰일 경우에 문장 맨 앞에 올 수 없으므로 양보의 의미를 나타내는 (B) Even if가 정답이다.

어휘 even if ~라 할지라도 make sure that 확실하게 ~하다, 꼭 ~하다 nevertheless 그럼에도 불구하고

66.

정답 (D)

해석 그린웨이 그로서리가 운영하는 소매 지점들 중에서, 웨스트파크 쇼핑몰에 있는 지점이 가장 수익성이 좋다.

해설 콤마 뒤에 최상급 표현 the most profitable과 함께 웨스트파크 쇼핑몰에 있는 지점이 가장 수익성이 좋다는 말이 쓰여 있어 빈칸 뒤에 위치한 복수명사구 the retail locations가 그 비교 대상이 포함된 범위에 해당된다는 것을 알 수 있다. 따라서 '~ 중에서'라는 의미로 최상급 표현과 어울리는 비교 대상 범위를 말할 때 사용하는 (D) Of가 정답이다.

어휘 retail 소매(업) location 지점, 위치 operate ~을 운영하다 profitable 수익성이 있는 during ~ 중에, ~ 동안 above (분리된 위치) ~ 위쪽에, (수량, 정도 등) ~을 넘어, ~ 보다 나은

Part 6

67-70.

그랜드뷰 아파트의 모든 세입자께

공용 수영장이 긴급 수리 작업으로 인해 4월 4일부터 4월 8일까지 폐쇄될 것이라는 점에 유의하시기 바랍니다. 이 **67** 작업은 매일 오전 10시에서 오후 5시 사이에 진행될 것입니다.

이 수영장이 수리되는 **68** 동안, 반드시 안전을 위해 아이들이 해당 구역에서 멀리 떨어져 있도록 해주시기 바랍니다. **69** 현장에 여러 가지 잠재적으로 위험한 공구들이 있을 것입니다. 추가로, 세입자들께 물품 보관실에서 어떤 귀중한 소지품이든 치우시도록 권해 드리는데, 수리 작업팀이 임시로 일부 장비를 보관하기 위해 이 공간을 이용해야 할 수도 있기 때문입니다.

이 수리 작업은 반드시 수영장이 시의 규정을 **70** 준수하도록 하는 데 필수적입니다. 여러분의 인내와 양해에 감사 드립니다.

어휘 tenant 세입자 take note that ~라는 점에 유의하다 communal 공용의 urgent 긴급한 take place (일, 행사 등이) 진행되다, 일어나다, 개최되다 under ~ 중인, ~의 영향을 받는 make sure that 반드시 하도록 하다, ~임을 확실히 해두다(= ensure that) be kept away from ~에서 멀리 떨어진 상태로 있다 be advised to do ~하도록 권고되다, ~하는 것이 좋다 valuable 귀중한, 소중한 belongings 소지품 storage 보관, 저장 crew (함께 작업하는) 팀, 조 temporarily 임시로, 일시적으로 regulation 규정, 규제 appreciate ~에 대해 감사하다 patience 인내(심)

67.

정답 (A)

해설 빈칸 뒤에 진행 시간대를 알리는 정보가 쓰여 있는데, 이는 앞선 문장에서 언급한 긴급 수리 작업이 실시되는 시간대로 볼 수 있다. 따라서 빈칸에 쓰일 명사는 urgent repairs를 대신할 수 있는 것이어야 하므로 '작업'을 뜻하는 (A) work이 정답이다.

68.

정답 (C)

해설 빈칸과 콤마 사이에는 주어와 동사가 포함된 절이, 콤마 뒤에는 명령문 구조의 절이 쓰여 있어 빈칸에 접속사가 필요하므로 (C) While과 (D) Yet 중에서 정답을 골라야 하는데, Yet이 접속사로 쓰일 경우 문장 맨 앞에 올 수 없으므로 (C) While이 정답이다.

어휘 even ad. 심지어 (~도), (비교급 강조) 훨씬 a. 평평한, 일정한 during ~ 중에, ~ 동안 while ~하는 동안, ~인 반면 yet 아직, 그런데도, (최상급과 함께) 지금까지 중에서

69.

정답 (D)

해석 (A) 여러분의 의견이 편의시설을 개선하는 데 있어 저희에게 도움이 되었습니다.
(B) 저희는 매주 수요일에 아동 수영 강습을 제공합니다.
(C) 안전 요원이 항상 수영장에 대기하고 있을 것입니다.
(D) 현장에 여러 가지 잠재적으로 위험한 공구들이 있을 것입니다.

해설 빈칸 앞에 반드시 안전을 위해 아이들이 작업 구역에서 멀리 떨어져 있도록 하라고 당부하는 말이 쓰여 있으므로 꼭 그렇게 해야 하는 이유로서 현장에 존재하는 잠재적 위험 요소를 알리는 (D)가 정답이다.

어휘 improve ~을 개선하다, ~을 향상시키다 amenities 편의시설 lifeguard 안전 요원, 인명 구조원 present 자리에 있는, 참석한 at all times 항상 potentially 잠재적으로 on site 현장에

70.

정답 (C)

해설 빈칸이 속한 that절에 주어와 빈칸, 그리고 전치사구만 쓰여 있어 빈칸이 that절의 동사 자리임을 알 수 있다. 따라서 선택지에서 유일한 동사로서 3인칭 단수 주어 the swimming pool과 수 일치되는 단수 동사 (C) complies가 정답이다.

어휘 comply (with) (~을) 준수하다 compliance 준수, 따름

71-74.

개별 식사 공간 대여

보네티 레스토랑이 새로운 개별 식사 룸을 선보입니다! 장관인 호숫가에서의 식사 경험을 **71** 여러분의 것으로 만들 수 있습니다! 모든 개별 식사 룸이 베넷 호수의 그림 같은 경치를 **72** 특징으로 합니다. 여러분께서는 갓 잡아 올린 다양한 해산물과 지역에서 나는 음식 재료들을 완전히 사적인 공간에서 즐기실 수 있습니다. 또한 군침이 도는 다양한 디저트들도 맛보실 수 있습니다. **73** 하지만, 이 디저트를 즐기실 배가 남아 있지 않을 수도 있습니다! 저희

> 보네티 레스토랑은 음식 양을 매우 넉넉하게 제공하기로 유명하므로, 메인 코스가 끝나면 배가 잔뜩 부를 수 있습니다! 저희 개별 식사 공간은 최대 25인 단체손님까지 예약하실 수 있습니다. **74** 특별한 상황이라면 더 많은 인원도 수용 가능합니다. 곧 저희 보네티 레스토랑에서 뵙기를 바랍니다!
>
> 앤드류 보네티 (555-0097), 레스토랑 총 지배인

어휘 private dining room 개별 식사 공간 for hire 대여 가능한, 유료로 이용하는 spectacular 장관을 이루는 lakeside 호숫가, 호반 picturesque 그림 같은 freshly-caught 갓 잡아 올린 locally-sourced 지역에서 공급 받는 total 전적인, 완전한 privacy 사적인 시간, 상태 mouth-watering 군침을 돌게 하는 have A left A가 남아 있다 room 여력, 여지 try ~을 한 번 먹어 보다 pride oneself on ~을 자랑으로 여기다 generous 넉넉한, 후한 portion size 음식 양, 1인분 full 배부른

71.
정답 (B)

해설 빈칸 앞 문장에 새로운 식사 공간을 제공하기 시작했다고 하므로 그 다음 문장의 멋진 경관을 보면서 식사하는 일은 새로운 공간에서 고객이 누리는 일이어야 한다. 따라서 '여러분의 것'이라는 의미를 나타내는 소유대명사 (B) yours가 정답이다.

72.
정답 (C)

해설 빈칸 앞뒤로 명사구들만 있으므로 빈칸은 문장의 동사 자리이며, 특정 장소의 경관이 그림 같은 것은 현재의 사실이므로 현재 시제 동사 (C) feature가 정답이다.

어휘 feature ~을 특징으로 하다, 포함하다

73.
정답 (A)

해설 빈칸 앞에서 맛있는 다양한 디저트들을 먹어 볼 수 있다고 했는데, 빈칸 뒤에는 그 디저트들을 즐기지 못할 가능성이 언급되므로 대조적인 내용 흐름임을 알 수 있다. 따라서 대조나 반대를 나타낼 때 사용하는 (A) However가 정답이다.

어휘 however 하지만 therefore 그러므로, 따라서 similarly 유사하게, 마찬가지로 consequently 결과적으로, 따라서

74.
정답 (D)

해석 (A) 그분들 모두가 저희의 여러 인상적인 요리들을 극찬하셨습니다.
(B) 저희는 이달 말까지 개조 공사가 완료될 것으로 예상하고 있습니다.
(C) 이것들은 여러분의 식사 관련 요건을 충족하도록 맞춤 제공될 수 있습니다.
(D) 특별한 상황이라면 더 많은 인원도 수용 가능합니다.

해설 바로 앞 문장에 최대 25인의 단체손님들을 받을 수 있다고 되어 있으므로 수용 인원과 관련되어 추가 정보를 제공하는 (D)가 정답이다.

어휘 praise ~을 칭찬하다 expect A to do A가 ~할 것으로 예상하다 by (기한) ~까지 customize ~을 맞춤 제공하다 dietary 식사의, 음식의 requirement 요건, 필수 조건 party 사람들, 일행 accommodate ~을 수용하다 circumstance 상황, (주변) 환경

Part 7

75-76.

> **윌슨 컴퓨터 매장**
>
> 이 쿠폰은 소지자에게 단일 상품 구매에 대한 1회 할인을 받을 수 있는 자격을 드립니다.
>
> 이 카드를 가지고, 저희 매장의 노트북 컴퓨터와 가정용 PC에 대해 10 퍼센트 할인, 모니터에 20퍼센트 할인, 또는 신제품인 휴대용 하드 드라이브에는 15퍼센트 할인을 받을 수 있습니다.
>
> **75** 컴퓨터 키보드, 헤드셋, 그리고 스피커는 이 할인에 포함되지 않습니다. **76** 이 쿠폰은 모든 윌슨 컴퓨터 매장 지점에서 사용 가능하며, 12월 말까지 사용되어야 합니다.

어휘 entitle ~에게 자격을 주다 bearer 소지자 new lines of ~의 신제품 portable 휴대용의 offer 할인 branch 지점, 지사

75. 할인이 제공되지 않는 것은 무엇인가?
(A) 노트북 컴퓨터
(B) 컴퓨터 키보드
(C) 외장 하드 드라이브
(D) 데스크탑 컴퓨터

정답 (B)

해설 지문 마지막 문단에서 컴퓨터 키보드, 헤드셋, 그리고 스피커는 할인에 포함되지 않는다고(Computer keyboards, headsets, and speakers are not included in this offer) 언급되어 있으므로 (B)가 정답이다.

어휘 external 외부의, 외부적인

76. 윌슨 컴퓨터 매장에 대해 명시된 것은 무엇인가?
(A) 12월에 새로운 지점을 열 것이다.
(B) 다수의 영업장을 가지고 있다.
(C) 신제품과 중고품을 모두 판매한다.
(D) 컴퓨터 신제품을 홍보하고 있다.

정답 (B)

해설 마지막 문장에서 쿠폰을 모든 윌슨 컴퓨터 매장 지점에서 사용할 수 있다고(This coupon can be used at all

Wilson's Computer Store branches) 언급되어 있으므로 (B)가 정답이다.

어휘 **multiple** 다수의, 많은 **business location** 영업장, 지점 **promote** ~을 홍보하다

77-79.

레베카 칼튼, 대표이사
볼콤 회사

칼튼 씨께,

저는 최근 <롱 비치 비즈니스 저널> 5월호에 최고 재무 이사 (CFO) 공석이 광고된 사실을 알게 되었습니다. 동봉해 드린 제 이력서에서 보실 수 있듯이, 저는 20년이 넘는 비즈니스 및 재무 경력을 지니고 있습니다. 저는 펜델 주식회사의 회계부에 5년 동안 고용된 후에 재무팀으로 옮겨졌습니다. **77** 이 부서에서의 첫 해에 회사 비용을 18퍼센트 절감하도록 도운 후에, 이 회사의 샌프란시스코 본사에서 재무팀장으로 승진되어, 이후 6년동안 회사 재무의 전략 기획 및 예산 편성을 책임지게 되었습니다.

78 저는 계속해서 9년 전에 와일리 건설 주식회사의 샌디에이고 본사에 재무이사로 입사했습니다. 그곳에서 이사로 재직한 기간에, 참신한 재무 운영 모델을 확립하고 시행하는 데 있어 중요한 역할을 했으며, 이는 그 회사가 더욱 정확한 재무 예측을 하고 더욱 효율적으로 자금을 할당할 수 있게 해주었습니다.

79 제 경험 및 해당 역할에 대한 적합성을 더욱 자세히 이야기할 수 있도록 직접 뵙고 귀하와 말씀 나눌 기회를 저에게 주실 수 있다면 감사하겠습니다. 인내심을 갖고 귀하의 답변을 기다리도록 하겠습니다.

안녕히 계십시오.

네이선 포그바

어휘 **notice** ~을 알아차리다 **vacancy** 공석 **enclosed** 동봉된 **be promoted to** ~로 승진되다 **go on to do** 계속해서 ~하다 **play a key role in** ~에 있어 중요한 역할을 하다 **establish** ~을 확립하다 **implement** ~을 시행하다 **novel** 참신한, 새로운 **operating model** 운영 모델 **make a projection** 예측하다 **allocate** ~을 할당하다, 배분하다 **funds** 자금 **in person** 직접 만나서 **suitability for** ~에 대한 적합성 **in more detail** 더 자세히 **patiently** 인내심을 갖고, 참을성 있게 **await** ~을 기다리다

77. 편지에 따르면, 왜 포그바 씨는 펜델 주식회사에서 승진되었는가?

(A) 회사가 연간 수익을 늘리도록 도움을 주었다.
(B) 혁신적인 재무 관리 모델을 만들어냈다.
(C) 회사 지출 비용의 감소에 기여했다.
(D) 회사의 고객 기반을 늘렸다.

정답 (C)

해설 첫 단락 후반부에 재무 팀에서 첫 해에 회사 비용을 18퍼센트

절감하도록 도운 후에 본사에서 재무팀장으로 승진되었다고(After helping to cut the company's costs by 18 percent within my first year in the department, I was promoted) 알리고 있다. 즉, 회사 지출 비용을 줄이는 데 기여한 것이므로 (C)가 정답이다.

어휘 **revenue** 수익, 수입 **innovative** 혁신적인 **contribute to** ~에 기여하다, 공헌하다 **lowering** 감소, 하락 **expenditure** 지출 비용 **customer base** 고객 기반, 고객층

78. 포그바 씨는 얼마나 오래 와일리 건설 주식회사에서 일해 오고 있는가?

(A) 5년
(B) 6년
(C) 9년
(D) 20년

정답 (C)

해설 두 번째 단락에 9년 전에 와일리 건설 주식회사의 샌디에이고 본사에 재무이사로 입사했다고(I went on to join Wiley Construction Inc. as the Director of Finance at its head office in San Diego nine years ago) 알리고 있고, 그 뒤로 다른 경력이 언급되지 않았으므로 (C)가 정답이다.

79. 포그바 씨는 왜 칼튼 씨에게 편지를 쓰는가?

(A) 한 프로젝트에 대해 협업하는 것을 제안하기 위해
(B) 상담 전문가로서 자신의 서비스를 제공하기 위해
(C) 더 많은 정보를 요청하기 위해
(D) 약속을 정하기 위해

정답 (D)

해설 마지막 단락에 자신의 경험 및 해당 역할에 대한 적합성을 더욱 자세히 이야기할 수 있도록 직접 만나 이야기 나눌 기회를 줄 수 있다면 감사할 것이라고(I would appreciate it if you could give me the opportunity to speak with you in person) 알리고 있다. 이는 포그바 씨가 면접을 보고 싶다는 의사를 밝힌 것이므로 만날 약속을 잡고 싶다는 뜻으로 쓰인 (D)가 정답이다.

어휘 **set up an appointment** 약속을 정하다

80-82.

수신: WalterSpiegel@whcc.com
발신: AlisonRiley@gomail.com
날짜: 8월 19일
제목: 잘못된 청구 요금

스피겔 씨께,

82 저는 수영장 이용과 테니스 레스, 그리고 운동 시설 이용 권한을 포함하는 소셜 멤버십 약정을 이용하고 있는 컨트리 클럽 회원입니다. — [1] —. 하지만, 제가 현재 5월에서 7월에 이르는 기간에 대한 청구서를 확인해보고 있는데, **80** 제가 965달러를 청구

받은 내용이 보입니다. 제가 잘못 알고 있는 것이 아니라면, 이는 일반적으로 기업 멤버십을 신청하는 사람들에게 적용되는 요금입니다. — [2] —.

8개월 전에 이 컨트리 클럽에 가입한 이후로, 저는 결코 한 번도 제 멤버십을 업그레이드한 적이 없습니다. — [3] —. 잠시 시간 내셔서 컴퓨터 데이터베이스를 확인해 보신다면, 분명 이 부분이 사실임을 아시게 될 것입니다. 현 시점까지, 저는 이 컨트리 클럽 및 시설에 매우 깊은 인상을 받아 왔으며, 회원들에 대해 귀하의 부서가 보여준 세심함을 언급할 필요도 없습니다. — [4] —. 저는 앞으로 몇 년간 귀하의 컨트리 클럽 회원으로 남아 있을 계획이므로, **81** 5월에서 7월까지의 기간에 대한 청구서를 수정해 새로운 청구서를 발송해 주실 수 있다면 감사하겠습니다. 어떤 정보든 필요하실 경우에 555-1192번으로 저에게 주저하지 마시고 연락 주시기 바랍니다.

신속히 이 문제를 해결해 주실 수 있다면 대단히 감사하겠습니다. 고맙습니다.

안녕히 계십시오.

앨리슨 라일리

어휘 **bill** 청구서, 고지서 **be charged A** (요금 등) A를 청구 받다 **Unless I am mistaken** 제가 잘못 알고 있는 것이 아니라면 **apply** ~을 적용하다 **at no time** 결코 ~하지 않다, 한 번도 ~하지 않다 **see that A is the case** A가 사실임을 알다 **up until this point** 현 시점까지 **be impressed with** ~에 깊은 인상을 받다 **not to mention** ~은 언급할 필요도 없이 **attentiveness** 세심함 **amend** ~을 수정하다 **resolve** ~을 해결하다 **swiftly** 신속히

80. 이메일은 왜 보내졌는가?
(A) 멤버십 옵션에 관해 문의하기 위해
(B) 좋은 서비스에 대해 감사 인사를 하기 위해
(C) 시설에 대한 이용을 요청하기 위해
(D) 청구 요금에 대한 불만을 제기하기 위해

정답 (D)

해설 첫 단락에 965달러를 청구 받은 내용이 보인다는 말과 함께 그것이 일반적으로 기업 멤버십을 신청하는 사람들에게 적용되는 요금이라고(I have been charged $965. ~ this is the fee normally applied to those who sign up for a Corporate Membership) 알리고 있다. 이는 잘못된 요금 청구에 대해 불만을 제기하는 것이므로 (D)가 정답이다.

어휘 **inquire about** ~에 관해 문의하다 **access to** ~에 대한 이용, 접근 **charge** n. 청구 요금

81. 라일리 씨는 컨트리 클럽이 무엇을 하도록 요청하는가?
(A) 전액 환불을 제공하는 일
(B) 지불 기한을 연장하는 일
(C) 자신의 멤버십을 업그레이드하는 일
(D) 자신에게 수정된 청구서를 보내는 일

정답 (D)

해설 두 번째 단락 후반부에 5월에서 7월까지의 기간에 대한 청구서를 수정해 새것을 발송해 달라고(I would appreciate it if you could amend the bill for the period of May to July and send a new one out) 요청하는 말이 쓰여 있으므로 (D)가 정답이다.

어휘 **issue a full refund** 전액 환불을 제공하다 **extend** ~을 연장하다 **revised** 수정된

82. [1], [2], [3], [4]로 표기된 위치들 중에서, 다음 문장이 들어가기에 가장 적절한 곳은 어디인가?

"저는 일반적으로 이러한 혜택들에 대한 모든 이용 서비스를 받기 위해 분기당 820달러를 지불합니다."

(A) [1]
(B) [2]
(C) [3]
(D) [4]

정답 (A)

해설 제시된 문장은 앞서 언급된 혜택들을(these benefits) 이용하는데 분기당 820달러를 지불한다는 의미를 담고 있다. 따라서 회원이 이용할 수 있는 몇 가지 서비스가 쓰여 있는 문장 뒤에 위치한 [1]에 들어가 그 서비스에 대해 지불하는 비용을 알리는 흐름이 되어야 자연스러우므로 (A)가 정답이다.

어휘 **typically** 일반적으로, 전형적으로 **full** 모든, 완전한, 전면적인 **benefit** 혜택, 이득

83-86.

게시일: 9월 1일

토론토 시내에서 이용 가능한 상업용 점포
임대료: 월 4,500달러

실버레이크 쇼핑 센터 내에 대형 상업용 공간이 이달 말에 자리를 비우게 됩니다. **83** 새로운 입주자께서는 10월 1일에 해당 점포에서 영업을 개시하실 수 있습니다. 이곳은 서쪽 출입구에서 가까운 1층에 편리하게 위치해 있어, 결과적으로 많은 유동 인구와 아주 많은 잠재 고객들이 생기는 곳입니다. **84** 또한 행사 무대나 푸드 코트 같이 분주한 구역들과 아주 가까운 거리에 위치해 있습니다. 이 쇼핑 센터 내에서 빈 점포를 찾아 보는 것이 매우 드문 일이며, 이곳의 상업용 공간들은 대단히 선호되는 곳입니다.

85 29만 평방미터의 실버레이크 쇼핑 센터는 시내 지역의 다른 쇼핑몰들보다 더 넓으며, 가장 많은 소비사들을 끌어들이고 있습니다. 해당 점포는 설치하시기를 바라는 어떤 진열 제품에 대해서도 충분한 공간을 지니고 있으며, 다수의 조절 가능한 선반들이 포함되어 있습니다. **86** 이 쇼핑몰에서 상업 공간을 임대하는 모든 매장 소유주들께서는 건물과 인접한 주차장에 지정 주차 공간을 배정 받습니다.

실버레이크 쇼핑 센터 매장 소유주들께서는 또한 쇼핑 센터 5층

에 위치한 피카딜리 영화관에서 많은 할인 서비스도 받습니다. 해당 점포는 쇼핑몰이 문을 닫는 일요일에 격주로 둘러보실 수 있으며, 첫 번째는 9월 7일 일요일에, 그 다음으로 2주 후인 9월 21일 일요일에 가능합니다. 둘러보실 시간을 마련하시거나 추가 정보를 얻으시려면, propertyoffice@silverlake.com으로 이메일 보내시기 바랍니다.

어휘 **commercial** 상업용의 **unit** (상가, 아파트 등의) 점포, 세대 **vacate** ~을 비우다, ~에서 떠나다 **tenant** 입주자 **result in** ~의 결과를 낳다, ~을 초래하다 **heavy** (양, 정도 등이) 많은, 심한 **footfall** 유동 인구, 고객 수 **vacancy** 빈자리 **desirable** (사람 들이) 선호하는, 바라는 **ample** 충분한 **room** (부정관사 없이) 공간 **adjustable** 조절 가능한 **assign A B** A에게 B를 배정하다, 할당하다 **adjacent to** ~와 인접한 **alternate** 번갈아 발생되는 **arrange** ~을 마련하다, 조치하다 **viewing** 둘러보기

83. 점포가 언제 임대로 이용 가능할 것인가?
(A) 9월 1일에
(B) 9월 7일에
(C) 9월 21일에
(D) 10월 1일에

정답 (D)

해설 지문 시작 부분에 새로운 입주자가 10월 1일에 해당 점포에서 영업을 개시할 수 있다고(A new tenant may open for business in the unit on October 1) 알리고 있으므로 (D)가 정답이다.

84. 해당 상업용 공간에 관해 암시된 것은 무엇인가?
(A) 최근에 개조되었다.
(B) 여러 방들로 구성되어 있다.
(C) 쇼핑몰 5층에 위치해 있다.
(D) 식당 시설과 가까이 있다.

정답 (D)

해설 첫 단락에 행사 무대나 푸드 코트 같이 분주한 구역들과 아주 가까운 거리에 위치해 있다는(It is also just a short distance from busy areas such as the event stage and food court) 특징이 제시되어 있으므로 (D)가 정답이다.

어휘 **be comprised of** ~로 구성되다 **dining** 식사 **establishment** (학교, 식당, 병원, 가게 등의) 시설(물)

85. 실버레이크 쇼핑 센터에 관해 언급된 것은 무엇인가?
(A) 시내 지역에서 가장 높은 건물이다.
(B) 지역 내 다른 쇼핑 센터들보다 더 크다.
(C) 현재 다수의 비어 있는 상업용 점포들이 있다.
(D) 주말마다 문을 닫는다.

정답 (B)

해설 지문 중반부에 29만 평방미터의 실버레이크 쇼핑 센터가 시내 지역의 나머지 다른 쇼핑몰들보다 더 넓다고(The

290,000-square-meter Silverlake Shopping Center is more expansive than the other malls in the downtown area) 알리는 내용이 쓰여 있으므로 이러한 규모의 차이를 언급한 (B)가 정답이다.

어휘 **structure** 구조(물) **vacant** 비어 있는

86. 해당 상업용 점포에 무엇이 딸려 있는가?
(A) 회원증
(B) 제품 진열
(C) 무료 영화 입장권
(D) 주차 공간

정답 (D)

해설 두 번째 단락에 해당 쇼핑몰에서 상업 공간을 임대하는 모든 매장 소유주들이 건물과 인접한 주차장에 지정 주차 공간을 배정 받는다는(All store owners renting commercial space in the mall are assigned a designated space in the parking lot) 혜택이 제시되어 있으므로 (D)가 정답이다.

어휘 **come with** ~가 딸려 있다, ~을 포함하다

87-90.

[오전 9:30]
닉: 안녕하세요 모두들, 무슨 일이에요?

[오전 9:31]
론: 모르겠어요. 톰 씨가 우리를 불렀어요.

[오전 9:38]
톰: 모두 안녕하세요. 늦어서 미안해요! 다루어야 할 긴급 사항이 있어요. **87** 엘리슨 씨에게 문자를 받았어요. 버스가 고장 나서 오늘 늦게 출근 한대요.

[오전 9:39]
닉: **90** 아, 안돼요! 저는 엘리슨 씨가 신규 고객들을 대상으로 프레젠테이션을 해줄 거라고 믿고 있었어요.

[오전 9:40]
론: 알아요! **88** 그리고 고객들은 30분 후에 도착할 거예요.

[오전 9:41]
닉: **89** 톰 씨, 그들에게 사무실을 좀 둘러보게 해주고 나서 먼저 사장님을 만나도록 하는게 어때요?

[오전 9:41]
론: 그러면 45분 정도 걸리겠네요.

[오전 9:42]
톰: 좋았어요! 그 후에, 또 어쩌면 두 분이 고객들을 아래층에 있는 커피숍에 데려 가셔도 됩니다.

[오전 9:43]
론: 좋은 생각이에요! 그때쯤이면 엘리슨 씨가 올 거예요.

[오전 9:43]
닉: 또한 고객들에게는 우리가 어떻게 일하는지 보여주는 기회가 되기도 합니다.

어휘 delay 지체 emergency 긴급상황 break down 고장 나다 depend on ~에 의존하다 give a tour 둘러보게 하다, 견학시키다 take up ~을 차지하다 as well 또한 terrific 멋진

87. 글쓴이들이 주로 논의하고 있는 것은 무엇인가?

(A) 버스 노선 변경에 대해 무엇을 할지
(B) 커피 휴식을 어디서 할지
(C) 일정 지연을 어떻게 해결할지
(D) 그들의 이전 동료를 언제 만날지

정답 (C)

해설 지문 초반에 엘리슨 씨가 늦는다는 문자 내용을(I got a text from Alison. She says her bus broke down and she will be late coming in today) 전달한 뒤, 그로 인해 고객에게 하는 발표에 문제가 있다는 내용이 이어진다. 그 뒤에 닉 씨가 사무실을 둘러보게 하는 것이 어떤지와 같은 해결책을 제시하고 있으므로 (C)가 정답이다.

어휘 avoid ~을 피하다 coworker 동료 직원

88. 고객들은 언제 도착할 것인가?

(A) 15분 후
(B) 30분 후
(C) 45분 후
(D) 60분 후

정답 (B)

해설 오전 9시 40분에 론 씨가 보낸 메시지에서 고객들이 30분 후 도착할 것이라고(they are arriving in half an hour) 언급하고 있으므로 (B)가 정답이다.

89. 닉 씨가 톰 씨에게 요청하는 것은 무엇인가?

(A) 고객을 데리고 점심 먹으러 갈 것
(B) 발표를 할 것
(C) 지연을 설명해줄 것
(D) 고객들을 안내할 것

정답 (D)

해설 오전 9시 41분에 닉 씨가 보낸 메시지를 보면 고객들에게 사무실을 둘러보게 하자는(why don't you give them a tour of the office) 제안을 하고 있으므로 (D)가 정답이다.

어휘 show around 둘러보게 하다

90. 오전 9시 40분에 론 씨가 "I know!"라고 말한 의미는 무엇인가?

(A) 문제 해결방법을 안다.
(B) 발표에 대해 걱정한다.
(C) 1분 전 엘리슨 씨에게서 문자를 받았다.
(D) 고객과의 회의를 잘 대비하고 있다.

정답 (B)

해설 론 씨가 "알아요!"라고 말하기 바로 전에 닉 씨가 보낸 메시지에 엘리슨 씨가 신규 고객들을 대상으로 발표를 해줄 것을 믿고 있

었다며(I was depending on her to do the presentation for the new clients) 걱정을 나타내고 있다. 따라서, 론 씨가 걱정에 동조한다는 것을 알 수 있으므로 (B)가 정답이다.

어휘 solve ~을 해결하다 concerned 걱정하는 well prepared 잘 준비된

91-95.

레스토랑 평가 - 마호가니 비스트로
작성자: 새라 앨포드

메인 주, 포틀랜드의 오션 드라이브 1236번지에 위치한 건물은 지난 8년 동안 무려 6개나 되는 업체에 공간을 제공해 왔습니다. 그 중 일부인 크리스피 랍스터 하우스와 네모스 시푸드 뷔페 같은 곳은 겨우 1년밖에 버티지 못한 끝에 폐업했습니다.

하지만, 마호가니 비스트로는 최근의 임차 업체로서, 영업 초기의 조짐을 보면 이 레스토랑이 성공을 거둘 수 있을 것으로 나타나고 있습니다. 첫 번째로, **92** 마호가니는 근처의 루이스타운에서 가장 뛰어난 평가를 받는 식당들 중 두 곳인 10번가의 라벤티노 및 텐에 창업 자금을 제공한 곳과 동일한 소유 그룹에 속해 있습니다. 또한, **91** 대형 벽난로를 포함해, 지난달에 여러 매력적인 장식 요소를 추가하면서 한때 평범했던 장소를 세련된 식사 공간으로 탈바꿈시켰습니다.

92 전직 라벤티노 소속의 요리사 피터 매스터슨 씨는 확실히 애피타이저를 전문으로 합니다. 무를 곁들인 농어는 뛰어났으며, **95** 레몬 주스에 재워 놓은 가리비도 마찬가지였는데, 이는 여러 다른 식사 손님들도 주문하는 것을 확인했습니다. 오직 시저 샐러드만 약간 눅눅한 상추로 인해 기대에 미치지 못했습니다. 주 요리들이 애피타이저만큼 인상적이지 못할 수도 있긴 하지만, 구운 폭찹은 여전히 상당히 좋았습니다. 여기에 더해, **93** 이 레스토랑은 훌륭한 하우스 칵테일 목록과 아주 다양한 지역 양조 맥주, 그리고 항상 식사 손님들의 요구에 귀를 기울이는 친절한 종업원들을 자랑합니다.

어휘 house v. ~에 공간을 제공하다 no fewer than 무려 ~나 되는 go out of business 폐업하다 belong to ~에 속하다 ownership group 소유 그룹 start-up 시작의, 개시의 eatery 식당 nearby 근처의 decorative touches 장식적 요소 transform A into B A를 B로 탈바꿈시키다, A를 B로 변모시키다 unexceptional 평범한 sophisticated 세련된 dining 식사 formerly of 전에 ~에 있던 sea bass 농어 radish 무 outstanding 뛰어난, 우수한 as is A (앞서 언급된 것처럼) A도 마찬가지이다 scallop 가리비 marinate A in B A를 B에 재워 놓다, A를 B에 절여 놓다 fall short 기대에 미치지 못하다 soggy 눅눅한, 축축한 as A as B B만큼 A한 to top it all off 그에 더해, 게다가, 설상가상으로 boast ~을 자랑하다 locally-brewed 지역에서 양조한 attentive to ~에 귀를 기울이는, ~에 신경 쓰는

수신: 새라 앨포드 <sarahalford@mainetimes.com>
발신: 조쉬 휴이트 <jhewitt@gotmail.com>
제목: 마호가니 비스트로 평가
날짜: 4월 11일

앨포드 씨께,

어제 <더 메인 타임즈>에 실린 귀하의 평가를 정말 즐겁게 읽었으며, 마호가니 비스트로가 지역 식당 업계에 아주 큰 보탬이 되는 존재라는 점에 동의합니다. 비록 제가 그곳에서 한 번밖에 식사해 보지 못했지만, 다음 번엔 주 요리로 펜네 파스타를 `94` 한 번 드셔 보시도록 권해 드리고자 합니다. 제가 폭 립 대신 그 요리를 선택했는데, 좋은 선택이었다고 생각합니다. `95` 귀하께서 레몬 마리네이드로 만드는 애피타이저를 언급하신 것을 보고 기뻤습니다. 저도 같은 것을 주문했는데, 훌륭했습니다.

귀하의 다음 평가 기사를 읽어 볼 수 있기를 고대합니다!

안녕히 계십시오.

조쉬 휴이트

어휘 **agree that** ~라는 점에 동의하다 **addition** 보탬이 되는 것 **scene** 업계, 분야 **try** ~을 한 번 먹어 보다 **instead of** ~ 대신 **choice** 선택(권) **see A do** A가 ~하는 것을 보다 **marinade** 마리네이드(고기 등을 조리하기 전에 재워 놓을 때 사용하는 액체)

91. 마호가니 비스트로와 관련해 언급된 것은 무엇인가?
(A) 문을 열고 영업한지 1년이 되었다.
(B) 크리스피 랍스터 하우스 옆에 위치해 있다.
(C) 다수의 사업 지점을 부유하고 있다.
(D) 최근에 개조 공사를 거쳤다.

정답 (D)

해설 첫 지문 두 번째 단락에 대형 벽난로 및 여러 매력적인 장식 요소를 추가하면서 한때 평범했던 장소를 세련된 식사 공간으로 탈바꿈시켰다는(last month's addition of several attractive decorative touches, including a large fireplace, has transformed the once unexceptional venue into a sophisticated dining space) 사실이 언급되어 있다. 이는 해당 공간을 개조했다는 뜻에 해당되는 말이므로 (D)가 정답이다.

어휘 **next to** ~ 옆에 **multiple** 다수의 **location** 지점, 위치 **recently** 최근에 **undergo** ~을 거치다, ~을 겪다

92. 요리사 매스터슨 씨와 관련해 언급된 것은 무엇인가?
(A) 마호가니 비스트로의 공동 설립자이다.
(B) 전에 루이스타운에서 고용되었다.
(C) 현재 두 곳의 레스토랑에서 일한다.
(D) 요리로 상을 받은 적이 있다.

정답 (B)

해설 첫 지문 세 번째 단락에 매스터슨 씨가 전에 라벤티노 소속이었다고(Chef Peter Masterson, formerly of L'Aventino) 언

급되어 있고, 같은 지문 두 번째 단락에 라벤티노가 루이스타운에 위치한 곳임을 알리는(L'Aventino and Ten on 10th, two of the best reviewed eateries in nearby Lewistown) 말이 쓰여 있다. 따라서 매스터슨 씨가 과거에 루이스타운에 있는 라벤티노에서 일했다는 사실을 알 수 있으므로 (B)가 정답이다.

어휘 **cofounder** 공동 설립자 **previously** 이전에, 과거에 **win an award** 상을 받다

93. 앨포드 씨와 관련해 유추할 수 있는 것은 무엇인가?
(A) 다른 식사 손님들에게 가리비를 추천했다.
(B) 애피타이저보다 주 요리를 선호한다.
(C) 시저 샐러드가 칭찬 받을 가치가 있다고 생각했다.
(D) 음료의 다양함에 깊은 인상을 받았다.

정답 (D)

해설 첫 지문 마지막 단락에 훌륭한 하우스 칵테일 목록과 아주 다양한 지역 양조 맥주, 그리고 항상 식사 손님들의 요구에 귀를 기울이는 친절한 종업원들을 자랑한다고(the restaurant boasts an excellent house cocktail list, an extensive selection of locally-brewed beers) 쓰여 있다. 이는 다양한 음료 및 친절한 종업원에 좋은 인상을 받은 경우에 언급할 수 있는 말에 해당되므로 (D)가 정답이다.

어휘 **prefer** ~을 선호하다 **over** (비교) ~보다, ~에 비해 **worthy of** ~할 만한 가치가 있는 **praise** 칭찬 **be impressed with** ~에 깊은 인상을 받다 **variety** 다양함, 종류 **beverage** 음료

94. 이메일에서, 첫 번째 단락, 세 번째 줄의 단어 "try"와 의미가 가장 가까운 것은 무엇인가?
(A) 제안하다
(B) 노력하다
(C) 준비하다
(D) 시식하다

정답 (D)

해설 해당 문장에서 try는 추천하는 사항을 설명하는 that절에 속해 있으며, try 뒤에 목적어로 파스타의 한 종류를 뜻하는 명사구가 위치해 있어 그 파스타를 한 번 먹어 보도록 추천하는 문장이라는 것을 알 수 있다. 이는 시험 삼아 먹어 보도록 권하는 것과 같으므로 '시식하다' 등을 뜻하는 (D) sample이 정답이다.

95. 휴이트 씨는 어느 요리를 주문했을 것 같은가?
(A) 농어 요리
(B) 가리비 요리
(C) 시저 샐러드
(D) 폭 립

정답 (B)

해설 두 번째 지문 후반부에 앨포드 씨가 레몬 마리네이드로 만드는 애피타이저를 언급한 것을 보고 기뻤다는 말과 함께 자신도 같은 것을 주문한 사실을(I was pleased to see you mention the appetizer with the lemon marinade. I ordered the same thing) 언급하고 있다. 이 애피타이저는 첫 지문 세 번째 단락에 제시된 레몬 주스에 재워 놓은 가리비를(the scallops marinated in lemon juice) 가리키므로 (B)가 정답이다.

96-100.

피에스타 트로피코 리조트 – 8월 게스트 활동 모든 활동은 달리 언급된 경우가 아니면 손님들에게 무료입니다.		
언제?	**무엇을?**	**누가?**
매주 월요일/ 수요일	100 스쿠버 다이빙 수업: 엘 니도를 둘러싸고 있는 파도 아래의 아름다운 수중 세계를 탐험해 보세요.	인솔자: 100 올리 갈베스
매주 화요일/ 금요일	99 해변가에서의 불춤: 강사님이 여러분에게 전통 불춤의 우아한 예술을 가르쳐 주실 것입니다.	인솔자: 99 이슬라 아구스틴
매주 수요일/ 토요일	**섬 호핑 투어:** 엘 니도 근처의 수많은 작은 섬들을 경험해 보시고, 보트에서 점심을 드세요.	인솔자: 리키 레예스
96 매주 목요일/ 일요일	**필리핀 요리:** 현지 필리핀 요리 조리법을 배워보세요. 96 (총 재료비는 게스트 청구서에 추가됩니다)	인솔자: 마틴 알론조

게스트 활동 사무소를 방문하여, 자세한 일정표를 받고 등록하세요.

어휘 free of charge 무료의 unless otherwise stated 달리 언급되지 않으면 explore ~을 탐험하다 underwater 수중의 beneath ~밑의 graceful 우아한 numerous 수많은 ingredient 재료 bill 청구서 timetable 시간표 register 등록하다

수신: 활동 팀원들 <activitiesteam@fiestatropico.com>
발신: 제니 킴 <jennykim@fiestatropico.com>
주제: 새로운 중요 소식
날짜: 8월 1일

안녕하세요, 여러분.

저는 여러분이 이달의 활동 프로그램에 주목하길 바랍니다. 99 저는 방금 이슬라 아구스틴 씨와 마틴 알론조 씨가 8월 7일부터 8월 13일까지 상급 훈련 워크샵에 참여할 것이라는 것을 98 알게 됐습니다. 그래서 그분들은 그 기간 동안 자신들의 활동을 이끌지 못할 것입니다. 97 99 따라서, 이슬라 씨의 활동은 제가 이끌 것이고, 제인 곤잘레스 씨가 마틴 씨의 활동을 이끌 것입니다. 이슬라 씨와 마틴 씨가 8월 14일에 직장에 복귀하고 나면, 모든 것은 평소처럼 진행될 것입니다.

안녕히 계십시오.

제니 킴
활동 팀 매니저
피에스타 트로피코 리조트

어휘 development 새로운 사실 draw attention 관심을 끌다 advanced 상급의 unavailable 이용이 불가한 respective 각각의 therefore 따라서, 그래서 come back 되돌아 오다 as normal 정상적으로

피에스타 트로피코 리조트

이름: 99 캐시 베링거
날짜: 8월 15일
게스트 인원: 4명
체류일: 99 8월 8일 – 8월 12일
피드백:
귀하의 리조트에서 제공된 훌륭한 서비스에 대해서 감사를 드리고자 합니다. 저는 최근에 가족과 함께 그곳에 머물렀고, 우리 모두는 제공되는 활동들에 참여하여 매우 많이 즐거웠습니다. 저는 레예스 씨와 하는 여행에는 함께 할 수 없었지만, 저와 함께 여행하는 동행자들은 좋은 시간을 보낸 것 같았습니다. 99 남편과 저는 불춤 수업이 대단히 재미 있다고 생각했고, 그는 곤잘레스 씨의 수업에서 배운 몇 가지 기술을 우리 집의 주방에서 활용할 계획을 하고 있습니다. 또한, 100 저의 어머니와 아버지는 갈베스 씨와 멋진 시간을 보냈습니다. 그들은 10월에 발리로의 여행 동안 모든 유용한 정보와 기술을 사용할 것입니다.

어휘 recently 최근에 have fun -ing ~하는 데 즐거움을 가지다, 재미있게 ~하다 excursion (짧은) 여행 companion 동료, 동행자 seem to do ~해 보인다 use ~을 사용하다

96. 추가 요금을 포함하는 활동은 언제 하는가?
(A) 매주 수요일
(B) 매주 금요일
(C) 매주 토요일
(D) 매주 일요일

정답 (D)

해설 첫 번째 지문에 도표 가장 마지막에 있는 요리 활동을 보면 총 재료비는 게스트 청구서에 추가된다는(Total cost of ingredients added to guests' bill) 내용이 언급되어 있다. 이 요리 활동은 매주 목요일과 일요일에 있기 때문에 (D)가 정답이다.

어휘 include ~을 포함하다 extra 추가적인 take place 일어나다, 발생하다

97. 이 이메일의 목적은 무엇인가?
(A) 두 명의 신입직원을 추천하기 위해서
(B) 몇 가지 일정 변경을 간략히 설명하기 위해서
(C) 직원들이 워크숍에 참여하도록 장려하기 위해서

(D) 게스트를 위한 새로운 활동들을 소개하기 위해서

Diving Lesson)임을 알 수 있으므로 (C)가 정답이다.

정답 (B)

해설 두 번째 지문에서 이슬라 씨와 마틴 씨가 특정일에 참가가 불가능해서 발신자인 제니 킴 씨를 포함한 다른 사람이 그들이 맡은 일정을 대신할 것(I will lead Isla's activities and Jane Gonzales will lead Martin's)이라는 변경 사항을 알리고 있다. 따라서 (B)가 정답이다.

어휘 take a tour 여행을 하다 traditional 전통의

어휘 outline ~을 대략적으로 설명하다 encourage ~을 장려하다

98. 이메일에서 첫째 단락, 첫째 줄에 있는 표현 "found out"과 의미가 가장 가까운 것은 무엇인가?

(A) 찾아 다녔다
(B) 위치를 알아냈다
(C) 쳐다보았다
(D) 알게 되었다

정답 (D)

해설 제시된 단어가 포함된 문장은 동료 직원 두 명이 다른 일정이 있다는 것을 이제 막 알게 되었다는 의미이다. 따라서 어떠한 사실을 '알게 되었다'라는 의미로 사용되었으므로 동일한 뜻을 가진 (D) learned가 정답이다.

99. 누가 베링거 씨에게 불춤을 추는 방법을 가르쳐 주었는가?

(A) 갈베스 씨
(B) 킴 씨
(C) 레예스 씨
(D) 알론조 씨

정답 (B)

해설 베링거 씨의 이름이 제시된 세 번째 지문에서 자신과 자신의 남편이 불춤 수업을 즐겼다는(My husband and I thought the fire dancing class was a lot of fun) 사실이 제시되어 있고, 그들의 체류기간이(Date of stay) 8월 8일-8월 12일인 것을 확인할 수 있다. 또한, 두번째 지문에서 이슬라 아구스틴 씨가 8월 7일부터 8월 13일까지 워크샵 참석으로 킴 씨가 대신 그녀의 수업을 담당할 것이라고(I will lead Isla's activities) 언급하고 있으므로 (B)가 정답이다.

100. 베링거 씨의 부모들은 발리에서 무엇을 하기를 의도하고 있는가?

(A) 몇 군데 섬을 둘러본다
(B) 토속 춤을 배운다
(C) 스쿠버 다이빙을 즐긴다
(D) 전통적 음식을 만든다

정답 (C)

해설 세 번째 지문 마지막 부분에 그의 부모들이 갈베스 씨와 멋진 시간을 보냈고, 배운 것을 10월에 발리에서 이용하려 한다는 (my mom and dad had a great time with Mr. Galvez. ~ during their trip to Bali) 말이 나온다. 따라서 첫 번째 지문에서 갈베스 씨가 지도한 수업이 스쿠버 다이빙(Scuba

DAY 04 LC+RC Half Test

LC

1. (A)	**2.** (C)	**3.** (A)	**4.** (C)	**5.** (B)
6. (A)	**7.** (B)	**8.** (C)	**9.** (A)	**10.** (B)
11. (B)	**12.** (C)	**13.** (B)	**14.** (A)	**15.** (C)
16. (C)	**17.** (A)	**18.** (A)	**19.** (B)	**20.** (B)
21. (B)	**22.** (C)	**23.** (A)	**24.** (C)	**25.** (D)
26. (A)	**27.** (B)	**28.** (C)	**29.** (C)	**30.** (A)
31. (D)	**32.** (D)	**33.** (B)	**34.** (D)	**35.** (C)
36. (B)	**37.** (B)	**38.** (C)	**39.** (B)	**40.** (C)
41. (A)	**42.** (C)	**43.** (A)	**44.** (A)	**45.** (C)
46. (C)	**47.** (C)	**48.** (A)	**49.** (A)	**50.** (C)

RC

51. (A)	**52.** (A)	**53.** (D)	**54.** (C)	**55.** (C)
56. (B)	**57.** (C)	**58.** (D)	**59.** (A)	**60.** (A)
61. (C)	**62.** (A)	**63.** (B)	**64.** (A)	**65.** (D)
66. (B)	**67.** (D)	**68.** (A)	**69.** (B)	**70.** (C)
71. (B)	**72.** (D)	**73.** (C)	**74.** (C)	**75.** (A)
76. (C)	**77.** (A)	**78.** (C)	**79.** (A)	**80.** (C)
81. (B)	**82.** (B)	**83.** (A)	**84.** (D)	**85.** (B)
86. (D)	**87.** (B)	**88.** (C)	**89.** (B)	**90.** (D)
91. (B)	**92.** (B)	**93.** (D)	**94.** (B)	**95.** (D)
96. (C)	**97.** (B)	**98.** (D)	**99.** (D)	**100.** (D)

Part 1

1. **(A) She's clearing off a windshield.**
(B) She's shoveling snow.
(C) She's reaching through a window.
(D) She's exiting a vehicle.

(A) 여자가 전면 유리를 닦아내고 있다.
(B) 여자가 눈을 삽으로 치우고 있다.
(C) 여자가 창문을 통해 팔을 뻗고 있다.
(D) 여자가 차량 밖으로 나가고 있다.

해설 (A) 여자가 자동차 전면 유리의 눈을 치우고 있으므로 정답.
(B) 여자가 눈을 삽으로 퍼내는 모습이 아니므로 오답.
(C) 여자가 창문을 통과해 팔을 뻗은 것이 아니므로 오답.
(D) 여자가 차량에서 내리는 모습이 아니므로 오답.

어휘 clear off ~을 깨끗이 치우다 shovel v. ~을 삽으로 퍼내다 reach 팔을 뻗다 exit ~의 밖으로 나가다 vehicle 차량

2. (A) One of the women is pointing at a poster.
(B) One of the women is writing on a notepad.
(C) Papers are pinned to a notice board.
(D) Some products are displayed for sale.

(A) 여자들 중 한 명이 포스터를 가리키고 있다.
(B) 여자들 중 한 명이 메모지에 뭔가 쓰고 있다.
(C) 종이들이 게시판에 핀으로 고정되어 있다.
(D) 몇몇 제품들이 판매용으로 진열되어 있다.

해설 (A) 무엇을 가리키는 동작을 하는 사람은 없으므로 오답.
(B) 메모지에 뭔가 쓰는 동작을 하고 있지 않으므로 오답.
(C) 게시판에 종이들이 붙어 있으므로 정답.
(D) 판매용으로 진열된 제품은 보이지 않으므로 오답.

어휘 point at ~을 가리키다 notepad 메모지 pin v. ~을 핀으로 고정하다 notice board 게시판 display ~을 진열하다, ~을 전시하다 for sale 판매용의

Part 2

3. Where do we keep the stamps and envelopes?
(A) In the third drawer of Harrison's desk.
(B) It's just down the street by the grocery store.
(C) No, we usually throw them out when we're done.

우리가 우표와 봉투를 어디에 두나요?
(A) 해리슨 씨의 책상 세 번째 서랍 안에요.
(B) 바로 길 저쪽 식료품점 옆에 있어요.
(C) 아뇨, 우리는 보통 그것들을 다 쓰고 나면 버려요.

해설 우표와 봉투를 두는 곳을 묻는 질문이므로 구체적인 위치를 알려주는 (A)가 정답이다. (B)도 Where와 어울리는 위치 표현이기는 하지만 우표와 봉투를 보관하는 곳으로 맞지 않으므로 오답이다. (C)는 의문사 의문문에 맞지 않는 No로 대답하는 오답이다.

어휘 stamp 우표 envelope 봉투 drawer 서랍 down ~ 저쪽에, ~을 따라 grocery store 식료품점 usually 보통, 일반적으로 throw out ~을 버리다 be done 다 처리하다, 쓰다

4. Why will you be out of town next week?
(A) I'm not sure when it is.
(B) Yes, I'm going to Japan.
(C) To attend a medical conference.

다음 주에 왜 다른 지역에 가세요?
(A) 언제인지 모르겠습니다.

(B) 네, 저 일본에 가요.
(C) 의학 컨퍼런스에 참석하려고요.

해설 다른 지역에 가는 이유를 묻고 있으므로 목적을 말할 때 사용하는 to부정사 구문을 이용해 '학회에 참석하기 위해서'라고 대답하는 (C)가 정답이다. (A)는 시점에 대해 묻는 When 의문문에 적절한 응답이다. 의문사 의문문에 (B)처럼 Yes로 대답할 수 없으므로 오답이다.

어휘 **be out of town** 다른 지역에 가 있다 **attend** ~에 참석하다 **medical** 의학의 **conference** 총회, 컨퍼런스

5. Which exit is for emergencies?
(A) No, it's standard procedure.
(B) The red door at the back.
(C) I'll call an ambulance.

어느 출구가 비상용이죠?
(A) 아뇨, 그건 표준 절차입니다.
(B) 뒤쪽의 붉은 색 문입니다.
(C) 제가 구급차를 부르겠습니다.

해설 Which exit을 한 단어처럼 들어야 한다. 어떤 출구가 비상용인지 묻고 있으므로, 빨간색 문이라는 특징을 알려주는 (B)가 정답이다. 의문사 의문문에 (A)처럼 No로 대답할 수 없다. (C)는 emergencies에서 쉽게 연상되는 ambulance를 이용한 오답이다.

어휘 **exit** 출구 **emergency** 비상 (상황) **standard** 표준의 **procedure** 절차

6. You've seen this month's sales figures, haven't you?
(A) No, I've been on vacation.
(B) Usually once a month.
(C) He checks all my figures.

이달의 월간 매출 수치를 보신 적 있으시죠, 그렇죠?
(A) 아뇨, 저는 휴가 가 있었어요.
(B) 보통 한 달에 한 번이요.
(C) 그분이 모든 제 수치들을 확인합니다.

해설 부가 의문문을 통해 상대방의 경험 여부를 확인하는 질문이므로 부정을 뜻하는 No와 함께 '휴가 중이었다'라는 말로 월간 매출 수치를 보지 못한 이유를 설명하는 (A)가 정답이다. (B)는 빈도와 관련된 응답으로 How often ~? 의문문에 적절한 반응이며, (C)는 화자 자신이 아닌 다른 사람(He)에 대해 말하고 있어 어울리지 않는 반응이다.

어휘 **sales figures** 매출 수치 cf. figures 수치, 숫자 **on vacation** 휴가 중인 **usually** 보통, 일반적으로

7. Who do I talk to about getting reimbursement for my travel expenses?
(A) My trip to Beijing was not successful.
(B) Call the accounting department.

(C) It won't be very expensive.

제 출장 경비를 상환 받는 것에 대해 누구에게 이야기하나요?
(A) 저의 베이징 출장이 성공적이지 못했습니다.
(B) 경리부에 전화해보세요.
(C) 많이 비싸진 않을 것입니다.

해설 출장 경비 상환에 대해 누구에게 이야기해야 하는지 묻는 질문에 대해 경리부에 전화해보라고 알려주는 (B)가 가장 자연스러운 대답이다. 이렇게 Who 질문에 대해 사람 이름이나 직책 대신 부서명이나 회사명으로 답하는 경우도 종종 나온다. (A)는 travel expenses에서 연상되는 trip to Beijing으로 혼동을 유발하는 함정이며, 질문의 요지와 거리가 먼 응답이다. (C)는 expenses - expensive 유사 발음 혼동을 노린 오답이다.

어휘 **reimbursement** 상환 **travel expenses** 여행[출장] 경비 **accounting department** 경리부, 회계부

8. Why did Ms. Whitman resign from her position?
(A) She left early on Wednesday.
(B) She signed it sometime yesterday.
(C) I wasn't aware that she had.

휘트먼 씨가 왜 자리에서 물러났나요?
(A) 그분은 수요일에 일찍 갔어요.
(B) 그분은 어제 중에 서명했어요.
(C) 저는 그분이 그만뒀는지 몰랐어요.

해설 휘트먼 씨가 일을 그만둔 이유를 묻는 질문이다. 회사를 그만둔 이유를 밝히는 대신 '그만뒀는지 몰랐다'는 말로 놀라움과 함께 자리에서 물러난 이유를 알지 못한다는 뜻을 나타내는 (C)가 정답이다. (C)는 I wasn't aware that she had resigned from her position에서 질문의 정보와 중복되는 resigned from her position을 생략한 문장이다. (B)는 질문의 resign과 발음이 유사한 sign을 이용한 함정이다.

어휘 **resign from** ~에서 물러나다, 그만두다 **sign** ~에 서명하다 **be aware that** ~임을 알다, 인식하다

9. How many application forms did we receive for the lab technician position?
(A) Almost one hundred, I guess.
(B) She's very experienced.
(C) I mailed out over 40.

우리가 실험실 기사직에 지원하는 지원서를 얼마나 많이 받았죠?
(A) 거의 100부 정도인 것 같아요.
(B) 그녀는 매우 경험이 많습니다.
(C) 제가 40부 넘게 우편으로 보냈어요.

해설 핵심은 How many application forms와 receive이다. 이력서 몇 부를 받았냐고 묻는 질문이므로 '거의 100부'라는 대략적인 수량을 밝히는 (A)가 정답이다. 단, 동사 부분(did we receive)을 놓치면 '이력서를 몇 부 보냈는가'라는 질문으로 착각하고 (C)를 고를 수도 있으므로 주의해야 한다.

어휘 application form 지원서 lab 연구소, 실험실(= laboratory) technician 기술자 experienced 경험이 많은 mail out ~을 우편으로 보내다 over ~ 넘게

10. Carol has an appointment now, doesn't she?

(A) If you called the dentist in advance.

(B) Not that I'm aware of.

(C) Yes, I can see her point.

캐롤 씨가 지금 약속이 있죠, 그렇죠?

(A) 당신이 치과에 미리 전화했다면요.

(B) 제가 알기로는 아니에요.

(C) 네, 그녀가 말하는 핵심을 알겠어요.

해설 캐롤에게 약속이 있는지를 확인하기 위한 부가 의문문이며, '그렇지 않은 것으로 알고 있다'라는 말로 부정의 의미를 나타내는 (B)가 알맞은 대답이다. Not that I'm aware of나 Not that I know of는 정답으로 종종 등장하는 표현이므로 하나의 덩어리로 기억해 둔다. (C)는 appointment와 일부 발음이 유사한 point를 활용해 혼동을 유발하는 오답이다.

어휘 appointment 약속, 예약 dentist 치과의사 in advance 미리 Not that I'm aware of 제가 알기로는 아니에요 see one's point ~의 요점을 알다

11. Should we pass the complaints on to Mr. Wu?

(A) I think he'll love any color we choose.

(B) He's too busy to be bothered right now.

(C) He's always complaining about something.

우리가 불만 사항들을 우 씨에게 전달해 드려야 하나요?

(A) 제 생각에 그분은 우리가 고르는 어떤 색이든 아주 좋아할 거예요.

(B) 지금 그분을 방해하기엔 너무 바쁘세요.

(C) 그분은 항상 뭔가에 대해 불평을 해요.

해설 pass A on to B는 어떤 문제를 누군가에게 전달하는 상황에 쓰이는 표현이므로 불만 사항을 Wu 씨에게 말해야 하는지를 묻는 질문에 해당된다. 따라서, 그렇게 하지 말아야 하는 이유를 말하는 (B)가 정답이다. (A)는 대답의 초점이 색(color)에 맞춰져 있으므로 질문과의 의미 연결이 자연스럽지 않다. (C)는 complaint와 발음이 유사한 동사 complain을 이용한 오답이며, 질문의 의도에 어울리지 않는 대답이다.

어휘 pass A on to B A를 B에게 전달하다 complaint n. 불만 사항, 불평 cf. complain 불평하다 choose ~을 선택하다 too 형용사 to do ~하기에는 너무 …하다 bother ~을 방해하다

12. When should we notify the staff of changes in employee benefits?

(A) Please call the department heads.

(B) No, I wasn't notified.

(C) Why don't we wait until it's official?

우리가 언제 직원 혜택의 변동 사항을 직원들에게 알려야 하나요?

(A) 부서장님들에게 전화해주세요.

(B) 아뇨, 저는 통보 받지 못했어요.

(C) 공식적인 사항이 될 때까지 기다리는 게 어때요?

해설 직원 혜택 변동 사항을 언제 알릴지 묻는 When 의문문이다. 이에 대해 공식화될 때까지 기다리는 게 어떨지 되묻는 것으로 나중에 알려야 한다는 뜻을 나타내는 (C)가 정답이다. (A)는 질문의 employee에서 연상할 수 있는 departmet heads(부서장들)을 이용한 오답이며, (B)는 의문사 의문문에 맞지 않는 No로 답변하는 오답이다.

어휘 notify A of B A에게 B를 통보하다, 알리다 benefits 혜택, 이점 department head 부서장 official 공식적인

13. Should we begin the presentation now, or wait for Mr. Jones?

(A) No, later this week.

(B) There's a lot to cover, so let's get started.

(C) I've been waiting in line for 25 minutes.

발표를 지금 시작해야 하나요, 아니면 존스 씨를 기다려야 하나요?

(A) 아뇨, 이번 주 후반에요.

(B) 다뤄야 할 것이 많으니, 시작합시다.

(C) 저는 25분 동안 줄 서서 기다리고 있어요.

해설 발표를 시작하는 시점에 대해 '지금 또는 나중'을 선택하는 의문문이며, now라는 시점을 '시작합시다(let's get started)'라는 말로 대체해 표현한 (B)가 정답이다. 질문 내용이 발표 직전에 할 수 있는 말에 해당되므로 한참 후의 미래 시점을 이야기하는 (A)는 어울리지 않는다.

어휘 cover (주제 등) ~을 다루다 get started 시작하다 in line 줄 서서

14. Can you help me move these chairs to the basement?

(A) I have a meeting in 5 minutes.

(B) He seems to be very busy.

(C) Let's go to see a movie this weekend.

이 의자들을 지하실로 옮기도록 저 좀 도와 주시겠어요?

(A) 제가 5분 후에 회의가 있어요.

(B) 그는 매우 바쁜 것 같아요.

(C) 이번 주말에 영화 보러 갑시다.

해설 도움을 줄 수 있는지 묻는 말에 대해 No를 생략하고 5분 후에 회의가 있다는 말로 간접적으로 거절의 뜻을 나타내는 (A)가 정답이다. (B)는 질문과 관계 없는 인물 He를 언급한 오답이며, (C)는 질문의 move와 발음이 유사한 movie를 이용한 함정이다.

어휘 help A do ~하도록 A를 돕다 basement 지하실 in 시간 ~ 후에 seem to do ~하는 것 같다

15. It seems darker than usual in the office today.

    (A) Tomorrow makes more sense if you ask me.

    (B) It's normal for me to be left out of these decisions.

    (C) Sorry. I closed the blinds.

오늘 사무실이 평소보다 더 어두운 것 같아요.
(A) 제가 볼 때는 내일이 더 나을 거 같아요.
(B) 이런 결정 사항에 대해 저는 보통 제외됩니다.
(C) 죄송해요. 제가 블라인드를 내렸어요.

해설   사무실이 어두운 것 같다는 의견을 제시하는 평서문이다. 이에 대해 블라인드를 내렸다는 말로 어두운 이유를 밝히는 (C)가 정답이다. (A)에서는 today와 대비되는 의미로 tomorrow가 쓰였는데, 대화의 핵심은 시점이 아니므로 어울리지 않는 반응이다. (B)는 사무실이 어두운 것과 전혀 관련 없는 내용이다.

어휘   **seem** 형용사 ~한 것 같다 **than usual** 평소보다 **make sense** 이치에 맞다, 앞뒤가 맞다, 이해가 되다 **if you ask me** 제가 볼 때, 제 생각에 **normal** 보통의 **be left out of** ~에서 제외되다 **decision** 결정

16. We're five minutes ahead of schedule.

    (A) Sorry. We lost track of time.

    (B) Let's organize it for November 30.

    (C) I guess we'll need to wait for the others to arrive.

우리는 일정보다 5분 빨리 온 상태에요.
(A) 죄송합니다. 우리가 시간 가는 줄 몰랐어요.
(B) 그 일정을 11월 30일로 잡읍시다.
(C) 다른 분들이 도착할 때까지 기다려야 할 것 같아요.

해설   '일정보다 5분 빠르다'라는 의미로 five minutes ahead of schedule이라는 말이 쓰였는데, 선택지를 듣는 동안 이 내용과 의미 관계가 가장 잘 맞아 떨어지는 것이 무엇인지 재빨리 파악하는 것이 중요하다. 일정보다 이른 시점인 것에 대해 뭔가를 함께 시작하는 장소에서 나머지 사람들이 도착할 때까지 기다리자고 제안하는 말이 가장 자연스러운 반응이므로 (C)가 정답이다. (A)에 쓰인 lost track of time은 '시간 가는 줄 모르다'라는 뜻이므로 의미가 자연스럽게 연결되지 않는다. (B)는 schedule에서 연상되는 특정 날짜를 언급하고 있으나, it이 무엇인지 불분명하고 의미 관계도 어울리지 않는다.

어휘   **ahead of schedule** 일정보다 빠른 **lose track of time** 시간 가는 줄 모르다 **organize** ~의 일정을 잡다, ~을 마련하다 **wait for A to do** A가 ~하기를 기다리다 **arrive** 도착하다

17. Have you considered hiring a professional consultant?

    (A) Yes, but I haven't made up my mind yet.

    (B) Just a little higher.

    (C) Three or four business days.

전문 컨설턴트를 고용하는 건 고려해 보셨나요?
(A) 네, 하지만 아직 결정을 내리진 못했어요.
(B) 조금 더 높게요.
(C) 영업일로 3~4일 정도요.

해설   과거의 경험이나 동작의 완료를 묻는 현재완료시제 동사가 쓰인 의문문이다. 전문 컨설턴트 고용을 고려했는지 묻고 있으므로 Yes라고 긍정한 다음, 아직 결정하지 못했다는 말로 자신의 상황을 언급한 (A)가 정답이다. (B)는 질문의 hiring과 발음이 유사한 higher를 이용한 함정이다.

어휘   **consider -ing** ~하는 것을 고려하다 **consultant** n. 컨설턴트, 상담가 **make up one's mind** 결정하다 **business day** 영업일

18. You are an instructor at this gym, aren't you?

    (A) Yes, I teach yoga classes.

    (B) Those instructions are hard to follow.

    (C) It's next door to the library.

이 체육관에서 근무하는 강사 맞으시죠, 그렇죠?
(A) 네, 요가 수업을 가르칩니다.
(B) 그 안내 사항들은 따라 하기 힘들어요.
(C) 도서관 옆 건물입니다.

해설   체육관에 근무하는 강사인지 확인하고자 하는 질문이므로 Yes라고 긍정의 뜻을 나타낸 다음, 자신이 가르치는 구체적인 강좌를 말하는 (A)가 정답이다. (B)는 instructor와 발음이 유사한 instructions를 이용한 함정이다. (C)는 위치를 묻는 Where 의문문에 어울리는 답변이므로 오답이다.

어휘   **instructor** 강사 **gym** 체육관 **instructions** 안내, 지시, 실명 **follow** ~을 따르다 **next door to** ~의 옆 건물에

19. Is the client's office on a subway line or should we take a taxi?

    (A) Take the elevator in the lobby.

    (B) It's on Line 4.

    (C) Yes, he's on his way.

고객의 사무실이 지하철 노선상에 있나요, 아니면 우리가 택시를 타야 할까요?
(A) 로비에서 엘리베이터를 타세요.
(B) 4호선에 있어요.
(C) 네, 그가 가는 중이에요.

해설   고객의 사무실이 지하철 노선상에 있는지 아니면 택시를 타야 하는지 묻는 선택 의문문이다. 이에 대해 4호선에 있다는 말로 지하철을 타고 갈 수 있다는 뜻을 나타낸 (B)가 정답이다. (A)는 질문에 나온 동사 take를 반복한 함정으로 질문에 나온 내용과 전혀 관련이 없지만, 질문을 제대로 못 들은 경우에 이러한 함정에 속기 쉬우므로 주의해야 한다.

어휘   **take** (교통편) ~을 타다, ~을 이용하다 **be on one's way** 가는[오는] 중이다

20. I'm going to need some color printer ink.

(A) Yes, I made numerous copies.

(B) I'll order some later today.

(C) The cartridge is the wrong size.

제가 컬러 프린터 잉크가 좀 필요할 거예요.

(A) 네, 다수의 사본을 만들어 두었습니다.

(B) 오늘 이따가 좀 주문할게요.

(C) 카트리지 사이즈가 달라요.

해설 I'm going to need ~'는 필요한 것이 있으니 부탁한다는 요청의 의미를 나타낸다. 여기서는 프린터 잉크가 필요하다는 요청에 대해 이따가 주문하겠다는 말로 요청을 수락하는 의미를 나타내는 (B)가 정답이다. (A)와 (C)는 printer에서 연상 가능한 내용을 말하고 있으나 평서문으로 말하는 요청에 대한 반응으로 어울리지 않는다.

어휘 **make a copy** 복사하다 **numerous** 다수의, 많은 수의 **order** ~을 주문하다

Part 3

Questions 21-23 refer to the following conversation.

M: Hello, Michelle. Did you hear that **21** the Crows are playing this weekend in Auckland baseball stadium? It should be a really competitive game against the Lions. Do you want to come? I'm planning to get tickets later today.

W: Oh, really? I love the Crows. I've supported them since I was young. **22** But I'm surprised that the tickets haven't sold out already. I thought a match between those two popular teams would sell out almost immediately.

M: Well, as a member of the fan club, it's easier for me to get seats at home games. So, what do you think? If you want me to get you a ticket, **23** let me know before the end of the day where in the stadium you would like to sit.

남: 안녕하세요, 미셸. 크로우즈가 이번 주말에 오클랜드 야구장에서 경기한다는 얘기 들었어요? 라이언즈를 상대로 정말 치열한 경기가 될 거예요. 같이 보러 가실래요? 오늘 오후에 입장권을 살 생각이에요.

여: 아, 그래요? 제가 크로우즈를 정말 좋아해요. 제가 어렸을 때부터 응원한 팀이에요. 그런데 입장권이 벌써 매진된 게 아니

라니 놀랍네요. 그 두 팀처럼 인기 있는 팀들 간의 경기는 거의 곧바로 매진될 줄 알았는데요.

남: 그게, 저는 팬클럽 회원이라서 홈경기에서 자리를 구하는 게 더 수월하거든요. 그래서 어떻게 생각하세요? 제가 입장권을 구하길 원하시면, 오늘 안으로 경기장 내에 어느 자리에 앉고 싶으신지 알려 주세요.

어휘 **competitive** 경쟁을 하는 **against** ~를 상대로 **plan to do** ~할 계획이다 **support** ~을 응원하다 **sell out** 매진되다 **match** 경기 **immediately** 곧바로, 즉시 **seat** 좌석, 자리 **get A B** A에게 B를 구해주다, 갖다 주다 **would like to do** ~하고 싶다, ~하고자 하다

21. 남자는 어떤 행사에 참석할 계획인가?

(A) 음악 축제

(B) 스포츠 행사

(C) 지역 박람회

(D) 미술 전시회

해설 남자가 초반부에 여자에게 Did you hear that the Crows are playing this weekend in Auckland baseball stadium?이라고 묻는 질문과 It should be a really competitive game against the Lions라는 말을 통해 Crows와 Lions 팀들의 야구 경기임을 알 수 있으므로 (B)가 정답이다.

어휘 **community** 지역 (사회) **fair** 박람회, 축제 마당 **exhibition** 전시(회)

22. 여자는 왜 놀라는가?

(A) 공연이 취소되었다.

(B) 행사 장소가 변경되었다.

(C) 입장권이 여전히 구입 가능하다.

(D) 주차비가 무료일 것이다.

해설 surprised가 핵심이므로 여자의 말에서 관련 표현이 제시되는 부분을 잘 찾아 들어야 한다. 남자의 제안을 들은 여자는 But I'm surprised that the tickets haven't sold out already라는 말로 아직 구입 가능한 티켓이 있다는 점에 대해서 놀라움을 표현하고 있으므로 (C)가 정답이다.

어휘 **performance** 공연, 연주(회) **cancel** ~을 취소하다 **relocate** ~을 이전하다 **available** 구입 가능한 **free** 무료의

Paraphrase the tickets haven't sold out already
→ Tickets are still available.

23. 오늘 안으로 여자는 무엇을 해야 하는가?

(A) 앉을 자리를 정해야 한다.

(B) 회원 가입 신청을 해야 한다.

(C) 웹 사이트를 확인해야 한다.

(D) 남자에게 입장권을 사줘야 한다.

해설 by the end of the day라는 특정 시점이 언급되어 있으므로 해당 시점이 제시되는 부분을 놓치지 말고 들어야 한다. 여자의 말을 들은 남자가 대화 후반부에 let me know before the end of the day where in the stadium you would like to sit라고 말하는 부분에서 해당 시점을 확인할 수 있는데, 앉고자 하는 자리를 알려 달라고 여자에게 말하는 내용이므로 (A)가 정답이다.

어휘 decide on ~에 대해 결정하다 apply for ~을 신청하다, ~에 지원하다

Paraphrase let me know ~ where in the stadium you would like to sit
→ Decide on seats

Questions 24-26 refer to the following conversation.

W: Hello, my name is Jane Gable. **24** My colleague ordered some of your chicken wings about 20 minutes ago over the phone. Are they ready, or should I come back later?

M: Okay. I think **24** I have an order here under the name of Catherine Smith. Is that right? The chicken wings are all ready, **25** but I'm still preparing some of the side dishes. I'm sorry about this. Do you mind waiting another five or ten minutes?

W: Okay, that's our order. I don't mind waiting. **26** I'll go and get a coffee across the road at Star Café. I'll be back soon.

여: 안녕하세요, 제 이름은 제인 게이블입니다. 제 직장 동료가 약 20분 전에 전화로 치킨 윙을 주문했습니다. 준비가 됐나요, 아니면 이따가 다시 와야 하나요?

남: 알겠습니다. 여기에 캐서린 스미스라는 분의 이름으로 주문된 게 있는 것 같네요. 맞으세요? 치킨 윙은 모두 준비가 됐는데, 사이드 메뉴가 여전히 준비 중입니다. 죄송합니다. 5분에서 10분 정도 기다리실 수 있으세요?

여: 네, 저희가 주문한 게 맞아요. 기다리는 건 상관 없습니다. 저쪽 길 건너편에 있는 스타 카페에 가서 커피를 사 올게요. 금방 오겠습니다.

어휘 colleague 직장 동료 over the phone 전화상에서 under the name of ~의 이름으로 prepare ~을 준비하다 Do you mind -ing? ~해도 괜찮으세요? another five minutes 5분 더 across the road 길 건너편에

24. 남자는 누구일 가능성이 큰가?
(A) 슈퍼마켓 직원
(B) 커피숍 주인
(C) 레스토랑 직원

(D) 상점 청소부

해설 대화를 시작하는 여자가 My colleague ordered some of your chicken wings about 20 minutes ago over the phone과 같이 음식을 주문한 상황을 알리자, 이에 대해 남자가 주문이 되어 있다고 확인해 주고(I have an order here under the name of Catherine Smith) 있으므로 남자는 식당 직원일 것이라고 짐작할 수 있다. 따라서, (C)가 정답이다.

25. 남자는 왜 사과하는가?
(A) 고객에게 비용이 과다 청구되었다.
(B) 배달 주소가 잘못되었다.
(C) 엉뚱한 음식을 준비했다.
(D) 주문한 것이 아직 준비되지 않았다.

해설 man, apologize가 핵심이므로 남자의 말에서 사과의 표현이 나타나는 부분을 잘 찾아내야 하며, 이때 함께 제시되는 사과의 이유를 놓치지 말고 들어야 한다. 남자의 말에서 사과하는 내용을 들을 수 있는 부분은 I'm still preparing some of the side dishes. I'm sorry about this이며, 여전히 음식을 준비하는 상황인 점에 대해 사과하는 것이므로 (D)가 정답이다.

어휘 apologize 사과하다 overcharge ~에게 과다 청구하다 incorrect 잘못된, 부정확한

Paraphrase still preparing some of the side dishes
→ An order is not ready yet.

26. 여자는 대화에 이어 무엇을 할 것인가?
(A) 다른 매장을 방문한다.
(B) 상사와 이야기한다.
(C) 주문한 것을 취소한다.
(D) 영수증을 복사한다.

해설 will, next가 핵심이므로 대화 마지막 부분에 특히 집중해 들어야 한다. 여자는 주문한 음식이 준비될 때까지 기다릴 수 있다고 말하면서 다른 곳에 가서 커피를 사오겠다고(I'll go and get a coffee across the road at Star Café) 알리고 있으므로 이러한 의미에 해당되는 (A)가 정답이다.

어휘 business 매장, 상점 supervisor 상사, 책임자 make a copy of ~을 복사하다 receipt 영수증

Questions 27-29 refer to the following conversation.

W: Excuse me, **27** is this the platform for the train going to Baltimore?

M: Yes, it is.

W: Oh, great. **27** I have an audition there this afternoon. Is there a dining car where I can eat on my way there?

M: There is a dining car, but **28** the kitchen is only open for lunch and dinner hours. You wouldn't be able to order breakfast there.

W: Oh, really? That's too bad. I was in a rush coming to the station this morning and **29** didn't get a chance to eat.

M: Well, the train to Baltimore doesn't leave for another half hour.

W: **29** Then I can visit a café here in the station first. Thank you!

여: 실례합니다, 여기가 볼티모어 행 열차 플랫폼인가요?
남: 네, 맞습니다.
여: 아, 다행이네요. 제가 오늘 오후에 거기서 오디션이 있거든요. 거기로 가는 중에 식사를 할 수 있는 식당칸이 있나요?
남: 식당칸이 있긴 하지만, 주방이 점심과 저녁 식사 시간에만 열어요. 아침 식사는 주문하실 수 없을 거예요.
여: 아, 정말요? 아쉽네요. 오늘 아침에 기차역에 서둘러 오느라 먹을 기회가 없었거든요.
남: 음, 볼티모어 행 열차는 삼십 분이나 더 있어야 출발해요.
여: 그럼 먼저 여기 기차역의 카페에 들를 수 있겠네요. 감사합니다!

어휘 **dining car** (기차의) 식당칸 **be able to do** ~할 수 있다 **order** ~을 주문하다 **be in a rush** 서두르다 **get a chance to do** ~할 기회가 있다 **half hour** 30분

27. 여자는 왜 볼티모어에 가는가?
(A) 공연을 위해
(B) 오디션을 위해
(C) 고객과의 회의를 위해
(D) 가족 휴가를 위해

해설 여자가 볼티모어 행 기차 플랫폼이 맞는지 묻자 남자가 맞다고 알려주고, 이에 그곳에서 오디션이 있다고(I have an audition there this afternoon) 밝히고 있다. 따라서, 정답은 (B)이다.

28. 남자는 식당칸에 대해 뭐라고 말하는가?
(A) 아침 식사를 제공하지 않는다.
(B) 미리 예약된 식사만 제공한다.
(C) 일반석보다 비싸다.
(D) 식사가 제공되는 데 오래 걸린다.

해설 여자가 식당칸이 있는지 묻자 남자는 식당칸이 있긴 하지만 점심과 저녁 식사 시간에만 열고 아침 식사는 주문할 수 없다고(~ the kitchen is only open for lunch and dinner hours. You wouldn't be able to order breakfast there) 알려주고 있다. 따라서, (A)가 정답이다.

어휘 **serve** (음식 등) ~을 제공하다 **meal** 식사 **reserved** 예약된 **in advance** 미리 **regular** 일반의 **seating** 좌석

Paraphrase You wouldn't be able to order breakfast → It does not serve breakfast.

29. 남자가 "볼티모어 행 열차는 삼십 분이나 더 있어야 출발해요"라고 말할 때 의미하는 것은 무엇인가?
(A) 출발 안내판이 부정확하다.
(B) 엔진 이상이 생겼다.
(C) 여자가 음식을 먹을 시간이 있다.
(D) 여자가 급행 열차를 타야 한다.

해설 해당 문장 앞뒤 부분의 내용 흐름을 잘 파악해야 한다. 여자가 급하게 오느라 먹을 시간이 없었다는 말을 하자 남자가 "볼티모어행 열차는 삼십 분이나 더 있어야 출발한다"고 알리고 있다. 이에 대해 여자가 그렇다면 카페에 먼저 들르겠다고 말하고 있으므로, 여자가 기차를 타기 전에 음식을 먹을 시간이 있다고 알려주는 것임을 알 수 있다. 따라서, (C)가 정답이다.

어휘 **departure** 출발 **board** 안내판 **inaccurate** 부정확한 **malfunction** 기능 이상, 오작동 **occur** 발생하다

Questions 30-32 refer to the following conversation with three speakers.

W: **30** I can't wait to hear Leeroy Cole sing the songs from his new album, *Twilight Melody*. I think I must be his biggest fan!

M1: I know how you feel. I just hope we get there on time. This traffic is really slowing us down.

M2: It shouldn't be too bad once we get out of the downtown area. **31** Some of the streets are shut down for the city festival this weekend.

M1: Oh, that's right. Well, once we get onto the expressway, it'll just take us about twenty minutes to reach the venue. And, we saved some time by buying tickets online.

W: True, but **32** I hope there are still some spaces for us to park. I heard that all the tickets have sold out, so it's going to be really busy.

여: 리로이 콜 씨가 자신의 새 앨범인 <트와일라잇 멜로디>에 담긴 노래들을 부르는 것을 빨리 들어 보고 싶어요. 저는 그의 열성 팬이 틀림 없는 것 같아요!

남1: 어떤 느낌인지 압니다. 저는 우리가 그곳에 제때 갈 수 있기를 바라고 있어요. 지금 이 차량들 때문에 너무 느리게 움직이고 있어요.

남2: 시내 지역만 벗어 나면 그렇게 나쁘지 않을 거예요. 일부 거리들이 이번 주말에 있을 도시 축제 때문에 폐쇄되어 있거든요.

남1: 아, 그렇네요. 저, 고속도로에 진입하기만 하면, 행사 장소에 도착하는 데 약 20분 정도 밖에 걸리지 않을 거예요. 그리고 우리는 온라인으로 티켓을 구매해서 시간을 절약했어요.

여: 맞아요, 하지만 우리가 주차할 공간이 여전히 있으면 좋겠어요. 제가 듣기로는 모든 티켓이 매진되었기 때문에 정말로 붐빌 거예요.

어휘 can't wait to do 빨리 ~하고 싶다 biggest fan 열성 팬 on time 제시간에, 제때 traffic 차량, 교통량 slow A down A를 느리게 만들다, 둔화시키다 once (일단) ~하는 대로, ~하자마자 get out of ~에서 벗어 나다 shut down 폐쇄하다, 닫다 get onto ~로 들어서다, 진입하다 expressway 고속도로 it takes A B(시간) to do A가 ~하는 데 B의 시간이 걸리다 reach ~에 도착하다, 도달하다 venue 행사 장소 park 주차하다 sell out 매진되다 busy 붐비는, 분주한

30. 화자들은 무슨 종류의 행사에 참석하는가?
(A) 음악 콘서트
(B) 연극 공연
(C) 스포츠 경기 대회
(D) 영화제

해설 여자가 대화 시작 부분에 리로이 콜이 새 앨범 <트와일라잇 멜로디>의 곡들을 부르는 것을 빨리 들어 보고 싶다고 (I can't wait to hear Leeroy Cole sing the songs from his new album, Twilight Melody) 말하고 있는데, 이와 같은 일이 가능한 장소는 콘서트 행사장이므로 (A)가 정답이다.

어휘 theater play 연극 공연 competition 경기 대회, 경연 대회

31. 시내 지역에 교통 흐름이 왜 좋지 못한가?
(A) 사고가 발생했다.
(B) 일부 건물들이 공사 중이다.
(C) 거리 한 곳이 수리 중이다.
(D) 일부 도로들이 행사로 인해 폐쇄되어 있다.

해설 시내 지역에 교통 흐름이 좋지 못한 이유를 묻고 있으므로 이와 같은 내용과 함께 그 이유가 제시될 것임을 예상하고 들을 수 있다. 대화 중반부에 남자 한 명이 차량이 느리게 움직이는 것과 관련해 일부 거리들이 주말에 있을 도시 축제 때문에 폐쇄되어

있다고(Some of the streets are shut down for the city festival this weekend) 알리고 있으므로 (D)가 정답임을 알 수 있다.

어휘 accident 사고 occur 발생하다 construct ~을 공사하다, 짓다 closed 폐쇄된

Paraphrase streets are shut down / city festival
→ roads are closed / event

32. 여자는 무엇에 대해 걱정하는가?
(A) 티켓을 구입하는 일
(B) 연주자를 만나는 일
(C) 행사장 위치를 찾는 일
(D) 주차 자리를 찾는 일

해설 대화 마지막 부분에 여자는 주차할 공간이 여전히 있으면 좋겠다는 말과 함께 모든 티켓이 매진되어서 정말로 붐빌 것이라는(I hope there are still some spaces for us to park. ~ so it's going to be really busy) 걱정을 말하고 있다. 따라서, 주차 자리를 찾는 문제에 해당되는 (D)가 정답이다.

어휘 be concerned about ~에 대해 걱정하다 performer 연주자 locate ~의 위치를 찾다 spot 자리, 위치, 지점

Paraphrase spaces for us to park
→ parking spot

Questions 33-35 refer to the following conversation and list.

W: Hi, Mark. **33** I'm in the middle of organizing our department's weekend excursion to Gale Lake, but I'm not sure which cottage to choose.

M: Well, just make sure it has an outdoor patio, because it's supposed to be sunny this weekend. **34** The only thing that worries me is our budget. The HR department has reduced it this year.

W: I know, but I still think we have enough. So, which one of these cottages should we pick?

M: Hmm... well, **35** we definitely need at least five beds. And, try to save as much money as possible so that we can spend it on food and activities.

여: 안녕하세요, 마크. 제가 게일 호수로 떠나는 우리 부서의 주말 야유회를 준비하는 중인데, 어느 산장을 선택해야 할지 모르겠어요.

남: 저, 이번 주말에 날씨가 화창할 것으로 예상되기 때문에, 반드시 옥외 테라스가 있는 곳으로 하세요. 제가 걱정하는 유일한 것은 예산입니다. 인사부에서 올해 예산을 줄였거든요.

여: 알고 있어요, 하지만 여전히 우리에게 충분히 있다고 생각해요. 그래서 이 산장들 중에서 어느 것을 골라야 할까요?

남: 흠... 저, 우리가 최소한 침대 5개는 꼭 필요해요. 그리고 우리가 음식과 활동에 소비할 수 있도록 가능한 한 많은 비용을 아끼도록 해 보세요.

대여 가능한 산장	1박당 요금	침대 개수
데이지 코티지	200달러	3개
주니퍼 코티지	300달러	4개
아이비 코티지	400달러	6개
파인 코티지	500달러	7개

어휘 **in the middle of** ~하는 중인 **organize** ~을 준비하다, 조직하다 **excursion** 야유회 **cottage** 산장, 오두막 **choose** ~을 선택하다 **make sure (that)** 반드시 ~하도록 하다 **outdoor** 옥외의 **patio** 테라스 **be supposed to do** ~할 예정이다 **worry** ~을 걱정시키다 **budget** 예산 **HR department** 인사부 **reduce** ~을 줄이다, 감소시키다 **pick** ~을 고르다, 선택하다 **definitely** 분명히, 확실히 **at least** 최소한, 적어도 **as much A as possible** 가능한 한 많은 A **spend A on B** A를 B에 소비하다 **for rent** 대여용의 **rate** 요금 **per night** 1박당

33. 화자들은 무엇을 논의하고 있는가?
(A) 교육 세미나
(B) 직원 야유회
(C) 고객 방문
(D) 건물 개조 공사

해설 대화 시작 부분에 여자가 부서의 주말 야유회를 준비하는 중인데 어느 산장을 선택해야 할지 모르겠다고(I'm in the middle of organizing our department's weekend excursion ~) 알리고 있다. 뒤이어 이에 대한 장소 선정 및 비용과 관련된 대화가 이어지고 있으므로 excursion과 같은 의미에 해당되는 (B)가 정답이다.

어휘 **property** 건물, 부동산 **renovation** 개조, 보수
`Paraphrase` our department's weekend excursion
→ company trip

34. 남자는 왜 걱정하는가?
(A) 악천후가 예상되고 있다.
(B) 건물이 수리를 필요로 한다.
(C) 교통편을 이용할 수 없다.
(D) 예산이 부족할 수도 있다.

해설 대화 중반부에 남자는 자신의 유일한 걱정 거리가 예산이며, 인사부에서 예산을 줄였다고(The only thing that worries me is our budget. The HR department has reduced it this year) 알리고 있으므로 예산 부족을 언급한 (D)가 정답이다.

어휘 **inclement weather** 악천후 **transportation** 교통편 **unavailable** 이용할 수 없는 **inadequate** 부족한, 부적당한

35. 시각자료를 보시오. 여자는 어느 산장을 선택할 것 같은가?
(A) 데이지 코티지
(B) 주니퍼 코티지
(C) 아이비 코티지
(D) 파인 코티지

해설 선택하려는 산장의 조건으로 대화 마지막 부분에 남자가 최소한 침대 5개는 꼭 필요하지만 가능한 한 비용을 아끼라고(we definitely need at least five beds. And, try to save as much money as possible ~) 언급하고 있다. 따라서, 시각자료에서 침대 개수가 5개 이상인 곳 중에서 비용이 더 저렴한 곳에 해당되는 (C)가 정답이다.

Questions 36-38 refer to the following conversation and map.

M: Hello, **36** I'd like to sell some T-shirts and hats during the town festival next month. I heard that I need to apply for a permit here at City Hall.

W: That's correct. First, I'd like you to choose a spot where you'll set up your stall. You can see the vacant spaces on this map.

M: Let's see. Hmm... **37** I'll take the spot at the end of the street, next to the fruit smoothie stand.

W: Okay, **38** now I just need you to fill out this application before I can issue your permit.

M: No problem. And... how many days will it take for the permit to be sent out to me?

W: You should get it in two or three days.

남: 안녕하세요, 제가 다음 달에 열릴 도시 축제 기간 중에 티셔츠와 모자를 판매하고자 합니다. 제가 듣기로는 이곳 시청에서 허가증을 신청해야 한다고 하던데요.

여: 맞습니다. 우선, 가판대를 설치하실 위치를 선택해 주시기 바랍니다. 이 안내도에서 빈 자리를 확인하실 수 있습니다.

남: 어디 보자. 흠.... 거리 끝 쪽에 과일 스무디 판매대 옆에 있는 자리로 하겠습니다.

여: 좋습니다, 이제 제가 허가증을 발급해 드리기 전에 이 신청서를 작성해 주시기 바랍니다.

남: 알겠습니다. 그리고... 허가증이 제게 발송되는 데 며칠이나 걸릴까요?

여: 2~3일 후에는 받게 되실 겁니다.

빈자리 왼편 #1	판매상: 밥스버거	판매상: 과일 스무디	빈자리 왼편 #4

메인 스트리트

판매상: 프로즌 요거트	빈자리 오른편 #2	빈자리 오른편 #3	판매상: 점보 프레젤

어휘 **during** ~ 동안 **apply for** ~을 신청하다 **permit** 허가증 **city hall** 시청 **correct** 맞는, 옳은 **would like A to do** A에게 ~하기를 원하다 **choose** ~을 선택하다 **spot** 위치, 자리, 지점 **set up** ~을 설치하다 **stall** 가판대 **vacant** 비어 있는 **at the end of** ~의 끝에 **next to** ~ 옆에 **stand** 판매대 **need A to do** A에게 ~하기를 원하다 **fill out** ~을 작성하다 **application** 신청(서) **issue** ~을 발급하다 **it takes 시간 for A to do** A가 ~하는 데 …의 시간이 걸리다 **send out** ~을 발송하다 **in 기간** ~ 후에 **vendor** 판매업자

36. 남자는 무슨 종류의 제품을 판매하고 싶어 하는가?
   (A) 음료
   (B) 의류
   (C) 간식
   (D) 포스터

해설 남자가 판매하려는 물품을 찾아야 하므로 남자의 말에서 특정 불품의 명칭이나 특성 등이 제시될 것임을 예상하고 들어야 한다. 대화 시작 부분에 남자는 도시 축제 기간 중에 티셔츠와 모자를 판매하려 한다고(I'd like to sell some T-shirts and hats during the town festival next month) 알리고 있으므로 의류를 의미하는 (B)가 정답이다.

어휘 **beverage** 음료 **clothing** 의류
Paraphrase T-shirts and hats → Clothing

37. 시각자료를 보시오. 남자는 어느 빈 자리에 자신의 가판대를 설치하고 싶어 하는가?
   (A) 왼편 1번
   (B) 왼편 4번
   (C) 오른편 2번
   (D) 오른편 3번

해설 배치도가 시각자료로 제시되어 있으므로 위치 관련 표현에 특히 주의해 들어야 한다. 대화 중반부에 남자는 자신이 원하는 위치와 관련해, 거리 끝 쪽에 과일 스무디 판매대 옆에 있는 자리로 하겠다고(I'll take the spot at the end of the street, next to the fruit smoothie stand) 언급하고 있다. 따라서, 시각자료에서 과일 스무디 판매대 옆에 빈 자리로 표기된 왼편 4번 자리에 설치하고 싶어 한다는 것을 알 수 있으므로

(B)가 정답이다.

38. 여자는 남자에게 무엇을 하도록 요청하는가?
   (A) 회의에 참석할 것
   (B) 제품 샘플을 제공할 것
   (C) 양식을 작성할 것
   (D) 신분증을 제시할 것

해설 여자가 요청하는 일을 묻고 있으므로 여자의 말에서 요청 관련 표현이 제시되는 부분을 파악해야 한다. 가판대 설치 위치를 정한 남자에게 여자는 대화 후반부에 허가증을 발급해 주기 전에 신청서를 작성해 달라고(now I just need you to fill out this application before I can issue your permit) 요청하고 있으므로 (C)가 정답이다.

어휘 **complete** ~을 작성하다 **form** 양식, 서식 **present** ~을 제시하다
Paraphrase fill out this application
→ Complete a form

Part 4

Questions 39-41 refer to the following introduction.

Welcome, ladies and gentlemen, to today's talk by the CEO of Lerkens Motors, Mr. David Denton. **39** Mr. Denton will be talking to us about Lerkens' new sedan that is set to change the face of the automobile industry forever. **40** Mr. Denton wanted to speak to the media here today before the car's unveiling next month, so that you may accurately write about the new car with as much insider information as possible. The speech will focus on the car's fuel efficiency and environmentally-friendly features. Mr. Denton has a busy schedule today, **41** but he has promised to answer some quick questions in the lobby after the talk. So, make your way there at the end if you wish to ask him any questions.

오늘 러큰스 모터스 사의 데이빗 덴튼 대표이사님께서 진행하시는 연설에 오신 신사 숙녀 여러분 환영합니다. 덴튼 대표님께서는 자동차 업계의 형세를 완전히 뒤바꿀 것으로 예상되는 러큰스 사의 새로운 세단 차량을 소개해 주실 것입니다. 덴튼 대표님께서는 다음 달에 있을 신차 공개에 앞서 오늘 이 자리에서 언론을 대상으로 이야기하시길 원하셨으며, 이에 따라 여러분께서는 가능한 한 많은 내부 정보를 가지고 신차에 대해 정확하게 기사를 쓰실 수 있을 겁니다. 오늘 회견은 신차의 연비 및 환경 친화적인 특징들에 초점을 맞출 것입니다. 덴튼 대표님께서는 오늘 일정이 바쁘시긴 하지만, 회견을 마치고 로비에서 간단한 질문에 답변해 주시기로 약속하셨습니다. 그러므로 질문이 있으신 분들은 마지막에 그쪽으로 이동해 주시기 바랍니다.

어휘 **sedan** 세단(형 자동차) **be set to do** ~할 예정이다, ~할 준비가 되다 **face** 형세, 국면 **automobile industry** 자동차 업계 **the media** 언론, 매체 **unveiling** 공개 **so that** (결과) 따라서, 그래서, (목적) ~할 수 있도록 **accurately** 정확하게 **as much insider information as possible** 가능한 한 많은 내부 정보 **focus on** ~에 초점을 맞추다 **fuel efficiency** 연비 **environmentally-friendly** 환경 친화적인 **feature** n. 특징, 특색 **make one's way there** 그곳으로 가다, 이동하다

39. 덴튼 씨의 연설 주제는 무엇인가?
(A) 가전제품
(B) 신차 모델
(C) 내비게이션 시스템
(D) 제조 공장

해설 문제를 통해 Mr. Denton이라는 사람이 뭔가에 대해 이야기를 한다는 것을 미리 확인하고 듣는다. 화자는 Mr. Denton을 소개한 후에 그가 이야기하게 될 내용에 대해 Mr. Denton will be talking to us about Lerkens' new sedan that is set to change the face of the automobile industry forever라고 알리고 있으므로 이를 통해 그 대상이 새로 출시될 차량임을 알 수 있다. 따라서, 이를 new car model이라고 제시한 (B)가 정답이다.

어휘 **electrical appliance** 가전제품

40. 담화를 듣는 대상은 누구인가?
(A) 마케팅 임원들
(B) 자동차 기술자들
(C) 전문 언론인들
(D) 포커스 그룹 구성원들

해설 화자는 담화의 목적을 Mr. Denton wanted to speak to the media here today before the car's unveiling next month, so that you may accurately write about the new car ~와 같이 설명하면서 청중들을 you로 가리켜 이들이 할 수 있는 일을 you may accurately write about the new car라고 말하고 있다. 따라서, 담화를 듣는 이들은 기자라는 것을 알 수 있으며, 이를 Media professionals라고 표현한 (C)가 정답이다.

어휘 **executive** n. 임원 **professional** n. 전문가 **focus group** (시장 조사나 여론 조사를 위한) 포커스 그룹, 소비자 그룹

41. 청중들은 무엇을 하라는 요청을 받는가?
(A) 회견 후에 로비로 갈 것
(B) 발표 중에 질문할 것
(C) 안내 책자 묶음을 가져갈 것
(D) 환경 단체에 가입할 것

해설 청중들이 요청을 받는 일을 묻고 있으므로 화자의 말에서 명령문 형태의 요청이나 당부 등의 표현이 나타나는 부분이 있는지 확인해 봐야 한다. 화자는 담화 마지막에 he has promised

to answer some quick questions in the lobby after the talk. So, make your way there at the end if you wish to ask him any questions라고 말하는 부분에서 there(lobby)로 이동하라고 알리고 있으므로 (A)가 정답이다.

어휘 **pick up** ~을 가져가다[오다] **information packet** 안내 책자 묶음 **environmental** 환경의 **organization** 단체, 기관

Questions 42-44 refer to the following excerpt from a meeting.

The main issue on today's agenda is **42** the assembly of our new Fit Guru 600 treadmill. Unfortunately, we have already received several complaints from customers who experienced problems when trying to put the machine together. When we designed the product, we made sure that it is very lightweight, and we advertised this as its best feature. **43** We hoped that this would make it easier for customers to assemble the device, but... it hasn't helped. So, I asked Francis in product design to create a new instruction manual that we'll start including with the product. **44** I'll hand out copies of that now so that you can familiarize yourselves with it.

오늘 의제의 주요 사안은 우리의 새로운 핏 구루 600 러닝 머신의 조립 문제입니다. 안타깝게도, 이 기계를 조립하려 할 때 문제점을 겪으신 고객들로부터 이미 여러 차례 불만을 접수했습니다. 우리가 이 제품을 디자인했을 때, 반드시 매우 가볍게 만들도록 했고, 이를 이 제품의 가장 큰 특징으로 광고했습니다. 우리는 이 점이 고객들께서 기기를 더 쉽게 조립하도록 만들어 주기를 바랐지만... 별 소용이 없었습니다. 따라서, 저는 이 제품에 포함하기 시작할 새로운 사용 설명서를 만들어 달라고 제품 디자인팀의 프랜시스 씨에게 요청했습니다. 여러분께서 이 설명서의 내용을 숙지하실 수 있도록 지금 사본을 나눠 드리도록 하겠습니다.

어휘 **main** 주요한 **issue** 사안, 문제 **agenda** 의제, 안건 **assembly** 조립 **treadmill** 러닝 머신 **unfortunately** 안타깝게도, 아쉽게도 **complaint** 불만 **experience** ~을 겪다, 경험하다 **put A together** A를 조립하다 **make sure that** 반드시 ~하도록 하다 **lightweight** 가벼운, 경량의 **advertise** ~을 광고하다 **feature** 특징, 기능 **make it** 형용사 **for A to do** A가 ~하는 것을 …하게 만들다 **assemble** ~을 조립하다 **device** 기기, 장치 **instruction manual** 사용 설명서 **include** ~을 포함하다 **hand out** ~을 나눠 주다, 배부하다 **copy** 사본, 한 부, 한 장 **familiarize oneself with** ~에 익숙해 지다, ~을 숙지하다

42. 무슨 종류의 제품이 논의되고 있는가?

(A) 주방용품
(B) 오디오 장치
(C) 운동 기계
(D) 공사 도구

해설　논의되는 제품을 찾아야 하므로 특정 물품의 명칭이나 특성, 또는 기능 등이 제시되는 부분에서 단서를 파악해야 한다. 화자는 담화 시작 부분에 회의 안건으로 새로운 핏 구루 600 러닝 머신의 조립 문제(the assembly of our new Fit Guru 600 treadmill)를 언급하고 있으므로 운동 기계를 의미하는 (C)가 정답이다.

어휘　kitchen appliance 주방용품　construction 공사, 건설　tool 도구, 공구

43. 화자가 "별 소용이 없었습니다"라고 말할 때 의미하는 것은 무엇인가?

(A) 고객들이 어려움을 겪고 있다.
(B) 제품들이 늦게 배송되고 있다.
(C) 직원들이 추가 교육을 받아야 한다.
(D) 한 가지 절차가 유익했다.

해설　해당 문장은 담화 중반부에 화자가 광고에 언급된 특징으로 인해 고객들이 기기를 더 쉽게 조립하게 되길 바랐다고(We hoped that this would make it easier for customers to assemble the device) 언급한 다음에 들을 수 있다. 따라서, 도움이 되지 못했다는 말은 고객들이 쉽게 조립하지 못하게 된 것과 같으므로 이와 같은 의미에 해당되는 (A)가 정답이다.

어휘　have difficulty 어려움을 겪다　require ~을 필요로 하다　further 추가의　procedure 절차　beneficial 유익한

44. 화자는 곧이어 무엇을 할 것 같은가?

(A) 문서를 배부한다.
(B) 제품을 시연한다.
(C) 동료 직원 한 명을 소개한다.
(D) 고객 실문 조사 내용을 이야기한다.

해설　화자는 담화 마지막 부분에 새로운 사용 설명서를 언급하면서 그 내용을 숙지할 수 있도록 지금 사본을 나눠 주겠다고 (I'll hand out copies of that now so that you can familiarize yourselves with it) 알리고 있으므로 문서 배부를 의미하는 (A)가 정답이다.

어휘　distribute ~을 나눠 주다, 배부하다　demonstrate ~을 시연하다, 시범을 보이다　colleague 동료 직원　survey 설문 조사

Paraphrase　hand out copies of that(instruction manual)
　　　　　→ Distribute a document

Questions 45-47 refer to the following telephone message.

Hello, **45** this is Veronica, the head of the marketing team. I'm calling about the design for the product packaging, which we sent to your team in the art department last week. First of all, thanks for creating a sample of the product packaging well before the deadline I had set. Overall, the design on the packaging looks great. However, **46** it looks like you used a different font from the one we wanted, and, **47** I'm sorry, but, umm... I'd like you to change it. I know you have a lot going on right now. I'd be happy to send my assistant, Gina, down to help you correct the matter, if you'd like.

여보세요, 저는 마케팅 팀장인 베로니카입니다. 지난 주에 저희가 미술 부서 내의 당신 팀으로 보내 드린 제품 포장지용 디자인에 관해 전화 드렸습니다. 가장 먼저, 제가 정해 드렸던 마감 시한 전에 제품 포장지 샘플을 잘 만들어 주신 것에 대해 감사드립니다. 전반적으로, 해당 포장지 디자인은 아주 좋아 보입니다. 그런데 저희가 원했던 것과 다른 서체를 사용하신 것 같아서, 죄송하지만, 음... 이것을 바꿔 주셨으면 합니다. 현재 하셔야 할 일이 많다는 것을 알고 있습니다. 괜찮으시다면, 이 문제를 바로잡는 데 도움이 될 수 있도록 제 담당 보조인 지나 씨를 기꺼이 그쪽으로 보내 드리겠습니다.

어휘　head 부서장, 팀장, 책임자　packaging 포장(지)　first of all 가장 먼저, 우선　deadline 마감시한　set ~을 정하다, 설정하다　overall 진반직으로　look 형용사: ~하게 보이다　look like ~한 것 같다　font 서체　would like A to do A에게 ~하기를 원하다　have a lot going on 진행되는 많은 일이 있다　be happy to do 기꺼이 ~하다　send A down A를 그쪽으로 보내다　correct v. ~을 바로잡다, 고치다　matter 문제, 일　if you'd like 괜찮으시다면

45. 화자는 무슨 부서에서 근무하는가?

(A) 인사부
(B) 웹 디자인부
(C) 마케팅부
(D) 총무부

해설　화자는 담화 시작 부분에 자신을 마케팅 팀장이라고(the head of the marketing team) 소개하고 있으므로 (C)가 정답임을 알 수 있다.

어휘　human resources 인사(부)　administration 총무(부)

46. 화자는 무슨 문제점을 언급하는가?

(A) 마감시한이 연장될 수 없다.
(B) 디자인이 늦게 제출되었다.
(C) 잘못된 서체가 사용되었다.
(D) 소포가 도착하지 않았다.

해설 화자가 언급하는 문제점을 찾아야 하므로 부정적인 정보가 제
시되는 부분이 있음을 예상하고 들어야 한다. 담화 중반부에 화
자는 자신이 원했던 것과 다른 서체를 사용한 것 같다는 말과
함께(it looks like you used a different font from the
one we wanted) 이것을 바꿔 달라고 요청하고 있다. 따라서,
이에 대해 언급한 (C)가 정답이다.

어휘 extend ~을 연장하다 submit ~을 제출하다 incorrect
잘못된, 부정확한 package 소포

47. 화자가 "현재 하셔야 할 일이 많다는 것을 알고 있습니다"라고
말하는 이유는 무엇인가?

(A) 청자의 일정에 관해 문의하기 위해
(B) 한 가지 업무를 연기하도록 제안하기 위해
(C) 요청을 하는 것에 대해 유감의 뜻을 나타내기 위해
(D) 청자에게 회의에 참석하도록 요청하기 위해

해설 해당 문장은 담화 중반부에 미안하지만 잘못된 것을 바꿔 달라고
고(I'm sorry, but, umm... I'd like you to change it) 요청
한 말 다음에 들을 수 있다. 즉 바쁜 상황에 요청하는 것이 미안
하다는 의미로 쓰인 것이므로 이와 같은 뜻에 해당되는 (C)가
정답이다.

어휘 inquire about ~에 관해 문의하다 postpone ~을 연기
하다 task 업무, 일 express regret 유감의 뜻을 나타내
다 make a request 요청하다

Questions 48-50 refer to the following telephone
message and graph.

Thanks for taking the time to attend this urgent
meeting. The store owner has expressed concerns
about our profits in the first part of the year. **48**
She specifically wants to know what happened
during the month we recorded our lowest profits.
If we continue to have months where profits are
that low, the store will struggle to stay in business.
As you know, **49** we will open a new branch on
Sutherland Street next month, so it's important
that we identify ways to keep profits high. So,
during this meeting, **50** I'd like you all to give me
your ideas on how to maintain our daily profits at
approximately 800 dollars per day, all year round.

이번 긴급 회의에 참석하기 위해 시간 내어 주셔서 감사드립니
다. 사장님께서 올 상반기 동안 우리가 거둔 수익에 관해 우려를
나타내셨습니다. 특히 우리가 가장 낮은 수익을 기록한 달에 무
슨 일이 있었는지 알고 싶어 하십니다. 수익이 이 정도로 낮은 달
이 지속될 경우에, 우리 매장은 사업을 유지하기 위해 발버둥쳐
야 할 것입니다. 아시다시피, 우리는 다음 달에 서덜랜드 스트리
트에 신규 지점을 열 예정이므로 수익을 높게 유지할 방법을 찾는

것이 중요합니다. 따라서, 이번 회의 중에, 저는 여러분께서 일년
내내 하루에 약 800달러의 수준으로 일일 수익을 유지할 방법에
대한 아이디어를 내 주셨으면 합니다.

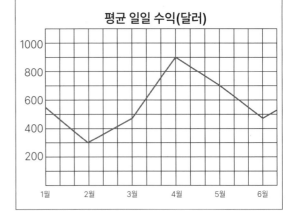

어휘 take the time to do ~할 시간을 내다 urgent 긴급한
owner 소유주 express (감정 등) ~을 표현하다, 나타내
다 concern 우려, 걱정 profit 수익 specifically 특히
record ~을 기록하다 continue to do 지속적으로 ~하다
that ad. 그렇게, 그만큼 struggle to do ~하기 위해 발버
둥치다 stay in business 사업을 유지하다 branch 지점,
지사 identify ~을 찾아 내다, 알아 내다 way to do ~하
는 방법 keep A 형용사 A를 ~하게 유지하다 maintain
~을 유지하다 daily 매일의 approximately 약, 대략
per day 하루에 all year round 일년 내내 average
평균

48. 시각자료를 보시오. 화자는 어느 달에 관해 이야기하고 있는가?
(A) 2월
(B) 3월
(C) 4월
(D) 5월

해설 담화 시작 부분에 화자는 사장님이 우려하는 점과 관련해, 가
장 낮은 수익을 기록한 달에 무슨 일이 있었는지 알고 싶어 한
다고(She specifically wants to know what happened
during the month we recorded our lowest profits) 알
리고 있다. 따라서, 그래프에서 가장 낮은 수익이 기록된 달로
표기된 (A)가 정답이다.

49. 업체는 다음 달에 무엇을 할 것인가?
(A) 매장을 하나 더 개장한다.
(B) 신제품을 출시한다.
(C) 더 많은 직원을 고용한다.
(D) 진열 공간을 확장한다.

해설 다음 달에 하려는 일이 질문의 핵심이므로 해당 시점 표현이 제
시되는 부분에서 단서를 찾아야 한다. 담화 중반부에 화자는 다
음 달에 서덜랜드 스트리트에 신규 지점을 열 예정이라고(we
will open a new branch on Sutherland Street next

month) 알리고 있으므로 (A)가 정답이다.

어휘 release ~을 출시하다 enlarge ~을 확장하다, 넓히다
display 진열, 전시

Paraphrase open a new branch on Sutherland Street
→ Open another store

50. 화자는 청자들에게 무엇을 하도록 요청하는가?

(A) 교육 강좌에 참석할 것
(B) 고객들에게 설문 조사를 할 것
(C) 제안 사항을 전달할 것
(D) 매출 수치 자료를 검토할 것

해설 담화 마지막 부분에 일년 내내 하루에 약 800달러의 수준으로
일일 수익을 유지할 방법에 대한 아이디어를 내 달라고(I'd like
you all to give me your ideas for how to maintain our
daily profits ~) 요청하고 있다. 이는 제안을 하는 일을 의미하
므로 (C)가 정답이다.

어휘 survey ~에게 설문 조사를 하다 provide ~을 제공하다
review ~을 검토하다 sales 매출, 판매(량) figure 수치,
숫자

Paraphrase give me your ideas on how to maintain our
daily profits
→ Provide suggestions

Part 5

51.
정답 (A)

해석 딜런 홈 인테리어 사는 소형 아파트에 거주하는 사람들을 위해
고안된 다양한 가구들을 보유하고 있습니다.

해설 빈칸은 전치사 for의 목적어 자리이며, 뒤에 이어지는 관계대명
사절의 수식을 받아야 한다. 인칭대명사도 빈칸에 들어갈 수 있
지만 빈칸 앞에 가리킬 수 있는 대상이 없고, 의미로 보아 빈칸
에 들어갈 단어는 사람을 가리켜야 하므로 '사람들'을 뜻하는
(A) those가 정답이다.

어휘 a large selection of 다양한 (종류의) design A for B
B를 위해 A를 고안하다, 디자인하다 reside in ~에 거주하
다 condominium 아파트

52.
정답 (A)

해석 행사 개최 장소에 대한 전체 좌석 배치도는 저희 웹 사이트에서
온라인으로 보실 수 있습니다.

해설 빈칸 앞에 위치한 형용사 available은 to부정사와 결합해 그 행
위의 발생 가능성과 관련된 의미를 나타내므로 (A) to view가
정답이다.

어휘 seating chart 좌석 배치도 venue 개최 장소, 행사장
available 이용 가능한, 구입 가능한 view v. ~을 보다 n.

경치, 시야, 관점

53.
정답 (D)

해석 낡은 기계를 완전히 새로운 기계로 교체한 것이 제조 공장의 가
동 효율을 크게 향상시켜 왔다.

해설 빈칸이 소유격과 형용사 뒤에 위치해 있으므로 빈칸은 이 둘
의 수식을 동시에 받을 수 있는 명사 자리이다. 따라서 (D)
efficiency가 정답이다.

어휘 machinery 기계 brand new 완전히 새로운 greatly
크게, 대단히, 매우 improve ~을 향상시키다, ~을 개선
하다 manufacturing 제조 operating 가동의, 운영
의, 조작상의 efficient 효율적인 efficiently 효율적으로
efficiency 효율(성)

54.
정답 (C)

해석 경영진은 올해의 업무 효율 경연대회 우승자가 500달러의 보
너스를 받았다고 발표했다.

해설 선택지가 4형식 동사 grant의 다양한 형태로 구성되어 있고,
빈칸 바로 뒤에 직접목적어가 제시되어 있다. 따라서 간접목적
어가 주어 자리에 있는 것으로 볼 수 있으므로 수동태 (C) was
granted가 정답이다.

어휘 management 경영진, 운영진 announce that ~라고
발표하다 work efficiency 업무 효율 grant A B A에게
B를 주다, 수여하다

55.
정답 (C)

해석 쿡빌에 있는 많은 기업들은 각자의 창고에 대해 보안 담당 직원
들을 긴급하게 필요로 하고 있다.

해설 빈칸 앞에 전치사가 있고 빈칸 뒤에는 명사가 있으므로 빈칸에
명사를 수식할 형용사가 필요하나. 따라서 (C) urgent가 정답
이다.

어휘 in need of ~을 필요로 하는 urgent 긴급한 personnel
직원 urgency 긴급함 urgently 긴급하게

56.
정답 (B)

해석 도시 계획부는 허스트 에비뉴의 울퉁불퉁한 보도를 평탄화하는
공사에 대한 자금을 마침내 할당했다.

해설 빈칸 앞에 위치한 leveling은 '평탄화, 평준화' 등을 의미하며,
빈칸 뒤에 위치한 울퉁불퉁한 보도가 그 대상으로서 목적어와
같은 역할을 한다. 따라서 이와 같은 행위 대상 또는 목적물 관
계를 나타낼 때 사용하는 (B) of가 정답이다.

어휘 urban planning 도시 계획 finally 마침내, 결국
allocate ~을 할당하다, 배정하다 leveling 평탄화, 평준화
uneven 울퉁불퉁한, 평평하지 않은 sidewalk 보도, 인도

57.

정답 (C)

해석 대표이사는 두 회사가 옥외 광고판을 이용한 광고 프로젝트에 대해 전통적으로 협업해 왔다고 언급했다.

해설 현재완료 시제를 구성하는 have와 과거분사 collaborated 사이에 위치한 빈칸은 과거분사를 수식할 부사 자리이므로 (C) traditionally가 정답이다.

어휘 traditionally 전통적으로, 일반적으로 billboard 옥외 광고판 traditionalism 전통주의

58.

정답 (D)

해석 우리 회사의 새로운 판매 수수료 체계에 관한 모든 문의는 인사팀의 코크런 씨에게 보내져야 합니다.

해설 빈칸 뒤에 위치한 전치사구들이 새로운 판매 수수료 체계에 관한 문의를 받아 처리하는 담당자인 것으로 판단할 수 있으므로 메시지 등과 관련해 '~을 보내다'를 뜻하는 동사 direct의 과거분사 (D) directed가 정답이다.

어휘 query 문의 commission (판매나 서비스 등의 대가로 받는) 수수료 structure 체계, 구조(물) HR 인사(부) limit ~을 제한하다 assert ~라고 주장하다 direct (메시지 등) ~을 보내다

59.

정답 (A)

해석 특별 보너스가 보통 정규직 직원들에게만 지급되지만, 올해는 시간제 직원들도 받을 것이다.

해설 빈칸 뒤에 주어와 동사를 포함한 두 개의 절이 있으므로 빈칸은 접속사 자리이다. 해석상 '보통 정규직 직원들에게 지급되지만 올해에는 시간제 직원들도 받을 것'이라는 양보의 의미를 나타내는 문장이 되는 것이 자연스러우므로 (A) Although가 정답이다.

어휘 full-time employee 정규직 직원 part-time worker 시간제 직원 whether (A or B와 함께) ~이든 …이든 moreover 더욱이

60.

정답 (A)

해석 경쟁이 줄어드는 덕분에, 래쉬드 드라이 클리너는 서비스를 받는 고객들의 숫자의 급격한 증가를 경험했다.

해설 빈칸은 현재분사 decreasing의 수식을 받으며 전치사 to의 목적어 역할을 할 명사 자리이다. 선택지에서 명사는 불가산명사인 (A) competition과 가산명사인 (D) competitor인데, 빈칸 앞에 관사가 없으므로 불가산명사 (A) competition이 정답이다.

어휘 decreasing 점점 줄어드는, 감소하는 sharp 급격한 rise in ~의 증가 serve ~에게 서비스를 제공하다 compete 경쟁하다 competitive 경쟁력 있는

61.

정답 (C)

해석 그 고객께서 우리에게 어떤 애피타이저와 주 요리를 제공하기를 원하시는지를 결정하시는 대로, 디저트에 대한 여러 가지 선택권을 고려하실 것입니다.

해설 빈칸 뒤에 복수명사가 쓰여 있으므로 '여럿의, 몇몇의'라는 의미로 복수명사를 수식할 때 사용하는 복수 수량형용사 (C) several이 정답이다.

어휘 once ~하는 대로, ~하자마자 provide ~을 제공하다 consider ~을 고려하다 another 또 다른 하나의 either 둘 중의 하나 several 여럿의, 몇몇의 whichever ~하는 어느 것이든

62.

정답 (A)

해석 동물 보호소에서 자원봉사를 하는 것과 지역 재즈 밴드에서 피아노를 연주하는 것이 그의 여러 취미들 중에 속해 있다.

해설 두 개의 동명사구가 and로 연결되어 있고 동사 다음에 빈칸과 명사구가 위치한 구조이다. 빈칸 뒤의 명사구는 '여러 취미들'을 의미하므로 주어로 쓰인 동명사구들이 속하는 범위를 나타낸다. 따라서, '~ 중에, ~에 포함된'라는 의미로 복수명사를 목적어로 취해 범위를 나타낼 때 사용하는 (A) among이 정답이다.

어휘 shelter 보호소 among ~ 중에, ~ 사이에 considering ~을 고려하면, 감안하면 regarding ~ 와 관련해, ~에 관해

63.

정답 (B)

해석 요즘 대다수의 사람들은 현금으로 지불하는 대신 신용카드를 사용하는 것을 선호한다.

해설 빈칸 앞에는 신용카드를 사용하는 것을 선호한다는 절이 쓰여 있고, 빈칸 뒤에는 또 다른 지불 방식에 해당되는 동사구가 위치해 있다. 따라서, '~ 대신, ~가 아니라'는 의미로 쓰이면서 문법적으로 동일한 두 가지 요소를 연결한 병렬 구조를 구성해 선택이나 비교 등을 나타낼 때 사용하는 상관접속사 (B) rather than이 정답이다.

어휘 prefer to do ~하는 것을 선호하다 only if 오직 ~하는 경우에만, ~하는 경우에 한해 rather than ~ 대신, ~가 아니라 in case (that) ~하는 경우에 (대비해) so that (목적) ~하도록, (결과) 그래서, 그러므로

64.

정답 (A)

해석 콜 씨는 모든 재무 자료를 모았을 뿐만 아니라, 직접 정산표에 그 자료를 입력하기까지 했다.

해설 대동사 did 다음에 명사가 있고 바로 다음에 동사 gather가 나타나 있으므로 도치 구조임을 알 수 있다. 따라서 문장 맨 앞에 위치한 빈칸에 부정어가 와야 하므로 (A) Not only가 정답이다.

어휘 **not only A but also B** A뿐만 아니라 B도 **gather** ~을 모으다 **enter A into B** A를 B에 입력하다 **spreadsheet** 정산표, 스프레드시트 **oneself** (부사적으로) 직접 **in addition** 게다가 **besides** ~ 외에도, 게다가 **above** ad. 위로 prep. ~ 보다 위에

65.

정답 (D)

해석 저희는 모든 고용주들께 저희 웹 사이트에 게시하시기 전에 공석 광고 내용을 신중히 교정 보시도록 권해 드립니다.

해설 전치사 prior to와 목적격 대명사 them 사이에 위치한 빈칸은 이 목적격 대명사를 목적어로 취함과 동시에 전치사의 목적어 역할을 할 동명사 자리이므로 (D) posting이 정답이다.

어휘 **advise A to do** A에게 ~하도록 권하다, A에게 ~하도록 조언하다 **proofread** ~을 교정 보다 **job vacancy** 공석 **carefully** 신중히, 조심스럽게 **prior to** ~ 전에, ~에 앞서

66.

정답 (B)

해석 여러분의 출품작이 제출 마감 기한 이후에도 여전히 접수되도록 확실히 해두시려면, 대회 조직위원회에 전화로 직접 연락하십시오.

해설 수동태 동사를 구성하는 be동사와 과거분사 accepted사이에 빈칸이 위치해 있으므로 be동사와 과거분사 사이에 위치해 과거분사를 수식할 수 있는 부사 (B) still이 정답이다.

어휘 **ensure that** ~임을 확실히 해두다, ~임을 보장하다 **accept** ~을 받아들이다, ~을 수락하다 **submission** 제출 (되는 것) **deadline** 마감 기한

Part 6

67-70.

트리니티 어드버타이징의 제3회 연례 직원 회의에 오신 것은 환영합니다. **67** 우리는 올해 500명이 넘는 직원의 참석으로 이전 기록을 깰 예정입니다. 그렇게 많은 수의 직원들이 참여하므로, 우리는 모든 활동을 반드시 제 시각에 완료하기 위해서 행사 중 **68** 엄격한 일정표대로 운영할 것입니다.

이점을 염두에 두고, 저희는 여러분에게 예정된 행사를 불참하는 것을 **69** 삼갈 것을 부탁드립니다. 여러분 모두 각각의 행사에 참석하는 것이 얼마나 중요한지 이미 알고 있을 것입니다.

오늘 밤, 우리는 저녁 만찬을 위해 무도회장에 모일 것이며, 그 뒤에 연례 시상식이 이어질 것입니다. 내일은 일련의 연설자와 워크숍이 있을 것입니다. 워크숍 사이에 점심이 제공되지 않을 것이라는 점에 대해 사과 드립니다. **70** 하지만, 로비에 있는 자판기에서 샌드위치와 음료는 구입하실 수 있습니다.

어휘 **timetable** 일정표 **ensure** 반드시 ~하게 하다, 확실하게

하다 **complete** ~을 완료하다 **on time** 제 시각에, 정시에 **miss** ~에 빠지다, ~을 놓치다 **vital** 중요한 **followed by** 그 뒤로 ~가 이어지는 **awards ceremony** 시상식 **a series of** 일련의 **in between** ~사이에 **vending machine** 자판기 **beverage** 음료

67.

정답 (D)

해석 (A) 귀하가 저희 업체에서 숙박하신 것이 즐거운 일이었기를 바랍니다.
(B) 우리의 손님들을 따뜻하게 환영해주시고, 그들을 편하게 있도록 해주시기 바랍니다.
(C) 행사 중에 논의 될 주제들 중에 몇 가지를 설명해드리겠습니다.
(D) 우리는 올해 500명이 넘는 직원의 참석으로 이전 기록을 깰 예정입니다.

해설 바로 뒤에 그렇게 많은 수의 직원들의 참가라는 내용에서 such가 언급되어 있으므로 빈칸에 들어갈 문장에 이미 많은 수의 직원이 참가한다는 내용이 언급되어야 한다는 것을 알 수 있다. 따라서 빈칸에는 500명이 넘는 직원들의 참석이 언급된 (D)가 정답이다.

어휘 **make A feel at home** A를 편안하게 있게 하다 **be set to do** ~하게 되어 있다, ~할 예정이다 **break records** 기록을 깨다

68.

정답 (A)

해설 빈칸 뒤에 많은 활동들을 제 시각에 완료해야 한다는 내용이 있으므로, 일정표대로 일정을 완료하기 위해 행사가 엄격하게 운영될 것이라는 것을 알 수 있다. 따라서 '엄격한'이라는 의미의 (A) rigorous가 정답이다.

어휘 **rigorous** 엄격한 **numerous** 매우 많은 **hazardous** 위험한

69.

정답 (B)

해설 빈칸 뒤에 목적어가 없고 전치사 from이 있으므로 빈칸에는 from -ing와 함께 쓰이는 자동사가 들어가야 한다. 문맥상 각각의 행사가 모두 중요하므로 놓치지 말라는 내용이므로 '금지하다, 삼가다'라는 의미의 (B) prevent가 정답이다.

어휘 **obtain A from B** B로부터 A를 얻다 **refrain from -ing** ~하는 것을 삼가다 **prevent A from -ing** A가 ~하지 못하게 방지하다, 예방하다 **mind** ~을 꺼려하다

70.

정답 (C)

해설 빈칸 앞에는 점심을 제공하지 못해 죄송하다는 내용이고, 빈칸 뒤에는 샌드위치와 음료와 같은 가벼운 먹거리가 자판기에서 판매된다는 내용이 있으므로 서로 반대되는 내용이다. 따라서

역접의 의미를 나타내는 (C) However가 정답이다.

어휘 for instance 예를 들어 in addition 게다가 however 그러나 otherwise 그렇지 않으면

71-74.

치솟는 덜위치 관광 산업 관련 수치

덜위치 (12월 28일) - 우리 덜위치의 지역 호텔 및 레스토랑 소유주들이 사업에서의 상당한 증진을 71 경험하고 있습니다. 매직 월드 놀이공원이 6월에 개장한 이후로 줄곧, 방문객들이 이 새로운 명소를 방문하기 위해 우리 도시로 계속 모여들고 있습니다. 관광 안내소에 따르면, 50만 명이 넘는 관광객들이 7월과 12월 사이에 덜위치를 방문했습니다. 72 이는 작년 상반기에 기록된 숫자의 세 배입니다. 전문가들은 이러한 상향 추세가 내년으로 접어들어도 지속될 것으로 예상하고 있습니다.

관광 산업의 호황은 호텔과 레스토랑 73 같은 지역 업체들에게 긍정적인 영향을 미쳐 왔습니다. 오크필드 호텔의 소유주 미치 해스킨 씨는 이러한 관광 산업의 증진이 매직 월드의 개장뿐만 아니라, 덜위치 시의회가 74 마케팅에 더 많은 중점을 둔 것에도 기인한다고 생각합니다. 해스킨 씨의 말에 따르면, "의회에서 만든 온라인 광고와 홍보 캠페인이 덜위치에 있는 모든 업체에 직접적으로 혜택이 되어 왔습니다."

어휘 soar 치솟다 owner 소유주 significant 상당한, 중요한 ever since ~한 이후로 줄곧 flock to ~로 모여들다 attraction 명소, 인기 장소 according to ~에 따르면 expert 전문가 upward 상향의 move into + 시점 ~로 접어들다 boom 호황, 대유행, 붐 have a positive effect on ~에 긍정적인 영향을 미치다 attribute A to B A가 B에 기인한다고 생각하다, A의 원인이 B라고 생각하다 increased 더 많아진, 늘어난, 증가된 focus on ~에 대한 중점, ~에 대한 초점 promotional 홍보의 directly 직접적으로, 곧장 benefit ~에 혜택을 주다, ~에 유익하다

71.

정답 (B)

해설 주어 뒤로 빈칸이 있고, 그 뒤에 명사구와 전치사구들만 쓰여 있어 빈칸이 문장의 동사 자리임을 알 수 있다. 또한, 다음 문장에 쓰인 현재완료진행시제 동사에서 알 수 있듯이 계속 많은 방문객이 찾는 상황을 나타내는 동사가 빈칸에 필요하므로 현재진행 중인 일을 말할 때 사용하는 현재진행시제 동사 (B) are experiencing이 정답이다.

72.

정답 (D)

해석 (A) 덜위치는 여러 역사적인 명소들로 알려져 있습니다.
(B) 시의회가 힘겨워하는 업체들을 돕겠다고 약속했습니다.
(C) 매직 월드는 그 작업이 완료되고 3월에 재개장할 것입니다.
(D) 이는 작년 상반기에 기록된 숫자의 세 배입니다.

해설 빈칸 앞 문장에 50만 명이 넘는 관광객들이 7월과 12월 사이에 덜위치를 방문했다는 말이 쓰여 있으므로 이 수치를 This로 지칭해 작년의 특정 기간에 해당되는 수치와 비교하는 내용을 담은 (D)가 정답이다.

어휘 be known for ~로 알려지다 landmark 명소, 주요 지형지물 promise to do ~하겠다고 약속하다 struggling 힘겨워하는 complete ~을 완료하다 triple the + 명사 ~의 세 배

73.

정답 (C)

해설 빈칸 뒤에 위치한 호텔과 레스토랑은 빈칸 앞에 위치한 지역 업체들의 범주에 속하는 곳으로서, 긍정적인 영향을 받은 업체들의 예시에 해당되므로 '~와 같은'이라는 의미로 예시를 나타낼 때 사용하는 (C) such as가 정답이다.

어휘 throughout (장소) ~ 전역에 걸쳐, (기간) ~ 동안 내내 between ~ 사이에 such as ~와 같은 ahead of (위치, 시점 등) ~보다 앞서, ~보다 빨리

74.

정답 (C)

해설 빈칸에 쓰일 명사는 전치사 on의 목적어로서 시의회가 더 많이 중점을 둔 사항을 나타내야 한다. 뒤에 이어지는 문장에 온라인 광고 및 홍보 캠페인이 큰 영향을 미쳤음을 나타내는 말이 쓰여 있어 광고 및 홍보와 관련된 사항에 중점을 두었다는 말이 되어야 자연스러운데, 이는 '마케팅'에 해당되므로 (C) marketing이 정답이다.

어휘 hiring 고용 investment 투자 construction 공사, 건설

Part 7

75-76.

가레스 볼드 (오후 12:40) 안녕하세요, 비키 씨. 제가 발표 유인물을 기다리느라 여전히 인쇄소에 있습니다. 75 발표에 필요한 것들을 준비하기 시작해 주시겠어요? 노트북 컴퓨터는 제 사무실에 있고, 그 슬라이드는 문서 폴더에 저장되어 있습니다.

비키 무니 (오후 12:41) 알겠습니다.

가레스 볼드 (오후 12:43) 75 좋습니다. 발표가 오후 2시 30분이나 되어야 시작하기는 하지만, 반드시 노트북 컴퓨터가 그 방에 놓여 있고 슬라이드가 모두 보여질 준비가 되어 있도록 했으면 합니다.

비키 무니 (오후 12:44) 76 발표가 3층에 있는 회의실에서 열리는 게 맞죠?

가레스 볼드 (오후 12:46) 네, 그리고 그 다음에 우리가 잠재 투자자들께 연구 실험실을 둘러보시게 해 드릴 겁니다. 처음 도착할 때는 그곳에 출입하실 수 없을 겁니다. 먼저 출입증을 받으실 수 있도록 경비실로 모시고 가야 할 겁니다.

비키 무니 (오후 12:47) 아, 물론입니다. 그럼, **76** 저는 준비하는 일을 시작하겠습니다.

가레스 볼드 (오후 12:48) 감사합니다, 비키 씨. 곧 돌아 가겠습니다.

어휘   **printing shop** 인쇄소   **presentation** 발표(회)   **handout** 유인물   **get A p.p.** A를 ~되게 하다, A를 ~해놓다   **On it** 알겠습니다, 제가 할게요   **not A until B** B나 되어야 A하다   **be ready to do** ~할 준비가 되다   **give A a tour of B** A에게 B를 둘러보게 하다, A에게 B를 견학시키다   **potential** 잠재적인   **investor** 투자자   **laboratory** 실험실   **be able to do** ~할 수 있다   **access** ~에 출입하다, ~을 이용하다   **take A to B** A를 B에 데리고 가다   **organize** ~을 준비하다, ~을 조직하다   **appreciate** ~에 대해 감사하다

75. 오후 12시 41분에, 무니 씨가 "On it"이라고 쓸 때 무엇을 의미할 것 같은가?

    (A) 볼드 씨에게 도움을 제공할 수 있다.
    (B) 일부 유인물이 준비될 것으로 확신한다.
    (C) 노트북 컴퓨터가 사무실에 있다고 확신한다.
    (D) 볼드 씨의 발표가 성공할 것으로 생각한다.

정답   (A)

해설   12시 40분 메시지에 볼드 씨가 발표에 필요한 것들을 준비하기 시작해 달라고 요청한(Can you start getting things set up for the presentation?) 것에 대해 무니 씨가 "On it"이라고 답변하자, 볼드 씨도 좋다고(Excellent) 말하는 흐름이다. 이를 통해 무니 씨가 볼드 씨의 요청을 수락했다는 것을 알 수 있으며, 이는 발표를 준비하는 일을 돕겠다는 뜻을 나타내는 것이므로 (A)가 정답이다.

어휘   **lend A a hand** A에게 도움을 제공하다   **be positive that** ~임을 확신하다

76. 무니 씨가 곧이어 어디로 갈 것 같은가?

    (A) 경비실로
    (B) 인쇄 업체로
    (C) 회의실로
    (D) 연구 실험실로

정답   (C)

해설   무니 씨가 12시 47분 메시지에 준비를 시작하겠다고(I'll start getting things organized) 알리고 있는데, 이는 12시 44분 메시지에 언급된 회의실에서(The presentation will be in the third floor conference room, won't it?) 발표에 필요한 준비를 하겠다는 뜻이므로 (C)가 정답이다.

77-79.

수신: 지그프리드 코퍼레이션 전 직원
발신: 노먼 팔쿠스
제목: 파파야 6X 스마트폰 행사
79 날짜: 3월 22일

직원 여러분,

77 여러분 모두에게 업계 선두주자들 중의 한 곳이 최신 기기를 발표하는 것을 지켜 볼 수 있는 흥미로운 기회를 알려 드리고자 합니다. 타미야 일렉트로닉스가 파파야 6X 스마트폰의 출시를 기념하기 위한 업계 행사를 4월 15일에 개최합니다. 이 행사는 **78** 틀림없이 매우 흥미로울 것이며, 특히 제품 개발 및 마케팅과 관련된 분들께 그럴 것입니다. 물론, 우리는 타미야 사와 함께 그곳의 최첨단 터치 스크린 기술을 개발하는데 도움을 주기 위해 일했기 때문에, 그 제품이 마침내 시장에 진입하는 것을 보게 되어 매우 자랑스럽습니다.

우리의 기여에 대한 감사의 표시로, 타미야 일렉트로닉스가 우리에게 이 행사에 대한 25장의 초대권을 제공해 주었으며, 이는 선착순으로 할당될 것입니다. **79** 관심 있는 모든 분들께서는, 반드시 이달 말까지 저에게 알려 주시기 바랍니다. 우리는 4월 8일까지 타미야 사에 전체 참석자 명단을 제출해야 합니다. 이 행사는 타미야 일렉트로닉스처럼 시장의 선두주자가 되기를 꿈꾸는 이곳 지그프리드 코퍼레이션에 근무하는 분들께 영감의 원천으로서 역할을 할 것입니다.

안녕히 계십시오.

노먼 팔쿠스

어휘   **witness** ~을 지켜 보다, 목격하다   **unveil** ~을 발표하다, 공개하다   **gadget** 기기   **mark** ~을 기념하다   **be bound to do** 틀림없이 ~하다   **alongside** ~와 함께   **cutting-edge** 최첨단의   **enter the market** 시장에 진입하다   **as a token of** ~의 표시로   **appreciation** 감사   **contribution** 기여, 공헌   **allocate** ~을 할당하다, 배분하다   **on a first-come, first-served basis** 선착순으로   **serve as** ~로서 역할을 하다   **inspiration** 영감(을 주는 것)

77. 이 회람의 목적은 무엇인가?

    (A) 직원들에게 행사에 참석하는 것을 제안하기 위해
    (B) 제품 개발자들에게 감사의 뜻을 표하기 위해
    (C) 직원들에게 프로젝트 일정을 간략히 설명하기 위해
    (D) 직원들에게 행사 입장권을 구입하도록 상기시키기 위해

정답   (A)

해설   첫 단락 초반부에 업계 선두주자들 중의 한 곳이 최신 기기를 발표하는 것을 지켜 볼 수 있는 흥미로운 기회를 알린다고 (I'd like to inform you all of an exciting opportunity to witness one of the industry leaders unveiling its latest gadget) 언급하면서 특정 행사 개최와 관련된 정보를 제공하고 있다. 이는 해당 행사에 참석하도록 권하는 것이므로 (A)가 정답이다.

어휘　gratitude 감사(의 마음)　outline ~을 간략히 설명하다
　　　remind A to do A에게 ~하도록 상기시키다

78. 첫 번째 단락, 세 번째 줄의 단어 "bound"와 의미가 가장 가까운 것은 무엇인가?

　　(A) 굳은
　　(B) 자제하는
　　(C) 분명한
　　(D) 강요된

정답　(C)

해설　해당 문장에서 bound 뒤로 '매우 흥미롭다'를 뜻하는 to be very interesting이 쓰여 있는 것으로 볼 때, 분명히 흥미로운 행사임을 나타내는 말인 것으로 판단할 수 있으므로 '분명한'을 의미하는 (C) certain이 정답이다.

79. 직원들은 행사 참석과 관련해 언제 팔쿠스 씨에게 알려야 하는가?

　　(A) 3월 31일까지
　　(B) 4월 8일까지
　　(C) 4월 15일까지
　　(D) 4월 30일까지

정답　(A)

해설　두 번째 단락에서 행사 참석에 관심 있는 사람들은 반드시 이 달 말까지 자신에게 알려달라고(For all those who are interested, please make sure to inform me by the end of the month) 언급하고 있으며, 지문 상단의 회람 작성 날짜가 3월 22일이므로(Date: March 22) 3월 말, 즉 3월 31일까지 알려야 한다는 것을 알 수 있다. 따라서 (A)가 정답이다.

80-82.

---

　80 블레이즈컴 케이블 & 인터넷 서비스 구독 갱신
　연속해서 구독서비스를 이용하시기 바랍니다!

　고객 성명: 조던 크랜스턴
　자택 주소: 552 스팰딩 드라이브, 올랜도, FL, 32803
　전화 번호: 301-555-3907
　이메일 주소: jcranston@blazecom.net
　고객 서명: 조던 크랜스턴
　구독 갱신 후 첫 납입액: 99.99달러

일반 패키지:	프리미엄 패키지:
매월 89.99달러 본 12개월짜리 패키지에는 96개의 케이블TV 채널과 가장 빠른 저희 인터넷 서비스가 포함됩니다. 가입자께서는 다음 서비스를 이용하실 수 있습니다. - 추가 비용 없는 HD 채널들 - **81(A)** 모바일 기기에서 이용 가능한 무료 TV 로밍 서비스 - **81(C)** 최대 150 Mbps의 다운로드 속도 - **81(D)** 블레이즈컴 상품에 붙는 10달러 상당의 포인트	매월 109.99달러 본 18개월짜리 패키지에서는 122개의 케이블TV 채널과 가장 빠른 저희 인터넷 서비스가 포함됩니다. **82** 일반 패키지 제공 서비스에 더해, 추가 비용 없이 신작 개봉영화들로 구성된 저희 전체 라이브러리 이용권도 받게 됩니다.

기술지원 상담 전화: 저희 기술지원팀을 고객들께서는 하루 종일, 연중 무휴로 이용하실 수 있습니다. 555-3892로 전화 주시기 바랍니다.

신작 개봉영화: 저희 신작 개봉영화 서비스를 통해 구입하신 영화들의 요금은 프리미엄 패키지를 이용하지 않는 분들의 월간 고지서에 부과될 것입니다.

어휘　renewal 갱신　uninterrupted 끊임 없는, 중단 없는　payment 지불 금액　due 예정된　upon ~할 때, ~하자마자　subscriber 서비스 가입자, 구독자　following 다음, 아래　at no extra charge 추가 요금 없이　up to 최대 ~의　credit (매장 등의) 포인트　merchandise 상품　in addition to ~에 더해, ~뿐만 아니라　offering 제공 서비스　access 이용 (권한), 접근 (권한)　hotline 상담 전화 서비스　available to ~가 이용할 수 있는　through ~을 통해　bill 고지서, 청구서

80. 크랜스턴 씨에 관해 암시된 것은 무엇인가?

　　(A) 새로운 케이블TV 패키지에 관해 문의했다.
　　(B) 인터넷 연결 문제를 겪은 적이 있다.
　　(C) 현재 블레이즈컴 사의 서비스에 가입되어 있다.
　　(D) 최근에 새로운 자택 주소로 이사했다.

정답　(C)

해설　계약서에 해당되는 이 지문의 제목이 '블레이즈컴 사의 케이블 & 인터넷 서비스 구독 갱신(Blazecom Cable & Internet Service Subscription Renewal)'이라고 되어 있는데, Subscription Renewal은 구독 중인 서비스의 계약 연장을 의미하므로 (C)가 정답이다.

어휘　inquire about ~에 관해 문의하다　connection 연결, 접속　currently 현재

81. 일반 패키지에 속하지 않는 것은 무엇인가?

　　(A) 휴대전화로 TV를 시청할 수 있는 옵션
　　(B) 100개가 넘는 텔레비전 채널 이용 권한

(C) 150 Mbps의 최대 다운로드 속도

(D) 블레이즈컴 상품에 붙는 포인트

정답 (B)

해설 지문 중반부의 왼쪽 표를 보면 모바일 기기에서 이용 가능한 무료 TV 로밍 서비스를(Free Roam TV on your mobile devices) 뜻하는 부분에서 (A)를, 150 Mbps의 최대 다운로드 속도를(Up to 150 Mbps download speed) 뜻하는 부분에서 (C)를, 블레이즈컴 상품에 붙는 10달러 상당의 포인트를($10 credit on Blazecom merchandise) 의미하는 부분에서 (D)를 확인할 수 있다. 하지만 100개가 넘는 텔레비전 채널을 이용할 수 있다는 정보는 프리미엄 패키지(Premium Package)에 속하는 것이므로 (B)가 정답이다.

82. 일반에서 프리미엄 상품으로 업그레이드함으로써 고객은 어떤 추가 혜택을 받을 수 있는가?

(A) 더 빠른 인터넷 속도

(B) 무료 신작 개봉영화들

(C) 온라인 기술지원 서비스

(D) 하드웨어에 대한 품질 보증 서비스

정답 (B)

해설 프리미엄 패키지의 서비스가 언급된 오른쪽 표를 보면, 추가 비용 없이 신작 개봉영화들로 구성된 라이브러리 이용권도 받는다고(you will receive access to our full library of Box Office movies at no extra charge) 나오므로 (B)가 정답이다.

어휘 benefit 혜택, 이점 warranty 품질 보증(서)

83-86.

83 피에스타 크루즈 라인의 최신 선박으로 3,785명의 승객을 태우는 피에스타 제미니는 지금까지 중에서 의심의 여지 없이 이 회사의 가장 인상적인 배입니다. 여객선 업계의 최신 경향을 따라, 피에스타는 제미니에서 제공되는 식사 및 오락 서비스를 확대해 승객들에게 과거 그 어느 때보다 더 많은 선택권을 제공합니다.

저는 "할 것은 너무 많고, 시간은 너무 적다!"는 말로 10박으로 이뤄진 제 여객선 여행을 요약할 수 있습니다. 제가 가장 좋아했던 활동들 중에는 84(C) 미니 골프 코스와 볼링장, 그리고 84(A) 아이맥스 영화관이 있었습니다. 저는 또한 행사 공연장 중앙 무대에서 있었던 마술 공연과 곡예 공연도 아주 마음에 들었지만, 바쁜 제 일정으로 인해 코미디 공연은 놓쳤습니다. — [1] —.

84(B) 제공된 라이브 음악의 양과 질은 매우 인상적이었습니다. 선상에서 들려 주는 라이브 음악의 양을 몇 년 동안 점차적으로 줄여 온 끝에, 피에스타는 고객 의견을 듣고 콘서트를 다시 도입했습니다. 톱 데크 플라자와 많은 바에서, 그리고 심지어 카지노에서도 라이브 밴드들을 찾을 수 있습니다! — [2] —.

85 이 선박에 어떤 것이든 정말로 단점이 있다면, 그건 중앙의 식당에서 제공되는 아침 식사 뷔페입니다. — [3] —. 저는 메뉴가 너무 자주 반복된다는 느낌을 받았으며, 그 중 많은 것이 원래 그래야 하는 것만큼 신선하지 않았습니다. 86 하지만 제미니

에 대해 제가 가장 좋아하는 점은 친절한 승무원들이었습니다. — [4] —. 객실 관리 직원들에서부터 활동을 기획하는 분들까지, 모두 항상 따뜻한 미소로 저를 맞이해 주셨습니다.

후기 작성자: 그레타 맨슬

어휘 vessel 선박 undoubtedly 의심의 여지 없이 yet (최상급과 함께) 지금까지 중에서 sum A up A를 요약하다 acrobatics 곡예 on offer 제공되는 gradually 점차적으로 re-introduce ~을 다시 도입하다 should have p.p. (원래) ~했어야 했다 crew 승무원 housekeeping 객실 관리, 시설 관리 greet ~을 맞이하다, 인사하다

83. 피에스타 제미니 여객선에 관해 암시된 것은 무엇인가?

(A) 최근 전체 선박에 추가된 것이다.

(B) 전 세계에 있는 여행지들을 방문한다.

(C) 업계 내의 여러 상을 받았다.

(D) 승객용 선실이 개조되었다.

정답 (A)

해설 첫 문장에 피에스타 크루즈 라인의 최신 선박으로(Fiesta Cruise Line's newest vessel) 3,785명의 승객을 태운다는 말로 피에스타 제미니를 소개하고 있다. 최신 선박이라는 말은 그 업체에서 보유한 전체 선박에 최근 추가된 것임을 나타내므로 (A)가 정답이다.

어휘 destination 여행지, 목적지 addition 추가(된 것) fleet (한 업체가 보유한) 전체 선박, 전체 차량 cabin 선실, 객실

84. 맨슬 씨가 여객선 여행 중에 즐긴 활동이 아닌 것은 무엇인가?

(A) 영화 관람

(B) 음악 공연 참석

(C) 미니 골프 경기

(D) 코미디언 얘기 듣기

정답 (D)

해설 두 번째 단락에서 가장 좋아했던 활동들 중에는 미니골프 코스와 볼링장, 그리고 아이맥스 영화관이 있었다는(Among my favorite activities were the mini-golf course, the bowling alley, and the IMAX movie theater) 부분에서 (A)와 (C)를, 다음 단락에 제공된 라이브 음악의 양과 질이 매우 인상적이었다는(The quantity and quality of live music on offer was very impressive) 부분에서 (B)를 확인할 수 있다. 하지만 두 번째 단락에서 코미디 공연을 놓쳤다고(I missed the comedy show) 알리고 있으므로 (D)가 정답이다.

85. 맨슬 씨는 무엇이 개선되어야 한다고 생각하는가?

(A) 선실의 청결도

(B) 식당 메뉴

(C) 야외 좌석 구역

(D) 라이브 음악의 양

정답 (B)

해설 개선되어야 할 단점이 언급되는 마지막 단락에 어떤 것이든 정말로 단점이 있다면 식당에서 제공되는 아침 식사 뷔페라고 (If the ship has any real weakness, it's the breakfast buffet in the main dining room) 알리고 있으므로 (B)가 정답이다.

어휘 cleanliness 청결도

86. [1], [2], [3], [4]로 표기된 위치들 중에서, 다음 문장이 들어가기에 가장 적절한 곳은 어디인가?

"그 중 많은 분들께서 만난 지 불과 며칠 만에 저희들의 이름을 아시게 되었습니다."

(A) [1]
(B) [2]
(C) [3]
(D) [4]

정답 (D)

해설 제시된 문장은 앞서 언급된 복수명사를 them으로 가리키면서 그 중 많은 사람들이 며칠 만에 사람들의 이름을 알게 되었다는 의미를 나타낸다. 따라서 the friendly crew와 함께 승무원들을 언급한 문장 뒤에 위치한 [4]에 들어가 그 승무원들이 사람들의 이름을 금방 알게 되었다는 흐름이 되어야 자연스러우므로 (D)가 정답이다.

어휘 get to do ~하게 되다

87-90.

야외 최적화

최근 연구에서는 인류가 우리가 알고 있는 것 이상으로 야외에서 일하고 사는 데 적합하다는 결론을 내렸다. 몇 가지 흥미로운 사실들이 밝혀지고 있다.

우리 모두는 초기의 농부들과 노동자들이 그랬던 것처럼 부족사회 사람들이 대부분 야외에서 살았다는 것을 알고 있다. 88 전기의 출현 전까지, 사람들의 삶은 주로 햇빛과 어둠의 순환에 의해 지배되었고, 아무도 창문에서 멀리 떨어진 곳에서 일하지 않았다. 우리가 위대한 야외로의 연결을 87 유지할 때, 우리는 최선을 다하도록 진화한 것으로 보인다. 최근에 실시된 몇몇 연구들이 이것을 보여준다.

한 연구는 복잡한 도시 거리들이 두뇌에 미치는 영향을 조사했다. 실험 대상자들은 혼잡한 거리를 따라 한시간 동안 걷도록 요구 받았으며, 반면에 다른 사람들은 한시간 동안 큰 공원에서 걷도록 지시 받았다. 그 직후에 그들의 뇌가 측량되었을 때, 공원에서 걸었던 사람들이 불안감을 보이는 뇌의 영역에서 덜 활발하다는 것이 밝혀졌다.

또 다른 연구는 도시 내부의 빈민가 지역에서, 90 몇 그루의 나무만 있어도 그 지역의 폭력 범죄율을 낮출 수 있다는 것을 보여주었다. 특히, 가정 폭력 신고 건수가 감소한다.

우리의 마음과 두뇌가 잘 기능하기 위해서는 우리의 환경에 녹색의 자라나는 것들이 필요한 것처럼 보인다. 89 고용주들과 사업가들은 이것을 기억하는 것이 좋을 것이다.

어휘 optimize ~을 최적화하다 conclude ~의 결론을 내리다 suited 적합한 come to light 밝혀지다 tribal 부족의 advent 출현, 도래 it appears that ~인 것 같다 evolve 진화하다 subject (의학) 실험 대상자, 피실험자 map ~을 측량하다, ~의 지도를 만들다 afterward 그 후에 anxiety 걱정, 불안 inner-city 도시 내부 slum 슬럼, 빈민가 presence 존재 violent 폭력적인 in particular 특히 do well to do ~하는 편이 낫다, ~하는 것이 현명하다

87. 두 번째 문단, 세 번째 줄에 있는 단어 "maintain"과 의미가 가장 가까운 것은 무엇인가?

(A) 수리하다
(B) 유지하다
(C) 믿다
(D) 주장하다

정답 (B)

해설 두 번째 문단에서 인간이 진화한 것은 자연과 가까이 있었기 때문이고, 창문은 주거 환경에서도 자연과 이어져 있음을 알리고 있다. 따라서 '유지하다'라는 의미로 '위대한 야외로의 연결을 유지하다(maintain some link to the great outdoors)'라는 내용을 나타내므로 (B) keep이 정답이다.

88. 전기가 발명되기 전에 시대에 대해 언급된 것은 무엇인가?

(A) 근로자들에게 더 많은 휴식이 주어졌다.
(B) 사람들은 더 빠르게 진화하고 있었다.
(C) 창문들이 더 중요했다.
(D) 근로장소는 덜 편했다.

정답 (C)

해설 두 번째 문단에 전기가 발명되기 전에 아무도 창문에서 멀리 떨어진 곳에서 일을 하지 않았다고(no one worked far from a window) 언급되어 있다. 이는 전기가 없던 시절에 창문을 통해 들어오는 자연광이 있어야만 작업이 가능했다는 뜻이므로 (C)가 정답이다.

어휘 break 휴식 workplace 근로장소, 작업장

89. 이 기사글은 신문의 어떤 섹션에서 발견될 수 있는가?

(A) 조경
(B) 비즈니스
(C) 부동산
(D) 여행

정답 (B)

해설 지문 전반적으로 자연이 인간에게 주는 이점에 대해서 언급하고 있다. 그런데 마지막 문장을 보면 고용주와 사업가들은 이점을 기억하는 게 현명할 것이라고(Employers and business owners would do well to remember this) 언급하고 있다. 따라서 이 글은 근무 환경 개선을 위한 내용이라 볼 수 있고 이는 신문의 비즈니스 부분에 나오므로 (B)가 정답이다.

90. 기사에서 사람들이 나무 주변에 있을 때 일어나는 일은 무엇이라고 암시하는가?

(A) 잠 자는 것이 더 쉽다고 여긴다.
(B) 그들의 뇌 기능이 빨라진다.
(C) 더 고품질 작업물을 생산해낸다.
(D) 덜 폭력적이 된다.

정답 (D)

해설 네 번째 단락에 몇 그루의 나무만 있어도 폭력 범죄율을 낮출 수 있다고(just the presence of a few trees will lower the rates of violent crime) 제시되어 있다. 따라서 (D)가 정답이다.

어휘 function 기능 aggressive 폭력적인

91-95.

8월 17일
호텔 지배인
버던트 호텔, 필딩 드라이브 552번지
인디애나폴리스, IN 46225

관계자께,

제가 지난주에 귀하의 호텔에서 숙박하면서, **92** 8월 11일에 체크인했다가 8월 14일에 체크아웃했습니다. **91** 유감스럽게도, 저는 귀하의 시설에서 제공 받은 드라이 클리닝 서비스에 만족하지 못했습니다. 제가 세탁을 위해 제 비즈니스 정장을 건넸지만, 제 객실로 다시 돌려 받았을 때, 가슴 쪽 주머니에 큰 얼룩이 있다는 사실을 알게 되었습니다. 제가 이 사실을 프런트 데스크 책임자이신 리차드 씨께 언급해 드렸고, **93** 이분께서 세탁 담당 책임자께 이 옷을 다시 세탁하도록 지시하셨습니다. 하지만, 페레즈 씨의 노력은 성공적이지 못했으며, 저는 오후 1시에 있었던 제 비즈니스 회의에 앞서 한 정장 매장을 방문해 새 정장을 구입할 수밖에 없었습니다.

비록 그 상황을 바로잡으려 했던 페레즈 씨의 노력에 감사하기는 하지만, 제 정장에 대한 손상은 제가 결국 새 것을 구입하는 데 300달러를 지불하게 되었다는 사실을 의미했습니다. 오직 제 재킷만 손상되었기 때문에, **95** 이 정장 한 벌 전체에 원래 총 400 달러가 늘었지만, 자켓에 대한 200달러만 보상받기를 요청드립니다.

안녕히 계십시오.

리차드 월러

어휘 unfortunately 유감스럽게도, 안타깝게도 establishment 시설, 기관 hand in ~을 건네다, ~을 내다 stain 얼룩 mention A to B A를 B에게 언급하다 instruct A to do A에게 ~하도록 지시하다 garment 옷, 의류 have no choice but to do ~하는 수밖에 없다 formalwear store 정장 매장 appreciate ~에 대해 감사하다 rectify ~을 바로잡다 end up -ing 결국 ~하게 되다 be compensated 보상받다 cost A B A가 B의 비용을 들이다 in total 총, 전부 합쳐

수신: 리차드 월러 <rwaller@berninc.com>
발신: 사이먼 헨리 <shenley@verdanthotel.com>
날짜: 8월 21일
제목: 정장 보상

월러 씨께,

귀하께서 저희 호텔에서 겪으셨던 최근의 문제와 관련해 사과의 말씀 드립니다. 이는 귀하께 큰 불편함뿐만 아니라 상당한 지출 비용까지 초래했습니다. 비록 귀하께서는 정장 재킷에 대해 200달러의 보상만 **94** 원하시고 계시지만, **95** 손상된 정장 한 벌 전체에 대한 원래의 총 비용을 변상해 드리고자 합니다. 제가 오늘 이따가 수표를 보내 드리겠습니다.

안녕히 계십시오.

사이먼 헨리
지배인, 버던트 호텔

어휘 Please accept my apologies 사과의 말씀 드립니다 regarding ~와 관련해 cause A B A에게 B를 초래하다 inconvenience 불편함 significant 상당한, 많은 expense 지출 (비용), 경비 reimburse A B A에게 B를 변상하다, A에게 B를 환급하다 check n. 수표

91. 편지의 목적은 무엇인가?
(A) 업체를 칭찬하는 것
(B) 문제를 설명하는 것
(C) 예약을 취소하는 것
(D) 가격에 대해 불만을 제기하는 것

정답 (B)

해설 첫 지문 첫 단락에 자신이 숙박했던 호텔에서 제공 받은 드라이 클리닝 서비스에 만족하지 못한 사실을 언급하면서 (Unfortunately, I was not satisfied with the dry cleaning service provided at your establishment) 자신의 옷에 어떤 문제가 있었는지 알리고 있다. 따라서 자신이 겪은 문제를 설명하는 것이 목적임을 알 수 있으므로 (B)가 정답이다.

어휘 praise ~을 칭찬하다 describe ~을 설명하다 cancel ~을 취소하다 reservation 예약

92. 월러 씨는 얼마나 오래 버던트 호텔에 머물렀는가?
(A) 2박 동안
(B) 3박 동안
(C) 4박 동안
(D) 5박 동안

정답 (B)

해설 첫 지문 첫 단락에 8월 11일에 체크인했다가 8월 14일에 체크아웃했다고(checking in on August 11th and checking out on August 14th) 알리고 있는데, 이는 3박을 했다는 뜻이므로 (B)가 정답이다.

93. 페레즈 씨는 누구일 것 같은가?

(A) 의류 매장 책임자
(B) 프런트 데스크 책임자
(C) 호텔 지배인
(D) 세탁 담당 책임자

정답 (D)

해설 첫 지문 첫 단락에 프런트 데스크 책임자가 세탁 담당 책임자에게 옷을 다시 세탁하도록 지시했지만 페레즈 씨의 노력은 성공적이지 못했다는(she instructed the dry cleaner manager to clean the garment again. However, Mr. Perez's efforts were unsuccessful) 말이 쓰여 있다. 따라서 세탁 담당 책임자인 페레즈 씨가 다시 세탁했음에도 문제가 바로잡히지 않았다는 것을 알 수 있으므로 (D)가 정답이다.

94. 이메일에서, 첫 번째 단락, 세 번째 줄의 단어 "seeking"과 의미가 가장 가까운 것은 무엇인가?

(A) 보는
(B) 요청하는
(C) 찾는
(D) 노력하는

정답 (B)

해설 두 번째 지문 해당 문장에서 even though절의 동사 are seeking 앞뒤로 주어 you와 '200달러의 보상'을 뜻하는 명사구 compensation of $200가 각각 위치해 있다. 따라서 상대방인 고객이 그 정도 금액의 보상을 원하고 있다는 의미임을 알 수 있으며, 이는 그러한 보상을 요청하는 것과 같으므로 '요청하다'를 뜻하는 request의 현재분사 (B) requesting이 정답이다.

95. 헨리 씨가 월러 씨에게 얼마나 많은 돈을 보낼 것인가?

(A) 100달러
(B) 200달러
(C) 300달러
(D) 400달러

정답 (D)

해설 두 번째 지문 후반부에 손상된 정장 한 벌 전체에 대한 원래의 총 비용을 변상해 주겠다고(I would like to reimburse you the original total cost of the full suit that was damaged) 알리는 말이 쓰여 있다. 이와 관련해, 첫 지문 마지막 문장에 정장 한 벌 전체가 비용이 400달러였다고(the full suit originally cost me $400 in total) 언급되어 있으므로 (D)가 정답이다.

96-100.

수신: 사이클 트레이더 프로 <inquiries@ctp.com>
발신: 데스 언하트 <desearnhardt@realmail.com>
제목: 구입 가능한 오토바이
날짜: 10월 16일

안녕하세요,

특정 유형의 오토바이를 찾도록 도와 주실 수 있기를 바랍니다. 제가 찾고 있는 것은 클래식 밴가드 오토바이로, 1978년과 1987년 사이에 제조된 것을 선호합니다. [96] 그게 제가 타는 법을 배웠던 오토바이 종류였습니다. [97] 오토바이가 검은색이어야 하고 1,340cc의 엔진 크기를 지니고 있어야 합니다. 에볼 엔진이든 아니면 V 헤드 엔진이든 상관없습니다. 또한, 너무 많은 마일을 주행한 오토바이는 원하지 않습니다. [97] 2만 미만의 주행 거리로 된 것이어야 합니다. 마지막으로, 1만 달러 넘게 소비하고 싶진 않습니다. 답장 받아 볼 수 있기를 기대하고 있겠습니다. 미리 감사의 말씀 드립니다!

데스 언하트

어휘 available 구입 가능한, 이용 가능한 specific 특정한, 구체적인 search for ~을 찾다, ~을 검색하다 preferably 선호하여 manufacture ~을 제조하다 cycle 오토바이 whether A or B A이든 아니면 B이든 (상관없이) mileage 주행 거리 reply 답장, 대답 in advance 미리, 사전에

사이클 트레이더 프로
아넛 스트리트 5167번지, 러틀랜드, VT 05701
전화 번호: 555-8276

저희 사이클 트레이더 프로에 찾아 오셔서 아주 다양한 오토바이를 한 번 살펴 보시기 바랍니다! 예를 들어, 저희는 현재 구입 가능한 이 네 가지 놀라운 밴가드 오토바이를 보유하고 있습니다!

	제조 연도	엔진 크기	엔진 유형	대략적인 주행 거리	본체 색상	가격
밴가드 로드 킹	1986	1,340	V-헤드	26,400	블랙	$9,200
[97] 밴가드 일렉트라	1983	[97] 1,340	에볼	[97] 14,100	[97] 블랙	$9,400
밴가드 하드 그립	1981	1,340	에볼	9,700	실버	$8,200
[99] 밴가드 바이슨	[99] 1979	1,200	V-헤드	13,200	블랙	$7,100

어휘 take a look at ~을 한 번 보다 one's wide selection of 아주 다양한 currently 현재 available for purchase 구입 가능한

수신: 데스 언하트 <desearnhardt@realmail.com>
발신: 레이첼 맥도웰 <rachelmcd@ctp.com>
제목: **회신:** 구입 가능한 오토바이
날짜: 10월 17일

언하트 씨께,

저희 차고에 현재 오직 네 대의 밴가드 모델이 있는 것 같습니다. 사실, 저희가 최근에 이 네 대의 특정 오토바이를 기재한 전단을 인쇄해 **98** 배부했습니다. 하지만, **99** 이 전단에 기재된 가장 오래된 모델이 최근 판매되었고, 1986년 모델은 몇 가지 사소한 수리를 필요로 합니다.

저희 차고에 찾아 오셔서 이 오토바이들을 시운전해 보셔도 좋습니다. 그리고 마음에 드시는 것을 찾으시면, 즉시 가져가실 수 있습니다! 저희가 모든 주요 신용카드를 받고 있기는 하지만, **100** 현금을 사용해 전액 지불하시는 경우, 기재된 가격에서 기꺼이 100달러를 깎아 드릴 것입니다. 저희가 현재 현금 자동 입출금기 또는 온라인을 이용한 은행 계좌 이체는 받지 않습니다.

안녕히 계십시오.

레이첼 맥도웰
사이클 트레이더 프로

어휘 **I'm afraid** (부정적인 일에 대해) ~인 것 같습니다, 유감이지만 ~입니다 **lot** 차고, 주차장 **in fact** 사실, 실제로 **circulate** ~을 배부하다 **flyer** 전단 **particular** 특정한 **require** ~을 필요로 하다 **minor** 사소한 **take A for a test ride** A를 시운전하다 **take A away** A를 가져가다 **immediately** 즉시 **accept** ~을 받아들이다, ~을 수락하다 **in full** 전액, 전부 **knock A off B** B에서 A만큼 깎아주다 **bank transfer** 은행 계좌 이체

96. 언하트 씨와 관련해 유추할 수 있는 것은 무엇인가?
(A) 사이클 트레이더 프로의 영업 지점에서 멀리 떨어진 곳에 산다.
(B) 사이클 트레이더 프로에 여러 번 이메일을 보냈다.
(C) 자신이 익숙한 모델을 찾고 있다.
(D) 자신의 오토바이에 생긴 기술적 결함을 경험했다.

정답 (C)

해설 첫 지문 초반부에 자신이 원하는 오토바이를 설명하면서 자신이 타는 법을 배운 오토바이였다고(That was the kind of motorcycle I learned to ride on) 언급하는 부분이 있다. 이는 타 본 적이 있어서 익숙한 오토바이를 찾는다는 말과 같으므로 (C)가 정답이다.

어휘 **far from** ~에서 멀리 떨어져 **location** 지점, 위치 **look for** ~을 찾다 **be used to do** ~에 익숙하다 **fault** 결함, 흠

97. 전단에 기재된 모델들 중 어느 것에 대해 언하트 씨가 관심이 있을 것 같은가?
(A) 로드 킹

(B) 일렉트라
(C) 하드 그립
(D) 바이슨

정답 (B)

해설 첫 지문에서 언하트 씨가 언급하는 조건은 검은색에 1,340cc의 엔진, 그리고 2만 미만의 주행 거리이다(The cycle should be black and have an engine size of 1,340cc. ~ It should have a mileage of less than 20,000). 이와 관련해, 두 번째 지문의 도표에서 이 조건에 해당되는 오토바이가 두 번째 줄에 1,340/14,100/Black의 순서로 엔진 크기와 주행 거리, 그리고 색상이 기재된 Vanguard Elektra이므로 (B)가 정답이다.

98. 두 번째 이메일에서, 첫 번째 단락, 두 번째 줄의 단어 "circulated"와 의미가 가장 가까운 것은 무엇인가?
(A) 감쌌다
(B) 둘러쌌다
(C) 출판했다
(D) 배부했다

정답 (D)

해설 해당 문장에서 동사 circulated는 바로 앞에 and로 연결된 또 다른 동사 printed와 함께 홍보용 전단(flyer)과 관련해 할 수 있는 일을 나타낸다. 전단을 인쇄한 후에는 사람들이 볼 수 있도록 배부해야 하므로 '배부했다'를 뜻하는 (D) distributed가 정답이다.

99. 밴가드 바이슨과 관련해 언급된 것은 무엇인가?
(A) 최근에 개조되었다.
(B) 가격이 할인되었다.
(C) 수리를 필요로 한다.
(D) 더 이상 구매할 수 없다.

정답 (D)

해설 두 번째 지문 도표에서 맨 아래에 기재된 밴가드 바이슨은 제조 연노가 1979년으로 표기되어 있어 나머지 세 개의 모델보다 더 오래되었다는 점을 알 수 있다. 이와 관련해, 세 번째 지문 첫 단락에 전단에 기재된 가장 오래된 모델이 최근 판매되었다는 말이 쓰여 있어(the oldest model listed on the flyer has recently been sold) 더 이상 구매할 수 없다는 사실을 알 수 있으므로 (D)가 정답이다.

어휘 **modify** ~을 개조하다, ~을 수정하다 **in need of** ~을 필요로 하는 **no longer** 더 이상 ~ 않다

100. 언하트 씨는 어떻게 오토바이에 대해 할인 받을 수 있는가?
(A) 특정 신용카드를 이용함으로써
(B) 은행 계좌 이체를 통해 지불함으로써
(C) 온라인으로 구입함으로써
(D) 전액 현금으로 지불함으로써

정답 (D)

해설 세 번째 지문 두 번째 단락에 전액 현금으로 지불하면 100달

러를 깎아 주겠다고(if you use cash to pay in full, we would be happy to knock a hundred dollars off the listed price) 언급하고 있으므로 (D)가 정답이다.

어휘   **specific** 특정한, 구체적인 **via** ~을 통해

LC+RC Half Test

<table>
<tr><td colspan="5">LC</td></tr>
<tr><td>1. (D)</td><td>2. (C)</td><td>3. (A)</td><td>4. (C)</td><td>5. (C)</td></tr>
<tr><td>6. (B)</td><td>7. (B)</td><td>8. (B)</td><td>9. (C)</td><td>10. (A)</td></tr>
<tr><td>11. (B)</td><td>12. (C)</td><td>13. (C)</td><td>14. (A)</td><td>15. (A)</td></tr>
<tr><td>16. (A)</td><td>17. (A)</td><td>18. (B)</td><td>19. (A)</td><td>20. (C)</td></tr>
<tr><td>21. (B)</td><td>22. (C)</td><td>23. (A)</td><td>24. (D)</td><td>25. (A)</td></tr>
<tr><td>26. (A)</td><td>27. (A)</td><td>28. (C)</td><td>29. (B)</td><td>30. (C)</td></tr>
<tr><td>31. (A)</td><td>32. (D)</td><td>33. (B)</td><td>34. (C)</td><td>35. (B)</td></tr>
<tr><td>36. (A)</td><td>37. (D)</td><td>38. (B)</td><td>39. (B)</td><td>40. (D)</td></tr>
<tr><td>41. (B)</td><td>42. (D)</td><td>43. (D)</td><td>44. (C)</td><td>45. (B)</td></tr>
<tr><td>46. (C)</td><td>47. (D)</td><td>48. (C)</td><td>49. (C)</td><td>50. (D)</td></tr>
<tr><td colspan="5">RC</td></tr>
<tr><td>51. (A)</td><td>52. (C)</td><td>53. (C)</td><td>54. (A)</td><td>55. (C)</td></tr>
<tr><td>56. (D)</td><td>57. (B)</td><td>58. (A)</td><td>59. (C)</td><td>60. (A)</td></tr>
<tr><td>61. (B)</td><td>62. (A)</td><td>63. (A)</td><td>64. (D)</td><td>65. (B)</td></tr>
<tr><td>66. (D)</td><td>67. (B)</td><td>68. (D)</td><td>69. (A)</td><td>70. (A)</td></tr>
<tr><td>71. (D)</td><td>72. (C)</td><td>73. (A)</td><td>74. (B)</td><td>75. (C)</td></tr>
<tr><td>76. (D)</td><td>77. (C)</td><td>78. (A)</td><td>79. (D)</td><td>80. (B)</td></tr>
<tr><td>81. (D)</td><td>82. (C)</td><td>83. (D)</td><td>84. (C)</td><td>85. (D)</td></tr>
<tr><td>86. (B)</td><td>87. (C)</td><td>88. (B)</td><td>89. (B)</td><td>90. (B)</td></tr>
<tr><td>91. (D)</td><td>92. (B)</td><td>93. (C)</td><td>94. (D)</td><td>95. (C)</td></tr>
<tr><td>96. (B)</td><td>97. (D)</td><td>98. (B)</td><td>99. (D)</td><td>100. (C)</td></tr>
</table>

Part 1

1. (A) She's tying her apron.
(B) She's stirring a pot.
(C) She's wiping a counter.
(D) She's pouring liquid into a mug.

(A) 여자가 앞치마를 매고 있다.
(B) 여자가 냄비를 젓고 있다.
(C) 여자가 조리대를 닦아내고 있다.
(D) 여자가 액체를 머그잔에 붓고 있는 중이다.

해설 (A) 앞치마를 매는(tying) 모습이 아니므로 오답.
(B) 냄비(pot)는 보이지 않으므로 오답.
(C) 조리대를 닦는 동작이 아니므로 오답.
(D) 머그잔에 액체를 붓고 있는 동작을 묘사한 정답.

어휘 tie ~을 묶다, 매다 apron 앞치마 counter 조리대 pour A into B A를 B에 붓다, 따르다 liquid 액체 mug 머그잔

2. (A) All of the chairs are occupied.
(B) Some papers are being distributed.
(C) They have gathered for a meeting.
(D) They are adjusting electrical equipment.

(A) 모든 좌석이 다 찼다.
(B) 종이가 배부되고 있다.
(C) 사람들이 회의로 모여 있다.
(D) 사람들이 전기 기구를 조정하고 있다.

해설 (A) 의자 하나에는 사람이 앉아 있지 않으므로 오답.
(B) 종이를 배부하는 사람은 보이지 않으므로 오답.
(C) 사람들이 테이블에 모여 이야기를 나누는 모습이므로 정답.
(D) electrical equipment (전기 기구)는 보이지 않으므로 오답.

어휘 occupied 사용 중인, 점유된 distribute ~을 분배하다, 나눠주다 gather (사람들이) 모이다 adjust ~을 조정[조절]하다 electrical equipment 전기 기구 cf. electrical 전기의 equipment 장비, 기기

Part 2

3. When is Mr. Boone's new movie supposed to come out?
(A) It won't be released until the summer.
(B) No, I've never seen that film.
(C) He prefers to work from home.

분 씨의 새 영화는 언제 나올 예정인가요?
(A) 여름에나 개봉될 겁니다.
(B) 아뇨, 전 그 영화를 본 적이 없어요.
(C) 그는 자택에서 근무하는 걸 선호해요.

해설 영화가 나오는 시점을 묻는 질문이므로, '~나 되어야 한다'라는 의미로 쓰이는 not ~ until 구문과 함께 summer라는 특정 시점을 언급하는 (A)가 정답이다. not ~ until 구문을 알고 있어야 질문과 알맞은 의미 관계가 형성되는 답변이라는 것을 알 수 있다. 의문사 의문문은 (B)처럼 Yes/No로 답할 수 없다.

어휘 not A until B B가 되어서야 A하다 release ~을 개봉하다, 출시하다 prefer to do ~하는 것을 선호하다 work from home 재택 근무하다

4. Where can I get a copy of the survey results?
(A) Many of our customers participated.
(B) Try the coffee shop on the first floor.
(C) I'll e-mail you one immediately.

설문조사 결과 사본 한 부를 어디에서 얻을 수 있을까요?
(A) 우리 고객들이 많이 참여했어요.
(B) 1층에 있는 커피점에 가보세요.
(C) 제가 이메일로 한 부 바로 보내드리겠습니다.

해설 특정 서류를 어디에서 얻을 수 있는지 묻는 질문이다. 문서를 받을 수 있는 장소나 사람을 알려주는 대답이 일반적이지만, 자신이 한 부 보내주겠다고 말하는 (C)가 정답이다. 이와 같이 의문사에 어울리는 직접적인 대답 대신 상황에 어울리는 의외의 대답이 정답이 되는 경우가 종종 나오므로 이러한 반응에도 대비해야 한다. (A)는 survey에서 연상할 수 있는 동사 participate(참여하다)를 활용한 혼동 보기이다. (B)는 copy-coffee의 발음 혼동을 노린 오답이다.

어휘 **copy** 사본 **survey** 설문조사 **result** 결과 **participate** 참여하다, 참가하다 **immediately** 즉시

5. How would you feel about switching seats today?
(A) Today is not a good day for organizing meetings.
(B) It's being repaired as we speak.
(C) I don't really care where I sit.

오늘은 서로 자리를 바꾸는 게 어때요?
(A) 오늘은 회의를 준비하기 좋은 날이 아니에요.
(B) 우리가 얘기하는 동안 수리되고 있어요.
(C) 전 어디에 앉든지 별로 신경 안 써요.

해설 How would you feel about ~?이 무엇을 제안하는 표현이라는 것을 알아차려야 정답을 고를 수 있다. 자리를 바꾸는 것에 대해 어떻게 생각하는지 정중히 묻는 질문으로, 이는 한 마디로 말해 자리를 바꾸자는 뜻이다. 따라서 이에 대해 수락이나 거절의 응답이 오는 것이 자연스러운데, '어디 앉든지 상관없다'라고 말하는 (C)는 제안을 수락하는 의미이므로 질문에 적절한 응답이 된다.

어휘 **switch seats** 자리를 바꾸다 **organize** ~을 조직하다, 준비하다

6. Should we all have to work this weekend?
(A) You all have different strengths.
(B) If we want to meet the deadline, yes.
(C) I forgot to schedule it.

우리 모두 이번 주말에 일해야 하는 건가요?
(A) 여러분은 모두 각기 다른 장점을 갖고 있어요.
(B) 마감 기한을 맞추려면, 그래요.
(C) 일정을 잡는 걸 깜빡했어요.

해설 모두가 주말에 일해야 하는 게 맞는지 확인하고자 하는 조동사 의문문이므로, 이에 대해 마감 기한을 맞추려면 그렇게 해야 한다고 말하는 (B)가 가장 자연스러운 응답이다. (A)는 질문의 요지와 거리가 먼 응답이고 (C)는 질문의 weekend에서 연상할 수 있는 schedule(일정)을 이용한 함정이다.

어휘 **strength** 강점, 장점 **meet the deadline** 마감기한을 맞

추다 **forget to do** ~할 것을 잊다 **schedule** ~의 일정을 잡다

7. Do you have the architect's business card?
(A) Several company cars.
(B) Check my top drawer.
(C) He is working on the blueprints.

그 건축가가 준 명함을 갖고 계세요?
(A) 몇몇 회사 차량이요.
(B) 제 책상 맨 위 서랍을 확인해 보세요.
(C) 그가 지금 도면 작업을 하고 있어요.

해설 특정한 사람이 준 명함을 갖고 있는지를 묻는 질문이므로 해당 명함을 찾을 수 있는 곳을 알려주는 (B)가 적절한 응답이다. 이와 같이 '~에게 물어봐라', '~를 확인해봐라'와 같은 의미를 나타내는 유형의 대답은 어떤 질문에도 답이 될 가능성이 높으므로 반드시 미리 알아두어야 한다. (A)는 질문의 card와 발음이 유사한 cars를 이용한 소리 오답이다. (B)는 architect에서 연상할 수 있는 blueprint를 이용한 오답이다.

어휘 **architect** 건축가 **business card** 명함 **several** 몇몇의, 여럿의 **drawer** 서랍 **blueprint** 도면, 청사진

8. Why isn't there an information booth in this train station?
(A) It comes with very detailed instructions.
(B) I think there is one on the second floor.
(C) You can buy train tickets in advance.

이 역에는 왜 안내 부스가 없는 거죠?
(A) 매우 상세한 안내가 딸려 있어요.
(B) 2층에 하나 있는 것 같은데요.
(C) 기차표를 미리 구매하실 수 있어요.

해설 역내에 안내 부스가 없는 이유를 묻고 있다. 이에 대해 2층에 하나 있는 것 같다며 그 위치를 직접 말해주는 (B)가 어울리는 응답이다. (A)는 information과 관련성 있어 보이는 내용을 말하는 오답으로 안내 부스 존재 여부와 관련이 없는 내용이다. (C)는 train station에서 연상 가능한 train tickets를 이용한 오답이다.

어휘 **booth** 부스, 칸막이 공간 **come with** ~가 딸려 있다, ~가 함께 나온다 **detailed** 상세한 **instructions** 안내, 지시사항 **in advance** 미리

9. This cell phone comes with a free mini portable speaker, doesn't it?
(A) Yes, it plays video files.
(B) I'll check the microphone.
(C) No, this model doesn't.

이 휴대전화기는 무료 미니 휴대용 스피커가 함께 딸려 나오지 않나요?
(A) 네, 동영상 파일을 재생할 수 있어요.

(B) 제가 마이크를 확인할게요.
(C) 아뇨, 이 모델은 그렇지 않습니다.

해설 휴대전화기와 함께 딸려 나오는 제품에 대해 묻는 부가 의문문으로 This cell phone을 this model로, comes를 대신하는 does를 사용해 부정하는 내용을 말하는 (C)가 정답이다. 동영상 재생 여부를 묻는 것이 아니므로 질문의 핵심에서 벗어난 (A)는 오답이다. (B)는 질문의 speaker(스피커)와 의미상 연관 지을 수 있는 microphone(마이크)를 이용한 함정이다.

어휘 **come with** ~이 딸려 나오다 **portable** 휴대용의

10. Doesn't this hotel have any movie channels?
(A) It does, but you have to pay extra.
(B) The game is on channel six.
(C) I think it's within walking distance.

이 호텔에 영화 채널이 있지 않나요?
(A) 있어요, 하지만 추가 비용을 내야 합니다.
(B) 그 경기는 6번 채널에서 볼 수 있어요.
(C) 제 생각에 걸어서 갈 수 있는 거리에 있어요.

해설 호텔에서 영화 채널을 제공하는지를 묻는 부정 의문문으로 조동사 does를 이용해 긍정한 후 해당 채널을 이용할 수 있는 조건을 언급하는 (A)가 정답이다. (B)는 영화 채널 시청 가능성을 묻는 질문인데 game을 볼 수 있는 채널을 말하고 있어 의미 연결이 되지 않는 대답이다. (C)는 How far ~? 의문문에 어울리는 응답이다.

어휘 **pay extra** 추가 비용을 내다 **within walking distance** 걸어서 갈 수 있는 거리에 있는

11. Would you still like me to try to fix your watch?
(A) Let's watch it together sometime.
(B) Oh, I've already thrown it out.
(C) Maybe you should get a new one.

당신의 시계를 여전히 제가 수리해 드리길 원하세요?
(A) 언제 같이 봐요.
(B) 아, 그 시계는 이미 버렸어요.
(C) 아마 새로 하나 사야 할 거예요.

해설 Would you like me to ~?의 형태로 질문자가 상대방을 위해 뭔가를 해줄지를 묻는 제안/요청 의문문이다. 질문에서 시계를 고치는 일을 해주는 것에 대해 묻고 있으므로 이에 대해 이미 버렸다는 말로 그럴 필요가 없음을 나타내는 (B)가 정답이다. (A)는 watch를 반복한 소리 오답으로 질문에 제시된 것과 달리 동사로 쓰였다. (C)는 화자 자신의 시계에 대한 내용이 아니라 오히려 상대방이 쓸 시계에 대해 말하고 있어 어울리지 않는 반응이다.

어휘 **Would you like me to do?** 제가 ~해드릴까요? **fix** ~을 수리하다 **sometime** 언젠가 **throw out** ~을 버리다

12. Should I take these packages to the mailroom?
(A) No, this is the cafeteria.

(B) I really hope it gets here on time.
(C) Yes, that would be very helpful.

이 소포들을 우편물실로 가져갈까요?
(A) 아뇨, 여기는 구내식당이에요.
(B) 그게 여기로 정말 제때 왔으면 해요.
(C) 네, 그래 주시면 정말 도움이 될 거예요.

해설 소포를 옮기는 것에 대한 상대방의 의견을 묻는 질문이므로 Yes와 함께 감사의 뜻을 나타내는 (C)가 적절한 반응이다. (A)는 화자가 있는 특정 장소를 말하는 내용이므로 질문의 의도에 어울리지 않는 대답이다. (B)에서는 질문의 핵심인 these packages를 가리키는 대명사가 it으로 잘못 제시되었을 뿐만 아니라 질문자가 소포를 옮기는 것에 대한 의견이 제시되어 있지 않다.

어휘 **take A to B** A를 B로 가져가다, 옮기다 **mailroom** 우편물실 **cafeteria** 구내식당 **get here** 여기로 오다, 도착하다 **on time** 제때, 제 시간에 **helpful** 도움이 되는

13. Would you rather choose your own hotel or should I make the arrangements?
(A) A hotel would suit me fine.
(B) I was happy with the amenities.
(C) I'd appreciate it if you could help.

머무를 호텔을 직접 고르시겠어요, 아니면 제가 예약을 해 드릴까요?
(A) 저는 호텔이 잘 맞을 것 같아요.
(B) 그곳의 편의시설 때문에 즐거웠어요.
(C) 도와주실 수 있다면 감사하겠습니다.

해설 호텔을 직접 예약할 것인지 아니면 질문자가 대신 해도 되는지를 묻는데, 이 중에서 도와주면(예약해주면) 고맙겠다는 말로 두 번째 선택사항에 대해 답하는 (C)가 정답이다. '문장 or 문장' 선택 의문문으로 나올 것에 대비해 끝까지 질문에 집중해야 하며, 두 문장 중 하나라도 들었다면 or not을 붙인 의미로 이해하고 풀 수 있는 문제이다. (A)는 hotel이 반복된 보기로 예약을 하는 주체와 전혀 관련이 없는 내용이다. (B)는 hotel에서 연상 가능한 amenities를 이용한 오답이다.

어휘 **choose** ~을 고르다 **make an arrangement** 예약하다 **be happy with** ~때문에 즐겁다 **amenities** 편의시설 **appreciate** ~에 대해 감사하다

14. Do you have a user's manual, or should I ask a technician to help?
(A) I've operated this device before.
(B) It hasn't been used much.
(C) It was lucky that you did.

사용자 설명서를 가지고 계신가요, 아니면 제가 기술자에게 도와달라고 부탁할까요?
(A) 전에 이 기기를 다뤄본 적 있어요.
(B) 그건 많이 사용되지 않았어요.

(C) 해내셨다니 다행이었네요.

해설 질문 유형은 어느 정도 암기를 통해 해결할 수도 있지만, 답변 유형은 다양하게 제시되기 때문에 모든 가능성을 열어 두고 적절한 답변으로 가능한 모든 상황을 생각해 보는 연습을 해야 한다. 이 질문의 선택사항인 '사용자 설명서를 갖고 있는 것'과 '기술자를 부르는 것' 중의 하나가 아닌 다른 내용, 즉 '이미 사용해 본 적이 있다'는 말로 두 가지 선택사항 중 하나가 아닌 제 3의 의견을 제시한 (A)가 정답이다. (B)는 user와 비슷한 used를 이용한 소리 오답이다. (C)는 질문 내용과 어울리지 않게 과거 시점의 일을 언급하고 있으므로 오답이다.

어휘 **user's manual** 사용자 설명서 **technician** 기술자 **operate** ~을 조작하다, 다루다 **device** 기기, 장치

15. I thought you were taking this Friday off.

   (A) I wanted to, but we have a deadline to meet.
   (B) I usually save the beach for the weekends.
   (C) It's Friday the 17th of March to be exact.

이번 금요일에 쉬시는 줄 알았는데요.
   (A) 그러고 싶었지만 마감이 걸려 있어서요.
   (B) 저는 보통 기다렸다가 주말에 해변에 가요.
   (C) 정확히 3월 17일, 금요일이에요.

해설 상대방이 금요일에 쉬는 것으로 알았다는 사실을 말하는 평서문으로, 이에 대해 마감 때문이라는 말로 쉬지 않는 이유를 언급한 (A)가 적절한 대답이다. (B)에는 take Friday off에서 연상 가능한 beach가 제시되었는데 해변에 가는 시점을 말하는 내용이어서 어울리지 않는 대답이다. (C)는 질문의 Friday를 반복하여 혼동을 주는 동일어휘 반복 오답이다.

어휘 **take a day off** 하루 쉬다 **deadline** 마감시한 **meet** ~을 충족시키다 **save A for B** B를 위해 A를 아끼다, 남겨 두다 **to be exact** 정확히 말해, 엄밀히 말하면

16. This new photocopier does not work the way it is supposed to.

   (A) The previous model was more reliable.
   (B) He's supposed to make extra copies.
   (C) It's a photo from the staff outing.

이 새 복사기가 원래 방식대로 작동하지 않아요.
   (A) 이전 모델이 더 믿을 만했어요.
   (B) 그가 추가 사본을 만들기로 되어 있었어요.
   (C) 그건 직원 야유회에서 찍은 사진이에요.

해설 new photocopier와 not work가 핵심어이다. 새 복사기가 지닌 문제점에 대해 말하는 내용이므로 이에 동의하는 의미로 이전 모델이 더 좋았다는 의견을 말하는 (A)가 적절한 반응이다. 여기서는 복사기와 관련된 본인의 의견을 제시하는 내용이 정답이지만, We should talk to the manager와 같이 해결을 위한 방법을 제안하는 식의 답변도 정답으로 자주 출제된다.

어휘 **photocopier** 복사기 **work** (기계 등이) 작동하다 **be supposed to do** ~하기로 되어 있다 **reliable** 믿을 만한 **make a copy** ~을 복사하다 **extra** 추가의, 별도의

outing 야유회

17. Has Ms. Lopez left for the business trip?

   (A) Yes, but she will be back tomorrow.
   (B) There are leftovers in the kitchen.
   (C) A conference in Germany.

로페즈 씨가 출장을 떠났나요?
   (A) 네, 하지만 내일 돌아올 겁니다.
   (B) 부엌에 남은 음식이 있어요.
   (C) 독일에서 열리는 컨퍼런스입니다.

해설 Ms. Lopez라는 제 3의 인물이 출장을 떠났는지 묻는 조동사 의문문이므로 Yes라고 긍정한 뒤 내일 돌아올 것이라고 부가 정보를 주는 (A)가 정답이다. leave for the business trip, be out of town 등과 함께 출장 여부를 묻는 질문의 경우, be back이나 return 등의 표현을 통해 돌아오는 정보를 알려주는 답변이 정답으로 흔히 제시된다.

어휘 **leave** 떠나다 **business trip** 출장 **leftover** (음식 등) 남은 것

18. The theater seems rather empty, doesn't it?

   (A) It does look like we should refill it.
   (B) Yes, we can easily find a good seat.
   (C) Just the standard ticket price.

극장이 좀 빈 것 같아 보여요, 안 그런가요?
   (A) 확실히 그걸 다시 채워야 할 것 같아 보이네요.
   (B) 네, 좋은 자리를 쉽게 찾을 수 있겠네요.
   (C) 일반 티켓 가격이면 됩니다.

해설 극장에 사람이 없어 보이지 않느냐는 내용의 질문이므로 긍정을 나타내는 Yes와 함께 앉을 자리와 관련된 예측을 추가로 언급하는 (B)가 적절한 반응이다. (A)는 empty에서 연상 가능한 refill을, (C)는 theater에서 연상 가능한 ticket price를 이용한 오답이다.

어휘 **seem** ~인 것 같이 보이다 **rather** 다소, 약간 **empty** 비어 있는, 없는 **look like** ~인 것 같다 **refill** ~을 보충하다, 다시 채우다 **standard** 보통의, 표준의

19. Why don't you come to the gym with us this evening?

   (A) I already made plans.
   (B) It's free for members.
   (C) It was open this morning.

오늘 저녁에 저희랑 체육관에 가는 게 어때요?
   (A) 저는 이미 계획이 있어요.
   (B) 회원들에게는 무료입니다.
   (C) 거긴 오늘 아침에 열려 있었어요.

해설 Why don't you ~? (~하는 게 어때?)라고 제안을 하는 질문이므로, 그 제안에 대한 수락 여부를 말하는 내용의 대답을 골라

야 한다. 따라서 체육관에 같이 가자는 제안에 대해 계획이 있다며 간접적으로 거절하는 (A)가 정답이다.

어휘 gym 체육관 make a plan 계획을 세우다, 짜다

20. I'll print out an up-to-date schedule of our art classes for you.

(A) Yes, I'll pay for an upgrade.
(B) Whichever day is most suitable.
(C) Thanks. I'd appreciate it.

저희 미술 강좌 최신 일정을 한 부 출력해 드리겠습니다.
(A) 네, 업그레이드 비용을 지불하겠습니다.
(B) 가장 적합한 날이면 언제든지요.
(C) 고맙습니다. 그렇게 해주시면 감사하겠습니다.

해설 일정표를 출력해 주겠다는 말에 감사의 뜻을 나타내는 말로 응답한 (C)가 정답이다. 평서문 문제에서는 유사 발음 함정을 잘 확인해 소거하는 것만으로도 정답을 쉽게 찾을 수 있다. (A)에서는 up-to-date와 유사한 upgrade가, (B)에서도 up-to-date의 일부가 date가 유사 발음 함정으로 사용되었다.

어휘 print out ~을 출력하다, 인쇄하다 up-to-date 최신의 pay for ~에 대한 비용을 지불하다 whichever ~하는 어느 것이든 suitable 적합한 appreciate ~에 대해 감사하다

Part 3

Questions 21-23 refer to the following conversation.

W: Hi, Jacob. I think **21** I might have found a company that can deliver some affordable fitness club equipment. I've only seen the equipment on the company's Web site, so **21** I'll need to meet with the supplier today to check the merchandise in person.

M: Great! All the other equipment suppliers we have tried have been too expensive. **22** I think we are allready for the weight lifting competition tomorrow, so just take today off for the meeting, and give me a call afterwards.

W: Oh, I didn't know we were all prepared. I'll give you a call when I finish the meeting then. By the way, do you need me to bring anything with me tomorrow?

M: No, **23** just do me a favor and check that our advertisement is up and running on our Web site. It's the only way we are publicizing the event, so I need to make sure people can see it.

여: 안녕하세요, 제이콥 씨. 제가 저렴한 가격의 피트니스 클럽용 장비를 배송해 줄 수 있는 회사를 찾아냈을지도 모르겠네요. 이 회사의 웹 사이트에서만 장비를 봤기 때문에, 오늘 공급업자를 직접 만나서 물품을 확인해 봐야겠어요.

남: 좋아요! 우리가 그동안 알아본 다른 모든 장비 공급업체들은 너무 비쌌어요. 제 생각에 내일 있을 역도 경기대회 준비가 다 된 것 같으니 오늘은 그 회의를 위해 쉬고 이따가 제게 전화 한 통 해주세요.

여: 아, 저는 우리가 준비가 다 된 줄 몰랐어요. 그럼 회의를 마칠 때 전화 드릴게요. 그런데, 내일 제가 챙겨 와야 하는 게 있나요?

남: 아뇨, 우리 웹 사이트에 광고가 잘 올라가 있는지 확인하는 것만 부탁 좀 드릴게요. 이 광고가 행사를 홍보하는 유일한 방법이라서 사람들이 잘 볼 수 있는지 확실히 해 두어야 해서요.

어휘 might have p.p. ~했을지도 모르다 affordable (가격이) 알맞은, 저렴한 equipment 장비 supplier 공급업체[업자] merchandise 상품 in person 직접 weight lifting 역도 competition 경기대회 take A off A만큼 쉬다 give A a call A에게 전화하다 afterwards 나중에 prepared 준비된 by the way (화제를 바꿀 때) 그런데, 그건 그렇고 do A a favor A의 부탁을 들어 주다 up and running 운영 중인, 가동 중인 way 방법 publicize ~을 알리다, 홍보하다 make sure (that) 반드시 ~하도록 하다

21. 여자는 누구를 만나야 한다고 말하는가?
(A) 웹 사이트 디자이너
(B) 체육관 장비 공급업자
(C) 마케팅 이사
(D) 헬스 클럽 소유주

해설 문제를 통해 여자의 말에서 누군가를 만나는 일이 언급되는 부분이 있다는 것을 알 수 있다. 여자는 적절한 가격에 피트니스 클럽 장비를 구입할 수 있는 회사(a company that can deliver some affordable fitness club equipment)를 찾았다는 말과 함께 오늘 그 공급업자를 직접 만나 장비를 확인해 봐야겠다고(I'll need to meet with the owner today to check the merchandise in person) 알리고 있다. 이를 종합해 보면 여자가 만날 사람으로 (B)가 정답이다.

어휘 gym 체육관 owner 소유주, 주인

22. 화자들은 어떤 행사를 준비하고 있는가?
(A) 제품 시연회
(B) 연말 기념 행사
(C) 스포츠 경기대회
(D) 월간 세일 행사

해설 event와 preparing for가 핵심이므로 대화 속에서 화자들이 언급하는 특정 행사를 찾아내야 한다. 화자들은 피트니스 장비에 대한 이야기를 하면서 대화 중간에 I think we are all ready for the weight lifting competition tomorrow라는 말로 역도 경기대회 준비 상황에 대해 말하고 있으므로 이 대회를 A sports competition이라고 바꿔 표현한 (C)가 정

답이다.

어휘 demonstration 시연(회) end-of-year 연말의
celebration 기념 행사, 축하 행사 monthly 월간의, 달마
다의

Paraphrase weight lifting competition
→ sports competition

23. 행사는 어디에서 홍보되고 있는가?
(A) 인터넷에서
(B) 라디오 방송에서
(C) 옥외 광고판에서
(D) 텔레비전에서

해설 행사 홍보 방법을 묻는 문제이므로 선택지를 먼저 확인한 뒤에
대화에 언급되는 방식과 같은 것을 골라야 한다. 대화 후반부에
남자가 여자에게 just do me a favor and check that our
advertisement is up and running on our Web site와
같이 부탁하는 부분에서 웹 사이트를 통해 행사 홍보가 이루어
지고 있음을 알 수 있으므로 (A)가 정답이다.

어휘 billboard (옥외의) 광고판

Paraphrase on our Web site
→ On the Internet

Questions 24-26 refer to the following conversation.

M: Hello. I just saw the advertisement you have on
Bargains.com. **24** I was wondering if you've
sold your car yet. I love Makda convertibles,
and yours looks like it's in good condition.

W: Yes. It's definitely still on the market. And you're
right; it's in great condition. **25** But what's really
special about it is that there were only ten
of them made in 1999. It's a collector's item.
Would you like to take it for a drive?

M: I sure would. **26** Can I come and take it for a
drive sometime tomorrow?

W: **26** No problem. Come to my apartment at 3
o'clock and we'll go for a drive together.

- -

남: 여보세요. Bargains.com에 올리신 광고를 제가 방금 확인했
는데요. 혹시 광고하신 차량이 벌써 팔렸는지 궁금합니다. 제
가 매크다 컨버터블을 아주 좋아하는데, 광고하신 차량이 상태
가 좋아 보여서요.

여: 네. 아직 확실히 그대로 있습니다. 그리고 상태가 좋다는 말씀
이 맞습니다. 하지만 이 차량이 정말 특별한 이유는 1999년에
10대 밖에 만들어지지 않았다는 것이죠. 수집가들의 흥미를
끄는 제품입니다. 운전을 한 번 해 보시겠습니까?

남: 물론 그럴 겁니다. 내일 중으로 가서 운전해 볼 수 있을까요?

여: 좋습니다. 3시에 제 아파트로 오셔서 같이 시운전하러 가시죠.

어휘 advertisement 광고 wonder if ~인지 궁금하다
convertible n. 컨버터블(지붕을 접었다 폈다 할 수 있는 승
용차) look like ~인 것 같다 be in good condition
상태가 좋다 definitely 확실히, 분명히 on the market
시장에 나온, 팔려고 내놓은 collector's item 수집가들의
흥미를 끄는 것 Would you like to do? ~하시겠어요?,
~하고 싶으신가요? take A for a drive A를 운전해 보다

24. 남자는 자동차와 관련해 무엇을 물어보는가?
(A) 차량이 시중에 나와 있었던 기간
(B) 차량이 위치해 있는 장소
(C) 차량이 만들어진 때
(D) 차량이 판매되었는지의 여부

해설 남자는 대화를 시작하면서 광고에서 본 것과 관련해 I was
wondering if you've sold your car yet이라는 말로 자신
이 궁금해하는 점을 말하고 있다. 이는 차량이 판매되었는지를
궁금해 하는 것이므로 (D)가 정답이다.

어휘 be located 위치해 있다 whether ~인지 (아닌지)

25. 차량은 무엇이 특이한가?
(A) 매우 희귀한 것이다.
(B) 색상이 흔치 않다.
(C) 매우 비싸다.
(D) 복원되었다.

해설 차량에 대해 묻는 남자의 질문에 답변하는 여자의 말에서 차량
의 특징을 확인할 수 있는데, 1999년에 제작된 10대 중의
하나(there were only ten of them made in 1999)라
는 점이 특징으로 언급되고 있다. 10대 중의 하나라는 특징을
very rare라는 말로 바꿔 표현한 (A)가 정답이다.

어휘 unique 특이한, 독특한 rare 희귀한 unusual 흔치 않은,
드문 restore ~을 복원하다

26. 남자는 내일 무엇을 할 것 같은가?
(A) 자동차 시운전하기
(B) 광고 게시하기
(C) 예약 취소하기
(D) 주문품 배송하기

해설 man, tomorrow가 키워드이다. 대화 마지막 부분에 남자가
내일 시운전을 하러 가도 되는지 묻자(Can I come and take
it for a drive ~) 여자가 좋다고 말하며 자신의 아파트로 3시
에 오라고 알리고 있으므로 (A)가 정답이다.

어휘 test drive ~을 시운전하다 post ~을 게시하다 cancel
~을 취소하다 appointment 예약, 약속 order n. 주문
(품)

Paraphrase take it for a drive
→ Test drive a car

Questions 27-29 refer to the following conversation.

M: Hi, **27** I want to buy a new computer monitor, and I think I've narrowed it down to these two. Could you help me choose?

W: Of course. They are both good choices, really. The XMT-2000 has a higher resolution, though the Corgo Advanced has a larger screen area.

M: Yeah, I noticed that. Honestly, a few of the other options look appealing, too. **28** I might need to think about it some more.

W: Take your time, sir. But, we're closing in 20 minutes.

M: Oh, really? Let's see... I'll just get the Corgo then.

W: Great. **29** We're also offering a two-year warranty on that one. I'd recommend purchasing it.

남: 안녕하세요, 제가 새 컴퓨터 모니터를 구입하려고 하는데, 이 두 가지로 범위를 좁힌 것 같아요. 제가 선택할 수 있도록 도와주시겠어요?

여: 물론입니다. 그 두 가지 모두 좋은 선택권입니다, 정말로요. XMT-2000 제품은 화면 해상도가 더 좋은 반면에, 콜고 어드밴스드 제품은 화면 공간이 더 넓습니다.

남: 네, 그 점은 저도 알고 있습니다. 솔직히, 몇 가지 다른 옵션들도 흥미로운 것 같아요. 조금 더 생각해 봐야 할 것 같아요.

여: 천천히 생각해 보세요, 고객님. 하지만 저희는 20분 후에 영업을 종료합니다.

남: 아, 그래요? 어디 보자... 그럼 그냥 콜고 제품으로 구입할게요.

여: 좋습니다. 그 제품에 대해서는 2년 기간의 품질 보증 서비스도 제공해 드리고 있습니다. 이것을 구입하시도록 추천해 드리고 싶습니다.

어휘 **narrow A down to B** A의 범위를 B로 좁히다 **help A do** ~하도록 A를 돕다 **choose** ~을 선택하다 **resolution** 해상도 **screen area** 화면 공간 **notice** ~을 알게 되다, ~을 알아 차리다 **honestly** 솔직히 **a few of** ~중의 몇몇 **option** 옵션, 선택권 **look** 형용사 ~한 것 같다, ~하게 보이다 **appealing** 흥미로운, 매력적인 **Take your time** 천천히 하세요 **in** 시간 ~ 후에 **warranty** 품질 보증(서) **recommend -ing** ~하도록 권하다, 추천하다

27. 화자들은 어디에 있을 것 같은가?
  (A) 전자 제품 매장에
  (B) 기술 박람회에
  (C) 인쇄소에
  (D) 컴퓨터 수리소에

해설 대화 장소를 묻는 문제이므로 대화 중에 언급되는 특정 업무 및 서비스, 활동 등과 관련된 내용을 파악해야 한다. 남자가 대화를 시작하면서 새 컴퓨터 모니터를 구입하려 한다고(I want to buy a new computer monitor) 말하고 있으므로 해당 제품을 구입할 수 있는 장소인 (A)가 정답이다.

어휘 **electronics** 전자제품 **expo** 박람회 **repair shop** 수리소

28. 여자가 "저희는 20분 후에 영업을 종료합니다"라고 말할 때 암시하는 것은 무엇인가?
  (A) 영업이 잘 안되고 있다.
  (B) 남자가 온라인 구매를 완료할 수 있다.
  (C) 결정이 빨리 내려져야 한다.
  (D) 다른 매장이 여전히 문을 연 상태이다.

해설 해당 문장은 대화 중반부에 남자가 조금 더 생각해 봐야 할 것 같다고(I might need to think about it some more) 말한 후에 들을 수 있다. 이에 대해 20분 후에 영업을 종료한다고 말하는 것은 생각할 시간이 많지 않다는 뜻으로 빨리 구매 제품을 결정하도록 요청하는 것과 같으므로 (C)가 정답이다.

어휘 **business** 사업, 영업 **slow** 저조한, 한산한 **complete** ~을 완료하다 **purchase** 구매(품) **make a decision** 결정을 내리다

29. 여자는 무엇을 제안하는가?
  (A) 배송 서비스를 이용할 것
  (B) 품질 보증 서비스를 구입할 것
  (C) 신용카드로 비용을 지불할 것
  (D) 매장 회원으로 등록할 것

해설 대화의 마지막 부분에 여자가 2년 기간의 품질 보증 서비스도 제공하고 있다는 말과 함께 이것을 구입하도록 추천한다고(We're also offering a two-year warranty on that one. I'd recommend purchasing it) 제안하고 있으므로 (B)가 정답이다.

어휘 **sign up for** ~에 등록하다, ~을 신청하다

Questions 30-32 refer to the following conversation with three speakers.

M: Thanks for coming, Sarah and Tina. The marketing team asked if we could push up **30** the release date of our next mobile game, Treasure Drive 3. How's it coming along?

W1: The programming is nearly finished, but **31** a lot of the audio is still missing. Tina, has the recording team set a date with the voice actors yet?

W2: I'm afraid not. The people we usually work with have very busy schedules. We might need to hire some new talent.

M: Okay. I want this project to be ready, so **32** I'll speak with an acting agency we've used in the past. It can set us up with the right people.

남: 와 주셔서 감사합니다, 새라 씨 그리고 티나 씨. 마케팅 팀에서 우리의 다음 모바일 게임인 <트레저 드라이브 3>의 출시 날짜를 앞당길 수 있는지 물어 왔습니다. 어떻게 되어 가고 있나요?

여1: 프로그래밍 작업은 거의 끝났는데, 많은 분량의 오디오가 여전히 빠져 있습니다. 티나 씨, 혹시 녹음 팀에서 성우들과의 일정을 잡았나요?

여2: 그런 것 같지 않아요. 우리가 보통 함께 작업하는 분들께서 일정이 너무 바쁘세요. 능력 있는 새로운 분들을 고용해야 할 필요가 있을지도 모르겠어요.

남: 알겠습니다. 저는 이 프로젝트가 준비되기를 원하기 때문에, 우리가 과거에 이용했던 성우 에이전시와 이야기해 보겠습니다. 그곳에서 우리를 위해 좋은 분들을 준비해 주실 수 있을 겁니다.

어휘 **push up a date** 날짜를 앞당기다 **release** 출시, 발매, 공개 **How's A coming along?** A는 어떻게 되어 가고 있나요? **nearly** 거의 **missing** 빠진, 사라진 **set a date** 날짜를 정하다 **voice actor** 성우 **I'm afraid not** (앞서 언급된 것에 대해) 그런 것 같지 않다 **usually** 보통, 일반적으로 **might need to do** ~해야 할지도 모르다 **hire** ~을 고용하다 **talent** 능력 있는 사람, 재능 있는 사람 **agency** 에이전시, 대행업체 **in the past** 과거에 **set A up with B** A에게 B를 준비해 주다, 마련해 주다

30. 화자들은 무엇을 맡아 작업하는 중인가?
(A) 애니메이션 영화
(B) 텔레비전 프로그램
(C) 비디오 게임
(D) 뮤직 비디오

해설 화자들이 하는 일의 종류를 묻고 있으므로 업무의 특성이나 제품 또는 서비스 관련 정보를 파악하는 데 집중해야 한다. 대화 시작 부분에 남자가 모바일 게임 <트레저 드라이브 3>의 출시 날짜(the release date of our next mobile game, Treasure Drive 3)를 언급하고 있으므로 (C)가 정답임을 알 수 있다.

어휘 **work on** ~을 맡아 작업하다 **animated movie** 애니메이션 영화

31. 여자들은 무엇을 기다리고 있는가?
(A) 음성 녹음
(B) 구매 확인서
(C) 제품 이용 후기
(D) 컴퓨터 하드웨어

해설 여자들이 기다리는 것을 찾는 문제이므로 여자들의 말에서 공통적으로 언급되는 대상을 파악해야 한다. 대화 중반부에 한 여

자가 많은 분량의 음성이 여전히 빠져있다는 사실과 함께 녹음 팀에서 성우들과의 일정을 잡았는지(~ a lot of the audio is still missing. Tina, has the recording team set a date with the voice actors yet?) 묻고 있으므로 음성 녹음을 뜻하는 (A)가 정답이다.

어휘 **voice recording** 음성 녹음 **confirmation** 확인(서) **review** 후기, 평가, 의견

32. 남자는 무엇을 할 것이라고 말하는가?
(A) 마감 시한을 연장할 것이다.
(B) 예산을 늘릴 것이다.
(C) 보도 자료를 만들 것이다.
(D) 에이전시에 연락할 것이다.

해설 대화 마지막 부분에 남자가 과거에 이용했던 성우 에이전시와 이야기해 보겠다고(I'll speak with an acting agency we've used in the past) 알리고 있으므로 (D)가 정답이다.

어휘 **extend** ~을 연장하다 **deadline** 마감 시한 **budget** 예산 **press release** 보도자료 **contact** ~에게 연락하다

Paraphrase speak with an acting agency
→ Contact an agency

Questions 33-35 refer to the following conversation and receipt.

M: Hi, this is Samuel Jenkins. **33** I recently booked a week-long vacation on Lime Island, and I've scheduled a half-day rock climbing adventure with your organization.

W: Hello, Mr. Jenkins. Let me look up your information real quick. Got it. How can I help you?

M: Well, I was e-mailed a receipt, and **34** I'm wondering if I could get a cost removed. You see, I'm actually borrowing my friend's climbing shoes for the trip.

W: Oh, no problem. I'll make that change right now.

M: Great. And just to confirm, you'll pick me up at my hotel, right?

W: Yes. We'll meet you out front at 8 A.M. **35** I suggest having a good breakfast before we depart.

남: 안녕하세요, 저는 새뮤얼 젠킨스입니다. 제가 최근에 라임 아일랜드에서 일주일 기간으로 보낼 휴가를 예약했는데, 반나절 동안 진행되는 귀사의 암벽 등반 모험 행사 일정을 잡아 두었습니다.

여: 안녕하세요, 젠킨스 씨. 제가 아주 빨리 귀하의 정보를 찾아 보겠습니다. 됐습니다. 무엇을 도와 드릴까요?

남: 저, 제가 이메일로 영수증을 받았는데, 한 가지 비용을 제외할 수 있는지 궁금합니다. 그게, 사실은 제가 그 등산 여행을 위해 친구의 등산화를 빌릴 예정이라서요.

여: 아, 괜찮습니다. 지금 바로 그 변경 사항을 적용해 드리겠습니다.

남: 잘됐네요. 그리고 확인을 위해서 여쭤 보는 건데, 제 호텔로 저를 데리러 오시는 것이 맞으시나요?

여: 네, 오전 8시에 건물 입구 쪽에서 만나 뵐 겁니다. 출발하시기 전에 아침을 든든히 드시기를 권해 드립니다.

```
               영수증
-------------------------------------
반나절 패키지          --- 55달러

수강료                --- 15달러

신발 대여             --- 10달러

보험                 --- 8달러
-------------------------------------
              총액: 88달러
```

어휘 recently 최근에 book ~을 예약하다 week-long 일주일 기간의 schedule ~의 일정을 정하다 half-day 반나절의 rock climbing 암벽 등반 organization 단체, 기관 look up (정보 등) ~을 찾아 보다 real quick 아주 빨리 receipt 영수증 wonder if ~인지 궁금하다 get A p.p. A를 ~되게 하다 cost 비용 remove ~을 없애다, 제거하다 borrow ~을 빌리다 make a change 변경하다 pick A up (차로) A를 데리러 가다, 태우러 가다 out front 입구 쪽에서 suggest -ing ~하도록 권하다, 제안하다 depart 출발하다, 떠나다 instruction fee 수강료 rental 대여 insurance 보험

33. 남자는 최근에 무엇을 했는가?
(A) 사업을 시작했다.
(B) 여행을 예약했다.
(C) 신발을 구매했다.
(D) 사내 행사를 준비했다.

해설 남자가 최근에 한 일을 묻고 있으므로 질문에 포함된 recently를 비롯해 가까운 과거 시점을 나타내는 표현과 함께 언급되는 일을 찾아야 한다. 대화 시작 부분에 남자가 최근에 라임 아일랜드에서 일주일 기간으로 보낼 휴가를 예약했다고(I recently booked a week-long vacation on Lime Island) 알리고 있으므로 (B)가 정답이다.

어휘 organize ~을 준비하다, 조직하다

34. 시각자료를 보시오. 영수증에서 얼마의 액수가 제외될 것인가?
(A) 55달러
(B) 15달러
(C) 10달러

(D) 8달러

해설 제외되는 액수를 파악해야 하므로 질문에 포함된 remove를 비롯해 이와 유사한 의미를 나타내는 말이 제시되는 부분을 찾아야 한다. 남자가 대화 중반부에 한 가지 비용을 제외할 수 있는지 궁금하다는 말과 함께 친구의 등산화를 빌릴 예정이라고 (I'm wondering if I could get a cost removed. ~ I'm actually borrowing my friend's climbing shoes for the trip) 알리고 있다. 따라서, 시각자료에서 신발 대여 항목에 해당되는 비용인 (C)가 정답이다.

35. 여자는 무엇을 권하는가?
(A) 보험에 등록할 것
(B) 식사를 할 것
(C) 차량을 대여할 것
(D) 동영상을 시청할 것

해설 여자가 권하는 일을 묻고 있으므로 여자의 말에서 권고 또는 제안 등과 관련된 표현이 제시되는 부분에서 단서를 찾아야 한다. 대화의 마지막에 I suggest having a good breakfast before we depart라는 말로 출발 전에 아침 식사를 꼭 하도록 권하고 있으므로 이에 대해 언급한 (B)가 정답이다.

어휘 register for ~에 등록하다 rent ~을 대여하다 vehicle 차량

`Paraphrase` having a good breakfast
→ Eating a meal

Questions 36-38 refer to the following conversation and calendar.

W: Hello, **36** I'm calling to check on an order I placed on your Web site. It's been more than 40 minutes.

M: I'm sorry, ma'am. If you just tell me your name, I can look it up for you.

W: It should be under Kim Malone.

M: Ah, I see. We're working on it, but **37** a driver called off tonight, so we're a bit short-staffed. Hmm... Just to double check, what kind of pizza did you order?

W: I bought two of the daily specials, without onions.

M: Okay, **38** those two barbecue chicken pizzas are in the oven right now. I'll send them with the next driver. Again, sorry for the delay.

여: 안녕하세요, 귀사의 웹 사이트를 통해 주문한 사항을 확인하기 위해 전화 드렸습니다. 주문한지 40분이 넘어서요.

남: 죄송합니다, 고객님. 성함을 말씀해 주시면, 제가 찾아 보겠습니다.

여: 킴 말론이라는 이름으로 되어 있을 거예요.

남: 아, 알겠습니다. 현재 준비 중이기는 하지만, 배달 기사 한 명이 오늘밤에 휴무를 요청하는 바람에, 저희가 일손이 약간 부족한 상태입니다. 흠... 다시 한 번 확인해 드리려고 하는데, 무슨 종류의 피자를 주문하셨죠?

여: 오늘의 특별 메뉴로 두 개 구매했어요, 양파 없이요.

남: 알겠습니다, 그 바비큐 치킨 피자 두 개는 지금 오븐에 있습니다. 다음 배달 기사를 통해 보내 드리겠습니다. 다시 한 번 지연된 것에 대해 사과 드립니다.

스미티스 피자 – 10월 일일 특별 메뉴			
화요일	수요일	목요일	금요일
페퍼로니	바비큐	하와이안	디럭스 슈프림

어휘 check on ~에 대해 확인하다 place an order 주문하다 more than ~가 넘는 look A up (정보를 얻기 위해) A를 찾아 보다 under 이름 (주문, 예약 등) ~의 이름으로 된 work on ~을 준비하다, ~에 대해 작업하다 call off 취소하다, 철회하다 a bit 약간, 조금 short-staffed 일손이 부족한, 직원이 부족한 double check 다시 한 번 확인하다 order ~을 주문하다 daily special 오늘의 특별 메뉴 without ~ 없이 delay 지연, 지체 deal 거래 (제품), 거래 조건

36. 여자는 왜 전화를 거는가?

(A) 주문 사항에 관해 문의하기 위해
(B) 매장 영업 시간을 확인하기 위해
(C) 출장 요리 서비스를 요청하기 위해
(D) 할인을 요청하기 위해

해설 전화를 거는 목적은 대화 시작 부분에서 찾아야 하므로 대화가 시작될 때 집중해야 한다. 여자가 대화 시작 부분에 웹 사이트를 통해 주문한 사항을 확인하기 위해 전화했다는 말과 함께 주문한지 40분이 넘었다고(I'm calling to check on an order I placed on your Web site. It's been more than 40 minutes) 알리고 있다. 따라서, 주문 사항에 관해 문의하는 일을 의미하는 (A)가 정답이다.

어휘 inquire about ~에 관해 문의하다 store hours 매장 영업 시간 catering 출장 요리(업)

37. 남자는 무슨 문제점을 언급하는가?

(A) 주문이 잘못되어 있다.
(B) 컴퓨터 시스템이 작동되지 않고 있다.
(C) 주소가 포함되어 있지 않다.
(D) 직원 한 명이 결근 상태이다.

해설 남자가 언급하는 문제점을 찾아야 하므로 남자의 말에서 부정적인 정보가 제시될 것임을 예상하고 들어야 한다. 대화 중반부에 남자가 배달 기사 한 명이 오늘밤에 휴무를 요청해서 일손

이 약간 부족한 상태라는(~ a driver called off tonight, so we're a bit short-staffed) 문제점을 알리고 있으므로 직원 한 명이 결근했다는 의미로 쓰인 (D)가 정답이다.

어휘 incorrect 잘못된, 부정확한 down (기기 등이) 작동되지 않는 include ~을 포함하다 absent 결근한, 부재 중인

Paraphrase a driver called off
→ An employee is absent.

38. 시각자료를 보시오. 일정표에 따르면, 오늘은 무슨 요일인가?

(A) 화요일
(B) 수요일
(C) 목요일
(D) 금요일

해설 남자가 대화 마지막 부분에 여자가 오늘의 특별 메뉴로 주문한 바비큐 치킨 피자 두 개가 지금 오븐에 있다고(~ those two barbecue chicken pizzas are in the oven right now) 확인해 주는 내용을 통해 여자가 바비큐 치킨 피자를 주문했음을 알 수 있다. 따라서, 시각자료에서 해당 음식이 적힌 요일인 (B)가 정답이다.

Part 4

Questions 39-41 refer to the following talk.

Well, I have to say that I am overwhelmed with how well you have all done this past week. This is not an easy workshop, but you've all learned the skills in no time at all. **39** Learning to paint is not at all easy, so you should all be proud of yourselves. **39** **40** What really impresses me is your ability to paint human shapes. It's very difficult. Anyway, now that the classes have ended, **41** I'd like to take you all out for coffee so that we can have a chance to have a conversation. Please follow me.

자, 지난간 이번 한 주 동안 여러분 모두 너무 잘해주셔서 제가 크게 감동 받았다는 말씀을 꼭 드리고 싶습니다. 이번 워크샵이 쉬운 과정은 아니었지만, 여러분 모두가 정말 짧은 시간 안에 기술을 익혔습니다. 그림 그리는 법을 배우는 것은 절대 쉬운 일이 아니므로 여러분 모두가 자신에 대해 자랑스럽게 여기시기 바랍니다. 제가 정말로 깊은 인상을 받은 것은 여러분이 인간의 형상을 그리는 능력입니다. 이는 정말 어려운 일입니다. 어쨌든, 강좌가 모두 종료되었기 때문에, 대화를 나눌 시간을 가질 수 있도록 여러분 모두를 모시고 함께 커피를 마시러 나갔으면 합니다. 저를 따라 오세요.

어휘 be overwhelmed with ~에 압도되다, (감정 등) ~에 휩싸이다 skill 기술, 능력 in no time (at all) 즉시, 지체하지 않고 learn to do ~하는 법을 배우다 not at all 전혀 ~가 아니다 be proud of ~을 자랑스러워 하다 impress ~에게 깊은 인상을 남기다 ability to do ~할 수 있는 능력

shape 형상, 형태 **anyway** 어쨌든 **now that** (이제) ~이므로 **take A out** A를 밖으로 데리고 가다 **so that** (목적) ~하도록 **have a conversation** 대화를 나누다

socialize (사람들과) 어울리다, 교류하다 **present** ~을 발표하다, 제시하다 **pay for** ~에 대한 값을 지불하다

Paraphrase have a chance to have a conversation
→ socialize

39. 워크숍의 주제는 무엇인가?

(A) 일자리를 찾는 것
(B) 예술적인 능력을 배우는 것
(C) 집안을 꾸미는 것
(D) 소기업을 운영하는 것

해설 화자는 워크숍을 통해 배울 수 있는 것을 Learning to paint is not at all easy와 같이 언급하고 있으며, 그 이후에 What really impresses me is your ability to paint human shapes와 같이 그림을 그리는 것이 핵심임을 밝히고 있다. 따라서, 이를 artistic skill로 바꿔 그러한 능력을 배우는 일을 의미하는 (B)가 정답이다.

어휘 **employment** 일자리, 고용 **artistic** 예술적인 **decorate** ~을 꾸미다 **run** ~을 운영하다 **small business** 소기업

Paraphrase learning to paint
→ Learning an artistic skill

40. 워크숍 참가자들과 관련해서 무엇이 화자에게 깊은 인상을 주었는가?

(A) 모든 참가자들이 가진 좋은 태도
(B) 참가자들이 작업을 하는 속도
(C) 효과적으로 의사 소통하는 능력
(D) 어려운 기술을 활용하는 능력

해설 화자에게 깊은 인상을 준 것이 무엇인지를 묻는 문제이므로 화자의 말에서 impress와 유사한 표현 또는 놀라움 등을 나타내는 부분을 잘 찾아 들어야 한다. 화자는 담화 중반부에 What really impresses me라는 말로 자신에게 깊은 인상을 준 부분에 대해 언급하고 있는데, 사람의 모습을 그리는 능력에 깊은 인상을 받았으며, 그것이 정말 어려운 일이라고 말하고 있으므로 이를 하나로 묶어 간단히 바꿔 표현한 (D)가 정답이다.

어휘 **participant** 참가자 **attitude** 태도, 사고 방식 **communicate** 의사 소통하다 **effectively** 효과적으로 **perform** ~을 수행하다, 실시하다

41. 참가자들은 담화에 이어 무엇을 할 가능성이 큰가?

(A) 설문 조사를 완료한다.
(B) 밖에 나가 서로 어울린다.
(C) 작품을 발표한다.
(D) 수강료를 지불한다.

해설 화자는 마지막 부분에서 함께 나가 커피를 마시면서 이야기를 하자고 제안하면서(I'd like to take you all out for coffee so that we can have a chance to have a conversation) 자신을 따라 오라고(Please follow me) 말하고 있다. 따라서, 함께 이야기를 나눌 시간을 가질 것임을 알수 있으며, 이를 socialize라고 바꿔 표현한 (B)가 정답이다.

어휘 **complete** ~을 완료하다 **survey** 설문 조사(지)

Questions 42-44 refer to the following announcement.

Before the game starts, **42** I have an announcement for all season pass ticket holders. I'm sorry to inform you that the finals of the All-Star basketball tournament will no longer be held at the Falcon Arena, but will now take place at the Nolan Center in Charleston. This means that the season pass will not apply to the last five games of the tournament. **43** These tickets will need to be bought separately, and they're selling quickly. We're aware that access to the finals was a major draw to purchasing season passes, so we'll be adding extra benefits for those ticket holders to make up for it. **44** Please check our Web site at www.falconarena.com to stay up-to-date on these new offers.

경기를 시작하기에 앞서, 모든 시즌 입장권 소지자 여러분께 알리는 공지 사항이 있습니다. 올스타 농구 토너먼트의 본선 경기들이 더 이상 팔콘 아레나에서 개최되지 않을 것이며, 이제 찰스턴에 있는 놀란 센터에서 열린다는 점을 알려 드리게 되어 유감스럽게 생각합니다. 이는 시즌 입장권이 토너먼트의 마지막 다섯 경기에는 적용되지 않을 것임을 의미합니다. 이 경기들의 입장권은 별도로 구매하셔야 할 것이며, 빠르게 판매됩니다. 저희는 본선 경기 관람이 시즌 입장권을 구매하는 것에 대한 가장 큰 매력이었음을 인지하고 있으므로, 이를 보상해 드릴 수 있도록 해당 입장권 소지자들을 위한 별도의 혜택을 추가해 드릴 예정입니다. 이 새로운 제공 서비스에 관한 최신 정보를 얻으시려면 저희 웹 사이트 www.falconarena.com을 확인해 보시기 바랍니다.

어휘 **season pass** 시즌 입장권 **holder** 소지자, 보유자 **inform A that** A에게 ~라고 알리다 **final** 본선 경기, 결승전 **no longer** 더 이상 ~가 아니다 **hold** ~을 개최하다 **take place** (일, 행사 등이) 개최되다, 발생되다 **apply to** ~에 적용되다 **separately** 별도로, 따로 **be aware that** ~임을 인지하다, 알고 있다 **access to** ~에 대한 출입, 접근, 이용 **major** 주요한 **draw** 매력, 인기 거리 **add** ~을 추가하다 **extra** 별도의, 추가의, 여분의 **benefit** 혜택 **make up for** ~에 대해 보상하다, ~을 만회하다 **stay** 형용사 ~한 상태를 유지하다 **up-to-date** 최신의 **offer** n. 제공(되는 것)

42. 청자들은 누구일 것 같은가?

(A) 사업가들

(B) 운동 선수들
(C) 기자들
(D) 스포츠 팬들

해설 담화 시작 부분에 화자가 모든 시즌 입장권 소지자에게 알리는 공지라고 언급하고 있고(I have an announcement for all season pass ticket holders), 뒤이어 농구 토너먼트 경기 장소의 변경을 알리는 내용이 제시되고 있다(~ the finals of the All-Star basketball tournament will no longer be held at the Falcon Arena). 따라서, 스포츠 경기를 즐기는 팬들을 대상으로 하는 공지임을 알 수 있으므로 (D)가 정답이다.

어휘 owner 소유주, 주인 athlete 운동 선수

43. 남자가 "빠르게 판매됩니다"라고 말하는 이유는 무엇인가?
(A) 한 업체의 성공을 설명하기 위해
(B) 신제품이 인기가 많다는 것을 암시하기 위해
(C) 청자들에게 빠르게 조치하도록 권하기 위해
(D) 대안을 추천하기 위해

해설 해당 문장은 담화 중반부에 화자가 별도로 구매되어야 하는 입장권을 언급한 후에(These tickets will need to be bought separately) 이어지고 있다. 따라서, 구매를 서두르도록 권하기 위해 사용한 말이라는 것을 알 수 있으며, 이는 빠르게 조치하도록 권하는 것과 같으므로 (C)가 정답이 된다.

어휘 describe ~을 설명하다 suggest (that) ~임을 암시하다 encourage A to do A에게 ~하도록 권하다, 장려하다 act 조치하다, 움직이다 alternative n. 대안

44. 남자의 말에 따르면, 청자들은 왜 웹 사이트를 방문해야 하는가?
(A) 환불을 요청하기 위해
(B) 일정을 확인해 보기 위해
(C) 새로운 정보를 확인하기 위해
(D) 상품을 구입하기 위해

해설 웹 사이트를 방문하는 이유를 찾아야 하므로 웹 사이트 관련 정보가 제시될 것임을 예상하고 들어야 한다. 담화 마지막 부분에 새로운 제공 서비스에 관한 최신 정보를 얻으려면 웹 사이트를 확인하라고(Please check our Website at www.falconarena.com to stay up-to-date about these new offers) 알리고 있으므로 정보 확인을 언급한 (C)가 정답이다.

어휘 refund 환불 check for ~을 확인하다 merchandise 상품

Paraphrase check ~ to stay up-to-date
→ check for updates

Questions 45-47 refer to the following telephone message.

Hello, Mr. Flores. This is Mina from Sierra Gardening. **45** My crew was supposed to install a flower bed in your front yard tomorrow, but it has been raining hard all day. **45** So, how about Monday morning instead? You don't have to be present for it. My crew can handle everything. All you have to do is **46** use the small orange flags that we gave you to mark where you want us to plant the seedlings. And one more thing. **47** Could you send a map that specifically shows your property line? I don't want to disturb your neighbor's land.

안녕하세요, 플로어스 씨. 저는 시에라 가드닝의 미나입니다. 저희 작업팀이 내일 귀하의 앞마당에 화단을 설치할 예정이었으나, 종일 비가 많이 오고 있습니다. 그래서, 대신에 월요일 오전은 어떠신가요? 그 자리에 계실 필요는 없습니다. 저희 작업팀이 다 처리해 드릴 수 있습니다. 귀하께서는 저희 팀이 묘목을 심기 원하시는 곳에 저희가 드린 작은 오렌지 색 깃발을 이용해 표시해 주시기만 하면 됩니다. 그리고 한 가지다 더 말씀 드리겠습니다. 귀하의 건물 경계선을 명확히 보여주는 지도를 하나 보내주시겠습니까? 이웃분의 토지를 침범하고 싶지 않습니다.

어휘 crew (함께 작업하는) 팀, 조 be supposed to do ~하기로 되어 있다, ~할 예정이다 install ~을 설치하다 flower bed 화단 front yard 앞마당 hard (정도 등) 많이, 심하게 how about ~? ~는 어떤가요? present 있는, 참석한 handle ~을 처리하다, 다루다 All you have to do is do ~하시기만 하면 됩니다 flag 깃발 mark ~을 표시하다 plant ~을 심다 seedling 묘목 specifically 명확하게, 분명히 property 건물, 부동산 disturb ~을 방해하다, ~에 지장을 주다 neighbor 이웃

45. 남자가 "종일 비가 많이 오고 있습니다"라고 말할 때 의미하는 것은 무엇인가?
(A) 제때 끝내려면 추가 비용이 청구될 것이다.
(B) 일부 작업이 예정대로 완료될 수 없다.
(C) 스포츠 경기대회가 개최될 수 없었다.
(D) 추가 장비가 필요할 것이다.

해설 화자가 내일 화단을 설치할 예정이었다고(My crew was supposed to install a flower bed in your front yard tomorrow ~) 알리면서 '종일 비가 많이 오고 있다고 언급한 후에 월요일이 어떤지(~ how about Monday morning instead?) 제안하는 상황이다. 이는 날씨로 인해 예정된 작업을 제때 완료할 수 없음을 의미하는 것이므로 (B)가 정답이다.

어휘 extra 추가의, 별도의 fee 요금, 수수료 charge ~을 청구하다 on time 제때 as scheduled 예정대로, 일정대로 competition 경기대회 hold ~을 개최하다 additional 추가의 equipment 장비

46. 화자의 말에 따르면, 작은 깃발들은 어디에 쓰일 것인가?

    (A) 건물 경계선을 명시하기 위해
    (B) 팀을 응원하기 위해
    (C) 식물 위치를 지정하기 위해
    (D) 사람들에게 한 구역에 들어가지 말라고 경고하기 위해

해설 질문에 제시된 small flags가 핵심 정보이므로 이것이 언급되는 곳에서 단서를 찾아야 한다. 담화 중반부에 use the small orange flags ~ to mark where you want us to plant the seedlings라는 말로 작은 깃발들을 이용해서 묘목을 심고 싶은 곳에 표시하라고 알리고 있다. 이는 식물을 심을 위치를 지정해 달라는 뜻이므로 (C)가 정답이다.

어휘 specify ~을 명시하다 support 응원, 지원, 지지 designate ~을 지정하다 location 위치 warn A not to do A에게 ~하지 말라고 경고하다

Paraphrase to mark where you want us to plant the seedlings
    → designate plant locations

47. 화자는 청자에게 무엇을 보내주기를 원하는가?

    (A) 수정된 일정표
    (B) 서명한 계약서
    (C) 착수금
    (D) 건물 지도

해설 화자가 청자에게 원하는 일을 묻고 있으므로 요청 표현이 제시되는 부분에서 단서를 파악해야 한다. 담화 후반부에 화자가 Could you send a map that specifically shows your property line?이라는 말로 건물 경계선을 보여주는 지도를 보내 달라고 요청하고 있으므로 (D)가 정답이다.

어휘 revise ~을 수정하다 contract 계약(서) down payment 착수금, 계약금

Questions 48-50 refer to the following announcement and sign.

Hello, shoppers, and welcome to Wibley's Grocery. Here are a few announcements to keep in mind as you shop. First, **48** Wibley's will be staying open an hour later every night next month to accommodate the holiday shopping season. We'll be here for you when you need that last-minute ingredient! Also, **49** please note that there is a mistake on the flyer for our weekly specials. The "buy two, get one free" offer should read "buy one, get one free." What a deal! And finally, **50** if you see our cashier Rodney Wells today, be sure to congratulate him. He'll be retiring this week after 25 years of service. So from all of us at Wibley's, thank you Rodney!

쇼핑객 여러분, 안녕하세요, 그리고 위블리즈 식료품점에 오신 것을 환영합니다. 쇼핑하시면서 명심하셔야 할 몇 가지 안내 사항들이 있습니다. 우선, 저희 위블리즈는 연휴 쇼핑 시즌에 편의를 도모하기 위해 다음 달에 매일 밤 한 시간 더 늦은 시간까지 문을 열 예정입니다. 여러분께서 마지막 순간의 요리 재료가 필요하실 때 저희가 여기 있을 것입니다! 또한, 저희 주간 특가 상품을 위한 전단에 오류가 있다는 점에 유의하시기 바랍니다. "2개 구입 시, 1개 무료"라고 되어 있는 제공 서비스는 "1개 구입 시, 1개 무료"가 되어야 합니다. 정말 좋은 구매 조건이지 않습니까! 그리고 마지막으로, 오늘 저희 계산 담당 직원인 로드니 웰즈 씨를 보시게 될 경우, 꼭 축하 인사를 전해 주시기 바랍니다. 이분께서 25년 동안 근무해 오신 끝에, 이번 주에 퇴직하실 예정입니다. 따라서, 저희 위블리즈 직원 일동은 감사의 인사를 전해 드립니다, 로드니 씨!

위블리즈 식료품점
-"가족, 친구, 그리고 식품"

주간 특가 상품

소프트 터치 티슈	쿠폰 사용 시 무료*
델모어 샤프 체다	10퍼센트 할인
리플스 핫 칩스	2개 구입 시, 1개 무료
스톡스 쉐이빙 크림	15퍼센트 할인

* 고객 1인당 1개로 제한

어휘 keep A in mind A를 명심하다 stay open 문을 연 상태로 있다, 계속 영업하다 accommodate ~에 대한 편의를 도모하다 holiday shopping season 연휴 쇼핑 시즌 last-minute 마지막 순간의 ingredient (음식) 재료, 성분 note that ~라는 점에 유의하다 flyer 전단 special n. 특가 상품, 특별 메뉴 read (문서 등에) ~라고 적혀 있다 free 무료로 offer 제공(되는 것) deal 거래 (조건), 거래 제품 cashier 계산원 be sure to do 꼭 ~하다 congratulate ~에게 축하 인사를 하다 retire 퇴직하다, 은퇴하다 limit v. 제한하다 n. 제한

48. 화자의 말에 따르면, 다음 달에 어떤 변화가 시행될 것인가?

    (A) 신제품들이 판매될 것이다.
    (B) 또 다른 지점이 문을 열 것이다.
    (C) 매장 영업 시간이 연장될 것이다.
    (D) 배송 서비스가 시작될 것이다.

해설 다음 달이라는 미래 시점이 질문의 핵심이므로 해당 시점 표현이 제시되는 부분에서 단서를 찾아야 한다. 화자는 담화 시작 부분에 첫 번째 공지 사항으로 다음 달에 매일 밤 한 시간 더 늦은 시간까지 문을 연다고(Wibley's will be staying open an hour later every night next month ~) 알리고 있으므

로 (C)가 정답이다.

어휘 implement ~을 시행하다 location 지점, 위치 store hours 매장 영업 시간 extend ~을 연장하다

Paraphrase staying open an hour later every night next month
→ Store hours will be extended.

49. 시각자료를 보시오. 어느 제품이 잘못된 제공 서비스를 포함하고 있는가?

(A) 소프트 터치 티슈
(B) 델모어 샤프 체다
(C) 리플스 핫 칩스
(D) 스톡스 쉐이빙 크림

해설 화자는 담화 중반부에 정보 오류에 관해 언급하면서, "2개 구입 시, 1개 무료"라고 되어 있는 제공 서비스가 "1개 구입 시, 1개 무료"가 되어야 한다고(The "buy two, get one free" offer should read "buy one, get one free.") 알리고 있다. 따라서, 시각자료에서 이와 같은 혜택으로 언급된 제품인 (C)가 정답이다.

어휘 incorrect 잘못된, 부정확한

50. 로드니 웰즈 씨에 관해 무엇이 언급되는가?

(A) 신임 매니저이다.
(B) 무료 샘플을 나눠 주고 있다.
(C) 조리 음식 코너에서 근무한다.
(D) 곧 퇴직한다.

해설 Rodney Wells라는 이름이 제시되는 부분에서 함께 언급되는 정보에 집중해 들어가야 한다. 화자는 담화 후반부에 Rodney Wells 씨의 이름과 함께 축하 인사를 전하도록 당부하면서 25년 간의 근무 끝에 퇴직한다는 사실을 알리고 있다(He'll be retiring this week after 25 years of service). 따라서 (D)가 정답이 된다.

어휘 give away ~을 나눠 주다 deli 조리 음식 매장, 조제 식품점

Part 5

51.

정답 (A)

해석 해마다, 우리 정규직 직원들은 각자의 업무 능력에 대한 30분 길이의 평가 시간에 참석한다.

해설 빈칸이 부정관사와 형용사 역할을 하는 thirty-minute 뒤에 위치해 있으므로 이 둘의 수식을 받으면서 타동사 attend의 목적어 역할을 할 명사가 필요하다. 부정관사는 단수명사 앞에 사용하므로 (A) review가 정답이다.

어휘 attend ~에 참석하다 performance 수행 능력, 실력, 성과, 실적, 공연 review n. 평가, 후기 v. ~을 검토하다, ~을 살펴보다

52.

정답 (C)

해석 최근에 나온 그 책을 적극적으로 홍보함으로써, 출판사는 판매량이 증가할 것으로 기대하고 있다.

해설 빈칸 앞에는 전치사가, 빈칸 뒤에는 동명사가 위치해 있으므로 빈칸은 동명사를 수식할 부사 자리이다. 따라서 (C) actively가 정답이다.

어휘 actively 적극적으로 latest 최신의 active 활발한

53.

정답 (C)

해석 월간 잡지 칼럼에서, 경제 전문가인 길스 도킨스 씨는 소매업부문에서의 소비 경향을 분석한다.

해설 전치사구와 콤마 뒤로 주어와 빈칸이 있고 그 뒤로 명사구와 전치사구만 있으므로 빈칸이 문장의 동사 자리임을 알 수 있다. 따라서 (C) analyzes가 정답이다.

어휘 column 칼럼 (기사) analyze ~을 분석하다 spending 소비 retail 소매(업) sector 분야, 부문 analysis 분석 analyzer 분석가

54.

정답 (A)

해석 다양한 대학의 학생들이 이번 여름에 페이스 주식회사의 인턴쉽에 지원할 수 있을 것이다.

해설 빈칸 앞에는 전치사가, 빈칸 뒤에는 명사가 위치해 있으므로 빈칸은 명사 앞에서 명사를 수식할 형용사 자리이다. 따라서 (A) various가 정답이다.

어휘 various 다양한, 여러 가지의 apply for ~에 지원하다 variously 다양하게 variety 다양함 variation 변화, 변동

55.

정답 (C)

해석 도시 탄생 150주년 기념 행사에 대한 예산이 칼드웰 금융회사의 경험 많은 회계사에 의해 검토되었다.

해설 빈칸 앞에 부정관사와 형용사가 있으므로 빈칸은 이 둘의 수식을 받을 단수명사 자리이다. 그런데 의미상 experienced의 수식을 받을 수 있는 것은 사람이어야 하므로 단수 사람명사 (C) accountant가 정답이다.

어휘 celebration 기념 행사, 축하 행사 experienced 경험 많은 accountant 회계사 account 계좌, 계정 accounting 회계

56.

정답 (D)

해석 3개월의 시용 기간 후에, 대부분의 신입 직원들은 회사로부터 정규직 자리를 제안받았다.

해설 빈칸과 콤마 사이에 명사구가 위치해 있어 이 명사구를 목적어

로 취할 전치사가 필요하므로 (D) Following이 정답이다.

어휘 **following** ~이후에 **trial** 사용, 시범, 시도 **permanent** 영구적인, 정규직의 **position** 일자리

57.
정답 (B)

해석 개조 공사 기간 동안, 해당 직원들은 다른 부서로 재배치될 것입니다.

해설 동사 relocate는 대상의 장소를 다른 곳으로 옮긴다는 뜻인데 빈칸 뒤에 옮겨갈 장소인 other departments가 제시되어 있으므로 빈칸에 목적지 이동을 나타내는 전치사가 들어가야 한다. 따라서 (B) to가 정답이다.

어휘 **duration** 기간, 지속 **affected** 영향을 받은, 해당되는 **relocate A to B** A의 장소를 B로 옮기다

58.
정답 (A)

해석 마감일인 3월 15일이 지나서 기사를 받았기 때문에, 그 기사는 건축 저널의 4월 호에 실리지 않을 것이다.

해설 콤마를 기준으로 주어와 동사를 갖춘 두 개의 완전한 절이 제시되어 있으므로 빈칸은 접속사 자리이다. 그런데 의미상 마감일이 지나서 기사를 받은 것이 잡지에 실리지 않는 이유에 해당되므로 (A) Since가 정답이다.

어휘 **feature** ~을 특집으로 다루다 **edition** (잡지 등의) ~호, ~판 **as if** 마치 ~인 것처럼 **nearly** 거의

59.
정답 (C)

해석 저희 잡지의 광고 자리를 구매하려는 신규 광고자들은 제출에 대해 저희 웹 사이트에서 이용 가능한 지침을 참고할 것이 요청됩니다.

해설 빈칸에는 동사 consult의 목적어로 의미상 적절한 명사가 들어가야 하는데 문맥상 잡지에 광고를 싣고자 하는 광고주에게 요청하는 내용이므로 광고주들이 참고할 문서로는 '지침'이 적절하다. 따라서 (C) guidelines가 정답이다.

어휘 **seek to do** ~하려고 하다, ~하기 위해 애쓰다 **be asked to do** ~하도록 요청 받다 **consult** ~을 참고하다 **available** 이용가능한 **reference** 참조

60.
정답 (A)

해석 요즘에는, 슈퍼마켓이나 쇼핑몰뿐만 아니라 지역 내 편의점에서도 ATM 기기를 흔히 찾아볼 수 있다.

해설 문맥상 ATM을 찾아볼 수 있는 장소가 빈칸 앞뒤로 세 가지가 제시되어 있다. 따라서 빈칸 앞뒤에 위치한 장소 명사들을 연결하며 '~뿐만 아니라 …도'라는 의미를 나타내는 병렬 구조를 만들 수 있는 (A) as well as이 정답이다.

어휘 **ATM** 현금 자동 입출금기 **commonly** 흔히

61.
정답 (B)

해석 신규 회원들을 유치하기 위해, 베니스 체육관은 때때로 건물을 지나가는 사람들에게 1일 무료 체험 회원권을 제공한다.

해설 빈칸에 쓰일 부사는 현재시제로 된 동사 offers를 수식해야 하므로 현재시제와 어울리는 부사인 (B) occasionally가 정답이다.

어휘 **attract** ~을 유치하다, 끌어 들이다 **occasionally** 때때로 **one-day trial** 1일 무료 체험 **walk by** ~를 지나 가다 **previously** 이전에, 예전에 **hardly** 거의 ~ 않다

62.
정답 (A)

해석 저희 수영장에 오시는 방문객들께서는 탈의실 내 사물함에 소지품을 안전하게 보관하실 수 있습니다.

해설 빈칸에 쓰일 동사는 빈칸 뒤 명사구를 목적어로 취해 사물함이 있는 탈의실에서 소지품과 관련해 할 수 있는 일을 나타내야 하므로 '~을 안전하게 보관하다'를 뜻하는 (A) secure가 정답이다.

어휘 **belongings** 소지품, 소유물 **secure** v. ~을 안전하게 보관하다, ~을 안전하게 지키다 **attain** ~을 달성하다, ~을 이루다 **preserve** ~을 보존하다, ~을 보호하다

63.
정답 (A)

해석 좋지 않은 기상 여건에도 불구하고, 지난주의 '평화, 사랑 & 음악과 함께' 행사에 많은 사람들이 참석했다.

해설 수동태를 이루는 be동사와 과거분사 사이에 들어가 과거분사를 수식할 수 있는 것이 필요한데, 동사 was attended의 의미로 보아 사람들의 참석 정도를 나타내야 하므로 (A) well이 정답이다.

어휘 **despite** ~에도 불구하고 **unfavorable** 불리한 **conditions** 여건 **well attended** 아주 많이 참석한 **quite** 꽤, 상당히

64.
정답 (D)

해석 길 크리스트 씨는 파라곤 주식회사에서 거의 20년 동안 근무를 해왔지만, 회사 내에서 한 번도 책임자 직책을 제안 받은 적이 없다.

해설 빈칸 이하로 주어와 동사가 포함된 두 개의 절이 이어져 있으므로 빈칸에 접속사가 와야 한다. 20년 가까이 오래 일했음에도 책임자로서 일하도록 제안 받지 않았다는 대조적인 의미가 되어야 자연스러우므로 '비록 ~이지만, ~라 하더라도'라는 의미로 쓰이는 (D) Although가 정답이다.

어휘 **although** 비록 ~이지만, ~라 하더라도 **supervisory** 관리의, 감독의 **once** 일단 ~하면, ~하는 대로 **despite** ~에도 불구하고

65.

정답 (B)

해석 비록 마틴 크로스 씨와 제니 유 씨가 종종 마케팅 전략에 대해 의견이 엇갈리기는 하지만, 두 사람 모두 서로 프로젝트에 쏟아 붓는 집중력과 창의성을 존중한다.

해설 부사절이 끝나는 콤마 다음에 빈칸과 동사가 이어져 있으므로 빈칸이 주절의 주어 자리임을 알 수 있다. 그런데 빈칸에는 앞서 언급된 두 명의 특정 인물을 대상으로 하는 대명사가 쓰여야 의미가 알맞으므로 '둘 모두'를 의미하는 (B) both가 정답이다.

어휘 even though 비록 ~이기는 하지만 over ~에 대해 strategy 전략 both 둘 모두 focus 집중(력) the other (둘 중 하나를 제외한) 다른 하나 bring A to B A를 B에 초래하다, 불러 일으키다 either 둘 중 어느 것이든 less a. 더 적은 ad. 더 적게

66.

정답 (D)

해석 CWA 문학상의 수상자 발표까지 불과 며칠을 앞두고, 심사 위원들은 어느 작가가 올해 최고의 책을 발간했는지를 결정해야 한다.

해설 빈칸 이하는 타동사인 decide의 목적어 역할을 하는 절이 되어야 하는데, 빈칸 다음에 바로 명사가 있으므로 이를 수식하는 역할이 가능한 (D) which가 정답이다.

어휘 with (부대적인 상황) ~하여, ~한 채로 announcement 발표 judge 심사위원 author 작가

Part 6

67-70.

> 뉴욕, 10월 15일 - 프리빌 영화사는 3분기에 35 퍼센트 상승이라는 기록적인 이익을 보고하였다. 이 같은 수익 **67** 증가는 이 회사가 최근에 경쟁사인 스타라이트 픽쳐스 사를 매입한 덕분이라 할 수 있다. 이 합병 거래 **68** 이래로, 프리빌 영화사는 북아메리카에서 가장 큰 영화사가 되었다. **69** 그럼에도 불구하고, 영화업계의 전망은 전반적으로 그렇게 밝지 않다. 수익의 증가에도 불구하고, 저조한 경제는 영화관 관객수의 감소로 이어졌다. **70** 그 결과로, 이 회사는 최근에 확장 계획을 내년까지로 연기하기로 결정하였다.

어휘 record a. 기록적인 n. 기록 v. ~을 기록하다 be attributed to ~탓이다, ~덕분이다 merger 합병 outlook 전망 as a whole 전체적으로, 전반적으로 upswing 증가, 상승 attendance 참석자 수, 관객 수

67.

정답 (B)

해설 빈칸 앞에 정관사가 있으므로 빈칸의 어휘는 앞에서 언급된 내

용을 지칭하는 명사가 되어야 한다. 빈칸 앞 문장에서 35 퍼센트 증가(a rise of 35 percent)라는 기록적인 수익 증가를 언급하였으므로 rise와 의미가 같은 (B) increase가 정답이다.

어휘 downturn 하강, 침체 leveling 평준화

68.

정답 (D)

해설 빈칸 앞에 콤마로 이어진 전치사구에서 '~이후로'라는 의미의 Since가 쓰였음을 알 수 있다. since가 '~이후로'라는 의미로 쓰이면 주절에는 현재완료시제 동사가 함께 쓰이므로 (D) has become이 정답이다.

69.

정답 (A)

해설 빈칸 앞에는 합병 이후로 가장 큰 회사가 되었다는 내용이, 빈칸 뒤에는 전망이 밝지 않다는 반대의 내용이 나오고 있다. 따라서 '그럼에도 불구하고'라는 의미를 가져 대조되는 내용의 두 문장을 연결할 수 있는 (A) Nonetheless가 정답이다.

어휘 likewise 이와 유사하게 as a result 그 결과

70.

정답 (A)

해석 **(A) 그 결과로, 이 회사는 최근에 확장 계획을 내년까지로 연기하기로 결정하였다.**
(B) 그 새 영화는 휴가철의 시작에 맞추어 출시될 것으로 예상된다.
(C) 프리빌 영화사가 잘못된 결정을 내리는 것으로 절대 볼 수 없다.
(D) 스타라이트 픽쳐스 사가 지속적으로 경쟁력이 있을지는 두고 봐야 한다.

해설 빈칸 앞 문장에서 경기 침체로 인해서 극장의 관객 수가 줄어들었다는 언급이 나와 있으므로 극장의 관객 수 감소와 어울리는 내용이 들어가야 한다. 관객 수 감소는 수입 감소의 결과를 낳게 되고 이는 비용 절감 조치를 요구하게 되므로 확장 계획의 연기를 언급한 (A)가 정답이다.

어휘 postpone ~을 연기하다 expansion 확장 release ~을 출시하다 in time for ~와 때를 맞춰서 competitive 경쟁의, 경합하는

71-74.

수신: 버드하우스 퍼블리싱 전 직원
발신: 캐런 체임벌린, 대표이사

직원 여러분께,

우리 버드하우스 퍼블리싱이 모두의 취미 및 관심사를 파악하기 위해 전 **71** 직원들을 대상으로 설문 조사를 실시합니다. 이는 이번 주 목요일에 있을 주간 회의 직후에 여러분께 이메일로 보내질 것입니다. **72** 우리의 궁극적인 목표는 다양한 친목 동호회를 만들기 위해 그 데이터를 이용하는 것입니다. 반드시 이 양식을 작성 완료해 금요일 오후 5시까지 인사부로 다시 보내주시기 바랍니다.

과거에, 우리 회사는 직원들에게 한 자리에 모여 배드민턴과 등산, 그리고 자전거 타기 같은 다양한 활동을 즐길 수 있게 해준 여러 모임이 있었습니다. 이는 팀원들이 유대 관계를 형성하는 데 도움을 주어, 업무 만족도와 생산성을 **73** 높여 주었습니다. 우리는 새로운 모임들이 유사한 영향을 미치길 바랍니다!

인사부에서 모든 양식을 받는 대로, 그 데이터를 모아 정리하고 평가할 것입니다. 인사부장님께서 **74** 그 후에 어느 활동들이 직원 여러분을 위해 선택되었는지 공지해 주실 것입니다.

안녕히 계십시오.

캐런

어휘 **carry out** ~을 실시하다, ~을 수행하다 **find out** ~을 파악하다, ~을 알아내다 **interests** 관심사 **shortly after** ~ 직후에 **complete** ~을 완료하다 **form** 양식, 서식 **HR** 인사(부) **by** (기한) ~까지 **allow A to do** A에게 ~할 수 있게 해주다 **bond** 유대 관계를 형성하다 **satisfaction** 만족(도) **productivity** 생산성 **have an effect** 영향을 미치다 **once** ~하는 대로, ~하자마자 **compile** (자료 등) ~을 모아 정리하다 **assess** ~을 평가하다 **announce** ~을 공지하다, ~을 발표하다

71.

정답 (D)

해설 빈칸에 쓰일 명사는 전치사 of의 목적어로서 설문 조사 대상에 해당되는 사람들을 나타내야 한다. 또한, 다음 문장에 설문 조사용 양식을 작성해 인사부로 제출하는 사람을 이 회람의 수신인인 you로 지칭하고 있는데, 상단의 수신인 항목에 회사 전 직원이 이 회람을 받는 사람으로 표기되어 있어 직원들을 대상으로 하는 설문 조사임을 알 수 있으므로 '직원들'을 뜻하는 (D) employees가 정답이다.

어휘 **supplier** 공급업체 **publication** 출간(물)

72.

정답 (C)

해석 (A) 이 신제품들에 관한 더 많은 정보가 회의 시간에 제공될 것입니다.

(B) 어떤 휴무든 요청하시는 경우, 최소 2일 전에 미리 저희에게 알려 주십시오.

(C) 우리의 궁극적인 목표는 다양한 친목 동호회를 만들기 위해 그 데이터를 이용하는 것입니다.

(D) 하지만, 그 회의는 3층에 있는 대회의실로 옮겨질 수 있습니다.

해설 빈칸 앞에는 설문 조사지를 보내는 시점과 방식을 알리는 말이, 빈칸 뒤에는 작성한 설문 조사지를 보내는 곳과 제출 마감 시한을 알리는 말이 쓰여 있다. 따라서 설문 조사 실시 및 그 양식 작성과 관련된 의미를 지닌 문장이 빈칸에 쓰여야 흐름이 자연스러우므로 설문 조사 목적을 밝히는 (C)가 정답이다.

어휘 **require** ~을 필요로 하다 **time off work** 휴무 (시간) **inform** ~에게 알리다 **at least** 최소한, 적어도 **in advance** 미리, 사전에 **ultimate** 궁극적인 **however** 하지만, 그러나

73.

정답 (A)

해설 빈칸 앞에 주어와 동사, 명사구 목적어, 그리고 to부정사구로 구성된 완전한 절이 쓰여 있어 빈칸이 동사 자리가 아니라는 것을 알 수 있으므로 선택지에 제시된 동사 boost는 준동사의 형태로 빈칸에 들어가야 한다. 따라서 선택지에서 분사의 형태인 (A) boosting과 (B) boosted 중에서 하나를 골라야 하는데, 빈칸 뒤에 위치한 명사구 목적어를 취할 수 있는 것은 현재분사이므로 (A) boosting이 정답이다.

어휘 **boost** ~을 높이다, ~을 증진하다, ~을 촉진하다

74.

정답 (B)

해설 빈칸이 속한 문장은 인사부장이 어느 활동들이 선택되었는지 공지할 것이라는 의미를 나타내는데, 이는 앞선 문장에서 말하는 데이터를 정리하고 평가하는 과정을 거친 이후에 발생 가능한 일이다. 따라서, '그 후에, 그런 다음' 등의 의미로 다음 순서에 해당되는 일을 말할 때 사용하는 (B) then이 정답이다.

어휘 **quite** 꽤, 상당히 **then** 그 후에, 그런 다음, 그때, 그렇다면 **instead** 대신 **otherwise** 그렇지 않으면, 그 외에는

Part 7

75-76.

> **수신:** 마케팅 부서 전 직원
> **제목:** 컴퓨터 활용 워크숍
> **날짜:** 11월 14일
>
> 안녕하세요,
>
> 저는 방금 IT부의 로저 로스 씨와 회의를 했습니다. 우리는 다가오는 컴퓨터 활용 워크숍에 대해 논의하였으며 **75** 우리의 워크숍 기간을 몇 주 뒤로 미루는 것이 우리에게 최선일 것이라고 결정하였습니다. 다들 아시다시피, 우리 마케팅부에서는 이번 달에 긴급한 마감 기한이 몇 개 있습니다. 따라서, 고객 서비스부가 11월 24일부터 시작하는 주의 워크숍에 참가할 것이며, 우리는 12월 1일에 시작하는 주에 참가할 것입니다. **76** 회사 메시지를 통해 새로운 워크숍 일정에 관한 좀 더 자세한 메시지를 여러분들 모두에게 보내드릴 테니 살펴보시고 워크숍에 관한 질문이 있으시면 저에게 알려주시기 바랍니다.
>
> 감사합니다.
>
> 메이 나이트
> 마케팅 부장
> 코스그로브 푸드 주식회사

어휘 computing 컴퓨터 활용, 컴퓨터 사용 upcoming 다가오는 push back 미루다 pressing 긴급한 deadline 마감 기한 detailed 자세한, 상세한 via ~을 통하여

75. 회람의 목적은 무엇인가?
(A) 직원들에게 예정된 컴퓨터 관리에 대해 통보하는 것
(B) 교육 시간에 대한 직원들의 피드백을 요청하는 것
(C) 직원들에게 일정 변경에 대해 알리는 것
(D) 두 개 부서의 합병을 논의하는 것

정답 (C)

해설 지문 초반부에서 워크숍 일정을 몇 주 뒤로 미룬다고(push our session back by a couple of weeks) 알리고 있으므로 직원들에게 워크숍 일정이 변경되었음을 알리는 내용인 (C)가 정답이다.

어휘 notify ~을 알리다, 통보하다 planned 예정된, 계획된 maintenance 유지, 관리 merge ~을 합병하다, 합치다

76. 직원들은 무엇을 하도록 권고 받는가?
(A) 온라인으로 워크숍에 등록하는 것
(B) 로슨 씨에게 메시지를 보내는 것
(C) 우선시 되는 일자를 선택하는 것
(D) 회사의 메시지를 확인하는 것

정답 (D)

해설 지문 후반부에서 직원들에게 새로운 일정에 대한 정보를 회사

메시지로 보낼 것이라고 말하며 메시지를 확인해 볼 것을 당부하고 있다. 따라서 (D)가 정답이다.

어휘 be advised to do ~하도록 권고 받다 register 등록하다, 기재하다 preferred 우선의

77-79.

> **저희는 언제나 기쁜 마음으로 기부금을 받습니다!**
>
> **77 78** 저희 놀우드 컨트리 대저택 & 정원은 대연회장과 서재, 그리고 가치 있는 여러 미술품들이 소장되어 있는 중앙 식당을 포함해 방문객들께서 무료로 저희 대저택의 모든 공간들을 출입하실 수 있도록 보장하기 위해 전념하고 있습니다. 저희 대저택의 실내를 지속적으로 복원하고 유지 관리하기 위해, 저희는 후원해 주시는 분들의 너그러운 기부금에 일부 의존하고 있습니다. 후원자가 되셔서 건물 유지 관리에 도움을 주실 의향이 있으신 분은, 대연회장 내의 안내데스크 직원에게 말씀해 주시기 바랍니다.
>
> 후원을 통해 **79(C)** 저희 기념품 매장의 모든 제품들에 대한 상당한 액수의 할인과 놀우드 대저택의 모습의 **79(B)** 역사적인 사진들로 만든 특별 책자, 그리고 정원에서 **79(A)** 매년 개최되는 경축 행사에 대한 초청장 등과 같은 다양한 혜택을 누리실 수 있습니다. 저희 웹 사이트 www.norwoodmanor.co.uk를 방문하시면 후원에 따른 혜택들에 관해 더 많은 정보를 확인해 보실 수 있습니다.

어휘 donation 기부(금) be committed to -ing ~하는 데 전념하다 ensure that ~임을 보장하다, ~하는 것을 확실히 하다 access ~에 출입하다, 접근하다 manor 대저택 at no cost 무료로 including ~을 포함해 grand ballroom 대연회장 house v. ~을 소장하다, 보관하다 valuable 가치 있는, 소중한 continually 지속적으로 restore ~을 복원하다, 복구하다 maintain ~을 유지 관리하다 depend on ~에 의존하다 partly 일부, 부분적으로 patron 후원자 be willing to do ~할 의향이 있다 upkeep 유지 관리 perks 혜택 substantial 상당한, 많은 saving 할인, 절약 gala 경축 행사 benefit 혜택, 이점

77. 이 전단은 어디에서 배부될 것 같은가?
(A) 학술 기관에서
(B) 미술관에서
(C) 역사적인 건물에서
(D) 공공 도서관에서

정답 (C)

해설 첫 번째 문단에 대연회장과 서재, 가치 있는 많은 미술품들이 있는 식당을 포함하는 대저택을 무료로 방문하는 일이 소개되고 있으므로(Norwood Country Manor & Gardens ~ the grand ballroom, the library, and the main dining room, which houses several valuable works of art) 이와 같은 건물을 대신 지칭할 수 있는 것으로 '역사적인 건물'을 뜻하는 (C)가 정답이다.

어휘 institute 기관, 단체

78. 건물의 실내에 관해 무엇이 언급되어 있는가?

(A) 입장료가 무료이다.
(B) 최근에 개조되었다.
(C) 골동품 가구를 포함하고 있다.
(D) 일부 방에는 출입할 수 없다.

정답 (A)

해설 첫 번째 문단에 방문객들이 무료로 출입할 수 있다는(visitors are able to access all of the rooms in the manor at no cost) 정보가 제시되어 있으므로 (A)가 정답이다.

어휘 contain ~을 포함하다 antique 골동품의 inaccessible 출입할 수 없는, 접근할 수 없는

79. 후원자들이 받는 혜택으로 언급되지 않은 것은 무엇인가?

(A) 행사 초청장
(B) 사진이 들어 있는 책자
(C) 기념품 매장 할인
(D) 웹 사이트 이용자 계정

정답 (D)

해설 두 번째 단락에서 기념품 매장의 모든 제품들에 대해 상당한 액수의 할인 혜택을(savings on all items in our gift shop) 언급한 부분에서 (C)를, 역사적인 사진들로 만든 특별 책자(a special book of historical photographs)에서 (B)를, 정원에서 매년 개최되는 경축 행사에 대한 초청장을 받을 수 있다는(an invitation to the gala) 부분에서 (A)를 찾을 수 있다. 하지만 웹 사이트 이용자 계정은 언급되어 있지 않으므로 (D)가 정답이다.

80-82.

벨링햄스
81 이제는 454 토렌스 드라이브에서도 (파스텔 미술용품 옆)
피츠버그, PA 15213
555-9237

영업 시간:
오전 9시부터 오후 5시, 월요일에서 금요일
오전 9시부터 오후 6시, 토요일

100달러 이상 구매 시 크리스탈 꽃병 무료 증정
81 (킹스웨이 플라자 지점만 해당)
81 영업 첫 주 축하 기념:
80 모든 양탄자와 카펫 15% 할인
커튼 20% 할인 (순수 린넨 제품만)
모든 사진 액자 25% 할인

상기 할인은 5월 2일에서 5월 8일까지 제공됩니다.

1년에 30달러만으로, 벨링햄스의 고객 보상 카드를 신청할 수 있고 저희 토렌스 드라이브 지점 또는 베르트랑 스트리트에 있는 대형 상점에서 구매하시는 모든 상품에 대해 5%의 추가할인을 받으실 수 있습니다.

82 또한, 5월 8일까지, www.bellinghams.com에서 침구류 어떤 것이든 바로 주문하고 10% 할인을 받으세요!

어휘 business hours 영업시간 vase 화병 celebrate ~을 축하하다 plain 순수한 frame 액자 above 위의 sign up for ~에 등록하다 reward 보상 flagship store 플래그쉽 스토어(대형 상점) bedding 침구류 directly 직접, 곧장

80. 벨링햄스는 무슨 종류의 상품을 파는가?

(A) 건축 자재
(B) 가정용 물품
(C) 미술용품
(D) 꽃

정답 (B)

해설 지문의 중간 부분에서 할인되는 품목들이 양탄자와 카펫, 커튼, 액자 등임을(all rugs and carpets, curtains, picture frames) 알 수 있다. 이러한 것들을 한 마디로 종합할 수 있는 (B)가 정답이다.

81. 벨링햄스에 대해서 명시된 것은 무엇인가?

(A) 한군데 이상의 도시에 가게들을 가지고 있다.
(B) 일주일 내내 영업한다.
(C) 중고 상품을 취급한다.
(D) 새로운 지점을 오픈 한다.

정답 (D)

해설 지문 초반부에서 이제는 토렌스 지점에서도(Now also at Torrance)라는 광고 문구와 이 가게의 영업 첫 주를 기념하기 위해(To celebrate this store's first week) 할인을 제공한다고 언급하는 것을 통해 신규 지점 오픈 세일 광고임을 알 수 있다. 따라서 (D)가 정답이다.

어휘 second-hand 중고의 location 지점

82. 고객들이 온라인으로만 할인을 받을 수 있는 품목은 어떤 것인가?

(A) 욕실 러그
(B) 장식용 꽃병
(C) 침대 커버
(D) 커튼 세트

정답 (C)

해설 지문 후반부에 웹 주소가 나오면서, 그 사이트에서 바로 침구류를 구매하고 10%할인을 받으라고(bedding directly from www.bellinghams.com and get 10% off) 정보를 알리고 있다. 따라서 (C)가 정답이다.

83-86.

---

[84] 레진 버틀러, 이사
어반 네온 의류 회사

버틀러 씨께,

[83] 저는 이곳 원 러브 재단의 모두를 대신해 저희가 귀하께 분명 감사의 빚을 지고 있다고 말씀 드립니다. — [1] —. [86] 저희는 귀하 및 귀하의 회사가 지난주에 길드포드 지역 문화 센터에서 열린 저희 패션쇼에서 사용할 수 있도록 옷을 기부해 주실 수 있었던 점에 대해 기쁘게 생각합니다. — [2] —.

작년과 재작년에, 저희는 인기 있는 의류 디자이너들로부터 의류 기부를 받도록 간청 드리느라 힘겨웠습니다. — [3] —. 결과적으로, 참가자 수가 저희 기대치를 밑돌면서, 입장권 판매 측면에서 거의 성공이라고 말할 수 없었습니다. — [4] —. 귀사와 같이 사람들의 이목을 끄는 회사로부터 받은 후한 기부 물품은 [85] 올해 저희에게 입장권 가격을 올리고 훨씬 더 많은 손님들을 끌어들일 수 있게 해 주었으며, 이로 인해 저희가 더 많은 자금을 마련해 평소에 선택적으로 제공하던 지역 자선 단체들 사이에서 배분하는 데 도움이 되었습니다.

진심으로, 저희 노력에 대한 귀하의 지원에 많은 감사 드립니다.

안녕히 계십시오.

대니얼 알론소, 행사 진행 책임

어휘 foundation 재단 owe A B A에게 B를 빚지다, 신세 지다 debt 빚, 부채 gratitude 감사(의 마음) contribute ~을 기부하다, 기여하다 garment 옷, 의복 struggle to do ~하느라 힘겨워하다 solicit ~을 간청하다 contribution 기부(품), 기여 turnout 참석자 수 hardly 거의 ~ 않다 high-profile 사람들의 이목을 끄는 raise ~을 끌어올리다, 높이다, (돈 등) ~을 모으다 thereby 그로 인해, 그렇게 함으로써 distribute ~을 배분하다, 나눠주다 selection 선택 (가능한 것) endeavor 노력

83. 편지는 왜 쓰여졌는가?
(A) 최근의 문의에 대해 답변하는 것
(B) 회사에 기부를 요청하는 것
(C) 기금 마련 단체를 홍보하는 것
(D) 도움에 대해 감사의 뜻을 표하는 것

정답 (D)

해설 첫 단락 시작 부분에 원 러브 재단의 모두를 대신해 상대방에게 분명 감사의 빚을 지고 있다는(I am sure that I speak for everyone here at the One Love Foundation when I say we owe you a debt of gratitude) 말로 인사하면서 그 이유를 설명하는 내용으로 지문이 전개되고 있으므로 (D)가 정답이다.

어휘 respond to ~에 답변하다, 대응하다 inquiry 문의 fundraising 기금 마련, 모금

84. 버틀러 씨는 누구일 것 같은가?
(A) 지역 자선 단체의 책임자
(B) 원 러브 재단의 회원
(C) 한 의류 회사의 임원
(D) 지역 문화 센터의 부서장

정답 (C)

해설 지문 상단에 이사(Director)라는 직책과 어반 네온 의류 회사(Urban Neon Clothing Company)라는 업체 이름이 쓰여 있으므로 (C)가 정답이다.

어휘 executive 임원, 이사

85. 편지에 따르면, 올해의 행사는 어떻게 예년의 행사들과 다른가?
(A) 상대적으로 입장권 판매량이 저조했다.
(B) 다른 장소에서 개최되었다.
(C) 더 많은 자선 단체들을 포함했다.
(D) 참석하는 데 더 많은 비용이 들었다.

정답 (D)

해설 두 번째 단락 중반부에 기부 물품으로 인해 올해 입장권 가격을 올리고 훨씬 더 많은 손님들을 끌어들일 수 있게 해 주었다는(enabled us to raise the ticket price this year and attract even more guests) 사실이 쓰여 있다. 이는 입장권 가격이 올라 올해의 행사에 참석하는 데 더 많은 돈이 들었다는 뜻이므로 (D)가 정답이다.

어휘 relatively 상대적으로, 비교적 poor 형편 없는, 저조한

86. [1], [2], [3], [4]로 표기된 위치들 중에서, 다음 문장이 들어 가기에 가장 적절한 곳은 어디인가?

"행사는 대단한 성공이었으며, 저희는 지역 자선 단체들을 위한 많은 액수의 자금을 마련했습니다."

(A) [1]
(B) [2]
(C) [3]
(D) [4]

정답 (B)

해설 제시된 문장은 특정 행사를 지칭하는 The event와 함께 이 행사가 성공을 거둬 많은 돈을 모금한 긍정적인 결과를 언급하고 있다. 따라서 특정 행사가 처음 언급되는(our fashion show at Guildford Community Center) 문장 뒤에 위치한 [2]에 들어가 해당 행사의 결과를 언급하는 문맥이 되어야 자연스러우므로 (B)가 정답이다.

87-90.

> 밥 보우반 [오후 3:43] 안녕하세요, 파인 페이퍼 주식회사에 오신 것을 환영합니다. 무엇을 도와 드릴까요?
>
> 재니스 심즈 [오후 3:43] 안녕하세요, 밥 씨. 87 제가 지난주에 주문한 용지 제품과 관련해 도와 주실 수 있기를 바랍니다.
>
> 밥 보우반 [오후 3:44] 물론입니다. 주문번호를 말씀해 주시겠습니까?
>
> 재니스 심즈 [오후 3:44] 99554620입니다.
>
> 밥 보우반 [오후 3:44] 감사합니다. 잠시만 기다려 주십시오. 주문 상세 정보에 접속하겠습니다.
>
> 밥 보우반 [오후 3:46] 네, 2월 4일에 화이트 카드스톡 5통을 주문하신 것으로 확인됩니다.
>
> 재니스 심즈 [오후 3:47] 네. 87 그 주문품이 어제 도착하기로 되어 있었는데, 받지 못했어요. 88 도와 주실 수 있으세요?
>
> 밥 보우반 [오후 3:48] 물론입니다. 88 괜찮으시면, 배송 관리 책임자에게 채팅방에 입장하도록 요청하겠습니다.
>
> 재니스 심즈 [오후 3:48] 그럼 아주 좋을 것 같아요.
>
> 데미 디미트로프 [오후 3:51] 안녕하세요, 저는 데미입니다. 무엇이 문제인 것 같으신가요?
>
> 밥 보우반 [오후 3:51] 안녕하세요, 데미 씨. 심즈 씨께서 며칠 전에 카드스톡을 좀 주문하셨는데, 아직 배송되지 않았습니다.
>
> 데미 디미트로프 [오후 3:51] 잠시 시간을 주시면, 무슨 일인지 알아보겠습니다.
>
> 재니스 심즈 [오후 3:51] 감사합니다!
>
> 데미 디미트로프 89 [오후 3:54] 네, 트럭이 어제 고장 나는 바람에 제때 배송을 완료할 수 없었던 것으로 보입니다. 89 그 기사 분께서 오후 5시까지 주문품을 전달해 주실 것으로 예상하고 계십니다. 괜찮으신가요?
>
> 재니스 심즈 [오후 3:55] 오늘은 곧 퇴근해야 하지만, 90 저희 안내 담당 직원이 배송 물품을 받아 놓을 수 있을 거예요.
>
> 밥 보우반 [오후 3:55] 좋습니다. 제가 내일 아침에 이메일로 확인서를 보내 드리겠습니다.

어휘 **make an order** 주문하다(= place an order) **access** ~에 접속하다, ~을 이용하다 **details** 상세 정보, 세부 사항 **cardstock** 카드스톡(인쇄 용지의 하나) **be supposed to do** ~하기로 되어 있다, ~할 예정이다, ~해야 하다 **absolutely** (강한 긍정) 물론입니다, 당연합니다 **invite A to do** A에게 ~하도록 요청하다 **find out** ~을 알아내다, ~을 파악하다 **what's going on** 무슨 일인지, 어떻게 되어가고 있는지 **it appears that** ~인 것으로 보이다, ~인 것 같다 **break down** 고장 나다 **complete** ~을 완료하다 **on time** 제때 **have A to B** A를 B에게 전달하다 **leave for the day** 퇴근하다 **receptionist** 안내 담당 직

---

87. 심즈 씨가 왜 파인 페이퍼 주식회사에 연락하는가?
(A) 용지에 대한 할인을 요청하기 위해
(B) 용지 제품과 관련해 더 알아보기 위해
(C) 빠진 주문품에 관해 파악하기 위해
(D) 용지 제품을 구입하기 위해

정답 (C)

해설 심즈 씨가 3시 43분에 작성한 메시지에 지난주에 주문한 용지 제품과 관련해 도와 달라고(help me with a paper order I made last week) 요청하고 있으며, 3시 47분 메시지에 그 주문품을 아직 받지 못한(The order was supposed to be delivered yesterday, but I haven't received it) 사실을 알리는 말도 쓰여 있다. 이 메시지들을 통해 빠진 주문품과 관련해 알아보는 상황임을 알 수 있으므로 (C)가 정답이다.

어휘 **ask for** ~을 요청하다 **learn more about** ~에 관해 더 알아보다 **missing** 빠진, 없는, 사라진

---

88. 오후 3시 48분에, 보우반 씨가 "Absolutely"라고 쓸 때 무엇을 의미하는가?
(A) 심즈 씨의 제안을 고려할 것이다.
(B) 빠른 배송을 보장할 수 있다.
(C) 배송품의 위치를 확인해주고 있다.
(D) 기꺼이 심즈 씨를 도울 것이다.

정답 (D)

해설 심즈 씨가 3시 47분에 도와줄 수 있는지(Can you help?) 묻자, 보우반 씨가 "Absolutely"라고 대답하면서 배송 관리 책임자에게 채팅방에 입장하도록 요청하겠다고(I'll invite the shipping manager to join the chat) 알리고 있다. 이는 심즈 씨를 돕기 위한 조치에 해당되는 것으로 볼 수 있으므로 (D)가 정답이다.

어휘 **suggestion** 제안, 의견 **guarantee** ~을 보장하다 **package** 배송품, 소포, 포장물 **be willing to do** 기꺼이 ~하다, ~할 의향이 있다

---

89. 배송 기사가 언제 심즈 씨의 직장에 도착할 것으로 예상되는가?
(A) 5분 후에
(B) 약 1시간 후에
(C) 오전에
(D) 내일 오후에

정답 (B)

해설 디미트로프 씨가 3시 54분에 작성한 메시지에 배송 기사가 오후 5시까지 주문품을 전달할 것으로 예상하고 있다는(The driver expects to have your order to you by 5:00 P.M) 말이 쓰여 있다. 이는 메시지 작성 시간 기준으로 약 1시간 후에 해당되는 시점이므로 (B)가 정답이다.

어휘 **arrive** 도착하다 **in + 시간** ~ 후에

---

90. 심즈 씨가 제안된 배송 조치와 관련해 무슨 말을 하는가?

(A) 자신의 사무실이 오후 5시까지 문을 닫을 것이다.
(B) 한 직원이 배송품을 받을 것이다.
(C) 기사가 더 빨리 도착하기를 원하고 있다.
(D) 다른 곳에서 기사를 만날 것이다.

정답 (B)

해설 심즈 씨가 3시 55분에 작성한 메시지에 자신은 곧 퇴근하지만 안내 담당 직원이 배송 물품을 받아 놓을 수 있을 거라고(our receptionist will be able to take the delivery) 알리고 있으므로 (B)가 정답이다.

어휘 suggested 제안된 arrangement 조치, 마련, 조정 by (기한) ~까지 want A to do A가 ~하기를 원하다

91-95.

> **오크라 코퍼레이션 - 주말의 모험 행사**
> 5월 16일 토요일과 5월 17일 일요일에, 전 직원이 우리 오크라 코퍼레이션의 94 연례 주말의 모험 행사에 참가하기 위해 러너 캠프장으로 떠날 것입니다. 이는 해마다 5월에 개최되는 흥미로운 행사로서, 91 우리 회사의 전 직원 사이에서 소통과 교류를 향상시키는 것을 목적으로 합니다. 이전의 행사들이 팀원들 간의 관계를 강화하는 데 있어 대단히 효과적이었습니다.
>
> **숙소/식사**
> 모든 행사 참석자들은 러너 캠프장에 자리잡고 있는 대형 오두막에서 머무를 것입니다. 각 오두막은 10~12명 사이의 인원을 93 수용합니다. 92(C) 아침과 점심, 그리고 저녁 식사가 직원들에게 추가 비용 없이 제공될 것입니다.
>
> **활동**
> 여러 가지 단체 및 개인 활동이 진행될 것입니다. 여기에는 축구와 배구, 피구, 카약, 그리고 수상 스키가 포함될 것입니다. 92(D) 우승 팀들에게 트로피와 보상이 제공됩니다. 매일 특별 손님께서 진행하시는 92(A) 영감을 주는 강연으로 하루가 마무리될 것입니다. 어느 부서장님이시든 이 행사를 진행하는 데 도움을 주실 의향이 있으신 분은 총무부의 니나 시먼스 씨에게 연락하시기 바랍니다.

어휘 participate in ~에 참가하다 take place (일, 행사 등이) 개최되다, 일어나다, 발생되다 be intended to do ~하는 것을 목적으로 하다, ~하기 위한 것이다 interaction 교류, 상호 작용 previous 이전의, 과거의 effective 효과적인 strengthen ~을 강화하다 situated at ~에 자리잡고 있는, ~에 위치한 accommodate ~을 수용하다 expense 지출 (비용), 경비 reward 보상, 상 inspirational 영감을 주는 be willing to do ~할 의향이 있다, 기꺼이 ~하다 coordinate ~의 진행을 책임지다, ~을 편성하다

수신: 니나 시먼스 <nsimmons@okracorp.net>
발신: 그랜트 우드 <gwood@okracorp.net>
제목: 주말의 모험 행사
날짜: 4월 27일

안녕하세요, 니나 씨,

이곳 마케팅부에 있는 모든 직원이 다음 달에 있을 주말의 모험 행사를 정말로 고대하고 있습니다. 자원해서 행사 진행 담당자가 될 사람이 필요하다고 언급하셨는데, 경험 부족에도 불구하고, 제가 해 보고 싶습니다.

분명 아시겠지만, 94 제가 지난번 주말의 모험 행사에 참석하진 않았는데, 당시에는 아직 회사에 입사하지 않았기 때문입니다. 따라서, 전화 통신 판매 사무실에서 우리와 함께 하실 예정인 분들에 대한 95 직원 기록을 저에게 전송해 주실 수 있다면 감사하겠습니다. 러너 캠프장에서 처음으로 만나기 전에 적어도 제가 그분들의 이름과 얼굴, 그리고 직책을 알고 있으면 좋을 것 같습니다.

곧 연락 주시기를 바랍니다.

그랜트

어휘 look forward to ~을 고대하다 mention that ~라고 언급하다 coordinator 진행 책임자, 편성 담당자 despite ~에도 불구하고 lack 부족, 결핍 present 참석한, 있는 therefore 따라서, 그러므로 would appreciate it if ~한다면 감사할 것이다 forward v. ~을 전송하다 at least 적어도, 최소한 position 직책, 일자리

91. 공지 내용에 따르면, 행사의 목적은 무엇인가?
(A) 업체로 신규 고객을 끌어들이는 것
(B) 직원들에게 추가 교육을 제공하는 것
(C) 회사에 입사하는 신입 사원을 환영하는 것
(D) 직원들 사이에서 팀워크를 장려하는 것

정답 (D)

해설 첫 지문 첫 단락에 행사의 목적으로 전 직원 사이에서 소통과 교류를 향상시키는 것을 목적으로 한다고 알리면서 과거의 행사들이 팀원들 간의 관계를 강화하는 데 대단히 효과적이었다는 사실을(is intended to improve communication and interaction between all of our workers. ~ extremely effective in strengthening relationships between team members) 언급하고 있다. 이는 직원들의 팀워크를 장려하는 것이 목적임을 알리는 말이므로 (D)가 정답이다.

어휘 attract ~을 끌어들이다 new recruit 신입 사원 encourage ~을 장려하다, ~을 권장하다

92. 행사에서 있을 것으로 예상되지 않는 일은 무엇인가?
(A) 동기를 부여하는 연설이 진행될 것이다.
(B) 음악 공연이 열릴 것이다.
(C) 무료 식사가 제공될 것이다.
(D) 최고의 팀들에게 상품이 수여될 것이다.

정답 (B)

전송해 줄 수 있다면 감사할 것이라는(I would appreciate it if you could forward me the employee records) 말로 요청 사항을 언급하고 있으므로 (C)가 정답이다.

어휘 **directions** 길 안내 **location** 장소, 지점, 위치 **contact details** 연락처

96-100.

www.circusofbeijing.com/home			
홈	회원	투어 날짜	입장권

서커스 오브 베이징은 공중 그네 예술가에서부터 쿵푸 달인에 이르기까지 그 공연에 있어 아주 다양한 특별 요소들을 포함합니다. 서커스 주요 공연자들은 모두 고도로 훈련 받은 중국인 곡예사들이며, **96** 순 한차오 씨는 자국 내에서 가장 널리 알려져 있으면서 많은 존경을 받는 공연자들 중 한 명입니다. 다가오는 6월 17일부터 6월 27일까지 펼쳐지는 저희 영국 투어 공연들은 저희 단체의 수석 예술 코디네이터이신 양 텡롱 씨에 의해 연출될 것이며, **97** 몽골의 작곡가 타미르 알타산 씨의 열렬한 오케스트라 음악 작품이 동반됩니다.

2007년에 가오 지펭 씨에 의해 설립된 이후로, 서커스 오브 베이징은 페루와 핀란드만큼 멀리 떨어진 국가와 120개가 넘는 도시에서 공연을 제공해 왔습니다. 저희 단체의 공연자들과 운영 관리팀은 수년 동안에 걸쳐 다수의 상을 수상한 바 있습니다. 가장 주목할 만한 것은, **99** 리아오 리셍 씨께서 숨이 멎을 듯한 레이저 및 불빛 공연으로 **98** 인정 받으시면서 작년에 파블로프 우수상을 수상한 것이었습니다.

어휘 **specialty** 특별함, 특수함 **act** (공연) 요소 **trapeze** 공중 그네 **principal** 주요한 **highly trained** 고도로 훈련 받은 **acrobat** 곡예사 **highly respected** 많은 존경을 받는 **upcoming** 다가오는, 곧 있을 **direct** (공연 등) ~을 연출하다, 감독하다 **accompanied by** ~을 동반한 **composer** 작곡가 **rousing** 열렬한 **orchestral score** 오케스트라 음악 작품 **far-flung** 멀리 떨어진 **most notably** 가장 주목할 만하게 **be recognized for** ~로 인정 받다 **breathtaking** 숨이 멎을 듯한 **be presented with** ~을 받다, 제공 받다

보도 자료용
연락 담당자: 장 리우
zhangliu@beijingcircus.com

(6월 6일) - 곧 있을 저희 서커스 오브 베이징 영국 투어의 모든 공연 날짜가 발표된 지 불과 며칠 만에 매진되었기 때문에, 저희 공연 단체에서 수요를 충족하기 위해 별도로 4일의 날짜를 추가 하기로 결정했습니다. 이번 투어는 애초에 6월 17일에 버밍엄에서 시작해 6월 27일에 런던에서 종료될 예정이었지만, 이제 7월 4일까지 지속될 것입니다. 아래에서 추가 날짜를 확인해 보시기 바랍니다.

해설 첫 지문 세 번째 단락에 영감을 주는 강연으로 하루를 마무리한다는(inspirational talk by a special guest) 부분에서 (A)를, 두 번째 단락에 아침과 점심, 그리고 저녁 식사가 직원들에게 추가 비용 없이 제공될 것이라는(Breakfast, lunch, and dinner will be provided at no extra expense to staff) 부분에서 (C)를, 세 번째 단락에 우승 팀들에게 트로피와 보상이 제공된다는(Winning teams will be given trophies and rewards) 부분에서 (D)를 확인할 수 있다. 하지만 음악 공연과 관련된 정보는 제시되어 있지 않으므로 (B)가 정답이다.

어휘 **motivational** 동기를 부여하는 **complimentary** 무료의 **award** ~을 수여하다, ~을 주다

93. 공지에서, 두 번째 단락, 두 번째 줄의 단어 "accommodates"와 의미가 가장 가까운 것은 무엇인가?

(A) 머무르다
(B) 보관하다
(C) **수용하다**
(D) 나르다

정답 (C)

해설 해당 문장에서 동사 accommodates 앞뒤에 위치한 주어 Each cabin과 between 10 and 12 individuals는 각각 오두막과 인원수를 나타낸다. 따라서 오두막이 그 정도의 인원을 수용한다는 의미임을 알 수 있으므로 '수용하다'를 뜻하는 (C) hold가 정답이다.

94. 우드 씨와 관련해 유추할 수 있는 것은 무엇인가?

(A) 회사 야유회를 준비하는 데 경험이 많다.
(B) 시먼스 씨와 같은 부서에서 근무한다.
(C) 전화 통신 판매를 했던 경력이 있다.
(D) **오크라 사에서 근무한지 일년이 채 되지 않았다.**

정답 (D)

해설 두 번째 지문 두 번째 단락에 지난번 주말의 모험 행사에 참석하지 않은 사실과 함께 당시에 아직 입사하지 않은 상태였다고(I wasn't present at the previous Adventure Weekend because I hadn't yet joined the company at that time) 알리는 말이 쓰여 있다. 이와 관련해, 첫 지문 첫 단락에 이 행사가 해마다 열리는 행사라는(annual Adventure Weekend) 말이 쓰여 있어 우드 씨가 1년 전에 같은 행사가 열린 뒤에 입사했다는 사실을 알 수 있으므로 (D)가 정답이다.

어휘 **experienced** 경험 많은 **outing** 야유회 **background** 경력, 배경

95. 우드 씨가 요청하는 것은 무엇인가?

(A) 행사 장소로 가는 길 안내 정보
(B) 행사 활동들을 담은 일정표
(C) **직원들에 관한 정보**
(D) 시먼스 씨의 연락처

정답 (C)

해설 두 번째 지문 두 번째 단락에 행사에 참석할 예정인 직원 기록을

날짜	위치	장소
6월 28일	에든버러	머레이 브리지 경기장
6월 30일	뉴캐슬	윌크스 컨벤션 센터
7월 2일	100 맨체스터	100 소프 시티 파크
7월 4일	요크	노덤 컨벤션 센터

어휘 sell out 매진되다 add ~을 추가하다 extra 별도의
meet demand 수요를 충족하다

수신: 그랜트 무어 <gmoore@epco.com>
발신: 데비 도날드슨 <ddonaldson@epco.com>
날짜: 6월 28일
제목: 서커스 오브 베이징 공연

그랜트 씨께,

제가 아까 로드 씨와 이야기하고 있었는데, 100 저희 둘 모두 금요일에 소프 시티 파크에서 열리는 서커스 오브 베이징 공연을 보러 가고 싶어하는 것으로 결정되었습니다. 저희와 함께 가시겠어요? 100 이 공원이 사무실에서 불과 몇 블록 밖에 되지 않는 곳에 있어서, 저희 계획은 퇴근 후에 택시를 타고 빨리 가는 것입니다. 제가 듣기로는 행사장에 핫도그 및 버거 판매대가 많이 있기 때문에, 저녁 식사를 위해 다른 곳에 들르지 않아도 됩니다.

저는 이 공연이 요즘 전 세계에서 가장 인상적인 서커스 공연이라고 들었습니다. 실제로, 공연자들 외에, 이 서커스는 가장 놀라운 레이저 쇼를 포함할 예정입니다. 99 제가 최근에 <글로벌 익스피리언스 매거진>에서 그 모든 조명 효과를 만들어내는 일을 책임지고 있는 남자분에 관한 기사를 읽었습니다. 장관을 이루는 쇼가 될 겁니다! 관심 있으신지 알려 주세요.

데비

어휘 fancy -ing ~하고 싶다 leave work 퇴근하다 stand 판매대 stop off ~에 들르다 impressive 인상적인 apart from ~ 외에(도) be supposed to do ~할 예정이다, ~하기로 되어 있다 light effects 조명 효과 spectacular 장관을 이루는

96. 순 한차오 씨에 관해 언급된 것은 무엇인가?
   (A) 서커스 오브 베이징의 설립자들 중 한 명이었다.
   (B) 중국에서 최고의 곡예사들 중 한 명으로 여겨지고 있다.
   (C) 작년에 우수상을 받았다.
   (D) 서커스 공연 연출을 책임지고 있다.

정답 (B)

해설 첫 지문 첫 단락에 순 한차오 씨를 자국 내에서 가장 널리 알려져 있으면서 많은 존경을 받는 공연자들 중 한 명이라고 (Sun Hanchao being one of the most widely known and highly respected performers in his home country) 소개하고 있으므로 (B)가 정답이다.

어휘 be regarded as ~로 여겨지다

97. 곧 있을 서커스 오브 베이징 투어에 관해 언급된 것은 무엇인가?
   (A) 애초에 예정된 것보다 약 일주일 늦게 시작될 것이다.
   (B) 그 단체가 120개가 넘는 도시를 이동해야 할 것이다.
   (C) 핀란드와 페루에서 진행되는 여러 공연을 포함할 것이다.
   (D) 몽골의 작곡가가 쓴 음악을 특징으로 할 것이다.

정답 (D)

해설 첫 지문 첫 단락에 몽골의 작곡가 타미르 알타산 씨의 열렬한 오케스트라 음악 작품이 동반된다고(accompanied by Mongolian composer Tamir Altasan's rousing orchestral score) 쓰여 있으므로 (D)가 정답이다.

어휘 than originally scheduled 애초에 예정된 것보다 feature ~을 특징으로 하다, 포함하다

98. 웹 페이지에서, 두 번째 단락, 세 번째 줄의 단어 "recognized"와 의미가 가장 가까운 것은 무엇인가?
   (A) 설명된
   (B) 영예를 얻은
   (C) 간략히 말한
   (D) 특징을 이룬

정답 (B)

해설 해당 문장에서 recognized 뒤에 이유를 나타내는 전치사구가 있고, 상을 받았다는 사실이 함께 제시되어 있다. 따라서 레이저 및 불빛 공연으로 상을 받은 것에 대해 인정 받았다는 뜻을 나타내기 위해 recognized가 쓰였음을 알 수 있으며, 이는 영예를 얻는 것과 같은 의미이므로 (B) honored가 정답이다.

99. 도날드슨 씨는 한 잡지 기사에서 누구에 관해 읽었는가?
   (A) 양 텡롱
   (B) 타미르 알타산
   (C) 가오 지펭
   (D) 리아오 리셍

정답 (D)

해설 세 번째 지문 두 번째 단락에 최근에 <글로벌 익스피리언스 매거진>에서 모든 조명 효과를 만들어내는 일을 책임지고 있는 남자에 관한 기사를 읽었다고(I read about the man responsible for creating all the light effects in Global Experience Magazine recently) 알리고 있다. 이는 첫 지문 두 번째 단락에서 레이저 및 불빛 공연으로 상을 받은 리아오 리셍 씨를(Liao Lisheng was recognized for his breathtaking laser and light show) 가리키는 것이므로 (D)가 정답이다.

100. 도날드슨 씨의 직장은 어디에 있을 것 같은가?
   (A) 에든버러에
   (B) 뉴캐슬에
   (C) 맨체스터에
   (D) 요크에

정답 (C)

해설 세 번째 지문 첫 단락에 금요일에 소프 시티 파크에서 열리는 서커스 오브 베이징 공연을 보러 가고 싶어하는 것으로 결정된(we both decided we'd like to go and see the Circus of Beijing at Thorpe City Park on Friday) 사실이 언급되어 있고, 또한 소프 시티 파크가 사무실에서 불과 몇 블럭 밖에 되지 않는 곳에 있다고(The park is only a few blocks from the office) 언급되어 있다. 그리고 두 번째 지문의 표에서 소프 시티 파크는 맨체스터에 있는 것으로(July 2, Manchester, Thorpe City Park) 쓰여 있으므로 (C)가 정답이다.

시원스쿨 LAB

LC

1. (B)	**2.** (A)	**3.** (B)	**4.** (B)	**5.** (B)
6. (C)	**7.** (B)	**8.** (A)	**9.** (A)	**10.** (A)
11. (C)	**12.** (C)	**13.** (C)	**14.** (C)	**15.** (C)
16. (A)	**17.** (A)	**18.** (A)	**19.** (A)	**20.** (C)
21. (B)	**22.** (A)	**23.** (D)	**24.** (B)	**25.** (A)
26. (D)	**27.** (B)	**28.** (D)	**29.** (A)	**30.** (C)
31. (B)	**32.** (B)	**33.** (C)	**34.** (C)	**35.** (B)
36. (A)	**37.** (C)	**38.** (B)	**39.** (D)	**40.** (C)
41. (A)	**42.** (B)	**43.** (D)	**44.** (B)	**45.** (A)
46. (B)	**47.** (C)	**48.** (C)	**49.** (A)	**50.** (D)

RC

51. (A)	**52.** (C)	**53.** (C)	**54.** (A)	**55.** (A)
56. (B)	**57.** (B)	**58.** (A)	**59.** (B)	**60.** (A)
61. (D)	**62.** (B)	**63.** (D)	**64.** (D)	**65.** (C)
66. (A)	**67.** (D)	**68.** (B)	**69.** (D)	**70.** (C)
71. (D)	**72.** (D)	**73.** (B)	**74.** (A)	**75.** (C)
76. (D)	**77.** (C)	**78.** (B)	**79.** (D)	**80.** (C)
81. (A)	**82.** (B)	**83.** (D)	**84.** (C)	**85.** (D)
86. (C)	**87.** (D)	**88.** (B)	**89.** (B)	**90.** (A)
91. (A)	**92.** (A)	**93.** (B)	**94.** (C)	**95.** (B)
96. (B)	**97.** (C)	**98.** (C)	**99.** (D)	**100.** (D)

Part 1

1. (A) A woman is sipping from a cup.
(B) A woman is taking some notes.
(C) A woman is typing on a laptop.
(D) A woman is looking at a mobile phone.

(A) 여자가 컵으로 조금씩 마시고 있다.
(B) 여자가 필기를 하고 있다.
(C) 여자가 노트북 컴퓨터에 타이핑을 하고 있다.
(D) 여자가 휴대폰을 보고 있다.

해설 (A) 컵으로 마시고 있지 않으므로 오답.
(B) 노트에 뭔가를 쓰고 있으므로 정답.
(C) 타이핑을 하고 있는 모습이 아니므로 오답.
(D) 휴대폰을 보고 있지 않으므로 오답.

어휘 **sip** 음료를 조금씩 마시다 **take notes** 필기를 하다

2. **(A) A sidewalk runs along the street.**
(B) Some lampposts are being fixed.
(C) A path is being paved with bricks.
(D) Pedestrians are crossing at an intersection.

(A) 인도가 도로를 따라 이어지고 있다.
(B) 몇몇 가로등이 수리되는 중이다.
(C) 길이 벽돌로 포장되고 있다.
(D) 보행자들이 교차로에서 도로를 건너고 있다.

해설 (A) 인도(sidewalk)가 도로를 따라 나 있는 모습을 묘사한 정답.
(B) 가로등을 수리 중인 모습은 보이지 않으므로 오답.
(C) 길은 이미 포장되어 있으므로 오답.
(D) 보행자나 교차로가 보이지 않으므로 오답.

어휘 **sidewalk** 인도, 보도 **run** (길 등이) 이어지다, 연결되다 **along** ~을 따라 **lamppost** 가로등 **pave** (길 등을) 포장하다 **pedestrian** 보행자 **cross** 길을 건너다 **intersection** 교차로

Part 2

3. How did Monica react when her architecture design won the award?

(A) Everyone plans to go.
(B) She was extremely pleased.
(C) At a ceremony downtown.

모니카 씨는 자신의 건축 디자인이 상을 받았을 때 어떻게 반응했나요?
(A) 모든 사람들이 갈 계획입니다.
(B) 아주 기뻐했어요.
(C) 시내에서 열린 축하 행사에서요.

해설 방법/상태를 묻는 How의문문이다. 동사 react와 함께 상을 받은 후의 반응을 묻고 있으므로 대명사 She 및 감정 표현으로 답변하는 (B)가 정답이다. (A)는 질문의 Monica가 아닌 다른 사람을 언급하고 있고, (C)는 장소 표현이므로 Where 의문문에 어울리는 답변이다.

어휘 **react** 반응하다 **architecture** 건축 **win an award** 상을 받다 **extremely** 아주 **pleased** 기뻐하는 **ceremony** 축하 행사 **downtown** 시내에서

4. I wonder where the new storage room is.

(A) The room is not large enough.
(B) It's right next to the old one.
(C) For storing all our supplies.

새 창고가 어디에 있는지 궁금하네요.
(A) 방이 충분히 크지 않아요.
(B) 예전 창고 바로 옆에 있어요.
(C) 우리의 모든 비품들을 보관하기 위해서요.

해설 평서문의 형태를 취하고 있지만 새 창고가 어디에 있는지를 묻는 Where 의문문이다. 문장 중간에 위치한 where를 놓치지 말아야 한다. 이에 대해 예전 창고 바로 옆에 있다며 그 위치를 알려주는 (B)가 정답이다. (A)와 (C)는 storage room과 관련 있는 내용으로 혼동을 유도한 오답이다.

어휘 **storage room** 창고 **right next to** ~ 바로 옆에 **store** ~을 저장하다, 보관하다 **supplies** 자재, 비품

5. What should I bring to the orientation?
(A) It was more difficult than I expected.
(B) Why don't you e-mail them and check?
(C) In the training center.

오리엔테이션에 무엇을 가져가야 하죠?
(A) 제가 예상한 것보다 더 어려웠어요.
(B) 그쪽에 이메일을 보내서 확인해 보는 게 어때요?
(C) 교육 센터에서요.

해설 What, bring to the orientation을 꼭 들어야 한다. 오리엔테이션에 무엇을 가져가야 하는지를 묻는 질문이므로 가져가야 할 물품을 말해주는 대신 전화해서 확인해 보라고 권하는 (B)가 가장 자연스러운 응답이다. (A)는 orientation만 듣고 어땠냐는 질문으로 착각하면 고를 수 있는 오답이다. (C)는 의문사를 제대로 듣지 못하고 orientation이 열리는 장소를 묻는 질문으로 착각할 경우 고를 수 있는 오답이다.

어휘 **bring** ~을 가져가다[오다] **expect** ~을 기대하다, 예상하다

6. How much is this going to cost after tax?
(A) We take cash or credit card for your convenience.
(B) Yes, that includes 15% sales tax.
(C) Let me get out my calculator to find out.

세금 공제하고 난 후 이게 얼마쯤 될까요?
(A) 저희는 여러분의 편의를 위해 현금이나 신용카드를 받습니다.
(B) 네, 그건 15%의 판매세를 포함하고 있습니다.
(C) 제가 계산기를 꺼내 알아보겠습니다.

해설 How much, cost가 핵심어이다. 세금 공제 후 가격이 얼마인지 묻는 질문이므로 가격을 말해주는 대답을 예상할 수 있으나, 정작 답은 계산기로 알아보겠다는 (C)이다. 질문에 대한 직접적인 대답을 하지 않고 알아보겠다며 우회적으로 답하는 전형적인 유형이다.

어휘 **cost** (비용이) ~가 들다, ~이다 **cash** 현금 **for one's convenience** ~의 편의를 위해 **include** ~을 포함하다 **sales tax** 판매세 **get out** ~을 꺼내다 **find out** 알아보다, 알아내다

7. Why didn't you locate the file I asked you for?
(A) No, I'm afraid she didn't.
(B) Actually I did, but I forgot to bring it.
(C) You should've left it up to me.

제가 요청 드린 파일을 왜 찾지 못하셨나요?
(A) 아뇨, 그녀가 안 했어요.
(B) 사실 찾았는데, 가져오는 걸 깜빡했어요.
(C) 그걸 제게 맡겨 주셨어야 했는데요.

해설 파일을 찾지 못한 이유를 묻는 Why 의문문이다. 그 이유를 밝히는 응답을 예상하겠지만 막상 정답은 '찾았는데 가져오는 걸 깜빡했다'고 말하는 (B)이다. Part 2의 난이도 높은 문제 유형으로, 질문에 대한 직접적인 응답이 아니라 상황에 맞는 다른 제 3의 내용이 정답이 되는 경우이다.

어휘 **locate** ~의 정확한 위치를 찾아내다 **I'm afraid (that)** 유감이지만 ~이다 **should have p.p.** ~했어야 했다 **leave A up to B** A를 B에게 맡기다

8. Why don't you come over after lunch to check out the renovations?
(A) I probably won't arrive until 3.
(B) I don't mind where we eat.
(C) The check-out time is 12, I believe.

점심 식사 후에 오셔서 개조 상태를 확인해 보시겠어요?
(A) 저는 아마 3시나 되어야 도착할 것 같습니다.
(B) 어디서 먹든 상관없습니다.
(C) 체크아웃 시간이 12시인 걸로 알고 있습니다.

해설 일정 시점에 올 것을 제안하고 있으므로 수락하거나 거절하는 대답이 와야 한다. 이때 직접적으로 Yes/No를 쓰기보다는 다른 말로 돌려서 수락이나 거절의 표현을 하는 선택지가 정답으로 잘 나온다. (A)가 그러한 경우로, '3시 전에는 갈 수 없을 것 같다'는 말로 제안에 대해 완곡한 거절의 의미를 전달하고 있다.

어휘 **come over** (말하는 이가 있는 쪽으로) 오다 **check out** ~을 확인하다 **renovation** 개조(공사) **probably not A until B** B가 되어서야 A하다 **I don't mind + 명사절** ~이든지 상관없다, ~에 대해 신경 쓰지 않는다

9. Has Mr. Roy reviewed the contract with the food company?
(A) He hasn't had a chance yet.
(B) The view is lovely.
(C) I'll get the ingredients.

식품회사와 맺은 계약서를 로이 씨가 검토했나요?
(A) 그는 아직 그럴 기회가 없었어요.
(B) 경치가 멋지네요.
(C) 제가 음식 재료를 구해올게요.

해설 특정 인물의 이름을 언급하며 그 사람이 한 일을 묻는 조동사 의문문이므로 No를 생략하고 대명사 he와 함께 '그럴 기회가 없었다'라는 말로 부정의 의미를 나타내는 (A)가 정답이다. (B)

는 review와 일부 발음이 비슷한 view를 이용한 오답이다. (C)는 food에서 연상 가능한 ingredients(재료)를 이용한 오답이다.

어휘 **review** ~을 검토하다 **contract** 계약(서) **view** 경치, 경관 **lovely** 멋진, 아름다운 **ingredient** 재료, 원료

10. Doesn't the library close at around 3 today?

(A) No, just on Sundays.
(B) Actually, it's quite far.
(C) I will go there just after 4.

도서관이 오늘 3시쯤에 문을 닫지 않나요?
(A) 아뇨, 일요일에만 그래요.
(B) 사실, 꽤 멀어요.
(C) 저는 4시가 넘는 대로 그리 갈게요.

해설 도서관이 문 닫는 시간을 확인하는 부정 의문문인데, not을 빼고 긍정형 문장으로 해석해야 쉽다. 3시에 문을 닫는지 묻고 있으므로, No와 함께 일요일에만 그렇다는 말로 질문자가 알고 있는 정보가 잘못되었음을 나타내는 (A)가 정답이다.

어휘 **at around 3** 3시쯤에 **quite** 꽤, 상당히

11. Would you like me to pick up your clothes at the cleaner's on my way home?

(A) It's hard to pick one out.
(B) Yes, twice before.
(C) Only if you have time.

집으로 가는 길에 제가 세탁소에서 당신 옷을 찾아올까요?
(A) 하나를 고르기가 정말 어렵네요.
(B) 네, 전에 두 번이요.
(C) 시간이 있으실 경우에만요.

해설 Would you like me to ~?로 묻고 있으므로 제안/요청 의문문이다. 뒤에 이어지는 표현에서 옷을 대신 찾아가는 것에 대해 묻고 있음을 알 수 있으므로 '시간이 있을 경우에'라는 조건을 내세워 긍정의 의미를 나타내는 (C)가 정답이다. (A)는 질문의 동사 pick을 반복한 함정이고, (B)는 Yes로 대답하지만 미래의 일에 대해 제안을 하는 질문과 달리 과거에 있었던 일에 대한 횟수를 언급하는 대답이므로 의미 관계가 적절하지 않다.

어휘 **pick up** ~을 가져가다[오다] **the cleaner's** 세탁소 **on one's way home** 집으로 가는 길에 **it is hard to do** ~하기 어렵다 **pick out** ~을 고르다, 선택하다 **only if** ~할 경우에만

12. Can you give me a lift home from work today?

(A) Go ahead and ask her yourself.
(B) I've had back pain since moving day.
(C) I'd love to, but my car is in the shop.

오늘 회사에서 집까지 저를 차로 태워주실 수 있으신가요?
(A) 얼른 가셔서 그녀에게 직접 물어보세요.
(B) 이사한 날 이후로 요통이 생겼어요.

(C) 저도 그러고 싶지만, 제 차가 수리소에 있어요.

해설 give ~ a lift는 차로 누군가를 태워다 주는 것을 의미하며, 상대방에게 그것이 가능한지를 묻는 질문이므로 정중히 거절할 때 사용하는 I'd love to but과 함께 그 이유를 언급하는 (C)가 정답이다. (A)는 질문과 관계없는 her에 대해 이야기하고 있으므로 어울리지 않는 반응이다. (B)는 lift와 home에서 연상 가능한 moving day(이사일)를 이용한 오답이다.

어휘 **give A a lift home** A를 차로 집까지 태워 주다 **go ahead** 어서 ~하세요 **oneself** (부사적으로) 직접 **back pain** 허리통증, 요통 **moving** 이사

13. I'd like to rent some camera equipment.

(A) Your rent is overdue by three days.
(B) I don't remember seeing your pictures.
(C) I'll get a customer service representative.

카메라 장비를 대여했으면 합니다.
(A) 집세 내는 날이 3일 지나셨어요.
(B) 당신의 사진을 본 기억이 없어요.
(C) 고객 서비스 담당 직원을 불러 드리겠습니다.

해설 장비 대여를 요청하는 내용으로, 대여에 대해 논의하도록 담당 직원을 불러주겠다고 알리는 (C)가 적절한 반응이다. (A)는 rent가 반복된 선택지로, 여기서 rent는 집세를 뜻하며 이미 기한이 지난 것에 대해 이야기하고 있어 대화 상황에 어울리지 않는다. (B)는 camera에서 연상 가능한 pictures를 이용한 오답으로 장비 대여와는 전혀 상관 없는 내용이다.

어휘 **I'd like to do** ~하고 싶습니다 **rent** v. ~을 대여하다 n. 집세, 임차료 **overdue** 기한이 지난 **remember -ing** ~한 것을 기억하다 **customer service representative** 고객 서비스 담당 직원

14. I think we should reschedule for a later date so that more people will show up.

(A) We can discuss who's going to be in charge later.
(B) I didn't expect such a large turnout, either.
(C) Sure. How about two weeks from today?

제 생각엔 더 많은 사람들이 올 수 있도록 일정을 나중으로 재조정해야 해요.
(A) 나중에 누가 책임자가 될 지 논의해 봐요.
(B) 저도 그렇게 많은 수의 참가자를 기대하진 않았어요.
(C) 좋아요. 오늘부터 2주 후가 어떠세요?

해설 I think we should ~라는 표현을 통해 제안을 나타내는 말인데, 일정을 나중으로 재조정하자는 내용이므로 그에 해당하는 구체적 시점을 다시 제안하는 (C)가 적절한 대답이다. (A)는 later가 반복된 오답으로 일정 조정이 아닌 책임자에 대해 말하는 내용이어서 어울리지 않는다. (B)에서 turnout은 '참가자의 수'를 의미하므로 more people과 연관성 있게 들릴 수도 있지만 과거 시점의 일에 대해 말하고 있어 어울리지 않는 반응이다.

어휘 **reschedule** (일정 등) ~을 재조정하다 **so that** (목적) ~ 할 수 있도록 **show up** 나타나다 **in charge** 담당하는 **turnout** 참가자 수

15. When do you plan to have lunch today?
(A) No, it was yesterday.
(B) How about the bakery?
(C) As soon as I'm done with this report.

오늘 언제 점심 식사를 하실 계획이세요?
(A) 아뇨, 그건 어제였어요.
(B) 제과점은 어때요?
(C) 이 보고서를 완료하는 대로요.

해설 때를 묻는 When 의문문이므로 As soon as와 함께 대략적인 시점을 나타내는 (C)가 정답이다. (A)는 의문사 의문문에 맞지 않는 No로 답변하는 오답이며, (B)는 시점이 아닌 장소와 관련해 되묻고 있으므로 오답이다.

어휘 **plan to do** ~할 계획이다 **How about ~?** ~는 어때요? **as soon as** ~하는 대로, ~하자마자 **be done with** ~을 완료하다, 끝내다 **report** 보고(서)

16. What's your opinion about the new PR manager?
(A) I think she'll be an asset to us.
(B) I appreciated your suggestions.
(C) She told me the same thing.

새로운 홍보 매니저에 대한 당신의 의견은 어떤가요?
(A) 그녀가 우리에게 꼭 필요한 인재가 될 거라고 생각합니다.
(B) 당신의 제안에 감사드립니다.
(C) 그녀는 같은 것을 말했어요.

해설 What's your opinion ~?은 상대의 의견을 묻는 질문이므로, 자신의 생각을 말하는 (A)가 정답이다. 이와 같은 의미의 질문인 What do you think about ~?도 종종 출제된다. (B)는 opinion(의견)과 관련 있을 법한 어휘인 suggestion(제안)을 이용한 오답이고, (C)는 your opinion을 묻는 질문에 she를 주어로 대답하여 틀렸다.

어휘 **opinion** 의견 **PR manager** 홍보 매니저 cf. PR 홍보 (public relations) **asset** 자산, 인재

17. You need me to pick up more stationery, don't you?
(A) Have we already run out?
(B) No, he didn't pick up when I called.
(C) Yes, they are waiting at the station.

제가 문구용품을 더 가져와야 하죠, 안 그런가요?
(A) 벌써 다 떨어졌어요?
(B) 아뇨, 제가 전화했을 때 그는 받지 않았어요.
(C) 네, 그들이 역에서 기다리고 있어요.

해설 문구용품을 더 가져올지를 묻는 부가 의문문이다. 이에 대한 대답으로 '(문구용품이) 벌써 다 떨어졌나요?'라고 되묻는 (A)가 정답이다. (B)는 pick up을 반복하였지만 전혀 다른 의미로 쓰인 경우이고 (C)는 stationery와 발음이 유사한 station을 이용한 소리 오답이다.

어휘 **pick up** ~을 가져오다[가다], 전화를 받다 **stationery** 문구용품 **run out** (물품 등이) 다 떨어지다

18. Weren't you going to replace that office chair?
(A) I figured I'd just keep it.
(B) No, I tried a different place.
(C) An office furniture store.

그 사무용 의자는 교체하려던 것 아니었어요?
(A) 그냥 사용하기로 했습니다.
(B) 아뇨, 다른 곳에 한 번 가봤어요.
(C) 사무용 가구 매장입니다.

해설 부정어가 포함된 부정 의문문이지만 긍정형으로 문장을 해석한다. 사무실 의자를 교환할지 묻고 있으므로 No를 생략하고 의자를 그냥 갖고 있겠다는 뜻을 나타낸 (A)가 정답이다. (B)는 질문의 replace와 발음이 유사한 place를 이용한 함정이고 (C)는 질문의 office를 반복한 함정이다.

어휘 **replace** ~을 교체하다 **figure (that)** ~라고 생각하다, 판단하다 **try** ~을 시험해 보다, 도전해 보다 **office furniture** 사무용 가구

19. Should I file these financial statements, or do you want to see them?
(A) You can leave them on my desk.
(B) I stayed up late last night with a stack of files.
(C) He said they were.

이 재무제표들을 철해서 보관해 둘까요, 아니면 확인해 보실 건가요?
(A) 제 책상에 놓아 두세요.
(B) 파일 더미와 씨름하느라 어제 밤늦게까지 못 자고 있었어요.
(C) 그가 말하길 그것들이 그러했대요.

해설 서류를 파일로 철해 둘지 확인할 건지 물어보는 선택 의문문이다. 이 중에서 살펴보겠다는 의미로 leave them on my desk라고 달리 표현한 (A)가 적절한 반응이다. (B)는 질문의 file을 반복하였으나 여기에서는 명사로 쓰인 함정이고, (C)는 질문의 핵심과 상관없는 he에 대해 말하고 있어 오답이다.

어휘 **financial statement** 재무제표 **leave A on B** A를 B 위에 놓다, 두다 **stay up late** 늦게까지 자지 않고 있다 **a stack of** ~ 더미

20. Please call me if there's anything urgent while I'm on vacation.

    (A) It's good news for the company.
    (B) Yes, he called me last night.
    (C) Will you have your cell phone with you?

제가 휴가를 떠난 동안 긴급한 일이 생기면 전화주세요.
(A) 회사에게는 좋은 소식이네요.
(B) 네, 그가 어젯밤에 제게 전화했어요.
(C) 휴대전화기를 가지고 계실 건가요?

해설   문제가 있을 경우 전화로 연락 달라는 요청의 뜻을 담고 있으므로 이를 수락하거나 거절하는 답변을 예상할 수 있는데, 그보다는 휴대폰을 가져갈 것인지 되묻는 (C)가 적절한 답변이다.

어휘   **urgent** 긴급한   **on vacation** 휴가 중인

Part 3

Questions 21-23 refer to the following conversation.

M: Hi, Melanie. **21** I just found out that I will be conducting the interviews for the human resources intern position tomorrow instead of Friday. I know we have four candidates coming in, and I was told that you have their résumés and applications. Can you write summaries of all four candidates and make sure they are on my desk before the end of the day?

W: **22** I'm really sorry, but I have to meet with the management today. If you'd like, I can write them when I get home and send them to you by e-mail later tonight. Would that be all right?

M: Yes, that will be fine. **23** I'll have time to go over them either tonight or in the morning before the candidates arrive. Thanks for your help.

남: 안녕하세요, 멜라니 씨. 제가 금요일이 아니라 내일 인사부 인턴직에 지원한 분들과 면접이 있다는 걸 방금 알았어요. 네 명의 후보자가 온다는 것은 알고 있고, 당신이 그들의 이력서와 지원서를 가지고 있다고 들었어요. 네 사람 모두에 대해 간략히 요약을 해서 오늘 안으로 제 책상에 꼭 좀 놓아 줄래요?
여: 정말 죄송하지만, 제가 오늘 경영진 임원들을 만나 뵈어야 합니다. 괜찮으시다면, 제가 집에 가서 작성한 후에 오늘 밤에 이메일로 보내 드릴 수 있습니다. 그렇게 해도 될까요?
남: 네, 괜찮아요. 오늘 밤이나 내일 아침에 지원자들이 도착하기 전에 훑어볼 시간이 있을 거예요. 도와줘서 고마워요.

어휘   **find out that** ~임을 알게 되다   **conduct** ~을 실시하다, 시행하다   **human resources** 인사부   **instead of** ~ 대신에   **candidate** 후보자, 지원자   **be told that** ~라고 듣다

résumé 이력서   **application** 지원(서)   **summary** 요약(본)   **make sure** 꼭 ~하다, 반드시 ~하다   **meet with** (약속하여) ~와 만나다   **management** 경영진   **if you'd like** 괜찮다면   **get home** 집에 가다[오다]   **go over** ~을 살펴보다   **either A or B** A 또는 B 둘 중의 하나

21. 남자에 따르면, 무엇이 바뀌었는가?

    (A) 회사 내 절차
    (B) 면접 날짜
    (C) 구직 지원자들의 수
    (D) 직책에 대한 지원 자격

해설   문제를 읽어 보면 남자의 말에서 변경사항이 언급될 것임을 알 수 있으므로 남자의 말에 집중해야 한다. 남자는 대화를 시작하면서 I just found out that I will be conducting the interviews for the human resources manager position tomorrow instead of Friday라는 말로 면접을 보는 요일이 달라졌음을 말하고 있으므로 (B)가 정답이다.

어휘   **procedure** 절차   **candidate** 후보자   **requirement** 자격 요건

22. 여자는 무슨 문제에 대해 언급하는가?

    (A) 다른 약속이 있다.
    (B) 엉뚱한 장소로 갔다.
    (C) 서류를 둔 곳을 잊어버렸다.
    (D) 어떤 직책에 대해 자격 미달이다.

해설   면접과 관련해 남자가 부탁하는 일을 들은 여자는 I'm really sorry, but I have to meet with the management today라는 말로 이미 선약이 있음을 알리고 있으므로 이를 간단히 줄여 말한 (A)가 정답이다.

어휘   **engagement** 약속   **wrong location** 다른 장소, 엉뚱한 곳   **misplace** ~을 둔 곳을 잊다   **document** 서류, 문서   **underqualified** 자격미달인

Paraphrase   I have to meet with the management → She has another engagement.

23. 남자는 무엇을 할 시간이 있을 것이라고 말하는가?

    (A) 보고서를 쓰는 일
    (B) 취업 박람회에 참석하는 일
    (C) 몇몇 지원자들에게 전화하는 일
    (D) 어떤 정보를 읽어보는 일

해설   대화 마지막 부분에 남자는 여자가 보내주겠다는 파일과 관련해 I'll have time to go over them either tonight or in the morning before the candidates arrive라고 말하고 있다. 파일들을 검토할 시간이 있다고 하므로 이를 다른 말로 바꿔 표현한 (D)가 정답이다.

어휘   **job fair** 취업 박람회   **applicant** 지원자

Paraphrase   go over them → Read some information

Questions 24-26 refer to the following conversation.

W: Hi, William. **24** I heard that you will be handling the orientation session on Wednesday for the new staff that are coming in. How's it going? Can I help you with anything?

M: Well, I'll be running through rules and procedures for most of the afternoon. But, **25** in the morning, I think I might present the new workers to all the company's employees. Then we can take them out to lunch.

W: That's a great idea. Have you thought about taking them to the city center? **26** There are so many good lunch spots there. I can find one for you if you'd like. I know that area really well.

여: 안녕하세요, 윌리엄 씨. 새로 입사하는 신입직원들을 위해 수요일에 열리는 오리엔테이션을 맡는다고 들었어요. 어떻게 되어가나요? 제가 도와줄 일이라도 있나요?

남: 음, 오후 시간에는 대부분 규정과 절차에 대해 이야기할 겁니다. 하지만 오전 시간에는 신입직원들을 사내 전 직원들에게 소개할까 해요. 그리고는 데리고 나가서 점심 식사 하려고요.

여: 좋은 생각이네요. 혹시 시내로 데리고 갈 생각은 해봤나요? 그곳에 가면 점심 먹기 좋은 식당들이 정말 많거든요. 괜찮으면 제가 한 곳 알아볼 수 있어요. 제가 그쪽 지역을 정말 잘 알거든요.

어휘 **handle** ~을 처리하다, 다루다 **How's it going?** 어떻게 되어 가나요? **help A with B** A가 B하는 것을 돕다 **run through** ~을 훑어보다 **procedure** 절차 **present A to B** A를 B에게 소개하다 **take A out to lunch** A를 데리고 나가 점심을 먹다 **spot** 위치, 장소

24. 여자는 무엇에 대해 묻고 있는가?
(A) 절차상의 변화
(B) 직원 오리엔테이션
(C) 직책에 대한 자격 요건
(D) 근무 시작일

해설 여자가 묻는 내용이 무엇인지를 찾는 문제이다. 여자는 대화를 시작하면서 I heard that you will be handling the orientation session on Wednesday for the new staff that are coming in. How's it going?과 같이 신입직원을 대상으로 하는 오리엔테이션을 언급하며 어떻게 되어가고 있는지 묻고 있으므로 (B)가 정답이다.

어휘 **requirement** 자격 요건

25. 남자는 수요일 점심 식사 전에 무엇을 할 것인가?
(A) 신입직원들을 소개한다.
(B) 시내에 간다.

(C) 문서를 나눠준다.
(D) 교육용 동영상을 보여준다.

해설 on Wednesday before lunch가 문제의 핵심이다. 대화를 시작하는 여자의 말에서 수요일은 신입직원 오리엔테이션이 열리는 날임을 먼저 파악해야 하며, 이날 있을 일정과 관련해 남자가 오전에 신입직원들을 다른 이들에게 소개하겠다고(in the morning, I think I might present the new workers to all the company's employees) 밝히고 있으므로 (A)가 정답이다.

어휘 **distribute** ~을 나눠주다, 배포하다 **instructional** 교육용의

Paraphrase before lunch → in the morning
present the new workers
→ Introduce the new staff

26. 여자가 하겠다고 제안하는 일은 무엇인가?
(A) 교육 프로그램을 여는 일
(B) 유인물을 준비하는 일
(C) 프레젠테이션을 하는 일
(D) 식사 장소를 찾는 일

해설 오리엔테이션과 관련된 대략적인 일정을 들은 여자는 대화 마지막 부분에 점심 식사 장소에 대해 There are so many good lunch spots there. I can find one for you if you'd like라고 말하고 있는데, 식사 장소를 찾아주겠다고(I can find one for you ~) 제안하고 있으므로 (D)가 정답이다.

어휘 **hold** ~을 열다, 개최하다 **handout** n. 유인물 **give a presentation** 프레젠테이션을 하다, 발표하다

Paraphrase lunch spots
→ a place to eat

Questions 27-29 refer to the following conversation.

W: Oh, Philip, I've been hoping to run into you. **27** I didn't get the chance to talk to you after your art exhibit last weekend.

M: Hi, Cindy. I'm sorry I didn't see you there. What did you think?

W: Honestly, I don't know what to say. **28** Your sculptures were so beautiful, especially with how you positioned them in the lighting.

M: Oh, wow. It means a lot hearing that from you. I was really nervous the entire night.

W: I was thinking, **29** you should enter a submission for the Talon Award. It's a nation-wide competition, but I really think you'd have a shot at winning.

여: 오, 필립 씨, 당신과 마주치기를 바라고 있었어요. 지난 주에 있었던 당신의 미술 전시회 후에 이야기를 나눠 볼 기회가 없었거든요.

남: 안녕하세요, 신디 씨. 그곳에서 보지 못해서 미안해요. (전시회는) 어땠나요?

여: 솔직히, 무슨 말을 해야 할지 모르겠어요. 당신의 조각품들은 정말 아름다웠는데, 특히 조명 아래에 그 작품들을 배치해 두신 방식이 훌륭했어요.

남: 오! 그런 말을 듣는 것은 정말 큰 힘이 돼요. 저는 그날 밤 내내 정말로 긴장했었거든요.

여: 전 당신이 탤론 어워드에 작품을 제출해야 한다고 생각했어요. 전국적인 규모의 대회인데, 상을 받도록 한 번 시도해 봐야 한다고 진심으로 생각해요.

어휘 run into (우연히) ~와 마주치다 get the chance to do ~할 기회를 얻다 exhibit 전시(회) honestly 솔직히 sculpture 조각품 especially 특히 position A in B A를 B에 놓다, 두다 lighting 조명 it means a lot 큰 힘이 되다, 큰 의미가 되다 nervous 긴장한 entire 전체의 enter a submission 작품을 제출하다 nation-wide 전국 규모의 competition 경연대회 have a shot at ~을 한 번 시도해 보다 win (상 등을) 받다, 타다

27. 대화는 주로 무엇에 관한 것인가?
   (A) 디자인 강좌
   (B) 미술 전시회
   (C) 박물관 개장
   (D) 초청 연주자

해설 대화 시작 부분에 여자가 상대방의 미술 전시회 후에 이야기를 나눠 볼 기회가 없었다고(I didn't get the chance to talk to you after your art exhibit last weekend) 언급한 후로 해당 전시회에 관한 내용으로 대화가 이어지고 있으므로 (B)가 정답이다.

어휘 visiting (초청 받아) 방문하는 performer 연주자

28. 여자가 "무슨 말을 해야 할지 모르겠어요"라고 말할 때 암시하는 것은 무엇인가?
   (A) 질문에 대해 준비가 되지 않았다.
   (B) 주제를 이해하지 못했다.
   (C) 남자를 도와 줄 수 없다.
   (D) 작품에 대해 깊은 인상을 받았다.

해설 대화 중반부에 여자가 이 말을 하면서 조각품들이 정말 아름다웠다고(Your sculptures were so beautiful, ~) 언급하고 있으므로 작품에 대한 긍정적인 의견에 해당하는 (D)가 정답임을 알 수 있다.

어휘 be unprepared for ~에 대해 준비가 되어 있지 않다 assist ~을 돕다 be impressed by ~에 대해 깊은 인상을 받다 work (글, 그림, 음악 등) 작품

29. 여자는 무엇을 추천하는가?
   (A) 콘테스트에 참가할 것
   (B) 강연에 참석할 것
   (C) 프로젝트를 변경할 것
   (D) 행사를 취소할 것

해설 대화의 마지막에 여자는 특정 경연대회에 작품을 제출해 보도록 권하고 있으므로(you should enter a submission for the Talon Award. ~) (A)가 정답이 된다.

어휘 enter ~에 참가하다 lecture 강연 revise ~을 변경하다, 수정하다

Paraphrase enter a submission for the Talon Award / competition
→ Entering a contest

Questions 30-32 refer to the following conversation with three speakers.

M: I called this meeting to discuss **30** which famous individual we should hire to endorse our new line of sunglasses. So, any ideas?

W1: Well, I think a popular actor would be best. They tend to have a broader appeal than athletes and musicians do.

W2: Yes, my team has been carrying out an extensive survey on the topic. It does seem that actors are more likely to drive up product sales.

M: Can you tell us about the survey findings in more detail, **31** Sophie?

W2: **31** I'm going to compile the data into a report and send it by e-mail later today.

M: That sounds great. Well, whoever we choose, **32** I hope that we'll be able to boost our sales next year with their help.

남: 우리가 선글라스 신제품 라인을 광고하는 데 어느 유명인을 고용해야 할지 논의하기 위해 이 회의를 소집했습니다. 그럼, 어떤 아이디어라도 있으신가요?

여1: 음, 제 생각엔 인기 배우가 최선일 것 같아요. 배우들이 운동선수나 음악가들보다 더 폭넓은 매력을 지니고 있는 경향이 있습니다.

여2: 네, 저희 팀에서 이 주제로 폭넓은 설문 조사를 실시해 오고 있습니다. 분명 배우들이 제품 판매량을 끌어올릴 가능성이 더 큰 것으로 보입니다.

남: 그 설문 조사 결과와 관련해 더 자세히 얘기해 주시겠어요, 소피 씨?

여2: 제가 자료를 모아 보고서로 정리해서 오늘 이따가 이메일로 보내 드릴 예정입니다.
남: 아주 좋은 것 같습니다, 음, 우리가 누구를 선택하든, 우리가 그 사람들의 도움을 받아 내년에 판매량을 높일 수 있기를 바랍니다.

어휘 **call a meeting** 회의를 소집하다 **individual** n. 사람, 개인 **endorse** ~을 유명인이 광고하다 **line** 제품 라인, 제품군 **tend to do** ~하는 경향이 있다 **broad** 폭넓은, 광범위한(= extensive) **appeal** 매력 **athlete** 운동 선수 **carry out** ~을 실시하다, ~을 수행하다 **survey** 설문 조사(지) **It seems that** ~하는 것처럼 보이다, ~하는 것 같다 **be likely to do** ~할 가능성이 있다 **drive up** ~을 끌어올리다 **sales** 판매(량), 영업, 매출 **findings** 결과(물) **in detail** 자세히 **compile** (자료 등) ~을 모아 정리하다 **whoever** 누구를 ~하든, ~하는 누구든 **boost** ~을 높이다, ~을 촉진하다

---

30. 화자들이 무엇을 이야기하고 있는가?
(A) 제품 디자인
(B) 개장 기념 행사
(C) 유명인 출연 광고
(D) 옥외 광고판 광고

해설 남자가 대화를 시작하면서 선글라스 신제품 라인을 광고하는 데 어느 유명인을 고용해야 할지(~ which famous individual we should hire to endorse our new line of sunglasses) 언급한 뒤로 특정 유명인 선정 방식과 관련해 이야기하고 있으므로 (C)가 정답이다.

어휘 **celebrity** 유명인 **endorsement** (유명인이 출연하는) 광고, 홍보 **billboard** 옥외 광고판

Paraphrase which famous individual we should hire to endorse
→ celebrity endorsement

---

31. 소피 씨는 자신이 무엇을 할 것이라고 말하는가?
(A) 동료 직원과 상의하는 일
(B) 보고서를 준비하는 일
(C) 업무 일정표를 이메일로 보내는 일
(D) 몇몇 문서를 출력하는 일

해설 Sophie라는 이름이 언급되는 부분에서 계획이나 앞으로의 일정 등과 관련해 말하는 정보를 파악해야 한다. 남자가 대화 후반부에 여자 한 명을 Sophie라고 부르자, 그 여자가 자료를 모아 보고서로 정리할 것이라고(I'm going to compile the data into a report ~) 알리고 있으므로 (B)가 정답이다.

어휘 **consult with** ~와 상의하다, ~와 상담하다 **prepare** ~을 준비하다

Paraphrase compile the data into a report
→ Prepare a report

---

32. 남자가 내년에 무슨 일이 있기를 바라는가?
(A) 제품이 출시될 것이다.
(B) 판매량이 증가할 것이다.
(C) 직원이 고용될 것이다.
(D) 합병이 있을 것이다.

해설 남자가 내년에 무슨 일이 있기를 바라는지 묻고 있으므로 남자의 말에 집중해 들어야 하며, 질문에 제시된 next year와 함께 언급되는 바람이나 긍정적인 요소를 찾아야 한다. 남자가 대화 마지막 부분에 내년에 판매량을 높일 수 있기를 바란다는 말로(~ I hope that we'll be able to boost our sales next year with their help) 내년에 대한 희망 사항을 밝히고 있으므로 (B)가 정답이다.

어휘 **launch** ~을 출시하다, ~을 시작하다 **merger** 합병, 통합 **take place** (일, 행사 등이) 일어나다, 발생되다, 개최되다

Paraphrase boost our sales
→ Sales will increase

Questions 33-35 refer to the following conversation and price list.

M: Good afternoon. **33** I have an important banking conference for my work next month, and I'd like to get a new suit made for it. Would it be ready by then?

W: Sure, that's plenty of time. What kind of material are you considering?

M: Well, I don't want to spend too much, so I think a linen suit would be fine.

W: Hmm... **34** Keep in mind that it's winter, and the temperatures have been breaking record lows lately. You might want a warmer material.

M: I didn't think about that. **35** The wool-blend would be best, then.

W: **35** That's a good choice. Did you bring your measurements, or should we take them here?

남: 안녕하세요. 제가 다음 달에 업무와 관련된 중요한 금융 컨퍼런스가 있는데요, 이를 위해 새로운 정장을 한 벌 맞추려고 합니다. 그때까지 준비될 수 있을까요?
여: 그럼요, 시간은 충분합니다. 무슨 종류의 소재를 고려하고 계신가요?
남: 저, 비용을 너무 많이 소비하고 싶지는 않기 때문에 린넨으로 된 정장이면 좋을 것 같습니다.
여: 흠... 지금은 겨울이라는 점을 명심하세요, 그리고 최근에 최저 기온 기록이 계속 깨지고 있습니다. 더 따뜻한 소재로 된 것이 필요하실 겁니다.
남: 그 점을 생각하지 못했네요. 그럼 울 혼방 소재가 가장 좋겠

네요.

여: 좋은 선택이십니다. 치수는 알아 오셨나요, 아니면 여기서 저희가 측정해 드릴까요?

설리번 테일러즈 - 맞춤 정장 전문	
소재	가격
면	500달러
울 혼방	400달러
폴리에스테르	350달러
린넨	300달러

어휘 **banking** 금융 (업무) **get A p.p.** A가 ~되게 하다 **suit** 정장 **plenty of** 충분한, 많은, 풍부한 **material** 소재, 재료, 자재 **consider** ~을 고려하다 **spend too much** 너무 많이 소비하다 **keep in mind that** ~라는 점을 명심하다 **temperature** 기온 **break** (기록 등) ~을 깨트리다 **record lows** 기록적인 최저 기온 **lately** 최근에 **take measurements** 치수를 재다 **tailor** (양복) 재단사 **custom** 맞춤 제작의

33. 남자는 다음 달에 무슨 행사가 있는가?
    (A) 동창회
    (B) 구직 면접
    (C) 업무 관련 컨퍼런스
    (D) 시상식 만찬

해설 next month라는 미래 시점이 질문의 핵심이므로 남자의 말에서 해당 시점 표현이 제시되는 부분에서 단서를 찾아야 한다. 대화 시작 부분에 남자가 일 때문에 중요한 금융 컨퍼런스가 다음 달에 있다고(I have an important banking conference for my work next month) 알리고 있으므로 (C)가 정답임을 알 수 있다.

어휘 **reunion** 동창회 **awards dinner** 시상식 만찬

34. 여자는 무슨 문제점을 언급하는가?
    (A) 마감시한에 맞출 수 없다.
    (B) 일부 비용이 더 높을 것이다.
    (C) 날씨가 춥다.
    (D) 한 가지 제품이 품절되었다.

해설 여자가 언급하는 문제점을 찾아야 하므로 여자의 말에서 부정적인 정보가 제시되는 부분이 있음을 예상하고 들어야 한다. 대화 중반부에 여자가 겨울이라는 점을 명심하라는 말과 함께 최저 기온 기록이 계속 깨지고 있다고(Keep in mind that it's winter, and the temperatures have been breaking record lows lately) 알리고 있으므로 추운 날씨를 언급한 (C)가 정답이다.

어휘 **meet a deadline** 마감시한에 맞추다 **cost** 비용 **item** 제품, 물품, 품목 **sold out** 품절된, 매진된

Paraphrase the temperatures have been breaking record lows → The weather is cold.

35. 시각자료를 보시오. 남자는 얼마를 소비할 것인가?
    (A) 500달러
    (B) 400달러
    (C) 350달러
    (D) 300달러

해설 추운 날씨에 관한 얘기를 들은 남자가 대화 후반부에 울 혼방 소재가 가장 좋겠다고 말하자(The wool-blend would be best, then) 여자도 이에 동의하고 있다(That's a good choice). 따라서 시각자료에서 울 혼방 소재의 가격에 해당되는 (B)가 정답임을 알 수 있다.

Questions 36-38 refer to the following conversation and graph.

W: Good morning, Shane. 36 Have you heard anything about what our next advertising project will be?

M: Actually, since our last few campaigns have been so successful, the marketing director is leaving the decision to us. That's why I'm checking the most recent sales report.

W: Wow, look at those numbers. Sales are still on the rise for Black Cherry. Considering this report, though, 37 I think we should try to increase the sales of the lowest-performing product.

M: That's what I was thinking. I still have some ideas we never used from last time. 38 I'll go ahead and e-mail them to you. Then we can start our planning from there.

여: 안녕하세요, Shane. 우리의 다음 광고 프로젝트가 무엇이 될 것인지에 관해 들은 얘기 없으세요?

남: 실은, 지난 몇 번의 캠페인들이 아주 성공적이었기 때문에 마케팅 부장님께서 저희에게 결정권을 주셨어요. 이것이 바로 제가 가장 최근의 매출 보고서를 확인하고 있는 이유입니다.

여: 와우, 이 수치들 좀 보세요. Black Cherry에 대한 매출은 여전히 상승세네요. 그런데 이 보고서를 감안하면, 가장 실적이 저조한 제품에 대한 매출을 높이도록 노력해야 할 것 같다고 생각해요.

남: 저도 그렇게 생각하고 있었어요. 저에게 지난 번 작업에서 아직 한 번도 활용하지 않은 아이디어가 좀 있어요. 제가 어서 가서 이메일로 보내 드릴게요. 그럼 그 부분부터 기획을 시작할 수 있을 거예요.

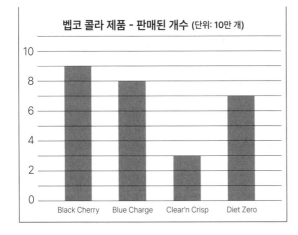

벱코 콜라 제품 - 판매된 개수 (단위: 10만 개)

어휘 advertising 광고 (활동) leave a decision to ~에게 결정을 맡기다 recent 최근의 sales 매출, 판매(량) on the rise 상승세인, 증가세인 considering ~을 감안하면, 고려하면 lowest-performing 실적이 가장 저조한 go ahead 어서 하다, 어서 가다 planning 기획 unit (제품의) 한 개, 구성 단위

36. 화자들은 무슨 부서에서 근무하고 있을 것 같은가?
   (A) 광고부
   (B) 제품 개발부
   (C) 고객 서비스부
   (D) 영업부

해설 대화를 시작하면서 여자가 자신들의 다음 광고 프로젝트가 무엇이 될 것인지에 관해 들은 얘기가 없는지(Have you heard anything about what our next advertising project will be?) 묻는 내용을 통해 (A)가 정답임을 알 수 있다.

어휘 development 개발, 발전

37. 시각자료를 보시오. 화자들은 어느 제품에 초점을 맞출 것인가?
   (A) Black Cherry
   (B) Blue Charge
   (C) Clear 'n Crisp
   (D) Diet Zero

해설 화자들이 주력할 제품이 질문의 핵심이므로 시각자료에 나타나 있는 판매량과 관련해 언급되는 특징을 찾아야 한다. 대화 중반부에 여자가 실적이 가장 저조한 수준의 제품에 대한 매출을 높이도록 노력해야 할 것이라고(I think we should try to increase the sales of the lowest-performing product) 알리고 있으므로 시각자료에서 가장 낮은 수치로 표기된 (C)가 정답이다.

어휘 focus on ~에 초점을 맞추다

38. 남자는 곧이어 무엇을 할 것인가?
   (A) 일부 장비를 구입한다.
   (B) 이메일을 보낸다.
   (C) 보고서를 작성한다.
   (D) 책임자와 얘기한다.

해설 대화가 끝난 후에 남자가 할 일을 묻고 있으므로 대화의 끝부분에 집중해야 하며, 미래 표현이나 의지 등을 나타내는 말과 함께 곧 있을 일로 언급되는 내용을 찾아야 한다. 대화의 마지막에 남자가 자신의 아이디어와 관련해 이메일로 보내 알려 주겠다고(I'll go ahead and e-mail them to you) 언급하고 있으므로 (B)가 정답이다.

어휘 equipment 장비

Paraphrase e-mail → Send an e-mail

Part 4

Questions 39-41 refer to the following news report.

> And now it's time for *Radio Four*'s **39** weekly music report. This Saturday marks the beginning of the biggest jazz festival in the country. If you are a fan of jazz, this year's festival will be a good one for you, as the world's best jazz bands will be here. **40** Unfortunately, however, the headlining performer, John Miles, will not be able to appear at this year's festival due to an unspecified illness. And to all of my listeners who plan on going, **41** I suggest you bring sunscreen and some kind of hat, as it looks like it's going to be very hot at the festival this week.
>
> ---
>
> 지금은 라디오 포의 주간 음악 소식입니다. 이번 토요일은 전국 최대 규모의 재즈 페스티벌이 시작되는 날입니다. 재즈를 좋아하는 팬이시라면, 올해 열리는 페스티벌이 좋은 기회가 될 텐데요, 세계 최고의 재즈 밴드들이 이곳에 오기 때문입니다. 하지만 아쉽게도, 주요 연주자인 존 마일즈 씨는 원인 불명의 질병으로 인해 올해 페스티벌에 참가할 수 없을 것입니다. 그리고 공연을 보러 갈 계획이신 모든 청취자 여러분께서는, 이번 주 페스티벌 현장 날씨가 매우 더울 것으로 보이므로 자외선 차단제와 모자같은 것을 챙겨 가시길 권해 드립니다.

어휘 mark (날짜 등이) ~을 나타내다, 가리키다 unfortunately 아쉽게도, 안타깝게도 headline v. (공연 등에) 주 연주자로 나오다 performer 연주자, 공연자 unspecified 규명되지 않은, 불특정한 illness 병, 아픔 sunscreen 자외선 차단제

39. 보도의 주제는 무엇인가?
   (A) 코미디 쇼
   (B) 음식 축제
   (C) 극장 공연 작품
   (D) 음악 행사

해설 　주제를 묻는 문제이므로 담화의 초반부에 특히 집중해 듣되, 만일의 경우에 대비해 담화의 큰 흐름을 함께 파악하면서 들어야 한다. 화자는 담화를 시작하면서 weekly music report라는 말로 음악과 관련된 내용이 보도될 것임을 밝히고 있고, 뒤이어 This Saturday marks the beginning of the biggest jazz festival in the country라는 말로 재즈 페스티벌이 열리는 것에 대해 알리고 있으므로 (D)가 정답이다.

어휘 　**production** (극장에서 상연되는) 작품
`Paraphrase` jazz festival
　　　　　　→ musical event

40. 화자는 어떤 문제점을 언급하는가?
　　(A) 장소가 변경되었다.
　　(B) 남은 티켓이 없다.
　　(C) 주 연주자가 취소를 했다.
　　(D) 행사 주최자가 아프다.

해설 　problem에 대해 묻는 문제이므로 담화에서 어떤 부정적인 내용이 언급되는지를 잘 찾아야 한다. 화자는 재즈 페스티벌이 개최된다는 내용을 소개한 후에 Unfortunately라는 표현을 이용해 부정적인 내용을 언급하고 있는데, 그 내용이 however, the headlining performer, John Miles, will not be able to appear at this year's festival due to an unspecified illness, 즉 주요 연주자가 올 수 없다는 것이므로 (C)가 정답이다.

어휘 　**venue** 장소, 개최지 **cancel** 취소하다 **organizer** 주최자, 조직자
`Paraphrase` headlining performer
　　　　　　→ main performer

41. 화자는 청자들에게 무엇을 하도록 권하는가?
　　(A) 햇빛으로부터 스스로를 보호할 것
　　(B) 돈을 충분히 가져갈 것
　　(C) 장소에 일찍 도착할 것
　　(D) 일기예보를 확인할 것

해설 　마지막 부분에 I suggest you ~라는 표현과 함께 제안하는 내용을 말하고 있는데, 여기서 화자는 bring sunscreen and some kind of hat, as it looks like it's going to be very hot at the festival this week라는 말로 햇빛으로부터 보호할 수 있는 방법을 권하고 있으므로 이를 다른 말로 적절히 바꿔 표현한 (A)가 정답이다.

어휘 　**protect** ~을 보호하다 **plenty of** 많은 양의 **weather forecast** 일기예보
`Paraphrase` bring sunscreen
　　　　　　→ Protect themselves from the sun

Questions 42-44 refer to the following telephone message.

Hello, Mr. Russel. This is Ji-Soo returning your call about the investment opportunity with the Wellington Foundation. I thought about it, and 42 I'd like to meet with you to discuss the details some more. I'm in the city for the next few days attending a tech conference. It ends tomorrow, so I'll be free in the evening. I would like it if we could meet at the Ember Bistro. 43 I'll be tired after the conference, and it's right next to my hotel. Just to let you know, I'm definitely interested, but 44 I'm a little worried, too. I've lost a big investment in a construction venture like this before. Anyway, I'm looking forward to learning more.

안녕하세요, 러셀 씨. 저는 지수라고 하며, 웰링턴 재단과 함께 하는 투자 기회와 관련된 귀하의 전화에 답변 드립니다. 제가 그 일에 대해 생각해 봤는데, 세부 사항을 좀 더 논의할 수 있도록 귀하를 만나 뵀었으면 합니다. 제가 기술 컨퍼런스에 참석하느라 앞으로 며칠 동안 이 도시에 있을 예정입니다. 이 행사는 내일 종료되기 때문에 저녁에 시간이 있습니다. 앰버 비스트로에서 만나 뵐 수 있다면 좋을 것 같습니다. 컨퍼런스를 마친 후에 피곤할 것 같은데, 해당 장소가 제 호텔 바로 옆에 있습니다. 간단히 알려 드리자면, 저는 분명히 관심이 있기는 하지만 약간 걱정되기도 합니다. 예전에 이번과 같은 건설 사업에서 많은 투자액을 잃은 적이 있거든요. 어쨌든, 조금 더 알아볼 수 있기를 고대합니다.

어휘 　**return one's call** ~의 전화에 답신 전화하다 **investment** 투자(액) **opportunity** 기회 **tech conference** 기술 컨퍼런스 **free** 시간이 있는 **right next to** ~ 바로 옆에 있는 **definitely** 분명히, 확실히 **venture** 벤처 기업, 벤처 사업 **anyway** 어쨌든 **look forward to -ing** ~하기를 고대하다

42. 전화의 목적은 무엇인가?
　　(A) 요청을 거절하는 것
　　(B) 회의 일정을 잡는 것
　　(C) 약속을 취소하는 것
　　(D) 교통편을 마련하는 것

해설 　화자는 담화 시작 부분에 투자 기회를 언급하면서 세부 사항을 좀 더 논의할 수 있도록 상대방과 만나고 싶다고(I'd like to meet with you to discuss the details some more) 알리고 있다. 이는 회의 일정을 정하자는 말과 같으므로 (B)가 정답이 된다.

어휘 　**decline** ~을 거절하다 **request** 요청 **set up** ~의 일정을 잡다, ~을 준비하다 **appointment** 약속, 예약 **arrange** ~을 마련하다, 조치하다 **transportation** 교통편

Paraphrase meet with you to discuss
→ set up a meeting

43. 여자가 "해당 장소가 제 호텔 바로 옆에 있습니다."라고 말하는 이유는 무엇인가?

(A) 자신이 일찍 도착할 것으로 예상하고 있다.
(B) 자신이 너무 가까이 있는 것에 놀라워하고 있다.
(C) 남자에게 길을 알려 주고 있다.
(D) 편리한 위치에 있는 곳을 선호한다.

해설 해당 문장은 담화 중반부에 화자가 컨퍼런스를 마친 후에 피곤할 것 같다고(I'll be tired after the conference) 말한 후에 들을 수 있는 말이다. 이로부터 자신이 가기 편리한 장소에서 만나고 싶다는 의미로 사용된 말이라는 것을 알 수 있으므로 이와 같은 의미에 해당하는 (D)가 정답이다.

어휘 **expect to do** ~할 것으로 예상하다 **be surprised to do** ~해서 놀라다 **give A directions** A에게 길을 알려 주다 **prefer** ~을 선호하다 **convenient** 편리한

44. 여자는 왜 걱정하는가?

(A) 남자가 다시 전화를 하지 않았다.
(B) 다른 프로젝트가 형편없이 진행되었다.
(C) 경기가 좋지 않았다.
(D) 비용이 너무 높다.

해설 화자는 담화 후반부에 걱정된다는 말과 함께 예전에 건설 사업에서 많은 투자액을 잃은 적이 있다고(I'm a little worried, too. I've lost a big investment in a construction venture like this before) 언급하고 있다. 따라서 이와 같은 상황에 대해 다른 프로젝트가 형편없었다는 말로 표현한 (B)가 정답이다.

어휘 **call back** 다시 전화하다 **poorly** 형편 없이, 저조하게 **economy** 경기, 경제

Paraphrase lost a big investment in a construction venture like this before
→ Another project went poorly.

Questions 45-47 refer to the following telephone message.

Good morning, Jennifer. As you know, **45** our company's new branch will be opening next month in Montgomery, and my HR team has been busy hiring and training the new staff members who will work there. The thing is, **46** we haven't found a great candidate for the regional manager position, and we only have a few interviews left. I was thinking about our options, and I was curious if there is someone we could promote from within the company. **47** Since you have the most

experience with our current employees, I thought you could make some recommendations. If you have anyone in mind, I'd appreciate it if you would have him or her call me at extension #5545.

안녕하세요, 제니퍼 씨. 아시다시피, 우리 회사의 신규 지점이 다음 달에 몽고메리에서 개장할 예정인데, 제 인사팀이 그곳에서 근무할 신입 사원들을 고용하고 교육하느라 계속 바빴습니다. 문제는, 지부장직을 맡을 뛰어난 지원자를 찾지 못한데다, 겨우 몇 번의 면접만 남아 있는 상태입니다. 제가 다른 선택사항에 대해 생각해 봤는데요, 회사 내부에서 승진시킬 수 있는 사람이 있는지 궁금합니다. 당신이 현재 근무 중인 직원들과 관련해 가장 많은 경험을 갖고 있기 때문에, 추천을 좀 해 주실 수 있을 거라고 생각했습니다. 마음에 두고 있는 사람이 있을 경우, 그 사람이 내선번호 5545로 제게 전화하도록 해 주시면 감사하겠습니다.

어휘 **branch** 지점, 지사 **HR team** 인사팀 **be busy -ing** ~하느라 바쁘다 **The thing is** 문제는 ~라는 것이다 **candidate** 지원자, 후보자 **regional manager** 지부장 **have A left** A가 남아 있다 **option** 선택 사항 **be curious if** ~인지 궁금하다 **promote** ~을 승진시키다 **from within** ~ 내부로부터 **make a recommendation** 추천하다 **have A in mind** A를 마음에 두다 **I'd appreciate it if** ~라면 감사하겠습니다 **have A do** A가 ~하게 하다 **extension** 내선 전화 (번호)

45. 화자의 말에 따르면, 다음 달에 무슨 행사가 있을 것인가?

(A) 지점 개장식
(B) 기업 합병
(C) 은퇴 기념 만찬
(D) 사내 야유회

해설 담화에서 질문의 next month가 언급되는 부분을 특히 주의 깊게 들어야 한다. 담화 시작 부분에 화자는 회사의 신규 시설이 나음 날에 Montgomery에서 개장한다고(our company's new branch will be opening next month in Montgomery) 알리고 있으므로 (A)가 정답이 된다.

어휘 **merger** 합병 **retirement** 은퇴, 퇴직

46. 화자가 "겨우 몇 번의 면접만 남아 있는 상태입니다"라고 말하는 이유는 무엇인가?

(A) 연장을 요청하기 위해
(B) 우려를 나타내기 위해
(C) 변명을 하기 위해
(D) 지연 상황을 설명하기 위해

해설 해당 문장은 담화 중반부에 화자가 지부장 직책에 대한 뛰어난 지원자를 찾지 못했다고(we haven't found a great candidate for the regional manager position) 알리는 말 다음에 들을 수 있다. 따라서 적합한 지원자를 찾지 못할 가능성에 대한 걱정을 나타내기 위해 사용한 말이라는 것을 알 수

있으므로 (B)가 정답이 된다.

어휘 **extension** 연장, 확장 **express** (감정 등) ~을 나타내다, 표현하다 **concern** 우려, 걱정 **make an excuse** 변명하다 **delay** 지연, 지체

47. 화자는 청자에게 무엇을 하도록 요청하는가?
(A) 사용 설명서를 작성할 것
(B) 다른 사무실로 이전할 것
(C) 추천을 해 줄 것
(D) 교육 시간을 진행할 것

해설 담화 후반부에 화자는 지원자를 내부에서 찾는 일과 관련해 상대방이 직원들을 잘 알기 때문에 누군가를 추천해 주면 좋겠다고(~ I thought you could make some recommendations) 요청하고 있다. 따라서 추천을 하는 일이라는 의미로 쓰인 (C)가 정답이다.

어휘 **manual** 사용 설명서, 안내서 **relocate to** ~로 이전하다 **lead** ~을 진행하다, 이끌다 **session** (특정 활동을 위한) 시간

Questions 48-50 refer to the following excerpt from a meeting and sign.

> Good morning, everyone. First, 48 I'd like to thank you all for volunteering to assist the attendees of this Winter Festival. In a moment, we'll assign each of your tasks. I guess 49 we'll begin with the location that will require the most people, so I'll need 6 of you there. Oh, and there's one thing I should make clear before dividing you into your teams. 50 We would really appreciate it if all of you could stay after at the end of the day to help us pick up any garbage that has been left around the park. Okay, with that said, let's get started.
>
> ---
>
> 안녕하세요, 여러분. 먼저, 이번 겨울 페스티벌의 참가자들을 돕기로 자원해주신 여러분 모두에게 감사 드립니다. 곧 여러분 각자의 업무를 배정할 것입니다. 가장 많은 인원이 필요한 곳부터 시작하도록 하겠습니다. 그곳에서는 6명이 필요할 것입니다. 아, 그리고 여러분을 팀으로 나누기 전에 확실하게 해 둘 것이 하나 있습니다. 여러분 모두 하루 일정이 끝나고 난 뒤에도 남아 주셔서 공원 주변에 버려진 쓰레기를 줍는 일을 도와 주신다면 정말 감사하겠습니다. 자 이제 말씀을 드렸으니, 시작하겠습니다.
>
> | 위치 | 담당 인원 |
> | --- | --- |
> | 간식 판매대 | 6 |
> | 주차장 | 5 |
> | 안내 센터 | 4 |
> | 티켓 판매처 | 3 |

어휘 **Thank A for B** A에게 B에 대해 감사하다 **volunteer to do** ~하겠다고 자원하다 **assist** ~을 돕다 **attendee** 참가자 **in a moment** 잠시 후에, 곧 **assign** ~을 배정하다, 할당하다 **task** 일 **make clear** 분명히 하다 **divide A into B** A를 B로 나누다 **appreciate** ~에 대해 감사하다 **pick up** ~을 줍다, 집어 올리다 **garbage** 쓰레기 **with that said** 그렇게 말하고, 그것으로써

48. 화자는 왜 청자들에게 감사 인사를 하는가?
(A) 일찍 도착해서
(B) 피드백을 제공해서
(C) 행사에 자원해서
(D) 업무를 빨리 마쳐서

해설 감사의 인사로 담화를 시작하고 있다. I'd like to thank you all for volunteering to assist the attendees ~에서 행사 참가자들을 돕기로 자원해 준 것에 대해 감사하고 있으므로 (C)가 정답이다.

어휘 **complete** ~을 마치다

Paraphrase volunteering to assist the attendees of this Winter Festival
→ volunteering for an event

49. 시각자료를 보시오. 어느 위치의 업무가 먼저 배정될 것인가?
(A) 간식 판매대
(B) 주차장
(C) 안내 센터
(D) 티켓 판매처

해설 업무 배정을 하겠다고 하면서 we'll begin with the location that will require the most people, so I'll need 6 of you there라고 말하고 있다. 사람이 가장 많이 필요한 곳부터 할 예정인데, 그곳은 6명의 인원이 필요하다고 덧붙이므로, 시각자료에서 6명이 필요한 곳을 찾으면 (A) Refreshment stands가 정답이다.

어휘 **assignment** 임무, 과제

50. 화자는 청자들에게 하루 일이 끝나고 무엇을 할 것을 요청하는가?
(A) 전시물을 해체하기
(B) 근무 시간 기록지에 서명하기
(C) 트럭에 짐 싣기
(D) 쓰레기 치우기

해설 the end of the day가 질문의 핵심이므로 이 표현이 언급되는 부분을 놓치지 말고 잘 듣도록 한다. 담화 마지막 부분에서 We would really appreciate if all of you could stay after at the end of the day to help us pick up any garbage라고 한다. 하루 일이 끝나고 남아서 쓰레기를 치우는 일을 도와 달라고 하므로 (D)가 정답이다.

어휘 **dismantle** ~을 해체하다 **time sheet** 출퇴근 시간 기록 용지 **load up** ~에 짐을 가득 싣다 **clean up** ~을 치우다

trash 쓰레기
Paraphrase pick up any garbage
→ Clean up trash

Part 5

51.
정답 (A)

해석 건축 허가를 받으려면, 모든 신청서들은 상세한 건축 도면을 포함해야 한다.

해설 빈칸은 부정관사의 수식을 받으며, 빈칸 앞에 있는 building과 함께 복합명사를 구성해 to부정사로 쓰인 타동사 obtain의 목적어 역할을 할 수 있는 명사 자리이다. 따라서 단수 가산명사인 (A) permit이 정답이다

어휘 obtain ~을 얻다, 획득하다 building permit 건축 허가(서) detailed 상세한 architectural 건축의, 건축물의 plan 도면

52.
정답 (C)

해석 성공으로 가는 길은 당신의 약점을 인정할 수 있고, 스스로 나타나는 기회들을 활용할 수 있는 것을 포함한다.

해설 빈칸 앞에 to부정사로 쓰인 타동사 recognize가, 빈칸 뒤에는 명사가 있으므로 이 명사를 수식할 수 있는 소유격 대명사가 빈칸에 들어가야 한다. 따라서 (C) your가 정답이다.

어휘 path to ~로의 길 involve ~을 포함하다 recognize ~을 인정하다 weakness 약점 capitalize on ~을 활용하다 present oneself 나타나다, 출두하다

53.
정답 (C)

해식 더 부드러운 작동을 보장하기 위해, 표준 규격의 종이만 복사기에 올려놓아야 합니다.

해설 빈칸 뒤에 명사구가 있고, 콤마 뒤로 완전한 구성의 문장이 나와 있으므로 빈칸과 명사구는 부사의 역할을 해야 한다. 따라서 빈칸 뒤 명사구를 목적어로 취하면서 규격 용지를 사용하는 이유 또는 그 목적을 나타낼 수 있는 to부정사 (C) To ensure가 정답이다.

어휘 ensure ~을 보장하다, 확보하다 smooth 원활하게 움직이는, 부드러운 operation 작동, 가동 standard-sized 표준 규격인 load ~을 올려놓다, 싣다

54.
정답 (A)

해석 셀리숍에서는 판매직원이 항상 표기된 가격이 정확하도록 이중으로 확인합니다.

해설 빈칸 앞에 정관사가 있고, 빈칸 뒤에 명사가 있으므로 빈칸은 형용사 자리이다. 선택지에 형용사가 없으므로 형용사 역할이 가능한 분사 (A) marked와 (C) marking 중에서 골라야 하는데, 가격은 사람에 의해 표시되는 대상이므로 '표기된'이라는 수동의 의미로 쓰이는 과거분사 (A) marked가 정답이다.

어휘 sales associate 영업사원, 판매직원 double-check 이중으로 확인하다 make sure that ~하는 것을 확실하게 하다 mark v. ~을 표시하다 n. 자국, 흔적

55.
정답 (A)

해석 우리가 지난 10년에 걸쳐 발전시켜 온 사업 관계들이 우리가 주내에서 선도적인 회계법인이 되는 데 도움이 되어 왔다.

해설 빈칸은 문장의 주어인 The business relationships를 수식하는 관계사절의 동사 자리이며, 빈칸 다음에 제시된 과거에서 현재까지 이어지는 기간을 나타내는 표현인 over the past decade가 있으므로 현재완료 (A) have developed가 정답이다.

어휘 relationship 관계 leading 선두의, 일류의 accounting firm 회계법인 province (행정 단위) 주

56.
정답 (B)

해석 일단 티켓을 받고 나면, 지정된 게이트로 가서 출발 준비를 하십시오.

해설 빈칸 뒤에 주어와 동사가 있고, 콤마 뒤에 명령문 형식의 절이 있으므로 빈칸은 접속사 자리이다. 티켓을 받아야 게이트로 갈 수 있으므로 '일단 ~하면'이라는 뜻의 선행 조건을 나타내는 (B) Once가 정답이다.

어휘 proceed to ~로 나아가다, ~에 이르다 designated 지정된 departure 출발 owing to ~때문에

57.
정답 (B)

해석 우리의 새로운 광고시리즈가 잘못된 정보를 포함하고 있다고 생각하는 고객들로부터 몇몇 건의 불만 사항을 접수하였다.

해설 빈칸 뒤에 위치한 advertisements를 가리킬 일종의 범주에 해당되는 명사가 필요하므로 '시리즈'를 뜻하는 (B) series가 정답이다.

어휘 incorrect 잘못된, 올바르지 않은 process 과정, 절차 series 시리즈, 일련, 연쇄 operation 작동, 수술, 조작

58.
정답 (A)

해석 젊은 전문가들을 끌어들이기 위해 제이미슨 & 손스 사는 신입사원들이 회사와 3년 계약을 맺을 경우에 학자금 대출에 대하여 5천 달러를 지불할 것이다.

해설 회사가 지급하는 5천 달러가 학자금 대출을 갚는 데 사용될 것이므로 기부 또는 원조 대상을 나타내며, 돈의 이동 방향을 나타

내는 (A) toward가 정답이다.

어휘 **loan** 대출 **provided that** ~라면, ~을 조건으로 한다면, ~할 경우에 **sign a contract** 계약서에 서명하다, 계약을 맺다 **toward** ~용도로, ~을 위하여, ~에 쓰도록

59.
정답 (B)

해석 우리의 등산화의 인기가 급격히 증가해 왔으며, 특히 전문 등산인들 사이에서 그러하다.

해설 주어와 동사를 포함한 하나의 절이 끝나고 콤마와 함께 전치사구가 추가된 구조이다. 이 전치사구 앞에 빈칸이 있으므로 빈칸에 전치사구를 수식할 수 있는 부사가 쓰여야 알맞다. 따라서 (B) particularly가 정답이다.

어휘 **rise** 증가하다, 오르다 **dramatically** 급격히 **mountaineer** 등산인 **particularly** 특히 **among** ~ 사이에서 **particular** 특정한, 특별한 **particularize** ~을 자세히 다루다, 특별한 예를 들다 **particularity** 특이성

60.
정답 (A)

해석 침체된 경제에 적응하려는 회사의 지속적 노력에도 불구하고, 경영진은 조심스럽게 기업 구조조정을 고려 중이다.

해설 빈칸 뒤에 명사구와 이 명사구를 수식하는 to부정사구, 그리고 콤마가 있으므로 빈칸은 명사구 목적어를 취할 수 있는 전치사 자리이다. 따라서 선택지 중 유일한 전치사인 (A) Despite가 정답이다.

어휘 **continuous** 지속적인 **adapt to** ~에 적응하다 **cautiously** 주의 깊게 **now that** ~때문에 **nonetheless** 그럼에도 불구하고 **yet** conj. 그러나 adv. 아직

61.
정답 (D)

해석 생산성 향상을 위해 즉각적 조치가 취해져야 한다고 공장 관리자들이 만장일치로 동의하긴 하지만, 그들 중에서 힐 씨에 의해 가장 최근에 제안된 일정을 지지하는 사람은 거의 없다.

해설 부사 어휘 문제로 빈칸 뒤 동사 agree와 어울리는 어휘를 골라야 한다. '동의하다'라는 의미와 어울리는 부사는 '만장일치로'라는 의미를 가진 부사가 적절하므로 (D) unanimously가 정답이다.

어휘 **immediate** 즉각적인, 즉석의 **take action** 조치를 취하다 **productivity** 생산성 **concurrently** 동시에 **feasibly** 실행할 수 있게 **unanimously** 만장일치로

62.
정답 (B)

해석 시장은 잠재적인 침수 문제로 인해 틸러슨 에비뉴를 폐쇄하는 것이 필수적이라고 여기고 있다.

해설 빈칸 앞에 쓰인 동사 consider는 5형식 동사로서 「consider

+ 목적어 + 목적격보어」의 구조로 쓰이므로 빈칸은 목적격 보어 자리이다. 따라서 목적격보어 자리에 쓰일 수 있는 형용사 (B) necessary가 정답이다.

어휘 **mayor** 시장 **flooding** 침수, 홍수 **necessity** 필요, 필수 (품) **necessitate** ~을 필요하게 만들다 **necessarily** 필연적으로

63.
정답 (D)

해석 린 디자인 사는 직원들에게 재택 근무를 할 것인지 또는 사무실에서 근무할 것인지 선택하는 데 있어 유연성을 제공할 것임을 발표하게 되어 기쁩니다.

해설 빈칸 앞에는 주어와 동사를 포함한 절이, 빈칸 다음에 to부정사가 있으므로 선택지에서 to부정사와 어울릴 수 있는 접속사 (D) whether가 정답이다.

어휘 **announce that** ~을 발표하다, 알리다 **flexibility** 유연성, 융통성 **telecommute** 재택근무를 하다 **in that** ~이므로 **while** ~하는 반면에

64.
정답 (D)

해석 회사 본사는 작년에 거의 50퍼센트 정도 수익이 감소한 지사 한 곳의 문을 닫는다는 사실을 발표했다.

해설 빈칸 뒤의 내용은 빈칸 앞에 제시된 명사 branch에 대한 설명이므로 빈칸은 관계대명사 자리인데, 빈칸 다음의 명사 earnings가 branch에 속하는 것으로 볼 수 있으므로 소유격 대명사 (D) whose가 정답이다.

어휘 **corporate** 기업의 **announce** ~을 발표하다 **closure** 문을 닫음, 폐쇄 **earnings** 수익

65.
정답 (C)

해석 공사장 인부들은 초고층건물의 상층에서 일하는 것이 예상했던 것보다 더 어렵다는 것을 알았다.

해설 현재완료 5형식 동사 find가 빈칸 앞에 있으므로 동명사구가 목적어로 쓰인 것을 알 수 있다. 따라서 빈칸은 목적보어 자리이므로 형용사가 필요한데, 빈칸 다음에 than이 있으므로 비교급 (C) more difficult가 정답이다.

어휘 **construction worker** 공사장 인부 **upper** 상부의, 더 위에 있는 **skyscraper** 초고층건물 **difficultly** 어려움

66.
정답 (A)

해석 우드슨 퍼니처는 최대 10명까지 사람을 앉히도록 연장시킬 수 있는 조절 가능한 식탁을 제조한다.

해설 빈칸에 쓰일 형용사는 바로 뒤에 위치한 dining tables를 수식해 그 특징에 해당되는 의미를 나타내야 한다. that절에 최대 10명까지 사람을 앉히도록 연장시킬 수 있다는 특징과 관련되

어야 자연스러우므로 '조절 가능한'을 뜻하는 (A) adjustable 이 정답이다.

어휘 **extend** ~을 연장하다, ~을 늘리다 **up to** 최대 ~까지 **adjustable** 조절 가능한, 조정 가능한 **renewable** 갱신 가능한 **improbable** 있을 것 같지 않은, 사실 같지 않은 **reachable** 도달 가능한, 닿을 수 있는

Part 6

67-70.

> 연예 및 패션 뉴스
>
> 인기 가수 크리스티나 카카 씨가 이번 여름 말에 "심포니"라는 이름의 새 향수를 출시할 예정입니다. 최근 23살이 되었으며 벌써 3집 앨범을 출시할 계획 중인 카카 씨는 이 **67** 향수가 생기 넘치고 매혹적이라고 밝혔습니다.
>
> 처음에는, 이 향수가 **68** 오직 www.christinakaka.com에서만 구매 가능하겠지만, 처음 출시되고 몇 주 후에 주요 소매 판매점에도 소개될 것입니다. **69** 그 정확한 날짜에 대해서는 아직 아무 소식도 없습니다.
>
> "심포니"에 대한 대대적인 광고 캠페인이 이미 시작된 관계로, 이 제품은 출시 후 베스트셀러 제품이 될 것으로 **70** 예상되고 있습니다.

어휘 **be set to do** ~할 예정이다 **release** v. ~을 출시하다, 공개하다 n. 출시, 공개 **turn** (나이가) ~살이 되다 **fragrance** 향수, 향기 **vibrant** 생기 넘치는 **alluring** 매혹적인 **at first** 처음에는 **extensive** 대대적인, 광범위한 **in place** 준비가 된, 제자리에 있는

67.

정답 (D)

해설 빈칸에는 정관사와 함께 앞서 언급된 특정 대상을 가리킬 명사가 쓰여야 하는데, '생기 넘치고 매혹적인'이라는 특징으로 설명 가능한 것이어야 하므로 새로 출시할 계획인 향수를 가리켜야 알맞다. 따라서 perfume과 동일한 의미를 지니는 (D) fragrance가 정답이다.

어휘 **outfit** 옷, 복장

68.

정답 (B)

해설 빈칸 이하의 but절을 읽어보면, 처음 출시되고 몇 주 후에 주요 판매점에도 소개될 것이라는 말이 쓰여 있다. 따라서 처음에는 빈칸 뒤에 제시된 웹 사이트에서만 판매된다는 의미가 되어야 흐름이 자연스러우므로 '오직'을 의미하는 (B) only가 정답이다.

69.

정답 (D)

해석 (A) 그 앨범은 13곡의 원곡과 여러 게스트 아티스트를 특징으로 할 것입니다.
　　(B) 카카 씨는 히트곡 "도도 버드"로 유명해졌습니다.
　　(C) 일부 수익금은 카카씨의 자선 단체 '솔 뮤직'에 돌아갈 것입니다.
　　(D) 그 정확한 날짜에 대해서는 아직 아무 소식도 없습니다.

해설 바로 앞 문장에 여름에 출시할 향수 제품 구매 방법이 설명되어 있으므로 빈칸에도 제품 구매와 관련된 정보를 담은 문장이 쓰여야 흐름이 자연스럽다. 따라서 주요 판매점에도 소개되는 시점과 관련해 아직 정확한 날짜를 알 수 없다는 의미로 쓰인 (D)가 정답이다.

어휘 **feature** ~을 특징으로 하다, 포함하다 **proceeds** 수익(금) **charity** 자선 단체

70.

정답 (C)

해설 빈칸 앞에 위치한 향수를 가리키는 대명사 it은 사람에 의해 예상되는 대상이므로 빈칸에 들어갈 동사 expect는 수동태로 쓰여야 한다. 또한, 지문 시작 부분에 여름에 출시될 예정이라고 한 것으로 볼 때 베스트셀러 제품이 되는 것도 출시 이후의 시점, 즉 미래의 일이므로 현재 시점에 예상되는 일이어야 알맞다. 따라서 현재시제 수동태인 (C) is expected가 정답이다.

71-74.

> 수신: 레지 클라이드
> 발신: 데니스 강
> 주제: 주차 변경
> 날짜: 3월 10일
>
> 클라이드 씨께,
>
> **71** 유감스러운 소식을 가지고 연락 드리게 되있습니다. 이제 더 이상 귀하의 고객들이 주차장 앞에 주차할 수 없을 것입니다. **72** 안타깝게도, 그 토지가 강제 수용 명령 하에 지자체에 인수되었습니다. 시립 주차장이 그곳에 건설될 예정이며, 새로운 학교가 바로 옆에 위치하게 될 것으로 생각합니다. 충분한 안내를 해드리지 못해 죄송합니다만, 이 모든 일이 지난 며칠 **73** 동안 아주 갑자기 벌어졌습니다.
>
> 다른 주차 장소를 알아보시는 데 **74** 큰 어려움이 없으시기를 바랍니다.
>
> 안녕히 계십시오.
>
> 데니스 강

어휘 **no longer** 더 이상 ~않는 **lot** 주차장 **acquire** ~을 인수하다 **compulsory purchase** (정부에 의한 토지 및 재산의) 강제 수용 **assumption** 추정 **notice** 통지, 예고 **rather** 아주, 꽤 **suddenly** 갑자기, 급작스럽게 **have difficulty**

-ing ~하는 데 어려움을 겪다 **arrangement** 준비, 예약

71.

정답 (D)

해석 (A) 귀하의 주차 허가증 요청을 접수하였습니다.
(B) 저희 서비스 이용에 대한 관심에 감사 드립니다.
(C) 저희 주차장은 개조 작업을 위해 폐쇄될 예정입니다.
(D) 유감스러운 소식을 가지고 연락 드리게 되었습니다.

해설 빈칸 뒤에 더 이상 주차를 할 수 없다는 내용이 제시되고 있는데 이는 다소 좋지 않은 소식에 해당한다. 그러므로 부정적인 소식을 예고하는 (D)가 정답이다.

어휘 **parking permit** 주차 허가증 **interest** 관심 **be scheduled to do** ~할 예정이다 **renovation** 개조작업, 내부공사 **regrettable** 유감스러운

72.

정답 (D)

해설 빈칸 앞 문장은 더 이상 주차가 불가능할 것이라는 부정적인 내용이며, 빈칸 뒤에는 구체적 이유에 해당하는 지역 당국의 강제 수용 명령에 대해 말하고 있다. 그러므로 좋지 않은 소식에 대한 감정을 나타내는 부사로 '안타깝게도'라는 의미의 (D) Unfortunately가 정답이다.

어휘 **surprisingly** 놀랍게도 **initially** 초기에, 애초에 **alternatively** 또는, 아니면 **unfortunately** 안타깝게도, 불행히도

73.

정답 (B)

해설 선택지가 모두 전치사로 구성되어 있고, 빈칸 뒤에 기간을 나타내는 명사구가 있으므로 기간 명사구와 함께 쓰이는 (B) over가 정답이다.

74.

정답 (A)

해설 빈칸 뒤에 위치한 단수명사를 수식할 수 있으면서 부정어 not과 함께 쓰일 수 있는 (A) any가 정답이다.

Part 7

75-76.

북잇에 모든 것을 맡기세요!

75 항공편을 알아보고, 호텔을 예약하고 관광 일정을 계획하는 것은 어렵고, 스트레스 받는 일이죠, 그렇다면 북잇이 모든 걸 처리하도록 해 보는 게 어때세요? 웹 사이트를 확인해보고 책을 찾아보고, 그리고 가격을 비교하느라 여러분의 소중한 시간을 낭비하지 마세요. **76** 뛰어난 자격을 갖춘 저희 여행 전문가 팀은

여러분이 그저 앉아서 휴가를 기대하는 동안 필요한 모든 준비를 해 드릴 수 있습니다. 저희 사무실로 오셔서 여러분이 어떤 여행을 희망하는지 정확히 말씀해 주세요, 그러면 저희가 여러분의 기대를 뛰어 넘을 수 있도록 최선을 다하겠습니다. 그럼, 왜 망설이시나요? 미들위치의 리폼 스트리트 125번지로 방문해 주시거나 555-9900으로 전화주세요!

어휘 **search for** ~을 찾다 **sightseeing** 관광 **itinerary** 여행 일정표 **consult** (정보 확인을 위해) ~을 찾아보다, 참고하다 **highly-qualified** 뛰어난 자격을 갖춘, 잘 훈련된 **arrangement** 준비, 마련 **look forward to** ~을 기대하다 **surpass** ~을 능가하다, 뛰어넘다

75. 북잇은 어떤 종류의 기업인가?

(A) 온라인 서점
(B) 호텔 체인점
(C) 여행사
(D) 항공사

정답 (C)

해설 첫 문장에 비행편을 알아보거나 호텔을 예약하거나 관광일정을 짜는 등의 일을 북잇에게 처리하도록 하는 것이 어떤지(Searching for flights, booking hotel rooms, and planning sightseeing itineraries can be difficult and stressful, so why not let Bookit handle everything for you) 광고하고 있는데 이는 여행사가 하는 일이므로 (C)가 정답이다.

어휘 **chain** (상점, 호텔 등의) 체인점 **travel agency** 여행사

76. 북잇에 대해 명시된 것은 무엇인가?

(A) 상대적으로 새로운 회사이다.
(B) 최근에 이전하였다.
(C) 주로 온라인에서 광고를 한다.
(D) 직원들이 능숙하다.

정답 (D)

해설 지문 중간 부분에 뛰어난 자격을 갖춘 여행 전문가 팀을(Our highly-qualified team of travel experts) 언급한 부분에서 직원들이 숙련된 여행 전문가임을 알 수 있으므로 (D)가 정답이다.

어휘 **relatively** 상대적으로 **relocate** 이전하다 **experienced** 경험이 많은, 능숙한

77-79.

변화 예정인 프랑코 스트리트

77 미들섹스 시 의회는 차량 운전자, 자전거 이용자, 그리고 보행자들 사이의 충돌 횟수를 줄이기 위한 노력으로 프랑코 스트리트의 자전거 도로에 변화를 만들고 있다.

이 계획의 첫 단계로, 리치몬드 스트리트의 교차로와 로톤 에비뉴의 교차로 사이의 프랑코 스트리트 남쪽 방향 자전거 도로는

노란색으로 칠해질 것이다. — [1] —. **78** 또한, 프랑코 스트리트의 북쪽 방향과 남쪽 방향 양쪽의 자전거 도로를 지정하는 선들은 차량 운전자들이 자전거 도로선이 더 잘 보이도록 약 15센티미터 더 두껍게 칠해질 것이다. — [2] —.

이 계획의 두 번째 단계는 솔턴 로드와 메이필드 스트리트가 만나는 프랑코 스트리트에 자전거 박스가 추가되는 것이다. — [3] —. 이 박스들은 자전거 운전자들이 좌회전을 하는 데 도움을 줄 것이다. 자전거 박스는 운전자와 자전거 운전자가 도로를 좀 더 안전하게 공유할 수 있게 해주는 아주 새로운 유형의 도로 표시이다. 이 상자들은 빨간 신호에 멈춰 선 차량 앞쪽에 공간을 지정한다. **79** 자전거 운전자들은 이 공간에서 기다리는 것이 허용되며, 녹색 불이 켜지면 먼저 출발할 수 있다. — [4] —.

이러한 변화들을 통해, 시 의회는 자전거 도로를 좀 더 눈에 잘 띄게 하고, 도로 이용자들이 교차로에서 각별히 주의하도록 하며, 회전하는 차량들이 속도를 늦추고 자전거 운전자들과 보행자들을 포함한 다른 도로 이용자들을 잘 살피도록 하고자 한다.

어휘 **lane** 좁은 길, 차선 **collision** 충돌 **pedestrian** 보행자 **intersection** 교차로 **designate** ~을 지정하다 **thick** 두꺼운 **approximately** 대략, 거의 **visible** 가시적인, 볼 수 있는 **fairly** 상당히, 꽤 **proceed** 앞으로 나아가다, 진행하다

77. 시 의회의 계획의 목적은 무엇인가?
(A) 프랑코 스트리트의 교통 혼잡을 완화하기
(B) 자전거 이용자들의 수를 줄이기
(C) 사고의 빈도를 감소시키기
(D) 자전거 전용 도로를 만들기

정답 (C)

해설 첫 번째 문단 초반부에 차량 운전자, 자전거 이용자, 그리고 보행자들 사이의 충돌 횟수를 줄이기 위해 자전거 도로에 변화를 만들고 있다는(The City Council of Middlesex is making changes to Franco Street bike lanes in an effort to reduce the number of collisions between motorists, cyclists, and pedestrians) 부분에서 사고를 줄이려 한다는 것을 알 수 있다. 따라서 (C)가 정답이다.

어휘 **alleviate** ~을 완화시키다 **congestion** 혼잡 **frequency** 빈도

78. 이 계획의 첫 단계로 언급된 것은 무엇인가?
(A) 자전거 박스의 추가
(B) 도로 표시의 확장
(C) 프랑코 스트리트의 부분적 폐쇄
(D) 낡은 신호등 교체

정답 (B)

해설 두 번째 문단에 변화를 위한 첫 단계가 제시되었는데, 특정 자전거 도로를 표시하는 선들을 더 잘 보이게 하기 위해 두껍게 칠할 것이라는(lines designating the bicycle lanes ~ will be painted thicker, by approximately 15 centimeters, to

make the bike lanes more visible to motorists) 계획이 언급되어 있으므로 (B)가 정답이다.

어휘 **widening** 확장, 넓히기 **partial** 부분적인 **replacement** 교체

79. [1], [2], [3], [4]로 표기된 위치들 중에서, 다음 문장이 가장 잘 어울리는 곳은 어디인가?

"자전거 운전자들이 먼저 출발하는 것을 방해하는 차량 운전자들은 벌금 부과 대상이 될 것이다."

(A) [1]
(B) [2]
(C) [3]
(D) [4]

정답 (D)

해설 벌금이 부과된다는 것은 해당 문장이 들어갈 위치 앞에 특수한 상황을 제시했다는 뜻인데, 이는 자전거 운전자들이 먼저 출발하는 것과 관련된다. 그러므로 자전거와 차량의 출발 순위를 규정하는 내용을 지문에서 찾아야 한다. [4]의 앞을 보면 자전거 운전자들이 차량보다 먼저 출발할 수 있는 구간을(Cyclists are permitted to wait in this space and proceed first when the light turns green) 얘기하고 있으므로 (D)가 정답이다.

80-82.

81 게시일: 3월 19일

모든 수험자들에게:

80 저희의 연례 어학 능력 시험을 준비하기 위해, 저희는 시험에 등록한 모든 직원들을 위한 워크샵을 개최할 것입니다.

이 워크샵은 4월 9일부터 15일까지 카막 강당에서 개최됩니다. 능력 시험에 등록한 모든 직원들은 워크샵에 참여할 수 있습니다. 82 이 어학 시험을 처음 보는 사람들은 반드시 참석해야 합니다. 워크샵에 대한 비용은 없습니다. 하지만, 다음 주에는 선택적 보충 과정이 있을 것입니다. 보충 과정에 등록하는 직원들은 매일 밤 연습 시험을 보게 될 것입니다. 비용은 100달러가 될 것입니다.

81 만약 이 보충 과정에 관심이 있으시면, 다음 달 초 이전에 결제해 주십시오. 이것은 4월 18일 오후 6시에 시작할 예정입니다.

어휘 **exam taker** 수험자 **in preparation for** ~에 대한 준비로 **proficiency** 유능함, 숙련도 **supplementary** 보충하는 **enroll in** ~에 등록하다

80. 누가 워크샵에 참석할 수 있는가?
(A) 모든 회사 직원들
(B) 최근에 회사에 들어온 직원들
(C) 시험에 등록한 직원들
(D) 지난번 시험에 실패한 직원들

정답 (C)

해설 첫 문단에 시험에 등록한 모든 직원들을 위한 워크샵을 개
최할 것이라고(we will be hosting a workshop for all
employees who have registered for the test) 하므로 전
직원이 아닌 테스트에 등록한 직원들이 워크샵에 참석할 것을
알 수 있다. 따라서 (C)가 정답이다.

81. 보충 과정의 수강료를 낼 수 있는 마지막 날은 언제인가?

(A) 3월 31일
(B) 4월 1일
(C) 4월 18일
(D) 4월 30일

정답 (A)

해설 마지막 단락에 보충 과정에 관심 있는 사람은 다음 달 초 전까지
(If you are interested in the supplementary course,
please submit your payment before the beginning of
next month) 수강료를 내야 한다고 쓰여져 있다. 지문의 상단
을 보면 공지를 게시한 시점이 3월 19일이므로 다음 달 1일 전
까지가 기한이라면 3월 31일까지 수강료를 내야 함을 알 수 있
다. 따라서 (A)가 정답이다.

82. 시험을 처음 치르는 직원들에 대해서 알 수 있는 것은 무엇인
가?

(A) 반드시 온라인 등록을 해야 한다.
(B) 반드시 워크샵을 참석해야 한다.
(C) 반드시 등록을 위해 100달러를 내야 한다.
(D) 반드시 보충 과정을 들어야 한다.

정답 (B)

해설 두 번째 단락 중반부에 어학 시험을 처음 보는 사람은 반드시
워크샵에 참석해야 한다고(Those who are taking the
language test for the first time must attend. There is
no cost for the workshop) 명시되어 있으므로 (B)가 정답
이다.

83-86.

라샤드 클레먼즈 [오전 9:07] 안녕하세요, 여러분. 83 제가 5층
대회의실에 있는데, 이곳에 있는 노트북 컴퓨터를 작동할 수가없
어요. 우리가 이것 없이는 직원 오리엔테이션을 진행할 수 없어요.
좋은 아이디어 있으신 분 계신가요?

개리 샌들러 [오전 9:08] 아, 저도 그것 때문에 문제가 좀 있었어
요. 몇몇 불필요한 배경 프로그램들을 닫아 보도록 해 보세요.

캐롤 글리슨 [오전 9:10] 84 그 회의실이 오늘 아침 9시 15분까
지 완전히 준비되어 있기로 되어 있지 않았나요? 83 우리가 발표
슬라이드와 동영상을 보여 줄 수 없다면 신입 사원들을 제대로 교
육할 수 없을 거예요.

라샤드 클레먼즈 [오전 9:12] 84 네, 제가 우리 인턴 사원인 리
반즈 씨에게 그렇게 하도록 요청했는데, 그분이 오늘 아침 일찍

전화로 병가를 냈어요. 그게 바로 제가 일찍 이곳으로 올라와 의자
와 탁자들을 설치한 이유예요. 지금은, 이 노트북 컴퓨터만 작동시
키면 돼요...

라샤드 클레먼즈 [오전 9:13] 85 개리 씨, 이게 계속 멈추고 작동
이 되지 않고 있어요. 시간 좀 있으세요?

개리 샌들러 [오전 9:14] 그리로 바로 가겠습니다.

캐롤 글리슨 [오전 9:15] 또 도움이 필요하신 다른 일이라도 있으
세요? 기억하셔야 할 점은, 참석자들이 정확히 9시 30분에 그곳
에 도착할 거예요.

라샤드 클레먼즈 [오전 9:17] 아뇨, 일단 노트북 컴퓨터만 제대로
작동되면 전부 준비가 돼요. 여러분은 모두 각자의 발표 자료와 유
인물만 챙겨 오시면 됩니다.

캐롤 글리슨 [오전 9:19] 좋습니다. 86 제가 10시에 그곳으로 가
서 순서를 이어 받아 회사 정책을 이야기할 거예요. 모든 게 준비가
되어서 잘 진행되기를 바랍니다.

어휘 **get A to work** A를 작동시키다 **run** ~을 진행하다, 운영
하다 **be supposed to do** ~하기로 되어 있다 **fully** 완전
히, 전적으로 **new hires** 신입 사원들 **properly** 제대로,
적절히 **call in sick** 전화로 병가를 내다 **freeze** (기계, 프
로그램 등이) 멈추다 **crash** (기계, 프로그램 등이) 작동되
지 않다 **sharp** (시간 뒤에 쓰여) 정확히 ~시에, ~시 정각에
once 일단 ~하면, ~하는 대로 **up and running** 제대로
작동되는 **take over from** (순서, 자리 등) ~로부터 이어
받다

83. 클레먼즈 씨는 무엇을 하려고 준비 중인가?

(A) 시상하는 일
(B) 고객과 만나는 일
(C) 일부 장비를 설치하는 일
(D) 신입 직원을 교육하는 일

정답 (D)

해설 클레먼즈 씨가 첫 메시지에서 5층 대회의실에 있는 노트북 컴퓨
터를 작동할 수가 없다는 말과 함께 그것 없이는 직원 오리엔테
이션을 진행할 수 없다고(I can't get the laptop in here to
work. We can't run the employee orientation without
it) 언급하였다. 그리고 9시 10분에 글리슨 씨가 발표 슬라이드
와 동영상을 보여줄 수 없다면 신입 사원들을 제대로 교육시킬
수 없다고(We can't train our new hires properly if we
can't show them the presentation slides and videos)
하였으므로 오리엔테이션 대상이 신입 직원인 것을 알 수 있다.
따라서 (D)가 정답이다.

84. 회의실이 왜 오전 9시 15분까지 준비되어 있지 않았는가?

(A) 반즈 씨가 또 다른 업무가 있었기 때문에
(B) 그 회의실이 사용 중이었기 때문에
(C) 반즈 씨가 결근한 상태이기 때문에
(D) 한 행사 일정이 재조정되었기 때문에

정답 (C)

해설 글리슨 씨가 9시 10분에 회의실이 오늘 아침 9시 15분까지 완전히 준비되어 있기로 되어 있지 않았는지(Wasn't the room supposed to be fully prepared by 9:15 this morning?) 묻자, 클레먼즈 씨가 인턴 사원인 리 반즈 씨에게 그렇게 하도록 요청했는데, 오늘 아침 일찍 전화로 병가를 냈다고(Yes, I asked our intern, Lee Barnes, to do it, but he called in sick early this morning) 알리고 있으므로 (C)가 정답이다.

어휘 **absent** 결근한, 부재 중인 **reschedule** ~의 일정을 재조정하다

85. 오전 9시 14분에, 샌들러 씨가 "Be right there"라고 쓸 때, 무엇을 의미할 것 같은가?
(A) 5층으로 노트북 컴퓨터 하나를 올려 보낼 것이다.
(B) 수리 기사에게 연락할 것이다.
(C) 클레먼즈 씨가 다른 방으로 가기를 원하고 있다.
(D) 클레먼즈 씨에게 도움을 제공할 것이다.

정답 (D)

해설 클레먼즈 씨가 9시 13분에 개리 씨에게 노트북 컴퓨터가 계속 멈추고 작동이 되지 않고 있다면서 시간 좀 있는지(Gary, it keeps freezing and crashing. Are you free?) 묻자 '그리로 바로 가겠습니다'라고 대답하는 상황이다. 이는 도와주러 가겠다는 뜻이므로 (D)가 정답이다.

86. 오전 10시에 무슨 일이 있을 것 같은가?
(A) 클레먼즈 씨가 방을 말끔히 치울 것이다.
(B) 클레먼즈 씨가 몇몇 직원들을 맞이할 것이다.
(C) 글리슨 씨가 연설을 시작할 것이다.
(D) 글리슨 씨가 샌들러 씨와 만날 것이다.

정답 (C)

해설 오전 10시라는 시간이 언급되는 9시 19분 메시지에, 글리슨 씨가 10시에 가서 순서를 이어 받아 회사 정책을 이야기할 것이라고 알리고 있다. 이는 연설을 한다는 뜻이므로 (C)가 정답이다.

어휘 **tidy up** ~을 말끔히 치우나

87-90.

수신: 전 직원
발신: 재스민 랴오
날짜: 8월 27일

직원 여러분,

87 연말이 다가오고 있으니, 모든 휴가는 반드시 12월 말 이전에 쓰여야 한다는 것을 기억해 두십시오. 안타깝게도, 저희는 직원들이 휴가를 내년으로 넘기는 것을 허용할 수 없기 때문에, 휴가를 다 쓰지 않으면 그 휴가들을 잃게 됩니다.

또한 휴가 요청은 반드시 고위 경영진에 의해 한달 전에 미리 서면으로 접수되어야 한다는 것을 알려 드립니다. 요청은 적절한

양식에 따라 이루어져야 하며, 양식의 사본은 이 회람에 첨부되어 있습니다. 89 특별한 상황에서는, 막바지에 가는 휴가도 허용될 수 있습니다. 그런 요청들에 대해서는 저에게 직접 말씀해 주십시오.

88 그리고 마지막으로, 휴가는 선착순으로 일정이 잡힌다는 것을 기억하십시오. 90 여러분 중 많은 사람들이 며칠, 심지어 몇 주나 남아 있는 휴가 기간을 가지고 있습니다. 반드시 휴가 요청을 부서장님에게 미리 전달하여 실망하는 일이 없도록 하십시오.

남은 올해의 멋진 4개월에 행운이 있기를 바랍니다. 계속 수고하시고, 여러분 자신에게 마땅한 휴식의 시간으로 보상하는 것을 잊지 마십시오.

재스민

어휘 **approach** 접근하다 **carry over** ~을 이월하다, 끝내지 않고 넘기다 **in writing** 서면으로 **in advance** 미리 **attach** ~을 첨부하다 **last-minute** 막판의, 막바지의 **grant** ~을 허가하다 **in person** 직접 **on a first-come, first-served basis** 선착순으로 **remaining** 남아 있는 **avoid** ~을 피하다 **disappointment** 실망 **Here's to** ~에게 행운이 있기를 **reward** ~에게 보상하다 **well-deserved** 마땅한

87. 회람의 주요 목적은 무엇인가?
(A) 직원들이 열심히 일한 것에 감사를 표하기 위해서
(B) 다가오는 해에 대한 공휴일을 발표하기 위해서
(C) 휴가를 내년으로 옮기는 방법을 설명하기 위해서
(D) 직원들에게 휴가시간을 요청할 것을 상기시키기 위해서

정답 (D)

해설 첫 단락에 모든 휴가는 올해가 가기 전에 다 쓰라고(please remember that all holidays must be taken before the end of December) 알리고 있으므로 (D)가 정답이다.

어휘 **gratitude** 감사함 **public holiday** 공휴일 **transfer** ~을 옮기나 **remind** ~에게 상기시키다 **request** ~을 요청하다

88. 휴가 정책으로 나열되지 않은 것은 무엇인가?
(A) 휴가는 연말 전에 다 쓰여야만 한다.
(B) 휴가 시간은 선임 직원에게 우선적으로 허가되어진다.
(C) 휴가 시간은 반드시 경영진에 의해 승인되어야만 한다.
(D) 휴가 요청은 한달 전에 미리 이루어져야 한다.

정답 (B)

해설 세 번째 문단에 휴가는 선착순으로 일정이 잡힌다는 것을 기억하라고(And finally, remember that holidays are scheduled on a first-come, first-served basis) 상기시키고 있으므로 (B)가 정답이다.

어휘 **use up** ~을 다 써버리다 **seniority** 상급자임, 선임자임 **approve** ~을 승인하다

89. 직원이 왜 재스민 씨와 직접 이야기를 할 수도 있는가?

    (A) 휴가를 연장하기 위해

    (B) 휴가를 급하게 요청하기 위해

    (C) 휴가에 대한 승인을 얻기 위해

    (D) 휴가 양식을 받기 위해

정답 (B)

해설 두 번째 문단 후반부에 특별한 상황에서는 막바지에 가는 휴가도 허용될 수 있는데, 그런 요청들에 대해서는 직접 재스민 씨에게 말하라고(In special circumstances, a last-minute holiday may be granted. Speak to me in person for such requests) 언급하고 있으므로 (B)가 정답이다.

어휘 in person 직접 (만나서) extend ~을 연장하다 at short notice 급하게 통지하여

90. 이 회람에서 암시된 것은 무엇인가?

    (A) 많은 직원들은 휴일을 남겨두고 있다.

    (B) 직원들이 적합한 양식을 작성하고 있지 않다.

    (C) 부서장들이 휴가 요청 양식을 업데이트 했다.

    (D) 신입 직원들은 새해에 휴가에 대한 자격이 된다.

정답 (A)

해설 세 번째 문단에서 직원들이 며칠씩, 심지어 몇 주씩 남은 휴가가 있다는 사실을 알려주면서 꼭 사용하라고 권하고(A lot of you have several days, even weeks, of holiday time remaining) 있다. 따라서 (A)가 정답이다.

어휘 left over 남겨진 fill out ~을 작성하다 be eligible for ~에 대한 자격이 되다

91-95.

> **월간 인더스트리얼 푸드**
> **특별 설문 조사**
>
> 저희는 구독자 여러분께 앞으로의 월간 인더스트리얼 푸드 발행본에서 무엇을 읽어보고 싶으신지 여쭤보고 있습니다. **91 92** 여러분의 의견이 전국에 각지에 위치한 수천 곳의 슈퍼마켓 체인 관리책임자들께서 읽으시는 저희 출판물을 위한 올바른 콘텐츠를 선정하는 데 도움이 될 것입니다.
>
> 1. 앞으로의 발행본에서 어떤 종류의 기사를 읽어보고 싶으신가요?
>   A. 더 많은 정보성 기사
>   B. 더 많은 문제 해결 관련 이야기
>   C. 현재의 콘텐츠에 만족합니다.
>
> 2. 편집자 논평이 얼마나 마음에 드시나요?
>   A. 현재의 분량이 딱 알맞다.
>   B. 더 적으면 더 좋을 것 같다.
>   C. 더 많으면 더 좋을 것 같다.
>
> **93** 3. 다른 국가의 혁신에 관한 기사를 더 많이 원하시나요?
>   A. 네
>   B. 아니오

4. 잡지에 판매업체 광고가 더 많이 있어야 하나요?
  A. 네
  B. 아니오

어휘 issue (출판물 등의) 발행본, 호 input 의견(의 제공) help A do A가 ~하는 데 도움이 되다 right 올바른, 알맞은, 맞는 publication 출판(물) thousands of 수천의 informational 정보성의, 정보를 제공하는 problem-solving 문제 해결의 narrative 이야기 be satisfied with ~에 만족하다 editorial comment 편집자 논평 amount 분량, 수량 innovation 혁신(성) vendor 판매업체, 판매업자

> **월간 인더스트리얼 푸드**
> **독자 의견 설문 조사 결과**
>
> 저희 잡지의 향후 운영 방향에 영향을 미칠 몇몇 특정 주제와 관련해 독자 여러분을 대상으로 여론 조사를 하기 위해 올해 초에 설문 조사가 실시되었습니다.
>
> 저희는 두 번째와 네 번째 질문에 대한 응답에 85%의 저희 독자들께서 저희 출판물에 담긴 판매업체 광고 및 편집자 논평 관련 내용의 분량에 만족하시는 것으로 드러났다는 점을 알게 되어 기뻤습니다. 한 가지 저희를 놀라게 한 것은 **93** 약 63%의 독자들께서 세 번째 질문에 대해 "네"라고 답변하셨다는 점이었습니다. 분명, 점점 커져가는 세계 시장이 일부 우려를 초래하고 있습니다. 마지막으로, **94** 77%라는 엄청나게 많은 독자들께서 더 많은 문제 해결 관련 이야기를 보시기를 원하고 계십니다. 이는 집필진이 정보 제공용 조사 및 과학적 조사에서 어떻게 특정 회사들과 업체 소유주들이 고유의 문제를 해결했는지에 관한 흥미로운 사례 연구 역사로 초점을 전환해야 한다는 것을 의미합니다. **95** 다음 달에, 저희가 이를 시작할 수 있는 방법과 관련해 재정 후원자들과 함께 하는 브레인스토밍 워크숍을 계획하고 있습니다.

어휘 conduct ~을 실시하다, ~을 수행하다 poll ~에게 여론 조사를 하다 specific 특정한, 구체적인 affect ~에 영향을 미치다 direction 방향 find (that) ~임을 알게 되다 readership 독자들, 독자층 apparently 분명히, 보아 하니 growing 점점 커져가는, 성장하는 marketplace 시장 cause A B A에게 B를 초래하다 concern 우려, 걱정 huge 엄청난 mean that ~임을 의미하다 shift A from B to C A를 B에서 C로 전환하다 case history 사례 연구 역사 solve ~을 해결하다 financial 재정의, 재무의 backer 후원자 get started on ~을 시작하다

91. 설문 조사의 목적은 무엇인가?

    (A) 앞으로의 콘텐츠를 결정하는 일을 돕는 것

    (B) 전 세계적인 독자들을 늘리는 것

    (C) 광고주들의 요구를 평가하는 것

    (D) 잡지의 성공을 평가하는 것

정답 (A)

해설 첫 지문 첫 단락에 설문 조사를 통한 의견 제공이 출판물을 위

한 올바른 콘텐츠를 선정하는 데 도움이 될 것이라고(Your input will help us select the right content for our publication) 언급하는 부분이 목적에 해당된다. 이는 앞으로 출판물에 실을 콘텐츠를 결정하는 데 도움이 될 것이라는 뜻이므로 (A)가 정답이다.

어휘 **determine** ~을 결정하다, ~을 밝혀내다 **worldwide** 전 세계적인 **assess** ~을 평가하다 **advertiser** 광고주 **rate** ~을 평가하다, ~의 등급을 매기다

92. 설문 조사가 누구를 대상으로 하는 것 같은가?
(A) 식료품점 체인의 관리 책임자들
(B) 레스토랑 프랜차이즈의 소유주들
(C) 출판사 직원들
(D) 광고 관련 거래처 임원들

정답 (A)

해설 첫 지문 첫 단락에 설문 조사가 잡지 콘텐츠를 정하는 데 도움이 된다는 말과 함께 전국에 있는 수천 곳의 슈퍼마켓 체인 관리 책임자들이 읽는다는(which is read by thousands of supermarket chain managers across the country) 말이 쓰여 있다. 이는 독자인 슈퍼마켓 체인 관리 책임자들을 대상으로 하는 설문 조사임을 나타내는 말이므로 (A)가 정답이다.

어휘 **be intended for** ~을 대상으로 하다 **grocery store** 식료품점 **publishing company** 출판사 **account** 거래처, 고객사, 계좌

93. 독자들 중 몇 퍼센트가 외국의 혁신에 관해 더 알고 싶다고 말했는가?
(A) 40%
(B) 63%
(C) 77%
(D) 85%

정답 (B)

해설 첫 번째 지문에서 3번 질문이 외국의 혁신에 관해 알고 싶은지 묻는(Do you want more articles on innovations from other countries?) 내용으로 되어 있다. 이 3번 질문과 관련해, 두 번째 지문 두 번째 단락에 약 63%의 독자들이 세 번째 질문에 "네"라고 답변했다는(about 63% of the readers answered "yes" to the third question) 설문조사 결과를 알리고 있으므로 (B)가 정답이다.

94. 잡지의 기사와 관련해 언급된 것은 무엇인가?
(A) 대부분의 사람들이 너무 많은 광고와 관련해 불만을 제기했다.
(B) 소수의 독자들이 세계 시장에 관심을 갖고 있다.
(C) 독자들이 일반적으로 다른 사람들의 해결책에 관해 알아보는 것을 좋아한다.
(D) 대다수의 구독자들이 집필진의 전반적인 의견에 동의하지 않는다.

정답 (C)

해설 두 번째 지문 두 번째 단락에 77%라는 엄청나게 많은 독자들이 더 많은 문제 해결 관련 이야기를 읽어보기를 원하고 있다는(a huge 77% of our readers would like to see more problem-solving narratives) 내용이 쓰여 있다. 이는 독자들이 문제 해결책들과 관련된 정보를 얻고 싶어한다는 뜻이므로 (C)가 정답이다.

어휘 **typically** 일반적으로, 전형적으로 **solution** 해결책 **a majority of** 대다수의, 대부분의 **agree with** ~에 동의하다

95. 다음 달에 무슨 일이 있을 것인가?
(A) 새로운 설문 조사가 완료될 것이다.
(B) 투자자 대상 회의가 개최될 것이다.
(C) 새로운 해설식 광고가 개발될 것이다.
(D) 집필진 대상 워크숍이 개최될 것이다.

정답 (B)

해설 두 번째 지문 마지막 문장에 다음 달에 재정 후원자들과 함께 하는 브레인스토밍 워크숍을 계획하고 있다고(Next month, we are planning a brainstorming workshop with our financial backers) 알리고 있다. 이는 재정 후원자들, 즉 투자자들이 참석하는 아이디어 회의가 열린다는 의미이므로 (B)가 정답이다.

어휘 **occur** 일어나다, 발생되다 **investor** 투자자 **take place** (일, 행사 등이) 개최되다, 일어나다, 발생되다 **infomercial** n. 해설식 광고(광고처럼 보이지 않도록 길게 정보를 제공하는 방식)

96-100.

수신: 메리 가르시아 <mgarcia@fivehillsmanila.com>
발신: 마틴 볼러 <mvoller@fivehillsbali.com>
제목: 푸켓에서 열리는 컨벤션
날짜: 6월 12일

안녕하세요, 메리 씨,

다음 달에 푸켓에서 개최되는 '여행, 관광, 그리고 접객업 컨벤션'과 관련해 **96** 제가 이메일에서 요청 드린 상세 정보를 보내 주셔서 감사합니다. 안타깝게도, 제가 직접 이 컨벤션 행사에 갈 수 없을 것처럼 보이기 때문에, 저희 프런트 데스크 직원들 중에서 두 명의 선임 직원이 저 대신 참석할 것입니다. **98** 행사 마지막 날에 하시게 되는 연설이 성공적이기를 바랍니다. **97** 비행기를 타고 마닐라로 돌아가시기 전에 7월 21일에 저희 직원 두 명과 함께 저녁 식사하시면 어떠실 것 같으신가요? 괜찮으시다면, 자리를 마련하실 수 있도록 그분들의 이메일 주소를 전달해 드리겠습니다.

안녕히 계십시오.

마틴 볼러
고객 서비스부장
파이브 힐즈 리조트
발리, 인도네시아

---

http://www.pecc.com/tthconvention

여행, 관광, 그리고 접객업 컨벤션
푸켓 전시 및 컨퍼런스 센터, [98] 7월 17일-20일

전체 일정	연설 일정	워크숍 일정	자주 하는 질문

컨벤션 기간에 매일 특별 워크숍이 있을 것입니다. 공간이 각 시간에 대해 100명의 참가자로 제한되므로, 이 페이지 하단에서 미리 등록하시도록 권해 드립니다. 모든 시간은 대강당에서 오후 5시 30분부터 오후 8시 30분까지 진행될 것입니다.

1일차 "업무 공간 말끔하게 유지하기" 진행자, 마크 코니쉬	2일차 "효과적으로 시간 관리하기" 진행자, 샐리 노먼
3일차 "수익 극대화하기" 진행자, 에바 윌튼	4일차 [99] "고객을 최우선시하기" 진행자, 그랜트 벨

온라인 등록 페이지

수신: 마틴 볼러 <mvoller@fivehillsbali.com>
발신: 메리 가르시아 <mgarcia@fivehillsmanila.com>
제목: 회신: 푸켓에서 열리는 컨벤션
날짜: 6월 14일

마틴 씨께,

이메일 감사합니다. 아주 좋은 아이디어 같습니다. 그런데, 귀하의 직원들을 워크숍 중 하나에 등록하시는 것을 고려해야 보셔야 할 것 같습니다. 저는 그분들께서 에바 윌튼 씨의 시간을 통해 많은 통찰력을 얻으실 것으로 생각하지 않는데, 이 시간이 업체 소유주 및 기업가들에게 더 많이 [100] 맞춰져 있고, 첫째 날과 둘째 날에 열리는 워크숍은 꽤 기본적입니다. 하지만, [99] 그랜트 벨 씨의 시간에 많은 것을 얻으실 수도 있습니다. 이분이 그 업계에서 손꼽히는 교육 전문가들 중의 한 분이기 때문에, 귀하의 직원들이 이분의 전문 지식으로부터 뭔가 얻을 수 있는 좋은 기회입니다.

안녕히 계십시오.

메리

---

96. 첫 번째 이메일에서 가르시아 씨와 관련해 암시된 것은 무엇인가?

(A) 최근에 파이브 힐스 리조트에 고용되었다.
(B) 앞서 볼러 씨의 연락을 받았다.
(C) 추가 프런트 데스크 직원을 모집할 생각이다.
(D) 주로 푸켓을 기반으로 활동한다.

정답 (B)

해설 첫 번째 이메일인 첫 지문 시작 부분에 작성자인 볼러 씨 자신이 이메일을 통해 요청한 상세 정보를 보내준 것에 대해 가르시아 씨에게 감사 인사를(Thanks for sending me the details I asked for in my e-mail) 전하는 말이 쓰여 있다. 이를 통해 볼러 씨가 먼저 이메일을 통해 연락했다는 사실을 알 수 있으므로 (B)가 정답이다.

어휘 **previously** 앞서, 이전에, 과거에 **intend to do** ~할 생각이다, ~할 작정이다 **recruit** ~을 모집하다 **be based in** ~을 기반으로 하다 **primarily** 주로

97. 볼러 씨는 가르시아 씨에게 무엇을 하도록 제안하는가?

(A) 인도네시아에 있는 자신의 리조트를 방문하는 일
(B) 발표회 날짜를 변경하는 일
(C) 자신의 직원들과 만나는 일
(D) 한 워크숍에 등록하는 일

정답 (C)

해설 첫 지문 후반부에 7월 21일에 자신의 직원 두 명과 함께 저녁 식사하면 어떨지 묻는 말이 쓰여 있는데(How would you feel about having dinner with my two employees on July 21st), 이는 자신의 직원들과 만나도록 제안하는 것이므로 (C)가 정답이다.

98. 가르시아 씨는 언제 연설할 것인가?

(A) 7월 17일
(B) 7월 18일
(C) 7월 20일
(D) 7월 21일

정답 (C)

해설 첫 지문 중반부에 볼러 씨가 가르시아 씨에게 행사 마지막 날에 하는 연설이 성공적이기를 바란다고(I hope that the talk that you will give on the final day of the event is successful) 알리고 있고, 두 번째 지문에 제시된 행사 일정표 상단에 마지막 날이 7월 20일로(July 17-20) 표기되어 있으므로 (C)가 정답이다.

99. 가르시아 씨는 어느 워크숍을 볼러 씨에게 추천하는가?

(A) 업무 공간 말끔하게 유지하기
(B) 효과적으로 시간 관리하기
(C) 수익 극대화하기
(D) 고객을 최우선시하기

정답 (D)

해설 마지막 지문에 불러 씨의 직원들을 워크숍 중 하나에 등록시키는 일을 제안하면서 그랜트 벨 씨의 시간을 통해 많은 것을 얻을 수 있을 것이라고(they might get a lot out of Grant Bell's session) 알리고 있다. 두 번째 지문의 행사 일정표에서 4일차에 표기된 "고객을 최우선시하기"가 그랜트 벨 씨의 연설 주제이므로("Putting the Customer First", Led by Grant Bell) (D)가 정답이다.

100. 두 번째 이메일에서, 첫 번째 단락, 세 번째 줄의 단어 "geared"와 의미가 가장 가까운 것은 무엇인가?

(A) 교대된
(B) 접근된
(C) 갖춰진
(D) 대상이 된

정답 (D)

해설 해당 문장에서 geared가 속한 which절은 바로 앞에 언급된 Eva Wilton's session을 수식하는 역할을 한다. 또한, geared 뒤에 위치한 toward 전치사구에 업체 소유주들 및 기업가들을 뜻하는 명사구가 위치해 있어 에바 윌튼 씨의 시간이 그 사람들을 대상으로 한다는 뜻을 나타내기 위해 geared가 쓰인 것으로 볼 수 있다. 따라서, '대상이 된' 등을 뜻하는 (D) targeted가 정답이다.

LC

1. (C)	**2.** (C)	**3.** (C)	**4.** (A)	**5.** (C)
6. (C)	**7.** (B)	**8.** (A)	**9.** (C)	**10.** (C)
11. (A)	**12.** (B)	**13.** (C)	**14.** (A)	**15.** (C)
16. (B)	**17.** (A)	**18.** (C)	**19.** (B)	**20.** (A)
21. (D)	**22.** (B)	**23.** (C)	**24.** (B)	**25.** (C)
26. (D)	**27.** (C)	**28.** (C)	**29.** (A)	**30.** (C)
31. (A)	**32.** (D)	**33.** (C)	**34.** (C)	**35.** (C)
36. (D)	**37.** (C)	**38.** (D)	**39.** (A)	**40.** (D)
41. (C)	**42.** (C)	**43.** (A)	**44.** (B)	**45.** (C)
46. (C)	**47.** (A)	**48.** (B)	**49.** (A)	**50.** (B)

RC

51. (A)	**52.** (D)	**53.** (B)	**54.** (C)	**55.** (B)
56. (C)	**57.** (D)	**58.** (B)	**59.** (D)	**60.** (C)
61. (B)	**62.** (D)	**63.** (D)	**64.** (D)	**65.** (D)
66. (C)	**67.** (A)	**68.** (C)	**69.** (C)	**70.** (D)
71. (D)	**72.** (B)	**73.** (A)	**74.** (D)	**75.** (D)
76. (D)	**77.** (D)	**78.** (D)	**79.** (C)	**80.** (B)
81. (B)	**82.** (B)	**83.** (D)	**84.** (D)	**85.** (B)
86. (B)	**87.** (C)	**88.** (D)	**89.** (D)	**90.** (D)
91. (C)	**92.** (D)	**93.** (D)	**94.** (C)	**95.** (C)
96. (B)	**97.** (C)	**98.** (C)	**99.** (C)	**100.** (D)

Part 1

1. (A) A dock is crowded with tourists.
(B) Some boats are sailing on the lake.
(C) Some buildings are located near a hill.
(D) A bridge crosses over a waterway.

(A) 부두가 관광객들로 붐비고 있다.
(B) 보트들이 호수에 떠 있다.
(C) 몇몇 건물들이 언덕 근처에 위치해 있다.
(D) 다리가 수로 위에 가로질러 있다.

해설 (A) 부두에 많은 사람들이 보이지 않으므로 오답.
(B) 호수에 보트가 떠 있는 모습이 보이지 않으므로 오답.
(C) 언덕 근처에 건물들이 있으므로 정답.
(D) 수로 위를 가로지르는 다리도 보이지 않으므로 오답.

어휘 **be crowded with** ~로 붐비다 **tourist** 관광객 **sail** 항해
하다 **hill** 언덕 **lake** 호수 **cross over** ~ 위를 가로지르다
waterway 수로

2. (A) A woman is holding a map.
(B) A woman is zipping her jacket.
(C) Some signs are posted along a trail.
(D) Some bushes are being planted.

(A) 여자가 지도를 들고 있다.
(B) 여자가 재킷의 지퍼를 채우고 있다.
(C) 표지판이 산책길을 따라 게시되어 있다.
(D) 관목이 심어지고 있다.

해설 (A) 여자가 손에 뭔가를 들고 있지 않으므로 오답.
(B) 여자가 재킷의 지퍼를 채우는 동작을 하고 있지 않으므로
오답.
(C) 산길을 따라 표지판이 세워져 있으므로 정답.
(D) 관목을 심는 모습이 아니므로 오답.

어휘 **zip** ~의 지퍼를 채우다 **post** ~을 게시하다 **trail** 산길, 오
솔길 **bush** 관목, 덤불

Part 2

3. When should we start painting the walls in the
waiting room?

(A) That's an attractive color.
(B) I've been in line for 30 minutes.
(C) How about on Friday night?

대기실 벽에 언제 페인트칠을 시작해야 하나요?
(A) 그거 매력적인 색상이네요.
(B) 저는 30분 동안 줄을 서고 있어요.
(C) 금요일 저녁에 하는 게 어때요?

해설 페인트칠을 언제 해야 하는지를 묻는 질문에 대해 How about
~? 구문을 이용해 특정 시점을 제안하고 있는 (C)가 정답이다.
(A)는 painting에서 연상 가능한 내용으로, That이 특정 색상
을 가리켜야 하는데 질문에서 언급된 색이 없으므로 어울리지
않는다. (B)는 waiting에서 연상 가능한 be in line(줄을 서다)
이라는 표현을 제시해 혼동을 유발하는 선택지다.

어휘 **waiting room** 대기실 **attractive** 매력적인 **be in line**
줄 서 있다

4. Who should I talk to about leaving the office
early?

**(A) I think everybody is supposed to work a full
shift.**
(B) Leave them on my desk.
(C) The office usually closes at 6.

일찍 퇴근하는 것에 대해 누구에게 얘기해야 하죠?

(A) 전원 종일 근무하도록 되어 있는 것 같은데요.
(B) 그것들을 제 책상 위에 두세요.
(C) 사무실은 보통 6시에 닫아요.

해설 일찍 퇴근하는 문제에 대해 누구에게 이야기하면 되는지 묻는 질문이다. 이에 대해 부서나 사람 이름을 대는 직접적인 응답 대신 '전원 종일 근무를 해야 하는 것 같다'라는 말로 일찍 퇴근하는 것이 어려울 것임을 암시하는 (A)가 가장 적절한 대답이다. 대화가 이루어지는 상황 자체를 이해해야 풀 수 있는, 난이도가 꽤 높은 문제이다.

어휘 **shift** 교대 근무 **leave** ~을 놓다, 두다

5. What are your plans this evening?
(A) At 9 p.m. at the pancake restaurant.
(B) No, what do you have in mind?
(C) Just the usual family dinner.

오늘 저녁 계획이 어떻게 됩니까?
(A) 밤 9시에 팬케이크 식당에서요.
(B) 아뇨, 생각해 둔 것 있어요?
(C) 그냥 일상적인 가족 식사요.

해설 핵심어는 What, plans이다. 오늘 저녁에 계획한 일이 무엇인지 묻는 질문이므로, 평소처럼 가족들과 식사를 할 것이라고 답하는 (C)가 가장 자연스러운 응답이다. (A)는 질문의 evening에서 연상할 수 있는 9 p.m.(9시)를 이용한 혼동 선택지고, (B)는 의문사 의문문에 맞지 않는 No로 답하고 있으므로 오답이다.

어휘 **have A in mind** A를 마음에 두다 **usual** 일상적인, 평소의

6. How long have you been waiting in line?
(A) Yes, if you have an item to return.
(B) I just can't seem to log on.
(C) For at least an hour or so.

얼마나 오랫동안 줄 서서 기다리신 거예요?
(A) 네, 반품할 물건이 있으시다면요.
(B) 전 그저 로그온이 안 되는 것 같아요.
(C) 적어도 한 시간 정도요.

해설 기간을 묻는 How long ~? 의문문으로, how long과 waiting을 챙겨 들어야 한다. 얼마 동안 기다렸는지 묻고 있으므로 기간을 나타내는 전치사 for를 이용하여 '적어도 한 시간 동안'이라고 답하는 (C)가 가장 잘 어울린다. (A)는 의문사 의문문에 Yes/No로 답할 수 없으므로 오답이며, (B)는 소요시간을 묻는 질문에 적절한 대답이 아니다.

어휘 **wait in line** 줄서서 기다리다 **return** ~을 반품하다 **seem to do** ~하는 것 같다 **log on** 로그온하다 **at least** 적어도 **or so** ~ 쯤, ~ 정도

7. Why don't you e-mail me when you hear the final results?
(A) I called you right away.
(B) Yes, I will let you know immediately.
(C) You should have listened to me.

최종 결과를 듣게 되면 제게 이메일로 알려주시겠어요?
(A) 제가 당신에게 바로 전화했습니다.
(B) 네, 제가 즉시 알려드리겠습니다.
(C) 당신은 제 말을 들었어야 해요.

해설 Why don't you ~?는 권유나 제안하는 의미의 표현이다. 결과가 나오면 이메일을 보내달라는 뜻이므로, 그렇게 하겠다고 답하는 (B)가 가장 잘 어울리는 응답이다. Yes를 통해 확실한 수락의 의미를 전달한 뒤 즉시 알려주겠다고 덧붙이고 있다. (A)는 시제가 맞지 않아 오답이고, (C)는 질문의 내용에 어울리는 응답이 아니다.

어휘 **final result** 최종 결과 **right away** 곧바로 **immediately** 즉시 **should have p.p** ~했어야 했다

8. Is Mary Gomez staying at this hotel?
(A) We don't have any guests by that name.
(B) Yes, I had a comfortable stay.
(C) This is the reception area.

메리 고메즈 씨가 이 호텔에 묵고 있나요?
(A) 그런 이름의 손님은 없는데요.
(B) 네, 편안히 머물렀습니다.
(C) 여긴 접수 구역입니다.

해설 특정인의 이름을 대면서 그 사람이 호텔에 묵고 있는지를 묻는 be동사 일반의문문으로 이를 확인해주는 대답이 와야 한다. (A)는 그런 이름의 손님이 없다는 말로, 질문에 대한 적절한 응답이 된다. (B)에서 Yes는 긍정을 나타내나, 뒤에 이어지는 내용이 질문과 어울리지 않는다. (C)는 hotel에서 연상하기 쉬운 reception을 이용한 오답이다.

어휘 **stay** v. 머물다, 묵다 n. 세류 **by that name** 그런 이름을 가진 **comfortable** 안락한, 편안한 **reception** 접수

9. Have you completed the building blueprint?
(A) He printed it in a different color.
(B) No, in a different building.
(C) I'm almost done.

건물 설계도 작업을 완료하셨나요?
(A) 그는 그것을 다른 색으로 인쇄했어요.
(B) 아뇨, 다른 건물에서요.
(C) 거의 다 했어요.

해설 설계도 완성 여부를 묻는 질문이므로 '거의 다 했다'라는 말로 완료 정도를 알리는 (C)가 적절한 반응이다. 완료시제가 사용되는 문제에서는 과거분사로 사용되는 동사의 발음에 주의해야 해야 함을 꼭 기억하자. (A)는 질문에 나온 blueprint의 print를 반복하고 있으며, 누군지 알 수 없는 he에 대해 말하고 있어

어울리지 않는 대답이다. (B)는 building이 반복된 선택지며, 장소에 대한 질문이 아니므로 핵심을 벗어난 대답이다.

어휘 **complete** ~을 완료하다 **blueprint** 설계도, 청사진 **almost** 거의

10. Don't you think the volume on the sound system is too low?

(A) I haven't heard of that person.
(B) They've already been placed in a row.
(C) Yes, especially in a room this big.

음향 시스템의 볼륨이 너무 작다고 생각하지 않으세요?
(A) 그 분에 대해 들어본 적이 없어요.
(B) 이미 그것들은 한 줄로 놓여 있어요.
(C) 네, 특히 이 정도로 큰 방에서는요.

해설 음향의 볼륨 크기에 대한 상대방의 생각을 묻는 부정 의문문으로, Yes라고 답하는 것으로 자신도 소리가 작다고 생각한다고 말한 뒤 부연 설명을 붙이는 (C)가 정답이다. (A)는 사람에 대해 이야기하고 있어 대화 주제에 벗어나는 오답이다. (B)는 low와 발음이 비슷하게 들리는 row를 이용한 함정이다.

어휘 **sound system** 음향 시스템 **hear of** ~에 대해 듣다 **in a row** 한 줄로 **especially** 특히 **this big** 이렇게 큰

11. Could you work overtime this weekend? We need some extra help.

(A) I have a family event, but Sally said she'd come in.
(B) No, I am available.
(C) I'm glad we got it finished before the deadline.

이번 주말에 시간외 근무를 하실 수 있으세요? 추가로 도움이 필요해서요.
(A) 저는 집안일이 있지만, 샐리 씨가 올 거라고 말했어요.
(B) 아뇨, 저는 시간이 됩니다.
(C) 마감시한 전에 일을 끝내서 기쁩니다.

해설 Could you ~?를 통해 상대방에게 제안을 하는 상황이며, 시간외 근무를 하는 것에 대해 묻고 있다. 따라서 집안일이 있다는 이유를 들어 간접적인 거절 의사를 밝힌 후, 샐리 씨가 올 것이라는 말로 대안을 제시하는 (A)가 적절한 반응이다. (B)는 부정을 나타내는 No와 긍정을 나타내는 available(시간을 낼 수 있는)이 질문 상황과 어울리지 않는다. (C)는 과거에 끝난 일에 대해 말하고 있으므로 미래의 일에 대해 제안하는 질문에 어울리는 반응이 아니다.

어휘 **work overtime** 시간외 근무를 하다 **extra** 추가의, 별도의 **available** (사람이) 시간이 있는 **get A p.p.** A가 ~되게 하다 **deadline** 마감시한

12. Do I need to use a ladder to reach the book?

(A) Try the non-fiction section.
(B) The shelf is quite high.
(C) I'm a big fan of that author.

그 책에 손이 닿으려면 사다리를 이용해야 하나요?
(A) 비소설 코너에 한 번 가 보세요.
(B) 그 책장은 꽤 높습니다.
(C) 저는 그 작가의 열성 팬입니다.

해설 책에 손이 닿도록 하기 위해 사다리를 이용해야 하는지 묻는 의문문이므로 책장이 높다는 말로 사다리를 이용해야 함을 알리는 (B)가 정답이다. (A)와 (C)는 book에서 연상 가능한 non-fiction section과 author를 각각 활용한 오답이다.

어휘 **ladder** 사다리 **reach** ~에 손이 닿다, 미치다 **try ~**에 한 번 가 보다, ~을 한 번 해 보다 **non-fiction** 비소설 **section** (특정 제품의) 코너, 섹션 **shelf** 책장, 선반 **quite** 꽤, 상당히 **big fan** 열성 팬 **author** 작가, 저자

13. Is she going to educate the staff about our new product this week or next?

(A) Yes, it is educational.
(B) Probably only some members.
(C) This Friday, I think.

그녀가 이번 주에 우리 신제품에 대해 직원들을 교육할 건가요, 아니면 다음 주에 하나요?
(A) 네, 교육적이에요.
(B) 아마 일부 회원에 한해서 일 거예요.
(C) 제 생각에 이번 금요일이에요.

해설 직원 교육을 실시할 미래 시점 중의 하나를 선택하는 의문문이다. 선택지 중에서 this week를 더욱 구체적으로 언급한 (C)가 정답이다. (A)는 선택 의문문에 Yes로 응답하므로 오답이다. (B)는 staff와 연관 지을 수 있는 대상 members를 이용한 혼동 선택지다.

어휘 **educate** ~을 교육하다 **staff** 직원들 **educational** 교육적인

14. How do I get into the gym's sauna?

(A) Just use your membership card.
(B) Yes, on the second floor.
(C) There are towels available.

체육관 사우나에 어떻게 들어 갈 수 있죠?
(A) 갖고 계신 회원 카드를 이용하시면 됩니다.
(B) 네, 2층에요.
(C) 이용 가능한 타월들이 있습니다.

해설 체육관 사우나 출입 방법을 묻는 How 의문문이므로 회원 카드를 사용해 출입할 수 있는 방법을 알리는 (A)가 정답이다. (B)는 의문사 의문문에 맞지 않는 Yes로 답변하는 오답이며, (C)는 sauna에서 연상 가능한 towels를 활용한 오답이다.

어휘 **get into** ~로 들어 가다 **gym** 체육관

15. Who's responsible for booking Mr. Hamill's limousine?

(A) From the airport.
(B) Yes, it's a great book.
(C) Joseph will take care of it.

해밀 씨의 리무진 예약을 누가 맡고 있죠?
(A) 공항에서부터요.
(B) 네, 그건 아주 좋은 책입니다.
(C) 조셉 씨가 처리할 겁니다.

해설 특정한 일을 책임지고 있는 사람을 묻는 Who 의문문이므로 담당자의 이름을 언급하는 (C)가 정답이다. (A)는 limousine에서 연상 가능한 airport를 활용한 오답으로 Where 의문문에 어울리는 답변이며, (B)는 의문사 의문문에 맞지 않는 Yes로 답변하는 오답이다.

어휘 **be responsible for** ~을 맡고 있다, 책임지고 있다 **book** ~을 예약하다 **take care of** ~을 처리하다

16. Let's check our facts first before we publish the article.

(A) I got $500 up front for it.
(B) That sounds like a good idea.
(C) It's my third assignment.

기사를 내기 전에 사실을 먼저 확인해 봅시다.
(A) 그 일에 대해 500달러를 선불로 받았어요.
(B) 좋은 생각인 거 같아요.
(C) 그게 제 세 번째 업무예요.

해설 사실 관계를 먼저 확인해 보자고 제안하는 것에 대해 동조하는 의미를 나타내는 (B)가 정답이다. That sounds like a good idea류의 문장은 동의할 때 자주 쓰이는 표현이므로 꼭 기억해 두자. (A)는 비용과 관련된 내용이 전혀 아니다. (C)는 업무 순서에 대한 내용이 아니므로 어울리지 않는 반응이다.

어휘 **fact** 사실 **publish** ~을 출간하다, 발행하다 **article** (신문 등의) 기사 **up front** 선불로 **assignment** 업무, 할당(된 일)

17. We have until 5 p.m. to hand in our expense reports, don't we?

(A) Actually, they were due yesterday.
(B) No, I didn't receive any handouts.
(C) At least 500 dollars a week.

오후 5시까지 비용 보고서를 제출해야 해요, 안 그런가요?
(A) 실은, 어제가 제출 기한이었어요.
(B) 아뇨, 저는 어떤 유인물도 받지 않았어요.
(C) 적어도 일주일에 500달러요.

해설 hand in, expense reports가 질문의 핵심이며, 시점을 나타내는 until 5 p.m.이 문장 중간에 삽입된 구조임을 재빨리 파악해야 하는 어려운 문제이다. 특정 기한을 확인하기 위한 의도로 묻는 부가 의문문이므로 이미 그 기한이 지났음을 말하

는 (A)가 정답이다. (A)처럼 actually가 사용된 답변은 질문과의 의미 연결이 적절하기만 하면 정답일 확률이 매우 높은 유형 중의 하나이다. (B)는 질문의 hand가 단어 일부에 포함된 handout을 이용한 함정이고, (C)는 질문의 expense(비용)에서 연상할 수 있는 500 dollars를 이용해 혼동을 주는 오답이다.

어휘 **hand in** ~을 제출하다 **expense report** 지출 보고서 **actually** 실은, 사실은 **due** ~가 기한인, 예정인 **receive** ~을 받다 **handout** 유인물, 인쇄물 **at least** 적어도, 최소한

18. Won't it be too expensive to remodel the reception area?

(A) I think it was held at the Noblesse Hotel.
(B) Yes, I got the newer model.
(C) Not if we stick to our budget.

접수 구역을 개조하는 데 너무 비용이 많이 들지 않을까요?
(A) 노블레스 호텔에서 열렸던 거 같은데요.
(B) 네, 더 최신의 모델을 샀어요.
(C) 예산에 맞게만 하면 그렇지 않을 거예요.

해설 비용이 너무 많이 드는 것은 아닐지 묻는 부정 의문문이다. 이에 대한 적절한 답변은 Not if(~라면 그렇지 않다)가 쓰인 (C)로, 예산에 맞게만 하면 비용이 많이 들지 않을 것이라는 뜻을 나타낸다. Will not의 축약형 Won't와 주어 it이 곧바로 이어져 연음되는 부분을 제대로 듣지 못하면 당황하기 쉬우므로 여러 번 듣고 익숙해지도록 한다. 또한 조건으로 말하는 답변에 Not if가 종종 쓰이므로 그 의미와 쓰임을 알아두자.

어휘 **too … to do** 너무 …해서 ~하다 **remodel** ~을 개조하다 **be held** 개최되다, 열리다 **stick to** ~을 고수하다 **budget** 예산

19. Will you be dropping by the coffee shop or the bakery?

(A) No, they weren't there.
(B) Both of them.
(C) At least ten copies.

커피숍에 들르실 건가요, 아니면 제과점에 들르실 건가요?
(A) 아뇨, 그것들은 거기에 없었어요.
(B) 두 군데 모두요.
(C) 최소한 10부요.

해설 핵심 선택 대상인 coffee shop or bakery 뿐만 아니라 질문에 쓰인 동사 drop by까지 챙겨 들을 수 있으면 더욱 좋다. 두 가지 선택 사항에 대해 '둘 다'라는 의미를 나타내는 (B)가 적절한 반응이다. (A)는 질문에 쓰인 동사와 달리 과거 시점의 일을 나타내기 때문에 어울리지 않는 답변이며, (C)는 coffee-copies의 유사한 소리를 이용한 오답 선택지다.

어휘 **drop by** ~에 들르다 **bakery** 제과점 **both of them** 둘 다 **at least** 최소한

20. You can use my office phone while I'm out meeting my client.

(A) Great. I'm not sure what's wrong with mine.
(B) Yes, feel free to hold it in my office.
(C) Any time after 2 P.M. would be good.

제가 고객을 만나러 나가 있는 동안 제 사무실 전화를 쓰셔도 됩니다.

(A) 잘됐네요. 제 전화기가 뭐가 문제인지 모르겠어요.
(B) 네, 마음 놓고 제 사무실에 보관하세요.
(C) 오후 2시 이후에는 아무 때나 좋습니다.

해설 사무실 전화를 써도 좋다는 제안의 의미를 갖는 평서문이다. 제안에 대한 답변은 크게 승낙과 거절로 나뉘는데, 여기서는 자신의 사무실 전화기를 사용할 것을 제안하는 내용에 대해 '잘됐다'고 한 뒤 자신의 전화에 문제가 있음을 덧붙인 (A)가 적절한 반응이다. (B)는 질문의 office를 반복한 오답이고, (C)는 질문의 meeting을 듣고 만남의 시간을 묻는 것으로 착각하고 고를 수 있는 오답이다.

어휘 **be out** 밖에 있다 **what's wrong with** ~에 뭐가 문제인지 **feel free to do** 마음껏 ~하다 **hold** ~을 보관하다, 수용하다 **any time after** ~ 이후에는 언제든지

Part 3

Questions 21-23 refer to the following questions.

> M: Hi, Melissa. Len told me **21** you were at the Changing World of Travel seminar last week, and that you filmed the entire event. Would you be able to put together a video to put up on the company's Web site?
>
> W: Yes. I filmed it, but the footage is all in pieces at the moment. Unfortunately, **22** I don't have very good editing skills. Perhaps I should find someone who can put them all together for me. What do you think about that?
>
> M: Actually, I have another idea. **23** Bring me what you have, and maybe I can teach you how to do it.
>
> W: **23** Okay, that sounds like a good idea. I'll come to your office on Friday so we can do it together.
>
> ---
>
> 남: 안녕하세요, 멜리사. 렌이 그러는데 지난 주에 열렸던 '변화하는 여행 업계' 세미나에 가서 행사 전체를 촬영해 오셨다면서요. 혹시 하나의 동영상으로 편집하셔서 회사 웹 사이트에 올려주실 수 있으세요?
>
> 여: 네. 촬영해 오긴 했지만, 지금은 영상들이 모두 여러 조각으로 되어 있어요. 안타깝게도, 제 편집 기술이 그렇게 좋은 편

은 아니에요. 아마 이 영상들을 모두 한 군데 모아줄 수 있는 사람을 찾아봐야 할 것 같네요. 어떻게 생각하세요?
남: 사실, 저한테 다른 생각이 있어요. 갖고 계신 것을 가져오시면, 제가 편집하는 방법을 가르쳐 드릴 수 있을 거예요.
여: 그래요, 좋은 생각 같아요. 금요일에 사무실로 찾아갈테니 함께 해봐요.

어휘 **world** (특정 분야·직업 등에 관련된) 세계, ~계 **film** ~을 촬영하다, 녹화하다 **entire** 전체의 **put together** (부분, 요소 등) ~을 조립하다 **put A up on B** A를 B에 올리다 **footage** 동영상, 자료 영상 **in pieces** 조각조각으로 **at the moment** 지금은, 현재 **unfortunately** 안타깝게도, 아쉽게도 **editing skill** 편집 기술 **bring A B** A에게 B를 가져오다[가다] **what you have** 당신이 가지고 있는 것

21. 여자는 최근에 무슨 행사에 참석했는가?
(A) 아이들을 위한 자선 행사
(B) 경제 변화에 대한 프레젠테이션
(C) 텔레마케터들을 위한 컨퍼런스
(D) 여행과 관련된 강연회

해설 남자는 대화를 시작하면서 you were at the Changing World of Travel seminar last week라는 말로 여자가 지난주에 참석했던 행사에 대해 언급하고 있다. 이 부분을 통해 참석한 seminar가 여행에 관련된 것임을 알 수 있고, 이를 talk regarding travel로 바꿔 말한 (D)가 정답이다.

어휘 **charity event** 자선행사 **economic** 경제의 **regarding** ~와 관련된

22. 여자가 제안하는 일은 무엇인가?
(A) 동영상을 텔레비전 방송국에 파는 것
(B) 다른 사람에게 영상 편집을 부탁하는 것
(C) 주말에 본인이 직접 영상을 편집하는 것
(D) 다른 행사를 촬영하는 것

해설 woman과 suggest가 문제의 핵심이므로 여자의 말에서 제안 관련 내용을 찾아야 한다. 여자는 대화 중반에 자신은 편집 기술이 좋지 않아서 자신을 대신해 동영상 편집을 해줄 사람을 찾아야 될 것 같다고(I don't have very good editing skills. Perhaps I should find someone who can put them all together for me) 언급하고 있다. 이어서 What do you think about that?라고 물으며 남자의 의견을 구하고 있으므로, 편집해줄 다른 사람을 찾아보는 게 어떤지 제안하고 있음을 알 수 있으므로 정답은 (B)이다.

어휘 **television station** 텔레비전 방송국 **by oneself** 혼자, 스스로 **over** (기간) ~에 걸쳐

23. 화자들은 무엇을 하는 데 동의하는가?
(A) 편집 프로그램을 구입하는 것
(B) 도와줄 다른 사람을 찾는 것
(C) 공동으로 작업하는 것

(D) 프로젝트 마감시한을 연기하는 것

해설 agree to do가 문제의 핵심이므로 두 사람의 의견이 일치되는 부분을 찾아야 한다. 여자의 제안을 들은 남자가 Bring me what you have, and maybe I can teach you how to do it이라며 편집하는 방법을 가르쳐주겠다는 의사를 나타내자 여자가 이에 흔쾌히 동의하고 있다. 이어서 여자가 함께 작업하기 위해 금요일에 사무실로 가겠다고 말하는 내용이 나오므로(I'll come to your office on Friday so we can do it together) (C)가 정답임을 알 수 있다.

어휘 collaborate on ~을 공동으로 작업하다 postpone ~을 연기하다

Paraphrase do it together
→ collaborate

Questions 24-26 refer to the following conversation.

M: Hi, Lisa. I heard you just started a new company. Jake told me that **24** you offer business advice to owners of up-and-coming small businesses.

W: Yeah, we just started last month. Unfortunately, it has not gone as well as we had hoped. **25** The economy has been really poor this year, so we think that might be the reason for our slow start. If it picks up in the next few months, maybe our business will improve, too.

M: I think you will be okay. I heard the economy looks like it is going to improve soon. **26** I have a friend who owns a similar business. Would you like to meet him? He might be able to give you some advice. I think he struggled in the beginning, as well.

남: 안녕하세요, 리사 씨. 새로운 회사를 막 시작하셨다고 들었어요. 제이크 씨가 그러는데 전도 유망한 소기업들의 소유주들에게 사업 관련 자문 서비스를 제공하신다면서요.
여: 네, 지난 달에 막 시작했어요. 아쉽게도 우리가 바랐던 것만큼 잘 되고 있진 않네요. 올해 경제 상황이 너무 좋지 않아서, 그게 저희 사업 초반이 느린 이유가 아닐까 생각해요. 앞으로 몇 달 후에 경기가 회복되면 아마 저희 사업도 나아지겠죠.
남: 좋아지실 거라고 생각해요. 경기가 곧 괜찮아질 것으로 보인다는 얘기를 들었어요. 저에게 비슷한 사업을 하는 친구가 있어요. 한 번 만나 보시겠어요? 제 친구가 아마 조언을 해 줄 수 있을지도 모르죠. 그 친구도 마찬가지로 초반에 고생을 했던 것 같아요.

어휘 owner 소유주 up-and-coming 전도 유망한 small business 소기업 pick up 회복되다, 개선되다 in the next few months 앞으로 몇 달 후에 improve 개선되다,

향상되다 struggle 애쓰다, 분투하다, 발버둥을 치다 in the beginning 초기에, 초반에 as well 마찬가지로, 또한

24. 여자는 무슨 종류의 사업을 운영하고 있는가?
(A) 컴퓨터 회사
(B) 컨설팅 회사
(C) 여행사
(D) 회계 법인

해설 대화 시작 부분에서 남자는 여자가 새로 사업을 시작했음을 언급하며 you offer business advice for up-and-coming small businesses라는 말로 여자가 하는 사업 내용이 offer business advice임을 밝히고 있으므로 여자의 회사는 (B) A consulting firm일 것이라고 짐작할 수 있다.

어휘 business 사업(체), 회사 run ~을 운영하다 firm n. 회사 accounting 회계

25. 여자는 무엇이 자신의 회사에 도움이 될 수 있을 거라고 말하는가?
(A) 신제품 출시
(B) 회사 위치 이전
(C) 경기 회복
(D) 마케팅 전략 수정

해설 여자가 자신의 회사에 도움이 되는 것(help her business)으로 말하는 내용이 무엇인지를 묻고 있으므로 여자의 말에서 긍정적인 요소로 언급되는 것을 찾아야 한다. 여자는 대화 중반부에 사업이 아주 잘 진행되는 것은 아니라는 말과 함께 If it picks up in the next few months maybe our business will improve, too라는 희망사항을 언급하고 있다. 앞서 언급한 economy를 it으로 받아 경기가 나아지는 경우(If it picks up ~)에 회사가 좋아질 것이라고 말하고 있으므로 이를 improvement in the economy로 표현한 (C)가 정답이다.

어휘 release n. 출시, 공개, 발표 relocation (위치 등) 이전, 재배치 Improvement 개선, 향상 strategy 선략

26. 남자가 제안하는 일은 무엇인가?
(A) 여자의 직원들을 교육하는 것
(B) 고객과 만날 약속을 잡는 것
(C) 여자의 회사에 투자하는 것
(D) 여자를 친구에게 소개하는 것

해설 남자의 제안을 들을 수 있는 부분은 대화 마지막 부분에 나타나는데, 남자는 I have a friend who owns a similar business와 같이 친구의 이야기를 꺼내면서 Would you like to meet him?이라고 제안하고 있으므로 (D)가 정답이다. 자신의 친구를 만나보지 않겠냐고 묻고 있으므로 (D)의 introduce와 같은 의미임을 알 수 있다. (B)의 arrange a meeting도 같은 의미이지만 그 대상이 client로 나타나 있으므로 혼동하지 않도록 주의해야 한다.

어휘 arrange ~을 예정하다, 준비하다 invest in ~에 투자하다

introduce A to B A를 B에게 소개하다

Questions 27-29 refer to the following conversation.

W: Good morning. It's my manager's birthday today, and we're having a party for him later in the office. A colleague told me that **27** **28** your bakery makes the best chocolate fudge cake in town. **28** But, I'm not sure if you can make one on such short notice.

M: **That's our specialty.** We can bake and customize a cake for our clients in three hours as part of our express service. What time is the party?

W: It's at 1 o'clock this afternoon. **29** Will the cake be ready for pick-up at around 12:30?

M: **29** Yes, definitely. I'll see you then.

여: 안녕하세요. 오늘이 저희 부장님 생신이시라서 이따가 사무실에서 생일 파티를 해 드릴 예정입니다. 이 제과점이 우리 시에서 최고의 초콜릿 퍼지 케이크를 만든다고 제 동료 직원 한 명이 알려 주었습니다. 그런데 이렇게 갑작스럽게 말씀드리는데도 만들어 주실 수 있는지 모르겠어요.

남: 그건 저희 전문 제품입니다. 저희는 신속 서비스의 일환으로 3시간 안에 고객들을 위해 케이크를 굽고 맞춤 제작해 드리고 있습니다. 파티가 몇 시에 있으시죠?

여: 오늘 오후 1시입니다. 12시 30분쯤에 케이크를 가져 갈 수 있도록 준비될 수 있을까요?

남: 네, 물론입니다. 그때 뵙겠습니다.

어휘 **colleague** 동료 직원 **on such short notice** 갑작스런 연락에도, 급한 공지에도 **specialty** 특제품, 특산품 **bake** ~을 굽다 **customize** ~을 맞춤 제작하다 **as part of** ~의 일환으로 **express** 신속한, 급행의 **be ready for** ~에 대한 준비가 되다 **pick-up** 가져 가기, 가져 오기 **at around + 시간** ~쯤에 **definitely** 물론입니다, 당연합니다, 확실합니다

27. 화자들은 어디에 있을 것 같은가?
(A) 패스트푸드 매장에
(B) 사무실에
(C) 제과점에
(D) 호텔 주방에

해설 대화 시작 부분에 여자가 부서장의 생일을 언급하면서 이 제과점이 최고의 초콜릿 퍼지 케이크를 만든다고 들은 얘기를 하고 있으므로(your bakery makes the best chocolate fudge cake in town) (C)가 정답임을 알 수 있다.

28. 남자가 "그건 저희 전문 제품입니다"라고 말할 때 암시하는 것은 무엇인가?
(A) 할인된 가격을 제공할 것이다.
(B) 한 가지 종류의 제품만 판매한다.
(C) 서비스를 제공해 줄 수 있다.
(D) 여자에게 감사의 뜻을 전하고 있다.

해설 해당 문장에서 specialty는 주특기나 특별히 잘 만든 상품 등을 가리킨다. 이 말은 바로 앞서 여자가 최고의 초콜릿 퍼지 케이크를 만드는 제과점이라서 왔는데 시간이 짧아 케이크 제작이 가능할지 모르겠다고(your bakery makes the best chocolate fudge cake ~ if you can make one on such short notice) 언급한 다음에 들을 수 있다. 따라서 해당 제품을 이용할 수 있음을 확인해 주기 위한 말이라는 것을 알 수 있으므로 이와 같은 뜻으로 쓰인 (C)가 정답이다.

어휘 **reduced** 할인된 **appreciate** ~에 대해 감사하다 **business** 거래 **express** (감정 등) ~을 표현하다 **gratitude** 감사(의 마음)

29. 여자는 12시 30분경에 무엇을 할 것인가?
(A) 케익을 찾아온다.
(B) 파티를 주최한다.
(C) 예약을 한다.
(D) 특별 제품을 주문한다.

해설 대화 후반부에 여자가 제품을 가지러 올 수 있는 시간으로 12시 30분이 가능한지 묻자(Will the cake be ready for pick-up at around 12:30?) 남자가 그렇다고 답변하고 있으므로 (A)가 정답이다.

어휘 **host** ~을 주최하다 **make a reservation** 예약하다

Questions 30-32 refer to the following conversation with three speakers.

M1: Welcome to Live Well Fitness Center.

M2: Hi, **30** I'm Martin Rodriguez. I called this morning to ask about looking around the gym. **30** I just moved into an apartment nearby, so I'm considering becoming a member here.

M1: Oh, of course. Actually, here comes our members services manager now. Ms. Parker, this is Martin Rodriguez. He's just moved to the area and is interested in a gym membership.

W: Hi, Martin. We're always happy to welcome new members. It's a good time to join, because **31** we're starting several new exercise classes next week.

M2: That sounds good. **32** Are there any free gifts for signing up?

W: **32** Yes, when you start a membership, you get a bag you can use to carry your sports gear around.

남1: 리브 웰 피트니스 센터에 오신 것을 환영합니다.

남2: 안녕하세요, 저는 마틴 로드리게즈입니다. 체육관을 둘러보는 것에 관해 여쭤보려고 오늘 오전에 전화드렸어요. 제가 근처 아파트로 이제 막 이사해서, 이곳의 회원이 되는 것에 대해 고려하고 있습니다.

남1: 아, 물론입니다. 실은, 회원 서비스 매니저님이 여기 오셨네요. 파커 씨, 이분은 마틴 로드리게즈 씨입니다. 이분은 이 지역으로 이제 막 이사오셨고 체육관 멤버십에 관심이 있으세요.

여: 안녕하세요, 마틴 씨. 저희는 새 회원분이 오시는 것을 늘 환영합니다. 저희가 다음 주에 여러 새로운 운동 수업을 시작할 예정이기 때문에 지금 등록하기에 좋은 때입니다.

남2: 좋습니다. 등록하면 어떤 사은품이라도 있습니까?

여: 네, 회원으로 등록하시면, 운동 용품을 담아서 가지고 다니실 수 있는 가방을 하나 드립니다.

어휘 **look around** ~을 둘러보다 **move into** ~로 이사하다 **nearby** 근처에 **consider -ing** ~하는 것을 고려하다 **several** 몇몇의 **free gift** 무료 선물, 사은품 **sign up** 등록하다 **carry A around** A를 가지고 다니다 **gear** 장비, 용품

30. 로드리게즈 씨는 최근에 무엇을 했다고 말하는가?
(A) 작업 프로젝트를 끝냈다.
(B) 새로운 일을 시작했다.
(C) 새 집으로 이사했다.
(D) 수업에 등록했다.

해설 로드리게즈 씨가 자신이 했다고 말하는 부분에 주목해서 들어야 한다. 대화 초반부에 로드리게즈 씨가 자신을 소개하면서 최근에 근처 아파트로 이사했다고(~, I'm Martin Rodriguez. ~ I just moved into an apartment nearby) 언급하고 있으므로 (C)가 정답이다.

어휘 **recently** 최근에 **move into** ~로 이사하다 **enroll in** ~에 등록하다

31. 피트니스 센터가 다음 주에 하기로 계획하는 것은 무엇인가?
(A) 추가 수업을 제공하는 일
(B) 운동 공간을 확장하는 일
(C) 새 강사들을 고용하는 일
(D) 회비를 인하하는 일

해설 대화 중반부에 여자가 next week를 언급하고 있으므로 그 부분을 주목해서 들어야 한다. 다음 주에 여러 새로운 운동 수업을 시작할 예정이라고(we're starting several new exercise classes) 언급하고 있으므로 여러 새로운 운동 수업을 추가 수업으로 표현한 (A)가 정답이다.

어휘 **offer** ~을 제공하다 **additional** 추가적인 **expand** ~을

확장하다 **instructor** 강사 **reduce** (가격을) 낮추다, 인하하다

Paraphrase we're starting several new exercise classes
→ Offer additional classes

32. 여자에 따르면, 새 회원은 어떤 무료 선물을 받는가?
(A) 물병
(B) 운동용 타월
(C) 티셔츠
(D) 스포츠 가방

해설 대화의 마지막 부분에서 여자가 회원으로 등록하면 운동 용품을 담아서 가지고 다닐 수 있는 가방을 하나 받게 된다고(when you start a membership, you get a bag you can use to carry your sports gear around) 언급하고 있다. 따라서 (D)가 정답이다.

어휘 **complimentary** 무료의

Paraphrase a bag you can use to carry your sports gear around
→ a sports bag

Questions 33-35 refer to the following conversation and list.

W: Hello, Mr. Boyle. This is Donna Mumford calling from Meadow Supermarket. **33** I'm sorry to tell you this, but we'll need to move your interview from Wednesday to Friday.

M: Oh, really? Well, that's okay. I'll need to ask my current boss for time off, though.

W: Once again, I apologize for the inconvenience. **34** I made a mistake when I was scheduling appointment times. We have too many candidates coming in on Wednesday.

M: No problem. So, **35** should I come to your office when I arrive on Friday?

W: There's no need to do that. **35** Just go straight to the sales department and find the manager there.

M: Okay, thanks for your help.

여: 안녕하세요, 보일 씨. 메도우 수퍼마켓에서 전화 드리는 도나 멈포드입니다. 이런 말씀 드리기 죄송하지만, 면접을 수요일에서 금요일로 옮겨야 할 것 같습니다.

남: 아, 그렇습니까? 저, 괜찮습니다. 하지만 지금 있는 곳의 상사에게 휴무를 요청해야 할 겁니다.

여: 다시 한 번 불편함을 끼쳐 드려 사과 드립니다. 면접 약속 일정을 정할 때 제가 실수를 했습니다. 수요일에 오시는 지원자들이 너무 많아서요.

남: 괜찮습니다. 그럼, 금요일에 도착하면 귀하의 사무실로 찾아 가면 되는 건가요?

여: 그러실 필요는 없습니다. 영업부로 곧바로 가셔서 그곳의 부서장님을 찾으시기만 하면 됩니다.

남: 알겠습니다, 도와 주셔서 감사합니다.

부서	부서장
인사부	Donna Mumford
광고부	Olivia Benton
영업부	Harriet Blanc
회계부	Gerard Nesbitt

어휘 **ask A for B** A에게 B를 요청하다 **current** 현재의 **time-off** 휴무, 휴가 **apologize for** ~에 대해 사과하다 **inconvenience** 불편 **make a mistake** 실수하다 **appointment** 약속, 예약 **candidate** 지원자 **come in** 도착하다, 들어오다 **straight** 곧장 **sales** 영업, 판매

33. 대화의 주제는 무엇인가?
  (A) 근무 정책
  (B) 슈퍼마켓 세일 행사
  (C) 구직 면접
  (D) 고객 불만 사항

해설 대화 주제를 묻고 있으므로 대화가 시작될 때 특히 주의해 들어야 한다. 대화 시작 부분에 여자가 자신을 소개하면서 면접을 수요일에서 금요일로 옮겨야 할 것 같다고(I'm sorry to tell you this, but we'll need to move your interview from Wednesday to Friday) 알리고 있다. 따라서 구직 면접을 뜻하는 (C)가 정답임을 알 수 있다.

어휘 **policy** 정책, 방침 **complaint** 불만

34. 여자는 무슨 문제점을 언급하는가?
  (A) 매니저가 다른 지역에 가 있다.
  (B) 특가 제공 서비스가 종료되었다.
  (C) 일정 상의 오류가 발생되었다.
  (D) 한 부서가 일시적으로 폐쇄되어 있다.

해설 여자가 언급하는 문제점을 찾아야 하므로 여자의 말에서 부정적인 정보가 제시되는 부분이 있음을 예상하고 들어야 한다. 일정 변경을 언급한 여자는 대화 중반부에 면접 일정을 정할 때 자신이 실수를 했다고(I made a mistake when I was scheduling appointment times) 언급하고 있으므로 (C)가 정답이다.

어휘 **out of town** 다른 지역에 가 있는 **special offer** 특가 제공 서비스 **scheduling error** 일정 상의 오류 **occur** 발생되다, 일어나다 **temporarily** 일시적으로

35. 시각자료를 보시오. 남자는 금요일에 누구를 만날 것 같은가?
  (A) Donna Mumford
  (B) Olivia Benton
  (C) Harriet Blanc
  (D) Gerard Nesbitt

해설 대화 중반부에 남자가 금요일에 상대방의 사무실로 가는 것인지 묻자(should I come to your office when I arrive on Friday?) 여자는 이에 대해 영업부로 가서 그곳의 부서장을 찾으라고(Just go straight to the sales department and find the manager there) 알려 주고 있다. 따라서 시각자료에서 영업부 책임자로 표기되어 있는 (C)가 정답이 된다.

어휘 **meet with** (약속하여) ~와 만나다

Questions 36-38 refer to the following conversation and newspaper layout.

M: Hi, Maggie. How's everything going with tomorrow's edition of our newspaper?

W: Everything is looking great! **36** I had a meeting with the editor-in-chief this morning, and we finalized the front page layout for tomorrow.

M: Great! Do you mind if I take a look? This is the first time one of my articles will be featured on the front page!

W: Sure. Here's the layout... **37** You can see that your article will go directly beneath headline four.

M: I can't wait to see it once it's printed. I really enjoyed traveling to London to research the article.

W: Oh, **38** don't forget to send me the form for your travel expenses. You can get reimbursed for them sometime next month.

남: 안녕하세요, 매기. 내일 자 우리 신문 작업은 어떻게 되어 가고 있으신가요?

여: 모든 일이 잘 되고 있는 것 같아요! 오늘 아침에 편집장님과 회의를 했는데, 내일 신문의 1면 배치 방식을 최종 확정했어요.

남: 잘됐네요! 제가 한 번 봐도 괜찮을까요? 제 기사들 중의 하나가 1면에 특집으로 실리는 게 처음이거든요!

여: 그럼요. 여기 배치도입니다... 4번째 헤드라인 바로 아래에 당신의 기사가 들어 간다는 것을 아실 수 있을 거예요.

남: 인쇄되는 대로 빨리 보고 싶어요. 기사 취재를 위해 런던으로 출장 간 것이 정말로 즐거웠거든요.

여: 아, 당신의 출장 지출 비용에 대한 양식을 잊지 말고 제게 보내 주세요. 다음 달 중으로 그 비용을 돌려 받으실 수 있을 거예요.

어휘 **How's everything going with A?** A는 잘 되어 가고 있나요? **edition** (출판물의) 판, 호 **editor-in-chief** 편집장 **finalize** ~을 최종 확정하다 **front page** 1면 **layout** 배치 (도) **Do you mind if ~?** ~해도 될까요? **take a look** 살펴보다 **article** (신문 등의) 기사 **feature** ~을 특집으로 싣다 **directly beneath** ~ 바로 아래에 **headline** 헤드라인, 표제 **can't wait to do** 빨리 ~하고 싶다 **travel to** ~로 출장 가다, 여행 가다 **research** ~을 조사하다 **expense** 지출 (비용) **get reimbursed** 환급 받다 **local** 지역의, 현지의

36. 여자는 오늘 아침에 무엇을 했는가?
(A) 새로운 편집자를 고용했다.
(B) 사진을 몇 장 찍었다.
(C) 계약서에 서명했다.
(D) 회의에 참석했다.

해설 대화 시작 부분에 여자는 오늘 아침에 편집장과 회의를 했다는 사실을(I had a meeting with the editor-in-chief this morning) 알리고 있다. 따라서 회의 참석을 뜻하는 (D)가 정답이다.

어휘 **take a photograph** 사진을 찍다 **sign** ~에 서명하다 **contract** 계약(서)

Paraphrase had a meeting with
→ attended a meeting

37. 시각자료를 보시오. 남자는 어느 기사를 작성했는가?
(A) 스포츠 기사

(B) 여행 기사
(C) 비즈니스 기사
(D) 지역 뉴스 기사

해설 배치도가 시각자료로 제시되어 있으므로 배치도 안의 특정 명칭 및 위치 관련 표현에 집중해 들어야 한다. 대화 중반부에 1면 기사 배치 작업을 한 여자가 남자에게 4번째 헤드라인 바로 아래에 기사가 들어 간다고(You can see that your article will go directly beneath headline four) 알리고 있다. 시각자료에서 4번 헤드라인 바로 아래는 비즈니스 기사 자리로 되어 있으므로 (C)가 정답이 된다.

38. 여자는 남자에게 무엇을 하도록 상기시키는가?
(A) 일부 장비를 반납할 것
(B) 일정표를 확인할 것
(C) 기사를 교정 볼 것
(D) 양식을 제출할 것

해설 대화 후반부에 여자가 남자에게 출장 지출 비용에 대한 양식을 잊지 말고 보내 달라고(don't forget to send me the form for your travel expenses) 당부하고 있으므로 양식 제출을 의미하는 (D)가 정답이다.

어휘 **remind A to do** A에게 ~하도록 상기시키다 **return** ~을 반납하다, 반환하다 **equipment** 장비 **proofread** ~을 교정 보다 **submit** ~을 제출하다

Paraphrase send me the form
→ Submit a form

Part 4

Questions 39-41 refer to the following announcement.

Welcome, everybody. We are honored to have so many people in attendance today. **39** **40** It's an important night, as we are celebrating the election win of a well-known town council member, Sean Newton. After years of hard work, he finally made it. Mr. Newton will take on the role of town mayor this coming September. Tonight, I'd like you to show your gratitude for all the great work that Mr. Newton has already done in our town. He has promised to continue doing his best to help our town to flourish. **41** Now, I'd like you all to stand up and put your hands together as Mr. Newton comes up to the stage.

여러분, 환영합니다. 오늘 정말 많은 분들께서 참석해 주셔서 영광으로 생각합니다. 오늘밤은 저명하신 시의원인 션 뉴튼 의원님께서 선거에서 승리하신 것을 축하하는 자리이기 때문에 중요한 시간입니다. 몇 년 동안 힘들게 노력해 오신 끝에 의원님께서 드디어 이뤄내셨습니다. 뉴튼 의원님께서는 오는 9월부터 시장

으로 일하시게 됩니다. 오늘 밤, 우리 시를 위해 의원님께서 이미 해오신 모든 훌륭한 일들에 대해 여러분께서 감사의 뜻을 보여 주실 수 있기를 바랍니다. 의원님께서는 우리 시가 번영하는 데 도움이 될 수 있도록 계속해서 최선을 다하시겠다고 약속하셨습니다. 자, 뉴튼 의원님께서 무대에 올라오실 때 모두 일어서서 박수로 맞이해 주시기 바랍니다.

어휘 **be honored to do** ~하게 되어 영광이다 **in attendance** 참석한 **celebrate** ~을 축하하다 **election** 선거 **well-known** 잘 알려진 **council member** 시의원 **make it** 해내다 **take on** (일, 책임 등) ~을 맡다 **role** 역할 **mayor** 시장 **gratitude** 감사(의 뜻) **promise to do** ~하기로 약속하다 **continue -ing** 계속 ~하다 **flourish** 번영하다 **put one's hands together** 박수 치다

39. 무슨 종류의 특별 행사가 열리는가?
  (A) 승리 축하 행사
  (B) 퇴직 기념 만찬
  (C) 시의 기념일 파티
  (D) 시상식

해설 화자는 담화를 시작하는 부분에 행사의 목적을 It's an important night, as we are celebrating the election win of a well-known town council member, Sean Newton과 같이 밝히고 있는데, 이를 통해 선거에서 이긴 것을 기념하는 행사임을 알 수 있으므로 (A)가 정답이다.

어휘 **celebration** 축하(행사) **retirement** 퇴직, 은퇴 **anniversary** 기념일

40. 션 뉴튼은 누구인가?
  (A) 학교 교사
  (B) 자선단체 직원
  (C) 지역 사업가
  (D) 시 공직자

해설 Sean Newton이라는 사람이 언급되는 부분을 놓치지 말고 들어야 한다. 담화의 목적을 밝히는 초반부 a well-known town council member, Sean Newton 부분을 통해 시 의원임을 알 수 있으므로 (D)가 정답이다. 이후 Mr. Newton will take on the role of town mayor ~에서 시장으로서의 역할도 겸하는 것을 알 수 있다.

어휘 **charity** 자선 단체 **official** 공무원, 임원

41. 담화에 이어 무슨 일이 있을 가능성이 큰가?
  (A) 공연이 시작될 것이다.
  (B) 양식이 배부될 것이다.
  (C) 당선자가 환영을 받을 것이다.
  (D) 청자들이 자리에 앉을 것이다.

해설 담화 이후에 있을 일에 대해 묻는 문제이므로 담화의 마지막 부분에 특히 집중해 들어야 한다. 화자는 담화 마지막 부분에 가서 Now, I'd like you all to stand up and put your hands

together as Mr. Newton comes up to the stage라는 말로 무대에 오르는 Sean Newton을 박수로 맞아 줄 것을 부탁하고 있으므로 (C)가 정답이다.

어휘 **performance** 공연, 연주(회) **form** 양식, 서식 **distribute** ~을 나눠주다, 배포하다 **election winner** 당선자 **welcome** ~을 환영하다

Paraphrase stand up and put your hands together
  → be welcomed

Questions 42-44 refer to the following talk.

Hello everyone, and **42** welcome to the Northern California's Annual Real Estate Seminar. As usual, I'd like to start off by congratulating one of our members. For those of you who don't already know, **43** Maria Weizmann has recently started her own agency to service clients in and around the city of Redding. Her office is located in the city center. Be sure to congratulate her when you get a chance. Now, **44** let's move on to the legal changes that have been made in the past year. This may take a while.

안녕하세요, 여러분, 북 캘리포니아 지역의 연례 부동산 세미나에 오신 것을 환영합니다. 평소처럼, 저는 우리 회원분들 중 한 분께 축하 인사를 하는 것으로 시작하겠습니다. 아직 모르시는 분들을 위해 말씀드리면, 마리아 웨이즈만 씨가 레딩 시와 근교 지역의 고객들에게 서비스를 제공하고자 자신의 중개업체를 시작하셨습니다. 그분의 사무실은 시내 중심부에 위치해 있습니다. 기회가 되시면 마리아 씨께 축하 인사를 해주세요. 이제, 지난 해에 있었던 법률적인 변경 사항들에 대한 내용으로 넘어가겠습니다. 이는 시간이 좀 걸릴 수 있습니다.

어휘 **anual** 연례의 **real estate** 부동산 **start off** 시작하다 **congratulate** ~에게 축하하다 **one's own** ~만의 **agency** 대리점, 사무소 **service** ~에게 서비스를 제공하다 **be sure to do** 반드시 ~하다 **get a chance** 기회가 생기다 **move on to** (순서 등) ~로 넘어가다 **legal** 법률적인 **take a while** 시간이 좀 걸리다

42. 청자들은 누구일 것 같은가?
  (A) 이벤트 기획자들
  (B) 회사 변호사들
  (C) 부동산 중개업자들
  (D) 고객 서비스 직원들

해설 화자는 담화 첫 부분에서 welcome to the Northern California's Annual Real Estate Seminar라고 인사하고 있다. 부동산 세미나에 참석했을 사람은 부동산 중개인일 것이므로 (C)가 정답이다.

어휘 **corporate** 기업의, 회사의 **real estate agent** 부동산 중개인 **representative** 직원

43. 화자는 마리아 웨이즈만 씨가 무엇을 했다고 말하는가?

(A) 자신의 사업을 시작했다.
(B) 퇴직을 발표했다.
(C) 계약서를 검토했다.
(D) 상을 탔다.

해설 Maria Weizmann이라는 이름이 언급되는 곳을 잘 들어야 한다. Maria Weizmann has recently started her own agency에서 마리아 씨가 자신의 사무소를 시작했다고 알리고 있으므로 (A)가 정답임을 알 수 있다.

어휘 **retirement** 퇴직 **award** 상

Paraphrase started her own agency
→ Opened her own business

44. 화자는 왜 "이는 시간이 좀 걸릴 수 있습니다"라고 말하는가?

(A) 잠시 쉴 것을 제안하기 위해
(B) 많은 것들이 변경되었음을 강조하기 위해
(C) 시간 부족에 대한 우려를 나타내기 위해
(D) 복잡한 법적인 문제에 대해 불만을 표하기 위해

해설 법적인 변경 사항들에 대해 다루겠다고 한 뒤 시간이 좀 걸릴 것이라고 말하는 것은 변경 사항들이 꽤 많기 때문일 것이라고 추측할 수 있다. 따라서 (B)가 정답이다.

어휘 **take a break** 잠깐 쉬다 **emphasize that** ~임을 강조하다 **concern** 걱정, 우려 **lack** 부족 **complicated** 복잡한 **legal issue** 법적인 문제

Questions 45-47 refer to the following announcement.

Attention, all passengers waiting to board the 9:30 bus to Kyoto. **45** Unfortunately, a mechanical problem means that the bus will be departing approximately 30 minutes behind schedule. **46** Our engineers are working hard to fix the problem as quickly as possible. Please bear with us. **46** While you wait, please enjoy some snacks at our brand new coffee shop in the main terminal building. **47** If you would like to find out more details about the amenities available in our bus terminal, please speak with an employee in the ticket office. Thank you for your patience, and enjoy your journey with Onyudo Bus Services.

교토 행 9시 30분 버스 탑승을 기다리고 계신 모든 승객께 알립니다. 안타깝게도, 기계적인 문제로 인해 해당 버스가 일정보다 약 30분 늦게 출발할 예정입니다. 저희 기술자들이 가능한 한 빨리 이 문제를 바로잡기 위해 열심히 노력하고 있습니다. 양해 부탁드립니다. 기다리시는 동안, 중앙 터미널 건물 내에 있는 새로운 저희 커피 매장에서 간식을 즐기시기 바랍니다. 저희 버스 터미널에서 이용 가능한 편의 시설에 관한 추가 상세 정보를 알아보시고자 하는 경우, 매표소에 있는 직원에게 말씀하시기 바랍니다. 여러분의 인내에 감사드리며, 저희 오뉴도 버스 서비스와 함께 즐거운 여행 되시기 바랍니다.

어휘 **Attention** 알립니다, 주목하세요 **passenger** 승객 **board** ~에 탑승하다 **unfortunately** 안타깝게도 **mechanical** 기계적인 **depart** 출발하다, 떠나다 **approximately** 약, 대략 **behind schedule** 일정보다 늦게 **fix** ~을 바로잡다, 고치다 **as quickly as possible** 가능한 한 빨리 **bear with** ~을 참고 기다리다 **while** ~하는 동안 **brand new** (완전히) 새로운 **find out** ~을 알아보다, 확인해 보다 **details** 상세 정보 **amenities** 편의 시설 **patience** 인내

45. 무엇이 주로 공지되고 있는가?

(A) 여행의 취소
(B) 버스 터미널 관련 정책
(C) 지연된 출발
(D) 새로운 이동 경로

해설 화자는 담화 시작 부분에 버스에 발생된 문제로 인해 30분 늦게 출발한다고(Unfortunately, ~ the bus will be departing approximately 30 minutes behind schedule) 알리고 있다. 이는 출발이 지연된 상황임을 알리는 것이므로 (C)가 정답이다.

어휘 **cancelation** 취소 **policy** 정책 **delayed** 지연된 **departure** 출발 **route** 경로

Paraphrase departing approximately 30 minutes behind schedule
→ delayed departure

46. 화자가 "양해 부탁드립니다"라고 말하는 이유는 무엇인가?

(A) 청자들에게 탑승 준비를 하도록 요청하기 위해
(B) 청자들에게 좌석이 이용 가능함을 알리기 위해
(C) 청자들의 협조를 요청하기 위해
(D) 청자들에게 티켓을 구매하도록 권하기 위해

해설 해당 문장은 직역하면 "(우리가 일하는 동안) 인내심을 갖고 기다려달라"는 의미로, 양해를 부탁한다는 말이다. 이 문장은 담화 중반부에 기술자들이 가능한 한 빨리 문제를 바로잡기 위해 노력하고 있다고(Our engineers are working hard to fix the problem as quickly as possible) 알리는 말 다음에 들을 수 있다. 버스 수리로 인해 출발이 지연되는 상황에 대해 승객들의 양해를 구하려는 의도이므로 청자들의 협조를 요청하기 위해서라는 말로 바꿔 표현한 (C)가 정답이 된다.

어휘 prepare for ~을 준비하다 boarding 탑승 inform
A that A에게 ~라고 알리다 request ~을 요청하다
cooperation 협조 recommend that ~하도록 권하다

47. 화자의 말에 따르면, 청자들은 어떻게 추가 정보를 얻을 수 있는
가?

(A) 매표소를 방문함으로써
(B) 또 다른 공지를 기다림으로써
(C) 일정표를 확인함으로써
(D) 정보 안내 책자를 읽음으로써

해설 추가 정보를 얻는 방법이 질문의 핵심이므로 추가 정보가 언급
되는 부분이 있음을 예상하고 들어야 한다. 담화 후반부에 화
자는 이용 가능한 편의 시설에 관한 추가 상세 정보가 필요하면
매표소 직원에게 얘기하라고(If you would like to find out
more details ~, please speak with an employee in
the ticket office) 알리고 있다. 따라서 (A)가 정답이다.

Paraphrase speak with an employee in the ticket office
→ visiting a ticket office

Questions 48-50 refer to the following excerpt from a
meeting and chart.

I'd like to start the meeting by thanking all of you
for your recent hard work. We just went through a
particularly busy period here at Attica Publishing,
and **48** as a result, you had to put in a lot of
overtime on weekends so that we could meet
our deadlines. Management wants to reward you
all for your efforts, so **49** you'll each receive an
envelope containing 300 dollars at the end of this
meeting. But first we need to discuss our typical
expenses, and think of ways to reduce them. **50**
We'll start by discussing the largest portion of
our publishing expenses. Please don't hesitate to
speak up if you have any good suggestions.

여러분 모두가 최근에 보여 주신 노고에 대해 감사드리는 것으로
회의를 시작하고자 합니다. 우리 애티카 출판사는 특히 바쁜 시기
를 막 보냈으며, 결과적으로 마감시한에 맞추기 위해 여러분은 주
말마다 많은 초과 근무를 하셔야 했습니다. 우리 경영진은 여러분
모두의 노력에 대해 보상해 드리기를 원하고 있으므로 이번 회의
가 끝날 때 각자 300달러가 들어 있는 봉투를 받게 되실 것입니
다. 하지만 우선, 우리의 일반적인 지출 비용에 관해 논의하고, 이
를 줄일 수 있는 방법을 생각해 봐야 합니다. 출판 관련 지출 비용
의 가장 큰 부분에 관해 논의하는 것으로 시작해 보겠습니다. 어느
것이든 좋은 제안 사항이 있으시면 주저하지 마시고 크게 말씀해
주시기 바랍니다.

도서 출판 지출 비용

- 제본 작업 29%
- 용지 및 인쇄 작업 36%
- 저자 인세 24%
- 판촉 활동 11%

어휘 go through ~을 거치다, 겪다 particularly 특히 as a
result 결과적으로 put in overtime 초과 근무를 하다
meet a deadline 마감시한에 맞추다 management
경영(진) reward A for B B에 대해 A에게 보상해 주다
effort 노력 contain ~을 포함하다 typical 일반적인,
전형적인 expense 지출 (비용) portion 부분, 일부
publishing 출판 hesitate to do ~하기를 주저하다
speak up 크게 말하다 book binding 제본 author 저
자 royalty 인세, 저작권 사용료 promotion 판촉, 홍보

48. 화자는 왜 청자들에게 감사하는가?
(A) 연간 수익을 증대시켰다.
(B) 추가 근무를 했다.
(C) 유용한 아이디어를 제공했다.
(D) 신규 독자들을 끌어 들였다.

해설 담화 시작 부분에 화자는 청자들의 노고에 감사한다는 말과 함
께 마감시한에 맞추기 위해 많은 초과 근무를 했다고(~ you
had to put in a lot of overtime on weekends so that
we could meet our deadlines) 언급하고 있다. 따라서 이
와 같은 직원들의 노력을 말한 (B)가 정답이다.

어휘 annual 연간의, 해마다의 profit 수익 additional 추가의
attract ~을 끌어 들이다

Paraphrase put in a lot of overtime on weekends
→ worked additional hours

49. 청자들은 무엇을 받을 것인가?
(A) 현금 보너스
(B) 별도의 휴가
(C) 상품권
(D) 연봉 인상

해설 담화 중반부에 화자는 포상으로 300달러가 들어 있는 봉
투를 받게 된다고(you'll each receive an envelope
containing 300 dollars ~) 밝히고 있다. 이는 현금으로 보
너스를 주는 것을 의미하므로 (A)가 정답이다.

어휘 extra 별도의, 추가의 gift certificate 상품권 salary 연
봉 raise 인상, 증가

an envelope containing 300 dollars
→ A cash bonus

50. 시각자료를 보시오. 화자는 곧이어 어느 사안에 관해 이야기할 것인가?

(A) 제본 작업
(B) 용지 및 인쇄 작업
(C) 판촉 활동
(D) 저자 인세

해설 화자는 담화 마지막에 지출 비용의 가장 큰 부분에 관해 논의하는 것으로 시작하겠다고(We'll start by discussing the largest portion of our publishing expenses) 알리고 있다. 따라서 시각자료에서 가장 큰 비율인 36퍼센트에 해당되는 항목인 (B)가 정답이 된다.

Part 5

51.

정답 (A)

해석 전자 도서에 대한 최근의 수요 감소로 인해, 모비우스 주식회사는 자사의 일부 전자책 리더기 모델들을 단종시킬 것이다.

해설 빈칸이 전치사 in과 for 사이에 위치해 있으므로 빈칸은 전치사 in의 목적어 역할을 할 명사 자리임을 알 수 있다. 따라서 (A) demand가 정답이다.

어휘 demand n. 수요 v. ~을 요구하다 discontinue ~을 단종시키다 e-reader 전자책 리더기 demanding 부담이 큰, 힘든

52.

정답 (D)

해석 피트니스 강사는 요가 강좌 회원들을 위해 완전히 새로운 일정을 만들 것이다.

해설 부정관사와 형용사 사이에 빈칸이 위치해 있으므로 빈칸은 형용사를 수식할 부사 자리이다. 따라서 (D) completely가 정답이다.

어휘 instructor 강사 completely 완전히, 전적으로 completion 완료, 완성 complete a. 완전한, 완료된 v. ~을 완료하다

53.

정답 (B)

해석 쉴튼 씨는 저널리스트로서 높이 평가 받고 있기 때문에, 기고 중인 신문 칼럼을 수십 만 명의 사람들이 읽고 있다.

해설 빈칸이 속한 주절의 주어로 쓰인 명사구를 앞에서 수식할 대명사가 필요하므로 소유격 대명사 (B) her가 정답이다.

어휘 highly regarded 높이 평가 받는 as (자격, 신분) ~로서 hundreds of thousands of 수십 만 명의, 수십 만 개의

54.

정답 (C)

해석 시 의회 토론회는 마벨 빌딩에서 개최되었던 기획 회의와 유사하게 구성될 것이다.

해설 빈칸이 be동사와 부사 사이에 위치해 있으므로 빈칸은 주격 보어 자리이다. 따라서 보어의 역할을 할 수 있는 형용사를 정답으로 골라야 하는데, 시 의회 토론회는 사람에 의해 구성되는 것이므로 과거분사 (C) structured가 정답이다.

어휘 structured 구성된, 구조가 있는 planning n. 기획, 계획 structure n. 구조 v. ~을 구성하다 structural 구조적인, 구조상의

55.

정답 (B)

해석 모든 케이크들이 너무 매력적으로 디자인되었기 때문에 예식을 위해 하나만 고르는 것이 거의 불가능했다.

해설 빈칸 앞에 원인이나 이유를 나타내는 「so + 부사 + 형용사」가 있으므로 이 구조와 함께 결과의 의미를 나타내는 절 앞에 쓰이는 (B) that이 정답이다.

어휘 so ~ that 너무 ~해서 …하다 attractively 매력적으로 ceremony 예식, 행사

56.

정답 (C)

해석 사진 촬영 강좌는 아마추어나 전문직 종사자들에게 똑같이 열려 있으므로 강좌 등록의 제약은 없다.

해설 빈칸이 속한 절의 문장 구성이 완전하므로 빈칸에는 부사가 필요한데, 누구나 등록할 수 있다는 뜻을 지닌 문장이므로 두 부류의 사람들에게 동등하다는 의미를 나타낼 수 있는 (C) alike가 정답이다.

어휘 photography 사진 촬영 amateur 아마추어 professional n. 전문직 종사자 alike ad. 동등하게, 똑같이 enrollment 등록 restriction 제약

57.

정답 (D)

해석 크리스 최 씨와 비비안 리우 씨는 세계 인터넷 마케팅 경연대회에서 조별 최종 결선에 진출할 것으로 예상된다.

해설 제시된 문장에 조별 결선에 진출한다는 내용이 나왔는데, 빈칸 앞에 나온 '세계 인터넷 마케팅'만으로는 결선 진출을 하는 장소의 의미가 부족하므로 '경연대회'를 뜻하는 명사 (D) competition이 정답이다.

어휘 reach ~에 다다르다, 이르다 final group stage 조별 결선 compete 경쟁하다, 출전하다 competition 경연대회, 경기

58.

정답 (B)

해석 <더 선 타임즈>는 그들의 가장 강력한 독자층이 15세에서 30세 사이의 연령이라는 것을 확인했다.

해설 빈칸 뒤에 and로 두 나이대가 연결되어 있으므로 이 구조와 함께 사용할 수 있는 (B) between이 정답이다.

어휘 identify A as B A를 B로 확인하다, 동일시하다 readership 독자, 독자층 along ~을 따라 between ~사이에 through ~을 통해서 among ~중에서

59.
정답 (D)

해석 이번 주에 연구 논문을 내지 않은 학생은 누구든 이 과목을 통과할 수 없을 것입니다.

해설 선택지가 모두 관계대명사로 구성되어 있으므로 문장 구조 분석을 통해 알맞은 것을 골라야 한다. 빈칸 앞에 선행사가 있고 빈칸 뒤에 주어와 동사가 있는 절이 있으므로 소유격인 (D) whose가 정답이다.

어휘 research 연구, 조사 paper 논문, 숙제, 리포트 pass ~을 통과하다 course 과목

60.
정답 (C)

해석 건물 내의 계단에 페인트칠 작업이 진행되는 동안, 3층 구내식당에 대한 출입은 오직 엘리베이터를 통해서만 가능합니다.

해설 빈칸 뒤에 제시된 전치사 to와 어울리며 구내식당과 엘리베이터의 관계를 나타낼 수 있는 명사가 빈칸에 와야 하므로 '~에 대한 출입, 접근, 이용'을 뜻하는 (C) access가 정답이다.

어휘 while ~하는 동안 stairways 계단 access to ~로의 출입, 접근, 이용 direction 지시, 감독, 길 안내 reservation 예약, 지정

61.
정답 (B)

해석 <핸디맨의 핸드북>은 기본적인 주택 유지 관리 프로젝트 및 수리 작업에 대한 가장 종합적인 가이드북이다.

해설 정관사와 명사 사이에 빈칸이 있으므로 빈칸이 형용사 자리임을 알 수 있다. 따라서 the와 결합해 명사를 수식하는 형용사의 최상급 형태인 (B) most comprehensive가 정답이다.

어휘 comprehensive 종합적인, 포괄적인 maintenance (시설 등의) 유지 관리 compression 압축(된 상태), (글 등의) 요약 comprehensively 종합적으로, 포괄적으로

62.
정답 (D)

해석 화재경보 소리가 들리자마자, 즉시 건물 밖으로 대피하여 추후 통보가 있을 때까지 지정된 모임 장소에 계시기 바랍니다.

해설 빈칸에는 화재 경보가 울리면 건물에서 어떻게 대피할 것인지를 나타낼 수 있는 부사가 와야 한다. 따라서 '즉시'라는 뜻을 가진 (D) promptly가 정답이다.

어휘 as soon as ~하자마자 evacuate ~을 떠나다, 대피하다 designated 지정된 currently 현재 previously 이전에 forcefully 강제로, 강력히 promptly 즉시

63.
정답 (C)

해석 귀하께서 사업차 또는 즐거움 위해 여행을 하던지 간에, 저희는 분명히 귀하의 숙박이 즐겁도록 만들 것입니다.

해설 빈칸은 콤마 앞뒤로 제시된 주어와 동사를 포함한 두 개의 절을 연결할 접속사 자리이므로 선택지 중 유일한 접속사인 (C) Whether가 정답이다.

어휘 for pleasure 즐거움으로, 재미를 위해 certainly 분명히 stay 숙박, 머무름 enjoyable 즐거운

64.
정답 (D)

해석 여러 손꼽히는 음식 평론가들이 10번 애비뉴에 위치한 요리사 크레이그 놀란의 새 레스토랑을 적극 추천했다.

해설 빈칸에 쓰일 과거분사는 강조 부사 highly와 어울릴 수 있으면서 평론가들이 레스토랑에 대해 할 수 있는 일과 관련되어야 하므로 '~을 추천하다'를 뜻하는 recommend의 과거분사 (D) recommended가 정답이다.

어휘 leading 손꼽히는, 선도적인 critic 평론가, 비평가 highly 크게, 대단히, 매우 consume ~을 소비하다, ~을 먹다 nominate ~을 후보로 지명하다 publish ~을 출간하다

65.
정답 (D)

해석 체육관 회원들은 각자의 개인 소지품들이 탈의실 내에 방치되도록 하지 말아야 한다는 점을 명심하시기 바랍니다.

해설 빈칸 뒤에 형용사 unattended가 위치해 있는데, 선택지에 제시된 동사 leave가 형용사와 함께 쓰이는 경우는 「leave + 목적어 + 목적격보어」와 같이 5형식 동사로 쓰일 경우이다. 그런데 빈칸 바로 다음에 목적어 없이 형용사만 남아 있으므로 leave가 수동태로 쓰여야 한다는 것을 알 수 있다. 조동사 다음에는 동사원형이 쓰여야 하므로 수동태 동사원형 (D) be left가 정답이다.

어휘 keep in mind that ~라는 점을 명심하다 belongings 소지품 unattended 방치되어 있는 changing room 탈의실

66.
정답 (C)

해석 윙 씨는 다양한 캠페인을 통해 도시의 이미지를 높이기 위한 뛰어난 노력으로 표창을 받았다.

해설 빈칸 뒤에 to부정사가 쓰였으므로 '~하기 위한 노력'이라는 의미로 to부정사의 수식을 받을 수 있는 (C) efforts가 정답이다.

어휘 **recognize** ~을 인정하다, 표창하다 **outstanding** 뛰어난, 우수한 **response** 반응, 응답 **attention** 주의, 돌봄, 관심

Part 6

67-70.

> 수신: 유지보수 담당 직원들
> 발신: 카리사 뎀시, 유지보수 관리자
> 날짜: 2월 21일
> 주제: 사우스 랜드 병원 지점
>
> 친애하는 직원들에게,
>
> 우선, 여러분 모두 우리 모든 지점에서 67 훌륭하게 일을 하고 계시다고 말씀 드립니다. 저는 우리가 고용되어 일하는 회사들과 단체로부터 호평을 자주 받고 있습니다.
>
> 최근 몇 주 동안, 사우스 랜드 병원에서 일하고 있는 직원분들이 베이직 브론즈 패키지에서 제공되고 있는 것 외의 서비스를 제공해 달라는 요청을 받아왔다는 것을 알게 되었습니다. 그런 요청은 쓰레기를 쓰레기통으로 가져 가는 것과, 대기실 의자들을 닦는 것, 그리고 커피 포트를 씻는 것을 포함합니다. 이 모든 경우에서, 우리 직원들은 이런 68 추가적인 일들을 수행했습니다.
>
> 여러분이 우리의 고객을 기쁘게 하고자 하는 바람은 이해하지만, 계약서에 서명이 되었던 당시에 우리가 합의한 것만 제공하는 것은 중요한 일입니다. 69 이것이 우리의 다른 고객들에게 시간을 뺏는 것을 방지할 것입니다. 여러분이 우리 패키지에 포함된 서비스에 대해 우려나 질문이 있다면, 제가 70 기꺼이 처리해 드리겠습니다. 거리낌없이 제 사무실에 언제든 들러 주시고 계속 열심히 근무해주시기 바랍니다.
>
> 안녕히 계십시오.
>
> 카리사 뎀시, 유지보수 관리자

어휘 **first of all** 우선, 무엇보다도 **regularly** 정기적으로, 자주 **come to one's attention that** ~라는 사실을 알게 되다 **dumpster** 대형 쓰레기통 **wipe** ~을 문지르다, 닦다 **coffee pot** 커피 포트 **perform** ~을 수행하다 **concern** 걱정, 우려 **address** ~을 처리하다 **feel free to do** 거리낌없이 ~하다, 마음껏 ~하다

67.

정답 (A)

해설 빈칸 뒤에 제시된 문장에서 다른 데서 긍정적인 말을 듣고 있다는 내용으로 보아, 직원들이 일을 잘 하고 있음을 알 수 있다. 따라서, 긍정적인 의미를 가진 어휘로서 '훌륭한, 모범적인'이라는 뜻의 (A) exemplary가 정답이다.

어휘 **exemplary** 모범적인, 훌륭한 **accessible** 접근 가능한, 접근할 수 있는 **eventual** 궁극적인

68.

정답 (C)

해설 빈칸이 한정사 these와 명사 tasks 사이에 위치해 있으므로 빈칸은 명사를 수식할 수 있는 형용사 자리이다. 따라서 (C) additional이 정답이다.

69.

정답 (C)

해석 (A) 이런 방식으로, 여러분의 도움은 인정받을 것입니다.
(B) 그래서, 저는 여러분이 모두 양식서에 서명하길 바랍니다.
(C) 이것이 우리의 다른 고객들에게 시간을 뺏는 것을 방지할 것입니다.
(D) 이러한 서비스 추가는 일시적일 것입니다.

해설 빈칸 앞에서 계약서에 합의된 것 외의 일을 하지 말라는 언급이 있으므로 빈칸에는 계약서 이외의 일을 하면 안 되는 당위성이나 이유를 설명하는 말이 오는 것이 문맥상 자연스럽다. 따라서 다른 고객들의 시간을 뺏지 않는다는 내용의 (C)가 정답이다.

어휘 **assistance** 도움, 보조 **appreciate** ~을 인정하다, ~의 진가를 알아보다 **avoid** ~을 방지하다, 피하다 **take away** ~을 빼앗아 가다 **addition** 추가

70.

정답 (C)

해설 빈칸 뒤에 언제든 자신의 사무실에 들러도 된다는 언급이 있으므로 be동사와 to부정사와 함께 '기꺼이 문제를 해결해 주겠다'고 말하는 것이 자연스러우므로 (C) willing이 정답이다.

어휘 **plain** 명백한, 평이한 **hesitant** 망설이는 **willing** 기꺼이 ~하는

71-74.

> 집을 71 임대하는데 지치셨나요? 언젠가는 단독집이나 타운하우스를 자신의 것으로 가지는 꿈을 가지고 있으신가요? 그렇다면 계속 읽어보세요!
>
> 시중에 나와 있는 집은 많고, 이자는 역사적으로 낮은, 지금이 구매하기에 가장 좋은 시기입니다! 노 워리스 부동산에서는 12명의 부동산 중개업자가 있으며, 72 모두 최소한 10년의 경험을 가지고 있습니다. 다른 몇몇 회사들과는 달리, 저희는 단지 판매를 이루기 위해서 여러분에게 맞지 않는 주택을 구매하도록 설득하려 하지 않을 것입니다.
>
> 저희의 절차는 여러분이 원하는 집을 여러분이 지불할 수 있는 가격에 찾아드리도록 만들어져 있습니다. 우선, 여러분은 선호하는 지역, 욕실의 개수, 공간의 크기, 물론 가격도 물어보는 자세한 질문지를 작성할 것입니다. 73 그리고 나서, 여러분의 중개업자가 여러분의 판단기준에 충족하는 주택으로만 여러분을 데려갈 것입니다.

여러분이 구매할 준비가 되면, 저희가 모든 서류작업을 처리해 드릴 것이며, 여러분이 주택 74 점검을 하는 것을 도와드릴 것입니다. 여러분은 짐을 꾸려서 이사만 하시면 됩니다!

633-435-4505로 전화해서 첫 주택을 찾는 흥미진진한 과정을 시작해보세요!

어휘 tired of ~에 지친 dream of ~을 꿈꾸다 bungalow 단독주택 on the market (팔려고) 시장에 나와있는 agent 중개업자 convince ~을 확신시키다, 설득시키다 process 과정, 절차 afford (금전적인) 여유가 되다 fill out ~을 작성하다 detailed 자세한 questionnaire 질문지 preferred 선호되는 take care of ~을 돌보다, 처리하다 inspection 조사, 점검

71.

정답 (D)

해설 빈칸이 전치사와 명사구 목적어 사이에 있으므로 전치사의 목적어 역할을 하면서 목적어를 취할 수 있는 동명사가 빈칸에 와야 한다. 따라서 (D) renting이 정답이다.

72.

정답 (B)

해설 빈칸에는 문맥상 직원 모두를 대신할 대명사가 필요한데, 빈칸 뒤에 복수동사가 있으므로 (B) all이 정답이다.

73.

정답 (A)

해석 **(A) 그리고 나서, 여러분의 중개업자가 여러분의 판단기준에 충족하는 주택으로만 여러분을 데려갈 것입니다.**
(B) 귀하의 주문은 접수되었고, 이제 저희 중개업자에 의해 처리되고 있는 중입니다.
(C) 일단 저희가 이 정보를 가지게 되면, 저희는 최선을 다해서 귀하에게 적합한 직업을 찾는 것을 도와드릴 것입니다.
(D) 저희 노 워리스 부동산은 귀하가 저희와 함께 집을 매매로 내놓아 주신 것을 감사드립니다.

해설 빈칸 앞에는 집을 사기 위해 원하는 조건들을 적는 양식에 관한 이야기가 있으므로 빈칸 뒤에는 그 양식에 나온 조건들에 맞는 집을 보여주겠다는 언급이 있는 것이 자연스럽다. 따라서 (A)가 정답이다.

어휘 criteria 판단 기준 (단수형은 criterion) process ~을 가공하다, 처리하다 suitable 적합한 list (팔 물건으로) 내놓다

74.

정답 (D)

해설 빈칸 앞에 '~을 하다, 마련하다'라는 뜻의 타동사 arrange가 있는데, 문맥상 '주택 점검을 하는 것을 도와주겠다'라고 해석하는 것이 자연스러우므로 빈칸 앞에 위치한 명사 home과 함께 복합명사를 구성할 명사 (D) inspection이 정답이다.

Part 7

75-76.

> **픽쳐 퍼펙트**
> 142 햄프쉬어 드라이브, 앨런데일, MI 49401
> 3002 브릭스 에비뉴, 앨런데일, MI 49404
>
> 75 결혼식이나 졸업식과 같은 특별한 행사에서 오래 지속되는 기억을 원하시든, 여권이나 사원증을 위해 잘 나온 사진 한 장이 필요하시든 관계없이, 픽쳐 퍼펙트는 이 지역에서 최상의 결과를 제공해드릴 것입니다. 저희 전문 직원들이 자연스러운 모습을 포착하거나, 런웨이 상의 모델처럼 보이게 만들어 드릴 수 있습니다. 저희 본사로 오시거나 지난달 브릭스 에비뉴에 문을 연 스튜디오를 방문해 주십시오. 50장 이상의 사진을 주문을 하시면 10퍼센트 할인을 제공해드리며, 76 약간의 추가 요금을 지불하시면, 3일 신속 인화 서비스를 요청하실 수 있습니다.

어휘 whether A, or (simply) B, C A하든 B하든 관계없이, C할 것이다 long-lasting 오래 지속되는 company ID card 사원증 professional 전문적인 capture ~을 포착하다 look like ~처럼 보이다 catwalk 런웨이, 패션 무대 main location 본사 stop by ~에 방문하다 minimal 아주 적은, 최소의 rapid 빠른 processing service 인화 서비스

75. 픽쳐 퍼펙트는 어떤 종류의 업체인가?
(A) 카메라 제조사
(B) 모델 에이전시
(C) 미술 용품 매장
(D) 사진 스튜디오

정답 (D)

해설 지문 초반부에 특별한 행사에서 오래 지속되는 기억을 원하거나 여권이나 사원증을 위한 사진이 필요할 경우 최상의 결과를 제공할 것이라고(Whether you wish to make long-lasting memories of a special event ~ Picture Perfect will provide the best results in town) 소개하고 있는데 이는 사진관에서 하는 일이므로 (D)가 정답이다.

어휘 manufacturer 제조사 modeling agency 모델 에이전시 art supply 미술 도구

76. 픽쳐 퍼펙트에 대하여 명시된 것은 무엇인가?
(A) 적어도 세 개의 지점을 가지고 있다.
(B) 본사 이전을 계획하고 있다.
(C) 재구매 고객에게 무료 선물을 준다.
(D) 특별한 신속 서비스를 제공한다.

정답 (D)

해설 마지막 문장에 약간의 추가 요금을 지불하면 3일 신속 인화 서비스를 요청할 수 있다는(for a minimal extra fee you can request our rapid 3-day processing service) 내용이 있

다. 따라서 (D)가 정답이다.

어휘 **at least** 최소한, 적어도 **relocate** ~로 이전하다 **main branch** 본사 **express service** 빠른 배송 서비스

77-79.

http://www.facemotors.com/comments

회사 소개	뉴스	상품	의견	연락처

77 귀사의 제품 중 하나인 페이스 GT-20의 품질에 대해 항의하고자 글을 씁니다. 제 차량이 잘못 조립된 좌석이나 형편없게 설계된 연료 라인 결합과 같은 문제들로 인해 여러 번 회수 조치를 받았는데, 둘 다 모두 매우 위험하지만 쉽게 예방할 수 있는 상황입니다.

이 글을 쓰고 있는 동안에도, 제 차는 다시 한번 회수 조치로 인해 귀사의 서비스 센터에 들어가 있습니다. **78** 페이스 사가 EGR 밸브를 고치도록 하려고 저는 또 다시 하루 결근을 해야 합니다. 사소한 문제로 보일 수도 있지만, 고치는 데 하루 종일 걸릴 것이며, 저는 수리를 마치고 자동차 등록증을 갱신하는 인증서를 수령해야 합니다. 다시 한번, 저는 제가 선택한 자동차에 대해 벌금을 내야 할 처지에 놓여 있습니다. **79** 제가 서비스센터 직원에게 직장에 꼭 출근해야 하는데 결함 있는 부품 때문에 결근할 처지라고 설명을 했지만, 그분은 모든 사람에게 당일 대체용 차량을 빌려준다면 수백 대의 차량이 필요하다고 주장하며 완전히 무시했습니다. 그 결과, 저는 교통수단이 없기 때문에 수리 작업이 진행되는 동안 이곳 귀사의 서비스센터에 갇혀 있습니다.

존 알프레드슨

어휘 **namely** 즉 **recall** ~을 회수하다 **frighteningly** 무섭게 **preventable** 예방할 수 있는 **due to** ~때문에 **yet another** 또 한차례의 **obtain** ~을 얻다, 획득하다 **certificate** 인증서 **registration** 등록 **be faced with** ~에 직면하다 **penalty** 벌금 **as a result of** ~의 결과로 **dismiss** ~을 거절하다, 무시하다 **replacement** 대체 **means of transportation** 교통수단 **duration** 지속 기간

77. 의견의 목적은 무엇인가?
(A) 제품을 향상시킬 방안을 제시하기
(B) 고객서비스센터 직원을 칭찬하기
(C) 대체용 자동차 부속품을 주문하기
(D) 제품에 대한 불만을 제기하기

정답 (D)

해설 첫 문단 첫째 줄에 제품 중 하나의 품질에 대해 항의하고자 글을 쓴다고(I'm writing to complain about the quality of one of your products) 목적을 밝히고 있으므로 (D)가 정답이다.

어휘 **improve** ~을 향상시키다 **praise** ~을 칭찬하다 **dissatisfaction** 불만족

78. 알프레드슨 씨가 언급하는 문제점은 무엇인가?
(A) 수리 비용을 낼 여유가 없다.
(B) 부속품을 며칠 기다려야 한다.
(C) 운전 중 부상을 입었다.
(D) 근무를 하루 종일 빠져야만 했다.

정답 (D)

해설 두 번째 문단에서 페이스 사가 알프레드슨 씨의 차를 고치게 하려고 또 다시 하루 결근을 해야 한다(I'm missing yet another day of work so that FACE can correct an EGR valve) 사실을 말하고 있으므로 (D)가 정답이다.

어휘 **afford** ~할 여유가 있다 **suffer** (고통을) 겪다 **injury** 부상

79. 의견에 따르면, 알프레드슨 씨가 서비스 센터 직원에게 요청했던 것은 무엇인가?
(A) 직원의 사과
(B) 연장된 보증
(C) 임시 차량
(D) 수리에 대한 할인

정답 (C)

해설 두 번째 문단 후반부에 알프레드슨 씨가 서비스센터 직원에게 상황을 설명하며 당일 대체 차량을 빌려달라고 요청했지만 무시당했다고(Although I explained to the serviceman that it was very important that I get to work and ~ they'd have to give out hundreds of cars) 밝히고 있으므로 (C)가 정답이다.

80-82.

수신: 고객 서비스 직원들
발신: 로사 홈즈, 이사
주제: 12월 초과 근무
날짜: 11월 15일

안녕하세요 여러분,

다시 한 해의 그 시기가 되었네요! 11월 25일부터 시작해서 고객 서비스 시간을 연장하여 제공할 것입니다. 우리는 전화선을 주중에는 오전 7시에, 주말에는 오전 8시에 열 것입니다. 전화선은 매일 저녁 9시까지 열려 있습니다. **81** 우리는 1월 5일까지 보통의 일정으로 돌아가지 않을 것입니다. **82** 늘 그랬듯이, 초과근무에 대해서는 1.5배 특별 수당이 지급될 것입니다(주당 40시간 초과 시).

제가 여러분의 개인 일정은 알지 못하므로, **80** 고객 서비스 부서의 일정에 여러분의 초과 근무 요청을 등록해 주십시오. 여러분 중 많은 사람들이 해마다 이 시기에 가족과 함께 해야 할 의무가 있다는 것을 알고 있지만 여러분 중 많은 분들이 또한 추가급여를 벌 수 있는 기회를 즐기기도 합니다. 저는 원하지 않는 직원들이 추가 근무를 하도록 강요하지 않고도 이러한 요구가 채워지기를 기대합니다.

어휘 **extended** 연장된 **stay open** 열어두다 **time-and-a-half** 1.5배의 초과 근무 수당 **overtime work** 초과 시간 근무 **sign up with** ~에 등록하다 **obligation** 의무, 마 땅히 해야 할 일 **earn** 돈을 벌다 **force A to do** A가 ~하 기를 강제하다, 억지로 ~하게 하다 **unwilling** 꺼려하는, 마 지못해 하는

80. 이메일은 왜 쓰여졌는가?

(A) 정규직 일자리 공석을 설명하기 위해
(B) 사람들에게 자원하도록 요청하기 위해
(C) 휴일에 대한 인사말을 전하기 위해
(D) 프로그램에 가입할 기회를 알리기 위해

정답 (B)

해설 두번째 문단에서 바뀐 운영시간에 따라 초과 근무를 희망하는 사람에게 등록하라는(please sign up with your overtime requests) 내용이 언급되어 있는데, 이를 통해 초과 근무는 의 무가 아닌 지원자들에 의해서 시행될 것임을 알 수 있다. 따라서 사람들에게 초과 근무를 지원할 것을 요청하는 것이라 볼 수 있 으므로 (B)가 정답이다.

어휘 **describe** ~을 설명하다 **full-time** 정규직의 **vacancy** 공석(일자리) **extend best wishes** 안부 인사를 전하다

81. 고객서비스 부서는 언제 정규 근무 시간제로 돌아갈 것인가?

(A) 11월 25일
(B) 1월 5일
(C) 1월 15일
(D) 1월 25일

정답 (B)

해설 첫 문단에서 1월 5일 전까지 보통의 일정으로 돌아가지 않을 것 이라고(We won't return to our routine schedule until January 5) 언급되어 있으므로, 정규 근무 시간제로 돌아가는 것은 1월 5일임을 알 수 있다. 따라서 (B)가 정답이다.

82. 초과 근무에 대해 암시된 것은 무엇인가?

(A) 주말은 포함되지 않을 것이다.
(B) 추가 금액이 지불될 것이다.
(C) 한 달 동안만 요구될 것이다.
(D) 모든 직원들에게 의무적이다.

정답 (B)

해설 첫 번째 문단 후반부에 주 40시간의 정규 근무 이외의 근무에 대해서 1.5배 초과 근무 수당을 제공한다고(time-and-a-half will be paid for any overtime work) 언급된 부분에 초과 근무에 대해 추가 수당이 주어질 것이라고 했으므로 (B)가 정답 이다.

어휘 **required** 요구되는 **mandatory** 의무적인

83-86.

보르샤 주식회사
신제품을 발표하다

베를린 85 (4월 4일) – 안드레아스 슈미트 보르샤 주식회사 대표 이사가 어제 열린 기자회견에서 이 회사의 새로운 최첨단 제품 라 인 출시 계획에 관해 이야기했습니다. 보르샤에서 마지막으로 출 시한 제품은 NX560이었습니다. — [1] —. 84 86 보르샤의 임 원과 전자 제품 업계의 전문가들에게 아주 놀랍게도, 이 모델은 작년 7월의 출시 이후에 겨우 약 54만대만 판매되어 왔습니다. — [2] —. 이 실망스러운 일을 감안해, 이 회사는 NX600 제품 라 인의 개발을 가속화했으며, 이 제품들은 올 6월에 시장에 출시될 예정입니다. 85 다음 달에 베를린에 문을 여는 완전히 새로운 제 조 공장과 함께, 보르샤 주식회사는 분명 높은 수준의 수요를 기대 하고 있으며, 생산량을 늘릴 계획입니다.

슈미트 씨는 NX600 단말기가 83 개선된 메뉴 배치와 더욱 강력 한 카메라, 비드토크 일대일 영상 통화 기능, 그리고 더 높은 화면 해상도를 갖출 것이라고 밝혔습니다. — [3] —. 또한, 이전 모델들 과 달리, 신제품은 유럽 시장뿐만 아니라 아시아 시장에서도 출시 된다는 점도 언급했습니다. 소매가는 약 750유로가 될 것으로 예 상됩니다. — [4] —.

어휘 **press conference** 기자회견 **release** ~을 출시하다, ~을 발매하다 **cutting-edge** 최첨단의 **much to the surprise to** ~에게 놀랍게도 **unit** (기계의) 한 대, 한 개 **launch** 출시, 공개, 시작 **in light of** ~을 감안해 (볼 때), ~에 비추어 (볼 때) **disappointment** 실망(스러운 일) **accelerate** ~을 가속화하다 **be scheduled to do** ~할 예정이다 **manufacturing** 제조 **clearly** 분명히, 확실히 **anticipate** ~을 기대하다, ~을 예상하다 **intend to do** ~할 계획이다, ~할 작정이다 **production capacity** 생산 량, 생산 능력 **state that** ~라고 말하다 **handset** 단말기 **face-to-face** 마주보고 하는, 대면하는 **function** 기능 **resolution** 해상도 **note that** ~라고 언급하다 **retail** 소 매(업) **be expected to do** ~할 것으로 예상되다

83. 보르샤 주식회사가 무엇을 생산할 것 같은가?

(A) LED 텔레비전
(B) 팩스 기계
(C) 디지털 카메라
(D) 휴대전화기

정답 (D)

해설 두 번째 단락에 개선된 메뉴 배치와 더욱 강력한 카메라, 비드 토크 일대일 영상 통화 기능, 그리고 더 높은 화면 해상도라는 (an improved menu layout, a more powerful camera, a VidTalk face-to-face call function, and a higher screen resolution) 특징들이 제시되어 있다. 이러한 특징 은 휴대전화기에서 찾아 볼 수 있으므로 (D)가 정답이다.

84. NX560과 관련해 유추할 수 있는 것은 무엇인가?

(A) 1년도 더 이전에 출시되었다.
(B) 소비자들로부터 많은 찬사를 받았다.
(C) 보르샤 주식회사가 출시한 첫 제품이었다.
(D) 예상보다 덜 인기 있는 것으로 드러났다.

정답 (D)

해설 첫 단락 중반부에 작년 7월의 출시 이후에 오직 약 54만대만 판매되어서 보르샤의 임원과 전자 제품 업계의 전문가들이 놀라워했다는(Much to the surprise of Vorsha executives and experts in the electronics industry, only around 540,000 units of that model have been sold) 말이 쓰여 있다. 이는 생각보다 판매량이 저조한 상태를 나타내는 말이므로 (D)가 정답이다.

어휘 **praise** 찬사, 칭찬 **prove to be A** A한 것으로 드러나다

85. 보르샤 주식회사가 언제 새 생산 시설을 열 것인가?
(A) 4월에
(B) 5월에
(C) 6월에
(D) 7월에

정답 (B)

해설 첫 단락 후반부에 다음 달에 베를린에 완전히 새로운 제조 공장이 문을 연다는(With its brand new manufacturing plant opening in Berlin next month) 말이 쓰여 있고, 지문 시작 부분에 기사 작성 날짜가 4월 4일(April 4)로 표기되어 있어 5월에 새 생산 시설이 문을 연다는 사실을 알 수 있으므로 (B)가 정답이다.

86. [1], [2], [3], [4]로 표기된 위치 중에서, 다음 문장이 들어가기에 가장 적절한 곳은 어디인가?

"이는 전 세계적으로 수백만 달러를 들인 광고 캠페인에도 불구하고 일어난 일입니다."

(A) [1]
(B) [2]
(C) [3]
(D) [4]

정답 (B)

해설 제시된 문장은 특정한 일을 지칭하는 This와 함께 수백만 달러를 들인 광고 캠페인에도 불구하고 그러한 일이 나타났다는 의미를 지니고 있으며, 이는 엄청난 돈을 들인 광고에도 불구하고 좋지 못한 결과를 얻은 경우에 할 수 있는 말에 해당된다. 따라서 NX560 모델의 저조한 판매량을 언급한 문장 뒤에 위치한 [2]에 들어가 제품 홍보를 위해 노력했던 일을 말하는 흐름이 되어야 자연스러우므로 (B)가 정답이다.

어휘 **in spite of** ~에도 불구하고 **multi-million-dollar** 수백만 달러의 **worldwide** 전 세계적인

87-90.

루이즈 드리스콜 [오후 4:30] **87** 저와 같은 마음을 갖고 계신 등산 애호가 분들께 조언을 좀 요청 드리고자 합니다. 제 남편과 제가 다음 주말에 셔먼산으로 등산을 갈 계획입니다. 도시에서 멀리 있다는 것을 알지만, 여러분 중에서 가 보신 분 계신가요?

트로이 팍스 [오후 4:32] 몇몇 제 친구들이 그곳에 갔었는데, 등산로가 잘 관리되어 있고 경치도 믿을 수 없을 정도라고 말하더군요.

루이즈 드리스콜 [오후 4:34] 저도 같은 얘기를 들었어요. **88** 그래서 저는 그곳이 너무 붐빌까봐 조금 걱정돼요.

질 핀들레이 [오후 4:35] 제가 올해 초에 제 등산 동호회와 함께 그곳에 갔었는데, 실망하시지 않을 거예요. 등산로가 꽤 비어 있었는데, 그 공원이 아주 크기 때문이에요.

루이즈 드리스콜 [오후 4:36] 아주 좋은 것 같네요! 그리고 셔먼산에 캠핑 시설이 있나요? 저희가 그곳에서 잠도 자고 이틀 기간으로 등산하고 싶어요.

트로이 팍스 [오후 4:37] 그쪽에서 야영객들에 대한 야간 요금을 없애지 않았나요, 질 씨?

질 핀들레이 [오후 4:38] 네, 사실이에요. **89** 캠핑장과 캠핑 시설이 전부 완전히 무료입니다.

루이즈 드리스콜 [오후 4:39] 와우! 헨리산에 대해서도 같은 얘기가 있으면 좋겠어요.

딘 말로우 [오후 4:41] 그리고, **90** 잊지 마시고 공원 관리 사무소를 방문해 보세요. 제가 듣기로는 여름 기간 중에 무료로 생수를 나눠준다고 하더라고요.

루이즈 드리스콜 [오후 4:42] 아주 좋은 팁이네요, 감사합니다! 여러분 모두 큰 도움이 되어 주셨어요.

어휘 **like-minded** 같은 마음을 가진 **trekker** 등산객, 여행하는 사람 **well-maintained** 잘 유지된 **incredible** 믿을 수 없을 정도의 **crowded** 붐비는 **trail** 등산로, 산길 **be tempted to do** ~하고 싶다 **get rid of** ~을 없애다, 제거하다 **overnight** 야간의 **indeed** 사실인, 정말인 **give out** ~을 나눠주다

87. 드리스콜 씨는 누구와 얘기하고 있었을 것 같은가?
(A) 셔먼산 근처에 살고 있는 사람들
(B) 자신과 함께 여행할 사람들
(C) 자주 등산 가는 사람들
(D) 캠핑 용품을 판매하는 사람들

정답 (C)

해설 드리스콜 씨가 채팅을 시작하면서 자신과 같은 마음을 갖고 있는 등산 애호가들에게 조언을 요청한다고(I'd like to ask my likeminded mountain trekkers for some advice) 알리고 있다. 따라서 등산 애호가들, 즉 자주 등산 가는 사람들과 이야기했다는 것을 알 수 있으므로 (C)가 정답이다.

88. 드리스콜 씨는 무엇에 대해 우려하고 있는가?

    (A) 좋지 못한 날씨
    (B) 셔먼산에 도달하는 방법
    (C) 혼잡한 등산로
    (D) 등산로의 난이도

정답 (C)

해설 드리스콜 씨가 4시 34분 메시지에서 너무 붐빌까 조금 걱정된 다는(I'm just a bit worried that it'll be too crowded) 말을 하고 있는데, 이는 사람들이 많아 혼잡할까봐 걱정된다는 뜻이므로 (C)가 정답이다.

89. 오후 4시 39분에, 드리스콜 씨가 "If only the same could be said for Mount Henry"라고 쓸 때, 무엇을 의미할 것 같은가?

    (A) 헨리산의 캠핑 시설이 좋지 못한 수준이다.
    (B) 헨리산의 경관이 전혀 감동적이지 못하다.
    (C) 헨리산의 등산로가 열악하게 유지된다.
    (D) 헨리산의 캠핑장이 요금을 부과한다.

정답 (D)

해설 오후 4시 38분에 핀들레이 씨가 캠핑장과 캠핑 시설이 전부 완전히 무료라고(The campground and camping facilities are all completely free) 말하자, 드리스콜 씨가 '헨리산에 대해서도 같은 얘기가 있으면 좋겠어요'라고 답변하는 상황이다. 이는 헨리산의 캠핑장은 무료가 아니라 요금을 부과하고 있다는 뜻이므로 (D)가 정답이다.

어휘 **underwhelming** 전혀 감동적이지 않은

90. 말로우 씨에 따르면, 공원 관리 사무소에서 무엇을 얻을 수 있는가?

    (A) 등산로 지도
    (B) 주차 허가증
    (C) 무료 음료
    (D) 캠핑용 장비

정답 (C)

해설 말로우 씨가 4시 41분에 작성한 메시지에, 잊지 말고 공원 관리 사무소를 방문하라고 알리면서 여름 기간 중에 무료로 생수를 나눠준다는(they give out free bottles of water during the summer) 정보를 제공하고 있으므로 (C)가 정답이다.

어휘 **permit** 허가증 **complimentary** 무료의

91-95.

> **저희에게 새로운 모습에 대한 의견을 주시고 경품을 받으세요!**
>
> 라이브 랜드스케이프 디자인 사는 새로운 모습을 원하며, 여러분의 도움이 필요합니다. 저희 회사를 위해 새로운 로고를 디자인하시고, 여러분의 정원을 새롭게 단장하고 95 이탈리아, 프랑스, 스페인의 유명한 정원을 방문하기 위한 10,000달러의 여행을 하기 위해 참가하세요.
>
> 여러분은 저희 회사의 이미지를 반영하는 과감한 로고를 디자인하셔야 합니다. 저희는 자연을 보존하고 사람들이 그들의 조경 디자인 목표를 달성하는 것을 돕는 것에 헌신하고 있습니다. 그 로고는 한 장의 A4 사이즈 크기의 페이지에 제출되어야 하며, 92 또한 로고의 의미를 설명하는 500단어의 글을 포함하셔야 합니다. 저희는 그 로고의 컬러와 흑백 버전 모두 필요합니다.
>
> 만약 당신이 대회에서 우승한다면, 당신의 사진이 출간되는 것에 동의해야 함을 알아 두십시오. 91 18세를 초과해야 참가 자격이 됩니다.
>
> 11월 21일에서 12월 30일 사이에 언제든지 참가하실 수 있습니다. 93 우승자는 1월 15일에 발표될 것입니다.
>
> l.penny@livelandscape.com으로 릴리 페니에게 이메일로 참가작들을 보내주십시오.

어휘 **makeover** 수선, 단장 **bold** 대담한, 과감한 **be committed to -ing** ~에 전념하다, 헌신하다 **preserve** ~을 보존하다 **submission** 제출 **notify** ~을 통지하다 **entry** 참가작, 참가자

> **수신:** 릴리 페니 <l.penny@livelandscapes.com>
> **발신:** 헌터 존스 <hjones@hunterdesign.co.uk>
> **날짜:** 11월 23일
> **주제:** 공모전 질문사항
>
> 페니 씨에게,
>
> 최근에 광고하신 로고 디자인 공모전에 관하여 이메일을 드립니다. 당신이 저를 위해 답변해 주셨으면 하는 몇 가지 질문 사항들이 있습니다.
>
> 94(D) 혹시 이 공모전에 아마추어 디자이너들만 참가 가능한가요, 아니면 전문 디자이너들도 참가작을 제출할 수 있나요? 저는 한 조경 회사에서 디자이너로 일하고 있어서 이런 질문을 드리는 것입니다. 94(B) 또한, 혹시 이 공모전에 미국 시민들만 참가할 수 있나요, 아니면 다른 국가의 거주자들 또한 참가할 수 있나요? 94(A) 참가작을 늦게 제출하는 것이 허용되나요?
>
> 저는 귀하께서 저의 질문들에 답변하실 수 있기를 바라며 제가 그 공모전에 참가할 수 있기를 바랍니다. 95 저는 그 해외 여행상을 꼭 받고 싶은데 왜냐하면 저는 언제나 그 국가들을 방문하는 것을 즐기기 때문입니다.
>
> 안녕히 계십시오,
>
> 헌터 존스

어휘 **professional** 전문적인, 직업의 **resident** 거주민 **accept** ~을 허용하다, 받아들이다 **overseas** 해외로

91. 이 대회에 참가하기 위한 하나의 필수 조건은 무엇인가?
(A) 미국 시민이어야만 한다.
(B) 경험 있는 정원사여야 한다.
(C) 적어도 19세는 되어야 한다.
(D) 전문 디자이너이어야 한다.

정답 (C)

해설 첫 지문 세 번째 문단에 18세를 넘어야 이 공모전에 참가할 수 있다고(You need to be over 18 years of age to enter) 언급되어 있으므로 (C)가 정답이다.

어휘 **experienced** 경험 있는 **at least** 적어도

92. 참가작과 함께 포함되어야 하는 것은 무엇인가?
(A) 컬러 사진
(B) 추천장
(C) 자세한 이력서
(D) 서면 설명

정답 (D)

해설 첫 번째 지문 두 번째 단락에서 로고의 의미를 설명하는 500단어로 된 글을 제출해야 한다는(need to include a 500-word submission which explains the meaning of the logo) 내용이 언급되어 있다. 따라서 (D)가 정답이다.

어휘 **recommendation** 추천 **detailed** 자세한 **written** 글로 쓰인, 서면의 **description** 설명, 묘사

93. 참가자들은 본인이 우승했는지 언제 알 수 있는가?
(A) 11월 21일에
(B) 11월 23일에
(C) 12월 30일에
(D) 1월 15일에

정답 (D)

해설 첫 번째 지문 네 번째 문단에 우승자는 1월 15일에 발표될 것(The winner will be notified on January 15)이라고 언급되어 있다. 따라서 (D)가 정답이다.

94. 존스 씨에 의해 요청된 정보가 아닌 것은 무엇인가?
(A) 자신의 작품을 마감일 이후에 보낼 수 있는지
(B) 미국 시민이 아니어도 경연에 참여할 수 있는지
(C) 상이 현금으로 교환 가능한지
(D) 전문가들이 참가할 자격이 되는지

정답 (C)

해설 두 번째 지문 두 번째 단락에 전문가들도 참가작을 제출할 수 있는지 묻는(Is the competition only open to amateur designers, or can professional designers also submit entries?) 부분에서 (D)를, 공모전에 미국 시민들만 참가할 수 있는지 묻는(Also, is the competition only open to US residents, or can residents of other countries enter

the competition?) 부분에서 (B)를, 그리고 마감일 이후에 작품을 늦게 제출하는 것이 허용되는지 묻는(Are late entries accepted?) 부분에서 (A)를 확인할 수 있다. 하지만 해당 상을 현금으로 교환할 수 있는지에 대해서는 문의하고 있지 않으므로 (C)가 정답이다.

95. 존스 씨에 대해 알 수 있는 것은 무엇인가?
(A) 라이브 랜드스케이프 디자인 사의 직원이다.
(B) 지금 현재 정원을 가지고 있지 않다.
(C) 전에 프랑스로 여행간 적이 있다.
(D) 경연 참가작들을 심사하는데 도울 것이다.

정답 (C)

해설 두 번째 지문 마지막 문단을 보면 존스 씨는 언제나 그 국가들을 방문하는 것을 즐긴다는(as I always enjoy visiting those countries) 내용이 언급되고 있다. 이와 관련해, 첫 번째 지문 첫 문단에 이탈리아, 프랑스, 스페인이 언급되어 있으므로(a $10,000 trip to visit famous gardens in Italy, France and Spain) 존스 씨가 이 국가들에 가본 경험이 있을 거라고 유추할 수 있고, 이 중 한 나라를 언급한 (C)가 정답이다.

어휘 **currently** 현재 **assist in** ~하는데 돕다 **judge** ~을 판단하다, 심사하다

96-100.

> 레지나 뉴섬 씨
> 뱅크스 애비뉴 306번지
> 휴스턴, TX 77003
>
> 뉴섬 씨께,
>
> 저희가 올해의 '아프리카계 미국인 미술 전시회'를 준비하는 과정에 있으며, 이는 8월 12일부터 8월 25일까지 메트로폴리탄 미술관에서 개최될 것입니다. **99** 작년 8월에 열린 전시회의 경우와 마찬가지로, 참가하시는 모든 미술가들께서 각자의 작품 사진과 함께 저희 웹 사이트에서 프로필을 통해 소개되실 것입니다. **96** 저는 귀하께서 이번 행사에 몇몇 조각품을 전시하시길 원하셨으면 하는 희망을 갖고 편지를 씁니다. 저희는 해당 건물의 미술관 네 곳을 모두 활용할 예정입니다.
>
> 등록 절차는 대체로 예년과 동일하지만, 두 가지 작은 변동 사항이 있습니다. 참가자들께서는 여전히 반드시 행사 개막일보다 최소한 달 전에 참가 등록하셔야 합니다. 이제 주된 차이점을 말씀 드리자면 **97** 양식을 우송하시는 것이 아니라, 저희 웹 사이트를 통해 등록하셔야 한다는 점입니다. 또한, 올해부터, 저희가 국가에서 발급한 신분증 또는 운전 면허증 둘 중 하나를 스캔하신 사본이 필요할 것입니다.
>
> 안녕히 계십시오.
>
> 마커스 페인
> 회장
> LOLA 미술 협회

어휘 in the process of ~하는 과정에 있는 exhibition 전시(회) as is the case with ~의 경우와 마찬가지로 participating 참가하는 alongside ~와 함께 in the hope that ~라는 희망을 갖고 display ~을 전시하다, ~을 진열하다 sculpture 조각품 utilize ~을 활용하다 registration 등록 procedure 절차 previous 이전의, 과거의 register 등록하다 take part 참가하다 prior to ~ 전에, ~보다 앞서 via ~을 통해 scanned 스캔된

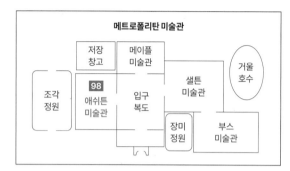

어휘 storage 보관, 저장 warehouse 창고

수신: 마커스 페인 <mpayne@lolaart.com>
발신: 레지나 뉴섬 <rnewsome@artism.com>
제목: 아프리카계 미국인 미술 전시회
날짜: 6월 4일

페인 씨께,

'아프리카계 미국인 미술 전시회'와 관련해 편지 보내 주셔서 감사합니다. 참가자로서 직접 등록하기 위해 웹 사이트에 가기 전에, 귀하께 확인해 보고자 하는 것이 있습니다. 제가 참가하는 데 관심이 있기는 하지만, 제 작품의 아름다움과 복잡함을 100 돋보이게 하는 환경에서 선보일 수 있는 경우에 한해 그렇게 할 것입니다. 제 조각품이 자연광에서 더 좋아 보이기 때문에, 아주 많은 햇빛을 받는 미술관에 배치될 수 있기를 바랍니다. 99 작년에 있었던 전시회에 제 작품을 전시했을 때, 메이플 미술관에 제공되었던 조명이 만족스럽지 않았으며, 거울 호수 옆에 있는 미술관들도 자연적으로 충분히 밝지 않았던 것 같았습니다. 98 제 생각엔 조각 정원을 내려다보는 공간이 제 작품에 훨씬 더 많이 적합할 것 같습니다.

감사합니다, 그리고 8월에 미술관에서 뵐 수 있기를 고대합니다.

레지나 뉴섬

어휘 regarding ~와 관련해 be interested in ~에 관심이 있다 highlight ~을 돋보이게 하다, ~을 강조하다 intricacy 복잡함 place v. ~을 배치하다, ~을 놓다 a great deal of 아주 많은 (양의) display ~을 전시하다, ~을 진열하다 be satisfied with ~에 만족하다 next to ~ 옆에 overlook (건물 등이) ~을 내려다보다 be suitable for ~에 적합하다, ~에 어울리다

---

96. 페인 씨가 왜 뉴섬 씨에게 편지를 썼는가?
(A) 행사 개최 장소가 변경되었음을 알리기 위해
(B) 행사에 참가하도록 권하기 위해
(C) 전시회를 준비하도록 도운 것에 대해 감사하기 위해
(D) 새 미술관이 곧 개장할 것임을 알리기 위해

정답 (B)

해설 첫 지문 첫 단락에 행사 개최 정보와 함께 이번 행사에 몇몇 조각품을 전시하길 원했으면 하는 희망을 갖고 편지를 쓴다고(I am writing to you in the hope that you would like to display some of your sculptures at the event) 알리는 말이 편지를 쓰는 목적에 해당된다. 이는 전시 행사에 참가하도록 권하는 말에 해당되므로 (B)가 정답이다.

어휘 inform A that A에게 ~라고 알리다(= notify A that) venue 개최 장소, 행사장 encourage A to do A에게 ~하도록 권하다

97. 행사 등록 절차가 어떻게 변경되었는가?
(A) 참가자들이 미리 등록해야 한다.
(B) 등록이 행사 개최 장소에서 진행될 것이다.
(C) 등록이 오직 온라인에서만 실시될 수 있다.
(D) 참가자들이 반드시 두 가지 종류의 신분증을 제출해야 한다.

정답 (C)

해설 첫 지문 두 번째 단락에 양식을 우송하는 것이 아니라 웹 사이트를 통해 등록해야 한다고(you have to sign up via our Web site, not by mailing a form) 언급하고 있다. 이는 온라인으로만 등록할 수 있다는 뜻이므로 (C)가 정답이다.

어휘 be required to do ~해야 하다, ~할 필요가 있다 take place (일, 행사 등이) 진행되다, 개최되다, 일어나다 carry out ~을 실시하다, ~을 수행하다 identification 신분 확인(증)

98. 뉴섬 씨가 어디에 자신의 전시품을 전시하고 싶어 하는가?
(A) 샐튼 미술관
(B) 메이플 미술관
(C) 애쉬튼 미술관
(D) 부스 미술관

정답 (C)

해설 세 번째 지문 후반부에 조각 정원을 내려다보는 공간이 자신의 작품에 적합할 것이라고(I think the space overlooking the sculpture garden would be much more suitable for my works) 언급되어 있다. 두 번째 지문인 배치도에서 왼편에 위치한 조각 정원을 내려다보는 위치에 있는 미술관이 바로 옆에 있는 애쉬튼 미술관(Ashton Gallery)이므로 (C)가 정답이다.

99. 뉴섬 씨와 관련해 암시된 것은 무엇인가?
(A) 일부 미술품에 대해 페인 씨와 협업했다.
(B) 한 달 안에 페인 씨와 만날 것이다.

(C) 작년에 미술관 웹 사이트에서 간략히 설명되었다.

(D) 행사 등록에 대해 할인을 받을 것이다.

정답 (C)

해설 세 번째 지문 중반부에 뉴섬 씨가 작년에 있었던 전시회에 자신의 작품을 전시했다고(When I displayed my works at last year's exhibition) 언급하는 것으로 작년 참가 사실을 알리고 있다. 이와 관련해, 첫 번째 지문 첫 단락에 작년 8월에 열린 전시회의 경우와 마찬가지로 참가하는 미술가들이 웹 사이트에서 프로필을 통해 소개된다는(As was the case with last August's exhibition, all participating artists will be profiled on our Web site) 말이 쓰여 있다. 따라서 작년에도 미술관 웹 사이트에서 프로필을 통해 간략히 설명된 것으로 볼 수 있으므로 (C)가 정답이다.

어휘 **briefly** 간략히, 잠깐

---

100. 이메일에서, 첫 번째 단락, 네 번째 줄의 단어 "highlights"와 의미가 가장 가까운 것은 무엇인가?

(A) 비추다

(B) 미리 설명하다

(C) 요약하다

(D) 두드러지게 하다

정답 (D)

해설 해당 문장에서 highlights는 명사 environment를 수식하는 that절에 속해 있으며, highlights의 목적어로 쓰인 명사구 their beauty and intricacy는 작품이 지닌 아름다움과 복잡함을 가리킨다. 따라서, 그러한 특징들을 잘 드러나게 하는 환경이라는 의미가 구성되어야 자연스러우므로 '두드러지게 하다'를 뜻하는 (D) accentuates가 정답이다.

LC

1. (D)	**2.** (A)	**3.** (B)	**4.** (A)	**5.** (A)
6. (B)	**7.** (A)	**8.** (B)	**9.** (B)	**10.** (B)
11. (C)	**12.** (C)	**13.** (A)	**14.** (A)	**15.** (C)
16. (A)	**17.** (C)	**18.** (A)	**19.** (C)	**20.** (C)
21. (C)	**22.** (D)	**23.** (C)	**24.** (C)	**25.** (D)
26. (B)	**27.** (B)	**28.** (C)	**29.** (A)	**30.** (B)
31. (B)	**32.** (C)	**33.** (C)	**34.** (D)	**35.** (B)
36. (C)	**37.** (C)	**38.** (D)	**39.** (B)	**40.** (D)
41. (D)	**42.** (D)	**43.** (B)	**44.** (B)	**45.** (A)
46. (C)	**47.** (C)	**48.** (D)	**49.** (D)	**50.** (C)

RC

51. (A)	**52.** (C)	**53.** (A)	**54.** (D)	**55.** (B)
56. (A)	**57.** (C)	**58.** (A)	**59.** (D)	**60.** (A)
61. (A)	**62.** (D)	**63.** (B)	**64.** (C)	**65.** (A)
66. (D)	**67.** (B)	**68.** (C)	**69.** (C)	**70.** (A)
71. (C)	**72.** (B)	**73.** (A)	**74.** (D)	**75.** (C)
76. (C)	**77.** (D)	**78.** (C)	**79.** (D)	**80.** (C)
81. (C)	**82.** (D)	**83.** (A)	**84.** (D)	**85.** (A)
86. (C)	**87.** (A)	**88.** (B)	**89.** (D)	**90.** (D)
91. (B)	**92.** (A)	**93.** (A)	**94.** (D)	**95.** (C)
96. (C)	**97.** (D)	**98.** (B)	**99.** (C)	**100.** (C)

Part 1

1. (A) A refrigerator is being installed.
(B) A tool has been propped against a wall.
(C) The man is assembling some shelves.
(D) The man is bending over an oven.

(A) 냉장고가 설치되는 중이다.
(B) 도구 하나가 벽에 기대어져 있다.
(C) 남자가 몇몇 선반을 조립하는 중이다.
(D) 남자가 오븐 위로 몸을 구부리고 있다.

해설 (A) 냉장고를 설치하는 동작을 하고 있지 않으므로 오답.
(B) 벽에 기대어 있는 도구를 찾아볼 수 없으므로 오답.
(C) 선반을 조립하는 동작을 하고 있지 않으므로 오답.
(D) 오븐 위로 몸을 구부린 자세를 묘사하고 있으므로 정답.

어휘 refrigerator 냉장고 install ~을 설치하다 tool 도구, 공구 be propped against ~에 기대어져 있다 assemble ~을 조립하다 bend over ~ 위로 몸을 구부리다, 숙이다

2. **(A) Park maintenance work is being carried out.**
(B) A worker is inspecting a tool.
(C) Some equipment has been left next to a tree.
(D) A worker is repairing some light fixtures.

(A) 공원 유지 관리 작업이 실시되는 중이다.
(B) 한 작업자가 도구 하나를 점검하는 중이다.
(C) 일부 장비가 나무 옆에 놓인 채로 있다.
(D) 한 작업자가 일부 조명 기구를 수리하는 중이다.

해설 (A) 공원에서 남자가 장비를 이용해 하는 일을 공원 유지 관리 작업으로 묘사하고 있으므로 정답.
(B) 장비를 들여다보며 점검하는 동작이 아니므로 오답.
(C) 나무 옆에 놓인 장비를 찾아볼 수 없으므로 오답.
(D) 조명 기구를 수리하는 동작이 아니므로 오답.

어휘 maintenance 유지 관리 carry out ~을 실시하다, 수행하다 inspect ~을 점검하다 equipment 장비 leave ~을 놓다, 두다(leave-left-left) light fixture 조명 기구

Part 2

3. When do you think the renovations will be completed?

(A) The cafeteria and meeting room.
(B) By the end of the month.
(C) No, I need some more time.

개조 작업이 언제 완료될 것이라고 생각하세요?
(A) 구내식당과 회의실입니다.
(B) 이달 말까지요.
(C) 아니요, 전 시간이 좀 더 필요합니다.

해설 개조 작업이 완료되는 시점을 묻는 When 의문문에 대해 전치사 By를 사용하여 대략적인 시점으로 질문에 답하는 (B)가 정답이다.

어휘 renovation 수리, 개조 cafeteria 구내식당, 카페테리아

4. Who was honored at the company banquet?

(A) Bill received an award.
(B) There's a bank around the corner.
(C) Yes, it was a great honor.

회사 연회에서 누가 상을 받았나요?
(A) 빌 씨가 상을 받았어요.
(B) 모퉁이를 돌면 은행이 있어요.
(C) 네, 그건 굉장한 영광이었어요.

해설 상을 받은 사람이 누구인지 묻는 Who 의문문에 사람 이름을 언급하며 상을 받은 사람을 말하는 것으로 질문에 답하는 (A)

가 정답이다. (B)는 banquet과 발음이 유사하게 들리는 bank 를 이용한 오답이다.

어휘 **be honored** 상을 받다, 영광을 차지하다 **banquet** 연회
honor 영광, 영예

5. Is Mr. Harris supposed to be joining us for the meeting?

(A) **Not that I know of.**
(B) Yes, it was nice to meet him.
(C) He enjoyed it, too.

해리스 씨가 우리와 함께 회의에 참석하기로 되어 있나요?
(A) **제가 알기로는 그렇지 않습니다.**
(B) 네, 그를 만나게 되어 좋았습니다.
(C) 그도 즐거워했습니다.

해설 해리스 씨가 회의에 함께 할 것인지를 묻는 일반 의문문이므로
Yes/No 답변이나 그에 준하는 다른 표현을 통해 참석 여부를
언급하는 응답이 적절하다. 따라서 본인이 알기로는 그렇지 않
다는 말로 해리스 씨가 회의에 참석하기로 되어 있지 않다는 의
미를 표현하며 질문에 답하는 (A)가 정답이다.

어휘 **be supposed to do** ~하기로 되어 있다, ~해야 한다
Not that I know of 내가 알기로는 아니다

6. Which advisor are you hiring?

(A) No, sadly not.
(B) **Rosa, from Entrue Consulting.**
(C) We just have.

어느 자문위원을 고용할 겁니까?
(A) 아니요, 안타깝지만 아닙니다.
(B) **엔트루 컨설팅에 근무하는 로사 씨요.**
(C) 저희는 이제 막 했어요.

해설 명사와 함께 나오는 Which 의문문의 경우 바로 뒤의 명사까지
놓치지 않고 들어야 하며, which 뒤에 사람에 해당하는 어휘가
있으므로 Who 의문문과 동일한 의미를 나타낸다. 따라서 사람
이름과 소속을 말하며 질문에 답하는 (B)가 정답이다.

어휘 **advisor** 고문, 자문위원 **hire** ~을 고용하다

7. Are you going to be here until 7 this evening?

(A) **I might leave around 6:30.**
(B) I didn't hear from her.
(C) Usually in the morning.

오늘 저녁에 7시까지 여기 계실 건가요?
(A) **저는 6시 30분쯤에 나갈 수도 있어요.**
(B) 저는 그녀에게서 아무 말도 듣지 못했어요.
(C) 대개 아침에요.

해설 특정 시간까지 머물 것인지 묻고 있으므로 대략적인 시간을 언
급하면서 그 전에 떠날 수도 있다는 말로 질문에 답하는 (A)가
정답이다. (C)는 질문에서 말하는 앞으로의 계획과는 달리 평

소에 하는 일에 대한 답변이므로 오답이다.

어휘 **hear from** ~로부터 소식을 듣다

8. Should we present the awards now or wait until after the meal?

(A) For outstanding employees.
(B) **Let's do it later.**
(C) We usually gather once a year.

상을 지금 수여해야 하나요, 아니면 식사 후까지 기다려야 할
까요?
(A) 뛰어난 직원들을 위해서입니다.
(B) **나중에 하도록 합시다.**
(C) 우리는 보통 1년에 한 번 모입니다.

해설 상을 지금 수여하는지, 아니면 식사 후까지 기다려야 하는지를
묻는 선택 의문문에 나중에 하자는 말로 식사 후까지 기다리라
는 것을 선택하여 답하는 (B)가 정답이다. (A)는 awards에서
연상 가능한 수여 대상을 언급한 오답이다.

어휘 **outstanding** 뛰어난

9. How long is Mr. Jensen going to be off work with the flu?

(A) It'll be done within an hour.
(B) **At least a week, I think.**
(C) He's worked here for five years.

젠슨 씨는 독감으로 얼마나 쉴 예정입니까?
(A) 한 시간 안에 완성될 예정입니다.
(B) **제 생각으로는 적어도 일주일입니다.**
(C) 그는 이곳에서 5년 동안 일해 왔습니다.

해설 기간을 묻는 How 의문문에 자신이 추측하는 바를 표현하는 I
think를 덧붙여 최소 기간을 언급하며 질문에 답하는 (B)가 정
답이다. (C)에도 for five years라는 기간이 언급되지만 젠슨
씨의 근무 기간은 질문과 맞지 않는 내용이므로 오답이다.

어휘 **flu** 독감 **at least** 최소한, 적어도

10. How can I find the research report for the Rasmussen account?

(A) I can count it again for you.
(B) **I'll let you know in a second.**
(C) We should tell the client about it.

라스무센 고객사에 대한 조사 보고서를 어떻게 찾을 수 있나
요?
(A) 제가 다시 세어 드릴 수 있습니다.
(B) **제가 금방 알려 드릴게요.**
(C) 우리는 그 고객에게 그것에 대해 말해주어야 합니다.

해설 방법을 묻는 How 의문문에 방법을 직접 알려주는 대신 잠시
후에 알려주겠다는 말로 조금만 기다려 달라고 답하는 (B)가
정답이다.

어휘 account 고객사, 거래처, 계좌, 계정 count ~을 셈하다, 세다 in a second 금방, 순식간에

11. Hasn't she been featured in our magazine before?

(A) It has lots of interesting articles.
(B) No, she doesn't have a subscription.
(C) Yes, but not for a few years.

그녀가 전에 우리 잡지에서 특종으로 다루어진 적이 있지 않습니까?
(A) 그것에는 재미있는 기사들이 많이 있습니다.
(B) 아니요, 그녀는 구독하지 않습니다.
(C) 네, 하지만 지난 몇 년 동안은 아니었습니다.

해설 특정 인물이 잡지에서 특종으로 다루어진 적이 있는지 확인하는 부정 의문문이다. 이에 긍정을 나타내는 Yes와 함께 다루어진 적이 있기는 하지만 최근 몇 년 동안은 그렇지 않았다는 말로 질문에 답하는 (C)가 정답이다. (A)에서 It이 our magazine을 지칭하여 질문에 긍정하는 것으로 잘못 생각하기 쉽지만, 질문에서 묻고 있는 특종 여부에 적절한 응답이 아니므로 오답이다.

어휘 feature (신문이나 잡지에) ~을 특종으로 다루다, 특징으로 삼다 have a subscription 구독하다

12. I didn't know Maria had moved to the Lansing branch.

(A) Start packing up all your things.
(B) There aren't any vacancies right now.
(C) Yes, they gave her a big pay raise.

마리아 씨가 랜싱 지사로 옮겼는지 몰랐어요.
(A) 당신의 모든 짐을 싸기 시작해 주세요.
(B) 현재 빈 자리가 전혀 없어요.
(C) 네, 그들은 그녀에게 연봉을 크게 인상해주었습니다.

해설 마리아 씨가 랜싱 지사로 옮겼다는 사실을 몰랐다고 말하는 평서문이다. 이에 Yes로 긍정하며 부가 정보를 제시하는 (C)가 정답이다. (B)는 전근/이직과 관련하여 연상할 수 있는 vacancy(공석, 빈 자리)를 이용한 오답이다.

어휘 start –ing ~하기 시작하다 pack up 짐을 싸다 vacancy 공석, 빈 자리 give A a pay raise A에게 급여를 인상해주다

13. Are they holding the wedding indoors or outdoors?

(A) It'll take place by the river.
(B) Guests should arrive by 10 a.m.
(C) Yes, I received an invitation.

그들은 결혼식을 실내에서 하나요, 아니면 야외에서 하나요?
(A) 강가에서 열릴 겁니다.
(B) 손님들은 오전 10시까지 도착해야 해요.
(C) 네, 초대장을 받았습니다.

해설 결혼식을 하는 장소를 묻는 선택 의문문에 강가에서 열릴 것이라는 말로 outdoors를 선택하여 질문에 답하는 (A)가 정답이다. (B)와 (C)는 wedding에서 연상 가능한 guests와 invitation을 각각 이용했으나 결혼식 장소와 관련 없는 오답이다.

어휘 indoors 실내(에서) outdoors 야외(에서) take place (행사가) 열리다, 개최되다

14. Isn't there a newer model of that cell phone?

(A) I think that's the latest version.
(B) Thanks, I'm pleased with it.
(C) The news is on after this program.

저 휴대폰의 좀 더 신형 모델은 없나요?
(A) 그게 가장 최신 버전인 것 같아요.
(B) 고마워요, 전 그것에 만족해요.
(C) 이 프로그램 다음에 뉴스가 나옵니다.

해설 휴대폰의 최신형 모델이 있는지 확인하는 부정 의문문이다. 이에 부정을 나타내는 No를 생략하고 I think를 이용해 그것이 가장 최신 버전인 것 같다는 말로 질문에 답하는 (A)가 정답이다. (B)는 물건을 받은 입장에서 할 수 있는 응답이므로 질문에 적절하지 않은 오답이다.

어휘 newer 더 새로운, 더 신형의 be pleased with ~에 만족하다, 기쁘다

15. How many clients does Richard deal with?

(A) That's an important business deal.
(B) Mostly business accounts.
(C) It changes from week to week.

리차드 씨는 얼마나 많은 고객을 응대하나요?
(A) 그건 중요한 사업 거래입니다.
(B) 대부분 기업 고객입니다.
(C) 매주 바뀝니다.

해설 응대하는 고객의 규모를 묻는 How 의문문에 매주 바뀐다는 말로 응대하는 고객의 수가 일정하지 않다는 의미로 질문에 답하는 (C)가 정답이다. (B)는 응대하는 고객의 종류를 말하므로 규모와는 관련 없는 오답이다.

어휘 deal with ~을 응대하다, ~을 처리하다, ~을 다루다 deal 거래 (조건), 거래 제품 account 고객(사), 거래처, 계정, 계좌 from week to week 매주, 주마다

16. Will your gallery be displaying work by local artists?

(A) This pamphlet lists all our featured exhibits.
(B) About an hour by bus.
(C) A recently renovated building.

당신의 미술관에서 지역 미술가들의 작품을 전시할 예정인가요?

(A) 이 팸플릿에 저희의 모든 특별 전시회 목록이 있습니다.
(B) 버스로 약 한 시간이요.
(C) 최근 개조된 건물이요.

해설   지역 미술가들의 작품을 전시할 예정인지 묻는 질문에 팸플릿을 언급하면서 관련 정보를 확인할 수 있는 방법을 알려주는 (A)가 정답이다. (C)는 질문에서 묻는 지역 미술가들의 작품 전시가 열리는 장소로 잘못 생각할 수 있지만, 단순히 장소만을 언급하는 답변이므로 오답이다.

어휘   **display** ~을 전시하다, ~을 진열하다 **work** 작품, 작업물 **list** ~을 목록에 올리다, ~을 목록에 기재하다 **featured** 특별히 포함된, 특색으로 하는 **renovated** 개조된, 보수된

17. You've made the logo too small, haven't you?
(A) We might have that in a large.
(B) Try the marketing team.
(C) The client asked for it this way.

그 로고를 너무 작게 만드시지 않았나요?
(A) 우리가 그걸 큰 사이즈로 할지도 몰라요.
(B) 마케팅팀에 한 번 알아보세요.
(C) 고객께서 이렇게 하도록 요청하셨어요.

해설   로고를 너무 작게 만든 게 아닌지 묻는 부가 의문문이다. 이에 the logo를 it으로, made the logo too small을 this way로 각각 지칭해 고객의 요청에 따라 그렇게 만들었다는 말로 질문에 답하는 (C)가 정답이다. (B)는 제3자 또는 타팀에 문의해 보라는 말로 정보를 확인할 수 있는 방법을 알려주는 답변이라고 잘못 생각할 수 있지만, 질문을 듣는 사람이 만든 로고의 크기에 대한 응답으로 적절하지 않으므로 오답이다.

어휘   **make A B** A를 B하게 만들다 **in a large** 큰 사이즈로 **ask for** ~을 요청하다

18. The local theater is organizing a film festival.
(A) Are tickets on sale yet?
(B) He's one of my favorite actors.
(C) It was my pleasure to help.

지역 영화관이 영화제를 준비하고 있어요.
(A) 혹시 입장권이 판매 중인가요?
(B) 그는 제가 가장 좋아하는 배우들 중 한 명입니다.
(C) 도와 드릴 수 있어서 제가 기뻤습니다.

해설   지역 영화관이 영화제를 준비하고 있다는 정보를 전달하는 평서문에 입장권이 판매 중인지 되묻는 것으로 답하는 (A)가 정답이다. (C)는 감사 표현에 답하는 표현이므로 영화제 준비 사실과는 관련 없는 오답이다.

어휘   **organize** ~을 준비하다, ~을 조직하다 **yet** (의문문) 혹시, 벌써, (부정문) 아직, (최상급과 함께) 지금까지 중에서

19. You sent Greg Findlay the invitation to our

product launch, didn't you?
(A) Yes, I'm looking forward to attending.
(B) Thanks, but I already had lunch.
(C) I'll be seeing him in person tomorrow.

그렉 핀들레이 씨에게 우리 제품 출시 행사 초대장을 보내시지 않았나요?
(A) 네, 저는 참석하기를 고대하고 있습니다.
(B) 감사합니다만, 저는 이미 점심 식사를 했습니다.
(C) 내일 그분을 직접 만나 뵐 예정입니다.

해설   그렉 핀들레이 씨에게 제품 출시 행사 초대장을 보내지 않았는지 묻는 부가 의문문이다. 이에 그렉 핀들레이 씨를 him으로 지칭해 내일 직접 만난다는 말로 초대장 전달 방법을 알리는 (C)가 정답이다. (A)는 긍정을 나타내는 Yes 뒤에 오는 말이 행사 초대장 발송 여부와 관련 없는 내용이므로 오답이다.

어휘   **send A B** A에게 B를 보내다 **invitation** 초대(장) **launch** 출시 (행사), 공개, 시작 **look forward to -ing** ~하기를 고대하다 **attend** 참석하다 **in person** 직접 (가서)

20. We're choosing new wallpaper for the waiting area.
(A) I'll wait for you at the main entrance.
(B) I normally don't read any newspapers.
(C) Eddy's Home Décor has a good selection.

저희가 대기실에 필요한 새 벽지를 선택하고 있습니다.
(A) 정문에서 당신을 기다리고 있을게요.
(B) 저는 보통 어떤 신문도 읽지 않습니다.
(C) 에디스 홈 데코에 다양한 제품이 있습니다.

해설   대기 구역에 필요한 새 벽지를 선택하고 있다는 정보를 전달하는 평서문에 특정 매장명과 함께 제품 선택의 폭이 넓은 곳이 있다는 말로 답하는 (C)가 정답이다.

어휘   **wallpaper** 벽지 **normally** 보통, 일반적으로 **have a good selection** 다양한 제품이 있다

Part 3

Questions 21-23 refer to the following conversation.

W: Hi, Shawn. **21** How are the arrangements going for this Saturday's fine art seminar?

M: Well, I'm still deciding where we should hold it. We usually use the gallery's main exhibition hall, but it's completely filled with exhibits right now. What do you think about using Exhibition Room 3 instead?

W: **22** I'm not sure about that. Exhibition Room 3 is a little dim and I think we'll need more light in order to display some artworks during the seminar.

M: Good point. Actually, **23** the seminar speaker is stopping by for a meeting after lunch. I'll ask him for his opinion on the matter.

여: 안녕하세요, 숀 씨. 이번 주 토요일에 있을 미술 세미나 준비 작업은 어떻게 되어가고 있나요?

남: 음, 어디서 개최해야 할지 여전히 결정하는 중입니다. 저희는 보통 미술관의 본관 전시홀을 이용하는데, 지금은 전시물로 완전히 가득 차 있어요. 대신 3 전시실을 이용하는 건 어떻게 생각하세요?

여: 저는 잘 모르겠어요. 3 전시실이 좀 어둑한 곳이라서, 제 생각에 세미나가 진행되는 동안 몇몇 미술품을 전시하려면 조명이 더 필요할 것 같아요.

남: 좋은 지적입니다. 사실, 세미나 연설자께서 점심 시간 후에 회의하러 들르실 거예요. 제가 이 문제와 관련해 그분께 의견을 여쭤볼게요.

어휘 **How is A going?** A가 어떻게 되어가고 있나요? **arrangement** 준비, 조치, 조정 **hold** ~을 개최하다, ~을 열다 **be filled with** ~로 가득 차 있다 **dim** 어둑한, 흐릿한 **in order to do** ~하려면, ~하기 위해 **display** ~을 전시하다, ~을 진열하다 **during** ~ 중에, ~ 동안 **stop by** (잠깐) 들르다 **matter** 문제, 사안

21. 화자들은 어디에서 근무할 것 같은가?
(A) 영화관에서
(B) 과학 박물관에서
(C) 미술관에서
(D) 호텔에서

해설 대화 초반부에 여자가 미술 세미나 준비 작업이 어떻게 되어가고 있는지(How are the arrangements going for this Saturday's fine art seminar?) 묻고 있으므로 (C)가 정답이다.

22. 여자는 왜 우려하는가?
(A) 일부 장비가 무거울 수도 있다.
(B) 한 공간이 현재 개조되는 중이다.
(C) 일부 전시품이 설치되지 않았다.
(D) 방 한 곳이 충분히 밝지 않다.

해설 대화 중반부에 여자가 불확실성을 언급하는 말과 함께 3 전시실이 좀 어둑해서 조명이 더 필요하다고(I'm not sure about that. Exhibition Room 3 is a little dim and I think we'll need more light ~) 알리고 있으므로 (D)가 정답이다.

어휘 **equipment** 장비 **currently** 현재 **renovate** ~을 개조하다, ~을 보수하다 **display** n. 전시(품), 진열(품) **set up** ~을 설치하다, ~을 마련하다

Paraphrase a little dim / need more light
→ not be bright enough

23. 남자가 오늘 이따가 무엇을 할 것인가?
(A) 여자와 함께 점심 식사하는 일
(B) 일정표를 업데이트하는 일
(C) 연설자와 만나는 일
(D) 공지를 하는 일

해설 남자가 오늘 이따가 무엇을 할 것인지 묻고 있으므로 남자의 말에서 later today 또는 이와 유사한 시점 표현과 함께 계획이나 앞으로의 일정, 제안 사항 등을 알리는 부분에서 정보를 찾아야 한다. 대화 마지막 부분에 남자가 세미나 연설자가 점심 시간 후에 회의하러 들른다는(~ the seminar speaker is stopping by for a meeting after lunch) 사실을 알리고 있으므로 (C)가 정답이다.

어휘 **meet with** (약속하고) ~와 만나다 **make an announcement** 공지하다, 발표하다

Paraphrase seminar speaker is stopping by for a meeting
→ Meet with a speaker

Questions 24-26 refer to the following conversation.

M: Bianca, how is the development going on **24** our new line of dining tables?

W: Great! The design we chose is fantastic. They're going to look so stylish and sophisticated.

M: Definitely. But, **25** I just hope they aren't too complicated for our customers to set up. Even with the instruction manual, **25** it seems like it's very difficult to put all the parts together.

W: Well, we still have time to make some changes. **26** The products won't be in shops until June, so that gives us six more months to improve them.

남: 비앙카 씨, 우리의 새 식탁 제품 라인에 대한 개발 작업은 어떻게 되어가고 있나요?

여: 아주 좋습니다! 우리가 선택한 디자인이 환상적이에요. 아주 감각적이고 세련되어 보일 겁니다.

남: 물론입니다. 하지만, 우리 고객들께서 설치하시기에 너무 복잡하지만 않으면 좋겠어요. 심지어 안내 설명서가 있어도, 모든 부품을 조립하는 게 아주 어려운 것 같아요.

여: 음, 여전히 몇 가지 변경할 시간이 있습니다. 제품들이 6월이나 되어야 매장에 나갈 것이기 때문에, 개선할 수 있는 시간이 6개월이나 있어요.

어휘 **development** 개발, 발전 **line** 제품 라인, 제품군 **stylish** 감각적인, 멋진 **sophisticated** 세련된 **Definitely** (강한 긍정) 물론입니다, 당연하죠 **too 형용사 to do** ~하기엔 …한 **complicated** 복잡한 **set up** ~을 설치하다, ~을 마련하다 **instruction manual** 안내 설명서 **put A together** A를 조립하다 **part** 부품 **not A until B** B나 되어야 A하다 **improve** ~을 개선하다, ~을 향상시키다

24. 화자들은 어떤 종류의 제품을 이야기하고 있는가?
(A) 의류
(B) 가전 제품
(C) 가구
(D) 컴퓨터 부대용품

해설 화자들이 어떤 종류의 제품을 이야기하는지 묻고 있으므로 제품명이나 특징, 기능 등과 관련된 정보를 찾는 데 집중해야 한다. 대화 초반부에 남자가 자사의 새 식탁 제품 라인(our new line of dining tables) 개발 작업을 언급한 뒤로 그 제품과 관련해 이야기하고 있으므로 (C)가 정답이다.

Paraphrase dining tables → Furniture

25. 남자는 제품의 어떤 측면을 우려하는가?
(A) 내구성
(B) 가격
(C) 외관
(D) 조립 용이성

해설 대화 중반부에 남자가 설치 작업의 복잡함(I just hope they aren't too complicated ~ to set up) 및 부품 조립의 어려움과(~ it's very difficult to put all the parts together) 관련해 언급하고 있으므로 조립 용이성을 뜻하는 (D)가 정답이다.

어휘 **aspect** 측면, 양상 **be concerned about** ~을 우려하다, ~을 걱정하다 **durability** 내구성 **appearance** 외관, 모습 **ease** 용이함, 쉬움 **assembly** 조립

26. 6월에 무슨 일이 있을 것인가?
(A) 몇몇 직원들이 고용될 것이다.
(B) 몇몇 제품이 출시될 것이다.
(C) 광고 캠페인이 시작될 것이다.

(D) 소매 지점이 개장될 것이다.

해설 6월에 무슨 일이 있을 것인지 묻고 있으므로 June이라는 시점 표현과 함께 언급되는 정보를 찾는 데 집중해야 한다. 대화 후반부에 여자가 제품들이 6월이나 되어야 매장에 나갈 것이라고 (The products won't be in shops until June ~) 알리고 있는데, 이는 6월에 제품이 출시된다는 뜻이므로 (B)가 정답이다.

어휘 **hire** ~을 고용하다 **launch** ~을 출시하다, ~을 공개하다 **advertising** 광고 (활동) **retail** 소매(업)

Paraphrase The products won't be in shops until June → Some products will be launched

Questions 27-29 refer to the following conversation.

M: Hello, **27** thank you for calling Cascade Travel Agency.

W: Hi, this is Sabrina Mitchell. I booked a trip next month to Brazil through one of your agents, and I was wondering if there is a fee to postpone it.

M: Yes, normally there is.

W: Well, the thing is, my passport is about to expire.

M: Before the trip? **28** We should have checked that...

W: Yeah, that's what I thought too.

M: It's alright. **28** I can waive the fee this time. Also, **29** I'll send some links to your e-mail address. One with steps for renewing your passport, and the other to reschedule your trip.

W: I really appreciate that. **29** I'll take a look at it now.

남: 안녕하세요, 캐스케이드 여행사에 전화 주셔서 감사합니다.
여: 안녕하세요, 저는 사브리나 미첼입니다. 제가 귀사의 직원 한 분을 통해 다음 달에 브라질로 가는 여행을 예약했는데, 그걸 연기하는 데 수수료가 있는지 궁금합니다.
남: 네, 일반적으로 있습니다.
여: 음, 문제는, 제 여권이 막 만료되려 한다는 거예요.
남: 여행 전에요? 저희가 그걸 확인했어야 했는데요...
여: 네, 저도 그렇게 생각했어요.
남: 그럼 괜찮습니다. 이번엔 수수료를 철회해 드릴 수 있습니다. 그리고, 제가 고객님 이메일 주소로 링크를 좀 보내 드리겠습니다. 하나는 여권을 갱신하시는 단계에 대한 것이고, 다른 하나는 여행 일정을 재조정하시는 것에 대한 것입니다.
여: 정말 감사합니다. 지금 한 번 확인해 볼게요.

어휘 **agent** 직원, 대리인 **postpone** ~을 연기하다, ~을 미루다

be about to do 막 ~하려 하다, ~하려는 참이다 **expire**
만료되다 **waive** ~을 철회하다, (권리 등) ~을 포기하다
renew ~을 갱신하다 **reschedule** ~의 일정을 재조정하
다 **appreciate** ~에 대해 감사하다

27. 남자는 누구일 것 같은가?

(A) 택시 기사
(B) 여행사 직원
(C) 호텔 지배인
(D) 항공기 승무원

해설 대화 초반부에 남자가 캐스케이드 여행사에 전화주셔서 감사하
다고(~ thank you for calling Cascade Travel Agency)
말하고 있으므로 남자가 여행사에 소속된 직원임을 알 수 있다.
따라서 (B)가 정답이다.

28. 여자가 "저도 그렇게 생각했어요"라고 말할 때 무엇을 암시하는
가?

(A) 한 가지 결정이 재고되어야 한다.
(B) 마감기한이 다가오고 있다.
(C) 수수료가 철회되어야 한다.
(D) 여행이 취소될 것이다.

해설 대화 중반부에 남자가 자신들이 제대로 확인하지 못한 사실을
인정하는(We should have checked that...) 말을 하자, 여
자가 자신도 그렇게 생각했다고 언급한 뒤로 남자가 이번엔 수
수료를 철회해 주겠다고(I can waive the fee this time) 알
리고 있다. 이는 여자도 남자와 동일하게 여자 자신의 잘못이 아
니므로 수수료를 내지 않아도 된다는 생각을 했음을 나타내는
말이므로 (C)가 정답이다.

어휘 **reconsider** ~을 재고하다 **approach** 다가오다, 다가가다

29. 여자는 곧이어 무엇을 할 것인가?

(A) 자신의 이메일을 확인하는 일
(B) 지불 금액을 내는 일
(C) 여행 상세 정보를 제공하는 일
(D) 몇몇 서류를 작성하는 일

해설 대화 후반부에 남자가 여자의 이메일 주소로 링크를 보내겠다
고(I'll send some links to your e-mail address) 말하
자, 여자가 그것을 지금 확인해 보겠다고(I'll take a look at it
now) 대답하고 있으므로 (A)가 정답이다.

어휘 **payment** 지불(액) **details** 상세 정보, 세부 사항 **fill out**
~을 작성하다

Paraphrase e-mail address / take a look at it
→ Check her e-mail

Questions 30-32 refer to the following conversation with
three speakers.

W: I just wanted to say thanks for helping me
get settled in with the new job today. I really
appreciate it.

M1: Don't mention it. **30** We're happy to have you
join our accounting team.

M2: And someone as experienced as you will really
help us out.

W: Well, the job is great so far. **31** I'm still a little
worried about the commute, though. It's a long
drive from Daubeny.

M1: You know, **32** you should try to find someone
to carpool with. Doesn't Angelina live in
Daubeny?

M2: Yeah. She works in accounting, too, though she
left early today. **32** I'll give you her number,
and you can just send her a message later.

여: 제가 새로운 일에 적응할 수 있도록 도와주신 것에 대해 감사하
다는 말씀을 드리고 싶었어요. 진심으로 감사드립니다.
남1: 별 말씀을요. 저희는 당신이 우리 회계팀에 들어오게 되어 기
쁩니다.
남2: 그리고 당신만큼 경험 많은 분은 저희에게 정말로 큰 도움이
될 거예요.
여: 저, 일은 지금까지 아주 좋습니다. 하지만 여전히 통근 문제에
대해 조금 걱정이 돼요. 도베니에서부터 장거리 운전을 해야 하
거든요.
남1: 있잖아요, 카풀을 함께 할 사람을 찾아보세요. 안젤리나 씨가
도베니에 살지 않나요?
남2: 네. 오늘은 일찍 퇴근하기는 했지만, 그분도 회계팀에서 근무
합니다. 제가 전화번호를 알려드릴 테니 나중에 그분께 문자
메시지를 보내시면 됩니다.

어휘 **get settled in** 적응하다 **appreciate** ~에 대해 감사하다
as A as B B만큼 A한 **experienced** 경험 많은 **so far**
지금까지 **commute** 통근 **long drive** 장거리 운전

30. 화자들은 어떤 부서에서 근무하는가?

(A) 인사부
(B) 회계부
(C) 마케팅부
(D) 기술 지원부

해설 화자들의 근무 장소를 묻는 문제이므로 대화 중에 언급되는 특
정 부서명이나 업무 및 서비스, 활동 등과 관련된 내용을 파악해
야 한다. 대화 초반부에 남자 한 명이 여자에게 자신들의 회계팀
에 들어오게 되어 기쁘다고(We're happy to have you join

our accounting team) 알리는 부분을 통해 화자들이 회계부에서 근무한다는 것을 알 수 있다. 따라서 (B)가 정답이다.

31. 여자는 어떤 문제점을 언급하는가?
  (A) 해당 분야에서 경험이 없다.
  (B) 장거리 통근을 한다.
  (C) 또 다른 문서가 필요하다.
  (D) 사무실 주변에 익숙하지 않다.

해설 여자가 언급하는 문제점을 찾아야 하므로 여자의 말에서 부정적인 정보가 제시되는 부분이 있음을 예상하고 들어야 한다. 대화 중반부에 여자가 통근 문제에 대해 아직도 조금 걱정이 된다면서 장거리 운전을 해야 한다고(I'm still a little worried about the commute, though. It's a long drive from Daubeny) 언급하고 있으므로 (B)가 정답이다.

Paraphrase commute / a long drive
→ a long commute

32. 남자들은 무엇을 제안하는가?
  (A) 일찍 도착할 것
  (B) 세미나에 등록할 것
  (C) 다른 직원에게 연락해 볼 것
  (D) 회의를 준비할 것

해설 장거리 통근 얘기를 들은 남자 중 한 명이 카풀을 권하면서(you should try to find someone to car pool with) 특정 직원의 이름을 언급하고, 다른 남자가 그 사람의 전화번호를 알려줄 테니 메시지를 보내 보라고 제안하고(I'll give you her number, and you can just send her a message later) 있다. 따라서 (C)가 정답이다.

어휘 register for ~에 등록하다 organize ~을 마련하다, 조직하다

Paraphrase send her a message
→ contacting

Questions 33-35 refer to the following conversation and label.

W: Hi, Mr. Marino. Are you all done fixing the leak?

M: **33** I found the pipe that was leaking and replaced it with a new one. Actually, it seems like the pipe was defective because it was poorly made.

W: If that's the case, do you think the same thing might happen in other apartments in this complex?

M: It's possible. Perhaps **34** the contractor that you hired to renovate it used parts that were too cheap to save on costs. You might want to bring that issue up with them.

W: **34** I'll be sure to file a complaint with them.

M: Okay, now I'll need to file a report on this. Could you read me the code on the label there? The one that starts with K C.

W: Alright. **35** K C 1 0 3.

여: 안녕하세요, 마리노 씨. 새는 부분을 고치는 작업을 모두 완료하셨나요?
남: 새는 파이프를 찾아서 새것으로 교체했습니다. 실은, 이 파이프가 좋지 못하게 만들어져서 결함이 있었던 것 같습니다.
여: 그런 경우라면, 이 단지 내의 다른 아파트 동에도 같은 문제가 일어날 수도 있다고 생각하세요?
남: 가능합니다. 아마 보수하기 위해 고용하셨던 계약업체가 비용을 절약하기 위해 너무 저렴한 부품을 사용했을 겁니다. 이 문제에 관한 얘기를 그쪽에 꺼내 보시는 게 좋겠어요.
여: 저는 분명히 그쪽에 불만을 제기할 겁니다.
남: 알겠습니다, 이제 제가 이에 관해 보고해야 할 겁니다. 거기 라벨이 있는 코드를 읽어 주시겠습니까? K C로 시작하는 것이요.
여: 좋아요. K C 1 0 3입니다.

일련 번호	PF-3646
제조사 ID	KC-103
모델 종류	24 와이드
제품 구분	90 스탠다드

어휘 be done -ing ~하는 것을 완료하다 leak n. (물, 가스 등의) 새는 부분, 누출 v. 새다, 누출되나 replace A with B A를 B로 교체하다 defective 결함이 있는 poorly 좋지 못하게, 형편 없이 If that's the case 그런 경우라면, 그렇다면 complex (건물) 단지, 복합 건물 contractor 계약업체, 계약자 renovate ~을 보수하다, ~을 개조하다 part 부품 You might want to do ~하시는 게 좋겠습니다 bring A up with B A에 관한 얘기를 B에게 꺼내다 file a complaint 불만을 제기하다 file a report on ~에 관해 보고하다 serial number 일련 번호 manufacturer 제조사 category 구분, 범주, 항목

33. 남자는 누구일 것 같은가?
  (A) 공사장 인부
  (B) 부동산 중개인
  (C) 배관공
  (D) 보안 직원

해설 특정 화자의 신분을 묻는 문제의 경우, 특정 업무나 활동, 전문 지식, 제공 서비스 등과 관련된 정보를 통해 단서를 파악해야 한다. 대화 초반부에 남자가 새는 파이프를 찾아서 새것으로 교체했다는(I found the pipe that was leaking and replaced it with a new one) 말을 하고 있는데, 이는 배관공이 하는 일에 해당되므로 (C)가 정답이다.

34. 여자는 자신이 무엇을 처리할 것이라고 말하는가?

    (A) 거래내역서 비용을 지불하는 것
    (B) 문서를 파일로 정리하는 것
    (C) 다른 아파트를 점검하는 것
    (D) 계약업체에 불만을 제기하는 것

해설 남자가 대화 중반부에 여자가 고용한 계약업체와(the contractor that you hired) 관련된 문제를 언급하자, 여자가 그 업체를 them으로 지칭해 분명히 불만을 제기할 것이라고(I'll be sure to file a complaint with them) 말하고 있으므로 이를 언급한 (D)가 정답이다.

어휘 **handle** ~을 처리하다, ~을 다루다 **invoice** 거래내역서 **file** ~을 파일로 정리하다 **paperwork** 문서 (작업) **inspect** ~을 점검하다, ~을 조사하다 **complain** v. 불만을 제기하다

> Paraphrase contractor / file a complaint with them
> → Complaining to a contractor

35. 시각자료를 보시오. 여자는 남자에게 어떤 정보를 읽어 주는가?

    (A) 일련 번호
    (B) 제조사 ID
    (C) 모델 종류
    (D) 제품 구분

해설 대화 후반부에 여자가 남자의 요청에 따라 KC 103이라는 코드를 읽어 주고 있다. 시각자료에서 이 코드는 두 번째 줄에 위치한 Manufacturer ID에 해당되므로 (B)가 정답이다.

Questions 36-38 refer to the following conversation and chart.

W: Hi, Donald. You might remember me from your interview. **36** I'm Nancy Travis, the head of the hiring committee. Welcome to your first day at Freshco Manufacturing.

M: Hello, Ms. Travis. I'm excited to start learning the ropes.

W: Well, you have a busy day ahead. I'll be training you on company policies this morning, and then you'll meet with **37** your department manager, Mr. Smith, after lunch.

M: Sounds great. I was wondering... is there somewhere I can leave my bag and coat?

W: Oh, of course! **38** Let's head over to the staff room and I'll show you where the lockers are. You can store your belongings in there.

여: 안녕하세요, 도널드 씨. 면접 시간에 저를 보신 기억이 있으실지 모르겠네요. 저는 고용 위원회장 낸시 트래비스입니다. 프레시코 제조사에서의 첫 출근일에 오신 것을 환영합니다.

남: 안녕하세요, 트래비스 씨. 일하는 요령을 터득하기 시작하는 것이 기쁩니다.

여: 음, 오늘 바쁜 하루를 앞두고 있으십니다. 제가 오늘 오전에 회사 정책에 관해 교육해 드릴 예정이고, 그 후에는 소속 부서장님이신 스미스 씨를 점심 식사 후에 만나시게 될 겁니다.

남: 아주 좋은 것 같습니다. 궁금한 게 있었는데... 제 가방과 코트를 놓아둘 수 있는 곳이 있나요?

여: 아, 물론이죠! 직원 휴게실로 같이 가서 사물함이 어디 있는지 알려 드릴게요. 거기에 소지품을 보관하시면 됩니다.

부서장	부서
베이커 씨	마케팅
웰스 씨	고객 서비스
스미스 씨	회계
카터 씨	홍보

어휘 **hiring committee** 고용 위원회 **learn the ropes** 일하는 요령을 터득하다 **have A ahead** A를 앞두고 있다, A가 앞에 놓여 있다 **leave** ~을 놓아두다, ~을 남겨놓다 **head over to** ~ 쪽으로 가다, ~ 쪽으로 향하다 **show A B** A를 B에게 알려 주다, A를 B에게 보여 주다 **belongings** 소지품

36. 여자는 누구일 것 같은가?

    (A) 신입 직원
    (B) 회사 소유주
    (C) 고용 책임자
    (D) 영업 사원

해설 대화 초반부에 여자가 자신을 소개하면서 이름과 함께 고용 위원회장이라고(I'm Nancy Travis, the head of the hiring committee) 알리고 있다. 이는 여자가 고용 책임자임을 나타내는 말이므로 (C)가 정답이다.

> Paraphrase head of the hiring committee
> → hiring manager

37. 시각자료를 보시오. 남자는 어느 부서에서 근무하는가?

    (A) 마케팅부
    (B) 고객 서비스부
    (C) 회계부
    (D) 홍보부

해설 대화 중반부에 여자가 남자의 소속 부서장을 스미스 씨라고(your department manager, Mr. Smith) 언급하고 있다. 시각자료에서, 이 사람의 이름이 있는 세 번째 줄에 기재된 부서명은 Accounting이므로 (C)가 정답이다.

38. 화자들은 곧이어 어디로 갈 것인가?

    (A) 본사로
    (B) 수납장으로
    (C) 구내식당으로
    (D) 직원 휴게실로

해설 대화 후반부에 여자가 직원 휴게실로 함께 가서 사물함이 있는 곳을 알려 주겠다고(Let's head over to the staff room ~) 말하고 있으므로 (D)가 정답이다.

Part 4

Questions 39-41 refer to the following telephone message.

Hello. My name is Max Linberg, and **39** I'm calling about a pair of shoes I purchased from your online store. I received an e-mail today notifying me that I didn't send enough money. I'm sorry, I was sure that I had sent the right amount. I thought I read that they were 60 dollars, but now I see that they were actually 80. **40** I'll make sure I send the remaining 20 dollars this afternoon. **41** I also need to know when the shoes will arrive. Can you e-mail me right after you send them to me? I apologize for any inconvenience I've caused you.

안녕하세요. 제 이름은 맥스 린버그이며, 귀하의 온라인 매장에서 구매한 신발에 대해 전화 드립니다. 제가 오늘 이메일을 받았는데, 제가 충분한 돈을 보내지 않았다고 알리는 것이었습니다. 죄송해요, 제가 맞는 금액을 보냈다고 생각했어요. 60달러라고 읽었던 것 같은데 지금 보니 사실 80달러네요. 남은 20달러를 오늘 오후에 꼭 보내도록 하겠습니다. 저는 신발이 언제 도착할지도 알고 싶습니다. 신발을 보내시자마자 제게 이메일을 주시겠습니까? 불편을 끼쳐드려 죄송합니다.

어휘 **notify A that** A에게 ~라고 알리다 **remaining** 남은, 남아 있는 **apologize for** ~에 대해 사과하다 **inconvenience** 불편 **cause** ~을 초래하다, 야기하다

39. 화자는 무엇에 대해 전화하는가?

    (A) 제품에 대한 환불
    (B) 온라인 구매
    (C) 과다 청구
    (D) 너무 큰 제품

해설 담화 초반부에 화자가 자신을 소개하며 전화를 건 목적으로 온라인 매장에서 구매한 신발을 언급하고(I'm calling about a pair of shoes I purchased from your online store) 있다. 따라서 (B)가 정답이다.

40. 화자는 오후에 무엇을 하기로 약속하는가?

    (A) 제품을 매장에 반품하는 일
    (B) 다른 스타일을 주문하는 일
    (C) 신발 사이즈를 바꾸는 일
    (D) 나머지 금액을 보내는 일

해설 화자는 담화 중반부에 afternoon을 언급하는데, 신발 금액이 60달러인줄 알고 보냈는데 사실 80달러가 맞기에 오후에 나머지 금액을 보내겠다고(I'll make sure I send the remaining 20 dollars this afternoon) 약속하고 있다. 따라서 이를 언급한 (D)가 정답이다.

41. 청자는 무엇을 할 것을 요청 받는가?

    (A) 고객의 주문을 바꾸는 일
    (B) 고객의 전화에 답신 전화를 하는 일
    (C) 돈을 환불하는 일
    (D) 최신 배송 정보를 제공하는 일

해설 담화 마지막 부분에서 화자는 신발이 언제 도착하는지 알고 싶다며 신발을 보내자마자 이메일을 보내줄 것을 요청하고(Can you e-mail me right after you send them to me?) 있다. 이는 최신 배송 정보를 받고자 하는 것이므로 (D)가 정답이다.

어휘 **return one's call** ~에게 답신 전화를 하다 **shipping update** 배송 관련 최신 정보

Paraphrase e-mail me right after you send them to me
    → Provide a shipping update

Questions 42-44 refer to the following tour information.

Welcome to Richmond, everyone! During today's tour, we'll be visiting the Old Town District of the city **42** to see several locations where popular film scenes and television dramas were filmed. I'm sure you'll recognize a lot of the landmarks. However, **43** due to flooding, we can't visit the Market District today. Fortunately, the Theater District has several sites of interest. Don't forget that you can sign up for a wide variety of tours with our company. And, **44** if you write a review on our Web site, you'll get 25 percent off the next tour you sign up for.

리치몬드에 오신 것을 환영합니다, 여러분! 오늘 투어 중에, 우리는 인기 영화의 장면들과 텔레비전 드라마들이 촬영된 여러 장소를 보기 위해 도시의 구시가지를 방문할 예정입니다. 분명 많은 명소를 알아보시게 될 것입니다. 하지만, 침수 문제로 인해, 오늘 시장 구역은 방문할 수 없습니다. 다행히, 극장가에 여러 흥미로운 곳이 있습니다. 저희 회사의 아주 다양한 투어에 등록하실 수 있으시다는 점을 잊지 마시기 바랍니다. 그리고, 저희 웹 사이트에서 후기를 작성하시면, 다음 번에 등록하시는 투어에서 25퍼센트 할인 받으시게 될 것입니다.

Old Town District 구시가지 location 장소, 위치 film v. ~을 촬영하다 recognize ~을 알아보다, ~을 인식하다 landmark 명소 flooding 침수, 홍수 fortunately 다행히 of interest 흥미로운 a wide variety of 아주 다양한

42. 화자의 말에 따르면, 투어의 초점이 무엇인가?

(A) 역사적인 전쟁터
(B) 현대적인 사회 기반 시설
(C) 고대의 인공 유물
(D) 촬영 장소

해설 투어의 초점이 무엇인지 묻는 것은 투어의 목적을 묻는 것과 같으며, 이는 담화 초반부에 제시될 가능성이 높으므로 담화가 시작될 때 특히 집중해 들어야 한다. 담화 초반부에 화자가 투어 장소를 알리면서 인기 영화의 장면들과 텔레비전 드라마들이 촬영된 여러 장소를 보러 가는 것을(~ to see several locations where popular film scenes and television dramas were filmed) 목적으로 언급하고 있으므로 (D)가 정답이다.

어휘 battleground 전쟁터 infrastructure 사회 기반 시설 ancient 고대의 artifact 인공 유물

Paraphrase locations where popular film scenes and television dramas were filmed
→ Filming locations

43. 화자는 왜 "극장가에 여러 흥미로운 곳이 있습니다"라고 말하는가?

(A) 한 프로그램을 추천하기 위해
(B) 다른 장소를 제안하기 위해
(C) 자원봉사자를 요청하기 위해
(D) 빡빡한 마감 기한과 관련해 주의시키기 위해

해설 담화 중반부에 화자가 침수 문제로 인해 오늘 시장 구역을 방문할 수 없다는(~ due to flooding, we can't visit the Market District today) 문제를 알리면서, 해당 문장을 말한다. 이는 시장 구역 대신 방문할 수 있는 장소로 대안을 제시하는 흐름에 해당되므로 (B)가 정답이다.

어휘 warn about ~와 관련해 주의시키다, ~와 관련해 경고하다 tight (기한, 예산 등) 빡빡한, 빠듯한

44. 청자들은 어떻게 할인을 받을 수 있는가?

(A) 업체를 방문함으로써
(B) 후기를 작성함으로써
(C) 콘테스트에 참가함으로써
(D) 몇몇 사진을 공유함으로써

해설 담화 마지막 부분에 화자가 웹 사이트에서 후기를 작성하면 다음 번 투어에서 25퍼센트 할인 받는다고(if you write a review on our Web site, you'll get 25 percent off the next tour ~) 알리고 있으므로 청자들이 할인을 받을 수 있는 방법은 후기를 작성하는 것임을 알 수 있다. 따라서 (B)가 정답이다.

Questions 45-47 refer to the following instructions.

Hello! **45** I hope you're all excited to have our first woodworking class at Waterford Community College. Before we begin, everyone has been assigned a locker in the back of the room where you can store your safety gear when it isn't being used. In addition, I know the class finishes late in the evening, but **46** please expect to stay an extra 15 minutes to help clean up. The program fee doesn't cover cleaning staff. And finally, **47** be sure to write your phone number and e-mail address on the paper on my desk before heading home. That way I can let you know about any schedule changes.

안녕하세요! 여러분 모두 우리 워터포드 커뮤니티 컬리지에서 열리는 첫 번째 목공예 강좌를 수강하시는 것이 즐거우시길 바랍니다. 시작하기 전에, 모든 분들께 강의실 뒤쪽에 있는 사물함이 하나씩 배정되었으며, 안전 장비를 사용하지 않으실 때 이곳에 보관하실 수 있습니다. 추가로, 강좌가 저녁 늦게 끝난다는 것을 알고 있기는 하지만, 청소를 도와주실 수 있도록 15분 동안 더 남아 계셔야 할 것으로 예상해 주십시오. 프로그램 수강료에는 청소 직원에 대한 비용이 포함되어 있지 않습니다. 그리고 마지막으로, 댁으로 돌아가시기 전에 제 책상에 놓여 있는 종이에 여러분의 전화번호와 이메일 주소를 꼭 적어 주시기 바랍니다. 그렇게 하시면 어떠한 일정 변경에 관해서도 알려드릴 수 있습니다.

어휘 woodworking 목공예 assign A B A에게 B를 배정하다, 할당하다 store ~을 보관하다 safety gear 안전 장비 in addition 추가로 expect to do ~할 것으로 예상하다 cover ~을 포함하다, 충당하다 head ~로 가다, 향하다 let A know about B A에게 B에 관해 알려 주다

45. 화자는 무엇을 가르치는가?

(A) 엔진 수리
(B) 목공예
(C) 원예
(D) 춤

해설 화자가 가르치는 것을 찾아야 하므로 각 선택지의 강좌 명칭을 미리 확인해 둔 후에 담화 중에서 언급되는 것을 골라야 한다. 담화를 시작하면서 화자가 첫 번째 목공예 강좌를 수강하는 것에 대해(I hope you're all excited to have our first woodworking class) 언급하고 있으므로 (B)가 정답이다.

46. 화자는 왜 "프로그램 수강료에는 청소 직원에 대한 비용이 포함되어 있지 않습니다"라고 말하는가?

(A) 기부를 요청하기 위해
(B) 비용에 대한 이유를 설명하기 위해
(C) 청소의 필요성을 강조하기 위해

(D) 정책에 대한 불만을 표현하기 위해

해설 담화 중반부에 화자가 청소를 할 수 있도록 15분 정도 더 남아 있어 달라고(please expect to stay an extra 15 minutes to help clean up) 부탁하는 말 다음에 해당 문장을 들을 수 있다. 이는 함께 남아서 청소해야 한다는 점을 강조하기 위한 말이므로 (C)가 정답이다.

어휘 **donation** 기부(금) **emphasize** ~을 강조하다 **dissatisfaction** 불만 **policy** 정책, 방침

47. 청자들은 나가기 전에 무엇을 하도록 상기되는가?
(A) 또 다른 강좌에 등록하는 일
(B) 설문 조사에 참가하는 일
(C) 각자의 연락처를 공유하는 일
(D) 과제를 준비하는 일

해설 화자의 말에서 요청이나 당부 등의 표현이 제시되는 부분에서 단서를 찾아야 한다. 담화 후반부에 화자가 자신의 책상에 놓여 있는 종이에 전화번호와 이메일 주소를 꼭 적어 달라고(be sure to write your phone number and e-mail address on the paper on my desk ~) 요청하는 부분이 있다. 이는 연락처를 공유하는 것이므로 (C)가 정답이다.

어휘 **sign up for** ~에 등록하다, ~을 신청하다 **another** 또 다른 하나의 **participate in** ~에 참가하다 **assignment** 과제, 할당(된 일)

Paraphrase be sure to write your phone number and
e-mail address on the paper
→ Share their contact information

Questions 48-50 refer to the following excerpt from a meeting and flow chart.

48 As we decided last week, we will hold management meetings more frequently to discuss operations in our clothing factory. This will allow us to address minor problems swiftly before they become major ones. For instance, today we need to discuss the large number of flaws found in a recent batch of garments. We investigated 49 the defects, and 49 they seem to have resulted from a problem with our steam presses. So, I want some workers to disassemble the machines and then 50 clean the parts thoroughly. Make sure that gets done as soon as we wrap up this meeting. We'll need to get the machines up and running again quickly.

지난 주에 결정한 바와 같이, 우리 의류 공장의 운영 문제를 논의하기 위해 경영진 회의를 더 자주 열 것입니다. 이로 인해 우리는 사소한 문제들이 중대한 문제가 되기 전에 신속하게 처리할 수 있게 될 것입니다. 예를 들어, 오늘 우리는 최근의 일괄 제공 의류에서 발견된 다수의 결함에 관해 이야기해야 합니다. 우리가 이 결함을 조사했는데, 우리의 스팀 다림 기계에 생긴 문제에서 초래된 것으로 보입니다. 따라서, 저는 몇몇 직원들께서 이 기계들을 분해한 다음, 부품들을 철저히 세척해 주셨으면 합니다. 반드시 우리가 이 회의를 마무리하는 대로 그 작업이 완료되도록 하시기 바랍니다. 빨리 이 기계들이 다시 정상 가동되도록 해야 할 것입니다.

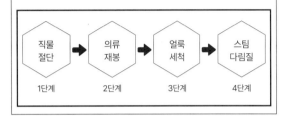

직물 절단	의류 재봉	얼룩 세척	스팀 다림질
1단계	2단계	3단계	4단계

어휘 **management** 경영(진), 운영(진) **operation** 운영, 영업, 가동, 작동 **clothing** 의류(= garment) **allow A to do** A에게 ~할 수 있게 해 주다 **address** v. (문제 등) ~을 처리하다, ~을 다루다 **swiftly** 신속하게, 빠르게(= quickly) **major** 중대한, 주요한 **the large number of** 다수의, 수많은 **flaw** 결함, 흠(= defect) **batch** 일괄 제공(량), 한 회분 **investigate** ~을 조사하다 **result from** ~에서 초래되다, ~의 결과로 생기다 **steam press** 스팀 다림 기계 **disassemble** ~을 분해하다 **thoroughly** 철저히 **wrap up** ~을 마무리하다
up and running 정상 가동되는, 잘 운영되는 **sewing** 재봉 **spot** 얼룩, 점

48. 지난 주에 어떤 결정이 내려졌는가?
(A) 공장이 안전 점검 과정을 거칠 것이다.
(B) 공장이 일부 제품의 생산을 중단할 것이다.
(C) 청자들이 반드시 주간 보고서를 제출해야 한다.
(D) 청자들이 반드시 더 자주 회의에 참석해야 한다.

해설 화자는 담화를 시작하면서 지난 주에 결정한 대로 경영진 회의를 더 자주 열 것이라고(As we decided last week, we will hold management meetings more frequently ~) 알리고 있다. 이는 회의에 더 자주 참석해야 한다는 뜻이므로 (D)가 정답이다.

어휘 **undergo** ~을 거치다, ~을 겪다 **inspection** 점검, 조사 **discontinue** ~을 중단하다, ~을 단종시키다 **production** 생산, 제작

Paraphrase hold management meetings more frequently
→ attend meetings more frequently

49. 시각자료를 보시오. 화자는 어느 단계에서 문제가 일어났다고 생각하는가?

(A) 1단계
(B) 2단계
(C) 3단계
(D) 4단계

해설 담화 중반부에 화자가 특정 결함(the defects)을 they로 지칭해 결함이 스팀 다림 기계에 생긴 문제에서 초래된 것으로 보인다고(~ they seem to have resulted from a problem with our steam presses) 알리고 있다. 화자가 언급하는 steam presses로 하는 작업은 시각자료 맨 오른쪽에 표기된 STEP 4의 STEAM PRESSING에 해당되므로 (D)가 정답이다.

50. 회의 후에 무슨 일이 있을 것인가?

(A) 일부 장비가 배송될 것이다.
(B) 일부 직원들이 교육을 받을 것이다.
(C) 일부 기계 부품들이 세척될 것이다.
(D) 일부 의류가 점검될 것이다.

해설 담화 후반부에 화자가 부품들을 철저히 세척하는 일을 언급하면서 그 일이 회의가 마무리되는 대로 완료되도록(~ clean the parts thoroughly. Make sure that gets done as soon as we wrap up this meeting) 요청하고 있으므로 (C)가 정답이다.

어휘 equipment 장비 inspect ~을 점검하다, ~을 조사하다

Part 5

51.

정답 (A)

해석 한슨 씨가 휴가를 떠난 동안 이다시 씨가 모든 고객 불만사항을 처리할 것이다.

해설 주절에 동사가 없으므로 빈칸에 동사가 들어가야 하는데 while이 이끄는 시간부사절에 쓰인 현재시제 is는 미래를 대신할 수 있으므로 주절의 동사 자리인 빈칸에는 미래시제가 와야 한다. 따라서 (A) will take가 정답이다.

어휘 take care of ~을 처리하다, 수습하다 while ~하는 동안 be on vacation 휴가 중이다

52.

정답 (C)

해석 조립라인이 첫 회계 분기에 가동될 것으로 예상된다.

해설 빈칸 앞에 2형식 동사 become이 있으므로 빈칸은 보어 자리이다. 명사 보어가 빈칸에 올 경우에는 주어와 동격이 되어야 하므로 형용사 (C) operational이 정답이다.

어휘 assembly line 조립 라인 operational 가동 중인 fiscal 회계 상의 operate ~을 가동하다, 운영하다 operation 가동, 작동

53.

정답 (A)

해석 제과제빵 수업에 관여된 강사들은 모든 학생들과 기술 그리고 전문 지식을 공유할 필요가 있다.

해설 빈칸 앞뒤로 명사 두 개가 나열되어 있으므로 같은 품사를 연결하는 등위접속사 (A) and가 정답이다.

어휘 involved in ~에 관여된, 포함된 expertise 전문 지식

54.

정답 (D)

해석 퍼거슨 씨가 최근에 채용된 영업사원들을 대상으로 한 교육에 대해 도움을 요청하고 있다.

해설 문장의 동사 다음에 빈칸이 있으므로 동사의 목적어로 쓰일 명사가 빈칸에 와야 한다. 선택지에서 명사는 (A) assistant와 (D) assistance인데, 빈칸 앞에 부정관사가 없으므로 '도움'을 뜻하는 추상명사 (D) assistance가 정답이다.

어휘 request ~을 요청하다 assistance 도움, 보조 recently 최근에

55.

정답 (B)

해석 설문 조사에 참여한 대부분의 소비자들은 식료품 쇼핑을 할 때 제품의 영양 정보를 면밀하게 확인한다고 말했다.

해설 빈칸이 생략되어 있는 that절의 주어와 동사 사이에 위치해 있으므로 빈칸에 동사를 수식하는 부사가 와야 한다. 따라서 (B) closely가 정답이다.

어휘 poll ~에게 여론 조사를 하다 closely 면밀하게, 자세하게 examine ~을 확인하다, 점검하다 nutritional 영양의 groceries 식료품

56.

정답 (A)

해석 각각의 신입직원은 첫 근무일 전에 개인 프로필 서식과 최근의 세금 정보를 제출해야 한다.

해설 빈칸 앞뒤로 명사구가 있으므로 빈칸은 전치사 자리이다. 빈칸 뒤에 제시된 명사구가 개인 프로필 서식과 최근 세금 정보를 제출해야 하는 기한에 해당되므로 '~전에'란 뜻의 (A) prior to가 정답이다.

어휘 up-to-date 최근의 prior to ~이전에 as long as ~이기만 하면, ~하는 한 until ~까지 afterward 그 후에

57.

정답 (C)

해석 많은 손님들이 그 호텔 로비의 기분 좋은 모습과 프런트 데스크 직원들의 친절함에 관해 언급했다.

해설 소유격과 명사 사이에 위치한 빈칸은 소유격과 함께 명사를 수식할 형용사가 필요한 자리이다. 또한, appearance가 사람을 기분 좋게 만드는 주체에 해당되므로 '기분 좋게 만드는' 등을 뜻하는 (C) pleasing이 정답이다.

어휘 comment 언급하다, 발언하다 appearance 모습, 외관 helpfulness 친절함, 도움이 됨 please ~을 기쁘게 하다 pleasingly 기쁘게, 기분 좋게 pleasing 기쁘게 만드는, 기분 좋게 만드는 pleased (사람이) 기쁜, 즐거운

58.

정답 (A)

해석 안타깝게도, 유지관리부장 직 채용에서 적합한 자격을 갖춘 후보자 수가 많았기 때문에 귀하는 합격하지 못하였습니다.

해설 빈칸에는 빈칸 앞뒤로 제시된 합격하지 못한 결과와 원인인 다수의 적격한 후보자들과의 관계를 나타내는 전치사가 필요하므로 (A) due to가 정답이다.

어휘 regrettably 안타깝게도 maintenance 유지보수 except for ~을 제외하고 regarding ~에 관하여 in spite of ~에도 불구하고

59.

정답 (D)

해석 한 회사의 주가의 변동은 항상 그 회사의 판매 실적이나 고객들 사이에서의 인기에 달려있지는 않다.

해설 빈칸 앞뒤에 be동사와 전치사 on이 있으므로 이와 어울려 쓰이면서 '~에 달려 있다, 의존하다'라는 의미를 구성하는 (D) dependent가 정답이다.

어휘 fluctuation 변동 stock price 주가 popularity 인기 cause ~을 초래하다, 야기하다 indicative of ~을 나타내는

60.

정답 (A)

해석 노트북 컴퓨터에 결함이 있는 고객들은 알타톤이나 판매에 있는 저희 기술 지원 센터 중에서 더 편리한 곳을 방문하시면 됩니다.

해설 콤마 앞에는 주어와 동사를 포함한 완전한 절이, 콤마 뒤에는 동사와 형용사가 이어지고 있으므로 빈칸을 포함한 절이 부사절인 것을 알 수 있다. 따라서 부사절을 이끌 수 있는 복합관계대명사 (A) whichever가 정답이다.

어휘 faulty 결함이 있는

61.

정답 (A)

해석 이번 주의 전례 없이 많은 주문은 우리 신제품이 금방 성공을 거둘 것임을 보여주고 있다.

해설 빈칸 앞에 제시된 a number of는 복수명사와 결합하는 수량 형용사이다. 따라서 빈칸에는 복수명사가 와야 하므로 (A)

orders가 정답이다.

어휘 unprecedented 전례 없는 suggest that ~임을 나타내다, 보여주다 instant 즉각적인

62.

정답 (D)

해석 비록 직원들이 1년에 한 번만 무료로 시외의 활동에 참여하도록 제한되어 있지만, 정보 기술 워크숍 참석은 권장된다.

해설 빈칸 앞뒤로 주어와 동사를 포함한 완전한 절이 있으므로 빈칸은 접속사 자리이다. 빈칸 앞에서는 워크숍 참석을 장려한다는 말이, 빈칸 뒤에는 1년에 1회 무료 활동으로 제한되어 있다는 말이 쓰여 있으므로 서로 상반되는 내용이다. 따라서 '비록 ~ 하지만'이라는 의미의 (D) although가 정답이다.

어휘 attendance 참석, 출석 be limited to ~로 제한된다 out-of town 시외의, 마을 바깥의 such as 예를 들어, ~와 같은 nevertheless 그럼에도 불구하고

63.

정답 (A)

해석 사내 채팅 시스템의 목적은 다른 부서에서 근무하는 직원들이 서로 연락할 수 있게 하기 위한 것이다.

해설 빈칸 앞에 전치사가 있으므로 빈칸은 전치사의 목적어 자리이다. 따라서 목적어 역할을 할 수 있으면서 전치사 with과 함께 '서로'라는 의미를 나타내는 (A) one another가 정답이다.

어휘 aim 목적 internal 내부의 allow A to do A가 ~할 수 있게 하다 keep in contact 연락하다 one another 서로

64.

정답 (C)

해석 메르소프트 사에서 10년 동안 일한 후에, 오마르 윌리스는 자신의 사업을 경영하기 위해 그만두었다.

해설 빈칸과 전치사구 뒤로 콤마와 완전한 절이 이어지고 있으므로 빈칸과 전치사구가 분사구문이 되어야 한다. 10년간 어떤 회사에서 일한 것은 자신의 사업을 하기 위해 퇴사하기 전의 일이므로, 주절보다 앞선 시제를 나타내야 한다. 따라서 (C) Having worked가 정답이다.

어휘 quit 그만두다 run 운영하다, 관리하다

65.

정답 (A)

해석 과제를 제출할 수 없는 사람은 적어도 3일 전에 러실로 씨에게 보고해야 합니다.

해설 빈칸 뒤에 숫자 표현 부사구 three days가 있으므로 그 앞에 쓸 수 있는 (A) at least가 정답이다.

어휘 hand in ~을 제출하다 assignment 과제, 숙제 report to ~에게 보고하다 in advance 미리, 앞서 at least 적어도 instead of ~ 대신 by means of ~에 의하여, ~을 써서 so that ~하기 위하여

66.

정답 (D)

해석 식기 세척기에서 최고의 결과를 얻기 위해서, 제품 설명서에 명확하게 언급된 세제들만 사용하세요.

해설 빈칸에 들어갈 부사는 빈칸 뒤에 제시된 과거분사구를 수식해야 하는데, 제품 설명서에 언급되어 있는 상태를 나타내야 하므로 '명확하게'라는 뜻의 (D) specifically가 정답이다.

어휘 result 결과, 성과 detergent 세제 mention ~을 언급하다, 말하다 courteously 예의 바르게 reflectively 반사적으로 relatively 상대적으로

Part 6

67-70.

공항 내 공황 사태의 주범으로 밝혀진 컴퓨터 오작동

뉴어크 국제 공항이 어제 이 공항의 컴퓨터화된 레이더 시스템에 발생된 문제로 인해 여러 시간 동안 폐쇄되었습니다. 거의 50편의 **67** 항공편이 일정이 재조정되거나 심지어 취소되어야 했습니다. **68** 8,000명이 넘는 여행객들이 영향을 받았습니다.

어제 오전의 인터뷰에서, 이 공항의 최고 책임자는 공항이 적정한 정도의 문제들을 겪어 오기는 했지만, 어제 있었던 일과 같은 규모는 아니었다고 말했습니다. 다음 달 정도의 기간 중에, 전 세계에서 최고의 능력을 갖춘 컴퓨터 기술자들이 소집되어 향후에 유사한 문제를 **69** 방지하기 위해 프로그램에 대해 작업할 것입니다.

어제 있었던 공항 사태 및 혼란으로 인해, 공항 직원들은 일종의 사이버 공격이 아닐까 우려해 관계 당국에 즉시 전화를 걸었습니다. 경찰관들이 여전히 오작동의 원인을 **70** 조사 중이기는 하지만, 지금까지 이 문제가 단순히 컴퓨터 장비 측면의 작동 오류였으며, 다행히도 더 불길한 일은 아닌 것으로 여겨지고 있습니다. 기자 회견이 다음 주로 예정되어 있습니다.

어휘 malfunction 오작동 culprit 주범 panic 공황 close down 폐쇄되다 due to ~로 인해 computerized 컴퓨터화된 nearly 거의 affect ~에 영향을 미치다 fair share of 적정한 정도의 scale 규모 or so (명사 뒤에서) ~ 정도 best and brightest 최고의 능력을 갖춘 prevent ~을 방지하다 confusion 혼란 proper authorities 관계 당국 of some sort (명사 뒤에서) 일종의 investigate ~을 조사하다 cause 원인 on the part of ~의 측면에서 thankfully 다행히도 sinister 불길한, 해로운 press conference 기자 회견 be scheduled for + 시점 ~로 예정되다

67.

정답 (B)

해설 빈칸 앞 문장에 공항의 특정 장비와 관련된 문제가 발생된 사실이 쓰여 있으므로 빈칸이 속한 문장에서 숫자 50으로 수식할 수

있으면서 일정이 재조정되거나 취소되었다고 말할 수 있는 대상은 항공편이어야 알맞다. 따라서 (B) flights가 정답이다.

어휘 possession 소유(물)

68.

정답 (C)

해석 (A) 업데이트된 항공 일정표를 보실 수 있도록 이메일을 확인하십시오.
(B) 고속도로 운전자들 또한 혼잡한 교통 상태를 겪었습니다.
(C) 8,000명이 넘는 여행객들이 영향을 받았습니다.
(D) 해당 조종사의 답변은 들을 수 없었습니다.

해설 앞서 공항에서 발생된 문제와 관련된 상황이 언급되는 흐름이 되어야 가장 자연스러우므로 8,000명이 넘는 여행객들이 영향을 받은 사실을 말하는 (C)가 정답이다.

어휘 itinerary 여행 일정(표) congested 혼잡한 available for comment 답변할 수 있는, 의견을 말할 수 있는

69.

정답 (C)

해설 빈칸 앞에 위치한 in order는 to부정사와 결합해 '~하기 위해'라는 목적의 의미를 나타내므로 (C) to prevent가 정답이다.

70.

정답 (A)

해설 빈칸이 속한 절의 주어가 경찰관들이므로 경찰이 오작동의 원인과 관련해 할 수 있는 일을 나타낼 동사의 현재분사가 필요하다. 따라서 '~을 조사하다'를 뜻하는 investigate의 현재분사 (A) investigating이 정답이다.

어휘 protest ~에 항의하다, 이의를 제기하다

71-74.

11월 9일
척 멀그루
척스 샌드위치숍
웨스트 핀치 에비뉴
토론토, ON M1B 5K7

멀그루 씨께,

11월 5일에 전화로 요청하신 바와 같이, 귀하가 11월 2일에 저희 웹 사이트에서 제출하신 월간 식품 공급 주문서를 확인해 보았습니다. 말씀해 주신 바와 같이, 정말로 그 주문서에 귀하께서 명시하셨던 것보다 10병이 더 많은 마요네즈가 포함되어 있었습니다. **71** 그 결과, 11월 8일에, 저희는 이 문제를 처리해 드렸으며, 이것이 저희의 실수였음을 인정합니다. 그날, 저희는 귀하의 주문서에서 10개를 **72** 뺐습니다. 이달의 주문에 대한 변경사항을 **73** 반영하기 위해 귀하의 거래내역서가 수정되었으며, 이 편지에 동봉되어 있습니다. **74** 부디 이 실수에 대한 저희의 사과를 받아 주시기 바랍니다. 귀하의 주문품은 요청하신 바처럼 11월 15일까지 도

착할 것입니다.

안녕히 계십시오.

프라이스 라이트 푸드 서플라이즈

어휘 over the phone 전화 상에서 supplies 공급 물품, 용품 through ~을 통해 note 특별히 언급하다, 주목하다 indeed 실제로, 정말로 jar 병, 통 specify ~을 명시하다 address (문제 등) ~을 처리하다, 해결하다 acknowledge ~을 인정하다 fault 실수, 잘못 unit (상품) 한 개, 구성 단위 invoice 거래 내역서, 송장 modify ~을 수정하다

71.

정답 (C)

해설 빈칸 앞 부분을 보면 11월 2일의 주문 사항과 관련해 주문자가 11월 5일에 문제를 제기하여 오류를 확인한 내용이 나오고, 빈칸 뒤에는 11월 8일에 그 문제를 처리하였다고 나온다. 문제 확인과 처리는 원인과 결과의 흐름으로 판단할 수 있으므로 결과를 나타내는 접속부사 (C) As a result가 정답이다.

어휘 furthermore 더욱이, 게다가 in addition 추가로, 게다가 as a result 그 결과, 결과적으로 on the contrary 대조적으로

72.

정답 (B)

해설 빈칸 앞에 앞서 언급한 특정 날짜를 지칭하는 부사구 On that date가 있는데, that은 앞 문장에서 조치를 취한 날짜로 언급된 8 November를 가리킨다. 이 시기가 편지 작성 날짜인 9 November보다 과거 시점이므로 과거시제 (B) deducted가 정답이다.

어휘 deduct ~을 공제하다, 제하다

73.

정답 (A)

해설 빈칸 앞에 주어와 수동태 동사가 제시되어 있어 이미 구성이 완전한 상태이다. 따라서, 빈칸 이하는 부가적인 요소가 되어야 하며, 거래 내역서가 수정된 목적을 나타내야 하므로 to부정사인 (A) to reflect가 정답이다.

어휘 reflect ~을 반영하다 reflection 반영, 반사, 심사숙고 reflect on ~을 반성하다, 되돌아 보다

74.

정답 (D)

해석 (A) 모든 저희 물품들은 온라인 카탈로그에서 보실 수 있습니다.
(B) 대량으로 주문함으로써, 추가 비용 절약 혜택을 누리실 수 있습니다.

(C) 배송 중에 야기된 손상에 대해 저희는 책임을 지지 않습니다.
(D) 부디 이 실수에 대한 저희의 사과를 받아 주시기 바랍니다.

해설 빈칸 앞 부분에 전반적으로 업체 측에서 잘못 처리한 일과 관련해 확인 및 조치한 일을 고객에게 알리는 내용을 담고 있으므로 이와 같은 실수를 the error로 지칭해 사과하는 의미로 쓰인 (D)가 정답이다.

어휘 in bulk 대량으로 enjoy savings 비용 절약 혜택을 누리다 further 추가의 be responsible for ~에 대한 책임이 있다 cause ~을 야기하다, 초래하다 accept ~을 받아 들이다, 수용하다

Part 7

75-76.

니먼스 백화점
50달러 상품권

75 우리 팀의 새로운 팀원으로서 당신을 환영하는 방식의 일환으로, 이 상품권을 당신의 오리엔테이션 팩에 포함시켰습니다. 니먼스는 몇 가지 직원 우대를 제공하므로 만약 새 직책에서 좋은 성과를 낸다면, 당신은 이와 같은 유사한 혜택들을 받을 수 있을 것입니다.

매장 방침에 따라, 이 상품권은 온라인에서 출력 가능한 상품권과 신문의 상품권을 포함한 다른 어떤 상품권과도 함께 사용될 수 없습니다. 또한, 현재 세일 중인 상품을 구매하는 데에도 사용될 수 없습니다. 마지막으로, **76** 이 상품권은 현금으로 바꾸실 수 없습니다.

상품권 수령인: 트리스탄 하퍼

유효기간: 4월 30일

어휘 gift voucher 상품권 inccntive 우대혜택, 장려금 benefit 혜택 role 역할 in accordance with ~에 따라 in conjunction with ~와 함께 printable 출력 가능한 mark down 가격을 인하하다 redeem 현금으로 교환하다 recipient 받는 사람, 수령인 valid 유효한

75. 왜 하퍼 씨에게 상품권이 주어졌을 것 같은가?
(A) 그가 매장 멤버십에 가입했기 때문이다.
(B) 그가 매장에 새로운 고객을 소개했기 때문이다.
(C) 그가 업체에 채용되어 일을 시작했기 때문이다.
(D) 그가 4월에 뛰어나게 업무를 수행하였기 때문이다.

정답 (C)

해설 첫 단락 첫 문장에 팀의 새로운 팀원으로서 환영하는 방식의 일환으로 상품권을 오리엔테이션 팩에 포함시켰다고(As one of our ways of welcoming you as a new member of our team, we have included this gift voucher in your orientation pack) 언급하고 있으므로 상품권이 새로 입사한

하퍼 씨의 환영 선물임을 알 수 있다. 따라서 (C)가 정답이다.

어휘 refer A to B A를 B에게 소개하다 exceptionally 월등히, 특별히

76. 이 상품권에 대해 사실인 것은?
  (A) 다른 상품권과 함께 사용이 가능하다.
  (B) 웹 사이트에서 출력될 수 있다.
  (C) 돈으로 교환될 수 없다.
  (D) 할인 물품을 구매하는 데에만 사용 가능하다.

정답 (C)

해설 두 번째 문단 마지막 문장에 현금으로는 교환되지 않는다는(it may not be redeemed for cash) 사실이 쓰여 있으므로 (C)가 정답이다.

어휘 be combined with ~와 결합되다 exchange ~을 교환하다

77-79.

> ### 건강한 신체가 생산적 사고를 낳는다
>
> 4월 5일 – **77** 몬타나의 불더에 본사를 둔 자동차 보험 회사인 이 슈런스 온라인 사는 자사의 직원들이 더 많은 운동을 할 수 있도록 금전적 보상을 제공할 예정이다. 직원들이 매주 회사의 대회의실 에서 열리는 1시간 길이의 피트니스 시간에 최소 3회 참석할 경우 에 매달 150달러의 추가 비용을 지급 받게 된다.
>
> — [1] —. 헬스장 회원권 비용이 점점 증가하고 있는 것을 고려하 면, 이는 회사가 시행하기에 굉장히 후한 정책이다. 이슈런스 온라 인 사는 요가와 스피닝, 그리고 에어로빅과 같은 다양한 강좌들을 이끌 전임 피트니스 강사를 채용했다. 이슈런스 온라인 사의 인사 부장 피터 셀비 씨의 말에 따르면, 이 피트니스 강좌에 등록하는 것은 전혀 의무가 아니지만, 대다수의 직원들이 이 기회와 추가 비 용을 활용할 것으로 예상되고 있다. — [2] —. 이 새로운 정책은 건강한 신체 상태가 직장에서 열심히 집중하는 능력에 얼마나 긍 정적으로 영향을 미치는지를 보여주는 최근의 연구를 바탕으로 하 고 있다. 이 연구를 주도한 과학자의 말에 따르면, **78** 주기적인 운 동을 통해 건강한 신체 상태를 유지하는 직원들이 각자의 업무를 더 빠르게, 그리고 더 뛰어난 수준으로 완료해 낼 수 있다. — [3] —.
>
> 또한, 이 연구는 **79** 좀처럼 운동을 하지 않아 좋지 않은 신체 상태 를 지닌 직원은 자신이 지닌 잠재적 효율성의 불과 50퍼센트 수준 밖에 일하지 못한다고 주장한다. — [4] —. 직원 건강에 대한 이슈 런스 온라인 사의 새로운 정책은 회사의 인력과 전반적인 업무 성 과 모두에 이득이 되도록 하는 것이 목적이다.

어휘 insurance company 보험 회사 based in ~에 본사를 둔 get more exercise 더 많이 운동하다 considering ~을 고려하면 tremendously 굉장히, 엄청나게 implement ~을 시행하다 according to ~에 따르면 enrollment in ~에의 등록 by no means 결코 ~가 아니 다 mandatory 의무적인 take advantage of ~을 이

용하다 be based on ~을 바탕으로 하다, 기반으로 하다 affect ~에 영향을 미치다 maintain ~을 유지하다 get A done A를 완료하다 to a higher standard 더 높은 수준 으로 furthermore 게다가, 더욱이 claim that ~라고 주 장하다 rarely 좀처럼 ~ 않다 efficiency 효율(성) aim to do ~하는 것이 목적이다 benefit ~에게 이득이 되다, 혜택을 주다 workforce 인력 overall 전반적인

77. 기사의 목적은 무엇인가?
  (A) 지역 체육관과의 합작 투자 사업을 발표하는 것
  (B) 직원들에게 워크숍 참석을 권하는 것
  (C) 회사가 최근에 거둔 성공을 설명하는 것
  (D) 회사의 새로운 정책을 설명하는 것

정답 (D)

해설 첫 문단 첫 문장에 한 보험회사가 직원들이 더 많은 운동을 할 수 있도록 금전적 보상을 제공할 예정임을 밝히고 있는데(is offering its workers a financial incentive to get more exercise) 이는 회사가 새롭게 실시하는 정책에 해당하므로 (D)가 정답이다.

어휘 joint venture 합작 투자 사업 advise A to do A에게 ~하도록 권하다, 조언하다

78. 기사는 직원들에게 더 규칙적으로 운동하도록 장려하는 것과 관련해 무엇을 언급하는가?
  (A) 직장에서 사람들을 더 피곤하게 만들 수 있다.
  (B) 직원들 사이에서 의사 소통이 더 잘 되도록 촉진한다.
  (C) 사람들이 업무를 더 효율적으로 완수하는 데 도움을 준다.
  (D) 직원들이 중요한 마감 시한을 충족하지 못하게 한다.

정답 (C)

해설 두 번째 단락의 후반부에 업무를 더 빠르고 더 뛰어난 수준으 로 완료할 수 있다고(workers who exercise regularly ~ can get their work done more quickly and to a higher standard) 알리고 있으므로 효율적인 업무 완수에 도움이 된 다는 의미로 쓰인 (C)가 정답이다.

어휘 make A do A가 ~하게 만들다 accomplish ~을 완수하 다, 달성하다 efficiently 효율적으로 prevent A from -ing A가 ~하지 못하게 하다, 방지하다

79. [1], [2], [3], [4]로 표기된 위치들 중에서, 다음 문장이 가장 잘 어울리는 곳은 어디인가?

  "이는 회사의 생산성을 상당히 감소시킬 수 있다."

  (A) [1]
  (B) [2]
  (C) [3]
  (D) [4]

정답 (D)

해설 제시된 문장은 생산성의 감소가 초래되는 결과를 언급하고 있으므로 앞에서 부정적인 내용이 제시되는 위치를 고르면

된다. 따라서 신체 상태가 좋지 않은 직원이 잠재적 효율성의 50퍼센트 수준으로 일한다는(a worker who rarely exercises ~ works at only 50% of his or her potential efficiency) 내용 뒤에 위치한 [4] 자리에 들어가는 것이 가장 적절하므로 (D)가 정답이다.

어휘 **result in** ~을 초래하다, ~라는 결과를 낳다 **significant** 상당한, 많은 **productivity** 생산성

80-82.

22 크레이포드 스트리트
몽고메리, AL 36043
7월 2일

코너스 씨께,

저희는 당신이 새로운 식당을 설립하시는 데 도움을 드릴 수 있도록 저희 서비스를 제공하게 되어 기쁘게 생각합니다. 식당에 일반적인 고정 설비와 디자인을 포함한 몇몇 샘플 인테리어를 포함했습니다. 로고 혹은 그림과 같은 맞춤형 장식은 선택 사항이지만, **81** 개조 비용을 전체적으로 20% 높일 것입니다. 7월 13일 오후 3시부터 오후 7시까지 저희 본사에서 이러한 인테리어 모델들을 갖춘 오픈 하우스를 열 예정입니다.

80 **82** 저희가 공사를 마치는 데 한 달의 시간을 가질 수 있도록 8월 12일까지 귀하의 식당에 어떤 스타일의 인테리어를 원하는지 귀하의 결정 사항을 저희에게 알려 주십시오. 질문이 있으시면 저에게 205-555-1388로 전화 주십시오.

안녕히 계십시오.

카일 랭글리
창업자, 스토어프론트 인테리어

동봉물

어휘 **set up** ~을 세우다, 설립하다 **fixture** 고정 설비 **optional** 선택적인 **overall** 전반적인 **feel free to do** 자유로이 ~하다, 마음 놓고 ~하다

80. 이 편지는 왜 보내졌는가?
(A) 오픈 하우스에 오는 길 안내를 하려고
(B) 복구 서비스에 대한 납부를 요청하려고
(C) 맞춤 디자인 레이아웃을 요청하려고
(D) 주문 절차에 대해서 알리려고

정답 (C)

해설 두 번째 단락에서 어떤 스타일의 인테리어를 원하는지 알려달라고(We ask that you let us know your decision on what style) 요청하는 말을 보면, 고객 맞춤형 디자인을 위한 결정사항을 알려 달라는 것으로 이해할 수 있으므로 (C)가 정답이다.

어휘 **give directions to** ~로 오는 길 안내를 하다 **restoration** 복구 **custom design** 맞춤 디자인 **procedure** 절차

81. 스토어프론트 인테리어의 맞춤 디자인에 대해 암시된 것은 무엇인가?
(A) 건축 규제사항들을 반드시 지켜야만 한다.
(B) 대개장 행사에서 보여질 것이다.
(C) 표준 디자인보다 더 비싸다.
(D) 유명한 디자이너들에 의해 만들어진다.

정답 (C)

해설 첫 번째 단락 중반부에 맞춤형 장식은 개조 비용을 전체적으로 20% 높일 것이라고(Custom decorations ~ will increase the overall cost ~ by 20%) 언급되어 있으므로 표준 디자인보다 비싼 것으로 생각할 수 있다. 따라서 (C)가 정답이다.

어휘 **adhere to** ~을 따르다 **well-known** 유명한

82. 코너스 씨의 식당이 문을 여는 것은 언제인가?
(A) 7월 2일에
(B) 7월 13일에
(C) 8월 12일에
(D) 9월 12일에

정답 (D)

해설 두 번째 문단에서 공사를 마치는 데 한 달의 시간을 가질 수 있도록 8월 12일까지 원하는 스타일의 인테리어를 알려달라고(We ask that you let us know your decision on what style of interior you would like for your restaurant by August 12, so that we have one month to finish the construction) 요청하고 있으므로 8월 12일로부터 한 달 뒤에 코너스 씨의 식당이 문을 여는 것으로 예상할 수 있다. 따라서 (D)가 정답이다.

83-86.

299달러만으로 골드코스트에서의 일주일을 즐기세요!

여름 휴일 보너스 할인행사로, 홀리데이 트레블 다이렉트 사는 인기 있는 골드코스트 휴가 패키지의 가격을 100달러 할인하고 있습니다. **83** 이 특별 상품을 이용하기 위해서는, 7월 10일까지 예약해야 하고 7월 31까지 여행하셔야 합니다.

이런 가격은 다시 없을 것이므로, 실망하지 않도록 지금 저희에게 전화하세요! 아래 도시들 중 어디서든 출발하실 수 있습니다.
· **84** 뉴욕 *
· 디트로이트
· 시카고
· 휴스턴

85 모든 패키지는 3성급 숙박 시설과 이코노미 항공편을 포함합니다. 환승 및 모든 점심식사 또한 포함되어 있습니다. 모든 날짜에 이용 가능한 것은 아니며, 항공세와 그 밖의 항공사 요금은 포함되어 있지 않다는 것을 알아두세요. 아동 비행 요금은 반값입니다. 저희는 모든 주요 신용카드를 받습니다만, 수표는 받지 않습니다. 단체, 기업 고객, 그리고 저희 고객 보상 프로그램에 가입하신 분들에 대해서는 추가 할인이 적용 가능합니다.

어휘 **cut off** ~을 삭감하다 **travel** 이동하다, 여행하다 **repeat** ~을 반복하다 **avoid** ~을 피하다 **disappointment** 실망 **depart** 출발하다 **accommodation** 숙박 **transfer** 환승 **accept** ~을 받아들이다 **surcharge** 추가 요금 **complimentary** 무료의, 공짜의

83. 이 광고에 나온 특별 패키지에 대해 암시된 것은 무엇인가?
(A) 7월 10일 이후에 가격이 인상될 것이다.
(B) 휴일 시즌에 대한 신상 패키지이다.
(C) 50달러를 추가하여 일등석 티켓을 구매할 수 있다.
(D) 여행자들은 어떤 지불 수단도 이용할 수 있다.

정답 (A)

해설 첫 문단을 보면 이 특별 상품을 이용하기 위해서는 7월 10일까지 예약해야 한다는(To get these special deals, you must make a booking by July 10) 내용이 제시되어 있다. 따라서 7월 10일 이후에는 가격이 올라간다는 것을 유추할 수 있으므로 (A)가 정답이다.

어휘 **brand-new** 완전히 새로운 **payment method** 지불 방식

84. 뉴욕에서 출발하는 비행편에 대한 특별한 것은 무엇인가?
(A) 좌석 이용이 제한적이다.
(B) 직항편이 아니다.
(C) 비행기가 더 작다.
(D) 추가 요금이 필요하다.

정답 (D)

해설 두 번째 문단과 네 번째 문단에 * 표시가 된 부분을 보면 뉴욕에서 출발하는 비행기는 50달러 추가 요금이 있다는(There is a $50 surcharge for flights departing from New York.) 내용이 나와 있으므로 (D)가 정답이다.

어휘 **limited** 제한된 **direct flight** 직항

85. 패키지 비용에 포함되지 않은 것은 무엇인가?
(A) 항공세
(B) 숙박
(C) 환승
(D) 점심식사

정답 (A)

해설 세번째 단락에서 패키지에 포함된 것에 대한 내용이 언급되어 있는데, 3성급 숙박시설과 이코노미 항공편, 환승과 점심식사가 포함되어 있지만 항공세와 항공사 요금은 포함되어 있지 않다고(All of the packages include 3-star accommodation and economy flights. Transfers and

all lunches are also included. ~ flight tax and other airline charges are not included) 서술되어 있으므로 (A)가 정답이다.

86. 7월 5일까지 예약하고 결제하면 무엇을 받게 되는가?
(A) 무료 수화물 취급
(B) 아동 할인
(C) 무료 식사
(D) 특별 회원 카드

정답 (C)

해설 지문 마지막 부분에 7월 5일까지 예약하고 결제하면 무료조식 1회와 여행가방을 받을 것이라고(If you book ~ by July 5, you will receive a complimentary breakfast and a travel bag) 언급되어 있으므로 (C)가 정답이다.

어휘 **handling** 취급

87-90.

어휘 **brown rice** 현미 **permit** ~을 허락하다 **diet** 식단조절 **have access to** ~에 접근하다 **complex carbohydrates** 복합 탄수화물 **misplace** ~을 잘못 놓다 **access** ~에 접근하다

87. 조슈아 씨가 이 프로그램에 대해서 암시하는 것은 무엇인가?
(A) 효과적이다.
(B) 적정한 가격이다.

(C) 널리 인기가 있다.

(D) 시간 소모적이다.

정답 (A)

해설 조슈아 씨가 보낸 첫 메시지를 보면 4파운드가 빠졌고 자신의 결과에 기쁘다고(I have lost four pounds this week. I am pleased with my results so far) 말하고 있다. 따라서 이 프로그램이 효과적이라 생각한다고 볼 수 있으므로 (A)가 정답이다.

88. 시반 씨가 조슈아씨가 해야 한다고 제안하는 것은 무엇인가?

(A) 다이어트 수업에 참여하기

(B) 새로운 음식을 맛보기

(C) 책을 구입하기

(D) 이메일을 보내기

정답 (B)

해설 3시 24분에 시반 씨가 조슈아 씨에게 먹어야 한다고(You should) 말한 부분 앞에 조슈아 씨가 브로콜리 쌀밥을 한 번도 먹어 본 적이 없다고(Broccoli rice? I have never tried that before) 밝히고 있다. 따라서 시반 씨가 조슈아 씨에게 먹어 본 적 없는 음식을 먹어야 한다고 제안한 것이므로 (B)가 정답이다.

89. 오후 3시 26분에, 조슈아 씨가 "I've actually misplaced those"라고 말할 때 의미하는 것은 무엇인가?

(A) 그가 브로콜리 쌀밥 패키지를 받지 않았다.

(B) 그는 영수증을 찾을 수 없다.

(C) 환영 이메일이 도착하지 않았다.

(D) 안내책자가 분실되었다.

정답 (D)

해설 제시된 메시지가 보내지기 전에 3시 24분에 시반 씨가 보낸 메시지에 식사 안내서를 볼 수 있냐고 묻고 있는데(Do you have access to the dietary guidebook?) 이에 대해 조슈아 씨가 안내책자를 잃어버렸다고 답하는 상황이므로 (D)가 정답이다.

어휘 **missing** 분실한

90. 이 다음에 어떤 일이 일어날 것 같은가?

(A) 시반 씨가 이 상품의 웹 사이트를 확인할 것이다.

(B) 조슈아 씨가 약간의 흰 쌀밥을 준비할 것이다.

(C) 시반 씨가 조슈아 씨를 위해 무엇인가를 요리할 것이다.

(D) 시반 씨가 조슈아 씨에게 이메일을 보낼 것이다.

정답 (D)

해설 가장 마지막 메시지에 시반 씨가 이메일 주소를 알려 주면 식사 안내서를 보내주겠다고(Please let me know your e-mail address and I will send them to you) 말하고 있으므로 (D)가 정답이다.

91-95.

3월 5일

필딩 씨께,

91 제가 3월 9일 수요일 오전 10시 30분에 <무비 비즈>와 귀하의 인터뷰와 사진 촬영 일정을 잡았다는 점을 알아 두십시오. 귀하의 새로운 영화가 얼마나 많은 언론의 관심을 받고 있는지에 대해 놀랐습니다. 작년에 <무비 비즈>는 귀하를 인터뷰하는 것을 거절했는데, 올해는 이 기사에 자사의 최고 사진사와 최고 작가를 배정했습니다.

92 <무비 비즈>는 4월 중으로, 월말에 스타 어워즈 페스티벌이 시작되기 전에 기사를 실을 계획입니다. 귀하를 인터뷰하고 기사를 작성할 분인 알렉사 해밀턴 씨가 이 축제에 대한 귀하의 기대감에 대해 질문할 것입니다. 몇 가지 적절한 답변을 검토할 시간을 정합시다. **94** 귀하가 그들에게 그 상을 얼마나 받고 싶은지 밝히지 않았으면 합니다. 저희는 그들이 귀하를 겸손하다고 생각하기를 바랍니다.

요한나 비슨

데미안 필딩 씨의 홍보담당

어휘 **make a note that** ~을 알아두다 **amazed** 감탄한 **attention** 관심 **decline to do** ~하기를 거절하다 **assign** ~을 할당하다, 배정하다 **story** 기사 **go over** ~을 검토하다 **appropriate** 적정한 **response** 응답 **modest** 겸손한

<서클 오브 플레임즈>

직성자: 일렉사 해밀턴

93 바로 지난달에 <서클 오브 플레임즈>를 개봉하기 전까지, 데미안 필딩 씨는 8개의 영화를 감독했지만, 어떤 것도 언론의 관심을 끌지 못했다. 여배우 수산나 왈라스 씨는 필딩 감독이 주목을 받는 데 기여한 **95** 공적이 있다. "저는 그분의 초기 작품들 중 하나인 <피시스>를 봤는데, 그분의 뛰어난 감독 능력에 감명을 받았습니다."라고 그녀가 말했다. "저는 즉시 그분과 함께 작업을 하고 싶었습니다."

95 왈라스 씨 같은 유명 여배우가 <서클 오브 플레임즈>의 주연을 맡으면서, 필딩 씨는 갑자기 유명해졌다. 한 연예 잡지에 따르면, 그는 스타 어워즈 페스티벌의 가장 유력한 최우수 감독상 후보로 꼽히고 있다. **94** "저는 상을 받기 위해 영화를 만들지 않는다는 것을 분명히 밝혀 두고 싶습니다."라고 필딩 씨가 말한다. "하지만, 물론, 스타 어워즈를 받게 된다면 영광일 것입니다."

자연스럽게, <서클 오브 플레임즈>의 관람평들은 관객들로 하여금 그의 이전 영화들을 다시 보게끔 권했고, 그들은 신선한 놀라움을 느꼈다. 비록 그 영화들이 흥행하지는 못했지만, 그들은 <서클 오브 플레임즈>와 같은 고품질의 감독 수준을 보여 준다. 필딩 씨는 상당한 지지층을 모으고 있다. 그는 틀림없이 우리가 대작들을 볼 수 있을 그런 사람이다.

어휘 | release ~을 출시하다 direct ~을 감독하다 be credited with ~에 공이 있다 impressed 감동받은 brilliant 훌륭한 immediately 즉시, 즉각 well-known 유명한 star 주연을 맡다 encourage ~을 장려하다 pleasantly 기분 좋게 significant 상당한 규모의 following 추종자들, 지지층

91. 비슨 씨가 필딩 씨에게 메모를 쓴 이유는 무엇인가?
(A) 그가 수상한 것을 알리려고
(B) 그에게 인터뷰 준비를 시키려고
(C) 그에게 오디션 통과하는 방법을 조언하려고
(D) 그를 영화제에 초대하려고

정답 (B)

해설 첫 번째 지문 첫째 줄에 요한나 씨가 인터뷰와 사진 촬영 일정을 잡았다고(Please make a note that I've scheduled your interview and photo shoot with Movie Biz for Wednesday) 알리고 있으므로 필딩 씨에게 그의 인터뷰 일정을 알리고 그에 대한 준비를 시키는 것이 목적임을 알 수 있다. 따라서 (B)가 정답이다.

92. 기사가 실리는 것은 언제인가?
(A) 스타 어워즈 페스티벌 전에
(B) <서클 오브 플레임즈>의 개봉 전에
(C) <무비 비즈> 창간 10주년에
(D) <서클 오브 플레임즈>시사회 중에

정답 (A)

해설 첫 번째 지문 둘째 단락에서 <무비 비즈>는 4월 중으로 월말에 스타 어워즈 페스티벌이 시작되기 전에 기사를 실을 계획이라는(Movie Biz plans to print your article in April, prior to the start of the Star Awards Festival at the end of the month) 말로 시기를 언급하고 있으므로 (A)가 정답이다.

어휘 release 개봉 premiere 시사회

93. 기사의 목적은 무엇인가?
(A) 필딩 씨의 최신 영화를 축하하기 위해
(B) 왈라스 씨가 왜 배역을 맡았는지 설명하기 위해
(C) 스타 어워즈 페스티벌을 홍보하기 위해
(D) 필딩 씨의 이전 영화들을 강조하기 위해

정답 (A)

해설 두 번째 지문의 첫 단락을 보면 바로 지난달에 영화를 출시하기 전까지 8편의 영화가 관심을 못 받았으나, 이번 영화는 유명 여배우의 출연으로 조명을 받게 되었다는(Prior to releasing Circle of Flames just last month, ~ can be credited with helping to bring Fielding into the spotlight) 사실을 밝히고 있다. 이는 필딩 씨의 최신 영화가 주목받은 것을 축하하는 것이라고 볼 수 있으므로 (A)가 정답이다.

어휘 latest 최신의 accept ~을 받아들이다 highlight ~을 강조하다

94. 필딩 씨에 대해서 유추할 수 있는 것은 무엇인가?
(A) 인터뷰 동안에 마음이 편하지 않았다.
(B) 전에 왈라스 씨와 일했다.
(C) 이미 새로운 영화를 작업하고 있다.
(D) 홍보담당자의 조언을 따르고 있다.

정답 (D)

해설 첫 번째 지문 후반부에 홍보담당자가 상을 얼마나 받고 싶은지 밝히지 않았으면 한다는(I don't want you to tell them how much you want to win that award) 충고를 전하고 있고, 두 번째 지문 두 번째 단락에 필딩 씨가 조언대로 상을 받기 위해 영화를 만들지 않는다는 것을 분명히 밝혀 두고 싶다고(I don't make movies for awards) 말했으므로 충고를 잘 따랐다고 볼 수 있다. 따라서 (D)가 정답이다.

어휘 previously 전에 work on ~에 대해 작업하다 publicist 홍보담당자

95. 기사에서 첫째 단락, 둘째 줄에 있는 단어 "credited"와 의미가 가장 가까운 것은 무엇인가?
(A) 빚을 진
(B) 보상 받은
(C) 공을 인정 받은
(D) 상을 받은

정답 (C)

해설 해당 문장 다음 단락에 필딩 씨의 영화에 출연한 여배우 덕분에 유명해지게 되었다는(With a well-known actress like Wallace starring in Circle of Flames, Fielding has suddenly become famous) 내용이 언급되어 있으므로 이 여배우가 감독이 유명해지는 데에 대한 공이 있다고 할 수 있다. 따라서 '공을 인정 받은'이라는 뜻의 (C) recognized가 정답이다.

96-100.

스트랫포드 지역 축제 마당 행사 일정표
6월 29일, 토요일 (애쉬베리 농장 곳곳의 다양한 장소)

지역 축제 마당 주최자들을 위한 임시 일정표		
시간	행사/활동	행사장/위치
오전 8:30	- 뷔페 아침 식사	출장 요리 제공용 텐트
오전 9:30	- 96(D) 가장 큰 채소 경연대회 - 경품 추첨 티켓 배부 - 96(B) 강아지 및 고양이 경연대회 - 96(A) 어린이 페이스 페인팅	중앙 들판
오전 11:30	- 98 짐 리 코미디 쇼 - 98 포고 더 클라운 쇼	98 공연용 텐트
오후 12:30	- 샌드위치 및 간식	출장 요리 제공용 텐트

| 100 오후 1:30 | - 100 음악 공연 | 야외 공연 무대 |
| 오후 4:00 | - DJ와 댄스
- 경품 추첨 당첨자 발표 | 출장 요리 제공용 텐트 |

97 일단 모든 행사가 종료되는 대로, 지역 축제 마당 주최자들과 자원 봉사자 작업자들께서는 부지 입구에서 랄프 피츠 씨와 만나 청소 및 해체 업무와 관련된 안내 사항을 전달 받으셔야 합니다.

어휘 **fair** 축제 마당, 박람회 **location** 장소, 위치, 지점 **provisional** 임시의, 잠정적인 **organizer** 주최자, 조직자 **raffle** 경품 추첨 **distribution** 배부, 배포 **refreshments** 간식, 다과 **announcement** 발표, 공지 **venue** 행사장, 개최 장소 **catering** 출장 요리 제공(업) **once** 일단 ~하는 대로, ~하자마자 **instructions** 안내, 설명, 지시 **regarding** ~와 관련해 **clean-up** 청소 **dismantling** (구조물 등의) 해체 **task** 업무, 일

수신: 일레인 오워 <eower@stratford.gov>
발신: 도널드 이건 <donegan@stratford.gov>
제목: 스트랫포드 지역 축제 마당
날짜: 6월 17일

안녕하세요, 일레인 씨,

지역 축제 마당에서 도와 주시겠다고 제안해 주셔서 대단히 감사합니다. 98 리사 멀럼바 씨께서 주최자로서의 직무를 이행하실 수 없을 것이라는 이야기를 듣고 유감스러웠지만, 당신이 그 자리를 대신하는 데 동의해 주셔서 기쁩니다. 98 6월 29일, 토요일에, 코미디 쇼와 클라운 쇼를 준비하시는 일을 책임지시게 될 것입니다. 선임 행사 진행 책임자들 중의 한 분이신 랄프 피츠 씨께서 반드시 일이 순조롭게 99 진행되도록 도와 주실 것입니다.

안녕히 계십시오.

도널드 이건
회장
스트랫포드 행사 기획 위원회

어휘 **offer to do** ~하겠다고 제안하다 **help out** 돕다 **fulfill** ~을 이행하다, ~을 수행하다 **duty** 직무, 임무 **agree to do** ~하는 데 동의하다 **take one's place** ~을 대신하다 **be responsible for** ~에 대한 책임을 지다 **coordinator** 진행 책임자, 편성 책임자 **make sure (that)** 반드시 ~하도록 하다, ~임을 확실히 해두다 **run** 진행되다, 운영되다 **smoothly** 순조롭게

수신: 도널드 이건 <donegan@stratford.gov>
발신: 일레인 오워 <eower@stratford.gov>
제목: 회신: 스트랫포드 지역 축제 마당
날짜: 6월 18일

안녕하세요, 도널드 씨,

저에게 전혀 감사하실 필요 없습니다. 저는 항상 우리 지역 행사를 기꺼이 도울 준비가 되어 있고, 도울 의향도 되어 있습니다. 저에게 지역 사회에 봉사할 수 있는 기회를 주실 뿐만 아니라, 다양한 공연도 즐길 수 있게 해 주셨습니다! 다가오는 축제 마당에서, 100 저는 오후 3시쯤에 야외 공연 무대 쪽으로 건너갈 시간이 있기를 정말로 바라고 있습니다. 엘리엇 스펜서 씨가 대단히 재능이 뛰어나서 분명 훌륭한 공연을 하실 것입니다!

안녕히 계십시오.

일레인

어휘 **absolutely** 전적으로, 절대적으로, (부정문에서) 전혀 **be ready to do** ~할 준비가 되어 있다 **be willing to do** 기꺼이 ~하다, ~할 의향이 있다 **help out with** ~을 돕다 **serve** ~에 봉사하다, ~에 서비스를 제공하다 **allow A to do** A에게 ~할 수 있게 해 주다 **upcoming** 다가오는, 곧 있을 **have time to do** ~할 시간이 있다 **get over to** ~ 쪽으로 건너가다, ~로 넘어가다 **around** ~쯤, ~경에 **extremely** 대단히, 매우 **talented** 재능 있는 **be sure to do** 분명 ~하다

96. 6월 29일 오전에 있을 일이 아닌 것은 무엇인가?
(A) 아이들이 얼굴에 그림을 그릴 것이다.
(B) 반려동물들이 대회에 참가할 것이다.
(C) 추첨 행사 경품을 나눠줄 것이다.
(D) 농산물이 크기에 대해 심사될 것이다.

정답 (C)

해설 첫 지문에 포함된 일정표의 오전 시간대에 제시된 가장 큰 채소 경연대회(Largest vegetable competition) 부분에서 (D)를, 강아지 및 고양이 경연대회(Dog and cat competition) 부분에서 (B)를, 그리고 어린이 페이스 페인팅(Children's face painting) 부분에서 (A)를 확인할 수 있다. 하지만 추첨 행사 경품을 나눠주는 일은 오후 4시에 있을 행사로 표기되어 있으므로 (C)가 정답이다.

어휘 **take place** (일, 행사 등이) 일어나다, 발생되다, 개최되다 **have A p.p.** A를 ~되게 하다, A를 ~해놓다 **enter A into B** A를 B에 참가시키다 **produce** n. 농산물 **judge** ~을 심사하다

97. 지역 축제 마당 자원 봉사자들과 관련해 알려진 것은 무엇인가?
(A) 행사 후에 함께 식사하기 위해 모일 것이다.
(B) 감사의 표시로 무료 선물을 받을 것이다.
(C) 도널드 이건 씨와 함께 기획 회의에 참석할 것이다.
(D) 당일 행사 종료 시에 말끔히 정리해야 할 것이다.

정답 (D)

해설 첫 지문 마지막 단락에 모든 행사가 종료되는 대로 지역 축제 마당 주최자들과 자원 봉사자 작업자들이 랄프 피츠 씨와 만나 청소 및 해체 업무와 관련된 안내 사항을 전달 받아야 한다고(Once all the events have ended, community fair organizers and volunteer workers ~ to receive instructions regarding clean-up and dismantling tasks) 알리고 있으므로 청소 업무에 해당되는 일을 언급한 (D)가 정답이다.

어휘 gather 모이다 as a token of ~의 표시로 gratitude 감사(의 마음) planning 기획 be required to do ~해야 하다, ~할 필요가 있다 tidy up 말끔히 정리하다

98. 리사 멀럼바 씨는 어디에서 일하기로 되어 있었을 것 같은가?

(A) 출장 요리 제공용 텐트에서

(B) 공연용 텐트에서

(C) 중앙 들판에서

(D) 야외 공연 무대에서

정답 (B)

해설 두 번째 지문에 리사 멀럼바 씨의 불참 사실을 언급하면서 6월 29일에 코미디 쇼와 클라운 쇼를 준비하는 일을 대신 책임지게 될 것이라고(On Saturday, June 29, you will be responsible for organizing the comedy show and the clown show) 수신인인 일레인 씨에게 알리고 있다. 첫 지문의 일정표를 보면, 오전 11시 30분에 코미디 쇼와 클라운 쇼가 표기되어 있고, 장소는 performance Tent로 쓰여 있으므로 (B)가 정답이다.

어휘 be supposed to do ~하기로 되어 있다, ~할 예정이다, ~해야 하다

99. 첫 번째 이메일에서, 첫 번째 단락, 네 번째 줄의 단어 "run"과 의미가 가장 가까운 것은 무엇인가?

(A) 전력 질주하다

(B) 여행하다

(C) 운영되다

(D) 도착하다

정답 (C)

해설 해당 문장에서 run 앞뒤로 관련 '업무' 등을 가리키는 things와 '순조롭게'를 의미하는 부사 smoothly가 쓰여 있어 run이 일을 순조롭게 진행되도록 한다는 의미를 지니고 있다는 것을 알 수 있다. 이는 순조롭게 운영되는 것과 같으므로 '운영되다' 등을 뜻하는 (C) operate이 정답이다.

100. 엘리엇 스펜서 씨가 누구일 것 같은가?

(A) 코미디언

(B) 행사 주최자

(C) 음악가

(D) 위원회장

정답 (C)

해설 세 번째 지문에 일레인 씨가 오후 3시쯤에 야외 공연 무대 쪽으로 갈 수 있기를 정말로 바라고 있다는 말과 함께 엘리엇 스펜서 씨가 분명 훌륭한 공연을 할 것이라는 기대를 나타내고 있다(to get over to the outdoor performance stage at around 3 p.m. Elliot Spencer is extremely talented and is sure`to give a great performance!). 첫 지문의 일정표를 보면, 오후 3시는 1시 30분에 시작되는 음악 공연(Musical performances)이 진행되는 시점이어서 엘리엇 스펜서 씨가 음악가임을 알 수 있으므로 (C)가 정답이다.

LC

1. (C)	**2.** (D)	**3.** (C)	**4.** (B)	**5.** (B)
6. (A)	**7.** (B)	**8.** (B)	**9.** (B)	**10.** (A)
11. (B)	**12.** (C)	**13.** (A)	**14.** (A)	**15.** (B)
16. (C)	**17.** (B)	**18.** (C)	**19.** (A)	**20.** (C)
21. (C)	**22.** (A)	**23.** (D)	**24.** (D)	**25.** (B)
26. (C)	**27.** (C)	**28.** (C)	**29.** (A)	**30.** (A)
31. (C)	**32.** (A)	**33.** (B)	**34.** (B)	**35.** (D)
36. (B)	**37.** (C)	**38.** (D)	**39.** (C)	**40.** (D)
41. (B)	**42.** (C)	**43.** (A)	**44.** (C)	**45.** (B)
46. (B)	**47.** (B)	**48.** (C)	**49.** (C)	**50.** (C)

RC

51. (B)	**52.** (A)	**53.** (D)	**54.** (D)	**55.** (D)
56. (A)	**57.** (D)	**58.** (D)	**59.** (C)	**60.** (A)
61. (C)	**62.** (A)	**63.** (D)	**64.** (A)	**65.** (A)
66. (A)	**67.** (D)	**68.** (D)	**69.** (B)	**70.** (B)
71. (D)	**72.** (A)	**73.** (B)	**74.** (C)	**75.** (B)
76. (D)	**77.** (B)	**78.** (D)	**79.** (A)	**80.** (D)
81. (B)	**82.** (A)	**83.** (B)	**84.** (D)	**85.** (A)
86. (D)	**87.** (D)	**88.** (C)	**89.** (C)	**90.** (D)
91. (D)	**92.** (A)	**93.** (B)	**94.** (D)	**95.** (C)
96. (C)	**97.** (C)	**98.** (D)	**99.** (B)	**100.** (D)

Part 1

1. (A) Some people are waiting for a bus.
(B) Lines are being painted on a street.
(C) A bus is being driven down a road.
(D) A woman is getting into her car.

(A) 몇몇 사람들이 버스를 기다리는 중이다.
(B) 길에 선이 그려지고 있다.
(C) 버스 한 대가 도로를 따라 운행되는 중이다.
(D) 한 여자가 차에 오르고 있다.

해설 (A) 버스를 기다리는 사람들을 찾아볼 수 없으므로 오답.
(B) 선은 이미 그려져 있는 상태이므로 오답.
(C) 도로에서 이동하고 있는 버스를 묘사하고 있으므로 정답.
(D) 차를 타는 동작을 하는 여자는 보이지 않으므로 오답.

어휘 **get into a car** 차에 오르다, 차에 타다

2. (A) Bicycles have been propped against a wall.
(B) Some passengers are boarding a boat.
(C) A railing is being installed around a lake.
(D) A bridge crosses over a waterway.

(A) 자전거들이 벽에 기대어 있다.
(B) 몇몇 승객들이 보트에 탑승하는 중이다.
(C) 난간이 호수 주위에 설치되고 있다.
(D) 다리 하나가 물길 위를 가로지르고 있다.

해설 (A) 다리가 이미 지어져 있는 상태이므로 오답.
(B) 보트에 탑승하는 사람들을 찾아볼 수 없으므로 오답.
(C) 난간은 이미 설치되어 있으므로 오답.
(D) 물 위로 가로질러 설치되어 있는 다리를 묘사하고 있으므로 정답.

어휘 **be propped against** ~에 기대어 있다 **passenger** 승객 **board** ~에 탑승하다 **railing** 난간 **cross** ~을 가로지르다, 건너다 **waterway** 물길, 수로

Part 2

3. When can I catch a flight to Los Angeles?
(A) West Coast Airlines.
(B) From San Francisco.
(C) There's one at 2:35.

로스앤젤레스로 가는 비행기를 언제 탈 수 있을까요?
(A) 웨스트 코스트 항공입니다.
(B) 샌프란시스코에서요.
(C) 2시 35분에 하나 있습니다.

해설 의문사 When으로 시점을 묻는 질문이므로 그에 맞게 구체적인 시간/시점을 언급하는 대답이 정답이 된다. LA 행 비행기 시간을 묻고 있으므로 2시 35분에 비행기가 하나 있다고 말하는 (C)가 정답이다.

어휘 **catch a flight** 비행기를 타다

4. You will remember to proofread my article, won't you?
(A) It was in a magazine.
(B) I already did that.
(C) Can I borrow it when you're done?

제 기사를 교정 봐주시기로 한 것 기억하실 거죠, 그렇죠?
(A) 그것은 잡지에 있었어요.
(B) 이미 했어요.
(C) 당신이 다 끝내면 이걸 빌릴 수 있을까요?

해설 기사를 교정 봐주기로 한 것을 기억해 달라고 확인하는 부가 의
문문이다. 이에 대해 이미 그 일을(proofread) 했다고 말하는
(B)가 가장 자연스러운 응답이다. (A)는 질문 속 article(기사)
을 듣고 magazine(잡지)를 연상하게끔 한 오답이며, (C)는 묻
는 내용과 전혀 상관없는 오답이다.

어휘 **proofread** ~을 교정보다 **article** (신문, 잡지의) 글, 기사
magazine 잡지 **borrow** ~을 빌리다

5. What did Mr. Parker have to say about our sales
figures?

(A) They are currently on sale.
(B) He thought they were impressive.
(C) That's not what he told me.

파커 씨는 우리 매출액에 대해서 뭐라고 말했죠?
(A) 그것들은 현재 판매 중입니다.
(B) 인상적이라고 생각했답니다.
(C) 그건 그가 제게 했던 말이 아닙니다.

해설 Parker 씨가 매출액에 대해 뭐라고 말했는지, 매출액에 대한
Parker 씨의 의견을 묻는 질문이다. 이에 대해 '그는 ~라고 생
각 했다'라는 표현으로 매출액에 대한 Parker 씨의 생각을 전
하는 (B)가 정답이다.

어휘 **sales figure** 판매액, 매출액 **currently** 최근에 **on sale**
판매 중인 **impressive** 인상적인

6. Did you talk to our CEO, or was he busy?
(A) Actually, he's away all week.
(B) Well, let me know when you are free.
(C) Mr. Sawyer might know.

우리 대표이사님께 말씀 드렸나요, 아니면 그분이 바빴나요?
(A) 사실, 주중 내내 부재중이세요.
(B) 음, 당신이 시간이 될 때 제게 알려 주세요.
(C) 쏘여 씨가 아마 알고 있을 거예요.

해설 선택 의문문에서 가장 가능성이 큰 답변은 질문에 제시된 A or
B 중 하나를 택해 다른 말로 돌려 표현하는 것이다. CEO에게
말할 기회가 있었는지 혹은 CEO가 바빴는지를 묻고 있으므로,
CEO가 주중 내내 부재중이었다고 하는 (A)가 가장 잘 어울린
다. 참고로, Actually가 나오는 응답은 정답이 될 확률이 매우
높다.

어휘 **CEO** 최고 경영자(= Chief Executive Officer) **be away**
떠나 있다, 부재중이다 **be free** 여유가 있다, 시간이 있다

7. Where can I see a play in the downtown area?
(A) Around 30 dollars per ticket.
(B) You have lots of options.
(C) Rent is much higher there.

시내에서 연극을 볼 수 있는 곳은 어딘가요?
(A) 티켓당 약 30달러입니다.
(B) 많은 선택 사항이 있어요.

해설 연극을 볼 수 있는 장소를 묻는 Where 의문문이다. 구체적인
장소를 말해주는 대신 '선택할 수 있는 곳이 많다'라고 말하는
(B)가 가장 자연스러운 응답이다. (A)는 티켓 가격을 말하는 오
답이고, (C)는 downtown area에서 연상하기 쉬운 rent(임
대료)를 이용한 오답이다.

어휘 **downtown** 시내(에서) **per** ~당, ~마다 **option** 선택 사
항, 선택할 대상 **rent** 임대료

8. The Mexican restaurant across the road has
great tacos.

(A) Flights are expensive, though.
(B) Maybe I'll try some at lunchtime.
(C) It normally closes at 10.

길 건너편에 있는 멕시코 식당에 타코가 아주 훌륭해요.
(A) 그렇지만 항공편 가격이 비싸요.
(B) 점심 시간에 좀 먹어봐야겠네요.
(C) 거긴 보통 10시에 닫아요.

해설 건너편 식당에 음식이 훌륭하다는 말에 점심에 가서 먹어봐야
겠다고 말하는 (B)가 가장 자연스러운 응답이다. (A)는 제시문
내용과 관련 없는 flights를 언급했지만 주어를 제대로 듣지 못
하면 expensive, though만 듣고 식당 음식에 대해 하는 말
인 줄 착각하고 고를 수 있으므로 주의해야 한다.

어휘 **across the road** 길 건너에 **taco** 타코(얇은 부침개 같은
것에 고기, 야채 등을 싸 먹는 멕시코 음식) **flight** 항공편, 항
공기 **try** ~을 먹어보다 **normally** 보통(= usually)

9. Should we book a room in advance, or just hope
that there is one available?

(A) The payment is overdue.
(B) Let's call the Olive Hotel now.
(C) For our business trip.

방을 미리 예약해야 할까요, 아니면 그저 이용 가능한 방이 있
길 바라야 할까요?
(A) 지불이 연체되었습니다.
(B) 지금 올리브 호텔에 전화해 봅시다.
(C) 출장을 위해서입니다.

해설 선택 의문문으로 book a room in advance(미리 예약하다)
와 hope that there is one available(방이 있길 바라다)의
두 가지 선택사항을 제시하고 있다. 둘 중 하나를 택하는 대답이
정답이 될 확률이 높은데, 지금 호텔에 전화해 보자고 하는 (B)
는 book a room in advance를 돌려서 표현한 말로서 정답
이다.

어휘 **book** ~을 예약하다 **in advance** 사전에, 미리 **available**
이용 가능한 **payment** 지불 **overdue** 연체된, 기한이
지난

10. Would you like to travel to the convention

together?

(A) I'm not sure I'll be able to make it.
(B) I've traveled to several countries.
(C) Yes, we decided to take the same flight.

컨벤션에 함께 가시겠어요?
(A) 제가 갈 수 있을지 모르겠어요.
(B) 몇몇 나라들에 여행을 가본 적이 있어요.
(C) 네, 우리는 같은 항공편을 타기로 결정했어요.

해설 Would you like to ~?는 '~하시겠어요?'라는 의미로, 무엇을 할 것을 정중히 권하는 말이다. 컨벤션에 함께 갈 것을 청하고 있으므로 Yes/No로 수락이나 거절을 하는 답을 하는 것이 기본이지만 Yes/No를 언급하지 않고 간접적으로 수락이나 거절을 하는 답변도 있으므로 주의한다. '갈 수 있을지 모르겠다, 못 갈 수도 있다'라고 말하는 (A)는 간접적인 거절의 답변으로 정답이다. make it(어떤 곳에 시간에 맞춰 가다)이라는 표현을 알고 있어야 정답을 고를 수 있다.

어휘 **convention** 컨벤션, 총회 **travel to** ~로 이동하다, 여행하다

11. Where do you think I can find an affordable apartment?

(A) It sounds like you got a great deal.
(B) Try the Beach Hill neighborhood.
(C) Yes, it's a two-bedroom condominium.

제가 어디서 가격이 적당한 아파트를 찾을 수 있다고 생각하세요?
(A) 당신은 굉장히 좋은 계약을 한 것 같네요.
(B) 비시 힐 지역에 한번 가 보세요.
(C) 네, 그건 침실 2개짜리 아파트입니다.

해설 Where do you think ~?는 장소에 관해 상대방의 의견을 물어 보는 표현이며, 가격이 적당한(affordable) 아파트를 찾을 수 있는 곳을 물어보고 있다. 따라서 아파트 장소와 관련된 대답이 적절한 답변이 될 것이다. (A)에서 deal은 '거래, 계약'을 의미하며, 상대방이 좋은 계약을 얻은 것 같다는 표현이므로 적절한 답변이 아니다. (B)에서는 neighborhood라는 단어를 통해 Beach Hill이 지명이라는 것을 유추할 수 있으며, try가 try finding을 의미하므로 적절한 답변이다.

어휘 **affordable** 가격이 적당한, 감당할 수 있는
neighborhood 지역, 근처, 인근 **condominium** 아파트

12. Isn't there an additional fee for overnight delivery?

(A) It arrived really quickly.
(B) No, it wasn't free.
(C) Yes, it's an extra 5 dollars.

익일 배송에 대한 추가 요금이 있지 않나요?
(A) 이것은 정말 빠르게 도착했습니다.
(B) 아니요, 그것은 무료가 아니었습니다.
(C) 네, 추가 5달러입니다.

해설 부정 의문문의 경우 not을 빼고 생각한다. 익일 배송에 추가 요금이 있는지를 묻는 질문이므로 Yes라고 긍정한 뒤 5달러라고 가격을 말해주는 (C)가 적절한 응답이다. 일반 의문문의 경우에는 첫 다섯 단어 정도만 들어도 문제를 풀 수 있다. 이 질문 역시 Isn't there an additional fee까지만 들어도 정답을 고를 수 있다. (B)의 경우 추가 요금이 있는지 묻는 질문에 No라고 말하면 추가 요금이 없다는 뜻인데 뒤에 이어지는 내용이 이와 맞지 않다.

어휘 **additional fee** 추가 요금 **overnight delivery** 익일 배송 **extra** 추가의

13. Would you mind taking notes for me at the seminar?

(A) I wasn't planning on going.
(B) Thanks, I'll sit here instead.
(C) As soon as you can.

세미나에서 절 위해 노트 필기 좀 해 주시겠어요?
(A) 전 가지 않을 계획이었어요.
(B) 감사합니다, 제가 대신 여기 앉을게요.
(C) 최대한 빨리요.

해설 Would you mind –ing?는 무엇을 해달라고 정중히 부탁하는 표현이다. 세미나에서 노트 필기를 해달라는 부탁에 대해 '(세미나에) 갈 계획이 없다'고 말하는 (A)가 가장 잘 어울리는 대답이다.

어휘 **Would you mind -ing?** ~해주시겠습니까? **take notes** 메모하다, 필기하다 **plan on -ing** ~할 계획이다

14. I heard that someone in this department was having computer trouble.

(A) That would be Gary.
(B) Remember to back up your work.
(C) Check if it's out of ink.

이 부서에 누군가가 컴퓨터 문제를 겪고 있다고 들었어요.
(A) 그건 개리 씨일 거예요.
(B) 당신이 한 작업물을 꼭 백업하도록 하세요.
(C) 잉크가 다 떨어졌는지 확인해 보세요.

해설 컴퓨터 문제를 겪는 사람이 있다는 것을 들은 사실을 밝히는 말이므로 '그 사람은 Gary일 것이다'라는 말로 당사자를 알리는 (A)가 정답이다.

어휘 **department** 부서 **trouble** 문제 **back up** (예비로) 저장하다, (파일을) 백업하다 **be out of** ~가 다 떨어지다, ~을 다 쓰다

15. Which water pipe connects to the bathroom sink?
(A) No, I don't think so.
(B) The white plastic one.
(C) With running water.

어느 배수도관이 욕실 배수구와 연결되어 있나요?
(A) 아뇨, 전 그렇게 생각하지 않아요.
(B) 흰색 플라스틱으로 된 거요.
(C) 흐르는 물로요.

해설 Which 의문문에서는 Which와 함께 제시되는 명사를 놓치지 않고 들어야 한다. 그 명사와 관련해 특징적인 요소를 언급하는 보기를 찾아내면 되는데, 이때 대명사 one을 쓰는 경우가 많기 때문에 one이 들어간 보기를 고르면 정답일 확률이 매우 높다. 여기서도 Which water pipe(어느 배수도관)라는 질문에 '흰색 플라스틱으로 된 거요(The white plastic one)'라고 답하는 (B)가 정답이다.

어휘 **water pipe** 수도관 **connect to** ~에 연결되다 **running water** 흐르는 물

16. How does Mr. Chen like the company he works for?
(A) He can take a bus instead.
(B) No, he's too busy.
(C) Well, he's been there 20 years.

첸 씨께서 자신이 근무하는 회사를 마음에 들어 하나요?
(A) 그분께서 대신 버스를 타실 수 있습니다.
(B) 아뇨, 그분께서 너무 바쁘세요.
(C) 음, 그분께서 그곳에 계신지 20년 됐어요.

해설 첸 씨가 자신이 근무하는 회사를 마음에 들어 하는지 묻고 있으므로 Mr. Chen을 he로 지칭해 20년 동안 그곳에 있었다고 알리는 것으로 마음에 들어 한다는 뜻을 나타낸 (C)가 정답이다. (B)는 의문사 의문문에 맞지 않는 No로 대답하고 있으므로 오답이다.

어휘 **work for** ~에 근무하다 **take** (교통편, 도로 등) ~을 타다, ~을 이용하다 **instead** 대신

17. Did they have a grand opening for this department store?
(A) It opens every day at 9.
(B) There was a big event on Sunday.
(C) I just moved into the apartment.

그 사람들이 이 백화점을 위한 개장 기념 행사를 열었나요?
(A) 매일 9시에 문을 엽니다.
(B) 일요일에 큰 행사가 있었어요.
(C) 저는 막 그 아파트로 이사했어요.

해설 백화점을 위한 개장 기념 행사를 열었는지 묻고 있으므로 일요일에 큰 행사가 있었다는 말로 개장을 기념하는 행사를 열었다는 뜻을 나타낸 (B)가 정답이다. (A)는 opening과 발음이 유사한 opens를, (C)는 department와 일부 발음이 유사한 apartment를 각각 활용해 혼동을 유발하는 오답이다.

어휘 **grand opening** 개장 기념 행사 **move into** ~로 이사하다

18. Why does the air conditioner keep making a noise?
(A) Yes, it's getting hot in here.
(B) I'll try to keep my voice down.
(C) Does it need to be cleaned?

에어컨에서 왜 계속 소음이 나는 거죠?
(A) 네, 이 안이 더워지고 있어요.
(B) 제 목소리를 낮추도록 하겠습니다.
(C) 청소해야 하나요?

해설 에어컨이 왜 계속 소음을 내는지 묻고 있으므로 청소해야 하는지 묻는 것으로 답변자 자신이 생각하는 문제에 따른 해결책을 되묻는 것으로 답변하는 (C)가 정답이다. (A)는 의문사 의문문에 맞지 않는 Yes로 답변하는 오답이며, (B)는 keep을 반복함과 동시에 keep making a noise에서 연상 가능한 keep my voice down을 활용해 혼동을 유발하는 오답이다.

어휘 **keep -ing** 계속 ~하다 **make a noise** 소음을 내다 **get A** A한 상태가 되다 **keep A down** (소리 등) A를 낮추다

19. Are we closing down our branch on Bleeker Street?
(A) It hasn't been making money.
(B) At 6 P.M. on weekdays.
(C) It's only a few blocks from here.

블리커 스트리트에 있는 우리 지점을 닫게 되나요?
(A) 그곳이 계속 수익을 내지 못하고 있거든요.
(B) 평일 오후 6시에요.
(C) 이곳에서 몇 블록밖에 되지 않아요.

해설 블리커 스트리트에 있는 지점을 닫는 것인지 묻고 있으므로 branch on Bleeker Street을 It으로 지칭해 수익을 내지 못하고 있다는 말로 지점 폐쇄 이유를 밝히는 (A)가 정답이다. (B)는 closing에서 연상 가능한 영업 종료 시간 At 6 P.M.을, (C)는 Street에서 연상 가능한 거리 관련 표현 only a few blocks from here를 각각 활용해 혼동을 유발하는 오답이다.

어휘 **close down** ~을 닫다, ~을 폐쇄하다 **branch** 지점, 지사 **make money** 수익을 내다, 돈을 벌다

20. Ms. Hegarty usually parks in the East Parking Lot, doesn't she?
(A) It's the nicest park in town.
(B) No, I'll be coming by bus.
(C) It's already full today.

헤거티 씨가 평소에 동쪽 주차장에 주차하지 않나요?
(A) 우리 도시에서 가장 좋은 공원입니다.
(B) 아뇨, 저는 버스로 갈 예정입니다.
(C) 오늘은 이미 만차입니다.

해설 헤거티 씨가 평소에 동쪽 주차장에 주차하지 않는지 묻고 있으므로 East Parking Lot을 It으로 지칭해 이미 만차인 상태라고 밝히는 것으로 그곳에 주차하지 않았을 가능성을 언급하는

(C)가 정답이다. (A)는 park의 다른 의미(주차하다, 공원)를 활용해 혼동을 유발하는 오답이며, (B)는 부정을 나타내는 No 뒤에 이어지는 말이 헤거티 씨가 아닌 답변자 자신과 관련된 말이므로 핵심에서 벗어난 오답이다.

어휘 **parking lot** 주차장 **full** 가득한, 꽉 찬

Part 3

Questions 21-23 refer to the following conversation.

M: Lydia, I met with a Web designer from the IT company this morning. He said there are several improvements we could make to **21** our hotel's Web site.

W: Great! **22** I'd really like him to improve the way our guests reserve rooms here. The current site is so complicated, and many guests have complained about the process.

M: Exactly, so I already mentioned that to the designer. **23** I'm going to look at the guest comment cards today to find out what other changes they think we should make. Then I'll speak with the designer again.

남: 리디아 씨, 제가 오늘 아침에 그 IT 회사에서 근무하시는 웹 디자이너 한 분과 만났어요. 그분께서 우리 호텔 웹 사이트에 할 수 있을 만한 몇 가지 개선 사항을 이야기해 주셨습니다.

여: 잘됐네요! 저는 우리 고객들께서 이곳에 객실을 예약하시는 방법을 그분께서 꼭 개선해 주셨으면 좋겠어요. 현재 이용 중인 사이트가 너무 복잡해서, 많은 고객들께서 그 과정과 관련해 불만을 제기하셨어요.

남: 맞아요, 그래서 제가 이미 그 디자이너 분께 그 부분을 언급해 드렸어요. 사람들이 다른 어떤 것을 변경해야 한다고 생각하는지 알아보기 위해 제가 오늘 고객 의견 카드를 살펴볼 예정입니다. 그 후에 그 디자이너 분과 다시 얘기하겠습니다.

어휘 **meet with** (약속하고) ~와 만나다 **make an improvement** 개선하다, 향상시키다 **would like A to do** A에게 ~하기를 원하다 **the way (that)** ~하는 방법 **reserve** ~을 예약하다 **current** 현재의 **complicated** 복잡한 **complain about** ~에 관해 불만을 제기하다 **process** 과정 **Exactly** (강한 긍정) 맞아요, 바로 그거예요 **mention** ~을 언급하다 **comment** 의견 **find out** ~을 알아보다, ~을 파악하다 **make a change** 변경하다, 바꾸다 **then** 그 후에, 그런 다음, 그렇다면, 그때

21. 화자들이 어디에서 일하는가?
(A) 레스토랑에서
(B) 컴퓨터 매장에서
(C) 호텔에서
(D) 대여점에서

해설 대화 초반부에 남자가 our hotel's Web site를 언급하는 것으로 소속 업체를 밝히고 있으므로 (C)가 정답이다.

어휘 **rental** 대여, 임대

22. 여자가 무엇을 하고 싶어 하는가?
(A) 예약 과정을 변경하는 일
(B) 광고를 만드는 일
(C) 건물을 개조하는 일
(D) 일부 가격을 낮추는 일

해설 여자가 대화 중반부에 객실을 예약하는 방법을 개선해 주면 좋겠다는 말과 함께 너무 복잡하다는 문제를(I'd really like him to improve the way our guests reserve rooms here. The current site is so complicated ~) 언급하고 있다. 이는 예약 과정을 변경하는 일을 의미하므로 (A)가 정답이다.

어휘 **create** ~을 만들어내다 **renovate** ~을 개조하다, ~을 보수하다 **lower** v. ~을 낮추다, ~을 내리다

Paraphrase improve the way our guests reserve rooms
→ Change a reservation process

23. 남자는 자신이 오늘 무엇을 할 것이라고 말하는가?
(A) 웹 사이트를 업데이트하는 일
(B) 일부 장비를 수리하는 일
(C) 제품 샘플을 주문하는 일
(D) 일부 의견을 확인하는 일

해설 남자가 오늘 무엇을 할 것이라고 말하는지 묻고 있으므로 남자의 말에 집중해 단서를 파악해야 하며, 질문에 제시된 today 또는 이와 유사한 시점 표현과 함께 언급되는 정보에 귀 기울여 들어야 한다. 남자가 대화 후반부에 오늘 고객 의견 카드를 살펴볼 생각이라고(I'm going to look at the guest comment cards today ~) 알리고 있으므로 (D)가 정답이다.

어휘 **repair** ~을 수리하다 **equipment** 장비 **order** ~을 주문하다 **feedback** 의견

Questions 24-26 refer to the following conversation.

W: Kyle, you are responsible for **24** updating the social media page for our store, right?

M: Yes. The store manager put me in charge of it last month, because **25** he liked the online advertisement I created. A lot of our customers really liked it too.

W: You did a great job on it. Well, I have an idea that you might want to consider. **26** How about putting more pictures of our products on the page? I think that would really help us attract new customers.

M: You're probably right. We don't really show enough photos of products at the moment. Thanks for the advice.

W: No problem. I'm happy to help.

여: 카일 씨, 당신이 우리 매장 소셜 미디어 페이지를 업데이트하는 일을 책임지고 계시는 게 맞죠?

남: 네. 점장님께서 지난 달에 저에게 그 일에 대한 책임을 맡기셨는데, 제가 만든 온라인 광고를 마음에 들어 하셨기 때문입니다. 많은 우리 고객들께서도 아주 좋아하셨고요.

여: 그 일에 대해 정말 수고가 많으셨네요. 음, 고려해 보기를 원하실 수도 있는 아이디어가 하나 있어요. 그 페이지에 우리 제품 사진을 더 많이 올리면 어떨까요? 제 생각에 그렇게 하면 우리가 신규 고객을 끌어들이는 데 정말 도움이 될 것 같아서요.

남: 그 말씀이 아마 맞을 겁니다. 우리가 지금은 제품 사진을 정말 충분히 보여주고 있지 않습니다. 조언 감사합니다.

여: 별 말씀을요. 도와 드릴 수 있어서 기쁩니다.

어휘 **be responsible for** ~을 책임지고 있다 **put A in charge of B** A에게 B에 대한 책임을 맡기다 **advertisement** 광고 **create** ~을 만들어내다 **do a great job on** ~을 아주 잘 해내다 **consider** ~을 고려하다 **at the moment** 지금, 현재

24. 대화가 주로 무엇에 관한 것인가?
(A) 계절 할인 행사
(B) 제품 카탈로그
(C) 잡지 기사
(D) 소셜 미디어 페이지

해설 여자가 대화를 시작하면서 매장 소셜 미디어 페이지를 업데이트하는 일을(updating the social media page for our store) 언급한 뒤로 해당 작업과 관련해 이야기하고 있으므로 (D)가 정답이다.

어휘 **seasonal** 계절적인, 계절에 따른 **article** (잡지 등의) 기사

25. 남자가 광고와 관련해 무슨 말을 하는가?
(A) 유명인을 특징으로 한다.
(B) 좋은 평가를 받았다.
(C) 많은 비용이 들어갔다.
(D) 시간 소모적이었다.

해설 대화 초반부에 남자가 자신이 만든 온라인 광고를 점장과 많은 고객들이 마음에 들어 했다고(~ he liked the online advertisement I created. A lot of our customers really liked it too) 알리고 있다. 이는 좋은 평가를 받았다는 뜻이므로 (B)가 정답이다.

어휘 **feature** ~을 특징으로 하다 **celebrity** 유명인 **well received** 좋은 평가를 받은 **cost** ~의 비용이 들다 **time-consuming** 시간 소모적인

Paraphrase he liked the online advertisement / A lot of our customers really liked it too
→ well received

26. 여자가 무엇을 하도록 제안하는가?
(A) 일부 고객에게 설문 조사하는 일
(B) 매장 운영 시간을 변경하는 일
(C) 일부 사진을 추가하는 일
(D) 신제품을 출시하는 일

해설 여자가 무엇을 하도록 제안하는지 묻고 있으므로 여자의 말에 집중해 제안 표현과 함께 제시되는 정보를 찾아야 한다. 여자가 대화 중반부에 제품 사진을 더 많이 올리면 어떨지(How about putting more pictures of our products on the page?) 제안하고 있으므로 (C)가 정답이다.

어휘 **suggest -ing** ~하도록 제안하다 **survey** v. ~에게 설문 조사하다 **add** ~을 추가하다 **launch** ~을 출시하다, ~을 시작하다

Paraphrase putting more pictures
→ Adding some pictures

Questions 27-29 refer to the following conversation with three speakers.

W1: Annie, **27** the plan we've been creating for Wallis Corporation's fundraising banquet is almost complete. But, I'm not sure they've given us a large enough budget for the live band they requested.

W2: I was thinking the same thing. It already cost a lot just to reserve the venue and provide catering.

M: Wait a minute... I don't mean to interrupt, but **28** don't forget that the client said they could make the budget bigger if necessary. They might pay a little bit extra.

W2: Oh, that's a good point, Brad. We should speak to the client about it, Lara. But, **29** let's go out and grab a bite to eat first.

W1: **29** Sure. I know a good place nearby.

여1: 애니 씨, 우리가 월리스 코퍼레이션의 기금 마련 연회를 위해 만들어 오고 있는 계획이 거의 완료된 상태입니다. 하지만, 그쪽에서 요구한 라이브 밴드에 대해 충분히 많은 예산을 우리에게 제공했는지 잘 모르겠습니다.

여2: 저도 같은 생각을 하고 있었어요. 행사장을 예약하고 출장 요리를 제공하는 데에만 이미 많은 비용이 들었어요.

남: 잠시만요... 방해하고 싶은 생각은 아니지만, 그 고객사에서 필요할 경우에 예산을 더 늘릴 수 있다고 말한 것을 잊지 마세요. 그쪽에서 조금 더 추가 비용을 지불할 수도 있습니다.

여2: 아, 좋은 지적입니다, 브래드 씨. 우리가 이 부분과 관련해서 고객사와 얘기해 봐야 해요, 라라 씨. 하지만, 우선 밖에 나가서 간단히 뭐 좀 먹죠.

여1: 좋아요. 근처에 있는 좋은 곳을 알아요.

어휘 create ~을 만들어내다 fundraising 기금 마련, 모금 banquet 연회 complete 완료된 budget 예산 request ~을 요구하다, ~을 요청하다 think the same thing 같은 생각을 하다 cost ~의 비용이 들다 reserve ~을 예약하다 venue 행사장, 개최 장소 provide ~을 제공하다 catering 출장 요리 제공(업) mean to do ~할 생각이다 interrupt 방해하다, (대화 등) ~에 끼어들다 forget that ~임을 잊다 make A B A를 B하게 만들다 if necessary 필요할 경우에 extra 추가(되는 것), 여분(의 것) that's a good point 좋은 지적입니다 grab a bite to eat 간단히 먹다 nearby 근처에

27. 화자들이 어떤 업계에서 일하고 있는 것 같은가?
(A) 제조
(B) 온라인 마케팅
(C) 행사 기획
(D) 재무 컨설팅

해설 여자 한 명이 대화를 시작하면서 자신들이 월리스 코퍼레이션의 기금 마련 연회를 위해 만들어 오고 있는 계획을(~ the plan we've been creating for Wallis Corporation's fundraising banquet ~) 언급하고 있다. 이는 행사 기획 업무를 말하는 것이므로 (C)가 정답이다.

어휘 financial 재무의, 재정의, 금융의 consulting 컨설팅, 상담, 자문

Paraphrase plan we've been creating for Wallis Corporation's fundraising banquet
→ Event planning

28. 남자가 왜 여자들의 대화에 끼어드는가?
(A) 마감 기한 연장을 요청하기 위해
(B) 할당된 업무를 도와주기 위해
(C) 예산 증대에 대해 상기시키기 위해
(D) 행사 장소와 관련해 문의하기 위해

해설 남자가 왜 여자들의 대화에 끼어드는지 묻고 있으므로 남자의 말에 집중해 대화 중간에 끼어들면서 언급하는 정보를 파악해야 한다. 남자가 대화 중반부에 여자들에게 필요할 경우에 예산을 더 늘릴 수 있다고 말한 것을 잊지 말라고(~ don't forget that the client said they could make the budget bigger if necessary) 언급하고 있다. 이는 예산이 늘어날 가능성과 관련해 여자들에게 상기시키는 것이므로 (C)가 정답이다.

어휘 deadline 마감 기한 extension 연장 assist A with B B에 대해 A를 돕다 assignment 할당(된 일) remind A that A에게 ~임을 상기시키다 location 장소, 위치, 지점

29. 여자들이 곧이어 무엇을 할 것인가?
(A) 음식을 조금 먹는 일
(B) 고객과 만나는 일
(C) 보고서를 준비하는 일
(D) 몇몇 가격을 비교하는 일

해설 대화 후반부에 여자 한 명이 밖에 나가서 뭐 좀 먹자고(Let's go out and grab a bite to eat first) 제안하자, 다른 여자도 Sure라고 동의하고 있으므로 (A)가 정답이다.

어휘 meet with (약속하고) ~와 만나다 prepare ~을 준비하다 compare ~을 비교하다

Paraphrase grab a bite to eat
→ Eat some food

Questions 30-32 refer to the following conversation.

W: Hi, Malcolm. Have you heard anything about **30** the ingredients we ordered from the supplier?

M: You mean the herbs and spices we use in many of our dishes?

W: Yes. **31** I was hoping to increase the amounts for some of the items on the order.

M: Oh, it's already on its way.

W: That's too bad. I just realized we might need more oregano and parsley starting next week.

M: I forgot about that, too. **32** A lot of the new dishes we're adding to the menu next week will include oregano. Well, we might have to just make an extra order.

여: 안녕하세요, 말콤 씨. 우리가 공급업체에서 주문한 재료와 관련해 무슨 얘기라도 들으셨나요?

남: 많은 우리 요리에 사용하는 허브와 양념 말씀하시는 거죠?

여: 네. 저는 주문 사항에 일부 제품에 대한 양을 늘릴 수 있기를 바라고 있었어요.

남: 아, 이미 오는 중이네요.

여: 너무 아쉽네요. 다음 주부터 오레가노와 파슬리가 더 필요할지도 모른다는 사실을 막 알게 되었어요.

남: 저도 그 부분에 대해 잊고 있었어요. 우리가 다음 주에 메뉴에 추가하는 많은 새 요리가 오레가노를 포함할 겁니다. 음, 그냥 추가 주문을 해야 할지도 모르겠네요.

어휘 ingredient (음식) 재료, 성분 order v. ~을 주문하다 n. 주문(품) supplier 공급업체 spice 양념 increase ~을 늘

리다, ~을 증가시키다 **amount** 양, 수량 **on one's way** 오는 중인, 가는 중인 **realize (that)** ~라는 사실을 알게 되다, ~임을 깨닫다 **starting + 시점** ~부터 **forget about** ~에 대해 잊다 **add A to B** A를 B에 추가하다 **include** ~을 포함하다 **make an order** 주문하다 **extra** 추가의, 여분의

---

30. 화자들이 무엇을 주문했는가?
(A) 재료
(B) 기구
(C) 식탁보
(D) 접시

해설 화자들이 무엇을 주문했는지 묻고 있으므로 질문에 제시된 order가 언급되는 부분에서 해당 물품의 종류 및 특성 등과 관련된 정보를 찾아야 한다. 여자가 대화 초반부에 자신들이 재료를 주문한(the ingredients we ordered) 사실을 언급하고 있으므로 (A)가 정답이다.

어휘 **utensil** 기구, 도구

31. 남자가 "이미 오는 중입니다"라고 말할 때 무엇을 의미하는가?
(A) 배송 물품이 엉뚱한 주소로 갔다.
(B) 행사가 계획대로 진행될 것이다.
(C) 주문이 수정될 수 없다.
(D) 회의 일정이 재조정되었다.

해설 대화 중반부에 여자가 일부 제품에 대한 양을 늘릴 수 있기를 바라고 있었다고(I was hoping to increase the amounts for some of the items on the order) 알리자, 남자가 '이미 오는 중입니다'라고 대답하는 흐름이다. 이는 이미 배송이 진행 중인 상태이기 때문에 주문량을 늘릴 수 없다는 뜻을 나타내는 말에 해당되므로 (C)가 정답이다.

어휘 **go ahead** 진행되다 **as planned** 계획대로 **amend** ~을 수정하다 **reschedule** ~의 일정을 재조정하다

32. 화자들이 다음 주에 무엇을 할 계획인가?
(A) 새로운 제품을 소개하는 일
(B) 사업을 시작하는 일
(C) 할인을 제공하는 일
(D) 사업 계약을 취소하는 일

해설 화자들이 다음 주에 무엇을 할 계획인지 묻고 있으므로 질문에 제시된 시점 표현 next week과 함께 제시되는 정보를 찾아야 한다. 남자가 대화 후반부에 자신들이 다음 주에 많은 새 요리를 메뉴에 추가한다고(A lot of the new dishes we're adding to the menu next week ~) 언급하고 있다. 이는 새로운 제품을 소개한다는 뜻이므로 (A)가 정답이다.

어휘 **introduce** ~을 소개하다, ~을 도입하다 **launch** ~을 시작하다, ~을 출시하다 **offer** ~을 제공하다 **cancel** ~을 취소하다 **contract** 계약(서)

Paraphrase new dishes we're adding to the menu
→ Introduce new items

Questions 33-35 refer to the following conversation and catalog page.

M: Hi, I'm looking at sports vests in your product catalog, and I'd like to order one hundred for the employees at my company. **33** I'm organizing a sports day to raise money for charity on July 21st, so I'll need them by then.

W: No problem. I'll be able to fill that order for you. Did you choose a specific design for the vests?

M: Yes, **34** I want the one with the large number in a large square in the middle of the vest. I'll just check the product number for you...

W: There's no need for that. I can see the design you mean. By the way, **35** because you're buying so many items, you'll get 15 percent off the total amount.

남: 안녕하세요, 제가 귀사의 제품 카탈로그에서 스포츠 조끼를 살펴보는 중인데, 저희 회사 직원들을 위해 100장 주문하고자 합니다. 제가 7월 21일에 있을 자선 기금 마련을 위한 운동회를 준비하고 있기 때문에, 그때까지 필요할 겁니다.
여: 좋습니다. 그 주문 사항을 이행해 드릴 수 있을 겁니다. 특정 조끼 디자인을 선택하셨나요?
남: 네, 조끼 중앙에 위치한 큰 사각형 안에 큰 숫자가 있는 것을 원합니다. 그 제품 번호를 바로 확인해 드릴게요...
여: 그러실 필요 없습니다. 말씀하시는 디자인을 볼 수 있습니다. 그건 그렇고, 아주 많은 제품을 구입하시기 때문에, 총액에서 15퍼센트 할인을 받으시게 될 것입니다.

스포츠 조끼 디자인

| #124 | #147 | #154 | #172 |

어휘 **vest** 조끼 **organize** ~을 준비하다, ~을 조직하다 **raise money** 돈을 모으다, 모금하다 **charity** 자선 (단체) **then** 그때, 그렇다면, 그런 다음, 그 후에 **fill** ~을 이행하다, ~을 충족하다 **specific** 특정한, 구체적인 **square** 사각형 **by the way** (화제 전환 시) 그건 그렇고, 그런데 **get A percent off B** B에서 A만큼 할인 받다 **total amount** 총액

33. 남자의 말에 따르면, 7월에 무슨 일이 있을 것인가?
(A) 휴가를 떠난다.

(B) 모금 행사를 주최한다.

(C) 교육 과정에 참석한다.

(D) 새로운 사업을 시작한다.

해설 July라는 시점 표현과 함께 제시되는 정보를 찾아야 한다. 남자가 대화 초반부에 7월 21일에 자선 기금을 마련하기 위해 여는 운동회를 준비하고 있다고(I'm organizing a sports day to raise money for charity on July 21st ~) 알리고 있으므로 모금 행사 주최를 뜻하는 (B)가 정답이다.

어휘 **go on vacation** 휴가를 떠나다 **host** ~을 주최하다 **fundraising** 모금, 기금 마련 **launch** ~을 시작하다, ~을 출시하다

Paraphrase organizing a sports day to raise money
→ hosting a fundraising event

34. 시각자료를 보시오. 남자가 어느 제품을 주문할 것인가?

(A) #124

(B) #147

(C) #154

(D) #172

해설 대화 중반부에 남자가 조끼 중앙에 위치한 큰 사각형 안에 큰 숫자가 있는 것을 원한다는(I want the one with the large number in a large square in the middle of the vest) 말로 제품 특징을 설명하고 있다. 시각자료에서 중앙 부분에 큰 사각형이 있고 숫자가 크게 쓰여 있는 것이 왼쪽에서 두 번째에 위치한 #147 제품이므로 (B)가 정답이다.

35. 여자가 남자에게 어떤 제공 서비스와 관련해 말하는가?

(A) 제품이 주문 제작될 수 있다.

(B) 주문이 무료 배송 대상이다.

(C) 무료 선물을 받게 될 것이다.

(D) 구입품이 할인 대상이다.

해설 여자가 대화 맨 마지막 부분에 아주 많은 제품을 구입하기 때문에 총액에서 15퍼센트 할인을 받게 된다고(~ because you're buying so many items, you'll get 15 percent off the total amount) 언급하고 있다. 이는 할인을 받을 수 있는 자격을 충족했다는 뜻이므로 (D)가 정답이다.

어휘 **customize** ~을 주문 제작하다, ~을 맞춤 제작하다 **be eligible for** ~에 대한 대상이다, ~에 대한 자격이 있다(= qualify for) **free** 무료의(= complimentary)

Paraphrase you're buying so many items, you'll get 15 percent off the total amount
→ purchase qualifies for a discount

Questions 36-38 refer to the following conversation and map.

W: Good morning. Welcome to Morrison Manufacturing.

M: Hi. My name is Jerry Sanders. **36** I'm here to fix a faulty printer in your sales department.

W: Yes, we've been expecting you. The sales department is up on the fourth floor, so you'll probably want to take an elevator. **37** I'd suggest taking the one right beside the vending machines, as it goes straight to the sales department.

M: Thanks for the advice.

W: I'll let the sales manager know that you're on your way up. Also, **38** before you go, I'll need you to attach this visitor's tag to your clothing.

여: 안녕하세요. 모리슨 제조사에 오신 것을 환영합니다.

남: 안녕하세요. 제 이름은 제리 샌더스입니다. 귀사 영업부에 결함이 있는 프린터를 고치러 왔습니다.

여: 네, 계속 기다리고 있었습니다. 영업부가 위쪽 4층에 있기 때문에, 아마 엘리베이터를 이용하시는 게 좋을 겁니다. 자판기 바로 옆에 있는 것을 이용하시도록 권해 드리고자 하는데, 영업부로 곧장 가기 때문입니다.

남: 조언 감사합니다.

여: 올라가시는 중이라고 영업부장님께 알려 드리겠습니다. 그리고, 가시기 전에, 옷에 이 방문자 출입증을 부착해 주셔야 할 겁니다.

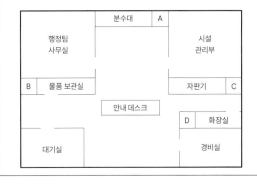

어휘 **fix** ~을 고치다, ~을 바로잡다 **faulty** 결함이 있는, 흠이 있는 **expect** (오기로 한 사람 등) ~을 기다리다 **right** (강조) 바로 **beside** 옆에 **vending machine** 자판기 **go straight to** ~로 곧장 가다 **let A know that** A에게 ~라고 알리다 **on one's way** 가는 중인, 오는 중인 **need A to do** A가 ~할 필요가 있다 **attach** ~을 부착하다, ~을 붙이다 **clothing** 옷, 의류 **administration** 행정 **storage** 보관, 저장 **water fountain** 분수대 **reception desk** 안

36. 남자가 왜 모리슨 제조사를 방문하는가?

(A) 면접에 참석하기 위해

(B) 기기를 수리하기 위해

(C) 용품을 배송하기 위해

(D) 견학하기 위해

해설 대화 초반부에 남자가 영업부에 결함이 있는 프린터를 고치러 왔다는 말로(I'm here to fix a faulty printer in your sales department) 찾아 온 목적을 밝히고 있으므로 (B)가 정답이다.

어휘 **device** 기기, 장치 **supplies** 용품, 물품 **take a tour** 견학하다, 둘러보다

Paraphrase fix a faulty printer

→ repair a device

37. 시각자료를 보시오. 여자가 어느 엘리베이터를 추천하는가?

(A) 엘리베이터 A

(B) 엘리베이터 B

(C) 엘리베이터 C

(D) 엘리베이터 D

해설 여자가 대화 중반부에 자판기 바로 옆에 있는 것을 이용하도록 권한다고(I'd suggest taking the one right beside the vending machines ~) 알리고 있다. 시각자료에서 오른쪽 중앙 부분에 Vending Machines와 함께 C가 표기되어 있으므로 (C)가 정답이다.

38. 남자가 곧이어 무엇을 할 것 같은가?

(A) 옷을 갈아입는 일

(B) 지문을 스캔하는 일

(C) 서명을 제공하는 일

(D) 방문자 출입증을 부착하는 일

해설 대화 맨 마지막 부분에 여자가 남자에게 가기 전에 옷에 방문자 출입증을 부착해야 한다고(~ before you go, I'll need you to attach this visitor's tag to your clothing) 알리고 있으므로 (D)가 정답이다.

어휘 **provide** ~을 제공하다 **signature** 서명 **put on** (몸에) ~을 붙이다, ~을 착용하다

Paraphrase attach this visitor's tag to your clothing

→ Put on a visitor's tag

Part 4

Questions 39-41 refer to the following recorded message.

Thank you for calling the 39 **Albertville tourist information line**. We are happy to help you with any inquiries you might have regarding Albertville and the many activities we have here in our town. 40 **Please be aware that the downtown area is currently undergoing extensive development, and this construction work may cause some disruption to our normal services.** The project is expected to last until August 14. 41 **Please continue to hold if you wish to speak with one of our customer service operators**, who will be happy to provide you with more information about our amenities and landmarks.

앨버트빌 관광 안내 전화에 전화해 주셔서 감사합니다. 저희 앨버트빌 지역 및 이곳 저희 지역의 많은 체험 활동들에 대해 여러분께서 궁금해하시는 것들과 관련해 도와드리게 되어 기쁩니다. 시내 지역에는 현재 광범위한 개발 공사가 진행중이며, 이 공사 작업이 저희의 평소 서비스에 지장을 줄 수도 있다는 점에 유의하시기 바랍니다. 작업은 8월 14일까지 계속될 것으로 예상됩니다. 고객 서비스 상담원 중 한 명과 이야기하고 싶으시면 끊지 말고 기다리시기 바라며, 상담원이 여러분께 저희 지역의 편의시설 및 명소들에 관해 더 많은 정보를 기꺼이 제공해 드릴 것입니다.

어휘 **tourist information line** 관광 안내 전화 **be happy to do** ~하게 되어 기쁘다, 기꺼이 ~하다 **inquiry** 질문, 문의 **regarding** ~에 관하여 **activity** 활동 **town** 소도시, 고장 **be aware that** ~라는 것을 알다, 인식하다 **downtown** 시내 **area** 지역 **currently** 현재 **undergo** ~을 겪다 **extensive** 광범위한 **development** 개발 **construction** 건설 공사 **cause** ~을 야기하다 **disruption** 방해, 중단 **normal** 평소의, 정상적인 **be expected to do** ~할 것으로 예상되다 **last** v. 지속되다 **continue to do** 계속해서 ~하다 **hold** (전화상에서) 기다리다 **operator** 전화 교환원 **provide A with B** A에게 B를 제공하다 **amenities** 편의 시설 **landmark** 주요 장소, 명소

39. 이 메시지는 누구를 대상으로 하겠는가?

(A) 지역 주민들

(B) 여행사 직원들

(C) 잠재 관광객들

(D) 기업 소유주들

해설 메시지 처음에 Albertville tourist information line이라고 밝히며 Albertville 지역 및 그 지역에서 할 수 있는 활동들에 대한 문의사항(any inquiries you might have regarding Albertville and the many activities)에 대해 도와주겠다

고 말하는 것으로 보아 이 메시지는 관광 정보 안내 전화로서 관광객들을 대상으로 한다는 것을 알 수 있다. 따라서 정답은 (C)다.

어휘 **local** 지역의 **resident** 주민 **travel agent** 여행사 직원 **potential** 잠재적인 **tourist** 관광객 **owner** 소유주

40. 화자는 시내 지역에 대해 뭐라고 말하는가?
(A) 매우 붐빈다.
(B) 모든 차량에 대해 폐쇄되어 있다.
(C) 여러 명소를 포함하고 있다.
(D) 공사 중이다.

해설 downtown area가 키워드이므로 이 표현이 언급되는 부분을 놓치지 말아야 한다. 메시지 중반의 Please be aware that the downtown area is currently undergoing extensive development에 downtown area가 언급되는데, 이 부분에서 현재 도시 개발이 진행중임을 알 수 있으므로 (D)가 정답이다.

어휘 **crowded** 붐비는 **closed** 닫힌, 폐쇄된 **vehicle** 차량 **contain** ~을 포함하다 **under construction** 공사 중인

Paraphrase undergoing extensive development
→ under construction

41. 청자들은 더 많은 정보를 알려면 무엇을 해야 하는가?
(A) 이메일을 보낸다.
(B) 전화를 끊지 않고 기다린다.
(C) 웹 사이트를 방문한다.
(D) 다른 번호로 전화한다.

해설 메시지 마지막 부분에서 더 많은 정보를 제공해 줄 고객서비스 직원과 통화하려면 전화를 끊지 말고 기다리라고(continue to hold) 안내하고 있으므로, (B)가 정답이다.

어휘 **stay on the phone[line]** 전화를 끊지 않고 기다리다

Paraphrase continue to hold
→ Stay on the phone

Questions 42-44 refer to the following advertisement.

Boost Nutrition sells a wide variety of products at unbeatable prices. We'll be opening our brand new retail outlet inside the Gateway Mall on February 20, and we hope you stop by to browse our merchandise. **42** You can find all the top brands of vitamins, minerals, and other supplements that will keep you healthy. And, **43** only in our new location, you can find many products from foreign suppliers that you cannot typically find here. So, there's no need to import these yourself anymore. And, **44** if you come down on our opening day, you'll get 10% off anything you purchase.

저희 부스트 뉴트리션은 아주 다양한 제품을 타의 추종을 불허하는 가격에 판매하고 있습니다. 저희가 2월 20일에 게이트웨이 몰 내부에 완전히 새로운 소매 판매점을 개장할 예정이며, 저희 상품을 둘러보실 수 있도록 들러보시기 바랍니다. 여러분을 건강하게 유지해 드릴 최고의 비타민, 무기질, 그리고 기타 보충제 브랜드를 모두 찾으실 수 있습니다. 그리고, 오직 저희 신규 지점에 한해, 일반적으로 이곳에서 찾으실 수 없는 해외 공급업체 제품도 많이 찾으실 수 있습니다. 따라서, 더 이상 이 제품들을 직접 수입하실 필요가 없습니다. 그리고, 개장일에 찾아오시는 경우, 구입하시는 어떤 제품이든 10퍼센트 할인 받으시게 될 것입니다.

어휘 **a wide variety of** 아주 다양한 **unbeatable** 타의 추종을 불허하는, 더 이상 좋을 수 없는 **brand new** 완전히 새로운 **retail outlet** 소매 판매점 **stop by** (잠깐) 들르다 **browse** ~을 둘러보다 **merchandise** 상품 **mineral** 무기질 **supplement** 보충(제) **keep A B** A를 B한 상태로 유지하다 **location** 지점, 위치 **supplier** 공급업체 **typically** 일반적으로, 전형적으로 **no ~ anymore** 더 이상 ~ 아니다 **import** ~을 수입하다 **oneself** (부사처럼 쓰여) 직접, 스스로 **get ~ percent off A** A에서 ~만큼 할인 받다

42. 해당 회사에서 어떤 종류의 제품을 판매하는가?
(A) 스포츠 의류
(B) 피트니스 장비
(C) 건강 보충제
(D) 조리 기구

해설 화자가 담화 중반부에 제품 종류를 언급하면서 비타민, 무기질, 그리고 기타 보충제 브랜드를 모두 찾을 수 있다는(You can find all the top brands of vitamins, minerals, and other supplements ~) 사실을 알리고 있다. 이는 건강 보충제에 해당되는 제품을 말하는 것이므로 (C)가 정답이다.

어휘 **clothing** 의류, 옷 **equipment** 장비 **utensil** 기구, 도구

Paraphrase vitamins, minerals, and other supplements
→ Health supplements

43. 화자의 말에 따르면, 신규 매장과 관련해 무엇이 특별한가?
(A) 수입된 제품을 판매한다.
(B) 보상 프로그램을 제공한다.
(C) 교육 강좌를 제공한다.
(D) 무료로 제품을 배송한다.

해설 담화 중반부에 화자가 신규 지점에 한해 일반적으로 찾을 수 없는 해외 공급업체 제품도 많이 찾을 수 있다고(~ only in our new location, you can find many products from foreign suppliers ~) 언급하는 부분이 있다. 이는 해외에서 수입한 제품을 판매한다는 말과 같으므로 (A)가 정답이다.

어휘 **unique** 특별한, 독특한 **provide** ~을 제공하다(= offer) **reward** 보상 **for free** 무료로

find many products from foreign suppliers
→ sells imported items

44. 청자들이 어떻게 할인 받을 수 있는가?

(A) 대량으로 주문함으로써
(B) 온라인 매장을 방문함으로써
(C) 특정한 날에 쇼핑함으로써
(D) 회원 프로그램에 가입함으로써

해설 화자가 담화 맨 마지막 부분에 개장일에 오면 어떤 제품이든 10퍼센트 할인 받는다고(~ if you come down on our opening day, you'll get 10% off anything you purchase) 알리고 있다. 이는 특정한 날에만 쇼핑할 경우에 적용되는 혜택을 말하는 것이므로 (C)가 정답이다.

어휘 **place an order** 주문하다 **bulk** 대량의 **specific** 특정한, 구체적인

Paraphrase come down on our opening day / you'll get 10% off anything
→ shopping on a specific day

Questions 45-47 refer to the following telephone message.

Hi, Tim. This is Nancy from the personnel department. I've been checking out various car rental firms based at the airport you'll be arriving at on your business trip. Once I compare their different rates and benefits, **45** I'll go ahead and rent a car for you. **46** I know you asked me to get you a nice one, but please try to understand, we have a limited budget. Oh, and by the way, **47** I'll be out of the office tomorrow, so if you need to get in touch with me, just give me a call on my mobile phone.

안녕하세요, 팀 씨. 저는 인사부의 낸시입니다. 출장 가시는 날에 도착하실 예정인 공항을 기반으로 하는 다양한 자동차 대여 업체들을 계속 확인해 보는 중입니다. 일단 제가 서로 다른 요금 및 혜택들을 비교하는 대로, 어서 진행해서 자동차를 한 대 대여해 드리겠습니다. 저에게 좋은 것으로 구해 달라고 요청하신 건 알지만, 양해해 주셨으면 하는 점은, 우리가 예산이 제한적이라는 사실입니다. 아, 그건 그렇고, 제가 내일 사무실에 있지 않을 것이기 때문에, 저에게 연락하셔야 하는 경우, 그냥 제 휴대전화기로 전화 주시기 바랍니다.

어휘 **personnel** 인사(부) **check out** ~을 확인하다 **various** 다양한 **rental** 대여, 임대 **firm** 업체, 회사 **based at** ~을 기반으로 하는, ~에 본사를 둔 **once** 일단 ~하는 대로, ~하자마자 **compare** ~을 비교하다 **rate** 요금, 비율, 등급, 속도 **benefit** 혜택, 이득 **go ahead and do** 어서 진행해서 ~하다 **rent** ~을 대여하다, ~을 임대하다 **get A B** A에게

B를 구해 주다, A에게 B를 갖다 주다 **try to do** ~하려 하다 **limited** 제한적인, 한정된 **budget** 예산 **by the way** (화제 전환 시) 그건 그렇고, 그런데 **get in touch with** ~와 연락하다 **give A a call** A에게 전화하다

45. 화자는 청자가 무엇을 하는 데 도움을 주는가?

(A) 항공편을 예약하는 일
(B) 차량을 대여하는 일
(C) 객실을 예약하는 일
(D) 고객에게 연락하는 일

해설 화자가 청자에게 어떤 도움을 주는지 묻고 있으므로 상대방을 위해 하는 일과 관련된 정보를 찾는 데 집중해야 한다. 화자가 현재 진행 중인 업무를 언급하면서 상대방을 위해 자동차를 한 대 대여해 주겠다고(I'll go ahead and rent a car for you) 알리고 있으므로 (B)가 정답이다.

어휘 **book** ~을 예약하다 **vehicle** 차량 **reserve** ~을 예약하다 **contact** ~에게 연락하다

Paraphrase rent a car
→ Rent a vehicle

46. 화자가 "우리가 예산이 제한적이라는 사실입니다"라고 말할 때 무엇을 암시하는가?

(A) 청자가 할인을 신청해야 한다.
(B) 청자가 더 저렴한 선택권을 예상해야 한다.
(C) 지출 수당이 제공될 것이다.
(D) 티켓이 이코노미 좌석용이다.

해설 화자가 담화 중반부에 청자에게 좋은 것으로 구해 달라고 요청한 사실을 언급한 뒤로(I know you asked me to get you a nice one), 양해를 구하는 말과 함께 '예산이 제한적입니다'라고 알리는 흐름이다. 이는 비용이 많이 드는 것을 선택할 수 없다는 뜻으로 하는 말이므로 (B)가 정답이다.

어휘 **apply for** ~을 신청하다, ~에 지원하다 **expect** ~을 예상하다 **spending** 지출, 소비 **allowance** 수당 **provide** ~을 제공하다

47. 화자가 왜 휴대전화기로 연락하도록 요청하는가?

(A) 자신의 이메일 비밀 번호를 잊어버렸다.
(B) 사무실에 있지 않을 것이다.
(C) 사무실 전화기가 결함이 있다.
(D) 컴퓨터가 오작동했다.

해설 담화 마지막 부분에 화자가 내일 사무실에 있지 않을 것이기 때문에 연락해야 하는 경우에 휴대전화기로 전화해 달라고(~ I'll be out of the office tomorrow, so if you need to get in touch with me, just give me a call on my mobile phone) 요청하고 있으므로 (B)가 정답이다.

어휘 **request to do** ~하도록 요청하다 **forget** ~을 잊다 **faulty** 결함이 있는, 흠이 있는 **malfunction** 오작동하다

Paraphrase I'll be out of the office
→ She will not be in the office.

Questions 48-50 refer to the following instructions and flowchart.

Let's start with some good news. The online store we just launched has already increased our overall sales by 15%, and **48** **our Coolwave lamps were even featured in a major design magazine.** With this success, though, we need to make a change to the online payment process. On the flowchart you'll notice **49** **we've added a step between submitting shipping information and choosing a payment option.** This step will better protect our customers, though they will need to provide some extra information to their user profiles. **50** **There has been some concern over the increased risk of identity theft,** so this additional step should ensure that our customers have no need to worry when shopping on our site.

좋은 소식으로 시작해 보겠습니다. 우리가 막 시작한 온라인 매장이 이미 우리의 전반적인 매출을 15퍼센트만큼 증가시켰으며, 우리의 쿨웨이브 램프 제품은 심지어 주요 디자인 잡지 한 곳에 특집으로 실리기도 했습니다. 하지만 이와 같은 성공과 함께, 우리는 온라인 비용 지불 과정에 변화를 줘야 합니다. 순서도를 보시면 배송 정보를 제출하는 것과 지불 방식을 선택하는 것 사이에 한 단계를 추가했음을 알 수 있으실 겁니다.
우리 고객들은 각자의 사용자 프로필에 일부 추가 정보를 제공해야 하겠지만 이 단계가 그들을 더 잘 보호해 줄 것입니다. 신분 도용에 대한 위험성이 증가된 것에 관한 우려가 있어 왔기 때문에 이 추가적인 단계는 고객들이 우리 사이트에서 쇼핑할 때 걱정할 필요가 없다는 점을 확실히 해줄 것입니다.

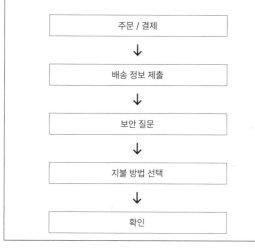

어휘 **launch** ~을 시작하다, ~에 착수하다 **overall** 전반적인 **even** 심지어 **feature** ~을 특집으로 싣다 **make a change to** ~을 변경하다, 바꾸다 **payment** 비용 지불 **process** 과정 **flowchart** 순서도 **notice** ~을 알아차리

다, 인식하다 **add** ~을 추가하다 **step** 단계 **between A and B** A와 B 사이에 **shipping** 배송 **option** 선택(권) **protect** ~을 보호하다 **extra** 추가의, 별도의 **concern** 우려, 걱정 **over** ~에 대해 **risk** 위험(성) **identity theft** 신분 도용 **additional** 추가적인 **ensure that** ~임을 확실히 하다 **worry** 걱정하다 **checkout** 계산대, (웹페이지) 주문/결제 **confirmation** 확인

48. 화자는 쿨웨이브 램프에 관해 무슨 말을 하는가?
(A) 생산하기에 더 저렴해졌다.
(B) 디자인 경연대회에서 우승했다.
(C) 잡지에 소개되었다.
(D) 모든 지점에서 품절되었다.

해설 Coolwave lamp라는 명칭이 질문의 핵심이므로 이 명칭이 제시되는 부분에서 단서를 찾아야 한다. 담화 시작 부분에 Coolwave lamps 제품이 주요 디자인 잡지 한 곳에 특집으로 실렸다는 사실을(our Coolwave Lamps were even featured in a major design magazine) 알리고 있으므로 (C)가 정답임을 알 수 있다.

어휘 **produce** ~을 생산하다 **win** ~에서 우승하다 **appear** 나타나다, 보이다 **sell out** 품절되다, 매진되다 **location** 지점, 위치

Paraphrase were featured in a major design magazine
→ It appeared in a magazine.

49. 시각자료를 보시오. 화자의 말에 다르면, 최근에 어느 단계가 추가되었는가?
(A) 주문/결제
(B) 배송 정보 제출
(C) 보안 관련 질문
(D) 지불 방식 선택

해설 새로 추가된 단계를 묻고 있으므로 미리 각 단계를 확인해 둔 후에 담화에서 특별히 언급되는 단계의 순서를 파악해야 한다. 담화 중반부에 배송 성보를 제출하는 것과 지불 방식을 선택하는 것 사이에 한 단계를 추가했다고(we've added a step between submitting shipping information and choosing a payment option) 한다. 시각자료에서 이 두 단계 사이에 위치한 것이 Security Question이므로 (C)가 정답이다.

어휘 **recently** 최근에

50. 화자는 무슨 우려 사항을 언급하는가?
(A) 해외 배송 비용이 너무 비싸다.
(B) 일부 제품들이 재고가 없다.
(C) 신분 도용 위험이 높아졌다.
(D) 계산 과정이 너무 헷갈린다.

해설 우려 사항을 묻고 있으므로 질문에 제시된 concern을 비롯해 걱정을 나타내는 표현이 제시되는 부분에서 단서를 찾아야 한다. 담화의 끝부분에 신분 도용에 대한 위험성이 증가된 것에 관

한 우려가 있다고(There has been some concern over the increased risk of identity theft) 말하는 부분을 통해 (C)가 정답임을 알 수 있다.

어휘 out of stock 재고가 없는 confusing 헷갈리게 하는, 혼란스럽게 하는

Paraphrase increased risk
→ higher risk

Part 5

51.
정답 (B)

해석 만약 그 직무에 관심이 있으시다면, 귀하의 이력서를 사무엘 존슨 씨 에게 보내주십시오.

해설 타동사 send 뒤에 명사 목적어가 있으므로 빈칸에는 이 명사를 수식할 수 있는 대명사가 들어가야 한다. 따라서 소유격 (B) your이 정답이다.

어휘 be interested in ~에 관심이 있다 position 직무, 일자리 résumé 이력서

52.
정답 (A)

해석 올해 열리는 자동차 박람회에 대해 다른 행사 장소가 보통 사용된 곳에 대한 대안으로 제안되었다.

해설 부정관사와 전치사 사이에 빈칸이 있으므로 빈칸은 단수명사 자리이다. 따라서 (A) alternative가 정답이다.

어휘 venue 행사 장소 auto expo 자동차 박람회 alternative n. 대안 a. 대체 가능한 alternatively 그 대신에 alternativeness 대안이 있음, 대체 가능함

53.
정답 (D)

해석 오찬 행사를 준비하는 데 어떤 직원이라도 자원한다면, 출장 요리 서비스를 이용할 필요가 없어서 운영비를 절감할 수 있을 것이다.

해설 접속사와 명사 사이에 빈칸이 있으므로 빈칸은 명사를 수식할 형용사 자리이다. 그런데 빈칸 뒤에 제시된 명사가 단수이므로 단수 명사를 수식할 수 있는 부정형용사 (D) any가 정답이다.

어휘 volunteer to do ~하도록 자원하다, 자원해서 ~하다 luncheon 오찬 not have to do ~할 필요가 없다 catering 출장 요리 (서비스) save ~을 절약하다 operating costs 운영비

54.
정답 (D)

해석 회사 대표는 새 사무실 부지로 제안된 장소가 너무 불편한 곳에 위치해 있다는 이유로 거절했다.

해설 빈칸이 부사와 과거분사 사이에 위치해 있으므로 빈칸은 부사의 수식을 받으면서 과거분사를 수식할 수 있는 부사 자리이다. 따라서 (D) inconveniently가 정답이다.

어휘 reject ~을 거절하다, 거부하다 proposed 제안된 site 부지, 장소 inconveniently 불편하게 located 위치한, 자리잡은

55.
정답 (D)

해석 존스 씨는 향후 참고용으로 안전한 장소에 보관해 두기 위해서, 그의 고객에게 계약서를 인쇄해 두어야 한다고 조언했다.

해설 빈칸 앞에 주장/명령/요구/제안/충고 등의 의미를 나타내는 동사 advise가 있으므로 that절의 동사 자리인 빈칸에 동사원형이 와야 한다. 따라서 (D) print가 정답이다.

어휘 advise ~에게 조언하다 client 고객 reference 참조

56.
정답 (A)

해석 그 소프트웨어 개발팀이 몇 주 동안 추가 시간을 들였기 때문에, 그들은 빠듯한 마감기한을 충족할 수 있었다.

해설 콤마 앞뒤로 주어와 동사를 포함한 두 개의 절이 연결되어 있으므로 빈칸은 접속사 자리이다. 소프트웨어 개발팀이 열심히 노력한 것은 원인에, 마감기한을 충족한 것은 결과에 해당하므로 이유를 나타내는 (A) Because가 정답이다.

어휘 put in ~을 넣다, 담다 tight 빡빡한, 빠듯한 although 비록 ~일지라도 despite ~임에도 불구하고

57.
정답 (D)

해석 킴&청 어소시에이츠의 변호사들은 중국에서 신규 고객들을 유치하기 위해 새로운 법률 서비스를 마케팅하는 것을 고려했다.

해설 동사 considered 다음에 빈칸이 있고 빈칸 다음에 명사구가 이어지고 있다. 동사 consider는 동명사를 목적어로 취하는 동사이므로 (D) marketing이 정답이다.

어휘 market v. 홍보하다, 시장 활동을 벌이다 n. 시장 legal 법률의, 합법적인 attract ~을 끌어 모으다, ~의 마음을 끌다

58.
정답 (D)

해석 불리한 상황에서 매우 훌륭하게 수행하는 그 팀의 능력은 회장에게 정말로 깊은 인상을 주었다.

해설 빈칸 앞에 있는 동사 perform은 자동사와 타동사 둘 다 가능하므로 빈칸에는 부사 또는 명사가 올 수 있다. 명사 exception을 목적어 자리에 넣어 해석하면 '예외를 수행하다'라는 의미가 되어 어색해지므로 부사 (D) exceptionally가 정답이다.

어휘 perform 수행하다 adverse 불리한, 부정적인 circumstance 상황 exceptional 훌륭한 exception

예외 **except** v. ~을 제외하다 prep. ~을 제외하고는 conj. ~라는 점만 제외하면, ~라는 것 외에는

59.

정답 (C)

해석 페가수스 노트북 컴퓨터는 여러 최고급 부품을 포함하고 있음에도 불구하고 가격이 알맞다.

해설 빈칸에 쓰일 형용사는 노트북 컴퓨터 제품이 지닌 특징과 관련된 의미를 나타내야 하며, 전치사 despite 이하 부분에서 말하는 여러 최고급 부품을 포함하고 있다는 점과 대비되는 특징에 해당되어야 하므로 '가격이 알맞은' 등을 뜻하는 (C) affordable이 정답이다.

어휘 **despite** ~에도 불구하고 **top-of-the-line** 최고급의, 최상급의 **component** 부품 **confident** 확신하는, 자신감 있는 **knowledgeable** 아는 것이 많은, 박식한 **affordable** 가격이 알맞은, 구입할 수 있는 **apparent** 분명한, 명백한

60.

정답 (A)

해석 마케팅 부장들은 최신 시장 경향을 잘 알아 두기 위해서 주기적으로 비즈니스 잡지를 읽어야 한다.

해설 타동사 read 뒤에 명사 목적어 business가 위치해 있으나 그 의미가 '사업을 읽다'라는 의미가 되어 어색하므로, business와 빈칸이 복합명사로서 하나의 목적어가 되어야 한다. 따라서 선택지 중 타동사 read의 대상이 될 수 있는 명사가 필요하므로 '신문, 잡지'라는 의미의 (A) journals가 정답이다.

어휘 **periodically** 주기적으로, 정기적으로 **journal** 신문, 잡지 **keep abreast of** ~의 최근 정황을 잘 챙겨 알아 두다 **journalism** 저널리즘 **journalist** 기자 **journalistic** 기자의

61.

정답 (C)

해석 그랜트 씨가 내년에 위글러 사에서 은퇴할 때쯤이면, 그는 회사에서 33년 동안 일하게 되는 것이다.

해설 「By the time 주어 + 동사」 구문에서 현재시제 동사 (retires)가 쓰이면 주절에는 미래완료시제 동사를 사용해야 한다. 따라서 (C) will have served가 정답이다.

어휘 **retire from** ~에서 은퇴하다 **serve** 근무하다

62.

정답 (A)

해석 오늘 강연자께서는 광고팀 직원들이 새로운 텔레비전 광고에 관한 자신의 생각들을 임원진과 나누는 방법들에 대해 논의할 예정입니다.

해설 문장에 이미 동사가 있으므로 빈칸은 준동사 자리이다. 또한, for 전치사구로 행위 주체를 나타낼 때 그 뒤에 to부정사로 행

위를 말하므로 (A) to share가 정답이다.

어휘 **discuss** ~을 논의하다 **way to do** ~하는 방법 **share** ~을 나누다, 공유하다 **commercial** 광고 (방송) **executive** 임원, 간부

63.

정답 (D)

해석 모든 부서들은 조달계약에 관한 새로운 정책들을 숙지하고, 반드시 각자의 내부 문서를 업데이트해야 한다.

해설 빈칸 앞에 완전한 문장이 있고, 빈칸과 명사구, 그리고 접속사 and와 명령문 형식의 절로 문장이 구성되어 있다. 따라서 빈칸은 빈칸 앞뒤에 위치한 두 개의 명사구를 연결할 전치사 자리인데 문맥상 '~에 관한 정책'이 자연스러우므로 (D) concerning이 정답이다.

어휘 **be aware of** ~을 알다 **procurement** 조달, 입수 **make sure to do** 반드시 ~하다 **internal** 내부의 **documentation** 서류, 문서 **whereas** ~인 반면에 **besides** prep. ~뿐만 아니라 adv. 게다가

64.

정답 (A)

해석 일류 통신 회사로서의 평판을 유지하기 위해, 우리는 시장의 현재 경향을 아주 자세히 주시해야 한다.

해설 빈칸 뒤에 제시된 '현재 경향'을 목적어로 취할 수 있으면서 의미가 어울리는 타동사가 빈칸에 와야 하는데 '경향을 자세히 주시하다'라는 뜻이 가장 자연스러우므로 (A) monitor가 정답이다.

어휘 **maintain** ~을 유지하다 **reputation** 평판 **leading** 선두적인, 일류의 **monitor** ~을 관찰하다, 감시하다, 주시하다 **current** 현재의 **extremely** 매우, 극도로 **closely** 자세히 **focus** 집중하다 **adhere** 들러붙다, 고착되다 **achieve** ~을 이루다, 달성하다

65.

정답 (A)

해석 최고 재무담당관으로서, 부르노 씨는 회사에서 지출하고 입금된 모든 금전 기록을 유지해야만 한다.

해설 빈칸 뒤에 명사구와 콤마, 그 뒤로 주어와 동사로 구성된 완전한 절이 있으므로 빈칸은 전치사 자리이다. 최고 재무담당관은 브루노 씨의 신분을 나타내므로 '~로서'라는 신분이나 자격을 나타내는 (A) As가 정답이다.

어휘 **chief** 주요한 **keep track of** ~의 진로를 쫓다, 놓치지 않고 따라가다 **throughout** ~내내, 도처에

66.

정답 (A)

해석 대다수의 기조 연설자들은 다가오는 기술 컨퍼런스에서 소셜 네트워킹 발전에 대해서 연설할 것이다.

어휘 integrate ~을 통합하다 afford ~할 여유가 있다

69.

정답 (B)

해석 (A) 우승 상품은 고급 호텔에서의 2박 서비스가 될 것입니다.

(B) **페르난데즈 씨께서는 또한 매력적인 테라스 공사도 총괄 하도록 의뢰 받으셨습니다.**

(C) 그 건축 회사가 한 백화점에 대한 설계도를 개발하고 있습니다.

(D) 최고의 디자인에 대한 연례 시상식 행사가 있을 것입니다.

해설 빈칸 앞 문장에는 페르난데즈 씨가 디자인을 구상한 사실이, 빈칸 뒤에는 방문객들이 테라스에서 즐길 수 있는 일이 언급되어 있다. 따라서 추가 접속부사 also와 함께 페르난데즈 씨가 테라스 공사를 의뢰 받은 사실을 말하는 문장이 자연스러우므로 (B)가 정답이다.

어휘 winning prize 우승 상품 luxurious 고급의 plan 설계도 awards ceremony 시상식

70.

정답 (B)

해설 빈칸 앞뒤에 위치한 명사구 the remodeling과 the main exhibition hall 사이의 의미 관계로 볼 때 '전시회장의 개조 공사'라는 뜻이 되어야 알맞으므로 '~의, ~에 대한' 등의 의미로 소유나 대상 등을 나타낼 때 사용하는 (B) of가 정답이다.

71-74.

이제 당신은 집의 편안함을 떠나지 않고서 대부분의 쇼핑을 할 수 있다. 다양한 회사들의 온라인 안내 책자에서 가전이나 가구를 구매할 수 있다. 책을 온라인으로 주문할 수 있고, 혹은 심지어 책을 당신의 전자책 장치에 **71** 직접 다운로드할 수도 있다.

72 그러나, 점점 더 많은 판매자들이 그들의 웹 사이트에 온라인 쇼핑을 추가하고 있는 반면에, 많은 이들은 여전히 사이버 공간에 뛰어드는 것을 꺼려하고 있다. 예를 들어, 어떤 이들은 새로운 소파를 인터넷을 통해 사려고 하겠지만, 대다수 사람들은 아마도 그것을 직접 보고, 실제 구매를 실행하기 전에 시험 삼아 앉아 보기를 원할 것이다. 몇몇 기업에게는 온라인 쇼핑 제공이 추가적인 배달 비용의 발생을 포함할 수 있는데, 그것은 이익을 감소시키거나, 매장에서 지불하는 것보다 온라인 주문에 대해 더 많은 금액을 고객들에게 청구하는 것을 의미한다.

온라인 쇼핑으로 이동하는 것은 또한 인구학적 현실에 의해 늦추어 질 수 있다. **73** 여러 서구 국가에는 대부분 노령화 인구가 있다. 몇몇 나라에서는, 시민 대다수가 은퇴연령에 다가가거나 혹은 지났다. 이런 사람들은 종종 기술을 아주 잘 알지 **74** 못하지만, 그들은 많은 기업 고객층의 상당 부분을 차지한다.

어휘 without -ing ~하지 않고서 comfort 안락, 편안함 appliances 가전(제품들) vendor 판매자 be reluctant

---

해설 빈칸 앞뒤에 두 개의 명사구가 제시되어 있으므로 빈칸은 전치사 자리이다. 컨퍼런스는 연설을 하는 장소의 개념이므로 장소를 나타내는 전치사 (A) at이 정답이다.

어휘 the majority of 대다수의 keynote speaker 기조 연설자 upcoming 다가오는

Part 6

67-70.

빌바오에 위치한 뮤지오 델 소롤라의 신임 관장 마누엘 살리나스와 프란체스카 살리나스가 예술을 사랑하는 모든 분들께 이 미술관 재개장에 함께 하시도록 요청 드립니다. 미술관 관장은 뮤지오 델 소롤라에 대대적인 변화를 **67** 만들어냈습니다.

유명 건축가 호세 페르난데즈에 의해 구상된 새로운 실내 구조 설계는 전통적인 바스크 석조물이 **68** 통합된 현대적인 디자인 장식을 특징으로 합니다. **69** 페르난데즈 씨께서는 또한 매력적인 테라스 공사도 총괄하도록 의뢰 받으셨습니다. 뮤지오 델 소롤라 방문객들께서는 미술관의 다채로운 정원을 내려다보는 동안 이 테라스에서 음료와 엄선된 간식을 즐기실 수 있을 것입니다.

게다가, **70** 중앙 전시회장의 개조 공사로 인해 현대적이면서도 미묘한 전시 조명과 대형 채광 창문들이 도입되었습니다.

이번 행사 입장권은 미술관 웹 사이트에서 구매 가능합니다.

어휘 join ~와 함께 하다 make a change 변화를 주다, 변경하다 structural design 구조 설계 conceive ~을 구상하다 renowned 유명한 feature ~을 특징으로 하다 flourishes n. 장식 stonework 석조물 commission v. ~을 의뢰하다 oversee ~을 감독하다 selected 엄선된, 선택된 overlook ~을 내려다보다 A yet B A하면서도 B한 subtle 미묘한, 미세한 skylight window 채광창

67.

정답 (D)

해설 주어 뒤로 빈칸과 명사구, 그리고 전치사구만 있으므로 빈칸에는 문장의 동사가 필요하다. 또한 뒤에 이어지는 내용을 보면 특정한 특징을 갖춘 사실과 함께 테라스와 조명과 채광 창문들이 설치된 점을 설명하고 있다. 따라서 이미 변화가 만들어진 상태임을 알 수 있으므로 과거에 발생되어 현재까지 지속되어 온 상태를 나타낼 때 사용하는 현재완료시제 (D) have made가 정답이다.

68.

정답 (A)

해설 빈칸 바로 앞뒤 부분을 보면 건물의 특징으로 현대적인 디자인 요소와 전통적인 디자인 요소가 언급되어 있으므로 이 두 가지 요소들이 통합되어 있다는 의미가 되어야 가장 자연스럽다. 따라서 '~을 통합하다'를 뜻하는 integrate의 과거분사인 (A)

to do ~하기를 꺼려하다 **for instance** 예를 들어 **say** (감탄사) 여, 이봐요 **in person** 직접 **commit** ~을 실행하다 **incur** ~을 초래하다, 발생하다 **charge** 요금을 청구하다 **shift** 이동 **demographic** 인구통계의, 인구학의 **savvy** 잘 아는, 상식 있는 **make up** ~을 차지하다 **bulk** 대부분

71.

정답 (D)

해설 동사의 목적어와 전치사 사시에 위치한 빈칸은 전치사를 수식할 부사 자리이므로 (D) directly가 정답이다.

72.

정답 (A)

해설 빈칸 앞에는 인터넷 쇼핑이 다양하고 활발하다는 내용이, 빈칸 뒤에는 온라인 쇼핑의 어려움과 단점이 부각되어 나온다. 따라서 상반된 내용을 이끌 수 있는 '그러나'라는 뜻의 (A) However가 정답이다.

어휘 **however** 그러나 **therefore** 따라서, 그래서 **in fact** 사실 **in addition** 게다가

73.

정답 (B)

해석 (A) 예를 들어, 고속 인터넷은 몇몇 지역에서는 이용이 불가하다.
(B) 여러 서구 국가에는 대부분 노령화 인구가 있다.
(C) 이것은 몇몇 고객들에 대해서 더 비싸게 만든다.
(D) 매년 출시된 신제품의 수는 증가하고 있다.

해설 빈칸 앞에는 인구학적 현실이, 빈칸 뒤에 내수 인구가 은퇴연령에 다가가거나 넘어 섰다는 내용이 제시되어 있으므로 빈칸에 들어갈 내용은 노령화 인구와 관련된 내용이어야 한다. 따라서 서구 국가에 노령화 인구가 있다는 사실을 언급한 (B)가 정답이다.

어휘 **available** 이용 가능한 **mostly** 대부분, 대개 **aging** 노화하는, 나이가 들어가는

74.

정답 (C)

해설 빈칸 앞뒤로 주어와 동사를 포함한 두 개의 절이 있기 때문에 빈칸에 접속사가 와야 한다. 따라서 선택지 중 유일한 접속사인 (C) yet이 정답이다.

어휘 **otherwise** 그렇지 않으면 **still** 여전히 **despite** ~에도 불구하고

Part 7

75-76.

리드버그 타임즈

랜싱 재단에서 지역주민들을 봄 음악 축제에 초대합니다.
에이미 딕슨 작성

5월 26일 일요일, 음악 페스티벌이 리드버그 시내에 있는 아름다운 풍경의 필그림 공원에서 개최될 것입니다.

'봄 멜로디 축제'라는 이름의 이 행사는 리드버그 지역과 주변 마을 및 도시들의 많은 문제들을 해결하고자 열심히 노력해 온 랜싱 재단에 의해 준비되고 있습니다. **75** 이 축제의 티켓 수익금은 딜버리 초등학교와 롬포드 고등학교의 새 컴퓨터 구입에 쓰여질 것입니다.

이 지역의 상공인이자 기업가인 키스 렛저 씨가 축제의 개회사를 할 것입니다. 렛저 씨는 이 재단의 노력에 대한 지원을 아주 확실하게 언급해 왔습니다. **76** 그의 연설은 리드버그 도시 안팎의 사회적이고 경제적인 문제에 대해서 더욱 관심을 가지도록 지역공동체의 많은 주민들을 고무시켰습니다.

이 축제의 티켓은 행사 당일에 필그림 공원에서 구매 가능합니다.

어휘 **foundation** 재단 **beautifully-landscaped** 아름다운 풍경의 **organize** ~을 준비하다, ~을 조직하다 **surrounding** 주변의 **proceeds** 수익금 **entrepreneur** 기업가 **outspoken** 확실하게 말하는, 당당하게 말하는 **endeavor** 노력, 시도 **inspire** 영감을 주다 **take interest in** ~에 관심을 가지다

75. 이 기사는 주로 무엇에 관한 것인가?
(A) 조경사업 계획
(B) 모금 행사
(C) 공예 박람회
(D) 길거리 퍼레이드

정답 (B)

해설 두 번째 단락에 축제 공연 수익금이 고등학교 새 컴퓨터를 구입하는데 쓰일 것이라고(Proceeds from festival tickets will go toward buying new computers) 언급되었으므로 모금 행사에 대한 기사라는 것을 알 수 있다. 따라서 (B)가 정답이다.

어휘 **landscaping** 조경 **arts and crafts fair** 공예 박람회 **fundraising** 모금

76. 기사에 따르면, 렛저 씨는 어떻게 랜싱 재단에 도움을 주었는가?
(A) 몇 가지 지역 행사를 조직했다.
(B) 지역 학교를 위해 새로운 컴퓨터를 구매했다.
(C) 리드버그 타임즈에 지지하는 기사를 썼다.
(D) 지역 문제에 대한 대중의 인식을 끌어올렸다.

정답 (D)

해설 세 번째 단락에 렛저 씨의 연설이 리드버그의 시민들에게 영감을 주고 주변 문제에 관심을 갖게 했다는(His speeches have inspired many members of the community to take more interest in social and economic problems in and around Reedburg) 말이 있는데 이는 대중의 인식을 끌어 올렸다고 여길 수 있으므로 (D)가 정답이다.

어휘 organize ~을 조직하다 supportive 지지하는 public awareness 대중 인식

77-79.

> 79 존 사익스 시 의원 귀하
>
> 시청,
> 파버빌, OH 45820
>
> 사익스 씨에게,
>
> 제가 메인 스트리트의 교통 흐름 패턴을 변경하고자 하는 제안을 지지한다는 점을 알려드리고 싶습니다. 제 식당은 도심 중심구역에 있으며, 저는 그곳에 있는 모든 업체들이 이 변화를 통해 혜택을 볼 것이라고 믿습니다.
>
> 제가 이해하기로는, 우리 시는 도심을 형성하는 네 블록을 위해 메인 스트리트를 일방 통행로로 만들자고 제안하고 있습니다. 여기에는 거리를 좁혀서 각도 주차가 이루어지게 하는 방안도 포함될 것이고, 그런 주차 방식은 물론 더 많은 차들을 수용할 공간을 만들어 줄 것입니다. 인도 또한 넓어질 수 있습니다.
>
> 제 견해는 도심 지역에 주차 공간이 너무 부족하다는 것이며, 이 상황에 도움이 될 만한 것은 무엇이든 환영 받을 것입니다. 저는 또한 78 보행자 통행량을 더 늘리는 것이 경기를 부양하는 데 도움이 될 것이라고 믿습니다. 77 주로 관광 도시로서, 우리의 경제의 대부분이 가볍게 들르는 방문객들에게 의존하고 있으며, 그들이 걸어 다니도록 장려하면 그들이 더 많은 것을 발견하고 더 많이 구매하게 됩니다.
>
> 시 외곽 센테니얼 스퀘어 지역의 식당가에서 사업을 하는 지인들이 몇 있는데, 그들 모두 도보 통행량이 증가하면서 자신들의 사업이 커졌다고 말합니다. 그것은 그들이 중앙 주차 공간을 늘리고 보행자 전용 구역을 설치함으로써 가능했습니다. 그들은 또한 더 많은 나무들을 심고 화단을 조성하기 시작했습니다.
>
> 이런 점에서 볼 때, 저는 이 거리들에 대한 어떠한 변화도 우리가 내는 재산세를 사용하는 훌륭한 방법이 될 것이라 믿으며, 79 의원님께서 다음 주 회의에서 변경 제안에 대해 찬성표를 던져 주시도록 요청 드리는 바입니다. 이 문제에 관심을 가져 주셔서 감사합니다.
>
> 안녕히 계십시오.
>
> 로날드 그린
> 웨스트 사이드 그릴 소유주

어휘 proposed 제안된 traffic flow 교통 흐름 profit from ~로부터 혜택을 입다 comprise ~을 구성하다 angle

parking 각도 주차, 비스듬한 주차 institute ~을 실행에 옮기다 result in ~라는 결과를 낳다 sidewalk 인도 pedestrian 보행자 boost ~을 증대하다 depend on ~에 의존하다 casual visitor 어쩌다 오는 손님, 우연한 방문객 associate 동료 flower box 화단 property tax 재산세 vote for ~에 찬성표를 던지다

77. 파버빌에 대해 암시된 것은 무엇인가?
(A) 주차 요금이 최근 인상되었다.
(B) 손님들을 잘 끌어들이지 못한다.
(C) 많은 업체들이 문을 닫고 있다.
(D) 열악한 대중 교통 시스템을 가지고 있다.

정답 (B)

해설 세 번째 문단에 파버빌이 주로 관광 도시로서 경제 대부분이 가볍게 들르는 방문객들에게 의존하고 있다고(As a mainly tourist town, most of our business depends on casual visitors) 알리는 부분을 보면 이 도시의 수입이 주로 관광업에서 나오는 것을 알 수 있으므로 (B)가 정답이다.

어휘 attract ~을 끌어 모으다

78. 그린 씨는 무엇이 사업을 증대시킬 것이라고 생각하는가?
(A) 시의 관광명소들을 광고하기
(B) 시의 모든 공원을 재건하기
(C) 더 많은 업체들에 투자하기
(D) 사람들이 돌아다니도록 장려하기

정답 (D)

해설 세 번째 단락에서 더 많은 보행자 통행량을 늘리는 것이 사업을 증대하는 데 도움이 될 것이라고(encouraging more pedestrian traffic will help boost business) 언급하고 있으므로 (D)가 정답이다.

어휘 revitalize ~을 재건하다, 소생시키다 encourage ~을 장려하다

79. 다음 주에 무슨 일이 있을 것 같은가?
(A) 시 의회 모임
(B) 나무와 꽃 심기
(C) 일련의 도로 작업
(D) 주차장 개발

정답 (A)

해설 마지막 문단에서 의원에게 다음 주 회의에서 변경 제안에 대해 찬성표를 던지도록 요청하고(I ask you to please vote for ~ changes at the meeting next week) 있고, 지문 상단에 수신인이 시 의원이므로 (A)가 정답이다.

80-82.

> **수신:** 셔먼 트레이딩 직원들
> **발신:** 브루노 레스너, 대표이사
> **제목:** 뉴스 발표
> **날짜:** 7월 3일
>
> **80** 이미 아실 수도 있겠지만, 레이첼 뮤네즈 신임 마케팅 이사께서 곧 본사로 합류하실 것입니다. **81** 우리는 7월 23일 월요일에 메르세데스 비스트로에서 셔먼 트레이딩에 첫 출근하시는 뮤네즈 씨를 위한 환영 오찬을 가질 예정입니다. 여러분 모두의 참석을 환영합니다.
>
> **80** **82** 이와 관련된 내용으로, 현 마케팅 이사님께서 우리 셔먼 트레이딩의 이사회를 떠나시는 대로 캘리포니아로 이사를 가십니다. 티모시 힐튼 씨는 7월 20일에 공식적으로 자리에서 물러나실 예정입니다. 힐튼 씨께서는 우리 회사에서 26년 동안 재직하시면서 회사의 성공과 번영에 중요한 역할을 해 주셨습니다. 이와 같은 훌륭한 경력을 마무리하시고 업계에서 아주 떠나, 부동산 중개업자로 일하셨던 부인과 함께 오렌지 카운티로 이사 가실 계획입니다.
>
> 힐튼 씨께서는 7월 20일에 있을 회의에서 짐 랑에 회장님으로부터 작별 선물을 전달 받으실 것입니다. 회의 후에는 각 부서를 방문하시면서 모든 직원들에게 직접 작별 인사를 하실 것입니다. 오전 11시와 오후 12시 사이에 여러분의 자리에서 업무를 보시다가 애정 어린 작별 인사를 하시기 바랍니다.

어휘 **headquarters** 본사 **welcome luncheon** 환영 오찬 **be welcome to do** ~하는 것을 환영하다, ~해도 좋다 **on a similar note** 유사한 내용으로, 유사한 부분으로 **once** 일단 ~하면, ~하자마자 **leave** ~에서 떠나다, 그만 두다 **officially** 공식적으로 **step down** 물러 나다 **play a significant role in** ~에 있어 중요한 역할을 하다 **prosperity** 번영, 번창 **distinguished** 훌륭한, 저명한 **for good** 영원히 **real estate agent** 부동산 중개업자 **be presented with** ~을 전달 받다, 제공 받다 **farewell** 작별 (인사) **following** ~ 후에 **in person** 직접 (만나) **bid A a farewell** A에게 작별 인사를 하다

80. 메모는 무엇을 알리는가?
(A) 채용 기회
(B) 회사 이전
(C) 기업 합병
(D) 인사 이동

정답 (D)

해설 첫 번째 문단에서 레이첼 뮤네즈 신임 마케팅 이사가 곧 합류한다는(our new Director of Marketing, Rachel Munez, will soon be joining) 내용이, 그리고 두 번째 문단에서 현 마케팅 이사가 회사를 떠난다는(our current Director of Mar-keting will be moving to California once he leaves his position) 사실이 언급되고 있다. 따라서 인사 이동을 뜻하는 (D)가 정답이다.

어휘 **employment opportunity** 고용 기회 **relocation** 이전 **merger** 합병, 통합

81. 회람 내용에 따르면, 7월 23일에 무슨 일이 있을 것인가?
(A) 레스너 씨가 지원자들을 면접할 것이다.
(B) 뮤네즈 씨가 특별 식사 시간에 참석할 것이다.
(C) 힐튼 씨가 교육 시간을 진행할 것이다.
(D) 랭어 씨가 선물을 받을 것이다.

정답 (B)

해설 첫 번째 문단에서 7월 23일 월요일에 메르세데스 비스트로에서 뮤네즈 씨를 위한 환영 오찬을 가진다고(We will have a welcome luncheon at Mercedes Bistro on Monday, July 23, for Ms. Munez's first day) 쓰여 있으므로 (B)가 정답이다.

어휘 **candidate** 지원자, 후보자 **lead** ~을 진행하다, 이끌다

82. 힐튼 씨는 누구인가?
(A) 퇴임하는 이사회 임원
(B) 신임 마케팅부장
(C) 부동산 중개업자
(D) 채용 전문가

정답 (A)

해설 두 번째 단락에 현 마케팅 이사가 이사 직에서 물러나 캘리포니아로 이사 간다고 하면서 다음 문장에 티모시 힐튼 씨가 7월 20일에 공식적으로 자리에서 물러날 것이라고(Timothy Hilton will be officially stepping down on July 20) 언급하므로 (A)가 정답이다.

어휘 **board member** 이사회 임원 **recruitment** 직원 모집, 채용

83-86.

> **짐 [오후 4:32]** 혹시 제가 금요일 회의를 위해 만든 프리젠테이션을 검토해 보셨습니까?
>
> **테드 [오후 4:36]** 네, 매우 좋은 것 같아요. **83** 저희가 그 잡지에 광고를 한 이후로 페인트가 30% 더 팔렸다는 것은 인상적인 일이에요. 이번 달 페인트 판매량을 포함할 것도 계획 중인가요?
>
> **짐 [오후 4:40]** 그럴 계획이었는데, 3월까지의 수치들만 접근이 가능해요. 저희의 4월 판매량은 아직 데이터베이스에서 이용이 불가해요.
>
> **테드 [오후 4:44]** **84** 제 생각에 4월 판매량을 프리젠테이션에 포함시키는 것은 중요한 것 같아요. 사실 제가 1시간 후에 앤소니 씨와 회의가 있는데, **85** 제가 그에게 당신이 발표하기 전에 정보를 얻을 수 있도록 데이터베이스를 업데이트 하라고 요청할게요.
>
> **짐 [오후 4:45]** 그가 그렇게 할 수 있을 줄 몰랐네요. 고마워요.
>
> **테드 [오후 4:46]** 별거 아니에요.

짐 [오후 4:50] 혹시 프리젠테이션을 개선할 수 있는 다른 제안을 해 주시겠어요?

테드 [오후 4:55] 사실, 저라면 한가지 작은 세부사항을 바꿀 거예요. **86** 우리 동료들이 검은 배경 위의 파란 글씨를 읽는 것이 어려울 수도 있어요. 아마도 배경을 흰색으로 변경하거나 글꼴을 더 밝은 색으로 만들 수 있을 거예요.

짐 [오후 4:58] 좋아요. 배경을 흰색으로 할게요. 감사합니다.

어휘 **look through** ~을 검토하다 **include** ~을 포함하다 **access** 접근하다 **available** 이용 가능한 **realize** ~을 깨닫다 **improve** ~을 향상시키다, 개선하다 **actually** 사실, 실제로

83. 테드 씨와 짐 씨의 회사가 판매하는 것은 무엇인가?
(A) 잡지
(B) 페인트
(C) 광고
(D) 달력

정답 (B)

해설 테드 씨의 첫 번째 메시지를 보면 광고 이후 페인트 판매량이 30%늘었다는(we have sold 30% more paint since we advertised in that magazine) 말이 쓰여 있어 페인트 판매 회사임을 알 수 있다. 따라서 (B)가 정답이다.

어휘 **commercial** 광고

84. 앤소니 씨는 무엇을 하도록 요청 받을 것 같은가?
(A) 짐 씨에게 정보를 이메일로 보내는 것
(B) 짐 씨의 프리젠테이션을 편집하는 것
(C) 데이터베이스에 대해 논의하는 것
(D) 판매 정보를 업데이트하는 것

정답 (D)

해설 테드 씨가 4시 44분에 작성한 메시지에 4월 판매량을 발표 내용에 넣는 것이 중요하고 1시간 후 앤소니 씨와 회의가 있으니 그때 그에게 요청하겠다는(it's important to include our April sales in your presentation. Actually, I have a meeting with Anthony in an hour and I will ask him to) 부분에서 앤소니 씨는 누락된 판매 정보를 업데이트하도록 요청 받을 것을 알 수 있다. 따라서 (D)가 정답이다.

85. 오후 4시 45분에, 짐 씨가 "I didn't realize he could do that"라고 말한 의미는 무엇인가?
(A) 앤소니 씨의 역할을 잘못 이해했다.
(B) 테드 씨가 회의를 했음을 잊었다.
(C) 앤소니 씨가 로그인을 할 수 없다고 생각했다.
(D) 데이터베이스에 대해 들어본 바 없다.

정답 (A)

해설 오후 4시 45분 이전에 보내진 테드 씨의 메시지에서 앤소니 씨에게 누락 정보 업데이트를 부탁할 것이라는 말이 언급되어 있는데, 이에 대해 짐 씨가 '그가 그렇게 할 수 있을 줄 몰랐네요'라고 대답하는 상황이다. 따라서 짐 씨는 앤소니 씨가 무엇을 하는 사람인지 정확히 알지 못했다는 것을 알 수 있으므로 (A)가 정답이다.

어휘 **misunderstand** ~을 오해하다 **hear of** ~에 대해 들어보다

86. 테드 씨는 프리젠테이션의 디자인에 대해 무슨 말을 하는가?
(A) 폰트가 너무 작다.
(B) 인상적으로 디자인되었다.
(C) 모든 사실과 수치들을 포함하고 있다.
(D) 색상 선택에 문제가 있다.

정답 (D)

해설 테드 씨가 보낸 마지막 메세지에 글자가 안 보일 수 있는 원인으로 배경과 글자의 색상 조합을 지적하고 있으므로(It might be difficult for our colleagues to read blue letters over the black background) (D)가 정답이다.

어휘 **fact** 사실 **problematic** 문제의, 문제가 있는

87-90.

등산화는 지저분해지도록 만들어져 있지만, 그것이 등산화를 깨끗하게 그리고 훌륭한 상태로 유지하는 일을 등한시해도 된다는 뜻은 아닙니다. **87** 적절한 관리와 유지를 통해, 새로 구입하신 트렉 로드 등산화를 오랫동안 즐겁게 사용하실 수 있습니다.

등산화를 닦으시기에 앞서, 끈을 제거하셔야 합니다. 그런 다음, 솔을 이용해 등산화와 끈에 묻은 먼지와 흙을 부드럽게 제거해 주십시오.

더욱 철저한 세척이 필요하실 경우, 흐르는 물과 적합한 신발 세척제를 이용하시기 바랍니다. **88** 대부분의 신발 세척제가 다양한 재질에 사용될 수 있기는 하지만, 갖고 계신 세척제가 여러분의 트렉 로드 등산화에 적합한지 항상 확인하시기 바랍니다.

손상을 피하기 위해, 절대로 세탁기에 등산화를 넣지 마시기 바라며, 비누 또는 세제를 사용하지 마셔야 하는데, 이 제품들 중 많은 것이 가죽 또는 방수 재질에 유해할 수 있는 화학 물질을 함유하고 있기 때문입니다. 트렉 로드 등산화는 구입할 때 이미 방수 상태인 제품이므로, 물방울이 더 이상 표면에 구슬처럼 맺히지 않는 상태임을 인식하기 시작하실 때까지 방수 물질을 다시 바르는 것을 기다려 주십시오.

또한 등산화를 올바르게 건조하고 보관하는 것도 중요합니다. – [1] –. 먼저 깔창 부분을 꺼내 등산화와 별도로 자연 건조하셔야 합니다. – [2] –. 습도가 높은 곳을 피해 실온에서 등산화를 건조 하십시오. 벽난로나 라디에이터 같은 열 방출원을 활용하는 것을 삼가셔야 하는데, 높은 온도가 접착제를 약하게 만들고 가죽을 노화시키기 때문입니다. – [3] –. **89** 건조 과정을 가속화하시려면, 선풍기를 이용하시거나 등산화 안쪽에 신문지를 넣어 두십시오.

90 등산화의 부드러운 가죽 부분들이 말라 보이거나 갈라져 보이면, 컨디셔너를 활용하십시오. – [4] –. 가죽은 수분이 유지된 상태일 때 최상으로 기능하지만, 과도한 컨디셔너는 등산화를 너무 부드럽게 만들거나 발목 및 발바닥 지지 부분을 약화시킵니다.

어휘 **get + 형용사** ~한 상태가 되다 **neglect** ~을 등한시하다 **in excellent condition** 훌륭한 상태인 **proper** 적절한, 제대로 된 **laces** 신발 끈 **gently** 부드럽게 **thorough** 철저한 **running water** 흐르는 물 **detergent** 세제 **chemical** n. 화학 물질 **no longer** 더 이상 ~ 않다 **bead up** 구슬 모양으로 맺히다 **insole** 깔창, 안창 **air-dry** 자연 건조하다 **room temperature** 실온 **humidity** 습기 **refrain from -ing** ~하는 것을 삼가다 **heat source** 열 방출원 **weaken** ~을 약화시키다 **adhesive** n. 접착제 **age** v. ~을 노화시키다 **accelerate** ~을 가속화하다 **cracked** 갈라진 **function** v. 기능하다, 작용하다 **excess** 과도한

87. 정보를 어디에서 찾아 볼 수 있을 것 같은가?
(A) 알림판에서
(B) 등산 잡지에서
(C) 홍보용 전단에서
(D) 제품 포장 내부에서

정답 (D)

해설 첫 단락에 적절한 관리와 유지를 통해 새로 구입한 트렉 로드 등산화를 오랫동안 즐겁게 사용할 수 있다고(With proper care and maintenance, you can enjoy using your newly-purchased Trek Lord boots) 언급하면서 그 관리 방법을 소개하고 있다. 이는 제품을 구입한 사람이 갖고 있을 수 있는 물품에 적힌 정보인 것으로 볼 수 있으므로 (D)가 정답이다.

어휘 **notice board** 알림판, 게시판 **flyer** 전단

88. 트렉 로드에 관해 언급된 것은 무엇인가?
(A) 여분의 신발 끈과 함께 판매된다.
(B) 구입 후에 방수 처리 작업을 필요로 한다.
(C) 특정 세척제를 필요로 한다.
(D) 세탁기 세척을 할 수 있다.

정답 (C)

해설 두 번째 단락을 보면 대부분의 신발 세척제가 다양한 재질에 사용될 수 있기는 하지만 갖고 있는 세척제가 트렉 로드 등산화에 적합한지 항상 확인하라고(always check that your cleaner is suitable for use on your Trek Lord boots) 당부하고 있다. 이는 적합한 세척제, 즉 특정 종류의 세척제만 사용하라는 말이므로 (C)가 정답이다.

어휘 **extra** 여분의 **specific** 특정한, 구체적인

89. 트렉 로드 등산화는 어떻게 건조되어야 하는가?
(A) 라디에이터 근처에 놓아 둠으로써

(B) 신문지 위에 놓아 둠으로써
(C) 선풍기 앞에 놓아 둠으로써
(D) 어두운 방에 놓아 둠으로써

정답 (C)

해설 네 번째 단락에 건조 과정의 가속화를 위해 선풍기를 이용하거나 등산화 안쪽에 신문지를 넣어 두라고 (To accelerate the drying process, use a fan, or place newspaper inside the boots) 알리고 있으므로 이 중 하나에 해당되는 (C)가 정답이다.

90. [1], [2], [3], [4]로 표기된 위치들 중에서, 다음 문장이 들어 가기에 가장 적절한 곳은 어디인가?

"너무 많이 바르지 않도록 주의하시기 바랍니다."

(A) [1]
(B) [2]
(C) [3]
(D) [4]

정답 (D)

해설 마지막 단락에 가죽 부분이 말라 보이거나 갈라져 보일 때 바르는 제품에 해당되는 컨디셔너가 언급된 문장 뒤에 위치한 [4]에 들어가 컨디셔너 사용량과 관련해 주의시키는 흐름이 되어야 알맞으므로 (D)가 정답이다.

어휘 **take care not to do** ~하지 않도록 주의하다 **apply** ~을 바르다, 칠하다

91-95.

수신: 프랭크 크루즈 <fcruise@primeedu.com>
발신: 샐리 불러드 <sbullard@primeedu.com>
주제: 이사회 회의
날짜: 3월 20일

프랭크 씨에게,

91 94 이사회의 가장 신참으로서, 다음 회의에 참석해 주시기를 부탁 드립니다. 3월 27일 수요일, 7층의 이사회실에서 열릴 예정입니다.

당신의 특정 전문 분야가 매출 트렌드라는 것을 알기에, 지난 12개월 동안은 다룬 프리젠테이션과 향후 12개월 동안의 기대치를 다룬 프리젠테이션을 준비하여 와 주시기를 바랍니다. 저희는 내년에는 시장 점유율을 높일 수 있기를 바라고 있으며, 바로 이번 회의에서 그렇게 하기 위한 아이디어를 냈으면 합니다.

의제에 오른 다른 **92** 항목들로는 직원들의 사기, 경력 개발, 그리고 교육이 포함되어 있습니다. 만약 이런 주제에 대해 어떠한 생각이라도 가지고 있으시면, 저희는 그 어떤 모든 제안을 환영합니다. 고려하셔야 할 몇 가지 구체적인 질문들은 다음과 같습니다.

1. 현재 사기가 어떻다고 평가하시나요? 그리고 개선을 위해 무엇을 할 수 있을까요?

2. 우리가 좀 더 경쟁력을 갖추려면 무엇을 해야 할까요?

93 3. 우리는 현 직원들을 외부에서 고용하기보다는 조직 내에서 승진할 수 있도록 교육시키고 싶습니다. 생산성을 저해하지 않고 어떻게 이런 교육을 제공할 수 있을까요?

참석을 확정하기 위해 답변 주십시오.

어휘 **board of executives** 이사회 **attendance** 참석, 출석 **expertise** 전문 지식 **cover** ~을 다루다 **improve** ~을 향상시키다 **brainstorm** 아이디어를 짜내다 **specific** 구체적인 **assess** ~을 평가하다 **morale** 사기, 의욕 **competitive** 경쟁력 있는 **move up** 승진하다 **rather than** ~보다는 차라리 **hinder** ~을 방해하다, 저해하다 **productivity** 생산성

수신: 샐리 불러드 <sbullard@primeedu.com>
발신: 프랭크 크루즈 <fcruise@primeedu.com>
주제: 회신: 이사회 회의
날짜: 3월 20일

샐리 씨께,

3월 27일 이사회 회의에 저의 참석을 확정하고자 메일 드립니다. 저는 많은 조사를 해왔고, 시장 점유율을 높이기 위한 주제에 대한 저의 연구 결과를 여러분 모두와 공유할 것입니다. 저는 우리가 경험하고 있는 몇몇 문제 분야를 설명해 주는 수치를 공유하고자 하며, 저는 우리가 이러한 문제들을 함께 해결해 나갈 수 있다고 확신합니다. 또한 다른 문제들도 고려해 볼 것이며, **93** 특히 당신이 이 메일에서 언급하신 세 번째 질문에 대한 제 생각을 나누는 것을 기대하고 있습니다. 매우 생산적인 회의가 될 것이라고 생각합니다.

95 또한 저를 신임해주시고 이사회에 저를 지명해 주신 데 대해서도 감사 드리고 싶습니다. 이것은 저에게 엄청난 기회이고 당신을 실망시키지 않겠습니다!

어휘 **confirm** ~을 확정하다 **a great deal of** 대단히 많은 **illustrate** ~을 설명하다, 묘사하다 **confident** 자신 있는 **address problems** 문제를 해결하다 **take A into consideration** A를 고려하다 **productive** 생산적인 **confidence in** ~에 대한 신뢰, 확신 **nominate** ~을 지명하다 **tremendous** 엄청난 **let A down** A를 실망시키다

91. 첫 이메일의 목적은 무엇인가?

(A) 작업 보고를 요청하려고
(B) 크루즈 씨에게 일자리 기회를 알려주려고
(C) 크루즈 씨를 이사회에 후보지명 하려고
(D) 크루즈 씨를 모임에 초대하려고

정답 (D)

해설 첫 번째 문단에 이사회의 가장 신임으로서 회의에 참석해 주기를 부탁한다고(As the newest member of the board of executives, your attendance is requested at our next meeting) 요청하고 있으므로 (D)가 정답이다.

어휘 **request** ~을 요청하다

92. 첫 번째 이메일에서, 셋째 단락, 첫째 줄의 단어 "items"와 의미가 가장 가까운 것은 무엇인가?

(A) 문제들
(B) 제품들
(C) 특징들
(D) 공지사항들

정답 (A)

해설 해당 문제에 쓰인 items를 해석해보면 '의제에 오른 다른 항목들'이라는 뜻인데 이는 회의에서 다룰 문제들이라 할 수 있으므로 (A) issues가 정답이다.

93. 크루즈 씨가 회의에서 논의하길 가장 기대하는 것은 무엇인가?

(A) 사기를 향상시킬 방안
(B) 현재 직원들을 교육시킬 방안
(C) 더욱 경쟁력을 갖출 수 있는 방안
(D) 공장 생산량을 증대하기 위한 방안

정답 (B)

해설 두 번째 이메일에서 크루즈 씨는 세 번째 질문에 대한 생각을 나누는 것을 기대하고 있다고(especially looking forward to sharing my ideas with you regarding the third question) 말하고 있다. 이와 관련해, 첫 번째 이메일에서 세 번째 질문이 무엇인지 보면 현 직원들 교육(train our current staff)과 관련 있는 것이므로 (B)가 정답이다.

어휘 **existing** 현존하는 **boost** ~을 증대하다

94. 크루즈 씨에 대해 유추할 수 있는 것은 무엇인가?

(A) 다가오는 승진의 기회에 관심을 보였다.
(B) 불러드 씨와 3월 27일 회의 전에 만날 것이다.
(C) 경쟁사들 중 한 곳을 떠나 최근에 입사했다.
(D) 이것이 그가 이사회에 처음 하게 되는 회의이다.

정답 (D)

해설 첫 지문 첫 단락에 이사회의 가장 신참으로서 회의에 참석해 주기를 부탁한다는(As the newest member of the board of executives, your attendance is requested at our next meeting) 부분에서 크루즈 씨가 회의에 처음 참석한다는 것을 알 수 있다. 따라서 (D)가 정답이다.

어휘 **upcoming** 다가오는 **promotion** 승진, 홍보 **prior to** ~보다 이전에

95. 크루즈 씨가 불러드 씨에게 감사하는 이유는 무엇인가?

(A) 그가 매출 트렌드를 조사하는 데 도움을 줘서
(B) 프리젠테이션 요령에 관한 조언을 해줘서
(C) 자신을 이사회에 추천해 줘서
(D) 자신을 프로젝트 책임자가 되도록 해줘서

정답 (C)

해설 두 번째 지문 마지막 문단에서 크루즈 씨가 이사회에 본인을 지명해 준 것에 대해 감사 인사를 전하고(thank you for nominating me to the board) 있으므로 (C)가 정답이다.

어휘 **recommend** ~을 추천하다 **put A in charge of B** A를 B의 담당자로 두다

96-100.

드라이든 온 텐스

웨스트 10번 애비뉴 1402번지, 밴쿠버, BC V6H 1J6
96(D) 영업 시간 화-목 오전 11시에서 오후 10시 / 금-일 오전 11시에서 오후 11시

지난 달에, 마침내 저희 레스토랑에 대한 대대적인 개조 공사를 끝마쳤으며, 실내 장식 작업이 숙련된 디자이너 홀든 스펜서 씨에 의해 처리되었습니다. **97** 원래 1층 건물이었던 저희 레스토랑이 이제 2층을 자랑하고 있으며, 주요 식사 공간 좌석 수용 규모를 253석으로 끌어올렸습니다. **100** 위층에는, 저희가 1층에 보유하고 있는 네 곳에 더해, 여섯 곳의 새로운 개별 식사 공간을 보유하고 있습니다. 경험 많은 저희 진 듀퐁 주방장님께서 여러분께 인기 있는 요리를 제공해 드리기 위해 기다리고 계십니다!

96(A) 지역 내에 있는 업체에서 근무하시는 경우, 받으실 자격이 있는 할인과 관련해 저희에게 문의하십시오. 저희 회사 목록에 등록되어 있는 업체 소속 직원들께서는 계산서에서 최대 15% 할인을 받으실 수 있습니다.

www.drydenontenth.ca를 방문하셔서 저희 메뉴도 살펴보시고 저녁 식사 예약도 하시기 바랍니다. **96(B)** 저희 레스토랑에서는 어떤 반바지나 민소매 셔츠도 착용하시지 말아야 한다는 점에 유의하시기 바랍니다.

어휘 **extensive** 대대적인, 광범위한, 폭넓은 **renovation** 개조, 보수 **with A p.p.** A가 ~되어, A가 ~된 채로 **decoration** 장식(물) **handle** ~을 처리하다, ~을 다루다 **skilled** 숙련된 **originally** 원래, 애초에 **one-story** 1층으로 된 **boast** ~을 자랑하다 **raise** ~을 끌어올리다, ~을 높이다 **seating capacity** 좌석 수용 규모 **upstairs** 위층에 **in addition to** ~에 더해, ~뿐만 아니라 **experienced** 경험 많은 **serve A B** (음식 등) A에게 B를 제공하다, A에게 B를 내오다 **local** 지역의, 현지의 **be eligible to do** ~할 자격이 있다 **receive** ~을 받다 **register** ~을 등록시키다 **directory** (주소와 연락처 등이 있는) 안내 목록, 안내 책자 **up to** 최대 ~의 **bill** 계산서, 청구서 **view** ~을 보다 **make a reservation** 예약하다 **note that** ~임에 유의하다, ~임에 주목하다 **shorts** 반바지 **sleeveless** 소매 없는

---

http://www.drydenontenth.ca/dinnermenu

저녁 식사 메뉴

애피타이저	주 요리	디저트
프렌치 어니언 수프 $8.50	허브 로스티드 치킨 $15.50	라즈베리 치즈케이크 $8.50
게살 샐러드 $12.50	**98** 버터 포치드 랍스터 $17.50	주방장 특선 티라미수 $9.50
갈릭 브레드 $6.50	구운 연어 $16.50	리치 초콜릿 케이크 $7.50

BC 리빙 매거진 – 7월호

이달의 특집 레스토랑 – 드라이든 온 텐스
작성, 브리짓 카일

제가 최근에 드라이든 온 텐스를 방문했을 때 가장 먼저 주목했던 점은 이 레스토랑이 홀든 스펜서 씨에 의해 다시 디자인된 뒤로 얼마나 더 좋아 보이는가 하는 점이었습니다. 주요 식사 공간은 현재 250명을 약간 넘는 식사 손님들이 앉을 좌석이 있으며, 이 레스토랑은 이제 개별 파티에 이용될 수 있는 **100** 총 여섯 곳의 개별 식사 공간을 자랑합니다.

드라이든 온 텐스의 음식은 늘 그렇듯이 더없이 훌륭합니다. **98** 저는 특히 주 요리로 랍스터를 즐겼고, 진 듀퐁 주방장님의 대표적인 프렌치 어니언 수프는 전채 요리로 이상적인 선택이며, 라즈베리 치즈케이크는 뛰어났습니다. **99** 식사 손님들은 메뉴 가격이 지역 내 재료의 이용 가능성 및 연중 시기에 따라 변동될 수 있다는 점에 유의하셔야 합니다.

드라이든 온 텐스는 일주일에 6일, 오전 11시에 문을 열며, 매주 금요일과 토요일, 그리고 일요일에는 더 늦게까지 문을 열고 영업합니다.

어휘 **feature** ~을 특집으로 하다, ~을 특징으로 하다 **notice** ~에 주목하나, ~을 알아차리나 **look A** A하게 보이다, A한 것 같다 **seat** v. ~을 앉힐 좌석이 있다 **diner** 식사 손님 **a total of** 총 ~의 **as A as B** B만큼 A한 **exquisite** 더없이 훌륭한 **especially** 특히 **ideal** 이상적인 **outstanding** 뛰어난, 우수한 **note that** ~라는 점에 유의하다 **fluctuate** 변동을 거듭하다 **depending on** ~에 따라, ~에 달려 있는 **availability** 이용 가능성

96. 드라이든 온 텐스와 관련해 언급되지 않은 것은 무엇인가?
(A) 기업 할인을 제공한다.
(B) 복장 규정 정책이 있다.
(C) 점심 식사 예약을 필요로 한다.
(D) 매주 월요일에 문을 닫는다.

정답 (C)

해설 첫 번째 지문 상단의 영업 시간에서 월요일이 휴무일임을
(Open 11 a.m. to 10 p.m., Tue – Thu / 11 a.m. to 11 p.m.

Fri – Sun) 알 수 있으므로 (D)를 확인할 수 있다. 또한, 두 번째 단락에서 지역 내 업체에서 근무한다면 할인을 받을 수 있다는(If you work at a business in the local area, ask us about the discounts that you are eligible to receive) 부분에서 (A)를 확인할 수 있으며, 마지막 단락에 반지나 민소매 셔츠를 착용할 수 없다는(Please note that no shorts or sleeveless shirts should be worn inside our restaurant) 부분을 통해 (B)도 확인할 수 있다. 하지만 점심 식사 예약과 관련된 정보는 제시되어 있지 않으므로 (C)가 정답이다.

어휘 **corporate** 기업의 **dress code** 복장 규정 **policy** 정책, 방침 **require** ~을 필요로 하다

97. 광고에 따르면, 레스토랑에서 최근 무슨 일이 있었는가?
(A) 옥외 공간이 지어졌다.
(B) 새 주방장이 고용되었다.
(C) 한 층이 더 추가되었다.
(D) 메뉴가 확대되었다.

정답 (C)

해설 첫 번째 지문 첫 단락에 원래 1층 건물이었던 레스토랑이 이제 2층을 자랑하고 있다는(Originally a one-story building, our restaurant now boasts a second floor) 말이 쓰여 있다. 이는 앞서 언급한 개조 공사로 인해 1개 층이 추가되었음을 의미하는 말이므로 (C)가 정답이다.

어휘 **hire** ~을 고용하다 **add** ~을 추가하다 **expand** ~을 확대하다, ~을 확장하다

98. 카일 씨가 자신의 주 요리에 대해 얼마를 청구 받았을 것 같은가?
(A) $8.50
(B) $12.50
(C) $16.50
(D) $17.50

정답 (D)

해설 세 번째 지문 두 번째 단락에 주 요리로 랍스터를 즐긴 사실이(I especially enjoyed the lobster for my main dish) 언급되어 있다. 이와 관련해, 두 번째 지문 중간 부분에 랍스터 요리가 $17.50으로(Butter Poached Lobster, $17.50) 표기되어 있으므로 (D)가 정답이다.

어휘 **charge A B** A에게 B를 청구하다

99. 기사에서, 레스토랑의 가격과 관련해 언급된 것은 무엇인가?
(A) 경쟁 업체들의 가격보다 더 낮다.
(B) 계절에 따라 변동될 수 있다.
(C) 웹 사이트에 다르게 기재되어 있을 수 있다.
(D) 수년 동안에 걸쳐 상당히 인상되었다.

정답 (B)

해설 세 번째 지문 두 번째 단락에 메뉴 가격이 지역 내 재료의 이용 가능성 및 연중 시기에 따라 변동될 수 있다는 점에 유의하도록

알리는(menu prices may fluctuate depending on the availability of local ingredients and the time of year) 말이 쓰여 있다. 이는 재료 확보 여부나 일년 중의 계절에 따라 가격이 바뀔 수 있다는 뜻이므로 (B)가 정답이다.

어휘 **competitor** 경쟁사, 경쟁자 **list** v. ~을 기재하다, ~을 목록에 올리다 **significantly** 상당히, 많이

100. 카일 씨가 어떤 정보를 부정확하게 설명했는가?
(A) 실내 디자이너의 이름
(B) 주요 식사 공간의 수용 규모
(C) 레스토랑의 영업 시간
(D) 개별 식사 공간의 수

정답 (D)

해설 세 번째 지문 첫 단락에 카일 씨가 해당 레스토랑에 총 여섯 곳의 개별 식사 공간이 있다고 언급하고 있는데(the restaurant now boasts a total of six private dining rooms), 첫 지문 첫 단락에는 1층에 있는 네 곳에 더해 2층에 여섯 곳의 개별 식사 공간이 있다고(Upstairs, we have six new private dining rooms, in addition to the four we have on the ground floor) 쓰여 있다. 따라서 카일 씨가 개별 식사 공간의 숫자와 관련해 잘못된 정보를 제공했다는 것을 알 수 있으므로 (D)가 정답이다.

어휘 **incorrectly** 부정확하게

DAY 05 LC+RC Half Test

LC

1. (B)	**2.** (C)	**3.** (C)	**4.** (A)	**5.** (C)
6. (B)	**7.** (C)	**8.** (C)	**9.** (A)	**10.** (B)
11. (B)	**12.** (A)	**13.** (B)	**14.** (C)	**15.** (B)
16. (C)	**17.** (A)	**18.** (C)	**19.** (A)	**20.** (C)
21. (C)	**22.** (C)	**23.** (D)	**24.** (B)	**25.** (B)
26. (C)	**27.** (B)	**28.** (B)	**29.** (C)	**30.** (A)
31. (C)	**32.** (B)	**33.** (C)	**34.** (A)	**35.** (C)
36. (D)	**37.** (C)	**38.** (C)	**39.** (D)	**40.** (B)
41. (A)	**42.** (C)	**43.** (D)	**44.** (C)	**45.** (B)
46. (A)	**47.** (B)	**48.** (D)	**49.** (B)	**50.** (D)

RC

51. (D)	**52.** (B)	**53.** (B)	**54.** (D)	**55.** (A)
56. (C)	**57.** (B)	**58.** (B)	**59.** (D)	**60.** (B)
61. (A)	**62.** (B)	**63.** (C)	**64.** (B)	**65.** (C)
66. (A)	**67.** (B)	**68.** (D)	**69.** (D)	**70.** (D)
71. (B)	**72.** (C)	**73.** (B)	**74.** (D)	**75.** (C)
76. (D)	**77.** (B)	**78.** (C)	**79.** (D)	**80.** (B)
81. (A)	**82.** (D)	**83.** (D)	**84.** (B)	**85.** (B)
86. (D)	**87.** (D)	**88.** (B)	**89.** (B)	**90.** (D)
91. (D)	**92.** (A)	**93.** (A)	**94.** (D)	**95.** (C)
96. (D)	**97.** (B)	**98.** (D)	**99.** (C)	**100.** (B)

Part 1

1. (A) The woman is carrying a suitcase on the platform.
(B) **A structure extends over the railroad tracks.**
(C) The station is under construction.
(D) Passengers are boarding a train.

(A) 여자가 승강장에서 여행 가방을 옮기는 중이다.
(B) **철로 위를 가로질러 구조물이 이어져 있다.**
(C) 역이 공사 중이다.
(D) 승객들이 열차에 탑승하는 중이다.

해설 (A) 여자가 여행 가방을 옮기는 동작을 하는 것이 아니므로 오답.
(B) 철로 위쪽에 지붕 같은 구조물이 있는 것을 묘사하고 있으므로 정답.
(C) 역에 공사가 진행되는 상황이 아니므로 오답.
(D) 열차에 탑승하는 승객을 찾아볼 수 없으므로 오답.

어휘 carry ~을 나르다, 옮기다, 휴대하다 suitcase 여행 가방 structure 구조물 extend 이어지다, 뻗어 있다, 펼쳐지다 railroad track 철로 under construction 공사 중인 passenger 승객 board ~에 탑승하다

2. (A) A wooden panel is leaning against a wall.
(B) A car is parked behind the truck.
(C) **Some items have been loaded onto a truck.**
(D) Some boxes are piled on the ground.

(A) 나무로 된 판자가 벽에 기대어져 있다.
(B) 트럭 뒤에 자동차 한 대가 주차되어 있다.
(C) **몇몇 물품들이 트럭 위에 실려 있다.**
(D) 몇몇 상자들이 땅바닥에 쌓여 있다.

해설 (A) 벽에 기대어진 나무 판자를 찾아볼 수 없으므로 오답.
(B) 트럭 뒤에 주차된 차량을 찾아볼 수 없으므로 오답.
(C) 트럭에 물건이 실려 있는 상태를 묘사하고 있으므로 정답.
(D) 땅바닥에 쌓여 있는 상자를 찾아볼 수 없으므로 오답.

어휘 **wooden panel** 나무 판자 **lean against** ~에 기대다 **behind** ~ 뒤에 **load A onto B** A를 B에 싣다 **pile** ~을 쌓다

Part 2

3. Who will give the first talk at the advertising seminar?
(A) I'd be happy to help you practice.
(B) At the Halford Conference Hall.
(C) **I heard it'll be Jack Colt.**

광고 세미나에서 누가 첫 번째로 강연을 할 건가요?
(A) 당신이 연습하는 걸 도와줄게요.
(B) 핼포드 컨퍼런스 홀에서요.
(C) **잭 콜트 씨일 거라고 들었어요.**

해설 의문사 Who를 이용해 '누구'인지를 묻는 질문이므로, 구체적인 인물의 이름을 언급하고 있는 답변이 정답일 가능성이 높다. 따라서 Jack Colt라는 인물의 이름을 언급하며 그 사람일 것이라고 말한 (C)가 정답이다.

어휘 **give a talk** 강연하다 **practice** 연습하다, 훈련하다

4. Where am I supposed to pick up the clients?
(A) **Right in front of their hotel.**
(B) Yes, I suppose you should.
(C) At 10:30 tomorrow morning.

제가 어디서 고객을 태우기로 되어 있나요?
(A) 그분들의 호텔 바로 앞에서요.
(B) 네, 저는 당신이 그래야 한다고 생각합니다.
(C) 내일 아침 10시 30분에요.

해설 장소나 위치를 묻는 Where 의문문이다. be supposed to do는 '~하기로 되어 있다', '~해야 하다'라는 의미로 예정이나 의무를 나타내는 표현이므로, '어디에서 고객을 태워야 하나요?'라는 뜻의 질문이 된다. 이에 대해 고객을 태울 장소를 말해주는 (A)가 가장 적절한 응답이다.

어휘 **pick up** ~ 을 (차에) 태우다 **client** 고객, 의뢰인
suppose ~라고 생각하다, 추정하다

5. Why haven't the tablecloths been put on the tables yet?
(A) You can wear whatever you like.
(B) Just leave them by the door.
(C) They're still being cleaned.

왜 아직도 식탁보가 식탁에 놓이지 않았나요?
(A) 당신은 좋아하는 무엇이든 입을 수 있습니다.
(B) 문 옆에 그것들을 놓아두세요.
(C) 그것들은 아직도 세탁되고 있습니다.

해설 의문사와 부정 의문문 형태, 현재완료 시제와 수동태가 혼합된 고난도 질문이다. 게다가, haven't the clothes는 연음되어 haven't 가 제대로 들리지 않기 때문에 웬만한 듣기 실력으론 질문을 알아듣기가 쉽지 않다. 이럴 땐 단편적으로라도 들은 정보들을 조합해 의미를 유추해 보아야 한다. Why, haven't, tablecloths, put 정도는 꼭 들어야 하는데, 이로부터 유추해볼 수 있는 질문의 의미는 '왜 테이블보가 놓여지지 않았나?'라는 것이다. 이에 어울리는 답변을 찾기 위해 오답을 하나하나 소거해 보면, '테이블보가 아직 세탁 중이어서'라고 그 이유를 설명하는 (C)가 정답이다.

어휘 **tablecloth** 식탁보, 테이블보 **yet** 아직도 **wear** ~을 입다, 걸치다 **whatever + 주어 + 동사** 주어가 ~하는 무엇이든 **leave** 놓다, 두다

6. Will you have the work schedules completed soon or do you need more time?
(A) It's for the marketing department.
(B) Can I finish them tomorrow?
(C) She will get here by 4 at the latest.

업무 일정표를 곧 완료하실 건가요, 아니면 시간이 더 필요하세요?
(A) 마케팅 부서를 위한 거예요.
(B) 내일 끝내도 될까요?
(C) 그녀는 늦어도 4시까지 여기로 올 거예요.

해설 두 개의 질문이 들어 있는 선택 의문문이다. 두 개의 질문을 간추려 보면 A(work schedules 작성을 지금 완료할 것인가)와 B(시간이 더 필요한가)이다. 이에 대해 내일 완료해도 되는지 묻

는 (B)는 시간이 더 필요하다는 의미를 간접적으로 나타내는 대답으로, 주어진 선택 의문문에 적절한 응답이다.

어휘 **have A completed** A를 완료하다 **get here** 여기로 오다 **at the latest** 늦어도

7. Make sure there are enough seats for all attendees.
(A) Everyone showed up on time.
(B) It was very informative.
(C) I already set up at least fifty.

모든 참석자들의 좌석이 충분하도록 해두세요.
(A) 모두가 제시간에 왔어요.
(B) 아주 유익했어요.
(C) 제가 이미 적어도 50개는 준비해 뒀습니다.

해설 동사원형으로 시작하는 명령문으로서 Make sure ~(~을 확실하게 하다)는 상대방에게 당부를 할 때 쓰는 표현이다. 좌석이 충분하도록 확실히 해두라고 당부하는 말에 이미 좌석을 준비해 뒀다고 답하는 (C)가 가장 어울리는 응답이다.

어휘 **make sure (that)** ~임을 확실히 하다 **attendee** 참석자 **show up** 나타나다 **set up** ~을 마련하다, 준비하다 **at least** 적어도

8. You're going to the music festival, aren't you?
(A) There were a lot of bands.
(B) That's a nice song.
(C) Only if I can get time off work.

음악 축제에 가실 거죠, 그렇지 않나요?
(A) 많은 밴드들이 있었습니다.
(B) 그건 좋은 노래입니다.
(C) 제가 일을 쉴 수 있을 경우에만요.

해설 부가 의문문은 상대방에게 사실을 확인하는 의도로 쓰인다. 때문에 Yes/No로 답하는 것이 기본이지만 제 3의 대답도 할 수 있다는 것을 늘 염두에 두자. (C)는 '일을 쉴 수만 있다면 가겠다'라는 의미로, 질문에 대한 대답으로 적절하다. only if(~일 경우에만)이라는 구문을 알고 있어야 정답을 제대로 고를 수 있다.

어휘 **band** (대중 음악) 밴드 **only if** ~하기만 한다면, ~일 경우에만 **get time off work** 일을 쉬다

9. When will Ms. Doyle distribute the pay slips?
(A) Not until tomorrow.
(B) Some important information.
(C) Thanks, I'll let her know.

도일 씨는 급여 명세서를 언제 배부할 것인가요?
(A) 내일은 되어야 배부할 것입니다.
(B) 일부 중요한 정보입니다.
(C) 감사합니다, 제가 그녀에게 알려 줄게요.

해설 급여 명세서를 언제 배부할지를 묻는 질문이므로 배부 시점으

로 답하는 것이 기본이다. 단, not until ~이라는 표현에 익숙해져야 할 필요가 있는데, 「not until + 시점」은 '~이 되어서야 비로소'라는 뜻으로 Part 2에서 난이도 높은 When 질문에 대한 대답으로 잘 나온다. 따라서 '내일이나 되어야 배부할 것'이라는 의미인 (A)가 정답이다.

어휘 **distribute** ~을 배부하다 **pay slip** 급여 명세서 **not until + 시점** ~이나 되어야 비로소

10. Did you have any problems locating the baseball stadium?

(A) There's a game this Saturday.
(B) No, there were lots of signs.
(C) Let's meet at the north gate.

야구 경기장을 찾는 데 어떤 문제라도 있었나요?
(A) 이번 주 토요일에 경기가 있습니다.
(B) 아뇨, 표지판이 많이 있었습니다.
(C) 북문에서 만납시다.

해설 「have problems -ing」는 '~하는 데 문제가 있다'라는 표현이며, locate는 '~의 위치를 찾다'라는 동사이다. 따라서 이 문제는 야구 경기장을 찾는 데 어려움이 있었는지 묻는 질문이다. 이에 대한 대답으로 어렵지 않았다고(No) 말하며, 표지판이 많았다고 그 이유를 덧붙이는 (B)가 적절하다.

어휘 **have problems –ing** ~하는 데 문제가 있다 **locate** ~의 위치를 찾다 **lots of** 많은 **sign** 표지판 **at the north gate** 북문에서

11. How long is Serena going to be working at the Epsom branch?

(A) Since 10 a.m. this morning.
(B) Just until the end of this week.
(C) Yes, it's on the other side of town.

세레나 씨는 엡솜 지사에서 얼마나 오래 일할 예정인가요?
(A) 오늘 아침 10시부터요.
(B) 이번 주말까지만요.
(C) 네, 그것은 마을의 반대편에 있습니다.

해설 얼마나 오래 일할 것인지를 묻고 있으므로 언제까지 일할 것인지 그 구체적인 시점을 밝히는 대답이 가장 적절하다. 따라서 '이번 주가 끝날 때까지만'이라고 답하는 (B)가 정답이다. (A)의 since는 '~이후로 계속'이라는 의미로서, 과거의 한 시점부터 현재까지의 계속을 나타내기 때문에 질문의 미래시제와 맞지 않다. 의문사 의문문에 Yes/No로 답할 수 없으므로 (C)는 오답이다.

어휘 **branch** 지사, 지점

12. Were you able to get a refund for the jacket?
(A) I exchanged it instead.
(B) It looks quite expensive.
(C) I'd be able to help you.

그 재킷에 대해 환불 받을 수 있었나요?
(A) 그 대신에 교환했어요.
(B) 그것은 꽤 비싸 보이네요.
(C) 제가 도와드릴 수 있을 겁니다.

해설 환불을 받을 수 있었느냐는 질문에 대신 교환을 했다고 말하는 (A)가 가장 자연스러운 응답으로, 앞에 No가 생략되어 있다. (B)는 jacket과 관련하여 연상할 수 있는 expensive를 이용한 함정이며, (C)는 질문에 쓰인 표현을 그대로 쓴 함정이다.

어휘 **get a refund for** ~을 환불 받다 **exchange** ~을 교환하다 **quite** 꽤, 상당히

13. Does Mr. Daley know that the office supply order was changed?

(A) No, he wasn't surprised.
(B) He's been informed.
(C) I didn't know he had changed offices.

데일리 씨가 사무용품 주문이 변경되었다는 걸 알고 있나요?
(A) 아니요, 그는 놀라지 않았어요.
(B) 그는 통보를 받았어요.
(C) 저는 그가 사무실을 변경했다는 걸 몰랐어요.

해설 Does로 시작하는 일반 의문문이므로 Yes/No로 답하거나 또는 Yes/No를 의미하는 다른 말로 답해야 한다. 'Daley 씨가 ~라는 사실을 알고 있느냐'는 질문에 대해 He's been informed라고 답하는 (B)는 '그에게 그 내용이 알려졌다'라는 뜻으로, Yes를 의미하는 자연스러운 응답이다. inform은 '~에게 알리다'라는 뜻의 타동사로서 수동태로 쓰이면 '주어가 알고 있다, 주어에게 알려주었다'라는 뜻이 된다.

어휘 **office supply** 사무용품 **be informed** 알고 있다, 통보 받다

14. I'll be with you in just a moment.
(A) No, I haven't seen her.
(B) It was a nice surprise.
(C) There's no need to hurry.

잠시 후에 당신에게 가겠습니다.
(A) 아뇨, 저는 그녀를 본 적이 없습니다.
(B) 그것은 뜻밖의 기쁜 소식이었습니다.
(C) 서두르실 필요 없습니다.

해설 I'll be with you는 '당신에게 가겠다, 가서 도와주겠다'라는 뜻으로, '잠시 후에'라는 뜻의 in a minute[moment] 등과 같은 표현과 잘 쓰인다. '곧 가겠다'라는 말에 대한 반응으로 적절한 것은 서두를 필요가 없다는 뜻인 (C)이다. 의문사 의문문과 달리 평서문은 문장 전체를 다 듣고 상황을 파악해야 답을 고를 수 있기 때문에 난이도가 높다.

어휘 **in just a moment** 잠시 후에, 곧 **nice surprise** 뜻밖의 기쁜 소식, 깜짝 놀랄 만한 좋은 소식 **hurry** 서두르다

15. How many employees attended the Christmas

party?

(A) I'd love to go.

(B) Almost everyone.

(C) Yes, it starts at 6.

얼마나 많은 직원들이 크리스마스 파티에 참석했나요?

(A) 꼭 가고 싶어요.

(B) 거의 모두 다요.

(C) 네, 6시에 시작해요.

해설 '얼마나 많은'이라는 의미로 수량을 묻는 How many ~? 의 문문이므로, 정확한 숫자는 아니더라도 숫자를 대략적으로 추측해서 말할 수 있는 표현인 'almost(거의, 대부분)'가 들어간 (B)가 정답이다. 그리고 갈지 안 갈지 의사를 물어본 질문이 아니므로 (A)는 오답, 의문사 의문문에 Yes/No로 답할 수 없으므로 (C) 또한 오답이다.

어휘 **I'd love to do** 꼭 ~하고 싶다 **almost** 거의, 대부분

16. Have you spoken to the new intern yet?

(A) The keynote speech.

(B) Check the contract terms.

(C) We had a brief chat.

새로 온 인턴과 이야기해보셨습니까?

(A) 기조연설입니다.

(B) 계약조건을 확인해보세요.

(C) 잠시 대화를 했습니다.

해설 Have you 과거분사 ~?는 '~을 했습니까'라고 묻는 일반 의문문이다. '새로 온 인턴과 이야기를 해보았는지'를 묻고 있으므로 Yes나 No로 답하는 것이 자연스러운데, (C)는 Yes를 생략하고 '잠시 이야기를 해 보았다'는 말로 질문에 긍정하고 있으므로 잘 어울리는 대답이다.

어휘 **contract terms** 계약 조건 **brief chat** 짧은 대화

17. Can you tell Judy Walker about the schedule conflict, or shall I?

(A) Why don't I take care of it?

(B) I'm afraid we are overbooked.

(C) Judy tries to avoid conflict.

주디 워커 씨에게 일정이 겹치는 문제에 대해 말씀하실 수 있나요, 아니면 제가 할까요?

(A) 제가 처리하는 게 어떨까요?

(B) 유감스럽게도 저희는 예약이 초과된 상태입니다.

(C) 주디 씨는 충돌을 피하기 위해 노력하고 있어요.

해설 '문장 or 문장' 선택 의문문이지만, 두 번째 문장에서 반복되는 부분을 생략하고 조동사와 주어만 제시된 형태이다. 질문의 핵심은 질문자와 응답자 중에 누가 Judy에게 얘기할 것인지이므로 응답자가 자신이 하는 게 어떤지 제안하기 위해 되묻는 (A)가 정답이다.

어휘 **schedule conflict** 일정의 겹침 cf. conflict 충돌, 상충

take care of ~을 처리하다 I'm afraid (that) 유감이지만 ~이다 overbook 예약을 초과해 받다 try to do ~하려 노력하다 avoid ~을 피하다

18. You are planning on signing up for the bowling club, aren't you?

(A) Maybe I'll order another bowl.

(B) Yes, I like those designs.

(C) I'm waiting to see who else joins.

당신은 볼링 클럽에 가입할 계획이죠, 그렇지 않나요?

(A) 아마 전 한 그릇 더 주문할 것 같아요.

(B) 네, 저는 그 디자인들을 좋아합니다.

(C) 그밖에 누가 가입하는지 보려고 기다리고 있습니다.

해설 볼링 클럽에 가입할 계획인지 확인하는 질문이므로 그럴 계획이라면 Yes, 아니라면 No로 답하는 것이 보통이나, Yes/No를 언급하지 않고 그러한 의미를 전달할 수도 있으므로, 무조건 Yes/No만 기다릴 것이 아니라 상황에 맞는 대답이 나오면 정답으로 택하도록 한다. (C)는 '누가 가입하는지 보려고 기다리고 있다'는 뜻으로 아직 볼링 클럽에 가입할 계획은 아니라는 의미이며, 질문에 어울리는 응답이다.

어휘 **sign up** 등록하다, 가입하다 **bowling** 볼링 **bowl** (움푹한) 그릇

19. Ron has offered to lead the computer skills workshop.

(A) That will be a great help.

(B) Try turning it off and then on again.

(C) It's open to all staff.

론 씨가 컴퓨터 활용 능력 워크숍을 진행하겠다고 제의했어요.

(A) 그럼 정말 큰 도움이 될 거예요.

(B) 껐다가 다시 켜보세요.

(C) 그건 모든 직원에게 열려있어요.

해설 평서문은 의문문과 달리 정보를 요구하기보다는 정보나 문제 사항을 전달하는 기능을 한다. 여기서도 'Ron이 워크숍을 진행하겠다고 했다'는 정보를 전달하고 있다. 이에 대해 '그럼 큰 도움이 될 것이다'라며 자신의 의견을 말하는 (A)가 가장 잘 어울리는 답변이다.

어휘 **offer to do** ~하겠다고 제의하다 **lead** ~을 이끌다

20. Mr. Pietro is presenting at the board meeting tomorrow.

(A) No, I thought it was boring.

(B) It was very nice meeting you.

(C) Does he have the updated sales figures?

피에트로 씨가 내일 이사진 회의에서 발표를 할 거예요.

(A) 아뇨, 전 그게 지루하다고 생각했어요.

(B) 만나서 반가웠습니다.

(C) 그가 최신 매출 수치를 갖고 있나요?

해설 피에트로 씨가 내일 발표를 할 것이라고 말하는 것에 대해 그 (피에트로 씨)의 발표와 관련해 최신 매출 자료를 갖고 있는지 확인하는 (C)가 자연스러운 응답이다. 이렇게 상대방의 말에 대해 질문하는 응답 유형은 정답일 확률이 높다.

어휘 **present** 발표하다 **board meeting** 이사진 회의 **boring** 지루한 **updated** 최신의 **sales figures** 매출액, 매출 수치

Part 3

Questions 21-23 refer to the following conversation.

> **M:** Hi, Claire. Have you started getting things ready for **21** the charity event to raise money for the children's hospital?
>
> **W:** Yes, I've spoken with the event organizers about the job. **22** They want us to provide a wide range of sandwiches and cakes, plus tea, coffee, and soft drinks. I'll ask our team to set up our food tables at 5 P.M., one hour before the guests arrive.
>
> **M:** Sounds good. **23** We have a small problem, though. Two of our team will be away for training that day, so we might not have enough workers.
>
> **W:** Hmm, maybe you and I will need to help out at the event then.
>
> ┄┄┄┄┄┄┄┄┄┄┄┄┄┄┄┄┄┄┄┄┄┄┄┄┄┄┄
>
> 남: 안녕하세요, 클레어 씨. 아동 병원을 위해 모금하는 자선 행사에 필요한 일은 준비하기 시작하셨나요?
> 여: 네, 그 일과 관련해 행사 주최 측과 이야기했습니다. 그쪽에서 우리에게 아주 다양한 샌드위치와 케이크뿐만 아니라 차와 커피, 그리고 청량 음료를 제공해 주길 원하고 있습니다. 제가 손님들이 도착하기 한 시간 전인 오후 5시에 음식 테이블을 설치하도록 우리 팀에 요청할 겁니다.
> 남: 좋습니다. 하지만, 작은 문제가 하나 있습니다. 우리 팀에서 두 분이 그날 교육 때문에 자리를 비우게 될 것이기 때문에, 직원이 충분하지 않을지도 모릅니다.
> 여: 흠, 아마 그럼 당신과 제가 행사장에서 도와야 할 겁니다.

어휘 **get things ready for** ~에 대한 일을 준비하다 **charity** 자선 (단체) **raise money** 모금하다, 돈을 모으다 **organize** 주최하다, 조직하다 **a wide range of** 아주 다양한 **plus** ~뿐만 아니라, ~에 더해 **set up** ~을 설치하다, ~을 마련하다 **arrive** 도착하다 **be away** 자리를 비우다 **help out** 돕다 **then** 그럼, 그렇다면, 그때, 그런 다음

21. 화자들이 어떤 종류의 행사를 이야기하고 있는가?

(A) 세미나
(B) 시상식 연회
(C) 모금 행사
(D) 개장 기념 행사

해설 남자가 대화를 시작하면서 아동 병원을 위해 모금하는 자선 행사를(the charity event to raise money) 언급한 뒤로 이 행사 준비와 관련해 이야기 나누고 있으므로 (C)가 정답이다.

어휘 **banquet** 만찬, 연회 **fundraiser** 모금 행사

Paraphrase charity event to raise money
→ fundraiser

22. 화자들이 어떤 업계에서 일하고 있는 것 같은가?

(A) 회계
(B) 교육
(C) 출장 요리 제공
(D) 엔지니어링

해설 대화 중반부에 여자가 행사 주최 측을 They로, 자신의 소속 업체를 us로 각각 지칭하면서 다양한 샌드위치와 케이크뿐만 아니라 차와 커피, 그리고 청량 음료를 제공하는 일을(They want us to provide a wide range of sandwiches and cakes, plus tea, coffee, and soft drinks) 언급하고 있다. 이는 음식을 제공하는 업체에서 하는 일이므로 (C)가 정답이다.

어휘 **industry** 업계

23. 남자의 말에 따르면 무엇이 문제인가?

(A) 교육 시간이 취소되었다.
(B) 일부 제품이 현재 품절된 상태이다.
(C) 행사 일정표가 업데이트되지 않았다.
(D) 일부 직원이 시간이 나지 않을 것이다.

해설 대화 후반부에 여자가 문제가 하나 있음을 언급하면서 두 명의 직원이 자리를 비우게 되어 직원이 충분하지 않을 수도 있다는 점을(We have a small problem, though. Two of our team will be away ~ we might not have enough workers) 알리고 있다. 이는 일부 직원이 시간이 나지 않는 문제를 말하는 것이므로 (D)가 정답이다.

어휘 **currently** 현재 **out of stock** 품절된, 재고가 없는 **unavailable** (사람) 시간이 없는, (사물) 구입할 수 없는, 이용할 수 없는

Paraphrase Two of our team will be away / not have enough workers
→ Some workers will be unavailable

Questions 24-26 refer to the following conversation.

M: Dave's Dog Training School. What can I do for you?

W: Hi, **24** I saw an ad for your company on TV recently. I recently got a dog, and I think I need some help with training him.

M: Sure. Can you tell me some details about your dog?

W: Well, he was a stray, and I got him from an animal shelter. **25** He gets quite scared and aggressive around people, so I'm having trouble training him.

M: Oh, I see that kind of thing all the time.

W: Great!

M: In fact, if you'd like to see the work I've done in similar cases, **26** I can forward some video clips to you.

W: I'd be interested in seeing them. Thanks.

남: 데이브의 반려견 훈련 학교입니다. 무엇을 도와 드릴까요?
여: 안녕하세요, 제가 최근에 TV에서 귀하의 회사에 대한 광고를 봤습니다. 저한테 최근에 개가 한 마리 생겼는데, 제 생각에 훈련시키는 데 도움이 좀 필요한 것 같아서요.
남: 네. 그 개와 관련해 상세 정보를 좀 말씀해 주시겠습니까?
여: 음, 떠돌이 개였는데, 동물 보호소에서 데려 왔어요. 사람들 주변에서 꽤 겁을 먹고 공격적인 상태가 되기 때문에, 훈련시키는 데 어려움이 있습니다.
남: 아, 저는 그런 종류의 일을 항상 봅니다.
여: 잘됐네요!
남: 사실, 유사한 경우에 대해 제가 했던 일을 확인해 보고 싶으신 경우, 몇몇 동영상을 전송해 드릴 수 있습니다.
여: 관심 있게 보게 될 거예요. 감사합니다.

어휘 **ad** 광고 **recently** 최근에 **help with** ~에 대한 도움 **details** 상세 정보, 세부 사항 **stray** 떠돌이 동물, 길 잃은 동물 **shelter** 보호소, 쉼터 **get A** A한 상태가 되다 **quite** 꽤, 상당히 **scared** 겁 먹은 **aggressive** 공격적인 **have trouble -ing** ~하는 데 어려움이 있다 **all the time** 항상 **in fact** 사실, 실제로 **similar** 유사한 **case** 경우, 사례 **forward** ~을 전송하다 **video clip** 동영상

24. 여자가 회사와 관련해 어떻게 듣게 되었는가?
(A) 가족을 통해서
(B) TV 광고를 통해서
(C) 회사 동료를 통해서
(D) 홍보용 전단을 통해서

해설 여자가 회사와 관련해 어떻게 듣게 되었는지 묻고 있으므로 여자의 말에 집중해 정보를 얻게 된 방식이나 과정과 관련해 언급하는 내용을 파악해야 한다. 여자가 대화 초반부에 최근에 TV에서 남자의 회사 광고를 본 사실을(~ I saw an ad for your company on TV recently) 언급하고 있으므로 (B)가 정답이다.

어휘 **promotional** 홍보의 **flyer** 전단
Paraphrase ad for your company on TV
→ TV advertisement

25. 남자가 "저는 그런 종류의 일을 항상 봅니다"라고 말할 때 무엇을 의미하는가?
(A) 최근에 개를 한 마리 새로 샀다.
(B) 한 가지 상황에 대한 지식이 있다.
(C) 한 가지 제안에 동의하지 않는다.
(D) 자신의 일정에 비는 시간이 없다.

해설 여자가 대화 중반부에 자신의 개가 사람들 주변에서 겁을 먹고 공격적인 상태가 된다는 점과 그래서 훈련시키는 데 어려움이 있다는(He gets quite scared and aggressive ~ I'm having trouble training him) 사실을 알리자, 남자가 '그런 종류의 일을 항상 봅니다'라고 말하는 흐름이다. 이는 그런 상황을 많이 겪어봐서 대처 방법을 알고 있다는 뜻에 해당되는 말이므로 이러한 의미로 쓰인 (B)가 정답이다.

어휘 **knowledge** 지식 **situation** 상황 **disagree with** ~에 동의하지 않다 **suggestion** 제안, 의견 **opening** 빈 시간, 빈 자리

26. 남자가 무엇을 보내겠다고 제안하는가?
(A) 몇몇 팸플릿
(B) 몇몇 웹 사이트 주소
(C) 몇몇 동영상
(D) 몇몇 길 안내 정보

해설 남자가 무엇을 보내겠다고 제안하는지 묻고 있으므로 남자의 말에 집중해 제안 표현과 함께 제시되는 정보를 찾아야 한다. 대화 후반부에 남자가 몇몇 동영상을 전송해 줄 수 있다고(I can forward some video clips to you) 알리고 있으므로 (C)가 정답이다.

어휘 **pamphlet** 팸플릿, 안내 책자 **directions** 길 안내 정보

Questions 27-29 refer to the following conversation.

M: Thanks for calling Pegasus Event Planning. This is Mike Rodgers.

W: Good morning, Mike. This is Rachel Lee calling. Thanks for **27** inviting me and my kitchen staff to this year's International Food Fair.

M: Hi, Rachel. I'm sure all the attendees will love 27 the food you cook today. Did the event staff help you set up 28 your booth?

W: That's why I'm calling, actually. 28 It hasn't been set up, and I can't see any of your staff here.

M: Oh, I'm sorry about that. They might be busy having a morning meeting before getting started. 29 I'll call one of our event managers and ask him to help you out right away.

남: 페가수스 행사 기획사에 전화 주셔서 감사합니다. 저는 마이크 로저스입니다.

여: 안녕하세요, 로저스 씨. 저는 레이첼 리입니다. 저와 저희 주방 직원을 올해의 국제 식품 박람회에 초대해 주셔서 감사합니다.

남: 안녕하세요, 레이첼 씨. 분명 모든 참석자들께서 오늘 요리해 주시는 음식을 아주 좋아하실 겁니다. 행사 직원이 부스를 설치하시는 데 도움을 드렸나요?

여: 실은, 그게 전화 드리는 이유입니다. 설치가 되어 있지 않고, 이곳에 직원이 한 분도 보이지 않습니다.

남: 아, 그 부분에 대해 사과 드립니다. 그 직원들이 일을 시작하기 전에 오전 회의를 하느라 바쁠지도 모릅니다. 제가 저희 행사 관리 책임자들 중 한 명에게 전화해서 즉시 도와 드리도록 요청하겠습니다.

어휘 **This is A calling** (전화상에서) 저는 A입니다 **invite** ~을 초대하다 **fair** 박람회 **attendee** 참석자 **help A do** A가 ~하는 데 도움을 주다 **set up** ~을 설치하다, ~을 마련하다 **booth** (행사장 등에서 임시로 설치하는) 부스, 칸막이 공간 **actually** 실은, 사실 **be busy -ing** ~하느라 바쁘다 **get started** 시작하다 **help A out** A를 돕다 **right away** 즉시, 당장

27. 여자가 누구일 것 같은가?
(A) 행사 기획자
(B) 요리사
(C) 음악가
(D) 미술가

해설 특정 화자의 신분을 묻는 문제의 경우, 특정 업무나 활동, 전문 지식, 제공 서비스 등과 관련된 정보를 통해 단서를 파악해야 한다. 여자가 대화 초반부에 자신과 주방 직원을(inviting me and my kitchen staff) 언급하고 있고, 남자가 곧이어 여자가 요리하는 음식을(the food you cook today) 말하는 것으로 볼 때, 요리사임을 알 수 있으므로 (B)가 정답이다.

28. 여자가 어떤 문제를 언급하는가?
(A) 행사가 연기되었다.
(B) 부스가 준비되지 않았다.
(C) 일부 장비가 고장 났다.

(D) 일부 행사 참석자가 불만을 제기했다.

해설 남자가 대화 중반부에 여자의 부스와(your booth) 관련된 질문을 한 뒤로 여자가 booth를 It으로 지칭해 아직 설치되지 않은 사실(It hasn't been set up ~) 알리고 있다, 이는 해당 부스가 아직 준비되지 않았다는 뜻이므로 (B)가 정답이다.

어휘 **postpone** ~을 연기하다, ~을 미루다 **prepare** ~을 준비하다 **equipment** 장비 **break down** 고장 나다 **complain** 불만을 제기하다

Paraphrase booth / It hasn't been set up
→ A booth has not been prepared

29. 남자가 곧이어 무엇을 할 것 같은가?
(A) 회의 시간을 마련하는 일
(B) 문서를 보내는 일
(C) 동료 직원에게 연락하는 일
(D) 일부 용품을 주문하는 일

해설 대화 마지막 부분에 남자가 소속 업체의 행사 관리 책임자들 중 한 명에게 전화하겠다고(I'll call one of our event managers ~) 알리는 부분이 있는데, 이는 회사 동료 직원에게 연락하는 일을 뜻하므로 (C)가 정답이다.

어휘 **organize** ~을 마련하다, ~을 조직하다 **contact** ~에게 연락하다 **colleague** 동료 (직원) **supplies** 용품, 물품

Paraphrase call one of our event managers
→ Contact a colleague

Questions 30-32 refer to the following conversation with three speakers.

M1: We're glad you found some time to meet with us today, Sarah. We know you must be busy preparing for your upcoming concert tour.

W: Yes, 30 I've been rehearsing the songs with my band all week. But that's okay... I'm excited to meet with you about our collaboration.

M1: We're very glad you've agreed to write music for our new movie.

M2: Yes, so 31 we're here today to go over the terms of the contract with you.

W: Well, I want to work with you because 32 I was a big fan of the TV show you both directed. I watched it every Friday. I never missed it!

M2: That's nice to hear. We hope our movie will be just as successful. So, let's take a look at the terms in the agreement.

남1: 오늘 저희와 만나실 수 있는 시간이 있으셨다니 기쁩니다, 새라 씨. 다가오는 콘서트 투어를 준비하시느라 틀림없이 바쁘신 것으로 알고 있습니다.

여: 네, 일주일 내내 제 밴드와 함께 노래들을 계속 예행 연습하고 있습니다. 하지만 괜찮습니다... 공동 작업과 관련해 만나 뵙게 되어 기쁩니다.

남1: 저희 신작 영화를 위해 곡을 쓰시는 데 동의해 주셔서 아주 기쁩니다.

남2: 네, 그래서 저희가 함께 계약서 조항을 살펴보기 위해 오늘 이곳에 왔습니다.

여: 음, 제가 두 분과 함께 작업하고 싶은 이유는 제가 두 분께서 연출하신 TV 프로그램을 아주 좋아하는 팬이었기 때문입니다. 금요일마다 시청했거든요. 절대 놓치지 않았어요!

남2: 그 말씀을 들으니 좋습니다. 저희는 저희 영화가 딱 그만큼만 성공적이기를 바라고 있습니다. 자, 함께 계약서 조항을 한 번 살펴보시죠.

어휘 **find time to do** ~할 시간을 내다 **meet with** (약속하고) ~와 만나다 **prepare for** ~을 준비하다 **upcoming** 다가오는, 곧 있을 **rehearse** ~을 예행 연습하다 **collaboration** 공동 작업, 협업 **agree to do** ~하는 데 동의하다 **go over** ~을 살펴보다, ~을 검토하다 **term** (계약서 등의) 조항, 조건 **contract** 계약(서) **direct** ~을 연출하다, ~을 감독하다 **miss** ~을 놓치다, ~을 지나치다 **just as** 딱 ~하는 만큼 **take a look at** ~을 한 번 보다 **agreement** 계약(서), 합의(서)

30. 여자가 누구일 것 같은가?
(A) 음악가
(B) 배우
(C) 작가
(D) 모델

해설 특정 화자의 신분을 묻는 문제의 경우, 특정 업무나 활동, 전문 지식, 제공 서비스 등과 관련된 정보를 통해 단서를 파악해야 한다. 대화 초반부에 여자가 계속 노래들을 예행 연습하고 있다고(I've been rehearsing the songs with my band all week) 알리는 부분을 통해 음악가임을 알 수 있으므로 (A)가 정답이다.

31. 회의의 목적이 무엇인가?
(A) 일부 공연자를 평가하는 것
(B) 마케팅 캠페인을 만드는 것
(C) 비즈니스 계약을 논의하는 것
(D) 상을 제공하는 것

해설 회의의 목적이 무엇인지 묻는 경우, 대화의 목적을 묻는 것과 같을 수 있으므로 주제나 목적이 드러날 가능성이 높은 초반부에 우선적으로 집중해 들어야 한다. 하지만, 종종 배경 설명 후에 중반부나 후반부에 가서 실제 목적이 언급되는 흐름으로 진행되는 대화도 있으므로 주의해야 한다. 대화 중반부에 남자 한 명이 함께 계약서 조항을 살펴보기 위해 왔다고(~ we're here

today to go over the terms of the contract with you) 언급하는 부분이 회의 목적에 해당되며, 이는 계약 사항을 논의하는 일을 뜻하므로 (C)가 정답이다.

어휘 **evaluate** ~을 평가하다 **performer** 공연자, 연주자 **create** ~을 만들어내다 **present** ~을 제공하다, ~을 제시하다 **award** 상

Paraphrase go over the terms of the contract
→ discuss a business contract

32. 여자가 한 TV 프로그램과 관련해 무슨 말을 하는가?
(A) 흥미롭지 않다고 생각했다.
(B) 주기적으로 시청했다.
(C) 주연 배우와 친하다.
(D) 한 배역에 대해 오디션을 봤다.

해설 여자가 대화 후반부에 남자들이 연출한 TV 프로그램을 아주 좋아해서 금요일마다 시청했다고(I was a big fan of the TV show you both directed. I watched it every Friday ~) 말하고 있다. 이는 주기적으로 시청했다는 말과 같으므로 (B)가 정답이다.

어휘 **find A B** A를 B하다고 생각하다 **be friends with** ~와 친하다, ~와 스스럼 없는 사이다 **uninteresting** 흥미롭지 않은 **regularly** 주기적으로, 규칙적으로 **audition** v. 오디션을 보다

Paraphrase watched it every Friday
→ watched it regularly

Questions 33-35 refer to the following conversation and design options.

W: Hi, Antony. I'm trying to make sure **33** everything is organized for our job fair next month. Did you already design the job fair Web site like I asked?

M: Yes, and it's almost ready to be launched online. The one thing I haven't decided yet is which logo to use for the event. I'm trying to decide between these four logos.

W: Hmm... **34** Let's go with the one with the two hands. It looks very professional.

M: That's my favorite, too. Oh, and **35** I haven't added the event dates to the Web site yet. Can you send those to me, if they've been finalized?

W: Of course. I'll send them in a moment.

여: 안녕하세요, 안토니 씨. 다음 달에 열릴 우리 취업 설명회에 필요한 모든 것이 준비된 상태인지 확실히 해두려는 중입니다. 제가 요청 드린 것처럼 취업 설명회 웹 사이트를 이미 디자인하셨나요?

남: 네, 그리고 이미 온라인으로 공개될 준비가 되어 있습니다. 제가 아직 결정하지 못한 한 가지는 어느 로고를 이 행사에 사용할 것인가 하는 점입니다. 저는 이 네 가지 로고 중에서 결정하려 하고 있습니다.

여: 음... 두 손으로 되어 있는 것으로 합시다. 아주 전문적으로 보여요.

남: 저도 그게 가장 좋습니다. 아, 그리고 제가 웹 사이트에 행사 날짜들을 아직 추가하지 않았습니다. 최종 확정된 상태라면, 저에게 보내 주시겠어요?

여: 물론입니다. 잠시 후에 보내 드릴게요.

로고 1 　　로고 2 　　로고 3 　　로고 4

어휘 **try to do** ~하려 하다 **make sure (that)** ~임을 확실히 해두다, 반드시 ~하도록 하다 **organize** ~을 준비하다, ~을 조직하다, ~을 체계화하다 **job fair** 취업 설명회, 직업 박람회 **be ready to do** ~할 준비가 되다 **launch** ~을 공개하다, ~을 시작하다, ~을 출시하다 **decide** ~을 결정하다 **go with** (결정) ~로 하다 **look A** A하게 보이다, A한 것 같다 **professional** 전문적인 **favorite** 가장 좋아하는 것 **add A to B** A를 B에 추가하다 **finalize** ~을 최종 확정하다 **in a moment** 잠시 후에

33. 화자들이 무엇을 계획하는가?
(A) 회사 야유회
(B) 시상식
(C) 직원 모집 행사
(D) 교육 세미나

해설 화자들이 무엇을 계획하는지 묻고 있으므로 특정 행사나 활동 및 그 특징과 관련된 정보를 찾아야 한다. 여자가 대화를 시작하면서 자신들이 준비하고 있는 취업 설명회를(everything is organized for our job fair) 언급하고 있다. 이는 직원을 모집하기 위한 행사에 해당되므로 (C)가 정답이다.

어휘 **outing** 야유회 **recruitment** (직원 등의) 모집 **training** 교육, 훈련

Paraphrase job fair
→ recruitment event

34. 시각자료를 보시오. 여자가 어느 로고를 마음에 들어 하는가?
(A) 로고 1
(B) 로고 2
(C) 로고 3
(D) 로고 4

해설 제품 그림이나 디자인적 요소가 시각자료로 제시되는 경우, 형태나 기호, 배치 방식 등과 같은 특징을 파악하는 것이 중요하며, 항목별로 각 선택지와 짝을 이루는 정보가 담화 중에 단서로 제시된다는 점에 유의해야 한다. 대화 중반부에 여자가 두 손으로 되어 있는 것으로 하자고 언급하면서 아주 전문적으로 보인다고(Let's go with the one with the two hands. It looks very professional) 알리고 있다. 시각자료에서 손 모양 그림으로 되어 있는 것이 맨 왼쪽에 있는 Logo 1이므로 (A)가 정답이다.

35. 남자가 여자에게 무엇을 보내도록 요청하는가?
(A) 이메일 주소
(B) 행사장 위치
(C) 몇몇 행사 날짜
(D) 몇몇 이미지 파일

해설 남자가 여자에게 무엇을 보내도록 요청하는지 묻고 있으므로 남자의 말에 집중해 요청 표현과 함께 제시되는 정보를 찾아야 한다. 대화 후반부에 남자가 웹 사이트에 행사 날짜들을 아직 추가하지 않은 상태임을 언급하면서 그 날짜들을 보내 달라고(I haven't added the event dates to the Web site yet. Can you send those to me, ~?) 요청하고 있으므로 (C)가 정답이다.

어휘 **venue** 행사장, 개최 장소 **location** 위치, 장소, 지점

Questions 36-38 refer to the following conversation and invoice.

M: Ms. Coleman, the **36** sandwiches have arrived for the office party, **36** but some of them smell bad. **37** Do you want me to call Regal Catering and complain about it?

W: Yes, if there's something wrong with the sandwiches, we can't accept them. **37** Perhaps we shouldn't have contacted such a new company. We should've stuck with our usual local caterer.

M: I guess so. Well, **38** I'll give them a call and ask them to come and pick up the egg salad sandwiches immediately.

W: Thanks, Paul. And make sure they refund us the fifty dollars we already paid for them.

남: 콜만 씨, 사무실 파티를 위한 샌드위치가 도착했는데, 일부 샌드위치에서 안 좋은 냄새가 나요. 제가 리걸 케이터링 사에 전화해서 불만을 제기할까요?

여: 네, 샌드위치에 잘못된 것이 있다면, 받아들일 수 없죠. 아마 그곳과 같이 새로 생긴 업체에 연락하지 말았어야 했던 것 같아요. 우리가 평소에 이용하던 지역 내 출장 요리 업체를 계속 이용해야 했어요.

남: 저도 그렇게 생각해요. 그럼, 제가 전화를 해서 이곳에 와서 계란 샐러드 샌드위치를 즉시 가져가도록 요청할게요.

여: 고마워요, 폴 씨. 그리고 우리가 이미 지불한 50달러를 반드시 환불 받도록 하세요.

리걸 케이터링 주식회사 고객 거래 내역서 #2817		
품목	수량	가격
치즈 샌드위치	25	50달러
햄 샌드위치	30	60달러
계란 샐러드 샌드위치	20	50달러
참치 마요네즈 샌드위치	15	45달러
	총액:	205달러

어휘 complain about ~에 대해 불만을 제기하다 accept 받아들이다, 수락하다 should(n't) have p.p. ~했어야(하지 말았어야) 했다 contact ~에게 연락하다 stick with ~을 고수하다, ~을 계속해서 이용하다 usual 평상시의, 흔히 하는 caterer 출장 요리 제공 업체 give A a call A에게 전화하다 immediately 즉시 make sure (that) 반드시 ~하다, 꼭 ~하다 refund 환불해 주다 pay for ~을 값을 지불하다 invoice 거래 내역서 quantity 수량 item 물품, 품목 total amount 총액

36. 화자들은 무슨 문제점에 관해 이야기하고 있는가?
(A) 일부 물품이 배송되지 않았다.
(B) 출장 요리를 제공 받는 행사가 취소되었다.
(C) 회사가 가격을 인상했다.
(D) 일부 물품이 만족스럽지 못하다.

해설 남자의 첫 대사에서 알 수 있다. 샌드위치를 배달 받았는데 상한 냄새가 난다는(some of them smell bad) 것이다. 이를 unsatisfactory라고 돌려 표현한 (D)가 정답이다.

어휘 cater ~에 출장 요리 서비스를 제공하다 raise ~을 인상하다, 올리다 unsatisfactory 불만족스러운

Paraphrase sandwiches / some of them smell bad
→ Some items are unsatisfactory.

37. 여자는 리걸 케이터링에 대해 무엇을 언급하는가?
(A) 기업 할인 서비스를 제공한다.
(B) 현지의 재료만을 사용한다.
(C) 비교적 새로 생긴 회사이다.
(D) 직원들이 매우 경험이 많다.

해설 Regal Catering Co.는 샌드위치를 배달한 업체이다. 이를 두고 여자가 Perhaps we shouldn't have contacted such a new company(그런 새로 생긴 업체에 전화하지 말았어야 해)라고 말하는 것에서 이 회사가 신생 업체임을 알 수 있다. 따라서 (C)가 정답이다.

어휘 corporate discount 기업 할인 local 지역의, 현지의 ingredient 재료, 성분 relatively 비교적, 상대적으로 highly 매우 experienced 경험[경력]이 많은

Paraphrase new company
→ new business

38. 시각자료를 보시오. 얼마나 많은 샌드위치가 반품될 것인가?
(A) 25개
(B) 30개
(C) 20개
(D) 15개

해설 대화 후반부에 남자가 I'll give them a call and ask them to come and pick up the egg salad sandwiches immediately 라고 말한다. 계란 샐러드 샌드위치를 반품하겠다고 하는데, 주어진 주문 확인서에서 계란 샐러드 샌드위치 수량을 확인해 보면 20개이므로 (C)가 정답이다.

어휘 return ~을 반품하다

Part 4

Questions 39-41 refer to the following excerpt from a meeting.

I called this meeting to discuss the rising number of customer complaints. I've noticed that many of you are having difficulty resolving problems **39 when you deal with customers on the phone or at the service desk.** I think it's because some of you don't have enough knowledge about the products our company manufactures. So, I've invited our company's lead product developer, **40 Roberta Simmons,** to come and explain specific features and functions of our products. She'll be here in about 30 minutes, so **41 I'd like you to think of some things you'd like to ask her when she arrives.**

숫자가 증가하고 있는 고객 불만 문제를 논의하기 위해 이 회의를 소집했습니다. 여러분 중 많은 분들이 전화상으로 또는 서비스 데스크에서 고객들을 응대하실 때 문제를 해결하시는 데 어려움을 겪고 계신다는 사실을 알게 되었습니다. 제 생각엔 여러분 중 일부가 우리 회사에서 제조하는 제품들과 관련된 지식을 충분히 갖고 계시지 않기 때문인 것 같습니다. 따라서, 저는 우리 회사의 선임 제품 개발 책임자인 로버타 시먼스 씨께 이 자리에 오셔서 우리 제품들의 구체적인 특징 및 기능을 설명하시도록 요청 드렸습니다. 약 30분 후에 이곳에 오실 것이기 때문에, 도착하시면 여쭤 보고자 하시는 몇 가지 사항들을 생각해 보셨으면 합니다.

어휘 call a meeting 회의를 소집하다 discuss ~을 논의하다, ~을 이야기하다 rising 증가하는, 상승하는 complaint 불만, 불평 notice that ~임을 알게 되다, ~임을 알아차리다 have difficulty -ing ~하는 데 어려움을 겪다 resolve ~을 해결하다 deal with ~을 응대하다, ~을 처

리하다, ~을 다루다 **manufacture** ~을 제조하다 **invite A to do** A에게 ~하도록 요청하다 **developer** 개발자, 개발업체 **explain** ~을 설명하다 **specific** 구체적인, 특정한 **feature** 특징 **function** 기능 **in** 시간 ~ 후에 **about** 약, 대략

39. 청자들이 누구일 것 같은가?
(A) 영업 사원
(B) 광고 이사
(C) 창고 직원
(D) 고객 서비스 직원

해설 청자들의 신분을 묻고 있으므로 특정 업무나 활동, 전문 지식, 제공 서비스 등과 관련된 정보를 통해 단서를 파악해야 한다. 화자가 담화 초반부에 청자들을 you로 지칭해 전화상으로 또는 서비스 데스크에서 고객들을 응대하는 경우를(~ when you deal with customers on the phone or at the service desk) 언급하고 있다. 이는 고객 서비스 직원들이 하는 일에 해당되므로 (D)가 정답이다.

어휘 **sales** 영업, 판매(량), 매출 **representative** 직원, 대표자 **advertising** 광고 (활동) **executive** 이사, 임원 **warehouse** 창고 **agent** 직원, 대리인

40. 로버타 시먼스 씨가 무엇에 관해 이야기할 것인가?
(A) 마케팅 전략
(B) 제품 특징
(C) 비용 절감 조치
(D) 프로젝트 관리

해설 담화 중반부에 화자가 로버타 시먼스 씨를 언급하면서 이 사람이 와서 제품들의 구체적인 특징과 기능을 설명할 것이라고(~ Roberta Simmons, to come and explain specific features and functions of our products) 알리고 있으므로 (B)가 정답이다.

어휘 **strategy** 전략 **cost-saving** 비용을 절감하는 **measures** 조치

41. 화자가 청자들에게 무엇을 하도록 요청하는가?
(A) 몇몇 질문을 준비하는 일
(B) 몇몇 양식을 작성 완료하는 일
(C) 일정표를 확인하는 일
(D) 제품을 시연하는 일

해설 화자가 담화 맨 마지막 부분에 시먼스 씨가 도착하면 물어보고 싶은 것들을 생각해 놓으라고(~ I'd like you to think of some things you'd like to ask her when she arrives) 요청하고 있다. 이는 질문할 내용을 준비하고 있으라는 뜻이므로 (A)가 정답이다.

어휘 **prepare** ~을 준비하다 **complete** ~을 완료하다 **form** 양식, 서식 **demonstrate** ~을 시연하다, ~을 시범 보이다

Paraphrase think of some things you'd like to ask her
→ Prepare some questions

Questions 42-44 refer to the following telephone message.

Hello. **42** **This is Ken from Far East Tours.** I'm calling about the vacation package you booked for your trip to Indonesia and Malaysia. You mentioned that you were interested in joining a guided tour to Mount Bromo. Well, even though it was on short notice, I managed to find a tour that you could join. However, **43** you'll need to pay the registration fee in advance in order to secure your place. **44** If you would like to sign up for this activity, please get back to me at your earliest convenience. Keep in mind, there is likely to be high demand.

안녕하세요. 저는 파 이스트 투어스의 켄입니다. 귀하께서 인도네시아와 말레이시아로 떠나시는 여행을 위해 예약하신 휴가 패키지와 관련해 전화 드립니다. 귀하께서 브로모 산으로 가는 가이드 동반 투어에 참가하시는 데 관심이 있으시다고 언급하셨습니다. 음, 촉박한 통보였기는 하지만, 참가하실 수 있는 투어를 하나 찾아냈습니다. 하지만, 자리를 확보하시려면 미리 등록비를 지불하셔야 할 것입니다. 이 활동을 신청하시고자 하는 경우, 가급적 빨리 저에게 다시 연락 주십시오. 명심하셔야 하는 부분은, 수요가 높을 가능성이 있다는 점입니다.

어휘 **book** ~을 예약하다 **mention that** ~라고 언급하다 **join** ~에 참가하다, ~에 합류하다 **guided** 가이드를 동반하는 **even though** (비록) ·이기는 하지만 **short notice** 촉박한 통보 **manage to do** (간신히) ~해내다 **registration** 등록 **fee** 요금, 수수료 **secure** v. ~을 확보하다 **sign up for** ~을 신청하다, ~에 등록하다 **get back to** ~에게 다시 연락하다 **at your earliest convenience** 가급적 빨리 **keep in mind** 명심하다 **be likely to do** ~할 가능성이 있다 **demand** 수요, 요구

42. 화자가 누구일 것 같은가?
(A) 호텔 지배인
(B) 항공기 조종사
(C) 여행사 직원
(D) 공원 경비원

해설 화자가 담화 시작 부분에 소속 업체를 Far East Tours라고 밝히면서 상대방이 예약한 여행 패키지를(This is Ken from Far East Tours. I'm calling about the vacation package you booked for your trip ~) 언급하고 있다. 이는 여행사 직원이 할 수 있는 말에 해당되므로 (C)가 정답이다.

어휘 **agent** 직원, 대리인 **ranger** (공원 등의) 경비원, 관리원

43. 어떤 요건이 언급되는가?

(A) 운전 면허증
(B) 차량 대여
(C) 방문객 허가증
(D) 선금

해설 어떤 요건이 언급되는지 묻고 있는데, 요건은 충족해야 하는 조건을 말하는 것이므로 반드시 해야 하는 조건이나 요구 사항 등을 찾아야 한다. 담화 중반부에 화자가 청자에게 자리를 확보하려면 미리 등록비를 내야 한다고(~ you'll need to pay the registration fee in advance in order to secure your place) 알리고 있다. 이는 선금을 지불해야 한다는 조건을 말하는 것이므로 (D)가 정답이다.

어휘 requirement 요건, 필수 조건 vehicle 차량 rental 대여, 임대 permit 허가증 advance 사전의, 미리 하는

Paraphrase pay the registration fee in advance
→ advance fee

44. 화자가 "수요가 높을 가능성이 있다는 점입니다"라고 말할 때 무엇을 의미하는가?

(A) 일부 객실이 더 이상 이용할 수 없을 것이다.
(B) 일부 정보가 부정확했다.
(C) 청자가 빠른 결정을 내려야 한다.
(D) 청자가 대안을 고려해야 한다.

해설 담화 후반부에 화자가 특정 활동을 신청하려면 가급적 빨리 자신에게 다시 연락하라고(If you would like to sign up for this activity, please get back to me at your earliest convenience) 알리면서 '수요가 높을 가능성이 있습니다'라고 언급하는 흐름이다. 이는 높은 수요로 인해 빨리 마감될 수 있기 때문에 청자가 신속히 결정해야 한다는 뜻으로 하는 말이므로 (C)가 정답이다.

어휘 no longer 더 이상 ~ 않다 incorrect 부정확한 make a decision 결정을 내리다 consider ~을 고려하다 alternative n. 대안

Questions 45-47 refer to the following talk.

Thank you all for coming in early for this meeting. First of all, I'm glad to say that **45** our latest office desk sets have been selling well. We've actually sold more of them than our bed frames and sofas for the first time this quarter. **46** I am concerned about one thing, though. The lamps that go with that set have a frame that can crack easily, so you need to be very careful when handling those boxes. Be sure to warn customers about that. **47** I'd like to post a warning, but it should really catch people's attention. Does anyone have anything?

이 회의를 위해 일찍 와 주셔서 여러분 모두에게 감사드립니다. 가장 먼저, 우리의 최신 사무용 책상 세트가 계속 잘 판매되고 있다는 사실을 말씀 드리게 되어 기쁩니다. 우리가 사실 이번 분기에 처음으로 우리 침대 프레임과 소파들보다 그 제품을 더 많이 판매했습니다. 하지만, 저는 한 가지 우려되는 것이 있습니다. 그 세트에 딸려 나가는 전등이 쉽게 깨질 수 있는 프레임으로 되어 있기 때문에, 그 상자를 다루실 때 아주 조심하셔야 합니다. 꼭 고객들께 그 부분에 관해 주의시켜 드리십시오. 저는 주의 사항을 게시했으면 하는데, 정말로 사람들의 주의를 끌어야 합니다. 무엇이든 생각나는 게 있으신 분 있나요?

어휘 latest 최신의 actually 사실, 실은 for the first time 처음으로 quarter 분기 be concerned about ~을 우려하다, ~을 걱정하다 though (문장 끝이나 중간에서) 하지만 crack 깨지다, 금이 가다 careful 조심하는, 신중한 handle ~을 다루다, ~을 처리하다 be sure to do 꼭 ~하다, 반드시 ~하다 post ~을 게시하다 warning 주의 사항, 경고(문) catch one's attention ~의 주의를 끌다, ~의 관심을 끌다

45. 청자들이 어디에서 근무하고 있을 것 같은가?

(A) 인쇄소에서
(B) 가구 매장에서
(C) 이삿짐 회사에서
(D) 유통 센터에서

해설 담화 초반부에 화자가 소속 회사를 our로 지칭해 자사의 최신 사무용 책상 세트를(our latest office desk sets) 언급하고 있다. 이는 가구 제품에 해당되므로 (B)가 정답이다.

어휘 distribution 유통, 배부

46. 화자가 무엇을 우려하는가?

(A) 깨지기 쉬운 제품을 다루는 일
(B) 분기 목표를 충족하는 일
(C) 프로젝트 마감 기한을 연기하는 일
(D) 고객 불만 사항을 처리하는 일

해설 담화 중반부에 화자가 우려 사항이 있다는 사실을 말하면서 세트에 딸려 나가는 전등이 쉽게 깨질 수 있는 프레임으로 되어 있어서 조심스럽게 다뤄야 한다는 점을(~ The lamps that go with that set have a frame that can crack easily, so you need to be very careful when handling ~) 알리고 있으므로 (A)가 정답이다.

어휘 fragile 깨지기 쉬운, 취약한 meet (요구, 조건 등) ~을 충족하다 quarterly 분기의 postpone ~을 연기하다, ~을 미루다 deadline 마감 기한 deal with ~을 처리하다, ~을 다루다 complaint 불만, 불평

Paraphrase a frame that can crack easily
→ fragile items

47. 화자가 "무엇이든 생각나는 게 있으신 분 있나요?"라고 말하는 이유는 무엇인가?

(A) 불만을 표현하기 위해
(B) 의견을 요청하기 위해
(C) 일부 용품을 요청하기 위해
(D) 결정에 대해 동의하지 않기 위해

해설 화자가 담화 후반부에 주의 사항을 게시하고 싶다는 말과 함께 그것이 정말로 사람들이 주의를 끌어야 한다고(I'd like to post a warning, but it should really catch people's attention) 언급한 뒤에 '무엇이든 생각나는 게 있나요?'라고 묻는 흐름이다. 이는 주의 사항 게시와 관련된 좋은 아이디어가 있는지 묻는 것이므로 (B)가 정답이다.

어휘 express (감정, 생각 등) ~을 표현하다 frustration 불만, 좌절감 request ~을 요청하다 input 의견(의 제공) ask for ~을 요청하다 supplies 용품, 물품 disagree with ~에 동의하지 않다 decision 결정

Questions 48-50 refer to the following telephone message and schedule.

Hello, Ms.Gordon. This is Anthony Costas calling from Europa Travel Agency. **48** As you requested, I changed the date of your Zeus Airlines flight. **49** You'll be taking the flight that departs at 11:35 A.M., instead of the one that leaves at 4:55 P.M. Your ticket is still for economy class, and the same baggage allowance applies. You can print your ticket at the airport by using the self-service check-in booths in the departure terminal. **50** However, I'd recommend just checking in on the Zeus Airlines Web site 24 hours before your flight. It's a very quick and convenient process. I hope you have a safe flight and an enjoyable vacation.

안녕하세요, 고든 씨. 저는 앤서니 코스타스이며 유로파 여행사에서 전화 드립니다. 귀하께서 요청하신 대로, 귀하의 제우스 항공 비행편에 대한 날짜를 변경하였습니다. 귀하는 오후 4시 55분에 출발하는 비행편 대신 오전 11시 35분에 출발하는 비행편을 이용하실 것입니다. 귀하의 항공권은 여전히 이코노미 클래스이며, 동일한 수하물 허용 범위가 적용됩니다. 귀하는 공항 출발 터미널 내에 있는 셀프 서비스 체크인 부스를 이용해 항공권을 출력하실 수 있습니다. 하지만 비행편이 출발하기 24시간 이전에 제우스 항공 웹 사이트에서 체크인하시기 바랍니다. 매우 빠르고 편리하게 처리될 것입니다. 안전한 여행과 즐거운 휴가 보내시기 바랍니다.

제우스 항공 – 일일 항공편		
항공기 번호	출발	도착
021편	오전 9:25	오후 12:35
024편	오전 11:35	오후 2:45
032편	오후 1:30	오후 4:35
035편	오후 4:55	오후 8:05

어휘 request 요청하다 take (교통편, 도로 등) ~을 타다, ~을 이용하다 depart 출발하다 instead of ~ 대신 baggage allowance 수하물 허용 범위 apply 적용되다 by (방법) ~해서, ~함으로써 booth 부스, 칸막이 공간 however 하지만, 그런데 convenient 편리한 process (처리) 과정 departure 출발, 떠남 arrival 도착

48. 화자가 전화를 건 이유는 무엇인가?

(A) 새로운 항공사를 홍보하기 위해
(B) 업그레이드 서비스를 제공하기 위해
(C) 여행의 지연에 대해 설명하기 위해
(D) 여행 일정을 확인해주기 위해

해설 화자는 여행사 소속임을 밝힌 후 상대방의 요청으로 처리한 항공편 일정 변경에 대해(I changed the date of your Zeus Airlines flight. You'll be taking the flight that departs at 11:35 A.M., instead of the one that leaves at 4:55 P.M.) 상세히 말해주고 있다. 따라서 전화를 건 이유는 여행 일정을 확인해주는 것으로 볼 수 있으므로 (D)가 정답이다. 내용을 제대로 듣지 않으면 담화에 언급된 airline이나 flight 등에서 연상할 수 있는 travel delay에 속기 쉬우므로 주의해야 한다.

어휘 promote ~을 홍보하다 delay 지연, 지체, 연착 confirm ~을 확인해주다 itinerary 여행 일정(표)

49. 시각자료를 보시오. 청자가 탈 제우스 에어라인의 항공편은 어떤 것인가?

(A) 021편
(B) 024편
(C) 032편
(D) 035편

해설 화자가 You'll be taking the flight that departs at 11:35 A.M., instead of the one that leaves at 4:55 P.M.이라고 했으므로 시각자료에서 11:35 A.M에 해당하는 항공편을 찾아보면 (B)가 정답이다.

50. 청자는 무엇을 하도록 권고 받는가?

(A) 공항에 일찍 도착할 것
(B) 숙박 시설을 예약할 것
(C) 패키지 여행을 신청할 것
(D) 온라인 체크인 서비스를 이용할 것

해설 화자는 I'd recommend(~하기를 권한다)라는 표현을 써서 I'd recommend just checking in on the Zeus Airlines Web site 24 hours before your flight라고 권하고 있다. 비행 예정 24시간 전에 항공사 웹 사이트에서 체크인을 하라고 하므로 (D)가 정답이다.

어휘 book ~을 예약하다 accommodation 숙박 시설 sign up for ~을 신청하다, ~에 등록하다

Paraphrase checking in on the Zeus Airlines Web site → Use an online check-in service

Part 5

51.
정답 (D)

해석 재택 근무하는 모든 직원들은 오후 5시에 그들의 상사에게 일일 업무 보고서를 보내야 한다.

해설 빈칸 앞에 제시된 telecommuting이 보고서를 보내는 주체일 수 없으며, 그 주체는 재택 근무하는 모든 직원들이 되어야 하므로 사람명사가 빈칸에 필요하다, 또한, All의 수식을 받을 복수 명사가 쓰여야 하므로 (D) employees가 정답이다.

어휘 telecommuting 재택 근무하는 daily work report 일일 업무 보고서 supervisor 상사, 감독관

52.
정답 (B)

해석 20년 이상 회사와 함께 해온 조지 라모스 씨의 은퇴를 기념하기 위해서 저희와 함께 해주시기 바랍니다.

해설 빈칸 앞에 관계대명사 who가 있고 빈칸 뒤에 전치사가 있으므로 빈칸은 관계대명사절의 동사 자리이다. 또한, 빈칸 뒤에 기간을 나타내는 표현이 있으므로 빈칸에는 현재완료시제 동사가 필요한데 선행사가 3인칭 단수명사이므로 단수동사 (B) has been이 정답이다.

어휘 join ~에 참가하다, 함께 하다 celebrate ~을 기념하다 retirement 은퇴

53.
정답 (B)

해석 전략 기획팀의 도움으로, 우리 이사님은 매출을 증대하고 비용을 줄일 창의적인 방법들을 구상해 오고 있다.

해설 빈칸 앞에는 동사가, 빈칸 뒤에는 명사가 있으므로 명사를 수식할 수 있는 형용사 (B) creative가 정답이다.

어휘 with the help from ~의 도움으로 strategic 전략적인 brainstorm ~을 구상하다 revenue 매출

54.
정답 (D)

해석 사용자들은 기기에 대해 잘 알 수 있도록 제품 사용 설명서를 읽어야 합니다.

해설 빈칸이 타동사 뒤에 위치해 있으므로 빈칸은 목적어 자리이다. 따라서 목적어 역할을 할 대명사가 들어가야 하는데, 주어인 they(= Users)와 동일한 대상을 가리켜야 하므로 재귀대명사가 쓰여야 한다. 따라서 (D) themselves가 정답이다.

어휘 manual 사용 설명서 familiarize oneself with ~을 잘 알다, ~에 정통하다 device 기기

55.
정답 (A)

해석 지난달 시카고행 출장에 대한 변제 요청은 아직 처리되지 않았는데, 차량 임대에 대한 영수증이 누락되었기 때문이다.

해설 빈칸 앞뒤로 has와 to부정사가 위치해 있으므로 yet과 함께 '아직 ~하지 않다'라는 숙어를 구성해야 한다. 따라서 (A) yet이 정답이다.

어휘 reimbursement 변제 process ~을 가공하다, 처리하다 missing 빠진, 잃어버린

56.
정답 (C)

해석 국제관계사무소 소장인 알바레스 씨는 모든 영어로 쓰여진 고객과의 통신 내용을 번역하는 일을 맡고 있다.

해설 빈칸이 전치사와 명사구 목적어 사이에 있으므로 선택지에 제시된 동사 translate은 전치사의 목적어 역할과 명사 목적어를 취할 수 있는 동명사 형태가 되어야 한다. 따라서 (C) translating이 정답이다.

어휘 head 책임자, 부서장 be responsible for ~에 대한 책임을 지다, ~을 담당하다 translate ~을 번역하다 written 쓰여진

57.
정답 (B)

해석 부서장은 지속되는 결근 문제에 주안점을 두고 직원들과 관련된 여러 가지 사안들을 논의했다.

해설 빈칸 앞뒤로 전치사가 있으므로 빈칸은 전치사 with의 목적어 역할을 할 명사 자리이다. 따라서 (B) emphasis가 정답이다.

어휘 regarding ~와 관련된 with emphasis on ~에 주안점을 두고, ~을 강조해 persistent 지속되는, 반복되는 absenteeism 결근 emphatic 강조하는, 단호한

58.
정답 (B)

해석 우리 고객들과의 모든 연락이 전문적이도록 하기 위해, 이메일과 유선 연락에 관련된 지침을 준수하는 것이 중요하다.

해설 선택지가 모두 다른 명사로 구성되어 있으므로 해석을 통해 의미상 알맞은 어휘를 골라야 하는데, 빈칸에는 빈칸 뒤에 제시된 with our guidelines와 함께 '지침을 준수하는 것'이라는 의미를 구성하는 것이 자연스러우므로 (B) compliance가 정답이다.

어휘 ensure that 반드시 ~하도록 하다 crucial 중요한 disclosure 폭로, 공개 compliance 준수 enthusiasm 열정 connection 연결

59.

정답 (D)

해석 회사의 구내식당에서 제공되는 디저트들은 단지 믿을 수 없을 정도로 맛있을 뿐 아니라, 또한 건강에도 좋고 아름답게 제공되기도 한다.

해설 빈칸 뒤에 이미 문장의 동사가 있으므로 빈칸에는 준동사가 와야 하는데 선택지에 제시된 동사 offer가 타동사이므로 동명사나 현재분사 또는 to부정사로 쓰일 경우에는 뒤에 목적어가 필요하다. 따라서 과거분사로 쓰여 빈칸 앞에 제시된 명사를 수식하는 구조가 되어야 하므로 (D) offered가 정답이다.

어휘 incredibly 믿을 수 없을 정도로 present ~을 선사하다, 제시하다

60.

정답 (B)

해석 수개월간의 협상 후에, 케네스 씨는 JM 로지스틱스 사와 합의에 도달했는데, 그곳의 후원은 그가 하는 사업의 경제 상황 회복에 중요하다.

해설 빈칸 앞에 제시된 선행사 JM Logistics Co.와 빈칸 뒤에 제시된 명사 support가 소유 관계를 나타내야 자연스러우므로 소유격 관계대명사 (B) whose가 정답이다.

어휘 negotiation 협상 reach an agreement 협의에 도달하다 support 후원, 지지

61.

정답 (A)

해석 귀하의 이메일 주소는 저희의 홍보 목적으로만 사용될 것이며, 귀하의 서면 허가 없이는 제3자에게 절대 공개되지 않을 것이라는 점을 알아 두시기 바랍니다.

해설 빈칸 뒤에 명사구가 있으므로 빈칸은 전치사 자리이다. 개인정보인 이메일 주소가 제3자에게 공개되지 않을 것이라는 내용이 있으므로 '서면 허가' 앞에는 '~없이는'이라는 의미의 제외 전치사가 오는 것이 자연스러우므로 (A) without이 정답이다.

어휘 promotional 홍보의 disclose ~을 드러내다, 공개하다 third party 제3자 permission 허락, 허가 within ~이내에 except ~을 제외하고 unless ~하지 않으면

62.

정답 (B)

해석 우리는 새 컴퓨터들을 살 예산은 가지고 있지만, 구식 복사기가 올해 후반까지는 교체될 수 없다는 것을 유감스럽게 생각한다.

해설 콤마를 기준으로 주어와 동사를 포함한 두 개의 절이 있으므로 빈칸은 접속사 자리이다. 빈칸 앞에는 컴퓨터를 살 예산은 있다는 내용이, 빈칸 뒤에는 구형 복사기를 교체할 수 없다는 상반되는 내용이 제시되어 있으므로 '~인 반면에, ~이지만'이라는 의미를 지닌 (B) While이 정답이다.

어휘 regret that ~을 유감스럽게 생각하다 outdated 구식의 replace ~을 교체하다

63.

정답 (C)

해석 약 90 퍼센트의 회사 직원들이 행사에 참석하였으므로, 부사장의 퇴직 만찬은 성공이었다.

해설 빈칸 뒤에 90이라는 숫자 표현이 있으므로 '대략'이라는 의미로 숫자 표현 앞에 사용하는 (C) approximately가 정답이다.

어휘 retirement 은퇴 vice president 부사장 normally 보통, 정상적으로 generously 관대하게, 후하게 evenly 균일하게, 평평하게

64.

정답 (B)

해석 우리 공장이 몇 개월 전에 기술적 어려움을 겪은 이래로, 생산량이 지속적으로 최저치를 경신하며 하락하고 있다.

해설 선택지가 모두 다른 동사로 구성되어 있는데 빈칸 뒤에 제시된 목적어인 technical difficulties와의 의미를 연결해보면 '어려움을 겪는다'라는 뜻을 나타내는 것이 적절하므로 (B) experienced가 정답이다.

어휘 since ~이래로 output 생산량, 산출량 continuously 지속적으로 low n. 최저치 excuse ~을 용서하다, 실례하다 exhaust ~을 다 써버리다, 고갈시키다 experiment ~을 실험하다

65.

정답 (C)

해석 올해의 건축상 수상자가 다음 달에 심사위원단에 의해 결정될 것이다.

해설 빈칸에 쓰일 과거분사는 건축상 수상자와 관련해 심사위원단이 하는 일에 해당되는 의미를 나타내야 하므로 '~을 결정하다'를 뜻하는 determine의 과거분사 (C) determined가 정답이다.

어휘 architecture 건축(술), 건축 양식 panel of judges 심사위원난 preserve ~를 보존하다, ~을 보호하다 determine ~을 결정하다, ~을 밝혀내다 situate ~을 위치시키다, ~을 놓다

66.

정답 (A)

해석 지난주 직원회의에서 언급된 대로, 5월 1일부터 직원들에게 피트니스 활동에 참가할 기회를 주기 위해 점심식사 시간이 30분 연장될 것입니다.

해설 빈칸 뒤에 과거분사구가 제시되어 있으므로 빈칸은 분사구문을 이끌 수 있는 접속사 자리이다. '지난주 직원회의에서 언급된 대로'라는 뜻이 자연스러우므로 (A) As가 정답이다.

어휘 mention ~을 언급하다, 말하다 beginning + 날짜 ~부터, ~을 시작으로 extend ~을 연장하다 participate in ~에 참가하다

Part 6

67-70.

인피니티 프로덕션 사는 직원들에게 그들의 다양한 업무를 역할을 수행할 때 발생한 여행 경비를 변제해 줄 것입니다. 여행 경비는 출장 동안에 소비된 교통, 숙박 그리고 식사 **67** 비용을 포함합니다.

비용에 대한 변제를 요청하는 직원들은 늦어도 매달 1일까지 비용 보고서를 제출해야 합니다. **68** 각 항목은 별개로 입력되어야 하며, 날짜와 총액, 비용 사유, 그리고 스캔된 영수증 사본을 포함해야 합니다. 변제는 월급과 함께 매달 15일에 직원들의 은행계좌로 **69** 직접 입금될 것입니다.

70 입금이 15일보다 늦어질 가능성이 있는 경우 여러분에게 통보될 것입니다.

인피니티 프로덕션 사에 대한 여러분의 지속적인 헌신에 감사드립니다.

어휘 **reimburse** ~을 변제하다 **incur** ~을 초래하다, 발생하다 **function** 역할, 기능, 행사 **travel expenses** 출장 경비 **accommodation** 숙박 **duration** 기간 **file** (서류를) 제출하다 **no later than** 늦어도 ~까지 **separately** 별개로, 분리하여 **deposit** ~을 예금하다 **along with** ~와 함께 **commitment to** ~의 헌신

67.

정답 (B)

해설 빈칸이 포함된 문장의 주어인 Travel expenses가 빈칸에 들어갈 명사를 포함하는 것이므로 빈칸 뒤의 교통, 숙박, 식사와 어울려서 경비의 개념과 유사한 '비용'이란 뜻의 (B) cost가 정답이다.

어휘 **length** 길이 **cost** 비용 **share** 주식

68.

정답 (D)

해설 빈칸 뒤에 제시된 단수명사 item을 꾸며줄 수 있는 알맞은 형용사를 골라야 하므로 단수명사 앞에 사용하는 (D) Each가 정답이다.

어휘 **such** 그러한 **each** 각각의

69.

정답 (D)

해설 수동태 동사와 전치사 사이에 위치한 빈칸은 동사 또는 전치사를 수식할 부사 자리이므로 (D) directly가 정답이다.

어휘 **direct** a. 직접적인, 직행의 v. ~을 감독하다, 지시하다 **direction** 방향, 지시, 감독 **directly** 즉시

70.

정답 (D)

해석 (A) 여러분의 여행 일정표 사본을 이번 주에 꼭 보내주세요.
(B) 유효한 영수증을 지참 시에만 반품될 수 있다는 것을 잊지 마세요.
(C) 우리가 월별 사업 경비를 줄이도록 도와 주셔서 감사합니다.
(D) 입금이 15일보다 늦어질 가능성이 있는 경우 여러분에게 통보될 것입니다.

해설 빈칸 앞에 매달 15일에 변제 금액이 은행계좌로 입금될 것이라는 내용이 있으므로 빈칸에는 이와 관련된 추가 정보가 제공되는 것이 적절하다. 따라서 15일 이후에 입금될 경우 통보될 것이라는 내용의 (D)가 정답이다.

어휘 **ensure** ~을 확실하게 하다 **itinerary** 일정표 **valid** 유효한 **be likely to do** ~할 것 같다, ~할 가능성이 있다 **later than** ~보다 늦은

71-74.

수신: 아이다 피츠제럴드 <ifiz@daox.net>
발신: 제니퍼 러쉬모어 <jrushmore@tvnradio.com>
주제: 감사드립니다.

피츠제럴드 씨께,

약 10년 전에 저는 라디오 방송국으로 현장학습을 갔습니다. 저는 생방송으로 방송되고 있는 목소리와 음악에 매료되었습니다. **71** 그 때 이후로, 제 청소년 시절 내내 라디오 아나운서가 되는 것이 제 가장 큰 소원이 되었습니다. 그러나 저는 그것이 이루는 것이 거의 불가능한 꿈임을 알았습니다.

어느 날, 저는 충분한 용기를 갖고 제 담임 선생님인 당신에게 그것에 대해 여쭤봤습니다. 당신은 저에게 "수천 마일의 여정도 오직 한 걸음으로 **72** 시작한다"라고 말하면서 많은 좋은 조언을 주었습니다. 선생님은 또한 라디오 방송국에 친구가 있다고 말씀하셨고, 저에게 그분의 핸드폰 번호를 주셨습니다. 만약 선생님이 안 계셨더라면, 저는 절대 **73** 그러한 기회를 얻지 못했을지도 모릅니다. 지금, 저는 그 방송국에서 일하고 있고 전문적인 라디오 아나운서가 되는 방법을 배우고 있는 중입니다. **74** 제가 제 꿈을 추구하도록 격려해 주셔서 감사합니다.

안녕히 계십시오.

제니퍼 러쉬모어

어휘 **field trip** 현장 학습 **fascinate** ~을 매료시키다 **broadcast** 방송하다 **on air** 방송 중인 **through** ~동안 내내, ~을 통해 **adolescence** 청소년기 **achieve** ~을 이루다, 달성하다 **build up** ~을 세우다, 쌓다 **courage** 용기 **offer** ~을 제공하다 **advice** 조언 **journey** 여정 **professional** 전문적인

71.

정답 (B)

해설 빈칸 뒤의 문장에서 동사의 시제가 현재완료 has been이므로 현재완료 시제와 어울리는 부사가 빈칸에 들어가야 한다. 따라서 '그 이후로'라는 의미의 (B) Since then이 정답이다.

어휘 specifically 분명히, 명확하게 likewise 이와 같이, 비슷하게 rather 꽤, 상당히, 오히려

72.

정답 (C)

해설 빈칸이 속한 문장은 only with a single step라는 부사구를 강조하기 위해 문장 앞으로 이동시킨 도치 구문이다. 일반 동사인 begins 대신에 조동사 does가 부사구 뒤에 이어진 구조이므로 빈칸에는 동사원형이 쓰여야 한다. 따라서 (C) begin이 정답이다.

73.

정답 (B)

해설 빈칸 앞뒤로 동사 had와 목적어 an opportunity가 있으므로 빈칸은 an opportunity를 수식할 수 있는 것이 와야 한다. 따라서 선택지 중 빈칸 뒤에 위치한 「a + 명사」 구조와 함께 쓰일 수 있는 (B) such가 정답이다.

74.

정답 (D)

해석 (A) 당신의 작품은 정말로 저에게 영감을 주는 것이었습니다.
(B) 저는 당신의 방송국에서 당신과 함께 참여하는 것을 꿈꾸어 왔습니다.
(C) 저를 고용하기로 선택해 주셔서 정말로 기쁩니다.
(D) 제가 제 꿈을 추구하도록 격려해 주셔서 감사합니다.

해설 글 전반적으로 예전 선생님에게 학생이었던 글쓴이가 꿈을 이루게 조언을 해준 것에 대해 감사하는 내용이다. 따라서 지문 마지막에 위치한 빈칸에는 글쓴이가 선생님이 해준 조언에 대한 감사를 표현하는 흐름이 되어야 자연스러우므로 (D)가 정답이다.

어휘 inspiration 영감, 영감을 주는 것 grateful 기쁜, 감사한 employ ~을 고용하다 encourage A to do A가 ~하도록 격려하다 pursue ~을 추구하다

Part 7

75-76.

> **펀리 교육 위원회**
> **구직 기회**
>
> 펀리 교육 위원회는 펀리 고등학교에서 정규직으로 일할 근면 성실한 사람을 구하고 있습니다. **75** 합격자는 주로 학교 건물의 모든 공간을 깨끗하고 깔끔하게 유지하는 일을 맡게 됩니다. 이 일은 교실, 구내식당/주방, 그리고 과학실이 포함됩니다. 간혹 무거운 짐을 드는 일이 필요해서 합격한 지원자는 반드시 **76** 강인하고 건강해야 합니다. 지원자는 파손된 책상, 의자, 문과 같은 단순한 물건들을 고칠 수 있어야 합니다. 고등학교 졸업장이나 대학 학위는 필요하지 않습니다. 하지만, 합격한 지원자는 최소 12개월 간의 시설 관리 유사 경력이 있어야 합니다. 관심이 있으신 분들은 펀리 고등학교(위스콘신 54487, 펀리, 세븐 옥스 크레센트 3901번지)의 존 스키너 교장에게 이력서와 자기 소개서를 제출하셔야 합니다.

어휘 board of education 교육 위원회 seek ~을 찾다, 구하다 hard-working 근면 성실한 primarily 주로 be responsible for ~을 맡다, ~에 대한 책임이 있다 tidy 정돈된, 깔끔한 occasionally 가끔씩 object 사물, 물체 diploma 졸업장 candidate 후보자, 지원자 janitorial 시설 관리의 cover letter 자기 소개서

75. 어떤 일자리가 제공되고 있는가?
(A) 교사
(B) 실험실 기술자
(C) 시설 관리자
(D) 주방 보조

정답 (C)

해설 지문 초반부에서 학교 건물의 모든 공간을 깨끗하고 깔끔하게 유지하는 일을 맡게 될 것이라고(The successful applicant will primarily be responsible for keeping all rooms in the school buildings clean and tidy) 언급하였으므로 광고되고 있는 일자리는 건물 관리인 혹은 청소부임을 알 수 있다. 따라서 (C)가 정답이다.

어휘 technician 기술자 janitor 시설 관리자

76. 이 일자리에 대한 자격 요건으로 기재되지 않은 것은 무엇인가?
(A) 이전의 직업 경험
(B) 기본적인 수리 기술
(C) 양호한 신체적 조건
(D) 학문적인 자격

정답 (D)

해설 지문 중반부에 지원자의 고등학교 졸업장이나 대학 학위는 필요하지 않다고(A high school diploma or college degree is not necessary) 하였으므로 학문적인 자격은 요구되지 않는다는 내용의 (D)가 정답이다.

어휘 **requirement** 자격 요건, 요구사항 **prior** 이전
의 **physical** 신체적인 **academic** 학문의, 학문적인
qualification 자격

77-79.

어휘 **expand** ~을 확장하다 **carry out** ~을 실행하다
measurement 측정 **observation** 관찰 **post-secondary** 고등교육의, 중고등 이후의 **enroll in** ~에 등록하다 **fine** 섬세한 **delicate** 정교한 **occasionally** 때때로 **flexible** 유동성 있는 **be commensurate with** ~와 비례하다 **noncompete and secrecy declarations** 경쟁사 취업 금지 및 비밀유지 서약

77. 비바랩스에서 신규 직원들을 채용하는 이유로 언급된 것은 무엇인가?

(A) 많은 직원들이 사직했다.
(B) 신규 시설을 개장한다.
(C) 판매량 증가가 예상된다.
(D) 최근에 이전했다.

정답 (B)

해설 첫 문단 첫 문장에 새로 추가된 연구소에서 일할 실험실 기사를 채용하고 있다는(We are an expanding biotech company that is hiring three new part-time lab technicians to work in our newly-added research laboratories) 부분을 보아 신규 시설을 열고 있어서 인력이 필요함을 알 수 있다. 따라서 (B)가 정답이다.

어휘 **resign** ~을 사직하다, 그만두다 **relocate** 이전하다

78. 해당 업무의 일부분으로 언급된 것은 무엇인가?

(A) 실험 샘플 운반
(B) 현장 연구팀 운영
(C) 실험실 실험 수행
(D) 연구 결과 출간

정답 (C)

해설 첫 문단 마지막 부분에 신규 실험실 기사들이 하게 될 일들의 예시들이 제시되고 있는데(will carry out a variety of tasks, including performing tests and measurements, recording data and observation results, and writing reports) 이 중 실험 수행 업무가 있으므로 (C)가 정답이다.

79. 근무 여건에 대해서 언급된 것은 무엇인가?

(A) 학력에 따라 근로시간이 다르다.
(B) 합격한 지원자들은 반드시 서로 다른 두 곳에서 일해야 한다.
(C) 연구는 다양한 동물 실험을 필요로 한다.
(D) 약간의 초과 근무가 필요하다.

정답 (D)

해설 세 번째 문단에 가끔 주말과 저녁 근무가 요구된다는 (Weekend and evening work required occasionally) 사실이 제시되어 있으므로 가끔 초과 근무를 하는 경우가 있다는 것을 알 수 있다. 따라서 (D)가 정답이다.

어휘 **depend on** ~에 달려있다 **overtime** 초과 근무

80-82.

어휘 **go over** ~을 검토하다 **addition** 추가 **input** 의견 제시 **B as well as A** A 뿐만 아니라 B 도 **make it** 약속을 지키다, 성공하다, 해내다

80. 점심 회의를 하는 이유는 무엇인가?

(A) 사무실 증축을 설계하기 위해

(B) 발표 내용을 편집하기 위해

(C) 새로운 프로젝트를 논의하기 위해

(D) 제안서를 쓰기 위해

정답 (B)

해설 첫 단락에 발표에 추가할 내용들에 대한 의견을 바란다고(I want your input on the details) 언급되어 있다. 따라서 발표에 내용을 추가할 작업을 점심 회의 때 할 것으로 예상되므로 (B)가 정답이다.

어휘 edit ~을 편집하다 proposal 제안서

---

81. 이 발표에 대해 추론될 수 있는 것은 무엇인가?

(A) 여러 회사들이 참석할 것이다.

(B) 메리 씨는 기꺼이 에런 씨를 도울 것이다.

(C) 더 립 하우스에서 열릴 것이다.

(D) 상당히 더 오래 진행되어야 한다.

정답 (A)

해설 두번째 문단에서 미란다 프로덕트와 블루 릿지 어소시에이츠에서 발표에 관심이 있는 사람들을 보낼 것이라는(Blue Ridge Associates will be sending someone to the presentation, as well as Miranda Products, who are interested) 부분을 통해 언급된 회사들의 직원이 참석한다는 것을 알 수 있다. 따라서 (A)가 정답이다.

어휘 be willing to do 기꺼이 ~하다 assist ~을 돕다 take place (행사 등이) 열리다, 일어나다 considerably 상당히

---

82. 메리 씨는 어느 단체와 함께 일한 경험이 있는가?

(A) 더 립 하우스

(B) 블루 릿지 어소시에이츠

(C) 미란다 프로덕트

(D) 브라운 & 손스

정답 (D)

해설 첫 단락에서 이메일의 작성자인 메리 씨가 수신자인 애런 씨에게 브라운 & 손스에서 프로젝트를 본인보다 더 오래 작업했다고(You have worked on projects for Brown & Sons longer than I have) 말하고 있으므로 두 사람이 브라운 & 손스에서 함께 작업한 경험이 있다는 것을 알 수 있다. 따라서 (D)가 정답이다.

83-86.

축하 드립니다! 네이처 링크 비타민을 주문하기로 결정하셨을 때, 귀하는 훌륭한 결정을 하신 것입니다. 왜냐하면 우리 제품은 평생 보증이 되기 때문입니다. 맞습니다. 마음에 들지 않으시면, 어떤 제품이든 언제든지 저희에게 반품 하실 수 있습니다. 그리고 아래 지시사항을 따라 주시면, 저희는 기꺼이 구매하신 것을 환불해 드리거나 대체할 수 있는 물건을 제공해 드립니다.

[83] 주문하신 물건을 받으신 후 한달 이내에 전액을 지불해 주시기 바랍니다. — [1] —. [84] 만약 구매가 만족스럽지 않다면, 저희 친절한 직원에게 무료 전화 569-555-0129로 전화하세요.

— [2] —. 저희는 어떤 문제든 빠르게 처리해 드릴 것이고, [85] 저희 안내책자에 있는 대체품을 제공해 드리거나, 귀하에서 원하신다면 다른 상품을 구매하실 수 있는 매장 포인트를 제공해 드리겠습니다. 물론, 전액 환불 또한 가능합니다. 무엇을 하고 싶은 지 선택하는 것은 전적으로 귀하에게 달려 있습니다.

[86] 제품을 반납하실 때는, 물건을 원래의 포장에 넣어 보내주시고, 송장과 영수증을 포함시켜 주시기 바랍니다. — [3] —. 저희는 기꺼이 모든 표준 우편 요금을 환불해 드릴 것입니다. — [4] —. 저희 고객은 저희에게 중요한 분들이며, 저희는 고객 만족을 보장합니다!

어휘 place an order 주문하다 life-time 평생의 gladly 기꺼이 alternative 대안의 pay in full 완납하다 toll-free 요금 무료의 replacement 대체품 store credit 매장 크레딧(매장에서 고객에게 주는 혜택 점수) full refund 전액 환불 up to ~에 달려있는 ensure that 반드시 ~하게 하다 invoice 송장 postage 우편 요금 guarantee ~을 보장하다

---

83. 상품이 결제되어야 하는 것은 언제인가?

(A) 주문할 때

(B) 물품이 배달된 직후에

(C) 월말이 되기 이전에

(D) 상품을 받은 지 한 달 이내에

정답 (D)

해설 두 번째 문단 첫째 줄에서 주문품을 받은 한 달 이내에 완납해 주기를 요청한다고(We request that you pay for your goods in full within a month of receiving your order) 설명하고 있다. 따라서 (D)가 정답이다.

어휘 immediately after 직후에

---

84. 이 공지에 따르면, 고객이 만족하지 않으면 무엇을 해야 하는가?

(A) 웹 사이트에 메시지를 남긴다.

(B) 회사에 전화를 한다.

(C) 보증서를 읽는다.

(D) 제품을 즉각 반송한다.

정답 (B)

해설 두 번째 문단 둘째 줄에서 만족 못하면 무료 전화로 걸라는(If you're not satisfied with your purchase, please call our friendly staff at our toll-free number 569-555-0129) 내용이 나온다. 따라서 (B)가 정답이다.

어휘 leave ~을 남기다 send back ~을 되돌려 보내다

---

85. 불만족한 고객에게 제공되지 않는 것은 무엇인가?

(A) 반품된 물건에 대한 보상

(B) 우선 배송비

(C) 교체품

(D) 매장 포인트

정답 (B)

해설 두 번째 단락에서 안내책자에 있는 대체품을 제공하거나 고객이 원한다면 다른 상품을 구매할 수 있는 매장포인트를 제공할 수 있으며, 전액 환불 또한 가능하다고(either provide you with a replacement item from our catalog, or if you want, we will give you store credit with which you can buy an alternative item. Of course, a full refund is also possible) 말하는 부분에서 (C)와 (D), 그리고 (A)를 확인할 수 있다. 따라서 언급되지 않은 (B)가 정답이다.

어휘 compensation 보상 priority 우선 shipping fee 배송비

86. [1], [2], [3], [4]로 표기된 위치들 중에서, 다음 문장이 가장 잘 어울리는 곳은 어디인가?

"이것은 우리가 최고 품질의 고객 만족을 믿기 때문입니다."

(A) [1]
(B) [2]
(C) [3]
(D) [4]

정답 (D)

해설 제시된 문장 앞에는 고객 서비스에 대한 장점이나 자부할 수 있는 내용이 언급되어야 한다. [1], [2], [3] 모두 고객 서비스 측면에서 자랑할 만한 내용이지만, 삽입 문장의 내용은 최고 품질의 고객 만족에 대한 전체적인 이유를 나타내는 것이기 때문에 모든 고객 만족의 서비스가 모두 언급된 후, 마지막 부분에 넣는 것이 자연스럽다. 따라서 (D)가 정답이다.

87-90.

> **세스 [오전 9:21]**
> 팀에 온 것을 환영합니다, 무스타파 씨. 당신의 교육은 점심 먹고 오후 1시 30분에 시작합니다.
>
> **무스타파 [오전 9:24]**
> 고맙습니다. 준비하기 위해 제가 할 수 있는 게 있을까요?
>
> **세스 [오전 9:30]**
> 89 데이터베이스를 잘 알아두도록 하세요. 이 프로그램을 사용해서 신규 87 환자들을 등록하고, 그들의 의료 기록들과 88 신용카드 세부 내역을 입력합니다. 임시 사용자 이름인 GUEST와 비밀번호 Health4U로 로그인하십시오.
>
> **무스타파 [오전 9:32]**
> 바로 시작하겠습니다.
>
> **세스 [오전 9:35]**
> 90 또한 환자, 예상 환자, 그리고 방문객들이 자주 묻는 질문 목록을 이메일로 보내 드리겠습니다. 한 번 보십시오. 응대 절차에 대해서는 교육 중에 자세히 논의하게 될 것입니다.
>
> **무스타파 [오전 9:38]**
> 고맙습니다. 고대하고 있습니다.

어휘 familiarize oneself with ~에 익숙해지다 register 등록하다 enter ~을 입력하다 temporary 임시의 prospective 미래의, 기대되는 procedure 절차 in detail 자세하게

87. 무스타파 씨가 어디에서 근무할 것 같은가?
(A) 기차역
(B) 방문객 센터
(C) 공공 도서관
(D) 병원

정답 (D)

해설 세스 씨의 두 번째 메시지에서 환자들과 의료 기록들을 언급한(You will be using this program to register new patients and enter their health histories and credit card details) 부분을 보고 근무지가 병원임을 알 수 있다. 따라서 (D)가 정답이다.

88. 세스 씨가 데이터베이스에 대해서 하는 말은 무엇인가?
(A) 이용하기 쉽다.
(B) 금융 정보를 보관한다.
(C) 개인화된 비밀번호를 필요로 한다.
(D) 하루에 한 번씩 업데이트된다.

정답 (B)

해설 세스 씨의 두 번째 메시지에서 신용카드 세부 내역을 입력한다는(You will be using this program to register new patients and enter their health histories and credit card details) 말을 보면, 데이터베이스에 신용카드 내역과 같은 금융 정보가 보관됨을 알 수 있다. 따라서 (B)가 정답이다.

어휘 personalized 개인화된

89. 오전 9시 32분에, 무스타파 씨가 "I'll get right on it"라고 쓸 때, 무엇을 의미하는가?
(A) 몇몇 고객들에게 연락할 것이다.
(B) 프로그램 이용 연습을 할 것이다.
(C) 어떤 정보를 제출할 것이다.
(D) 새로운 이용자 정보를 만들 것이다.

정답 (B)

해설 세스 씨가 데이터베이스를 잘 알아두라고(You may familiarize yourself with our database) 한 말에 대해서 무스타파 씨가 응답한 상황이다. 따라서 무스타파 씨가 해당 프로그램을 잘 알기 위해 연습을 할 것임을 알 수 있으므로 (B)가 정답이다.

90. 세스 씨가 다음에 할 것 같은 일은 무엇인가?
(A) 참가자 목록을 만들 것이다.
(B) 무스타파 씨의 이메일 계정을 만들 것이다.
(C) 급여 명단 데이터베이스를 업데이트할 것이다.
(D) 무스타파 씨에게 문서 하나를 보낼 것이다.

정답 (D)

해설 세스 씨가 보낸 가장 마지막 메시지를 보면 자주 묻는 질문 목록을 이메일로 보내겠다고(e-mail you a list of questions commonly asked) 했으므로 따라서 (D)가 정답이다.

어휘 account 계정 payroll 급여 대상자 명단

91-95.

> 7월 29일 준정장 행사에 개인 투자자이자
> JL 파이낸셜의 대표이사인 제임스 임 씨와 함께 해주세요.
>
> 태평양의 기슭에 위치한
> 핑크 호라이즌 인 앤 스파에서 열립니다.
>
> 손님들은 국제적으로 호평을 받는 세 가지 식사를 즐기게 되고,
> 그 후에는 카디날 베이에서 일몰 크루즈를 즐기게 될 것입니다.
>
> 하루 묵기를 바라시는 분들을 위해서,
> 각 손님당 2인 1박 서비스가 예약되어 있습니다.
>
> 각 커플은 또한 스파 상품권을 받게 되며,
> 이 모든 것은 임 씨가 제공합니다.
>
> **91** 이 저녁 행사는 선호 고객들만 해당됩니다.
> 올해 임 씨에게 10명 이상의 신규 고객을 소개해 주심에
> 감사드립니다.
> **93** 6월 21일까지 임 씨의 비서에게 회신 바랍니다.

어휘 black tie 준정장 bank 기슭 acclaim ~을 갈채하다 treat ~을 대접하다 accommodation 숙박 voucher 상품권 courtesy 호의, 예절 바름 preferred 선호되는 refer ~을 소개하다 RSVP 회신바람

> **93** 재스민 박 씨에게,
>
> **93** 임 씨의 준정장 행사에 초대해 주셔서 감사합니다. 저는 이 초대장을 받게 되어 꽤나 놀랐습니다. 제가 투자 은행가에게 이런 식으로 인정 받은 것은 처음입니다. **92** 이는 분명 제가 "선호 고객"으로 남도록 할 것입니다. 현명한 사업적 **94** 한 수입니다!
>
> **95** 안타깝게도, 저는 선약 때문에 행사에 참석할 수 없습니다. 저는 제 사업의 유일한 경영자이기 때문에, 매우 바쁘게 지내고 있고, 행사가 열리는 날 밤에는 해외에 있을 것입니다. 제 아내 또한 그날 저녁에 참석하지 못하고 임 씨 부인을 만날 기회를 놓치게 되어 유감으로 생각하고 있습니다. 저희가 올해 빠진 것을 만회하기 위해 내년에 초대 받을 수 있을까요? 만약 이 행사가 임 씨가 정기적으로 하시는 일이라면, 저는 다음에 참석하는 것을 영광으로 생각할 것입니다. 향후에는, 제가 이런 행사에 꼭 참석할 수 있기 위해서는 3주 전이 아닌, 적어도 2달 전에 통지를 해주시길 바랍니다.
>
> 초대해 주셔서 다시 한번 감사 드립니다. 저는 임 씨와 투자하기로 한 저의 결정에 매우 기쁘고, 앞으로 당신을 만나기를 고대합니다.
>
> 안녕히 계십시오,
>
> 다니엘 수젝
> 수젝 컨설팅 사장

어휘 recognize ~을 인정하다 move 움직임, 이동, (체스 등의) 한 수 engagement 약속, 관여 sole 유일한 proprietor 경영자, 소유자 make up for ~을 메우다, 보상하다, 만회하다 be honored to do ~하게 되어 영광이다 instead of ~대신에 make a commitment to ~에 헌신하다, 전념하다

91. 이 행사의 목적은 무엇인가?
(A) 한 회사의 창업일을 기념하기 위해
(B) 잠재적 투자자들을 한 프로젝트에 끌어 모으기 위해
(C) 한 대표이사의 은퇴를 기념하기 위해
(D) 고객들에게 소개를 해준 것에 대해 감사하기 위해

정답 (D)

해설 첫 지문 후반부에 행사의 목적은 임 씨에게 10명 이상의 신규 고객을 소개해 주심에 감사드린다는(Thank you for referring over 10 new clients) 부분에서 확인할 수 있으므로 (D)가 정답이다.

어휘 mark ~을 표시하다, 기념하다 referral 소개

92. 수젝 씨가 이 행사에 대해 암시하는 것은 무엇인가?
(A) 사업을 성장하기 위한 특별한 방법이다.
(B) 단지 사업가들만을 포함한다.
(C) 열악하게 조직되고 있다.
(D) 주말에 열릴 것이다.

정답 (A)

해설 두 번째 지문 첫 단락에 수젝 씨가 행사에 초대 받아 기분이 좋다는 말을 건네면서 분명 선호 고객으로 남도록 할 것이라며 현명한 사업적 한 수라는(It will certainly encourage me to remain a "preferred client." Smart business move) 표현을 쓰고 있다. 따라서 이러한 행사가 고객을 유지하기 위한 것임을 알 수 있으므로 (A)가 정답이다.

어휘 poorly 열악하게

93. 재스민 박 씨는 누구인가?
(A) 제임스 임 씨의 비서
(B) 다니엘 수젝 씨의 부인
(C) JL 파이낸셜의 투자자
(D) 핑크 호라이즌의 접수원

정답 (A)

해설 첫 번째 지문 마지막 문장에서 행사에 참석할 사람들은 임 씨의 비서에게 회신하기 바란다는(Kindly RSVP by June 21 to Mr. Leem's secretary) 내용이 제시되어 있는데, 두 번째 지문인 편지의 상단에 수신자가 Jasmine Park으로 쓰여 있고, 첫 문장에 초대에 감사하다는 인사를 하는 것으로 회신하는 말이 쓰여 있어 재스민 박씨가 제임스 임 씨의 비서임을 알 수 있으므로 (A)가 정답이다.

어휘 secretary 비서

94. 편지에서, 첫째 단락 셋째 줄의 단어 "move"와 의미가 가장 가

까운 것은 무엇인가?

(A) 위치
(B) 충고
(C) 진도
(D) 전략

정답 (D)

해설 제시된 단어가 속한 단락을 보면 뜻밖의 초대를 받아 감동을 받고, 계속 선호 고객으로 남고 싶은 마음이 들게 하는 것을 가리켜 move라고 했는데, 이것은 사업적으로 좋은 전략이라 바꾸어 말할 수 있다. 따라서 (D) strategy가 정답이다.

95. 수젝 씨가 이 행사에 참여할 수 없는 이유는 무엇인가?

(A) 사업 관련 회의가 있어서
(B) 아내가 선약이 있어서
(C) 해외로 출장 갈 것이라서
(D) 컨벤션에 참여할 것이라서

정답 (C)

해설 두 번째 지문 둘째 단락에 행사가 열리는 날 밤에 해외에서 선약이 있다며(I am unable to attend the event due to a prior business engagement. Because I am the sole proprietor of my business, I am kept quite busy, and I will be overseas the night of the event) 행사에 불참하는 이유를 언급하고 있으므로 (C)가 정답이다.

어휘 **prior** 사전의 **abroad** 해외로

96-100.

국제 생태계 저널
- 2월호 -
여전히 위험한 상태인 이르탁 강의 오염 수준
작성자, 앤드류 파솔리니

1986년에, 100 우즈베키스탄의 알타이 시에 위치한 한 섬유 공장이 많은 양의 유독성 화학 폐기물을 이르탁 강에 방류하면서, 96 대부분의 자연 수생 생물 종을 죽음에 빠뜨렸습니다. 비록 이 공장이 2007년에 문을 닫기는 했지만, 많은 양의 화학 물질이 강바닥을 비롯해 주변의 강둑 및 들판의 토양에 남아 있습니다.

영향을 받은 토양 대부분이 알타이와 토볼 저수지 사이에 위치한 이 강의 20킬로미터에 이르는 구간에 걸쳐 펼쳐져 있습니다. 하지만, 비가 수위를 상승하게 97 만드는 경우에, 오염된 토양이 강 하류 쪽으로 70킬로미터 넘게 옮겨지면서, 광범위한 문제를 만들어냅니다. 98 현재, 135만 입방 미터의 오염된 토양이 강바닥에 존재하는 것으로 추정됩니다.

어휘 **ecology** 생태계 **pollution** 오염 **remain A** 여전히 A한 상태이다, 계속 A한 상태로 남아 있다 **hazardous** 위험한 **textile** 섬유, 직물 **discharge** ~을 방출하다, ~을 배출하다 **toxic** 유독한 **chemical** a. 화학의 n. 화학 물질 **aquatic** 수생의, 물에서 사는 **species** (동식물의) 종 **riverbed** 강바닥 **surrounding** 주변의 **riverbank**

강둑 **affect** ~에 영향을 미치다 **spread** ~을 펼치다 **stretch** (길게 뻗은) 구간, 지역 **contaminate** ~을 오염시키다(= pollute) **carry** ~을 옮기다 **downriver** 강 아래로 **widespread** 광범위한, 폭넓은 **estimated** 추정되는 **cubic meters** 입방 미터

국제 생태계 저널
- 12월호 -
순조롭게 진행 중인 이르탁 강 프로젝트
작성자, 앤드류 파솔리니

7월에 시작된 이르탁 강 프로젝트의 주 목적은 이르탁 강 안팎의 심각한 오염 물질을 정화함으로써 그 지역에 거주하는 사람들의 행복 수준을 향상시키고, 그로 인해 지역 사람들에게 안전한 수자원과 경작 가능한 토지를 제공하는 것입니다.

현재까지, 98 약 100만 입방 미터의 오염된 토양이 해당 부지에서 신중히 제거되어 위험 폐기물 매립지에 안전하게 버려졌습니다.

99 이 프로젝트의 전체적인 비용은 오염된 토양의 처리와 관련해 예기치 못한 문제들로 인해 처음 할당된 27.75백만 달러에서 29.25백만 달러로 증가했습니다. 하지만, 프로젝트 진행 책임자들의 말에 따르면, 이 프로젝트는 예상대로 여전히 내년 11월까지 완료되도록 정상 궤도에 올라 있습니다.

어휘 **progress** 진행되다, 진척되다 **smoothly** 순조롭게 **primary** 주된, 주요한 **objective** 목적 **welfare** 행복, 복지 **reside** 거주하다 **clean up** ~을 정화하다 **thereby** 그로 인해, 그에 따라 **farmable** 경작 가능한 **to date** 현재까지, 지금까지 **take away** ~을 제거하다, ~을 치우다 **dump** ~을 버리다 **landfill** 매립지 **allocate** ~을 할당하다 **unforeseen** 예기치 못한, 뜻밖의 **complication** 문제 **regarding** ~와 관련해 **disposal** 처리, 처분 **on track** (진행 등이) 정상 궤도에 오른, 착착 진행 중인

수신: 앤드류 파솔리니 <apasolini@ije.com>
발신: 크레이그 톰린슨 <craigtomlinson@onemail.net>
제목: 최근의 기사
날짜: 12월 20일

파솔리니 씨께,

저는 아주 큰 관심을 갖고 귀하의 12월 기사를 읽었으며, 이르탁 강 프로젝트가 지금까지 성공적인 것으로 드러났다는 얘기를 듣게 되어 매우 기쁘게 생각합니다. 전직 세계 환경 협회(WEA) 조사관으로서, 100 저는 그 화학 물질 누출 근원지를 방문했습니다. 저희는 물 샘플을 채취하고 현장 분석을 실시하는 일을 맡았습니다. 그곳은 매우 비참한 모습이었습니다. 저는 그 강에서 오염원을 근절하기 위한 적절한 조치가 마침내 취해졌다는 사실을 알게 되어 그저 기쁜 마음입니다. 귀하의 보도에 감사 드리며, 계속 수고해 주시기 바랍니다.

안녕히 계십시오.

크레이그 톰린슨

96. 이르탁 강과 관련해 유추할 수 있는 것은 무엇인가?

    (A) 수위가 과거에 그랬던 것보다 더 낮다.

    (B) 길이가 20킬로미터에 이른다.

    (C) 2007년에 처음 오염되었다.

    (D) 어류 개체수가 감소했다.

정답 (D)

해설 첫 지문 첫 단락에 섬유 공장이 많은 유독성 화학 폐기물을 강에 방류해 대부분의 자연 수생 생물 종을 죽음에 이르게 했다는 (killing off the majority of native aquatic species) 말이 쓰여 있다. 이를 통해 물고기 개체수가 감소한 것으로 판단할 수 있으므로 (D)가 정답이다.

어휘 **used to do** 전에 ~했다 **population** 개체수, 개체군 **decline** 감소하다, 하락하다

97. 첫 번째 기사에서, 두 번째 단락, 두 번째 줄의 단어 "makes"와 의미가 가장 가까운 것은 무엇인가?

    (A) 만들어내다

    (B) 초래하다

    (C) 만나다

    (D) 용이하게 하다

정답 (B)

해설 makes가 속한 when절을 보면, 주어 rain 뒤로 동사 makes와 목적어 the water level, 그리고 목적보어의 역할을 하는 원형부정사 rise가 이어져 있다. 이렇게 동사 make가 「make + 목적어 + 원형부정사」의 구조로 쓰일 때 '~을...하게 만들다'라는 의미로 쓰이는데, 이는 그러한 일이 발생되도록 초래하는 것과 같으므로 '초래하다'를 뜻하는 (B) causes가 정답이다.

98. 이르탁 강 프로젝트의 결과로 언급된 것은 무엇인가?

    (A) 토볼 저수지에서 물이 빠져 나갔다.

    (B) 지역 농장의 작물 수확량이 증가했다.

    (C) 이르탁 강이 넓어졌다.

    (D) 대부분의 오염된 토양이 제거되었다.

정답 (D)

해설 두 번째 지문 첫 단락에 약 100만 입방 미터의 오염된 토양이 해당 부지에서 신중히 제거되었다고(To date, approximately one million cubic meters of the contaminated soil has been carefully taken away) 언급되어 있다. 이는 첫 지문 두 번째 단락에서 135만 입방 미터의 토양이 오염된 것

으로 추정된다고(there is an estimated 1,350,000 cubic meters of polluted soil in the riverbed) 알린 정보와 비교할 때 대부분의 오염된 토양이 제거된 상태인 것으로 볼 수 있는 수준이므로 (D)가 정답이다.

어휘 **drain** ~에서 물을 빼내다 **crop yields** 작물 수확량 **widen** ~을 넓히다

99. 어떤 요인이 예산 증가로 이어졌는가?

    (A) 지역 주민들의 반대

    (B) 프로젝트 일정상의 충돌

    (C) 토양 처리에 대한 문제

    (D) 계절에 맞지 않게 좋지 못한 날씨

정답 (C)

해설 두 번째 지문 마지막 단락에 프로젝트의 전체적인 비용이 오염된 토양의 처리와 관련해 예기치 못한 문제들로 인해 처음 할당된 27.75백만 달러에서 29.25백만 달러로 증가했다고 (The overall cost of the project increased ~ due to unforeseen complications regarding the disposal of contaminated soil) 알리고 있으므로 (C)가 정답이다.

어휘 **lead to** ~로 이어지다 **opposition** 반대 **conflict** 충돌, 겹침 **unseasonably** 계절에 맞지 않게

100. 톰린슨 씨와 관련해 유추할 수 있는 것은 무엇인가?

    (A) 환경 단체를 설립했다.

    (B) 알타이에서 근무하면서 시간을 보냈다.

    (C) 해당 저널에 기사를 제출했다.

    (D) WEA에 의해 시작된 청원에 서명했다.

정답 (B)

해설 세 번째 지문 중반부에 자신이 조사관으로서 해당 화학 물질 누출 근원지를 방문한 사실과 함께 샘플을 채취하고 분석하는 일을 했다고(I visited the source of the chemical leak. We were tasked with taking water samples and performing on-site analysis) 알리고 있다. 이 오염 장소가 첫 번째 지문 시작 부분에 언급된 우즈베키스탄의 알타이 지역이며(the city of Altai, Uzbekistan) 톰린슨 씨가 그곳에 직접 가서 조사관으로서 근무한 것이므로 (B)가 정답이다.

어휘 **found** ~을 설립하다 **spend time -ing** ~하면서 시간을 보내다 **petition** 청원(서)

시원스쿨 **LAB**

WEEK 08

PART 1

Directions: For each question in this part, you will hear four statements about a picture in your test book. When you hear the statements, you must select the one statement that best describes what you see in the picture. Then find the number of the question on your answer sheet and mark your answer. The statements will not be printed in your test book and will be spoken only one time.

1.

2.

PART 2

Directions: You will hear a question or statement and three responses spoken in English. They will not be printed in your test book and will be spoken only one time. Select the best response to the question or statement and mark the letter (A), (B), or (C) on your answer sheet.

3. Mark your answer on your answer sheet.

4. Mark your answer on your answer sheet.

5. Mark your answer on your answer sheet.

6. Mark your answer on your answer sheet.

7. Mark your answer on your answer sheet.

8. Mark your answer on your answer sheet.

9. Mark your answer on your answer sheet.

10. Mark your answer on your answer sheet.

11. Mark your answer on your answer sheet.

12. Mark your answer on your answer sheet.

13. Mark your answer on your answer sheet.

14. Mark your answer on your answer sheet.

15. Mark your answer on your answer sheet.

16. Mark your answer on your answer sheet.

17. Mark your answer on your answer sheet.

18. Mark your answer on your answer sheet.

19. Mark your answer on your answer sheet.

20. Mark your answer on your answer sheet.

PART 3

Directions: You will hear some conversations between two or more people. You will be asked to answer three questions about what the speakers say in each conversation. Select the best response to each question and mark the letter (A), (B), (C) or (D) on your answer sheet. The conversations will not be printed in your test book and will be spoken only one time.

21. According to the man, what has changed?

    (A) A company procedure
    (B) An interview date
    (C) The number of job candidates
    (D) The requirements for a job

22. What problem does the woman mention?

    (A) She has another engagement.
    (B) She went to the wrong location.
    (C) She misplaced some documents.
    (D) She is underqualified for a position.

23. What does the man say he will have time to do?

    (A) Write a report
    (B) Attend a job fair
    (C) Call some applicants
    (D) Read some information

24. What does the woman ask about?

    (A) A change in procedure
    (B) An employee orientation
    (C) The requirements for a position
    (D) The start date for a job

25. What will the man do on Wednesday before lunch?

    (A) Introduce the new staff
    (B) Go to the city center
    (C) Distribute some documents
    (D) Show an instructional video

26. What does the woman offer to do?

    (A) Hold a training session
    (B) Prepare some handouts
    (C) Give a presentation
    (D) Find a place to eat

27. What is the conversation mainly about?

    (A) A design class
    (B) An art exhibit
    (C) A museum opening
    (D) A visiting performer

28. What does the woman imply when she says, "I don't know what to say"?

    (A) She was unprepared for a question.
    (B) She didn't understand a topic.
    (C) She cannot assist the man.
    (D) She was impressed by some work.

29. What does the woman recommend?

    (A) Entering a contest
    (B) Attending a lecture
    (C) Revising a project
    (D) Cancelling an event

30. What are the speakers discussing?

    (A) A product design
    (B) A grand opening event
    (C) A celebrity endorsement
    (D) A billboard advertisement

31. What does Sophie say she will do?

    (A) Consult with a colleague
    (B) Prepare a report
    (C) E-mail a work schedule
    (D) Print some documents

32. What does the man hope will happen next year?

    (A) Products will be launched.
    (B) Sales will increase.
    (C) Employees will be hired.
    (D) A merger will take place.

Sullivan Tailors – Custom Suit	
Material	**Cost**
Cotton	$500
Wool-blend	$400
Polyester	$350
Linen	$300

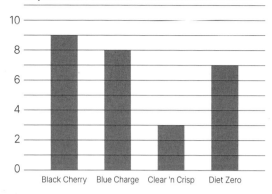

Bepco Cola Products - Units Sold (per 100,000)

33. What event does the man have next month?

(A) A reunion
(B) A job interview
(C) A work conference
(D) An awards dinner

34. What problem does the woman mention?

(A) A deadline cannot be met.
(B) Some costs will be higher.
(C) The weather is cold.
(D) An item is sold out.

35. Look at the graphic. How much will the man spend?

(A) $500
(B) $400
(C) $350
(D) $300

36. What department do the speakers most likely work in?

(A) Advertising
(B) Product development
(C) Customer service
(D) Sales

37. Look at the graphic. Which product will the speakers focus on?

(A) Black Cherry
(B) Blue Charge
(C) Clear 'n Crisp
(D) Diet Zero

38. What will the man do next?

(A) Purchase some equipment
(B) Send an e-mail
(C) Write a report
(D) Speak with a manager

PART 4

Directions: You will hear some talks given by a single speaker. You will be asked to answer three questions about what the speakers say in each conversation. Select the best response to each question and mark the letter (A), (B), (C) or (D) on your answer sheet. The conversations will not be printed in your test book and will be spoken only one time.

39. What is the main topic of the report?

(A) A comedy show
(B) A food festival
(C) A theater production
(D) A musical event

40. What problem does the speaker mention?

(A) The venue has been changed.
(B) There are no tickets left.
(C) The main performer cancelled.
(D) The event organizer is sick.

41. What does the speaker suggest listeners do?

(A) Protect themselves from the sun
(B) Bring plenty of money
(C) Arrive at a venue early
(D) Check the weather forecast

42. What is the purpose of the call?

(A) To decline a request
(B) To set up a meeting
(C) To cancel an appointment
(D) To arrange transportation

43. Why does the woman say, "it's right next to my hotel"?

(A) She expects to arrive early.
(B) She is surprised to be so close.
(C) She is giving the man directions.
(D) She prefers a convenient location.

44. Why is the woman worried?

(A) The man has not called back.
(B) Another project went poorly.
(C) The economy has been bad.
(D) A cost was too high.

45. According to the speaker, what event is occurring next month?

(A) A branch opening
(B) A company merger
(C) A retirement dinner
(D) A company trip

46. Why does the speaker say, "we only have a few interviews left"?

(A) To ask for an extension
(B) To express concern
(C) To make an excuse
(D) To explain a delay

47. What does the speaker ask the listener to do?

(A) Write a manual
(B) Relocate to another office
(C) Make a recommendation
(D) Lead a training session

Location	Positions
Refreshment Stands	6
Parking Lot	5
Information Center	4
Ticket Booth	3

48. Why does the speaker thank the listeners?

(A) For arriving early
(B) For providing feedback
(C) For volunteering for an event
(D) For completing a task quickly

49. Look at the graphic. Which location assignments will be given out first?

(A) Refreshment Stands
(B) Parking Lot
(C) Information Center
(D) Ticket Booth

50. What does the speaker ask the listeners to do at the end of the day?

(A) Dismantle some displays
(B) Sign a time sheet
(C) Load up a truck
(D) Clean up trash

This is the end of the Listening test. Turn to Part 5 in your test book.

READING TEST

In the Reading test, you will read a variety of texts and answer several different types of reading comprehension questions. The entire Reading test will last 75 minutes. There are three parts, and directions are given for each part. You are encouraged to answer as many questions as possible within the time allowed. You must mark your answers on the separate answer sheet. Do not write your answers in your test book.

PART 5

Directions: A word or phrase is missing in each of the sentences below. Four answer choices are given below each sentence. Select the best answer to complete the sentence. Then mark the letter (A), (B), (C), or (D) on your answer sheet.

51. In order to obtain a building -------, every application must include detailed architectural plans.

(A) permit
(B) permitting
(C) permits
(D) permitted

52. The path to success involves being able to recognize ------- weaknesses and capitalize on opportunities that present themselves.

(A) you
(B) yourself
(C) your
(D) yours

53. ------- smoother operation, only standard-sized paper should be loaded into the copy machine.

(A) Ensure
(B) Ensures
(C) To ensure
(D) Ensured

54. At Selly's Shop, the sales associates always double-check to make sure that the ------- prices are correct.

(A) marked
(B) mark
(C) marking
(D) marks

55. The business relationships we ------- over the past decade have helped us become a leading accounting firm in the province.

(A) have developed
(B) developing
(C) will develop
(D) develop

56. ------- you have picked up your tickets, please proceed to your designated gate and prepare for departure.

(A) Before
(B) Once
(C) Should
(D) Owing to

57. We've received several complaints from customers who think our new ------- of advertisements have incorrect information.

(A) process
(B) series
(C) course
(D) operation

58. To attract young professionals, Jamieson and Sons will pay $5,000 ------- new employees' student loans, provided that they sign a three-year contract with the company.

(A) toward
(B) above
(C) by
(D) on

59. The popularity of our outdoor shoes has been rising dramatically, ------- among professional mountaineers.

(A) particular
(B) particularly
(C) particularize
(D) particularity

60. ------- the company's continuous effort to adapt to the slow economy, management is cautiously considering a corporate restructuring.

(A) Despite
(B) Now that
(C) Nonetheless
(D) Yet

61. While plant managers ------- agree that immediate action must be taken to improve productivity, few of them support the schedule most recently proposed by Mr. Hill.

(A) concurrently
(B) feasibly
(C) extremely
(D) unanimously

62. The mayor of the city is considering it ------- to close Tillerson Avenue due to potential flooding.

(A) necessity
(B) necessary
(C) necessitate
(D) necessarily

63. Lynn Design is pleased to announce that we are giving employees flexibility in choosing ------- to telecommute from home or work in the office.

(A) in that
(B) that
(C) while
(D) whether

64. Corporate headquarters announced the closure of a branch ------- earnings last year decreased by almost 50 percent.

(A) which
(B) that
(C) who
(D) whose

65. The construction workers have found working on the upper floors of the skyscraper ------- than they had expected.

(A) difficult
(B) difficulty
(C) more difficult
(D) much difficult

66. Woodson Furniture manufactures ------- dining tables that can be extended to seat up to ten people.

(A) adjustable
(B) renewable
(C) improbable
(D) reachable

PART 6

Directions: Read the texts that follow. A word, phrase, or sentence is missing in parts of each text. Four answer choices for each question are given below the text. Select the best answer to complete the text. Then mark the letter (A), (B), (C) or (D) on your answer sheet.

Questions 67-70 refer to the following article.

Entertainment and Fashion News

Popular singer Christina Kaka is set to release a new perfume called "Symphony" later this summer. Ms. Kaka, who turned 23 recently and is already planning to release her third album, has stated that the ------- is vibrant and alluring.
67.

At first, the perfume will be available ------- on www.christinakaka.com, but will be introduced to major
68.
retail stores a couple of weeks after its original release. -------.
69.

With an extensive advertising campaign already in place for "Symphony", it ------- to be a best-selling
70.
product upon its release.

67. (A) announcement
    (B) outfit
    (C) song
    (D) fragrance

68. (A) ever
    (B) only
    (C) since
    (D) almost

69. (A) The album will feature 13 original songs and several guest artists.
    (B) Ms. Kaka became famous with her hit song "Dodo Bird."
    (C) Some proceeds will go to Ms. Kaka's charity, Sole Music.
    (D) There is still no word on an exact date.

70. (A) expected
    (B) is expecting
    (C) is expected
    (D) was expected

Questions 71-74 refer to the following e-mail.

To: Reggie Clide

From: Dennis Kang

Subject: Parking changes

Date: March 10

Dear Mr. Clide,

-------. It will be no longer possible to allow your customers to park their cars in front of the lot. -------,
  71.   72.
the land has been acquired by the local government under a compulsory purchase order.

It is my best assumption that a city park is scheduled to be built there, and a new school will be right
next to it. I am sorry that I am not giving you much notice, but this has all happened rather suddenly
-------- the past few days.
  73.

I hope that you will not have ------- difficulty making other parking arrangements.
                                  74.

Sincerely,

Dennis Kang

---

71. (A) I received your request for a parking permit.
    (B) Thanks for your interest in using our services.
    (C) Our parking lot is scheduled to be closed for renovations.
    (D) I am contacting you with some regrettable news.

72. (A) Surprisingly
    (B) Initially
    (C) Alternatively
    (D) Unfortunately

73. (A) by
    (B) over
    (C) upon
    (D) with

74. (A) any
    (B) many
    (C) every
    (D) such

PART 7

Directions: In this part you will read a selection of texts, such as magazine and newspaper articles, e-mails, and instant messages. Each text or set of texts is followed by several questions. Select the best answer for each question and mark the letter (A), (B), (C), or (D) on your answer sheet.

Questions 75-76 refer to the following advertisement.

Let Bookit Take Care of Everything!

Searching for flights, booking hotel rooms, and planning sightseeing itineraries can be difficult and stressful, so why not let Bookit handle everything for you? Don't waste your precious time checking Web sites, consulting books, and comparing prices. Our highly-qualified team of travel experts can make all the necessary arrangements for you while you just sit back and look forward to your vacation. Come down to our offices and tell us exactly what type of trip you are hoping for, and we will do our best to surpass your expectations. So, why wait? Visit us at 125 Reform Street, Middlewich, or call us at 555-9900!

75. What kind of business is Bookit?

(A) An online bookstore
(B) A hotel chain
(C) A travel agency
(D) An airline

76. What is indicated about Bookit?

(A) It is a relatively new company.
(B) It recently relocated.
(C) It mainly advertises online.
(D) Its staff is experienced.

Franco Street to Undergo Changes

The City Council of Middlesex is making changes to Franco Street bike lanes in an effort to reduce the number of collisions between motorists, cyclists, and pedestrians.

In the first stage of the plan, Franco Street southbound bike lanes will be painted yellow between the intersection at Richmond Street and the intersection at Lawton Avenue. — [1] —. Also, lines designating the bicycle lanes in both the northbound and southbound directions of Franco Street will be painted thicker, by approximately 15 centimeters, to make the bike lanes more visible to motorists. — [2] —.

The second stage of the plan will see bicycle boxes added to Franco Street at the intersections at Salton Road and Mayfield Street. — [3] —. These will help people riding bikes to make left-hand turns. Bicycle boxes are a fairly new type of on-street marking that enables motorists and cyclists to share the road more safely. The boxes designate a space in front of cars at the red light. Cyclists are permitted to wait in this space and proceed first when the light turns green. — [4] —.

With these changes, the council aims to make bicycle lanes more visible, encourage road users to use extra caution at intersections, and remind turning vehicles to slow down and watch for other road users, including cyclists and pedestrians.

77. What is the purpose of the city council's plan?

    (A) To alleviate traffic congestion on Franco Street
    (B) To reduce the number of bike riders
    (C) To decrease the frequency of accidents
    (D) To create bicycle-only routes

78. What is mentioned as part of the first stage of the plan?

    (A) The addition of bicycle boxes
    (B) The widening of road markings
    (C) The partial closure of Franco Street
    (D) The replacement of old traffic lights

79. In which of the positions marked [1], [2], [3], and [4] does the following sentence best belong?

    "Motorists who fail to let cyclists start first will be subject to a fine."

    (A) [1]
    (B) [2]
    (C) [3]
    (D) [4]

Date posted: March 19

To all exam takers:

In preparation for our annual language proficiency test, we will be hosting a workshop for all employees who have registered for the test.

The workshop will be held at the Camak Auditorium from April 9 to 15. All employees who have registered for the proficiency test can participate in the workshop. Those who are taking the language test for the first time must attend. There is no cost for the workshop. However, there will be an optional supplementary course the following week. Employees who enroll in the supplementary course will take a practice exam every night. The cost will be $100.

If you are interested in the supplementary course, please submit your payment before the beginning of next month. It is scheduled to start on April 18 at 6:00 P.M.

80. Who may attend the workshop?
    (A) All company staff
    (B) Employees who recently joined the company
    (C) Staff who have signed up for a test
    (D) Employees who failed a previous test

81. What is the last day that individuals may pay for the supplementary course?
    (A) March 31
    (B) April 1
    (C) April 18
    (D) April 30

82. What is indicated about employees who are taking the test for the first time?
    (A) They must register online.
    (B) They must attend a workshop.
    (C) They must pay $100 to register.
    (D) They must take the supplementary course.

Questions 83-86 refer to the following online chat discussions.

Rashad Clemons	[9:07 A.M.]	Good morning, everyone. I'm in the 5th floor conference room, but I can't get the laptop in here to work. We can't run the employee orientation without it. Any ideas?
Gary Sandler	[9:08 A.M.]	Oh, I had some issues with it, too. Try closing down some of the unnecessary background programs.
Carole Gleason	[9:10 A.M.]	Wasn't the room supposed to be fully prepared by 9:15 this morning? We can't train our new hires properly if we can't show them the presentation slides and videos.
Rashad Clemons	[9:12 A.M.]	Yes, I asked our intern, Lee Barnes, to do it, but he called in sick early this morning. That's why I got here early to set up the chairs and tables. Now, I just need this laptop to work...
Rashad Clemons	[9:13 A.M.]	Gary, it keeps freezing and crashing. Are you free?
Gary Sandler	[9:14 A.M.]	Be right there.
Carole Gleason	[9:15 A.M.]	Do you need a hand with anything else? Remember the attendees will be there at 9:30 sharp.
Rashad Clemons	[9:17 A.M.]	No, I'm all set once the laptop is up and running. All you guys need to do is bring your own presentations and handouts.
Carole Gleason	[9:19 A.M.]	Great. I will be there at 10 to take over from you and discuss company policies. I hope everything will be ready and working fine.

83. What is Mr. Clemons preparing to do?

(A) Present awards
(B) Meet with a client
(C) Install some equipment
(D) Train new staff

84. Why was the meeting room not prepared by 9:15 A.M.?

(A) Because Mr. Barnes had another task
(B) Because the room was being used
(C) Because Mr. Barnes is absent from work
(D) Because an event has been rescheduled

85. At 9:14 A.M., what does Mr. Sandler most likely mean when he writes, "Be right there"?

(A) He will send a laptop up to the 5th floor.
(B) He will contact a repair technician.
(C) He wants Mr. Clemons to go to a different room.
(D) He will provide Mr. Clemons with assistance.

86. What will most likely happen at 10 A.M.?

(A) Mr. Clemons will tidy up a room.
(B) Mr. Clemons will welcome some employees.
(C) Ms. Gleason will begin a talk.
(D) Ms. Gleason will meet with Mr. Sandler.

Questions 87-90 refer to the following memorandum.

To: All Staff
From: Jasmine Liao
Date: August 27

Dear staff,

As we approach the end of the year, please remember that all holidays must be taken before the end of December. Unfortunately, we cannot allow staff to carry over holiday time to the next year, so if you do not use up all your holidays, you will lose them.

A reminder also that time off must be received by senior management, in writing, one month in advance. Requests should be made on the proper form, a copy of which has been attached to this memorandum. In special circumstances, a last-minute holiday may be granted. Speak to me in person for such requests.

And finally, remember that holidays are scheduled on a first-come, first-served basis. A lot of you have several days, even weeks, of holiday time remaining. Make sure you get your holiday request in to your manager well in advance to avoid disappointment.

Here's to a great last four months this year. Keep up the good work, and don't forget to reward yourselves with some well-deserved time off!

Jasmine

87. What is the main purpose of the memorandum?

    (A) To express gratitude to staff for their hard work

    (B) To announce public holidays for the coming year

    (C) To explain how to transfer holiday time to next year

    (D) To remind staff to request vacation time

88. What is NOT listed as a holiday policy?

    (A) Holidays must be used up before the end of the year.

    (B) Holiday time is granted first to employees with seniority.

    (C) Holiday time must be approved by management.

    (D) Holiday requests must be made one month in advance.

89. Why might a staff member speak with Jasmine in person?

    (A) To extend a vacation

    (B) To request a holiday at short notice

    (C) To get approval for a holiday

    (D) To receive the vacation form

90. What is implied in the memorandum?

    (A) Many employees have holiday time left over.

    (B) Employees are not filling out the proper form.

    (C) Managers have updated the vacation request form.

    (D) New employees are eligible for holidays in the new year.

Industrial Foods Monthly
Special Survey

We are asking our subscribers what they would like to see in future issues of Industrial Foods Monthly. Your input will help us select the right content for our publication, which is read by thousands of supermarket chain managers across the country.

1. What types of articles would you like to see in future issues?
A. More informational articles
B. More problem-solving narratives
C. I am satisfied with the current content.

2. How much editorial comment do you like?
A. The current amount is just right.
B. Less would be better.
C. More would be better.

3. Do you want more articles on innovations from other countries?
A. Yes
B. No

4. Should the magazine have more vendor advertisements?
A. Yes
B. No

Industrial Foods Monthly
Reader opinion survey results

A survey was conducted earlier this year to poll our readers on some specific topics that will affect our future direction.

We were pleased to find the responses to the second and fourth questions showed that 85% of our readership is happy with the amount of vendor advertising and editorial material in our publication. One thing that surprised us was that about 63% of the readers answered "yes" to the third question. Apparently, the growing global marketplace is causing them some concern. Lastly, a huge 77% of our readers would like to see more problem-solving narratives. This means that writers need to shift their focus from informational and scientific research to interesting case histories of how specific companies and business owners solved their unique problems. Next month, we are planning a brainstorming workshop with our financial backers on how to get started on this.

91. What is the purpose of the survey?

    (A) To help determine future content
    (B) To increase worldwide readership
    (C) To assess advertisers' needs
    (D) To rate the magazine's success

92. Who is the survey most likely intended for?

    (A) Managers of grocery store chains
    (B) Owners of restaurant franchises
    (C) Publishing company employees
    (D) Advertising account executives

93. What percentage of readers said they wanted to learn more about foreign innovations?

    (A) 40%
    (B) 63%
    (C) 77%
    (D) 85%

94. What is mentioned about the magazine's articles?

    (A) Most people complained about too much advertising.
    (B) A small number of readers are interested in the global market.
    (C) Readers typically like learning about other people's solutions.
    (D) A majority of subscribers do not agree with the writers' general opinions.

95. What will occur next month?

    (A) A new survey will be completed.
    (B) A meeting for investors will take place.
    (C) A new infomercial will be developed.
    (D) A workshop for writers will be held.

To:	Mary Garcia <mgarcia@fivehillsmanila.com>
From:	Martin Voller <mvoller@fivehillsbali.com>
Subject:	Convention in Phuket
Date:	June 12

Hi Mary,

Thanks for sending me the details I asked for in my e-mail regarding the Travel, Tourism, and Hospitality Convention taking place in Phuket next month. Unfortunately, it looks as though I won't be able to go to the convention in person, so two senior members of my front desk staff will attend on my behalf. I hope that the talk that you will give on the final day of the event is successful. How would you feel about having dinner with my two employees on July 21st before you have to fly back to Manila? If this suits you, I'll pass on their e-mail addresses to you so that you can make arrangements.

Best regards,

Martin Voller
Customer Service Manager
Five Hills Resort
Bali, Indonesia

---

http://www.pecc.com/tthconvention

Travel, Tourism, and Hospitality Convention
@ Phuket Exhibition & Conference Center, July 17-20

Full Schedule	Talk Schedule	Workshop Schedule	FAQ

There will be a special workshop on each day of the convention. Space is limited to one hundred participants for each session, so you are advised to register in advance at the foot of the page. All sessions will take place in the main auditorium from 5:30 P.M. to 8:30 P.M.

Day 1	Day 2
"Keeping Your Workspace Tidy"	"Managing Your Time Effectively"
Led by Mark Cornish	Led by Sally Noman
Day 3	Day 4
"Maximizing Your Revenue"	"Putting the Customer First"
Led by Eva Wilton	Led by Grant Bell

Online Registration Page

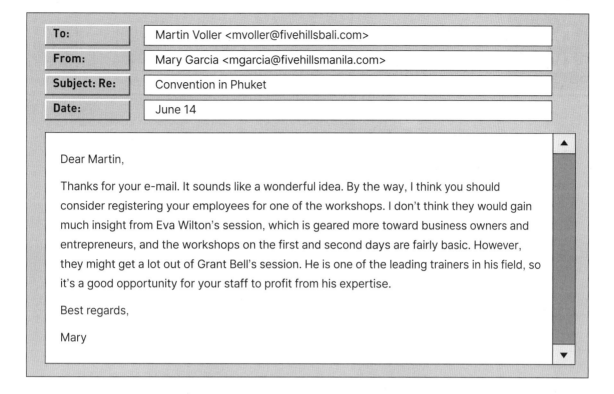

To:	Martin Voller <mvoller@fivehillsbali.com>
From:	Mary Garcia <mgarcia@fivehillsmanila.com>
Subject: Re:	Convention in Phuket
Date:	June 14

Dear Martin,

Thanks for your e-mail. It sounds like a wonderful idea. By the way, I think you should consider registering your employees for one of the workshops. I don't think they would gain much insight from Eva Wilton's session, which is geared more toward business owners and entrepreneurs, and the workshops on the first and second days are fairly basic. However, they might get a lot out of Grant Bell's session. He is one of the leading trainers in his field, so it's a good opportunity for your staff to profit from his expertise.

Best regards,

Mary

96. What is suggested about Ms. Garcia in the first e-mail?

(A) She was recently hired by Five Hills Resort.
(B) She was previously contacted by Mr. Voller.
(C) She intends to recruit more front desk staff.
(D) She is primarily based in Phuket.

97. What does Mr. Voller suggest that Ms. Garcia do?

(A) Visit his resort in Indonesia
(B) Change the date of a presentation
(C) Meet with members of his staff
(D) Register for a workshop

98. When will Ms. Garcia give a talk?

(A) On July 17
(B) On July 18
(C) On July 20
(D) On July 21

99. Which workshop does Ms. Garcia recommend to Mr. Voller?

(A) Keeping Your Workspace Tidy
(B) Managing Your Time Effectively
(C) Maximizing Your Revenue
(D) Putting the Customer First

100. In the second e-mail, the word "geared" in paragraph 1, line 3, is closest in meaning to

(A) alternated
(B) accessed
(C) equipped
(D) targeted

DAY 02

LC+RC
Half Test

제한 시간 60분

MP3 바로듣기

강의 바로보기

정답 및 해설 p. 26

PART 1

Directions: For each question in this part, you will hear four statements about a picture in your test book. When you hear the statements, you must select the one statement that best describes what you see in the picture. Then find the number of the question on your answer sheet and mark your answer. The statements will not be printed in your test book and will be spoken only one time.

1.

2.

PART 2

Directions: You will hear a question or statement and three responses spoken in English. They will not be printed in your test book and will be spoken only one time. Select the best response to the question or statement and mark the letter (A), (B), or (C) on your answer sheet.

3. Mark your answer on your answer sheet.

4. Mark your answer on your answer sheet.

5. Mark your answer on your answer sheet.

6. Mark your answer on your answer sheet.

7. Mark your answer on your answer sheet.

8. Mark your answer on your answer sheet.

9. Mark your answer on your answer sheet.

10. Mark your answer on your answer sheet.

11. Mark your answer on your answer sheet.

12. Mark your answer on your answer sheet.

13. Mark your answer on your answer sheet.

14. Mark your answer on your answer sheet.

15. Mark your answer on your answer sheet.

16. Mark your answer on your answer sheet.

17. Mark your answer on your answer sheet.

18. Mark your answer on your answer sheet.

19. Mark your answer on your answer sheet.

20. Mark your answer on your answer sheet.

Directions: You will hear some conversations between two or more people. You will be asked to answer three questions about what the speakers say in each conversation. Select the best response to each question and mark the letter (A), (B), (C) or (D) on your answer sheet. The conversations will not be printed in your test book and will be spoken only one time.

21. What event has the woman recently attended?

    (A) A charity event for children
    (B) A presentation on economic change
    (C) A conference for telemarketers
    (D) A talk regarding travel

22. What does the woman suggest?

    (A) Selling the video to a television station
    (B) Letting another person edit the film
    (C) Editing the film by herself over the weekend
    (D) Filming a different event

23. What do the speakers agree to do?

    (A) Buy an editing program
    (B) Find another person to help them
    (C) Collaborate on some work
    (D) Postpone a project deadline

24. What kind of business does the woman run?

    (A) A computer company
    (B) A consulting firm
    (C) A travel agency
    (D) An accounting business

25. What does the woman say would help her business?

    (A) The release of a new product
    (B) The relocation of the company
    (C) An improvement in the economy
    (D) A change in marketing strategy

26. What does the man offer to do?

    (A) Train the woman's staff
    (B) Arrange a meeting with a client
    (C) Invest in the woman's company
    (D) Introduce the woman to a friend

27. Where most likely are the speakers?

    (A) In a fast food store
    (B) In an office
    (C) In a bakery
    (D) In a hotel kitchen

28. What does the man imply when he says, "That's our specialty"?

    (A) He will offer a reduced price.
    (B) He sells a single item.
    (C) He is able to provide a service.
    (D) He is expressing gratitude to the woman.

29. What will the woman probably do at around 12: 30?

    (A) Pick up a cake
    (B) Host a party
    (C) Make a reservation
    (D) Order a special product

30. What does Mr. Rodriguez say he recently did?

    (A) Finished a work project
    (B) Started a new job
    (C) Moved into a new home
    (D) Enrolled in a course

31. What is the fitness center planning to do next week?

    (A) Offer additional classes
    (B) Expand an exercise area
    (C) Hire new instructors
    (D) Reduce membership fees

32. According to the woman, what complimentary gift do new members receive?

    (A) A water bottle
    (B) A gym towel
    (C) A T-shirt
    (D) A sports bag

Department	Manager
Human Resources	Donna Mumford
Advertising	Olivia Benton
Sales	Harriet Blanc
Accounting	Gerard Nesbitt

33. What is the topic of the conversation?

(A) A work policy
(B) A supermarket sale
(C) A job interview
(D) A customer complaint

34. What problem does the woman mention?

(A) A manager is out of town.
(B) A special offer has ended.
(C) A scheduling error occurred.
(D) A department is temporarily closed.

35. Look at the graphic. Who will the man most likely meet with on Friday?

(A) Donna Mumford
(B) Olivia Benton
(C) Harriet Blanc
(D) Gerard Nesbitt

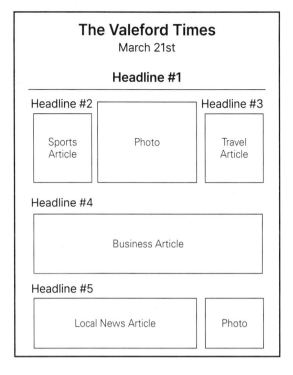

36. What did the woman do this morning?

(A) She hired a new editor.
(B) She took some photographs.
(C) She signed a contract.
(D) She attended a meeting.

37. Look at the graphic. Which article did the man write?

(A) The sports article
(B) The travel article
(C) The business article
(D) The local news article

38. What does the woman remind the man to do?

(A) Return some equipment
(B) Check a schedule
(C) Proofread an article
(D) Submit a form

Directions: You will hear some talks given by a single speaker. You will be asked to answer three questions about what the speakers say in each conversation. Select the best response to each question and mark the letter (A), (B), (C) or (D) on your answer sheet. The conversations will not be printed in your test book and will be spoken only one time.

39. What type of special event is being held?

    (A) A victory celebration
    (B) A retirement dinner
    (C) A town's anniversary party
    (D) An awards ceremony

40. Who is Sean Newton?

    (A) A school teacher
    (B) A charity worker
    (C) A local businessman
    (D) A town official

41. What will most likely happen next?

    (A) A performance will begin.
    (B) Forms will be distributed.
    (C) An election winner will be welcomed.
    (D) The listeners will take their seats.

42. Who most likely are the listeners?

    (A) Event planners
    (B) Corporate lawyers
    (C) Real estate agents
    (D) Customer service representatives

43. What does the speaker say that Maria Weizmann has done?

    (A) Opened her own business
    (B) Announced her retirement
    (C) Reviewed a contract
    (D) Received an award

44. Why does the speaker say, "This may take a while"?

    (A) To suggest taking a break
    (B) To emphasize that a lot has changed
    (C) To express concerns about a lack of time
    (D) To complain about a complicated legal issue

45. What is mainly being announced?

    (A) A trip cancelation
    (B) A bus terminal policy
    (C) A delayed departure
    (D) A new travel route

46. Why does the speaker say, "Please bear with us"?

    (A) To ask the listeners to prepare for boarding
    (B) To inform the listeners that seats are available
    (C) To request the listeners' cooperation
    (D) To recommend that the listeners purchase tickets

47. According to the speaker, how can the listeners receive more information?

    (A) By visiting a ticket office
    (B) By waiting for another announcement
    (C) By checking a schedule
    (D) By reading an information pamphlet

Book Publishing Expenses

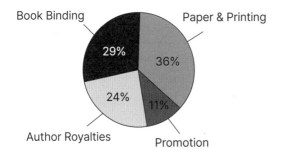

48. Why does the speaker thank the listeners?
    (A) They increased annual profits.
    (B) They worked additional hours.
    (C) They provided useful ideas.
    (D) They attracted new readers.

49. What will the listeners receive?
    (A) A cash bonus
    (B) An extra vacation day
    (C) A gift certificate
    (D) A salary raise

50. Look at the graphic. Which issue will the speaker discuss next?
    (A) Book Binding
    (B) Paper & Printing
    (C) Promotion
    (D) Author Royalties

This is the end of the Listening test. Turn to Part 5 in your test book.

READING TEST

In the Reading test, you will read a variety of texts and answer several different types of reading comprehension questions. The entire Reading test will last 75 minutes. There are three parts, and directions are given for each part. You are encouraged to answer as many questions as possible within the time allowed. You must mark your answers on the separate answer sheet. Do not write your answers in your test book.

PART 5

Directions: A word or phrase is missing in each of the sentences below. Four answer choices are given below each sentence. Select the best answer to complete the sentence. Then mark the letter (A), (B), (C), or (D) on your answer sheet.

51. Due to the recent decrease in ------- for e-books, Mobius Inc. will discontinue some of its e-reader models.

   (A) demand
   (B) demanded
   (C) demanding
   (D) to demand

52. The fitness instructor will create a ------- new schedule for members of the yoga class.

   (A) completion
   (B) completes
   (C) completing
   (D) completely

53. Because Ms. Shilton is highly regarded as a journalist, ------- newspaper column is read by hundreds of thousands of people.

   (A) she
   (B) her
   (C) hers
   (D) herself

54. The city council debate session will be ------- similarly to the planning meeting held in the Mabel Building.

   (A) structure
   (B) structural
   (C) structured
   (D) structuring

55. All of the cakes were so attractively designed ------- it was almost impossible to choose one for the ceremony.

   (A) until
   (B) that
   (C) even
   (D) after

56. The photography course is open to amateurs and professionals -------, so there are no enrollment restrictions.

   (A) ahead
   (B) around
   (C) alike
   (D) along

57. Kris Choi and Vivian Liu are expected to reach the final group stage at the global Internet marketing -------.
    (A) competes
    (B) competing
    (C) competed
    (D) competition

58. *The Sun Times* has identified its strongest readership market as those aged ------- 15 and 30 years old.
    (A) along
    (B) between
    (C) through
    (D) among

59. Any student ------- research paper is not received this week will be unable to pass the course.
    (A) that
    (B) which
    (C) who
    (D) whose

60. While the stairways in the building are being painted, ------- to the third-floor cafeteria is by elevator only.
    (A) direction
    (B) reservation
    (C) access
    (D) order

61. *The Handyman's Handbook* is the ------- guide for basic home maintenance projects and repairs.
    (A) compression
    (B) most comprehensive
    (C) comprehensive
    (D) most comprehensively

62. As soon as the fire alarm sounds, please evacuate the building ------- and stay at the designated meeting point until further notice.
    (A) currently
    (B) previously
    (C) forcefully
    (D) promptly

63. ------- you travel for business or for pleasure, we will certainly make your stay enjoyable.
    (A) Either
    (B) Then
    (C) Whether
    (D) In spite of

64. Several leading food critics have highly ------- Chef Craig Nolan's new restaurant on Tenth Avenue.
    (A) consumed
    (B) nominated
    (C) published
    (D) recommended

65. Gym members should keep in mind that their personal belongings should not ------- unattended in the changing room.
    (A) leave
    (B) have left
    (C) was left
    (D) be left

66. Ms. Wong was recognized for her outstanding ------- to promote the Image of the city through a variety of campaigns.
    (A) talents
    (B) responses
    (C) efforts
    (D) attention

PART 6

Directions: Read the texts that follow. A word, phrase, or sentence is missing in parts of each text. Four answer choices for each question are given below the text. Select the best answer to complete the text. Then mark the letter (A), (B), (C) or (D) on your answer sheet.

Questions 67-70 refer to the following memo.

To: Maintenance Staff
From: Carissa Dempsey, Maintenance Manager
Date: February 21
Subject: Re: South Land Hospital Location

Dear Staff,

First of all, let me say that all of you are doing an ------- job at all of our locations. I regularly receive
67.
positive comments from the companies and organizations we work for.

In recent weeks, it has come to my attention that staff working at the South Land Hospital have been
asked to provide services that are outside what is offered in our Basic Bronze package. Such requests
have included taking the garbage to the dumpster, wiping off chairs in the waiting room, and cleaning
out coffee pots. In every case, our staff members performed these ------- tasks.
68.

While I understand your desire to please our clients, it's important to provide only what we agreed to
at the time the contract was signed. -------. If you have any concerns or questions about the services
69.
included in any of our packages, I am ------- to address them. Please feel free to stop by my office any
70.
time, and keep up the great work.

Sincerely,

Carissa Dempsey, Maintenance Manager

---

67. (A) exemplary
    (B) frequent
    (C) accessible
    (D) eventual

68. (A) addition
    (B) additions
    (C) additional
    (D) additionally

69. (A) In this way, your assistance will be
    appreciated.
    (B) So, I want you all to sign the form.
    (C) This will avoid taking time away from our
    other clients.
    (D) This addition to the service will be only
    temporary.

70. (A) plain
    (B) hesitant
    (C) willing
    (D) possible

Tired of ------- your home? Dreaming of one day having a bungalow or townhouse to call your own?
71.
Then read on!

With plenty of homes on the market and interest rates at historic lows, NOW is the best time to buy! At
No Worries Realty, we have a staff of twelve real estate agents, and ------- have at least 10 years of
72.
experience. Unlike some other companies, we won't try to convince you to purchase a home that's not
right for you just to make a sale.

Our process is designed to find you exactly the home you want at a price you can afford. First, you'll
fill out a detailed questionnaire that asks you about your preferred area, number of bathrooms, floor
space, and of course cost. -------.
73.

When you're ready to buy, we'll take care of all the paperwork and help you arrange a home -------. All
74.
you'll need to do is just pack and move in!

Call us at 633-435-4505 to begin the exciting process of searching for your first home!

71. (A) rent
(B) rents
(C) rented
(D) renting

72. (A) everyone
(B) all
(C) each
(D) any

73. (A) Then, your agent will take you to only those
homes that meet your criteria.
(B) Your order has been received and is now
being processed by an agent.
(C) Once we have this information, we will do
our best to find you a suitable job.
(D) We at No Worries Realty appreciate your
listing your home with us.

74. (A) inspect
(B) inspected
(C) inspecting
(D) inspection

PART 7

Directions: In this part you will read a selection of texts, such as magazine and newspaper articles, e-mails, and instant messages. Each text or set of texts is followed by several questions. Select the best answer for each question and mark the letter (A), (B), (C), or (D) on your answer sheet.

Questions 75-76 refer to the following advertisement.

Picture Perfect
142 Hampshire Drive, Allendale, MI 49401

3002 Briggs Avenue, Allendale, MI 49404

Whether you wish to make long-lasting memories of a special event such as a wedding or graduation ceremony, or simply need a nice shot for your passport or company ID card, Picture Perfect will provide the best results in town! Our professional employees can capture a natural look, or make you look like a model on the catwalk. Come on down to our main location, or stop by the studio we opened on Briggs Avenue last month. We offer 10 percent off when you order 50 photographs or more, and for a minimal extra fee you can request our rapid 3-day processing service.

75. What type of business is Picture Perfect?

(A) A camera manufacturer
(B) A modeling agency
(C) An art supply store
(D) A photography studio

76. What is indicated about Picture Perfect?

(A) It has at least three locations.
(B) It is planning to relocate its main branch.
(C) It gives free gifts to returning customers.
(D) It offers a special express service.

Questions 77-79 refer to the following Web page.

http://www.facemotors.com/comments

About	News	Products	Comments	Contact

I'm writing to complain about the quality of one of your products, namely the FACE GT-20. My car has been recalled numerous times for things such as poorly-attached seats and poorly designed fuel line couplings, which are both frighteningly dangerous and easily preventable conditions.

As I'm writing this, my car is, once again, at your service center due to a recall. I'm missing yet another day of work so that FACE can correct an EGR valve. This would seem to be a minor thing, but it will take all day to fix, and I must have this corrected and obtain a certificate to renew my car's registration. Once again, I'm faced with paying the penalty for my choice of automobile. Although I explained to the serviceman that it was very important that I get to work and that I was missing work as a result of a defective part, he dismissed me completely with the argument that if they gave everyone a replacement car for the day, they'd have to give out hundreds of cars. As a result, I have no means of transportation and am stuck here in your service center for the duration of the repair work.

John Alfredson

77. What is the purpose of the comment?

(A) To suggest ways to improve a product
(B) To praise a customer service representative
(C) To order replacement automobile parts
(D) To express dissatisfaction with a product

78. What problem does Mr. Alfredson mention?

(A) He cannot afford repair costs.
(B) He must wait several days for parts.
(C) He suffered an injury while driving.
(D) He had to miss a full day of work.

79. According to the comment, what did Mr. Alfredson request from a service center worker?

(A) An apology from an employee
(B) An extended warranty
(C) A temporary vehicle
(D) A discount on repairs

Questions 80-82 refer to the following e-mail.

To:	Customer Service Employees
From:	Rosa Holmes, Director
Subject:	December overtime
Date:	November 15

Hi everyone,

It is that time of year again! We will be offering extended customer service hours starting November 25. We will open the phone lines at 7:00 A.M. on weekdays and 8:00 A.M. on weekends. Lines will stay open until 9:00 P.M. every day. We won't return to our routine schedule until January 5. As always, time-and-a-half will be paid for any overtime work (over 40 hours a week).

I don't know your personal schedules, so please sign up with your overtime requests on the schedule with the Customer Service Department. I know many of you have family obligations at this time of year, but many of you also enjoy the opportunity to earn a little extra. I expect to fill these needs without forcing any unwilling staff to work extra hours.

Happy holiday season, everyone!

Rosa

80. Why was the e-mail written?

(A) To describe a full-time vacancy
(B) To ask people to volunteer
(C) To extend best wishes for the holiday
(D) To announce an opportunity to join a program

81. When will the Customer Service Department return to its regular work hours?

(A) November 25
(B) January 5
(C) January 15
(D) January 25

82. What is suggested about the overtime work?

(A) It will not include weekends.
(B) Extra money will be paid.
(C) It will only be required for one month.
(D) It is mandatory for all employees.

Questions 83-86 refer to the following article.

Vorsha Inc.
Announces New Products

Berlin (April 4) – Andreas Schmidt, CEO of Vorsha Inc., spoke at a press conference yesterday about the firm's plans to release a new line of cutting-edge products. The last product released by Vorsha was the NX560. — [1] —. Much to the surprise of Vorsha executives and experts in the electronics industry, only around 540,000 units of that model have been sold since its launch last July. — [2] —. In light of this disappointment, the company has accelerated development of its NX600 line, and these products are scheduled to be released onto the market this June. With its brand new manufacturing plant opening in Berlin next month, Vorsha Corporation clearly anticipates a high level of demand and intends to increase its production capacity.

Mr. Schmidt stated that the NX600 handsets will have an improved menu layout, a more powerful camera, a VidTalk face-to-face call function, and a higher screen resolution. — [3] —. He also noted that, unlike previous models, the new products will be launched not only in European markets, but also in Asian markets. The retail price is expected to be approximately €750. — [4] —.

---

83. What does Vorsha Inc. most likely produce?

(A) LED televisions
(B) Fax machines
(C) Digital cameras
(D) Cell phones

84. What can be inferred about the NX560?

(A) It was launched more than one year ago.
(B) It received a lot of praise from consumers.
(C) It was the first product to be released by Vorsha Inc.
(D) It proved to be less popular than expected.

85. When will Vorsha Inc. open its new production facility?

(A) In April
(B) In May
(C) In June
(D) In July

86. In which of the positions marked [1], [2], [3], and [4] does the following sentence best belong?

"This is in spite of a multi-million-dollar worldwide advertising campaign."

(A) [1]
(B) [2]
(C) [3]
(D) [4]

Questions 87-90 refer to the following online chat discussions.

Louise Driscoll	[4:30 P.M.]	I'd like to ask my like-minded mountain trekkers for some advice. My husband and I are planning to hike Mount Sherman next weekend. I know it's far from the city, but have any of you ever been?
Troy Parks	[4:32 P.M.]	Some friends of mine went there and they said the trails are well-maintained and the views are incredible.
Louise Driscoll	[4:34 P.M.]	I've heard the same. So, I'm just a bit worried that it'll be too crowded.
Jill Findlay	[4:35 P.M.]	I went there with my hiking club earlier this year, and you won't be disappointed. The trails were quite empty because the park is so huge.
Louise Driscoll	[4:36 P.M.]	Sounds great! And does Mount Sherman have camping facilities? We're tempted to sleep there and make it a two-day trek.
Troy Parks	[4:37 P.M.]	Didn't they just get rid of overnight fees for campers, Jill?
Jill Findlay	[4:38 P.M.]	Yes, indeed. The campground and camping facilities are all completely free.
Louise Driscoll	[4:39 P.M.]	Wow! If only the same could be said for Mount Henry.
Dean Marlowe	[4:41 P.M.]	Also, don't forget to visit the park ranger office. I heard they give out free bottles of water during the summer.
Louise Driscoll	[4:42 P.M.]	Great tip, thanks! You've all been a lot of help.

87. With whom was Ms. Driscoll most likely chatting?

(A) People who live near Mount Sherman
(B) People who will join her on a trip
(C) People who often go hiking
(D) People who sell camping supplies

88. What is Ms. Driscoll concerned about?

(A) Poor weather
(B) How to reach Mount Sherman
(C) Busy trails
(D) The difficulty of a hiking route

89. At 4:39 P.M., what does Ms. Driscoll most likely mean when she writes, "If only the same could be said for Mount Henry"?

(A) Mount Henry's camping facilities are poor quality.
(B) Mount Henry's views are underwhelming.
(C) Mount Henry's trails are poorly maintained.
(D) Mount Henry's campground charges a fee.

90. According to Mr. Marlowe, what can be obtained at the park ranger office?

(A) A map of the trails
(B) A permit for parking
(C) Complimentary beverages
(D) Camping equipment

Give us a new look and be entered to win!

Live Landscape Design wants a new look and we need your help. Design a new logo for our company and be entered to win a makeover for your garden and a $10,000 trip to visit famous gardens in Italy, France and Spain.

You need to design a bold logo that reflects our company image. We are committed to preserving nature and helping people achieve their landscape design goals. The logo should be submitted on an A4-sized page and you will also need to include a 500-word submission which explains the meaning of the logo. We require both a color and black and white version of the logo.

Be aware that if you win the competition, you must agree to a photograph of yourself being published. You need to be over 18 years of age to enter.

You may enter anytime between November 21 and December 30. The winner will be notified on January 15.

Please submit your entries by e-mail to Lily Penny at l.penny@livelandscape.com.

To:	Lily Penny <l.penny@livelandscape.com>
From:	Hunter Jones <hjones@hunterdesign.co.uk>
Date:	November 23
Subject:	Competition questions

Dear Ms. Penny,

I am writing regarding your recently advertised logo design competition. I have a few questions that I hope you can answer for me.

Is the competition only open to amateur designers, or can professional designers also submit entries? I work as a designer at a landscape company, so that is why I am asking this question. Also, is the competition only open to US residents, or can residents of other countries enter the competition? Are late entries accepted?

I hope you will be able to answer my questions and that I will be able to enter the competition. I'd love to win the trip overseas, as I always enjoy visiting those countries.

Yours sincerely,

Hunter Jones

91. What is a requirement to enter the competition?

    (A) You must be an American citizen.
    (B) You must be an experienced gardener.
    (C) You must be at least 19.
    (D) You must be a professional designer.

92. What needs to be included with the entry?

    (A) A color photograph
    (B) A letter of recommendation
    (C) A detailed résumé
    (D) A written description

93. When will participants find out if they have won?

    (A) On November 21
    (B) On November 23
    (C) On December 30
    (D) On January 15

94. What information is NOT requested by Mr. Jones?

    (A) Whether he can send his entry after the closing date
    (B) Whether non-US residents may enter the competition
    (C) Whether the prize can be exchanged for cash
    (D) Whether professionals are eligible to participate

95. What is indicated about Mr. Jones?

    (A) He is an employee of Live Landscape Design.
    (B) He does not currently have a garden.
    (C) He has traveled to France before.
    (D) He will assist in judging competition submissions.

Ms. Regina Newsome
306 Banks Avenue
Houston, TX 77003

Dear Ms. Newsome,

We are in the process of organizing this year's African American Art Exhibition, which will be held at the Metropolitan Art Gallery from August 12 to August 25. As was the case with last August's exhibition, all participating artists will be profiled on our Web site alongside images of their work. I am writing to you in the hope that you would like to display some of your sculptures at the event. We will be utilizing all four of the building's galleries.

The registration procedure is largely the same as in previous years, with a couple of small changes. Participants must still register to take part at least one month prior to the opening day of the event. The main difference now is that you have to sign up via our Web site, not by mailing a form. Also, starting from this year, we will need a scanned copy of either your national ID card or your driver's license.

Sincerely,

Marcus Payne
Chairman
LOLA Art Organization

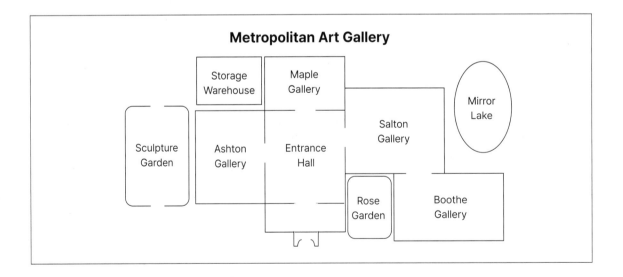

Metropolitan Art Gallery

Storage Warehouse

Maple Gallery

Mirror Lake

Salton Gallery

Sculpture Garden

Ashton Gallery

Entrance Hall

Rose Garden

Boothe Gallery

To:	Marcus Payne <mpayne@lolaart.com>
From:	Regina Newsome <rnewsome@artism.com>
Subject:	African American Art Exhibition
Date:	June 4

Dear Mr. Payne,

Thank you for writing to me regarding the African American Art Exhibition. Before I go to the Web site to register myself as a participant, I would like to check something with you. Although I am interested in participating, I will only do so if my works can be shown in an environment that highlights their beauty and intricacy. As my sculptures look better in natural lighting, I was hoping they could be placed in a gallery that receives a great deal of daylight. When I displayed my works at last year's exhibition, I was not satisfied with the lighting that was provided in the Maple Gallery, and the galleries next to Mirror Lake did not seem naturally bright enough either. I think the space overlooking the sculpture garden would be much more suitable for my works.

Thanks, and I look forward to seeing you at the gallery in August.

Regina Newsome

96. Why did Mr. Payne write to Ms. Newsome?
(A) To inform her that an event venue has been changed
(B) To encourage her to participate in an event
(C) To thank her for helping to organize an exhibition
(D) To notify her that a new art gallery will open soon

97. How has the procedure for event registration changed?
(A) Participants are required to register in advance.
(B) Registration will take place at the event venue.
(C) Registration can only be carried out online.
(D) Participants must submit two forms of identification.

98. Where does Ms. Newsome wish to display her exhibits?
(A) The Salton Gallery
(B) The Maple Gallery
(C) The Ashton Gallery
(D) The Boothe Gallery

99. What is suggested about Ms. Newsome?
(A) She has collaborated with Mr. Payne on some artwork.
(B) She will meet with Mr. Payne in a month.
(C) She was briefly described on the gallery's Web site last year.
(D) She will receive a discount on event registration.

100. In the e-mail, the word "highlights" in paragraph 1, line 4, is closest in meaning to
(A) illuminates
(B) previews
(C) summarizes
(D) accentuates

PART 1

Directions: For each question in this part, you will hear four statements about a picture in your test book. When you hear the statements, you must select the one statement that best describes what you see in the picture. Then find the number of the question on your answer sheet and mark your answer. The statements will not be printed in your test book and will be spoken only one time.

1.

2.

PART 2

Directions: You will hear a question or statement and three responses spoken in English. They will not be printed in your test book and will be spoken only one time. Select the best response to the question or statement and mark the letter (A), (B), or (C) on your answer sheet.

3. Mark your answer on your answer sheet.

4. Mark your answer on your answer sheet.

5. Mark your answer on your answer sheet.

6. Mark your answer on your answer sheet.

7. Mark your answer on your answer sheet.

8. Mark your answer on your answer sheet.

9. Mark your answer on your answer sheet.

10. Mark your answer on your answer sheet.

11. Mark your answer on your answer sheet.

12. Mark your answer on your answer sheet.

13. Mark your answer on your answer sheet.

14. Mark your answer on your answer sheet.

15. Mark your answer on your answer sheet.

16. Mark your answer on your answer sheet.

17. Mark your answer on your answer sheet.

18. Mark your answer on your answer sheet.

19. Mark your answer on your answer sheet.

20. Mark your answer on your answer sheet.

PART 3

21. Where do the speakers most likely work?

    (A) At a theater
    (B) At a science museum
    (C) At an art gallery
    (D) At a hotel

22. Why is the woman concerned?

    (A) Some equipment might be heavy.
    (B) A space is currently being renovated.
    (C) Some displays have not been set up.
    (D) A room may not be bright enough.

23. What will the man do later today?

    (A) Have lunch with the woman
    (B) Update a schedule
    (C) Meet with a speaker
    (D) Make an announcement

24. What kind of product are the speakers discussing?

    (A) Clothing
    (B) Home appliances
    (C) Furniture
    (D) Computer accessories

25. What aspect of the product is the man concerned about?

    (A) The durability
    (B) The price
    (C) The appearance
    (D) The ease of assembly

26. What will happen in June?

    (A) Some employees will be hired.
    (B) Some products will be launched.
    (C) An advertising campaign will begin.
    (D) A retail location will be opened.

27. Who most likely is the man?

    (A) A taxi driver
    (B) A travel agent
    (C) A hotel manager
    (D) A flight attendant

28. What does the woman imply when she says, "that's what I thought too"?

    (A) A decision should be reconsidered.
    (B) A deadline is approaching.
    (C) A fee should be waived.
    (D) A trip will be canceled.

29. What will the woman do next?

    (A) Check her e-mail
    (B) Submit a payment
    (C) Provide travel details
    (D) Fill out some documents

30. What department do the speakers work in?

    (A) Human resources
    (B) Accounting
    (C) Marketing
    (D) Technical assistance

31. What problem does the woman mention?

    (A) She isn't experienced in the field.
    (B) She has a long commute.
    (C) She needs another document.
    (D) She doesn't know her way around the office.

32. What do the men suggest?

    (A) Arriving early
    (B) Registering for a seminar
    (C) Contacting another employee
    (D) Organizing a meeting

Serial Number	PF-3646
Manufacturer ID	KC-103
Model Type	24 Wide
Category	90 Standard

Manager	Department
Mr. Baker	Marketing
Ms. Wells	Customer Service
Mr. Smith	Accounting
Ms. Carter	Public Relations

33. Who most likely is the man?

(A) A construction worker
(B) A real estate agent
(C) A plumber
(D) A security guard

34. What does the woman say she will handle?

(A) Paying an invoice
(B) Filing some paperwork
(C) Inspecting other apartments
(D) Complaining to a contractor

35. Look at the graphic. Which piece of information does the woman read to the man?

(A) The serial number
(B) The manufacturer ID
(C) The model type
(D) The category

36. Who most likely is the woman?

(A) A new employee
(B) A company owner
(C) A hiring manager
(D) A sales representative

37. Look at the graphic. What department does the man work in?

(A) Marketing
(B) Customer Service
(C) Accounting
(D) Public Relations

38. Where will the speakers go next?

(A) To the main office
(B) To the storage closet
(C) To the cafeteria
(D) To the staff room

PART 4

Directions: You will hear some talks given by a single speaker. You will be asked to answer three questions about what the speakers say in each conversation. Select the best response to each question and mark the letter (A), (B), (C) or (D) on your answer sheet. The conversations will not be printed in your test book and will be spoken only one time.

39. What is the speaker calling about?

(A) A refund for an item
(B) An online purchase
(C) An overcharge
(D) An oversized product

40. What does the speaker promise to do in the afternoon?

(A) Return the item to the store
(B) Order a different style
(C) Change the shoe size
(D) Send the remaining amount

41. What is the listener asked to do?

(A) Change the customer's order
(B) Return the customer's call
(C) Refund some money
(D) Provide a shipping update

42. According to the speaker, what is the focus of the tour?

(A) Historic battlegrounds
(B) Modern infrastructure
(C) Ancient artifacts
(D) Filming locations

43. Why does the speaker say, "the Theater District has several sites of interest"?

(A) To recommend a show
(B) To suggest a different location
(C) To ask for volunteers
(D) To warn about a tight deadline

44. How can the listeners receive a discount?

(A) By visiting a business
(B) By writing a review
(C) By entering a contest
(D) By sharing some photos

45. What does the speaker teach?

(A) Engine repair
(B) Woodworking
(C) Gardening
(D) Dancing

46. Why does the speaker say, "The program fee doesn't cover cleaning staff"?

(A) To request a donation
(B) To explain the reason for a cost
(C) To emphasize the need to clean
(D) To express dissatisfaction with a policy

47. What are the listeners reminded to do before leaving?

(A) Sign up for another class
(B) Participate in a survey
(C) Share their contact information
(D) Prepare an assignment

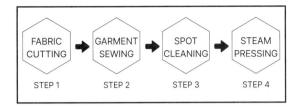

| FABRIC CUTTING | GARMENT SEWING | SPOT CLEANING | STEAM PRESSING |
| STEP 1 | STEP 2 | STEP 3 | STEP 4 |

48. What decision was made last week?

(A) The factory will undergo a safety inspection.
(B) The factory will discontinue production of some items.
(C) The listeners must submit weekly reports.
(D) The listeners must attend meetings more frequently.

49. Look at the graphic. During which step does the speaker think a problem occurred?

(A) Step 1
(B) Step 2
(C) Step 3
(D) Step 4

50. What will happen after the meeting?

(A) Some equipment will be delivered.
(B) Some employees will be trained.
(C) Some machine parts will be cleaned.
(D) Some clothing will be inspected.

This is the end of the Listening test. Turn to Part 5 in your test book.

READING TEST

In the Reading test, you will read a variety of texts and answer several different types of reading comprehension questions. The entire Reading test will last 75 minutes. There are three parts, and directions are given for each part. You are encouraged to answer as many questions as possible within the time allowed. You must mark your answers on the separate answer sheet. Do not write your answers in your test book.

PART 5

Directions: A word or phrase is missing in each of the sentences below. Four answer choices are given below each sentence. Select the best answer to complete the sentence. Then mark the letter (A), (B), (C), or (D) on your answer sheet.

51. Ms. Idassi ------- care of all the customer complaints while Mr. Hanson is on vacation.

    (A) will take
    (B) had taken
    (C) taking
    (D) to take

52. The assembly line is expected to become ------- in the first fiscal quarter.

    (A) operate
    (B) operating
    (C) operational
    (D) operation

53. Teachers involved in the baking course need to share their skills ------- expertise with all students.

    (A) and
    (B) because
    (C) after
    (D) as

54. Mr. Ferguson is requesting ------- in the training of the recently hired sales representatives.

    (A) assistant
    (B) assist
    (C) assisted
    (D) assistance

55. Most consumers polled said they ------- examine products' nutritional information when shopping for groceries.

    (A) close
    (B) closely
    (C) closest
    (D) closer

56. Each new employee must submit a personal profile form and up-to-date tax information ------- their first day of work.

    (A) prior to
    (B) as long as
    (C) until
    (D) afterward

57. Many guests have commented on the hotel lobby's ------- appearance and the helpfulness of the front desk staff.

(A) please
(B) pleasingly
(C) pleasing
(D) pleased

58. Regrettably, your application was unsuccessful ------- the high number of qualified candidates for the position of maintenance manager.

(A) due to
(B) except for
(C) regarding
(D) in spite of

59. Fluctuations in a company's stock prices are not always ------- on the firm's sales performance or popularity among customers.

(A) caused
(B) relevant
(C) indicative
(D) dependent

60. Customers with faulty laptops can visit our technical support centers in Allerton or Farnham, ------- is more convenient.

(A) whichever
(B) everyone
(C) other
(D) both

61. An unprecedented number of ------- this week suggest that our new product will be an instant success.

(A) orders
(B) ordering
(C) order
(D) ordered

62. Attendance in information technology workshops is encouraged, ------- staff members are limited to one free out-of-town session per year.

(A) such as
(B) nevertheless
(C) because
(D) although

63. The aim of the internal chat system is to allow employees in different departments to keep in contact with -------.

(A) one another
(B) the other
(C) another
(D) other

64. ------- for the Mersoft Corporation for ten years, Omar Willis quit in order to run his own business.

(A) Had worked
(B) Worked
(C) Having worked
(D) Works

65. Anyone who is unable to hand in the assignment must report to Mr. Russilo ------- three days in advance.

(A) at least
(B) instead of
(C) by means of
(D) so that

66. To get the best results from your dishwasher, use only those detergents ------- mentioned in the product manual.

(A) courteously
(B) reflectively
(C) relatively
(D) specifically

PART 6

Directions: Read the texts that follow. A word, phrase, or sentence is missing in parts of each text. Four answer choices for each question are given below the text. Select the best answer to complete the text. Then mark the letter (A), (B), (C) or (D) on your answer sheet.

Questions 67-70 refer to the following article.

Computer Malfunction Found To Be Culprit In Airport Panic

Newark International Airport closed down yesterday for several hours due to a problem with the airport's computerized radar system. Nearly 50 -------- needed to be either rescheduled, or even
67.
cancelled. --------.
68.

In an interview this morning, the head of the airport said that the airport has seen its fair share of problems, but nothing on the scale of yesterday's event. During the course of the next month or so, the best and brightest computer technicians from all over the country will be called to work on programs in order -------- similar problems in the future.
69.

During yesterday's panic and confusion, airport employees immediately called the proper authorities, worrying that it was a cyber-attack of some sort. Although police officers are still -------- the cause of
70.
the malfunction, so far it is believed to have been simply a computing error on the part of computer equipment and, thankfully, not something more sinister. A press conference is scheduled for next week.

67. (A) workers
(B) flights
(C) possessions
(D) tickets

68. (A) Check your e-mail for an updated flight itinerary.
(B) Highway drivers also experienced congested traffic.
(C) Over 8,000 travelers were affected.
(D) The pilot was not available for comment.

69. (A) prevented
(B) prevents
(C) to prevent
(D) to be prevented

70. (A) investigating
(B) protesting
(C) removing
(D) contacting

9 November

Chuck Mulgrew

Chuck's Sandwich Shop

West Finch Avenue

Toronto, ON M1B 5K7

Dear Mr. Mulgrew,

As you requested over the phone on 5 November, we checked the monthly order of food supplies you submitted through our Web site on 2 November. As you had noted, the order did indeed include ten jars of mayonnaise more than you had specified. -------, on 8 November, we addressed this issue, which
71.
we acknowledge was our fault. On that date, we ------- ten units from your order. Your invoice has
72.
been modified ------- the change to this month's order, and has been enclosed with this letter. -------.
73.   74.
Your items should arrive by 15 November as you requested.

Best regards,

Price Rite Food Supplies

71. (A) Furthermore
    (B) In addition
    (C) As a result
    (D) On the contrary

72. (A) deduct
    (B) deducted
    (C) will deduct
    (D) are deducting

73. (A) to reflect
    (B) reflecting in
    (C) a reflection of
    (D) that reflect on

74. (A) All of our items can be viewed in our online
        catalog.
    (B) By ordering in bulk, you can enjoy further
        savings.
    (C) We are not responsible for damage caused
        during shipping.
    (D) Please accept our apologies for the error.

PART 7

Directions: In this part you will read a selection of texts, such as magazine and newspaper articles, e-mails, and instant messages. Each text or set of texts is followed by several questions. Select the best answer for each question and mark the letter (A), (B), (C), or (D) on your answer sheet.

Questions 75-76 refer to the following voucher.

Neimann's Department Store
$50 GIFT VOUCHER

As one of our ways of welcoming you as a new member of our team, we have included this gift voucher in your orientation pack. Neimann's offers several staff incentives, so you may receive similar benefits like this if you perform well in your new role.

In accordance with store policy, this voucher may not be used in conjunction with any other vouchers, including printable online vouchers and newspaper vouchers. Also, it may not be used to purchase goods currently marked down in price. Finally, it may not be redeemed for cash.

Voucher Recipient: Tristan Harper

Valid Until: April 30

---

75. Why was the gift voucher most likely given to Mr. Harper?

(A) He signed up for a store membership.
(B) He referred a new customer to the store.
(C) He started employment at the business.
(D) He performed exceptionally at work in April.

76. What is true about the gift voucher?

(A) It can be combined with other vouchers.
(B) It can be printed from a Web site.
(C) It cannot be exchanged for money.
(D) It can only be used to purchase sale items.

A Healthy Body Leads to a Productive Mind

5 April – Esurance Online, a vehicle insurance company based in Boulder, Montana, is offering its workers a financial incentive to get more exercise. Employees will be paid an extra $150 each month if they attend at least three 1-hour fitness sessions in the company's conference rooms each week.

— [1] —. Considering the rising cost of gym memberships, this is a tremendously generous policy for the company to implement. Esurance Online has hired a personal fitness instructor who will lead a variety of classes such as yoga, spinning, and aerobics. According to Esurance Online's personnel manager, Peter Selby, enrollment in fitness sessions is by no means mandatory, but the vast majority of workers are expected to take advantage of the opportunity and the extra money. — [2] —. This new policy is based on a recent study that shows how a healthy physical condition can positively affect one's ability to focus well in the workplace. According to the scientist who led the study, workers who exercise regularly and maintain a healthy physical condition can get their work done more quickly and to a higher standard. — [3] —.

Furthermore, the study claims that a worker who rarely exercises and is in poor physical condition works at only 50% of his or her potential efficiency. — [4] —. Esurance Online's new policy on staff fitness aims to benefit both its workforce and its overall business performance.

---

77. What is the purpose of the article?

(A) To announce a joint venture with a local gym
(B) To advise employees to attend a workshop
(C) To explain a company's recent success
(D) To describe a company's new policy

78. What does the article state about encouraging staff to exercise more regularly?

(A) It can make people feel more tired in the workplace.
(B) It encourages more communication between staff members.
(C) It helps people to accomplish tasks more efficiently.
(D) It prevents staff from meeting important deadlines.

79. In which of the positions marked [1], [2], [3], and [4] does the following sentence best belong?

"This can result in a significant reduction in productivity for a company."

(A) [1]
(B) [2]
(C) [3]
(D) [4]

22 Crayford Street
Montgomery, AL 36043
July 2

Dear Mr. Connors,

We are very happy to provide our services in helping you set up your new restaurant. I've included some sample interiors including fixtures and designs that are standard for restaurants. Custom decorations, such as logos or paintings, are optional, but will increase the overall cost of the renovations by 20%. We will have an open house with models of many of these interiors at our headquarters on July 13 from 3 P.M. to 7 P.M.

We ask that you let us know your decision on what style of interior you would like for your restaurant by August 12, so that we have one month to finish the construction. Feel free to call me with any questions at 205-555-1388.

Best wishes,

Kyle Langley
Founder, Storefront Interiors

Enclosures

---

80. Why was the letter sent?

(A) To give directions to an open house
(B) To request payment for restoration services
(C) To ask for a custom design layout
(D) To inform about ordering procedures

81. What is suggested about Storefront Interiors' custom designs?

(A) They must adhere to construction regulations.
(B) They will be shown at a grand opening.
(C) They are more expensive than standard designs.
(D) They are made by well-known designers.

82. When will Mr. Connors' restaurant open?

(A) On July 2
(B) On July 13
(C) On August 12
(D) On September 12

Enjoy a week on the Gold Coast for only $299!

As a summer holiday bonus deal, Holiday Travel Direct Ltd. is cutting $100 off the price of our popular Gold Coast holiday package. To get these special deals, you must make a booking by July 10 and travel by July 31.

These prices won't be repeated, so call us now to avoid disappointment! You can depart from any of these cities:

- New York *
- Detroit
- Chicago
- Houston

All of the packages include 3-star accommodation and economy flights. Transfers and all lunches are also included. Please be aware that not all dates are available and that flight tax and other airline charges are not included. Children fly for half price. We accept all major credit cards, but do not accept checks. Additional discounts are available for groups, corporate customers and those who join our loyalty program.

* There is a $50 surcharge for flights departing from New York.

Free gift: If you book and pay for your package by July 5, you will receive a complimentary breakfast and a travel bag.

83. What is suggested about the special package in the advertisement?

(A) The price will be raised after July 10.
(B) It is a brand-new package for the holiday season.
(C) First-class tickets can be purchased for an extra $50.
(D) Travelers can use any payment method.

84. What is special about flights departing from New York?

(A) There are limited seats available.
(B) They aren't direct flights.
(C) The aircraft is smaller.
(D) An extra charge is needed.

85. What is NOT included in the cost of the package?

(A) Flight taxes
(B) Accommodations
(C) Transfers
(D) Lunches

86. What will you receive if you book and pay by July 5?

(A) Free baggage handling
(B) A discount for children
(C) A free meal
(D) A special membership card

Questions 87-90 refer to the following online chat discussion.

Sivan	[3:12 P.M.]	Hello. This is Sivan, your customer service representative for Lose Weight, Feel Great. How may I help you today?
Joshua	[3:15 P.M.]	Hi, Sivan. I have lost four pounds this week. I am pleased with my results so far. I wanted to know if I could eat white rice with my dinner tonight.
Sivan	[3:18 P.M.]	Brown rice is permitted on this diet, but white rice is not. Broccoli rice is also allowed.
Joshua	[3:20 P.M.]	Broccoli rice? I have never tried that before.
Sivan	[3:24 P.M.]	You should. It is healthy and delicious! Do you have access to the dietary guidebook? Complex carbohydrates are explained in the paperwork that you should have received in your welcome package.
Joshua	[3:26 P.M.]	I've actually misplaced those.
Sivan	[3:29 P.M.]	Not a problem. Please let me know your e-mail address and I will send them to you. You can also access them online at our Web site.

87. What does Joshua imply about the program?

   (A) It is effective.
   (B) It is affordable.
   (C) It is widely popular.
   (D) It is time-consuming.

88. What does Sivan recommend that Joshua do?

   (A) Attend a dieting class
   (B) Try a new food
   (C) Purchase a book
   (D) Send an e-mail

89. At 3:26 P.M., what does Joshua mean when he says, "I've actually misplaced those"?

   (A) He didn't receive the package of broccoli rice.
   (B) He cannot find his receipt.
   (C) The welcome e-mail didn't arrive.
   (D) A handbook is missing.

90. What will most likely happen next?

   (A) Sivan will check the product's Web site.
   (B) Joshua will prepare some white rice.
   (C) Sivan will cook something for Joshua.
   (D) Sivan will e-mail Joshua.

March 5

Dear Mr. Fielding,

Please make a note that I've scheduled your interview and photo shoot with Movie Biz for Wednesday, March 9 at 10:30 A.M. I am amazed at how much media attention your new movie is getting. Last year, Movie Biz declined to interview you; this year, they have assigned their top photographer and top writer for the story.

Movie Biz plans to print your article in April, prior to the start of the Star Awards Festival at the end of the month. Alexa Hamilton, the lady who will be interviewing you and writing your story, is likely going to ask you questions about your expectations for the festival. Let's set a time to go over some appropriate responses. I don't want you to tell them how much you want to win that award. We want them to think you're modest.

Johanna Beeson
Publicist for Damien Fielding

Circle of Flames
By Alexa Hamilton

Prior to releasing *Circle of Flames* just last month, Damien Fielding had directed eight films, but none ever received much media attention. Actress Susannah Wallace can be credited with helping to bring Fielding into the spotlight. "I saw *Pieces*, one of his earlier films, and was impressed with his brilliant direction," she said. "I wanted to work with him immediately."

With a well-known actress like Wallace starring in *Circle of Flames*, Fielding has suddenly become famous. According to an entertainment magazine, he is the first choice for the Star Awards Festival's Best Director prize. "I want to be clear that I don't make movies for awards," Fielding comments. "But, of course, I would be honored to receive a Star Award."

Naturally, reviews of *Circle of Flames* have encouraged viewers to re-watch his older films and they've been pleasantly surprised. Though the films did not do very well at the box office, they exhibit the same high-quality direction as *Circle of Flames*. Fielding is developing a significant following. He is someone from whom we are sure to see great things.

91. Why did Ms. Beeson write a memo to Mr. Fielding?

(A) To inform him that he has won an award
(B) To prepare him for an interview
(C) To advise him on how to pass an audition
(D) To invite him to a film festival

92. When will the article be published?

(A) Before the Star Awards Festival
(B) Before the release of *Circle of Flames*
(C) At the tenth anniversary of Movie Biz
(D) During the premiere of *Circle of Flames*

93. What is the purpose of the article?

(A) To celebrate Mr. Fielding's latest film
(B) To explain why Ms. Wallace accepted the role
(C) To promote the Star Awards Festival
(D) To highlight Mr. Fielding's previous films

94. What can be inferred about Mr. Fielding?

(A) He did not feel comfortable during the interview.
(B) He previously worked with Ms. Wallace.
(C) He is already working on a new movie.
(D) He follows the advice of his publicist.

95. In the article, the word "credited" in paragraph 1, line 2, is closest in meaning to

(A) indebted
(B) compensated
(C) recognized
(D) honored

Stratford Community Fair Event Schedule
Saturday, June 29 (Various locations around Ashbury Farm)

Provisional Schedule for Community Fair Organizers		
Time	Event/Activity	Venue/Location
8:30 a.m.	- Breakfast buffet	Catering Tent
9:30 a.m.	- Largest vegetable competition - Raffle ticket distribution - Dog and cat competition - Children's face painting	Main Field
11:30 a.m.	- Jim Lee comedy show - Pogo the clown show	Performance Tent
12:30 p.m.	- Sandwiches and refreshments	Catering Tent
1:30 p.m.	- Musical performances	Outdoor Performance Stage
4:00 p.m.	- DJ and dancing - Raffle winners announcement	Catering Tent

Once all the events have ended, community fair organizers and volunteer workers should meet with Ralph Fitts at the site entrance to receive instructions regarding clean-up and dismantling tasks.

To: Elaine Ower <eower@stratford.gov>

From: Donald Egan <donegan@stratford.gov>

Subject: Stratford Community Fair

Date: June 17

Hi Elaine,

Thank you so much for offering to help out at the community fair. We were sorry to hear that Lisa Mulumba would be unable to fulfill her duties as an organizer, but we are glad that you have agreed to take her place. On Saturday, June 29, you will be responsible for organizing the comedy show and the clown show. Ralph Fitts, one of the senior event coordinators, will assist you to make sure things run smoothly.

Best wishes,

Donald Egan
Chairman
Stratford Events Planning Committee

Hi Donald,

There is absolutely no need to thank me. I'm always ready and willing to help out with our local events. Not only does it give me an opportunity to serve the community, but it allows me to enjoy the various performances! At the upcoming fair, I really hope I have time to get over to the outdoor performance stage at around 3 p.m. Elliot Spencer is extremely talented and is sure to give a great performance!

Regards,

Elaine

---

96. What will NOT take place in the morning on June 29?

(A) Kids will have their faces painted.

(B) Pets will be entered into a contest.

(C) Raffle prizes will be handed out.

(D) Produce will be judged on its size.

97. What is indicated about community fair volunteers?

(A) They will gather together for a meal after the event.

(B) They will receive a free gift as a token of gratitude.

(C) They will attend a planning meeting with Donald Egan.

(D) They will be required to tidy up at the end of the day.

98. Where was Lisa Mulumba most likely supposed to be working?

(A) In the catering tent

(B) In the performance tent

(C) In the main field

(D) At the outdoor performance stage

99. In the first e-mail, the word "run" in paragraph 1, line 4, is closest in meaning to

(A) sprint

(B) travel

(C) operate

(D) arrive

100. Who most likely is Elliot Spencer?

(A) A comedian

(B) An event organizer

(C) A musician

(D) A committee chairman

DAY 04 LC+RC Half Test

PART 1

Directions: For each question in this part, you will hear four statements about a picture in your test book. When you hear the statements, you must select the one statement that best describes what you see in the picture. Then find the number of the question on your answer sheet and mark your answer. The statements will not be printed in your test book and will be spoken only one time.

1.

2.

PART 2

Directions: You will hear a question or statement and three responses spoken in English. They will not be printed in your test book and will be spoken only one time. Select the best response to the question or statement and mark the letter (A), (B), or (C) on your answer sheet.

3. Mark your answer on your answer sheet.

4. Mark your answer on your answer sheet.

5. Mark your answer on your answer sheet.

6. Mark your answer on your answer sheet.

7. Mark your answer on your answer sheet.

8. Mark your answer on your answer sheet.

9. Mark your answer on your answer sheet.

10. Mark your answer on your answer sheet.

11. Mark your answer on your answer sheet.

12. Mark your answer on your answer sheet.

13. Mark your answer on your answer sheet.

14. Mark your answer on your answer sheet.

15. Mark your answer on your answer sheet.

16. Mark your answer on your answer sheet.

17. Mark your answer on your answer sheet.

18. Mark your answer on your answer sheet.

19. Mark your answer on your answer sheet.

20. Mark your answer on your answer sheet.

PART 3

Directions: You will hear some conversations between two or more people. You will be asked to answer three questions about what the speakers say in each conversation. Select the best response to each question and mark the letter (A), (B), (C) or (D) on your answer sheet. The conversations will not be printed in your test book and will be spoken only one time.

21. Where do the speakers work?
    (A) At a restaurant
    (B) At a computer store
    (C) At a hotel
    (D) At a rental agency

22. What does the woman want to do?
    (A) Change a reservation process
    (B) Create an advertisement
    (C) Renovate a building
    (D) Lower some prices

23. What does the man say he will do today?
    (A) Update a Web site
    (B) Repair some equipment
    (C) Order product samples
    (D) Check some feedback

24. What is the conversation mostly about?
    (A) A seasonal sale
    (B) A product catalog
    (C) A magazine article
    (D) A social media page

25. What does the man say about an advertisement?
    (A) It features a celebrity.
    (B) It was well received.
    (C) It cost a lot of money.
    (D) It was time-consuming.

26. What does the woman suggest doing?
    (A) Surveying some customers
    (B) Changing store hours
    (C) Adding some pictures
    (D) Launching new products

27. What industry do the speakers most likely work in?
    (A) Manufacturing
    (B) Online marketing
    (C) Event planning
    (D) Financial consulting

28. Why does the man interrupt the women?
    (A) To request a deadline extension
    (B) To assist them with an assignment
    (C) To remind them about a budget increase
    (D) To inquire about the location of an event

29. What will the women do next?
    (A) Eat some food
    (B) Meet with a client
    (C) Prepare a report
    (D) Compare some prices

30. What did the speakers order?
    (A) Ingredients
    (B) Utensils
    (C) Tablecloths
    (D) Dishes

31. What does the man mean when he says, "It's already on its way"?
    (A) A delivery went to the wrong address.
    (B) An event will go ahead as planned.
    (C) An order cannot be amended.
    (D) A meeting has been rescheduled.

32. What do the speakers plan to do next week?
    (A) Introduce new items
    (B) Launch a business
    (C) Offer discounts
    (D) Cancel a business contract

Sports Vest Designs

| #124 | #147 | #154 | #172 |

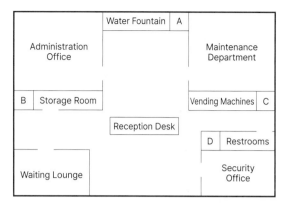

33. According to the man, what is happening in July?

(A) He is going on vacation.
(B) He is hosting a fundraising event.
(C) He is attending a training course.
(D) He is launching a new business.

34. Look at the graphic. Which product will the man order?

(A) #124
(B) #147
(C) #154
(D) #172

35. What offer does the woman tell the man about?

(A) An item can be customized.
(B) An order is eligible for free shipping.
(C) He will receive a complimentary gift.
(D) His purchase qualifies for a discount.

36. Why is the man visiting Morrison Manufacturing?

(A) To attend an interview
(B) To repair a device
(C) To deliver supplies
(D) To take a tour

37. Look at the graphic. Which elevator does the woman recommend?

(A) Elevator A
(B) Elevator B
(C) Elevator C
(D) Elevator D

38. What will the man most likely do next?

(A) Change his clothing
(B) Scan his fingerprints
(C) Provide his signature
(D) Put on a visitor's tag

PART 4

Directions: You will hear some talks given by a single speaker. You will be asked to answer three questions about what the speakers say in each conversation. Select the best response to each question and mark the letter (A), (B), (C) or (D) on your answer sheet. The conversations will not be printed in your test book and will be spoken only one time.

39. Who most likely is the message intended for?
    (A) Local residents
    (B) Travel agents
    (C) Potential tourists
    (D) Business owners

40. What does the speaker say about the downtown area?
    (A) It is very crowded.
    (B) It is closed to all vehicles.
    (C) It contains several landmarks.
    (D) It is under construction.

41. What should listeners do to find out more information?
    (A) Send an e-mail
    (B) Stay on the phone
    (C) Visit a Web site
    (D) Call another number

42. What type of products does the company sell?
    (A) Sports clothing
    (B) Fitness equipment
    (C) Health supplements
    (D) Cooking utensils

43. According to the speaker, what is unique about the new store?
    (A) It sells imported items.
    (B) It provides a reward program.
    (C) It offers educational classes.
    (D) It delivers items for free.

44. How can the listeners receive a discount?
    (A) By placing a bulk order
    (B) By visiting an online store
    (C) By shopping on a specific day
    (D) By joining a membership

45. What is the speaker helping the listener do?
    (A) Book a flight
    (B) Rent a vehicle
    (C) Reserve a room
    (D) Contact a client

46. What does the speaker imply when she says, "we have a limited budget"?
    (A) The listener should apply for a discount.
    (B) The listener should expect a cheaper option.
    (C) A spending allowance will be provided.
    (D) A ticket is for economy class.

47. Why does the speaker request to be contacted by mobile phone?
    (A) She forgot her e-mail password.
    (B) She will not be in the office.
    (C) Her office phone is faulty.
    (D) Her computer has malfunctioned.

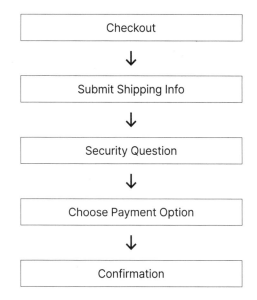

Checkout
↓
Submit Shipping Info
↓
Security Question
↓
Choose Payment Option
↓
Confirmation

48. What does the speaker say about the company's Coolwave lamp?

(A) It has become cheaper to produce.
(B) It won a design contest.
(C) It appeared in a magazine.
(D) It sold out at every location.

49. Look at the graphic. According to the speaker, which step was recently added?

(A) Checkout
(B) Submit Shipping Info
(C) Security Question
(D) Choose Payment Option

50. What concern does the speaker mention?

(A) International shipping costs are too high.
(B) Some products are out of stock.
(C) There is a higher risk of identity theft.
(D) The checkout process is too confusing.

This is the end of the Listening test. Turn to Part 5 in your test book.

READING TEST

In the Reading test, you will read a variety of texts and answer several different types of reading comprehension questions. The entire Reading test will last 75 minutes. There are three parts, and directions are given for each part. You are encouraged to answer as many questions as possible within the time allowed. You must mark your answers on the separate answer sheet. Do not write your answers in your test book.

PART 5

Directions: A word or phrase is missing in each of the sentences below. Four answer choices are given below each sentence. Select the best answer to complete the sentence. Then mark the letter (A), (B), (C), or (D) on your answer sheet.

51. If you are interested in the position, please send ------- résumé to Mr. Samuel Johnson.

   (A) you
   (B) your
   (C) yours
   (D) yourself

52. A different venue for this year's auto expo has been proposed as an ------- to the one typically used.

   (A) alternative
   (B) alternatively
   (C) alternatives
   (D) alternativeness

53. If ------- employee volunteers to organize the luncheon, we won't have to order catering, saving operating costs.

   (A) few
   (B) all
   (C) one another
   (D) any

54. The company head rejected the proposed site for the new office because it was too ------- located.

   (A) inconvenience
   (B) inconvenienced
   (C) inconvenient
   (D) inconveniently

55. Mr. Jones advised his client that he ------- the contract in order to keep it in a safe place for future reference.

   (A) printed
   (B) prints
   (C) printing
   (D) print

56. ------- the software development team put in extra hours for several weeks, they were able to meet the tight deadline.

   (A) Because
   (B) Although
   (C) Despite
   (D) Until

57. Lawyers from Kim & Chung Associates considered ------- their new legal services to attract new clients in China.

(A) market
(B) marketable
(C) marketed
(D) marketing

58. The team's ability to perform ------- well in adverse circumstances has really impressed the president.

(A) exceptional
(B) exception
(C) except
(D) exceptionally

59. Pegasus laptop computers are ------- despite including several top-of-the-line components.

(A) confident
(B) knowledgeable
(C) affordable
(D) apparent

60. Marketing managers should periodically read business ------- to keep abreast of market trends.

(A) journals
(B) journalism
(C) journalists
(D) journalistic

61. By the time Mr. Grant retires from Wigler Inc. next year, he ------- the company for 33 years.

(A) served
(B) has served
(C) will have served
(D) will served

62. Today's speaker will discuss ways for the advertising team members ------- their ideas for our new television commercials with executives.

(A) to share
(B) have shared
(C) sharing
(D) will share

63. All departments should be aware of the new policies ------- procurement contracts and make sure to update their internal documentation.

(A) that
(B) whereas
(C) besides
(D) concerning

64. To maintain our reputation as a leading communications company, we must ------- current trends in the marketplace extremely closely.

(A) monitor
(B) focus
(C) adhere
(D) achieve

65. ------- chief financial officer, Ms. Berno must keep track of all money spent and received in the company.

(A) As
(B) At
(C) Throughout
(D) Except

66. The majority of the keynote speakers will be talking about social networking developments ------- the upcoming technology conference.

(A) at
(B) as
(C) though
(D) of

PART 6

Questions 67-70 refer to the following advertisement.

Manuel and Francesca Salinas, the new directors of the Museo del Sorolla in Bilbao, invite all art lovers to join them for the art gallery's grand reopening. The gallery directors ------- major changes to the
67.
Museo del Sorolla.

The new structural design of the interior, conceived by renowned architect Jose Fernandez, features modern design flourishes ------- with traditional Basque stonework. -------. Visitors to the Museo
68. **69.**
del Sorolla will be able to enjoy beverages and selected snacks on the terrace while overlooking the gallery's colorful garden.

Furthermore, the remodeling ------- the main exhibition hall has introduced modern yet subtle exhibit
70.
lighting and large skylight windows.

Tickets for the event are available from the gallery's Web site.

67. (A) will make
(B) make
(C) to make
(D) have made

68. (A) integrated
(B) exchanged
(C) recruited
(D) afforded

69. (A) The winning prize will be two nights in a luxurious hotel.
(B) Mr. Fernandez was also commissioned to oversee construction of an attractive terrace.
(C) The architecture company is developing a plan for a department store.
(D) There will be an annual awards ceremony for the best designs.

70. (A) since
(B) of
(C) about
(D) up

Questions 71-74 refer to the following article.

You can now do most of your shopping without ever leaving the comfort of your own home. You can purchase appliances and furniture from various companies' online catalogues. You can order books online, or even download them ------- to your e-reader device.
71.

-------, while more and more vendors are adding online shopping to their Web sites, many are still
72.
reluctant to make the jump to cyberspace. For instance, while some might be willing to buy, say, a new sofa over the Internet, most people probably want to see it in person and try sitting in it before committing to buying it. For some businesses, offering online shopping involves incurring extra delivery expenses, which means either making less profit or charging customers more for online orders than they would pay in store.

The shift to online shopping has also been slowed by demographic realities. -------. In some, the
73.
majority of citizens are approaching or past retirement age. These people are often not very tech savvy, ------- they make up the bulk of many businesses' customer bases.
74.

71. (A) directed
    (B) directing
    (C) direction
    (D) directly

72. (A) However
    (B) Therefore
    (C) In fact
    (D) In addition

73. (A) For instance, high-speed Internet is not available in some areas.
    (B) Western countries mostly have aging populations now.
    (C) This makes it expensive for some of the customers.
    (D) The number of new products released each year is increasing.

74. (A) otherwise
    (B) still
    (C) yet
    (D) despite

Directions: In this part you will read a selection of texts, such as magazine and newspaper articles, e-mails, and instant messages. Each text or set of texts is followed by several questions. Select the best answer for each question and mark the letter (A), (B), (C), or (D) on your answer sheet.

Questions 75-76 refer to the following article.

The Reedburg Times

Lansing Foundation Invites Residents to Enjoy the Spring Melody Festival
By Amy Dickson

On Sunday, May 26, a music festival will be held at the beautifully-landscaped Pilgrim Park in downtown Reedburg.

The event, named the Spring Melody Festival, is being organized by the Lansing Foundation, a group which has worked hard to fix many problems in Reedburg and the surrounding towns and cities. Proceeds from festival tickets will go toward buying new computers for Dillbury Elementary School and Romford High School.

Local businessman and entrepreneur Keith Ledger will give an opening speech at the festival. Mr. Ledger has been very outspoken in his support of the foundation's endeavors. His speeches have inspired many members of the community to take more interest in social and economic problems in and around Reedburg.

Tickets for the festival may be purchased at Pilgrim Park on the day of the event.

75. What is the article mainly about?

(A) A landscaping project
(B) A fundraising event
(C) An arts and crafts fair
(D) A street parade

76. According to the article, how has Mr. Ledger helped the Lansing Foundation?

(A) He organized several community events.
(B) He purchased new computers for local schools.
(C) He wrote a supportive article in The Reedburg Times.
(D) He raised public awareness about local issues.

Mr. John Sykes, City Councilor
City Hall,
Farberville, OH 45820

Dear Mr. Sykes,

I would like to inform you of my support for the proposed changes to the traffic flow patterns on Main Street. My restaurant is in the middle of the downtown section and I believe all the businesses there would profit from the changes.

As I understand it, the city is proposing to make the street a one-way street for the four blocks that comprise the downtown area. This would include narrowing the street so that angle parking may be instituted, which of course will result in spaces for more cars. The sidewalks may also be widened.

It is my view that there is far too little parking in the downtown area, and anything that can help the situation is to be welcomed. I also believe that encouraging more pedestrian traffic will help boost business. As a mainly tourist town, most of our business depends on casual visitors, and encouraging them to walk around means they notice more and will shop more.

I have several associates in the restaurant industry in the Centennial Square area on the edge of town, and they all report that their business increased when foot traffic was increased. They did this by creating more central parking spaces and instituting pedestrian-only areas. They have also started planting more trees and adding flower boxes.

In view of this, I believe that any changes along these lines would be a good way to spend our property tax dollars, and I ask you to please vote for the proposed changes at the meeting next week. Thank you for your attention to this matter.

Yours sincerely,

Ronald Green
Owner, West Side Grill

---

77. What is suggested about Farberville?

(A) Its parking fees have recently increased.
(B) It attracts few shoppers.
(C) Many of its businesses are closing.
(D) It has a poor public transportation system.

78. What does Mr. Green think will increase business?

(A) Advertising the town's attractions
(B) Revitalizing all the town parks
(C) Investing in more companies
(D) Encouraging people to walk around

79. What will most likely take place next week?

(A) A city council meeting
(B) Tree and flower planting
(C) Several road modifications
(D) A parking lot development

To: Sherman Trading Staff
From: Bruno Lesnar, CEO
Subject: News Announcement
Date: July 3

As you may already know, our new director of marketing, Rachel Munez, will soon be joining us at our headquarters. We will have a welcome luncheon at Mercedes Bistro on Monday, July 23, for Ms. Munez's first day at Sherman Trading. You are all welcome to join.

On a similar note, our current director of marketing will be moving to California once he leaves his position on the board here at Sherman Trading. Timothy Hilton will be officially stepping down on July 20. Mr. Hilton has served our company for 26 years and played a significant role in its success and prosperity. After such a distinguished career, he plans to leave the field for good and move to Orange County with his wife, a former real estate agent.

Mr. Hilton will be presented with a farewell gift by the company president, Jim Lange, at a meeting on July 20. Following the meeting, he will visit each department to say goodbye in person to all staff. Please try to be available at your workstations between 11 A.M. and 12 P.M. to bid him a fond farewell.

80. What is the memo announcing?

(A) An employment opportunity
(B) A company relocation
(C) A corporate merger
(D) A personnel change

81. According to the memo, what will happen on July 23?

(A) Mr. Lesnar will interview candidates.
(B) Ms. Munez will attend a special meal.
(C) Mr. Hilton will lead a training session.
(D) Mr. Lange will receive a gift.

82. Who is Mr. Hilton?

(A) A retiring board member
(B) A new marketing manager
(C) A real estate agent
(D) A recruitment expert

Jim	[4:32 P.M.]	Did you have a chance to look through the presentation I created for Friday's meeting?
Ted	[4:36 P.M.]	Yes. I think it's great. It's impressive that we have sold 30% more paint since we advertised in that magazine. Were you planning on including this month's paint sales?
Jim	[4:40 P.M.]	I planned to, but I can only access the numbers through March. Our April sales are still not available on the database.
Ted	[4:44 P.M.]	I think it's important to include our April sales in your presentation. Actually, I have a meeting with Anthony in an hour and I will ask him to update the database so you can have the information before your presentation.
Jim	[4:45 P.M.]	I didn't realize he could do that. Thanks.
Ted	[4:46 P.M.]	No problem.
Jim	[4:50 P.M.]	Could you give me any other suggestions that might improve the presentation?
Ted	[4:55 P.M.]	Actually, I would change one small detail. It might be difficult for our colleagues to read blue letters over the black background. Perhaps you could change the background to white, or make the font a lighter color.
Jim	[4:58 P.M.]	Okay. I'll make the background white. Thanks.

83. What does Ted and Jim's company sell?

(A) Magazines
(B) Paints
(C) Commercials
(D) Calendars

84. What will Anthony most likely be asked to do?

(A) E-mail Jim the information
(B) Edit Jim's presentation
(C) Discuss the database
(D) Update the sales information

85. At 4:45 P.M., what does Jim mean when he writes, "I didn't realize he could do that"?

(A) He misunderstood Anthony's role.
(B) He forgot Ted had a meeting.
(C) He thought Anthony couldn't log in.
(D) He hadn't heard of the database.

86. What does Ted say about the presentation's design?

(A) The font is too small.
(B) It is impressively designed.
(C) It includes all the facts and figures.
(D) The color selection is problematic.

Questions 87-90 refer to the following information.

Hiking boots are designed to get dirty, but that doesn't mean you should neglect to keep them clean and in excellent condition. With proper care and maintenance, you can enjoy using your newly-purchased Trek Lord boots for many years.

Prior to cleaning your boots, you should remove the laces. Then, use a brush to gently remove dust and dirt from the boots and the laces. If a more thorough cleaning is required, use running water and a suitable boot cleaner. Although most footwear cleaners can be used on a range of materials, always check that your cleaner is suitable for use on your Trek Lord boots.

To avoid damage, never put your boots in the washing machine, and do not use soaps or detergents, as many of these contain chemicals that can be harmful to leather or waterproof materials. Your Trek Lord boots are already waterproof when you purchase them, so wait until you start to notice that water drops no longer bead up on the surface to re-apply a waterproofing material.

It is also important to dry and store your boots correctly. — [1] —. You should first remove the insoles and let them air-dry separately from the boots. — [2] —. Dry the boots at room temperature away from high humidity. Refrain from using a heat source such as a fireplace or radiator, as high temperatures weaken adhesives and age leather. — [3] —. To accelerate the drying process, use a fan, or place newspaper inside the boots.

When your boots' smooth leather parts appear dry or cracked, use a conditioner. — [4] —. Leather functions best when moisturized, but excess conditioner makes boots too soft and weakens ankle and foot support.

87. Where would the information most likely be found?

 (A) On a notice board
 (B) In a hiking magazine
 (C) On a promotional flyer
 (D) Inside product packaging

88. What is indicated about Trek Lord boots?

 (A) They are sold with extra laces.
 (B) They need waterproofing after purchase.
 (C) They require specific cleaners.
 (D) They can be machine-washed.

89. How should the Trek Lord boots be dried?

 (A) By placing them near a radiator
 (B) By placing them on top of newspaper
 (C) By placing them in front of a fan
 (D) By placing them in a dark room

90. In which of the positions marked [1], [2], [3], and [4] does the following sentence best belong?

 "Take care not to apply too much."

 (A) [1]
 (B) [2]
 (C) [3]
 (D) [4]

Questions 91-95 refer to the following e-mails.

To:	Frank Cruise <fcruise@primeedu.com>
From:	Sally Bullard <sbullard@primeedu.com>
Subject:	Meeting of the board of executives
Date:	March 20

Dear Frank,

As the newest member of the board of executives, your attendance is requested at our next meeting. It will be held on Wednesday, March 27, at 1:00 in the board room on the seventh floor.

I know that your particular area of expertise is trends in sales, so I would like to request that you come prepared with a presentation covering the past twelve months and expectations for the next twelve months. We are hoping to improve our market share in the coming year, and I would like for us to brainstorm ideas for doing just that at this meeting.

Other items on the agenda include staff morale, career development, and training. If you have any thoughts on these topics, we welcome any and all suggestions. A few specific questions for you to consider are as follows:

1. How would you assess morale currently, and what can be done to make improvements?
2. What can we do to be more competitive?
3. We would like to train our current staff to move up in our organization rather than hiring from outside. How can we provide such training without hindering productivity?

Please respond to confirm your attendance.

To: Sally Bullard <sbullard@primeedu.com>
From: Frank Cruise <fcruise@primeedu.com>
Subject: Re: Meeting of the board of executives
Date: March 20

Dear Sally,

I am writing to confirm my attendance at the March 27 meeting of the executive board. I have done a great deal of research and will share my findings with you all on the topic of improving our market share. I have some figures to share that illustrate some problem areas we are experiencing, and I feel confident that we can address these problems together. I will also take the other questions into consideration, and I am especially looking forward to sharing my ideas with you regarding the third question you mentioned in your e-mail. I think that this is going to be a very productive meeting.

I also wanted to thank you for your confidence in me and for nominating me to the board of executives. This is a tremendous opportunity for me and I will not let you down!

91. What is the purpose of the first e-mail?

(A) To request a work report
(B) To inform Mr. Cruise of a job opportunity
(C) To nominate Mr. Cruise to the board
(D) To invite Mr. Cruise to a meeting

92. In the first e-mail, the word "items" in paragraph 3, line 1, is closest in meaning to

(A) issues
(B) products
(C) traits
(D) notices

93. What topic is Mr. Cruise most looking forward to discussing at the meeting?

(A) Ways to improve morale
(B) Ways to train existing staff
(C) Ways to be more competitive
(D) Ways to boost factory production

94. What can be inferred about Mr. Cruise?

(A) He has shown interest in an upcoming promotion opportunity.
(B) He will meet with Ms. Bullard prior to the meeting on March 27.
(C) He recently joined the company from one of its competitors.
(D) This will be his first meeting with the board of executives.

95. Why does Mr. Cruise thank Ms. Bullard?

(A) For helping him research sales trends
(B) For providing advice on presentation techniques
(C) For recommending him to the board
(D) For putting him in charge of a project

Questions 96-100 refer to the following advertisement, Web page, and article.

Dryden on Tenth

1402 West 10th Avenue, Vancouver, BC V6H 1J6

Open 11 a.m. to 10 p.m., Tue – Thu / 11 a.m. to 11 p.m. Fri – Sun

Last month, we finally finished extensive renovations to our restaurant, with the interior decoration handled by the skilled designer Holden Spencer. Originally a one-story building, our restaurant now boasts a second floor, raising our main dining area seating capacity to 253. Upstairs, we have six new private dining rooms, in addition to the four we have on the ground floor. Our experienced head chef, Jean Dupont, is waiting to serve you his popular dishes!

If you work at a business in the local area, ask us about the discounts that you are eligible to receive. Employees at businesses registered in our company directory may receive up to 15% off their bill.

Visit www.drydenontenth.ca to view our menus and make a dinner reservation. Please note that no shorts or sleeveless shirts should be worn inside our restaurant.

http://www.drydenontenth.ca/dinnermenu

Dinner Menu

Appetizers	Main Dishes	Desserts
French Onion Soup	Herb Roasted Chicken	Raspberry Cheesecake
$8.50	$15.50	$8.50
Crab Salad	Butter Poached Lobster	Chef's Special Tiramisu
$12.50	$17.50	$9.50
Garlic Bread	Baked Salmon	Rich Chocolate Cake
$6.50	$16.50	$7.50

BC Living Magazine – July Edition

Featured Restaurant of the Month – Dryden on Tenth
By Bridgette Kyle

The first thing I noticed during my recent visit to Dryden on Tenth was how much better the restaurant looks after being redesigned by Holden Spencer. The main dining area now seats just over 250 diners, and the restaurant now boasts a total of six private dining rooms, which are available for private parties.

The food at Dryden on Tenth is as exquisite as ever. I especially enjoyed the lobster for my main dish, while head chef Jean Dupont's signature French onion soup was an ideal choice for a starter, and the raspberry cheesecake was outstanding. Diners should note that menu prices may fluctuate depending on the availability of local ingredients and the time of year.

Dryden on Tenth opens at 11 a.m., six days a week, and stays open later on Fridays, Saturdays, and Sundays.

96. What is NOT indicated about Dryden on Tenth?

(A) It offers corporate discounts.
(B) It has a dress code policy.
(C) It requires bookings for lunch.
(D) It is closed on Mondays.

97. According to the advertisement, what has recently happened at the restaurant?

(A) An outdoor area was built.
(B) A new head chef was hired.
(C) An extra floor was added.
(D) A menu was expanded.

98. How much was Ms. Kyle probably charged for her main dish?

(A) $8.50
(B) $12.50
(C) $16.50
(D) $17.50

99. In the article, what is stated about the restaurant's prices?

(A) They are lower than those of its competitors.
(B) They may change depending on the season.
(C) They may be listed differently on its Web site.
(D) They have increased significantly over the years.

100. What information did Ms. Kyle describe incorrectly?

(A) The name of the interior designer
(B) The capacity of the main dining room
(C) The business hours of the restaurant
(D) The number of private dining rooms

PART 1

Directions: For each question in this part, you will hear four statements about a picture in your test book. When you hear the statements, you must select the one statement that best describes what you see in the picture. Then find the number of the question on your answer sheet and mark your answer. The statements will not be printed in your test book and will be spoken only one time.

1.

2.

PART 2

Directions: You will hear a question or statement and three responses spoken in English. They will not be printed in your test book and will be spoken only one time. Select the best response to the question or statement and mark the letter (A), (B), or (C) on your answer sheet.

3. Mark your answer on your answer sheet.

4. Mark your answer on your answer sheet.

5. Mark your answer on your answer sheet.

6. Mark your answer on your answer sheet.

7. Mark your answer on your answer sheet.

8. Mark your answer on your answer sheet.

9. Mark your answer on your answer sheet.

10. Mark your answer on your answer sheet.

11. Mark your answer on your answer sheet.

12. Mark your answer on your answer sheet.

13. Mark your answer on your answer sheet.

14. Mark your answer on your answer sheet.

15. Mark your answer on your answer sheet.

16. Mark your answer on your answer sheet.

17. Mark your answer on your answer sheet.

18. Mark your answer on your answer sheet.

19. Mark your answer on your answer sheet.

20. Mark your answer on your answer sheet.

PART 3

Directions: You will hear some conversations between two or more people. You will be asked to answer three questions about what the speakers say in each conversation. Select the best response to each question and mark the letter (A), (B), (C) or (D) on your answer sheet. The conversations will not be printed in your test book and will be spoken only one time.

21. What type of event are the speakers discussing?

    (A) A seminar
    (B) An awards show
    (C) A fundraiser
    (D) A grand opening

22. What industry do the speakers most likely work in?

    (A) Accounting
    (B) Education
    (C) Catering
    (D) Engineering

23. According to the man, what is the problem?

    (A) A training session has been cancelled.
    (B) Some items are currently out of stock.
    (C) An event schedule has not been updated.
    (D) Some workers will be unavailable.

24. How did the woman hear about a company?

    (A) From a family member
    (B) From a TV advertisement
    (C) From a work colleague
    (D) From a promotional flyer

25. What does the man mean when he says, "I see that kind of thing all the time"?

    (A) He recently bought a new dog.
    (B) He has knowledge of a situation.
    (C) He disagrees with a suggestion.
    (D) He has no openings in his schedule.

26. What does the man offer to send?

    (A) Some pamphlets
    (B) Some Web site addresses
    (C) Some videos
    (D) Some directions

27. Who most likely is the woman?

    (A) An event planner
    (B) A chef
    (C) A musician
    (D) An artist

28. What problem does the woman mention?

    (A) An event has been postponed.
    (B) A booth has not been prepared.
    (C) Some equipment has broken down.
    (D) Some event attendees have complained.

29. What will the man most likely do next?

    (A) Organize a meeting
    (B) Send a document
    (C) Contact a colleague
    (D) Order some supplies

30. Who most likely is the woman?

    (A) A musician
    (B) An actor
    (C) A writer
    (D) A model

31. What is the purpose of the meeting?

    (A) To evaluate some performers
    (B) To create a marketing campaign
    (C) To discuss a business contract
    (D) To present an award

32. What does the woman say about a TV show?

    (A) She found it uninteresting.
    (B) She watched it regularly.
    (C) She is friends with the lead actor.
    (D) She auditioned for a role in it.

Logo 1

Logo 2

Logo 3

Logo 4

33. What are the speakers planning?

(A) A company outing
(B) An awards ceremony
(C) A recruitment event
(D) A training seminar

34. Look at the graphic. Which logo does the woman like?

(A) Logo 1
(B) Logo 2
(C) Logo 3
(D) Logo 4

35. What does the man ask the woman to send?

(A) An e-mail address
(B) A venue location
(C) Some event dates
(D) Some image files

Regal Catering Co. Customer Invoice #2817		
Item	Quantity	Price
Cheese Sandwiches	25	$50.00
Ham Sandwiches	30	$60.00
Egg Salad Sandwiches	20	$50.00
Tuna Mayo Sandwiches	15	$45.00
	TOTAL AMOUNT:	$205.00

36. What are the speakers discussing?

(A) Some items have not been delivered.
(B) A catered event has been canceled.
(C) A company has raised its prices.
(D) Some items are unsatisfactory.

37. What does the woman mention about Regal Catering?

(A) It provides corporate discounts.
(B) It uses only local ingredients.
(C) It is a relatively new business.
(D) Its workers are highly experienced.

38. Look at the graphic. How many sandwiches will likely be returned?

(A) 25
(B) 30
(C) 20
(D) 15

PART 4

Directions: You will hear some talks given by a single speaker. You will be asked to answer three questions about what the speakers say in each conversation. Select the best response to each question and mark the letter (A), (B), (C) or (D) on your answer sheet. The conversations will not be printed in your test book and will be spoken only one time.

39. Who most likely are the listeners?

(A) Sales representatives
(B) Advertising executives
(C) Warehouse employees
(D) Customer service agents

40. What will Roberta Simmons talk about?

(A) Marketing strategies
(B) Product features
(C) Cost-saving measures
(D) Project management

41. What does the speaker ask the listeners to do?

(A) Prepare some questions
(B) Complete some forms
(C) Check a schedule
(D) Demonstrate products

42. Who most likely is the speaker?

(A) A hotel manager
(B) An airline pilot
(C) A travel agent
(D) A park ranger

43. What requirement is mentioned?

(A) A driver's license
(B) A vehicle rental
(C) A visitor's permit
(D) An advance fee

44. What does the speaker mean when he says, "there is likely to be high demand"?

(A) Some rooms may no longer be available.
(B) Some information was incorrect.
(C) The listener should make a quick decision.
(D) The listener should consider an alternative.

45. Where do the listeners most likely work?

(A) At a print shop
(B) At a furniture store
(C) At a moving company
(D) At a distribution center

46. What is the speaker concerned about?

(A) Handling fragile items
(B) Meeting a quarterly goal
(C) Postponing a project deadline
(D) Dealing with customer complaints

47. Why does the speaker say, "Does anyone have anything?"

(A) To express frustration
(B) To request some input
(C) To ask for some supplies
(D) To disagree with a decision

Zeus Airlines – Daily Flights		
Flight Number	Departure	Arrival
Flight 021	09:25 AM	12:35 PM
Flight 024	11:35 AM	2:45 PM
Flight 032	1:30 PM	4:35 PM
Flight 035	4:55 PM	8:05 PM

48. Why is the speaker calling?

(A) To promote a new airline
(B) To offer an upgrade
(C) To explain a travel delay
(D) To confirm an itinerary

49. Look at the graphic. Which Zeus Airlines flight will the listener take?

(A) Flight 021
(B) Flight 024
(C) Flight 032
(D) Flight 035

50. What is the listener advised to do?

(A) Arrive at the airport early
(B) Book accommodations
(C) Sign up for a package tour
(D) Use an online check-in service

This is the end of the Listening test. Turn to Part 5 in your test book.

READING TEST

In the Reading test, you will read a variety of texts and answer several different types of reading comprehension questions. The entire Reading test will last 75 minutes. There are three parts, and directions are given for each part. You are encouraged to answer as many questions as possible within the time allowed. You must mark your answers on the separate answer sheet. Do not write your answers in your test book.

PART 5

Directions: A word or phrase is missing in each of the sentences below. Four answer choices are given below each sentence. Select the best answer to complete the sentence. Then mark the letter (A), (B), (C), or (D) on your answer sheet.

51. All telecommuting ------- must send a daily work report to their supervisor at 5 P.M.

    (A) employment
    (B) employable
    (C) employer
    (D) employees

52. Please join us to celebrate the retirement of George Ramos, who ------- with the company for over twenty years.

    (A) have been
    (B) has been
    (C) having been
    (D) is being

53. With the help from the strategic planning team, our director has been brainstorming ------- ways to increase revenue and cut costs.

    (A) creatively
    (B) creative
    (C) creation
    (D) create

54. Users must read the product manual so they can familiarize ------- with the device.

    (A) they
    (B) their
    (C) them
    (D) themselves

55. The reimbursement request for your trip last month to Chicago has ------- to be processed because there is a missing receipt for the car rental.

    (A) yet
    (B) already
    (C) after
    (D) too

56. Mr. Alvarez, the head of the International Relations Office, is responsible for ------- all client communication written in English.

    (A) translate
    (B) translated
    (C) translating
    (D) translation

57. The department supervisor discussed several issues regarding staff with ------- on persistent absenteeism.

   (A) emphatic
   (B) emphasis
   (C) emphasize
   (D) emphasized

58. To ensure that all contact with our clients is professional, ------- with our guidelines regarding e-mail and phone communication is crucial.

   (A) disclosure
   (B) compliance
   (C) enthusiasm
   (D) connection

59. The desserts ------- in the company cafeteria are not only incredibly delicious, but healthy and beautifully presented, too.

   (A) offering
   (B) offers
   (C) to offer
   (D) offered

60. After months of negotiations, Mr. Kenneth has reached an agreement with JM Logistics Co., ------- support is crucial for his business' economic recovery.

   (A) which
   (B) whose
   (C) that
   (D) what

61. Please be aware that your e-mail address will only be used for our promotional purposes and will never be disclosed to third parties ------- written permission from you.

   (A) without
   (B) within
   (C) except
   (D) unless

62. ------- we have the budget to buy new computers, we regret that our outdated photocopier cannot be replaced until later this year.

   (A) But
   (B) While
   (C) Before
   (D) However

63. The retirement dinner for the vice president was a success, as ------- 90 percent of the company's workers attended the event.

   (A) normally
   (B) generously
   (C) approximately
   (D) evenly

64. Since our factory ------- technical difficulties several months ago, its output has been continuously dropping to new lows.

   (A) excused
   (B) experienced
   (C) exhausted
   (D) experimented

65. The winner of this year's architecture award will be ------- by a panel of judges next month.

   (A) preserved
   (B) continued
   (C) determined
   (D) situated

66. ------- mentioned during the staff meeting last week, beginning May 1, lunch time will be extended by 60 minutes to give employees the chance to participate in fitness activities.

   (A) As
   (B) If
   (C) After
   (D) For

PART 6

Questions 67-70 refer to the following notice.

Infinity Productions will reimburse employees for travel expenses incurred when performing the various functions of their jobs. Travel expenses include the ------- of transportation, accommodation, and
67.
meals consumed over the duration of the business trip.

Employees seeking reimbursement for expenses must file an expense report no later than the first day of each month. ------- item should be entered separately and include the date, the amount, the reason
68.
for the expense, and a scanned copy of the receipt. Reimbursements will be deposited ------- into
69.
employees' bank accounts on the fifteenth day of each month, along with regular pay.

-------.
70.

Thank you for your continued commitment to Infinity Productions.

67. (A) length
    (B) cost
    (C) share
    (D) content

68. (A) All
    (B) Which
    (C) Such
    (D) Each

69. (A) direct
    (B) directs
    (C) direction
    (D) directly

70. (A) Please ensure that you send a copy of your
        trip itinerary this week.
    (B) Don't forget that products may only be
        returned with a valid receipt.
    (C) Thank you for helping us to reduce our
        monthly business expenses.
    (D) You will be notified if payments are likely to
        be later than the 15th.

To: Ida Fitzgerald <ifiz@daox.net>

From: Jennifer Rushmore <jrushmore@tvnradio.com>

Subject: My gratitude

Dear Ms. Fitzgerald,

About a decade ago, I took a field trip to a radio station. I was fascinated by the voices and music that were being broadcast on air. ------- , it has been my greatest wish to become a radio announcer,
71.
all the way through my adolescence. However, I knew it would be an almost impossible dream to achieve.

One day, I built up enough courage to ask you, my homeroom teacher, about it. You offered me a lot of good advice, saying, "Only with a single step does a journey of a thousand miles -------." You
72.
also said that you had a friend at a radio station and gave me his phone number. Had it not been for you, I might never have had ------- an opportunity. Now, I work at the station and am learning how to
73.
become a professional radio announcer. -------.
74.

Sincerely,

Jennifer Rushmore

71. (A) Specifically
(B) Since then
(C) Likewise
(D) Rather

72. (A) began
(B) begun
(C) begin
(D) begins

73. (A) great
(B) such
(C) each
(D) too

74. (A) Your work has truly been an inspiration to me.
(B) I have been dreaming of joining you at your station.
(C) I am truly grateful that you chose to employ me.
(D) Thanks for encouraging me to pursue my dream.

PART 7

Directions: In this part you will read a selection of texts, such as magazine and newspaper articles, e-mails, and instant messages. Each text or set of texts is followed by several questions. Select the best answer for each question and mark the letter (A), (B), (C), or (D) on your answer sheet.

Questions 75-76 refer to the following job listing.

Fernlea Board of Education
Employment Opportunity

The Fernlea Board of Education is seeking a hard-working individual to fill a full-time position at Fernlea High School. The successful applicant will primarily be responsible for keeping all rooms in the school buildings clean and tidy. This includes the classrooms, the cafeteria/kitchen, and the science labs. Heavy lifting may occasionally be required, so the successful applicant must be strong and fit. He or she must also be able to fix simple objects, such as damaged desks, chairs, and doors. A high school diploma or college degree is not necessary. However, the successful candidate must have worked in a similar janitorial role for a minimum of 12 months. Interested individuals should submit their resume and cover letter to Principal John Skinner at Fernlea High School, 3901 Seven Oaks Crescent, Fernlea, WI 54487.

75. What position is being offered?

(A) Teacher
(B) Lab technician
(C) Janitor
(D) Kitchen assistant

76. What is NOT a listed requirement of the position?

(A) Prior job experience
(B) Basic repair skills
(C) A good physical condition
(D) An academic qualification

Lab Techs Required - Vivalabs

We are an expanding biotech company that is hiring three new part-time lab technicians to work in our newly-added research laboratories. The technicians will work at either our Dallas or Fort Worth sites, and will carry out a variety of tasks, including performing tests and measurements, recording data and observation results, and writing reports. Working with animals is not required.

Applicants will be expected to have a minimum of three years of related work experience, which may include medical or chemical laboratory experience. Post-secondary studies in biology and/or chemistry are required, and a master's degree is preferred, although students currently enrolled in a degree program will also be considered.

The work includes some writing, so basic word processing skills are required, along with the ability to use fine instruments and perform delicate experiments. Weekend and evening work is required occasionally and hours are flexible. The starting date is November 4.

Salary will be commensurate with education and experience. Non-compete and secrecy declarations are required. For further information, or to apply and send your résumé, please e-mail us at humanresources@vivalabs.com.

---

77. What is indicated as a reason for Vivalabs hiring new workers?

(A) Many employees have resigned.
(B) It is opening new facilities.
(C) Sales are expected to increase.
(D) It has recently relocated.

78. What is mentioned as being part of the job?

(A) Transporting lab samples
(B) Leading a field research team
(C) Conducting laboratory tests
(D) Publishing research results

79. What is stated about the working conditions?

(A) The number of hours worked will depend on education level.
(B) Successful applicants must work at two different sites.
(C) Research requires various animal tests.
(D) Some overtime work is required.

To:	Mary Engels
From:	Aaron Blackmore
Date:	February 18
Subject:	Lunch meeting

Do you think we can meet for lunch tomorrow? We need to go over the additions we should make to the slide presentation we are giving later this week. You have worked on projects for Brown & Sons longer than I have, and I want your input on the details.

I understand that Blue Ridge Associates will be sending someone to the presentation, as well as Miranda Products, who are already interested. Do you have any background information about this new company?

I have booked a table at The Rib House for lunch tomorrow. Expect it to be a long lunch. Please let me know if you cannot make it.

Thanks.

80. What is the reason for the lunch meeting?

(A) To design an office addition
(B) To edit a presentation
(C) To discuss a new project
(D) To write a proposal

81. What can be inferred about the presentation?

(A) Several companies will be attending it.
(B) Mary is willing to assist Aaron with it.
(C) It will take place at The Rib House.
(D) It needs to be made considerably longer.

82. Which organization does Mary have work experience with?

(A) The Rib House
(B) Blue Ridge Associates
(C) Miranda Products
(D) Brown & Sons

Questions 83-86 refer to the following notice.

Congratulations! You made a wonderful decision when you decided to place an order for Nature Link vitamins, because our products come with a life-time guarantee. That's right, if you're not happy, you can return any product to us at any time and we will gladly refund your purchase price or provide an alternative product as long as you follow the instructions below.

We request that you pay for your goods in full within a month of receiving your order. — [1] —. If you're not satisfied with your purchase, please call our friendly staff at our toll-free number 569-555-0129. — [2] —. We'll deal with any problems quickly and either provide you with a replacement item from our catalog, or if you want, we will give you store credit with which you can buy an alternative item. Of course, a full refund is also possible. It's completely up to you to choose what you'd like to do.

When you return a product, please ensure that you send it in the original packaging and include your invoice and receipt. — [3] —. We'll gladly refund any standard postage charges. — [4] —. Our customers are important to us and we guarantee customer satisfaction!

83. When should the goods be paid for?

(A) At the time the order is placed
(B) Immediately after the item is delivered
(C) Before the end of the month
(D) Within a month of receiving them

84. According to the notice, what should customers do if they are not satisfied?

(A) Leave a message on a Web site
(B) Call the company
(C) Read their guarantee
(D) Send the products back immediately

85. What is NOT offered to dissatisfied customers?

(A) Compensation for the returned goods
(B) Priority shipping fees
(C) A replacement item
(D) Store credit

86. In which of the positions marked [1], [2], [3], and [4] does the following sentence best belong?

"This is because we believe in the highest quality of customer service."

(A) [1]
(B) [2]
(C) [3]
(D) [4]

Questions 87-90 refer to the following online chat discussion.

Seth	[9:21 A.M.]	Welcome to the team, Moustapha. Your training will begin after lunch at 1:30 P.M.
Moustapha	[9:24 A.M.]	Thank you. Is there anything I can do to prepare?
Seth	[9:30 A.M.]	You may familiarize yourself with our database. You will be using this program to register new patients and enter their health histories and credit card details. Please log in with the temporary username GUEST and password Health4U.
Moustapha	[9:32 A.M.]	I'll get right on it.
Seth	[9:35 A.M.]	I will also e-mail you a list of questions commonly asked by patients, prospective patients, and visitors. Please have a look. We will discuss the response procedures in detail during your training.
Moustapha	[9:38 A.M.]	Thank you. I look forward to it.

87. Where most likely does Moustapha work?

(A) In a train station
(B) In a visitor's center
(C) In a public library
(D) In a medical office

88. What does Seth say about the database?

(A) It is easy to use.
(B) It stores financial information.
(C) It requires a personalized password.
(D) It is updated once per day.

89. At 9:32 A.M., what does Moustapha mean when he writes, "I'll get right on it"?

(A) He will contact some clients.
(B) He will practice using a program.
(C) He will submit some information.
(D) He will create new user information.

90. What will Seth most likely do next?

(A) He will make a list of participants.
(B) He will create Moustapha's e-mail account.
(C) He will update the payroll database.
(D) He will send a document to Moustapha.

Questions 91-95 refer to the following invitation and letter.

You are invited to join James Leem, personal investor and Chief Executive Officer
at JL Financial, for a Black Tie event on July 29 at the Pink Horizon Inn and Spa
on the banks of the Pacific Ocean.

Guests will enjoy an internationally-acclaimed three-course meal,
after which they will be treated to a sunset cruise on Cardinal Bay.

For those who would like to stay the night,
one night's accommodation for two has been reserved for each guest.

Each couple will also receive a voucher for the spa, all courtesy of Mr. Leem.

This evening is for preferred clients only.
Thank you for referring over 10 new clients to Mr. Leem this year.
Kindly RSVP by June 21 to Mr. Leem's secretary.

Dear Ms. Jasmine Park,

Thank you for the invitation to Mr. Leem's Black Tie event. I must say I was quite surprised to receive it. It is the first time I have been recognized in this way by an investment banker. It will certainly encourage me to remain a "preferred client." Smart business move!

Unfortunately, I am unable to attend the event due to a prior business engagement. Because I am the sole proprietor of my business, I am kept quite busy, and I will be overseas the night of the event. My wife is also sorry she will miss out on the evening and the chance to meet with Mrs. Leem. I wonder if we will be invited next year to make up for our absence this year. I would be honored to attend another time, if this is the sort of thing Mr. Leem does regularly. In the future, I need at least two months' notice instead of three weeks in order to make a commitment to an event such as this one.

Thank you again for the invitation. I am pleased with my decision to invest with Mr. Leem and look forward to meeting you in the future.

Regards,

Daniel Sujek
President, Sujek Consulting

91. What is the purpose of the event?

 (A) To mark a company's founding day
 (B) To attract potential investors to a project
 (C) To celebrate a CEO's retirement
 (D) To thank clients for their referrals

92. What does Mr. Sujek suggest about the event?

 (A) It is a unique way to grow business.
 (B) It includes only business owners.
 (C) It is being poorly organized.
 (D) It should be held on a weekend.

93. Who is Jasmine Park?

 (A) James Leem's secretary
 (B) Daniel Sujek's wife
 (C) An investor at JL Financial
 (D) The receptionist at Pink Horizon

94. In the letter, the word "move" in paragraph 1, line 3, is closest in meaning to

 (A) location
 (B) advice
 (C) progress
 (D) strategy

95. Why is Mr. Sujek unable to attend the event?

 (A) He has a business meeting.
 (B) His wife has a prior appointment.
 (C) He will be traveling abroad.
 (D) He will be attending a convention.

Questions 96-100 refer to the following articles and e-mail.

International Journal of Ecology
- FEBRUARY ISSUE -
Pollution Levels Remain Hazardous in Irtak River
By Andrew Pasolini

In 1986, a textiles factory in the city of Altai, Uzbekistan, began to discharge large quantities of toxic chemical waste into the Irtak River, killing off the majority of native aquatic species. Although the factory closed in 2007, large amounts of chemicals remain in the riverbed and in the soil of the surrounding riverbanks and fields.

Most of the affected soil is spread across a 20-kilometer stretch of the river located between Altai and the Tobol Reservoir. However, when rain makes the water level rise, contaminated soil is carried over 70 kilometers downriver, creating a widespread problem. Currently, there is an estimated 1,350,000 cubic meters of polluted soil in the riverbed.

International Journal of Ecology
- DECEMBER ISSUE –
Irtak River Project Progressing Smoothly
By Andrew Pasolini

The primary objective of the Irtak River Project, which began in July, is to improve the welfare of those residing in the region by cleaning up the serious pollution in and around the Irtak River, thereby providing a safe source of water and farmable land for locals.

To date, approximately one million cubic meters of the contaminated soil has been carefully taken away from the site and safely dumped in a hazardous waste landfill.

The overall cost of the project increased from the originally allocated $27.75 million to $29.25 million due to unforeseen complications regarding the disposal of contaminated soil. However, according to project coordinators, the project is still on track to be completed by November next year, as expected.

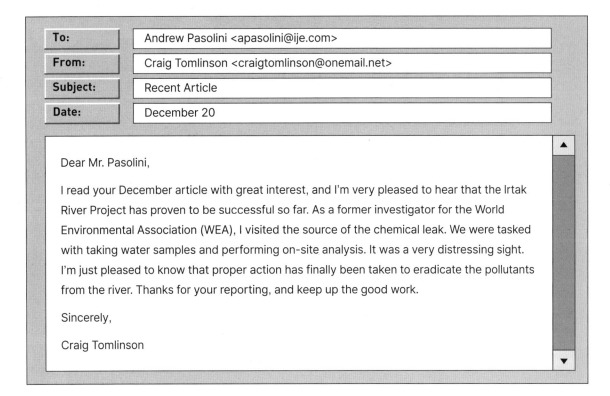

To:	Andrew Pasolini <apasolini@ije.com>
From:	Craig Tomlinson <craigtomlinson@onemail.net>
Subject:	Recent Article
Date:	December 20

Dear Mr. Pasolini,

I read your December article with great interest, and I'm very pleased to hear that the Irtak River Project has proven to be successful so far. As a former investigator for the World Environmental Association (WEA), I visited the source of the chemical leak. We were tasked with taking water samples and performing on-site analysis. It was a very distressing sight. I'm just pleased to know that proper action has finally been taken to eradicate the pollutants from the river. Thanks for your reporting, and keep up the good work.

Sincerely,

Craig Tomlinson

96. What can be inferred about the Irtak River?

(A) Its water level is lower than it used to be.
(B) It is twenty kilometers in length.
(C) It first became polluted in 2007.
(D) Its fish populations have declined.

97. In the first article, the word "makes" in paragraph 2, line 2, is closest in meaning to

(A) creates
(B) causes
(C) meets
(D) facilitates

98. What is a stated result of the Irtak River Project?

(A) The Tobol Reservoir has been drained.
(B) Crop yields of local farms have increased.
(C) The Irtak River has been widened.
(D) Most of the polluted soil has been removed.

99. What factor led to a budget increase?

(A) Opposition from local residents
(B) Conflicts in a project schedule
(C) Problems with soil disposal
(D) Unseasonably bad weather

100. What can be inferred about Mr. Tomlinson?

(A) He founded an environmental organization.
(B) He has spent time working in Altai.
(C) He submitted an article to the journal.
(D) He signed a petition started by the WEA.

시원스쿨 LAB